KU-440-487

Alcohol-induced mood disorder
Alcohol-induced anxiety disorder
Alcohol-induced sexual dysfunction
Alcohol-induced sleep disorder
Alcohol-related disorder NOS

Amphetamine (or Amphetamine-Like)–Related Disorders

Amphetamine Use Disorders
Amphetamine dependence
Amphetamine abuse

Amphetamine-Induced Disorders
Amphetamine intoxication
Amphetamine withdrawal
Amphetamine intoxication delirium
Amphetamine-induced psychotic disorder
  With delusions
  With hallucinations
Amphetamine-induced mood disorder
Amphetamine-induced anxiety disorder
Amphetamine-induced sexual dysfunction
Amphetamine-induced sleep disorder
Amphetamine-related disorder NOS

Caffeine-Related Disorders

Caffeine-Induced Disorders
Caffeine intoxication
Caffeine-induced anxiety disorder
Caffeine-induced sleep disorder
Caffeine-related disorder NOS

Cannabis-Related Disorders

Cannabis Use Disorders
Cannabis dependence
Cannabis abuse

Cannabis-Induced Disorders
Cannabis intoxication
Cannabis intoxication delirium
Cannabis-induced psychotic disorder
  With delusions
  With hallucinations
Cannabis-induced anxiety disorder
Cannabis-related disorder NOS

Cocaine-Related Disorders

Cocaine Use Disorders
Cocaine dependence
Cocaine abuse

Cocaine-Induced Disorders
Cocaine intoxication
Cocaine withdrawal
Cocaine intoxication delirium
Cocaine-induced psychotic disorder
  With delusions
  With hallucinations
Cocaine-induced mood disorder
Cocaine-induced anxiety disorder
Cocaine-induced sexual dysfunction
Cocaine-induced sleep disorder
Cocaine-related disorder NOS

Hallucinogen-Related Disorders

Hallucinogen Use Disorders
Hallucinogen dependence
Hallucinogen abuse

Hallucinogen-Induced Disorders
Hallucinogen intoxication
Hallucinogen persisting perception disorder (flashbacks)
Hallucinogen intoxication delirium
Hallucinogen-induced psychotic disorder
  With delusions
  With hallucinations
Hallucinogen-induced mood disorder
Hallucinogen-induced anxiety disorder
Hallucinogen-related disorder NOS

Inhalant-Related Disorders

Inhalant Use Disorders
Inhalant dependence
Inhalant abuse

Inhalant-Induced Disorders
Inhalant intoxication
Inhalant intoxication delirium
Inhalant-induced persisting dementia
Inhalant-induced psychotic disorder
  With delusions
  With hallucinations
Inhalant-induced mood disorder
Inhalant-induced anxiety disorder
Inhalant-related disorder NOS

Nicotine-Related Disorders

Nicotine Use Disorder
Nicotine dependence

Nicotine-Induced Disorder
Nicotine withdrawal
Nicotine-related disorder NOS

Opioid-Related Disorders

Opioid Use Disorders
Opiod dependence
Opiod abuse

Opioid-Induced Disorders
Opioid intoxication
Opioid withdrawal
Opioid intoxication delirium
Opioid-induced psychotic disorder
  With delusions
  With hallucinations
Opioid-induced mood disorder
Opioid-induced sexual dysfunction
Opioid-induced sleep disorder
Opioid-related disorder NOS

Phencyclidine (or Phencyclidine-Like)–Related Disorders

Phencyclidine Use Disorders
Phencyclidine dependence
Phencyclidine abuse

Phencyclidine-Induced Disorders
Phencyclidine intoxication
Phencyclidine intoxication delirium
Phencyclidine-induced psychotic disorder
  With delusions
  With hallucinations
Phencyclidine-induced mood disorder
Phencyclidine-induced anxiety disorder
Phencyclidine-related disorder NOS

Sedative-, Hypnotic-, or Anxiolytic-Related Disorders

Sedative, Hypnotic, or Anxiolytic Use Disorders
Sedative, hypnotic, or anxiolytic dependence
Sedative, hypnotic, or anxiolytic abuse

Sedative-, Hypnotic-, or Anxiolytic-Induced Disorders
Sedative, hypnotic, or anxiolytic intoxication
Sedative, hypnotic, or anxiolytic withdrawal
Sedative, hypnotic, or anxiolytic intoxication delirium
Sedative, hypnotic, or anxiolytic withdrawal delirium
Sedative-, hypnotic-, or anxiolytic-induced persisting dementia
Sedative-, hypnotic-, or anxiolytic-induced persisting amnestic disorder
Sedative-, hypnotic-, or anxiolytic-induced psychotic disorder
  With delusions
  With hallucinations
Sedative-, hypnotic-, or anxiolytic-induced mood disorder
Sedative-, hypnotic-, or anxiolytic-induced anxiety disorder
Sedative-, hypnotic-, or anxiolytic-induced sexual dysfunction
Sedative-, hypnotic-, or anxiolytic-induced sleep disorder
Sedative-, hypnotic-, or anxiolytic-related disorder NOS

(continued on inside back cover)

Abnormal Psychology

FRASERBURGH ACADEMY LIBRARY

M01601(3)

DATE DUE

150

05 JAN 2005
- 9 OCT 2014
24 APR 2015
26 OCT 2015
16 FEB 2017
- 7 DEC 2017
17 MAY 2021
20 Sep 2022
23 AUG 2023
21 SEP 2023

W/D

GAYLORD PRINTED IN U.S.A.

Abnormal Psychology

third edition

Ronald J. Comer
Princeton University

W. H. Freeman and Company
New York

To Hadaso and David Slotkin,
Always loving, always supportive,
always there

Executive Editor: *Susan Finnemore Brennan*
Development Editor: *John Haber*
Project Editor: *Kate Ahr*
Text and Cover Designer: *Blake Logan*
Cover Illustration: *Janet Hamlin*
Illustration Coordinator: *Susan Wein*
Illustration: *Academy Art Works, Inc.; Network Graphics; Patrice M. Rossi*
Photo Researchers: *Kathy Bendo, Larry Marcus*
Production Coordinator: *Maura Studley*
Composition: *Progressive Information Technologies*
Manufacturing: *Von Hoffman Press, Inc.*
Senior Marketing Manager: *Kate Steinbacher*

Excerpt from *An Unquiet Mind* by Kay Redfield Jamison. Copyright © 1995 by Kay Redfield Jamison. Reprinted by permission of Alfred A. Knopf, Inc.

Library of Congress Cataloging-in-Publication Data

Comer, Ronald J.
Abnormal psychology / Ronald J. Comer.—3rd ed.
p. cm.
Includes bibliographical references and index.
ISBN 0-7167-3089-8 (alk. paper)
1. Psychology, Pathological. I. Title
RC454.C634 1998 97-25100
616.89—dc21 CIP

© 1992, 1995, 1998 by W. H. Freeman and Company. All rights reserved.

No part of this book may be reproduced by any mechanical, photographic, or electronic process, or in the form of a phonographic recording, nor may it be stored in a retrieval system, transmitted, or otherwise copied for public or private use, without written permission from the publisher.

Printed in the United States of America

First printing, 1997

Contents in Brief

Contents

M016015

Preface

Writing a preface is actually the final stage of a long process. As I reach this point, I experience great exhilaration and, at the same time, a sense of barely making it—like a marathon runner crawling to the finish line. But most of all, I feel great satisfaction. This book, I believe, can truly open the doors of abnormal psychology for students. I think it will help them experience my own excitement and fascination with the field, my respect for its practitioners and researchers, and my deep regard for individuals faced with psychological problems.

Continuing Strengths

In writing each new edition, I have introduced new features, topics, and insights, and I have updated the book completely. My goal has also been to maintain the strengths of early editions:

- ***Breadth and balance*** The many theories, studies, disorders, and treatments are presented completely and accurately. *All* major models—psychological, biological, and sociocultural—receive objective, balanced, up-to-date coverage, without bias toward any single approach.

- ***Humanity*** The subject of abnormal psychology is people—very often people in great pain. I have therefore tried to write always with humanity and to affect students. The book speaks with a single voice, in clear and straightforward language—the main advantage of a single-author book.

Of course, I am slightly biased, but I believe that the new edition achieves these goals, and reviewers of draft manuscript, who have themselves been so very helpful, echo this belief. Let me therefore briefly highlight the features continued from previous editions:

Community Therapy: The Sociocultural Model in Action Persons who are traumatized by disasters, victimization, or accidents may profit from many of the treatments applied to survivors of combat stress. In addition, because their traumas occur in their own community, where mental health resources are close at hand, these individuals may respond well to immediate, active community interventions. Compelling examples are the rapidly mobilized community care programs now offered by mental health professionals across the United States to victims of large-scale disasters.

For years the American Red Cross has provided food, shelter, and clothing needed by survivors of disasters such as hurricanes and earthquakes, and the federal

p. 228

■ ***Integrated treatment*** Treatment is an essential part of the field—and the part that often interests readers most—and I therefore carefully integrate it throughout the book. I again give a complete overview of treatment in the opening chapters. Students then learn about treatment in the context of each mental disorder.

■ ***Cross-cultural and gender coverage*** The text examines cross-cultural and gender issues in diagnosis, treatment, and research, as well as legal and economic influences on clinical practice. For that reason, I integrate sociocultural models on an equal footing with the other major models of psychological abnormality, beginning in Chapter 4.

1993, 1987). In the following statement a woman who survived her leap from a tall building describes her dichotomous thinking at the time. She saw death as the only alternative to her pain:

> I was so desperate. I felt, my God, I couldn't face this thing. Everything was like a terrible whirlpool of confusion. And I thought to myself: There's only one thing to do. I just have to lose consciousness. That's the only way to get away from it. The only way to lose consciousness, I thought, was to jump off something good and high. . . .

p. 315

■ ***Chapters of special interest*** I devote full chapters to eating disorders and suicide. Both are of enormous importance to college-age readers.

■ ***Rich case material*** I integrate numerous clinical examples, to bring theoretical and clinical issues to life.

■ ***Adaptability*** Chapters are self-contained, so that they can be assigned in whatever order makes sense to the professor. They can also be made optional without affecting a student's grasp of basic concepts.

■ ***Consistent pedagogical aids*** Each chapter begins with a topical outline and an overview, contains summary tables, and concludes with a detailed summary. For this edition I have rewritten concluding summaries in outline form, to help students sort out the key questions.

TABLE 7-1 **Anxiety Disorders Profile**

	One-year prevalence	*Female : male ratio*	*Typical age at onset*	*Prevalence among close relatives*
Panic disorder	2.3%	5:2	15–35 years	Elevated
Obsessive compulsive disorder	2.0%	1:1	4–25 years	Elevated
Acute and posttraumatic stress disorders	0.5%	1:1	Variable	Unknown

Source: APA, 1994; Kessler et al., 1994; Regier et al., 1993; Blazer et al., 1991; Davidson et al., 1991; Eaton et al., 1991.

p. 199

■ ***Boxes*** Students should have the chance to think critically about concepts and issues as they apply in ordinary life. For that reason, I again include many boxes, often on controversial topics making the news.

■ ***Stimulating illustrations*** Chapters illustrate concepts, disorders, treatment, and applications with many photographs, diagrams, and graphs. I supply detailed captions, to make the point of illustrations clear, interesting, and self-contained. All graphs and tables, many new to this edition, reflect the most up-to-date data available.

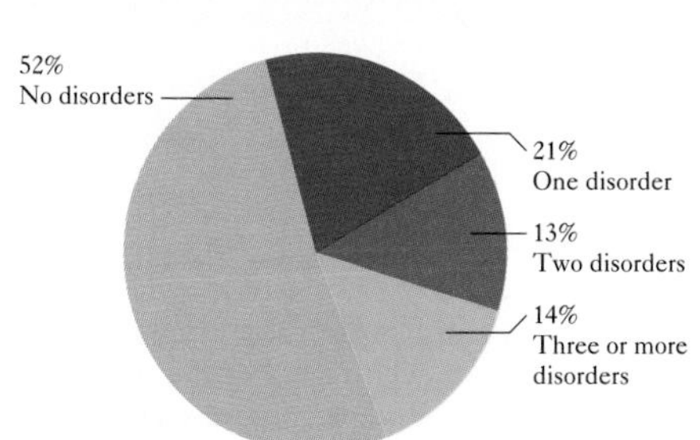

Figure 5-7 *How many people in the United States qualify for a DSM diagnosis during their lives? Almost half, according to one survey. In fact, 27 percent meet the criteria for two or more different disorders. In some cases these individuals even experience their disorders simultaneously, an occurrence known as "comorbidity." (Adapted from Kessler et al., 1994.)*

p. 139

Features New to This Edition

"If it ain't broke, don't fix it." That bit of wisdom also applies to psychology textbooks, but only up to a point. When a book is so well received, it is tempting to approach changes cautiously. Yet new pedagogical insights emerge almost daily. I have tried to listen carefully to professors and students using previous editions. I have reworked chapters sentence by sentence so that students can more easily follow important points. I have also introduced fresh strategies to help them find their way through their study of abnormal psychology and to assess its beliefs and practices critically.

■ ***"Thought and Afterthought"*** At the end of each chapter, a full page presents a fresh look at events in the world around us. This feature challenges readers to *think critically* about what they have learned and *apply it* in their own world. Each chapter's "Thought and Afterthought" opens with stories from today's headlines. Among them are the suicides by the Heaven's Gate cult, the epidemic of Mad Cow Disease, and charges of sexual harassment against a six-year-old. After each story, an "afterthought" poses critical questions, in an exciting context that helps students to understand, use, and retain what they have learned.

Thought and Afterthought

The David Helfgott Story: When Labels Fail

The Australian pianist David Helfgott burst onto the world stage during the winter of 1997. The story of his journey from a boy piano prodigy to a deeply troubled and dysfunctional young man and finally to an inspirational concert performer was told in the popular movie *Shine*. People everywhere were moved and fascinated by his plight, and many attended his sold-out concerts in cities throughout the world.

Everyone who has seen *Shine* is familiar with Helfgott's symptoms, including his repeated hugs, hyperspeed commentary, and self-addressed pep talk—for example, "It's awesome it's awesome it's awesome," (Chang & Gates, 1997, p. 62).

Less clear to everyone is what these symptoms add up to. Stories about Helfgott speak vaguely of a "mental, or nervous, breakdown." His wife, Gillian, describes him as "delightfully eccentric." His psychiatrist notes, "He's not autistic, not schizophrenic, and may be manic only in the colloquial rather than the clinical sense," (Chang & Gates, 1997, p. 63). The absence of a clear diagnostic label does not seem to trouble anyone, however. If anything, it adds to Helfgott's charm and to the public's fascination with him.

Afterthoughts: Why is a clear diagnostic label of Helfgott's problem so elusive? . . . How may the lack of a diagnostic label be helping people to see Helfgott as a person rather than a disorder? . . . Does the public's fascination with Helfgott and attendance at his concerts reflect their empathy and admiration, or, as some claim, simple curiosity?

p. 153

Crossroads

The tendency to combine concepts and interventions from various models has been even more apparent with regard to the remaining anxiety disorders—panic disorder, obsessive-compulsive disorder, and stress disorders. Over the past fifteen years truly enormous progress has been made in the understanding and treatment of these disorders. We shall turn to this very promising work in Chapter 7.

p. 193

■ ***"Crossroads"*** A concluding section in each chapter also brings together the principles and findings of the various models of abnormality. A "Crossroads" is a place where roads come together. It is also where we stand on the brink of a new journey. The new section, which falls just before the chapter summary, will serve as both. It asks whether the competing models can work together, in a more integrated approach. It clarifies what every chapter already implies—that competing models can often complement each other to produce deeper insights and more effective treatment. It helps students sort out critically the strengths and limitations of apparently conflicting ideas. Finally, it conveys a sense of where the field stands and where it may well be going.

Personal Pathways

Albert Ellis: Clinician Heal Thyself

Rational-emotive therapy teaches clients to challenge and change their irrational assumptions. And who was the first client treated by Albert Ellis, the founder of the approach? Why, none other than Albert Ellis (Warga, 1988, p. 56):

p. 170

■ ***"Personal Pathways"*** This feature offers a first-hand look at personal events that have shaped the lives and careers of some of the field's most distinguished figures. "Personal Pathways" discuss Albert Ellis and his self-treatment for social anxiety, Kay Jamison and her triumph over bipolar disorder, E. Fuller Torrey and his compassion for his sister with schizophrenia, and other practitioners.

Changes in Coverage and Organization

The clinical field itself is not content with modest change. It grows by leaps and bounds with each year, and readers need to learn about the exciting new directions right along with the old. I have therefore made significant changes to help readers better appreciate abnormal psychology:

■ ***A fully updated text*** I have thoroughly updated and, where appropriate, rewritten the third edition. Data, studies, theories, topics, and trends that have emerged during the last three years are added throughout. New topics in text and boxes include college binge drinking, the rise in Ritalin use, "treatment" on the Internet, Munchausen's syndrome by proxy, the melatonin craze, and the psychology of serial murderers. This is, without question, a textbook that accompanies the field into the twenty-first century.

■ ***Expanded sociocultural coverage*** I have further emphasized the text's special attention to sociocultural issues. Chapters now designate sociocultural explanations and treatments more explicitly. Additional coverage and boxes focus on the historical use of labeling to suppress groups of individuals (Chapters 5 and 20), gender and depression (Chapter 8), race differences in body image and eating behavior (Chapter 12), and other issues.

BOX 2-2 Gender, Race, and Age Bias in Research

Sometimes mistakes are committed by an entire community of researchers. Blinded by their own social biases, investigators may consistently err in their efforts to design appropriate studies. For example, for many years scientists in Western society have favored the use of young white men as subjects for research on human functioning (Blumenthal, 1996; Gannon et al., 1992; Stark-Adamek, 1992). Only recently have researchers come to appreciate the extent to which some of

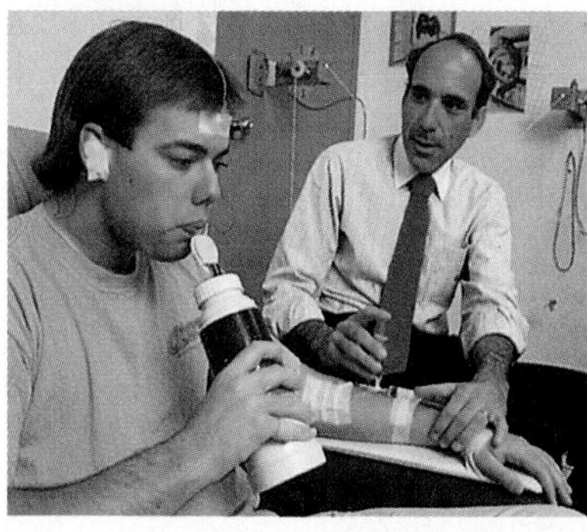

Over the years, most medical and psychological studies have used young white men as subjects. Findings from these studies may not, however, always apply to women, elderly persons, or

and foreign-born Asians metabolize the antipsychotic drug haloperidol (Haldol), prescribed for many people with schizophrenia, much faster than white Americans do (Goodman, 1992). This finding suggests that Asian American patients require lower doses of this drug in order to achieve the same effect, yet until recent years they have been started on the same dosage as white Americans.

The need to correct this kind of research bias is much more than a mere academic

p. 42

■ ***Earlier integration of treatment*** Treatment is now integrated into the text from the outset, rather than occupying a separate introductory chapter that some classes might have to omit. Chapter 1 defines treatment along with psychological abnormality and discusses past views of treatment. Chapters 3 and 4 then discuss the different approaches to treatment along with the models of abnormality. Chapter 5 concludes with an extensive overview of how (and whether) treatment works. The new arrangement is more efficient for the classroom and clearer for students. It prepares them fully for coverage of treatment in chapters on particular disorders.

■ ***More coverage of stress disorders*** I have separated coverage of anxiety disorders into two chapters. The new division recognizes the growing importance of stress and the stress disorders, as well as sociocultural and gender issues increasingly relevant to both. Chapter 6 takes up generalized anxiety disorder and phobias, and Chapter 7 considers panic, obsessive-compulsive, and stress disorders, including stress caused by victimization and abuse. Treatment is now integrated into each of these chapters, rather than separated as in previous editions.

■ ***A life-span chapter*** I have streamlined coverage of life-span problems, perhaps most obviously by combining childhood disorders and problems of old age into a single chapter.

■ ***Sole authorship*** I have written the coverage of sexual disorders, previously contributed by Joseph LoPiccolo of the University of Missouri, Columbia, and the coverage of the problems of aging, previously contributed by Dolores Gallagher-Thompson and Larry Wolford Thompson, both of Stanford University and the Palo Alto Veteran Affairs Medical Center. However, I have continued to rely on them for guidance, and am most especially grateful to Joe for his careful review.

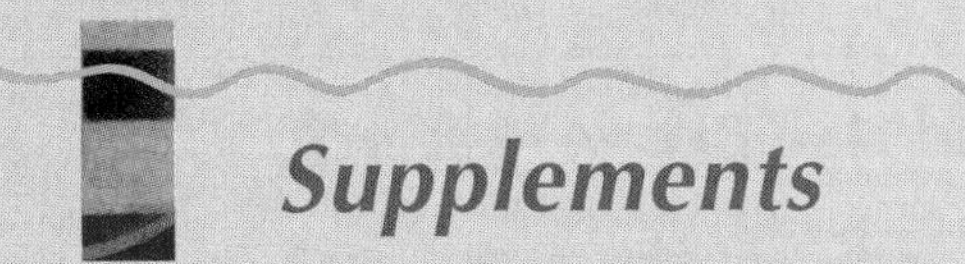

Supplements

The response to supplements accompanying previous editions has been gratifying. This edition is able to retain them, and also to add new ones—including two innovative multimedia supplements. Like the textbook, the entire package can therefore look to the coming century:

■ Our unique new ***Student CD-ROM*** adds depth to the students' understanding of abnormal psychology. The CD offers intriguing "video investigations" running three to five minutes each. Videos usually center on a person with a disorder that is discussed in the text. The students first view the video and then answer a series of thought-provoking questions about it. Their answers can be entered directly on screen and then saved to a disk or printed out to be handed in. Additionally, the CD contains a multiple-choice self-quiz for every chapter. Quizzes have built-in instructional feedback for every option and a page reference for each question. Another useful CD feature is a comprehensive set of web links relating to the content of each chapter of the text. With the user's web browser, the links launch the user directly to these web sites. The link feature ties the CD to the book's *Web Site* (please see below). It will offer updates to the web links as well as many other features for the lifetime of the text's Third Edition.

■ The inspiration for our *Student CD* was our remarkably popular ***Video Segments for Abnormal Psychology*** created for instructors using the Second Edition of the text. The warm response has made it a pleasure to add a third cassette of *Video Segments* for the new edition, bringing our total number of offerings to over 70 video segments. I selected the new clips in response to instructors' suggestions for topics they would like to see added to the series. Like the original clips, the new segments are designed to introduce an added dimension to lectures in one- to eight-minute bursts. They illustrate key aspects of abnormal psychology that are sometimes difficult to describe with words and static visual materials alone—including clinical topics, pathologies, current and historical treatments, laboratory experiments, clinical dilemmas, and the client/therapist relationship. A special *Video Guide* to using the segments is included in the *Instructor's Manual* (please see below).

■ A comprehensive printed ***Test Bank,*** by Melvyn B. King of the State University of New York at Cortland, Debra E. Clark of the New Medico Rehabilitation Center of Cortland, and me, offers roughly 2000 multiple-choice and 400 fill-in questions. We have graded each question according to difficulty, identified it as factual or applied, and keyed it to the page in the text where the source information appears.

■ ***Computerized Test Banks*** provide the questions in both Windows and Macintosh test-making software.

■ A new full-color ***Overhead Transparency Set*** makes fifty key diagrams and graphs from the text available for use in lectures. Additionally, there are many black-and-white transparency masters of text tables and DSM-IV criteria listings available in the *Instructor's Manual.*

■ Abnormal psychology is a field in which important new information appears continually. This is why we offer adopters of the text periodic ***Update Newsletters*** prepared by Greg Neimeyer of the University of Florida. The *Newsletters* provide timely updates in research in the context of the book's coverage.

■ The ***Student Workbook,*** by Katherine M. Nicolai of Rockhurst College, actively involves students in the text material, using a variety of engaging exercises. Students who complete the exercises can better organize and apply what they have studied.

■ The ***Instructor's Manual and Video Guide,*** by Fred W. Whitford of Montana State University and me, ties together this wide-ranging supplements package for instructors and their teaching assistants. It offers strategies for using the *Video Segments, Student CD-ROM, Web Site,* and transparencies. It also includes detailed chapter outlines, lists of principal learning objectives, and ideas for lectures and launching class discussions. In response to many requests, it also lays out precise DSM-IV criteria for each of the disorders discussed in the text and offers most of this material in transparency masters. The *Video Guide* material was specially prepared. It describes each of the *Video Segments* and offers recommendations for their use.

■ Finally, our new ***Web Site*** offers an ever-expanding set of resources for both students and instructors. In addition to the web links and the coverage updates described above (please see *Student CD* and *Newsletters*), the site offers a variety of other features including another multiple-choice self-quiz for every chapter with

built-in instructional feedback (the *Student CD* has the other self-quizzes) and potential research questions utilizing the web links for each chapter. The Web offers exciting possibilities, and we will take advantage of this by continually updating our *Web Site* and expanding its features. We welcome you to regularly visit it during your use of this book. New and updated material will be specially marked. The address is:
http://www.whfreeman.com/abnormalpsychology

Acknowledgments

I am enormously grateful to the many people who have contributed to writing and producing this book. To begin, my sincere gratitude goes to Meath Bowen, Gretchen Rickards, John Beaver, Greg Comer, and Amy Dierberger, all extremely talented individuals who did research and helped with drafts of boxes and sections of the book. Their accomplishments were truly outstanding. I also greatly appreciate the hard work of the book's conscientious research assistants, including Linda Chamberlin, Jon Comer, and Amy Chris.

I particularly thank Marlene Comer (whose last name is more than a coincidence) for her never-ending, superb work on every aspect of the manuscript, from editorial judgments to typing. In addition, I am greatly indebted to Marion Kowalewski for her outstanding work on the manuscript, Marlene Catania, for her fine work on the references, as well as to the wonderful help of Arlene Kronewitter, Vera Sohl, Arlene Kerch, Elaine Russo, Carol Zaffarese, and Bernie VanUiter.

Throughout three editions, I have received valuable feedback from academicians and clinicians, who have reviewed portions of the manuscript and commented on its clarity, accuracy, and completeness. Their collective knowledge, and their willingness to share it with me, have in large part shaped the third edition. I am of course indebted to those who reviewed the manuscript of the new edition:

E. M. Coles, *Simon Fraser University*
Frederick L. Coolidge, *University of Colorado, Colorado Springs*
Mary Dozier, *University of Delaware*
Morton G. Harmatz, *University of Massachusetts*
William G. Iacono, *University of Minnesota*
Kimberlyn Leary, *University of Michigan*
Arnold D. LeUnes, *Texas A&M University*
Mary Margaret Livingston, *Louisiana Technical University*
Joseph LoPiccolo, *University of Missouri, Columbia*
Jerald J. Marshall, *University of Central Florida*
Janet R. Matthews, *Loyola University*
F. Dudley McGlynn, *Auburn University*
Lily D. McNair, *University of Georgia*
Daniel Paulson, *Carthage College*
Lynn P. Rehm, *University of Houston*
Sandra T. Sigmon, *University of Maine, Orono*
John M. Spores, *Purdue University, South Central*

I also wish to thank the many professors and clinicians around the country who offered special counsel on the third edition, through personal communication with me and reviews of the second edition: Eric W. Corty, Pennsylvania State University at Erie; Lenore E. DeFonso, Indiana University, Purdue University at Indianapolis; Marilyn S. Denninger, Monmouth University; Victoria Follette, University of Nevada; Jon E. Frew, Washington State University at Vancouver; Robert W. Hill, Appalachian State University; Carolin Keutzer, University of Oregon; Kenneth McGill, William Patterson College; Jeffrey Scott Mio, California State University, Pomona; Joseph Palladino, University of Southern Indiana; Patricia Port, Paradise Valley Community College; Roger N. Reeb, University of Dayton; Patricia J. Sawyer, Middlesex Community Technical College; George W. Shardlow, City College of San Francisco; David E. Silber, George Washington University; Susan Williams-Quinlan, University of Scranton; and Amy R. Wolfson, College of the Holy Cross. I would also like to express special thanks to E. Fuller Torrey for contributing his personal experiences and insights for the *Personal Pathways* feature in Chapter 16.

I acknowledge once again the reviewers of earlier editions. Their contributions remain integral to the quality of the revision: Kent G. Bailey, Virginia Commonwealth University; Marna S. Barnett, Indiana University of Pennsylvania; Otto A. Berliner, Alfred State College; Allan Berman, University of Rhode Island; Douglas Bernstein, University of Toronto, Mississauga; Sarah Cirese, College of Marin; Victor B. Cline, University of Utah; S. Wayne Duncan, University of Washington, Seattle; Morris N. Eagle, York University;

Alan Fridlund, University of California, Santa Barbara; Stan Friedman, Southwest Texas State University; Lawrence L. Galant, Gaston College; David A. Hoffman, University of California, Santa Cruz; Bernard Kleinman, University of Missouri, Kansas City; Alan G. Krasnoff, University of Missouri, St. Louis; Robert D. Langston, University of Texas, Austin; Harvey R. Lerner, Kaiser-Permanente Medical Group; Michael P. Levine, Kenyon College; Robert J. McCaffrey, State University of New York, Albany; Katherine M. Nicolai, Iowa State University; Paul A. Payne, University of Cincinnati; David V. Perkins, Ball State University; Norman Poppel, Middlesex County College; David E. Powley, University of Mobile; Max W. Rardin, University of Wyoming, Laramie; Leslie A. Rescorla, Bryn Mawr College; Vic Ryan, University of Colorado, Boulder; A. A. Sappington, University of Alabama, Birmingham; Roberta S. Sherman, Bloomington Center for Counseling and Human Development; Janet A. Simons, Central Iowa Psychological Services; Jay R. Skidmore, Utah State University; Thomas A. Tutko, San Jose State University; Norris D. Vestre, Arizona State University; Joseph L. White, University of California, Irvine; and Amy C. Willis, Washington, D.C., Veterans Administration Medical Center.

The authors of the book's support package have my thanks for again doing splendid jobs with their respective supplements. They are: Melvyn B. King, of the State University of New York at Cortland, and Debra E. Clark for the Test Bank and Web Site; Katherine M. Nicolai, of Rockhurst College for the Student Workbook; Greg Neimeyer, of the University of Florida, for the Newsletters; and Fred W. Whitford, of Montana State University, for the Instructor's Manual, Web Site, and Student CD-ROM. My thanks also go to Janet A. Simons, of the University of Iowa, for her outstanding work on the Instructor's Manual to the first two editions of the text.

Many at W. H. Freeman have worked tirelessly and diligently to produce this book. John Haber, the development editor, has been a close friend, wise advisor, and gifted teacher over two years. I have especially appreciated his caring and gentle manner, superior insights, and writing skills. He has taught me much about writing, and the book and I are both better for his guidance. Kate Ahr, the project editor, has displayed a remarkable mix of intelligence, energy, and grace under fire. Guiding a book through production is one of life's most difficult jobs, and Kate's ability and delightful personality were ever present. Blake Logan, the book's designer, has made the book beautiful, stimulating, and enriching. Every page reflects her taste and artistic skill. Kathy Bendo, the book's photo researcher, worked with energy, organization, and talent to find just the right photographs to bring the subject to life. I appreciate her tireless efforts and commitment to excellence. Susan Finnemore Brennan, Freeman's psychology editor, managed every aspect of the new edition, once again with her extraordinary skill, enthusiasm, and commitment. Oh, and while doing that she gave birth to another project as well, named Katie.

In addition, I would like to thank Elizabeth Widdicombe, president of W. H. Freeman; Robert L. Biewen, chairman of the Scientific American/St. Martin's College Publishing Group; Mary Shuford, director of development; Philip McCaffrey, managing editor; Barbara Salazar, copy editor; Louise Ketz and Bernice Soltysik, indexers; Eleanor Wedge, proofreader; Beverly Wehrli, reference editor; Larry Marcus, assistant photo editor, who just keeps digging and digging until he gets his photo; Nancy Giraldo Walker, rights and permissions manager; Maura Studley, production coordinator; Susan Wein, illustration coordinator; and Diana Gill, Maia Holden, and Jon Dowling, editorial assistants. I wish to mention in particular Patrick Shriner, supplements editor, whose astute pedagogical insights have led once again to an extraordinary and innovative supplements package, and Robert Christie, associate supplements editor, who has worked so effectively on the current package. I also wish to thank Marie Schappert, vice-president and director of sales; Kate Steinbacher, senior marketing manager; and Freeman's sales representatives, who have enthusiastically embraced each edition of this book and brought it skillfully to the attention of professors across North America. I want particularly to note the talents of those special people in the sales organization who have worked with me since the book's inception—Carol Gainsforth, Julie Hirshman, Dave Kennedy, Patti Mallardi, Sandy Manly, Chris Spavins, and Cindi Weiss. I deeply appreciate their astute judgments and warm friendship. Finally, I wish to mention, all too briefly, members of the core team from previous editions, particularly Linda Chaput, Moira Lerner, Diane Maass, Jonathan Cobb, and Travis Amos. Their work continues to live on in this one—and in my heart.

Like all previous editions, a project of this magnitude would be impossible in the absence of a loving and supportive family, and I am truly grateful to mine. I again thank my mother, Claire; sister, Pam; and brother, Steve, whose love and respect have been an enduring and motivating presence in my life; and my very special parents-in-law, Hadaso and David Slotkin. Similarly, I thank my wonderful sons, Greg and Jon, who continue to fill my life with pride, laughter, joy, and love. And, of course, I thank Annie, my dog, who has taught me the virtues of unconditional love, loyalty, and patience.

This is the fourth time I have sat down to write the book's preface, counting three editions and my shorter textbook, *Fundamentals of Abnormal Psychology*. In the first edition, I noted the thrill of watching my children grow. In the second, I stated my admiration for my father and the life he led. Here I'd like to say briefly to my wife, Marlene Slotkin Comer, how much I love and appreciate her. I know at the age of 50, more than I could ever have recognized at age 21, how fortunate I am that she is my partner in life. My life is always enriched, my joys enhanced, and my sorrows softened by her presence and her gentle, generous spirit.

Ronald J. Comer
Princeton University
September 1997

Topic Overview

Chapter 1

Abnormal Psychology: Past and Present

"Psychological abnormality" is a loose term for the wide spectrum of problems that seem to have their roots in the human brain or mind. It crosses all boundaries—cultural, economic, emotional, and intellectual. It affects the famous and the obscure, the rich and the poor, the upright and the perverse. Politicians, actors, writers, and other public icons of the present and the past have struggled with psychological problems. Such problems can bring great suffering, but they can also be the source of inspiration and energy.

Because they are so ubiquitous and so personal, psychological problems capture the interest of us all. Hundreds of novels, plays, films, and television programs have explored what many people see as the dark side of human nature, and self-help books flood the market. Psychologists and psychiatrists are popular guests on both television and radio, and some even have their own shows and encourage troubled people to call or to appear for instant advice.

The Surgeon, *by Jan Saunders van Hemessen, reminds us that demonological beliefs dominated the study and treatment of abnormal behavior until recent times. As far back as the Stone Age, people viewed abnormality as the work of evil spirits, and "practitioners" sometimes opened a person's skull to release the spirits.*

The field devoted to the scientific study of the abnormal behavior we find so fascinating is usually called ***abnormal psychology.*** As in the other sciences, workers in this field, called ***clinical scientists,*** gather information systematically so that they may describe, predict, explain, and exert some control over the phenomena they study. The knowledge that they acquire is then used by a wide variety of ***clinical practitioners*** to detect, assess, and treat abnormal patterns of functioning.

Although their general goals are similar to those of other scientific professionals, clinical scientists and practitioners confront problems that make their work especially difficult. One of the most troubling problems is that psychological abnormality is extremely hard to define.

Defining Psychological Abnormality

Miriam cries herself to sleep every night. She is certain that the future holds nothing but misery. Indeed, this is the only thing she does feel certain about. "I'm going to die and my daughters are going to die. We're doomed. The world is ugly. I detest every moment of this life." She has great trouble sleeping. She is afraid to close her eyes, afraid that she will never wake up, and what will happen to her daughters then? When she does drift off to sleep, her dreams are nightmares filled with blood, dismembered bodies, thunder, decay, death, destruction.

One morning Miriam has trouble getting out of bed. The thought of facing another day overwhelms her. Again she wishes she were dead, and she wishes her daughters were dead. "We'd all be better off." She feels paralyzed by her depression and anxiety, too tired to move and too afraid to leave her house. She decides once again to stay home and to keep her daughters with her. She makes sure that all shades are drawn and that every conceivable entrance to the house is secured. She is afraid of the world and afraid of life. Every day is the same, filled with depression, fear, immobility, and withdrawal. Every day is a nightmare.

During the past year Brad has been hearing mysterious voices that tell him to quit his job, leave his family, and prepare for the coming invasion. These voices have brought tremendous confusion and emotional turmoil to Brad's life. He believes that they come from beings in distant parts of the universe who are somehow wired to him. Although it gives him a sense of purpose and specialness to be the chosen target of their communications, they also make him tense and anxious. He dreads the coming invasion. When he refuses an order, the voices insult and threaten him and turn his days into a waking nightmare.

Brad has put himself on a sparse diet against the possibility that his enemies may be contaminating his food. He has found a quiet apartment far from his old haunts where he has laid in a good stock of arms and ammunition. His family and friends have tried to reach out to Brad, to understand his problems, and to dissuade him from the disturbing course he is taking. Every day, however, he retreats further into his world of mysterious voices and imagined dangers.

Miriam and Brad are the kinds of people we think of when abnormal behavior is mentioned. Most of us would probably label their emotions, thoughts, and behavior as abnormal, reflections of a state sometimes called *psychopathology, maladjustment, emotional disturbance,* or *mental illness.*

But are the responses of Miriam and Brad abnormal, and if so, why? What is it about their thoughts, emotions, and behavior that might lead us to this conclusion? Many definitions of abnormal mental functioning, or psychological abnormality, have been proposed over the years, but none of them has won universal acceptance. Still, most of the definitions do have common features, often called "the four D's": deviance, distress, dysfunction, and danger. That is, patterns of mental dysfunctioning are those that, in a given context, are ***deviant***—different, extreme, unusual, perhaps even bizarre; ***distressful,*** or unpleasant and upsetting to the individual; ***dysfunctional,*** or disruptive to the person's ability to conduct daily activities in a constructive manner; and possibly ***dangerous.*** This definition provides a useful starting point from which to explore the phenomena of psychological abnormality. As we shall see, however, it has significant limitations.

Deviance

Abnormal mental functioning is functioning that is *deviant,* but deviant from what? Miriam's behavior, thoughts, and emotions are different from those that are considered normal in our place and time. We do not expect normal people to cry themselves to sleep every night, to wish themselves dead, or to endure paralyzing depression and anxiety. Similarly, Brad's obedience to voices that no one else can hear contradicts our expectation that normal people perceive only the material world accessible to everyone's five senses.

In short, abnormal behavior, thoughts, and emotions are those that violate a society's ideas about proper functioning. Each society establishes ***norms***—explicit

Along the Niger River, men of the Wodaabe tribe don elaborate makeup and costumes to attract women. In Western society, the same behavior would violate behavioral norms and probably be judged abnormal.

and implicit rules for appropriate conduct. Behavior that violates legal norms is called criminal. Behavior, thoughts, and emotions that violate norms of psychological functioning are called abnormal. Typically, the norms of psychological functioning focus on conduct that is common in a society, such as our society's expectations that people will remember important events in their lives. Sometimes, however, a society may value certain psychological deviations, such as superior intelligence and extreme selflessness, and may include these forms of functioning within its norms.

This focus on social values as a yardstick for measuring deviance suggests that judgments of abnormality vary from society to society. A society's norms emerge from its particular ***culture***—its history, values, institutions, habits, skills, technology, and arts. Thus a society whose culture places great value on competition and assertiveness may accept aggressive behavior, whereas one that highly values courtesy, cooperation, and gentleness may consider aggressive behavior unacceptable and even abnormal. A society's values may also change over time, causing its views of what is psychologically abnormal to change as well. In Western society, for example, a woman's participation in the business or professional world was considered inappropriate and strange a hundred years ago, but today the same behavior is valued.

Judgments of abnormality depend on *specific circumstances* as well as on psychological norms. The description of Miriam, for example, might lead us to conclude that she is functioning abnormally. Certainly her unhappiness is more intense and pervasive than that of most of the people we encounter every day. Before you conclude that this woman's emotions and behaviors are abnormal, however, consider that Miriam lives in Lebanon, a country pulled apart by years of combat. The happiness she once knew with her family vanished when her husband and son were killed. Miriam used to tell herself that the fighting had to end soon, but as year follows year with only temporary respites, she has stopped expecting anything except more of the same.

In this light, Miriam's reactions do not seem inappropriate. If anything is abnormal here, it is her situation. Sometimes overwhelming or unusual situations elicit reactions that appear abnormal out of context but are understandable in the surroundings in which they occur. Many things in our world elicit intense reactions—large-scale catastrophes and disasters, rape, child abuse, war, terminal illness, and chronic pain (Turner & Lloyd, 1995). Is there an "appropriate" way to react to such things? Should we ever call reactions to them abnormal?

As we shall see in Chapter 5, today's leading diagnostic system holds that some people's reactions to traumatic events are indeed excessive, and assigns such cases to the category of either *acute stress disorder* or *posttraumatic stress disorder.* Many theorists deny the merits of these categories, however, arguing that there is no such thing as an excessive reaction to brutality or catastrophe.

Distress

Even functioning that is considered unusual and inappropriate in a given context does not necessarily qualify as abnormal. According to many clinical theorists, one's behavior, ideas, or emotions usually have to cause one *distress* before they can be labeled abnormal. Consider the Ice Breakers, a group of people in Michigan who go swimming in lakes throughout the state every weekend from November through February. The colder the weather, the better they like it. One man, a member of the group for seventeen years, says he loves the challenge. Man against the elements. Mind over matter. A 37-year-old lawyer believes that the weekend shock is good for her health. "It cleanses me," she says. "It perks me up and gives me strength for the week ahead." Another avid Ice Breaker likes the special feelings the group brings to him. "When we get together, we know we've shared something special, something no one else understands. I can't even tell most of the people I know that I'm an Ice Breaker. They wouldn't want anything to do with me. A few people think I'm a space cadet."

Certainly these people are different from most of us, but is this behavior abnormal? Far from experiencing distress, they feel invigorated and challenged. Their lack

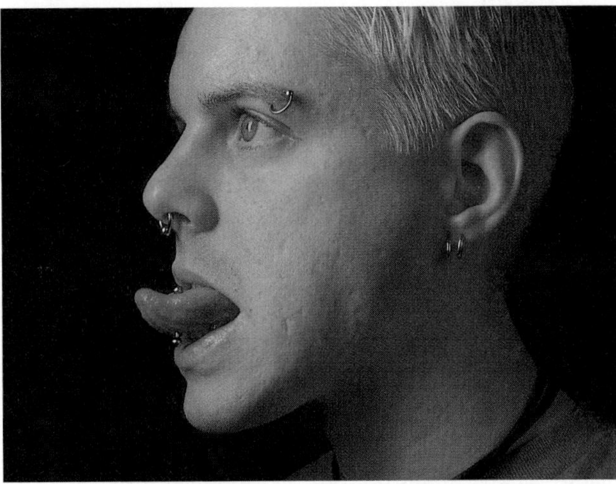

As society's norms change, so do its judgments of abnormality. A decade ago, extreme body piercing was considered a form of self-mutilation, and deemed abnormal. In today's fashion world, clinicians must pause before drawing such conclusions.

of internal distress must cause us to hesitate before we conclude that these people are functioning abnormally.

Should we conclude, then, that feelings of distress must always be present before a person's functioning can be considered abnormal? Not necessarily. Some people who function abnormally may maintain a relatively positive frame of mind. Consider once again Brad, the young man who hears mysterious voices. Brad does experience severe distress over the coming invasion and the changes he feels forced to make in the way he lives. But what if he felt no such anxiety? What if he greatly enjoyed listening to the voices, felt honored to be chosen, and looked forward to the formidable task of saving the world? Shouldn't we still consider his functioning abnormal? As we shall discover in Chapter 8, people whose behaviors are described as manic often feel just wonderful, yet still are diagnosed as psychologically disturbed. Indeed, in many cases it is their euphoria and disproportionate sense of well-being that make them candidates for this diagnosis.

Dysfunction

Abnormal behavior tends to be *dysfunctional;* that is, it interferes with daily functioning. It so upsets, distracts, or confuses its victims that they cannot care for themselves properly, participate in ordinary social relationships, or work effectively. Brad, for example, has quit his job, left his family, and prepared to withdraw from the productive and meaningful life he once led to an empty and isolated existence in a distant apartment.

Here again one's culture plays a role in the definition of abnormality. Our society holds that it is important to carry out daily activities in an effective, self-enhancing manner. Thus Brad's behavior is likely to be regarded as abnormal and undesirable, whereas that of the Ice Breakers, who continue to perform well at their jobs and maintain appropriate family and social relationships, would probably be considered unusual but not a sign of psychological abnormality.

Of course, dysfunction alone does not necessarily indicate psychological abnormality. Some people (Gandhi, Dick Gregory, and Cesar Chavez, for example) fast or in other ways deprive themselves of things they need as a means to protest social injustice. Far from receiving a clinical label of some kind, they are widely viewed as caring, sacrificing, even heroic.

Danger

Perhaps the ultimate in psychological dysfunctioning is behavior that becomes *dangerous* to oneself or others. A pattern of functioning that is marked by carelessness,

In the Val d'Isère, France, these students bury themselves in snow up to their necks. Far from experiencing distress, they are engaging in a Japanese practice designed to open their hearts and enlarge their spirits, so diagnosticians are unlikely to judge them to be abnormal.

poor judgment, hostility, or misinterpretation can jeopardize one's own well-being and that of many other people. Brad, for example, seems to be endangering himself by his diet and others by his stockpile of arms and ammunition.

Although danger to oneself or others is usually cited as a criterion of abnormal psychological functioning, research suggests that it is more often the exception than the rule (Junginger, 1996; Monahan, 1993, 1992; Swanson et al., 1990). Despite popular misconceptions, most people struggling with anxiety, depression, and even bizarre behavioral patterns pose no immediate danger to themselves or to anyone else.

Psychological Abnormality: An Elusive Concept

Efforts to define psychological abnormality typically raise as many questions as they answer. The major difficulty is that the very concept of abnormality is relative: it depends on the norms and values of the society in question. A society selects general criteria for defining abnormality and then interprets them in order to judge the normality or abnormality of each particular case.

Calling the concept of mental illness a "myth," the psychiatrist Thomas Szasz believes that societies apply the label to persons whose deviant behaviors confuse other people and may seem to threaten their emotional and physical well-being. According to Szasz (1961), "looking for evidence of illness is like searching for evidence of heresy: Once the investigator gets into the proper frame of mind, anything may seem to him to be a symptom of mental illness."

One clinical theorist, Thomas Szasz (1997, 1987, 1961), places such emphasis on society's role that he finds the whole concept of mental illness to be invalid, a myth of sorts. According to Szasz, the deviations that society calls abnormal are simply "problems in living," not signs of something inherently wrong within the person. Societies, he is convinced, invent the concept of mental illness to justify their efforts to control or change people whose unusual patterns of functioning threaten the social order. In extreme cases the category even serves to justify the removal of those individuals from society.

Even if we assume that psychological abnormality is a valid concept and that abnormalities are unhealthy, we may be unable to agree on a definition and to apply it consistently. If a behavior—excessive consumption of alcohol among college students, say—is common enough, society may fail to recognize it as deviant, distressful, dysfunctional, and dangerous. Thousands of college students throughout the United States are so dependent on alcohol that it interferes greatly with their personal and academic functioning, causes them significant discomfort, places their health in jeopardy, and even endangers them and the people around them. Yet their problem often goes unnoticed, certainly undiagnosed, by college administrators, other students, and health professionals. Alcohol consumption is so much a part of the college subculture that it is easy to overlook drinking behavior that has become abnormal.

Conversely, a society may have trouble distinguishing an abnormality that requires intervention from ***eccentricity,*** individuality that others have no right to interfere with. From time to time we see or hear about people who behave in ways we consider strange—a woman who keeps dozens of cats in her apartment or a man who lives alone and rarely talks to anyone. Their behavior is deviant, and it may well be distressful and dysfunctional, yet most professionals think of them as eccentric rather than abnormal (see Box 1-1).

In short, while we may agree that abnormal patterns of functioning are those that are deviant, distressful, dysfunctional, and sometimes dangerous in a given context, we should always be aware of the ambiguity and subjectivity of this definition. When is an unusual pattern deviant, distressful, dysfunctional, and dangerous *enough* to be considered abnormal? The question may be impossible to answer. Few of the current categories of abnormality that we will meet are as clear-cut as they may seem, and most of them continue to be debated within the clinical community (APA, 1994).

BOX 1-1 Marching to a Different Drummer: Eccentrics

Darla Shaw believes that it's immoral to throw anything away, so she still owns everything she has ever purchased or been given. In addition to vast amounts of what most people would consider to be ordinary garbage, she owns a good stock of theatrical costumes, a life-sized Santa on skis, a papier-mâché mermaid, stuffed alligators, and a portable shower that doubles as a telephone booth. Darla's hoard of earthly possessions finally grew to such vast proportions that she bought an abandoned opera house in order to have room for everything. Among her many other hobbies, Darla plays in a kazoo band. In winter, she wears a fireman's coat.

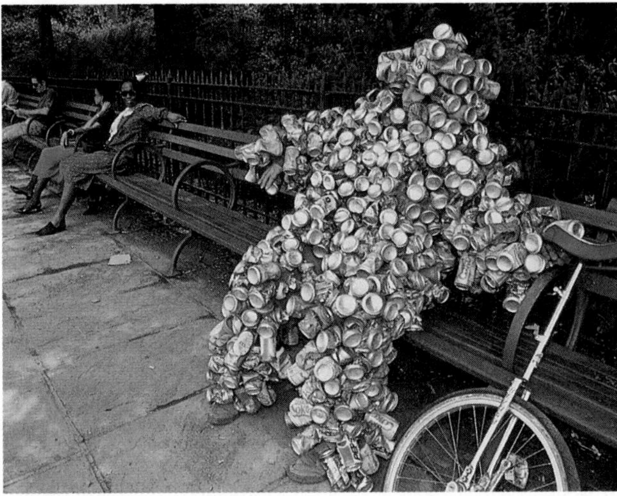

Gene Pool, a 37 year old carpenter, journeys repeatedly around New York City wearing an outfit made of 500 empty cans. The reason? To make a statement about the need for recycling and *to be noticed. He also wears other outfits—one made of grass, another of forks. Here he takes a much-needed break on a city park bench.*

Gary Holloway, an environmental planner in San Francisco, keeps a veritable stable of hobbyhorses. He is also fascinated by Martin Van Buren. . . . He discovered that Van Buren was the only U.S. president not to have a society dedicated to his memory, so he promptly founded the Van Buren Fan Club. Holloway is a lifelong devotee of St. Francis of Assisi, and frequently dresses in the habit of a Franciscan monk. "It's comfortable, fun to wear, and I like the response I get when I wear it," he explains. "People always offer me a seat on the bus."

John Slater is the only person ever to have walked from Land's End to John o'Groats in his bare feet, wearing only his striped pajamas and accompanied by his pet labrador Guinness. The dog, unlike his master, was shod, with two pairs of suede booties. Slater has been a Royal Marine bandsman, a truck driver, steward on a luxury yacht, social worker, salesman, insurance broker, waiter, driftwood artist, painter and decorator and fundraiser. He once volunteered to spend six months in a cage in London Zoo as a human exhibit, to help raise funds for the conservation of the panda, but the zoo authorities "foolishly declined." For most of the past ten years, Slater has lived in a cave, which is flooded with seawater at high tide. He says that he enjoys the "cathedral-like silence in caves, which helps me to think and work things out. . . . I'm nursing all this terrific idealism, always thinking about what I can do next."

(Weeks & James, 1995, pp. 29, 36-37, 189-190)

Darla Shaw, Gary Holloway, and John Slater may all be considered eccentrics. The dictionary defines an eccentric as a person who deviates from an established behavior pattern, or exhibits odd or whimsical behavior. But how can we differentiate between a psychologically healthy person who has unusual habits and a person whose oddness is a symptom of psychopathology? Is there a continuum of human behavior, with "normal" conformity at one end, eccentric nonconformity in the middle, and pathological deviance at the other end? Until recently, little psychological research existed on the nature of emotionally healthy eccentrics, but a lighthearted study by the researcher David Weeks (Weeks & James, 1995) has perhaps started the ball rolling. He estimates that as many as 2 in 10,000 people may be accounted "classic, full-time eccentrics," with equal distribution among the sexes.

After conducting in-depth interviews and administering IQ tests, personality questionnaires, and other diagnostic tests to 1,000 eccentrics over a ten-year period, he concluded that although eccentrics may be "loosely wrapped," they do not suffer from mental disorders. Both eccentrics and seriously disturbed persons display aberrant behavior, but the strangeness of persons with mental disorders is thrust upon them and typically causes them suffering, whereas eccentric behavior is chosen freely and provides pleasure. In short, "neurotics are miserable because they think they're not as good as everyone else, while eccentrics know they're different and glory in it" (Weeks & James, 1995, p. 14).

Similarly, while the workings of the eccentric mind may be peculiar, they are not the seriously disrupted thought processes of persons with severe mental disorders, and they do not make the eccentric dysfunctional. And while eccentrics may be passionate about their hobbies or causes, their interests are not compulsions but sources of fun and pleasure. Although the eccentrics in Weeks's study were not immune to mental disorders, they had a lower overall incidence of such problems than the general population. Perhaps being an "original" is good for mental health. The eccentrics in the study were also physically healthier than usual; on average, they visited a doctor only once every eight years.

Weeks concludes that most eccentrics, despite their deviant behavior—perhaps even because of it—are happy, well-adjusted, and joyful people. Since nonconformists are relieved of the stress of trying to meet other people's expectations, they are free to plunge through life in their own optimistic, individualistic way, undeterred by criticism or convention. In a culture that increasingly values homogeneity over uniqueness, the offbeat and spirited personalities of eccentrics are often a refreshing change.

Are You Eccentric?

David Weeks identifies the following fifteen descriptions (in descending order of importance) as applicable to eccentrics. Although the first five characterizations are most definitive, possessing any ten of the fifteen may qualify one as an eccentric.

- Nonconforming
- Creative
- Strongly curious
- Idealistic
- Happily obsessed with a hobby (often more than one)
- Aware from early childhood of being different from others
- Intelligent
- Opinionated and outspoken
- Noncompetitive
- Unusual eating or living habits
- Not interested in the opinions or company of others
- Mischievous sense of humor
- Single
- Eldest or only child
- Bad speller

Top Ten Places to Find Eccentrics

The Eccentrics in Weeks's study congregated in the West. The largest number of eccentrics appear to live in California.

1. California
2. Colorado
3. Minnesota
4. Texas
5. New Mexico
6. Oklahoma
7. Utah
8. Arizona
9. Montana
10. Alaska, Florida (tie)

(Based on Peterson, 1995)

Famous Eccentrics

James Joyce always carried a tiny pair of woman's bloomers, which he waved in the air to demonstrate approval.

Emily Dickinson always wore white, never left her room, and hid her poems in tiny boxes.

Benjamin Franklin took "air baths" for his health, sitting naked in front of an open window.

Alexander Graham Bell covered the windows of his house to keep out the rays of the full moon. He also tried to teach his dog how to talk.

Herbert Spencer, who coined the term "survival of the fittest," wore velvet earplugs and a self-designed bulky one-piece garment when he was at home. Friends said he resembled a "deaf bear."

(Weeks & James, 1995)

Defining Treatment

Once practitioners have identified a case of psychological abnormality, they want to treat it. ***Treatment*** is a procedure to help change abnormal behavior into more normal behavior; it, too, requires careful definition. For clinical scientists, the problem is closely related to defining abnormality. Consider the case of Bill:

> *February:* He cannot leave the house; Bill knows that for a fact. Home is the only place where he feels safe—safe from humiliation, danger, even ruin. If he were to go to work, his co-workers would somehow reveal their contempt for him. A pointed remark, a quizzical look—that's all it would take for him to get the message. If he were to go shopping at the store, before long everyone would be staring at him. Surely others would see his dark mood and thoughts; he wouldn't be able to hide them. He dare not even go for a walk alone in the woods—his heart would probably start racing again, bringing him to his knees and leaving him breathless, incoherent, and unable to get home. No, he's much better off staying in his room, trying to get through another evening of this curse called life.
>
> *July:* Bill's life revolves around his circle of friends: Bob and Jack, whom he knows from the office, where he was recently promoted to director of customer relations, and Frank and Tim, his weekend tennis partners. The gang meets for dinner every week at someone's house, and they chat about life, politics, and their jobs. Particularly special in Bill's life is Janice, with whom he has a promising relationship. They go to movies, restaurants, and shows together. She thinks Bill's just terrific, and Bill finds himself beaming whenever she's around. In fact, most people think Bill is terrific. They are eager to be with him and earn his respect, and Bill appreciates their admiration. He looks forward to work each day and his one-to-one dealings with customers. He is enjoying life and basking in the glow of his many activities and relationships.

Bill's thoughts, feelings, and behavior were so debilitating in February that they affected all aspects of his life. Most of his symptoms had disappeared by July, and he returned to his previous level of functioning. All sorts of factors may have contributed to Bill's improvement. Friends and family members may have offered support or advice. A new job or vacation may have lifted his spirits. Perhaps he changed his diet or started to exercise. Any or all of these things may have been useful to Bill, but they could not be considered ***therapy.*** That term is usually reserved for special, systematic processes for helping people overcome their psychological difficulties.

What makes Bill's improvement a case of clinical treatment? According to the clinical theorist Jerome Frank, all forms of therapy have three essential features:

> 1. A sufferer who seeks relief from the healer.
> 2. A trained, socially sanctioned healer, whose healing powers are accepted by the sufferer and his social group or an important segment of it.
> 3. A circumscribed, more or less structured series of contacts between the healer and the sufferer, through which the healer, often with the aid of a group, tries to produce certain changes in the sufferer's emotional state, attitudes, and behavior.
>
> *(Frank, 1973, pp. 2–3)*

Despite Frank's straightforward definition, clinical treatment is surrounded by conflict and confusion. Carl Rogers, a pioneer in the modern clinical field whom we will meet in Chapter 3, noted that "therapists are not in agreement as to their goals or aims. . . . They are not in agreement as to what constitutes a successful outcome of their work. They cannot agree as to what constitutes a failure. It seems as though the field is completely chaotic and divided." For clinicians who view abnormality as an illness, therapy is a procedure that corrects the illness. For clinicians who see abnormality as a maladaptive way of behaving or thinking, therapists are *teachers* of more functional behavior and thought.

Clinicians even differ on what to call the person undergoing therapy: those who see abnormality as an illness speak of the *patient,* while those who view abnormality as a maladaptive mode of behaving or thinking refer to the *client.* Because both terms are so common, this book will use them more or less interchangeably. Despite their many differences, most clinicians do agree that large numbers of people need therapy of one kind or another. In Chapter 5, after we have surveyed the practice of therapy more fully, we shall present evidence that therapy is indeed often helpful.

Past Views and Treatments

The facts and figures on psychological abnormality are almost numbing. In any given year as many as 30 percent of the adults and 20 percent of the children and adolescents in the United States are believed to display serious mental disturbances and to be in need of clinical treatment (Friedman et al., 1996; Kessler et al., 1996, 1994; Kazdin, 1993; Regier et al., 1993). It is estimated that at least thirteen of every hundred adults have a significant anxiety disorder, six suffer from profound depression, five display a personality disorder (inflexible and maladaptive personality traits), one has schizophrenia (loses touch with reality for an extended period of time), one experiences the brain deterioration of Alzheimer's disease, and close to ten abuse alcohol or other drugs. Add to these figures as many as 600,000 suicide attempts, 500,000 rapes, and 3 million cases of child abuse in this country each year, and it becomes apparent that abnormal psychological functioning is a pervasive problem in our society (Frankel, 1995; U.S. Department of Justice, 1995; Koss, 1993; McCurdy & Daro, 1993; Regier et al., 1993). Furthermore, most people have difficulty coping at various points in their lives and experience high levels of tension, demoralization, or other forms of psychological discomfort. At such times, they too experience at least some of the distress associated with psychological disorders.

It is tempting to conclude that such emotional maladjustment is linked to something in today's world—rapid technological change, perhaps, or a decline in religious, community, family, or other support systems (see Figure 1-1). Although the special pressures of modern life probably do contribute to psychological dysfunctioning, they are hardly its primary cause. Every society, past and present, has contended with psychological abnormality. Perhaps, then, the proper place to begin our examination of abnormal behavior and treatment is in the past.

As we look back, we can ask what features remain constant in human societies, and which vary from place to place and from time to time. We can look at how each society has struggled to understand and treat psychological problems, and see that many present-day ideas and treatments can be traced to the past. A look backward makes it clear that progress in the understanding and treatment of mental disorders has hardly been a steady movement forward. Many of the inadequacies and controversies that characterize the clinical field today parallel those of the past. At the same time, looking back can help us to appreciate the full significance of recent breakthroughs, as well as the importance of the journey that lies ahead.

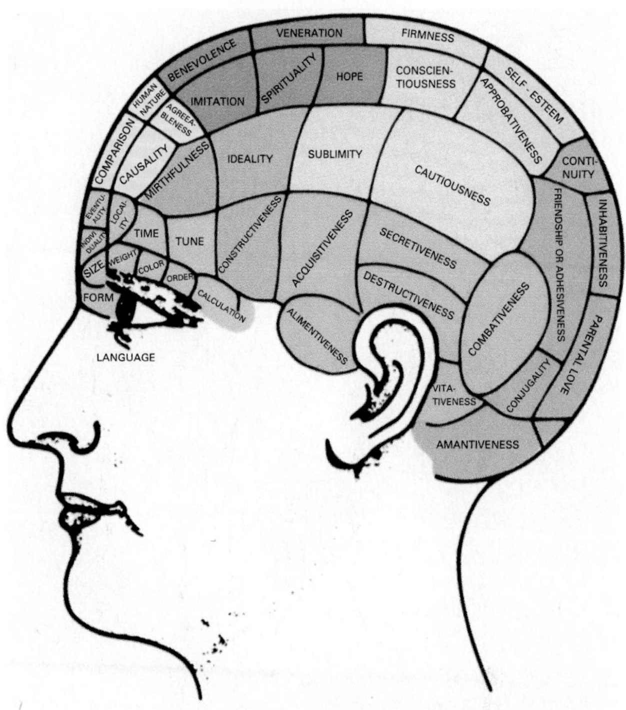

Past efforts to understand abnormal behavior have not always been scientifically sound. One hypothesis was called "phrenology." Franz Joseph Gall (1758–1828) and his followers held that the brain consisted of discernible portions, each responsible for some aspect of personality. Phrenologists tried to assess personality by feeling bumps and indentations on a person's head.

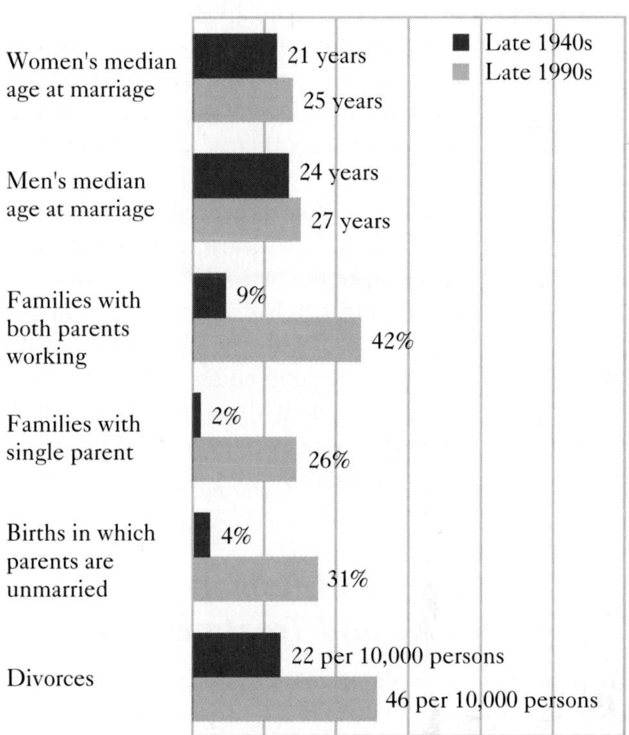

Figure 1-1 *The changing family. Family patterns have shifted dramatically during the past fifty years. Persons now get married later and divorced more often, and families are more likely to be headed by a single parent or to have both parents working. Some clinicians suggest that these changes leave millions of persons, particularly children, with fewer personal resources for coping with stress (Stacey, 1996; National Center for Health Statistics, 1995; U. S. Bureau of the Census).*

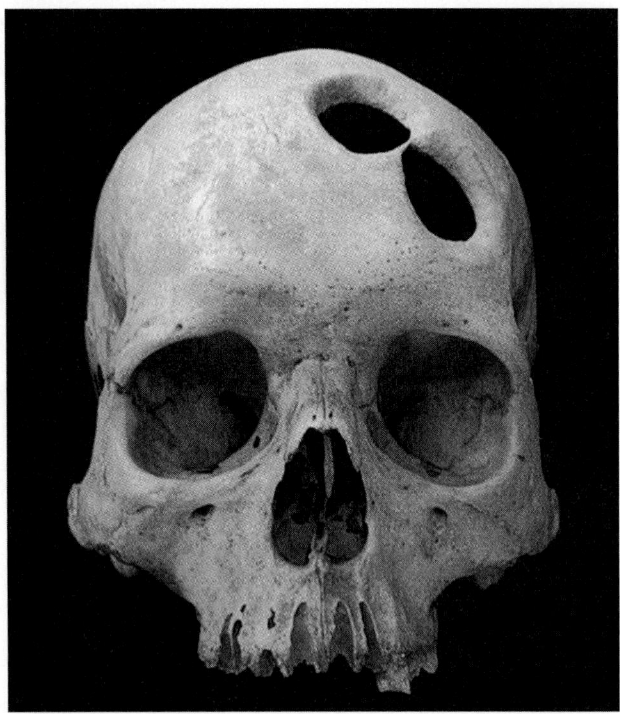

The skulls of some Stone Age people show evidence of trephination, possibly for the purpose of releasing evil spirits and thus remedying abnormal psychological functioning. Signs of bone regrowth around the two holes in this skull suggest that this patient survived two trephinations.

Ancient Views and Treatments

Most of our knowledge of prehistoric societies has been acquired indirectly and is based on inferences made from archaeological discoveries. Historians scrutinize the unearthed bones, artwork, artifacts, and other remnants of ancient societies to find clues to people's customs, beliefs, and daily life. Any conclusions are at best tentative and are always subject to revision in the face of new discoveries.

Thus our knowledge of how ancient societies viewed and treated people with mental disturbances is limited. Historians have concluded that prehistoric societies probably viewed abnormal behavior as the work of evil spirits. People in these early societies apparently explained the phenomena around and within them as resulting from the actions of magical, sometimes sinister beings who shaped and controlled the world. In particular, they viewed the human body and mind as sites of battle between external forces, and they viewed behavior, both normal and abnormal, as the outcome of battles between good and evil spirits, positive forces and demons, or good and bad gods. Abnormal behavior was often interpreted as a victory by evil spirits, and the cure for such behavior was to force the spirits to leave the person's body.

A supernatural view of abnormality may have begun as far back as the Stone Age, a half-million years ago. Some skulls from that period recovered by archaeologists in Europe and South America show evidence of an operation called ***trephination,*** in which a stone instrument, or ***trephine,*** was used to cut away a circular section of the skull. Some historians surmise that this operation was performed as a treatment for severe abnormal behavior—either hallucinatory experiences, in which people saw or heard things not actually present, or melancholic reactions, characterized by extreme sadness and immobility. The purpose of opening the skull was to release the evil spirits that were supposedly causing the problem (Selling, 1940).

In recent years, some historians have questioned whether Stone Age people actually believed that evil spirits caused abnormal behavior. Trephination may instead have been used to remove bone splinters or blood clots caused by stone weapons during tribal warfare (Maher & Maher, 1985). Either way, later societies clearly did attribute abnormal behavior to demonic possession. The early writings of the Egyptians, Chinese, and Hebrews, for example, all account for psychological deviance this way. The Bible describes how an evil spirit from the Lord affected King Saul and how David feigned madness in order to convince his enemies that he was inhabited by divine forces.

These early societies often practiced ***exorcism*** as a treatment for abnormality. The idea was to coax the evil spirits to leave or to make the person's body an uncomfortable place for the spirits to live. A ***shaman,*** or priest, might recite prayers, plead with the evil spirits, insult them, perform magic, make loud noises, or have the person drink noxious solutions. If these techniques failed, the shaman employed a more extreme form of exorcism, such as whipping or starvation.

Greek and Roman Views and Treatments

In the years from, roughly, 500 B.C. to A.D. 500, when the Greek and Roman civilizations flourished, philosophers and physicians described a number of mental disorders. Heading the list were ***melancholia,*** a condition marked by unshakable sadness; ***mania,*** a state of euphoria and frenzied activity; ***dementia,*** a general intellectual decline; ***hysteria,*** a physical ailment with no apparent physical cause; ***delusions,*** blatantly false beliefs; and ***hallucinations,*** the experience of imagined sights or sounds as if they were real. Although demonological views concerning mental and physical illness were still widespread, philosophers and physicians began to offer alternative explanations during this period. They even proposed that mental disorders were capable of inspiring creativity (see Box 1-2).

Hippocrates (460–377 B.C.), often called the father of modern medicine, taught that illnesses had natural causes rather than metaphysical ones. He saw abnormal behavior as a disease caused by internal physical problems rather than by conflicts between gods or spirits. Specifically, he believed that some form of brain pathology was the culprit, and that it resulted—like all other forms of disease, in his view—from an imbalance of four fluids, or ***humors,*** that flowed through the body: *yellow bile, black bile, blood,* and *phlegm.* An excess of yellow bile, for example, caused mania; an excess of black bile was the source of melancholia.

To treat psychological dysfunctioning, Hippocrates sought to correct the underlying physical pathology. He believed, for instance, that the excess of black bile underlying melancholia could be reduced by a quiet life, a vegetable diet, temperance, exercise, celibacy, and even bleeding.

Hippocrates' focus on internal causes for abnormal behavior was shared by the great Greek philosophers Plato (427–347 B.C.) and Aristotle (384–322 B.C.) and later was extended by influential Greek and Roman physicians. The physician Aretaeus (A.D. 50–130), for example, suggested that emotional problems could also cause abnormal behavior. The physician Galen (A.D. 130–200) systematically distinguished emotional causes, such as financial worries and loss of love, from medical ones, such as head injuries and alcohol abuse.

These theories led Greek and Roman physicians to treat mental illnesses with a mixture of physical and psychological techniques. Before resorting to such extreme methods as bleeding patients or restraining them with mechanical devices, many Greek physicians first prescribed a warm and supportive atmosphere, music, massage, exercise, and baths. Roman physicians were even more emphatic about the need to soothe and comfort patients who had mental disorders.

Europe in the Middle Ages: Demonology Returns

The enlightened views of noted physicians and scholars during the Greco-Roman period were not enough to shake many people's belief in demons. And with the decline of Rome, demonological views and practices enjoyed a strong resurgence, as a growing distrust of science spread throughout Europe.

In the years from A.D. 500 to 1350, the period known as the Middle Ages, the power of the clergy increased

Hippocrates believed that imbalances of the four humors affected personality and caused mental disorders. In these depictions of two of the humors, yellow bile (left) drives a choleric husband to beat his wife; black bile (right) renders a man melancholic and sends him to bed.

Box 1-2 Madness and the Muse

The nineteenth century poet Lord Byron endured what he called "savage moods." From childhood on, he careened between periods of wretched despondency and fiery, increasingly irrational urges and thoughts. His volatile temperament frequently set off sparks of poetic imagination, inspiring him at one point to write of "the apostle of affliction, he who threw enchantment over passion, and from woe wrung overwhelming eloquence."

(Bower, 1995).

"Men have called me mad," wrote Edgar Allan Poe, "but the question is not yet settled, whether madness is or is not the loftiest intelligence—whether much that is glorious—whether all that is profound—does not spring from disease of thought—from moods of mind exalted at the expense of the general intellect."

(Jamison, 1995).

Creativity and abnormal psychological functioning have intuitively been linked for centuries. The ancient Greeks believed that various forms of "divine madness" inspired creative acts, from poetry to performance (Ludwig, 1995). In the eighteenth century, romantic notions of the "mad genius" emerged, and asylum superintendents, believing that madness brought access to previously dormant creative talents, often encouraged their patients to write (Gamwell & Tomes, 1995). Even today many people expect creative geniuses to be unconventional at best, psychologically disturbed at worst. Indeed, a popular image of the artist includes a glass of liquor, a cigarette, and a tormented expression. Classic examples include the writer William Faulkner, who suffered from alcoholism and received electroconvulsive therapy for depression; the poet Sylvia Plath, who experienced a lifetime of depression and eventually committed suicide; and the dancer Vaslav Nijinsky, who suffered from schizophrenia and spent many years in institutions.

But is it true that madness and creativity are linked? For every Sylvia Plath, are there not many more stable, "sane" artists, such as Henri Matisse and Edgar Degas? In fact, a number of investigations indicate that creative people *are* somewhat more likely than others to suffer from mental disorders, and they may also experience psychological difficulties for longer periods of time (Ludwig, 1995). Some studies have found that as many as 80 percent of examined writers report suffering from episodes of depression—8 to 10 times the rate found in the general population (Jamison, 1995; Andreasen, 1987). Still other investigations have found that artists and writers suffer from high levels of anxiety, panic disorder, substance abuse, and eating disorders (Ludwig, 1994).

Patterns of mental dysfunctioning may vary systematically among the creative professions. Poets seem to be particularly prone to mood disorders and psychosis, musicians and actors to substance abuse, and artists and composers to alcoholism and depression. One study of over 1,000 creative individuals revealed that 87 percent of the poets experienced a mental disorder at some point during their lives, compared to 73 percent of artists, 68 percent of musicians, and 74 percent of actors (Ludwig, 1995).

Why are creative people burdened with mental disorders? One study suggests that they may be *predisposed* to mental disorders

greatly. The church rejected secular studies and scientific forms of investigation, and it controlled all education. Religious beliefs—themselves highly superstitious and demonological at this time—came to dominate all aspects of life. Personal experience and conduct were often interpreted as a conflict between good and evil, God and the devil; and deviant behavior, particularly mental dysfunctioning, was seen as evidence of an association with Satan. Although some scientists and physicians still argued for medical explanations and treatments, their views carried little weight in an atmosphere of rigid religious doctrine.

The Middle Ages were centuries of great stress and anxiety, times of war, urban uprisings, and plagues. People blamed the devil for these hard times and feared being possessed by him. The incidence of abnormal behavior apparently increased dramatically during this stressful period. In addition, there were outbreaks of ***mass madness,*** in which large numbers of people apparently shared the same delusions and hallucinations. Two prevalent forms were tarantism and lycanthropy.

Tarantism (also known as ***St. Vitus's dance***) was a form of mania that occurred throughout Europe between A.D. 900 and 1800. Groups of people would sud-

long before they begin their artistic careers (Ludwig, 1995). Many creative people have a family history of psychological problems. The poet Alfred, Lord Tennyson, suffered from the "taint of blood of the Tennysons"; nearly all the Tennysons had bipolar disorders, alternating between episodes of depression and periods of mania (Jamison, 1995). Many other creative people have experienced psychological trauma during childhood. Virginia Woolf, for example, endured sexual abuse as a child.

Another reason for the link between madness and creativity may be that creative endeavors create emotional turmoil or dredge up unresolved conflicts that are overwhelming. Truman Capote said that writing *In Cold Blood* "killed" him psychologically. Before writing that powerful book, he considered himself "a stable person. . . . Afterward something happened to me" (Ludwig, 1995). Artists who pour their tormented souls into their work may be rewarded with a product of special passion, intensity, and insight—but some of them "may find it hard" to restore their psychological balance after the work is done (Ludwig, 1995).

Yet a third possibility is that the creative professions may offer a welcome climate for people with psychological disturbances. Emotive expression, vivid imagery, and personal turmoil may be sources of inspiration and success for poets, painters, and actors (Ludwig, 1995). In addition, creative professions usually lack the regimentation, established work hours, and other restrictions that make it difficult for persons suffering from mental disorders to work in traditional fields. Finally, odd behavior typically is not stigmatized in the artistic professions. The arts can thus be a haven for nonconformists and persons with emotional disturbances (Ludwig, 1995).

Clearly, much remains to be learned about the relationship between emotional turmoil and creativity, but work in this area has already clarified two important points. First, psychological disturbance is hardly a prerequisite to creativity. Many "creative geniuses" are, in fact, psychologically stable and happy throughout their lives. Second, creative achievement is more closely related to *mild* psychological disturbances than to severe disorders. For example, mild patterns of mania, called *hypomania,* often stimulate creative thinking and increase creative output (Jamison, 1995; APA, 1994). Similarly, emotional pain often provides insight that enhances creativity (Ludwig, 1995). Mild disturbances of this kind, however, often worsen with time and provide little creative benefit in the long run. In fact, extreme disturbances, such as severe mania, severe depression, and alcoholism, tend to *reduce* the quality and quantity of creative work and have ruined many careers (Ludwig, 1995). The nineteenth-century composer Robert Schumann produced twenty-seven works during one hypomanic year, but generated very few compositions during the years in which he was severely depressed and suicidal (Jamison, 1995).

Some artists fear that if their psychological suffering is eliminated, their creativity will go along with it. In fact, research suggests that successful treatment for severe mental disorders can actually improve the creative process (Ludwig, 1995; Whybrow, 1994). Often treatment eases the extremes of destructive psychopathology without dulling the artist's psychological experiences (Jamison, 1995). Clearly, romantic notions aside, mental disorders—particularly severe ones—have little redeeming value, in the arts or anywhere else.

denly start to jump around, dance, and go into convulsions (Sigerist, 1943). They might bang into walls or roll on the ground. Some dressed oddly; others tore off their clothing. All were convinced that they had been bitten and possessed by a wolf spider, now called a tarantula, and they sought to cure their disorder by performing a dance called a *tarantella.* The dance was thought to have originated in the town of Taranto in southern Italy, which gave it its name.

People with ***lycanthropy*** thought they were possessed by wolves or other animals. They acted wolflike and imagined that fur was growing all over their bodies. Stories of lycanthropes, more popularly known as ***werewolves,*** have been passed down to us and continue to capture the imagination of writers, moviemakers, and their audiences.

Many earlier demonological treatments for psychological abnormality reemerged in the Middle Ages. Once again the key to a cure was to rid the person's body of the devil that possessed it, and techniques of exorcism were revived. Clergymen, who generally were in charge of treatment during this period, would plead, chant, or pray to the devil or evil spirit. They might also administer holy water or bitter-tasting concoctions, and if these techniques did not work, they might try to insult the devil and attack his pride (Satan's great weakness, they believed). These milder forms of exorcism were sometimes supplemented by torture in the form of starvation, whipping, scalding, or stretching.

As the Middle Ages drew to a close, demonology and its methods began to lose favor. Cities throughout Europe grew larger, and municipal authorities gained more power and increasingly took over the secular activities of the church. Among other responsibilities, they began to administer hospitals and direct the care of sick people, including those with mental illness. Medical views of psychological abnormality started to gain prominence once again. In the British lunacy trials of the late thirteenth century, held to determine the sanity of persons, a natural cause such as a "blow to the head" or "fear of one's father" might be held responsible for an individual's unusual behavior (Neugebauer, 1979, 1978). During these same years, many people with mental disturbances were treated in medical hospitals. The Trinity Hospital in England, for example, was established to treat "madness" along with other kinds of illness, and to keep the mad "safe until they are restored to reason" (Allderidge, 1979, p. 322).

The Renaissance and the Rise of Asylums

Demonological views of abnormality continued to decline in popularity during the first half of the Renaissance (approximately 1400–1700), a period of flourishing cultural and scientific activity. The German physician Johann Weyer (1515–1588) apparently became the first medical practitioner to specialize in mental illness. Weyer believed that the mind was as susceptible to sickness as the body. He is now considered the founder of the modern study of psychopathology, another term for mental dysfunction.

Belief in demonological possession persisted into the Renaissance. A great fear of witchcraft swept Europe during the fifteenth and sixteenth centuries. Tens of thousands of people, most of them women, were thought to have made a pact with the devil. Some of the accused appear to have had mental disorders that caused them to act strangely (Zilboorg & Henry, 1941). This individual is being "dunked" repeatedly in water until she confessed to witchery.

Care for many people with mental disorders continued to improve in this atmosphere. In England many such individuals were kept at home, and their families were given extra funds by the local parish. Across Europe religious shrines became consecrated to the humane and loving treatment of persons with mental illness. Perhaps the best-known such shrine was actually established centuries earlier at Gheel in Belgium. Beginning in the fifteenth century, however, people with mental problems ranging from melancholia to hallucinations came from all over the world to visit it for psychic healing. Local residents welcomed them into their homes, and many pilgrims stayed on to form the world's first "colony" of mental patients. This colony set the stage for many of today's community mental health and foster care programs, and Gheel continues to demonstrate that people with mental disorders can respond to loving care and respectful treatment (Aring, 1975, 1974). Many patients still live in foster homes there until they recover, interacting with and accepted by the town's other residents.

Unfortunately, the improvements in care for persons with psychological disorders began to fade by the mid–sixteenth century. Municipal authorities eventually discovered that only a small percentage of those with severe mental disorders could be accommodated in private homes and community residences, and that medical hospitals were too few and too small. Increasingly, officials in cities across the world converted hospitals and monasteries into ***asylums,*** institutions to which people with mental illness could be sent. These institutions apparently began with the best of intentions—to provide genuine care for patients. As the asylums started to overflow with patients, however, they became virtual prisons. Patients came to be held in filthy and degrading conditions and treated with unspeakable cruelty.

The first asylum was founded in Muslim Spain in the early fifteenth century, but the idea did not gain full momentum until the next century. In 1547 the Bethlehem Hospital in London was given to the city by Henry VIII for the exclusive purpose of confining the mentally ill. Here patients, restrained in chains, cried out their despair for all to hear. The hospital actually became a popular tourist attraction; people were eager to pay to look at the howling and gibbering inmates. The hospital's name, pronounced "Bedlam" by the local people, became synonymous with a chaotic uproar. Asylums later founded in Mexico, France, Russia, the United States, and

London's Bethlehem Hospital, or Bedlam, was typical of insane asylums from the sixteenth to the nineteenth centuries. In his eighteenth-century work from A Rake's Progress, *William Hogarth depicted the asylum as a chaotic place where ladies and gentlemen of fashion came to marvel at the strange behavior of the inmates.*

Austria offered similar forms of "care." In the Lunatics' Tower in Vienna, for example, patients were kept in narrow hallways by the outer walls, so that tourists outside could look up and see them. In La Bicêtre in Paris, patients were shackled to the walls of cold, dark, dirty cells with iron collars and given spoiled food that could be sold nowhere else (Selling, 1940).

The inability of municipal authorities to address the needs of large numbers of patients was not the only reason for the poor quality of care in asylums. Large segments of the population still feared and had grave suspicions of persons with mental disorders—concerns that were alleviated by the restraints and confinement of asylums. Moreover, the "medical" cures developed for use in asylums during this period were themselves misguided and unintentionally cruel. In the eighteenth century, no less a figure than Benjamin Rush (1745–1813), often called the father of American psychiatry, treated some patients by drawing blood from their bodies, a technique also used at that time to treat bodily illnesses. This treatment was meant to lower an excessively high level of blood in the brain, which Rush believed was causing the patient's abnormal behavior (Farina, 1976). Thus suspicion, ignorance, and erroneous medical theory conspired to keep asylums a shameful form of care until the late eighteenth century.

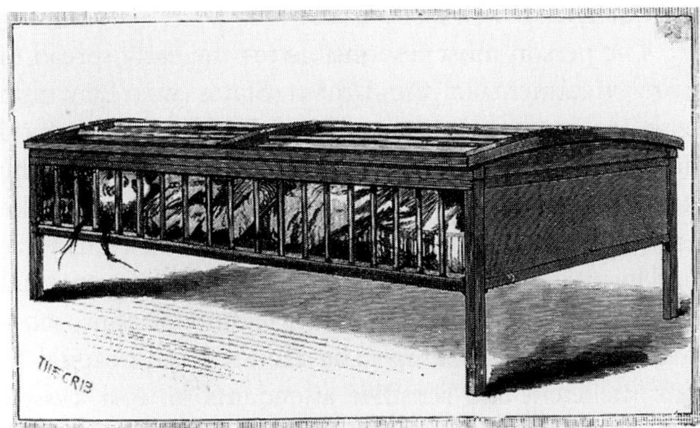

Outrageous devices and techniques were used in asylums and continued to be used even during the reforms of the nineteenth century. Many patients, particularly violent ones, were repeatedly placed in the "crib," a precursor to the straitjacket.

The Nineteenth Century: Reform and Moral Treatment

As 1800 approached, the treatment of people with mental disorders began to change for the better once again. Historians usually point to La Bicêtre, an asylum in Paris for male patients, as the initial site of asylum reform. In 1793, during the French Revolution, Philippe Pinel (1745–1826) was named the chief physician there. Influenced by the humane work of Jean-Baptiste Pussin, the hospital's superintendent of incurable patients, Pinel began a series of reforms. He argued that the patients were sick people whose mental illnesses should be treated with support and kindness rather than with chains and beatings. He would not allow patients to be abused and

A popular feature of moral treatment was the "lunatic ball." Hospital officials would bring male and female patients together to dance and enjoy themselves. The artist George Bellows depicted one such ball in this painting, Dance in a Madhouse.

tortured. He unchained them and gave them the liberty of the hospital grounds, replaced the dark dungeons with sunny, well-ventilated rooms, and offered patients support and advice.

Pinel's new approach did indeed prove remarkably successful. Many patients who had been locked away in darkness for decades were now enjoying fresh air and sunlight and being treated with dignity. Some improved significantly over a short period of time and were released. Pinel and Pussin were later commissioned to reform a mental hospital in Paris for female patients, La Salpetrière, and had excellent results there as well. Jean Esquirol (1772–1840), Pinel's student and successor, followed his teacher's lead and went on to help establish ten new mental hospitals that operated by the same principles.

Meanwhile an English Quaker named William Tuke (1732–1819) was bringing similar reforms to northern England. In 1796 he founded the York Retreat, a rural estate where about thirty mental patients were lodged as guests in quiet country houses and treated with a combination of rest, talk, prayer, and manual work.

The Spread of Moral Treatment The methods espoused by Pinel and Tuke, called ***moral treatment*** by their contemporaries because of their emphasis on moral guidance and on humane and respectful intervention, caught on throughout Europe and the United States. Increasingly, patients with psychological disorders were perceived not as possessed, but as potentially productive human beings whose mental functioning had broken down under overwhelming personal stresses. These unfortunate people were considered deserving of individualized care, including discussions of their problems, constructive activities, work, companionship, and quiet.

The person most responsible for the early spread of moral treatment in the United States was Benjamin Rush. As we have seen, some of Rush's early medical views were naive and harsh by today's standards, but he fully embraced the concept of moral treatment when he learned about it. As an eminent physician at Pennsylvania Hospital, he limited his practice and study to mental illness, and he developed innovative, humane approaches to treatment. For example, he required the hospital to hire intelligent and sensitive attendants to work closely with patients, reading and talking to them and taking them on regular walks. He also suggested that it would be of therapeutic value for doctors to give small gifts to their patients now and then.

Rush wrote the first American treatise on mental illness and organized the first American course in psychiatry. However, it was a Boston schoolteacher named Dorothea Dix (1802–1887) who made humane care a public and political concern in the United States. In fact, she was largely responsible for the passage of new laws to mandate humane treatment. In 1841 Dix had gone to teach Sunday school at a local prison and been shocked by the conditions she saw there. Her interest in prison conditions broadened to include the plight of poor and mentally ill people throughout the country. A powerful campaigner, Dix went from state legislature to state legislature speaking of the horrors she had observed and calling for reform. In an address to the Massachusetts legislature, she proclaimed that people with mental disorders were being "confined within this Commonwealth, in cages, closets, cellars, stalls, pens; chained, naked, beaten with rods, and lashed into obedience" (Deutsch, 1949, p. 165). She told the Congress of the United States that mentally ill people across the country were still being "bound with galling chains, bowed beneath fetters and heavy iron balls attached to drag chains, lacerated with ropes, scourged with rods and terrified beneath storms of execration and cruel blows" (Zilboorg & Henry, 1941, pp. 583–584).

Dix's campaign, which spanned the decades from 1841 until 1881, led to new laws and the appropriation of funds to improve the treatment of people with mental disorders. Each state was made responsible for developing effective public mental hospitals. Dix personally helped establish thirty-two of these ***state hospitals,*** all intended to offer moral treatment (Bickman & Dokecki, 1989; Viney & Zorich, 1982). Similar government-funded hospitals for people with mental disorders were established throughout Europe and run according to humanitarian principles.

For years the moral treatment movement improved the care of people with mental disorders. By the 1850s, a number of mental hospitals throughout Europe and North America reported that many of their patients were recovering and being released (Bockoven, 1963). Unfortunately, social changes at the end of the nineteenth century once again altered this promising situation for the worse.

The Decline of Moral Treatment As we have observed, the treatment of abnormality has followed a crooked path. Over and over again, relative progress has been followed by serious decline. Viewed in this context, the decline of moral treatment in the late nineteenth century is disappointing but not surprising.

Several factors contributed to this decline (Bockoven, 1963). One was the reckless speed with which the moral treatment movement had advanced. As mental hospitals multiplied, severe money and staffing shortages developed, and recovery rates declined. Fewer and fewer patients left the hospitals each year, and admissions continued unabated; overcrowding became a major problem. Under these conditions it was impossible to provide the individual care and genuine concern that were the cornerstones of moral treatment.

The basic assumptions of moral treatment also contributed to its downfall. The major one was that patients would begin to function normally if they were treated with dignity and if their physical needs were met. For some patients this was indeed the case. Others, however, needed more effective treatments than any that had yet been developed. Many of these people remained hospitalized till they died.

A further reason for the decline of moral treatment was the emergence of a new wave of prejudice against people with mental disorders. As more and more patients disappeared into the large, distant mental hospitals, the public once again came to view them as strange and dangerous. In turn, people were less open-handed when it came to making donations or allocating government funds. Moreover, by the end of the nineteenth century,

From 1841 to 1881 the Boston schoolteacher Dorothea Dix tirelessly campaigned for more humane forms of treatment in mental hospitals throughout the United States. Her efforts led to new laws providing for the establishment of public mental hospitals, supported and administered by the states.

many of the patients entering public mental hospitals in the United States were impoverished foreign immigrants and so were already subjected to considerable prejudice. The public had little interest in helping people from other countries; even the hospital personnel were less conscientious in their care of them.

By the early twentieth century, the moral treatment movement had ground to a halt in both the United States and Europe. Public mental hospitals provided minimal custodial care and medical interventions that did not work, and became more overcrowded and less effective every year. Long-term hospitalization became the norm once again.

This state of affairs was powerfully described in 1908 by Clifford Beers (1876–1943) in *A Mind That Found Itself,* an autobiographical account of his severe mental disturbance and of the "treatment" he received in three mental institutions. Beers revealed that he and other patients were repeatedly restrained, beaten, choked, and spat on in these places, all in the name of treatment. His moving account aroused both public and professional sympathy, and he went on to found the National Committee for Mental Hygiene, dedicated to educating the public about mental illness and the need for proper treatment. Unfortunately, although Beers's work brought considerable attention to the terrible conditions in public mental hospitals, these institutions were not to improve significantly for forty more years.

The Somatogenic Perspective The late nineteenth century also saw a dramatic resurgence of the ***somatogenic perspective,*** the view that abnormal psychological functioning has physical causes. This perspective had at least a 2,300-year history—remember Hippocrates' view that abnormal behavior resulted from brain maladies and an imbalance of humors, or bodily fluids—yet it had never before been so widely accepted.

Two factors were responsible for this resurgence. One was the work of Emil Kraepelin (1856–1926), a German researcher who took particular interest in the relation between abnormal psychological functioning and such physical factors as fatigue, and who measured the effects of various drugs on abnormal behavior. In 1883 Kraepelin published an influential textbook, expounding the view that physical factors are responsible for mental dysfunctioning. In addition, as we shall see in Chapter 5, he constructed the first "modern" system for classifying abnormal behavior. He identified various ***syndromes,*** or clusters of symptoms, listed their organic causes, and discussed their expected course (Jablensky, 1995).

Biological and anatomical discoveries also spurred the rise of the somatogenic perspective. One of the most important discoveries was that an organic disease, syphilis, led to ***general paresis,*** an irreversible, progressive disorder with both physical and mental symptoms, including paralysis and delusions of grandeur. The organic basis of this partly mental disorder had been suspected as early as the mid–nineteenth century, but concrete evidence did not emerge until decades later.

In 1897 Richard von Krafft-Ebing (1840–1902), a German neurologist, established a direct link between general paresis and syphilis. He inoculated paretic patients with matter from syphilis sores and found that none of the patients developed symptoms of syphilis. Their immunity could have been caused only by an earlier case of syphilis. Since all paretic patients were now immune to syphilis, Krafft-Ebing theorized that it had been the cause of their general paresis. Finally, in 1905, Fritz Schaudinn (1871–1906), a German zoologist, discovered that the microorganism *Treponema pallida* was responsible for syphilis, which in turn was responsible for general paresis.

The work of Kraepelin and the new understanding of general paresis led many researchers and practitioners to suspect that organic factors were responsible for many mental disorders, perhaps all of them. These theories and the possibility of quick and effective medical solutions for mental disorders were especially welcomed by those who worked in mental hospitals, where patient populations were now growing at an alarming rate.

Despite the general optimism, the biological approach yielded largely disappointing results throughout the first half of the twentieth century. True, many medical treatments were developed for patients in mental hospitals during that time, but most of the techniques proved ineffectual. Physicians tried extraction of teeth, tonsillectomy, hydrotherapy (alternating hot and cold baths to soothe excited patients), insulin coma shock (a "therapeutic" convulsion induced by lowering a patient's blood sugar level with insulin), and lobotomy (a surgical severing of certain nerve fibers in the brain). Not until the 1950s, when a number of effective medications were finally discovered, did the somatogenic perspective truly begin to pay off for patients with mental disorders.

The Psychogenic Perspective Yet another important trend to unfold in the late nineteenth century was the emergence of the ***psychogenic perspective,*** the view that the chief causes of abnormal functioning are psychological. This perspective, too, had a long history. The Roman statesman and orator Cicero (106–43 B.C.) held that psychological disturbances could cause bodily ailments, and the Greek physician Galen believed that many mental disorders are caused by fear, disappointment in love, and other psychological events. However, the psychogenic perspective did not command a significant following until the late nineteenth century, when studies of hypnotism demonstrated the potential of this line of inquiry.

Hypnotism is the inducing of a trancelike mental state in which a person becomes extremely suggestible. Its use as a means of treating psychological disorders actually dates back to 1778. In that year an Austrian physician named Friedrich Anton Mesmer (1734–1815) established a clinic in Paris where he employed an unusual treatment for patients with ***hysterical disorders,*** mysterious bodily ailments that had no apparent physical basis. Mesmer's patients would sit in a darkened room filled with music. In the center of the room, a tub held bottles of chemicals from which iron rods protruded. Suddenly Mesmer would appear in a flamboyant costume, withdraw the rods, and touch them to the troubled area of each patient's body. A surprising number of patients did seem to be helped by this treatment. Their pain, numbness, or paralysis disappeared.

Mesmer's treatment, at first called ***mesmerism,*** was so controversial that eventually he was banished from Paris. But few could deny that at least some patients did indeed improve after being mesmerized. Several scientists believed that Mesmer was inducing a trancelike state in his patients, and that this state caused their symptoms to disappear. In later years the technique was developed further and relabeled *neurohypnotism,* later shortened to *hypnotism* (from *hypnos,* the Greek word for sleep).

It was not until years after Mesmer died, however, that many researchers had the courage to investigate hypnotism and its effects on hysterical disorders. By the late nineteenth century, two competing views had emerged. That a technique that enhanced the power of suggestion could alleviate hysterical ailments indicated to one group of scientists that hysterical disorders must be caused by the power of suggestion—that is, by the mind—in the first place. Another group of scientists believed that hysterical disorders had subtle physiological causes. Jean Charcot (1825–1893), an eminent Paris neurologist, argued that hysterical disorders were the result of degeneration in portions of the brain.

The experiments of two physicians practicing in the city of Nancy in France finally seemed to settle the matter. Hippolyte-Marie Bernheim (1840–1919) and Ambroise-Auguste Liébault (1823–1904) showed that hysterical disorders could actually be induced in otherwise normal subjects while they were under the influence of hypnosis. That is, they could make normal people experience deafness, paralysis, blindness, or numbness by means of hypnotic suggestion—and they could remove

Friedrich Anton Mesmer, standing at the back and to the right in this painting, works with hysterical patients in his Paris clinic. He believed that hysterical ailments were caused by an improper distribution of magnetic fluid in the body, and that touching an ailing part of the body with an iron rod would correct the problem.

these artificially induced symptoms by the same means. In short, they established that a *mental* process—hypnotic suggestion—could both cause and cure a physical dysfunction. Most leading scientists, including Charcot, finally embraced the idea that hysterical disorders were largely psychological in origin.

Among those who studied the effects of hypnotism on hysterical disorders was a Viennese doctor named Josef Breuer (1842–1925). He discovered that his hypnotized patients sometimes awoke free of hysterical symptoms after speaking freely about past traumas under hypnosis. During the 1890s Breuer was joined in his work by another Viennese physician, Sigmund Freud (1856–1939). As we shall see in greater detail in Chapter 3, Freud's work eventually led him to develop the theory of ***psychoanalysis,*** which holds that many forms of abnormal and normal psychological functioning are psychogenic. He believed that conflict between powerful psychological processes operating at an unconscious level is the source of much abnormal psychological functioning. Freud also developed the *technique* of psychoanalysis, a form of discussion in which psychotherapists help troubled people acquire insight into their psychological conflicts. Such insight, he believed, would help the patients overcome their psychological problems.

To many observers, Freud's psychogenic perspective seemed the antithesis of the increasingly influential somatogenic view of mental dysfunctioning. Thus his ideas were initially criticized and rejected. Freud persevered, however, and by the early twentieth century psychoanalytic theory and treatment were widely accepted

BOX 1-3 The Moon and the Mind

As time passes, every society undergoes changes that redefine both the range of behavior considered normal and the explanations for behavior that deviates from the norm. The belief in demonic possession as a cause of abnormal behavior has been replaced by the assumption that biological, psychological, and sociocultural explanations can be found; yet some ancient theories still have a hold on us today. One is the persistent belief that the phases of the moon have a direct effect on personality and behavior.

> It is the very error of the
> moon;
> She comes more near the
> earth than she was wont,
> And makes men mad.

When Shakespeare put these words into the mouth of Othello, he was expressing the thoughts of people of centuries past and centuries to come. Primitive societies believed that the moon had magical, mystical powers and that its changes portended events of many kinds. The moon had the power to impregnate women, to make plants grow, and to drive people crazy. Later societies also credited the power of the moon to affect behavior, and they applied the terms "lunatic" and "lunacy" to the person and the behavior to capture their lunar, or moonlike, qualities. Today many respected institutions and people actively support the idea that behavior is affected by the phases of the moon. The belief that bizarre behavior increases when the moon is full is so prevalent that a successful lunar newsletter serves a number of hospitals and law enforcement officials, warning them to be wary on nights of a full moon (Gardner, 1984).

Anecdotal evidence abounds: New York City police officers note more violent and bizarre crimes during the full moon, and hospitals claim to experience an increase in births. One hospital has linked the full moon to the onset of ulcers and heart attacks. A Wall Street broker has for years used the schedule of the full moon as a guide in giving investment advice—successfully (Gardner, 1984).

Scientists, who generally rely on explanations other than the inherent mystical prowess of the moon, have advanced many theories to make sense of a lunar effect on human behavior. Some say that since the moon causes the tides of the oceans, it is reasonable to expect that it has a similar effect on the bodily fluids of human beings (whose composition is more than 80 percent water). The increase in births might therefore be explained by the force of the moon on the expectant mother's amniotic fluid. Similar tidal and gravitational effects have been posited to explain the increase in bizarre behavior in people who may already be viewed as disturbed. Aside from the abundant anecdotal evidence, a study of clams by the biologist Frank Brown is often cited to show the ubiquitous power of the moon over the behavior of creatures of the earth throughout the Western world. Indeed, it would be difficult to name another school of thought that has had greater influence on Western culture.

Freud and his followers applied the psychoanalytic treatment approach primarily to patients with relatively modest mental disorders, problems of anxiety or depression that did not require hospitalization. These patients visited psychoanalytic therapists in their offices for sessions of approximately an hour and then went about their daily activities—a format of treatment now known as ***outpatient therapy.***

The psychoanalytic approach had little effect on the treatment of severely disturbed patients in mental hospitals, however. This type of therapy requires levels of clarity, insight, and verbal skill beyond the capabilities of most such patients. Moreover, psychoanalysis often takes years to be effective, and the overcrowded and understaffed public mental hospitals could not accommodate such a leisurely pace.

Current Trends

It would hardly be accurate to say that we now live in a period of widespread enlightenment or dependable treatment (see Box 1-3). Indeed, a relatively recent survey found that 43 percent of respondents believe that people bring on mental disorders themselves, and 35 percent consider the disorders to be caused by sinful behavior (Murray, 1993). Nevertheless, the past fifty years have

(Gardner, 1984). Brown reports moving a group of clams gathered in Connecticut to a laboratory in the landlocked city of Evanston, Illinois. At first the clams opened up to receive food during the times of high tide in Connecticut, as they had done all of their lives. After two weeks, however, the clams adopted an eating pattern that followed what would have been the schedule of high tides in Evanston—if Evanston had actually had any tides.

Moonstruck maidens dance in the town square in this eighteenth-century French engraving.

This evidence may seem to be compelling, but any hypothesis devised to explain the alleged effects of the moon is only a tentative assumption; none has been substantiated. Some researchers, less moonstruck, have performed rigorous statistical analyses of the actual numbers of births, crimes, and incidents of unusual behavior that occur during the full moon. Only a few have found evidence supporting the influence of the moon on various scales of human behavior (de Castro & Pearcy, 1995; Byrnes & Kelly, 1992; Kelly et al., 1990; Culver, Rotton, & Kelly, 1988). In view of the weakness of support for the popular lunacy theory, some scientists have suggested that we drop the entire question. Other researchers, undissuaded, claim that the lack of statistical evidence is not the problem—the problem has been the researchers' failure to look at the right variables, to use the appropriate measures, or to look at enough days both before and after the full moon. It has been suggested, for example, that studies of mental hospital admissions should take a lag time into account because the moon-induced behavior may not be identified or the individuals may not be processed until a week or more after the full moon (Cyr & Kalpin, 1988).

Most clinicians remain convinced that moon-induced abnormality is a myth, yet some people do exhibit strange behavior when the moon is full, or report strange sensations or increased sexual desire. The simplest explanation for these phenomena is most likely the most accurate. Personal belief, superstition, and bias can be powerful motivators of behavior. For people who already exhibit abnormal behavior or are searching for an excuse or a cue to break with society's behavioral norms, the historical belief in the power of the moon provides a convenient outlet. One waives personal responsibility by attributing one's behavior to the moon. The cause of lunacy may lie far less in the heavens than in our minds.

In state hospitals across the United States during the early twentieth century, overcrowding and limited funding led to the formation of back wards, throwbacks to the asylums of earlier times. Many patients languished in these wards for years, without therapy or hope of recovery.

With the discovery and application of these drugs, many patients who had languished for years in mental hospitals began to show signs of significant improvement. Hospital administrators, encouraged by the effectiveness of the drugs and pressured by a growing public outcry over the high cost of care and the terrible conditions in public mental hospitals, began to discharge patients almost immediately.

Since the discovery of these medications, mental health professionals in most of the developed nations of the world have followed a policy of ***deinstitutionalization,*** and hundreds of thousands of patients have been released from public mental hospitals. On any given day in 1955, close to 600,000 people were confined in public mental institutions across the United States (see Figure 1-2). Today the daily patient population in the same hospitals is around 80,000 (Torrey, 1997).

In short, outpatient care has now become the primary mode of treatment for people with severe psychological disturbances as well as for those with more moderate problems. When severely impaired people do require institutionalization, the current practice is to provide them with *short-term* hospitalization (Thompson et al., 1995). As in the past, today's private

brought significant changes in the understanding and treatment of abnormal functioning. There are more theories and types of treatment, more research studies, more information, and, perhaps for these reasons, more disagreements about abnormal functioning today than at any time in the past. In some ways the study and treatment of mental disorders have made great strides, but in other respects, clinical scientists and practitioners are still struggling to make a difference. The current era of abnormal psychology can be said to have begun in the 1950s.

Severe Disturbances and Their Treatment

In the 1950s researchers discovered a number of new ***psychotropic medications***—drugs that primarily affect the brain and alleviate many symptoms of mental dysfunctioning. They included the first *antipsychotic drugs,* to correct grossly confused and distorted thinking; *antidepressant drugs,* to lift the mood of severely depressed people; and *antianxiety drugs,* to help reduce tension and anxiety.

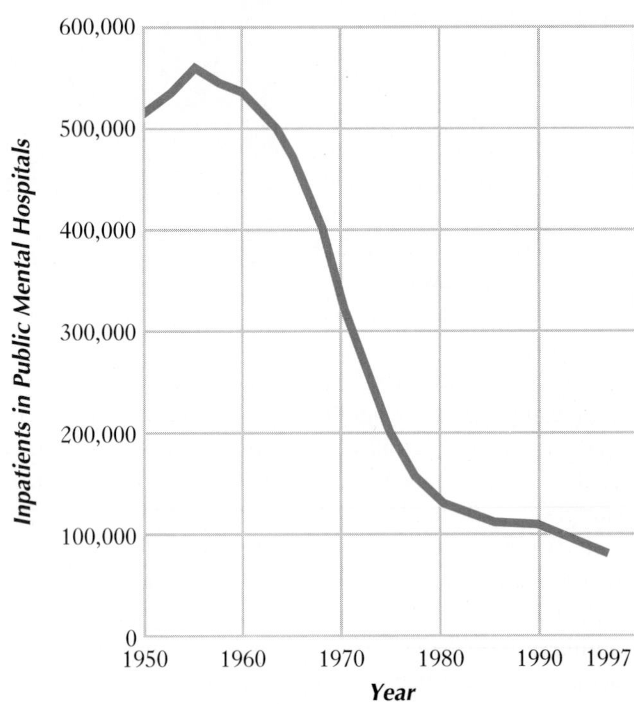

Figure 1-2 *The number of patients (80,000) now hospitalized in public mental hospitals in the United States is a small fraction of the number hospitalized in 1955. (Adapted from Torrey, 1997, 1988; Manderscheid & Sonnenschein, 1992.)*

institutions usually offer better facilities, more trained staff members per patient, and more varied treatments than public institutions (Redick et al., 1992). Ideally, after release from a hospital, patients are provided with outpatient psychotherapy and medication monitoring in community mental health centers. Other community programs such as supervised residences (halfway houses) and vocational rehabilitation centers may also be available (Thompson et al., 1995).

Chapters 4 and 16 will look more closely at this recent emphasis on community care for people with severe psychological disturbances, called the ***community mental health approach.*** The approach has helped many patients, but unfortunately too few community facilities and programs are available to address the needs of severely disturbed people in the United States. As a result, hundreds of thousands fail to make lasting recoveries and are shuffled back and forth between the mental hospital and the community. After they are released from the hospital, they receive at best minimal care and often wind up living in decrepit rooming houses or on the streets. In fact, an estimated 150,000 or more persons with severe psychological disturbances are currently homeless on any given day. Even more are inmates of jails and prisons (Torrey, 1997; Manderscheid & Rosenstein, 1992; NIMH, 1992). Their virtual abandonment is truly a national disgrace.

Less Severe Disturbances and Their Treatment

The treatment picture for people with less severe psychological disturbances has been more positive since the 1950s. Outpatient care has continued to be the preferred mode of treatment for these people, and the number and types of facilities that offer such care have expanded to meet the need (Redick et al., 1996).

Before the 1950s, almost all outpatient care took the form of ***private psychotherapy,*** an arrangement by which an individual directly pays a psychotherapist for counseling services. This tended to be an expensive form of treatment, available almost exclusively to the affluent. Since the 1950s, however, many medical health insurance plans have expanded coverage to include private psychotherapy, so that this service is now more widely available to people with more modest incomes (Levin, 1992). In addition, outpatient therapy has become increasingly available in a variety of relatively inexpensive settings—community mental health centers, crisis intervention centers, family service centers, and other social service agencies (Redick et al., 1996; Olfson, Pincus, & Dial, 1994). The new settings have spurred a dramatic increase in the number of persons seeking outpatient care for psychological problems. The growth in the use of outpatient services, from roughly 23 percent of people treated for psychological disturbances in 1955 to about 94 percent today, is seen in Figure 1-3.

Therapy for people with mild or moderate psychological disturbances is widely available today in individual, group, and family formats. It can be obtained privately or in less expensive government-subsidized mental health centers and agencies.

Nationwide surveys of adults suggest that between 16 and 22 million people in the United States now receive therapy for psychological problems in the course of a year (Kessler et al., 1994; Narrow et al., 1993). This figure represents approximately 12 percent of the entire adult population. It has become increasingly common for children to be treated for psychological problems, too (Kazdin, 1993).

During the past several decades, outpatient treatments have also become available for more and more problems. When Freud and his colleagues first began to conduct therapy, most of their patients suffered from anxiety or depression. These problems still dominate therapy today; almost half of all clients suffer from them. However, people with other kinds of disorders are also receiving therapy (Narrow et al., 1993). In addition, large numbers of people with milder psychological problems, sometimes called "problems in living," are also in outpatient therapy. Surveys suggest that approximately 25 percent of clients enter therapy because of problems with marital, family, job, peer, school, or community relationships.

Yet another change in outpatient care since the 1950s has been the development of specialized programs that focus exclusively on one kind of psychological problem. We now have, for example, suicide prevention centers, substance abuse programs, eating disorder programs,

1950s (1.7 Million Cases)

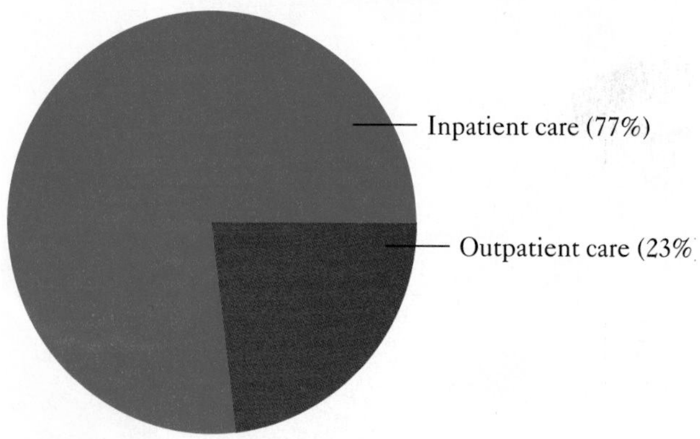

Today (22 Million Cases)

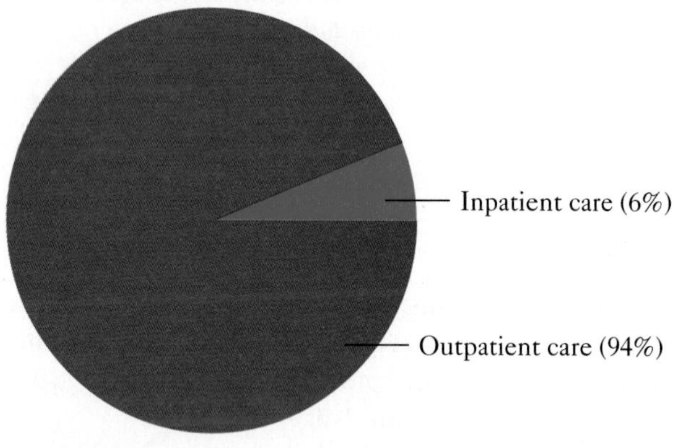

Figure 1-3 *The percentage of mental health patients who are treated on an outpatient basis has grown steadily since the 1950s. "Inpatient care" refers to treatment in state, county, and private mental hospitals, general hospitals, and Veterans Administration hospitals. "Outpatient care" refers to treatment by community mental health agencies, private therapists, day-care centers, and specialists in social and vocational rehabilitation. (Adapted from Narrow et al., 1993; Regier et al., 1993; Witkin et al., 1990; NIMH, 1983.)*

phobia clinics, and sexual dysfunction programs. Practitioners in these programs acquire the kind of expertise that can come only by concentrating one's efforts in a single area.

Today's Perspectives and Professionals

One of the most significant developments in the understanding and treatment of abnormal psychological functioning has been the emergence of numerous theoretical perspectives. Before the 1950s, the *psychoanalytic* perspective, with its emphasis on unconscious conflicts as the cause of psychopathology, was dominant. Then the discovery of effective psychotropic drugs brought new stature to the somatogenic, or *biological,* view of abnormality. As we shall see in Chapters 3 and 4, other influential perspectives that have emerged since the 1950s are the *behavioral, cognitive, humanistic-existential,* and *sociocultural* schools of thought. At present no single perspective dominates the clinical field as the psychoanalytic perspective once did. Indeed, the various perspectives often conflict and compete with one another; yet, as we shall be observing, they may in some instances complement one another and collectively provide more comprehensive explanations and interventions for mental disorders (Gabbard & Goodwin, 1996).

In addition, a variety of professional practitioners now offer help to people with psychological problems (Peterson et al., 1996; Murstein & Fontaine, 1993). Before the 1950s, psychotherapy was the exclusive province of ***psychiatrists,*** physicians who complete three to four additional years of training after medical school (a *residency*) in the treatment of abnormal mental functioning. After World War II, however, the demand for mental health services expanded more rapidly than the ranks of psychiatrists, so other professional groups stepped in to fill the need (Humphreys, 1996).

Prominent among those other groups are ***clinical psychologists***—professionals who earn a doctorate in clinical psychology by completing four or five years of graduate training in abnormal functioning and its treatment and also complete a one-year internship at a mental hospital or mental health agency. Before their professional responsibilities expanded into the area of treatment, clinical psychologists were principally assessors and researchers of abnormal functioning. Some of them still specialize in those activities.

Psychotherapy and related services are also provided by ***counseling psychologists, educational and school psychologists, psychiatric nurses, marriage therapists, family therapists,*** and—the largest group—***psychiatric social workers*** (see Table 1-1). Each of these specialties requires completion of its own graduate training program (Neimeyer, 1996; Peterson et al., 1996). Theoretically, each specialty conducts therapy in a distinctive way, but in reality there is considerable overlap in the ways practitioners of the various specialties work. Indeed, the individual differences within a given professional group are sometimes much greater than the general differences between groups.

One final important development in the study and treatment of mental disorders since World War II has been a heightened appreciation of the need for effective research. As numerous theories and forms of treatment have been proposed, clinical researchers have tried to single out the concepts that best explain and predict abnor-

TABLE 1-1 Profiles of Mental Health Professionals

	Degree	Began to Practice	Current Number	Median Age	Percent Male
Psychiatrists	M.D.	1840s	33,486	52	75%
Psychologists	Ph.D., Psy.D., Ed.D.	Late 1940s	69,817	48	56%
Social workers	M.S.W., D.S.W.	Early 1950s	188,792	47	23%
Marriage and family therapists	Various	1940s	46,227	52	45%

(Sources: Peterson et al., 1996; Knowlton, 1995.)

mal behavior, to determine which treatments are most effective, and to discover whether they should be modified and, if so, how. Today well-trained clinical researchers are conducting studies in academic institutions, laboratories, mental hospitals, mental health centers, and other clinical settings throughout the world. Their work has already yielded important discoveries and changed many of our ideas about abnormal psychological functioning. Just as important, it repeatedly demonstrates that properly conducted research is essential for continued progress in the study and practice of abnormal psychology.

Organization of the Text

The study and treatment of abnormal psychological functioning are exciting and confusing in equal measure. New ideas, discoveries, and refinements are continually being introduced, and the proliferating theories and treatment approaches can be difficult to evaluate and compare.

How, then, should we proceed in our examination of the various kinds of psychological abnormality? To begin with, we need to appreciate the basic tools and perspectives that today's scientists and practitioners find most useful. This is the task we turn to in the next several chapters. Chapter 2 helps us to understand how abnormal functioning is studied today—the research tools and strategies that are currently used. Chapters 3 and 4 then examine the range of views that dominate the thinking and practice of today's professionals. Finally, Chapter 5 examines how abnormal behaviors are assessed, diagnosed, and treated today.

Later chapters examine the major categories of psychological abnormality as well as the leading explanations and treatments for each of them. In the final chapter we shall see how the science of abnormal psychology and its professionals address current social issues and interact with legal, social, and other institutions in today's society.

Chapter Review

1. ***The field*** The field devoted to the scientific study of abnormal behavior is called *abnormal psychology.* Its goals are to understand and to treat abnormal patterns of functioning.

2. ***Defining psychological abnormality and treatment*** Abnormal patterns of psychological functioning are generally considered to be those that are *deviant, distressful, dysfunctional,* and *dangerous.* However, behavior must be considered in the context in which it occurs; behavior considered deviant in one set of circumstances may be the norm in another. *Treatment* is a procedure to help change abnormal behavior into more normal behavior. It requires a *sufferer,* a *sanctioned healer,* and a *series of contacts* between the two.

3. ***Abnormality in ancient times*** The history of human societies over the millennia provides many clues to the nature of psychological abnormality.

A. ***Prehistoric societies*** Historians have concluded that prehistoric societies probably viewed abnormal behavior as the work of evil spirits. There is evidence that Stone Age peoples used *trephination,* a primitive form of brain surgery, to treat abnormal behavior. People of early societies also sought to drive out evil spirits by *exorcism.*

B. ***Greeks and Romans*** Physicians of ancient Greece and Rome offered alternative explanations of mental disorders. Hippocrates believed that abnormal behavior was due to an imbalance of the four bodily fluids, or *humors:* black bile, yellow bile, blood, and phlegm. Treatment for mental disorders consisted of correcting the underlying physical pathology through diet and lifestyle.

4. ***Europe in the Middle Ages: demonology returns*** In the Middle Ages, Europeans resurrected the demonological explanation of abnormal behavior. The combination of great strife in the Western world and the preeminence of the clergy contributed to the view that mental disorders were the work of the devil. As the Middle Ages drew to a close, physical explanations and treatments for psychological abnormality started to gain prominence, and many people with mental disorders were treated in hospitals instead of by the clergy.

5. ***The Renaissance and the rise of asylums*** Care of the people with mental disorders continued to improve during the Renaissance, highlighted by religious shrines dedicated to the humane treatment of such individuals. By the middle of the sixteenth century, however, persons with mental disorders were being warehoused in *asylums.*

6. ***Moral treatment*** Care of people with mental disorders started to improve again in the nineteenth century. At La Bicêtre asylum in Paris, Philippe Pinel started the movement toward *moral treatment* by treating inmates as people suffering from an illness that required support and kindness. Similar reforms were brought to England by William Tuke.

The moral treatment methodology was adopted in the United States by Benjamin Rush. In the mid- and late nineteenth century in Massachusetts, Dorothea Dix spearheaded a movement to ensure legal rights and protection for people with mental disorders and to establish state hospitals for their care.

Unfortunately, moral treatment was costly and not always effective. As a result, the system disintegrated by the late nineteenth century and mental hospitals again became warehouses where the inmates received minimal care.

7. ***The somatogenic perspective*** The late nineteenth century saw the return of the *somatogenic perspective,* the view that abnormal psychological functioning is rooted primarily in physical causes. This development was precipitated in part by the work of Emil Kraepelin and the finding that *general paresis* was caused by the organic disease syphilis.

8. ***The psychogenic perspective*** The late nineteenth century also saw the emergence of the *psychogenic perspective,* the view that the chief causes of abnormal functioning are psychological. One of the key developments at this time was the use of *hypnotism* to treat patients with hysterical disorders. Another was the finding by the Viennese doctor Josef Breuer that some patients who spoke candidly about past traumas during hypnosis awoke free of hysterical symptoms. These developments influenced the subsequent work of Sigmund Freud, whose *psychoanalytic* approach eventually gained wide acceptance and influenced future generations of researchers and practitioners.

9. ***Current trends*** The past fifty years have brought significant changes in the understanding and treatment of abnormal functioning.

A. ***Severe disturbances and their treatment*** In the 1950s, researchers discovered a number of new drugs that affected perceptions and emotions. The success of these *psychotropic drugs* contributed to a policy of *deinstitutionalization,* under which hundreds of thousands of patients were released from public mental hospitals.

B. ***Less severe disturbances and their treatment*** One result of the deinstitutionalization movement was a focus on *outpatient treatment* as the primary approach for most persons with mental disorders. The wider availability of outpatient care and private therapy has also led to a dramatic increase in treatment for patients suffering less severe psychological disturbances.

C. ***Today's perspectives and professionals*** Numerous theoretical perspectives have emerged over the past fifty years. Each explains and treats abnormality in a distinctive way. In addition, a variety of professionals now offer help to people with psychological problems. Each specialty requires completion of its own graduate training. Finally, many well-trained clinical researchers investigate the various concepts of abnormal behavior and treatments for them.

Thought and Afterthought

Beware the Evil Eye

In rural Pakistan many parents apply special makeup around the eyes of their young children, as their ancestors have done for centuries. A paste of hazelnut powder and several oils, known as *surma*, is applied, partly to protect the eyes from the smoke given off by home heating fires and partly to cool and clean the eyes (Smolan, Moffitt, & Naythons, 1990). But another, less acknowledged reason is to ward off *nazar*, the evil eye, thought to be responsible for the many deaths among infants and for poor health and behavioral problems in those who survive.

Afterthoughts: The widespread belief in the evil eye indicates that many people still rely on demonology to explain or remedy undesirable or abnormal events or behaviors. What other demonological explanations or treatments are still around today?... Why do they continue?... Are some people more likely than others to adopt them?

Frankly Speaking

The more [patients] resist our efforts to serve them, the more they have need of our services.

—**Benjamin Rush,** father of American psychiatry

We are all here on earth to help others; what on earth the others are here for, I don't know.

—**W. H. Auden,** *The Dyer's Hand and Other Essays* (1968)

Afterthoughts: While Benjamin Rush believed that therapists have a right and an obligation to treat patients—even to impose treatment on them—the poet W. H. Auden suggested that such notions, when carried to an extreme, are presumptuous and self-serving.

As the study and treatment of abnormal behavior have expanded in the past fifty years, which of these statements reflects the view of practitioners? . . . What dangers may accompany the enormous increase and influence of the clinical field during the past half century?

Ascending to a Higher Kingdom

In 1997 the world was shocked to learn of the incredible beliefs propounded by the Heaven's Gate cult when thirty-nine of its members committed suicide at an expensive house outside San Diego. Videotapes left behind, written tracts, and postings on the Internet revealed that the members had believed that they were infused with higher heavenly spirits, that their bodies were mere "containers" or "vehicles," and that a UFO was hiding in the slipstream of the comet Hale-Bopp, coming to take them home to "their world." Ultimately, they believed, their death would free them to ascend on a cloud of light to a higher kingdom.

The public was particularly captivated by two aspects of this tragedy. One was the striking similarities between the strange beliefs and behaviors of the Heaven's Gate cult and those of various groups at earlier points in history. Through the ages a number of groups have sought to speed their entry into heaven before the arrival of the end times predicted in Revelation. In the sixteenth century, for example, villages of Christian "saints" burned themselves to death in a quest for salvation.

A second area of interest was the key role that the mass media and modern communication systems apparently played in the rise and spread of Heaven's Gate. In 1993, trying to generate interest in the group, its leader, Marshall Herff Applewhite (above), ran an ad in *USA Today* that described the cult's philosophical bonds with other millennial groups. Beyond this "conventional" form of publicity, the cult members became experts on the Internet and used it to learn about UFO sightings and other signs of "higher life." In addition, cult members apparently recruited new members by sending messages out to Internet newsgroups focused on suicide, depression, and substance abuse.

Afterthoughts: What features do the beliefs, behaviors, and circumstances of the Heaven's Gate cult share with past forms of "mass madness", such as tarantism and lycanthropy? . . . What features distinguish Heaven's Gate from these past forms of mass madness? . . . Does the Internet pose special dangers of the emergence and spread of new forms of "mass madness"?

Topic Overview

Chapter 2

Research in Abnormal Psychology

Schizophrenia is a severe disorder that causes people to lose contact with reality. Sufferers' thoughts, perceptions, and emotions become distorted and disorganized. Their behavior can look bizarre, and they often withdraw socially as well. As we shall see in Chapter 15, for the first half of this century most clinical theorists traced the disorder primarily to inappropriate parenting. They believed that people with schizophrenia were reared by ***schizophrenogenic*** ("schizophrenia-causing") ***mothers***—cold and domineering women who were impervious to their children's needs. This widely held belief turned out to be wrong.

In the 1940s, clinical practitioners developed a surgical procedure that supposedly cured schizophrenia. In this treatment procedure, called a ***lobotomy,*** a pointed instrument was inserted into the frontal lobe of the brain and rotated, destroying a considerable amount of brain tissue. Reports soon spread that lobotomized patients showed near-miraculous improvement, and clinical practitioners administered the procedure to tens of thousands of mental patients. This impression, too, turned out to be wrong: far from curing schizophrenia, lobotomies caused irreversible brain damage that left many patients withdrawn, excessively subdued, and even stuporous.

Like the travelers in M. C. Escher's Relativity, *1953, clinical researchers find that all paths lead somewhere, yet many paths lead in unexpected directions.*

These errors underscore the importance of sound research in abnormal psychology. Theories and treatment procedures that seem reasonable and effective in individual instances may prove disastrous when they are applied to large numbers of people or situations. Only by testing a theory or technique on representative groups of subjects can its accuracy or utility be determined. It was only through such testing that the notion of schizophrenogenic mothers was finally challenged and the indiscriminate use of lobotomies stopped.

Clinical researchers subject the ideas of clinical theorists and the techniques of clinical practitioners to systematic testing. Research is the key to accuracy and progress in all fields of study, and it is particularly important in abnormal psychology, because inaccurate beliefs here can cause or prolong enormous suffering. Until clinical researchers conducted relevant studies, for example, millions of parents, already heartbroken by their children's schizophrenic disorders, were additionally stigmatized as the primary cause of the disorders; and countless people with schizophrenia, already debilitated by their symptoms, were made permanently apathetic and spiritless by a lobotomy.

Unfortunately, although effective and rigorous research is essential for progress in abnormal psychology, the nature of the issues under study makes such research particularly difficult. Researchers must figure out ways to measure such elusive concepts as unconscious motives, private thoughts, mood change, and human potential, and they must also address such ethical issues as the rights of subjects, both human and animal.

Fortunately, research in this field has taken giant steps forward, especially during the last thirty-five years. In the past, many clinical researchers had only limited skills. Now graduate clinical programs train large numbers of students to conduct appropriate studies on clinical topics. Their development of new research tools and methods has greatly improved our understanding of psychological function and dysfunction.

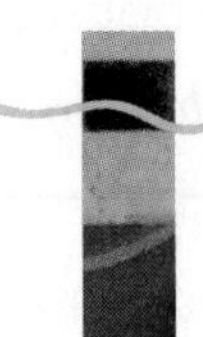

The Task of Clinical Researchers

Clinical researchers, also called clinical scientists, try to discover universal *laws*, or principles, of abnormal psychological functioning. They search for general, or ***nomothetic,*** truths about the nature, causes, and treatments of abnormality ("nomothetic" is derived from the Greek *nomothetis,* "lawgiver"). They do not typically assess, diagnose, or treat individual clients; that is the job of clinical practitioners, who seek an ***idiographic,*** or individualistic, understanding of abnormal behavior (Stricker & Trierweiler, 1995). We shall explore the work of practitioners in Chapters 3, 4, and 5.

"You want proof? I'll give you proof!"

To gain a nomothetic understanding of abnormal psychology, clinical researchers, like scientists in other fields, rely primarily on the ***scientific method***—that is, they systematically acquire and evaluate information through observations (Beutler et al., 1995). Such observations in turn enable them to identify and explain relationships between variables. Simply stated, a ***variable*** is any characteristic or event that can vary, whether from time to time, from place to place, or from person to person. Age, sex, and race are human variables. So are eye color, occupation, and social status. Clinical researchers are particularly interested in variables such as childhood traumas and other life experiences, moods, levels of social and occupational functioning, and responses to treatment. They want to know whether two or more such variables change together and whether a change in one variable causes a change in another. Will the death of a parent, for example, cause a child to become depressed? If so, will a given treatment reduce that depression?

Such questions cannot be answered by logic alone. Reasoning is only as accurate as the information available to reason with, so numerous observations are often needed to establish a factual basis on which to build a conclusion. Even then, reasoning may fail to serve the scientific enterprise. Although human beings are marvelously sophisticated and complex, they are prone to frequent errors in thinking (NAMHC, 1996). Witness the false impressions we often form of others and the many times we jump to wrong conclusions.

To acquire valid information about abnormal behavior and minimize errors in reasoning, clinical researchers depend primarily on three methods of investigation: the *case study,* which typically observes but one individual, and the *correlational method* and *experimental method,* approaches that usually observe many individuals. As we shall see, each method is best suited to certain circumstances and questions (Beutler et al., 1995). Collectively, the methods enable scientists to formulate and test hypotheses, or hunches, that certain variables are related in certain ways, and to draw broad conclusions as to why. More properly, a ***hypothesis*** is a tentative explanation advanced to provide a basis for an investigation.

The Case Study

A ***case study*** is a detailed and often interpretive description of one person. It describes the person's background, present circumstances, and symptoms. It may also describe the application and results of a particular treatment, and it may speculate about how the person's problems developed.

In his famous case study of Little Hans (1909), Sigmund Freud discusses a 4-year-old boy who has developed a fear of horses. Freud gathered his material from detailed letters sent him by Hans's father, a physician who had attended lectures on psychoanalysis, and from Freud's own limited interviews with the child. Freud's study covers 140 pages in his *Collected Papers,* so only key excerpts will be reproduced here.

> One day while Hans was in the street he was seized with an attack of morbid anxiety. . . . [Hans's father wrote:] "He began to cry and asked to be taken home. . . . Till the evening he was cheerful, as usual. But in the evening he grew visibly frightened; he cried and could not be separated from his mother. . . . [When taken for a walk the next day], again he began to cry, did not want to start, and was frightened. . . . On the way back from Schönbrunn he said to his mother, after much internal struggling: 'I was afraid a horse would bite me.' . . . In the evening he . . . had another attack similar to that of the previous evening. . . . He said, crying: 'I know I shall have to go for a walk again tomorrow.' And later: 'The horse'll come into the room.' . . ."
>
> But the beginnings of this psychological situation go back further still. . . . The first reports of Hans date from a period when he was not quite three years old. At that time, by means of various remarks and questions, he was showing a quite peculiarly lively interest in that portion of his body which he used to describe as his 'widdler' [his word for penis]. . . .
>
> When he was three and a half his mother found him with his hand to his penis. She threatened him in these words: 'If you do that, I shall send for Dr. A. to cut off your widdler. And then what'll you widdle with?' . . . This was the occasion of his acquiring [a] 'castration complex.' . . .
>
> [At the age of four, Hans entered] a state of intensified sexual excitement, the object of which was his mother. The intensity of this excitement was shown by . . . two attempts at seducing his mother. [One such attempt, occurring just before the outbreak of his anxiety, was described by his father:] "This morning Hans was given his usual daily bath by his mother and afterwards dried and powdered. As his mother was powdering round his penis and taking care not to touch it, Hans said: 'Why don't you put your finger there? . . .'"
>
> . . . The father and son visited me during my consulting hours. . . . Certain details which I now learnt—to the effect that [Hans] was particularly bothered by what horses wear in front of their eyes and by the black round their mouths—were certainly not to be explained from what we knew. But as I saw the two of them sitting in front of me and at the same time heard Hans's description of his anxiety-horses, a further piece of the solution shot through my mind, and a piece which I could well understand might escape his father. I asked Hans jokingly whether his horses wore eyeglasses, to which he replied that they did not. I then asked him whether his father wore eyeglasses, to which, against all the evidence, he once more said no. Finally I asked him whether by 'the black round the mouth' he meant a moustache; and I then disclosed to him that he was afraid of his father, precisely because he was so fond of his mother. It must be, I told him, that he thought his father was angry with him on that account; but this was not so, his father was fond of him in spite of it, and he might admit everything to him without any fear. Long before he was in the world, I went on, I had known that a little Hans would come who would be so fond of his mother that he would be bound to feel afraid of his father because of it. . . .
>
> By enlightening Hans on this subject I had cleared away his most powerful resistance against allowing his unconscious thoughts to be made conscious. . . . There was a plentiful flow of material; the little patient summoned up courage to describe the details of his phobia, and soon began to take an active share in the conduct of the analysis.
>
> . . . It was only then that we learnt what the objects and impressions were of which Hans was afraid. He was not only afraid of horses biting him—he was soon silent upon that point—but also of carts, of furniture-vans, and of buses [their common quality being, as presently became clear, that they were all heavily loaded], of horses that started moving, of horses that looked big and heavy, and of horses that drove quickly. The meaning of these specifications was explained by Hans himself: he was afraid of horses falling down, and consequently incorporated in his phobia everything that seemed likely to facilitate their falling down.

> It was at this stage of the analysis that he recalled the event, insignificant in itself, which immediately preceded the outbreak of the illness and may no doubt be regarded as the exciting cause of the outbreak. He went for a walk with his mother, and saw a bus-horse fall down and kick about with its feet. This made a great impression on him. He was terrified, and thought the horse was dead; and from that time on he thought that all horses would fall down. His father pointed out to him that when he saw the horse fall down he must have thought of him, his father, and have wished that he might fall down in the same way and be dead. Hans did not dispute this interpretation; and a little while later he played a game consisting of biting his father, and so showed that he accepted the theory of his having identified his father with the horse he was afraid of. From that time forward his behavior to his father was unconstrained and fearless, and in fact a trifle overbearing.
>
> It is especially interesting . . . to observe the way in which the transformation of Hans's libido into anxiety was projected on to the principal object of his phobia, on to horses. Horses interested him the most of all the large animals; playing at horses was his favorite game with the older children. I had a suspicion—and this was confirmed by Hans's father when I asked him—that the first person who had served Hans as a horse must have been his father. . . . When repression had set in and brought a revulsion of feeling along with it, horses, which had till then been associated with so much pleasure, were necessarily turned into objects of fear.
>
> [Hans later reported] two concluding phantasies, with which his recovery was rounded off. One of them, that of [a] plumber giving him a new and . . . bigger widdler, was . . . a triumphant wish-phantasy, and with it he overcame his fear of castration. . . . His other phantasy, which confessed to the wish to be married to his mother and to have many children by her . . . corrected that portion of those thoughts which was entirely unacceptable; for, instead of killing his father, it made him innocuous by promoting him to a marriage with Hans's grandmother. With this phantasy both the illness and the analysis came to an appropriate end.
>
> *(Freud, 1909)*

Most clinicians take notes and keep records in the course of treating their patients, and some, like Freud, further organize such notes into a formal study to be shared with other professionals. Faced with the task of helping someone, a clinician must first gather all relevant information and search through it for factors that may have brought about the person's problems (Stricker & Trierweiler, 1995). The clues provided by the case study may also have direct implications for the person's treatment. But case studies also play nomothetic roles that go far beyond the individual clinical case (Beutler et al., 1995; Smith, 1988).

Contributions of the Case Study

Case studies often serve as a *source of ideas* about behavior and "open the way for discoveries" (Bolgar, 1965). Freud's own theory of psychoanalysis was based mainly on the cases he saw in private practice. He pored over case studies, such as the one he wrote about Little Hans, to ferret out what he believed to be universal psychological processes and principles of development. Second, a case study may provide *tentative support* for a theory. Once again, Freud used case studies in precisely this way, as preliminary evidence for the accuracy of his ideas. Conversely, case studies may serve to *challenge theoretical assumptions* (Kratochwill, 1992; Kratochwill et al., 1984).

One of the most celebrated case studies in abnormal psychology is a study of identical quadruplets, all of whom developed schizophrenic disorders in their 20s. At the National Institute of Mental Health (NIMH) in Washington, D.C., where these sisters underwent extensive study (Rosenthal, 1963), they were given the pseudonyms Nora, Iris, Myra, and Hester (after the initials NIMH) and the family name Genain (after the Greek words for "dire birth").

Case studies also may serve as sources of ideas for *new therapeutic techniques* or as examples of unique applications of existing techniques. The psychoanalytic principle that patients may benefit by discussing their problems and underlying psychological issues, for example, has roots in the famous case study of Anna O., presented by Freud's collaborator Josef Breuer, a case we shall explore in Chapter 3. Similarly, Freud believed that the case study of Little Hans demonstrated the therapeutic potential of a verbal approach for children as well as for adults.

Finally, case studies may offer opportunities to study *unusual problems* that do not occur often enough to permit a large number of observations and comparisons (Lehman, 1991). For years information about multiple personality disorders was based almost exclusively on case studies, such as the famous *Three Faces of Eve*, a clinical account of a woman who displayed three alternating personalities, each having a distinct set of memories, preferences, and personal habits (Thigpen & Cleckley, 1957).

Some twenty-five years after the initial case study of the Genain sisters, the four women returned to NIMH for a follow-up study that used new technology to detect brain activity and structure (Buchsbaum & Haier, 1987). Marked variations in the sisters' levels of functioning corresponded to variations found in their brain activity and structure, suggesting that biological factors or interactions of biological and environmental factors may contribute to schizophrenia.

Limitations of the Case Study

Although case studies are useful in many ways, they have limitations. To begin with, they are reported by *biased observers* (Lehman, 1991). Therapists are participants in the healing process as well as observers of it, and they have a personal stake in seeing their treatments succeed (Stricker & Trierweiler, 1995). They must choose what to include in a case study, and their choices may be unsystematic and perhaps self-serving, however well intended.

A related limitation is that case studies rely upon *subjective evidence.* Is a client's dysfunction really caused by the events that the therapist or client says are responsible? After all, those are only a fraction of the events that may have contributed to the person's predicament. An investigator ultimately hopes to show that of a host of possible causes, all but one can be ruled out. If that aim is met, a study is said to have internal accuracy, or ***internal validity.*** Obviously, case studies rate low on that score.

A famous case study of identical quadruplets called the Genain sisters illustrates the problem of internal validity. These women of identical genetic makeup all developed schizophrenia, suggesting that this disorder may be genetically transmitted. Careful investigation also revealed, however, that the quadruplets shared more than their DNA. They were all kept in the hospital for the first six weeks of their lives, severely restricted in their interactions with others during childhood, and raised by a hostile and accusatory father. Any of these environmental factors could have contributed to their disorders. The case study could not confirm or clarify the relevance of either the genetic or environmental factors.

Finally, case studies provide little basis for *generalization.* Even if we agree that Little Hans did develop a dread of horses because he was terrified of castration and feared his father, how can we be confident that other people's phobias are rooted in the same kinds of causes? Factors or treatment techniques that seem important in one case may be of no help at all in efforts to understand or treat others. When the findings of an investigation can be generalized beyond the immediate study, the investigation is said to have external accuracy, or ***external validity.*** Case studies rate low on external validity, too (Lehman, 1991) (see Table 2-1).

The limitations of the case study are largely addressed by two other methods of investigation: the *correlational method* and the *experimental method.* They do not offer the richness of detail that makes case studies so interesting, but they do help investigators to draw broad conclusions and to pinpoint the occurrence and characteristics of abnormality in the population at large. Three characteristics of these methods enable clinical investigators to gain nomothetic insights:

1. Researchers typically observe *many* individuals. That way, they can collect enough information, or ***data,*** to support a conclusion.

2. Researchers apply carefully prescribed procedures *uniformly.* Therefore other researchers can repeat, or ***replicate,*** the study to see whether it consistently gives the same findings.

3. Researchers apply *statistical tests* to analyze the results of a study. These tests can help indicate whether broad conclusions are justified.

TABLE 2-1 Relative Strengths and Weaknesses of Research Methods

	Provides Individual Information (Idiographic)	*Provides General Information (Nomothetic)*	*Provides Causal Information*	*Statistical Analysis Is Possible*	*Replicable*
Case study	Yes	No	No	No	No
Correlational method	No	Yes	No	Yes	Yes
Experimental method	No	Yes	Yes	Yes	Yes

The correlational and experimental methods were used only occasionally to study abnormal functioning earlier in this century, but they are now the preferred methods of investigation (Pincus et al., 1993).

The Correlational Method

Correlation is the degree to which events or characteristics vary in conjunction with each other. The ***correlational method*** is a research procedure used to determine this "co-relationship" between variables. This method can, for example, answer the question "Is there a correlation between the amount of life stress people confront and the degree of depression they display?" That is, as people repeatedly experience stressful events, are they increasingly likely to become depressed?

To test this question, researchers must first find a way to measure the two variables *life stress* and *depression.* They do so by translating the variables into events they can observe, a process called ***operationalization.*** Life stress has been operationalized in some studies as the number of threatening events that a person experiences during a specified period of time (Veiel et al., 1992). A significant health problem or the loss of a job could each count as one such event. Similarly, depression has been operationalized as obtaining a high score on a special depression questionnaire. The questionnaire may include such questions as how often one feels like crying or how often one feels tired and fatigued.

Once the variables being examined are operationalized, researchers can measure them in a large number of individuals. Only then can they determine whether a general correlation between the variables does indeed exist. The people who are chosen for a study are its ***subjects,*** or ***participants,*** collectively called the ***sample.*** A sample must be representative of the larger population that the researchers wish to understand (Sandelowski, 1995). Otherwise the relationship found in the study may not apply elsewhere in the real world. If researchers found a correlation between life stress and depression in a group of very young subjects, for example, they might still be able to say little about what, if any, correlation exists among adults.

The Direction of Correlation

Suppose we use the correlation method to conduct a study of depression. We collect life stress scores and depression scores for ten subjects, and we plot the scores on a graph, as shown in Figure 2-1. As you can see, the subject named

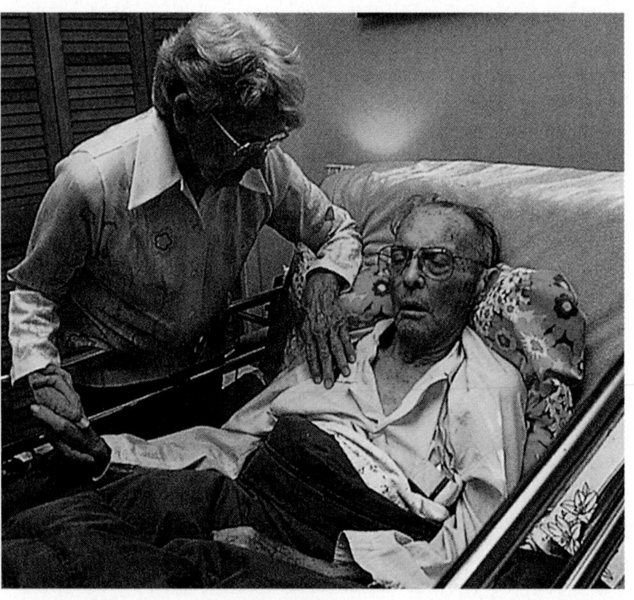

Numerous studies have found a correlation between life stress and depression. The pressures of caring for a chronically-ill spouse, for example, have been linked to depression in caretakers. It is not clear, however, whether the stress of caretaking causes *depression, or whether increases in depression and caretaking are each independently caused by the deteriorating condition of a loved one.*

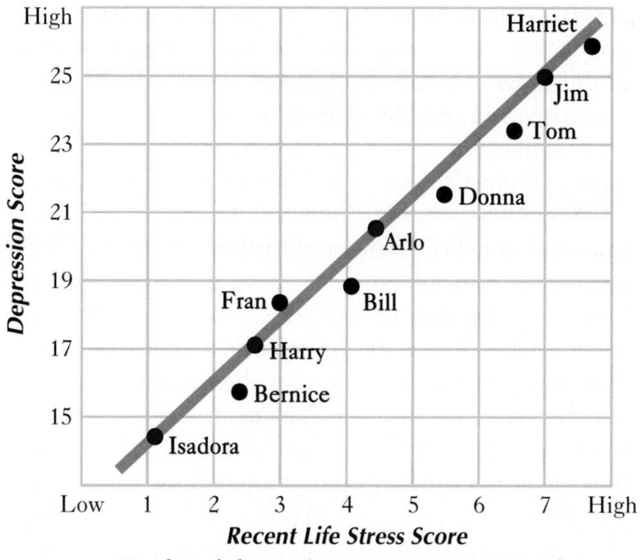

Figure 2-1 *The relationship between the amount of recent stress and feelings of depression shown by this hypothetical sample of ten subjects is a near-perfect "positive" correlation.*

Jim has a recent life stress score of 7, meaning seven threatening events over the past three months; he also has a depression score of 25. Thus he is "located" at the point on the graph where these two scores meet. The graph can show us what results like this mean visually. Here, notice that the data points all fall roughly along a straight line that slopes upward. We draw the line so that each data point is as close to the line as possible. The one line that best fits all the data points is called the ***line of best fit.***

The line of best fit in Figure 2-1 slopes upward and to the right, indicating that the variables under examination are increasing or decreasing together. That is, the greater someone's life stress score, the higher his or her score on the depression scale. When variables change the same way, the correlation is said to have a positive direction, and the correlation is referred to as a ***positive correlation.*** Most studies have indeed found a positive correlation between recent life stress and depression (Paykel & Cooper, 1992).

Correlations can have a negative rather than a positive direction. In a ***negative correlation,*** as the value of one variable increases, the value of the other variable decreases. Researchers have found, for example, a negative correlation between depression and activity level. The greater one's depression, the lower the number of one's activities. When the subjects' scores of a negative correlation are plotted, they produce a downward-sloping graph, like the one shown in Figure 2-2.

There is still a third possible relationship in a correlational study. Two variables may well be ***unrelated,*** meaning that there is no systematic relationship between them. As the measures of one variable increase, those of the other variable sometimes increase and sometimes decrease. If subjects' scores are uncorrelated, the graph of their relationship looks like Figure 2-3. Here the line of best fit is horizontal, with no slope at all. Studies have found that depression and intelligence are unrelated, for example.

The Magnitude of Correlation

In addition to knowing the direction of a correlation, researchers need to know its ***magnitude,*** or ***strength.*** That is, how closely do the two variables correspond? Does one *always* vary along with the other, or is their relationship less precise? When the points are plotted on a graph, how close do the points fall to the line of best fit?

To appreciate the strength of a correlation, look again at Figure 2-1. In this graph of a positive correlation between depression and life stress, the data points all fall very close to the line of best fit. Here researchers can predict each person's score on one variable with a high degree of confidence if they know his or her score on the other. But what if the graph of the correlation between depression and life stress looked more like Figure 2-4? Now the data points are loosely scattered around the upward-sloping line of best fit rather than hugging it closely. In this case, researchers could not predict with as much accuracy a subject's score on one variable from the score on the other variable. Because the correlation in Figure 2-1 allows researchers to make more accurate predictions than the one in Figure 2-4, it is stronger, or greater in magnitude.

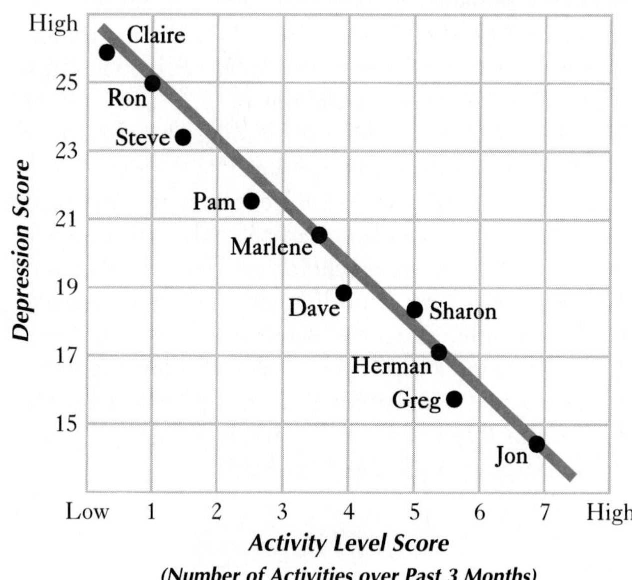

Figure 2-2 *The relationship between the number of activities and feelings of depression shown by this hypothetical sample is a near-perfect "negative" correlation.*

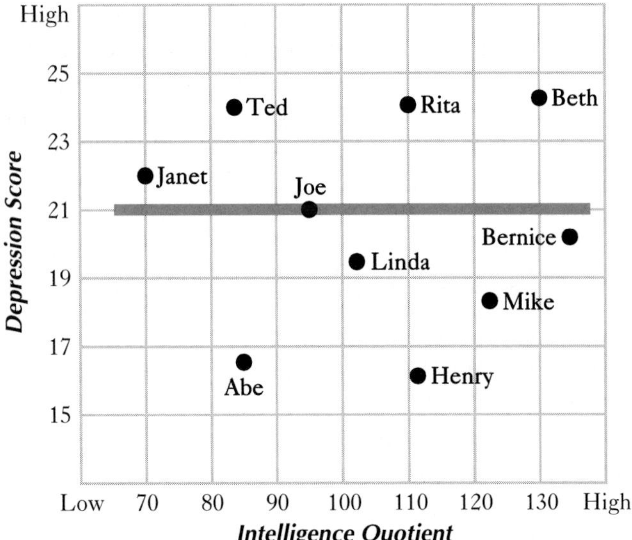

Figure 2-3 *The relationship between intelligence quotient and feelings of depression shown by this hypothetical sample is a "near-zero" correlation.*

The Correlation Coefficient

The direction and magnitude of a correlation can also be stated numerically and expressed by a statistical term called the ***correlation coefficient,*** symbolized by the letter ***r*** (statisticians call it the *Pearson product moment correlation coefficient,* after the man who devised it, Karl Pearson). The correlation coefficient can vary from +1.00, which conveys a perfect positive correlation between two variables, down to −1.00, which represents a perfect negative correlation. The *sign* of the coefficient (+ or −) signifies the *direction* of the correlation; the *number* represents its *magnitude.* An *r* of .00 reflects a zero correlation, or no relationship between variables. The closer *r* is to .00, the weaker, or lower in magnitude, the correlation. Thus correlations of +.75 and −.75 are of equal magnitude and equally strong, whereas a correlation of +.25 is weaker than either.

Everyone's behavior is subject to change, and many human responses can be measured only approximately. Most correlations in psychological research, therefore, fall short of a perfect positive or negative correlation. One study of life stress and depression, with a sample of 68 adults, found a correlation of +.53 (Miller, Ingraham, & Davidson, 1976). Although hardly perfect, a correlation of this magnitude with a sample of this size is considered large in psychological research.

Statistical Analysis of Correlational Data

When scientists first determine a correlation between variables, they cannot immediately conclude a nomothetic truth. They must still decide whether the correlation accurately reflects the relationship that exists in the general population: Is the sample used in the study representative of the larger population? Could the observed correlation have occurred only by chance? Perhaps in actuality no such connection exists in the population at large, or perhaps a connection exists but with a different magnitude.

Scientists can never know for certain, but they can test their conclusions by a ***statistical analysis*** of their data, using principles of probability. In essence, they ask how likely it is that the study's particular findings have occurred by chance. If the statistical analysis suggests that chance is a likely reason for the correlation, the researchers have no basis for drawing broader conclusions from the sample. But if the statistical analysis indicates that chance is unlikely to account for the relationship they found, the researchers may conclude that their findings reflect a real correlation in the general population.

A cutoff point helps researchers make this decision. By convention, if there is less than a 5 percent probability that a study's findings are due to chance (signified as $p < .05$), the findings are said to be ***statistically significant.*** The researcher may then conclude that they do reflect the larger population. In the life stress study described earlier, a statistical analysis indicated a probability of less than 5 percent that the +.53 correlation found in the sample was due to chance (Miller et al., 1976). Therefore, the researchers concluded with some confidence that among adults in general, depression does tend to rise along with the amount of recent stress in a person's life. Generally, our confidence increases with the number of subjects and the magnitude of the correlation. The larger they are, the more likely it is that a correlation will be statistically significant.

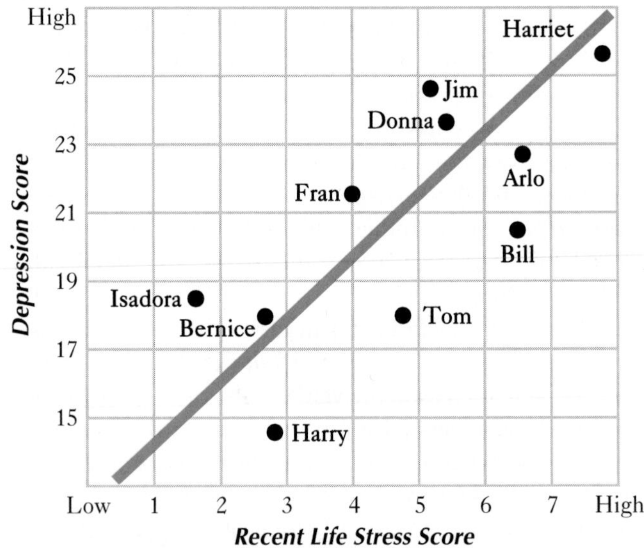

Figure 2-4 *The relationship between the amount of recent stress and feelings of depression shown by this hypothetical sample is a "moderately positive" correlation.*

Strengths and Limitations of the Correlational Method

Unlike case studies, correlational studies typically exhibit high *external validity*. Because researchers quantify their variables in such studies, observe numerous subjects, and apply statistical analyses, they are in a better position to generalize their findings. Researchers are also able to repeat correlational studies on new samples of subjects, so that they can corroborate the results of such studies.

On the other hand, correlational studies, like case studies, lack *internal validity* (Goodwin, 1995). Although correlations give researchers predictive power by describing the relationship between two variables, they do not *explain* the relationship. When we look at the positive correlation found in many life stress studies, we may be tempted to conclude that increases in recent life stress *cause* people to feel more depressed. In fact, however, the two variables may be correlated for any one of three reasons: (1) life stress may cause depression; (2) depression may cause people to experience more life stress (for example, a depressive approach to life may cause people to mismanage their money, be less effective at work, or let social relationships deteriorate); or (3) depression and life stress may each be caused by yet a third variable, such as poverty.

In short, correlation says nothing about causation. Internal validity is not always a problem for clinicians. Sometimes it's enough to know that two variables tend to occur together. Clinicians need to know that suicide attempts increase as people become more depressed, for example. That way, when they work with severely depressed clients they keep on the lookout for symptoms of suicidal thinking (Beck, 1993, 1967). It doesn't necessarily make a difference to them whether depression directly causes suicidal behavior. Perhaps a third variable, such as a sense of hopelessness, causes both depression and suicidal thoughts. Still, as soon as the clinicians identify intense feelings of depression, they can stand ready to take measures to prevent suicide (such as hospitalization).

Often, however, clinicians do want to know whether one variable causes another. Do parents' marital conflicts cause their children to be more anxious? Does job dissatisfaction lead to feelings of depression? Will a given treatment help people to cope more effectively in life? Questions about causality call for the experimental method, as we shall see.

Special Forms of Correlational Research

Two kinds of correlational research that are used widely by clinical researchers warrant special consideration—epidemiological studies and longitudinal studies. ***Epidemiological studies*** determine the incidence and prevalence of a disorder in a particular population (Weissman, 1995). ***Incidence*** is the number of *new* cases that emerge during a given period of time. ***Prevalence*** is the *total* number of cases in the population during a given time period; prevalence includes both existing and newly emerging cases.

Over the past twenty years clinical researchers across the United States have worked on the most comprehensive epidemiological study ever conducted. In the Epidemiologic Catchment Area Study, under the sponsorship of the National Institute of Mental Health, they interviewed more than 20,000 people in five cities to determine the prevalence of numerous mental disorders in this country and the treatment programs available (Regier et al., 1993; Robins & Regier, 1991). Another large-scale epidemiological study, the National Comorbidity Survey, has surveyed more than 8,000 young and middle-aged adults across the United States (Anthony et al., 1995, 1994; Kessler et al., 1994). These extraordinary studies have also been compared with well-conducted epidemiological studies done in other countries, to see how the rates of mental disorders and treatment programs vary around the world (Weissman, 1995; Compton et al., 1991).

These epidemiological studies have helped investigators identify groups at risk for particular disorders. Women, it turns out, have a higher prevalence rate of anxiety disorders and depression than men, while men have a higher rate of alcoholism than women. Elderly people have a higher rate of suicide than younger people, African Americans have a higher rate of high blood

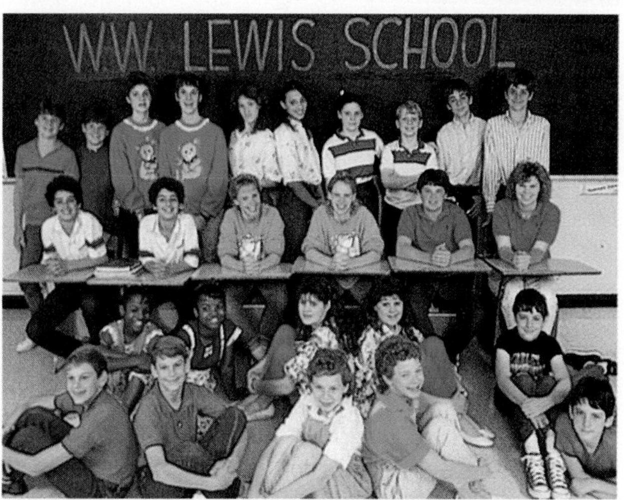

Correlational studies of many pairs of twins have suggested a possible relationship between genetic factors and certain psychological disorders. Identical twins (twins who, like those pictured here, have identical genes) display a higher correlation for some psychopathologies than do fraternal twins (twins whose genetic makeup is not identical).

pressure than white Americans, and persons in some non-Western countries (such as Taiwan) have a higher rate of mental disorders than people in Western countries (such as the United States). These trends may lead researchers to suspect that something unique about certain groups or settings is helping to cause particular disorders (Rogers & Holloway, 1990). Declining health in elderly people, for example, may make them more likely to commit suicide than younger people, or cultural pressures or attitudes prevalent in one country may be responsible for a rate of mental dysfunctioning that is higher than that found in another country. Yet, as in other forms of correlational research, such suspicions can be confirmed only by the experimental method.

In correlational studies of another kind, ***longitudinal studies*** (also called ***high-risk*** or ***developmental studies***), researchers observe the same subjects on many occasions over a long period of time. In several well-known longitudinal studies, investigators observed the progress over the years of normally functioning children whose mothers or fathers manifested schizophrenia (Parnas, 1988; Griffith et al., 1980; Mednick, 1971). These normal children were considered to be at particular risk for schizophrenia. The researchers found, among other things, that the children of the parents with the most severe cases of schizophrenia were more likely to develop a psychological disorder and to commit crimes at later points in their development. Because longitudinal studies document the *order* of events, they provide clues about which events may be causes and which may be the consequences. But they still do not pinpoint causation. Are the psychological problems that these high-risk children encountered later in their lives actually caused by a genetic factor, inherited from their severely disturbed parents? Or was the cause their parents' inadequate coping behaviors, the loss of their parents to extended hospitalization, or some other factor? Again, only experimental studies can supply an answer.

The Experimental Method

The French playwright Molière created a character who was astonished to learn that he had been speaking prose all his life. Similarly, most of us perform experiments throughout our lives without knowing that we are behaving so scientifically. In an ***experiment*** researchers manipulate a situation and observe the effect.

Suppose that we go to a party on campus to celebrate the end of midterm exams. As we mix with people at the party, we begin to notice that many of them are becoming quiet and depressed. The more we talk, the more distraught they become. As the party deteriorates before our eyes, we decide we must do something, but what? Before we can eliminate the problem, we need to know what's causing it.

Our first hunch may be that something we're doing is responsible. Perhaps our incessant chatter about academic pressures is upsetting everyone. We decide to change the topic to skiing in the mountains of Colorado, and we watch for signs of depression in our next round of conversations. The problem seems to clear up; most people now smile and laugh as they converse with us. As a final check on our thinking, we could go back to talking about school with the next several people we meet. Their dark and hostile reaction would probably convince us that the academic focus of our discussion was indeed the cause of the problem.

We have performed an experiment, testing our hypothesis about a causal relationship—between our discussions of academic matters and the depressed mood of the people around us. We manipulated the variable that we suspected to be the cause (the topic of discussion) and then observed the effect of that manipulation on the variable that we suspected was the effect (the mood of the people around us). In scientific experiments, the manipulated variable is called the ***independent variable,*** and the variable being observed is called the ***dependent variable.***

Confounds

The goal of an experiment is to isolate and identify a cause. If we cannot separate the true, or primary, cause from a host of other possible causes, then the experiment gives us very little information. It would not be very helpful, for instance, to find out that the depressed mood of subjects is caused *either* by our talk of school *or* by some other factor, such as the music at the party or midterm fatigue.

The major obstacles to isolating the true cause in an experiment are ***confounds***—variables other than the independent variable that are also acting on the dependent variable. When there are confounds in an experiment, the experimenter cannot confidently attribute the results to the independent variable under investigation. It may actually be the confounding variables that are causing the observed changes (Goodwin, 1995).

Confounds may, for example, make it difficult to answer a question that clinical scientists frequently ask: "Does a particular therapy relieve the symptoms of a given disorder?" (Lambert & Bergin, 1994). Because this question is about a causal relationship, it requires an experiment. Let us suppose that we have developed a new treatment called "buttermilk therapy" to alleviate anxiety in our clients. Our first thought might be to measure our

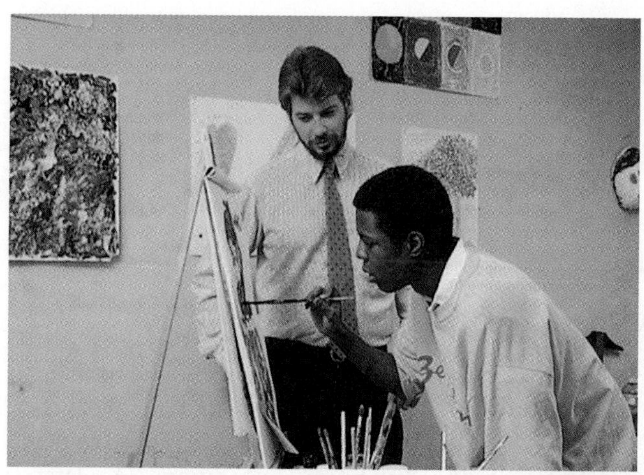

It has been estimated that as many as 400 different kinds of therapies are currently used for psychological problems. In one approach, art therapy, *clients find, express, and work out their feelings through drawings. Researchers must use experimental designs to determine whether this or any form of treatment actually causes clients to improve.*

clients' anxiety levels both before and after we give them a large glass of buttermilk, to see whether the anxiety levels decrease with treatment. In doing so we would be manipulating an independent variable (the presence or absence of buttermilk therapy) and observing its effect on a dependent variable (the clients' anxiety). But if we perform this experiment and observe a decrease in anxiety, what can we actually conclude?

Not much. Without realizing it, we have allowed our independent variable, buttermilk therapy, to change right along with the ever-present confound of time. The clients clearly became less anxious during the hour they spent in the therapist's office, but it is possible that the simple passage of time was responsible. We cannot tell whether the decrease in our clients' anxiety is due to the independent variable that we manipulated or to the confound we overlooked. Because we have not separated the effects of the independent variable from the effects of the confound, we do not know which one was the cause of the change in the dependent variable.

Other confounds also may have been present in our experiment. The location of the therapy office (a quiet country setting) or its soothing color scheme may have had an effect. Perhaps the subjects in our experiment had extraordinarily high expectations that the therapy would work, which accounted for their improvement. Or perhaps the supportive tone of voice of the assistant who served the buttermilk actually made the subjects more relaxed. To minimize the influence of potential confounds, researchers incorporate three important features into their experiments—a control group, random assignment, and a blind design (Goodwin, 1995).

The Control Group

A ***control group*** is a group of subjects who are *not* exposed to the independent variable under investigation. Otherwise their experience is similar to that of the ***experimental group,*** the subjects who *are* exposed to the independent variable. By comparing the two groups, an experimenter can better determine the effect of the manipulated variable.

To study the effectiveness of therapy, for example, experimenters typically divide clients into two groups. The experimental group may come into an office and receive the therapy in question for an hour, while the control group may simply come into the office for an hour. If the experimenters find later that the clients in the experimental group improve more than the clients in the control group, they may conclude that therapy was effective, above and beyond the effects of time, the office setting, and any other confounds. To guard against confounds, experimenters try to provide all subjects, both control and experimental, with experiences that are identical in every way—except for the independent variable.

Random Assignment

Researchers must also watch out for systematic differences that may exist between subjects in the experimental and control groups before a study, since these differences may also confound a study's results. Let's suppose that in setting up our buttermilk therapy study, we allow the subjects themselves to choose the group they wish to join. It is likely that those who love buttermilk will choose the buttermilk group and those who detest it will choose the control group. Their self-selection can result in quite a long list of differences between the control group and the experimental group. The two groups may differ not only in the therapy they receive but in many other ways as well. Suppose people who like buttermilk are healthier, stronger, older, more affectionate, and smarter than those who detest it. All these factors would become confounded with the independent variable, so it could not be known with certainty which was responsible for the improvements later found among the experimental subjects.

To reduce the possibility that preexisting systematic differences are causing the differences observed between groups, experimenters typically use ***random assignment.*** This is the general term for any selection procedure that ensures that every subject in the experiment is as likely to be placed in one group as the other. We might, for example, try flipping a coin or picking names out of a hat. (Box 2-1 shows what can happen when assignment is not random.) Of course, even if subjects are randomly

BOX 2-1 Confounding the Experts: Stress and the Executive Monkey

Every so often an experiment yields results so compelling that the thinking of an entire generation is affected by them. But beware: an experiment that influences our view of the world may later prove to have serious flaws that have gone unnoticed. Even the best-intentioned and most painstaking researchers are only human. They do not always recognize every possible confound. Usually journal reviewers catch the mistake before the research is published; or if it is published, it does not become particularly influential and is lost in the crowd. If such an experiment passes journal review and is then seen as important, however, the consequences can be both embarrassing to the researcher and harmful to the discipline. Consider the "executive monkey study."

What happens if you take two monkeys, put them in separate wire cages, and then give them shocks every 20 seconds for 6 hours—shocks that one of the monkeys can terminate (for itself and the other monkey) by pressing a lever? The psychologist J. V. Brady predicted that the monkeys who did not have a lever to press would develop ulcers because they had no control over the shocks (Brady et al., 1958). In his experiment, exactly the opposite happened. In each of four pairs of monkeys, the "executive" monkey—the one who was able to stop the shocks—developed duodenal ulcers and died. The other monkey in each pair was not affected. This result ran counter to predictions offered by contemporary theories that the monkeys without control would suffer a greater number of problems than those in control of the shocks. Nevertheless, the research community and the public embraced the new finding, partly because it supported the intuitive notion that high-level business executives, people who make important decisions every day, were susceptible to ulcers. For thirteen years Brady's results exerted great influence on psychological views about the relationship between environment and stress.

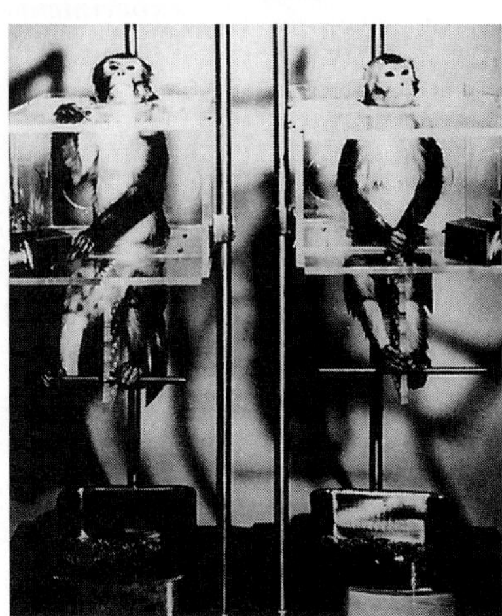

The executive monkey (left) learns that it can prevent shocks by pressing a lever with its hand. The control monkey (right) is given no control over the shocks and appears to lose interest in both the lever and its surroundings.

To "replicate" an experiment is to repeat it exactly as it was done the first time and get the same results. The executive monkey study could not be replicated. Investigators who attempted and failed, including Brady himself, looked carefully at the original procedure and finally found a glaring mistake. It turned out that Brady had failed to consider the importance of assigning his subjects at *random* to each of the conditions in the experiment. Before the experiment, he had pretested all eight monkeys by giving them shocks. The first four monkeys to press the lever were assigned to the "executive" condition. A later study found that animals with a higher response rate (animals that would press the lever first in Brady's pretest) were more likely to develop ulcers (Weiss, 1977). It appeared that their higher emotionality was responsible for both the response rate and the ulcers. In later executive monkey studies in which the subjects were assigned at random, the animals *without control* over the shocks suffered more than those with control. Brady's finding had been an ***artifact***—a product of his own activity, not the monkeys'.

Brady was an outstanding researcher who had made an honest mistake. His result was the opposite of his expectations and surprised him as much as anyone else. Unfortunately, it also was generally accepted and cited for more than a dozen years. Nevertheless, the erroneous experiment has proved to be valuable: it spurred an enormous amount of research that has ultimately led to a more accurate understanding of stress and how it relates to health. It also taught the scientific community a great lesson. Inadvertent mistakes are always possible in research. The only way to minimize them is to train researchers as carefully as possible and to review critically each study that is announced.

assigned to the groups in our buttermilk therapy experiment, we may still end up with all the strongest, smartest, and most affectionate subjects accidentally grouped together, but the chances of this outcome are greatly reduced (Goodwin, 1995).

Blind Design

A final confound problem is ***bias,*** on the part of either the subjects or the people conducting the experiment (see Box 2-2). Subjects may bias an experiment's results by trying to please or help the experimenter. For instance, if subjects who receive buttermilk know the purpose of the study and know which group they are in, they may consciously or unconsciously try to feel better, in an effort to fulfill the experimenter's expectations. If so, ***subject bias*** rather than therapy could be causing their improvement.

To prevent subject bias, experimenters can prevent subjects from finding out which group they are in. This strategy is called a ***blind design*** because subjects are blind as to their assigned group. In a study to determine whether a particular therapy is effective, for example, control subjects could receive a ***placebo*** (Latin for "I shall please"), something that looks or tastes like real therapy but has none of its key ingredients (Addington, 1995). This "imitation" therapy is called ***placebo therapy.*** If the experimental (true therapy) subjects then improve more than the control (placebo therapy) subjects, experimenters may more confidently conclude that the true therapy has caused their improvement.

An experiment may also be invalidated by ***experimenter bias*** (Margraf et al., 1991). That is, experimenters may have expectations that they subtly and unintentionally transmit to their subjects. When we hand subjects buttermilk, for example, we may talk in a particularly promising tone of voice. This confound source is referred to as the ***Rosenthal effect*** (Rosenthal, 1966). Experimenters can eliminate the potential effects of their own bias by contriving to be blind themselves. In a drug therapy study, for example, an aide could make sure that the real medication and the placebo look identical. The experimenter could then administer treatment without knowing which subjects were receiving true medications and which were receiving false medications.

While the subjects *or* the experimenter may be kept blind in an experiment, it is best that *both* be blind—a ***double-blind design.*** In fact, most medication experiments now use double-blind designs to test the efficacy of promising drugs (Morin et al., 1995). Many experiments also arrange for a group of judges to assess the patients' improvement independently, and the judges, too, are blind to the group each patient is in—a ***triple-blind design.***

Statistical Analysis of Experimental Data

The findings of experiments, like those of correlational studies, must be analyzed statistically. In any experiment, no matter how well designed, differences observed between the experimental and control groups may have occurred simply by chance. A statistical analysis can again determine how likely it is that the pattern of changes in the dependent variable is due to chance. If the likelihood is less than 5 percent ($p<.05$), the observed differences are considered to be statistically significant, and the experimenter may conclude with some confidence that they are due to the independent variable. Generally, the larger the sample of subjects in an experiment, the greater the differences observed between groups, and the smaller the range of scores within each group, the more likely it is that the findings will be statistically significant.

Variations in Experimental Design

It is not easy to devise an experiment that is both well controlled and enlightening. The goal of manipulating a single variable without inadvertently manipulating others—that is, controlling every possible confound—is rarely attained in practice. Moreover, because psychological experiments must involve living beings, ethical and practical considerations limit the kinds of manipulations one can do. Clinical experimenters must often settle for a less than optimal experimental design. The most common variations are the quasi-experimental design, the natural experiment, the analogue experiment, and the single-subject experiment.

Quasi-Experimental Design In ***quasi-experiments*** investigators do not randomly assign subjects to control and experimental groups. Instead they make use of groups that already exist in the world at large (Kazdin, 1994; Bawden & Sonenstein, 1992). Because such groups already differ before the experiment, the investigator is technically "correlating" their existing differences with other variables and manipulations in the study. Thus some researchers refer to this research method as a ***mixed design.*** Research into the psychological impact of child abuse illustrates the use of a quasi-experimental design (Bertolli, Morgenstern, & Sorenson, 1995).

Because investigators cannot inflict abuse on a randomly chosen group of children, they instead compare children who already have a history of abuse with children who do not. Because this strategy violates the rule of random assignment, it introduces possible confounds into the study. Children who receive physical

BOX 2-2 Gender, Race, and Age Bias in Research

Sometimes mistakes are committed by an entire community of researchers. Blinded by their own social biases, investigators may consistently err in their efforts to design appropriate studies. For example, for many years scientists in Western society have favored the use of young white men as subjects for research on human functioning (Blumenthal, 1996; Gannon et al., 1992; Stark-Adamek, 1992). Only recently have researchers come to appreciate the extent to which some of science's broad conclusions about human functioning are, in fact, sometimes inaccurate generalizations drawn from this select sample of subjects. In short, the findings of studies that use only young white male subjects are seriously lacking in external validity: their findings may not be relevant to persons of a different sex, race, or age. Such bias may, we are now learning, lead to some very serious misconceptions about the symptoms, causes, course, and treatment of various psychological disorders.

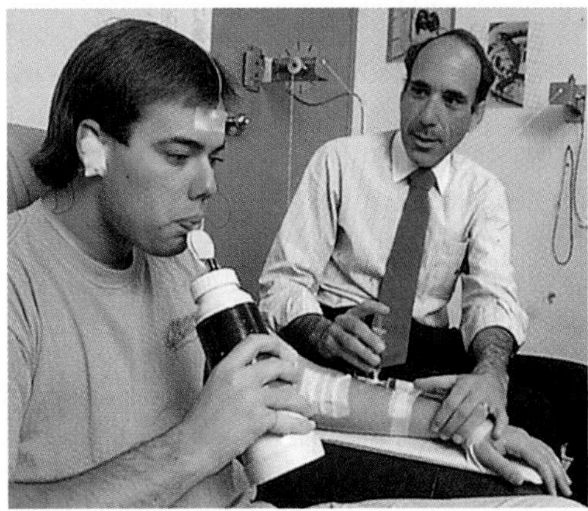

Over the years, most medical and psychological studies have used young white men as subjects. Findings from these studies may not, however, always apply to women, elderly persons, or members of other races. Here a subject drinks various substances to help determine whether the effects of alcohol are linked to genetic factors.

One review of past studies on schizophrenia, for example, revealed that male subjects outnumbered female subjects by more than 2 to 1 (Wahl & Hunter, 1992), despite the fact that this disorder is as prevalent in women as in men. How can we be sure that the psychological and biological insights gleaned from these studies are valid for all persons with schizophrenia rather than just men with this disorder?

In a similar vein, medications for psychological disorders have been tested on groups made up largely of young white male subjects, and on that basis alone have been made available to all patients. Often, however, such medications have turned out to act differently, sometimes dangerously so, in elderly, female, or nonwhite populations (Wolfe et al., 1988). The psychiatrist Keh-Ming Lin has found, for example, that Asian Americans and foreign-born Asians metabolize the antipsychotic drug haloperidol (Haldol), prescribed for many people with schizophrenia, much faster than white Americans do (Goodman, 1992). This finding suggests that Asian American patients require lower doses of this drug in order to achieve the same effect, yet until recent years they have been started on the same dosage as white Americans.

The need to correct this kind of research bias is much more than a mere academic formality. It is tied closely to such important issues as scientific credibility, public health, and even sexism, racism, and ageism. Although recent reviews show that researchers are doing better each year—becoming more aware of gender, race, and age, and designing more appropriate studies—it is also clear that more improvement is needed (Sue et al., 1994; Gannon et al., 1992). The American Psychological Association and the Canadian Psychological Association have offered guidelines to help enlighten their members about the problem and its remedies (Stark-Adamek, 1992). They are aware that when research is biased in these ways, knowledge is limited, progress is stifled, and everyone loses.

punishment, for example, usually come from poorer and larger families than children who are punished verbally. Any differences found later in mood or self-concept may be due to differences in wealth or family size rather than to the abuse.

Some child-abuse researchers have addressed the confound problems of quasi-experiments by further using ***matched control groups.*** That is, they match the experimental subjects with control subjects who share with them several of the same potentially confounding variables, including age, sex, race, birth order, number of children in the family, socioeconomic status, and type of neighborhood (Kinard, 1982). In short, for every abused child in the experimental group, they choose an unabused child with the same characteristics for the control group. When the data from studies of this kind have shown that children in experimental groups are typically sadder and think less of themselves than children in the control groups, the investigators have been able to conclude with some confidence that abuse is causing the differences (Kinard, 1982).

Natural Experiment In ***natural experiments*** nature itself manipulates the independent variable, while the experimenter systematically observes the effects. Natural experiments must be used for studying the psychological effects of unusual and unpredictable events, such as floods, earthquakes, plane crashes, and fires. Because their subjects are selected by an accident of fate rather than by conscious design, natural experiments are actually a kind of quasi-experiment.

On February 26, 1972, a dam gave way in the town of Buffalo Creek, West Virginia, releasing 132 million gallons of black slag, mud, and water into the valley below. The black swirling waters carried with them houses, trailers, cars, bridges, and human beings. The disaster killed 125 people, injured hundreds more, and left thousands homeless. In presiding over a settlement that required the persons responsible for maintaining the dam to pay the survivors many millions of dollars, the court found that the flood had caused psychological impairment in many survivors. Accordingly, the tragedy has received considerable attention from investigators in psychology, including a comprehensive natural experiment conducted by Goldine Gleser and her colleagues (1981).

The Great Flood of 1993 brought destruction and homelessness to thousands of people in America's Midwest, including this man on Front Street in Clarksville, Missouri. Natural experiments conducted in the aftermath of this and other natural catastrophes have found that many survivors experience lingering feelings of anxiety and depression.

The experimenters collected data from 381 survivors approximately eighteen months after the flood. They used extensive interviews, self-report checklists, surveys, and physical examinations. Survivors scored significantly higher on anxiety and depression measures (dependent variables) than did a control group of people who lived elsewhere. Similarly, the survivors experienced more difficulty falling asleep or staying asleep and had more nightmares (additional dependent variables) than the control subjects did. Finally, the study found more severe psychological disturbances among older children who survived than among preschool-age survivors.

Because natural experiments rely on unexpected occurrences in nature, they cannot be repeated at will. Also, because each natural event is unique in some ways, broad generalizations drawn from a single study could be incorrect. Nevertheless, catastrophes have provided opportunities for hundreds of natural experiments over the years, and findings obtained repeatedly have enabled clinical scientists to identify reactions that may often occur in such situations. We shall be discussing these patterns—*acute stress disorders* and *posttraumatic stress disorders*—in Chapter 7.

Analogue Experiment There is one way in which investigators can freely manipulate independent variables while avoiding many of the ethical and practical limitations of clinical research: they can conduct ***analogue experiments.*** These experiments induce laboratory subjects to behave in ways that seem to resemble real-life abnormal behavior. The investigators then conduct experiments on the laboratory-created, analogous form of abnormality, hoping to shed light on its real-life counterpart.

Experimenters often use animals as subjects in analogue studies. Animal subjects are easier to gather and manipulate than human subjects, and they present fewer ethical problems. While the needs and rights of animal subjects must be considered, most experimenters are willing to subject animals to more manipulation and discomfort than human subjects. They believe that the insights gained from such experimentation outweigh the discomfort of the animals as long as that discomfort is not excessive (Plous, 1996; Overmier, 1992). In addition, experimenters can, and often do, use human subjects in analogue experiments.

As we shall see in Chapter 8, the investigator Martin Seligman (1975) has used analogue studies with great success to investigate the causes of human depression. Seligman has theorized that people become depressed when they believe they no longer have any control over the good and bad things that happen in their lives. His strategy for investigating this hypothesis has been to

Chimpanzees and human beings share more than 90 percent of their genetic material, but the brains and bodies of the two species are enormously different, as are their perceptions and experiences. Other animals are even more different from human beings. Thus abnormal-like behavior produced in animal analogue experiments may differ in key ways from the human abnormality under investigation, and the conclusions drawn from such studies may be incorrect.

gather a group of subjects, attempt to change their perceptions of control (manipulate the independent variable), and see whether their moods change accordingly (observe the dependent variable). He has, for example, subjected dogs to random electrical shocks—unpleasant events over which they have absolutely no control. Seligman has found that the dogs typically react with symptoms suspiciously similar to those of human depression. In contrast to the control subjects in his studies, who are allowed to escape or avoid shocks, the experimental subjects become exceedingly passive, socially and sexually withdrawn, and slow moving, their demeanor resembling the sadness and pessimism of depression. In short, under laboratory conditions Seligman has created a pattern of behavior—he calls it ***learned helplessness***—that he believes to be an analogue of human depression.

Seligman and his colleagues have also conducted some analogue studies on *human* subjects. They have exposed laboratory subjects randomly to unpleasant and unavoidable stimuli, such as loud noises or failures on cognitive tasks. These subjects, too, display symptoms of learned helplessness, including temporary passivity, pessimism about their effectiveness at future tasks, and sadness (Young & Allin, 1992; Miller & Seligman, 1975).

It is important to recognize that Seligman's analogue experiments are enlightening only to the extent that the laboratory-induced condition of learned helplessness is indeed analogous to human depression. If it turns out that this laboratory phenomenon is only superficially similar to depression, then the clinical inferences drawn from such experiments may be wrong and misleading. This, in fact, is the major limitation of all analogue research (Vredenburg, Flett, & Krames, 1993). Researchers can never be certain that the phenomena they see in the laboratory are the same as the psychological disorders they are investigating. For this reason, researchers such as Seligman usually conduct many variations of an analogue study in hopes of demonstrating consistent parallels between the laboratory analogue and the real-life phenomenon. The more parallels they demonstrate, the more compelling their analogue findings are.

Single-Subject Experiment Sometimes scientists do not have the luxury of experimenting on numerous subjects. They may, for example, be investigating a disorder so rare that few subjects are available. Experimentation is still possible, however. ***Single-subject,*** or ***single-case, experimental designs*** observe a single subject both before and after the manipulation of an independent variable (Goodwin, 1995; Kazdin, 1994). Single-subject experiments first rely on ***baseline data***—data gathered during the observation, or baseline, period. The data reveal what a subject's behavior is like without any manipulations or interventions, and thus they establish a standard with which later changes may be compared. The experimenter next introduces the independent variable and observes the subject's behavior once again. Any changes in behavior are attributed to the effects of the independent variable. Common single-subject experimental designs are the *ABAB* and *multiple-baseline designs* (Goodwin, 1995).

ABAB Design In an ***ABAB,*** or ***reversal, design,*** a subject's reactions are measured and compared not only during a baseline period (condition A) and after the introduction of the independent variable (condition B) but once again after the independent variable has been removed (condition A) and yet again after it has been reintroduced (condition B). If the subject's responses change back and forth systematically with changes in the independent variable, the experimenter may conclude that the independent variable is causing the shifting responses (Kratochwill, 1992). Essentially, in an ABAB design a subject is compared with himself or herself under different conditions rather than with control subjects. Subjects, therefore, serve as their own controls.

Clinical researchers are likely to resort to an ABAB design when they wish to determine the effectiveness of a particular form of therapy on a client but are unable to obtain other clients with similar problems for a properly controlled experiment. One researcher used this design to determine whether a reinforcement treatment program was helping to reduce a teenage boy's habit of disrupting his special education class with loud talk (Deitz, 1977). The reinforcement program consisted of rewarding the boy, who suffered from mental retardation, with extra teacher time whenever he managed to go 55 minutes without talking in class more than three times. When the student's level of talking was measured during a baseline period, it was found to consist of frequent verbal disruptions. Next the boy was given a series of teacher reinforcement sessions (the independent variable); as expected, his loud talk soon decreased dramatically. Then the reinforcement treatment was stopped, and the student's loud talk was found to increase once again. Apparently the independent variable had indeed been the cause of the improvement.

To be more confident about this conclusion, the therapist introduced the teacher reinforcement treatment yet again. Once again the subject's behavior improved. This reintroduction of the independent variable helped rule out the possibility that some confounding factor had actually been causing the boy's improvement. Therapy, rather than the onset of magnificent spring weather or a present from a relative, had indeed been the key factor.

Multiple-Baseline Design A ***multiple-baseline design*** does not employ the reversals found in an ABAB design. Instead, the experimenter selects two or more behaviors displayed by a subject and observes the effect that the manipulation of an independent variable has on each of the behaviors (Balk, 1995; Herz et al., 1992; Morley, 1989). Let us say that the teenage boy in the ABAB study exhibited *two* kinds of inappropriate behavior—the disruptive talk during class and odd grimaces. In a multiple-baseline design, the experimenter would first collect baseline data on both the frequency of the boy's disruptive talk and the frequency of his facial grimaces during a 55-minute period. In the next phase of the experiment, the experimenter would reward the boy with extra teacher time whenever he cut down his verbalizations but not when he cut down his grimaces. The experimenter would then measure changes in the boy's verbal and grimacing behaviors, expecting the verbal interruptions to decrease in frequency but the grimacing to remain about the same as before. In the final phase of the experiment, the experimenter would also reward the boy with extra teacher attention whenever he reduced his grimacing, expecting that this manipulation would now reduce the frequency of grimacing as well.

If the expected pattern of changes was found, it would be reasonable to conclude that the manipulation of the independent variable (teacher reinforcement), rather than some other factor, was responsible for the changes in the two behaviors. Had some extraneous factor such as an improvement in the weather or a gift from a relative been the cause of the boy's improvement, it would probably have caused improvements in both kinds of behavior in earlier phases of the study, not just in the final phase. In short, by choosing more than one behavioral baseline for observation, an experimenter can systematically eliminate confounding variables from his or her interpretations of the findings.

Obviously, single-subject experiments—both ABAB and multiple-baseline designs—are similar to individual case studies in their focus on one subject. In the single-subject experiment, however, the independent variable is systematically manipulated so that the investigator can draw conclusions about the cause of an observed effect. The single-subject experiment therefore has greater internal validity than the case study (Lehman, 1991; Smith, 1988).

At the same time, single-subject designs, like case studies, have only limited external validity. Because only one subject is studied, the experimenter cannot be sure that the subject's reaction to the independent variable is typical. Other subjects might react differently. In the single-subject designs described here, for example, there is no basis for concluding that other adolescents with similar behavior problems would respond successfully to the same reinforcement programs.

"Oh, not bad. The light comes on, I press the bar, they write me a check. How about you?"
(Drawing by Cheney; © 1993 The New Yorker Magazine, Inc.)

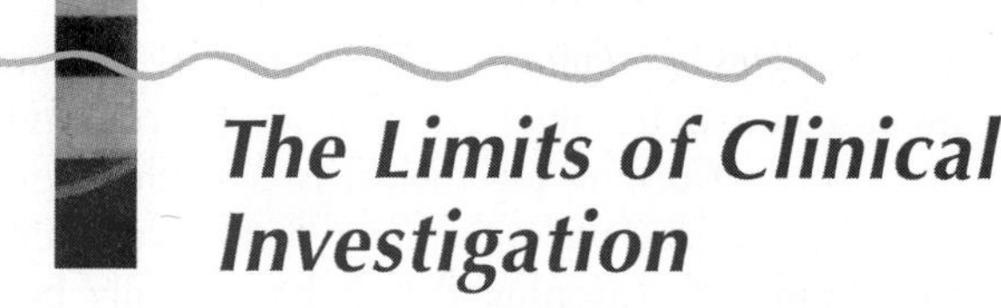

The Limits of Clinical Investigation

As we noted at the beginning of this chapter, clinical scientists look for general laws that will help them to understand, prevent, and treat psychological disorders. Various circumstances may impede their progress, however (de Groot & Kennedy, 1995; Stricker & Trierweiler,

BOX 2-3 Human Subjects Have Rights

There is no question that research is necessary if we are to understand and treat psychological disorders, or that this is a worthy goal—in fact, an essential one. The design of meaningful research, however, is fraught with ethical pitfalls. Should people be given experimental treatments that could be harmful? Is it right to withhold treatment from one group of patients to compare them with another group receiving a new therapy? When does the benefit to many outweigh the suffering of a few? These are but some of the questions facing researchers, patients, and society. To produce dependable results, an experiment must be conducted according to the scientific method. When this method conflicts with standards of ethical treatment, society—not researchers alone—must decide the answer.

Obtaining *informed consent* from subjects recruited to participate in a study is perhaps the most fundamental ethical safeguard in clinical human research. A dilemma arises, however, when one must obtain consent from people who suffer from disorders that may affect their judgment (de Groot & Kennedy, 1995; High & Doole, 1995). Does a mental disorder such as schizophrenia or severe depression render people unable to make this decision for themselves?

Some researchers argue that when a therapy is not considered harmful, it is not a violation of patients' rights to involve them in studies in which they receive treatment, whether or not they are able to make an informed decision to participate. Although this position may seem reasonable at first glance, it has opened the door to some isolated, highly publicized instances of professional misconduct. Large-scale, government-sanctioned abuse of patients occurred in the 1950s and 1960s, for example, when almost 100 people unknowingly became subjects in "depatterning" experiments meant to test the feasibility of mind control. Both the Canadian government and the United States CIA funded experiments in a variety of research settings. These experiments took place during the height of the Cold War, and the two governments wanted to learn more about mind control before potential foes mastered the technique. Most research subjects emerged from the experiments emotionally disabled, with limited memories of the life they had lived before they entered the hospital.

Linda Macdonald was one of those subjects. In 1963 she checked into a Canadian institution to be treated for fatigue and depression. Six months later, she couldn't read, write, cook a meal, or make a bed. She did not remember her husband, her five children, or any of the first twenty-six years of her life. During her stay, Ms. Macdonald was given massive doses of various drugs, put into a drug-induced sleep for 86 days, given more than 100 electroconvulsive treatments, and ex-

1995). We have already noted some of them. The most problematic are summarized below.

1. *Clinical subjects have needs and rights that investigators are obliged to respect.* Clinical scientists must respect the human and civil rights of their human subjects (Balk, 1995; Sigmon, 1995). Ethical considerations significantly limit the kinds of investigations that clinical scientists can conduct (see Box 2-3).

2. *The origins of human functioning are very complex.* Because human behavior generally results from multiple factors working together, it is difficult to pinpoint its precise causes. So many factors can influence human functioning that it has actually been easier to unravel the complexities of energy and matter than to understand human sadness, stress, and anxiety.

3. *Human beings are changeable.* Moods, behaviors, and thoughts fluctuate. Is the person clinical scientists are studying today truly the same as the individual they were investigating yesterday? Variability in a single person, let alone the normal variations from person to person, limits the kinds of conclusions researchers can draw about abnormal functioning.

4. *Human self-awareness may influence the results of clinical investigations.* When human subjects know they are being studied, their behavior often changes (Harris & Lahey, 1986). They may try to respond in expected ways or present themselves in a favorable light. The attention they receive from investigators may also affect their perceptions and feelings, often increasing their optimism and improving their mood. It is an axiom of science that the very act of measuring an object distorts the object to some degree. Nowhere is this more true than in the study of human beings.

posed to "psychic driving," a technique in which repetitive taped messages were played for her 16 hours a day. The purpose was not to treat this woman's depression but to gather information about the causes and effects of brainwashing (Davis, 1992; Powis, 1990).

Later many of the victims, including Macdonald, sued the Canadian and United States governments for subjecting them to these experiments without their permission. In 1988 the United States government agreed to compensate Macdonald and eight others about $100,000 each, and in 1992, without admitting any legal or moral responsibility but acknowledging "a collective sense of accountability for events which took place in good faith with ill effect," the government of Canada agreed to pay each of the eighty living victims $100,000.

Such instances highlight the ethical necessity to obtain informed consent. Regulations that now govern the conduct of experimenters, written by the U.S. Department of Health and Human Services, include guidelines for making sure that potential human subjects are well informed on eight basic issues:

1. That they are participating in an experiment and what procedures will be used.
2. Any potential or foreseeable risks.
3. Any benefits to themselves or others.
4. Any alternative procedures available to the patient.
5. Whether or not their participation and performance are confidential.
6. Whether or not they will receive any compensation if they are harmed during the experiment.
7. Whom they may contact to ask questions about the experiment.
8. That their participation is voluntary and that they face no penalty if they refuse to participate.

These guidelines are eminently reasonable, but there are no accompanying guidelines for establishing whether or not a potential subject is competent to understand these issues and make a truly informed decision. As a result, in some circumstances researchers are permitted to alter or waive the requirements—a questionable practice.

Today, largely as a result of government regulations, research facilities establish committees to oversee the well-being of research subjects. But even a consensus among well-educated, concerned, ethical individuals does not answer the underlying question: How does one weigh the suspension of individual rights against the potential benefit to others? This has become such a difficult and important issue that universities now train ethicists, who confer with philosophers, psychologists, physicians, civil rights experts, and people from all sectors of society in an effort to develop acceptable guidelines. Though the system is not perfect, it reflects the value our society places on maintaining a balance between scientific advances and an individual's rights.

5. *Clinical investigators have a special link to their subjects.* Clinical scientists too have mood changes, troubled thoughts, and family problems. They may identify with the pain of their subjects; they may also have personal opinions about the causes and implications of their problems. These feelings can bias their attempts to understand abnormality.

In short, human behavior is so complex that clinical scientists must use a variety of methods to study abnormality. Each method addresses some of the problems inherent in investigating human behavior, but no one method overcomes them all. For example, case studies allow investigators to consider a broader range of causes, but experiments pinpoint causes more precisely. It is best to view each method of investigation as part of a battery of approaches that collectively may shed light on abnormal human functioning.

When more than one of these methods has been used to investigate a disorder, we should ask whether all the results point in the same direction. If they do, we are probably that much closer to a clear understanding of that disturbance or an effective treatment for it. Conversely, if the methods produce conflicting results, we must admit that our knowledge in that particular area is still limited.

Before accepting any research findings, however, students of the clinical field must review the details of the studies with a very critical eye. In an experiment, for example, have the variables been properly controlled? Was the choice of subjects representative, was the sample large enough to be meaningful, and have subject and experimenter bias been eliminated? Are the investigator's conclusions justified? How else might the results be interpreted? Only after such scrutiny can we conclude that a truly informative investigation has taken place.

Chapter Review

1. ***Clinical research*** The history of abnormal psychology shows that theories and treatment procedures may seem reasonable and effective in some cases but prove useless and even harmful in others. Only through research can the dangers be discovered and the benefits clarified.

2. ***The task of clinical researchers*** Researchers use the *scientific method* to uncover *nomothetic,* or general, principles of abnormal psychological functioning. They attempt to identify and examine relationships between variables to determine whether two or more variables change together and whether change in one variable causes a change in another. Researchers depend primarily on three methods of investigation.

3. ***The case study*** The *case study* is a detailed account of a person's life and psychological problems.

   A. ***Contributions of the case study*** It can serve as a source of ideas about behavior, provide tentative support for a theory, challenge theoretical assumptions, clarify new therapeutic techniques, or offer an opportunity to study an unusual problem.

   B. ***Limitations of the case study*** The observer may be biased and therefore may be subjective about what is included in the case study. In addition, case studies tend to have *low internal validity* and *low external validity.*

4. ***The correlational method*** The *correlational method* is a procedure for systematically observing the extent to which events or characteristics vary together. This method allows researchers to draw broad conclusions about abnormality in the population at large.

   A. ***Correlation*** A *correlation* is the degree to which variables change in accordance with one another. When two variables increase or decrease together, the correlation has a *positive direction.* When the value of one variable goes up as the other goes down, the correlation is *negative.* If the variables have no systematic relationship, they are said to be *unrelated.* The more closely the two variables change together, the greater the *magnitude,* or *strength,* of the correlation.

   B. ***The correlation coefficient*** A correlation can be calculated numerically and expressed by the *correlation coefficient (r).*

   C. ***Statistical analysis of correlational data*** When a correlation has been found, the scientist wants to know if it is truly characteristic of the larger population. To find out, he or she does a *statistical analysis* of the data to determine whether the correlation may be due to chance.

   D. ***Strengths and limitations of the correlational method*** Correlational studies generally have high external validity but lack internal validity. They allow researchers to describe the relationship between variables but not to explain that relationship.

   E. ***Special forms of correlational research*** Two widely used forms of the correlation method are *epidemiological studies,* which determine the incidence and prevalence of a disorder in a given population, and *longitudinal studies,* which observe the characteristics or behavior of the same subjects over a long period of time.

5. ***The experimental method*** When it is important to understand the *causal* relationship between variables, researchers generally turn to the *experimental method.* In this type of study, the investigators manipulate suspected causes to see whether expected effects will result. The variable that is manipulated is called the *independent variable* and the variable that is expected to change as a result is called the *dependent variable.*

   A. ***Confounds*** *Confounds* are variables other than the independent variable that are also acting on the dependent variable. They can be major obstacles to efforts to isolate the true cause of an effect. To minimize the possible influence of confounds, researchers use *control groups, random assignment,* and *blind designs.*

   B. ***Statistical analysis of experimental data*** The findings of experiments, like those of correlational studies, must be analyzed statistically.

   C. ***Variations in experimental design*** For ethical and practical reasons, it is difficult to formulate and carry out an ideal experiment in human psychology. Clinical experimenters must often settle for imperfect variations of the optimal experimental design, including the *quasi-experimental design,* the *natural experiment,* the *analogue experiment,* and the *single-subject experiment.* Two versions of the single-subject experiment are the *ABAB design* and the *multiple-baseline design.*

6. ***The limits of clinical investigation*** Because human subjects have rights that must be respected, the origins of behavior are complex, and behavior varies, it can be difficult to assess the findings of clinical research. Also, researchers must take into account their own biases and a study's unintended impact on subjects' usual behavior.

Thought and Afterthought

Animals Have Rights, Too

For years researchers have gathered insights about abnormal human behavior from experiments with animals. Animals have sometimes been shocked, prematurely separated from their parents, and starved; they have had their brains surgically altered and even been killed, or sacrificed, so that researchers could autopsy them. Are such actions always ethically acceptable?

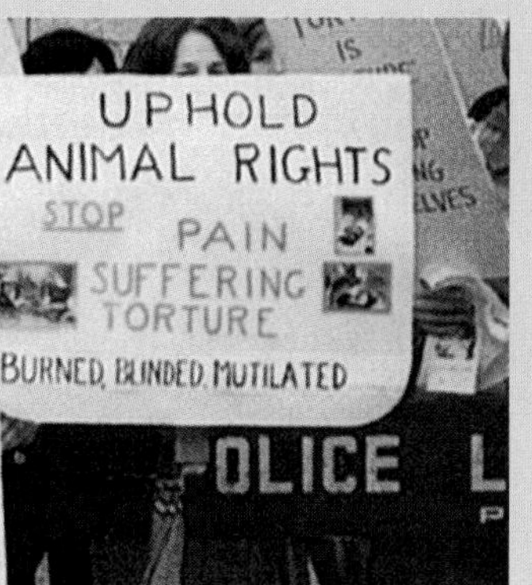

Animal rights activists say no. They have called the undertakings cruel and unjustified, and have fought many forms of animal research with legal maneuvers and demonstrations. Some have even harassed scientists and vandalized their labs. In turn, some researchers accuse the activists of caring more about animals than about human beings.

Many clinicians and scientists find themselves somewhere in the middle on this issue. According to a recent survey, most psychologists disapprove of experiments that cause pain or death, yet generally support animal research, including the caging and manipulation of animals (Plous, 1996).

In response to this issue, some state courts have ruled that university researchers must publicly disclose their research proposals to help ensure the well-being of animal subjects. Similarly, government agencies and the American Psychological Association have issued rules and guidelines for animal research. Their regulations define, for example, the circumstances in which animals may be killed, and limit the number of surgeries that can be performed on a single animal. Still the battle goes on.

Afterthoughts: *Do restrictions on animal research curtail necessary investigations and thus foreclose potential gains for human beings? Or do the current regulations still fail to adequately protect the rights and needs of animal subjects? . . . Is there a way to address the concerns of both activists and scientists?*

The Rise and Fall of Halcion

In 1982 Halcion *(triazolam)* was approved by the Food and Drug Administration (FDA), and was quickly heralded as the perfect sleeping pill. Sales skyrocketed, but soon many users were reporting undesired effects such as confusion, memory loss, depression, agitation, aggression, paranoid thinking, and physical dependence on the drug.

At first the drug's manufacturer, the Upjohn Company, claimed that such case reports were misleading. By the late 1980s, however, the company was defending itself against a number of well-publicized suits brought by persons who blamed the drug for various problems, including homicide. The controversy escalated in 1991, when Upjohn acknowledged that it had inadvertently underreported some undesired effects in an early study.

Recent studies have yielded mixed results regarding these various effects. Nevertheless, the FDA has greatly reduced the recommended maximum dosage of Halcion and has recommended stronger warnings on its package. Five countries, including Great Britain, have banned it altogether. By 1994, sales in the United States had dropped by half.

Afterthoughts: *What roles may public sentiment, business interests, and legal procedures play in the conduct and impact of mental health research? . . . How can clinical drug research be made purer and more objective? . . . When research findings are mixed, how should clinicians and policy makers proceed?*

Frankly Speaking

The temptation to form premature theories upon insufficient data is the bane of our profession.

—**Sherlock Holmes,**
in Arthur Conan Doyle's
The Valley of Fear (1914)

Afterthoughts: *Clinicians once believed that women who are abused by their partners are masochistic and that heroin is not addictive. What problems may have resulted from these and other mistaken conclusions? . . . What beliefs and conclusions about mental dysfunction currently thrive despite a lack of adequate data to support them? . . . What harm may such beliefs be causing if they are incorrect?*

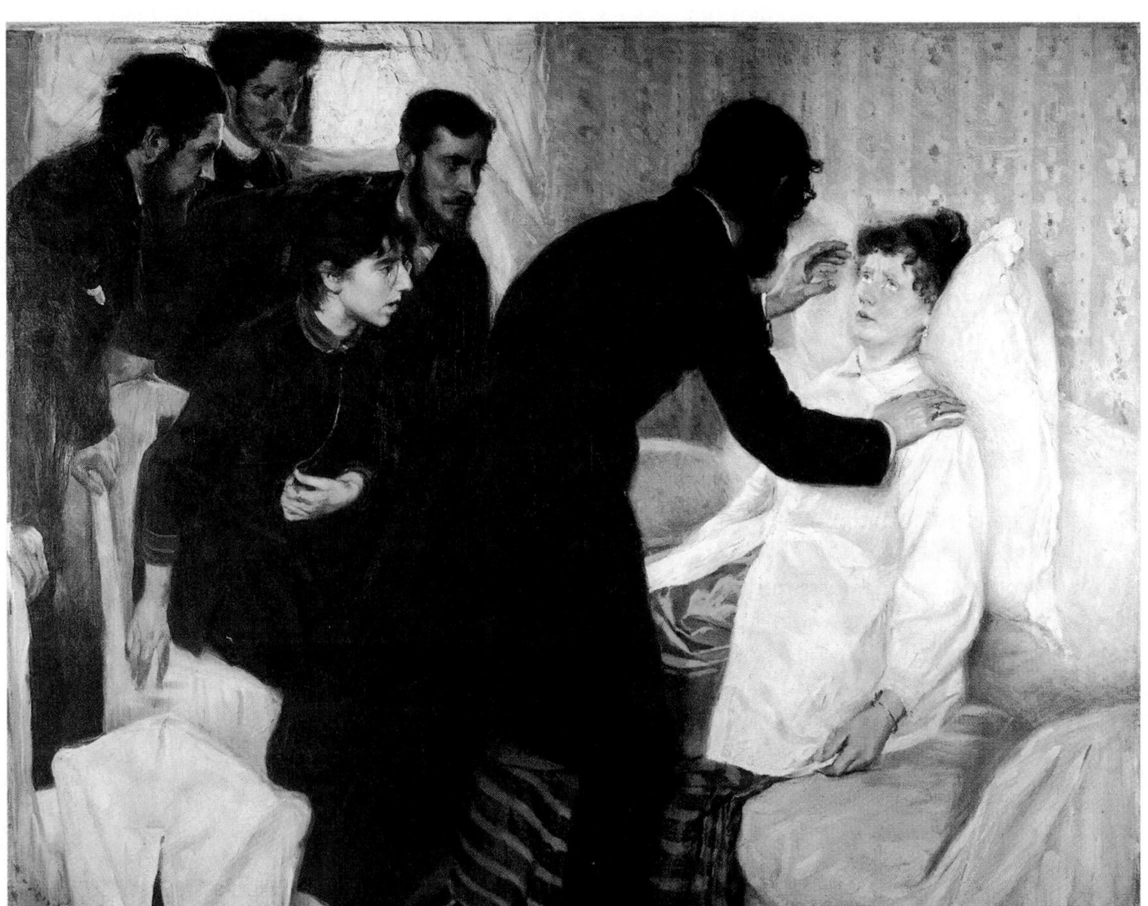

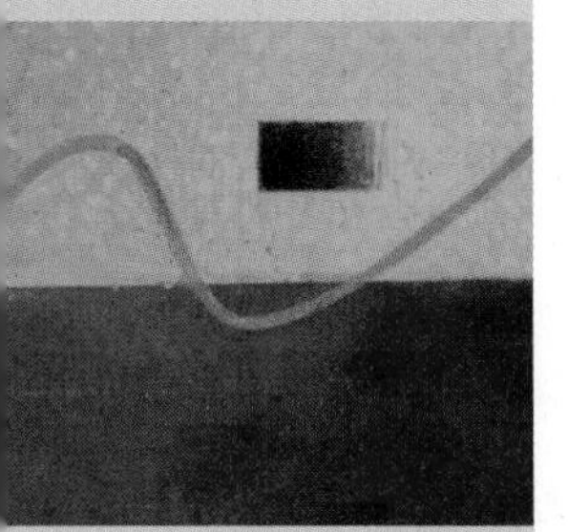

Topic Overview

Chapter 3

The Psychological Models of Abnormality

In Richard Bergh's Hypnotic Seance, *1887, even the clinicians seem awed by the power of hypnotism, like so many others in the late nineteenth century. The study of this technique gave rise to the psychogenic perspective, the view that abnormal functioning is often the result of psychological factors.*

Philip Berman, a 25-year-old single unemployed former copy editor for a large publishing house, . . . had been hospitalized after a suicide attempt in which he deeply gashed his wrist with a razor blade. He described [to the therapist] how he had sat on the bathroom floor and watched the blood drip into the bathtub for some time before he telephoned his father at work for help. He and his father went to the hospital emergency room to have the gash stitched, but he convinced himself and the hospital physician that he did not need hospitalization. The next day when his father suggested he needed help, he knocked his dinner to the floor and angrily stormed to his room. When he was calm again, he allowed his father to take him back to the hospital.

The immediate precipitant for his suicide attempt was that he had run into one of his former girlfriends with her new boyfriend. The patient stated that they had a drink together, but all the while he was with them he could not help thinking that "they were dying to run off and jump in bed." He experienced jealous rage, got up from the table, and walked out of the restaurant. He began to think about how he could "pay her back."

Mr. Berman had felt frequently depressed for brief periods during the previous several years. He was especially critical of himself for his limited social life and his inability to have managed to have sexual intercourse with a woman even once in his life. As he related this to the therapist, he lifted his eyes from the floor and with a sarcastic smirk said, "I'm a 25-year-old virgin. Go ahead, you can laugh now." He has had several girlfriends to date, whom he described as very attractive, but who he said had lost interest in him. On further questioning, however, it became apparent that Mr. Berman soon became very critical of them and demanded that they always meet his every need, often to their own detriment. The women then found the relationship very unrewarding and would soon find someone else.

During the past two years Mr. Berman had seen three psychiatrists briefly, one of whom had given him a drug, the name of which he could not remember, but that had precipitated some sort of unusual reaction for which he had to stay in a hospital overnight. Another gave him three treatments with electroconvulsive therapy (ECT) because he complained that he was suicidal. These had no effect on his mood but, according to him, caused significant memory loss. He saw the third psychiatrist for three months, but while in treatment he quit his job and could no longer afford the therapy. When asked why he quit, he said, "The bastards were going to fire me anyway." When asked whether he realized he would have to drop out of therapy when he quit his job, he said, "What makes you think I give a damn what happens to therapy?" Concerning his hospitalization, the patient said that "It was a dump," that the staff refused to listen to what he had to say or to respond to his needs, and that they, in fact, treated all the patients "sadistically." The referring doctor corroborated that Mr. Berman was a difficult patient who demanded that he be treated as special, and yet was hostile to most staff members throughout his stay. After one angry exchange with an aide, he left the hospital without leave, and subsequently signed out against medical advice.

Mr. Berman is one of two children of a middle-class family. His father is 55 years old and employed in a managerial position for an insurance company. He perceives his father as weak and ineffectual, completely dominated by the patient's overbearing and cruel mother. He states that he hates his mother with "a passion I can barely control." He claims that his mother used to call him names like "pervert" and "sissy" when he was growing up, and that in an argument she once "kicked me in the balls." Together, he sees his parents as rich, powerful, and selfish, and, in turn, thinks that they see him as lazy, irresponsible, and a behavior problem. When his parents called the therapist to discuss their son's treatment, they stated that his problem began with the birth of his younger brother, Arnold, when Philip was 10 years old. After Arnold's birth Philip apparently became an "ornery" child who cursed a lot and was difficult to discipline. Philip recalls this period only vaguely. He reports that his mother once was hospitalized for depression, but that now "she doesn't believe in psychiatry."

Mr. Berman had graduated from college with average grades. Since graduating he had worked at three different publishing houses, but at none of them for more than one year. He always found some justification for quitting. He usually sat around his house doing very little for two or three months after quitting a job, until his parents prodded him into getting a new one. He described innumerable interactions in his life with teachers, friends, and employers in which he felt offended or unfairly treated, . . . and frequent arguments that left him feeling bitter . . . and spent most of his time alone, "bored." He was unable to commit himself to any person, he held no strong convictions, and he felt no allegiance to any group.

The patient appeared as a very thin, bearded, and bespectacled young man with pale skin who maintained little eye contact with the therapist and who had an air of angry bitterness about him. Although he complained of depression, he denied other symptoms of the depressive syndrome. He seemed preoccupied with his rage at his parents, and seemed particularly invested in conveying a despicable image of himself. When treatment was discussed with Mr. Berman, the therapist recommended frequent contacts, two or three per week, feeling that Mr. Berman's potential for self-injury, if not suicide, was rather high. The judgment was based not so much on the severity of Mr. Berman's depression as on his apparent impulsivity, frequent rages, childish disregard for the consequences of his actions, and his pattern of trying to get other people to suffer by inflicting injury on himself. Mr. Berman willingly agreed to the frequent sessions, but not because of eagerness to get help. "Let's make it five sessions a week," he said. "It's about time my parents paid for all that they've done to me."

(Spitzer et al., 1983, pp. 59–61)

Philip is clearly a troubled person, but how did he come to be that way? How do we explain and correct his many problems? In confronting these questions, we must acknowledge their complexity. First, we must appreciate the wide range of complaints we are trying to understand: Philip's depression and anger, his social failures, his lack of employment, his distrust of the people around him, and the problems within his family. Second, we must sort through all kinds of potential primary causes—internal and external, biological and interpersonal, past and present. Which, if any, is having the biggest impact on Philip's behavior? Every investigator of abnormal psychology faces the same challenges, whether in research or in clinical practice. This chapter looks at the kinds of answers most frequently given today.

Although we may not recognize it, we all use implicit theoretical frameworks as we read about Philip. Most of us probably attempt to explain Philip's conduct to ourselves. Over the course of our lives, each of us has developed a perspective that helps us make sense of the things other people say and do. Our perspective helps us to explain other people's behavior to our own satisfaction.

In science, the perspectives used to explain phenomena are known as ***paradigms*** or ***models.*** Each model makes explicit the scientist's basic assumptions, gives structure to the field under study, and sets forth guidelines for its investigation (Kuhn, 1962). It influences what the investigators observe. It also affects the questions they ask, the information they consider legitimate, and how they interpret this information (Nietzel et al., 1994; Lehman, 1991). To understand how a clinical scientist or practitioner explains and treats a specific pattern of symptoms, such as Philip's pattern, we must appreciate the model that shapes his or her view of abnormal functioning (see Figure 3-1).

Until recent times the models used by clinicians were usually monolithic and culturally determined. That is, one model was paramount in a particular place at a particular time, couched in the metaphors of the prevalent worldview. Recall the demonological model used to explain and treat abnormal functioning in Europe during the Middle Ages. It borrowed heavily from medieval society's preoccupation with religion, superstition, and warfare. Each person was viewed as a battleground where the devil challenged God. Abnormal behavior signaled the devil's victory.

Medieval practitioners would have seen the devil's guiding hand in Philip Berman's efforts to commit suicide. They would have pointed to possession by the devil as the ultimate explanation for Philip's feelings of depression, rage, jealousy, and hatred. Actually, some might have disagreed on the immediate cause of Philip's abnormal behavior, arguing that he was possessed not by the devil but by a tarantula or a wolf, but they would not have doubted that an evil spirit of some kind was responsible. Similarly, while medieval practitioners might have employed any of a variety of treatments to help Philip overcome his difficulties, from prayers to bitter concoctions to whippings, all would have had a common purpose—to drive a foreign spirit from his body. Few would have been brazen enough to offer an explanation or treatment outside of the accepted demonological model. To do so would have brought harsh criticism for failure to appreciate the fundamental issues at stake.

Whereas one model was dominant during the Middle Ages, several models are employed to explain and treat abnormal functioning today. This variety has resulted from shifts in values and beliefs over the past half century, as well as better clinical research. At one end of the spectrum is the ***biological model,*** which cites organic processes as the key to human behavior. At the other end is the ***sociocultural model,*** which scrutinizes the effects of society and culture on individual behavior. In between

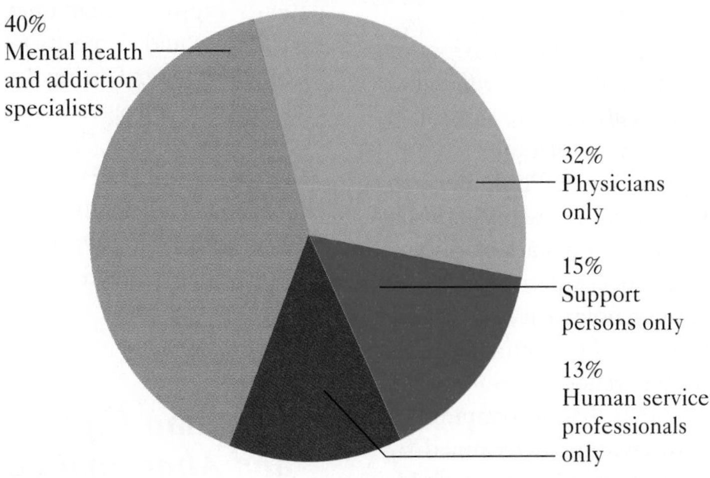

Figure 3-1 *Where do people with psychological problems seek help today? Approximately 40 percent of the Americans who receive treatment see mental health or addiction specialists. Another 32 percent see a physician only; 13 percent work exclusively with a human service professional, such as a religious or social service counselor; and 15 percent discuss their problems only with support persons, such as a self-help group, family member, or friend. (Adapted from Regier et al., 1993.)*

are four models that focus on more psychological and personal dimensions of human functioning: the ***psychodynamic model*** looks at people's unconscious internal dynamics and conflicts; the ***behavioral model*** emphasizes ingrained behavior and the ways in which it is learned; the ***cognitive model*** concentrates on the process and content of the thinking that underlies behavior; and the ***humanistic-existential model*** stresses the role of values and choices in determining human individuality and fulfillment. We shall examine the psychological models in this chapter and explore the biological and sociocultural models in Chapter 4.

Rooted as they are in different assumptions and concepts, the models are sometimes in conflict. Proponents of one perspective often scoff at the "naive" interpretations, investigations, and treatment efforts of the rest. Yet none of the models is complete in itself. Each focuses primarily on one aspect of human functioning, and none can explain the entire spectrum of abnormality.

The Psychodynamic Model

The psychodynamic model is the oldest and most famous of the modern psychological models. Psychodynamic theorists believe that a person's behavior, whether normal or abnormal, is determined to a large extent by underlying psychological forces of which the person is not consciously aware. These internal forces are considered *dynamic*—that is, they interact with one another; and their interaction gives shape to an individual's behavior, thoughts, and emotions. Abnormal behaviors or symptoms are viewed as the consequences of *conflicts* between these forces, as unconscious attempts to solve such conflicts and lessen some painful inner turmoil.

Psychodynamic theorists would view Philip Berman as a person in conflict. They would ask how his underlying needs and motives came to be in a state of disharmony. They would want to explore his past experiences because, in their view, people's psychological conflicts are related to their early relationships and to traumatic experiences during their early years. Psychodynamic theories rest on the *deterministic* assumption that no symptom or behavior is "accidental." All behavior is determined by past experiences, particularly the experiences of childhood. Thus Philip's hatred for his mother, his recollections of her as cruel and overbearing, the weakness and ineffectuality of his father, and the birth of a younger brother when Philip was 10 may all be relevant.

The psychodynamic model was first formulated by the Viennese neurologist Sigmund Freud (1856–1939) at the turn of the twentieth century. After studying hypnosis in Paris under the famous neurologist Jean Charcot in 1885, Freud returned to Vienna to work with Josef Breuer (1842–1925). This physician had been conducting experiments on hypnosis and hysterical illnesses—mysterious physical ailments with no apparent medical cause. In a famous case, Breuer had treated a woman he called "Anna O.," whose extensive hysterical symptoms included paralysis of the legs and right arm, deafness, and disorganized speech. Breuer placed the woman under hypnosis, expecting that suggestions made to her in that state would help rid her of her hysterical symptoms. While she was under hypnosis, however, she began to talk about traumatic past events and to express deeply felt emotions. This venting of repressed memories seemed to enhance the effectiveness of the treatment. Anna O. referred to it as her "talking cure." Breuer himself called it the "cathartic method," borrowing the term from the Greek *katharsis,* purgation.

Breuer and Freud collaborated on a number of case studies in the 1890s. Together they proposed that hysterical illnesses are caused by psychological conflicts, principally sexual in origin, of which the patient is not consciously aware. These conflicts would exert less negative influence if some treatment could bring them into consciousness, and that is what hypnosis and the cathartic method did.

Over the course of the next several decades, Freud developed and expanded these ideas. His general theory, ***psychoanalysis,*** proposed that "unconscious" conflicts account for *all* forms of normal and abnormal psychological functioning. Freud also formulated a corresponding method of treatment, a conversational approach. As patients explored their unconscious with a psychoanalyst, they would come to terms with the conflicts they discovered there. During the early 1900s, Freud and several of his colleagues in the Vienna Psychoanalytic Society—including Carl Gustav Jung (1875–1961) and Alfred Adler (1870–1937)—became the most influential clinical theorists in the Western world. Freud's twenty-four volumes on psychoanalytic theory and treatment are still widely studied today.

Freudian Explanations of Normal and Abnormal Functioning

As Freud studied the lives and problems of his patients, he came to believe that three central forces shape or "constitute" the personality: instinctual needs, rational thinking, and moral standards. All these forces, he believed, operate at the *unconscious* level, unavailable to immediate, cognizant awareness; and he believed them to

Freud's office is dominated by the key tools of his therapy: a couch, a desk, and a writing pad. Freud had patients lie on the couch during therapy, while he sat behind them taking notes. He believed that this arrangement heightened concentration and facilitated recall.

be dynamic, or interactive, components whose jostling for expression molds the person's behavior, feelings, and thoughts. Freud called these three forces the *id, ego,* and *superego.*

The Id Freud used the term ***id*** to denote instinctual needs, drives, and impulses. He believed that people are motivated primarily by the id, which he described as "a cauldron of seething excitement" (Freud, 1933, pp. 103-104). The id operates in accordance with the ***pleasure principle;*** that is, it always seeks gratification. One source of id gratification is direct, or ***reflex,*** activity, as when an infant seeks and receives milk from the mother's breast to satisfy its hunger. Another source, ***primary process thinking,*** consists of activation of a memory or image of the desired object. When a hungry child's mother is not available, for example, the child may imagine her breast. Gratification of id instincts by primary process thinking is called ***wish fulfillment.***

Freud also believed that all id instincts tend to be sexual, noting that from the very earliest stages of development a child's gratification has sexual dimensions, as much of its pleasure is derived from nursing, defecating, and masturbating. Freud created the concept of ***libido*** to represent the sexual energy that fuels not only the id but the other forces of personality as well.

The Ego During our early years we come to recognize that our environment will not meet every instinctual need. Our mother, for example, is not always available to provide nurturance at our bidding. Thus a part of the id becomes differentiated into a separate force called the ***ego.*** Like the id, the ego unconsciously seeks gratification, but it does so in accordance with the ***reality principle,*** the knowledge we acquire through experience and from the people around us that it can be dangerous or unacceptable to express our id impulses outright. The ego, employing reason and deliberation, guides us to recognize when we can and cannot express those impulses without negative consequences. The ego's mode of operation, called ***secondary process,*** is to assess new situations, weigh in past experiences, anticipate consequences, and plan how best to obtain gratification.

The ego develops basic strategies, called ***ego defense mechanisms,*** to control unacceptable id impulses and avoid or reduce the anxiety they arouse. The most basic defense mechanism, ***repression,*** prevents unacceptable impulses from ever reaching consciousness. There are many other ego defense mechanisms, and each of us tends to favor some over others (see Box 3-1).

The Superego The ***superego*** grows from the ego, just as the ego grows out of the id. As we learn from our parents that many of our id impulses are unacceptable, we unconsciously incorporate, or ***introject,*** our parents' values. We identify with our parents and judge ourselves by their standards. When we uphold their values, we feel good; when we go against them, we feel guilty.

The superego has two components, the conscience and the ego ideal. The ***conscience*** is always reminding us that certain behaviors, feelings, or thoughts are good or bad, right or wrong. The ***ego ideal*** is a composite image of the values we have acquired, the kind of person we believe we should strive to become. Parents are usually the chief source of this ideal when children are young. As children grow older, however, they may come to identify with other people, too; then those people's values become incorporated in the ego ideal.

According to Freud, these three parts of the personality—the id, ego, and superego—are often in conflict, so that we seem impelled to act, think, and feel in contradictory ways. A healthy personality is one in which an effective working relationship, a stable and acceptable compromise, has been established among the three forces. If the id, ego, and superego are in excessive conflict, the person's behavior may show signs of dysfunction. Freudians would therefore view Philip Berman as someone whose personality forces have a poor working relationship. His rational, constructive ego is unable to control his id impulses, which lead him repeatedly to act in impulsive and often dangerous ways—suicide gestures, jealous rages, job resignations, outbursts of temper, frequent arguments. At the same time, his superego

BOX 3-1 The Defense Never Rests

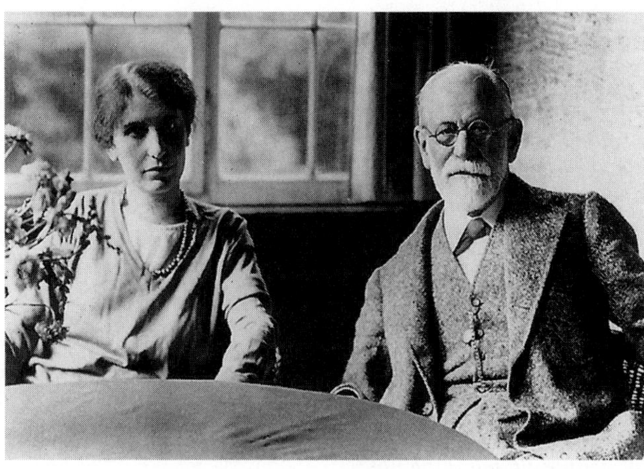

Anna Freud, the last of Sigmund Freud's six children, studied psychoanalysis with her father and then opened a practice next door to his. (They shared a waiting room.) Her work on defense mechanisms, other ego activities, and child development earned her a distinct identity.

Sigmund Freud claimed that the ego tries to defend itself from the anxiety arising out of the conflicts created by unacceptable desires. His daughter Anna Freud (1895–1982) extended the concept of the ego defense mechanism beyond her father's reliance on repression as the key means for defense of the ego. Though repression is the cornerstone of the psychodynamic model of abnormality, it is but one of many methods by which the ego is thought to protect itself from anxiety. Some of these mechanisms are described below.

Repression is the central focus of the psychoanalytic approach to therapy. All other defense mechanisms grow out of it. The person who engages in repression avoids anxiety by simply not allowing painful or dangerous thoughts to become conscious. Once thoughts have been repressed, other ego defense mechanisms may be employed to provide additional insulation.

Example: An executive's desire to run amok and kill his boss and colleagues at a board meeting is denied access to awareness.

Denial is an extreme sort of self-protection. A person who denies reality simply refuses to acknowledge the existence of an external source of anxiety.

Example: You have a final exam in an abnormal psychology course tomorrow and you are entirely unprepared for it, but you tell yourself that it's not actually an important exam and that there's no good reason not to go to a movie or to a concert tonight.

Fantasy is the use of imaginary events to satisfy unacceptable, anxiety-producing desires that would otherwise go unfulfilled.

Example: Pulling into the parking lot at school, a student finds the space he was about to enter suddenly filled by an aggressive, unpleasant person in an expensive sports car. Instead of confronting the offender, the student later fantasizes about getting out of his car and beating the other man to a pulp in front of admiring onlookers, who laud him for his courage and righteousness.

Projection is the attributing of one's own unacceptable motives or desires to others. Rather than admit to having an anxiety-producing impulse, such as anger toward another person, the individual represses the feelings and sees the other person as being the angry one.

Example: The disturbed executive who repressed his murderous desires may project his anger onto his employer and claim that it is actually the boss, not he, who is hostile.

Rationalization, one of the most common defense mechanisms, is the construction of a socially acceptable reason for an action that actually reflects unwor-

seems to be poorly formulated and largely ineffective. Having had weak and ineffectual parental models, Philip never incorporated an effective set of values, a positive ego ideal that might have helped to channel and guide his id impulses.

Developmental Stages Freud proposed that the forces of personality are called to action throughout one's development, beginning in early infancy. At each stage of development, from infancy to maturity, new events and pressures challenge the child and threaten thy motives. Freud explained rationalization as an attempt to explain our behavior to ourselves and to others even though much of our behavior is motivated by unconscious drives that are irrational and infantile.

Example: A student explains away poor grades one semester to her concerned parents by citing the importance of the "total experience" of going to college and claiming that an overemphasis on grades would reduce the overall goal of a well-rounded education. This rationalization may hide an underlying fear of failure and lack of self-esteem.

Reaction formation is the adoption of behavior that is the exact opposite of impulses that one dare not express or even acknowledge.

Example: A man experiences homosexual feelings and responds by taking a strong antihomosexual stance in front of his colleagues.

Displacement, like projection, is a transferral of repressed desires and impulses. In this case one displaces one's hostility away from a dangerous object and onto a safer substitute.

Example: The student whose parking spot was taken may release his pent-up anger by going home and starting a fight with his girlfriend.

In **intellectualization (isolation)** one represses the emotional component of a reaction and resorts to a determinedly logical treatment of the problem at hand. Such an attitude is exemplified by Mr. Spock of the *Star Trek* television series, who believes that emotional responses interfere with analysis of an event.

Example: A woman who has been raped gives a detached, methodical description of the effects that the ordeal is known to have on a victim.

Undoing, as the name suggests, is an attempt to atone for unacceptable desires or acts, frequently through ritualistic behavior.

Example: A woman who has murderous thoughts about her husband ceremoniously dusts and repositions their wedding photograph every time such thoughts occur to her.

Regression is a retreat from an anxiety-producing conflict to a developmental stage at which no one is expected to behave maturely and responsibly.

Example: A boy who is unable to cope with the anger he feels toward an unfeeling and rejecting mother reverts to infantile behavior, ceasing to take care of his basic needs and soiling his clothes, for instance.

Identification is the opposite of projection. Rather than attribute one's thoughts or feelings to someone else, one tries to increase one's sense of self-worth by taking on the values and feelings of the person who is causing the anxiety.

Example: In concentration camps during World War II, some prisoners adopted the behavior and attitudes of their oppressors, even to the point of harming other prisoners. By identifying with their captors, these prisoners were attempting to reduce their own fear.

Overcompensation is an attempt to cover up a personal weakness by focusing on another, more desirable trait.

Example: A very shy young woman overcompensates for her lack of social abilities and the problems that her awkwardness causes by spending many hours in the gym trying to perfect her physical condition.

Sublimation is the expression of sexual and aggressive energy in a way that is acceptable to society. This is a unique defense mechanism in that it can actually be quite constructive and beneficial to both the individual and the community. Freud saw love as sublimation at its best: it allows for the expression and gratification of sexual energy in a way that is socially acceptable.

Example: High achievers in our society—athletes, artists, surgeons, and other highly dedicated and skilled people—may be seen as reaching such high levels of accomplishment by directing other energies into their work.

his or her habitual way of doing things. The clashes require adjustments in the id, ego, and superego. If the adjustments are successful, they foster personal growth.

Under certain pressures, the id, ego, and superego may not mature properly or interact effectively, and the child becomes ***fixated,*** or entrapped, at an early stage of development. Then all subsequent development suffers, and the child may well be headed for some form of abnormal functioning in the future. Because parents provide the primary environmental input during the early years of life, they are often seen as the cause of improper development.

Freud distinguished most stages of normal development by the body area, or ***erogenous zone,*** that he considered central to the child's sexual drives and conflicts at that time. He called the stages the *oral, anal, phallic, latency,* and *genital stages.*

The earliest developmental stage embraces the first 18 months of life. It is called the ***oral stage*** because the infant's main libidinal gratification comes from the body parts involved in feeding—the mouth, lips, and tongue. The most significant threat during the oral stage is the possibility that the mother who feeds and comforts the child will disappear. Children whose mothers consistently fail to gratify their oral needs may become fixated at the oral stage and fail to grow beyond their oral needs. They will display an "oral character" throughout their lives: extreme dependence or extreme mistrust. An oral character may include habits such as pencil chewing, constant talking, or overindulgence in eating, smoking, and drinking.

During the second 18 months of life, the ***anal stage,*** the child's focus of pleasure shifts to the anus. Libidinal gratification comes from retaining and passing feces, and the child becomes very interested in this bodily function.

Freud believed that toilet training is a critical developmental experience. Children whose training is too harsh may become "fixated" at this stage and develop an "anal character."

If parental toilet-training techniques during this stage are too severe, an anal fixation may result, and the child may develop into an adult with an "anal character"—stubborn, contrary, stingy, or overcontrolling.

During the ***phallic stage,*** between the third and fourth years, the focus of sexual pleasure shifts to the genitals—the penis for boys and the clitoris for girls. Boys become attracted to their mother as a fully separate sexual object. They see their father as a rival they would like to push aside, a pattern of desires called the ***Oedipus complex.*** (Oedipus is a character in a Greek tragedy who unknowingly kills his father and marries his mother.)

The phallic conflict for girls is somewhat different. During this stage, girls become aware that they do not have a penis—an organ that, according to Freud, they value and desire (so-called ***penis envy***). They develop a sexual attraction to their father, rooted in the fantasy that by seducing him they can have a penis—a pattern of desires called the ***Electra complex.*** (Electra is a character in another Greek tragedy who conspires to kill her mother to avenge her father's death.)

Both boys and girls fear that they will be punished for their phallic impulses, and so they repress these desires and identify with the parent of their own sex. Boys aspire to be like their fathers and girls to be like their mothers in every way. If children are punished too harshly for sexual behavior during this stage, or if they are subtly encouraged to pursue their desire for the parent of the opposite sex, they may later develop a sexual orientation different from the norm, fear sexual intimacy, be overly seductive, or have other difficulties in romantic relationships.

When children identify with the parent of the same sex during the phallic stage, they particularly identify with that parent's moral standards. Thus it is during this stage that the superego is formed. The superego can be a constructive or a destructive force. It may generate self-praise, self-affection, and high self-esteem; or it may call for self-condemnation, self-punishment, and reparation. Children who become fixated at the phallic stage may suffer pervasive feelings of guilt throughout their lives.

At 6 years of age children enter the ***latency stage,*** in which their sexual desires apparently subside and their libidinal energy is devoted to developing new interests, activities, and skills. They seek friends of the same sex, express dislike for the opposite sex, and are embarrassed by sexual displays. The broader process of socialization, of learning one's roles in family and society, takes place during latency.

At approximately the age of 12, with the onset of puberty and adolescence, the child's sexual urges emerge once again. Now, in what is termed the ***genital stage,*** sexual pleasure begins to be found in heterosexual relationships. Adolescents become increasingly capable of genuine affection and caring for others, and in the normal course of events learn to participate fully in loving and altruistic relationships. The genital stage ends when sexual, social, and vocational maturity is achieved.

Other Psychodynamic Explanations

Personal and professional differences between Freud and his colleagues led to a split in the Vienna Psychoanalytic Society early in the twentieth century. Carl Jung, Alfred Adler, and others left to develop new theories. They perpetuated Freud's basic belief that all human functioning is shaped by dynamic (interacting) psychological forces, though they departed from his model in other respects. Accordingly, all such theories, including Freud's psychoanalytic theory, are referred to as ***psychodynamic.*** Three of today's most influential psychodynamic theories are *ego theory, self theory,* and *object relations theory.*

Ego Theory ***Ego psychologists*** believe that the ego is a more independent and powerful force than Freud recognized. They contend that the ego grows independently of the id and has autonomous, "conflict-free" functions in addition to its id-related responsibilities. The ego guides memory and perception. It also strives for mastery and competence independent of the id. Both the conflict-free and conflict-resolving activities of the ego must be considered if psychological functioning is to be explained properly.

Self Theory Another modern movement in psychodynamic theory has focused on the role of the *self*—the unified personality that defines one's sense of identity—rather than on the various components of personality, such as the id, ego, and superego. In the theory of ***self psychology*** developed by Heinz Kohut (1913–1981), the self is conceptualized as an independent, integrating, and self-motivating force, and the basic human motive is to preserve and enhance its wholeness (Lachmann & Beebe, 1995; Kramer & Akhtar, 1994; Kohut, 1977). Other persons—called ***selfobjects*** in this theory—help the self to define itself, address its needs, and grow. Thus a healthy self requires relationships with empathic and affirming selfobjects throughout life.

Object Relations Theory Relationships play an even more central role in ***object relations theory.*** In classical Freudian theory, *objects* can be either people or things; they acquire their importance because they help to satisfy fundamental drives. In object relations theory, in contrast, objects are exclusively human, and they are important because people are motivated *primarily* by a need to establish relationships with others.

The psychoanalytic notion of the "Electra complex" holds that 4-year-old girls repress threatening desires for their fathers and identify with their mothers, trying to emulate them by dressing, acting, and talking as their mothers do.

Object relations theorists focus on relationships as central to personality development and to the emergence of psychopathology (Kernberg, 1997; Grotstein, 1996, 1995). Children must have appropriate relationships with their parents to progress effectively through the stages of development. Each stage, these theorists believe, is characterized by processes of *attachment* and *separation,* or the building and breaking of bonds (Settlage, 1994). Severe deficiencies in the relationship between child and caregiver may result in fixation, abnormal development, and psychological problems.

Psychodynamic Therapies

Psychodynamic therapies range from classical *Freudian psychoanalysis* to modern therapies based on *self theory* or *object relations theory.* All seek to uncover past traumatic events and the inner conflicts that have resulted from them. All share the goals of helping clients to resolve, or settle, those conflicts and to resume interrupted personal development. Because awareness is the key, psychodynamic therapy is considered an "insight therapy."

According to psychodynamic therapists, the process of gaining insight cannot typically be rushed or imposed. If therapists were simply to tell clients about their inner conflicts, the explanations would sound "off the wall," and the clients would not accept them. Thus therapists must subtly guide the therapeutic discussions so that the patients discover their underlying problems for themselves. To help them do so, psychodynamic therapists rely on such techniques as *free association, therapist interpretation, catharsis,* and *working through.* Naturally, psychodynamic therapists of different theoretical persuasions focus on different underlying problems. An object relations therapist, for example, focuses primarily on problems in early relationships, whereas a Freudian therapist spends more time discussing unresolved psychosexual conflicts. Still, all psychodynamic therapists rely on essentially these same techniques (Kernberg, 1997).

Free Association In psychodynamic therapies the patient is responsible for initiating and leading each discussion. The therapist tells the patient to describe any thought, feeling, or image that comes to mind, even if it seems unimportant or irrelevant. This is the process known as ***free association.*** The therapist probes the patient's associations, expecting that they will eventually reveal unconscious events and unearth the dynamics underlying the individual's personality. Notice how free association helps this New Yorker to discover threatening impulses and conflicts within her.

> *Patient:* So I started walking, and walking, and decided to go behind the museum and walk through Central Park. So I walked and went through a back field and felt very excited and wonderful. I saw a park bench next to a clump of bushes and sat down. There was a rustle behind me and I got frightened. I thought of men concealing themselves in the bushes. I thought of the sex perverts I read about in Central Park. I wondered if there was someone behind me exposing himself. The idea is repulsive, but exciting too. I think of father now and feel excited. I think of an erect penis. This is connected with my father. There is something about this pushing in my mind. I don't know what it is, like on the border of my memory. *(Pause)*
>
> *Therapist:* Mm-hmm. *(Pause)* On the border of your memory?
>
> *Patient: (The patient breathes rapidly and seems to be under great tension.)* As a little girl, I slept with my father. I get a funny feeling. I get a funny feeling over my skin, tingly-like. It's a strange feeling, like a blindness, like not seeing something. My mind blurs and spreads over anything I look at. I've had this feeling off and on since I walked in the park. My mind seems to blank off like I can't think or absorb anything.
>
> *(Wolberg, 1967, p. 662)*

Therapist Interpretation Although psychodynamic therapists allow the patient to generate the discussion, they are listening carefully, looking for clues, and drawing tentative conclusions. They share their interpretations with the patient when they think the patient is ready to hear them. Otto Fenichel (1945), a highly respected psychodynamic theorist, once said that psychodynamic therapists should propose what is already apparent to the patient—"and just a little bit more." The interpretation of three phenomena that occur during therapy is particularly important: *resistance, transference,* and *dreams.*

Patients demonstrate ***resistance*** when they encounter a block in their free associations or change the subject so as to avoid a potentially painful discussion. Through the entire course of therapy, the therapist remains on the lookout for resistance, which is usually unconscious, and may point it out to the patient and interpret it.

Psychodynamic therapists also believe that patients act and feel toward the therapist as they did toward important figures in their childhood, especially their parents and siblings. By interpreting this ***transference*** behavior, therapists may better understand how a patient unconsciously feels toward a parent or some other significant person in the patient's life. Consider again the woman who walked in Central Park. As she continues talking, the therapist helps her to explore some transference issues:

> *Patient:* I get so excited by what is happening here. I feel I'm being held back by needing to be nice. I'd like to blast loose sometimes, but I don't dare.
>
> *Therapist:* Because you fear my reaction?
>
> *Patient:* The worst thing would be that you wouldn't like me. You wouldn't speak to me friendly; you wouldn't smile; you'd feel you can't treat me and discharge me from treatment. But I know this isn't so, I know it.
>
> *Therapist:* Where do you think these attitudes come from?
>
> *Patient:* When I was nine years old, I read a lot about great men in history. I'd quote them and be dramatic. I'd want a sword at my side; I'd dress like an Indian. Mother would scold me. Don't frown, don't talk so much. Sit on your hands, over and over again. I did all kinds of things. I was a naughty child. She told me I'd be hurt. Then at fourteen I fell off a horse and broke my back. I had to be in bed. Mother told me on the day I went riding not to, that I'd get hurt because the ground was frozen. I was a stubborn, self-willed child. Then I went against her will and suffered an accident that changed my life, a fractured back. Her attitude was, "I told you so." I was put in a cast and kept in bed for months.
>
> *(Wolberg, 1967, p. 662)*

Because the therapist's interpretations play such a major role in psychodynamic therapy, psychodynamic therapists must make every effort to listen and interpret without bias. This is easier said than done. Therapists are human beings, with feelings, histories, and values that can subtly and unintentionally influence the way they listen to their patients' problems. These personal biases are called ***countertransference.*** To prevent them from contaminating their interpretations, psychodynamic therapists (particularly Freudian therapists) undergo therapy with a ***training analyst*** during their training.

Finally, many psychodynamic therapists try to help patients interpret their ***dreams.*** Freud (1924) called dreams the "royal road to the unconscious." He believed that repression and other defense mechanisms operate less completely during sleep. Thus a patient's dreams, correctly interpreted, can reveal unconscious instincts, needs, and wishes (see Box 3-2).

Freud defined two kinds of dream content, manifest and latent. ***Manifest content*** is the consciously remembered dream, ***latent content*** its symbolic meaning. To interpret a dream, therapists must translate its manifest content into its latent content. Psychodynamic therapists believe that some types of manifest content are universal and have much the same meaning in everybody's dreams. For example, a house's basement, downstairs, upstairs, attic, and front porch are often symbols of anatomical parts of the body (Lichtenstein, 1980).

Catharsis Insight must be an emotional as well as intellectual process. Psychodynamic therapists believe that patients must experience ***catharsis,*** a reliving of past repressed feelings, if they are to settle internal conflicts and overcome their problems. Only when catharsis accompanies intellectual insight is genuine progress achieved.

Working Through A single session of interpretation and catharsis will not change a person. For deep and lasting insight to be gained, the patient and therapist must examine the same issues over and over in the course of many sessions, each time with new and sharper clarity. This process is called ***working through.*** Because working through a disorder can take a long time, psychodynamic treatment is usually a long-term proposition, often lasting years. When psychodynamic treatment is offered once a week—as most forms of it now are—it is properly known as ***psychodynamic,*** or ***psychoanalytic, therapy.*** The term ***psychoanalysis,*** or simply ***analysis,*** is reserved for therapy given on a daily basis.

Short-Term Psychodynamic Therapies In recent years, several therapists have developed a short version of psychodynamic therapy (Sifneos, 1992, 1987; Davanloo, 1980). They ask their patients to identify a single problem or issue—a ***dynamic focus***—early in therapy, such as difficulty getting along with certain persons or a marital problem. The therapist helps the patient remain attentive to this focus throughout treatment and helps him or her work only on psychodynamic issues, such as an unresolved Oedipal conflict, that relate to it. Resolution of this focus is expected to generalize to other important life situations.

"Don't worry. Fantasies about devouring the doctor are perfectly normal."

(Drawing by Lorenz; © 1993 The New Yorker Magazine, Inc.)

From the beginning the therapist tells the patient that therapy will last for a fixed number of sessions, usually fewer than thirty. The time limit requires the therapist sometimes to be anxiety-provoking or confrontational in interpreting what the patient says. Freud himself tried short-term therapy with some of his patients and judged it to be relatively effective "provided that one hits the right time at which to employ it." Only a limited number of studies have been conducted, but they do suggest that the newer short-term psychodynamic approaches are sometimes quite helpful to patients (Crits-Christoph, 1992; Messer et al., 1992).

Assessing the Psychodynamic Model

Freud and his followers have helped change the way abnormal functioning is understood (Nietzel et al., 1994). Their theories of personality and abnormality are eloquent and comprehensive. Largely because of their groundwork, a wide range of theorists today look for answers and explanations outside the confines of biological processes.

Psychodynamic theorists have also helped us to understand that abnormal functioning may be rooted in the same processes as normal functioning. Psychological conflict, for example, is a universal experience; it leads to abnormal functioning, the psychodynamic theorists say, only if the conflict becomes excessive.

BOX 3-2 Perchance to Dream

All people dream; so do dogs, and maybe even fish. But what purpose do dreams serve? Some people claim that dreams reveal the future; others see them as inner journeys or alternative realities. The Greek philosopher Plato saw dreams as reflections of inner turmoil and wish fulfillment,

> desires which are awake when the reasoning and taming and ruling power of the personality is asleep; the wild beast in our nature, gorged with meat and drink, starts up and walks about naked, and surfeits at his will . . . In all of us, even in good men, there is such a latent wild beast nature, which peers out in sleep.
>
> *(Phaedrus, c. 380 B.C.)*

Psychodynamic therapists consider dreams to be highly revealing. Rather like Plato, Sigmund Freud (1900) contended that dreaming is a mechanism with which we express and attempt to fulfill the unsatisfied desires we spend our lives pursuing. His colleague Carl Jung (1909) also believed dreams to be expressions of the unconscious psyche. And another colleague, Alfred Adler, believed that dreams serve to prepare us for waking life by providing a medium for solving the problems we anticipate: they give us a setting in which to rehearse new behavior patterns or alert us to internal problems of which we have not been aware (Kramer, 1992). All of these theorists claimed that patients would benefit from interpreting their dreams in therapy and understanding the underlying needs, aspirations, and conflicts they symbolized.

The Nightmare *by Johann Heinrich Füssli*

Biological theorists offer a different, though not entirely incompatible, view of dreams. In 1977 J. Allan Hobson and Robert McCarley proposed an ***activation-synthesis*** model of dreams. They claimed that during ***REM sleep*** (the stage of sleep characterized by rapid eye movement, or REM), memories are elicited by random signals from the brain stem—in evolutionary terms, a very old region of the brain. The brain's cortex, the seat of higher cognitive functioning, attempts to make sense of this random bombardment of electrical activity. The result is a dream, often irrational or weird, but the best fit given the variety of signals received by the cortex (Begley, 1989). Hobson later revised the theory to include the idea that the resulting dream, far from being arbitrary, is influenced by the dreamer's drives, fears, and ambitions.

More recently the neuroscientist Jonathan Winson of Rockefeller University contended that dreams are a "nightly record of a basic mammalian process: the means by which animals form strategies for survival and evaluate current experience in light of those strategies" (Winson, 1990). By recording electrical activity in the brains of sleeping and awake nonprimate mammals, Winson found that the brain waves of animals as they dreamed were similar to their brain waves when they were engaged in survival activities. Thus Winson concluded that dreams are a means of reprocessing information necessary for an animal's survival. The information is "accessed again and integrated with past experience to provide an ongoing strategy for behavior" (Winson, 1990). In essence, dreams rehash, reprocess, and reevaluate the day's activities in preparation for the next day's struggle for survival.

Surveys and studies of the contents of human dreams have revealed some interesting patterns (Domhoff, 1996). For example, two-thirds of people's dreams involve unpleasant material, such as aggression, threats, rejection, confusion, or an inability to communicate (Van de Castle, 1993). Dreamers are commonly pursued or in some way attacked by a threatening figure. Such chase dreams have often been taken to mean that the dreamers are running from internal fears or issues that they do not want to face, or from someone in their lives whom they do not trust.

Eighty percent of college students report having had dreams of falling. Some theorists think such dreams occur when our sense of security is threatened or when we are in fear of losing control. Many people say falling dreams are the first ones they can remember, although people can have them at any stage of life (Van de Castle, 1993; Cartwright & Lamberg, 1992).

In some studies, one-third of subjects claim to have had dreams in which they have the ability to fly (Van de Castle, 1993); in a laboratory study, however, flying occurred in only one of 635 dreams (Hennager 1993; Snyder, 1970). These results are not necessarily contradictory; even if flying dreams occur infrequently, they may still occur at least once in the lives of many people. Dreams of flying tend to be associated with positive feelings. Freud considered them to be a symbol of sexual desire; others see them as an expression of freedom, like "being on top of the world" (Hennager, 1993; Jung, 1967; Adler, 1931, 1927).

Another common theme is public nudity. The incidence of such dreams appears to vary across cultures. One study found that 43 percent of American college-age subjects reported having them, but only 18 percent of Japanese subjects did so (Vieira, 1993; Griffith et al., 1958). Freud (1900) viewed dreams of nudity as an unconscious wish to exhibit oneself. Other theorists contend that these dreamers may be afraid of being seen for who they really are (Van de Castle, 1993).

Dreams are also distinguished by gender. Some observers have said that the dreams of American women have more in common with the dreams of Australian Aboriginal women than with those of American men (Kramer, 1989). In a landmark dream study in 1951, the researcher Calvin Hall found that men dreamed twice as often about men as they did about women, whereas women dreamed about men and women in equal proportions. In addition, most male dreams took place in outdoor settings, whereas women's dreams were more often set in their homes or elsewhere indoors. Men's sexual dreams were more likely to include women they did not know, whereas women dreamed more often about men they cared for. In 1980 Hall and his colleagues compared the dream content of college-age men and women with the data he had recorded in 1951 and found no significant changes (Van de Castle, 1993). Other researchers are finding that dreams of men and women are becoming more androgynous, that the dreams of women now take place outdoors more than they did in the past, and that women are now as likely as men to behave aggressively in their dreams (Kramer, 1989).

Finally, the research on dreams has succeeded in putting some myths to rest (Walsh & Engelhardt, 1993):

Myth 1: Some people never dream. Actually, all human beings experience three to six periods of REM sleep each night, and they probably dream in every one.

Myth 2: Most people dream in black and white. Laboratory studies show that everyone dreams in color.

Myth 3: All the places in your dreams are places you have been. Many people dream about places or things they have never seen. Some researchers believe these images represent compilations of things that are familiar to us.

Myth 4: If you die in a dream, you will die in actuality. There are people who have reported dying in their dreams, and, thank goodness, remain alive to tell about it.

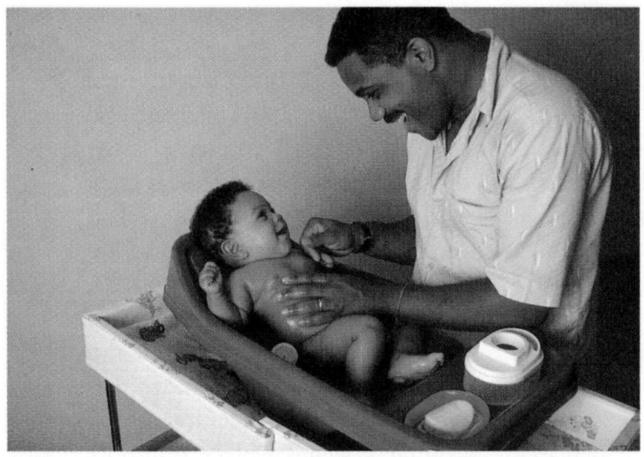

Because mothers provided almost all infant care in his day, Freud pointed largely to maternal influences to explain the development of personality and psychological problems. Today, many fathers also actively nurture their young children, and contemporary psychodynamic theorists have modified their explanations accordingly. It turns out that fathers and mothers are more similar than different when it comes to nurturing.

Freud and his many followers have also had a most significant impact on the treatment of abnormal psychological functioning. They were the first to apply theory and techniques systematically to treatment. They were the first to underscore the potential of psychological, as opposed to biological, treatment, and their notions have served as starting points for many other psychological treatments.

At the same time, the psychodynamic model has shortcomings and limitations. Its concepts can be difficult to define and to research (Nietzel et al., 1994; Erdelyi, 1992, 1985). Because processes such as id drives, ego defenses, and fixation are abstract and supposedly operate at an unconscious level, it is often impossible to determine if they are occurring. Not surprisingly, then, psychodynamic explanations have received little research support, and psychodynamic theorists have been forced to rely largely on individual case studies (Teller & Dahl, 1995).

Similarly, systematic research has often failed to support the effectiveness of psychodynamic therapies. For the first half of the twentieth century, these therapies, too, found their principal support in the case studies of enthusiastic psychodynamic clinicians and uncontrolled research studies. Controlled investigations have been conducted only since the 1950s, and only a minority of those have found psychodynamic therapies to be more effective than no treatment or than placebo treatments (Nietzel et al., 1994; Prochaska & Norcross, 1994). Some recent studies, however, do suggest that the newer, short-term psychodynamic approaches are often quite helpful to some patients (Crits-Christoph, 1992; Messer et al., 1992).

Critics also argue that psychodynamic treatment is impractical for millions of troubled people. With the

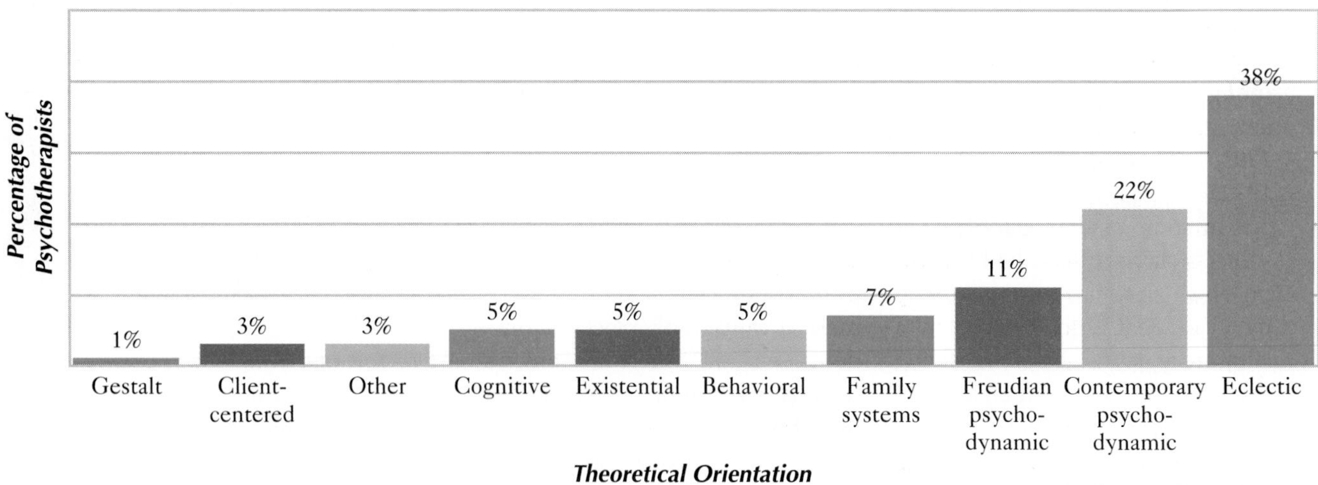

Figure 3-2 *Theoretical orientations of today's clinicians. In one survey, almost 40 percent of 818 psychologists, counselors, psychiatrists, and social workers labeled themselves as primarily "eclectic." The cross-professional percentages in this figure fail to reveal that psychologists and counselors are even more likely to follow a behavioral or cognitive model, psychiatrists a Freudian psychodynamic model or an eclectic model, and social workers a family systems model. (Adapted from Prochaska & Norcross, 1994; Norcross et al., 1988; Norcross & Prochaska, 1986.)*

exception of the short-term approaches, it simply takes too long and costs too much (Simons, 1981). Psychodynamic therapists respond that the necessary steps of free association, therapist interpretation, catharsis, and working through cannot always be rushed if lasting change is to occur.

Partly in response to these problems, other psychological models have emerged over the past several decades. Nevertheless, 11 percent of today's therapists continue to identify themselves principally as Freudian psychodynamic therapists (see Figure 3-2) and 22 percent as contemporary psychodynamic therapists (Prochaska & Norcross, 1994). And, interestingly, many practitioners of other models report that when they seek help for their own problems, psychodynamic therapy is their choice (Norcross & Prochaska, 1984).

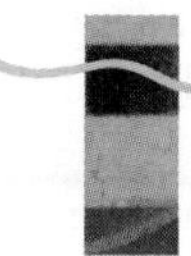

The Behavioral Model

Like psychodynamic theorists, behavioral theorists hold a deterministic view of human functioning: they believe that our actions are determined largely by our experiences in life. However, behavioral theorists concentrate on ***behaviors,*** the responses that an organism makes to its environment. Behaviors can be external (going to work, say) or internal (having a feeling or thought). In the behavioral view, people are the sum total of their learned behaviors. Behavioral theorists, therefore, seek ***principles of learning,*** the processes by which these behaviors change in response to the environment.

Many learned behaviors are constructive and adaptive. They help people to cope with daily challenges and to lead happy, productive lives. However, abnormal and undesirable behaviors also can be learned. Behaviorists who try to explain Philip Berman's problems would concentrate on his inappropriate behaviors and on the principles of learning by which he acquired them. They might view him as a man who has received improper training in life. He has learned behaviors that alienate and antagonize others, behaviors that repeatedly work against him. He does not know how to engage other people, express his emotions constructively, or enjoy himself.

Whereas the psychodynamic model had its origins in the clinical work of physicians, the behavioral model was conceived in laboratories. There psychologists were conducting experiments on ***conditioning,*** simple forms of learning. The scientists manipulated stimuli and rewards, then observed how their manipulations affected their experimental subjects' responses.

Since the turn of the twentieth century, conditioning has been one of experimental psychology's chief areas of study. The work of eminent conditioning theorists such as Ivan Pavlov (1849–1936), B. F. Skinner (1904–1990), and Neal Miller (b. 1909) has pointed to three principles of conditioning: *classical conditioning, operant* (or *instrumental*) *conditioning,* and *modeling.*

Researchers tried to modify abnormal behaviors by means of conditioning as early as the 1920s (Jones, 1924). During the 1950s, practitioners finally applied these principles in clinical practice. Many clinicians were growing disenchanted with what they viewed as the vagueness, slowness, and imprecision of the psychodynamic model. Looking for an alternative approach, some of them began to apply the principles of conditioning to the study and treatment of psychological problems (Wolpe, 1997, 1987). Their efforts gave rise to the behavioral model of psychopathology.

Classical Conditioning

Classical conditioning is a process of learning by *temporal association.* When two events repeatedly occur close together in time, they become fused in a person's mind, and before long the person responds in the same way to both events. If one event elicits a response of joy, the other brings joy as well; if one event brings feelings of relief, so does the other.

Ivan Pavlov, the Russian physiologist, first demonstrated classical conditioning. His early animal studies illustrate the process well. Pavlov placed a bowl of meat powder before a dog, eliciting the innate response that all dogs have to meat: they start to salivate (see Figure 3-3). Next Pavlov inserted an additional step: just before

Figure 3-3 *In Ivan Pavlov's experimental device, the dog's saliva was collected in a tube as it was secreted, and the amount was recorded on a revolving cylinder called a kymograph. The experimenter observed the dog through a one-way glass window.*

presenting the dog with meat powder, he sounded a metronome. After several such pairings of metronome tone and presentation of meat powder, Pavlov observed that the dog began to salivate as soon as it heard the metronome. The dog had learned to salivate in response to a sound.

In the vocabulary of classical conditioning, the meat in this demonstration is an ***unconditioned stimulus (US).*** It elicits the ***unconditioned response (UR)*** of salivation (that is, a natural response the dog is born with). The sound of the metronome is a ***conditioned stimulus (CS),*** a previously neutral stimulus that comes to be associated with meat in the dog's mind. As such, it too elicits a salivation response. When the salivation response is elicited by the conditioned stimulus rather than by the unconditioned stimulus, it is called a ***conditioned response (CR).***

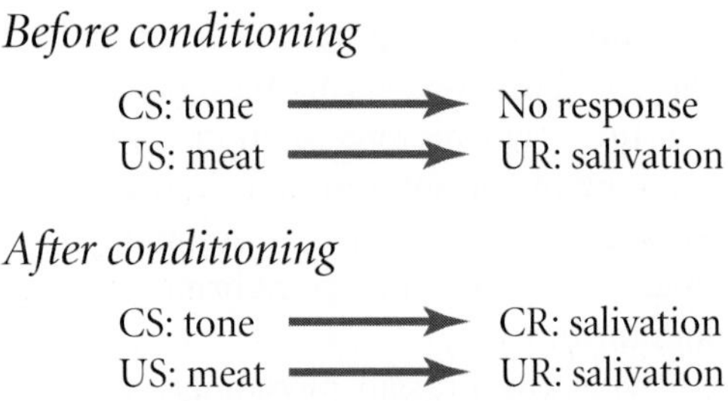

If, after conditioning, the conditioned stimulus is repeatedly presented alone, without being paired with the unconditioned stimulus, it will eventually stop eliciting the conditioned response. When Pavlov stopped pairing the metronome tone and meat powder, for example, the dog salivated less and less in response to the tone. The conditioned response was undergoing ***extinction*** (see Figure 3-4).

Classical conditioning accounts for many familiar animal behaviors. It explains, for example, this ad in the lost-and-found column of a local newspaper: "Lost: female calico cat that answers to the sound of an electric can opener" (Hart, 1985). According to behaviorists, many human behaviors are also acquired through classical conditioning. The amorous feelings a young man experiences when he smells his girlfriend's perfume, say, may represent a conditioned response. Initially this perfume may have had no emotional effect on him, but because the fragrance was present during several romantic encounters, it too came to elicit an amorous response.

The Classical Conditioning of Abnormal Behavior Abnormal behaviors, too, can be acquired by classical conditioning. Consider a young boy who is repeatedly frightened by a neighbor's large German shepherd dog. Whenever the child walks past the neighbor's front yard, the dog barks loudly and lunges at him, stopped only by a rope tied to the porch. In this unfortunate situation, the boy's parents are not surprised to discover that he develops a fear of dogs. They are mystified, however, by another intense fear the child displays, a fear of sand. They cannot understand why he cries whenever they take him to the beach, refuses to take a single step off the beach blanket, and screams in fear if sand even touches his skin.

Where did this fear of sand come from? The answer is found in the principle of classical conditioning. It turns out that a big sandbox is set up in the neighbor's front yard for the fearsome dog to play in. Every time the dog barks and lunges at the boy, the sandbox is there too. After repeated associations of this kind, the child comes to fear sand as much as he fears the dog. Through a simple process of conditioning, the child develops a fear response that may persist throughout his life. The child may be so successful at avoiding sand that he never learns how harmless it is.

Treatments Based on Classical Conditioning Behavioral therapy first aims to identify the behaviors that are causing the client's problems. It then tries to manipulate and replace them with more appropriate ones. The therapist's attitude toward the client is that of teacher rather than healer. Unlike psychodynamic ther-

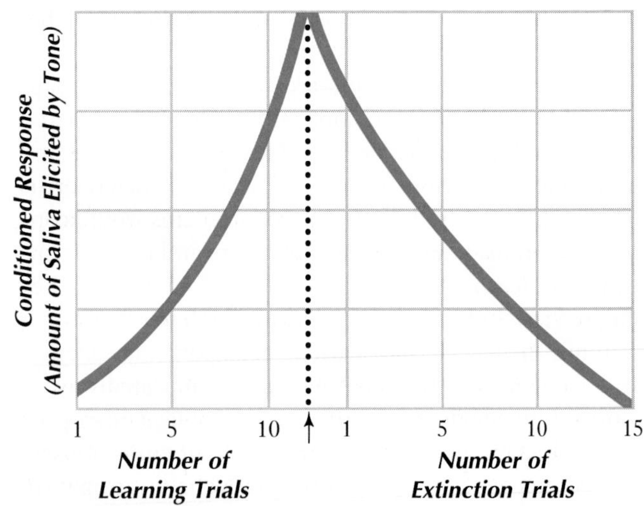

Figure 3-4 *Classical conditioning. During learning trials, a stimulus such as a loud tone is repeatedly paired with another stimulus such as meat. The dog learns to salivate in response to the tone, just as it naturally salivates whenever it sees meat. During extinction trials, the tone is no longer paired with the meat, and the dog eventually stops salivating in response to the tone.*

apy, it need not focus on a client's early life. That history matters only for the clues it can provide to current conditioning processes.

Classical conditioning treatments are intended to change clients' dysfunctional reactions to stimuli (Wolpe, 1997, 1987; Emmelkamp, 1994). Consider ***systematic desensitization,*** a treatment often used for clients with phobias, specific unreasonable fears. This step-by-step procedure teaches them to react calmly instead of with intense fear to the objects or situations they dread (Wolpe, 1990, 1987, 1958). It begins with teaching the skill of deep muscle relaxation over the course of several sessions. Next, the clients construct a ***fear hierarchy,*** a list of feared objects or situations, starting with those that are less feared and ending with the ones that are most fearsome. Here is the hierarchy developed by a man who was afraid of criticism, especially about his mental stability:

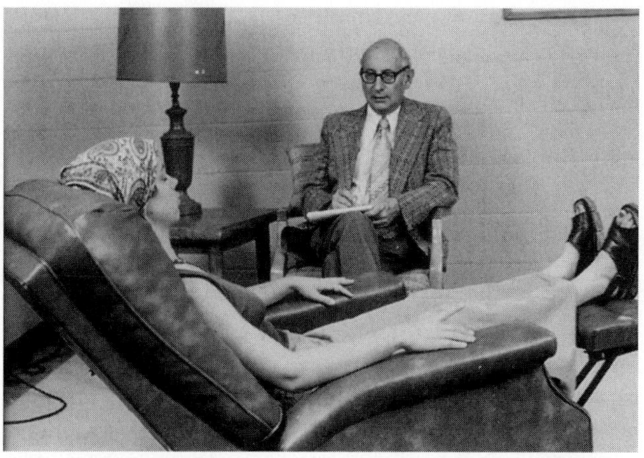

Joseph Wolpe, the psychiatrist who developed the behavioral treatment of systematic desensitization, first teaches a client to relax, then guides her to confront feared objects or situations, real or imagined, while she remains relaxed.

1. Friend on the street: "Hi, how are you?"
2. Friend on the street: "How are you feeling these days?"
3. Sister: "You've got to be careful so they don't put you in the hospital."
4. Wife: "You shouldn't drink beer while you are taking medicine."
5. Mother: "What's the matter, don't you feel good?"
6. Wife: "It's just you yourself, it's all in your head."
7. Service station attendant: "What are you shaking for?"
8. Neighbor borrows rake: "Is there something wrong with your leg? Your knees are shaking."
9. Friend on the job: "Is your blood pressure okay?"
10. Service station attendant: "You are pretty shaky, are you crazy or something?"

(Marquis & Morgan, 1969, p. 28)

Desensitization therapists next have clients either imagine or physically confront each item in the hierarchy while they are in a state of deep relaxation. In step-by-step pairings of feared items and relaxation, clients move up the hierarchy until at last they can relax in the presence of all the items.

As we shall see in Chapter 6, research has repeatedly found systematic desensitization and other classical conditioning techniques to reduce phobic reactions more effectively than placebo treatments or no treatment at all (Wolpe, 1997; Emmelkamp, 1994). These approaches have also been helpful in treating other problems, including sexual dysfunctions, posttraumatic stress disorder, and asthma attacks (Emmelkamp, 1994).

In sharp contrast to desensitization, ***aversion therapy*** helps clients to *acquire* anxiety responses to stimuli that they have been finding too attractive. This classical conditioning therapy has been used with people who want to stop excessive smoking, for example (Blanchard, 1994). In repeated sessions the clients may be given an electric shock, a nausea-producing drug, or some other noxious stimulus whenever they reach for a cigarette. After numerous pairings of this kind, clients are expected to develop an unpleasant emotional reaction to cigarettes. Studies show, however, that the effects of this approach are often short-lived.

Aversion therapy has also been used to help eliminate such undesirable behavior as self-mutilation, sexual deviance, and alcoholism (Emmelkamp, 1994). In the following case, it was used successfully with a man who felt repeated urges to make obscene phone calls.

> **H**e was a married, 32-year-old police officer who made up to twenty obscene telephone calls a week to young women in his community. Therapy consisted of the client making an obscene call to a female listener in another office who was instructed to listen and answer questions in a passive but noncomplying manner. Two young, attractive women listeners were part of the treatment; they were instructed not to hang up first. After each telephone contact, the client and listener shared their feelings. This exchange evoked a great deal of anxiety, shame, and embarrassment on the part of the client. The therapist also was present at each of the meetings. Under these circumstances the client experienced the telephone calls as extremely unpleasant.

These feelings apparently generalized to the client's real-life situation. For nine months after the brief three-week treatment, the client reported no strong urges to make an obscene call and the authorities in the community were not notified of any such calls.

(Adapted from Boudewyns, Tanna, & Fleischman, 1975, pp. 704–707)

Operant Conditioning

In ***operant conditioning,*** humans and animals learn to behave in certain ways because they receive ***reinforcements*** from their environment whenever they do so. Behavior that leads to satisfying consequences, or rewards, is likely to be repeated, whereas behavior that leads to unsatisfying, or aversive, consequences is unlikely to be repeated. Children acquire manners by receiving praise, attention, or treats for desirable behaviors and censure for undesirable ones. Adults work at their jobs because they are paid when they do and fired when they do not.

Operant conditioning was first elucidated by the eminent psychologists Edward L. Thorndike and B. F. Skinner. They taught animal subjects a wide range of behaviors (see Figure 3-5), from pulling levers and turning wheels to navigating mazes and even playing Ping-Pong (Skinner, 1948). To teach complex behaviors, experimenters typically employ ***shaping***—rewarding successive approximations of the desired behavior.

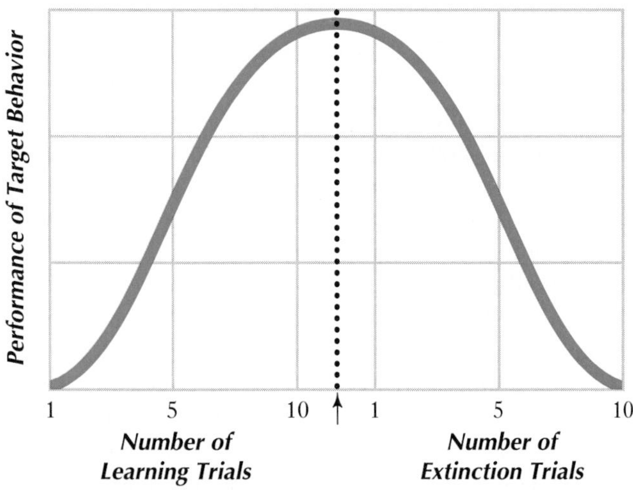

Figure 3-5 *Operant conditioning. During learning trials, a target behavior (such as lifting a paddle) is repeatedly rewarded, and the subject increasingly performs the target behavior. During extinction trials, the target behavior is no longer rewarded, and the subject steadily stops performing the target behavior.*

The public was introduced to aversion therapy by the 1971 movie A Clockwork Orange. *In the film, clinicians tried to change the violent sexual thoughts and behavior of the main character, Alex. They gave him a drug that induced stomach spasms and nausea and had him watch scenes of violence while he experienced these symptoms. The character's severe reactions to the drug and the imprecision of the procedure left a bad taste in the mouths of movie-goers, making it difficult for behaviorists to further develop and apply aversion therapy.*

The Operant Conditioning of Abnormal Behavior Behaviorists also claim that many abnormal behaviors develop as a result of reinforcements (Kohlenberg et al., 1996). Some people learn to abuse alcohol and drugs because initially the drug-related behaviors brought them calm, comfort, or pleasure (Carey & Carey, 1995; Hughes et al., 1995). Others may exhibit bizarre, psychotic behaviors because they enjoy the attention they get when they do so.

Some of Philip Berman's maladaptive behaviors may have been acquired through operant conditioning. When he first became "ornery" at the age of 10, how did his parents react? Perhaps they unintentionally reinforced his rebellious behavior by giving him more attention. Rather than teaching him alternative ways to express his needs, perhaps they simply gave in and let him have his way.

Treatments Based on Operant Conditioning Therapists who rely on operant conditioning consistently provide rewards for appropriate behavior and withhold rewards for inappropriate behavior. This technique has been employed frequently, and often successfully, with people experiencing psychosis (Emmelkamp, 1994; Ayllon & Azrin, 1965). When these patients talk coherently and behave normally, they are rewarded with food, privileges, attention, or something else they value. Conversely, they receive no rewards when they speak bizarrely or display other psychotic behaviors.

In addition, parents, teachers, and therapists have successfully used operant conditioning techniques to change problem behaviors in children, such as repeated tantrums, and to teach skills to individuals with mental retardation (Kazdin, 1994; Schloss & Smith, 1994). Rewards have included meals, recreation time, hugs, and statements of approval.

As we shall see in Chapter 16, operant conditioning techniques typically work best in institutions or schools, where a person's behavior can be reinforced systematically throughout the day. Often a whole ward or classroom is converted into an operant conditioning arena. Such programs are referred to as ***token economy*** programs because desirable behavior is reinforced with tokens that can later be exchanged for food, privileges, or other rewards.

One token economy program was applied in a classroom where children were behaving disruptively and doing poorly at their studies (Ayllon & Roberts, 1974). The children earned tokens whenever they did well on daily reading tests or successfully performed other targeted behaviors. They could then exchange their tokens for a reward, such as extra recess time or a movie. Under this system, reading accuracy increased from 40 to 85 percent, and the proportion of time spent in disruptive behavior decreased from 50 percent to 5 percent.

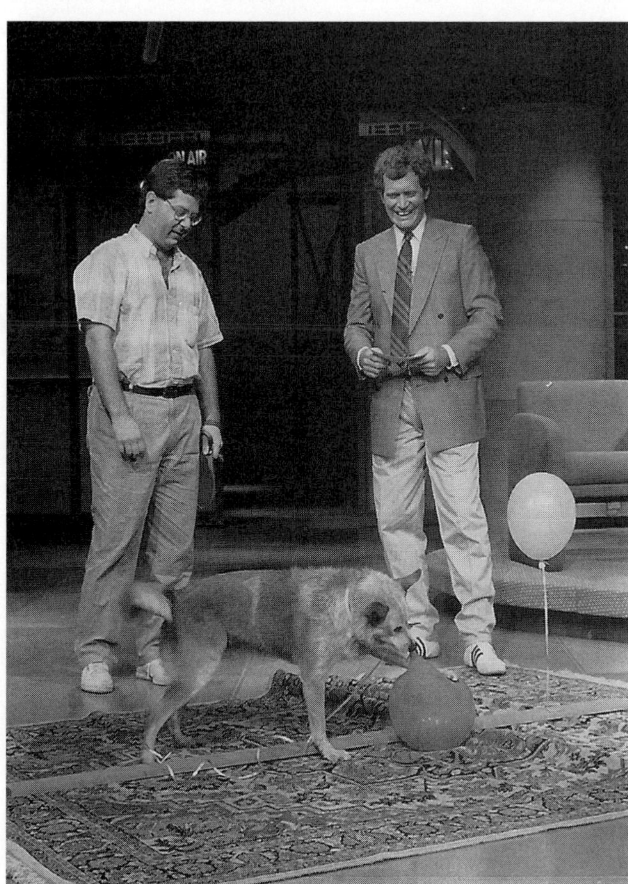

Pet owners have discovered that they can teach animals a wide assortment of tricks through shaping—rewarding successive approximations of a desired behavior.

Modeling

Modeling is a form of conditioning through *observation* and *imitation* (Bandura, 1986, 1977, 1976, 1969). Individuals acquire responses by observing other people (the ***models***) and repeating their behaviors. Observers are especially likely to imitate models they find important or who are themselves being rewarded for the behaviors.

Behaviorists believe that many everyday human behaviors are learned through modeling. Children may acquire language, facial expressions, tastes in food, and the like by imitating the words, expressions, and eating behaviors of their parents. Similarly, adults may acquire interpersonal skills or vocational interests by imitating the behaviors and preferences of important people in their lives.

The Modeling of Abnormal Behavior Modeling, too, can lead to abnormal behaviors. A famous study had young children observe adult models who were acting very aggressively toward a doll (Bandura, Ross, & Ross, 1963). Later, in the same setting, many of the children behaved in the same highly aggressive manner. Other children who had not observed the adult models behaved much less aggressively.

Similarly, children of poorly functioning people may themselves develop maladaptive reactions because of their exposure to inadequate parental models. Certainly the selfish and demanding behaviors displayed by Philip Berman's mother could have served as the model for his own self-centered and hypercritical style. Just as his mother was repeatedly critical of others, Philip was critical of every person with whom he developed a close relationship. Similarly, the severe depressive symptoms exhibited by his mother, which led her to be hospitalized, could have been a model for Philip's own depression and discontent.

Treatments Based on Modeling Modeling therapy was first developed by the pioneering social learning theorist Albert Bandura (1977, 1969). In this approach, therapists demonstrate appropriate behaviors for clients. Through a process of imitation and rehearsal, the clients then acquire the ability to perform the behaviors in their own lives. In some cases, therapists even model new emotional responses for clients. Therapists have calmly handled snakes, for example, to show clients with snake phobias that it is possible to be relaxed in their presence (Bandura, 1977, 1971). After several modeling sessions, clients themselves are encouraged to handle the snakes. As we shall see in Chapter 6, the modeling of emotion can be quite effective in the treatment of phobias (Bandura, 1986; Bandura et al., 1977).

Behavioral therapists have also used modeling in combination with other techniques to help people acquire or improve their social skills and assertiveness. In ***social skills training,*** therapists point out the social deficits of clients and then role-play social situations with the clients. In some enactments the therapist may take the role of the client and demonstrate appropriate social behaviors; in others, the client may try out and rehearse the behaviors, always receiving feedback from the therapist. Ultimately the client practices the behaviors in real-life situations. Consider the case of a male college student who has difficulty making dates:

> *Client:* By the way (*pause*), I don't suppose you want to go out Saturday night?
>
> *Therapist:* Up to actually asking for the date, you were very good. However, if I were the girl, I think I might have been a bit offended when you said, "By the way." It's like your asking her out is pretty casual. Also the way you phrased the question, you were kind of suggesting to her that she doesn't want to go out with you. Pretend for the moment I'm you. Now, how does this sound: "There is a movie at the Varsity Theater this Saturday that I want to see. If you don't have other plans, I'd very much like to take you."
>
> *Client:* That sounded good. Like you were sure of yourself and liked the girl, too.
>
> *Therapist:* Why don't you try it.
>
> *Client:* You know that movie at the Varsity? Well, I'd like to go, and I'd like to take you Saturday, if you don't have anything better to do.
>
> *Therapist:* Well, that certainly was better. Your tone of voice was especially good. But the last line, "if you don't have anything better to do," sounds like you don't think you have too much to offer. Why not run through it one more time?
>
> *Client:* I'd like to see the show at the Varsity Saturday, and, if you haven't made other plans, I'd like to take you.
>
> *Therapist:* Much better. Excellent, in fact. You were confident, forceful, and sincere.
>
> *(Rimm & Masters, 1979, p. 74)*

Using a combined strategy of modeling, rehearsal, feedback, and practice, therapists have successfully taught social and assertion skills to shy, passive, or socially isolated people. They have helped as well people who have a pattern of bursting out in rage or violence after building up resentment over perceived social slights (Emmelkamp, 1994). As we shall note in later chapters, the approach has also been used to improve the social skills of people who are depressed, alcoholic, obese, or anxious (Cooney et al., 1991; Hersen et al., 1984).

Assessing the Behavioral Model

The number of behavioral clinicians has grown steadily since the 1950s, and the behavioral model has become a powerful force in the clinical field. Various schools of behavioral thought have emerged over the years, and many treatment techniques have been developed. Approximately 5 percent of today's therapists report that their approach is primarily behavioral (Prochaska & Norcross, 1994).

Perhaps the most prominent appeal of the behavioral model is that it can be tested in the laboratory, whereas psychodynamic theories generally cannot. The behaviorists' basic concepts—stimulus, response, and reinforcement—can be observed and measured. Even more important, the results of research have lent considerable support to the behavioral model (Wolpe, 1997; Emmelkamp, 1994). Experimenters have successfully used the principles of conditioning to create clinical symptoms in laboratory subjects, suggesting that psychological disorders may indeed develop the same way.

Similarly, behavioral treatments have been effective in clinical practice for specific fears, social deficits, mental retardation, and other problems (Juster et al., 1996; Emmelkamp, 1994; Bierman & Furman, 1984). Their effectiveness is, in fact, all the more impressive in view of the relatively short duration and low overall cost of these therapies.

At the same time, research has revealed weaknesses in the behavioral model. Certainly behavioral researchers have induced specific symptoms in subjects, but are these symptoms *ordinarily* acquired in this way? There is still no indisputable evidence that most people with mental disorders are victims of improper conditioning.

Similarly, behavioral therapies have limitations. First, the improvements noted in the behavioral therapist's office cannot necessarily be counted on to extend to the client's real life. Nor do improvements necessarily maintain themselves without continued therapy (Nietzel et al., 1994; Stokes & Osnes, 1989). Second, as we shall observe in later chapters, behavioral therapies do not appear to be particularly effective with psychological disorders that

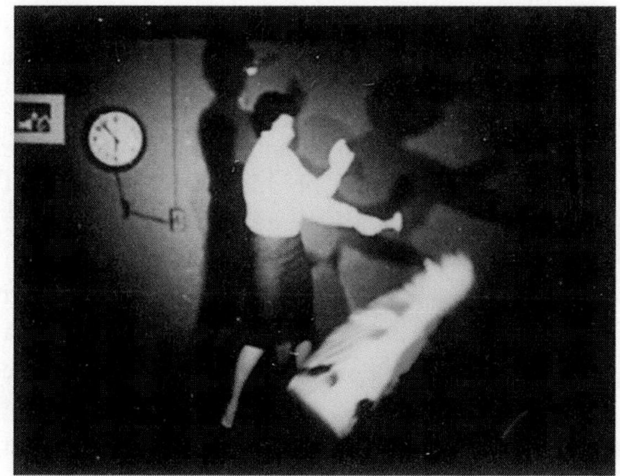

Modeling may account for some forms of abnormal behavior. A well-known study by Albert Bandura and his colleagues (1963) demonstrated that children learned to abuse a doll by observing an adult model hit it. Children who had not been exposed to the adult model did not mistreat the doll.

are pervasive, such as generalized anxiety disorder (O'Leary & Wilson, 1987). Third, some people have raised ethical questions about the behavioral approaches (Kipnis, 1987). It troubles them that token economy programs and other operant conditioning techniques are imposed on many clients without their permission. In addition, they are concerned that aversion therapy inflicts pain or at least discomfort on clients.

Finally, some critics hold that the behavioral perspective is too simplistic, that its concepts and principles fail to capture the complexity of human behavior. In 1977 Albert Bandura, who earlier had identified modeling as a key conditioning process, argued that in order to feel happy and function effectively people must develop a positive sense of ***self-efficacy,*** a judgment that they can master and perform needed behaviors whenever necessary. Other behaviorists of the 1960s and 1970s similarly recognized that human beings engage in ***cognitive behaviors,*** such as anticipating, interpreting, and perceiving; these ways of thinking were being largely ignored in behavioral theory and therapy. Accordingly, they developed ***cognitive-behavioral theories*** that also took unseen cognitive behaviors into account (Meichenbaum, 1993; Goldiamond, 1965).

Cognitive-behavioral theorists bridge the behavioral model and cognitive model, the perspective that we shall be turning to next. On the one hand, their explanations are firmly entrenched in behavioral principles. They believe, for example, that cognitive processes are acquired and maintained by classical conditioning, operant conditioning, and modeling. At the same time, cognitive-behavioral theorists share with other kinds of cognitive theorists a belief that the ability to think is the most important aspect of both normal and abnormal human functioning (Wilson, Hayes, & Gifford, 1997). Given this central concern with human thought, cognitive-behavioral theories and therapies are now often seen as a special category of the cognitive model (Dougher, 1997).

The Cognitive Model

Philip Berman, like the rest of us, has ***cognitive*** abilities—special intellectual capacities to think, remember, and anticipate. These cognitive abilities serve him in all his activities and can help him accomplish a great deal in life. Yet they can also work against him (see Box 3-3). As he cognitively organizes and records his experiences, Philip may be developing false ideas. He may misinterpret experiences in ways that lead to counterproductive decisions, maladaptive responses, and unnecessarily painful emotions.

According to the cognitive model, to understand human behavior we must understand the content and process of human thought. What assumptions and attitudes color a person's perceptions? What thoughts run through that person's mind, and what conclusions do they lead to? When people display abnormal patterns of

BOX 3-3 Slips of the Tongue

"It happens quite often. Right before an exam a student calls to ask for a postponement, giving one of several familiar excuses. It is easy to be skeptical when this happens, but I recall one occasion when my doubt was underscored with a curious slip of the tongue. The student said that she wanted the postponement because '. . . last night my grandmother lied—I mean died!'"

(Motley, 1987, p. 25).

"Good morning, beheaded—uh, I mean beloved." (Drawing by Fradon; © 1983 The New Yorker Magazine, Inc.)

What could have caused this student's unfortunate slip? Sigmund Freud would have considered it a classic case of ***parapraxis,*** popularly known as a ***Freudian slip,*** a repressed thought, feeling, or motive that fights its way to the surface (Gossy, 1995). According to Freud's theory, a verbal slip is *never* a simple mistake. He considered it evidence of the unconscious mind at work.

Freud might have agreed that the embarrassed student was lying to her professor, and her conflicted feelings caused the slip. Or perhaps the lie raised repressed guilt about an old lie to her grandmother. Or perhaps the flummoxed student was really telling the truth; she just worried that her professor would think she was lying (Motley, 1987).

Most modern researchers dismiss Freud's theory. Many focus on cognitive factors to explain slips of the tongue. One explanation holds that verbal slips result from the constant, automatic choices we make between words. When more than one linguistically acceptable word is available, a verbal slip may result (Motley, 1987). Competition between "perchance" and "perhaps," for example, may result in "perchaps." Researchers note that verbal slips are more common when people are nervous, as during a job interview or when they beg a professor to postpone an exam. When we are tense we may not devote the usual attention to resolving competition between word choices.

Michael Motley (1987), a professor of rhetoric and communication, has studied verbal slips. According to Motley, competition among words may be explained by the ***spreading activation theory.*** This cognitive theory proposes that in a person's mental dictionary, each word is connected with other words by meaning, sound, or grammar. The mental dictionary, then, looks more like a spider web than a list of words. As we speak, our thoughts spread along the lines of the web to activate related words. The word that ends up with the most accumulated activation is the one we utter. If two words have equal levels of activation, as "perhaps" and "perchance" might, a verbal slip could result.

Some research has focused on how this verbal network may be affected by *hidden* thoughts—the same hidden thoughts that Freud believed were the basis of parapraxis. In one experiment, men were asked to complete a series of sentences. One group of unsuspecting men sat in a room with a seductively dressed, attractive woman, while the other group worked with a man. The experimenters found that the aroused men completed their sentences with sexual words almost twice as often as the other men did. They said, for example, "Tension mounted at the end, when the symphony reached its *climax,*" rather than "finale" or "conclusion" (Motley, 1987). Presumably sets of sexual words were activated in the mental dictionaries of the men who worked with the attractive woman. When those words also had meanings that would fit the sentence, they were activated a second time, and so were selected. Thus this study provided evidence that unconscious or hidden thoughts could indeed activate the verbal network and influence the choice of words. Later research has further indicated that hidden thoughts can lead to spreading activation *competition* between words, causing the type of verbal slips that Freud described.

In short, after being disparaged for so long, Freud's explanation of verbal slips, particularly his emphasis on unconscious processes, has found some support in the laboratories of cognitive psychologists. What an intersecting—that is, *interesting*—development!

"Stimulus, response! Stimulus, response! Don't you ever *think*?"

The Far Side © Farworks, Inc. Reprinted with permission of Universal Press Syndicate. All rights reserved.

functioning, cognitive theorists assume that cognitive problems are to blame.

The roots of the cognitive model of abnormal psychology can be traced to the late 1950s and to the field of social psychology. This branch of experimental psychology studies the individual's interactions with the social environment. Social psychologists became interested in how we explain the things we see going on around us. They proposed that we rely on ***attributions;*** that is, we attribute events to particular causes, and our causal attributions then influence the way we feel about ourselves and others (Heider, 1958, 1944).

While attributions were becoming a dominant focus in social psychology, the movement toward a more cognitively oriented behaviorism was gaining strength in the clinical community. These two developments set the stage for the emergence of the cognitive model of abnormal psychology.

In the early 1960s two clinicians, Aaron Beck and Albert Ellis, proposed cognitive theories of abnormality. Building on earlier work (Kelley, 1955; Rotter, 1954), these theorists claimed that cognitive processes are at the center of behavior, thought, and emotions and that we can best understand abnormal functioning by looking to the cognitive realm. Other theorists and therapists soon incorporated and expanded upon the ideas and techniques of Beck and Ellis.

Cognitive Explanations of Abnormal Behavior

To cognitive theorists, we are all artists. We reproduce and create our worlds in our minds as we try to understand the events going on around us. If we are effective artists, our cognitive representations tend to be accurate (agreed upon by others) and useful (adaptive). If we are ineffective artists, however, we may create a cognitive inner world that is alien to others and painful and harmful to ourselves. Abnormal functioning can result from several kinds of cognitive problems: *maladaptive assumptions or attitudes, specific upsetting thoughts,* and *illogical thinking processes* (see Table 3-1).

Maladaptive Assumptions Albert Ellis (1997, 1992, 1962) proposes that each of us holds a unique set of assumptions about ourselves and our world. Unfortunately, some people's assumptions are largely irrational, guiding them to act and react in ways that are inappropriate and that prejudice their chances of happiness and success. Ellis calls these ***basic irrational assumptions.***

Some people, for example, irrationally assume that they are abject failures if they are not loved or approved of by virtually every person they know. Such people constantly seek approval and repeatedly feel rejected. All their interactions and interpretations are affected. An otherwise successful presentation in the classroom or boardroom can make them sad or anxious because one listener seems bored, or an evening with friends can leave them dissatisfied because the friends do not offer enough compliments. The basic irrational assumption sets the stage for a life hampered by tension or disappointment.

Ellis (1962) suggested other common irrational assumptions:

- The idea that one must be thoroughly competent, adequate, and achieving in all possible respects if one is to consider oneself worthwhile.
- The idea that it is awful and catastrophic when things are not the way one would very much like them to be.
- The idea that human unhappiness is externally caused and that people have little or no ability to control their sorrows and disturbances.

TABLE 3-1 Comparing the Psychological Models

	Psychodynamic	*Behavioral*	*Cognitive*	*Humanistic*	*Existential*
Cause of dysfunction	Underlying conflicts	Maladaptive learned behaviors	Maladaptive thinking	Self-deceit	Avoidance of responsibility
Research support	Modest	Strong	Strong	Weak	Weak
Consumer designation	Patient	Client	Client	Patient or client	Patient or client
Therapist role	Interpreter	Teacher	Persuader	Observer	Collaborator
Key therapist technique	Free association and interpretation	Conditioning	Reasoning	Reflection	Varied
Therapy goal	Broad psychological change	Functional behaviors	Adaptive thinking	Self-actualization	Authentic life

- The idea that one needs someone stronger than oneself to rely on.
- The idea that one's past is an all-important determinant of one's present behavior, and that because something once strongly affected one's life, it will affect it in the same way indefinitely.
- The idea that there is invariably a right, precise, and perfect solution to human problems and that it is catastrophic if this perfect solution is not found.

Philip Berman often seems to hold the basic irrational assumption that his past history has inexorably determined his present behavior, so something that once affected his life will have the same effect indefinitely. Philip believes he was victimized by his parents and that he is now doomed by his oppressive past. He seems to approach all new experiences and relationships with expectations of failure and disaster.

Specific Upsetting Thoughts Cognitive theorists believe that specific upsetting thoughts may also contribute to abnormal functioning. As we confront the myriad situations that arise in life, numerous thoughts come into our minds, some comforting, others upsetting. Aaron Beck has called these unbidden cognitions ***automatic thoughts.*** If a person's stream of automatic thoughts is overwhelmingly negative, Beck would expect that person to become depressed (Beck, 1997, 1991, 1976; Philpot et al., 1995). Philip Berman has made it clear what fleeting thoughts and images keep popping into his mind as he interacts with others: "My old girlfriend wants to jump into bed with her date. . . . I'm a 25-year-old virgin. . . . The therapist wants to laugh at me. . . . My boss wants to fire me. . . . My parents think I'm lazy and irresponsible." Certainly such automatic thoughts are contributing to his pervasive feelings of despondency.

The clinical theorist Donald Meichenbaum (1993, 1986, 1977) speaks similarly of ***self-statements,*** or inadvertent thoughts about ourselves. He suggests that people who suffer from anxiety have learned to generate counterproductive self-statements during stressful situations. As a result, they react to any difficult situation with automatic fear and anxiety. When Philip Berman met his old girlfriend and her date, his mind may have been flooded with self-statements: "Oh, no, I can't stand this. . . . I look like a fool. . . . I'm getting sick. . . . Why do these things always happen to me?" These statements may have fueled his anxiety and rage and prevented him from handling the encounter constructively.

Illogical Thinking Processes Cognitive theorists also point to illogical thinking processes to explain abnormal functioning. Beck (1993, 1991, 1967) has found that some people habitually think in illogical ways and keep drawing self-defeating and even pathological con-

clusions. As we shall see in Chapter 8, Beck has identified a number of illogical thought processes characteristic of depression, including *selective perception,* or seeing only the negative features of an event, and *overgeneralization,* or drawing broad negative conclusions on the basis of a single insignificant event. One depressed student couldn't remember the date of Columbus's third voyage to America during a history class. Overgeneralizing, she spent the rest of the day in despair over her invincible ignorance.

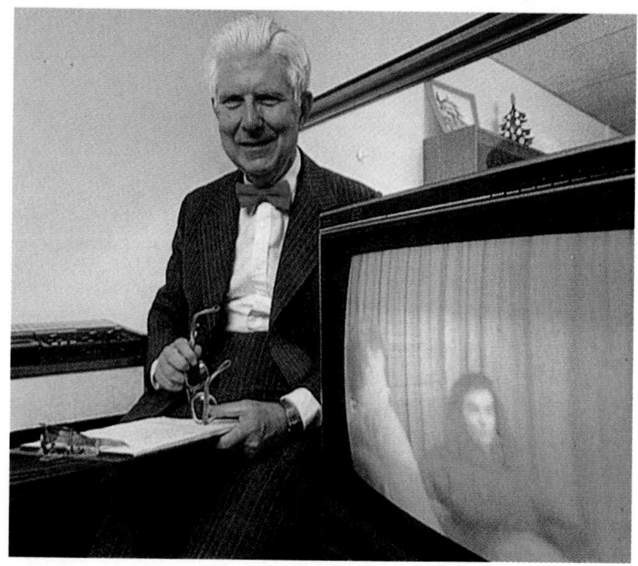

Aaron Beck proposes that many forms of abnormal behavior can be traced to cognitive factors, such as upsetting thoughts and illogical thinking.

Cognitive Therapies

According to cognitive theorists, people with psychological disorders can overcome their difficulties by developing new, more functional ways of thinking. Because different forms of abnormality may involve different kinds of cognitive dysfunctioning, cognitive therapists have developed a variety of cognitive strategies.

Ellis's Rational-Emotive Therapy In line with his belief that irrational assumptions give rise to abnormal functioning, Albert Ellis has developed an approach called ***rational-emotive therapy*** (Ellis, 1997, 1991, 1962). Therapists help clients to discover the irrational assumptions that govern their emotional responses. Therapy can then change their assumptions into constructive ways of viewing themselves and the world.

In his own practice, Ellis is a direct, active therapist. He points out clients' irrational assumptions in a blunt, confrontational, often humorous way and then models the use of alternative assumptions. After criticizing a man's perfectionistic standards, for example, he might say, "So what if you did a lousy job on your project? It's important to realize that one lousy project simply means one lousy project, and no more than that!" Ellis also gives clients homework assignments. He may require them to observe how their assumptions operate in everyday life and to think of ways to test the assumptions' rationality.

A number of studies have found that rational-emotive therapy often proves helpful to clients (Altrows, 1995; Kopec, 1995; Smith & Lombardo, 1995). As we shall observe in Chapter 6, anxious clients in particular who are treated with this therapy improve more than anxious clients who receive no treatment or placebo treatment.

Beck's Cognitive Therapy Aaron Beck has independently developed a system of therapy that is similar to Ellis's rational-emotive therapy. Called simply ***cognitive therapy,*** Beck's approach has been most widely used in cases of depression (Beck, 1997, 1993, 1976, 1967). Cognitive therapists help clients to recognize the negative thoughts, biased interpretations, and errors in logic that pervade their thinking and, according to Beck, cause them to feel depressed. The therapists also guide clients to challenge their dysfunctional thoughts, try out new interpretations, and ultimately apply alternative ways of thinking in their daily lives. As we shall see in Chapter 9, people with depression who are treated with Beck's approach improve significantly more than those who receive no treatment (Hollon & Beck, 1994; Young, Beck, & Weinberger, 1993). In recent years Beck's cognitive therapy has also been successfully applied to panic disorders and other anxiety disorders (Beck, 1997, 1993).

Here a cognitive therapist guides a depressed 26-year-old graduate student to see the relationship between the way she interprets her experiences and the way she feels and to question the accuracy of her interpretations:

> *Patient:* I agree with the description of me but I guess I don't agree that the way I think makes me depressed.
>
> *Therapist:* How do you understand it?
>
> *Patient:* I get depressed when things go wrong. Like when I fail a test.
>
> *Therapist:* How can failing a test make you depressed?
>
> *Patient:* Well, if I fail I'll never get into law school.
>
> *Therapist:* So failing the test means a lot to you. But if failing a test could drive people into clinical depression,

wouldn't you expect everyone who failed the test to have a depression? . . . Did everyone who failed get depressed enough to require treatment?

Patient: No, but it depends on how important the test was to the person.

Therapist: Right, and who decides the importance?

Patient: I do.

Therapist: And so, what we have to examine is your way of viewing the test (or the way that you think about the test) and how it affects your chances of getting into law school. Do you agree?

Patient: Right.

Therapist: Do you agree that the way you interpret the results of the test will affect you? You might feel depressed, you might have trouble sleeping, not feel like eating, and you might even wonder if you should drop out of the course.

Patient: I have been thinking that I wasn't going to make it. Yes, I agree.

Therapist: Now what did failing mean?

Patient: *(Tearful)* That I couldn't get into law school.

Therapist: And what does that mean to you?

Patient: That I'm just not smart enough.

Therapist: Anything else?

Patient: That I can never be happy.

Therapist: And how do these thoughts make you feel?

Patient: Very unhappy.

Therapist: So it is the meaning of failing a test that makes you very unhappy. In fact, believing that you can never be happy is a powerful factor in producing unhappiness. So, you get yourself into a trap—by definition, failure to get into law school equals "I can never be happy."

(Beck et al., 1979, pp. 145–146)

Meichenbaum's Self-Instruction Training The clinical innovator Donald Meichenbaum (1993, 1986, 1977, 1975) has developed a kind of cognitive training to help people solve problems and cope with stress more effectively. In ***self-instruction training,*** therapists teach clients to make helpful statements to themselves—*positive self-statements*—and to apply them in difficult circumstances. The therapists begin by explaining and modeling effective self-statements. They then have clients practice and apply the statements in stressful situations.

Using self-instruction training, Meichenbaum has taught anxious clients to make self-statements like these as they try to cope with anxiety-arousing situations:

Just think about what you can do about it. That's better than getting anxious.

Just "psych" yourself up—you can meet this challenge. One step at a time: you can handle the situation.

Relax; you're in control. Take a slow deep breath.

Don't try to eliminate fear totally; just keep it manageable.

(Meichenbaum, 1974)

In comparison with no treatment and placebo treatment, Meichenbaum's self-instruction training has been found helpful for people with impulsive disorders, social anxiety, test anxiety, pain, and problems with anger (Meichenbaum, 1993; Jay et al., 1987; Novaco, 1976, 1975). It is not clear, however, how long the new cognitive problem-solving skills are retained (Schlichter & Horan, 1981).

Assessing the Cognitive Model

The cognitive model has had very broad appeal. In addition to the many behaviorists who have incorporated cognitive concepts into their theories about learning, a great many clinicians believe that thinking processes are much more than conditioned reactions. Cognitive theory, research, and treatments have developed in so many interesting ways that the model is now viewed as distinct from the behavioral school that spawned it.

Approximately 5 percent of today's therapists identify their orientation as cognitive (Prochaska & Norcross, 1994). This overall percentage actually reflects a split in the clinical community. A full 10 percent of psychologists and other counselors employ cognitive therapy primarily, compared to only 1 percent of psychiatrists and 4 percent of social workers (Prochaska & Norcross, 1994; Norcross, Prochaska, & Farber, 1993). Moreover, surveys suggest that the number of professionals who embrace cognitive approaches is continuing to rise.

There are several reasons for the cognitive model's appeal. First, it focuses on the most singular of human processes, thought. Just as our special cognitive abilities

Personal Pathways

Donald Meichenbaum and a Mother's Wisdom

Donald Meichenbaum theorized that people under stress make counterproductive self-statements. *In* self-instruction training *he encourages clients to make helpful self-statements instead. Where did this approach come from? Meichenbaum (1993) points to his mother:*

"On a recent occasion she related [how] a coworker . . . asked her to help move some files. As the story unfolded, my mother not only conveyed what had happened to her, but she also commented on how she felt and thought in complying with this request.

"So, what should I say? I did what she asked. I'm a nice person. Who would know that the files would be so heavy and I could hurt my back? . . . Now, I start getting angry—not with Sadie, but getting down on myself. . . .

"You know it's bad enough I lifted something that I shouldn't have. I decided I shouldn't get upset too. I noticed that I was working myself up. I caught myself and thought, look you've got choices. You don't have to get yourself down because you made a mistake."

As she was telling me her story, I realized that I had listened to such tales throughout my entire childhood and adolescence. . . . Free of charge, my mother . . . conveyed how we could "notice," "catch," "interrupt," "choose" different thoughts and behaviors. . . .

In a moment of insight, I realized that my entire research career, which has been spent trying to understand and measure how adults and children think and how their thoughts influence their feelings and behavior, had its origins at my family's dinner table. My mother was an "undaunted psychologist," coping and teaching us to cope with the normal and not so normal perturbations of life."

are responsible for so many human accomplishments, they may also be responsible for the special problems that characterize human functioning. Thus many theorists of varied backgrounds find themselves drawn to a model that views thought as the primary contributor to normal and abnormal behavior.

Cognitive theories also lend themselves to investigation. Researchers have found that people often do exhibit the assumptions, specific thoughts, and thinking processes that supposedly contribute to abnormal functioning, and these cognitive phenomena do seem to operate in many cases of pathology. When experimental subjects are manipulated into adopting unpleasant assumptions or thoughts, for example, they become more anxious and depressed (Rimm & Litvak, 1969). Similarly, many people with psychological disorders display maladaptive assumptions, thoughts, or thinking processes (Whisman & McGarvey, 1995; Gustafson, 1992).

Yet another reason for the popularity of the cognitive model is the impressive performance of cognitive therapies. They have proved to be very effective for treating depression and sexual dysfunctions, for example, and moderately effective for anxiety problems (Hollon & Beck, 1994; Carey et al., 1993). They also adapt well to new technologies, as we see in Box 3-4.

Nevertheless, the cognitive model, too, has its drawbacks (Beck, 1997, 1991; Meichenbaum, 1997, 1992). First, although cognitive processes seem to be involved in many forms of abnormality, their precise role has yet to be determined. The maladaptive cognitions seen in psychologically troubled people could well be a consequence rather than a cause of their difficulties. Certainly a process so central to human functioning as thought must be highly vulnerable to disturbances of any kind.

Second, although cognitive therapies are clearly of help to people with various kinds of problems, they are far from a panacea. After an initial wave of enormous enthusiasm, research findings have begun to suggest limitations. Is it enough to alter cognitive features in cases of psychological dysfunctioning? Can such specific kinds of thought changes make a general and lasting difference in the way a person feels and behaves? These and related questions are now receiving considerable attention and analysis.

Finally, like the other models, the cognitive model has been criticized for its narrowness. Although cognition is a very special human dimension, it is still only one part of human functioning. Aren't human beings more than the sum of their fleeting thoughts, emotions, and behaviors? For those who believe that they are, explanations of human functioning must at least sometimes embrace broader issues. They must look at how people approach life, what they get from it, and how they deal with the question of life's meaning. This is the contention of the humanistic-existential perspective.

BOX 3-4 What's New in "Treatment"?

Each day seems to bring some new approach to helping people with psychological problems. In New York, a former stockbroker offers a "playshop" to help people learn to be less serious and more outrageous. Her technique, called "chutzpah therapy," consists of three days of charades, body-movement exercises, coloring with crayons, improvisation, and dressing up in costumes (Kaufman, 1993). Elsewhere in the city, on Saturdays, the three "Advice Ladies" stand on a corner giving advice to passers-by (Bellafante, 1993). Interventions such as these may capture the attention of reporters, but professionals do not always take them seriously. Three unconventional approaches that clinical professionals *are* giving serious consideration are treatments that make use of the great outdoors, the telephone, and the computer.

Outward Bound offers special programs to meet psychological needs. The well-known wilderness program traditionally focuses on the development of outdoor skills, self-esteem, and positive group dynamics. In its special programs, however, participants confront mental as well as physical challenges, both in groups and alone. In the "solo" period, for example, when participants are given limited food supplies and left alone for seventy-two hours, they can learn they have more strengths than they knew, and they may increase their sense of self-reliance and control.

In one study, juvenile offenders who participated in an Outward Bound program showed a one-year reduction in delinquency, but the reduction was not sustained at a two-year follow-up (Castellano & Soderstrom, 1992). Similarly, follow-up studies reveal only limited systematic changes in self-concept over the long term (Ewert, 1988; Marsh, Richards, & Barnes, 1986).

Bedridden, physically disabled, and hospitalized patients are the targets of ***telephone therapy.*** Although visual and nonverbal cues are lost when therapist and client speak by telephone rather than face to face, some clinicians suggest that the very anonymity of telephone therapy may actually enhance the psychotherapeutic process (Mermelstein & Holland, 1991). Phone therapy has apparently also been helpful for individuals who suffer from agoraphobia, a fear of leaving one's home (Cox, Fergus, & Swinson, 1993).

Other clinicians are looking to the ***computer*** and the ***Internet.*** Using the principles behind telephone therapy, some therapists have established on-line services

The Humanistic-Existential Model

Philip Berman is more than psychological conflicts, learned behaviors, and cognitions. Being human, he also has the ability to confront self-awareness, values, meaning, and choice, and to incorporate them in his life. And according to humanistic and existential theorists, Philip's problems can be understood only in the light of those complex and challenging philosophical issues. Humanistic and existential theorists are usually grouped together because of their common focus on these broader dimensions of human existence. At the same time, there are some important differences between them.

Humanists, the more optimistic of the two groups, believe that human beings are born with a natural inclination to be friendly, cooperative, and constructive. People, these theorists propose, are driven to ***self-actualize***—that is, to fulfill this potential for goodness and growth. They will be able to do so, however, only if they can honestly appraise and accept their weaknesses as well as their strengths and establish a satisfying system of personal values to live by.

Existentialists agree that human beings must have an accurate awareness of themselves and live subjectively meaningful—they say "authentic"—lives in order to be psychologically well adjusted. These theorists do not believe, however, that people are naturally inclined to live constructively. They believe that from birth we have total freedom, either to face up to our existence and give meaning to our lives or to shrink from that responsibility. Those who choose to "hide" from responsibility and choice will view themselves as helpless and weak and may live empty, inauthentic, and dysfunctional lives as a consequence.

which encourage persons with problems to e-mail questions and concerns. Although services like these are not intended to replace in-person therapy, they have raised concerns about confidentiality and the quality of care provided (Foderaro, 1994). The American Psychological Association is currently trying to formulate guidelines for psychologists who offer these services (Sleek, 1995).

In addition to on-line professional services, there are now chat groups on the Internet for everything from depression to substance abuse, anxiety, and eating disorders. Users of these groups communicate their feelings with others in similar situations. Advice and empathy are freely traded. Of course, people who pursue "chat group therapy," as it were, do not know who is on the other end of the computer connection or whether the advice given is at all appropriate. Distasteful or insulting responses are not uncommon (Ehrman, 1995).

Finally, there are computer software programs on the market that profess to offer help for emotional distress (Oldenburg, 1995; Wiegner, 1995). Supporters suggest that people may find it easier to reveal sensitive personal information to a computer than to a live therapist (Greist & Klein, 1980). The computer offers them the freedom to express their thoughts and emotions without fear of being judged (Lawrence, 1986). The computer therapist is never tired, angry, or bored (Colby et al., 1979). It does not make grimaces, gestures, or harrumphing noises that signal surprise, approval, or dismay. It is always available, it can reach a large number of people, and its fees are modest. These are all attractive attributes in a therapist.

Numerous computer programs have been designed, and some have been found to be helpful (Elias, 1995; Ghosh & Greist, 1988; Ghosh & Marks, 1987). One simulates a client-centered therapy session. The patient types in a response to a question, and the computer selects the next question on the basis of key words that appear in the response. Another helps people articulate their problems in "if–then" statements, a basic technique used by cognitive therapists (Binik et al., 1988). Still another program offers a form of cognitive therapy to depressed persons, and in the process quotes from such authors as Leo Tolstoy and Bertrand Russell.

Computers may never substitute fully for the judgment of a trained therapist, nor will they ever be able to simulate the interpersonal patient-therapist relationship, which some therapists believe to be the foundation of recovery. Yet, as researchers and practitioners learn more about the nature of psychological disorders and create more complex and humanlike computer programs, computer therapies may at least find a place as adjuncts to other forms of treatment.

The humanistic and existential views of abnormality both date back to the 1940s. At that time Carl Rogers (1902–1987), often considered the pioneer of the humanistic perspective, developed *client-centered therapy,* a warm and supportive approach that contrasted sharply with the influential psychodynamic principles of the day. Moreover, he proposed a humanistic theory of personality that deemphasized irrational instincts and conflicts. About the same time, other humanistic theories developed by Abraham Maslow (1908–1970) and Fritz Perls (1893–1970) also received widespread attention. They all emphasized a special, positive potential inherent in human beings.

The existential view of personality and abnormality came into prominence during this same period. It derived from the ideas of nineteenth-century European existential philosophers who had held that human beings are constantly defining their existence through their actions, and that the meaning of individual existence lies in these efforts at definition. In the late 1950s a book titled *Existence,* now considered a classic work on the clinical existential perspective, described all the major existential ideas and treatment approaches of the time and captured widespread attention (May, Angel, & Ellenberger, 1958).

The humanistic and existential theories were extremely popular during the 1960s and 1970s, years of considerable soul-searching and social upheaval in Western society. Humanistic theories reaffirmed the human spirit, and existential theories challenged people to take charge of their lives. They both seemed perfect remedies for the alienation and spiritual emptiness that had become common in the face of burgeoning technology and bureaucracy. The humanistic-existential model lost some of its popularity in the 1980s, but it continues to influence the ideas of many clinicians and the treatments they offer.

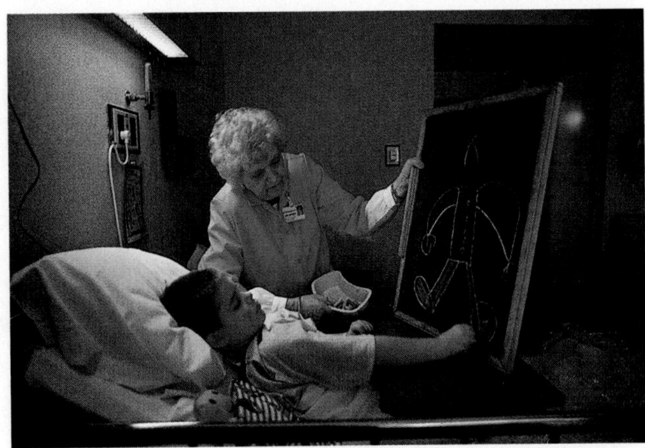

Humanists suggest that self-actualized people, such as this hospital volunteer, show concern for the welfare of humanity. They are also thought to be highly creative, spontaneous, independent, and humorous.

Rogers's Humanistic Theory and Therapy

According to Carl Rogers (1987, 1961, 1951), the road to dysfunction begins in infancy. We all have a basic need to receive *positive regard* from the significant other people in our lives (primarily from our parents). Those who receive *unconditional* (nonjudgmental) *positive regard* early in life are likely to develop *unconditional self-regard.* That is, they come to recognize their worth as persons, even while recognizing that they are not perfect. They feel comfortable about themselves and are able to evaluate themselves in a clear-sighted way. Such people are in a good psychological position to actualize their inherent positive potential.

Unfortunately, some children are repeatedly made to feel that they are not worthy of positive regard. As a result, they acquire *conditions of worth,* standards that tell them they are lovable and acceptable only when they conform to the guidelines they have been exposed to, and they constantly judge themselves accordingly. In order to maintain positive self-regard, these people have to look at themselves very selectively, denying or distorting thoughts and actions that do not measure up to their conditions of worth. They thus acquire a distorted view of themselves and their experiences.

The constant self-deception makes it impossible for these people to self-actualize. They do not know what they are truly feeling, what they genuinely need, or what values and goals would be meaningful for them. Moreover, they spend so much energy trying to protect their self-image that little is left to devote to self-actualizing. Problems in functioning are then inevitable.

Carl Rogers might view Philip Berman as a man who has gone astray. Rather than striving to fulfill his positive human potential, he drifts from job to job, relationship to relationship, outburst to outburst. In every interaction he is defending himself, trying to interpret events in ways he can live with. He always considers his problems to be someone else's fault, and he keeps presenting himself as a strong person who cares little about what other folks may think. Yet his constant efforts at self-defense and self-enhancement are only partially successful. His basic negative self-image and his assumption that others will think badly of him keep breaking through. Rogers would probably ascribe this problem to the way Philip was treated as a child. Rather than offer him unconditional positive regard, his mother apparently kept calling him a "pervert" and a "sissy," bullied him, and even abused him. Small wonder that Philip never learned to accept and value himself unconditionally.

Clinicians who practice Rogers's ***client-centered therapy*** try to create a supportive climate. They wish clients to look at themselves honestly and accept what they discover themselves to be (Raskin & Rogers, 1995; Rogers, 1987, 1967, 1951). The therapist must display three important qualities throughout the therapy—*unconditional positive regard* for the client, *accurate empathy,* and *genuineness.*

Therapists show ***unconditional positive regard*** by conveying full and warm acceptance no matter what clients say, think, or feel. They show ***accurate empathy*** by accurately hearing what clients are saying and sensitively communicating it back to them. They neither interpret what clients are saying nor try to teach them; rather, they listen, and help their clients listen to themselves as well. Finally, therapists must convey ***genuineness,*** also referred to as ***congruence,*** to clients. Unless therapists' communications are honest and sincere, clients may perceive them as mechanical and false. The following interaction shows the therapist using all these qualities to move the client toward greater self-awareness:

> *Client:* Yes, I know I shouldn't worry about it, but I do. Lots of things—money, people, clothes. In classes I feel that everyone's just waiting for a chance to jump on me. It's like they were breathing down my neck waiting for a chance to find something wrong. At school there were fellows like that waiting for me. I can't stand people laughing at me. I can't stand ridicule. That's why I'm afraid of kids. When I meet somebody I wonder what he's actually thinking of me. Then later on I wonder how I match up to what he's come to think of me.
>
> *Therapist:* You feel that you're pretty responsive to the opinions of other people.

Client: Yes, but it's things that shouldn't worry me.

Therapist: You feel that it's the sort of things that shouldn't be upsetting, but they do get you pretty much worried anyway.

Client: Just some of them. Most of those things do worry me because they're true. The ones I told you, that is. But there are lots of little things that aren't true. And time bothers me, too. That is, when I haven't anything to do. Things just seem to be piling up, piling up inside of me. When I haven't anything to do I roam around. I feel like—at home when I was at the theater and nobody would come in, I used to wear it off by socking the doors. It's a feeling that things were crowding up and they were going to burst.

Therapist: You feel that it's a sort of oppression with some frustration and that things are just unmanageable.

Client: In a way, but some things just seem illogical. I'm afraid I'm not very clear here but that's the way it comes.

Therapist: That's all right. You say just what you think.

(Snyder, 1947, pp. 2–24)

In such an atmosphere, clients can be expected increasingly to feel accepted by their therapist. They then may be able to look at themselves with honesty and acceptance—a process called ***experiencing.*** That is, they begin to value their own emotions, thoughts, and behaviors, and so they are freed from the insecurities and doubts that prevented their self-actualization.

Client-centered therapy has not fared particularly well in research. Although people who receive this therapy do seem to improve more than control subjects in some studies (Greenberg et al., 1994; Stuhr & Meyer, 1991), they show no such superiority in many others (Dircks et al., 1980; Rudolph et al., 1980).

All the same, Rogers's therapy has had a positive influence on clinical practice. It was the first major alternative to psychodynamic therapy, and so it helped open up what had been a highly complacent field to new approaches. Second, Rogers helped open up the practice of psychotherapy to psychologists; it had previously been considered the exclusive province of psychiatrists. Third, Rogers's commitment to clinical research has strengthened the position of those who argue for the importance of systematic research into treatment (Rogers & Sanford, 1989; Sanford, 1987). Approximately 3 percent of today's therapists report that they employ the client-centered approach (Prochaska & Norcross, 1994).

Gestalt Theory and Therapy

Gestalt theory and therapy, another humanistic approach, was developed in the 1950s by a charismatic clinician named Frederick (Fritz) Perls (1893–1970). Like Rogers, Perls believed that people experience psychological difficulties when they are unaware of their needs or unwilling to accept or express them. Troubled individuals act only to protect themselves from perceived threats and do little to actualize their potential.

Gestalt therapists, like client-centered therapists, try to move clients toward self-recognition and self-acceptance (Nietzel et al., 1994; Yontef & Simkin, 1989). But unlike client-centered therapists, they often try to achieve this goal by challenging and even frustrating clients. Their techniques are meant also to make the therapy process considerably shorter than it is in client-centered therapy. Some of Perls's favorite techniques were *skillful frustration, role playing,* and numerous *rules, exercises,* and *games.*

In the technique of ***skillful frustration,*** gestalt therapists refuse to meet their clients' expectations or even their outright demands. This use of frustration is meant to help clients see how they try to manipulate others into meeting their needs. Perls describes his use of skillful frustration with a male client:

> The first six weeks of therapy—more than half the available time—were spent in frustrating him in his desperate attempts to manipulate me into telling him what to do. He was by turn plaintive, aggressive, mute, despairing. He tried every trick in the book. He threw the time barrier up to me over and over again, trying to make me responsible for his lack of progress. If I had yielded to his demands, undoubtedly he would have sabotaged my efforts, exasperated me, and remained exactly where he was.
>
> *(Perls, 1973, p. 109)*

Another way gestalt therapists may try to promote self-awareness is by instructing clients to ***role-play***—that is, to act out various roles assigned by the therapist. Clients may be told to be another person, an object, an alternative self, or even a part of the body (Polster, 1992). They are instructed to talk as the other would talk and to feel what the other would feel. Role playing can become intense, as clients are encouraged to be uninhibited in feeling and expressing emotions. Many cry out, scream,

Gestalt therapists may guide their clients to express their needs and feelings in their full intensity through role playing, banging on pillows, and other exercises. These techniques are expected to enable clients to "own" needs and feelings they previously were unaware they had, overcome fears of being judged, and stop behaving defensively. In a gestalt therapy group, members may help each other to "get in touch" with their needs and feelings.

kick, or pound. Through this experience they gradually come to "own" (accept) feelings that were previously unknown to them.

Perls also developed a list of ***rules*** to ensure that clients will look at themselves more closely. In some versions of gestalt therapy, for example, clients may not ask "why" questions. If they ask, "Why do you do that?" therapists make them change the question into a statement, such as "I hate it when you do that." Similarly, clients may be required to use "I" language rather than "it" language. They must say, "I am frightened," rather than "The situation is frightening." Yet another common rule requires clients to stay in the *here and now.* They have needs now, are camouflaging their needs now, and must observe them now. Gestalt therapists who favor this rule may continually refocus discussions by asking, "What are you feeling about that person now?" or "What are you doing now, as you speak?"

Finally, Perls enjoyed using ***exercises and games.*** In the *exaggeration game,* clients must repeatedly exaggerate some gesture or verbal behavior, perhaps a phrase that they use regularly. This "game" is intended to help clients recognize the depth of their feelings, the meaning of particular behaviors, and the effect of their behavior on others. Perls employs this strategy with a client named Jane:

> *Fritz:* Now talk to your Top Dog! Stop nagging.
>
> *Jane: (Loud, pained)* Leave me alone.
>
> *Fritz:* Yah, again.
>
> *Jane:* Leave me alone.
>
> *Fritz:* Again.
>
> *Jane: (Screaming it and crying)* Leave me alone!
>
> *Fritz:* Again.
>
> *Jane: (She screams it, a real blast)* Leave me alone! I don't have to do what you say! *(Still crying)* I don't have to be that good! . . . I don't have to be in this chair! I don't have to. You make me. You make me come here! *(Screams)* Aarhhh! You make me pick my face *(Crying)*, that's what you do. *(Screams and cries)* Aarhhh! I'd like to kill you.
>
> (Perls, 1969, p. 293)

Approximately 1 percent of clinicians describe themselves as gestalt therapists (Prochaska & Norcross, 1994). Because they believe that subjective experiences and self-awareness defy objective measurement, controlled research has rarely been conducted on the gestalt approach (Greenberg et al., 1994).

Existential Theories and Therapy

Like humanists, existentialists believe that psychological dysfunctioning is caused by self-deception; but existentialists are talking about a kind of self-deception in which people hide from life's responsibilities and fail to recognize that it is up to them to give meaning to their lives and that they have the capacity and freedom to do so. According to existentialists, people start to hide from personal responsibility and choice when they become engulfed in the constant change, confusion, and emotional strain of present-day society, as well as in the particular stresses of their immediate environment. Overwhelmed by these pressures, many people look to others for guidance and authority, and conform excessively to social standards. Others may build resentment toward society. Either way, they overlook their personal freedom of choice and avoid responsibility for their lives and decisions (May & Yalom, 1995, 1989; May, 1987, 1961). This abdication of responsibility and choice may offer a form of refuge, but at a cost. Such people are left with empty, inauthentic lives. Their prevailing emotions are anxiety, frustration, alienation, and depression.

Thus existentialists might view Philip Berman as a man who considers himself incompetent to resist the forces of society. He views his parents as "rich, powerful, and selfish," and he sees teachers, acquaintances, and employers as perpetrators of abuse and oppression. Overwhelmed, he fails to appreciate his choices in life and his capacity to find meaning and direction. Quitting becomes a habit with him—he leaves job after job, ends every romantic relationship, flees difficult situations, and even tries suicide. For existentialists, Philip's problems are best summarized by the part of the case description that states, "He spent most of his time alone, 'bored.' He was unable to commit himself to any person, he held no strong convictions, and he felt no allegiance to any group."

In existential therapy clients are encouraged to accept responsibility for their lives and for their problems. They are helped to recognize their freedom, so they may choose a different course and live an *authentic life,* one full of meaning and values (May & Yalom, 1995, 1989). Like humanistic therapists, existential therapists emphasize the individual's subjective view of things (van den Berg, 1971) and the here and now (May, 1987). For the most part, however, these therapists care more about the *goals* of therapy than any specific therapeutic technique, and their methods and the length of treatment vary greatly from practitioner to practitioner (Johnson, 1997; May & Yalom, 1995, 1989). At the same time, most do place great emphasis on the relationship between therapist and client, and strive for an atmosphere in which the two are open to each other, work hard together, and share, learn, and grow (Frankl, 1975, 1963). Here an existential therapist uses a highly confrontational approach to try to help a patient to accept responsibility for her choices both in therapy and in life:

> *Patient:* I don't know why I keep coming here. All I do is tell you the same thing over and over. I'm not getting anywhere.
>
> *Doctor:* I'm getting tired of hearing the same thing over and over, too. [Doctor refusing to take responsibility for the progress of therapy and refusing to fulfill the patient's expectations that he cure her.]
>
> *Patient:* Maybe I'll stop coming. [Patient threatening therapist; fighting to maintain role as therapist's object.]
>
> *Doctor:* It's certainly your choice. [Therapist refusing to be intimidated; forcing patient-as-subject.]
>
> *Patient:* What do you think I should do? [Attempt to seduce therapist into role of subject who objectifies patient.]
>
> *Doctor:* What do you want to do?
>
> *Patient:* I want to get better.
>
> *Doctor:* I don't blame you.
>
> *Patient:* If you think I should stay, ok, I will.

Emphasizing the need to accept responsibility, recognize one's choices, and live an authentic life, existential therapists guide clients to reject feelings of victimhood. (Calvin and Hobbes © 1993 Watterson. Reprinted with permission of Universal Press Syndicate. All rights reserved.)

> *Doctor:* You want me to tell you to stay? [Confrontation with patient's evasion of the decision and calling attention to how patient is construing the therapy.]
>
> *Patient:* You know what's best; you're the doctor. [Patient's confirmation of how she is construing the therapy.]
>
> *Doctor:* Do I act like a doctor?
>
> *(Keen, 1970, p. 200)*

Existential therapists do not believe that experimental methods can adequately test the effectiveness of their treatment interventions (May & Yalom, 1995, 1989). They believe that research that reduces patients to test measures or scale scores serves only to dehumanize them. Not surprisingly, then, virtually no controlled research has been conducted on the effectiveness of existential therapy (Prochaska & Norcross, 1994). A lack of empirical data does not, however, constitute evidence of ineffectiveness. Indeed, surveys suggest that as many as 5 percent of today's therapists use an approach that is primarily existential (Prochaska & Norcross, 1994).

Assessing the Humanistic-Existential Model

The humanistic-existential model appeals to many people in and out of the clinical field. First, the model focuses on broad human issues rather than on a single aspect of psychological functioning. In recognizing the special features and challenges of human existence, humanistic and existential theorists tap into a dimension of psychological life that is typically missing from the other models (Fuller, 1982). Moreover, the factors that they say are essential to effective psychological functioning—self-acceptance, personal values, personal meaning, and personal choice—are undeniably lacking in many people with psychological disturbances.

The optimistic tone of the humanistic-existential model is also an attraction. Humanistic and existential theorists offer great hope when they assert that despite the often overwhelming pressures of modern society, we can make our own choices, determine our own destiny, and accomplish much.

Still another attractive feature of the model is its emphasis on health rather than illness (Cowen, 1991). Unlike proponents of some of the other models who see individuals as patients with psychological illnesses, humanists and existentialists view them simply as people whose special potential has yet to be fulfilled. And although they acknowledge the impact of past events on present behavior, they do not hold a deterministic view of behavior. They believe our behavior can be influenced by our innate goodness and potential, and by our willingness to take responsibility, more than by any factor in our past.

Although appealing in these ways, the humanistic-existential focus on abstract issues of human fulfillment gives rise to a significant problem: these issues are resistant to research. In fact, with the notable exception of Rogers, who spent years empirically testing his psychotherapeutic methods, humanists and existentialists tend to reject the investigative approaches that now dominate the field. They believe that such methods cannot accurately evaluate their ideas. Thus humanists and existentialists have tried to establish the merits of their views by appealing primarily to logic, introspection, and individual case histories. Although they are sincere and

While imprisoned in Nazi concentration camps from 1942 to 1945, the psychotherapist Viktor Frankl observed that the victims who found some spiritual meaning in their suffering were able to resist despair and to survive. He later developed "logotherapy" (from the Greek, logos, *word or thought), an existential therapy that helps clients assign values and spiritual meaning to their existence. Frankl's positive attitude toward life is shown by his choice of leisure activities.*

true to their principles in taking this position, the result is that the model has received limited empirical examination or support.

A final problem is the model's heterogeneity. Theories and therapies called humanistic or existential are so numerous and so varied that it is almost misleading to lump them together into a single category. Still, this extremely varied group of theorists and practitioners does share a belief that human beings are self-determining. They all agree that people have an enormous potential for growth and that self-exploration is the key to this growth.

Chapter Review

1. ***Models of psychological abnormality*** Scientists use paradigms to understand abnormal behavior. Each paradigm, or *model,* is a set of basic assumptions that influences what questions are asked, what information is considered legitimate, and how that information is interpreted.
   A. The principles and techniques of treatment used by a clinical practitioner correspond to his or her preferred model.
   B. Today's leading psychological models are the *psychodynamic, behavioral, cognitive,* and *humanistic-existential* models.
   C. The *biological* and *sociocultural* models are also influential.

2. ***The psychodynamic model*** Supporters of the psychodynamic model believe that a person's behavior, whether normal or abnormal, is determined by underlying psychological forces. They consider psychological conflicts to be rooted in early parent-child relationships and traumatic experiences. The psychodynamic model was formulated by Sigmund Freud, who developed a general theory of *psychoanalysis* as well as a treatment approach.
   A. Freud envisioned three dynamic forces—the *id, ego,* and *superego*—that constitute the personality and interact to mold thought, feeling, and behavior.
   (1) The id operates in accordance with the *pleasure principle.* Like the other dynamic forces, it is fueled by the *libido.*
   (2) The ego is guided by the *reality principle.* It develops *ego defense mechanisms* to avoid or reduce anxiety.
   (3) The superego has two components, the *conscience* and the *ego ideal.*
   B. Psychodynamic theorists believe that people pass through *stages* as they develop. Each stage presents challenges and conflicts. Freud identified the *oral, anal, phallic, latency,* and *genital* stages.
   C. Other psychodynamic theories are *ego theory, self theory,* and *object relations theory.*
   (1) Ego theorists view the ego as a more independent and powerful force of personality.
   (2) Self theorists emphasize the role of the self—the unified personality that defines one's sense of identity.
   (3) Object relations theorists believe that people are motivated primarily by a need to establish relationships with others.
   D. *Psychodynamic therapists* help patients uncover past traumatic events and the inner conflicts that have resulted from those events. They use such techniques as *free association* and interpretations of psychological phenomena such as *resistance, transference,* and *dreams. Short-term psychodynamic therapies* have also been developed in recent years.

3. ***The behavioral model*** Theorists who espouse the behavioral model concentrate on a person's *behaviors,* which they believe develop in accordance with the *principles of learning.* They hold that three types of conditioning—*classical conditioning, operant conditioning,* and *modeling*—account for all behavior, whether normal or dysfunctional.
   A. Classical conditioning is a process of learning by temporal association. Fears, for example, may be learned through this process.
   B. In operant conditioning, people and animals learn to behave in certain ways because they receive *reinforcements* from their environment when they do so.
   C. Modeling is a form of conditioning through *observation* and *imitation.*
   D. The goal of the *behavioral therapies* is to identify the client's problem-causing behaviors and replace them with more appropriate ones. Behavioral therapists use techniques that follow the principles of classical conditioning, operant conditioning, or modeling, alone or in combination.

4. ***The cognitive model*** According to the cognitive model, we must understand the content and process of human thought to understand human behavior. When people display abnormal patterns of functioning, cognitive theorists point to cognitive problems, including *maladaptive assumptions, specific upsetting thoughts,* and *illogical thinking processes.*

A. Maladaptive assumptions, called *basic irrational assumptions* by Albert Ellis, guide people to act and react in ways that are inappropriate and that prejudice their chances of happiness and success.

B. Specific upsetting thoughts, called *automatic thoughts* by Aaron Beck and *self-statements* by Donald Meichenbaum, may pervade and negatively influence one's functioning.

C. Illogical ways of thinking may, according to Beck, lead to self-defeating conclusions.

D. *Cognitive therapists* try to help people recognize and change their faulty ideas and thinking processes. Among the most widely used cognitive therapies are Ellis's *rational-emotive therapy, Beck's cognitive therapy,* and Meichenbaum's *self-instruction training.*

5. ***The humanistic-existential model*** Proponents of the humanistic-existential model focus on the human ability to confront complex and challenging philosophical issues such as self-awareness, values, meaning, and choice, and to incorporate them in one's life.

A. *Humanists* Humanists believe that people are driven to *self-actualize,* that is, to fulfill their potential for goodness and growth. When this drive is interfered with, abnormal behavior may result.

(1) Carl Rogers proposed that people may fail to develop *unconditional positive regard* for themselves and may instead develop *conditions of worth.* These lead to self-denial and self-deception, and make it difficult to self-actualize. Rogers's therapy, *client-centered therapy,* tries to create a very supportive climate in which clients can look at themselves honestly and begin to accept what they discover themselves to be, thus opening the door to self-actualization.

(2) Fritz Perls developed *gestalt theory* and *therapy,* which emphasize that people who develop psychological problems may be unaware of their needs or unable to accept or express them. *Gestalt therapists* try to move clients to recognize and accept their needs through more active techniques such as *skillful frustration* and *role playing.*

B. *Existentialists* Existentialists, in contrast, believe that all of us have total freedom either to face up to our existence and give meaning to it or to shrink from that responsibility. Abnormal behavior is seen as the result of hiding from life's responsibilities. Existential therapists encourage clients to accept their responsibility to recognize their freedom to choose a different course, and to choose to live an authentic life.

Thought and Afterthought

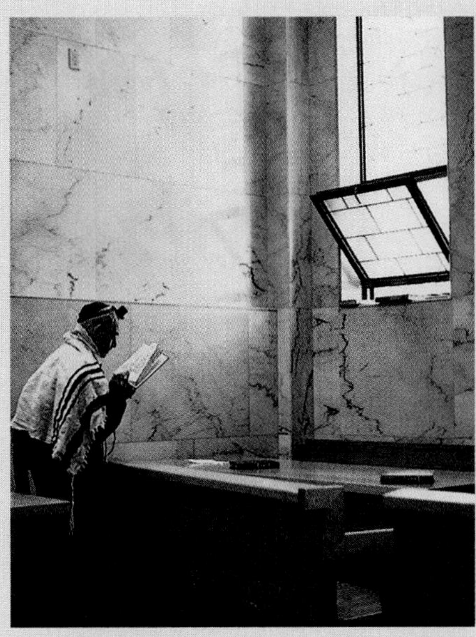

Faith Linked to Mental Health

For years many clinical theorists and practitioners have viewed religion as a negative factor in mental health (Clay, 1996; Neeleman & Persaud, 1995). They have suspected that people with strong religious beliefs are often more superstitious, guilt-ridden, and unstable than others, and less able to cope. Recently, however, a growing body of research has indicated that these views are wrong. Religious faith and mental health are often closely linked.

Studies have examined the mental health of persons who view God as warm, caring, helpful, and dependable (Clay, 1996). Repeatedly, these persons are found to be less lonely, depressed, or anxious than those who consider God cold and unresponsive or those without any religious belief. Believers also seem to cope better with major life stresses, from illness to war, and they are less likely to abuse drugs.

Afterthoughts: Why might positive religious beliefs be linked to mental health? . . . Why have so many mental health professionals been suspicious of religious beliefs for so long? . . . Are some psychological models of abnormality more likely than others to view religion negatively?

Frankly Speaking

I think Freud has been a wholesale disaster for psychology and what we can learn from him is how not to do things.

—Hans J. Eysenck

We all have much to learn . . . from Freud's willingness to study his own dreams, reexamine his theories and persist in a lifelong exploration.

—Jerome L. Singer

Afterthoughts: What might each of these influential clinical scientists be referring to in his critique of Freud? . . . Some persons have called Freud's theories sexist and even dangerous when psychotherapists seek to apply them. What are the merits of their assessment? . . . Are the criticisms leveled at Freud better aimed at the amateur Freudians who toil in literature, the movies, and everyday conversation?

Maternal Instinct

On an August day in 1996, a 3-year-old boy climbed over a barrier at the Brookfield Zoo in Illinois and fell 24 feet onto the cement floor of the gorilla enclosure. An 8-year-old, 160-pound gorilla named Binti-Jua picked up the child and cradled his limp body in her arms. The child's mother, fearing the worst, screamed out, "The gorilla's got my baby!" But Binti protected the little boy as if he were her own. She held off the other gorillas, rocked him gently, and carried him to the entrance of the gorilla area where rescue workers were waiting. Within hours, the incident was seen on videotape around the world, and Binti was being hailed for her maternal instinct.

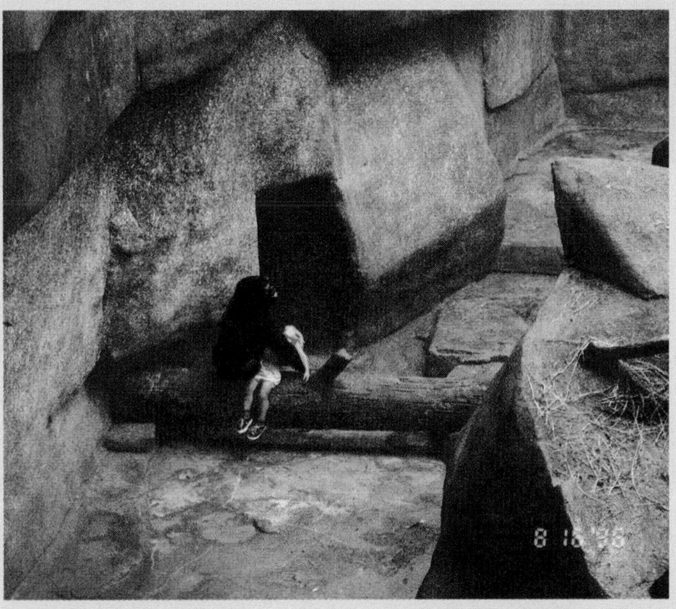

In fact, when Binti was herself an infant, she had to be separated from her mother because her mother was not producing enough milk to keep her alive. To make up for this loss, keepers at the zoo worked around the clock to raise Binti, constantly holding her in their arms. When Binti later became pregnant at age 6, trainers were afraid that her early separation from her own mother would leave her ill prepared to raise her own infant. So they gave her mothering lessons and taught her to nurse and carry around a stuffed doll.

Afterthoughts: What was responsible for the gorilla's surprisingly gentle and nurturing care for the hurt child? . . . Was it, as object relations theorists might hold, an expression of attachment and bonding, already experienced with her own 17-month-old daughter? . . . Was it her observations of nurturing behavior by human models during her own infancy, as behaviorists might claim? . . . Or might it have been the parent training she received during her pregnancy?

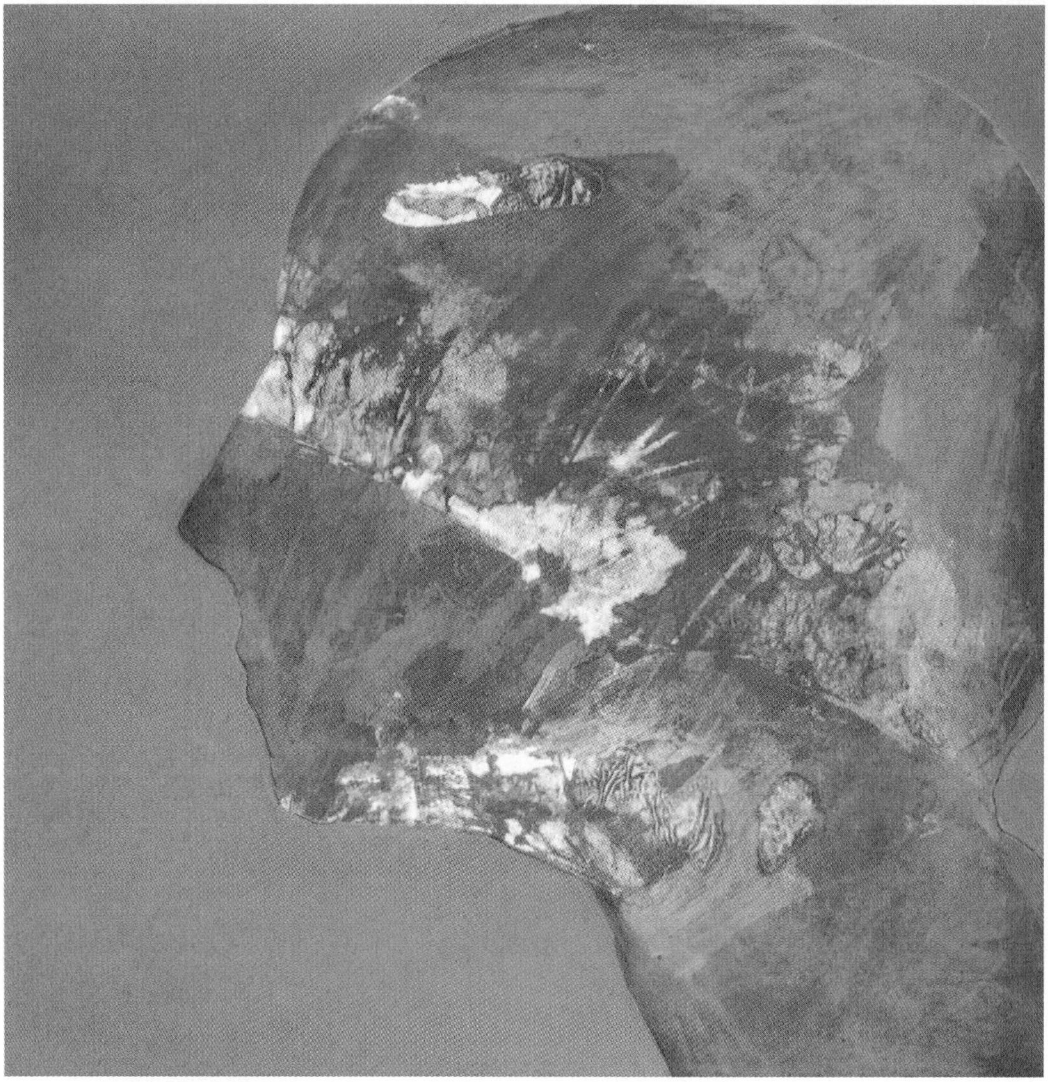

Topic Overview

The Biological Model
Biological Explanations
Biological Therapies

The Sociocultural Model
Sociocultural Explanations
Sociocultural Therapies

Crossroads

Chapter 4

The Biological and Sociocultural Models of Abnormality

The painting Unseeing, *by Karen Poulson, reminds us that much activity occurs within the human head, yet the activity is undirected and incomplete without a social context.*

According to the models discussed in Chapter 3, normal and abnormal mental functioning are rooted in psychological events. These models explore a person's thoughts, memories, needs, and personal experiences. But surely we answer to other forces too: we are also biological and social beings. We operate by means of physiological processes throughout our bodies. These processes, which owe much to the genes we inherit, are also influenced by the rules and structure of our society, including the behavior and opinions of its members. Thus two other models of abnormal functioning—the *biological* and *sociocultural* models—have also gained prominence during this century. Each favors its own special principles and concepts, explanations, and treatments. Yet their views are, as we shall see, often quite compatible with the psychological models.

The Biological Model

Think back to the case of Philip Berman in Chapter 3. Philip is a biological being. His thoughts and feelings are the results of complex biochemical and bioelectrical processes throughout his brain and body. Biological theorists believe that a full understanding of his thoughts, emotions, and behavior must include an understanding of their biological basis. Not surprisingly, they believe that the most effective treatments for Philip's problems will then be biological ones.

As we saw in Chapter 1, the roots of the biological model of abnormal psychology actually stretch back thousands of years. The model's influence, however, has been especially strong since the 1950s. At that time researchers produced several effective ***psychotropic drugs,*** drugs that have their dominant effect on emotions or thought processes. These drugs were found to alleviate some symptoms of mental dysfunctioning. Antianxiety, antidepressant, antipsychotic, and other psychotropic medications have changed the treatment picture for persons with mental disorders. Today these drugs are used frequently, either as an adjunct to other forms of therapy or as the dominant form of treatment.

Biological Explanations of Abnormal Behavior

Adopting a medical perspective, biological theorists view abnormal behavior as an illness brought about by malfunctioning parts of the organism. Specifically, they point to a malfunctioning brain as the primary cause of abnormal behavior (Gershon & Rieder, 1992). So much is being learned about the brain and its functions that in 1990 President George Bush declared the 1990s the "Decade of the Brain."

Mental disorders that have clear physical causes were long called ***organic mental disorders.*** In the past they were distinguished from ***functional mental disorders,*** abnormal behavior patterns without clear links to physical abnormalities in the brain. Years of research, however, have demonstrated that many so-called functional disorders, including anxiety disorders, depression, and schizophrenia, are also related to physical dysfunctions in the brain. In fact, the terms "organic" and "functional" are no longer used to designate mental disorders included in the leading diagnostic and classification systems (APA, 1994).

Biological theorists believe that mental disorders are usually linked to problems in brain-cell functioning, just as lung and kidney disorders result from problems in the cells of those organs. The problems may be largely

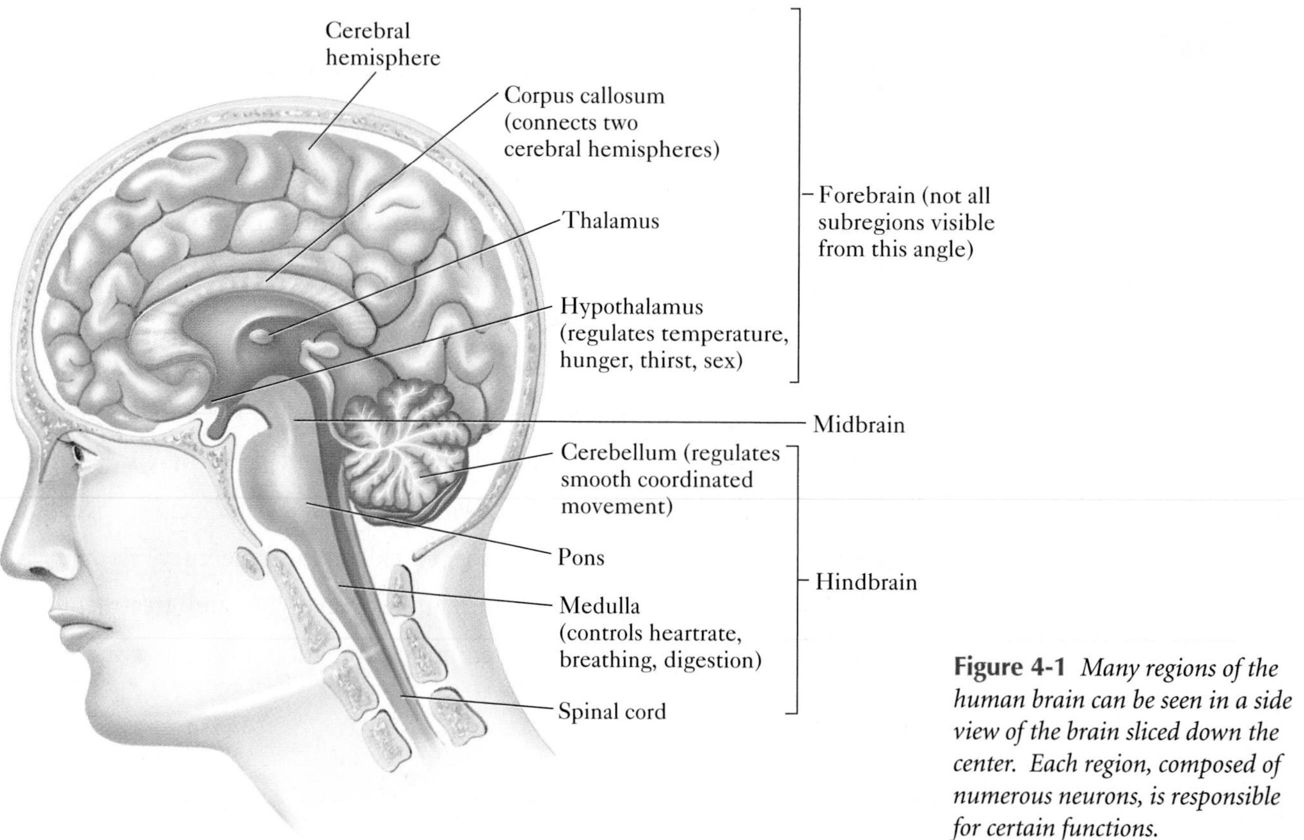

Figure 4-1 *Many regions of the human brain can be seen in a side view of the brain sliced down the center. Each region, composed of numerous neurons, is responsible for certain functions.*

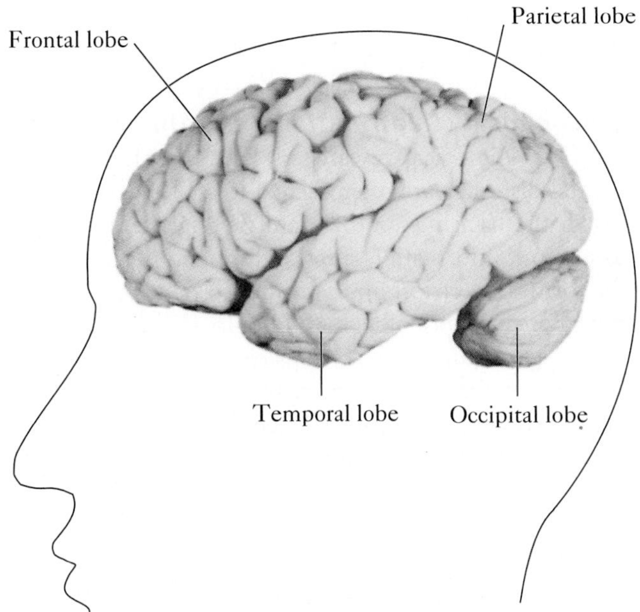

Figure 4-2 *Researchers have estimated that the cortex, the gray outer layer of the cerebrum, contains at least 70 percent of all neurons in the central nervous system and is responsible for the highest levels of cognitive and perceptual analysis, including reasoning, speaking, reading, hearing, and seeing. Anatomists recognize four regions, called lobes, in the cortex of each hemisphere.*

Anatomical Contributions to Abnormal Behavior Researchers now know that the brain comprises approximately 100 billion nerve cells, called ***neurons,*** and thousands of billions of support cells, called ***glia*** (the Greek word for glue) (Fishbach, 1992). Within the brain large groups of neurons form anatomically distinct areas, or ***brain regions.*** To read an anatomical map of the brain more easily, let us imagine these regions as continents, countries, and states.

At the bottom of the brain is the "continent" known as the ***hindbrain,*** which in turn is composed of countrylike regions called the *medulla, pons,* and *cerebellum* (see Figure 4-1). In the middle of the brain is the "continent" called the ***midbrain.*** And at the top is the "continent" called the ***forebrain,*** which is composed of countrylike regions called the *cerebrum* (the two cerebral hemispheres), the *thalamus,* and the *hypothalamus,* each in turn made up of statelike regions. The cerebrum, for instance, consists of the *cortex* (see Figure 4-2), *corpus callosum, basal ganglia, hippocampus,* and *amygdala.* The neurons in each of these brain regions control important functions. The hippocampus helps regulate emotions and memory, for example.

Using a variety of research techniques, clinicians have discovered unambiguous connections between some mental disorders and problems in specific areas of

anatomical or *biochemical.* In the case of anatomical, or structural, problems, the size or shape of certain brain regions may be abnormal. If instead the problem is biochemical, then the chemicals that enable brain cells to operate may not work properly. Anatomical and biochemical problems may result from factors encountered in the course of living, such as excessive stress, infections, allergies, tumors, inadequate blood supply, and physical injury (Haroutunian, 1991). Alternatively, they may be the result of genetic factors. That is, people may *inherit* many of the biological abnormalities that figure in mental disorders.

Largely as a result of insights gained from the study of the psychotropic medications, biological researchers initially came to believe that most or all mental disorders have some physical basis (Gershon & Rieder, 1992). By studying where these drugs go and what they do in the brain, they learned much about the mental disorders the drugs alleviate and where in the brain the disorders arise. In recent years the sophisticated scanning techniques that we shall encounter in Chapter 5 have added to the understanding of the physical underpinnings of abnormal behavior. These techniques, such as *computerized axial tomography (CAT scanning), positron emission tomography (PET scanning),* and *magnetic resonance imaging (MRI),* produce "photographs" of the living brain.

"That's a lie, Morty! . . . Mom says you might have got the brains in the family, but I got the looks!"

(THE FAR SIDE © 1987 FARWORKS, INC./Dist. by UNIVERSAL PRESS SYNDICATE. Reprinted with permission. All rights reserved.)

the brain. One such disorder is ***Huntington's disease,*** a degenerative disorder marked by violent emotional outbursts, memory loss and other cognitive difficulties, suicidal thinking, involuntary body movements, and absurd beliefs. This disease has been traced to a loss of cells in the basal ganglia.

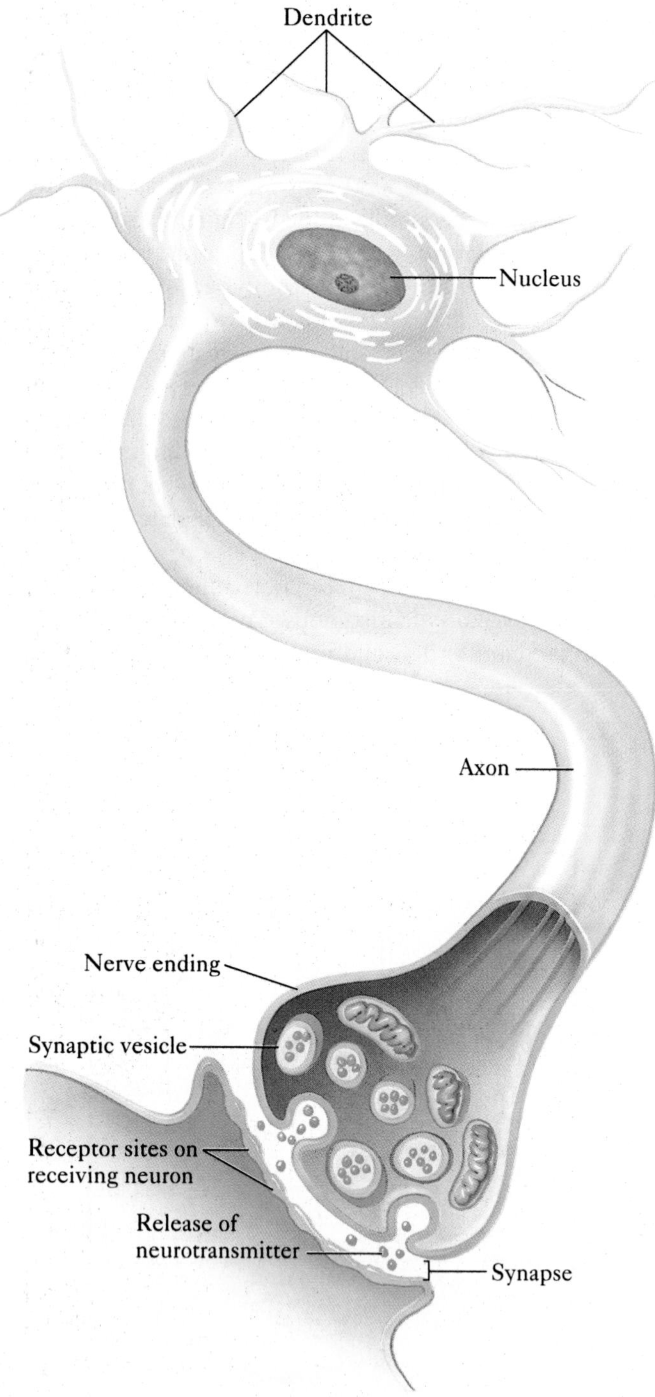

Figure 4-3 *A typical neuron. A message travels down the neuron's axon to the nerve ending, where neurotransmitters carry the message across the synaptic space to a receiving neuron. (Adapted from Bloom, Lazerson, & Hofstadter, 1985, p. 35.)*

Biochemical Contributions to Abnormal Behavior Biological researchers have also learned that mental disorders are often related to subtle dysfunctioning in the transmission of brain messages from neuron to neuron. Information spreads throughout the brain in the form of electrical impulses that travel from one neuron to one or more others. An impulse is first received by a neuron's ***dendrites,*** extensions (or antennae) located at one end of the neuron. From there it travels down the neuron's ***axon,*** a long fiber extending from the neuron body. Finally, it is transmitted to other neurons through the ***nerve endings,*** at the other end of the neuron (see Figure 4-3).

But how do messages get from the nerve endings of one neuron to the dendrites of another neuron? After all, the neurons do not actually touch each other. A tiny space, called a ***synapse,*** separates one neuron from the next, and the message must somehow move across that space. When an electrical impulse reaches a neuron's ending, the nerve ending is stimulated to release a chemical, called a ***neurotransmitter,*** which travels across the synaptic space to ***receptors*** (actually proteins) on the dendrites of the adjacent neurons. Some neurotransmitters in turn lead the receiving neurons to "fire" or trigger another electrical impulse. Other neurotransmitters instead cause the receiving neurons to cease firing. Obviously, neurotransmitters play a key role in moving information through the brain.

Researchers have identified dozens of neurotransmitters in the brain, and they have learned that each neuron uses only certain kinds (Barondes, 1993). Neurological studies indicate that abnormalities in the activity of certain neurotransmitters can lead to specific mental disorders (Gershon & Rieder, 1992). Anxiety disorders, for example, have been linked to insufficient activity of the neurotransmitter ***gamma aminobutyric acid (GABA),*** schizophrenia to excessive activity of the neurotransmitter ***dopamine,*** and depression to low activity of the neurotransmitter ***serotonin.*** Indeed, biological theorists might point to deficient serotonin activity to account for Philip Berman's pattern of depression and rage.

In addition to focusing on neurons and neurotransmitter activity, biological researchers have learned that mental disorders are sometimes related to abnormal chemical activity in the body's ***endocrine system.*** Endocrine glands, located throughout the body, work in conjunction with neurons to regulate such vital activities as growth, reproduction, sexual activity, heart rate, body temperature, energy, and responses to stress. Under various conditions, the glands release chemicals directly into

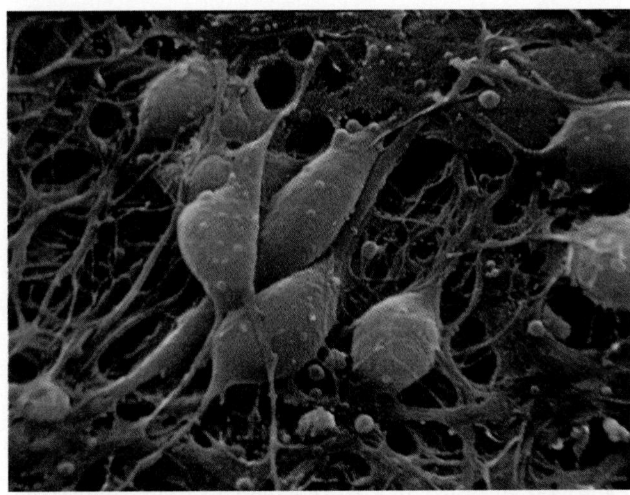

State-of-the-art electron microscopes and color-enhancement techniques highlight the complex network of cell bodies, axons, and dendrites that make up the brain.

the bloodstream. These chemicals, called ***hormones,*** in turn propel body organs into action. During times of stress, for example, the ***adrenal glands,*** located on top of the kidneys, secrete ***cortisol,*** a hormone that stimulates body organs to greater activity.

Genetic Contributions to Abnormal Behavior

Each cell throughout the human brain and body contains 23 pairs of ***chromosomes.*** Each of these structures contains numerous ***genes***— molecules of ***deoxyribonucleic acid (DNA)*** that control the characteristics and traits we inherit. The chromosomes (and genes) are inherited; each chromosome in a pair is inherited from one of our parents. Scientists have known for years that genes help determine such physical characteristics as hair color, height, and eyesight. Genes can make people more prone to heart disease, cancer, or diabetes and perhaps to develop artistic skill or musical aptitude. In recent years, researchers have discovered that genes may also influence an individual's behavior, including the development of many abnormal patterns of behavior.

Apparently, whenever a particular gene is activated, an intermediary molecule called ***messenger ribonucleic acid (MRNA)*** is produced, and this messenger molecule in turn sets in motion the production of other chemicals, ***proteins*** (Griffiths et al., 1996). Each protein carries out particular functions such as helping to produce hormones, muscles, bones, or neurotransmitters. If a person inherits abnormal or defective genes, they will affect the production of corresponding proteins, which in turn may disrupt the normal operation of important neurotransmitters or hormones. In that case, the stage may be set for such psychological problems as depression or schizophrenia (Lesch et al., 1996; Greenspan, 1995).

Researchers have successfully linked genetic factors to mood disorders, schizophrenia, mental retardation, Alzheimer's disease, and other mental disorders (Cadoret, 1995; Winokur et al., 1995; Gottesman, 1991). They have not, however, been able to identify the specific genes that are the culprits. Nor do they yet know how much genetic factors contribute to various mental disorders. It appears that in most cases no single gene is responsible for a behavior or mental disorder. Many genes combine to help bring about our various behaviors and emotional reactions, both functional and dysfunctional. That complexity demands a range of research strategies. Most genetic researchers who investigate abnormal behavior rely on *family studies, twin studies, adoption studies, genetic linkage studies,* and *molecular biology studies.*

Family pedigree studies survey the biological relatives of patients. Researchers pinpoint how many and which of the relatives have the same disorder as the patient. Many family studies have demonstrated, for example, that the closer one's biological relationship to someone with severe depression, the greater the risk of experiencing that disorder (Winokur et al., 1995; Gottesman, 1991).

Twin studies examine the rates of mental disorders in *monozygotic (identical) twins,* twins whose genes are all identical, and *dizygotic (fraternal) twins,* some but not all of whose genes are identical. If the tendency to

Studies of twins suggest that some aspects of behavior and personality are influenced by genetic factors. These identical twins were separated at birth and raised apart. Yet when reunited at age 31, they discovered that they had each chosen to be a firefighter. Many separated identical twins have been found to make similar life choices, behave in similar ways, and even develop similar abnormal behaviors.

develop a mental disorder is inherited, then identical twins should be more likely to share a disorder than fraternal twins. After looking at nearly two hundred pairs of twins, for example, researchers determined that when an identical twin had depression, there was a 46 percent chance that the other twin would have the same disorder. When a fraternal twin had depression, the other twin had only a 20 percent chance of developing the disorder (McGuffin et al., 1996).

Adoption studies determine whether the biological relatives of persons suffering from a mental disorder are more likely than adoptive relatives to have it too. Such studies have suggested, for example, that genetic inheritance often plays an important role in the development of alcoholism. Biological relatives of persons with alcoholism indeed have higher rates of this disorder than adoptive relatives (Cadoret et al., 1995).

Genetic linkage studies select extended families that have exhibited high rates of a particular disorder over several generations. Researchers observe the pattern of the disorder among family members to determine whether it closely follows the distribution of family traits (called *genetic markers*) that are already known to be genetically transmitted. Some established genetic markers are color blindness, hair color, and particular medical syndromes. Say that all the family members with a mood disorder also have a genetically transmitted skin condition, but normal family members do not. Researchers might conclude that a predisposition to the mood disorder is linked to a predisposition to the skin condition, and so the two predispositions must be carried by genes located close together on the same chromosome. Genetic linkage studies have tied bipolar disorders—disorders characterized by both manic and depressive episodes—to genetic factors (Stine et al., 1995; Egeland et al., 1987).

Finally, using new techniques from the field of ***molecular biology,*** researchers can now isolate DNA from the blood samples of persons with mental disorders. By "cutting" the DNA into segments, researchers can compare gene segments from different people and better identify the genes underlying particular characteristics, physical or psychological. With this and related technology in hand, investigators began the ***human genome project*** in 1990, designed to map *all* of the genes in the human body (Mandel et al., 1992). So far they have located about half of the suspected 80,000 human genes, although they do not yet know what all of the discovered genes do or how they work (Begley, 1995). Moreover, they have been able to link more than 3,200 kinds of gene *defects* to medical diseases such as cystic fibrosis and certain forms of cancer, as well as to mental disorders such as Huntington's disease, schizophrenia, some forms of mental retardation, and Alzheimer's disease (Glausiusz, 1997, 1996; Begley, 1995). Again, however, *multiple* gene defects, rather than a single gene defect, usually seem to be needed to set the stage for a mental disorder.

Biological Therapies

Given their orientation, practitioners of the biological school look for certain kinds of clues when they try to understand a person's abnormal behavior. Does the family have a history of that behavior, and hence a possible genetic predisposition to it? (Philip Berman's case history mentions that his mother was once hospitalized for

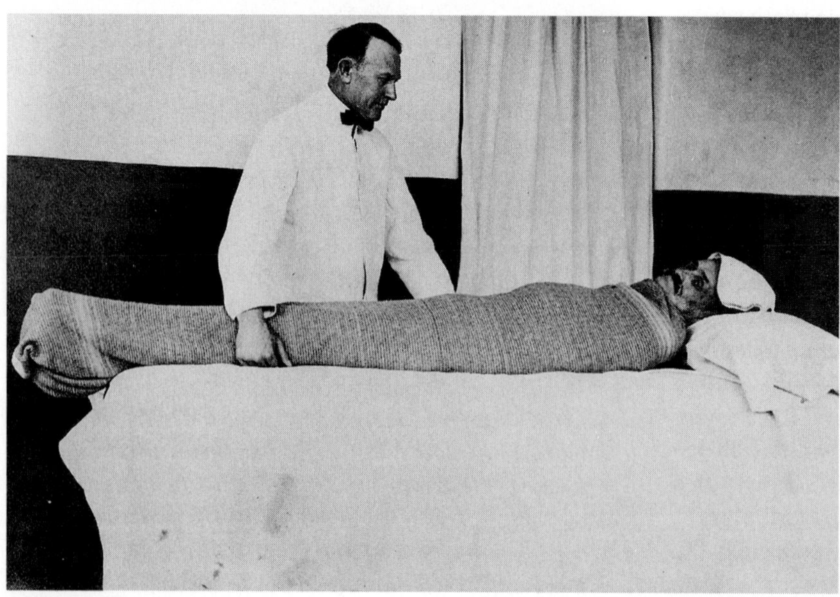

Before effective psychotropic drugs were developed, clinicians in mental institutions used techniques such as the "wet pack," designed for calming excited patients.

depression.) Does the disorder seem to follow its own course, irrespective of situational changes? (Philip's depressed feelings were described as periodic; they seemed to come and go over the course of several years.) Is the behavior heightened by events that could have had a physiological effect? (Philip was having a drink when he flew into a jealous rage at the restaurant.) Once clinicians have pinpointed a presumed organic dysfunction, they are in a better position to choose a course of biological treatment.

The three principal kinds of biological interventions used today are *drug therapy, electroconvulsive therapy,* and *psychosurgery.* Drug therapy is by far the most common approach, whereas psychosurgery is relatively infrequent.

Drug Therapy As we observed earlier, in the 1950s researchers discovered several kinds of effective psychotropic drugs. These drugs have radically changed the outlook for a number of mental disorders and are now used widely, either alone or with another form of therapy. Unfortunately, the psychotropic drug revolution has also been accompanied by significant problems. Some of the drugs have serious undesirable effects that must be weighed against the good the drugs can do. Also, when clinicians and patients become seduced by the possibility of rapid change, the drugs are often overused. Finally, while the drugs are effective in many cases, they do not help everyone. Four major groups of psychotropic drugs are used in therapy: *antianxiety, antidepressant, antibipolar,* and *antipsychotic drugs.*

Antianxiety drugs, also called ***minor tranquilizers*** or ***anxiolytics*** (from "anxiety" and the Greek *lytikos,* able to loosen or dissolve), reduce tension and anxiety. These drugs include *alprazolam* (trade name Xanax) and *diazepam* (trade name Valium). Although often very helpful, the drugs have been overused and even misused. As we shall see in Chapter 6, they can induce physical dependence if they are taken in high dosages over an extended period of time (Hyman & Cassem, 1994; Murphy, Owen, & Tyrer, 1984). Thus the drugs alone do not provide a long-term solution in most cases of anxiety.

Antidepressant drugs help lift the spirits of many people who are depressed. There are three kinds of antidepressants: the *MAO inhibitors,* the *tricyclics,* and the recently developed *second generation antidepressants,* which include *fluoxetine hydrochloride* (Prozac). The drugs seem to help around 60 percent of patients with depression but may also produce undesired effects (Frank, 1997; Montgomery & Kasper, 1995). Today antidepressant drugs are prescribed for thousands of patients with depression. Indeed, their very trade names often imply a significant elevation of mood (see Table 4-1). Research suggests that some forms of psychotherapy, such as Beck's cognitive therapy, are able to equal the impressive

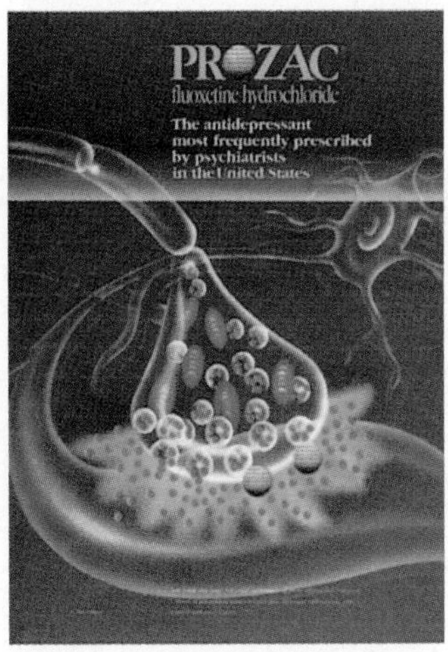

Unfortunately, a clinician's choices among the psychotropic drugs available for prescription may be influenced not only by research literature but by a pharmaceutical company's promotional campaigns. Enticing ads for drugs fill the journals read by psychiatrists and other physicians.

TABLE 4-1 The Name Game

The trade names of psychotropic medications often seem to advertise the drug's intended effect.

Trade Name	*Linguistic Connotation*
Antianxiety	
Halcion	Halcyon (pleasingly calm or peaceful)
Equanil	Equanimity
Unisom	Unified somnolence
Librium	Equilibrium (balance)
Antidepressant	
Elavil	Elevate
Sinequan	Sine qua non (the one essential thing)
Vivactil	Vivacious
Asendin	Ascend
Zoloft	Lofty
Antipsychotic	
Serentil	Serenity
Thorazine	Thor (powerful Norse god of thunder)
Anti-Parkinsonian	
Symmetrel	Symmetry
Anti-Alzheimer's	
Cognex	Cognizant

effectiveness of this biological treatment (Hollon & Beck, 1994, 1986). On the other hand, a combination of antidepressant drugs and cognitive therapy is often more effective than either treatment alone (Hollon et al., 1993, 1991, 1985).

Antibipolar drugs help stabilize the moods of persons with a bipolar mood disorder, a disorder marked by mood swings from mania to depression. As we shall see in greater detail in Chapter 9, the most effective antibipolar drug is ***lithium,*** a metallic element that occurs in nature as a mineral salt. This drug is helpful in approximately 60 percent of cases of bipolar disorders (Klerman et al., 1994; Prien, 1992). The dosage of lithium must be carefully monitored, however (Mondimore, 1993; Jefferson & Greist, 1989). Too high a concentration may dangerously alter the body's sodium level and even threaten the patient's life.

Antipsychotic drugs alleviate the confusion, hallucinations, and delusions of psychosis, a loss of contact with reality. Common antipsychotic drugs are *chlorpromazine* (trade name Thorazine), *haloperidol* (Haldol), and *clozapine* (Clozaril). Research has repeatedly shown that antipsychotic drugs are more effective than any other single form of treatment for schizophrenia and related psychotic disorders, reducing symptoms in at least 65 percent of patients (Lieberman et al., 1996; Klerman et al., 1994). For many patients with schizophrenia the drugs alone are not sufficient treatment, but when drug therapy is combined with appropriate community programs and adjunct psychotherapy, many of these patients, too, can return to a reasonably normal life.

Unfortunately, some patients with psychosis fail to improve even when drugs are combined with psychotherapy and community care. Worse, antipsychotic drugs may also cause serious harm. In fact, they are also called *neuroleptic* drugs because their undesired effects in many patients are similar to the symptoms of neurological disease. The most troubling are ***extrapyramidal effects,*** movement problems such as severe shaking, bizarre-looking contractions of the face and body, and extreme restlessness. These effects are believed to result from the drugs' action on the "extrapyramidal" areas of the brain, just beneath the cortex. One such effect, called ***tardive dyskinesia*** (meaning "late-appearing movement disorder"), emerges in some patients after they have taken antipsychotic drugs for a few years. Tardive dyskinesia is not always reversible even when patients stop taking antipsychotic drugs. Fortunately, some of the newer antipsychotic drugs do not appear to produce these unpleasant and dangerous extrapyramidal effects (Gerlach et al., 1996; Borison 1995; Meltzer, 1993).

Electroconvulsive Therapy Another form of biological treatment used widely today, primarily on depressed patients, was first developed in the 1930s by two Italian physicians, Ugo Cerletti and Lucio Bini. In

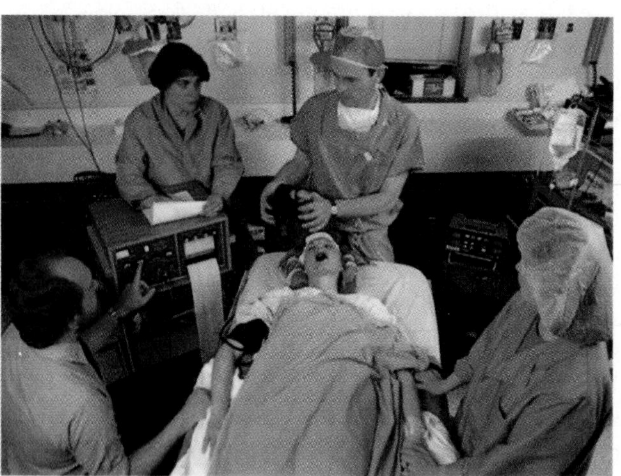

A patient who receives electroconvulsive therapy experiences a brain seizure as an electric current passes through electrodes attached to the head.

electroconvulsive therapy (ECT), two electrodes are attached to a patient's forehead and an electrical current of 65 to 140 volts is briefly passed through the brain. The current causes a brain seizure, or ***convulsion,*** that lasts up to a few minutes. After an average of seven to nine ECT sessions, each spaced two or three days apart, many patients feel considerably less depressed.

ECT is able to help approximately 60 percent of depressed subjects to improve (APA, 1993; Wechsler et al., 1965). Accordingly, the procedure is used on tens of thousands of depressed persons annually (Foderaero, 1993). Although administered less often today than it was in the past, ECT is still applied when people have a severe depressive episode that is unresponsive to other forms of treatment (Buchan et al., 1992). Arguments against and in favor of its use are discussed at length in Chapter 9.

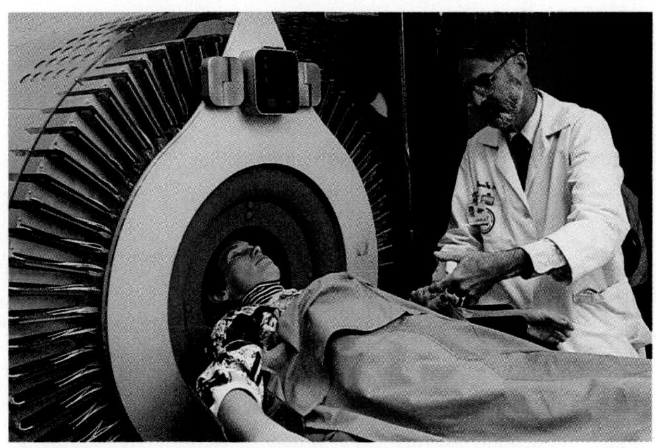

Elaborate biological tests such as positron emission tomography (PET) are often administered to help detect abnormalities that may be causing psychological problems. A PET scan produces moving pictures of metabolic activity at sites throughout the brain, thus revealing problems in functioning as opposed to anatomical abnormalities.

Psychosurgery Brain surgery as a treatment for mental disorders is thought to have roots as far back as trephining, the prehistoric practice of chipping a hole in the skull of a person who behaved strangely. Modern forms of psychosurgery are derived from a technique first developed in the late 1930s by a Portuguese neuropsychiatrist, Antonio de Egas Moniz. In that procedure, known as a ***lobotomy,*** a surgeon cut the connections between the cortex of the brain's frontal lobes and the lower centers of the brain.

As we shall observe in Chapter 16, it became clear by the late 1950s that lobotomies were not so effective as many psychosurgeons had been claiming. Even more disturbing, many lobotomized patients suffered terrible and irreversible effects—seizures, extreme listlessness, stupor, and in some cases death (Barahal, 1958). Thus the procedure declined in popularity during the 1960s. Today's psychosurgery procedures are much more precise than the lobotomies of the past (Beck & Cowley, 1990). They have fewer unwanted effects and are apparently beneficial in some cases of severe depression, anxiety, and obsessive-compulsive disorder. Even so, they are considered experimental and are used infrequently, usually only after a severe disorder has continued for years without responding to any other form of treatment (Goodman et al., 1992).

Assessing the Biological Model

Today the biological model enjoys considerable prestige. First, the model serves to remind us that psychological processes, however complex and subtle, have biological causes worthy of examination and study. Second, thanks to sophisticated procedures developed over centuries of experimentation, biological research often produces valuable new information in a relatively short time. Finally, biological treatments have often afforded significant relief for abnormal functioning when other approaches have failed.

At the same time, the biological model has characteristic limitations and problems. Some of its proponents seem to expect that all human behavior can be explained in biological terms and treated with biological methods. This narrow view has encouraged many people to expect miracles from unproven preparations (see Box 4-1). It also can limit rather than enhance our understanding of abnormal functioning. Although biological processes certainly do affect our behavior, thoughts, and emotions, they are just as certainly affected by our behavior, thoughts, and emotions. Our mental life is an interplay of biological and nonbiological factors, and it is important to explore that interplay in both our theories and our treatments rather than to focus exclusively on biological variables (Kleinman & Cohen, 1997).

A second problem is that much of the evidence for biological explanations is incomplete or inconclusive. Many neurological studies, for example, must be conducted on animals in whom apparent symptoms of depression, anxiety, or some other abnormality have been induced by drugs, surgery, or behavioral manipulation. Researchers can never be certain that the animals are experiencing the human disorder under investigation. Similarly, the family and related studies often cited in support of biological and genetic explanations are open to alternative interpretations. Evidence that close relatives are more likely to develop certain disorders than more distant relatives may simply mean that close relatives are more likely to have had similar "psychological" experiences early in their lives.

BOX 4-1 Melatonin: Miracle Hormone or Hype?

Cleopatra bathed in sour milk and Ponce de León spent years searching in vain for the fountain of youth. Today an army of baby boomers is turning to "herbal" supplements and "natural" hormones to stave off the inevitable signs of aging and to cure life's everyday aches and pains. ***Melatonin,*** a hormone secreted by the brain's pineal gland, is one example.

At least five best-selling books on melatonin have been published since 1995. Their jackets call melatonin "the most exciting medical breakthrough of our time!" and claim that it can actually "reverse the effects of aging." They say it can lift depression, strengthen the immune system, lower cholesterol, reverse aging, extend the life span, increase energy, improve sleep, reduce stress, cure jet lag, and even enhance sexual desire and performance. It can supposedly prevent cancer, heart disease, cataracts, ulcers, Parkinson's disease, Alzheimer's disease, and pregnancy as well.

Melatonin may not live up to all of these claims, but one thing is certain: it sells extraordinarily well. Source Naturals, one of more than a dozen suppliers of melatonin supplements, shipped over 10 million bottles in 1995 alone (Kiester & Kiester, 1996). The nationwide General Nutrition Centers sell about 4,000 bottles of melatonin every day, more than even the old standard vitamin C (Bonn, 1996; DeVita, 1996). Demand for melatonin is so great that some health food stores have trouble keeping it in stock, and limit customers to a few bottles each to avoid shortages. But does the reality live up to the hype? What does melatonin actually do?

Melatonin is one of life's most common hormones, found in organisms as diverse as algae, rats, and primates (Cowley, 1995). It was identified in the 1950s, when researchers discovered that the brain's pea-sized pineal gland, which had been considered a useless organ, is a part of the endocrine system. As darkness falls, the absence of light triggers the pineal gland to secrete melatonin. Melatonin then triggers other chemical changes in the brain, making us drowsy. Melatonin levels off at dawn, as light slows the pineal gland's activity, and we wake up. In this way the hormone regulates our ***circadian rhythm,*** or "body clock." Melatonin plays an important role in the hibernation of animals, their breeding cycles, and even their migration and molting.

Melatonin levels peak during childhood and begin a steady decline in young adulthood, eventually dropping precipitously in middle age, as the pineal gland begins to calcify. By age 70, melatonin levels may be almost undetectable (Turek, 1996). The age-related decline in melatonin led some researchers to wonder whether sleep difficulties and other problems common in the elderly might be helped by doses of melatonin. Research supports some, but certainly not all, of their expectations.

Small doses of melatonin apparently do induce restful sleep in some healthy adults (Wurtman, 1995; Waldhauser et al., 1990). Studies show that small doses can also alleviate jet lag by resetting the body's internal clock, essentially tricking the body into believing that it is still nighttime (Bonn, 1996). Melatonin supplements can also be useful for night shift workers and the blind, whose circadian rhythms may be out of synch. Although melatonin is often an effective sleep aid, ideal doses have not yet been established, and in fact excessive doses often occur. Too much melatonin produces drowsiness, a dangerous consequence for airline pilots or night shift workers who operate heavy machinery (Arendt, 1994).

There are some indicators that melatonin may have potential as a birth control pill. An ongoing study of 1,500 women in

The Sociocultural Model

Philip Berman is also a social being. He is surrounded by people and by institutions, he is a member of a family and a society, and he participates in social and professional relationships. Thus external social forces are always operating on Philip, setting rules and expectations that guide and at times pressure him, helping to shape his behavior, thoughts, and emotions as surely as any internal biological or psychological mechanism.

According to the sociocultural model of psychology, abnormal behavior is best understood in the light of the social and cultural forces brought to bear on an individ-

the Netherlands is investigating whether large doses can reliably prevent ovulation. Efforts are also underway to develop a melatonin-based male contraceptive (Raloff, 1995). Unfortunately, it is unlikely that melatonin will prove to be much of an aphrodisiac, as some promotional materials would have us believe. Some animal studies have even found it to reduce sexual functioning (Turek, 1996).

Can melatonin boost immunity or cure disease? No studies have established any effect of melatonin on heart disease or cholesterol levels (Turek, 1996). Some small studies on animals have indicated that it may have an antioxidant effect, which theoretically could reduce the risk of cancer or inhibit the growth of tumors (Bonn, 1996; Ralof, 1995), but this effect has not been reliably demonstrated in humans. Still other research indicates that melatonin may help keep the immune system active during extreme stress (Maestroni, 1993; Guerrero & Reiter, 1992; Maestroni & Conti, 1991). Overall, however, the interactions between the immune system and melatonin are not well understood, and further research is necessary before immunity-boosting claims can be substantiated.

No reliable evidence exists for melatonin as a fountain of youth, either. Its longevity claims are based primarily on a study in which researchers exchanged the calcified pineal glands of old mice with healthy pineals from young mice. The old mice given the healthy pineals lived longer than the normal life span, and the young mice given the calcified pineals aged quickly and died earlier than normal. At first glance this finding seems to indicate that melatonin, produced by an active pineal gland, is prolonging the life span. Other researchers have argued, however, that the type of mouse used in the study normally does not produce melatonin at all. Thus any life-extending effects from the switching of pineals must be due to some other factor (Turek, 1996; Ebihara et al., 1986).

Even if the benefits of melatonin are unproved, some people say, "it can't hurt to try it." Or can it? Few serious undesirable effects of melatonin have been reported, and it is not toxic in the short term (Raloff, 1995); but many of its actions and its potential long-term dangers have not been investigated. Melatonin is a potent hormone, not a simple vitamin, and hormones may take years to reveal their effects. There is no well-established dosing schedule for melatonin, and too much of it could cause not only drowsiness but decreases in body temperature and in immunity (Chase, 1996). Melatonin's effects during pregnancy and puberty and its interactions with other drugs are unknown (Bonn, 1996).

The over-the-counter sale of melatonin is banned in Canada, Britain, and France, and it is strictly regulated in other countries (Chase, 1996). In the United States, however, melatonin supplements are classified as "dietary supplements" rather than drugs, so the Food and Drug Administration does not regulate them. Consumers have no guarantee that the product they purchase is pure, safe, or effective, or even that it contains any melatonin at all. It appears that until melatonin is better understood and better regulated, *caveat emptor* applies.

ual. What are the norms and values of the person's society? What roles does the person play in the social environment? What kind of family structure is this person exposed to? And how do other people view and react to him or her?

The sociocultural view of abnormality derives its basic assumptions from two fields that first emerged in the nineteenth century. One is ***sociology,*** the study of human relationships and social groups. The other, ***anthropology,*** studies human cultures and institutions.

Sociologists have proposed that societies themselves are capable of generating abnormal behavior in their members. Certain communities, for example, may be so disorganized that many members are forced to engage in odd behavior; it is how they adapt to the community's norms or standards. Even stable societies may help produce and maintain abnormal behavior in some members by the common practice of identifying certain individuals as unusual; by reacting to them in special ways, the society may expect and encourage them to take on the roles assigned to abnormal people (Scheff, 1966; Becker, 1964).

Anthropologists have found that some patterns of abnormality vary from society to society, from culture to culture (Stix, 1996). The disorder of *windigo,* for example, an intense fear of being turned into a cannibal by a flesh-eating monster, was found only among Algonquin Indian hunters. Similarly, *koro,* a fear that one's penis will withdraw into the abdomen, was found only in Southeast Asia. Each of these abnormal patterns seemed to be tied to the society's particular history and culture (see Box 4-2).

For years these sociological and anthropological notions influenced the study and treatment of abnormal psychology. Finally, in the 1950s, a new clinical model—the sociocultural model—emerged, marked by three key events. One was the publication in 1958 of a major study, *Social Class and Mental Illness,* by August Hollingshead and Frederick Redlich. They found that psychotic, aggressive, and rebellious behavior is much more common in the lower socioeconomic classes than in the upper classes. A second event was the development of family theory and therapy during the 1950s. A third factor in the emergence of the sociocultural model was the influential work of Thomas Szasz (1997, 1987, 1961). This outspoken psychiatrist launched an attack against the mental health system, challenged the

Box 4-2 Culture-Bound Abnormality

Red Bear sits up wild-eyed, his body drenched in sweat, every muscle tensed. The horror of the dream is still with him; he is choked with fear. Fighting waves of nausea, he stares at his young wife lying asleep on the far side of the wigwam, illuminated by the dying embers.

His troubles began several days before, when he came back from a hunting expedition empty-handed. Ashamed of his failure, he fell prey to a deep, lingering depression. Others in the village, noticing a change in Red Bear, watched him nervously, afraid that he was becoming bewitched by a windigo. Red Bear was frightened too. The signs of windigo were all there: depression, lack of appetite, nausea, sleeplessness and, now, the dream. Indeed, there could be no mistake.

He had dreamed of the windigo—the monster with a heart of ice—and the dream sealed his doom. Coldness gripped his own heart. The ice monster had entered his body and possessed him. He himself had become a windigo, and he could do nothing to avert his fate.

Suddenly, the form of Red Bear's sleeping wife begins to change. He no longer sees a woman, but a deer. His eyes flame. Silently, he draws his knife from under the blanket and moves stealthily toward the motionless figure. Saliva drips from the corners of his mouth, and a terrible hunger twists his intestines. A powerful desire to eat raw flesh consumes him.

With the body of the "deer" at his feet, Red Bear raises the knife high, preparing to strike. Unexpectedly, the deer screams and twists away. But the knife flashes down, again and again. Too late, Red Bear's kinsmen rush into the wigwam. With cries of outrage and horror, they drag him outside into the cold night air and swiftly kill him.

(Lindholm & Lindholm, 1981, p. 52)

Red Bear was suffering from *windigo,* a disorder once common among Algonquin Indian hunters. They believed in a supernatural monster that ate human beings and had the power to bewitch them and turn them into cannibals. Red Bear was among the few afflicted hunters who actually did kill and eat members of their households.

Windigo is one of several unusual mental disorders discovered around the world, each unique to a particular culture, each apparently growing from that culture's pressures, history, institutions, and ideas (Lindholm & Lindholm, 1981; Kiev, 1972; Lehmann, 1967; Yap, 1951). Proponents of the sociocultural model cite such exotic disorders as evidence that societies often help to produce abnormal behavior in their members.

Susto, a disorder found among members of Indian tribes in Central and South America and Hispanic natives of the Andean highlands of Peru, Bolivia, and Colombia, is most likely to occur in infants and young children. The symptoms are extreme anxiety, excitability, and depression, along with loss of weight, weakness, and rapid heartbeat. The culture holds that this disorvery concept of mental illness, and took the extreme position that all mental disorders are the creations of society.

Sociocultural Explanations of Abnormal Behavior

Because behavior is shaped by social forces, sociocultural theorists hold, we must examine the social context if we are to understand abnormal behavior in individual cases (Kleinman & Cohen, 1997; NAMHC, 1996) (see Table 4-2). Their explanations focus on *family structure and communication, social networks, societal stress,* and *societal labels and reactions.*

Family Structure and Communication According to ***family systems theory,*** the family is a *system* of interacting parts, the family members, who relate to one another in consistent ways and are governed by implicit rules unique to each family (Rolland & Walsh, 1994; Nichols, 1992). The parts interact in ways that enable the system to maintain itself and survive—a state known as ***homeostasis.*** Family systems theorists believe that the structure, rules, and communication patterns of some families actually force individual members to behave in a way that the society at large may define as abnormal. If the individual members were to behave normally, they would severely strain the family's boundaries, implicit rules, and homeostasis and actually increase their own and their family's turmoil. The responses by other family

der is caused by contact with supernatural beings or with frightening strangers, or by bad air from cemeteries and other supposedly dangerous places. Treatment includes rubbing certain plants and animals against the skin.

Amok, a disorder found in Malaya, the Philippines, Java, and some parts of Africa, is more likely to occur in men than in women. Those who are afflicted jump around violently, yell loudly, grab knives or other weapons, and attack any people and objects they encounter. This behavior is usually preceded by social withdrawal and some loss of contact with reality. The periods of violent behavior are followed by depression and by amnesia concerning the outburst. Within the culture, amok is thought to be caused by stress, severe shortage of sleep, alcohol consumption, and extreme heat.

Peasant women are overcome by the psychological disorder St. Vitus' dance *in this engraving, based on a fifteenth-century painting by Pieter Brueghel. The disorder, marked by manic dancing and jumping around, was unique to Europe during the Middle Ages, and seems to have been caused by a combination of the demonological beliefs and political and social strife that marked that period.*

Koro is a pattern of anxiety found in Southeast Asia in which a man suddenly becomes intensely fearful that his penis will withdraw into his abdomen and that he will die as a result. Cultural lore holds that the disorder is caused by an imbalance of "yin" and "yang," two natural forces believed to be the fundamental components of life. Accepted forms of treatment include having the individual keep a firm hold on his penis until the fear passes, often with the assistance of family members or friends, and clamping the penis to a wooden box.

Latah is a disorder found in Malaya, usually among uneducated middle-aged or elderly women. Certain circumstances (hearing someone say "snake" or being tickled, for example) trigger a fright reaction that is marked by repeating the words and acts of other people, uttering obscenities, and doing the opposite of what others ask.

members would quickly extinguish such "normal" behavior. Thus a dysfunctional family system may both create and maintain an individual's abnormal behavior (Szapocznik & Kurtines, 1993).

Family systems theory portrays certain family systems as particularly likely to produce abnormal functioning in individual family members (Becvar & Becvar, 1993; Nichols, 1992, 1984). Some families, for example, are so *inflexible* that it is virtually impossible for the children to grow into healthy adults. These families may be resistant to almost all external influences or may fail to adapt appropriately to internal changes, as when a new child is born or an older one enters adolescence. Other families have a rigidly *enmeshed* structure in which the members are grossly overinvolved in each other's activities, thoughts, and feelings. Children in this kind of family may have great difficulty establishing autonomy. Conversely, some families display a structure of *disengagement,* which is characterized by overly rigid boundaries between the members. Children in these families may find it hard to function interdependently and may have difficulty giving or requesting support when it is needed. And finally, some families are characterized by *pathological triangular relationships* in which the parents avoid dealing with their own serious conflicts by always involving the children in their discussions or activities. These children have great difficulty developing into autonomous, separate individuals. Problematic family patterns are often passed on from one generation to the next.

Philip Berman's angry and impulsive personal style can be seen as the product of a disturbed family structure. According to family systems theorists, the whole family—mother, father, Philip, and his brother Arnold—relates in such a way as to maintain Philip's behavior. Family theorists might be particularly interested in the conflict between Philip's mother and father and the imbalance between their parental roles. They might see Philip's behavior as both a reaction to and stimulus for his parents' behaviors, and consider his "ornery" behavior, like his mother's critical comments and his father's weak and ineffectual actions, as functioning to preserve the parents' troubled marriage and stabilize the family. With Philip acting out the role of the misbehaving child, or "scapegoat," his parents may have little need or time to question their own relationship. Family systems theorists would also seek to clarify issues such as the precise nature of Philip's relationship with each parent. Is he enmeshed with his mother and disengaged from his father? They would ask too for the implicit rules governing the sibling relationship in the family, the relationship between the parents and Philip's brother, and the nature of parent-child relationships in previous generations of the family.

Social Networks and Supports Sociocultural theorists are also concerned with the broader social networks in which people operate. What is the nature of their social and professional relationships? How well do they communicate with others? What kind of signals do they send to or receive from others?

Repeatedly researchers have found ties between social networks and abnormal functioning. They have noted, for example, that people who are isolated and lack social support or intimacy in their lives are more likely to become depressed when they are under stress and to remain depressed longer than are people with supportive spouses or warm friendships (Sherbourne, Hays, &

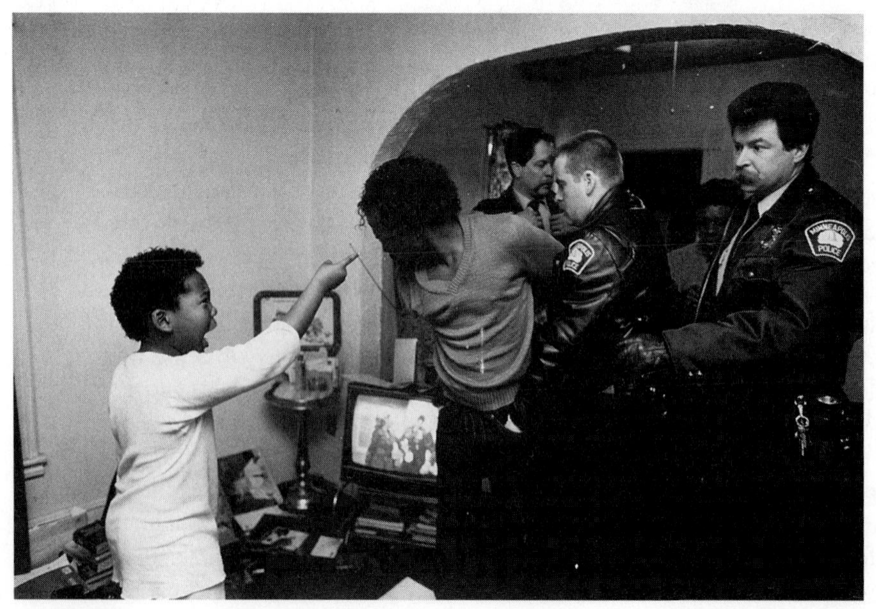

People from dysfunctional families may be particularly vulnerable to the development of psychological problems. They often face special pressures, and, in addition, may be called upon to behave and think in ways that are personally maladaptive. Children from families characterized by domestic violence are a case in point. This eight-year-old had to call the police when he saw his father attacking his mother with a knife. The child's rage, frustration, and emotional pain are apparent.

TABLE 4-2 Comparing the Biological and Sociocultural Models

	Biological Model	*Sociocultural Model*
Cause of dysfunction	Biological malfunction	Family or social stress
Research support	Strong	Moderate
Consumer designation	Patient	Client
Therapist role	Doctor	Social facilitator
Key therapist technique	Biological intervention	Social intervention
Therapy goal	Biological repair	Effective family or social system

Wells, 1995; Paykel & Cooper, 1992). Similarly, individuals who have inadequate social supports are particularly vulnerable to developing a posttraumatic stress disorder in the face of traumatic experiences such as being raped or caught in a devastating hurricane (Perry et al., 1992).

Societal Stress The unique characteristics of a given society may create special stresses that heighten the likelihood of abnormal functioning in its members (Kleinman & Cohen, 1997). Studies have found correlations between rates of abnormal functioning and such factors as widespread social change, social class, ethnic and national background, race and sex, and cultural institutions and values. As a consequence, clinicians are becoming increasingly sensitive to the "hidden injuries" that result from racism, sexism, and poverty, as well as from less obvious societal stressors such as urbanization and cultural change (Vega & Rumbaut, 1991).

Social Change When a society undergoes major change, the mental health of its members can be greatly affected. In societies undergoing rapid urbanization, for example, the prevalence of mental disorders often rises, although it is not known which features of urbanization—overcrowding, technological change, social isolation—are most to blame (Gamwell & Tomes, 1995; Ghubash, Hamdi, & Bebbington, 1992). Similarly, a society in the throes of economic depression is likely to show a significant rise in rates of clinical depression and suicide (Hammer, 1993), which may be explained in part by an increase in unemployment and the resulting loss of self-esteem and personal security.

Social Class Studies have found that rates of psychological abnormality, especially severe psychological abnormality, are higher in the lower socioeconomic classes than in the higher ones (NAMHC, 1996; Dohrenwend et al., 1992; Eron & Peterson, 1982). Perhaps the special pressures of lower-class life help explain this relationship (Adler et al., 1994). The higher rates of crime, unemployment, overcrowding, and even homelessness, the inferior medical care, and the limited educational opportunities that often characterize lower-class life may place great stress on members of these groups (Zima et al., 1996; Ensminger, 1995). Of course, other factors could also be to blame. People who suffer from significant mental disturbances may be less effective at work, earn less money, and as a result drift downward to settle in a lower socioeconomic class.

Ethnic, Religious, and National Background Ethnic, religious, and national groups have distinctive traditions that may influence the kinds of abnormal functioning to which they are vulnerable and the kinds of relief they seek. Alcoholism, for example, is more prevalent in groups that tolerate heavy drinking (Catholics, Irish, Western Europeans, Eastern Europeans) than in groups that frown on it (Jews, Protestants) (Kohn & Levav, 1994; Barry, 1982).

Racial and Sexual Prejudice Prejudice and discrimination may also contribute to some forms of abnormal functioning (NAMHC, 1996). Most societies have one or more "out-groups," whose members are deprived of many of the opportunities and comforts available to the "in-group." The out-groups—often smaller than the in-group and different in ethnicity, race, or gender—are sometimes called "minority groups" or "ethnic minorities" (Phinney, 1996). In the United States these terms typically refer to all nonwhite groups.

The number of people who are members of ethnic minorities is both substantial and growing in the United States. At present a fifth of the U.S. population has minority status, and that proportion will rise to almost half by the year 2050. White Americans themselves encompass many ethnic groups. No wonder the term "ethnic minority" in the United States is inaccurate in many eyes (Phinney, 1996). Nevertheless, largely because of their minority status, people in these groups continue to be confronted each day with prejudice, pressures, and difficulties beyond life's usual stresses. These pressures all make it particularly hard to achieve physical and psychological health and life satisfaction.

Women in Western society receive diagnoses of anxiety and depressive disorders at least twice as often as men (Culbertson, 1997). African Americans experience unusually high rates of anxiety disorders (Blazer et al., 1991; Eaton, Dryman, & Weissman, 1991). Hispanic persons, particularly young men, have higher rates of alcoholism than members of most other ethnic groups (Helzer, Burnam, & McEvoy, 1991). And Native Americans display unusually high rates of alcoholism and suicide (Kinzie et al., 1992). Although many factors may combine to produce these differences, racial and sexual prejudice and the struggles and limitations they impose may contribute to pathological patterns of tension, unhappiness, low self-esteem, and escape (NAMHC, 1996; Sue, 1991).

Cultural Institutions and Values Disorders such as windigo and koro are thought to grow out of the institutions and values of the cultures where they arise. So is *anorexia nervosa*, a disorder particularly prevalent among young women in Western society (Fombonne, 1995; Russell, 1995; Szmukler & Patton, 1995). As we will see in Chapter 12, people with this disorder intentionally deprive themselves of food and lose dangerous amounts of weight. Many theorists believe that the current emphasis on thinness as the female aesthetic ideal in Western societies is largely responsible for anorexia nervosa's high incidence there. Studies have found a growing preference for very thin female frames in North American and European magazines, movies, and advertisements over the past two decades, the same period of time in which the rates of anorexia nervosa have risen significantly.

Societal Labels and Reactions Sociocultural theorists also believe that abnormal functioning is influenced greatly by the diagnostic labels given to troubled people and by the ways other people react to those labels (Szasz, 1997, 1987, 1963; NAMHC, 1996; Rosenhan, 1973). The theorists hold that when people violate the norms of their society, the society categorizes them as deviant and assigns them labels such as "mentally ill." This label then tends to stick. The person is condemned to be viewed in stereotyped ways, reacted to as "crazy," and expected and subtly encouraged to be incapacitated. According to sociocultural theorists, the person gradually learns to accept and play the assigned role, functioning and behaving in an increasingly disturbed manner. Ultimately the label seems fully justified.

A famous and controversial study by the clinical investigator David Rosenhan (1973) supports this position. Eight normal people presented themselves at various mental hospitals, complaining that they had been hearing voices say the words "empty," "hollow," and "thud." On the basis of this complaint alone, each "pseudopatient" was diagnosed as having schizophrenia and admitted to the hospital. According to Rosenhan, labeling con-

The pressures and uncertainty of living in a war-torn environment may contribute to the development of psychological problems. An environment's ongoing violence may leave some individuals feeling numb and confused. This child seems to hardly notice the burning bombed truck behind him as he bicycles through Northern Ireland.

People in the lower socioeconomic classes have higher rates of psychological dysfunctioning than those in the middle and upper classes. Conditions of chronic poverty, such as experienced by these Irish "travelers," may contribute.

tinued to distort the patients' diagnosis and care for weeks. First, it was hard to get rid of the label. The length of hospitalization ranged from seven to fifty-two days, even though the pseudopatients behaved normally as soon as they were admitted to the hospital. Second, the schizophrenic label kept influencing the way staff viewed and dealt with the pseudopatients. A pseudopatient who paced the corridor out of boredom, for example, was said to be "nervous." Third, pseudopatients reported that the staff's attitudes and reactions toward patients in general were often authoritarian, limited, and counterproductive. Overall, the pseudopatients came to feel powerless, depersonalized, and bored. Their treatment in the hospital seemed to undermine their mood.

Sociocultural Therapies

As we have seen, clients often see therapists in *individual therapy.* In this time-honored format the two meet alone for sessions that last from fifteen minutes to two hours, depending on the client's problem and the therapist's orientation. Sociocultural theories have also spurred the growth of several other therapy formats and settings. Therapists may see a client with other clients who have similar problems, in *group therapy;* with family members, in *family* and *couple therapy;* or in the client's natural habitat, in *community treatment.*

Therapists with any of the theoretical orientations that we have discussed can work with clients in these broad formats and still apply the techniques and principles of their preferred models (Stone, 1996). In such instances the therapy is not "purely" sociocultural. More and more of the practitioners who use these formats, however, believe that psychological problems emerge in a social setting and are best addressed in such a setting (see Box 4-3). They are embracing a sociocultural position, and many have developed special sociocultural strategies specifically for use in group, family, couple, and community treatments.

Group Therapy At the turn of the twentieth century, a physician in Boston named Joseph Pratt brought tuberculosis patients together in groups to teach them about their illness and encourage them to provide emotional support for one another. This appears to have been the first clinical application of group therapy (Rosenbaum & Berger, 1963). American and British clinicians continued to experiment with group processes over the next fifty years, but it was not until after World War II that group therapy became a popular format for treating people with psychological problems. At that time, a growing demand for psychological services forced therapists throughout the United States and Europe to look for alternatives to individual therapy. Many who tried the group format found it to be efficient, time-saving, and relatively inexpensive. They also found that group therapy was often as helpful as individual therapy.

Thousands of therapists now specialize in group therapy, and countless others conduct therapy groups as a part of their practice. A survey of 481 clinical psychologists, for example, has revealed that almost a third of them devote some portion of their practice to group therapy (Norcross et al., 1993).

Typically, members of a therapy group meet together with a therapist and discuss the problems of one or more

Box 4-3 Ethnic Minorities in the Mental Health System

Researchers and clinicians have become interested in the experiences of members of ethnic minority groups who need psychological services (Commander et al., 1997; Lippincott & Mierzwa, 1995). What are their use rates and dropout rates? We now know, for example, that African Americans and Native Americans use mental health services as often as white Americans, but that Asian Americans and Hispanic Americans do not (Flaskerud & Hu, 1992; Sue, 1991, 1977). Among people who abuse drugs and alcohol, however, African Americans are less likely to seek or complete treatment than white Americans (Booth et al., 1992; Longshore et al., 1992).

What keeps some ethnic minority groups from seeking out mental health services? Cultural beliefs, a language barrier, and lack of information all play their parts. People who need treatment for a psychological problem may be more stigmatized in some cultures than in others. Furthermore, many members of minority groups simply do not trust the establishment (Nickerson, Helms, & Terrell, 1994). Some rely instead on traditional remedies. Some Hispanic persons, for example, believe that bad spirits can enter the body and cause mental disorders, and that good spirits can drive them out (Rogler, Malgady, & Rodriguez, 1989). Since these beliefs are incompatible with Western beliefs about mental disorders, the individuals may shun therapists and seek help from folk healers, family members, and friends.

Studies have also found that African Americans, Native Americans, Asian Americans, and Hispanic Americans all have higher therapy dropout rates than white Americans (Wierzbicki & Pekarik, 1993). This finding may be due to the fact that the dropout rate is higher among poorer clients, and ethnic minorities are overrepresented in lower-income groups. In addition, members of ethnic minority groups may terminate treatment because they do not feel that they are benefiting from it. Ethnic and cultural differences may also keep them from establishing rapport with their therapist (Atkinson et al., 1996; Sue, 1991).

Asian American and Hispanic American *adolescents* also appear to be underrepresented in the mental health system, though African American adolescents are not (Bui & Takeuchi, 1992; Mason & Gibbs, 1992). Moreover, Hispanic American, Asian American, and African American adolescents are more likely to be treated in public hospitals, whereas white American adolescents are more likely to be treated in private mental hospitals (Mason & Gibbs, 1992). A partial explanation for this difference is that more white American families have private insurance, and thus can more readily afford treatment in private hospitals. In addition adolescents from ethnic minority groups typically have shorter hospitalizations than white American teens (Mason & Gibbs, 1992).

of the members. Groups are often created with particular client populations in mind; for example, there are groups for people with alcoholism, for those who are physically handicapped, and for people who are divorced, abused, or bereaved (Bednar & Kaul, 1994; DeAngelis, 1992). The group format has also been used for purposes that are educational rather than therapeutic, such as "consciousness raising" and spiritual inspiration.

On the basis of his own work and other investigations, the group therapy theorist Irvin Yalom suggests that successful forms of group therapy share certain "curative" features (Vinogradov & Yalom, 1994; Yalom, 1985):

1. *Guidance:* they usually provide information and advice for members.
2. *Identification:* they provide models of appropriate behavior.
3. *Group cohesiveness:* they offer an atmosphere of solidarity in which members can learn to take risks and accept criticism.
4. *Universality:* members discover that other people have similar problems.
5. *Altruism:* members develop feelings of self-worth by helping others.
6. *Catharsis:* members develop more understanding of themselves and of others and learn to express their feelings.
7. *Skill building:* members acquire or improve social skills.

Some clinicians have developed *culture-sensitive therapies,* designed to address the unique pressures faced by minority groups, especially pressures that contribute to emotional problems (Richardson & Molinaro, 1996; Prochaska & Norcross, 1994; Watkins-Duncan, 1992). These clinicians focus on (1) making clients aware of the impact of the dominant culture and their own culture on their behavior and self-image, (2) helping clients express suppressed anger and come to terms with their pain, (3) helping clients make choices that work for them, and (4) developing a self-awareness of the cultural bias that they may hold as therapists. These approaches can help clients achieve the bicultural identity and balance that feels right for them.

Researchers have also begun to intensify their investigations into treatments for members of ethnic minority groups. This body of research is still very limited, but a few preliminary trends have emerged (Ramirez et al., 1996; Prochaska & Norcross, 1994; Sue et al., 1994):

1. Ethnic minority groups are generally underserved in the mental health field.

2. Clients from ethnic minority groups appear to improve as much as white Americans in some studies, but less in others.

3. Members of ethnic minority groups tend to prefer therapists who are ethnically similar to themselves, and such a therapist sometimes improves the outcome of treatment, certainly when the client's primary language is not English.

4. The effectiveness of treatment is enhanced when the therapist is sensitive to cultural issues and includes cultural morals and models in the treatment, especially when the client is a child or an adolescent. Treatment is also helped by pre-therapy intervention programs in which clients are initially introduced to what psychotherapy is and what to expect.

5. Clinical researchers often make the mistake of lumping together subjects from different ethnic groups and failing to consider the important individual differences between the groups. Similarly, some studies fail to consider the important individual differences that exist within each minority group.

This research makes clear the urgency of efforts to address ethnic minority issues in both research and practice, to increase the number of ethnic minority clinicians, and to increase the sensitivity of all mental-health-care providers to the cultures and needs of clients from ethnic minority groups. In those cities where the specific needs of the various ethnic groups have been addressed, the numbers of persons from these groups who use mental health services have increased, the clients report being more satisfied with the services they receive, and they are also more likely to continue treatment (O'Sullivan et al., 1989; Rodriguez, 1986).

It has been difficult to assess the effectiveness of groups (Bednar & Kaul, 1994). They vary widely in type and conduct (MacKenzie, 1996), as well as in the characteristics of their leaders and members; and group interactions can be complex, Moreover, many group studies have failed to use proper research methodology (Sadock, 1989; Lubin, 1983).

Research does seem to suggest, however, that group therapy is of help to many clients, often as helpful as individual therapy (Bednar & Kaul, 1994; Vinogradov & Yalom, 1994). Candid feedback is usually useful for group members as long as a balance is struck between positive and negative feedback. Moreover, skilled group leaders are usually able to screen out those prospective members who need more individual attention or who would not be able to tolerate the demands of the group experience (Rice, 1996; Sadock, 1989).

Over the years, various specialized kinds of group therapy have been developed. Two of the most influential are *psychodrama* and *self-help groups.*

Psychodrama In the 1920s Jacob Moreno, a Viennese psychiatrist and the first person to use the term "group psychotherapy," developed the therapy known as ***psychodrama.*** Here group members act out dramatic roles as if they are improvising a play. The atmosphere of structured fantasy is expected to make the participants feel secure enough to express their feelings and thoughts, explore new behavior and attitudes, and empathize with the feelings and perspectives of others. Often the group

"Encounter groups" or "sensitivity groups," designed to help members develop greater self-awareness and skill in human relationships through intense interactions, became very popular in the 1960s and 1970s. Perhaps the most controversial of these groups was the nude encounter group, which was thought to help lower the participants' defenses (Bindrim, 1968). Sexual expression was forbidden.

members act on a stage and even in front of an audience. The acting is guided by the therapist, or "director," who also provides feedback about each participant's performance. The audience, too, may give useful feedback.

Although relatively few of today's therapists limit their groups' activities to psychodrama alone, many have incorporated its role-playing techniques and principles into their practice (Mitchell, 1996). As we saw earlier, many behavioral and humanistic therapists now use role playing to teach assertiveness and social skills and to facilitate interactions among members of their groups. Similarly, psychodrama's emphasis on spontaneity and empathy has permeated most group therapies (Lubin, 1983).

Self-Help Groups In ***self-help groups*** (or ***mutual help groups***), people who have similar problems come together to help and support one another without the direct leadership of a professional clinician. These groups have become increasingly popular over the last two decades, and today there are about 500,000 such groups attended by 15 million people in the United States alone. The groups address issues that range from alcoholism and other forms of substance abuse to compulsive gambling, bereavement, overeating, phobias, child abuse, medical illnesses, rape victimization, unemployment, and divorce (Fehre & White, 1996).

Self-help groups are popular for several reasons. Some of the participants are looking for inexpensive and interesting alternatives to traditional kinds of treatment and find self-help groups in their search. Others have simply lost confidence in the ability of clinicians and social institutions to help with their particular problems (Silverman, 1992). Alcoholics Anonymous, the well-known network of self-help groups for people dependent on alcohol, was developed in 1934 in response to the general ineffectiveness of clinical treatments for alcoholism. Still other people are drawn to self-help groups because they find them less threatening and less stigmatizing than therapy groups. Finally, the popularity of self-help groups may be related to the decline of the extended family and other traditional sources of emotional support in Western society (Bloch, Crouch, & Reibstein, 1982).

Self-help groups encourage more helping among members than therapy groups do (Silverman, 1992). Often new members are assigned to veteran members who take a special interest in them and help integrate them into the group. In addition, self-help groups encourage members to exchange information more than other groups do. People who are newly bereaved, for example, can obtain information about funeral arrangements and business matters. Their group can also suggest what feelings to expect and how to cope with them.

Many clinicians consider self-help groups a form of therapy despite the absence of a therapist-leader (Christensen & Jacobson, 1994). At the very least, therapists usually view the groups as compatible with traditional forms of therapy. They often urge clients to participate in self-help groups as part of a broader treatment program for problems such as alcoholism, eating disorders, and victimization.

Thousands of self-help groups around the world help people cope with a variety of problems. Here members of an AIDS support group participate in a group exercise.

Family Therapy In the sociocultural view, disturbances in social structure often cause disturbances in individual functioning. Hence several clinicians in the 1950s developed ***family therapy,*** a format in which therapists meet with all members of a family, point out problematic behavior and interactions between the members, and help the whole family to change (Minuchin, 1997, 1993, 1992; Ackerman, 1965; Bowen, 1960). Most family therapists meet with family members as a group, but some choose to see them separately. Either way, the family is viewed as the unit under treatment. Here is a typical interaction between family members and a therapist:

The family therapy pioneer Virginia Satir (1916-1988) first recognized the importance of subtle communication in families during a series of sessions with a 28-year-old woman and her mother. "I noticed the tilting of a head, or an arm moving, or a voice drop, and then I would see a reaction. It didn't seem to have anything to do with the words. The words could be 'I love you' but all the rest of it was something else" (Satir, 1987, p. 67).

> "I just don't understand. We have had a happy family all along until Tommy started acting up." Bob Davis was visibly exasperated. . . .
>
> "We have tried so hard to be good parents to both of the children," Bob glanced at his wife, "but Tommy just doesn't respond anymore. I wish he was more like his little sister. She is so well behaved and is a joy to have around."
>
> Tommy sat motionless in a chair gazing out the window. He was fourteen and a bit small for his age. He looked completely disinterested in the proceedings.
>
> Sissy was eleven. She was sitting on the couch between her Mom and Dad with a smile on her face. Across from them sat Ms. Fargo, the family therapist.
>
> Ms. Fargo spoke. "Could you be a little more specific about the changes you have seen in Tommy and when they came about?"
>
> Mrs. Davis answered first. "Well, I guess it was about two years ago. Tommy started getting in fights at school. When we talked to him at home he said it was none of our business. He became moody and disobedient. He wouldn't do anything that we wanted him to. He began to act mean to his sister and even hit her."
>
> "What about the fights at school?" Ms. Fargo asked.
>
> This time it was Mr. Davis who spoke first. "Ginny was more worried about them than I was. I used to fight a lot when I was in school and I think it is normal. I had a lot of brothers and sisters in my family and I learned early that I had to fight for whatever I could; it's part of being a boy. But I was very respectful to my parents, especially my Dad. If I ever got out of line he would smack me one."
>
> "Have you ever had to hit Tommy?" Ms. Fargo inquired softly.
>
> "Sure, a couple of times, but it didn't seem to do any good."
>
> All at once Tommy seemed to be paying attention, his eyes riveted on his father. "Yeah, he hit me a lot, for no reason at all!"
>
> "Now, that's not true, Thomas." Mrs. Davis has a scolding expression on her face. "If you behaved yourself a little better you wouldn't get hit. Ms. Fargo, I can't say that I am in favor of the hitting, but I understand sometimes how frustrating it may be for Bob."
>
> "You don't know how frustrating it is for me, honey." Bob seemed upset. "You don't have to work all day at the office and then come home to contend with all of this. Sometimes I feel like I don't even want to come home."
>
> Ginny gave him a hard stare. "You think things at home are easy all day? I could use some support from you. You think all you have to do is earn the money and I will do everything else. Well, I am not about to do that anymore." . . .
>
> There was a long tense silence.
>
> "What about you, Sissy," Ms. Fargo looked at the little girl, "what do you think about what's happening at home?"
>
> "I think Tommy is a bad boy. I wish he would stop hitting me. I liked him before when he was nice."
>
> Tommy began to fidget and finally he got up from his chair and started to walk around the room.
>
> "Sit down, son," Mr. Davis demanded in a firm voice.

Tommy ignored him.

"Sit down before I knock you down!"

Tommy reluctantly sat down in a chair in the far corner of the room.

Mrs. Davis began to cry. "I just don't know what to do anymore. Things just seem so hopeless. Why can't people be nice in this family anymore? I don't think I am asking too much, am I?"

Ms. Fargo spoke thoughtfully. "I get the feeling that people in this family would like things to be different. Bob, I can see how frustrating it must be for you to work so hard and not be able to relax when you get home. And, Ginny, your job is not easy either. You have a lot to do at home and Bob can't be there to help because he has to earn a living. And you kids sound like you would like some things to be different too. It must be hard for you, Tommy, to be catching so much flack these days. I think this also makes it hard for you to have fun at home too, Sissy."

She looked at each person briefly and was sure to make eye contact. "There seems to be a lot going on. What I would like to do is talk with you together and then see the parents for a while and then maybe you kids alone, to hear your sides of the story. I think we are going to need to understand a lot of things to see why this is happening. . . . What I would like everyone to do is to think about how each of you, if you could, would change the other family members so that you would be happier in the family. I will want everyone to tell me that and I want you all to listen to what the others have to say."

(Sheras & Worchel, 1979, pp. 108–110)

Like group therapists, family therapists may subscribe to any of the major theoretical models, but more and more of them are embracing the sociocultural principles of *family systems theory.* As we noted earlier, this theory holds that each family has its own implicit rules, relationship structure, and communication patterns that shape the behavior of the individual members. Indeed, 7 percent of today's therapists identify themselves primarily as family systems therapists—13 percent of all social workers, 7 percent of psychologists and counselors, and 1 percent of psychiatrists (Prochaska & Norcross, 1994).

In one family systems approach, ***structural family therapy,*** therapists pay particular attention to the family power structure, the role each member plays, and the alliances between family members (Minuchin, 1997, 1987, 1974). The goal of therapy is to build a new family structure in which a working balance, or *homeostasis,* is achieved without the need for any member to adopt a sick role. In the case of the Davis family, Tommy's misbehavior was interpreted as a shift in roles that was upsetting the family's homeostasis, forcing other family members also to change their roles and expectations:

As Tommy grew into adolescence and desired to have more independence in his family, his role began to change. He did not want to be treated as "Mommy's little boy." He began to fight frequently at school so that she would have to see his role differently. Mrs. Davis, however, still saw Tommy as her little boy who was now acting like a "bad" boy instead of the model child she expected him to be. Since what she expected from Tommy and what she observed in him were not the same behaviors, she had to change her behavior to treat him differently in an attempt to change his behavior. This also produced a change in Mr. Davis' behavior. Everyone in the system was affected by the change that began with Tommy's desire for independence.

(Sheras & Worchel, 1979, p. 121)

In another family systems approach, ***conjoint family therapy,*** the therapist focuses primarily on communication in the family, helping members recognize harmful patterns of communication, appreciate the impact of such patterns on other family members, and change the patterns (Satir, 1987, 1967, 1964). Here a therapist helps a mother, father, and son identify their communication difficulties:

Therapist: (To husband) I notice your brow is wrinkled, Ralph. Does that mean you are angry at this moment?

Husband: I did not know that my brow was wrinkled.

Therapist: Sometimes a person looks or sounds in a way of which he is not aware. As far as you can tell, what were you thinking and feeling just now?

Husband: I was thinking over what she *[his wife]* said.

Therapist: What thing that she said were you thinking about?

Husband: When she said that when she was talking so loud, she wished I would tell her.

Therapist: What were you thinking about that?

Husband: I never thought about telling her. I thought she would get mad.

Therapist: Ah, then maybe that wrinkle meant you were puzzled because your wife was hoping you would do something and you did not know she had this hope. Do you suppose that by your wrinkled brow you were signaling that you were puzzled?

Husband: Yeh, I guess so.

Therapist: As far as you know, have you ever been in that same spot before, that is, where you were puzzled by something Alice said or did? . . .

Wife: He never says anything.

Therapist: (Smiling, to Alice) Just a minute, Alice, let me hear what Ralph's idea is of what he does. Ralph, how do you think you have let Alice know when you are puzzled?

Husband: I think she knows.

Therapist: Well, let's see. Suppose you ask Alice if she knows.

Husband: This is silly.

Therapist: (Smiling) I suppose it might seem so in this situation, because Alice is right here and certainly has heard what your question is. She knows what it is. I have the suspicion, though, that neither you nor Alice are very sure about what the other expects, and I think you have not developed ways to find out. Alice, let's go back to when I commented on Ralph's wrinkled brow. Did you happen to notice it, too?

Wife: (Complaining) Yes, he always looks like that.

Therapist: What kind of message did you get from that wrinkled brow? . . .

Wife: (Exasperated and tearfully) I don't know.

Therapist: Well, maybe the two of you have not yet worked out crystal-clear ways of giving your love and value messages to each other. Everyone needs crystal-clear ways of giving their value messages. *(To son)* What do you know, Jim, about how you give your value messages to your parents?

(Satir, 1967, pp. 97–100)

Research indicates that family therapies of various kinds are indeed useful for certain persons and problems (Pinsoff & Wynne, 1995; Shadish et al., 1995, 1993; Alexander, Holtzworth-Munroe, & Jameson, 1994). Studies have found that the overall improvement rate for families that undergo this form of therapy is between 50 and 65 percent, compared to 35 percent for those in control groups (Gurman et al., 1986; Todd & Stanton, 1983). Some studies also show that the involvement of the father in family therapy substantially increases the likelihood of a successful outcome.

Couple Therapy In ***couple therapy,*** or ***marital therapy,*** the therapist works with two people who are in a long-term relationship. Often they are husband and wife, but the couple need not be married or even living together. Like family therapy, couple therapy focuses on the structure and communication patterns in the relationship. It is usually used when a relationship is unsatisfying or in conflict (Epstein, Baucom, & Rankin, 1993). Also, a couple approach may be employed rather than family therapy when a child's psychological problems are traced to problems between the parents (Fauber & Long, 1992).

Although some degree of conflict is inevitable in any long-term relationship, there is growing evidence that many adults in our society experience serious marital discord (Bradbury & Karney, 1993; Markman & Hahlweg, 1993) (see Figure 4-4). The divorce rate in Canada, the United States, and Europe is now close to 50 percent of the marriage rate and has been climbing steadily in recent decades (Inglehart, 1990; Doherty & Jacobson, 1982). Only a third of Americans who married in the early 1970s are still married and proclaiming their marriages "very happy" (Glenn, 1989). Many couples who live together without marrying seem to have similar levels of disharmony in the relationship (Greeley, 1991).

Some complaints are particularly common among the people who enter couple therapy. The most common complaints by women include feeling unloved (66 percent), constantly belittled (33 percent), and repeatedly criticized (33 percent) (Kelly, 1982). Men complain of being neglected (53 percent) and unloved (37 percent), or they sense some long-standing incompatibility (39 percent). Approximately a third of both women and men also complain that they are sexually deprived and that their partner is chronically angry or nasty.

"I've been a cow all my life, honey. Don't ask me to change now."
(Drawing by Ziegler; © 1992 The New Yorker Magazine, Inc.)

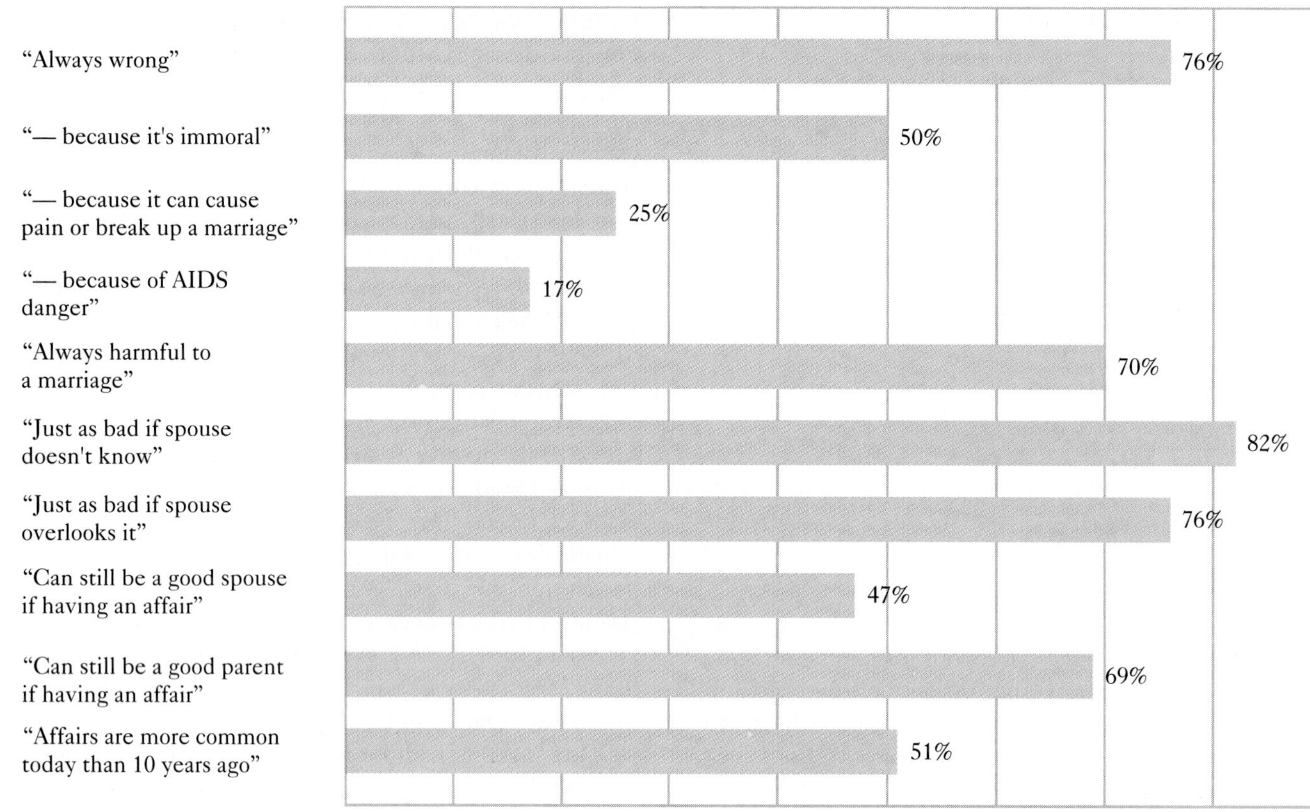

Figure 4-4 *Attitudes toward extramarital affairs. The discovery of an extramarital affair often leads to couple therapy. Surveys suggest that 21 to 35 percent of married men and 11 to 26 percent of married women have had extramarital relationships (National Opinion Research Center, 1994; Janus & Janus, 1993). Nevertheless, most people look down on such affairs and believe them to be harmful–an attitude that has held steady for at least 25 years. (Adapted from Princeton Research Associates, 1996).*

Couple therapy, like family and group therapy, may be incorporated in any of the major therapy orientations (Livingston, 1995; Epstein et al., 1993; Goldman & Greenberg, 1992). A version that has been employed widely, ***behavioral marital therapy,*** uses many techniques from the behavioral perspective (Cordova & Jacobson, 1993; Jacobson, 1989). Therapists help spouses identify and change problem behaviors largely by teaching specific communication and problem-solving skills. Spouses may be instructed to follow such guidelines as these when they discuss their problems with each other:

- Always begin with something positive when stating the problem.
- Discuss only one problem at a time; that is, be aware of sidetracking.
- Use specific behaviors to describe what is bothersome rather than derogatory labels or overgeneralizations.
- Admit one's own role in the development of the problem.

The approach also suggests how to take action to solve the problem:

- Focus on solutions by brainstorming as many solutions as possible.
- Focus on mutuality and compromise by considering solutions that involve change by both partners.
- Offer to change something in one's own behavior.
- Accept, for a beginning, a change less than the ideal solution.

(Margolin, 1983, pp. 265–266; Jacobson & Margolin, 1979)

To help increase a couple's intimacy, behavioral marital therapists may show them how to reestablish *core symbols* in their marriage—events, places, rituals, or objects that have special meaning for them (Stuart, 1975). The spouses may be told to reserve Friday nights for "dates" with each other, wear special clothes for each other, or regularly go to favorite places together. The therapist may also have the spouses perform considerate behaviors. In the technique of "caring days," each spouse devotes a day to doing things the other has requested (Stuart, 1980). Similarly, in the "love days" technique, spouses must double the number of their pleasing actions on a designated day of the week (Weiss, Hops, & Patterson, 1973).

Some practitioners of behavioral marital therapy have expanded the approach beyond skill building. Their treatment, called ***integrative behavioral couple therapy,*** has a broader, more sociocultural focus. It is designed to help partners accept behaviors that they cannot change and to embrace the whole relationship nevertheless (Cordova & Jacobson, 1993). Partners are asked to see such behaviors as an understandable consequence of basic differences between them. During this part of therapy, the partners learn not to blame either themselves or their partner for the relationship problems. As they come to empathize with the other's emotional pain, they can stop trying to change the partner, reinterpret marital differences as complementary, and recognize the positive features of certain "problem" behaviors. Thus a wife may be guided to see her husband's "stodginess" as the quality of stability that she was initially attracted to. Or a husband may learn to reinterpret his wife's overinvolvement with friends as the quality of gregariousness that he once valued.

Couples treated with behavioral marital therapy or integrative behavioral couple therapy apparently do indeed develop more effective interpersonal skills and greater tolerance for each other. Research suggests that they typically feel greater satisfaction than couples who receive no treatment at all (Cordova & Jacobson, 1993; Jacobson & Addis, 1993).

More generally, research suggests that couples treated by most forms of couple therapy show greater improvement in their relationships than couples with similar problems who fail to receive treatment, but no one form of couple therapy stands out as superior to others (Bray & Jouriles, 1995; Alexander et al., 1994). At the same time, only around 50 percent of treated couples are "happily married" at the end of couple therapy. Moreover, the few long-term studies that have been conducted suggest that as many as 38 percent of successfully treated couples may relapse within two to four years after couple therapy (Snyder, Wills, & Grady-Fletcher, 1991). Couple approaches that help clients to develop insight into their marital problems seem to have a lower relapse rate (Snyder et al., 1991). Couples who are younger, well adjusted, and less rigid in their gender roles tend to have the best results (Bray & Jouriles, 1995).

Community Treatment Following sociocultural principles, ***community mental health treatment*** programs work with people in nearby and familiar surroundings as they try to recover. In 1963 President Kennedy called for such a "bold new approach" to the treatment of mental disorders—a community approach that would enable most people with psychological difficulties to receive mental health services from nearby publicly funded agencies. Soon after Kennedy's proclamation, Congress passed the Community Mental Health Act, launching the ***community mental health movement*** across the United States.

A key feature of the community movement is ***prevention*** (Lamb, 1994). The mandate to prevent, or at least minimize, mental disorders has encouraged clinicians to actively seek out clients. This attitude contrasts with the passive posture of traditional therapists, who typically wait for clients to seek treatment. Research suggests that prevention efforts are often very successful (Heller, 1996; Muñoz, Mrazek, & Haggerty, 1996; Mrazek & Haggerty, 1994). Community workers may pursue three types of prevention: *primary, secondary,* and *tertiary.*

Primary prevention consists of efforts to improve community attitudes and policies. Its goal is to prevent mental disorders altogether (Burnette, 1996; Martin, 1996; Martin & Murray, 1996). Community workers may lobby for better recreational programs or child-care facilities in the community, consult with a local school board to help formulate a curriculum, or offer public workshops on stress reduction.

Community workers engaged in ***secondary prevention*** try to identify and treat mental disorders at their earliest stages of development, before they become

Abuse hot-line operators in New York City receive calls from victims of abuse, or from their relatives or neighbors, and set in motion community programs to help the victims and prevent further abuse.

Some sociocultural theorists believe that intense social stressors may produce outbreaks of "mass madness" such as the Los Angeles riots of 1992. In a vicious cycle, the riots, which occurred against a backdrop of poverty, unemployment, and prejudice, produced further stress for members of the community, such as Joe and Joyce Wilson, who survey the damage to their business, "Pop's Restaurant."

serious. Workers may, for instance, consult with schoolteachers, ministers, or police to help them recognize the early signs of psychological dysfunction and teach them how to help people find appropriate treatment (Newman et al., 1996; Zax & Cowen, 1976, 1969). Similarly, communities may offer hot lines or walk-in clinics that encourage people to seek help before their psychological problems get worse.

Community workers who practice ***tertiary prevention*** target moderate or severe mental disorders. They seek to prevent the disorders from becoming long-term problems by providing appropriate and effective treatment when it is needed. Tertiary care has been provided for millions of people with moderate psychological problems, such as anxiety disorders, through traditional therapy at community mental health centers across the country. Community programs have often failed, however, to provide the tertiary services needed for hundreds of thousands of persons with severe disturbances—***day centers*** (or ***day hospitals***), treatment facilities that provide day-long activities and treatment; ***halfway houses,*** residential group homes where live-in staff offer support, guidance, and practical advice; and ***sheltered workshops,*** protected and supervised workplaces that offer clients occupational training (Leshner et al., 1992).

Why has the community mental health approach fallen short for so many people with severe disturbances? One of the major reasons is lack of funding. In 1981, when only 750 of the planned 2,000 community mental health centers were in place, virtually all federal funding was withdrawn and replaced with smaller financial grants to the states. As a result, the existing centers have been forced to focus much of their effort on financial survival (Humphreys & Rappaport, 1993).

Whether this trend will continue in the twenty-first century depends on how health care is reformed (Kiesler, 1992) and on how state legislatures allocate the hundreds of millions of dollars saved by the closing of large state hospitals (Torrey, 1997). Mental health advocates urge politicians to put those savings, which exceed $200 million in New York alone, into community-based programs, but so far their advice has not been heeded. Until it is, the enormous promise of community mental health and prevention programs will remain unfulfilled.

Assessing the Sociocultural Model

The sociocultural model has added greatly to the understanding and treatment of abnormal functioning. Today most clinicians take into account family, social, and societal issues, factors that were largely overlooked just thirty years ago (NAMHC, 1996). Moreover, clinicians have become more sensitive to the negative impact of clinical labels. Finally, as we have just observed, sociocultural treatment formats sometimes succeed where more traditional approaches have failed (Heller, 1996).

At the same time, the sociocultural model, like other models, leaves some questions unanswered and problems unresolved. To begin with, studies often fail to support certain key predictions of the sociocultural model. Although some forms of abnormality are indeed uniquely associated with certain societies, as the model predicts (Kleinman & Cohen, 1997), other forms, particularly the most severe ones, appear to be universal, and their incidence and symptoms are much the same the world over. Schizophrenia, for example, occurs throughout the world, regardless of a country's values and pressures. Approximately 1 percent of people everywhere appear to exhibit this disorder's central symptoms of confusion, distorted ideas, and hallucinations; and every society considers these symptoms abnormal (Regier et al., 1993; Strauss, 1979; Murphy, 1976).

Still another problem is that sociocultural research findings are often difficult to interpret. Research may reveal a relationship between sociocultural factors and a mental disorder, yet still fail to establish that they are its cause. Studies show a link between family conflict and schizophrenia, for example, but that finding does not necessarily mean that family dysfunction causes schizophrenia (Miklowitz et al., 1995; Velligan et al., 1995; Goldstein, 1990). It is equally possible that family functioning is disrupted by the tension and conflict created by the schizophrenic behavior of a family member (Eakes, 1995).

Perhaps the most serious limitation of the sociocultural model is its inability to predict psychopathology in specific individuals. If, say, the current emphasis on thinness in women is a major reason for the growing incidence of anorexia nervosa in Western nations, why do only a small percentage of the women in these countries manifest this disorder? Are still other factors necessary for the disorder to develop? In response to such limitations, most clinicians choose to view sociocultural explanations as going hand in hand with biological or psychological explanations. They agree that sociocultural variables may be responsible for a climate favorable to the development of certain mental disorders. They believe, however, that biological or psychological conditions or both must also be present before the mental disorders unfold.

Crossroads

The models we have examined in this chapter and in Chapter 3 vary widely. They look at behavior differently, are based on different assumptions, reach different conclusions, and adopt different treatments. Many of their proponents go beyond claiming that their particular model is the most enlightened; they criticize the other models as misleading or plain foolish (Marmor, 1987). Yet none of the models has proved consistently superior. Each helps us appreciate a critical dimension of human functioning, and each has important strengths as well as serious limitations.

In fact, the conclusions of the different models are often compatible (Friman et al., 1993). Certainly our understanding and treatment of abnormal behavior are more complete if we appreciate the biological, psychological, *and* sociocultural aspects of a person's problem rather than only one of those aspects. Even the various psychological models can be compatible at times. In cases of sexual dysfunction, for example, psychodynamic causes, such as internal conflicts in childhood, behavioral causes, such as learning incorrect sexual techniques, and cognitive causes, such as misconceptions about sex, often seem to combine to produce the problem.

The models also can be compatible when each emphasizes a different kind of causal factor. When some theorists talk about a disorder's cause, they are referring to *predisposing factors,* events that occurred long before the disorder appeared and set the stage for it. Meanwhile other theorists may be suggesting *precipitating factors,* events that actually triggered the disorder, or *maintaining factors,* events that are keeping it going. When models focus on different kinds of causal factors, their explanations may be far from contradictory.

In fact, many clinicians now embrace explanations of abnormal behavior that consider more than one kind of causal factor at a time. In the ***diathesis-stress*** view, for example, to develop and maintain some forms of abnormality a person must first have a biological, psychological, or sociocultural predisposition to the disorder and must then also be subjected to an immediate form of stress. If we were to explore a case of depression, we might well find a neurotransmitter dysfunction as a predisposing factor, a major loss as a precipitating factor, and errors in logic as a maintaining factor.

As different kinds of disorders are presented throughout this book, we will see how the proponents of today's models explain each disorder, and how each model's practitioners treat people with the disorder. We will also ask how well these explanations and treatments are supported by research. Just as important, we will be observing not only how the explanations and treatments differ, but also how they may build upon and illuminate each other.

Chapter Review

1. ***The biological and sociocultural models*** Many theorists and practitioners focus primarily on biological or sociocultural factors to explain or treat abnormal behavior. Those with a biological bent look inward at the biological processes of human functioning. Sociocultural theorists, in contrast, look outward at the social rules, pressures, and related factors that influence all members of a society.

2. ***Biological explanations*** Biological theorists believe that psychological disorders are linked to anatomical or biochemical problems in the brain. Researchers have found that abnormalities in the activity of certain *neurotransmitters*—chemicals released into the *synapse* between two *neurons*—are often connected with specific psychological disorders.

3. ***Biological therapies*** Biological therapies comprise physical and chemical methods developed to help people overcome their psychological problems. The principal kinds of biological interventions are *drug therapy, electroconvulsive therapy,* and, on rare occasions, *psychosurgery.*

4. ***Sociocultural explanations*** Some sociocultural theorists focus on *family structure and communication;* they see the family as a system of interacting parts in which structure, rules, and patterns of communication may force family members to behave in abnormal ways. Others focus on *social networks* and *supports* and how they may affect a person's psychological functioning. Still others examine *societal stress* and consider the unique characteristics of a given society that may create special problems for its members and heighten the likelihood of abnormal functioning. Finally, some theorists focus on *societal labels and reactions;* they hold that society categorizes certain people as "crazy" or "mentally ill," and that the label produces expectations that influence the way the person behaves and is treated.

5. ***Sociocultural therapies*** Sociocultural principles are on display in such therapy formats as group, family, couple, and community therapy. Many therapists continue to apply the explanations and concepts of other models when they work with clients in these broader formats. Increasingly, however, practitioners who use such formats are embracing a sociocultural view of abnormal functioning and are using special sociocultural strategies in their work.

A. ***Group therapy*** has helped many clients. The feedback and support that group members experience is usually beneficial. Two specialized forms of group therapy are *psychodrama* and the *self-help group.*

B. ***Family therapy*** is a format in which therapists meet with all members of a family, point out problematic behavior and interactions, and help the whole family to change. In ***couple therapy,*** the therapist works with two people who share a long-term relationship. An increasing body of research on the effectiveness of various family and couple therapies suggests that they are useful for some problems and in some circumstances.

C. In ***community treatment,*** therapists try to work in settings close to their clients' homes, schools, or workplaces. Their goal is either to prevent mental disorders altogether by improving community attitudes and policies *(primary prevention),* to prevent disorders from deteriorating by early identification and treatment *(secondary prevention),* or to prevent moderate or severe disorders from becoming long-term problems by providing appropriate and effective treatment *(tertiary prevention).*

6. ***Relationship between the models*** The models vary widely yet their conclusions are often compatible, suggesting that our understanding of abnormal behavior is more complete if we appreciate the biological, psychological, *and* sociocultural aspects of the problem. Clinicians are increasingly embracing the *diathesis-stress* view, that people must first have a biological, psychological, or sociocultural predisposition to a disorder and must then be subjected to an immediate psychological stress to develop and maintain certain forms of abnormality.

Thought and Afterthought

Politics, Psychology, and Public Perceptions

When George McGovern ran for president of the United States in 1972, word leaked out that his running mate, Senator Thomas Eagleton (left), had once suffered from depression and had received electroconvulsive therapy. The news, as well as the perception that Eagleton may have tried to hide his past problems, led to Eagleton's withdrawal from the race and no doubt contributed to McGovern's overwhelming defeat. Similarly, when General Colin Powell was being touted as a possible presidential candidate in 1996, rumors emerged that his wife, Alma, had suffered from depression. During a news conference announcing his decision not to run, Powell straightforwardly acknowledged his wife's past episode of depression, discussed her successful response to antidepressant drug treatment, and encouraged everyone with this problem to seek treatment. In this instance, the public responded with admiration and respect. Indeed, support for Powell seemed to rise.

Afterthoughts: Do the different public reactions suggest that labels of psychological dysfunctioning are less problematic and less enduring in our society today than they were a generation ago? . . . Might a persons own perception of his or her psychological problems influence the reactions of others? . . . . If Colin Powell himself, rather than his wife, had experienced a bout of depression, would the public reaction have been more similar to that accorded Senator Eagleton?

Frankly Speaking

All happy families resemble one another; every unhappy family is unhappy in its own fashion.

—**Leo Tolstoy,** *Anna Karenina*

Afterthoughts: What did Tolstoy mean by this statement? . . . Would family systems theorists agree with him? . . . Why are people so affected by the functioning of their families?

Prozac du Jour

In 1996 the French government launched a campaign to curb an outbreak of psychotropic drug use throughout France—where it was once considered chic to be blue. A scathing report found that clinical practitioners in France prescribe twice as many antidepressants and tranquilizers as those in Italy, and three times as many as those in Britain and Germany (Patel, 1996, 1995). More than 400,000 French people take Prozac, and 2 million take other psychotropic drugs (Mabry, 1995). To combat what it sees as excessive reliance on drugs, the government proposed to print warnings on all drug packages.

Afterthoughts: Why might some countries have more emotional problems than others? . . . Why might countries differ in their preferences for certain treatments? . . . A leading French psychiatrist worries that psychotropic drugs constrain behavior, destroy individuality, and divert people's attention from societal ills. Are such concerns justified?

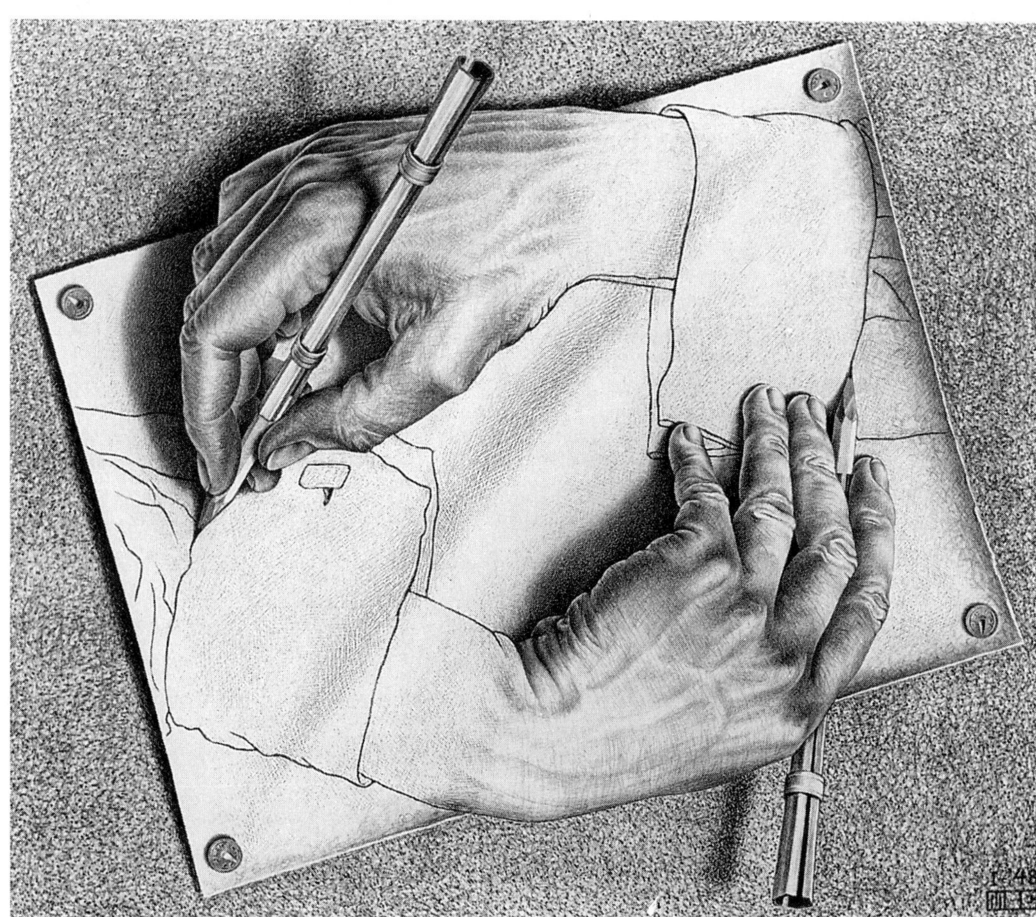

Topic Overview

Clinical Assessment
Clinical Interviews
Clinical Tests
Clinical Observations

Diagnosis
Classification Systems
DSM-IV

Treatment
Treatment Decisions
Is Treatment Effective?

Crossroads

Chapter 5

Clinical Assessment, Diagnosis, and Treatment

Angela Savanti was 22 years old, lived at home with her mother, and was employed as a secretary in a large insurance company. She . . . had had passing periods of "the blues" before, but her present feelings of despondency were of much greater proportion. She was troubled by a severe depression and frequent crying spells, which had not lessened over the past two months. Angela found it hard to concentrate on her job, had great difficulty falling asleep at night, and had a poor appetite. . . . Her depression had begun after she and her boyfriend Jerry broke up two months previously.

(Leon, 1984, p. 109)

Eventually Angela Savanti made an appointment with a therapist at a local counseling center. The first step the clinician took toward helping Angela was to learn as much as possible about her disturbance. Who is she, what is her life like, and what precisely are her symptoms? This information was expected to throw light on the causes and the probable course of her present dysfunction and help the clinician decide what kinds of treatment strategies would be likely to help her. The treatment program could then be tailored to Angela's unique needs and to her particular pattern of abnormal functioning.

Like the body parts in M. C. Escher's lithograph Drawing Hands, *1948, a client's personality, needs, emotions, and behavior take form during clinical assessment.*

In Chapters 2, 3, and 4 we saw how theorists and researchers in abnormal psychology seek a nomothetic, or broad, understanding of abnormal functioning. Clinical practitioners, in contrast, are interested in compiling ***idiographic,*** or individual, information about their clients. If practitioners are to help people overcome their problems, they must have the fullest possible understanding of those people and know the nature and origins of their problems. Although they also apply general information in their work, they can determine its relevance only after they have thoroughly examined the person who has come for treatment (Stricker & Trierweiler, 1995). Idiographic information about the client is arrived at through *assessment* and *diagnosis.* With this information in hand, practitioners can implement *treatment.* In this chapter we shall examine the primary tasks of clinical practitioners—assessment, diagnosis, and treatment.

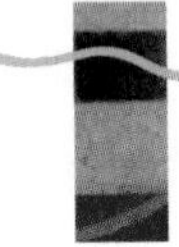

Clinical Assessment

Assessment is simply the collecting of relevant information about a subject. It goes on in every realm of life. We make assessments when we shop for groceries or vote for president. College admissions officers, who have to predict which students will succeed in college, depend on academic records, recommendations, achievement test scores, interviews, and application forms to give them information about prospective students. Employers, who have to decide which applicants are most likely to be effective workers, collect information about them from résumés, interviews, references, and perhaps on-the-job observations.

Clinical assessment is used to determine how and why a person is behaving abnormally and how that person may be helped. It also allows clinicians to evaluate clients after they have been in treatment for a while, to see what progress they are making and whether the treatment ought to be modified.

Clinicians' selection of specific assessment techniques and tools depends on their theoretical orientation. Psychodynamic clinicians, for example, use assessment methods that provide information about a person's personality and any unconscious conflicts he or she may be experiencing (Butler & Satz, 1989). This kind of assessment, called a ***personality assessment,*** enables them to piece together a clinical picture in accordance with the principles of their model. Behavioral and many cognitive clinicians, in contrast, use assessment methods that provide detailed information about specific dysfunctional behaviors and cognitions (Haynes, 1990; Kendall, 1990). The goal of this kind of assessment, called ***behavioral assessment,*** is to carry out a ***functional analysis*** of the person's behaviors—an analysis of how the behaviors are learned and reinforced.

Hundreds of assessment techniques and tools have been developed from all theoretical perspectives. They fall into three general categories: *clinical interviews, tests,* and *observations.* If these tools are to be highly useful, they must be *standardized,* and they must have *reliability* and *validity.*

It is best that all clinicians follow the same procedures when they employ a particular technique of assessment. They may accomplish this by ***standardizing*** the technique, establishing common standards to be followed whenever it is administered. Similarly, clinicians must standardize the scores of an assessment tool in order to be able to interpret each individual person's score. They may, for example, administer a particular test to a group of subjects whose performance then serves as a common standard, or norm, against which any individual's score can be measured. The group that initially took the test is called the ***standardization sample.*** This sample must be representative of the larger population the test is intended for. If an aggressiveness test meant for the public at large were standardized on a group of Marines, for example, the "norm" might turn out to be misleadingly high. Factors such as age, gender, and education level must also be considered in selecting a standardization sample.

Reliability refers to the *consistency* of assessment measures. A good assessment tool will always yield the same results in the same situation (Barker, Pistrang, & Elliott, 1994; Kline, 1993). For example, an assessment tool has high ***test–retest reliability,*** one kind of reliabilty, if it yields the same results when it is given again to the same people. If a woman's responses on a particular test indicate that she is a heavy drinker, the test should produce the same result when she takes it again a week later. To measure test–retest reliability, the scores subjects earn on two occasions are correlated. The higher the correlation (see pp. 34–37), the greater the reliability.

An assessment tool shows high ***interrater*** (or ***interjudge***) ***reliability,*** another kind of reliability, if different evaluators independently agree on how to score and interpret it. True–false and multiple-choice tests yield consistent scores no matter who evaluates them, but other tests require the evaluator to make a judgment, and three evaluators may come up with three different scores. Consider a test that requires the subject to produce a copy of a picture, which a judge then rates for accuracy. Different judges may give different ratings to the same copy. A test's interrater reliability may be determined by the level of agreement among several evaluators who score a single person's test performance.

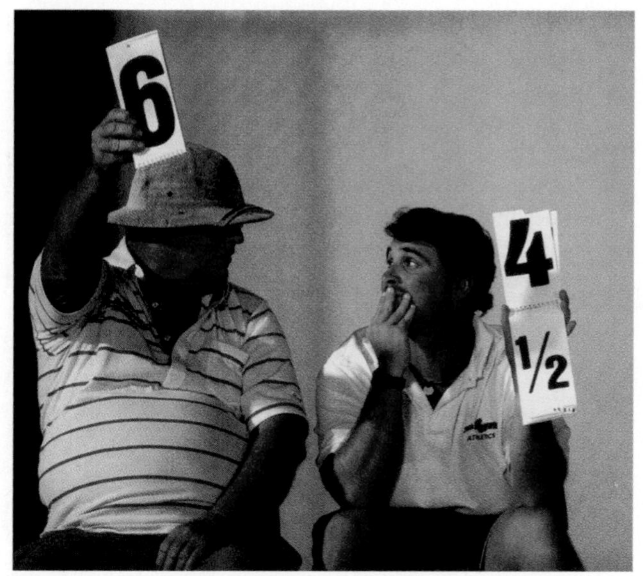

These judges of a high school diving competition arrive at very different assessments of the same diver. The low interrater reliability may reflect ambiguities in the scoring procedure, or it may be the result of evaluator bias. The judges are coaches from the opposing teams.

Finally, an assessment tool must show high ***validity:*** it must *accurately* measure what it is supposed to be measuring (Barker et al., 1994; Kline, 1993). Suppose a weight scale reads 12 pounds every time a 10-pound bag of sugar is placed on it. Although the scale is reliable because its readings are consistent, those readings are not valid, or accurate.

Some assessment techniques appear to be valid because they *seem* to make sense. This sort of validity, called ***face validity,*** does not by itself establish an instrument's trustworthiness. A test for depression, for example, might include questions about how often an individual cries. Because it makes sense that depressed people would cry, these test questions would have face validity. It turns out, however, that many people cry a great deal for reasons other than depression, and some extremely depressed people fail to cry at all. Thus, an assessment tool should not be used unless it has been successfully subjected to more exacting measures, such as predictive or concurrent validity (Goodwin, 1995).

Predictive validity is a tool's ability to predict a person's future characteristics or behavior. Let us say that a test gathers information about the parents of elementary school children, their personal characteristics, and their attitudes toward smoking. On that basis, clinicians might try to identify children who will take up cigarette smoking in junior high school. To establish the test's predictive validity, we could administer it to a group of elementary school students, wait until they were in junior high school, and then check to see which children actually did become smokers.

Concurrent validity is the degree to which an instrument's measures agree with measures obtained from other assessment techniques. Subjects' scores on a new test designed to measure anxiety, for example, should correlate highly with their scores on other anxiety tests, or with their performance during clinical interviews.

Before any assessment technique can be fully useful, it must meet the requirements of standardization, reliability, and validity (see Box 5-1). No matter how insightful or clever a technique may be, clinicians cannot profitably use its results if they are uninterpretable, inconsistent, or inaccurate (Nietzel et al., 1994). Unfortunately, more than a few clinical assessment tools fall short, suggesting that at least some clinical assessments, too, miss their mark (Shedler, Mayman, & Manis, 1993).

Clinical Interviews

Most of us feel instinctively that the best way to get to know people is to meet with them. In face-to-face interactions we can see other persons' reactions to our questions. We can observe as well as listen as they answer, watch them observing us, and generally get a sense of who they are. The clinical interview is the same sort of face-to-face encounter (Nietzel et al., 1994; Wiens, 1990). If a woman becomes markedly restless and avoids eye contact when she talks about men, the clinician may suspect that she feels some anxiety in her heterosexual relationships. If a man says that the death of his mother saddened him but looks as happy as can be, the clinician may suspect that the man actually has conflicting emotions about this loss. Almost all practitioners use clinical interviews as part of the assessment process.

Conducting The Interview The interview is often the first contact between client and clinician. Harry Stack Sullivan, the renowned American psychiatrist, said that the interviewer's primary task is to "discover who the client is—that is, he must review what course of events the client has come through to be who he is, what he has in the way of background and experience" (Sullivan, 1954, pp. 17–18). Correspondingly, clinicians usually seek detailed information about the person's current problems and feelings, current life situations and relationships, and personal history. They may also examine the person's expectations of therapy and motives for seeking it. The clinician who worked with Angela Savanti began with a face-to-face interview:

Angela was dressed neatly when she appeared for her first interview. She was attractive, but her eyes were puffy and ringed with dark circles. She answered questions and related information about her life history in a slow, flat tone of voice, which had an impersonal quality to it. She sat stiffly in her chair with her hands in her lap, and moved very little throughout the entire interview.

The client stated that the time period just before she and her boyfriend terminated their relationship had been one of extreme emotional turmoil. She was not sure whether she wanted to marry Jerry, and he began to demand that she decide either one way or the other. Mrs. Savanti did not seem to like Jerry and was very cold and aloof whenever he came to the house. Angela felt caught in the middle and unable to make a decision about her future. After several confrontations with Jerry over whether she would marry him or not, he told her he felt that she would never decide, so he was not going to see her anymore. . . .

Angela stated that her childhood was a very unhappy period. Her father was seldom home, and when he was present, her parents fought constantly. Sometimes the arguments became quite severe and her father would throw things and shout. Mrs. Savanti usually became sullen and withdrawn after an argument, refused to speak to her husband, and became uncommunicative with her daughters. Angela remembered that many times as a child she was puzzled because it seemed that her mother was angry at her, too. Sometimes after an argument, Mrs. Savanti told her daughters that she had ruined her life by marrying their father. . . .

Angela recalled feeling very guilty when Mr. Savanti left. . . . She revealed that whenever she thought of

BOX 5-1 Tests, Lies, and Videotape: The Public Misuse of Assessment

In movies, criminals being grilled by the police reveal their guilt by sweating, shaking, cursing, or twitching. When they are hooked up to a ***polygraph*** (or lie detector), the needles bounce all over the paper. This image has been with us since World War I, when some clinicians developed the theory that certain detectable physiological changes occur in people who are being deceptive (Marston, 1917).

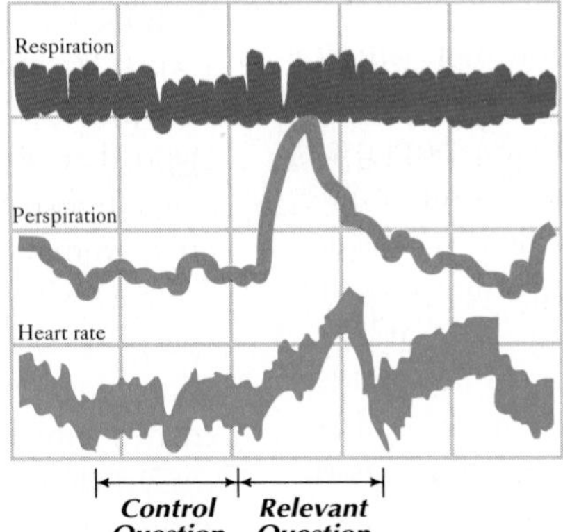

The logic and design of a lie detector test are straightforward. A subject's respiration level, perspiration level, and heart rate are recorded while he or she answers questions. The clinician observes these physiological responses while the subject answers yes to *control questions*—questions whose answers are known to be yes, such as "Are your parents both alive?" Then the clinician observes the subject's physiological responses to the test questions, such as "Did you commit this robbery?" If (as shown here) breathing, perspiration, and heart rate have increased, the subject may be lying (Raskin, 1982). The danger of relying on such tests, however, is that there is no compelling evidence that they work (Steinbrook, 1992).

It is crucial that a test be valid if it is to be used as a diagnostic tool. Yet polygraph tests have enjoyed widespread popularity for many years despite an almost total lack of evidence that they are meaningful. Only recently has this inconvenient fact reduced reliance on these tests. In 1984 the U.S. Office of Technology Assessment reviewed all available literature on the polygraph and concluded that the test *lacked* validity. It failed to find clear evidence of a unique physiological response associated with deception (Saxe, Dougherty, & Cross, 1985). As a result, the House of Representatives voted to restrict the use of the polygraph in preemployment screening. In 1986 the American Psychological Association concluded that polygraphs were inaccurate, for much the same reason.

With the polygraph's popularity in decline, businesses and governments found themselves in need of a test to replace it. They were losing billions of dollars to theft, low productivity, and other dishonest behavior, and so they desired a new screening tool

her father, she always felt that she had been responsible in some way for his leaving the family. Angela had never communicated this feeling to anyone, and her mother rarely mentioned his name.

Angela described her mother as the "long-suffering type" who said that she had sacrificed her life to make her children happy, and the only thing she ever got in return was grief and unhappiness. Angela related that her mother rarely smiled or laughed and did not converse very much with the girls. . . . When Angela and [her sister] Doreen began dating, Mrs. Savanti . . . commented on how tired she was because she had waited up for them. She would make disparaging remarks about the boys they had been with and about men in general. . . .

Angela revealed that she had often been troubled with depressed moods. During high school, if she got a lower grade in a subject than she had expected, her initial response was one of anger, followed by depression. She began to think that she was not smart enough to get good grades, and she blamed herself for studying too little. Angela also became despondent when she got into an argument with her mother or felt that she was being taken advantage of at work. However, these periods of depression usually lasted only about a day, and passed when she became involved in some other activity.

The intensity and duration of the [mood change] that she experienced when she broke up with Jerry were much more severe. She was not sure why she was so depressed, but she began to feel it was an effort to walk around and go out to work. Talking with others became difficult. Angela found it hard to concentrate, and she began to forget things she was supposed to do. It took

---

for employment. ***Integrity tests*** seemed to be the answer. These personality tests seek to measure whether test takers are generally honest or dishonest—and whether it is safe to hire them for a particular job. More than forty of these written tests are now in use, supposedly revealing such broad characteristics as dependability, deviance, social conformity, wayward impulses, and hostility to rules. Here again, however, research suggests that the tests have virtually no theoretical foundation. They show limited validity at best, are easy to fake, are often interpreted by unqualified testers, and, most important, yield high rates of false accusations (Camara & Schneider, 1994; Guastello & Rieke, 1991).

Other psychological tests too have caused uproars. In Old Town, Maine, a police officer lost his job after he refused to take a ***penile plethysmograph test,*** a test meant to evaluate his sexual impulses. The police officer had been accused of child sexual abuse. Although he was not indicted and the charges were never confirmed, the police department required him to see a therapist and to undergo further testing in order to retain his job.

To administer a penile plethysmograph test, a clinician places a rubber tube filled with mercury around a subject's penis and then shows him videotapes or slides of naked adults and children. When the subject becomes sexually aroused, the band stretches and the mercury registers the arousal. Clinicians can chart the results on a computer program to determine whether a subject is more aroused by adults than by children, by males than by females, or by coerced than by consensual sex.

Psychologists point out that although the test does accurately report sexual arousal, it has no predictive validity—it cannot predict whether a person will act on those feelings (Barker & Howell, 1992). Researchers also note that of all the people who may be sexually attracted to children, few actually try to satisfy those desires. The test therefore cannot determine whether anyone has committed a sexual offense or predict whether he is likely to do so.

The officer in Maine charged the city of Old Town with violation of his civil rights. No government agency, he claimed, had the right to make such an intimate physical test a condition of employment. An employment arbitrator ordered the police department to reinstate the officer. In addition, an appeals court ruled that he could proceed to sue the city of Old Town for damages in a federal court.

Lives can be changed dramatically when people are labeled, whether the label be "dishonest," "criminal," "depressive," or "sexually deviant." People who administer psychophysiological, personality, or other tests have an obligation to consider the consequences carefully, particularly before they make any results public. Such questionable devices as polygraph, integrity, and plethysmograph tests may violate more than the basic tenets of science. They can also violate civil rights and hurt innocent people.

> her a long time to fall asleep at night, and when she finally did fall asleep, she sometimes woke up in the midst of a bad dream. She felt constantly tired, and loud noises, including conversation or the television, bothered her. She preferred to lie in bed rather than be with anyone, and she often cried when alone.
>
> *(Leon, 1984, pp. 110–115)*

Beyond gathering basic interview data of this kind, clinical interviewers give special attention to whatever topics they consider most important. Psychodynamic interviewers try to learn about the person's needs and fantasies, elicit relevant memories about past events and relationships, and observe the way the person molds the interview (Shea, 1990; Pope, 1983). Behavioral interviewers have an acronym, SORC, for the kinds of information they gather in order to do a functional analysis: relevant information about the *stimuli* that trigger the abnormal functioning, about the *organism* or person (such as a low self-opinion), about the precise nature of the abnormal *responses,* and about the *consequences* of those responses (Reyna, 1989; O'Leary & Wilson, 1987). Cognitive interviewers try to discover assumptions, interpretations, and cognitive coping skills that influence the way the person acts and feels (Kendall, 1990). Humanistic clinicians ask about the person's self-concept and try to learn about his or her unique perceptions (Aiken, 1985; Brown, 1972). Biological clinicians use the interview to help pinpoint signs of any biochemical or neurological dysfunction. And sociocultural interviewers ask about relevant family, social, and cultural issues.

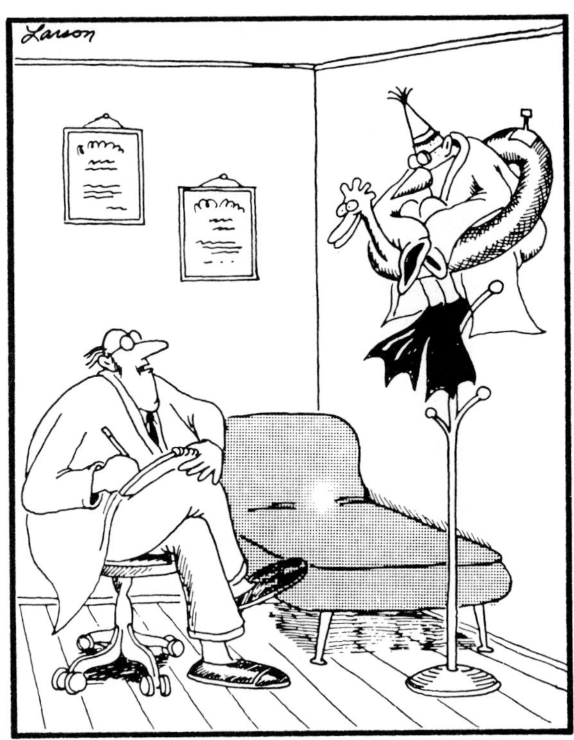

"So, Mr. Fenton . . . Let's begin with your mother."

In a structured interview, clinicians gather information by asking a set of standard questions irrespective of the client's particular symptoms. (The Far Side cartoon by Gary Larson is reprinted by permission of Chronicle Features, San Francisco, CA. All rights reserved.)

Interview Formats Interviews can be either unstructured or structured (First et al., 1995; Barker et al., 1994). In an ***unstructured interview,*** the clinician asks open-ended questions, perhaps as simple as "Would you tell me about yourself?" The lack of structure allows clinicians to follow interesting leads, including important topics that they could not anticipate before the interview. Because it places few constraints on what the client can discuss, it gives clinicians a better appreciation of the issues that are important to the client.

In a ***structured interview,*** clinicians ask a series of prepared questions. Sometimes they use a published ***interview schedule***—a standard set of questions designed for use in all interviews. Structured interviews often include a ***mental status exam,*** questions and observations that systematically probe a client's awareness of what is going on, orientation with regard to time and place, attention span, memory, judgment and insight, thought content and processes, mood, and appearance. A structured format ensures that clinicians will cover the same kinds of important issues in all interviews and enables them to compare the responses of different individuals.

Although most clinical interviews have both structured and unstructured portions, many clinicians favor one kind over the other (Nietzel et al., 1994; Leon, Bowden, & Faber, 1989). Unstructured interviews typically appeal to pschodynamic clinicians because they allow interviewers to search freely for underlying issues and conflicts. They are also popular among humanists because they allow clinicians to guide the conversation in any direction the clients's ideas and experiences indicate (Pope, 1983). Structured formats, on the other hand, are more widely used by behavioral clinicians, who need to do a systematic review of many pieces of information to complete a functional analysis of a person's behaviors (Pope, 1983). Structured formats are equally popular among cognitive interviewers because they can point to certain characteristic attitudes or thinking processes, and among biological interviewers because they can help clinicians search systematically for indicators of biological dysfunctioning.

Limitations of Clinical Interviews Both structured and unstructured interviews yield valuable information about a client, but there are limits to what the clinical interview can accomplish. One problem centers on the validity, or accuracy, of this assessment technique. An interview can gather only the information that a client chooses to reveal. Clients may try to present themselves in the best light or feel reluctant to introduce embarrassing topics (Barker et al., 1994; Nietzel et al., 1994). Alternatively, they may be unable to provide accurate information. People who suffer from depression, for example, take an unduly pessimistic view of themselves. Some describe themselves inaccurately as incompetent at their jobs or inadequate as parents (Beck, 1997, 1991, 1967; Hewitt, Flett, & Ediger, 1996).

Interviewers, too, may make subjective judgments that skew the information they gather. They usually rely too heavily on first impressions, for example, and give too much weight to unfavorable information about a client (Aiken, 1985; Meehl, 1960). The interviewers' biases, including gender and race biases, may also influence the way they interpret what a client says (Nietzel et al., 1994).

Finally, clients respond differently to different interviewers. Because clients feel uncomfortable with clinicians who are cold and distant, they apparently offer less information to them than to clinicians who are warm and supportive (Eisenthal, Koopman, & Lazare, 1983). A clinician's race, sex, age, and appearance may also influence the client's responses (Paurohit, Dowd, & Cottingham, 1982).

In these circumstances, different clinicians can obtain different answers and draw different conclusions, even when they ask the same questions of the same person (Langwieler & Linden, 1993). Accordingly, some researchers believe that interviewing, a time-honored approach to assessment, should be discarded. This might be a reasonable suggestion if there were any problem-free techniques to use instead. As we shall see, however, the two other kinds of clinical assessment methods also have serious limitations.

Clinical Tests

More than 500 clinical tests are currently used throughout the United States. ***Tests*** are devices for gathering information about a few aspects of a person's psychological functioning, from which broader information about that person can be inferred (Goldstein & Hersen, 1990). A test may reveal subtle information that might not become apparent during an interview or observation.

On the surface, it may appear relatively simple to design an effective clinical test. Every month in magazines and newspapers we come across new tests that purport to tell us about ourselves, our relationships, our sex lives, our stresses, our ability to succeed in business, and more. These tests can seem convincing, but most of them lack reliability, validity, and standardization. That is, they do not yield consistent, accurate information or say anything meaningful about where we stand in comparison with others. The tests that clinicians find most useful and use most frequently are of six kinds: *projective tests, personality inventories, response inventories, psychophysiological tests, neuropsychological tests,* and *intelligence tests.*

Projective Tests

Projective tests require subjects to interpret relatively vague stimuli, such as inkblots or ambiguous pictures, or just to follow open-ended instructions such as "Draw a person." Theoretically, when clues and instructions are so vague, subjects "project" aspects of their own personality into the task. As we observed in Chapter 3, psychodynamic theorists believe projection to be a common defense mechanism in which people project their own inner wishes onto others. Thus projective tests are used primarily by psychodynamic clinicians to help them assess the unconscious personality drives and conflicts that they believe to be at the root of abnormal functioning. The most widely used projective tests are the *Rorschach test,* the *Thematic Apperception Test, sentence-completion tests,* and *drawings.*

Rorschach Test In 1911 Hermann Rorschach, a Swiss psychiatrist, experimented with the use of inkblots in clinical diagnosis. He made thousands of blots by dropping ink on paper, folding the paper in half, and then unfolding it to reveal a symmetrical but wholly accidental composition, such as the one shown in Figure 5-1. Rorschach found that everyone saw images in these blots. Moreover, the images viewers perceived corresponded in important ways with their psychological condition. People diagnosed with schizophrenia, for example, tended to see images that differed radically from those that people with anxiety disorders saw.

Rorschach selected ten inkblots and published them in 1921 with instructions for their use in assessment. This set of ten inkblots was called the Rorschach Psychodynamic Inkblot Test. Rorschach died just eight months later, at the age of 37, but his colleagues continued his work, and his inkblots have taken their place among the most widely used projective tests of the twentieth century.

Clinicians administer the ***Rorschach,*** as it is commonly called, by presenting one inkblot card at a time to subjects and asking them what they see, what the inkblot seems to be, or what it reminds them of. The subjects are encouraged to give more than one response. In the following exchange, a tense 32-year-old woman who complains of feeling unworthy and lacking in confidence responds to one Rorschach inkblot.

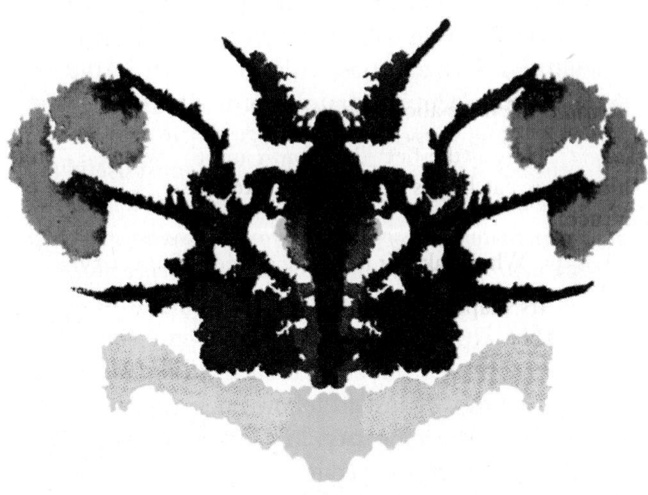

Figure 5-1 *An inkblot similar to those used in the Rorschach Test. When subjects tell what they see in a Rorschach inkblot, testers are interested both in the "thematic" content of the response (the images they see) and in its "style" (for example, whether the subject sees movement in the inkblot).*

> *Subject:* Oh, dear! My goodness! O.K. Just this [upper] part is a bug. Something like an ant—one of the social group which is a worker, trying to pull something. I think this is some kind of food for the rest of the ants. It's a bee because it has wings, a worker bee bringing up something edible for the rest of the clan.
>
> *Clinician:* Tell me about the bee.
>
> *Subject:* Here is the bee, the mouth and the wings. I don't think bees eat leaves but it looks like a leaf or a piece of lettuce.
>
> *Clinician:* What makes it look like a piece of lettuce?
>
> *Subject:* Its shape and it has a vein up the middle. It is definitely a bee.
>
> *(Klopfer & Davidson, 1962, p. 164)*

In the early years, Rorschach testers paid special attention to the themes, images, and fantasies that the inkblots evoked, called the ***thematic content.*** Subjects who saw numerous water images, for example, were often thought to be grappling with alcoholism, whereas those who saw bizarre images or saw themselves in the blots might be suffering from schizophrenia. Testers now pay more attention to the ***style*** of subjects' responses: Do the subjects view the design as a whole or see specific details? Do they focus on the blots or on the white spaces between them? Do they use or ignore the shadings and colors in several of the cards? Do they see human movement in the designs, animal movement, animals engaged in human actions, or inanimate objects? Here is how the clinician interpreted the bug responses of the 32-year-old woman:

> The bee may reflect the image she has of herself as a hard worker (a fact noted by her supervisor). In addition, the "bee bringing up something edible for the rest of the clan" suggests that she feels an overwhelming sense of responsibility toward others.
>
> This card frequently evokes both masculine and feminine sexual associations, either in direct or symbolic form. Apparently [this woman] is not able to handle such material comfortably either overtly or in a more socialized manner, and so both sexual symbols are replaced by the oral symbolism of providing food.
>
> *(Klopfer & Davidson, 1962, pp. 182–183)*

Thematic Apperception Test The ***Thematic Apperception Test (TAT)*** is a pictorial projective test developed by the psychologist Henry A. Murray at the Harvard Psychological Clinic in 1935. People who take the TAT are commonly shown thirty black-and-white pictures of individuals in vague situations, and are asked to make up a dramatic story about each one. They must tell what is happening in the picture, what led up to it, what the characters are feeling and thinking, and what the outcome of the situation will be.

Clinicians who use the TAT believe that people identify with one of the characters on each card, called the

"RORSCHACH! WHAT'S TO BECOME OF YOU?"

hero. In their stories, people are thought to express their own circumstances, needs, environmental demands, emotions, and perceptions of reality and fantasy. For example, a female client seems to be identifying with the hero and revealing her own feelings in this story about the TAT picture shown in Figure 5-2, one of the few TAT pictures permitted for display in textbooks:

> This is a woman who has been quite troubled by memories of a mother she was resentful toward. She has feelings of sorrow for the way she treated her mother, her memories of her mother plague her. These feelings seem to be increasing as she grows older and sees her children treating her the same way that she treated her mother.
>
> *(Aiken, 1985, p. 372)*

As with Rorschach tests, clinicians evaluate TAT responses by looking not only at the content of the stories but also at the style of response to the cards (Cramer, 1996; Aiken, 1985). Slow or delayed responses, for example, are thought to indicate depression. Overcautiousness and preoccupation with details are thought to suggest obsessive thoughts and indecisiveness.

Figure 5-2 *A picture used in the Thematic Apperception Test. One client who made up a story about this card seemed to be revealing resentment toward her mother, regret over the way she had treated her mother, and sadness over her relationship with her children.*

Sentence-Completion Test The ***sentence-completion test,*** first developed in the 1920s (Payne, 1928), asks people to complete a series of unfinished sentences, such as "I wish______" or "My father______." The test can be taken without an examiner present. It is considered a good springboard for discussion and a quick and easy way to pinpoint topics to explore.

Drawings On the assumption that a drawing tells us something about its creator, clinicians often ask clients to draw human figures and talk about them. Evaluations of these drawings are based on the quality and shape of the drawing, solidity of the pencil line, location of the drawing on the paper, size of the figures, features of the figures, use of background, and comments made by the respondent during the drawing task.

The *Draw-a-Person Test (DAP)* is the most popular drawing test among clinicians (Machover, 1949). Subjects are first told to draw "a person"; that done, they are told to draw another person of the opposite sex. Some clinicians hold that a disproportionately large or small head may reflect problems in intellectual functioning, social balance, or control of body impulses, and that exaggerated eyes may indicate high levels of suspiciousness. Here is how a clinical assessor evaluated the DAP drawing in Figure 5-3, produced by a depressed man:

> He drew the large figure first; then when he saw that he could not complete the entire figure on the page, he drew the smaller figure. He momentarily paused, looked at both figures, said that the larger figure lacked a collar, picked up the pencil he had laid down, and drew the "collar" by slashing the pencil across the throat of the drawn male. It was almost as if . . . the patient were committing suicide on paper.
>
> *(Hammer, 1981, p. 170)*

The Value of Projective Tests Until the 1950s, projective tests were the dominant technique for assessing a client's personality. In recent years, however, clinicians and researchers have treated these tests more as sources of "supplementary" insights (Clark, 1995; Lerner & Lerner, 1988). One reason for this shift is that practitioners from the younger models have found these kinds of tests less useful than have psychodynamic clinicians and investigators (Kline, 1993). Even more important, the tests have rarely demonstrated impressive reliability or validity (Weiner, 1995; Lanyon, 1984).

In reliability studies, different clinicians have tended to score the same person's projective test quite differently (Little & Shneidman, 1959). Standardized procedures for

Figure 5-3 *Drawing by a depressed man on the Draw-a-Person Test. (From Hammer, 1981, p.171.)*

administering and scoring the tests have been developed and might improve their consistency if all practitioners used them (Exner, 1997, 1993; Franklin & Cornell, 1997; Weiner, 1995), but none has gained wide acceptance (Kline, 1993).

Research has also challenged the validity of projective tests (Kline, 1993). When clinicians are asked to describe a client's personality and feelings on the basis of responses to projective tests, their conclusions often fail to match those of the client's psychotherapist or those gathered from an extensive case history (Golden, 1964; Sines, 1959; Kostlan, 1954).

Another validity problem is that projective tests are sometimes biased against minority ethnic groups. People are, for example, supposed to identify with the characters in the Thematic Apperception Test (TAT) when they make up stories about them, yet no members of minority groups are depicted. In response to this problem, some clinicians have developed other TAT-like tests with African American or Hispanic figures (Ritzler, 1996; Constantino et al., 1988).

Personality Inventories An alternative way to understand individual clients is to ask them to assess themselves. The ***personality inventory*** asks respondents a wide range of questions about their behavior, beliefs, and feelings. The typical personality inventory consists of a series of statements, and subjects are asked to indicate whether or not each statement applies to them. Clinicians then use the responses to draw broad conclusions about the person's traits and psychological functioning.

Minnesota Multiphasic Personality Inventory By far the most widely used personality inventory is the ***Minnesota Multiphasic Personality Inventory*** (***MMPI***) (Colligan & Offord, 1992). Two versions of this test are available—the original test, published in 1945, and the ***MMPI-2,*** a 1989 revision. Currently the two versions are competing for clinicians' favor.

The traditional MMPI consists of 550 self-statements, to be labeled "true," "false," or "cannot say." Respondents describe their physical concerns; mood; morale; attitudes toward religion, sex, and social activities; and possible tendencies toward psychological dysfunctioning, such as phobias and hallucinations.

The inventory was constructed by a method called ***criterion keying.*** Statements were gathered from existing scales of personal and social attitudes, from textbooks, from medical and neurological case-taking procedures, and from psychiatric examination forms. The authors then asked 724 "normal" people (hospital visitors) and 800 hospitalized mental patients to indicate whether or not each statement was true for them. Only statements that differentiated the hospitalized subjects from normal subjects were incorporated in the inventory.

The items in the MMPI make up ten clinical scales:

HS (hypochondriasis) Items showing abnormal concern with bodily functions ("I have chest pains several times a week").

Drawing tests are commonly used to assess the functioning of children. Two popular tests are the House-Tree-Person test, in which subjects draw a house, tree, and person; and the Kinetic Family Drawing test, in which subjects draw their household members engaged in some activity ("kinetic" means "active").

Clinicians often view works of art as informal projective tests in which artists reveal their conflicts and mental stability. The sometimes bizarre cat portraits of the early twentieth-century artist Louis Wain, for example, have been interpreted as reflections of the psychosis with which he struggled for many years. Others believe such interpretations to be incorrect, however, and note that the decorative patterns in some of his later paintings were actually based on textile designs.

D (depression) Items showing extreme pessimism and hopelessness ("I often feel hopeless about the future").

Hy (conversion hysteria) Items from patients who use physical or mental symptoms as a way of unconsciously avoiding difficult conflicts and responsibilities ("My heart frequently pounds so hard I can feel it").

PD (psychopathic deviate) Items showing a repeated and flagrant disregard for social customs and an emotional shallowness ("My activities and interests are often criticized by others").

Mf (masculinity-femininity) Items that are thought to differentiate between male and female respondents ("I like to arrange flowers").

Pa (paranoia) Items that show abnormal suspiciousness and delusions of grandeur or persecution ("There are evil people trying to influence my mind").

Pt (psychasthenia) Items that show obsessions, compulsions, abnormal fears, and guilt and indecisiveness ("I save nearly everything I buy, even after I have no use for it").

Sc (schizophrenia) Items that show bizarre or unusual thoughts or behavior, including extreme withdrawal, delusions, or hallucinations ("Things around me do not seem real").

Ma (hypomania) Items that show emotional excitement, overactivity, and flight of ideas ("At times I feel very 'high' or very 'low' for no apparent reason").

Si (social introversion) Items that show shyness, little interest in people, and insecurity ("I am easily embarrassed").

Scores for each scale can range from 0 to 120. When people score above 70, their functioning on that scale is considered deviant. When the scores are connected on a graph, a pattern called the person's ***profile*** takes shape, indicating the person's general personality style and underlying emotional needs (Graham, 1993; Meehl, 1951). Figure 5-4 shows the MMPI profile of J. A. K., a depressed 27-year-old man. It suggests that he is very depressed, feels anxious and threatened, is socially withdrawn, and is prone to somatic complaints.

Each person approaches a personality inventory such as the MMPI with a particular ***response set,*** a tendency to respond in fixed ways. Some people tend to respond affirmatively to statements irrespective of their content ("yea-sayers"). Others try to answer in ways that they believe are socially desirable. Obviously, their MMPI scores will be misleading (Rogers et al., 1995). For this reason additional scales have been built into the MMPI to detect response sets (Berry et al., 1995; Iverson, Franzen, & Hammond, 1995).

The ***L scale,*** or lie scale, consists of items that test whether a person is answering dishonestly. People who keep answering true to such items as "I smile at everyone I meet" and false to items like "I gossip a little at times" receive a high L score. Similarly, the MMPI includes items that help indicate whether people are *careless* test takers (the ***F scale***) or *defensive* test takers who keep trying to protect their own image (***K scale***). If an individual scores high on the L, F, or K scale, clinicians may alter their MMPI conclusions or pronounce the test results invalid.

MMPI-2 A new version of the MMPI contains 567 items—many identical to those in the original, some rewritten to reflect contemporary language ("upset stomach," for instance, replaces "acid stomach"), and

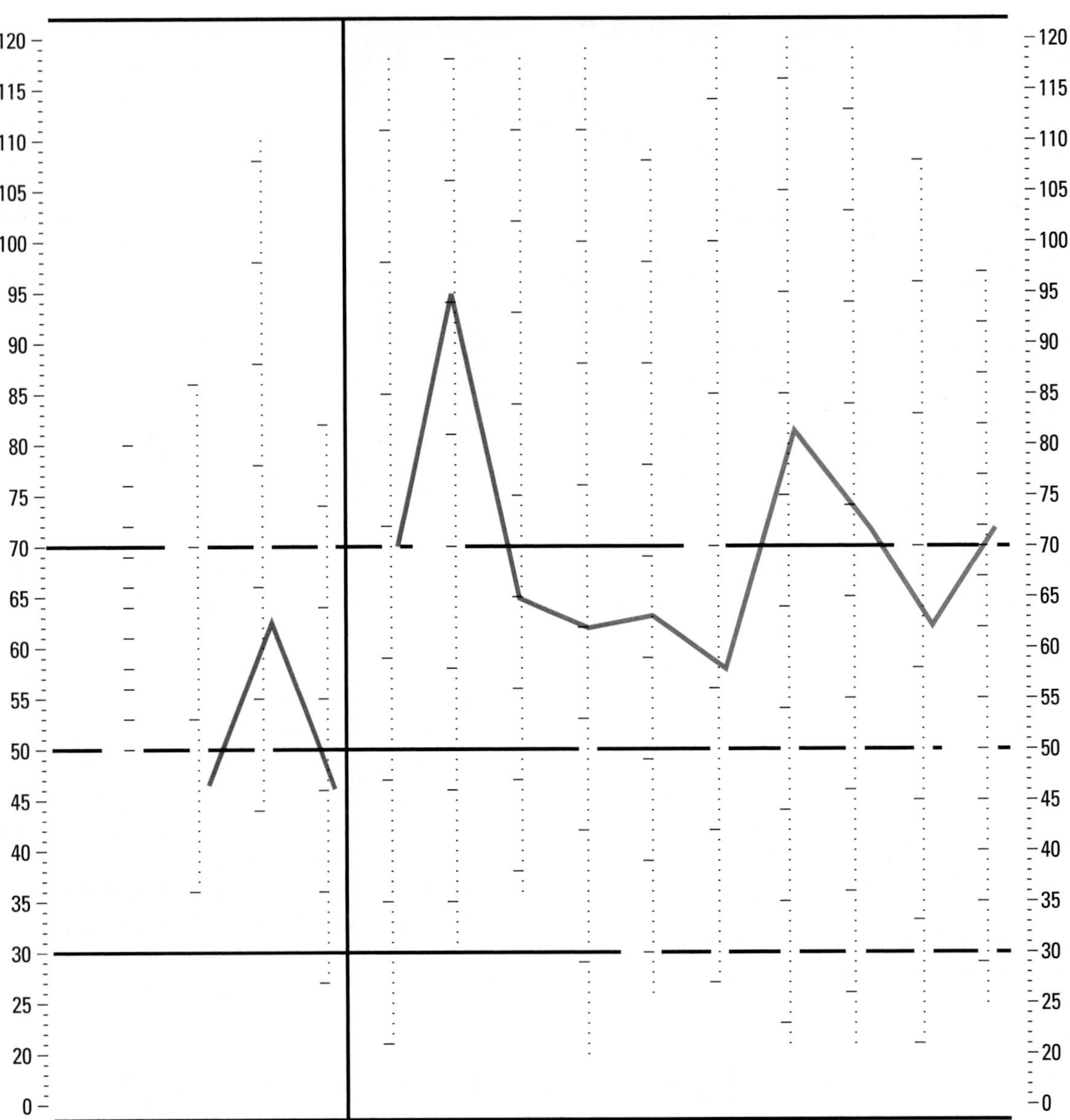

Figure 5-4 *The MMPI profile of J. A. K., a 27-year-old man, suggests that he is depressed. He also appears to be anxious, prone to somatic complaints, indecisive, introverted, and insecure. (From Graham, 1977, p. 164.)*

others that are new. To the ten basic scales, which are the same as in the original, the MMPI-2 adds several new scales that measure such things as a vulnerability to eating disorders, a tendency to abuse drugs, and poor functioning at work.

Many clinicians have welcomed the MMPI–2 as a valuable improvement and appropriate update. Others, however, believe that the new test may never be an adequate substitute for the original and that the large body of research conducted on the original MMPI may not be applicable to the MMPI–2 (Humphrey & Dahlstrom, 1995). Any decision to shelve one of the versions awaits the outcome of current research (Johnson et al., 1996; Bagby et al., 1995).

The Value of Personality Inventories The MMPI and other personality inventories have several advantages over projective tests. They are paper-and-pencil tests that do not take much time to administer, and they are objectively and easily scored. In addition, they are usually standardized, so that one person's scores can be compared with many others'. Moreover, they usually display greater test–retest reliability than projective tests. For example, people who take the MMPI a second time after an interval of less than two weeks receive approximately the same scores; studies have found the reliability correlation to be as high as .85 (Graham, 1987, 1977).

Although personality inventories also appear to have greater validity, or accuracy, than projective tests (Graham & Lilly, 1984), they can hardly be considered *highly* valid. When clinicians use these tests alone, they have not typically been able to judge a subject's personality accurately (Johnson et al., 1996; Shedler et al., 1993). One problem is that the personality traits that the tests seek to measure cannot be verified directly. How can we fully know a person's character, emotions, and needs from his or her words and actions alone?

Another problem is the tests' inability to take cultural differences into consideration. Test responses suggesting a mental disorder in one culture may be normal responses in another. In Puerto Rico, for example, where it is common to practice spiritualism, it would be normal to answer "true" to the MMPI item "Evil spirits possess me at times." In most U.S. residents, that response may indicate psychopathology (Rogler, Malgady, & Rodriguez, 1989).

Despite their limited validity, personality inventories continue to be popular assessment tools (Archer, 1997). Research indicates that they can help clinicians draw clearer pictures of people's characteristics and disorders as long as they are used *in combination* with interviews or other assessment tools (Levitt, 1989).

Response Inventories Like personality inventories, ***response inventories*** ask people to provide detailed information about themselves, but these tests focus on one specific area of functioning. They may, for example, measure affect (emotion), social skills, or cognitive processes. Clinicians can then better determine the role these factors play in the person's disorder.

Affective inventories measure the severity of such emotions as anxiety, depression, and anger (Beidel, Turner, & Morris, 1995). In one of the most widely used affective inventories, the Beck Depression Inventory, shown in Table 5-1, people rate how sad they feel and how depressed their functioning is across a number of spheres. ***Social skill inventories,*** used particularly by behavioral and sociocultural clinicians, ask respondents to indicate how they would react in a variety of social situations (Wiggins & Trobst, 1997). ***Cognition inventories*** disclose a client's typical thoughts and assumptions, uncovering counterproductive patterns of thinking that may be at the root of abnormal functioning (Burgess & Haaga, 1994). They are, not surprisingly, often used by cognitive therapists and researchers.

Because response inventories collect information directly from the subjects themselves, they have strong face validity. As a consequence, both the number of these tests and the number of clinicians who use them have increased steadily in the past two decades. At the same time, however, these inventories have significant limitations (Shedler et al., 1993). Unlike the personality inventories, they rarely include questions to indicate whether people are being careless or inaccurate in their accounts. Moreover, with the notable exception of the Beck inventory and some other tests, only some of the response

TABLE 5-1 Sample Items from the Beck Depression Inventory

Items		*Inventory*
Suicidal ideas	0	I don't have any thought of killing myself.
	1	I have thoughts of killing myself but I would not carry them out.
	2	I would like to kill myself.
	3	I would kill myself if I had the chance.
Work inhibition	0	I can work about as well as before.
	1	It takes extra effort to get started at doing something.
	2	I have to push myself very hard to do anything.
	3	I can't do any work at all.
Loss of libido	0	I have not noticed any recent change in my interest in sex.
	1	I am less interested in sex than I used to be.
	2	I am much less interested in sex now.
	3	I have lost interest in sex completely.

inventories have been subjected to rigorous standardization, reliability, and validity procedures (Sanderman & Ormel, 1992). Often they are improvised as the need for them arises, without being tested for accuracy and consistency.

Psychophysiological Tests A number of clinicians use ***psychophysiological tests,*** which measure physiological responses (Stoyva & Budzynski, 1993). The interest in these measures began when several studies suggested that states of anxiety are regularly accompanied by physiological changes, particularly increases in heart rate, body temperature, blood pressure, electrical resistance in the skin (*galvanic skin response*), and muscle contraction. Because measures of these changes were often more precise indicators of anxiety than interviews, projective tests, personality inventories, or response inventories, behavioral and cognitive clinicians began using them in their functional analyses (Cook et al., 1988; Lang, 1985). The measuring of physiological changes has since become integral to the assessment of many psychological disorders.

Psychophysiological tests are used widely to help assess sexual disorders. The ***vaginal plethysmograph,*** for example, is used to measure sexual arousal in women. This test instrument, a small tampon-shaped probe with a light at its end, is placed in a woman's vagina to measure the amount of light reflected by the vaginal wall. The reflected light increases when the wall arteries receive additional blood—that is, when the woman is sexually aroused. Studies find that this instrument does detect a difference when female subjects are watching erotic films (Wincze & Lange, 1981; Heiman, 1977). As Box 5-1 indicated, a ***penile plethysmograph,*** sometimes called a *strain gauge,* is used to measure sexual arousal in men.

Psychophysiological tests have also been used to help assess and treat medical problems, such as headaches and hypertension (high blood pressure), which might be related to a person's psychological state. As we shall see in

BOX 5-2 Taking Pictures of the Brain

For many years X rays and surgery were the only means scientists had of looking at a living brain. Both methods reveal aspects of a brain's structure, but neither provides much information about its actual functioning. Moreover, surgery is highly "invasive" (the surgeon cuts open the skull and perhaps cuts into—and damages—healthy tissue), and X rays do not provide detailed views of the brain's structure. In the past several decades other techniques have emerged to permit researchers and clinicians to obtain detailed recordings of the brain's physical makeup and activity without invading the tissue (Olfson, 1992).

Electroencephalogram (EEG)

The EEG is a record of the electrical activity of the brain. Electrodes placed on the scalp send brain-wave impulses to a machine called an oscillograph, which amplifies and records them. When the encephalogram reveals an abnormal brain-wave pattern, or ***dysrhythmia,*** clinicians suspect the existence of abnormalities such as brain lesions, and they proceed to use more precise and sophisticated techniques to ascertain the nature and scope of the problem.

Computerized Axial Tomography (CAT)

The CAT scan is a widely used procedure that has proved invaluable for locating brain structures. A machine passes a beam of X rays through the brain, and this beam is recorded by an X-ray detector on the other side of the patient's head. This procedure creates a thin, horizontal picture of a single cross section of the brain. The procedure is repeated many times over the patient's entire head. A computer then combines the many cross-sectional views to construct a complete three-dimensional picture of the brain. Though the CAT scan does not provide information about the activity of the brain, it is extremely useful for identifying the precise locations, sizes, and shapes of various structures. It reveals tumors, injuries, and anatomical abnormalities much more clearly than a conventional X ray, providing researchers and clinicians with important information about the correlation between a person's behavior and the physical characteristics of his or her brain. Diagnosticians have found that the scans of persons who suffer from psychological disorders often deviate noticeably from the CAT scans of people who display no behavioral abnormality.

Positron Emission Tomography (PET)

The development of PET has made it possible to watch the brain in action. A harmless radioactive isotope is injected into the patient's bloodstream and travels to the

Chapter 6, clinical researchers have discovered that these problems can sometimes be helped by ***biofeedback,*** a technique in which clients are given systematic information about key physiological responses as they occur and learn gradually to control them (Blanchard, 1994; Norris & Fahrion, 1993; Stoyva & Budzynski, 1993). When people who have frequent tension headaches, for example, are given detailed feedback about the levels of tension in their head muscles, many can learn to relax those muscles at will, and the frequency of their headaches declines.

Like other kinds of clinical tests, however, psychophysiological tests pose problems for clinicians. One is logistical. Many psychophysiological tests require expensive recording equipment that must be carefully maintained and expertly calibrated (Nelson, 1981). Moreover, psychophysiological measurements can be inaccurate and unreliable. The laboratory equipment itself—impressive, unusual, and sometimes frightening—may arouse a subject's nervous system and thus alter a subject's typical physiological responses. Physiological responses may also change when they are measured repeatedly in a single session. Galvanic skin responses, for example, often decrease upon repeated testing, and genital arousal responses may lessen because of fatigue.

Neuropsychological Tests

Some problems in personality or behavior are caused primarily by neurological damage in the brain or alterations in brain activity. Head injuries, brain tumors, brain malfunctions, alcoholism, infections, and other disorders can all cause such organic impairment. If a psychological dysfunction is to be treated effectively, it is important to know whether it stems primarily from some physiological abnormality in the brain (see Box 5-2).

Neurological problems can sometimes be detected through brain surgery and biopsy; brain X rays; a ***computerized axial tomogram (CAT scan),*** in which X rays

---

brain. The isotope also emits subatomic particles—positrons—that collide with electrons to produce photons. The photons are detected by a sensitive electronic device and recorded in a computer. The more physically active parts of the brain receive more of the isotope than the less active regions and produce a greater number of photons. The computer translates these data into a moving picture of the brain in which levels of blood flow and brain activity are represented by various colors. Studies have demonstrated some fascinating correlations between specific kinds of brain activity and specific psychological disorders. PET scans of patients with obsessive-compulsive disorder, for example, show increased activity in the caudate nuclei structures, and those of patients with a bipolar disorder tend to show increased activity in the right temporal region during manic episodes.

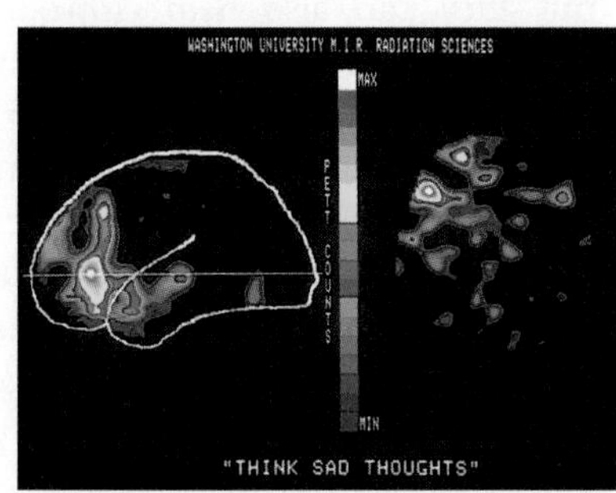

A PET scan of a person thinking sad thoughts reveals which areas of brain activity (shown in red, orange, and yellow) are related to such mood changes.

A high-speed "echo-planar" MRI reveals the reaction of a patient with an obsessive-compulsive disorder to "an envelope soiled with illicit drugs."

Magnetic Resonance Imaging (MRI)

MRI, the most recent development in brain-imaging techniques, provides information on both the structure and the function of the brain and does not require any form of radiation. In this highly complex and elegant procedure a person lies on a machine that creates a magnetic field around his or her head, causing the hydrogen atoms in the brain to line up. When the magnet is turned off, the atoms return to their normal positions, emitting magnetic signals in the process. The signals are recorded, read by a computer, and translated into a detailed and accurate picture of the brain. In many cases MRI is so precise that the image it produces looks more like a photograph of the brain than a typical computer-produced image. MRI is believed to reflect the composition of cells and may be critical in detecting damaged areas of the brain containing different concentrations of hydrogen.

of the brain are taken at different angles; an ***electroencephalogram (EEG),*** a recording of electrical impulses in the brain gathered by wires attached to the scalp; a ***positron emission tomogram (PET scan),*** a computer-produced motion picture of rates of metabolism throughout the brain; or ***magnetic resonance imaging (MRI),*** a complex procedure that uses the magnetic property of certain atoms in the brain to create a detailed picture of the brain's structure.

Subtle brain abnormalities, however, may escape detection by these techniques. Clinicians have therefore developed less direct but sometimes more revealing ***neuropsychological tests.*** These tests measure a person's cognitive, perceptual, and motor performances and interpret abnormal performances as indicators of broader neurological problems (Butters et al., 1995; Matarazzo, 1992). Neurological damage is especially likely to affect visual perception, recent memory, and visual-motor coordination, and so neuropsychological tests focus particularly on these areas of performance.

The ***Bender Visual-Motor Gestalt Test*** (Bender, 1938), one of the most widely used neuropsychological tests, consists of nine cards, each displaying a simple design (see Figure 5-5). Test subjects look at the designs one at a time and copy each one on a piece of paper. Later they try to reproduce the designs from memory. By the age of 12, most people can remember and copy the designs accurately. Notable errors in the accuracy of the drawings are thought to reflect organic brain impairment.

Electrodes pasted to a patient's scalp detect electrical impulses from the brain. The impulses are then amplified and converted into ink tracings on a roll of graph paper to produce an electroencephalogram (EEG). The EEG, used here to measure the brain waves of a 4-month-old being stimulated with toys, is only a gross indicator of the brain's activity.

The test can *generally* distinguish people with organic impairments in approximately 75 percent of cases, suggesting relatively high validity (Heaton, Baade, & Johnson, 1978). However, no single neuropsychological test can consistently distinguish one *specific* kind of neurological impairment from another (Goldstein, 1990). This is the major limitation of all the neuropsychological tests. At best they are rough and general screening devices for neurological impairment.

To achieve greater precision and accuracy, clinicians frequently use a comprehensive series, or ***battery,*** of neuropsychological tests, each targeting a specific neurological skill. The highly regarded *Halstead-Reitan Neuropsychology Battery* consists of numerous tests that measure sensorimotor, perceptual, and memory skills. The shorter *Luria-Nebraska Battery* is also widely used by today's clinicians (Reitan & Wolfson, 1985; Halstead, 1947).

Intelligence Tests

There is little agreement about the precise nature of intelligence, although most educators and clinicians agree in a general way with an early definition of intelligence as "the capacity to judge well, to reason well, and to comprehend well" (Binet & Simon, 1916, p. 192). Because intelligence is an inferred quality rather than a specific physical process or entity, it can be measured only indirectly. In 1905 the French psychologist Alfred Binet and his associate Theodore Simon produced an ***intelligence test*** consisting of a series of tasks that require people to use various verbal and nonverbal skills. The general score derived from this and subsequent intelligence tests is termed an ***intelligence quotient,*** or ***IQ,*** so called because initially it represented the ratio of a person's "mental" age to his or her "chronological" age, multiplied by 100 (see Figure 5-6).

There are now more than 100 intelligence tests, including the widely used *Wechsler Adult Intelligence Scale, Wechsler Intelligence Scale for Children,* and *Stanford-Binet Intelligence Scale.* As we shall discuss in Chapter 19, intelligence tests play a large role in the diagnosis of mental retardation, but they can also help clinicians identify other problems, such as neurological disorders (Hackerman et al., 1996; Skelton, Boik, & Madero, 1995).

Intelligence tests are among the most carefully constructed of all clinical tests. Large standardization samples have been used to calibrate the major ones, so that clinicians have a good idea how each person's score compares with the performance of the population at large. These tests have also demonstrated very high reliability: people who take the same IQ test years apart receive approximately the same scores (Kline, 1993). Finally, the major IQ tests appear to have relatively high validity: children's IQ scores correlate fairly highly with their performance in school, for example (Neisser et al., 1996).

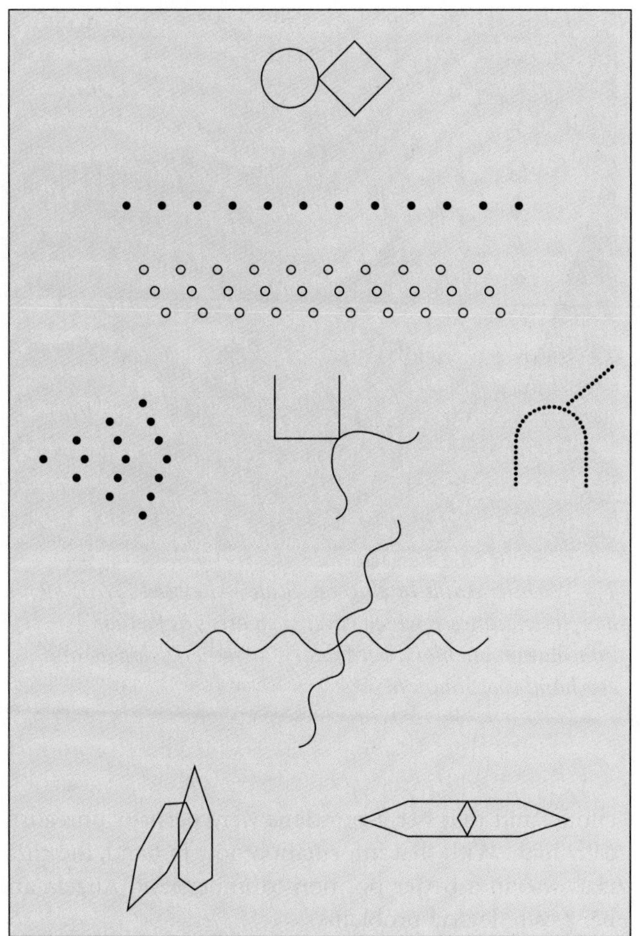

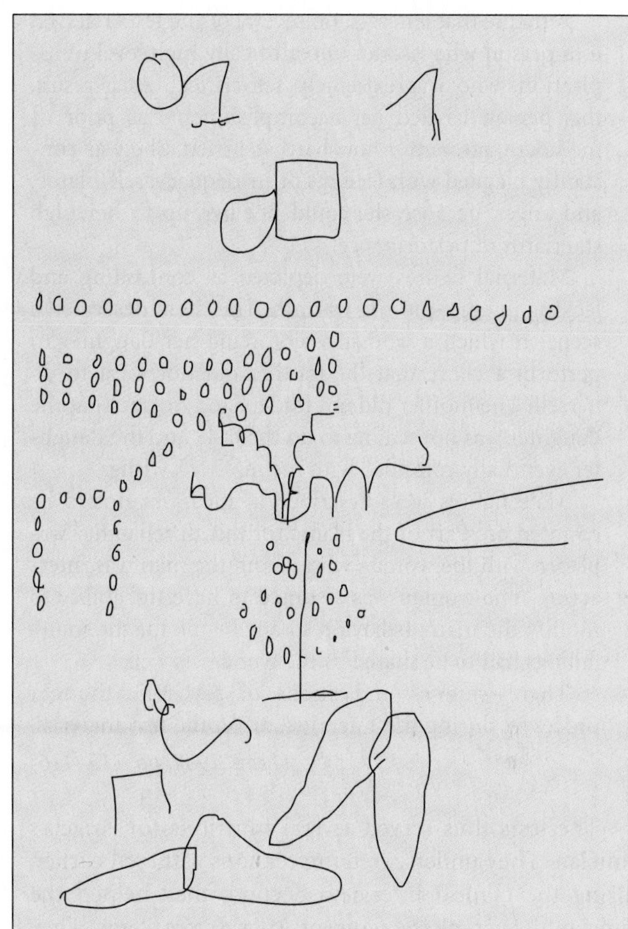

Figure 5-5 *In the Bender Gestalt Test subjects copy each of nine designs on a piece of paper, then produce them again from memory. Sizable errors in a drawing (as in the one on the right, which was done by a person with brain damage) may reflect organic brain dysfunction of some kind. (Adapted from Lacks, 1984, p. 33.)*

Nevertheless, intelligence tests have some significant shortcomings. Factors that have nothing to do with intelligence, such as low motivation and high anxiety, can greatly influence a person's performance (Van der Molen et al., 1995; Frederiksen, 1993, 1986). In addition, IQ tests may contain culturally biased language, items, or tasks that place people of one background at an advantage over those of another (Keitel et al., 1996; Neisser et al., 1996; Helms, 1992; Puente, 1990). Similarly, members of some minority groups may have relatively little experience with this kind of test, or they may be uncomfortable with test examiners of a majority ethnic background. Either way, their performances may well suffer.

Integrating Test Data It is unwise to put too much faith in any one clinical test. Most fall short on one or more of the three key criteria of standardization, reliability, and validity. Clinicians therefore usually administer a battery of tests to assess psychological functioning (Watkins et al., 1995), typically to clarify and supplement clinical interviews and observations.

Let us return to Angela Savanti, the depressed young woman we met at the beginning of the chapter. After interviewing Angela, her clinician collected additional data from a battery of tests, including the TAT, the MMPI, a depression inventory, and an intelligence test. The result was a detailed test report:

> The client scored in the average range of intelligence. The long reaction times to verbal stimuli and the slowness of her motor responses suggested an impairment in intellectual functioning. This slowness in verbal and motor behavior is consistent with the performance observed in persons who are depressed. The client's affect [feeling or emotion], as interpreted from the test material, was constricted and controlled. She appeared to react strongly to some of the events occurring around her, but she controlled her emotions so that other people were not aware of how she felt. . . .

> A theme that emerged on several of the tests referred to a person who had an unrealistically high level of aspiration, who was extremely self-critical. As a result, this person labeled her accomplishments as poor or mediocre, no matter how hard she tried. She was constantly plagued with feelings of inadequacy, self-blame, and anger, because she could not live up to her high standards of performance.
>
> Maternal figures were depicted as controlling and lacking in empathy and warmth. The client described a scene in which a woman was forcing her daughter to perform a chore that the mother did not want to do herself. The mother did not understand or care that the daughter was not willing to do the task, and the daughter eventually complied with the mother's wishes.
>
> Male figures were described as nice, but not to be counted on. Part of the blame for this unreliability was placed with the woman with whom the man was interacting. The woman was assumed to have the ability to modify the man's behavior, so any blame for the man's failings had to be shared by the woman as well.
>
> There were no indications of psychotic thought processes during the interview or on the test material.
>
> *(Leon, 1984, pp. 115–116)*

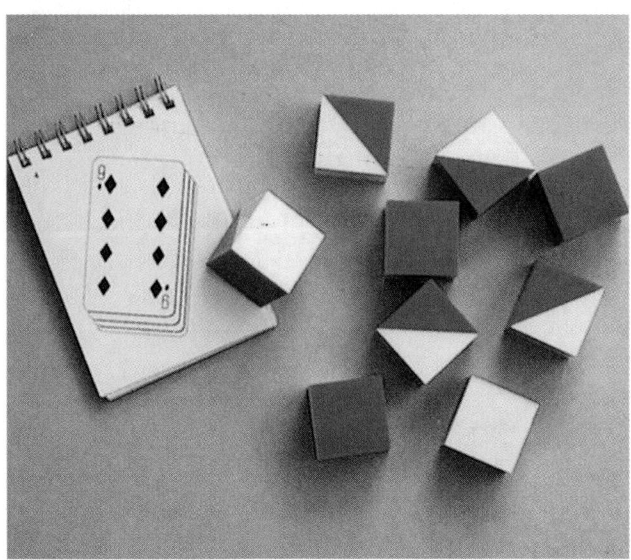

The Wechsler Adult Intelligence Scale—Revised (WAIS–R) has eleven subtests, which cover such areas as factual information, memory, vocabulary, arithmetic, design, and eye-hand coordination.

The tests thus served several functions for Angela's clinician. They underscored impressions gathered earlier, during the clinical interview. Second, they helped the clinician determine the scope of Angela's problems. They indicated, for example, that her depression was so pervasive that it even retarded her verbal and motor behavior, and her feelings of inadequacy, self-criticism, and anger were more enduring than the interview alone conveyed. Finally, the test data revealed that Angela's intellectual functioning was at least average, that she was not psychotic, and that her aspirations were perhaps unrealistically high. With that information now in hand, the clinician was in a better position to understand Angela and her psychological problems.

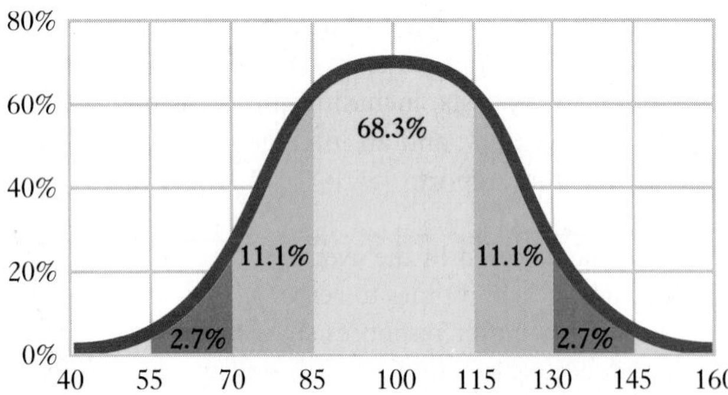

Figure 5-6 *The distribution of IQ scores in the population follows a "bell-shaped curve," an idealized graph in which the* mode, *or the most frequent score (in this case 100) is in the middle, and less frequent scores fall evenly on each side. More than two-thirds of all people score between 85 and 115 on IQ tests.*

Clinical Observations

In addition to interviewing and testing people, clinicians may follow specific strategies for observing their behavior (Stricker & Trierweiler, 1995). In one such technique, called ***naturalistic*** or ***in vivo*** (literally, "in the living") ***observation,*** clinicians observe clients in their everyday environments. ***Structured observation,*** in contrast, takes place in an artificial setting created in the clinician's office or laboratory. Finally, clients may observe themselves by ***self-monitoring.***

Naturalistic and Structured Observations

Most naturalistic clinical observations take place in homes, schools, institutions such as hospitals and prisons, and community settings. Observations have usually focused on parent-child, sibling-child, or teacher-child interactions and on fearful, aggressive, or disruptive behavior. Most often such observations are made by ***participant observers,*** key persons in the client's environment, and reported to the clinician.

When naturalistic observation is impractical, clinicians may choose to observe some clients in a structured setting. Interactions between parents and their children, for example, may be observed in an office or laboratory on videotape or from behind a one-way mirror (Field, 1977). Similarly, clinicians have used observation rooms to monitor married couples engaging in a disagreement, speech-anxious people giving a speech, alcoholic people drinking, and fearful people approaching an object they find frightening (Floyd, O'Farrell, & Goldberg, 1987).

Although it is helpful for a clinician actually to watch behavior that may be leading to a person's disturbances, these methods have several disadvantages as well. For one thing, clinical observations are not always reliable (Banister et al., 1994; Foster & Cone, 1986). It is quite possible for various clinicians who observe the same person to focus on different aspects of behavior, evaluate the person differently, and draw different conclusions. Careful training of observers and the use of observer checklists do, however, help increase the reliability of observations (Goodwin, 1995).

Second, observers may make errors that affect the validity, or accuracy, of their observations (Banister et al., 1994; Nietzel et al., 1994; Foster & Cone, 1986). The observer may suffer from ***overload*** and be unable to see or record all relevant behavior and events. Or the observer may experience ***observer drift,*** a steady deterioration in accuracy as a result of fatigue or of a gradual unintentional change in the criteria used when observations continue over a long period of time (O'Leary & Kent, 1973). Another possibility is ***observer bias***—the observer's judgments may be inappropriately influenced by information and expectations he or she already has about the client (Goodwin, 1995; Shuller & McNamara, 1980).

A subject's ***reactivity*** may also limit the validity of clinical observations; that is, his or her behavior may be affected by the very presence of the observer (Goodwin, 1995; Barker et al., 1994; Harris & Lahey, 1982). If schoolchildren are aware that someone special is watching them, for example, they may alter their usual classroom behavior, perhaps in the hope of impressing the observer.

Finally, clinical observations may lack ***cross-situational,*** or ***external, validity.*** A child who behaves aggressively in school is not necessarily aggressive at home or with friends after school. Because behavior is often specific to particular situations, observations in one setting cannot always be applied to other settings (Simpson & Halpin, 1986).

Self-Monitoring Earlier we considered personality and response inventories, assessment instruments in which subjects report their own behaviors, feelings, or cognitions. In a related procedure, ***self-monitoring,*** persons observe themselves and carefully record the frequency of certain behaviors, feelings, or cognitions *as they occur* throughout the day (Nietzel et al., 1994; Bornstein, Hamilton, & Bornstein, 1986). How *frequently,* for instance, does a drug user have an urge for drugs or a headache sufferer have a headache? What are the *circumstances* surrounding their responses?

Self-monitoring offers several advantages (Barker et al., 1994). First, it may be the only way to observe behavior that occurs relatively infrequently. Second, it is useful for behaviors—for example, smoking, drinking, or other drug use—that occur so frequently that any other comprehensive observation of them would be impossible. Third, self-monitoring may be the only way to observe and count private thoughts or perceptions. In one study a woman was having *auditory hallucinations,* hearing voices and sounds that were not really occurring around her. She monitored the hallucinations for her clinician by raising a finger and keeping it raised throughout each such experience (Turner, Hersen, & Bellack, 1977).

Like all other clinical assessment procedures, however, self-monitoring has drawbacks. Here too validity is often a problem (Barker et al., 1994). Clients do not always receive proper instruction in this form of observation; nor are they always motivated to record their observations accurately. Furthermore, when clients try to monitor themselves, they often do not behave as they normally do. Smokers, for example, often smoke fewer cigarettes than usual when they are monitoring themselves (Kilmann, Wagner, & Sotile, 1977), drug users take drugs less frequently (Hay, Hay, & Angle, 1977), and teachers give more positive and fewer negative comments to their students (Nelson, 1977).

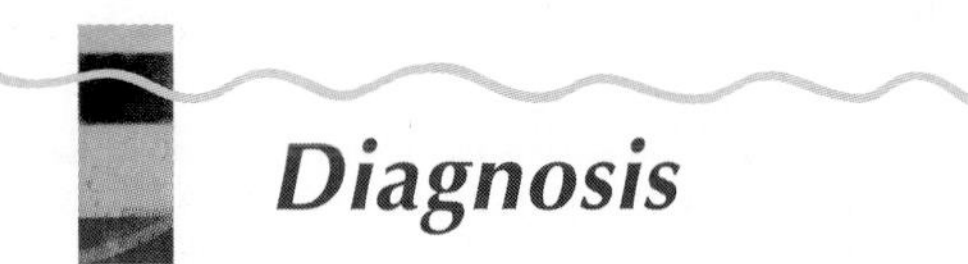

Diagnosis

Once clinicians complete their interviews, tests, and observations, they are in a position to draw broad conclusions about clients (Stricker & Trierweiler, 1995). These conclusions take the form of a ***clinical picture,*** an integrated picture of the various factors that are causing and sustaining the person's disturbed functioning.

Each clinician uses his or her own implicit rules to form a clinical picture (Ganzach, 1995; Nietzel et al., 1994). Some, for example, use an *additive,* or *linear, model* (Hammond & Summers, 1965); that is, they base their conclusions on how many assessment responses point in the same direction. As the number of concurring responses increases, the likelihood of a given conclusion increases as well.

The conclusions drawn by clinicians are also influenced by their theoretical orientation. The clinician who worked with Angela Savanti held a cognitive-behavioral view of abnormality, so the clinical picture of her emphasized modeling and reinforcement principles as well as the client's expectations, assumptions, and interpretations:

> Angela was rarely reinforced for any of her accomplishments at school, but she gained her mother's negative attention for what Mrs. Savanti judged to be poor performance at school or at home. Mrs. Savanti repeatedly told her daughter that she was incompetent, and any mishaps that happened to her were her own fault. . . . When Mr. Savanti deserted the family, Angela's first response was that somehow she was responsible. From her mother's past behavior, Angela had learned to expect that in some way she would be blamed. At the time that Angela broke up with her boyfriend, she did not blame Jerry for his behavior, but interpreted this event as a failing solely on her part. As a result, her level of self-esteem was lowered still more.
>
> The type of marital relationship that Angela saw her mother and father model remained her concept of what married life is like. She generalized from her observations of her parents' discordant interactions to an expectation of the type of behavior that she and Jerry would ultimately engage in. . . .
>
> Angela's uncertainties intensified when she was deprived of the major source of gratification she had, her relationship with Jerry. Despite the fact that she was overwhelmed with doubts about whether to marry him or not, she had gained a great deal of pleasure through being with Jerry. Whatever feelings she had been able to express, she had shared with him and no one else. Angela labeled Jerry's termination of their relationship as proof that she was not worthy of another person's interest. She viewed her present unhappiness as likely to continue, and she attributed it to some failing on her part. As a result, she became quite depressed.
>
> *(Leon, 1984, pp. 123–125)*

With the assessment data and clinical picture in hand, clinicians are able to make a ***diagnosis*** (from Greek for "a discrimination")—that is, a determination that a person's psychological problems constitute a particular disorder. When clinicians decide, through diagnosis, that a client's pattern of dysfunction reflects a particular disorder, they are saying that the pattern is basically the same as one that has been displayed by many other people, has been observed and investigated in a variety of studies, and perhaps has responded to particular forms of treatment (Bourgeois, 1995). If their diagnosis is correct, clinicians can fruitfully apply what is generally known about the disorder to the particular person they are trying to help. They can, for example, better predict the future course of the client's problem and the treatment strategies that are likely to be helpful.

Classification Systems

The principle behind diagnosis is straightforward. When certain symptoms regularly occur together (a cluster of symptoms is called a ***syndrome***) and follow a particular course, clinicians agree that those symptoms constitute a particular mental disorder. When people display this particular cluster and course of symptoms, diagnosticians assign them to that category. A comprehensive list of such categories, with a description of the symptoms characteristic of each and guidelines for assigning individuals to categories, is known as a ***classification system.***

As we saw in Chapter 1, Emil Kraepelin developed the first modern classification system for abnormal behavior in 1883. By collecting thousands of case studies of patients in mental hospitals, he was able to identify various syndromes and to describe each syndrome's apparent cause and expected course (Zilboorg & Henry, 1941). The categories of disorders established by Kraepelin have formed the foundation for the psychological part of the ***International Classification of Diseases,*** the classification system now used by the World Health Organization (Jablensky, 1995). This system, which covers both medical and psychological disorders, is currently in its tenth revision, known as ***ICD-10.***

Kraepelin's work has also been incorporated into the ***Diagnostic and Statistical Manual of Mental Disorders (DSM),*** a classification system developed by the Ameri-

Emil Kraepelin developed a system for classifying mental disorders, on which today's classification systems are built.

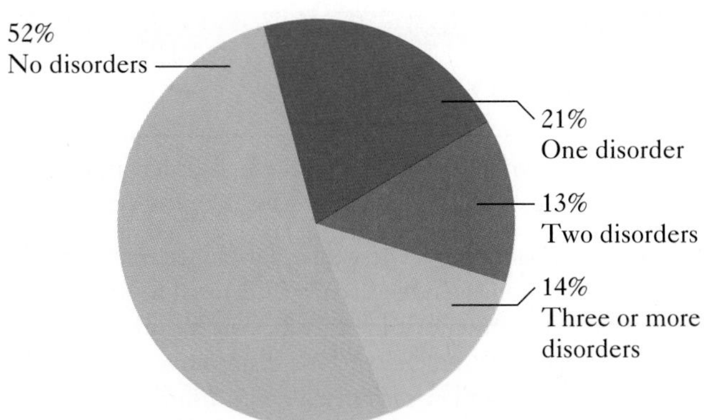

Figure 5-7 *How many people in the United States qualify for a DSM diagnosis during their lives? Almost half, according to one survey. In fact, 27 percent meet the criteria for two or more different disorders. In some cases these individuals even experience their disorders simultaneously, an occurrence known as "comorbidity." (Adapted from Kessler et al., 1994.)*

can Psychiatric Association. The DSM, like the ICD, has been changed over time. The current edition, ***DSM-IV,*** is by far the most widely used classification system in the United States today. The descriptions of mental disorders presented throughout this book adhere to the categories and distinctions in DSM-IV (see Figure 5-7).

Classification systems must be revised periodically as new findings emerge and perspectives change in the clinical field. The DSM was first published in 1952 (DSM-I) and has undergone major revisions in 1968 (DSM-II), 1980 (DSM-III), 1987 (DSM-III-R), and 1994 (DSM-IV). In a sense, then, a classification system actually freezes in time one moment in the history of a constantly changing clinical field (Talbott & Spitzer, 1980). This is not to say, however, that all clinicians agree whenever a new system or new categories are developed. Indeed, today's clinicians actively debate the merits of DSM-IV, just as clinicians continually argued over past versions of the DSM.

DSM-IV

DSM-IV lists close to 300 mental disorders. Each entry describes the criteria for diagnosing the disorder and its essential clinical features—the features that are invariably present. It also describes associated features, which are often but not invariably present, and age, culture, or gender trends. Finally, it includes a disorder's prevalence and risk, course, complications, predisposing factors, and family patterns.

The criteria in DSM-IV are more detailed and objective than those of the early versions of the DSM. DSM-IV focuses entirely on *verifiable* symptoms, for example, and stipulates that a person's dysfunction must include the specified symptoms if it is to qualify for a diagnosis. DSM-I and DSM-II, in contrast, required diagnosticians to infer the underlying cause of a disorder in order to make a diagnosis. To make a diagnosis of "anxiety neurosis" according to DSM-II, for example, diagnosticians first had to conclude that a person was experiencing internal conflicts and defending against anxiety. In DSM-IV such inferences are not required.

When clinicians use DSM-IV to make a diagnosis, they must evaluate a client's condition on five separate ***axes,*** or branches of information. This requirement forces diagnosticians to review and use a broad range of observations and data. First, clinicians must decide whether the client is displaying one or more of the disorders on ***Axis I,*** an extensive list of florid clinical syndromes that typically cause significant impairment (see Table 5-2). Some of the most common disorders listed on Axis I are the anxiety disorders and mood disorders—problems that we shall discuss at length in later chapters:

Anxiety disorders Anxiety is the predominant disturbance in this group of disorders. People with anxiety disorders may experience broad feelings of anxiety and worry (*generalized anxiety disorder*), anxiety concerning a specific situation or object (*phobia*), discrete periods of panic (*panic disorder*), persistent and recurrent thoughts or repetitive behaviors or both (*obsessive-compulsive disorder*), or lingering anxiety reactions to extraordinarily traumatic events (*acute stress disorder* and *posttraumatic stress disorder*).

Mood disorders Disorders in this group are marked by severe disturbances of mood. They cause people to feel extremely and inappropriately sad or elated for extended periods of time. These disorders include *major depressive disorder* and *bipolar disorder* (in which episodes of mania alternate with episodes of depression).

Next, diagnosticians must decide whether the client is displaying one of the disorders on ***Axis II,*** long-standing problems that are frequently overlooked in the presence of the disorders on Axis I. There are only two major categories of Axis II disorders, mental retardation and personality disorders. We shall also be observing these patterns again in later chapters:

Mental retardation People with this disorder display significant subaverage intellectual function-

TABLE 5-2 Axis I Disorders in DSM-IV

Disorders Usually First Diagnosed in Infancy, Childhood, and Adolescence Disorders in this group tend to emerge and sometimes dissipate before adult life. They include *pervasive developmental disorders* (such as *autism*), *learning disorders, attention-deficit hyperactivity disorder, conduct disorder,* and *separation anxiety disorder.*

Delirium, Dementia, Amnestic, and Other Cognitive Disorders These disorders are dominated by impairment in cognitive functioning. They include *Alzheimer's disease* and *Huntington's disease.*

Mental Disorders Due to a General Medical Condition These are mental disorders that are caused primarily by a general medical disorder. They include *mood disorder due to a general medical condition.*

Substance-Related Disorders These disorders are brought about by the use of substances that affect the central nervous system, such as *alcohol use disorders, opioid use disorders, amphetamine use disorders, cocaine use disorders,* and *hallucinogen use disorders.*

Schizophrenia and Other Psychotic Disorders In this group of disorders, functioning deteriorates until the patient reaches a state of *psychosis,* or loss of contact with reality.

Mood Disorders Disorders in this group are marked by severe disturbances of mood that cause people to feel extremely and inappropriately sad or elated for extended periods of time. They include *major depressive disorder* and *bipolar disorders.*

Anxiety Disorders Anxiety is the predominant disturbance in this group of disorders. They include *generalized anxiety disorder, phobias, panic disorder, obsessive-compulsive disorder, acute stress disorder,* and *posttraumatic stress disorder.*

Somatoform Disorders These disorders, marked by physical symptoms that apparently are caused primarily by psychological rather than physiological factors, include *conversion disorder, somatization disorder,* and *hypochondriasis.*

Factitious Disorders People with these disorders intentionally produce or feign physical or psychological symptoms.

Dissociative Disorders These disorders are characterized by significant changes in the usually integrated functions of consciousness, memory, identity, or perception, without a clear physical cause. They include *dissociative amnesia, dissociative fugue,* and *dissociative identity disorder (multiple personality disorder).*

Eating Disorders People with these disorders display abnormal patterns of eating that significantly impair their functioning. The disorders include *anorexia nervosa* and *bulimia nervosa.*

Sexual Disorders and Gender Identity Disorder These disorders in sexual functioning, behavior, or preferences include *sexual dysfunctions, paraphilias,* and *gender identity disorder.*

Sleep Disorders People with these disorders display chronic sleep problems. The disorders include *primary insomnia, primary hypersomnia, sleep terror disorder,* and *sleepwalking disorder.*

Impulse-Control Disorders People with these disorders are chronically unable to resist impulses, drives, or temptations to perform certain acts that are harmful to them or to others. The disorders include *pathological gambling, kleptomania, pyromania,* and *intermittent explosive disorders.*

Adjustment Disorders The primary feature of these disorders is a maladaptive reaction to a clear stressor such as divorce or business difficulties that occurs within three months after the onset of the stressor.

Other Conditions That May Be a Focus of Clinical Attention This category consists of conditions or problems that are worth noting because they cause significant impairment, such as *relational problems, problems related to abuse or neglect, medication-induced movement disorders,* and *psychophysiological disorders.*

ing by 18 years of age and concurrent deficits or impairment in adaptive function.

Personality disorders People with these disorders display an enduring, pervasive, inflexible, and maladaptive pattern of inner experience and outward behavior. People with *antisocial personality disorder,* for example, have a history of continuous and chronic disregard for and violation of the rights of others. People with *dependent personality disorder* manifest submissive, clinging behavior, along with fears of separation; they have an excessive need to be taken care of.

NORMAL

DOMINANT SYMPTOMATOLOGY: Characterized by unimpaired occupational, social, and sexual functioning for a period of one year or more. During this time individuals are free of neurotic or psychotic symptoms, i.e., anxiety, depression, hallucinations, or delusional thinking. Judgment is good, self-esteem high. Age onset: birth. More commonly diagnosed in the early twentieth century, this condition is rarely seen today.

As the list of mental disorders grows ever longer, some clinical observers believe that normal behavior is increasingly being viewed as the somewhat drab absence of abnormal functioning.

Although people usually receive a diagnosis on *either* Axis I or Axis II, they may receive diagnoses on both axes. Angela Savanti would first receive a diagnosis of *major depressive disorder* on Axis I (one of the mood disorders). Compare her pattern of dysfunction with the DSM-IV criteria:

> **A.** At least five symptoms of depression (for example, daily depressed mood, daily diminished interest in almost all activities, daily loss of energy) have been present during the same two-week period and represent a change from previous functioning.
>
> **B.** The symptoms cause clinically significant distress or impairment in social, occupational, or other important areas of functioning.

Let us suppose that the diagnostician judged that Angela had also displayed a life history of chronic dependent behavior. Perhaps she had submitted and clung to others, required them to take care of her, and subordinated her own needs to those of others. In this case, she would also receive an Axis II diagnosis of *dependent personality disorder.*

The remaining axes of DSM-IV guide diagnosticians to recognize and report other relevant information. ***Axis III*** information includes any relevant general medical condition from which the person is currently suffering. ***Axis IV*** information includes pertinent psychosocial or environmental problems the person is facing, such as school or housing problems. And ***Axis V*** information is a *global assessment of functioning (GAF),* the diagnostician's rating of the person's overall level of psychological, social, and occupational functioning.

If Angela Savanti had diabetes, for example, the clinician might include that under Axis III information. Angela's recent breakup with her boyfriend would be noted on Axis IV. And because she seemed moderately impaired at the time of diagnosis, Angela's global assessment of functioning would probably be rated approximately 55 on Axis V, in accordance with DSM-IV's *Global Assessment of Functioning Scale* (see Table 5-3). The complete diagnosis for Angela Savanti would then be:

Axis I: Major depressive disorder

Axis II: Dependent personality disorder

Axis III: Diabetes

Axis IV: Problem related to the social environment (termination of engagement)

Axis V: GAF = 55 (current)

TABLE 5-3 Global Assessment of Functioning (GAF) Scale

Consider psychological, social, and occupational functioning on a hypothetical continuum of mental health–illness. Do not include impairment in functioning due to physical (or environmental) limitations

Code	*Functioning*
100–91	Superior functioning in a wide range of activities, life's problems never seem to get out of hand, is sought out by others because of his or her many positive qualities. No symptoms.
90–81	Absent or minimal symptoms (e.g., mild anxiety before an exam), good functioning in all areas, interested and involved in a wide range of activities, socially effective, generally satisfied with life, no more than everyday problems or concerns (e.g., an occasional argument with family members).
80–71	If symptoms are present, they are transient and expectable reactions to psychosocial stressors (e.g., difficulty concentrating after family argument); no more than slight impairment in social, occupational, or school functioning (e.g., temporarily falling behind in schoolwork).
70–61	Some mild symptoms (e.g., depressed mood and mild insomnia) **or** some difficulty in social, occupational, or school functioning (e.g., occasional truancy, or theft within the household), but generally functioning pretty well, has some meaningful interpersonal relationships.
60–51	Moderate symptoms (e.g., flat affect and circumstantial speech, occasional panic attacks) **or** moderate difficulty in social, occupational, or school functioning (e.g., few friends, conflicts with peers or co-workers).
50–41	Serious symptoms (e.g., suicidal ideation, severe obsessional rituals, frequent shoplifting) **or** any serious impairment in social, occupational, or school functioning (e.g., no friends, unable to keep a job).
40–31	Some impairment in reality testing or communication (e.g., speech is at times illogical, obscure, or irrelevant) **or** major impairment in several areas, such as work or school, family relations, judgment, thinking, or mood (e.g., depressed man avoids friends, neglects family, and is unable to work; child frequently beats up younger children, is defiant at home, and is failing at school).
30–21	Behavior is considerably influenced by delusions or hallucinations **or** serious impairment in communication or judgment (e.g., sometimes incoherent, acts grossly inappropriately, suicidal preoccupation) **or** inability to function in almost all areas (e.g., stays in bed all day; no job, home, or friends).
20–11	Some danger of hurting self or others (e.g., suicide attempts without clear expectation of death; frequently violent; manic excitement) **or** occasionally fails to maintain minimal personal hygiene (e.g., smears feces) **or** gross impairment in communication (e.g., largely incoherent or mute).
10–1	Persistent danger of severely hurting self or others (e.g., recurrent violence) **or** persistent inability to maintain minimal personal hygiene **or** serious suicidal act with clear expectation of death.
0	Inadequate information.

Note: Use intermediate codes when appropriate; e.g., 45, 68, 72.

Source: APA, 1994.

Because DSM-IV uses several kinds of diagnostic information, each defined by a different "axis," it is known as a ***multiaxial*** system. The diagnoses arrived at under this classification system are expected to be more informative and more carefully considered than those derived from the early DSMs.

Reliability and Validity in Classification

A diagnostic classification system, like an assessment method, is judged by its reliability and validity. Here *reliability* means that different diagnosticians agree that a given pattern of observed behavior should be assigned to a given category. If different diagnosticians keep arriving at different diagnoses after observing the same behavior, the classification system is not very reliable.

Early versions of the DSM were only moderately reliable (Nietzel et al., 1994). In the early 1960s, four clinicians, each relying on DSM-I, independently interviewed 153 patients recently admitted to a mental hospital (Beck et al., 1962). Only 54 percent of their diagnoses were in agreement. Because all four clinicians were experienced diagnosticians, their failure to agree suggested deficiencies in the DSM-I classification system. To improve reliability, later versions of the DSM sought to remove vague descriptions of categories and categories defined by underlying causes. Yet even with the clearer and more objective criteria provided by DSM-III and DSM III-R, studies rarely found more than 70 percent agreement among diagnosticians (DiNardo et al., 1993; Kirk & Kutchins, 1992).

DSM-IV appears to have greater reliability than any of its predecessors (APA, 1994). Its framers began with comprehensive reviews of relevant research, so that they could pinpoint which categories in past DSMs were indeed producing low reliability (Livesley, 1995; APA, 1994). After developing new diagnostic criteria and categories, they conducted extensive *field trials* with 6,000 subjects at more than 70 sites to make sure that the new criteria and categories were indeed reliable. Still, many clinicians suggest that we must wait until DSM-IV is more widely used and tested by the clinical community at large before making any assumptions about its reliability (Klein, 1995; Kirk & Kutchins, 1992).

The *validity* of a classification system is the accuracy of the information that a diagnostic category provides about the people assigned to that category and about their symptoms. Categories are of most use to clinicians when they demonstrate ***predictive validity***—that is, when they help predict future symptoms or events. A common symptom of major depressive disorder, for example, is insomnia or hypersomnia (excessive sleep). When clinicians give Angela Savanti a diagnosis of major depressive disorder, they expect that she may eventually develop this symptom even though she does not manifest it now. Moreover, they expect her to respond to treatments that are effective for other depressed persons. The more often such predictions are accurate, the greater a given category's predictive validity.

DSM-IV's framers tried to maximize the validity of this newest version of the DSM by again conducting

The power of labeling is revealed in this late nineteenth-century photograph of a baseball team at the State Homeopathic Asylum for the Insane, in Middletown, New York. Most observers assume that the players are patients, and they "see" depression or confusion in the players' faces and posture. In fact, the players are members of the asylum staff, some of whom even sought their jobs in order to play for the hospital team.

BOX 5-3 The Battle over Premenstrual Dysphoric Disorder

Some categories of mental dysfunctioning are much more controversial than others. Clinicians and the public battle over their usefulness and appropriateness. After long and heated discussions almost two decades ago, for example, DSM-III dropped *homosexuality* as a category of mental dysfunctioning, citing a lack of evidence and concern about the social implications of calling this sexual orientation abnormal. Battles were equally fierce in 1987 when many practitioners wanted to include *self-defeating* (or *masochistic*) *personality disorder* in DSM to describe persons who are drawn repeatedly to relationships or situations in which they suffer. Critics saw this as a female-targeted category that perpetuated the stereotype of abused women as the instigators of damaging relationships rather than the victims of them. The framers of DSM-III-R postponed a decision, designating the category as one "for further study." DSM-IV has dropped it altogether.

Perhaps the biggest controversy in the development of DSM-IV centered on the category *premenstrual dysphoric disorder (PMDD).* After years of study, a DSM work group recommended in 1993 that PMDD be formally listed as a new and distinct kind of depressive disorder. The category was to be applied when a woman was regularly impaired by at least 5 of 11 symptoms during the week before her menses: sad or hopeless feelings; tense or anxious feelings; marked mood changes; frequent irritability or anger and increased interpersonal conflicts; decreased interest in her usual activities; lack of concentration; lack of energy; changes in appetite; insomnia or sleepiness; a subjective feeling of being overwhelmed or out of control; and physical symptoms such as swollen breasts, headaches, muscle pain, a "bloated" sensation, or weight gain.

The work group claimed that since women with this pattern of symptoms do not respond well to treatments used for other kinds of depression, such as antidepressant drugs, PMDD should be a separate category. If it were not included, they argued, problems of women who are severely impaired by these symptoms would not be fully investigated, properly understood, or effectively treated.

This recommendation set off an uproar. Many clinicians (including some dissenting members of the work group), several national organizations, interest groups, and the media voiced their concern that this diagnostic category would "pathologize" severe cases of *premenstrual syndrome,* or *PMS,* the premenstrual discomforts that are common and normal (Chase, 1993; DeAngelis, 1993). The National Organization for Women (NOW) argued that 42 percent of all women experience the vague and general symptoms of PMDD, and could qualify for a diagnosis (Chase, 1993), although the DSM work group estimated that only 5 percent of women would meet the criteria. NOW also argued that a diagnosis of PMDD would cause women's behavior in general to be attributed largely to "raging hormones" (a stereotype that society is finally rejecting), stigmatizing women and inviting discrimination in courtrooms, in the workplace, and during child custody hearings.

Opponents of the proposed category also argued that there were insufficient data to include it. In addition, they pointed out, clinicians have paid far less attention to the possible relationships between male hormones and men's mental health.

Again the DSM framers worked out a compromise to resolve this controversy. PMDD is not listed as a formal category in DSM-IV, but clinicians can include it under the broad category of *depressive disorder not otherwise specified,* and the pattern and its criteria are listed in the DSM appendix, with the suggestion that it be studied more thoroughly in the coming years. Whether this category, too, will quietly disappear is anyone's guess at this point. Meanwhile, the issue of PMDD illustrates the many important factors—scientific, social, political, and personal—that come into play in the development of a diagnostic system.

comprehensive reviews of the most recent literature and directing many field studies to the issue of validity (see Box 5-3). Thus the new criteria and categories of DSM-IV probably have stronger validity than those of earlier versions of the DSM, but like DSM-IV's reliability, its validity has yet to be broadly tested (Clark, Watson, & Reynolds, 1995; McGorry et al., 1995). It is reasonable to expect that it too will prove to have at least some validity problems, given current areas of uncertainty in the field.

Problems of Clinical Misinterpretation

Even with trustworthy assessment data and reliable and valid classification categories, clinicians will sometimes arrive at a wrong conclusion (Stricker & Trierweiler, 1995; Nietzel et al., 1994). Numerous factors can adversely affect their thinking (see Box 5-4).

First, like all human beings, clinicians are flawed information processors. They often give too much weight to the data they encounter first and too little to data they acquire later (Meehl, 1960). They may sometimes pay too much attention to certain sources of information, such as a parent's report about a child, and too little to others, such as the child's point of view (McCoy, 1976). Finally, their judgments can be distorted by any number of personal biases—gender, age, race, and socioeconomic status, to name just a few (Strakowski et al., 1995; Jenkins-Hall & Sacco, 1991). In a recent study, for example, white American therapists were asked to watch a videotaped clinical interview and then to evaluate either an African American or a white American woman who either was or was not depressed. Although the therapists rated the nondepressed African American woman much the same as the nondepressed white American woman, they rated the depressed African American woman with more negative adjectives and judged her to be less socially competent than the depressed white American woman.

Second, clinicians may bring various misconceptions about methodology to the decision-making process (Nietzel et al., 1994; Reisman, 1991). Many think, for example, that the more assessment techniques they use, the more accurate their interpretations will be—a belief that is not borne out by research (Kahneman & Tversky, 1973; Golden, 1964).

A third factor that can distort clinicians' interpretations is their expectations about the client. They may assume, for example, that any person who consults them professionally must have some disorder. Because they are looking for abnormal functioning, clinicians may overreact to assessment data that suggest abnormality, a phenomenon that has been called the "reading-in syndrome" (Phares, 1979).

It is small wonder that investigations periodically uncover shocking errors in diagnosis, especially in hospitals (Chen, Swann, & Burt, 1996). In one study a clinical team was asked to reevaluate the records of 131 randomly selected patients at a mental hospital in New York, conduct interviews with many of the patients, and arrive at a diagnosis for each patient (Lipton & Simon, 1985). The researchers then compared the team's diagnoses with the original ones. Although 89 of the patients had originally received a diagnosis of schizophrenia, only 16 received it upon reevaluation. And whereas 15 patients originally had been given a diagnosis of mood disorder, 50 received it now. Obviously, it is important for clinicians to be aware that huge diagnostic disagreements can occur.

Dangers of Diagnosing and Labeling

Classification is intended to help clinicians understand, predict, and change abnormal behavior, but it can have some unfortunate and unintended consequences. As we observed in Chapter 4, for example, many sociocultural theorists believe that diagnostic labels become self-fulfilling prophecies (Scheff, 1975; Rosenhan, 1973). When persons are diagnosed as mentally disturbed, they may be viewed and treated in stereotyped ways. If others view them as deficient and expect them to take on a sick role, they may begin to consider themselves sick as well and act accordingly. As the prophecy fulfills itself, the label "patient" seems justified.

Furthermore, sociocultural theorists point out, our society attaches a stigma to abnormality (Raguram et al., 1996). People labeled mentally ill may find it difficult to get a job, especially a position of responsibility, or to enter into social relationships. Once a label has been applied, it may stick for a long time. Clinicians, friends, relatives, and the people themselves may all continue to apply the label long after the disorder has disappeared.

Because of these problems, some clinicians would like to do away with diagnoses. Others disagree. Although they too recognize the unfortunate consequences of labeling, they believe that the best remedy is to increase what is known about mental disorders and improve diagnostic techniques (Chen et al., 1996; Akiskal, 1989). They hold that classification and diagnosis yield information that is critical for understanding and treating people in distress (Reid, 1997).

Treatment

Over the course of ten months, Angela Savanti received extensive treatment for depression and related symptoms. She improved significantly during that time, as the following report describes.

BOX 5-4 Oppression, Slavery, and Mental Health: The Politics of Labeling

Throughout history, governments have applied the label of mental illness in efforts to control or change people whose views threaten the social order. This was a common practice in the former Soviet Union. There political dissent was considered a self-evident symptom of abnormal mental functioning, and many dissidents were committed to mental hospitals.

A country's cultural values often influence diagnostic categories more subtly. Mental health practitioners deem certain behaviors or ways of thinking abnormal primarily because they are different from the society's cultural norms. A vicious cycle unfolds in which cultural beliefs define a clinical category and the application of the category helps maintain the cultural belief. The role of cultural values is not necessarily apparent at the time, but it becomes obvious to historians who later look back on the period.

When the historians Lynn Gamwell and Nancy Tomes (1995) reviewed mental health practices in the United States, they noted the widespread belief in the nineteenth century that freedom would drive such "primitive" people as Native Americans insane. In fact, medical experts of that time announced that the forcible movement of tribal groups onto reservations was in their best interest: it would save them from the madness that awaited them in free society. The medical officer who supervised the "removal" of the Cherokee from their homeland to Oklahoma was later pleased to report that during the whole time he oversaw the migration of 20,000 Cherokee (over 4,000 of whom died), he had not observed a single case of insanity.

Frederick Douglass (1818–1895) became a leading abolitionist after he escaped slavery. His eloquent autobiography, My Bondage and My Freedom, *provided a powerful description of slavery and of its impact on individuals, thus challenging many nineteenth-century myths.*

Angela's depression eased as she began to make progress in therapy. A few months before the termination of treatment, she and Jerry resumed dating. Angela discussed with Jerry her greater comfort in expressing her feelings and her hope that Jerry would also become more expressive with her. They discussed the reasons why Angela was ambivalent about getting married, and they began to talk again about the possibility of marriage. Jerry, however, was not making demands for a decision by a certain date, and Angela felt that she was not as frightened about marriage as she previously had been. . . .

Psychotherapy provided Angela with the opportunity to learn to express her feelings to the persons she was interacting with, and this was quite helpful to her. Most important, she was able to generalize from some of the learning experiences in therapy and modify her behavior in her renewed relationship with Jerry. Angela still had much progress to make in terms of changing the characteristic ways she interacted with others, but she had already made a number of important steps in a potentially happier direction.

(Leon, 1984, pp. 118, 125)

Clearly, treatment helped Angela, and by its conclusion she was a happier, more functional person than the woman who had first sought help ten months earlier. But how did her therapist decide on the treatment program that proved so helpful to Angela? The therapist began, of course, with assessment information. Knowing the nature, causes, and context of Angela's problem, the clinician could make informed decisions about therapy. The therapist also took into account the diagnostic informa-

Slave owners, too, liked to believe that slaves were psychologically comfortable with their situation, and that those who tried to escape either were or would soon become disturbed. In fact, Secretary of State John Calhoun of South Carolina pointed to the 1840 census, conducted by his office, as evidence: the census identified almost *no* insane slaves in the South, but many insane former slaves in the North. Based on this finding—later proved to be inaccurate—an article published in *The American Journal of Insanity* in 1851 concluded, "Who would believe it without the facts in black and white . . . that every fourteenth colored person in the state of Maine is either an idiot, or lunatic" (Gamwell & Tomes, 1995). Calhoun asserted in a letter to the Speaker of the House in 1845, "The data on insanity revealed in this census is unimpeachable. From it our nation must conclude that the abolition of slavery would be to the African a curse instead of a blessing."

The work of Samuel Cartwright, a professor of medicine who specialized in "diseases of the Negro," lent further support to this belief. Cartwright claimed that several kinds of mental disorders were unique to African Americans, including "drapetomania" (from the Latin *drapeta,* fugitive), an obsessive desire for freedom that drove some slaves to try to flee from captivity. Any slave who tried to run away more than twice, Cartwright held, was insane.

Frederick Douglass, the former slave who escaped to become a world-famous lecturer and to hold influential posts in the federal government, dispelled the notion that freedom would cause psychological damage to African Americans. In his autobiography he described the emotional strength and mental clarity he felt after fighting back when Covey, his owner, flogged him:

> He only can understand the effect of this combat on my spirit, who has himself incurred something, hazarded something, in repelling the unjust and cruel aggressions of a tyrant. Covey was a tyrant, and a cowardly one, withall. After resisting him, I felt as I had never felt before. It was a resurrection from the dark and pestiferous tomb of slavery, to the heaven of comparative freedom. I was no longer a servile coward, trembling under the frown of a brother worm of the dust, but, my long-cowed spirit was roused to an attitude of manly independence. I had reached the point at which I was not afraid to die.
>
> *(Douglass, 1855, p. 247)*

Drapetomania is long forgotten, but cultural views continue to define psychological categories. Indeed, many clinicians have argued that categories such as homosexuality, sexual frigidity, and masochistic personality—each of which entered and departed from the classification system during the twentieth century—exemplify all too well the recurring impact of cultural beliefs on clinical categorizations and diagnoses.

tion, and selected treatment techniques that are known to be helpful in cases of depression.

Therapists are also influenced by other factors when making decisions about treatment. For example, their treatment plan typically reflects their orientation and how they have learned to conduct therapy. As we observed in Chapters 3 and 4, each model has strategies and techniques that its practitioners must learn. As therapists apply their favored model, they become increasingly familiar and comfortable with its principles and techniques, and they tend to hold on to them in their future work (Goldfried & Wolfe, 1996).

Therapists may also consider the research literature in designing a treatment program. Most clinicians say that they value research as a guide to practice (Beutler et al., 1995). Not all, however, actually read about recent findings on clinical disorders and treatments, and so they cannot be readily influenced by them (see Figure 5-8). Because research articles tend to be written for other researchers, their technical language is not typically accessible to clinicians or other kinds of readers (Goldfried & Wolfe, 1996). As a result, today's therapists gather most of their information about the latest developments in the field from colleagues, professional newsletters, workshops, conferences, books, and the like (Goldfried & Wolfe, 1996; Beutler et al., 1995; Cohen, Sargent, & Sechrest, 1986; Morrow-Bradley & Elliott, 1986). Unfortunately, the accuracy and usefulness of these sources varies widely.

Finally, clinicians are influenced by the state of knowledge in the clinical field when making therapy decisions. What does the field currently know about

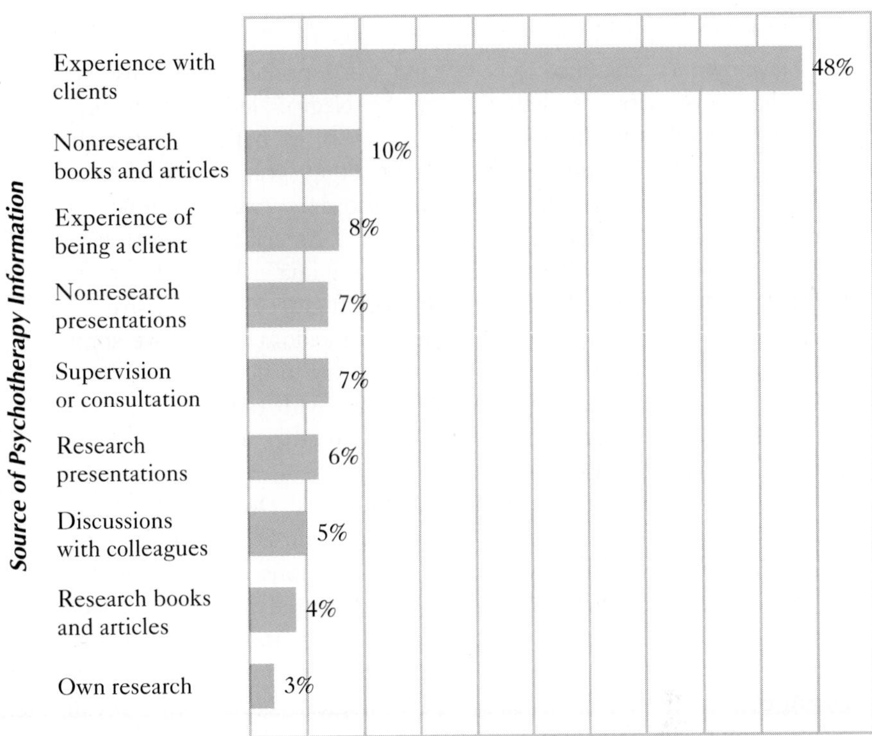

Figure 5-8 *Which sources of information about psychotherapy do clinical practitioners find most useful? According to one survey, almost half of all clinicians rely most often on their ongoing experiences with clients. Although practitioners value research in principle, relatively few depend primarily on psychotherapy research presentations, books, or articles, or on their own research work. (Adapted from Morrow-Bradley & Elliot, 1986.)*

treatment and treatment effectiveness? And what implications does this have for the treatment of particular clients and problems? The answers to such questions are often far from clear.

Investigating the Effectiveness of Treatment

Altogether, as many as 400 forms of therapy are practiced in the clinical field today (Garfield & Bergin, 1994; Karasu, 1992). Thus, probably the most important question to ask about treatment is whether it does what it is supposed to do (Lichtenberg & Kalodner, 1997). Does a particular treatment really help people cope with and overcome their psychological problems? On the surface, the question may seem simple. In fact, it is one of the most difficult questions for clinical researchers to answer (Strupp, 1996; Persons, 1991).

The first problem is how to *define* a "successful" treatment (Strupp, 1996, 1989). If, as Angela's therapist suggests, she still has much progress to make at the conclusion of therapy, should her recovery be considered successful? Different clinical researchers would answer this question differently. Because definitions of success vary from investigator to investigator, it is not always appropriate to combine the results from different treatment studies and use them to draw general conclusions (Kazdin, 1994).

The second problem is how to *measure* improvement (Sechrest, McKnight, & McKnight, 1996; Strupp, 1996). Should researchers give equal weight to the reports of clients, friends, relatives, therapists, and teachers? Should they use rating scales, inventories, checklists, therapy insights, behavior observations, adjustment scores, or some other measure? The various measures of improvement correlate only moderately with one another (Lambert & Hill, 1994).

Perhaps the biggest problem is the *range* and *complexity* of the treatments currently in use. Clients differ in their problems, personal styles, and motivation for therapy; therapists differ in skill, experience, orientation, and personality; and therapies differ in theory, format, and setting. Because a client's progress in therapy is influenced by all these factors and more, the findings of a particular study will not always apply to other clients and therapists.

Proper research procedures address some of these problems, as we observed in Chapter 2. By using control groups, random assignment, matched subjects, and the like, clinicians can draw certain conclusions about various therapies. Even in studies that are well designed, however, the enormous complexity of treatment sets limits on the conclusions that can be reached (Kazdin, 1994).

Despite these difficulties, the job of evaluating therapies must be done, and clinical researchers have plowed ahead with it (Lambert & Bergin, 1994). Thousands of studies have been conducted on various treatments, and numerous reviewers have tried to draw conclusions. The studies typically ask one of three questions:

1. Is therapy *in general* effective?
2. Are *particular* therapies generally effective?
3. Are *particular* therapies effective for particular problems?

Is Therapy Generally Effective?

Studies suggest that therapy is often more helpful than no treatment or than placebos (Hollon, 1996; Seligman, 1995; Lambert & Bergin, 1994). In 1970 a pioneering review that covered many kinds of therapies and mental disorders found therapy to be more effective than no therapy in more than 80 percent of adequately controlled studies (Meltzoff & Kornreich, 1970). Later a still broader review examined 375 controlled studies, covering a total of almost 25,000 clients seen in a wide assortment of therapies (Smith, Glass, & Miller, 1980; Smith & Glass, 1977). The reviewers combined the findings of these studies by standardizing their results, a statistical technique called a "meta-analysis." They rated the level of improvement in each treated person and in each untreated control subject and computed the average difference between those two groups. According to this meta-analysis, the average person who received treatment was better off than 75 percent of the untreated control subjects (see Figure 5-9). Still other meta-analyses have revealed a similar relationship between treatment and improvement (Lambert, Weber, & Sykes, 1993; Crits-Cristoph et al., 1991).

The widely read *Consumer Reports* also conducted a survey a few years back. Relying on the clinical researcher Martin Seligman as the principal consultant, the magazine asked its readers about their experiences and satisfaction in therapy, whether from a mental health professional, family doctor, or support group (Seligman, 1995). More than 4,000 readers responded. Although their detailed responses have received considerable attention and aroused debate among both clinical professionals and the public (Jacobson & Christensen, 1996; Seligman, 1996; VandenBos, 1996), they suggest once again that therapy is often helpful, or at least satisfying. Around 54 percent of those respondents who had felt "very poor" when they first began therapy reported that therapy "made things a lot better." Their responses also indicated that treatments by psychologists, psychiatrists, and social workers were of equal effectiveness, and that these treatments in turn were more effective than those by family doctors.

Some clinicians have concerned themselves with an important related question: Can therapy be harmful? In his book *My Analysis with Freud* the psychoanalyst Abraham Kardiner (1977) wrote, "Freud was always infuriated whenever I would say to him that you could not do harm with psychoanalysis. He said: 'When you say

(Drawing by Shanahan; © 1992 The New Yorker Magazine, Inc.)

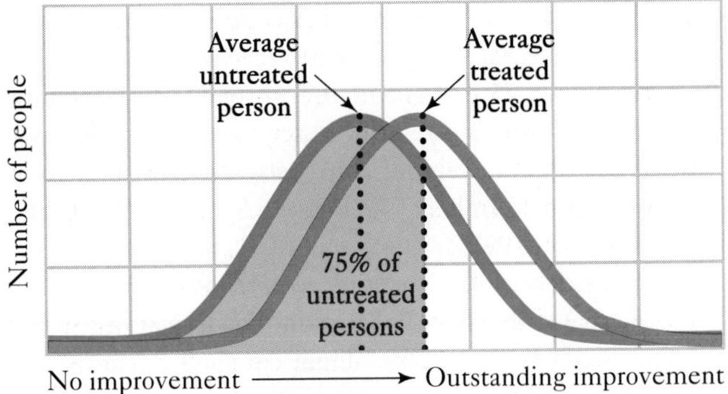

Figure 5-9 *Combining subjects and results from hundreds of studies, investigators have determined that the average person who receives psychotherapy experiences greater improvement than do 75 percent of all untreated people with similar problems. (Adapted from Lambert, Weber, and Sykes, 1993; Smith, Glass, & Miller, 1980; Smith & Glass, 1977.)*

that, you also say it cannot do any good. Because if you cannot do any harm, how can you do good?'" Studies conducted since the 1950s agree with Freud that some patients actually seem to get worse because of therapy (Lambert & Bergin, 1994; Mays & Franks, 1985).

The deterioration may take the form of a general worsening of symptoms or the development of new ones, including a sense of failure, guilt, low self-concept, or hopelessness over one's inability to profit from therapy (Lambert, Shapiro, & Bergin, 1986; Hadley & Strupp, 1976). The numbers have varied from study to study, but between 5 and 10 percent of clients appear to decline as a result of therapy (Nietzel et al., 1994; Ogles et al., 1993; Smith et al., 1980).

Are Particular Therapies Effective?

The studies we have looked at so far have lumped all therapies together to consider their general effectiveness. Many researchers, however, consider it inappropriate to treat all therapies alike. One critic suggested that these studies were operating under a *uniformity myth*—a false belief that all therapies are equivalent despite differences in the therapists' training, experience, theoretical orientations, and personalities (Kiesler, 1995, 1966).

An alternative approach examines the effectiveness of particular therapies. Most such studies show each of the major forms of therapy to be superior to no treatment or to placebo treatment. Psychodynamic therapies and client-centered therapy have fared well occasionally in therapy outcome studies (Prochaska & Norcross, 1994: Stuhr & Meyer, 1991; Svartberg & Stiles, 1991), while behavioral, cognitive, biological, and sociocultural therapies have frequently demonstrated considerable effectiveness (Emmelkamp, 1994; Hollon & Beck, 1994; Apter, 1993).

Studies have also compared particular therapies with one another, but no one form of therapy generally stands out over others (Seligman, 1995; Nietzel et al., 1994; Luborsky et al., 1975). In a classic comparative study, researchers assigned ninety-four clients with anxiety, depressive, and personality disorders to one of three treatment conditions: psychodynamic therapy, behavioral therapy, or a "waiting list" control group (Sloane et al., 1975). The subjects in each group were matched on such variables as age, sex, and severity of symptoms. Six highly experienced therapists then provided treatment in weekly hour-long sessions. The researchers found that after four months, the clients who had been receiving either form of psychotherapy had improved to a similar degree, significantly more than the control clients. Approximately 80 percent of the clients in each therapy group had improved, but only 48 percent of the waiting-list clients.

If different kinds of therapy have similar successes, might they have something in common? A ***rapprochement movement*** has tried to delineate a set of common therapeutic strategies that may characterize the work of all effective therapists, regardless of their particular orientation (Prochaska & Norcross, 1994; Beutler, Machado, & Neufeldt, 1994). A survey of highly successful therapists suggests, for example, that most provide feedback to patients, help patients focus on their own thoughts and behavior, pay attention to the way they and their patients are interacting, and try to promote self-mastery in their patients. In short, effective therapists of any type may practice more similarly than they preach (Korchin & Sands, 1983).

Are Particular Therapies Effective for Particular Disorders?

People with different disorders may respond differently to the various therapeutic systems, formats, and settings (Barlow, 1996; Zettle, Haflich, & Reynolds, 1992). Gordon Paul, an influential clinical theorist, said some years back that the most appropriate question regarding the effectiveness of therapy may be "*What* specific treatment, by *whom*, is most effective for *this* individual with *that* specific problem, and under *which* set of circumstances?" (Paul, 1967, p. 111). Researchers therefore have investigated how effective particular therapies are at treating particular disorders (Kazdin, 1994; Beutler, 1991). Their studies have often found sizable differences among the various therapies (Seligman, 1994). Behavioral therapies, for example, appear to be the most effec-

tive of all in the treatment of phobias (Wolpe, 1997; Emmelkamp, 1994), whereas drug therapy is the single most effective treatment for schizophrenia (Meltzer, 1992).

Studies have also revealed that some clinical problems may respond better to combined approaches than to any one therapy alone (Beitman, 1996, 1993; Seligman, 1994; Sander & Feldman, 1993). Drug therapy is sometimes combined with certain forms of psychotherapy, for example, to better treat depression. In fact, it is becoming common for clients to be seen by two therapists—a **psychopharmacologist** (or **pharmacotherapist**), a psychiatrist who only prescribes medications, and a psychologist, social worker, or other therapist who conducts psychotherapy (Woodward, Duckworth, & Gutheil, 1993). A combination of therapies seems to be particularly in order in cases of **comorbidity**—the occurrence of two or more psychological disorders simultaneously (Clarkin & Kendall, 1992).

Determining how particular therapies fare with particular disorders can help therapists and clients alike make better decisions about treatment (Beutler, 1991, 1979). It can also lead researchers to a better understanding of therapy processes and ultimately of abnormal functioning. Thus this is a question to which we shall keep returning as we examine the disorders the therapies have been devised to combat.

Crossroads

In Chapters 3 and 4, we observed that today's leading models of abnormal behavior differ widely in their assumptions, conclusions, and treatments. Thus, it should not surprise us that clinicians also show great diversity in their approaches to assessment and diagnosis. Nor that clinicians who prefer certain assessment techniques often scoff at the naiveté of those who use other approaches. However, no one yet has bragging rights in the realm of clinical assessment and diagnosis. Each of the hundreds of available tools has significant limitations, and each produces at best an incomplete picture of how and why a person is behaving.

Some assessment procedures have, of course, received more research support than others, and clinicians should pay great attention to such findings when choosing their assessment tools. However, given the present diversity and limitations of clinical assessment and diagnosis, it seems inappropriate to rely exclusively on any one approach. This is, in part, why more and more clinicians now use batteries of assessment tools in their work.

Attitudes toward clinical assessment have fluctuated over the past several decades (Nietzel et al., 1994). For many years, assessment, particularly testing, was a highly regarded part of clinical practice. However, as the clinical models grew in number during the 1960s and 1970s, proponents of each model advocated some tools and not others, and the field of assessment became increasingly fragmented. Meanwhile, research began to reveal that many tools were imprecise, inaccurate, or inconsistent. In this atmosphere, a number of clinicians lost confidence in systematic assessment and diagnosis, and some even came to approach these tasks casually. Nevertheless, interest in assessment and diagnosis has begun to rise once again in recent years. One reason for the renewed interest is the development of more precise diagnostic criteria for use in DSM-IV. Another is the drive by researchers for more standardized tests to help identify subjects for clinical studies. Still another factor is the clinical field's growing awareness that certain disorders—for example, Alzheimer's disease—can be properly identified only after wide-ranging assessment procedures.

Along with the heightened interest in assessment has come increased research (Exner, 1997; Cramer, 1996; Butcher, 1995). Today's researchers are actively investigating the merits of the various assessment techniques, so that clinicians can perform their tasks with more precision, accuracy, and consistency. Indeed, every major kind of assessment tool—from projective tests to personality inventories—is now undergoing careful scrutiny. This expansion of research, and more generally, the return to prominence of systematic clinical assessment, is welcome news for both clients and the clinicians who wish to help them.

Chapter Review

1. ***The practitioner's task*** Clinical practitioners are interested primarily in compiling *idiographic,* or individual, information about their clients. They seek a full understanding of the specific nature and origins of a client's problems through *assessment,* the gathering of information about the person's problems, and *diagnosis,* the process of determining whether the person's dysfunction constitutes a particular psychological disorder.

2. ***Clinical assessment*** To be useful, assessment tools must be *standardized, reliable,* and *valid.* Most clinical

assessment methods fall into three general categories: clinical interviews, tests, and observations.

A. *Clinical interviews* A clinical interview permits the practitioner to interact with a client and generally get a sense of who he or she is. The clinician may conduct either an *unstructured* or a *structured* interview.

B. *Clinical tests* Clinical tests are devices that gather information about a few aspects of a person's psychological functioning from which broader information about that person can be inferred. They include *projective tests, personality inventories, response inventories, psychophysiological tests, neuropsychological tests,* and *intelligence tests.* Because each type of test falls short on one or more of the key criteria of standardization, reliability, and validity, clinicians generally administer a *battery* of tests to assess psychological functioning.

C. *Clinical observations* Two strategies for observing people's behavior are *naturalistic observation* and *structured observation.* Practitioners also employ the related procedure of *self-monitoring:* subjects observe themselves and carefully record designated behavior, feelings, or cognitions as they occur throughout the day.

3. *Diagnosis* After collecting and interpreting the assessment information, clinicians form a *clinical picture* and reach a diagnosis. The diagnosis is chosen from a *classification system,* which lists recognized disorders and describes the symptoms characteristic of each. The classification system developed by the American Psychiatric Association is the *Diagnostic and Statistical Manual of Mental Disorders (DSM).*

4. *DSM-IV* The most recent version of the DSM, known as DSM-IV, lists close to 300 disorders. Clinicians who use it to make a diagnosis must evaluate a client's condition on five *axes,* or categories of information. Because DSM-IV is new, its reliability and validity have yet to receive broad clinical review.

5. *Problems of clinical misinterpretation* Even with trustworthy assessment data and reliable and valid classification categories, clinicians will not always arrive at the correct conclusion. Many factors can mar their judgment. Clinicians are human and so fall prey to various biases, misconceptions, and expectations.

6. *Dangers of diagnosing and labeling* Sociocultural theorists suggest that diagnosing a patient often does more harm than good, because the labeling process and the prejudices that labels arouse may be damaging to the person who is diagnosed.

7. *Treatment* The treatment decisions of therapists may be influenced by assessment information, the diagnosis, the clinician's theoretical orientation, research literature, and the field's state of knowledge.

8. *Is therapy effective?* Determining the effectiveness of treatment is difficult because therapists differ in their ways of defining and measuring success. Moreover, the diversity and complexity of today's treatments present a problem. The critical question to be asked about the various treatments is whether they actually help people cope with and overcome their psychological problems. Three general conclusions have been reached:

A. People in therapy are usually better off than people with similar problems who receive no treatment.

B. The various therapies do not appear to differ dramatically in their general effectiveness.

C. Certain therapies do appear to be more effective than others for certain disorders, and often a particular combination of approaches is more effective than a single approach in the treatment of certain disorders.

Thought and Afterthought

The David Helfgott Story: When Labels Fail

The Australian pianist David Helfgott burst onto the world stage during the winter of 1997. The story of his journey from a boy piano prodigy to a deeply troubled and dysfunctional young man and finally to an inspirational concert performer was told in the popular movie *Shine*. People everywhere were moved and fascinated by his plight, and many attended his sold-out concerts in cities throughout the world.

Everyone who has seen *Shine* is familiar with Helfgott's symptoms, including his repeated hugs, hyperspeed commentary, and self-addressed pep talk—for example, "It's awesome it's awesome it's awesome," (Chang & Gates, 1997, p. 62).

Less clear to everyone is what these symptoms add up to. Stories about Helfgott speak vaguely of a "mental, or nervous, breakdown." His wife, Gillian, describes him as "delightfully eccentric." His psychiatrist notes, "He's not autistic, not schizophrenic, and may be manic only in the colloquial rather than the clinical sense," (Chang & Gates, 1997, p. 63). The absence of a clear diagnostic label does not seem to trouble anyone, however. If anything, it adds to Helfgott's charm and to the public's fascination with him.

Afterthoughts: *Why is a clear diagnostic label of Helfgott's problem so elusive? . . . How may the lack of a diagnostic label be helping people to see Helfgott as a person rather than a disorder? . . . Does the public's fascination with Helfgott and attendance at his concerts reflect their empathy and admiration, or, as some claim, simple curiosity?*

Diagnosing van Gogh: Still Labeling After All These Years

Vincent van Gogh led a turbulent and unhappy life. In a legendary incident the artist cut off one of his ears. He also was admitted to a mental institution and ultimately committed suicide. For years diagnosticians have speculated that van Gogh suffered from a mood disorder, schizophrenia, or both. Since the mid-1980s, however, these posthumous assessments have been challenged.

A Harvard neurologist has suggested that van Gogh in fact suffered from *Geschwind's syndrome*, technically known as *interictal personality disorder*, caused by brain seizure disorder, or epilepsy. Van Gogh exhibited many of its symptoms—excessive drawing (hypergraphia), hyperreligiosity, aggression, and more (Trotter, 1985).

In contrast, medical specialists in Colorado have concluded that van Gogh suffered from an extreme form of *Menière's syndrome*, a disorder characterized by an excessive buildup of fluid in the inner ear. The enormous pressure may produce nausea, vertigo, poor balance, pain, deafness, and constant buzzing or ringing sensations. Perhaps van Gogh cut off his ear in an effort to reduce the pain. And perhaps his other problems and pains arose from the severe secondary psychological problems that can accompany Menière's syndrome (Scott, 1990).

Vincent van Gogh, a self-portrait.

Afterthoughts: *Would people react to van Gogh's work differently if they thought of him as having had an ear disorder rather than a psychological disorder? . . . Why do people find it fascinating to diagnose famous people, particularly those in the arts, long after their death? . . . Do works of art reveal more about the artists who produce them or about the art lovers who interpret their meaning?*

Topic Overview

Stress, Coping, and the Anxiety Response

Generalized Anxiety Disorder

Phobias
Agoraphobia
Social Phobias
Specific Phobias

Crossroads

Chapter 6

Generalized Anxiety Disorder and Phobias

The outward appearance of anxiety may take various forms. Like the subject in Diane Kepford's Alex #10, *1995, some people with generalized anxiety disorder reveal only a trace of apprehension, but underneath they are grappling with repeated worries and constant tension.*

Think about a time when your breathing quickened, your muscles tensed, and your heart pounded with a sudden sense of dread. Was it when your car almost skidded off the road in the rain? When your professor announced a pop quiz? What about when the person you most cared about went out with someone else, or your boss suggested that your job performance ought to improve? Any time you confront what seems to be a serious threat to your well-being, you may react with the state of alarm known as ***fear.*** Sometimes, though, you cannot pinpoint a specific cause for alarm, but still you feel tense and edgy, as if something unpleasant were going to happen. The ominous sense of being menaced by an unspecified threat is usually termed ***anxiety,*** and it has the same clinical features—the same acceleration of breathing, muscular tension, perspiration, and so forth—as fear (Strelau, 1992; Barlow, 1988).

Although everyday experiences of fear and anxiety are not pleasant, they have an adaptive function: they prepare us for action—for "fight or flight"—when danger threatens. They may motivate us to drive more cautiously in a storm, keep up with our reading assignments, treat our date more sensitively, and work harder at our job (Millar & Millar, 1996). Unfortunately, some people suffer such continuous and disabling fear and anxiety that they cannot lead a normal life. Their discomfort is too severe or too frequent; it lasts too long; it is triggered too readily by what the sufferers themselves recognize as minimal, unspecified, or nonexistent threats. These people are said to have an ***anxiety disorder.***

Anxiety disorders are the most common mental disorders in the United States (Zajecka,1997). In any given year between 15 and 17 percent of the adult population—23 million people—suffer from one or another of the six anxiety disorders identified by DSM-IV (Kessler et al., 1994; Regier et al., 1993; Davidson et al., 1991). Collectively, these disorders cost society close to $50 billion each year in health-care expenses, lost wages, and lost productivity (Hales, Hilty, & Wise, 1997; Du Pont et al., 1993).

People with ***generalized anxiety disorder*** experience general and persistent feelings of anxiety. People with ***phobias*** experience a persistent and irrational fear of a specific object, activity, or situation. People with ***panic disorder*** have recurrent attacks of terror. Those with ***obsessive-compulsive disorder*** are beset by recurrent and unwanted thoughts that cause anxiety or by the need to perform repetitive and ritualistic actions to reduce anxiety. People with ***acute stress disorder*** and ***posttraumatic stress disorder*** are tormented by fear and related symptoms well after a traumatic event (military combat, rape, torture) has ended. Typically a client will be assigned only one of these diagnoses at a time, but most people with a primary diagnosis of one anxiety disorder also meet the criteria for a secondary diagnosis of another anxiety disorder (Goisman et al., 1995; Hunt & Andrews, 1995; Merikangas & Angst, 1995).

In this chapter we shall investigate generalized anxiety disorder and phobias, disorders whose central symptom is fear or anxiety. These are the most common anxiety disorders and the ones with the longest history of study (Magee et al., 1996). In the other anxiety disorders—panic disorder, obsessive-compulsive disorder, and stress disorders—anxiety plays a prominent role, but other features or symptoms are just as important or even more so. Recurrent thoughts, for example, are as prominent in obsessive-compulsive disorder as the anxiety they generate. These *anxiety-related* problems, which have received increased attention and study during the past decade (Norton et al., 1995), are the subjects of Chapter 7. It is only in recent years that they have come to be understood and successfully treated.

Early editions of the DSM included anxiety disorders in Freud's category of the neuroses. A ***neurosis,*** according to Freud, was a disorder in which a person's ego defense mechanisms were incapable of preventing or reducing intense anxiety aroused by unconscious conflicts. The resultant struggle with anxiety could take any of several malfunctional forms. In some neurotic disorders (phobic, anxiety, and obsessive-compulsive neuroses) the anxiety was apparent. In others (hysterical, neurasthenic,

Living and working in a complex, highly technological society produces stress in many people, and sometimes leads to experiences of fear or anxiety.

depersonalization, depressive, and hypochondriacal neuroses) the anxiety was thought to be hidden and "controlled unconsciously and automatically by conversion, displacement, and various other psychological mechanisms" (APA, 1968, p. 9).

Because the DSM now defines disorders by symptoms and without reference to possible causes, the category of neurosis has been dropped and the neurotic disorders have been distributed among other categories. Those disorders in which anxiety is a key symptom are now simply called anxiety disorders. Several others of the so-called neurotic disorders, now defined as mood disorders, somatoform disorders, and dissociative disorders, are described in Chapters 8, 11, and 17, respectively.

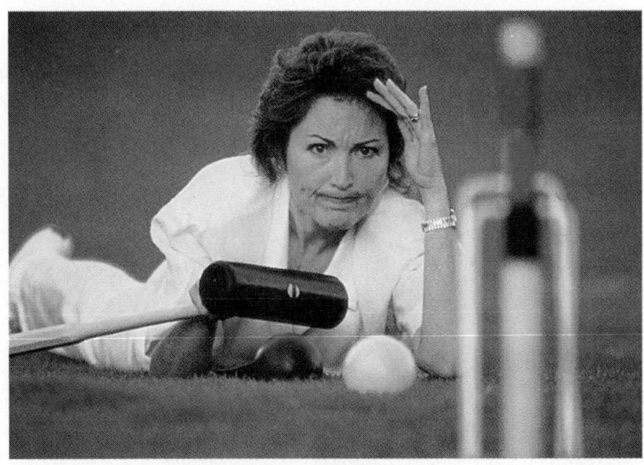

Stress has two components: a stressor and one's appraisal of it. Even mild events, such as a game of croquet, can feel stressful if they are interpreted as important, threatening, or beyond one's ability.

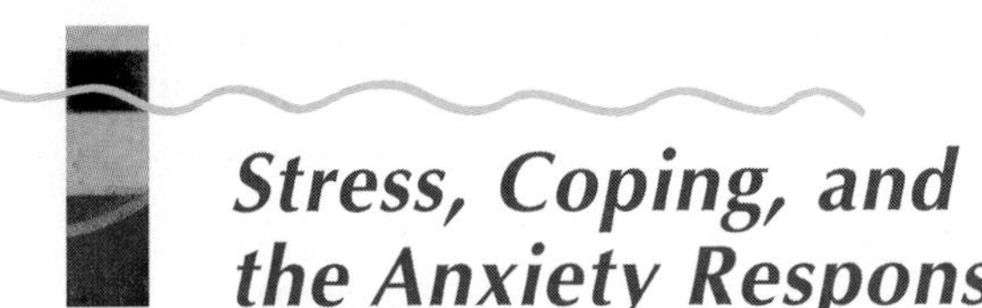

Stress, Coping, and the Anxiety Response

Before we examine the various anxiety disorders, we need to take a closer look at the kinds of situations that normally cause us to feel threatened and the kinds of changes we experience in response to them. Actually, we feel some degree of threat—a state of ***stress***—whenever we are confronted with demands or opportunities that require us to change in some manner. A state of stress has two components: a ***stressor,*** the event that creates the demands, and a ***stress response,*** a person's idiosyncratic reactions to the demands.

The stressors of life may take the form of daily hassles, such as rush-hour traffic or the appearance of unexpected company; major life events or transitions, such as college graduation or marriage; chronic problems, such as poverty, poor health, or overcrowded living conditions; or traumatic events, such as catastrophic accidents, assaults, tornados, or military combat.

Our response to such stressors is influenced by the way we *appraise* both the events and our capacity to react to them in an effective way. Two stages of appraisal are often distinguished: ***primary appraisal,*** in which we interpret a situation as threatening or harmless; and ***secondary appraisal,*** in which we weigh what kind of response is needed and assess whether we have the ability and the personal and social resources to cope with it (Lazarus & Folkman, 1984). People who sense that they have sufficient ability and resources to cope are more likely to take stressors in stride. They can respond constructively and avoid negative emotional, behavioral, and cognitive reactions. In short, one's response does not depend just on the nature of the stressor. It reflects one's own past experience, behavioral skills, self-concept, social support, and biological makeup.

When we appraise a stressor as threatening, a key reaction is fear. Fear is actually a package of responses—physical, emotional, and cognitive. Physically, we perspire, our breathing quickens, our muscles tense, and our hearts beat faster. We may turn pale and develop goose bumps, our lips may tremble, and we may feel nauseated. If the situation is extremely threatening, we may feel such emotions as horror, dread, and even panic. And fear can interfere with our ability to concentrate and distort our view of the world. We may exaggerate the harm that actually threatens us or remember things incorrectly after the threat has passed.

These features of the fear and anxiety response are generated by the action of the body's ***autonomic nervous system (ANS),*** the extensive network of nerve fibers that connects the ***central nervous system*** (the brain and spinal cord) to all the other organs of the body. The ANS helps regulate the *involuntary* activities of these organs—breathing, heartbeat, blood pressure, perspiration, and the like (see Figure 6-1).

When our brain interprets a situation as dangerous, it excites a special group of ANS fibers that quickens our heartbeat and produces the other changes that we experience as fear or anxiety. The ANS nerve fibers specifically responsible for these activities are referred to collectively as the ***sympathetic nervous system*** (in a sense, these nerve fibers are "sympathetic" to our emergency needs). The sympathetic nervous system is also called the *fight-or-flight system,* precisely because it prepares us for some kind of action in response to danger. When a perceived danger passes, a second group of ANS nerve fibers, the ***parasympathetic nervous system,*** returns our heartbeat and other body processes to normal. Together, these two

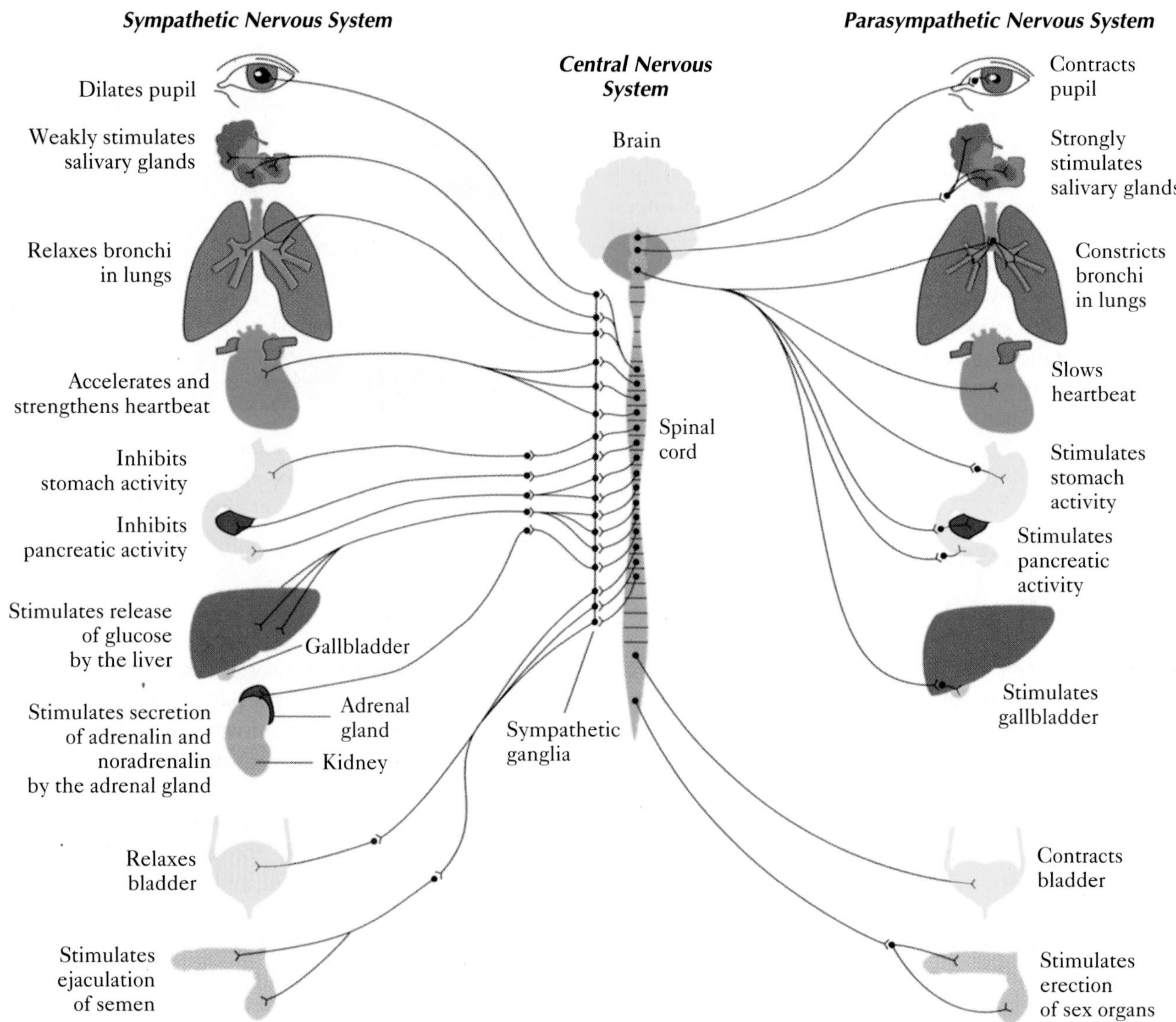

Figure 6-1 *The autonomic nervous system (ANS) regulates the involuntary functions of the body. When the sympathetic division of the ANS is activated, it stimulates some organs and inhibits others. The result is a state of general arousal. In contrast, the parasympathetic division's stimulation and inhibition of various organs have an overall calming effect.*

parts of the ANS help regulate our fear and anxiety reactions, as well as other responses to stress. They enable our body to maintain both the stability and the adaptability essential to life.

The ANS regulates our fear reactions through several channels (Thayer, Friedman, & Borkovec, 1996), but one of the most important is the body's *endocrine system.* As we observed in Chapter 4, the endocrine system consists of endocrine glands located throughout the body. Under various conditions, the glands release chemicals called *hormones* into the bloodstream, and various body organs are propelled into action. When we are confronted by stressors, the ANS triggers the *adrenal glands,* located on top of the kidneys, and these glands secrete a group of hormones called ***corticosteroids,*** including the hormone *cortisol.* These corticosteroids in turn stimulate various body organs as well as certain parts of the brain, setting in motion the rise and fall of anxiety reactions. Eventually the corticosteroids stimulate the ***hippocampus,*** the brain part that seems to regulate emotional memories, and it helps to turn off the body's anxiety reaction.

We all have our own patterns of ANS and endocrine functioning and our own ways of experiencing fear and anxiety. One person may respond to a threat by perspiring profusely and being gripped by a sense of dread; another may breathe faster and have difficulty concentrating, yet perspire very little. Similarly, we all have our own level of *ongoing* anxiety. Some people are always relaxed, while others almost always feel some tension, even when no threat is apparent. A person's general level of anxiety is sometimes called ***trait anxiety,*** because it seems to be a trait or characteristic that each of us brings to the events in our life (Rafferty, Smith, & Ptacek, 1997; Spielberger, 1985, 1972, 1966). Some psychologists believe that our trait anxiety reflects our early childhood experience—the atmosphere of safety or insecurity that surrounded us at that time. But others have found that enduring differences in trait anxiety can be noted soon after birth (Kalin, 1993; Pekrun, 1992; Kagan, 1983).

People also differ in their sense of which situations are threatening (Weiner, 1985; Stattin & Magnusson, 1980). Walking through a forest may be fearsome for one person but relaxing for another. Similarly, flying in an airplane may arouse terror in some people and boredom in others. Such variations are called differences in ***situation,*** or ***state, anxiety.*** The fear and anxiety most of us have experienced, however, are quite different from the disproportionate, frequent, and enduring waves of tension and dread experienced by persons who suffer from an anxiety disorder.

Generalized Anxiety Disorder

Bob Donaldson was a 22-year-old carpenter referred to the psychiatric outpatient department of a community hospital. . . . During the initial interview Bob was visibly distressed. He appeared tense, worried, and frightened. He sat on the edge of his chair, tapping his foot and fidgeting with a pencil on the psychiatrist's desk. He sighed frequently, took deep breaths between sentences, and periodically exhaled audibly and changed his position as he attempted to relate his story:

Bob: It's been an awful month. I can't seem to do anything. I don't know whether I'm coming or going. I'm afraid I'm going crazy or something.

Doctor: What makes you think that?

Bob: I can't concentrate. My boss tells me to do something and I start to do it, but before I've taken five steps I don't know what I started out to do. I get dizzy and I can feel my heart beating and everything looks like it's shimmering or far away from me or something—it's unbelievable.

Doctor: What thoughts come to mind when you're feeling like this?

Bob: I just think, "Oh, Christ, my heart is really beating, my head is swimming, my ears are ringing—I'm either going to die or go crazy."

Doctor: What happens then?

Bob: Well, it doesn't last more than a few seconds, I mean that intense feeling. I come back down to earth, but then I'm worrying what's the matter with me all the time, or checking my pulse to see how fast it's going, or feeling my palms to see if they're sweating.

Doctor: Can others see what you're going through?

Bob: You know, I doubt it. I hide it. I haven't been seeing my friends. You know, they say "Let's stop for a beer" or something after work and I give them some excuse—you know, like I have to do something around the house or with my car. I'm not with them when I'm with them anyway—I'm just sitting there worrying. My friend Pat said I was frowning all the time. So, anyway, I just go home and turn on the TV or pick up the sports page, but I can't really get into that either.

Bob went on to say that he had stopped playing softball because of fatigability and trouble concentrating. On several occasions during the past two weeks he was unable to go to work because he was "too nervous."

(Spitzer et al., 1983, pp. 11–12)

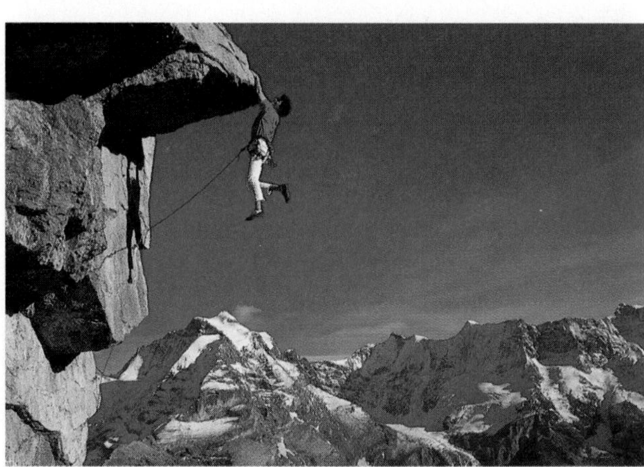

Although most people are terrified by the very thought of climbing a mountain, some are stimulated by the experience and others are even calmed by it. Such individual reactions represent differences in situation, or state, anxiety.

BOX 6-1 Fears, Shmears: The Odds Are Usually on Our Side

People with anxiety disorders have many unreasonable fears. Moreover, millions of others worry about disaster every day. Most of the events that we fear are, thank goodness, not probable, and we learn to live in accordance with *probability* rather than *possibility.* In fact, that ability may be what distinguishes the fearless from the fearful. What are the odds, then, that commonly feared events will happen? The range of probability is wide, but the odds are usually heavily in our favor.

A city resident will be a victim of a violent crime.	1 in 60
A suburbanite will be a victim of a violent crime.	1 in 1,000
A small-town resident will be a victim of a violent crime.	1 in 2,000
A child will suffer a high-chair injury this year.	1 in 6,000
The IRS will audit you this year.	1 in 100
You will be bumped off any given airline flight.	1 in 4,000
You will be struck by lightning.	1 in 9,100
You will be murdered this year.	1 in 12,000
You will be killed on your next bus ride.	1 in 500 million
You will be hit by a baseball at a major-league game.	1 in 300,000
You will drown in the tub this year.	1 in 685,000
You will be killed in an air crash.	1 in 4.6 million
Your plane will arrive late.	1 in 6
Your house will have a fire this year.	1 in 200
You will die in a fire this year.	1 in 40,200
Your carton will contain a broken egg.	1 in 10
You will develop a tooth cavity.	1 in 6
A young child will develop a tooth cavity.	1 in 10
You will contract AIDS from a blood transfusion.	1 in 100,000
Any given miner will be injured while working this year.	1 in 23

Bob suffers from ***generalized anxiety disorder.*** Like Bob, people with this disorder experience excessive anxiety and worry about numerous events or activities (see Box 6-1). Given the scope of their worries, their problem is often described as ***free-floating anxiety.***

Generalized anxiety disorder is relatively common in our society. Surveys suggest that up to 3.8 percent of the United States population have the symptoms of it in any given year (APA, 1994; Kessler et al., 1994; Blazer et al., 1991). Although the disorder may emerge at any age, it most commonly first appears in childhood or adolescence. Women diagnosed with it outnumber men 2 to 1.

Like Bob, people with generalized anxiety disorder typically feel restless, keyed up, or on edge, are easily fatigued, have difficulty concentrating, are irritable, experience muscle tension, and have sleep problems. The symptoms last at least six months (APA, 1994). The majority of people with this disorder also develop another anxiety disorder, such as a phobia, at some point in their lives (Roy-Byrne & Katon, 1997; Blazer et al., 1991) (see Figure 6-2). Many experience depression as well (Sherbourne et al., 1996; Kendler et al., 1995, 1992). Nevertheless, most individuals with this disorder are able, with some difficulty, to maintain adequate social relationships and occupational activities.

Pervasive anxiety is often difficult for friends and relatives to accept. It's unpleasant for them to see a loved one so anxious and tense, and it's a burden to be contin-

Cruise ships do occasionally run into trouble, but the likelihood of disaster is low enough that these passengers might consider taking off their life preservers while resting in the ship's lounge.

Any given construction worker will be injured at work this year.	1 in 27
Any given factory worker will be injured at work this year.	1 in 37
Any given farmer will be injured while working this year.	1 in 19
You will die in a fall.	1 in 200,000
You will be attacked by a shark.	1 in 4 million
You will receive a diagnosis of cancer this year.	1 in 8,000
A woman will develop breast cancer during her lifetime.	1 in 9
You will develop a brain tumor this year.	1 in 25,000
A business owner will become insolvent or declare bankruptcy this year.	1 in 55
A piano player will eventually develop lower back pain.	1 in 3
You will be killed on your next automobile outing.	1 in 4 million
You will eventually die in an automobile accident.	1 in 140
Condom use will eventually fail to prevent pregnancy	1 in 10
An IUD will eventually fail to prevent pregnancy.	1 in 10
Coitus interruptus will eventually fail to prevent pregnancy.	1 in 5

(Adapted from Krantz, 1992)

ually reassuring. Sometimes they accuse the anxious person of "wanting" to worry, "looking" for things to worry about, and being "happy" only when worrying. These characterizations are unfair and certainly foreign to the subjective experience of the sufferers themselves. People with a generalized anxiety disorder hardly feel happy. They feel that they are in a constant struggle, always threatened and defending themselves, and always trying to escape their pain (Roemer et al., 1995).

A variety of factors has been cited to explain the development of generalized anxiety disorder. We shall observe here the views and treatments offered by proponents of the sociocultural, psychodynamic, humanistic-existential, cognitive, and biological models. The behavioral perspective will be examined later, when we turn our attention to phobias, because that model's approach to generalized anxiety disorder and phobias is essentially the same.

The Sociocultural Perspective

According to sociocultural theorists, generalized anxiety disorder is most likely to develop in people who are confronted with societal pressures and situations that pose real danger. Studies have found that people in highly threatening environments are indeed more likely to develop the general feelings of tension, anxiety, and fatigue,

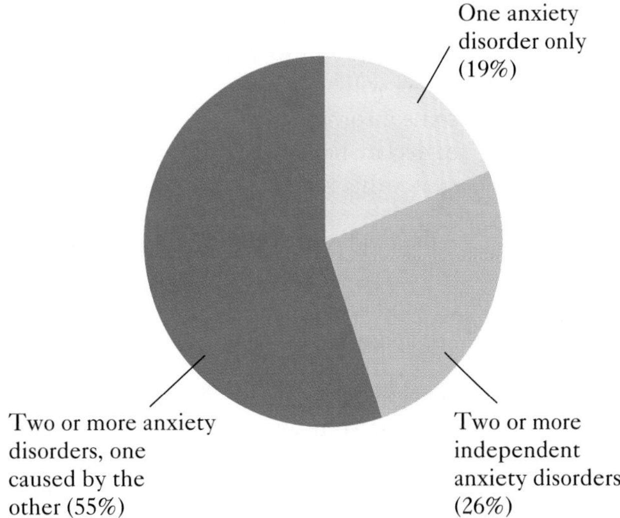

Figure 6-2 *People with one anxiety disorder usually experience another as well, either simultaneously or at another point in their lives. One study of persons with anxiety disorders found that 26 percent suffered from multiple independent disorders, and another 55 percent suffered from multiple disorders, one of which helped cause the others. Only 19 percent had but one anxiety disorder. (Adapted from Hunt & Andrews, 1995.)*

the exaggerated startle reactions, and the sleep disturbances that characterize this disorder (Staples, 1996; Turner & Lloyd, 1995; Baum & Fleming, 1993).

Take the psychological impact of living near the Three Mile Island nuclear power plant in the aftermath of the nuclear reactor accident of March 1979 (Baum, 1990; Bromet et al., 1984, 1982). In the months after the accident, mothers of preschool children living in the vicinity were found to display five times as many anxiety or depression disorders as mothers of comparable age and family structure living elsewhere. Although many of their disorders subsided during the next year, the Three Mile Island mothers still displayed elevated levels of anxiety or depression a year later.

Societal Changes Stressful changes have occurred in our society over the past several decades. Older workers have felt increasingly threatened by the introduction of computer technology, parents by the increased media attention to child abuse and abduction, and travelers by the heightened incidence of terrorism. In addition, public concern about the dangers of nuclear energy has intensified. As sociocultural theorists might predict, these societal stresses have been accompanied by steady increases in the prevalence of generalized anxiety disorder throughout the United States.

A 1975 survey indicated that 2.5 percent of the population suffered from generalized anxiety disorder (Weissman et al., 1978). That rate has now increased to 3.8 percent (Regier et al., 1993; Blazer et al., 1991; Eaton et al., 1991). Moreover, the prevalence of generalized anxiety disorder is typically higher in urbanized countries that have greater numbers of stressful changes than in less urbanized countries (Compton et al., 1991). Similarly, studies across the world (Japan, Britain, Canada, Taiwan, Poland, India, France, Italy, Chile, Israel, and Nigeria) suggest that the prevalence of anxiety symptoms often increases along with societal changes caused by war, political oppression, modernization, and related national events (Compton et al., 1991; Hwu, Yeh, & Chang, 1989).

Poverty and Race One of the most direct indicators of societal stress is poverty. People without sufficient

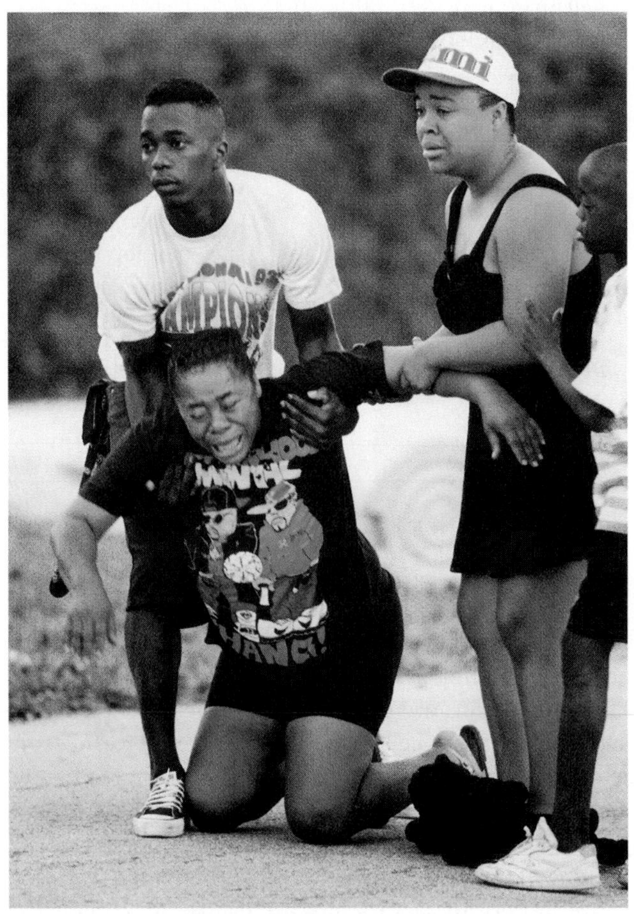

Upon learning that her son was a victim of a drive-by shooting, a woman collapses in the arms of relatives at the scene. People who live in dangerous environments experience greater anxiety and have a higher prevalence of generalized anxiety disorder than those residing in other settings.

means typically live in homes that are more run down and communities with higher crime rates, and have fewer educational and job opportunities and more job instability. They are also at greater risk for health problems. As sociocultural theorists would predict, research indicates that poorer people have a higher rate of generalized anxiety disorder. In the United States, the rate is twice as high among people with incomes of less than $10,000 a year as among those with higher incomes (Blazer et al., 1991). Indeed, as job income decreases in this country, the rate of generalized anxiety disorder steadily increases.

Since race is closely related to income and job opportunity in the United States (Belle, 1990), it is not surprising that the prevalence of generalized anxiety disorder is also tied to race (see Figure 6-3). In any given year, approximately 6 percent of all African Americans suffer from this disorder, compared to 3.5 percent of white Americans. African American women, perhaps the most socially stressed group in this country (Bennett, 1987), have the highest rate of all (6.6 percent).

Although poverty and other societal pressures may establish a climate in which generalized anxiety disorder is more likely to develop, sociocultural variables are not the only factors at work. After all, most people in poor, war-torn, politically oppressed, or endangered communities or societies do not develop anxiety disorders. Even granting the broad influence of sociocultural factors, theorists still must explain why some people develop these disorders and others do not. The psychodynamic, humanistic-existential, cognitive, and biological schools of thought have each tried to explain why and have offered corresponding treatments.

The Psychodynamic Perspective

Sigmund Freud (1933, 1917) formulated the initial psychodynamic explanation of generalized anxiety disorder. To begin with, he distinguished three kinds of anxiety that are experienced by all people: realistic, neurotic, and moral. We experience ***realistic anxiety*** when we confront genuine external dangers. We experience ***neurotic anxiety*** when we are repeatedly prevented, by our parents or by circumstances, from expressing our id impulses. And we experience ***moral anxiety*** when we are punished or threatened for expressing our id impulses, come to perceive the id impulses themselves as threatening, and so become anxious whenever we feel those impulses. In addition, as we saw in Chapter 3, Freud proposed that people try to control unacceptable impulses and accompanying neurotic and moral anxiety by employing *ego defense mechanisms.*

Psychodynamic Explanations Freud suggested that generalized anxiety disorder occurs when a person's defense mechanisms break down under stress and are overrun by neurotic or moral anxiety. It may be that the person's level of anxiety is just too high. Say that a young boy is spanked every time he cries for milk as an infant, messes his pants as a 2-year-old, and explores his genitals as a toddler. He may eventually come to believe that his various id impulses are extremely dangerous, and he may experience overwhelming anxiety whenever he has such impulses. Or perhaps the ego defense mechanisms are too weak or inadequate to cope with the resulting anxiety. Overprotected children, shielded by their parents from all frustrations and sources of anxiety, have little opportunity to develop effective defense mechanisms. Later, when they encounter the inevitable pressures of adult life, their defense mechanisms may be too weak to cope with the resulting anxieties.

Although contemporary psychodynamic theorists often disagree with some of Freud's specific notions, they too believe that generalized anxiety disorder can be traced to inadequacies in the early relationships between children and their parents. *Object relations theorists,* for example, believe that the children of overly strict or overly protective parents develop a fear of being attacked by "bad objects" (particularly their parents) or losing "good objects." If they carry this internalized anxiety state into adulthood, they may form a generalized anxiety disorder (Cirese, 1993; Zerbe, 1990). Similarly, *self-theorists* believe that children whose parents fail to treat them in a confident, relaxed, and supportive manner develop *disintegration anxiety:* they experience the self as lacking all support and set up lifelong defensive structures to sooth and repair their damaged self (Zerbe, 1990). Such makeshift structures are typically overwhelmed by the stresses of adulthood, causing a state of self-fragmentation, or "coming apart at the seams," marked by repeated outbreaks of anxiety (Diamond, 1987).

Researchers have looked for ways to test the psychodynamic explanations of generalized anxiety disorder. First, they have tried to show that people in general are inclined to use defense mechanisms excessively during fearful situations. In some studies, experimenters have exposed subjects to an apparent threat and have then measured how well the subjects remember the fear-arousing event. In accord with psychodynamic expectations, researchers have found that subjects often forget—that is, repress—many aspects of the upsetting events. In a famous study of this kind, Saul Rosenzweig (1943, 1933) arranged for subjects to fail half of the problems on an important test. He found that they later remembered less about the problems they had answered incorrectly than about those they had answered successfully.

Still other psychodynamic researchers have tried to demonstrate that people who have generalized anxiety disorder are particularly prone to use defense mechanisms. Evaluators who have studied the transcripts of early therapy sessions with anxious patients have noted that when the patients were asked to discuss anxiety-arousing experiences, they did often react defensively. They quickly forgot (repressed) what they were just talking about, changed the direction of the discussion, or denied negative feelings (Luborsky, 1973).

Others have studied cases of extreme punishment for early id impulses. In accord with the psychodynamic claim, they have found higher levels of anxiety at later points in life (Chiu, 1971). In cultures where children are regularly punished and threatened, adults seem to have more fears and anxieties (Whiting et al., 1966). In addi-

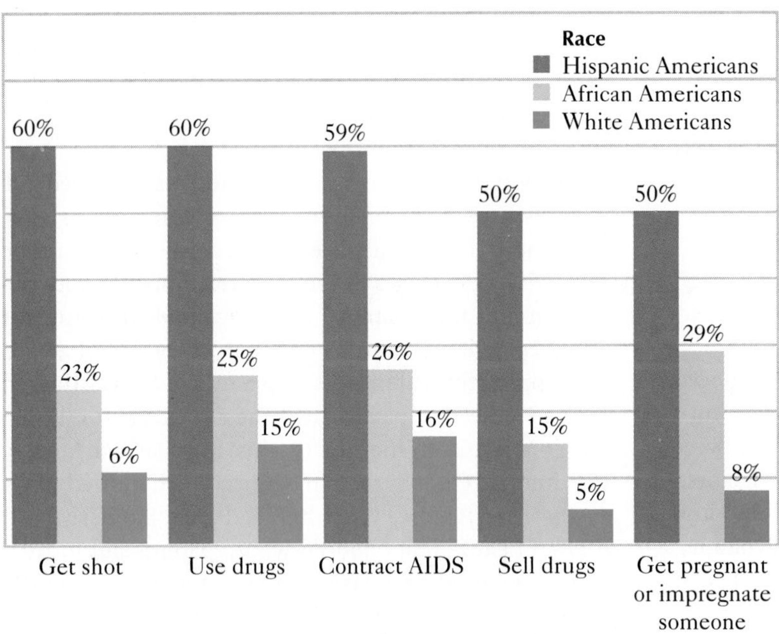

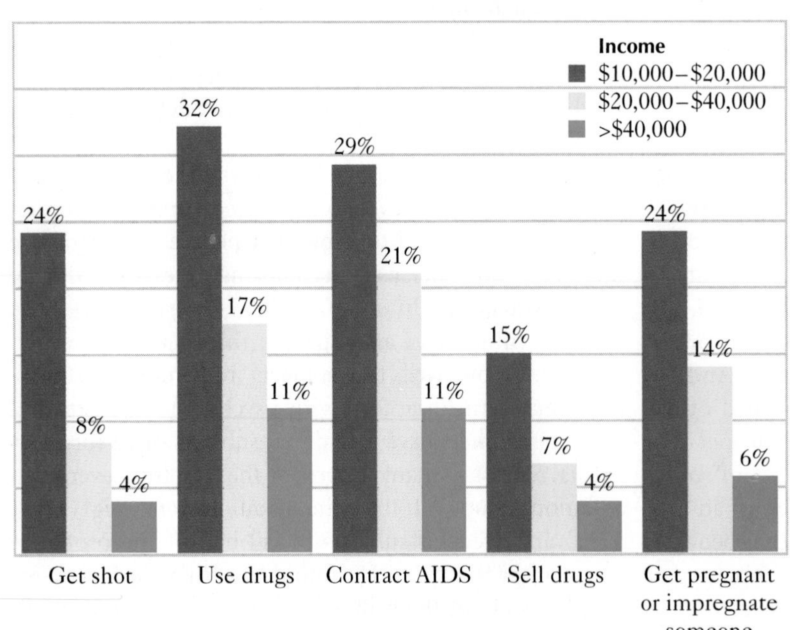

Figure 6-3 *According to a survey of 1,738 parents in the United States, African Americans and Hispanic Americans are much more likely than white Americans to worry significantly about their children's safety, future, and survival. Similarly, poorer parents are much more likely than wealthier parents to worry greatly about their children's welfare, irrespective of race. The higher anxiety levels of racial minorities, then, may be largely a matter of living in poorer, more deprived, or more dangerous environments. (Adapted from National Commission on Children, 1991.)*

tion, several studies have supported the psychodynamic position that extreme protectiveness by parents may also lead to heightened anxiety in their children (Jenkins, 1968; Eisenberg, 1958).

Although these studies are consistent with psychodynamic explanations, they have been criticized on several grounds. First, some scientists question whether these studies show what they claim to show. When people are reluctant to talk about upsetting events early in therapy, they are not necessarily repressing those events. They may be consciously focusing on the positive aspects of their lives, or they may be too embarrassed to share personal negative events until they develop trust in the therapist. Similarly, when studies show a correlation between parenting styles and individual anxiety, they are not necessarily establishing a *causal* relationship. It could be instead that high levels of anxiety in children lead some parents to develop an overcontrolling or overprotective parenting style.

Another problem is that some research studies and clinical reports have actually contradicted the psychodynamic explanations. In one, sixteen people with generalized anxiety disorder were interviewed to obtain histories of their upbringing (Raskin et al., 1982). They reported relatively little of the excessive discipline or disturbed childhood environments that psychodynamic therapists might expect for people with this disorder.

Psychodynamic Therapies As we observed in Chapter 3, psychodynamic therapies approach all psychological problems in a similar manner. They use free association and the therapist's interpretations of transference, resistance, and dreams to help patients overcome their problems. With these techniques, *Freudian psychodynamic therapists* try to help clients with generalized anxiety disorder become less afraid of their id impulses and able to control them successfully. Other psychodynamic therapists, such as *object relations therapists,* focus more on helping anxious patients identify and resolve the anxiety-provoking childhood relationship problems that they seem to be repeating in adulthood. And *self therapists* seek to help anxious patients build a cohesive self from the fragmented self that these therapists believe keeps generating anxiety (Compton, 1992; Zerbe, 1990; Diamond, 1987).

"Why do you think you cross the read?"
(Drawing by A. Levin; © 1993 The New Yorker Magazine, Inc.)

Psychodynamic therapists guide clients with anxiety disorders (and other disorders as well) to uncover hidden motives, feelings, and needs.

Here a therapist uses classic psychodynamic techniques and interpretations to help a client overcome his generalized anxiety disorder. The client, a financially successful young man, was unable to enjoy his success, felt inferior to others, and had a very limited social life:

> In the course of analysis many facts were revealed that explained his inability to enjoy his financial success, and his despair of having an intimate relationship with a respectable girl. Briefly stated these difficulties were all rooted in guilt arising from unresolved oedipal conflicts and incestuous feelings for his sisters. Material success and becoming the sole support of the family symbolized for him the childhood wish to replace and surpass his father. Hence when he accomplished his wholehearted desire to give his mother every comfort to compensate for her many years of hardship, he was faced with an acute conflict.
>
> He had always retained his strong attachment to his mother, since she was the only understanding and mild person in his whole miserable environment. He also had very tender feelings for his two young sisters. Toward the male members of his family who had always abused him he felt hatred, rebellion, and a desire to excel them. . . .
>
> [Over the course of treatment] he saw clearly how much his business was responsible for creating actual conflicts and neurotic difficulties because it was a stepping stone to realizing his competitive drives. Apart from the conscious reasons he also recognized the unconscious motivations for his ambitions to be an independent, successful businessman, the center of this being more powerful materially than his brothers and father and to have power over them, make them dependent, if he could, on him. He became also more aware as analysis progressed why he gradually became tired of the business, lost his ambition, began to have anxieties that grew worse. By realizing his ambitions to be more successful than the older brothers and father, he also realized his childhood and puberty period ambitions,

> which then carried the oedipal desire and so were charged with a powerful sense of guilt. The adult success revived the early striving and brought forth the early repressed guilt feeling that accompanied these strivings, and this chaos created his desire to run away from it all, in the neurosis and illness. . . .
>
> With this [insight] and working through of aggressiveness the patient began to achieve self-confidence in his business, social, and family relations. He became less afraid of his business associates and began to develop genuine feelings of affection for, or at least understanding of, various members of his family. He started meeting young people of college training and even putting up brave arguments against their opinions. At this period he bought a better car, which he had hitherto avoided doing, and he also began to interest himself in sports. He became ambitious to make up his lack of education, began to study, and went to the theater. Finally he decided to sell his business, to rest for a period.
>
> *(Lorand, 1950, pp. 37–43)*

Controlled research has not consistently supported the effectiveness of psychodynamic approaches in cases of generalized anxiety disorder (Svartberg & Stiles, 1991; Nemiah, 1984; Prochaska, 1984). The bulk of evidence suggests that psychodynamic therapy is at best of modest help to people suffering from this disorder and of little help for those with other anxiety disorders, such as phobias and obsessive-compulsive disorder.

"Just because you're Attila the Hun, Dad, doesn't mean I have to be Attila the Hun."

Humanists and existentialists believe that people must be fully aware and accepting of their own thoughts, emotions, and behaviors. If they are unduly influenced by the standards of others and fail to address their own needs, they will develop a generalized anxiety disorder or another kind of psychological problem.

The Humanistic and Existential Perspectives

Humanistic and existential theorists propose that a generalized anxiety disorder, like other mental disorders, arises when people stop looking at themselves honestly and acceptingly. Instead, they deny and distort their true thoughts, emotions, and behavior. Their defensive postures ultimately serve to make them extremely anxious and incapable of fulfilling their potential as human beings.

Humanistic Explanations and Treatments The humanistic position on why people develop a generalized anxiety disorder is best illustrated by Carl Rogers's explanation. As we observed in Chapter 3, Rogers believed that some people develop a defensive way of functioning when as children they fail to receive ***unconditional positive regard*** from significant others. They, in turn, become overly critical of themselves and develop harsh self-standards, what Rogers called ***conditions of worth.*** They try to meet these standards by repeatedly distorting and denying their true experiences. Using such defensive techniques, these people succeed only partially in feeling good about themselves; threatening self-judgments persist in breaking through and causing intense anxiety. This foundation of anxiety sets the stage for a generalized anxiety disorder or some other form of psychological dysfunctioning.

Practitioners of Rogers's treatment approach, ***client-centered therapy,*** try to show unconditional positive regard for their clients and to empathize with them. These therapists expect that an atmosphere of genuine acceptance and caring will provide the security that clients need to recognize their true inner needs, thoughts, and emotions (Raskin & Rogers, 1995). The therapists' goal is to help clients "experience" themselves—that is, become completely trusting of their instincts and honest and comfortable with themselves. Their anxiety or other symptoms of psychological dysfunctioning will then subside.

Here Rogers describes the progress made by a client named Mrs. Oak, who was experiencing anxiety and related symptoms:

> Mrs. Oak was a housewife in her late thirties who was in a deeply discordant relationship with her husband and also much disturbed in her relationship with her adolescent daughter, who had recently been through a serious illness which had been diagnosed as psychoso-

matic. Mrs. Oak felt she must be to blame for this illness. She herself was a sensitive person, eager to be honest with herself and to search out the causes of her problems. She was a person with little formal education, though intelligent and widely read.

By the fifth interview any specific concentration on her problems had dropped out and the major focus of therapy had shifted to an experiencing of herself and her emotional reactions. . . . She was unusually sensitive to the process she was experiencing in herself. To use some of her expressions, she was feeling pieces of a jigsaw puzzle, she was singing a song without words, she was creating a poem, she was learning a new way of experiencing herself which was like learning to read Braille. Therapy was an experiencing of herself, in all its aspects, in a safe relationship. At first it was her guilt and her concern over being responsible for the maladjustments of others. Then it was her hatred and bitterness toward life for having cheated and frustrated her in so many different areas, particularly the sexual, and then it was the experiencing of her own hurt, of the sorrow she felt for herself for having been so wounded. But along with these went the experiencing of self as having a capacity for wholeness, a self which was not possessively loving toward others but was "without hate," a self that cared about others. This last followed what was, for her, one of the deepest experiences in therapy . . . the realization that the therapist cared, that it really mattered to him how therapy turned out for her, that he really valued her. She experienced the soundness of her basic directions. She gradually became aware of the fact that, though she had searched in every corner of herself, there was nothing fundamentally bad, but rather, at heart she was positive and sound. She realized that the values she deeply held were such as would set her at variance with her culture, but she accepted this calmly. . . .

One of the outstanding characteristics of the interviews was the minimal consideration of her outside behavior. Once an issue was settled in her, the behavioral consequences were mentioned only by chance. After she had "felt" her way through her relationship with her daughter, there was little mention of her behavior toward the daughter until much later when she casually mentioned that the relationship was much better. . . .

When she left therapy, it was with the feeling that a process was going on in her which would continue to operate. She felt that the relationship with the therapist had been very meaningful and in a psychological sense would never stop, even though she walked out of the office for good. She felt ready, she thought, to cope with her life, though she realized it would not be easy.

(Rogers, 1954, pp. 261–264)

In spite of such optimistic case reports, controlled studies have only sometimes found client-centered therapy more effective than placebo therapy or no therapy at all (Greenberg et al., 1994; Prochaska & Norcross, 1994). Moreover, researchers have found at best limited support for Rogers's explanation of generalized anxiety disorder and other forms of abnormal behavior. Nor have other humanistic theories and treatment received much research support. Indeed, most humanistic theorists believe that traditional research methods cannot provide a fair test for their explanations and treatments, and thus they have not even tried to test their work empirically.

Existential Explanations and Treatments Existentialists believe that generalized anxiety disorder grows out of ***existential anxiety,*** a universal human fear of the limits, freedom, and responsibilities of one's existence (May & Yalom, 1995; Tillich, 1952). We experience existential anxiety, they say, because we know that life is finite and we fear the death that awaits us. We also know that our actions and choices may hurt others unintentionally. Finally, we suspect that our own personal existence may ultimately lack meaning.

According to existentialists, people can confront their existential anxiety head on by taking responsibility for their actions, making decisions, making their lives meaningful, and appreciating their own uniqueness, or they can shrink from this confrontation. Caught up in the change, confusion, and strain of our highly organized, competitive technological civilization, some people choose to lead "inauthentic lives": they deny their fears, overlook their freedom of choice, avoid taking responsibility, and conform excessively to the guidelines imposed by society (Bugental, 1992, 1965; May, 1967). According to existentialists, such a lifestyle inevitably fails to reduce a person's existential anxiety, which continues to erupt in the form of generalized and other anxiety disorders.

Existential therapists use a variety of techniques, from supportive to confrontational, to help anxious clients take more responsibility and live more meaningfully. However, little systematic research has been conducted on these treatments, or on the existential explanations, for that matter. Like most humanists, existentialists believe that traditional research methods miss subtle, internal experiences by looking only at what can be observed and defined objectively (Bugenthal, 1997, 1992). Thus existentialists resort instead to reason, introspection, and individual case examples as evidence for their views and approaches.

The Cognitive Perspective

As we observed in Chapter 3, proponents of the cognitive model suggest that maladaptive ways of thinking are often the cause of psychological problems. Given that

Children visiting the Hiroshima Peace Memorial Museum stare in horror at wax figures depicting the pain and destruction caused by the atomic bomb dropped in 1945. While it is important to transmit cultural and personal history, research suggests that parental and societal descriptions of horrific events can sometimes heighten children's anxiety and even result in anxiety disorders (Bower, 1996). Cognitive theorists suggests that the children may learn from such acccounts that the world is dangerous and threatening.

excessive worry is a defining characteristic of generalized anxiety disorder, it is not surprising that cognitive theorists have had much to say about the causes and treatments for this disorder in particular.

Cognitive Explanations Several influential cognitive theories suggest that a generalized anxiety disorder is caused by ***maladaptive assumptions.*** As we saw in Chapter 3, Albert Ellis believes that some people hold basic irrational assumptions that color their interpretations of events and lead to inappropriate emotional reactions (Ellis, 1997, 1977, 1962). According to Ellis, people with generalized anxiety disorder often hold the following assumptions:

> "It is a dire necessity for an adult human being to be loved or approved of by virtually every significant other person in his community."
>
> "It is awful and catastrophic when things are not the way one would very much like them to be."
>
> "If something is or may be dangerous or fearsome, one should be terribly concerned about it and should keep dwelling on the possibility of its occurring."
>
> "One should be thoroughly competent, adequate, and achieving in all possible respects if one is to consider oneself worthwhile."
>
> *(Ellis, 1962)*

When people with these basic assumptions are faced with a stressful event, such as an exam or a blind date, they are likely to interpret it as highly dangerous and threatening, to overreact, and to experience fear. As they apply the assumptions to more and more life events, they may begin to develop a generalized anxiety disorder.

In a similar cognitive theory, Aaron Beck holds that people with generalized anxiety disorder constantly hold unrealistic silent assumptions that imply that they are in imminent danger (Beck, 1997, 1991, 1976; Beck & Emery, 1985):

> "Any strange situation should be regarded as dangerous."
>
> "A situation or a person is unsafe until proven to be safe."
>
> "It is always best to assume the worst."
>
> "My security and safety depend on anticipating and preparing myself at all times for any possible danger."
>
> *(Beck & Emery, 1985, p. 63)*

According to Beck, such silent assumptions lead people to experience ***automatic thoughts***—persistent anxiety-provoking images and thoughts. In social situations, for example, they may think, "I'll make a fool of myself"; "I won't know what to say"; "People will laugh at me"; and so on. Similarly, when they work on important tasks, they may be plagued by automatic thoughts such as "What if I fail?"; "I won't have enough time to do a good job"; "I'm falling behind."

Research has provided support for Ellis's and Beck's notion that maladaptive assumptions can induce anxiety. In several studies, nonanxious subjects who were manipulated into adopting negative views of themselves later developed signs of anxiety. For example, when normal college students were instructed to read to themselves such sentences as "My grades may not be good enough" and "I might flunk out of school," they temporarily showed greater respiratory changes and emotional arousal than did control subjects who read neutral sentences (Rimm & Litvak, 1969).

Other studies have suggested that people who tend to worry and have upsetting thoughts and images typically experience such features of anxiety as general nervous tension, muscle tension, upset stomach, and a sinking and heavy feeling in the stomach (Borkovec et al., 1993, 1983). Such worriers also experience more intrusions of negative thoughts and are more distracted than nonworriers when they try to concentrate on tasks.

Other investigations have found that many people with generalized anxiety disorder do indeed hold dysfunctional assumptions (Ellis, 1995; Hollon & Beck, 1994). One study found that thirty-two subjects with generalized anxiety disorder held exaggerated notions of possible harmful events or consequences (Beck et al., 1974). Each subject reported upsetting assumptions, images, and automatic thoughts about at least one of the following danger areas: physical injury, illness, or death; mental dysfunctioning; psychological impairment or loss of control; failure and inability to cope; and rejection, depreciation, and domination. Indeed, 70 percent of them feared three or more of these possibilities. Related studies have also found that people with generalized anxiety symptoms are more attentive to threatening cues than to other kinds of cues (Calvo, Eysenck, & Castillo, 1997; Mathews et al., 1995; Moog et al., 1995).

What kinds of people are likely to have inflated expectations of danger and experience a generalized anxiety disorder? Some cognitive theorists point to people whose lives have been punctuated by numerous *unpredictable* negative events. These individuals become generally fearful of the unknown and always wait for the boom to drop (Pekrun, 1992). In order to avoid being "blindsided," they keep trying to predict the occurrence of new unforeseen negative events, looking everywhere for signs of danger. Ironically, they wind up "reading" such signs into most of the situations that they encounter, and they see danger everywhere, thus setting up a life of anxiety. In accord with this notion, numerous laboratory studies have demonstrated that animal and human subjects respond more fearfully to unpredictable negative events than to predictable ones (Mineka, 1985). Subjects also choose to predict and control such negative events when given the option (Weinberg & Levine, 1980). However, researchers have yet to perform the difficult task of determining whether people with generalized anxiety disorder have experienced an unusual number of unpredictable negative events in life.

Cognitive Therapies Two kinds of cognitive approaches are commonly used in cases of generalized anxiety disorder. In one, based on the theories of Ellis and Beck, therapists help clients change the maladaptive assumptions that are supposedly at the root of their disorder. In the other, therapists teach clients how to cope during stressful situations.

Changing Maladaptive Assumptions In Ellis's technique of *rational-emotive therapy,* which we first observed in Chapter 3, the practitioner's role is to point out the irrational assumptions held by clients, offer alternative (more realistic) assumptions, and assign homework that gives clients practice at challenging old assumptions and applying new ones (Ellis, 1997, 1995, 1962). The approach is illustrated in the following discussion between Ellis and an anxious client who fears failure and disapproval at work, especially over a testing procedure that she has developed for her company.

Client: I'm so distraught these days that I can hardly concentrate on anything for more than a minute or two at a time. My mind just keeps wandering to that damn testing procedure I devised, and that they've put so much money into; and whether it's going to work well or be just a waste of all that time and money. . . .

Ellis: Point one is that you must admit that you are telling yourself something to start your worrying going, and you must begin to look, and I mean really look, for the specific nonsense with which you keep reindoctrinating yourself. . . . The false statement is: "If, because my testing procedure doesn't work and I am functioning inefficiently on my job, my co-workers do not want me or approve of me, then I shall be a worthless person". . . .

Client: But if I want to do what my firm also wants me to do, and I am useless to them, aren't I also useless to me?

Ellis: No—not unless you *think* you are. You are frustrated, of course, if you want to set up a good testing procedure and you can't. But need you be desperately unhappy because you are frustrated? And need you deem yourself completely unworthwhile because you can't do one of the main things you want to do in life?

(Ellis, 1962, pp. 160–165)

Beck has developed a similar but more systematic treatment for generalized anxiety disorder (Beck, 1997, 1991; Hollon & Beck, 1994; Beck & Emery, 1985). He starts therapy by trying to alter the numerous automatic thoughts that he says arise from the maladaptive assumptions of anxiety-prone persons and bombard their

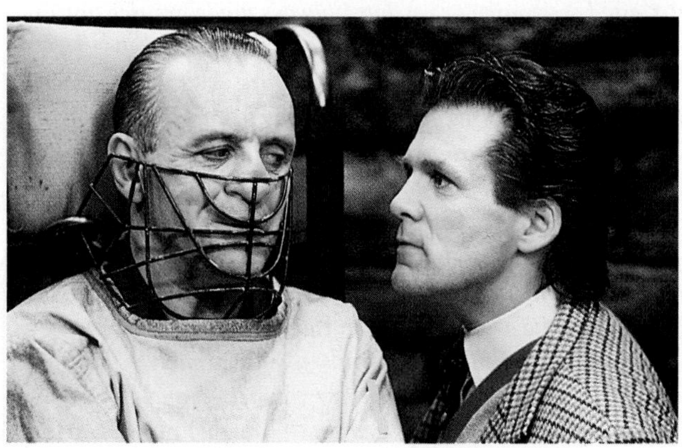

Cognitive researchers have found that people respond less fearfully to negative events when they can predict and control their onset. In fact, many people enjoy the feeling of fear as long as it occurs under controlled circumstances, as when they are safely viewing the sinister plots of Hannibal Lecter or other movie villians.

Personal Pathways

Albert Ellis: Clinician Heal Thyself

Rational-emotive therapy teaches clients to challenge and change their irrational assumptions. And who was the first client treated by Albert Ellis, the founder of the approach? Why, none other than Albert Ellis (Warga, 1988, p. 56):

At 19 Ellis became active in a political group but was hampered by his terror of public speaking. Confronting his worst demons in the first of many "shame-attacking" exercises he would devise, Ellis repeatedly forced himself to speak up in any political context that would permit. . . . "Instead of just getting good at this, I found I was very good at it. And now you can't keep me away from a public platform."

[Next] Ellis decided to work on the terrors of more private communication. "I was always violently interested in women, . . . but I always made excuses not to talk to them and was terrified of being rejected.

"Since I lived near The New York Botanical Garden in the Bronx, I decided to attack my fear and shame with an exercise in the park. I vowed that whenever I saw a reasonably attractive woman up to the age of 35, . . . I would sit next to her with the specific goal of opening a conversation within one minute. I sat next to 130 consecutive women who fit my criteria. Thirty of the women got up and walked away, but about 100 spoke to me—about their knitting, the birds, a book, whatever. I made only one date out of all these contacts—and she stood me up. . . . But I realized that throughout this exercise no one vomited, no one called a cop and I didn't die. The process of trying new behaviors and understanding what happened in the real world instead of in my imagination led me to overcome my fear of speaking to women."

thinking in situation after situation. The therapist helps the client recognize automatic thoughts, observe the faulty logic and assumptions underlying them, and test their validity. As a result, the client becomes less prone to see danger where there is none.

Beck's cognitive treatment for generalized anxiety disorder is really a recent adaptation of his influential and very effective treatment for depression (which is discussed in Chapter 9). Researchers are already finding that it often reduces generalized anxiety to more tolerable levels (Beck, 1997; Hollon & Beck, 1994; Barlow et al., 1992). Indeed, some observers suggest that it may turn out to be the single most helpful treatment for generalized anxiety disorder (Chambless & Gillis, 1993; Borkovec & Costello, 1992).

Teaching Clients to Cope As we saw in Chapter 3, Donald Meichenbaum (1997, 1993, 1992, 1975) has developed a cognitive technique for coping with stress called ***self-instruction training,*** or ***stress inoculation training.*** It teaches clients to rid themselves of thoughts that heighten their anxiety. These negative "self-statements," as he calls them, are similar to Beck's automatic thoughts.

In Meichenbaum's approach, clients are taught coping self-statements that they can apply during the various stages of a stressful situation—say, talking to their boss about a raise. First, they learn to say things to themselves that prepare them for the situation. They also learn self-statements that enable them to cope with the stressful situation as it is occurring, the kind of self-statements that can help them when they are actually in the boss's office. Third, they learn self-statements that will help them through the very difficult moments when the situation seems to be going badly, as when the boss glares at them as they ask for more money. And finally, they learn to make self-congratulatory self-statements after they have coped effectively. Here are a few examples of these four kinds of self-statements:

Preparing for a stressor

What is it you have to do?

You can develop a plan to deal with it.

Just think about what you can do about it. That's better than getting anxious.

Confronting and handling a stressor

Just psych yourself up—you can meet this challenge.

This tenseness can be an ally—a cue to cope.

Relax: you're in control. Take a slow, deep breath.

Coping with the feeling of being overwhelmed

When fear comes, just pause.

Keep the focus on the present. What is it you have to do?

You should expect your fear to rise.

Don't try to eliminate fear totally. Just keep it manageable.

Reinforcing self-statements

It worked! You did it.

It wasn't as bad as you expected.

You made more out of your fear than it was worth.

Your damn ideas—that's the problem. When you control them, you control your fear.

Once clients are skilled at using self-statements, therapists may subject them to stressful experiences in therapy and instruct them to apply what they have learned. The therapist may employ unpredictable electric shocks, imaging techniques, or stress-inducing films, or have the clients role-play unpleasant and embarrassing situations (Meichenbaum, 1977).

Self-instruction training has proved to be of modest help in cases of generalized anxiety disorder (Sanchez-Canovas et al., 1991; Ramm et al., 1981) and moderately helpful to people who suffer from test-taking and performance anxiety, stress associated with life change, and mild forms of anxiety (Fausel, 1995; Meichenbaum, 1993, 1992, 1972; Kirkland & Hollandsworth, 1980). It has also been adapted with some success to help athletes compete better and to encourage people to behave less impulsively, control anger, and control pain (Meichenbaum, 1997, 1993; Crocker, 1989; Novaco, 1977).

In view of the limited effectiveness of self-instruction training in treating anxiety disorders, Meichenbaum (1972) himself has suggested that it should be used to supplement other treatments. In fact, anxious people treated with a combination of self-instruction training and rational-emotive therapy improve more than people treated by either approach alone (Glogower, Freinouw, & McCroskey, 1978).

The Biological Perspective

Biological theorists believe that generalized anxiety disorder is related to biological factors and that these factors must be corrected to help people with this disorder. For years these claims were supported primarily by family risk studies. If biological tendencies toward generalized anxiety disorder are inherited, people who are biologically related should have more similar probabilities of developing this disorder. Studies have in fact found that blood relatives of persons with a generalized anxiety disorder are more likely than nonrelatives to have the disorder too (Kendler et al., 1992; Carey & Gottesman, 1981). Approximately 15 percent of the relatives of people with the disorder display it themselves—proportionally more than the 4 percent found in the general population. And the closer the relative (an identical twin, for example, as opposed to a fraternal twin or other sibling), the greater the likelihood that he or she will also have the anxiety disorder (Marks, 1986; Slater & Shields, 1969).

Of course, investigators cannot have full confidence in genetic and biological interpretations of these studies. The findings could also be suggesting that generalized anxiety disorder is caused by environmental experiences. Because relatives are likely to share aspects of the same environment, their shared disorders may be reflecting similarities in environment and upbringing rather than similarities in biological makeup. Indeed, the closer the relatives, the more similar their environmental experiences are likely to be. Because identical twins are more physically alike than fraternal twins, they may even experience more similarities in their upbringing (Tambs, Harris, & Magnus, 1995).

In recent decades important discoveries by brain researchers have offered more compelling evidence that generalized anxiety disorder is indeed related to biological factors, in particular to biochemical dysfunction in the brain (Brawman-Mintzer & Lydiard, 1997).

Biological Explanations The first discovery that helped open the door to a biological understanding of generalized anxiety disorder was made in the 1950s. Researchers determined that ***benzodiazepines,*** the family of drugs that includes diazepam (Valium), alprazolam (Xanax), and chlordiazepoxide (Librium), provide relief from anxiety. No one understood, however, why they were effective.

It was not until the late 1970s that newly developed radioactive techniques enabled researchers to pinpoint the exact sites in the brain that are affected by benzodiazepines (Mohler & Okada, 1977; Squires & Braestrup, 1977). Apparently certain neurons have receptor molecules that receive the benzodiazepines, just as a lock receives a key. Particularly high concentrations of these receptors are located in the brain's limbic system and hypothalamus, brain areas known to be heavily involved in controlling emotional states. Investigators soon discovered that these same receptors ordinarily receive ***gamma-aminobutyric acid (GABA),*** a common and important neurotransmitter in the brain (Haefely, 1990; Costa et al., 1978, 1975). As we saw in Chapter 4, neurotransmitters are chemicals that carry messages from one neuron to another. GABA carries *inhibitory* messages:

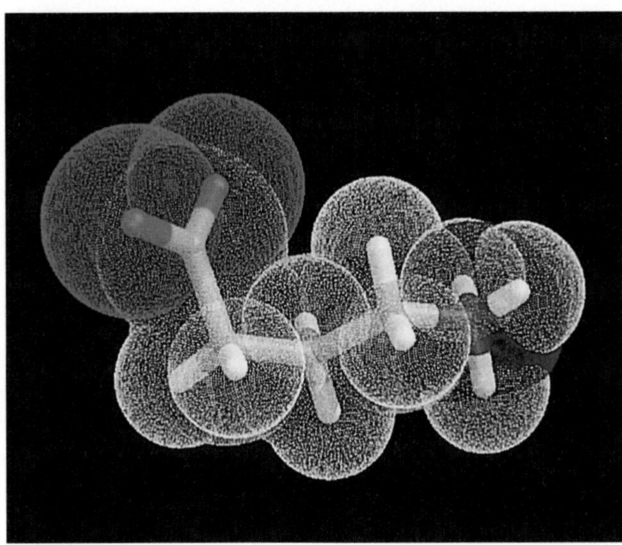

A computer-drawn molecule of gamma-aminobutyric acid (GABA), the neurotransmitter that carries an inhibitory message to neuron receptors. Neurons that receive GABA stop firing, reducing the brain's excitability and the overall experience of anxiety.

when GABA is received at a receptor, it causes the neuron to stop firing.

Researchers have studied the possible role of GABA and GABA receptors in fear reactions and have pieced together a scenario. In normal fear reactions, key neurons throughout the brain fire more rapidly, triggering the firing of still more neurons and creating a general state of hyperexcitability throughout the brain and body. Perspiration, breathing, and heartbeat increase. This state is experienced as fear or anxiety. After neuron firing continues for a while, it triggers a feedback system that reduces the level of excitability. Some neurons throughout the brain release the neurotransmitter GABA, which then binds to GABA receptors on receiving neurons and essentially instructs those neurons to stop firing. The state of excitability is thereby reduced, and the experience of fear or anxiety subsides (Costa, 1995, 1983; Sanders & Shekhar, 1995).

Researchers believe that a problem in the feedback system can cause fear or anxiety to go unchecked (Lloyd, Fletcher, & Minchin, 1992). In fact, when some investigators reduced the capacity of GABA to bind to GABA receptors, they found that animal subjects reacted with heightened anxiety (Costa, 1985; Mohler, Richards, & Wu, 1981). This finding suggests that people with a generalized anxiety disorder may have ongoing problems in their anxiety feedback system. Perhaps their brain supplies of GABA are too low. Perhaps they have too few GABA receptors, or their GABA receptors do not readily bind the neurotransmitters. Or perhaps their brain releases an excess of other chemicals that reduce GABA's activity at receptor sites. Indeed, researchers have identified some natural brain chemicals that seem able to promote anxiety by doing just that (Barondes, 1993).

This explanation of generalized anxiety disorder is promising, but it has problems. One is that further biological discoveries seem to complicate the picture. It has been found, for example, that GABA is only one of several body chemicals that can bind to the important GABA receptors (Bunney & Garland, 1981). Could these other chemicals, operating either alone or in conjunction with GABA, be critical factors in the brain's control of anxiety? Moreover, we now know that GABA is very widely distributed in the brain: it is released at about 40 percent of the synapses there. So it is difficult to identify precisely where in the brain it produces its effect on anxiety (Barondes, 1993).

Another problem is that much of the research on the biological regulation of anxiety has been done on laboratory animals. When researchers generate fear responses in animals, they are assuming that the animals are experiencing something that approximates human anxiety, but it is impossible to be certain (Newman & Farley, 1995). The animals may be experiencing a high level of arousal that is quite distinct from human anxiety.

Finally, biological theorists are faced with the problem of establishing a causal relationship. Although biological studies implicate physiological functioning in generalized anxiety disorder, they do not usually establish that the physiological events *cause* the disorder. The biological responses of chronically anxious adults may be the result rather than the cause of their anxiety disorders. Perhaps chronic anxiety eventually leads to poorer GABA reception, for example.

Biological Treatments The leading biological approach to treating generalized anxiety disorder is to prescribe *antianxiety drugs.* Indeed, it would be hard to find someone in our society who is not familiar with the words "tranquilizer," "Valium," and the like. Other biological interventions are *relaxation training,* in which people learn to relax the muscles throughout their bodies, and *biofeedback,* in which clients learn to control underlying biological processes that may be contributing to their problems.

Antianxiety Drugs Until the 1950s, a family of drugs labeled ***barbiturates*** were the major biological treatment for anxiety disorders (Ballenger, 1995; Nishino, Mignot & Dement, 1995). These drugs were used to sedate people at low doses and help them fall asleep at higher doses, and so they were generally known as ***sedative-hypnotic drugs.*** However, barbiturates created serious problems. They made people very drowsy, too high a dose could lead to death, and those who took them over an extended period could become physically dependent on them.

In the late 1940s, however, Frank Berger, a pharmacologist who was trying to develop a more effective antibiotic, developed a compound called ***meprobamate.*** Testing showed that meprobamate relaxed subjects' muscles and reduced their anxiety (Cole & Yonkers, 1995; Berger, 1970). In the 1950s it was released as a new kind of sedative-hypnotic medication under the brand name Miltown. This drug was less dangerous and less addictive than barbiturates, but it still caused drowsiness, so researchers continued to search for more satisfactory antianxiety medications.

Finally, in the late 1950s Lowell Randall found that a drug named *chlordiazepoxide,* a member of the family of drugs called ***benzodiazepines*** (see Table 6-1), tranquilized animals without making them extremely tired (Randall, 1982; Sternbach, 1982). This drug had actually been developed in the 1930s and put aside as seemingly useless. It was soon marketed under the brand name Librium. Several years later another benzodiazepine drug, *diazepam,* was developed and marketed under the brand name Valium.

Prior to the passage of food and drug laws in the early twentieth century, drug companies in the United States did not have to prove the safety or efficacy of their products. "Brain Salt," a patent medicine for anxiety and related difficulties, promised to cure nervous disability, headaches, indigestion, heart palpitations, and sleep problems, among other psychological and medical problems.

From the beginning, researchers were able to confirm that benzodiazepines reduced anxiety both in animals and in humans (Rickels, 1978). The drugs quickly became popular among health professionals, because they seemed to reduce anxiety without making people exceptionally tired. They also appeared relatively nontoxic even in large doses (Lader, 1992). By reducing tension at bedtime, they were able to help individuals fall asleep, and so they also gained wide use as sleeping medications. Doctors and patients alike viewed benzodiazepines as a totally safe kind of sedative-hypnotic drug, and the drugs soon became the most widely prescribed medications in the United States (Strange, 1992).

Only years later did researchers begin to understand the reasons for the effectiveness of benzodiazepine drugs. As we noted earlier, in 1977 researchers discovered specific neuron sites in the brain that receive benzodiazepines (Mohler & Okada, 1977; Squires & Braestrup, 1977). These are the same receptor sites that ordinarily receive GABA, the neurotransmitter that inhibits neuron firing, slows physical arousal, and reduces anxiety (Primus et al., 1996; Luddens & Korpi, 1995; Sanders & Shekhar, 1995). When benzodiazepines bind to these neuron receptor sites, particularly those receptors known as *GABA-A receptors,* they increase the ability of GABA to bind to them as well, and so apparently improve GABA's ability to slow neuron firing and reduce bodily arousal (Ballenger, 1995).

Benzodiazepines are prescribed for generalized anxiety disorder more than for most other kinds of anxiety disorders (Uhlenhuth et al., 1995). Controlled studies reveal that they do sometimes provide temporary and at least modest relief for this disorder (Ballenger, 1995; Taylor, 1995; Leonard, 1992). However, in recent years clinicians have begun to realize the potential dangers of these drugs (Schweizer & Rickels, 1996; Lader, 1992; Rickels & Schweizer, 1990). It has become clear that benzodiazepines alone are not a long-term solution for anxiety. When the medications are stopped, many clients' anxieties return and are as strong as ever (Ballenger, 1995; Taylor, 1995). Second, we now know that people who take benzodiazepines in large doses for an extended time can become physically dependent on them. Third, they can develop significant undesired effects such as drowsiness, lack of coordination, impaired memory, depression, or aggressive behavior (Elsesser et al., 1996;

TABLE 6-1 Drugs That Reduce Anxiety

Class/Generic Name	*Trade Name*	*Usual Daily Dose (mg)*	*Speed of Onset*
Benzodiazepines			
Alprazolam	Xanax	0.50–4.0	Rapid
Chlordiazepoxide	Librium	5–100	Moderate
Clonazepam	Klonopin	0.50–10	Very rapid
Clorazepate dipotassium	Tranxene	3.75–60	Very rapid
Diazepam	Valium	2.50–40	Very rapid
Lorazepam	Ativan	0.50–6	Moderate
Oxazepam	Serax	15–90	Moderate
Prazepam	Centrax	5–120	Slow
Azaspirones			
Buspirone	BuSpar	15–60	Slow
Beta blockers			
Propanolol	Inderal	10–40	Rapid
Atenolol	Tenormin	50–100	Rapid

Source: Hedaya, 1996; Physician's Desk Reference, *1994; Shader & Greenblatt, 1993, p. 1399; Leaman, 1992, p. 236; Silver & Yudofsky, 1988, pp. 807–809.*

Primus et al., 1996; Gold et al., 1995). Fourth, long-term use of these drugs may impair a person's cognitive and psychomotor functioning, and these effects may continue even after the drugs are stopped (Foy et al., 1995; Gorenstein et al., 1995). Fifth, animal studies suggest that long-term use of benzodiazepines may gradually erode one's ability to cope with stress, thus producing a greater dependence on the drug over the years (Roy-Byrne & Wingerson, 1992). And finally, although benzodiazepines are not toxic themselves, clinicians have learned that they do *potentiate,* or multiply, the effects of other toxic drugs, such as alcohol (Ballenger, 1995; Uhlenhuth et al., 1995; Allen & Lader, 1992). Respiration can slow dangerously, sometimes fatally, if people on these antianxiety drugs drink even small amounts of alcohol.

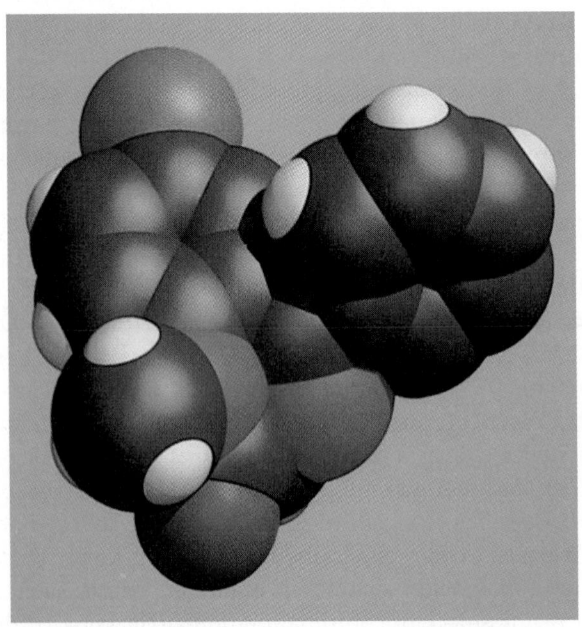

A computer-drawn molecule of the antianxiety drug "diazepam," known by the trade name Valium.

Several new kinds of antianxiety drugs have also been applied to generalized anxiety disorder (Roy-Byrne & Wingerson, 1992). One group, called ***beta blockers,*** bind to receptors in the brain called ***b-adrenergic receptors*** and in turn reduce specific *physical* symptoms of anxiety, such as palpitations and tremors (Tyrer, 1992). Apparently, however, beta blockers bring only minor improvement at best to people with generalized anxiety disorder (Meibach, Mullane, & Binstok, 1987). They are generating more enthusiasm as a treatment for performance anxiety; they have, for example, sometimes helped the performances of anxious bowlers, musicians, and public speakers (Taylor, 1995). Another antianxiety drug, ***buspirone***—a member of a group of drugs called ***azaspirones,*** which bind to yet different receptors in the brain—has received more research support than beta blockers. This drug is often as effective as benzodiazepines for generalized anxiety, yet appears less likely to lead to physical dependence (Schweizer & Rickels, 1997; Cole & Yonkers, 1995). While these various new drugs undergo further investigation, benzodiazepines continue to be the drugs most widely prescribed to curb broad anxiety symptoms (Ballenger, 1995; Shader & Greenblatt, 1993).

Relaxation Training A biological technique that has been commonly used in cases of generalized anxiety disorder is ***relaxation training.*** Here therapists teach clients to relax the muscles throughout the body. They expect that physical relaxation will inevitably lead to a state of psychological relaxation. Over the course of several sessions and homework assignments, clients learn to identify individual muscle groups, tense them, release the tension, and ultimately relax the whole body. With continued practice, they can bring on a state of deep muscle relaxation at will.

The therapist's instructions in relaxation training typically include the following points:

Identifying and Tensing the Muscle Groups

> . . . Now, what I want you to do is, with your left hand, hold the arm of your chair quite tight. I want you to observe certain things that are a result of your holding this chair tight. First of all, there are certain sensations. To begin with, you have sensations . . . in your hand and you may have other sensations. With your right hand, point out to me all the places where you get any kind of feeling which seems to be a result of holding the chair tightly.

Relaxing the Muscle Groups

> . . . I'm going to hold your wrist again and ask you to pull against it. When you pull, you will notice that the muscle becomes tight again. Then I will say to you, "Let go gradually." Now, when you let go, I want you to notice two things. The tight feeling will become less and I want you also to notice that the letting go is something that you do—something active that you put in the muscle. Well, your forearm will eventually come down to rest on the arm of the chair and ordinarily that would seem to you as though that's the end of the matter. You have let go. But it will not really be quite the end, because some of the muscle fibers will still be contracted, so that when your forearm has come down to the chair I will say to you, "Keep on letting go. Go on doing that in the muscle, that activity which you were doing while it was coming down. . . . Try and make it go further and further."
>
> (*Wolpe, The Case of Mrs. Schmidt*)

It is expected that anxious clients who complete relaxation training will be able to relax during stressful situations, thus reducing or preventing anxiety. Sometimes therapists actually create stressful situations during therapy sessions so that the clients can practice relaxing under stress (Suinn & Richardson, 1971). Suggestion, imagery, exercise, hyperventilation, and even short-acting drugs may be used to induce anxiety for this purpose (Mathews, 1985).

Research indicates that relaxation training is more effective than no treatment or placebo treatment in cases of generalized anxiety disorder (Bernstein & Carlson, 1993; Barlow et al., 1992; Barlow, 1989). The improvement it produces, however, tends to be modest (Butler et al., 1991), and other techniques that are known to induce relaxation, such as *meditation,* often seem to be equally effective in reducing anxiety (Kabat-Zinn et al., 1992; Mathews, 1984). Relaxation training is apparently of greatest help to people with generalized anxiety disorder when it is combined with cognitive therapy or with biofeedback (Taylor, 1995; Brown, Hertz, & Barlow, 1992; Butler et al., 1991, 1987).

Biofeedback Therapists who use ***biofeedback*** train people to control their physiological processes, such as heart rate or muscle tension. Clients are connected to a monitoring device that gives them continuous information

The muscular tension experienced by this client is detected by electrodes attached to her body and displayed on the nearby monitor. Electromyograph biofeedback training has proved modestly helpful in reducing anxiety.

about their bodily activities. By attending to the therapist's instructions and the signals from the monitor, they gradually learn to control even seemingly involuntary physiological processes. Therapists have taught clients to reduce at will the brain-wave activity underlying brain seizures, the change in heart rate characteristic of cardiac arrhythmias, and the high blood pressure levels of hypertension (Chen & Cui, 1995; Wittrock et al., 1995; Blanchard, 1994; McGrady & Roberts, 1992).

Biofeedback has also been used to reduce muscular tension and so feelings of anxiety (Somer, 1995; Stoyva & Budzynski, 1993; Hurley & Meminger, 1992). The most widely applied method uses a device called an ***electromyograph (EMG),*** which provides feedback about the level of muscular tension in the body. Electrodes are attached to the client's muscles—usually the *frontalis,* or forehead, muscles—where they detect the minute electrical activity that accompanies muscle contraction (see Figure 6-4). The device then amplifies and converts electric potentials coming from the muscles into an image, such as lines on a screen, or into a tone whose pitch and volume vary along with changes in muscle tension. Thus clients "see" or "hear" when their muscles are becoming more or less tense. After repeated trial and error, they become skilled at voluntarily reducing muscle tension and, theoretically, at reducing tension and anxiety in everyday stressful situations.

Research indicates that EMG biofeedback training helps both normal and anxious subjects reduce their anxiety somewhat (Hurley & Meminger, 1992; Rice & Blanchard, 1982). According to direct comparisons, EMG biofeedback training and relaxation training have similar effects on anxiety levels (Brown, Hertz, & Barlow, 1992; Andrasik & Blanchard, 1983). The subjects given EMG feedback are better able than relaxation-trained subjects to reduce their EMG readings (Canter et al., 1975; Coursey, 1975), but the two techniques produce similar results on all other indicators of anxiety (Canter et al., 1975).

In efforts to reduce anxiety, biofeedback therapists have also used an ***electroencephalograph (EEG),*** which records electrical activity in the brain. With this device they try to teach clients to produce *alpha waves* voluntarily. Our brain-wave patterns—that is, the rhythmic electrical discharges in our brains—vary with our activities. Alpha waves occur when we are in a relaxed, wakeful state. It has been suggested that biofeedback-induced increases in alpha-wave activity will lead to greater relaxation and be of help to anxious people (Hardt & Kamiya, 1978). Unfortunately, the production of alpha waves does not promote relaxation consistently, and so the method seems to have only limited potential as a treatment for generalized anxiety disorder (Blanchard et al., 1992; Andrasik & Blanchard, 1983).

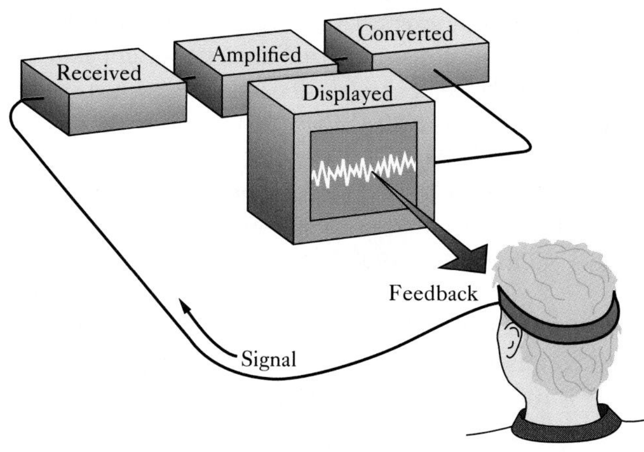

Figure 6-4 *This biofeedback system is recording tension in the forehead muscle of a headache sufferer. The system receives, amplifies, converts, and displays information about the tension, allowing the client to "observe" it and to try to reduce his tension responses.*

In the 1960s and 1970s, many people hailed biofeedback training as an approach that would change clinical treatment. This early expectation has not been fulfilled. So far, biofeedback procedures have tended to be more cumbersome, less efficient, and less productive than mental health clinicians had envisioned (Wittrock & Blanchard, 1992; Blanchard & Epstein, 1978). The techniques have proved most helpful as a complement to other treatments and have had their greatest impact on physical problems—headaches, back pain, gastrointestinal disorders, seizure disorders, and such neuromuscular disorders as cerebral palsy (Labbe, 1995; Naring, 1995; Newton et al., 1995; Blanchard et al., 1992, 1982).

Phobias

Most of us are none too eager to visit the dentist (Poulton et al., 1997; Litt, 1996), but few of us have such dread of the drill as this woman:

> At the age of twelve, my eye teeth came through very crooked and high up in the gum. I remember my mother dragging me along to the dentist and both of them standing behind me saying I would have to go into the hospital to have them out. . . . After that I would make up any excuse to get out of going. . . . I managed to bluff my way through school and it was such a relief when I actually left, as I knew no school dentist could come round wondering why I hadn't kept an appointment. Also, when I was at school we were al-

ways given a note asking us whether we would like to use the school dentist or the family one, and I always managed to forge my mother's signature stating the latter.

For the next ten years my life was unbearable. Looking back on it now, I honestly don't know how I didn't go off my head. I loved going out with boys, but most of them must have thought I was very shy or a miserable person: I could never laugh in public, only half-smile and bow my head. I could never relax, not even for a minute. Parties were unbearable, especially when someone told me a joke. And worst of all was the fact that I knew I would have to go to the dentist sometime in the future. As the years went by, my teeth got worse and I become more withdrawn. When I was twenty I did meet someone, and I knew if anyone would understand, it would be him, but I still could not bring myself to tell him, and on I went with my head bowed down and all the time thinking that I mustn't open my mouth too much and knowing that I had to go the dentist in the end.

We became engaged on my twenty-first birthday, and a year later we got married. You can imagine my wedding day was unbearable for me. The wedding photos were a nightmare, with the photographers asking me to put my head up and smile, and the whole time I was in a cold sweat. Anyway, we moved to the south coast, my husband got a good job and I could stay at home and not talk to anyone, so therefore I didn't have to open my mouth at all. Then I became pregnant and of course I was petrified I would have a full medical check-up and would have to open my mouth. I told my husband that I had been to the doctor, but at seven months I was afraid that by not going I might endanger the baby, so eventually I went, and as luck would have it, nobody even bothered to look. . . .

I had always wondered when my husband went to the dentist why he never mentioned that I never went, but I certainly wasn't going to. Every night I would lie in a cold sweat thinking about it, and as my son got older I knew I had to do something. Each night got worse; I couldn't sleep; I would wait until my husband was asleep and go downstairs and cry my eyes out. I honestly thought I was going mad. On one of my bad nights my husband came down, and I was in such a state that I managed to blurt the whole lot out. In the morning he got up and went to work, and . . . he came back at lunch time and said that he had had a long talk [with] the dentist and he understood how I felt and would see me the next day. That afternoon, and until 10:45 the next day, was unbearable. I was sick, I had diarrhea, I had a temperature and I certainly didn't sleep a wink. I took four tranquilizers that night and six the next morning, and in the end my husband had to practically carry me in. . . . Anyway, he told me I had left it so long that the roots were all twisted and that the front six teeth would have to come out. I still had about seven other fillings that needed doing, and I knew if I wanted the front ones done it would be no good not turning up for the other treatment. Each visit was a nightmare. Every time I went, my husband had to take hours off work, as if he hadn't been there I certainly wouldn't have turned up.

Eventually the dentist said that on the next visit he would take out the front six. My husband took the day off, and we went together. I had gas, and it was all over in a few seconds. I managed to get to the car and just sat there, and my husband handed me a present: a mirror. At first I was too afraid to look, but when I did I couldn't believe how radiant I looked. But I will never get over my phobia. In fact I am ashamed to admit I have not been back to the dentist since that last visit. I will walk half a mile out of my way rather than pass the door in case he sees me.

(Melville, 1978, pp. 151–153)

A ***phobia*** (from the Greek for "fear") is a persistent and unreasonable fear of a particular object, activity, or situation. People with a phobia become fearful if they even think about the object or situation they dread (Thorpe & Salkoviskis, 1995), but they usually remain comfortable and functional as long as they avoid the object or thoughts about it. Most are well aware that their fears are excessive and unreasonable. Many have no idea how their fears started.

We all have our areas of special fear, and it is normal for some things to upset us more than other things, perhaps even different things at different stages of our life. A survey of residents of a community in Burlington, Vermont, found that fears of crowds, death, injury, illness, and separation were more common among people in their 60s than in other age groups (Agras, Sylvester, & Oliveau, 1969). Among 20-year-olds, fears of snakes, heights, storms, enclosures, and social situations were much more prevalent (see Figure 6-5).

How do these common fears differ from phobias? How, for instance, does a "normal" fear of snakes differ from a snake phobia? DSM-IV indicates that phobic fear is more intense and persistent, and the desire to avoid the object or situation is more compelling (APA, 1994). People with phobias experience such distress that their fears often interfere dramatically with their personal, social, or occupational functioning.

Phobias are common in our society (see Box 6-2). Surveys suggest that 10 to 11 percent of the adult population in the United States suffer from a phobia in any given year (Magee et al., 1996; Regier et al., 1993; Eaton et al., 1991). More than 14 percent develop a phobia at some point in their lives. These disorders are more than twice as common in women as in men.

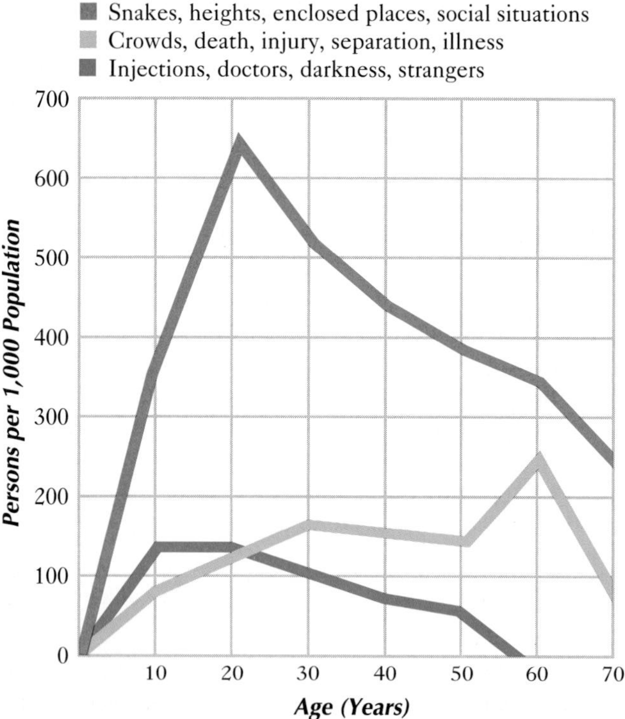

Figure 6-5 *Certain age groups are particularly likely to have certain fears. Close to 70 percent of all 20-year-olds surveyed in Burlington, Vermont—more than in any other age group—feared snakes and heights. People 60 years old, by contrast, were more likely than younger persons to be afraid of crowds and of death, and 10-year-olds were more likely than their elders to fear injections and doctors. (Adapted from Agras, Sylvester, & Oliveau, 1969, p. 153.)*

Types of Phobias

Some phobias share particular themes. Thus DSM-IV distinguishes three categories: agoraphobia, social phobias, and specific phobias. *Agoraphobia* (from the Greek for "fear of the marketplace") is a fear of venturing into public places, especially when one is alone. *Social phobias* are fears of social or performance situations in which embarrassment may occur. All other phobias are classified as *specific phobias.*

Agoraphobia

People with ***agoraphobia*** avoid public places or situations in which escape might be difficult or help unavailable should they develop symptoms of panic, such as dizziness, palpitations, diarrhea, or nausea (APA, 1994). It is a pervasive and complex phobia. In any given year between 2 and 4 percent of the adult population experience this problem, women twice as frequently as men (Magee et al., 1996; Kessler et al., 1994; Eaton et al., 1991). People typically develop agoraphobia in their 20s or 30s, as Veronica did:

> For several months prior to her application for treatment Veronica had been unable to leave her home. . . . "It is as if something dreadful would happen to me if I did not immediately go home." Even after she would return to the house, she would feel shaken inside and unable to speak to anyone or do anything for an hour or so. However, as long as she remained in her own home or garden, she was able to carry on her routine life without much problem. . . . Because of this agoraphobia, she had been unable to return to her position as a mathematics teacher in the local high school after the summer vacation.
>
> . . . [Veronica] stated that she had always been a somewhat shy person who generally preferred keeping to herself, but that up until approximately a year ago she had always been able to go to her job, shop, or go to church without any particular feelings of dread or uneasiness. It was difficult for her to recall the first time . . . but it seemed to her that the first major experience was approximately a year before, when she and her mother had been Christmas shopping. They were standing in the middle of a crowded department store when she suddenly felt the impulse to flee. She left her mother without an explanation and drove home as fast as she could. . . . After the Christmas vacation she seemed to recover for a while and was at least able to return to her classroom duties without any ill effect. During the ensuing several months she had several similar experiences, usually when she was off duty; but by late spring these fears were just as likely to occur in the classroom. . . . In thinking further about the occurrence of her phobia, it seemed to Veronica that there was actually no particular stress which might account for her fear. Often it seemed to come over her when she was momentarily relaxed, although always when she was in public.
>
> *(Goldstein & Palmer, 1975, pp. 163–164)*

It is typical of people with agoraphobia to avoid entering crowded streets or stores, driving through tunnels or on bridges, traveling on public transportation, and using elevators. If they venture out of the house at all, it is usually only in the company of close relatives or friends. Some people with agoraphobia further insist that family members or friends stay with them at home, but even at home and in the company of others they may continue to feel anxious.

In many cases the intensity of the agoraphobia fluctuates, as it did for Veronica. In severe cases, people become virtual prisoners in their own homes. Their social life dwindles, and they cannot hold a job. Persons with agoraphobia may also become depressed, sometimes as a result of the severe limitations that their phobia places on their lives.

Many people with agoraphobia are in fact prone to experience extreme and sudden explosions of fear, called *panic attacks,* when they enter public places. In such cases, the agoraphobic pattern is considered a type of panic disorder, ***panic disorder with agoraphobia,*** because the disorder involves much more than an overblown fear of venturing away from home and developing a few symptoms of panic. This disorder, which will be discussed in the next chapter's section on panic disorders, is thought to have different origins from the phobia under discussion here, technically labeled ***agoraphobia without history of panic disorder*** (Pollard et al., 1996; Hoffart, Thornes, & Hedley, 1995).

Social Phobias Many people have qualms about interacting with others or talking or performing in front of others. The opera singer Maria Callas often shook with fear while waiting in the wings to perform, and Harold MacMillan, the former British prime minister, typically felt nauseated before question time in Parliament (Marks, 1987). Such normal social fears are inconvenient, but the people who have them manage to function adequately, some at a very high level.

By contrast, people with a ***social phobia*** have severe, persistent, and irrational fears of social or performance situations in which embarrassment may occur. A social phobia may be specific, such as a fear of talking or performing in public, eating in public, using a public bathroom, or writing in front of others, or it may be a broader fear of social situations, such as a general fear of functioning inadequately or inappropriately when others are watching (Norton et al., 1997). In both forms, people repeatedly evaluate themselves as performing more poorly than they actually do (Rapee & Hayman, 1996; Alden & Wallace, 1995). The distinguishing characteristic that sets social phobias off from normal social fears is the person's degree of self-consciousness, overestimation of social catastrophe, level of discomfort, and constant avoidance of the feared situation (Makris & Heimberg, 1996; Poulton & Andrews, 1996).

A social phobia can be highly incapacitating (Stein et al., 1994; Liebowitz, 1992). A person who is unable to interact with others or speak in public may fail to perform important scholastic or professional responsibilities. One who cannot eat in public may reject dinner invitations and other social engagements. Since most people with this phobia keep their fears secret, their social reluctance is often misinterpreted as snobbery, disinterest, or stubbornness. Consider this 28-year-old woman who was terrified that her hands would tremble in front of others:

> She therefore didn't like giving to or accepting from strangers a drink or cup of tea or coffee. The first time this happened was when she was nineteen and was

George Tooker's painting Subway *expresses the sense of threat, entrapment, and disorientation that many people with agoraphobia experience when they enter public places.*

BOX 6-2 Phobias, Familiar and Not So Familiar

Air	Aerophobia
Animals	Zoophobia
Beards	Pogonophobia
Bees	Apiphobia, melissophobia
Being afraid	Phobophobia
Being alone	Autophobia, monophobia, eremophobia
Being buried alive	Tapophobia
Being dirty	Automysophobia
Being stared at	Scopophobia
Blood	Hematophobia
Books	Bibliophobia
Cancer	Cancerophobia, carcinomatophobia
Cats	Ailurophobia, gatophobia
Children	Pediophobia
Choking	Pnigophobia
Churches	Ecclesiaphobia
Cold	Psychrophobia, frigophobia
Corpse	Necrophobia
Crossing a bridge	Gephyrophobia
Crowds	Ochlophobia
Darkness	Achluophobia, nyctophobia
Daylight	Phengophobia
Death	Necrophobia, thanatophobia
Demons or devils	Demonophobia
Dirt	Mysophobia, rhypophobia
Disease	Nosophobia, pathophobia
Dogs	Cynophobia
Dolls	Pediophobia
Dreams	Oneirophobia
Drugs	Pharmacophobia
Empty rooms	Kenophobia
Enclosed space	Claustrophobia
England and things English	Anglophobia
Eyes	Ommatophobia
Failure	Kakorraphiaphobia
Feces	Coprophobia
Fire	Pyrophobia
Flood	Antlophobia
Flowers	Anthophobia
Flying	Aerophobia
Fog	Homichlophobia
Food	Sitophobia, cibophobia
Foreigners	Xenophobia
France and things French	Gallophobia
Fur	Doraphobia
Germany and things German	Germanophobia
Germs	Spermophobia
Ghosts	Phasmophobia
God	Theophobia
Graves	Taphophobia
Heart disease	Cardiophobia
Heat	Thermophobia
Heights	Acrophobia
Home	Domatophobia
Homosexuality	Homophobia
Horses	Hippophobia
Human beings	Anthropophobia
Ice, frost	Cryophobia
Illness	Nosemaphobia
Imperfection	Atelophobia

taken home by her boyfriend to meet his parents. Both this relationship and a succeeding one failed, and from then on she was conscious of her "phobia." She found her fears gradually spreading and affecting her work as a secretary. "At one time I found it difficult to take dictation and type it back if it was given to me just before I was due to leave the office, or if the work was needed urgently and my boss was waiting for it; I would panic and my fingers would just seize up. . . . I know everybody has some dread of something, but people accept somebody who has an aversion to mice or flies. If you don't like giving somebody a drink, though, they think you are antisocial and, if your hands shake, that you must either be 'on the bottle' or a complete wreck. It's strange, really, as I strike everybody as a confident person, but with certain people, regardless of whether they are 'ordinary' or 'impressive,' I become very self-conscious."

(Melville, 1978, pp. 78–79)

Social phobias are apparently more common than agoraphobia. As many as 8 percent of the population—around three women for every two men—experience this problem in any given year (Magee et al., 1996; APA, 1994; Kessler et al., 1994). The disorder often begins in late childhood or adolescence and may persist for many years, although its intensity may fluctuate over the years

Infection	Mysophobia, molysmophobia	Pain	Algophobia, odynephobia	Speed	Tachophobia
Injections	Trypanophobia	Physical love	Erotophobia	Spiders	Arachnophobia
Insanity	Lyssophobia, maniaphobia	Pleasure	Hedonophobia	Stings	Cnidophobia
Insects	Entomophobia	Poison	Toxiphobia	Strangers	Xenophobia
Light	Photophobia, phengophobia	Poverty	Peniaphobia	Sun	Heliophobia
Lightning	Astrapophobia, keraunophobia	Pregnancy	Maieusiophobia	Surgery	Ergasiophobia
Machinery	Mechanophobia	Punishment	Poinephobia	Swallowing	Phagophobia
Marriage	Gamophobia	Railways	Siderodromophobia	Teeth	Odontophobia
Meat	Carnophobia	Rain	Ombrophobia	Thunder	Keraunophobia, tonitrophobia
Men	Androphobia	Ridicule	Katagelophobia	Touching or being touched	Haphephobia
Mice	Musophobia	Rivers	Potamophobia	Travel	Hodophobia
Mirrors	Eisoptrophobia	Robbers	Harpaxophobia	Trees	Dendrophobia
Missiles	Ballistophobia	Russia and things Russian	Russophobia	Vehicles	Amaxophobia, ochophobia
Money	Chrometophobia	Satan	Satanophobia	Venereal disease	Cypridophobia, venereophobia
Nakedness	Gymnophobia	School	Scholionophobia, didaskaleinophobia	Wasps	Spheksophobia
Night	Nyctophobia	Sexual intercourse	Coitophobia, cypridophobia	Water	Hydrophobia
Noise or loud talking	Phonophobia	Shadows	Sciophobia	Wind	Anemophobia
Novelty	Cainophobia, neophobia	Sharp objects	Belonophobia	Women	Gynophobia
Odors	Osmophobia	Skin	Dermatophobia	Words	Logophobia
Odors (body)	Osphresiophobia	Skin diseases	Dermatosiophobia	Work	Ergasiophobia, ponophobia
Open spaces	Agoraphobia, cenophobia, kenophobia	Sleep	Hypnophobia	Worms	Helminthophobia
		Snakes	Ophidiophobia	Wounds, injury	Traumatophobia
		Snow	Chionophobia	Writing	Graphophobia

(Melville, 1978, pp. 196–202)

(Magee et al., 1996; Lepine & Lellovich, 1995; APA, 1994).

Specific Phobias A ***specific phobia*** is a persistent fear of a specific object or situation—other, of course, than being in public places (agoraphobia) or in socially embarrassing situations (social phobia). When they are exposed to or anticipate being exposed to the object or situation they dread, people with this disorder invariably experience immediate fear. Common specific phobias are intense fears of specific animals or insects, heights, enclosed spaces, and thunderstorms. Here are a few first-hand descriptions (all in Melville, 1978):

Spiders (arachnophobia) Seeing a spider makes me rigid with fear, hot, trembling and dizzy. I have occasionally vomited and once fainted in order to escape from the situation. These symptoms last three or four days after seeing a spider. Realistic pictures can cause the same effect, especially if I inadvertently place my hand on one. (p. 44)

Flying (aerophobia) We got on board, and then there was the take-off. There it was again, that horrible feeling as we gathered speed. It was creeping over me again, that old feeling of panic. I kept seeing everyone as puppets, all strapped to their seats with no control over their destinies, me included. Every time the plane did a variation of speed or route, my heart would leap and I would hurriedly ask what was happening. When the plane started to lose height, I was terrified that we were about to crash. (p. 59)

Thunderstorms (tonitrophobia) At the end of March each year, I start getting agitated because summer is coming and that means thunderstorms. I have been afraid since my early twenties, but the last three years have been the worst. I have such a heartbeat that for hours after a storm my whole left side is painful. . . . I say I will stay in the room, but when it comes I am a jelly, reduced to nothing. I have a little cupboard and I go there, I press my eyes so hard I can't see for about an hour, and if I sit in the cupboard over an hour my husband has to straighten me up. (p. 104)

Each year as many as 9 percent of the United States population have the symptoms of a specific phobia (APA, 1994; Kessler et al., 1994) (see Table 6-2). Eleven percent develop a specific phobia sometime during their lives, and many people have more than one specific phobia at a time (Magee et al., 1996; Eaton et al., 1991). Women with this disorder outnumber men by at least 2 to 1—a gender difference that holds in studies across the United States, Canada, and Europe (Fredrikson et al., 1996; Magee et al., 1996; Weissman, 1988).

The impact of a specific phobia on a person's life depends on what arouses the fear. Some things are easier to avoid than others. People whose phobias center on dogs, insects, or water will repeatedly encounter or expect to encounter the objects they dread. Their efforts to avoid them must be elaborate and may impose great restrictions on their lives. People with snake phobias have a much easier time. As we see in Figure 6-6, the vast majority of people with a specific phobia—almost 90 percent of them—do not seek treatment, concentrating instead on avoiding the objects they fear (Regier et al., 1993).

Specific phobias can develop at any time of life, although some, such as animal phobias, tend to begin during childhood and may disappear on their own before adulthood (APA, 1994). Among the children and adolescents with specific phobias observed in the Vermont study (Agras et al., 1969), most improved to some degree over the course of five years without any treatment at all, and 40 percent became totally free of symptoms. Phobias that last into or begin during adulthood, however, tend to hold on stubbornly and usually lessen only under treatment.

Explanations of Phobias

Each of the models has offered explanations for phobias that are consistent with its concepts and principles. Freud's psychodynamic explanation was once the most influential, but in recent years behavioral explanations have received much more attention.

Psychodynamic Explanations Freud believed that phobias result when people make excessive use of the defense mechanisms of ***repression*** and ***displacement*** to control underlying anxiety. Such persons repeatedly push their anxiety-producing impulses deeper into unconsciousness (repression) and transfer their fears to neutral objects or situations (displacement) that are easier to cope with and control. Although the new objects they come to fear are often related to the threatening impulses, the person is not aware of the relationship.

Consider once again Freud's (1909) famous case study of Little Hans, the child with a fear of horses, who was discussed in Chapter 2. Freud proposed that Hans became afraid of his own id impulses during the third and fourth years of his life, which Freud called the Oedipal stage. At that time, he began to express sexual feelings toward his mother by handling his penis and asking his mother to place her finger on it. She responded with a threat to cut off his penis and stressed that his desires were totally improper. According to Freud, this threat so frightened Hans that he became unconsciously afraid

TABLE 6-2 Anxiety Disorders Profile

	One-Year Prevalence	*Female : Male Ratio*	*Typical Age at Onset*	*Prevalence Among Close Relatives*
Generalized anxiety disorder	3.8%	2:1	0–20 years	Elevated
Agoraphobia without panic disorder	2.8%	2:1	20–40 years	Unknown
Social phobias	8.0%	3:2	10–20 years	Elevated
Specific phobias	9.0%	2:1	Variable	Elevated

Source: APA, 1994; Kessler et al., 1994; Regier et al., 1993; Blazer et al., 1991; Davidson et al., 1991; Eaton et al., 1991.

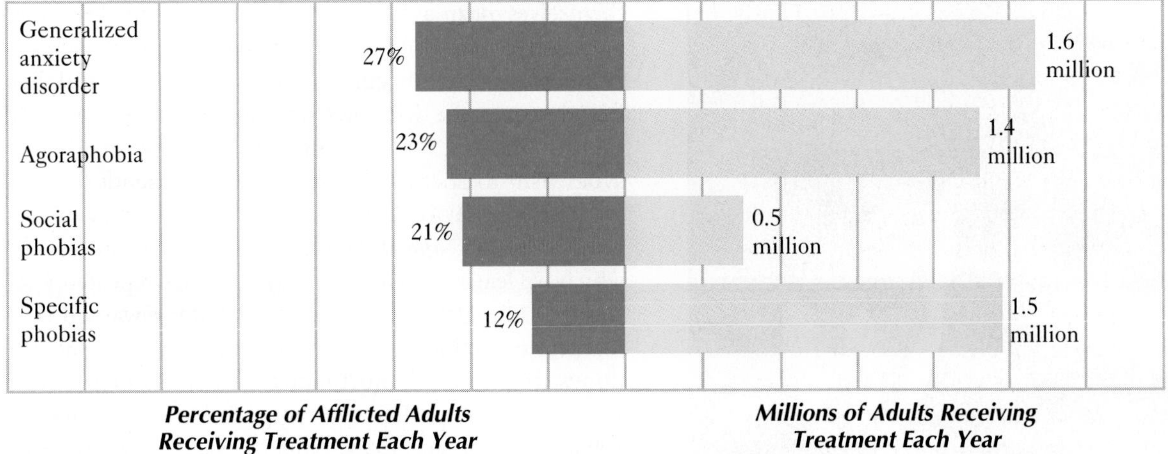

Figure 6-6 *Who receives treatment for their anxiety disorder? More than a quarter of all persons who have a generalized anxiety disorder in the United States receive professional treatment each year, but only about one-eighth of those with a specific phobia, a less disabling disorder, receive treatment. Because the prevalence rates of these disorders differ, however, approximately equal numbers of people receive treatment for each. (Adapted from Regier et al., 1993; Blazer et al., 1991; Boyd et al., 1990.)*

that his father, too, would learn of his desires and castrate him. In short, Hans came to develop high levels of neurotic and moral anxiety. However, he did not consciously fear his id impulses, his mother, or his father. Instead, Hans repressed the impulses and displaced his fears onto a neutral object—horses. Hans chose horses, Freud maintained, because he had come to associate them with his father.

Freud's explanation of phobias, like his explanation of generalized anxiety disorder, has received very limited research support over the years. Similarly, contemporary psychodynamic, humanistic, cognitive, and biological theorists have been unable to shed much light on why people develop phobias. In contrast, the explanations offered by *behavioral theorists* have received considerable research support and are today the most influential in the clinical field.

Behavioral Explanations

Behaviorists believe that people with phobias first learn to fear certain objects, situations, or events through conditioning. Once the fears are acquired, the individuals keep avoiding the dreaded object or situation, so that the fears become all the more entrenched.

Learning to Fear and Avoid Behaviorists propose ***classical conditioning*** as a common way of acquiring fear reactions to objects or situations that are not inherently dangerous. Here, two events that occur close together in time become closely associated in a person's mind, and, as we saw in Chapter 3, the person soon reacts similarly to both of them. If one event triggers a fear response, the other may also.

In the 1920s a clinician described the case of a young woman who apparently acquired a phobic fear of running water through classical conditioning (Bagby, 1922). As a child of 7 she went on a picnic with her mother and aunt, and ran off by herself into the woods after lunch. While she was climbing over some large rocks, her feet became deeply wedged between two of them, and the harder she tried to free herself, the more firmly trapped she became. No one heard her screams, and she became more and more terrified. In the terminology of behaviorists, the entrapment was eliciting a fear response.

Entrapment ⟶ Fear response

As she struggled to free her feet, the girl heard a waterfall nearby. The sound of the running water became linked in her mind to her terrifying encounter with the rocks, and she developed a fear of running water as well.

Running water ⟶ Fear response

Eventually the aunt found the screaming child, freed her from the rocks, and gave her comfort and reassurance; but significant psychological damage had been done. From that day forward, the girl was terrified of running water. For years family members had to hold her down to bathe her. When she traveled on a train, friends had to cover the windows so that she would not have to look at any streams. The young woman had apparently acquired a phobia through classical conditioning.

In conditioning terms, the entrapment was an ***unconditioned stimulus*** (US) that understandably elicited an ***unconditioned response*** (UR) of fear. The running

Ophidiophobia, an extreme fear of snakes, is one of the most common specific phobias. Thus, clinical researchers have little difficulty finding subjects with this problem when they are conducting research on the nature, cause, and treatment of phobias.

water represented a ***conditioned stimulus*** (CS), a formerly neutral stimulus that became associated with entrapment in the child's mind and came to elicit a fear reaction. The newly acquired fear was a ***conditioned response*** (CR).

CS: Running water ⟶ CR: Fear
US: Entrapment ⟶ UR: Fear

Another way of acquiring fear reactions is through ***modeling,*** that is, through observation and imitation (Bandura & Rosenthal, 1966). A person may observe that others are afraid of certain objects or events and develop fears of the same objects or events (Fredrikson, Annas, & Wik, 1997). Consider a young boy whose mother is afraid of illnesses, doctors, and hospitals. If she frequently expresses those fears, before long the boy himself may fear illnesses, doctors, and hospitals.

Why should one fear-provoking experience develop into a long-term phobia? Shouldn't the trapped girl later have seen that running water would bring her no harm? Shouldn't the boy later see that illnesses are temporary and doctors and hospitals helpful? Behaviorists agree that fears will indeed undergo ***extinction*** if a person is repeatedly exposed to the feared object and sees that it brings no harm. After acquiring a fear response, however, people try to *avoid* what they fear. Whenever they find themselves near a fearsome object, they quickly move away. They may also plan ahead to ensure that such encounters will not occur. Remember that the girl had friends cover the windows on trains so that she could avoid looking at streams. Similarly, the boy may try to avoid visits to doctors, hospitals, and sick friends.

In the behavioral view, such avoidance behaviors develop through ***operant conditioning,*** the process by which we learn to behave in ways that are repeatedly rewarded. The girl and boy are repeatedly rewarded by a marked reduction in anxiety whenever they avoid the things they fear. Unfortunately, such avoidance also serves to preserve their fear responses (Kim & Hoover, 1996; Wells et al., 1995; Miller, 1948; Mowrer, 1947, 1939). People with phobias do not get close to the dreaded objects often enough to learn that they are really quite harmless.

It is worth noting that behaviorists propose that specific learned fears will blossom into a generalized anxiety disorder when a person acquires a large number of them. This development is presumed to come about through ***stimulus generalization:*** responses to one stimulus are also elicited by similar stimuli. The fear of running water acquired by the girl in the rocks could have generalized to such similar stimuli as milk being poured into a glass or even the sound of bubbly music. Perhaps a person experiences a series of upsetting events, each event produces one or more feared stimuli, and the person's reactions to each of these stimuli generalize to yet other stimuli. That person may then build up a large number

When people observe others (models) being afraid of or victimized by an object or situation, they themselves may develop a fear of the object. Alfred Hitchcock's film The Birds *led to an increase in the incidence of ornithophobia (fear of birds) during the 1960s.*

of fears and eventually develop a generalized anxiety disorder.

Investigating the Behavioral Explanations Behavioral studies have indicated that fear reactions can indeed be acquired through conditioning. Some *analogue experiments,* for example, have found that laboratory animals can be taught to fear objects through classical conditioning (Miller, 1948; Mowrer, 1947, 1939). Experimenters typically place an animal in a shuttle box—a two-compartment box in which the animal can jump over a barrier from one compartment to the other—and shock the animal through the floor after a few seconds. Most animals react by running in circles, urinating, defecating, and crying out. After repeated trials, the animals show this reaction the moment they are placed in or even near the shuttle box, before the onset of shock. Because of its temporal association with shock, the box itself becomes a conditioned stimulus capable of eliciting conditioned fear responses.

The same studies have also demonstrated that animals can learn to *avoid* the shock of a shuttle box. While running around the box, most animals eventually cross the barrier into the other side, where they are safe from shock. Usually they discover that this is the road to safety, and henceforth jump over the barrier and escape to the safe side whenever they are shocked. Eventually the animals learn to avoid the threatening side altogether and go directly to the safe compartment before the current is even turned on. When experimenters use extremely traumatic stimuli (that is, high levels of shock), fear and avoidance reactions are learned more rapidly—often in one trial—and are particularly hard to extinguish (Solomon, Kamin, & Wynne, 1953).

Analogue studies with human beings have sometimes yielded similar results. In a famous report, the psychologists John B. Watson and Rosalie Rayner (1920) described how they taught a baby boy called Little Albert to fear white rats. For weeks Albert was allowed to play with a white rat and appeared to enjoy doing so. One time when Albert reached for the rat, however, the experimenter struck a steel bar with a hammer, making a very loud noise that upset and frightened Albert. The next several times that Albert reached for the rat, the experimenter again made the loud noise. Albert acquired a fear and avoidance response to the rat. As Watson (1930) described it, "The instant the rat was shown, the baby began to cry . . . and began to crawl away so rapidly that he was caught with difficulty before he reached the edge of the mattress" (p. 161). According to some reports, Albert's fear of white rats also generalized to such objects as a rabbit, human hair, cotton, and even a Santa Claus mask.

Research has also supported the behavioral position that fears can be acquired through modeling. The psychologists Albert Bandura and Theodore Rosenthal (1966), for example, had human subjects observe a person apparently being shocked by electricity whenever a buzzer sounded. The victim was actually the experimenter's accomplice—in research terminology, a ***confederate***—who pretended to experience pain by twitching, writhing, and yelling whenever the buzzer went on. After the unsuspecting subjects had observed several such episodes, they themselves experienced a fear reaction whenever they heard the buzzer. The process of acquiring fear reactions through modeling in this way is called ***vicarious conditioning.***

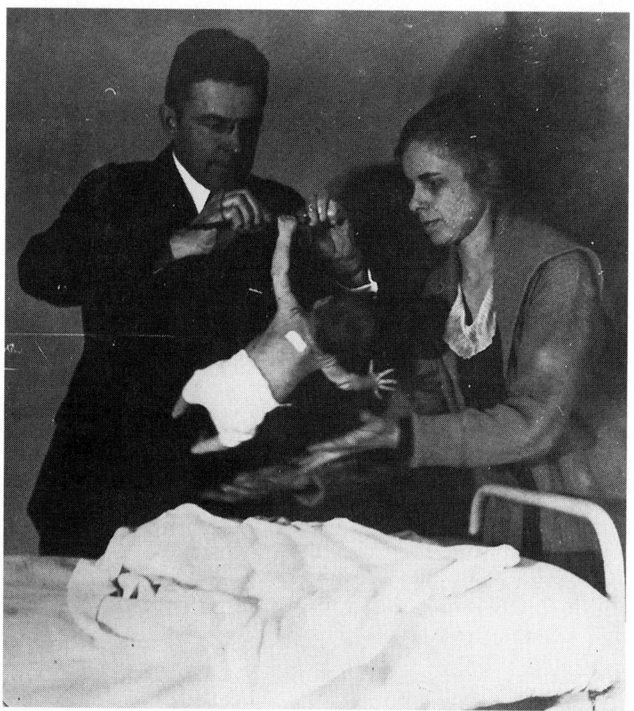

John B. Watson, pioneer of the American behaviorist movement, tests the grasping reflex of an infant. Watson never replicated the study in which he and his colleague Rosalie Rayner conditioned Little Albert to fear white rats. There is also some question as to whether the infant's fear reaction approached the strength of a phobia.

Similar modeling results have been obtained in a study of rhesus monkeys. Laboratory-reared adolescent monkeys, who had no fear of snakes, observed their wild-reared parents, who had a pronounced fear of snakes, behaving fearfully in the presence of real, toy, and model snakes. After six relatively short sessions of observation, the adolescent monkeys also demonstrated an intense fear of snakes (Mineka et al., 1984). A follow-up study three months later revealed that the adolescent monkeys were still afraid of snakes, real and simulated.

Although these studies support behaviorists' explanations of phobias, other research has called those expla-

nations into question (Graham & Gaffan, 1997; Marks, 1987; Samelson, 1980). Several laboratory studies with children and adult subjects have attempted but failed to condition fear reactions (Hallam & Rachman, 1976; Bancroft, 1971). Similarly, clinical case reports and questionnaires only sometimes find specific incidents of classical conditioning or modeling (Hofman, Ehlers, & Roth, 1995; Mellman, 1995; Marks, 1987). Thus researchers have found that phobias *can* be acquired by classical conditioning or modeling and retained by avoidance responses, but they have not established that the disorder is *ordinarily* acquired in this way.

A Behavioral-Biological Explanation Some phobias are much more common than others (Bixler, Floyd, & Hgammitt, 1995). Phobic reactions to animals, heights, and darkness are more common than phobic reactions to meat, grass, and houses. Behaviorists often account for this uneven distribution of fears by proposing that human beings, as a species, have a *predisposition* to develop certain fears (Ohman & Soares, 1993; Seligman, 1971). This idea is referred to as ***preparedness,*** because human beings, theoretically, are "prepared" to acquire some phobias and not others. The point is highlighted in the following case description by I. M. Marks (1977):

> A four-year-old girl was playing in the park. Thinking that she saw a snake, she ran to her parents' car and jumped inside, slamming the door behind her. Unfortunately, the girl's hand was caught by the closing car door, the results of which were severe pain and several visits to the doctor. Before this, she may have been afraid of snakes, but not phobic. After this experience, a phobia developed, not of cars or car doors, but of snakes. The snake phobia persisted into adulthood, at which time she sought treatment from me. (p. 192)

Marks concludes, "Certain stimuli seem to act as magnets for phobias . . . as if human brains were preprogrammed to make these preferential connections easily" (p. 194).

In a series of important tests of preparedness, the psychologist Arne Ohman and his colleagues have conditioned different kinds of fears in two groups of human subjects (Ohman & Soares, 1993; Ohman, Erixon, & Lofberg, 1975). In one such study they showed all subjects slides of faces, houses, snakes, and spiders. One group received electric shocks whenever they observed the slides of faces and houses, while the other group was shocked during their observations of snakes and spiders. Were subjects more prepared to fear snakes and spiders? Using the subjects' galvanic skin responses (GSRs) as a measure of fear, the experimenters found that both groups learned to fear the intended objects after repeated shock pairings. But then they noted an interesting distinction: after a short shock-free period, the subjects who had learned to fear faces and houses stopped registering high GSRs in the presence of those objects. Subjects who had learned to fear snakes and spiders continued to show high GSRs in response to them for a long while. One interpretation is that animals and insects are stronger candidates for human phobias than faces or houses.

Clinical researchers who use laboratory animals to test their theories and treatments must be careful when interpreting their findings. This infant monkey was considered "fearful" after being separated from its mother. But it may have been feeling another emotion entirely, such as depression, or experiencing a level of arousal that does not correspond to either human emotion.

Researchers do not know whether human predispositions to fear are imposed biologically or culturally. Proponents of a biological predisposition argue that a propensity to fear has been transmitted genetically through the evolutionary process (Graham & Gaffan, 1997; Ohman, 1993; DeSilva, Rachman, & Seligman, 1977). They suggest that the objects of common phobias represented real dangers to our ancestors. The ancestors who more readily acquired a fear of animals, darkness, heights, and the like were more likely to survive long enough to reproduce. Proponents of a cultural predisposition disagree. They argue that experiences teach us early in life that certain objects are legitimate sources of fear, and this training predisposes many people to acquire corresponding phobias (Carr, 1979). Research has supported each of these perspectives (Gray, 1987; McNally, 1986). As is so often the case in such circumstances, we may find that both biological and cultural factors are involved.

Treatments for Phobias

Practitioners of each major school of thought have developed interventions for phobias, but behavioral approaches have predominated. Research has shown them

to be highly effective and to fare better than other approaches in most head-to-head comparisons (Wolpe, 1997; Emmelkamp, 1994, 1982). Thus our discussion will focus primarily on the leading behavioral interventions for specific phobias, agoraphobia, and social phobias.

Treatments for Specific Phobias

Specific phobias were among the first anxiety disorders to be treated successfully. The major behavioral approaches to these phobias are *desensitization, flooding,* and *modeling.* Collectively, these approaches are called ***exposure treatments,*** because in all of them clients are exposed to the object or situation they dread (Rothbaum et al., 1996; Whitby, 1996).

Systematic Desensitization Clients treated by ***systematic desensitization*** learn to relax while they are confronted with the objects or situations they fear. Since relaxation and fear are incompatible, the new relaxation response is thought to substitute for the fear response. As we first noted in Chapter 3, this technique was developed by Joseph Wolpe (1997, 1987, 1969). As a military medical officer in 1944, he conducted classical conditioning experiments on cats. In the first phase of these experiments, he sounded a buzzer while hungry cats were eating. When he later sounded the buzzer at random times, the cats sought out food and ate it. Next he sounded a buzzer while the same cats were receiving electric shocks. Now the cats showed fear in response to the buzzer and would not eat while it sounded. Wolpe concluded that eating and fear were incompatible responses and that the stronger fear response had now substituted for the eating response. He had replaced the old bond (buzzer : eating) with a new bond (buzzer : fear). He labeled this process ***reciprocal inhibition,*** a term then in use by physiologists (Sherrington, 1906), because he believed that he was dealing with a physiological incompatibility between the responses of eating and fear.

Wolpe believed that this process of inhibition should work both ways. Just as he could stop an animal's eating response by teaching it a more powerful fear response, he should be able to replace the fear response with a different mode of behavior. He decided upon the relaxation response, and went on to develop the technique now known as systematic desensitization. Systematic desensitization is taught in three phases: *relaxation training,* construction of a *fear hierarchy,* and *graded pairing* of feared objects and relaxation responses.

Desensitization therapists first use relaxation training (see p. 175) to help clients release all of the tension in their bodies. With continued practice, the clients are able to bring on a state of deep muscle relaxation at will. In addition, they are ready for the other phases of desensitization.

During the early sessions of desensitization, therapists help clients to make a ***fear hierarchy,*** a list of specific situations in which their phobia is aroused. The situations are ranked in ascending order, ranging from circumstances that evoke only a trace of fear to those that the clients consider extremely frightening (see Table 6-3).

Next the clients learn how to pair relaxation with the objects they fear. While they are in a state of relaxation, the therapist has them confront the event at the bottom of their fear hierarchy. This may be an actual physical confrontation, a process called ***in vivo desensitization.*** A person who fears heights, for example, may stand on a chair or climb a stepladder. Alternatively, the confrontation may be imagined, a process called ***covert desensitization.*** In this case, the client creates a mental image of the frightening event while the therapist describes it.

The clients move through the entire list, pairing their relaxation responses with each feared item in the hierarchy. Because the first item is only mildly frightening, it is usually only a short while before they are able to relax totally when they confront it. Over the course of several sessions, clients move up the ladder of their fears until they reach and overcome the one that frightens them most of all. At this point they can relax in the face of all items in the hierarchy.

Flooding Another behavioral treatment for specific phobias is ***flooding.*** Flooding therapists believe that clients will stop fearing things when they are exposed to them repeatedly and made to see that they are actually quite harmless. The therapists force people with phobias

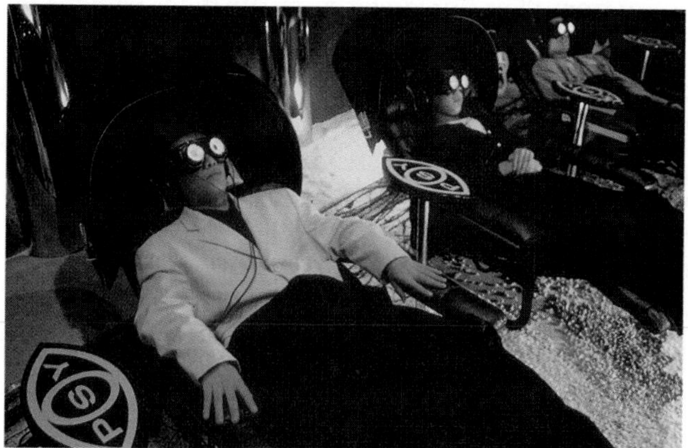

Behaviorists teach relaxation to clients with phobias as part of the treatment approach of systematic desensitization. But relaxation techniques may also be used to help reduce or prevent general feelings of tension and anxiety. At the Brain Mind Gym, business executives receive synchronized pulsations of light and sound from goggles and headphones, which are meant to lull their brain into deep relaxation.

TABLE 6-3 Sample "Fear of Flying" Hierarchy

(read from the bottom up)

- The plane starts down the runway, and the motors get louder as the plane increases speed and suddenly lifts off.
- The plane encounters turbulence.
- The plane has taken off from the airport and banks as it changes direction. I am aware of the "tilt."
- The plane is descending to the runway for a landing. I feel the speed and see the ground getting closer.
- I am looking out the window and suddenly the plane enters clouds and I cannot see out the window.
- I notice the seat-belt signs light up, so I fasten my seat belt and I notice the sound of the motors starting.
- I am now inside the plane. I move in from the aisle and sit down in my assigned seat.
- I walk down the ramp leading to the plane and enter the door of the plane.
- I hear my flight number announced, and I proceed to the security checkpoint with my hand luggage.
- I am entering the terminal. I am carrying my bags and tickets.
- I am driving to the airport for my flight. I am aware of every plane I see.
- It is ten days before the trip, and I receive the tickets in the mail.
- I have called the travel agent and told him of my plans.
- A trip has been planned, and I have decided "out loud" to travel by plane.

Source: Adapted from Martin & Pear, 1988, p. 380; Roscoe et al., 1980.

to confront their feared objects or situations without relaxation training and without a graduated approach. The flooding procedure, like desensitization, can be either in vivo (Leitenberg & Callahan, 1973; Crow et al., 1972) or covert (Levis & Carrera, 1967; Stampfl & Levis, 1967).

When therapists guide clients in imagining the feared objects or situations, they often embellish and exaggerate the description so that the clients experience intense emotional arousal. In the case of a woman who had a phobic reaction to snakes, the therapist had her imagine the following scenes, among others:

> Close your eyes again. Picture the snake out in front of you, now make yourself pick it up. Reach down, pick it up, put it in your lap, feel it wiggling around in your lap, leave your hand on it, put your hand out and feel it wiggling around. Kind of explore its body with your fingers and hand. You don't like to do it, make yourself do it. Make yourself do it. Really grab onto the snake. Squeeze it a little bit, feel it. Feel it kind of start to wind around your hand. Let it. Leave your hand there, feel it touching your hand and winding around it, curling around your wrist.
>
> Okay, now put your finger out towards the snake and feel his head coming up. Its head is towards your finger and it is starting to bite at your finger. Let it, let it bite at your finger. Put your finger out, let it bite, let it bite at your finger, feel its fangs go right down into your finger. Oooh, feel the pain going right up your arm and into your shoulder.
>
> Okay, feel him coiling around your hand again, touching you, slimy, now he is going up on your shoulder and he crawls there and he is sitting on your chest and he is looking you right in the eye. He is big and he is black and he is ugly and he's coiled up and he is ready to strike and he is looking at you. Picture his face, look at his eyes, look at those long sharp fangs. . . . He strikes out at you. (Therapist slaps hand.) Feel him bite at your face. Feel him bite at your face, let him bite; let him bite; just relax and let him bite; let him bite at your face, let him bite; let him bite at your face; feel his

> fangs go right into your cheeks; and the blood is coming out on your face now . . . feel it biting your eye and it is going to pull your eye right out and down on your cheek. It is kind of gnawing on it and eating it, eating at your eye. Your little eye is down on your cheek and it is gnawing and biting at your eye. Picture it. Now it is crawling into your eye socket and wiggling around in there, feel it wiggling and wiggling up in your head.
>
> *(Hogan, 1968, pp. 423–431)*

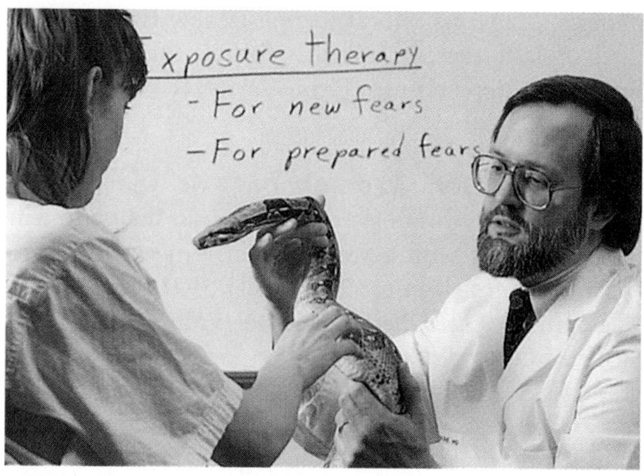

In the behavioral exposure technique of participant modeling, a therapist treats a client with a snake phobia by first handling a snake himself and demonstrating its harmlessness, then encouraging the client to touch and handle it.

Modeling In ***modeling,*** or ***vicarious conditioning,*** it is the therapist who confronts the feared object or situation while the fearful client observes (Bandura, 1977, 1971; Bandura, Adams, & Beyer, 1977). The behavioral therapist essentially acts as a model, to demonstrate that the client's fear is groundless or highly exaggerated. After several sessions clients can therefore hope to approach the object or situation with relative composure.

The most effective modeling technique is ***participant modeling,*** or ***guided participation,*** in which the therapist and client first construct a fear hierarchy, just as in desensitization. Then, while the client observes, the therapist experiences the least feared item in the hierarchy. Eventually the client is encouraged to join in, and they move up the hierarchy until the client is able to confront the most feared object or situation on the list.

Effectiveness of Treatments for Specific Phobias Clinical researchers have repeatedly found that the behavioral exposure therapies help with specific phobias (Wolpe, 1997; Wolpe et al., 1994; Emmelkamp, 1994). Moreover, in most cases once a phobia has been successfully treated by a behavioral method, new symptoms do not arise to replace it, as some psychodynamic theorists had predicted they would.

The first controlled experiment on desensitization measured the progress of two groups of subjects with snake phobias (Lang & Lazovik, 1963). One group received desensitization therapy; the control group received no therapy at all. After treatment, the desensitized subjects showed significantly less fear of snakes than the control subjects did. Even six months later, the desensitized subjects were less fearful of snakes. Overall, close to 75 percent of people with specific phobias improve with desensitization therapy (McGrath et al., 1990).

Flooding, too, helps people overcome specific phobias. A single session of flooding was administered to twenty-one subjects who were extremely fearful of rats. The therapist had them imagine scenes in which they touched rats, had their fingers nibbled by rats, were clawed by rats, and the like (Hogan & Kirchner, 1967). After this treatment, twenty of the subjects were able to open a rat's cage, and fourteen could actually pick up the rat. A control group of twenty-two subjects was instructed to imagine irrelevant and neutral scenes while relaxing. Only three of them could later open a rat's cage, and seven refused even to enter the room.

Modeling has also proved to be an effective treatment for specific phobias. The psychologist Albert Bandura and his colleagues (1969) used modeling to treat students who had snake phobias. One group of students went through a procedure consisting of live modeling and guided participation. A second group was treated by ***symbolic modeling;*** that is, they observed films of people who were safely and comfortably interacting with snakes. Yet another group was treated with covert desensitization, while a control group received no treatment at all. Ninety-two percent of the subjects treated with live modeling and guided participation overcame their fear of snakes. Many of the symbolic modeling and covert desensitization subjects also improved, but not nearly so much as the guided participation subjects. The untreated control subjects showed virtually no improvement.

The key to success with a behavioral approach appears to be actual contact with the feared object or situation (Hellstrom & Ost, 1996; Emmelkamp, 1994; Arntz & Lavy, 1993). In vivo desensitization, for example, is more effective than covert desensitization. Similarly, in vivo flooding is more effective than imaginal flooding, and participant modeling is more helpful than vicarious modeling (Menzies & Clarke, 1993). This finding explains the apparent superiority of participant modeling over covert desensitization in Bandura's study of snake phobias: real exposure simply outdid imaginal exposure.

Overall, desensitization, flooding, and modeling appear to be equally effective treatments for specific

phobias. Many behavioral therapists now combine features of each, making sure they include the critical feature of in vivo exposure (Flynn, Taylor, & Pollard, 1992; Ritchie, 1992).

Treatments for Agoraphobia As with specific phobias, behaviorists have led the way in the treatment of agoraphobia with a variety of in vivo exposure approaches (Emmelkamp, 1994; Gelder, 1991; Rose, 1990). Therapists typically help clients to venture farther and farther from their homes and to enter outside places gradually. Sometimes the therapists use rewards, support, reasoning, and coaxing to get clients to confront the outside world. Praise was the primary reward in the treatment of this young woman with agoraphobia:

> To measure the patient's improvement, we laid out a mile-long course from the hospital to downtown, marked at about 25-yard intervals. Before beginning . . . we asked the patient to walk as far as she could along the course. Each time she balked at the front door of the hospital. Then the first phase . . . began: We held two sessions each day in which the patient was praised for staying out of the hospital for a longer and longer time. The reinforcement schedule was simple. If the patient stayed outside for 20 seconds on one trial and then on the next attempt stayed out for 30 seconds, she was praised enthusiastically. Now, however, the criterion for praise was raised—without the patient's knowledge—to 25 seconds. If she met the criterion she was again praised, and the time was increased again. If she did not stay out long enough, the therapist simply ignored her performance. To gain the therapist's attention, which she valued, she had to stay out longer each time.
>
> This she did, until she was able to stay out for almost half an hour. But was she walking farther each time? Not at all. She was simply circling around in the front drive of the hospital, keeping the "safe place" in sight at all times. We therefore changed the reinforcement to reflect the distance walked. Now she began to walk farther and farther each time. Supported by this simple therapeutic procedure, the patient was progressively able to increase her self-confidence. . . .
>
> Praise was then thinned out, but slowly, and the patient was encouraged to walk anywhere she pleased. Five years later, she was still perfectly well. We might assume that the benefits of being more independent maintained the gains and compensated for the loss of praise from the therapist.
>
> *(Agras, 1985, pp. 77–80)*

Figure 6-7 demonstrates the progress of another client treated by this approach.

Exposure therapy for people with agoraphobia often makes use of support groups (Rose, 1990) and home-based self-help programs (Emmelkamp et al., 1992). In the ***support group approach,*** a small number of people with the disorder go out together for exposure sessions, which can last for several hours. The group members support and encourage one another; eventually they even coax one another to move away from the safety of the group and perform exposure tasks on their own. In ***home-based self-help programs,*** clinicians give clients and their families detailed instructions for carrying out exposure treatments themselves.

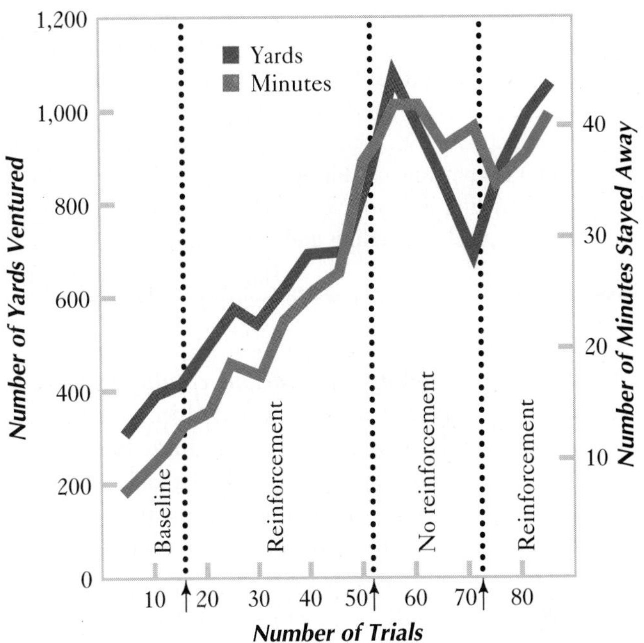

Figure 6-7 *When a patient with agoraphobia was increasingly reinforced for walking out of the hospital and staying away from the front door, she ventured increasingly farther and stayed away longer. When reinforcements were then stopped, she initially ventured even farther and stayed away even longer ("extinction burst"), but then steadily decreased the distance and time spent away from the hospital. When reinforcements were reinstated, she again ventured farther and stayed away longer. (Adapted from Agras et al., 1968.)*

Exposure treatment has had considerable success with agoraphobia. Between 60 and 80 percent of clients who receive this treatment find it at least somewhat easier to enter public places, and their improvement persists for years (Craske & Barlow, 1993; O'Sullivan & Marks, 1991). Unfortunately, these improvements are often partial rather than complete, and as many as 50 percent of clients suffer relapses. Fortunately, these individuals readily recapture previous gains if they are treated again (O'Sullivan & Marks, 1991). People whose agoraphobic symptoms accompany a panic disorder benefit less than others from exposure therapy alone. We shall take a

closer look at this group in Chapter 7, when we discuss panic disorder.

Treatments for Social Phobias Clinicians have only recently begun to have consistent success in treating social phobias (Heimberg et al., 1995; Herbert, 1995). This progress is due in part to the growing recognition that social phobias have two distinct components that may feed each other: (1) people with the phobias may have incapacitating social fears, and (2) they may lack skill at initiating conversations, communicating their needs, or addressing the needs of others. Armed with this insight, clinicians now treat social phobias according to the client's needs. They may try to reduce social fears, provide training in social skills, or both (Juster, Heimberg, & Holt, 1996).

Reducing Social Fears Clinicians are increasingly prescribing various psychotropic medications to reduce social fears. Most studies of their effectiveness, however, have been small and uncontrolled, so it is not yet clear which drugs are truly helpful (van Vliet et al., 1997; den Boer, van Vliet, & Westenberg, 1995; Taylor, 1995). Not surprisingly, then, today's clinicians rely primarily on psychotherapeutic techniques to treat social phobias.

In recent years, behaviorists have effectively employed exposure techniques to reduce social fears (Juster et al., 1996; Scholing & Emmelkamp, 1996, 1993; Mersch, 1995). The therapists guide, encourage, and persuade clients to expose themselves to dreaded social situations and to remain until their fear subsides. Usually exposure is gradual, beginning with social situations that clients find least frightening and moving up the hierarchy from there. Often the exposure approach includes a home-based self-help feature so that clients can better confront social situations on their own (Edelman & Chambless, 1995; Heimberg et al., 1990).

Group therapy often provides an ideal setting for exposure treatments, enabling people to confront head on the social situations they fear in an atmosphere of support and concern (Juster et al., 1996; Scholing & Emmelkamp, 1996; Hope, Heimberg, & Bruch, 1995). One woman who was afraid of blushing in front of people had to sit in front of other group members with her blouse slightly opened until her fear dissipated (Emmelkamp, 1982). Similarly, a man who was afraid that his hands would tremble in the presence of others had to write on a blackboard in front of the group and serve tea to the other members.

Cognitive interventions have also been widely employed in the treatment of social fears, often in combination with behavioral techniques (Woody, Chambless, & Glass, 1997). In the following discussion, Albert Ellis uses rational-emotive therapy to help a client who fears that he will be rejected if he speaks up at gatherings. True to his approach, Ellis points out and challenges the client's irrational assumptions and offers more realistic alternatives. The client's homework assignment had been to observe and identify his self-defeating thoughts and beliefs. Ellis also had asked that he force himself to say anything he had on his mind in social situations, no matter how stupid it might seem to him.

> After two weeks of this assignment, the patient came into his next session of therapy and reported: "I did what you told me to do. . . . [Every] time, just as you said, I found myself retreating from people, I said to myself: 'Now, even though you can't see it, there must be some sentences. What are they?' And I finally found them. And there were many of them! And they all seemed to say the same thing."
>
> "What thing?"
>
> "That I, uh, was going to be rejected."
>
> "If you spoke up and participated with others, you mean?"
>
> "Yes, if I related to them I was going to be rejected. And wouldn't that be perfectly awful if I was to be rejected. And there was no reason for me, uh, to take that, uh, sort of thing, and be rejected in that awful manner."
>
> "So you might as well shut up and not take the risk?"
>
> "Yes, so I might as well shut my trap and stay off in my corner, away from the others."
>
> "So you did see it?"
>
> "Oh, yes! I certainly saw it. Many times, during the week."
>
> "And did you do the second part of the homework assignment?"
>
> "The forcing myself to speak up and express myself?"
>
> "Yes, that part."
>
> "That was worse. That was really hard. Much harder than I thought it would be. But I did it."
>
> "And?"
>
> "Oh, not bad at all. I spoke up several times; more than I've ever done before. Some people were very surprised. Phyllis was very surprised, too. But I spoke up."
>
> . . .
>
> "And how did you feel after expressing yourself like that?"
>
> "Remarkable! I don't remember when I last felt this way. I felt, uh, just remarkable—good, that is. It was really something to feel! But it was so hard. I almost didn't make it. And a couple of other times during the week I had to force myself again. But I did. And I was glad!"
>
> *(Ellis, 1962, pp. 202–203)*

As the case shows, Ellis also uses in vivo exposure techniques to help clients change their assumptions. He asks, "Unless phobic individuals act against their irrational beliefs that they must not approach fearsome objects or situations . . . , can they ever really be said to have overcome such beliefs?" (Ellis, 1979, p. 162). Behaviorists might argue that exposure is playing a more direct and influential role in this cognitive treatment than Ellis acknowledges (Scholing & Emmelkamp, 1993).

Numerous studies indicate that rational-emotive therapy and similar cognitive approaches help reduce social fears (Woody et al., 1997; Juster et al., 1996; Leung & Heimberg, 1996). Moreover, these reductions are still apparent up to five years after treatment (Heimberg et al., 1993, 1991; Mersch, Emmelkamp, & Lips, 1991). Ellis's therapy has been applied to other psychological disorders, but nowhere does it perform better than as a treatment for social phobias. At the same time, research also suggests that cognitive therapy, like exposure treatment, rarely enables clients to overcome social phobias fully (Poulton & Andrews, 1996). Although it does reduce social fear, it does not consistently help people perform effectively in the social realm (Gardner et al., 1980). This is where social skills training has come to the forefront.

Social Skills Training In ***social skills training,*** therapists combine several behavioral techniques to help people improve their social skills. They usually model appropriate social behaviors and encourage their clients to try them out. Typically clients role-play with the therapists, rehearsing their new social behaviors until they become proficient. Throughout the process, therapists provide candid feedback and reinforce (praise) the clients for effective social performances.

Social reinforcement from others with the disorder is often more powerful than reinforcement from a therapist alone. In ***social skills training groups*** and ***assertiveness training groups,*** members try out and rehearse new social behavior with or in front of other group members. The group can also provide a consensus on what is socially appropriate.

Some practitioners have devised special exercises to help group members develop social skills (Mersch et al., 1991; Wlazlo et al., 1990; Rimm & Masters, 1979). One beginning exercise focuses on *greetings.* Each member turns to a neighbor and says, "Hello, how are you?" The neighbor replies, "Fine, how are you?" This exchange is to be made with warmth, good eye contact, and a strong, assertive tone of voice. *Exchanging compliments* is another exercise designed to help group members who have difficulty giving and receiving compliments. One person turns to another and delivers a warm and emphatic compliment, such as "Gee, I really like the way you're wearing your hair today." The recipient is encouraged to respond with an acknowledgment, such as "Thank you, that makes me feel good," or "Thanks, I thought I'd try something different."

Social skills training helps many people to perform better in social situations (Emmelkamp, 1994; Mersch et al., 1991). Some clients, however, continue to experience uncomfortable levels of fear despite such treatments (Juster et al., 1996; Marks, 1987).

No single approach—exposure treatment, cognitive therapy, or social skills training—consistently causes social phobias to disappear, and none has been shown to be superior to the others (Wlazlo et al., 1990; Mattick et al., 1989; Gardner et al., 1980). Yet each is helpful, and when the approaches are combined, the results have been espe-

Bound & Gagged

Contrary to popular belief, the goal of assertiveness training groups is to teach people to express their needs in socially acceptable ways, not to encourage them to lash out at others without restraint. Thus the approach may be useful for people who are generally hostile as well as for those who are socially anxious. (Copyright 1993 Tribune Media Services, Inc. All rights reserved.)

cially encouraging (Hope & Heimberg, 1993). One study compared the progress of four treatment groups: people who received social skills training, people who received social skills training combined with rational-emotive therapy, people in a consciousness-raising group, and control subjects on a waiting list (Wolfe & Fodor, 1977). The group that received the combined treatment showed significantly more improvement in both fear reduction and social performance than the other three groups.

Crossroads

Obviously, clinicians and researchers have generated many facts and ideas about generalized anxiety disorder and phobias. At times, however, the sheer quantity of concepts and findings makes it difficult to grasp what is and what is not really known about the disorders.

Of the two disorders, phobias are the better understood and more successfully treated. As we have observed, the behavioral perspective in particular has offered many insights into phobias, and behavioral interventions are often effective in treating specific phobias, agoraphobia, and (in combination with cognitive therapy) social phobias.

It is fair to say that clinicians do not yet have a clear understanding of generalized anxiety disorder. The various models of psychopathology all offer explanations for this disorder, but each is weakened by its model's characteristic limitations. Similarly, the many treatments applied to this disorder have had at best modest success. Partly because of this limited progress, there is a growing belief among researchers that the disorder is best understood when the various perspectives are considered in unison. It may well be that people develop a generalized anxiety disorder only when biological, psychological, and sociocultural factors are *all* operating. That is, the individuals must have a biological vulnerability toward experiencing anxiety that is brought to fruition by psychological and sociocultural influences.

In this regard, researchers have found that some infants become physically aroused very quickly while others remain placid in the face of the same degree of stimulation (Thomas et al., 1963). The former infants may have inherited deficiencies in GABA functioning or other biological limitations that predispose them to a generalized anxiety disorder (Kalin, 1993). If, over the course of their lives, they also learn to interpret the world as a dangerous place and confront significant societal pressures, they may be more likely still to develop a generalized anxiety disorder.

In fact, clinicians who treat people with phobias and generalized anxiety disorder have already begun to combine principles and techniques from the various models. As we noted earlier, many treat social phobias with a combination of medications, exposure therapy, cognitive therapy, and social skills training. Similarly, cognitive techniques such as self-instruction training are now often combined with relaxation training or biofeedback in the treatment of generalized anxiety disorder—a package known as ***stress management programs.***

The tendency to combine concepts and interventions from various models has been even more apparent with regard to the remaining anxiety disorders—panic disorder, obsessive-compulsive disorder, and stress disorders. Over the past fifteen years truly enormous progress has been made in the understanding and treatment of these disorders. We shall turn to this very promising work in Chapter 7.

Chapter Review

1. ***Anxiety and anxiety disorders*** *Fear* is a state of alarm that occurs in response to a serious threat. *Anxiety* is a broader reaction that occurs when our sense of threat is diffuse or vague. People with *anxiety disorders* experience ongoing fear and anxiety that prevent them from leading a normal life.

2. ***Generalized anxiety disorder*** People with generalized anxiety disorder experience excessive anxiety and worry about numerous events or activities. Up to 3.8 percent of the United States population suffer from this disorder in any given year, women twice as often as men.

3. ***Explanations and treatments for generalized anxiety disorder*** A variety of factors may contribute to the development of generalized anxiety disorder. Proponents of the various models have focused on different factors and offered different explanations and treatments. These explanations and treatments have received only limited research support, although recent cognitive and biological efforts seem to be promising.

   A. ***The sociocultural perspective*** According to the *sociocultural* view, increases in societal dangers and pressures may establish a climate in which generalized anxiety disorder is more likely to develop.

B. *The psychodynamic perspective* Freud, the initial formulator of the *psychodynamic* view, held that a generalized anxiety disorder develops when defense mechanisms break down and function poorly. Psychodynamic therapists use free association, interpretation, and related psychodynamic techniques to help patients overcome this problem.

C. *The humanistic and existential perspectives* Carl Rogers, the leading *humanistic* theorist, believed that people with generalized anxiety disorder fail to receive *unconditional positive regard* from significant others during their childhood and so become overly critical of themselves. He employed *client-centered therapy* to help clients become more self-accepting and less anxious.

Existentialists believe that generalized anxiety disorder results from the *existential anxiety* people experience because they know that life is finite and suspect it may have no meaning. Existential therapists help anxious clients take more responsibility and live more meaningfully.

D. *The cognitive perspective* *Cognitive* theorists believe that generalized anxiety disorder is caused by *maladaptive assumptions* that lead persons to view most life situations as dangerous. Cognitive practitioners treat clients by helping them to change such assumptions and by teaching them how to cope during stressful situations.

E. *The biological perspective* *Biological* theorists argue that generalized anxiety disorder results from deficient activity of the neurotransmitter GABA. The most common biological treatment is *antianxiety drugs,* particularly *benzodiazepines. Relaxation training* and *biofeedback* are also applied in many cases.

4. *Phobias* A *phobia* is a persistent and unreasonable fear of a particular object, activity, or situation. As many as 11 percent of the adult population in the United States suffer from this disorder in any given year. There are three main categories of phobias. *Agoraphobia* is a fear of venturing into public places in which escape might be difficult or help unavailable should symptoms of panic develop. A *social phobia* is a severe, persistent, and irrational fear of social or performance situations in which embarrassment may occur. All other phobias are called *specific phobias.*

5. *Explanations and treatments for phobias*

A. *Behavioral* explanations of phobias have been the most influential over the years. Behaviorists believe that phobias are learned from the environment through *classical conditioning* and through *modeling,* and then are maintained because of *avoidance behaviors.*

B. Behaviorists have treated specific phobias successfully by using *exposure techniques* in which clients confront the objects they fear. The exposure may be gradual and relaxed (*desensitization*), intense (*flooding*), or vicarious (*modeling*).

C. Behaviorists have also used exposure techniques successfully to treat agoraphobia. They help clients to venture farther and farther from their homes and to enter outside places gradually. The therapists may use rewards, support, reasoning, and coaxing.

D. Therapists typically distinguish two components of social phobias: *social fears* and lack of specific *social skills.* The therapists may try to reduce social fears by exposure techniques, group therapy, and various cognitive interventions. They may try to improve social skills with *social skills training,* a procedure that combines a number of behavioral techniques, including modeling and role playing. Often a combination of exposure techniques, cognitive therapy, and social skills training is used.

Thought and Afterthought

Flying the Fearful Skies

The sports commentator John Madden suffers from it. So do Bob Newhart, Wayne Gretzky, Maureen Stapleton, and Aretha Franklin (Zeman, 1989). The television producer Aaron Spelling, the journalist Sally Quinn, and the "Incredible Hulk," Lou Ferrigno, also admit to it. Their common problem? A fear of flying, or *aerophobia*, a phobia shared by millions of people worldwide. Airlines lose an estimated $1.5 billion a year to this problem. Several even offer exposure therapy programs for sufferers, such as USAir's Fearful Flyer's Program (left).

Afterthoughts: Many persons with aerophobia have never even been in a plane. Where might their fear have come from? . . . When famous people speak openly and graphically about their phobias, do their confessions help people with similar problems, or might they actually help generate such fears? . . . If such phobias are responsive to treatment, why do so many famous and wealthy persons continue to endure them?

Sour Notes

Two of every ten orchestra musicians in Great Britain use psychotropic drugs to soothe their nerves, according to a recent survey of 1,600 professional musicians (Hull, 1997). Overall, 22 percent of the musicians report long stretches of anxiety and 28 percent experience depression. Around 40 percent have trouble sleeping through the night. Many hyperventilate.

Three-quarters of the surveyed musicians feel such anxiety about performing that it affects their playing. As a result, one in ten takes *beta blockers*, the drugs that are believed to help performance by slowing the heartbeat and stopping shaking. Around 6 percent drink alcohol before a performance.

Afterthoughts: Why do so many professional performers seem particularly vulnerable to social anxiety? . . . Wouldn't their repeated exposure to audiences lead to a reduction in fear? . . . Is it possible that in many cases their fears of performing preceded their choice of profession?

The Imaginary Spotlight

Many people with anxiety disorders worry about how they appear in other people's eyes. They may worry about sounding foolish, looking unattractive, or seeming insensitive. It turns out that they are wrong—not about how they are being viewed, but that they are being viewed at all. People who are not excessively anxious often make the same mistake. Thomas Gilovich and his colleagues at Cornell University (1996) found that other people rarely notice our behaviors or appearance as much as we think they do. When these researchers asked a group of Cornell students to wear a Barry Manilow T-shirt, their embarrassed subjects predicted that at least half of all observers would snicker at the shirt the minute they walked into a room. Only a quarter of the observers actually did. Similarly, skiers overestimated the percentage of chair-lift riders who would be watching and judging their skiing prowess as they skied by the lift.

Afterthoughts: Why might people, including those with anxiety disorders, be so inclined to think that others are intensely interested in them? . . . Why do people, in fact, take such little notice of the actions and appearance of others?

Topic Overview

Panic Disorder
Biological Perspective
Cognitive Perspective

Obsessive-Compulsive Disorder
Psychodynamic Perspective
Behavioral Perspective
Cognitive Perspective
Biological Perspective

Stress Disorders
Acute Stress Disorder
Posttraumatic Stress Disorder

Crossroads

Chapter 7

Panic, Obsessive-Compulsive, and Stress Disorders

During most of the twentieth century, clinical practitioners and researchers paid much more attention to generalized anxiety disorder and phobias than to the other anxiety disorders. Panic, obsessive-compulsive, and stress disorders appeared to be less common. Explanations for them seemed more elusive and treatments less effective. This situation has changed drastically in the past 15 years.

Recent studies have revealed that panic, obsessive-compulsive, and stress disorders are more common than anyone had realized, although they still seem to be less prevalent than generalized anxiety disorder and phobias. Moreover, researchers have uncovered very promising clues to the origins of these disorders, and therapists have developed treatments for them that are very helpful indeed. Accordingly, this is where investigators of anxiety disorders are now focusing most of their attention (Norton et al., 1995).

Here again anxiety plays a key role, although it is less central to panic, obsessive-compulsive, and stress disorders than to generalized anxiety disorder and phobias. As we noted in Chapter 6, people with *panic disorder* have recurrent attacks of terror. Those with *obsessive-compulsive disorder* are beset by recurrent and unwanted thoughts that cause anxiety or by the need to perform repetitive actions to reduce anxiety. And people with *acute stress disorder* and *posttraumatic stress disorder* are tormented by fear and related symptoms well after a traumatic event has ended.

In George Scholz's Nightly Noise, *1919, the subject cries out into the night, reflecting a sense of terror and excitement. Similarly, people with an anxiety disorder may graphically express their fears in forms such as panic, compulsions, or lingering symptoms of terror.*

Panic Disorder

Sometimes an anxiety reaction accelerates into a smothering, nightmarish panic. When that happens to people, they lose control of their behavior, are practically unaware of what they are doing, and feel a sense of imminent doom. Anyone can react with panic when a real, immense threat looms up suddenly. Some people, however, experience ***panic attacks***—periodic, discrete bouts of panic that occur abruptly and reach a peak within ten minutes.

These attacks consist of at least four symptoms of panic. Most common are palpitations of the heart, tingling in the hands or feet, shortness of breath, sweating, hot and cold flashes, trembling, chest pains, choking sensations, faintness, dizziness, and a feeling of unreality (APA, 1994). Small wonder that during a panic attack many people fear they will die, go crazy, or lose control. Here a woman describes her episode:

> **I** was inside a very busy shopping precinct and all of a sudden it happened: in a matter of seconds I was like a mad woman. It was like a nightmare, only I was awake; everything went black and sweat poured out of me—my body, my hands and even my hair got wet through. All the blood seemed to drain out of me; I went as white as a ghost. I felt as if I were going to collapse; it was as if I had no control over my limbs; my back and legs were very weak and I felt as though it were impossible to move. It was as if I had been taken over by some stronger force. I saw all the people looking at me—just faces, no bodies, all merged into one. My heart started pounding in my head and in my ears; I thought my heart was going to stop. I could see black and yellow lights. I could hear the voices of the people but from a long way off. I could not think of anything except the way I was feeling and that now I had to get out and run quickly or I would die. I must escape and get into the fresh air.
>
> *(Hawkrigg, 1975)*

Typically a person must reach a certain level of physical or cognitive maturity before experiencing a full-blown panic attack. One research team found that over 5 percent of the 754 sixth- and seventh-grade girls whom they interviewed had experienced a panic attack (Hayward, 1992). In the subgroup of girls rated most physically immature, none reported panic attacks, but 8 percent of those who had completed puberty did report having them.

People who suffer from any of the anxiety disorders may experience a panic attack when they confront something they dread (APA, 1994). Some people, however, experience panic attacks recurrently and unpredictably without apparent provocation. They may receive a diagnosis of ***panic disorder.***

According to DSM-IV, a diagnosis of panic disorder is warranted if a person's behavior changes dysfunctionally and markedly for a month or more after an unexpected panic attack. Some people worry persistently about having another attack. Others worry about the implications or consequences of the attack. They may fear they are going crazy or having a heart attack. Still others plan their behavior around the possibility of a future attack.

In any given year, as many as 2.3 percent of people suffer from panic disorder (Weissman et al., 1997; Kessler et al., 1994; Regier et al., 1993). Most people develop the disorder between late adolescence and their mid-30s, and the diagnosis is at least twice as common among women as among men (APA, 1994) (see Table 7-1). Many other people experience panic attacks that are not severe or frequent enough to be diagnosed as a panic disorder (Katon et al., 1995; Eaton et al., 1994). In one survey of Australian adolescents, 43 percent reported having experienced at least one panic attack (King et al., 1993). In another study, 36 percent of normal young adults reported that they had had one or more attacks during the previous year (Norton et al., 1986).

Many people mistakenly believe that they have a general medical problem when they first experience a panic attack (Ballenger, 1997; Stahl & Soefje, 1995). Conversely, certain medical problems such as ***mitral valve prolapse,*** a cardiac malfunction marked by periodic episodes of heart palpitations, and ***thyroid disease*** may initially be misdiagnosed as panic disorder and nothing else (Carter et al., 1997; Schmidt & Telch, 1997; Pollock et al., 1996).

A panic disorder is often accompanied by agoraphobia, the fear of venturing into public places, a pattern that DSM-IV terms ***panic disorder with agoraphobia.*** In such cases, the agoraphobic pattern usually seems to emerge from the panic attacks (Beck & Weishaar, 1995; Guisman et al., 1995; McNally, 1994). After experiencing unpredictable and recurrent panic attacks, people become fearful of having one someplace where help is unavailable or escape difficult (Cox, Endler, & Swinson, 1995). Anne Watson was one such person:

> **M**s. Watson reported that until the onset of her current problems two years ago, she had led a normal and happy life. At that time an uncle to whom she had been extremely close in her childhood died following a sud-

TABLE 7-1 Anxiety Disorders Profile

	One-year Prevalence	*Female: Male Ratio*	*Typical Age at Onset*	*Prevalence Among Close Relatives*
Panic disorder	2.3%	5:2	15–35 years	Elevated
Obsessive compulsive disorder	2.0%	1:1	4–25 years	Elevated
Acute and posttraumatic stress disorders	0.5%	1:1	Variable	Unknown

Source: APA, 1994; Kessler et al., 1994; Regier et al., 1993; Blazer et al., 1991; Davidson et al., 1991; Eaton et al., 1991.

den unexpected heart attack. Though she had not seen her uncle frequently in recent years, Anne was considerably upset by his death. Nevertheless, after two or three months her mood returned to normal. Six months after his death she was returning home from work one evening when suddenly she felt that she couldn't catch her breath. Her heart began to pound, and she broke out into a cold sweat. Things began to seem unreal, her legs felt leaden, and she became sure she would die or faint before she reached home. She asked a passerby to help her get a taxi and went to a nearby hospital emergency room. The doctors there found her physical examination, blood count and chemistries, and electrocardiogram all completely normal. . . . By the time the examination was finished Anne had recovered completely and was able to leave the hospital and return home on her own. The incident had no effect on her daily life.

Four weeks later Ms. Watson had a second similar attack while preparing dinner at home. She made an appointment to see her family doctor, but again, all examinations were normal. She decided to put the episodes out of her mind and continue with her normal activities. Within the next several weeks, however, she had four attacks and noticed that she began to worry about when the next one would occur. . . .

She then found herself constantly thinking about her anxieties as attacks continued; she began to dread leaving the house alone for fear she would be stranded, helpless and alone, by an attack. She began to avoid going to movies, parties, and dinners with friends for fear she would have an attack and be embarrassed by her need to leave. When household chores necessitated driving she waited until it was possible to take her children or a friend along for the ride. She also began walking the twenty blocks to her office to avoid the possibility of being trapped in a subway car between stops when an attack occurred.

(Spitzer et al., 1983, pp. 7–8)

Many clinicians now believe that most cases of panic disorder are accompanied by agoraphobia, although the findings are not clear (McNally, 1994; Basoglu, 1992). Many also believe that most cases of agoraphobia are precipitated by panic attacks (Goisman et al., 1995). Nevertheless, DSM IV continues to distinguish these disorders. Cases of panic disorder without the symptoms of agoraphobia are designated ***panic disorder without agoraphobia*** in DSM-IV. As we observed earlier, cases of agoraphobia without panic origins are labeled ***agoraphobia without history of panic disorder.***

Until recently panic disorder was explained and treated very much like generalized anxiety disorder. Together these problems were called "anxiety neurosis." This strategy yielded few insights, however, and treatment was rarely successful. All that has now changed. In fact, 54 percent of all persons with a panic disorder in the United States currently receive treatment, often very successfully (Beamish et al., 1996; Narrow et al., 1993; Regier et al., 1993). Biological theorists and therapists initially led the way in distinguishing this disorder from generalized anxiety disorder. In recent years cognitive researchers and practitioners have built upon the insights gathered from biological research.

The Biological Perspective

Biological explanations and treatments for panic disorder had their beginning in the 1960s with the surprising discovery that people with this problem were helped not so much by benzodiazepine drugs, the drugs sometimes effective in treating generalized anxiety disorder, but by certain ***antidepressant drugs,*** drugs that are usually used to alleviate the symptoms of depression (Klein, 1964; Klein & Fink, 1962). Researchers then reasoned that panic attacks and generalized anxiety may involve different biological processes (Klein & Klein, 1989; Redmond, 1985; Klein, 1964).

Biological Explanations To understand the biology of panic disorder, researchers worked backward from their understanding of the effective antidepressant drugs, just as they had worked backward from their knowledge of benzodiazepines to understand the biochemical underpinnings of generalized anxiety disorder. They knew that the antidepressant drugs in question primarily alter the activity of ***norepinephrine,*** a neurotransmitter that carries messages from neuron to neuron in the brain. If that change also eliminated panic attacks, researchers wondered, might it be that panic disorder is caused in the first place by abnormal norepinephrine activity?

They have gathered evidence that norepinephrine activity may indeed be irregular in people who experience panic attacks (Levy et al., 1996; Gorman, Papp, & Coplan, 1995; Charney et al., 1992, 1990). For example, the ***locus ceruleus*** is a brain area rich in neurons that use norepinephrine (see Figure 7-1). When this area is electrically stimulated in monkeys, the monkeys display a paniclike reaction. Conversely, when this norepinephrine-rich brain area is surgically damaged, monkeys show virtually no reactions at all, even in the face of unmistakable danger. These findings suggest that panic reactions may be related to changes in norepinephrine activity in the locus ceruleus (Redmond, 1981, 1979, 1977).

In another line of research, scientists have induced panic attacks in human beings by administering chemicals known to alter the activity of norepinephrine (Bourin et al., 1995; Basoglu, 1992). When low doses of one such chemical, ***yohimbine,*** are given to subjects who suffer from panic disorder, many of them immediately experience a panic attack (Charney et al., 1990, 1987). Placebos administered to the same subjects have no such effects. Some studies have successfully used yohimbine to induce panic symptoms even in people with no history of panic (Charney et al., 1992, 1984, 1983). Such findings strongly implicate norepinephrine in panic attacks, because yohimbine alters norepinephrine functioning, particularly in the locus ceruleus, without affecting the other neurotransmitters at all (Charney et al., 1990; Den Boer, Westenberg, & Verhoeven, 1990).

Still other drugs known to alter norepinephrine activity in the locus ceruleus have been tested and shown to *reduce* panic symptoms. A blood pressure medication called ***clonidine,*** for example, has been shown to reduce the symptoms of panic disorder, as well as overall anxiety levels, significantly more than a placebo does (Levy et al., 1996; Charney et al., 1992, 1990; Uhde et al., 1989, 1984, 1982).

Just what goes wrong in panic attacks, however, is still not fully understood. It is not clear, for example,

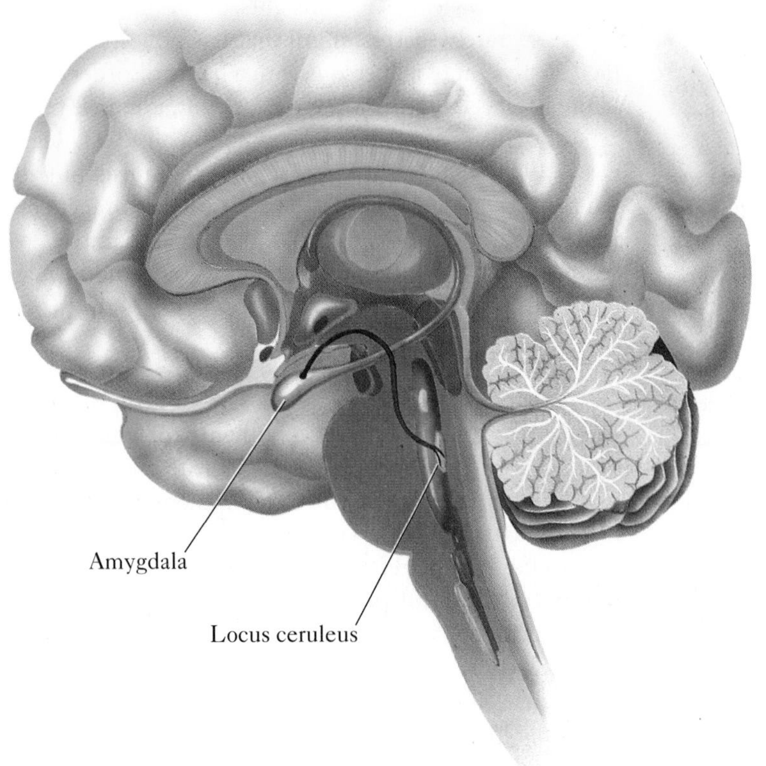

Figure 7-1 *The locus ceruleus, a small area in the brain stem, sends its major messages to the amygdala, a structure in the brain's limbic system that is known to trigger emotional reactions. The neurons of the locus ceruleus use norepinephrine, a neurotransmitter implicated in panic disorder and in depression.*

whether the culprit is excessive activity, deficient activity, or some other form of dysfunctioning involving norepinephrine. Moreover, there is some evidence that other neurotransmitters may also play important roles in panic disorder (Gorman et al., 1995; Stein & Uhde, 1995; Zaleman, 1995).

Nor do investigators know why some people develop the biological abnormalities that have been implicated in panic disorder. One possibility is that a predisposition is inherited (Goldstein et al., 1997; Kendler et al., 1995; Torgersen, 1990, 1983). If a genetic factor is indeed at work, close relatives should have higher rates of panic disorder than more distant relatives. Sure enough, one study found that among identical twins (twins who share all of their genes), if one twin had a panic disorder, the other twin had the same disorder in 24 percent of cases. Among fraternal twins, in contrast, if one twin had a panic disorder, the other twin had the same disorder in only 11 percent of cases (Kendler et al., 1993). Like all other siblings, fraternal twins share only half of their genes on average. Other analyses of twin studies, however, have not always yielded such clear trends with respect to panic disorder (Stein & Uhde, 1995). Thus the issue of genetic predisposition is still open to debate (Knowles & Weissman, 1995; Hollander et al., 1994; McNally, 1994).

Almost anyone is capable of experiencing panic in the face of a clear and overwhelming threat that unfolds at breakneck speed. Uncontrollable crowds led to panic when a wall collapsed at the European Cup soccer finals in Brussels in 1985. Thousands of persons were injured and thirty-eight were killed.

Drug Therapies In 1962 Donald Klein and Max Fink discovered that antidepressant drugs could prevent panic attacks or reduce their frequency. This surprising finding was a clinical breakthrough. Since then, studies across the world have repeatedly confirmed that certain antidepressant drugs bring relief to many people with panic disorder. In fact, the drugs seem to be helpful whether or not the panic disorder is accompanied by depressive symptoms (Jefferson, 1997; Hirschfeld, 1996, 1992; Villarreal, 1995). The antidepressant drugs apparently act to restore appropriate activity of the neurotransmitter norepinephrine, particularly at neurons in the locus ceruleus (Gorman et al., 1996; Levy et al., 1996; Redmond, 1985).

Altogether, studies conducted around the world indicate that these antidepressant drugs bring at least some improvement to 80 percent of patients who have panic disorder (Taylor, 1995; Hirschfeld, 1992). Approximately 40 percent reach full recovery or improve markedly, and the improvements can last four years or more. Recently ***alprazolam (Xanax)*** and a few other powerful benzodiazepine drugs have also proved very effective, yielding similar success rates (Davidson, 1997; Ballenger, 1995; Rickels et al., 1993).

Clinicians have also found antidepressant drugs or alprazolam to be helpful in most cases of panic disorder with agoraphobia (Uhlenhuth et al., 1995; Rickels et al., 1993; Hirschfeld, 1992). The drugs apparently help break the cycle of attack, anticipation, and fear. As the drugs eliminate or reduce their panic attacks, clients become confident enough to venture out into public places once again (Maddock et al., 1993).

At the same time, some studies suggest that an antidepressant drug or alprazolam alone is not always sufficient to relieve panic disorder with agoraphobia. In some cases the prescribed dosage may have been too low (Roy-Byrne & Wingerson, 1992). Often, however, the client's anticipatory anxiety has become so severe that fears continue even after the panic attacks are gone (Marks & Swinson, 1992; Klein et al., 1987, 1983). For these clients, a combination of antidepressant drugs and behavioral exposure treatments may be more effective than either treatment alone (deBeurs et al., 1995; Mavissakalian, 1993; Nagy et al., 1993).

The Cognitive Perspective

In recent years some cognitive theorists and practitioners have come to think that biological difficulties are but the first step on the path leading to panic attacks (Cox, 1996; Salkovskis, Clark, & Gelder, 1996; Ehlers, 1993). They argue that full panic reactions are experienced only by people who misinterpret or overreact to internal, physiological events, and they have focused their theories and treatments primarily on such misinterpretations.

The Cognitive Explanation Cognitive theorists believe that panic-prone people may be highly sensitive to certain bodily sensations and misinterpret them as signs of an imminent catastrophe. Rather than understanding the probable cause of their sensations as "something I ate" or "a fight with the boss," the panic-prone grow increasingly worried about losing control, fear the worst, lose all perspective, and rapidly plunge into panic. Expecting that their "dangerous" sensations may return at any time, they set themselves up for future misinterpretations and panic attacks.

Why might some people be prone to such misinterpretations? Clinicians have pointed to a variety of factors (Ehlers, 1993; Barlow, 1989, 1988). Perhaps the individuals have inadequate coping skills or lack social support. Perhaps their childhood was characterized by unpredictability, lack of control, chronic illnesses in the family, and overreactions by parents to their somatic symptoms. Dysfunctioning by the locus ceruleus, the brain area that we just discussed, may itself produce such misinterpretations. The British psychologist Jeffrey Gray has proposed that this area of the brain is part of a brain circuit, labeled the ***behavioral inhibition system (BIS),*** which alerts people to possible danger (Gray & McNaughton, 1996; Gray, 1995, 1985, 1982). When signs of danger occur, such as major changes in our body's functioning, this brain circuit ordinarily increases its production of neurotransmitters, which carry messages of the impending danger to yet other brain areas. People then stop what they are doing, experience fear, and assess their situations to determine how much danger they are in. Clearly, abnormal functioning in the locus ceruleus, such as that found in panic-prone people, could lead to dysfunctions in the BIS, resulting in overattentiveness to one's bodily changes, overassessments of actual danger, or both.

Whatever the precise causes, research suggests that panic-prone individuals have a high degree of ***anxiety sensitivity:*** they are preoccupied with their bodily sensations, lose their ability to assess them logically and knowledgeably, and interpret them as potentially harmful (Cox, Endler, & Swinson, 1995; Taylor, 1995). One study found that subjects who scored high on an anxiety sensitivity survey were five times more likely than other subjects to develop a panic disorder (Maller & Reiss, 1992). Other studies have found that people with panic disorder are indeed more aware of and frightened by bodily sensations than other people (Pauli et al., 1997; Taylor, Koch, & McNally, 1992) and that these fears often remain strong between panic attacks (Zoellner, Craske, & Rapee, 1996).

According to cognitive theorists, people with high anxiety sensitivity are likely to experience and misinterpret certain kinds of sensations in particular. Many seem to "overbreathe," or hyperventilate, in stressful situations. Apparently the abnormal breathing makes them think they are in danger or even dying of suffocation, so they panic (Rapee, 1995; Margraf, 1993). Other physical sensations that can be misinterpreted include euphoric excitement, respiratory discomfort, fullness in the abdomen, acute anger, and sudden tearing in the eyes (McNally, Hornic, & Donnell, 1995; Verburg et al., 1995; Sokol-Kessler & Beck, 1987). One patient, on learning that her artwork had been accepted for exhibit at a gallery, became so excited that she experienced "palpitations of the heart." Misinterpreting them as a sign of a heart attack, she panicked. Another patient was told of a relative's death and felt tears spring to his eyes. Fearing that he was about to cry uncontrollably, he too began to panic.

In ***biological challenge tests,*** researchers induce hyperventilation or other biological sensations by administering drugs or by instructing subjects to breathe, to exercise, or simply to think in certain ways (Bertani et al., 1997; Dowden & Allen, 1997; Faravelli et al., 1997). People with panic disorder do indeed experience greater anxiety during these tests than people without this disorder, particularly when they believe that their bodily sensations are dangerous or out of control (Rapee, 1995, 1993; Whittal & Goetsch, 1995).

Although the cognitive explanation of panic disorder is relatively new, it already has received considerable attention and empirical support. As we have noted, research clearly indicates that the panic-prone may interpret bodily sensations in ways that are not at all common. Precisely how different their misinterpretations are and how they interact with biological factors need to be answered more fully in the coming years.

Cognitive Therapy Cognitive therapists try to correct the misinterpretations of body sensations that they believe are leading to a client's panic attacks. Aaron Beck, for example, tries to teach patients that their physical sensations are harmless (Beck & Weishaar, 1995; Beck, 1988). Initially he briefs clients on the general nature of panic attacks, the actual causes of their bodily sensations, and their tendency to misinterpret them. For example, clients who experience sudden faintness before a panic attack are taught that this sensation stems from faulty adjustment of their blood pressure as they change posture. By applying more accurate interpretations of this kind, clients come to short out the panic sequence at an early point. Over the course of therapy, clients may also learn to distract themselves from their sensations—by starting a conversation, for example.

Cognitive therapists may also use biological challenge procedures to induce panic sensations in therapy, so that clients can develop their new skills under watchful supervision. Clients whose attacks are ordinarily triggered by a rapid heart rate, for example, may be told to jump up and down for several minutes or to run up a flight of stairs (Clark, 1993; Rapee, 1993). They can then practice interpreting sensations appropriately and not dwelling on them.

According to research, cognitive treatments often help people with panic disorder (Barlow, 1997; Craske et al., 1997; Taylor et al., 1996). In international studies, 85 percent of subjects given cognitive treatments were free of panic for as long as two years or more, compared to only 13 percent of control subjects (Ost & Westling, 1995; Chambless & Gillis, 1993).

Furthermore, cognitive therapy has proved to be at least as helpful as antidepressant drugs or alprazolam in the treatment of panic disorder, sometimes more so (Margraf et al., 1993; Brown et al., 1992; Clark et al., 1992, 1990). In view of the effectiveness of *both* cognitive and drug treatments, many clinicians have tried combining them (Craske, 1996; Rosenbaum et al., 1996). It is not yet clear, however, whether this strategy is more effective than cognitive therapy alone (Barlow, 1997; Taylor, 1995; Clum et al., 1993).

Obsessive-Compulsive Disorder

Obsessions are persistent thoughts, ideas, impulses, or images that seem to invade a person's consciousness. ***Compulsions*** are repetitive and rigid behaviors or mental acts that a person feels compelled to perform in order to prevent or reduce anxiety or distress. Minor obsessions and compulsions are familiar to almost everyone (Muris, Murckelbach, & Clavan, 1997). We may find ourselves preoccupied with thoughts about an upcoming performance, date, examination, or vacation; worry that we forgot to turn off the stove or lock the door; or be haunted for days by the same song, melody, or poem. We may feel better when we avoid stepping on cracks, turn away from black cats, follow a strict routine every morning, or arrange our closets in a carefully prescribed manner.

Minor obsessions and compulsions can play a helpful role in life. Distracting tunes or little rituals often calm us during times of stress. A man who repeatedly clicks his pen, hums a tune, or taps his fingers during a test may be releasing tension and thus improving his performance. Many people find it comforting to repeat religious or cultural rituals, such as touching a mezuzah, sprinkling holy water, or fingering rosary beads.

According to DSM-IV, a diagnosis of ***obsessive-compulsive disorder*** is appropriate when obsessions or compulsions feel excessive, unreasonable, intrusive, and inappropriate; are hard to dismiss; cause significant distress; are very time-consuming; or interfere with daily functions. Obsessive-compulsive disorder is classified as an anxiety disorder because the victims' obsessions cause intense anxiety, while their compulsions are aimed at preventing or reducing anxiety. Moreover, their anxiety intensifies if they try to resist their obsessions or compulsions. The obsessive-compulsive pattern displayed by Georgia is described by her husband:

> You remember that old joke about getting up in the middle of the night to go to the john and coming back to the bedroom to find your wife has made the bed? It's no joke. Sometimes I think she never sleeps. I got up one night at 4 A.M. and there she was doing the laundry downstairs. Look at your ash tray! I haven't seen one that dirty in years! I'll tell you what it makes me feel like. If I forget to leave my dirty shoes outside the back door she gives me a look like I had just crapped in the middle of an operating room. I stay out of the house a lot and I'm about half-stoned when I do have to be home. She even made us get rid of the dog because she said he was always filthy. When we used to have people over for supper she would jitterbug around everybody till they couldn't digest their food. I hated to call them up and ask them over because I could always hear them hem and haw and make up excuses not to come over. Even the kids are walking down the street nervous about getting dirt on them. I'm going out of my mind but you can't talk to her. She just blows up and spends twice as much time cleaning things. We have guys in to wash the walls so often I think the house is going to fall down from being scrubbed all the time. About a week ago I had it up to here and told her I couldn't take it any more. I think the only reason she came to see you was because I told her I was going to take off and live in a pig pen just for laughs.
>
> ■
>
> Georgia's obsessive concern with cleanliness forced her to take as many as three showers a day, one in the morning, one before supper, and one before going to bed, and on hot days the number of showers would rise in direct proportion to the temperature. . . .
>
> Georgia was aware, in part, of the effect she was having on her family and friends, but she also knew that when she tried to alter her behavior she got so nervous that she felt she was losing her mind. She was frightened by the possibility that "I'm headed for the funny-farm." As she said,

> I can't get to sleep unless I am sure everything in the house is in its proper place so that when I get up in the morning, the house is organized. I work like mad to set everything straight before I go to bed, but, when I get up in the morning, I can think of a thousand things that I ought to do. I know some of the things are ridiculous, but I feel better if I get them done, and I can't stand to know something needs doing and I haven't done it. I never told anybody but once I found just one dirty shirt and washed, dried, and ironed it that day. I felt stupid running a whole wash for one shirt but I couldn't bear to leave it undone. It would have bothered me all day just thinking about that one dirty shirt in the laundry basket.
>
> *(McNeil, 1967, pp. 26–28)*

Like Georgia, most (but not all) people with obsessive-compulsive disorder display *both* obsessions and compulsions. In fact, Georgia's obsessive worries about becoming dirty or disordered seemed to fuel her compulsive cleaning rituals.

Close to 2 percent of the population in the United States suffer from obsessive-compulsive disorder in any given year (APA, 1994; Regier et al., 1993). It is equally common in males and females and usually begins in childhood, adolescence, or the early 20s (Douglass et al., 1995; APA, 1994; Flament, 1990). As with Georgia, the disorder typically persists for many years, the symptoms and their severity fluctuating over time (Flament et al., 1991). Many people with an obsessive-compulsive disorder are also depressed, and some have an eating disorder (Crino & Andrews, 1996; APA, 1994; Rapoport, Swedo, & Leonard, 1992). Only around 41 percent of those with the disorder receive treatment each year (Narrow et al., 1993; Regier et al., 1993) (see Figure 7-2).

Captain Ahab's preoccupation with the great white whale in Herman Melville's Moby Dick *(1851) is one of literature's most famous presentations of obsessive thinking.*

Obsessions

Obsessions are not the same as excessive worries about real problems. They are thoughts that feel both intrusive ("ego dystonic") and foreign ("ego alien") to the people who experience them. Attempts to ignore or resist these thoughts may arouse even more anxiety, and before long they come back more strongly than ever. Like Georgia, people with obsessions are usually quite aware that their cognitions are excessive, inappropriate, and in fact products of their own minds, and many experience them as repugnant and torturous.

Clinicians have found it useful to distinguish various kinds of obsessions, although a single person may have several kinds that overlap and complement one another. Obsessions often take the form of obsessive *wishes* (for example, repeated wishes that one's spouse would die), *impulses* (e.g., repeated urges to yell out obscenities at work or church), *images* (e.g., fleeting visions of forbidden sexual scenes), *ideas* (e.g., notions that germs are lurking everywhere), or *doubts* (e.g., concerns that one has made or will make a wrong decision). Here a clinician describes a 20-year-old college junior who experienced obsessive doubts.

> He now spent hours each night "rehashing" the day's events, especially interactions with friends and teachers, endlessly making "right" in his mind any and all regrets. He likened the process to playing a videotape of each event over and over again in his mind, asking himself if he had behaved properly and telling himself that he had done his best, or had said the right thing every step of the way. He would do this while sitting at

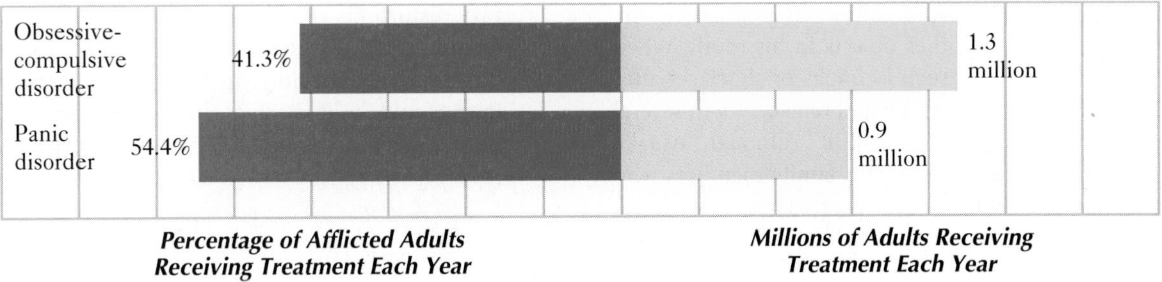

Figure 7-2 *Who receives treatment for anxiety disorders? More than half of all persons who have a panic disorder and more than 40 percent of those with an obsessive-compulsive disorder in the United States receive professional treatment each year, a total of 2.2 million people in all. (Adapted from Regier et al., 1993; Blazer et al., 1991; Boyd et al., 1990.)*

his desk, supposedly studying; and it was not unusual for him to look at the clock after such a period of rumination and note that, to his surprise, two or three hours had elapsed.

(Spitzer et al., 1981, pp. 20–21)

Certain basic themes permeate the thoughts of most people troubled by obsessive thinking (APA, 1994). The most common theme appears to be *dirt* or *contamination.* Other common ones are *violence* and *aggression, orderliness, religion,* and *sexuality* (Rachman & Hodgson, 1980, 1974; Aktar et al., 1975).

Compulsions

Although compulsive behaviors are technically under voluntary control, the people compelled to do them have little sense of choice in the matter. They believe something terrible, often unspecified, will happen if they don't act on their compulsion. Many, but not all, such people recognize at the same time that their behavior is excessive and unreasonable (Foa & Kozak, 1995). Typically they try to resist their compulsions at first but give in when anxiety overcomes them. Afterward they usually feel less anxious for a short while. Aside from this release of tension, however, they derive no pleasure from the compulsive act itself (APA, 1994).

Some people develop the act into a ***compulsive ritual,*** detailed and often elaborate. They must go through the ritual in exactly the same way every time, according to carefully observed rules. Failure to complete it properly will generate so much anxiety that they will have to start the ritual over again.

Like obsessions, compulsions take various forms and center on a variety of themes (Ball, Baer, & Otto, 1996). *Cleaning compulsions* are very common (Tallis, 1996). Like Georgia, people with these compulsions feel compelled to keep cleaning themselves, their clothing, or their homes. The cleaning may follow ritualistic rules and be repeated dozens or hundreds of times a day. The requirements of the cleaning ritual may be so detailed, bizarre, and time-consuming that a normal life is virtually impossible:

Ruth complained that her life was extremely restricted because she was spending most of her time engaged in some type of behavior she felt driven to carry out. In addition, each ritual activity was becoming more involved and time consuming. At the time of the interview, she was washing her hands at least three or four times an hour, showering six or seven times a day, and thoroughly cleaning her apartment at least twice a day. . . .

Ruth stated that she felt frustrated and tired most of the time, due to the amount of effort involved in these rituals. She experienced a great deal of pain in her hands because the outer layer of skin was virtually rubbed off. Nonetheless, she felt compelled to thoroughly wash her hands and repeatedly clean her apartment each time she felt that she or her environment was contaminated in some way.

(Leon, 1977, pp. 127–132)

People with *checking compulsions* check the same things over and over, such as door locks, gas taps, ashtrays, or important papers. Another common compulsion is displayed by people who repeatedly *seek symmetry, order,* or *balance* in their actions and surroundings. They must place certain items (such as clothing, books, or foods) in perfect order in accordance with strict rules.

Ted is a 13-year-old referred to a Midwestern inpatient psychiatric research ward because of "senseless rituals and attention to minutiae." He can spend 3 hours "centering the toilet paper roll on its holder or rearranging his bed and other objects in his room. When placing objects down, such as books or shoelaces after tying them, he picks them up and replaces them several times until they seem "straight." Although usually placid, he becomes abusive with family members who try to enter his room for fear they will move or break his objects. When he is at school, he worries that people may disturb his room. He sometimes has to be forced to interrupt his routine to attend meals. Last year he hid pieces of his clothing around the house because they wouldn't lie straight in his drawers. Moreover, he often repeats to himself, "This is perfect; you are perfect."

(Spitzer et al., 1983, p. 15)

BOX 7-1 Samuel Johnson and Howard Hughes: Famous Case Studies in Obsessive-Compulsive Behavior

Samuel Johnson, famous during his lifetime for his *Dictionary of the English Language* and his celebrated series of *Rambler* essays, was born to a struggling bookseller in Lichfield, England, in 1709. Johnson's courageous personality, prolific works, and philosophical commentaries on English life continue to fascinate biographers and scholars today. To clinicians, however, it is his reputation for having been a quirky, compulsive, and largely melancholic man that makes him most interesting. His letters and the detailed descriptions of his friend and famed biographer, James Boswell, show him to have been prone to depression, obsessive-compulsive behavior, and hypochondriasis. As Johnson wrote on March 30, 1777, "When I survey my past life I discover nothing but a barren waste of time with some disorders of the body, and disturbances of the mind, very near to madness" (Boswell, 1953).

Contemporaries described him as a "noisy beehive of crackpot mannerisms" (Davis, 1989; Malamud, 1979), muttering to himself, keeping count as he walked, touching posts anxiously, and ritually gesticulating with his hands and feet.

He had another particularity, of which none of his friends ever ventured to ask an explanation. It appeared to me some superstitious habit, which he had contracted early, and from which he had never called upon his reason to disentangle him. This was his anxious care to go out or in at a door or passage by a certain number of steps from a certain point, or at least so as that either his right or his left foot (I am not certain which) should constantly make the first actual movement when he came close to the door or passage. . . . It is requisite to mention, that while talking or even musing as he sat in his chair, he commonly held his head to one side towards his right shoulder, and shook it in a tremendous manner, moving his body backwards and forwards, and rubbing his left knee in the same direction, with the palm of his hand. In the intervals of articulating he made various sounds with his mouth, sometimes as if ruminating, or what is called chewing the cud, sometimes giving a half whistle, sometimes making his tongue play backwards from the roof of his mouth, as if clucking like a hen, and sometimes protruding it against his upper gums in front as if pronouncing quickly under his breath, too, too, too: all this accompanied sometimes with a thoughtful look, but more frequently with a smile.

(Boswell, 1933, pp. 301–302)

These descriptions are evidence of an obsessive-compulsive disorder. It is interesting, however, that despite his notable oddities, Johnson was able to make an enormous success of his professional life. In the words of William Blake, "though he looked like a mad hatter, [he] inspired men to reason and courage. He had learned from life" (Davis, 1989; Malamud, 1979).

■

Howard Hughes was born on December 24, 1905, and died on April 5, 1976, aboard a private jet bound for a hospital in Texas. Hughes's career is legendary. After inheriting a company that made drill bits used in drilling for oil, he went on to become a successful movie producer and record-setting flyer, to build the world's largest flying boat, and to found an international airline, TWA.

Hughes's personal habits are also legendary. He vanished from view in 1951 and lived his last twenty-five years in isolation, dominated by obsessive fears of contamination and the compul-

Still other common compulsions are those involving *touching* (repeatedly touching or avoiding touching certain items), *verbal rituals* (repeating expressions or chants), or *counting* (constant counting of the things one sees throughout the day). The two famous men who are described in Box 7-1 exhibited compulsions that are commonly seen in people with obsessive-compulsive disorder.

The Relationship Between Obsessions and Compulsions

Although some people with an obsessive-compulsive disorder experience obsessions only or compulsions only, most of them experience both (Jenike, 1992). In fact, as we noted earlier, their compulsive acts are often a response to their obsessive thoughts.

sion to carry out bizarre cleaning rituals. James Phelan, an investigative reporter, wrote a biography of Hughes, gathering his information from Hughes's closest aides. As the following excerpts show, Howard Hughes, one of the richest and most powerful men in the world, was at the same time a sad figure imprisoned by his obsessive-compulsive disorder:

When Howard Hughes was flying around the world setting records, starting an international airline, and running several businesses at once, no one suspected that he would one day become a near-helpless prisoner of phobias and an obsessive-compulsive disorder.

Stewart [a barber] was admitted by a man who introduced himself as John Holmes. Holmes gave Stewart detailed instructions. He was to scrub up, doctor-style, in the bathroom before beginning the hair cutting. Then he was to put on a pair of rubber surgical gloves. He was to have no foreign objects, such as pencils or pens, on his person. And, finally, he was not to speak to the man whose hair he would cut. . . .

Finally Holmes said, "Okay, Mr. Hughes will see you now," and took him into the bedroom. What he found stunned him.

"I found a skinny, bare-assed naked man sitting on an unmade three-quarter bed. His hair hung about a foot down his back. His beard was straggly and down to his chest. I tried not to act surprised, as if I was used to meeting naked billionaires sitting on unmade beds.

"I started to put my case with the barber tools on a chair. Hughes shouted, 'No, no! Not on the chair!'"

Hughes turned to Holmes and said, "Get some insulation for our friend to put his equipment on." Holmes got a roll of paper towels and laid out a layer on a nearby sideboard. The sideboard was already covered with a sheet, and so was the other furniture in the bedroom. . . .

Barbering Hughes took three hours. There was a series of special procedures, which Hughes outlined in detail. Stewart was to use one set of combs and scissors to cut his beard, but a different set to cut his hair. Before Stewart began, Hughes ordered a series of wide-mouthed jars filled with isopropyl alcohol. When Stewart used a comb he was to dip it into the alcohol before using it again, to "sterilize" it. After using a comb a few times, he was to discard it and proceed with a new comb.

While Stewart was trimming his hair on either side of his head, Hughes carefully folded his ears down tight "so none of that hair will get in me."

Stewart trimmed his beard to a short, neat Vandyke and gave his hair a tapered cut well above the collar line.

When he finished, Hughes thanked him and Holmes escorted him out. A few days later an emissary came down to Huntington Park and gave Stewart an envelope. In it was $1000. . . .

(Phelan, 1976, pp. 27–28, 44–46, 82)

One investigation found that in 61 percent of the cases reviewed, a subject's compulsions seemed to represent a *yielding* to obsessive doubts, ideas, or urges (Akhtar et al., 1975). A man who keeps doubting that his house is secure may yield to that obsessive doubt by repeatedly checking locks and gas jets. Or a man who obsessively fears contamination may yield to that fear by performing cleaning rituals. In 6 percent of the cases reviewed, the compulsions seemed to serve to *control* obsessions. A man who is beset by obsessive sexual images and urges, say, may try to distract himself by repetitive verbal rituals. Here a teenager describes how she tried to control her obsessive fears of contamination by performing counting and verbal rituals:

> *Patient:* If I heard the word, like, something that had to do with germs or disease, it would be considered something bad, and so I had things that would go through my mind that were sort of like "cross that out and it'll make it okay" to hear that word.
>
> *Interviewer:* What sort of things?
>
> *Patient:* Like numbers or words that seemed to be sort of like a protector.
>
> *Interviewer:* What numbers and what words were they?
>
> *Patient:* It started out to be the number 3 and multiples of 3 and then words like "soap and water," something like that; and then the multiples of 3 got really high, and they'd end up to be 124 or something like that. It got real bad then. . . .
>
> (*Spitzer et al., 1981, p. 137*)

Many people with obsessive-compulsive disorder worry that they will act out their obsessions. A man with obsessive images of mutilated loved ones may worry that he is but a step away from committing murder; or a woman with obsessive urges to yell out in church may worry that she will one day give in to them and embarrass herself. Most of these concerns are unfounded. Although many obsessions lead to compulsive acts—particularly to cleaning and checking compulsions—they do not usually lead to violence or immoral conduct.

Explanations and Treatments for Obsessive-Compulsive Disorder

Obsessive-compulsive disorder, like panic disorder, was once among the least understood of the psychological disorders. In recent years, however, researchers, particularly in the biological realm, have begun to learn more about it. The most influential explanations and treatments come from the psychodynamic, behavioral, cognitive, and biological models.

The Psychodynamic Perspective As we have observed, psychodynamic theorists believe that an anxiety disorder develops when children come to fear their own id impulses and use ego defense mechanisms to lessen the resulting anxiety. What distinguishes obsessive-compulsive disorder from other anxiety disorders in their view is that here the battle between anxiety-provoking id impulses and anxiety-reducing defense mechanisms is played out in explicit thoughts and actions, rather than unconsciously. The id impulses usually take the form of obsessive thoughts, and the ego defenses appear as counterthoughts or compulsive actions. A woman who keeps imagining her mother lying broken and bleeding, for example, may counter those thoughts with repeated safety checks throughout the house. Similarly, a man might distance himself from forbidden sexual thoughts by constantly washing or by meticulously avoiding sexual content in his conversations.

Psychodynamic Explanations According to psychodynamic theorists, three ego defense mechanisms are particularly common in obsessive-compulsive disorder: isolation, undoing, and reaction formation (Hollander et al., 1994). People who resort to ***isolation*** isolate and disown undesirable and unwanted thoughts, and experience them as foreign intrusions. People who engage in ***undoing*** perform acts that implicitly cancel out their undesirable impulses. People who wash their hands repeatedly or conduct elaborate symmetry rituals may be symbolically undoing their unacceptable id impulses. People who develop a ***reaction formation*** take on a lifestyle that directly opposes their unacceptable impulses. One person may live a life of compulsive kindness and devotion to others to counteract unacceptably aggressive impulses. Another may lead a life of total chastity to counteract obsessive sexual impulses.

Sigmund Freud believed that during the anal stage of development (occurring at about 2 years of age) some children experience intense rage and shame that fuel the battle between id and ego. He theorized that children at this period derive psychosexual pleasure from their bowel movements. When their parents try to toilet train them, they must learn to delay their anal gratification. If parents are premature or too harsh in their toilet training, the children may feel such rage that they develop aggressive id impulses, antisocial impulses that repeatedly seek expression. They may soil their clothes all the more frequently and become generally destructive, messy, or stubborn.

If parents handle the child's aggressiveness by further pressure and embarrassment, the child may also feel ashamed, guilty, and dirty. The aggressive impulses will now be countered by the child's strong desire to control them; the child who wants to soil will also have a competing desire to retain. If this intense conflict between the id and the ego continues, it may eventually blossom into an obsessive-compulsive disorder.

In accord with Freud's explanation, there is evidence that many people who develop obsessive-compulsive disorder have rigid and demanding parents. However, most of the studies have been poorly designed (Fitz, 1990). Moreover, this disorder also occurs in people whose family backgrounds are very different from the kind Freud anticipated.

Not all psychodynamic theorists agree with Freud's explanation of obsessive-compulsive disorder. Some *object relations* theorists, for example, propose that disturbed relationships early in life leave some people with a split view of the world. Believing that thoughts, emotions, actions, and persons are either all good or all bad, they must resort to ego-alien obsessions in order to tolerate the negative aspects of their thinking or feelings (Oppenheim & Rosenberger, 1991). In another departure from Freud, some *ego psychologists* interpret the aggressive impulses experienced by people with this disorder as an unfulfilled need for self-expression. These people are trying to overcome feelings of vulnerability or insecurity rather than poor toilet-training experiences (Salzman, 1968; Erikson, 1963; Sullivan, 1953; Horney, 1937). Each theory, however, agrees with Freud that a person with this disorder has intense aggressive impulses and a competing need to control them.

Psychodynamic Therapies Psychodynamic therapists try to help patients with obsessive-compulsive disorder uncover and overcome their underlying conflicts and defenses, using—once again—the techniques of free association and the therapist's interpretation. Research has offered little evidence, however, that a traditional psychodynamic approach is of much help to people with this disorder (Salzman, 1980).

In fact, there is some suspicion that psychodynamic therapy may actually add to these patients' difficulties (Salzman, 1980). Free association and interpretation may inadvertently play into their tendency to ruminate and overinterpret (Noon, 1971). Thus some psychodynamic therapists now prefer to treat these patients with ***short-term psychodynamic therapies,*** which, as we observed in Chapter 3, are more direct and action-based than the classical techniques. In one approach, the therapist directly advises clients that their compulsions are defense mechanisms and urges them to stop acting compulsively (Salzman, 1985, 1980).

The Behavioral Perspective Behaviorists have concentrated on explaining and treating compulsions rather than obsessions. Although the behavioral explanation itself has received at best limited support, behavioral treatments for compulsive behaviors have been highly successful and have helped change the once gloomy treatment picture for this disorder.

The Behavioral Explanation Behaviorists propose that people initially happen upon their compulsions quite randomly. In an anxiety-provoking situation, they happen just coincidentally to wash their hands, say, or dress a certain way. When the threat lifts, they link the improvement to that particular action.

After repeated chance associations, they believe that their actions brought them good luck or actually changed the situation, and so they perform the same actions again and again in similar situations. The acts become a primary method of avoiding or reducing anxiety (Steketee et al., 1996). This explanation, however, has nothing to say about why some people go on to develop compulsions and others do not. Certainly everyone experiences some chance associations, yet relatively few become compulsive.

The influential clinical theorist and investigator Stanley Rachman and his associates have shown that compulsions do appear to be rewarded by a reduction in anxiety. In one experiment, twelve persons who had compulsive hand-washing rituals were placed in contact with objects that they considered contaminated (Hodgson & Rachman, 1972). As behaviorists would predict, the hand-washing rituals of these subjects seemed to lower their anxiety. Similarly, a study of persons with compulsive checking rituals found that subjects' anxiety levels dropped significantly after they completed their checking rituals (Roper et al., 1973). Of course, although such studies suggest that compulsions may now be rewarded by a reduction in anxiety, they do not address the origins of the behaviors.

Behavioral Therapy In the mid-1960s, when V. Meyer (1966) was treating two patients with chronic obsessive-compulsive disorder, he instructed the hospital staff to supervise them around the clock and prevent them from performing their compulsive acts. The patients' compulsive behavior improved significantly, and the improvement was still apparent after fourteen months. In the 1970s Stanley Rachman dropped the supervision: he simply instructed clients to try to restrain themselves from their compulsive acts (Rachman, 1985; Rachman & Hodgson, 1980; Rachman, Hodgson, & Marks, 1971).

In Rachman's procedure, ***exposure and response prevention,*** clients are repeatedly exposed to objects or situations that elicit anxiety, obsessive fears, and compulsive behaviors, but they are instructed to refrain from the behaviors they feel compelled to perform. Because clients find it very difficult to stop, the therapists often set an example. As the clients watch, the therapists interact with the objects without performing any compulsive actions, and then they encourage the clients to do the same. That is, the therapists rely on *participant modeling.*

Many behavioral therapists now use Rachman's procedure. Some of them believe that after several therapy sessions, clients can and should carry out *self-help* procedures at home (Knox, Albano, & Barlow, 1996; Emmelkamp, 1994). There they can do homework assignments in exposure and response prevention, such as these given to a woman with a cleaning compulsion:

- Do not mop the floor of your bathroom for a week. After this, clean it within three minutes, using an ordinary mop. Use this mop for other chores as well without cleaning it.
- Buy a fluffy mohair sweater and wear it for a week. When taking it off at night do not remove the bits of fluff. Do not clean your house for a week.
- You, your husband, and children all have to keep shoes on. Do not clean the house for a week.
- Drop a cookie on the contaminated floor, pick the cookie up and eat it.
- Leave the sheets and blankets on the floor and then put them on the beds. Do not change these for a week.

(*Emmelkamp, 1982, pp. 299–300*)

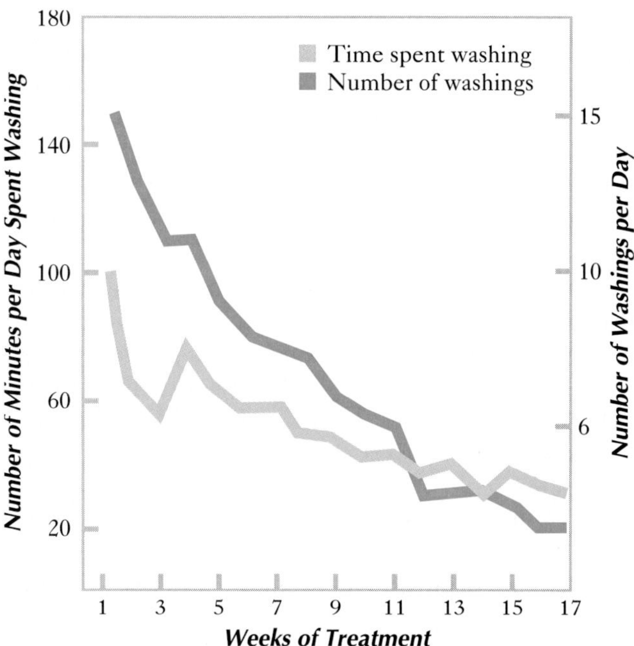

Figure 7-3 *When treated for his compulsive cleaning rituals by exposure and response prevention, a client showed a steady decline in the frequency of his daily washings and in the total amount of time he spent at them. Over the course of seventeen weeks of sessions, he went from washing himself fifteen times a day (1 hour and 40 minutes) to twice a day (31 minutes). (Adapted from Rachman, Hodgson, & Marzillier, 1970, p. 390.)*

Eventually the woman's therapist was able to help her determine a reasonable schedule for cleaning herself and her home on her own.

Exposure and response prevention has been applied in both individual and group therapy. Between 60 and 90 percent of clients with obsessive-compulsive disorder have been found to improve considerably with this approach (Kobak, Rock, & Greist, 1995; Fals-Stewart, Marks, & Schafer, 1993; Riggs & Foa, 1993). They perform fewer compulsive acts and suffer less from anxiety and obsessive thinking (see Figure 7-3). They also improve their family, social, and work lives. Moreover, these improvements continue to be observed years later (Bolton, Luckie, & Steinberg, 1995; Marks & Swinson, 1992; O'Sullivan et al., 1991).

The effectiveness of this approach suggests to many behaviorists that people with obsessive-compulsive disorder are like the superstitious man in the old joke who keeps snapping his fingers to keep elephants away. When someone points out, "But there aren't any elephants around here," the man replies, "See? It works!" One review concludes, "With hindsight, it is possible to see that the obsessional individual has been snapping his fingers, and unless he stops (response prevention) and takes a look around at the same time (exposure), he isn't going to learn much of value about elephants" (Berk & Efran, 1983, p. 546).

Despite the impressive showing of this approach, it does have certain limitations. Relatively few clients who receive the treatment overcome all their symptoms, and as many as one-quarter apparently fail to improve at all (Marks & Swinson, 1992; Greist, 1990). The approach also does relatively little to help people who have obsessions but no compulsions (Jenike, 1992). After all, this treatment gets at obsessions only by blocking compulsive acts. Finally, the approach's results come primarily from studies of cleaning and checking compulsions, leaving its effectiveness with other kinds of compulsions or with multiple compulsions less certain (Ball, Baer, & Otto, 1996).

The Cognitive Perspective Cognitive theorists have developed a promising explanation and several treatments for obsessive-compulsive disorder. Because their theory and intervention techniques also make use of behavioral principles, many observers prefer to describe the approach as cognitive-behavioral.

The Cognitive Explanation The cognitive explanation of obsessive-compulsive disorder begins with the premise that everyone has repetitive, unwanted, unpleasant, and intrusive thoughts. Anyone can have thoughts of harming others, engaging in unacceptable sexual acts, or being contaminated by germs, but most people dismiss or ignore them with ease (Salkovskis et al., 1997, 1995; Rachman, 1993; Salkovskis, 1989, 1985). Those who develop an obsessive-compulsive disorder, however, typically blame themselves for such thoughts, and they expect terrible consequences.

These people find the intrusive thoughts so repulsive and stressful that they try to eliminate or avoid them. They ***neutralize***—think or behave in ways calculated to put matters right internally, to make amends for the unacceptable thoughts. Neutralizing includes requesting special reassurance from others, deliberately thinking "good" thoughts, washing hands, or checking for possible sources of danger (Freeston & Ladouceur, 1997).

When a neutralizing strategy brings a temporary reduction in discomfort, it becomes reinforced; thus it is likely to be employed again. Eventually the neutralizing thought or act is employed so often that it becomes, by definition, an obsession or compulsion. At the same time, because the neutralizing strategy was effective, the individual becomes convinced that the initial intrusive thought must indeed have been dangerous and in need of elimination. That thought now feels even more reprehensible and worrisome; as a result, it begins to occur so frequently that it too becomes an obsession.

While everyone has undesired thoughts, only some people go on to develop an obsessive-compulsive disorder. Why do they find such normal thoughts so disturbing to begin with? Researchers have uncovered several factors:

1. *Depressed mood.* People prone to obsessive-compulsive disorder tend to be more depressed than other people. Research has shown that depressed mood increases the number and intensity of unwanted thoughts (Clark & Purdon, 1993; Conway et al., 1991; Rachman & Hodgson, 1980).

2. *Strict code of acceptability.* Many of the people who develop obsessive-compulsive disorder have exceptionally high standards of conduct and morality. They find their unwanted thoughts, especially aggressive or sexual ones, more unacceptable than other persons. Such people also tend to believe that "bad" thoughts are the same as bad acts: thinking about hurting a child is the same as doing so (Rachman, 1993; Rachman & Hodgson, 1980).

3. *Dysfunctional beliefs about responsibility and harm.* People who develop an obsessive-compulsive disorder typically believe that their intrusive negative thoughts are capable of harming them or others. Since they feel responsible for the danger they imagine, they also feel responsible for eliminating it (Ladouceur, Rhéaume, & Aublet, 1997; Lopatka & Rachman, 1995). Several studies confirm that persons who have a generally excessive sense of responsibility do indeed feel greater discomfort over intrusive thoughts than others do (Freeston, Rheaume, & Ladouceur, 1996; Ladouceur et al., 1995; Rheaume et al., 1995).

4. *Dysfunctional beliefs about the control of thoughts.* People who develop obsessive-compulsive disorder have inaccurate and maladaptive ideas about how thinking works (Freeston et al., 1992). They think

People who yield to compulsions, such as the compulsion to avoid stepping on cracks, typically believe that something terrible will happen if they don't act on them. (The Far Side © FARWORKS Inc. Reprinted with permission of Universal Press Syndicate. All rights reserved.)

that they can and should have perfect control over all of their thoughts; otherwise they will have no control over their behavior either, or will "go crazy" (Clark & Purdon, 1993; Rachman, 1993).

Other aspects of this cognitive theory have also received support from research. Several investigators have found that frequent intrusive thoughts are, as the theory suggests, quite normal (Niler & Beck, 1989; Clark & deSilva, 1985). In one study, 84 percent of normal subjects reported unwanted and repetitive intrusive thoughts (Rachman & deSilva, 1978). Still other investigations have confirmed that many people with obsessive-compulsive disorder do have more intrusive thoughts than other people (Clark, 1992). One study found that the higher a patient's score on an obsessive-compulsive scale, the more frequent the intrusive thoughts (Clark, 1992). Finally, studies have confirmed that people who develop obsessive-compulsive disorder resort, at least sometimes, to more elaborate neutralizing strategies than other people do in efforts to suppress their unwanted thoughts (Freeston et al., 1992). Moreover, such neutralizing strategies seem to reduce their discomfort temporarily (Roper, Rachman, & Hodgson, 1973; Hodgson & Rachman, 1972).

Still, some aspects of the cognitive theory remain unclear. Precisely how important, for example, are neutralizing thoughts and actions in the development of the disorder? While some theorists believe that they are the key (Salkovskis et al., 1997; Salkovskis, 1989, 1985), others point instead to an inability to dismiss intrusive thoughts in the first place or to dysfunctional notions about the need to control unpleasant thoughts (Clark & Purdon, 1993). And might other factors play a complementary role in the development of obsessive-compulsive disorder? Perhaps people who develop this disorder are driven by biological events to experience more intrusive thoughts, become more upset by them, and attempt to neutralize them.

Cognitive Therapies Several interventions that combine cognitive and behavioral techniques have been used to treat people with obsessive-compulsive disorder (Freeston, Rheaume, & Ladouceur, 1996; van Oppen & Arntz, 1994; Riggs & Foa, 1993). Therapists who use ***habituation training*** try to *evoke* a client's obsessive thoughts again and again. They expect that with intense exposure, the thoughts will no longer seem so threatening, will generate less anxiety, and so will trigger fewer new obsessive thoughts or compulsive acts.

In one version of habituation training, clients are simply instructed to summon the obsessive thought or image to mind and then to hold it for a while (Rachman & Hodgson, 1980). In another version, clients spend up to an hour once or twice a day listening to their own voices on tape, stating their obsessional thoughts again and again (Salkovskis & Westbrook, 1989; Salkovskis, 1985).

For clients who experience obsessions only, habituation training is often the entire plan of treatment (Rachman & Hodgson, 1980). For other clients, however, therapists may add ***covert-response prevention:*** they teach clients to prevent or distract themselves from carrying out any other obsessive thoughts or compulsive actions that may emerge during habituation training.

So far, the bulk of support for these approaches has come from case studies rather than empirical investigations (James & Blackborn, 1995; Ladouceur et al., 1995; Salkovskis & Westbrook, 1989). Moreover, cognitive theorists themselves have sometimes raised questions about the approaches. Some worry, for example, that habituation training and covert-response prevention fail to address the client's underlying dysfunctional beliefs. The psychologists David A. Clark and Christine Purdon (1993) suggest that to reduce obsessions or compulsions, therapists must also help clients to challenge and change their basic beliefs that unwanted negative thoughts are terrible, abnormal, and in need of control. This alternative view, however, also awaits broad empirical testing.

The Biological Perspective Partly because obsessive-compulsive disorder was so difficult to explain in the past, researchers repeatedly have tried to identify hidden biological factors that may contribute to it (Zaleman, 1995; Jenike, 1992). Their efforts have been rewarded in recent years, and promising biological interventions have been developed as well.

Biological Explanations Two intersecting lines of research now offer great promise in explaining the biology of obsessive-compulsive disorder. One points to abnormally low activity of the neurotransmitter serotonin in people with the disorder, the other to abnormal functioning in key regions of their brains (Gross-Isseroff et al., 1996; Swoboda & Jenike, 1995).

Serotonin, like GABA and norepinephrine, is a brain chemical that carries messages from neuron to neuron. It first became implicated in obsessive-compulsive disorder by the action of antidepressant drugs. Clinical researchers discovered unexpectedly that two such drugs, *clomipramine* and *fluoxetine* (Anafranil and Prozac), reduced obsessive and compulsive symptoms (Klerman et al., 1994; Rapoport, 1991, 1989; Ananth, 1983). Since these drugs also increase serotonin activity, some researchers have concluded that the disorder is associated with low serotonin activity (Altemus et al., 1993; Flament et al., 1985). In fact, *only* those antidepressant drugs that increase serotonin activity alleviate obsessive-compulsive disorder; antidepressants that primarily affect other neurotransmitters have no effect on it (Jenike, 1992).

Another line of research links obsessive-compulsive disorder to abnormal brain functioning in two parts of the brain: the *orbital region* of the frontal cortex, just above each eye, and the *caudate nuclei,* parts of the basal ganglia that lie under the cerebral cortex. Together, these parts set up a brain circuit that controls the conversion of sensory input into cognitions and actions (see Figure 7-4). The circuit begins in the orbital region, where impulses involving excretion, sexuality, violence, and other primitive activities normally arise. Nerve fibers then carry these impulses down into the caudate nuclei for possible translation into action. These nuclei serve as a filter that allows only the most powerful impulses to reach the *thalamus,* the next stop on the circuit. If the thalamus receives the impulses, the person is driven to think further about them. Many biological theorists now believe that either the orbital region or the caudate nuclei of some people function too actively, leading to a constant breakthrough of troublesome thoughts and actions (Salloway & Cummings, 1996; Swedo et al., 1992; Rapoport, 1991).

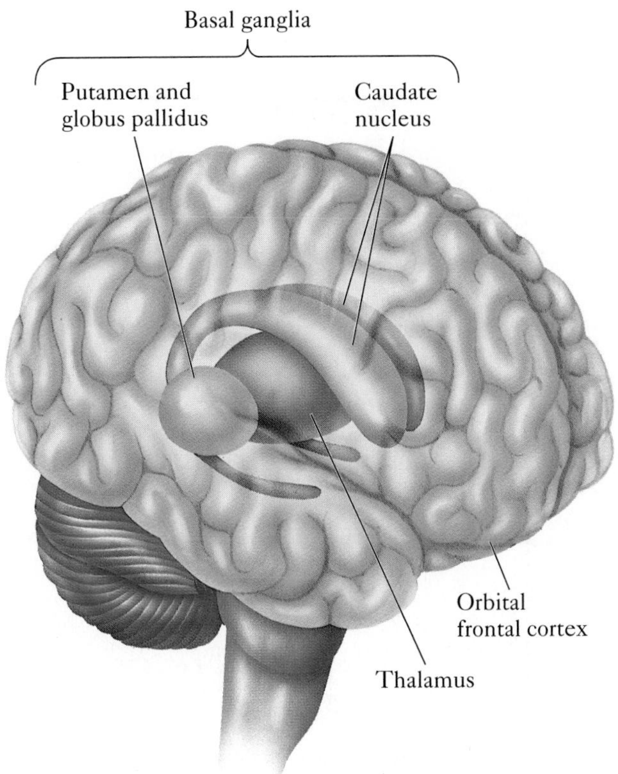

Figure 7-4 *A three-dimensional view of the human brain (with parts shown as they would look if the overlying cerebral cortex were transparent) clarifies the locations of the orbital frontal cortex and the basal ganglia–areas implicated in obsessive-compulsive disorder. Among the basal ganglia's structures are the caudate nuclei, which filter powerful impulses that arise in the orbital frontal cortex so that only the most powerful ones reach the thalamus. Perhaps the orbital frontal cortex or the caudate nuclei or both are so active in people with obsessive-compulsive disorder that numerous impulses reach the thalamus, generating obsessive thoughts or compulsive actions. (Adapted from Rapoport, 1989, p. 85.)*

In fact, it has been observed for years that obsessive-compulsive symptoms do sometimes arise or subside after the orbital region, caudate nuclei, or related brain areas are damaged by accident or illness (Max et al., 1995; Paradis et al., 1992; McKeon et al., 1984). In one well-publicized case, a patient with obsessive-compulsive disorder tried to commit suicide by shooting himself in the head. Although he survived the shot, he did considerable damage to the brain areas in question. Perhaps as a result of the injury, his obsessive and compulsive symptoms declined dramatically.

In recent years researchers have started to look directly at the activity of these brain regions by means of *positron emission tomography* (Goleman, 1995). As we saw in Chapter 5, PET scans show the brain in action. Scans have revealed that the caudate nuclei and the orbital region of patients with obsessive-compulsive disorder are more active than those of control subjects (Baxter et al., 1990). Moreover, patients whose symptoms respond well to treatment then show lower activity in these brain areas than do patients who are unaffected by treatment (Baxter et al., 1992; Swedo et al., 1992).

In sum, obsessive-compulsive disorder has been linked both to low serotonin activity and to heightened brain functioning in key areas. These two sets of findings may themselves be linked. It turns out that the neurotransmitter serotonin plays a very active role in the operation of the orbital region and the caudate nuclei, so low serotonin activity might well be expected to disrupt the proper functioning of these areas. Many researchers now believe that such abnormalities set up some kind of biological predisposition for the development of this disorder (Rapoport, 1991, 1989; Turner et al., 1985). The precise roles of these factors, however, are not yet fully understood.

Biological Therapies As we have seen, researchers have learned that certain antidepressant drugs are very useful in the treatment of obsessive-compulsive disorder (Greist et al., 1995; Klerman et al., 1994; Rapoport, 1991, 1989). Not only do these drugs increase brain serotonin activity; they also establish more normal activity in the orbital region and caudate nuclei, the brain areas that have been implicated in the disorder (Baxter et al., 1992; Swedo et al., 1992). Several studies have found that *clomipramine, fluoxetine,* and *fluvoxamine* (Anafranil, Prozac, and Luvox) bring improvement to between 50 and 80 percent of subjects with obsessive-compulsive disorder, whereas placebos bring improvement to as few as 5 percent of similar subjects (Black et al., 1997; Taylor, 1995; Orloff et al., 1994) (see Figure 7-5). The obsessions and compulsions of people who take these antidepressant drugs do not usually disappear totally, but on average they are cut almost in half within eight weeks of treatment (DeVeaugh-Geiss et al., 1992; Greist, 1990). People whose improvement is based on the drugs alone, however, tend to relapse if the medication is discontinued (Taylor, 1995; Michelson & Marchione, 1991). Not surprisingly, then, in head-to-head comparisons drug treatments do not fare so well as exposure and response prevention for long-term effectiveness (Stanley & Turner, 1995).

Obviously, the treatment picture for obsessive-compulsive disorder, like that for panic disorder, has improved over the past decade. Once a very stubborn problem, obsessive-compulsive disorder now appears to be helped by several forms of treatment, particularly exposure and response prevention and antidepressant drugs, often used in combination (Riggs & Foa, 1993; Greist, 1992). Moreover, at least two important studies suggest that the behavioral and biological approaches may ultimately have the same effect on the brain: in each study, a group of subjects who responded to exposure and response prevention and a group who responded to antidepressant drugs both showed marked reductions in activity in the caudate nuclei (Schwartz et al., 1996; Baxter et al., 1992). These were the first times that psychotherapy for a mental disorder had so directly been tied to an observable change in brain function.

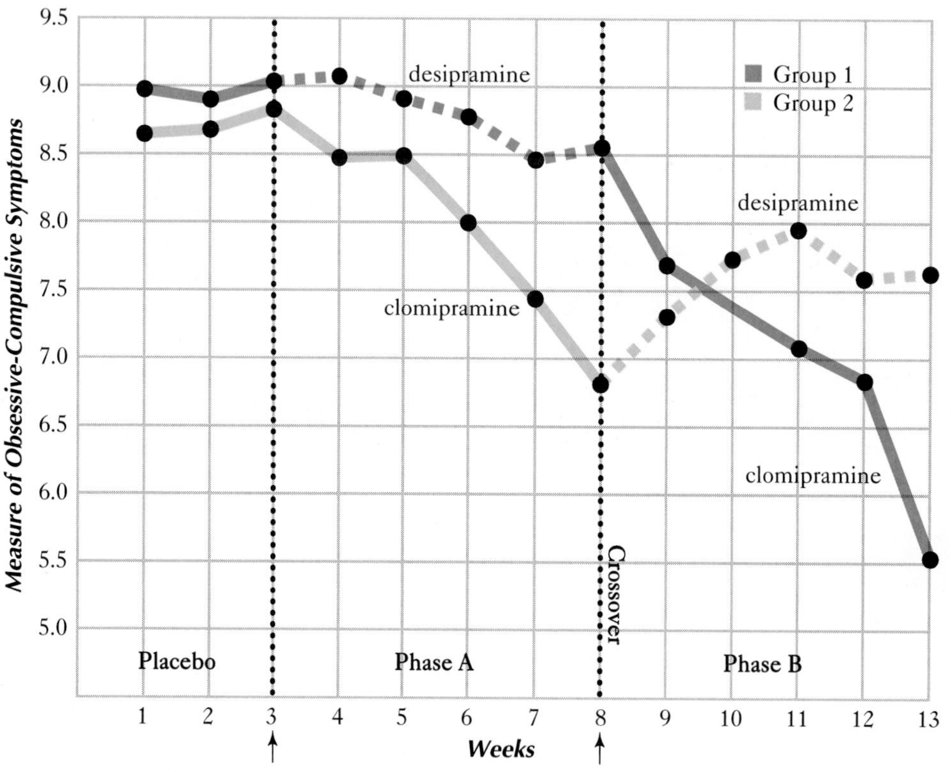

Figure 7-5 *Obsessive-compulsive disorder is improved only by antidepressants that increase serotonin activity, not by those that increase norepinephrine activity. The obsessive-compulsive symptoms of all patients in this "crossover" study stayed the same while the patients were given placebos for the first three weeks. Then, in phase A, the symptoms of patients who were given the serotonin enhancer clomipramine for five weeks declined significantly, while the symptoms of the patients given desipramine, a norepinephrine enhancer, stayed the same. Next, in phase B, when the clomipramine patients were switched (crossed over) to five weeks on desipramine, their symptoms returned; by contrast, when desipramine patients were switched to five weeks of clomipramine, their symptoms decreased significantly. (Rapoport, 1989.)*

Stress Disorders

Mark remembers his first "firefight" and encountering the VC [Viet Cong] for the first time. He lost all bladder and bowel control—in a matter of a few minutes. In his own words, "I was scared and literally shitless; I pissed all over myself, and shit all over myself too. Man, all hell broke loose. I tell you, I was so scared, I thought I would never make it out alive. I was convinced of that. Charlie had us pinned down and [was] hitting the shit out of us for hours. We had to call in the napalm and the bombing." During the first fight, Mark, an infantryman, experienced gruesome sights and strange sounds in battle. He witnessed headless bodies. "One guy said to me, 'Hey, Mark, new greenhorn boy, you saw that head go flying off that gook's shoulder. Isn't that something?'" Within 2 weeks Mark saw the head of a running comrade blown off his shoulders, the headless body moving for a few feet before falling to the ground. Mark, nauseous and vomiting for a long time, couldn't see himself surviving much longer: "I couldn't get that sight out of my head; it just kept on coming back to me in my dreams, nightmares. Like clockwork, I'd see R's head flying, and his headless body falling to the ground. I knew the guy. He was very good to me when I first got to the unit. Nobody else seemed to give a damn about me; he broke me in. It's like I would see his head and body, you know, man, wow!" Mark often found himself crying during his first weeks of combat. "I wanted to go home. I was so lonely, helpless, and really scared. But I knew I could not go home until my year was up."

(Brende & Parson, 1985, pp. 23–24)

Mark's reaction to combat experience is normal and understandable. During or immediately after a traumatic situation, many people become highly anxious and depressed. For some, however, anxiety and depression persist well after the situation is over. These people may be suffering from ***acute stress disorder*** or ***posttraumatic stress disorder,*** distinct patterns that arise in reaction to a psychologically traumatic event (Sharan et al., 1996; APA, 1994). The event usually involves actual or threatened serious injury or threatened death to the person or to a family member or friend. Unlike other anxiety disorders, which typically are triggered by objects or situations that most people would not find threatening, situations that cause acute stress disorder or posttraumatic stress disorder—combat, rape, an earthquake, an airplane crash—would be traumatic for anyone.

Soldiers often react to combat with severe anxiety or depression or both, reactions shown by these soldiers in Vietnam. These immediate responses to battle have at various times been called "shell shock," "combat fatigue," or most recently "acute stress disorder."

According to DSM-IV, if the anxiety-linked symptoms begin within four weeks of the traumatic event and last for less than a month, the pattern is diagnosed as *acute stress disorder* (APA, 1994). If the symptoms continue longer than a month, a diagnosis of *posttraumatic stress disorder* is appropriate. The symptoms of a posttraumatic stress disorder may begin either shortly after the traumatic event or months or years afterward. Some cases of acute stress disorder lead to posttraumatic stress disorder (Koopman et al., 1995). Aside from the differences in onset and duration, the symptoms of these two anxiety disorders are almost identical (Hartmann, 1996; Morgan et al., 1996; Wilmer, 1996):

1. *Reexperiencing the traumatic event.* The person may have recurring recollections, dreams, or nightmares about the event. A few relive the event so vividly in their minds that they think they are back in the traumatic situation.

2. *Avoidance.* The person will usually avoid activities or situations that are reminiscent of the traumatic event, and will try to avoid thoughts, feelings, or conversations associated with it.

3. *Reduced responsiveness.* Reduced responsiveness to the external world, often called "psychic numbing" or "emotional anesthesia," may begin during or soon after the traumatic event. The person feels detached or estranged from other people or loses interest in activities that once brought enjoyment. The ability to experience such intimate emotions as tenderness and sexuality is often impaired. Reduced

The symptoms of posttraumatic stress disorder appear after combat (or after another traumatic event), often when the individual is safely back home. The pain displayed by tens of thousands of veterans at the unveiling of the Vietnam War Memorial in Washington, D.C., more than a decade after the war ended, revealed that the war and its psychological effects were far from over for many people. Pilgrimages to the Memorial appear to be therapeutic for most veterans (Watson et al., 1995).

responsiveness is particularly prominent in acute stress disorder, where it may extend to signs of *dissociation,* or psychological separation: dazedness, loss of memory, derealization (feeling that the environment is unreal or strange), or depersonalization (feeling that one's thoughts or body are unreal or foreign).

4. *Increased arousal, anxiety, and guilt.* People with these disorders may experience hyperalertness, an exaggerated startle response, sleep disturbances, or other signs of increased arousal, and may also have trouble concentrating or remembering things. They may feel extreme guilt because they survived the traumatic event while others did not. Some also feel guilty about what they may have had to do to survive.

We can see these symptoms in the recollections of Vietnam combat veterans years after they returned home:

> Alan: I can't get the memories out of my mind! The images come flooding back in vivid detail, triggered by the most inconsequential things, like a door slamming or the smell of stir-fried pork. Last night I went to bed, was having a good sleep for a change. Then in the early morning a storm-front passed through and there was a bolt of crackling thunder. I awoke instantly, frozen in fear. I am right back in Vietnam, in the middle of the monsoon season at my guard post. I am sure I'll get hit in the next volley and convinced I will die. My hands are freezing, yet sweat pours from my entire body. I feel each hair on the back of my neck standing on end. I can't catch my breath and my heart is pounding. I smell a damp sulfur smell.
>
> *(Davis, 1992)*

> Ron: You get tired of being shot at again, over and over and over again. How many times do I gotta get blown up. I'm tired of seeing bullets hit me. I'm tired of seeing my friends get shot at. I'm tired. . . . I grew up and died right there [at the scene of battle]. And the last ten years have just been a space. I've just occupied space, just space. I've accomplished nothing. Nothing but occupied space.
>
> *("The War Within," 1985)*

> Lucas: [My wife] said that I wasn't the loving guy she used to know and love, that something horrible must have happened to me over there to change me so completely. . . . She said that the look in my eyes was the look of a deeply terrorized person, with a long-distance stare, looking off into the beyond—not into the present with her at this time. She also mentioned that my frightened look and pallid complexion, my uptight way of sitting, talking, walking, you name it, my aloofness, and all that, made her too uncomfortable for us to continue our relationship. . . . Finally, as time went on, I realized that so many people couldn't be wrong about me. The change in me began to seem deep to me—deeper than I would ever have imagined to be the case.
>
> *(Brende & Parson, 1985, pp. 46–47)*

An acute or posttraumatic stress disorder can occur at any age, even in childhood, and can cause mild to severe impairment in one's personal, family, social, or occupational functioning (Putnam, 1996; Jordan et al., 1992). Clinical surveys show that approximately 0.5 percent of the total population experience one of the disorders in any given year; as many as 7.8 percent will suffer from one of them within their lifetime (Kessler et al., 1995; Davidson et al., 1991). Still another 6 to 15 percent experience some of the symptoms of these disorders. Women are twice as likely as men to develop the disorders (Kessler et al., 1995). Around 20 percent of women who are exposed to a serious trauma develop one of them, compared to 8 percent of men (Kessler et al., 1995).

While any traumatic event can precipitate a stress disorder, some are particularly likely to do so. Among the most common precipitants are combat, disasters, and abuse and victimization (see Figure 7-6).

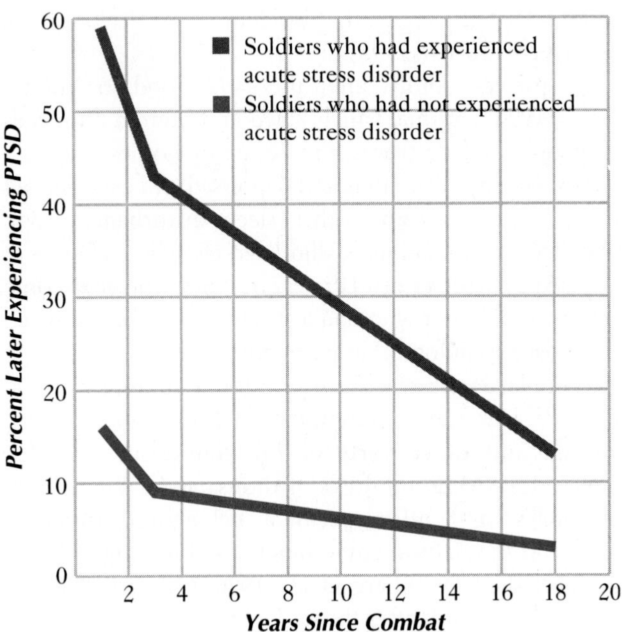

Figure 7-6 *According to research conducted in Israel, soldiers who experience acute stress symptoms during combat are more likely than soldiers without this initial reaction to later develop and maintain a posttraumatic stress disorder (PTSD). One year after combat, 59 percent of those who had experienced an acute stress disorder now qualified for a diagnosis of PTSD, compared to 16 percent of other soldiers. The rate of PTSD decreased for both groups over the years, but even 18 years later, the former soldiers had a higher rate of PTSD (13 percent) than the latter soldiers (3 percent). (Adapted from Solomon, 1995, 1993; Solomon et al., 1994.)*

Stress Disorders Caused by Combat

For years clinicians have recognized that many soldiers develop symptoms of severe anxiety and depression *during* combat (Oei, Lim, & Hennessy, 1990). The pattern of symptoms was called "nostalgia" during the American Civil War because it was considered to be the result of extended absence from home (Bourne, 1970). The syndrome was called "shell shock" during World War I because it was thought to result from minute brain hemorrhages or concussions caused by explosions during battle. During World War II and the Korean War, it was referred to as "combat fatigue" (Figley, 1978). Not until after the Vietnam War, however, did clinicians come to recognize that a great many soldiers, perhaps as many as 29 percent, also experience serious psychological symptoms *after* combat. This proportion is even greater, as much as 80 percent, among soldiers who were prisoners of war (Sutker, Allain, & Winstead, 1993).

In the first years after the Vietnam War, the psychological problems of combat veterans were generally overlooked, perhaps in part because of the nation's desire to put reminders of this unpopular war behind it. By the late 1970s, however, it had become apparent to staff members in veterans' hospitals throughout the United States that many Vietnam combat veterans were still experiencing war-related psychological problems that had been delayed in onset or previously ignored (Williams, 1983). Some signs of these disturbances were that one-quarter of the 1.5 million combat soldiers who returned from Vietnam had been arrested within two years of returning, and approximately 200,000 had become dependent on drugs. The divorce rate among Vietnam veterans was nearly double that of the general population, and their suicide rate was nearly 25 percent higher.

We now know that as many as 29 percent of all persons, male and female, who served in Vietnam subsequently suffered an acute or posttraumatic stress disorder, while another 22 percent suffered from at least some of the symptoms of these disorders (Weiss et al., 1992). In fact, 10 percent of the veterans of this war still experience significant posttraumatic stress symptoms, including flashbacks, night terrors, nightmares, and persistent images and thoughts (Williams, 1983; Goodwin, 1980). Such symptoms may be triggered by simple events that remind the veterans of conditions in Vietnam—a sudden downpour of summer rain or a rise in temperature to 80 degrees or more (DeFazio, Rustin, & Diamond, 1975)—or by combat scenes in news reports, novels, movies, or television shows. Similarly, in a study of combat veterans of the Persian Gulf War, over a third reported six months later that they were experiencing nightmares and were drinking more than before (Labbate & Snow, 1992). In addition to psychological symptoms, traumatic combat exposure has been linked to long-term health problems such as heightened rates of arthritis, bronchitis, and migraine headaches (Wolfe et al., 1994).

Stress Disorders Caused by Disasters

Acute and posttraumatic stress disorders may also follow *natural* and *accidental disasters* such as earthquakes, floods, tornados, fires, airplane crashes, and serious car accidents. Some studies have found that 10 to 40 percent of victims of serious traffic accidents may qualify for a diagnosis of posttraumatic stress disorder within six months of their accident (Blanchard et al., 1996; Brom, Kleber, & Hofman, 1993).

Eighteen months after the 1972 flood in Buffalo Creek, West Virginia, which killed and injured hundreds of people and destroyed thousands of homes, the survivors were more anxious and depressed and experienced more nightmares and other sleep disturbances than matched control subjects who lived elsewhere (Green et al., 1990; Gleser et al., 1981). The ones who had come closest to dying or who had lost family members showed the most psychological impairment.

Similar stress reactions were found among the survivors of Hurricane Andrew, the 1992 storm that ravaged Florida and other parts of the southeastern United States, destroying hundreds of thousands of homes, automobiles, and other personal belongings, wreaking havoc on the natural environment, and leaving millions impoverished (Vernberg et al., 1996; Gelman & Katel, 1993). By a month after the storm the number of calls received by the domestic violence hot line in Miami and the number of women applying for police protection had doubled (Treaster, 1992). Moreover, hundreds of mental health professionals who went from door to door shortly after the storm seeking to help victims throughout Florida reported seeing an extraordinary number of symptoms of acute and posttraumatic stress, including edginess, sleep difficulties, spontaneous crying, flashbacks, depression, disorientation, and even short-term memory loss. By six months after the storm it was clear that many elementary school-age children were also victims of posttraumatic stress disorder, their symptoms ranging from disruptive behavior in school to failing grades and problems with sleep (Vernberg et al., 1996; Gelman & Katel, 1993). One child said months afterward, "When I go to sleep, I think the storm is going to come, so I can't go to sleep." Another recalled, "I was sleeping, and I thought it was coming again" (Gelman & Katel, 1993, p. 65).

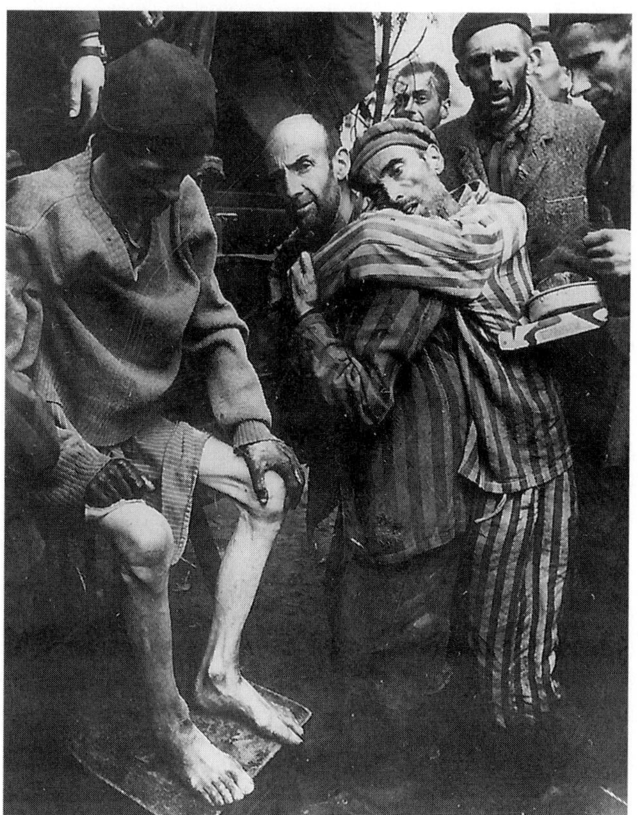

Many survivors of Nazi concentration camps faced a long road back to psychological health. Because knowledge of posttraumatic stress disorder was nonexistent until recent years, most survivors had to find their way back without professional help.

Stress Disorders Caused by Abuse and Victimization

Acute and posttraumatic stress disorders may also follow incidents of *abuse* and *victimization.* Lingering stress symptoms have been observed, for example, in survivors of Nazi concentration camps years after their liberation (Kuch & Cox, 1992; Eitinger, 1973, 1969, 1964). One study of 149 concentration camp survivors found that twenty years later 97 percent still experienced anxiety symptoms and feared that family members might be in danger when they were out of their sight; 71 percent had nightmares about their captivity and dreamed that their children, born afterward, were now imprisoned with them; 80 percent felt guilty that they had survived while other family members and friends had not; and 92 percent blamed themselves for not saving their relatives and friends (Krystal, 1968). A recent retrospective study of 124 Holocaust survivors found that 46 percent eventually met the diagnostic criteria for posttraumatic stress disorder (Kuch & Cox, 1992).

A common form of victimization in our society is sexual assault. ***Rape*** is forced sexual intercourse or another sexual act upon a nonconsenting person or underage person. Surveys suggest that more than 500,000 persons in the United States are victims of rape each year (U.S. Dept. of Justice, 1995). One sign of the trauma they experience is that only about 100,000 such attacks are reported to law enforcement authorities (FBI, 1991). Many victims are reluctant to report a rape because they are ashamed, or because they are intimidated by the rapist's threats of retaliation. Victims may also feel that dealing with police and the courts will compound their trauma.

Most rapists are men, and most victims are women. In fact, rates of reported rape and other sexual assaults against women are 10 times higher than the equivalent rates against men (U.S. Dept. of Justice, 1995). Studies estimate that between 8 and 25 percent of all women are raped or are the victims of some sexual assault at some time during their lives (Koss, 1993). Surveys also suggest that most rape victims are young: 29 percent are under 11 years old, 32 percent are between the ages of 11 and 17, and 29 percent are between 18 and 29. Approximately 18 percent of the victims are raped by strangers, the rest by acquaintances or relatives (U.S. Dept. of Justice, 1995; Koss, 1992; Youngstrom, 1992).

Spouse rape has received special attention during the past decade. It appears that 26 percent of rapes and sexual assaults are committed by the victim's husband, boyfriend, ex-husband, or ex-boyfriend (U.S. Dept. of Justice, 1995). Until recently the law presumed that sexual intercourse was a contractual part of marriage, and a woman could not accuse her husband of rape. That situation changed in 1982, when a Florida man was convicted of the crime of raping his wife. Half of the states have now eliminated the legal exemption for marital rape. Still other states remain ambivalent on the issue and offer the husband the benefit of the doubt unless there is convincing evidence of abuse.

"Date rape" has also been of special interest in recent years. Surveys of college students suggest that 15 percent of women may have been forced into intercourse against their will by acquaintances, either in high school or in college (Koss et al., 1988; Muehlenhard & Linton, 1987). Clinical research suggests that women who are raped by their husbands or dates are as likely to fear injury or death during the rape as are women who are raped by strangers (NVC, 1992).

The psychological impact of rape on a victim is immediate and may last a long time. Rape victims typically experience enormous distress during the week after the assault. Stress continues to rise for the next three weeks, maintains a peak level for another month or so, and then starts to improve over the next few months (Koss, 1993). Indeed, in one study, 94 percent of rape victims fully qualified for a clinical diagnosis of acute stress disorder when they were observed an average of twelve days after

Many people eventually overcome the effects of traumatic stress. During a reunion, these concentration camp survivors proudly display their tattooed camp identification numbers as symbols of their triumph over their psychological wounds.

their assault (Rothbaum et al., 1992). Although the majority of rape victims improve psychologically within three or four months, the effects may persist for up to eighteen months or longer (see Figure 7-7). Most victims continue to experience elevated levels of fear, anxiety, suspiciousness, depression, self-esteem problems, self-blame, flashbacks, sleep problems, and sexual dysfunction (Foa & Riggs, 1995; Koss, 1993). Even years after the assault, women who were raped are more likely than others to qualify for diagnoses of posttraumatic stress disorder, depression, or a substance-related disorder (Moncrieff et al., 1996; Koss, 1993). The lingering psychological impact of rape is apparent in the following case description:

> Mary Billings is a 33-year-old divorced nurse, referred to the Victim Clinic at Bedford Psychiatric Hospital for counseling by her supervisory head nurse. Mary had been raped two months ago. The assailant gained entry to her apartment while she was sleeping, and she awoke to find him on top of her. He was armed with a knife and threatened to kill her and her child (who was asleep in the next room) if she did not submit to his demands. He forced her to undress and repeatedly raped her vaginally over a period of 1 hour. He then admonished her that if she told anyone or reported the incident to the police he would return and assault her child.
>
> After he left, she called her boyfriend, who came to her apartment right away. He helped her contact the Sex Crimes Unit of the Police Department, which is currently investigating the case. He then took her to a local hospital for a physical examination and collection of evidence for the police (traces of sperm, pubic hair samples, fingernail scrapings). She was given antibiotics as prophylaxis against venereal disease. Mary then returned home with a girlfriend who spent the remainder of the night with her.
>
> Over the next few weeks Mary continued to be afraid of being alone and had her girlfriend move in with her. She became preoccupied with thoughts of what had happened to her and the possibility that it could happen again. Mary was frightened that the rapist might return to her apartment and therefore had additional locks installed on both the door and the windows. She was so upset and had such difficulty concentrating that she decided she could not yet return to work. When she did return to work several weeks later, she was still clearly upset, and her supervisor suggested that she might be helped by counseling.
>
> During the clinic interview, Mary was coherent and spoke quite rationally in a hushed voice. She reported recurrent and intrusive thoughts about the sexual assault, to the extent that her concentration was impaired and she had difficulty doing chores such as making meals for herself and her daughter. She felt she was not able to be effective at work, still felt afraid to leave her home, to answer her phone, and had little interest in contacting friends or relatives.
>
> The range of Mary's affect was constricted. She talked in the same tone of voice whether discussing the assault or less emotionally charged topics, such as her work history. She was easily startled by an unexpected noise. She also was unable to fall asleep because she kept thinking about the assault. She had no desire to eat, and when she did attempt it, she felt nauseated. Mary was repelled by the thought of sex and stated that she did not want to have sex for a long time, although she was willing to be held and comforted by her boyfriend.
>
> *(Spitzer et al., 1983, pp. 20–21)*

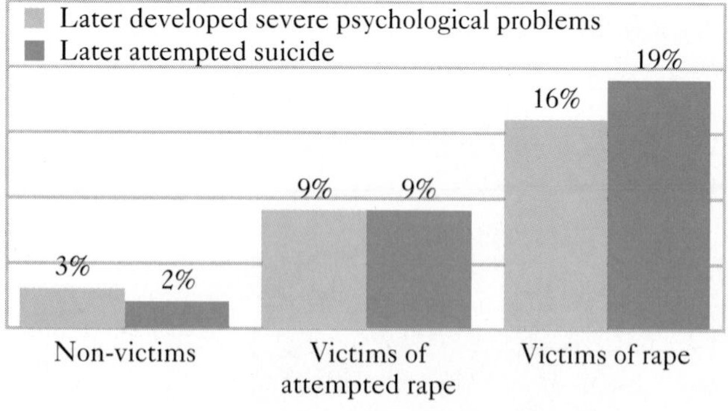

Figure 7-7 *Many rape victims develop symptoms of posttraumatic stress disorder. In one study, 19 percent of those surveyed by telephone revealed that they attempted suicide at some point after being raped, compared to 2 percent of nonvictims. (Adapted from Kilpatrick et al., 1985.)*

Rape victims may also experience somatic problems as a result of their assault. Many suffer physical trauma during the assault, although only half of those injured receive the kind of formal medical care afforded Mary (Beebe, 1991; Koss, Woodruff, & Koss, 1991). Between 4 and 30 percent of victims develop a sexually transmitted disease (Koss, 1993; Murphy, 1990) and 5 percent become pregnant (Beebe, 1991; Koss et al., 1991). Shockingly, a broad national survey of women has revealed that 60 percent of rape victims received no pregnancy testing or prophylaxis and 73 percent received no information or testing for exposure to HIV (National Victims Center, 1992).

Victims of rape and other crimes are also much more likely than other women to suffer serious long-term health problems (Leserman et al., 1996; Golding, 1994; Koss & Heslet, 1992). Interviews with 390 women revealed that victims of rape or assault had poorer physical well-being for at least five years after the crime, made twice as many visits to physicians, and incurred two and a half times more medical expenses. It is not yet clear why rape and other assaults lead to these long-term health problems.

As we can see in Box 7-2, ongoing victimization and abuse in the family have also been linked to stress symptoms (Lemieux & Coe, 1995; McNew & Abell, 1995). Moreover, spouse and child abuse often extend over a very long term and violate family roles and trust—special features that may lead to a still wider range of symptoms and disorders (Kemp et al., 1995; Mancini, Van Ameringen, & MacMillan, 1995; Mathias, Mertin, & Murray, 1995).

Finally, living in a violent neighborhood can be a source of ongoing trauma that triggers stress reactions. A study of one neighborhood found that fully 14 percent of fifth- and sixth-graders had witnessed a shooting and 43 percent had observed a mugging. These children showed more symptoms of stress than other children (Martinez & Richters, 1993; Richters & Martinez, 1993).

Explanations of Stress Disorders

Obviously, extraordinary trauma can cause an acute or posttraumatic stress disorder. The stressful event alone, however, is not a complete explanation. Although everyone who experiences an unusual trauma is affected by it, we do not yet understand why only some people develop one of these disorders. Researchers have looked at the survivors' biological processes, childhood experiences, personality, social support system, and the severity of the trauma.

Biological and Genetic Factors Biological researchers have gathered evidence that traumatic events trigger changes in the brain and body which may lead to severe stress reactions and, in some cases, to stress disorders. Much of this work has centered on changes in the activity of neurotransmitters and hormones (Bremner et al., 1997, 1993; Mason et al., 1996; Putnam, 1996). When subjects in the laboratory face various types of stressful stimuli, they show a rise in norepinephrine activity, particularly in key brain regions such as the locus ceruleus, hippocampus, amygdala, and hypothalamus (Charney et al., 1993). In addition, when young animals and young humans are separated from their parents, they display abnormal responses of cortisol and related hormones (Suomi, 1991; Breire et al., 1988). Indications of similar abnormal biochemical activity appear in the urine and blood of combat soldiers, raped women, concentration camp survivors, and persons subjected to other severe stresses (Resnick et al., 1995; Yehuda et al., 1995, 1994, 1993, 1992; DeBellis et al., 1994).

Perhaps people whose biochemical reactions to stress are particularly strong are more likely than others to develop acute and posttraumatic stress disorders. But why would some people have such unusually strong biological reactions to trauma? Some clinicians propose that they inherit a genetic predisposition to do so. One study of approximately 4,000 pairs of twins who had served in the Vietnam War found that if one twin developed stress symptoms after combat—flashbacks, say, or hyperarousal symptoms—an identical twin was more likely than a fraternal twin to develop the same problems (True et al., 1993). Of course, once again, the more similar vulnerabilities among identical twins do not necessarily reflect genetic influences. Their childhood experiences, personalities, and support systems may be more similar, too.

Childhood Experiences A recent wave of studies has uncovered childhood events that seem to leave some people vulnerable to acute and posttraumatic stress disorders if they later have traumatic experiences. People whose childhoods have been characterized by poverty appear more likely to develop stress disorders in the face of later trauma. So do individuals whose parents separated or divorced before the child was 10, whose family members suffered from psychological disorders, or who experienced assault, abuse, or catastrophe at an early age (Putnam, 1996; Astin et al., 1995; Bremner et al., 1993). Theorists have speculated on the reasons for a tie between early life experiences and later stress disorders. Both psychodynamic and behavioral theorists suggest that abused children tend to *dissociate,* or psychologically separate themselves, from the experience and memory of abuse. This may then become a habitual way of dealing with other traumatic events as well, thus setting the stage for the development of an acute or posttraumatic stress disorder (Bremner et al., 1993).

Personality Some studies suggest that people with certain personality profiles or attitudes are more likely to develop stress disorders (Kessler et al., 1995; Clark et al., 1994). In the aftermath of Hurricane Hugo, for example, children who had previously demonstrated anxiety were more likely than other children to develop severe stress reactions (Lonigan et al., 1994). Similarly, people who had psychological problems before they were raped, or who were struggling with stressful life situations, appear to be especially vulnerable (Darvres-Bornoz et al., 1995). So are war veterans who had psychological problems or poor relationships before they went into combat (Orsillo et al., 1996; Chemtob et al., 1990). Similarly, people who generally view life's aversive events as beyond their control develop more severe stress symptoms after criminal assaults than people who feel in greater control over life

BOX 7-2 Spouse Abuse: Victimization in the Family

Ruth

He told me that he was never going to let me go. He said that he married me, and whether he loved me or not, and whether I loved him or not, I was going to stay with him, and if I tried to leave him, he was going to kill me—one day at a time, like dripping water on a rock, until I broke apart. Although I never knew exactly what he would do, I knew that he was capable of torture. He broke my arm once and dangled it in front of me, playing with it, telling me it wasn't broken.

(Jones & Schechter, 1992)

Diane

"Being married to this man was like being a prisoner of war. I was not allowed to visit my family. I couldn't go out on my own. He wouldn't even let me cry. If I did, it started an 'episode.'"

*(*Time*, September 5, 1983, p. 23)*

As these cases reveal, ***spouse abuse,*** the physical mistreatment or misuse of one spouse by the other, can take various forms, from shoving to battering (Sadock, 1989). Ninety-three percent of abused spouses are women, married or cohabitating (National Crime Victimization Survey, 1993). It is estimated that spouse abuse occurs in at least 4 million homes in the United States each year and that as many as a third of all U.S. women have been abused at least once by their husbands (AMA, 1992). The U.S. surgeon general has ranked spouse abuse as the leading cause of injuries to women between the ages of 15 and 44.

Spouse abuse cuts across all races, religions, educational levels, and socioeconomic groups (U.S. Dept. of Justice, 1995; Mollerstrom, Patchner, & Milner, 1992). Some experts believe that the most violent abuse, particularly murder, occurs more often at lower socioeconomic levels (Bureau of Justice Statistics, 1995; Straus & Gelles, 1986). Others suggest that members of the middle class are simply less likely to report abuse, and point to the wider spacing of middle-class homes, which prevents neighbors from detecting violence and calling the police (Glazer, 1993; Sherman, 1992).

For years this behavior was viewed as a private matter; until 1874 a husband actually had a legal right to beat his wife in the United States. Even after that time, abusers were rarely arrested or prosecuted. Police were reluctant to do anything other than calm down domestic violence, the number-one source of police fatalities. And the courts rarely prosecuted an abuser.

Thanks to the civil rights movement in the 1970s and the efforts of women's groups, state legislatures have recently passed laws to empower the courts to prosecute abusers and protect victims. The police, in turn, have become more oriented toward intervention. In fact, nearly half of U.S. police departments now have special units to deal with spouse abuse (LEMAS, 1990), and twenty-five states have laws that require the police to make an arrest when they are called to a scene. Arrests do not necessarily lead to convictions, however, nor do convictions always result in sentences that deter the abuser in the future.

The Abusers

Clinical researchers have also increased their studies of spouse abuse. They have identified the abuser's need to assert power and control over his wife as a major theme in most cases. An abusive husband is often very emotionally dependent on his wife and fearful of losing her (Murphy et al., 1994). Many consider their wives to be their personal property and become most assaultive when the wife shows independence. They often are extremely jealous and possessive, and some inflict more abuse when their wives pursue outside friendships, attempt to work outside the home, or even attend to their children's needs first. The husbands may also belittle and isolate their wives, and make them feel inept, worthless, and dependent. Such repeated emotional abuse can have severe effects on the victim's sense of self and reality.

An abusive husband may show remorse for a time after beating his wife (Walker, 1984, 1979). A "honeymoon phase" seems to be common in abusive relationships. The husband, concerned that the last violent incident may cause his wife to leave him, acts with kindness and contrition, and promises that the abuse will never happen again (Jones & Schechter, 1992). Unfortunately, in most cases the abuse does happen again, and over time battering may even increase in severity and frequency.

Many persons who abuse their spouses have alcohol-related or other substance-related problems (Mollerstrom et al., 1992; Saunders, 1992). Yet these problems are not usually the primary cause of battering, and treating only an abuser's substance abuse seldom stops the violence

(ADVTP, 1996; Jones & Schechter, 1992). Clinicians consider spouse abuse primarily a learned behavior and a choice behavior in most cases, with a chosen victim as the target (ADVTP, 1996). Many abusers were themselves beaten as children or saw their mothers beaten (Peterson, 1996; Saunders, 1992; Pagelow, 1981). Often they suffer from low self-esteem and feel generally stressed and frustrated with their lives (Russell & Hulson, 1992).

The Victims

As a result of physical abuse, deprivation, threats, and intimidation, a victim of abuse typically feels very dependent on her husband and unable to function on her own. This sense of dependence and the feeling that she is helpless to change the situation typically keeps her in the relationship despite the obvious physical dangers. Such women are not masochistic, as many clinical theorists once believed (Walker, 1984; Finkelhor et al., 1983). In fact, 80 percent of them attempt to defend themselves either physically or verbally during abusive incidents—the same proportion as that of women who are assaulted by a stranger (U.S. Dept. of Justice, 1994).

Many victims also stay with their husbands out of economic need. Research shows that a woman's standard of living usually drops significantly after a divorce (Glazer, 1993; Heise & Chapman, 1990). Still others stay for fear of what their husbands will do if they leave. This fear is often justified: violence against the victim increases by as much as 75 percent when she attempts to leave the relationship (Hart, 1992; U.S. Dept. of Justice, 1992). One study found that half of all women murdered by their husbands are killed after they have left home (Hart, 1992). Victims of spouse abuse may also be justifiably afraid of reporting the abuse and asking for help (U.S. Dept. of Justice, 1994).

About 50 percent of victims of spouse abuse grew up in homes where they or their mothers were abused, and most come from families in which male and female roles conform to the stereotypes. Many victims have very low self-esteem, at least partly as a result of their ongoing abuse (Cornell & Gelles, 1983). They often blame themselves for the abuse, and agree when their husband accuses them of provoking it. Usually the pattern of abuse does not emerge until after the couple is married.

Interventions for Spouse Abuse

Clinicians used to propose couple therapy as the treatment of choice for spouse abuse, but they have learned that as long as a woman continues to be abused at home, this intervention is only a charade. In fact, couple therapy sometimes *increases* the victim's risk of serious injury or death (ADVTP, 1996; Jones & Schechter, 1992).

The treatment now preferred has three steps: (1) providing a woman with a safe place to live, separate from her abusive husband and situation; (2) counseling for the victim to help her recognize her plight, see her options, and experience a more positive self-image and greater autonomy; and (3) counseling for the abuser to help him cope with life more effectively, develop more appropriate attitudes toward his wife, and develop more appropriate avenues for expressing anger and frustration (Saunders, 1982; Ganley, 1981). A variety of community programs have been set up to provide these intervention services—hot lines, emergency shelters or "safe houses" for women, and public organizations and self-help groups to aid abused women and provide education about the problem (Page, 1996; Sullivan et al., 1992). There are about 1,500 shelters for abused women in the United States (Schneider, 1990).

Duluth, Minnesota, the first jurisdiction to adopt a mandatory arrest policy in cases of spouse abuse, has been a leader in addressing the problem. It has a comprehensive spouse abuse program in which a first-time offender is jailed overnight and released into a twenty-six-week batterers' program. If he fails to attend three consecutive classes, he goes back to jail. In the history of the program, Duluth has not reported one case of domestic homicide. On the one hand, over 60 percent of the men who completed the program were no longer abusing their wives when studied up to eighteen months later (Edelson & Eiskovitz, 1989). On the other hand, at least 40 percent of the men treated in the program committed the same offense within five years, either against the same woman or against a new partner (Sherman, 1992). It is clear to today's clinicians that effective treatment for spouse abuse must directly address the abuser rather than focus exclusively on the victim.

Although much progress has been made, spouse abuse remains a difficult and poorly understood problem. Nevertheless, the very fact that treatment programs now exist is an important development for both victims and our society, and most clinicians believe that many of these programs are on the right track.

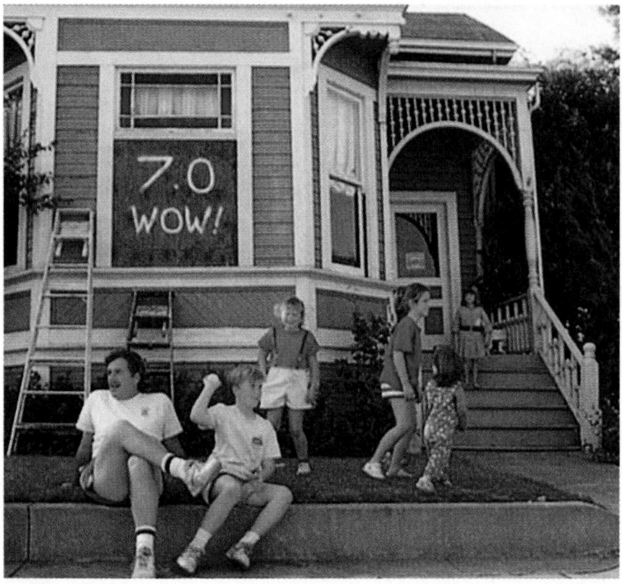

Millions reacted to the San Francisco earthquake of 1989 with dread and panic, but some laid-back individuals thrived on all the excitement. Their hardy personality styles may have helped to protect them from the development of stress disorders.

events (Kushner et al., 1992). These findings are reminiscent of another: that many people respond to stress with a set of positive attitudes, collectively called ***hardiness,*** that enables them to carry on their lives with a sense of fortitude, control, and commitment (Kobasa, 1990, 1987, 1979).

Social Support It has been found that people whose support systems are weak after a traumatic event are also more likely to develop a stress disorder (Pickens et al., 1995; Perry et al., 1992). Rape victims who feel loved, cared for, valued, and accepted by their friends and relatives recover more successfully. So do those treated with dignity and respect by the criminal justice system (Davis, Brickman, & Baker, 1991; Sales, Baum, & Shore, 1984). In contrast, clinical reports suggest that weak social support systems have contributed to the development of posttraumatic stress disorder in some Vietnam veterans (Figley & Leventman, 1990). This man's return home was, sadly, not at all unusual:

> Next morning my sisters went to school as usual, while my brother went to college. Everything seemed the same to them, real routine, you know. I didn't feel "routine." I felt out of it. I felt nervous, tense, jittery, even shaky. I wasn't able to fall asleep, so I got up at 10:00 A.M. I was home alone. So I walked down to the package store and bought me some liquor to help me out—you know, with the nervousness, and my anger about everything. . . .
>
> In spite of all my efforts to avoid having anyone see me, a long-time friend saw me and really welcomed me home. It was really nice. Then, like out of nowhere, six guys showed up on the scene; I knew most of them. They wanted to know about the "good dope" in Vietnam. They didn't seem interested in me as a person. They had heard of the Thai red, the opium, and all that stuff. They asked me about the Vietnamese whores; and how many times I caught the clap [gonorrhea].
>
> They also wanted to know what it was like having sex with Vietnamese women. One of them yelled out, "How many babies you've burned, man? How many young children don't have their fathers because of guys like you? Yeah, you killers, man; you heard me." Before I knew what had happened the cops were there. I had beaten four guys up severely; three had to be taken to the hospital. I seemed to have lost my head totally. I didn't want to hurt anybody. I had done a lot of killing in the 'Nam; I just wanted to be left alone, now. . . . I came back to my room, and began really drinking. I just kept thinking to myself that the streets of Cholon, Saigon, Nha Trang, and other cities and villages in Vietnam were probably safer for me than back in the United States.
>
> *(Brende & Parson, 1985, pp. 49–50)*

Severity of Trauma As one might expect, the severity and nature of traumatic events also help determine whether persons will develop stress disorders. Events can be so extremely traumatic that they override even a positive childhood, hardy personality, and supportive social context. One study followed 253 Vietnam prisoners of war five years after their release. Some 23 percent warranted a clinical diagnosis, though all had been effective Air Force officers, and all had been evaluated as well adjusted before their imprisonment (Ursano, Boydstun, & Wheatley, 1981).

Generally, the more severe the trauma, the greater the likelihood of a stress disorder (Putnam, 1996; Shaler et al., 1996; Lee et al., 1995). Among the Vietnam prisoners of war, for example, it was the men who had been imprisoned longest and treated most harshly who had the highest percentage of disorders. Mutilation and significant physical injury in particular seem to increase the risk of stress reactions, as do observations of other people being injured or killed (Putnam, 1996; Kessler et al., 1995; March, 1992). Biological, childhood, personal, and social variables notwithstanding, it is, as a survivor of trauma once said, "hard to be a survivor" (Kolff & Doan, 1985, p. 45).

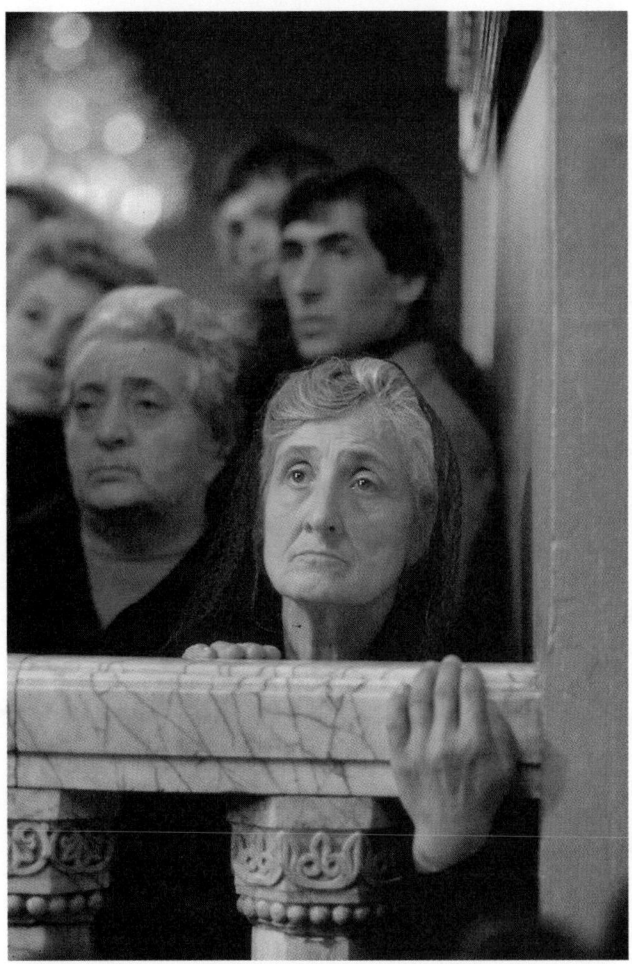

These Armenian citizens find solace in church after a devastating earthquake. Research indicates that people with strong institutional and social ties often recover more readily from the effects of disasters and other such traumatic events.

Treatments for Acute and Posttraumatic Stress Disorders

Treatment can make a major difference to a person with a stress disorder. One survey found that posttraumatic stress symptoms lasted an average of 3 years with treatment but 5.5 years without treatment (Kessler et al., 1995). The details of today's treatment programs for troubled survivors typically vary from trauma to trauma (Shalev, Bonne, & Eth, 1996; Marmar et al., 1993; McFarlane, 1991). Was it combat, sexual molestation, or a major accident? Yet all the programs share basic goals: they try to help survivors reduce or overcome their lingering symptoms, gain perspective on their traumatic experiences, and return to constructive living (see Box 7-3). Programs for combat veterans who suffer from posttraumatic stress disorder demonstrate how these issues may be addressed.

Treatment for Combat Veterans Therapists have used a variety of techniques to alleviate the posttraumatic symptoms of veterans (Shalev, Bonne, & Eth, 1996; Lawson, 1995). Among the most common are drug therapy, exposure techniques, insight therapy, family therapy, and group therapy. Typically, the approaches are combined, as no one of them successfully reduces all the symptoms of the disorder (Boudewins, 1996).

Antianxiety drugs have reduced the tension, hyperalertness, and exaggerated startle responses that many veterans experience (Marmar et al., 1993; Braun et al., 1990). In addition, antidepressant medications have sometimes lessened nightmares, flashbacks, intrusive recollections, and feelings of depression (Mirabella, Frueh, & Fossey, 1995; Marmar et al., 1993; Nagy et al., 1993).

Behavioral exposure techniques have also helped reduce specific symptoms of posttraumatic stress disorder, and they have often led to significant improvements in the overall adjustments of combat veterans with the disorder (Woodward et al., 1997; Boudewins, 1996; Frueh, 1995). Flooding, along with relaxation training, helped rid a 31-year-old veteran of his frightening combat flashbacks and nightmares (Fairbank & Keane, 1982). The therapist and client first singled out combat scenes that the veteran had been reexperiencing frequently. The therapist then helped the client to imagine one of these scenes in great detail and urged him to retain the image until his anxiety subsided. After each of these flooding exercises, the therapist switched to positive imagery and led the client through relaxation exercises. In response to this treatment, the man's flashbacks and nightmares diminished.

In recent years, a relatively new form of exposure therapy has been gaining attention. Clients treated with ***eye movement desensitization and reprocessing*** move their eyes in a *saccadic,* or rhythmic, manner from side to side while they flood themselves with images of phobic objects and situations (Shapiro, 1991, 1989). Case studies have reported dramatic improvements when this treatment has been applied to a variety of problems, including posttraumatic fears and memories. Some clients appear to improve after only one session (Lipke & Botkin, 1992; Puk, 1991). Controlled studies of the approach have been more modest in both number and results, but they do seem to suggest that this treatment can be effective (Boudewins et al., 1991; Shapiro, 1989).

Although drug therapy and exposure techniques bring about symptomatic and general relief, most clinicians believe that veterans with posttraumatic stress disorder cannot fully recover with these approaches alone: they must also develop insight into their combat experiences and the impact those experiences continue to have (Marmar et al., 1993; Weiss & Marmar, 1993). Sometimes

BOX 7-3 Preparing Victims for Rape's Aftermath

Mary Koss and Mary Harvey

Victims as well as significant others can benefit from some discussion of the usual symptomatic responses to rape, the psychological impact of rape, and the length of time required to feel recovered. Such information may prevent more serious problems from developing by making the expectations of involved others more realistic and by encouraging the victim to feel justified to seek help. The information that could be shared with victims and their families might be similar to the following comments. . . .

Rape is a trauma just like a major disaster such as a tornado or a bad car accident.

Physical Symptoms

Because of the shock that these events cause to your system, some physical problems usually develop afterwards. You may experience symptoms you usually associate with extreme fear, such as pounding heart, shortness of breath, or dizziness. You may find your appetite or sleeping is changed as when you're worried about a major traumatic event like a court appearance or are under a lot of pressure at work.

You may notice problems with sex that you've rarely experienced before. Often this is a signal that you're not ready to resume your former activities so quickly. It's perfectly okay to substitute other forms of feeling close and [to avoid] intercourse until you feel ready.

Even though these physical symptoms are typical, they will still upset you. Seek a doctor's care but be sure to tell him or her of your recent rape so that they can treat you properly.

Feelings

Nearly everyone experiences some psychological problems after a rape. Particularly upsetting are nightmares, flashbacks of the experience, and the feeling that you need to talk about your experience over and over again until everyone around you is fed up. These are normal psychological processes that operate after a major trauma. Their purpose is to gradually wear down the frightening impact of an experience. They will eventually help you put the experience behind you.

Even if you don't have any problems now, it's not unusual for some to crop up six months or a year from now. The problems that are most common are fears that you never had before or were never that pronounced, feeling bad about yourself and about life in general, conflicts in your intimate relationships, and problems getting back to your former enjoyment of sex.

You may find that the rape has affected your whole family. Don't be surprised if you develop negative feelings about someone that are stronger or different than you've ever had before. Try to talk your feelings over and be specific about what the other person can do to help you feel better. Family members may feel pretty impatient that it is taking you so long to get on top of things.

Availability of Services

You may find that although your enjoyment of life is less, you can live with your symptoms and cope. However, there may come a time when you feel that the toll is too great and you need relief. Or, you may notice that your important relationships are suffering or deteriorating. A number of people are available to help you at this point. I'm going to give you a sheet listing some of them so that you'll know who to call.

Besides counselors who could see you privately if you wanted, it is possible to become a member of a group made up of women who have been raped. It can often help to feel less crazy and alone if you know other people who share your experience and know what it's like.

Length of Recovery

It usually takes over a year to feel fully recovered from rape, to be able to think of your assault without crying, and to feel the same level of health you enjoyed previously. Going through a court process or anything else that reminds you of the assault may make you feel temporarily worse after you thought you were finally getting on top of things. It's not unusual for there to be ups and downs on the way to recovery.

If it's okay with you, I'd like to call you at home in a few days and see how you're doing. Then, or at a later time, I'd be glad to see you again or help you make an appointment with a counselor.

(Koss & Harvey, 1987, pp. 109–110)

Rap groups have helped many Vietnam veterans overcome the anxiety, depression, sleep problems, and flashbacks that still linger years after the war.

clinicians help clients to bring out deep-seated feelings, accept what they have done and experienced, become less judgmental of themselves, and learn to trust others once again. In related work, the psychologist James Pennebaker (1990) has found that talking (or even writing) about suppressed traumatic experiences can reduce lingering anxiety and tension.

Attempts to express feelings and develop insight are sometimes undertaken in couple or family therapy (Glynn et al., 1995; Johnson, Feldman, & Lubin, 1995). Indeed, the symptoms of posttraumatic stress disorder tend to be particularly apparent to family members, who may be directly affected by the individual's anxious responses, depressive mood, or angry outbursts. At the same time, family members may implicitly collude with the individual to keep unpleasant or grotesque events or memories hidden from family view, a pattern sometimes called a "conspiracy of silence" (VanDerHal, Tauber, & Gotresfeld, 1996). With the help and support of family members, individuals may identify feelings and issues that they are grappling with, examine their impact on others, learn to communicate better, and develop better problem-solving skills. Family therapy can also provide support, education, and guidance for family members who may themselves be experiencing considerable stress, confusion, and discord as a result of their relative's trauma and lingering symptoms.

In "rap groups," veterans meet to share experiences and feelings, develop insights, and give mutual support. This form of group therapy originated in 1971, when an organization called Vietnam Veterans Against the War decided that there was a pressing need for a forum in which veterans could discuss their experiences with other veterans and together heal their psychological wounds (Lifton, 1973). Many people find it easier to recall events and confront feelings they have been trying to avoid for years in an atmosphere of group trust, social support, and common experience (Sipprelle, 1992; Rozynko & Dondershine, 1991).

One of the major issues that rap groups deal with is guilt—guilt about things the members may have done to survive or about the very fact that they did survive while close friends died. Once the veterans are finally able to talk candidly about their combat experiences and guilt feelings, they may start to recover from them and gauge their responsibility for past actions more accurately

(Lifton, 1973). Rap groups can also address the rage that many veterans feel. Many veterans of the Vietnam War are intensely angry that they had to fight for a questionable cause, face unbearable conditions and tensions in Vietnam, and deal with an accusing society after they returned.

Today hundreds of small Veteran Outreach Centers across the country, as well as numerous treatment programs in Veterans Administration hospitals, specialize in rap groups. These agencies also offer individual therapy, counseling for the spouses and children of troubled veterans, family therapy, and assistance in securing employment, education, and benefits (Brende & Parson, 1985; Blank, 1982).

Because most Veteran Outreach Centers have existed only a relatively short time, research into their effectiveness is limited (Funari, Piekarski, & Sherwood, 1991). So far, clinical reports and empirical studies suggest that they offer an important, sometimes life-saving treatment opportunity. Julius's search for help upon his return from Vietnam was, unfortunately, an ordeal that many veterans have shared:

> When I got back from the 'Nam, I knew I needed psychotherapy or something like that. I just knew that if I didn't get help I was going to kill myself or somebody else. . . . I went to see this doctor; he barely looked at me. I felt he "saw me coming" and knew all about my sickness. I was the "sicky" to him. He just kept on asking me all that bullshit about how many children I had killed and was I guilty and depressed about it. He asked how it felt to kill people. He also kept on asking me about my brothers and sisters. But he never asked me about what my experiences were like in Vietnam. He never did. I saw him for treatment for about a month—about three visits, but I quit because we weren't getting anywhere. . . . He just kept on giving me more and more medications. I could've set up my own pharmacy. I needed someone to talk to about my problems, my real problems, not some bullshit about my childhood. I needed someone who wanted to help. The clinic later referred me to another shrink. . . . I guess she thought she was being honest with me, by telling me that she was not a veteran, was not in Vietnam, and did not know what was wrong with me. She also told me that she had no experience working with Vietnam veterans, and that I should go to the Veterans Administration for help. . . . I also became scared that there was something really wrong with me now. I just didn't want to go to the VA for help. . . . I blame the VA for my going to 'Nam anyway; I wanted no part of it.
>
> It was only in the last 3 years when my wife made an important phone call to a local Veterans Outreach Center that I started feeling I had hope, that something could be done for me. I received the help that I have always needed. Finally, I found it easier to hold a job and take care of my family. My nightmares are not as frightening or as frequent as they used to be. Things are better now; I am learning to trust people and give more to my wife and children.
>
> *(Brende & Parson, 1985, pp. 206–208)*

Community Therapy: The Sociocultural Model in Action Persons who are traumatized by disasters, victimization, or accidents may profit from many of the treatments applied to survivors of combat stress. In addition, because their traumas occur in their own community, where mental health resources are close at hand, these individuals may respond well to immediate, active community interventions. Compelling examples are the rapidly mobilized community care programs now offered by mental health professionals across the United States to victims of large-scale disasters.

For years the American Red Cross has provided food, shelter, and clothing needed by survivors of disasters such as hurricanes and earthquakes, and the federal government has helped such people find the financial resources to rebuild their ruined homes and businesses. But until recently no organization systematically addressed the psychological needs of disaster survivors, even though such survivors experience an estimated 17

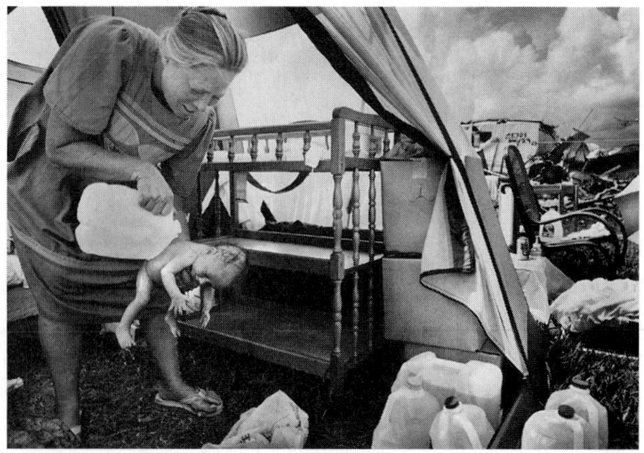

In the aftermath of Hurricane Andrew, a mother must wash her newborn baby with water from a jug, while the family takes up residence in a tent within sight of their former home. Mental health workers from the Disaster Response Network may initially help such individuals meet their basic needs, then increasingly provide counseling services.

percent increase in mental disorders and over half suffer from significant mental distress (Rubonis & Bickman, 1991; Roberts, 1990).

In 1991 the American Psychological Association, in collaboration with the American Red Cross, created the ***Disaster Response Network (DRN)*** to help provide the large numbers of mental health professionals needed after a disaster. The more than 2,500 psychologists in the network volunteer to provide free emergency mental health services at disaster sites throughout the United States (Peterson, 1996; Seppa, 1996; APA, 1991). They have been mobilized for such disasters as the Midwest's Great Flood of 1993, Hurricane Andrew in 1992, earthquakes in Southern California, the Oklahoma City bombing, the Los Angeles riots, the World Trade Center bombing, the explosion of TWA Flight 800, and shootings in business offices.

Traditional long-term mental health services are often not appropriate, not available, or not sought after a disaster, so the short-term community intervention provided by the Disaster Response Network fills a real need (Joyner & Swenson, 1993). The emotional support that survivors may receive from friends and relatives often breaks down within a few days or weeks. People soon get tired of hearing about the survivors' experiences and the stress of the disaster. Moreover, many survivors feel guilty about discussing their own losses if others' losses were greater, so they are reluctant to seek out professional help. And many survivors simply do not recognize their own emotional fragility immediately after a disaster (Michaelson, 1993). People who live in poverty are in particular need of community-level interventions. These survivors apparently have more psychological distress after disasters than survivors with higher incomes (Gibbs, 1989), they cannot afford private counseling, and they are less likely to know where to go to seek counseling.

Since psychological needs cannot be addressed if basic survival needs are not met, the first aim of disaster mental health professionals is to help survivors meet their basic needs as quickly as possible. During the Midwest flood of 1993, for example, mental health professionals worked in shelters and service centers and rode in Red Cross emergency vehicles to deliver food and water along with counseling services. Other counselors joined flood victims in piling sandbags to protect their homes from further damage. Counselors also used these early contacts with victims as an opportunity to determine which individuals were most in need of counseling. At this stage any counseling had to be brief, perhaps only a few minutes with each person, often in a highly distracting environment—a shelter, a sandbag brigade, a line at a water truck.

A fire captain cradles one-year-old Baylee Almon, a child killed in the bombing of the Oklahoma City federal building. This famous photograph reminds us that rescue workers are themselves subjected to enormous stress and trauma during disasters (Bryant & Harvey, 1995). Community intervention programs try to address their psychological needs along with those of the victims.

Once mental health volunteers become involved in the community, they may intervene more actively to meet the psychological needs of the survivors. Psychologists and other mental health workers often use a four-stage approach (Michaelson, 1993).

1. *Normalize people's responses to the disaster.* The counselors educate survivors about the symptoms they may experience, such as sleep or eating disturbances, difficulty concentrating, or feelings of grief, fear, or anger. Essentially, survivors are given permission to experience these emotions and told that these are normal responses to a disaster.

2. *Diffuse anxiety, anger, and frustration.* To diffuse the anxiety, anger, and frustration that survivors often feel after a disaster, counselors help them talk about their experiences and their feelings about the event.

3. *Teach self-helping skills.* Community professionals educate and train survivors to develop such self-

help skills as stress management. As part of this effort, they may hand out fliers on handling stress.

4. *Provide referrals.* The workers eventually may refer survivors to other professionals and agencies who can provide long-term counseling. It is estimated that between 15 and 25 percent of survivors need this specialized assistance. Some, however, may not seek help for months after the disaster.

Relief workers, too, can become overwhelmed by the traumas they witness. During the Los Angeles riots, for example, the primary responsibility of many counselors was to debrief Red Cross workers (Youngstrom, 1992)—to help them vent and normalize their feelings and teach them about acute and posttraumatic stress disorders and how to identify victims who need further treatment. Many mental health professionals who live in the disaster area need counseling themselves, since they, too, are survivors. The dual role they are thrown into may make it difficult for them to deal with their own experiences.

The needs of disaster survivors can also be met by ***paraprofessionals,*** lay persons who receive training and supervision from professionals. Graduate students at various schools in the Los Angeles area were enlisted to provide counseling for survivors of the riots. Some of them were actually more effective than professionals, because they were more familiar with the afflicted community and shared the survivors' socioeconomic and minority status.

Clearly, intervention at the community level is essential after a disaster. And sadly, our world seems to offer an ever-increasing number of opportunities for such interventions. In the wake of the 1995 Oklahoma City bombing, members of the Disaster Response Network were called upon to deliver death notices, to debrief rescue workers, medical personnel, police, and structural engineers, and to provide crisis counseling to hundreds of families (Peterson, 1996). Similarly, in the immediate aftermath of the explosion of TWA Flight 800, close to 500 mental health professionals were needed to counsel family members, flight crews, rescue personnel, and others affected by the disaster (Seppa, 1996). As Paul Ofman, a leader in the Disaster Response Network, has said, "Disaster mental health has a ripple effect. Everyone is affected by it" (Seppa, 1996, p. 38).

Crossroads

Panic, obsessive-compulsive, and stress disorders—once known in clinical circles simple as the "other" anxiety disorders—have received intense study over the past decade. Lessons can be learned from the history and current status of these disorders, not just about the disorders themselves, but about the general study and treatment of psychological abnormality.

First, we learn that perseverance pays off. For many years, the study and treatment of panic disorder and obsessive-compulsive disorder seemed to be getting nowhere. The explanations offered provided few genuine insights, and clinical interventions brought little change for people with these disorders. As we have seen, recent work in the biological, cognitive, and behavioral spheres has changed all that. Today research into these problems is flourishing, explanations are compelling, and treatment is highly productive.

A second lesson is that we can always improve on the identification and classification of psychological disorders. Panic disorder was not distinguished from generalized anxiety disorder until recent years, and the stress disorders did not even enter the diagnostic system until the 1980s. These recent classifications have been much more than clinical window dressing. Clinical theorists, researchers, and practitioners were able to make significant progress in understanding and treating these problems only after they were properly identified.

A third lesson is that insights and techniques associated with the various models not only *can* be combined, but often *should* be combined for greater clarity and effectiveness. Not until clinical theorists took a comprehensive look at the disorders discussed in this chapter were they able to develop explanations and treatments that were compelling, predictive, and effective. The productive cognitive explanation of panic disorder, for example, builds squarely on the biological idea that the disorder begins with unusual physiological sensations. And the promising cognitive explanation of obsessive-compulsive disorder considers biological and behavioral influences as well. Similarly, therapists have found that their interventions are often most effective when they combine medications with cognitive techniques to treat panic disorder, with behavioral techniques to treat obsessive-compulsive disorder, and with psychodynamic, humanistic, behavioral, or cognitive techniques to treat stress disorders. For the millions of people who suffer from these anxiety disorders, such integrated insights and interventions are most positive and momentous developments.

Finally, we can learn a lesson of caution from the recent work on these disorders. When problems are newly identified or heavily studied, it is common for researchers and clinicians to make claims and draw conclusions that sometimes prove to be overstated. Take posttraumatic stress disorder. Because its symptoms are many, because a variety of events can be construed as traumatic, and because the disorder has received so much attention, many people—perhaps too many—are now receiving this diagnosis. The accuracy and usefulness of this trend remains to be seen. We shall see this potential problem again when we look at attention-deficit hyperactivity disorder, repressed memories of childhood abuse, and multiple personality disorder. The line between enlightenment and overenthusiasm is often thin.

Chapter Review

1. ***Panic, obsessive-compulsive, and stress disorders*** Discoveries in recent years have shed new light on the causes of panic disorder, obsessive-compulsive disorder, and stress disorders, and promising treatment approaches have been developed for each of them.

2. ***Panic disorder*** *Panic attacks* are periodic, discrete bouts of panic that occur abruptly. Sufferers of *panic disorder* experience panic attacks frequently, unpredictably, and without apparent provocation. When the disorder is accompanied by agoraphobia, it is termed *panic disorder with agoraphobia.*

   A. ***The biological perspective*** Biological theorists believe that abnormal *norepinephrine* activity in the *locus ceruleus* is a key factor in panic disorder. Biological therapists use certain antidepressant drugs and benzodiazepine drugs such as *alprazolam* to treat many people with panic disorder. The drugs bring at least some improvement to most patients with panic disorder. Patients whose disorder is accompanied by agoraphobia may require a combination of drug therapy and behavioral exposure treatment.

   B. ***The cognitive perspective*** The cognitive position is that panic-prone people become preoccupied with some of their bodily sensations and mental states and often misinterpret them as indicative of imminent catastrophe.

   (1) Panic-prone individuals have a high degree of *anxiety sensitivity:* they are particularly attentive to bodily sensations and tend to interpret them as potentially harmful.
   (2) People with panic disorder experience greater anxiety during *biological challenge tests*—tests that induce various biological sensations—than do other people.
   (3) Cognitive therapists teach patients that the various physical sensations they experience are actually harmless.

3. ***Obsessive-compulsive disorder*** People with *obsessive-compulsive disorder* are beset by *obsessions*—repetitive and unwanted thoughts, ideas, impulses, or images that keep invading their consciousness and causing anxiety—or *compulsions*—repetitive and rigid actions or mental acts that they feel compelled to perform to reduce anxiety.

   A. Obsessions may have basic themes. Common themes are dirt or contamination and violence or aggression.
   B. Many compulsions center on cleaning. Other common compulsions involve checking, touching, verbal rituals, or counting.
   C. Most people with obsessive-compulsive disorder experience *both* obsessions and compulsions. The compulsions are often a response to the obsessive thoughts.
   D. ***Explanations and treatments*** Once poorly understood and ineffectively treated, obsessive-compulsive disorder is now receiving productive study by researchers and is often treated with considerable success.

   (1) ***The psychodynamic perspective*** According to the *psychodynamic* view, obsessive-compulsive disorder arises out of a battle between id impulses, which appear as obsessive thoughts, and ego defense mechanisms, which take the form of counterthoughts or compulsive actions. Psychodynamic therapists use free association, the therapist's interpretation, and related techniques to try to help people overcome their disorder.
   (2) ***The behavioral perspective*** *Behaviorists* believe that compulsive behaviors often develop through chance associations and operant conditioning. The leading behavioral approach combines prolonged *exposure* with *response prevention,* the blocking of compulsive behaviors.
   (3) ***The cognitive perspective*** *Cognitive* theorists believe that obsessive-compulsive disorder grows from a normal human tendency to have unwanted and unpleasant thoughts—a tendency that some people misinterpret as dangerous, reprehensible, and controllable. Their efforts to eliminate or avoid such thoughts inadvertently lead to the development of obsessions and compulsions. In a promising cognitive-behavioral approach, *habituation training,* therapists encourage clients to summon their obsessive thoughts to mind for a prolonged period, expecting that such prolonged exposure will cause the thoughts to seem less threatening and generate less anxiety.

(4) ***The biological perspective*** *Biological* researchers have identified two factors that may contribute to this disorder: low activity of the neurotransmitter *serotonin* and abnormal functioning in the brain's *orbital region* and *caudate nuclei. Antidepressant drugs* that raise serotonin activity are a useful form of treatment for this disorder.

4. ***Stress disorders*** People with *acute stress disorder* or *posttraumatic stress disorder* react with a distinct pattern of symptoms after a traumatic event: they reexperience the traumatic event, avoid related events, are markedly less responsive than normal, and experience increased arousal, anxiety, and guilt. The symptoms of acute stress disorder begin soon after the trauma and last less than a month. Those of posttraumatic stress disorder may begin at any time (even years) after the trauma, and may last for months or years.

A. These disorders can emerge in response to combat conditions, in the wake of disasters, and after stress that is intentionally inflicted.

(1) ***Combat*** For years clinicians have recognized that many soldiers develop symptoms of anxiety and depression *during* combat. Not until after the Vietnam War did they realize that many soldiers also experience stress symptoms *after* combat, in the form of acute stress disorder or posttraumatic stress disorder.

(2) ***Disasters*** The stress disorders may also follow natural and accidental disasters, such as earthquakes, floods, tornadoes, fires, airplane crashes, and serious car accidents.

(3) ***Abuse and victimization*** Lingering stress symptoms may follow incidents of abuse and victimization. They have been experienced, for example, by survivors of Nazi concentration camps, victims of rape, and persons exposed to ongoing trauma such as living in a violent neighborhood.

B. *Explanations* In attempting to explain why some people develop acute or posttraumatic stress disorder and others do not, researchers have focused on biological factors (excessive neurotransmitter or hormone reactions); childhood experiences (poverty, parent separation, or childhood abuse or trauma); personal variables (for example, a tendency to view life's aversive events as beyond one's control); social support (weak social support systems); and the severity of the traumatic event (more severe traumas present a higher probability of a stress disorder).

C. *Treatments* Techniques used for symptomatic relief of the stress disorders include drug therapy and exposure techniques. Clinicians may also use insight therapy, family therapy, and group therapy (including *rap groups* for combat veterans) to help sufferers develop insight and perspective regarding their continuing symptoms. *Community therapy,* such as that offered by the *Disaster Response Network,* can also be very helpful after large-scale disasters.

Thought and Afterthought

Working with Death

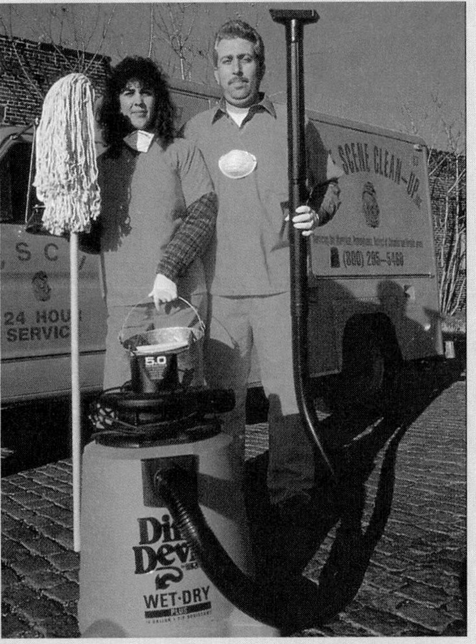

Some of the least pleasant jobs in our society are those which entail tying up loose ends after horrifying disasters or murders. Yet the jobs must be done, irrespective of the personal toll they may take on the individuals involved. It turns out that reactions to such responsibilities vary widely.

In 1993, eighty-three persons died in the famous fire at the Branch Davidian compound in Waco, Texas. Thirty-one dentists had to examine the dental remains of the dead. A study later revealed that these dentists had more symptoms of posttraumatic stress than did dentists who had not performed the upsetting deed (McCarroll et al., 1996).

Then there are Ray and Louise Barnes *(above)*, who run a business called Crime Scene Clean-Up. They and their staffers are hired by police departments, funeral homes, and grieving families to clean up after homicides, suicides, and accidents. They use latex gloves, mops, respirators, and other tools of the trade to "scrub away the detritus of human disaster" (Howe & Nugent, 1996). Ray Barnes says that his former jobs with a funeral home and a medical examiner's office helped prepare him for this work. While hardly indifferent to the grisly scenes, he has grown somewhat accustomed to them, and he and his wife now have a thriving business.

Afterthoughts: Why might the dentists and the Barneses react so differently to the situations they have encountered? . . . Is it possible to "adjust" to situations of horror over time, or might repeated exposure take a toll in other ways? . . . What other jobs in our society might be traumatizing?

Frankly Speaking

You cannot believe the savagery with which people attack toilets. They break the plumbing, they smash them. They go wild. I can see how people might injure schools or places where they've had difficulties, but I do not see how anyone can bear a grudge against a toilet.

—Parks Commissioner of New York City

Afterthoughts: Might psychodynamic theorists have a different view of the situation? . . . Would people who directly attack toilets or other remnants of toilet training be more or less likely to develop an obsessive-compulsive pattern?

Terror Behind the Smile

Many of today's college students grew up watching *Double Dare* and *Family Double Dare,* two of the messiest game shows in television history. Young contestants were regularly splattered with goo and immersed in slime and muck (Summers, 1996). All the while, the host, Marc Summers *(right)*, seemed to be having a great time, especially when the kids would pick him up and throw him into the mess as well. In 1996, however, Summers revealed that his years on the show had been a personal nightmare. He has an obsessive-compulsive disorder.

Summers says that his disorder dates back to the age of eight. He remembers cleaning his room for hours, removing and dusting every book in his bookcase. When he got the opportunity to host *Double Dare,* he couldn't turn down the career opportunity. But the price was high. After the shows, he would spend hours in the shower. "It was the most uncomfortable feeling in the world—a feeling of physical revulsion." Only recently has Summers recognized his disorder. He now takes medications for it and his symptoms are diminishing.

Afterthoughts: Might Summers have agreed to host this show to implicitly confront his fears and compulsions? . . . If it was a form of self-treatment, why did it not help? . . . What other examples of so-called counterphobic behavior pervade our culture?

Topic Overview

Unipolar Depression

Clinical Picture of Depression

Diagnosing Unipolar Depression

Explanations

Bipolar Disorders

Clinical Picture of Mania

Diagnosing Bipolar Disorders

Explanations

Crossroads

Chapter 8

Mood Disorders

Most people's moods are transient. Their feelings of elation or sadness are understandable responses to daily events and do not affect the overall tenor of their lives. The moods of people with mood disorders, in contrast, tend to last a long time, color all of the sufferer's interactions with the world, and disrupt normal functioning. Virtually all of such people's actions are dictated by their powerful moods.

Depression and mania are the dominating emotions in mood disorders. ***Depression*** is a low, sad state in which life seems bleak and its challenges seem overwhelming. ***Mania,*** the extreme opposite of depression, is a state of breathless euphoria, or at least frenzied energy, in which people have an exaggerated belief that the world is theirs for the taking. Most people with a mood disorder suffer exclusively from depression, a pattern often called ***unipolar depression.*** They have no history of mania and return to a normal or nearly normal mood state when their depression lifts. Others undergo periods of mania that alternate with periods of depression, a pattern called ***bipolar disorder*** or ***manic-depressive disorder.*** One might logically expect a third pattern of mood disorder, unipolar mania, in which people suffer exclusively from mania, but this pattern is so rare that there is some question as to whether it exists at all (APA, 1994) unless it is brought on by a medical condition.

Jacob Lawrence's Depression, *1950, illustrates the broad clinical picture of this mood disorder. The symptoms extend beyond sadness, and include a loss of energy, slumping posture, and slow movement, as well as a wide variety of other symptoms.*

Mood disorders have always captured people's interest, in part because so many prominent people have suffered from them. The Bible speaks of the severe depression of Nebuchadnezzar, Saul, and Moses. Queen Victoria of England and Abraham Lincoln seem to have experienced recurring depressions. Similarly, depression and sometimes mania have plagued such artists as George Frideric Handel, Ernest Hemingway, Eugene O'Neill, Virginia Woolf, Robert Lowell, and Sylvia Plath (Andreasen, 1980). The plight of these famous figures has been shared by millions, and the economic consequences (costs of treatment, hospitalization, work loss, and so on) amount to more than $40 billion each year (Simon & Katzelnick, 1997; Rupp, 1995; MIT, 1993). The human suffering these disorders cause is incalculable.

Unipolar Depression

People more unhappy than usual often say they are "depressed." Typically, they are responding to sad events, understandable fatigue, or unhappy thoughts. Unfortunately, this use of the term confuses a perfectly normal mood swing with a dysfunctional clinical syndrome. All of us experience dejection from time to time; only an unfortunate minority experience unipolar depression.

Normal dejection is seldom so severe as to alter daily functioning significantly, and it lifts within a reasonable period. Downturns in mood can even be beneficial. Periods spent in contemplation can lead us to explore ourselves, our values, and our situations, and we often emerge with a sense of greater strength, clarity, and resolve (see Figure 8-1).

Clinical depression, on the other hand, is a serious psychological disturbance with no redeeming characteristics. The psychological pain it brings is severe, long-lasting, and debilitating; it may intensify as the months go by. Persons with clinical depression may become unable to carry out the simplest of life's activities; some, in fact, try to end their lives.

Abraham Lincoln was one of many leaders who suffered from episodes of depression. In 1841 he wrote to a friend, "I am now the most miserable man living. If what I feel were equally distributed to the whole human family, there would be not one cheerful face on earth."

The Prevalence of Unipolar Depression

Surveys suggest that between 5 and 10 percent of adults in the United States suffer from a severe unipolar pattern of depression in any given year, while another 3 to 5 percent suffer from mild forms of the disorder (Kessler et al., 1994; Regier et al., 1993). Its prevalence is similar in Canada, England, and many other countries (Smith et al., 1995; Smith & Weissman, 1992). In fact, as many as 18 percent of all adults in the world may experience an episode of severe unipolar depression at some point in their lives (Angst, 1995).

A worldwide research project suggests that the risk of experiencing severe unipolar depression has steadily increased since 1915. The average age for the onset of severe depression, which is now 27 in the United States, has also dropped with each successive generation (Weissman et al., 1992, 1991; Klerman & Weissman, 1989).

In almost all industrialized countries, women are at least twice as likely as men to experience episodes of severe unipolar depression (Weissman et al., 1991) (see Box 8-1). As many as 26 percent of women may have a severe episode at some time in their lives, compared with 12 percent of men (APA, 1993). Women are also more likely than men to experience episodes of mild unipolar depression, although the difference in these rates is less extreme (Smith & Weissman, 1992; Weissman et al., 1991). Among children, the prevalence of unipolar depression is similar for girls and boys. All of these rates are similar across all socioeconomic classes (Weissman et al., 1991).

Relatively few differences in prevalence have been found among ethnic groups. White Americans between the ages of 30 and 64 have a somewhat higher rate than African Americans in that age range, but the rates for younger and older adults are the same in both populations (Weissman et al., 1991). Within both races, unipolar depression is again more than twice as common among women as among men.

Severe unipolar depression may begin at any age. Approximately two-thirds of people with this problem recover within six months, some without treatment (APA, 1994; Keller, 1988). However, most of those who recover have at least one subsequent episode of depression in their lifetime (Goldberg, 1995; Rao et al., 1995; APA, 1994, 1993).

The Clinical Picture of Depression

Some depressed people manage to function after a fashion, but their depression robs them of effectiveness and pleasure, as we see in the cases of Derek and Beatrice:

Derek has probably suffered from depression all of his adult life but was unaware of it for many years. Derek called himself a night person, claiming that he could not think clearly until after noon even though he was often awake by 4:00 A.M. He tried to schedule his work as editorial writer for a small town newspaper so that it was compatible with his depressed mood at the beginning of the day. Therefore, he scheduled meetings for the mornings; talking with people got him moving. He saved writing and decision making for later in the day.

Derek had always been a thoughtful person and was often preoccupied. His family and colleagues grew used to his apparent inattention and absentmindedness. He often failed to answer people when they spoke to him. Sometimes they were surprised to hear his slow, soft-spoken reply 20 or 30 seconds later. His wife tried to be patient when it took him 20 seconds to respond to "Do you want coffee or tea tonight?" Derek's private thoughts were rarely cheerful and self-confident. He felt that his marriage was a mere business partnership. He provided the money, and she provided a home and children. Derek and his wife rarely expressed affection for each other. Occasionally, he had images of his own violent death in a bicycle crash, in a plane crash, or in a murder by an unidentified assailant.

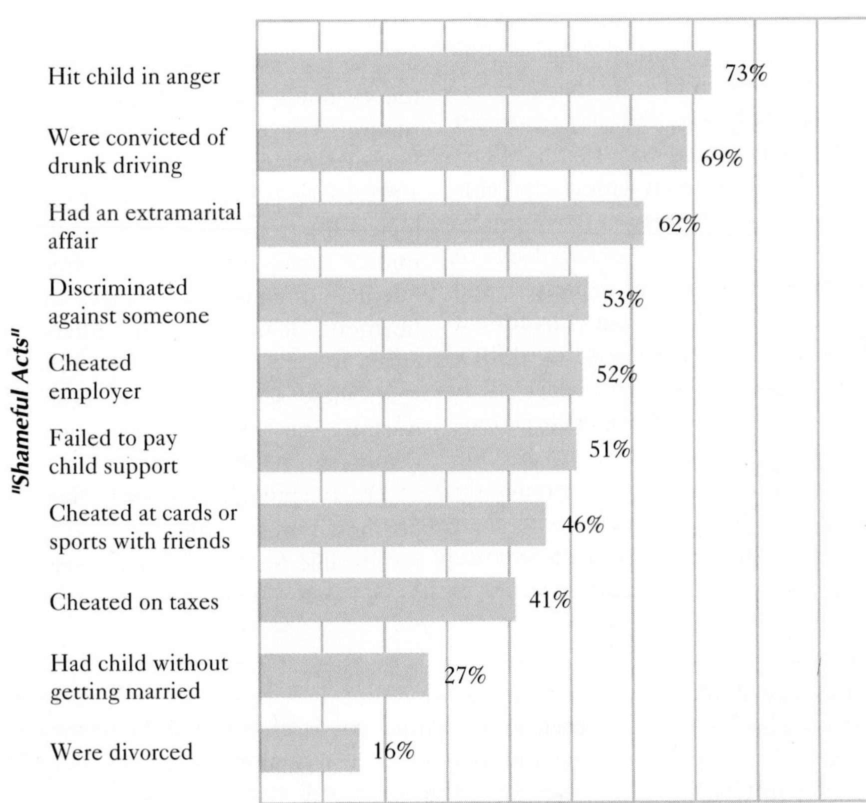

Figure 8-1 *What kinds of things make people feel ashamed? Although depressed people often experience excessive shame, most people feel this emotion from time to time. In a recent survey, the majority of respondents believed that people today would feel shame if they were discovered to have hit a child in anger or been convicted of drunk driving. Events that evoked shame for past generations, such as having a child out of wedlock or getting a divorce, are less likely to produce that reaction today. (Source:* Newsweek *Poll, 1995.)*

BOX 8-1 Depressing News for Women

More women than men are diagnosed with major unipolar depression. More women also report being mildly depressed. In fact, women in places as far apart as Paris, Beirut, New Zealand, and the United States are at least twice as likely as men to experience depression (Joiner & Black, 1995; Weissman & Olfson, 1995). Women also appear to be younger when depression strikes, to have more frequent and longer-lasting bouts, and to respond less successfully to treatment (Pajer, 1995; Weissman & Olfson, 1995). Why the huge difference between the sexes? Several explanations have been offered (Blehar & Oren, 1995; Brems, 1995; Nolen-Hoeksema, 1995, 1990, 1987).

Edvard Munch's painting Melancholy (Laura) *was inspired by his sister's bouts of severe depression.*

1. *The artifact theory.* One theory holds that women and men are equally prone to depression, but that gender differences arise because studies fail to detect depression in men. Perhaps men find it less socially acceptable to admit feeling depressed or to seek treatment. Or perhaps depressed women display more *emotional* symptoms, such as sadness and crying, which are easily diagnosed, while depressed men mask their depression behind traditionally "masculine" symptoms such as anger (Mirowsky & Ross, 1995).

Although the artifact explanation has an intuitive appeal, it lacks consistent research support (Fennig, Schwartz, & Bromet, 1994). It turns out that women are actually no more willing or able than men to identify their depressive symptoms and seek treatment (Nolen-Hoeksema, 1990). When men and women with comparable levels of depression were interviewed, they were equally likely to label themselves as depressed, and equally likely to seek treatment (Amenson & Lewinsohn, 1981). Similarly, the old adage that "women get sad and men get angry" appears to be a myth. One study found that while women do get depressed more often than men, they tend also to experience more anger (Mirowsky & Ross, 1995).

2. *The hormone theory.* Another theory holds that hormonal fluctuations trigger depression in genetically vulnerable women (Pajer, 1995; Parry, 1995). A woman's biological life from her early teens to middle age is characterized by frequent and significant changes in hormone levels. Gender differences in rates of depression also span these same years and peak during the childbearing years (Weissman & Olfson, 1995).

It is unlikely, however, that hormonal fluctuations are solely responsible for the elevated levels

Derek felt that he was constantly on the edge of job failure. He was disappointed that his editorials had not attracted the attention of larger papers. He was certain that several of the younger people on the paper had better ideas and wrote more skillfully than he did. He scolded himself for a bad editorial that he had written ten years earlier. Although that particular piece had not been up to his usual standards, everyone else on the paper had forgotten it a week after it appeared. But ten years later, Derek was still ruminating over that one editorial. . . .

Derek attributed his inability to enjoy himself and

of depression in women. Important sociocultural factors and life events also occur at puberty, pregnancy, and menopause. Besides, variations in hormone levels are not at all related to depression in adolescent girls, yet life events are strongly related to depression during the teenage years (Brooks-Gunn & Warren, 1989; Eccles et al., 1988). Thus it may be that hormonal changes serve primarily to exacerbate existing depression (Brems, 1995). Hormonal explanations have further been criticized as chauvinistic, since they imply that a woman's normal biology is flawed (Nolen-Hoeksema, 1990).

3. *The quality-of-life theory.* Women in our society on average confront more poverty, more menial jobs, less adequate housing, and more discrimination than men—all factors that have been linked to depression (Wu & DeMaris, 1996; Brems, 1995; Newmann, 1986). And in many homes, women also bear a disproportionate share of responsibility for child care and housework (Wu & DeMaris, 1996).

Some sociocultural theorists have further suggested that the millions of mothers who work outside the home may experience "role overload," which leaves them vulnerable to depression. This belief has gained wide acceptance, but it is not consistently supported by research. Though multiple roles certainly add complexity and stress to one's life, most studies find that outside employment may actually serve as a buffer against depression. It typically increases self-esteem, social status, and social support, and it does not by itself increase the likelihood of depression (Hyde, 1995; Hyde et al., 1995; Nolen-Hoeksema, 1990). One study even found that the level of depression declines with each hour a woman works outside the home (Wethington & Kesler, 1989). Few reliable studies support the "role overload" hypothesis (Brems, 1995; Hyde et al., 1995).

4. *The lack-of-control theory.* According to this theory, women are more vulnerable to depression because they are more likely than men to feel little control over their lives. Studies have, in fact, confirmed that women are more prone to develop learned helplessness in the laboratory than men. In one study, female college students were asked to unscramble anagrams that were actually insoluble. The students later experienced a greater sense of helplessness than male counterparts who had been subjected to the same conditions, and they performed more poorly at other tasks as well (Le Unes, Nation, & Turley, 1980).

In accord with the lack-of-control explanation, it has been found that victimization of any kind, from burglary to rape, often produces a general sense of helplessness and increases the symptoms of depression in both men and women. Unfortunately, women in our society are more likely than men to be victims, particularly of sexual assault and child abuse (Andrews et al., 1995; Brems, 1995; Pajer, 1995; Cutler & Nolen-Hoeksema, 1991). Despite these compelling correlations, researchers have yet to subject this idea to stringent tests (Nolen-Hoeksema, 1990, 1987).

5. *The "self-blame" theory.* Research indicates that women are more likely than men to blame their failures on lack of ability and to attribute their successes to luck—an attribution style that has also been linked to depression (Wolfe & Russianoff, 1997). Perhaps not so coincidentally, these gender differences in attribution begin to emerge during adolescence, about the same time that the gender differences in depression appear (Nolen-Hoeksema & Girgus, 1995).

Each of these explanations for the gender differences in unipolar depression offers food for thought. Each has gathered just enough supportive evidence to make it interesting, and at the same time has confronted just enough unsupportive evidence to raise questions about its usefulness. Moreover, this list of possibilities is hardly exhaustive. Thus no explanation of gender differences in depression has yet gained more influence than the others. Certainly, if one or more are finally seen to be more persuasive, they will have great influence on the way resources are allocated for the prevention and treatment of this debilitating problem.

his methodical, passionless marriage to his severe Anglo-Saxon Protestant upbringing. He had been taught that open expressions of affection were ill-mannered. He had never seen his own parents embrace in their fifty years of marriage. In his family, humility was valued more than self-confidence. He had been brought up to do the "right thing," not to enjoy himself. Raucous merrymaking was only for the irresponsible. Even a game of Go Fish had to be played in secret when he was a child.

Derek brushed off his morning confusion as a lack of quick intelligence. He had no way to know that it was a symptom of depression. He never realized that his death images might be suicidal thinking. People do not talk about such things. For all Derek knew, everyone had similar thoughts.

(Lickey & Gordon, 1991, pp. 183–185)

For several years, Beatrice had been irritable, but then for a six-month period, her irritability bordered on the irrational. She screamed in anger or sobbed in despair at every dirty dish left on the coffee table or on the bedroom floor. Each day the need to plan the dinner menu provoked agonizing indecision. How could all the virtues or, more likely, vices of hamburgers be accurately compared to those of spaghetti? A glass of spilled milk was an occasion for panic. Beatrice would bolt from her chair and run from the dining room. Ten minutes later, she would realize that the spilled milk was insignificant. She had her whole family walking on eggs. She thought they would be better off if she were dead.

Beatrice could not cope with her job. As a branch manager of a large chain store, she had many decisions to make. Unable to make them herself, she would ask employees who were much less competent for advice, but then she could not decide whose advice to take. Each morning before going to work, she complained of nausea. In public, she was usually able to control her feelings of panic and felt a little better when she actually arrived at work and was away from the wary eyes of her family.

Beatrice's husband loved her, but he did not understand what was wrong. He thought that she would improve if he made her life easier by taking over more housework, cooking, and child care. His attempt to help only made Beatrice feel more guilty and worthless. She wanted to make a contribution to her family. She wanted to do the chores "like normal people" did but broke down crying at the smallest impediment to a perfect job. Because Beatrice's volatility put a stress on her marriage, the couple went to a psychiatrist for marriage counseling. The psychiatrist failed to diagnose Beatrice's depression. He provided marriage counseling that was designed for healthy people. Consequently, the counseling failed. Months passed, and Beatrice's problem became more serious. Some days she was too upset to go to work. She stopped seeing her friends. She spent most of her time at home either yelling or crying. Finally, Beatrice's husband called the psychiatrist and insisted that something was seriously wrong.

(Lickey & Gordon, 1991, p. 181)

As these case descriptions indicate, depression has many symptoms other than sadness, and the symptoms often reinforce one another. Beatrice's indecisiveness, for example, led to her poor job performance, which in turn led to a lower self-image, less self-confidence, and still more indecisiveness. Moreover, depression can be somewhat different in different people. Its symptoms span five areas of functioning: the emotional, motivational, behavioral, cognitive, and physical.

Emotional Symptoms Most people who are depressed feel intensely sad and dejected. They describe themselves as feeling "miserable," "empty," and "humiliated." They report getting little pleasure from anything, and they tend to lose their sense of humor. Some depressed people also experience anxiety, anger, or agitation. This sea of misery may find expression in crying spells.

Many depressed people seem to lose their feelings of affection for friends and relatives (Gara et al., 1993). One woman said, "I envy everybody. I envy my own children. . . . I envy little girls who can play just like children" (Moriarty, 1967, p. 72). A depressed man said, "I feel I don't love anyone. I feel there are too many people demanding things of me—clinging to me" (Rowe, 1978, p. 49).

Motivational Symptoms Depressed people usually lose the desire to participate in their accustomed activities. Almost all report a lack of drive, initiative, and spontaneity, and they may have to force themselves to go to work, converse with friends, eat meals, or have sex (Buchwald & Rudick-Davis, 1993). Aaron Beck (1967) has described this state as a "paralysis of will." One indi-

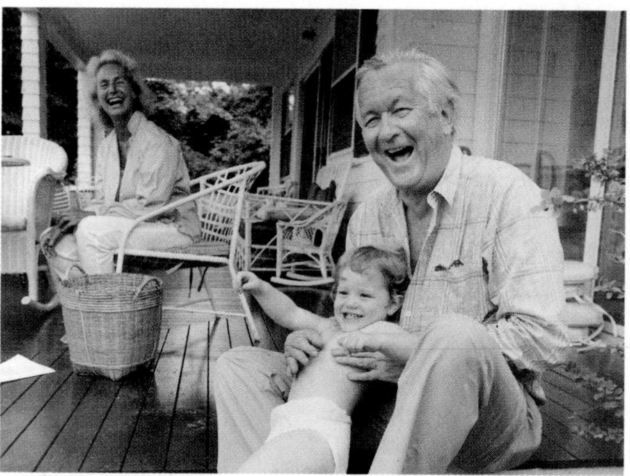

William Styron, the Pulitzer Prize–winning author of The Confessions of Nat Turner *and* Sophie's Choice, *describes the pessimism that characterized his own major depressive episode: "The pain is unrelenting, and what makes the condition intolerable is the foreknowledge that no remedy will come—not in a day, an hour, a month or a minute. It is hopelessness even more than pain that crushes the soul."*

vidual recalls, "I didn't want to do anything—just wanted to stay put and be let alone" (Kraines & Thetford, 1972, p. 20).

Suicide represents the ultimate escape from life's activities and pressures. As we shall see in Chapter 10, many depressed people become indifferent to life or wish to die; others wish that they could kill themselves, and some actually try. It has been estimated that between 7 and 15 percent of people who suffer from depression commit suicide (Rossow & Amundsen, 1995; Coryell & Winokur, 1992). Although people try to kill themselves for various reasons, approximately half of all suicides are committed by people who are depressed.

Behavioral Symptoms The activity of depressed people usually decreases dramatically. They do less and are less productive. They spend more time alone and may stay in bed for long periods. One man recalls, "I'd awaken early, but I'd just lie there—what was the use of getting up to a miserable day?" (Kraines & Thetford, 1972, p. 21).

Depressed people may also move more slowly, with seeming reluctance and lack of energy (Sobin & Sackeim, 1997; Buchwald & Rudick-Davis, 1993; Parker et al., 1993). Even their speech may be slow, quiet, and monotonal, delivered with eyes cast down and back bent. Researchers who videotaped and then evaluated admission interviews at a mental hospital found that depressed patients made less eye contact with their interviewers than did nondepressed patients and also turned down their mouths and hung their heads more (Waxer, 1974).

Cognitive Symptoms Depressed people hold decidedly negative views of themselves (Joiner et al., 1995). They consider themselves inadequate, undesirable, inferior, perhaps evil. They also blame themselves for nearly every negative event, even things that have nothing to do with them, and they rarely credit themselves for positive achievements.

Another cognitive symptom of depression is a negative view of the future. Depressed people are usually convinced that nothing will ever improve and they feel helpless to control or change any aspect of their lives (Dixon et al., 1993; Metalsky et al., 1993). Because they expect the worst, they are likely to procrastinate. Their sense of hopelessness also makes depressed people especially vulnerable to suicidal thinking. A successful businessman recalls, "Everything seemed black. The whole world was going to the devil, the country was going bankrupt, and my business was doomed to fail" (Kraines & Thetford, 1972, p. 20).

People with depression frequently complain that their intellectual ability is impaired. They feel confused, unable to remember things, easily distracted by outside

Some people mask their depression by smiling and looking happy most of the time. The movie star Marilyn Monroe was such a person. Emotion researcher Paul Ekman and his colleagues (1988) claim that certain facial and behavioral clues distinguish genuine happiness from masked depression, but that "we learn to ignore them, not wanting the burden of knowing the truth."

noises, and unable to solve even small problems. Research indicates that depressed subjects do indeed often perform more poorly than nondepressed subjects on laboratory tasks of memory, attention, and reasoning (Lemelin et al., 1996; Baker & Channon, 1995; Smith et al., 1995). Note, however, that these deficits may reflect motivational deficiencies rather than cognitive impairment per se (Lachner & Engel, 1994; Hartlage et al., 1993).

Physical Symptoms Depression is often accompanied by such physical ailments as headaches, indigestion, constipation, dizzy spells, unpleasant sensations in the chest, and generalized pain. In fact, many depressions are initially misdiagnosed as medical problems (Simon & Katzelnick, 1997; Coyne, Schwenk, & Fechner-Bates, 1995). Disturbances in appetite and sleep are particularly common, as are complaints of constant tiredness that is not relieved even when rest and sleep are increased (Kazes et al., 1994; Spoov et al., 1993). One patient recalls, "I slept poorly, so I began taking sleeping pills. I was tired most of the time even though I did far less work than usual" (Kraines & Thetford, 1972, p. 20). Depressed people usually get less sleep than others and awaken more frequently during the night. At the other end of the spectrum, however, approximately 9 percent of depressed people sleep excessively (Ballenger, 1988).

Diagnosing Unipolar Depression

DSM-IV describes several patterns of unipolar depression. People whose depressive symptoms do not fit into one of these patterns may experience just as much pain or dysfunction, but some patterns of clinical depression are particularly common (Gotlib, Lewinsohn, & Seely, 1995).

Individuals receive a diagnosis of ***major depressive disorder*** when they experience a *major depressive episode*—a period that lasts for two weeks or more, is characterized by at least five symptoms of depression, and is not caused by such factors as drugs or a general medical condition. In a small percentage of cases, the episode may include psychotic symptoms, in which the person loses contact with reality, experiencing *delusions*—bizarre ideas without foundation—or *hallucinations*—perceptions of things that are not actually present (Parker et al., 1997; Coryell et al., 1996; APA, 1994). A depressed man with psychotic symptoms may imagine that he "can't eat because my intestines are deteriorating and will soon stop working," or he may believe that he sees his dead wife.

DSM-IV further describes a major depressive disorder as ***recurrent*** if it has been preceded by previous depressive episodes; ***seasonal*** if it fluctuates with seasonal changes (for example, if the depression tends to recur each winter); ***catatonic*** if it is dominated by either immobility or excessive activity; ***postpartum*** if it occurs within four weeks of giving birth; or ***melancholic*** if the person is almost totally unaffected by pleasurable events, is more depressed in the morning, and suffers from significant motor disturbances, early-morning awakenings, appetite loss, and excessive guilt (Kendler, 1997; APA, 1994).

People who display a more chronic but less disabling pattern of unipolar depression may receive a diagnosis of ***dysthymic disorder*** (the term is from the Greek for "despondent") (see Table 8-1). Here depressed mood and only two or three other symptoms of depression are typically present and the depression persists for at least two years (or at least one year in children and adolescents). Periods of normal mood, lasting only days or weeks, may occasionally interrupt the depressed mood. When dysthymic disorder leads to a major depressive disorder, the sequence is called ***double depression*** (Donaldson et al., 1997; Hellerstein et al., 1994; APA, 1993).

Explanations of Unipolar Depression

Episodes of unipolar depression often seem to be triggered by stressful events (Brown, Harris, & Hepworth, 1995). The British psychiatric researcher Eugene Paykel and his colleagues found that depressed subjects experienced on average a greater number of stressful life events during the month just before the onset of their disorder than did nondepressed people during the same period of time (Paykel & Cooper, 1992). Stressful life events also appeared to precede other psychological disorders, but depressed people reported significantly more such events than anybody else.

Some clinicians consider it important to distinguish a ***reactive (exogenous) depression,*** which follows clear-cut precipitating events, from an ***endogenous depression,*** which unfolds without apparent antecedents and seems to be responding to internal factors. But how does one know whether a depression is reactive or not? Even if stressful events have occurred before the onset of depression, clinicians cannot be certain that the depression is reactive. The events could be a minor factor only or even a pure coincidence (Paykel, 1982). Conversely, even when a depression seems to emerge in the absence of stressful events, clinicians cannot be sure that it is endogenous

TABLE 8-1 Mood Disorders Profile

	One-year Prevalence	*Female: Male Ratio*	*Typical Age at Onset*	*Prevalence Among First-degree Relatives*
Major depressive disorder	5–10%	2:1	24–29 years	Elevated
Dysthymic disorder	2.5–5.4%	Between 3:2 and 2:1	10–25 years	Elevated
Bipolar I disorder	0.7%	1:1	15–44 years	Elevated
Bipolar II disorder	0.5%	1:1	15–44 years	Elevated
Cyclothymic disorder	0.4%	1:1	15–25 years	Elevated

Source: APA, 1994; Kessler et al., 1994; Regier et al., 1993; Weissman et al., 1991.

(Paykel, Rao, & Taylor, 1984). Perhaps a subtle stressor has escaped notice. Accordingly, today's clinicians usually concentrate on recognizing *both* the internal and the situational components of any given case of unipolar depression.

The current explanations of unipolar depression extend from biological and psychological causes to the broader societal context in which depression occurs. As we shall see, several of these explanations have received considerable research support. However, just as clinicians now recognize both internal and situational features in any given case of depression, many theorists believe that the various explanations must be viewed collectively if unipolar depression is to be fully understood.

The Biological View

Medical researchers have been aware for years that certain diseases, drugs, and toxins produce mood changes. Could clinical depression itself have a biological foundation? Compelling evidence over the past several decades suggests that biological abnormalities contribute to unipolar depression (Judd, 1995; Siever, Davis, & Gorman, 1991). Researchers have relied on genetic studies and on investigations that tie this pattern of depression directly to biochemical and hormonal dysfunction (see Box 8-2).

Genetic Factors Many theorists believe that some people inherit a predisposition to unipolar depression. Support for this view has come from several sources. Researchers who conduct *family pedigree studies* select people with unipolar depression as *probands* (the proband is the person who is the focus of a genetic study) and examine their close relatives to see whether depression also afflicts other members of the family. If a predisposition to unipolar depression is inherited, relatives should have a higher rate of depression than the population at large. Researchers have in fact found that as many as 20 percent of those relatives are depressed, compared to 5 to 10 percent of the general population (Harrington et al., 1993).

If a predisposition to unipolar depression is inherited, one would also expect more cases of depression among the probands' close relatives than among their distant relatives. *Twin studies* have found rates consistent with this expectation (Gershon & Nurnberger, 1995; Nurnberger & Gershon, 1992, 1984). One recent study looked at nearly 200 pairs of twins. When a monozygotic (identical) twin had unipolar depression, there was a 46 percent chance that the other twin would have the same disorder. In contrast, when a dizygotic (fraternal) twin had unipolar depression, the other twin had only a 20 percent chance of developing the disorder (McGuffin et al., 1996).

Finally, *adoption studies* have implicated a genetic factor, at least in severe unipolar depression. One study looked at the families of adopted persons who had been hospitalized for this disorder in Denmark. The biological parents of these adoptees turned out to have a higher incidence of severe depression (but not mild depression) than did the biological parents of a control group of nondepressed adoptees (Wender et al., 1986). Some theorists interpret these findings to mean that severe depression is more likely than mild depression to be caused by genetic factors.

Biochemical Factors As we have seen, neurotransmitters are the brain chemicals that carry messages from one nerve cell, or neuron, to another. ***Norepinephrine*** and ***serotonin*** are the two neurotransmitters whose reduced activity has been most strongly implicated in unipolar depression (Zaleman, 1995).

In the 1950s, several pieces of evidence pointed to low activity of both norepinephrine and serotonin as possible factors in depression. First, medical researchers discovered that *reserpine* and other medications used to treat high blood pressure may cause depression in some people (Ayd, 1956). Further research indicated that some of these medications lowered norepinephrine supplies and others lowered serotonin, thus suggesting to researchers that depression may be related to low activity of these neurotransmitters in the brain.

A second piece of evidence was the accidental discovery of two groups of effective antidepressant medications—***monoamine oxidase (MAO) inhibitors*** and ***tricyclics***—which we shall be examining more closely in Chapter 9. Researchers soon learned that these compounds increase either norepinephrine or serotonin activity. If this was the means by which the antidepressants alleviated depression, then depression could well be related to low activity of norepinephrine or serotonin.

Such findings led some theorists to conclude that unipolar depression is a product of low norepinephrine activity (Bunney & Davis, 1965; Schildkraut, 1965), and others to reason that depression is caused by low serotonin activity (Golden & Gilmore, 1990; Glassman & Platman, 1969). The investigators further concluded that lower activity of these neurotransmitters must reduce neuron firing, a concept that certainly fits the slow-motion picture of depression. Because norepinephrine belongs to the class of chemicals called catecholamines, the theory tying it to depression is known as the ***catecholamine*** theory. Correspondingly, the theory linking serotonin to depression is often called the ***indoleamine*** theory, because serotonin belongs to the class of chemicals known as indoleamines.

Over the past two decades an enormous amount of research has been devoted to sorting out the

BOX 8-2 When Body Clocks Need Resetting

Our lives are structured by cycles and rhythms—daily, monthly, seasonal, and yearly. The 24-hour day provides the cycle to which we adapt our most common activities—sleeping, eating, working, and socializing. Although our daily rhythms are imposed largely by our environment, they are also driven by a kind of internal clock, consisting of recurrent biological fluctuations, called ***circadian rhythms,*** which must be coordinated with one another and with both cyclic and transient changes in the environment.

The daily operation of our internal clock apparently is controlled by at least two self-sustained oscillators. One is strong and consistent, and it rigidly controls regular changes in body temperature, hormone secretions, and *rapid eye movement* (REM) sleep—the near-awake phase of sleep during which we dream. The other oscillator, weaker and more ready to adjust to changes, controls the sleep-wake cycle and activity-rest cycle. Most people can go to sleep late one night and early the next and have no trouble falling asleep quickly and sleeping soundly; but during this period their body temperature will rigidly follow its usual pattern, peaking at the same time each afternoon and bottoming out each morning.

A series of revealing studies conducted throughout the 1980s confirmed for many researchers that depression is often the result of an imbalance, or ***desynchronization,*** between the body's circadian rhythms and the rhythms of the environment (Healy & Williams, 1988; Zerssen et al., 1985). For example, the sleep cycle, the most basic rhythm in our lives, apparently is reversed in depressed people (Buysse et al., 1997, 1993; Thase et al., 1997, 1996, 1995). Unlike other people, they quickly move into REM sleep after falling asleep. They also experience longer stretches of REM sleep during the early parts of the sleep cycle and have shorter episodes of REM sleep toward the morning. Finally, they display more frequent rapid eye movements during REM sleep and less deep sleep overall. Thus some theorists think that the body's two oscillators, the rigid one that is in control of REM sleep and the flexible one in control of the sleep-wake cycle, may be out of harmony (Goodwin et al., 1982).

Hormones and Depression

Secretions of the hormone ***melatonin*** appear to play a particularly important role in depression. This hormone, nicknamed the Dracula hormone, is secreted by the brain's ***pineal gland*** when our surroundings are dark, but not when they are light. The role of melatonin in human biology is not entirely understood, but in animals it seems to help regulate hibernation, activity levels, and the reproductive cycle. As nights grow longer during the fall, animals secrete more and more melatonin, which has the effect of slowing them down and preparing them for an extended rest over the winter. When daylight hours lengthen in the spring, melatonin secretions decline, raising energy levels and setting the stage for reproduction.

Some theorists believe that our heightened melatonin secretions cause us to slow down, to have less energy, and to need more rest in the wintertime, much as hibernating animals do. Most people manage to adjust to these internal changes. Researchers believe, however, that some people are so sensitive to winter's heightened melatonin secretions that they find it impossible to carry on with business as usual (Dilsaver, 1990; Rosenthal & Blehar, 1989). Their slowdown takes the form of depression each winter, but a depression characterized by symptoms that are quite consistent with animal hibernation—a big appetite, a craving for carbohydrates, weight gain, oversleeping, and fatigue (Madden et al., 1996; Gupta, 1988). This pattern, often called ***seasonal affective disorder*** (Rosenthal & Blehar, 1989), or ***SAD,*** is now described in the DSM. Not surprisingly, the prevalence of this disorder seems to be lower in locations closer to the equator—that is, areas where days are longer in the winter months and melatonin secretions are presumably lower (Teng et al., 1995; Ito et al., 1992; Rosen et al., 1990).

Researchers believe that some people with SAD are also ex-

The importance of sunlight for physical health has been recognized for years. These children, who live 200 miles north of the Arctic Circle, receive a daily dose of ultraviolet light to compensate for the lack of midwinter sun. Otherwise they might experience severe deficiencies of Vitamin D and, hence, problems such as bone disease and tooth decay. Clinicians now know that light is also important to psychological health.

tremely sensitive to the drop in melatonin secretions that occurs during the longer days of summer. Some people, in fact, become overenergized and overactive and may display a hypomanic or manic pattern every summer (Faedda et al., 1993; Carney et al., 1988).

Light Therapy

If in fact darkness is the problem in SAD, the answer may be light. One of the most effective treatments for SAD turns out to be ***light therapy,*** or ***phototherapy,*** exposure to extra amounts of synthetic light throughout the winter. When seasonally depressed patients sit under special lights for several hours every winter day, their depression can be reduced or eliminated (Partonen et al., 1996; Thalen et al., 1995; Rosenthal et al., 1988).

Of course, there are more natural ways to get extra light. Some researchers have found that SAD patients are helped by morning walks outside (Wirz-Justice et al., 1996). Similarly, clinicians often recommend taking a winter vacation in a sunny place. Some theorists go so far as to suggest that people with wintertime blues, and certainly those with SAD, should spend a week or two just before winter begins in a location approximately 3 to 4 degrees north or south of the equator, where 70 percent more sunlight is available each day. The effectiveness of this form of "treatment" has yet to be investigated scientifically.

Clinicians have also searched actively for alternative ways to alter the body's melatonin level. One possibility is the enormously popular melatonin pills. Researchers are beginning to demonstrate that it isn't so much the amount of melatonin secreted that causes depression for SAD-prone people as the time of day it is secreted (Lewy et al., 1992). That is, the hormone's usual role may be to set the body's biological clock each day. Ill-timed secretions of it throughout the 24-hour period may disrupt the body's circadian rhythms, and so leave the person vulnerable to depression. A melatonin pill, given at key times in the day, might help readjust a patient's body clock and alleviate depression (Hätönen, Alila, & Laakso, 1996). Unfortunately, researchers have not yet pinpointed when those key times in the day might be, nor have they clarified the impact of melatonin pills on the body's circadian rhythms.

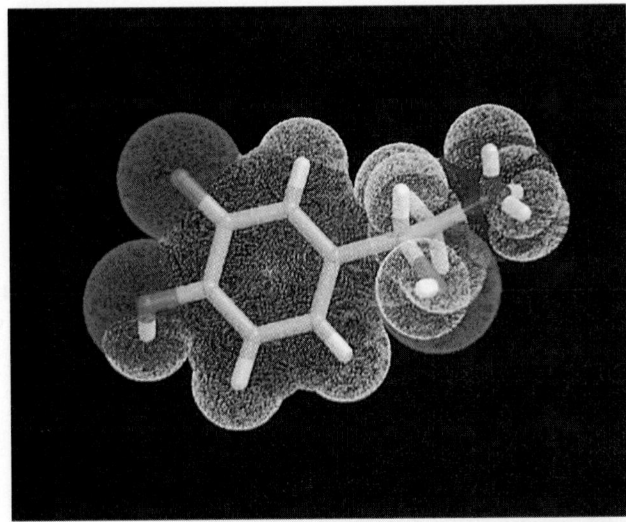

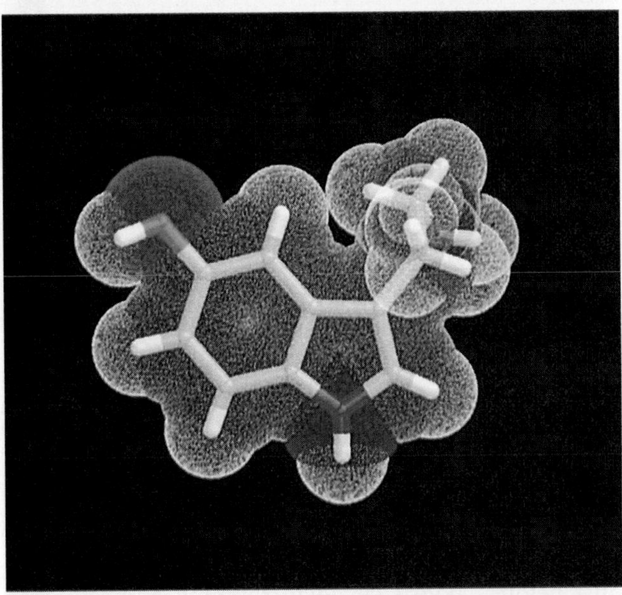

Computer-drawn molecules of the neurotransmitters norepinephrine (top) and serotonin (bottom). Low activity of these neurotransmitters has repeatedly been implicated in unipolar depression.

contributions of norepinephrine and serotonin to unipolar depression (Zaleman, 1995) (see Figure 8-2). On the basis of this work, theorists have offered a variety of proposals:

1. Unipolar depression occurs only when *both* norepinephrine and serotonin activity are low.
2. Low levels of *either* neurotransmitter can lead to unipolar depression.
3. Unipolar depression linked to low norepinephrine is qualitatively different from depression linked to low serotonin. The researcher Marie Asberg and her colleagues (1976) found, for example, that depressed subjects whose serotonin was depleted were more apathetic and suicidal than depressed subjects with normal serotonin activity. They also discovered that suicide attempts made by depressed patients with low serotonin were more frequent and more violent than those made by other depressed people.

Recent theories and investigations suggest that *interactions* between serotonin and norepinephrine systems, or between these systems and yet other neurotransmitter systems in the brain, rather than the operation of any one system, may account for unipolar depression. Some studies suggest, for example, that depressed people may have overall imbalances in the activity of serotonin, norepinephrine, *and* the neurotransmitters dopamine and acetylcholine (Ballenger, 1988; Risch & Janowsky, 1984). Some theorists further believe that serotonin helps regulate the other neurotransmitter systems, and that low serotonin activity disrupts the activity of the other neurotransmitters, thus leading to depression.

Hormonal Factors As we noted in Chapter 4, biological researchers have also investigated the body's endocrine system as a factor in abnormal behavior (see pp. 92–93). Under various conditions, endocrine glands throughout the body release hormones, chemicals that may in turn propel body organs and the brain itself into action. ***Cortisol,*** a hormone released by the *adrenal glands,* has been implicated in unipolar depression (Hedaya, 1996; Zaleman, 1995). This chemical is known as the *stress hormone* because it is largely secreted during times of stress. People who are depressed often have elevated levels of cortisol. This is not surprising, given that stressful events often seem to precipitate episodes of depression. Still another hormone that has been tied to depression is ***melatonin,*** sometimes called the Dracula hormone because it is released only in the dark (see Box 8-2).

Evaluating the Biological View The biological explanations of depression have deservedly generated much enthusiasm and investigation, but many questions are still unanswered. First, this research has relied to a large degree on analogue studies, which create depression-like symptoms in laboratory animals. As we have seen previously, researchers cannot be certain that symptoms produced in animals do in fact reflect the quality and substance of a human disorder (Overstreet, 1993).

Second, until recent years, the limitations of technology required most studies on human depression to measure brain activity indirectly, so investigators could never be quite certain of the actual biological events (Grossman, Manji, & Potter, 1993; Katz et al., 1993). Studies using newer technology, such as the PET and

MRI, should address such concerns in the coming years (Ketter et al., 1996; Mann et al., 1996).

These limitations notwithstanding, biological researchers seem to be closing in on some compelling insights into the biological underpinnings of unipolar depression. Their work has also opened the door to effective biological treatments for this disorder, an important turn of events that we shall be investigating in Chapter 9.

The Psychodynamic View Sigmund Freud and his student Karl Abraham developed the first psychodynamic explanation of depression (Freud, 1917; Abraham, 1916, 1911). They began by noting the similarity between clinical depression and grief in people who lose loved ones. Constant weeping, loss of appetite, difficulty sleeping, inability to find pleasure in life, and general withdrawal are common in both mourning and depression (Beutel et al., 1995; Stroebe et al., 1992) (see Box 8-3).

According to Freud and Abraham, a series of unconscious processes is set in motion when a loved one dies or is lost in some other way. At first, unable to accept the loss, mourners regress to the *oral* stage of development, the period when infants are so dependent that they cannot distinguish themselves from their parents. By regressing to this stage, the mourners fuse their own

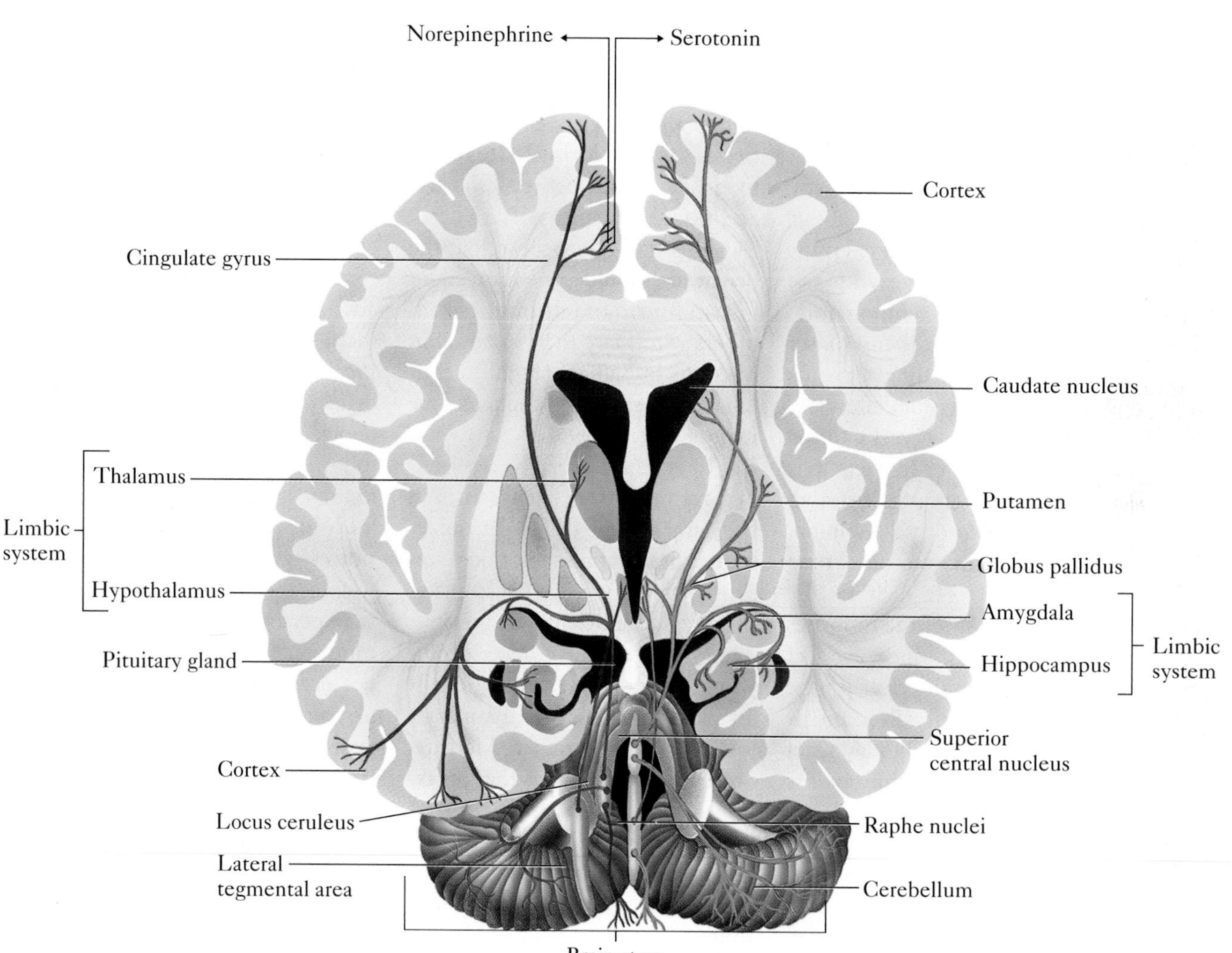

Figure 8-2 *The cell bodies of neurons that contain norepinephrine or serotonin are located throughout the brain stem. The cell bodies of norepinephrine neurons are found in the locus ceruleus and lateral tegmental area, while the serotonin-containing cell bodies are concentrated in the raphe nuclei. The axons of these neurons extend to various parts of the brain, particularly to the limbic system, the portion that regulates emotion. The norepinephrine pathways are indicated in blue, the serotonin pathways in green. (Adapted from Snyder, 1986, p. 108.)*

BOX 8-3 The Grieving Process

Each year more than 8 million people in the United States experience a death in their immediate family (Osterweis & Townsend, 1988). Many more lose a close friend or a more distant but still cherished relative. Reactions to such a painful loss can be so similar to clinical depression that Freud and Abraham based the psychoanalytic explanation of depression on them. But mourning is a natural process, and there are normal mechanisms for coping with it. Bereavement allows us eventually to come to grips with our loss and to resume our lives.

Unfortunately, there are many common misconceptions about grieving, and some of these errant beliefs actually interfere with the process. The most common mistake is to believe that there is a set timetable for mourning. Friends and acquaintances often allow the mourner only a few weeks to return to normal life. In fact, it is sometimes many months before a person is ready to do so (Gelman, 1983). The amount of time needed depends on such factors as the relationship of the mourner to the deceased, the age of the mourner, and, clearly, the mourner's personality. Even members of the same family may react differently to their common loss (Gilbert, 1996; Schwab, 1996). Much suffering would be avoided if people who wanted to offer support did not impose their own timetable on someone else's grief.

Some researchers suggest that the bereavement process is experienced differently in different cultural groups (Stroebe et al., 1992). Some cultures encourage lifelong ties to the deceased, while others try to forget the deceased as quickly as possible. Japanese Buddhists believe in maintaining contact with dead ancestors, and almost all homes have an altar dedicated to them. Offering food and speaking to the dead are common practices. The Hopi Indians, though, believe that contact with death brings pollution, so they quickly rid the home of all reminders of their deceased relatives. Hopi death rituals are meant to break all ties between mortals and the feared spirits of the dead. Muslims in Egypt believe that the bereaved should dwell on their loss and surround themselves with others who share their sorrow, but Muslims in Bali are taught to contain their grief, to laugh and be joyful (Wikan, 1991).

In Western society we view bereavement as an interference in the daily routine of life, a troublesome, debilitating emotional response that one must overcome as quickly and efficiently as possible. According to this view, people who continue to be emotionally attached to the dead are maladjusted. The researcher Margaret Stroebe refers to this as the "breaking bonds" approach to bereavement, because it requires the bereaved to form a new identity by finding rewards in new relationships.

But this type of bereavement was not always the norm in the United States. As recently as a century ago, Stroebe notes, Americans did *not* encourage the breaking of ties, and bereaved people commonly held on strongly to memories of their dead. In the mid–nineteenth century, communication with the dead through séances and mediums was popular. The amount of grief one felt after the death of a loved one was held to indicate the relationship's strength and significance, and the bereaved were expected to focus on a reunion with the deceased in heaven.

Despite individual variations in the duration of grief, research has shown that mourners in Western society today often do share certain experiences (Osterweis & Townsend, 1988). The bereavement process often begins with *shock:* the survivor has difficulty believing that the person has died. Shock and disbelief are frequently followed by a sense of *loss and separation,* a feeling that sometimes leads to misperceptions and illusions—glimpses of the dead person in the street or dreams that the person is alive. Once the mourner fully accepts the fact that the deceased is not coming back, *despair* may set in. Depression, irritability, guilt, and anger are natural responses at this stage. Social relationships may deteriorate at this time, as the mourner loses interest in the outside world and his or her customary activities. Some mourners may also begin to suffer from medical problems (Arnette, 1996).

The world watched, and even shared, the grief of those who lost relatives and friends in the 1995 bombing of the Oklahoma City federal building. The media focused in particular on Edye Smith and her ex-husband Tony Smith, here grieving the loss of their young sons Chase and Colton at the city's Rose Hill cemetery. Many parents who suffer the death of a child, one of life's most traumatic losses, are comforted by self-help groups for bereaved parents, such as "Bereaved Parents" (Klass, 1997).

Once the mourning process is complete, it then becomes possible to think of the deceased person without being overwhelmed by despair and a sense of loss. At this point, one is prepared to get on with one's life, although anniversaries and other special dates may cause flare-ups of mourning for many years to come.

Of course, not all people in Western society progress through the grieving process in the same way. Some experience *complicated grief*: their thoughts remain fixated on the dead person, and they cry frequently; they cannot reconcile themselves to the death, even after much time has passed. For others, the death of a loved one may also trigger a clinical depression well beyond the grief process (Arnette, 1996; Prigerson et al., 1995).

The normal mourning process is often disrupted, even prolonged, by others' reactions to one's grief. Anticipating that the widow or widower will feel like the odd person out, for example, friends may be reluctant to invite the surviving spouse to a social gathering. They may visit the mourner less frequently at this time, just when the person most needs support. And when friends do visit, they may take pains to avoid mentioning the bereaved person's loss, not realizing the great relief that sometimes comes from talking about one's pain.

Numerous self-help bereavement groups allow mourners opportunities to gather with others who have lost loved ones and discuss the emotional and practical problems they all face. Many of these groups are led by people who have completed a grieving process themselves and wish to offer insight and support to others. Group members do not avoid the topic of death, and no one promises or demands a speedy return to normal. Many mourners find this an ideal environment in which to confront and accept their loss. It allows a necessary process to proceed as it should—without pressure, misinterpretation, or judgment.

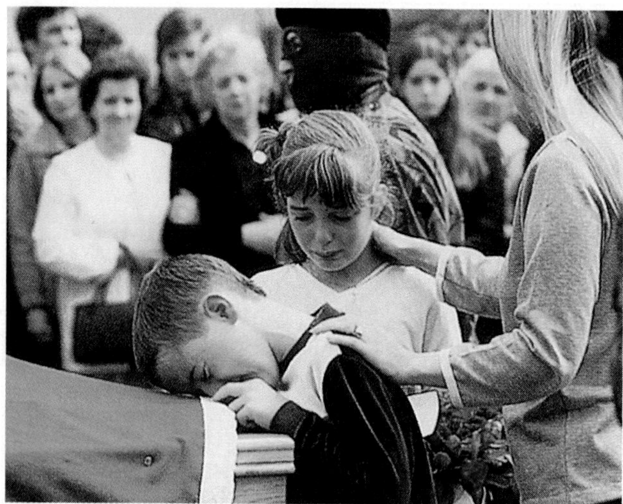

Psychodynamic theorists believe that depression is caused by the real or imagined loss of a loved one. Research has found that people who lose their parents as children have an increased likelihood of experiencing depression as adults.

identity with that of the person they have lost, symbolically regaining the lost person in the process. In other words, they ***introject*** the loved one and then experience all their feelings toward the loved one as feelings about themselves.

For most mourners, introjection is temporary and lasts only for the period of mourning. For some, however, grief intensifies. They feel empty, continue to avoid social relationships, and become more and more preoccupied with their sense of loss. They may introject feelings of anger toward the loved one for departing, or perhaps because of unresolved conflicts from the past. They therefore experience self-hatred, which leads to a negative mood, self-blame, and further withdrawal: they become depressed.

Freud and Abraham believed that two kinds of people are particularly prone to introjection and depression in the face of loss: those whose parents failed to nurture them and meet their needs during the oral stage of infancy and those whose parents gratified those needs excessively. Infants whose needs are inadequately met remain overly dependent on others throughout their lives, feel unworthy of love, and have low self-esteem. Those whose needs are excessively gratified find the oral stage so pleasant that they resist moving on to other stages in life. Either way, the individuals may devote their lives to others, desperately in search of love and approval (Bemporad, 1992). Such people are likely to experience a greater sense of loss when a loved one dies and greater anger toward the loved one for having departed.

Of course, many people become depressed without losing a loved one. To explain why, Freud invoked the concept of ***imagined,*** or ***symbolic, loss.*** A college student may, for example, experience failure in a calculus course as the loss of her parents, believing that they love her only when she excels academically.

Although many psychodynamic theorists have argued for changes in Freud and Abraham's theory of depression (Jacobson, 1971; Cohen et al., 1954; Bibring, 1953), the original theory continues to influence current psychodynamic thinking. *Object relations* theorists, for example—the psychodynamic theorists who emphasize relationships (Kernberg, 1997, 1976; Horner, 1991)—propose that depression results when people's relationships leave them feeling unsafe and insecure. Hence people whose parents pushed them toward either excessive dependence or excessive self-reliance are more likely to become depressed when they later confront complications or losses in their relationships.

The following description of a depressed middle-aged woman brings forth the psychodynamic concepts of dependence, loss of a loved one, symbolic loss, and introjection:

> Mrs. Marie Carls was in her middle fifties when she came for the first interview. . . . The patient had always felt very attached to her mother. As a matter of fact, they used to call her "Stamp" because she stuck to her mother as a stamp to a letter. She always tried to placate her volcanic mother, to please her in every possible way. The mother, however, did not fulfill her maternal role very well. . . .
>
> After marriage [to Julius], she continued her pattern of submission and compliance. Before her marriage she had difficulty in complying with a volcanic mother, and after her marriage she almost automatically assumed a submissive role. . . .
>
> Several months after beginning treatment, the patient reported a dream. Ignatius and she had decided not to see each other again. She would have to leave him forever. I asked who Ignatius was, because I had not heard the name until then. The patient replied almost with surprise, "But the first time I came to see you, I told you that in the past I had had an infatuation." She then told me that when she was thirty years old . . . the patient and her husband invited Ignatius, who was single, to come and live with them. Ignatius and the patient soon discovered that they had an attraction for each other. They both tried to fight that feeling; but when Julius had to go to another city for a few days, the so-called infatuation became much more than that. There were a few physical contacts. . . . There was an intense spiritual affinity. Ignatius understood her: he spoke her language, liked what she liked, and gave her the feeling of being alive. She remembered that before she married Julius, she had invented a slogan which she often emphatically repeated, "Long live

life"; but only with Ignatius could she believe in that slogan again. Ignatius suggested that they elope, but she did not take him seriously. A few months later everybody had to leave the city. Ignatius and Marie promised to keep in touch, but both of them were full of hesitation because of Julius, a devoted husband to Marie and a devoted friend to Ignatius. Nothing was done to maintain contact. Two years later, approximately a year after the end of the war, Marie heard that Ignatius had married. She felt terribly alone and despondent. . . .

Her suffering had become more acute as she realized that old age was approaching and she had lost all her chances. Ignatius remained as the memory of lost opportunities. . . . Her life of compliance and obedience had not permitted her to reach her goal. An Ignatius existed in the world, but she had lost him forever. . . .

For many years she had hoped she could make up for the loss of Ignatius, but now she could no longer do so. She could no longer scream, "Long live life!" She would rather think, "Down with life without Ignatius, a life which has lost its meaning."

When she became aware of these ideas, she felt even more depressed. . . . She felt that everything she had built in her life was false or based on a false premise. . . .

A life without love is an impoverished life. But love means many things, just as there are many types of love. For Marie it meant only romantic love, all passion and flame, like the one she had imagined with Ignatius. Life without that type of love is not at all a life characterized by lovelessness, and by no means to be equated with death: but it was so for her.

(Arieti & Bemporad, 1978, pp. 275–284)

Investigating the Psychodynamic View Studies by psychodynamic researchers have generally supported the ideas that depression is often triggered by a major loss and that people who experience early losses and early dependent relationships are more vulnerable to losses later in life (APA, 1993). In a famous study of 123 infants who were placed in a nursery after being separated from their mothers, René Spitz (1946, 1945) found that 19 of the infants became very weepy and sad upon separation, withdrew from their surroundings, ignored others, and lay passively in their cots. Later studies confirmed that separation from the mother before the age of 6 years often brings about a reaction of this kind, a pattern called ***anaclitic depression*** (Bowlby, 1980, 1969). Studies of infant monkeys who are separated from their mothers have noted a similar pattern of apparent depression (Harlow & Harlow, 1965).

Other research suggests that losses suffered early in life may also set the stage for depression in later years (Palosaari & Aro, 1995; Burbach & Borduin, 1986). When a depression scale was administered to 1,250 medical patients during visits to their family physicians, the patients whose fathers had died during their childhood averaged higher scores of depression (Barnes & Prosen, 1985). Likewise, several carefully controlled studies have found that more depressed adults than nondepressed adults have lost a parent before the age of 5 (Crook & Eliot, 1980).

A related body of research supports another of the psychodynamic propositions: people whose childhood needs were improperly addressed are particularly likely to become depressed after experiencing loss (Parker, 1992). In some studies, depressed subjects have filled out

Object relations theorists hold that people are more prone to develop depression if their childhood relationships were disrupted. These and other clinical theorists are particularly concerned about children who are returned to their biological parents after living, for an extended time, with adoptive parents. In 1995 "Baby Richard," as the courts referred to him, was removed from his adoptive parents and placed with his biological parents after a legal battle that spanned his entire four years.

a scale called the *Parental Bonding Instrument,* which indicates how much care and protection individuals feel they received as children. Many report that their parents displayed a child-rearing style identified as "affectionless control," consisting of a mixture of low care and high protection (Sato et al., 1997; Parker et al., 1995; Parker, 1992, 1983).

In yet another line of psychodynamic research, investigators have compared the dreams of depressed subjects with the dreams of nondepressed subjects to determine whether depression is indeed hostility turned inward. The evaluator, who is trained in dream analysis but does not know which dreams belong to which subjects, rates each dream for such factors as hostility and masochism (hostility toward oneself). Several studies have indicated that the dreams of depressed people do reflect higher levels of hostility and masochism than the dreams of nondepressed people (Hauri et al., 1974).

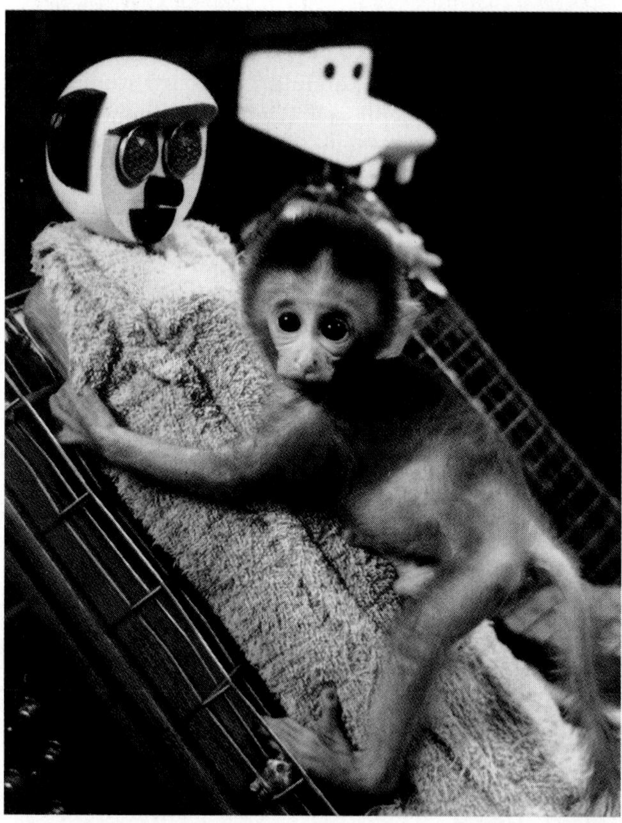

In their experiments with monkeys, Harry Harlow and his colleagues found that infant monkeys reacted with apparent despair to separation from their mothers. Even monkeys raised with surrogate mothers—wire cylinders wrapped with foam rubber and covered with terry cloth—formed an attachment to them, clung to them when anxious, and reacted with despair when separated from them.

Evaluating the Psychodynamic View These various studies offer general support for the psychodynamic view of depression, but it is important to be aware of their limitations. First, although the findings indicate that losses and inadequate parenting sometimes trigger depression, they do not establish that such factors are *typically* responsible for the disorder. In the studies of young children and young monkeys, for example, only some of the subjects who were separated from their mothers showed depressive reactions. Indeed, it is estimated that less than 10 percent of all people who experience major losses in life actually become depressed (Paykel & Cooper, 1992; Paykel,1982).

A second problem with the psychodynamic evidence is that many of the findings are inconsistent. For example, though many studies find evidence of a relationship between childhood loss and later depression, others do not (Parker, 1992; Owen, Lancee, & Freeman, 1986); and though some studies indicate that depressed people may exhibit covert hostility toward others and themselves, others, again, do not (Klerman, 1984).

A final drawback to this research is that some features of the psychodynamic explanation of depression are nearly impossible to test. Because symbolic loss, fixation at the oral stage, and introjection are said to operate at an unconscious level, it is difficult for researchers to determine if and when they are occurring. Similarly, other psychodynamic ideas can be measured only by retrospective self-reports. When subjects fill out the Parental Bonding Instrument, for example, how can we be sure that they are indicating their parents' actual behaviors?

The Behavioral View The psychologist Peter Lewinsohn has developed the leading behavioral explanation of unipolar depression (Lewinsohn et al., 1990, 1984). He suggests that some people perform fewer and fewer constructive behaviors when the rewards for such behaviors dwindle in their lives, and in turn they develop depression. The rewards of campus life, for example, may disappear when a young woman graduates from college and takes a job in the business world; or an aging baseball player may lose the rewards of high salary and adulation when his athletic skills deteriorate. Although many people manage to put such changes in perspective and fill their lives with other forms of gratification, some become disheartened. Their positive reinforcements decrease even more, and the decline in reinforcements leads to even fewer positive behaviors. In this manner, a person may spiral toward depression. In the same way, an increase in the number of punishing experiences (say, a hostile work environment) may lead to depression "by interfering with the person's engagement in and enjoyment of rewarding activities" (Lewinsohn & Arconad, 1981).

In a series of studies, Lewinsohn has found that the number of reinforcements a person receives is indeed related to the presence or absence of depression. Not only do depressed subjects report fewer positive reinforcements than nondepressed subjects, but when their reinforcements increase, their mood improves as well (Lewinsohn, Youngren, & Grosscup, 1979). Similarly, he has found that depressed people tend to have more unpleasant experiences than others do in such categories as health, finances, social interactions, and professional and academic pursuits (Lewinsohn, 1975).

Lewinsohn and other behaviorists believe that *social* reinforcements are particularly important (Peterson, 1993; Lewinsohn et al., 1984). Studies have indicated that depressed subjects tend to experience fewer positive social reinforcements than nondepressed subjects, and that as their mood improves, their positive social reinforcements increase. Although depressed people may be the victims of social circumstances, it is also possible that they are partly responsible for the decline in their social reinforcements (Davila et al., 1995; Segrin & Abramson, 1994). Phone callers in one study reported feeling worse than usual after a short conversation with a depressed person (Coyne, 1976), and subjects in another became less verbal, less supportive, and less cheerful than usual when they interacted with someone who was mildly depressed (Gotlib & Robinson, 1982).

Behaviorists have done an admirable job of compiling data to support these theories, but this research, too, has significant limitations. It has relied heavily on the self-reports of depressed subjects, and as we saw in Chapter 5, such measures can be biased and inaccurate; depressed people's reports may be influenced heavily by a gloomy mood and negative outlook (Youngren & Lewinsohn, 1980). It is also important to keep in mind that Lewinsohn's studies have been correlational and do not establish that decreases in reinforcing events are the initial causes of depression. A depressed mood in itself may lead to a decrease in activities and hence to fewer reinforcements.

Children whose parents are depressed are at greater risk of later experiencing depression than are children whose parents are not depressed. Modeling effects, the parent's behavior toward the child, or socioeconomic pressures may partly account for this relationship, but adoption studies suggest that genetic factors may also play a significant role in it (Beardslee et al., 1997; Cummings & Davies, 1994).

The Cognitive View Aaron Beck's work has led him to believe that negative thinking, rather than underlying conflicts or fewer positive reinforcements, lies at the heart of depression. Other cognitive theorists (Albert Ellis, for one) have also pointed to maladaptive thinking as the key to depression, but Beck's theory is the one most often associated with the disorder. According to Beck, *maladaptive attitudes,* the *cognitive triad, errors in thinking,* and *automatic thoughts* combine to produce pervasive negativity and lead to unipolar depression (Beck, 1997, 1991, 1967; Young, Beck, & Weinberger, 1993).

Maladaptive Attitudes Beck believes that children's attitudes toward themselves and the world are rooted in their own experiences, their family relationships, and the judgments of the people around them (see Figure 8-3). Unfortunately, some children develop negative attitudes, such as "My general worth is tied to every task I perform" and "If I fail, others will feel repelled by me." Many failures are inevitable in a full, active life, so such attitudes are inaccurate and self-defeating. The negative attitudes become templates, or schemas, against which the child evaluates every experience (Young et al., 1993; Beck et al., 1990).

The Cognitive Triad The negative cognitive schemas that develop during childhood may lie dormant for years, as long as life proceeds smoothly, without major disturbances or disappointments. But at any time a

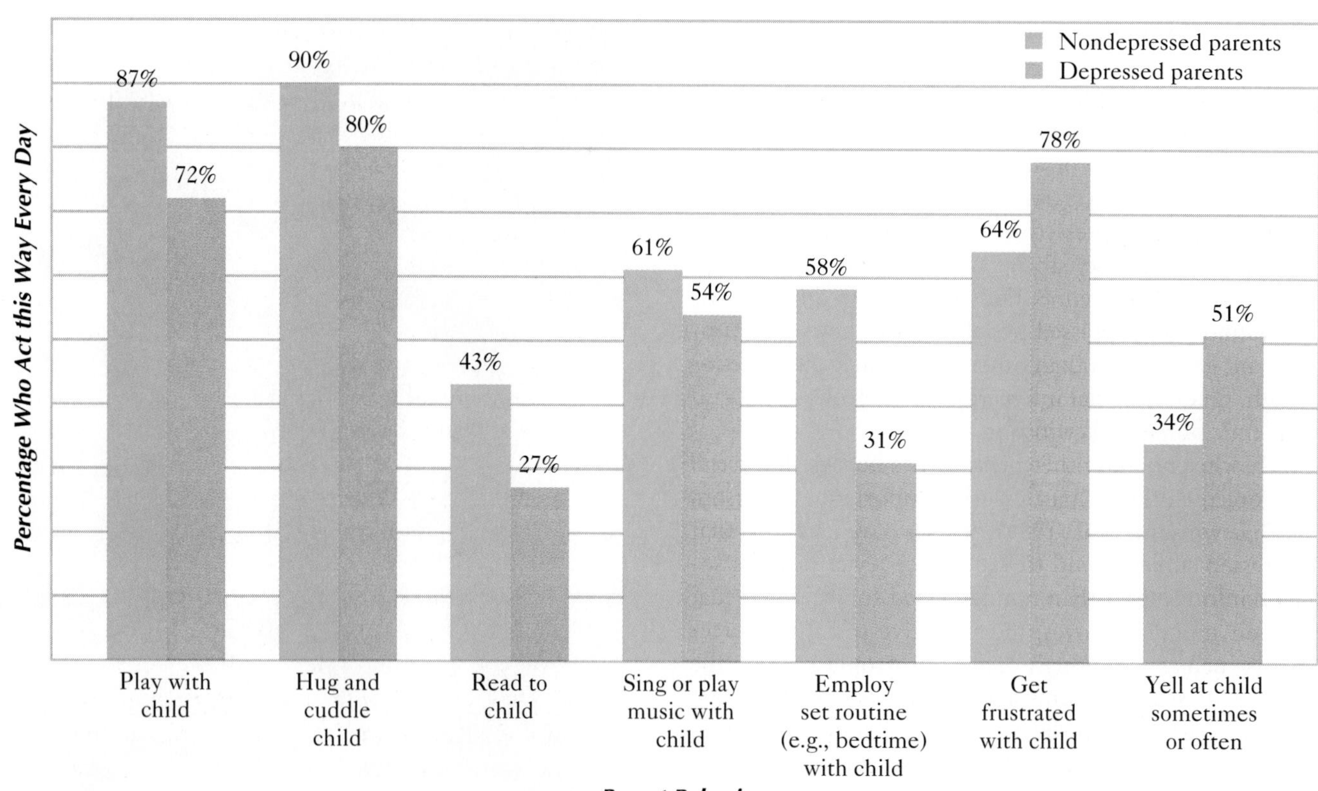

Figure 8-3 *Depressed parents and their children. Depressed parents act differently toward their babies and toddlers than do nondepressed parents. Depressed parents are less likely to play with, hug, read, or sing to their young children each day, or to employ the same routine each day. They are also more likely to get frustrated with their children on a daily basis. (Source: Princeton Survey Research Associates, 1996.)*

traumatic situation—particularly one reminiscent of early failure or loss—can trigger an extended round of pervasive negative thinking. According to Beck, such negative thinking typically takes three forms and is therefore termed the ***cognitive triad:*** the individuals repeatedly interpret (1) their *experiences,* (2) *themselves,* and (3) their *futures* in negative ways that lead them to feel depressed. That is, depressed people may interpret their experiences as burdens, obstacles, or traumas that repeatedly defeat, deprive, or disparage them. They may view themselves as deficient, undesirable, worthless, and inadequate. And they may regularly see the future as bleak, sure to be a never-ending series of hardships, miseries, frustrations, and failures. Such features of the cognitive triad are at work in the thinking of the following depressed person:

> **I** can't bear it. I can't stand the humiliating fact that I'm the only woman in the world who can't take care of her family, take her place as a real wife and mother, and be respected in her community. When I speak to my young son Billy, I know I can't let him down, but I feel so ill-equipped to take care of him; that's what frightens me. I don't know what to do or where to turn; the whole thing is too overwhelming. . . . I must be a laughing stock. It's more than I can do to go out and meet people and have the fact pointed up to me so clearly.
>
> *(Fieve, 1975)*

Errors in Thinking According to Beck, depressed people habitually employ errors of logic, forms of distorted thinking that help build and maintain the cognitive triad. In one common error of logic, they draw ***arbitrary inferences***—negative conclusions based on little or even contrary evidence. A man walking through the park, for example, passes a woman who is looking at nearby trees and flowers, and he concludes, "She's avoiding looking at me."

Similarly, depressed people often ***minimize*** the significance of positive experiences or ***magnify*** that of negative ones. A college student receives an A on a difficult English exam, for example, but concludes that the grade reflects the professor's generosity rather than her own ability (minimization). Later in the week the same student must miss an English class and is convinced that she will be unable to keep pace the rest of the semester (magnification).

Still other errors of logic commonly displayed by depressed people are ***selective abstraction,*** in which persons focus on one negative detail of a situation while ignoring the larger context; ***overgeneralization,*** in which they draw a broad conclusion from a single, perhaps insignificant event; and ***personalization,*** in which they incorrectly view themselves as the cause of negative events. A father is displaying personalization, for example, when he responds to a sudden rainstorm in the middle of a picnic by blaming himself for picking the wrong day for a family outing. Similarly, a woman is displaying personalization when she blames herself for her sister's divorce, believing that the infrequency of her visits and her lack of sensitivity were somehow responsible.

Automatic Thoughts Depressed people experience the cognitive triad in the form of ***automatic thoughts,*** a steady train of unpleasant thoughts that repeatedly remind them of their assumed inadequacy and the hopelessness of their situation. Beck labels these thoughts "automatic" because they seem to just happen, as if by reflex. In the course of only a few hours, depressed people may be visited by hundreds of such thoughts: "I'm worthless. . . . I'll never amount to anything. . . . I let everyone down. . . . Everyone hates me. . . . My responsibilities are overwhelming. . . . I've failed as a parent. . . . I'm stupid. . . . Everything is difficult for me. . . . I've caused problems for my friends. . . . Things will never change." One therapist says of a depressed client, "By the end of the day, she is worn out, she has lived a thousand painful accidents, participated in a thousand deaths, mourned a thousand mistakes" (Mendels, 1970).

Investigating the Cognitive View Beck's cognitive view of unipolar depression has received considerable research support. Several studies have confirmed that depressed people tend to hold such maladaptive attitudes as "People will probably think less of me if I make a mistake" and "I must be a useful, productive, creative person, or life has no purpose" (Whisman & McGarvey, 1995; Garber, Weiss, & Shanley, 1993). Moreover, the more of these maladaptive attitudes one holds, the more depressed one tends to be.

Other research has supported Beck's idea that depressed people exhibit the cognitive triad (Cole & Turner, 1993; Haaga & Beck, 1992). Various studies have found that depressed subjects recall unpleasant experiences more readily than positive ones (Lloyd & Lishman, 1975); rate themselves and their performances lower than nondepressed subjects do, even when they perform just as well (Slife & Weaver, 1992; Loeb, Beck, & Diggory, 1971); and tend to select pessimistic statements in storytelling tests, such as "I expect my plans will fail" and "I feel like I'll never meet anyone who's interested in me" (Weintraub, Segal, & Beck, 1974).

Beck's association of depression with errors in logic has also received research support (Cole & Turner, 1993; Yost, Cook, & Peterson, 1986). In one study, female subjects were asked to read paragraphs about women in difficult situations and then to answer multiple-choice questions about them. The women who were depressed chose a significantly greater number of responses reflecting errors in logic (such as arbitrary inference or magnification) than the nondepressed women did (Hammen & Krantz, 1976). Similarly, of 400 elementary school children, those who were depressed scored significantly higher on the Children's Negative Cognitive Error Questionnaire than those who were not depressed (Leitenberg et al., 1986).

Finally, investigations have supported Beck's claim that depressed people repeatedly experience negative automatic thoughts (Philpot, Holliman, & Madona, 1995; Garber et al., 1993). In one study, hospitalized depressed patients scored significantly higher on an Automatic Thought Questionnaire than other kinds of patients did (Ross et al., 1986). In another, nondepressed subjects who were manipulated into reading negative automatic thought-like statements about themselves became increasingly depressed (Strickland, Hale, & Anderson, 1975). Related investigations have revealed that people who consistently make ***ruminative responses*** during their depressed moods—that is, repeatedly think about their mood rather than acting to change it—experience longer periods of depressed mood and are more likely to develop a clinical depression than people who avoid such thoughts (Just & Alloy, 1997; Nolen-Hoeksema, 1995).

This body of research clearly indicates that negative cognitions are associated with depressive functioning, but it fails to establish that cognitive dysfunctioning represents the cause and core of unipolar depression. Most investigations leave open the possibility that a central mood problem leads to cognitive difficulties, which then take a further toll on mood, motivation, behavior, and physiology (Miranda & Persons, 1988).

Some studies have tried to establish that cognitive dysfunction does precede the negative mood of depressed people, as Beck claims. In one, investigators followed the progress of fifteen severely depressed women and interviewed them after their depressive symptoms had markedly declined to determine whether they still held maladaptive attitudes (Rush et al., 1986). The researchers found that the women who continued to hold such attitudes were more likely to develop depressive symptoms again six months later. That is, their negative schemas remained in place even during periods of improved mood, apparently setting the stage for renewed depressive functioning at a later point.

A Cognitive-Behavioral View: Learned Helplessness Feelings of helplessness emerge repeatedly in this account of a young woman's depression:

> Mary was 25 years old and had just begun her senior year in college. . . . Asked to recount how her life had been going recently, Mary began to weep. Sobbing, she said that for the last year or so she felt she was losing control of her life and that recent stresses (starting school again, friction with her boyfriend) had left her feeling worthless and frightened. Because of a gradual deterioration in her vision, she was now forced to wear glasses all day. "The glasses make me look terrible," she said, and "I don't look people in the eye much any more." Also, to her dismay, Mary had gained 20 pounds in the past year. She viewed herself as overweight and unattractive. At times she was convinced that with enough money to buy contact lenses and enough time to exercise she could cast off her depression; at other times she believed nothing would help. . . .
>
> Mary saw her life deteriorating in other spheres, as well. She felt overwhelmed by schoolwork and, for the first time in her life, was on academic probation. Twice before in the past seven years feelings of inadequacy and pressure from part-time jobs (as a waitress, bartender, and salesclerk) had caused her to leave school. She felt certain that unless she could stop her current downward spiral she would do so again—this time permanently. She despaired of ever getting her degree.
>
> In addition to her dissatisfaction with her appearance and her fears about her academic future, Mary complained of a lack of friends. Her social network consisted solely of her boyfriend, with whom she was living. Although there were times she experienced this relationship as almost unbearably frustrating, she felt helpless to change it and was pessimistic about its permanence. . . .
>
> *(Spitzer et al., 1983, pp. 122–123)*

Mary feels that she is "losing control of her life." Often she believes that she can do nothing to change what she considers to be her unattractive appearance and excess weight. She "despairs of ever getting her degree" and feels helpless to change her frustrating relationship with her boyfriend. According to the psychologist Martin Seligman, such feelings of helplessness are at the center of Mary's depression. Since the mid-1960s Seligman has been developing the ***learned helplessness*** theory of depression (Seligman 1992, 1975), which combines concepts from the behavioral and cognitive models. It holds that people become depressed when they think (1) that they no longer have control over the reinforcements in their lives and (2) that they themselves are responsible for this helpless state.

Seligman's theory first began to take shape when he and his colleagues were conducting conditioning studies with laboratory dogs, trying to teach them to escape and then avoid shocks. They placed each dog in a ***shuttle box,*** a box partitioned by a barrier over which the animal could jump to reach the other side (see Figure 8-4). Then they dimmed the lights as a warning signal and seconds later administered shocks to the dog. The shocks continued until the dog learned to escape them by jumping over the barrier.

Some of the dogs had been allowed to rest the day before (naive dogs); others had spent the previous day strapped into an apparatus called a hammock, in which they received inescapable shocks at random intervals. What fascinated Seligman was how these two groups then differed in their reactions to the shocks in the shuttle box. The naive dogs quickly learned to jump over the barrier in the shuttle box and escape the shocks. However, the dogs who had previously been given inescapable shock failed to learn anything in the shuttle box. After a flurry of activity, they simply "lay down and quietly whined."

Seligman concluded that the dogs who had previously received random inescapable shocks had learned

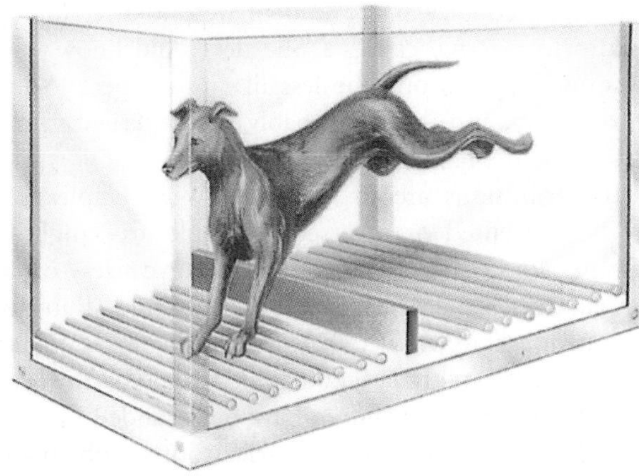

Figure 8-4 *Experimental animals learn to escape shocks that are administered in one compartment of a shuttle box by jumping to the other (safe) compartment. They may also learn to avoid the shocks altogether by jumping to the safe compartment in response to a warning, such as the dimming of a light.*

that they had no control over aversive reinforcements (shocks) in their lives. That is, they had learned that they were helpless to do anything to change negative situations. Thus, even when these dogs were later placed in a new situation where they could in fact control their fate, they continued to believe that they had no control. They continued to act helpless and failed to learn to escape painful shocks by jumping to the safe side of the shuttle box.

In subsequent experiments, Seligman and other investigators demonstrated that such helplessness effects can be generated in various animal species and under a variety of conditions (Hiroto & Seligman, 1975). Believing that the effects of learned helplessness greatly resemble the symptoms of human depression, he proposed that people in fact become depressed after developing the implicit belief that they have no control over reinforcements in their lives. Consequently, much of the helplessness research conducted during the past few decades has tried to demonstrate that helplessness in the laboratory is analogous to depression in the real world.

Investigating Learned Helplessness Many laboratory studies have found that both human and animal subjects who undergo helplessness training display reactions similar to depressive symptoms. Both display passivity, for example. In one helplessness study, nondepressed human subjects were pretreated in one of three ways: one group of subjects was exposed to a very loud noise that they could stop by pushing a button; a second group was also exposed to the loud noise but could do nothing to stop it; and a third group (naive subjects) heard no loud noise at all (Hiroto, 1974). All subjects were then placed in front of a *finger* shuttle box (a rectangular box with a handle on top) and subjected to a loud noise. Without the subjects' knowledge, the box was rigged so that the noise would stop when the handle was moved from one side to the other. Both the naive subjects and those who had previously had control over the loud noise quickly learned to move the handle and turn off the noise. The subjects who had been pretreated with unavoidable loud noise, however, failed to learn the simple task of moving the handle across the box. Most of them simply sat passively and accepted the abrasive sound.

Human and animal subjects who undergo helplessness training also display other reactions similar to depressive symptoms. When human subjects are given random aversive reinforcements, for example, they later score higher on a depressive mood survey than do subjects who are allowed control over their reinforcements (Miller & Seligman, 1975); and just as depressed people often show reductions in overt aggressive behavior, helplessness-trained subjects withdraw more and compete less in laboratory games (Kurlander, Miller, & Seligman, 1974). Similarly, animals subjected to inescapable shock eat little and lose weight, and they lose interest in sexual and social activities—common symptoms of human depression (Lindner, 1968). Finally, uncontrollable aversive events result in lower activity of the brain neurotransmitters norepinephrine and serotonin in rats (Neumaier et al., 1997; Hughes et al., 1984; Weiss, Glazer, & Pohorecky, 1976, 1974). As we observed earlier, this decreased activity has also been found in the brains of people with unipolar depression.

"I FEEL BETTER TODAY TOO, BUT AROUND HERE I'VE LEARNED NOT TO BE TOO OPTIMISTIC."

Learned Helplessness and Attributions During the past two decades, the learned helplessness explanation of depression has been further refined to reflect the importance of *attributions.* According to the revised theory, when people perceive events to be beyond their control, they implicitly ask themselves why (Abramson, Metalsky, & Alloy, 1989; Abramson, Seligman, & Teasdale, 1978). If they attribute their present lack of control to some ***internal*** cause that is both ***global*** and ***stable*** ("*I* am *inadequate* at everything and I *always* will be"), they may well feel helpless to prevent future negative outcomes and bereft of hope that anything positive will occur, and they may experience depression (see Table 8-2). If they make other kinds of attributions, this reaction is unlikely. The attribution factor helps explain why some people react helplessly and become depressed when they experience loss of control while others do not (Hilsman & Garber, 1995; Metalsky et al., 1993).

Consider a college student whose girlfriend breaks up with him. If he attributes this loss of control over a key source of gratification to an internal cause that is both global and stable—"It's my fault [internal], I ruin everything I touch [global], and I always will [stable]"—he then has reason to expect loss of control in the future and may therefore experience an enduring sense of helplessness. According to the learned helplessness view, he is a prime candidate for depression.

If the internal cause to which the student pointed were more *specific* ("The way I've behaved the past couple of weeks blew this relationship") and *unstable* ("I don't know what got into me—I don't usually act like that"), he would not be so likely to anticipate future loss of control. Similarly, if the student were to attribute the breakup to *external* causes ("She never did know what she wanted"), he would be less likely to expect to lose control again, and would probably not experience helplessness and depression.

If attributions are so important, then helplessness may be prevented or reversed if people are taught to attribute loss of control to external causes or to internal causes that are specific or unstable (Ramirez, Maldonado, & Martos, 1992). Helplessness has in fact been prevented in grade school children in just this way: in several studies the children have been guided to make alternative attributions for their classroom problems or failures (Gillham et al., 1995; Dweck, 1976).

Since the learned helplessness theory was revised, hundreds of studies have supported the relationship between styles of attribution, helplessness, and depressive functioning in both children and adults (Kinderman & Bentall, 1997; Gladstone & Kaslow, 1995; Whisman & McGarvey, 1995). In one study, a group of moderately depressed adults was asked to fill out an Attributional Style Questionnaire both before and after successful therapy (see Table 8-3). Before therapy, their relatively high levels of depression were accompanied by attribution styles that were highly internal, stable, and global. At the end of therapy and again one year later, their depression levels were lower and their attribution styles were significantly less internal, stable, and global (Seligman et al., 1988).

Finally, it is worth noting that several of the helplessness theorists have refined the model once again in recent years. They suggest that attributions are

TABLE 8-2 Internal and External Attributions

Event: "I failed my psych test today"

	Internal		*External*	
	Stable	*Unstable*	*Stable*	*Unstable*
Global	"I have a problem with test anxiety."	"Getting into an argument with my roommate threw my whole day off."	"Written tests are an unfair way to assess knowledge."	"No one does well on tests that are given the day after vacation."
Specific	"I just have no grasp of psychology."	"I got upset and froze when I couldn't answer the first two questions."	"Everyone knows that this professor enjoys giving unfair tests."	"This professor didn't put much thought into the test because of the pressure of her book deadline."

TABLE 8-3 Sample Item from the Attributional Style Questionnaire

You have been looking for a job unsuccessfully for some time.

1. Write down *one* major cause ______________________.
2. Is the cause of your unsuccessful job search due to something about you or something about other people or circumstances? (Circle one number.)

Totally due to other people or circumstances						Totally due to me	
1	2	3	4	5	6	7	***External vs. internal attribution***

3. In the future when looking for a job, will this cause again be present? (Circle one number.)

Will never again be present						Will always be present	
1	2	3	4	5	6	7	***Unstable vs. stable attribution***

4. Is the cause something that just influences looking for a job, or does it also influence other areas of your life? (Circle one number.)

Influences just this particular situation						Influences all situations in my life	
1	2	3	4	5	6	7	***Specific vs. global attribution***

5. How important would this situation be if it happened to you? (Circle one number.)

Not at all important						Extremely important
1	2	3	4	5	6	7

Source: Seligman et al., 1979.

likely to cause depression only when they produce a sense of *hopelessness* in an individual (Alloy et al., 1990; Abramson, Metalsky, & Alloy, 1989). By taking this factor into consideration, clinicians and researchers are often able to predict depressive states and disorders with still greater precision (Waikar & Craske, 1997).

Evaluating the Learned Helplessness Theory Although the learned helplessness model of unipolar depression is a promising and widely applied theory, it poses some problems. First, laboratory-induced helplessness does not parallel depression in every respect. Uncontrollable shocks administered in the laboratory, for example, invariably produce heightened anxiety along with the helplessness effects (Seligman, 1975), but human depression is not always accompanied by anxiety.

A second problem is the usual one for clinical research that relies to some degree on animal subjects. While the animals' passivity and social withdrawal in learned helplessness studies seem to correspond to symptoms of human depression, it is impossible to know whether they do in fact reflect the same psychological phenomena.

Finally, the attributional aspect of the learned helplessness theory raises difficult questions. What about the many dogs and rats who learn helplessness? Are they too *attributing* their lack of control to internal, global, and stable causes? Can animals make attributions, even implicitly? Or is this an area where animal and human helplessness part company? If so, how firmly has the explanation of human depression been supported?

These questions notwithstanding, Seligman's learned helplessness theory provides a compelling model of unipolar depression, and it has demonstrated an impressive capacity to grow in response to new findings and difficult questions. It has also inspired considerable research and thinking about human depression and human adaptation.

The Sociocultural View Sociocultural theorists propose that depression is often influenced by the broader social structure in which people live. As they would predict, stressful events often do trigger cases of depression, a finding that we observed earlier. However, the social context may have an impact on depression that extends even beyond this relationship.

On the one hand, depression is indeed a worldwide phenomenon: persons in all countries and cultures are at risk for it (Chen, Rubin, & Li, 1995). On the other hand, the precise character of depression varies from culture to culture. The symptoms of depression in non-Western countries tend to be more dominated by physical features such as fatigue, weakness, sleep disturbances, and weight loss (Manson & Good, 1993; Marsella, 1980). Depression in these countries is less often marked by such psychological feelings as self-blame and guilt. Moreover, as these countries become more Westernized, depression there takes on the more psychological character it has in the West.

The rates of depression also vary from subgroup to subgroup within a society. As we noted earlier, the prevalence of depression is much higher among women than men in almost all countries, and indeed, one sociocultural theory holds that the quality of women's roles in society makes them particularly vulnerable to depression (see Box 8-4). Similarly, although few differences in the *overall* prevalence of depression have been found between white Americans, African Americans, and Hispanic Americans (Weissman et al., 1991), striking differences are sometimes found when researchers look at depression in specific ethnic populations living under extraordinary circumstances. A study of one Native American village in the United States, for example, revealed that the lifetime risk of developing depression was 37 percent among women, 19 percent among men, and 28 percent overall, much higher than the risk in the general

BOX 8-4 Postpartum Depression: Sadness at the Happiest of Times

Women usually expect the birth of a child to be a happy though exhausting experience. But for 10 to 30 percent of new mothers, the weeks and months after childbirth bring significant depression (Terry, Mayocchi, & Hynes, 1996; Horowitz et al., 1995; Hopkins, Marcus, & Campbell, 1984). ***Postpartum depression*** begins within 4 weeks after the birth of a child (APA, 1994), and it is distinct from either simple "baby blues" or the rarer and more severe postpartum "psychosis."

The "baby blues" are so common—as many as 80 percent of women experience them—that many researchers consider them normal. Mothers have to respond not just to childbirth, but to a whole new lifestyle of interrupted sleep, added stress, and emotional drain. They may have crying spells, fatigue, anxiety, insomnia, and sadness for 3 to 7 days, but these symptoms usually subside completely within 10 days (Horowitz et al., 1995; Hopkins et al., 1984). At the other end of the spectrum, 2 of every 1,000 women experience postpartum psychosis, marked by delusions or hallucinations within a week or two of delivery. Some women have gone so far as to kill their infant under the delusion that the new baby is possessed or because hallucinations command its death (APA, 1994).

Postpartum depression falls between these two extremes. It is diagnosed when depressive symptoms do not subside after 10 days, and it may last up to a year (Terry et al., 1996). It has the symptoms of a major depressive episode (APA, 1994), including sadness, despair, tearfulness, insomnia, and feelings of inability to cope. Women with postpartum depression may also suffer from severe anxiety, panic attacks, and disinterest in their new baby (APA, 1994). The mother-infant relationship and the health of the child may also suffer. On the positive side, postpartum depression is often relatively mild, and suicidal thoughts appear to be less common than in other forms of depression (Terry et al., 1996; Horowitz et al., 1995).

Many clinicians view postpartum depression as biologically based, set off by the significant hormonal changes that accompany childbirth. All women experience a kind of "withdrawal" after delivery, as estrogen and progesterone levels, which rise as much as 50 times above normal during pregnancy, abruptly drop to levels far below normal (Horowitz et al., 1995). The levels of thyroid hormones, prolactin, and cortisol also change. Perhaps some women are particularly vulnerable to these dramatic hormone changes (Horowitz et al., 1995).

Other researchers suggest a genetic predisposition to postpartum depression. A woman with a family history of mood disorders appears to be at high risk, even if

United States population (Kinzie et al., 1992). Many sociocultural theorists explain heightened prevalence rates of this kind by pointing to the terrible social and economic pressures confronted by the people who live on Native American reservations.

Finally, the immediate social context in which people live appears to influence the likelihood of depression (Champion & Power, 1995). Across the United States, people who are separated or divorced display three times the depression rate of married or widowed persons and double the depression rate of people who have never been married (Weissman et al., 1991) (see Figure 8-5). In some cases, the depression displayed by one of the spouses may be a factor that leads to separation or divorce (Beach, Sandeen, & O'Leary, 1990); more often, however, it appears that the increased conflicts or low support experienced by persons in deteriorating relationships leads to depression (Bruce & Kim, 1992; Barnett & Gotlib, 1990).

Given such findings, it is not surprising that researchers have repeatedly found a link between low levels of social support and unipolar depression. People whose lives are isolated and without intimacy, for example, are more likely to become depressed at times of stress (Paykel & Cooper, 1992). Similarly, some highly publicized studies conducted in England a few decades ago revealed that women who had three or more young children, lacked a close confidante, and had no outside employment were more likely than other women to become depressed after experiencing stressful life events (Brown, 1988; Alloway & Bebbington, 1987; Brown & Harris, 1978). Studies also suggest that depressed people who lack social support tend to remain depressed longer than those who have a supportive spouse or warm

---

she herself has not previously had a mood disorder. So is a woman who has had previous episodes of postpartum depression (APA, 1994).

At the same time, psychosocial factors may play a very important role in the disorder. The birth of a baby requires enormous psychological, social, and interpersonal adaptation (Hopkins et al., 1984). A woman typically faces changes in her marital relationship, daily routines, and other roles, and further changes if she also decides to give up her career, even temporarily. Financial pressures may also increase, and sleep and relaxation time is likely to decrease as well. This accumulation of stressors may increase the risk of depression (Terry et al., 1996; Hobfoll et al., 1995). In addition some research indicates that mothers whose infants are sick or are temperamentally "difficult" are particularly at risk (Terry et al., 1996; Hopkins et al., 1984).

Not surprisingly, then, women who have greater coping skills (including high self-esteem) and those with stronger support systems may be less prone to develop postpartum depression (Fontaine & Jones, 1997; Terry et al., 1996). Supportive partners, helpful family members, and adequate financial resources may all act as buffers against the stress faced by a new mother (Hobfoll et al., 1997; Augusto et al., 1996; Zelkowitz & Milet, 1996).

Some theorists further suggest that postpartum depression may be "culture bound." To support their contention, they point out that the syndrome is relatively common in industrialized nations, yet is seldom reported elsewhere (Horowitz et al., 1995; Stern & Kruckman, 1983). In Western societies, the role of mother is not so highly prized as it once was, and the extended family is likely to be so far extended that no one may be around to give support.

Fortunately, treatment can make a big difference for most women with postpartum depression (Gilbert, 1996). Many respond well to the same approaches that are applied to other forms of unipolar depression—antidepressant medications, cognitive therapy, interpersonal psychotherapy, or a combination of them (Stowe et al., 1995). Some clinicians in Great Britain have even added an ***estrogen patch*** to the usual arsenal of treatment weapons: a skin patch theoretically delivers estrogen into the bloodstream. One study found that 80 percent of the women who wore the patch for three months overcame their postpartum depression (Gilbert, 1996; Gregoire et al., 1996).

Unfortunately, many women who would benefit from treatment are reluctant to seek help because they feel guilty about being sad at a time that is supposed to be joyous (APA, 1994). For them, and for the spouses and family members close to them, a large dose of *psychoeducation* is probably in order. Even positive events can be highly stressful and upsetting if they also bring significant change to one's life. Recognizing, acknowledging, and addressing such upsets is appropriate for everyone involved. This attitude can help ensure that the promise and pleasure of rearing children reach fruition.

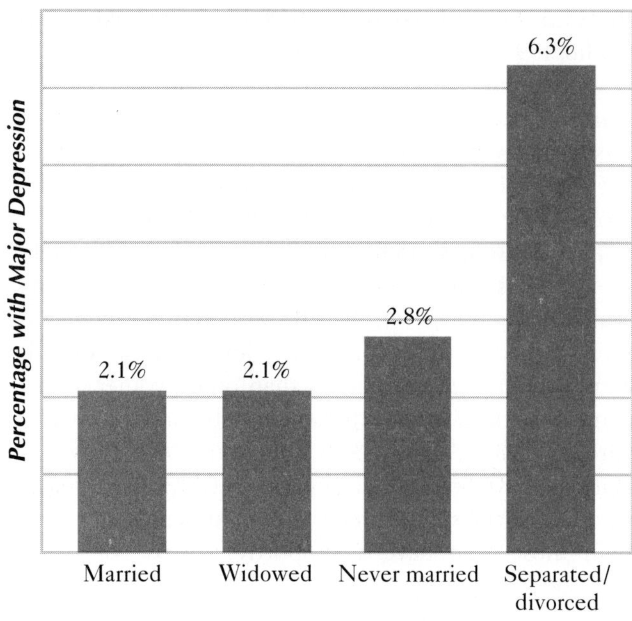

Figure 8-5 *The one-year prevalence rates of major depressive disorder make it clear that marital status is linked to major depression. Currently separated or divorced people are three times as likely to be depressed as people who currently are married. It may be that the stress of undergoing divorce precipitates depression, that depression puts intolerable stress on some marriages, or that marital problems lead to both depression and divorce. (Adapted from Weissman et al., 1991.)*

friendships (Goodyer et al., 1997; Sherbourne, Hays, & Wells, 1995; Paykel & Cooper, 1992). Similarly, persons who live with families that are very nagging, critical, and prone to emotional outbursts (that is, families with so-called *high expressed emotion*) are particularly likely to relapse after recovering from depression (Hooley & Teasdale, 1989; Hooley, Orley, & Teasdale, 1986). This growing emphasis on social support and on interpersonal relationships in unipolar depression has in recent years led to the development of ***interpersonal psychotherapy,*** a highly effective treatment that we shall be discussing in Chapter 9.

Bipolar Disorders

People with a bipolar disorder experience both the lows of depression and the highs of mania. Many describe their life as an emotional roller coaster. They shift back and forth between extreme moods (Goodwin & Jamison, 1990). This roller coaster ride and its impact on relatives and friends is dramatically seen in the following description:

> In his early school years he had been a remarkable student and had shown a gift for watercolor and oils. Later he had studied art in Paris and married an English girl he had met there. Eventually they had settled in London.
>
> Ten years later, when he was thirty-four years old, he had persuaded his wife and only son to accompany him to Honolulu, where, he assured them, he would be considered famous. He felt he would be able to sell his paintings at many times the prices he could get in London. According to his wife, he had been in an accelerated state, but at that time the family had left, unsuspecting, believing with the patient in their imminent good fortune. When they arrived they found almost no one in the art world that he was supposed to know. There were no connections for sales and deals in Hawaii that he had anticipated. Settling down, the patient began to behave more peculiarly than ever. After enduring several months of the patient's exhilaration, overactivity, weight loss, constant talking, and unbelievably little sleep, the young wife and child began to fear for his sanity. None of his plans materialized. After five months in the Pacific, with finances growing thin, the patient's overactivity subsided and he fell into a depression. During that period he refused to move, paint, or leave the house. He lost twenty pounds, became utterly dependent on his wife, and insisted on seeing none of the friends he had accumulated in his manic state. His despondency became so severe that several doctors came to the house and advised psychiatric hospitalization. He quickly agreed and received twelve electroshock treatments, which relieved his depressed state. Soon afterward he began to paint again and to sell his work modestly. Recognition began to come from galleries and critics in the Far East. Several reviews acclaimed his work as exceptionally brilliant.
>
> This was the beginning of the lifelong career of his moodswing. In 1952, while still in Honolulu, he once again became severely depressed. . . . Four years later he returned to London in a high. . . . When this manic period subsided and he surveyed the wreckage of his life, an eight-month interval of normal mood followed, after which he again switched into a profound depression.
>
> *(Fieve, 1975, pp. 64–65)*

The Clinical Picture of Mania

In contrast to the unrelieved gloom of depression, a person in a state of mania is governed by a dramatic, inappropriate, and disproportionate elevation of mood. The

Echoing Shakespeare's observation that "the lunatic, the lover, and the poet are all compact," clinical researchers Frederick Goodwin and Kay Jamison (1990) claim that some of our most famous poets, including Sylvia Plath, have experienced bipolar disorders. Plath committed suicide in 1963 at the age of 31.

symptoms of mania encompass the same areas of functioning—emotional, motivational, behavioral, cognitive, and physical—as those of depression, but mania affects those areas in an almost diametrically opposite way (see Table 8-4).

Mania is characterized by active, expansive *emotions* that seem to be looking for an outlet. The mood of euphoric joy and well-being is out of all proportion to the actual happenings in the person's life. One person with mania explained, "I feel no sense of restriction or censorship whatsoever. I am afraid of nothing and no one" (Fieve, 1975, p. 68). Another described his manic experience as "a sense of communion, in the first place with God, and in the second with all mankind" (Custance, 1952, p. 37). Not every person with mania is a picture of happiness, however. Some can also become irritable, angry, and annoyed (Verdoux & Bourgeois, 1993)—especially when others get in the way of their ambitions, activities, and plans—like this man:

> All by himself, he had been building a magnificent swimming pool for his country home in Virginia, working eighteen hours a day at it. He decided to make the pool public and open a concession stand at one end to help defray the mounting costs of the project. When his wife suggested that he might be going overboard, he became furious and threatened to leave her for another woman. Soon afterward, when his wife was out, he took many valuables from the house—his share, he claimed—and sold or pawned them. Complaining that his wife was a stick in the mud, he decided to throw a round-the-clock party, and he invited to the house almost everyone he passed on the street.
>
> *(Fieve, 1975, p. 148)*

In the *motivational* realm, people with mania seem to want constant excitement, involvement, and companionship. They enthusiastically seek out new friends and old, new interests and old, and have little awareness that their social style is overwhelming, domineering, and excessive:

TABLE 8-4 Mania and Depression

Mania	*Depression*
Emotional	
Elation	Depressed mood
Liking for self	Dislike of self
Increased mirth response	Loss of mirth response
Cognitive	
Positive self-image	Negative self-image
Positive expectations	Negative expectations
Tendency to blame others	Tendency to blame self
Denial of problems	Exaggeration of problems
Arbitrary decision making	Indecisiveness
Motivational	
Driven and impulsive behavior	Paralysis of the will
Action-oriented wishes	Wishes for escape
Drive for independence	Increased wishes for dependency
Desire for self-enhancement	Desire for death
Behavioral	
Hyperactivity	Inertia/agitation
Productivity	Lack of productivity
Loudness	Quietness
Physical	
Indefatigability	Easy fatigability
Increased libido	Loss of libido
Insomnia	Insomnia

Source: Beck, 1967, p. 91.

In recent years actress Patty Duke has talked and written about her roller coaster life with a bipolar disorder. Until her disorder was diagnosed and treated, she experienced recurrent episodes of suicidal depression alternating with episodes of normal mood or mania.

> He was interested in everything and everyone around him. He talked familiarly to patients, attendants, nurses, and physicians. He took a fancy to the woman physician on duty in the admission building, calling her by her first name and annoying her with letters and with his familiar, ill mannered, and obtrusive attentions. . . . He made many comments and asked many questions about other patients and promised that he would secure their discharge. He interfered with their affairs and soon received a blow on the jaw from one patient and a black eye from another.
>
> *(Kolb, 1973, p. 372)*

The *behavior* of people with mania is usually described as hyperactive. They move quickly, as though there were not enough time to do everything they want to do. They may talk rapidly and loudly, their conversations filled with jokes and efforts to be clever or, conversely, with complaints and hostile tirades. Flamboyance is another characteristic of manic functioning: dressing in flashy clothes, giving large sums of money to strangers, or even getting involved in dangerous activities. Several of these qualities are evident in the monologue delivered by Joe to the two policemen who escorted him to a mental hospital:

> You look like a couple of bright, alert, hardworking, clean-cut, energetic go-getters and I could use you in my organization! I need guys that are loyal and enthusiastic about the great opportunities life offers on this planet! It's yours for the taking! Too many people pass opportunity by without hearing it knock because they don't know how to grasp the moment and strike while the iron is hot! You've got to grab it when it comes up for air, pick up the ball and run! You've got to be decisive! decisive! decisive! No shilly-shallying! Sweat! Yeah, sweat with a goal! Push, push, push, and you can push over a mountain! Two mountains, maybe. It's not luck! Hell, if it wasn't for bad luck I wouldn't have any luck at all! Be there firstest with the mostest! My guts and your blood! That's the system! I know, you know, he, she or it knows it's the only way to travel! Get 'em off balance, baby, and the rest is leverage! Use your head and save your heels! What's this deal? Who are these guys? Have you got a telephone and a secretary I can have instanter if not sooner? What I need is office space and the old LDO [long-distance operator].
>
> *(McNeil, 1967, p. 147)*

In the *cognitive* realm, people with mania usually display poor judgment and planning, as if they feel too good or move too rapidly to consider consequences or possible pitfalls. Filled with optimism, they rarely listen when others try to slow them down, interrupt their buying sprees, or prevent them from investing money unwisely. They may also hold an inflated opinion of themselves, believing that there are few topics beyond their expertise and few tasks beyond their grasp. Sometimes their self-esteem approaches grandiosity (Silverstone & Hunt, 1992). Humboldt, a character created by the novelist Saul Bellow, displays the expansiveness and self-glorification of some persons during manic episodes:

> He was a great entertainer but going insane. The pathologic element could be missed only by those who were laughing too hard to look. Humboldt, that grand erratic handsome person with his wide blond face, that charming, fluent deeply worried man to whom I was so attached, passionately lived out the theme of Success. Naturally he died a Failure. What else can result from the capitalization of such nouns? Myself, I've always held the number of sacred words down. In my opinion Humboldt had too long a list of them—Poetry, Beauty, Love, Waste Land, Alienation, Politics, History, the Unconscious. And, of course, Manic and Depressive, always capitalized. According to him, America's great Manic Depressive was Lincoln. And Churchill with what he called his Black Dog moods was a classic case of Manic Depression. "Like me, Charlie," said Humboldt. "But think—if Energy is Delight and if Exuberance is Beauty, the Manic Depressive knows more about Delight and Beauty than anyone else. Who else has so much Energy and Exuberance? Maybe it's the strategy of the Psyche to increase Depression. Didn't Freud say that Happiness was nothing but the remission of Pain? So the more Pain the intenser the Happiness. But there is a prior origin to this, and the Psyche

makes Pain on purpose. Anyway, Mankind is stunned by the Exuberance and Beauty of certain individuals. When a Manic Depressive escapes from his Furies he's irresistible. He captures History. I think that aggravation is a secret technique of the Unconscious. As for great men and kings being History's slaves, I think Tolstoi was off the track. Don't kid yourself, kings are the most sublime sick. Manic Depressive heroes pull Mankind into their cycles and carry everybody away."

(Bellow, 1975)

People with mania are also easily distracted by random stimuli from the environment. Especially during the acute phases of mania, some have so much trouble keeping their thoughts on track that they become incoherent, even out of touch with reality (Double, 1991; Harrow et al., 1988). A number of individuals also report that their sensory impressions seem sharper, brighter, more colorful, and more pleasurable than when they are not in a state of mania.

Finally, in the *physical* realm, people with mania feel remarkably energetic. They typically get little sleep, yet feel and act wide awake (Silverstone & Hunt, 1992). Even if they miss a night or two of sleep, their energy level may remain high. Clifford Beers (1908) wrote:

> For several weeks I believe I did not sleep more than two or three hours a night. Such was my state of elation, however, that all signs of fatigue were entirely absent; and the sustained and abnormal mental and physical activity in which I then indulged has left on my memory no other than a series of very pleasant impressions.

Diagnosing Bipolar Disorders

DSM-IV considers people to be experiencing a full *manic episode* when they display for at least one week an abnormally elevated, expansive, or irritable mood, along with at least three other symptoms of mania. Such episodes may vary from moderate to extreme in severity and may include such psychotic features as delusions or hallucinations. When the symptoms of mania are less severe (causing no marked impairment) and perhaps shorter in duration, the person is said to be experiencing a *hypomanic episode* (APA, 1994).

DSM-IV distinguishes two general kinds of ***bipolar disorders***—bipolar I and bipolar II disorders. People with ***bipolar I*** disorder have full manic and major depressive episodes. Most of them experience an *alternation* of the episodes; some, however, have *mixed episodes,* in which they swing from manic to depressive symptoms on the same day. In ***bipolar II*** disorder, hypomanic—that is, mildly manic—episodes alternate with major depressive episodes over the course of time. Only people who have never had a full manic episode receive this diagnosis.

If people experience four or more episodes of mood disturbance within a one-year period, their disorder, whether a bipolar I or bipolar II pattern, is further classified as *rapid cycling.* If their episodes vary with the seasons, the bipolar disorder is further classified as *seasonal.*

Surveys conducted around the world indicate that between 1 and 1.5 percent of all adults suffer from a bipolar disorder at any given time. Bipolar I disorder is somewhat more common than bipolar II disorder (Babbington & Ramana, 1995; Kessler et al., 1994; Regier et al., 1993). According to most studies, bipolar disorders are equally common in women and men. However, women may experience more depressive and fewer manic episodes than men (Leibenluft, 1996), and rapid cycling is more common among women (Leibenluft, 1996; Smith & Weissman, 1992; Weissman et al., 1991). Research conducted in the United States suggests that bipolar disorders are equally common in all socioeconomic classes and ethnic groups (APA, 1994; Weissman

"EVER HAVE ONE OF THOSE GREAT DAYS WHEN YOU'RE JUST BETWEEN MANIC AND DEPRESSIVE?"

et al., 1991). The disorders usually begin between the ages of 15 and 44 years.

In most untreated cases of bipolar disorder, the manic and depressive episodes last for several months each. Periods of normal mood last for two or more years in many cases, only briefly in others (Weissman & Boyd, 1984). Also, in the absence of treatment, manic and depressive episodes tend to recur for people with either type of bipolar disorder (Goldberg et al., 1995; APA, 1994; Goodwin & Jamison, 1990). Generally, as episodes recur, the intervening periods of normality grow shorter and shorter (Goodwin & Jamison, 1984).

When individuals experience numerous periods of *hypomanic* symptoms and *mild* depressive symptoms, DSM-IV assigns a diagnosis of ***cyclothymic disorder.*** The milder symptoms of this form of bipolar disorder continue for two or more years, interrupted occasionally by normal moods that may last for only days or weeks. This disorder, like the more severe bipolar I and bipolar II disorders, usually begins in adolescence or early adulthood and is equally common among women and men. At least 0.4 percent of the population develops cyclothymic disorder (APA, 1994). In some cases, the milder symptoms eventually blossom into a bipolar I or II disorder.

Explanations of Bipolar Disorders

Throughout the first half of the twentieth century, the study of bipolar disorders made little progress. Various theories were proposed to explain mood swings, but research did not support their validity. Psychodynamic theorists, for example suggested that mania, like depression, emerges from the loss of a love object. Whereas some people introject the lost object and become depressed, others deny the loss and become manic. They avoid the terrifying conflicts generated by the loss by escaping into a dizzy style of activity (Lewin, 1950). Although some psychodynamic clinicians have cited case reports that fit this explanation (Krishnan et al., 1984; Cohen et al., 1954), few controlled studies have been able to find any systematic relationship between recent loss (real or imagined) and the onset of a manic episode (Dunner & Hall, 1980).

Lately some promising clues from the biological realm have led to better understanding of bipolar disorders. These biological insights come from research into *neurotransmitter activity, sodium ion activity,* and *genetic factors.*

Neurotransmitters If low norepinephrine activity may lead to depression, could overactivity of norepinephrine be related to mania? When researchers first proposed the catecholamine theory, they argued exactly that (Schildkraut, 1965). Subsequent research has offered some support for this claim. One team of investigators measured the norepinephrine level in subjects' spinal fluid, on the assumption that this measure would reflect the norepinephrine activity in the brain (Post et al., 1980, 1978). They found the norepinephrine levels of patients with mania to be significantly higher than those of depressed or control subjects. In another study patients with a bipolar disorder were given reserpine, the blood pressure drug known to reduce norepinephrine activity in the brain, and the manic symptoms of some of the subjects subsided (Telner et al., 1986).

Because serotonin activity often parallels norepinephrine's in unipolar depression, theorists expected that a high level of serotonin activity would also be related to manic functioning, but no such correspondence has been found. Instead, research has indicated that mania, like depression, may be associated with *low* serotonin activity (Price, 1990). Indeed, researchers have found that the drug *lithium* often seems to increase brain serotonin activity (Price, 1990; Bunney & Garland, 1984). As we shall see in Chapter 9, lithium is by far the most effective treatment for bipolar disorders. Somehow, depression and mania both seem to be related to low levels of serotonin activity.

In an effort to make sense of these seemingly contradictory findings, some researchers have proposed a "permissive theory" of mood disorders (Mandell & Knapp, 1979; Prange et al., 1974, 1970). According to this theory, low serotonin activity sets the stage for a mood disorder and permits the brain's norepinephrine activity (or the activity of yet other neurotransmitters) to define the particular form of the disorder. Low serotonin activity accompanied by low or normal norepinephrine activity may lead to depression. This idea is consistent with some of the neurotransmitter theories of unipolar depression discussed earlier (pp. 243–246). Conversely, low serotonin activity accompanied by high norepinephrine activity may lead to mania. Although not all researchers are convinced that norepinephrine and serotonin interact in this particular way to produce bipolar disorders, a number of them do believe that the disorders reflect some form of abnormal functioning by both of the neurotransmitter systems (Baraban, Worley, & Snyder, 1989).

Sodium Ion Activity On both sides of the cell membrane of every neuron are positively charged *sodium ions* that play a critical role in sending incoming messages down the axon to the nerve endings (see Figures 8-6 and 8-7). When the neuron is at rest, most of the sodium ions sit on the outer side of the membrane. When the neuron is stimulated by an incoming message at its receptor site, however, the sodium ions from the outer side of the membrane travel across to the inner side. This, in turn, starts a wave of electrochemical activity that continues down the length of the axon and results in the "firing" of the neuron. This activity is followed by a flow of *potassium ions* from the inside to the outside of the neuron, thus helping the neuron to return to its original resting state.

If brain messages are to be transmitted properly, the sodium ions must travel properly back and forth between the outside and the inside of the neural membrane. Some theorists believe that *improper transport* of these ions may cause neurons to fire too easily, thus resulting in mania, or to be too resistant to firing, thus resulting in depression. Such defects in the transport of sodium ions may result in shifting misalignments along neural membranes and consequent fluctuations from one mood extreme to the other (Kato et al., 1993; Meltzer, 1991).

Researchers have found clear indications of defective sodium ion transportation at certain neuron membranes in the brains of people with bipolar disorders. They have, for example, observed abnormal functioning in the proteins that help transport sodium ions back and forth across a neuron's membrane during firing (Kato et al., 1993; Meltzer, 1991). Some studies further suggest that people with bipolar disorders may have an extensive membrane defect that causes these problems in the sodium transport mechanisms (El-Mallakh & Wyatt, 1995; Kato et al., 1993; Meltzer, 1991).

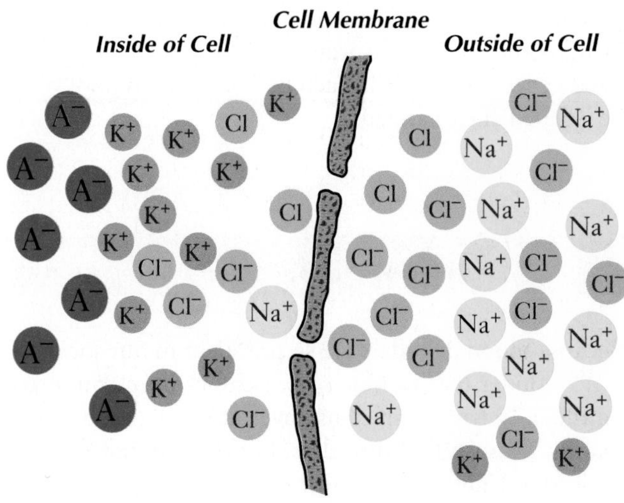

Figure 8-6 *The cell membrane, composed of protein and fat, contains small pores that allow the passage of water, sodium ions (Na^+), chloride ions (Cl^-), potassium ions (K^+), and large protein molecules (A^-). Potassium and chloride ions diffuse freely through the pores, but it is much more difficult for the larger sodium ions to do so, and protein molecules can hardly diffuse at all. (Adapted from Julien, 1985, p. 229.)*

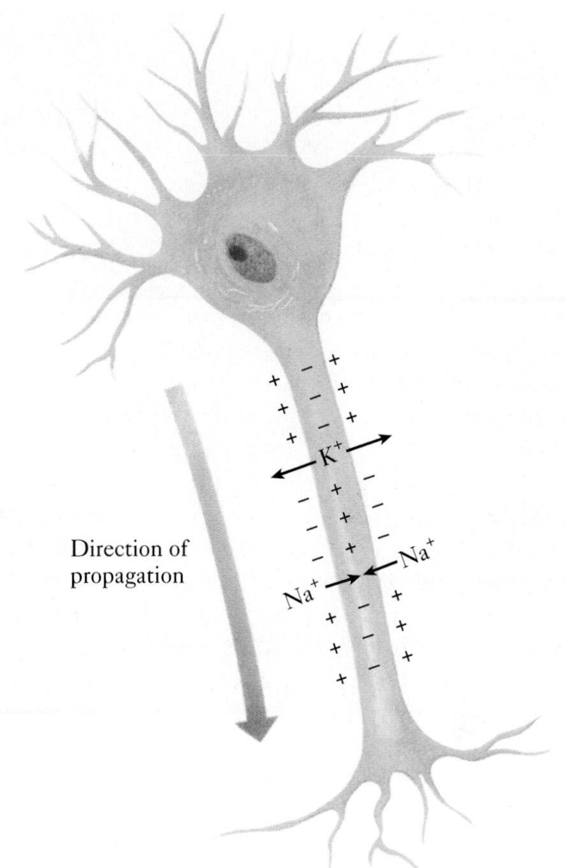

Figure 8-7 *Neurons relay messages in the form of electrical impulses that begin in the cell body and travel down the axon toward the nerve endings. As an impulse travels along the axon, it reduces the difference in voltage between the interior and exterior of the cell. This allows sodium ions (Na^+) to flow in. The inflow of sodium propagates the impulse. As sodium flows in, potassium ions (K^+) flow out, thus helping the membrane's electrical potential to return to its resting state, ready for the arrival of a new impulse. (Adapted from Snyder, 1986, p. 7.)*

Genetic Factors Many theorists have argued that people inherit a predisposition to develop the biological abnormalities that underlie bipolar disorders (Winokur et al., 1995; Blehar et al., 1988). *Family pedigree studies* have provided strong evidence that this is so. Close relatives of people with a bipolar disorder have been found to have a 4 to 25 percent likelihood of developing the same disorder, compared to the 1 percent prevalence rate in the general population (Gershon & Nurnberger, 1995; APA, 1994; Nurnberger & Gershon, 1992). While the relatives of people with bipolar disorders are also more likely than those in the general population to

Closely knit families in which there is little intermarriage across the generations are attractive candidates for genetic linkage studies, which seek to identify possible patterns in the inheritance of disorders. The possible genetic patterns of bipolar disorders have, for example, been studied in some Amish families in Pennsylvania.

experience unipolar depression, such relatives are particularly likely to develop a bipolar disorder (Winokur et al., 1995). Moreover, the more similar the genetic makeup of two people, the more similar their tendency to develop a bipolar disorder.

Researchers have also conducted *genetic linkage studies* to identify possible patterns in the inheritance of bipolar disorders. As we observed in Chapter 4, such studies select extended families that have exhibited high rates of a disorder over several generations, observe the pattern of distribution of the disorder among family members, and determine whether it closely follows the distribution pattern of genetically transmitted family traits (called *genetic markers*) such as color blindness, red hair, or a particular medical syndrome. After studying the records of Israeli, Belgian, and Italian families that had shown high rates of bipolar disorders across several generations, one team of researchers seemed for a while to have linked bipolar disorders to genes on the X chromosome (Baron et al., 1987; Mendlewicz et al., 1987, 1980, 1972).

Another team, however, used techniques from *molecular biology* (see p. 94) to examine Old Order Amish families in Pennsylvania, and determined that bipolar disorders can be traced to an area on chromosome 11 (Egeland et al., 1987, 1984). Still other studies have linked bipolar disorders to genes on chromosomes 18, 4, 6, 13, and 15 (Berrettini et al., 1997; Blackwood et al., 1996; Ginns et al., 1996).

Some theorists have interpreted these contradictory findings to mean that the logic behind the genetic studies is faulty. And, in fact, repeated failures to replicate some of the findings have raised further questions about the validity and implications of these studies (Nurnberger & Gershon, 1992; Kelsoe et al., 1989). On the other hand, perhaps a variety of genetic abnormalities combine to bring about bipolar disorders. Either way, the hypothesized genes pointed to in each line of research have yet to be isolated and analyzed.

Crossroads

Because mood disorders are so prevalent in our society, it is no wonder that so much research has been conducted on them. In truth, clinicians have gathered a lot of information about mood disorders, but they do not yet fully understand all that they know.

Over the past thirty years investigators have done a remarkable job of identifying factors that accompany the mood disorders. Biological factors have consistently been implicated in bipolar disorders, and most clinical theorists now believe that biological abnormalities, perhaps inherited and perhaps precipitated by life stress, cause these disorders. Unipolar patterns of depression, however, are apparently much more complex.

Several factors appear to be closely tied to unipolar depression, including biological abnormalities, a reduction in positive reinforcements, negative ways of thinking, a perception of helplessness, and sociocultural influences. In some cases life stresses, such as the loss of a loved one, also seem to precipitate the disorder. Precisely how these factors relate to unipolar depression is, to say the least, unclear. It may be that each factor helps cause a distinct depressive disorder (Kendler et al., 1996). Alternatively, the different patterns of unipolar depression may be variations of a single basic disorder (Flett, Vredenburg, & Krames, 1997). If so, the factors uncovered by researchers may relate to this disorder in any of several ways:

1. One of the factors may indeed be the key cause of unipolar depression. That is, one theory may be more useful than any of the others for predicting and understanding how unipolar depression unfolds. If so, cognitive and biological factors are leading candidates, for each have been found by at least a few researchers to precede and predict depression.

2. Any of the leading factors may be capable of initiating unipolar depression. This initial cause may then trigger problems in other areas of functioning, and so establish a full syndrome of unipolar depression. Some people may begin with low serotonin activity, for example, which may predispose them to react helplessly in stressful situations, interpret events negatively, and enjoy fewer pleasures in life. Others may first suffer a severe loss, which sets off helplessness reactions, low serotonin activity, and reductions in positive reinforcements. Regardless of the initial cause, these people may all move toward a "final common pathway" of unipolar depression.

3. An interaction between two or more factors may be necessary to create an episode of unipolar depression (Klocek, Oliver, & Ross, 1997). Perhaps people will become depressed only if they have low serotonin activity, feel helpless to control their reinforcements, *and* repeatedly blame themselves for negative events in their lives. This would help explain why only some helplessness-trained subjects actually come to exhibit helplessness in laboratory studies, and why only some people with low serotonin activity become depressed.

4. The various factors may play different roles in unipolar depression. Some may *cause* the disorder, some may *result* from it, and some may help *maintain* it. Peter Lewinsohn and his colleagues (1988) assessed more than 500 nondepressed subjects on several of the factors that have been linked to depression. They then assessed the subjects again eight months later to see who had in fact become depressed and which of the factors had predicted depression. Negative cognitions, life stress, and self-dissatisfaction were found to precede and predict depression; impoverished social relationships and reductions in positive reinforcements did not. The research team concluded that the former factors help cause unipolar depression, while the latter simply accompany or result from depression, and perhaps help maintain it.

Investigations into the mood disorders have been very fruitful. They have produced compelling evidence that a variety of factors are tied to the disorders. In fact, more contributing factors have been associated with mood disorders than with most other psychological disorders. Now that clinical researchers have gathered so many important puzzle pieces, their task is to put the pieces together into a meaningful picture that will suggest even better ways to predict, prevent, and treat the mood disorders.

Chapter Review

1. ***Mood disorders*** People with mood disorders have moods that tend to last for months or years, dominate their interactions with the world, and disrupt their normal functioning.

2. ***Unipolar depression*** People with *unipolar depression,* the most common pattern of mood disorder, suffer exclusively from depression. Women are more likely than men to experience unipolar depression. The symptoms of depression span five areas of functioning: emotional, motivational, behavioral, cognitive, and physical. Depressed people are also at greater risk for suicidal behavior.

A. ***The biological view*** According to the biological perspective, deficiencies in two chemical neurotransmitters, *norepinephrine* and *serotonin,* may cause depression. Hormonal factors may also be at work. The genetic view suggests that an inherited predisposition to biological abnormalities underlies unipolar depression.

B. ***The psychodynamic view*** According to the psychodynamic perspective, people who experience real or imagined losses may *introject* feelings for the lost object and may come to feel anger toward themselves and depression.

C. ***The behavioral view*** In the behavioral view, when people experience significant reductions in their total rate of positive reinforcements, they display fewer positive behaviors. This leads to still a lower rate of positive reinforcements, to yet fewer positive behaviors, and eventually to depression.

D. ***The cognitive view*** The leading cognitive explanations of unipolar depression focus on maladaptive thinking and learned helplessness.

(1) ***Maladaptive thinking*** According to Beck, *maladaptive attitudes,* the *cognitive triad, errors in thinking,* and *automatic thoughts* help generate unipolar depression.

(2) ***A cognitive-behavioral view: learned helplessness*** According to Seligman's *learned helplessness theory,* people become depressed when they perceive a loss of control over the reinforcements in their lives and when they attribute their loss of control to causes that are internal, global, and stable.

E. ***The sociocultural view*** Sociocultural theorists propose that unipolar depression is influenced by the social structure in which people live. In support of this position, research finds that stressful events often seem to trigger depression, the character and prevalence of depression can vary from culture to culture, and a low level of social support is linked to depression.

3. ***Bipolar disorders*** In *bipolar disorders,* episodes of mania alternate or intermix with episodes of depression.

A. ***Mania*** People in a state of *mania* experience dramatic, inappropriate, or disproportionate elevations in mood. As with depression, five areas are affected in mania: the emotional, motivational, behavioral, cognitive, and physical. Manic episodes almost always indicate a bipolar disorder, one in which depressive episodes also occur.

B. ***Diagnosing bipolar disorders*** Bipolar disorders are much less common than unipolar depression, afflict women and men equally, and tend to recur if they are not treated. People who experience manic and major depressive episodes receive a diagnosis of *bipolar I* disorder. People who experience mild manic, or *hypomanic,* episodes and major depressive episodes receive a diagnosis of *bipolar II* disorder. And those whose mood swings consist of mild depressive and mild manic episodes receive a diagnosis of *cyclothymic disorder.*

C. ***Explanations of bipolar disorders*** Mania has been related to *high norepinephrine activity* along with a low level of serotonin activity. Researchers also suspect that in persons with bipolar disorders, *sodium ions,* and perhaps other ions, are improperly transported back and forth between the outside and the inside of the neuron's membrane. Finally, some studies have suggested that people may inherit a *genetic predisposition* to the biological abnormalities that underlie bipolar disorders.

Thought and Afterthought

The Color of Depression

People often use color adjectives to describe depression. The deeper the depression, the darker the color. Even Winston Churchill referred to his episodes of depression as "the black dog." Researchers at Louisiana State University in Shreveport have found that the relationship between color choice and mood may extend deep into the minds of persons with depression (Nolan, Dai, & Stanley, 1995).

The investigators asked 261 college students to answer such questions as "Which color is your favorite?" The subjects who chose black were more depressed than those who chose blue, red, yellow, white, or green. Similarly, when they were asked, "Which color best describes your current mood?" those who answered black or brown were more depressed.

Afterthoughts: Why might people who are depressed actually prefer dark colors? . . . When people describe their mood as black, might that label in turn influence their mood? . . . Where might our associations between mood and color come from?

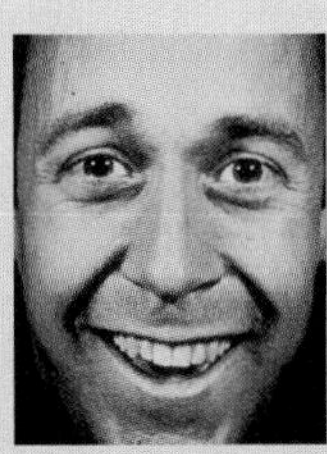
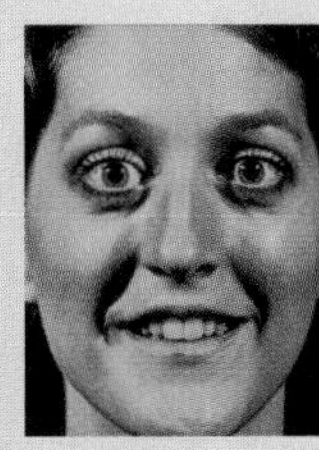
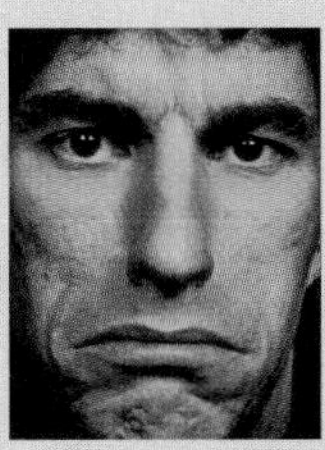
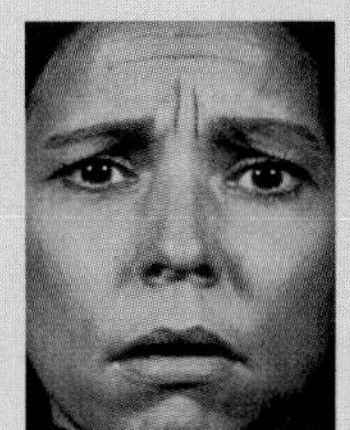

Spotting Depression: A Matter of Gender?

In 1994 a team of researchers at the University of Pennsylvania asked subjects to look at a series of photographs of people and judge whether the faces reflected happiness or sadness (Gur et al., 1994). Everyone identified happy faces correctly, but female and male subjects differed significantly in their ability to identify sadness.

Women picked out sad faces correctly 90 percent of the time, whether the faces were male or female. Men had similar success at picking out sad male faces, but on average they made more errors when the faces were female.

Afterthoughts: How might clinical theorists account for these findings? . . . How might the findings tie in with the gender differences in depression? . . . Do the findings have possible implications for interpersonal relationships or therapy interactions?

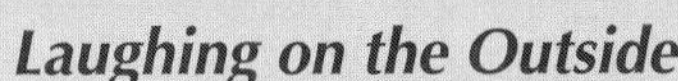

Laughing on the Outside

Millions of people across the United States tune in each week to watch Drew Carey *(left)* play a department store personnel director in the television show that bears his name. The reason? They want to laugh, and the comedian more than helps them to do so. Yet Carey, also a successful stand-up comedian, reveals that he suffered from severe depression for much of his life (Fields-Meyer & Wagner, 1995). By the age of 23 he had twice tried to kill himself.

He believes various traumas and circumstances contributed to his problem, including the sudden death of his father when Carey was 8. He says his life turned around when he entered the Marines in 1980 and became more anchored and self-disciplined. He has worked hard and successfully to develop a positive outlook. His work has included reading psychology books, listening to tapes on positive thinking, and applying insights to his own life.

Afterthoughts: Carey is one of many comedians who have grappled with depression. Is there something about being depressed that might make them more adept at thinking or acting funny? . . . Is there something about performing that might address their depressive feelings?

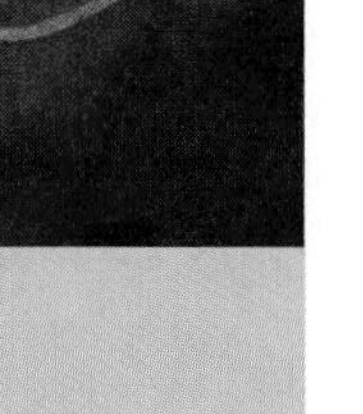

Topic Overview

Treatments for Unipolar Depression

- Psychodynamic Therapy
- Behavioral Therapy
- Cognitive Therapy
- Interpersonal Psychotherapy
- Electroconvulsive Therapy
- Antidepressant Drugs

Treatments for Bipolar Disorders

- Lithium Therapy
- Adjunctive Psychotherapy

Crossroads

Chapter 9

Treatments for Mood Disorders

What does it mean to overcome a mood disorder? When should treatment for depression be considered successful? Is it when symptoms are reduced, or must they be eliminated? Perhaps it is enough for the client to learn how to function in the face of some sadness and pessimism. The answers depend partly on the perspective of the therapist and partly on the needs of the client. Here Stan describes his "triumph" over depression:

> Everything used to overwhelm me. From big problems to the smallest of things. I'd get upset and feel dejected. I'd just know that things were never going to get better. And all the while I blamed myself. I stayed awake nights, and drove my wife up the wall. Therapy has helped to change all that. My wife says I seem to be a different person. And I feel like a different person. I rarely get upset, certainly not over little things. Oh, sure, if there's an illness or accident, or a problem at work, I'll get concerned and maybe down. But it doesn't get out of hand. I can still smile and look forward to things. I'm really enjoying my life again.

And Howard says:

> I'm feeling better since I first started treatment, but it's a long way from perfect. I still feel blue a lot of the time. Sometimes I think I'm going to slip into it again—the depression. Probably, that worries me the most. It's hard enough to feel bad without also worrying that I'm gonna sink into all that pain again.

Persons suffering from depression typically feel hopeless about their future. Yet, like the subject in Winsook Kim Linton's Rowing, *most eventually find their way out of the disorder and its darkness. A variety of treatment approaches, including cognitive, interpersonal, and drug therapies, are able to help persons overcome depression.*

> But I never seem to sink all the way anymore and I always bounce back pretty fast. I have more of a handle on things now. At least, I don't hang my head so often. And, I don't blame myself for everything. I even have some evenings when I feel pretty good. It's a battle. I have to work at it. But at least I'm no longer down every second.

Although Stan and Howard are talking about different kinds of success, they both believe they have made significant progress in their battles against depression. And in each case progress has been aided by a systematic treatment approach. Stan and Howard are among the 15 million adults in the United States with a mood disorder. More than 41 percent of them receive treatment in the hope of regaining some measure of control over their moods (Shelton et al., 1997; Regier et al., 1993) (see Figure 9-1). Most are successful; many, however, suffer a relapse sooner or later (APA, 1994, 1993).

"I'd like to talk about my abandonment issues."

Unlike the missing therapist in this cartoon, psychodynamic therapists try to help depressed patients recall and address early losses or instances of abandonment.

Treatments for Unipolar Depression

A large and diverse group of therapists treat unipolar depression. An average of 10 percent of the clients of psychiatrists, psychologists, and social workers have this disorder (Knesper et al., 1985). Many other clients experience depressed feelings as part of another disorder, such as an eating disorder, or as part of broader difficulties that they are encountering in life.

A variety of treatment approaches are now employed in cases of unipolar depression. We shall first consider the psychological approaches and focus on the psychodynamic, behavioral, and cognitive therapies. We will turn next to the sociocultural approaches, including a very promising intervention called interpersonal psychotherapy. And finally we will consider two effective biological interventions, electroconvulsive therapy and antidepressant drugs. Over the course of our travels, we shall see that unipolar patterns of depression are among the most successfully treated of all psychological disorders.

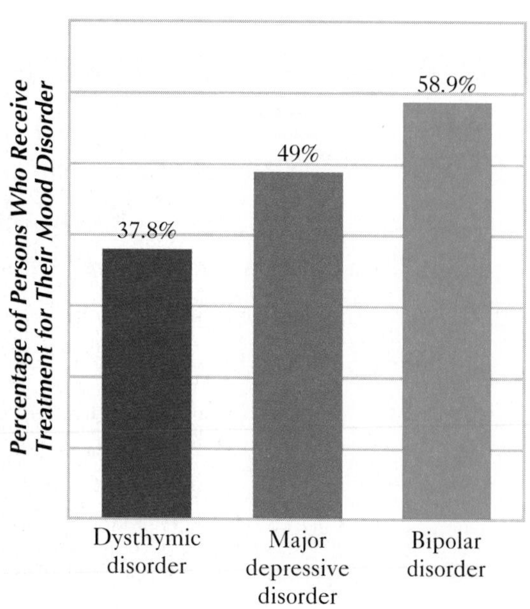

Figure 9-1 *People with mood disorders are more likely to receive treatment than those with most other mental disorders. As one might expect, the more disruptive the mood disorder (bipolar or major depressive disorder), the more likely the person is to be in treatment. (Adapted from Regier et al., 1993; Weissman et al., 1991.)*

Psychological Approaches

The psychodynamic, behavioral, and cognitive therapies are the psychological treatments that have been applied to unipolar depression most often. Psychodynamic therapy is the oldest of the modern approaches. As we shall see, research has not offered strong support for its effectiveness with depression, but it continues to be used widely. Behavioral therapy is effective primarily for mild or moderate depression. It is practiced less often today than it was in past decades. Cognitive therapy has performed so well in research that it has a large and growing following among clinicians.

Psychodynamic Therapies Believing that unipolar depression results from unconscious grief over real or imagined losses compounded by excessive dependence on other people, psychodynamic therapists try to help depressed clients bring those processes to consciousness, so they can understand the source of their pain and learn to leave it behind them. The therapists use the same basic psychodynamic procedures with depressed clients that they use with others: they encourage the client to associate freely during therapy; suggest interpretations of the client's associations, dreams, and displays of resistance and transference; and help the client reexperience and reevaluate past events and feelings. Free association helped one patient recall the early experiences of loss that, according to his therapist, had set the stage for his depression:

> Among his earliest memories, possibly the earliest of all, was the recollection of being wheeled in his baby cart under the elevated train structure and left there alone. Another memory that recurred vividly during the analysis was of an operation around the age of five. He was anesthetized and his mother left him with the doctor. He recalled how he had kicked and screamed, raging at her for leaving him.
>
> *(Lorand, 1968, pp. 325–326)*

In the following case, the therapist interpreted a depressed client's dream and traced his mood problem to early dependence and to real and symbolic losses:

> The patient reported a dream in which he was at his father's gravesite, in which his dead father was lying. In the dream the patient was crying and others were trying to comfort him. He had the feeling that everyone close to him was sick. He woke from the dream crying. In his associations this patient remembered the actual death of his father, stating that at the time, "I felt as if my purpose in life had been extinguished." The patient had had a quasi-symbiotic relationship with his father, who had preferred him over the other children. He followed his father's orders to the letter, in return for which his father lavished praise on him and gave him substantial sums of money. He never dared to cross his father since he had the experience of witnessing what had occurred to his brothers when they disagreed even slightly with the father. This patient had grown up in a rural area where the father, a wealthy and influential businessman, had ruled over a large estate like a small monarch. Although he had slavishly followed his father's instructions, the patient often had been irresponsible in his own affairs, and had lost moderate sums of money because of his naiveté. He had the dream after losing a considerable sum of money at cards. The dream may have represented an awareness that he was now on his own, yet there remained within him a desperate desire to be taken care of once again by a powerful other. The dream showed his characteristic turning to others to make things right, as his father had done in the past whenever he was in trouble.
>
> *(Arieti & Bemporad, 1978, p. 300)*

At times psychodynamic therapists must adjust their usual procedures, because depressed clients may pose special problems. If a client is too dejected even to associate freely at first, the therapist may have to take a more active role than usual (Bose, 1995; Spiegel, 1965; Kolb, 1956). By the same token, psychodynamic therapists must deal particularly carefully with the transference behavior of depressed clients (APA, 1993). Because of their extreme dependence on important people in their lives, depressed clients may seek guidance and relief from the therapist even more than other clients do, and expect the therapist to take care of them (Bose, 1992; Kolb, 1956).

Psychodynamic therapists expect that in the course of treatment depressed clients will eventually become less dependent on others, cope with losses more effectively, make corresponding changes in their daily lives, and join the majority of people who describe themselves as happy (see Box 9-1). The psychodynamic approach to depression is seen in the case of a middle-aged executive:

> He had functioned well in the context of a favored status relationship with his boss. However, he had been transferred to another department where his new boss was aloof and gave his colleagues little feedback. This new superior simply expected everyone to do their jobs

Old age is often accompanied by the loss of good health, close relatives and friends, and control over one's life. Both psychodynamic and behavioral therapists link such losses to depression among the elderly. Yet depression is not inevitable as people age. Although depression among the elderly received little clinical attention in the past, therapists of various orientations now have considerable success treating it.

BOX 9-1 Happiness: More Common Than We Think

Clinicians and popular opinion have long suspected that a general state of happiness may help prevent depression. If people enjoy life, and feel upbeat and enriched, perhaps they will not so readily succumb to the maladaptive thinking, personal losses, social stress, or biological events that mark depression.

But are many people really happy, and if so, why? Judging from the evening news and the proliferation of self-help books, one would think that happiness is a rare commodity. Even psychologists seem far more interested in heartache than in happiness. In the last twenty years, researchers have produced over 42,000 articles on depression, 30,000 on anxiety, 8,500 on suicide, and nearly 6,000 on suffering. Only 1,436 articles have mentioned happiness, and a mere 835 cheerful articles address joy. One study found that 79 percent of college psychology majors believed that people who live in poverty are unhappy most of the time, and 95 percent believed unemployed men to be consistently unhappy. Half of the students believed that elderly persons are chronically unhappy (Diener & Diener, 1996).

But there's good news. Research indicates that most people's lives are more upbeat than we think. In fact, most people around the world say they're happy—including those who are poor, unemployed, elderly, and disabled. Over 90 percent of people with quadriplegia say they're glad to be alive, and overall people with spinal cord injuries report feeling only slightly less happy than other people (Diener & Diener, 1996; Brickman, Coates & Janoff-Bulman, 1978). Worldwide surveys yield the same finding: people are generally happy, regardless of their age, socioeconomic status, race, educational level, health, gender, or physical attractiveness (Myers & Diener, 1996). Men and women are equally likely to declare themselves satisfied or very happy. Even members of generation X are not as angst-ridden as they may appear. There is truth too to the old adage "Money can't buy happiness." Wealthy people appear only slightly happier than those of modest means, and people whose income has increased

---

and was not concerned with personal niceties. The patient found himself becoming more and more depressed when he failed to elicit the needed reassurance from his new superior. . . . In therapy, he was able to connect his current plight to his childhood experience of devoting himself to pleasing his father. The latter rarely gave praise and was harshly critical of all the children, but the patient remembered feeling euphoric and important when the father did acknowledge some achievement.

The patient's father was still living and in a nursing home, where the patient visited him regularly. On one occasion, he went to see his father full of high expectations, as he had concluded a very successful business transaction. As he began to describe his accomplishments to his father, however, the latter completely ignored his son's remarks and viciously berated him for wearing a pink shirt, which he considered unprofessional. Such a response from the father was not unusual, but this time, as a result of the work that had been accomplished in therapy, the patient could objectively analyze his initial sense of disappointment and deep feeling of failure for not pleasing the older man. Although this experience led to a transient state of depression, it also revealed to the patient his whole dependent lifestyle—his use of others to supply him with a feeling of worth. This experience added a dimension of immediate reality to the insights that had been achieved in therapy and gave the patient the motivation to change radically his childhood system of perceiving himself in relation to paternal transference figures. This clinical vignette illustrates one of the major objectives of the working-through process: one must perceive usual situations in a new way and then use such insights for the purpose of change.

(Bemporad, 1992, p. 291)

over the past decade are no happier than those whose income has remained stagnant (Diener et al., 1993).

Only 1 in 10 reports being "not too happy" (Diener & Diener, 1996; Myers & Diener, 1996). Exceptions in this worldful of happy people include, according to surveys, the very poor, prison inmates, persons institutionalized with alcoholism, new psychotherapy clients, and victims of oppressive governments (Myers & Diener, 1996).

Although people aren't elated every day, most seem able to bounce back well from disappointments. Happy people also seem to remain happy from decade to decade, regardless of job changes, relocations, and family changes (Myers & Diener, 1996). Some research indicates that happiness is only briefly affected by events in life (Suh, Diener, & Fujita, 1996). Happy people are able to adapt to negative events and return to their usual cheerful state within a few months (Diener et al., 1992; Costa et al., 1987). Conversely, unhappy people are not cheered in the long term even by positive events. They too adapt—and return to their discontent.

Levels of happiness have sometimes been linked to two factors: marital status and religious activity. In one large longitudinal survey, 39 percent of married men and women rated themselves as very happy, compared to 24 percent of those who had never married and 12 percent of divorced people. Some surveys have found, too, that happiness tends to increase with frequency of attendance at religious services (Myers & Diener, 1996). Religious affiliation, like marriage, may provide a social support that encourages happiness.

But why are people happy? If gender, race, income, and life events have a limited effect on long-term happiness, what makes people so enduringly upbeat? Some research indicates that happiness is dependent on enduring personality characteristics and cognitive interpretive styles. Happy people are generally optimistic and extroverted, and they tend to have several close friends (Myers & Diener, 1995; Diener et al., 1992). Happy people also have high self-esteem and believe that they have control over their lives. Perhaps lack of control explains the unhappiness of the very poor, prison inmates, and subjects of oppressive governments.

Some researchers believe that people have a genetically determined "happiness set point" to which they consistently return, despite life's ups and downs. An investigation of 2,300 twins suggested to the researchers who conducted the study that as much as half of one's sense of happiness is related to genetic factors (Lykken & Tellegen, 1996).

A better understanding of the roots of happiness may emerge from the present flurry of research, perhaps providing useful solutions to those who are not so happy. Future studies of happiness may also help clinicians better understand, prevent, and treat clinical depression. In the meantime, we have the comfort of knowing that the human condition isn't quite as unhappy as news stories (and textbooks on abnormal psychology) may make it seem.

Despite successful reports such as this one, researchers have found long-term psychodynamic therapy to be helpful only occasionally in cases of unipolar depression (APA, 1993; Prochaska, 1984). Two features of the approach have been cited to explain its limited effectiveness. First, as we noted earlier, depressed clients may be too passive and feel too fatigued to participate fully in therapy discussions and to exercise the subtle insight that psychodynamic therapy requires. Second, clients may become discouraged and end treatment too early when this long-term approach is unable to provide the quick relief that they desperately seek. Short-term psychodynamic approaches have shown somewhat greater promise, although investigations have been limited and results modest (Jefferson & Greist, 1994; APA, 1993; Svartberg & Stiles, 1991). Despite researchers' findings that psychodynamic therapies are of limited help in treating depression, these approaches continue to be employed widely to combat it. Many therapists believe that, at the very least, the therapies may be useful in cases of depression that clearly involve a history of childhood loss or trauma, a chronic sense of emptiness, perfectionism, extreme self-criticism, or stringent self-expectations (Blatt, 1995; APA, 1993).

Behavioral Therapy Peter Lewinsohn has developed a behavioral treatment for unipolar depression (Lewinsohn et al., 1990, 1982; Teri & Lewinsohn, 1986). As we have seen, he traces depression to a drop in the number of positive reinforcements in a person's life. Therapists who take this approach therefore reintroduce clients to pleasurable events and activities, systematically reinforce nondepressive behavior, and help clients improve their social skills.

Reintroducing Pleasurable Events Guided by a client's responses on a Pleasant Events Schedule and an Activity Schedule (see Table 9-1), a therapist selects activities that the client considers pleasurable, such as going shopping or taking photographs, and encourages the client to set up a weekly schedule for engaging in them. Studies have shown that the reintroduction of positive activities does indeed lead to increased participation in the world and to a better mood (Leenstra, Ormel, & Giel, 1995; Teri & Lewinsohn, 1986). The following case description exemplifies this process:

> This patient was a forty-nine-year-old housewife whose children were grown and no longer living at home. Her major interest in life was painting, and indeed she was an accomplished artist. She developed a depression characterized by apathy, self-derogation, and anxiety while she was incapacitated with a severe respiratory infection. She was unable to paint during her illness and lost interest and confidence in her art work when she became depressed. Her therapist thought that she could reinstitute her sources of "reinforcement" if she could be motivated to return to the easel. After providing a supportive relationship for a month, the therapist scheduled a home visit to look at her paintings and to watch and talk with her while she picked up her brush and put paint to canvas. By the time he arrived, she had already begun to paint and within a few weeks experienced a gradual lessening of her depression.
>
> *(Liberman & Raskin, 1971, p. 521)*

Reinforcing Nondepressive Behavior Behaviorists argue that when people become depressed, their negative behaviors serve to keep others at a distance, reducing opportunities for positive reinforcement. Old adaptive behavior, such as going to work, may be replaced by complaining, crying, or self-deprecation. To combat this pattern, therapists may use a ***contingency management*** approach: they systematically ignore a client's depressive behavior while giving attention and other rewards to constructive statements and behavior. Therapists may also use family members and friends as part of this approach (see Table 9-2), instructing them to ignore the client's depressive behaviors and reward adaptive behaviors (Liberman & Raskin, 1971).

Teaching Social Skills To combat depressive behaviors and to prevent the further loss of social reinforcements, Lewinsohn and other behavioral therapists also train clients in effective social skills. In one group therapy program, called ***personal effectiveness training,*** group members work with one another to improve "expressive" behaviors such as eye contact, facial expression, tone of voice, and posture. Studies indicate that the social interactions of depressed clients improve under such techniques (Hersen et al., 1984; King et al., 1974).

Effectiveness of Behavioral Treatment Lewinsohn's behavioral techniques seem to be of only limited help when but one of them is applied. A group of depressed people who were instructed to increase their pleasant activities showed no more improvement than a control group of depressed subjects who were told simply to monitor their activities (Hammen & Glass, 1975).

Treatment programs that *combine* several of these techniques, however, do appear to reduce depressive symptoms, particularly if the depression is mild or moderate (Lewinsohn et al., 1990, 1984; Teri & Lewinsohn, 1986). Such programs appear to be effective in either individual or group formats. They help as many as 80 percent of mildly or moderately depressed clients, especially when the treatments are systematically offered along with lectures, classroom activities, homework assignments, and an explanatory guidebook (Teri & Lewinsohn, 1986; Lewinsohn et al., 1984, 1982).

Cognitive Therapy

In Chapter 8 we saw that Aaron Beck views unipolar depression as the result of a chain of cognitive errors. Beck believes that depressed people have *maladaptive attitudes* that lead to negatively biased ways of viewing themselves, the world, and their future—the so-called *cognitive triad.* These biased views combine with *illogical thinking* to produce *automatic thoughts,* unrelentingly negative thoughts that flood the mind and generate the symptoms of depression.

Beck has developed the leading cognitive treatment for unipolar depression, designed to help clients recognize and change their dysfunctional cognitive processes

Behaviorists propose that people need to maintain pleasurable events in their lives in order to thrive and to avoid depression. With this in mind, more and more activities, such as the Senior Olympics, are being made available to elderly persons, providing important rewards, stimulation, and satisfaction.

TABLE 9-1 Sample Items in a Behavioral Activity Schedule

Make check mark(s) within the parentheses to correspond to the activities of this day.
Only activities that were at least a little pleasant should be checked.

Activity	*Frequency Check*	*Activity*	*Frequency Check*
1. Buying things for myself	( )	17. Having a lively talk	( )
2. Going to lectures or hearing speakers	( )	18. Having friends come to visit	( )
3. Saying something clearly	( )	19. Giving gifts	( )
4. Watching TV	( )	20. Getting letters, cards, or notes	( )
5. Thinking about something good in the future	( )	21. Going on outings (to the park, a picnic, or a barbecue, etc.)	( )
6. Laughing	( )	22. Photography	( )
7. Having lunch with friends or associates	( )	23. Reading maps	( )
8. Having a frank and open conversation	( )	24. Wearing clean clothes	( )
9. Working on my job	( )	25. Helping someone	( )
10. Being helped	( )	26. Talking about my children or grandchildren	( )
11. Wearing informal clothes	( )	27. Meeting someone new of the opposite sex	( )
12. Being with friends	( )	28. Seeing beautiful scenery	( )
13. Reading essays or technical, academic, or professional literature	( )	29. Eating good meals	( )
14. Just sitting and thinking	( )	30. Writing papers, essays, articles, reports, memos, etc.	( )
15. Social drinking	( )	31. Doing a job well	( )
16. Seeing good things happen to my family or friends	( )	32. Having spare time	( )

Source: Lewinsohn et al., 1976, p. 117.

and thus to improve both their mood and their behavior (Beck, 1997, 1985, 1967). The treatment, which usually requires twelve to twenty sessions, is similar to Albert Ellis's rational-emotive therapy (discussed in Chapters 3 and 6), but it is tailored to the specific cognitive errors found in depression. Beck's approach follows four successive phases. Inasmuch as the early stage of treatment incorporates behavioral techniques, it is probably more accurate to consider this a cognitive-behavioral approach rather than a purely cognitive intervention (Jacobson et al., 1996).

Phase 1: Increasing Activities and Elevating Mood Therapists set the stage for cognitive therapy by encouraging clients to become more active and confident. Clients spend time during each session preparing a detailed schedule of hourly activities for the coming week (see Figure 9-2). As clients become more active from week to week, their mood is expected to improve. Obviously, this aspect of treatment is similar to Lewinsohn's behavioral approach. Beck, however, believes that the increases in activity produced by this approach will not by themselves lead a person out of depressive functioning; cognitive interventions must follow.

Phase 2: Examining and Invalidating Automatic Thoughts Once clients are somewhat active again and feeling some relief from their depression, cognitive

TABLE 9-2 Contract with Friend or Relative to Increase Positive Activities

My goal for the coming week is to increase the number of pleasant activities which I engage in by .... events or activities. I have explained to .... why this is important for improving my disposition and he/she has agreed to help.

I promise to forfeit .... (put here the amount of money, a valued possession, or a service you might perform for your friend or relative) if I don't achieve the goal of increased activity which I have stated above.

Signed ....
(your name)

I understand that .... (your name) is attempting to increase his/her activity in the coming week and I agree to help. Specifically, I agree to provide warmth and encouragement when .... (your name) tells me about activities or events which have occurred, and to give .... (specify some event, amount of money, or other reward you think will motivate you to achieve your goal) to .... (your name) if he/she achieves the goal which he/she has established.

Signed..
(friend's name)

Source: Lewinsohn, Biglan, & Zeiss, 1976, p. 110.

therapists help educate them about their unrelenting negative automatic thoughts, assigning "homework" in which the clients must recognize and record the thoughts as they occur. In session after session, therapist and client test the objective reality behind the thoughts and often conclude that they are groundless. Beck offers the following exchange as an example of this sort of review.

> *Therapist:* Why do you think you won't be able to get into the university of your choice?
>
> *Patient:* Because my grades were really not so hot.
>
> *Therapist:* Well, what was your grade average?
>
> *Patient:* Well, pretty good up until the last semester in high school.
>
> *Therapist:* What was your grade average in general?
>
> *Patient:* A's and B's.
>
> *Therapist:* Well, how many of each?
>
> *Patient:* Well, I guess, almost all of my grades were A's but I got terrible grades my last semester.
>
> *Therapist:* What were your grades then?
>
> *Patient:* I got two A's and two B's.
>
> *Therapist:* Since your grade average would seem to me to come out to almost all A's, why do you think you won't be able to get into the university?
>
> *Patient:* Because of competition being so tough.
>
> *Therapist:* Have you found out what the average grades are for admissions to the college?
>
> *Patient:* Well, somebody told me that a B+ average would suffice.
>
> *Therapist:* Isn't your average better than that?
>
> *Patient:* I guess so.
>
> *(Beck et al., 1979, p. 153)*

Phase 3: Identifying Distorted Thinking and Negative Biases As clients begin to recognize the fallacies in their automatic thoughts, cognitive therapists show them how illogical thinking processes may be contributing to these thoughts. The depressed student, for example, was using *dichotomous* (all-or-nothing) thinking when she concluded that any grade lower than A was "terrible." The therapists also guide clients to recognize that almost all their interpretations of events have a negative bias and to change that biased style of interpretation.

Phase 4: Altering Primary Attitudes In the final phase of treatment, therapists help clients to change their primary attitudes, the central beliefs that have predisposed them to depression in the first place. As part of the process, therapists often encourage clients to test their attitudes, as in the following therapy discussion:

> *Therapist:* On what do you base this belief that you can't be happy without a man?
>
> *Patient:* I was really depressed for a year and a half when I didn't have a man.
>
> *Therapist:* Is there another reason why you were depressed?
>
> *Patient:* As we discussed, I was looking at everything in a distorted way. But I still don't know if I could be happy if no one was interested in me.

Therapist: I don't know either. Is there a way we could find out?

Patient: Well, as an experiment, I could not go out on dates for a while and see how I feel.

Therapist: I think that's a good idea. Although it has its flaws, the experimental method is still the best way currently available to discover the facts. You're fortunate in being able to run this type of experiment. Now, for the first time in your adult life you aren't attached to a man. If you find you can be happy without a man, this will greatly strengthen you and also make your future relationships all the better.

(Beck et al., 1979, pp. 253–254)

Effectiveness of Cognitive Therapy Over the past three decades, literally hundreds of studies have concluded that cognitive therapy helps with depression (Beck, 1997, 1991; Hollon & Beck, 1994; Pace & Dixon, 1993). Mildly to severely depressed people who receive this therapy improve significantly more than those who receive placebos or no treatments at all, and approximately 50 to 60 percent show a total elimination of depressive symptoms.

	Monday	Tuesday	Wednesday	Thursday	Fr
9–10		Go to grocery store	Go to museum	Get ready to go out	
10–11		Go to grocery store	Go to museum	Drive to Doctor's appointment	
11–12	Doctor's appointment	Call friend	Go to museum	Doctor's appointment	
12–1	Lunch	Lunch	Lunch at museum		
1–2	Drive home	Clean front room	Drive home		
2–3	Read novel	Clean front room	Washing		
3–4	Clean bedroom	Read novel	Washing		
4–5	Watch TV	Watch TV	Watch TV		
5–6	Fix dinner	Fix dinner	Fix dinner		
6–7	Eat with family	Eat with Family	Eat with family		
7–8	Clean kitchen	Clean kitchen	Clean kitchen		
8–12	Watch TV, read novel, sleep	Call sister, watch TV, read novel, sleep	Work on rug, read novel, sleep		

Figure 9-2 *In the early stages of cognitive therapy for depression, the client and therapist prepare a weekly activity schedule such as this. Activities as simple as watching television and calling a friend are specified. (Adapted from Beck et al., 1979, p. 122.)*

Sunlight can sometimes play an important role in recovery from depression. This may be because light inspires hope, or because it affects individuals biologically. One study found that depressed patients who stayed in sunny hospital rooms recovered faster than similar patients in dull rooms (Beauchemin & Hayes, 1996). Here a whisper of sun reaches a woman in a spare room at an Alabama mental hospital. This wing of the hospital was recently closed.

Clients who respond display steady improvements in their cognitive functioning over the course of therapy, including progressively less pessimism and positive changes in self-concept; and their improvements correlate strongly with improvements in depression (Pace & Dixon, 1993).

In view of this strong research support, increasing numbers of therapists have adopted the cognitive approach (Hollon et al., 1993). Some have developed group programs to make the therapy more readily available to greater numbers of people (Bristow & Bright, 1995; Eidelson, 1985). Thus far, however, research suggests that cognitive therapy may be less effective in groups than in individual sessions (Rush & Watkins, 1981).

Sociocultural Therapies

As we observed in Chapter 8, sociocultural theorists propose that depression can often be traced to the broader social structure in which people live and the roles they are required to play. Perhaps the most effective sociocultural approach to unipolar depression is ***interpersonal psychotherapy (IPT),*** a treatment developed during the 1980s by clinical researchers Gerald Klerman and Myrna Weissman. Another important approach is ***couple therapy.*** The concepts and techniques used in these approaches often borrow from the psychodynamic, humanistic, behavioral, and cognitive perspectives, but they

are used primarily to clarify and address the critical social context (Klerman & Weissman, 1992; Klerman et al., 1984; Weissman et al., 1982).

Interpersonal Psychotherapy IPT holds that any of four interpersonal problem areas may lead to depression and must be addressed: interpersonal loss, interpersonal role dispute, interpersonal role transition, and interpersonal deficits. Over the course of twelve to sixteen sessions, IPT therapists cover each area that is contributing to a client's depression.

First, depressed persons may, as psychodynamic theorists suggest, be experiencing a grief reaction over ***interpersonal loss,*** the loss of a significant loved one. In such cases, IPT therapists encourage clients to explore their relationship with the lost person and express angry feelings toward the departed. Eventually, clients formu-

BOX 9-2 Role Transitions: "Suddenly I'm the Adult?"

Richard Cohen

In this essay, which originally appeared in Psychology Today, *May 1987, Richard Cohen discusses the feelings that have accompanied significant changes in his life. Although Cohen handles the changes with humor and perspective, the interpersonal role transitions posed by such changes may, according to interpersonal psychotherapists, cause depression for some people and even require treatment.*

Several years ago, my family gathered on Cape Cod for a weekend. My parents were there, my sister and her daughter, too, two cousins, and, of course, my wife, my son and me. We ate at one of those restaurants where the menu is scrawled on a blackboard held by a chummy waiter and had a wonderful time. With dinner concluded, the waiter set the check down in the middle of the table. That's when it happened. My father did not reach for the check.

In fact, my father did nothing. Conversation continued. Finally, it dawned on me. Me! I was supposed to pick up the check. After all these years, after hundreds of restaurant meals with my parents, after a lifetime of thinking of my father as the one with the bucks, it had all changed. I reached for the check and whipped out my American Express card. My view of myself was suddenly altered. With a stroke of a pen, I was suddenly an adult.

Some people mark off their life in years, others in events. I am one of the latter, and I think of some events as rites of passage. I did not become a young man at a particular year, like 13, but when a kid strolled into the store where I worked and called me "mister," I turned around to see whom he was calling. He repeated it several times—"Mister, mister"—looking straight at me. The realization hit like a punch: Me! He was talking to me. I was suddenly a mister.

There have been other milestones. The cops of my youth always seemed to be big, even huge, and of course they were older than I was. Then one day they were neither. In fact, some of them were kids—short kids at that. Another milestone.

The day comes when suddenly you realize that all the football players in the game you're watching are younger than you. Instead of being big men, they are merely big kids. With that milestone goes the fantasy that someday, maybe, you too could be a player—maybe not a football player but certainly a baseball player. I had a good eye as a kid—not much power, but a keen eye—and I always thought I could play the game. One day I realized that I couldn't. Without having ever reached the hill, I was over it.

For some people, the most momentous milestone is the death of a parent. This happened recently to a friend of mine. With the burial of his father came the realization that he had moved up a notch. Of course, he had known all along that this would happen, but until the funeral, the knowledge seemed theoretical at best. As long as one of your parents is alive, you stay in some way a kid. At the very least, there remains at least one person whose love is unconditional.

For women, a milestone is reached when they can no longer have children. The loss of a life, the inability to create one—they are variations on the same theme. For a childless woman who could control everything in life but the clock, this milestone is a cruel one indeed.

I count other, less serious milestones—like being audited by the Internal Revenue Service. As the auditor caught mistake after mistake, I sat there pretending that really knowing about taxes was for adults. I, of course, was still a kid. The auditor was buying none of it.

late new ways of remembering the lost person, and they are also expected to develop new relationships to "fill the empty space."

Second, depressed people often find themselves in the midst of an ***interpersonal role dispute.*** Role disputes occur when two people have different expectations of their relationship and of the role each should play. Such disputes may lead to smoldering resentments and to depressed feelings. IPT therapists help clients to explore any role disputes they may be involved in and to develop strategies for solving them.

Depressed people may also be experiencing ***interpersonal role transition,*** brought about by significant life changes such as divorce or the birth of a child. They may feel unable to cope with the role change that accompanies the life change (see Box 9-2). In such cases IPT therapists help clients review and evaluate their old roles, explore the opportunities offered by the new roles,

I was a taxpayer, an adult. She all but said, Go to jail.

There have been others. I remember the day when I had a ferocious argument with my son and realized that I could no longer bully him. He was too big and the days when I could just pick him up and take him to his room/isolation cell were over. I needed to persuade, reason. He was suddenly, rapidly, older. The conclusion was inescapable: So was I.

One day you go to your friends' weddings. One day you celebrate the birth of their kids. One day you see one of their kids driving, and one day those kids have kids of their own. One day you meet at parties and then at weddings and then at funerals. It all happens in one day. Take my word for it.

I never thought I would fall asleep in front of the television set as my father did, and as my friends' fathers did, too. I remember my parents and their friends talking about insomnia and they sounded like members of a different species. Not able to sleep? How ridiculous. Once it was all I did. Once it was what I did best. I never thought that I would eat a food that did not agree with me. Now I meet them all the time. I thought I would never go to the beach and not swim. I spent all of August at the beach and never once went into the ocean. I never thought I would appreciate opera, but now the pathos, the schmaltz and, especially, the combination of voice and music appeal to me. The deaths of Mimi and Tosca move me, and they die in my home as often as I can manage it.

I never thought I would prefer to stay home instead of going to a party, but now I find myself passing parties up. I used to think that people who watched birds were weird, but this summer I found myself watching them, and maybe I'll get a book on the subject. I yearn for a religious conviction I never thought I'd want, exult in my heritage anyway, feel close to ancestors long gone and echo my father in arguments with my son. I still lose.

One day I made a good toast. One day I handled a headwaiter. One day I bought a house. One day—what a day!—I became a father, and not too long after that I picked up the check for my own. I thought then and there it was a rite of passage for me. Not until I got older did I realize that it was one for him, too. Another milestone.

and develop the social support system and skills the new roles require.

The fourth interpersonal problem area that may accompany depression is the existence of some ***interpersonal deficits,*** such as extreme shyness, insensitivity to others' needs, and social awkwardness. According to Klerman and Weissman, many depressed people have experienced severely disrupted relationships as children and have failed to establish intimate relationships as adults. IPT therapists may use psychodynamic procedures to help these clients recognize and overcome the past traumas that have inhibited their social development. They may also use behavioral techniques such as social skills training and assertiveness training to improve clients' social effectiveness. In the following therapy discussion, the therapist encourages the client to recognize the effect his demeanor has on others.

> *Client:* *(After a long pause with eyes downcast, a sad facial expression, and slumped posture)* People always make fun of me. I guess I'm just the type of guy who really was meant to be a loner, damn it. *(Deep sigh)*
>
> *Therapist:* Could you do that again for me?
>
> *Client:* What?
>
> *Therapist:* The sigh, only a bit deeper.
>
> *Client:* Why? *(Pause)* Okay, but I don't see what . . . okay. *(Client sighs again and smiles)*
>
> *Therapist:* Well, that time you smiled, but mostly when you sigh and look so sad I get the feeling that I better leave you alone in your misery, that I should walk on eggshells and not get too chummy or I might hurt you even more.
>
> *Client:* *(A bit of anger in his voice)* Well, excuse me! I was only trying to tell you how I felt.
>
> *Therapist:* I know you felt miserable, but I also got the message that you wanted to keep me at a distance, that I had no way to reach you.
>
> *Client:* *(Slowly)* I feel like a loner, I feel that even you don't care about me—making fun of me.
>
> *Therapist:* I wonder if other folks need to pass this test, too?
>
> *(Young & Beier, 1984, p. 270)*

Many studies indicate that IPT and related interpersonal approaches are effective treatments for mild to severe cases of unipolar depression (Stuart & O'Hara, 1995; Elkin, 1994; Mason et al., 1994). In these studies, symptoms have almost totally disappeared in 50 to 60 percent of depressed clients who receive IPT treatment, a success rate similar to that achieved by cognitive therapy (see Table 9-3). One study compared the progress of depressed clients who received sixteen weeks of IPT with that of control clients who did not (Klerman & Weissman, 1992; Weissman et al., 1979). In addition to experiencing a greater reduction of depressive symptoms than the control clients, the IPT clients were functioning more effectively in their social and family activities a year later. On the basis of such findings, IPT is considered appropriate for use with depressed clients, particularly those who are struggling with social conflicts or who are negotiating a transition in their career or social role (APA, 1993).

Couple Therapy As we observed in Chapter 8, depression can often be the result of marital discord, and recovery from depression is often slower for persons who do not have a supportive spouse (Bruce & Kim, 1992; Barnett & Gotlib, 1988). In fact, as many as half of all depressed clients may be in a dysfunctional relationship. Thus it is not surprising that ***couple therapy*** has also been used in many cases of depression.

Therapists who engage in ***behavioral marital therapy*** help spouses identify and change detrimental marital behavior by teaching them specific communication and problem-solving skills (Lebow & Gurman, 1995). Research suggests that this and similar approaches may be as effective as individual cognitive therapy and interpersonal psychotherapy in alleviating depression when the client's marriage is indeed laden with conflict (Prince & Jacobson, 1995; Teichman et al., 1995; Jacobson et al., 1993). Moreover, such clients are more likely than clients in individual therapy to express a significant improvement in marital satisfaction after treatment.

Biological Treatments

Like several of the psychological and sociocultural therapies, biological treatments often bring great relief to people with unipolar depression. In most cases, biological treatment means antidepressant drugs, but for many depressed persons—especially those who do not respond to other forms of treatment—it sometimes means electroconvulsive therapy.

Electroconvulsive Therapy One of the most controversial forms of treatment for depression is ***electroconvulsive therapy,*** or ***ECT*** (Fink, 1992; Breggin, 1979). One patient describes his experience:

Strapped to a stretcher, you are wheeled into the ECT room. The electroshock machine is in clear view. It is a solemn occasion; there is little talk. The nurse, the attendant, and the anesthetist go about their preparation methodically. Your psychiatrist enters. He seems quite matter-of-fact, businesslike—perhaps a bit rushed. "Everything is going to be just fine. I have given hundreds of these treatments. No one has ever died." You flinch inside. Why did he say that? But there is no time to dwell on it. They are ready. The electrodes are in place. The long clear plastic tube running from the bottle above ends with a needle in your vein. An injection is given. Suddenly—terrifyingly—you can no longer breathe; and then. . . . You awaken in your hospital bed. There is a soreness in your legs and a bruise on your arm you can't explain. You are confused to find it so difficult to recover memories. Finally, you stop struggling in the realization that you have no memory for what has transpired. You were scheduled to have ECT, but something must have happened. Perhaps it was postponed. But the nurse keeps coming over to you and asking, "How are you feeling?" You think to yourself: "It must have been given"; but you can't remember. Confused and uncomfortable, you begin the dread return to the ECT room. You have forgotten, but something about it remains. You are frightened.

(Taylor, 1975)

Clinicians and patients alike vary greatly in their opinions of ECT (see Table 9-4). Some consider it a safe biological procedure with minimal risks; others believe it to be an extreme measure that can cause striking memory loss and even neurological damage. Despite this heated controversy, ECT is still used, because it is an effective and fast-acting intervention for severe unipolar depression (APA, 1993; Weiner & Coffey, 1988).

The Treatment Procedure In an ECT procedure, two electrodes are attached to the patient's head, and an electrical current of 65 to 140 volts is sent through the brain for half a second or less. In ***bilateral ECT*** one electrode is applied to each side of the forehead, and the current passes through the brain's frontal lobes. A method used increasingly in recent years is ***unilateral ECT,*** in which the electrodes are placed so that the current passes through only one side of the brain.

The electrical current causes a ***convulsion,*** or brain seizure, that lasts from 25 seconds to a few minutes. The convulsion itself, not any accompanying pain, appears to be the key to ECT's effectiveness (Ottosson, 1985, 1960; Weiner, 1984). Patients can therefore be put to sleep with barbiturates before ECT is administered with no reduction of therapeutic impact. Use of a muscle relaxant is also routine, to minimize the danger of physical injury from flailing about during the convulsion. Patients awaken approximately ten minutes after the current is applied. A typical program of ECT for depressed persons consists of six to nine treatments administered over two to four weeks (Lerer et al., 1995). Most patients then feel

TABLE 9-3 Mood Disorders and Treatment

Disorder	*Most Effective Treatments*	*Average Length of Treatment*	*Percent Improved by Treatment*
Major depressive disorder	Cognitive or interpersonal psychotherapy	20 weeks	60
	Antidepressant drugs	20 weeks	60
	ECT	2 weeks	60
Dysthymic disorder	Cognitive or interpersonal psychotherapy	20 weeks	60
	Antidepressant drugs	20 weeks	60
Bipolar I disorder	Antibipolar drugs	Indefinite	60
Bipolar II disorder	Antibipolar drugs	Indefinite	60
Cyclothymic disorder	Psychotherapy or antibipolar drugs	20 weeks to Indefinite	Unknown

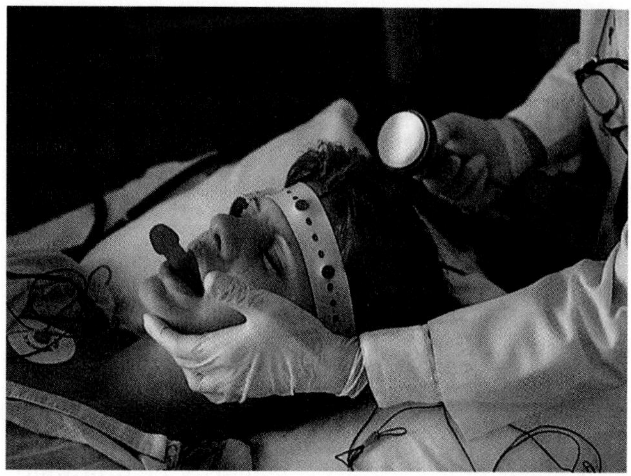

Patients given ECT today are administered barbiturate drugs to help them sleep, muscle relaxants to prevent convulsive jerks of the body and broken bones, and oxygen to guard against brain damage. To reduce memory loss, applications of electricity are often unilateral rather than bilateral.

less depressed than before the treatment was started (Fink, 1992).

The Origins of ECT The discovery that electric shock can be therapeutic was made by accident. Its history can be traced to 1785, when Dr. W. Oliver, physician to England's royal family, was treating a patient with "mental difficulties." He accidentally gave the man an overdose of *camphor*, a widely used stimulant, and the patient went into a coma and had convulsions. When the patient awakened, he seemed quite improved. This accident led a few doctors at the time to conclude that convulsions can cure psychological problems, and they began to give large doses of camphor to other patients with mental disturbances.

In a similar vein, a Hungarian physician named Joseph von Meduna came to believe in the early 1930s that people with schizophrenia or other psychotic disorders rarely suffered from epilepsy and that people with epilepsy rarely were psychotic. Believing that the convulsions of epilepsy somehow prevented psychosis, Meduna reintroduced camphor-caused convulsions as a form of treatment for psychosis.

Meduna was leaping to conclusions. A correlation between convulsions and lack of psychotic symptoms does not necessarily imply that one event causes the other. Moreover, subsequent research has challenged his observation that psychosis is inversely related to epilepsy. Nevertheless, Meduna pursued the treatment. Because camphor was slow acting, very powerful, and often unpredictable in its impact, sometimes even causing death, Meduna eventually changed to a derivative of camphor, ***metrazol.*** But metrazol, too, was very dangerous for some patients and unreliable for others.

TABLE 9-4 Arguments for and Against Electroconvulsive Therapy

Arguments For ECT	*Arguments Against ECT*
Theory of ECT is based on correcting a malfunctioning neurophysiological mechanism.	ECT is not corrective and works to the contrary, causing serious neurological destruction.
ECT's immediate effectiveness is supported by a large body of well-documented research.	An equally large body of contradictory research can be juxtaposed; ECT's long-term application is associated with a high incidence of relapse.
Undesired effects are much less troublesome from ECT than from medication in many instances; such effects are typically transient and dissipate over time.	Undesired effects are more profound than acknowledged; potential exists for cognitive dysfunction, personality alteration, and permanent organic changes with repeated treatment.
ECT is a useful intervention in life-threatening situations such as suicidal intent.	No data exist to defend ECT's utility in life-threatening situations.
State regulations regarding voluntary informed consent are too restrictive and legally impede the necessary administration of ECT under certain conditions.	Specific guidelines for ensuring full informed consent are actually inconsistent from state to state and do not necessarily provide the patient with all essential details surrounding treatment effects and outcome.

Source: Taylor & Carroll, 1987, p. 755.

About the same time, Manfred Sakel, a Viennese physician, developed another technique for inducing convulsions in psychotic patients—***insulin coma therapy*** (Sakel, 1938). When he gave his patients large doses of insulin, their blood sugar dropped so dramatically that they went into a coma. This treatment, too, was helpful to some patients, but again quite dangerous, causing intense bodily stress, physical complications, and sometimes death.

A few years later, an Italian psychiatrist named Ugo Cerletti discovered that he could induce seizures in dogs by attaching electrodes to their mouths and rectums and applying voltage. Still, he feared that placing electrodes on their heads, or on the heads of human beings, would be fatal. One day, however, he visited a slaughterhouse and observed that before slaughtering hogs with a knife, butchers clamped the animals' heads with metallic tongs and applied an electrical current. The hogs fell unconscious and had convulsions, but they did not die from the current itself. Their comas merely made it easier for the butchers to kill them by other means. Cerletti wrote, "At this point I felt we could venture to experiment on man." Cerletti and his colleague Lucio Bini (1938) soon developed electroconvulsive therapy as a treatment for psychosis. As one might expect, much uncertainty and confusion accompanied their first clinical application of ECT. Did experimenters have the right to impose such an untested treatment against a patient's will?

> The schizophrenic arrived by train from Milan without a ticket or any means of identification. Physically healthy, he was bedraggled and alternately was mute or expressed himself in incomprehensible gibberish made up of odd neologisms. The patient was brought in but despite their vast animal experience there was great apprehension and fear that the patient might be damaged, and so the shock was cautiously set at 70 volts for one-tenth of a second. The low dosage predictably produced only a minor spasm, after which the patient burst into song. Cerletti suggested another shock at a higher voltage, and an excited and voluble discussion broke out among the spectators. . . . All of the staff objected to a further shock, protesting that the patient would probably die. Cerletti was familiar with committees and knew that postponement would inevitably mean prolonged and possibly permanent procrastination, and so he decided to proceed at 110 volts for one-half second. However, before he could do so, the patient who had heard but so far not participated in the discussion sat up and pontifically proclaimed in clear Italian without hint of jargon, "Non una seconda! Mortifera!" (Not again! It will kill me!). Professor Bini hesitated but gave the order to proceed. After recovery, Bini asked the patient "What has been happening to you?" and the man replied "I don't know; perhaps I've been asleep." He remained jargon-free and gave a complete account of himself, and was discharged completely recovered after 11 complete and 3 incomplete treatments over a course of 2 months.
>
> *(Brandon, 1981, pp. 8–9)*

ECT soon became popular and was applied to a wide range of psychological problems, as new techniques so often are. Its effectiveness with depressive disorders in particular became quite apparent. Ironically, however, doubts were soon raised concerning its usefulness for psychosis, and many researchers have judged it ineffective for most psychotic disorders (Taylor & Carroll, 1987).

Changes in ECT Procedures Although Cerletti gained international fame for this procedure, eventually he abandoned ECT and spent his later years seeking alternative treatments for mental disorders (Karon, 1985). The reason: he abhorred the broken bones, memory loss, confusion, and neural damage that the convulsions caused. Other clinicians have stayed with the procedure, however, and have modified it to reduce undesirable consequences (Kevube et al., 1996; Fink, 1992, 1987). As we noted earlier, today's practitioners give patients muscle relaxants to reduce the danger of fractures or dislocations. They also use short-term anesthetics (barbiturates) to put patients to sleep during the procedure, thus reducing their terror (Fink, 1992). As a result of these changes, ECT is medically more complex than it used to be, but also less dangerous and somewhat less frightening (Fink, 1992; Hamilton, 1986).

Patients who receive ECT, particularly bilateral ECT, typically have difficulty remembering the periods of time just before and after their ECT treatments, but most of this memory loss usually clears up in a matter of months (Calev et al., 1995, 1991; Squire & Slater, 1983). Some patients may also experience gaps in more distant memory, and this form of amnesia can be permanent (Squire, 1984, 1977). Understandably, the relatively small number of people who have suffered significant permanent memory losses are often left embittered.

Effectiveness of ECT Research indicates that ECT is an effective treatment for unipolar depression. Most studies find that patients who receive ECT improve significantly more than those who receive placebos (APA, 1993; Sackeim, 1990; Wechsler et al., 1965). Overall, these studies suggest that between 60 and 70 percent of ECT patients improve (Rey & Walter, 1997). The procedure may be most effective in severe cases of depression characterized by delusions (O'Leary et al., 1995; Buchan et al., 1992).

It is not clear why ECT reduces depression. After all, it delivers a broad insult to the brain that causes neurons

BOX 9-3 ECT and the Law

Since its introduction in the 1930s, electroconvulsive therapy has increasingly come under the scrutiny of courts and state legislatures throughout the United States. The primary reason: the clinical field has done a poor job of regulating the use of this powerful and frightening procedure. When self-regulation fails, the government and legal system typically step in.

During ECT's first decade, psychiatrists and clinical researchers were left on their own to apply, experiment with, and modify the procedure (Winslade, 1988). Although this work often yielded impressive results, it also led to numerous complaints by patients and some clinicians (Rothman, 1985). In 1947 a psychiatric task force, the Group for the Advancement of Psychiatry, finally conducted an investigation into "shock therapy" and issued a critical report noting that ECT was being used indiscriminately and excessively, often to punish and control uncooperative patients (GAP, 1947). The next official report on ECT did not appear until 1978, more than thirty years later. Then the American Psychiatric Association issued an endorsement of ECT for severe depression when drugs have failed, and made detailed recommendations for informing patients about the procedure and obtaining their consent to it (Winslade, 1988; Winslade et al., 1984). Subsequent psychiatric reports have continued to endorse ECT for people with severe unipolar depression, particularly that accompanied by delusions (APA, 1993, 1990; Fink, 1992).

Legal regulation of ECT did not begin in earnest until the mid-1970s, when the California state legislature, responding to criticism from patients and former patients, passed a law restricting its use (Senter et al., 1984). All competent mental patients in California, both voluntary and involuntary, were granted the right to be informed about the nature of ECT and to refuse to undergo it. Many other states have since passed laws regulating ECT use. Some states require a second independent opinion by a professional that ECT is appropriate and necessary, and mandate a court hearing to determine whether an involuntary patient is competent to consent to ECT. Other states have less restrictive laws that allow hospital staff to override a patient's refusal of ECT simply by documenting that it is being applied for "good cause" (Senter et al., 1984).

Probably the most significant federal court decision regarding ECT has been *Wyatt* v. *Hardin*, which defined the legal standards for ECT treatments in Alabama, specifically forbidding some uses of ECT and establishing fourteen rules that severely restrict its practice (Winslade et al., 1984). This decision dictates, for example, that two psychiatrists (with the hospital director's concurrence) decide in each case that ECT is the most appropriate treatment, that a physical and neurological examination be conducted ten days before ECT, that anesthesia and muscle relaxants be used, that a psychiatrist and anesthesiologist be present during ECT, and that a single series of treatments be limited to twelve ECT sessions at most in a twelve-month period. In an effort to standardize the safe practice of ECT, the American Psychiatric Association and the National Institutes of Health have devised similar guidelines (APA, 1990, 1978; NIH, Consensus Conference, 1985).

Legal and judicial restrictions on the use of ECT have stirred heated debate in the clinical community (Cauchon, 1995). Many theorists believe that such protective measures are long overdue (Tenenbaum, 1983; Friedberg, 1975; Tien, 1975). Indeed, some of them would like to make it harder for administrators to override a patient's refusal of ECT, and some would require that all patients be given a complete description of ECT's effects before their consent is obtained, including a clear statement about the risk of some permanent memory loss (Fink, 1992; Friedberg, 1975). They are particularly disturbed by a growing trend to use ECT on elderly patients, the group most vulnerable to undesired medical effects. In fact, women in their seventies receive more ECT today than any other group (Cauchon, 1995). Other theorists believe that the laws and courts have gone too far, that such requirements as voluntary consent, professional board approval, and full disclosure often slow or prevent the therapeutic administration of ECT, leaving many patients unnecessarily depressed (Greenblatt, 1984; Tenenbaum, 1983; Kaufmann & Roth, 1981; Tien, 1975). Like the debate over the value and humaneness of ECT itself, this argument continues with no end in sight.

all over the brain to fire and all kinds of neurotransmitters to be released, and it affects many other systems throughout the body as well (Fink, 1992; Sackeim, 1988; Holaday et al., 1986).

Although research has repeatedly established the effectiveness of ECT, and although ECT techniques have improved markedly, the use of this procedure has generally declined since the 1950s. Apparently more than 100,000 patients a year underwent ECT during the 1940s and 1950s. Today as few as 30,000 to 50,000 per year are believed to receive it (Cauchon, 1995; Foderaero, 1993). Several factors have contributed to ECT's decline, including the frightening nature of the procedure and the attractive medical alternative now offered by antidepressant drugs. Yet another factor is the emergence of government restrictions guiding its use (see Box 9-3).

Antidepressant Drugs In the 1950s, two kinds of drugs were discovered that seemed to alleviate depressive symptoms: ***MAO (monoamine oxidase) inhibitors*** and ***tricyclics*** (see Table 9-5). These antidepressant drugs have recently been joined by a third group, the so-called ***second-generation antidepressants.*** Before the discovery of antidepressant drugs, the only drugs that brought any relief for depression were amphetamines. Amphetamines stimulated some depressed people to greater activity, but they did not result in greater joy.

MAO Inhibitors The effectiveness of MAO inhibitors as a treatment for unipolar depression was discovered accidentally. Physicians noted that ***iproniazid,*** a drug being tested on patients with tuberculosis, had an interesting effect on many such patients: it seemed to make them happier (Sandler, 1990). It was found to have the same effect on depressed patients (Kline, 1958; Loomer, Saunders, & Kline, 1957). Iproniazid damaged the liver, however, and sometimes caused death. Fortunately, researchers were able to create similar drugs, such as *phenelzine* (trade name *Nardil*), *isocarboxazid (Marplan)*, and *tranylcypromine (Parnate)*, that were less toxic than iproniazid but equally powerful in fighting depression. What these drugs all had in common biochemically was that they slowed the body's production of the enzyme *monoamine oxidase (MAO)*. Thus they were called ***MAO inhibitors.*** Approximately half of the mild to severely depressed patients who take MAO inhibitors are helped by them (Thase, Trivedi, & Rush, 1995; Davis, 1980; Davis et al., 1967).

During the past few decades, scientists have learned how MAO inhibitors operate on the brain and how they alleviate depression. Apparently, when the enzyme MAO interacts chemically with molecules of norepinephrine, it breaks down the neurotransmitter. MAO inhibitors block MAO from carrying out this destructive activity and thereby stop the destruction of norepinephrine. The result is a heightened level of norepinephrine activity and, in turn, the disappearance of depressive symptoms.

As clinicians have gained experience with the MAO inhibitors, they have learned that the drugs can also create serious medical problems. Apparently many of the foods we eat—including cheeses, bananas, and some wines—contain ***tyramine,*** a chemical that can raise blood pressure dangerously if too much of it accumulates (Davidson, 1992; Silver & Yudofsky, 1988). The body's enzyme MAO normally serves the beneficial role of quickly breaking tyramine down into another chemical, hence keeping blood pressure under control. Unfortunately, when MAO inhibitors are taken to combat depression, they also block the production of MAO in the liver

TABLE 9-5 Drugs That Reduce Unipolar Depression

Class/ Generic Name	*Trade Name*	*Usual Daily Maximum Oral Dose (mg)*
Monoamine oxidase inhibitors		
Isocarboxazid	Marplan	50
Phenelzine	Nardil	90
Tranylcypromine	Parnate	90
Tricyclics		
Imipramine	Tofranil	300
Amitriptyline	Elavil	300
Doxepin	Adapin Sinequan	300
Trimipramine	Surmontil	150
Desipramine	Norpramin Pertofrane	300
Nortriptyline	Aventyl Pamelor	150
Protriptyline	Vivactil	45
Second-generation antidepressants		
Maprotiline	Ludiomil	225
Amoxapine	Asendin	500
Trazodone	Desyrel	500
Clomipramine	Anafranil	225
Fluoxetine	Prozac	80
Sertraline	Zoloft	200
Paroxetine	Paxil	20
Venlafaxine	Effexor	375
Fluvoxamine	Luvox	300
Nefazodone	Serzone	600
Bupropion	Wellbutrin	450

Source: Hedaya, 1996; Physician's Desk Reference, *1994; APA, 1993.*

Regular exercise has been found to be positively linked to one's level of happiness, and exercise may help prevent or reduce feelings of depression (Diener, 1984). It is not clear, however, whether this relationship is the result of changes in biology, activity level, or cognition, or a combination of factors.

and intestines. This action allows tyramine to accumulate and puts the person in great danger of high blood pressure and perhaps sudden death (Blackwell et al., 1967).

Thus people who take MAO inhibitors must avoid any of the long list of foods that contain tyramine. These restrictions, along with other dangers associated with MAO inhibitors, have reduced clinicians' enthusiasm for these medications, especially since researchers have succeeded in developing other types of antidepressants that are safer and often more effective (Montgomery et al., 1993). Some of this lost enthusiasm has been recaptured in recent years with the discovery of new MAO inhibitors that affect only norepinephrine breakdown, not tyramine breakdown, thus reducing the dietary dangers of traditional MAO inhibitors (Lecrubier, 1995; Paykel, 1995). Some of these so-called *reversible selective MAO inhibitors* are now available in Canada and Europe but have yet to be approved for use in the United States.

Tricyclics The discovery of tricyclics in the 1950s was also accidental. Researchers were looking for a new drug to combat schizophrenia when they came upon a drug called ***imipramine*** (Kuhn, 1958). Imipramine did not turn out to be an effective treatment for schizophrenia, but it did relieve unipolar depression in many people. Imipramine (trade name *Tofranil*) and related drugs became known as ***tricyclic antidepressants*** because they all share a three-ring molecular structure. Other well-known tricyclics are *amitriptyline (Elavil), nortriptyline (Aventyl),* and *doxepin (Sinequan).*

Research has repeatedly demonstrated the effectiveness of tricyclics for treating unipolar patterns of depression. In hundreds of studies, mildly to severely depressed patients taking tricyclics have improved significantly more than similar patients taking placebos (APA, 1993; Montgomery et al., 1993). About 60 to 65 percent of patients who take these drugs are helped by them (Keller et al., 1995; Davis, 1980). The drugs improve both psychological symptoms, such as excessive guilt, and physical symptoms, such as poor appetite (Worthington et al., 1995). Numerous case reports have also described the successful impact of these drugs. The case of Derek, whom we met in Chapter 8, is typical of the glowing reviews tricyclics often receive:

> Derek might have continued living his battleship-gray life had it not been for the local college. One winter Derek signed up for an evening course called "The Use and Abuse of Psychoactive Drugs" because he wanted to be able to provide accurate background information in future newspaper articles on drug use among high school and college students. The course covered psychiatric as well as recreational drugs. When the professor listed the symptoms of affective mood disorders on the blackboard, Derek had a flash of recognition. Perhaps he suffered from depression with melancholia.
>
> Derek then consulted with a psychiatrist, who confirmed his suspicion and prescribed imipramine. A week later, Derek was sleeping until his alarm went off. Two weeks later, at 9:00 A.M. he was writing his column and making difficult decisions about editorials on sensitive topics. He started writing some feature stories on drugs just because he was interested in the subject. Writing was more fun than it had been in years. His images of his own violent death disappeared. His wife found him more responsive. He conversed with her enthusiastically and answered her questions without the long delays that had so tried her patience.
>
> *(Lickey & Gordon, 1991, p. 185)*

Studies also suggest that depressed people who stop taking tricyclics immediately after obtaining relief have as much as a 50 percent chance of relapse within a year (Montgomery et al., 1993). If, however, patients continue to take the drugs at full dose for around five months after being free of depressive symptoms ("continuation therapy"), their chances of relapse decrease considerably (Kocsis et al., 1995; Montgomery et al., 1993, 1988). In fact, several recent studies have revealed that patients who take these antidepressant drugs at full dosage for at least three to five years after initial improvement ("maintenance therapy") may reduce their risk of relapse even more. As a result, many clinicians keep certain patients on antidepressant drugs indefinitely (Franchini et al., 1997; Kupfer, 1995; Frank et al., 1992).

Many researchers have concluded that tricyclics alleviate depression by acting on neurotransmitter "reuptake" mechanisms (Goodwin, 1992; McNeal & Cimbolic, 1986). We saw earlier that a message is carried from a sending neuron across the synaptic space to a receiving neuron by means of a neurotransmitter released from the nerve ending of the sending neuron. However, there is a complication in this process. While the nerve ending is releasing a neurotransmitter, a pumplike mechanism in the same ending is trying to recapture it. The purpose of this mechanism is to prevent the neurotransmitter from remaining in the synapse too long and repeatedly stimulating the receiving neuron. This pumplike reuptake mechanism may be too successful in some people, causing too great a reduction of norepinephrine or serotonin activity and hence of neural firing. These reductions may, in turn, result in a clinical picture of depression. Studies have indicated that tricyclics act to *block* this reuptake process (see Figure 9-3), thus increasing neurotransmitter activity (Goodwin, 1992; Iversen, 1965).

While many researchers believe that this is why tricyclics are able to alleviate unipolar depression, others have questioned whether the reuptake mechanism is indeed the key to the drugs' effectiveness (Charney & Heninger, 1983; Sulser et al., 1978). Critics have observed that although tricyclics inhibit the reuptake process immediately upon being absorbed into the blood, the symptoms of depression usually continue unabated for at least seven to fourteen days after drug therapy is initiated. If the drugs act immediately to increase norepinephrine and serotonin efficiency, why the lag in clinical improvement?

There is now growing evidence that when tricyclics are first ingested, they actually *slow down* the activity of the neurons that use norepinephrine and serotonin (Gardner, 1996; Blier & de Montigny, 1994). Granted, the reuptake mehanisms of these cells are immediately corrected, thus opening the door for more efficient transmission of the neurotransmitters, but the neurons them-

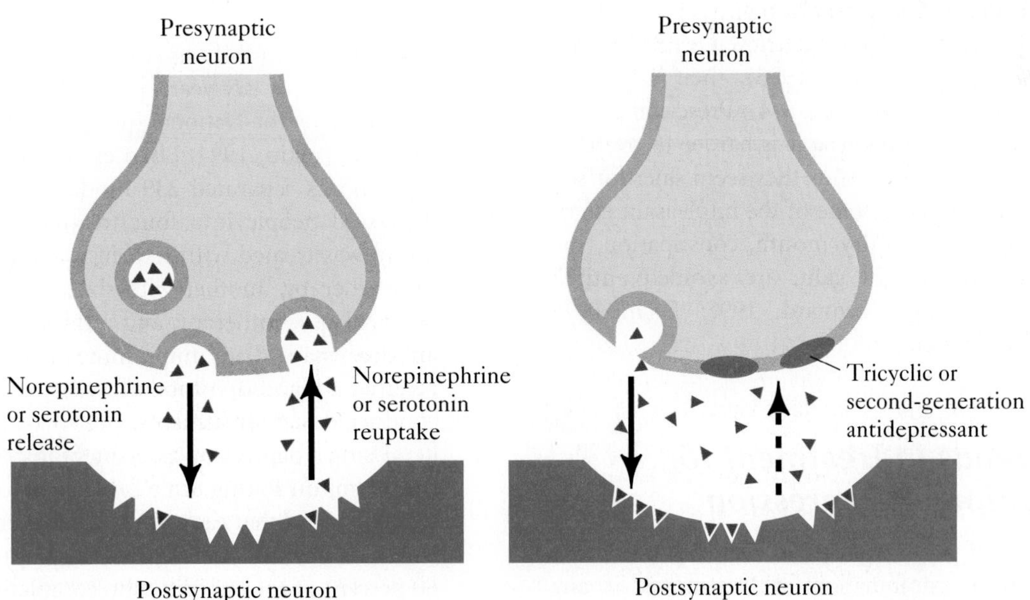

Figure 9-3 *(Left) When a neuron releases norepinephrine or serotonin from its endings, a pumplike reuptake mechanism immediately begins to recapture some of the neurotransmitter molecules before they are received by the postsynaptic (receptor) neuron. (Right) Tricyclic and most second-generation antidepressant drugs block this reuptake process, enabling more norepinephrine or serotonin to reach, and thus fire, the postsynaptic (receptor) neuron. (Adapted from Snyder, 1986, p. 106.)*

selves stop releasing as many neurotransmitters. After a week or two, the neurons adapt to the tricyclic drugs and start releasing normal amounts of the neurotransmitters once again. Now the corrections in the reuptake mechanisms can indeed help the neurotransmitters to reach receptor neurons in greater numbers, hence triggering more neural firing and producing a decrease in depression.

Today tricyclics are prescribed more often than MAO inhibitors, primarily for two reasons. First, they are less dangerous than most MAO inhibitors, and they do not require dietary restrictions (Montgomery et al., 1993). Second, patients taking tricyclics typically show higher rates of improvement than those taking MAO inhibitors (Swonger & Constantine, 1983). On the other hand, some patients respond better to MAO inhibitors and they continue to be given these drugs (Paykel, 1995; Thase et al., 1995; Goodwin, 1993).

Second-Generation Antidepressants Finally, new and effective antidepressant drugs, structurally different from the MAO inhibitors and tricyclics, have been discovered during the past several years. Most of these ***second-generation antidepressants*** have been labeled ***selective serotonin reuptake inhibitors (SSRIs),*** as they are thought to alter serotonin activity specifically, without affecting norepinephrine or other neurotransmitters or other biochemical processes (Singh & Lucki, 1993). The drugs include *fluoxetine* (trade name *Prozac*), *paroxetine (Paxil),* and *sertraline (Zoloft).*

Although the second-generation antidepressants are about equal in effectiveness to the tricyclics (Tollefson et al., 1995; Workman & Short, 1993), their sales have zoomed (see Figure 9-4 and Box 9-4). Prescribing clinicians often prefer them because it is harder to overdose on them than on tricyclics. Thus they seem safer for suicidal patients. In addition, some of the unpleasant effects of the tricyclics, such as dry mouth, constipation, impaired vision, and weight gain, are avoided entirely with the newer drugs (Leonard, 1997; Bech, 1995; Montgomery & Kasper, 1995).

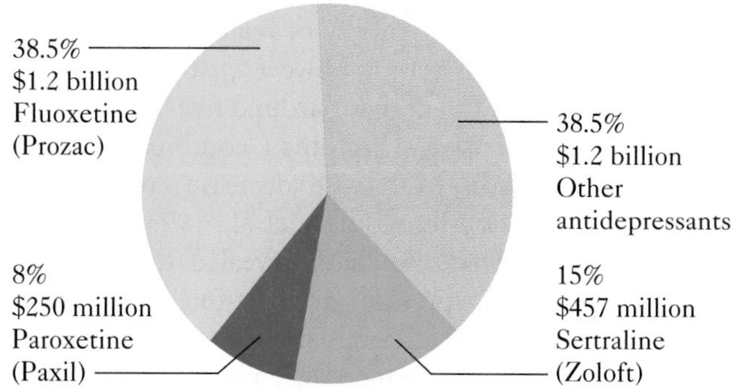

Figure 9-4 *The leading second-generation antidepressant drugs are Prozac, Zoloft, and Paxil. Introduced within the last decade, they now account for more than 60 percent of antidepressant drug sales. (Adapted from Cowley, 1994.)*

Trends in Treatment for Unipolar Depression

For most kinds of psychological disorders, no more than one treatment or combination of treatments, if any, emerges as highly successful. Unipolar depression seems to be an exception. This pattern may be effectively treated by any of several approaches: cognitive, interpersonal, or biological, as well as behavioral or couple therapy in certain circumstances. During the past decade researchers have conducted several comparative outcome studies to determine whether any of these approaches is more effective than the others. Several trends have emerged:

1. Cognitive, interpersonal, and biological therapies appear to be the most successful treatments for unipolar depression, from mild to severe. In most head-to-head comparisons, they seem to be equally and highly effective at reducing depressive symptoms (Elkin, 1994; Haaga & Beck, 1992; Elkin et al., 1989). There are indications, however, that some subpopulations of depressed patients respond better to one therapy than to another (Stewart et al., 1993).

   The most ambitious study of depression therapy to date was a six-year, $10 million investigation sponsored by the National Institute of Mental Health (NIMH) (Elkin, 1994; Elkin et al., 1989, 1985). Experimenters separated 239 moderately and severely depressed people into four treatment groups. One group was treated with sixteen weeks of Beck's cognitive therapy, another with sixteen weeks of interpersonal psychotherapy, and a third group with the antidepressant drug imipramine. The fourth group received a placebo. A total of twenty-eight therapists conducted these treatments.

   Using a depression assessment instrument called the Hamilton Rating Scale for Depression, the investigators found that each of the three therapies almost completely eliminated depressive symptoms in 50 to 60 percent of the subjects who completed treatment, whereas only 29 percent of those who received the placebo showed such improvement—a trend that also held, although somewhat less powerfully, when other assessment measures were used. These findings are consistent with those of most other comparative outcome studies (Stravynski & Greenberg, 1992; Frank et al., 1991, 1990).

The NIMH study found that drug therapy reduced depressive symptoms more quickly than the cognitive and interpersonal therapies did, but these psychotherapies had matched the drugs in effectiveness by the final four weeks of treatment. In addition, some recent studies suggest that cognitive therapy may be more effective than drug therapy at preventing relapses or recurrences of depression except when drug therapy is continued for an extended period of time (Beck, 1997; Hollon & Beck, 1994; Haaga & Beck, 1992) (see Figure 9-5). Despite the comparable or even superior showing of cognitive therapy, the 1980s and 1990s have witnessed a significant increase in the number of physicians prescribing antidepressants. The number of office visits in which an antidepressant was prescribed grew from 2.5 million in 1980 to 4.7 million in 1987 (Olfson & Klerman, 1993). That trend has continued in the 1990s with the emergence of second-generation antidepressants. Prozac alone has been prescribed for millions of people worldwide.

2. In head-to-head comparisons, depressed people who receive behavioral therapy have shown less improvement than those who receive cognitive, interpersonal, or biological therapy. Behavioral therapy has, however, proved more effective than placebo treatments or no attention at all (Emmelkamp, 1994; Shaw, 1977, 1976). Also, as we have seen, behavioral therapy is of less help to people who are severely depressed than to those with mild or moderate depression.

3. Research suggests that psychodynamic therapies are less effective than these other therapies in treating all levels of unipolar depression (Svartberg & Stiles, 1991; McLean & Hakstian, 1979). Many psychodynamic clinicians argue, however, that this system of therapy simply does not lend itself to empirical research, and its effectiveness should be judged by therapists' reports of individual recovery and progress (Bemporad, 1992).

4. Most studies have found that a combination of psychotherapy (usually cognitive or interpersonal) and drug therapy is at best modestly more helpful to depressed people than either treatment alone (Karp & Frank, 1995; Paykel, 1995; Hollon et al., 1993, 1991; Klerman & Weissman, 1992).

5. Among the biological treatments, antidepressant drugs and ECT appear to be equally effective for reducing depression, although ECT seems to act more

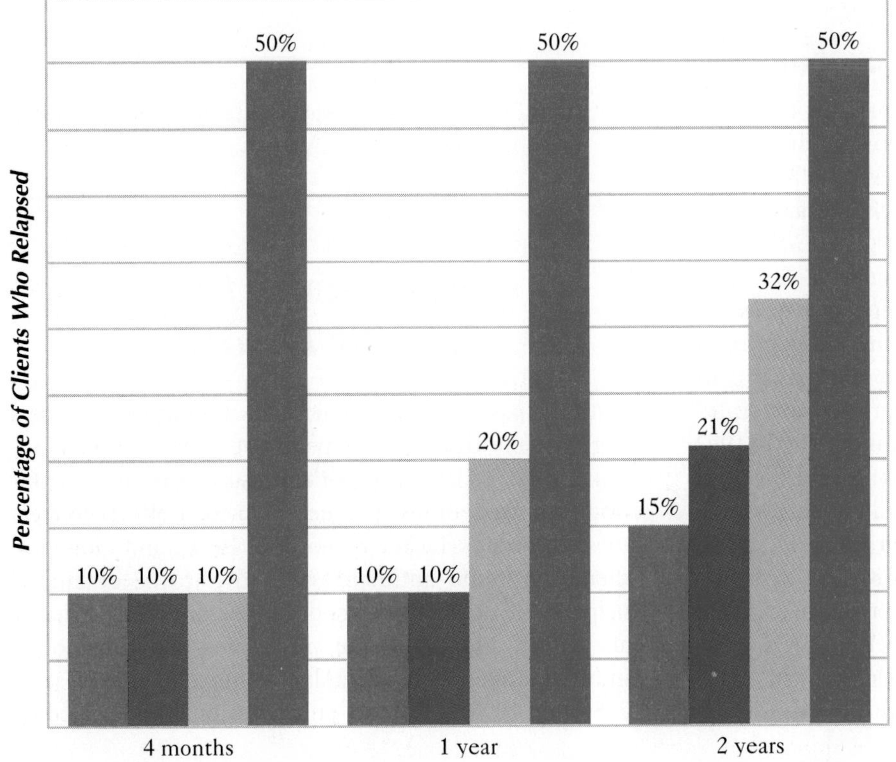

Figure 9-5 *What is the relationship between type of treatment and relapse? In one study, therapy for three groups of depressed clients was terminated after 12 weeks. The clients had received either cognitive therapy, antidepressant drug therapy, or combined cognitive-drug therapy—all deemed successful. A fourth group of clients continued to receive a year of drug therapy even after responding successfully to antidepressant drugs. After two years, subjects whose drug therapy had been stopped after initial improvement continued to have a higher relapse rate than all other subjects. (Adapted from Evans et al., 1992.)*

BOX 9-4 Flying with Prozac

First approved by the FDA late in 1987, ***fluoxetine***, better known by its trade name, ***Prozac***, has now been prescribed for millions of people throughout the world. Its enormous popularity is attributable to two factors. First, it has fewer undesired effects than MAO inhibitors and tricyclics. Thus many depressed people are able to benefit from an antidepressant drug for the first time in their lives. Second, Prozac also appears to be an effective treatment for other problems, such as eating disorders and obsessive-compulsive disorder.

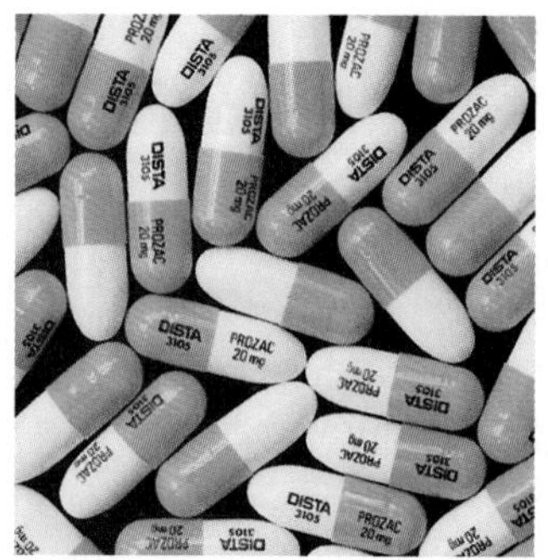

Prozac's enormous popularity has caused considerable concern in the clinical community. Many people believe that it is being glamorized and overused, and that its possible dangers have been largely ignored. The first major professional attack on Prozac came in 1990, when Martin Teicher and several colleagues at Harvard Medical School reported on six patients who had developed intense and violent suicidal tendencies after taking Prozac for two to seven weeks. The report hit the field like a tornado. It stirred an intense debate among clinicians and the public, and inspired some patients to sue the drug's manufacturer for damages. Subsequent empirical research found no clear link between Prozac and intensified suicidal thinking (Ashleigh & Fesler, 1992), but the negative publicity loosened Prozac's grip on the antidepressant drug marketplace. Tricyclic antidepressants regained some of their lost popularity, and other second-generation antidepressants, including sertraline (Zoloft) and paroxetine (Paxil), were soon being prescribed in numbers beyond their manufacturers' expectations.

The hype surrounding Prozac had begun to die down when the publication of Dr. Peter Kramer's book *Listening to Prozac* (1993) reignited interest in it. Kramer, a Rhode Island psychiatrist and a professor at Brown University, described case studies in which Prozac not only alleviated the symptoms of clinical depression but actually transformed some of his patients' personalities. Some patients were completely unaffected by the drug, but others, with long histories of social difficulties, low self-esteem, and a despondent outlook, were, according to

quickly (Fogel, 1986). Half of all patients treated by either intervention, however, relapse within a year unless the initial treatment is followed up by continuing drug treatment or by psychotherapy (Fink, 1992; Prien, 1992).

When clinicians today consider a biological treatment for mild to severe unipolar depression, they generally prescribe one of the antidepressant medications. They are not likely to refer patients for ECT unless they are severely depressed and unresponsive to all other forms of treatment (Fink, 1992, 1988). Studies suggest that ECT is helpful for 50 to 80 percent of the severely depressed patients who do not respond to antidepressant drugs (APA, 1993; Avery & Lubrano, 1979; Fink, 1978). If a depressed patient seems to be a high suicide risk, the clinician may consider referring him or her for ECT treatment even sooner (Fink, 1992; Brown, 1974; Hurwitz, 1974). Yet no studies have clearly indicated that ECT actually thwarts suicide (Frankel, 1984; Friedberg, 1975).

Treatments for Bipolar Disorders

Until the past few decades, people with bipolar disorders were usually destined to spend their lives on an emotional roller coaster. Psychotherapists of varying orientations reported almost no success in their efforts to treat these disorders (Lickey & Gordon, 1991), and biological therapists found antidepressant drugs to be of limited help for the depressive episodes of the disorders (Prien et al., 1974). Moreover, the antidepressant drugs often induced a manic episode (Altshuler et al., 1995; Dilsaver & Swann, 1995). ECT, too, only occasionally alleviated ei-

Kramer, able to adopt new patterns of interacting with the world.

Within weeks of starting Prozac, Tess settled into a satisfying dating routine. I'd never seen a patient's social life reshaped so rapidly and dramatically. Low self-worth and poor interpersonal skills—the usual causes of social awkwardness—are so deeply ingrained and difficult to influence that ordinarily change comes gradually, if ever. But Tess blossomed all at once.

Although Kramer reports twinges of uneasiness about prescribing Prozac for extended periods of time, he, like a growing number of clinicians, believes he would be withholding the bounties of science from his patients if he did not. Kramer suggests that the authentic self is revealed only as the depressive mask is removed. If Tess no longer feels like her "self" when she goes off the medication, and decides to continue taking the drug indefinitely, who is he to claim she should be naturally unhappy?

The public's enthusiastic response to Kramer's book has alarmed many clinical professionals. Some are concerned that Kramer is overstating Prozac's effectiveness. They argue that the drug is no more effective than any other antidepressant and hardly changes anyone's personality; it just has fewer undesired effects than the others. As one person said after taking Prozac for depression, "I have my ability to not snap at people back, my energy back . . . [but] I don't feel like Superman, and I still can't stand parties" (Toufexis, 1993). Others are concerned that extended Prozac therapy may interfere with the adaptive aspects of suffering or even despair. Finally, some professionals are concerned that Prozac will do away with the human vulnerabilities that people need in order to create and to grow.

Kramer's response is that by increasing some people's resilience, Prozac enables them to participate more fully in life. He finds the chemical's success both exciting and unnerving, as it infringes on the realm that once belonged to the psychotherapist alone. In many cases he has found a combination of traditional person-to-person psychotherapy and drug therapy to be the most effective treatment, and he believes that these patients would not have done so well on drugs alone. Nevertheless, he has observed in some of his patients "a kernel of vulnerability that the psychotherapy did not touch" but that responded to drug intervention.

Vulnerability, anxiety, guilt, sadness . . . are these essential parts of what it means to be a human being? Dr. Peter Kramer says perhaps they are not. Conceding that the moral implications of Prozac are complex, he argues that its discovery will be as impossible to ignore as Freud's discovery of the unconscious. At the very least, this drug is proving to be just as controversial.

ther the depressive or manic episodes of bipolar disorders (Jefferson & Greist, 1994; Black et al., 1987).

Lithium Therapy

The substance ***lithium*** has so dramatically changed this gloomy picture that many people view the silvery-white element—found in various simple mineral salts throughout the natural world—as a true miracle drug. The case of Anna, which dates from the 1960s, when lithium was still considered an experimental drug, shows the extraordinary impact this drug can have.

> Anna was a 21-year-old college student. Before she became ill, Anna was sedate and polite, perhaps even a bit prim. During the fall of her sophomore year at college, she had an episode of mild depression that began when she received a C on a history paper she had worked quite hard on. The same day she received a sanctimonious letter from her father reminding her of the financial hardships he was undergoing to send her to college. He warned her to stick to her books and not to play around with men. Anna became discouraged. She doubted that she deserved her parents' sacrifice. Anna's depression did not seem unusual to her roommate, to her other friends, or even to Anna herself. It seemed a natural reaction to her father's unreasonable letter and her fear that she could not live up to the standards he set. In retrospect, this mild depression was the first episode of her bipolar illness.
>
> Several months later, Anna became restless, angry, and obnoxious. She talked continuously and rapidly, jumping from one idea to another. Her speech was filled with rhymes, puns, and sexual innuendoes. During Christmas vacation, she made frequent and unwelcome sexual overtures to her brother's friend in the presence of her entire family. When Anna's mother asked her to behave more politely, Anna began to cry and then slapped her mother across the mouth. Anna

did not sleep that night. She sobbed. Between sobs she screamed that no one understood her problems, and no one would even try. The next day, Anna's family took her to the hospital. She was given chlorpromazine which calmed her. When she was discharged two weeks later, she was less angry and no longer assaultive. But she was not well and did not go back to school. Her thought and speech were still hypomanic. She had an exaggerated idea of her attractiveness and expected men to fall for her at the first smile. She was irritated when they ignored her attentions. Depressive symptoms were still mixed with the manic ones. She often cried when her bids for attention were not successful or when her parents criticized her dress or behavior.

Anna returned to school the following fall but suffered another depressive episode, followed by another attack of mania within seven months. She had to withdraw from school and enter the hospital. This time, Anna was fortunate to enter a research unit that was authorized to use lithium. The psychiatrists diagnosed her illness as bipolar disorder. Because she was so agitated, they began treatment with chlorpromazine as well as lithium. The initial sedative action of the chlorpromazine rapidly calmed her agitation, and this drug was discontinued after only a few days. As the effects of chlorpromazine subsided, the lithium began to take effect. After seventeen days on lithium, Anna's behavior was quite normal. She was attractively and modestly dressed for her psychiatric interviews. Earlier, she had been sloppily seductive; hair in disarray, half-open blouse, smeared lipstick, bright pink rouge on her cheeks, and bright green make-up on her eyelids. With the help of lithium, she gained some ability to tolerate frustration. During the first week of her hospital stay, she had screamed at a nurse who would not permit her to read late into the night in violation of the ward's 11:00 P.M. "lights out" policy. On lithium, Anna was still annoyed by this "juvenile" rule, but she controlled her anger. She gained some insight into her illness, recognizing that her manic behavior was destructive to herself and others. She also recognized the depression that was often mixed with the mania. She speculated that the mania was an attempt to cover up depression. She admitted, "Actually, when I'm high, I'm really feeling low. I need to exaggerate in order to feel more important."

Because Anna was on a research ward, the effectiveness of lithium had to be verified by removal of the drug. When she had been off lithium for four to five days, Anna began to show symptoms of both mania and depression. She threatened her psychiatrist, and as before, the threats were grandiose with sexual overtones. In a slinky voice, she warned, "I have ways to put the director of this hospital in my debt. He crawled for me before and he'll do it again. When I snap my fingers, he'll come down to this ward and squash you under his foot." Soon afterward, she threatened suicide. She later explained, "I felt so low last night that if someone had given me a knife or gun, POW." By the ninth day off lithium, Anna's speech was almost incomprehensible: "It's sad to be so putty, pretty, so much like water dripping from a faucet. . . . " Lithium therapy was reinstituted, and within about sixteen days, Anna again recovered and was discharged on lithium.

(Lickey & Gordon, 1991, pp. 236–239)

Determining the correct lithium dosage for a given patient is a delicate process, requiring regular analyses of blood and urine samples and other laboratory tests (Schou, 1997; Johnson et al., 1984). Too low a dose will have little or no effect on the bipolar mood swings, but too high a dose of lithium can result in lithium intoxication (literally, poisoning), which can cause nausea, vomiting, sluggishness, tremors, dizziness, slurred speech, and sodium imbalance, and in extreme cases seizures, kidney dysfunction, and even death (Mondimore, 1993; Abou-Saleh, 1992; Kondziela, 1984). With the correct dose, however, lithium may produce a noticeable change in mood within five to fourteen days, as it did for Anna. Some patients respond better to ***carbamazepine*** (Tegretol) or ***valproate*** (Depake), antiseizure drugs that have been discovered also to have therapeutic effects in bipolar disorders, or to a combination of antibipolar drugs and yet other drugs (Post et al., 1997; Frye et al., 1996; Guay, 1995).

Origins of Lithium Treatment The discovery that lithium effectively reduces bipolar symptoms was, like so many other medical discoveries, quite accidental. In 1949 an Australian psychiatrist, John Cade, hypothesized that manic behavior is caused by a toxic level of uric acid in the body. He set out to test this theory by injecting guinea pigs with uric acid, but first he combined it with lithium to increase its solubility.

To Cade's surprise, the guinea pigs became not manic but quite lethargic after their injections. Cade suspected that the lithium had produced this effect. When he later administered lithium to ten human beings who had mania, he discovered that it calmed and normalized their mood. Although many countries began using lithium for bipolar disorders soon after, it was not until 1970 that the U.S. Food and Drug Administration approved it.

Effectiveness of Lithium All manner of research has attested to lithium's effectiveness in treating manic episodes (Klerman et al., 1994; Prien, 1992, 1978; Bunney & Garland, 1984). Numerous studies have found lithium to be much more effective than placebos. Improvement rates of patients with mania range upward from 60 percent.

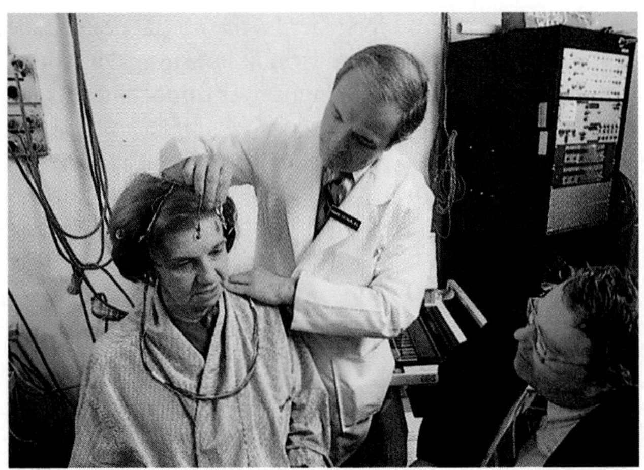

The sleep cycle is often disturbed in people with depression, either unipolar or bipolar (Thase et al., 1997, 1996, 1995). Thus, electroencephalogram recordings taken of patients while they sleep sometimes help clinicians to assess the patients more precisely and treat them more effectively.

Another frequent finding is that patients with recurrent mania undergo fewer new episodes as long as they are taking lithium (Suppes et al., 1995, 1991; Prien, 1992). Between 40 and 60 percent of patients with bipolar disorders avoid recurrences of the disorder while taking lithium (Keller et al., 1993; Prien & Potter, 1990). One study found that the risk of relapse is 28 times greater if patients stop taking lithium (Suppes et al., 1991). These findings suggest that lithium may also be a *prophylactic* drug, a drug that actually helps prevent symptoms from developing (Schou, 1997). Accordingly, today's clinicians usually recommend that patients continue some level of lithium treatment even after their manic episodes subside (Jefferson & Greist, 1994; Goodwin & Jamison, 1990).

Research indicates that lithium also alleviates the depressive episodes of bipolar disorders. Moreover, maintenance doses of lithium apparently decrease the risk of future depressive episodes, just as they seem to prevent the recurrence of manic episodes (Klerman et al., 1994; Abou-Saleh, 1992).

These findings have led researchers to wonder whether lithium might also be helpful in cases of unipolar depression. Here the results have been mixed. A few studies suggest that lithium helps some patients with unipolar depression (Jefferson & Greist, 1994; Abou-Saleh, 1992) and occasionally prevents recurrences of unipolar depression (Coppen, 1994; Abou-Saleh, 1992). Of course, it may be that the "unipolar" patients helped by lithium actually have a bipolar disorder whose manic phase has yet to appear.

At the same time, lithium often seems to enhance the effectiveness of antidepressant drugs prescribed for unipolar depression (Katona, 1995; Katona et al., 1995; Stein & Bernadt, 1993). In one study, up to two-thirds of "tricyclic nonrespondent" patients were converted to "responders" when lithium was added to their antidepressant drug therapy (Joffe et al., 1993).

Lithium's Mode of Operation Researchers do not really understand how lithium operates, but they suspect that it alters synaptic activity in neurons, though not in the same way as antidepressant drugs. Recent research indicates that the firing of a neuron actually consists of several phases that unfold at lightning speed. After the neurotransmitter binds to a receptor site on the receiving neuron, a series of cellular changes in the receiving neuron set the stage for firing. These changes are often called ***second messengers*** because they intervene between the reception of the original message and the actual firing of the neuron (Snyder, 1986).

The second-messenger events cause the neuron's ions (which sit along the neural membrane) to cross the neuron's membrane. This in turn results in a change in the electrical charge of the neuron, the transmission of the message down the cell's axon, and the firing of the neuron (see Figure 8-7 in Chapter 8). Whereas antidepressant drugs affect the initial reception of neurotransmitters by neurons, lithium appears to affect the second-messenger systems in certain neurons and in so doing it may correct the neuron abnormalities that lead to bipolar disorders.

Various second-messenger systems are at work in different neurons. In one of the most important systems, chemicals called ***phosphoinositides*** (consisting of sugars and lipids) are produced after neurotransmitters are received (Baraban et al., 1989). Lithium apparently affects this particular messenger system (Belmaker et al., 1995; Goodwin & Jamison, 1990). That is, the synaptic activity at any neuron that uses this second-messenger system may be altered by lithium.

Alternatively, it may be that lithium effectively treats bipolar functioning by directly altering sodium ion activity in neurons (Swonger & Constantine, 1983). In Chapter 8 we saw that lithium is related to sodium, and we considered the theory that bipolar disorders are triggered by unstable alignments of sodium ions along the membranes of certain neurons in the brain. If this instability is indeed the key to bipolar problems, one would expect lithium to have a direct effect of some kind on the activity of sodium ions.

Several studies do in fact suggest that lithium ions often substitute, although imperfectly, for sodium ions (Baer et al., 1971), and others suggest that lithium directly alters the transport mechanisms that move

Personal Pathways

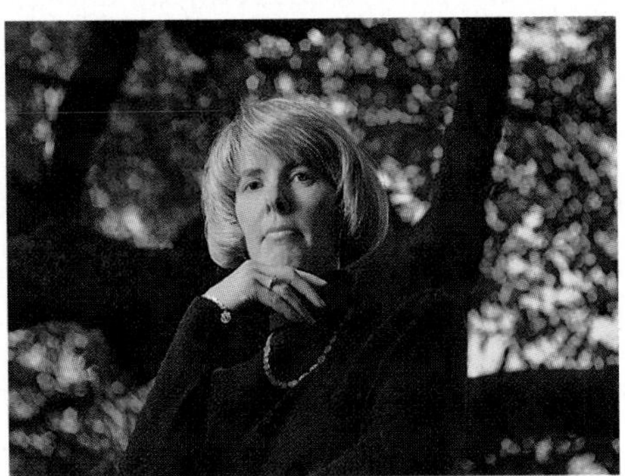

Kay Redfield Jamison
An Unquiet Mind

Kay Redfield Jamison, one of the world's leading experts on bipolar disorders, recently revealed in an autobiography, An Unquiet Mind *(1995, pp. 4–8), that she herself suffers from a bipolar disorder.*

"For as long as I can remember I was frighteningly, although often wonderfully, beholden to mood. Intensely emotional as a child, mercurial as a young girl, first severely depressed as an adolescent, and then unrelentingly caught up in the cycles of manic-depressive illness by the time I began my professional life, I became, both by necessity and intellectual inclination, a student of moods. It has been the only way I know to understand, indeed to accept, the illness I have; it also has been the only way I know to try and make a difference in the lives of others who also suffer from mood disorders. . . .

. . . My manias, at least in their early and mild forms, were absolutely intoxicating states that gave rise to great personal pleasure, an incomparable flow of thoughts, and a ceaseless energy that allowed the translation of new ideas into papers and projects. Medications not only cut into these fast-flowing, high-flying times, they also brought with them seemingly intolerable side effects. It took me far too long to realize that lost years and relationships cannot be recovered, that damage done to oneself and others cannot always be put right again, and that freedom from the control imposed by medication loses its meaning when the only alternatives are death and insanity. . . .

. . . I have no idea what the long-term effects of discussing such issues so openly will be on my personal and professional life, but, whatever the consequences, they are bound to be better than continuing to be silent. . . . one of the advantages of having had manic-depressive illness for more than thirty years is that very little seems insurmountably difficult."

sodium ions back and forth across the neural membrane as the neuron is firing (Goodwin & Jamison, 1990; Bunney & Garland, 1984). Of course, it is important to keep in mind that while lithium may in fact affect sodium ion activity, its effect on yet other important ions may be the reason for its effectiveness in relieving bipolar disorders (Dubovsky et al., 1992, 1991; Goodwin & Jamison, 1990).

Adjunctive Psychotherapy

Clinicians rarely treat bipolar patients with psychotherapy alone (Klerman et al., 1994). The well-known psychiatrist Ronald Fieve has written, "When the primary treatment of manic depression . . . has required the patient to talk with me about his problems . . . in my experience not very much has happened" (Fieve, 1975, p. 2). At the same time, clinicians have learned that lithium therapy alone is not always sufficient either. As we saw earlier, 30 percent or more of patients with bipolar disorders may not respond to lithium or a related drug, may not receive the proper dose, or may relapse while taking it (Solomon et al., 1995; Abou-Saleh, 1992).

In view of these problems, many clinicians now advocate individual, group, or family therapy as an adjunct to lithium treatment (Scott, 1995; Graves, 1993). The concerns most commonly addressed in these forms of psychotherapy are:

1. *Medication management* The importance of continuing proper lithium treatment is emphasized during therapy, and adherence to the medication regimen may be monitored (Goodwin & Jamison, 1990; Kripke & Robinson, 1985). Patients are also encouraged to discuss their reasons for disliking or rejecting lithium. They may be bothered by the drug's unwanted effects, be feeling too well to recognize the need for ongoing medication, miss the feelings of euphoria they used to have, or complain of being less productive and creative when they take lithium (Goodwin & Jamison, 1990; Wulsin et al., 1988; Jamison, 1987).

2. *Family and social relationships* Patients with bipolar disorders who return to critical and overinvolved families are more likely to relapse than those patients who live in a more supportive and less intrusive family atmosphere (Honig et al., 1995; Goodwin & Jamison, 1990). Thus helping patients cope with family members and improving family functioning are common focuses in psychotherapy (Honig et al., 1995).

As they recover, patients with bipolar disorders often experience major interpersonal and social difficulties, including the loss of friends who have been frightened away during the bipolar episodes (Wulsin et al., 1988; Aleksandrowicz, 1980; Donnelly et al., 1978). Psychotherapists may encourage patients to develop social skills and support systems, recognize their social limitations, and reduce social overstimulation and distress (Klerman & Weissman, 1992; Frank et al., 1990). One study of sixty patients with bipolar disorders who were stabilized on lithium found that social support was the factor most strongly linked to a good treatment outcome (O'Connell et al., 1985).

3. *Education* Many patients and their families may actually know very little about their bipolar disorder and need to be given information about causes, common patterns, and practical implications. Psychotherapists may provide such information and also encourage members of therapy groups to share what their firsthand experiences have taught them (Van Gent & Zwart, 1991; Wulsin et al., 1988).

4. *Problem solving* Bipolar disorders can create problems in all aspects of life. A person may, for example, be unable to stay in school or to hold a job when manic or depressive symptoms strike. Thus one role of therapy may be to help clients develop solutions for the particular difficulties they encounter (APA, 1993; Kripke & Robinson, 1985).

Few controlled studies have tested the effectiveness of psychotherapy as an adjunct to drug therapy for patients with severe bipolar disorders, but a growing number of clinical reports suggest that it reduces hospitalization, improves social functioning, and increases clients' ability to get and hold a job (Scott, 1995; Solomon et al., 1995; Werder, 1995). Although lithium or alternative medications are clearly the chief agents of improvement, it is becoming apparent that these drugs are most effective when they are combined with other forms of therapy.

Psychotherapy apparently plays a more central role in the treatment of *cyclothymic disorder,* the mild bipolar pattern that we observed in Chapter 8. Patients with this problem typically receive psychotherapy either alone or in combination with lithium. Few studies, however, have investigated whether such approaches help people who experience this pattern (Klerman et al., 1994).

Crossroads

Mood disorders are among the most treatable of all psychological disorders. The choice of treatment for bipolar disorders is narrow and simple: lithium (or a related drug), perhaps combined with psychotherapy, is the single most successful approach. The picture for unipolar depression is broader and more complex, although no less promising. Cognitive therapy, interpersonal psychotherapy, and antidepressant drugs are all helpful in cases of any severity; couple therapy is helpful in select cases; behavioral therapy helps in mild to moderate cases; and ECT is useful and effective in severe cases.

Why should several very different approaches be highly effective in the treatment of unipolar depression? Although clinicians do not yet know the answer, two explanations have won adherents. First, if many factors contribute to unipolar depression, one triggering others, it seems plausible that removal of any one of them may improve all areas of functioning. In fact, studies have found that when a therapy is effective, clients do function better in all spheres (Elkin, 1994). When antidepressant drugs are effective, for instance, they ultimately lead to the same cognitive improvements that Beck's cognitive therapy produces (Fava et al., 1994; Reda et al., 1985).

The second explanation proposes that there are various kinds of unipolar depression, and each responds to a different kind of therapy. Researchers have found, in fact, that interpersonal psychotherapy may be more helpful in depressions brought on by social problems than in depressions that seem to occur spontaneously (Thase et al., 1997; Prusoff et al., 1980). Similarly, antidepressant medications seem more helpful than other treatments in cases characterized by appetite and sleep problems, acute onset, and a family history of depression (McNeal & Cimbolic, 1986; Schatzberg et al., 1982; Byrne & Stern, 1981).

Whatever the ultimate explanation, the treatment picture is promising both for people with unipolar depression and for those with bipolar disorders. The odds are that one or a combination of the therapies now in use will alleviate their symptoms. Yet the sobering fact remains that as many as 40 percent of people with a mood disorder do not improve under treatment, and must suffer their mania or depression until it has run its course.

Chapter Review

1. ***Treatments for mood disorders*** Mood disorders are among the most treatable of all mental disorders. More than 60 percent of people with these disorders can be helped.

2. ***Treatments for unipolar depression*** A wide range of approaches has been employed in the treatment of unipolar depression.

A. ***Psychodynamic therapy*** Psychodynamic therapists try to help clients with unipolar depression become aware of and work through their real or imagined losses and excessive dependence on others. Although research has not shown psychodynamic therapies to be consistently helpful in cases of unipolar depression, they are still widely employed.

B. ***Behavioral therapy*** Therapists who take the behavioral approach reintroduce their clients to events and activities that the clients once found pleasurable. They also reinforce nondepressive behaviors and teach effective interpersonal skills. This approach is effective primarily for people who are mildly to moderately depressed.

C. ***Cognitive therapy*** Cognitive therapy helps depressed clients identify and change their dysfunctional cognitive processes. This is one of the most effective approaches. It is successful in up to 60 percent of cases, from mild to severe.

D. ***Sociocultural therapies*** Sociocultural theorists trace depression to the social structure in which people live and the social roles that they are required to play.

(1) ***Interpersonal psychotherapy (IPT)*** Interpersonal therapists assume that depression stems from social problems. They try to help clients develop insight into their interpersonal problems, change them, and learn skills to protect themselves in the future. Research suggests that IPT is effective in up to 60 percent of mild to severe cases.

(2) ***Couple therapy*** Couple therapy may be employed when depressed persons are in a dysfunctional relationship. It is often as effective as the individual therapies in such cases.

E. ***Biological treatments*** Most biological interventions consist of antidepressant drugs, but electroconvulsive therapy is still used to treat some severe cases of depression.

(1) ***Electroconvulsive therapy (ECT)*** ECT remains a controversial procedure, although it is a fast-acting intervention that is particularly effective when depression is severe, unresponsive to other kinds of treatment, or characterized by delusions.

(2) ***Antidepressant medications*** There are three kinds of antidepressant drugs—*MAO inhibitors, tricyclics,* and *second-generation antidepressants.*

(a) ***MAO inhibitors*** MAO inhibitors block the destruction of norepinephrine, allowing the levels of this neurotransmitter to build up and alleviate depressive symptoms. People taking MAO inhibitors must avoid eating foods with *tyramine.*

(b) ***Tricyclics*** Tricyclics have a higher success rate than MAO inhibitors. They seem to alleviate depression by blocking neurotransmitter reuptake mechanisms, thereby increasing the activity of norepinephrine and serotonin.

(c) ***Second-generation antidepressants*** The second-generation antidepressants—often called *SSRIs,* for *selective serotonin reuptake inhibitors*—selectively increase the activity of serotonin. As these drugs are as effective as tricyclics and have fewer undesired effects, they are rapidly gaining popularity.

F. ***Trends in treatments for unipolar depression*** The cognitive, interpersonal, and biological therapies appear to be the most successful for mild to severe depression. Couple therapy is helpful in select cases. Behavioral therapy is helpful in mild to moderate cases. And ECT is effective in severe cases. Combinations of psychotherapy and drug therapy tend to be modestly more helpful than any one approach on its own.

3. ***Treatments for bipolar disorders*** *Lithium* (or certain alternative drugs) has proved to be effective in alleviating and preventing both the manic and the depressive episodes of bipolar disorders. It is helpful in 60 percent or more of cases.

A. ***Lithium therapy*** Researchers suspect that lithium may reduce bipolar symptoms by affecting *second messenger systems* in certain neurons throughout the brain. Alternatively, lithium may directly alter the activity of *sodium ions.*

B. ***Adjunctive psychotherapy*** In recent years it has become clear that patients may fare better when lithium is supplemented by psychotherapy. The issues most commonly addressed by psychotherapists are medication management, family and social relationships, education, and problem solving.

Thought and Afterthought

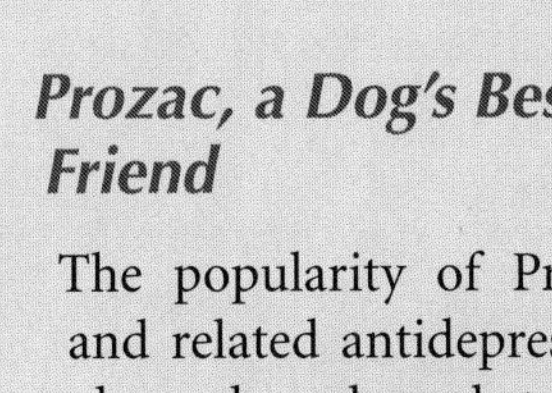

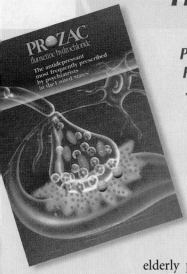

Prozac, a Dog's Best Friend

The popularity of Prozac and related antidepressant drugs has skyrocketed in the 1990s. Many clinicians argue that Prozac is being prescribed much too often. They worry in particular about its inappropriate use with chidren, elderly people, and people whose psychological concerns are relatively minor. Now they have been given something else to worry about: Prozac is also being given to *dogs* with mood or behavioral problems (Millward, 1996).

In a 1996 article for *Dogs Today* magazine, Dr. Peter Neville, an expert on animal behavior, described dogs given Prozac. Jannie, a pointer with a shadow-chasing problem, was prescribed the drug for an obsessive-compulsive disorder. George, a Staffordshire bull terrier, was given it to combat "sustained rage assaults" on other dogs. And Henry, an English bull terrier, kept pinning his owner every time she tried to leave home (Millward, 1996).

Afterthoughts: Is there something odd or wrong about human beings serving as a testing ground for a medication that is later given to animals? . . . What other human treatments (psychological or medical) are applied to pets? . . . Is the prescription of Prozac for troubled pets an excessive or inappropriate practice?

It Keeps On Ticking

There's a new product on the market, a digital timepiece called Timisis LifeClock. Once set, this pyramid-shaped desk clock ticks off the amount of time supposedly remaining in your life—in hours, minutes, seconds, and even tenths of a second—based on average life expectancies for men and women. You merely enter your age and gender, and the countdown begins. Tens of thousands of these timepieces have been sold at close to $100 each.

Afterthoughts: Cognitive therapists believe that people who think in certain ways are prone to develop depression. At the risk of overanalyzing a novelty item, what might they conclude about people interested in this product? . . . Are there ways in which this same product could be used to help people to think more positively *about their lives and their future, much as a glass that is half empty can be considered half full?*

Cheer Up, by the Numbers

In the movie *Say Anything,* Lloyd Dobler's sister says, "Get in a good mood! How hard can it be just to decide to be in a good mood and then be in a good mood?" It turns out that it's not always so easy. Researchers have found that people tend to use some strategies more than others to help rid themselves of their bad moods (Larsen, 1993; O'Brien, 1993; Tice, 1992). Among the more common ones:

1. Act to solve one's problems.
2. See the good as well as the bad in upsetting situations.
3. Remind oneself of personal successes in life.
4. Compare oneself to others who have it worse.
5. Socialize.
6. Drink alcohol.
7. Cry.
8. Distract oneself with TV, a book, a movie, or the like.
9. Isolate oneself.
10. Blame others for one's problems.

Afterthoughts: Be aware that some of these strategies do not necessarily work. Which of them might be counter-productive? . . . Which of these mood-altering techniques are similar to successful approaches to clinical depression? . . . Some techniques that help nondepressed people to cheer up may not be useful to people suffering from depression. Why not?

"Why don't you just go and see this summer's feel-good movie?"

(Drawing by Mankoff; © 1993 The New Yorker Magazine, Inc.)

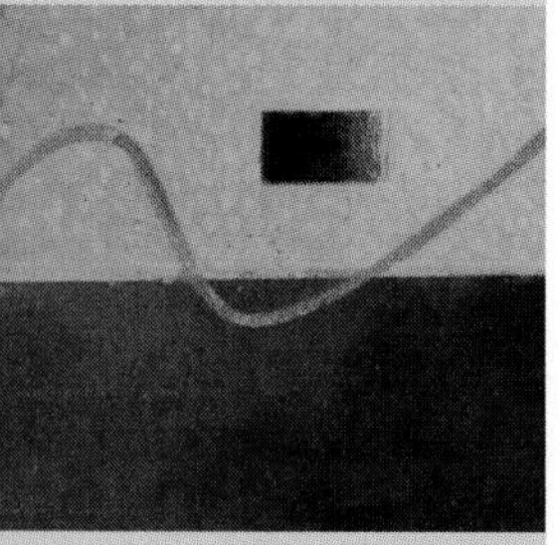

Topic Overview

What Is Suicide?

Factors That Precipitate Suicide

Explanations of Suicide

Suicide in Different Age Groups

Treatment and Suicide

Treatment After a Suicide Attempt

Suicide Prevention

Crossroads

Chapter 10

Suicide

I had done all I could and I was still sinking. I sat many hours seeking answers, and all there was a silent wind. The answer was in my head. It was all clear now: Die. . . .

The next day a friend offered to sell me a gun, a .357 magnum pistol. I bought it. My first thought was: What a mess this is going to make. That day I began to say goodbye to people: not actually saying it but expressing it silently.

Friends were around, but I didn't let them see what was wrong with me. I could not let them know lest they prevent it. My mind became locked on my target. My thoughts were: Soon it will all be over. I would obtain the peace I had so long sought. The will to survive and succeed had been crushed and defeated. I was like a general on a battlefield being encroached on by my enemy and its hordes: fear, hate, self-depreciation, desolation. I felt I had to have the upper hand, to control my environment, so I sought to die rather than surrender. . . .

I was only aware of myself and my plight. Death swallowed me long before I pulled the trigger. The world through my eyes seemed to die with me. It was like I was to push the final button to end this world. I committed myself to the arms of death. There comes a time when all things cease to shine, when the rays of hope are lost.

I placed the gun to my head. Then, I remember a tremendous explosion of lights like fireworks. Thus did the pain become glorious, an army rallied to the side of death to help destroy my life, which I could feel leaving my body with each rushing surge of blood. I was engulfed in total darkness.

(Shneidman, 1987, p. 56)

In The Suicide of Dorothy Hale, *1938–1939, the artist Frida Kahlo captures the mystery and surrealism of suicidal behavior, as well as its harsh and very real outcome. Researchers have yet to fully understand why some individuals choose to take their own life.*

The animal world is filled with seemingly self-destructive behavior. Worker bees lose their stingers and die after attacking intrusive mammals. Salmon die after the exhausting swim upstream to spawn. Lemmings are said to rush to the sea and drown. In each of these cases a creature's behavior leads to its death, but it would be inaccurate to say the animal or insect is trying to die. If anything, its actions are in the service of life. They are instinctual responses that help the species to survive in the long run. Only in the *human* act of suicide do beings knowingly end their own lives.

Suicide has been observed throughout history. It has been recorded among the ancient Chinese, Greeks, and Romans. King Saul's suicide is reported in the Old Testament. Cato threw himself upon his sword. And in more recent times, suicides by such famous people as Ernest Hemingway, Marilyn Monroe, and the rock star Kurt Cobain have both shocked and fascinated the public. Similarly, people have been confused and captivated by the mass suicides of the Branch Davidians in 1993 and the members of the Heaven's Gate cult in 1997.

A tiny male redback spider prepares to be eaten by his large female partner during copulation, and even aids in his own demise. While placing his intromittent organ into his partner, he also spins around and dangles his enticing abdomen in front of her mouth. The male may be shortsighted but he is not intending or trying to die. In fact, by keeping his partner busy devouring him, he can deposit a maxium amount of sperm, thus increasing the chances of reproduction and the birth of an offspring with similar proclivities (Andrade, 1996).

Today suicide ranks among the top ten causes of death in Western society. According to the World Health Organization (WHO) (1992), at least 160,000 people die by suicide each year, more than 30,000 in the United States alone. Those deaths, 12 of every 100,000 Americans, account for around 2 percent of all deaths in the nation (Stillion & McDowell, 1996; NCHS, 1994, 1988; McIntosh, 1991). It is estimated that each year more than 2 million other people throughout the world—600,000 in the United States—make unsuccessful attempts to kill themselves; these unsuccessful attempts are called ***parasuicides*** (McIntosh, 1991). These numbing statistics come to life every day:

> Before you finish reading this page, someone in the United States will try to kill himself. At least 60 Americans will have taken their own lives by this time tomorrow. . . . Many of those who attempted will try again, a number with lethal success.
>
> *(Shneidman & Mandelkorn, 1983)*

Actually, it is difficult to obtain accurate figures on suicide. Many investigators believe that the estimates are low (Diekstra, Kienhorst, & de Wilde, 1995; Smith, 1991). Because suicide is stigmatized in our society, relatives and friends may refuse to acknowledge that loved ones have taken their own lives. Moreover, it can be difficult for coroners to distinguish suicides from accidental drug overdoses, automobile crashes, drownings, and the like (O'Donnell & Farmer, 1995; Peck & Warner, 1995). Since relatively few of those who commit suicide actually leave notes (see Box 10-1), only the most obvious cases are categorized appropriately (Smith, 1991; Shneidman, 1981).

Suicide is not classified as a mental disorder by DSM-IV, but it does typically involve important clinical issues, such as a breakdown of coping skills, emotional turmoil, and distorted perspective. Although clinicians often address this topic in conjunction with mood disorders, at least half of all suicides result from other mental disorders, such as alcohol dependence or schizophrenia, or involve no clear mental disorder at all.

Despite the prevalence and long history of suicide, people have traditionally been misinformed about its symptoms and causes. A decade ago, when researchers administered a suicide fact test to several hundred undergraduates, the average score was only 59 percent correct (McIntosh, Hubbard, & Santos, 1985). Fortunately, as suicide has become a major focus of the clinical field, our insights are improving, and more recent scores on a similar test by students in both Canada and the United States have been higher (Leenaars & Lester, 1992) (see Table 10-1).

BOX 10-1 Suicide Notes

Dear Bill: I am sorry for causing you so much trouble. I really didn't want to and if you would have told me at the first time the truth probably both of us would be very happy now. Bill I am sorry but I can't take the life any more, I don't think there is any goodness in the world. I love you very very much and I want you to be as happy in your life as I wanted to make you. Tell your parents I am very sorry and please if you can do it don't ever let my parents know what happened.

Please, don't hate me Bill, I love you.

Mary

(Leenaars, 1991)

Many suicides pass undetected or remain shrouded in mystery because the only people who could tell us the truth have been lost to the world. Many other people who commit suicide, however—an estimated 12 to 34 percent—leave notes that provide unequivocal proof of their intentions and a unique record of their psychological state only hours or minutes before they died (Black, 1993; Leenaars, 1992, 1989).

Each suicide note is a personal document, unique to the writer and the circumstances (Leenaars, 1989). Some are barely a single sentence, others run several pages. People who leave notes clearly wish to make a powerful statement to those they leave behind (Leenaars, 1989), whether the message be "a cry for help, an epitaph, or a last will and testament" (Frederick, 1969, p. 17). Most suicide notes are addressed to specific individuals.

Survivors' reactions to suicide notes vary (Leenaars, 1989). A note can clarify the cause of death, thus saving relatives the ordeal of a lengthy legal inquiry. Friends and relatives may also find that it eases their grief to know the person's reasons for committing suicide (Chynoweth, 1977). Yet some suicide notes add to the guilt and horror that survivors commonly experience, as in the following case:

Rather than permit his wife to leave him, twenty-year-old Mr. Jefferson hanged himself in the bathroom, leaving a note on the front door for his wife, saying, "Cathy I love you. You're right, I am crazy . . . and thank you for trying to love me. Phil." Mrs. Jefferson felt and frequently insisted that she "killed Phil." She attempted suicide herself a week after. . . .

(Wallace, 1981, p. 79)

Traditionally, suicide notes have been private documents, read only by relatives, the police, or the courts (Frederick, 1969). During the past several decades, however, researchers have asked to study suicide notes. They hope to find clues about suicide by investigating differences between genuine and fake suicide notes; such dimensions as the age and sex of note writers; the grammatical structure of notes; the type and frequency of words used; the conscious and unconscious contents; emotional, cognitive, and motivational themes; and even handwriting (Leenaars, 1989).

One important finding is that suicide notes vary significantly with age. Younger persons express more self-directed hostility and interpersonal problems in their notes; those between 40 and 49 report being unable to cope with life; those between 50 and 59 rarely cite a reason for their suicide; and those over 60 are motivated by such problems as illness, disability, and loneliness.

Studies of notes have also revealed that the nature of suicide has changed little since the 1940s. Suicide notes written in the 1940s and 1950s are similar in content to modern notes, with one exception: modern notes show less ambivalence and more constricted thinking.

A note necessarily provides only a partial picture of the writer's experiences, perceptions, thoughts, and emotions. Moreover, as Edwin Shneidman points out, the writers may not be fully aware of their motives; their cognitive constriction prevents them from being truly insightful. Suicide notes are "not the royal road to an easy understanding of suicidal phenomena" (Shneidman, 1973, p. 380), but in conjunction with other sources they can point clinicians and researchers in the right direction (Black, 1995).

TABLE 10-1 Facts on Suicide Quiz (Revised)

Circle the Answer You Feel Is Most Correct for Each Question. "T" (true), "F" (false), or "?" (don't know)

T F ? 1. People who talk about suicide rarely commit suicide. [73%]*

T F ? 2. The tendency toward suicide is not genetically (i.e., biologically) inherited and passed on from one generation to another. [46%]

T F ? 3. The suicidal person neither wants to die nor is fully intent on dying. [38%]

T F ? 4. If assessed by a psychiatrist, everyone who commits suicide would be diagnosed as depressed. [57%]

T F ? 5. If you ask someone directly "Do you feel like killing yourself?," it will likely lead that person to make a suicide attempt. [95%]

T F ? 6. A suicidal person will always be suicidal and entertain thoughts of suicide. [76%]

T F ? 7. Suicide rarely happens without warning. [63%]

T F ? 8. A person who commits suicide is mentally ill. [70%]

T F ? 9. A time of high suicide risk in depression is at the time when the person begins to improve. [47%]

T F ? 10. Nothing can be done to stop people from making the attempt once they have made up their minds to kill themselves. [92%]

T F ? 11. Motives and causes of suicide are readily established. [58%]

T F ? 12. A person who has made a past suicide attempt is more likely to attempt suicide again than someone who has never attempted. [80%]

T F ? 13. Suicide is among the top 10 causes of death in the U.S. [83%]

T F ? 14. Most people who attempt suicide fail to kill themselves. [74%]

T F ? 15. Those who attempt suicide do so only to manipulate others and attract attention to themselves. [64%]

T F ? 16. Oppressive weather (e.g., rain) has been found to be very closely related to suicidal behavior. [26%]

T F ? 17. There is a strong correlation between alcoholism and suicide. [68%]

T F ? 18. Suicide seems unrelated to moon phases. [49%]

19. What percentage of suicides leaves a suicide note? [40%]
a. 15–25% b. 40–50% c. 65–75%

20. Suicide rates for the U.S. as a whole are ____ for the young. [8%]
a. lower than b. higher than c. the same as

21. With respect to sex differences in suicide attempts: [65%]
a. Males and females attempt at similar levels.
b. Females attempt more often than males.
c. Males attempt more often than females.

**Note: The percentages in brackets following each question refer to the proportion of 331 undergraduates enrolled in general psychology who correctly answered the item.*

What Is Suicide?

Not every self-inflicted death is a suicide. A man who crashes his car into a tree after falling asleep at the steering wheel is hardly trying to kill himself. Thus Edwin Shneidman (1993, 1981, 1963), one of the most influential writers on this topic, defines ***suicide*** as an intentioned death—a self-inflicted death in which one makes an intentional, direct, and conscious effort to end one's life. Most theorists agree that the term "suicide" should be limited to deaths of this sort.

Intentioned deaths may take various forms. Consider the following three imaginary instances. Although all of these people intended to die, their precise motives, the personal issues involved, and their suicidal actions differed greatly.

TABLE 10-1 Facts on Suicide Quiz (Revised) *(continued)*

22. Suicide rates among the young are ____ those for the old. [7%]
    a. lower than b. higher than c. the same as
23. Men kill themselves in numbers ____ those for women. [67%]
    a. similar to b. higher than c. lower than
24. Suicide rates for the young since the 1950s have: [97%]
    a. increased b. decreased c. changed little
25. The most common method employed to kill oneself in the U.S. is: [28%]
    a. hanging b. firearms c. drugs and poison
26. The season of highest suicide risk is: [11%]
    a. winter b. fall c. spring
27. The day of the week on which most suicides occur is: [60%]
    a. Monday b. Wednesday c. Saturday
28. Suicide rates for non-whites are ____ those for whites. [35%]
    a. higher than b. similar to c. lower than
29. Which marital status category has the lowest rates of suicide? [59%]
    a. married b. widowed c. single, never married
30. The ethnic/racial group with the highest suicide rate is: [15%]
    a. Whites b. Blacks c. Native Americans
31. The risk of death by suicide for a person who has attempted suicide in the past is ____ that for someone who has never attempted. [80%]
    a. lower than b. similar to c. higher than
32. Compared to other Western nations, the U.S. suicide rate is: [21%]
    a. among the highest b. moderate c. among the lowest
33. The most common method in attempted suicide is: [63%]
    a. firearms b. drugs and poisons c. cutting one's wrists
34. On the average, when young people make suicide attempts, they are ____ to die compared to elderly persons. [41%]
    a. less likely b. just as likely c. more likely
35. As a cause of death, suicide ranks ____ for the young when compared to the nation as a whole. [86%]
    a. the same b. higher c. lower
36. The region of the U.S. with the highest suicide rates is: [36%]
    a. east b. midwest c. west

Answer key: true items—2, 3, 7, 9, 12, 13, 14, 17, and 18; false items—1, 4, 5, 6, 8, 10, 11, 15, and 16. Items for which the correct answer is "a": 19, 22, 24, 27, 29, and 34. Items for which the correct answer is "b": 21, 23, 25, 32, 33, and 35. Items for which the correct answer is "c": 20, 26, 28, 30, 31, and 36.
Source: Hubbard & McIntosh, 1992, p. 164.

Dave: Dave was a successful man. By the age of 50 he had risen to the vice presidency of a small but profitable office machine firm. He was in charge of marketing and sales. True, he had invested most of his time in his work, and as a result had not developed close family relationships. Still, he was content. He had a devoted wife and two teenage sons who respected him. They lived in an upper-middle-class neighborhood, had a spacious house, and enjoyed a comfortable life. Dave was proud of his professional accomplishments, pleased with his family, and happy in the role of family provider.

In August of his fiftieth year, everything changed. Dave was fired. Just like that, after many years of loyal and effective service. The firm's profits were down and the president wanted to try new, fresher marketing approaches. He wanted to try a younger person in Dave's position.

Dave was shocked. The experience of rejection, loss, and emptiness was overwhelming. He looked for another position, but found only low-paying jobs for which he was overqualified. He began to fear that he would never find a position with the status and salary he was accustomed to.

Each day as he looked for work Dave became more depressed, anxious, and desperate. He was convinced that his wife and sons would not love him if he could not maintain their lifestyle. Even if they did, he could not love himself under such circumstances. He sank into hopelessness and withdrew from others.

Six months after losing his job, Dave began to consider ending his life. The pain was too great, the humiliation unending. He hated the present and dreaded the future. He believed his family would be better off if he were dead; he was certain he would be better off. He became increasingly convinced that suicide was a plausible, even desirable notion.

Throughout February he went back and forth. On some days he was sure he wanted to die. On other days, an enjoyable evening or uplifting conversation might change his mind temporarily. On a Monday late in February he heard about a job possibility and the anticipation of the next day's interview seemed to lift his spirits. But at Tuesday's interview, things did not go well. It was clear to him that he would not be offered the job. He went home, took a recently purchased gun from his locked desk drawer, and shot himself.

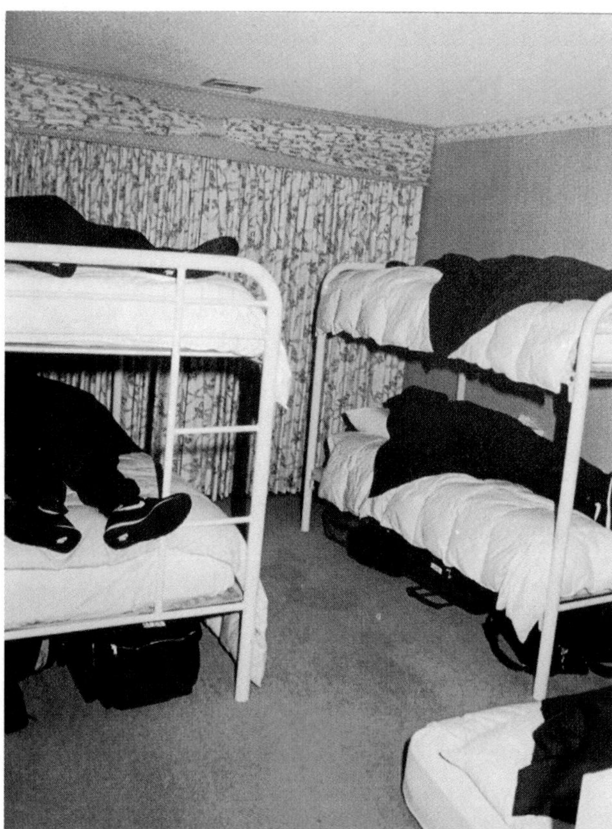

The nation will not soon forget the suicides by 39 members of the Heaven's Gate cult near San Diego, California, nor the eerie death scene. Each member lay neatly in new black sneakers, under a diamond-shaped purple shroud. Nearby was an overnight bag, packed with clothes, a notebook, and lip balm.

Billy: Billy never truly recovered from his mother's death. He was only 7 years old and unprepared for a loss of such magnitude. His father sent him to live with his grandparents for a time, to a new school with new kids and a new way of life. In Billy's mind, all these changes were for the worse. He missed the joy and laughter of the past. He missed his home, his father, and his friends. Most of all he missed his mother.

He did not really understand her death. His father said that she was in heaven now, at peace, happy. That she had not wanted to die or leave Billy, that an accident had taken her life. His father explained that life would be very hard for a while but that someday Billy would feel better, laugh again, enjoy things again. Billy waited for that day, but it didn't seem to come. As his unhappiness and loneliness continued day after day, he put things together in his own way. He believed that he would be happy again if he could join his mother. He felt that she was waiting for him, waiting for him to come to her. These thoughts seemed so right to him; they brought him comfort and hope. One evening, shortly after saying good night to his grandparents, Billy climbed out of bed, went up the stairs to the roof of their apartment house, and jumped to his death. He was frightened but at the same time happy as he jumped. In his mind he was joining his mother in heaven.

Margaret: Margaret and Bob had been going together for a year. It was Margaret's first serious relationship; it was her whole life. She confided all of her feelings to Bob, all of her hopes, ideas, and plans. She loved sharing and doing things with him. She felt that Bob shared these feelings. He said as much and acted like a person who cared. Thus when Bob told Margaret that he no longer loved her and was leaving her for someone else, Margaret was shocked and shaken.

As the weeks went by, Margaret was filled with two competing feelings—depression and anger. Several times she called Bob, begged him to reconsider, and pleaded for a chance to win him back. At the same time, she felt hatred toward Bob. She didn't deserve this treatment. It was he who deserved to suffer, not she. Sometimes when she was talking to him, her pleas would change to demands, her cries to yells.

Margaret's friends became more and more worried about her. At first they understood her pain, sympathized with it, and assumed it would soon subside. But as time went on, her depression and anger actually intensified. Then Margaret began to act strangely. She started drinking heavily and casually mixing her drinks with all kinds of pills. She constantly seemed to flirt with danger.

One night Margaret went into her bathroom, reached for a bottle of sleeping pills, and swallowed a handful of them. She wanted to make her pain go away and she wanted Bob to know just how much pain he had caused her. She continued swallowing pill after pill, crying and swearing as she gulped them down. When she began to feel drowsy, she decided to call her close friend Cindy. She was not sure why she was calling, perhaps to say good-bye, to explain her actions, or to make sure that Bob was told; or perhaps to be talked out of it. Cindy pleaded with Margaret, pointed out the irrationality of her actions, and tried to motivate her to live. Margaret was trying to listen, but she became less and less coherent. She had taken so many pills. She was beyond helping herself. Cindy hung up the phone and quickly called Margaret's neighbor and the police. When reached by her neighbor, Margaret was already in a coma. Seven hours later, while her friends and family waited for news in the hospital lounge, Margaret died.

While Margaret seemed ambivalent about her death, Dave was clear in his wish to die. And whereas Billy viewed death as a trip to heaven, Dave saw it as an end to his existence. Such differences can be important in efforts to assess, understand, and treat suicidal clients. Accordingly, Shneidman has distinguished four kinds of people who intentionally end their lives: the *death seeker, death initiator, death ignorer,* and *death darer.*

Death seekers have a clear intention of ending their lives at the time they attempt suicide. This singleness of purpose is usually of short duration. It can change to ambivalence the very next hour or day, and then return again in an equally short time.

Dave, the middle-aged executive, was a death seeker. Granted, he had many misgivings about suicide and was ambivalent about it for weeks. Had he been unable to carry out his action on Tuesday, Wednesday might have brought a different frame of mind and perhaps a different ending. On Tuesday, however, he was a death seeker—clear in his desire to die and acting in a manner that virtually guaranteed a fatal outcome.

Although ***death initiators*** also clearly intend to end their lives, they act out of a conviction that the process of death is already under way and that they are simply hastening the process. Some expect that they will die in a matter of days or weeks. Sometimes they believe that by killing themselves now, they are avoiding the loss of control or suffering that otherwise awaits them. As we shall see later, many suicides among the elderly and sick fall into this category (Valente & Saunders, 1995). The robust novelist Ernest Hemingway developed grave concerns about his failing body—concerns that some observers believe were at the center of his suicide.

Death ignorers do not believe that their self-inflicted death will mean the end of their existence. They believe they are trading their present life for a better or happier existence. Many child suicides, like Billy, fall into this category, as do adult believers in a hereafter who commit suicide to reach another form of life. The 1997 suicides by thirty-nine members of the Heaven's Gate cult also fall into this category. They acted out of the belief that their deaths would liberate their spirits and enable them to ascend to a "Higher Kingdom."

Death darers are ambivalent in their intent to die even at the moment of their attempt, and they show this ambivalence in the act itself. Although to some degree they wish to die, and they often do die, they take actions that do not guarantee death. The person who plays Russian roulette—that is, pulls the trigger of a revolver randomly loaded with one bullet—is a death darer. So is the person who walks along the ledge of a tall building. Death darers often are as interested in gaining attention, making someone feel guilty, or expressing anger as in dying per se (Brent et al., 1988; Hawton et al., 1982).

Margaret might be considered a death darer. Although her unhappiness and anger were pronounced, she was not sure that she wanted to die. Even while taking pills, she called her friend, reported her actions, and listened to her friend's pleas. She remained in conflict until her death.

When individuals play *indirect, covert, partial,* or *unconscious* roles in their own deaths, Schneidman classifies them in a suicide-like category called ***subintentional***

A sky surfer tries to ride the perfect cloud over Sweden. Thrill-seekers often progress from one dangerous activity to another, giving rise in recent years to such "sports" as white-water rafting, bungie jumping, and rock climbing. Are these people daredevils searching for new highs, as many of them claim, or are some actually death darers?

death (Shneidman, 1993, 1981). Seriously ill people who consistently mismanage their medicines may belong in this category. In related work, the influential clinical theorist Karl Menninger (1938) distinguished a category called ***chronic suicide.*** These people behave in life-endangering ways over an extended period of time, perhaps consuming excessive alcohol, abusing drugs, or indulging in risky activities or occupations. Although their deaths may represent a form of suicide, their true intent is unclear. In this chapter the term "suicide" refers only to deaths in which the victims intentionally, directly, and consciously end their own lives.

The Study of Suicide

Suicide researchers are faced with a major problem: their subjects are no longer alive. How can investigators draw accurate conclusions about the intentions, feelings, and circumstances of people who are no longer available to explain their actions? Two major research strategies have been used, each with its limitations.

One strategy is ***retrospective analysis,*** a kind of psychological autopsy in which clinicians and researchers piece together data from the person's past (Roberts, 1995; Jacobs & Klein, 1993). Relatives, friends, or therapists may remember past statements, conversations, and behavior that shed light on a suicide. Retrospective data may also be provided by the suicide notes that some victims leave behind. Unfortunately, these sources of information are not always available. Less than a quarter of all suicide victims have been in psychotherapy (Fleer & Pasewark, 1982), and less than a third leave notes (Black, 1993; Leenaars, 1992, 1989). Nor is retrospective information necessarily valid. A grieving, perhaps guilt-ridden relative may be incapable of objective and accurate recollections.

Because of these limitations, many researchers also use a second strategy—*studying people who survive their suicide attempts.* Of course, people who survive suicide may differ in important ways from those who actually do kill themselves (Diekstra et al., 1995; Lester, 1994; Stengel, 1974, 1964). Among adolescents, for example, attempted suicides outnumber fatal suicides by as many as 100 to 1 (Diekstra et al., 1995). Many of them do not want to die. Nevertheless, suicide researchers have found it useful and informative to study survivors of suicide, and we shall consider those who attempt suicide and those who commit suicide as more or less alike.

For most people, the subject of suicide evokes the image of a determined man sitting with a gun, much like the subject of Alex Colville's striking painting Target Pistol and Man, *1988. This image is often accurate—men commit suicide more than women and they usually use a firearm.*

Patterns and Statistics

Suicide researchers have gathered many statistics regarding the broader social and societal context of suicide. They have found, for example, that suicide rates vary from country to country. Hungary, Germany, Austria, Denmark, and Japan have very high rates, more than 20 suicides annually per 100,000 persons; conversely, Egypt, Mexico, Greece, and Spain have relatively low rates, fewer than 5 per 100,000. The United States and Canada fall in between, each with a suicide rate of between 12 and 13 per 100,000 persons, and England has a rate of around 9 per 100,000 (NCHS, 1994; WHO, 1992).

One factor often cited to account for these national differences is religious affiliation and beliefs (Shneidman, 1987). In Japan, for example, where religious beliefs are rooted in Shinto and Buddhist traditions, people's attitudes toward death tend to be quite different from those prevailing in Judeo-Christian communities (see Box 10-2). Furthermore, countries that are predominantly Catholic, Jewish, or Muslim tend to have lower suicide rates than predominantly Protestant countries. Perhaps in the first three cases, relatively strict proscriptions against suicide and heavy integration of members into religious and communal life deter many people from committing suicide. Yet there are exceptions to this tentative rule. Austria, for example, a predominantly Roman Catholic country, has one of the highest suicide rates in the world.

BOX 10-2 Suicide Among the Japanese

According to a comparison of American and Japanese medical students, Americans tend to regard suicide as an expression of anger or aggression, whereas the Japanese view it as normal, reasonable behavior (Domino & Takahashi, 1991). The sociologist Mamoru Iga (1993) holds that this difference reflects the cultures' religious and philosophical understandings of life and death.

The Shinto and Buddhist traditions stress eternal change and the transient nature of life. In the Buddhist view, life is sorrowful and death is a way of freeing oneself from illusion and suffering. Furthermore, the highest aim of many Japanese is complete detachment from earthly concerns, total self-negation. Within this framework, death can be seen as beautiful, as an expression of sincerity *(makoto),* or as an appropriate reaction to shame. Thus, according to Iga, "In Japan, suicide has traditionally been an accepted, if not a welcomed, way of solving a serious problem. . . . Suicide is not a sin in Japan; it is not punishable by God. Suicide is not viewed as a social or national issue but a personal problem."

Iga also points to the absence of the West's humanistic tradition in Japan. Self-expression, self-love, and self-enhancement are prominent values in the West, and out of such a tradition comes the impulse to prevent suicide. Japanese society, however, values the subjugation of the individual to the social order and stresses harmony between humanity and nature: humans must bow to nature. Thus no deep-rooted principle in Japan requires that people be stopped from taking their own lives.

Finally, Iga points to several important sociocultural factors that may further contribute to the high rate of suicide in Japan. One is a long-standing, pervasive sexism in Japanese culture. Others are increasing academic stresses on young people and increasing work pressures on middle-aged men.

Of course, in today's world East and West meet regularly, and in fact interactions between the cultures have had an impact on Japanese attitudes in one area of suicide—suicide prevention. After visiting the Los Angeles Suicide Prevention Center, some Japanese psychologists and psychiatrists opened the first suicide prevention center in Japan in 1971. They were apprehensive at first that shame would deter the Japanese from seeking help, but the center was so successful that by 1990 it was operating branches in thirty-three Japanese cities.

In fact, research is beginning to suggest that it may not be religious *doctrine* that helps prevent suicide but rather the degree of an individual's *devoutness.* Irrespective of their particular persuasion, very religious people may be less likely to commit suicide (Holmes, 1985; Martin, 1984). Similarly, it seems that people who hold a greater reverence for life are less prone to contemplate or attempt self-destruction (Lee, 1985).

The suicide rates of men and women also differ (see Figure 10-1). Three times as many women attempt suicide as men, yet men succeed at more than three times the rate of women in both North America and Western Europe (Stillion & McDowell, 1996; Kushner, 1995; McIntosh, 1991). Almost 19 of every 100,000 men in the United States kill themselves each year; the suicide rate for women, which has been increasing in recent years, is less than 5 per 100,000 (Stillion & McDowell, 1996; NCHS, 1994, 1990, 1988).

One reason for these differing rates appears to be the different methods used by men and women (Kushner, 1995). Men tend to use more violent methods, such as shooting, stabbing, or hanging themselves, whereas women use less violent methods, such as drug overdose. Indeed, firearms account for close to two-thirds of the male suicides in the United States, compared to 40 percent of the female suicides (Canetto & Lester, 1995; NCHS, 1990).

Why do men and women choose different ways of killing themselves? Some observers believe that more men than women are clear in their wish to die, and that this firmness of purpose accounts for the differential use of these methods. Others argue that because men have traditionally been stereotyped as more decisive and strong and less expressive than women, they are not permitted in their own minds to make less serious attempts or to call for help once they are in danger. Research has in fact found that male and female college students perceive completed suicide to be more powerful and more "masculine" than attempted suicide (Jack, 1992; Linehan, 1973).

Suicide is also related to marital status (see Figure 10-2). Married people, especially those with children, have a relatively low suicide rate; the single and widowed

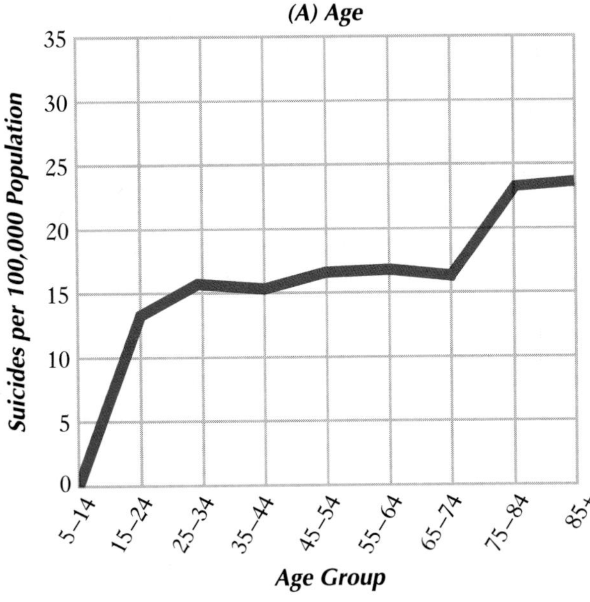

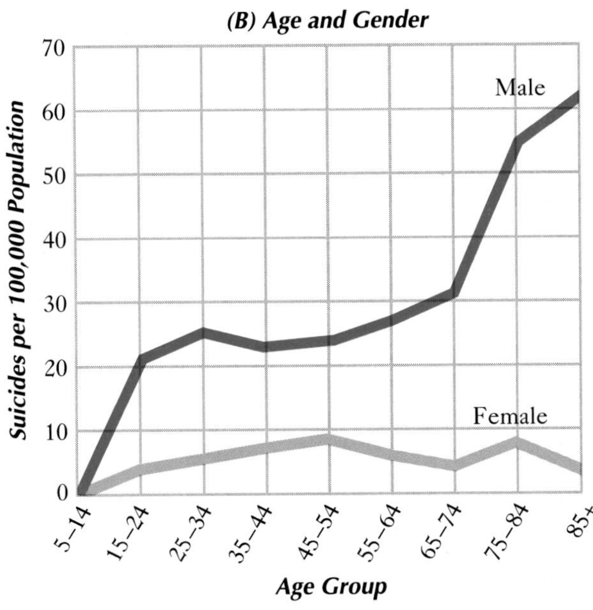

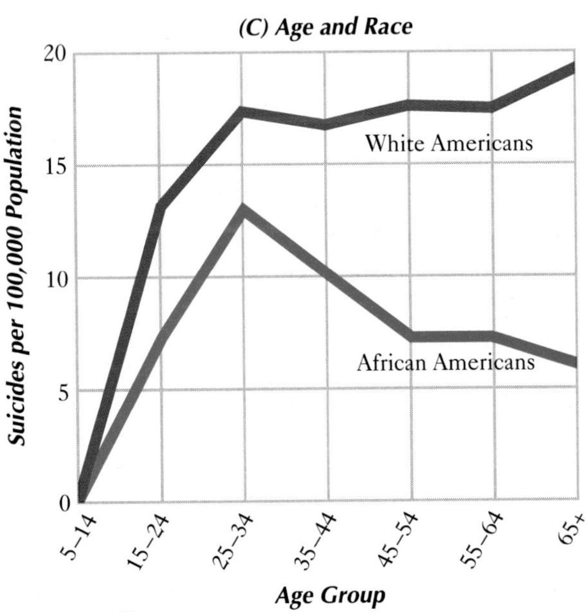

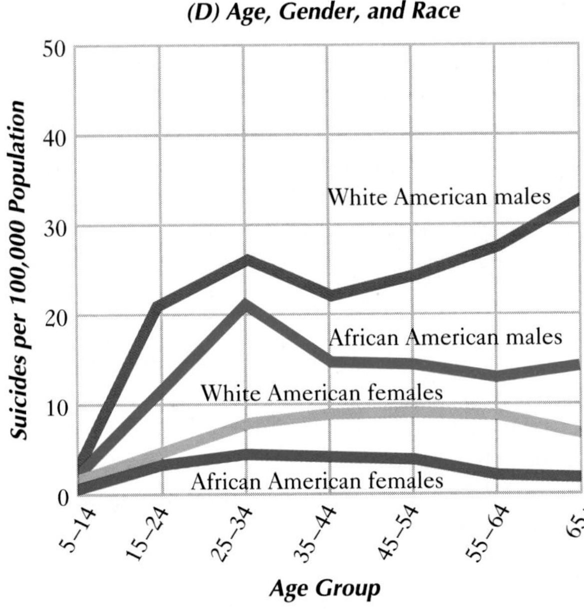

Figure 10-1 *Current U.S. suicide rates: (A) People over the age of 65 are more likely to commit suicide than those in any other age group; (B) males commit suicide at higher rates than females of corresponding ages; (C) white Americans commit suicide at higher rates than African Americans of corresponding ages; (D) elderly white American men have the highest risk of suicide. (Adapted from Stillion & McDowell, 1996; U.S. Bureau of the Census, 1994, 1990; McIntosh, 1991, pp. 62–63.)*

have higher rates; and divorced people have the highest rate of all (Canetto & Lester, 1995; Li, 1995; NCHS, 1988). One study compared ninety persons who committed suicide with ninety psychologically troubled patients matched for age, gender, and schooling who had never attempted suicide (Roy, 1982). Only 16 percent of the suicide subjects were married or cohabiting at the time of the suicide, compared to 30 percent of the control subjects. Similarly, an analysis conducted in Canada over three decades has revealed a strong positive correlation between national divorce rates and suicide rates (Trovato, 1987).

Finally, in the United States at least, suicide rates seem to differ markedly among the races (see Figure 10-1). The suicide rate of white Americans, 12 per 100,000 persons, is almost twice as high as that of

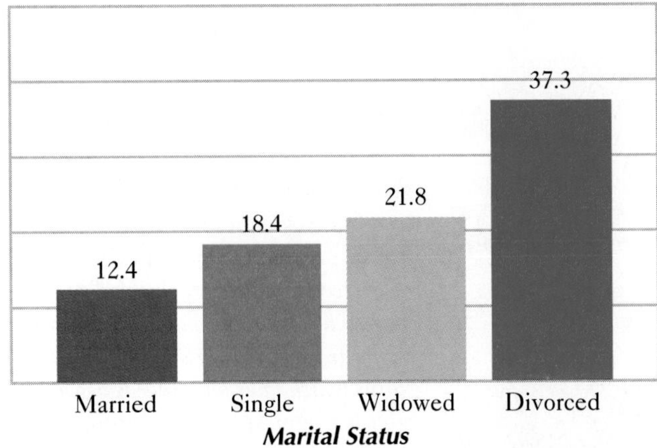

Figure 10-2 *Approximately 37 of every 100,000 divorced persons commit suicide, more than three times the rate of married persons. (Adapted from McIntosh, 1991, p. 64.)*

African Americans and members of other racial groups (Stillion & McDowell, 1996; NCHS, 1994; McIntosh, 1991). A major exception to this pattern is the very high suicide rate of Native Americans (Berlin, 1987). Their overall suicide rate is twice the national average; some Native American groups even display rates as high as four to ten times the national average (Berlin, 1987; Willard, 1979). Although the extreme poverty of many Native Americans may account in part for such trends, studies reveal that such factors as alcohol use, modeling, and availability of firearms may also be involved (Berman & Jobes, 1995, 1991; Young, 1991). Studies with Native Americans in Canada have similar implications (Strickland, 1997; Bagley, 1991).

It is worth noting that some of the statistics on suicide have been called into question by researchers in recent years. One analysis suggests that the actual rate of suicide may be 15 percent higher for African Americans and 6 percent higher for women than usually reported (Phillips & Ruth, 1993). Members of these groups, more often than other persons, use methods of suicide that can be mistaken for causes of accidental death: poisoning, drug overdose, single car crashes, pedestrian accidents.

Factors That Precipitate Suicide

Suicidal acts often are tied to contemporaneous events or conditions. Though these factors may not fully account for suicide, they can precipitate it. Common kinds of precipitating factors are stressful events and situations, mood and thought changes, alcohol and other drug use, mental disorders, and modeling.

Stressful Events and Situations

Researchers have repeatedly counted more undesirable events in the recent lives of suicide attempters than in those of matched control subjects (Isometsa et al., 1995; Heikkinen, Aro, & Lonnqvist, 1992; Paykel, 1991). In one study, suicide attempters reported twice as many stressful events in the year before their attempt as nonsuicidal depressed patients or patients with other kinds of psychological problems (Cohen-Sandler et al., 1982). One of the most common kinds of *recent stress* in cases of suicide is loss of a loved one by death, divorce, breakup, or rejection (Heikkinen et al., 1992; Paykel, 1991). Another is loss of a job (Heikkinen et al., 1992; Snyder, 1992). Indeed, the unemployment rate and the suicide rate in the United States rose and fell together from 1940 to 1984 (Yang, Stack, & Lester, 1992), and the rate of suicide among U.S. farmers tends to rise during a declining farm economy (Ragland & Berman, 1991). Finally, the stress of hurricanes and other natural disasters is sometimes linked to suicidal acts, even among very young children (Cytryn & McKnew, 1996).

A suicide attempt may be precipitated by a series of recent events that have a combined impact rather than by a single event, as in the following case:

> Sally's suicide attempt took place in the context of a very difficult year for the family. Sally's mother and stepfather separated after 9 years of marriage. After the father moved out, he visited the family erratically. Four months after he moved out of the house, the mother's boyfriend moved into the house. The mother planned to divorce her husband and marry her boyfriend, who had become the major disciplinarian for the children; a fact that Sally intensely resented. Sally also complained of being "left out" in relation to the closeness she had with her mother. Another problem for Sally had been two school changes in the last 2 years which left Sally feeling friendless. In addition, she failed all her subjects in the last marking period.
>
> *(Pfeffer, 1986, pp. 129–130)*

People may also attempt suicide in response to *long-term* rather than recent stress. Four long-term stressors are commonly implicated—serious illness, abusive environment, occupational stress, and role conflict.

Serious Illness As we noted earlier, a painful or disabling illness is at the center of many suicide attempts (Lester, 1992; Allebeck & Bolund, 1991). Individuals with such problems may come to feel that their death is

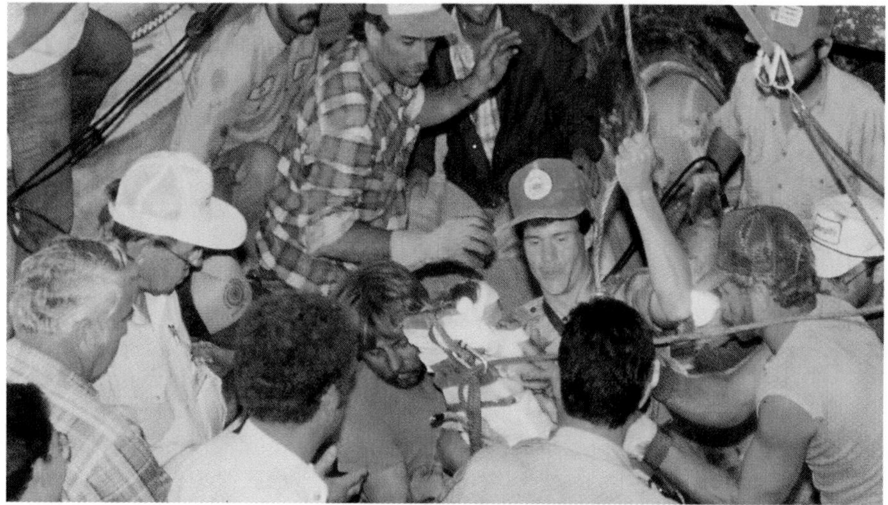

While the world watched in 1987, paramedic Robert O'Donnell squirmed down a narrow rescue shaft in Midland, Texas, and reached 2-year-old Jessica McClure, who had been trapped for two days after tumbling down an old unused well. He edged her to safety, then handed her to the rescue workers seen in this famous photograph. Some friends say that O'Donnell never really recovered from the "quicksilver" fame he won as one of the child's rescuers, nor from the inevitable loss of celebrity status which later followed. A decade after his heroic act, he shot himself to death with a shotgun.

unavoidable and imminent. Or they may believe that the suffering and problems caused by their illness are more than they can endure. One study found that 37 percent of the subjects who died by suicide had been in poor physical health (Conwell, Caine, & Olsen, 1990). Similarly, an analysis of the medical records of eighty-eight cancer patients who had died by suicide in Sweden revealed that nearly two-thirds were in an advanced or terminal phase of the disease and had severe symptoms (Bolund, 1985).

Illness-linked suicides have a long history, but they have become more prevalent and controversial in recent years. Medical progress is partly responsible. Although physicians can now apply life-sustaining techniques that keep seriously ill people alive much longer, they often fail to maintain the quality and comfort of the patients' lives. In such situations some persons try to end their slow and painful decline (Werth, 1995).

Abusive Environment Victims of an abusive or repressive environment from which they have little or no hope of escape sometimes commit suicide. Some prisoners of war, inmates of concentration camps, abused spouses, abused children, and prison inmates have attempted to end their lives (Fondacaro & Butler, 1995; Rodgers, 1995; Shaunesey et al., 1993) (see Figure 10-3). Like those who have serious illnesses, these people may have felt that they could endure no more suffering and believed that there was no hope for improvement in their condition.

Occupational Stress Some jobs create ongoing feelings of tension or dissatisfaction that can precipitate suicide attempts. Research has often found particularly high suicide rates among psychiatrists and psychologists, physicians, dentists, lawyers, and unskilled laborers (Holmes & Rich, 1990; Stillion, 1985). Of course, these correlations do not establish that occupational pressures are in fact pushing the suicide rate up. There are alternative interpretations. Unskilled workers may be responding to financial insecurity rather than job stress when they attempt suicide. Similarly, rather than reacting to the emotional strain of their work, suicidal psychiatrists and psychologists may have long-standing emotional problems that stimulated their career interest in the first place (Johnson, 1991).

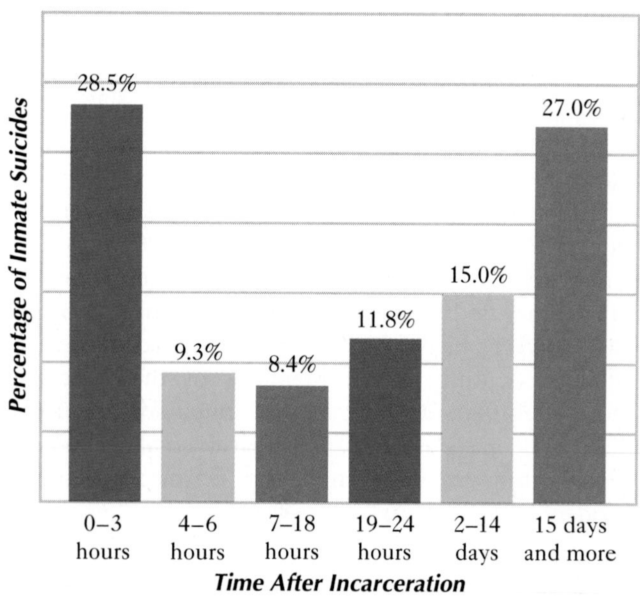

Figure 10-3 *Approximately 107 of every 100,000 inmates in U.S. jails commit suicide each year—many times the national prevalence rate. More than half of these suicides occur during the first day of incarceration. Almost 29 percent take place during the first three hours. (Adapted from Bonner, 1992; Hayes & Rowan, 1988.)*

Role Conflict Everyone occupies a variety of roles in life—spouse, employee, parent, and colleague, to name a few possibilities. These roles may conflict, cause considerable stress, and increase the risk of suicide. For years, clinical theorists believed that married women who held jobs outside of the home displayed higher suicide rates, perhaps because of conflicts between the demands of their family and their job (Stack, 1987; Stillion, 1985). As we noted earlier (see Box 8-1), however, recent studies call these notions into question. Some reviews even suggest that work outside the home may be linked to *lower* suicide rates among women, just as it is among men (Yang & Lester, 1995).

At the same time, women in certain professions—for example, chemists, psychologists, professors, and physicians—do appear to have elevated suicide rates (Yang & Lester, 1995). Here the higher rates may be related, at least in part, to the troubling experience of many professional women, including a high degree of discrimination, minority status, and stereotyping (Yang & Lester, 1995; Canetto, 1993).

Suicides by celebrities who had projected a happy and carefree image often leave fans feeling particularly shocked and unsettled. The self-inflicted deaths of Marilyn Monroe in 1963 and young comedian Freddie Prinze in 1978 had such an effect. So too did the 1996 death of comedian Ray Combs, whose playful interactions with contestants on the television show Family Feud *from 1988 to1994 had entertained millions and made him an honorary member of many families. Combs hanged himself after a series of personal and professional setbacks.*

Mood and Thought Changes

Many suicide attempts are preceded by a shift in mood and thought. Although these shifts may not be severe enough to warrant a diagnosis of a mental disorder, they typically represent a significant change from the person's past mood or point of view.

The mood change most often linked to suicide is an increase in sadness (Kienhorst et al., 1995; Tishler, McKenry, & Morgan, 1981). Also common are heightened feelings of anxiety, tension, frustration, anger, or shame (Kienhorst et al., 1995; Pine, 1981). Indeed, Shneidman (1993, 1991) characterizes the key to suicide as "psychache," a feeling of "psychological pain experienced as intolerable, caused by unfulfilled psychological needs." He states, "Pain is what the suicidal person seeks to escape" (1987, p. 56).

In the cognitive realm, many people on the verge of suicide have become preoccupied with their problems, lose perspective, and see suicide as the only effective solution to their difficulties (Shneidman, 1993, 1987). They develop a sense of ***hopelessness***—a pessimistic belief that their present circumstances, problems, and negative mood will not change (Klingman & Hochdorf, 1993). Some clinicians believe that a feeling of hopelessness is the single most sensitive indicator of suicidal intent, and they take special care to look for signs of hopelessness when they assess the risk of suicide (Hewitt et al., 1997; Levy, Jurkovic, & Spirito, 1995; Weishaar & Beck, 1992)(see Table 10-2).

Another cognitive characteristic of people who attempt suicide is ***dichotomous thinking,*** viewing problems and solutions in rigid either/or terms (Shneidman, 1993, 1987). In the following statement a woman who survived her leap from a tall building describes her dichotomous thinking at the time. She saw death as the only alternative to her pain:

> **I** was so desperate. I felt, my God, I couldn't face this thing. Everything was like a terrible whirlpool of confusion. And I thought to myself: There's only one thing to do. I just have to lose consciousness. That's the only way to get away from it. The only way to lose consciousness, I thought, was to jump off something good and high. . . .
>
> *(Shneidman, 1987, p. 56)*

TABLE 10-2 Hopelessness Scale

Hopelessness Is Indicated When People Answer:

True

I might as well give up because there's nothing I can do about making things better for myself.

I can't imagine what my life would be like in ten years.

My future seems dark to me.

I just don't get the breaks, and there's no reason to believe I will in the future.

All I can see ahead of me is unpleasantness rather than pleasantness.

I don't expect to get what I really want.

Things just won't work out the way I want them to.

I never get what I want so it's foolish to want anything.

It is very unlikely that I will get any real satisfaction in the future.

The future seems vague and uncertain to me.

There's no use in really trying to get something I want because I probably won't get it.

False

I look forward to the future with hope and enthusiasm.

When things are going badly, I am helped by knowing that they can't stay that way forever.

I have enough time to accomplish the things I most want to do.

In the future I expect to succeed in what concerns me most.

I happen to be particularly lucky and I expect to get more of the good things in life than the average person.

My past experiences have prepared me well for my future.

When I look ahead to the future I expect I will be happier than I am now.

I have great faith in the future.

I can look forward to more good times than bad times.

Source: Beck et al., 1974.

Alcohol and Other Drug Use

Studies indicate that as many as 60 percent of the people who attempt suicide drink alcohol just before the act (Suokas & Lonnqvist, 1995; Hirschfeld & Davidson, 1988). Autopsies reveal that about one-fourth of these people are legally intoxicated at the time of death (Flavin et al., 1990; Abel & Zeidenberg, 1985). In fact, the excessive use of alcohol just before suicide is probably much higher; coroners are more likely to classify deaths as accidental when they detect high alcohol consumption (Crompton, 1985). Such statistics suggest to many clinical researchers that alcohol consumption often contributes to suicidal behavior (Wasserman, 1992).

Some theorists believe that alcohol's disinhibiting effects allow people who are contemplating suicide to overcome the fears that would otherwise restrain them (Patel et al., 1972). Others suggest that alcohol contributes to suicide by lowering an individual's inhibitions against violence and helping to release underlying aggressive feelings (Whitlock & Broadhurst, 1969). Yet another possibility is that alcohol further impairs a suicidal person's judgment and problem-solving abilities (Rogers, 1992).

Research suggests that the use of other kinds of drugs may have a similar tie to suicide, particularly in teenagers and young adults (Garrison et al., 1993; Marzuk et al., 1992). We shall return to this point later.

Mental Disorders

As we noted earlier, people who attempt suicide do not necessarily have a mental disorder. Although they are troubled or anxious, their feelings may not add up to any disorder defined in DSM-IV. On the other hand, more than half of all suicide attempters do display a mental disorder (Harris & Barraclough, 1997; Moscicki, 1995; Brent et al., 1993).

The mental disorders linked most strongly to suicide are mood disorders (unipolar and bipolar depression), substance-related disorders (particularly alcoholism), and schizophrenia (see Table 10-3). Research suggests that as many as 15 percent of people with each of these disorders try to kill themselves (Krausz et al., 1995; Rossow & Amundsen, 1995; Black & Winokur, 1990). People who are both depressed and dependent on alcohol seem particularly vulnerable to suicidal impulses (Cornelius et al., 1995). Panic disorder too has been linked to suicide, but in most cases this disorder occurs in conjunction with one of the other disorders (King et al., 1995; Norton et al., 1993).

Mood Disorders In Chapter 8 we observed that most people with a major depressive disorder experience suicidal thoughts as part of their syndrome. Those whose disorder includes a particularly strong sense of hopelessness seem most likely to attempt suicide (Fawcett et al., 1987). Even when depressed people are showing improvement in mood, they may remain high suicide risks.

In fact, among those who are severely depressed, the risk of suicide may actually increase as their mood improves and they have more energy to act on their suicidal wishes. One program in Sweden was able to reduce the community suicide rate by teaching physicians how to recognize and treat depression at an early stage (Rihmer, Rutz, & Pihlgren, 1995).

Even when a suicidal person has a severe physical illness, major depression may play a key role in the attempt (Henriksson et al., 1995; Brown et al., 1986) (see Box 10–3). In one case, a depressed 26-year-old woman with cerebral palsy initially fought to compel a psychiatric hospital to assist her in committing suicide; when the woman's depression later lifted, she reversed her position (Bursztajn et al., 1986). Similarly, a study of forty-four patients with terminal illnesses revealed that fewer than a quarter of them had thoughts of suicide or wished for an early death, and that those who did were all suffering from a major depressive disorder (Brown et al., 1986).

Substance-Related Disorders Many people who commit suicide after drinking alcohol have actually had a long history of abusing alcohol or some other substance (Jones, 1997; Hawton et al., 1993; Merrill et al., 1992). The basis for the link between substance-related disorders and suicide is not clear. It may be that the tragic lifestyle that results from the long-term use of alcohol or other drugs or the sense of being hopelessly trapped by a drug leads to suicidal thinking. Alternatively, both substance abuse and suicidal thinking may be caused by a third factor—by psychological pain, for instance, or desperation (Frances & Franklin, 1988). Such people may in fact be caught in a downward spiral: they are driven toward substance use by psychological pain or loss, only to find themselves caught in a pattern of substance abuse that aggravates rather than solves their problems (Downey, 1991; Miller et al., 1991). Nor should the medical complications of chronic substance abuse be overlooked. Many suicides by people with alcoholism, for example, occur in the late stages of the disorder, when cirrhosis of the liver and other medical complications arise. At least some of these people may be acting as "death initiators" in the belief that a journey toward death has already begun (Miles, 1977; Barraclough et al., 1974).

TABLE 10-3 Common Predictors of Suicide

1. Depressive disorder and certain other mental disorders
2. Alcoholism and other forms of substance abuse
3. Suicide ideation, talk, preparation; certain religious ideas
4. Prior suicide attempts
5. Lethal methods
6. Isolation, living alone, loss of support
7. Hopelessness, cognitive rigidity
8. Being an older white male
9. Modeling, suicide in the family, genetics
10. Economic or work problems; certain occupations
11. Marital problems, family pathology
12. Stress and stressful events
13. Anger, aggression, irritability
14. Physical illness
15. Repetition and comorbidity of factors 1–14

Source: Adapted from Maris, 1992.

Schizophrenia People with schizophrenia, as we shall see in Chapter 15, may hear voices that are not actually present (hallucinations) or hold beliefs that are blatantly false and even bizarre (delusions). There is a popular belief that persons with schizophrenia who kill themselves are typically responding to imagined voices commanding them to do so or to a delusion that suicide is a grand and noble gesture. Research indicates, however, that such suicides more often reflect feelings of demoralization (Krausz et al., 1995; Haas et al., 1993). For example, many young and unemployed people with schizophrenia who have experienced relapses over several years come to believe that the disorder will forever disrupt their lives (Peuskens et al., 1997; Drake, Gates, & Cotton, 1986, 1984). Suicide is the leading cause of death among such individuals (Haas et al., 1993).

Modeling: The Contagion of Suicide

It is not unusual for people, particularly teenagers, to try to commit suicide after observing or reading about someone who has done so (Phillips et al., 1992; Phillips & Carstensen, 1988). Perhaps these people have been struggling with major problems and the other person's suicide seems to reveal a possible solution; or they have been contemplating suicide and the other person's suicide seems to give them permission or finally persuades them to act. Whatever the specific mechanism, one suicidal act apparently serves as a model for another.

Three kinds of models in particular seem to trigger suicides: suicides by celebrities, highly publicized suicides, and suicides by co-workers or colleagues.

BOX 10-3 The Right to Commit Suicide

In the fall of 1989, a Michigan doctor, Jack Kevorkian, built a "suicide device." A person using it could, at the touch of a button, change a saline solution being fed intravenously into the arm to one containing chemicals that would bring unconsciousness and a swift death. The following June, under the doctor's supervision, Mrs. J. Adkins took her life. She left a note explaining: "This is a decision taken in a normal state of mind and is fully considered. I have Alzheimer's disease and I do not want to let it progress any further. I do not want to put my family or myself through the agony of this terrible disease." Mrs. Adkins believed that she had a right to choose death and that her choice was rational; indeed, her husband supported her decision. Dr. Kevorkian believed that the "device" could be valuable in assisting persons with compelling grounds for suicide. Michigan authorities, however, promptly prohibited further use of the device.

(Adapted from Belkin, 1990; Malcolm, 1990)

Is there a right to commit suicide, or does society have a right to intervene (Clay, 1997; West, 1993)? Dr. Kevorkian's continuing court battles have made many people ask just that.

To ask how a society views suicide is to probe its very perceptions of life and death (Battin, 1993). The ancient Greeks, for example, valued physical and mental well-being in life and dignity in death. Therefore, individuals with a grave illness or mental anguish had legal recourse to suicide. Athenians could obtain official permission from the Senate to take their own lives, and magistrates were authorized to dispense hemlock (Humphry & Wickett, 1986).

The Bible does not explicitly censure the taking of one's own life, but in the fifth century St. Augustine declared that suicide broke the commandment "Thou shalt not kill." Soon after, the church announced that persons who attempted suicide would be excommunicated (Fletcher, 1981). Later, in Britain and other countries, suicide was considered a crime against the king or state, a failure to fulfill one's obligations to society (Siegel, 1988).

American traditions, too, discourage suicide, appealing to the sanctity of life (Ester, 1981). We speak of "committing" suicide, as though it were a criminal act (Barrington, 1980), and we allow the state to use force, including involuntary commitment to a mental hospital, to prevent it (Grisez & Boyle, 1979). But times and attitudes are changing. Today the idea of a "right to suicide" and "rational suicide" is receiving increasing support from the public, psychotherapists, and physicians. In fact, surveys suggest that half of today's physicians believe that suicide can be rational in some circumstances (Duberstein et al., 1995).

Public support for a right to suicide seems strongest in connection with great pain, suffering, and terminal illness (Werth, 1996; Siegel, 1988). In the United States, the Society for the Right to Die presses for legislation to prevent the "unnecessary prolongation of life"; Concern for Dying educates the public on these issues; and the Hemlock Society supports "self-deliverance" for the terminally ill (Burek, 1990; Siegel, 1988). Polls suggest that about half or more of all Americans believe that terminally ill persons should be free to take their lives or to seek a physician's assistance to do so (Drane, 1995; Duberstein et al., 1995; Siegel, 1988). There is also evidence that doctors and patients are acting on these beliefs. A recent survey found that half of doctors specializing in AIDS had helped patients commit suicide by writing prescriptions for lethal amounts of narcotics (Mitchell, 1996). And, in a now common practice, a legally competent person can write a "living will," declaring in advance the treatment that would be desired or refused in the event of terminal illness (Miesel, 1989; Siegel, 1988; Humphry & Wickett, 1986).

Common law traditionally affirms a person's right to self-determination (Miesel, 1989), and some people argue that this right extends to the "liberty right" to end one's life (Siegel, 1988; Battin, 1982). Others consider suicide a "natural right," comparable to the rights to life, ownership of property, and freedom of speech (Battin, 1982). Most such proponents, however,

Celebrities When the researcher Steven Stack (1987) analyzed U.S. suicide data spanning 1948 to 1983, he found that suicides by entertainers and political figures are regularly followed by unusual increases in the number of suicides across the nation. During the week after the suicide of Marilyn Monroe in 1963, for example, the national suicide rate rose 12 percent (Phillips, 1974). Similarly, in 1994, a depressed 28-year-would restrict this right to situations in which the act of suicide is indeed "rational," a reasonable alternative chosen when life stops being an enriching and fulfilling experience (Weir, 1992; Eser, 1981; Grisez & Boyle, 1979). Most do not believe that suicide is appropriate in "irrational" cases, those motivated by mental disorders such as depression (Clay, 1997; Weir, 1992; Battin, 1982, 1980).

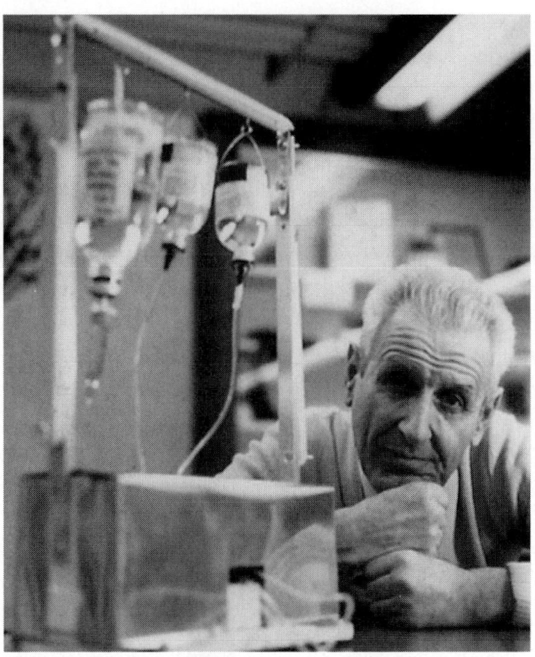

Dr. Kevorkian and his suicide device.

It turns out that even in cases of severe illness it is difficult to determine whether a person's wish to commit suicide is rational. Is the hopelessness of an AIDS patient realistic, or a symptom of depression? Healthy people tend to feel sorry for those who are very sick, elderly, or disabled, and may see their condition as "unbearable" and their depression as "just the way I would feel if it happened to me" (Sullivan & Younger, 1994). But, according to many psychotherapists, this interpretation may lead observers to mislabel a patient's depressive symptoms as "reasonable." In one study, physicians who had inadequate knowledge about suicide and depression were inclined to support the suicidal wishes of their terminally ill patients when those wishes were in fact caused by depression (Duberstein et al., 1995).

Some research suggests that cancer and AIDS patients' interest in suicide often springs largely from psychological and social distress (Breitbart, Rosenfeld, & Passik, 1996). Indeed, half or more of these patients who are suicidal may be clinically depressed (Chochinov et al., 1995; Brown et al., 1986). In fact, there seems to be little or no direct relationship between interest in suicide and physical pain or level of symptoms (Breitbart et al., 1996).

Clearly, reliable clinical criteria for recognizing depression will be essential if the "right to die" becomes legally established (Werth & Cobia, 1995). In some cases, people might benefit more from help in coming to terms with terminal illness than from a license to end it. Hospice care, psychotherapy, and antidepressant medications might provide pain management and emotional support (Sullivan & Younger, 1994; Van Bommel, 1992).

Finally, some clinicians worry that the right to suicide could be experienced more as a "duty to die" than as the ultimate freedom (Seale & Addington-Hall, 1995). Elderly people might feel unjustified in expecting relatives to support and care for them when suicide is a socially approved alternative (Sherlock, 1983). Indeed, many already feel that they are "too old" and have become burdens to their families (Breitbart et al., 1996; Seale & Addington-Hall, 1995).

Furthermore, if suicide is accepted as rational, some people argue, it might be all too easy to accept forced euthanasia and infanticide as well (Annas, 1993; Battin, 1982). As care for the terminally ill grows ever more costly, would suicide be subtly encouraged among the poor and disadvantaged? Could assisted suicide become a form of medical cost control (SHHV Task Force, 1995)? In the Netherlands, where assisted suicide and euthanasia are legal, "termination of the patient without explicit request" (or involuntary euthanasia) has occurred in at least 1,000 cases (Hendin, 1995; Seale & Addington-Hall, 1995).

How are these conflicts to be resolved? Understanding and preventing suicide remain challenges for the future, and so do questions about whether and when we should stand back and do nothing. Whatever one's position on this issue, it is a matter of life and death.

old fan mourned the suicide of Nirvana's Kurt Cobain at a large outdoor Seattle candlelight vigil, then went home and, like Cobain, killed himself with a shotgun.

Highly Publicized Cases If a suicide has any bizarre or unusual aspects, the news media tend to focus on it. Such highly publicized accounts may trigger suicides that are similar in method or circumstance (Ishii,

1991). During the year after a widely publicized suicide by self-immolation in England, for example, eighty-two other people set themselves on fire, with equally fatal results (Ashton & Donnan, 1981). Inquest reports revealed that most of those people had histories of emotional problems and that none of the suicides had the political motivation of the publicized suicide. In short, the imitators seemed to be responding to their own problems in a manner precipitated by the suicide they had observed or read about.

Even a media program that is clearly intended to educate and help viewers may have the paradoxical effect of spurring imitators. One study found a dramatic increase in the rate of suicide among West German teenagers after the airing of a television documentary showing the suicide of a teenager who jumped under a train (Schmidtke & Häfner, 1988). The number of railway suicides by male teenagers increased by 175 percent after the program was aired.

Some clinicians argue that more responsible reporting could reduce the frightening impact of well-publicized suicides (Mulder, 1996; Motto, 1967), as in the case of MTV's coverage of Kurt Cobain's suicide in 1994. Its repeated theme was "Don't do it!" In fact, thousands of young people called MTV and other radio and television stations in the hours after his death, distraught, worried, and in some cases suicidal. Some of the stations responded by posting the phone numbers of suicide prevention centers, presenting interviews with suicide experts, and offering counseling services and advice directly to callers. Some clinicians believe that these media actions held down the number of modeled suicides.

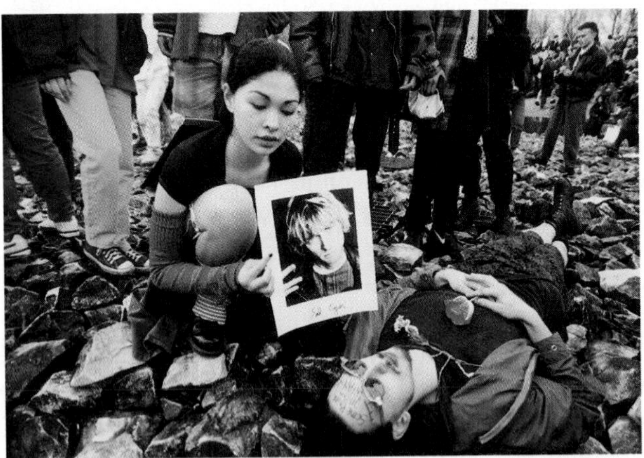

The suicide of Nirvana's Kurt Cobain in April 1994 shocked millions of young rock fans throughout the world and led to widespread grief and confusion. In Seattle, Cobain's hometown, a candlelight vigil was attended by about 5,000 people, including these two fans. Just a month before his death, Cobain had overdosed on a combination of painkillers and alcohol. Although it was called an accident at the time, a friend later observed, "You don't take fifty pills by accident" (Jones, 1994).

Co-workers and Colleagues The word-of-mouth publicity that attends suicides in a school, workplace, or small community may trigger suicide attempts. The suicide of a recruit at a U.S. Navy training school, for example, was followed within two weeks by another and by an attempted suicide at the school. To head off what threatened to become a suicide epidemic, the school initiated a program of staff education on suicide and group therapy sessions for recruits who had been close to the suicide victims (Grigg, 1988).

Explanations of Suicide

Most people who encounter difficult situations never try to kill themselves. In an effort to explain why some people are more prone to suicide than others, theorists have proposed still broader factors that may set the stage for self-destructive action. The leading theories come from the psychodynamic, biological, and sociocultural perspectives. Unfortunately, as we shall see, these explanations have received limited empirical support, and they fail to address all kinds of suicidal acts. Thus it would be inaccurate to conclude that the clinical field currently has a satisfactory understanding of suicide.

The Psychodynamic View

Many psychodynamic theorists believe that suicide usually results from depression and anger at others that is redirected at oneself. This theory was first stated by Wilhelm Stekel at a meeting in Vienna in 1910, when he proclaimed that "no one kills himself who has not wanted to kill another or at least wished the death of another" (Shneidman, 1979). Some years later Sigmund Freud (1920) wrote, "No neurotic harbors thoughts of suicide which he has not turned back upon himself from murderous impulses against others."

As we saw in Chapter 8, Freud (1917) and Abraham (1916, 1911) proposed that when people experience the real or symbolic loss of a loved one, they come to "introject" the lost person; that is, they unconsciously incorporate the person into their own identity and feel toward themselves as they had felt toward the other. For a short while, negative feelings toward the loved one are experienced as self-hatred. Extreme anger toward the lost loved one may turn into unrelenting anger against oneself, and finally into a broad depressive reaction. Suicide is an extreme expression of this self-hatred. The following description of a suicidal patient demonstrates how such dynamics may operate:

> A 27-year-old conscientious and responsible woman took a knife to her wrists to punish herself for being tyrannical, unreliable, self-centered, and abusive. She was perplexed and frightened by this uncharacteristic self-destructive episode and was enormously relieved when her therapist pointed out that her invective described her recently deceased father much better than it did herself.
>
> *(Gill, 1982, p. 15)*

In support of Freud's view, researchers have found a relationship between childhood losses and later suicidal behaviors (Paykel, 1991). One examination of 200 family histories found the incidence of early parental loss to be much higher among suicide attempters (48 percent) than among nonsuicidal control subjects (24 percent) (Adam, Bouckoms, & Streiner, 1982). Common forms of loss were death of the father and divorce or separation of the parents, especially during either the early years of life or late adolescence. Of course, although such findings coincide with Freud's view, they are correlational and do not establish the causality suggested in his model.

Late in his career, Freud proposed that human beings have a basic "death instinct." He called this instinct ***Thanatos,*** and proposed that it functions in opposition to their "life instinct." According to Freud, while most people learn to redirect their death instinct toward others, suicidal people, caught in a web of self-anger, direct the instinct squarely upon themselves (Freud, 1955).

Sociological findings are consistent with this explanation of suicide. National suicide rates have been found to drop significantly in times of war, when, one could argue, people are encouraged to direct their self-destructive energy against "the enemy." In addition, societies with high rates of homicide tend to have low rates of suicide, and vice versa (Somasundaram & Rajadurai, 1995). On the other hand, research has failed to establish that suicidal people are in fact dominated by intense feelings of anger. Although hostility is an important element in some suicides, several studies find that other emotional states are even more common (Linehan & Nielsen, 1981; Shneidman, 1979).

By the end of his career, Freud himself expressed dissatisfaction with his theory of suicide. Other psychodynamic theorists have modified his ideas over the years; yet themes of loss and self-directed aggression usually remain at the center of their explanations (Bose, 1995; Kincel, 1981).

Every summer thousands of walrus bulls congregate along the beaches of Bristol Bay in Alaska and, like those in this photograph, sun and feed themselves. In recent years, however, dozens of them have interrupted their summer leisure and climbed together to the top of a nearby cliff, waddled over the edge, and one by one plunged 100 feet to the rocks below. Although the walruses are not acting with the intent of mass suicide, some scientists believe that much can be learned from the social behavior, patterns, and biology of animals and insects who display suicide-like behavior.

The Sociocultural View

Just before the turn of the century, Emile Durkheim (1897–1951), a sociologist, developed the first comprehensive theory of suicidal behavior. Today this theory continues to be influential.

According to Durkheim, the probability of suicide is determined by how embedded a person is in such social groups as the family, religious institutions, and the community. The more thoroughly a person belongs, the lower the risk of suicide. Conversely, people who are removed from or have poor relationships with their society are at greater risk of killing themselves. He defined three categories of suicide based on the individual's relationship with society.

Egoistic suicides are committed by people over whom society has little or no control. These people are not concerned with the norms or rules of society, nor are they integrated into the social fabric. According to Durkheim, this kind of suicide is more likely in people who are isolated, alienated, and nonreligious. The larger the number of such people living in a society, the higher that society's suicide rate.

Altruistic suicides, in contrast, are committed by people who are so well integrated into the social structure that they intentionally sacrifice their lives for the well-being of society. Soldiers who threw themselves on top of a live grenade to save others, Japanese kamikaze pilots who gave their lives in air attacks, and Buddhist monks and nuns who protested the Vietnam War by setting themselves on fire—all were committing altruistic suicide. According to Durkheim, societies that encourage altruistic deaths and deaths to preserve one's honor (as Far Eastern societies do) are also likely to have higher suicide rates.

Anomic suicides, Durkheim's third category, are committed by people whose social environment fails to provide stable structures, such as family and religion, to support and give meaning to life. Such a societal state, called *anomie* (literally, "without law"), leaves individuals without a sense of belonging and brings about what Durkheim called a heightened "inclination for suicide." Unlike egoistic suicide, which is the act of a person who rejects the structures of a society, anomic suicide is the act of a person who has been let down by a disorganized, inadequate, often decaying society.

Durkheim argued that when societies go through periods of anomie, their suicide rates increase. Historical research supports this claim. Periods of economic depression and social disintegration bring about relative anomie in a country, and national suicide rates tend to rise (Yang et al., 1992; Lester, 1991). Periods of population change and increased immigration, too, tend to bring about a state of anomie, and again suicide rates rise (Ferrada et al., 1995). Steven Stack (1981) examined suicide rates and immigration increases in thirty-four countries. After controlling for age and other factors that affect suicide, he found that each 1 percent increase in immigration was associated with an increase of 0.13 percent in the suicide rate.

According to Emile Durkheim, people who intentionally sacrifice their lives for others are committing altruistic suicide. Betsy Smith, a heart transplant recipient who was warned that she would probably die if she did not terminate her pregnancy, elected to have the baby and died giving birth to a healthy daughter.

A profound change in an individual's immediate surroundings, rather than general societal deficiencies, can also lead to anomic suicide. People who suddenly inherit a great deal of money, for example, may go through a period of anomie as their relationships with social, economic, and occupational structures are upset or altered. Thus Durkheim predicted that societies with greater opportunities for change in individual wealth or status would have higher suicide rates, and this prediction, too, is supported by research (Lester, 1985).

Durkheim's theory of suicide highlights the potential importance of social and societal factors—a dimension that clinicians sometimes overlook. Today's sociocultural theorists do not necessarily embrace Durkheim's ideas about egoistic, altruistic, and anomic suicides, but they do agree that societal structure and cultural stress often play major roles in suicide. In fact, the sociocultural perspective currently pervades the study of suicide. We saw its impact earlier when we observed the extensive literature linking suicide to broad factors such as religious affiliation, marital status, gender, race, and societal stress. We will see it in action later when we consider the ties between suicide and age.

Despite the impact of sociocultural theories, they cannot by themselves explain why some people who experience societal pressures commit suicide when the majority do not. Durkheim himself concluded that the final explanation probably involves an interaction between societal and individual factors.

The Biological View

For years biological theorists relied largely on *family pedigree studies* to support their position that biological factors contribute to suicidal behavior. Researchers have repeatedly found higher rates of suicidal behavior among the parents and close relatives of suicidal people than among those of nonsuicidal people (Brent et al., 1996). Indeed, one study found that over one-third of teenage subjects who committed suicide had a close relative who had attempted or completed suicide (Gould, Shaffer, & Davies, 1990). Such findings may suggest that genetic, and so biological, factors are at work (Roy, 1992; Garfinkel, Froese, & Golombek, 1979).

Studies of twins also have been consistent with this view of suicide. Researchers who investigated twins born in Denmark between 1870 and 1920, for example, located nineteen identical pairs and fifty-eight fraternal pairs in which at least one twin had committed suicide (Juel-Nielsen & Videbech, 1970). In four of the identical pairs the other twin also committed suicide (21 percent), while none of the other twins among the fraternal pairs had done so.

Of course, as with all family pedigree research, nonbiological interpretations can also be offered. Psychodynamic clinicians might argue that children whose close relatives commit suicide are prone to depression and suicide because they have lost a loved one at a critical stage of development. And behavioral theorists might emphasize the modeling role played by parents or close relatives who attempt suicide. Clearly, a genetic or biological conclusion is inappropriate on the basis of family research findings alone.

In the past decade laboratory research has provided more direct support for a biological view of suicide. The activity level of the neurotransmitter *serotonin* is often found to be low in people who commit suicide (Mann & Malone, 1997; Malmquist, 1996; Stanley, 1991). The first indication of this relationship came from a study by the psychiatric researcher Marie Asberg and her colleagues (1976). These investigators measured the level of *5-hydroxyindoleactic acid (5-HIAA)*—a chemical that is a *metabolite,* or by-product, of brain serotonin—in sixty-eight depressed patients. Twenty of the patients had particularly low levels of 5-HIAA (and presumably low levels of serotonin activity), while in the remaining forty-eight the 5-HIAA levels were higher. The researchers found that the low 5-HIAA subjects made a total of eight suicide attempts (two lethal), whereas the much larger group of relatively high 5-HIAA subjects made only seven. The researchers interpreted this finding to mean that low serotonin activity may be "a predictor of suicidal acts." Later studies found that suicide attempters with low 5-HIAA levels are ten times more likely to make a repeat attempt and succeed than are suicide attempters with high 5-HIAA levels (Roy, 1992; Asberg et al., 1976).

Studies that examine the autopsied brains of suicide victims point in the same direction (Stanley et al., 1986, 1982). Such studies usually measure serotonin activity by determining the number of imipramine receptor sites in the brain. Recall that imipramine is an antidepressant drug that binds to certain neural receptors throughout the brain (see Chapter 9). It is believed that the degree of imipramine binding reflects the usual activity level of serotonin; the less imipramine binding, the less serotonin activity (Langer & Raisman, 1983). Fewer imipramine binding sites are found in the brains of persons who die by suicide than in the autopsied brains of nonsuicides—in fact, approximately half as many binding sites is the usual finding.

At first glance, these studies may appear to tell us only that many depressed people attempt suicide. After all, as we discussed in Chapter 8, depression is itself related to low serotonin activity. On the other hand, there is evidence of low serotonin activity even among suicidal subjects who have no history of depression (Van Praag, 1983; Brown et al., 1982). That is, low serotonin activity seems also to have a role in suicide unassociated with depression.

How, then, might low serotonin activity act to increase the likelihood of suicidal behavior? One possibility is that low serotonin helps cause aggressive behavior (Linnoila & Virkkunen, 1992). It has been found, for example, that 5-HIAA levels are significantly lower in highly aggressive men than in less aggressive men (Brown et al., 1992, 1979), and that serotonin activity is often low in those who commit such aggressive acts as arson and murder (Bourgeois, 1991). Moreover, lower 5-HIAA levels have been found in people who used guns and other violent means to commit suicide than in those who used nonviolent methods, such as drug overdose (Edman & Asberg, 1986; Van Praag, 1983, 1982). And finally, one study found that depressed patients with lower

5-HIAA levels both tried to commit suicide more often and scored higher in hostility on various personality inventories than did depressed patients with higher 5-HIAA levels (Van Praag, 1986).

This pattern of findings suggests to many theorists that low serotonin activity produces aggressive feelings and impulsive behavior (Volavka, 1995; Bourgeois, 1991). In people who are clinically depressed, low serotonin activity may produce aggressive and impulsive tendencies that leave them particularly vulnerable to suicidal thinking and action. Even in the absence of a depressive disorder, however, people with low serotonin activity may develop such aggressive feelings that they are dangerous to themselves or others.

Suicide in Different Age Groups

The likelihood of committing suicide generally increases with age, although people of all ages may try to kill themselves (see Figure 10-4). Recently particular attention has been focused on self-destruction in three age groups: *children,* partly because suicide at a very young age contradicts society's perception that childhood is an enjoyable period of discovery and growth; *adolescents* and *young adults,* because of the steady and highly publicized rise in their suicide rate; and the *elderly,* because suicide is more prevalent in this age group than in any other. Although the characteristics and theories of suicide discussed throughout this chapter apply to all age groups, each group faces unique problems that help account for patterns of self-destruction among its members.

Children

Tommy [age 7] and his younger brother were playing together, and an altercation arose that was settled by the mother, who then left the room. The mother recalled nothing to distinguish this incident from innumerable similar ones. Several minutes after she left, she considered Tommy strangely quiet and returned to find him crimson-faced and struggling for air, having knotted a jumping rope around his neck and jerked it tight.

(French & Berlin, 1979, p. 144)

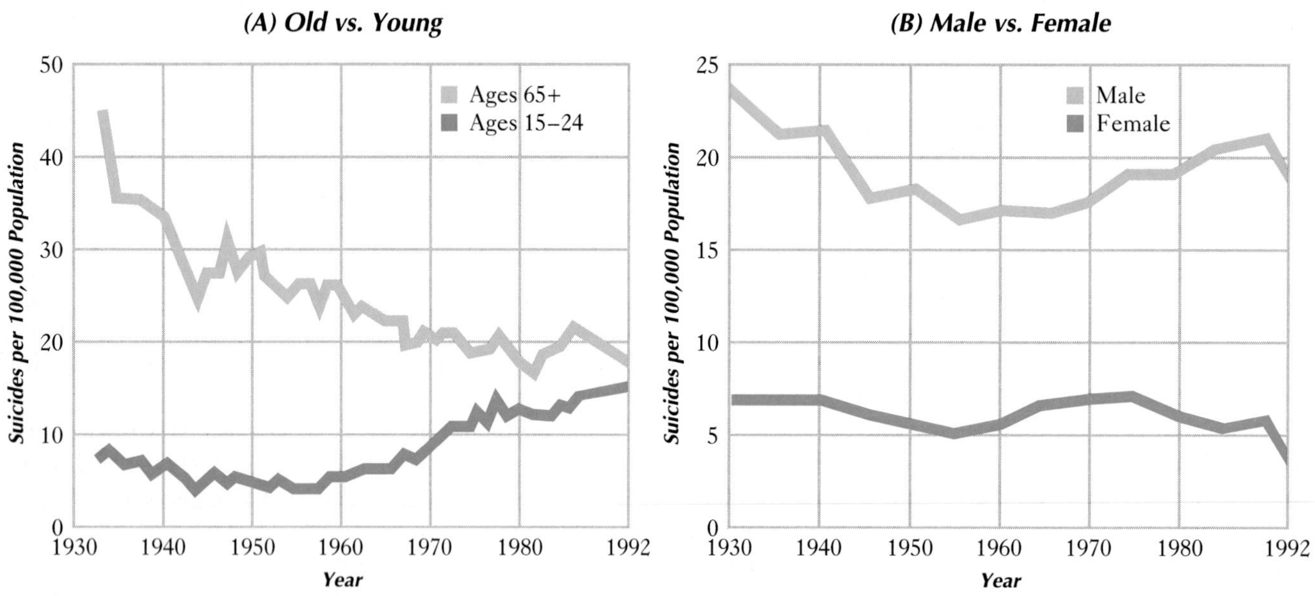

Figure 10-4 *Changing suicide rates over the years: (A) The suicide rate of elderly people has been generally declining for at least a half-century, while that of young adults is increasing. Still, older people continue to be at higher risk for suicide. (B) Conversely, the suicide rates of males and females have remained rather steady over the years, as has the greater prevalence of suicide among males than among females. (Adapted from McIntosh, 1996, 1991, 1987; Stillion & McDowell, 1996; NCSH, 1994; Buda & Tsuang, 1990; U.S. Bureau of the Census, 1968, 1947.)*

Dear Mom and Dad,

I love you. Please tell my teacher that I cannot take it anymore. I quit. Please don't take me to school anymore. Please help me. I will run away so don't stop me. I will kill myself. So don't look for me because I will be dead. I love you. I will always love you. Remember me.

Help me.

Love Justin [age 10]

(Pfeffer, 1986, p. 273)

Although suicide is relatively infrequent among children, it has been increasing rapidly during the past several decades. Approximately 300 children under 14 years of age in the United States now commit suicide each year—around 0.5 per 100,000 in this age group, a rate nearly 800 percent higher than that of 1950 (Stillion & McDowell, 1996; NCHS, 1993). Boys outnumber girls by 3 to 1. Moreover, it has been estimated that as many as 12,000 children may be hospitalized in the United States each year for deliberately self-destructive acts, such as stabbing, cutting, burning, overdosing, or jumping from high places (NIMH, 1986).

One study of suicide attempts by children revealed that the majority had taken an overdose of drugs at home, half were living with only one parent, and a quarter had attempted suicide before (Kienhorst et al., 1987). Recent studies further suggest that the use of guns is increasing among children who attempt suicide (Cytryn & McKnew, 1996).

Researchers have found that suicide attempts by the very young are commonly preceded by such behavioral patterns as running away from home, accident-proneness, acting out, temper tantrums, self-deprecation, social withdrawal and loneliness, psychophysiological disorders (discussed in Chapter 11), extreme sensitivity to criticism, low tolerance of frustration, morbid fantasies and daydreams, marked personality change, and preoccupation with death and suicide (Cytryn & McKnew, 1996; McGuire, 1982). Studies have further linked child suicides to the recent or anticipated loss of a loved one, family stress and parental unemployment, abuse by parents, and a clinical level of depression (Cytryn & McKnew, 1996; Kovacs, Goldston, & Gatsonis, 1993; Pfeffer et al., 1993).

Most people find it hard to believe that children fully comprehend the implications of a suicidal act. They argue that because a child's cognitive powers are so limited, children who attempt suicide fall into Shneidman's category of "death ignorers," like Billy, who sought to join his mother in heaven (Fasko & Fasko, 1991). Many child suicides, however, are in fact based on a clear understanding of death and on a clear wish to die (Carlson et al., 1994; Pfeffer, 1993, 1986).

Suicidal thinking among even normal children is apparently more common than most people once believed (Kovacs et al., 1993; Pfeffer et al., 1984). Clinical interviews with schoolchildren have revealed that between 6 and 33 percent have contemplated suicide (Culp, Clyman, & Culp, 1995; Jacobsen et al., 1994; Kashani et al., 1989). It is not clear whether suicidal thinking among young children represents a new phenomenon or was previously undetected.

Adolescents and Young Adults

Dear Mom, Dad, and everyone else,

I'm sorry for what I've done, but I loved you all and I always will, for eternity. Please, please, please don't blame it on yourselves. It was all my fault and not yours or anyone else's. If I didn't do this now, I would have done it later anyway. We all die some day, I just died sooner.

Love,
John

(Berman, 1986)

The suicide of John, age 17, was not an unusual occurrence. Suicidal actions become much more common after the age of 14 than at any earlier age. In the United States close to 5,000 adolescents and young adults kill themselves each year; that is, more than 13 of every 100,000 persons between the ages of 15 and 24 (Stillion & McDowell, 1996; NCHS, 1994). Because fatal illnesses are relatively rare among the young, suicide has become the third leading cause of death among adolescents and young adults, after accidents and homicides (Diekstra et al., 1995; Berman, 1986). In contrast, suicide accounts for less than 2 percent of deaths in the total population. About 75 percent of adolescents who commit suicide are male.

Unlike the rates for other age groups, suicide rates in the 15-to-24-year-old group are becoming more similar across the races in the United States. Although young white Americans continue to be considerably more prone to suicide than young African Americans, the rates are converging (Berman, 1986). This trend may reflect converging pressures on young African Americans and young white Americans—competition for grades and college opportunities, for example, is now intense for both groups. The growing suicide rate for young African Americans may also be linked to increasing unemployment among them, the numerous anxieties of inner-city life, and the rage felt by many young African Americans over racial inequities in our society (Lipschitz, 1995; Hendin, 1987).

Although analyses of suicide typically lump 15-to-24-year-olds together, it is also important to look separately at teenagers (15-to-18-year-olds) and college students (18-to-22-year-olds). These groups often confront very different pressures, which in turn produce different profiles of suicide.

Teenagers Over 2,000 teenagers, or 11 of every 100,000, commit suicide in the United States each year, and as many as 250,000 teenagers may make attempts (NCHS, 1991; U.S. Bureau of the Census, 1990). Moreover, as many as half of all teenagers surveyed have thought about killing themselves (Diekstra et al., 1995). Thus many school counselors have requested guidelines for dealing with suicidal adolescents (Coder, Nelson, & Aylward, 1991).

Some of the major warning signs of suicide in teenagers are tiredness and sleep loss, loss of appetite, mood changes, decline in school performance, withdrawal, increased smoking or drug or alcohol use, increased letter writing to friends, and the giving away of valued possessions (Smith, 1995; Peach & Reddick, 1991; Berman, 1986). Drug overdose is the technique by which most adolescents attempt suicide (Diekstra et al., 1995).

About half of teenagers' suicides, like those of people in other age groups, have been linked to clinical depression, low self-esteem, and feelings of hopelessness (Harter & Marold, 1994; Kashden et al., 1993), but many teenagers who try to kill themselves also appear to struggle with anger and impulsivity (Kashden et al., 1993; Hoberman & Garfinkel, 1988). In addition, adolescents who contemplate or attempt suicide are often under considerable stress (de Man et al., 1992; de Wilde et al., 1992). Many of them experience long-term pressures such as missing or poor parental relationships, family conflict, inadequate peer relationships, and social isolation (Garnefski & Diekstra, 1997; Diekstra et al., 1995; Ho et al., 1995). Their actions also may be triggered by more immediate stressors, such as a parent's unemployment, financial setbacks for the family, or difficulties with a boyfriend or girlfriend (Diekstra et al., 1995; de Wilde et al., 1992; Pfeffer, 1990, 1988).

Stress at school seems to be a particularly common problem for teenagers who attempt suicide (Ho et al., 1995; Brent et al., 1988). Some have trouble keeping up at school, while others may be high achievers who feel pressured to be perfect and to stay at the top of the class (Delisle, 1986; Leroux, 1986).

Nowhere is academic stress a more visible factor in suicide than in Japan. The Japanese suicide rate is very high in the late teenage years (Hawton, 1986). Research suggests that this high rate may be related to *shiken jigoku,* or "examination hell," an extremely competitive testing period that many Japanese teenagers must go through to enter a university. Some Japanese students who are unsuccessful in these critical tests try to take their lives.

The intense training and testing characteristic of Japan's educational system produce high levels of stress in many students. The students in this classroom are participating in summer juku, *a camp where they receive remedial help, extra lessons, and exam practice eleven hours a day.*

Some theorists believe that adolescent life itself produces a climate conducive to suicidal action (Harter & Marold, 1994; Maris, 1986). Adolescence is a period of rapid growth and development, and in our society it is often marked by conflicts, depressed feelings, tensions, and difficulties at home and school. Adolescents also tend to react to events more sensitively, angrily, dramatically, and impulsively than people in other age groups, so that the likelihood of suicidal actions during times of stress is increased (Kaplan, 1984; Taylor & Stansfeld, 1984). Finally, the suggestibility of adolescents and their eagerness to imitate others, including others who attempt suicide, may help set the stage for suicidal action (Hazell & Lewin, 1993; Berman, 1986). One study has found that 93 percent of adolescent suicide attempters knew someone who had attempted suicide previously (Conrad, 1992).

It is important to note that far more teenagers attempt suicide than actually kill themselves. As we observed earlier, some theorists believe that the ratio of attempts to fatalities may be as high as 100 to 1 (Diekstra et al., 1995). The unusually large number of incomplete attempts by teenagers may mean that they tend to be more ambivalent than older persons who make such attempts. While some do indeed wish to die, many may simply want to make others understand how desperate they are, get help, or teach others a lesson (Hawton, 1986; Hawton et al., 1982). Up to half of teenage attempters go on to make more suicide attempts, and as many as 14 percent eventually die by suicide (Diekstra et al., 1995; Diekstra, 1989; Spirito et al., 1989).

College Students For many years it was believed that the suicide rate was higher for college students than for other young people in the 18-to-22-year-old age range, but recent investigations have challenged this notion (Hawton et al., 1995; Schwartz & Whitaker, 1990). Again, female students are more likely to attempt suicide, but fatal suicides are more numerous among males. Furthermore, studies suggest that as many as 20 percent of college students have suicidal thoughts at some point in their college years (Carson & Johnson, 1985).

One factor underlying college suicides is academic pressure (Cytryn & McKnew, 1996; Hawton et al., 1995; Lyman, 1961). Examinations and the competition for grades undoubtedly place stress on a student. So do relationship problems, the loss of social support felt by those who have moved away from their families and friends, and the rapid shift in values that some students experience during their college years (Hawton et al., 1995; Carson & Johnson, 1985).

Some clinicians suggest that the college students who consider suicide are those who never learned how to deal with personal problems and emotions before they entered college. Their past problems may complicate the already difficult task of dealing with college-linked pressures and situations (Hendin, 1987; Berkovitz, 1985). Indeed, a third of college students interviewed in one study reported having suicidal thoughts before they entered college (Sherer, 1985). A study of 218 undergraduates also found that suicidal students did not necessarily experience more stress than other students; they simply had fewer resources for dealing with problems and intense emotions (Carson & Johnson, 1985).

Because so many aspects of college life are stressful, suicide among college students is difficult to interpret. Research in England, for example, has indicated that the number of college suicides increases along with the prestige of the school (Stengel, 1974; Seiden, 1969). How are we to understand this finding? Certainly academic pressures are intense at prestigious schools, but the number of students living far from home usually is greater in these schools as well. These schools also encourage students to work independently, and perhaps the lack of structure contributes to the high rate of suicide.

Evidence suggests that students are helped in their efforts to cope with college by the friendships of people with whom they can share their experiences and problems (Arnstein, 1986). Friends, support personnel, and other forms of personal and social support can thus reduce the pressures of college life that sometimes contribute to depression and suicidal behavior.

Rising Suicide Rate In countries across the world, the suicide rate among adolescents and young adults is not only high but increasing (Diekstra et al., 1995). Overall, the suicide rate for this age group has more than doubled since 1955 (McIntosh, 1996, 1991; U.S. Bureau of the Census, 1994, 1990). In the United States, the rate for young persons peaked in 1977, when 13.6 of every 100,000 adolescents and young adults committed suicide, leveled off to 11.9 per 100,000 by 1983, then increased again to more than 13 in the 1990s. This latest upswing suggests that suicide among the young may be on the rise once again.

Several theories, most pointing to societal changes, have been proposed to explain the dramatic rise in the suicide rate among adolescents and young adults. (1) Paul Holinger and his colleagues have suggested that the competition for jobs, college positions, and academic and athletic honors keeps intensifying for this age group, leading increasingly to shattered dreams and frustrated ambitions (Holinger & Offer, 1993, 1991, 1984, 1982; Holinger, 1988; Holinger et al., 1987) (see Figure 10-5). (2) Many studies suggest that depression is on the rise among teenagers and young adults, perhaps leaving them particularly vulnerable to suicidal thoughts and actions (Carlson et al., 1991; Robins & Regier, 1991; Weissman et al., 1991). (3) Following Durkheim's idea of anomic suicide, some theorists hold that weakening ties in the nuclear family during the past few decades have provoked feelings of alienation and rejection in many of today's young people—emotions that may contribute to suicidal thoughts and actions (Peck, 1982). (4) The increased availability of drugs and pressure to use them may also be factors (Jones, 1997; de Man & Leduc, 1995; Schuckit & Schuckit, 1991). In accord with this view, two studies found that 70 percent of teenage suicide attempters abused drugs or alcohol to some degree (Miller et al., 1991; Shafii et al., 1985). (5) The mass media coverage of suicide attempts by teenagers and young adults may contribute to the rise in the suicide rate among the young (Myatt & Greenblatt, 1993; Gould et al., 1990; Phillips & Carstensen, 1988, 1986). As we observed earlier, highly publicized suicides often trigger others. The detailed descriptions of teenage suicide that the media and arts have offered in recent years may serve as models for young people who are contemplating suicide. Within days of the highly publicized suicides of four adolescents in a garage in Bergenfield, New Jersey, in 1987, dozens of teenagers across the United States took similar actions (at least twelve of them fatal)—two in the same garage just one week later.

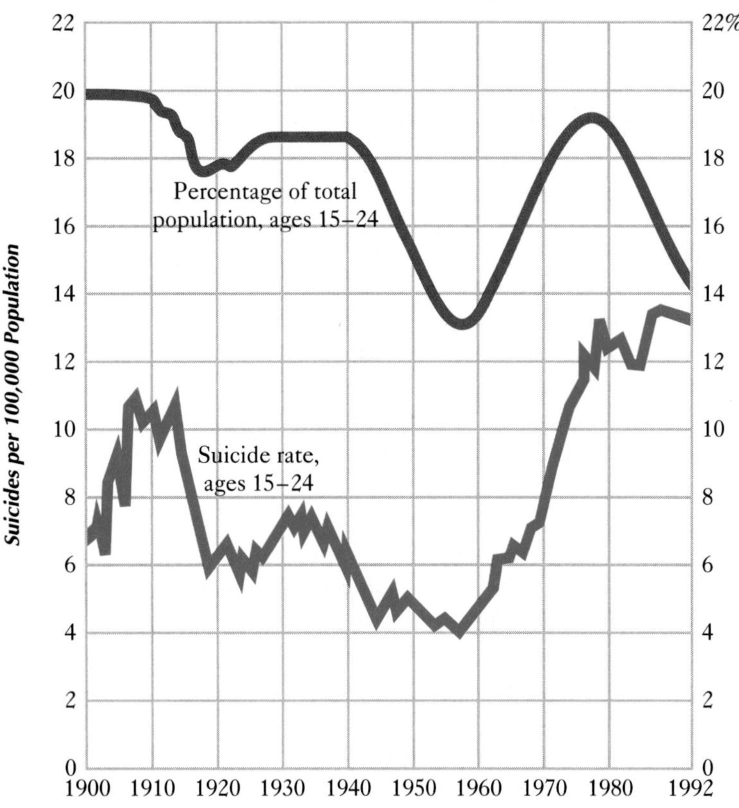

Figure 10-5 *Over the years, whenever the proportion of adolescents and young adults in the general population has increased, the suicide rate of this age group has risen as well. (Adapted from Stillion & McDowell, 1996; U.S. Bureau of the Census, 1994; Holinger & Offer, 1991.)*

As the rise in suicide rates among young persons reminds us, societal change does not necessarily lead to social progress. Our advances in medical, industrial, and communication technology during the past several decades are undeniably impressive. But often there is a significant price to pay for rapid change, and that price may include the mental health and survival of all too many young people.

The Elderly

Rose Ashby walks to the dry cleaner's to pick up her old but finest dinner dress. Although shaken at the cost of having it cleaned, Rose tells the sympathetic girl behind the counter, "Don't worry. It doesn't matter. I won't be needing the money any more."

Walking through the streets of St. Petersburg, Florida, she still wishes it had been Miami. The west coast of the fountain of youth peninsula is not as warm as the east. If only Chet had left more insurance money, Rose could have afforded Miami. In St. Petersburg, Rose failed to unearth de León's promised fount.

Last week, she told the doctor she felt lonely and depressed. He said she should perk up. She had everything to live for. What does he know? Has he lost a husband like Chet, and his left breast to cancer all in one year? Has he suffered arthritis all his life? Were his ovaries so bad he had to undergo a hysterectomy? Did he have to suffer through menopause just to end up alone without family or friends? Does he have to live in a dungeon? Is his furniture worn, his carpet threadbare? What does he know? Might his every day be the last one for him?

As Rose turns into the walk to her white cinderblock apartment building, fat Mrs. Green asks if she is coming to the community center that evening. Who needs it? The social worker did say Rose should come. Since Rose was in such good health, she could help those not so well as she.

Help them do what? Finger-paint like little children? Make baskets like insane people? Sew? Who can see to sew? Besides, who would appreciate it? Who would thank her? Who could she tell about her troubles? Who cares?

When she told the doctor she couldn't sleep, he gave her the prescription but said that all elderly people have trouble sleeping. What does he know? Does he have a middle-aged daughter who can only think about her latest divorce, or grandchildren who only acknowledge her birthday check by the endorsement on the back? Are all his friends dead and gone? Is all the money from his dead husband's insurance used up? What does he know? Who could sleep in this dungeon?

Back in her apartment, Rose washes and sets her hair. It's good she has to do it herself. Look at this hair. So thin, so sparse, so frowsy. What would a hairdresser think?

Then make-up. Base. Rouge. Lipstick. Bright red. Perfume? No! No cheap perfume for Rose today. Remember the bottles of Joy Chet would buy for her? He always wanted her to have the best. He would boast that she had everything, and that she never had to work a day in her life for it.

"She doesn't have to lift her little finger," Chet would say, puffing on his cigar. Where is the Joy now? Dead and gone. With Chet. Rose manages a wry laugh at the play on words.

Slipping into her dinner dress, she looks into the dresser mirror. "It's good you can't see this face now, Chet. How old and ugly it looks."

Taking some lavender notepaper from the drawer, she stands at the dresser to write. Why didn't anyone warn her that growing old was like this? It is so unfair. But they don't care. People don't care about anyone except themselves.

Leaving the note on the dresser, she suddenly feels excited. Breathing hard now, she rushes to the sink—who could call a sink in the counter in the living room a kitchen?—and gets a glass of water.

Trying to relax, Rose arranges the folds in her skirt as she settles down on the chaise. Carefully sipping the water as she takes all the capsules so as to not smear her lipstick, Rose quietly begins to sob. After a lifetime of tears, these will be her last. Her note on the dresser is short, written to no one and to everyone.

You don't know what it is like
to have to grow old and die.

(Gernsbacher, 1985, pp. 227–228)

In Western society the elderly are more likely to commit suicide than people in any other age group (Osgood & Eisenhandler, 1995) (see Figures 10-1 and 10-4). About 19 of every 100,000 persons over the age of 65 in the United States commit suicide (McIntosh, 1995, 1992). Elderly persons committed over 19 percent of all suicides in the United States during the 1980s, yet they accounted for only 12 percent of the total population (McIntosh, 1992).

Many factors contribute to the high suicide rate among the elderly (Canetto, 1995; Cattell & Jolley, 1995) As people grow older, all too often they become ill, lose close friends and relatives, lose control over their lives, and lose status in our society. Such experiences may result in feelings of hopelessness, loneliness, depression, or inevitability among aged persons, and so increase the likelihood that they will attempt suicide (Canetto, 1995; McIntosh, 1995; Osgood, 1987). In one study 44 percent of elderly people who committed suicide gave some indication that their act was prompted by the fear of being placed in a nursing home (Loebel et al., 1991). Too, the suicide rate of people who have lost a spouse is disproportionately high (Li, 1995; McIntosh, 1995, 1992). The risk is greatest during the first year of bereavement, but it remains elevated in later years as well.

Elderly persons are typically more resolute than younger persons in their decision to die, so their success rate is much higher (McIntosh, 1992). Apparently one of every four elderly persons who attempts suicide succeeds (McIntosh, 1992, 1987). Given the greater resolve of aged persons and their obvious physical decline, many people argue that older persons who want to die are clear in their thinking and should be allowed to carry out their wishes. At the same time, however, clinical depression appears to play an important role in as many as 60 percent of suicides among the elderly, suggesting that more elderly persons should be receiving treatment for their depressive disorders than is typically the case (Cattell & Jolley, 1995; McIntosh, 1995).

The suicide rate among elderly people in the United States is lower in some minority groups. Although Native Americans have the highest overall suicide rate, for example, the rate among elderly Native Americans is quite low (McIntosh & Santos, 1982). Similarly, the suicide rate is only one-third as high among elderly African Americans as among elderly white Americans (McIntosh, 1992).

Elderly persons are held in high esteem in many traditional societies because of the store of knowledge they have accumulated over the years. Perhaps not so coincidentally, suicides among the elderly seem to be less common in these cultures than in those of many modern industrialized nations.

Why are suicide rates for the elderly particularly low in some minority groups? The respect afforded elderly Native Americans may help account for their low rate (McIntosh & Santos, 1982). The aged are held in high esteem by Native Americans and looked to for the wisdom and experience they have acquired over the years. This heightened status is in sharp contrast to the loss of status often experienced by elderly white Americans (Butler, 1975).

One theory about the low suicide rate among elderly African Americans points paradoxically to the pressures African Americans live under: "only the strongest survive" (Seiden, 1981). Those who reach an advanced age have overcome significant adversity and often feel proud of what they have accomplished. Because advancement to old age is not in itself a form of success for white Americans, it leaves them with a different attitude toward life and age. Another suggestion is that aged African Americans have successfully overcome the rage that prompts many suicides in younger African Americans.

Treatment and Suicide

Treatment of people who are suicidal falls into two major categories: *treatment after suicide has been attempted* and *suicide prevention.* Treatment may also be given to relatives and friends, whose feelings of bereavement, guilt, and anger after a suicide fatality or attempt can be intense (Moore & Freeman, 1995; Sapsford, 1995; Farberow, 1993, 1991), but the discussion here is limited to the treatment afforded suicidal people themselves.

Treatment After a Suicide Attempt

After a suicide attempt, most victims' primary need is medical care. Some are left with severe injuries, brain damage, or other medical problems. Once the physical damage is reversed or at least stabilized, psychotherapy

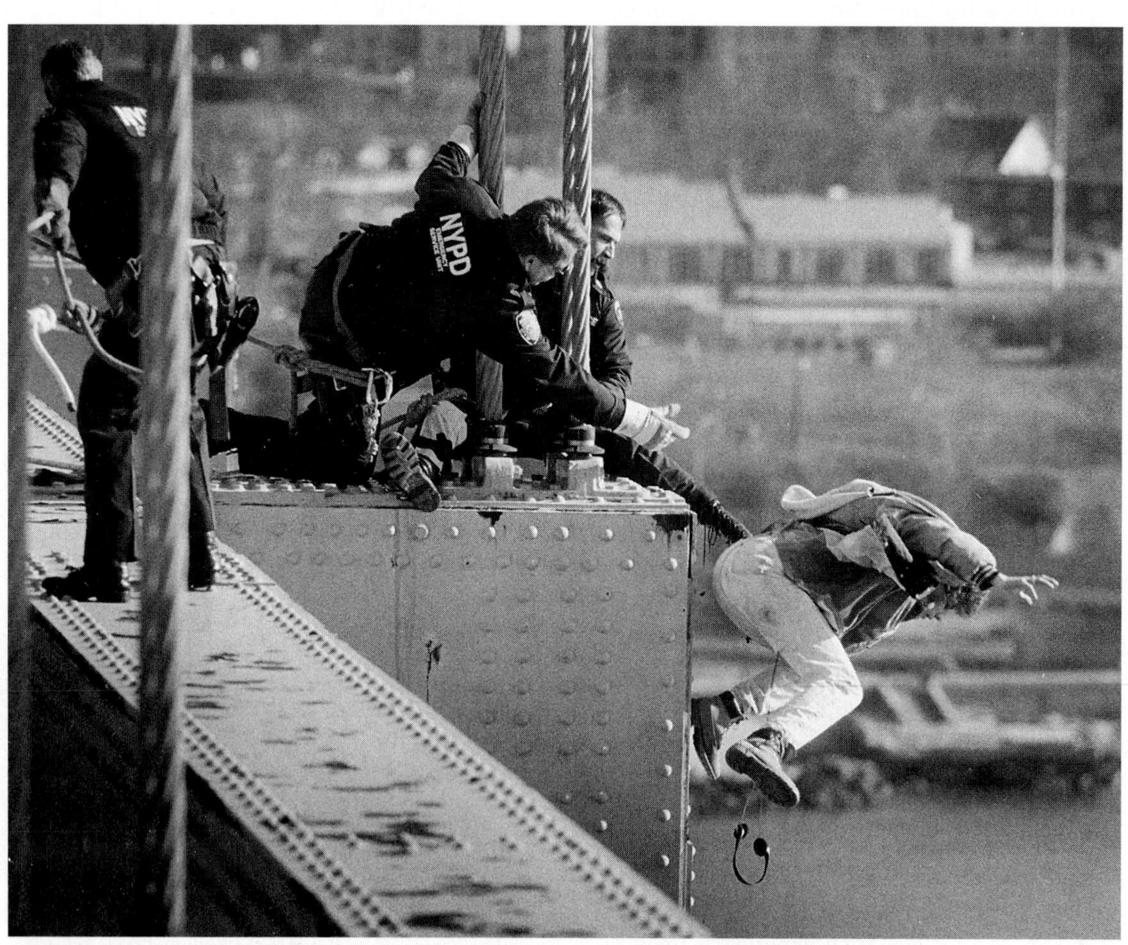

An individual breaks free from police and falls from a bridge in New York City. The scene reminds us that many kinds of professionals are confronted by suicidal behavior. Police departments typically provide special crisis intervention training so that officers can develop the skills to address suicidal individuals.

or drug therapy may begin. This treatment may be either inpatient or outpatient.

Unfortunately, even after trying to kill themselves, most suicidal people fail to receive systematic psychotherapy. In a random survey of several hundred teenagers, 9 percent were found to have made at least one suicide attempt, and of those only half had received subsequent psychological treatment (Harkavy & Asnis, 1985). In some cases, health-care professionals are at fault. One study found that 46 percent of people treated for attempted suicide in a Helsinki general hospital were not given even a psychological consultation (Suokas & Lonnqvist, 1991). In other cases, persons who attempt suicide refuse follow-up therapy. One study of adolescents who had attempted to kill themselves found that 40 percent failed to attend follow-up outpatient treatment (Piacentini et al., 1995).

The goal of therapy is to keep the clients alive, help them achieve a nonsuicidal state of mind, and guide them to develop more constructive ways of handling stress and solving problems (Shneidman, 1993; Möller, 1990). Various therapy systems and formats have been employed, including drug, psychodynamic, cognitive, group, and family therapies (Berman & Jobes, 1995, 1991; Canetto, 1995; Rotheram-Borus et al., 1994). Therapy appears to help. Studies suggest that at least 16 percent of patients in each kind of treatment make further suicide attempts, but as many as 30 percent of suicide attempters who do not receive treatment try again (Nordstrom, Samuelsson, & Asberg, 1995; Allard et al., 1991; Liberman & Eckman, 1981). It is not clear, however, whether any of these approaches are more effective than the others (Canetto, 1995; Salkovskis et al., 1990; Streiner & Adams, 1987).

Suicide Prevention

During the past thirty years emphasis in both North America and Western Europe has shifted from suicide treatment to suicide prevention (Rihmer et al., 1995; Silverman & Felner, 1995; Tanney, 1995). In some respects this change is most appropriate: the last opportunity to keep many potential suicide victims alive comes before the first attempt.

The emphasis on suicide prevention began in earnest during the mid-1950s. The first ***suicide prevention program*** in the United States was founded in Los Angeles by Norman Farberow and Edwin Shneidman in 1955; the first in England, called the Samaritans, was founded by the Reverend Chad Varah in 1953. There are now more than 200 independent, locally funded suicide prevention centers in the United States and over 100 in England, and the numbers are still growing (Lester, 1989; Roberts, 1979). In addition, many mental health centers, hospital emergency rooms, pastoral counseling centers, and poison control centers now include suicide prevention programs among their services.

There are also more than 1,000 ***suicide hot lines,*** 24-hour-a-day telephone services, in the United States (Garland, Shaffer, & Whittle, 1989). Callers reach a counselor, typically a ***paraprofessional,*** a person trained in counseling but without a formal degree, who provides services under the supervision of a mental health professional (Neimeyer & Bonnelle, 1997).

Suicide prevention programs and hot lines define suicidal people as people *in crisis*—that is, under great stress, unable to cope, feeling threatened or hurt, and interpreting their situations as unchangeable. Accordingly, the programs engage in ***crisis intervention:*** they try to help suicidal people perceive their situations more accurately, make better decisions, act more constructively, and overcome their crises (Frankish, 1994). Because crises can occur at any time, the centers advertise their hot lines and also welcome clients who walk in without appointments.

Although specific features vary from center to center, the general approach used by the Los Angeles Suicide Prevention Center reflects the goals and techniques of many such organizations (Litman, 1995; Maris & Silverman, 1995). During the initial contact, the counselor has several tasks: establishing a positive relationship with the caller, understanding and clarifying the problem, assessing the caller's suicide potential, assessing and mobilizing the caller's resources, and formulating a plan for overcoming the crisis (Shneidman & Farberow, 1968).

Establishing a positive relationship Obviously, callers must trust counselors if they are to confide in them and follow their suggestions. Thus counselors try to set a positive and comfortable tone for discussion. They convey the message that they are listening, understanding, interested, nonjudgmental, and available.

Understanding and clarifying the problem Counselors first try to understand the full scope of the caller's crisis, then help the person see the crisis in clear and constructive terms. In particular, counselors try to help callers identify the central issues and the transient nature of their crises and recognize the alternatives to suicidal action.

Assessing suicide potential Crisis workers at the Los Angeles Suicide Prevention Center fill out a questionnaire, often called a "lethality scale," to estimate the caller's potential for suicide. It helps them to determine the degree of stress the caller is under, relevant personality characteristics, how detailed the suicide plan is, the severity of symptoms, and the coping resources available to the caller.

Assessing and mobilizing the caller's resources Although they may view themselves as ineffectual and helpless, people who are suicidal usually have many strengths and resources, including relatives and friends. It is the counselor's job to recognize, point out, and activate those resources.

Formulating a plan Together the crisis worker and caller formulate a plan of action. In essence, they are agreeing on a way out of the crisis, a constructive alternative to suicidal action. Most plans include a series of follow-up counseling sessions over the next few days or weeks, either in person at the center or by phone. Each plan also usually requires the caller to take certain actions and make certain changes in his or her personal life. Counselors usually negotiate a "no suicide" contract with the caller—a promise not to attempt suicide, or at least a promise to reestablish contact if the caller again contemplates suicide. Family members and friends may be included in some plans. If callers are in the midst of a suicide attempt, counselors will also try to ascertain their whereabouts and get medical help to them immediately.

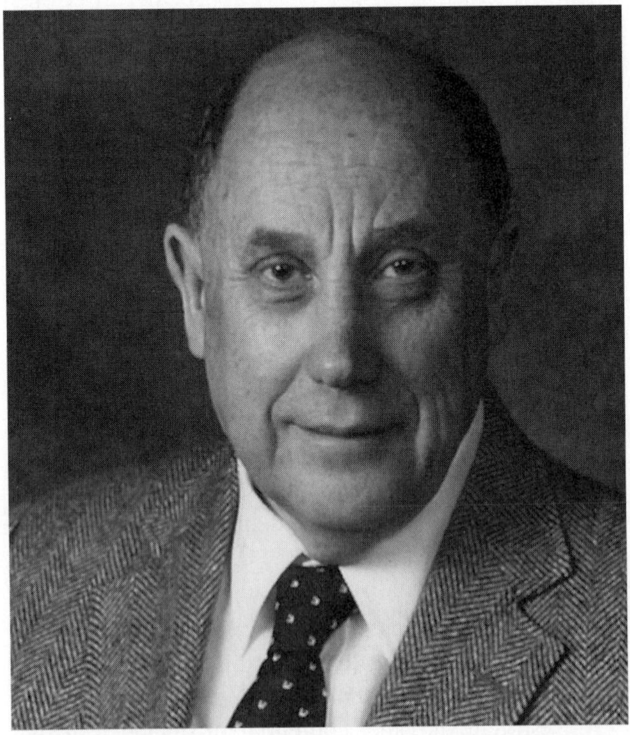

The psychologist Edwin Shneidman, who helped found America's first suicide prevention center in 1955, has developed techniques to assess the risk of suicide, identified various types of suicide, and corrected numerous myths about it.

Although crisis intervention appears to be sufficient treatment for some suicidal people (Hawton, 1986), longer-term therapy is needed for most of them (Berman & Jobes, 1995; Litman, 1995). If the crisis intervention center does not offer this kind of therapy, the counselors will refer the individuals elsewhere.

As the suicide prevention movement spread during the 1960s, many clinicians concluded that crisis intervention techniques should also be applied to problems other than suicide. They reasoned that nonsuicidal people may also be immobilized by crises and may benefit from an active, problem-solving form of intervention. Crisis intervention has emerged during the past three decades as a respected form of treatment for such wide-ranging problems as teenage confusion, drug and alcohol abuse, rape victimization, and spouse abuse (Lester, 1989; Bloom, 1984).

Yet another way to help prevent suicide may be to reduce the public's access to common means of suicide (Ohberg et al., 1995). In 1960, for example, around 12 of every 100,000 persons in Britain killed themselves by inhaling coal gas (which contains carbon monoxide). In the 1960s Britain replaced coal gas with natural gas (which contains no carbon monoxide) as an energy source, and by the mid-1970s, the rate of coal gas suicide fell to zero (Diekstra et al., 1995). Moreover, England's overall rate of suicide, at least for older people, dropped as well. On the other hand, the Netherlands' drop in gas-induced suicides was compensated for by an *increase* in other methods, particularly drug overdoses. Thus, while it is hoped that such measures as gun control, safer medications, and car emission controls may lower suicide rates, there is no guarantee that they will (Lester, 1992).

The Effectiveness of Suicide Prevention

It has been difficult for researchers to assess the effectiveness of suicide prevention programs (Maris & Silverman, 1995; Eddy et al., 1987). There are many kinds of programs, each with its own procedures and serving populations that vary in number, age, economic stability, and environmental pressures. Communities with high suicide risk factors, such as an elderly population or economic strife, may continue to have higher suicide rates than other communities regardless of the effectiveness of their local prevention centers.

Do suicide prevention centers reduce the number of suicides in a community? Clinical researchers do not know (Canetto, 1995; Dew et al., 1987). Studies comparing local suicide rates before and after the establishment of community prevention centers have yielded very different findings. Some find a decline in suicide rates (Dashef, 1984; Miller et al., 1984), others no change

(Dew et al., 1987; Lester, 1974, 1972), and still others an increase in suicide rates (Weiner, 1969). It is important to note, however, that the increase in suicide rates found in some studies may reflect society's overall increase in suicidal behavior. One investigator found that although suicide rates did increase in some cities with prevention programs, they increased even more in cities without such programs (Lester, 1991, 1974).

Do suicidal people contact prevention centers? Apparently only a small percentage do. Moreover, the typical caller to an urban prevention center appears to be young, African American, and female, whereas the greatest number of suicides are committed by elderly white men (Canetto, 1995; Lester, 1989, 1972).

At the same time, prevention programs do seem to avert many suicides among those high-risk people who do call. Norman Farberow and Robert Litman (1970) identified 8,000 high-risk individuals who contacted the Los Angeles Suicide Prevention Center. Approximately 2 percent of these callers later committed suicide, compared to the 6 percent suicide rate usually found in similar high-risk groups.

Clearly, then, centers need to be more visible to and approachable by people who are harboring thoughts of suicide. The growing number of advertisements and announcements in newspapers and on television, radio, and billboards attest to a movement in this direction.

Partly because of the many suicide prevention programs and the data they have generated, today's clinicians have a better understanding of suicide and greater ability to assess its risk than those of the past (Clum & Yang, 1995; McIntosh et al., 1985). Studies reveal that the professionals who are most knowledgeable about suicide are psychologists, psychiatrists, and personnel who actually work in prevention programs (Domino & Swain, 1986). Other professionals whom suicidal persons might contact, such as members of the clergy, are sometimes less well informed (Domino & Swain, 1986; Domino, 1985).

Shneidman (1987) has called for broader and more effective *public education* about suicide as the ultimate form of prevention. And at least some suicide education programs—most of them concentrating on teachers and students—have begun to emerge (Stillion & McDowell, 1996; Klingman & Hochdorf, 1993; Leenaars & Wenckstern, 1991). The curriculum for such programs has been the subject of considerable debate and the programs' merits have yet to be broadly investigated (Kalafat & Elias, 1995; Garland & Zigler, 1993). Nevertheless, most clinicians agree with the intent behind these programs and, more generally, with Shneidman when he states:

> The primary prevention of suicide lies in education. The route is through teaching one another and . . . the public that suicide can happen to anyone, that there are verbal and behavioral clues that can be looked for . . . , and that help is available. . . .
>
> In the last analysis, the prevention of suicide is everybody's business.
>
> *(Shneidman, 1985, p. 238)*

Crossroads

Once a mysterious and hidden problem, hardly acknowledged by the public and barely investigated by professionals, suicide today is a focus of attention for the public and researchers alike. During the past two decades in particular, investigators have learned a great deal about this staggering problem.

In contrast to most other problems examined in this textbook, suicide has received much more clarification from the sociocultural model than from any other. The explanations offered by the psychological and biological models have received only limited research support. Meanwhile, sociocultural theorists have highlighted the importance of societal change and stress, national and religious affiliation, marital status, gender, race, and the mass media. Unfortunately, although such factors certainly shed light on the context and precipitants of suicide, they typically leave us unable to predict when such attempts will be made. When all is said and done, clinicians do not yet fully comprehend why some people kill themselves while others under similar circumstances manage to find alternative ways of addressing their problems. Psychological and biological insights must catch up to the sociocultural insights if clinicians are truly to explain and understand suicide.

Treatments for suicide also pose some difficult problems. Clinicians have yet to develop indisputably successful interventions for suicidal persons. Suicide prevention programs have been embraced by the clinical community and certainly reflect its commitment to helping suicidal persons, but, as we have noted, it is not yet clear how much such programs actually reduce the overall risk or rate of suicide.

At the same time, the growing research on suicide offers great promise. And perhaps most promising of all, clinicians and educators are now enlisting the public in the fight against this problem. Most believe that suicide rates can be reduced only if people recognize the enormous scope of this problem and learn how to identify and respond to suicide risks. They are calling for broader public education about suicide—programs aimed at both young and old.

It is reasonable to expect that the current commitment by the clinical field to investigate, publicize, and overcome the phenomenon of suicide will lead to a better understanding of it and to more successful interventions. Clearly such goals are of importance to everyone. Although suicide itself is typically a lonely and desperate act, the implications and impact of such acts are very broad indeed.

Chapter Review

1. ***What is suicide?*** Suicide is a self-inflicted death in which one makes an *intentional, direct,* and *conscious* effort to end one's life.
   A. Edwin Shneidman has distinguished four kinds of people who intentionally end their lives: the *death seeker,* the *death initiator,* the *death ignorer,* and the *death darer.*
   B. Shneidman has also distinguished a suicide-like category called *subintentioned death,* in which people play indirect, covert, partial, or unconscious roles in their own deaths.

2. ***Research strategies*** Two major strategies are used in the study of suicide: *retrospective analysis,* a kind of psychological autopsy; and the study of people who survive suicide attempts, on the assumption that they are similar to those who commit fatal suicides. Each strategy has limitations.

3. ***Patterns and statistics*** Suicide ranks among the top ten causes of death in Western society.
   A. Suicide rates vary from country to country. One reason seems to be cultural differences in religious affiliation, beliefs, or degree of devoutness.
   B. Suicide rates also vary according to race, sex, and marital status.

4. ***Factors that precipitate suicide*** Many suicidal acts are tied to contemporaneous events or conditions. Common precipitating factors include *stressful events and situations, mood and thought changes, alcohol and other drug use, mental disorders,* and events that inspire *modeling.*

5. ***Explanations of suicide*** The leading explanations come from the psychodynamic, biological, and sociocultural models.
   A. ***Psychodynamic*** theorists believe that suicide usually results from depression and self-directed anger. Freud also proposed that human beings have a basic death instinct, which he called *Thanatos.*
   B. Emile Durkheim's ***sociocultural*** theory defined three categories of suicide based on the person's relationship with society: *egoistic suicides, altruistic suicides,* and *anomic suicides.*
   C. The ***biological*** view of suicide has focused on the finding that the activity of the neurotransmitter *serotonin* is often relatively low in individuals who commit suicide.

6. ***Suicide in different age groups*** The likelihood of suicide varies with age.
   A. Children Suicide is relatively infrequent among children, although it has been increasing rapidly in that group during the past several decades.
   B. Adolescents Suicide by adolescents is increasing. Suicide attempts by this age group are very numerous.
      (1) Adolescent suicide is often linked to clinical depression, anger, impulsivity, unusual stress, and adolescent life itself.
      (2) The rising suicide rate among adolescents and young adults may be related to the growing number and proportion of these young people in the general population, the rise in depression among young people, the weakening of ties in the nuclear family, the increased availability and use of drugs among the young, and the broad media coverage attending suicide attempts by the young.
   C. The elderly In Western society elderly persons are more likely to commit suicide than people in any other age group. The loss of health, friends, control, and status may produce feelings of hopelessness, loneliness, depression, or inevitability in this age group.

7. ***Treatment and suicide*** Treatment may follow a suicide attempt or may seek to prevent suicide.
   A. The goal of therapy after an attempted suicide is to help the client achieve a nonsuicidal state of mind and develop more constructive ways of handling stress and solving problems.
   B. Over the past thirty years, emphasis has shifted from suicide treatment to suicide prevention.
      (1) *Suicide prevention programs* include 24-hour-a-day hot lines and walk-in centers staffed largely by *paraprofessionals.*
      (2) During their initial contact with a suicidal person, counselors seek to establish a positive relationship, to understand and clarify the problem, to assess the potential for suicide, to assess and mobilize the caller's resources, and to formulate a plan for overcoming the crisis.
      (3) Such *crisis intervention* may be sufficient treatment for some suicidal people. Most, however, also need longer-term therapy.
      (4) Suicide education programs for the public are beginning to emerge.

Thought and Afterthought

Suicide in the Family

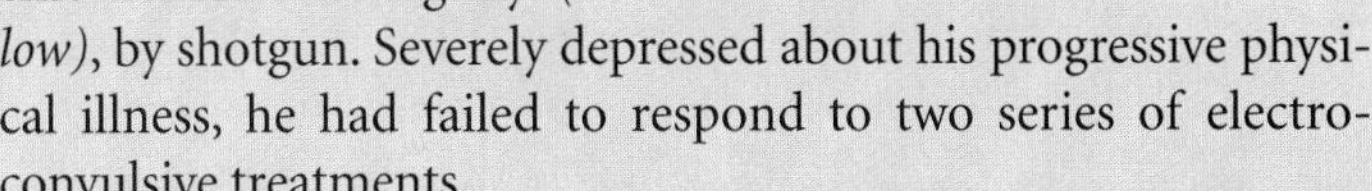

On July 1, 1996, the model and actress Margaux Hemingway killed herself by taking an overdose of barbiturates. She was the fifth person in four generations of her family to commit suicide. Her death came almost thirty-five years to the day after the suicide of her famous grandfather, the novelist Ernest Hemingway *(below)*, by shotgun. Severely depressed about his progressive physical illness, he had failed to respond to two series of electroconvulsive treatments.

Margaux Hemingway had suffered from severe depression, alcoholism, and bulimia nervosa. She had had a very successful modeling and acting career in the 1970s, but in recent years her work consisted primarily of making infomercials and low-budget movies. According to friends, she had tried for years to handle her anguish and problems with grace. "I was taught it was Hemingwayesque to take your blows and walk stoically through them."

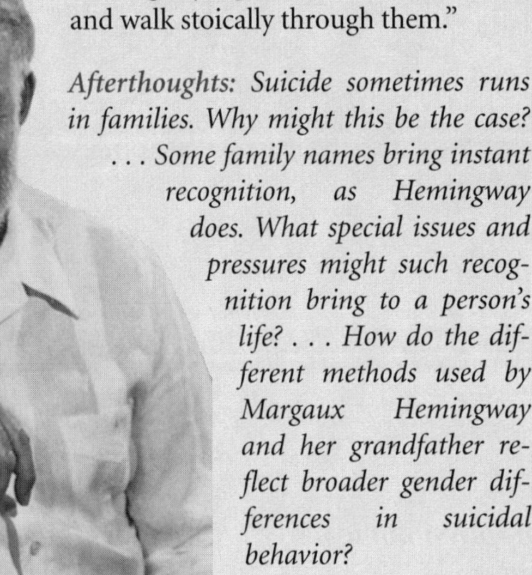

Afterthoughts: Suicide sometimes runs in families. Why might this be the case? . . . Some family names bring instant recognition, as Hemingway does. What special issues and pressures might such recognition bring to a person's life? . . . How do the different methods used by Margaux Hemingway and her grandfather reflect broader gender differences in suicidal behavior?

Even Success Feels Like Failure

Alasdair Clayre was a high achiever: brilliant enough to be compared with Sir Isaiah Berlin as a philosophy undergraduate at Oxford, a recipient of the prestigious Prize Fellowship of All Souls College. He also wrote a novel, performed his own songs as a folk singer and produced award-winning television programs.

And yet the day a book he had worked on for years —to accompany a television series—was to be published, Professor Clayre ended his life by jumping into the path of a train at an Underground station in North London. According to friends, he had been mortally fearful of what reviewers might say about his book.

(New York Times, May 1, 1996)

Clinicians have tied many cases of suicide, including that of Professor Clayre, to relentless perfectionism. Perfectionism may make even high achievers "implacable self-critics, vulnerable to overreacting to what they perceive as failure, often to the point of depression" (Goleman, 1996). Research confirms that perfectionistic depressed people have a higher suicide rate than depressed people who are less concerned with perfection (Hewitt et al., 1997).

Afterthoughts: Why might perfectionism be closely tied to suicide? . . . Is there something about our society that increases fear of failure or imperfection, especially among high-achieving people?

Attitudes Toward Suicide: Gender Plays a Role

We already know that men and women have different suicide rates and, on average, use different methods when they attempt suicide. It turns out that they also hold different attitudes toward people who try to kill themselves. Judith Stillion (1995) has reported, for example, that women tend to know more of the facts about suicidal behavior than men. They are more willing to discuss the subject with suicidal people, and they report feeling more sympathy for those who are contemplating suicide. Yet women are more disapproving of suicide as a "solution" to problems.

Afterthoughts: Why might women and men hold such different attitudes toward suicide? . . . How might these attitudes relate to patterns of suicidal behavior for women and men? . . . Are there implications here for suicide peer counseling and crisis intervention?

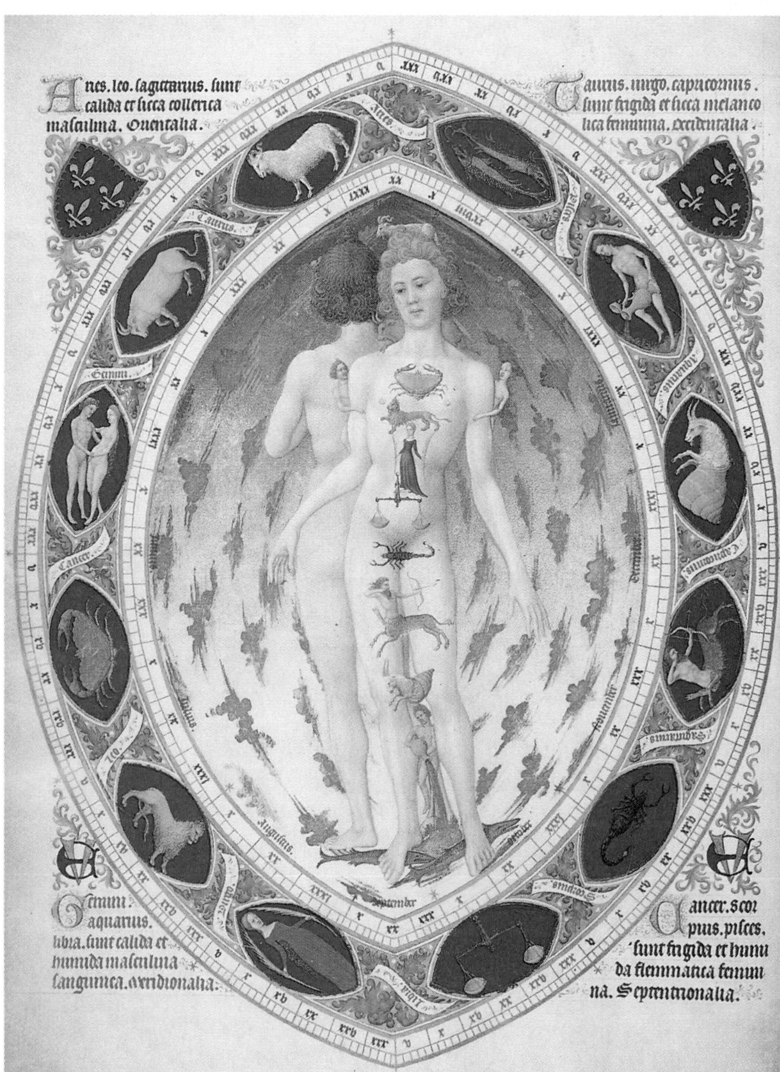

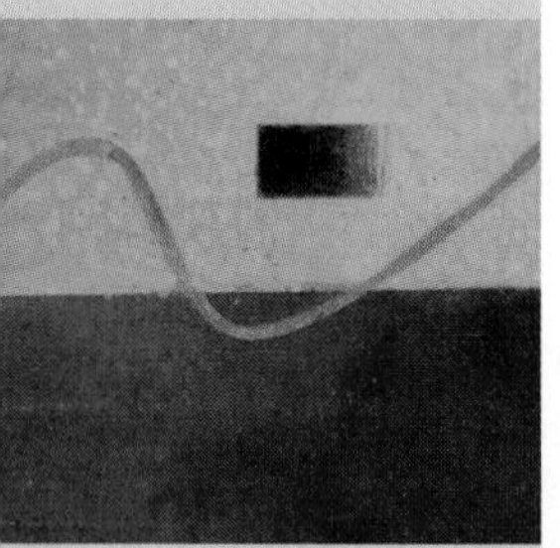

Topic Overview

Chapter 11

Psychosocial Factors in Physical Disorders

Throughout this text we have repeatedly encountered mental disorders that have physical causes. Abnormal neurotransmitter activity, for example, contributes to generalized anxiety disorder, panic disorder, and depression. Can it be surprising that somatic, or bodily, illnesses also have *psychosocial* causes—that is, causes that are psychological and sociocultural? Today's clinicians have come to recognize the wisdom of what Socrates said back in the fourth century B.C.: "You should not treat body without soul" (Fiester, 1986; Gentry & Matarazzo, 1981).

Psychosocial factors may contribute to medical illnesses in a variety of ways. Let's say that it's the morning of a midterm exam and Jerry awakens with severe dizziness. As the day progresses, his discomfort becomes progressively worse until finally he has to go to the student health center just an hour before the exam. There the physician on call has some possibilities to sort out. At one end, Jerry could be *faking* his dizziness to avoid taking a tough test. Alternatively, he may be *imagining* his illness, that is, faking himself out as much as anyone else. Then again, his physical symptoms could be very real, yet *triggered by stress:* whenever he feels extreme pressure, such as that produced by an important test, Jerry's blood pressure may rise and cause him to become dizzy. Finally, he may be coming down with the flu. Even this *purely medical problem,* however, could be linked to psychosocial factors. Perhaps a week of constant worry about the exam has weakened Jerry's body and left him incapable of

Throughout history, scientists and practitioners have cited a variety of factors that affect bodily health. This early fifteenth-century manuscript illustration from the Très Riches Heures de Jean, Duc de Berry, *for example, highlights the supposed astrological influences on the body. The importance of psychological and sociocultural factors has been recognized only in recent times.*

fighting off the flu virus. Clearly Jerry's state of mind and social environment are affecting his body in each of these scenarios. And the particular role played by psychosocial factors will in turn affect the way the physician decides to treat him.

The idea that psychological and sociocultural factors may contribute to somatic illnesses has ancient roots. Yet it held little appeal before the twentieth century. It was particularly unpopular during the Renaissance, when medicine first became a physical science and scientists became committed to the pursuit of objective "fact" (Gatchel & Baum, 1983). At that time the mind was the province of priests and philosophers, the body the realm of physicians and scientists. By the seventeenth century, the French philosopher René Descartes went so far as to claim that the mind, or soul, is separate from the body, and his position, called ***mind-body dualism,*** dominated medical theory for the next 200 years. After all, if the mind is totally separate from physical matter, how could it affect somatic processes?

During the past century, however, medical scientists have been steadily persuaded that many physical illnesses are ***psychogenic:*** contributed to by psychosocial factors such as family stress, worry, and unconscious needs. Some of these physical illnesses, called *factitious disorder* and *somatoform disorders* by today's professionals, are thought to be caused *primarily* by psychosocial factors. Others, called *psychophysiological disorders,* are believed to result from an *interaction* of biological, psychological, and sociocultural factors.

Factitious Disorder

Like Jerry, people who become physically sick usually go to a physician. Sometimes, however, an illness defies medical assessment, and physicians may suspect causes other than the physical factors they have been seeking. They may conclude, for instance, that the patient is ***malingering***—intentionally feigning illness to achieve some external gains, such as financial compensation or military deferment (Eisendrath, 1995).

Alternatively, a patient may intentionally produce or feign physical symptoms simply because he or she wishes to be a patient. That is, the motivation for assuming the sick role may be the role itself (APA, 1994). Physicians then say that the patient is manifesting a ***factitious disorder.*** A factitious disorder need not be a total fabrication. The physical symptoms may be self-inflicted or an exaggeration of a preexisting illness (APA, 1994):

> A 29-year-old female laboratory technician was admitted to the medical service via the emergency room because of bloody urine. The patient said that she was being treated for lupus erythematosus by a physician in a different city. She also mentioned that she had had Von Willebrand's disease (a rare hereditary blood disorder) as a child. On the third day of her hospitalization, a medical student mentioned to the resident that she had seen this patient several weeks before at a different hospital in the area, where the patient had been admitted for the same problem. A search of the patient's belongings revealed a cache of anticoagulant medication. When confronted with this information she refused to discuss the matter and hurriedly signed out of the hospital against medical advice.
>
> *(Spitzer et al., 1981, p. 33)*

People with a factitious disorder often go to extremes to create the appearance of illness. Many give themselves medications secretly. Some, like the woman just described, inject anticoagulants to cause bleeding disorders. Still others have bled themselves to simulate anemia or used laxatives to produce chronic diarrhea (Feldman, Ford, & Reinhold, 1994). High fevers are especially easy to create. In one study of patients with prolonged unidentifiable fever, more than 9 percent received a diagnosis of factitious disorder (Feldman et al., 1994).

Many people with a factitious disorder eagerly undergo painful testing or treatment, even surgery. They may develop real medical problems, such as the formation of scar tissue from unnecessary surgery, abscesses from numerous injections, or adverse reactions to drugs. If physicians confront them with evidence that their symptoms are factitious, they typically deny the charges and rapidly discharge themselves from the hospital; they may enter another hospital the same day.

People with this disorder usually are vague when pressed for details of their medical history, but some present an elaborate medical history, a fabrication called *pseudologia fantastica* (Bauer & Boegner, 1996). Their knowledge of medicine can be extensive.

Munchausen syndrome is the extreme and chronic form of factitious disorder. Like Baron Munchausen, an eighteenth-century cavalry officer who journeyed from tavern to tavern in Europe telling fantastical tales about his supposed military adventures, people with this syndrome travel from hospital to hospital reciting their supposed medical histories in great detail (Feldman et al., 1994; Zuger, 1993). In a related form of factitious disorder, ***Munchausen syndrome by proxy,*** parents fabricate or induce physical illnesses in their children, leading in some cases to numerous painful diagnostic tests, medication, and surgery (Feldman et al., 1994; McQuiston, 1993). When the children are removed from their parents and placed in the care of others, their symptoms disappear (see Box 11-1).

Clinical researchers have had great difficulty determining the prevalence of factitious disorder, since patients hide the true nature of their problem (Bauer & Boegner, 1996). It is believed, however, that the syndrome is more common among men than among women (APA, 1994). It usually begins during early adulthood and often prevents the person from holding a steady job.

The disorder seems to be most common among people who (1) as children received extensive medical treatment and hospitalization for a true physical disorder, (2) carry a grudge against the medical profession, (3) have worked as a nurse, laboratory technician, or medical paraprofessional, (4) had a significant relationship with a physician in the past, or (5) have underlying dependent, exploitive, or self-defeating personality characteristics (APA, 1994; Feldman et al., 1994). People with this disorder often have poor social support, few enduring social relationships, and limited family involvement (Feldman et al., 1994).

The precise causes of factitious disorder are not understood, although clinical reports have suggested such factors as depression, absent or unsupportive parental relationships during childhood, and an extreme need for social support that is not otherwise forthcoming (Feldman et al., 1994). The disorder has received little systematic study, and clinicians have not been able to develop standard effective treatments for it (Feldman & Feldman, 1995). Some individual cases, however, have responded to multidisciplinary treatment programs jointly conducted by psychotherapists and medical practitioners (Parker, 1993; Schwarz et al., 1993).

Clinical and medical practitioners often become annoyed or angry at people with a factitious disorder. They may feel that the individuals are wasting their time, or worse, in the case of Munchausen syndrome by proxy, jeopardizing the health of an innocent child. Yet, people with this disorder, like those with most other psychological disorders, feel little control over their problem, and they often experience considerable distress. Like others, they need effective therapy rather than scorn, treatment which is, unfortunately, not typically available to them.

Somatoform Disorders

When a physical illness eludes medical assessment, physicians may also suspect that the patient has a ***somatoform disorder,*** another pattern of physical complaints with predominantly psychosocial causes (Garralda, 1996; Kronenberger, Laite, & Laclave, 1995; Martin, 1995). In contrast to people with factitious disorder, patients with somatoform disorders do not consciously want or guide their symptoms, and they almost always believe that their problems are organic. As we shall see, some somatoform disorders, known as ***hysterical disorders,*** involve an actual loss or alteration of physical functioning. In others, the ***preoccupation disorders,*** people who are relatively healthy become preoccupied with the notion that something is wrong with them physically.

Hysterical Somatoform Disorders

People with hysterical disorders experience an actual loss or change in their physical functioning. These somatoform disorders are often difficult to distinguish from problems with an organic base (Kroenke et al., 1997; Labott et al., 1995). In fact, it is always possible that a diagnosis of hysterical disorder is a mistake, that the patient's problem actually has an organic base (Johnson et al., 1996; Sherman, Camfield, & Arena, 1995). The tools of medical science are too imprecise to eliminate organic factors completely (APA, 1994; Merskey, 1986). Some medical problems have particularly vague and

BOX 11-1 Munchausen Syndrome by Proxy

[Jennifer] had been hospitalized 200 times and undergone 40 operations. Physicians removed her gallbladder, her appendix and part of her intestines, and inserted tubes into her chest, stomach and intestines. [The 9-year-old from Florida] was befriended by the Florida Marlins and served as a poster child for health care reform, posing with Hillary Rodham Clinton at a White House rally. Then police notified her mother that she was under investigation for child abuse. Suddenly, Jennifer's condition improved dramatically. In the next nine months, she was hospitalized only once, for a viral infection. . . . Experts said Jennifer's numerous baffling infections were "consistent with someone smearing fecal matter" into her feeding line and urinary catheter.

(Katel & Beck, 1996)

Cases like Jennifer's have horrified the public in recent years and called attention to the disorder called ***Munchausen syndrome by proxy.*** In this factitious disorder, a caregiver, almost always the mother, induces illness in a child. The illness can take almost any form, but the most common symptoms are bleeding, seizures, comas, suffocation, diarrhea, vomiting, "accidental" poisonings, infections, fevers, and sudden infant death syndrome (Boros et al., 1995; Smith & Killam, 1994). The caregiver may use various techniques to produce such symptoms—give the child unprescribed drugs, tamper with medications, contaminate a feeding tube, or smother the child, for example.

Between 10 and 30 percent of the victims of Munchausen syndrome by proxy die as a result of their symptoms (Boros et al., 1995; Von Burg & Hibbard, 1995), and around 8 percent of those who survive are permanently disfigured or physically impaired (Von Burg & Hibbard, 1995). So is the child's psychological, educational, and physical development (Libow, 1995; Skau & Mouridsen, 1995). Jennifer missed so much school because of her induced illness that at age 9 she could barely read or write.

The syndrome is very difficult to diagnose. Indeed, the parent seems to be so devoted and caring that she too elicits sympathy and admiration. Yet the physical problems disappear only when the child is separated from the caregiver.

Unfortunately, Munchausen syndrome by proxy may be more common than clinicians once thought. Furthermore, in many

confusing symptoms (for example, hyperparathyroidism, multiple sclerosis, and lupus), and these problems have often been initially misdiagnosed as hysterical disorders. Moreover, the organic basis for some physical ailments has simply not yet been discovered. Whiplash, for example, was regularly diagnosed as a hysterical disorder in years past, because medical scientists had not yet uncovered the organic causes of this painful condition (Merskey, 1986).

Nevertheless, clinicians continue to believe that some physical problems have little or no organic base and qualify for categorization as one of the three hysterical somatoform disorders: *conversion disorder, somatization disorder,* or *pain disorder associated with psychological factors.*

Conversion Disorder

In a ***conversion disorder,*** a psychosocial conflict or need is *converted* into dramatic physical symptoms affecting voluntary motor or sensory functioning. The symptoms often appear neurological, such as paralysis, seizures, blindness, loss of feeling (anesthesia), or loss of speech (aphonia), and are often called "pseudoneurological" (Bowman & Markand, 1996; APA, 1994). One woman developed dizziness in apparent response to her unhappy marriage:

> A 46-year-old married housewife . . . described being overcome with feelings of extreme dizziness, accompanied by slight nausea, four or five nights a week. During these attacks, the room around her would take on a "shimmering" appearance, and she would have the feeling that she was "floating" and unable to keep her balance. Inexplicably, the attacks almost always occurred at about 4:00 P.M. She usually had to lie down on the couch and often did not feel better until 7:00 or 8:00 P.M. After recovering, she generally spent the rest of the evening watching TV; and more often than not, she would fall asleep in the living room, not going to bed in the bedroom until 2:00 or 3:00 in the morning.
>
> The patient had been pronounced physically fit by her internist, a neurologist, and an ear, nose, and throat specialist on more than one occasion. Hypoglycemia had been ruled out by glucose tolerance tests.

cases siblings of the sick child have also been victimized by the parent (Skau & Mouridsen, 1995; Smith & Killam, 1994; Schreier & Libow, 1993).

What kind of parent systematically inflicts pain and illness on her child? The typical Munchausen mother is emotionally needy. She thrives on the attention and praise she receives for the devoted care of her sick child. She may have little social support outside of the medical system, and her husband is often absent, physically or emotionally. She is often intelligent and may have a medical background—perhaps a former job in a doctor's office—and so she can provide a convincing medical history of her child's "illness."

Convalescent, *1994, by Frank Holl.*

Parents with Munchausen's syndrome by proxy typically deny their actions, even in the face of incontrovertible evidence, and refuse to participate in therapy. No wonder successful treatment has rarely been documented.

Law enforcement authorities are increasingly loath to consider Munchausen syndrome by proxy a psychological disorder and are treating it as a crime—a meticulously planned form of child abuse (Schreier & Libow, 1994). Treatment thus almost always requires the child to be permanently separated from the mother (Skau & Mouridsen, 1995; APA, 1994). At the same time, parents who resort to such actions are obviously experiencing profound psychological disturbances. Thus, while legal authorities grapple with the criminal aspects of this behavior, clinical researchers and practitioners must now work to develop clearer insights and more effective treatments for both the parents and their small victims.

When asked about her marriage, the patient described her husband as a tyrant, frequently demanding and verbally abusive of her and their four children. She admitted that she dreaded his arrival home from work each day, knowing that he would comment that the house was a mess and the dinner, if prepared, not to his liking. Recently, since the onset of her attacks, when she was unable to make dinner he and the four kids would go to McDonald's or the local pizza parlor. After that, he would settle in to watch a ballgame in the bedroom, and their conversation was minimal. In spite of their troubles, the patient claimed that she loved her husband and needed him very much.

(Spitzer et al., 1981, pp. 92–93)

Most conversion disorders emerge between late childhood and young adulthood; they are diagnosed at least twice as often in women as in men (APA, 1994; Tomasson, Kent, & Coryell, 1991). They usually appear suddenly, at times of extreme psychological stress, and last a matter of weeks (APA, 1994). Conversion disorders are thought to be quite rare, occurring in at most 3 of every 1,000 persons (APA, 1994).

Somatization Disorder Two women known as Ann and Sheila baffled medical specialists with the wide range of their symptoms:

Ann describes nervousness since childhood; she also spontaneously admits to being sickly since her youth with a succession of physical problems doctors often indicated were due to her nerves or depression. She, however, believes that she has a physical problem that has not yet been discovered by the doctors. Besides nervousness, she has chest pain, and has been told by a variety of medical consultants that she has a "nervous heart." She also goes to doctors for abdominal pain, and has been diagnosed as having a "spastic colon." She has seen chiropractors and osteopaths for backaches, for pains in the extremities, and for anesthesia of her fingertips. Three months ago she had vomiting, chest pain, and abdominal pain, and was admitted to a hospital for a hysterectomy. Since the hysterectomy she has had repeated anxiety attacks, fainting spells that she claims are associated with unconsciousness that lasts more than thirty minutes, vomiting, food intolerance, weakness, and fatigue. She has had several medical hospitalizations for workups of vomiting, colitis, vomiting blood, and chest pain. She has had a surgical procedure for an abscess of the throat. . . .

Sheila reported having abdominal pain since age 17, necessitating exploratory surgery that yielded no specific diagnosis. She had several pregnancies, each with severe nausea, vomiting, and abdominal pain; she ultimately had a hysterectomy for a "tipped uterus." Since age 40 she had experienced dizziness and "blackouts," which she eventually was told might be multiple sclerosis or a brain tumor. She continued to be bedridden for extended periods of time, with weakness, blurred vision, and difficulty urinating. At age 43 she was worked up for a hiatal hernia because of complaints of bloating and intolerance of a variety of foods. She also had additional hospitalizations for neurological, hypertensive, and renal workups, all of which failed to reveal a definitive diagnosis.

(Spitzer et al., 1981, pp. 185, 260)

Like Ann and Sheila, people with ***somatization disorder*** experience numerous long-lasting physical ailments that have little or no organic basis. This hysterical pattern, first described by Pierre Briquet in 1859, is also known as ***Briquet's syndrome.*** To receive this diagnosis, the person's multiple ailments must include pain symptoms at four sites of the body, two gastrointestinal symptoms (such as nausea and diarrhea), a sexual symptom (such as erectile or menstrual difficulties), and a pseudoneurologic symptom (such as double vision or paralysis)(Yutzy et al., 1995; APA, 1994).

Patients with somatization disorder usually go from doctor to doctor in search of relief (APA, 1994). They often describe their many symptoms in dramatic and exaggerated terms. Most also feel anxious and depressed (Fink, 1995; Hiller, Rief, & Fichter, 1995).

Between 0.2 and 2.0 percent of all women in the United States are believed to experience a somatization disorder in any given year, compared to less than 0.2 percent of men (APA, 1994; Regier et al., 1993). The disorder often runs in families; 10 to 20 percent of the close female relatives of women with the disorder also develop it. It usually begins between adolescence and young adulthood (Eisendrath, 1995; APA, 1994; Smith, 1992).

A somatization disorder lasts considerably longer than a conversion disorder, typically for many years (Kent, Tomasson, & Coryell, 1995). The symptoms may fluctuate over time but rarely disappear completely without psychotherapy (Smith, Rost, & Kashner, 1995). Two-thirds of the people diagnosed with this disorder in the United States receive treatment from a medical or mental health professional in any given year (Regier et al., 1993).

Pain Disorder Associated with Psychological Factors When psychosocial factors play a dominant role in the onset, severity, exacerbation, or maintenance of pain, patients may receive a diagnosis of ***pain disorder associated with psychological factors*** (APA, 1994). Patients with a conversion or somatization disorder may also experience pain, but in this disorder it is the central symptom.

Although the precise prevalence has not been determined, pain disorder associated with psychological factors appears to be relatively common, and more women than men seem to experience it. The disorder may begin at any age, and in some cases continues for years (APA, 1994). Often it develops after an accident or during an illness that has caused genuine pain, and then takes on a life of its own. Laura, a 36-year-old woman, reported pains that far exceeded the usual symptoms of her tubercular disease, called sarcoidosis:

Laura: Before the operation I would have little joint pains, nothing that really bothered me that much. After the operation I was having severe pains in my chest and in my ribs, and those were the type of problems I'd been having after the operation, that I didn't have before. . . . I'd go to an emergency room at night, 11:00, 12:00, 1:00 or so. I'd take the medicine, and the next day it stopped hurting, and I'd go back again. In the meantime this is when I went to the other doctors, to complain about the same thing, to find out what was wrong; and they could never find out what was wrong with me either. . . .

Doctor: With these symptoms on and off over the years, has that interfered with the way you've lived your life?

Laura: Yes. At certain points when I go out or my husband and I go out, we have to leave early because I start hurting. . . . A lot of times I just won't do things because my chest is hurting for one reason or another. . . . Two months ago when the doctor checked me and another doctor looked at the x-rays, he said he didn't see any signs of the sarcoid then and that they were doing a study now, on blood and various things, to see if it was connected to sarcoid. . . .

(Green, 1985, pp. 60–63)

Hysterical Versus Medical Symptoms Because it can be difficult to distinguish hysterical somatoform disorders from "true" medical problems (Janca et al., 1995), diagnosticians look especially for inconsistencies in the patient's medical picture. The symptoms of a hysterical disorder may conflict with the way the nervous system is known to work (Tiihonen et al., 1995; APA, 1994). In a conversion symptom called "glove anesthesia," for example, numbness begins abruptly at the wrist but extends right to the fingertips. As Figure 11-1 shows, real neurological damage is rarely as clearly defined or equally distributed. Even the numbness, tingling, and pain that characterize the neurological disease *carpal tunnel syndrome* rarely spread uniformly throughout the hand.

The physical consequences of hysterical disorders may also differ from those of corresponding medical problems (Levy, 1985). For example, when paralysis from the waist down, or *paraplegia,* is caused by damage to the spinal cord, a person's leg muscles may atrophy, or waste away, unless physical therapy is applied. People whose paralysis is the result of a conversion disorder, in contrast, do not ordinarily experience atrophy; presumably they exercise their muscles without being aware of what they are doing. Similarly, people with conversion blindness have fewer accidents than people who are organically blind, an indication that they have at least some vision even if they are unaware of it.

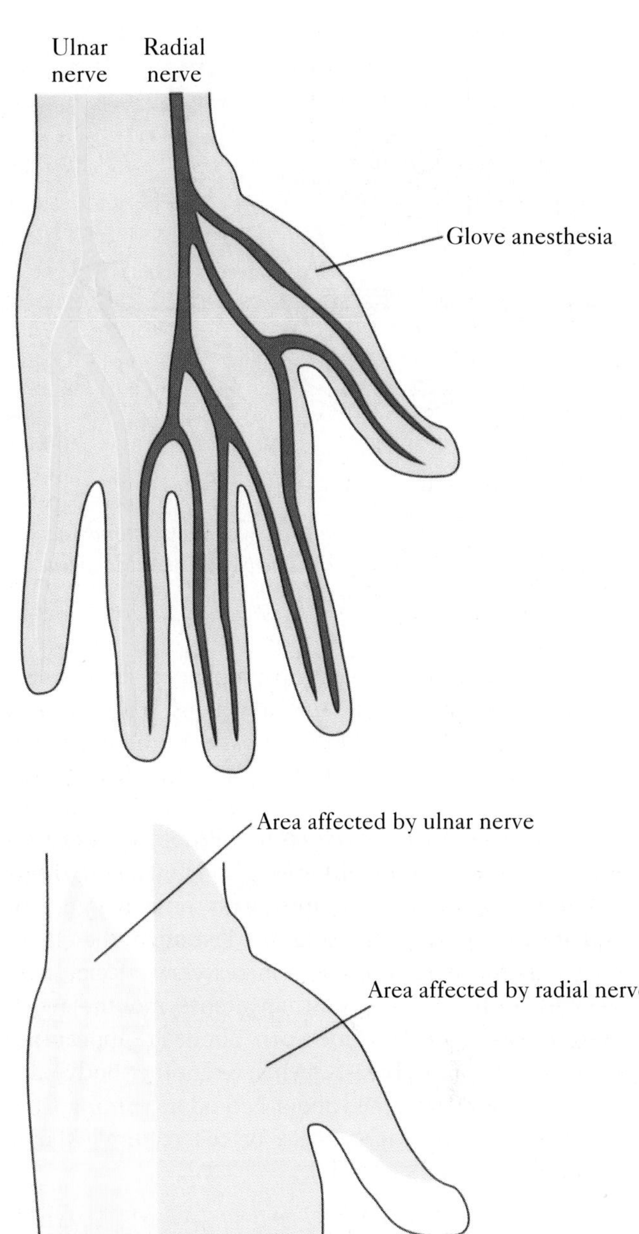

Figure 11-1 *In the conversion symptom called "glove anesthesia," the entire hand from fingertips to wrist becomes numb. Actual physical damage to the ulnar nerve, in contrast, causes anesthesia in the ring finger and little finger and beyond the wrist partway up the arm; and damage to the radial nerve causes insensitivity only in parts of the ring, middle, and index fingers and the thumb and partway up the arm. (Adapted from Gray, 1959.)*

Preoccupation Somatoform Disorders

Hypochondriasis and *body dysmorphic disorder* are ***preoccupation somatoform disorders.*** People with these disorders misinterpret and overreact to bodily symptoms or features no matter what friends, relatives, and physicians may say. Although preoccupation somatoform disorders cause considerable distress, they do not usually affect a person's social or occupational functioning so profoundly as hysterical disorders do (APA, 1994).

Hypochondriasis People who suffer from ***hypochondriasis*** unrealistically interpret bodily symptoms as signs of a serious illness. Often their symptoms are merely normal bodily changes, such as occasional coughing, sores, or sweating. Although some patients recognize that their concern is excessive, many do not (APA, 1994).

Hypochondriasis can present a picture very similar to that of a somatization disorder (Warwick, 1995). Each typically involves numerous physical symptoms and frequent visits to doctors, and each causes patients great concern. If the anxiety is great and the bodily symptoms are relatively minor, a diagnosis of hypochondriasis is probably in order; if the symptoms overshadow the patient's anxiety, they probably indicate a somatization disorder.

Although hypochondriasis can begin at any age, it emerges most commonly in early adulthood, among men and women in equal numbers (APA, 1994). Like

"He didn't really die of anything. He was a hypochondriac." (Drawing by Geo. Price; © 1970 The New Yorker Magazine, Inc.)

pain disorder associated with psychological factors, it is reportedly very familiar to physicians, but its exact prevalence is unknown. For most patients, the symptoms wax and wane over the years.

Body Dysmorphic Disorder People who experience a ***body dysmorphic disorder,*** also known as ***dysmorphophobia,*** become preoccupied with some imagined or minor defect in their appearance. Most often, they focus on wrinkles, spots on the skin, excessive facial hair, swelling of the face, or a misshapen nose, mouth, jaw, or eyebrow (APA, 1994). Some worry about the appearance of their feet, hands, breasts, penis, or another body part. Still others are concerned about bad odors coming from sweat, the breath, the genitals, or the rectum (Marks, 1987). Here we see such a case:

> **A** woman of 35 had for 16 years been worried that her sweat smelled terrible. The fear began just before her marriage when she was sharing a bed with a close friend who said that someone at work smelled badly, and the patient felt that the remark was directed at her. For fear that she smelled, for 5 years she had not gone out anywhere except when accompanied by her husband or mother. She had not spoken to her neighbors for 3 years because she thought she had overheard them speak about her to some friends. She avoided cinemas, dances, shops, cafes, and private homes. Occasionally she visited her in-laws, but she always sat at a distance from them. Her husband was not allowed to invite any friends home; she constantly sought reassurance from him about her smell; and strangers who rang the doorbell were not answered. Television commercials about deodorants made her very anxious. She refused to attend the local church because it was small and the local congregants might comment on her. The family had to travel to a church 8 miles away in which the congregants were strangers; there they sat or stood apart from the others. Her husband bought all her new clothes as she was afraid to try on clothes in front of shop assistants. She used vast quantities of deodorant and always bathed and changed her clothes before going out, up to 4 times daily.
>
> *(Marks, 1987, p. 371)*

People with body dysmorphic disorder become preoccupied with body areas that they imagine to be flawed; they, as well as others whose concerns are less extreme, may be greatly influenced by their culture. Whereas people in Western society tend to worry about facial features, women of the Padaung tribe in Burma focus on the length of their neck, and wear heavy stacks of brass rings to try to extend it. Although many such women are trying to make money as a tourist attraction, others are striving desperately to achieve what their culture has taught them is a perfect neck size. Said one, "It is most beautiful when the neck is really long. The longer it is, the more beautiful it is. I will never take off my rings. . . I'll be buried in them" (Mydans, 1996).

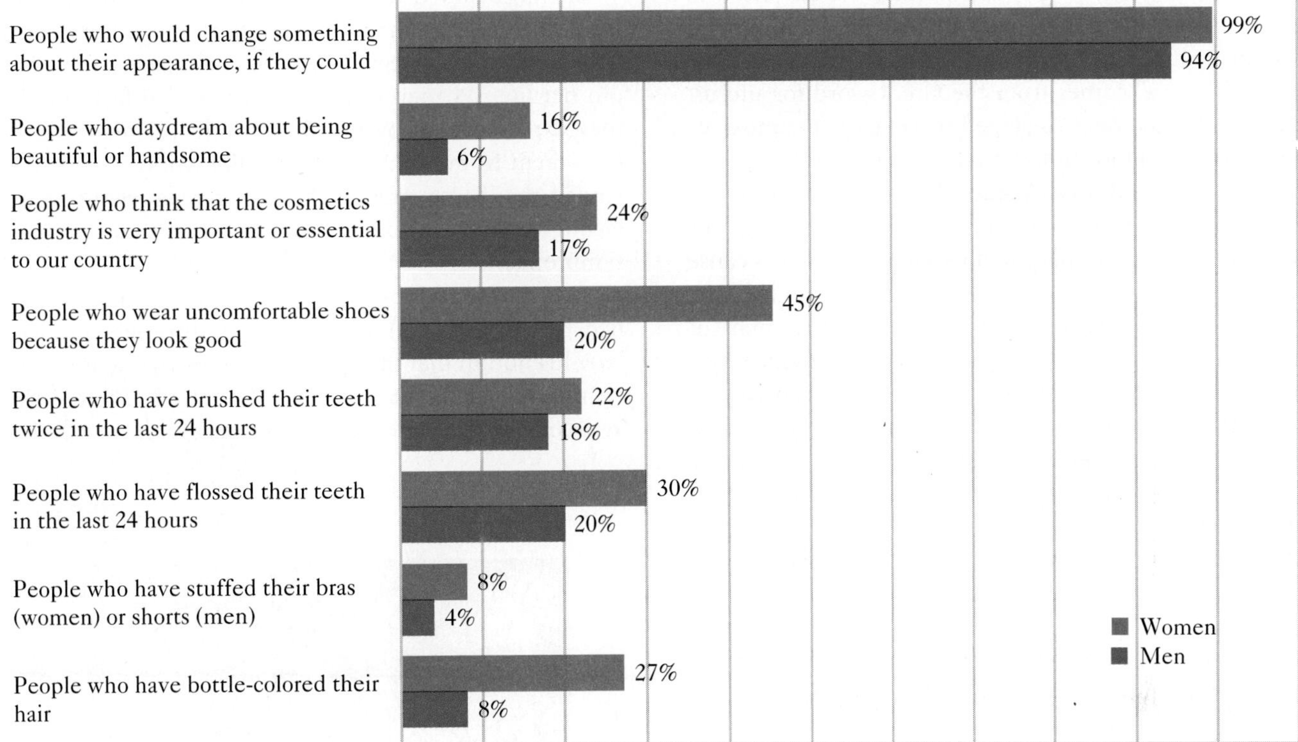

Figure 11-2 *"Mirror mirror on the wall. . . ." People with body dysmorphic disorder become preoccupied with imagined or exaggerated physical defects, but they are not the only ones who have concerns about their appearance. Indeed, it is estimated that 1.5 million Americans undergo "aesthetic surgery" each year. Surveys reveal that in our appearance-conscious society, a surprisingly large percentage of people regularly think about and try to alter the way they look. (Kimball, 1993; Poretz & Sinrod, 1991; Weiss, 1991; Simmon, 1990.)*

It is common in our society to be concerned about appearance (see Figure 11-2). Many adolescents and young adults worry about acne, for instance. The concerns of people with a body dysmorphic disorder, however, are extreme and disruptive. Sufferers may have difficulty looking others in the eye, or they may go to great lengths to conceal their "defect"—say, always wearing sunglasses to hide their supposedly misshapen eyes. Some seek plastic surgery (Bower, 1995). One study found that 30 percent of subjects with the disorder were housebound, and 17 percent had attempted suicide (Phillips et al., 1993). Most cases begin during adolescence and persist for an extended period. Often, people with the disorder go years without revealing their concerns. Researchers have not yet determined the prevalence of this disorder, but clinical reports suggest that it may be equally common among men and women (Bower, 1995; APA, 1994).

Views on Somatoform Disorders

Most theorists explain the preoccupation somatoform disorders much as they do anxiety disorders (discussed in Chapters 6 and 7) (Phillips, Kim, & Hudson, 1995). Behaviorists, for example, believe that the disproportionate fears displayed in hypochondriasis and body dysmorphic disorder have been acquired earlier in life through classical conditioning or modeling (Whitehead et al., 1994). Cognitive theorists suggest that people with the disorders are so acutely sensitive to bodily cues that they come to overinterpret them (Warwick, 1995; Karoly & Lecci, 1993; Barsky, 1992).

In contrast, the hysterical somatoform disorders—conversion, somatization, and pain disorders—are considered unique and in need of special explanations (Kirmayer, Robbins, & Paris, 1994). The ancient Greeks believed that only women had hysterical disorders. The uterus of a sexually ungratified woman was supposed to wander throughout her body in search of fulfillment, producing a physical symptom wherever it lodged. (Our word "hysteria" comes from the Greek word for uterus, *hustera.*) Hippocrates suggested marriage as the most effective treatment for hysterical disorders.

Work by Ambroise-Auguste Liébault and Hippolyte Bernheim in the late nineteenth century set the stage for today's prevailing opinion that psychosocial factors cause hysterical disorders. These researchers founded the Nancy School in Paris for the study and treatment of mental disorders. There they were able to produce hysterical symptoms in normal people—deafness, paralysis, blindness, and numbness—by hypnotic suggestion, and they could remove the symptoms by the same means (see Chapter 1). If hypnotic suggestion could both induce and reverse physical dysfunctioning, they concluded, hysterical disorders might themselves be caused by psychological processes.

Today's leading explanations for hysterical somatoform disorders come from the psychodynamic, behavioral, and cognitive models. None has received much research support, however, and the disorders are still poorly understood (Kirmayer et al., 1994).

The Psychodynamic View As we noted in Chapters 1 and 3, Freud's theory of psychoanalysis actually began with his efforts to account for hysterical symptoms. Indeed, he was one of the few clinicians of his day to treat patients with these symptoms seriously, as people with a genuine problem. After studying hypnosis in Paris and becoming acquainted with the work of Liébault and Bernheim, Freud became interested in the work of an older physician, Josef Breuer (1842–1925). Breuer had successfully used hypnosis to treat the woman he called Anna O., who suffered from hysterical deafness, disorganized speech, and paralysis. Although critics have since questioned whether Anna's ailments were entirely hysterical and whether Breuer's treatment helped her as much as he claimed (Ellenberger, 1972), the case seemed to confirm that hypnosis could be an effective treatment for hysterical ailments.

Freud (1894) came to believe that hysterical disorders represented a *conversion* of underlying emotional conflicts into physical symptoms. Observing that most of his patients with these disorders were women, he proposed that the underlying conflicts developed during a girl's phallic stage (ages 3 through 5), when he believed all girls develop an ***Electra complex:*** they experience strong sexual feelings for their father and come to recognize that they must compete with their mother for his affection. In deference to their mother's dominant position and to cultural taboos, they repress their sexual feelings and adopt a socially approved abhorrence of such desires.

Freud believed that if a child's parents overreact to her sexual feelings, the Electra conflict will go unresolved and the child may reexperience sexual anxiety throughout her life. Whenever events trigger sexual feelings, she may experience an overwhelming unconscious need to hide them from both herself and the world. Freud concluded that some women hide their reemerging sexual feelings by unconsciously converting them into physical symptoms.

Most of today's psychodynamic theorists have modified Freud's explanation of hysterical disorders, particularly his notion that the disorders can always be traced to an unresolved Electra conflict (Hess, 1995; Scott, 1995; Welldon, 1995). They continue to believe, however, that

Freud's explanation of hysterical disorders, indeed his entire theory of psychoanalysis, was greatly influenced by the case of Anna O. His colleague Joseph Breuer reported in 1895 that this patient and her hysterical symptoms had responded well to hypnotic techniques and a "talking cure." However, more than 75 years later, historians questioned both the nature of her symptoms and the effectiveness of Breuer's treatment (Ellenberger, 1972).

sufferers of these disorders experience unconscious conflicts that arouse anxiety and that the individuals convert this anxiety into "more tolerable" physical symptoms that symbolize the underlying conflicts.

Psychodynamic theories have distinguished two mechanisms at work in hysterical somatoform disorders—primary gain and secondary gain (Colbach, 1987). People achieve ***primary gain*** when their hysterical symptoms keep their internal conflicts out of awareness. During an argument, for example, a person who has underlying fears about expressing anger may develop a conversion paralysis of the arm, thus preventing a threatening rage reaction from reaching consciousness. People achieve ***secondary gain*** when their hysterical symptoms also enable them to avoid unpleasant activities or to receive kindness or sympathy from others. When, for example, a conversion paralysis allows a soldier to avoid combat duty or conversion blindness prevents the breakup of a relationship, secondary gain may be operating. Both forms of gain help to lock in the conversion symptoms. According to psychodynamic theorists, primary gains initiate hysterical symptoms; secondary gains are by-products of the symptoms. Although these psychodynamic ideas are widely accepted, they have received little research support.

The Behavioral View Behavioral theorists propose that the physical symptoms of hysterical disorders bring the sufferer rewards. Perhaps the symptoms keep the sufferer out of a difficult work situation or relationship, or elicit attention that is otherwise withheld (Whitehead et al., 1994; Mullins, Olson, & Chaney, 1992; Ullmann & Krasner, 1975). According to behaviorists, such reinforcements condition people into assuming the role of a physically impaired person. Behaviorists also hold that a person must be relatively familiar with an illness to be able to adopt its physical symptoms (Garralda, 1996). And, in fact, it has been found that hysterical symptoms often emerge after people have had similar medical problems or after close relatives or friends have experienced such maladies (Livingston, Witt, & Smith, 1995).

The behavioral focus on rewards is obviously similar to the psychodynamic idea of secondary gains. The key difference is that psychodynamic theorists view the gains as indeed secondary—that is, as rewards that come only after underlying dynamic conflicts produce the disorder. Behaviorists view them as the primary factor in the development of the disorder.

Like the psychodynamic explanation, the behavioral view of hysterical disorders has received limited research support. Even clinical case reports only occasionally support this position. In many cases the pain and upset that accompany the disorders seem to outweigh any rewards the symptoms may bring.

The Cognitive View Some theorists propose that hysterical disorders are forms of *communication:* through them people manage to express emotions that they cannot express otherwise (Lipowski, 1987). Like their psychodynamic colleagues, these theorists hold that the emotions of patients with hysterical disorders are being converted into physical symptoms. They suggest, however, that the purpose of the conversion is not to defend against anxiety but to communicate some distressing emotion—anger, fear, depression, guilt, jealousy—in a "physical language of bodily symptoms" that is familiar to the patient and therefore comfortable (Fry, 1993; Barsky & Klerman, 1983).

According to this view, people who have difficulty acknowledging their emotions or expressing them to others are candidates for a hysterical disorder, especially when they are in the midst of a difficult interpersonal situation. So are those who learn the language of physical dysfunction through firsthand experience with a genuine physical malady either in themselves or in a relative or friend; they may then adopt hysterical symptoms as a form of communication. Because children have less developed cognitive skills and less ability to express their emotions verbally, they are particularly likely to develop physical symptoms as a form of communication (Garralda, 1996).

This cognitive explanation of hysterical disorders is obviously broader than the other views. It allows, for example, that emotions other than anxiety may contribute to physical dysfunctioning, and that defensive functioning or particular rewards are less important than poor ability to communicate. Like the other explanations, however, it has not been widely tested or supported by research.

Treatments for Somatoform Disorders

People with somatoform disorders usually seek psychotherapy only as a last resort. They fully believe that their problems are somatic and initially reject all suggestions to the contrary. When a physician tells them that their problems have no physical basis, they simply go to another physician. Eventually, however, many patients with these disorders do try psychotherapy.

People with preoccupation somatoform disorders typically receive the kinds of treatment that are applied to anxiety disorders. In one study, seventeen patients with body dysmorphic disorder were treated with ***exposure and response prevention***—the behavioral approach that often helps persons with obsessive-compulsive disorder (see pp. 209–210). In daily sessions

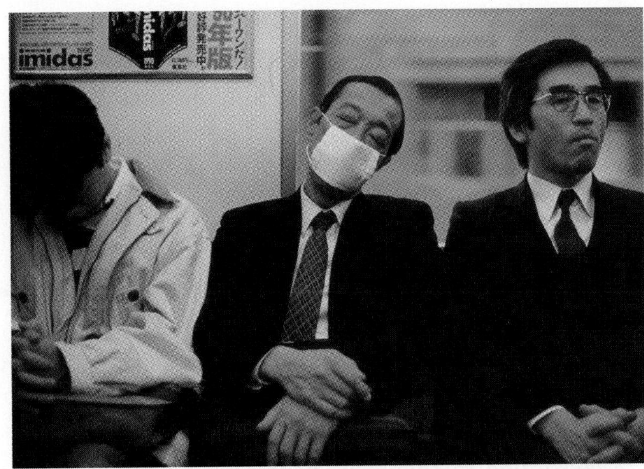

An extreme case of hypochondriasis? Not necessarily. After a 1918 flu epidemic killed 20 million people, people in Japan started wearing a masuku *to protect them from stray germs. Some individuals, like this commuter, continue the tradition during cold and flu season.*

over the course of four weeks, the clients were repeatedly exposed to their perceived physical defects and prevented from engaging in behaviors that would typically help reduce their discomfort (Neziroglu et al., 1996). By the end of treatment, clients were significantly less preoccupied with their imagined defects and spent less time checking their body parts, looking in the mirror, and avoiding social interactions. The effectiveness of such approaches, however, has yet to be tested broadly (Avia et al., 1996; Bower, 1995).

People with hysterical somatoform disorders typically receive interventions that stress either *insight, suggestion, reinforcement,* or *confrontation.* The most commonly applied *insight* approach has been psychodynamic therapy, which helps patients bring their anxiety-arousing conflicts into consciousness so they can work through them, theoretically eliminating the need to convert anxiety into physical symptoms. Therapists who employ *suggestion* tell patients persuasively that their physical symptoms will soon disappear (Bird, 1979) or suggest the same thing to them under hypnosis (Ballinger, 1987). Therapists who take a *reinforcement* approach arrange the removal of rewards for a client's "sick" behavior and an increase of positive rewards for nonsymptomatic behaviors (Donohue, Thevenin, & Runyon, 1997; Mullins et al., 1992). Finally, therapists who take a *confrontational* approach straightforwardly tell patients that their symptoms are without an organic foundation, hoping to force them out of the sick role (Brady & Lind, 1961).

Researchers have not yet clarified the effects of these various forms of psychotherapy on hysterical disorders (Ballinger, 1987). Case studies suggest, however, that conversion disorder and pain disorder respond better to psychotherapy than does somatization disorder, and that approaches that rely on insight, suggestion, and reinforcement bring more lasting improvement than the confrontation strategy.

Psychophysiological Disorders

Earlier in this century clinicians identified a group of physical illnesses that seemed to result from an *interaction* of psychosocial and physical factors (Dunbar, 1948; Bott, 1928). These illnesses differed from somatoform disorders in that both psychosocial and physical factors played significant causal roles and the illnesses themselves brought about actual physical damage. Whereas early versions of the DSM labeled these illnesses ***psychosomatic*** or ***psychophysiological disorders,*** DSM-IV uses the label ***psychological factors affecting medical condition.*** We shall use the more familiar term "psychophysiological" in discussing them (see Table 11-1).

"Traditional" Psychophysiological Disorders

Clinicians once believed that only a limited number of illnesses were psychophysiological. The best known and most prevalent of these disorders were ulcers, asthma, chronic headaches, hypertension, and coronary heart disease. Recent research, however, has taught clinicians that many kinds of physical illnesses—including bacterial and viral infections—may be caused by an interaction of psychosocial and physical factors. We will focus first on the "traditional" psychophysiological disorders, then look at the newer members of this category.

Ulcers are lesions, or holes, that form in the wall of the stomach (gastric ulcers) or of the duodenum (peptic ulcers), resulting in burning sensations or pain in the stomach, occasional vomiting, and stomach bleeding. This disorder is experienced by 5 to 10 percent of all persons in the United States and is responsible for more than 6,000 deaths each year (Suter, 1986). Ulcers are apparently caused by an interaction of psychosocial factors, such as environmental stress, intense feelings of anger or anxiety, or a dependent personality (Tennant, 1988; Weiner et al., 1957; Wolf & Wolff, 1947), and physiological factors, such as bacterial infections, excessive secretions of the gastric juices, or a weak lining of the stomach or duodenum (McDaniel et al., 1994; Fiester, 1986; Mirsky, 1958).

TABLE 11-1 Disorders That Have Physical Symptoms

Disorder	*Voluntary Control of Symptoms?*	*Symptoms Linked to Psychosocial Factor?*	*An Apparent Goal?*
Malingering	Yes	Maybe	Yes
Factitious disorder	Yes	Yes	No*
Somatoform disorder	No	Yes	Maybe
Psychophysiological disorder	No	Yes	Maybe
Physical illness	No	Maybe	No

**Except for medical attention.*
Source: Adapted from Hyler & Spitzer, 1978.

Asthma causes the body's airways (the trachea and bronchi) to constrict periodically, so that it is hard for air to pass to and from the lungs (Simeonsson et al., 1995). The resulting symptoms are shortness of breath, wheezing, coughing, and a terrifying choking sensation. Approximately 15 million people in the United States suffer from asthma, twice as many as 15 years ago (Weiss, 1997). Most victims are under 15 years of age at the time of the first attack (DeAngelis, 1994). Approximately 70 percent of all cases appear to be caused by an interaction of psychosocial factors, such as environmental stress, troubled family relationships, anxiety, and heightened dependency needs; and physiological factors, such as allergies to specific substances, a slow-acting sympathetic nervous system, and a weakness of the respiratory system traceable to respiratory infections or biological inheritance (Weiss, 1997; Carr, Lehrer, & Cochran, 1995; Simeonsson et al., 1995; Rees, 1964).

Chronic headaches are frequent intense aches of the head or neck that are not caused exclusively by a physical disorder. There are two types. ***Muscle contraction headaches*** (also called ***tension headaches***) bring pain at the back or front of the head or at the back of the neck (Peterson et al., 1995). These headaches occur when the muscles surrounding the skull contract, constricting the blood vessels. Approximately 40 million Americans suffer from these headaches. ***Migraine headaches*** are extremely severe and often immobilizing aches located on one side of the head, often preceded by a warning sensation called an ***aura,*** and sometimes accompanied by dizziness, nausea, or vomiting. Migraine headaches develop in two phases: (1) blood vessels in the brain constrict, so that the flow of blood to parts of the brain is reduced, and (2) the same blood vessels later dilate, so that blood flows through them rapidly, stimulating numerous neuron endings and causing pain. Migraines are suffered by about 12 million people in the United States. Research suggests that chronic headaches are caused by an interaction of psychosocial factors, such as environmental stress, a passive personality style, or chronic feelings of helplessness, hostility, anxiety, or depression (Marazziti et al., 1995; Merikangas, Stevens, & Angst, 1994); and physiological factors, such as serotonin dysfunction, vascular weakness, or musculoskeletal deficiencies (Raskin et al., 1987; Blanchard & Andrasik, 1982).

Hypertension is a state of chronic high blood pressure. That is, the blood pumped through the body's arteries by the heart produces too much pressure against the artery walls. Hypertension has few outward symptoms (Fahrenberg et al., 1995), but it plays havoc with the entire cardiovascular system, greatly increasing the likelihood of stroke, coronary heart disease, and kidney problems. It is estimated that 40 million people in the United States have hypertension, tens of thousands die directly from it annually, and millions more perish because of illnesses brought on by it (Johnson, Gentry, & Julius, 1992). Only 5 to 15 percent of all cases of hypertension are caused exclusively by physiological abnormalities; the vast majority are brought about by a combination of psychosocial and physiological factors and are often designated ***essential hypertension*** (McDaniel et al., 1994). Some of the leading psychosocial causes of essential hypertension are constant environmental danger, chronic feelings of anger or its inhibition, and an unexpressed need for power (Dubbert, 1995; Somova, Diarra, & Jacobs, 1995; McClelland, 1985, 1979). Leading physiological causes include a diet high in salt and dysfunctional ***baroreceptors***—sensitive nerves in the blood

Children who suffer from asthma may use an aerochamber, or inhaler, to help them inhale helpful medications. The child pumps the medication into the device's plastic tube, then inhales it.

vessels responsible for signaling the brain that blood pressure is becoming too high (Julius, 1992; Schwartz, 1977).

Coronary heart disease is caused by a blocking of the ***coronary arteries***—the blood vessels that surround the heart and are responsible for providing oxygen to the heart muscle. The term actually refers to any of several specific problems, including ***angina pectoris,*** extreme chest pain caused by a partial blockage of the coronary arteries; ***coronary occlusion,*** a complete blockage of a coronary artery that halts the flow of blood to various parts of the heart muscle; and ***myocardial infarction*** (a "heart attack"). Together such problems are the leading causes of death in men over the age of 35 and of women over 40 in the United States, accounting for close to 800,000 deaths each year, or 38 percent of all deaths in the nation (Blanchard, 1994; Matarazzo, 1984; NCHS, 1984). More than half of all cases of coronary heart disease are related to an interaction of psychosocial factors, such as job stress and high levels of hostility, and physiological factors, such as a high level of serum cholesterol, obesity, hypertension, the effects of smoking, and lack of exercise (NAMHC, 1996; Hugdahl, 1995; Friedman & Rosenman, 1974, 1959).

The Disregulation Model of Psychophysiological Disorders

By definition, psychophysiological disorders are caused by an interaction of psychosocial and physical factors. But how do these factors combine to produce a given illness? Gary Schwartz, a leading researcher, has proposed the ***disregulation model*** to account for this phenomenon (see Figure 11-3). Schwartz suggests that our brain and body ordinarily establish ***negative feedback loops*** that guarantee a smooth, self-regulating operation of the body (Schwartz, 1982, 1977). The brain receives information about external events from the environment, processes this information, and then stimulates body organs into action. Mechanisms in the organs then provide critical negative feedback, telling the brain that its stimulation has been sufficient and should now stop.

A typical feedback loop governs blood pressure (Egan, 1992; Julius, 1992). In one part of the loop the brain receives information that dangers exist in the environment, such as nearby lightning or cars speeding by. In the next part of the loop, the brain processes this information and alerts the nervous system to elevate the blood pressure. And in a later part of the loop, *baroreceptors,* the pressure-sensitive cells surrounding the body's blood vessels, alert the nervous system when the blood pressure rises too high, and the nervous system then lowers the blood pressure. In short, the various parts of the feedback loop work together to help maintain the blood pressure at an appropriate level.

According to Schwartz, if one part of a loop falters, the body will enter a state of disregulation rather than effective self-regulation, problems will occur throughout the loop, and a psychophysiological disorder may ultimately develop. Hypertension, for example, may result from problems in any part of the blood pressure feedback loop. Should information from the environment be excessive (as when one is faced with continuous job stress or extended unemployment), should information processing be faulty (as when one keeps misinterpreting

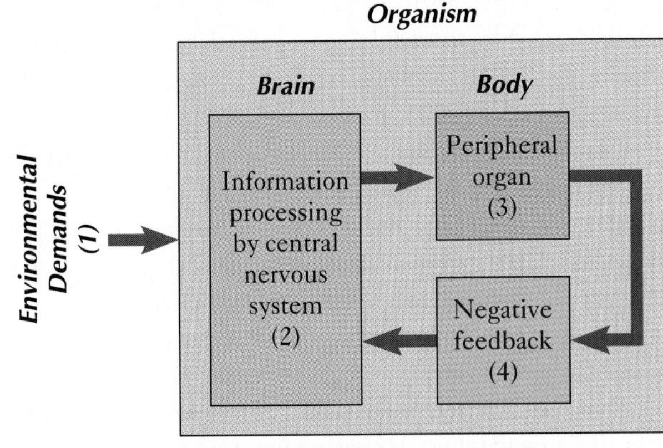

Figure 11-3 *In the normal process of regulation, according to Schwartz's disregulation model, the organism first receives environmental pressure (1). The brain processes information about this pressure (2) and then stimulates body organs into action (3). The organs then provide negative feedback to the brain, communicating that the stimulation has been sufficient and should cease (4). (Adapted from Schwartz, 1977.)*

or overreacting to everyday events), should a peripheral organ malfunction (as when the aorta narrows abnormally), or should a feedback mechanism fail (as when baroreceptors fail to inform the brain that blood pressure is rising too high), inaccurate information will be fed to the next part of the loop and relayed to the next, until every part in the loop has been stimulated to raise the blood pressure (Landsbergis et al., 1994).

Factors That Contribute to Psychophysiological Disorders Over the years, theorists have identified sociocultural, psychological, and biological variables that play important roles in the development of psychophysiological disorders. As Schwartz's disregulation model suggests, the variables help generate psychophysiological disorders by interacting with one another.

Sociocultural Factors Sometimes the demands placed on people by their society, social group, or family may lead to disregulation and set the stage for psychophysiological disorders. Such stress may be of various kinds. Wars, natural disasters, and other *wide-ranging stressors* can have a negative effect on a whole population. After the 1979 nuclear accident at Three Mile Island, for example, people who lived near the nuclear plant experienced an unusually large number of psychophysiological disorders (not radiation-linked illnesses), and they continued to do so for years (Schneiderman & Baum, 1992; Baum et al., 1983). Alternatively, stress can be generated by *chronic social circumstances* that produce persistent feelings of tension, such as living in a crime-ridden neighborhood or working in an unsatisfying job (Landsbergis et al., 1994). For example, hypertension is twice as common among African Americans as among white Americans (Johnson et al., 1992). Although physiological factors may have much to do with this difference, some theorists propose that it is also linked to the dangerous environments in which so many African Americans live and to the unsatisfying jobs at which so many must work (Anderson et al., 1992). Finally, stress may come from *transient stressors* such as a severe illness, a death in the family, or divorce (Levy et al., 1997). The stress of losing one's job, for example, has been tied to hypertension (Johnson et al., 1992; Kasl & Cobb, 1970).

Psychological Factors According to many theorists, certain needs, attitudes, emotions, and coping styles may increase a person's chances of developing psychophysiological disorders (Watten et al., 1997). Such factors cause some people to overreact repeatedly to stressors, thus setting the stage for physiological dysfunctioning. Researchers have found, for example, that men with a "repressive" coping style (reluctance to express discomfort, anger, or hostility) tend to experience a rise in blood pressure in response to mental stress tests (NAMHC, 1996; Vogele & Steptoe, 1993; Lai & Linden, 1992). Increased rates of asthma have also been found among those with a repressive coping style (DeAngelis, 1992).

A currency dealer shouts orders during trading at the Paris Stock Exchange. The stresses of working on the stock exchange and in similar high-pressure environments apparently increase a person's risk of developing a physical illness, including coronary heart disease.

Another personality style that has been linked to psychophysiological disorders is the ***Type A personality style,*** introduced by two cardiologists, Meyer Friedman and Raymond Rosenman (1959). People with this personality style are consistently hostile, cynical, driven, impatient, competitive, and ambitious. They interact with the world in a way that, according to Friedman and Rosenman, produces continual stress and often leads to coronary heart disease. People with a ***Type B personality style,*** by contrast, are thought to be more relaxed, less aggressive, and less concerned about time. They are less likely to experience cardiovascular deterioration. In reality, of course, most people fall between these two extremes, tending toward one or the other but exhibiting elements of both.

The link between Type A personality style and coronary heart disease has been supported by numerous studies (Rosenman, 1990; Williams, 1989). In one well-known investigation of more than 3,000 subjects, Friedman and Rosenman (1974) separated healthy men in their 40s and 50s into Type A and Type B categories and then followed the health of the men over the next eight years. They found that when physiological factors such as cholesterol level were controlled for, more than twice as many Type A men developed coronary heart disease. Later studies found that Type A functioning also relates to heart disease in women (Haynes, Feinleib, & Kannel, 1980).

Recent studies have found a weaker link between the Type A personality style and heart disease than earlier ones. It appears, however, that some of the characteristics associated with the Type A style, particularly hostility, are indeed related to heart disease (Miller et al., 1996; NAMHC, 1996; Hugdahl, 1995). In fact, one study has found that feelings of anger may directly impair the heart's pumping efficiency (Ironson et al., 1992).

Biological Factors We saw in Chapter 6 that when the brain stimulates body organs into action, it does so through the operation of the ***autonomic nervous system (ANS),*** consisting of the many nerve fibers that connect the central nervous system to the body's organs. If we see a frightening animal, for example, a group of ANS fibers identified as the *sympathetic nervous system* increases its activity. These nerve fibers prepare us for action by causing our heart to beat quickly, our respiration to speed up, and the like. As the danger passes, another group of ANS fibers known as the *parasympathetic nervous system* becomes more active in the reverse direction. These fibers slow our heartbeat, respiration, and other bodily functions. Essentially, the parasympathetic nervous system calms down our functioning. These two parts of the ANS are constantly working and complementing each other, helping our bodies to operate smoothly and stably—a condition called *homeostasis* (Cannon, 1927).

Hans Selye (1976, 1974), a leading researcher on the effects of stress, was one of the first to describe the relationship between stress and the ANS. He proposed that people typically respond to stress with a three-stage sequential reaction, which he called the ***general adaptation syndrome.*** In the presence of threat, the sympathetic nervous system increases its activity and arouses responses throughout the body *(alarm stage).* The parasympathetic nervous system next attempts to counteract these responses *(resistance stage).* Finally, if exposure to or perceptions of stress continue, the resistance may fail and organs controlled by the ANS may become overworked and break down *(exhaustion stage).*

Because it is at the center of stress reactions, ***defects in the ANS*** are believed to contribute to the development of psychophysiological disorders (Boyce et al., 1995; Hugdahl, 1995; Stanford & Salmon, 1993). If, for example, one's ANS is stimulated too easily, it may keep overreacting to situations that most people find only mildly stressful, so that certain organs eventually become damaged. A psychophysiological disorder may then develop (Boyce et al., 1995).

Local biological dysfunction also may contribute to psychophysiological disorders. People may, for example, have local somatic weaknesses—particular organs that are either defective or prone to dysfunction under stress (Rees, 1964). Those with a "weak" gastrointestinal system may be candidates for an ulcer. Those with a "weak" respiratory system may develop asthma.

Finally, psychophysiological disorders may also be caused by ***individual biological reactions*** to stress. Some people perspire in response to stress, others develop stomachaches, and still others experience a faster heartbeat or a rise in blood pressure (Fahrenberg, Foerster, & Wilmers, 1995). Although such variations are perfectly normal, the repeated activation of a "favored" system may wear it down and ultimately result in a psychophysiological disorder. Research has indicated, for example, that some individuals are more likely than others to experience temporary rises in blood pressure when stressed (McDaniel et al., 1994). It may be that they are also more likely to develop hypertension. Similarly, some infants secrete much more gastric acid under stress than other infants (Weiner, 1977; Mirsky, 1958). Perhaps over the years, this physical reaction wears down the mucous lining of the stomach or duodenum until an ulcer develops.

Clearly, sociocultural, psychological, and biological variables may combine to produce psychophysiological disorders. The interaction of such variables to produce medical problems was once considered an unusual occurrence. According to the disregulation model, however, the interaction of psychosocial and physical factors is the rule of bodily functioning, not the exception, and as the years have passed, more and more illnesses have been added to the list of traditional psychophysiological disorders.

"New" Psychophysiological Disorders

For years physicians and clinicians believed that psychosocial variables could impair physical health only in the form of traditional psychophysiological disorders, but in recent decades researchers have increasingly uncovered links between psychosocial stress and susceptibility to numerous physical illnesses. Let us look first at how these links were established and then at the area of study known as *psychoneuroimmunology,* a new discipline that further ties stress and illness to the body's *immune system.*

Stress and Susceptibility to Illness In 1967 Thomas Holmes and Richard Rahe developed the Social Adjustment Rating Scale (see Table 11-2), which assigns numerical values to the stresses that most people experience at some time in their lives. Answers given by a large sample of subjects indicated that the most stressful event on the scale is the death of a spouse, which receives a score of 100 *life change units (LCUs).* Lower on the scale

TABLE 11-2 Most Stressful Life Events

*Adults: "Social adjustment rating scale"**

1. Death of spouse	12. Pregnancy
2. Divorce	13. Sex difficulties
3. Marital separation	14. Gain of new family member
4. Jail term	15. Business readjustment
5. Death of close family member	16. Change in financial state
6. Personal injury or illness	17. Death of close friend
7. Marriage	18. Change to different line of work
8. Fired at work	19. Change in number of arguments with spouse
9. Marital reconciliation	20. Mortgage over $10,000
10. Retirement	21. Foreclosure of mortgage or loan
11. Change in health of family member	22. Change in responsibilities at work

Students: "Undergraduate stress questionnaire"†

1. Death (family member or friend)	12. Went into a test unprepared
2. Had a lot of tests	13. Lost something (especially wallet)
3. It's finals week	14. Death of a pet
4. Applying to graduate school	15. Did worse than expected on test
5. Victim of a crime	16. Had an interview
6. Assignments in all classes due the same day	17. Had projects, research papers due
7. Breaking up with boy-/girlfriend	18. Did badly on a test
8. Found out boy-/girlfriend cheated on you	19. Parents getting divorce
9. Lots of deadlines to meet	20. Dependent on other people
10. Property stolen	21. Having roommate conflicts
11. You have a hard upcoming week	22. Car/bike broke down, flat tire, etc.

**Full scale has 43 items.*
†Full scale has 83 items.
Source: Crandall et al., 1992; Holmes & Rahe, 1967.

is retirement (45 LCUs), and still lower is a minor violation of the law (11 LCUs). Even positive events, such as an outstanding personal achievement, are somewhat stressful (28 LCUs). This scale gave researchers a yardstick for measuring the total amount of stress a person has experienced over a period of time. If in the course of a year a businesswoman started a new business (39 LCUs), sent her son off to college (29 LCUs), moved to a new house (20 LCUs), and witnessed the death of a close friend in an automobile accident (37 LCUs), her stress score for the year would be 125 LCUs.

The researchers then proceeded to examine the relationship between life stress (as measured in LCUs) and the onset of illness. They found that the LCU scores of sick people during the year before they fell ill were much higher than those of healthy people (Holmes & Rahe,

1989, 1967). A particularly telling cutoff point was a score of 300 LCUs. If someone's life changes totaled more than 300 LCUs over the course of a year, that person was particularly likely to develop a serious health problem, in many cases a viral or bacterial infection.

The first investigations of this topic took the form of ***retrospective studies:*** subjects were asked to think back over the past year and remember their life events and illnesses. Investigators feared that in those circumstances, though, people's illnesses could be serving as time landmarks that actually helped their recall of particular life events. In other words, people who had been sick might be more likely to remember events that led up to their illnesses than healthy people were to remember events that occurred during the same span of time. To rule out this possibility, researchers began to conduct ***prospective studies*** as well, studies that predicted *future* health changes on the basis of current life events.

Rahe (1968) divided 2,500 healthy naval personnel into a high-risk group (the 30 percent with the highest LCU scores over the previous six months) and a low-risk group (the 30 percent with the lowest LCU scores), and he kept track of the subsequent health changes of the two groups when they went to sea. Twice as many high-risk as low-risk subjects developed illnesses during their first month at sea; furthermore, the high-risk group continued to develop more illnesses each month for the next five months.

Since Holmes and Rahe's pioneering work, stresses of various kinds have been tied to a wide range of diseases and physical conditions (see Figure 11-4), from trench mouth and upper respiratory infection to cancer (Pillow, Zautra, & Sandler, 1996; Kiecolt-Glaser et al., 1991). The greater the amount of life stress, the greater the likelihood of illness. Researchers have even found a relationship between significant stress and death. When, for example, investigators examined the medical records of 4,486 British widowers 55 years of age or older, they discovered that 213 of these men had died during the stressful first six months of their bereavement—a fatality rate significantly higher than usual for married men in this age range (Young, Benjamin, & Wallis, 1963). After six months the mortality rate of the widowers returned to a normal level. Another study of 903 close relatives of persons who had died in a community in Wales found that almost 5 percent of the relatives died during the stressful first year of their bereavement (Rees & Lutkin, 1967). The widows and widowers in this group had a mortality rate of 12 percent, compared to a rate of less than 1 percent for age-matched control subjects.

A particularly striking instance of death after the loss of a loved one is seen in the following case:

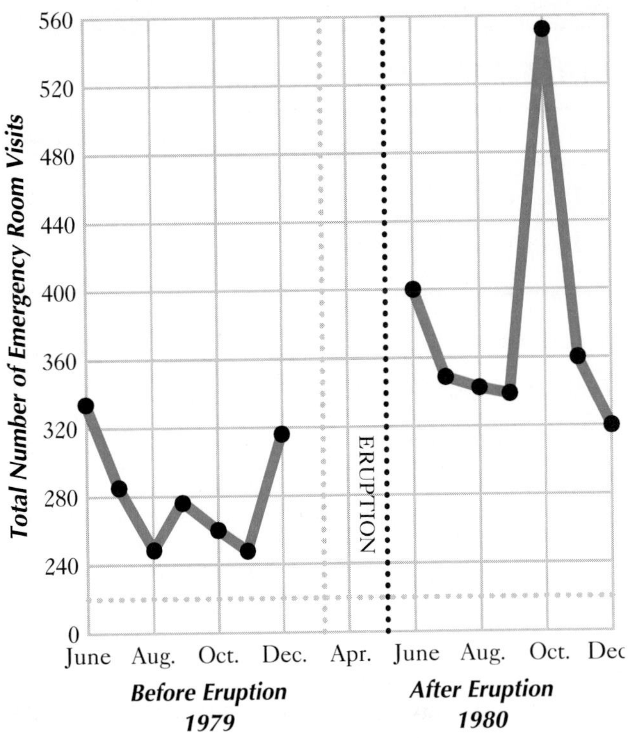

Figure 11-4 *A single catastrophic event may increase one's chances of developing a physical ailment. Paul and Gerald Adams (1984) found that during the months immediately after the eruption of Mount St. Helens on May 18, 1980, there was a 34 percent increase in emergency room visits and a 19 percent rise in deaths in nearby Othello, Washington.*

> Charlie and Josephine had been inseparable companions for 13 years. In a senseless act of violence Charlie, in full view of Josephine, was shot and killed in a melee with police. Josephine first stood motionless, then slowly approached his prostrate form, sunk to her knees, and silently rested her head on the dead and bloody body. Concerned persons attempted to help her away, but she refused to move. Hoping she would soon surmount her overwhelming grief, they let her be. But she never rose again; in 15 minutes she was dead. Now the remarkable part of the story is that Charlie and Josephine were llamas in the zoo! They had escaped from their pen during a snow storm and Charlie, a mean animal to begin with, was shot when he proved unmanageable. I was able to establish from the zoo keeper that to all intents and purposes Josephine had been normally frisky and healthy right up to the moment of the tragic event.
>
> *(Engel, 1968)*

One shortcoming of Holmes and Rahe's Social Adjustment Rating Scale is that it may not accurately mea-

sure the life stress of specific populations. In their development of the scale, the researchers used a sample composed predominantly of white Americans. Less than 5 percent of the subjects were African American. But since their ongoing life experiences often differ in significant ways, might not African Americans and white Americans differ in their stress reactions to various kinds of life events? One study indicates that indeed they do (Komaroff, Masuda, & Holmes, 1989, 1986). Both white and African Americans rank death of a spouse as the single most stressful life event, but African Americans experience greater stress from such events as a major personal injury or illness, a major change in work responsibilities, and a major change in living conditions than white Americans do. Such differences probably reflect differences in the impact and meaning of such events in the lives of persons of the two groups.

Similarly, college students often face stressors that are different from those listed in the Social Adjustment Rating Scale (Crandall et al., 1992). Instead of having marital difficulties, being fired, or applying for a job, a college student may have trouble with a roommate, fail a course, or apply to graduate school. When researchers developed special scales to measure life events more accurately in this population (see again Table 11-2), they found the expected correlations between stressful events and illness (Crandall et al., 1992).

Psychoneuroimmunology

How is a stressful event translated into a viral or bacterial infection? Researchers have increasingly focused on our body's immune system as the key to this relationship and have developed a new area of study called ***psychoneuroimmunology*** to examine the links between psychosocial stress, the immune system, and health.

The body's ***immune system*** is a complex network of cells that helps protect people from ***antigens***—foreign invaders, such as bacteria, viruses, fungi, and parasites—and from cancer cells. Most immune cells are located in the bone marrow, thymus, lymph nodes, spleen, tonsils, appendix, and small intestine (Cohen & Herbert, 1996). However, among the most important cells in the system are billions of ***lymphocytes,*** white blood cells that are manufactured in the lymph system and circulate throughout the bloodstream. Upon stimulation by antigens, lymphocytes spring into action to help the body overcome the invaders.

One group of lymphocytes, called ***helper T-cells,*** identify antigens and then multiply and trigger the production of still other kinds of immune cells. Another group, ***natural killer T-cells,*** seek out and destroy body cells that have already been infected by viruses, thus helping to stop the spread of a viral infection. A third group of lymphocytes, ***B-cells,*** produce ***antibodies*** (or ***immunoglobulins***), protein molecules that recognize and bind to a specific antigen, mark it for destruction, and prevent it from causing infection.

Researchers suspect that stress can interfere with the activity of lymphocytes, slowing them down and thus increasing a person's susceptibility to viral and bacterial infections (Ader, Felten, & Cohen, 1991). The idea has been supported by numerous studies. When laboratory animals are subjected to stressors of various kinds, their lymphocytes and antibodies reproduce more slowly than usual and destroy antigens less effectively (Hibma & Griffin, 1994; Maier et al., 1994). One study found that the immunological functioning of infant monkeys was reduced for up to two months after they had been separated from their mothers for a single day (Coe et al., 1987).

Studies of humans have told a similar story (Cohen & Herbert, 1996; Maier et al., 1994). Scientists who monitored Skylab astronauts during various phases of their extended space mission discovered that their T-cell reactions to

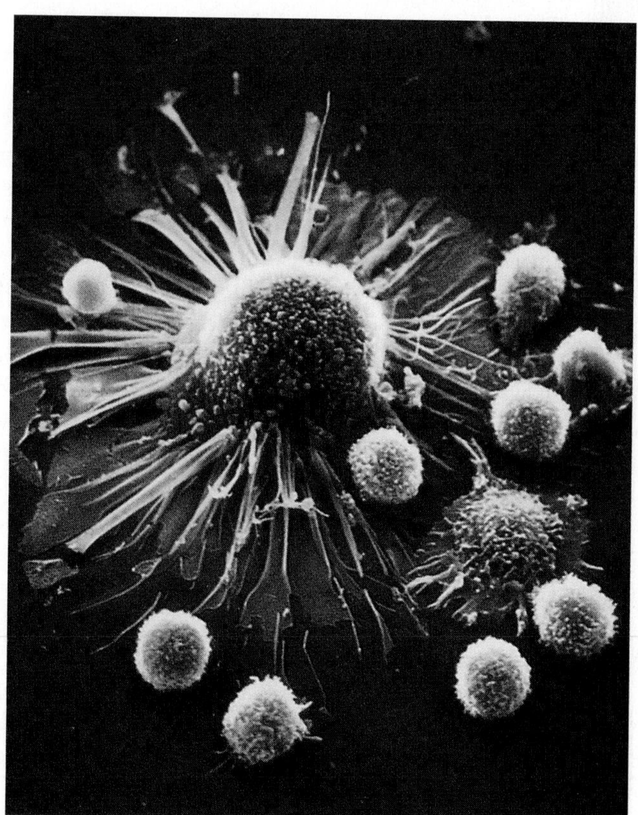

These killer T-cells surround a larger cancer cell and destroy it, thus helping to prevent the spread of cancer. Killer T-cells and other lymphocytes also help fight other illnesses by detecting and destroying bacteria and viruses throughout the body.

antigens decreased within a few hours after the stress of splashdown and returned to normal three days later (Kimzey et al., 1976; Kimzey, 1975). Similarly, the functioning of the immune systems of people who were exposed to simulated combat conditions in a laboratory for three days deteriorated significantly (Palmblad et al., 1976).

A relationship has also been found between *ordinary life stress* and poor immunologic functioning. In a landmark study, R. W. Bartrop and his colleagues (1977) in New South Wales, Australia, compared the immune systems of twenty-six people whose spouses had died eight weeks earlier with those of twenty-six matched controls whose spouses had not died. Blood samples revealed that lymphocyte functioning was significantly lower in the bereaved subjects than in the control subjects. Still other studies have found impaired immune functioning in persons who are exposed to *long-term stress*. For example, researchers have found poorer immune functioning among persons who face the challenge of providing ongoing care for a relative with Alzheimer's disease (Kiecolt-Glaser et al., 1996, 1991, 1987; Esterling et al., 1994).

Even *daily stresses* can affect the immune system. In one study, experimenters had subjects ingest a capsule containing a safe protein each day for twelve weeks (Stone et al., 1994). Because it was new to the subjects' bodies, the protein served as a novel antigen to which the immune system would respond by producing an antibody. The experimenters further collected samples of saliva from the subjects each day and analyzed them for the antibody ***secretory Immunoglobulin A (s-IgA).*** They found lower s-IgA antibody production—that is, poorer immune functioning—on the days when subjects re-

BOX 11-2 The Psychological Effects of HIV and AIDS

The ***human immunodeficiency virus (HIV)*** is a parasite that leads to the death of its host cell. This virus infects T-4 helper lymphocytes, the cells that normally protect the body from disease by telling the immune system which invaders to kill (Richardson, 1997; Batchelor, 1988). The lymphocytes in turn transport the killer deep into the immune system, where it wreaks further destruction. In many cases, HIV develops into ***acquired immune deficiency syndrome (AIDS).*** Most sufferers do not die of AIDS per se but instead succumb to opportunistic infections that would not survive in a healthy immune system. The psychological suffering of both people who are HIV-positive and people with AIDS, previously overlooked, is now being addressed by researchers and health-care workers (Taylor, Amodei, & Mangos, 1996; Lyketsos et al., 1996).

The progression from HIV infection to AIDS may take weeks, months, or years (Richardson, 1997; Travis, 1996; Kiecolt-Glaser & Glaser, 1988). Little is known about how and why persons who are infected with HIV develop AIDS, whether slowly or rapidly. One thing is certain, however: a weakened immune system is less able to defend itself against the virus, and extreme stress, psychological dysfunctioning, and environmental pressures can further reduce the ability of the immune system to ward off illness. A deadly interplay may unfold between the effect of the disease on the mental health of the HIV sufferer and the effect of declining mental health on the patient's physical well-being (Evans et al., 1997).

Psychological disorders associated with HIV may be caused by factors that are either primarily organic or primarily psychological. The HIV may invade the brain, for example, causing *AIDS dementia complex (ADC),* which can result in deep lethargy, manic-depressive symptoms, and psychosis. More commonly, there is a general decrement in cognitive functioning—it takes longer to think or remember (Maj et al., 1994). In a vicious and fatal cycle, the patient's psychological well-being diminishes, causing the immune system to weaken further. Not a great deal is known about ADC, but some researchers believe that it may affect the majority of AIDS sufferers and that it may be one of the earliest symptoms to develop (Price et al., 1988).

Although not all HIV sufferers will develop AIDS dementia complex, almost all are subjected to an array of environmental stressors that may lead to psychological problems and may weaken their ability to fight disease. Society does not provide AIDS sufferers with a supportive environment in which to wage their war. Indeed, it attaches considerable stigma to the disease and to those who contract it. Surveys show that a large part of the population continues to view AIDS as a proper punishment for gay men, intra-

ported stressful experiences, and greater production on the days filled with desirable events.

These studies seem to be telling a remarkable story. The subjects have all been healthy individuals who happened to experience unusual levels of stress. During the stressful periods, they remained healthy on the surface, but their experiences were apparently slowing their immune systems so that they became susceptible to illness. If stress affects our body's capacity to fight off illness in this way, we can see why researchers have repeatedly found a relationship between life stress and illnesses of various kinds (see Box 11-2).

But why does stress interfere with the immune system? Several factors have been implicated—biological factors such as *neurotransmitter stimulation* and *hormone activation;* psychological variables such as *behavioral changes* and *personality style;* and the sociocultural factor of *social support.*

Neurotransmitter Stimulation As we saw earlier, stress leads to increased activity by the sympathetic nervous system. Studies suggest that this increased autonomic arousal is accompanied by the release of the neurotransmitter *norepinephrine* throughout the brain and body. It appears that, beyond supporting the activity of the sympathetic nervous system, this chemical eventually helps slow the functioning of the immune system (Whitacre et al., 1994; Ader, Felton, & Cohen, 1991). Studies suggest that two kinds of norepinephrine receptors are located on the membranes of lymphocytes. One kind specifically receives *low* levels of norepinephrine and gives lymphocytes a message to increase their activity. Thus, during

---

venous drug users, and people who associate with them (Herek & Glunt, 1988). When Magic Johnson revealed that he had contracted HIV through means other than homosexual contact or intravenous drug use, AIDS activists hoped that this view would change. But even Magic Johnson was not safe from the repercussions of the public's angst over AIDS. This celebrated athlete lost lucrative endorsement contracts and found other professional players unwilling to face him on the basketball court for fear of contracting his disease.

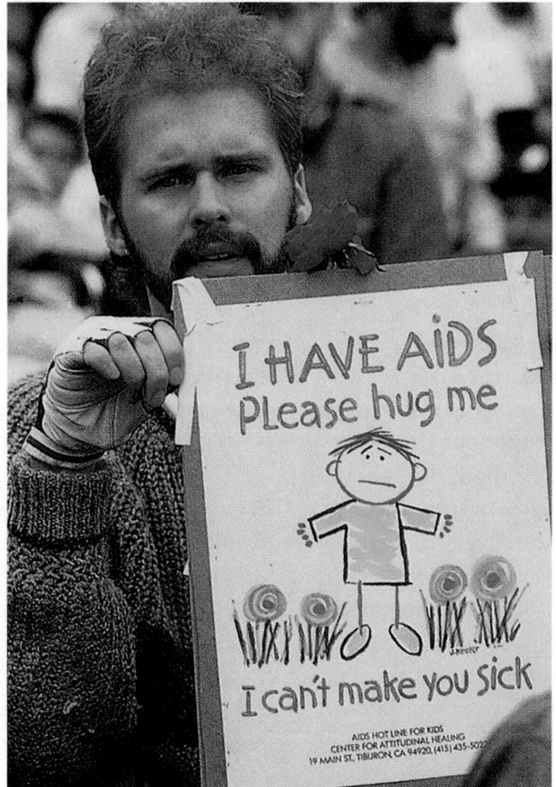

Experts agree that incidental contact with AIDS sufferers does not lead to infection (Herek et al., 1993). Yet prejudice and misunderstanding continue. Patients who are HIV positive may face discrimination and harassment, along with loss of their jobs, health insurance, and police protection (Tross & Hirsch, 1988). Many victims must also contend with the loss of friends who die of AIDS and others who succumb to social pressure, along with the prospect of their own death. The stress can lead to apathy, depression, preoccupation with the illness, anxiety-related disorders, and other problems (Lyketsos et al., 1996; Taylor et al., 1996). Once again, in a vicious and fatal cycle, all of these stressors can directly affect the ability of the immune system to fight off the disease (Fleishman & Fogel, 1994).

To reduce the psychologically based problems that accompany HIV, we must give its victims what is available to all other sufferers of a fatal illness: compassion and hope. We can do so only by educating the public about the facts. Today millions of dollars are spent to educate both youngsters and adults about AIDS (Jacobs, 1993). Yet it is extraordinarily difficult to overcome deeply felt prejudices—against people and against a mysterious and deadly disease. Only when sufferers are accepted as people in need of help and understanding will their environment serve to help their recovery rather than accelerate their death.

Laboratory animals are widely used in research on the immune system. The destruction of the immune systems of these mice, which has caused their hair to fall out, enables researchers to produce and investigate various invasive cells and viruses.

low or initial stress, when norepinephrine release is modest, immune system functioning actually intensifies. However, the other kind of norepinephrine receptor is stimulated by *higher* levels of norepinephrine and apparently gives lymphocytes an inhibitory message to reduce their activity. Thus, during high or chronic stress, when norepinephrine release is more extensive, the functioning of the immune system slows down.

Activation of Hormones As we have observed previously (see pp. 92–93), the body's endocrine system also plays a key biological role in mental and physical functioning. Endocrine glands located throughout the body help regulate activities such as growth, body temperature, and responses to stress. When stimulated, the glands release *hormones,* chemical messengers that propel various body organs into action.

Of particular interest in stress reactions is the chain of events leading from the brain's hypothalamus to the production of ***corticosteroids***—cortisone and other so-called stress hormones. This chain is known as the ***hypothalamic-pituitary-adrenal axis.*** When a person is under stress, the hypothalamus secretes a hormone called the *corticotropin releasing factor (CRF),* which in turn stimulates the nearby pituitary gland; the pituitary gland then secretes the *adrenocorticotropic hormone (ACTH),* which next stimulates the adrenal glands, located on top of each kidney; the adrenal glands then release the corticosteroids.

Initially, the body's release of corticosteroids stimulates body organs to greater activity. However, after stress continues for thirty minutes or more, the release of these stress hormones begins to intensify dramatically (Manuck et al., 1991). The stress hormones then travel to various receptor sites in the body and give *inhibitory* messages, which help calm down the overstressed body. One such group of receptor sites is located on lymphocytes. When the corticosteroids bind to these receptors, they give their inhibitory message and actually slow the production and activity of lymphocytes (Bellinger et al., 1994; Rabin et al., 1994; Zwilling et al, 1993). In short, the very hormones that otherwise help to stabilize persons under chronic stress also act to slow the immune system.

Behavior and Mood Changes Stress may slow immune system functioning indirectly by leading to certain behavioral changes. Some people under intense or chronic stress may, as we have observed in previous chapters, become anxious or depressed, perhaps even develop an anxiety or mood disorder. Many such individuals sleep or eat more poorly, exercise less, or increase their smoking or drinking of alcohol—behaviors known to adversely affect the functioning of the immune system (Cohen & Herbert, 1996; Cohen & Williamson, 1988; Kiecolt-Glaser & Glaser, 1988).

Mood changes may also affect the immune system more directly. It may be that the abnormal biochemical activity that accompanies depression also disrupts lymphocyte activity (Azar, 1996). In support of this theory, researchers have found that the immune systems of people with clinical levels of depression function much more poorly than those of other people (Schleifer et al., 1996). Even people who merely feel dejected experience some slowing of immune system functioning (Cohen & Herbert, 1996; Herbert & Cohen, 1993).

Personality Style Several theorists have proposed that people who generally respond to life stress with optimism, constructive coping strategies, and resilience may experience better immune system functioning and be better prepared to fight off illness (Everson et al., 1996; Dykema, Bergbower, & Peterson, 1995). As we observed in Chapter 7, some researchers have identified a "hardy" personality style, represented by people who welcome challenge and are willing to commit themselves and take control in their daily encounters (Kobasa, 1990, 1987, 1979; Maddi, 1990). According to studies of telephone company managers, army officers, bus drivers, printers, and lawyers, people with a hardy personality are less likely than others to become ill after stressful events (Kobasa, 1984, 1982). Conversely, those whose personality is less than hardy seem more susceptible to illness after stress. In fact, one study discovered that men with an abiding sense of hopelessness die at above-average rates from heart disease, cancer, and other causes (Everson et al., 1996).

In a related line of research, David McClelland and his associates have identified what they call the *inhibited power motive style* (McClelland, 1993, 1985). People who display this personality style are thought to have a strong need for power; they strive for prestige and influence over others. However, they have been taught to satisfy this need in indirect ways—by serving other people or worthy causes, for example, or by upholding high principles. Apparently, people with inhibited power motives are more likely than others to develop physical illnesses, particularly upper respiratory infections, in the face of academic and other power-related stresses (McClelland, 1993; Jemmott, 1987). According to McClelland, such stressors arouse the power needs of these people, and so trigger their sympathetic nervous system into action. All of this arousal, in turn, increases the release of norepinephrine, which, as we observed earlier, inhibits the functioning of the immune system (McClelland, 1993, 1979).

In one study designed to test this theory, sixty-four dental students were examined at five points in the school year: September, November, April, June, and July (Jemmott et al., 1983). September and July were considered to be periods of low academic stress, whereas November, April, and June—months filled with work and exams—were seen as periods of high academic stress. During each of these periods the experimenters collected samples of saliva from the subjects and analyzed them for s-IgA, the antibody mentioned earlier that typically helps defend people against upper respiratory infections: the lower the s-IgA readings, the poorer the functioning of the immune system.

As expected, the average s-IgA measures of the dental students were normal during the calm of September, dropped significantly during the stressful months of November, April, and June, and rebounded in July. In short, during periods of increased stress, the subjects' immune systems seemed less able to ward off upper respiratory infections. The investigators then looked separately at the s-IgA measures of those dental students who scored high in inhibited power motive style. Their s-IgA levels tended to be low even during the relatively calm periods of September and July. That is, these students remained highly susceptible to illness over a longer period of time than those with a low power motive. Their inhibited power drive, then, may account for the relatively high rates of illness among them.

Finally, some studies have also pointed to a correlation between certain personality characteristics and the prognoses of cancer patients (NAMHC, 1996; Anderson et al., 1994; Levy & Roberts, 1992; Greer, 1991). These studies have found that patients with certain forms of cancer who display a helpless coping style and who cannot readily express their feelings, particularly anger, have a worse prognosis than patients who do express their emotions. Other studies, however, have found no relationship between personality and cancer prognosis (Holland, 1996) (see Box 11-3).

Many people with cancer join a support group to share their experiences, concerns, and insights with others who have the same problem. Research indicates that membership in such groups significantly improves the prognosis of these persons.

Social Support Numerous studies have found that people who have few social supports and feel lonely have poorer immune functioning in the face of stress than people who do not feel lonely (Cohen & Herbert, 1996; Kiecolt-Glaser et al., 1988, 1987). In one such study, medical students were given the UCLA Loneliness Scale and then divided into "high" and "low" loneliness groups (Kiecolt-Glaser et al., 1984). The high-loneliness group showed lower lymphocyte responses during a final exam period.

Other studies have found that social support and affiliation actually help *protect* people from stress, poor immune system functioning, and subsequent illness (Uchino & Garvey, 1997; Cohen et al., 1992; Kiecolt-Glaser et al., 1991). In one study, hepatitis B vaccine inoculations were administered to forty-eight medical students on the last day of a three-day examination period (Glaser et al., 1992). The students who reported the greatest amount of social support had stronger immune responses to the hepatitis B vaccine. Similarly, some studies have suggested that patients with certain forms of

BOX 11-3 Psychological Factors in Physical Illness: Has the Pendulum Swung Too Far?

Benjamin Blech

(This essay originally appeared in Newsweek, *September 19, 1988.)*

It started with a terrible backache. That's when I realized how pervasive the new-age mentality has become. When I read that Shirley MacLaine, its leading practitioner, had convinced her devotees that people create their own reality—"You are God," she said—I assumed she meant nothing more by it than inspirational motivation. After all, isn't that what parents and preachers have been saying all along? Do your best. Aim high. Onward and upward. Every day in every way. . . . Be like the little engine that said it could.

Then I discovered the flip side of MacLaine's argument: if I'm sick, it must be my fault. If my life is a mess, I've failed to fulfill my potential. Real life isn't always perfect. Extrapolate from that to such realities as poverty and pestilence and you have what I view as a contemporary madness: for every misfortune in life, we seem too ready to blame the victim.

But first let me tell you what happened when my back went bad. Remember when sciatica could elicit at least a murmur of sympathy? Well, not anymore. Friends are now Freudians; everyone is "into" psychology. And when I shared the news that I have a herniated disc, all-knowing laymen looked at me and repeatedly asked: "Why are you letting stress get to you that much? Why are you doing this to yourself?"

Believe it or not, wear and tear, age and time, can actually cause damage to bodily parts and functions. Yet in these psychologically sophisticated times, the insight that illness is affected by the mind has so overwhelmed us that we often forget that it is also physical.

Some years ago Norman Cousins caused a considerable stir in medical circles when he attributed his recovery from a critical arthritic illness to extended exposure to humor. His conclusion deserved widespread circulation. Laughter is good medicine. Feelings can foster health. Attitude may mean the difference between life and death. But—and here is the crucial cautionary that's often lost in the upbeat literature of our day—disease is still a cruel killer. Cancer victims who truly want to live do nevertheless die. Wishing doesn't necessarily alter dreadful conditions. Yet those who suffer with courage are now stigmatized for failing to recover—even viewed as if they were committing suicide.

I cannot forget the pain of my best friend in the weeks before he died. Sam faced his imminent demise with dignity. He was able

cancer who receive social support in their personal lives or supportive therapy often have better immune system functioning and in turn a better prognosis than patients without such supports (Fawzy et al., 1995, 1993; Sleek, 1995; Classen, Hermanson, & Spiegel, 1994; Levy & Roberts, 1992).

Psychological Treatments for Physical Disorders

As clinicians have become more aware that psychosocial factors often contribute to physical disorders, they have increasingly used psychological interventions to help treat such disorders (Cassem & Hyman, 1995; Lehrer et al., 1993). The most common of these interventions are relaxation training, biofeedback training, meditation, hypnosis, cognitive interventions, and insight therapy. Initially these approaches were applied only to the traditional psychophysiological disorders, but today they are used for the fullest range of medical difficulties. The field of treatment that combines psychological and physical interventions to treat or prevent medical problems is known as ***behavioral medicine*** (Blanchard, 1994).

Relaxation Training As we saw in Chapter 6, people can be taught to relax their muscles at will, a process that also reduces feelings of anxiety. Given the effects of relaxation on the nervous system, clinicians believe that ***relaxation training*** can be of particular help in preventing or treating illnesses that are related to stress to bear almost everything but he could not forgive himself for his illness. He had been led to believe by the apostles of new ageism, friends who embraced this cultural perspective, that he had failed. Failed, because if he had really wanted to, the purveyors of these Mary Poppins–style miracles assured him, he would certainly recover. Failed because if he would only try a bit harder he would rid himself of the poisons that were destroying his body. Failed because as a husband and father, his will to live should have overpowered and overcome everything.

Hope is a wonderful tonic, but I fear that these days exhortation has overcome compassion. The result is a kind of indifference and unwillingness to face the fact that some misfortunes will always persist, in spite of our best efforts:

People can be poor not because they didn't try hard enough to pull themselves out of their ghettos but because society really stacked the deck against them so that they literally didn't have a chance.

People can be uneducated because the teachers were not there, because the help which should have been given was not offered, because the "system" failed to work.

People can require welfare and food stamps because, in the words of President Kennedy, life is not fair and there are times when tragedy strikes uninvited and unexpected, even unavoidably.

People can be hungry not because they don't want to work but because the world turns its back on those with unproductive skills and then calls them parasites.

People can even be sick and really need a medical doctor, not a holistic health healer.

Carlyle was of course quite correct when he said, "The greatest of faults is to be conscious of none." Self-awareness demands recognition of personal failings. But it seems we have allowed the pendulum to swing too far. From the blind extreme of "It's always their fault" to the delusionary and self-destructive "It's always my fault," we have veered from truth in equal measure.

Ironically, our obsession with self-incrimination is a product of those very movements which promised peace of mind through an emphasis on personal accountability. Of course in the spirit of est we must "take responsibility for our lives." But must we take as our identities the scripts that all too often are simply handed us?

If I slip on a banana peel that somebody else carelessly left on the ground, I can curse my bad luck and get on with my life. But if I drop the peel myself and was stupid enough to slip on it too, then I will never forgive myself.

Perhaps the time has come for us to call an amnesty in the war on ourselves. No matter what the comic-strip character Pogo may have said, there are times when we have met the enemy—and it isn't us.

When I was a small boy, I loved the story of the little engine that kept telling itself it could and it did. Growing up has taught me that there are times when it can't and maturity demands awareness not only of our abilities, but also of our limits.

and heightened activity of the autonomic nervous system.

Relaxation training, often in combination with medication, has been extensively used in the treatment of high blood pressure (Dubbert, 1995; Canino et al., 1994; Lehrer et al., 1993; Johnston, 1992). One study assigned hypertensive subjects to one of three forms of treatment: medication, medication plus relaxation training, or medication plus supportive psychotherapy (Taylor et al., 1977). Only those who received relaxation training in combination with medication showed a significant reduction in blood pressure. Still other studies have indicated that the positive effect of relaxation training on patients with hypertension persists for a year or more (Johnston, 1992; Agras et al., 1980). Relaxation training has also been of some help in treating headaches, insomnia, asthma, severe medical diseases, the undesired effects of cancer treatments, pain after surgery, and Raynaud's disease, a disorder of the vascular system characterized by throbbing, aching, and pain (Bliwise et al., 1995; Cassem & Hyman, 1995; Good, 1995; Bernstein & Carlson, 1993).

Biofeedback Training As we also observed in Chapter 6, patients given ***biofeedback training*** are connected to machinery that gives them continuous data about their involuntary body activities. This information enables them gradually to gain control over those activities. Moderately helpful in the treatment of anxiety disorders, the procedure has also been applied to a growing number of physical disorders.

In one study, *electromyograph (EMG)* feedback was used to treat sixteen patients who were experiencing fa-

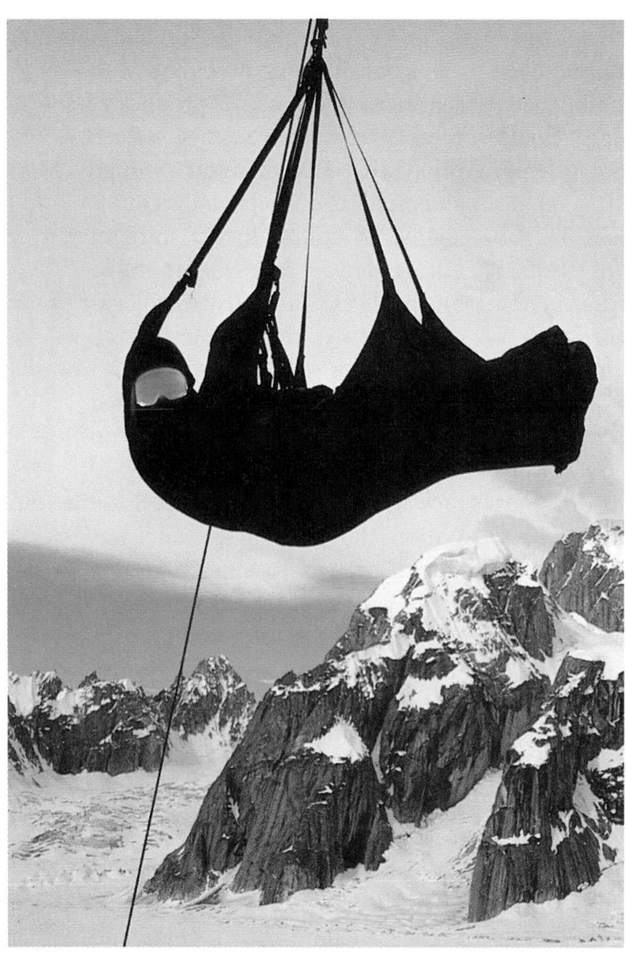

Clinicians are always developing new methods and tools to help people relax. A climber dangles from Alaska's Mount Barrile to demonstrate the use of "Tranquilite" sleep goggles, which are supposed to induce relaxation with blue light and a soothing "pink sound."

cial pain caused in part by tension in their jaw muscles (Dohrmann & Laskin, 1978). In an EMG procedure, electrodes are attached to a client's muscles so that the electrical activity that accompanies muscular contractions may be detected and converted into a tone for subjects to hear (see pp. 175–176). Changes in the pitch and volume of the tone indicate changes in muscle tension. After "listening" to EMG feedback repeatedly, the sixteen experimental subjects learned how to relax their jaw muscles at will and later reported a decrease in facial pain. In contrast, eight control subjects, who were wired to similar equipment and told that a low-grade electrical current was passing through the affected muscles, showed little improvement in muscle tension or pain.

EMG feedback has also been used successfully in the treatment of tension headaches and muscular disabilities caused by strokes or accidents (Blanchard, 1994; Phillips, 1991). Still other forms of biofeedback have been moderately helpful in the treatment of heartbeat irregularities (arrhythmia), asthma, migraine headaches, high blood pressure, stuttering, pain from burns, and Raynaud's disease (Chen & Cui, 1995; Hermann, Kim, & Blanchard, 1995; Labbe, 1995).

Meditation Although meditation has been practiced since ancient times, Western health-care professionals have only recently become aware of its effectiveness in relieving physical distress (Carrington, 1993). ***Meditation*** is a technique of turning one's concentration inward, achieving a slightly altered state of consciousness, and temporarily ignoring all stressors. In the most common approach, meditators go to a quiet place, assume a comfortable posture, utter or think a particular sound (called a ***mantra***) to help focus their attention, and allow their minds to turn away from all ordinary thoughts and concerns (Del Monte, 1995). Meditation is typically practiced in private for approximately 15 minutes twice a day. Many people who follow a regular schedule of meditation report feeling more peaceful, engaged, and creative; interacting more effectively with other people; and enjoying life more (Carrington, 1993, 1978; Schneider et al., 1992).

Meditation has been used to help manage pain in cancer patients (Goleman & Gurin, 1993) and to help treat high blood pressure, heart problems, asthma, the skin disorder psoriasis, diabetes, and even viral infections (Carrington, 1993, 1978; Shapiro, 1982). It has also been useful in relieving the stress-related problem of insomnia (Woolfolk et al., 1976) (see Box 11-4).

Hypnosis As we observed in Chapter 1, subjects who undergo ***hypnosis*** are guided by a hypnotist into a sleep-like, suggestible state during which they can be directed to act in unusual ways, to experience unusual sensations, to remember seemingly forgotten events, or to forget remembered events. With training some people are able to induce their own hypnotic state ***(self-hypnosis).*** Originally developed in the eighteenth century by Friedrich Anton Mesmer as a treatment for hysterical ailments, hypnosis is now used to supplement psychotherapy, to help conduct research, and to help treat many physical conditions (Barber, 1993, 1984).

Hypnosis is effectively used to help control pain, whether caused by a medical condition, such as shingles, or by medical procedures (Holroyd, 1996; Genuis, 1995; Labbe, 1995). One patient was reported to have undergone dental implant surgery under hypnotic suggestion: after a hypnotic state was induced, the dentist suggested to the patient that he was in a pleasant and relaxed setting listening to a friend describe his own success at undergoing similar dental surgery under hypnosis. The dentist then proceeded to perform a successful 25-minute operation (Gheorghiu & Orleanu, 1982).

Although only some people are able to undergo surgery when hypnotic procedures alone are used to control pain, hypnosis combined with chemical anesthesia is apparently beneficial to many patients (Wadden & Anderton, 1982). In addition to its use in painful medical procedures and pain disorders, hypnotic procedures have successfully helped combat such problems as skin diseases, asthma, insomnia, high blood pressure, warts, and other forms of infection (Barber, 1993; Agras, 1984).

Cognitive Interventions People with physical ailments have sometimes been taught new attitudes or cognitive responses toward their ailments as part of treatment (Davies, McKenna, & Hallam, 1995; Newton et al., 1995). In particular, ***self-instruction training*** has helped patients to cope with chronic and severe pain, including pain from burns, arthritis, surgical procedures, headaches, back disorders, ulcers, multiple sclerosis, and cancer treatment (Meichenbaum, 1997, 1993, 1977, 1975; Vlaeyen et al., 1995). As we saw in Chapter 6, self-instruction therapists systematically teach clients to rid themselves of negative self-statements ("Oh, no, I can't take this pain") and to replace them with coping self-statements ("When pain comes, just pause; keep focusing on what you have to do").

Researchers gave self-instruction training to eight burn victims over the course of five days, while eight other burn victims (control subjects) received only the routine services provided to burn patients, such as psychiatric consultation, instructions in general coping strategies, and pain medication (Wernick, 1983). The self-instruction subjects were taught to employ private coping statements whenever they experienced pain. The burn patients who received self-instruction training made significantly fewer requests for pain medication, while the requests of the control patients actually doubled over the course of the study. In addition, the self-instruction subjects later complied with other aspects of their treatment better than the control subjects did.

Insight Therapy and Support Groups If stress and anxiety often contribute to physical problems, therapy designed to reduce general levels of anxiety should help with such problems (House et al., 1988; Varis, 1987). Thus physicians often recommend insight therapy, support groups, or both, to patients as an adjunct to medical treatment. Some research suggests that the discussion of past and present traumas may indeed have beneficial effects on one's health (Lutgendorf et al., 1994; Francis & Pennebaker, 1992; Pennebaker et al., 1988, 1986). In addition, a few studies have indicated that asthmatic children who receive individual or family therapy often adjust better to their life situations, experience less panic during asthma attacks, have fewer and milder attacks, and miss fewer days of school (Simeonsson et al., 1995; Alexander, 1981). Finally, as we noted previously, recovery from cancer and certain other illnesses is often enhanced by participation in support groups (Classen et al., 1994).

Combination Approaches A number of studies have found that the various psychological interventions for physical problems often are equal in effectiveness (Newton et al., 1995; Wittrock et al., 1995; Lehrer et al., 1993). Relaxation and biofeedback training, for example, are equally helpful (and more helpful than placebos) in the treatment of high blood pressure, headaches, asthma, and Raynaud's disease.

Psychological interventions are often of greatest help when they are combined both with each other and with medical treatments (Canty, 1996; Dubbert, 1995; Hermann et al., 1995). In one study, ulcer patients who were given relaxation, self-instruction, and assertiveness training along with medical interventions were found to be more comfortable, have fewer symptoms, be less anxious, and have a better long-term outcome than patients who received medication only (Brooks & Richardson, 1980).

Combination interventions have also been helpful in changing Type A behavior patterns and in reducing

As part of his treatment at the Wellness Center in San Francisco, this man meditates and writes letters to his HIV virus. Research indicates that a combination of psychological interventions and medical treatment often brings greater improvement than a medical approach alone.

BOX 11-4 Sleep and Sleep Disorders

Sleep is crucial to health and well-being. Without it people behave oddly and have strange experiences. Sleep deprivation for 100 hours or more leads to hallucinations, paranoia, and bizarre behavior. When people who have gone without sleep attempt simple tasks, they find that their cognitive and motor functioning has deteriorated. Surprisingly, though, they can sometimes perform tasks demanding great concentration and skill with dexterity.

When people remain awake for over 200 hours, they frequently experience periods of "microsleep," naps lasting two to three seconds. The body simply refuses to be entirely deprived of sleep for long. The odd effects of sleep deprivation are completely eliminated once a person is allowed a period of recovery sleep.

To learn more about these phenomena, researchers bring people into the laboratory and record their activities as they sleep (Mendelson, 1990). They use three types of recording devices, usually simultaneously: the ***electroencephalograph (EEG),*** which records electrical activity in the brain; the ***electrooculograph,*** which records the movement of the eyes; and the ***electromyograph (EMG),*** which measures muscle tension and activity. One important discovery has been that eyes move rapidly about 25 percent of the time a person is asleep (Aserinsky & Kleitman, 1953), a phenomenon known as ***rapid eye movement, or REM.***

Research on eye movement and brain activity has helped identify five stages during the normal sleep cycle. During stages 1 through 4, generally referred to as non-REM (NREM), the eyes move slowly and regularly, if at all, in sharp contrast to the REM sleep of stage 5. As we cycle through the five stages of sleep several times over the course of a night, we typically experience four to six periods of REM sleep (stage 5). REM sleep is often called "paradoxical sleep" because it resembles both deep sleep and wakefulness. Despite small movements and muscle twitches, the body is immobilized—essentially paralyzed. At the same time, the eyes are darting back and forth. Blood flow to the brain increases and the EEG shows brain wave activity that is almost identical to that of a waking and alert person. Eighty percent of the subjects who are awakened from REM sleep report that they were dreaming.

When we are deprived of enough sleep or if the normal sleep cycle is disrupted, we suffer. DSM-IV distinguishes the ***dyssomnias***—sleep disorders involving disturbances in the amount, quality, or timing of sleep—from the ***parasomnias,*** which involve abnormal events that occur during sleep (Stores, 1996; APA, 1994).

Dyssomnias

Insomnia, or difficulty falling and staying asleep, is the most common dyssomnia. Over the course of each year between 30 and 40 percent of all adults experience it. For a diagnosis of ***primary insomnia,*** however, this problem must be the predominant complaint, last at least one month, and cause significant distress or impairment (APA, 1994). People with chronic insomnia experience periods of sleepiness or microsleep during the day, and their ability to function is often impaired. Insomnia has many causes.

1. *Biological factors.* A biological predisposition to be a very light sleeper or to have an overactive arousal system may interfere with sleep (Hobson, 1986). In addition, some medical disorders can contribute to insomnia (Mendelson, 1990).

2. *Psychological disorders.* Difficulty in falling and staying asleep accompanies many psychological disorders, including depression and schizophrenia.

3. *Lifestyle.* Sleeping late on weekends, sleeping in a room that is too hot or too cold, exercising just before going to sleep, ingesting too much caffeine, and other such habits may cause insomnia.

4. *Efforts to fall asleep.* People who have a hard time falling asleep may develop little rituals that they believe will produce the sleep they crave. Unfortunately, in some instances that behavior actually becomes a stimulus for postponing sleep. Preparing for bed, thinking about sleeping, even counting sheep may condition the person to stay awake.

5. *Substance misuse.* Many people believe that alcohol and other drugs will help them fall asleep. Sleeping pills and alcohol often have the opposite effect, however, leading to shallow sleep and abnormal REM periods.

In contrast to insomnia, the predominant problem of the person with ***primary hypersomnia,*** another kind of dyssomnia, is excessive sleepiness for at least a month. The disorder may take the form of prolonged sleep episodes or daytime sleep episodes that occur almost daily (APA, 1994).

Narcolepsy, a disorder characterized by more than three months of irresistible attacks of

REM sleep during waking hours, afflicts more than 200,000 people in the United States. The person's REM sleep is often brought on by strong emotion. Sufferers may find themselves suddenly experiencing REM sleep in the midst of an argument or during an exciting part of a football game. Treatment often includes amphetaminelike drugs.

Breathing-related sleep disorder disrupts sleep by depriving the brain of oxygen. ***Sleep apnea,*** the most common form of this disorder, is found among 1 to 10 percent of the adult population (APA, 1994). Its victims, predominantly overweight men who are heavy snorers, actually stop breathing for up to 30 or more seconds as they sleep. Hundreds of episodes may occur each night. During an episode, the trachea is partially or fully blocked and the diaphragm is unable to propel air out of the lungs, causing the heartbeat to slow and the brain to be deprived of oxygen. At the end of an episode, the person awakens very briefly and resumes normal breathing. Many sufferers are unaware of their disorder, but they may report extreme sleepiness during the day.

People with ***circadian rhythm sleep disorder*** experience excessive sleepiness or insomnia as a result of persistent or recurrent sleep disruptions brought about by a mismatch between the sleep-wake schedule of most other people in their environment and their own circadian sleep-wake pattern. Often the disorder appears as a pattern of falling asleep late and awakening late. This dyssomnia can be induced by night-shift work, frequent changes in work shifts, or repeated episodes of jet lag.

Parasomnias

Nightmare disorder is the most common of the parasomnias. Most people experience nightmares from time to time, but these frightening dreams are usually infrequent and short-lived and do not affect normal functioning. In some cases, however, nightmares become chronic and cause such great distress that they must be treated with psychotherapy or mild drug therapy. Such nightmares often increase under stress.

Persons with ***sleep terror disorder*** awaken suddenly during the first third of their evening sleep, screaming in extreme fear and agitation. They are in a state of panic, are often incoherent, and have a heart rate to match. Generally the sufferer does not remember the episode the next morning. Sleep terrors most often appear in children between ages 4 and 12 years, and disappear during adolescence. Approximately 1 to 6 percent of children experience them at some time (APA, 1994).

People with a ***sleepwalking disorder***—most of them are children—repeatedly leave their beds and walk around, without being conscious of the episode or remembering it later. The episodes occur in the first third of the night, and generally consist of getting out of bed and walking around, apparently with a specific purpose in mind. People who are awakened while sleepwalking are confused for several moments. If allowed to continue sleepwalking, they eventually return to bed. Sleepwalkers usually manage to avoid obstacles, climb stairs, and perform complex activities, always in a seemingly emotionless and unresponsive state. Accidents do happen, however: tripping, bumping into furniture, and even falling out of windows have all been reported. Approximately 1 to 5 percent of all children manifest this disorder for a period of time, and as many as 30 percent have isolated episodes. The causes of sleepwalking are unknown. It generally disappears by age 15 (APA, 1994).

Sleep and sleep disorders have caught the public interest in the last decade, and sleep research laboratories are now found in many major cities. Because sleep is such a crucial part of our lives, it is important to understand its underlying mechanisms. The results of sleep studies have implications not only for the treatment of sleep disorders and related psychological problems but for every human endeavor.

the risk of coronary heart disease among Type A people (Johnston, 1992; Roskies et al., 1986). In one study, 862 patients who had suffered a heart attack within the previous six months were assigned to one of two groups (Friedman et al., 1984). The control group was given three years of cardiological counseling regarding diet, exercise, and relevant medical and surgical information. The experimental group received the same counseling plus Type A behavioral counseling over the same period of time. They were taught to identify their Type A personality style and to recognize their excessive physiological, cognitive, and behavioral responses in stressful situations. They were also trained in relaxation and taught to change counterproductive attitudes (for example, the belief that their achievement was a measure of their worth).

The researchers found that the addition of the Type A behavioral counseling led to major differences in lifestyle and health. Type A behavior was reduced in almost 80 percent of the patients who received both Type A counseling and cardiological counseling for three years, compared to only 50 percent of those who received cardiological counseling only. Moreover, fewer of those who received the combined counseling suffered another heart attack—only 7 percent, compared to 13 percent of the subjects who had received cardiological counseling alone (see Figure 11-5).

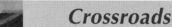

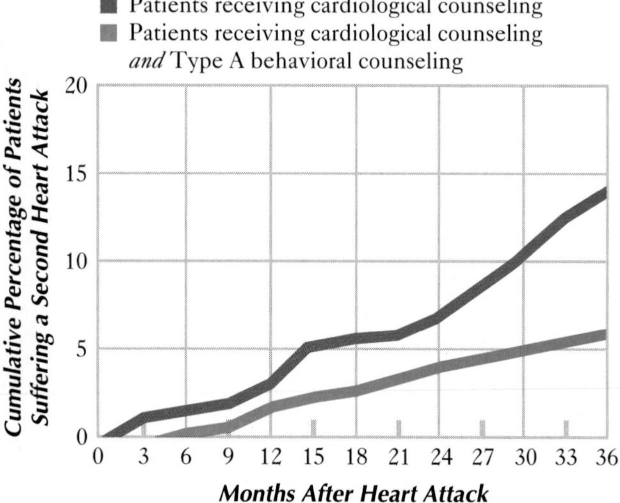

Figure 11-5 *Heart attack survivors who received behavioral counseling aimed at reducing their Type A behaviors experienced fewer repeat heart attacks during the 36 months after their attack than did survivors who received only standard medical counseling. (Adapted from Friedman et al., 1984.)*

Clearly, the treatment picture for physical illnesses has been changing. Medical interventions continue to predominate, but the use of psychological techniques as adjuncts is on the rise. As we have seen throughout this chapter, today's scientists and practitioners are traveling a course far removed from the path of mind-body dualism that once dominated medical thinking.

Crossroads

Once considered "outsiders" to the field of abnormal psychology, physical disorders are now seen as problems that fall squarely within its boundaries. Just as physical events have long been recognized as playing a role in abnormal mental functioning, psychosocial events are now considered important contributors to abnormal physical functioning. Indeed, today's clinicians believe that psychological and sociocultural factors contribute to the onset and course of virtually all physical ailments.

The number of studies devoted to this relationship has increased steadily during the past thirty years. What researchers once saw as a vague tie between stress and physical illness is now understood as a complex chain made up of many variables. Such factors as life stress, idiosyncratic psychological reactions, dysfunction of the autonomic nervous system, activation of neurotransmitters, and suppression of the immune system all play parts in disorders once considered purely physical.

Insights into treatment have been accumulating just as rapidly in this area. Psychological approaches such as relaxation training and cognitive therapy are being applied increasingly to physical ills, usually in combination with traditional medical treatments. Although such approaches have yielded only modest results so far, clinicians are becoming convinced that psychological interventions will eventually be integral parts of treatment for many physical ailments.

While the field's acknowledgment of psychosocial factors as contributors to physical illness is very promising indeed, perhaps most exciting is its growing emphasis on the *interrelationship* of the social environment, the brain, and the rest of the body. We have observed repeatedly that psychological disorders are often best understood and treated when sociocultural, psychological, and biological factors are all taken into consideration. We now know that their interaction also helps explain medical problems. We are again reminded that the brain is part of the body, and that both are part of a social context. For better and for worse, the three are inextricably linked.

Chapter Review

1. ***Somatic illness and psychosocial factors*** Before the twentieth century, medical theory was dominated by *mind-body dualism,* or the belief that the mind and body were totally separate entities. Today's clinicians recognize that somatic, or bodily, illnesses can have psychosocial causes.

2. ***Factitious disorder*** Patients with a factitious disorder feign physical disorders in order to assume the role of a sick person. *Munchausen syndrome* is the extreme and chronic form of factitious disorder. In *Munchausen syndrome by proxy,* a parent fabricates or induces a physical illness in his or her child.

3. ***Somatoform disorders*** Patients with somatoform disorders have physical complaints whose causes are predominantly psychosocial. Unlike people with a factitious disorder, these sufferers believe that their illnesses are organic.

   A. ***Hysterical somatoform disorders*** Hysterical somatoform disorders involve the actual loss or alteration of physical functioning. They include conversion disorder, somatization disorder (or Briquet's syndrome), and pain disorder associated with psychological factors.

   (1) In a *conversion disorder,* a psychosocial conflict or need is converted into dramatic physical symptoms affecting voluntary motor sensory functioning. It is thought to be rare.

   (2) People with *somatization disorder* experience long-lasting physical ailments that have little or no organic basis. It is more common and lasts longer than conversion disorder, and is more prevalent among women than among men.

   (3) When psychosocial factors play a dominant role in the onset, severity, exacerbation, or maintenance of pain, patients may receive a diagnosis of *pain disorder associated with psychological factors.*

   (4) Diagnosticians try to distinquish hysterical somatoform disorders from "true" medical problems by looking for inconsistencies in the patient's medical picture, such as an unusual pattern of symptoms.

   B. ***Preoccupation somatoform disorder:*** People with preoccupation somatoform disorders are preoccupied with the notion that something is wrong with them physically. In this category are hypochodriasis and body dysmorphic disorder.

   (1) *Hypochondriasis,* is characterized by fearful misinterpretations of bodily symptoms as signs of serious bodily diseases.

   (2) *Body dysmorphic disorder is* characterized by intense concern that some aspect of one's physical appearance is defective.

   C. ***Views on somatoform disorders*** Theorists explain preoccupation somatoform disorders much as they do anxiety disorders. Hysterical somatoform disorders, however, are viewed as unique disorders that are still poorly understood.

   (1) *Freud* developed the initial psychodynamic view of hysterical somatoform disorders. He proposed that the disorders represented a conversion of underlying emotional conflicts into physical symptoms.

   (2) According to *behaviorists,* the physical symtoms of hysterical disorders bring rewards to the sufferer, and such reinforcement helps maintain the symptoms.

   (3) Some *cognitive* theorists propose that hysterical somatoform disorders are forms of *communication,* and that people express their emotions through their physical symptoms.

   D. ***Treatments for somatoform disorders*** Therapy for preoccupation somatoform disorders includes exposure and response prevention and other treatments from the realm of anxiety disorders. Interventions for hysterical somatoform disorders emphasize either *insight, suggestion, reinforcement,* or *confrontation.*

4. ***Psychophysiological disorders*** Psychophysiological disorders are those in which psychosocial and physiological factors interact to cause a physical problem. These disorders have been explained by the *disregulation model,* which proposes that our brain and body ordinarily establish *negative feedback loops* that guarantee the smooth operation of the body. When this system fails to regulate itself properly, psychophysiological problems may result. Factors linked to these disorders are *sociocultural* factors, such as wide-ranging stressors or chronic social circumstances; *psychological* factors, such as particular needs, attitudes, or personality styles; and *biological* factors, such as defective functioning by the ANS or by a particular organ.

   A. ***"Traditional" psychophysiological disorders*** For years clinical researchers singled out a limited number of physical illnesses as psychophysiological. These "traditional" psychophysiological disorders include *ulcers, asthma, chronic headaches, hypertension,* and *coronary heart disease.*

   B. ***"New" psychophysiological disorders*** Recently many other psychophysiological disorders have been identified. Scientists have linked many physical illnesses to stress and have developed a new area of study called *psychoneuroimmunology.*

(1) ***Stress and susceptibility to illness*** Viral and bacterial infections and other health problems have been traced to high levels of stress.

(2) ***Psychoneuroimmunology*** The body's *immune system* consists of *lymphocytes* and other cells that fight off *antigens*—bacteria, viruses, and other foreign invaders.

(3) *Helper T-cells* are lymphocytes that identify antigens and then multiply and trigger the production of other immune cells. *Natural killer T-cells* are lymphocytes that seek out and destroy body cells that have already been infected. *B-cells* are lymphocytes that produce *antibodies,* chemicals that bind to antigens and mark them for destruction. Stress can slow lymphocyte activity, thereby interfering with the immune system's ability to protect against illness during times of stress. Factors implicated in the relationship between stress and immune system functioning include *neurotransmitter stimulation* (*norepinephrine* helps slow immune system functioning), *activation of hormones* (extended release of corticosteroids slows lymphocyte activity), *behavior and mood changes* (anxiety or depression can help slow immune system functioning, directly or indirectly), *personality style* (broad feelings of hopelessness or other counterproductive personality styles can affect the immune system), and *social support* (weak social support systems may contribute to poorer immune system functioning).

5. ***Psychological treatments for physical disorders*** *Behavioral medicine* combines psychological and physical interventions to treat or prevent medical problems. Psychological interventions such as relaxation training, biofeedback training, meditation, hypnosis, cognitive techniques, insight therapy, and support groups are increasingly being included in the treatment of various medical problems. They have been of some help in problems such as high blood pressure, headaches, pain during or after surgery, pain from burns or other problems, asthma, and cancer.

Thought and Afterthought

One More for the Road

People in Toronto are flocking to a new kind of bar, the O2 Spa Bar. There they pay $13 for a twenty-minute drink of fresh air. Customers hook up to oxygen tanks and inhale nearly pure oxygen. Patrons swear that repeated "drinks" of oxygen help them feel more energetic and less stressed. Many claim to be cured of everything from hangovers to hot flashes. Similar oxygen bars have been around for a while in Asian cities; they are just now getting started in North America.

Afterthoughts: *Why do people who respond positively to health-enhancement techniques, from oxygen bars to herbal medicines, invariably report that their psychological condition improves as well? . . . Is there something hypochondriacal about our society's constant search for more comfortable physical states, even if tens of thousands of people pursue them? . . . Might a placebo effect be operating for at least some of the people who respond so positively to health-enhancement techniques?*

Mind-Body Relationships

According to one study, women who work outside of the home have lower (that is, healthier) blood pressure levels than those who do not (Seachrist, 1995). Furthermore, today's employed women have lower blood pressure than employed women did in 1960.

Afterthoughts: *How might this relationship be explained? . . . Do these blood pressure findings among women contradict the many studies that link men's job stress to a rise in their blood pressure?*

He Ain't Heavy . . .

A few years ago, thirteen fifth-grade boys in San Marcos, California, went to a barbershop and proceeded to have their heads shaved. The purpose of this seemingly strange group action? To show support and compassion for their 11-year-old friend and classmate Ian O'Gorman. Ian was undergoing chemotherapy for cancer at the time and was beginning to lose his hair. His friends didn't want him to feel left out or further traumatized, so they undertook this selfless display of support. Their teacher, who had his head shaved too, said that the idea came from the boys, who nicknamed themselves the Bald Eagles. All parents gave their blessings to the group action. Ian gratefully reported, "What my friends did really made me feel stronger. It helped me get through all this. . . . I was really amazed that they would do something like this for me."

Afterthoughts: *No doubt the generous behavior by his friends had an enormous impact on Ian's state of mind. Might it also have affected his health and recovery? . . . Is our society more sensitive today than in the past to the psychosocial issues at work in illnesses such as Ian's? . . . How might psychologists account for the insight and empathy displayed by such very young boys?*

Topic Overview

Anorexia Nervosa

Bulimia Nervosa

Explanations

Societal Pressures

Family Environment

Ego Deficiencies and Cognitive Disturbances

Mood Problems

Biological Factors

Treatments for Eating Disorders

Chapter 12

Eating Disorders

Thinness has become a national obsession (see Figure 12-1). Most of us are as preoccupied with the quantity of the food we eat as with its taste and nutritional value. One need only count the articles about dieting in magazines and newspapers to be convinced that contemporary Western society equates thinness with health and beauty. Perhaps it is not coincidental that during the past three decades we have also witnessed an increase in two dramatic eating disorders at whose core is a morbid fear of gaining weight (Foreyt, Poston, & Goodrick, 1996; Russell, 1995). Sufferers of ***anorexia nervosa*** relentlessly pursue extreme thinness and lose so much weight that they may starve themselves to death. The term "anorexia," which means "lack of appetite," is actually a misnomer; sufferers usually continue to have strong feelings of hunger (Garfinkel & Garner, 1982). People with ***bulimia nervosa*** go on frequent eating binges during which they uncontrollably consume large quantities of food, then force themselves to vomit or take other strong steps to keep from gaining weight.

The news media have published many reports about anorexic or bulimic behavior. One reason for the surge in public interest is the frightening medical consequences that can result. The death in 1982 of Karen Carpenter, the popular singer and entertainer, from medical problems relating to anorexia nervosa serves as a reminder. Another widespread concern is the disproportionate prevalence of these disorders among adolescent girls and young women (Russell, 1995).

Wayne Thiebaud's painting Confections, *1962, presents the elegance and beauty of food. It is missing the ominous qualities of power and threat that food holds for many people.*

Clinicians and researchers have come to understand that the similarities between anorexia nervosa and bulimia nervosa can be as important as the

Percentage Dissatisfied with Their:

	1972 Females	1972 Males	1997 Females	1997 Males
Overall body	25%	15%	56%	43%
Weight	48%	35%	66%	52%
Muscle tone	30%	25%	57%	45%
Breast/Chest	26%	18%	34%	38%
Abdomen	50%	36%	71%	63%
Hips and upper thighs	49%	12%	61%	29%

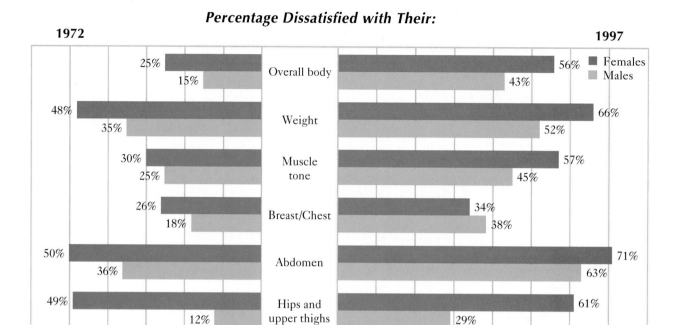

Figure 12–1 *According to surveys on body image, people in our society are much more dissatisfied with their bodies now than they were 25 years ago. Women are still more dissatisfied than men, but today's men are more dissatisfied with their bodies than the men of a generation past. Other data suggest that body dissatisfaction is actually accelerating. (Adapted from Garner, Cooke, & Marano, 1997, p. 42; Rodin, 1992, p. 57.)*

differences between them (van der Ham et al., 1997; Williams et al., 1996; APA, 1994). As we shall see, many people with anorexia nervosa binge as they persist in losing dangerous amounts of weight; some may even later develop bulimia nervosa (Mizes, 1995; Sharp & Freeman, 1993). Conversely, people with bulimia nervosa sometimes go on to develop anorexia nervosa.

Anorexia Nervosa

Janet Caldwell, 14 years old and in the eighth grade, displays many characteristic symptoms of anorexia nervosa, according to the DSM-IV classification: she refuses to maintain more than 85 percent of her normal body weight; intensely fears becoming overweight; has a disturbed view of her weight and shape; and has stopped menstruating (APA, 1994).

> Janet Caldwell was . . . five feet, two inches tall and weighed 62 pounds. . . . Janet began dieting at the age of 12 when she weighed 115 pounds and was chided by her family and friends for being "pudgy." She continued to restrict her food intake over a two-year period, and as she grew thinner, her parents became increasingly more concerned about her eating behavior. . . .
>
> Janet . . . felt that her weight problem began at the time of puberty. She said that her family and friends had supported her efforts to achieve a ten-pound weight loss when she first began dieting at age 12. Janet did not go on any special kind of diet. Instead, she restricted her food intake at meals, generally cut down on carbohydrates and protein intake, tended to eat a lot of salads, and completely stopped snacking between meals. At first, she was quite pleased with her progressive weight reduction, and she was able to ignore her feelings of hunger by remembering the weight loss goal she had set for herself. However, each time she lost the number of pounds she had set for her goal she decided to lose just a few more pounds. Therefore she continued to set new weight goals for herself. In this manner, her weight dropped from 115 pounds to 88 pounds during the first year of her weight loss regimen.
>
> Janet felt that, in her second year of dieting, her weight loss had continued beyond her control. . . . She became convinced that there was something inside of her that would not let her gain weight. . . . Janet commented that although there had been occasions over the past few years when she had been fairly "down" or unhappy, she still felt driven to keep on diet-

ing. As a result, she frequently went for walks, ran errands for her family, and spent a great deal of time cleaning her room and keeping it in a meticulously neat and unaltered arrangement.

When Janet's weight loss continued beyond the first year, her parents insisted that she see their family physician, and Mrs. Caldwell accompanied Janet to her appointment. Their family practitioner was quite alarmed at Janet's appearance and prescribed a high-calorie diet. Janet said that her mother spent a great deal of time pleading with her to eat, and Mrs. Caldwell planned various types of meals that she thought would be appealing to Janet. Mrs. Caldwell also talked a great deal to Janet about the importance of good nutrition. Mr. Caldwell, on the other hand, became quite impatient with these discussions and tended to order Janet to eat. Janet then would try to eat something, but often became tearful and ran out of the room because she could not swallow the food she had been ordered to eat. The youngster said that she often responded to her parents' entreaties that she eat by telling them that she indeed had eaten but they had not seen her do so. She often listed foods that she said she had consumed which in fact she had flushed down the toilet. She estimated that she only was eating about 300 calories a day.

Mrs. Caldwell indicated that Janet appeared quiet and withdrawn, in contrast to her generally active and cheerful disposition, at the time she began dieting. . . . Janet became very critical of her girlfriends, and Mrs. Caldwell felt that Janet behaved in an argumentative and stubborn manner with them. . . . In general, Janet seemed less spontaneous and talked less with her family and others than she had during any previous period that her parents could recall.

(Leon, 1984, pp. 179–184)

Like Janet, at least half of the people with anorexia nervosa reduce their weight by restricting their intake of food, a pattern called ***restricting type anorexia nervosa.*** At first they tend to cut out sweets and fattening snacks, then increasingly other foods (APA, 1994; Simon et al., 1993). Eventually, people with this kind of anorexia show almost no variability in diet. The pursuit of thinness becomes a personal test of self-discipline. Others, however, lose weight by forcing themselves to vomit after meals or by abusing laxatives or diuretics, and they may even engage in eating binges, a pattern called ***binge-eating/purging type anorexia nervosa,*** which we shall discuss in more detail when we examine bulimia nervosa (APA, 1994).

Approximately 90 to 95 percent of all cases of anorexia nervosa occur in females (see Box 12-1), and although the disorder can appear at any age, the peak age of onset is between 14 and 19 years (Fombonne, 1995; APA, 1994). Around 1 percent of adolescent girls and young women in Western countries develop the disorder, and many more display at least some of its symptoms. Moreover, anorexia nervosa seems to be on the increase in North America, Europe, and Japan (Battle & Brownell, 1996; Foreyt et al., 1996; Szmukler & Patton, 1995).

Typically the disorder begins after a person who is slightly overweight or of normal weight decides to "just lose a few pounds," and may follow a stressful event such as separation of the parents, a move away from home, or an experience of personal failure (Gowers et al., 1996; Horesh et al., 1995; APA, 1994). Although most victims recover, between 2 and 10 percent of them become so seriously ill that they die, usually from medical problems brought about by starvation or from suicide (Slade, 1995; Treasure & Szmukler, 1995).

The central features of anorexia nervosa are (1) a drive for thinness and a morbid fear of becoming

Perhaps the most publicized victim of anorexia nervosa during recent years was Karen Carpenter, the young singer who developed this disorder at the height of her career and died of related medical problems.

Box 12-1 Not For Women Only

The number of young men with eating disorders appears to be on the rise, and more men are now seeking treatment for these disorders than ever before (Gilbert, 1996). Nevertheless, males account for only 5 to 10 percent of all cases of eating disorders (Frasciello & Willard, 1995), and the reasons for this striking gender difference are not entirely clear.

One possible explanation is that men and women are subjected to different sociocultural pressures. For example, a survey of college men found that the majority selected "muscular, strong and broad shoulders" to describe the ideal male body, and "thin, slim, slightly underweight" to describe the ideal female body (Kearney-Cooke & Steichen-Asch, 1990). Of course, although the emphasis on a muscular, strong, and athletic body as the male ideal may decrease the likelihood of eating disorders in men, it may create other problems such as steroid abuse or excessive weight lifting to increase muscle mass and strength (Mickalide, 1990).

A second reason for the different rates of eating disorders may be the different methods of weight loss favored by men and women. According to some clinical observations, men are more likely to use exercise to lose weight, whereas women more often diet (Braun, 1996; Mickalide, 1990). Dieting helps bring on most cases of eating disorders.

Finally, eating disorders among men may be underdiagnosed. Some men do not want to admit that they have a traditionally "female problem." In addition, it may be more difficult for clinicians to identify eating disorders in men, because the clinical manifestations are different. An obvious symptom of anorexia nervosa among females, such as amenorrhea, is not available among men. It is much more difficult to test for male reproductive problems, such as low levels of testosterone (Andersen, 1990).

Men who do develop eating disorders often grapple with some of the same issues as women with these problems. Some report that they aspire to a "lean, toned, thin" shape similar to the ideal female body, rather than the strong muscular shape with broad shoulders of the typical male ideal (Kearney-Cooke & Steichen-Asch, 1990). In some cases, however, the triggers of male eating disorders are different from those of female eating problems. Most men with these disorders are overweight when they first start trying to lose weight (Andersen, 1995, 1990; Edwin & Andersen, 1990). Many report having been teased about their bodies and picked less often for athletic teams (Kearney-Cooke & Steichen-Asch, 1990). Women with eating disorders, by contrast, usually *feel* overweight when they begin dieting but may not actually be overweight according to objective measures (Edwin & Andersen, 1990).

Male athletes are particularly susceptible to eating disturbances because of the requirements and pressures of certain sports (Thompson & Sherman, 1993). According to one study, 37 percent of males with eating disorders had jobs or played sports for which weight control was important, compared to 13 percent of women (Braun, 1996). The highest rates of

overweight, (2) preoccupation with food, (3) certain cognitive disturbances, (4) psychological and mood problems, and (5) medical problems (APA, 1994). Table 12-1 demonstrates how these features are sometimes measured and assessed.

Becoming thin is life's central goal for persons with anorexia nervosa, but fear is at the root of their preoccupation (Russell, 1995). They are afraid of becoming obese, of giving in to their growing desire to eat, and more generally of losing control over the size and shape of their body. In fact, anorexia nervosa has been called a "weight phobia" (Crisp, 1967).

Despite this focus on thinness and the severe restrictions they may place on their food intake, people with anorexia are ***preoccupied with food.*** They may spend considerable time thinking and even reading about food and planning their limited meals (King, Polivy, & Herman, 1991). Many report that their dreams are filled with images of food and eating (Frayn, 1991; Levitan, 1981).

This preoccupation with food may in fact be the result of food deprivation rather than its cause. In a famous "starvation study" conducted in the late 1940s, thirty-six normal-weight conscientious objectors were put on a semistarvation diet for six months (Keys et al., 1950). Like people with anorexia nervosa, the volunteers became preoccupied with food and eating. They spent hours each day planning their small meals, talked more about food than about any other topic, studied cookbooks and recipes, mixed food in odd combinations, and eating disturbances have been found among jockeys, wrestlers, distance runners, body builders, and swimmers. Jockeys commonly spend up to four hours before a race in a sauna, shedding up to 7 pounds of weight at a time, and may restrict their food intake, abuse laxatives and diuretics, and induce vomiting (King & Mezey, 1987). Similarly, male wrestlers in high school and college commonly restrict their food intake for up to three days before a match in order to "make weight," often losing between 2 and 12 percent of their body weight. Some practice or run in several layers of warm or rubber clothing in order to lose up to 5 pounds of water weight before weighing in for a match (Thompson & Sherman, 1993).

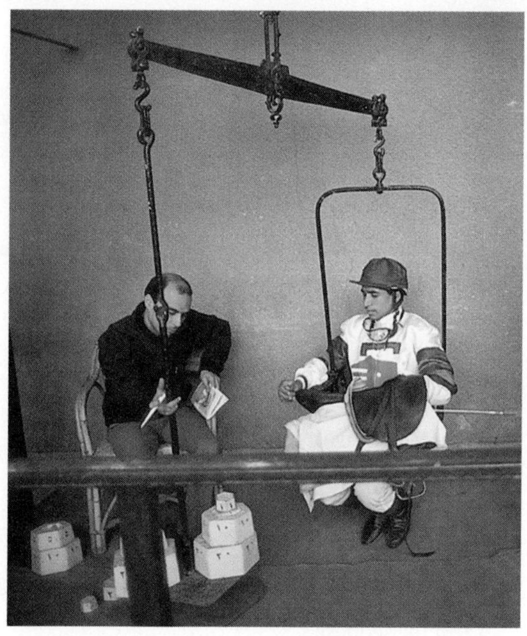

More than a third of males with eating disorders particpate in jobs or sports that require weight control. Although this jockey does not have an eating disorder, his pre-race weigh-in illustrates the weight standards and pressures to which these individuals are regularly subjected.

Whereas most women with eating disorders are obsessed with thinness at all times, wrestlers and jockeys are usually preoccupied with weight reduction only during their sport's season. After "making weight," many wrestlers go on eating and drinking binges in order to gain strength for the upcoming match, only to return to a weight-loss strategy after the match to get prepared for the next weigh-in. This cycle of losing and regaining weight each season has an adverse effect on the body, changing its metabolic activity and hindering future efforts at weight control (Steen, et al., 1988). In addition, weight reduction has anverse effect on an athlete's health (Mickalide, 1990).

Another gender difference that has been found is that male athletes with eating problems tend to estimate their body size more accurately than women with eating disorders do (Enns, Drewnowski, & Grinker, 1987). Research suggests, however, that this and other gender differences tend to disappear when the comparisons are between male and female athletes with these disorders (Prussin & Harvey, 1991).

As the number of males with eating disturbances increases, researchers are becoming more interested in understanding both the gender similarities *and* the gender differences in the disturbances (Andersen, 1992). Since eating disturbances cause problems for both men and women, researchers must unravel and address the relevant factors that operate across the gender divide.

dawdled over their meals. Many also had vivid dreams about food.

Persons with anorexia nervosa also exhibit ***cognitive dysfunction*** of various kinds. They usually have a low opinion of their body shape, for example, and consider themselves unattractive (Heilbrun & Witt, 1990). In addition, they are likely to overestimate their actual proportions. A 23-year-old patient said:

> **I** look in a full-length mirror at least four or five times daily and I really cannot see myself as too thin. Sometimes after several days of strict dieting, I feel that my shape is tolerable, but most of the time, odd as it may seem, I look in the mirror and believe that I am too fat.
>
> *(Bruch, 1973)*

The tendency to overestimate body size has been tested in the laboratory (Rushford & Ostermeyer, 1997; Waller & Hodgson, 1996; Gardner & Bokenkamp, 1995). In a popular assessment technique subjects look at a photograph of themselves through an adjustable anamorphic lens. They are asked to manipulate the lens until the image that they see matches their actual body size. The image can be made to vary from 20 percent thinner to 20 percent larger than actual appearance as the lens is adjusted. In one study, more than half of the subjects with anorexia nervosa were found to overestimate their body size, stopping the lens when the image was larger than they actually were. The majority of control subjects, in contrast, underestimated their body size (Garner et al., 1976).

TABLE 12-1 Sample Items From the Eating Disorder Inventory II

For each item, decide if the item is true about you ALWAYS (A), USUALLY (U), OFTEN (O), SOMETIMES (S), RARELY (R), or NEVER (N). Circle the letter that corresponds to your rating.

A	U	O	S	R	N	I think that my stomach is too big.
A	U	O	S	R	N	I eat when I am upset.
A	U	O	S	R	N	I stuff myself with food.
A	U	O	S	R	N	I think about dieting.
A	U	O	S	R	N	I think that my thighs are too large.
A	U	O	S	R	N	I feel ineffective as a person.
A	U	O	S	R	N	I feel extremely guilty after overeating.
A	U	O	S	R	N	I am terrified of gaining weight.
A	U	O	S	R	N	I get confused about what emotion I am feeling.
A	U	O	S	R	N	I feel inadequate.
A	U	O	S	R	N	I have gone on eating binges where I felt that I could not stop.
A	U	O	S	R	N	As a child, I tried very hard to avoid disappointing my parents and teachers.
A	U	O	S	R	N	I have trouble expressing my emotions to others.
A	U	O	S	R	N	I get confused as to whether or not I am hungry.
A	U	O	S	R	N	I have a low opinion of myself.
A	U	O	S	R	N	I think my hips are too big.
A	U	O	S	R	N	If I gain a pound, I worry that I will keep gaining.
A	U	O	S	R	N	I have the thought of trying to vomit in order to lose weight.
A	U	O	S	R	N	I think my buttocks are too large.
A	U	O	S	R	N	I eat or drink in secrecy.
A	U	O	S	R	N	I would like to be in total control of my bodily urges.

Source: Garner, Olmsted, & Polivy, 1991, 1984.

Another cognitive feature of anorexia nervosa is the development of maladaptive attitudes and misperceptions (DeSilva, 1995; Garner & Bemis, 1985, 1982). People with the disorder often hold such beliefs as "I must be perfect in every way"; "Weight and shape are the most important criteria for inferring one's own worth"; "I will become a better person if I deprive myself"; and "I can avoid guilt by not eating." Gertrude, who recovered from anorexia nervosa, recalls that at age 15 "my thought processes became very unrealistic. I felt I had to do something I didn't want to do for a higher purpose. That took over my life. It all went haywire" (Bruch, 1978, p. 17).

People with anorexia nervosa also display several ***psychological and mood problems.*** Again, studies of normal subjects placed on semistarvation diets have reported similar problems, suggesting that some such features may be the result of starvation (Fichter & Pirke, 1995; Keys et al., 1950). People with the disorder tend to be at least mildly depressed, have low self-esteem, and show symptoms of anxiety, such as social anxiety, beyond their specific fears about body weight (Halmi, 1995; APA, 1994). Some are also troubled by sleep disturbances such as insomnia (Casper, 1995; APA, 1994).

Anorexia nervosa is often accompanied by obsessive-compulsive patterns of behavior (Halmi, 1995; Thiel et

mented with laxatives at least once (Mitchell et al., 1982). Similarly, in a study of young working women, 41 percent reported bingeing (Hart & Ollendick, 1985). Only some of these subjects, however, fully satisfied the DSM-IV criteria for a diagnosis of bulimia nervosa: surveys in several countries suggest that between 1 and 4 percent of adolescent girls and young women develop the full syndrome (Foreyt et al., 1996; Szmukler & Patton, 1995; Halmi et al., 1994).

Like anorexia nervosa, bulimia nervosa usually occurs in females (again in 90 to 95 percent of the cases), begins in adolescence or young adulthood (most often between 15 and 21 years of age), and arises after a period of intense dieting (Fombonne, 1995; Szmukler & Patton, 1995; APA, 1994). It often lasts for several years, with intermittent letup.

The weight of people with bulimia nervosa usually stays within a normal range, although it may fluctuate noticeably within that range (APA, 1994). Some people with this disorder, however, become significantly underweight and may eventually qualify for a diagnosis of anorexia nervosa instead (see Figure 12-2). Still other individuals become overweight, largely as a result of their binge eating (Mitchell et al., 1990). Most overweight people, however, are not bulimic (see Box 12-2).

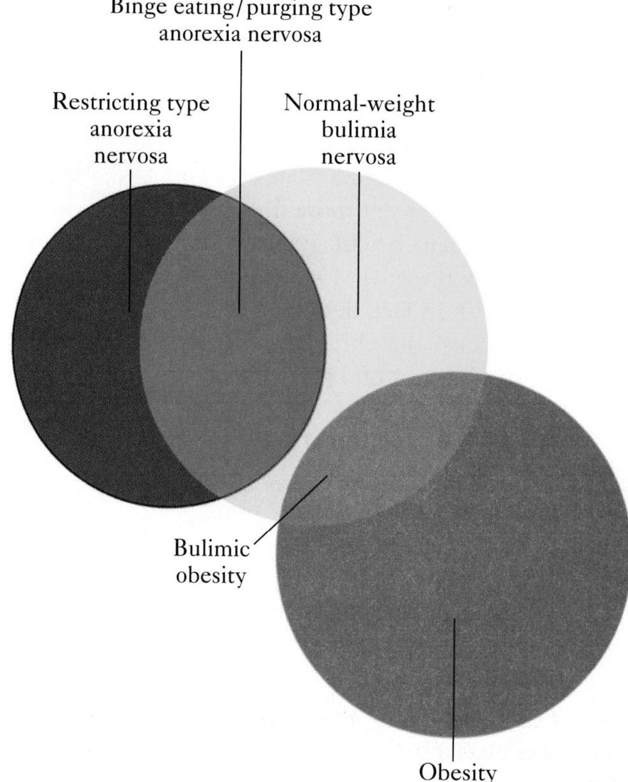

Figure 12–2 *Patterns of anorexia nervosa, bulimia nervosa, and obesity may overlap. Some people with anorexia nervosa binge and purge their way to weight loss. Similarly, some obese persons binge-eat. However, less than half of all people with anorexia purge, most people with bulimia are not obese, and most overweight people are not bulimic. (Adapted from APA, 1994; Garner & Fairburn, 1988; Russell, 1979.)*

Binges

People with bulimia nervosa may have 2 to 40 binge episodes per week, although around 10 per week is common (Mizes, 1993). As in the example above, binges are usually carried out in secret or as inconspicuously as possible. The person gobbles down massive amounts of food very rapidly, with minimal chewing, tending to select food with a sweet taste, high caloric content, and a soft texture, such as ice cream, cookies, doughnuts, and sandwiches. Although the term "bulimia" comes from the Greek *bous limos,* or "cattle hunger," the food is hardly tasted or thought about. Such persons commonly consume more than 1500 calories (often more than 3,000 calories) during a binge (Agras, 1995).

In the early stages of the disorder, the binges tend to be triggered by an upsetting event, depressed mood, hunger, concerns about one's weight or shape, or a desire to indulge in a forbidden food. Later the binge may become a carefully planned, even ritualistic event, with food bought expressly for that purpose.

Binges usually begin with feelings of unbearable tension (Johnson et al., 1995; Mizes, 1995). The individual feels irritable, removed from the scene, and powerless to control an overwhelming need to eat "forbidden" foods (Levine, 1987). During the binge, the person usually feels unable to stop eating. Although the binge itself may be experienced as pleasurable in the sense that it relieves the unbearable tension, it is followed by feelings of extreme self-reproach, guilt, and depression, and a fear of gaining weight and being discovered (Mizes, 1995; APA, 1994).

Compensatory Behaviors

After a binge people with bulimia nervosa try to compensate for and undo its effects. Many resort to vomiting. Actually, vomiting fails to prevent the absorption of half of the calories consumed during a binge. And ironically, repeated vomiting disrupts the body's satiety mechanisms, making people even hungrier and leading to more frequent and intense binges (Wooley & Wooley, 1985). Similarly, the compensatory use of laxatives or diuretics fails almost completely to undo the caloric effects of bingeing (Garner et al., 1985).

BOX 12-2 Obesity: To Lose or Not to Lose

By medical standards, one-third of adults in the United States weigh at least 20 percent more than people of their height typically do (Battle & Brownell, 1996; Foreyt et al., 1996). In fact, despite the public's focus on thinness, low-fat foods, and healthful lifestyles, obesity has become increasingly prevalent in the United States, and the average weight of U.S. adults has increased by eight pounds since 1980 (Kuczmarski et al., 1994).

Being overweight is not a mental disorder, nor in most cases is it the result of abnormal psychological processes. Nevertheless, it causes great anguish, and not just because of its physical effects. The media, people on the streets, and even many health professionals treat obesity as shameful. Indeed, obese people are often the unrecognized victims of discrimination in efforts to gain admission to college, jobs, promotions, and satisfaction in their personal relationships (Rothblum, 1992; Stunkard & Wadden, 1992). Society's disdain for obese people is tangled in a web of beliefs: that overweight people lack character or have personality defects; that they are significantly endangering their health; that dieting is the best means to lose weight; and that weight loss is the appropriate central goal of people who are overweight. These beliefs are either exaggerated or simply wrong.

Personality Defects?

Mounting evidence indicates that overweight persons are not to be sneered at as weak and out of control and that obesity results from multiple biological, social, and related factors. First, genetic and biological factors seem to play a large role in it. Researchers have found that children of obese biological parents are more likely to be obese than children whose biological parents are not obese, whether or not the people who raise those children are obese (Stunkard et al., 1986). Other researchers have identified a gene, the ***ob gene,*** that seems to be linked to obesity (Halaas et al., 1995). And still other investigators have identified at least two chemicals in the body—a hormone called ***leptin*** and a protein called ***glucagonlike peptide-1 (GLP-1)***—which apparently act as natural appetite suppressants when they are secreted by fat cells and bind to receptors in the brain (Turton et al., 1996; Tartaglia et al., 1995). Suspicion is growing that the brain receptors for these chemicals may be defective in overweight persons.

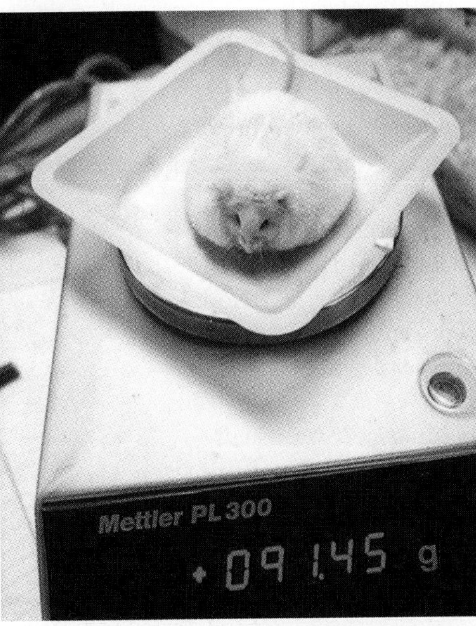

By stimulating parts of the hypothalamus or changing the activity of body chemicals such as leptin *or* GLP-1, *researchers can influence the eating behaviors and body size of animal subjects. This overweight rodent is a case in point.*

Environment also plays a causal role in obesity. Studies have shown that people eat more when they are in the company of others, particularly if the other people are eating (Logue, 1991). Moreover, researchers find that people of low socioeconomic environments are more likely to be obese than those of high socioeconomic backgrounds (Ernst & Harlan, 1991). The same distinction is found between highly developed and Third World countries. In countries where food is scarce, overweight is a sign of prosperity.

Health Risk?

Are mildly to moderately obese people at increased risk of coronary disease or cancer or some other disease? Investigations into this question have yielded conflicting and confusing results over the years (Troiano et al., 1996). Initially it was believed that any amount of excess weight presented a significant health hazard. Then studies conducted in the 1980s suggested that mild to moderate obesity was in fact unrelated to early death and that persons who were *underweight* actually bore a greater health risk (Robertson, 1992; Andres, 1980). As a result,

the weight guidelines published by the government and insurance companies raised their "acceptable" weights up to twenty pounds higher than those recommended thirty years earlier (DHHS, 1990).

More recently, some investigators have returned to the idea that excess weight is hazardous. One long-term study found that underweight female subjects had a relatively low likelihood of dying at an early age as long as their thinness could not be attributed to smoking or illness, while moderately overweight subjects had a 30 percent higher risk of early death (Manson et al., 1995). On the other hand, another recent study found that the mortality rate of underweight men was as elevated as that of overweight men, irrespective of smoking behavior or illness (Troiano et al., 1996). These fluctuating findings suggest that the jury is still out on this issue.

Dieting Works?

There are scores of diets and diet pills. There is virtually no evidence, however, that any diet yet devised can ensure long-term weight loss (Wilson, 1994). In fact, long-term studies generally reveal a *rebound effect,* a net gain in weight among obese people who have lost weight on very low-calorie diets. In addition to failing to keep weight off, such diets frequently are nutritionally deficient and physically dangerous (Wadden, Stunkard, & Liebschutz, 1988). Research also suggests that the feelings of failure and low self-efficacy that accompany diet rebounds may also lead to dysfunctional eating patterns, including binge-eating (Venditti et al., 1996).

One reason that dieting fails to achieve long-term weight loss is that the dieter is engaged in a losing battle against his or her own ***weight set point,*** the weight level that a particular body is organized to maintain. In response to weight loss below the set point, a dieter's body increasingly stores energy in its fat cells rather than in lean muscle mass. The person is thus likely to start gaining weight again, now more in the form of fat than before the dieting (Dulloo & Girardier, 1990). Furthermore, the body's metabolic rate (the rate at which it uses energy) decreases in the course of dieting and remains depressed after dieting stops. These physiological changes are compounded by the fact that many obese people already have lower metabolic rates and two to three times the number of fat cells that thin people have.

Most low-calorie dieters shift from weight loss to weight gain, then to loss again, and so on. In the end this yo-yo pattern may itself be a health risk, increasing the likelihood of high blood pressure and cardiovascular disease (Brownell & O'Neil, 1995, 1993; Lissner et al., 1991). As a result of these and other factors, people who are obese often feel that it is impossible to lose weight and to keep it off without existing in a permanent state of semistarvation (Garner & Wooley, 1991). In cases of extreme obesity, where weight is indeed a clear health hazard and weight loss is advisable, establishing a realistic, attainable goal rather than an unrealistic ideal appears to be the most promising path to long-term weight loss (Brownell & O'Neil, 1993; Brownell & Wadden, 1992).

Efforts are now under way to develop new kinds of drugs that will operate directly on the genes, hormones, and proteins that have been linked to obesity. Theoretically, these treatments will offset the metabolic reactions and other bodily changes that keep undermining efforts at dieting. Whether such interventions can provide safe and permanent weight loss remains to be seen.

Lower Body Weight Is the Proper Goal?

Some researchers contend that emphasis should shift away from weight loss toward improving general health and attitudes (Rosen et al., 1995). If poor eating habits can be corrected, if a poor self-concept and distorted body image can be improved, and if overweight persons can be educated about the myths and truths regarding obesity, perhaps everyone will be better off.

Accordingly, a growing number of theorists suggest that mild and perhaps even moderate obesity should be left alone, at least so far as weight loss is concerned; at the very least, weight loss should involve more modest and realistic goals, and should focus on physical and emotional well-being rather than on an arbitrary "ideal" weight. Even if this view is borne out by ongoing research, it will be a difficult task to reeducate a public that continues to associate obesity with negative personality traits. Regardless of the conclusion reached by scientists in laboratories, it is critical that the public overcome its prejudice against people who are overweight, for at worst obesity is a problem that requires treatment, and in fact it may simply be another version of the normal human condition.

Vomiting and other kinds of compensatory behavior may quickly relieve the uncomfortable physical feelings of fullness or temporarily reduce the feelings of anxiety, self-disgust, and lack of control attached to binge eating (DeSilva, 1995; Mizes, 1995), so that over time a cycle evolves in which purging allows more bingeing and bingeing necessitates more purging. The cycle eventually makes persons with this disorder feel generally powerless, useless, and disgusted with themselves (Kanakis & Thelen, 1995). Most recognize fully that they have an eating disorder, but their anxiety over gaining weight prevents them from interrupting the cycle.

The woman we met earlier recalls how the pattern of bingeing, purging, and self-disgust took hold while she was an adolescent in boarding school:

> **I** went away to boarding school at age fourteen with the nickname, Thunder Thighs. . . . Despite my nickname, I wasn't really obese. I weighed 142 pounds and was 5′6″ tall. But heavy legs and thighs were the most disgusting form of being overweight. Having a big chest still meant boys wanted to touch you, but being pear-shaped was an unspoken sin. I began to focus on my body as the source of all my unhappiness. Every bite that went into my mouth was a naughty and selfish indulgence, and I became more and more disgusted with myself. . . .
>
> The first time I stuck my fingers down my throat was during the last week of school. I saw a girl come out of the bathroom with her face all red and her eyes puffy. She had always talked about her weight and how she should be dieting even though her body was really shapely. I knew instantly what she had just done and I had to try it. . . .
>
> I chose to go to a college 3,000 miles from home in a blatant show of independence and bravery, but once alone in my dorm room, I was stunned by the isolation and the enemy relationship I had with my Self. I retreated into eating which was a numbing device in the past, and I learned how to throw up.
>
> I began with breakfasts which were served buffet-style on the main floor of the dorm. I learned which foods I could eat that would come back up easily. When I woke in the morning, I had to make the decision whether to stuff myself for half an hour and throw up before class, or whether to try and make it through the whole day without overeating. . . . I always thought people noticed when I took huge portions at mealtimes, but I figured they assumed that because I was an athlete, I burned it off. . . . Once a binge was under way, I did not stop until my stomach looked pregnant and I felt like I could not swallow one more time.
>
> That year was the first of my nine years of obsessive eating and throwing up. . . . I didn't want to tell anyone what I was doing, and I didn't want to stop. . . . [Though] being in love or other distractions occasionally lessened the cravings, I always returned to the food.
>
> *(Hall, 1980, pp. 9–12)*

As noted before, a bulimic pattern typically begins during or after a period of intense dieting in which the individual has tried to address a mild or moderate weight problem (Lowe et al., 1996; Szmukler & Patton, 1995; APA, 1994). Often that has been successful and earned praise from family members and friends. Research has found that normal subjects placed on very deficient diets also develop a tendency to binge. Some of the subjects in the conscientious objector "starvation study," for example, later engaged in bingeing when they were allowed to return to regular eating, and a number of them continued to be hungry even after large meals (Keys et al., 1950). A more recent study examined the binge-eating behavior of overweight subjects at the end of a very low calorie diet weight-loss program (Telch & Agras, 1993). Immediately after the program, 62 percent of the subjects, who had not previously been binge eaters, reported binge-eating episodes, although the episodes did decrease during the three months after treatment stopped. Thus the intense dieting that typically precedes the onset of bulimia nervosa may itself predispose some people to the disorder.

Bulimia Nervosa vs. Anorexia Nervosa

Bulimia nervosa is similar to anorexia nervosa in many ways. Both disorders typically unfold after a period of dieting by people who are fearful of becoming obese; driven to become thin; preoccupied with food, weight, and appearance; and grappling with feelings of depression, anxiety, and the need to be perfect (Joiner et al., 1997, 1995; Bastiani et al., 1995; Brewerton et al., 1995). Both groups of people believe that they weigh too much and look too heavy, regardless of their actual weight or appearance, and feel dominated by conflicts about what, when, and how much to eat (Mizes, 1995; Ledoux et al., 1993). And both disorders are often associated with disturbed attitudes toward eating (DeSilva, 1995; Williamson et al., 1991).

Yet the two disorders also differ in important ways (see Table 12-2). People with bulimia nervosa are much more likely to recognize that their behavior is pathological. They also tend to be more interested in pleasing others and to care more about being attractive to others and having intimate relationships (Striegel-Moore,

TABLE 12-2 Anorexia Nervosa vs. Bulimia Nervosa

Restricting Type Anorexia Nervosa	*Bulimia Nervosa*
Refusal to maintain a minimum body weight for healthy functioning	Underweight, normal weight, near normal weight, or overweight
Hunger and disorder denied; often proud of weight management and more satisfied with body	Intense hunger experienced and binge-purge considered abnormal; greater body dissatisfaction
Less antisocial behavior	Greater tendency to antisocial behavior and alcohol abuse
Amenorrhea of at least 3 months' duration common	Irregular menstrual periods common; amenorrhea uncommon unless body weight is low
Mistrust of others, particularly professionals	More trusting of people who wish to help
Tend to be obsessional	Tend to be dramatic
Greater self-control, but emotionally overcontrolled with problems experiencing and expressing feelings	More impulsivity and emotional instability
More likely to be sexually immature and inexperienced	More sexually experienced and sexually active
Females are more likely to reject traditional feminine role	Females are more likely to embrace traditional feminine role
Age of onset often around 14–19	Age of onset around 15–21
Greater tendency for maximum pre-disorder weight to be near normal for age	Greater tendency for maximum pre-disorder weight to be slightly greater than normal
Lesser familial predisposition to obesity	Greater familial predisposition to obesity
Greater tendency toward pre-disorder compliance with parents	Greater tendency toward pre-disorder conflict with parents
Tendency to deny family conflict	Tendency to perceive intense family conflict

Source: APA, 1994; Levine, 1987; Andersen, 1985; Garner et al., 1985; Neuman & Halvorson, 1983.

Silberstein, & Rodin, 1993; Muuss, 1986). Correspondingly, they are typically more sexually experienced and active than people with anorexia nervosa.

People with bulimia nervosa display fewer of the obsessive qualities that enable people with restricting type anorexia nervosa to regulate their caloric intake so rigidly (Halmi, 1995; Andersen, 1985). At the same time, sufferers of bulimia demonstrate several disturbed characteristics of their own. They may have long histories of mood swings, become easily frustrated or bored, and have difficulty coping effectively or controlling their impulses (Halmi, 1995; Yager, Rorty, & Rossotto, 1995). They tend to be ruled by their strong emotions, have to change friends and relationships frequently, and are also much more likely than the general population to abuse alcohol and other drugs, a pattern that often begins with the excessive use of diet pills (Wiederman & Pryor, 1996; Braun, Sunday, & Halmi, 1995; Tiller et al., 1995). More than one-third of people with bulimia nervosa display the characteristics of a personality disorder, a pattern we shall examine more closely in Chapter 18 (Braun et al., 1995; APA, 1994).

Finally, the medical complications of bulimia nervosa differ from those of anorexia nervosa (Keel & Mitchell, 1997). Only half of women with bulimia nervosa are amenorrheic or have very irregular menstrual periods, compared to almost all of those with anorexia nervosa (Treasure & Szmukler, 1995; Glassman et al., 1991). Moreover, repeated vomiting washes teeth and gums in hydrochloric acid, leading in some cases to serious dental problems—receding gums, breakdown of enamel, and even loss of teeth (Casper, 1995; Treasure &

Szmukler, 1995). People who vomit regularly or have chronic diarrhea may also develop a dangerous potassium deficiency, or ***hypokalemia,*** which may lead to weakness, paralysis, intestinal disorders, kidney disease, irregular heart rhythms, or heart damage (Halmi et al., 1994; Sharp & Freeman, 1993; Mitchell et al., 1991, 1990).

Explanations of Eating Disorders

For years traditional *psychodynamic explanations* of eating disorders dominated the clinical field (Dare & Crowther, 1995; Sayers, 1988). Some Freudian theorists suggested, for example, that unresolved *oral conflicts* lead to anorexia nervosa (Lerner, 1986; Sugarman, Quinlan, & Devenis, 1981; Meyer & Weinroth, 1957). They argued that some children are unable to separate themselves from their mothers at the appropriate time and become fixated at the oral stage. Such children were thought to become especially frightened when they approach adolescence and confront sexual maturity and separation from their parents, and they were thought to develop anorexic behavior in an unconscious attempt to return to the early oral relationship by undoing outward signs of maturity. Psychodynamic explanations of this kind, however, received little research support, and indeed, some contemporary psychodynamic theorists have instead proposed explanations that emphasize such factors as poor sense of self and difficulties in relationships (Dare & Crowther, 1995; Yarock, 1993; Steiger & Houle, 1991).

In recent years theorists and researchers have broadened their focus and identified yet other factors that seem to place persons at risk for eating disorders. Presumably the more of these factors that are present, the greater a person's risk of developing such a disorder (Lyon et al., 1997). This view, called the ***multidimensional risk perspective,*** cites factors from the sociocultural (societal and family pressures), psychological (ego, cognitive, and mood disturbances), and biological realms.

Societal Pressures

Many theorists believe that Western society's current emphasis on thinness has contributed to the recent increases in eating disorders (Abramson & Valene, 1991). Western standards of female attractiveness have changed throughout history and now favor a slender figure. As the clinical theorists Paul Garfinkel and David Garner (1982) point out, "Favor was shown for a buxom appearance in the early part of the century, followed by the flat chested flapper of the 1920s and the return of bustiness and an hour-glass figure in the 1950s. Recently, preference has once more returned to thinness as attractive for females" (p. 106).

The shift back to a thinner female frame has been steady since the 1950s. One investigation collected data on the height, weight, and age of contestants in the Miss America Pageant from 1959 through 1978 (Garner et al., 1980). After controlling for height differences, the investigators found an average decline of 0.28 pound per year among the contestants and 0.37 pound per year among winners. These same researchers examined data on all *Playboy* magazine centerfold models over the same 20-year span and found that the average weight, bust, and hip measurements of these women decreased significantly throughout that period. The researchers also found an increased emphasis on dieting when they examined five popular woman-oriented magazines from

"Seated Bather," by Pierre Auguste Renoir (1841–1919), like certain other works of art, shows that the aesthetically ideal woman of the past was considerably larger than today's ideal. Indeed, women of similar shape are now considered modestly overweight.

The thin frames of these dance students are apparent as they warm up for a class outside a rehearsal hall. Certain professionals, such as dancers, models, and athletes, have particularly high rates of eating concerns and disorders, largely because of their profession's emphasis on weight and size.

1959 through the late 1970s. A more recent study of Miss America contestants, *Playboy* centerfolds, and woman-oriented magazines indicates that each of these trends has continued into the 1990s (Wiseman et al., 1992).

Because thinness is especially valued and rewarded in the subcultures of fashion models, actors, dancers, and certain kinds of athletes, members of these groups are likely to be particularly concerned about their weight (Williamson et al., 1995; Morris et al., 1989; Silverstein et al., 1986). As sociocultural theorists would predict, these people are more vulnerable than others to eating disorders (Attie & Brooks-Gunn, 1992; Prussin & Harvey, 1991). One study compared the prevalence of anorexia nervosa among 183 ballet students, 56 students of fashion modeling, and 81 female university students. No cases of the disorder were found among the university students, but it did occur in 7 percent of the dancers and 7 percent of the modeling students (Garner & Garfinkel, 1980, 1978). Similarly, a survey of 1,443 athletes at 10 colleges around the United States revealed that more than 9 percent of female college athletes suffer from an eating disorder and another 50 percent admit to eating behaviors that put them at risk for such disorders (Johnson, 1995). A full 20 percent of the gymnasts surveyed manifested an eating disorder (see Figure 12-3).

Varying attitudes toward thinness in different socioeconomic and minority groups may help explain socioeconomic and racial differences in the prevalence of eating disorders (see Box 12-3). In the past, white American women of the upper socioeconomic classes expressed more concern about thinness and dieting than African American women or than white American women of the lower socioeconomic classes (Margo, 1985; Stunkard, 1975). Correspondingly, eating disorders were more common among white American women higher on the socioeconomic scale (Foreyt et al., 1996; Rosen et al., 1991). In more recent years concerns about thinness and dieting have increased to some degree in all classes and minority groups, and the prevalence of eating disorders has risen there as well (Rogers et al., 1997).

Cultural differences may also help explain the striking gender gap for eating disorders. Our society's emphasis on appearance has been aimed at women much more than men during most of our history (Nichter & Nichter, 1991; Rolls et al., 1991). Some theorists believe that this double standard of attractiveness has left women much more concerned about being thin, much more inclined to diet, and much more vulnerable to eating disorders (Rand & Kuldau, 1991). It is interesting to note an increased emphasis on male thinness and dieting in recent years—and, correspondingly, an apparent increase in the number of eating disorders among males (Seligmann, Rogers, & Annin, 1994; Striegel-Moore et al., 1986).

Western society not only glorifies thinness; it creates a climate of prejudice and hostility against overweight people, both young and old (Oliver & Thelen, 1996).

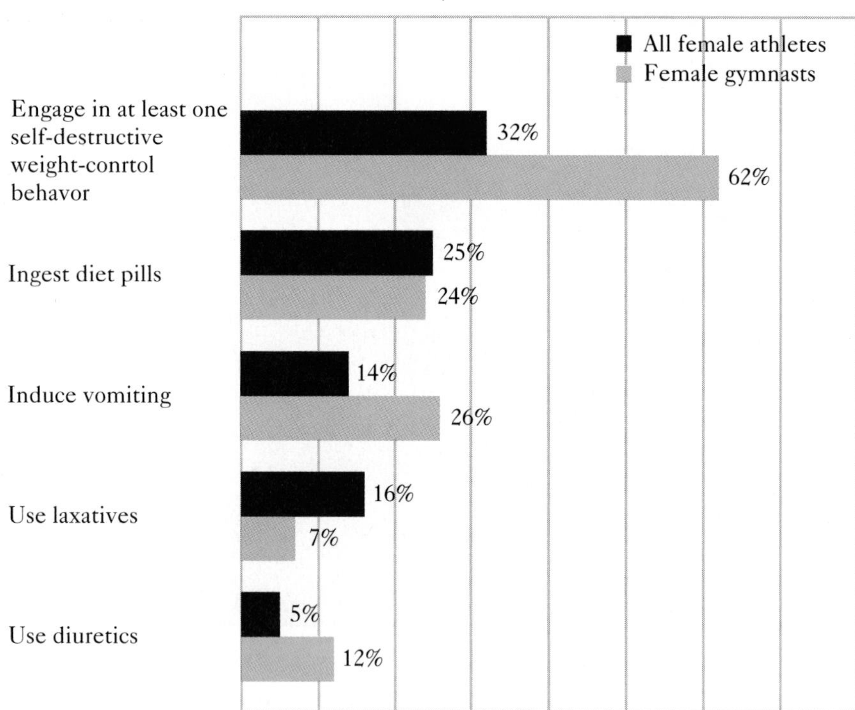

Figure 12–3 *According to surveys, in sports ranging from field hockey to gymnastics, almost a third of all female athletes engage in one or more self-destructive behaviors to control their weight. Close to two-thirds of female college gymnasts engage in at least one such behavior. (Adapted from Rosen & Hough, 1988; Rosen et al., 1986)*

Cruel comments and jokes about obesity are standard fare on television shows and in movies, books, and magazines, whereas similar slurs based on ethnicity, race, and gender are considered unacceptable. Research indicates that the prejudice against obese people is deep-rooted (Regan, 1997; Brownell & O'Neil, 1993; Wooley & Wooley, 1982, 1979). Prospective parents who were shown a picture of a chubby child and one of a medium-weight or thin child rated the former as less friendly, energetic, intelligent, and desirable than the latter. Preschool children who were given a choice between a chubby and a thin rag doll chose the thin one, although they could not say why. Similarly, college students who were asked to compare applicants for a job after reading a description of each candidate recommended a thin applicant over an obese one, even though the descriptions of the two applicants were the same otherwise. Given this bias against obesity, it is small wonder that as many as 40 percent of elementary school girls have tried to lose weight (Thelen, Lawrence, & Powell, 1992).

Some clinicians argue that physicians, insurance companies, and health organizations such as the American Heart Association may contribute to society's bias against obesity by issuing somewhat exaggerated warnings about the dangers of being overweight (Robertson, 1992; Wooley & Wooley, 1982). Although extreme obesity is indeed unhealthy, studies have not consistently found that mild or moderate obesity is dangerous to one's health. Indeed, the Department of Health and Human Services has revised its tables for "healthy" weights, allowing much more leeway for each level of height. Similarly, despite the claims of many psychologists, researchers have not found overweight people to be more disturbed psychologically than persons of normal weight (Garner et al., 1985). Nevertheless, such claims help establish a climate in which people seek thinness and fear weight gain, thus increasing the likelihood of developing eating disorders.

Family Environment

As a primary transmitter of societal values, the family may play a critical role in the development of eating disorders. Research suggests that as many as half of the families of people with eating disorders have a long history of emphasizing thinness, physical appearance, and dieting (Hart & Kenny, 1995; Lieberman, 1995; Thelen & Cormier, 1995).

Families may also set the stage for eating disorders by establishing abnormal and confusing family interactions and forms of communication. As we observed earlier, family systems theorists view each family as a system of interacting parts (the family members) that interrelate in consistent ways, operate by implicit rules, and maintain a certain balance, or homeostasis. Family systems theorists argue that the functioning of families of people who develop eating disorders is often disturbed to begin

Box 12-3 Body Image: A Matter of Race?

In the popular movie ***Clueless,*** Cher and Dionne, affluent teenage friends of different races, have similar tastes, beliefs, and values about everything from boys to schoolwork. In particular, they share the same kinds of eating habits and beauty ideals, and they are even similar in weight and physical form. But does the story of these young women accurately reflect that of white and African American females in our society? The answer, according to some recent investigations, appears to be a resounding no (Cash & Henry, 1995; Parker et al., 1995; Harris, 1994; Nichter & Vuckovic, 1994).

Although young African American women seem to be more concerned about thinness and dieting and more prone to develop eating disorders today than they were in past years, their values, aspirations, and behaviors in such realms nevertheless remain healthier than those of today's young white women. A recent investigation of this phenomenon conducted at the University of Arizona has gained enormous attention among clinicians and the public alike (Parker et al., 1995).

The study explored the body image ideals and dieting behaviors of 296 eighth- and ninth-grade girls during a three-year longitudinal study. Its findings: nearly 90 percent of the white respondents said they were *dissatisfied* with their weight and body shape, whereas nearly 70 percent of the African American teens were *satisfied* with their bodies. The African American teens expressed satisfaction regardless of their actual weight; even those who were overweight described themselves as happy.

Beauty Ideals

The study also suggests that white and African American adolescent girls have very different ideals of beauty. The white teens, asked to define the "perfect girl," described a girl of 5′7″ weighing between 100 and 110 pounds—proportions that mirror those of today's so-called supermodels. Attaining a perfect weight, many said, was the key to being "totally happy," and they indicated that thinness was a prerequisite for popularity. Several explained that "being skinny makes you fit in more."

In contrast, the African American respondents tended to emphasize personality traits over physical characteristics when they described the ideal girl. They defined the "perfect" African American girl as smart, fun, easy to talk to, not conceited, and funny; she did not necessarily need to be "pretty," as long as she was well groomed. The body dimensions the African American teens described were more attainable for the typical girl; they favored fuller hips, for example. Perhaps the key difference was the African American subjects' greater emphasis on true beauty as an inner quality. Two-thirds of them defined beauty as "the right attitude," and approximately the same percentage indicated that women become more beautiful as they age.

Health and Diet

Given such definitions of beauty, it is not surprising to find that the African American subjects were far less likely than the white American respondents to diet for extended periods. Although a full 52 percent of the African American teens had dieted at some point in the past year, they did not tend to stick to a strict diet, explaining that it is better to be a "little" overweight than underweight. Meanwhile, the white teens, 61 percent of whom had dieted in the past year, stressed dieting as a way both to become thinner and to gain control over other aspects of their lives, such as their social life. Body dissatisfaction and talk about feeling fat seemed to be a culturally appropriate way for the white teenagers to show that they were concerned about their appearance and were working toward their standard of beauty (Nichter & Vuckovic, 1994).

Although the African American teenagers in this study, and perhaps in settings across the country, hold positive feelings about their bodies and about beauty in general, the investigators who conducted this study warn us that pitfalls may lie ahead for them: "It remains to be seen whether they will be able to maintain these self-perceptions as they become older and obtain jobs in mainstream American society. . . . [They] may be more likely to deemphasize their black identities in order to get ahead. . . . Will this translate into body discipline in the form of dieting to obtain a thin body by girls who aspire to make it?" (Parker et al., 1995, p. 111).

with, and that the eating disorder of one member is simply a reflection of the larger dysfunction (Vandereycken, 1994; Lundholm & Waters, 1991).

The influential family theorist Salvador Minuchin, for example, believes that what he calls an ***enmeshed family pattern*** often leads to eating disorders (Minuchin, Rosman, & Baker, 1978). In an enmeshed system, family members are overinvolved with one another's affairs and overconcerned about the details of one another's lives. On the positive side, enmeshed families can be affectionate and loyal. On the negative side, they can be clinging and foster dependency. There is little room in them for individuality and autonomy. Parents are too involved in the lives of their children.

Minuchin argues that adolescence poses a special problem for these families. The adolescent child's normal push for independence threatens to disrupt the family facade of harmony and closeness. As the family implicitly searches for a solution, it subtly forces the child to take on a "sick" role—to develop an eating disorder or some other pattern such as chronic headaches or an ulcer. The child's disorder enables the family to maintain its illusion of living in harmony. A sick child needs her family, and family members can rally round and protect her.

Research support for the family systems explanation of eating disorders has run into some significant problems. First, much of it comes from case studies (Dare & Eisler, 1992). Empirical investigations, in contrast, have been limited and their findings open to alternative interpretations. One study tested the family systems prediction that the families of children with eating disorders would become unstable if the child were to improve (Crisp, Harding, & McGuinness, 1974). The investigators asked the parents of daughters with anorexia nervosa to fill out a psychological inventory before and after their daughters regained their lost weight. Before weight restoration, the parents' scores were comparable to those of parents of girls without anorexia nervosa. After the daughters regained weight, however, their parents showed a significant increase in depression and anxiety. This finding is consistent with family systems theory, but it is also possible that therapy and recovery—themselves sources of great conflict and tension—were causing the depressed and anxious feelings of family members (Colahan & Senior, 1995; Strober, 1992).

Another problem is that a growing number of controlled studies fail to show that a particular type of family pattern invariably sets the stage for the development of eating disorders (Wilson et al., 1996; Colahan & Senior, 1995; Eisler, 1995). In fact, the families of persons with either anorexia nervosa or bulimia nervosa often vary considerably. Moreover, when such families do, in fact, display heightened enmeshment or poorer communication, these differences are much less pronounced than family systems theory would seem to suggest (Eisler, 1995). In short, the actual role of the family in the development of eating disorders is not well understood.

Ego Deficiencies and Cognitive Disturbances

Hilde Bruch, a pioneer in the study and treatment of eating disorders, developed an influential theory that incorporates both psychodynamic and cognitive notions. She argued that disturbed mother–child interactions lead to serious *ego deficiencies* in the child (including a poor sense of autonomy and control) and to severe *perceptual and other cognitive disturbances* that jointly produce disordered eating patterns (Bruch, 1991, 1983, 1981, 1962).

According to Bruch, parents may respond to their children either effectively or ineffectively. *Effective parents* provide discriminating attention to their children's biological and emotional needs, giving them food when they are crying from hunger and comfort when they are crying out of fear. *Ineffective parents,* by contrast, fail to at-

Many clinicians believe that beauty contests for children harshly underline society's emphasis on appearance and thinness. The contests teach participants at a very young age that their appearance is key to pleasing others and that they may be judged by demanding aesthetic standards throughout their lives.

tend to their children's internal needs and instead arbitrarily decide when their children are hungry, cold, or tired, without correctly interpreting the children's actual condition. They may feed the children at times of anxiety rather than hunger, or comfort them at times of tiredness rather than anxiety. Children who are subjected to this kind of parenting may grow up confused and may be unable to differentiate between their own internal needs, not knowing when they are hungry or satiated and unable to identify their own emotions or levels of fatigue.

Unable to rely on internal standards, these children turn instead to external guides, such as their parents, and seem to be "model children"; but they fail to develop genuine self-reliance and "experience themselves as not being in control of their behavior, needs, and impulses, as not owning their own bodies" (Bruch, 1973, p. 55).

As adolescence approaches, these children are under increasing pressure to establish autonomy but feel unable to do so (Strauss & Ryan, 1987). To overcome their sense of helplessness, they seek extreme control over their body size and shape and over their eating habits. People who are "successful" in this attempt at control march toward restricting type anorexia nervosa. Those who are unsuccessful spiral instead toward a binge-purge pattern. Helen, an 18-year-old, describes her experience:

> There is a peculiar contradiction—everybody thinks you're doing so well and everybody thinks you're great, but your real problem is that you think that you are not good enough. You are afraid of not living up to what you think you are expected to do. You have one great fear, namely that of being ordinary, or average, or common—just not good enough. This peculiar dieting begins with such anxiety. You want to prove that you have control, that you can do it. The peculiar part of it is that it makes you feel good about yourself, makes you feel "I can accomplish something." It makes you feel "I can do something nobody else can do."
>
> *(Bruch, 1978, p. 128)*

Clinical reports and research have provided some support for Bruch's theory. Clinicians have repeatedly observed that the parents of adolescents with eating disorders tend to define their children's needs rather than allow them to define their own needs (Hart & Kenny, 1995; Steiner et al., 1991; Rowland, 1970). When Bruch interviewed the mothers of fifty-one patients with anorexia nervosa, for example, many proudly recalled that they had always "anticipated" their young child's needs, never permitting the child to "feel hungry" (Bruch, 1973).

Research has also supported Bruch's proposition that people with eating disorders perceive and distinguish internal cues inaccurately, including cues of hunger and

Personal Pathways

Hilde Bruch's Journey

Hilde Bruch (1904–1984), the preeminent pioneer in the modern study and treatment of eating disorders, achieved this status against a background of personal struggle and pain, according to a biography by Joanne Hatch Bruch, the wife of her nephew.

Born in a German hamlet, Bruch was exceptionally intelligent and intuitive as a child. When an authoritarian uncle told her, "Go study medicine, that is a good profession for you," she obediently entered medical school, and she became a pediatrician shortly before Hitler came to power. As a young Jewish physician, she soon felt the extreme prejudice and dangers of Nazi Germany. To save her life she fled to England, leaving home and loved ones behind, and eventually made her way to the United States. Here she rose to worldwide fame and influence, and her life was filled with great triumphs and rich relationships. At the same time, she was trying desperately from afar to help her family members escape from Nazi Germany. Despite her considerable efforts, her older brother, his wife, and their daughter perished in a concentration camp. Bruch later raised her brother's son.

Perhaps then it is not surprising that Bruch also suffered great emotional pain throughout her life, struggling, in particular, with episodes of severe depression. Indeed, at the age of 31 she was admitted to a hospital in a deep coma after a self-administered drug overdose. Inpatient treatment of depression lasted for months. Other episodes followed in later years. Some observers have suggested that Bruch's experiences of profound loss, separation, and depression helped her to identify the important role of family dynamics and emotional factors in eating disorders, factors previously not recognized.

emotion (Halmi, 1995; Halmi et al., 1989). Studies have found that persons with anorexia nervosa feel full sooner after they start to eat than others do and that subjects with bulimia nervosa often have trouble distinguishing hunger from other bodily needs or emotions (see Figure 12-4). When they are anxious or upset, for example, they mistakenly think they are also hungry, and they respond as they might respond to hunger—by eating (Rebert, Stanton, & Schwartz, 1991).

Finally, research has supported Bruch's argument that people with eating disorders rely excessively on the opinions, wishes, and views of others. They are more likely than other people to worry about how others view them, to seek approval, to be conforming, and to feel relatively little control over their lives (Vitousek & Manke, 1994; Striegel-Moore et al., 1993; Strober, 1983, 1981).

Mood Problems

Earlier we noted that many people with eating disorders, particularly those with bulimia nervosa, experience symptoms of depression, such as sadness, low self-esteem, shame, pessimism, and errors in logic (Paxton & Diggens, 1997; Sanftner et al., 1995; Ledoux et al., 1993). This finding has led some theorists to conclude that

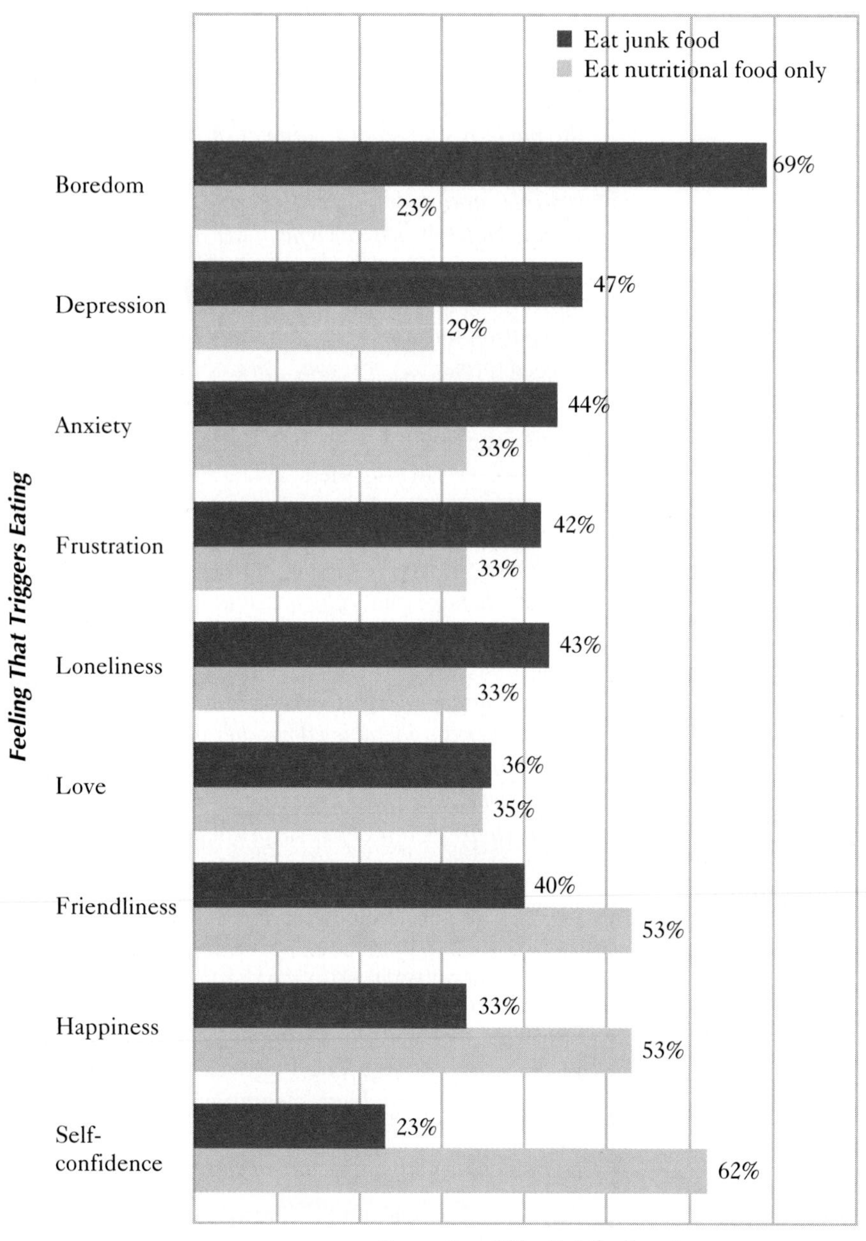

Figure 12–4 *When do people seek junk food? Apparently, when they feel bad. People who eat junk food when feeling bad outnumber those who eat nutritional food under similar circumstances. In contrast, more people seek nutritional food when feeling good. Apparently when in love, people can go either way. Relatively few individuals desire no food at all during intense emotional states. (Adapted from Lyman, 1982)*

mood disorders predispose some people to eating disorders (Hsu, Crisp, & Callender, 1992).

Their claim is supported by four kinds of evidence. First, many more people with an eating disorder qualify for a clinical diagnosis of major depression than do people in the general population. As many as 75 percent of those with bulimia nervosa may experience mood disorders, which are often present before the bulimic patterns (Brewerton et al., 1995; Pope & Hudson, 1984). Second, the close relatives of people with eating disorders apparently have a much higher rate of mood disorders than do close relatives of people without such disorders (APA, 1994; Johnson & Maddi, 1986). Third, persons with eating disorders, particularly bulimia nervosa, often display low activity of the neurotransmitter serotonin, similar to the serotonin depletions found in depressed people (Goldbloom et al., 1990; Wilcox, 1990). And finally, persons with eating disorders are often helped significantly by some of the same antidepressant drugs that alleviate depression (Advokat & Kutlesic, 1995; Mitchell & de Zwaan, 1993).

Although such findings are consistent with the notion that depression helps cause eating disorders, alternative explanations cannot be ruled out. It is possible, for example, that in some cases the pressure and pain of having an eating disorder help cause the mood disorder (Silverstone, 1990). Whatever the correct interpretation, it is clear that many people grappling with eating disorders also suffer from depression, among many other problems.

Biological Factors

Biological researchers have focused on the *hypothalamus* as a key to understanding the development and maintenance of eating disorders (Turton et al., 1996; Grossman, 1990, 1986; Garner et al., 1987). As we saw in Chapter 4, the ***hypothalamus*** is a part of the brain that helps maintain various bodily functions and affects the endocrine system. With its rich supply of blood vessels, it can detect changes in blood chemistry as well as respond to incoming neural information about what is happening throughout the body.

Researchers have located two separate centers in the hypothalamus that control eating (Grossman, 1990; Bray et al., 1980; Stellar, 1954). The ***lateral hypothalamus,*** or ***LH,*** consisting of the side areas of the hypothalamus, produces hunger when it is activated. When the LH of a laboratory animal is electrically stimulated, the animal eats, even if it has been fed recently. But if the LH is destroyed, the animal will refuse to eat, even if it has been starved by the experimenter. The ***ventromedial hypothalamus,*** or ***VMH,*** consisting of the bottom and middle of the hypothalamus, depresses hunger when it is activated. When the VMH is electrically stimulated, laboratory animals stop eating. When it is destroyed, the stomach and intestines of animals increase their rate of processing food, causing the animals to eat more often and eventually to become obese (Duggan & Booth, 1986; Hoebel & Teitelbaum, 1966).

These centers of the hypothalamus are apparently activated by chemicals that are released throughout the brain and body when individuals are being satiated or deprived of food. One such brain chemical is ***glucagon-like peptide-1 (GLP-1),*** which some scientists have hailed as the most potent natural appetite suppressant yet identified. In one study, researchers collected and injected GLP-1 into the brains of rats. The chemical then traveled to particular receptors in the hypothalamus and caused the rats to reduce their food intake up to 95 percent even though they had not eaten for 24 hours (Turton et al., 1996). Conversely, when "full" rats were injected with a substance that blocked the reception of GLP-1 in the hypothalamus, they more than doubled their food intake. Inasmuch as GLP-1 and its receptors are also found in the brains of human beings, scientists suspect that it is one of the chemicals that help the hypothalamus to regulate human eating behavior as well.

It is now believed that the LH and VMH and chemicals such as GLP-1 work together to help set up a "weight thermostat" in the body that predisposes individuals to keep their body at a particular weight level, called their ***weight set point*** (Garner et al., 1985; Keesey & Corbett, 1983). When a person's weight falls below his or her particular set point, the LH is activated and seeks to restore the lost weight by producing hunger. It also decreases the body's ***metabolic rate,*** the rate at which the body expends energy. When a person's weight rises above his or her set point, the VMH is activated, and it seeks to remove the excess weight by depressing hunger and increasing the body's metabolic rate.

In short, a person's weight set point reflects the range of body weight that is normal for that individual in accordance with such influences as genetic inheritance and early eating practices (Levine, 1987). If weight falls significantly below a person's set point, the hypothalamus will act to alter biological functioning, and thinking and behavior as well, in an effort to restore weight to the set point (Polivy & Herman, 1985; Wooley & Wooley, 1985).

According to weight set point theory, when people pursue a strict diet, their weight eventually moves below their set point and their brain begins to compensate. Hypothalamic activity leads to a preoccupation with food, a desire to binge, and bodily changes that make it harder and harder to lose weight, however little one eats (Hill & Robinson, 1991). These changes also make it easier to

The weight set point, the level of body weight that is normal for an individual, is influenced by a range of factors, from genetic to sociocultural. The Pima Native Americans in Arizona (left) share a common genetic background with their relatives in Mexico (right, during a holy week festival). Yet the Arizonan Pimas weigh more on average. High-fat foods dominate the diets of Arizonan Pimas, while Mexican Pimas subsist mainly on grains and vegetables.

gain weight no matter what one eats (Spalter et al., 1993).

Once the brain and body begin acting to raise weight to the set point, dieters actually enter into a battle against themselves. Some people are apparently "successful" in this battle; they manage to shut down and control their eating almost completely, and they move toward restricting type anorexia nervosa. For others, the battle spirals toward a binge-purge pattern.

Why do people with restricting type anorexia nervosa manage to attain control over the body's homeostatic weight mechanisms, while people with bulimia nervosa become caught in a cycle of bingeing and purging? Perhaps psychological differences are what matter. Maybe an obsessive style enables the former individuals to stick to a rigid regimen of dieting despite the brain's push for weight gain, while an impulsive style makes it impossible for the latter persons to resist increasing urges to eat. Alternatively, the two groups may differ in the level of conflict found in their families or in their biological predisposition. It is still unclear how best to account for the different courses of the eating disorders.

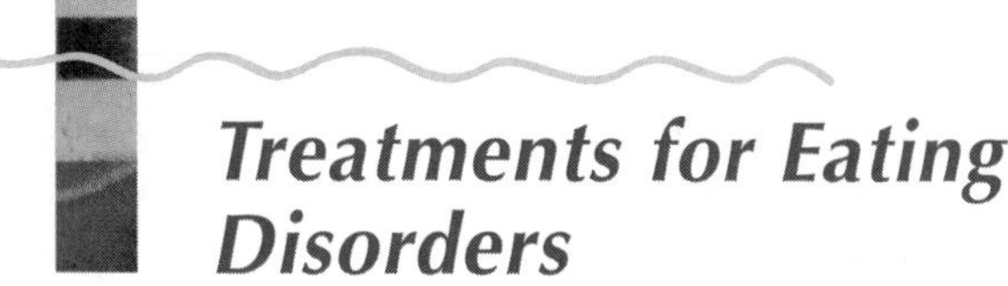

Treatments for Eating Disorders

Today's treatments for eating disorders have two dimensions. First, they seek to correct the pathological eating pattern as quickly as possible because it is endangering the client's health. Second, the therapist tries to address the broader psychological and situational factors that led to and now maintain the dysfunctional eating pattern. In addition, family and friends can play an important role in helping to overcome the disorder (Sherman & Thompson, 1990).

Treatments for Anorexia Nervosa

The immediate aim of treatment for anorexia nervosa is to help the individuals regain their lost weight, recover from malnourishment, and reestablish normal eating habits. Therapists must then help them to make psychological and perhaps family changes that enable them to maintain their immediate gains.

Weight Restoration and Resumption of Eating

A variety of methods is used to help patients with anorexia nervosa gain weight quickly and restore them to health in a matter of weeks. In the past the methods were almost always applied in a hospital, but now they are increasingly being offered in outpatient settings (Battle & Brownell, 1996; Treasure, Todd, & Szmukler, 1995; Garner, 1992).

In life-threatening cases, clinicians may provide nourishment directly by forcing *tube and intravenous feedings* on patients. Unfortunately, such feedings are often applied with minimal cooperation from a patient, breed the patient's distrust, and set up a power struggle (Treasure et al., 1995; Zerbe, 1993). Another approach, used in many cases, is *antidepressant drug therapy* (Wakeling, 1995; Kaye et al., 1991). And yet another weight-restoration intervention involves the use of *operant conditioning* (Yates, 1990; Halmi, 1985). Patients are given positive reinforcement when they eat properly or gain weight and no reinforcement when they eat improperly or fail to gain weight. Each of these approaches appears to be of limited value at best, helping to bring about quick weight gain but not a long-term solution.

In recent years, *supportive nursing care,* combined with a high-calorie diet, has become the most popular weight-restoration technique (Andersen, 1995; Treasure et al., 1995). In this approach, well-trained nurses gradually increase a patient's diet over the course of several weeks to between 3,000 and 4,000 calories a day. The nurses educate patients about the program, give them progress reports, provide encouragement, and help them recognize that their weight gain is proceeding in a controlled manner and that they will not go overboard into obesity. Studies suggest that patients on nursing care programs usually gain the necessary weight over eight to twelve weeks (Treasure et al., 1995; Garfinkel & Garner, 1982).

Broader Changes Clinical researchers have found that people with anorexia nervosa must address their underlying problems if they are to experience lasting improvement. Therapists typically offer a mixture of therapy and education to achieve this goal, using individual, group, and family formats (Andersen, 1995; Treasure et al., 1995). Such approaches have helped to bring about lasting change in many cases (Robin, Siegel, & Moye, 1995).

Building Autonomy and Self-Awareness One focus of treatment is on helping patients with anorexia nervosa *recognize their need for autonomy* and *exercise control in more appropriate ways* (Dare & Crowther, 1995; Robin et al., 1995; Bruch, 1988, 1986, 1983). Another is on helping them *recognize and trust their internal sensations and feelings* (Furumoto & Keating, 1995; Bruch, 1973). In the following exchange, a therapist tries to help a 15-year-old client identify and share her feelings:

> *Patient:* I don't talk about my feelings; I never did.
>
> *Therapist:* Do you think I'll respond like others?
>
> *Patient:* What do you mean?
>
> *Therapist:* I think you may be afraid that I won't pay close attention to what you feel inside, or that I'll tell you not to feel the way you do—that it's foolish to feel frightened, to feel fat, to doubt yourself, considering how well you do in school, how you're appreciated by teachers, how pretty you are.
>
> *Patient: (Looking somewhat tense and agitated)* Well, I was always told to be polite and respect other people, just like a stupid, faceless doll *(Affecting a vacant, doll-like pose).*
>
> *Therapist:* Do I give you the impression that it would be disrespectful for you to share your feelings, whatever they may be?
>
> *Patient:* Not really; I don't know.
>
> *Therapist:* I can't, and won't, tell you that this is easy for you to do. . . . But I can promise you that you are free to speak your mind, and that I won't turn away.
>
> *(Strober & Yager, 1985, pp. 368–369)*

Correcting Disturbed Cognitions Another focus of treatment is on helping people with anorexia nervosa *change their misconceptions and attitudes* about eating and weight—misconceptions that are all too common in

Cognitive treatments for eating disorders help individuals challenge and change misconceptions about body size that they have learned from society. Many young women, for example, must learn to relinquish aspirations of looking like the Barbie dolls with whom they have grown up. In fact, a 5-foot-2, 125 pound woman who wants to have Barbie's proportions would have to grow to be 7-foot-2, add 5 inches to her chest and 3.2 inches to her neck length, and lose 6 inches from her waist (Brownell & Napolitano, 1995).

TABLE 12-3 Social Attitudes Scale: How Do You Score?

Please read the following statements and indicate how strongly you agree or disagree with each.

1. A man would always prefer to go out with a thin woman than one who is heavy.

Strongly agree	Agree somewhat	Agree	Neither agree nor disagree	Disagree	Disagree somewhat	Strongly disagree
☐	☐	☐	☐	☐	☐	☐

2. Clothes are made today so that only thin people can look good.

Strongly agree	Agree somewhat	Agree	Neither agree nor disagree	Disagree	Disagree somewhat	Strongly disagree
☐	☐	☐	☐	☐	☐	☐

3. Fat people are often unhappy.

Strongly agree	Agree somewhat	Agree	Neither agree nor disagree	Disagree	Disagree somewhat	Strongly disagree
☐	☐	☐	☐	☐	☐	☐

4. It is not true that attractive people are more interesting, poised, and socially outgoing than unattractive people.

Strongly agree	Agree somewhat	Agree	Neither agree nor disagree	Disagree	Disagree somewhat	Strongly disagree
☐	☐	☐	☐	☐	☐	☐

5. A pretty face will not get you very far without a slim body.

Strongly agree	Agree somewhat	Agree	Neither agree nor disagree	Disagree	Disagree somewhat	Strongly disagree
☐	☐	☐	☐	☐	☐	☐

6. It is more important that a woman be attractive than a man.

Strongly agree	Agree somewhat	Agree	Neither agree nor disagree	Disagree	Disagree somewhat	Strongly disagree
☐	☐	☐	☐	☐	☐	☐

7. Attractive people lead more fulfilling lives than unattractive people.

Strongly agree	Agree somewhat	Agree	Neither agree nor disagree	Disagree	Disagree somewhat	Strongly disagree
☐	☐	☐	☐	☐	☐	☐

8. The thinner a woman is, the more attractive she is.

Strongly agree	Agree somewhat	Agree	Neither agree nor disagree	Disagree	Disagree somewhat	Strongly disagree
☐	☐	☐	☐	☐	☐	☐

9. Attractiveness decreases the likelihood of professional success.

Strongly agree	Agree somewhat	Agree	Neither agree nor disagree	Disagree	Disagree somewhat	Strongly disagree
☐	☐	☐	☐	☐	☐	☐

These items, developed by psychologist Judith Rodin (1992), test how much *you believe that appearance matters.* Score your responses as follows:

For items 1, 2, 3, 5, 7, and 8, give yourself a zero if you said "strongly disagree"; a 2 for "disagree"; up to a 6 for "strongly agree."

Items 4, 6, and 9 are scored in reverse. In other words, give yourself a zero for "strongly agree" and a 6 for "strongly disagree."

Add together your points for all nine questions. A score of 46 or higher means that you are vulnerable to being influenced by the great importance that current society places on appearance.

Western society (see Table 12–3). Using a cognitive approach, therapists may guide clients to focus on, challenge, and change maladaptive assumptions, such as "I must always be perfect" or "My weight and shape determine my value" (Freeman, 1995; Wilson & Fairburn, 1993; Garner & Bemis, 1985, 1982). The therapist may ask the client to gather evidence to support or refute the truth of such assumptions, weigh the advantages and disadvantages of living by them, and consider their consistency with other values. Here we see a therapist challenging an assumption common among people with anorexia nervosa:

> *Patient:* Once I reach my goal weight, or once I get into the habit of eating "non-dietetic" food, I will not be able to stop and I will catapult into obesity.
>
> *Therapist:* Are the only two options emaciation or obesity? If you have maintained "control" at this weight, where is the evidence that you will not be able to exert similar "control" at a normal weight? Recovered patients do not typically indulge in only high-calorie foods, and very few become obese. Could it be that you are feeling this way because you are currently starved—that once you get to a normal weight, you won't be sitting on a powder keg of hunger?
>
> *(Garner & Bemis, 1985, pp. 126–127)*

Therapists may also educate clients with anorexia nervosa about the body distortions typical of their disorder and train them to recognize that their own assessments of their size are incorrect (Freeman, 1995; Garner & Bemis, 1982; Garner & Garfinkel, 1981). Such education often paves the way for more accurate body perceptions. At the very least, a patient may reach a point where she says, "I know that a cardinal feature of anorexia nervosa is a misperception of my own size, so I can expect to feel fat no matter what size I really am," or "When I try to estimate my own dimensions, I'm like a color-blind person trying to coordinate her own wardrobe. I'll have to rely on objective data to determine my actual size."

Changing Interactions Within the Family Finally, family therapy is often used in cases of anorexia nervosa (Dare & Eisler, 1995; Vanderlinden & Vandereycken, 1991). As in other family therapy situations, the therapist meets with the family as a whole, points out dysfunctional family patterns, and helps the members make appropriate changes. In particular, family therapists may try to help the person with anorexia nervosa separate her feelings and needs from those of other family members.

> *Mother:* I think I know what [Susan] is going through: all the doubt and insecurity of growing up and establishing her own identity. *(Turning to the patient, with tears)* If you just place trust in yourself, with the support of those around you who care, everything will turn out for the better.
>
> *Therapist:* Are you making yourself available to her? Should she turn to you, rely on you for guidance and emotional support?
>
> *Mother:* Well, that's what parents are for.
>
> *Therapist: (Turning to patient)* What do you think?
>
> *Susan: (To mother)* I can't keep depending on you, Mom, or everyone else. That's what I've been doing, and it gave me anorexia. . . .
>
> *Therapist:* Do you think your mom would prefer that there be no secrets between her and the kids—an open door, so to speak?
>
> *Older sister:* Sometimes I do.
>
> *Therapist: (To patient and younger sister)* How about you two?
>
> *Susan:* Yeah. Sometimes it's like whatever I feel, she has to feel.
>
> *Younger sister:* Yeah.
>
> *Therapist: (To mother)* How does it make it better for you to be so close and involved with your kids?
>
> *Mother:* I don't see what's so wrong. You seem to be condemning me for being a conscientious parent. . . .
>
> *(Strober & Yager, 1985, pp. 381–382)*

As we observed earlier, the role of family factors in the development of anorexia nervosa has not really been clarified fully. Research does strongly suggest, however, that family therapy (or at least parent counseling) is often quite helpful in the treatment of this disorder (Dare & Eisler, 1995; Russell et al., 1992). Moreover, in some head-to-head comparisons with individual supportive therapy and individual psychodynamic therapy, family therapy appears to yield higher success rates (Dare & Eisler, 1995; Russell et al., 1992).

Combining the Approaches Today's therapists typically combine these various techniques for treating anorexia nervosa. The particular combination selected depends on the individual patient's situation and problems. Studies suggest that multiple approaches are indeed often helpful (Colahan, 1995; Tobin & Johnson, 1991; Garfinkel & Garner, 1982). Combination programs are now offered in mental health facilities and hospitals across the United States, Canada, and Europe.

The Aftermath of Anorexia Nervosa The development of multiple treatment approaches to anorexia nervosa has greatly improved the outlook for people with this disorder. Nevertheless, many of them still face significant obstacles on the road to recovery. Although the course and outcome of anorexia nervosa are highly variable (Miller, 1996), certain trends have emerged in numerous follow-up studies.

Many clinicians argue that society must also change if women are to avoid or overcome disturbed patterns of eating. For example, clothing ads might use models of more normal size and shape rather then images of thiness that are impossible for most women to attain.

On the positive side, weight is often quickly restored once treatment begins, although complete psychological and physical recovery may take several years (Treasure et al., 1995). Altogether, approximately 75 percent of patients continue to show improvement when they are examined several years or more after their initial recovery: as many as 45 percent are fully recovered and 30 percent considerably improved.

Most patients with anorexia nervosa are performing effectively at their jobs and express job satisfaction years after their recovery (Fombonne, 1995; Theander, 1970). Moreover, those who recover go on to marry or have intimate relationships at rates comparable to those of nonanorexic populations (Hsu, Crisp, & Harding, 1979; Theander, 1970).

In the medical realm, most females with anorexia nervosa menstruate again when they regain their weight. Others remain amenorrheic at least for a while (Fombonne, 1995; Crisp, 1981). Many of the other medical problems, such as reduced bone mineral density, improve correspondingly with weight gain and the return of menstruation (Iketani et al., 1995). Also encouraging, the death rate from anorexia nervosa seems to be declining (Treasure & Szmukler, 1995). Earlier diagnosis and safer and faster weight-restoration techniques may account for this trend. Deaths are usually caused by suicide, starvation, infection, gastrointestinal problems, or electrolyte imbalance (Treasure & Szmukler, 1995; APA, 1994; Andersen et al., 1985).

On the negative side, as many as 25 percent of persons with anorexia nervosa remain seriously impaired for years (APA, 1994; Halmi et al., 1991; Andersen et al., 1985). Moreover, recovery, when it does occur, is not typically a smooth or easy process (Murray, 1986). Anorexic behavior recurs in at least 15 percent of patients while they are recovering, usually precipitated by new stresses, such as marriage, pregnancy, or a major relocation (Sohlberg & Norring, 1992; Hsu et al., 1979). Even years later, many apparently recovered individuals continue to express concerns about their weight and appearance. Some continue to restrict their diets to some degree, experience anxiety when they eat with other people, or hold some distorted ideas about food, eating, and weight (Fichter & Pirke, 1995; Pirke et al., 1992; Clinton & McKinlay, 1986).

Around half of patients with anorexia nervosa continue to display some emotional problems—particularly depression, social anxiety, and obsessiveness–years after treatment. Such problems are particularly common in those who have not succeeded in attaining a fully normal weight (Halmi, 1995; Hsu et al., 1992; Halmi et al., 1991).

Similarly, family problems persist for approximately half of patients with anorexia nervosa (Hsu, 1980).

The more weight patients with anorexia nervosa lose and the longer they have the problem before treatment, the poorer their recovery rate (Steinhausen, 1997; Slade, 1995; Lewis & Chatoor, 1994). Those who display psychological, behavioral, or sexual problems before the onset of the disorder tend to have a poorer recovery rate than those without such a history (Lewis & Chatoor, 1994; Burns & Crisp, 1985). Adolescents seem to have a better recovery rate than older patients (Steinhausen, 1997; APA, 1994). Females have a better recovery rate than males.

Treatments for Bulimia Nervosa

Treatment programs tailored to the features of bulimia nervosa have been developed only in recent years, but they have risen meteorically in popularity. Most of these programs are offered in eating disorder clinics, and all share the immediate goal of helping clients to eliminate their binge–purge patterns and establish good eating habits; the broader goal is to address the underlying causes of bulimic patterns. The programs emphasize education as much as therapy (Davis et al., 1997; Button, 1993). Many programs combine several treatment strategies, including individual insight therapy, group therapy, behavioral therapy, and antidepressant drug therapy (Mizes, 1995; Wakeling, 1995; Fahy, Eisler, & Russell, 1993).

Individual Insight Therapy Psychodynamic and cognitive approaches have been the most common forms of individual insight therapy for clients with bulimia nervosa (Bloom et al., 1994; Fichter, 1990). Psychodynamic therapists use free association and interpretive techniques to help these clients uncover and resolve their frustrating tensions, lack of self-trust, need for control, and feelings of powerlessness (Dare & Crowther, 1995; Lerner, 1986). Only a few research studies have been conducted to test the effectiveness of psychodynamic therapy, but these studies are generally supportive (Garner et al., 1993; Yager, 1985).

Cognitive therapists try to help people with bulimia nervosa recognize and alter their maladaptive attitudes toward food, eating, weight, and shape, thus eliminating the kinds of thinking that raise anxiety and lead to bingeing (Freeman, 1995; Garner et al., 1993; Wilson & Pike, 1993). As in the treatment of anorexia nervosa, the therapists typically teach clients to identify and evaluate the dysfunctional thoughts that regularly precede their urge to binge—"I have no self-control," "I might as well give up," "I look fat" (Fairburn, 1985). The therapists may also guide clients to recognize, question, and eventually change their perfectionistic standards, sense of helplessness, and low self-concept (Freeman, 1995; Mizes, 1995).

Researchers have found cognitive therapy to be relatively effective in cases of bulimia nervosa, helping as many as 65 percent of patients to stop bingeing and purging (Walsh et al., 1997; Fairburn et al., 1995; Freeman, 1995). Approaches that mix cognitive and psychodynamic techniques also appear to be helpful (Brisman, 1992; Yager, 1985). In recent years, two other approaches have also been applied to bulimia nervosa with some degree of success: *interpersonal psychotherapy*—the treatment that is often effective in cases of depression (Fairburn et al., 1995, 1993)—and *self-care manuals* that contain extensive cognitive education and treatment strategies (Treasure et al., 1996; Schmidt & Treasure, 1993).

Group Therapy Most bulimia nervosa programs now include group therapy to give sufferers an opportunity to share their thoughts, concerns, and experiences with one another (McKisack & Waller, 1997; Lewis & Chatoor, 1994). Here they learn that their disorder is not unique or shameful, and they receive support and understanding from the other members, along with candid feedback and insights (Manley & Needham, 1995; Moreno, Fuhriman, & Hileman, 1995). They can also work directly on underlying fears of displeasing others or being criticized. In one group therapy technique, the ***group meal,*** clients plan and eat a meal together with the therapist, all the while discussing their thoughts and feelings as they occur (Franko, 1993). Research suggests that group therapy is somewhat helpful in as many as 75 percent of bulimia nervosa cases, particularly when it is combined with individual insight therapy (McKisack & Waller, 1997; Wilfley et al., 1993; Mitchell et al., 1985).

Behavioral Therapy Behavioral techniques are often employed in cases of bulimia nervosa along with individual insight therapy or group therapy. Clients may, for example, be asked to monitor and keep diaries of their eating behavior, their fluctuations of hunger and satiety, and other feelings and experiences (Goleman, 1995; Saunders, 1985; Greenberg & Marks, 1982). This strategy helps them to observe their eating patterns more objectively and to recognize the emotional triggers of their disorder.

Some behaviorists also use the technique of *exposure and response prevention* to help break the binge–purge cycle. As we saw in Chapter 7, this approach consists of exposing people to situations that would ordinarily raise anxiety and then preventing them from performing their usual compulsive acts until the clients learn that the situations are actually quite harmless and their compulsive acts unnecessary. In the realm of bulimia nervosa, behavioral therapists have clients eat particular kinds and amounts of food and then prevent them from vomiting until they come to see that eating can be a harmless and indeed constructive activity that needs no undoing (Rosen & Leitenberg, 1985, 1982). Studies have found that eating-related anxieties often decrease over the course of this treatment and that bingeing and vomiting decrease substantially (Kennedy, Katz, & Neitzert, 1995; Wilson et al., 1986).

Antidepressant Medications During the past decade, antidepressant drugs have often been added to the treatment packages for bulimia nervosa (Walsh et al., 1997; Wakeling, 1995; Mitchell & de Zwaan, 1993). In fact, in 1996 the antidepressant Prozac received formal approval by the U.S. Food and Drug Administration for specific use with this disorder. In one double-blind study an antidepressant drug was administered for 6 weeks to 20 women with bulimia nervosa, while a placebo was given to 10 others (Pope, Hudson, & Jonas, 1983). After treatment, 18 of the 20 women treated with the antidepressant showed a moderate to marked reduction of binge-eating. In fact, 7 stopped bingeing entirely. In contrast, only 1 of the 10 who were given placebos improved even moderately, 8 showed no improvement, and 1 became worse.

Although other studies have not always yielded such impressive results (Wakeling, 1995; Leitenberg et al., 1993), some do indicate that antidepressant medications help between 25 and 40 percent of patients to stop bingeing and purging. The drugs reduce an individual's bingeing an average of 67 percent and vomiting 56 percent. The medications are especially helpful in combination with other forms of therapy (Walsh et al., 1997; Agras, 1995, 1994; Advokat & Kutlesic, 1995).

The Aftermath of Bulimia Nervosa Left untreated, bulimia nervosa usually lasts for years, sometimes improving temporarily but then emerging again (APA, 1994). As with anorexia nervosa, relapses are usually precipitated by a new life stress, such as an impending examination, job change, illness, marriage, or divorce (Abraham & Llewellyn-Jones, 1984).

Approximately 40 percent of clients with bulimia nervosa show an outstanding response to treatment: they stop or greatly reduce their bingeing and purging and stabilize their eating habits and weight. Another 40 percent show a moderate response—decreased bingeing and purging. The remaining 20 percent show little improvement in their eating patterns (Keel & Mitchell, 1997; Fombonne, 1995; Button, 1993).

Relapse is a problem even among clients who respond successfully to treatment (Keel & Mitchell, 1997; Lewis & Chatoor, 1994; Keller et al., 1992). One study found that close to a third of recovered clients relapsed within two years of treatment, usually within 6 months (Olmsted, Kaplan, & Rockert, 1994). Relapse was more likely among persons who had established a pattern of frequent vomiting and those who maintained a high degree of interpersonal distrust even after treatment.

Research also suggests that treatment helps many people with bulimia nervosa make significant and lasting improvements in their psychological and social functioning (Yager, Rorty, & Rossotto, 1995; Herzog et al., 1990). Follow-up studies find former patients to be at least somewhat less depressed than they had been at the time of diagnosis (Halmi, 1995; Brotman et al., 1988; Fairburn et al., 1986). Such studies have also indicated that approximately a third of former patients interact more healthily at work, at home, *and* in social settings, while another third interact effectively in two of these areas (Hsu & Holder, 1986).

Crossroads

Throughout this book we have observed that it is often enlightening to consider sociocultural, psychological, and biological factors jointly in efforts to explain or treat various forms of abnormal functioning. Nowhere is the argument for combining these perspectives more compelling than in the case of eating disorders.

According to the ***multidimensional risk perspective*** embraced by the leading theorists and practitioners in this problem area, varied factors act together to encourage the development of eating disorders (Lyon et al., 1997; Gleaves, Williamson, & Barker, 1993; Garner & Garfinkel, 1980). One combination—for example, societal pressures, autonomy problems, the changes of adolescence, and hypothalamic overactivity—may bring about and maintain the disorder in one case. A different combination—say a dysfunctional family pattern, depression, and the effects of dieting—may account for another case.

Correspondingly, the most helpful treatment programs for eating disorders carefully combine sociocultural, psychological, and biological approaches. Inasmuch as several pathways may lead to eating disorders, it makes sense that treatment programs need to be multifaceted and flexible, tailored to the unique problems and features of the patient.

The multidimensional risk perspective that has been applied to eating disorders thus demonstrates that scientists and practitioners of very different models can indeed work together in an atmosphere of mutual respect and productivity. Of course, this perspective may not provide the best explanation or treatment for every psychological disorder, but in each case all possible factors must be considered before true insights can be achieved.

Despite the considerable achievements by eating disorder researchers and therapists, many questions remain unanswered. Indeed, every new discovery forces clinicians to adjust their theories and treatment programs. For example, bulimia nervosa was not even formally identified as a clinical disorder until the 1980s, and recently researchers have learned that people with this problem sometimes feel strangely positive toward their symptoms. A recovered patient said, "I still miss my bulimia as I would an old friend who has died" (Cauwels, 1983, p. 173). Only when feelings like these are understood will treatment programs become fully effective.

While clinicians and researchers strive for more answers about eating disorders, clients themselves have begun to take an active role. A number of patient-initiated organizations now provide information, education, and support through a national telephone hotline, professional referrals, newsletters, workshops, and conferences. The National Anorexic Aid Society, the American Anorexia and Bulimia Association, the National Association of Anorexia Nervosa and Associated Disorders, and Anorexia Nervosa and Related Eating Disorders, Inc., help counter the isolation and shame that people with eating disorders feel. They show countless sufferers that they are hardly alone or powerless against their eating disorders.

Chapter Review

1. Eating disorders. Eating disorders have increased dramatically since thinness has become a national obsession. Clinicians and researchers have learned that the two leading eating disorders, anorexia nervosa and bulimia nervosa, share many similarities.

2. ***Anorexia nervosa.*** Sufferers of anorexia nervosa relentlessly pursue extreme thinness and lose dangerous amounts of weight. They may follow a pattern of *restricting type anorexia nervosa* or *bing-eating/purging type anorexia nervosa.*

A. Anorexia nervosa most often appears between the ages of 14 and 19; over 90 percent of its sufferers are female; it strikes around 1 percent of the young female population.

B. Anorexia nervosa is characterized by five central features:

(1) Becoming thin is life's central goal. Individuals are afraid of becoming obese and of losing control over body size and shape.

(2) Individuals are preoccupied with food. This may be the result, in part, of starvation.

(3) Individuals exhibit cognitive dysfunctioning. They have a low opinion of their body shape, overestimate their body size, and develop maladaptive attitudes.

(4) Psychological and mood problems may occur, partly as a result of starvation. They include depression, low self-esteem, and anxiety, particularly obsessive-compulsive patterns.

(5) Medical problems include *amenorrhea,* lowered body temperature, low blood pressure, osteoporosis, and slow heart rate. Metabolic and electrolyte imbalances may also occur. Nutritional deficiencies may affect the skin, hands, and feet, and hair growth.

3. ***Bulimia nervosa.*** Sufferers of bulimia nervosa go on frequent eating binges, then compensate by such means as forcing themselves to vomit or taking laxatives to keep from gaining weight. They may follow a pattern of *purging type bulimia nervosa* or *nonpurging type bulimia nervosa.*

A. Bulimia nervosa, also known as the *binge–purge syndrome,* usually appears in females between the ages of 15 and 21 years, and is displayed by between 1 and 4 percent of them. Over 90 percent of its sufferers are female. These young women generally maintain their body weight within a normal range.

B. The binges of persons with bulimia nervosa often occur in response to growing tension. The binge episodes are followed by feelings of guilt and self-reproach.

C. Purging behavior is initially reinforced by the immediate relief from uncomfortable feelings of fullness or by temporary reduction of the feelings of anxiety, self-disgust, and loss of control attached to bingeing. Over time, however, people often feel increasingly disgusted with themselves, depressed, and guilty. People with bulimia nervosa may experience mood swings or have difficulty controlling their impulses. Some display a personality disorder. Around half are amenorrheic. A number develop dental problems. Some develop *hypokalemia.*

4. ***Explanations of eating disorders.*** Today's theorists usually apply a *multidimensional risk perspective* to explain eating disorders, and identify several key factors that place a person at risk for an eating disorder.

A. Society currently emphasizes thinness and is biased against obesity. Those whose jobs, sports, gender, or race especially value or reward thinness are particularly vulnerable to eating concerns and disorders.

B. Families may emphasize thinness and dieting, or establish dysfunctional family interactions and communication patterns. Theorists have particularly cited the *enmeshed* family pattern.

C. Hilde Bruch focused on ego deficiencies, including a poor sense of autonomy and control, and perceptual-cognitive disturbances, including an inability to differentiate between internal needs.

D. Mood disorders are often linked to and may help cause eating disorders.

E. Parts of the *hypothalamus* help control eating, along with natural appetite suppressants and other chemicals in the brain and body. Collectively, they help maintain a *weight set point,* the particular weight to which an individual is predisposed by genes and early eating practices. These brain areas and body chemicals may spring into action when weight deviates from the weight set point, trying to return it to the set point.

5. ***Treatments for eating disorders.*** Therapists aim first to help clients reestablish normal eating habits and regain their health; then they tackle the underlying problems that led to the disorder.

A. The first step in treating anorexia nervosa is to increase caloric intake and restore the person's weight quickly, using a strategy such as *supportive nursing care.* The second step is to address the underlying psychological and perhaps family problems, so that improvement may be lasting. Therapists typically offer a mixture of therapy and education.

B. About 75 percent of people with anorexia nervosa recover to a significant degree. Some of those who seem to recover relapse, many continue to be concerned about their weight and appearance, and half continue to experience some emotional or family problems. Most menstruate again when they regain weight. Most of those who recover from anorexia nervosa are later found to enjoy work and perform effectively at their jobs, and to marry or have intimate relationships at the usual rate.

C. Treatments for bulimia nervosa focus on eliminating the binge–purge pattern and addressing the underlying causes of the disorder. Often several treatment strategies are combined, including individual insight therapy, group therapy, behavioral therapy, and antidepressant medications.

D. Left untreated, bulimia nervosa may last for years. Approximately 40 percent of clients show an outstanding response to treatment, another 40 percent a moderate response. Relapse can be a problem and may be precipitated by a new stress. At the same time, research suggests that treatment leads to significant and lasting improvements in psychological and social functioning for many individuals.

Thought and Afterthought

And She Lived Happily Ever After?

In May 1996 Alicia Machado, a 19-year-old woman from Venezuela, was crowned Miss Universe. Then her problems began. During the first 8 months of her reign, her weight rose from 118 to 160 pounds, incurring the wrath of pageant officials and sparking rumors that she was about to be relieved of her crown. The "problem" received broad newspaper and television coverage and much ridicule on talk radio programs around the world.

Ms. Machado explained, "I was a normal girl, but my life has had big changes. I travel to many countries, eat different foods." Nevertheless, in response to all of the pressure, she undertook a special diet and an extensive exercise program to lose at least some of the weight she had gained. Her trainer claimed that a weight of 118 pounds was too low for her frame and explained that she had originally attained it by taking diet pills.

Afterthoughts: What does this whole episode suggest about the role of societal factors in the development of eating problems? . . . Why did so many people hold such strong, often critical opinions about Ms. Machado's weight? . . . What messages did the episode and the way it was resolved convey to women around the world?

A Big "McProblem"

If the aesthetic ideal is a small frame, if people want to restrict their eating, and if eating disorders are increasing, why are fast-food products getting bigger and bigger and more and more profitable? In fact, a Macho Meal at a restaurant of the Del Taco Mexican fast-food chain weighs almost 4 pounds – more than the Manhattan telephone book (Horovitz, 1996). A Double Gulp drink at a 7-Eleven store equals more than 5 cans of cola. Just four slices of Pizza Hut's Triple Decker pizza contain more than the average allowance of calories, salt, and saturated fat for an entire day. Meanwhile, McLean Deluxe lower-fat burgers and Taco Bell's Border Lights have struggled in the marketplace. Altogether, customers spent more than $2.5 billion on "big" fast-food products in 1996.

Afterthoughts: How may these large products be related to the increase in eating disturbances found throughout society? . . . Do these tempting products set a climate for bingeing and purging? . . . Or are people actually driven to such products by the effects of excessive concern about dieting and eating?

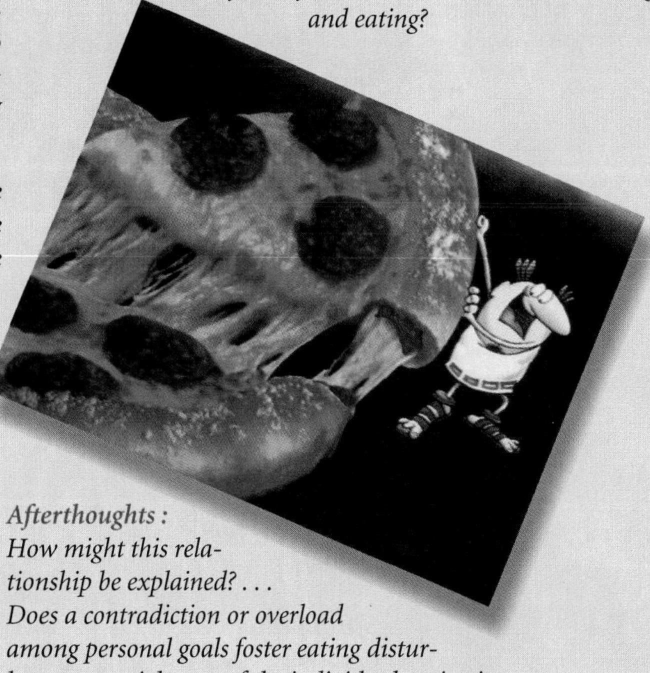

Superwoman, Super Cost

A new ideal has emerged in our society—the so-called **superwoman**, who is warm, nurturing, and attractive and at the same time competitive, accomplished, and successful (Gordon, 1990). Research suggests that young girls who aspire to be superwomen are more likely to have eating problems than those who reject the model (Steiner-Adair, 1986).

Afterthoughts: How might this relationship be explained? . . . Does a contradiction or overload among personal goals foster eating disturbances, or might one of the individual aspirations, such as striving for success, alone place individuals at risk?

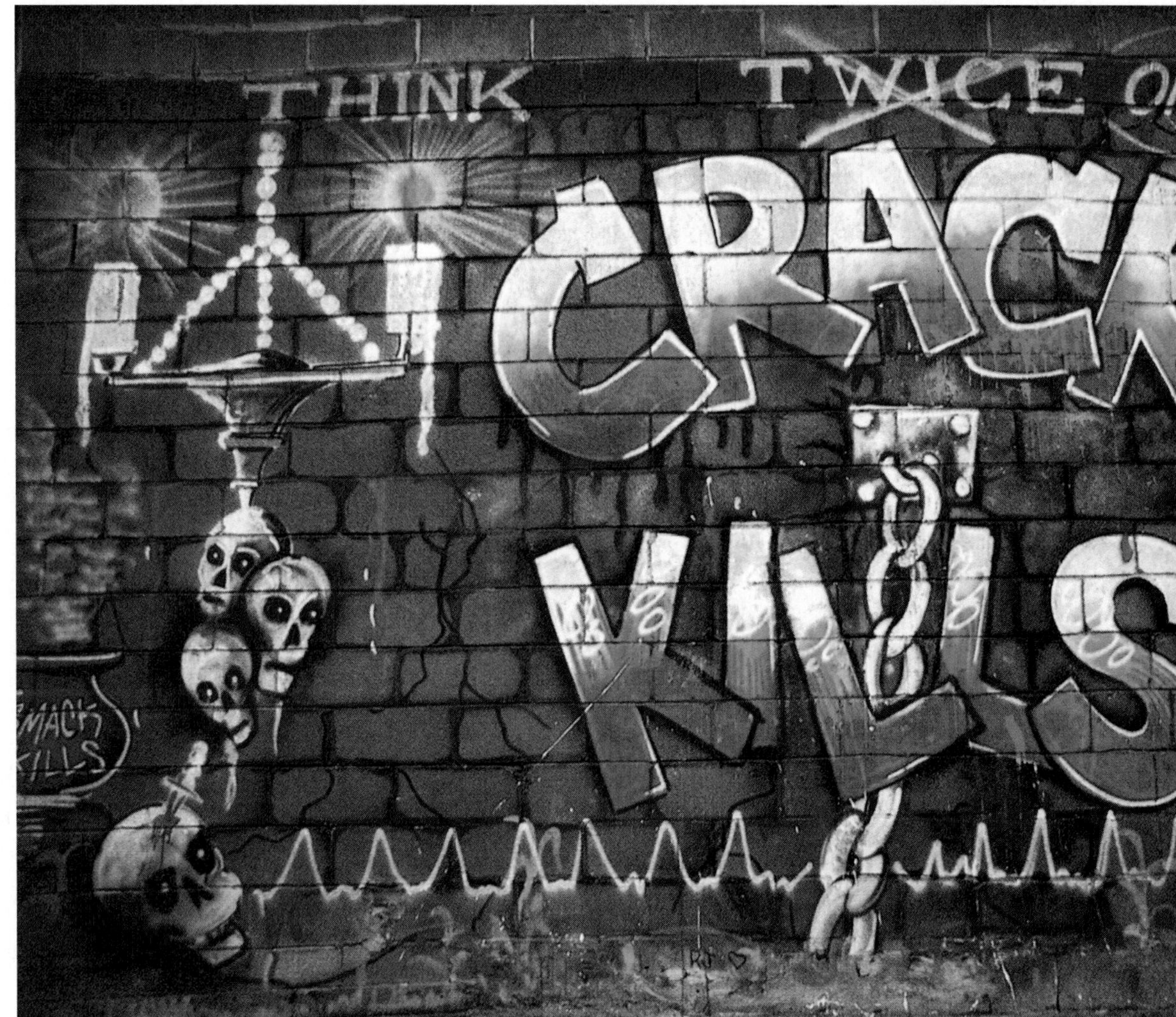

Topic Overview

Depressants
- Alcohol
- Sedative-Hypnotic Drugs
- Opioids

Stimulants
- Cocaine
- Amphetamines
- Caffeine

Hallucinogens

Cannabis

Combinations of Substances

Explanations of Substance-Related Disorders

Treatments for Substance-Related Disorders

Crossroads

Chapter 13

Substance-Related Disorders

Probably every substance on earth has been ingested by someone somewhere, at some time. Curious and adventuresome, humans have learned that a vast variety of substances are edible and nutritious when they are prepared in certain ways, and have developed a long list of acceptable foods and delicacies. Humans have likewise stumbled upon substances that have interesting effects—medicinal or pleasurable—on the brain and the rest of the body. We may swallow an aspirin to quiet a headache, an antibiotic to fight an infection, or a tranquilizer to calm us down. We may drink coffee to get going in the morning or wine to relax with friends. We may smoke cigarettes to soothe our nerves.

Many of the substances that humans have come across harm the body or adversely affect behavior or mood. Their misuse has become one of society's most disabling and expensive problems. It has been estimated that the annual cost of drug misuse is $238 billion in the United States alone (Nash, 1997; Kleber, 1995; Nemecek, 1995).

Technically, a drug is any substance other than food that affects our bodies or minds. It need not be a medicine or illegal. In recent years the term "substance" has gained favor as a substitute for "drug," partly because most people fail to see that substances like alcohol, tobacco, and caffeine are drugs, too.

These graffiti illustrate the danger of excessive drug use. The search for pleasure may become a psychological and physical prison from which escape is elusive and often painful.

The moment people ingest a drug—whether it be alcohol, cocaine, or marijuana—trillions of powerful molecules surge through the bloodstream and into the brain (Nash, 1997). Once there, the molecules set off an explosion of biochemical events—a chain reaction of sorts—that literally rearranges the normal anatomy and operation of the brain and body. Not surprisingly, then, drug misuse may lead to various kinds of abnormal functioning.

First, drugs may cause *temporary changes* in behavior, emotion, or thought. An excessive amount of alcohol, for example, may lead to ***intoxication*** (literally, "poisoning"), a temporary syndrome marked by impaired judgment, mood changes, irritability, slurred speech, and loss of coordination. Drugs such as LSD may produce a distinct form of intoxication, sometimes called ***hallucinosis,*** a state of perceptual distortions and hallucinations.

Some substances can also lead to *long-term problems.* People who regularly ingest them may develop patterns of maladaptive behavior and changes in their body's responses. They may come to rely on a drug excessively and chronically, a pattern called ***substance abuse,*** and so may seriously damage their family and social relationships, perform unreliably at work, and create physical hazards for themselves or others. People may further develop ***substance dependence,*** a more advanced substance-related pattern, popularly known as ***addiction.*** In addition to abusing the drug they acquire a *physical* dependence on it, marked by a *tolerance* for the drug, *withdrawal* symptoms, or both.

People who develop a ***tolerance*** for a substance need increasing doses of it in order to keep obtaining the desired effect. Those who experience ***withdrawal*** are confronted by unpleasant and even dangerous symptoms—cramps, anxiety attacks, sweating, nausea—when they suddenly stop taking the drug or reduce their dose of it. Withdrawal symptoms can begin within hours of the last dose and tend to intensify over several days before they subside. Over the course of a year, between 9.5 and 11.3 percent of all adults in the United States, more than 15 million people, display a substance-related disorder; only 20 percent of them receive treatment for it (Kessler et al., 1994; Regier et al., 1993).

Many drugs are available in our society, and new ones emerge almost every day. Some are found in nature, others are derived from natural substances, and still others are synthetically produced. Some, such as antianxiety drugs and barbiturates, require a physician's prescription for legal use. Others, such as alcohol and the nicotine found in cigarettes, are legally available to all adults. Still others, such as heroin, are illegal under any circumstance, yet are manufactured and sold in such quantities that they constitute major, albeit underground, industries. In 1962 only 4 million people in the United States had ever used marijuana, cocaine, heroin, or another illegal substance; today that number has climbed to more than 72 million (SAMHSA, 1996; Kleber, 1995). In fact, over 23 million people have used such a substance within the past year and 13 million are using it currently (SAMHSA, 1996). Eleven percent of teenagers have used an illicit drug within the past month (see Figure 13-1).

In this chapter we shall investigate some of today's most problematic substances and the abnormal patterns they may produce. Each has a specific profile and a unique impact on people and on society, yet the abnormal patterns they produce often have related causes and respond to similar treatments. We shall begin by examining the substances separately, then consider the causes and treatments of substance-related disorders together. The substances fall into four categories: those that act to *depress* the central nervous system, such as alcohol and opioids; *stimulants* of the central nervous system, such as cocaine and amphetamines; *hallucinogens,* such as LSD, which cause delusions, hallucinations, and other powerful changes in sensory perception; and *cannabis* substances, such as marijuana, which cause a mixture of hallucinogenic, depressant, and stimulant effects. As we shall see, many people also take more than one of these substances at a time, a condition known as *polydrug use.*

Depressants

Depressants are substances that slow the activity of the central nervous system. In sufficient doses they reduce tension and inhibitions and impair judgment, motor activity, and concentration. The three most widely used groups of depressants are *alcohol, sedative-hypnotics,* and *opioids.*

Alcohol

Two-thirds of the people in the United States drink alcohol-containing beverages, at least from time to time. Purchases of beer, wine, and liquor add up to tens of billions of dollars each year in the United States alone. More than 5 percent of all adults are heavy drinkers, consuming at least five drinks on at least five occasions during the past month (SAMHSA, 1996). Among heavy drinkers men outnumber women by more than 4 to 1, 9.4 percent to 2.0 percent (SAMHSA, 1996).

All alcoholic beverages contain ***ethyl alcohol.*** This chemical compound is rapidly absorbed into the blood through the lining of the stomach and the intestine, and it immediately begins to take effect. The ethyl alcohol is

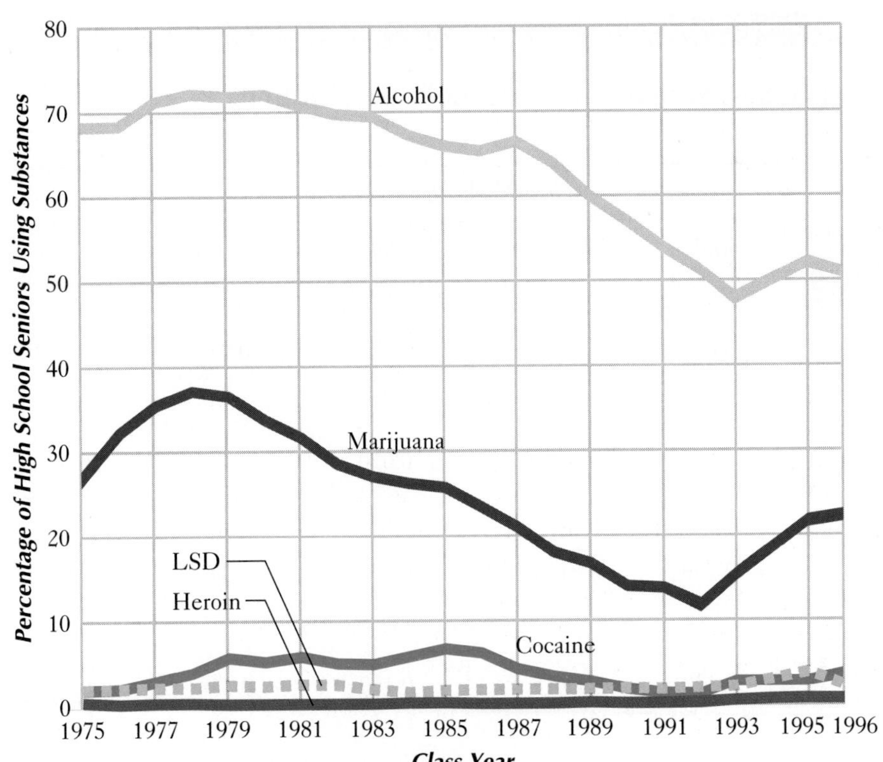

Figure 13-1 *The overall percentage of high school seniors who admitted to using substances illicitly at least once within 30 days of being surveyed rose in the 1970s, declined in the 1980s, and rose again in the 1990s (NIDA, 1996).*

carried in the bloodstream to the central nervous system (the brain and spinal cord), where it acts to *depress,* or slow, its functioning by binding to a variety of neurons. In particular, the alcohol binds to receptors on the neurons that normally receive the neurotransmitter *GABA* (Gordis, 1991). In Chapter 6 we observed that GABA gives an inhibitory message—a message to stop firing—when it is received at receptors (see pp. 171–172). Thus it plays a key role in reducing anxiety. When alcohol is received at receptors that usually receive GABA, it apparently helps GABA to operate more effectively in shutting down the neurons. As a result, it helps calm and relax the drinker.

At first ethyl alcohol depresses the higher centers of the central nervous system, those that control judgment and inhibition, and people become less constrained, more talkative, and often more friendly. As their inner control breaks down, they may feel relaxed, safe, self-confident, and happy. Alcohol's depression of these regions also impairs fine motor skills, increases sensitivity to light, and causes the small blood vessels of the skin to dilate, so that the face and neck become flushed and the person feels warm.

As more alcohol is ingested, it eventually depresses other areas in the central nervous system, causing changes that are even more problematic. Drinkers become still less restrained and more confused. Their ability to make rational judgments declines, their speech becomes less guarded and less coherent, and their memory falters (Fromme, Katz, & D'Amico, 1997; Goldstein, 1994). Many become loud, boisterous, and aggressive, their emotions exaggerated and unstable; mildly amusing remarks or situations may strike them as hilarious.

Motor impairment also becomes more pronounced as drinking continues, and reaction times slow. People at this stage are unsteady when they stand or walk and clumsy in performing even simple activities. They may drop things, bump into doors and furniture, and misjudge distances. Their vision becomes blurred, particularly peripheral vision, and they have trouble distinguishing between different intensities of light. Hearing is affected, too. As a result of such impairments, people who have drunk too much alcohol may have great difficulty driving or solving simple problems.

The extent of the effect of ethyl alcohol on body chemistry is determined by its concentration in the blood. Thus a given amount of alcohol will have less effect on a large person than on a small one because the large person has a greater volume of blood (see Table 13-1 and Figure 13-2). Other factors may also influence the concentration of ethyl alcohol in the blood. When size is held constant, for example, women become more intoxicated than men on equal doses of alcohol, since women have significantly less of the stomach enzyme ***alcohol dehydrogenase,*** which breaks down alcohol in the stomach before it enters the blood (NIAAA, 1992).

TABLE 13-1 Relationships Between Sex, Weight, Oral Alcohol Consumption, and Blood Alcohol Level

		Blood Alcohol Level (Percent)					
Absolute Alcohol (Ounces)	*Beverage Intake**	*Female (100 lb.)*	*Male (100 lb.)*	*Female (150 lb.)*	*Male (150 lb.)*	*Female (200 lb.)*	*Male (200 lb.)*
1/2	1 oz. spirits† 1 glass wine 1 can beer	0.045	0.037	0.03	0.025	0.022	0.019
1	2 oz. spirits 2 glasses wine 2 cans beer	0.090	0.075	0.06	0.050	0.045	0.037
2	4 oz. spirits 4 glasses wine 4 cans beer	0.180	0.150	0.12	0.100	0.090	0.070
3	6 oz. spirits 6 glasses wine 6 cans beer	0.270	0.220	0.18	0.150	0.130	0.110
4	8 oz. spirits 8 glasses wine 8 cans beer	0.360	0.300	0.24	0.200	0.180	0.150
5	10 oz. spirits 10 glasses wine 10 cans beer	0.450	0.370	0.30	0.250	0.220	0.180

** In 1 hour.*
† 100-proof spirits.
Source: Ray & Ksir, 1993, p. 194.

Levels of impairment are closely related to the concentration of ethyl alcohol in the blood. When alcohol constitutes 0.06 percent of the blood volume, a person usually feels relaxed and comfortable without yet being intoxicated. By the time the blood-alcohol concentration reaches 0.09 percent, however, the drinker crosses the line into intoxication. As the concentration of alcohol in the bloodstream further increases, the drinker becomes even more impaired. If the level goes as high as 0.55 percent, death will probably result. Most people, however, lose consciousness before they can drink enough to reach this level.

The effects of alcohol decline only as the alcohol concentration in the blood declines. Most of the alcohol is broken down, or ***metabolized,*** by the liver into carbon dioxide and water, which can be exhaled and excreted. The average rate of metabolizing is 10 to 15 percent of an ounce per hour, but different people's livers conduct this process at somewhat different speeds; thus rates of "sobering up" vary. Despite a popular misconception, neither drinking black coffee, splashing cold water on the face, nor "getting hold of oneself" can speed the process up. Only time and metabolism can make a person sober.

Alcohol Abuse and Dependence Though legal, alcohol is actually one of the most dangerous drugs. Many people develop patterns of long-term alcohol abuse or alcohol dependence—patterns collectively known as ***alcoholism.*** Surveys indicate that over a one-year period, between 7.2 and 9.7 percent of all adults in the United States abuse or are dependent on alcohol (Anthony et al., 1995; Kessler et al., 1994; Regier et al., 1993). Between 13 and 23 percent of the adult population will display one of these patterns at some time in their lives, with men outnumbering women by as much as 5 to 1 (Anthony et al., 1995; APA, 1994; Kessler et al., 1994; Helzer et al., 1991).

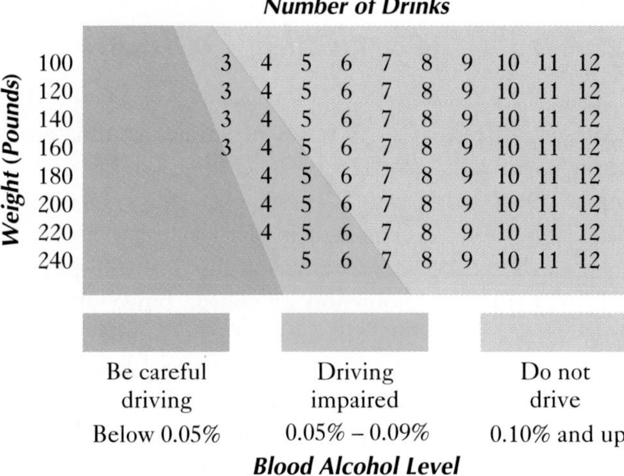

Number of Drinks
Weight (Pounds)
100 3 4 5 6 7 8 9 10 11 12
120 3 4 5 6 7 8 9 10 11 12
140 3 4 5 6 7 8 9 10 11 12
160 3 4 5 6 7 8 9 10 11 12
180 4 5 6 7 8 9 10 11 12
200 4 5 6 7 8 9 10 11 12
220 4 5 6 7 8 9 10 11 12
240 5 6 7 8 9 10 11 12
Be careful driving
Below 0.05%
Driving impaired
0.05% – 0.09%
Do not drive
0.10% and up
Blood Alcohol Level

Figure 13-2 *Counting a 12-ounce glass of beer as one drink, clinicians estimate that a 100-pound person will reach a state's legal limit for drunk driving, a blood alcohol level of 0.08 to 0.10 percent, after ingesting just four drinks, whereas a 240-pound person will usually reach this limit only after having about seven drinks. The ability to drive is somewhat impaired even when the blood alcohol level is below the legal limit. (Adapted from Frances & Franklin, 1988.)*

Alcohol abuse and dependence are also major problems among the young (Scheier & Botvin, 1997). Approximately 3.5 percent of high school seniors report that they drink every day (NIDA, 1995), and an estimated 5 million teenagers have experienced problems related to alcohol use (Beck, Thombs, & Summons, 1993). Even 8 to 12 percent of surveyed elementary school children admit to some alcohol use (Johnston et al., 1993; Hutchinson & Little, 1985). Alcohol abuse is a particular problem on college campuses (see Box 13-1).

The prevalence rate of alcoholism in a given year is around 7 percent for both white and African Americans and 9 percent for Hispanic Americans (Anthony et al., 1995; APA, 1994; Helzer et al., 1991). The men in these groups, however, show strikingly different age patterns in their rates of alcoholism. For white and Hispanic American men, the rate of alcoholism is highest—over 18 percent—during young adulthood, compared to 8 percent among African American men in that age group. For African American men, the rate is highest—15 percent—during late middle age, compared to 8 percent among white and Hispanic American men in that age group.

Alcohol Abuse People who abuse alcohol drink excessive amounts regularly and rely on it to enable them to do things that would otherwise make them anxious. Eventually the excessive drinking interferes with their socializing or with their cognitive ability and work performance. They may have frequent arguments with family members or friends, miss work repeatedly, and even lose their jobs (Coambs & McAndrews, 1994).

Precise patterns of alcohol abuse vary in important ways (Walker et al., 1996). One schema identifies three broad patterns of abuse. In one, the person drinks large amounts of alcohol every day, keeps drinking until intoxicated, and plans his or her daily life around drinking. In a second pattern, the individual may abstain from drinking for long periods of time, then go on periodic binges of heavy drinking that can last weeks or months. The drinker may remain intoxicated for days and later be unable to remember anything about the period. In a third pattern of alcohol abuse, drinking to excess is limited to

A society's attitudes toward alcohol help influence the drinking behavior of its members. Changes in attitudes may also influence historical recollections. An 1848 lithograph of George Washington saying farewell to his officers shows him drinking a toast with his compatriots. But the wine glasses and bottle are mysteriously absent in an edition released in 1876, when alcohol was out of favor. If alcohol was a sign of weakness or immorality, Washington could not possibly have been a drinker.

BOX 13-1 College Binge Drinking: An Extracurricular Problem

Binge drinking, consuming large quantities of alcohol at a single time, is a problem that plagues American society, particularly college campuses. Recent studies show that nearly half of all college students binge drink at times (Wechsler et al., 1994; Cage, 1992). Contrary to popular belief, the phenomenon is more common among college students than among people of the same age who are not in college. In fact, college students drink an estimated 430 million gallons of alcohol each year, and spend $5.5 billion to do so (Eigan, 1991).

In many circles, alcohol use is an accepted aspect of college life. But are we as a society taking the issue too lightly? Consider some of the following statistics:

- Alcohol is a factor in nearly 40 percent of academic problems and 28 percent of all college dropouts (Anderson, 1994).
- Although 84 percent of incoming freshmen see heavy alcohol use as a problem on campus, 68 percent drink during their first semester, at least half of them during their first week on campus (Harvard School of Public Health, 1995).
- The average student spends $466 a year on alcohol (Eigan, 1991).
- More undergraduates ultimately die of alcohol-related causes while still in school than the number who go on to earn MBA's and Ph.D.'s (Eigan, 1991).
- Binge drinking has been linked to acute health problems and serious injury, auto crashes, unplanned and unprotected sex, assaults and aggressive behaviors, and drinking-related psychological problems (Wechsler et al., 1995; Wechsler & Isaac, 1992).

These trends have led some educators to describe binge drinking as "the No. 1 public health hazard" for full-time college students (Wechsler et al., 1995). Correspondingly, researchers and clinicians have begun to approach the problem as a national health priority.

A series of studies conducted by Henry Wechsler and his colleagues (1995) at the Harvard School of Public Health have provided some insights into the phenomenon of college binge drinking. In one of the studies, the investigators looked at gender differences (Wechsler et al., 1995). They mailed a questionnaire to students at 140 college campuses around the United States and received close to 18,000 replies. The extensive questionnaire first probed the drinking patterns of the students, then whether the students had experienced negative outcomes—injuries, unsafe sex, forgetfulness, hangovers, missed classes—as a result of drinking. They found that the likelihood of these negative outcomes was as great for women who typically drank four drinks at a time as for men who usually drank five. The researchers concluded, "A lower standard of defining heavy or binge drinking needs to be used for women than for men" (1995, p. 984). Previously most researchers and drug agencies had defined binge drinking as an episode in-

weekends or evenings, or both. The actor Dick Van Dyke displayed this pattern of alcohol abuse.

> I didn't miss work ever because of drinking. And I never drank at work. Never drank during the day—only at home and only in the evenings. . . . I never craved a drink during the day. I was never a morning drinker—I didn't want one then. The idea made me as sick as it would make anyone else. But evening drinking is a form of alcoholism, just like periodic drinking is a form of alcoholism. . . .
>
> My wife had long gone to bed. I was sitting alone, drinking, lost in what I took to be deep thought. I realized suddenly, "Why I am thinking gibberish here—my mind is completely out of it." When I woke up the next morning, I got up and went to a hospital. Went straight into a treatment center.
>
> (HEW, 1976, p. 76)

Alcohol Dependence For many people, the pattern of alcoholism further includes physical dependence. As they use alcohol repeatedly, their body builds up a tolerance for it and they need to drink increasing amounts in order to feel any effects. They also experience withdrawal responses when they abstain from alcohol. When they try to stop drinking, within hours their hands, tongue, and eyelids begin to shake noticeably. They feel weak and nauseated. They sweat and vomit. Their heart beats volving five or more drinks in a row, for both men and women, despite the fact that women's bodies metabolize alcohol more slowly than men's.

By more properly defining binge drinking, researchers and the community at large can better estimate the prevalence of this behavior in women. In the Wechsler study alone, changing the cutoff increased the number of women identified as binge drinkers by 6 percent overall, from 33 percent to 39 percent. Moreover, the study's findings should probably alert college counselors to adjust their procedures and the advice they offer. The researchers suggest, "Women should be advised that they cannot drink at the same level as men without risking greater health and behavioral consequences [and] college alcohol educators should . . . alert women to the heightened risks they run in matching male drinking patterns" (Wechsler et al., 1995, p. 984).

Some cultures seem to encourage binge drinking. During Germany's 16-day "Oktoberfest," 5 million liters of beer are served to thousands of revelers.

Using the same sample, Wechsler and his colleagues (1995) tried to determine the individual correlates of college binge drinking. They found that the strongest predictors of this pattern were residence in a fraternity or sorority, commitment to a party-centered lifestyle, and engagement in risky behaviors, such as smoking marijuana, having multiple sex partners, and smoking cigarettes. Other variables—including being male, white, involved in athletics, and a business major—also raised the risk of binge drinking. As the researchers note, it is of great concern "that college binge drinking is tied to some of the most desired aspects of American college life—parties, social lives, dormitory living, athletics, and interaction with friends" (Wechsler et al., 1995, p. 925). Finally, the study found that students who were binge drinkers in high school were more likely than other students to follow the pattern in college.

Of course, the results of these studies are based on self-administered questionnaires, and thus may reflect biased responding. Perhaps binge drinkers were more likely than nondrinkers to respond to the questionnaire. Still, the implication of this and related work is clear: college drinking, certainly binge drinking, requires the attention of both higher education and public health administrators. The problem apparently extends to more persons, and causes more dysfunction and harm, than was previously recognized. At the very least, it is a problem whose research time has come.

rapidly and their blood pressure rises. They may also become anxious, depressed, unable to sleep, or irritable (Thompson et al., 1995).

A small percentage of people who are dependent on alcohol also experience a particularly dramatic withdrawal reaction, *alcohol withdrawal delirium,* or ***delirium tremens*** ("the DT's"). Beginning within three days after they stop or reduce drinking, they become delirious and have terrifying visual hallucinations. They may believe they are seeing small frightening animals or objects moving about rapidly, perhaps pursuing them or crawling on them. Mark Twain gave a classic picture of delirium tremens in Huckleberry Finn's description of his father:

> **I** don't know how long I was asleep, but . . . there was an awful scream and I was up. There was Pap looking wild, and skipping around every which way and yelling about snakes. He said they was crawling up on his legs; and then he would give a jump and scream, and say one had bit him on the cheek—but I couldn't see no snakes. He started and run round . . . hollering "Take him off! he's biting me on the neck!" I never see a man look so wild in the eyes. Pretty soon he was all fagged out, and fell down panting; then he rolled over . . . kicking things every which way, and striking and grabbing at the air with his hands, and screaming . . . there was devils a-hold of him. He wore out by and by. . . . He says . . .

> "Tramp-tramp-tramp: that's the dead; tramp-tramp-tramp; they're coming after me; but I won't go. Oh, they're here; don't touch me . . . they're cold; let go . . ."
>
> Then he went down on all fours and crawled off, begging them to let him alone. . . .
>
> *(Twain, 1885)*

Some people who experience delirium tremens also have seizures and lose consciousness and are vulnerable to strokes and other life-threatening problems. Like most other alcohol withdrawal symptoms, the DT's usually run their course in two to three days. However, as many as 5 percent of sufferers may die from this pattern or from a related severe withdrawal reaction (Cornish et al., 1995; Schuckit, 1987).

Another dramatic and relatively rare withdrawal reaction, *alcohol-induced psychotic disorder,* consists of *delusions,* ideas that have no basis in fact, or *auditory hallucinations,* such as imaginary voices that say demeaning or hostile things. Such reactions usually develop within two days after the person stops drinking and may last for weeks or months.

The Personal and Social Impact of Alcohol and Alcoholism Alcoholism destroys millions of families, social relationships, and careers. Medical treatment, lost productivity, and potential losses due to premature deaths from alcoholism have been estimated to cost society as much as $136 billion annually (Cornish et al., 1995). Alcohol is also a factor in more than a third of all suicides, homicides, assaults, rapes, and accidental deaths, including close to half of all fatal automobile accidents in the United States (Painter, 1992). Altogether, intoxicated drivers are responsible for 23,000 deaths each year—an average of one alcohol-related death every 23 minutes (OSAP, 1991). Similarly, intoxicated pedestrians are 4 times more likely than sober pedestrians to be hit by a car (Painter, 1992).

Alcoholism has serious effects as well on the 28 to 34 million children of persons with this disorder. They are likely to grow up in a family with disharmony and perhaps sexual and other physical abuse (Mathew et al., 1993; Velleman & Orford, 1993; Painter, 1992). During both childhood and adulthood, they are at increased risk for psychological problems, particularly anxiety, depression, phobias, and substance-related disorders (Hill & Muka, 1996). They may also display low self-esteem, poor communication skills, poor sociability, and an increased likelihood of marital instability (Kelly & Myers, 1996; Greenfield et al., 1993; Mathew et al., 1993).

Chronic and excessive alcohol consumption can also seriously damage one's physical health. It so overworks the liver, for example, that it can cause fatal damage. An excessive intake of alcohol results in a "fatty liver," or accumulation of excess fat. If excessive alcohol intake continues for years, a person may further develop an irreversible condition called ***cirrhosis,*** in which the liver becomes scarred, forms fibrous tissue, and begins to change its anatomy and functioning. Blood fails to flow through it properly, and major complications follow. Cirrhosis is the seventh most frequent cause of death in the United States, accounting for around 28,000 deaths each year (Ray & Ksir, 1993; ADAMHA, 1987); and a large percentage of these cases result from chronic alcohol use.

Alcohol abuse and dependence may cause other medical problems as well. Alcohol can depress heart functioning and damage heart muscle fibers and over time may lead to heart failure, irregularities of functioning, or blood clots. It can also impair the immune responses, increasing a person's susceptibility to cancer and to bacterial infections, and speeding the onset of AIDS after infection (NIAAA, 1992).

Chronic excessive drinking also poses major problems in nutrition. Alcohol satiates people and lowers their intake of other foods, but has virtually no food value itself. As a result, chronic drinkers are likely to become malnourished, their bodies weak, tired, and highly vulnerable to disease.

The vitamin and mineral deficiencies of persons with alcoholism may also cause certain mental disorders. An alcohol-related deficiency of vitamin B (thiamine), for example, may cause ***Wernicke's encephalopathy,*** a potentially fatal neurological disease characterized by confusion, excitement, delirium, double vision, and other eye-movement abnormalities (Dodd et al., 1996). Untreated, Wernicke's encephalopathy may develop into ***Korsakoff's syndrome*** (also called *alcohol-induced persisting amnestic disorder*), marked by extreme confusion, memory impairment, and other neurological symptoms (Kopelman, 1995). People with Korsakoff's syndrome cannot remember the past or learn new information, and may make up for their memory loss by ***confabulating***—spontaneously reciting made-up events to fill in the gaps.

Finally, women who drink during pregnancy place the health of their fetuses at risk. Even low alcohol use during pregnancy may cause a baby to be born with ***fetal alcohol syndrome,*** a pattern of abnormalities that can include mental retardation, hyperactivity, head and face deformities, heart defects and other organ malfunctions, and retarded growth (Goldstein, 1994; Ray & Ksir, 1993). It has been estimated that in the overall population fewer than 3 of every 1,000 births are characterized by this syndrome. The rate increases to as many as 29 of every 1,000 births among women who are problem drinkers (Ray & Ksir, 1993). Babies of women who drink heavily throughout their pregnancy are at greatest risk. In addition, heavy drinking early in pregnancy often leads to a miscarriage.

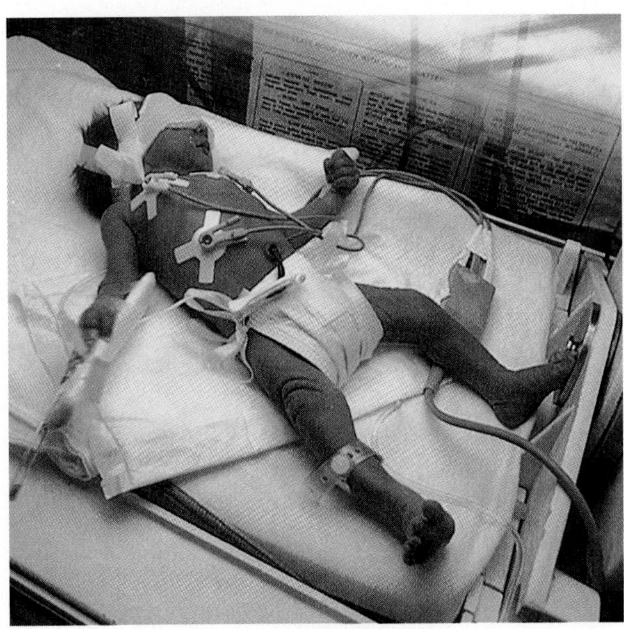

A woman who drinks during pregnancy risks harming her fetus. More than 50,000 babies are born with alcohol-related problems in the United States each year. Many of these babies suffer from "fetal alcohol syndrome." Ingestion of cocaine, heroin, and certain other drugs during pregnancy may also severely affect the psychological and physical development of babies.

Sedative-Hypnotic Drugs

Sedative-hypnotic drugs produce feelings of relaxation and drowsiness. At relatively low dosages, they have a calming or sedative effect. At higher ones, they are sleep inducers, or hypnotics. The drugs are also called ***anxiolytic*** (meaning "anxiety-reducing") ***drugs.*** They include *barbiturates* and *benzodiazepines.*

Barbiturates First discovered in Germany more than 100 years ago, ***barbiturates*** were widely prescribed throughout the first half of the twentieth century to combat anxiety and to help people sleep. Despite the emergence of the safer benzodiazepines, some physicians still prescribe them, especially for sleep problems. Many dangers attend the use of barbiturates, however, not the least of which is their potential for abuse and dependence (see Table 13-2). Several thousand deaths a year are caused by accidental or suicidal overdoses. Still other sedative-hypnotic drugs, including ***methaqualone*** (trade name Quaalude), act on the brain in barbiturate-like ways and can lead to similar forms of abuse or dependence.

Barbiturates are usually taken in pill or capsule form. In low doses they reduce a person's level of excitement in the same way that alcohol does, by binding to neuron receptors that normally receive the inhibitory neurotransmitter GABA and increasing GABA's synaptic activity at those receptors (Frey et al., 1995; Morgan & London, 1995). Not surprisingly, then, alcohol and its derivatives were used widely as sedative-hypnotic drugs before the development of barbiturates. People can get intoxicated from large doses of barbiturates, just as they do from alcohol. And, like alcohol, barbiturates are metabolized primarily in the liver (Nishino et al., 1995).

At high doses, barbiturates also depress the ***reticular formation,*** the body's arousal center, which is responsible for keeping people awake, thus causing the person to get sleepy. At still higher doses, they depress spinal reflexes and muscles and are often used as surgical anesthetics. At too high a level, they cause respiratory failure and low blood pressure and can lead to coma and death.

Even when physicians prescribe barbiturates for their hypnotic effects, patients soon discover their sedative qualities. As the patient starts taking the drug to help cope with daily problems, their use can become execssive and can quickly lead to abuse. A person may feel unable to stop or reduce the use of barbiturates and may spend much of the day intoxicated. Social and occupational functioning may be disrupted by quarrels, alienation, and poor job performance, all stemming from the effects of the drug.

Excessive barbiturate use can further lead to dependence. Tolerance for the drug increases very rapidly; increasing amounts become necessary to calm people down or help them to sleep. Moreover, abstaining from the drug may cause withdrawal symptoms that are similar to those seen in alcoholism, such as nausea, weakness, anxiety, depression, and sleep problems. In extreme cases the withdrawal reaction may resemble delirium tremens (here called *barbiturate withdrawal delirium*). Barbiturate withdrawal is one of the most dangerous forms of drug withdrawal, for it sends some people into convulsions.

One of the great dangers of barbiturate dependence is that the lethal dose of the drug remains the same even while the body is rapidly building up a tolerance for its other effects (Landry, 1994; Gold, 1986). In a common and tragic scenario, once the initial barbiturate dose prescribed by a physician stops working, a person decides independently to keep increasing it every few weeks. Eventually the person ingests a dose that may very well prove fatal.

Benzodiazepines As we saw in Chapter 6, ***benzodiazepines,*** the antianxiety drugs discovered in the 1950s, are the most popular sedative-hypnotic drugs available. Dozens are in clinical use, including Xanax, Valium, and Librium (Frey et al., 1995). Like alcohol and barbiturates, they calm people by binding to neuron receptors that normally receive the inhibitory neurotransmitter GABA and by increasing GABA's synaptic activity at those receptors. They can, however, relieve anxiety without

TABLE 13-2 Risks and Consequences of Drug Misuse

	Intoxication Potential	*Dependency Potential*	*Risk of Organ Damage or Death*	*Risk of Severe Social or Economic Consequences*	*Risk of Severe or Long-Lasting Mental and Behavioral Change*
Opioids	High	High	Low	High	Low to Moderate
Sedative-hypnotics					
Barbiturates	Moderate	Moderate to High	Moderate to High	Moderate to High	Low
Benzodiazepines	Moderate	Low	Low	Low	Low
Stimulants (cocaine, amphetamines)	High	High	Moderate	Low to Moderate	Moderate to High
Alcohol	High	Moderate	High	High	High
Cannabis	High	Low to Moderate	Low	Low to Moderate	Low
Mixed drug classes	High	High	High	High	High

Source: APA, 1994; Gold, 1986, p. 28.

making people as drowsy as other kinds of sedative-hypnotics. They are less likely to depress respiratory functioning, so they are less likely to cause death by overdose (Nishino et al., 1995).

When benzodiazepines first appeared, they seemed so safe and effective that physicians prescribed them readily, and their use proliferated. Eventually it became apparent that in high enough doses the drugs can cause intoxication and even lead to abuse or dependence (Ashton, 1995; Cornish et al., 1995; Palacios & Cortés, 1995). More than 1 percent of the adult population in the United States is estimated to abuse or become physically dependent on antianxiety drugs at some point in their lives (Anthony et al., 1995; APA, 1994) and thus become subject to some of the same dangers that researchers have identified in barbiturate misuse.

Opioids

Opioids include opium and the drugs derived from it, such as heroin, morphine, and codeine. A natural substance from the sap of the opium poppy, ***opium*** itself has been in use for thousands of years. In the past it was used widely in the treatment of medical disorders because of its ability to reduce both physical and emotional pain. Physicians eventually discovered, however, that the drug was physically addictive.

In 1804 a new substance, ***morphine,*** was derived from opium by the German chemist Frederic Serturner. It relieved pain even more effectively than opium. In addition, morphine helped quiet people and put them to sleep (thus its name, derived from Morpheus, the Greek god of sleep). Believing that morphine was free of opium's addictive properties, physicians began to use it widely. Unfortunately, as eventually became clear, repeated administrations of morphine could also lead to addiction. So many wounded soldiers in the United States received morphine injections during the Civil War that morphine addiction became known as "soldiers' disease."

In 1898 morphine was converted into yet another new pain reliever, ***heroin.*** For several years heroin was viewed as a wonder drug and was used as a cough medicine and for other medicinal purposes. Eventually, however, physicians recognized that heroin is even more addictive than the other opioids. By 1917 the U.S. Congress concluded that all drugs derived from opium were addictive and passed a law making opioids illegal except for medical purposes.

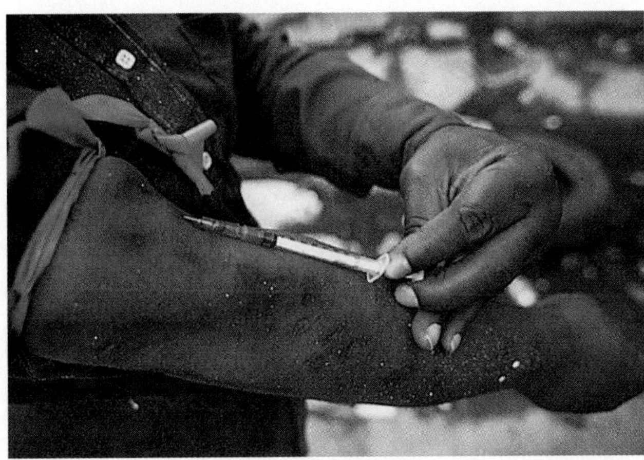

Opioids may be taken by mouth, inhaled, snorted, injected just beneath the surface of the skin, or, as here, injected intravenously. Those who share needles to inject themselves run the risk of developing AIDS or hepatitis; those who use unsterile equipment may develop skin abscesses.

New derivatives of opium have been discovered, and synthetic (laboratory-blended) opioids such as ***methadone*** have also been developed. All these various opioid drugs are known collectively as ***narcotics.*** Each has its own potency, speed of action, and tolerance level. Morphine and codeine have become the primary medical narcotics, usually prescribed to relieve pain. Heroin has remained illegal in the United States under all circumstances.

Narcotics may be smoked, inhaled, snorted, injected by needle just beneath the skin ("skin popped"), or injected directly into the bloodstream ("mainlined") (see Table 13-3). An injection quickly brings on a ***rush***—a spasm of warmth and ecstasy that is sometimes compared with orgasm. The brief spasm is followed by several hours of a pleasant feeling called a ***high*** or ***nod.*** During a high, the drug user feels relaxed and euphoric, and unconcerned about food, sex, or other bodily needs.

Heroin and other opioids create these effects by depressing the central nervous system, particularly the centers that generate emotion. The drugs are received at brain receptor sites that ordinarily receive ***endorphins***—neurotransmitters that help relieve pain and reduce emotional tension (Snyder, 1991, 1986; Trujillo & Akil, 1991) (see Figure 13-3). When neurons at these receptor sites receive opioids, they fire and produce pleasurable and calming feelings just as they would do if they were receiving endorphins. In addition to pain relief, sedation, and mood changes, opioids cause nausea, constriction of the pupils of the eyes ("pinpoint pupils"), and constipation, bodily reactions that can also be brought about by a heightened release of endorphins in the brain.

Heroin Abuse and Dependence

It takes only a few weeks of repeated heroin use for people to be caught in a pattern of abuse: the drug becomes the center of

TABLE 13-3 Methods of Taking Substances

Method	*Route*	*Time to Reach Brain*
Inhaling	Drug in vapor form is inhaled through mouth and lungs into circulatory system	7 seconds
Snorting	Drug in powdered form is snorted into the nose. Some of the drug lands on the nasal mucous membranes, is absorbed by blood vessels, and enters the bloodstream.	4 minutes
Injection	Drug in liquid form directly enters the body through a needle. Injection may be intravenous or intramuscular (subcutaneous).	20 seconds (intravenous) 4 minutes (intramuscular)
Oral ingestion	Drug in solid or liquid form passes through esophagus and stomach and finally to the small intestines. It is absorbed by blood vessels in the intestines.	30 minutes
Other routes	Drugs can be absorbed through areas that contain mucous membranes. Drugs can be placed under the tongue, inserted anally and vaginally, and administered as eyedrops.	Variable

Source: Landry, 1994, p. 24.

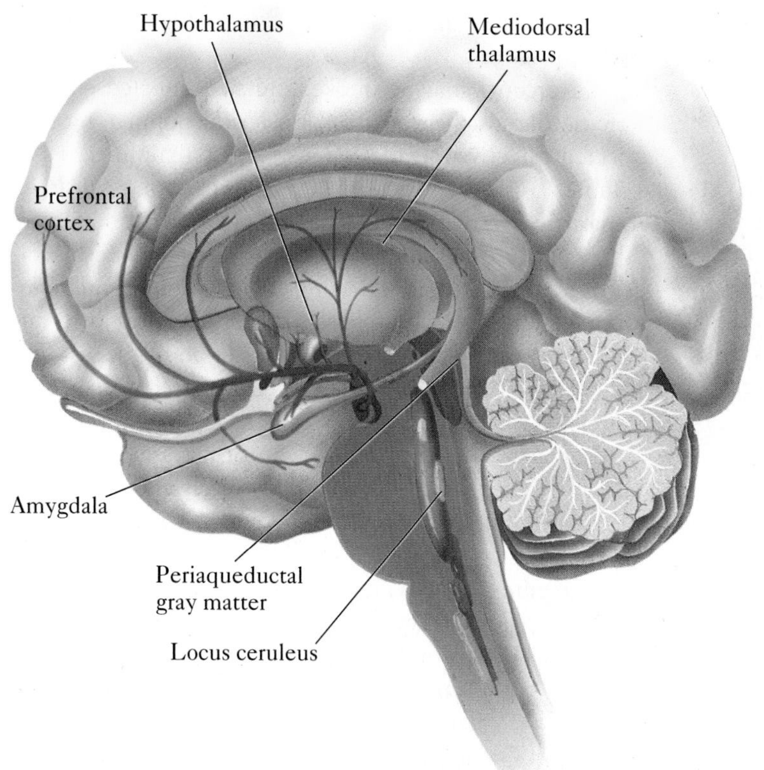

Figure 13-3 *The neural receptors to which opioids bind are most concentrated in the brain's emotion center, which includes the amygdala, hypothalamus, and locus ceruleus, and the pain center, which includes the mediodorsal thalamus and periaqueductal gray matter. (Adapted from Snyder, 1986, p. 49.)*

their lives, and social and occupational functioning deteriorates significantly. Most abusers also develop a dependence on heroin, quickly building up a tolerance for it and experiencing withdrawal symptoms when they abstain. The withdrawal symptoms initially are anxiety, restlessness, perspiration, and rapid breathing, and eventually include severe twitching, constant aches, painful gastrointestinal and muscle cramps, fever, acute vomiting and diarrhea, loss of appetite, high blood pressure, dehydration, and weight loss of up to 15 pounds.

Withdrawal distress usually peaks by the third day, then gradually subsides and disappears by the eighth day. A person in withdrawal can either wait the symptoms out (an extremely difficult and unpleasant ordeal) or end withdrawal by taking more heroin. Heroin taken at any time during withdrawal will quickly restore a feeling of physical and emotional well-being.

The character of drug taking eventually changes for people dependent on heroin. They soon need the drug just to maintain normal functioning and to avoid the distress of withdrawal, and they must continually increase their doses in order to achieve that state. The temporary high becomes less intense and less important (Goldstein, 1994). They may organize their lives around plans for getting their next dose. Many turn to criminal activities, such as theft and prostitution, to support their expensive "habit."

The Dangers of Heroin The most direct danger of heroin abuse is an overdose, which depresses the respiratory center in the brain, virtually paralyzing it and in many cases causing death. Death is particularly likely during sleep, when a person is unable to fight the effect by consciously working at breathing. People who resume the use of heroin after having abstained for a time often make the fatal mistake of taking the dose they used when they were last addicted. Because their bodies have been free of heroin for some time, however, they can no longer tolerate this high level. Each year approximately 1 percent of the untreated persons dependent on heroin and other opioids die under the drug's influence, usually from an overdose (APA, 1994).

Users run risks aside from the effects of the drug itself. Often profit-minded pushers mix heroin with a cheaper drug, such as a barbiturate or LSD, or even a deadly substance such as cyanide or battery acid. Addicted persons who use dirty needles and other unsterile equipment when they inject heroin are vulnerable to AIDS, hepatitis, and skin abscesses (O'Rourke, 1990; NIDA, 1987). In some areas of the United States the HIV infection rate among persons dependent on heroin is reported to be as high as 60 percent (APA, 1994). The drug *quinine* is often added to heroin to counteract potential infections. While quinine does help to some extent, too much of it may be lethal. Many deaths attributed to heroin may actually have been caused by a quinine-induced flooding of the lungs.

Surveys suggest that close to 1 percent of the adult population of the United States becomes addicted to heroin or other opioids at some time in their lives (APA, 1994). The number of addicted persons took a sharp turn upward during the 1960s and 1970s, and by the late 1970s it had reached more than half a million. Although this number declined in the 1980s, it apparently has risen again to more than 750,000 (Kleber, 1995; Elias, 1993). Of course, such statistics may well be understated, given the reluctance of many people to admit to an illegal activity (Maurer & Vogel, 1978).

Stimulants

Stimulants are substances that increase the activity of the central nervous system, resulting in increased blood pressure and heart rate and in an intensification of behavior, thought processes, and alertness. Among the most troublesome stimulants are cocaine and amphetamines, whose behavioral and emotional effects are virtually indistinguishable (Gawin & Ellinwood, 1988; Snyder, 1986). When users report different effects from the two, it is usually because they have ingested different amounts of the drugs. Two more widely used and legal stimulants are caffeine and nicotine (see Box 13-2).

Cocaine

Cocaine—the central active ingredient of the coca plant, found in South America—is the most powerful natural stimulant now known. The drug was first isolated from the plant in 1865. South American natives, however, have chewed the leaves of the plant since prehistoric times for the energy and alertness the drug content provides. Processed cocaine (*hydrochloride powder*) is an odorless, white, fluffy powder. For recreational use, it is most often snorted so that it is absorbed through the mucous membrane of the nose. Some users prefer the more powerful effects of injecting cocaine intravenously or smoking cocaine "base" in a pipe or cigarette.

> Sherlock Holmes took his bottle from the corner of the mantelpiece, and his hypodermic syringe from its neat morocco case. With his long white nervous fingers, he adjusted the delicate needle and rolled back his left shirtcuff. For some little time his eyes rested thoughtfully upon the sinewy forearm and wrist, all dotted and scarred with innumerable puncture-marks. Finally, he thrust the sharp point home, pressed down the tiny piston, and sank back into the velvet-lined armchair with a long sigh of satisfaction.
>
> Three times a day for many months I had witnessed this performance, but custom had not reconciled my mind to it. . . .
>
> "Which is it today," I asked, "morphine or cocaine?"
>
> He raised his eyes languidly from the old black-letter volume which he had opened.
>
> "It is cocaine," he said, "a seven-per-cent solution. Would you care to try it?"
>
> "No, indeed," I answered brusquely. "My constitution has not got over the Afghan campaign yet. I cannot afford to throw any extra strain upon it."
>
> He smiled at my vehemence. "Perhaps you are right, Watson," he said. "I suppose that its influence is physically a bad one. I find it, however, so transcendently stimulating and clarifying to the mind that its secondary action is a matter of small moment."
>
> "But consider!" I said earnestly. "Count the cost! Your brain may, as you say, be roused and excited, but it is a pathological and morbid process which involves increased tissue-change and . . . a permanent weakness. You know, too, what a black reaction comes upon you. Surely, the game is hardly worth the candle."
>
> *(Doyle, 1938, pp. 91–92)*

For years the prevailing opinion of cocaine was that it posed few significant problems aside from intoxication and occasional temporary psychosis. Like Sherlock Holmes, many people believed that the benefits outweighed the costs. Only in recent years have researchers recognized its potential for harm and developed a clearer understanding of how cocaine produces its effects. This insight was triggered by a dramatic increase in the drug's popularity and in problems related to its use. In the early 1960s an estimated 10,000 persons in the United States had tried cocaine; today more than 21 million people have tried it (SAMHSA, 1996). Indeed, one and a half million people are currently caught in a pattern of cocaine abuse or dependence—most of them teenagers or young adults (SAMHSA, 1996; Kleber, 1995) Altogether, close to 3 percent of the population have been dependent on cocaine at some point in their lives (Anthony et al., 1995).

Cocaine brings on a euphoric rush of well-being and confidence. Given a high enough dose, this rush can be almost orgasmic, like that produced by heroin. Initially cocaine stimulates the higher centers of the central nervous system, making its users feel excited, energetic, talkative, and even euphoric. As more is taken, it stimulates other centers of the central nervous system, producing a faster pulse, higher blood pressure, faster and deeper breathing, and further arousal and wakefulness. Cocaine apparently produces these effects by increasing supplies

BOX 13-2 Tobacco and Nicotine: A Powerful Addiction

Smoking tobacco has been an accepted practice for centuries, but its dangers are well documented. More than 410,000 people die each year in the United States as a result of smoking (Farley, 1994; Report of the Surgeon General, 1990, 1988). Pregnant women who smoke are more likely than nonsmokers to deliver prematurely and to have babies who are underweight (Goldstein, 1994). Smoking is directly associated with high blood pressure, coronary heart disease, lung disease, cancer, stroke, and other deadly medical problems. People who smoke two packs a day are twenty-two times as likely to die of lung cancer as nonsmokers. Moreover, nonsmokers who inhale cigarette smoke from the environment also have an elevated risk of lung cancer and other diseases (Report of the Surgeon General, 1987).

Approximately 29 percent of Americans over the age of 12 are regular smokers (SAMHSA, 1996). Although this rate represents a drop of 40 percent since the early 1960s, it is still alarming (Goldstein, 1994). Still more alarming is recent news that smoking may actually be increasing among teenagers. Surveys suggest that around 17 percent of all teenagers smoke regularly (Johnson et al., 1993), and 3,000 teens light up for the first time each day (Kessler, 1995). Over a third of teenagers report having smoked within the past month (Johnson et al., 1996).

Most adult smokers know that smoking is unhealthful and would rather not do it. So why do they continue to smoke? Because, as the surgeon general declared in 1988, ***nicotine,*** the active substance in tobacco and a stimulant of the central nervous system, is as addictive as heroin, perhaps even more so. Nicotine acts on the same reward center in the brain as amphetamines and cocaine do, mimicking their pleasurable but addictive effects (McGehee et al., 1995; Stolerman & Jarvis, 1995). Inhaling a puff of cigarette smoke delivers a dose of nicotine to the brain faster than it could be delivered by injection into the bloodstream, and it is believed to bind directly to receptors in the brain, which soon becomes dependent on it. When regular smokers abstain, they experience *withdrawal* symptoms—irritability, increased appetite, sleep disturbances, decreased metabolic rate, cognitive difficulties, and a powerful desire to smoke. Smokers also develop a tolerance for nicotine and must increase their consumption in order to achieve the same psychological and physiological results and to avoid withdrawal.

The acceptability of smoking is on the decline. Still, most people are comfortable admitting that they smoke and openly look for ways to quit. This situation has created a ready market for products and techniques to help people kick the habit. Most of these methods do not work very well; much depends on the motivation of the smoker. Most smokers who quit permanently are successful only after several failed attempts (Spanier et al., 1996). Too many smokers still seem to find that the immediate pleasure they experience outweighs the fears of long-term consequences. In fact, despite widespread antismoking campaigns, many smokers tend to underestimate the magnitude of the health risks they face (Gibbons, Eggleston, & Benthin, 1997; Strecher, Kreuter, & Kobrin, 1995). Whether the person succeeds at quitting also depends on factors such as stress, social support, family members who smoke, self-confidence, gender, and availability of information (Tunstal, Ginsberg, & Hall, 1985). Self-help kits, informational pamphlets, commercial programs, and support groups are at most modestly helpful. Most people who do stop smoking after receiving such interventions start smoking again within one year (Hall et al., 1985).

The most successful treatments for nicotine addiction have been behavioral therapies and biological interventions. Using *aversion therapy,* therapists have on the

of the neurotransmitter *dopamine* at key neurons throughout the brain (see Figure 13-4). More precisely, cocaine prevents the neurons that release dopamine from reabsorbing it, as they normally would do. So excessive amounts of dopamine travel to receiving neurons throughout the central nervous system and overstimulate them. In addition, cocaine appears to facilitate the release of the neurotransmitters *norepinephrine* and *serotonin* in certain areas of the brain (Volkow et al., 1997; Biegon et al., 1995; Meyer, 1995).

If a high dose of cocaine is taken, the stimulation of the central nervous system will result in poor muscle coordination, grandiosity, declining judgment, anger, aggression, compulsive behavior, anxiety, and confusion—

average been able to foster a two-year abstinence from smoking in about half of cases. The most common form of aversion therapy is ***rapid smoking.*** The smoker sits in a closed room and puffs quickly on a cigarette, as often as once every six seconds, until the smoker begins to feel ill and cannot take another puff. The feelings of illness become associated with smoking, and the smoker experiences an aversive reaction to cigarettes (Baker & Brandon, 1988).

An Albanian boy in Kosovo is already acquainted with the powers of nicotine.

A common intervention is the use of ***nicotine gum,*** which contains a high level of nicotine that is released as the smoker chews. Theoretically, people who ingest nicotine by chewing no longer need to smoke, and the reinforcing effects of smoking are removed. Research suggests that this approach does improve a smoker's chances of long-term abstinence, especially when it is combined with behavioral therapies (Fortmann & Killen, 1995). The more nicotine-dependent the smoker, the more effective the use of nicotine gum (Jarvik & Schneider, 1984).

A similar biological approach is the ***nicotine patch,*** which is attached to the skin like a Band-Aid. Its nicotine content is absorbed through the skin throughout the day, supposedly easing withdrawal and leaving the smoker with less need for nicotine. Research indicates that the patch often helps people abstain from or cut down on cigarette smoking (Stapleton et al., 1995; Goldstein, 1994). It may be particularly effective in conjunction with behavioral counseling and nicotine gum (Kornitzer et al., 1995).

Nicotine nasal spray is a new biological approach. The spray delivers nicotine much more rapidly than other replacement methods can, and may stimulate the rapid uptake of nicotine in the brain that occurs with smoking (Perkins et al., 1996). Nicotine nasal spray can be used several times an hour, whenever the craving for a cigarette arises. While the spray may be as effective as the patch or gum, it is also potentially addictive (FDA, 1996). Smokers who use a nicotine nasal spray may be trading one habit for another.

Nicotine patches, gum, and nasal sprays are all effective, but they have a big drawback—they do not automatically lead to a decrease in nicotine consumption. Some former smokers have trouble giving up their new sources of nicotine (Hurt et al., 1995). These treatments also have little or no effect on the critical component of nicotine withdrawal: the craving for a cigarette. Many smokers report that the craving is the most debilitating obstacle to quitting (Drobes & Tiffany, 1997; Paty et al., 1997).

The blood pressure drug *clonidine* has undergone testing as a possible means of reducing craving and other symptoms of withdrawal from nicotine and other addictive substances, and has shown some promise (Glassman et al., 1984), but it is no magic pill. The more one smokes, the harder it is to quit. On the positive side, however, former smokers' risk of disease and death decreases steadily the longer they abstain from smoking (Goldstein, 1994; Jaffe, 1985). For those who are able to take the long view, this assurance may be a powerful motivator. In the meantime, more than 1,000 people die of smoking-related diseases each day.

all symptoms of ***cocaine intoxication.*** Some people experience hallucinations or delusions, or both, a condition known as ***cocaine-induced psychotic disorder*** (Rosse et al., 1993; Yudofsky, Silver, & Hales, 1993).

> A young man described how, after free-basing, he went to his closet to get his clothes, but his suit asked him, "What do you want?" Afraid, he walked toward the door, which told him, "Get back!" Retreating, he then heard the sofa say, "If you sit on me, I'll kick your ass." With a sense of impending doom, intense anxiety, and momentary panic, the young man ran to the hospital where he received help.
>
> *(Allen, 1985, pp. 19–20)*

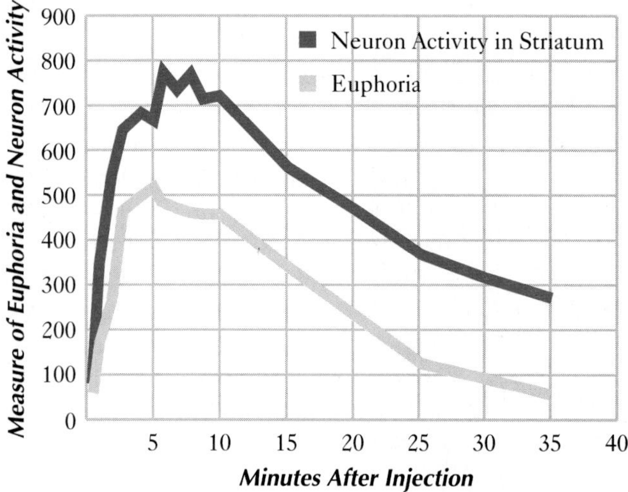

Figure 13-4 *Studies indicate that the subjective experiences of euphoria following a cocaine injection closely parallel cocaine's action at dopamine-using neurons in the brain's striatum region. The peak experience of euphoria seems to occur at around the same time as the peak of activity in the striatum (Fowler, Volkow, & Wolf, 1994, p. 110; Cook, Jeffcoat, & Perez-Reyes, 1985).*

As the symptoms caused by cocaine subside, the user often experiences a depression-like letdown, popularly called "crashing," which may be accompanied by headaches, dizziness, and fainting (Cornish et al., 1995). For occasional users, the effects of cocaine usually disappear within twenty-four hours. The effects may, however, last longer for those who have taken an excessive dose. They may sink into an extended stupor, deep sleep, or, in some cases, coma (Coambs & McAndrews, 1994).

Cocaine Abuse and Dependence

An extended period of cocaine use may lead to a pattern of abuse in which the person is intoxicated throughout the day and functions poorly in social and occupational spheres. Chronic abuse may also result in cognitive impairments such as short-term memory and attention deficits (Rosselli & Ardila, 1996; Washton & Gold, 1984). A physical dependence may also develop, so that more cocaine is needed to achieve the desired effects and abstinence results in significant feelings of depression, fatigue, sleep problems, irritability, and anxiety (APA, 1994). These withdrawal symptoms may last for weeks or even months.

Despite the pleasurable reinforcing properties of cocaine, in the past cocaine abuse and dependence were limited by its high cost. In addition, because it was usually snorted, its ingestion was limited by the constriction of nasal blood vessels and so had less powerful effects than either injection or smoking. Since 1984, however, newer, more powerful, and sometimes cheaper forms of cocaine have gained favor among users and have produced an enormous increase in abuse and dependence. Currently one user in five falls into a pattern of abuse or dependence. Many people now use the technique of ***free-basing,*** in which the pure cocaine basic alkaloid is chemically separated or "freed" from processed cocaine, vaporized by heat from a flame, and inhaled with a pipe. And millions more use crack, a powerful ready-to-smoke free-base cocaine.

Crack is cocaine that has been boiled down into crystalline balls. It is smoked with a special crack pipe. This form of cocaine makes a crackling sound when it is smoked, hence the name. Crack is sold in small quantities at a relatively low cost. Some cities have seen veritable crack epidemics among people who previously could not have afforded cocaine. Approximately one percent of high school seniors report using crack within the past year (NIDA, 1996). Although this rate represents a sizable drop from the 1986 rate of 4 percent, the crack epi-

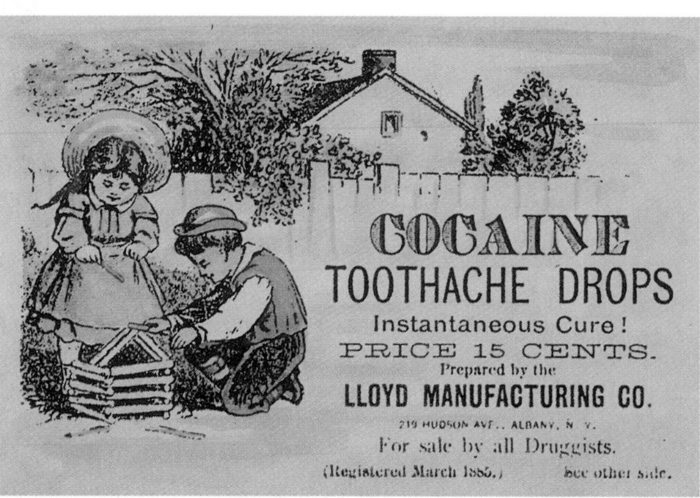

Legal in the United States until 1914, cocaine was an ingredient in various over-the-counter medicines, such as Cocaine Toothache Drops. This 1885 ad shows that it was used to treat children as well as adults. Similarly, cocaine was part of Coca-Cola's formula until 1903.

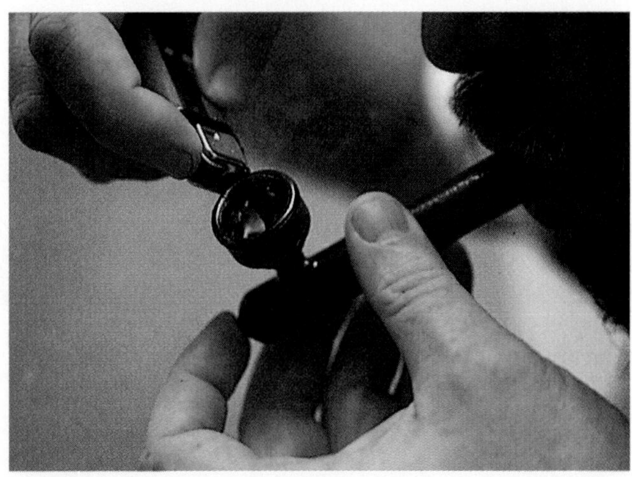

Crack, a powerful form of free-base cocaine, is produced by boiling cocaine down into crystalline balls and is smoked with a special crack pipe.

demic is still very disturbing, particularly because of the unusual degree of violent crime and risky sex-for-drugs exchanges reported in the crack-using population (Balshem et al., 1992). The crack epidemic is also problematic in that it is concentrated in poor urban areas (OSAP, 1991).

The Dangers of Cocaine Cocaine poses serious dangers. Aside from its effects on psychological functioning, cocaine turns out to be highly dangerous to one's physical well-being. Its widespread use in increasingly powerful forms has caused the annual number of cocaine-related emergency room incidents in the United States to multiply thirty-five times since 1982, from around 4,000 cases to more than 140,000 (DAWN, 1996). In addition, it has been linked to as many as 20 percent of all suicides by persons under 61 years of age (Marzuk et al., 1992).

The most obvious danger of cocaine comes from overdose. Excessive doses have a strong effect on the respiratory center of the brain, at first stimulating it and then depressing it, possibly to the point of respiratory failure and death. Cocaine also stimulates the brain center that controls body temperature. Because the drug both raises a person's temperature and constricts the blood vessels in the skin, the person cannot perspire sufficiently. The dangerously high body temperature that results can lead to death.

Cocaine can also create significant, even fatal heart problems. The heart beats rapidly and irregularly under the drug's influence and at the same time must work harder to pump blood through cocaine-constricted blood vessels. For some people, this strain on the heart causes a brain seizure that brings breathing or heart functioning to a sudden halt. These effects may be more common in people who have taken a high dose of cocaine and who have a history of cocaine abuse, but they also occur in casual cocaine users (Gold, 1986). Such was the case with Len Bias, the well-known college basketball player who died of these effects some years back, apparently after ingesting only a moderate amount of cocaine.

Pregnant women who use cocaine also run serious risks (DiPietro et al., 1995; Scherling, 1994). Because cocaine penetrates fetal brain tissue and also restricts blood supply to the placenta (depriving the fetus of oxygen), the baby may be born with ***fetal cocaine syndrome.*** This highly damaging syndrome is characterized by altered immune function, learning deficits, decreased activity in the brain's dopamine system, and abnormal thyroid size (Adler, 1992).

Amphetamines

The ***amphetamines*** are stimulant drugs that are manufactured in the laboratory. Some common ones are amphetamine (Benzedrine), dextroamphetamine (Dexedrine), and methamphetamine (Methedrine). First synthesized by the chemist Gordon Alles in the 1930s for use in the treatment of asthma, these drugs soon became popular among people trying to lose weight; athletes seeking an extra burst of energy; soldiers, truck drivers, and pilots trying to stay awake; and students studying for exams through the night. Today they are prescribed much more sparingly. The drugs are far too dangerous to be used so casually (Fawcett & Busch, 1995). At the same time, there are indications that the illicit use of amphetamines is currently increasing (Baberg, Nelesen, & Dimsdale, 1996).

Amphetamines are most often taken in pill or capsule form, although some people inject the drug intravenously for a quicker, more powerful impact. Others ingest the drug in such forms as "ice" and "crank," counterparts of free-basing cocaine and crack, respectively.

Like cocaine, amphetamines increase energy and alertness and reduce appetite in low doses; produce a rush, intoxication, and psychosis in high doses; and cause an emotional letdown as they leave the person's body. Also like cocaine, amphetamines stimulate the central nervous system by increasing the release of the neurotransmitters dopamine, norepinephrine, and serotonin from neurons throughout the brain, although amphetamines achieve this effect by somewhat different actions than cocaine (Fawcett & Busch, 1995; Nestler et al., 1995).

Tolerance to amphetamines builds so quickly that it is easy to become ensnared in a pattern of amphetamine dependence. People who start using the drug to reduce their appetite and weight may soon find they are as hungry as ever, and increase their dose in response. Similarly, athletes who use amphetamines to increase their energy may find before long that larger and larger amounts of the drug are needed. So-called speed freaks who pop pills all day for days at a time have built a tolerance so high that they now take as much as 200 times their initial amphetamine dose. When persons who chronically abuse the drug stop taking it, they enter the state of deep depression and extended sleep that also characterizes withdrawal from cocaine. Around 2 percent of the population in the United States have been dependent on amphetamines at some point in their lives (Anthony et al., 1995).

Caffeine

Caffeine is the world's most widely used stimulant (Chou, 1992). Seventy-five percent of all caffeine is taken in the form of coffee (from the coffee bean); the rest is consumed in tea (from the tea leaf), cola (from the kola nut), and chocolate (from the cocoa bean), and in its purified form in numerous prescription and over-the-counter medications, such as Excedrin (Chou, 1992; Johnson-Greene et al., 1988). Americans consume between 15 and 45 million pounds of caffeine annually (Chou, 1992; Julien, 1988).

Research has revealed that 99 percent of caffeine is absorbed by the body and that it reaches its peak concentration within an hour (Julien, 1988). It acts as a stimulant of the central nervous system, again producing a release of the neurotransmitters dopamine, serotonin, and norepinephrine in the brain (Benowitz, 1990). Thus it increases vigilance and arousal and general motor activity, and reduces fatigue. It also disrupts the performance of complex motor tasks and may interfere with both the duration and quality of sleep (Chou, 1992; Jacobson & Thurman-Lacey, 1992). Heart rate also decreases with moderate amounts of consumption, respiration increases, and the gastric acid secreted by the stomach increases (Benowitz, 1990; Levitt, 1975).

More than two to three cups of brewed coffee (250 milligrams of caffeine) can produce ***caffeine intoxication,*** which may include such symptoms as restlessness, nervousness, anxiety, stomach disturbances, twitching, and increased heart rate (APA, 1994). Grand mal seizures and fatal respiratory failure or circulatory failure can occur at doses in excess of 10 grams of caffeine (about 100 cups of coffee).

Research has increasingly linked caffeine to a withdrawal syndrome in some persons. Kenneth Silverman and his colleagues (1992) demonstrated that the abrupt cessation of caffeine by persons who consume even low amounts (two and a half cups of coffee daily or seven cans of cola) can cause significant withdrawal symptoms. In a six-day study the researchers had sixty-two adult subjects consume their usual caffeine-filled drinks and foods for two days, then refrain from all caffeine foods for two days while taking placebo pills that they thought contained caffeine, and then refrain from caffeine foods for two days while taking actual caffeine pills. More subjects experienced painful headaches (52 percent), depression (11 percent), anxiety (8 percent), and fatigue (8 percent) during the two-day placebo period than during the caffeine periods. In addition, more subjects reported using unauthorized medications (13 percent) and performed more slowly on a tapping task during the placebo period than during the caffeine periods.

The widespread and casual use of caffeine has spurred much debate on its effects. As public awareness of possible health risks has increased, researchers have observed a decline in caffeine consumption. The International Coffee Organization reports that around half of Americans now drink coffee, whereas 80 percent did so in 1983 (Chou, 1992).

Investigators often measure caffeine intake by coffee consumption, yet coffee also contains other chemicals that may be dangerous to one's health. Thus, although some studies hint at links between caffeine and cancer (particularly pancreatic cancer), clear evidence does not yet exist. Similarly, studies demonstrating correlations between caffeine consumption and heart rhythm irregularities (arrhythmias) or high cholesterol levels have proved unreliable (Hirsch et al., 1989; Rosmarin, 1989). Caffeine does, however, appear to cause at least a slight increase in blood pressure over time in regular caffeine users, and a larger but short-lived increase during the first few days of consumption by new users of caffeine (Friend, 1996; Shi et al., 1993).

Hallucinogens

Hallucinogens (from the Latin for "wander in mind") are substances that cause powerful changes primarily in sensory perception, including intensification of perceptions and the inducement of illusions and hallucinations. They produce sensations so novel that they are sometimes called "trips." The trips may be exciting or frightening, enhancing or dangerous, depending on how a person's mind interacts with the drugs. This interaction may vary greatly from person to person and even from time to time for the same person.

Also called ***psychedelic drugs,*** the hallucinogens include LSD (lysergic acid diethylamide), mescaline, psilocybin, MDMA ("ecstasy"), DOM, DMT, and morning-glory seeds (Strassman, 1995). Many of these substances come from plants or animals; others are laboratory-produced rearrangements of natural psychedelics.

LSD, one of the most famous and most powerful hallucinogens, was derived by the Swiss chemist Albert Hoffman in 1938 from a group of naturally occurring drugs called ***ergot alkaloids.*** For years LSD remained in limited use while researchers struggled to understand its action and medicinal value. Then during the 1960s, a decade of social rebellion and experimentation, it found a home. Millions of persons turned to the drug as a means of expanding their experience.

Within two hours of being swallowed, LSD brings on a state of ***hallucinogen intoxication,*** sometimes called ***hallucinosis,*** marked by a general intensification of perceptions, particularly visual perceptions, along with maladaptive psychological changes and physical symptoms. People may focus on minutiae—the pores of the skin, for example, or individual blades of grass. Colors may seem enhanced or take on a shade of purple. Illusions may be experienced in which objects seem distorted, and inanimate objects may appear to move, breathe, or change shape. A person under the influence of LSD may also hallucinate, seeing people, objects, or geometric forms that are not actually present.

Intoxication may also cause one to hear sounds more clearly, feel tingling or numbness in the limbs, or experience distorted sensations of hot and cold. Some people have been badly burned after touching flames that felt cool to them under the influence of LSD. The drug may also cause the senses to cross, an effect called ***synesthesia.*** A loud noise may be experienced as visible fluctuations in the air. Colors may be "heard" or "felt."

LSD can also cause emotional changes, ranging from euphoria to anxiety or depression. The perception of time may slow dramatically. Long-forgotten thoughts and feelings may resurface. Physical symptoms can include dilation of the pupils, sweating, palpitations, blurred vision, tremors, and loss of coordination. All these effects take place while the user is fully awake and alert, and wear off in about six hours.

It seems that LSD produces these symptoms by interfering with neurons that use the neurotransmitter *serotonin* (Jacobs, 1994, 1984). These neurons are ordinarily involved in the brain's transmission of visual information and (as we observed in Chapter 8) emotional experiences; thus LSD's interference produces a range of visual and emotional symptoms. Ordinarily when serotonin-containing neurons are activated, they release serotonin, whose action helps the brain to filter incoming sensory messages. Without the action of serotonin, the brain would be flooded by perceptual and emotional input—particularly visual input—and people would experience more sensations, see more details, distort visual images, and even see things not actually there. This is the very effect created by LSD, which apparently binds to the surface of serotonin-containing neurons and essentially prevents them from releasing serotonin (Jacobs, 1984).

Psychedelic art seemed all-pervasive in the 1960s. Displayed on advertisements, clothing, record albums, and book covers, it was inspired by the kinds of images and sensations produced by psychedelic drugs such as LSD.

More than 7 percent of all persons in the United States have used LSD at some point in their lives (SAMHSA, 1996). Although people develop minimal tolerance and do not experience withdrawal when they stop using the drug, it poses distinct dangers for both one-time and long-term users. First, LSD is so remarkably potent that any dose, no matter how small, is likely to elicit powerful perceptual, emotional, and behavioral reactions. Sometimes these reactions are extremely unpleasant, an experience described in the drug vernacular as a "bad trip":

> A 21-year-old woman was admitted to the hospital along with her lover. He had had a number of LSD experiences and had convinced her to take it to make her less constrained sexually. About half an hour after ingestion of approximately 200 microgm., she noticed that the bricks in the wall began to go in and out and that light affected her strangely. She became frightened when she realized that she was unable to distinguish her body from the chair she was sitting on or from her lover's body. Her fear became more marked after she thought that she would not get back into herself. At the time of admission she was hyperactive and laughed inappropriately. Her stream of talk was illogical and affect labile. Two days later, this reaction had ceased.
>
> *(Frosch, Robbins, & Stern, 1965)*

Reports of LSD users who injure themselves or commit suicide or murder usually involve a severe panic reaction of this kind.

Another danger is the extended impact that LSD has on some people. They may develop patterns of hallucinations and delusions *(hallucinogen-induced psychotic disorder),* extreme guilt and depression *(hallucinogen-induced mood disorder),* or severe fearfulness, tension, or restlessness *(hallucinogen-induced anxiety disorder).* Many fear that they have destroyed their brains and driven themselves crazy, and worry that they will never return to normal.

Finally, about a quarter of LSD users experience lingering effects called a *hallucinogen persisting perception disorder,* or simply ***flashbacks***—sensory and emotional changes that recur long after the LSD has left the body (APA, 1994). Flashbacks may occur days or even months after the last LSD experience. Although they typically may become less severe and disappear within several months, some people report flashbacks five years or more after taking LSD. Flashbacks are entirely unpredictable. A one-time LSD user may have multiple flashbacks, or a regular user with no history of flashbacks may suddenly start to experience them.

Cannabis

Cannabis sativa, the hemp plant, grows in warm climates throughout the world. The drugs produced from varieties of hemp are collectively called ***cannabis.*** The most powerful of them is ***hashish;*** drugs of intermediate strength include ***ganja;*** and the weaker ones include the best-known form of cannabis, ***marijuana,*** a mixture of the crushed leaves and flowering tops. Each of these drugs is found in various strengths because the potency of a cannabis drug is greatly affected by the climate in which the plant is grown, the way it was prepared, and the manner and duration of its storage.

Of the several hundred active compounds in cannabis, ***tetrahydrocannabinol (THC)*** appears to be the one most responsible for its effects. The greater the THC content, the more powerful the cannabis: hashish contains a large portion, while marijuana's is relatively small.

Cannabis is smoked. At low doses it typically produces feelings of joy and relaxation and may lead people to become either contemplative or talkative. Some smokers, however, feel anxious, suspicious, apprehensive, or irritated, especially if they have been in a bad mood or are smoking in an upsetting environment. Many smokers report sharpened perceptions and great preoccupation with the intensified sounds and sights around them. Time seems to slow down, and distances and sizes seem greater than they actually are. This overall "high" is technically called ***cannabis intoxication.***

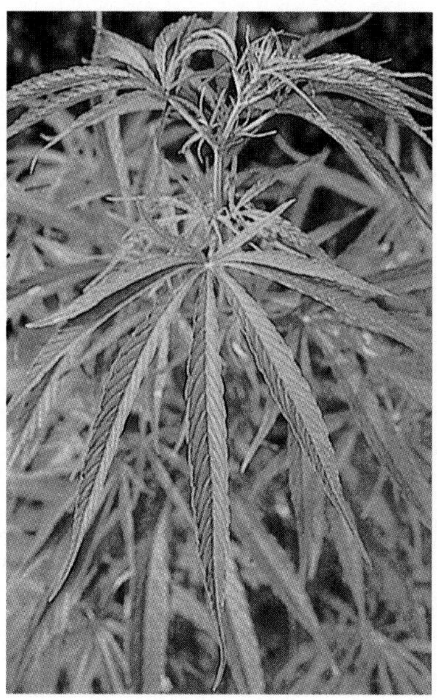

Marijuana is made from the leaves of the hemp plant, "Cannabis sativa." The plant is an annual herb, reaches a height of between 3 and 15 feet, and is grown in a wide range of altitudes, climates, and soils.

The physical changes induced by cannabis include reddening of the eyes (the blood vessels in the conjunctiva become engorged), a fast heartbeat, an increase in blood pressure and appetite, dryness in the mouth, and dizziness. Some people become drowsy and may fall asleep.

In high doses, cannabis produces visual distortions, alterations of body image, and hallucinations (Mathew et al., 1993). Smokers may become confused or impulsive; some panic and fear that they are losing their minds. Some smokers develop delusions that other people are trying to hurt them *(cannabis-induced psychotic disorder).* Most of the effects of cannabis last for three to six hours. The changes in mood, however, may continue longer (Chait, Fishman, & Schuster, 1985).

Marijuana Abuse and Dependence

Until the early 1970s, the use of the weak form of cannabis, marijuana, rarely led to a pattern of abuse or dependence. Today, however, many people, including large numbers of high school students, are caught in a pattern of marijuana abuse—getting high on marijuana regularly and finding their social and occupational or academic lives significantly affected by their heavy use of it (see Figure 13-5). Many chronic users also become physically dependent on marijuana. They develop a tolerance for it and may experience flulike withdrawal symptoms when they try to stop smoking, including hot flashes, loss of appetite, runny nose, sweating, diarrhea, and hiccups (Ray & Ksir, 1993; Jones & Benowitz, 1976). Around 4 percent of all persons in the United States have been dependent on marijuana at some point in their lives (Anthony et al., 1995).

Why have patterns of marijuana abuse and dependence emerged in the last two decades? Mainly because the drug has changed (see Box 13-3). The marijuana available in the United States today is two to ten times more powerful than that used in the early 1970s. The THC content of today's marijuana is as much as 10 to 15 percent, compared to 1 to 5 percent in the late 1960s (APA, 1994). Apparently, marijuana is now cultivated in places with a hot, dry climate, which increases the THC content (Weisheit, 1990).

The Dangers of Marijuana

As the strength and use of marijuana have increased, researchers have discovered that smoking it may pose some significant problems and dangers. It occasionally elicits panic reactions similar to the ones caused by hallucinogens (Ray & Ksir, 1993). People with emotional problems are thought to be more vulnerable to such reactions, but others may also experience them. Typically the panic reaction ends in three to six hours, along with marijuana's other effects.

Earlier research suggested that marijuana did not interfere with automobile driving as much as alcohol did (Crancer et al., 1969). It seems, however, that marijuana's impact on driving has increased along with its potency. Studies have implicated marijuana in numerous automobile accidents. Apparently cannabis intoxication interferes with the performance of complex sensorimotor tasks (Volkow et al., 1995; Goodman & Gilman, 1990; Yesavage et al., 1985).

Marijuana appears to interfere with cognitive functioning, too (Pope & Yurgelun-Todd, 1996; Coambs & McAndrews, 1994; Varma et al., 1988). People on a marijuana high often fail to remember information, especially recently acquired information, no matter how hard they try to concentrate. Clearly, heavy marijuana smokers are operating at a considerable disadvantage at school and in the workplace.

There are indications that chronic marijuana smoking may also lead to long-term problems. It may, for example, contribute to lung disease. Studies have indicated that marijuana smoking reduces one's ability to expel air from the lungs even more than tobacco smoking does. One marijuana cigarette is equivalent to at least sixteen tobacco cigarettes in this regard. In addition, research indicates that marijuana smoke contains significantly more tar and benzopyrene than tobacco smoke. Both of these substances have been linked to cancer (Ray & Ksir, 1993).

Another concern is the effect of chronic marijuana smoking on human reproduction. Studies since the late 1970s have discovered lower sperm counts and reduced spermatozoa activity in men who are chronic smokers of marijuana, and irregular and abnormal ovulation has

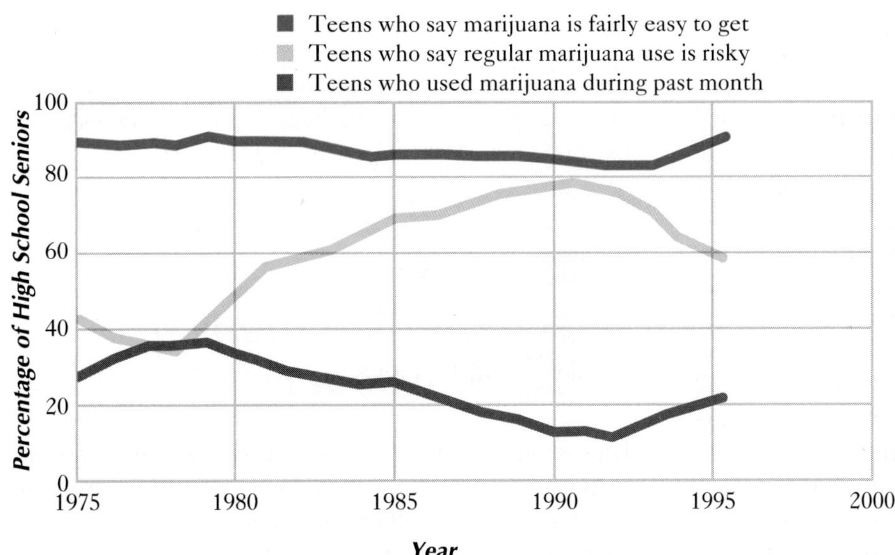

Figure 13-5 *Teenagers' attitudes toward and use of marijuana have changed over the years. The 1980s witnessed a steady rise in the percentage of high school seniors who considered regular marijuana use to be risky and, correspondingly, a steady fall in the percent regularly using it. That trend has reversed in the 1990s, however. Fewer seniors now consider marijuana use to be risky and more are using it. Either way, the substance has remained easy to obtain for decades (NIDA, 1996).*

BOX 13-3 Cannabis and Society

For centuries cannabis played a respected role in medicine. It was recommended as a surgical anesthetic by Chinese physicians 2,000 years ago and was used in other lands to treat cholera, malaria, coughs, insomnia, and rheumatism. In the mid–nineteenth century Western European physicians used it to treat neuralgia, menstrual pain, and migraine.

Cannabis entered the United States in the early twentieth century, mainly in the form of marijuana. The U.S. drug company Parke-Davis became a leading importer of marijuana and distributed it for medical purposes.

Early in the century, however, the positive view of cannabis began to change. For one thing, more effective medicines replaced it, and physicians placed less and less reliance on cannabis. Second, cannabis soon acquired some notoriety as a recreational drug, and its illegal distribution became a law enforcement problem. Authorities associated marijuana with alcohol and other disreputable drugs, assumed it was highly dangerous, and communicated this "fact" to the public. In 1937, when the "killer weed" was outlawed, the following magazine report was typical:

> In Los Angeles, Calif., a youth was walking along a downtown street after inhaling a marijuana cigarette. For many addicts, merely a portion of a "reefer" is enough to induce intoxication. Suddenly, for no reason, he decided that someone had threatened to kill him and that his life at that very moment was in danger. Wildly he looked about him. The only person in sight was an aged bootblack. Drug-crazed nerve centers conjured the innocent old shoe-shiner into a destroying monster. Mad with fright, the addict hurried to his room and got a gun. He killed the old man, and then, later, babbled his grief over what had been wanton, uncontrolled murder. . . .
>
> That's marijuana!
>
> *(Anslinger & Cooper, 1937, p. 153)*

Marijuana was not finished, however. The substance resurfaced with renewed vigor in the 1960s. It seemed to fit right in with that decade's disillusionment, protest, and self-exploration. Young people in particular discovered the pleasures of getting high, and smoking marijuana became a popular form of recreation. Many saw marijuana as a symbol of the government's low credibility: the drug was hardly the killer weed the government claimed it to be, and the harsh legal punishments for smoking it seemed unreasonable.

In the 1970s marijuana use continued to expand throughout the United States. By the end of the decade 16 million people reported using it at least once, 11 percent of the population identified themselves as recent users, and 11 percent of high school seniors said they smoked marijuana every day (NIDA, 1982).

These rates declined considerably during the 1980s. The marijuana that was imported to the United States became more pow-

been found among women (Nahas, 1984; Hembree, Nahas, & Huang, 1979). Finally, research has suggested that THC slows the functioning of the immune system, although the suppression is mild and temporary (Hollister, 1986).

Efforts to educate the public about the changing nature and impact of regular marijuana use appeared to be paying off as the 1990s unfolded. The percentage of high school seniors who smoked marijuana on a daily basis decreased from 11 percent in 1978 to 2 percent in 1992 (Johnston et al., 1993). Moreover, in 1992 about 77 percent of high school seniors believed that regular marijuana smoking poses a serious health risk, a much higher percentage than in earlier years (Johnston et al., 1993). However, marijuana use among the young has jumped back up during the past several years. Today more than 5 percent of high school seniors smoke marijuana daily and less than 60 percent believe that it is potentially harmful (Johnston et al., 1996; NIDA, 1995).

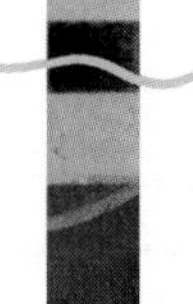

Combinations of Substances

Because people often take more than one drug at a time, researchers have had to study the ways in which drugs interact with one another. Two important concepts have emerged from this work: *cross-tolerance* and *synergistic effects.*

erful and dangerous than the earlier form, and people stopped using it so often and so casually. At the same time, marijuana and other forms of cannabis returned to their roots, so to speak, and once again found respect as a medical treatment.

In the 1980s cannabis researchers developed precise techniques for measuring and controlling THC content and for extracting pure THC from cannabis. They also developed synthetic forms of THC. These newly acquired abilities opened the door to new medical applications for cannabis (Ray & Ksir, 1993). Cannabis became helpful in treating glaucoma, a severe eye disease in which fluid from the eyeball is obstructed from flowing properly. Oral THC combats glaucoma by lowering the pressure of fluid in the eye. Cannabis was also found to help patients with asthma, by causing the bronchi to dilate. And because THC helps prevent nausea and vomiting, it gained use among cancer patients whose chemotherapy elicited such reactions (Plasse et al., 1991; Gunby, 1981). Similarly, some studies have suggested that THC might improve the appetites of AIDS patients and combat *wasting,* weight loss associated with AIDS and HIV (Johnson, 1996; Plasse et al., 1991).

In light of all this, organizations such as the National Organization for the Reform of Marijuana Laws (NORML) and Americans for Medical Rights have campaigned for the medical legalization of marijuana cigarettes. They have argued that doses of THC are more controllable in marijuana cigarettes than in THC pill form. In the late 1980s the Drug Enforcement Administration (DEA) considered classifying marijuana as a medically useful drug that can be prescribed by physicians. In 1992, however, the DEA finally decided against this move, and the Food and Drug Administration even terminated the process of reviewing requests for the "compassionate use" of marijuana cigarettes (Karel, 1992). They held that prescriptions of pure THC, available in a capsule called *dronabinol* (trade name Marinol), serve all needed medical functions.

Advocates for the medical use of marijuana challenged this position yet again during the November elections of 1996. Voter referendums, which have the force of law, were passed in California and Arizona, giving physicians the right to prescribe marijuana for "seriously ill" or "terminally ill" patients. Clearly displeased by the referendums, the federal government countered by threatening to revoke the prescription-writing privileges of any physician who prescribes marijuana, to exclude such physicans from participation in the Medicare and Medicaid programs, and even to prosecute them. Outraged by the government's intransigence on this complex issue, many more physicians have now openly joined the battle. In 1997 the *New England Journal of Medicine,* one of the world's most prestigious medical publications, published an editorial favoring the medical use of marijuana cigarettes. The journal further called the threat of government sanctions "misguided, heavy-handed, and inhumane." Clearly we have not heard the last of this issue.

Sometimes two or more drugs are so similar in their actions on the brain and the body that as people build up a tolerance for one drug, they are simultaneously developing a tolerance for the other, even if they have never taken the other. When users display such ***cross-tolerance,*** they can reduce the symptoms of withdrawal from one drug by taking the other. Because alcohol and antianxiety drugs are cross-tolerant, for example, it is sometimes possible to alleviate the alcohol withdrawal reaction of delirium tremens by administering benzodiazepines, along with vitamins and electrolytes (Kosten & McCance-Katz, 1995).

When different drugs are in the body at the same time, they may also potentiate, or enhance, each other's effects. The combined impact, called a ***synergistic effect,*** is often greater than the sum of the effects of each drug taken alone: a small dose of one drug mixed with a small dose of another can produce an enormous change in body chemistry.

One synergistic effect occurs when two or more drugs have *similar actions.* For instance, alcohol, benzodiazepines, barbiturates, and opioids—all depressants—may severely depress the central nervous system when mixed (Miller & Gold, 1990). Combining them, even in small doses, can lead to extreme intoxication, coma, and even death (Nishino et al., 1995). A young man may have just a few alcoholic drinks at a party, for example, and shortly afterward take a normal dose of barbiturates to help him fall asleep. He believes he has acted with restraint and good judgment—yet he may never wake up.

A different kind of synergistic effect results when drugs have *opposite (antagonistic) actions* (Braun, 1996).

Stimulant drugs, for example, interfere with the liver's usual disposal of barbiturates and alcohol. Thus people who combine barbiturates or alcohol with cocaine or amphetamines may build up toxic, even lethal levels of the depressant drugs in their systems. Students who take amphetamines to help them study late into the night and then take barbiturates to help them fall asleep are unwittingly placing themselves in serious danger.

Each year tens of thousands of people are admitted to hospitals with a multiple drug emergency, and several thousand of them die (DAWN, 1996). Sometimes the cause is carelessness or ignorance: a "wired" student who later takes sleeping pills may simply be unaware of the synergistic effects created by the combination. Often, however, people use multiple drugs precisely because they enjoy the synergistic effects. This kind of drug use, or ***polysubstance use,*** appears to be on the rise—so much so that ***polysubstance-related disorders*** are becoming as common as individual substance-related disorders in the United States, Canada, and Europe (Newcomb, 1994; Miller et al., 1990; Weisheit, 1990). Studies indicate that as many as 90 percent of persons who use one illicit drug are also using another to some extent (Cornish et al., 1995). Teenagers and young adults seem particularly likely to use drugs in combination (Wright, 1985). A look-in on a group therapy session for users of crack reveals that several of the group members have used substances in addition to crack:

> Okay. Now, can you give me a list of all the drugs you've used? Gary?
>
> *Gary:* Pot. Coke. Crack. Mescaline. Acid. Speed. Crystal meth. Smack. Base dust. Sometimes alcohol.
>
> *Dennis:* Alcohol. Pot. Coke. Mescaline. LSD. Amyl nitrate. Speed and Valium.
>
> *Davy:* Coke. Crack. Reefer. Alcohol. Acid. Mescaline. Mushrooms. Ecstasy. Speed. Smack.
>
> *Rich:* Alcohol. Pot. Ludes [Quaaludes]. Valium. Speed. Ups [amphetamines]. Downs [barbiturates]. Acid. Mescaline. Crack. Base. Dust. That's about it.
>
> *Carol:* Alcohol. Pot. Cocaine. Mescaline. Valium. Crack.
>
> *(Chatlos, 1987, pp. 30–31)*

Some famous people have been the victims of polysubstance use. Elvis Presley's delicate balancing act of stimulants and depressants eventually killed him. Janis Joplin's propensity for mixing wine and heroin was ultimately fatal. And John Belushi's and River Phoenix's liking for the combined effect of cocaine and opioids ("speedballs") also ended in tragedy.

Polysubstance use, particularly a mixture of cocaine and opioids, eventually proved fatal for the comedian John Belushi (left), who often made jokes about the use of drugs on "Saturday Night Live," and the actor River Phoenix (right), who was a practicing vegetarian and environmentalist. Their deaths were separated by years, at locations only blocks apart, from biological causes that were identical.

Explanations of Substance-Related Disorders

Clinical theorists have proposed sociocultural, psychological, and biological explanations for why people abuse or become dependent on various substances. None, however, has gained unqualified research support. Indeed, like so many other disorders, excessive and chronic drug use is increasingly being viewed as a consequence of a combination of these factors.

The Sociocultural View

Sociocultural theorists propose that the people most likely to develop substance abuse or dependence live in stressful socioeconomic circumstances. And in fact epidemiological studies have found that geographical regions with higher levels of unemployment have higher rates of alcoholism (Linsky, Strauss, & Colby, 1985). Similarly, hunting societies, in which people presumably experience greater danger, uncertainty, and tension, have more alcohol problems than agrarian societies (Bacon, 1973; Horton, 1943); city dwellers have higher alcoholism rates than residents of small towns and rural areas (Cisin & Calahan, 1970); and lower socioeconomic classes have higher substance abuse rates than other classes (Smith, North, & Spitznagel, 1993; Beauvais, 1992). Studies have similarly found higher rates of heroin addiction among people who live in stressful environments. About 40 percent of Army enlisted men used heroin at least once while serving in Vietnam, half of them so often that they had a withdrawal reaction when they stopped (Grinspoon & Bakalar, 1986).

Sociocultural theorists also propose that substance abuse is more likely to emerge in families and social environments that value, or at least tolerate, drug taking (see Table 13-4). Researchers have, in fact, found that problem drinking is more common among teenagers whose parents and peers drink, as well as among teenagers whose family environment is stressful and unsupportive (Shucksmith, Glendinning, & Hendry, 1997; Oostveen, Knibbe, & de Vries, 1996; Wills et al., 1996; Farrell, Barnes, & Banerjee, 1995). In addition, lower rates of alcohol abuse are found among Jews and Protestants, groups in which drinking is typically acceptable only so long as it remains within clearly defined boundaries, whereas alcoholism rates are relatively high among the Irish and Eastern Europeans, who do not tend to make as clear a distinction (Kohn & Levav, 1995; Vaillant & Milofsky, 1982; Calahan, Cisin, & Crossley, 1969; Snyder, 1955).

The sociocultural explanations of substance abuse and dependence have received support from epidemiological studies. As with sociocultural explanations of other problems, however, they fail to explain why only *some* people subjected to unfavorable social conditions develop substance-related disorders. Psychological (psychodynamic and behavioral) and biological explanations have tried to provide more insight into this issue.

The Psychodynamic View

Psychodynamic theorists believe that people who ultimately abuse substances have inordinate dependency needs traceable to their early years (Shedler & Block, 1990; Ward, 1985; Abadi, 1984). They theorize that when parents fail to satisfy a child's need for nurturance, the child is likely to go through life depending too much on others for help and comfort, in an effort to find the nurturance he or she did not receive as a child. If this search for external sources of support includes experimentation with a drug, the person is likely to develop a dependent relationship with the substance.

TABLE 13-4 **Alcohol Consumption Around the World***

	Wine	*Beer*	*Liquor*
France	63.5	40.1	2.5
Italy	58.0	25.1	0.9
Switzerland	46.0	65.0	1.7
Australia	15.7	102.1	1.2
Britain	12.2	100.0	1.5
U.S.A.	8.9	87.8	2.0
Russia	2.7	17.1	3.8
Czech Republic	1.7	140.0	1.0
Japan	1.0	55.0	2.1
Mexico	0.2	50.4	0.8

Source: Shapiro, 1996; World Drink Trends, 1994; World Health Organization; Wine Market Council; Adams/Jobson Publishing Corp.
**Consumption in liters per capita.*

Some psychodynamic theorists also believe that certain people develop a "substance abuse personality" that makes them particularly vulnerable to drugs. Personality inventories and patient interviews have indicated that people who abuse or depend on drugs tend to be more dependent, antisocial, impulsive, novelty-seeking, and depressive than other people (Mâsse & Tremblay, 1997; Calsyn et al., 1996; McMahon & Richards, 1995).

Do such personality styles actually *cause* substance abuse? A longitudinal study measured the characteristics of a large group of nonalcoholic young men and then kept track of each man's development (Jones, 1971, 1968). The profiles of those men who developed alcohol problems in middle age were compared with the profiles of those who did not. The men who developed alcohol problems had been more impulsive as adolescents and continued to be so in middle age, suggesting that impulsive men are indeed more prone to develop alcohol problems. Even some animal investigations seem to suggest that some personalities are more prone to abuse drugs. In one study, "impulsive" rats—those who generally had trouble delaying their rewards—were found to drink more alcohol than other rats (Poulos, Le, & Parker, 1995).

A major problem with these studies is that a suspiciously wide range of personality traits has been linked to substance-related disorders. In fact, different studies point to different "key" traits. Inasmuch as some people with a drug addiction are apparently dependent, others impulsive, and still others antisocial, researchers have been unable to conclude that any one personality trait or cluster of traits stands out as a factor in substance abuse or dependence (Rozin & Stoess, 1993).

Over the years, substances may rise and fall and rise again, as new generations discover their rewarding properties. During the 1980s, for example, heroin was associated with crime, immorality, and street life, and its use declined. In the 1990s, however, its popularity has risen greatly. The drug is prominently featured in the recent movie Trainspotting, *a film focusing on a group of young Scottish addicts.*

The Behavioral View

According to *operant conditioning* theorists, the temporary reduction of tension, raising of spirits, sense of well-being, or other positive effects produced by a drug has a reinforcing effect and increases the likelihood that the user will seek this reaction again (Cooney et al., 1997; Carey & Carey, 1995; Hughes et al., 1995). In support of this theory, studies have found that many subjects do in fact drink more alcohol or seek heroin when they feel tense (Cooney et al., 1997; Shaham, Rajabi, & Stewart, 1996; Stewart, Zeitlin, & Samoluk, 1996; Cooper, 1994). In one study, experimenters had individuals work on a difficult anagram task while another person unfairly criticized and belittled them (Marlatt, Kosturn, & Lang, 1975). These subjects were then asked to participate in an "alcohol taste task": their job was supposedly to compare and rate various alcoholic beverages. The harassed subjects drank significantly more alcohol during the taste task than did control subjects who had not been criticized. Another group of subjects were harassed while doing the anagrams but were given an opportunity to retaliate against their critics. These subjects drank relatively little during the tasting. Their retaliatory behavior had apparently reduced their tension and lessened their need for alcohol.

In a manner of speaking, the reinforcement theorists are arguing that many people take drugs to *medicate themselves* when they feel tense and upset (Anthony et al., 1995; Khantzian, 1985). If so, one would expect elevated rates of drug abuse and dependence among people with high levels of anxiety, depression, or anger. Consistent with this expectation, substance abuse and dependence appear to be relatively common among people with mood disorders. Indeed, one study of 835 clinically depressed patients found that more than one-fourth abused drugs during episodes of depression (Hasin, Endicott, & Lewis, 1985). In another study, the negative thoughts and biases of depressed subjects were found to improve significantly after the subjects drank alcoholic beverages (Stephens & Curtin, 1995). Similarly, studies have found a higher than usual rate of drug abuse among people with posttraumatic stress disorder (Brown, Stout, & Mueller, 1996; McFall, Mackay, & Donovan, 1992), eating disorders (Higuchi et al., 1993), schizophrenia (Regier et al., 1990), antisocial personality disorder (Brooner et al., 1997; Schuckit, 1994), histories of being abused (Yama et al., 1993; Hernandez, 1992), and yet other psychological problems (Kessler et al., 1997). One study found that a full 80 percent of the adolescent subjects who displayed a substance-related disorder also qualified for another clinical diagnosis (Rohde, Lewinsohn, & Seeley, 1996).

At the same time, however, a number of studies indicate that many people do not find drugs pleasurable or reinforcing when they first take them. Many people report that they do not get high the first time they smoke marijuana, for example. Similarly, at least some volunteers who were administered heroin in laboratory settings initially disliked the drug or felt indifferent to it (Alexander & Hadaway, 1982). In fact, some people dependent on opioids report that their initial experiences with these drugs were anything but pleasurable:

> We slept most of the day until late afternoon, and when I woke up she got up and got a tray out of the dresser drawer and brought it over and placed it on the bed. . . . She told me she was [an opium] smoker and asked me if I had ever smoked hop. I told her I never had and she said that I ought to try it once, as she was sure I would like it. . . . [After smoking it] I suddenly became very nauseated and had to leave to vomit. I vomited till there was nothing left on my stomach and I was still sick so I went to bed.
>
> *(Lindesmith, 1972, p. 85)*

Even when a drug does initially produce pleasant feelings and reward the user with a reduction in tension, the picture seems to change later when the person takes the drug excessively and chronically. As we saw earlier, many people become increasingly anxious and depressed over time as they take more and more drugs (Roggla & Uhl, 1995; Vaillant, 1993). Why, then, do they keep on taking them?

Some behaviorists use Richard Solomon's ***opponent-process theory*** to answer this question. Solomon (1980) held that the brain is structured in such a way that pleasurable emotions, such as drug-induced euphoria, inevitably lead to opponent processes—negative aftereffects—that leave the person feeling worse than usual. People who continue to use pleasure-giving drugs inevitably develop opponent aftereffects, such as cravings for more of the drug, withdrawal responses, and an increasing need for the drug. According to Solomon, the opponent processes eventually dominate and suppress the pleasure-giving processes, and avoidance of the negative aftereffects replaces pursuit of pleasure as the individual's primary motivation for taking drugs. Although a highly regarded theory, the opponent-process explanation has not received systematic research support (Peele, 1989).

Other behaviorists have proposed that *classical conditioning* may also contribute to certain aspects of drug abuse and dependence (Remington, Roberts, & Glautier, 1997; Zack & Vogel-Sprott, 1995; Childress et al., 1993, 1988, 1984). Objects present at the time drugs are taken may act as classically conditioned stimuli and come to elicit some of the same pleasure brought on by the drugs themselves. Just the sight of a hypodermic needle or a regular supplier, for example, has been known to comfort people who abuse heroin or amphetamines, and to relieve their withdrawal symptoms (Meyer, 1995; Childress et al., 1993, 1988, 1984).

In a similar manner, objects that are present during withdrawal distress may elicit withdrawal-like symptoms (Meyer, 1995; Childress et al., 1993, 1988, 1984). One individual who had formerly been dependent on heroin experienced nausea and other withdrawal symptoms when he returned to the neighborhood where he had gone through withdrawal in the past—a reaction that led him to start taking heroin again (O'Brien et al., 1975). Similarly, after eight addicted subjects were repeatedly exposed to a peppermint odor during their withdrawal reactions, they experienced withdrawal-like symptoms (tearing eyes, sick feelings, running nose) whenever someone near them ate peppermint candy (O'Brien et al., 1975).

Although these studies demonstrate that withdrawal responses can be classically conditioned, other studies suggest that conditioning is not at work in most cases. Of forty persons who had gone through heroin withdrawal, only eleven reported having withdrawal symptoms during later encounters with environments and objects associated with their withdrawal, and only five of those people actually relapsed into heroin use (McAuliffe, 1982). In short, the classical conditioning explanations of drug abuse and dependence, like the operant conditioning explanations, have received at best mixed support (Powell, Bradley, & Gray, 1992).

The Biological View

In recent years researchers have come to suspect that many cases of drug misuse may be related largely to biological processes. Their suspicions have been bolstered by research focusing on genetic predispositions and biochemical processes.

Genetic Factors For years researchers have conducted animal breeding experiments that implicate genetic predispositions in the development of drug dependence (Kurtz et al., 1996; Azar, 1995; George, 1990). In one line of research, investigators have selected animals that prefer alcohol to other beverages, mated them to one another, and found that their offspring display the same preference (Melo et al., 1996).

Similarly, research with human twins has suggested that people may inherit a predisposition to substance abuse and dependence (Kendler et al., 1994, 1992; Goodwin, 1984, 1976; Vaillant, 1983). In a classic study, an alcohol-abuse concordance rate of 54 percent was found in a group of identical twins. That is, in 54 percent of the cases in which one identical twin abused alcohol, the other twin also abused alcohol. In contrast, a group of fraternal twins had a concordance rate of only 28 percent (Kaij, 1960). Of course, as we have observed, such findings do not rule out other interpretations. For one thing, parents may act more similarly toward identical twins than toward fraternal twins.

A stronger indication that genetics may play a role in drug abuse and dependence has come from studies that examine the alcoholism rates of people who were adopted shortly after birth (Cadoret, 1995; Goldstein, 1994; Goodwin et al., 1973). These studies compare adoptees whose biological parents are dependent on alcohol to adoptees whose biological parents are not. By adulthood those whose biological parents are dependent on alcohol typically show significantly higher rates of alcohol abuse than those with nonalcoholic biological parents, suggesting once again that a predisposition to develop alcoholism may be inherited.

Finally by using "gene mapping" strategies (see Chapter 4), some investigators have found direct links between abnormal genes and substance-related disorders (Chen et al., 1996; Melo et al., 1996; Hill et al, 1995). One line of investigation has found that an abnormal form of the so-called ***dopamine-2 (D2) receptor gene*** is present in as many as 69 percent of subjects with alcohol dependence and 51 percent of subjects with cocaine dependence, but in less than 20 percent of nondependent subjects (Lawford et al., 1997; Blum & Noble, 1993; Blum et al., 1991). Still other studies have implicated other dopamine-linked genes in substance-related disorders (Nash, 1997). Debate on this issue is very heated (Gejman et al., 1994; Arinami et al., 1993; Turner et al., 1992), but these studies seem to provide strong evidence that genes play at least some role in the development of alcoholism, cocaine dependence, and other substance-related disorders.

Biochemical Factors During the past few decades, investigators have pieced together a general biological understanding of drug tolerance and withdrawal symptoms (Wise, 1996). As we have seen, when a particular drug is ingested, it increases the activity of certain neurotransmitters—neurotransmitters that normally act to sedate, alleviate pain, lift mood, or increase alertness. When people keep taking the drug, the brain apparently makes an adjustment and reduces its own production of the neurotransmitters (Goldstein, 1994). Because the drug acts to stimulate neurotransmitter activity, action by the brain is less necessary. As the drug intake is increased, the body's production of the corresponding neurotransmitters may continue to decrease, leaving the person in need of more and more of the drug to achieve its initial effects. In short, drug takers build tolerance for the drug. They become increasingly reliant on a drug rather than on their own mechanisms, and they must continue to ingest it in order to feel reasonably calm, comfortable, happy, or alert. If they suddenly stop taking the drug, for a time their supply of neurotransmitters will be deficient, and they will not feel well. In fact, they will feel terrible, and their withdrawal symptoms will continue until the brain resumes its normal production of the necessary neurotransmitters.

Which neurotransmitters are suppressed depends on the drug in use. A chronic and excessive use of alcohol or benzodiazepines may lower the brain's production of the inhibitory neurotransmitter GABA; a chronic use of opioids may reduce the brain's own production of endorphins; and a chronic use of cocaine or amphetamines may lower the brain's own production of dopamine (Fowler, Volkow, & Wolf, 1995). In addition, researchers appear very close to identifying a neurotransmitter that functions as the body's natural equivalent of THC; excessive use of marijuana may reduce the production of this neurotransmitter (Biegon & Kerman, 1995; Fackelmann, 1993; Nye et al., 1989, 1988, 1985).

Recent studies suggest that the craving for chocolate may be more than just a state of mind. Apparently, some chemicals in chocolate may bind to the same neuron receptors that receive cannabis substances (di Tomaso, Beltramo, & Piomelli, 1996). At the same time, however, a person would have to eat 25 pounds of chocolate in one sitting to experience a cannabis-like effect. Then again, for chocolate-lovers . . .

This model helps explain why people who chronically take substances experience tolerance and withdrawal reactions. But why do they turn to drugs in the first place? For years biological researchers deferred to their psychological and sociocultural colleagues on this question, but brain-imaging technology has recently guided them to a biological explanation that is creating an enormous stir in the clinical field (Volkow et al., 1997; Bardo, Donohew, & Harrington, 1996; Biegon & Volkow, 1995). The explanation is also highly compatible with the psychological and sociocultural propositions.

As we have noted, behavioral and sociocultural theorists believe that people take drugs because the substances bring pleasure or relieve tension. But why are drugs so rewarding? A recent flurry of biological research suggests that many, perhaps all, drugs eventually activate a single *reward center*, or "pleasure pathway," in the brain (Volkow et al., 1997). This reward center apparently extends from the brain's ***ventral tegmental area*** (in the midbrain) to the ***nucleus accubens*** and on to the ***frontal cortex*** (Korenman & Barchas, 1993). The key neurotransmitter in this pleasure pathway is *dopamine*. When dopamine is activated here, a person experiences pleasure. Music may activate dopamine in the reward center. So may a hug or a word of praise. And so may drugs.

Some drugs apparently activate the reward center directly. Remember that cocaine, amphetamines, and caffeine stimulate dopamine activity. Other drugs seem to activate it in roundabout ways. Research suggests that the biochemical activities triggered by alcohol, opioids, marijuana, and nicotine set in motion chemical events that eventually stimulate dopamine activity in the pleasure center (Volkow et al., 1997; Goldstein, 1994; Koob, 1992).

Such findings lead some theorists to suspect that people who abuse drugs suffer from a ***reward-deficiency syndrome:*** their reward centers are not readily activated by the usual events in their lives (Nash, 1997). So, they turn to drugs to stimulate their reward centers, particularly during times of stress. Abnormal genes, such as the abnormal D2 receptor gene, have already been suggested as a possible source for such deficiencies (Lawford et al., 1997).

Although these ideas have produced great enthusiasm among biological theorists and researchers, they are at the earliest stages of investigation and analysis, and indeed biological investigators themselves differ greatly on how to interpret the various findings. Nevertheless, this explanation of why drugs are so appealing and so habit-forming is gaining more and more recruits, and the theory is very likely to receive growing attention in the coming years.

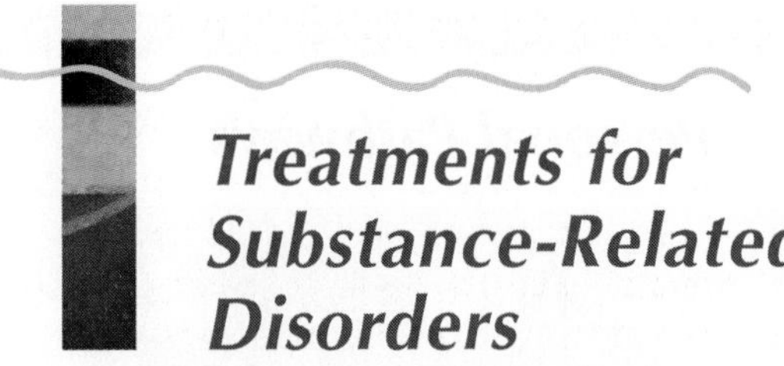

Treatments for Substance-Related Disorders

Clinicians have worked diligently to correct substance-related disorders. Most of the approaches fall into one of several groups: psychodynamic, behavioral, cognitive-behavioral, biological, and sociocultural therapies. Although these treatments sometimes meet with great success, more often they have had only moderate effectiveness (Azrin et al., 1996; Cornish et al., 1995; Prochaska, Di Clemente, & Norcross, 1992). Today the treatments are typically used in combination (Landry, 1994; Galanter, 1993), and may be applied on either an outpatient or an inpatient basis (McKay et al., 1995).

It can be extremely difficult to determine at any given time whether a treatment for substance abuse or dependence is succeeding, failing, or irrelevant to a given person's progress (Cornish et al., 1996; Carroll & Rounsaville, 1995; Prochaska et al., 1992). First, different substance-related disorders often pose different treatment problems. Second, some people recover without any intervention at all, while other people appear to recover and then relapse, or fail to recover from their disorder even after intensive treatment. Finally, as with other mental disorders, the different criteria and goals employed by different clinical researchers make it

Both public officials and clinical experts typically encourage people to use alternative substances that are more healthful and less addictive than alcohol or other such drugs. Such alternatives are even the main fare at some pubs, such as this juice bar in New York City.

Personal Pathways

Sigmund Freud

"A Big Wild Man Who Has Cocaine in His Body"

Sigmund Freud, like so many people before and after him, was played for a fool by a drug—in his case, cocaine. He prematurely concluded that cocaine was free of danger, largely because he enjoyed it and wanted it to be safe.

Early in his career Freud read about cocaine, and proceeded to test it on himself. He quickly experienced a powerful reaction, and seemed more than a little smitten with the drug when he wrote to his fiancée in 1885, "Woe to you my princess when I come. I will kiss you quite red and feed you until you are plump. And if you are forward, you shall see who is stronger, a gentle little girl who doesn't eat enough or a big wild man who has cocaine in his body" (Freud, 1885).

Freud studied the effects of cocaine on subjects and soon proclaimed to the medical community of Western Europe: "Cocaine brings about an exhilaration and lasting euphoria. . . . You perceive an increase of self-control and possess more vitality and capacity for work. . . . In other words, you are simply normal, and it is soon hard to believe that you are under the influence of any drug"(Freud, 1885).

Freud received a rude awakening after he recommended to a close friend, Erst Fleischl von Marxow, that he take cocaine to relieve him of his addiction to morphine. Fleischl injected himself with increasingly higher doses of cocaine until finally he became a victim of cocaine-induced psychosis. *This and other reports of cocaine psychosis led to severe criticism of Freud by the Continent's most eminent medical authorities and dealt a heavy blow to his reputation. It was not at all clear that he would be able to continue his medical career. But then he began to focus on psychoanalysis.*

difficult to draw broad conclusions about a treatment's effectiveness. How long, for example, must a person refrain from substance use in order to be categorized as a treatment success? And is total abstention the only criterion, or is a reduction of drug use considered significant?

Psychodynamic Therapies

Psychodynamic therapists try to help people with substance-related disorders become aware of and address the psychological factors that they believe contribute to the pattern of drug use (Jungman, 1985). They first help clients to uncover and resolve their underlying conflicts and then try to help them alter their substance-related styles of living (Hopper, 1995; Levinson, 1985). Although this approach is often applied to substance-related disorders, research has not found it to be highly effective (Cornish et al., 1995; Holder et al., 1991; Meyer et al., 1989). Its lack of success may indicate that drug abuse or dependence eventually becomes a stubborn and independent problem irrespective of its causes, and that the maladaptive pattern itself must be the primary target for change if people are to become drug-free. Thus psychodynamic therapy tends to be of greater help when it is combined with other approaches in a multidimensional treatment program. It has been combined successfully with behavioral and biological therapies (Carroll & Rounsaville, 1995; Galanter, 1993).

Behavioral Therapies

A widely used behavioral treatment for substance-related disorders is ***aversion therapy,*** the approach based on the principles of classical conditioning (Frawley & Smith, 1992). Here individuals are repeatedly presented with an unpleasant stimulus (for example, an electric shock) at the same time that they are taking a drug. After repeated pairings, the individuals are expected to start reacting negatively to the substance itself and to lose their craving for it.

Aversion therapy has been applied to alcohol abuse and dependence more than to other substance-use disorders (Clarke & Saunders, 1988; Callner, 1975). In the past, aversion therapy was sometimes drastic and controversial. In one treatment program people with alcoholism were injected with ***succinylcholine,*** a drug that actually paralyzed their bodies while they tasted alcoholic beverages (Sanderson, Campbell, & Laverty, 1963). These people did develop an aversion to alcohol, but many clinicians understandably worried about the safety and ethics of the program. Moreover, the effectiveness seemed to be short-lived. Electrical aversion therapy, which pairs electrical shock with drinking, also raised ethical questions and proved to have limited effectiveness (Wilson, 1987, 1978).

Today's aversion therapy techniques tend to be somewhat less severe. In one approach, drinking behavior is paired with drug-induced nausea and vomiting (Elkins, 1991; Cannon et al., 1986, 1981). Another, ***covert sensitization,*** requires people with alcoholism to *imagine* extremely upsetting, repulsive, or frightening scenes while they are drinking (Emmelkamp, 1994; Cautela, 1977, 1966). The supposition is that the pairing of these imagined scenes with liquor will elicit negative responses to liquor itself. Here are the kinds of scenes therapists may guide a client to imagine:

> I'd like you to vividly imagine that you are drinking and tasting (beer, whiskey, etc.). You are in a (restaurant, pub, etc.) where others are drinking. 'See' yourself there, having a drink. Capture the exact taste of it, the colour and the smell. Use all of your senses. Imagine that you are actually drinking it, tasting it, swallowing it, feel the glass in your hand; and be aware of its temperature, taste and smell, but especially the taste.
>
> As you swallow the drink, a man sitting not far from you gives a low groan, replaces his glass on the table and pushes it away. His head remains lowered as he grasps his stomach with both hands and continues moaning. His eyes are closed now as he grimaces and slowly shakes his head. His face has become a sickly pale colour, and his hands are trembling as he starts to make quick swallowing motions. He opens his eyes and claps both hands over his mouth, but he cannot hold it in and the vomit bursts out. You can see it so clearly. Pieces of food run down his face, soaking his clothes and even reaching his glass. He continues to throw up and particles of his last meal stick to his chin and the hot sticky smell of alcohol reaches you. He really is a disgusting sight. He's got the dry heaves now, there's nothing left to bring up, but his face is still pale and he continues moaning.

> I'd like you to vividly imagine that you are tasting the (beer, whiskey, etc.). See yourself tasting it, capture the exact taste, colour and consistency. Use all of your senses. After you've tasted the drink you notice that there is something small and white floating in the glass—it stands out. You bend closer to examine it more carefully, your nose is right over the glass now and the smell fills your nostrils as you remember exactly what the drink tastes like. Now you can see what's in the glass. There are several maggots floating on the surface. As you watch, revolted, one manages to get a grip on the glass and, undulating, creeps up the glass. There are even more of the repulsive creatures in the glass than you first thought. You realise that you have swallowed some of them and you're very aware of the taste in your mouth. You feel very sick and wish you'd never reached for the glass and had the drink at all.
>
> *(Clarke & Saunders, 1988, pp. 143–144).*

Another behavioral approach focuses on teaching ***alternative behaviors*** to drug taking (Azrin et al., 1996). This approach, too, has been applied to alcohol abuse and dependence more than to other substance-related disorders. Problem drinkers may be taught to reduce their tensions with relaxation, meditation, or biofeedback instead of alcohol (Rohsenow, Smith, & Johnson, 1985). Some are also taught assertiveness or social skills to help them both express their anger more directly and withstand social pressures to drink (Carroll & Rounsaville, 1995; Van Hasselt et al., 1993). Similarly, leisure education programs teach substance abusers positive "fun" alternatives to drug abuse (Aguilar & Munson, 1992).

A behavioral approach that has been effective in the short-term treatment of persons who abuse cocaine (a notoriously hard-to-treat group) and some other drugs is ***contingency training,*** which makes incentives (such as program privileges) contingent on the submission of drug-free urine specimens (Azrin et al., 1996; Carroll & Rounsaville, 1995; Stitzer et al., 1993). In one study of contingency training, 58 percent of cocaine abusers completed the full six months of treatment, and 68 percent achieved at least eight weeks of continuous abstinence. Since the length of time clients remain with a treatment program and the length of their abstinence are predictors of future freedom from substance abuse, the results are cause for some optimism (Higgins et al., 1993).

With some notable exceptions (Azrin et al., 1996), behavioral treatments for substance abuse and dependence have had at most limited success when they are the sole form of treatment (Carroll & Rounsaville, 1995; Meyer et al., 1989). One of the major problems with these approaches is that they can be successful only when subjects are sufficiently motivated to continue with them despite their unpleasantness or demands. In fact, behavioral treatments generally work best in combination with either biological or cognitive approaches (Whorley, 1996; Washton & Stone-Washton, 1990).

Cognitive-Behavioral Therapies

Two leading treatments combine cognitive and behavioral techniques to help people gain control over their substance-related behaviors. In one, ***behavioral self-control training (BSCT),*** typically applied to alcoholism, therapists first instruct clients to monitor their own drinking behavior (Miller et al., 1992; Miller, 1983). When clients record the times, locations, emotions, bodily changes, and other circumstances of their drinking, they become more sensitive to the cues that place them at risk for excessive drinking. They are then taught coping stategies to use when such cues arise. They learn, for example, to set appropriate limits on their drinking, to recognize when the limits are being approached, to control their rate of drinking (perhaps by spacing their drinks or by sipping them rather than gulping), and to apply relaxation responses and other coping behaviors in situations in which they would otherwise be drinking. Approximately 70 percent of the clients who complete this program have been assessed as showing some improvement (Miller & Hester, 1980). The program appears to be more effective with clients who are young and not physically dependent on alcohol (Miller et al., 1992; Meyer et al., 1989).

In ***relapse-prevention training,*** heavy drinkers do many of the same tasks as in BSCT (Kivlaham et al., 1990; Marlatt & Gordon, 1985, 1980). They are further taught to plan ahead of time how much drinking is appropriate, what they will consume, and under what circumstances. Here a therapist presents the basic principles of this approach to a client:

> We know that you would like to be totally abstinent for life, but our knowledge of alcoholics generally and of you in particular suggests that however hard you try, you are likely to drink on some occasion or occasions after you leave hospital. This is not being pessimistic, but simply realistic. We are not suggesting that your task is hopeless—far from it—but we do want you to anticipate future events and work out ways of coping. We have already told you that some drink will be given to you during your stay in hospital and that your aim is to stop after a certain amount when you feel like continuing. In this way we believe that you will gradually break the compulsion to continue and will develop your willpower. This should have two effects when you leave the hospital. First, when you attempt to drink, your experience of resisting temptation in the hospital will give you greater control. Second, if you do drink you will find it easier to pull out before you explode into a heavy-drinking binge. . . .
>
> *(Hodgson & Rankin, 1982, p. 213)*

Research indicates that this approach sometimes reduces the frequency of intoxication (Hollon & Beck, 1994; Annis et al., 1989). Like BSCT, relapse-prevention training is apparently more effective for people who abuse alcohol than for those who are physically dependent on it (Meyer et al., 1989). This approach has also been adapted, with some success, to the treatment of marijuana and cocaine abuse (Carroll & Rounsaville, 1995; Wells et al., 1994).

Biological Treatments

Biological techniques play a variety of roles in the treatment of substance-related disorders. They may be directed at helping people withdraw from substances, abstain from them, or simply maintain their current substance use without further escalation. Research suggests that biological approaches alone rarely lead to long-term improvement but can sometimes be a helpful component of broader treatment programs (Cornish et al., 1995; Kleber, 1995).

Detoxification ***Detoxification*** is systematic and medically supervised withdrawal from a drug. Many detoxification programs are set up in hospitals and clinics, as people who abuse drugs often seem more motivated to persevere through withdrawal in those settings. Inpatient detoxification programs of this kind may also offer individual and group therapy, a "full-service" institutional approach that has become increasingly popular.

One detoxification strategy, used most often to reduce dependence on sedative-hypnotic drugs, is to have clients withdraw gradually from the drug, taking ever-decreasing doses until they are off the drug completely. Another detoxification strategy is to administer other drugs that reduce the symptoms of withdrawal (Cornish et al., 1995; Kosten & McCance-Katz, 1995). Antianxiety drugs, for example, are sometimes used to reduce severe alcohol withdrawal reactions such as delirium tremens.

Detoxification programs have proved effective in helping motivated people to withdraw from drugs. For people who fail to pursue psychotherapy after withdrawal, however, relapse rates tend to be high (Pickens & Fletcher, 1991).

Antagonist Drugs After successful withdrawal from a drug, the challenge is to avoid a recurrence of drug abuse or dependence. In one biological technique, people with substance-related disorders are given ***antagonist drugs,*** drugs that block or change the effects of the addictive drug. ***Disulfiram (Antabuse),*** for example, is often given to people who are trying to refrain from drinking alcohol (Landry, 1994). By itself this drug is believed to have relatively few negative effects; but because disulfiram interferes with the body's metabolism of alcohol, a person who drinks alcohol while taking disulfiram will experience intense nausea, vomiting, blushing, faster heart rate, dizziness, and perhaps fainting. Theoretically, people who are taking disulfiram will refrain from alcohol because they know the terrible reaction that awaits them should they have even one drink. Disulfiram has proved helpful but again only with people who are highly motivated (Cornish et al., 1995; Meyer et al., 1989). After all, they can stop taking the disulfiram and return to alcohol at any time.

Narcotic antagonists, such as *naloxone* and *naltrexone*, are sometimes used with people who are dependent on opioids. These drugs attach to opioid receptor sites throughout the brain and make it impossible for the opioids to have their usual euphoric effect. Theoretically,

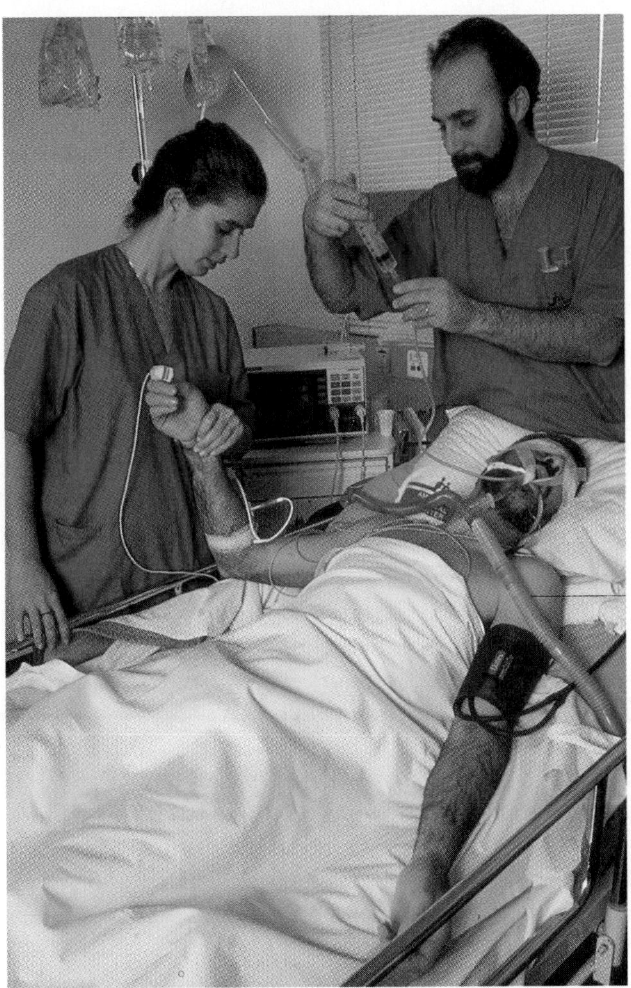

Because narcotic antagonists may throw persons with an addiction into severe and even dangerous withdrawal, most clinicians use moderate doses of antagonists. Some clinicians in Spain, Israel, and Mexico, however, check their patients into intensive-care units, place them under heavy sedation to shield them from pain, then use antagonists to induce "ultra-rapid detoxification" (Cowley, 1995).

without the rush or high, continued drug use becomes pointless. Although narcotic antagonists have been helpful in emergencies to rescue people from an overdose of opioids, some clinicians consider them too dangerous for regular treatment of opioid dependence. The antagonists must be administered very carefully because of their ability to throw a person with an addiction into severe withdrawal reactions (Rosen et al., 1996; Goldstein, 1994). In recent years, a so-called ***partial antagonist,*** *buprenorphine,* which produces less severe withdrawal symptoms, has been developed and apparently will be approved for treatment in the United States in the near future (Bickel & Amass, 1995). It has already been widely available in other countries for several years, and has been used with greater success than the full antagonists (Kosten & McCance-Katz, 1995; Shih et al., 1993).

Some recent studies indicate that narcotic antagonists may also have therapeutic value in alcohol and cocaine dependence (O'Malley at al., 1996; Nemecek, 1995). One study found, for example, that the narcotic antagonist naltrexone helped reduce the craving for alcohol. As a result, relapses were reduced to 23 percent in a group of patients who were taking naltrexone, compared to 54 percent in a traditional detoxification group (Volpicelli et al., 1992). A similar line of investigation found that excessive drinkers receiving naltrexone along with coping skills therapy attained three times the rate of abstinence achieved by control patients. Moreover, fewer than half of the naltrexone patients who later sampled one or two drinks experienced a full relapse, whereas the majority of the control patients relapsed (O'Malley et al., 1996, 1992). These and related studies led the U.S. Food and Drug Administration to approve naltrexone as a medication for alcoholism in 1995.

Initially these studies surprised and confused clinicians. Why should narcotic antagonists, which operate on endorphins, affect alcoholism, which has been tied largely to GABA activity? However, with research now suggesting that various drugs may ultimately stimulate the same pleasure pathway in the brain, it seems reasonable to expect that antagonists for one drug may in a roundabout way affect the rewarding impact of other drugs as well.

Finally, newly developed antibodies are under investigation as a possible cocaine antagonist. These antibodies seek cocaine molecules and break them into two inert byproducts. The new antibodies may eventually prove helpful to motivated cocaine abusers, enabling them to stay drug-free long enough to break the cycle of addiction (Landry, 1997; Landry et al., 1993). In related work, some researchers have developed a compound that seems to *immunize* rats against some of the stimulating effects of cocaine (Carrera et al., 1995).

Drug Maintenance Therapy A drug-related lifestyle may be a greater problem than the drug's direct effects. Much of the damage caused by heroin addiction, for example, comes from overdoses, unsterile needles, harmful contaminants, and an accompanying life of crime. Thus clinicians were initially very enthusiastic when ***methadone maintenance programs*** were developed in the 1960s to treat heroin addiction (Dole & Nyswander, 1967, 1965). In these programs, clients with an addiction are given the synthetic opioid methadone as a substitute for heroin. Although the clients then become dependent on methadone, their addiction is maintained under legal and safe medical supervision. The programs' creators believed methadone to be preferable to heroin because it can be taken orally, thus eliminating the dangers of needles, and it needs to be taken only once a day.

The initial methadone programs appeared to be very effective, and led to the establishment of numerous such programs throughout the United States, Canada, and England (Payte, 1989). These programs became less popular during the 1980s, however, largely because of the addictiveness and dangers of methadone itself (Peachey & Franklin, 1985; Etzioni, 1973). Many clinicians came to believe that substituting one addiction for another is not an acceptable "solution" for drug dependence, and many persons with an addiction complained that methadone addiction was creating an additional drug problem that simply complicated their original one, leaving them with a far from drug-free existence (Cornish et al., 1995). In fact, methadone is harder to withdraw from than heroin, because the withdrawal symptoms last nearly twice as long (Kleber, 1981).

Pregnant women maintained on methadone have the added concern of the drug's effect on their fetus. Methadone has been associated with severe and extensive withdrawal symptoms in newborns and with possible neurological symptoms. Methadone-exposed children may exhibit greater anxiety and aggression than their unexposed peers, and may be at increased risk of developing attention-deficit disorder and learning disorders (DeCubas & Field, 1993).

Despite such concerns, interest in methadone maintenance treatment (as well as treatment by a related substitute drug, *Levo-alpha-acetyl-methadol,* or *LAAM*) has increased in recent years, partly as a result of the rapid spread of the HIV virus among intravenous drug abusers and their sex partners and children (Cacciola et al., 1995; Cornish et al., 1995). More than a quarter of AIDS cases reported in the early 1990s were directly associated with intravenous drug abuse, and intravenous drug abuse is the ultimate causal factor in 60 percent of pediatric AIDS cases (Brown, 1993; NIDA, 1991). Intravenous drug abuse is risky not only because of the dangers of unsterile needle sharing but also because of the disinhibiting effects of drugs, which can lead to high-risk sexual behavior (Millstein, 1992). Thus some methadone maintenance programs have incorporated AIDS education and health-focused supportive psychotherapy in their treatment services (Batki, 1988).

Research suggests that methadone maintenance programs are most effective when they are combined with education, regular psychotherapy, family therapy, and employment counseling (McLellan et al., 1993). In such a treatment program, clinicians are often able to decrease the dosage of methadone gradually until the client is indeed drug-free.

Sociocultural Therapies

As we have observed, sociocultural theorists believe that psychological problems emerge in a social setting and are best treated in a social context. Three sociocultural approaches have been applied to substance-related disorders: (1) self-help programs, in which persons with addictions help each other; (2) culture-sensitive programs; and (3) community prevention programs.

Self-Help and Residential Treatment Programs

In view of the cost and limited success of clinical interventions, many people who abuse drugs have organized among themselves to help one another recover without professional assistance. The drug self-help movement dates back to 1935, when two men from Ohio with alcoholism met to discuss alternative treatment possibilities. The first discussion led to others and to the eventual formation of a self-help group for persons with alcoholism. The members discussed alcohol-related problems, traded ideas, and provided support. The organization became known as ***Alcoholics Anonymous (AA).***

Today AA has more than 2 million members in 89,000 groups across the United States and nearly 100 other countries (AA World Services, 1994). It provides peer support therapy with moral and spiritual features to help people overcome alcoholism. Different members apparently find different aspects of AA helpful. For some it is the peer support and identification (Galanter et al., 1990); for others it is the spiritual dimension. Meetings take place regularly, and members are available to help each other twenty-four hours a day.

All kinds of persons in all kinds of places now use the principles of self-help programs to help them overcome and control their problems with alcohol or other substances. Here sober bikers get together at "The Dry Gulch," a favorite spot in St. Paul, Minnesota.

BOX 13-4 Controlled Drug Use vs. Abstinence

Is total abstinence the only cure for drug abuse and dependence, or can people with substance-related disorders learn to keep drug use under control? This issue has been debated for years, especially when the drug in question is alcohol (Manning, 1996; Marriott et al., 1995; Sleek, 1995).

Some cognitive-behavioral theorists believe that people can continue to drink in moderation if they learn to set appropriate drinking limits, a principle that underlies moderate drinking programs such as Drink/Link and Moderation Management (MM). The advocates of controlled drinking argue that a goal of strict abstinence may in fact encourage people to abandon self-control entirely if they should have a single drink (Peele, 1989; Heather et al., 1982). Those who view alcoholism as a disease, in contrast, take the AA position of "Once an alcoholic, always an alcoholic," and hold that relapse is almost inevitable when people with alcoholism believe that they can safely take one drink (Pendery et al., 1982). This misguided belief, they hold, will sooner or later open the door to alcohol once again and lead back to uncontrollable drinking.

Feelings run so strongly that the people on one side have at times challenged the motives and integrity of those on the other (Sobell & Sobell, 1984, 1976, 1973; Pendery et al., 1982). Research indicates, however, that both controlled drinking and abstinence may be viable treatment goals, depending on the individual's personality and on the nature of the particular drinking problem. Studies suggest, for example, that abstinence is a more appropriate goal for people who have a long-standing dependence on alcohol, while controlled drinking can be helpful to younger drinkers whose pattern does not extend to physical dependence. They may in fact need to be taught a nonabusive form of drinking (Peele, 1992; Nathan, 1986; Marlatt, 1985; Miller, 1983, 1982). Studies also suggest that abstinence is appropriate for people who believe that abstinence is the only answer for them (Rosenberg, 1993). These individuals are more likely to relapse after having just one drink. The results of these studies may apply to other drug disorders as well.

Generally speaking, both abstinence and controlled drinking are extremely difficult for persons with alcoholism to achieve (Watson, 1987). Although treatment may help them to improve for a while, follow-up studies indicate that many of them relapse. A study that followed the progress of 110 individuals found that thirty years after treatment, 20 percent had become moderate drinkers, 34 percent had become abstinent, and the rest continued to have significant drinking problems (Vaillant, 1983). Some other alcoholism findings are even gloomier (Peele, 1989; Emrick & Hansen, 1983).

Such statistics serve as a harsh reminder that substance abuse and dependence continue to be among our society's most durable and disabling problems.

By establishing guidelines for living, the organization helps members abstain "one day at a time," urging them to accept as "fact" the idea that they are powerless over alcohol and that they must stop drinking entirely and permanently if they are to live normal lives (see Box 13-4). A related self-help organization, *Al-Anon,* offers support for people who live with and care about persons with alcoholism. In these groups people share their painful experiences and learn how to cope with and to stop reinforcing the drinking behavior of their relatives. Self-help programs, such as Narcotics Anonymous and Cocaine Anonymous, have also been developed for other substance-related disorders.

Many self-help programs, such as Daytop Village and Phoenix House, have expanded into ***residential treatment centers,*** or ***therapeutic communities,*** where people formerly dependent on drugs live, work, and socialize in a drug-free environment while undergoing individual, group, and family therapies and making a transition back to community life (Landry, 1994).

The actual success of the self-help and residential treatment programs has been difficult to determine (Ray & Ksir, 1993; Meyer et al., 1989). Some programs keep no records of members who failed to be helped and dropped out. Moreover, such programs are often distrustful of researchers and deal with them very selectively (Vaillant, 1983). The studies that have been conducted have offered favorable findings (Watson et al., 1997; Wells et al., 1994; Sheehan, Oppenheimer, & Taylor, 1993). The evidence that keeps these programs going, however, comes primarily in the form of individual testimonials. Many tens of thousands of persons have revealed that they are members of these programs and credit them with turning their lives around (Gleick, 1995; Galanter et al., 1990).

Culture-Sensitive Programs Many persons who abuse substances live in a poverty-stricken and violence-prone environment (NIDA, 1990). A growing number of today's treatment programs try to be sensitive to the special sociocultural pressures and unique problems faced by drug abusers who are poor, homeless, or members of ethnic minority groups (Gottfredson & Koper, 1996; Deitch & Solit, 1993; Wallace, 1993). Sensitivity to each patient's unique life challenges can be the best defense against the environmental and social stresses that can lead to relapse.

Similarly, therapists have become more aware that women often require treatment methods different from those designed for men (Lisansky-Gomberg, 1993). Women and men have different physical and psychological reactions to drugs, for example (Hamilton, 1991). In addition, treatment of women who abuse substances may be complicated by the impact of sexual abuse, the possibility that they may become pregnant while taking drugs, the stresses of raising children, and their fear of criminal prosecution for abusing drugs during pregnancy (Cornish et al., 1995; Roper, 1992; Wallen, 1992). According to some studies, as many as 70 percent of women with substance-related disorders have experienced sexual abuse before age 16 (Arbiter, 1991; Hagan, 1991; Worth, 1991). Thus many women with such disorders feel more comfortable seeking help at gender-sensitive clinics or at feminist-oriented residential programs that focus on empowerment and education and that allow children to live with their recovering mothers (Copeland & Hall, 1992; DeAngelis, 1992).

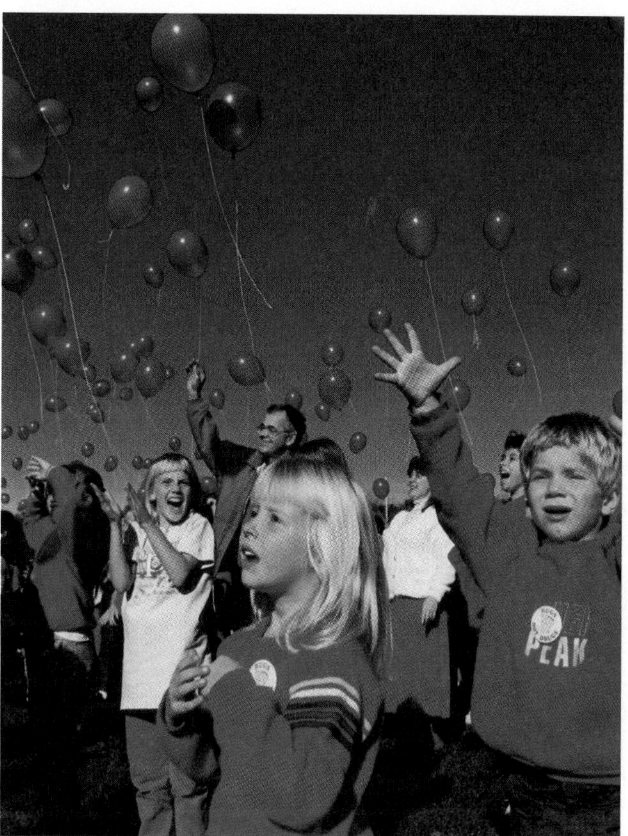
Community prevention programs for substance-related disorders often target very young children. Here children pledge abstinence from drug use on Red Ribbon Day by releasing balloons.

Community Prevention Programs Perhaps the most effective "treatment" for substance-related disorders is to prevent them (Anthony et al., 1995; Kleber, 1995). The first drug-prevention efforts took place in schools exclusively. To reach chronic truants, school dropouts, and older people, however, prevention programs are now also being conducted in workplaces, activity centers, and other community settings.

Some programs advocate total abstinence from drugs, while others advocate "responsible" use. Some seek to interrupt drug use; others, recognizing that early onset of drug use is strongly correlated with later abuse, seek to delay the age of experimentation with drugs. Similarly, programs may differ in whether they try to provide drug education, teach constructive alternatives to drug use, change the psychological state of the potential user, modify relationships with peers, or combine some of these techniques.

Prevention programs may focus on the *individual* (for example, by providing education about unpleasant drug effects), on the *family* (by teaching parenting skills and improving family functioning), on the *peer group* (by changing peer norms or teaching resistance to peer pressure), on the *school* (by establishing firm enforcement of drug policies), or on the *community* at large (by public service announcements such as the "Just say no" campaign). The most effective prevention efforts combine several such areas of focus to create a comprehensive and cooperative program that provides a consistent message about drug abuse in all areas of individuals' lives (NIDA, 1991).

Some prevention programs have even been developed for preschool children. *The Beginning Alcohol and Addiction Basic Education Studies (BABES)* program teaches preschool children decision-making skills, coping skills, and techniques for resisting peer pressure and dealing with feelings. It also provides information about alcohol and other drugs, and familiarizes children with sources of help. This program uses instructional puppets such as Buttons and Bows McKitty, whose parents are drug-dependent; Early Bird, who gives warning signals about self-destructive behaviors and about the effects of incorrect beliefs about drugs; Recovering Reggie, a recovering alcoholic dog who tells about his addiction and recovery; and Rhonda Rabbit, an abused child whose parents abuse drugs and who demonstrates coping skills (Abbott, 1987). The *Head Start* program has initiated a similar preschool prevention curriculum, targeting the disadvantaged children enrolled in Head Start and their parents (Oyemade, 1989). Although it seems sad that intensive efforts to prevent drug abuse must focus on preschool children, they may make a major positive difference in the course of a child's life.

Crossroads

In some respects the story of the misuse of drugs is the same today as in past years. Substance use is still rampant, and it still creates some of society's most prevalent and debilitating psychological disorders. New drugs keep emerging, and the public continues to go through periods of believing naively that they are "safe." Only gradually do people learn that these drugs, too, pose significant dangers. And treatments for substance-related disorders continue to have only limited effect.

Yet there are important new wrinkles in this familiar story. Researchers have begun to develop a clearer understanding of the way many drugs act on the brain and body. In the treatment sphere, self-help groups and rehabilitation programs are flourishing. Preventive education to make people aware of the seduction of drugs and the dangers of drug misuse is also on the upswing and seems to be making some difference in the public's drug behavior. And clinicians have discovered drug antagonists that seem to hold promise as forms of biological intervention.

One reason for this improved state of affairs is that proponents of the various models have stopped working in relative isolation. They have looked increasingly for intersections between their work and that from other models. This more integrated approach has brought new promise to the study and treatment of substance-related disorders, just as integrated approaches have enhanced work on other psychological disorders.

Perhaps the most important new insight is that several of the models were already on the right track. The societal climate, social pressures, addictive personalities, self-rewards, and genetic predispositions proposed by various theorists seem to play major roles in substance-related disorders, and they appear to operate together. For example, some people may inherit a deficient biological reward center, and so may need special doses of external stimulation—say, intense relationships, an abundance of certain foods, or drugs—to activate their reward centers. Their repeated reliance on external rewards may then suggest an addictive personality. The same individuals may be especially prone to try drugs, particularly when their subculture makes the drugs available or when they are subjected to social and personal stress. Finally, once the individuals start taking drugs, their deficient reward centers may help to insure a continuing need for more and more such drugs.

Just as each model offers important insights into substance-related disorders, each may make important contributions to treatment. As we have observed, the various treatments that have been proposed for these disorders each seem to work best when they are combined with approaches from the other models. Clearly, integrated treatment is the most productive approach.

These recent developments are encouraging. Meanwhile, however, enormous quantities of drugs are distributed and used, more every year. New drugs and drug combinations are discovered almost daily. And with them come new problems, new questions, and requirements for new research and new interventions. Perhaps the most valuable lesson is an old one: there is no free lunch. The pleasures associated with these substances come with high psychological and biological costs, some not yet even known.

Chapter Review

1. ***Substance misuse*** A drug is any substance other than food that changes our bodily and mental functioning. The misuse of *substances,* or *drugs,* may lead to temporary changes in behavior, emotion, or thought, such as *intoxication.* Chronic excessive use can lead to either *substance abuse,* a pattern in which people rely heavily on a drug and structure their lives around it, or *substance dependence,* in which they show the symptoms of substance abuse plus physical dependence on the drug. People who become physically dependent on a drug develop a *tolerance* to it or experience unpleasant *withdrawal symptoms* when they abstain from it, or both.

2. ***Depressants*** Depressants are substances that slow the activity of the central nervous system. Each of the

major depressants is associated with various problems and dangers.

A. *Alcohol* Alcoholic beverages contain *ethyl alcohol,* which is carried to the central nervous system, depressing its function and leading to impairment of fine motor skills and other physiological effects. *Intoxication* occurs when the concentration of alcohol in the bloodstream reaches 0.09 percent. Among other actions, alcohol facilitates the release of the neurotransmitter *GABA* at key sites in the brain. Excessive use may lead to abuse or dependence, also called *alcoholism,* as well as to accidents, health impairment, and certain psychological disorders.

B. *Sedative-hypnotic drugs* The sedative-hypnotic drugs, which produce feelings of relaxation and drowsiness, include *barbiturates* and *benzodiazepines.* Both increase the activity of GABA. Chronic and excessive use of these drugs, particularly barbiturates, may lead to abuse or dependence.

C. *Opioids* Opioids include *opium* and drugs derived from it, such as *morphine* and *heroin,* and various synthetic opioids. They all reduce tension and pain and cause other bodily reactions. Opioids operate by binding to neurons that ordinarily receive *endorphins.* Chronic and excessive use of opioids can lead to abuse or dependence.

3. *Stimulants* Stimulants are substances that increase the activity of the central nervous system, such as cocaine, amphetamines, and caffeine. They may lead to intoxication, abuse, and dependence, including a withdrawal pattern marked by depression, fatigue, and irritability. *Cocaine* produces a euphoric effect by stimulating the activity of *dopamine, norepinephrine,* and *serotonin* in the brain. *Amphetamines,* stimulant drugs that are manufactured in a laboratory, operate in a similar manner.

4. *Hallucinogens* Hallucinogens, such as *LSD,* are substances that cause powerful changes primarily in sensory perception. Perceptions are intensified and distorted and illusions and hallucinations can occur. LSD apparently causes such effects by disturbing the release of the neurotransmitter *serotonin.* LSD is extremely potent, and its ingestion may lead to a "bad trip" or to *flashbacks.*

5. *Cannabis* *Cannabis sativa* is a hemp plant whose main ingredient is *tetrahydrocannabinol (THC).* The most popular, and weakest, form of cannabis, *marijuana,* is more powerful today than it was in years past. It can cause intoxication, and regular use can lead to abuse and dependence.

6. *Combinations of substances* Many people take more than one drug at a time, and the drugs interact with each other. When different drugs enhance each other's effects, they have a combined impact known as a *synergistic effect.* The use of two or more drugs at the same time—*polysubstance use*—has become increasingly common. Similarly, *polysubstance-related disorders* have also become a significant problem.

7. *Explanations for substance-related disorders* A variety of explanations for substance abuse and dependence have been put forward. None has gained unqualified research support, but collectively they are beginning to shed light on the disorders.

A. The *sociocultural* view proposes that the people most likely to abuse drugs are those whose societies create an atmosphere of stress or whose families value or tolerate drug use. Epidemiological studies provide some support for these claims.

B. In the *psychodynamic view,* people who turn to substance abuse have excessive dependency needs traceable to the oral stage of life. Some theorists also believe that certain people have a "substance abuse personality" that makes them vulnerable to drugs.

C. The leading *behavioral* view proposes that drug use is initially reinforced because it reduces tension and raises spirits.

D. The *biological view* is supported by studies of twins and adoptees, which suggest that people may inherit a predisposition to substance dependence. Biological researchers have further learned that drug tolerance and withdrawal symptoms may be related to the brain's reduced production of particular neurotransmitters during excessive and chronic drug use. Finally, biological investigations suggest that many, perhaps all, drugs may ultimately lead to increased dopamine activity in the brain's *reward center.*

8. *Treatments for substance-related disorders* Treatments for substance abuse and dependence vary widely. Usually several approaches are combined.

A. *Psychodynamic therapies* try to help clients become aware of and address the underlying issues and needs that contribute to their use of drugs.

B. A common *behavioral technique* is *aversion therapy,* in which an unpleasant stimulus is paired with the drug that the person is abusing.

C. *Cognitive* and *behavioral techniques* have been combined in such forms as *behavioral self-control training (BSCT)* and *relapse-prevention training.*

D. *Biological treatments* include *detoxification, antagonist drugs,* and *drug maintenance therapy.*

E. *Sociocultural therapies* treat substance-related disorders in a social context. The leading approaches are *self-help groups,* such as Alcoholics Anonymous; *culture-sensitive treatments;* and *community prevention programs.*

"My Life's Great Big Secret"

On one of her shows in January 1995, the popular talk-show host Oprah Winfrey revealed, with great emotion, that she had been physically dependent on cocaine in the mid-1970s. "That is my life's great big secret that has been held over my head," she said. "I understand the shame. I understand the guilt."

Afterthoughts: Does drug abuse by a middle-aged, highly regarded person conjure up a different image than drug abuse by a younger, less famous individual? . . . What different kinds of issues might be confronted by drug abusers of different genders or different races? . . . Is society today more, or less accepting of admissions like Winfrey's than it might have been a generation ago? Why?

Chasing Highs Wherever They May Lead

Jonathan Melvoin, a backup keyboard player for the rock group Smashing Pumpkins, died of a heroin overdose in July of 1996. Word soon spread that the brand of heroin he had taken was Red Rum, a strain smuggled in from Colombia. Its name—*murder* spelled backward—comes from the Stephen King novel *The Shining*.

Within hours the demand for Red Rum rose precipitously on the streets of Manhattan's Lower East Side. "It's kind of sick," a narcotics officer told the *New York Times*. "But when people die from something or nearly die, all of a sudden there's this rush to get it."

Afterthoughts: Why might people actively pursue drugs that are known to endanger their lives? . . . What effects might the heightened use of drugs by some rock performers have on adolescents and young adults? . . . Who has the greater impact on the drug behaviors of teenagers and young adults: rock performers who speak out against drugs or rock performers who praise the virtues of drugs?

Police surround a drug suspect in rush-hour traffic.

Frankly Speaking

Outlawing drugs in order to solve the drug problem is much like outlawing sex in order to win the war against AIDS.

—**Ronald Siegel,** *Intoxication*, 1990

Afterthoughts: What point is Siegel making about interventions for substance-related disorders? . . . What are the merits and flaws of his argument? . . . Only a third of the $15 billion the U.S. government spends on drug abuse goes to prevention and treatment. Does the focus on the criminalization of drugs ultimately add to the stigma of drug abuse and, in turn, make effective treatment more elusive (Nash, 1997)?

Topic Overview

Sexual Dysfunctions
Sexual Desire Disorders
Sexual Excitement Disorders
Orgasm Disorders
Sexual Pain Disorders

Paraphilias
Fetishism
Transvestic Fetishism
Exhibitionism
Voyeurism
Frotteurism
Pedophilia
Sexual Masochism
Sexual Sadism

Gender Identity Disorder

Crossroads

Chapter **14**

Sexual Disorders and Gender Identity Disorder

Sexual behavior may add intimacy and joy to a relationship and may enhance feelings of love and tenderness between individuals, as we are reminded by the floating figures in Marc Chagall's Birthday, *1915. Conversely, problems in sexual functioning sometimes detract from a relationship and may bring feelings of anxiety or depression.*

Few areas of functioning are of more interest to human beings than sexual behavior. Sexual feelings are a crucial part of our development and daily functioning, sexual activity is tied to the satisfaction of our basic needs, and sexual performance is linked to our self-esteem. No wonder sexual behavior is a major focus of both private thoughts and public discussions (Becker & Segraves, 1995).

For the same reasons, abnormal sexual behavior is of more widespread interest than almost all other forms of abnormal functioning. Most people are fascinated by the sexual problems of others and worry about the normality of their own sexuality. Our society, too, is curious about abnormal sexual behavior and attaches enormous shame to it. Many people who have sexual disorders, or fear they do, are therefore burdened with feelings of anxiety, guilt, or self-disgust.

There are two kinds of sexual disorders: *sexual dysfunctions* and *paraphilias.* People with ***sexual dysfunctions*** are unable to function normally in their sexual responses. They may not be able to become sexually aroused, for example, or to achieve orgasm. People with ***paraphilias*** experience recurrent and intense sexual urges, fantasies, or behaviors in response to objects or situations that society deems inappropriate. They may be aroused by sexual activity with a child, for example, or by exposure of their genitals to strangers. Some may even act on those urges. In addition to these sexual disorders is ***gender identity disorder,*** a sexual-related disorder in which people persistently feel that they have been assigned to the wrong sex and in fact identify with the other gender.

Sexual Dysfunctions

Sexual dysfunctions make it difficult or impossible to have or enjoy coitus. The dysfunctions are typically very distressing to those who experience them, and they often lead to sexual frustration, guilt about failure, loss of self-esteem, and interpersonal problems with the sex partner. Often these dysfunctions are interrelated, so that many patients with one dysfunction manifest another as well (Segraves & Segraves, 1991). Sexual dysfunctioning will be described here for heterosexual couples in long-term relationships, because this is the context in which the majority of cases are seen in therapy. Homosexual couples are subject to the same dysfunctions, however, and therapists use the same basic techniques to treat them (LoPiccolo, 1995).

The human sexual response consists of a *cycle* with four phases: *desire, excitement, orgasm,* and *resolution* (see Figures 14-1, 14-2, and 14-3). Sexual dysfunctions affect one or more of the first three phases of the cycle. Resolution consists simply of the relaxation and decline in arousal that follow orgasm, and there are no sexual dysfunctions associated with it.

Some individuals have struggled with a sexual dysfunction their whole lives (labeled ***lifelong type*** in DSM-IV); in other cases the dysfunction was preceded by normal sexual functioning (***acquired type***). Similarly, in some cases the dysfunction is present during all sexual situations (***generalized type***); in others it is tied to particular situations (***situational type***) (APA, 1994).

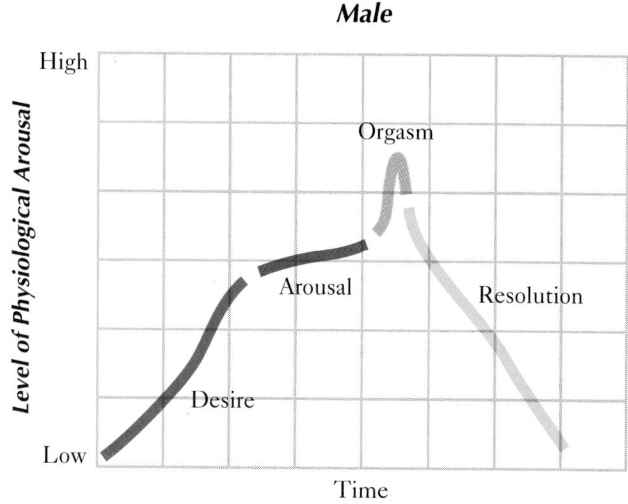

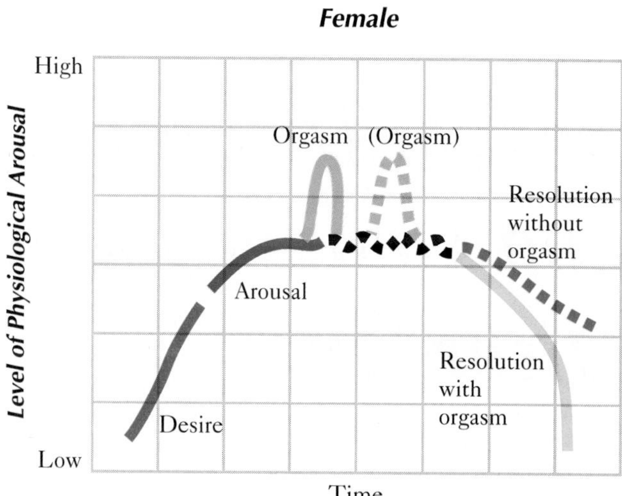

Figure 14-1 *Masters and Johnson found similar sequences of phases in the normal sexual response cycles of both males and females. Sometimes, however, women do not experience orgasm; in that case, the resolution phase is less abrupt. And sometimes women experience two or more orgasms in succession before the resolution phase. (Adapted from Kaplan, 1974; Masters & Johnson, 1970, 1966.)*

Disorders of the Desire Phase

The ***desire phase*** of the sexual response cycle consists of an urge to have sex, sexual fantasies or daydreams, and sexual attraction to others. Two dysfunctions—*hypoactive sexual desire* and *sexual aversion*—are associated with the desire phase. A client named Ms. Bryarton experiences both of these disorders:

> Mr. and Ms. [Bryarton] have been married for 14 years and have three children, ages 8 through 12. They are both bright and well educated. Both are from Scotland. . . . [They complain that Ms. Bryarton] has never enjoyed [sex] since they have been married.
>
> Before their marriage, although they had intercourse only twice, Ms. Bryarton had been highly aroused by kissing and petting and felt she used her attractiveness

to "seduce" her husband into marriage. She did, however, feel intense guilt about their two episodes of premarital intercourse; during their honeymoon, she began to think of sex as a chore that could not be pleasing. Although she periodically passively complied with intercourse, she had almost no spontaneous desire for sex. She never masturbated, had never reached orgasm, thought of all variations such as oral sex as completely repulsive, and was preoccupied with a fantasy of how disapproving her family would be if she ever engaged in any of these activities.

Ms. Bryarton is almost totally certain that no woman she respects in any older generation has enjoyed sex, and that despite the "new vogue" of sexuality, only sleazy, crude women let themselves act like "animals." These beliefs have led to a pattern of regular, but infrequent, sex that at best is accommodating and gives little or no pleasure to her or her husband. Whenever Ms. Bryarton comes close to having a feeling of sexual arousal, numerous negative thoughts come into her mind, such as "What am I, a tramp?" "If I like this, he'll just want it more often." Or "How could I look myself in the mirror after something like this?" These thoughts almost inevitably are accompanied by a cold feeling and an insensitivity to sensual pleasure. As a result, sex is invariably an unhappy experience. Almost

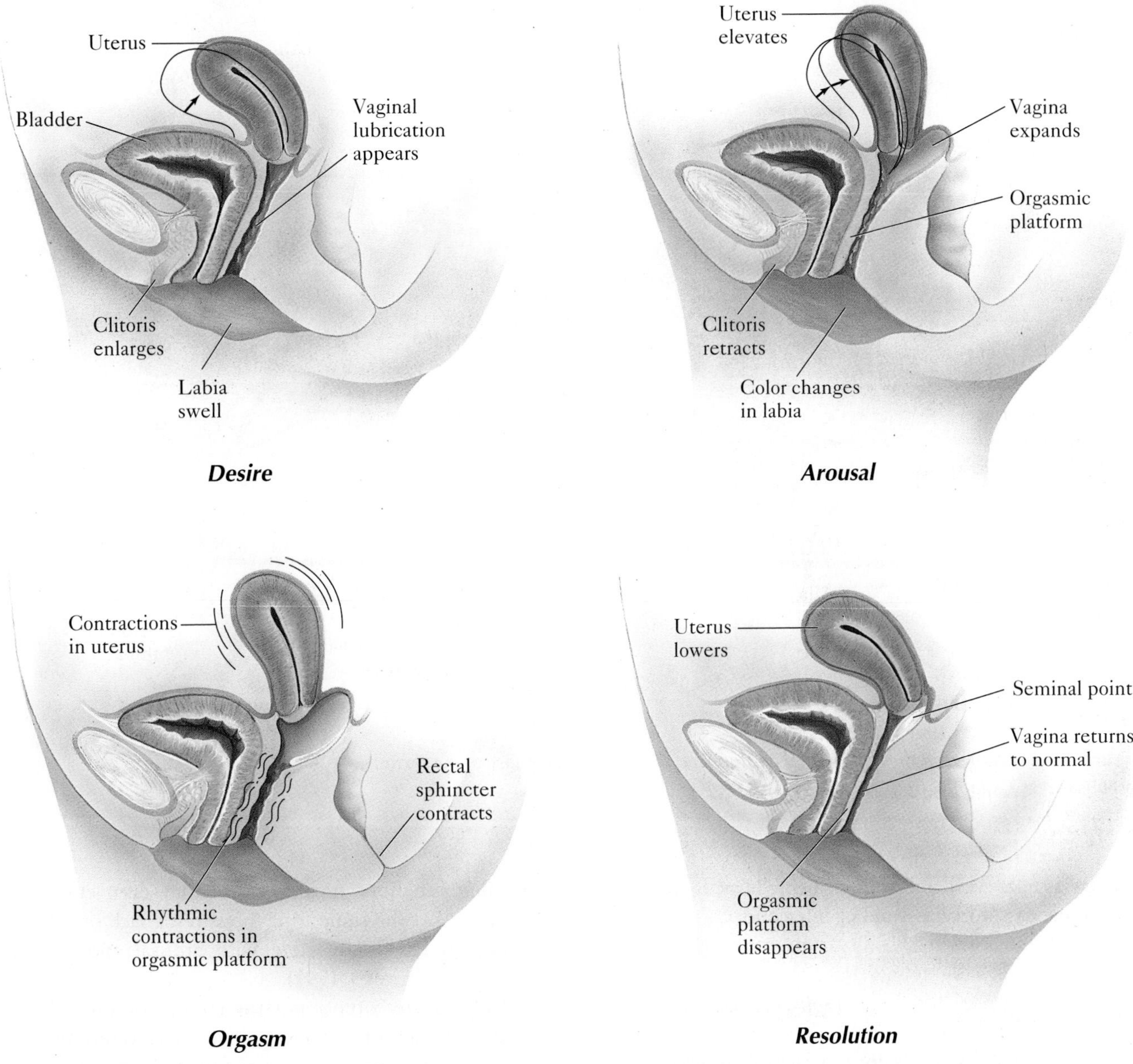

Figure 14-2 *Changes in the female sexual anatomy occur during each phase of the sexual response cycle. (Adapted from Hyde, 1990, p. 200.)*

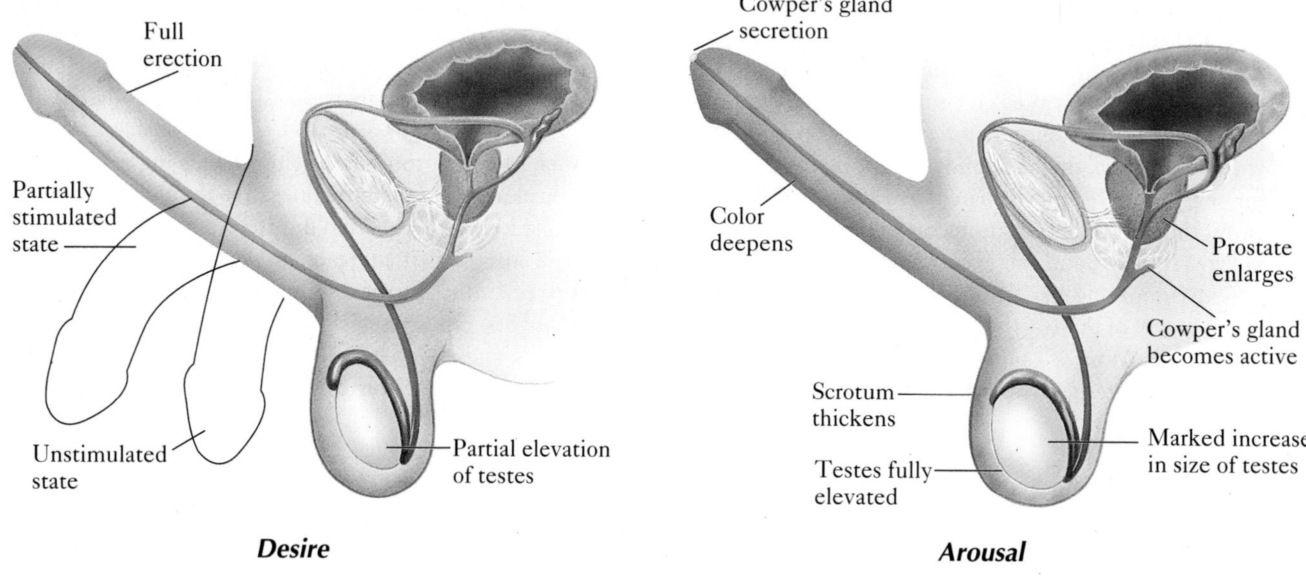

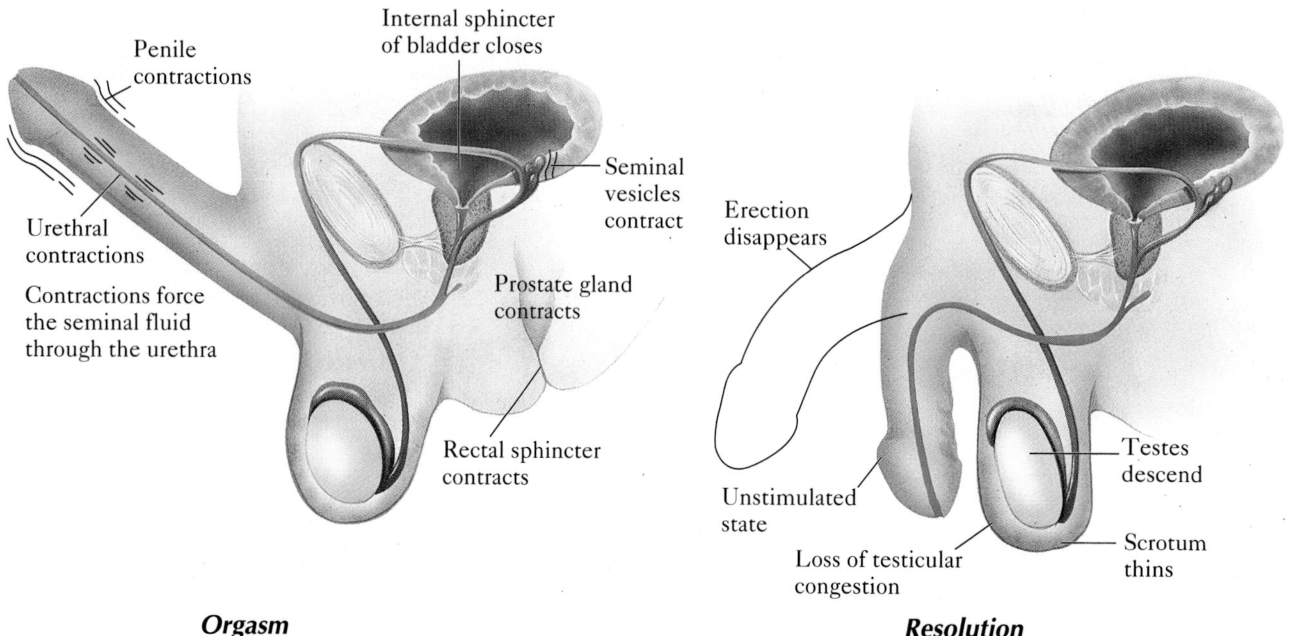

Figure 14-3 *Changes in the male sexual anatomy occur during each phase of the sexual response cycle. (Adapted from Hyde, 1990, p. 199.)*

> any excuse, such as fatigue or being busy, is sufficient for her to rationalize avoiding intercourse.
>
> Yet, intellectually Ms. Bryarton wonders, "Is something wrong with me?" . . .
>
> *(Spitzer et al., 1994, p. 251)*

Hypoactive sexual desire is a lack of interest in sex and a resulting low level of sexual activity. When a person with hypoactive sexual desire does have sex, he or she often functions normally and may even enjoy the experience. At the same time, however, a lack of interest in sex can readily interfere with arousal and orgasm (Segraves & Segraves, 1991).

Cultural stereotypes portray men as wanting all the sex they can get. In fact, hypoactive sexual desire may be found in as many as 15 percent of men (LoPiccolo, 1995; Rosen & Leiblum, 1995; Spector & Carey, 1990), and the number seeking therapy has increased markedly during the past decade (LoPiccolo & Friedman, 1988). Some theorists believe that the number of male cases is actually unchanged, but that men have become more likely to seek treatment for this problem. They may be prodded by partners who would not have asserted their own sexual needs years ago, when our society professed to believe that "nice women" were not interested in sex (LoPiccolo, 1995). According to estimates, hypoactive sexual desire may also be found in 20 to 35 percent of women (LoPiccolo, 1995; Rosen & Leiblum, 1995).

Precise figures on hypoactive sexual desire are elusive, however. DSM-IV defines this dysfunction as "deficient or absent sexual fantasies and desire for sexual activity," but it does not specify what a "deficient" level is (LoPiccolo, 1995). Age, number of years married, education, social class, race, and other factors may all influence the frequency of sex. Even frequency of occurrence does not necessarily indicate level of desire (Beck, 1995). In one survey ninety-three happily married couples were asked to report both the actual frequency of their sexual encounters and their desired frequency (see Table 14-1). The responses reveal that the typical desired frequency has a wide range, from once a day to twice a week. The findings suggest that a diagnosis of hypoactive sexual desire may not be warranted unless a patient desires sex less frequently than once every two weeks (LoPiccolo & Friedman, 1988).

People with ***sexual aversion*** find sex so unpleasant that any sexual advance may arouse revulsion, disgust, anxiety, and fear. Aversion to sex seems to be quite rare in men and somewhat more common in women, but precise prevalence rates are not known.

A person's sex drive is determined by a combination of biological, psychological, and sociocultural factors, and any of them may reduce sexual desire (Beck, 1995; Rosen & Leiblum, 1995). In most instances low sexual desire or sexual aversion is attributable primarily to sociocultural and psychological factors, but biological conditions can also lower sex drive significantly (Kresin, 1993).

Biological Causes A number of hormones are involved in sexual desire and activity, and abnormalities in their levels can lower the sex drive (Beck, 1995; Rosen & Leiblum, 1995; Kresin, 1993). A high level of the hormone ***prolactin,*** a low level of the male sex hormone ***testosterone,*** and either a high or low level of the female sex hormone ***estrogen*** can result in low sex drive. Low sex drive has, for example, been linked to the high levels of estrogen contained in some oral contraceptives.

TABLE 14–1 Desired vs. Actual Frequency of Sexual Intercourse for Males and Females in 93 Happily Married Couples*

	Percentage Reporting as "Desired"		*Percentage Reporting as "Actual"*	
Frequency	*Males*	*Females*	*Males*	*Females*
More than once a day	12.2%	3.3%	2.2%	1.1%
Once a day	28.9	19.8	2.2	1.1
3–4 times a week	42.4	50.6	35.6	39.6
Twice a week	12.2	16.5	30.0	24.2
Once a week	4.4	9.9	15.6	20.9
Once every 2 weeks	0	0	8.9	8.8
Once a month	0	0	2.2	2.2
Less than once a month	0	0	3.3	0
Not at all	0	0	0	0

** Mean age, 34 for men, 32 for women; married mean of 9 years; mean number of children, 2.6; mean family income, $33,000.*
Source: LoPiccolo & Friedman, 1988.

Conversely, it has also been tied to the low level of estrogen experienced by many postmenopausal women or women who have recently given birth. An abnormal hormone level, however, causes only a small percentage of cases of hypoactive sexual desire (Kresin, 1993; LoPiccolo & Friedman, 1988).

"When I touch him he rolls into a ball."

Some medications for pain relief and some psychotropic drugs may also suppress the sex drive (Beck, 1995; Segraves, 1995; Nitenson & Cole, 1993). Indeed, *most* of the psychotropic drugs currently in use in the United States are capable of causing sexual dysfunctions of one kind or another in some people (Segraves, 1995). Illicit drugs such as cocaine, marijuana, amphetamines, and heroin may also suppress the sex drive. Alcohol may enhance the sex drive at a low level, by lowering psychological inhibitions, yet diminish it at higher levels (Roehrich & Kinder, 1991). Meanwhile, centuries of searching have failed to find a true *aphrodisiac,* a substance that increases the sex drive (Henderson, Boyd, & Whitmarsh, 1995; Bancroft, 1989).

Not surprisingly, chronic physical illness can also suppress the sex drive (Schiavi et al., 1995; Kresin, 1993). A low sex drive can be caused directly by the illness, by the effect of medication, or by the stress, pain, and depression that may accompany a chronic illness.

Psychological Causes Research suggests that a general increase in anxiety or anger may reduce sexual desire in both men and women (Beck & Bozman, 1996; Bozman & Beck, 1991). More often, as cognitive theorists have noted, people with hypoactive sexual desire and sexual aversion hold particular attitudes or fears that contribute to their dysfunction (LoPiccolo, 1995). Some people who were raised in a strict religious culture have extreme antisexual attitudes. Some with an exaggeratedly hardworking, serious approach to life think of sex as self-indulgent. Others are so afraid of losing control over their sexual urges that they suppress them completely. And still others fear pregnancy.

Certain psychological disorders may also contribute to hypoactive sexual desire and sexual aversion. Even a mild level of depression can interfere with sexual desire, and some people with obsessive-compulsive characteristics find contact with another person's body fluids and odors to be aversive (LoPiccolo, 1995).

Sociocultural Causes The attitudes, fears, and psychological disorders that contribute to hypoactive sexual desire and sexual aversion arise within a social context, and indeed sociocultural factors have also been linked to these dysfunctions. Many sufferers are confronting situational pressures—divorce, a death in the family, job stress, infertility difficulties, having a baby (Burns, 1995; Letourneau & O'Donohue, 1993; Kaplan, 1979). Others may be responding to problems in their relationships (LoPiccolo, 1997; Beck, 1995; Speckens et al., 1995). Simply being in an unhappy, conflicted relationship may suppress the sex drive or make sex unpleasant. Similarly, persons who feel powerless in their relationships and very dominated by their partner can lose sexual interest. Even in generally happy relationships, if one partner is a very unskilled, unenthusiastic lover, the other can begin to lose interest in sex. And sometimes partners differ in their needs for closeness and "personal space." The one who needs more personal space may develop hypoactive sexual desire as a way of maintaining the critical distance (LoPiccolo, 1997, 1995).

Inappropriate cultural standards can also set the stage for hypoactive sexual desire and sexual aversion. Some men, having adopted our culture's double standard, are unable to feel sexual desire for a woman they love and respect. A man may lose sexual interest in his wife when she has their first child, as he cannot see a mother as a sexually exciting woman. More generally, because our society equates sexual attractiveness with youthfulness, many men and women lose interest in sex as their self-esteem and attraction to their partner diminish with age (LoPiccolo, 1995)(see Box 14-1).

The trauma of sexual molestation or assault is especially likely to result in sexual dysfunction (McCarthy, 1990; Browne & Finklehor, 1986). Sexual aversion is very common in victims of sexual abuse and persists for years, even decades (Jackson et al., 1990; Becker, 1989). In extreme cases, individuals may experience vivid flashbacks during adult sexual activity, when visual memories of the assault overwhelm them.

Disorders of the Excitement Phase

The ***excitement phase*** of the sexual response cycle is marked by general physical arousal; increases in heart rate, muscle tension, blood pressure, and respiration; and changes in the pelvic region. In men, blood pooling in the pelvis leads to erection of the penis; in women, it produces swelling of the clitoris and labia, as well as vaginal lubrication. Dysfunctions affecting the excitement phase are *female sexual arousal disorder* (once referred to as frigidity) and *male erectile disorder* (once called impotence).

Female Sexual Arousal Disorder Women with a ***sexual arousal disorder*** are repeatedly unable to attain or maintain adequate lubrication or genital swelling during sexual activity (APA, 1994). Understandably, many of them also experience an orgasm disorder or other sexual dysfunction. Indeed, this disorder is rarely diagnosed alone (Segraves & Segraves, 1991). Studies vary widely in their estimates of its prevalence, from 10 to 50 percent of women (Laumann et al., 1994; LoPiccolo, 1993; Rosen et al., 1993). This variability reflects the difficulty clinicians may have in distinguishing female sexual arousal disorder from other sexual dyfunctions (Segraves & Segraves, 1991). Too, the widespread use of vaginal lubricants may mask some cases (Rosen & Leiblum, 1995; Wincze & Carey, 1991).

Because lack of sexual arousal in women is so often tied to orgasmic dysfunction, researchers usually study and explain the two problems together. We shall follow their lead and examine the causes of these problems together when we consider female orgasmic disorder.

Male Erectile Disorder Men with an ***erectile disorder*** experience a persistent inability to attain or maintain an adequate erection during sexual activity (APA, 1994). This problem, also known in clinical circles as ***erectile failure*** and ***inhibited sexual arousal,*** occurs in about 10 percent of the general male population (Feldman et al., 1994). Carlos Domera is one such man:

> Carlos Domera is a 30-year-old dress manufacturer who came to the United States from Argentina at age 22. He is married to an American woman, Phyllis, also age 30. They have no children. Mr. Domera's problem was that he had been unable to have sexual intercourse for over a year due to his inability to achieve or maintain an erection. He had avoided all sexual contact with his wife for the prior five months, except for two brief attempts at lovemaking which ended when he failed to maintain his erection.
>
> The couple separated a month ago by mutual agreeement due to the tension that surrounded their sexual problem and their inability to feel comfortable with each other. Both professed love and concern for the other, but had serious doubts regarding their ability to resolve the sexual problem. . . .
>
> Mr. Domera conformed to the stereotype of the "macho Latin lover," believing that he "should always have erections easily and be able to make love at any time." Since he couldn't "perform" sexually, he felt humiliated and inadequate, and he dealt with this by avoiding not only sex, but any expression of affection for his wife.
>
> Ms. Domera felt "he is not trying; perhaps he doesn't love me, and I can't live with no sex, no affection, and his bad moods." She had requested the separation temporarily, and he readily agreed. However, they had recently been seeing each other twice a week. . . .
>
> During the evaluation he reported that the onset of his erectile difficulties was concurrent with a tense period in his business. After several "failures" to complete intercourse, he concluded he was "useless as a husband" and therefore a "total failure." The anxiety of attempting lovemaking was too much for him to deal with.
>
> He reluctantly admitted that he was occasionally able to masturbate alone to a full, firm erection and reach a satisfying orgasm. However, he felt ashamed and guilty about this, from both childhood masturbatory guilt and a feeling that he was "cheating" his wife. It was also noted that he had occasional firm erections upon awakening in the morning. Other than the antidepressant, the patient was taking no drugs, and he was not using much alcohol. There was no evidence of physical illness.
>
> *(Spitzer et al., 1983, pp. 105–106)*

Unlike Mr. Domera, most men with an erectile disorder are over the age of 50, largely because so many cases are associated with diseases that afflict older adults (Seidman & Rieder, 1995; Bancroft, 1989). Erectile failure is experienced by around 5 percent of all men who are 40 years old and increases to at least 15 percent at age 70 (Feldman et al., 1994). Moreover, according to surveys, half of all adult men experience some erectile difficulty during intercourse at least some of the time (Feldman et al., 1994). Erectile dysfunction accounts for more than 400,000 visits to physicians and more than 30,000 hospital admissions in the United States each year (Ackerman & Carey, 1995). In fact, the single largest group of men who seek services in sex therapy programs consists of men with erectile difficulties (Spector & Carey, 1990).

Many cases of erectile disorder—perhaps the majority—involve an interaction of biological, psychological, and sociocultural causes. Partial organic impairment of

BOX 14-1 Patterns of Sexual Behavior, Year by Year

Sexual dysfunctions are, by definition, different from the norm—or at least from the usual patterns of sexual functioning. But in the sexual realm, what is the usual? Surprisingly, this question did not receive much study until recently. In 1948 and 1953, Alfred Kinsey, a professor of biology at Indiana University, caused a national stir when he published the results of his extensive surveys on adult sexual behavior. Yet only a few similar surveys followed, and they focused mostly on adolescent sexuality and fertility (Seidman & Rieder, 1995).

Then came the mid-1980s and AIDS. Clinicians, finding their efforts to prevent the spread of this plague hampered by a dearth of available data, began to conduct large, well-designed surveys on sexual behavior. Collectively, the studies of the past decade provide a wealth of useful, sometimes eye-opening information on sexual patterns in the "normal" population (Seidman & Rieder, 1995; Laumann et al., 1994; Janus & Janus, 1993).

Teenagers

More than 90 percent of boys masturbate by the end of adolescence, compared to 50 percent of girls. For the vast majority of them, masturbation began by age 14. Males report masturbating an average of one to two times a week, females once a month.

Around 20 percent of teenagers have heterosexual intercourse by the age of 15, and 80 percent by age 19. Today's teenagers are having intercourse younger than those of past generations.

Most adolescents who are sexually experienced engage in only one sexual relationship at a time. Over the course of their teen years, however, most have at least two sex partners. Ten percent have five or more partners.

Extended periods of sexual abstinence are still common, even for teenagers in a relationship. Half of sexually experienced adolescent girls have intercourse once a month or less. Sexually experienced teenage boys spend an average of six months of the year without engaging in intercourse.

Condom use by teenagers has increased somewhat during the past decade, partly because of warnings about HIV. However, at most half of teenagers report having used a condom the last time they had sex. (Another third used a different method of contraception.) Less than a third of teenagers use condoms consistently and appropriately.

Early Adulthood (Ages 18–24)

More than 80 percent of unmarried young adults have intercourse in a given year. Of those who are sexually active, around a third have intercourse two or three times a month and another third engage in it two or three times a week. Masturbation remains rela-

the erection response typically makes the man more vulnerable to the psychosocial factors that inhibit erection (Ackerman & Carey, 1995; Rosen et al., 1994; LoPiccolo, 1985). One study found that only 10 of 63 cases of this disorder were caused by purely psychosocial factors, and only 5 were the result of organic impairment alone (LoPiccolo, 1991).

Biological Causes The same hormonal abnormalities that can cause hypoactive sexual desire can also produce an erectile disorder. Again, however, an abnormal level of testosterone, estrogen, prolactin, or thyroid hormone is found in only a small percentage of cases (Morales et al., 1991).

Vascular abnormalities are much more common biological causes of erectile disorder (Althof & Seftel, 1995; Carey et al., 1993). Since an erection occurs when the chambers in the penis fill with blood, any condition that reduces blood flow into the penis, such as heart disease or clogging of the arteries, may cause this disorder (LoPiccolo, 1997; Feldman et al., 1994; Huws, 1991). Leakage of blood out of the penile chambers through holes or tears can also cause erectile problems, as can damage to the nervous system caused by conditions as diverse as diabetes, spinal cord injuries, multiple sclerosis, kidney failure, and treatment with an artificial kidney machine (Dupont, 1995; Leiblum & Segraves, 1995; Schiavi et al., 1995). As with hypoactive sexual desire, medications for a variety of ailments and alcohol or other substance abuse may interfere with erections (LoPiccolo, 1997; Leiblum & Segraves, 1995). Erectile dysfunction is also more common among cigarette

tively common in young adulthood: close to 60 percent of men masturbate, a third of them at least once a week, and 36 percent of women masturbate, a tenth of them at least once a week.

Mid-Adulthood (Ages 25–59)

From the ages of 25 to 59, sexual relationships last longer and are more monogamous. More than 90 percent of men in this age range have sexual intercourse in a given year. Around 20 percent of the men who are married have two or more partners during that year. Half of the unmarried men have two or more partners, but by the time they turn 45, only a fourth of them have more than one sex partner in a given year.

Similarly, over 90 percent of married women in this age range have intercourse in a given year, relatively few of them with more than one partner. Around two-thirds of the unmarried women have sexual intercourse in a given year, around 25 percent with two or more partners.

Among sexually active adults, close to 60 percent of men have intercourse up to three times a week and around 60 percent of women once or twice a week.

Middle-aged adults are still masturbating. Half of all middle-aged men masturbate at least monthly. Half of all women between 25 and 50 masturbate at least monthly, but only a third of those between 51 and 64 do so.

Old Age (Over Age 60)

More and more people cease intercourse as the years go by—10 percent in their 40s, 15 percent in their 50s, 30 percent in their 60s, and 45 percent in their 70s.

The decline in men's sexual activity usually comes gradually as they advance in age and their health fails. Sexual activity is more likely to drop off precipitously for elderly women, commonly because of the death or illness of a partner. Elderly women also seem to lose interest in sex before elderly men do. Half of the women in their 60s report limited sexual interest, compared to fewer than 10 percent of the men.

Among elderly persons who remain sexually active, those in their 60s have intercourse an average of four times a month, those in their 70s two or three times a month. Around 70 percent of elderly men and 50 percent of elderly women continue to have sexual fantasies. Around half of men and a fourth of women continue to masturbate into their 90s.

Clearly sexual interests and behaviors remain an important part of life for many individuals, even as they grow older and as their sexual responses change to some degree.

smokers than nonsmokers; the heavier the smoker, the greater the degree of dysfunction (Condra et al., 1986; Hirshkowitz et al., 1992).

A variety of medical procedures have been developed for diagnosing biological causes of erectile disorder, including ultrasound recordings and blood tests (Ackerman & Carey, 1995). Measuring ***nocturnal penile tumescence (NPT),*** or erections during sleep, is particularly useful in assessing neurological causes (Althof & Seftel, 1995; Schiavi et al., 1993). Men typically have erections during *rapid eye movement (REM)* sleep, the phase of sleep that corresponds with dreaming (see p. 364). A healthy man will typically have two to five REM periods each night, and perhaps two to three hours of penile erections (see Figure 14-4). Abnormal or absent nightly erections usually (not always) indicate some organic basis for erectile failure (Mohr & Beutler, 1990). As a rough screening device, a patient may be instructed to fasten a simple "snap gauge" band around his penis before going to sleep and then check the next morning. A broken band indicates that penile erection has occurred during the night. An unbroken band indicates a lack of nighttime erections and suggests that the patient's general erectile dysfunction may have an organic basis (Mohr & Beutler, 1990).

Psychological Causes Any of the psychological causes of hypoactive sexual desire can interfere with arousal and lead to an erectile disorder. As many as 90 percent of all men with severe depression experience some degree of erectile dysfunction (Leiblum & Segraves, 1995).

An influential psychological explanation for erectile disorder is a cognitive theory developed by William Masters and Virginia Johnson (1970). This explanation, which highlights the mechanisms of ***performance anxiety*** and the ***spectator role,*** has received considerable research support (Barlow, 1986). Once a man begins to experience erectile problems, for whatever reason, he becomes fearful about failing to have an erection and worries during each sexual encounter. Instead of relaxing and enjoying the sensations of sexual pleasure, he remains somewhat distanced from the activity, watching himself and focusing on the goal of reaching erection. Instead of being an aroused participant, he becomes a self-evaluative spectator. Whatever the initial reason for the erectile dysfunction, the resulting anxious, self-evaluative spectator role becomes the reason for the ongoing problem. In this self-perpetuating vicious cycle, the original cause of the erectile failure becomes less important than fear of failure.

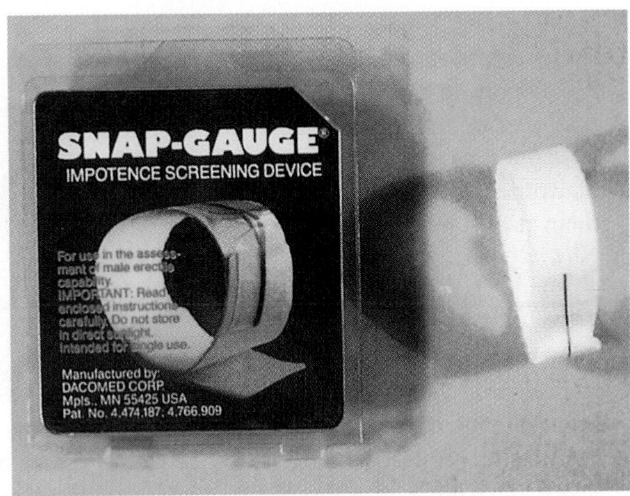

The snap gauge, worn around the penis at night, is a fabric band with three plastic filaments. If the filaments are broken in the morning, the man knows that he has experienced normal erections during REM sleep and that erectile failures during intercourse are probably due to psychological factors. If the filaments are still intact, his erection problems may be due to organic impairment.

Sociocultural Causes Each of the sociocultural factors that contribute to hypoactive sexual desire has also been tied to erectile disorder. Men who have lost their jobs and are under financial stress, for example, are more likely to develop erectile difficulties than other men (Morokoff & Gillilland, 1993). Marital stress, too, has been tied to this dysfunction. Two relationship patterns in particular may contribute to erectile failure (LoPiccolo, 1991). In one, the wife provides inadequate physical stimulation to her aging husband, who, as a normal part of aging, now requires more intense, direct, and lengthy physical stimulation of the penis for erection to occur. In the second relationship pattern, a couple believes that only intercourse can give the wife an orgasm. This idea increases the pressure on the man to have an erection and makes him more vulnerable to erectile dysfunction. If the wife reaches orgasm manually or orally, she does not depend on his erection for her sexual gratification, and his pressure to perform is reduced.

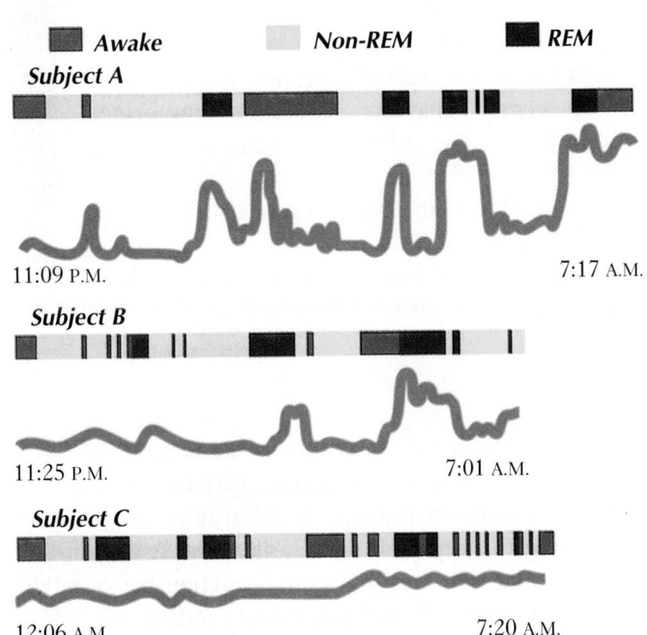

Figure 14-4 *Measurements of erections during sleep help reveal the sources of erectile problems. Subject A, a man without erectile problems, has normal erections during REM sleep. Subject B has erectile failure problems that seem to be at least partly psychogenic—otherwise he would not have any erections during REM sleep. Subject C's erectile disorder is related to organic problems, an interpretation supported by his lack of erections during REM sleep. (Adapted from Bancroft, 1985.)*

Disorders of the Orgasm Phase

During the ***orgasm phase*** of the sexual response cycle, an individual's sexual pleasure peaks and sexual tension is released as the muscles in the pelvic region contract rhythmically. The man's semen is ejaculated, and the outer third of the woman's vaginal wall contracts. Dysfunctions of this phase of the sexual response cycle are *premature ejaculation, male orgasmic disorder,* and *female orgasmic disorder.*

Premature Ejaculation Eddie is typical of many men in his experience of premature ejaculation:

> Eddie, a 20-year-old student, sought treatment after his girlfriend ended their relationship because his premature ejaculation left her sexually frustrated. Eddie had had only one previous sexual relationship, during his senior year in high school. With two friends he would drive to a neighboring town and find a certain prostitute. After picking her up, they would drive to a deserted area and take turns having sex with her, while the others waited outside the car. Both the prostitute and his friends urged him to hurry up because they feared discovery by the police, and besides, in the winter it was cold. When Eddie began his sexual relationship with his girlfriend, his entire sexual history consisted of this rapid intercourse, with virtually no foreplay. He found caressing his girlfriend's breasts and genitals and her touching of his penis to be so arousing that he sometimes ejaculated before complete entry of the penis, or after at most only a minute or so of intercourse.
>
> *(LoPiccolo, 1995, p. 495)*

A man with the dysfunction of ***premature ejaculation*** reaches orgasm and ejaculates with minimal sexual stimulation before, on, or shortly after penetration and before he wishes it (APA, 1994). Between 25 and 40 percent of men in the United States experience difficulties with premature ejaculation at some time (Laumann et al., 1994; St. Lawrence & Madakasira, 1992; Spector & Carey, 1990). It appears that the typical duration of intercourse in our society has lengthened dramatically over the past several decades, in turn increasing the distress of men who suffer from premature ejaculation, typically men under the age of 30 (Bancroft, 1989).

Psychological, particularly behavioral, explanations of premature ejaculation have received more research support than other kinds of explanations. This dysfunction seems to be typical of young, sexually inexperienced men such as Eddie, who simply have not learned to slow down, modulate their arousal, and prolong the pleasurable process of making love. In fact, premature ejaculation is very common when a young man has his first sexual encounter. With continued sexual experience, most men acquire greater control over their sexual responses. Men who have sex only infrequently are also prone to ejaculate prematurely (LoPiccolo, 1985).

Clinicians have also suggested that premature ejaculation may be related to heightened anxiety, rapid masturbation experiences during adolescence (in fear of being "caught" by parents), or inaccurate perceptions of one's own sexual arousal. However, none of these theories has received clear research support (Strassberg et al., 1990, 1987; Heiman et al., 1986). Attempts have been made to identify hormonal or other biological factors that may play a role in some cases of premature ejaculation, but these efforts, too, have produced limited results thus far (Assalian, 1994).

Male Orgasmic Disorder A man with ***male orgasmic disorder*** is repeatedly unable to reach orgasm or is significantly delayed in reaching orgasm after normal sexual excitement. The disorder, also referred to as ***inhibited male orgasm, inhibited ejaculation, ejaculatory incompetence,*** or ***retarded ejaculation,*** is relatively uncommon, occurring in only 1 to 3 percent of the male population (Dekker, 1993). It is typically a source of great frustration and upset when it does occur, as in the case of John:

> John, a 38-year-old sales representative, had been married for 9 years. At the insistence of his 32-year-old wife, the couple sought counseling for their sexual problem—his inability to ejaculate during intercourse. During the early years of the marriage, his wife had experienced difficulty reaching orgasm until he learned to delay his ejaculation for a long period of time. To do this, he used mental distraction techniques and regularly smoked marijuana before making love. Initially, John felt very satisfied that he could make love for longer and longer periods of time without ejaculation and regarded his ability as a sign of masculinity.
>
> About 3 years prior to seeking counseling, after the birth of their only child, John found that he was losing his erection before he was able to ejaculate. His wife suggested different intercourse positions, but the harder he tried, the more difficulty he had in reaching orgasm. Because of his frustration, the couple began to avoid sex altogether. John experienced increasing performance anxiety with each successive failure, and an increasing sense of helplessness in the face of his problem.
>
> *(Rosen & Rosen, 1981, pp. 317–318)*

A low testosterone level, certain neurological diseases, and some head or spinal cord injuries can interfere with ejaculation (LoPiccolo, 1997, 1995, 1985). Drugs that inhibit arousal of the sympathetic nervous system, such as alcohol, some medications for high blood pressure, some antidepressants, and many antianxiety and antipsychotic medications can also inhibit ejaculation (LoPiccolo, 1997; Segraves, 1995, 1993; Jacobsen, 1992; Bancroft, 1989). The widely prescribed antidepressant ***fluoxetine,*** or Prozac, appears to inhibit ejaculation in 15 to 25 percent of men who take it (Nitenson & Cole, 1993; Buffum 1992).

A leading psychological cause of male orgasmic disorder appears to be performance anxiety and the

spectator role, the cognitive factors also involved in male erectile disorder. Once a man begins to focus on reaching orgasm, he stops being an aroused participant in his sexual activity and instead becomes a sexually unaroused, self-critical, and fearful observer (LoPiccolo, 1995). A few studies also suggest that men who do not ejaculate have generally high levels of anxiety and hostility, but this relationship has not been found consistently in other research (Dekker, 1993).

Finally, inhibited ejaculation may also grow from hypoactive sexual desire (Rosen & Leiblum, 1995; LoPiccolo & Friedman, 1988). A man who engages in sex primarily because of pressure from his partner, without any real desire for it, simply may not get aroused enough to reach orgasm.

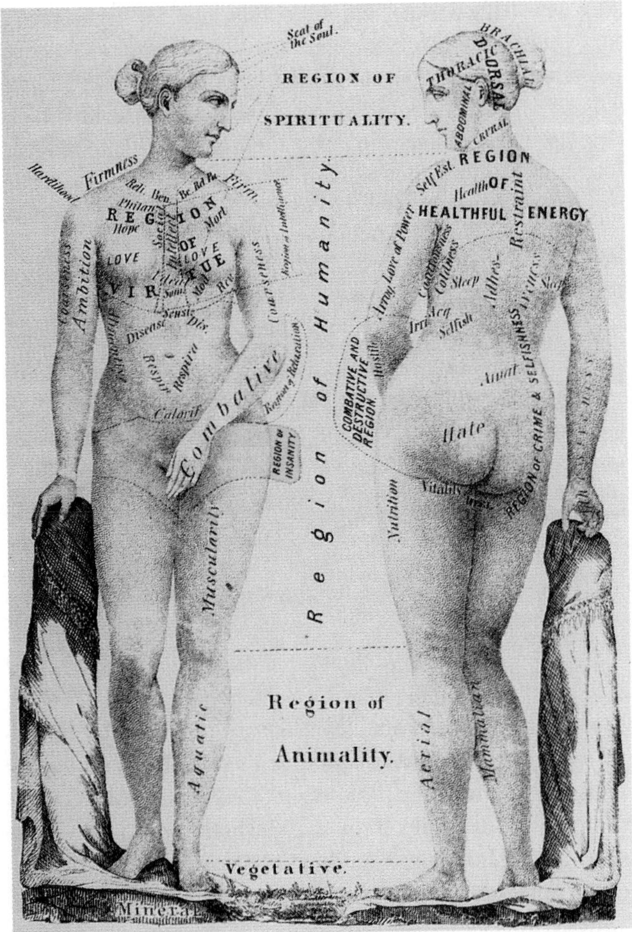

Women of the nineteenth century were expected to experience limited sexual arousal. In fact, medical authorities described "excessive passion" in Victorian women as both physically and psychologically dangerous, and a possible cause of insanity (Gamwell & Tomes, 1995). This illustration from a nineteenth century medical textbook even labels a woman's reproductive organs as her "region of insanity" (Buchanan, 1854).

Female Orgasmic Disorder Stephanie and Bill, married for three years, came for sex therapy because of her total lack of orgasm.

> Stephanie had never had an orgasm in any way, but because of Bill's concern, she had been faking orgasm during intercourse until recently. Finally she told him the truth, and they sought therapy together. Stephanie had been raised by a strictly religious family. She could not recall ever seeing her parents kiss or show physical affection for each other. She was severely punished on one occasion when her mother found her looking at her own genitals, at about age 7. Stephanie received no sex education from her parents, and when she began to menstruate, her mother told her only that this meant that she could become pregnant, so she mustn't ever kiss a boy or let a boy touch her. Her mother restricted her dating severely, with repeated warnings that "boys only want one thing." While her parents were rather critical and demanding of her (asking her why she got one B among otherwise straight A's on her report card, for example), they were loving parents and their approval was very important to her.
>
> *(LoPiccolo, 1995, p. 496)*

A woman with ***female orgasmic disorder,*** also called ***inhibited female orgasm,*** repeatedly experiences a very delayed orgasm or rarely has one at all (APA, 1994). Between 20 and 30 percent of women apparently have this problem—around 15 percent of premenopausal women and 35 percent of postmenopausal women (Rosen & Leiblum, 1995; Laumann et al., 1994; Rosen et al., 1993). Studies indicate that 10 to 15 percent of women today have never had an orgasm, either alone or during intercourse, and another 10 to 15 percent only rarely experience orgasm (LoPiccolo, 1995). Research also suggests that around 50 percent of women experience orgasm in intercourse at least fairly regularly (LoPiccolo & Stock, 1987). The ability to experience orgasm regularly has been related to sexual assertiveness (Hurlbert, 1991) and comfort with masturbation (Kelly, Stressberg, & Kircher, 1990).

Female orgasmic disorder appears to be higher among single women than among women who are married or living with someone (Laumann et al., 1994). Apparently it bears no relation to race, religion, education, or socioeconomic status (Laumann et al., 1994; Heiman & Grafton-Becker, 1989).

Most clinicians agree that orgasm during intercourse is not critical to normal sexual functioning. A woman can instead reach orgasm with her partner during direct stimulation of the clitoris (LoPiccolo, 1995). Although traditional psychoanalytic theory proposed that a lack of orgasm during intercourse is pathological (see Box 14-2),

BOX 14-2 The Vaginal Orgasm Controversy

Joseph LoPiccolo

Sigmund Freud (1905) began the controversy about what constitutes sexual health for women. According to his theory, a child's sexuality progresses through an innate, biologically programmed series of phases. During the oral phase, in infancy, sexual pleasure is focused on the mouth. Later, during the anal phase, about age 2, erotic feelings center on the anus. Around age 4 or so, in the phallic phase, the little girl's clitoris becomes erotically charged and is her main source of sexual arousal and pleasure.

During the phallic phase, the girl develops an Electra complex: she experiences sexual feelings for her father and rivalry with her mother. According to Freud, she believes women are inferior because they lack a penis, and develops *penis envy.* A girl who achieves a healthy resolution of the Electra complex identifies with her mother, accepts her femininity, and loses interest in her clitoris, which is essentially a small substitute for a penis. When she becomes a mature woman, she reaches the genital stage, and gets her sexual arousal from vaginal stimulation. Women who fail to make this shift in focus from the clitoris to the vagina, Freud taught, are fixated at an immature, neurotic, and masculine level. Classical psychoanalysts even considered them to be "frigid," since the orgasms they had from clitoral stimulation were not "mature" and "healthy" (Sherfey, 1973).

Where is the evidence to substantiate this theory? Essentially, it was pure speculation, with no experimental work to support it. During Freud's time, virtually nothing was known about the anatomy and physiology of female sexual response.

In the past 25 years the weight of evidence has been very heavily against Freud's theory. It has been shown that the vagina has far fewer nerve endings than the clitoris (Kinsey et al., 1953). The clitoris and penis both develop from the same structure in the embryo, so expecting a woman to lose clitoral sensitivity makes as much sense as expecting a man's sexual focus somehow to switch from his penis to his scrotum. Masters and Johnson, in their pioneering studies of the female sexual response (1966), showed that all orgasms are identical, regardless of the body part being stimulated. Furthermore, their research demonstrated that when orgasm occurs during vaginal intercourse, it does so primarily because of indirect stimulation of the clitoris. In essence, then, there actually is no difference between a "clitoral" and a "vaginal" orgasm. Finally, decades of research have failed to demonstrate any differences in mental health, maturity, femininity, or sexual adjustment between women who have orgasms during vaginal intercourse and those who have their orgasms during direct clitoral stimulation (Fisher, 1973; Sherfey, 1973; LoPiccolo & Stock, 1987). Modern sex therapists are virtually unanimous in rejecting Freud's ideas about clitoral and vaginal orgasms.

evidence suggests that women who rely on clitoral stimulation for orgasm are entirely normal and healthy (Stock, 1993; LoPiccolo & Stock, 1987).

As we observed earlier, female orgasmic disorder typically is linked to female sexual arousal disorder, and the two are investigated, explained, and treated together (APA, 1995). Once again, biological, psychological, and sociocultural factors have all been cited in these disorders.

Biological Causes A number of physiological conditions can affect a woman's arousal and orgasm. Diabetes can damage the nervous system in ways that interfere with arousal, vaginal lubrication, and orgasm. Lack of orgasm has sometimes been linked to multiple sclerosis and other neurological diseases, to the same medications and drugs that inhibit ejaculation in men, and to postmenopausal changes in skin sensitivity and in the structure of the clitoris and of the vaginal walls (LoPiccolo, 1997; Segraves, 1995; Morokoff, 1993, 1988). Several theorists have also tried to relate female orgasm to the size or location of the clitoris, the strength of the pelvic muscles, and other such factors, but research has failed to support these ideas (Stock, 1993; LoPiccolo & Stock, 1987).

Psychological Causes The various psychological causes of hypoactive sexual desire and sexual aversion may also

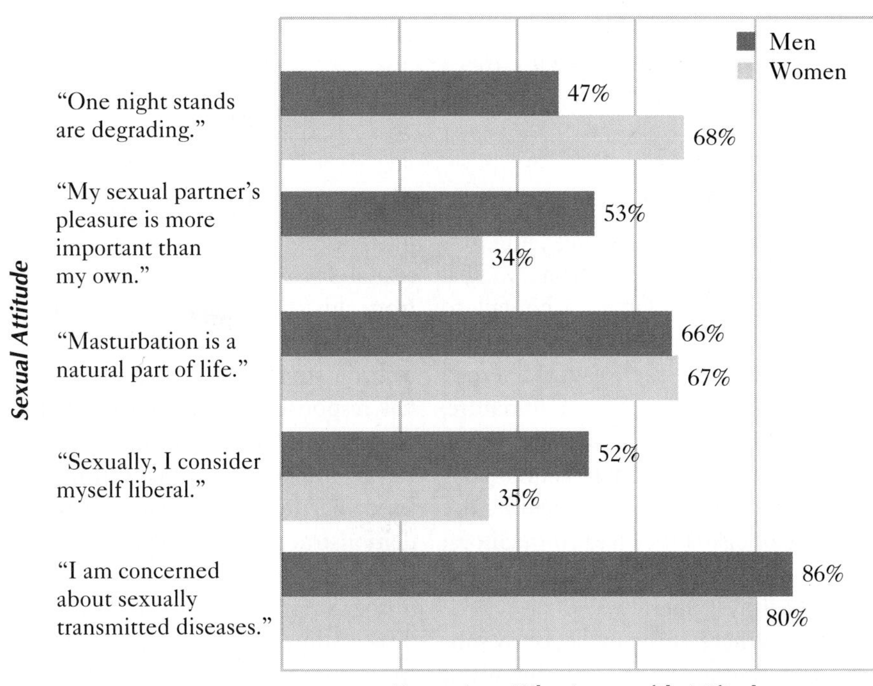

Figure 14-5 *Sexual attitudes and gender. According to surveys, women are more likely than men to consider "one-night-stands" degrading, whereas, contrary to stereotypes, men are more likely than women to say that their sex partner's pleasure is more important than their own. The vast majority of both men and women worry about sexually transmitted diseases. (Adapted from Janus & Janus, 1993.)*

contribute to the female arousal and orgasmic disorders. In addition, as psychodynamic theorists might predict, memories of childhood traumas and relationships have sometimes been associated with these disorders. In one large study, memories of an unhappy childhood or loss of a parent during childhood were associated with lack of orgasm in adulthood (Raboch & Raboch, 1992). In another, childhood memories of a positive relationship with one's mother, affection between the parents, the mother's positive personality qualities, and the mother's expression of positive emotions were all shown to be related to functional orgasm (Heiman et al., 1986).

Sociocultural Causes For years many clinicians have embraced the belief that female arousal and orgasmic disorders are largely the result of society's recurrent message to women that they should suppress and deny their sexuality. In support of this sociocultural explanation, most inorgasmic women in treatment report that they were raised in a sexually restrictive manner. Factors that may help cause orgasmic dysfunction include a strict religious upbringing, punishment for childhood masturbation, lack of preparedness for the onset of menstruation, restrictions placed on adolescent dating, and being told that "nice girls don't" (LoPiccolo, 1997; Masters & Johnson, 1970).

A sexually restrictive history, however, is just as common among sexually functional women (LoPiccolo, 1997; LoPiccolo & Stock, 1987; Heiman et al., 1986). Moreover, negative cultural messages about female sexuality have been declining in recent years (see Figure 14-5), while the prevalence of female arousal and orgasmic disorders remains stable. Why, then, do only some women and not others develop sexual arousal and orgasm dysfunctions? Researchers have looked to specific kinds of stressful events, traumas, or relationships. For example, 50 to 75 percent of women molested as children or raped as adults have arousal and orgasm dysfunctions (Browne & Finklehor, 1986).

Research has also linked orgasmic behavior to the nature of one's intimate relationships. One study found that the likelihood of reaching orgasm was tied to the degree of emotional involvement and the length of the relationship at the time of each subject's first experience of coitus, the pleasure the woman obtained during that experience, her current attraction to her partner's body, and marital happiness (Heiman et al., 1986). Interestingly, the same study found that sexual fantasies during sex with their current partner were much more common in orgasmic than in nonorgasmic women.

Sexual Pain Disorders

Two sexual dysfunctions do not fit neatly into a specific phase of the sexual response cycle. These are the sexual pain disorders, ***vaginismus*** and ***dyspareunia,*** marked by enormous physical dysfunctioning or discomfort when sexual activity is attempted.

Vaginismus In ***vaginismus,*** involuntary contractions of the muscles around the outer third of the vagina prevent entry of the penis. Severe cases can prevent a couple from ever having intercourse. Women with severe cases typically avoid gynecological examinations, too (Rosen & Leiblum, 1993). Few data are available on the prevalence of this disorder. Perhaps 20 percent of women occasionally experience pain during intercourse, but vaginismus probably occurs in less than 1 percent of the female population (LoPiccolo, 1995).

Most clinicians agree with the cognitive-behavioral explanation that vaginismus is typically a conditioned fear response, set off by anticipation that vaginal penetration will be painful and damaging. A variety of factors apparently can set the stage for this fear, including anxiety and ignorance about sexual intercourse, exaggerated stories about how painful and bloody the first occasion of intercourse is for women, trauma caused by an unskilled lover who forces his penis into the vagina before the woman is aroused and lubricated, and, of course, the trauma of childhood sexual abuse or adult rape (LoPiccolo, 1995).

Some women experience painful intercourse because of an infection of the vagina or urinary tract, a gynecological disease such as herpes simplex, or the physical consequences of menopause. They may in turn develop what is sometimes called "rational" vaginismus, in which the insertion of the penis will indeed cause them problems unless they receive medical treatment for these conditions (LoPiccolo, 1995).

Most women who have vaginismus also have other sexual dysfunctions, but not all such women. Some, in fact, enjoy sex greatly, have a strong sex drive, and reach orgasm with clitoral stimulation. Their negative emotions are specific to fear of vaginal penetration.

A teenage girl in the Samburu highlands of Kenya has her genitals (clitoris and labia) cut so that she may be admitted into the society of mature women. Educated women across Africa are increasingly condemning this tradition, practiced by ethnic groups in 28 countries throughout the continent (Dugger, 1996). They argue that the circumcision can lead to various sexual dysfunctions, deprives women of sexual pleasure, and also may create medical problems during childbirth.

Dyspareunia A person with ***dyspareunia*** (from Latin words meaning "painful mating") experiences severe pain in the genitals during sexual activity. Dyspareunia occasionally occurs in men, but it is much more common in women. Indeed, surveys suggest that 10 to 15 percent of women suffer from this problem to one degree or another (Rosen & Leiblum, 1995; Laumann et al., 1994; Rosen et al., 1993). Sufferers typically enjoy sex and get aroused, but find their sex life severely hindered by the pain that accompanies what used to be a positive event.

Dyspareunia in women usually has a physical cause (LoPiccolo, 1995; Steege & Ling, 1993). Among the most common are injury to the vagina, cervix, uterus, or pelvic ligaments during childbirth. Similarly, the scar left by an episiotomy (a cut often made to enlarge the vaginal entrance and ease delivery) can be a source of pain. Dyspareunia has also been linked to collision of the penis with remnants of the hymen; vaginal infection; wiry pubic hair that abrades the labia during intercourse; pelvic diseases; tumors; cysts; and allergic reactions to the chemicals in vaginal douches, contraceptive creams, the rubber in condoms or diaphragms, or the protein in semen (LoPiccolo & Stock, 1987).

Although relationship problems or the psychological aftereffects of sexual abuse may contribute to this disorder, dyspareunia that is caused *entirely* by psychological factors is rare. Most such diagnoses may even be mistaken (LoPiccolo, 1995; LoPiccolo & Stock, 1987). Those cases that are truly psychogenic in fact usually reflect a chronic lack of sexual arousal (Steege & Ling, 1993). That is, penetration into an unaroused, unlubricated vagina is painful.

Treatment of Sexual Dysfunctions

The last 25 years have brought a big change in the treatments for sexual dysfunctions. For the first half of the twentieth century, the major approach was long-term *psychoanalysis.* Clinicians assumed that sexual dysfunctioning was caused by failure to progress satisfactorily through the psychosexual stages of development. This approach, which sought to bring about broad personality changes, was typically unsuccessful (Bergler, 1951).

The extensive research, theories, and clinical reports of William Masters and Virginia Johnson have dramatically changed the way clinicians understand and treat sexual functioning and dysfunctioning.

In the 1950s and 1960s, *behavioral therapists* offered alternative treatments for sexual dysfunctions. Typically, they tried to reduce the anxieties that they believed were causing sexual dysfunctions by applying such procedures as relaxation and systematic desensitization (Lazarus, 1965; Wolpe, 1958). Such approaches were moderately successful, but they failed to work in cases marked by misinformation, negative attitudes, and lack of effective sexual technique (LoPiccolo, 1995).

A revolution in the treatment of sexual dysfunctions occurred with the publication of William Masters and Virginia Johnson's book *Human Sexual Inadequacy* in 1970. The "sex therapy" they introduced has evolved into a complex approach, including techniques from the various models, particularly cognitive, behavioral, and family systems therapies, and communication skill building (LoPiccolo, 1997).

General Components of Sex Therapy Modern sex therapy is short-term and directive, typically lasting fifteen to twenty sessions. As the eminent sex therapist and researcher Joseph LoPiccolo (1997, 1995) has explained, it centers on specific sexual problems rather than on broad personality issues. Carlos Domera, the Argentine man with an erectile disorder whom we met earlier, responded successfully to the multiple techniques of modern sex therapy:

> At the end of the evaluation session the psychiatrist reassured the couple that Mr. Domera had a "reversible psychological" sexual problem that was due to several factors, including his depression, but also more currently his anxiety and embarrassment, his high standards, and some cultural and relationship difficulties that made communication awkward and relaxation nearly impossible. The couple was advised that a brief trial of therapy, focused directly on the sexual problem, would very likely produce significant improvement within ten to fourteen sessions. They were reassured that the problem was almost certainly not physical in origin, but rather psychogenic, and that therefore the prognosis was excellent.
>
> Mr. Domera was shocked and skeptical, but the couple agreed to commence the therapy on a weekly basis, and they were given a typical first "assignment" to do at home: a caressing massage exercise to try together with specific instructions not to attempt genital stimulation or intercourse at all, even if an erection might occur.
>
> Not surprisingly, during the second session Mr. Domera reported with a cautious smile that they had "cheated" and had had intercourse "against the rules." This was their first successful intercourse in more than a year. Their success and happiness were acknowledged by the therapist, but they were cautioned strongly that rapid initial improvement often occurs, only to be followed by increased performance anxiety in subsequent weeks and a return of the initial problem. They were humorously chastised and encouraged to try again to have sensual contact involving caressing and nondemanding light genital stimulation, without an expectation of erection or orgasm, and to avoid intercourse.
>
> During the second and fourth weeks Mr. Domera did not achieve erections during the love play, and the therapy sessions dealt with helping him to accept himself with or without erections and to learn to enjoy sensual contact without intercourse. His wife helped him to believe genuinely that he could please her with manual or oral stimulation and that, although she enjoyed intercourse, she enjoyed these other stimulations as much, as long as he was relaxed.
>
> Mr. Domera struggled with his cultural image of what a "man" does, but he had to admit that his wife seemed pleased and that he, too, was enjoying the nonintercourse caressing techniques. He was encouraged to

view his new lovemaking skills as a "success" and to recognize that in many ways he was becoming a better lover than many husbands, because he was listening to his wife and responding to her requests.

By the fifth week the patient was attempting intercourse successfully with relaxed confidence, and by the ninth session he was responding regularly with erections. If they both agreed, they would either have intercourse or choose another sexual technique to achieve orgasm. Treatment was terminated after ten sessions, and follow-up three months later verified that the improvement had persisted and the couple was again living together.

(Spitzer et al., 1983, pp. 106–107)

As Mr. Domera's treatment reveals, modern sex therapy includes a variety of foci and techniques:

1. ***Assessment and conceptualization of the problem.*** Patients initially receive a medical examination and are interviewed concerning their "sex history" (Risen, 1995; Warren & Sampson, 1995)(see Figure 14-6). The emphasis during the interview is on understanding past life events and, in particular, current factors that are contributing to the dysfunction. Some clinicians also administer various psychological inventories to clients (Beck, 1995; Craig, Cannon, & Olson, 1995). Depending on the problem, assessment tools may also include interviews with the client's partner and psychophysiological tests such as the nocturnal penile tumescence test described earlier (Ackerman & Carey, 1995). Often a team of specialists, perhaps including a psychologist, urologist, and neurologist, is needed for a proper assessment.

2. ***Mutual responsibility.*** Therapists stress the principle of ***mutual responsibility.*** Both partners in the relationship share the sexual problem, regardless of who has the actual dysfunction, and treatment will be more successful when both are in therapy (Heiman et al., 1981).

3. ***Education about sexuality.*** Many patients who suffer from sexual dysfunctions know very little about the anatomy, physiology, and technique of sexual activity. Sex therapists supplement their

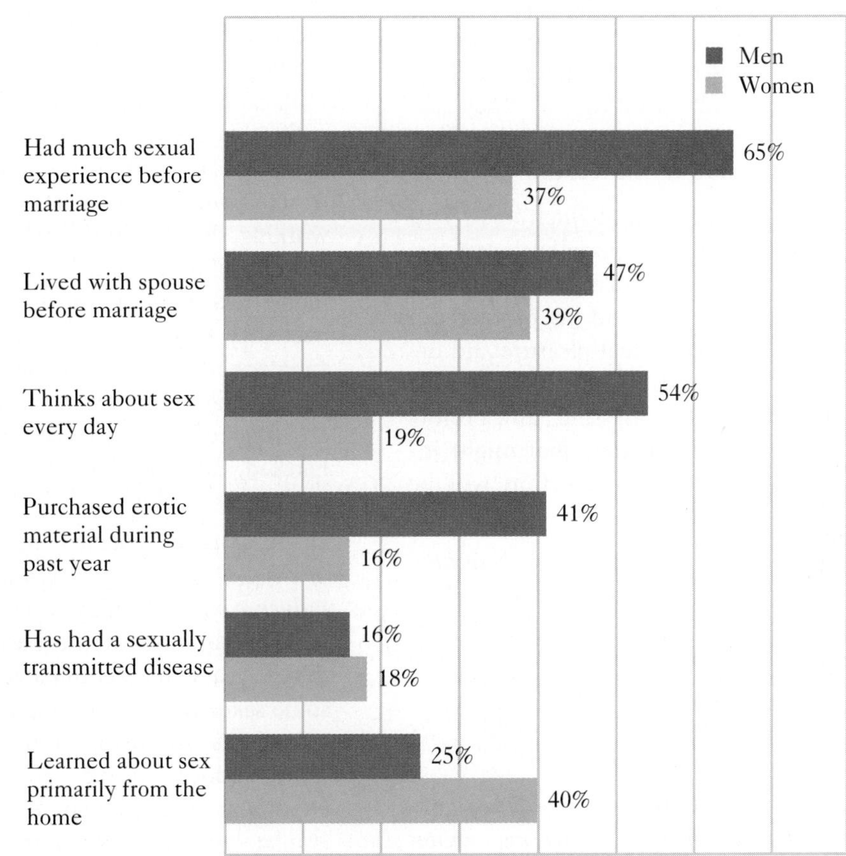

Figure 14-6 *Sexual behavior and gender. According to questionnaires, men are much more likely than women to think about sex on a daily basis and to have purchased sexual material, such as magazines, within the past year. Women are more likely to have learned about sex from the home. (Adapted from Michael et al., 1994; Janus & Janus, 1993.)*

patients' knowledge through discussions, instructional books and videotapes, and educational films.

4. ***Attitude change.*** Therapists help patients to examine and change the beliefs about sexuality that are preventing sexual arousal and pleasure (Rosen, Leiblum, & Spector, 1994). Family attitudes toward sex, past traumatic experiences, and the patients' own emotional reactions to dysfunction in themselves or in their partners can all create strongly negative thoughts and emotions that prevent sexual arousal and pleasure. Our socially imposed sex roles are accompanied by a set of myths or cognitive distortions that can also lead to sexual dysfunctions. Some widespread myths are examined in Box 14-3.

5. ***Elimination of performance anxiety and the spectator role.*** Therapists teach couples ***sensate focus*** and ***nondemand pleasuring,*** a graded series of sexual tasks, sometimes called "petting" exercises, in which the partners explore and caress each other's bodies at home, without demands to have intercourse or reach orgasm—demands that may be interfering with arousal. Initially, couples are told to refrain from intercourse or genital caressing at home and instructed that sexual activity is to be restricted

BOX 14-3 Sex-Role Myths

Myths of Male Sexuality

1. *Men should not have certain emotions.* Men believe they are supposed to be strong, aggressive, competitive, unemotional, and in control. All of these emotions interfere with the tenderness, closeness, sensuality, openness, and emotional expressiveness that contribute to good sex.

2. *In sex, it's performance that counts.* Men take a goal-oriented approach to sex, equating erections and orgasm with success, and are unable to relax and enjoy sex as a pleasurable process rather than as an end to be achieved.

3. *The man must take charge and orchestrate sex.* Men who think this way do not let the woman guide them to do what she likes to have done to her. This attitude also leads a man to focus on what he is doing to the woman, rather than learning to receive pleasure from what she does to him.

4. *A man always wants and is always ready to have sex.* This myth pressures men to try to have sex in situations or relationships in which they are not emotionally comfortable, with predictably unpleasant results.

5. *All physical contact must lead to sex.* This notion prevents men from simply enjoying kissing, hugging, cuddling, and caressing, as they see these activities as only a prelude to "the real thing."

6. *Sex equals intercourse.* This myth is especially destructive to men with erectile problems. If a man and his partner can derive sexual pleasure and orgasm from manual or oral genital caressing, any performance anxiety that might interfere with erection will be greatly reduced.

7. *Sex requires an erection.* This is a corollary to myth 6. The truth is that the penis is not the only sexual part of the man's body, and couples can have very pleasurable sex without an erection.

8. *Good sex is a linear progression of increasing excitement terminated only by orgasm.* Acceptance of this myth eliminates the pleasure of leisurely, playful sex, which may include breaks to talk, rest, and enjoy each other fully as people rather than as just genital organs.

9. *Sex should be natural and spontaneous.* This myth prevents couples from teaching each other what they like during sex. For today's typical couple, with both partners working, sharing child-rearing responsibilities, and living high-stress lives, it is often necessary to make very nonspontaneous plans for sex, designating a time when both are likely to be relaxed, not exhausted, and capable of responding sexually.

10. *In this enlightened age, myths 1–9 no longer have any influence on us.* While the sexual liberalization of the past thirty years has eliminated some sexual inhibitions, it has caused us to worry much more about being good enough at sex and to strive to emulate the supersexual role

to kissing, hugging, and sensual massage of various parts of the body, but not of the breasts or genitals. Over successive weeks, their sexual repertoire is gradually rebuilt, with a constant emphasis on enjoying the experience of sensual pleasure and not striving for results.

6. ***Increasing communication skills and the effectiveness of sexual technique.*** Couples are told to use their sensate focus sessions at home to try sexual positions in which the person being caressed can guide the other's hands and regulate the speed, pressure, and location of the caressing. Couples are also taught to give verbal instructions in a nonthreatening, informative manner ("It feels better over here, with a little less pressure"), rather than a threatening uninformative manner ("The way you're touching me doesn't turn me on").

7. ***Changing destructive lifestyles and problematic marital interactions.*** A therapist may encourage a couple to change their lifestyle or to improve a situation that is having a destructive influence on their relationship—to distance themselves from interfering in-laws, for example, or from the problems of their adult children, or to quit a job that requires

---

models in current literature, films, and music.

(Zilbergeld, 1978)

Myths of Female Sexuality

1. *Sex is only for women under 30.* Many women don't reach their peak of sexual responsiveness until their mid-30s, and there is no real decline thereafter.

2. *Normal women have an orgasm every time they have sex.* Even for easily orgasmic women, 70 to 80 percent of the time is the average rate of orgasm.

3. *All women can have multiple orgasms.* Research indicates that 20 percent of women are multiply orgasmic. There is no relationship between sexual adjustment or satisfaction and the number of orgasms a woman has each time she has sex.

4. *Pregnancy and delivery reduce women's sexual responsiveness.* While discomfort during the last months of pregnancy and just after delivery can temporarily inhibit sex, the increased blood supply to the pelvis that develops during pregnancy can actually increase sexual responsiveness.

5. *A woman's sex life ends with menopause.* While vaginal dryness can interfere with enjoyment of intercourse in some postmenopausal women who do not receive estrogen therapy, many women, freed from concerns about contraception and pregnancy, experience increased sexual arousal and interest after menopause.

6. *There are different kinds of orgasm related to a woman's personality.* Vaginal orgasms are more feminine and mature than clitoral orgasms. An orgasm is an orgasm, not a personality trait.

7. *A sexually responsive woman can always be turned on by her partner.* Fatigue, anger, worry, and many other emotions suppress sexuality in even the most responsive women.

8. *Nice women aren't aroused by erotic books or films.* Research indicates that women are just as aroused by erotica as men are.

9. *You are frigid if you don't like the more exotic forms of sex.* Many very sexual women aren't interested in oral or anal sex, sex toys such as vibrators, or group sex.

10. *If you can't have an orgasm quickly and easily, there's something wrong with you.* The threshold for orgasm varies naturally among women. Just as some women can run faster than others, some have orgasm more rapidly.

11. *Feminine women don't initiate sex or become wild and unrestrained during sex.* This is a holdover of the Victorian double standard.

12. *Double jeopardy: you're frigid if you don't have sexual fantasies and a wanton woman if you do.* Many, but not all, sexually responsive women do have sexual fantasies.

13. *Contraception is a woman's responsibility, and she's just making up excuses if she says contraceptive issues are inhibiting her sexually.* Many highly sexual women find their sexual enjoyment interfered with by contraceptive technology. Many couples who feel their families are complete find vasectomy to be a good solution.

(Heiman & LoPiccolo, 1988)

many hours. Similarly, if the couple's general relationship is lacking or in conflict, the therapist will help them restructure and improve it. LoPiccolo (1995) writes, "Just as marital therapists cannot ignore the sexual area in treating couples, the sex therapist cannot ignore these other important relationship issues when focusing upon a sexual dysfunction."

8. ***Addressing physical and medical factors.*** If sexual dysfunctions are related to a physical or medical problem, such as a disease, neurological condition, injury, hormonal irregularity, unwanted effects of medications, or alcohol or other substance abuse, therapists will address this problem as part of treatment. When antidepressant medications are causing a client's erectile disorder, for example, the clinician may reduce the dosage of the medication, change the time of day when the drug is taken, try an alternative medication, or prescribe an additional drug to counteract the antisexual effect of the first one (Segraves, 1995; Shrivastava et al., 1995). Such changes often lead to a return of sexual functioning, but of course they may also produce relapses of the psychological disorder under treatment (Segraves, 1995).

Problem-Focused Techniques In addition to the broad components of sex therapy, specific techniques can help in each of the sexual dysfunctions.

Hypoactive Sexual Desire and Sexual Aversion Hypoactive sexual desire and sexual aversion are among the most difficult dysfunctions to treat and require a longer treatment program than others (LoPiccolo, 1997, 1995; Beck, 1995; Rosen & Leiblum, 1995). The reason is the wide range of issues that can underlie them. Treatment typically relies on a combination of techniques (LoPiccolo & Friedman, 1988). In one technique, called ***affectual awareness,*** patients visualize sexual scenes to help uncover feelings of anxiety, vulnerability, and other negative emotions associated with sex. In another technique, patients receive cognitive ***self-instruction training*** to help them change their negative reactions to sex. They learn to generate "coping statements," such as "I can allow myself to enjoy sex; it doesn't mean I'll lose control."

Therapists may also use behavioral approaches to help heighten a patient's sex drive. They may have patients keep a "desire diary" in which they record sexual thoughts and feelings, read books and view films with erotic content, and develop sexual fantasies. Pleasurable shared activities such as dancing and walking together are also encouraged, to strengthen feelings of sensual enjoyment and sexual attraction (LoPiccolo, 1997, 1995).

For sexual aversion resulting from sexual assault or childhood molestation, yet additional procedures may be needed. Patients may be encouraged to remember, talk, and think about the assault until such memories no longer arouse fear or tension. Or the patient may be instructed to write letters to the molester or have a mock dialogue with the molester, in order to express at last the feelings of rage and powerlessness the assault created. Sensate focus is carefully structured so that the location, context, and sexual actions do not set off flashbacks to the assault (LoPiccolo, 1997, 1995).

These and related approaches apparently help both women and men with sexual desire and aversion disorders (Hurlbert, 1993). Most clients can eventually have intercourse more than once a week (Schover & LoPiccolo, 1982). However, properly controlled studies have been disappointingly few (Beck, 1995; O'Carroll, 1991). Finally, biological interventions, such as hormone treatments, have also been used, but have not received much support in research studies (Beck, 1995).

Erectile Disorder Treatment for erectile disorder includes special techniques to help reduce a man's performance anxiety and increase his stimulation (LoPiccolo, 1995). The couple are typically instructed to try the ***tease technique:*** if the man gets an erection, his partner stops caressing him until he loses it. This exercise teaches the couple that erections occur naturally in response to stimulation, as long as the couple doesn't focus on performance. When the couple is finally ready to resume intercourse, the ***stuffing technique*** can help: one of the partners pushes the man's nonerect penis into the woman's vagina while he lies on his back. The procedure frees him from having to have a rigid penis to accomplish entry. Finally, the couple may try to achieve the woman's orgasms through manual or oral sex (LoPiccolo, 1997, 1995). All these treatments aim to reduce pressure on the male to perform. It is therefore understandable that the best single predictor of how well men with erectile disorders will respond may be the couple's ability to communicate (Hawton et al., 1992).

When significant physical problems underlie erectile disorder, the man may need to turn to a physician, particularly a urologist or vascular surgeon (Ackerman & Carey, 1995). Surgical implantation of a ***penile prosthesis*** will produce an artificial erection. This approach is expensive (between $5,000 and $15,000, depending on the type), but over 25,000 of the devices are implanted each year in the United States (LoPiccolo, 1997, 1991; Krane et al., 1989). A less expensive ($300 to $600) nonsurgical aid for erectile disorder is the ***vacuum erection device (VED),*** consisting of a hollow cylinder that is placed over the penis. The man uses a hand pump to pump air out of the cylinder, in turn drawing blood into his penis and producing an erection (Cookson & Nadig, 1993; Aloni et al., 1992; Turner et al., 1991). Finally, oral or injected drugs to dilate the arteries in the penis or even vascular surgery may be useful (Ackerman & Carey, 1995; Althof & Seftel, 1995; Montorsi et al., 1994). Each of these physical interventions has been at least somewhat helpful to men whose erectile disorders have physical roots, and their use is on the rise (LoPiccolo, 1997; Ackerman & Carey, 1995). Yet few studies have assessed their long-term effectiveness and safety (Rosen & Leiblum, 1995).

Male Orgasmic Disorder Like treatment for male erectile disorder, sex therapy for male orgasmic disorder may include techniques to reduce performance anxiety and ensure adequate stimulation (LoPiccolo, 1997; Rosen & Leiblum, 1995). Often during sex the penis is caressed manually (and, if acceptable to the couple, orally) until the man is aroused, but the stimulation is stopped whenever he feels he might be close to having an orgasm. This instruction reduces goal-focused anxiety and allows the man to enjoy the sexual pleasure provided by the caressing (Shaw, 1990).

In another approach, a man with the disorder may be instructed to masturbate to orgasm in the presence of his partner or to masturbate just short of orgasm before inserting his penis for intercourse (Marshall, 1997). This increases the likelihood that he will ejaculate during intercourse. He then is instructed to insert his penis earlier and earlier during his masturbatory behavior.

When the male orgasmic disorder is caused by organic factors such as neurological damage or injury, treatment may include a drug to increase arousal of the sympathetic nervous system (Murphy & Lipshultz, 1988). Unfortunately, very few studies have systematically examined the effectiveness of these treatments (Rosen & Leiblum, 1995).

Premature Ejaculation Premature ejaculation has been treated for years with apparent success by direct behavioral retraining (Masters & Johnson, 1970; Semans, 1956). In the ***stop–start,*** or ***pause,*** procedure, the penis is manually stimulated until the man is fairly highly aroused. The couple then pauses until his arousal subsides, and then the stimulation is resumed. This sequence is repeated several times before stimulation is carried through to ejaculation, so the man ultimately experiences much more total time of stimulation than he has ever experienced before and learns to have a higher threshold for ejaculation (Lo Piccolo, 1995). The ***squeeze*** procedure is much like the stop–start procedure, except that when stimulation stops, the woman firmly squeezes just below the head of the penis to reduce arousal further.

After a few weeks of behavioral training, the necessity of pausing diminishes. The couple can then progress

Myths aside, people do not necessarily lose interest in sex as they age. Most middle-aged and elderly women and men remain fully capable of sexual performance and orgasms, although the speed and intensity of their sexual response may lessen somewhat.

to putting the penis in the vagina, making sure to withdraw it and to pause whenever the man becomes too highly aroused. According to clinical reports, after two or three months the couple are typically able to enjoy prolonged intercourse without any need for pauses or squeezes (LoPiccolo, 1997, 1995).

Although studies often find behavioral retraining to be a highly effective treatment for premature ejaculation, at least a few studies have had more modest results, and some have raised questions about the duration of the improvement achieved by such retraining (DeAmicis et al., 1995; Hawton et al., 1986). Therefore, some clinicians try instead to administer fluoxetine (Prozac) and other serotonin-enhancing antidepressant drugs. Because these drugs often reduce sexual arousal or orgasm, they may be helpful to men who experience chronic premature ejaculation. Although some studies have reported positive results (Althof, 1995; Althof et al., 1994; Segraves et al., 1993), researchers have yet to examine the long-term impact of these drugs on men with premature ejaculation. Nor have they determined whether drug therapy may be combined with psychological and relationship techniques to greater advantage (Rosen & Leiblum, 1995).

Female Arousal and Orgasmic Disorders Specific treatment techniques for female arousal and orgasm dysfunctions include self-exploration, body awareness, and directed masturbation training (LoPiccolo, 1997; Heiman

& LoPiccolo, 1988). These procedures are especially useful for women who have never had an orgasm under any circumstances. Biological interventions, such as hormone therapy, have not proved highly effective in research studies (Mathews et al., 1983).

In ***directed masturbation training,*** a woman is taught step by step how to masturbate effectively and eventually to reach orgasm during sexual interactions (Hulbert & Apt, 1995; Hulbert, 1993; Hulbert et al., 1993). The training includes the client's use of diagrams and reading material, private self-stimulation, erotic material and fantasies, "orgasm triggers" such as holding her breath or thrusting her pelvis, sensate focus with her partner, and sexual positioning that allows stimulation of the clitoris during intercourse.

Research suggests that this training program is highly effective: over 90 percent of women learn to have orgasm during masturbation, about 80 percent during caressing by their partner, and about 30 percent during intercourse (LoPiccolo, 1997; Heiman & LoPiccolo, 1988). It can also be administered in group therapy or through a self-help book and instructional videotape (LoPiccolo, 1990).

Therapists may treat *situational* lack of orgasm, such as failure to reach orgasm only during intercourse with one's partner, by helping a client to identify and increasingly apply to the intercourse situation techniques that she is already using during masturbation (McCabe & Delaney, 1992). However, this and other efforts to treat situational orgasm dysfunction have been less successful than efforts to treat *generalized* orgasm dysfunction (Rosen & Leiblum, 1995; McCabe & Delaney, 1992; Heiman & Grafton-Becker, 1989).

As we observed earlier, however, a lack of orgasm during intercourse is not necessarily a sexual dysfunction, provided the woman enjoys intercourse and can reach orgasm through caressing, either by her partner or by herself. For this reason some therapists believe that it may be best just to educate women whose only concern is situational lack of orgasm during intercourse, and reassure them that they are quite normal.

Vaginismus Treatment for vaginismus, spastic contractions of the muscles around the vagina, takes place on two fronts. First, a woman may practice contracting and relaxing the *pubococcygeal muscle,* which surrounds the vagina, until she attains voluntary control of her vaginal muscles (LoPiccolo, 1995; Rosen & Leiblum, 1995). Second, she may receive gradual behavioral exposure treatment to help her overcome her fear of penetration, beginning by inserting increasingly large dilators in her vagina at home and at her own pace, and eventually ending with the insertion of her partner's penis. The therapist keeps stressing the need for effective stimulation, so that the client learns to associate penetration with vaginal lubrication, pleasure, and arousal, instead of with fear (LoPiccolo, 1997, 1995). Understandably, the cooperation of a woman's partner and a strong relationship can greatly aid in treatment (Hawton & Catalan, 1990).

Over 90 percent of the women treated for vaginismus eventually have pain-free intercourse (Beck, 1993; LoPiccolo, 1990). Unfortunately many women with this problem report that they received ineffective or inaccurate forms of intervention when they first sought help from their physicians (Ogden & Ward, 1995).

Dyspareunia We saw earlier that the most common cause of dyspareunia, pain during intercourse, is physical, such as pain caused by scars or lesions. When the cause is known, a couple may learn intercourse positions that avoid putting pressure on the injured area. A medical or surgical intervention may also be tried (Meana & Binik, 1994), but it must still be supplemented by other sex therapy techniques (Leiblum, 1996; Schover, Youngs, & Gannata, 1992). After all, often years of anticipatory anxiety and lack of arousal have had time to build (Quevillon, 1993). Finally, because many cases of dyspareunia are actually caused by undiagnosed physical problems, it is very important that a client receive an expert gynecological exam (Reid & Lininger, 1993).

New Directions in Sex Therapy

Over the past 25 years, sex therapists have expanded upon the approach first developed by Masters and Johnson (LoPiccolo, 1997; Rosen & Leiblum, 1995). For example, today's sex therapists regularly treat persons who are cohabitating but not married (see Figure 14-7), and they also treat sexual dysfunctions that grow out of psychological disorders, including depression, mania, schizophrenia, and certain personality disorders (Rowlands, 1995). In addition, sex therapists no longer routinely screen out clients with severe marital discord, the elderly, the medically ill, or the physically handicapped (Donohue & Gebhard, 1995; Dupont, 1995; Rosen & Leiblum, 1995), or clients with a homosexual orientation or those who have no ongoing sex partner (Stravynski et al., 1997). Sex therapists have also increased their attention to excessive sexuality, sometimes called ***sexual addiction*** (Black et al., 1997; Rosen & Leiblum, 1995; Travin, 1995; Goodman & Carnes, 1991). And group therapy has emerged as an effective and viable format for sex therapy.

Many sex therapists currently worry about the sharp increase in the use of strictly medical interventions for sexual dysfunctions, particularly male erectile disorder and hypoactive sexual desire (Ackerman, 1995; Rosen & Leiblum, 1995; McCarthy, 1994). In part, this development reflects the trend toward the use of psychotropic drugs to treat anxiety, mood, and schizophrenic disorders, often to the exclusion of psychological and sociocultural interventions. And in part it reflects the relative

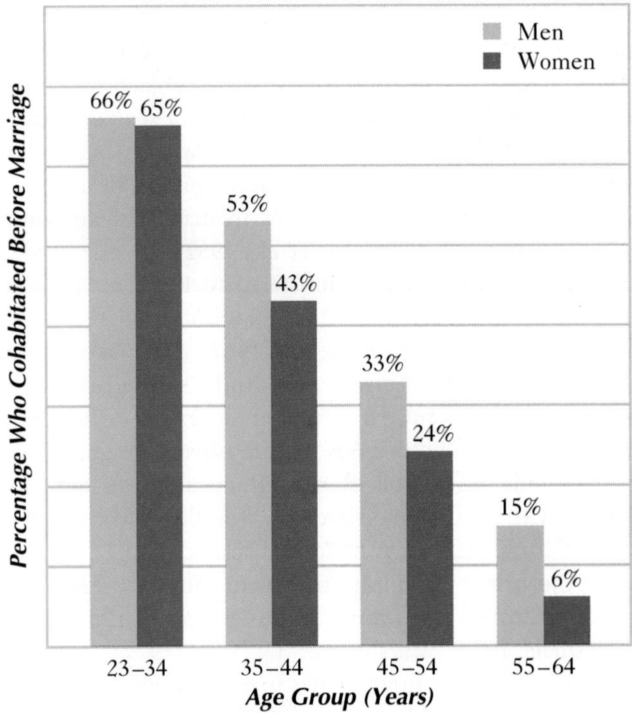

Figure 14-7 *The number of persons who live together prior to marriage increases generation by generation. Around two-thirds of young adults now live together before marrying, whereas less than a third of their parents did the same (Michael et al., 1994).*

scarcity of new psychological and sociocultural interventions for sexual dysfunctions in recent years (Ackerman, 1995; Schover & Leiblum, 1994). The concern is that therapists will increasingly choose the newly developed biological interventions rather than integrate biological, psychological, and sociocultural interventions to greater advantage (Hartmann & Langer, 1993; Althof et al., 1991). In fact, single, narrow interventions probably cannot satisfactorily address the complex factors that typically underlie sexual problems (Ackerman & Carey, 1995). It took sex therapists years to recognize the considerable advantages of an integrated approach to sexual dysfunctions. The development of new medical interventions should not lead to its abandonment.

Paraphilias

Paraphilias are disorders characterized by recurrent and intense sexual urges, fantasies, or behaviors involving either nonhuman objects, children, nonconsenting adults, or the experience of suffering or humiliation. Many people with a paraphilia can become aroused only when a paraphilic stimulus is present, acted out, or fantasized about. Others seem to need the paraphilic stimulus only occasionally, as during times of stress. Many people with one kind of paraphilia display others as well (Abel & Osborn, 1997).

According to DSM-IV, a diagnosis of paraphilia should be applied only when the urges, fantasies, or behaviors last at least six months. They must also cause great distress or produce impairment in one's social life or job (APA, 1994). Some clinicians hold that, with the exception of nonconsensual paraphilias, paraphilic activities should be considered a disorder only when they are the exclusive or preferred means of achieving sexual excitement and orgasm.

Actually, relatively few people receive a formal diagnosis of paraphilia, but the large market in paraphilic pornography and other items leads clinicians to suspect that the disorders may be quite prevalent (APA, 1994). People whose paraphilias involve children or nonconsenting adults often wind up in legal trouble and come to the attention of professionals in that way. Almost all of those who do receive a diagnosis are men.

Theorists have proposed various explanations for paraphilias, but research has revealed relatively little about the causes of most of these disorders (APA, 1994). A range of treatments have been applied to them, but none has yet received clear and systematic research support (Bradford, 1995; APA, 1994; Stein et al., 1992). Psychological and sociocultural treatments for paraphilias have been around the longest, but as in the treatment of sexual dysfunctions, biological interventions have received increased attention in recent years. Clinicians have, for example, administered drugs designed to reduce the sex drive by lowering the production of testosterone, the male sex hormone (Bradford, 1995). Research suggests that such drugs do indeed often reduce paraphilic patterns, but several of them reduce normal sexual behavior as well (Bradford, 1995). Thus the drugs are currently applied primarily to the paraphilias that are of most danger either to the individuals themselves or to other persons.

Clinical researchers have also become very interested in the possible use of second-generation antidepressant medications to treat persons with paraphilias (Bradford et al., 1995; Leo & Kim, 1995). Noting that the recurrent urges, fantasies, and behaviors found in paraphilias resemble the unwanted recurrent thoughts and behaviors of obsessive-compulsive disorder, these researchers have reasoned that the second-generation antidepressants may help reduce paraphilic patterns just as they help alleviate obsessive-compulsive patterns (Bradford, 1995, 1991). Case reports and early studies of such applications have been promising (Bradford, 1995; Fedoroff, 1993; Stein et al., 1992), but again considerably more research is needed to establish whether these medications can be consistently helpful in the treatment of paraphilias.

Fetishism

The key features of ***fetishism*** are recurrent intense sexual urges, sexually arousing fantasies, or behaviors that involve the use of a nonliving object, often to the exclusion of all other stimuli. Usually the disorder begins in adolescence (APA, 1994). Almost anything can be a fetish; women's underwear, shoes, and boots are particularly common (APA, 1994; Raphling, 1989). Some persons with fetishism commit petty theft for the purpose of collecting as many of the objects of their desire as possible. The objects may be touched, smelled, worn, or used in some other way while the person masturbates, or the individual may ask a partner to wear the object when they have sex. Several of these features are seen in the following case:

> A 32-year-old, single male . . . related that although he was somewhat sexually attracted by women, he was far more attracted by "their panties."
>
> To the best of the patient's memory, sexual excitement began at about age 7, when he came upon a pornographic magazine and felt stimulated by pictures of partially nude women wearing "panties." His first ejaculation occurred at 13 via masturbation to fantasies of women wearing panties. He masturbated into his older sister's panties, which he had stolen without her knowledge. Subsequently he stole panties from her friends and from other women he met socially. He found pretexts to "wander" into the bedrooms of women during social occasions, and would quickly rummage through their possessions until he found a pair of panties to his satisfaction. He later used these to masturbate into, and then "saved them" in a "private cache." The pattern of masturbating into women's underwear had been his preferred method of achieving sexual excitement and orgasm from adolescence until the present consultation.
>
> *(Spitzer et al., 1994, p. 247).*

Researchers have not been able to pinpoint the causes of fetishism (Wise, 1985). Psychodynamic theorists have proposed that fetishes are defense mechanisms to help the person avoid the anxiety associated with normal sexual contact. Their efforts to translate this explanation into an effective psychodynamic treatment, however, have met with relatively little success (LoPiccolo, 1992).

Behaviorists have proposed that fetishes are acquired through classical conditioning. In one behavioral study, male subjects were shown a series of slides of nude women interspersed with slides of boots (Rachman, 1966). After numerous trials, the subjects became aroused by the boot photos alone. If early sexual experiences similarly occur in conjunction with a particular object, the stage may be set for development of a fetish.

Behaviorists have sometimes treated fetishism with ***aversion therapy*** (Kilmann et al., 1982). In one study, an electric shock was administered to the arms or legs of subjects with fetishes while they imagined their objects of desire (Marks & Gelder, 1967). After two weeks of therapy all subjects in the study showed at least some improvement. In another aversion technique, *covert sensitization,* persons with fetishism are guided to imagine the pleasurable object and repeatedly to pair this image with an imagined aversive stimulus, until the object of erotic pleasure is no longer desired.

Another behavioral treatment for fetishism is ***masturbatory satiation*** (Quinsey & Earls, 1990; Marshall, 1979; Marshall & Lippens, 1977). In this method, the client masturbates to orgasm while fantasizing aloud about a sexually appropriate object, then switches to fantasizing in detail about fetishistic objects while masturbating again and continues to elaborate on the fetishistic fantasy for an hour. The procedure is meant to produce a feeling of boredom, which in turn becomes associated with the fetishistic object.

Yet another behavioral approach to fetishism, also used for other paraphilias, is ***orgasmic reorientation,*** which conditions clients to respond to more appropriate sources of erotic stimulation: they are shown conventional stimuli while they are responding to unconventional objects. A person with a shoe fetish, for example, may be instructed to obtain an erection from pictures of shoes and then to begin masturbating to a picture of a nude woman. If he starts to lose the erection, he must return to the pictures of shoes until he is masturbating effectively, then change back to the picture of the nude woman. All focus should be on the conventional stimulus when orgasm becomes imminent.

Transvestic Fetishism

Transvestic fetishism, also known as ***transvestism*** or ***cross-dressing,*** involves the recurrent need or desire to dress in clothes of the opposite sex in order to achieve sexual arousal. In the following passage, a 42-year-old married father describes his pattern:

> I have been told that when I dress in drag, at times I look like Whistler's Mother [laughs], especially when I haven't shaved closely. I usually am good at detail, and I make sure when I dress as a woman that I have my nails

> done just so, and that my colors match. Honestly, it's hard to pin a date on when I began cross dressing. . . . If pressed, I would have to say it began when I was about 10 years of age, fooling around with and putting on my mom's clothes. . . . I was always careful to put everything back in its exact place, and in 18 years of doing this in her home, my mother never, I mean *never,* suspected, or questioned me about putting on her clothes. I belong to a transvestite support group . . . , a group for men who cross dress. Some of the group are homosexuals, but most are not. A true transvestite—and I am one, so I know—is not homosexual. We don't discriminate against them in the group at all; hey, we have enough trouble getting acceptance as normal people and not just a bunch of weirdos ourselves. They are a bunch of nice guys . . . , really. Most of them are like me.
>
> Most of them have told their families about their dressing inclinations, but those that are married are a mixed lot; some wives know and some don't, they just suspect. I believe in honesty, and told my wife about this before we were married. We're separated now, but I don't think it's because of my cross dressing. She may have thought that she would get me to change after we married. That is silly; you have to accept a person as they are. . . . I have been asked many times why I cross dress, and it's hard to explain, other than it makes me feel good. There is something deep down that it gratifies. Some of my friends, when I was growing up, suggested psychotherapy, but I don't regard this as a problem. If it bothers someone else, then they have the problem. . . . I function perfectly well sexually with my wife, though it took her some time to be comfortable with me wearing feminine underwear; yes, sometimes I wear it while making love, it just makes it more exciting.
>
> *(Janus & Janus, 1993, p. 121)*

"Crossroads" is a self-help group for men with transvestic fetishism, a recurrent need to dress in women's clothing as a means to achieve sexual arousal. These men are not transsexual; they never question their identity as men and have no wish to be women.

Like this man, the typical person with transvestism, almost always a heterosexual male, begins cross-dressing in childhood or adolescence, usually but not always in private (Bradley, 1995; Schott, 1995; APA, 1994). He is the picture of characteristic masculinity in everyday life, and cross-dresses only in relative privacy. A small percentage of such men cross-dress to visit bars or social clubs. Some wear a single item of women's apparel, such as underwear or hosiery, under their masculine clothes. Others wear makeup and dress fully as women. Many married men with transvestism involve their wives in their cross-dressing behavior (Kolodny, Masters, & Johnson, 1979).

Research into the personality characteristics of those with transvestism reveals many to be fairly hostile and self-centered, with a limited capacity for intimacy (Wise et al., 1991). Many report high levels of marital discord, which transcends their cross-dressing behaviors (Wise et al., 1991). Transvestic fetishism is often confused with transsexualism, but, as we shall observe shortly, the two are separate disorders.

The development of transvestic fetishism sometimes seems consistent with the behavioral principles of operant conditioning. Their parents or other adults have openly encouraged these individuals to cross-dress as children. In one case, a woman was delighted to discover that her young nephew enjoyed dressing in girls' clothes. She had always wanted a niece, and she proceeded to buy him dresses and jewelry and sometimes dressed him as a girl and took him out shopping.

Exhibitionism

A person with ***exhibitionism*** has recurrent urges to expose his genitals to another person, almost always a member of the opposite sex, or perhaps a sexually arousing fantasy of doing so. He may also carry out those urges (APA, 1994; Abel, 1989), but rarely attempts sexual activity with the person to whom he exposes himself. More often, he wants to provoke shock or surprise. Sometimes a so-called flasher will expose himself in a particular neighborhood at particular hours. The urges typically intensify when the person has free time or is under significant stress (Abel, 1989).

Dressing in clothes of the opposite sex does not necessarily convey a paraphilia. The context of this and other sexual-like behaviors must be weighed. Male performers, for example, have long dressed as females to entertain nightclub patrons or theatergoers. Here members of Harvard University's Pudding Theatricals Club, known for staging musicals in which male undergraduates look and dress like women, flank actress Michelle Pfeiffer, the recipient of their Woman of the Year award.

Generally the disorder begins before age 18, and most such individuals are males (APA, 1994). Persons with exhibitionism are immature in their approaches to the opposite sex and have difficulty in interpersonal relationships. Over half of them are married, but their sexual relationships with their wives are not usually satisfactory (Blair & Lanyon, 1981; Mohr et al., 1964). Many have doubts or fears about their masculinity, and some apparently have a strong bond to a possessive mother.

Treatment is the same as that for other paraphilias, including aversion therapy and masturbatory satiation, possibly combined with orgasmic reorientation, social skills training, or psychodynamic intervention (LoPiccolo, 1992; McNally & Lukach, 1991). One unusual, apparently successful version of aversion therapy pairs the unpleasant smell of valeric acid with images of self-exposure (Maletzky, 1980). Clinicians have also reported some success with hypnotherapy (Epstein, 1983; Polk, 1983; Ritchie, 1968).

Voyeurism

A person who engages in ***voyeurism*** has recurrent and intense sexual desires to observe unsuspecting people in secret as they undress or to spy on couples engaged in intercourse. The individual generally does not seek to have sex with the person being spied on (APA, 1994). The risk of being discovered often adds to the person's excitement, as we see in the following statement by a man with this disorder:

> Looking at a nude girlfriend wouldn't be as exciting as seeing her the sneaky way. It's not just the nude body but the sneaking out and seeing what you're not supposed to see. The risk of getting caught makes it exciting. I don't want to get caught, but every time I go out I'm putting myself on the line.
>
> *(Yalom, 1960, p. 316)*

People with voyeurism may masturbate either during the act or when thinking about it afterward. The vulnerability of the people being observed and the probability that they would feel humiliated if they found out are often part of the individual's enjoyment. Voyeurism usually begins before the age of 15 and tends to be chronic (APA, 1994).

Elements of both exhibitionism and voyeurism can play a role in normal sexuality, but in such instances they are engaged in with the consent or understanding of the partner. The clinical disorder of voyeurism is marked by the repeated invasion of another person's privacy. Some people with voyeurism are unable to have normal sexual interplay; others, however, maintain normal sexual relationships apart from their voyeurism.

Many psychodynamic and cognitive clinicians believe that people with voyeurism are seeking by their actions to exercise power over others, possibly because they feel inadequate or are sexually or socially inhibited. Psychodynamic theorists have also explained voyeurism as an attempt to reduce castration anxiety, originally generated by the sight of an adult's genitals. Theoretically, those with voyeurism are repeating the behavior that produced the original fright, so that they can be reassured there is nothing to fear (Fenichel, 1945). Behaviorists explain the disorder as a learned behavior that can be traced to a chance and secret observation of a sexually arousing scene. If such observations are repeated on several occasions in conjunction with masturbation, a voyeuristic pattern may develop.

Frotteurism

A person who exhibits ***frotteurism*** has recurrent and intense sexual urges to touch and rub against a nonconsenting person, or sexually arousing fantasies of doing so. The person may also act on the urges. Individuals must further be distressed or impaired by the urges or behaviors to warrant a diagnosis. Frottage (from French *frotter*, to rub) is usually committed in a crowded place, such as a subway or a busy sidewalk (APA, 1994). The person, almost always a male, may rub his genitals against the victim's thighs or buttocks or fondle her genitalia or breasts with his hands. Typically he fantasizes during the act that he is having a caring relationship with the victim (APA, 1994).

Frotteurism usually begins in adolescence or earlier, often after the person observes others committing an act of frottage. After the person reaches the age of 25, the acts gradually decrease and often disappear (APA, 1994).

Pedophilia

A person who is subject to ***pedophilia,*** literally "love of children," obtains sexual gratification by watching, touching, or engaging in simple or complex sexual acts with prepubescent children, usually those 13 years old or younger. Some persons with this disorder are satisfied by child pornography or seemingly innocent material such as children's underwear ads; others are driven to watching, fondling, or engaging in sexual intercourse with children (Howitt, 1995; Barnard et al., 1989). Some persons with pedophilia are attracted only to children *(exclusive type);* others are attracted to adults as well *(nonexclusive type)* (APA, 1994).

One study found that 4 percent of pedophilia victims are 3 years old or younger, 18 percent are 4 to 7 years old, and 40 percent are 8 to 11 (Mohr et al., 1964). Victims usually know the persons who molest them; 15 to 30 percent of sexual molestation cases are incestuous (Gebhard et al., 1965; Mohr et al., 1964). Both boys and girls can be pedophilia victims, but there is some evidence that three-quarters of them are girls (Koss & Heslet, 1992).

People with pedophilia usually develop their disorder during adolescence. Many were themselves sexually abused as children (Howitt, 1995; McCormack et al., 1992). It is not unusual for them to be married and to have sexual difficulties or other frustrations in life that lead them to seek an arena in which they can be masters. Alcohol abuse figures prominently in many cases (Rada, 1976).

Immaturity may often be a primary cause of pedophilia (Groth & Birnbaum, 1978). Social and sexual skills may be underdeveloped, so that the person feels intense anxiety at the very thought of a normal sexual relationship. Some persons with pedophilia also display faulty thinking, such as "It's all right to have sex with children as long as they agree" (Abel et al., 1984).

Most pedophilic offenders are imprisoned or forced into treatment if they are caught. After all, they are committing child sexual abuse when they approach a child. Treatments include those already mentioned for other paraphilias, such as aversion therapy, masturbatory satiation, and orgasmic reorientation (LoPiccolo, 1992; Enright, 1989).

There is also a cognitive-behavioral treatment for pedophilia: ***relapse-prevention training,*** modeled after the relapse-prevention programs used in the treatment of substance dependence (see p. 434). In this approach, clients identify the problematic situations that typically trigger their pedophilic fantasies and actions (such as depressed mood or distorted thinking). They then learn strategies to avoid or cope more effectively with these situations (LoPiccolo, 1992; Pithers, 1990). Relapse-prevention training has shown success in this and some other paraphilias. One study of 147 people with pedophilia found only a 4 percent relapse rate over a five-year period among persons who received this treatment (Pithers & Cumming, 1989).

Sexual Masochism

A person with ***sexual masochism*** is intensely sexually aroused by the act or thought of being humiliated, beaten, bound, or otherwise made to suffer. Many people have fantasies of being forced into sexual acts against their will; only those who are markedly distressed or impaired by the fantasies receive this diagnosis (APA, 1994; Reik, 1989). Many people with the disorder act on the masochistic urges by themselves, perhaps binding, sticking pins into, or even mutilating themselves. Others have their sexual partners restrain, tie up, blindfold, spank, paddle, whip, beat, electrically shock, "pin and pierce," or humiliate them (APA, 1994).

A veritable industry of products and services has formed to address the desires of people with sexual masochism. Here a 34-year-old woman describes her work as the operator of a sadomasochism house:

> **I** get people here who have been all over looking for the right kind of pain they feel they deserve. Don't ask me why they want pain, I'm not a psychologist; but when they have found us, they usually don't go elsewhere. It may take some of the other girls an hour or even two hours to make these guys feel like they've had their treatment—I can achieve that in about 20 minutes. . . . Remember, these are businessmen, and they are not only buying my time, but they have to get back to work, so time is important.
>
> Among the things I do, that work really quickly and well, are: I put clothespins on their nipples, or pins in their [testicles]. Some of them need to see their own blood to be able to get off. . . .
>
> . . . All the time that a torture scene is going on, there is constant dialogue. . . . I scream at the guy, and tell him what a no-good rotten bastard he is, how

> this is even too good for him, that he knows he deserves worse, and I begin to list his sins. It works every time. Hey, I'm not nuts, I know what I'm doing. I act very tough and hard, but I'm really a very sensitive woman. But you have to watch out for a guy's health . . . you must not kill him, or have him get a heart attack. . . . I know of other places that have had guys die there. I've never lost a customer to death, though they may have wished for it during my "treatment." Remember, these are repeat customers. I have a clientele and a reputation that I value.
>
> *(Janus & Janus, 1993, p. 115)*

In one form of sexual masochism, ***hypoxyphilia,*** people strangle or smother themselves (or ask their partner to strangle them) in order to enhance their sexual pleasure. There have, in fact, been a disturbing number of clinical reports of ***autoerotic asphyxia,*** in which individuals, usually males and as young as 10 years old, inadvertently induce a fatal cerebral anoxia (lack of oxygen) by hanging, suffocating, or strangling themselves while masturbating. There is some debate as to whether the practice should be characterized as sexual masochism, but it is commonly accompanied by other acts of bondage (Blanchard & Hucker, 1991).

People with sexual masochism and those with sexual sadism often achieve satisfaction with each other. Although many such relationships stay within safe bounds and are often portrayed with humor in photos, novels, and movies, they can cross the line and result in severe physical or psychological damage.

Most masochistic sexual fantasies begin in childhood. The person does not act out the urges until later, usually by early adulthood. The disorder typically continues for many years. Some people practice more and more dangerous acts over time or during times of particular stress (APA, 1994).

In many cases sexual masochism seems to have developed through classical conditioning. One case study tells of a teenage boy with a broken arm who was caressed and held close by an attractive nurse as the physician set his fracture without anesthesia (Gebhard, 1965). The powerful combination of pain and sexual arousal he experienced then may have been the cause of his later masochistic urges and acts.

Sexual Sadism

A person with ***sexual sadism,*** usually male, is intensely sexually aroused by the act or thought of inflicting physical or psychological suffering on others, by dominating, restraining, blindfolding, cutting, strangling, mutilating, or even killing the victim. The label is derived from the name of the Marquis de Sade (1740–1814), who inflicted severe cruelty on others in order to satisfy his sexual desires. People who fantasize about sadism typically imagine that they have total control over a sexual victim who is terrified by the prospect of the sadistic act. Many carry out sadistic acts with a consenting partner, often a person with sexual masochism. Some act out their urges on nonconsenting victims. Some rapists, for example, manifest sexual sadism. In all cases, the real or fantasized victim's suffering is the key to arousal.

Fantasies of sexual sadism, like those of sexual masochism, may appear in childhood; the sadistic acts, when they occur, develop by early adulthood. The pattern is chronic (APA, 1994). The acts sometimes stay at the same level of cruelty, but more often they increase in severity over the years. Obviously, people with severe forms of the disorder may be highly dangerous to others (Dietz et al., 1990).

The pattern has been associated with a variety of causal factors. Behaviorists suggest that classical conditioning often plays a role in its development. While inflicting pain, perhaps unintentionally, on an animal or person, an adolescent may feel intense emotions and sexual arousal. The association between inflicting pain and being aroused sexually sets the stage for a pattern of sexual sadism. Behaviorists also propose that many cases result from modeling, when adolescents observe others achieving sexual satisfaction by inflicting pain. The many sexual magazines, books, and videotapes in our society make such models readily available. Indeed, according to one review, close to one-quarter of pornographic magazines and books contain an act of paraphilia, with sadomasochism overwhelmingly the most common type (Lebegue, 1991).

Psychodynamic and cognitive theorists have suggested that people with sexual sadism may have underlying feelings of sexual inadequacy or insecurity, and that they inflict pain in order to achieve a sense of power, which in turn increases their sexual arousal. Alternatively, some biological investigations have found signs of possible abnormal functioning in the endocrine systems of persons with sadism (Langevin et al., 1988). None of these explanations, however, has been systematically investigated or consistently supported by research (Breslow, 1989).

Sexual sadism has been treated by aversion therapy. As we have noted previously, the public's view of and perhaps distaste for this procedure has been influenced by Anthony Burgess's novel (later a movie) *A Clockwork Orange,* which describes simultaneous presentations of sadistic images and drug-induced stomach spasms to a sadistic and violent young man. It is not clear that aversion therapy is consistently helpful in cases of sexual sadism. However, relapse-prevention training, used in some criminal cases, seems somewhat effective (Vaillant & Antonowicz, 1992; Pithers & Cumming, 1989).

Societal Norms and Sexual Labels

The definitions of the various paraphilias, like those of sexual dysfunctions, are closely tied to the norms of the particular society in which they occur (Brown, 1983). It could be argued that except when people are hurt by them, many paraphilic behaviors are not disorders at all. Especially in light of the stigma associated with sexual disorders and the self-revulsion that many people experience when they believe they have such a disorder, we need to be very careful about applying such labels to others or to ourselves. Keep in mind that for years clinical professionals considered homosexuality a paraphilia, and their judgment was used to justify laws and even police actions against homosexual persons. Only when the gay rights movement helped change society's understanding of and attitudes toward homosexuality did clinicians stop considering it a disorder. In the meantime, the clinical field had inadvertently contributed to the persecution, anxiety, and humiliation of millions of people because of personal sexual behavior that differed from the conventional norms (see Box 14-4).

Gender Identity Disorder

One of the most fascinating disorders related to sexuality is ***gender identity disorder,*** or ***transsexualism,*** a disorder in which people persistently feel that a vast mistake has been made—they have been assigned to the wrong sex. Such persons are preoccupied with getting rid of their primary and secondary sex characteristics—many of them find their own genitals repugnant—and acquiring the characteristics of the other sex (APA, 1994). People with this problem often experience depression and have thoughts of suicide (Bradley, 1995).

People with gender identity disorder usually feel uncomfortable wearing the clothes of their own sex and dress instead in clothes of the opposite sex. Their condition is not, however, transvestism. People with that paraphilia cross-dress in order to become sexually aroused; persons with transsexualism have much deeper reasons for cross-dressing, reasons of gender identity (Bradley, 1995). In addition to cross-dressing, individuals with transsexualism often engage in roles and activities that are traditionally associated with the other sex (Brown et al., 1996).

Sometimes gender identity disorder emerges in children (Zucker, Bradley, & Sullivan, 1996; Sugar, 1995; APA, 1994). Like adults with this disorder, they feel uncomfortable about their assigned sex and yearn to be members of the opposite sex. In addition to seizing every opportunity for cross-dressing, these children usually prefer to play cross-sex roles in make-believe games, to participate in the stereotypical games of the other sex, and to play with children of the other sex.

This childhood pattern usually disappears by adolescence or adulthood, but in some cases it develops into adult transsexualism (Bradley, 1995). Thus many transsexual adults have had a childhood gender identity disorder (Tsoi, 1992), but most children with a gender identity disorder do not become transsexual adults. Some adults with transsexualism do not develop any symptoms until mid-adulthood.

Various psychological theories have been proposed to explain this disorder (Zucker et al., 1996; Gilmore, 1995; Sugar, 1995), but research in this area has been limited and generally weak. Some clinicians have long suspected that biological factors may play a significant role in the disorder, but studies over the years have failed

BOX 14-4 Homosexuality and Society

In 1948, when Alfred Kinsey and his associates conducted one of the first extensive studies of male sexuality, they found that 4 percent of the male population were exclusively homosexual and that 37 percent had had a homosexual experience that led to orgasm. Half of the unmarried men over the age of 35 had had a homosexual experience to the point of orgasm. In a later study they found the occurrence of homosexuality among women to be approximately one-half to one-third that of men (Kinsey et al., 1953). These findings shocked and astonished many people.

Homosexuality has always existed in all cultures. It is not new, nor is the controversy that surrounds it. Most cultures do not openly advocate homosexuality, but historically few have condemned it so fiercely as Western culture has done since the Victorian era. Nevertheless, research shows that a society's acceptance or rejection of people who engage in homosexual activity does not affect the incidence of homosexual behavior.

Before 1973, the DSM listed homosexuality as a sexual disorder. Protests by gay activist groups and many psychotherapists eventually led to its elimination from the manual as a sexual disorder per se, but for a while the DSM did retain a category called ***ego dystonic homosexuality***—the experience of extreme distress over one's homosexual orientation. Recent editions of the DSM have dropped even this category, and homosexuality is no longer mentioned. Most clinicians now accept homosexuality as a variant of normal sexual behavior and not a disorder.

Despite the growing acceptance of homosexuality by clinicians, many people in Western society continue to foster antihomosexual attitudes and to propagate myths about the lifestyles of homosexual persons. The research data show that homosexual persons do *not* suffer from gender confusion; they are *not* more prone to psychopathology than others; there is *not* an identifiable "homosexual personality."

To cope with the stress, discrimination, and even danger they encounter, many homosexual people have chosen to live on streets or in neighborhoods that are predominantly homosexual. Certain bars or restaurants serve as gathering places where gay persons exchange information and socialize. Organizations exist to support and lobby for issues affecting homosexual people, demanding equal treatment under the law and in society (Freiberg, 1994). This battle is being fought constantly.

One of the key issues affecting support for homosexual rights has been the debate over whether homosexual persons choose their lifestyle or whether it is a natural part of their physiological and psychological makeup. This debate is fueled by findings—pro and con—from the scientific community (Horgan, 1995). Several lines of research have suggested that sometimes homosexuality is not simply a lifestyle choice but linked to a physiological predisposition (Pillard & Bailey, 1995; Turner, 1995; Levay & Hamer, 1994), supporting the claim of the gay community that homosexuality is a naturally occurring phenomenon.

Some recent studies have, for example, suggested that homosexuality has a genetic component. Several studies of both male and female homosexual individuals have found genetic markers indicating that homosexuality may be passed on by the mother's genes (Hu et al., 1995; Hamer, 1993). Similarly, two studies found that when one identical twin was homosexual, his twin was also homosexual in more than 50 percent of the cases. The number dropped to less than 20 percent when the siblings were fraternal twins or nontwins and to under 10 percent when the children were adopted and biologically unrelated (Bailey & Pillard, 1993). Although environmental factors also have a major impact on homosexuality—otherwise all persons with a homosexual identical twin would be homosexual—genetics may play a key role in it.

Homosexual persons are represented in every socioeconomic group, every race, and every

to find consistent biological differences between persons with and persons without transsexualism. One recent biological study, however, is being hailed as a breakthrough (Zhou et al., 1995). Dutch investigators autopsied the brains of six people who had changed their sex from male to female. They found that a cluster of cells in the hypothalamus called the *bed nucleus of stria terminalis (BST)* was only half as large in these subjects as it was in profession. It is impossible to identify a characteristic that consistently separates them from the rest of the population other than their sexual orientation. Moreover, heterosexual and homosexual relationships do not differ dramatically. AIDS is currently affecting hundreds of thousands of homosexual males, moving an increasing number of previously promiscuous men toward monogamy in long-term relationships, but it is important to note that homosexual persons have always made commitments of this sort.

The homosexual community takes the position that since sexual orientation is the only behavioral variable that consistently distinguishes homosexual from heterosexual couples, gay couples should be accorded the same rights as heterosexual ones. Thus today marriages are sometimes performed for same-sex couples. Moreover, homosexual couples are increasingly demanding access to housing reserved for couples only and to health insurance "spouse" coverage, and recent court cases are supporting such rights. These issues affect the day-to-day lives of homosexual couples in the same way that they affect heterosexual couples.

In the early 1990s many issues regarding acceptance of homosexuality came to a head in the United States. Media coverage exposed numerous episodes of gay-bashing in which homosexual men and women were beaten, even killed. The practice of "outing," in which public figures who have not made their homosexuality known are exposed by gay activists, increased. And President Clinton reviewed the military's policy regarding homosexuality, an action that stirred a national debate.

Few events of 1997 received more attention than the announcement by actress Ellen DeGeneres that she and her television character Ellen Morgan are gay. The episode in which Morgan's sexual orientation was revealed showed a vast increase in viewership.

During his campaign, Clinton had received much support from the gay community for his support of AIDS research and his promise to review the military's policy of asking recruits their sexual preference, actively pursuing reports of homosexuality in its ranks, and discharging anyone suspected of being gay. Once Clinton was in office, the promised review dominated the news for months. Many military commanders and social conservatives argued that homosexuality was incompatible with military service. The gay community and its supporters argued that sexual orientation was unrelated to one's ability to serve one's country (Jones & Koshes, 1995). The military adopted a middle-of-the-road "Don't ask, don't tell" policy in 1993. The armed forces would not hunt out homosexual persons, but, if faced with incontrovertible evidence, they could discharge such individuals from the service.

One of the most important issues to emerge during the debate on homosexuality and the military was whether Americans—those in the armed services specifically, but throughout the country as well—could overcome prejudice against homosexuality. Despite the high emotions this issue evokes, reviews of relevant literature suggest that, through education and exposure, people can learn to accept and work with others who are different from them (Herek & Capitanio, 1993).

Obviously, homosexuality continues to be a lifestyle that many people adopt, whether through environment, genetics, or psychosocial development. Now that clinical concerns about homosexuality have been put aside, one of the key remaining issues is how society will deal with a significant proportion of its population that typically does not differ from the rest in any way other than sexual orientation. So far, Western society cannot claim to have dealt very effectively or fairly with this question, but at least a trend toward understanding and equality seems to be emerging.

a control group of normal men. Normally, a woman's BST is much smaller than a man's, so in effect the subjects with transsexualism were found to have a female-sized BST. Scientists do not know for certain what the BST does in humans, but they do know that it helps regulate the sexual behavior of male rats. Although alternative interpretations of these findings are possible, it may well be that men who develop transsexualism have a key

Feeling like a woman trapped in a man's body, the British writer James Morris (left) underwent sex-reassignment surgery, described in his 1974 autobiography, Conundrum. *Today Jan Morris (right) is the successful author of more than a dozen books and numerous travel articles and seems comfortable with her change of gender.*

biological difference that leaves them highly uncomfortable with their assigned sex characteristics.

Some adults with transsexualism alter their sexual characteristics by hormone treatments (Bradley, 1995). The hormone prescribed for men with this disorder, who apparently outnumber women by around 2 to 1, is the female sex hormone *estrogen.* It causes breast development, loss of body and facial hair, and change in the distribution of body fat. Similar treatments with the male sex hormone *testosterone* are given to women with transsexualism.

Hormone therapy and psychotherapy are sufficient to enable many persons with transsexualism to lead a satisfactory existence in the gender role that they believe represents their true identity. For others, however, this is not enough, and their dissatisfaction leads them to undergo one of the most controversial practices in medicine: *sex-change surgery* (Bradley, 1995).

The first sex-change operation took place in 1931, but the procedure did not gain acceptance among practitioners working on this problem until 1952, when an operation converted an ex-soldier named George Jorgensen into a woman, renamed Christine Jorgensen. This transformation made headlines around the world and sparked the interest of people everywhere.

By 1980, sex-reassignment surgery was routine in at least forty medical centers in the western hemisphere (Arndt, 1991). This surgery is preceded by one to two years of hormone therapy, after which the operation itself involves, for men, amputation of the penis, creation of an artificial vagina, and face-altering plastic surgery. For women, surgery may include bilateral mastectomy and hysterectomy. The procedure for creating a functioning penis, called ***phalloplasty,*** is performed in some cases, but it is not yet perfected. Doctors have also developed a silicone prosthesis that gives the patient the appearance of having male genitals (Hage & Bouman, 1992). Approximately 1,000 sex-change operations are performed each year in the United States. Studies in some European countries suggest that one person in every 350,000 believes he or she was born the wrong gender (Gorman, 1995) and that one of every 30,000 men and one of every 100,000 women seek sex-change surgery (APA, 1994).

Clinicians have heatedly debated the legitimacy of surgery as a treatment for gender identity disorder. Some consider it a humane solution, perhaps the most satisfying one to people with transsexualism (Cohen-Kettenis & van Goozen, 1997). Others argue that transsexual surgery is a "drastic nonsolution" for a purely psychological problem, akin to lobotomy (Restak, 1979). Research has not yet been able to settle the matter. The long-term psychological outcome of surgical sex reassignment, either by itself or in combination with psychotherapy and hormone treatments, is not well established. Many people seem to function well for years after such treatments (Bradley, 1995), but some have experienced psychological difficulties. Without any form of treatment, gender identity disorder among adults is usually chronic, but some cases of spontaneous remission have reportedly occurred.

Our gender is so fundamental to our sense of our identity that it is difficult for most of us to imagine wanting to change it, much less to imagine the feelings of conflict and stress experienced by those who question

their assigned gender. Whether the underlying cause is biological, psychologial, or sociocultural, gender identity disorder is a dramatic psychological dysfunction that shakes the foundations of the sufferer's existence.

Crossroads

For all the public interest in sexual disorders, clinical theorists and practitioners have only recently begun to understand the nature of sexual dysfunctions and to develop effective treatments for them. Moreover, they have made only limited progress in explaining and treating paraphilias and gender identity disorder.

People with sexual dysfunctions once were doomed to a lifetime of sexual frustration and distress. Over the past twenty-five years, however, sexual functioning has been broadly investigated, and systematic studies of various sexual dysfunctions have identified many of their psychological, sociocultural, and biological causes. Researchers are now trying to pinpoint the precise roles of these factors in sexual dysfunctioning.

As we have seen in regard to so many disorders, the various causes often seem to interact to produce a particular dysfunction, as in many cases of erectile disorder and female orgasmic disorder. In other cases, however, one causal factor alone is dominant, and an integrated approach could actually lead clinical theorists to less productive explanations. Premature ejaculation, for example, appears to have largely psychological causes, while dyspareunia usually has a physical cause.

The past few decades have also witnessed considerable progress in the treatment of sexual dysfunctions, and people with such problems are now often helped greatly by therapy. Today sex therapy is usually a complex program tailored to the particular problems and personality of an individual or couple. Once again, techniques from the various models may be combined in a given case, but sometimes the particular problem calls primarily for the implementation of one approach.

One of the most important insights to emerge from all this work is that education about sexual dysfunctions can be as important as private treatment. Myths are still taken so seriously that they often lead to feelings of shame, self-loathing, isolation, and hopelessness—feelings that contribute directly to sexual difficulty. Even a modest amount of proper education can help persons who are in treatment.

In fact, most people, not just those who seek treatment, can benefit from a more accurate understanding of sexual functioning. Public education about sexual functioning—through books, television and radio, school programs, group presentations, and the like—has become a major focus of clinical scientists. It is to be hoped that these efforts, too, will continue and increase in the coming years.

Chapter Review

1. ***Sexual dysfunctions*** Sexual dysfunctions are disorders that make it difficult or impossible for a person to have or enjoy coitus.

2. ***Disorders of the desire phase*** Disorders of the desire phase of the sexual response cycle are *hypoactive sexual desire disorder,* a lack of interest in sex and a corresponding low level of sexual activity; and *sexual aversion disorder,* a persistent revulsion to and active avoidance of sexual activity with a partner.
   - A. ***Biological causes*** cited in hypoactive sexual desire and sexual aversion include abnormal hormone levels, certain drugs, and some chronic illnesses.
   - B. ***Psychological and sociocultural causes*** include fears, situational pressures, relationship problems, and the trauma of having been sexually molested or assaulted.

3. ***Disorders of the excitement phase*** Disorders of the excitement phase of the sexual response cycle are *female sexual arousal disorder,* a persistent inability to attain or maintain adequate lubrication or genital swelling during sexual activity; and *male erectile disorder,* a persistent inability to attain or maintain an erection during sexual activity.
   - A. ***Biological causes*** of male erectile disorder include abnormal hormone levels, vascular abnormalities, medical conditions, and certain medications.
   - B. ***Psychological and sociocultural causes*** of male erectile disorder include *performance anxiety* and the *spectator role,* situational pressures such as job loss, and relationship problems.

4. ***Disorders of the Orgasm Phase*** Disorders of the orgasm phase of the sexual response cycle are *premature ejaculation, male orgasmic disorder,* and *female orgasmic disorder.*
   - A. ***Premature ejaculation,*** recurrently reaching orgasm and ejaculating before or shortly after penetration, has been related to behavioral causes, such as inappropriate early learning and inexperience.

B. ***Male orgasmic disorder,*** a repeated absence of or long delay in reaching orgasm, has been related to biological causes such as low testosterone levels, neurological diseases, head injuries, and certain drugs; and to psychological causes such as performance anxiety and the spectator role. The dysfunction may also grow from hypoactive sexual desire.

C. ***Female orgasmic disorder*** is a repeated absence of or long delay in orgasm. It, along with female sexual arousal disorder, has been tied to biological causes such as certain medical diseases, some drugs, and several postmenopausal changes; psychological causes such as memories of childhood traumas; and sociocultural causes such as society's mixed messages about female sexuality, the trauma of sexual molestation or assault, and relationship problems. Most clinicians agree that orgasm during intercourse is not critical to normal sexual functioning, provided a woman can reach orgasm with her partner during direct stimulation of the clitoris.

5. ***Sexual pain disorders*** In *vaginismus,* involuntary contractions of the muscles around the outer third of the vagina prevent entry of the penis. In *dyspareunia,* the person experiences severe pain in the genitals during sexual activity. Dyspareunia usually occurs in women and typically has a physical cause such as injury during childbirth.

6. ***Treatment of sexual dysfunctions*** In the 1970s the work of William Masters and Virginia Johnson led to the development of *sex therapy.* Its major components are careful assessment, education, attitude changes, sensate focus exercises to help eliminate *performance anxiety* and the *spectator role,* improvements in communication and sexual technique, and couple therapy. Specific techniques are also applied for each of the sexual dysfunctions.

7. ***Paraphilias*** Paraphilias are characterized by recurrent and intense sexual urges, fantasies, or behaviors involving either nonhuman objects, children, nonconsenting adults, or experiences of suffering or humiliation. The diagnosis is applied only when the urges, fantasies, or behaviors last at least six months and cause great distress or impairment.

A. These patterns are found primarily in men.

B. The paraphilias include *fetishism, transvestic fetishism (transvestism), exhibitionism, voyeurism, frotteurism, pedophilia, sexual masochism,* and *sexual sadism.*

8. ***Gender identity disorder*** People who manifest a *gender identity disorder,* or *transsexualism,* persistently feel that they have been assigned to the wrong sex and are preoccupied with acquiring the physical characteristics of the other sex. Males apparently outnumber females with this disorder by around 2 to 1.

A. The causes of gender identity disorder are not well understood.

B. Hormone treatments and psychotherapy have been used in many cases of this disorder. Sex-change operations have also been performed, but the appropriateness of surgery as a form of "treatment" has been hotly debated.

Thought and Afterthought

Improving a Dog's Life

A company in Buckner, Missouri, has developed a new product: artificial testicles for dogs. Called "neuticles," the testicle substitutes are slipped into a dog's scrotum immediately after neutering to protect the animal from psychological trauma. They are made of polypropylene, a material used to coat some human implants and surgical equipment. Over a thousand pairs were sold in 1996 alone. One dog owner explained, "A dog is like a kid. Same thing. Consideration for his feelings" (Steinberg, 1996). But many veterinarians have questioned "whether the plastic substitutes would improve a dog's esteem" (Uhlig, 1996).

Afterthoughts: Why might some pet owners believe that this product is necessary or useful? . . . Are pet owners sometimes too quick to project human discomforts and fears onto animals? . . . On the other hand, why are other people often so critical of the concerns, kindness, and affection that many people extend to their pets?

A Kiss Felt Round the World

In September 1996, 6-year-old Jonathan Prevette came home from school in Lexington, North Carolina, and admitted to his mother that he was in big trouble. His deed? Not truancy, teacher disrespect, or fighting. To his mother's disbelief, the school had charged little Jonathan with *sexual harassment* for kissing another child on the cheek, and suspended him for a day. The school later explained that by his kiss he had broken a rule prohibiting unwarranted and unwelcome touching of one student by another.

Within a day, Jonathan's photograph appeared in newspapers around the country. People everywhere wondered how a 6-year-old child could be charged with so serious an offense. For his part, Jonathan seemed understandably confused by his suspension—and more than a little saddened that he had missed an ice cream party at school.

Afterthoughts: Is a 6-year-old capable of understanding the sexual and social implications of planting an uninvited kiss on another person? . . . When school officials react so powerfully to behaviors that would be considered sexual in an adult, might they unintentionally be teaching the child and other onlookers that sex is dirty, undesirable, and even dangerous? . . . Does misapplying this label to the behavior of a young child trivialize the problem and implications of sexual harassment in the teenage and adult worlds?

Surfing for Sex on the Internet

On a given week, Internet users make hundreds of thousands of searches on the popular program Veronica. Which topic do they seek out most often? "Sex," by far. The second most-sought topic is "Erotica." Users search for these topics almost four times as often as "Games" and five times as often as "Music" (Foster, 1995).

Afterthoughts: Why might sex be such a popular commodity on the Internet? . . . Is the ready availability of sex chat groups and other sexual material on the Internet psychologically healthy or damaging? . . . Might proliferation of sexual material in our computerized world fuel abnormal sexual interests and behaviors, as some observers fear?

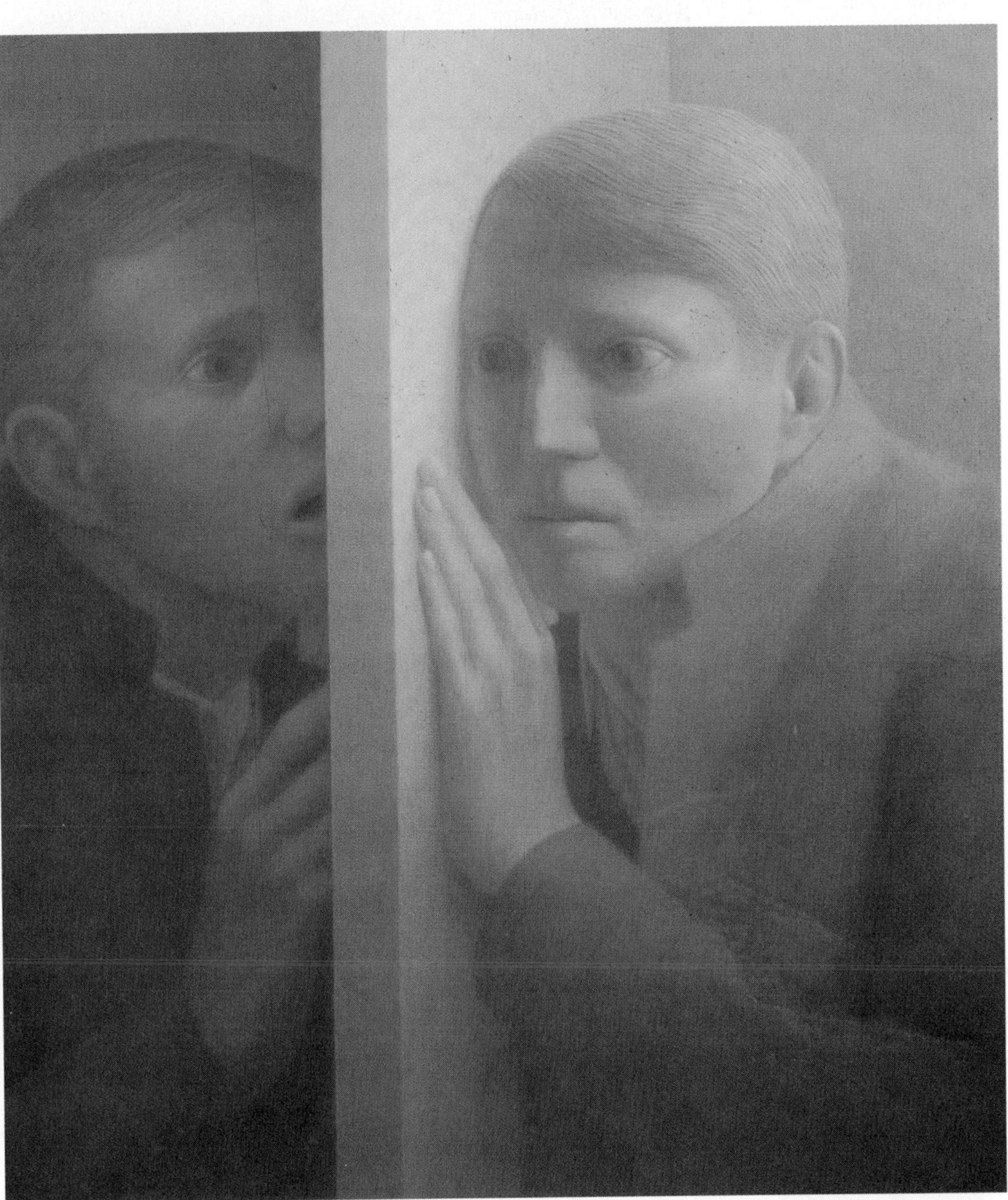

Topic Overview

Chapter 15

Schizophrenia

Psychosis is a condition characterized by loss of contact with reality. Often sufferers' capacity to perceive, process, and respond to environmental stimuli becomes so impaired and distorted that they may be unable to achieve even marginal adaptive functioning. Individuals in a state of psychosis may have *hallucinations* (false sensory perceptions) or *delusions* (false beliefs), or they may withdraw into a private world.

Psychosis may sometimes have an obvious immediate cause. As we noted in Chapter 13, taking LSD, abusing amphetamines or cocaine, or ingesting some other substances may produce psychosis. So may injuries to the brain and diseases that affect it. Most commonly, however, psychosis appears in the form of ***schizophrenia.*** People with this disorder find their previously adaptive personal, social, and occupational functioning deteriorating into a welter of distorted perceptions, disturbed thought processes, deviant emotional states, and motor abnormalities.

Like the subject of George Tooker's Voice I, *1963, some people with schizophrenia hear sounds and voices that may alarm or comfort them. Although the voices come from within, they seem real to the individuals and are often attributed to outside sources.*

> *W*hat . . . does schizophrenia mean to me? It means fatigue and confusion, it means trying to separate every experience into the real and the unreal and sometimes not being aware of where the edges overlap. It means trying to think straight when there is a maze of experiences getting in the way, and when thoughts are continually being sucked out of your head so that you become embarrassed to speak at meetings. It means feeling sometimes that you are inside your head and visualizing yourself walking over your brain, or watching another girl wearing your clothes and carrying out actions as you think them. It means knowing that you are continually "watched," that you can never succeed in life because the laws are all against you and knowing that your ultimate destruction is never far away.
>
> *(Rollin, 1980, p. 162)*

Schizophrenia appears to have been with us throughout history; it is one of the conditions commonly described as "madness" (Cutting, 1985). The Bible speaks of King Saul's mad rages and terrors. When David feigns madness in order to escape his enemies, he is mimicking some of the symptoms of schizophrenia. Hippocrates considered the syndrome to be caused by an imbalance of the body's humors. The Roman physician Galen (A.D. 130–200) blamed it on a reduction in the number and size of a person's normal "animal spirits."

In 1892, an artist who was a patient at a mental hospital claimed credit for this painting Self-Portrait as Christ. *Recent discoveries suggest that the portrait may in fact be an alteration of another artist's work. Either way, the patient was manifesting delusions of grandeur sometimes found in cases of schizophrenia.*

In 1865 a Belgian psychiatrist named Benedict Morel (1809–1873) applied the label ***démence précoce*** ("early dementia") to a 14-year-old-boy who showed the symptoms of this disorder. In 1899 Emil Kraepelin used the Latin form of Morel's label, ***dementia praecox.*** Finally, in 1911, the Swiss psychiatrist Eugen Bleuler (1857–1939) coined the term "schizophrenia" by combining Greek words that mean "split mind." To Bleuler the term implied (1) a fragmentation of thought processes, (2) a split between thoughts and emotions, and (3) a withdrawal from reality. He did not intend to convey a split into two or more personalities, as many people still misinterpret the term to mean (see Chapter 17).

Today we know that approximately one of every 100 people on earth meets the DSM-IV criteria for schizophrenia (APA, 1994; Regier et al., 1993). Thus more than 4 million people currently living in the United States have been or will be diagnosed as suffering from this disorder (Carson & Sanislow, 1993). The President's Commission on Mental Health (1978) brought such figures to life some years back with the observation "There are as many schizophrenics in America as there are people in Oregon, Mississippi and Kansas, or in Wyoming, Vermont, Delaware and Hawaii combined."

The financial cost of schizophrenia is enormous—estimated at more than $100 billion annually, including the costs of hospitalization, lost wages, and disability benefits (Black & Andreasen, 1994). The emotional cost of this disorder to families is even greater. Moreover, schizophrenia is associated with increased risk of suicide and of physical—often mortal—illness (Bruce et al., 1994; McGlashan, 1988). As we discussed in Chapter 10, it is estimated that up to 15 percent of persons with the disorder commit suicide (Fenton et al., 1997; Peuskens et al., 1997; Krausz et al., 1995).

Although schizophrenia appears in all socioeconomic groups, it is found more frequently in the lower socioeconomic classes (see Figure 15-1). Thus some theorists believe that the stress of poverty is itself a cause of the disorder. Alternatively, schizophrenia may cause its victims to migrate from a higher to a lower socioeconomic class or to remain poor because they are unable to function as before (Munk & Mortensen, 1992). This is sometimes called the "downward drift" theory.

Equal numbers of men and women receive a diagnosis of schizophrenia. In men, however, the age of onset is typically earlier and the course of the disorder more severe (Castle et al., 1995; Gorwood et al., 1995; Kulkarni et

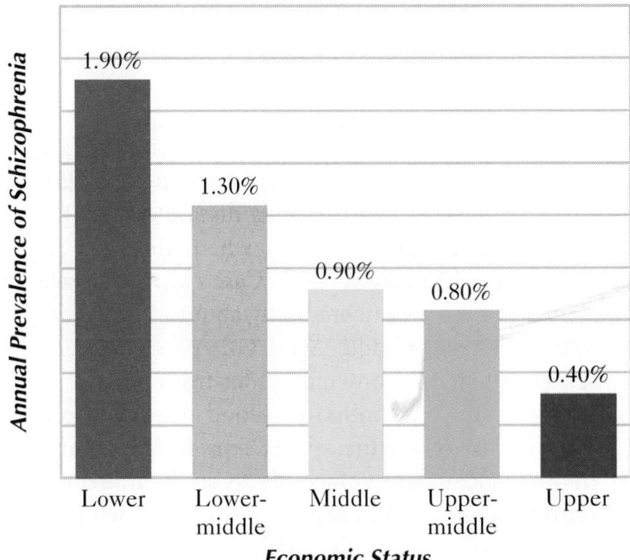

Figure 15-1 *According to surveys, poor people in the United States are much more likely than wealthy people to experience schizophrenia. This relationship may indicate that the stresses of poverty help cause schizophrenia, that the impairment of schizophrenia leads to poverty, or both. (Adapted from Keith et al., 1991.)*

al., 1995). Almost 3 percent of all divorced or separated persons suffer from the disorder over the course of their lives, compared to 1 percent of married people and 2 percent of people who remain single (Keith et al., 1991). Again, however, it is not clear whether marital discord is a cause of it or its result.

Approximately 2.1 percent of African Americans receive a diagnosis of schizophrenia at some time during their lives, compared to 1.4 percent of white Americans (Keith et al., 1991). However, African Americans are also more likely to be poor and to experience marital separation. When these factors are controlled for, the prevalence rates of schizophrenia are equal for the two races.

Let us now consider in depth the clinical picture of schizophrenia—a fascinating array of symptoms that have captured the interest of scientists and the imagination of artists. The general public, too, shows great interest in the disorder, flocking to movies (including the remarkably popular horror movies) and plays whose plots center on schizophrenia (see Box 15-1). Yet all too many people with this disorder are neglected in our country, and their needs are almost entirely ignored. Although effective interventions have been developed for schizophrenia, most sufferers live without adequate treatment and without nearly fulfilling their potential as human beings (Torrey, 1997).

The Clinical Picture of Schizophrenia

For years schizophrenia was a "wastebasket category" for diagnosticians. The disorder was defined especially broadly in the United States, where it often covered anyone who acted unpredictably or strangely. Some clinicians were known to say that "even a trace of schizophrenia is schizophrenia" (Lewis & Piotrowski, 1954).

Although the disorder is defined more precisely today, its symptoms do vary greatly, and so do its triggers, course, and responsiveness to treatment (APA, 1994). In fact, some clinicians believe that schizophrenia is actually a group of distinct disorders that happen to have some common features. To see the variety of forms schizophrenia may take, consider three people who were diagnosed as suffering from it. The cases are taken from the files of Silvano Arieti (1974), a prominent theorist on the disorder.

Ann, 26 years old

Ann graduated from high school and from a school for commercial art. She was a very persistent student, very punctual in her study habits, and even in her early childhood showed a talent for drawing and painting. . . . At the age of 18 she began going out with Henry. . . . They became engaged shortly thereafter and went out together frequently until their marriage. . . . Married life was considered a boring routine by both Ann and Henry. There was very little conversation between them. . . .

Ann's disappointment in Henry increased. They had nothing in common; she was artistically inclined, whereas he had only an ordinary, conventional outlook toward life. It was at this time that she started to go dancing and then met Charles. Her interest in him increased, but . . . a divorce was not compatible with the precepts of the Catholic church. Her conflict grew and put her in a state of great agitation. . . .

. . . One evening she came home from dancing and told her mother that she was going to give up her husband Henry, marry Charles, go to Brazil with him, and have twenty babies. She was talking very fast and saying many things, several of which were incomprehensible. At the same time she also told her mother that she was seeing the Virgin Mary in visions. She then went to her mother-in-law and told her to take back her son Henry, because he was too immature. The following day Ann went to work and tried to get the entire office down on their knees with her to recite the rosary. A few days later, her mother took her to a priest, whom

BOX 15-1 Howling for Attention

It's when I was bitten by a rabid dog. . . . When I'm emotionally upset, I feel as if I am turning into something else: my fingers go numb, as if I had pins and needles right in the middle of my hand; I can no longer control myself. . . . I get the feeling I'm becoming a wolf. I look at myself in the mirror and I witness my transformation. It's no longer my face; it changes completely. I stare, my pupils dilate, and I feel as if hairs are growing all over my body, as if my teeth are getting longer. . . . I feel as if my skin is no longer mine.

(Benezech, DeWitte, & Bourgeois, 1989)

Lycanthropy, the delusion of being an animal, is a rare psychological syndrome. The word "lycanthropy" comes from the Greek *lykos,* wolf, and *anthropos,* man. Accounts have been found all over the world of people who take on the characteristics and behavior of wolves or other animals. Belief in these tales has persisted for centuries, though the perceptions about causation have changed. In the Middle Ages, lycanthropy was attributed to demonic possession (Lehmann, 1985). In the sixteenth and seventeenth centuries, the accepted causes were physical illness and satanic influence. In some societies where lycanthropy was frequently reported, it occurred after special ointments, probably potent hallucinogenic drugs, were applied, often for religious purposes (Lévi-Strauss, 1977). In other societies, cases of lycanthropy were closely linked to mental disorders, including schizophrenia, severe mood disorders, and certain forms of brain damage.

Mention of lycanthropy continues to evoke an image of a werewolf baring its fangs at a terrified villager on a fog-shrouded Scottish moor, all because the former was bitten by another werewolf in the unbroken chain that passes on such a legacy, but there are now more plausible explanations for this type of behavior. One explanation is that some people afflicted with lycanthropy actually suffer from *congenital generalized hypertrichosis,* an extremely rare disease, characterized by excessive amounts of hair on the face and upper body (Maugh, 1995). Victims of this disease appear totally normal when the hair is shaved off. Case reports have numbered only about 50 since the Middle Ages. Others with lycanthropy may suffer from *porphyria,* an inherited blood disease whose victims sprout extra facial hair and are vulnerable to sunlight. People with porphyria can be treated successfully with blood pigment. Still another current explanation associates lycanthropy with a disturbance in the activity of the temporal lobe of the brain. The posterior region of the temporal lobe is close to other areas of the brain that are linked to visual functions and may be the source of visual hallucinations. Abnormal brain activity in the temporal lobe combined with a psychotic thought disorder may account for many of the symptoms of lycanthropy.

One of the most interesting contemporary instances of lycanthropy happens to differ somewhat from the classical mold. A

---

she "told off" in no uncertain terms. She finally spit at him. A psychiatrist was consulted, and he recommended hospitalization.

. . . When the patient was first seen in the ward by the examiner, she was dashing around the room, singing and laughing. She was markedly agitated; frequently she would cry one minute and then laugh in a silly, impulsive manner, or suddenly slump over and become mute. Her speech would be incoherent at one time because she mumbled and at another time she would shriek very loudly. She would be irrelevant, or circumstantial, and she frequently rambled, her thoughts being completely unrelated to one another. Her affect would vary from extreme lability to complete flatness. She was hallucinating in auditory and visual spheres quite vividly. She was saying:

I was judged insane and others felt that this was the place for me. I am too weak. You look to me like Uncle Joe, and he is so far away. He knew how much I loved him. We could always get along. I never meant to be disobedient to you. The darn son of a bitch, you couldn't smile at me. You are the Pope and I must be obedient to the Pope. He is the only one I must be obedient to. You didn't flinch when I said "son of a bitch." You are trying to help me. All the others are different. That I can't fake in your presence, my Lord. You will understand me as my friends didn't. Russia is the only Catholic country. Russia is to the rest of the world what God is to the Pope.

Later the patient became more agitated and required strong sedation. Her illness seemed to proceed toward

26-year-old man had been convinced that he was a cat for more than fifteen years at the time his case was reported. He was a research scientist who had a history of alcohol abuse, major depression, and several other problems. While being treated for these disorders, he revealed to the clinician that as a child he had discovered that he was a cat. He was able to communicate with other cats, he reported, and his true identity was confirmed by the family cat, Tiffany. It should be noted that this man had apparently been neglected, if not outright abused, by his parents. In addition, there was a history of severe psychological disorders in his immediate family.

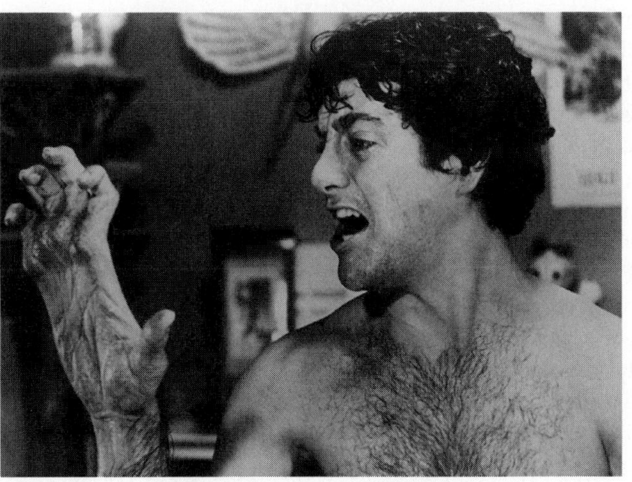

In the film An American Werewolf in London, *a possessed man watches in terror as his hand stretches into the forepaw of a wolf.*

When the boy made his discovery, he began to hunt with cats and to eat raw meat. He also reported that he had had a series of monogamous relationships with cats. At the age of 17 he refined his view of his feline existence and concluded that in fact he was a tiger. He fell in love with Dolly, a tiger at the zoo. His plans to orchestrate Dolly's escape from the zoo and live with her were dashed when she was sold to an Asian zoo, and he fell into a major depression.

At the time of the clinical interview, the young man looked normal except for his attire—striped clothes, primarily—and his long fingernails. He had a number of friends, and except for his cat delusions, his thought processes were normal.

The clinician's explanation for this extreme and persistent case of lycanthropy was that the patient had "failed to form an adequate self-identification with either parent, due to their own disturbances, and subsequently targeted his favorite cat as an idealized self-object during childhood. This process, perhaps superimposed on a medical or neurological vulnerability, may have produced his persistent lycanthropic delusion" (Kulick, Pope, & Keck, 1990, p. 136).

Modern cases of lycanthropy make a powerful point about human nature: ideas and beliefs play major roles in shaping behavior. Though our explanations for abnormal behavior evolve as we become more sophisticated about the workings of the human mind, age-old myths are difficult to put to rest.

more advanced disintegration. She laughed in an inappropriate manner, and her whole behavior appeared silly. She was restless, confused, and talked to imaginary persons.

(Arieti, 1974, pp. 173–177)

Richard, 23 years old

In high school, Richard was an average student. After graduation from high school, he was drafted into the army. . . . Richard remembered [the] period . . . after his discharge from the army . . . as one of the worst in his life, even worse than his childhood. . . . Any, even remote, anticipation of disappointment was able to provoke attacks of anxiety in him. He could never be indifferent or detached, but was very much involved in everything. . . .

Approximately two years after his return to civilian life, Richard left his job because he became overwhelmed by these feelings of lack of confidence in himself, and he refused to go look for another one. He stayed home most of the day. His mother would nag him that he was too lazy and unwilling to do anything. He became slower and slower in dressing and undressing and taking care of himself. When he went out of the house, he felt compelled "to give interpretations" to everything he looked at. He did not know what to do outside the house, where to go, where to turn. If he saw a red light at a crossing, he would interpret it as a message that he should not go in that direction. If he saw an arrow, he would follow the arrow interpreting it as a sign sent by God that he should go in that direction. Feeling lost and horrified, he would go home and stay there, afraid to go out because going out meant making decisions or choices that he felt unable to make. He reached the point where he stayed home most of the time. But even at home, he was tortured by his symptoms. He could not act; any motion that he felt like making seemed to him an insurmountable obstacle, because he did not know whether he should make it or not. He was increasingly afraid of doing the wrong thing. Such fears prevented him from dressing, undressing, eating, and so forth. He felt paralyzed and lay motionless in bed. He gradually became worse, was completely motionless, and had to be hospitalized.

. . . Even in the hospital, he had to interpret everything that occurred. If a doctor asked him a question, he had a sudden impulse to answer, but then feared that by answering he would do the wrong thing. He tried desperately to find signs that would indicate to him whether he should answer or not. An accidental noise, the arrival of another person, or the number of words the questions consisted of were indications of whether he should reply or not.

Being undecided, he felt blocked, and often would remain mute and motionless, like a statue, even for days.

(Arieti, 1974, pp. 153–155)

Laura, 40 years old

Laura's desire was to become independent and leave home [in Austria] as soon as possible. . . . She became a professional dancer at the age of 20 . . . and was booked for vaudeville theaters in many European countries. . . .

It was during one of her tours in Germany that Laura met her husband. . . . They were married and went to live in a small provincial town in France where the husband's business was. Laura felt like a stranger immediately; she was in an environment very different from her own and was not accepted by his family. There were realistic grounds for her feelings. They considered her a foreigner and could not forgive her for having been a dancer, and not a "regular girl." She spent a year in that town and was very unhappy. . . . [Finally] Laura and her husband decided to emigrate to the United States. . . .

They had no children, and Laura . . . showed interest in pets. She had a dog to whom she was very devoted. The dog became sick and partially paralyzed, and veterinarians felt that there was no hope of recovery. The dog required difficult care, and her husband, who knew how she felt about the animal, tolerated the situation for several weeks. But finally he broached the problem to his wife, asking her "Should the dog be destroyed or not?" From that time on Laura became restless, agitated, and depressed. . . .

. . . Later Laura started to complain about the neighbors. A woman who lived on the floor beneath them was knocking on the wall to irritate her. According to the husband, this woman had really knocked on the wall a few times; he had heard the noises. However, Laura became more and more concerned about it. She would wake up in the middle of the night under the impression that she was hearing noises from the apartment downstairs. She would become upset and angry at the neighbors. Once she was awake, she could not sleep for the rest of the night. The husband would vainly try to calm her. Later she became more disturbed. She started to feel that the neighbors were now recording everything she said; maybe they had hidden wires in the apartment. She started to feel "funny" sensations. There were many strange things happening, which she did not know how to explain; people were looking at her in a funny way in the street; in the butcher shop, the butcher had purposely served her last, although she was in the middle of the line. During the next few days she felt that people were planning to harm either her or her husband. . . . In the evening when she looked at television, it became obvious to her that the programs referred to her life. Often the people on the programs were just repeating what she had thought. They were stealing her ideas. She wanted to go to the police and report them.

(Arieti, 1974, pp. 165–168)

Symptoms of Schizophrenia

Ann, Richard, and Laura each regressed from a normal level of functioning to become ineffective in dealing with the world. Ann, a promising art student, became unhappy and discontented, and finally totally disoriented; Richard, a sensitive and talented young man, became so indecisive that he literally stopped moving; and Laura, once so independent and competent, became restless and agitated and eventually consumed by bizarre suspicions. Among them, these three individuals demonstrate the range of symptoms associated with schizophrenia. Although several such disturbances are usually present in any given case of schizophrenia, no single symptom is present in every case.

Over the years, clinicians have searched for meaningful links and distinctions between the symptoms of schizophrenia (Himelhoch et al., 1996; Arndt et al., 1995). Today many favor grouping the symptoms into three categories: ***positive symptoms,*** so named because they seem to represent "pathological excesses," bizarre additions to a normal repertoire of behavior; ***negative***

symptoms, which seem to reflect "pathological deficits," characteristics that are lacking; and ***psychomotor symptoms,*** which take such forms as motionlessness, odd gestures, and excited movements. Men with schizophrenia are more likely to display negative symptoms than women, but both sexes display equal numbers of positive symptoms (Shtasel et al., 1992).

Positive Symptoms The positive symptoms of schizophrenia include delusions, disorganized thinking and speech, heightened perceptions and hallucinations, and inappropriate affect.

Delusions Many people with schizophrenia develop ***delusions,*** ideas that they believe fervently but that have no basis in fact. Delusions may be elaborate and internally consistent or fragmented and capricious; they are often absurd. To the believer they may appear as either enlightening or confusing. Some people with schizophrenia hold a single delusion that dominates their life and behavior, while others have many delusions.

Delusions of persecution are the most common in schizophrenia (APA, 1994). People with this delusion believe that they are being plotted or discriminated against, spied on, slandered, threatened, attacked, or deliberately victimized. Laura believed that her neighbors were trying to irritate her and that other people were trying to harm her and her husband. Another woman with schizophrenia vividly recalled her delusions of persecution:

> I felt as if I was being put on a heavenly trial for misdeeds that I had done and was being held accountable by God. Other times I felt as if I was being pursued by the government for acts of disloyalty. . . . I felt that the government agencies had planted transmitters and receivers in my apartment so that I could hear what they were saying and they could hear what I was saying. I also felt as if the government had bugged my clothing, so that whenever I went outside my apartment I felt like I was being pursued. I felt like I was being followed and watched 24 hours a day.
>
> I would like to point out that these were my feelings then, and in hindsight I hold nothing against these government agencies. I now know that this constant monitoring was either punishment at the hands of God's servants for deeds I committed earlier in my life (sort of like being punished in hell but while I was still alive) or alternatively, but less likely, that I just imagined these things.
>
> *(Anonymous, 1996, p. 183)*

People with schizophrenia may also experience ***delusions of reference,*** when they attach special and personal significance to the actions of others, or to various objects or events (Richard, for example, interpreted arrows on street signs as indicators of the direction he should take); ***delusions of grandeur,*** when they believe themselves to be great inventors, religious saviors, or other specially empowered persons; and ***delusions of control,*** when they believe their impulses, feelings, thoughts, and actions are being controlled by other people. This man hospitalized for schizophrenia imagined he was being controlled by telepathy:

No, it's not "the King." But surveys indicate that as many as one of every eight Americans believes that Elvis Presley is still alive—a belief that has led to numerous Elvis sightings at 7-Eleven stores around the country and encouraged an army of Elvis impersonators. Clinicians stop short of calling such beliefs delusions, however, noting that the Elvis loyalists do not hold on to their beliefs with a high degree of conviction. Most can be persuaded that Elvis has indeed "left the building."

> The inmates, here, hate me extremely because I am sane. . . . They talk to me telepathically, continuously and daily almost without cessation, day and night. . . . By the power of their imagination and

> daily and continuously, they create extreme pain in my head, brain, eyes, heart, stomach and in every part of my body. Also by their imagination and daily and continuously, they lift my heart and stomach and they pull my heart, and they stop it, move it, twist it and shake it and pull its muscles and tissues. . . . By telepathy and imagination, they force me to say orally whatever they desire, whenever they desire and as long as they desire. I never said a word of my own. I never created a thought or image of my own.
>
> *(Arieti, 1974, pp. 404–405)*

Disorganized Thinking and Speech People with schizophrenia may be incapable of logical, rational thinking, and often present very peculiar speech. These ***formal thought disorders*** can cause the sufferer great confusion and make communication with others extremely difficult (Docherty, DeRosa, & Andreasen, 1996). Often they take the form of positive symptoms (that is, pathological excesses), as in loose associations, neologisms, perseveration, and clang.

People who display ***loose associations,*** or ***derailment,*** the most common formal thought disorder, rapidly shift from one topic to another, apparently believing that their inconsequential and incoherent statements make sense. One man with schizophrenia, asked about his itchy arms, responded:

> The problem is insects. My brother used to collect insects. He's now a man 5 foot 10 inches. You know, 10 is my favorite number. I also like to dance, draw, and watch television.

Note the oblique association between one block of words and the next. A single, perhaps unimportant word in one sentence becomes the focus of the next.

Some people with schizophrenia display a formal thought disorder that causes them to use ***neologisms,*** or made-up words. They typically have meaning only to the person using them:

> I am here from a foreign university . . . and you have to have a "plausity" of all acts of amendment to go through for the children's code . . . and it is no mental disturbance or "putenence" . . . it is an "amoriton" law . . . there is nothing to disturb me . . . it is like their "privatilinia" . . . and the children have to have this "accentuative" law so they don't go into the "mortite" law of the church.
>
> *(Vetter, 1969, p. 189)*

Persons with schizophrenia may also display the formal thought disorder of ***perseveration;*** that is, they repeat their words and statements again and again (Capleton, 1996). Finally, some use ***clang,*** or rhyme, as a guide to formulating thoughts and statements. When asked how she was feeling, one person with schizophrenia replied, "Well, hell, it's well to tell." Another described the weather as "So hot, you know it runs on a cot."

Formal thought disorders such as these are not unique to schizophrenia. Loose associations and perseverations are common in cases of severe mania, for example. Even people who function normally may organize statements loosely or may on occasion use words that others fail to understand, especially when they are fatigued or feeling ill; but the formal thought disorders of schizophrenia are much more severe and pervasive (Holzman, 1986). Research suggests that some disorganized speech or thinking may appear long before a full pattern of schizophrenia unfolds (Bilder et al., 1992; Harvey, 1991; Walker & Lewine, 1990).

Heightened Perceptions and Hallucinations The deranged protagonist in Edgar Allan Poe's "The Tell-Tale Heart" asks, "Have I not told you that what you mistake for madness is but the overacuteness of the senses?" Some people with schizophrenia similarly feel that their senses are being *flooded* by all the sights and sounds that surround them, so that it is almost impossible for them to attend to anything important:

> Everything seems to grip my attention although I am not particularly interested in anything. I am speaking to you just now, but I can hear noises going on next door and in the corridor. I find it difficult to shut these out, and it makes it more difficult for me to concentrate on what I am saying to you.
>
> *(McGhie and Chapman, 1961)*

Laboratory studies have repeatedly demonstrated such problems of perception and attention in schizophrenia (Bustillo et al., 1997; Finkelstein et al., 1997; Williams, 1996; Mirsky et al., 1995). In one study, subjects were instructed to listen for and identify a target syllable on a recording that also included background speech (Harris et al., 1985). As long as the background speech was kept simple, subjects with schizophrenia and those without the disorder were equally adept at picking out the target syllable; but when the background speech was made more distracting, the subjects with schizophrenia became less able than the others to identify the target syllable.

Deficiencies in ***smooth pursuit eye movement*** may be related to these attention problems. When asked to keep their head still and track a moving object back and forth with their eyes, many subjects with schizophrenia perform more poorly than those without schizophrenia (Sereno & Holzman, 1995). Studies suggest that the various perception and attention problems in schizophrenia may develop years before the onset of the actual disorder (Cornblatt & Keilp, 1994; Cornblatt & Erlenmeyer-Kimling, 1985).

Another kind of perceptual problem in schizophrenia consists of ***hallucinations,*** perceptions that occur in the absence of external stimuli. People who have *auditory* hallucinations, by far the most common kind in schizophrenia (APA, 1994; Mueser, Bellack, & Brady, 1990), hear sounds and voices that seem to come from outside their heads. The voices may be complimentary or critical; they may be heard frequently or only on occasion. They may talk directly to the hallucinator, perhaps giving commands or warning of dangers, or they may be experienced as overheard.

> The voices . . . were mostly heard in my head, though I often heard them in the air, or in different parts of the room. Every voice was different, and each beautiful, and generally, speaking or singing in a different tone and measure, and resembling those of relations or friends. There appeared to be many in my head, I should say upwards of fourteen. I divide them, as they styled themselves, or one another, into voices of contrition and voices of joy and honour.
>
> *("Perceval's Narrative" in Bateson, 1974)*

> For about almost seven years—except during sleep—I have never had a single moment in which I did not hear voices. They accompany me to every place and at all times; they continue to sound even when I am in conversation with other people, they persist undeterred even when I concentrate on other things, for instance read a book or a newspaper, play the piano, etc.; only when I am talking aloud to other people or to myself are they of course drowned by the stronger sound of the spoken word and therefore inaudible to me. But the well-known phrases recommence at once, sometimes in the middle of a sentence, which tells me that the conversation had continued during the interval, that is to say that those nervous stimuli or vibrations responsible for the weaker sounds of the voices continue even while I talk aloud.
>
> *(Schreber, 1955, p. 225)*

Auditory hallucinations are most likely to occur during times of idleness or inattention. As a patient once observed, "Isn't it funny, when I'm shoveling snow I don't hear voices" (Strauss et al., 1981). One study similarly noted increases in hallucinations during sensory isolation. In this study people with schizophrenia listened to a bland noise over headphones and wore goggles to restrict visual information (Margo, Hemsley, & Slade, 1981).

Research also suggests that people with auditory hallucinations actually produce sounds, hear them, and then attribute them to external sources. That is, their brain is generating sound during the hallucinations. One study measured cerebral blood flow in *Broca's area,* the region of the brain that helps people produce speech (McGuire et al., 1995, 1993). The researchers found increased blood flow in Broca's area while patients were experiencing auditory hallucinations.

A related study instructed six men with schizophrenia to press a button whenever they experienced an auditory hallucination (Silbersweig et al., 1995). PET scans revealed increased activity near the brain's surface, in the tissues that are needed for hearing. In sum, then, during auditory hallucinations the brain apparently both produces sounds and leads individuals to hear those sounds. In contrast, *Wernicke's area,* the brain region that helps people *comprehend* the language of others, is not particularly active during auditory hallucinations (Cleghorn et al., 1990).

Hallucinations can also involve any one of the other senses. *Tactile* hallucinations may take the form of tingling, burning, or electrical-shock sensations, or the feeling of insects crawling over one's body or just beneath the skin. *Somatic* hallucinations convey the sensation that something is happening inside the body, such as an organ shifting position or a snake crawling inside one's stomach. *Visual* hallucinations run the gamut from vague perceptions of colors or clouds to distinct visions

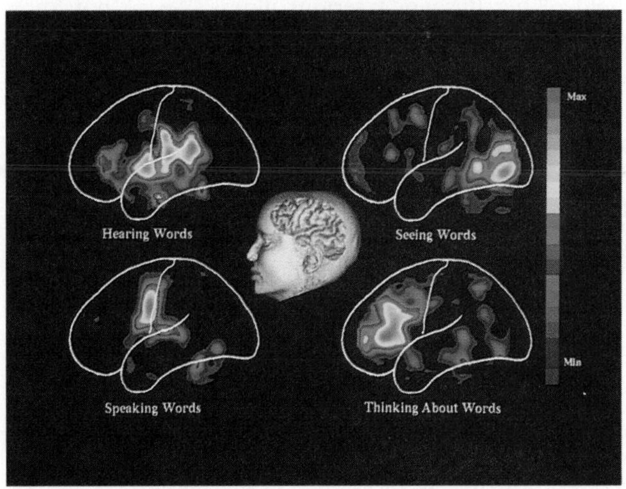

These PET scans of normal subjects show which brain areas are active under various circumstances. When people speak, Broca's area is particularly active (lower left scan). *When they listen to the words of others, activity rises in Wernicke's area* (upper left scan). *Apparently, when individuals are having auditory hallucinations, Broca's area is especially active, but Wernicke's area is not (McGuire et al., 1993). This suggests that the brain of a hallucinating individual produces actual sounds and thoughts during hallucinations, but the person does not recognize that the sounds are coming from within.*

of people, objects, or scenes that are not there. They are different from the range of normal mental images experienced by adults and children. People with *gustatory* hallucinations regularly find that their food or drink tastes strange, and people with *olfactory* hallucinations smell odors that no one else does, being haunted, for example, by the smell of poison, smoke, or decay.

Hallucinations and delusional ideas often go hand in hand. A woman who hears voices issuing commands, for example, may have the delusion that the commands are being placed in her head by someone else. Similarly, a man with delusions of persecution may hallucinate the smell of poison in his bedroom or the taste of poison in his coffee. Regardless of which comes first, the hallucination and delusion eventually feed into each other.

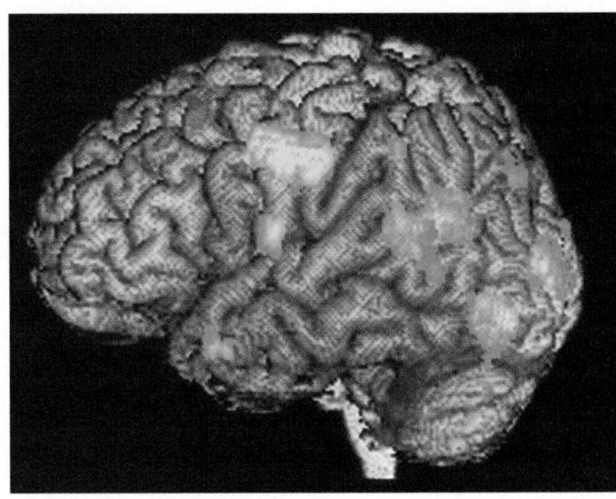

The human brain during hallucinations. This PET scan taken at the moment a subject was experiencing auditory and visual hallucinations shows heightened activity (orange) *in hearing-related tissues at the brain's* surface *and in deeper brain areas where current and past experiences and emotions are usually integrated (Silbersweig et al., 1995). Conversely, the front of the brain, which is responsible for assessing the source of sounds and other sensations, was quiet during the hallucinations. Thus, once again, people who are hallucinating seem to hear sounds generated by their own brain and make sense of them by tying them to various experiences and emotions, but their brain cannot recognize that the sounds are actually coming from within.*

Inappropriate Affect Many people with schizophrenia display ***inappropriate affect,*** emotions that are unsuited to the situation. They may smile inappropriately when making a somber statement or on being told terrible news, or become upset in situations that should make them happy. They may also undergo inappropriate shifts in mood. During a tender conversation with his wife, for example, a man with schizophrenia suddenly started yelling obscenities at her and complaining about her inadequacies.

In some cases, at least, these emotions may be merely a response to other positive symptoms of schizophrenia. Consider a woman with this disorder who smiles when told of her husband's serious illness. We do not know that she is indeed happy about the bad news; she may not be comprehending or even hearing it. She may be responding instead to another of the many stimuli flooding her senses, perhaps a joke she is hearing from an auditory hallucination.

Negative Symptoms

Negative symptoms of schizophrenia include poverty of speech, blunted and flat affect, loss of volition, and social withdrawal. These deficits make it difficult to participate in life's usual activities and interactions.

Poverty of Speech People with schizophrenia often display ***alogia,*** a decrease in speech or speech content, characterized by absent or empty replies. Some people with this negative kind of formal thought disorder think and say very little, particularly when their thoughts become *blocked* and seem to disappear from memory. One patient describes how this problem feels to him:

> I may be thinking quite clearly and telling someone something and suddenly I get stuck. You have seen me do this and you may think I am just lost for words or that I have gone into a trance, but that is not what happens. What happens is that I suddenly stick on a word or an idea in my head and I just can't move past it. It seems to fill my mind and there's no room for anything else. This might go on for a while and suddenly it's over. Afterwards I get a feeling that I have been thinking very deeply about whatever it was but often I can't remember what it was that has filled my mind so completely.
>
> *(McGhie & Chapman, 1961)*

Other persons with alogia may say quite a bit but still manage to convey little meaning (Chen et al., 1996; Baltaxe & Simmons, 1995), reflecting what is termed *poverty of content.* Vaslav Nijinsky, one of the century's great ballet dancers, wrote the following diary entry on February 27, 1919, as his schizophrenia was becoming increasingly apparent:

> I do not wish people to think that I am a great writer or that I am a great artist nor even that I am a great man. I am a simple man who has suffered a lot. I believe I suffered more than Christ. I love life and want to live, to cry but cannot—I feel such a pain in my soul—a pain which frightens me. My soul is ill. My soul, not

> my mind. The doctors do not understand my illness. I know what I need to get well. My illness is too great to be cured quickly. I am incurable. Everyone who reads these lines will suffer—they will understand my feelings. I know what I need. I am strong, not weak. My body is not ill—it is my soul that is ill. I suffer, I suffer. Everyone will feel and understand. I am a man, not a beast. I love everyone, I have faults, I am a man—not God. I want to be God and therefore I try to improve myself. I want to dance, to draw, to play the piano, to write verses, I want to love everybody. That is the object of my life.
>
> *(Nijinsky, 1936)*

Blunted and Flat Affect Many people with schizophrenia have a ***blunted affect***—they manifest less anger, sadness, joy, and other feelings than most people—and some show almost no emotions at all, a condition known as ***flat affect.*** The faces of these subjects are typically immobile, their eye contact is poor, and their voices are monotonous.

Blunted or flat affect may well reflect an actual absence of emotions. ***Anhedonia*** is just that, a general lack of pleasure or enjoyment. One young man told his father, "I wish I could wake up feeling really bad—it would be better than feeling nothing" (Wechsler, 1972, p. 17). In other cases, however, flat affect may simply reflect an inability to *express* emotions as others do. One study had subjects view highly emotional film clips. Those with schizophrenia showed less facial expression than other subjects; however, they reported feeling just as much positive and negative emotion as the other subjects, and in fact displayed greater skin arousal (Kring & Neale, 1996).

Loss of Volition As people with schizophrenia struggle to function in a grossly distorted world, many experience ***avolition,*** or apathy, feeling drained of energy and interest in normal goals and unable to initiate or complete a course of action (Lysaker & Bell, 1995). This problem is particularly common in people who have had the disorder for many years, as if they have been worn down by it. Similarly, the individuals may display ***ambivalence,*** or conflicted feelings, about most things. This feature was so common among the subjects Bleuler studied that he proclaimed it one of the central symptoms of schizophrenia. Richard, whose growing indecisiveness we observed earlier, was so overwhelmed by his avolition and indecisiveness that even eating, dressing, and undressing eventually became impossible ordeals.

Social Withdrawal People with schizophrenia often withdraw emotionally and socially from their environment and become totally preoccupied with their own ideas and fantasies (Bellack et al., 1989; Falloon et al., 1984). They may distance themselves from other people and avoid talking to them. Because their ideas are illogical and distorted, withdrawal helps distance them still further from reality. In fact, one study found that 75 percent of subjects with this disorder were less knowledgeable about everyday social issues than were people with other psychological disorders (Cutting & Murphy, 1990, 1988). The social withdrawal seems also to lead to a deterioration of social skills, including the ability to perceive other people's needs and emotions accurately (Penn et al., 1997; Mueser et al., 1996; Sayers et al., 1995).

Psychomotor Symptoms Loss of spontaneity in movement and the development of odd grimaces, gestures, and mannerisms are also symptoms of schizophrenia (Carnahan, Elliott, & Velamoor, 1996; APA, 1994). Such movements may be repetitive and sometimes seem to be purposeful, like a ritualistic or magical act.

The psychomotor symptoms of schizophrenia may take extreme forms, collectively called ***catatonia.*** People in a *catatonic stupor* become totally unaware of and unresponsive to their environment, remaining motionless and silent for long stretches of time. Recall how Richard would lie motionless and mute in bed for days. Some people show *catatonic rigidity,* maintaining a rigid, upright posture for hours and resisting efforts to be moved. Others exhibit *catatonic posturing,* assuming awkward, bizarre positions for long periods of time. They may spend hours holding their arms out at a 90-degree angle or balancing in a squatting position. Some also display *waxy flexibility,* indefinitely maintaining postures into which they have been placed by someone else.

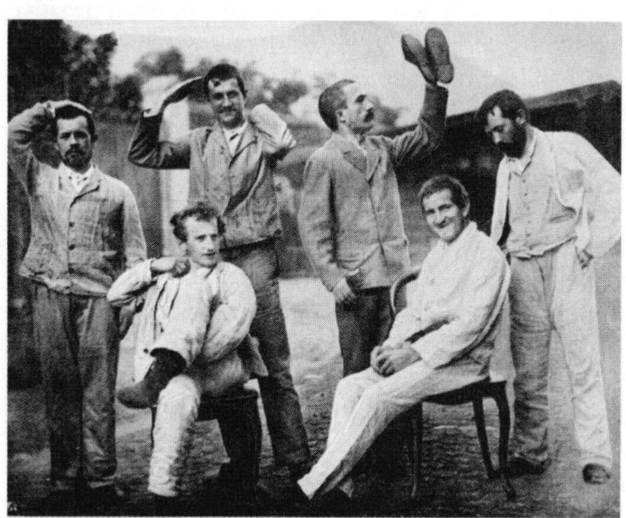

These patients, photographed at the turn of the century, display features of catatonia, including catatonic posturing, in which they assume bizarre positions for long periods of time.

If a nurse raises a patient's arm or tilts the patient's head, for example, the individual will remain in that position until moved again.

People who display ***catatonic excitement,*** a different form of catatonia, move excitedly, sometimes with wild waving of arms and legs. When such patients are extremely hyperactive and uncontrolled, they pose a danger to themselves and others. Some clinicians view catatonic excitement as just one more positive symptom and catatonic stupor, rigidity, and posturing as further negative symptoms.

The Course of Schizophrenia

Schizophrenia usually emerges between the late teens and the mid-30s (APA, 1994). Although the course of this disorder varies widely from person to person (Norman & Malla, 1995; APA, 1994), many patients seem to go through three phases—prodromal, active, and residual.

During the ***prodromal phase*** schizophrenic symptoms, particularly positive symptoms, are not yet prominent, but persons begin to deteriorate from previous levels of functioning. They may withdraw socially, speak in vague or metaphorical ways, develop strange ideas, or display some degree of blunted or inappropriate affect.

During the ***active phase,*** schizophrenic symptoms become pronounced. In some instances this phase is triggered by stress in the person's life. For Ann, the confused woman we read about earlier, the immediate precipitant was falling in love with a man she met dancing; for Laura, it was the loss of her cherished dog.

Finally, the ***residual phase*** is marked by a return to a prodromal-like level of functioning. The striking positive symptoms of the active phase recede, but often negative symptoms, such as blunted emotions, remain. The person is still unable to live a full life.

Each of the three phases may last for days or for years. Although as many as a quarter of patients with schizophrenia recover completely, the majority continue to show at least some residual impairment indefinitely (Putnam et al., 1996; Strange, 1992). After months or even years in a recovered or residual state, some people experience a new prodromal phase, which may in turn lead to another active phase if treatment is not available (Herz & Lamberti, 1995). A fuller recovery from schizophrenia is more likely in subjects who functioned quite adequately before the disorder (had good ***premorbid*** functioning), or when the disorder was initially triggered by stress, came on abruptly, or developed during middle age (Lindström, 1996; Tolbert, 1996; APA, 1994). Relapses are apparently more likely during times of stress (Hultman et al., 1997; Hirsch et al., 1996).

When schizophrenia is chronic, the symptoms typically change somewhat over the years (Black & Andreasen, 1994). A preponderance of positive symptoms in the early years of the disorder, for example, often gives way to a greater proportion of negative symptoms later (Lieberman, 1995).

Diagnosing Schizophrenia

Since the 1950s clinicians have worked carefully to specify the diagnostic criteria for schizophrenia. DSM-IV takes particular care to distinguish it from other psychotic disorders and from bipolar disorders (see Box 15-2). A diagnosis of schizophrenia is appropriate when signs of the disorder continue for six months or more. At least one of these months must be an active phase, marked by two or more major symptoms. In addition, work, social relations, self-care, or other functions must have deteriorated from a higher level.

Emil Kraepelin, writing in 1896, distinguished three patterns of schizophrenia: hebephrenic (what we would today term "disorganized"), catatonic, and paranoid schizophrenia. To these categories DSM-IV adds two others: undifferentiated and residual schizophrenia.

Disorganized Type The central symptoms of ***disorganized schizophrenia*** are confusion, incoherence, and flat or inappropriate affect. Formal thought disturbances and perceptual problems make for difficult communication, which leads in turn to extreme social withdrawal. Grimaces, odd mannerisms, and flat and inappropriate affect are common. Silliness is also a common feature; some patients giggle constantly without apparent reason. This is why the pattern was first called "hebephrenic," after Hebe, the Greek goddess of youth, who according to Greek mythology often acted like a clown to make the other gods laugh. Not surprisingly, people with disorganized schizophrenia are typically unable to take adequate care of themselves, to maintain social relationships, or to hold a job.

Catatonic Type The central feature of ***catatonic schizophrenia*** is a psychomotor disturbance of some sort. Some of the people in this category spend their time in a catatonic stupor, mute and unresponsive; others are seized with catatonic excitement, waving their arms and acting in an uncontrolled manner; in still other cases, the extremes of stupor and excitement alternate. Richard, the unemployed young man who became mute and statuelike, would receive a diagnosis of this type of schizophrenia.

Paranoid Type The most prominent symptom of ***paranoid schizophrenia*** is an organized system of delusions and auditory hallucinations that often guide the

BOX 15-2 A Diagnostic Dilemma

When we look at a close-up photograph of the moon, it is sometimes hard to say whether a formation on its surface is a mound or a crater. Sometimes diagnosing a mental disorder can also seem a matter more of perspective than of clear-cut differences in symptoms. Clinicians are frequently confronted with patients who display symptoms that suggest both *schizophrenia* and a *bipolar disorder.* Differentiating between these disorders is sometimes easier said than done.

People with schizophrenia often exhibit severe mood changes, and patients suffering from a bipolar disorder may have distorted perceptions and bizarre cognitive experiences. Yet if clinicians are fully to understand the nature and possible course of a client's problems and choose an appropriate treatment (at the earliest and most treatable stage), they must decide on one diagnosis. Schizophrenia will respond well to antipsychotic drugs, while a bipolar disorder will respond to lithium. There is growing evidence that clinicians frequently make mistakes when they diagnose these two disorders. Apparently many persons hospitalized for schizophrenia are actually experiencing a bipolar disorder, and vice versa (Carlson et al., 1994; Lipton & Simon, 1985).

What are clinicians to do in the face of such confusion? One solution is not to choose between schizophrenia and bipolar disorder at all when a clear choice cannot be made. DSM-IV lists *schizoaffective disorder* as a possible diagnosis when people exhibit both schizophrenic symptoms and signs of a mood disorder. This category is very controversial, however. Many clinicians argue that there is no such disorder and that the name should really be read as "I don't know."

Yet another way to distinguish schizophrenia from a bipolar disorder might be to observe how the patient responds to treatment. If lithium works, the problem is mania. If antipsychotic medication works, it is schizophrenia. Haphazard as this procedure may sound, some clinicians believe it to be the most efficient way to arrive at a correct diagnosis. They suggest that it is also a powerful means to learn to differentiate between disorders that appear not in black and white but in shades of gray. It is important to keep in mind, however, that diagnosis by treatment is always risky. Headaches caused by a brain tumor may be alleviated temporarily by aspirin, but people whose headaches respond to aspirin are not necessarily suffering from a brain tumor.

Today there is no totally satisfactory solution to the diagnostic dilemma. The problem exists because our current knowledge about these disorders is limited, and the situation will improve only as our knowledge of psychopathology grows. In the meantime, perhaps the most useful approach to the problem is for clinicians to pay close attention to the diagnostic standards of DSM-IV. Studies suggest that diagnoses of schizophrenia and bipolar disorder become at least somewhat more accurate when the established criteria are followed with meticulous care (Pulver et al., 1988).

person's life. Laura would receive this diagnosis. She believed that her neighbors, a past acquaintance, and people on the street were out to get her (delusions of persecution) and that people on television were supposedly stealing her ideas (delusions of reference). In addition, she heard noises from the apartment downstairs (auditory hallucinations) and experienced "funny sensations" that further supported her beliefs.

Undifferentiated Type When people with schizophrenia do not fall neatly into one category, the disorder is classified as ***undifferentiated type.*** Over the years, this vague diagnosis has been particularly misused by diagnosticians, and a range of schizophrenic and nonschizophrenic patterns have been incorrectly assigned to it.

Residual Type When the symptoms of schizophrenia lessen in intensity and number yet remain with the patient in a residual form, the diagnosis is usually changed to ***residual type*** of schizophrenia. As we noted earlier, people with this type of schizophrenia may continue to display blunted or inappropriate emotional reactions, social withdrawal, eccentric behavior, and some illogical thinking.

Other Categorizations of Schizophrenia Still other diagnostic distinctions have been proposed (Toomey et al., 1997; Keefe et al., 1996). Many researchers have recently found that a distinction between so-called Type I and Type II schizophrenia helps to predict the course of the disorder. ***Type I schizophrenia*** is

TABLE 15-1 Type I vs. Type II Schizophrenia

	Type I	Type II
Symptoms	Positive symptoms: Delusions Hallucinations Inappropriate affect Positive formal thought disorders	Negative symptoms: Avolition Social withdrawal Blunted and flat affect Alogia
Premorbid adjustment	Relatively good	Relatively poor
Responsiveness to traditional antipsychotic drugs	Good	Poor
Outcome of disorder	Fair	Poor
Biological features	Abnormal neurotransmitter activity	Abnormal brain structures

Source: Adapted from Crow, 1985, 1982, 1980.

dominated by positive symptoms, such as delusions, hallucinations, and positive formal thought disorders (Crow, 1995, 1985, 1982, 1980; Andreasen et al., 1985). ***Type II schizophrenia*** is characterized largely by negative symptoms, such as flat affect, poverty of speech, and loss of volition (see Table 15-1).

As we shall see shortly, Type I patients generally have a better premorbid adjustment, later onset of the disorder, greater likelihood of improvement, and better responsiveness to antipsychotic drugs than do Type II patients (Crow, 1995; Fenton & McGlashan, 1994). Moreover, the positive symptoms of Type I schizophrenia seem to be closely linked to biochemical abnormalities in the brain, while the negative symptoms of Type II schizophrenia have been tied to structural abnormalities in the brain (Crow, 1995; Andreasen et al., 1992).

Views on Schizophrenia

As with many other kinds of disorders, biological, psychological, and sociocultural theorists have proposed numerous explanations for schizophrenia. So far, the biological explanations have received by far the most research support. This is not to say that psychological and sociocultural factors play no role in the disorder. Rather, it appears that a biological predisposition to develop schizophrenia must often be accompanied by key psychological events, personal stress, or societal expectations in order for the disorder to unfold (Yank et al., 1993; Cutting, 1985).

Biological Views

What is arguably the most prolific and enlightening research on schizophrenia during the past few decades has come from the genetic and biological realms of inquiry. These studies have underscored the key roles of inheritance and brain activity in the development of this disorder and have opened the door to important changes in its treatment.

Genetic Factors Genetic researchers believe that some people inherit a biological predisposition to schizophrenia and, in accordance with a diathesis-stress model, come to develop the disorder when they are confronted by extreme stress of some kind, usually during late adolescence or early adulthood (Gottesman, 1991; Holzman & Matthysse, 1990). The genetic view has been supported by studies of (1) relatives of people with schizophrenia, (2) twins with this disorder, (3) people with schizophrenia who are adopted, and (4) chromosomal mapping.

Studies of Relatives Family pedigree studies have found repeatedly that schizophrenia is more common among relatives of people with the disorder (Kendler et al., 1994, 1993; Parnas et al., 1993; Gottesman, 1991). Moreover, the more closely related the relatives are to the person with schizophrenia, the greater their likelihood of developing the disorder (see Figure 15-2).

As we saw earlier, only 1 percent of the general population develops schizophrenia. The prevalence rises to 3 percent among second-degree relatives with this disorder—that is, half-siblings, uncles, aunts, nephews, nieces, and grandchildren (Gottesman, 1991; Gottesman

& Shields, 1982). And it reaches an average of 10 percent among first-degree relatives (parents, siblings, and children). Approximately 6 percent of the parents, 9 percent of the siblings, and 13 percent of the children of people with schizophrenia also manifest the disorder.

Of course, this trend by itself does not establish a genetic basis for the disorder. The prominent neuroscientist Solomon Snyder (1980) points out, "Attendance at Harvard University also runs in families but would hardly be considered a genetic trait." Family members are exposed to many of the same environmental influences as the person with schizophrenia, and it may be these influences that lead to the disorder.

Twins Studies Twins, who are among the closest of relatives, have received particular study by schizophrenia researchers. As we noted previously, if both members of a pair of twins have a particular trait, they are said to be *concordant* for that trait. If genetic factors are at work in schizophrenia, identical twins (who share identical genes) should have a higher concordance rate for this disorder than fraternal twins (who share only some genes). This expectation has been supported repeatedly by research (APA, 1994; Gottesman, 1991). Studies have found that if one identical twin develops schizophrenia, there is a 48 percent chance that the other twin will do so as well. If one fraternal twin has schizophrenia, in contrast, the other twin has approximately a 17 percent chance of developing the disorder.

Although the findings from twin studies are consistent with a genetic predisposition to schizophrenia, factors other than genetics may explain the heightened schizophrenia concordance rates of identical twins. For example, if one twin is exposed to a particular danger during the prenatal period, such as an injury or virus, the other twin is also very likely to be exposed to it (Davis & Phelps, 1995). This is especially true for identical twins, whose prenatal environment is shared even more closely than that of fraternal twins. In short, a predisposition to schizophrenia could be the result of a prenatal event, and twins, particularly identical twins, would still be expected to have a heightened concordance rate for the disorder.

Adoption Studies Adoption studies look at adults with schizophrenia who were adopted as infants and compare them with both their biological and their adoptive relatives. Because they were reared apart from their biological relatives, similar schizophrenic symptoms in those relatives would indicate genetic influences. Conversely, similarities to their adoptive relatives would suggest environmental influences.

Seymour Kety and his colleagues (1988, 1978, 1975, 1974, 1968) conducted an extensive adoption study in Copenhagen, Denmark, where detailed records of adoptions and mental disorders are available. In a sample of nearly 5,500 adults who had been adopted early in life, the researchers found 33 with schizophrenia. They then selected 33 matching control subjects from the same

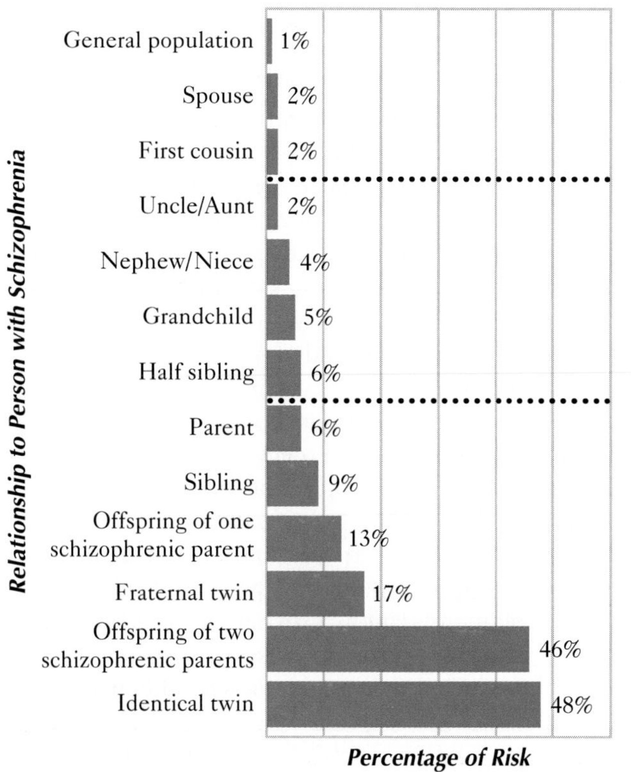

Figure 15-2 *People who are biologically related to individuals with schizophrenia have a heightened risk of developing the disorder during their lifetime. The closer the biological relationship (that is, the more similar the genetic structure), the greater the risk of developing the disorder. (Adapted from Gottesman, 1991, p. 96.)*

large sample—normal adoptees similar in age, sex, and schooling to the subjects with schizophrenia. Next the investigators located 365 biological and adoptive relatives of these 66 adoptees, including both parents and siblings, and separated the relatives into four groups: (1) biological relatives of adoptees with schizophrenia; (2) adoptive relatives of adoptees with schizophrenia; (3) biological relatives of normal adoptees; and (4) adoptive relatives of normal adoptees. The relatives were interviewed by psychiatrists and 37 were found to qualify for a clinical diagnosis of either *definite schizophrenia* or *uncertain schizophrenia* (psychotic patterns that did not fully warrant a clinical diagnosis of schizophrenia) (see Box 15-3).

Most of the 37 relatives with schizophrenic symptoms turned out to be *biological* relatives of the adoptees with schizophrenia, a result that strongly supports the hypothesis that there is a genetic factor in schizophrenia. In this sample, almost 14 percent of the biological relatives of the adoptees with the disorder were themselves classified as schizophrenic, whereas only 2.7 percent of their adoptive relatives received this classification. The biological and adoptive relatives of the normal adoptees had schizophrenia prevalence rates of 3.4 percent and 5.5 percent, respectively. Clearly the biological relatives of adoptees with schizophrenia were most likely to develop the disorder. More recent adoption studies in other countries have yielded similar findings (Wahlberg et al., 1997). Such studies have convinced many researchers that the genetic factor in schizophrenia is at least as important as that found in other illnesses with a clear genetic component, such as diabetes, hypertension, and coronary artery disease (Kendler, 1983).

BOX 15-3 An Array of Psychotic Disorders

"Schizophrenia" is often used as a synonym for "psychosis." Although schizophrenia is indeed the most common kind of psychosis, it is but one of several. Psychotic functioning—loss of contact with reality—actually comes in many sizes and shapes, and may be caused by a wide variety of factors. In addition to schizophrenia, DSM-IV distinguishes the following psychotic disorders.

Brief Psychotic Disorder

If psychotic symptoms appear suddenly and last anywhere from a day to a month (as opposed to six months in schizophrenia), a diagnosis of ***brief psychotic disorder*** may be called for. This disorder may occur either in response to a very stressful event, such as the loss of a loved one, or in the absence of a stressor. In a *postpartum* pattern of brief psychotic disorder, the symptoms emerge in women within four weeks after they have given birth.

Schizophreniform Disorder

People with ***schizophreniform disorder*** experience most of the key features of schizophrenia, but the symptoms last from one to five months. In short, this diagnosis applies if the disorder lasts longer than a brief psychotic disorder but is less persistent than schizophrenia. Emotional turmoil, fear, confusion, and very vivid hallucinations often characterize this psychotic pattern.

Schizoaffective Disorder

Sometimes people display prominent symptoms of both schizophrenia and a mood disorder. In such cases, they may receive a diagnosis of ***schizoaffective disorder.*** To receive this diagnosis, however, the individual must, during the course of the disorder, also have at least one episode of psychotic symptoms only.

Schizoaffective disorder appears to be equally common among men and women. The disorder is thought to be less common than schizophrenia, although the precise prevalence rate is unknown (APA, 1994). Some clinicians dislike this category, believing it to be a wastebasket category that is generally used when diagnosticians have a hard time determining whether a client's mood problems are resulting from schizophrenia or vice versa.

Delusional Disorder

People who have at least one month of persistent delusions that are not bizarre and not part of a larger schizophrenic pattern may receive a diagnosis of ***delusional disorder.*** Aside from their delusions, they do not act in a particularly odd way and rarely experience prominent hallucinations. *Persecutory, jealous, grandiose,* and *somatic* delusions are common in people who have this disorder (Manschreck, 1996).

It has been estimated that around 0.03 percent of the population experiences a delusional disorder. It is equally common in men and women, although the

Chromosomal Mapping As with bipolar disorders (see Chapter 8), researchers have conducted chromosomal mapping research to identify more precisely the possible genetic factors in schizophrenia (Bassett, 1992; Eaves et al., 1988). In this strategy, they select large families in which schizophrenia is unusually common, take blood and DNA samples from all members of the families, and then compare the gene segments taken from members with and without schizophrenia. Applying this procedure to families from Iceland and England, Hugh Gurling and his colleagues (1989) found that a particular area on chromosome 5 of schizophrenia sufferers had a different appearance from the same area on chromosome 5 of other family members. The researchers concluded that an abnormal gene or cluster of genes in this area of chromosome 5 establishes a predisposition to develop schizophrenia.

Although chromosomal research is promising, major problems remain to be solved (Holzman & Matthysse, 1990). For example, the area of chromosome 5 implicated in this study is very large, containing more than 1,000 genes. Researchers have yet to isolate the gene or cluster of genes that may contribute to schizophrenia. In addition, studies of large families in Sweden and Italy have failed to find a consistent discrepancy on chromosome 5 (Kendler & Diehl, 1993; Macciardi et al., 1992; Kennedy et al., 1988). And still other studies have recently identified possible gene defects on chromosomes 6, 9, 10, 11, 18, and 19, each of which may predispose individuals to develop schizophrenia (Leutwyler, 1996; Wang et al., 1995; Bassett, 1992; Garofalo et al., 1992).

These varied findings may indicate that some of the suspected gene sites do not contribute to schizophrenia

jealous type is apparently more common in men. The disorder generally begins in the middle or late adult years, but can appear earlier (APA, 1994).

Shared Psychotic Disorder

A person who embraces the delusions held by another individual may qualify for a diagnosis of ***shared psychotic disorder.*** Such individuals usually have a close relationship with a dominant person, such as a parent or sibling, whose psychotic thinking they come to share. When the disorder is found in a two-person relationship, as it usually is, it is also known as ***folie à deux.*** If the relationship with the inducer is broken, the second person's delusional beliefs usually subside or disappear. Sometimes the disorder occurs in a whole family or group.

In one or two of every 1,000 births, a mother suffers postpartum psychosis, *marked by hallucinations, severe depression, and, in some cases, impulses to kill herself or her child or both. This disorder appears to be either a* brief psychotic disorder *or* a major depressive episode with psychotic features. *It is different from the much more common* postpartum depression without psychotic features.

Substance-Induced Psychotic Disorder

If prominent hallucinations or delusions are caused by the direct physiological effects of a substance, the person is said to be suffering from a ***substance-induced psychotic disorder.*** The substance may be an abused drug such as alcohol, a hallucinogen, or cocaine, and the disorder may occur in association with either intoxication or withdrawal from the substance, depending on the substance. The symptoms may also be caused by a medication or a toxin such as nerve gas, carbon monoxide, carbon dioxide, fuel, or paint.

Psychotic symptoms may also be caused by a medical illness or brain damage. The individual may then receive a diagnosis of ***psychotic disorder due to a general medical condition.*** A variety of medical problems may cause such symptoms, including Huntington's disease, epilepsy, endocrine diseases, and metabolic diseases.

after all. Alternatively, different kinds of schizophrenia may be traced to different genes. The British subjects may, for example, have had a kind of schizophrenia caused by a chromosome 5 defect, while the symptoms in the Swedish or Italian families may have been caused by gene defects on one of the other implicated chromosomes. Finally, like a number of other physical and psychological disorders, schizophrenia may be a *polygenic disorder,* caused by a combination of gene defects located at various chromosome sites (Fowles, 1992; Gottesman, 1991).

How might genetic factors lead to the development of schizophrenia? Research has pointed to two kinds of biological abnormalities that apparently contribute to schizophrenia and could conceivably be inherited—biochemical abnormalities and abnormal brain structure.

Biochemical Abnormalities In Chapter 4, where we first discussed the role of neurons, neurotransmitters, and synapses, we saw that the brain consists largely of neurons. When an impulse (or "message") travels from neuron to neuron, it is received by a neuron's dendrites (antennae) and travels down the neuron's axon until it reaches the nerve ending. The nerve ending then releases a chemical neurotransmitter from its storage vessels, and these neurotransmitter molecules cross the synaptic space and attach to receptors on the dendrites of another neuron, thus relaying the message and causing that neuron to fire.

Over the past two decades, research has led to a ***dopamine hypothesis*** to explain schizophrenia: the neurons that use the neurotransmitter *dopamine* fire too often and transmit too many messages, thus producing the symptoms of the disorder. This hypothesis has faced challenges and undergone changes in recent years, but it is still the foundation for present biochemical insights into schizophrenia.

Like the biological explanations of anxiety, depression, and mania, the dopamine hypothesis of schizophrenia was arrived at by a mixture of serendipity, painstaking experimental work, and clever theorizing. The chain of events began with the accidental discovery of ***antipsychotic medications,*** drugs that help remove the symptoms of schizophrenia. As we shall see in Chapter 16, the first group of antipsychotic medications, the ***phenothiazines,*** were discovered in the 1950s by researchers who were looking for effective antihistamine drugs to combat allergies. Although phenothiazines failed as antihistamines, their effectiveness in reducing schizophrenic symptoms soon became apparent, and clinicians began to prescribe them widely.

Researchers soon learned that these drugs also produce troublesome muscular tremors, identical to those seen in *Parkinson's disease,* a disabling neurological disease that typically emerges after the age of 50. When patients with schizophrenia were given an antipsychotic drug, most seemed to develop Parkinsonian symptoms.

This unfortunate reaction to antipsychotic drugs gave researchers their first important clue to the biology of schizophrenia. Medical scientists already knew that people with Parkinson's disease have abnormally low levels of the neurotransmitter dopamine in some areas of the brain, as a result of the destruction of dopamine-containing neurons; and the insufficiency of dopamine is the reason for their uncontrollable shaking. In fact, the chemical ***L-dopa,*** a precursor of dopamine, is used to treat Parkinson's disease precisely because it raises dopamine levels.

If antipsychotic drugs generate Parkinsonian symptoms while alleviating schizophrenia, scientists reasoned, perhaps the drugs reduce dopamine activity. And if lowering dopamine activity alleviates the symptoms of schizophrenia, perhaps schizophrenia is related to excessive dopamine activity in the first place.

Establishing the Dopamine-Schizophrenia Link Since the 1960s, research has both supported and clarified the dopamine hypothesis. It has been found that some people with Parkinson's disease develop schizophrenic symptoms if they take too much L-dopa (Carey et al., 1995; Davis, Comaty, & Janicak, 1988). Presumably the L-dopa raises their dopamine activity to schizophrenia-inducing levels. Correspondingly, when patients with schizophrenia are given L-dopa, their symptoms sometimes worsen considerably (Angrist, Sathananthan, & Gershon, 1973). Presumably their high dopamine activity becomes even higher.

Support for the dopamine hypothesis has also come from research on *amphetamines,* drugs that, as we saw in Chapter 13, stimulate the central nervous system (Davis et al., 1988). Researchers first noticed during the 1970s that people who take high doses of amphetamines for a long time may develop ***amphetamine psychosis***—a syndrome that closely mimics schizophrenia and includes hallucinations and motor hyperactivity. They later found that antipsychotic drugs can correct amphetamine psychosis, just as they are able to alleviate the symptoms of schizophrenia, and that even small doses of amphetamines exacerbate the symptoms of schizophrenia (Janowsky & Davis, 1976; Janowsky et al., 1973). Researchers eventually found that amphetamines increase dopamine synaptic activity in the brain (Nestler et al., 1995; Snyder, 1976), thus inducing or exacerbating schizophrenic symptoms.

Researchers have also pinpointed sites in the brain that have high concentrations of dopamine receptors, and have found that antipsychotic drugs bind to many of them (Burt et al., 1977; Creese et al., 1977; Snyder et al.,

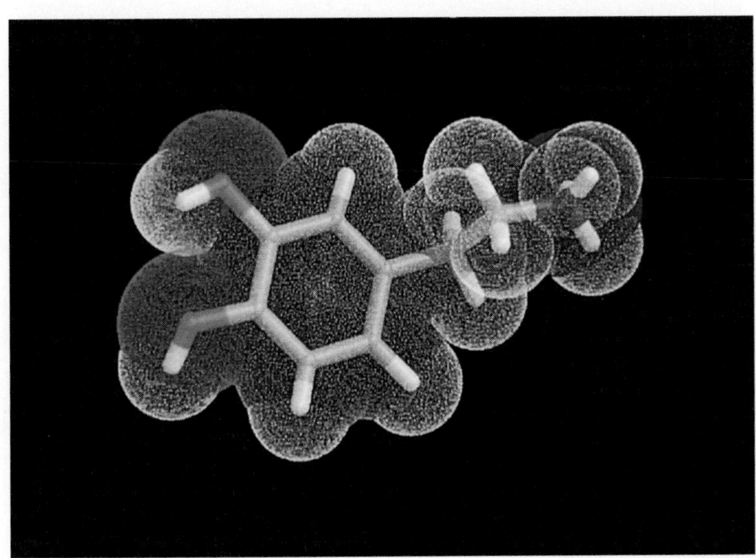

A computer-drawn molecule of dopamine. Excessive activity of this neurotransmitter has been linked to schizophrenia and to amphetamine and cocaine psychosis, while low dopamine activity has been related to Parkinson's disease.

1976). On the basis of this finding, they have concluded that phenothiazines and other antipsychotic drugs are ***dopamine antagonists***—drugs that bind to dopamine receptors, prevent dopamine from binding there, and so prevent dopamine-receiving neurons from firing (Iversen, 1975; Kebabian et al., 1972). Researchers have been able to distinguish five kinds of dopamine receptors in the brain—called the D-1, D-2, D-3, D-4, and D-5 receptors—and have found that phenothiazines bind most strongly to the D-2 receptors (Strange, 1992).

Overactive Dopamine Synapses All these findings suggest that certain dopamine synapses in people with schizophrenia are overactive. In other words, messages from dopamine-sending neurons to dopamine receptors on other neurons, particularly to the D-2 receptors, are transmitted too readily or too often (see Figure 15-3). This theory has an intuitive appeal because some dopamine-receiving neurons have been found to play an active role in guiding and sustaining attention (Cohen et al., 1988). People whose attention mechanisms are grossly impaired by biochemical irregularities might well be expected to suffer from the abnormalities of attention, perception, and thought that characterize schizophrenia.

Why might the dopamine synapses of people with schizophrenia be overactive? Researchers used to think that their neurons simply produce and store too much dopamine, but studies have failed to support this notion (Seidman, 1990; Carlsson, 1978; Van Praag, 1977). Instead, the cause of the synaptic overactivity may be an oversupply of D-2 receptors (Sedvall, 1990; Seidman, 1990; Owen et al., 1987). Remember that when dopamine carries a message to a receiving neuron, it binds to receptors on the membrane of the neuron. Inasmuch as more receptors will lead to more firing, an excessive number of D-2 receptors would ensure greater synaptic activity and overtransmission of dopamine messages in people with schizophrenia. Autopsies have in fact found an unusually large number of dopamine receptors in people with schizophrenia (Owen et al., 1987, 1978; Lee & Seeman, 1980).

Questioning the Dopamine Hypothesis Though compelling, the dopamine hypothesis is not without its problems. The biggest challenge has come with the discovery of a new group of antipsychotic drugs, referred to as ***atypical antipsychotics*** because their mechanism of action differs from that of the traditional drugs (Meltzer, 1992, 1987). As we shall see in Chapter 16, ***clozapine*** and ***resperidone,*** the most commonly prescribed atypical antipsychotic drugs, are often more effective than the traditional antipsychotic drugs.

One difference between the traditional and atypical antipsychotic drugs lies in their ability to bind to and block various dopamine receptors. The traditional drugs bind to most of the D-2 receptors in the brain, but to few or none of the D-1 receptors (Farde et al., 1992; Farde & Nordstrom, 1992). The atypical drugs do bind to many D-1 receptors (Meltzer, 1995; Gerlach & Hansen, 1992). This finding suggests to some researchers that D-2 receptors may be less important in schizophrenia and D-1 receptors more so than the dopamine hypothesis holds.

Even more challenging for the dopamine hypothesis is the finding that the atypical antipsychotic drugs also bind to many receptors for the neurotransmitter *serotonin* (Meltzer, 1995, 1992; Owen et al., 1993). This finding has led some researchers to suspect that schizophrenia may be related to *intersecting* activity of the serotonin and dopamine pathways in the brain, rather than to dopamine activity alone (Kapur & Remington, 1996;

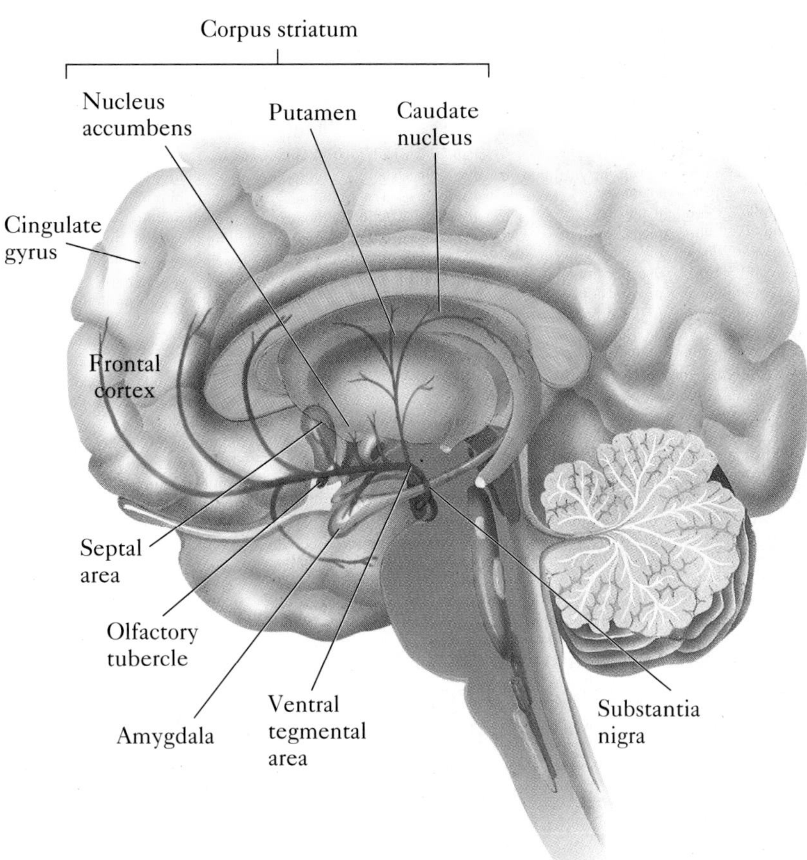

Figure 15-3 *Dopamine pathways. Some of the neurons that release the neurotransmitter dopamine have cell bodies in the substantia nigra with axons extending all the way to the corpus striatum, the part of the brain that functions to produce smooth coordination of movements in the arms and legs. When these neurons release too little dopamine, the muscular tremors and other symptoms of Parkinson's disease occur. Another group of neurons that release dopamine have cell bodies in the ventral tegmental area with axons extending to the olfactory tubercle, nucleus accumbens, amygdala, and cingulate gyrus—areas that apparently function to link sensory perceptions to memories and emotions. It may be that when dopamine released from these neurons is excessively active, the symptoms of schizophrenia result. (Adapted from Snyder, 1986, p. 85.)*

Sumiyoshi et al., 1996; Breier, 1995). Similarly, there is some evidence that dopamine interacts in important ways with still other neurotransmitters, such as glutamate and GABA (Busatto et al., 1997; Hirsch et al., 1997; Delini-Stula & Berdah-Tordjman, 1995).

Finally, in yet another challenge to the dopamine hypothesis, some theorists claim that excessive dopamine activity contributes only to Type I schizophrenia (Crow, 1995, 1989, 1985, 1980). As we saw earlier, cases of Type I schizophrenia are characterized by positive symptoms such as delusions and hallucinations, whereas Type II cases are marked by negative symptoms such as flat affect and loss of volition. It turns out that Type I cases are particularly responsive to the traditional antipsychotic drugs, which bind so strongly to D-2 receptors, whereas Type II cases are more responsive to the atypical antipsychotic drugs, which bind less strongly to D-2 receptors. Some researchers therefore suspect that the dopamine hypothesis is relevant only to Type I schizophrenia (Ragin et al., 1989; Crow, 1980). In fact, recent studies seem to be suggesting that Type II schizophrenia is related primarily to a very different kind of abnormality—abnormal brain structure.

Abnormal Brain Structure Ever since Kraepelin, clinicians have suspected that schizophrenia is caused by abnormalities in brain structure. Only during the past decade, however, have researchers been able to link this disorder, particularly Type II schizophrenia, to specific structural abnormalities (Strange, 1992; Buchsbaum & Haier, 1987). Improvements in postmortem tissue analyses and the development of the scanning technologies have opened the door to these new insights (Black & Andreasen, 1994).

Using the new technologies, researchers have found that many people with schizophrenia have ***enlarged ventricles***—the brain cavities that contain cerebrospinal fluid (Corey-Bloom et al., 1995; APA, 1994; Cannon & Marco, 1994; Hyde et al., 1991). The ventricles on the left side of their brains seem much larger than the ventricles on the right (Losonczy et al., 1986). Since these enlargements appear at the onset of schizophrenia, before treatment, they are not produced by antipsychotic drugs (Cannon & Marco, 1994; DeLisi et al., 1992; Weinberger et al., 1982).

Patients with enlarged ventricles tend to display more negative symptoms of schizophrenia, fewer positive symptoms, a poorer premorbid social adjustment, greater cognitive disturbances, and poorer responses to traditional antipsychotic drugs (Bornstein et al., 1992; Klausner et al., 1992). At the same time, enlarged ventricles are also found in cases of mood disorder and of alcoholism, so researchers cannot be certain about their precise relationship to schizophrenia (Pearlson et al., 1984).

Perhaps enlarged ventricles are only a sign that nearby parts of the brain have atrophied. These other parts may not have developed adequately or may have been damaged, and these problems may be the ones that help produce schizophrenia. Consistent with this notion, some studies suggest that patients with this disorder have smaller frontal lobes than other people (Gur & Pearlson, 1993; Suddath et al., 1990), smaller amounts of cortical gray matter (Barta et al., 1997; Lim et al., 1996; Sullivan et al., 1996), and, perhaps most important, a reduced blood flow in their brains (Zemishlany et al., 1996; Sagawa et al., 1990; Buchsbaum & Haier, 1987). Two investigations measured the rate at which blood was flowing to the frontal lobes of subjects with and subjects without schizophrenia while they were performing a card-sorting task (Berman et al., 1992; Weinberger, 1983). The rate of blood flow dropped sharply in many subjects with schizophrenia, whereas blood flow actually increased in most of the control subjects.

Viral Problems What might cause the structural abnormalities that accompany many cases of schizophrenia? Various studies have tied the abnormalities to genetic factors, poor nutrition, fetal development, birth complications, immune reactions, and toxins (Brown et al., 1996; Özcan et al., 1996; Susser et al., 1996).

One recent theory suggests that the brain abnormalities may result from exposure to viruses before birth. Proponents of this theory suggest that the viruses enter the fetus's brain and remain latent until puberty or young adulthood. At that time they are reactivated by hormonal changes or another viral infection, and cause schizophrenic symptoms (Torrey et al., 1993; Torrey, 1991).

Circumstantial evidence for the viral theory comes from the large number of persons with schizophrenia born during the winter (Takei et al., 1995; Tam & Sewell, 1995; Torrey, 1992). One study found that approximately 8 percent more persons with this disorder are born during the winter months than would be expected on the basis of birth rates (DeLisi, Crow, & Hirsch, 1986). The larger number of people with schizophrenia born during winter could be due to an increase in fetal or infant exposure to viruses at that time of year (Sponheim et al., 1997; Torrey, 1991; Barr et al., 1990) (see Figure 15-4).

The viral theory of schizophrenia has also received circumstantial support from investigations of fingerprints. Normally, identical twins have almost identical numbers of fingerprint ridges. Persons with schizophrenia, however, often have significantly more or fewer ridges than their nonschizophrenic identical twins (Van Os et al., 1997; Bracha et al., 1995, 1992; Torrey et al., 1994). Fingerprints form in the fetus during the second trimester of pregnancy, just when the fetus is most vulnerable to certain viruses (Torrey et al., 1994; Purvis-Smith et al., 1972, 1969). The fingerprint irregularities of some people with schizophrenia may in fact reflect a viral infection contracted during the prenatal period, an infection that also predisposed the individuals to schizophrenia.

More direct evidence for the viral theory of schizophrenia has come from closer examinations of viral reactions during and after pregnancy. Several studies have found that mothers of persons with schizophrenia were more often exposed to the influenza virus during pregnancy (particularly during the second trimester) than mothers of other persons (Torrey et al., 1994). Similarly, an investigation in the Netherlands has found a higher rate of schizophrenia among persons born during influenza epidemics than among those born during influenza-free periods (Takei, Os, & Murray, 1995). And finally, studies have found antibodies to *pestiviruses,* a particular group of viruses usually found in animals, in the blood of 40 percent of subjects with schizophrenia (Torrey et al., 1994; Yolken et al., 1993). The presence of

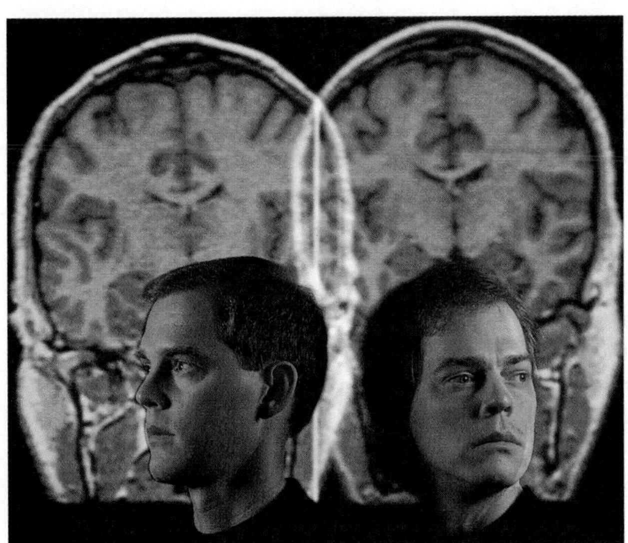

Not-so-identical twins. The man on the left is normal, while his identical twin, on the right, has schizophrenia. Magnetic resonance imaging (MRI), shown in the background, reveals that the brain of the twin with schizophrenia is smaller overall than his brother's and has larger ventricles, indicated by the dark butterfly-shaped spaces. These same differences in brain structure have been observed in many pairs of identical twins when one twin has schizophrenia and the other does not.

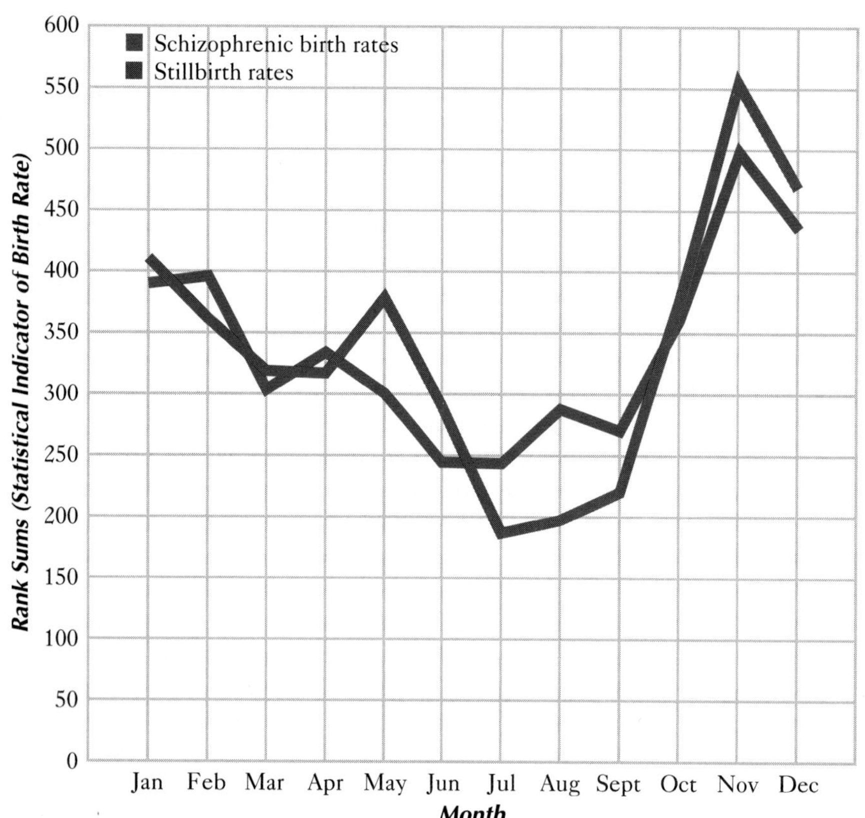

Figure 15-4 *The birth pattern of people who develop schizophrenia is very closely linked to that of stillbirths, yielding a correlation of 0.8. The incidence of stillbirths and the incidence of births of persons who later develop schizophrenia are highest during November and December and lowest during the summer. One interpretation of this finding is that fetuses are more exposed to certain infectious agents during the winter months, producing death in some cases and a viral infection that eventually causes schizophrenia in other cases. (Adapted from Torrey et al., 1993.)*

such antibodies suggests that the subjects have in fact been exposed to pestiviruses. The identical twins of these subjects do not have schizophrenia and do not have these antibodies in their blood.

Obviously, the biological underpinnings of schizophrenia are more complex and more subtle than anyone had imagined. Together the biochemical, brain structure, and viral findings are beginning to shed much light on the mysteries of this disorder. At the same time, it is important to recognize that many people who manifest these biological abnormalities never develop schizophrenia. Why not? Possibly, as we noted earlier, because biological factors merely set the stage for schizophrenia, while key psychological and sociocultural factors must be present for the disorder to unfold (Wahlberg et al., 1997).

Psychological Views

When investigators began to identify genetic and biological factors in schizophrenia during the 1950s and 1960s, many clinicians abandoned psychogenic explanations of the disorder. During the past decade, however, the tables have been turned once again and psychological factors are increasingly being considered important pieces of the puzzle of schizophrenia. This turnaround has occurred partly because biology alone has proved unable to account for schizophrenia and partly because research has increasingly provided some support for psychological theories. The leading psychological explanations of schizophrenia have come from the psychodynamic, behavioral, and cognitive perspectives.

The Psychodynamic View Freud (1924, 1915, 1914) believed that the development of schizophrenia involves a two-part psychological process: (1) *regression* to a pre-ego stage and (2) efforts to *restore* ego control. He explained that schizophrenia begins much like anxiety and depressive disorders: it stems from conflict between self-gratifying impulses and the demands of the real world. When the world is consistently harsh or withholding—for example, when parents are cold or unnurturing—people may regress to an early period in their functioning. Those who develop schizophrenia have egos that are less stable than those of people who develop anxiety and depressive disorders. They regress to the earliest point in their development, to the pre-ego state of *primary narcissism,* in which only their own needs are felt. Their near-total regression leads to self-indulgent symptoms such as neologisms, loose associations, and delusions of grandeur. Once people regress to such an infantile state, Freud further believed, they try to reestablish ego control and contact with reality. Their efforts give rise to yet other schizophrenic symptoms. Auditory hallucinations, for example, may represent an unconscious attempt to substitute for a lost sense of reality.

Years later, the noted psychodynamic clinician Frieda Fromm-Reichmann (1948) elaborated on Freud's proposition that cold or unnurturing parents may set in motion the dynamics of schizophrenia. She described the mothers of people who develop schizophrenia as cold, domineering, and impervious to their children's needs. According to Fromm-Reichmann, these mothers appear to be self-sacrificing but are actually using their children to address their own needs. At once overprotective and rejecting, they confuse their children and set the stage for schizophrenic functioning. She called them ***schizophrenogenic*** (schizophrenia-causing) ***mothers.***

Fromm-Reichmann did enormous amounts of work with sufferers of schizophrenia, but her theory, like Freud's, has received little research support. The majority of people with schizophrenia do *not* appear to have mothers who fit the schizophrenogenic description. In fact, some studies have suggested that quite a different personality style may prevail among their mothers. In one study the mothers of subjects with this disorder were found to be shy, inadequate, withdrawn, anxious, suspicious, or incoherent, while the mothers of normal control subjects seemed more likely to display what Fromm-Reichmann would have called a schizophrenogenic maternal style (Waring & Ricks, 1965).

The renowned ballet artist Vaslav Nijinsky, performing here in Schéhérazade, *developed severe schizophrenia and spent the last years of his life in a mental institution.*

The views of Freud and Fromm-Reichmann have not been retained by most of today's psychodynamic theorists. Although the contemporary theorists still use some of the early notions (Spielrein, 1995; Blatt & Wild, 1976), more and more of them are including biological factors in their explanations (Mosak & Goldman, 1995). Self theorists, for example, suggest that biological deficiences make it impossible for persons with schizophrenia to develop an integrated self. Their symptoms represent the expressions and coping efforts of a struggling fragmented self (Pollack, 1989; Kohut & Wolf, 1978).

The Behavioral View Behaviorists point primarily to *operant conditioning* to explain schizophrenia (Liberman, 1982; Ullmann & Krasner, 1975). They propose that most people learn in life to attend to social cues—for example, to other people's smiles, frowns, and comments. When they respond to these stimuli in a socially acceptable way, they are better able to satisfy their emotional needs and to achieve their goals. Some people, however, do not receive proper social cues or reinforcements, either because of unusual circumstances or because important figures in their lives are socially inadequate. As a result, they stop attending to social cues and focus instead on irrelevant cues—the brightness of light in a room, a bird flying above, or the sound of a word rather than its meaning. As they attend more and more to such cues, their responses become increasingly bizarre. Their responses in turn elicit heightened attention or other types of reinforcement, thus increasing the likelihood that they will be repeated.

Support for the behavioral position has been circumstantial. As we shall see in Chapter 16, researchers have found that patients with schizophrenia are often capable of learning more appropriate verbal and social behaviors if hospital personnel consistently ignore their bizarre responses and reinforce normal responses with cigarettes, food, attention, or other rewards (Belcher, 1988; Braginsky, Braginsky, & Ring, 1969; Ayllon & Michael, 1959). If bizarre verbal and social responses can be successfully altered by reinforcements, perhaps they were acquired through operant conditioning in the first place. Of course, as we already know, an effective treatment does not necessarily indicate the cause of a disorder.

Today the behavioral view is usually treated as only a partial explanation for schizophrenia. Although it may help explain why a given person displays more schizophrenic behavior in some situations than in others, it is too limited, in the opinion of many theorists, to account for schizophrenia's origins and its many symptoms.

The Cognitive View A leading cognitive explanation of schizophrenia agrees that biological problems cause strange sensory experiences for people with schizophrenia. According to this explanation, however, further features of the disorder emerge when the individuals attempt to understand their unusual experiences. When first confronted by voices, visions, or other sensations, these people turn to friends and relatives. But the friends are likely to deny the existence of the new sensory experiences. Eventually the sufferers come to believe that others are trying to hide the truth. They reject all feedback and may develop beliefs (delusions) that they are being persecuted (Garety, 1991; Maher, 1974). In short, people with schizophrenia take a "rational path to madness" (Zimbardo, 1976).

As we discussed earlier, researchers have documented that people with schizophrenia do indeed experience special sensory and perceptual problems. Many persons with the disorder have hallucinations, and most have trouble keeping their attention focused on anything (APA, 1994; Elkins & Cromwell, 1994). But researchers have yet to provide clear, direct support for the cognitive notion that misinterpretations of such sensory problems actually generate the schizophrenic syndrome.

Sociocultural Views

Sociocultural theorists contend that persons with mental disorders are victims of social forces. In the case of schizophrenia, these factors include *social labeling* and *family dysfunctioning*. As we shall see, the sociocultural explanations of schizophrenia have been influential, but research has not consistently supported their specific claims. Societal and family forces are today considered factors of probable importance in this disorder, but their specific roles have yet to be identified.

Social Labeling Many sociocultural theorists believe that the features of schizophrenia are influenced by the diagnosis itself (Modrow, 1992; Szasz, 1987, 1963). They propose that society assigns the label "schizophrenic" to people who deviate from certain behavioral norms. Once the label is assigned, justified or not, it becomes a self-fulfilling prophecy that promotes the development of many schizophrenic symptoms. Certainly sufferers of schizophrenia have attested to the power that labeling has had on their lives:

> Like any worthwhile endeavor, becoming a schizophrenic requires a long period of rigorous training. My training for this unique calling began in earnest when I was six years old. At that time my somewhat befuddled mother took me to the University of Washington to be examined by psychiatrists in order to find out what was wrong with me. These psychiatrists told my mother: "We don't know exactly what is wrong with your son, but whatever it is, it is very serious. We recommend that you have him committed immediately or else he will be completely psychotic within less than a year." My mother did not have me committed since she realized that such a course of action would be extremely damaging to me. But after that ominous prophecy my parents began to view and treat me as if I were either insane or at least in the process of becoming that way. Once, when my mother caught me playing with some vile muck I had mixed up—I was seven at the time—she gravely told me, "They have people put away in mental institutions for doing things like that." Fear was written all over my mother's face as she told me this. . . . The slightest odd behavior on my part was enough to send my parents into paroxysms of apprehension. My parents' apprehensions in turn made me fear that I was going insane. . . . My fate had been sealed not by my genes, but by the attitudes, beliefs, and expectations of my parents. . . . I find it extremely difficult to condemn my parents for behaving as if I were going insane when the psychiatric authorities told them that this was an absolute certainty.
>
> *(Modrow, 1992, pp. 1–2)*

Like this man, people who are called schizophrenic are viewed and reacted to as "crazy." Others typically expect and encourage them to display schizophrenic behaviors. They may come to accept their assigned role and learn to play it convincingly.

We have already seen the very real dangers of diagnostic labeling. The famous Rosenhan (1973) study, which we first encountered in Chapter 4, is a particularly influential demonstration of these dangers. Recall that eight normal people presented themselves at various mental hospitals, complaining that they had been hearing voices utter the words "empty," "hollow," and "thud." They were readily diagnosed as schizophrenic, and all eight were hospitalized. Although the pseudopatients then dropped all symptoms and proceeded to behave normally, they had great difficulty getting rid of the label.

The pseudopatients reported that staff members spent limited time interacting with patients, usually responded curtly to questions, and were frequently authoritarian. They treated patients as though they were invisible. Rosenhan reports, "A nurse unbuttoned her uniform to adjust her brassiere in the presence of an entire ward of viewing men. One did not have the sense that she was being seductive. Rather, she didn't notice us." The pseudopatients described feeling powerless, depersonalized, and bored, and often behaved in a listless and apathetic manner. The deceptive design and broad interpretations of this study have aroused the emotions of clinicians and researchers, pro and con. The investigation does demonstrate, however, that the label "schizophrenic" can have a negative effect on people—not just on how they are perceived, but on how they themselves feel and behave.

Family Dysfunctioning Theorists have suggested for years that certain patterns of family interactions help lead to—or at least maintain—schizophrenic symptoms. Family theories have pointed in particular to *double-bind communications* and particular *family alignments.*

Double-Bind Communications One of the best-known family theories is the ***double-bind hypothesis*** (Bateson, 1978; Bateson et al., 1956), which holds that some parents repeatedly communicate pairs of messages that are mutually contradictory. They place the children in double-bind situations: the children cannot avoid displeasing their parents, because nothing they do is right. In theory, the child's response to such double binds ultimately lead to schizophrenic symptoms.

Double-bind messages typically contain a contradiction between a verbal communication (the *primary* communication) and an accompanying nonverbal communication (the *metacommunication*). If one person says to another, "I'm glad to see you," yet frowns and avoids eye contact, the two aspects of the message are incongruent.

According to this theory, a child who is repeatedly exposed to double-bind communications will adopt a *special life strategy* for coping with them. One such strategy is always to ignore primary communications and respond only to metacommunications: be suspicious of what anyone is saying, wonder about its true meaning, and look for clues only in gestures or tones. People who increasingly respond to messages in this way may be on their way to manifesting symptoms of paranoid schizophrenia.

The double-bind hypothesis is closely related to the psychodynamic notion of a schizophrenogenic mother. When Fromm-Reichmann described schizophrenogenic mothers as overprotective and rejecting at the same time, she was in fact describing someone who is likely to offer double-bind communications. Like the schizophrenogenic mother theory, the double-bind hypothesis has been popular in the clinical field since its inception, but systematic investigations into it have been surprisingly few, and they have, in fact, been unsupportive (Chaika, 1990). In one study, clinicians read and evaluated letters written by parents to their children in the hospital (Ringuette & Kennedy, 1966). One group of parents had children with schizophrenia; the other had children without this disorder. Rating each letter, the clinicians found the letters of both groups of parents to offer similar degrees of double-bind communication.

Family Structure Theodore Lidz (1973, 1963) has proposed that still other disturbed patterns of family interaction and communication may push children toward schizophrenia. According to Lidz, either of two kinds of family alignment can lead to the disorder: *marital schism* or *marital skew.*

In families with a ***marital schism*** structure, the mother and father are in open conflict, with each spouse trying to undercut the other and compete for the loyalty of the child (usually a daughter). In families with ***marital skew,*** hostility is less overt, as the mother dominates family life and the father seemingly yields to her every wish. Here again, however, the parents implicitly compete for the affection and loyalty of the child (usually a son).

According to Lidz, the children become caught in the middle in either of these family structures. Any attempt to please one parent will be viewed as a rejection by the other. In defense, the children may adopt a posture of massive confusion that allows them to avoid acknowledging or resolving the conflict. In other words, they may retreat into schizophrenia.

Although Lidz's theory has attracted widespread interest, it is actually based on very small, possibly unrepresentative samples. He examined only forty families, all from the upper socioeconomic classes (Lidz, 1973, 1963; Lidz et al., 1965, 1957). Without wider sampling and appropriate control groups, it is impossible to know how common these family patterns are in cases of schizophrenia.

The Status of Family Theories Although the family explanations of schizophrenia have failed to receive compelling research support, studies do suggest that this disorder, like other mental disorders, is often linked to stressful family situations (Miklowitz et al., 1995; Velligan et al., 1995; Falloon & Liberman, 1983). Generally, parents of people with schizophrenia (1) display more conflict, (2) have greater difficulty communicating with one another, and (3) are more critical of and overinvolved with their children than other parents.

Certainly, family experiences of this kind may contribute to the onset of schizophrenia (Mavreas et al.,

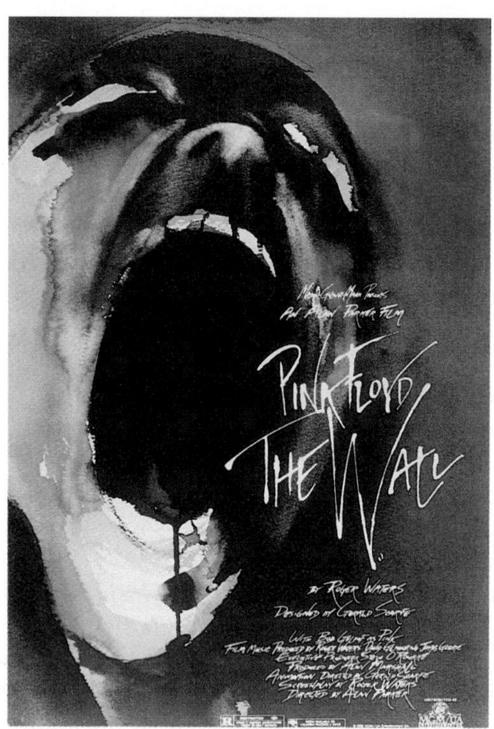

"Is there anybody out there?" R. D. Laing's theory that schizophrenia is an extended inward search undertaken by some persons in order to cure themselves of confusion and unhappiness caused by their family and society has been romanticized throughout the arts. It is the central theme of Pink Floyd's hugely popular album and movie The Wall.

1992; Vaughan et al., 1992; Goldstein, 1985). They may also help to maintain the disorder and contribute to relapses among recovering individuals. Family theorists have long recognized that some families are high in *expressed emotion*—that is, they frequently express criticism, disapproval, and hostility and are highly intrusive. It turns out that individuals who are trying to recover from schizophrenia are almost four times more likely to relapse if they live with such a family than if they live with one low in expressed emotion (Linszen et al., 1997; Parker & Hadzi-Pavlovic, 1990; Brown et al., 1962).

Does all this mean that family dysfunctioning helps cause and maintain schizophrenia? Not necessarily. It is also the case that individuals with schizophrenia disrupt family life. In so doing, they themselves may help cause the family problems that clinicians and researchers continue to observe (Woo, Goldstein, & Neuchterlein, 1997; Rosenfarb et al., 1995; Asarnow & Horton, 1990).

The Sociocultural-Existential View The final explanation of schizophrenia that we shall examine is also the most controversial. The clinical theorist R. D. Laing (1967, 1964, 1959) combined sociocultural principles with the existential philosophy that was his hallmark, and argued that schizophrenia is actually a constructive process in which people try to cure themselves of the confusion and unhappiness caused by their social and family environment. Laing believed that, left alone to complete this process, people with schizophrenia would indeed achieve a healthy level of integration.

According to Laing's existential principles, in order to give meaning to their lives, all human beings must be in touch with their true selves. Unfortunately, said Laing, it is difficult to achieve this inner discovery and lead a meaningful existence in present-day society. Typically, other people's expectations, demands, and standards require us to develop a *false self* rather than a true one.

Laing asserted that the people who develop schizophrenia have even greater obstacles to deal with. After a lifetime of paradoxical communications and demands from their families and community, they undertake out of desperation an inner search for a sense of strength and purpose. They withdraw from others as they try to recover their wholeness as human beings, and they attend increasingly to their own inner cues. Laing argued that these people would emerge stronger and less confused if they were simply allowed to continue this inner search. Instead, society and its clinicians tell them that they are sick. Yielding to society's expectations, the individuals assume the role of patient, submitting to efforts at treatment that actually serve to produce further schizophrenic symptoms. In attempting to cure these people, society dooms them to suspension in an inner world.

It is easy to understand why Laing's theory is so controversial. Most theorists reject his notion that schizophrenia is constructive. They see it as a problem that brings extensive suffering and no benefit. Many individuals with schizophrenia themselves reject the theory.

> "Schizophrenia's a reasonable reaction to an unreasonable society." It's great on paper. Poetic, noble, etc. But if you happen to be a schizophrenic, it's got some not-so-cheery implications. . . . One of R.D.'s worst sins is how blithely and misleadingly he glides over the suffering involved. . . . Pulling off a revolution and ushering in a new era in which truth and beauty reign triumphant seems unlikely when you're having trouble brushing your teeth or even walking.
>
> *(Vonnegut, 1974, p. 91)*

For the most part research has not resolved the controversy over Laing's explanation (Howells & Guirguis, 1985). His ideas do not lend themselves to empirical research (Hirsch & Leff, 1975), and the existentialists who embrace his view typically have little confidence in traditional research approaches.

Crossroads

Schizophrenia, one of our species' most bizarre and frightening disorders, has been studied intensively throughout the twentieth century. Only since the discovery of antipsychotic drugs, however, have clinicians gained significant insight into its causes. Although theories abounded before that time, they typically lacked empirical support. They also contributed to inaccurate stereotyping of people with schizophrenia and their parents, and they resulted in ineffective forms of treatment.

In the past three decades, investigators have at last begun to learn much about the nature and course of schizophrenia. As a result, the prevailing view of schizophrenia as a single disorder with numerous faces may be changing. Research increasingly suggests that the different types of schizophrenia may actually represent different disorders. And each may have a distinct course; distinct biological, genetic, and perhaps psychological and sociocultural origins; and a distinct response to treatment.

As with most other psychological disorders, clinical theorists now agree that schizophrenia, in whatever form, is probably caused by a combination of factors. Most hold a *diathesis-stress* perspective of the disorder. They believe that genetic and biological factors establish a predisposition to develop the disorder, but psychological and sociocultural factors then help bring it to fruition. A biological predisposition may lead to schizophrenia only among individuals who face personal traumas, inappropriate patterns of reinforcement, or family or social stress. Once schizophrenia emerges, the forces of social labeling or family dysfunction may help to exacerbate or maintain its symptoms.

Despite the growing acceptance of this diathesis-stress explanation of schizophrenia, researchers have been far more successful in identifying the biological culprits than the psychological and sociocultural factors. While biological investigations have homed in on specific genes, abnormalities in brain biochemistry and structure, and even viral infections, psychological and sociocultural research has been able to cite only general contributors, such as family conflict and the influence of diagnostic labeling. Clearly, researchers must identify psychological and sociocultural factors with greater precision if we are to gain a full understanding of schizophrenia. The exciting, at times spectacular progress now being made in the study of schizophrenia is indeed impressive. It must not blind us, however, to the significant gaps, uncertainties, and confusions that continue to obscure our view.

Chapter Review

1. ***The clinical picture of schizophrenia*** Schizophrenia is a disorder in which previously adaptive personal, social, and occupational functioning deteriorates into disturbed thought processes, distorted perceptions, deviant emotional states, and motor abnormalities. Approximately 1 percent of the world's population suffers from this disorder.

2. ***Symptoms of schizophrenia*** The symptoms associated with schizophrenia fall into three groupings: *positive symptoms, negative symptoms,* and *psychomotor symptoms.*

   A. The leading positive symptoms are *delusions, disorganized thinking and speech, hallucinations* and other disturbances in perception and attention, and *inappropriate affect.*

   B. Negative symptoms include *poverty of speech, blunted* and *flat affect, loss of volition,* and *social withdrawal.*

   C. The disturbances in psychomotor behavior are collectively called *catatonia.*

3. ***The course of schizophrenia*** Schizophrenia usually emerges during late adolescence or early adulthood and tends to progress through three phases: *prodromal, active,* and *residual.*

4. ***Diagnosing schizophrenia*** Patients may be placed in five categories of schizophrenia, according to DSM-IV criteria: *disorganized type, catatonic type, paranoid type, undifferentiated type,* and *residual type.* In addition, clinicians have distinguished between *Type I schizophrenia,* characterized by the predominance of positive symptoms, and *Type II schizophrenia,* whose symptoms are largely negative.

5. ***Views on schizophrenia*** Biological, psychological, and sociocultural factors seem to interact to cause schizophrenia.

   A. *Biological views* The biological explanations point to genetic, biochemical, structural, and viral factors.

   (1) ***Genetic factors*** The genetic view is supported by studies of relatives, twins, adoptees, and chromosomal mapping.

   (2) ***Biochemical abnormalities*** The predominant biochemical explanation focuses on an unusually high level of activity in neurons that use the neuro-

transmitter *dopamine.* The brains of people with schizophrenia may contain an unusually large number of dopamine receptors, particularly *D-2* receptors.

(3) ***Abnormal brain structure*** Modern brain-imaging techniques have detected *abnormal brain structures* in people with schizophrenia, including enlarged ventricles and unusual variations in blood flow in certain parts of the brain.

(4) ***Viral problems*** Research suggests that schizophrenia may be related to a *virus* contracted by the fetus, which lies dormant until puberty or young adulthood.

B. ***Psychological views*** Several psychological explanations have been proposed for schizophrenia, including psychodynamic, behavioral, and cognitive explanations.

(1) ***The psychodynamic view*** Freud believed that schizophrenia involves *regression* to a pre-ego state of *primary narcissism* and efforts to *restore* ego control. Fromm-Reichmann proposed that *schizophrenogenic mothers*—cold, domineering, and impervious to their children's needs—help produce this disorder. Neither theory has received much research support. Contemporary psychodynamic theorists point to a combination of biological and psychodynamic factors.

(2) ***The behavioral view*** Behaviorists theorize that people with schizophrenia fail to attend to relevant social cues and as a result develop bizarre responses to the environment.

(3) ***The cognitive view*** Cognitive theorists contend that when people with schizophrenia try to explain biologically induced hallucinations or other strange sensations, they develop delusional thinking.

C. ***Sociocultural views*** One sociocultural explanation holds that society expects persons who are *labeled* as having schizophrenia to behave in certain ways, and these expectations promote the further development of symptoms. Other sociocultural views point to *family dysfunctioning* as a cause of schizophrenia. They hold that the family environment contains confusing elements, such as *double-bind communications, marital schism,* and *marital skew.* Finally, R. D. Laing's theory states that schizophrenia is actually a constructive process by which people try to cure themselves of the confusion and unhappiness caused by their societal and family environment.

D. ***The diathesis-stress explanation*** Most clinical theorists now agree that schizophrenia can probably be traced to a combination of biological, psychological, and sociocultural factors. However, the biological factors have been more precisely identified.

Thought and Afterthought

Relationships of the Mind

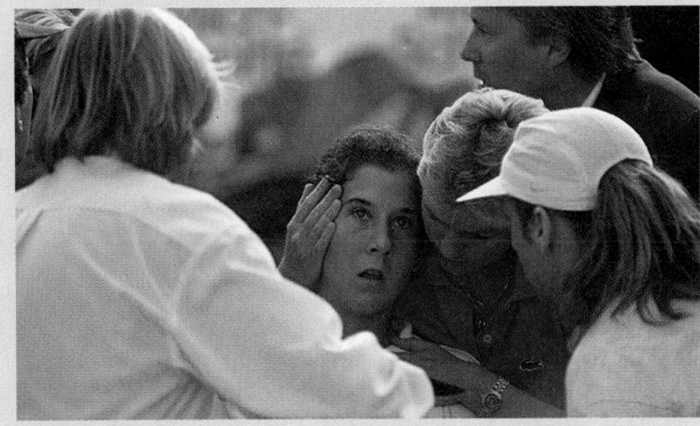

While playing in a professional tennis tournament in 1993, Monica Seles (right) was stabbed by a 38-year-old man from Germany. The attacker was obsessed with another tennis star, Steffi Graf, and believed that it was his responsibility to help Graf's career by striking down her rival. Seles did not return to professional tennis for two years.

In 1989 the actress Rebecca Shaeffer of the television show *My Sister Sam* was shot and killed outside her West Hollywood apartment by a fan. He had closely followed Shaeffer's career for months, and eventually he journeyed to her apartment building. When she failed to greet him warmly, he took her rebuff as a sign of arrogance and shot her.

At least 200,000 people are victims of stalkers in the United States each year (Corwin, 1993). Some stalkers manifest *erotomanic delusions*—they believe without any basis whatsoever that they are loved by someone who may actually be a casual acquaintance or a complete stranger (Anderson, 1993). Some persons with such delusions, like Shaeffer's and Graf's pursuers, develop fantasies in which they feel compelled to protect, harm, or even kill the object of their desire (Menzies et al., 1995).

Afterthoughts: Some experts believe that erotomanic delusions are more common today than they were in the past. Why might this be the case? . . . Do high-profile cases like these heighten or lower the probability that other cases of erotomanic delusions and stalking will emerge?

Looking into the Brain of Jeffrey Dahmer

In 1992 Jeffrey Dahmer was found guilty of killing at least 15 young men. In response to various delusions and possibly hallucinations, Dahmer drugged his victims and performed crude lobotomies on them. Apparently he was trying to create zombie-like companions for himself. He also dismembered his victims' bodies and stored parts to be eaten. In 1995, while serving his term in prison, Dahmer was beaten to death by another inmate.

Upon his death, Dahmer's body was cremated, except for his brain, which was stored in formaldehyde in a laboratory at the University of Wisconsin while a judge decided what to do with it. Dahmer's mother wanted it to be made available for scientists to study. His father, however, opposed such research, saying that his son had wanted all of his remains cremated.

Afterthoughts: Many important insights about the human brain have come from autopsies. Do scientists have a right to override personal wishes and conduct post-mortem studies on the remains of people who have behaved in grossly antisocial ways? . . . Most people with schizophrenia pose no threat to others. How might cases such as Dahmer's affect the way people with this and related disorders are perceived and treated?

Frankly Speaking

Insanity in individuals is something rare—but in groups, parties, nations, and epochs, it is the rule.

—Friedrich Wilhelm Nietzsche

Afterthoughts: What behaviors committed by groups or nations might be considered psychotic if an individual performed them? . . . What factors might cause groups or nations to act irrationally?

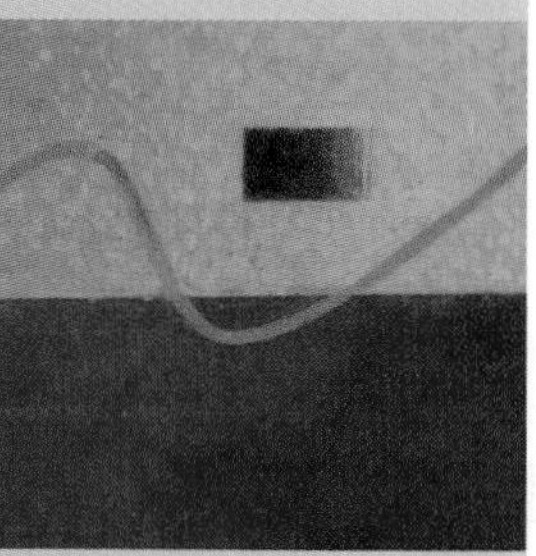

Topic Overview

Chapter 16

Treatments for Schizophrenia

How can a patient and a therapist communicate when they speak virtually different languages? For years, efforts at treating schizophrenia brought only frustration. Lara Jefferson, a young woman with this disorder, wrote of her treatment experience in the 1940s:

> They call us insane—and in reality they are as inconsistent as we are, as flighty and changeable. This one in particular. One day he derides and ridicules me unmercifully; the next he talks to me sadly and this morning his eyes misted over with tears as he told me of the fate ahead. Damn him and all of his wisdom!
>
> He has dinned into my ears a monotonous dirge—"Too Egotistical—too Egotistical—too Egotistical. Learn to think differently."—And how can I do it? How—how—can I do it? How the hell can I do it? I have tried to follow his suggestions but have not learned to think a bit differently. It was all wasted effort. Where has it got me?
>
> *(Jefferson, 1948)*

Jean Beraud's The Asylum, *1885, depicts an outdoor scene at a nineteenth-century public mental hospital. The stately and well-manicured grounds of such hospitals contradicted the chaotic thoughts and feelings of patients, as well as the overcrowded, unstimulating, and deplorable conditions that often existed within this hospital's walls.*

For much of human history, patients with schizophrenia were considered beyond help. The disorder is still extremely difficult to treat, but clinicians are much more successful today than they were in the past (Lindström, 1996). Much of the credit goes to antipsychotic drugs, medications that help many people with schizophrenia think rationally enough to engage in therapeutic programs that previously had a limited effect at best (Lieberman et al., 1996).

Most people with schizophrenia now live outside of institutions, and many of them profit from outpatient treatment and community programs.

As we shall see, each of the models offers treatments for schizophrenia, and all have been influential at one time or another. However, a mere delineation of the various approaches cannot convey the truly remarkable events and issues that have surrounded treatment for schizophrenia over the years. The approaches that have been developed offer enormous promise to people debilitated by the disorder, yet those people have been subjected to more mistreatment and indifference than perhaps any other group. Even today the majority of them do not receive adequate care, largely for reasons of economics and political priorities (Torrey, 1997). In an effort to convey their plight accurately, this chapter will depart from the usual format and discuss the various treatments as they have unfolded over the years. At the same time, we will be careful to identify the models that are linked to the various treatments. Ultimately, a look at how treatment has progressed over the years will help us understand the nature and implications of today's approaches to this debilitating disorder.

Past Institutional Care

For more than half of the twentieth century, society's response to schizophrenia was ***institutionalization,*** usually in a public facility. Because patients with this disorder failed to respond to traditional therapies, the principal goals of these establishments were restraint and custodial care (provision of food, shelter, and clothing). Patients rarely saw therapists and were largely neglected. Many were abused. Oddly enough, this tragic state of affairs unfolded in an atmosphere of good intentions.

The move toward institutionalization began in 1793, when the French physician Philippe Pinel "unchained the insane" from virtual imprisonment at La Bicêtre asylum and began the practice of "moral treatment" (as we saw in Chapter 1). For the first time in centuries, patients with severe disturbances were viewed as human beings who should be cared for with sympathy and kindness. As Pinel's ideas spread throughout Europe and the United States, they led to the creation of large mental hospitals rather than asylums to care for people with severe mental disorders (Goshen, 1967).

These new mental hospitals, typically located in isolated areas where land and labor were cheap, were to be havens from the stresses of daily life and offer a healthful psychological environment in which patients could work closely with therapists (Grob, 1966). It was believed that such institutional care should be available to both the poor and the rich, so states throughout the United States were required by law to establish public mental institutions, ***state hospitals,*** to supplement the private ones.

Eventually, however, the state hospital system developed serious problems. Wards became increasingly overcrowded, admissions kept rising, and state funding was unable to keep up with the increasing need for professional therapists. Too many aspects of treatment became

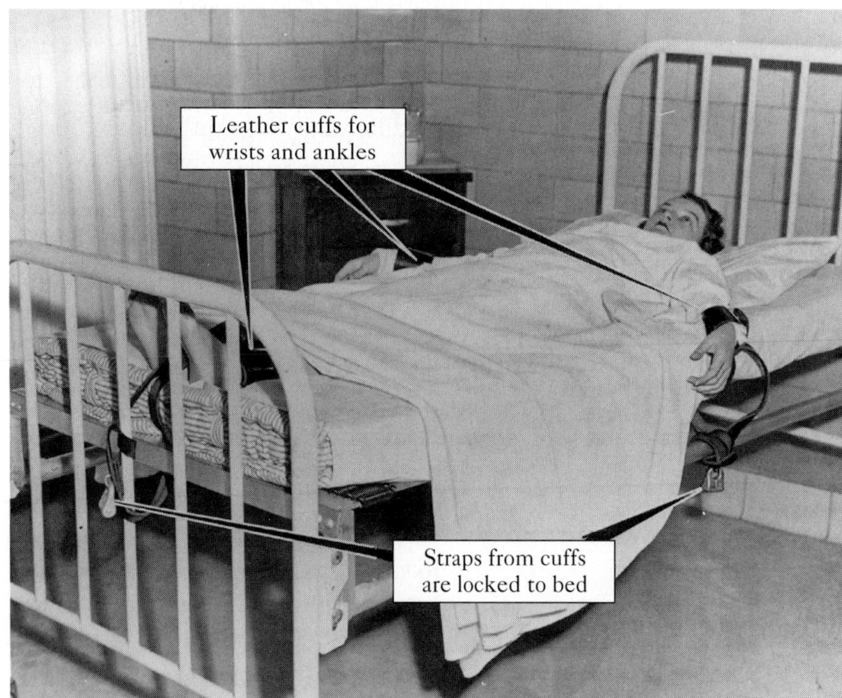

As state hospitals across the United States became overcrowded, they relied increasingly on mechanical restraints as a method of controlling patients. At Byberry State Hospital in Philadelphia, for example, violent patients were often tied to their beds, a procedure that was employed as late as the 1950s.

the responsibility of nurses and attendants, whose knowledge and experience at that time were limited. Between 1845 and 1955 the number of state hospitals and mental patients rose steadily while the quality of care declined. During this period close to 300 state hospitals were established in the United States. The number of hospitalized patients on any given day rose from 2,000 in 1845 to nearly 600,000 in 1955.

The priorities of the public mental hospitals changed during those 110 years. In the face of overcrowding and understaffing, the emphasis shifted from humanitarian care to order-keeping and efficiency. In a throwback to the asylum period, disruptive patients were physically restrained, isolated, and punished; individual attention diminished. Patients were transferred to chronic wards, or "back wards," if they failed to improve quickly (Bloom, 1984).

These back wards were in fact human warehouses shrouded in an aura of hopelessness. Staff members often relied on straitjackets and handcuffs to deal with difficult patients. More "advanced" forms of intervention included the medically debilitating approach of *lobotomy* (see Box 16-1). Most of the patients on these wards suffered from schizophrenia (Hafner & an der Heiden, 1988).

Many patients not only failed to improve under these conditions but developed additional symptoms, apparently as a result of institutionalization itself. The most common pattern of deterioration was the ***social breakdown syndrome:*** extreme withdrawal, anger, physical aggressiveness, and loss of interest in personal appearance and functioning (Gruenberg, 1980). Often more troublesome than the original symptoms of their disorders, this new syndrome made it impossible for patients to return to society even if they somehow recovered from the difficulties that had first brought them to the hospital.

Improved Institutional Care

In the 1950s, clinicians developed two institutional interventions that finally offered some help to patients who had been languishing in institutions for years (Bloom, 1984): *milieu therapy,* based primarily on humanistic principles, and the *token economy program,* based on behavioral principles. These approaches were particularly helpful in addressing the personal-care and self-image problems exacerbated by institutionalization. They were soon adopted by many institutions and are now standard features of institutional care.

Milieu Therapy

Humanistic theorists propose that institutionalized patients deteriorate mainly because they are deprived of opportunities to develop self-respect, independence, and responsibility and to engage in meaningful activity, all experiences basic to healthy human functioning. Thus the premise of ***milieu therapy*** is that the social milieu of institutions must change if patients are to make clinical progress, and that an institutional climate conducive to self-respect, individual responsibility, and meaningful activity must be established.

The pioneer of this approach was Maxwell Jones, a London psychiatrist who in 1953 converted a psychiatric ward of patients with various disorders into a ***therapeutic community.*** Patients were referred to as "residents" of the community, and they were treated as quite capable of running their own lives and making their own decisions. They participated in community government, working with staff members to establish rules and determine sanctions. In fact, patient-staff distinctions were almost eliminated in Jones's therapeutic community. Everyone was valued as an important therapeutic agent. The atmosphere was one of mutual respect, interdependence, support, and openness. Patients could also take on special projects, semipermanent jobs, occupational therapy, and recreational activities. In short, their daily schedule resembled life outside the hospital.

Milieu-style programs have since been developed in institutions throughout the Western world. The programs have varied from setting to setting, but at a minimum staff members try to facilitate interactions (especially group interactions) between patients and staff, keep patients active, and establish higher expectations of what patients should be able to accomplish.

Because milieu approaches vary so greatly among institutions and have been applied to patients with such a variety of disorders, researchers have had difficulty assessing their effectiveness. It does appear that patients with schizophrenia in some milieu hospital programs have improved and left the hospital at higher rates than patients in custodial programs (Paul & Lentz, 1977; Cumming & Cumming, 1962). Many of these patients remain impaired, however, and must live in sheltered settings after their release.

Despite these limitations, milieu therapy continues to be practiced in many institutions, often as a helpful adjunct to other hospital approaches (Dobson et al., 1995; Ciompi et al., 1992). It has also had an impact on community treatment programs. As we shall see, programs established at halfway houses to ease individuals with schizophrenia back into community residential life often incorporate resident self-government, work schedules, and other features of milieu therapy.

BOX 16-1 Lobotomy: How Could It Happen?

In 1949 a *New York Times* article reported on a medical procedure that appeared to offer hope to an enormous number of sufferers of severe mental disorders, people for whom it seemed no future was possible outside of very overcrowded state mental institutions:

> Hypochondriacs no longer thought they were going to die, would-be suicides found life acceptable, sufferers from persecution complex forgot the machinations of imaginary conspirators. Prefrontal lobotomy, as the operation is called, was made possible by the localization of fears, hates, and instincts [in the prefrontal cortex of the brain]. It is fitting, then, that the Nobel Prize in medicine should be shared by Hess and Moniz. Surgeons now think no more of operations on the brain than they do of removing an appendix.

We now know that the lobotomy was hardly a miracle treatment. Far from "curing" people with mental disorders, the procedure left thousands upon thousands withdrawn, excessively subdued, and even stuporous. Yet, in the twenty-five years after the introduction of the lobotomy by the Portuguese neuropsychiatrist Egas Moniz in 1935, clinicians around the world considered this approach to be an effective way to treat people suffering from schizophrenia and other severe mental disorders.

Moniz's particular lobotomy procedure, called a ***prefrontal leukotomy,*** consisted of drilling two holes in either side of the skull and inserting an instrument resembling an icepick into the brain tissue to cut or destroy nerve fibers. Moniz's theory was based on his belief that serious mental disorders were caused by "fixed thoughts" that interfered with mental functioning. The abnormal thought patterns could be altered, he believed, if the appropriate nerve pathways in the brain were cut.

In examining the factors that contributed to the widespread acceptance of the lobotomy in the 1940s and 1950s, the neuroscientist Elliot Valenstein (1986) considers one of the most important factors to have been the extreme overcrowding in mental hospitals at the time. This crowding was making it difficult to maintain decent standards in the hospitals. The problem was exacerbated by the multitude of returning World War II veterans who required treatment for emotional problems.

Valenstein also points to the personalities of the inventors and advocates of psychosurgery as important factors. Although he does not deny the fact that Moniz and his American counterpart, Walter Freeman, were gifted and dedicated physicians, Valenstein also calls attention to their desire for professional status. Just three months after seeing how the destruction of the prefrontal brain lobes in monkeys and chimpanzees had sedated them, Moniz performed the first prefrontal leukotomy on a human being.

Today it is hard to believe that respected physicians and scientists around the world would condone, much less applaud, this kind of impulsive experimentation on human beings. Moniz's prestige

The Token Economy

In the 1950s behaviorists had little status in mental institutions and were permitted to work only with patients whose problems seemed virtually hopeless. Among the "hopeless" were many patients with schizophrenia. Through years of experimentation, behaviorists discovered that the systematic application of *operant conditioning* techniques could help alter the dysfunctional patterns of these patients (Ayllon, 1963; Ayllon & Michael, 1959). Programs that apply such techniques are called ***token economy programs.***

In token economy programs patients are rewarded whenever they behave acceptably according to established criteria and are not rewarded when they behave unacceptably. The immediate rewards for acceptable behavior are often tokens that can later be exchanged for food, cigarettes, hospital privileges, and other desirable items; they thus create a "token economy." Among the acceptable behaviors that are typically targeted are caring for oneself (making one's bed, dressing oneself, and the like), working in a vocational program, speaking normally, abiding by ward rules, and exercising self-control.

To keep widening a patient's repertoire of appropriate behaviors, clinicians must periodically introduce new target behaviors and reinforcements. Some hospitals actually set up several token economy programs, called *leveled* programs, each representing a different level of difficulty. When patients learn to perform the target behaviors of one program consistently, they are transferred to another program that requires more demanding behaviors.

and capacity for diplomacy were so great, however, and the field of neurology was so small, that his work received relatively little criticism. Furthermore, for many people, this "cure" seemed to offer an economic and social relief that was just too desirable to resist (Swayze, 1995).

In the 1940s Walter Freeman and his surgical partner, James Watts, developed a second kind of psychosurgery called the ***transorbital lobotomy,*** in which the surgeon inserted a needle into the brain through the eye socket and rotated it in order to destroy the brain tissue.

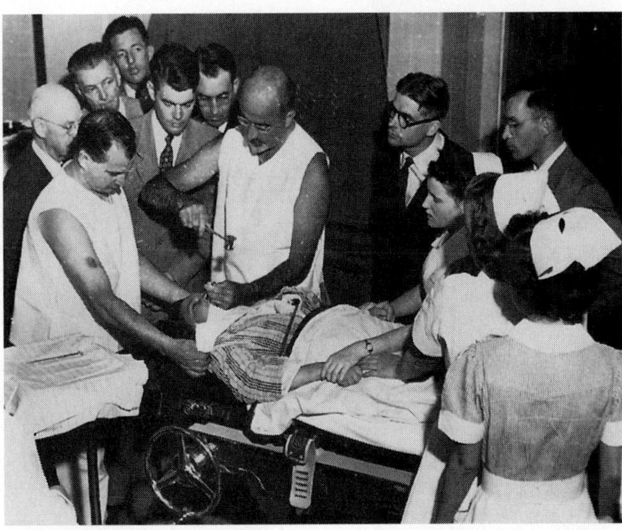

Neuropsychiatrist Walter Freeman performs a lobotomy in 1949 by inserting a needle through a patient's eye socket into the brain.

Physicians may have been misled by the initial outcome studies of lobotomy, which were methodologically flawed and offered no placebo comparison groups (Swayze, 1995; Valenstein, 1986). Apparently they were also captivated by glowing written reports of postoperative patient responses to lobotomy. By the 1950s, however, studies revealed that in addition to having a fatality rate of 1.5 to 6 percent, lobotomy resulted in objectionable physical consequences such as brain seizures, huge weight gain, loss of motor coordination, partial paralysis, incontinence, endocrine problems, and extreme intellectual and emotional unresponsiveness.

In the 1950s concern also developed that psychosurgery might be used to control the perpetrators of violent crimes, and lobotomy became a civil rights issue as well. Furthermore, with the discovery of antipsychotic drugs, the lobotomy began to look like an expensive, complicated, and inhumane way of treating mental disorders. By 1960 the number of lobotomies being performed had been drastically reduced.

Today psychosurgery of any kind is rare. It is, in fact, considered experimental, and it is used only as a last resort in the most severe cases of obsessive-compulsive disorder and depression (Goodman et al., 1992; Greist, 1992). Psychosurgical procedures have also been greatly refined, and hardly resemble the blind and brutal lobotomies that were performed forty and fifty years ago. Yet despite such improvements, many professionals believe that any kind of surgery aimed specifically at destroying brain tissue is unethical. They argue that even a limited use of psychosurgery keeps alive one of the clinical field's most shameful and ill-advised efforts at cure.

The Effectiveness of Token Economy Programs

Research suggests that token economies do help change schizophrenic and related behaviors (Emmelkamp, 1994; Belcher, 1988). In one of the most successful such programs, Gordon Paul and R. L. Lentz (1977) applied operant conditioning principles to twenty-eight patients with chronic schizophrenia. Their dysfunctional behaviors included mutism, repeated screaming, incontinence, smearing feces on walls, and physical assault.

Most patients in this program improved significantly. By the end of the program, four and a half years later, 98 percent of the subjects had been released, usually to sheltered care facilities. At a follow-up eighteen months later, only two patients had been rehospitalized. By comparison, 71 percent of patients treated in a milieu program and 45 percent of patients who received custodial care had been released by the end of four and a half years. It is no wonder that many hospitals use token economies (Emmelkamp, 1994).

Problems Facing Token Economies Some clinicians have raised questions about the effectiveness of token economy programs (Kazdin, 1983). One problem is that many token economy studies, unlike Paul and Lentz's, are uncontrolled. When administrators set up a token economy, they usually include all ward patients in the program rather than dividing the patients into a token economy group and a control group. As a result, patients' improvements can be compared only with their own past behaviors, and that comparison may be confounded by variables other than the operation of the token economy program. A new physical setting, for

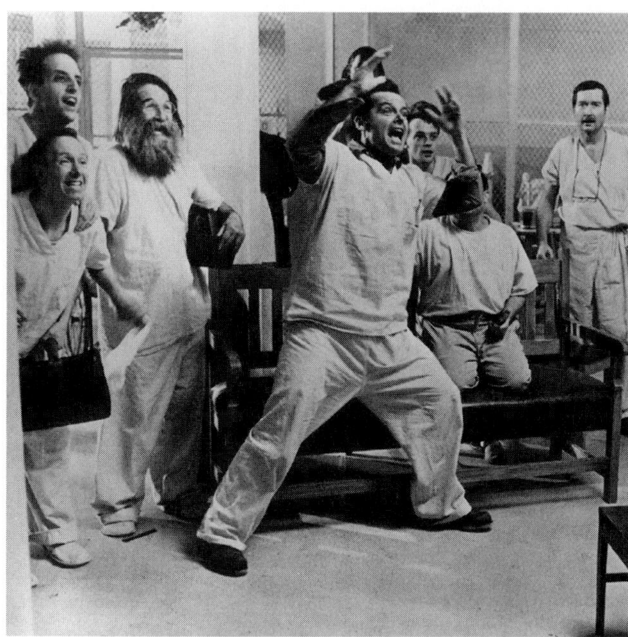

Francisco de Goya's early nineteenth-century painting The Madhouse, *depicting a typical mental hospital of his day, is strikingly similar to the portrayal in Ken Kesey's 1950s novel (later a play and film),* One Flew Over the Cuckoo's Nest. *Institutions of both the distant and the recent past were overcrowded, often negligent, and concerned primarily with keeping order.*

example, or a general increase in staff attention could also cause improvement.

Many clinicians also have raised ethical and legal concerns. If token economy programs are to be effective, administrators need to control the important reinforcements in a patient's life, perhaps including such basic rewards as food and a comfortable bed. But aren't there some things in life to which all human beings are entitled? Court decisions have now affirmed that patients have certain basic rights that clinicians cannot violate, irrespective of the positive goals of a treatment program. They have a right to free access to food, storage space, and furniture, as well as freedom of movement (Emmelkamp, 1994). Appropriate though such boundaries are, they have set limits on the scope and impact of many token economy programs.

Still other clinicians have questioned the quality of the improvement achieved under token economy programs. Are behaviorists altering a patient's psychotic thoughts and perceptions or simply improving the patient's ability to mimic normal behavior? This question is raised by the case of a middle-aged man named John, who had the delusion that he was the United States government. Whenever he spoke, he spoke as the government. "We are happy to see you. . . . We need people like you in our service. . . . We are carrying out our activities in John's body." When John's hospital ward was converted into a token economy, the staff members targeted his delusional statements, requiring him to identify himself properly to earn tokens. If he called himself John, he received tokens; if he maintained that he was the government, he received nothing.

After a few months on the token economy program, John stopped presenting himself as the government. When asked his name, he would say, "John." Although staff members were understandably pleased by his improvement, John himself had a different view of the situation. In a private discussion he said:

> We're tired of it. Every damn time we want a cigarette, we have to go through their bullshit. "What's your name? . . . Who wants the cigarette? . . . Where is the government?" Today, we were desperate for a smoke and went to Simpson, the damn nurse, and she made us do her bidding. "Tell me your name if you want a cigarette. What's your name?" Of course, we said, "John." We needed the cigarettes. If we told her the truth, no cigarettes. But we don't have time for this nonsense. We've got business to do, international business, laws to change, people to recruit. And these people keep playing their games.
>
> *(Comer, 1973)*

Critics of the behavioral approach would argue that John was still delusional and therefore as schizophrenic as before. Behaviorists, however, would argue that at the very least, John's judgment about the consequences of his behavior had improved. Learning to keep his delusion to himself might even be a step toward changing his private thinking.

Finally, it has often been difficult for patients to make a satisfactory transition from token economy hospital programs to community living. In an environment where rewards are contingent on proper behaviors, proper behaviors become contingent on continued rewards. Some patients who find that the real world doesn't reward them so concretely abandon their newly acquired behaviors.

Nonetheless, token economy programs have had a most important effect on the treatment of people with schizophrenia. They were among the first hospital treatments that actually helped change schizophrenic symptoms, got chronic patients moving again, and enabled some to be released from the hospital. Although no longer as popular as they once were (Glynn, 1990), token economies are still employed in many mental hospitals, usually along with medication, and in some community residences as well. The token economy approach has also been applied to other clinical problems, including mental retardation, delinquency, and hyperactivity, as well as in other fields, such as education and business.

Antipsychotic Drugs

Milieu therapy and token economy programs helped to improve the gloomy prognosis for schizophrenia, but it was the discovery of antipsychotic drugs in the 1950s that truly revolutionized its treatment. These drugs eliminate many symptoms of this disorder and today are almost always a part of treatment. What is more, as we noted in Chapter 15, they have also influenced the way clinicians view schizophrenia.

The discovery of antipsychotic medications dates back to the 1940s, when researchers developed the first ***antihistamine drugs*** to combat allergies. Although these drugs also produced considerable tiredness and drowsiness, they quickly became popular, and many antihistamines were developed. The French surgeon Henri Laborit soon discovered that one group of antihistamines, ***phenothiazines,*** were useful adjuncts to surgical anesthesia. They helped to calm patients before surgery while allowing them to remain awake. Laborit and others experimented with several phenothiazine antihistamines and became most impressed with one called ***chlorpromazine.*** Laborit reported, "It provokes not any loss of consciousness, not any change in the patient's mentality but a slight tendency to sleep and above all 'disinterest' for all that goes on around him."

Laborit suspected that chlorpromazine might also have a calming effect on persons with severe psychological disorders. The psychiatrists Jean Delay and Pierre Deniker (1952) soon tested the drug on six patients with psychotic symptoms and reported a sharp reduction in their symptoms. In 1954, after a series of laboratory and clinical tests, chlorpromazine went on the market in the United States as an antipsychotic medication under the trade name Thorazine.

Since the discovery of the phenothiazines, other kinds of antipsychotic drugs have been developed (see Table 16-1). Collectively they are known as ***neuroleptic drugs,*** because they often produce effects similar to the symptoms of neurological diseases. Some of the drugs, like chlorpromazine, are from the phenothiazine group, including *thioridazine* (Mellaril), *mesoridazine* (Serentil), *fluphenazine* (Prolixin), and *trifluoperazine* (Stelazine). Others, such as *haloperidol* (Haldol)

TABLE 16-1 Antipsychotic Drugs

Class/Generic Name	*Trade Name*	*Usual Daily Oral Dose (mg)*
Chlorpromazine	Thorazine	200–600
Risperidone	Risperdal	2–8
Triflupromazine	Vesprin	50–150
Thioridazine	Mellaril	200–600
Mesoridazine besylate	Serentil	150
Piperacetazine	Quide	20–40
Trifluoperazine	Stelazine	2–4
Fluphenazine hydrochloride	Prolixin Permitil	2.5–10
Perphenazine	Trilafon	16–64
Acetophenazine maleate	Tindal	60
Chlorprothixene	Taractan	75–200
Thiothixene	Navane	6–30
Haloperidol	Haldol	2–12
Loxapine	Loxitane	20
Molindone hydrochloride	Moban Lidone	15–60
Pimozide	Orap	2–10
Clozapine	Clozaril	300–900

Source: Hedaya, 1996, p. 249; Silver & Yudofsky, 1988, pp. 771–773.

and *thiothixene* (Navane), belong to different chemical classes.

As we saw in Chapter 15, these drugs apparently reduce the symptoms of schizophrenia at least in part by blocking excessive activity of the neurotransmitter dopamine, particularly at the brain's dopamine D-2 receptors (Holcomb et al., 1996; Kusumi et al., 1995; Strange, 1992). Remember that some studies suggest that persons with schizophrenia, particularly those with Type I schizophrenia, have an excessive number of receptors on their dopamine-receiving neurons, which may lead to extra dopamine activity at those sites and so to the symptoms of schizophrenia. After a patient takes antipsychotic drugs for a time, the dopamine-receiving neurons apparently grow additional dopamine receptors (Strange, 1992; Burt et al., 1977; Seeman et al., 1976). It is as if the neurons recognize that dopamine transmission is being blocked by the drugs at the usual receptors and compensate by developing new ones. Now the patient has two groups of dopamine receptors—the excessive number of original ones, which are blocked, and a normal number of new ones, which produce normal synaptic activity rather than schizophrenic symptoms.

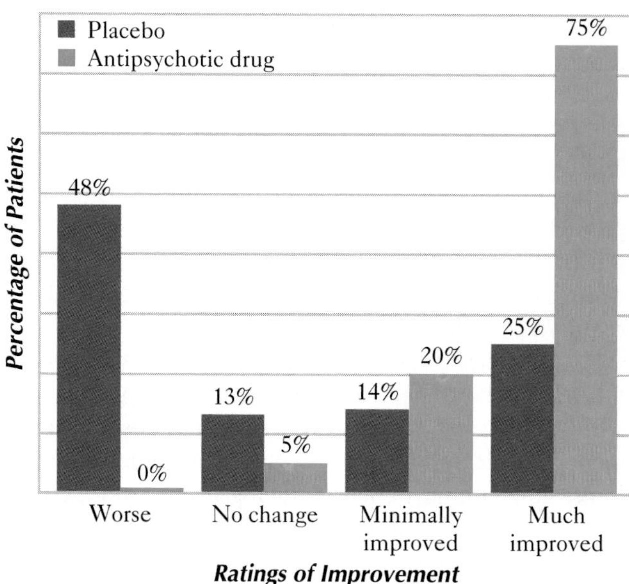

Figure 16-1 *An early influential study found that after six weeks of treatment, 75 percent of patients with schizophrenia who had been given antipsychotic drugs were much improved, compared to only 25 percent of patients given placebos. In addition, close to half of those on the placebos worsened. (Adapted from Cole et al., 1964.)*

The Effectiveness of Antipsychotic Drugs

Research has repeatedly shown that antipsychotic drugs reduce schizophrenic symptoms in the majority of patients (Lieberman et al., 1996; Strange, 1992) (see Figure 16-1). Moreover, the drugs have emerged as the single most effective intervention for schizophrenia in direct comparisons with other forms of treatment such as psychodynamic therapy, milieu therapy, and electroconvulsive therapy (May, Tuma, & Dixon, 1981; May & Tuma, 1964).

The drugs apparently produce the maximum improvement within the first six months of treatment (Szymanski et al., 1996). At the same time, symptoms may return if patients stop taking the drugs too soon (Davis et al., 1993). In one study, when the antipsychotic medications of people with chronic schizophrenia were changed to a placebo after five years, 75 percent of the patients relapsed within a year, compared to 33 percent of similar patients who continued to receive medication (Sampath et al., 1992).

As we noted in Chapter 15, antipsychotic drugs alleviate the *positive symptoms* of schizophrenia, such as hallucinations and delusions, more completely, or at least more quickly, than the *negative symptoms,* such as flat affect, poverty of speech, and loss of volition (Lieberman et al., 1996; Szymanski et al., 1996; Arndt et al., 1995; Dixon, Lehman, & Levine, 1995). Correspondingly, people dominated by positive symptoms (Type I schizophrenia) display generally higher recovery rates from schizophrenia, while those with negative symptoms (Type II schizophrenia) are less affected by drug treatment and have a poorer prognosis (Lindström, 1996; Lindström et al., 1992). Inasmuch as men with schizophrenia tend to have more negative symptoms than women, it is not surprising that they require higher doses and respond less readily to antipsychotic drugs (Szymanski et al., 1996, 1995; Angermeyer et al., 1990; Seeman, 1982).

Antipsychotic drugs have achieved widespread acceptance in the treatment of schizophrenia. Patients often dislike the powerful impact of these drugs, and some refuse to take them; but like Edward Snow, a writer who overcame schizophrenia, many are greatly helped by the medications.

> In my case it was necessary to come to terms with a specified drug program. I am a legalized addict. My dose: 100 milligrams of Thorazine and 60 milligrams of Stelazine daily. I don't feel this dope at all, but I have been told it is strong enough to flatten a normal person. It keeps me—as the doctors agree—sane and in good spirits. Without the brain candy, as I call it, I would go—zoom—right back into the bin. I've made the institution scene enough already to be familiar with what it's like and to know I don't want to go back.
>
> *(Snow, 1976)*

Unwanted Effects of Antipsychotic Drugs

Unfortunately, in addition to their impact on schizophrenic symptoms, antipsychotic drugs sometimes produce disturbing movement abnormalities that may affect appearance and functioning (Gerlach & Peacock, 1995) (see Figure 16-2). These effects are called ***extrapyramidal effects*** because they appear to be caused by the drugs' impact on the extrapyramidal areas of the brain, areas that regulate motor activity. They include Parkinsonian and related symptoms, neuroleptic malignant syndrome, and tardive dyskinesia. These undesired effects are so common that they are listed separately in DSM-IV as ***medication-induced movement disorders*** (APA, 1994).

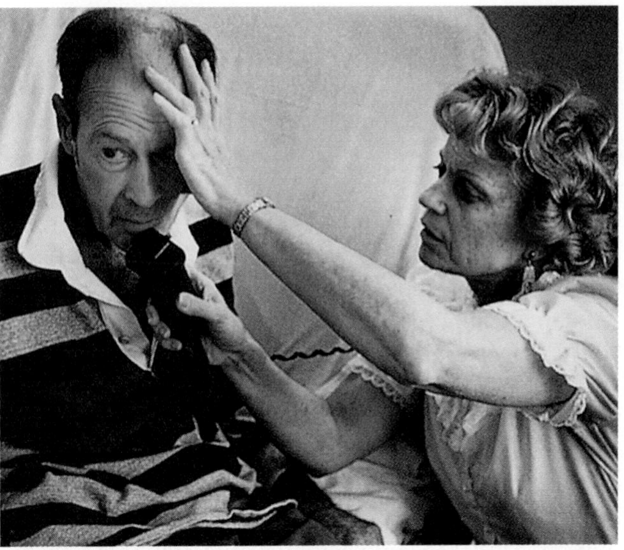

This man has a severe case of Parkinson's disease, a disorder caused by low dopamine activity, and his muscle tremors prevent him from shaving himself. The traditional antipsychotic drugs often produce similar Parkinsonian symptoms.

Parkinsonian and Related Symptoms As we saw in Chapter 15, antipsychotic drugs may produce ***Parkinsonian symptoms,*** reactions that closely resemble the features of the neurological disorder Parkinson's disease. From 20 to 40 percent of patients on the drugs experience severe and continuous muscle tremors and muscle rigidity; they shake, move very slowly, shuffle their feet, and show little facial expression (Strange, 1992). Related symptoms are ***dystonia,*** characterized by involuntary muscle contractions that cause bizarre and uncontrollable movements of the face, neck, tongue, and back (Khanna, Das, & Damodaran, 1992); and ***akathisia,*** marked by a very high degree of restlessness, agitation, and discomfort in the limbs, which causes individuals to move their arms and legs continually in search of relief.

These symptoms seem to be related to medication-induced reductions of dopamine activity in the *substantia nigra,* a part of the mid-brain that coordinates movement and posture (Pickar et al., 1991). In most cases, they can be reversed if an anti-Parkinsonian drug is taken along with the antipsychotic drug (Silver et al., 1995). Alternatively, clinicians may have to reduce the dose of the antipsychotic drug or stop it altogether.

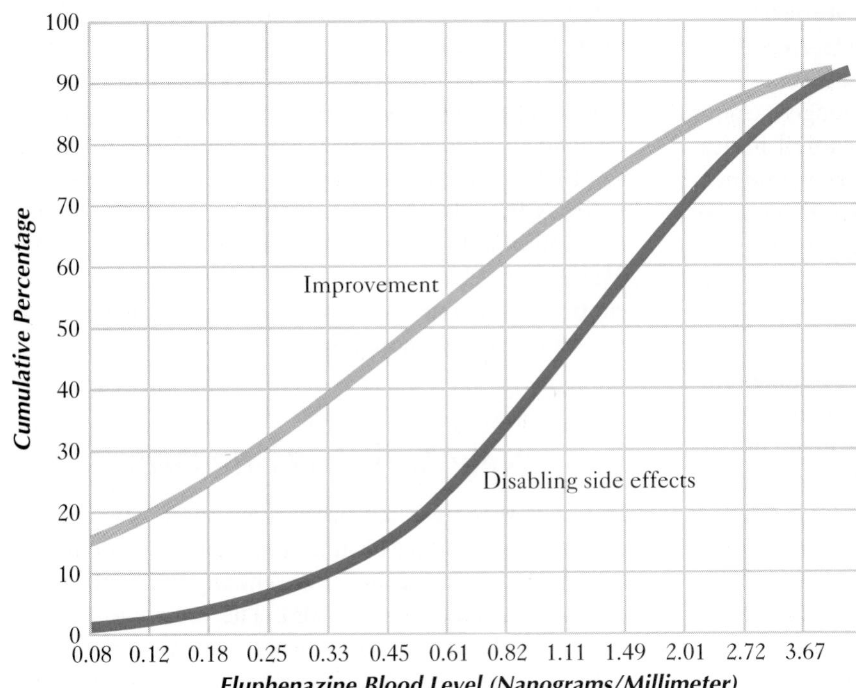

Figure 16-2 *The reactions of patients with schizophrenia to the traditional antipsychotic drug fluphenazine (Prolixin) demonstrate the close relationship between drug dosage, patient improvement, and serious unwanted drug effects. As the blood level of the drug increases, patients improve, but disabling effects of the drug increase as well. At higher levels of the drug, the benefits-risk trade-off becomes arguable. (Adapted from Barondes, 1993, p. 162.)*

Neuroleptic Malignant Syndrome In as many as 1 or 2 percent of patients, particularly elderly ones, antipsychotic drugs produce ***neuroleptic malignant syndrome,*** a severe, potentially fatal reaction marked by muscle rigidity, fever, altered consciousness, and autonomic dysfunction (Leipsic, Abraham, & Halperin, 1995; Raja & Miti, 1995; Hermesh et al., 1992). The syndrome, which is sometimes overlooked in its early stages, is treated by immediately stopping the antipsychotic drugs and intervening to reduce its symptoms (Velamoor et al., 1994; Levenson, 1985).

Tardive Dyskinesia ***Tardive dyskinesia*** means "late-appearing movement disorder." Whereas many of the other undesirable drug effects appear within days or weeks, tardive dyskinesia usually does not unfold until a person has taken antipsychotic drugs for more than a year. Sometimes it does not even appear until after the patient's medications are stopped (Schultz et al., 1995; Wyatt, 1995). The syndrome consists of involuntary writhing or ticlike movements of the tongue, mouth, face, or whole body, and may include involuntary chewing, sucking, and lip smacking and jerky, purposeless movements of the arms, legs, or entire body. It is sometimes accompanied by memory impairment (Sorokin et al., 1988).

Although most cases of tardive dyskinesia are mild and involve a single symptom such as tongue flicking, some are severe and include such features as continual rocking back and forth, irregular breathing, and grotesque contortions of the face and body. It is believed that over 20 percent of the people who take antipsychotic drugs for an extended time develop tardive dyskinesia to some degree, and the longer the drugs are taken, the greater the risk becomes (Chakos et al., 1996; APA, 1994; Strange, 1992). Patients over 45 years of age seem to be as much as six times more vulnerable than younger persons (Jeste et al., 1996). There are also some clinical indications that people with Type II schizophrenia, whose negative symptoms are relatively unresponsive to many of the antipsychotic drugs anyway, may be at greater risk of developing tardive dyskinesia; however, research findings are mixed on this issue (Yuen et al., 1996; Davis, Borde, & Sharma, 1992).

Tardive dyskinesia can be difficult, sometimes impossible to eliminate. If it is discovered early and the antipsychotic drugs are stopped immediately, it will usually disappear (APA, 1994; Pickar et al., 1991). Early detection, however, is elusive. Some of the symptoms are very similar to schizophrenic symptoms (Fenn et al., 1996; McCreadie et al., 1996), so clinicians may overlook them, continue antipsychotic drug therapy, and inadvertently create a more serious case of tardive dyskinesia. The longer patients continue taking antipsychotic drugs, the less likely it is that their tardive dyskinesia will disappear when the antipsychotic drugs are finally stopped. There is some evidence that treatment with vitamin E may reduce or help prevent symptoms of tardive dyskinesia, but the research results have been mixed (Gattaz, 1995; Ricketts et al., 1995). Researchers do not yet fully understand why antipsychotic drugs cause tardive dyskinesia, although they suspect that the syndrome is once again related, in part at least, to the drugs' effect on dopamine receptors in the substantia nigra.

Prescribing Antipsychotic Drugs Clinicians are now wiser and more careful in their prescription practices than they were in past years. In the past, when a patient did not respond to a neuroleptic drug, clinicians would keep increasing the dose (Kane, 1992); today they typically stop the drug in such cases (Safferman & Munne, 1992; Simhandl & Meszaros, 1992). Similarly, today's clinicians try to prescribe the lowest effective dose of antipsychotic drugs for each patient and to reduce or halt medication gradually weeks or months after the patient reestablishes nonpsychotic functioning (Dixon et al., 1995; Gerlach & Peacock, 1995; Gilbert et al., 1995; Kane, 1990, 1987). Unfortunately, as we noted earlier, many patients, particularly those whose disorders are chronic, cannot hold their own without medications (Gaebel, 1995; Gilbert et al., 1995; Lerner et al., 1995). They tend to be put back on medications rather quickly, and some wind up receiving higher doses than are recommended (Remington et al., 1993; Collins et al., 1992; Segal, Cohen, & Marder, 1992).

Researchers keep searching for ways to predict psychotic relapse, so that they may better determine when a patient's dose can be lowered or discontinued (van Kammen et al., 1996). One promising method for predicting relapse is to measure the *prolactin* level in the patient's blood; apparently patients with a low level of this chemical tend to relapse earlier (Lieberman, 1993; Coryell et al., 1990). Another method is to observe a recovered patient's behavioral changes after he or she is temporarily given a dopamine-enhancing drug such as *methylphenidate* (Lieberman, 1993). Patients who display psychotic-like symptoms after receiving methylphenidate apparently relapse more rapidly.

New Antipsychotic Drugs

In recent years research has yielded some new antipsychotic drugs that may be given to patients who do not respond to, cannot tolerate, or are endangered by the traditional drugs (Ereshefsky, 1995). The most effective and widely used of these new drugs are ***clozapine*** (trade name Clozaril) and ***risperidone*** (trade name Risperdole)

(Kopala et al., 1996; He & Richardson, 1995; Klieser et al., 1995; Buckley et al., 1994). As we discussed in Chapter 15, these drugs are considered *atypical* because their biological impact differs from that of traditional antipsychotic medications. They are received at fewer dopamine D-2 receptors and more D-1 and serotonin receptors than are traditional neuroleptic drugs (Gerlach, Lublin, & Peacock, 1996; Breier, 1995; Meltzer, 1995). They have been found to be significantly more effective than the traditional drugs, helping as many as 85 percent of persons with schizophrenia, including those with negative symptoms, as compared to the 65 percent helped by most of the traditional neuroleptics (Essock et al., 1996; Meltzer et al., 1996; Carpenter et al., 1995).

Another major benefit of these atypical antipsychotic drugs is that they cause few extrapyramidal symptoms, apparently because they do not block as many D-2 receptors as traditional neuroleptic drugs (Gerlach et al., 1996; Lindenmayer, 1995; Meltzer, 1995). Most important, few, if any, cases of tardive dyskinesia have been attributed to these new drugs, even after prolonged treatment (Borison, 1995; Meltzer, 1993; Safferman et al., 1991). In addition, tardive dyskinesia and other extrapyramidal symptoms are often reduced when patients with schizophrenia are switched from the traditional to the atypical drugs (Gerlach et al., 1996; Buchanan, 1995; Levin et al., 1992).

Yet these new drugs have some serious problems of their own. People who use clozapine, for example, have around a 1 percent risk of developing ***agranulocytosis,*** a life-threatening drop in white blood cells (Alvir, Lieberman, & Safferman, 1995). This risk may be even higher among elderly patients (Salzman et al., 1995). Since researchers have not yet developed a way to predict who is susceptible to this condition, patients who take clozapine need frequent blood tests so that it can be detected early and the drug stopped (Alvir & Lieberman, 1994; Krupp & Barnes, 1992). Unfortunately, several deaths have resulted from failure to detect agranulocytosis early. In addition, there are some indications that combining clozapine with antidepressant drugs, a common treatment strategy for patients with schizophrenia, can produce serious medical problems for some patients (Centorrino et al., 1996).

Because of the potential medical problems, the atypical antipsychotic drugs have been approved by the FDA only for patients who do not improve with traditional neuroleptic drugs. Some researchers argue, however, that all patients should be allowed to try these new drugs, even if they show some improvement on other drugs, because with the atypical antipsychotics there is less chance of extrapyramidal effects and because some patients improve more on them than on the traditional neuroleptic drugs (Meltzer et al., 1996; Meltzer, 1995, 1993; Meltzer & Okayli, 1995). Continuing their search for antipsychotic drugs that are both effective and safe, researchers are now testing dozens of other promising compounds (Loo et al., 1997; Tollefson et al., 1997; Beasley et al., 1996; Wetzel et al., 1995).

Psychotherapy

Before the discovery of antipsychotic drugs, psychotherapy was not really a viable option as a treatment for schizophrenia. Most patients with schizophrenia were simply too far removed from reality to profit from it (see Box 16-2). Only a handful of therapists, apparently blessed with extraordinary patience and skill, specialized in the treatment of this disorder and reported some success (Will, 1967, 1961; Sullivan, 1962, 1953; Fromm-Reichmann, 1950, 1948, 1943).

These therapists believed that the primary task of therapy was to win the trust of patients with schizophrenia and build a close relationship with them. Frieda Fromm-Reichmann, for example, would initially tell her patients that they could continue to exclude her from their private world and hold onto their disorder as long as they wished. She reported that eventually, after much

"I'M GLAD YOU CAME TO ME. VISIONS OF GHOSTS OF CHRISTMAS PAST, PRESENT AND FUTURE ARE CLEARLY DELUSIONS BASED ON UNDERLYING PSYCHOLOGICAL CONFLICTS."

BOX 16-2 "Being Personally Touched by Mental Illness Is Very Different from Treating It"

Keith Russell Ablow, M.D.

When clinicians work with people suffering from schizophrenia, they usually manage to put aside personal feelings and fears in order to accomplish their therapeutic tasks. But what happens when a clinician's family member or friend develops a severe mental disorder? The psychiatrist Keith Russell Ablow movingly conveys his own personal reaction in an essay originally published in the Washington Post, *Feb. 9, 1993.*

Late one night last year, a close friend from college called me at home. We had spent hours the previous night at dinner, discussing our careers and our families. While I spent years in medical school and psychiatric residency, he had become a very successful businessman.

But during that late-night phone call his tone was anything but friendly. "When we were talking last night, you asked me the name of my new business partner," he said. "Why did you want that information?"

My question had been routine; I barely remember having asked. "I didn't have any real reason," I replied. "I just thought if he was local I might know him."

"Keith, if you want to get involved in one of my business deals, all you have to do is ask," he said.

"I didn't want to be involved," I replied, stunned by his accusatory tone. "I was just wondering. What's the problem?"

There was a long silence. "Fine," he said coldly. "If you want to go head-to-head, we can do that. You play your game, and I'll play mine," he said, then hung up.

I called back immediately, perplexed and upset by his behavior.

"I'm only going to tell you this once," he said the moment he heard my voice. "If I want to talk to you, I'll call you. Other than that, I don't need or want to hear from you," he said, hanging up.

I almost called again, still not convinced that he meant what he had said. Instead, I called his father and a mutual friend of ours. Each of them had also been falsely accused, over the course of a few weeks, of trying to sabotage his business deals.

It quickly became clear that my friend was mentally ill. He was suffering from paranoid delusions, a form of psychosis, and saw us as his enemy. . . .

I found myself wishing that his paranoia had resulted from street drugs in the hope that it would go away soon, once the effects of the drug had worn off. But I was certain that he had never used street drugs in the 10 years I had known him.

Unfortunately, little has changed since that night. My friend has almost completely avoided psychiatric care. We have spoken only a few times for a few minutes. He still distrusts me and his family and views us as unwelcome intrusions in his life.

The last time I called him, I asked if we could get together and talk about our friendship. His response was the same as other times I had tried to reach him. "Why are you calling me?" he asked. "If I need to speak with you, I know where to find you," he said, hanging up.

Being personally touched by mental illness is very different from treating it. Over the past several months, I have experienced many of the emotions that relatives and friends of the mentally ill have described: guilt, fear, sorrow, a sense of loss and the inevitable question of whether something I did had somehow caused or triggered his illness.

It is easier now for me to understand the depth of guilt that families of mentally ill patients struggle to escape. I, after all, didn't have to wonder whether something I did or didn't do as a parent decades before might be

testing and acting out, the patients would accept, trust, and grow attached to her, and begin to examine relevant issues with her.

Although no consistent research was conducted on the effectiveness of such psychotherapeutic approaches, people who later recovered from schizophrenia often confirmed that trust and emotional bonding had been important to them throughout therapy. Here a woman tells her therapist how she had felt during their early interactions:

> At the start, I didn't listen to what you said most of the time but I watched like a hawk for your expression and the sound of your voice. After the interview, I would add all this up to see if it seemed to show love. The words were nothing compared to the feelings you

wrapped up in my friend's current suffering. I didn't have to trace the branches of my family tree looking for aberrant genes.

Yet what I felt most immediately and most intensely was guilt. I relived past events and wondered how I could have ignored what now seemed like signs of my friend's emotional instability. At the time, I regarded them as eccentricities.

On one occasion, for example, he had demanded from me an oath of allegiance to our friendship. "If we're going to be friends," he said, "I want us to be more like brothers, so we can count on each other no matter what."

He suggested we cut our fingers and, as a symbol of our bond, mix our blood. I laughed the idea off, thinking he was joking. In retrospect, I'm not so sure.

He made a great deal of the fact that he wanted only one or, at most, two very committed friends. I was flattered; his focus on trust made me feel he was especially trustworthy. I never recognized the underlying vulnerability and fear that his demands reflected.

I worried that maybe our competitiveness had damaged him and fueled his paranoia. Over the years, he and I had tended to measure our professional achievements against one another. We were both acutely aware of which of us was closer to achieving his goals. Did I covet his business deals, after all? Was there a kernel of truth to his paranoia?

His illness also revealed how much more unsettling it can be to relate to a psychotic individual on a personal—rather than a professional—level. In the office, I have treated many people who, having assaulted or murdered others, feel no remorse whatsoever.

But treating them frightened me less than the thought of encountering my friend in his current state. The truth was, I was afraid of him. He had turned on me before.

During what to me seemed a minor argument seven years earlier, my friend had threatened to use his many contacts in academia to derail my hopes for admission to medical school. We ultimately resolved our dispute, but I never forgot the seriousness with which he had leveled his threat.

I had watched him methodically, almost fanatically, undermine competitors. He kept extensive files on them, sometimes including damaging personal information.

If he had shown that degree of determination to overwhelm his competition in business while relatively well, I wondered, how far would he go now that he was sick to protect his business deal from me? Would he kill me if he felt he had to? I had to admit to myself that I would be hesitant to open my apartment door if he knocked on it unexpectedly. I wondered whether people he was doing business with might be in some danger and whether he should be committed against his will. . . .

. . . I felt inadequate: as a psychiatrist I thought I should be able to do something to intervene in his illness. I talked to his parents and tried to explain the possible disorders their son might be suffering from. I helped them get the names of prominent psychiatrists near his home.

Looking back, I worry that I could have helped him more. That night on the phone, I might instead have asked him what had shaken his confidence in me and apologized for the misunderstanding. I could have understood his accusation as a plea for reassurance that I would always stand by him. Slowly, perhaps over the course of many months or years, I could have urged him to examine his fear in psychotherapy.

But I was responding as a friend, not a psychiatrist. And I now have lost a friend, not a patient. The waves of grief come unexpectedly. I think of the time passing without contact like a wall being built between us. It is a bigger loss than if he had died.

I think often of the advice he gave me when I was unhappy and under great stress in medical school. "Remember," he told me, "you're still in complete control. You have all the cards. If you were to throw them in and leave that place tomorrow, you'd leave with your intelligence, your family and your friends."

I hope, ultimately, he will see that the same holds true for him.

showed. I sense that you felt confident I could be helped and that there was hope for the future. . . .

The problem with schizophrenics is that they can't trust anyone. They can't put their eggs in one basket. The doctor will usually have to fight to get in no matter how much the patient objects. . . .

Loving is impossible at first because it turns you into a helpless little baby. The patient can't feel safe to do this until he is absolutely sure the doctor understands what is needed and will provide it.

(Hayward & Taylor, 1965)

Psychotherapy is now successfully employed in many more cases of schizophrenia, thanks to the discovery and effectiveness of antipsychotic drugs. By helping to relieve thought and perceptual disturbances, the drugs enable people with schizophrenia to learn about their disorder, play an active role in the therapeutic process, think more clearly about themselves and their relationships, and make changes in their behavior (Atkinson et al., 1996; Falloon, Coverdale, & Brooker, 1996; Saper, Blank, & Chapman, 1995). Although psychotherapy tends to be of limited help during the earliest stages of the disorder, research suggests that it becomes very useful later on, particularly after medications have made an impact. The most helpful forms of psychotherapy include insight therapy and two broader, sociocultural therapies—family therapy and social therapy. Often these approaches are combined and tailored to the particular needs of patients (Jeffries, 1995; Prendergast, 1995).

Insight Therapy

A variety of insight therapies are now applied to schizophrenia (Chadwick & Trower, 1996; Bacon, 1995; Wasylenki, 1992). Studies suggest that insight therapists who are more experienced with schizophrenia have greater success, often regardless of their particular orientation (Karon, 1988, 1985; Lamb, 1982; Karon & Vandenbos, 1981). According to one study, therapists whose treatment is successful tend to take a more active role than less successful therapists, setting limits, expressing opinions, challenging patients' statements, and providing guidance (Whitehorn & Betz, 1975). At the same time, gaining a patient's trust remains a major part of therapy.

Family Therapy

Between 25 and 40 percent of community residents who are recovering from schizophrenia live with their parents, siblings, spouses, or children (Torrey, Wolfe, & Flynn, 1988; Bocker, 1984). Such unions create special pressures for both the patients and the family members.

Patients who are recovering from schizophrenia are greatly affected by the behavior and reactions of family members, even if family dysfunction was not a factor in the onset of the patients' disorder. Indeed, it has been found that persons with schizophrenia who have positive perceptions of their relatives do better in treatment (Lebell et al., 1993; Scott et al., 1993). Similarly, as we noted in Chapter 15, recovered patients living with relatives who display high levels of *expressed emotion*—that is, high levels of criticism, emotional overinvolvement, and hostility—often have a higher relapse rate than those living with cooler, less emotional relatives (Penn & Mueser, 1996; Fox, 1992; Vaughan et al., 1992). Whether expressed emotion *precedes* the onset of schizophrenia or *results from* the pressures of caring for a relative with schizophrenia, this family pattern does seem to hinder long-term recovery (Penn & Mueser, 1996; Fox, 1992).

Family members, for their part, are often greatly affected by the behavior of a relative with schizophrenia (Bloch et al., 1995). In an enlightening series of interviews, one team of investigators found many family members to be greatly disturbed by the social withdrawal and unusual behaviors of their relative (Creer & Wing, 1974). One family member complained, "In the evening you go into the sitting room and it's in darkness. You turn on the light and there he is just sitting there, staring in front of him."

To address such issues, clinicians now commonly include family therapy in their treatment of schizophrenia (Penn & Meuser, 1996; Dixon & Lehman, 1995; Goldstein, 1991, 1987). Family therapy provides family members with guidance, training, practical advice, education about schizophrenia ***(psychoeducation),*** and emotional support and empathy (Solomon et al., 1996; Goldstein, 1995; Goldstein & Miklowitz, 1995). It helps family members become more realistic in their expectations, more tolerant, less guilt-ridden, and more willing to try new patterns of interaction and communication. Over the course of treatment, family therapists also try to help the individual with schizophrenia cope with the pressures of family life, make better use of family resources, and avoid problematic interactions. Family therapy often succeeds in improving communication and reducing tensions within the family. In turn, it helps relapse rates to go down, particularly when it is combined with drug therapy (Penn & Mueser, 1996; Dixon & Lehman, 1995; Zastowny et al., 1992). The principles of this approach are at work in the following case:

> Mark was a 32-year-old single man living with his parents. He had a long and stormy history of schizophrenia with many episodes of psychosis, interspersed with occasional brief periods of good functioning. Mark's father was a bright but neurotically tormented man gripped by obsessions and inhibitions in spite of many years of psychoanalysis. Mark's mother appeared weary, detached, and embittered. Both parents felt hopeless about Mark's chances of recovery and resentful that needing to care for him would always plague their lives. They acted as if they were being intentionally punished. It gradually emerged that the father, in fact, was riddled with guilt and self-doubt; he suspected that his wife had been cold and rejecting toward Mark as an infant and that he had failed to intervene, due to his unwillingness to confront his wife and the demands of graduate school that distanced him from home life. He entertained the fantasy that Mark's illness was a punishment for this. Every time Mark did begin to show improvement—both in reduced symptoms and

in increased functioning—his parents responded as if it were just a cruel torment designed to raise their hopes and then to plunge them into deeper despair when Mark's condition deteriorated. This pattern was especially apparent when Mark got a job. As a result, at such times, the parents actually became more critical and hostile toward Mark. He would become increasingly defensive and insecure, finally developing paranoid delusions, and usually would be hospitalized in a panicky and agitated state.

All of this became apparent during the psychoeducational sessions. When the pattern was pointed out to the family, they were able to recognize their self-fulfilling prophecy and were motivated to deal with it. As a result, the therapist decided to see the family together. Concrete instances of the pattern and its consequences were explored, and alternative responses by the parents were developed. The therapist encouraged both the parents and Mark to discuss their anxieties and doubts about Mark's progress, rather than to stir up one another's expectations of failure. The therapist had regular individual sessions with Mark as well as the family sessions. As a result, Mark has successfully held a job for an unprecedented 12 months.

(Heinrichs & Carpenter, 1983, pp. 284–285)

Finally, the families of persons with schizophrenia may also need outside social support to be of most help to their troubled relatives (Perlick et al., 1992), and a number of ***family support groups*** and ***family psychoeducational programs*** have been organized (Buchkremer et al., 1995; Birchwood et al., 1992; Hyde & Goldman, 1992). In such programs, family members come together with others in the same situation, share their thoughts and emotions, receive support, and learn about schizophrenia. Although research has yet to determine the usefulness of these groups, the approach is becoming increasingly common as professionals try to address this long-neglected need.

Social Therapy

Many clinicians who treat persons with schizophrenia try to address all aspects of a client's life and recovery. They make practical advice and life adjustment a key focus of treatment, and also direct therapy toward such issues as problem solving, decision making, development of social skills, and management of medication (Penn & Mueser, 1996; Prendergast, 1995; Scott & Dixon, 1995). In addition, they may help their clients find work, financial assistance, and proper housing. This kind of intervention, called ***social therapy*** or ***sociotherapy*** (Hogarty et al., 1986, 1974), may be offered in group formats as well as in individual sessions (Wilson, Diamond, & Factor, 1990).

Research supports the belief that this practical, active, and broad treatment helps keep patients with schizophrenia out of the hospital. Gerard Hogarty and his colleagues (1986, 1974) compared the progress of four groups of chronic patients after their discharge from a state hospital. One group received both antipsychotic medications and social therapy in the community, while the other groups received medication only, social therapy only, or no treatment of any kind. The researchers' first finding was that chronic patients needed medication in the community to avoid rehospitalization. Over a two-year period, 80 percent of those who did not take medication needed to be hospitalized again, compared to 48 percent of those who received medication. They also found that among the patients on medication, those who also received social therapy adjusted to the community and avoided rehospitalization most successfully. Clearly, social therapy played an important role in their recovery.

The Community Approach

The broadest approach to schizophrenia is the *community approach*. Partly in response to the deplorable conditions in public mental institutions, President John F. Kennedy called for a "bold new approach" to mental disorders in 1963, and Congress passed the Community Mental Health Act. This act provided that patients with psychological disorders were to receive a range of mental health services—outpatient therapy, inpatient treatment, emergency care, preventive care, and aftercare—right in their communities rather than far from home. The act was intended to address a variety of psychological disorders, but patients with schizophrenia, especially those who had been institutionalized for years, were targeted and affected more than most (Hafner & an der Heiden, 1988). The government was ordering that these patients be released and treated in the community. Other countries around the world put similar sociocultural treatment programs into action shortly thereafter (Hafner & an der Heiden, 1988; Torrey, 1988).

Thus began three decades of ***deinstitutionalization,*** an exodus of hundreds of thousands of patients with schizophrenia and other chronic mental disorders from state institutions into the community. On a given day in 1955 close to 600,000 patients were living in state institutions; today only around 80,000 patients reside in mental health settings (Torrey, 1997).

Clinicians have learned that patients recovering from schizophrenia can profit greatly from community-based programs. Unfortunately, as we shall see in more detail later, the quality and funding of community care for these patients have been grossly inadequate throughout the United States. The result is a "revolving door" syndrome: many patients are repeatedly released to the community, readmitted to an institution within months, and released again, only to be admitted yet again (Geller, 1992).

Effective Community Care

Community residents recovering from schizophrenia need medication, psychotherapy, help in handling daily pressures and responsibilities, guidance in making decisions, training in social skills, residential supervision, and vocational counseling and training. Patients whose communities systematically address these needs make greater progress than patients living in other communities (Scott & Dixon, 1995; Hogarty, 1993). Some of the key elements in effective community care programs are coordination of patient services, short-term hospitalization, partial hospitalization, halfway houses, and occupational training.

Coordinated Services The government commission whose work led to the Community Mental Health Act originally proposed that the cornerstone of community care should be a ***community mental health center,*** a treatment facility that would provide medication, psychotherapy, and inpatient emergency care to people with severe disturbances. The community mental health center was also to *coordinate* the patient services offered by other community agencies. Each center was expected to serve a designated "catchment area," a geographic area with a population of 50,000 to 200,000 people.

When community mental health centers do in fact provide these services, patients with schizophrenia often

BOX 16-3 Mentally Ill Chemical Abusers: A Challenge for Treatment

A state appeals court yesterday ordered Larry Hogue, who has for years frightened residents of Manhattan's Upper West Side with his bizarre behavior, to remain in a state mental hospital until a hearing next week. . . . Before he was arrested, Mr. Hogue had attacked passers-by and cars in the area around West 96th Street and Amsterdam Avenue. . . .

. . . Mr. Hogue has been arrested 30 times and served at least six terms in prison, ranging from five days to a year, according to law-enforcement records. He now faces charges of criminal mischief for scraping the paint off a car last August.

(New York Times, *February 9, 1993*)

Larry Hogue, nicknamed the "Wild Man of West 96th Street" by his neighbors, is a ***mentally ill chemical abuser (MICA),*** an individual who suffers from both a mental disorder (in his case schizophrenia) and a substance-related disorder. Between 20 and 50 percent of all people who suffer from chronic mental disorders may be MICAs (Polcin, 1992).

MICAs tend to be young and male. They are often below average in social functioning and school achievement and above average in poverty, acting-out behavior, emergency room visits, and encounters with the criminal justice system (Bartels et al., 1993; O'Hare, 1992). MICAs commonly report greater distress and have poorer treatment outcomes than patients with mental disorders who do not abuse substances (Carey et al., 1991).

The relationship between substance abuse and mental dysfunctioning is complex. A mental disorder may precede substance abuse, and the drug may be a form of self-medication or a result of impaired judgment (Woody et al., 1995; Polcin, 1992). Conversely, substance abuse may cause or exacerbate psychopathology. Cocaine, for example, exacerbates the symptoms of psychosis and can quickly intensify the symptoms of schizophrenia (Shaner et al., 1993). Perhaps the most compelling theory is that substance abuse and mental disorders interact to create a unique problem that is, so to speak, greater than the sum of its parts (Boutros, Bonnet, & Mak, 1996; Robertson, 1992). The course and outcome of one problem can be significantly influenced by the other disorder.

Treatment of MICAs has been undermined by the tendency of patients to hide their drug abuse problem and for clinicians to underdiagnose substance abuse (Lehman et al., 1996). Unrecognized substance abuse may lead to the misdiagnosis of mental disorders or to misunderstanding of the make steady and significant progress (Scott & Dixon, 1995; Beiser et al., 1985). They are better reintegrated into the community and function more effectively than those who receive standard outpatient care (Madianos & Madianou, 1992). Coordination of services is particularly important for the so-called MICAs, patients who have a dual diagnosis of schizophrenia and substance abuse (see Box 16-3). It is estimated that at least half of all patients with schizophrenia also are dependent on alcohol or other drugs (Haywood et al., 1995; Westermeyer, 1992).

Short-Term Hospitalization When people first develop schizophrenic symptoms, today's clinicians first try to treat them on an outpatient basis, usually administering antipsychotic medication and perhaps psychotherapy (Marder, 1996). If these interventions prove inadequate, short-term hospitalization that lasts a few weeks, rather than months or years, may be tried (Davis et al., 1988). As soon as the patients are stabilized, they are released for a program of posthospitalization care and treatment, or ***aftercare,*** out in the community (Sederer, 1992; Lamb, 1988). Short-term hospitalization usually leads to a greater reduction of symptoms and a lower rehospitalization rate than extended institutional care (Caton, 1982; Herz et al., 1977, 1975). Countries throughout the world now favor this policy (Hafner & an der Heiden, 1988).

Partial Hospitalization For people whose needs fall somewhere between full hospitalization and outpatient therapy sessions, some communities offer ***day centers*** or ***day hospitals,*** programs in which patients with psychological disorders return home for the night (Clay, 1996; Goldberg, 1995; Kennedy, 1992; Hoge et al., 1988). Such programs originated in Moscow in 1933, when a

---

course and prognosis of a disorder (Shaner et al., 1993).

The treatment of MICAs is further complicated by the fact that many treatment facilities are designed and funded to treat *either* mental disorders or substance abuse; relatively few are equipped or willing to treat both. As a result, it is not uncommon for MICA patients to be rejected as inappropriate for treatment in both substance abuse and mental health programs. Many MICAs fall through the cracks in this way and find themselves in jail, like Larry Hogue, or in homeless shelters for want of the treatment they sought in vain (Polcin, 1992).

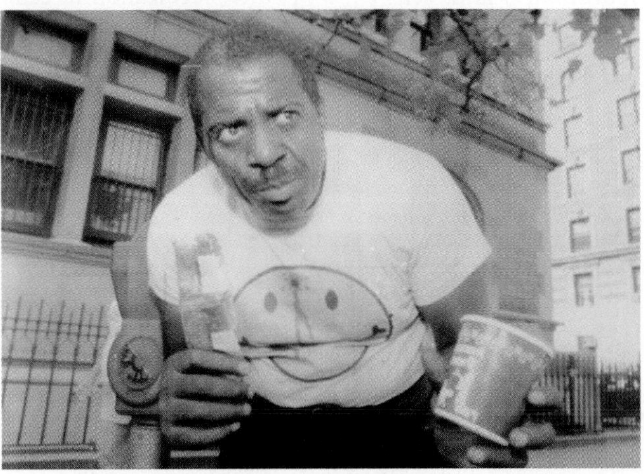

The case of Larry Hogue, the so-called "Wild Man of West 96th Street," helped bring the plight of MICAs to public attention.

The ideal MICA treatment program appears to be a safe and supportive therapeutic environment that adopts techniques to treat both mental disorders and substance abuse and takes into account the unique effects of both problems (Hellerstein, Rosenthal, & Miner, 1995; Fals & Schafer, 1992; Carey, 1989). One particularly inspiring development is the recent establishment of self-help groups for MICAs living in the community.

The problem of falling through the cracks is perhaps most poignantly seen in the case of homeless MICAs. Researchers estimate that 10 to 20 percent of homeless persons may be MICAs (Drake et al., 1991). MICAs typically are homeless longer than other homeless persons and are more likely to experience extremely harsh conditions, such as living on the winter streets rather than in a homeless shelter. They are also more likely to be jailed, to grant sexual favors for food or money, to share needles, to engage in unprotected sex, and to be victimized (Susser et al., 1996). It has been suggested that treatment programs for homeless MICAs should include intensive case management, with a commitment to build trust and provide long-term practical assistance (Drake et al., 1991). In short, treatment programs must be tailored to MICAs' unique combination of problems rather than expect them to adapt to traditional forms of treatment.

shortage of hospital beds necessitated the premature release of many patients. Canada and England later developed day hospitals as well, and so did the United States. Today's day centers provide patients with daily activities, therapy, and programs to improve social skills. People recovering from schizophrenia in day centers often do better than those in programs that provide extended hospitalization or traditional outpatient therapy (Takano et al., 1995; Creed, Black, & Anthony, 1989; Herz et al., 1971).

Halfway Houses ***Halfway houses*** are residences for people who do not require hospitalization but cannot live either alone or with their families. These residences, typically large houses in areas where housing is inexpensive, usually shelter between one and two dozen people. Although outside mental health professionals may be available to residents, the live-in staff usually consists of ***paraprofessionals***—lay people who have received some training in providing emotional support and practical guidance in matters of daily living. The houses are usually run with a milieu therapy philosophy that emphasizes support, resident responsibility, and self-government. Patients with schizophrenia are prominent among residents of halfway houses.

Research indicates that halfway houses help many people recovering from schizophrenia adjust to community life and avoid rehospitalization (Simpson, Hyde, & Faragher, 1989; Caton, 1982) (see Figure 16-3). Here is how one woman described living in a halfway house after ten hospitalizations in twelve years:

> The halfway house changed my life. First of all, I discovered that some of the staff members had once been clients in the program! That one single fact offered me hope. For the first time, I saw proof that a program could help someone, that it was possible to regain control over one's life and become independent. The house was democratically run; all residents had one vote and the staff members, outnumbered 5 to 22, could not make rules or even discharge a client from the program without majority sentiment. There was a house bill of rights that was strictly observed by all. We helped one another and gave support. When residents were in a crisis, no staff member hustled them off or increased their medication to calm them down. Residents could

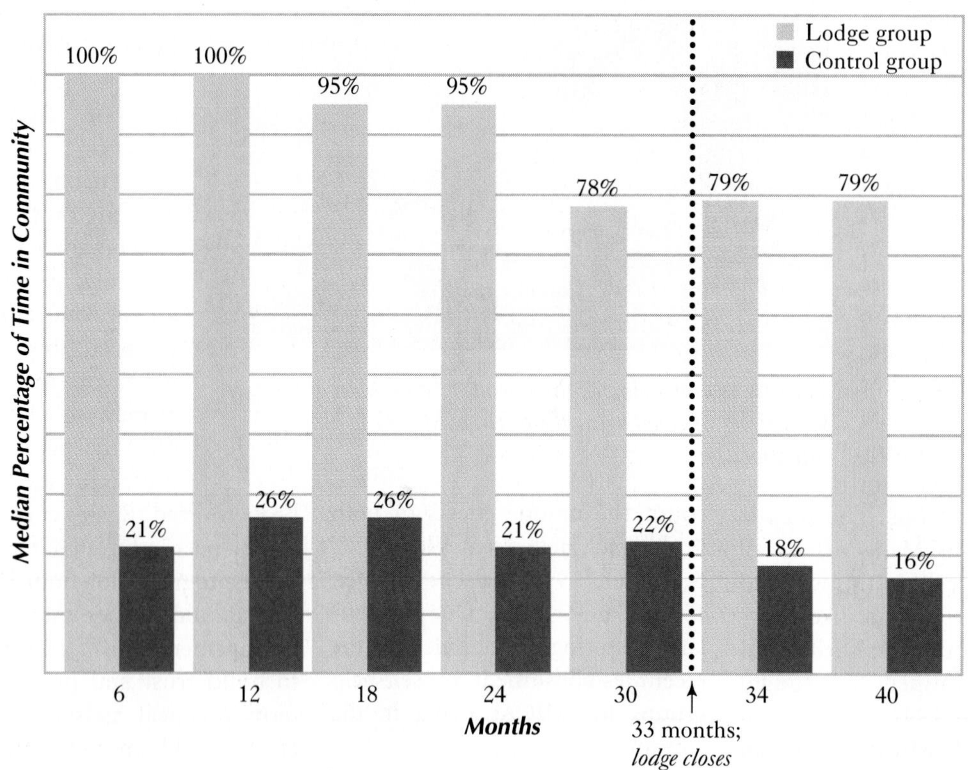

Figure 16-3 *In a famous study by George Fairweather and his associates (1969), patients with schizophrenia who were released from a hospital to a "lodge" (halfway house and business program) adjusted better than patients who were released directly to a boardinghouse or apartment. They also remained in the community longer, avoided rehospitalization more successfully, and continued this trend even after the lodge closed.*

> cry, be comforted and hugged until a solution could be found, or until they accepted that it was okay to feel bad. Even anger was an acceptable feeling that did not have to be feared, but could be expressed and turned into constructive energy. If you disliked some aspect of the program or the behavior of a staff member, you could change things rather than passively accept what was happening. Choices were real, and failure and success were accepted equally. . . . Bit by bit, my distrust faltered and the fears lessened. I slept better and made friends. . . . Other residents and staff members who had hallucinated for years and now were able to control their hallucinations shared with me some of the techniques that had worked for them. Things like diet, bioenergetic "grounding," and interpersonal relationships became a few of my tools.
>
> *(Lovejoy, 1982, pp. 605–609)*

Occupational Training Regular employment enables people to support themselves, exercise independence, gain self-respect, and learn to work with others. It also brings companionship and order to a person's daily life. For these reasons, occupational training and placement are important aspects of community treatment for people with schizophrenia (Bell, Lysaker, & Milstein, 1996; Drake et al., 1996; Lysaker, Bell, & Bioty, 1995).

Many people recovering from this disorder may receive occupational training in a ***sheltered workshop***—a protected and supervised workplace for employees who are not ready for competitive or complicated jobs. The workshop tries to establish a typical work environment: products such as toys, home furnishings, or simple appliances are manufactured and sold, workers are paid according to their performance, and all are expected to be at work regularly and on time. For some the sheltered workshop becomes a permanent workplace. For others it is an important step toward better-paying and more complex outside employment or a return to a previous job or its equivalent (Bell et al., 1996; Lehman, 1995).

Unfortunately, in the United States vocational rehabilitation is not consistently available to people with severe mental disorders (Drake et al., 1996). One study found that only 25 percent of such people are employed, fewer than 10 percent outside of sheltered workplaces (Mulkern & Manderscheid, 1989).

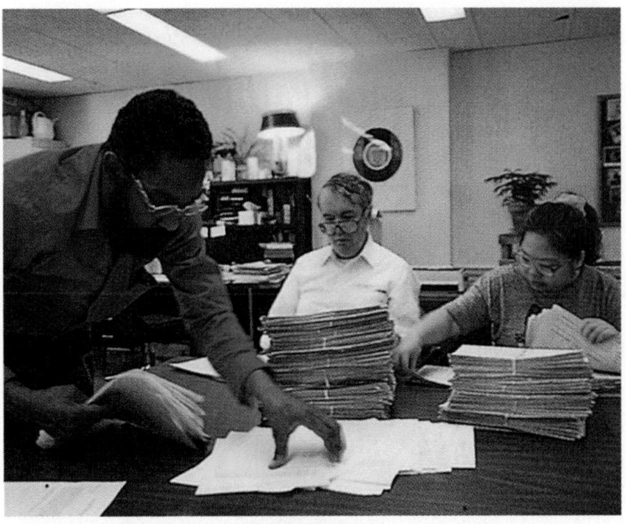

Sheltered workshops, such as the one at New York City's Fountain House, provide job training and employment and teach independence, self-respect, and social skills. Unfortunately, there is a severe shortage of such workshops for people with schizophrenia.

Inadequacies of Community Treatment

Effective community programs clearly can help patients with schizophrenia recover. Unfortunately, less than half of all people with schizophrenia receive appropriate community mental health services (Von Korff et al., 1985). Indeed, almost 40 percent of all people with this disorder fail to receive any treatment at all in any given year (Torrey, 1997; Regier et al., 1993). Two factors are primarily responsible: poor coordination of services and shortage of services.

Poor Coordination of Services The various mental health agencies in a community often fail to communicate with one another (Leshner et al., 1992). A day center and the community mental health center may, for example, dispense conflicting advice to a client. Similarly, there could be an opening at a nearby halfway house and the therapist at the community mental health center might not know about it. In addition, even within a community agency a patient may not have continuing contacts with the same staff members.

Poor communication between state hospitals and the state's various community mental health centers is another barrier to good mental health care (Torrey, 1997; Leshner et al., 1992; McShane & Redoutey, 1987). Sometimes community agencies are not even informed when patients are discharged from the hospital. This problem had its beginnings in the early days of deinstitutionalization, when hospitals were forced to discharge patients before many community mental health centers were open and ready to receive them. The habits of independence that hospitals developed then have continued to the present day. Moreover, institutional care is so expensive today that institutions often feel pressured to release patients before a discharge plan has been completed (Leshner et al., 1992).

Personal Pathways

E. Fuller Torrey

"Forty Years Later"

E. Fuller Torrey has been called the conscience of the mental health field, the profession's leading advocate for people with schizophrenia and their relatives. His work is rooted, once again, in very personal experiences.

"I was just about to begin my second year at Princeton University when my younger sister was initially diagnosed with schizophrenia. I had almost no idea what the word meant, but I did know that 17-year-old young women were not supposed to hear voices and have delusional ideas about a British invasion of our house. Accompanying my sister and mother to treatment facilities, I rapidly learned that nobody else, including putative world experts, knew much about the disease either. One of them even told my mother, with great confidence, that my sister's illness had been caused by the death of my father many years earlier. Even to the eye of a university student at that time, psychiatry looked like the last car on the medical train.

I was already committed to medicine at the time, but it was several more years before I decided to become a psychiatrist. The more I learned in medical school, the more I realized that the heart, liver, and pancreas were relatively known territory, while the brain was a great unknown. It seemed likely that during my lifetime the brain was the organ where the most exciting action was likely to take place.

That has proven to be true, and I have never regretted my decision to become a psychiatrist. It has provided me with an exciting research venue as well as the opportunity to advocate for better services for individuals like my sister. Forty years later she still has schizophrenia and lives in a group home with intermittent hospitalizations."

It is not surprising, then, that a growing number of community therapists are becoming *case managers* for people with schizophrenia (Wolff et al., 1997). Like the social therapists described earlier, they offer therapy and advice, teach problem solving and social skills, and help ensure that medications are being taken properly. In addition, they help clients to take advantage of available community services. They help coordinate such services, guide clients through the community system, and, perhaps most important, act as advocates for the clients. Case management appears to enhance the effectiveness of community treatment for people with schizophrenia. In fact, many professionals believe that effective case management is the key to success for a community program (Dozier, 1996).

Shortage of Services The number of community programs available to people with schizophrenia falls far short of the number needed. The roughly 800 community mental health centers now functioning in the United States are only a third of the number needed. Halfway houses and sheltered workshops are in similarly short supply.

Still more disturbing, the community mental health centers that do exist often fail to provide adequate services for people with severe disorders. They tend to devote their efforts and money to outpatient services for people with less disabling problems, such as anxiety and depressive disorders or problems in social adjustment. For the past fifteen years, only about 10 percent of the patients treated by community mental health centers have suffered from schizophrenia (Rosenstein et al., 1990, 1989; Torrey, 1988).

Why is there such a shortage of services for people with schizophrenia? First, it appears that most mental health professionals simply prefer to work with people whose problems are less severe and less chronic (Lee et al., 1993; Harding et al., 1992). Second, cultural and language barriers often make it difficult for patients who belong to racial and ethnic minorities to find adequate treatment in the community (Leshner et al., 1992). Third, people in the neighborhood often object to the presence of recovering mental patients, sometimes going so far as to picket, protest, and even vandalize community facilities (Leshner et al., 1992). This has been referred to as the "NIMBY" (not in my backyard) syndrome.

Perhaps the primary reason for the shortage of community care is economic. On the one hand, more public funds are allocated for people with mental disorders now than in the past. In 1963 a total of $1 billion was spent in this area, whereas today more than $61 billion is spent on people with mental disorders (Torrey, 1997, 1988; Redick et al., 1992). On the other hand, relatively little of this new money is going to community treatment programs for people with severe disorders. Much of it goes to monthly subsistence payments such as social security disability income, to subsidies for persons with mental disorders in nursing homes and general hospitals, and to community services for people who are less disturbed (Torrey, 1997, 1988; Stein, 1993). And a considerable amount still goes to state hospitals (even though the populations of these hospitals have decreased more than 80 percent since 1963). Today, much of the financial burden of providing community treatment for persons with chronic severe disorders falls on local governments and organizations rather than the federal or state government, and local resources are simply too limited to meet the challenge effectively.

Consequences of Inadequate Community Treatment What happens to persons with schizophrenia whose communities do not provide the services they need and whose families cannot afford private treatment? As we observed earlier, a large number receive no treatment at all; many others spend a short time in a state hospital and are then discharged prematurely, often without benefit of adequate follow-up treatment (Regier et al., 1993; Torrey et al., 1988). Many of those patients with schizophrenia who return to their families may receive medication and perhaps emotional and financial support, but little else in the way of treatment. Between 5 and 15 percent enter an alternative institution such as a nursing home or rest home, where they receive only custodial care and medication (Torrey, 1997; Smyer, 1989; Torrey et al., 1988). As many as 35 percent are placed in single-room-occupancy hotels, boardinghouses, or rooming houses, typically in run-down inner-city neighborhoods (Torrey et al., 1988). Many of these places offer only small rooms in conditions that are substandard and unsafe. At times a media report such as the following newspaper account focuses on the abominable conditions in such dwellings; usually they receive no public attention.

> Hundreds of mentally ill patients throughout Dade County are being packed into aging hotels and homes that are little better than slums, according to health officials, who say the appalling living conditions virtually ensure patients will sink deeper into insanity.
>
> Florida's policy of emptying its mental institutions, a paucity of appropriate "halfway houses," and lax inspections of existing homes have left many mentally ill without the care that might ease them back into normal life.
>
> It also has left them without protection. Released from hospitals into overburdened halfway houses, the indigent patients eventually are shunted to landlords, some of whom jam them, perhaps three to a room, into decaying and dangerous buildings and then collect their welfare payments as rent.
>
> The worst buildings, found scattered throughout Little Havana and the dying hotel district in South Miami Beach, contain the stuff of nightmares. Piles of trash and feces litter the floors. Half-naked men wander purposelessly through hallways, and doors swing open into hot and fetid rooms where others, gazing vacantly at the ceiling, lie neglected on dirty cots.
>
> In some cases, the state Department of Health and Rehabilitative Services places patients in substandard homes. HRS officials concede there is a problem, but say they are doing the best they can in an overloaded and underfunded system.
>
> In one instance, HRS released patients to a Little Havana house run by a landlord who three years earlier lost his state license to operate a group home because of its life-threatening conditions.
>
> The landlord . . . didn't apply for a license for his latest home at 218 SW Eighth Ave. Instead, he used plywood sheets to divide the coral rock house into 12-foot by 14-foot boxes and then told HRS workers he would take in the mentally ill.
>
> Each of the boxes, strung along trash-strewn passageways in the two-story house, contains a narrow bed, a fan and a chest of drawers. Hot meal containers and plastic forks fill waste bins. Most of the boxes also contained people like Vallant Garez, a timid 55-year-old whose bed sores attest to hours spent in bed, staring at a paint-chipped wall a foot from his pillow.
>
> (Miami Herald, *August 10, 1984*)

Most boardinghouse residents survive on government disability payments (Barker et al., 1992) and spend their days wandering through neighborhood streets. Thus it is often said that persons with schizophrenia are being dumped in the community, just as they were once warehoused in institutions.

Finally, and perhaps saddest of all, a great number of people with schizophrenia are forced to take refuge in hallways, subways, and vacant buildings, sleeping on park benches or heating grates (Adams et al., 1996; Susnick & Belcher, 1995; Leshner et al., 1992). Many of them have been released from hospitals. Others are young adults who have never been hospitalized in the first place. There are between 350,000 and 1 million homeless people in the United States, and approximately one-third apparently have a severe mental disorder, commonly schizophrenia (Torrey, 1997; DeAngelis, 1994; Manderscheid & Rosenstein, 1992). The "lucky" ones find beds in public shelters. Another 150,000 people with severe mental disorders wind up in prisons because their pathology has led them to break the law (Torrey, 1997; DeAngelis, 1994). Certainly deinstitutionalization and the community mental health movement have failed these people. Small wonder that many of them report actually feeling relieved if they are able to return to hospital life: they no longer have to search fruitlessly for housing, food, or treatment in the community (Drake & Wallach, 1992).

The Promise of Community Treatment

Despite these very serious problems, proper community care has demonstrated its potential for people recovering from schizophrenia, and both clinicians and many government officials continue to press for community services. In recent years the federal government has created the Task Force on Homelessness and Severe Mental Illness, whose job is to find more effective ways for the federal government, states, and local organizations, both public and private, to meet the housing, treatment, and support needs of people with severe disorders, with emphasis on the needs of the homeless among them (Leshner et al., 1992). In 1992 the task force proposed such major initiatives as Safe Havens, a program of low-cost, stable, and supervised housing for homeless people with mental disorders.

Another important development has been the formation of *national interest groups* to promote community treatment (Torrey, 1997; Rosenstein et al., 1989). One, the National Alliance for the Mentally Ill, began in 1979 with 300 members and has expanded to more than 160,000 members in 1,100 chapters (NAMI, 1997). Made up largely of family members of people with severe mental disorders (particularly schizophrenia, bipolar disorders, and major depression), this group has become a powerful lobbying force in state legislatures and has pressured community mental health centers to provide treatment for persons with schizophrenia.

Today community care is a major aspect of treatment for patients recovering from schizophrenia in countries throughout the world (Dencker & Dencker, 1995; Fog, 1995; Madianos & Economou, 1988). Some countries, learning from the problems of deinstitutionalization in the United States, have managed to introduce their community programs in a better organized, less disruptive, and more successful manner. Sweden, for example, in gradually dismantling its public mental hospitals, has taken care to have community resources available before releasing chronic patients and to give them adequate preparation for release (Perris, 1988). Clearly, both in the United States and abroad, wide-ranging and coordinated community treatment is viewed as an important part of the solution to the problem of schizophrenia.

Crossroads

After years of frustration and failure in efforts to treat schizophrenia, clinicians now have an arsenal of weapons to use against it—medication, institutional programs, psychotherapy, and community programs. It has become very clear that antipsychotic medications open the door

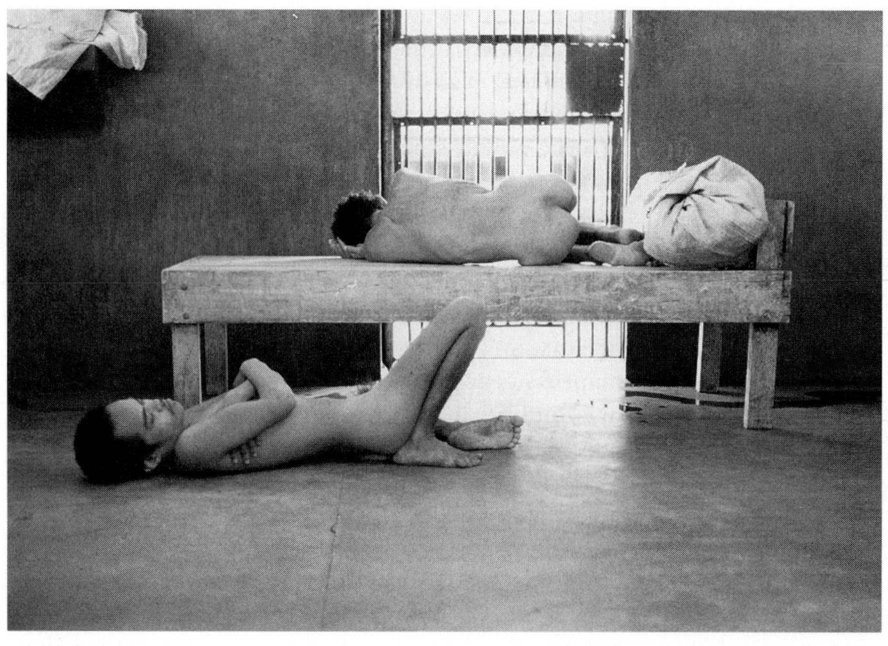

Even as countries around the world move away from long term institutional treatment and toward community mental health, the horrors of asylums and overcrowded public mental hospitals continue to live in parts of today's world. This heartwrenching scene inside a mental hospital in the southern Philippines clarifies the point.

for recovery from schizophrenia, but in most cases other kinds of treatment are then needed to help the recovery process along. Judicious combinations of approaches can best meet the specific needs of each individual.

Researchers and clinicians have thus been taught an important lesson in this area of treatment and study: no matter how compelling the biological evidence, a strictly biological approach to psychological disorders is a mistake more often than not. Largely on the basis of biological discoveries and the promise of biological treatments, clinical administrators released hundreds of thousands of patients with schizophrenia and other severe mental disorders to the community in the 1960s. As deinstitutionalization proceeded, scant attention was paid to the psychological and sociocultural needs of these individuals, and many of them have been caught in the web of their pathology ever since. Clinicians must remember this lesson, especially in today's economic and political climate, when managed care and government priorities often promote medication as the sole treatment for psychological problems.

When Kraepelin first described schizophrenia at the turn of the century, he estimated that only 13 percent of its sufferers ever improved and that the improvements were usually temporary. Today, even with the current shortages and inadequacies of community programs, many more individuals with this disorder show improvement (Eaton et al., 1992; Ram et al., 1992). As many as 25 percent are believed to recover from schizophrenia completely and permanently. An equal number return to relatively independent lives, although their occupational and social functioning may continue to fall short of earlier levels. Of the remaining half, some are able to maintain a degree of employment, although they need considerable help in managing for themselves; others continue to require hospitalization or intense supervision for large segments of their lives (Sultenfuss & Geczy, 1996).

Certainly the clinical field has advanced considerably in the treatment of schizophrenia since Kraepelin's days, yet it still has far to go. It is intolerable that the majority of people with this disorder receive few or none of the effective community interventions that have been developed over the past three decades, worse still that tens of thousands have become homeless vagrants deserted by society. Although many factors have contributed to this state of affairs, neglect by clinical practitioners has certainly played a big role in it. It is now the mandate of these professionals, prodded by the newly developed interest groups and task forces, to address the needs of all people with schizophrenia.

Chapter Review

1. ***Overview of treatment*** For years all efforts to treat schizophrenia brought only frustration. The disorder is still difficult to treat, but today's therapies are more successful than those of the past.

2. ***Past institutional care*** For more than half of the twentieth century the main treatment for schizophrenia was institutionalization and custodial care. Because people with schizophrenia failed to respond to traditional therapies, they were usually placed in overcrowded public institutions, typically in back wards where the primary goal was to restrain them. Between 1845 and 1955 the number of state hospitals and mental patients rose steadily while the quality of care declined.

3. ***Improved institutional care*** The development of two in-hospital interventions, based on humanistic and behavioral principles—*milieu therapy* and the *token economy program*—was particularly helpful in addressing the personal-care and self-image problems brought about by schizophrenia and by institutionalization itself.

4. ***Antipsychotic drugs*** The discovery of *antipsychotic drugs,* or *neuroleptic drugs,* in the 1950s revolutionized the treatment of schizophrenia. Today they are almost always a part of treatment. Theorists believe that the drugs operate by reducing excessive *dopamine* activity in the brain. The traditional antipsychotic drugs reduce the positive symptoms of schizophrenia more completely, or more quickly, than the negative symptoms.

   A. ***Unwanted effects of antipsychotic drugs*** Unfortunately, traditional antipsychotic drugs can also produce dramatic unwanted effects, particularly *extrapyramidal effects,* movement abnormalities that affect appearance and functioning. These effects include *Parkinsonian and related symptoms, neuroleptic malignant syndrome,* and *tardive dyskinesia.* It is believed that tardive dyskinesia is developed by over 20 percent of the people who take traditional antipsychotic drugs for an extended time, particularly people over 45 years of age. Tardive dyskinesia can be difficult—at times impossible—to eliminate, even when traditional antipsychotic drugs are stopped.

   B. ***New antipsychotic drugs*** Some *atypical* antipsychotic drugs (such as *clozapine* and *risperidone*) seem to be more effective and to cause fewer or no extrapyramidal effects. These new drugs do, however, pose new difficulties and dangers of their own.

5. ***Psychotherapy*** Today psychotherapy is often employed successfully in conjunction with antipsychotic drugs. The most helpful forms include *insight therapy, family therapy,* and *social therapy. Family support groups* and *family psychoeducational programs* are also growing in number.

6. ***The community approach*** A community approach to the treatment of schizophrenia was developed when a policy of *deinstitutionalization* brought about a mass exodus of hundreds of thousands of patients with schizophrenia and other severe problems from state institutions into the community. The number of persons living in mental health settings has decreased from nearly 600,000 on any given day in 1955 to 80,000 today.

A. ***Effective community care*** Among the key elements of effective community care programs are coordination of patient services by a *community mental health center, short-term hospitalization* (followed by *aftercare*), *day centers, halfway houses,* and *occupational training.*

B. ***Inadequacies of community treatment*** Unfortunately, the quality of and funding for community care for persons with schizophrenia has been grossly inadequate throughout the United States, often resulting in a "revolving door" syndrome. Two factors are primarily responsible for this state of affairs: *poor coordination of services* and *shortage of services.* One result of the inadequacy of community treatment is that many people with schizophrenia have become homeless. Approximately one-third of the homeless people in the United States suffer from a severe mental disorder, commonly schizophrenia. Still others live in nursing homes or rest homes, many live in boarding houses or single-room-occupancy hotels, and many thousands live in prisons because their disorder has led them to break the law.

C. ***The promise of community treatment*** The success and potential of proper community care for persons recovering from schizophrenia continue to capture the interest of both clinicians and government officials. One major development has been the formation of *national interest groups* that are successfully promoting community treatment for people with severe mental disorders.

Thought and Afterthought

Just Because You're Paranoid . . .

The atypical antipsychotic drug *clozapine* (brand name Clozaril) has enormous potential as an effective treatment for schizophrenia, but its early use in the United States brought frustration and heartache to hundreds of thousands of prospective users.

The problem began with the discovery that a small percentage of people who take this drug develop *agranulocytosis*, a life-threatening drop in white blood cell count. The U.S. Food and Drug Administration (FDA) thus released clozapine with the proviso that patients who take it must have their blood tested every week for signs of agranulocytosis.

Unfortunately, the drug's manufacturer further required that all clozapine users in the United States had to purchase an entire treatment package consisting of the medication *and* weekly testing by the drug company's own subsidiaries. Most patients in the United States could not afford the company's fee for this combination—a whopping $9,000 a year. What's more, their insurance companies refused to pay for it. Clearly patients were caught in the middle between big business and the health industry.

A flurry of lawsuits followed. So did federal investigations and hearings. After several years the drug's manufacturer agreed to sell clozapine separately, allowing patients to get blood tests elsewhere at lower costs. It also agreed to rebate $10 million to clozapine users, plus another $11 million to mental health agencies and patients who could not afford treatment. Sadly, however, many patients had already lost valuable time.

Afterthoughts: Why have people with schizophrenia been the victims of mistreatment (e.g., lobotomy, deinstitutionalization) more often than those with other disorders? . . . Should companies in the private sector have so much control over the cost and distribution of a critical breakthrough drug, one that could improve millions of lives? . . . Clozapine was available in Europe fifteen years before its approval in the United States. Might the FDA be too cautious in its approach to new drugs?

Coming Full Circle

During the past three decades patients with schizophrenia have journeyed from mental hospitals, where they received poor care, to the community, where many receive no care at all. E. Fuller Torrey describes the ultimate irony in this tragic state of affairs:

> For three quarters of a century . . . part of Manhattan State Hospital [served] patients with severe mental illnesses. Then, as more and more beds became vacant in the 1970s, the building was no longer needed and it was turned over to the City of New York, which reopened it in 1981 as a public shelter [the Keener Shelter] for homeless men. . . .
>
> In 1990, the Keener Shelter housed 800 homeless men. At least 40 percent of them were mentally ill and many had previously been patients at Manhattan State Hospital. One man with schizophrenia has been living in the Keener Shelter for seven years, the same period of time he had previously been there when it had been a hospital. . . . [The difference is] the Keener Shelter is merely a shelter and cannot deliver the psychiatric care needed by many of its inhabitants. Nor is the Keener Shelter unique. . . . For many of these homeless, it is like returning home.
>
> (Torrey, 1997, pp. 23–24)

Afterthoughts: How might patients react when they find themselves back in the same place where they were confined years earlier, under totally different circumstances? . . . Might the Keener Shelter, which is run humanely and efficiently by the Volunteers of America, be more therapeutic than the old state hospitals? . . . How might homeless shelters compare to the town of Gheel in Belgium, where local residents once welcomed people with mental disorders to live in their community?

Topic Overview

Dissociative Disorders

Dissociative Amnesia

Dissociative Fugue

Dissociative Identity Disorder (Multiple Personality Disorder)

Organic Memory Disorders

Amnestic Disorders

Dementias

Crossroads

Chapter 17

Disorders of Memory and Other Cognitive Functions

The importance of memory and attention are illustrated in the self-portraits of the German artist Anton Räderscheidt, which followed a stroke that temporarily damaged his right parietal lobe. In a portrait drawn shortly after his stroke, the artist omitted half of his face (upper left). Within nine months, however, he had recovered his cognitive skills and was able to complete all the details in his painting (lower right).

As we interact with the world, we usually experience a sense of wholeness. We feel like much more than isolated sensory experiences, feelings, and behaviors. We have an *identity,* a sense of who we are—a unique person with particular preferences, abilities, characteristics, and needs. Others reconize our particularities, and they expect certain things of us. Even more important, we recognize ourselves and develop our own expectations, values, and goals. We have an awareness of ourselves, a consciousnesss, a sense of where we fit in our environment.

Memory is a key contributor to this sense of wholeness and identity. Our memory links our past, present, and future. The recollection of past experiences, although not always precisely accurate, helps us make sense of and react to events and guides us in making decisions about the future. We recognize our friends and relatives, teachers and employers, and respond to them in appropriate and consistent ways. Without a memory we would always be starting over; with it, life has progression and continuity. The Spanish filmmaker Luis Buñuel wrote, "Our memory is our coherence, our reason, our feeling, even our action. Without it, we are nothing."

People sometimes experience a significant disruption of their memory. They may not be able to remember new information they just learned or old information they once knew well. When the alterations in memory lack a clear physical cause, they are, by tradition, called *dissociative disorders.* When the physical causes are clear, the memory disorder is called *organic.* Some memory difficulties reflect both psychological and organic causes.

Dissociative Disorders

People with ***dissociative disorders*** experience significant alterations in memory without a clear physical cause. Typically, one part of the person's memory is dissociated, or separated, from another. There are several different kinds of dissociative disorders. The principal symptom of *dissociative amnesia* is an inability to recall important personal events and information. A person with *dissociative fugue* not only forgets the past but travels to a new location and may assume a new identity. Individuals with *multiple personality disorder (dissociative identity disorder)* have two or more distinct identities that may not always recall each other's thoughts, feelings, and behavior.

Several memorable books and movies have dealt with these dissociative disorders. Two of the best known are *The Three Faces of Eve* and *Sybil,* each about women with multiple personalities. The topic is so intriguing that the majority of television drama series seem to include at least one case of dissociative functioning each season, creating the impression that the disorders are very common. Many clinicians, however, believe that they are quite rare.

Adults often forget or have distorted memories of events from early childhood. Factors such as the passage of time and intervening events play key roles in this loss of memory. Such lapses are, however, normal and universal, and do not reflect dissociative disorders—syndromes marked by significant and unusual alterations in memory.

DSM-IV also lists ***depersonalization disorder,*** persistent feelings of being detached from one's own mental processes or body, as a dissociative disorder. People with this disorder feel as though they are observing themselves from outside. Because memory impairment is not the central feature of this disorder, we shall not discuss it here.

Dissociative Amnesia

People with ***dissociative amnesia*** are suddenly unable to recall important information about their lives, usually of a traumatic or stressful nature (APA, 1994). The loss of memory is much more extensive than normal forgetting and cannot be attributed to an organic disorder. Very often the episode of amnesia is directly precipitated by a specific upsetting event (Classen, Koopman, & Spiegel, 1993).

> Brian was spending the day sailing with his wife, Helen. The water was rough but well within what they considered safe limits. They were having a wonderful time and really didn't notice that the sky was getting darker, the wind blowing harder, and the sailboat becoming more difficult to control. After a few hours of sailing, they found themselves far from shore in the middle of a powerful and dangerous storm.
>
> The storm intensified very quickly. Brian had trouble controlling the sailboat amidst the high winds and wild waves. He and Helen tried to put on the safety jackets they had neglected to wear earlier, but the boat turned over before they were finished. Brian, the better swimmer of the two, was able to swim back to the overturned sailboat, grab the side, and hold on for dear life, but Helen simply could not overcome the rough waves and reach the boat. As Brian watched in horror and disbelief, his wife disappeared from view.
>
> After a time, the storm began to lose its strength. Brian managed to restore the sailboat to its proper position and sail back to shore. Finally he reached safety, but the personal consequences of this storm were just beginning. The next days were filled with pain and further horror: the Coast Guard finding Helen's body . . . discussions with authorities . . . breaking the news to Helen's parents . . . funeral plans . . . the funeral itself . . . conversations with friends . . . self-blame . . . grief . . . and more—the start of a nightmare that wouldn't end.

Dissociative amnesia may be *localized, selective, generalized,* or *continuous.* Any of these kinds of amnesia can be triggered by a traumatic experience such as Brian's, but each represents a distinct pattern of forgetting.

Imagine that Brian awakened on the day after the funeral and could not recall any of the events of the past difficult days, beginning with the boating tragedy. He remembered everything that occurred before the accident. He could even recall everything from the morning after the funeral forward, but the intervening days remained a total blank. In this case, Brian would be suffering from ***localized,*** or ***circumscribed, amnesia,*** the most common type of dissociative amnesia. Here a person forgets only a limited period of time, beginning almost always with something very disturbing.

People with ***selective amnesia,*** the second most common form of dissociative amnesia, remember some, but not all, events during a circumscribed period of time. In this case, Brian might remember his conversations with friends and breaking the news to his in-laws, for example, but have no recollection of the funeral.

The forgotten or partially forgotten period is called the ***amnestic episode.*** During an amnestic episode, people sometimes act puzzled and confused, and they may even wander about aimlessly. They are already experiencing memory difficulties, but only when they try to recall the events of the amnestic episode are they aware of their memory disturbance.

In some cases the forgetting extends back for some time before the traumatic period. Brian might awaken after the funeral and find that, in addition to the preceding few days, he could not remember other events in his past life. In this case, he would be experiencing ***generalized amnesia.*** In extreme cases, Brian might not even remember who he was and fail to recognize relatives and friends.

In the forms of dissociative amnesia discussed so far, the period affected by the amnesia has an end. In ***continuous amnesia,*** however, forgetting continues into the present. Brian might forget new and ongoing experiences as well as what happened before the tragedy. He would be caught in a prolonged amnestic episode. Continuous forgetting of this kind is actually quite rare in cases of dissociative amnesia, but, as we shall see, not in cases of organic amnesia.

All of these forms of dissociative amnesia are similar in that the amnesia disrupts ***episodic memory*** primarily—a person's autobiographical memory of personal experiences and other highly personal material. ***Semantic memory***—memory for abstract, encyclopedic, or categorical information—remains largely intact. People with dissociative amnesia are as likely as anyone else to know the name of the president of the United States and how to write, read, drive a car, and so on.

Many cases of dissociative amnesia originate during significant threats to health and safety, as in wartime and natural disasters (APA, 1994; Kihlström et al., 1993). Combat veterans often report memory gaps of hours or days, and some forget personal information, such as their name and address (Bremner et al., 1993). In fact, at least 5 percent of all mental disorders that emerge during military combat are cases of dissociative amnesia. Close to half of these combat amnesia cases arise in soldiers who have endured enemy fire; soldiers whose experience has been confined to base camp make up only 6 percent of the cases (Sargent & Slater, 1941). Recently many cases of dissociative amnesia linked to child sexual abuse have also been reported (see Box 17-1).

Dissociative amnesia may also arise under more ordinary circumstances. The sudden loss of a loved one through rejection, abandonment, or death can lead to it (Spiegel, 1994; Loewenstein, 1991). So can guilt over behavior that a person considers immoral or sinful (such as an extramarital affair).

The personal impact of dissociative amnesia depends on what is forgotten. Obviously, an amnestic episode of two years is more disabling than one of two hours. Similarly, an amnestic episode during which a person undergoes major life changes causes more difficulties than one that is largely uneventful.

Dissociative Fugue

People with a ***dissociative fugue*** not only forget their personal identity and at least some details of their past life, but also flee to an entirely different location. Some establish a new identity (APA, 1994). The term "fugue" comes from the Latin for "flee."

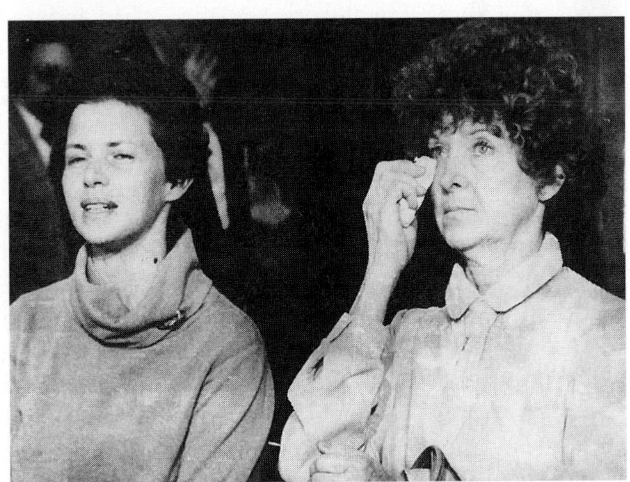

In 1980 a Florida park ranger found a woman naked and starving in a shallow grave. Unaware of her identity and in an apparent fugue state, she was hospitalized as "Jane Doe." Five months later, the woman was recognized on Good Morning, America *by Irene Tomiczek (right) as her 34-year-old daughter, Cheryl Ann, who had been missing for seven years. With the help of sodium amobarbital treatment and reunion with her family, Cheryl Ann's fugue at last began to lift.*

BOX 17-1 Repressed Childhood Memories or False Memory Syndrome?

In recent years, reports of ***repressed childhood memory of abuse*** have attracted enormous public attention. Adults with this type of dissociative amnesia seem to recover buried memories of sexual and physical abuse from their childhood.

A woman may claim, for example, that her father sexually molested her repeatedly between the ages of 5 and 7. Or a young man may remember that a family friend made sexual advances to him on several occasions when he was very young. Often the repressed memories begin to surface during a course of therapy, perhaps for an eating disorder or depression (Gudjonsson, 1997). The traumatic events that have been repressed are seen as partly responsible for the current disorder.

The recollections of traumatic events can be vivid and deeply felt. Many cases revolve around a single event. Others involve repeated abuse over several years. Some individuals have even reported memories of bloody satanic rituals that included forced sexual encounters and human sacrifices (Goodyear-Smith, Laidlaw, & Large, 1997; Loftus, 1997).

Many people who recall childhood sexual traumas confront their abusers. Some have brought criminal or civil charges (Pope & Brown, 1996), and hundreds of such cases are in the courts. Nineteen states have revised their laws to extend the statute of limitations on cases of this kind (Horn, 1993). The willingness of state legislatures and courtroom juries to decide in favor of the apparent victims indicates a growing acceptance of the ideas of repressed and recovered memories.

Society has become deeply divided on this issue (Schooler, 1996, 1994). Some people believe that recovered memories are just what they appear to be—horrific memories of abuse that have been buried in the deep recesses of a person's mind, to resurface only years later, in a more benign climate. Others believe that the memories are in fact damaging illusions—images and stories falsely constructed or embraced by confused and suggestible persons.

An organization called the False Memory Syndrome Foundation has been founded to assist people who claim to be falsely charged with abuse. Such counterclaims have themselves been gaining status in the courts. Recently, for example, a 23-year-old woman publicly accused her father of having sexually abused her when she was a child. He brought suit against her therapists, claiming that their treatment techniques had induced false memories and destroyed his reputation, his job, his marriage, and his family. He won the suit and was awarded a large financial judgment.

The clinical community is just as deeply divided on this issue (Barasch, 1996; Pope & Brown, 1996; Toglia, 1996). At least 200,000 to 300,000 children in the United States are victims of sexual abuse each year (Horn, 1993; AAPC, 1992). Few experiences bring more horror or shame, are kept more private, or have a more lingering impact (Nash et al., 1993; Briere, 1992). These experiences, proponents of the repressed memory position point out, make victims prime candidates for dissociative amnesia. Some studies even suggest that 18 to 59 percent of sexual abuse victims may have difficulty recalling at least some details of their traumas (Horn, 1993). Some children, proponents argue, may well repress their painful traumas altogether until therapy or life events trigger their memories.

Proponents also point out that hidden memory has been at the center of psychodynamic explanations and treatments for years, as the defense mechanism called *repression.* Moreover, DSM-IV formally acknowledges dissociative amnesia.

Other clinicians reject the idea of repressed memories. They agree that child sexual abuse is an enormous problem, but, they maintain, most victims remember it all too well. Systematic research has found few cases in which the events are completely wiped from memory (APA, 1996). A study that observed teenagers who had been sexually abused found no evidence of repression over a ten-year period (Loftus, 1993).

Opponents also note that many memories of childhood are illusory. Even memories of events that happen to us as adults are fallible. Eyewitness accounts of crimes, for example, often change over time and can be influenced by other people's suggestions (Loftus, 1993). Even when an event is as dramatic as the explosion of the space shuttle *Challenger,* people give inaccurate accounts of where they were at the time or who told them about it. Moreover, they seem certain of their recollections. In short, the opponents argue, the public's ready acceptance of so-called recovered memories is probably unwarranted.

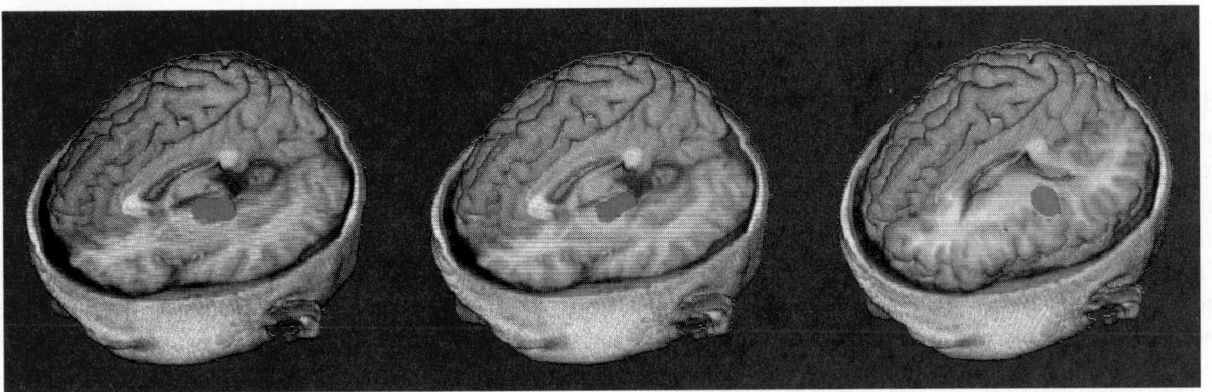

A recent study suggests that false memories may produce activity in some of the same areas of the brain as real memories, except for the area involved in sensory recall (Schacter et al., 1996). According to PET scans, activity in the medial temporal lobe increases whether subjects accurately remember words from a previously heard list (left) or inaccurately attribute other words to the list (center). However, only the accurately remembered words increase activity in the temporal parietal region (right) where sounds and speech are processed. Apparently, words must truly have been heard in order for this sensory area of the brain to be activated during recall. Such studies have focused on very short-term memory, however, and may have no implications for the long-term memories of concern to clinicians.

Actually, Freud himself disagreed with the interpretations now being made by proponents of repressed memories. True, he did at first believe that many of his patients had been sexually abused as children. He wrote in 1893 that their repressed memories had caused them to develop psychological problems. Over the next four years, however, Freud changed his mind. He came to believe that treatment was actually bringing to light repressed *fantasies* and *desires* rather than true recollections. The motives behind Freud's theoretical shift have been hotly debated, but the fact remains that his views can hardly be cited to support a belief in repressed childhood memories.

If the recovery of childhood memories is not what it appears to be, what is it? According to the opponents, a powerful case of suggestibility (Loftus, 1997). They hold that all the clinical and public attention has led some therapists to accept the diagnosis without evidence (Frankel, 1993). The therapists may actively seek indicators of early sexual abuse with some clients. They may even encourage clients to find repressed memories (Ganaway, 1989). Many use special *memory recovery techniques,* including hypnosis, journal writing, dream interpretation, and the interpretation of bodily symptoms (Lindsay, 1996, 1994; Lindsay & Read, 1994). It may be that clients oblige by unwittingly forming illusory memories of abuse.

Other factors in the therapy interaction too may further contribute to the creation of false memories: suggestions by a respected authority figure, long delays between the purported events and the surfacing of the memory, the plausibility of the events, and repetitive therapy discussions of the alleged abuse (Loftus, Hashtroudi, & Lindsay, 1993; Belli et al., 1992). In short, recovered memories may actually be *iatrogenic*—unintentionally caused by the therapist.

Of course, repressed memories of child sexual abuse do not surface only in clinical settings. Many individuals come forward on their own. They report flashbacks of sexual abuse and only then seek therapy. Such self-revelations are on the increase. Some clinical theorists point to all the popular books, articles, and television shows that take a strong stand in support of recovery of repressed memories (Loftus, 1993). Several books offer readers criteria for diagnosing the repression of memories of sexual abuse. Often the lists include symptoms that are actually rather common—not clinical symptoms at all, or symptoms that have not been reliably correlated with sexual abuse (Tavris, 1993). Nevertheless, readers who meet a number of these criteria may begin a search for repressed memories.

Of course, the heated debate over repressed childhood memories does not in any way diminish the enormity of the problem of child sexual abuse (APA, 1996; Pope & Brown, 1996). In fact, proponents and opponents alike are greatly concerned that the public may take this controversy to mean that clinicians have doubts about the scope of the problem of child sexual abuse. In a controversy filled with the potential for sad outcomes, that would be the most unfortunate result of all.

Some individuals travel only a short distance, their new identity is not a complete one, and they have few social contacts (APA, 1994). Their fugue is brief—a matter of hours or days—and ends suddenly. In other cases, however, the person may travel far from home, adopt a new name, establish a new identity, engage in complex social interactions, and even pursue a new line of work. The new identity may include personal characteristics never displayed before—usually more outgoing and less inhibited (APA, 1994). Some people have been known to travel to foreign countries thousands of miles away. This kind of fugue is seen in the case of the Reverend Ansel Bourne, described by the famous psychologist William James at the turn of the century:

> On January 17, 1887, [the Reverend Ansel Bourne, of Greene, R.I.] drew 551 dollars from a bank in Providence with which to pay for a certain lot of land in Greene, paid certain bills, and got into a Pawtucket horsecar. This is the last incident which he remembers. He did not return home that day, and nothing was heard of him for two months. He was published in the papers as missing, and foul play being suspected, the police sought in vain his whereabouts. On the morning of March 14th, however, at Norristown, Pennsylvania, a man calling himself A. I. Brown who had rented a small shop six weeks previously, stocked it with stationery, confectionery, fruit and small articles, and carried on his quiet trade without seeming to any one unnatural or eccentric, woke up in a fright and called in the people of the house to tell him where he was. He said that his name was Ansel Bourne, that he was entirely ignorant of Norristown, that he knew nothing of shopkeeping, and that the last thing he remembered—it seemed only yesterday—was drawing the money from the bank, etc. in Providence. . . . He was very weak, having lost apparently over twenty pounds of flesh during his escapade, and had such a horror of the idea of the candy-store that he refused to set foot in it again.
>
> The first two weeks of the period remained unaccounted for, as he had no memory, after he had once resumed his normal personality, of any part of the time, and no one who knew him seems to have seen him after he left home. The remarkable part of the change is, of course, the peculiar occupation which the so-called Brown indulged in. Mr. Bourne has never in his life had the slightest contact with trade. "Brown" was described by the neighbors as taciturn, orderly in his habits, and in no way queer. He went to Philadelphia several times; replenished his stock; cooked for himself in the back shop, where he also slept; went regularly to church; and once at a prayer-meeting made what was considered by the hearers a good address, in the course of which he related an incident which he had witnessed in his natural state of Bourne.
>
> *(James, 1890, pp. 391–393)*

Approximately 0.2 percent of the population experiences dissociative fugue. Like dissociative amnesia, a fugue usually follows a severely stressful event, such as a wartime experience or a natural disaster, though personal stress, such as financial or legal difficulties or episodes of depression, may also trigger it (APA, 1994; Kihlström et al., 1993). Some clinicians suspect that some adolescent runaways are in a state of fugue (Loewenstein, 1991). As in dissociative amnesia, primarily episodic memories from the past are impaired in fugues, while semantic knowledge remains intact (Kihlström et al., 1993).

Fugues tend to end abruptly. In some cases, as with the Reverend Mr. Bourne, the person "awakens" in an unfamiliar place, surrounded by strangers, and wonders how he or she got there. In other cases the lack of personal history may arouse curiosity or suspicion. Perhaps a traffic accident or legal difficulty leads police to discover the false identity, or friends search for and find the missing person (Kihlstrom et al., 1993). When people with this disorder are found, it may be necessary to ask them extensive questions about the details of their lives, repeatedly remind them who they are, and even begin psychotherapy before they recover their memories.

Most people who experience dissociative fugue regain most or all of their memories and never have a recurrence. Interestingly, though, as they recover their past, many of them forget the events of the fugue period (APA, 1994). Since fugues are usually brief and totally reversible, impairment and aftereffects are usually minimal (Keller & Shaywitz, 1986). People who have been away for months or years, however, often do have trouble adjusting to family, social, or occupational changes that have occurred during their flight. Moreover, some people commit illegal or violent acts in their fugue state and later must face the consequences.

Multiple Personality Disorder (Dissociative Identity Disorder)

Multiple personality disorder is as dramatic as it is disabling, as we see in the case of Eric:

> Dazed and bruised from a beating, Eric, 29, was discovered wandering around a Daytona Beach shopping mall on Feb. 9. He had no ID and acted so oddly that ambulance workers, who took him to a nearby hospital, assumed he was retarded. Transferred six weeks later to Daytona Beach's Human Resources Center, Eric began talking to doctors in two voices: the infantile rhythms of "young Eric," a dim and frightened child, and the measured tones of "older Eric," who told a tale of terror and child abuse. According to "older Eric," after his immigrant German parents died, a harsh stepfather and

> his mistress took Eric from his native South Carolina to a drug dealers' hideout in a Florida swamp. Eric said he was raped by several gang members and watched his stepfather murder two men.
>
> One day in late March an alarmed counselor watched Eric's face twist into a violent snarl. Eric let loose an unearthly growl and spat out a stream of obscenities. "It sounded like something out of *The Exorcist*," says Malcolm Graham, the psychologist who directs the case at the center. "It was the most intense thing I've ever seen in a patient." That disclosure of a new personality, who insolently demanded to be called Mark, was the first indication that Graham had been dealing with a rare and serious emotional disorder: true multiple personality. . . .
>
> Eric's other manifestations emerged over the next weeks: quiet, middle-aged Dwight; the hysterically blind and mute Jeffrey; Michael, an arrogant jock; the coquettish Tian, whom Eric considered a whore; and argumentative Phillip, the lawyer. "Phillip was always asking about Eric's rights," says Graham. "He was kind of obnoxious. Actually, Phillip was a pain."
>
> To Graham's astonishment, Eric gradually unfurled 27 different personalities, including three females. . . . They ranged in age from a fetus to a sordid old man who kept trying to persuade Eric to fight as a mercenary in Haiti. In one therapy session, reports Graham, Eric shifted personality nine times in an hour. "I felt I was losing control of the sessions," says the psychologist, who has eleven years of clinical experience. "Some personalities would not talk to me, and some of them were very insightful into my behavior as well as Eric's."
>
> (Time, *October 25, 1982, p. 70*)

Chris Sizemore, the subject of the book and film The Three Faces of Eve, *is now an accomplished author, artist, and mental health spokesperson who no longer manifests a multiple personality disorder. The variety of her portraits reflects the many subpersonalities Sizemore previously displayed.*

A person with ***multiple personality disorder*** displays two or more distinct personalities, often called ***subpersonalities,*** each with a unique set of memories, behaviors, thoughts, and emotions. At any given time, one of the subpersonalities dominates the person's consciousness and interactions with the environment. Usually one subpersonality, the ***primary,*** or ***host, personality,*** appears more often than the others.

The transition from one subpersonality to another, often called *switching,* is usually sudden (APA, 1994; Dell & Eisenhower, 1990). Eric, for example, twisted his face, growled, and yelled obscenities while changing personalities. Transitions are usually precipitated by a stressful event (APA, 1994), although hypnotic suggestion can also bring about the change (Smith, 1993; Brende & Rinsley, 1981).

Cases of multiple personality were first reported almost four centuries ago (Bliss, 1985, 1980). Most clinicians consider the disorder to be rare, but recent reports suggest that it may be more common than it was once thought to be (APA, 1994; Kluft, 1991). Most cases are first diagnosed in late adolescence or young adulthood, but the symptoms usually begin to develop in early childhood after episodes of abuse, typically before the age of 5 (Ross et al., 1991; Sachs, 1986). Indeed, studies suggest that as many as 97 percent of these patients have been physically, often sexually, abused during their early years (Ross et al., 1991, 1990, 1989; Dell & Eisenhower, 1990). The disorder is diagnosed in women at least three times as often as it is in men (APA, 1994). In some cases, the parents of people with multiple personality disorder appear to have themselves displayed some kind of dissociative disorder (Dell & Eisenhower, 1990; Ross et al., 1989).

The Subpersonalities

How subpersonalities relate to or recall one another varies from case to case. Generally, however, there are three kinds of relationships: mutually amnesic, mutually cognizant, and, most common of all, one-way amnesic.

In ***mutually amnesic*** relationships, the subpersonalities have no awareness of one another (Ellenberger, 1970). Conversely, in ***mutually cognizant*** patterns, each subpersonality is well aware of the rest. They may hear one another's voices and even talk among themselves. Some are on good terms, relating as friends would do and sharing opinions and goals. Others do not get along at all. Eric's subpersonalities were mutually cognizant:

> Most of the personalities interacted. Cye, a religious mystic, once left a comforting note for Eric. The pushy Michael, who loved rock music, hated Eric's classical records so much that he yanked the wires from a stereo. Eric defended the menacing Mark: "Mark never hurt anybody," he said one day. "He is just there to scare other people off when they get too close." Eric referred

> to his troupe of personalities as his "talking books." One of the characters was a librarian named Max who occasionally announced a sudden personality change by saying, "One of the books just fell off the shelf."
>
> (Time, *October 25, 1982, p. 70*)

Other patterns fall between these two extremes. In the ***one-way amnesic*** relationship, some subpersonalities are aware of others, but the awareness is not reciprocated. Those that are aware are called ***co-conscious subpersonalities.*** They are "quiet observers" who watch the actions and thoughts of the other subpersonalities but do not interact with them. Sometimes, while another subpersonality is dominating consciousness, they make themselves known through such indirect means as auditory hallucinations (for example, a voice giving commands) or "automatic writing" (the present personality finds itself writing down words over which it experiences no control).

A one-way amnesic relationship was at work in the case of Miss Christine Beauchamp, one of the earliest reported and most famous examples of multiple personality (Prince, 1906). In therapy, this woman initially manifested three subpersonalities. Her therapist labeled them the Saint (a religious, even-tempered subpersonality), the Woman (irreligious and bad-tempered), and the Devil (mischievous and cheerful). The Saint, Miss Beauchamp's primary personality, knew nothing of the Woman or the Devil. The Woman knew of the Saint but not of the Devil. The Devil knew of both the Saint and the Woman but in different ways: she had direct access to the Saint's thoughts, but her knowledge of the Woman was based solely on her observations of the Woman's behavior.

Investigators used to believe that cases of multiple personality disorder usually involved two or three subpersonalities. Studies now suggest, however, that the average number of subpersonalities per patient is much higher—fifteen for women and eight for men (APA, 1994; Ross et al., 1989). In fact, there have been cases in which 100 or more subpersonalities were observed (APA, 1994). Often the subpersonalities emerge in groups of two or three at a time.

In the case of "Eve White," made famous in the book and movie *The Three Faces of Eve,* a woman had three personalities—Eve White, Eve Black, and Jane (Thigpen & Cleckley, 1957). Eve White, the primary personality, was colorless, quiet, and serious; Eve Black was carefree, mischievous, and uninhibited; and Jane was mature and intelligent. According to the book, these three subpersonalities eventually merged into Evelyn, a stable and enduring personality who represented an integration of the other three.

The book was wrong, however: this was not to be the end of Eve's dissociation. In an autobiography twenty years later, she revealed that altogether twenty-two subpersonalities had emerged by the mid-1970s, including nine subpersonalities after Evelyn. Usually they emerged in groups of three, each group displaying a range of characteristics, abilities, and tastes. Because the authors of *The Three Faces of Eve* had worked with her during the ascendancy of one such group, they apparently never knew about her previous and subsequent subpersonalities. She has now overcome her disorder, has achieved a single, stable identity, and has been known as Chris Sizemore for over twenty years (Sizemore & Huber, 1988).

As in Chris Sizemore's case, subpersonalities often differ dramatically in their respective personalities. They may also have their own names and differ in *vital statistics, abilities and preferences,* and even *physiological responses* (Alpher, 1992; Dell & Eisenhower, 1990).

Vital Statistics The subpersonalities may differ in features as basic as age, sex, race, and family history (Coons, Bowman, & Milstein, 1988), as in the famous case of Sybil Dorsett. Sybil's multiple personality disorder has been described in fictional form (in the novel *Sybil*), but both the therapist and the patient have attested to its accuracy (Borch-Jacobsen, 1997; Schreiber, 1973). Sybil manifested seventeen subpersonalities, all with different identifying features. They included adults, a teenager, and a baby named Ruthie; two were male, named Mike and Sid.

Sybil's subpersonalities had distinct physical images of themselves and of each other. The subpersonality named Vicky, for example, saw herself as an attractive blonde, while another, Peggy Lou, was described as a pixie with a pug nose. Mary was plump with dark hair, and Vanessa was a tall redhead with a willowy figure. Mike's olive skin and brown eyes stood in contrast to Sid's fair skin and blue eyes.

Abilities and Preferences Although semantic memory is not affected by dissociative amnesia or fugue, it can often be disrupted by multiple personality disorder. It is not uncommon for the different subpersonalities to have different abilities: one may be able to drive, speak a foreign language, or play a musical instrument, while the others cannot (Coons et al., 1988). Their handwriting can also differ (Coons, 1980). In addition, the subpersonalities usually have different tastes in food, friends, music, and literature, as in Sybil's case.

> Among outsiders Vanessa claimed to like everybody who wasn't a hypocrite. Peggy Lou vented her spleen against what she called "showoffs like Sybil's mother." Vicky favored intelligent and sophisticated persons. Both Mary and Sybil had a special fondness for children. Mary, indicating oneness rather than autonomy, remarked about a woman they all knew, "None of us liked her."
>
> Excited by conversations about music, Peggy Lou often shut her ears in the course of other conversations.

> Bored by female conversation in general, Mike and Sid sometimes succeeded in making Sybil break an engagement or nagged throughout the visit.
>
> . . . Marjorie told Dr. Wilbur, "I go with Sybil when she visits her friends, but they talk about things they like and I don't care about—houses, furniture, babies. But when Laura Hotchkins comes, they talk about concerts, and I like that."
>
> *(Schreiber, 1973, p. 288)*

Chris Sizemore ("Eve") displayed such differences in abilities and preferences. She later pointed out, "If I had learned to sew as one personality and then tried to sew as another, I couldn't do it. Driving a car was the same. Some of my personalities couldn't drive" (1975, p. 4).

Physiological Responses Researchers have discovered that subpersonalities may also display physiological differences, as in autonomic nervous system activity, blood pressure levels, and menstrual cycles (Putnam, Zahn, & Post, 1990). One study investigated the brain activities of different subpersonalities by measuring their ***evoked potentials***—that is, the brain response patterns recorded on an electroencephalograph under varying conditions, such as while subjects observe a flashing light (Putnam, 1984). The brain pattern in response to a specific stimulus is usually stable and unique to a given individual. However, when an evoked potential test was administered to four subpersonalities of each of ten people with multiple personality disorder, the results were dramatic. The brain activity patterns of the subpersonalities differed greatly within each individual. They showed the kinds of variations usually found in totally different people.

The evoked potential study also used control subjects who *pretended* to have different subpersonalities. They were instructed to create and rehearse their alternate personalities in detail. The brain-reaction patterns of the control subjects' simulated subpersonalities did not vary. This finding suggests that simple faking cannot bring about the variations in brain reaction patterns found in cases of multiple personality.

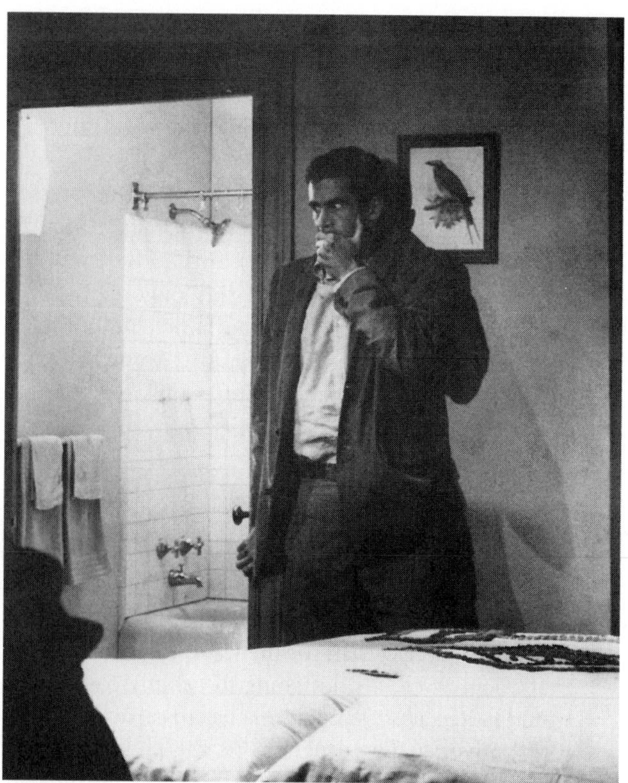

One of the cinema's best-known fictional sufferers of multiple personality disorder, Norman Bates, is horrified to discover his mother has stabbed a woman to death in the shower. Later in the movie Psycho *we learn that his mother died years ago and now "exists" as one of Bates's subpersonalities.*

The Prevalence of Multiple Personality Disorder As we noted earlier, multiple personality has traditionally been thought of as a rare disorder. Some researchers even argue that many or all cases are ***iatrogenic***—that is, unintentionally caused by practitioners. They believe that therapists create this disorder by subtly suggesting the existence of alternate personalities during therapy or by eliciting the personalities while patients are under hypnosis. In addition, they believe, a therapist who is looking for multiple personalities may reinforce these patterns by becoming more interested when the patient displays symptoms of dissociation (Frick, 1995; Merskey, 1995, 1992; Fahy, 1988).

These arguments seem to be supported by the fact that many cases do initially come to attention while a client is already being treated for a less serious problem (Allison, 1978). But not always: many other people seek treatment only after they have experienced losses of time throughout their lives or after relatives and friends have observed subpersonalities (Schacter, 1989; Putnam, 1988, 1985).

The number of people diagnosed with multiple personality disorder has been increasing. By 1970 only 100 cases had ever been reported in professional journals. By 1990, thousands of cases had been identified in the United States and Canada alone (Merskey, 1995; Ross et al., 1989; Kluft, 1987). Although the disorder is still relatively rare, its prevalence appears to be on the rise.

What accounts for this increase in the number of cases reported? At least two factors seem to be involved. First, belief in the authenticity of this disorder is growing, and willingness to diagnose it has increased accordingly (French, 1987). A second factor may be greater precision in diagnostic criteria. As we saw in Chapter 15, from 1910 to 1978 schizophrenia was one of the most popular clinical diagnoses (Rosenbaum, 1980). It was readily applied to a wide range of unusual and mysterious patterns of abnormality, perhaps including multiple

personality disorder. Under the stricter criteria of recent editions of the DSM, diagnosticians have applied the label of schizophrenia with greater accuracy, allowing more cases of multiple personality disorder to be recognized and assessed (Spiegel, 1994; Coons & Fine, 1990; French, 1987). In addition, several diagnostic scales and tests have been developed to help distinguish multiple personality disorder (Steinberg & Hall, 1997; Mann, 1995; Allen & Smith, 1993).

Despite such changes in professional perceptions, diagnostic practices, and assessment tools, many clinicians are still reluctant to make this diagnosis (McMinn & Wade, 1995; Saxe et al., 1993; McElroy, 1992). In fact, people suffering from this disorder still receive an average of four different diagnoses, such as schizophrenia or depression, and average nearly seven years of contact with health service providers before a diagnosis of multiple personality disorder is finally made (Putnam et al., 1986).

Psychodynamic theorists propose that people with dissociative disorders, like the individual in this cartoon, want and unconsciously seek to escape from their life situations and from themselves. Behaviorists believe that psychological escapes such as forgetting are happened upon accidentally, then are reinforced by bringing about a reduction in anxiety.

Explanations of Dissociative Disorders

Relatively few researchers have investigated the origins of the dissociative disorders, although a variety of theories have been offered to explain them. Proponents of the older perspectives especially, such as the psychodynamic and behavioral viewpoints, have gathered few systematic data. However, newer theories, which combine cognitive, behavioral, and biological principles and highlight such factors as state-dependent learning and self-hypnosis, have begun to capture the enthusiasm of clinical scientists (Doan & Bryson, 1994).

The Psychodynamic View Psychodynamic theorists believe that dissociative disorders represent extreme *repression,* the most fundamental defense mechanism: people ward off anxiety by unconsciously preventing painful memories, thoughts, or impulses from reaching awareness. Everyone uses repression to a degree, but people with dissociative disorders are thought to repress their memories excessively and dysfunctionally (Terr, 1988).

In the psychodynamic view, dissociative amnesia and fugue are single episodes of massive repression. In each, a person unconsciously blocks the memory of an extremely upsetting event to avoid the pain of confronting it (Noll & Turkington, 1994; Putnam, 1985). This reaction has its roots in childhood. When parents overreact to a child's expressions of id impulses (for example, to signs of sexual impulses), some children become excessively afraid of those impulses, defend against them, and develop a strict code prohibiting such "immoral" desires. Later in their lives, when they act in a manner that violates their moral code—by having an extramarital affair, for example—they are brought face to face with their most unacceptable impulses. They may be forced to repress the whole situation as the only means of protecting themselves from overwhelming anxiety.

If amnesia and fugue conceal a single repressed event, multiple personality disorder bespeaks a lifetime of excessive repression (Reis, 1993). Psychodynamic theorists believe that dependence on this ongoing style of coping is triggered by extremely traumatic childhood experiences, particularly abusive parenting. Young Sybil, for example, was repeatedly made to suffer unspeakable tortures by her disturbed mother, Hattie:

> A favorite ritual . . . was to separate Sybil's legs with a long wooden spoon, tie her feet to the spoon with dish towels, and then string her to the end of a light bulb cord, suspended from the ceiling. The child was left to swing in space while the mother proceeded to the water faucet to wait for the water to get cold. After muttering, "Well, it's not going to get any colder," she would fill the adult-sized enema bag to capacity and return with it to her daughter. As the child swung in space, the mother would insert the enema tip into the child's urethra and fill the bladder with cold water. "I did it," Hattie would scream triumphantly when her mission was accomplished. "I did it." The scream was followed by laughter, which went on and on.
>
> *(Schreiber, 1973, p. 160)*

According to psychodynamic theorists, children who are exposed to such traumas and abuses may come to fear the dangerous world they live in and take to flight symbolically by regularly pretending to be another person who is safely looking on from afar. This flight is much more desperate and pathological than the flights of fantasy and daydreaming that all people engage in on occasion. Sybil's psychotherapist concluded, "She had sought rescue from without until, finally recognizing that this rescue would be denied, she resorted to finding rescue from within. . . . Being a multiple personality was the ultimate rescue" (Schreiber, 1973, p. 158).

Abused children may also become afraid of the impulses that they believe are leading to their excessive punishments. They may strive to be "good" and "proper" all of the time and keep repressing the impulses they consider "bad" and "dangerous." Whenever "bad" thoughts or impulses do break through, such children may feel bound to disown and deny them, and may unconsciously assign all unacceptable thoughts, impulses, and emotions to other personalities. This situation would lead to an inhibited and drab primary personality that is accompanied by bold and colorful subpersonalities.

Most of the support for the psychodynamic position is drawn from case histories. They report such brutal childhood experiences as beatings, cuttings, burnings with cigarettes, imprisonment in closets, rape, and extensive verbal abuse. Yet the backgrounds of some individuals with multiple personality disorder do not seem to be markedly deviant (Bliss, 1980). Moreover, child abuse appears to be far more prevalent than multiple personality disorder. Why, then, do only a small fraction of abused children develop this form of dysfunctioning?

The Behavioral View Behaviorists believe that dissociation is a response acquired through *operant conditioning.* People who experience a horrifying event may later find temporary relief when their minds drift to other subjects. For some, this momentary forgetting, leading to a reduction in anxiety, increases the likelihood of future forgetting. In short, they are reinforced for the act of forgetting and learn—without being aware that they are learning—that forgetting lets them avoid or escape anxiety.

The behavioral explanation of dissociative disorders shares several features with the psychodynamic view. Both hold that dissociative disorders are precipitated by traumatic experiences, that the disorders represent ways of avoiding extreme anxiety, and that the individuals themselves are unaware that their disorder is actually protecting them from facing a painful reality. The explanations do, however, differ in some important ways. Psychodynamic theorists believe that the disorders represent attempts at forgetting that, although unconscious, are purposeful from the start, whereas behaviorists believe the initial development of dissociative reactions to be more accidental. Furthermore, behaviorists believe that a subtle reinforcement process rather than a hardworking unconscious is keeping the individual unaware that he or she is using dissociation as a means of escape.

Like proponents of the psychodynamic explanation, behaviorists have been forced to rely largely on case histories to support their position. While case descriptions do often support the behavioral view, they are equally consistent with other kinds of explanations as well, offering no evidence that one explanation is superior to the other. A case that seems to reflect the reinforcement of forgetting, for example, can usually also be interpreted as an instance of unconscious repression.

In addition, the behavioral explanation fails to explain precisely how temporary distractions from painful memories grow into acquired responses or why more people do not develop dissociative disorders. Nor has it yet described how reinforcement can account for the complicated interrelationships of subpersonalities found in multiple personality disorder. Two other theories, which focus on *state-dependent learning* and *self-hypnosis,* address some of the questions left unanswered by the psychodynamic and behavioral explanations.

State-Dependent Learning If people learn something when they are in a particular state or situation, they often remember it best when they are returned to that same state or situation. If they are given a learning task while under the influence of alcohol, for example, their later recall of it may also improve under the influence of alcohol (Overton, 1966). Similarly, if they smoke cigarettes while learning, they may later recall the material better when they are again smoking.

This association between state and recall is called ***state-dependent learning.*** It was initially observed in experimental animals who were administered certain drugs and then taught to perform certain tasks. Researchers repeatedly found that the animals' subsequent test performances were best in the same drug states (Pusakulich & Nielson, 1976; Overton, 1966, 1964).

Research with human subjects later showed that state-dependent learning can be associated with psychological states as well as physiological ones. Some studies have found mood to be influential (see Figure 17-1): material learned during a happy mood is recalled best when the subject is again happy, and sad-state learning is recalled best during sad states (Eich, 1995; Bower, 1981).

What causes state-dependent learning? One possibility is that *arousal levels* are an important part of memory processes. That is, a particular level of arousal will have a set of remembered events, thoughts, and skills attached to it. When a situation elicits that particular level of arousal, the person is more likely to recall the memories associated with it.

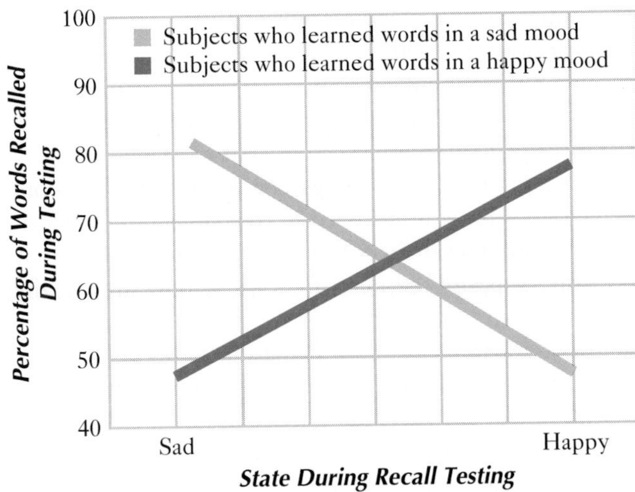

Figure 17-1 *State-dependent learning was demonstrated in a study by Bower (1981). Subjects who learned a list of words while in a hypnotically induced happy state remembered the words better if they were in a happy mood when tested later than if they were in a sad mood. Conversely, subjects who learned the words when in a sad mood recalled them better if they were sad during testing than if they were happy.*

Although people may remember certain events better in some states than in others, most can recall events across a range of arousal states. However, people prone to develop dissociative disorders may have state-to-memory links that are extremely rigid and narrow. Their thoughts, memories, and skills may be tied *exclusively* to particular states of arousal. They may recall past events only when they experience arousal states almost identical to the states in which the memory was acquired. When such people are calm, for example, they may forget what occurred during upsetting events, thus laying the groundwork for dissociative amnesia or fugue. Similarly, in multiple personality disorder, different arousal levels may elicit different clusters of memories, thoughts, and abilities—that is, different subpersonalities (Putnam, 1992). This could explain why personality transitions in multiple personality disorder tend to be rapid and stress-related.

Efforts to tie state-dependent learning to dissociative disorders keep running into a major problem: theorists do not yet agree about the precise relationship between arousal and memory. Many believe that arousal is no more important than any of a variety of cues that help to jog a person's memory. Researchers already know, for example, that cues such as familiar objects, smells, and sounds can help elicit memories of past events. It is possible that a state of arousal is just another such memory cue, albeit an internal one. If so, state-dependent learning has little new to say about memory itself—and less still about the active forgetting involved in dissociative disorders.

Self-Hypnosis As we first noted in Chapter 1, the word "hypnosis" describes the deliberate induction of a sleeplike state in which a person becomes highly suggestible. While in this state, the person can behave, perceive, and think in ways that would ordinarily seem impossible. Hypnotized subjects can, for example, be made to suspend their sensory functioning so that they become temporarily blind, deaf, or insensitive to pain (Fromm & Nash, 1992).

Hypnosis can help people remember events that occurred and were forgotten years ago, a capability of which many psychotherapists make frequent use. Conversely, it can also make people forget facts, events, and even their personal identity—the phenomenon of ***hypnotic amnesia*** (Allen, Law, & Laravuso, 1996; Spanos & Coe, 1992; Coe, 1989).

Most investigations of hypnotic amnesia follow similar formats. Subjects are asked to study a word list or other material until they are able to repeat it correctly. Under hypnosis, they are then instructed to forget the material until they receive a cancellation signal (such as

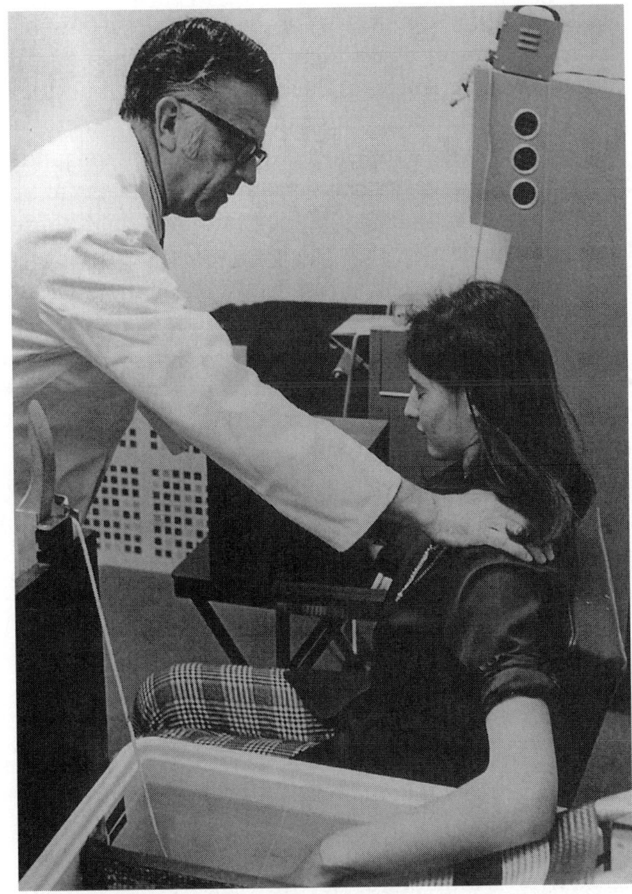

Ernest Hilgard hypnotizes subjects into experiencing tepid water as painfully cold or ice water as comfortably warm. Work by Hilgard and other researchers on hypnotic amnesia has convinced many clinicians that dissociative disorders represent a form of self-hypnosis.

the snap of a finger), at which time they will suddenly recall the learned material once again. Repeatedly these experiments have shown the subjects' memories to be severely impaired during the period of hypnotically suggested amnesia and then restored after the cancellation signal is given (Coe, 1989).

The parallels between hypnotic amnesia and dissociative disorders are striking (Bliss, 1980). Both are conditions in which people forget certain material for a period of time yet later recall it to mind. In both, the people forget without any insight into why they are forgetting or any awareness that something has been forgotten. Finally, in both situations, events are more readily forgotten than basic knowledge.

These parallels have led some theorists to conclude that dissociative disorders may represent a form of ***self-hypnosis:*** people actively induce themselves to forget unpleasant events (Bliss, 1985, 1980; Hilgard, 1977). Dissociative amnesia, for example, may occur in people who, consciously or unconsciously, go so far as to hypnotize themselves into forgetting horrifying experiences that have recently occurred in their lives. If the self-induced amnesia extends to all memories of a person's past and identity, that person may undergo a dissociative fugue. As in experimental hypnosis, the forgotten material is fully retrievable and is remembered completely when the fugue ends.

Self-hypnosis can also be used to explain multiple personality disorder. On the basis of several investigations, some theorists believe that multiple personality disorder often begins between the ages of 4 and 6, a time when children are generally very suggestible and excellent hypnotic subjects (Kluft, 1987; Bliss, 1985, 1980; Braun & Sachs, 1985) (see Figure 17-2). These theorists argue that some abused or otherwise traumatized children manage to escape their threatening world by self-hypnosis, mentally separating themselves from their body and its surroundings and fulfilling their wish to become some other person or persons. As one patient with multiple personality observed, "Now that I know what hypnosis is, I can say that I was in a trance often [during my childhood]. There was a little place where I could sit, close my eyes and imagine, until I felt very relaxed just like hypnosis" (Bliss, 1980, p. 1392).

There are different schools of thought about the nature of hypnosis, each with distinct implications for dissociative disorders. Some theorists see hypnosis as a *special process* or *trance,* an out-of-the-ordinary kind of functioning (Bowers & Woody, 1996; Hilgard, 1992, 1987, 1977). Other theorists believe that hypnotic behaviors, and hypnotic amnesia in particular, can be explained by *common social and cognitive processes* such as high motivation, attention, role enactments, and expectations (Spanos et al., 1995; Spanos & Coe, 1992). According to them, hypnotic phenomena consist simply of

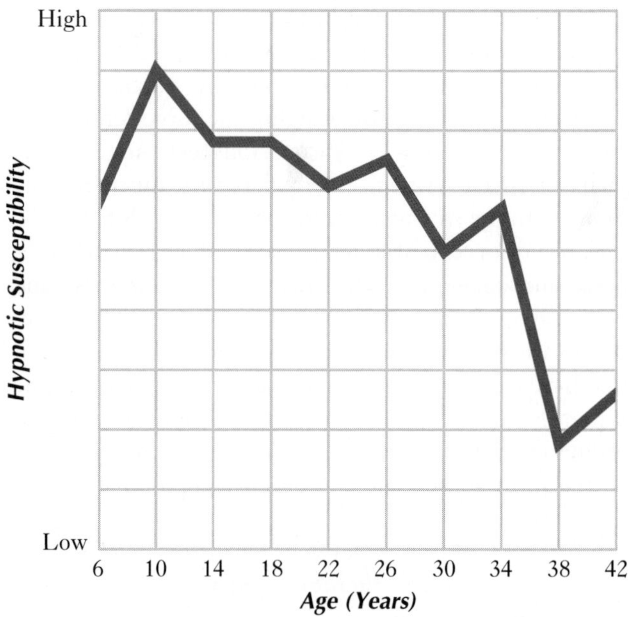

Figure 17-2 *Multiple personality disorder is thought to begin between the ages of 4 and 6, when the child's hypnotic susceptibility is on the rise. A person's hypnotic susceptibility steadily increases until just before adolescence, then generally declines with age. (Adapted from Morgan & Hilgard, 1973.)*

motivated people performing tasks that are asked of them. Yet, because of their strong belief in hypnosis, they fail to recognize their own contributions.

Special-process theorists contend that people with dissociative disorders place themselves in internal trances during which their conscious functioning is significantly altered. In contrast, common-process theorists hold that people with dissociative disorders provide themselves (or are provided by others) with powerful suggestions to forget and to imagine, and implicitly use social and cognitive principles to follow those suggestions.

Whether hypnosis involves special or common processes, hypnosis research effectively demonstrates the power and potential of our normal thought processes, while rendering the idea of dissociative disorders somewhat less remarkable. At the same time, hypnosis research leaves a number of questions unanswered (Kirsch & Lynn, 1995), and until these questions are addressed, the possible tie between hypnosis and dissociative disorders remains unsettled.

Treatments for Dissociative Amnesia and Fugue

As we saw earlier, cases of dissociative amnesia and fugue often end spontaneously in complete recovery. Sometimes, however, they linger and require treatment (Lyon, 1985). Several interventions have reported some success.

Psychodynamic therapy, for example, is commonly applied to both disorders (Loewenstein, 1991). Therapists guide patients to free-associate and search their unconscious in the hope of bringing the forgotten experiences back to the level of consciousness. Actually, the focus of psychodynamic therapy is very much in harmony with the treatment needs of people with these dissociative disorders. After all, people with dissociative amnesia and fugue need to recover lost memories, and psychodynamic therapists generally strive to uncover memories—as well as other psychological processes—that have been repressed. Thus many theorists, including some who do not espouse the psychodynamic perspective ordinarily, believe that psychodynamic therapy may be the most appropriate and effective approach for these disorders.

Another common treatment for dissociative amnesia and fugue is ***hypnotic therapy,*** or ***hypnotherapy.*** Therapists hypnotize patients and then guide them to recall the forgotten events (Spiegel, 1994; MacHovek, 1981; Bliss, 1980). Experiments have repeatedly indicated that hypnotic suggestion can successfully elicit forgotten memories, and experience has shown that people with dissociative disorders are usually highly susceptible to hypnosis (Frischholz et al., 1992; Putnam et al., 1986). Moreover, if, as some theorists argue, dissociative amnesia and fugue involve self-hypnosis, hypnotherapy may be a uniquely relevant intervention for them. It has been applied both alone and in combination with other approaches.

Sometimes intravenous injections of ***sodium amobarbital*** (Amytal) or ***sodium pentobarbital*** (Pentothal) are used to help patients regain lost memories (Ruedrich et al., 1985). The drugs are sometimes called "truth serum," but the key to their success is their capacity for sedating people and lowering their inhibitions, thus helping them to recall forgotten events (Kluft, 1988; Perry & Jacobs, 1982). Unfortunately, these drugs often fail to work (Spiegel, 1994); and when they do help people recall past events, the individuals may forget much of what they have said and experienced under the drug's influence. For these reasons, the drugs tend to be used in conjunction with other treatment approaches, if they are used at all.

Treatments For Multiple Personality Disorder

Unlike the victims of dissociative amnesia and fugue, people with multiple personality disorder rarely recover spontaneously (Spiegel, 1994). Therapists usually try to help people with this more chronic disorder to (1) recognize the full breadth of their disorder, (2) recover the gaps in their memory, and (3) integrate their subpersonalities into one (Spiegel, 1994; Kluft, 1992, 1991, 1983; Dell & Eisenhower, 1990).

Recognizing the Disorder Once a diagnosis of multiple personality disorder is made, therapists typically try to form a therapeutic alliance both with the primary personality and with each of the subpersonalities (Kluft, 1992). In general, these alliances are not easily achieved, owing to the history of abuse and mistrust of others.

Multiple personality patients are typically slow to recognize the full scope and nature of their disorder. The notion of having more than one personality may seem as strange to them as it does to everyone else. Thus treatment may begin with educating patients about their disorder (Allen, 1993). Some therapists actually introduce the subpersonalities to one another under hypnosis, and some have patients look at videotapes of their other personalities (Ross & Gahan, 1988; Sakheim, Hess, & Chivas, 1988).

Many therapists have also found that group therapy helps to educate patients. Being with a group of people who all have multiple personality disorder helps reduce a person's feelings of isolation and fears of being "crazy" (Buchele, 1993; Becker & Comstock, 1992). Family therapy is often used as an adjunct to individual therapy to help educate spouses and children about the disorder and to gather helpful information about the patient (Porter, Kelly, & Grame, 1993).

Recovering Memories To help these patients recover the missing pieces of their past, therapists use many of the approaches applied to the other dissociative disorders, including psychodynamic therapy, hypnotherapy, and sodium amobarbital (Smith, 1993; Kluft, 1991, 1985). These techniques work slowly for patients with multiple personality disorder, as some subpersonalities may persist in denying experiences that the others recall (Lyon, 1992). In many cases, a subpersonality assumes a "protector" role, to prevent the primary personality from suffering the pain of recollecting traumatic experiences. Indeed, some patients become self-destructive and violent during this phase of treatment (Kelly, 1993; Lamberti & Cummings, 1992; Young, Young, & Lehl, 1991).

Integrating the Subpersonalities The final goal of therapy is to help the person gain access to and merge the different subpersonalities. *Integration* is a continuous process that occurs throughout treatment as dissociative boundaries diminish, until patients have achieved continuous ownership of their behaviors, emotions, sensations, and knowledge. ***Fusion*** is the final merging of two or more subpersonalities. Many patients distrust this final treatment goal and their subpersonalities are likely to view integration as a form of death (Spiegel, 1994; Kluft, 1991, 1988). As one subpersonality said, "There are too many advantages to being multiple. Maybe we're being sold a bill of goods by therapists" (Hale, 1983).

Therapists have used a range of approaches to help integrate the personalities, including psychodynamic, supportive, cognitive, and drug therapies (Goldman, 1995; Fichtner et al., 1990; Caddy, 1985). One woman's primary personality was given assertiveness training: as she learned to express anger in more functional and satisfying ways, her aggressive and hostile subpersonality began to disappear. Some therapists have even conducted discussions and interactions between the subpersonalities, as if they were conducting group therapy.

Once the subpersonalities are integrated, further therapy is necessary to solidify the integrated personality and to provide social and coping skills to help prevent subsequent dissociations. Without continuous intervention, many patients are at risk for further dissociative responses to heightened stress in the future (Fink, 1992).

In case reports, some therapists report high success rates in treating multiple personality disorder (Kluft, 1993, 1984; Wilbur, 1984; Allison, 1978), but others find that most patients continue to resist full and final integration. A few therapists have in fact questioned the need for full integration. The relatively small number of reported cases has typically prevented researchers from gathering a large enough sample to assess the effectiveness of the various approaches.

Organic Memory Disorders

Changes in memory can also have clearly organic causes, including brain injury, medical conditions, and substance misuse. There are two kinds of organic memory disorders. *Amnestic disorders* primarily affect memory, while *dementias* affect both memory and other cognitive functions.

Before discussing the organic memory disorders, we need to know about the anatomical and chemical bases of memory. Much of this knowledge has emerged through studies of people who have suffered injuries to specific locations in the brain. Important information has also been gained through experiments in which lesions are produced in animals' brains and then their ability to learn new information is studied. Additionally, careful studies of neurons have begun to reveal the specific changes that occur in brain cells as memories form.

Memory Systems

In essence, there are two human memory systems, and they work together to help us learn and recall. ***Short-term memory,*** or ***working memory,*** collects new information. ***Long-term memory*** is the repository of all the information that we have stored over the years—information that first made its way through the short-term memory system. The information held in short-term memory must be *transformed,* or *consolidated,* into long-term memory if we are to retain it. The transformation usually occurs in steps. When short-term information becomes part of our long-term memory, it is said to have been ***encoded.*** Remembering such information thereafter involves ***retrieval,*** going into one's long-term memory to bring it out for use again in short-term, or working, memory (NIMH, 1996).

Information in long-term memory can be classified as either procedural or declarative. ***Procedural memories*** are learned skills we perform without needing to think about them, such as cutting with scissors or knowing how to solve a math problem. ***Declarative memory*** consists of information that is directly accessible to consciousness, such as names, dates, and other facts that have been learned. Most organic memory disorders disrupt declarative memory far more than procedural memory.

The Anatomy of Memory

Memories are difficult to locate. Researchers have searched for the place where the *content* of memory is stored, but they have concluded that no such well-defined storehouse exists. They now see memory as a *process* rather than a place, an activity that involves changes in cells throughout the brain; when the process begins, a memory is activated and comes forth. Occasionally, this process leads to errors or peculiarities of memory (see Box 17-2), but typically it operates in a remarkably effective manner.

Certain brain structures appear to be particularly important in short-term and long-term memory processes. Among the most important structures in short-term, or working, memory are the ***prefrontal lobes,*** located just behind the forehead (Goleman, 1995). When both animal and human subjects acquire new information, their prefrontal lobes display much more activity on PET and MRI scans (Cohen et al., 1997, 1995; Haxby et al., 1996; Goldman-Rakic & Friedman, 1995; Haxby, 1995; Friedman & Goldman-Rakic, 1994). Apparently, activity by neurons in the prefrontal lobes enables individuals to hold information temporarily (both brand-new information and information pulled back from long-term memory) and to continue working with the information as long as it is needed.

BOX 17-2 Peculiarities of Memory

Memory problems usually must cause significant distress and impairment before they are considered abnormal. But *peculiarities* of memory permeate our daily lives, and sometimes they cause concern. Memory investigators Richard Noll and Carol Turkington (1994) review a number of these phenomena—some familiar, some useful, some problematic—and none abnormal.

Absentmindedness Often we fail to register information because we are preoccupied with other thoughts: we are absentminded. This is not the same thing as being unable to recall information stored in our memory. We never registered the information in the first place, so of course we can't recall it. The only cure for absentmindedness is to find better ways to pay attention. If you always forget where you put your keys, for instance, try saying out loud, "I'm putting my keys down *here,*" and look hard at those keys.

Déjà vu Almost all of us have at some time had a haunting sense of recognition when we have come upon a scene we are seeing for the first time. We feel sure we have been there before. The sense of déjà vu, French for "already seen," is sometimes so vivid that it seems almost like a hallucination.

Jamais vu At other times we have the opposite experience: a situation or scene that is part of our daily lives seems suddenly unfamiliar. "I knew it was my car, but I felt as if I'd never seen it before." Jamais vu, French for "never seen," is less common than déjà vu. It may in fact have very different mechanisms, although both are anomalies of recognition.

Pseudopresentiment Related to both déjà vu and jamais vu, pseudopresentiment is the feeling that we knew beforehand that an event we are witnessing was going to happen. Not that we claim to have actually prophesied the event. The dreamlike feeling of having previously known about the event usually comes just as the event unfolds.

The tip-of-the-tongue phenomenon To have something on the tip of the tongue is an acute "feeling of knowing": we are unable to recall something, but we know that we know it. The brain contains such a tremendous store of information that not all of it can be retrieved at any given moment. Sometimes we can even recall related information—a person's face but not the name, say, or a name similar to it but not quite the one we are seeking. Apparently our search has activated networks in a way we can feel. If we try to remember the name MacDuff, for example, we may think of Scotland, because of the Scottish association of the prefix "Mac"; or Shakespeare's name may spring to mind, because MacDuff is a character in Shakespeare's *Macbeth.*

Eidetic images Some people experience an afterimage so strong that they can describe a picture in detail after looking at it just once. Fewer than 10 percent of children can form eidetic ("identical" or "duplicative") images of this kind; the ability is even rarer after adolescence. The image may be a memory of a picture, event, fantasy, or dream.

Memory while under anesthesia Some anesthetized patients may comprehend enough of what is said during surgery to affect their recovery. The ability to understand language has con-

Among the brain structures most important to long-term memory are the ***temporal lobes*** (including the *hippocampus* and *amygdala,* key structures that are embedded under the lobes) and the ***diencephalon*** (including the *mammillary bodies, thalamus,* and *hypothalamus*). These brain regions seem to be particularly involved in the transformation, or encoding, of short-term memory into long-term memory (Searleman & Hermann, 1994). Many cases of organic memory loss involve damage to one or more of these areas (Aggleton & Shaw, 1996).

tinued under anesthesia, even though the patient cannot explicitly recall it. Nearly all adequate anesthetics produce an amnesia that prohibits any recall after surgery, but auditory function is the last sense to fade under anesthesia.

Flashbacks during surgery Spontaneous recall can occur *during* surgery. Wilder Penfield discovered such flashbacks when he performed neurosurgery on a conscious patient in 1933. As his probe touched parts of the brain now thought to be associated with memory storage, it triggered distant memories in the patient. "The astonishing aspect of this phenomenon," Penfield wrote, "is that suddenly [the patient] is aware of all that was in his mind during an earlier strip of time. It is the stream of a former consciousness flowing again."

Memory for music Even as a small child, Mozart could memorize and reproduce a piece of music after having heard it only once. Since he learned to read music and started composing at almost the same time, he may have visualized the notes on the music staff as he was hearing them and later just recreated them in his mind. He could play a piece immediately after hearing it, which crystallized the memory when its trace was freshest. While no one yet has matched the genius of Mozart, many musicians can mentally hear whole pieces of music, so that they can rehearse anywhere, far from their instruments.

Visual memory Most people are predominantly visual when it comes to memorizing: they can easily visualize places, objects, faces, the pages of a book. They almost never forget a face, although they may well forget the name attached to it. They will recall that face even if they saw the person only once, ten years before. A sizeable minority of people have stronger verbal memories: they remember sounds or words, and the associations that come to their minds are often puns or rhymes.

Memory in myth The mythology of memory is very important in cultures that hold to the idea of reincarnation and rebirth. Some North American medicine men, for example, claim to remember elements of a prenatal existence, a faculty they believe is lost to "common" people. In addition, many practicing Buddhists claim to remember many lives, and a few—including Buddha himself—remember their very first existence.

In Indian myth, the veil of *maya* (illusion) prevents a person from remembering his or her true origin. The ancient Gnostics warned of a similar forgetfulness, which they believed should be resisted. Finally, the Greek goddess of memory, Mnemosyne, was believed to know the past, present, and future. As the mother of the Muses, she was responsible for all creativity.

These brain regions also have numerous connections between them. A structure known as the *fornix,* for example, connects the hippocampus with the mammillary bodies. Damage to the fornix has effects on memory, suggesting that newly learned information follows a circuit, and that disruption of this circuit may be the cause of some memory disorders (Aggleton & Shaw, 1996). There is also evidence, however, that memory processes are redundant; if one pathway is disrupted, alternate routes may be available. The multiple paths by which

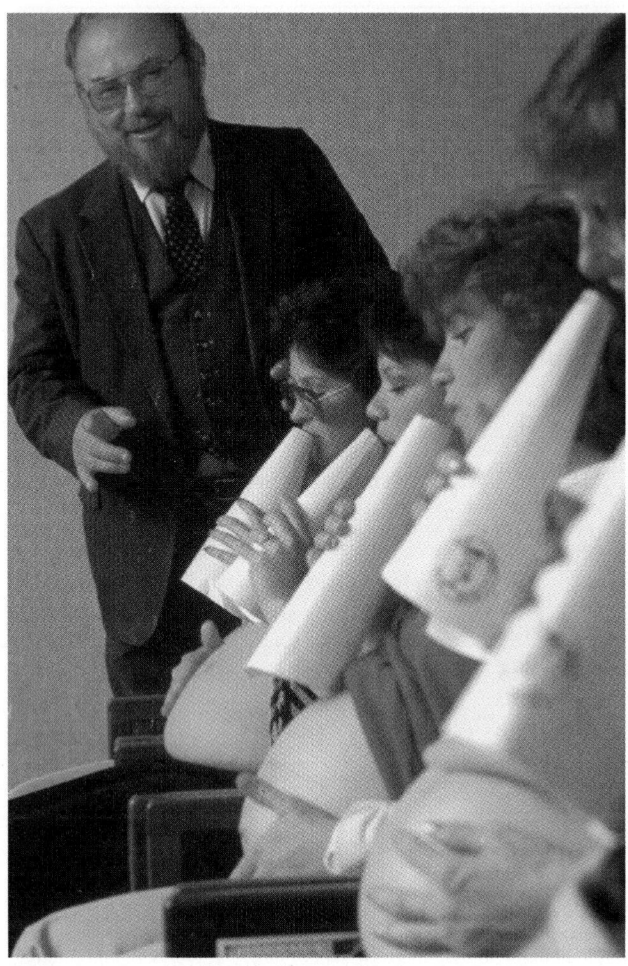

The mothers-to-be in this prenatal program are talking to their fetuses. Their goal is to establish an early relationship with their child and to improve the baby's interactive skills. Memory studies suggest that the babies will not remember these early interventions, however; humans apparently cannot intentionally recall events until sometime during their first or second year of life (Bauer, 1996; Mandler & McDonough, 1995).

new information may be processed and encoded make it difficult to identify the exact roles played by specific brain structures (Amaral, 1987).

The Biochemistry of Memory

So far we have identified structures within the brain that may mediate memory processes. But how do the brain cells actually create and store memories? Although no one has yet found the "engram"—the exact physical change in a cell that accounts for a memory—many relevant discoveries have been made about the electrical and chemical bases of learning and memory.

One of the most exciting of these findings is the role that ***long-term potentiation*** (LTP) may play in memory formation (Martinez & Derrick, 1996; Bliss & Gardner, 1973). Apparently, repeated stimulation of nerve cells in the brain significantly increases the likelihood that the cells will respond—and respond strongly—to future stimulation. This effect can last quite a long time (hence the name "long-term potentiation"), long enough to bea key mechanism in the formation of memories. Think of many sleds ridden in succession down a snowy slope, creating a groove that later sledders can easily find. LTP, too, may create a kind of groove that corresponds to the process of making a memory, so that one can easily retrieve that memory later by following the same path.

Memory researchers have also identified complicated biochemical changes within and between cells that apparently help in the formation of memories (Rosenzweig, 1996; Noll & Turkington, 1994). Most important, when new information is acquired, *protein production* increases in key brain cells. Since this increase in protein production appears to be essential to memory formation, the steps that bring it about are of corresponding importance. First, an individual's body organs receive new information and release neurotransmitters, particularly ***acetylcholine*** and ***glutamate,*** which carry the information to receptors on neurons located in key memory regions of the brain. Next the receptors trigger chemical changes—termed *second messengers*—within the receiving neurons. For example, those neurons increase their production of ***RNA (ribonucleic acid),*** a complex molecule, and of ***calcium,*** the most abundant mineral in the body. Each of these chemicals helps manufacture the proteins that help memories to form.

If any of these biological steps is disturbed, the formation of memories may be interrupted (Martinez & Derrick, 1996; Rosenzweig, 1996). If, for example, researchers chemically block neural receptors for the neurotransmitter glutamate (often called *NMDA receptors*), they may prevent both short-term memory and LTP. Similarly, if they administer drugs that block a receiving cell's production of RNA or of calcium, the formation of long-term memories is disrupted.

All these changes suggest that memory occurs as a result of real and observable changes within and between nerve cells. With this overview of the systems, anatomy, and biochemistry of memory, we can turn to the organic disorders that affect memory and other cognitive functions—the *amnestic disorders* and *dementias.*

Amnestic Disorders

Retrograde amnesia is a lack of memory of events that occurred before the event that caused the amnesia. ***An-***

TABLE 17-1 Comparison of Memory Disorders

	Anterograde (continuous) Amnesia	*Retrograde (localized, selective, and generalized) Amnesia*	*Declarative Memory Loss*	*Procedural Memory Loss*	*Organic Causes*
Dissociative amnesia	Sometimes	Yes	Yes	Sometimes	No
Dissociative fugue	Sometimes	Yes	Yes	Sometimes	No
Multiple personality disorder	Yes	Yes	Yes	Yes	No
Amnestic disorders	Yes	Sometimes	Yes	Sometimes	Yes
Dementias	Yes	Yes	Yes	Yes	Yes

terograde amnesia is an ongoing inability to recall new information that is acquired after the event. As we noted earlier, people with dissociative amnesia often suffer from retrograde amnesia and rarely suffer from anterograde amnesia. ***Amnestic disorders,*** organic disorders of which memory impairment is the primary symptom, are quite different. Here people *sometimes* suffer from retrograde amnesia, depending on the particular disorder, but they almost *always* exhibit anterograde amnesia (see Table 17-1).

In severe forms of anterograde amnesia, people newly met are forgotten almost immediately, and problems solved one day must be tackled again the next. Patients may not remember anything that has happened since the time of their organic trauma. A middle-aged patient who suffered a trauma more than twenty years ago, for example, may still believe that Jimmy Carter is president of the United States. The sufferer of anterograde amnesia may retain all other cognitive skills, including verbal skills and problem-solving abilities. The IQ is not changed.

In anterograde amnesia, it is as though information from short-term memory, the psychological "work space" that holds information for a few minutes or so, can no longer cross over into long-term memory. It is not surprising that the anterograde amnesia observed in amnestic disorders is often the result of damage to the brain's temporal lobes or diencephalon, the areas particularly responsible for transforming short-term memory into long-term memory.

Korsakoff's Syndrome (Alcohol-Induced Persisting Amnestic Disorder) Fred, a 69-year-old man was admitted to a mental hospital in a state of confusion and disorientation, the result of ***Korsakoff's syndrome,*** a disorder that causes its victims to keep forgetting newly learned information, although their general knowledge and intelligence remain intact:

> Fred . . . had a history of many years of heavy drinking, although he denied drinking during the past several years. When seen in the admitting ward, the patient was neatly dressed, but there was some deterioration of his personal habits. Although pleasant and sociable with the interviewer and ward personnel, he was definitely confused. He wandered about the ward, investigating objects and trying on other people's clothing. He talked freely, though his speech tended to be rambling and at times incoherent. Most of his spontaneous conversation centered on himself, and there were a number of hypochondriacal complaints. Fred was disoriented for time and place, although he was able to give his name. He could not give his correct address, said his age was 91, and was unable to name the day, the month, or the year. He did not know where he was, although he said he was sent here by his landlord because he had been drinking. He admitted that he had been arrested for fighting and drinking, but he said that he had never had an attack of delirium tremens. [Fred] showed the characteristic symptom picture of ***Korsakoff's syndrome,*** with disorientation, confusion,

> and a strong tendency toward confabulation. When asked where he was, he said he was in a brewery. He gave the name of the brewery, but when asked the same question a few minutes later, he named another brewery. Similarly, he said that he knew the examiner, called him by an incorrect name, and a little later changed the name again. When leaving the examining room, he used still another name when he said politely, "Goodbye, Mr. Wolf!"
>
> *(Kisker, 1977, p. 308)*

As we observed in Chapter 13, approximately 5 percent of people with chronic alcoholism develop the severe amnestic disorder known as Korsakoff's syndrome. Excessive drinking, combined with a lack of proper diet, lead to a deficiency of vitamin B (*thiamine*). The effect on portions of the diencephalon, among other areas, is dramatic.

Patients in the early stages of Korsakoff's syndrome, called *Wernicke's encephalopathy,* are extremely confused. Treated with large doses of thiamine, the syndrome subsides (APA, 1994). Untreated, it progresses to Korsakoff's syndrome. The memory deficit applies primarily to declarative knowledge; patients are still able to incorporate new procedural knowledge, such as the way to solve a particular kind of puzzle, and they also maintain their language skills (Verfaellie et al., 1990). This may explain why Korsakoff's patients often ***confabulate.*** Like Fred, they use their general intellectual and language skills to create elaborate stories and lies in efforts to compensate for the memories they keep losing.

In addition to profound anterograde amnesia, patients with Korsakoff's syndrome experience some retrograde amnesia. They have particular difficulty remembering events from the years immediately preceding the onset of the syndrome, as opposed to long-ago events (Albert et al., 1979). Damage to yet other brain areas may cause this feature of the syndrome; or heavy drinking during those hard-to-remember years could have interfered with encoding at that time (Goodwin, 1995).

Korsakoff's syndrome can also profoundly affect personality. Before its onset, individuals may be aggressive and boisterous; after the disorder has progressed, they often become more passive and unimposing.

Head Trauma and Brain Surgery Both *head injuries* and *brain surgery* are capable of causing amnestic disorders (Noll & Turkington, 1994). Either may destroy memory-related brain structures or cut the connections between memory-related areas of the brain.

Second only to the popularity of emotional trauma as a cause of amnesia in television shows and movies, bumps on the head are portrayed as a quick and easy way to lose one's memory. In fact, *mild* head trauma, such as a concussion that does not result in coma or a period of unconsciousness, usually leaves a person with only minimal memory dysfunction, which disappears within days or at most months (Levin et al., 1987; McLean et al., 1983).

Almost half of the cases of *severe* head trauma, in contrast, do result in some permanent learning and memory problems, both anterograde and retrograde, partly the results of damage to the temporal lobes and the structures embedded under them. The memories that do return often come back haphazardly, but older ones typically return first (Searlemen & Herrmann, 1994).

Surgical lesions create significantly more specific memory problems. The most famous case of memory loss as a result of brain surgery is that of H.M. (a man whose identity has been more or less protected for decades, despite his notoriety in the memory literature) (Ogden & Corkin, 1991; Corkin, 1984, 1968; Milner, 1971). H.M. suffered from severe epilepsy, a disorder that created seizures in his temporal lobes. To alleviate his symptoms, doctors removed parts of his temporal lobes, along with the amygdala and hippocampus. At that time the role of these brain areas in the formation of memories was not known. (Today temporal lobe surgery is generally restricted to either the right or left side of the brain). H.M. has experienced severe anterograde amnesia ever since the surgery. He keeps failing to recognize anyone he has met since the operation, although he is able to learn some types of procedural information, such as how to trace figures while looking at them in a mirror (a standard exercise used to test a person's ability to acquire a new skill) (Corkin, 1968) (see Figure 17-3).

Other Amnestic Disorders Other biological events can also damage memory-related regions of the brain. These include *vascular disease,* which affects the flow of blood to the brain (Gorelick et al., 1988); *heart attacks,* which interrupt the flow of oxygen to the brain (Volpe & Hirst, 1983); and certain *infectious diseases* (Hokkanen et al., 1995). Each may cause memory problems that vary in character and severity.

Dementias

Dementias, syndromes also associated with significant loss of memory, are sometimes difficult to distinguish from the amnestic disorders. The severe memory problems of ***dementia,*** however, are accompanied by impairment in at least one other cognitive function, such as abstract thinking, judgment, or language (APA, 1994). In addition, people with certain forms of dementia may undergo personality changes—they may begin to behave inappropriately, for example—and they may deteriorate progressively.

(A)

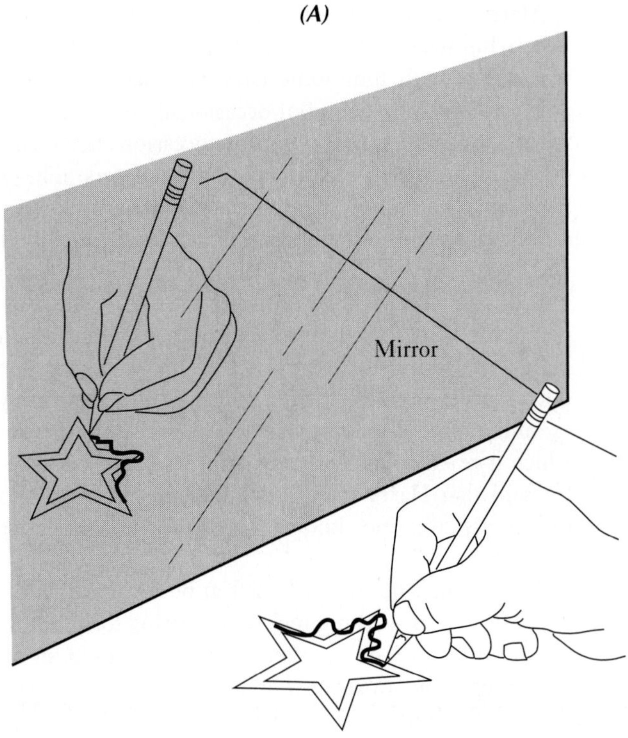

(B)

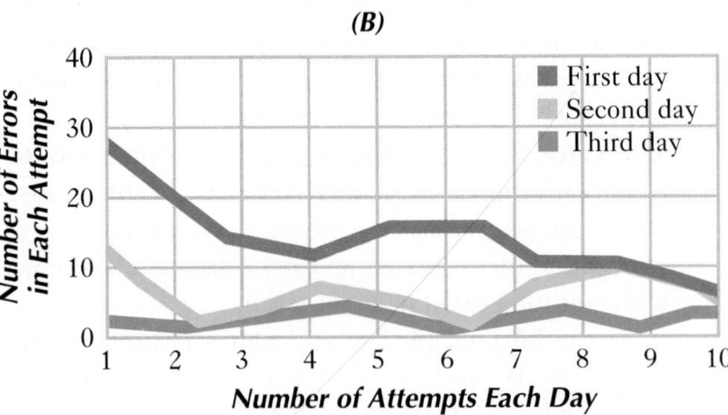

Figure 17-3 *The mirror-tracing task. (A) All subjects initially have difficulty tracing a line between two figures while observing their hand in a mirror (Kolb & Whishaw, 1990). (B) After repeated practice, however, they usually become quite proficient at this task, as did H.M., the famous subject whose amygdala and hippocampus were surgically removed, leaving him with severe anterograde amnesia (Milner et al., 1968).*

Fear that we are losing our memory and other mental abilities occasionally strikes all of us. Perhaps we have rushed out the door without our keys. Perhaps we meet a familiar person and cannot remember her name, or in the middle of a critical test our mind seems to go blank (Gallagher-Thompson & Thompson, 1995). At such times, we may well believe that we are on our way to dementia. Actually such mishaps are quite common and usually are a normal feature of aging. Typically, as people progress through middle age, memory difficulties and lapses of attention increase, and may occur regularly by the age of 60 or 70. Sometimes, however, people experience intellectual changes that are broad, severe, and excessive. They, like Harry, manifest a dementia.

Harry appeared to be in perfect health at age 58, except that for a few days he had had a nasty flu. He worked in the municipal water treatment plant of a small city, and it was at work that the first overt signs of Harry's mental illness appeared. While responding to a minor emergency, he became confused about the correct order in which to pull the levers that controlled the flow of fluids. As a result, several thousand gallons of raw sewage were discharged into a river. Harry had been an efficient and diligent worker, so after puzzled questioning, his error was attributed to the flu and overlooked.

Several weeks later, Harry came home with a baking dish his wife had asked him to buy, having forgotten that he had brought home the identical dish two nights before. Later that week, on two successive nights, he went to pick up his daughter at her job in a restaurant, apparently forgetting that she had changed shifts and was now working days. A month after that, he quite uncharacteristically argued with a clerk at the phone company; he was trying to pay a bill that he had already paid three days before.

By this time his wife had become alarmed about the changes in Harry. Thinking back, she began to piece together episodes that convinced her that his memory had actually been undependable for at least several months, perhaps much longer. . . . She insisted that he see a doctor. . . . The doctor did a physical examination and ordered several laboratory tests, including an electroencephalogram (a brain wave test). The examination results were normal, and the doctor thought the problem might be depression. . . .

Months passed and Harry's wife was beside herself. She could see that his problem was worsening. Not only had she been unable to get effective help, but Harry himself was becoming resentful and sometimes suspicious of her attempts. He now insisted there was nothing wrong with him, and she would catch him narrowly watching her every movement. From time to time he accused her of having the police watch him, and he would draw all the blinds in the house. Once he ripped the telephone out of the wall, convinced it was "spying." Sometimes he became angry—sudden little storms without apparent cause. . . . More difficult for his wife was Harry's repetitiveness in conversation: He often repeated stories from the past and sometimes repeated isolated phrases and sentences from more recent exchanges. There was no context and little continuity to his choice of subjects. He might recite the same story or instruction several times a day. His work was also a great cause of deep concern. His wife . . . began checking on him at his job at least once a day. Soon she was actually doing most of his work. His supervisor, an

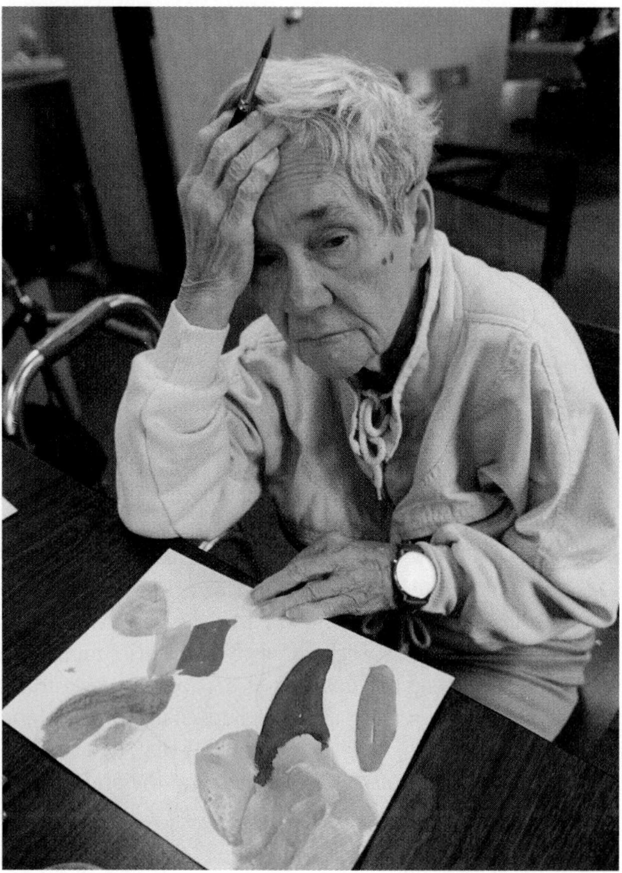

Because of their short-term memory problems, people with advanced cases of Alzheimer's disease are often unable to complete simple tasks such as painting a picture. In addition, their long-term memory deficits may prevent them from recognizing even close relatives or friends.

old friend of the family, looked the other way. Harry seemed grateful that his wife was there.

Two years after Harry had first allowed the sewage to escape, he was clearly a changed man. Most of the time he seemed preoccupied; he usually had a vacant smile on his face, and what little he said was so vague that it lacked meaning. He had entirely given up his main interests (golf and woodworking), and he became careless about his person. More and more, for example, he slept in his clothes. Gradually his wife took over getting him up, toileted, and dressed each morning.

One day the county supervisor stopped by to tell his wife that Harry just could not work any longer. . . . He was just too much of a burden on his co-workers. Harry himself still insisted that nothing was wrong, but by now no one tried to explain things to him. He had long since stopped reading. His days were spent sitting vacantly in front of the television, but he couldn't describe any of the programs he had watched.

Harry's condition continued to worsen slowly. When his wife's school was in session, his daughter would stay with him some days, and neighbors were able to offer some help. But occasionally he would still manage to wander away. On those occasions he greeted everyone he met—old friends and strangers alike—with "Hi, it's so nice." That was the extent of his conversation, although he might repeat "nice, nice, nice" over and over again. . . . When Harry left a coffee pot on a unit of the electric stove until it melted, his wife, desperate for help, took him to see another doctor. Again Harry was found to be in good health. This time the doctor ordered a CAT scan . . . a sophisticated x-ray examination that made a visual image of Harry's brain, which it revealed had actually shrunk in size. The doctor said that Harry had "Pick-Alzheimer disease" and that there was no known cause and no effective treatment.

Harry could no longer be left at home alone, so his daughter began working nights and caring for him until his wife came home after school. He would sit all day, except that sometimes he would wander aimlessly through the house. Safety latches at each entrance kept him from going outdoors, though he no longer seemed interested in that—or in much of anything else. He had no memory for events of the day and little recollection of occasions from the distant past, which a year or so before he had enjoyed describing. . . .

Because Harry was a veteran . . . [he qualified for] hospitalization in a regional veterans' hospital about 400 miles away from his home. . . . Desperate, five years after the accident at work, [his wife] accepted with gratitude [this] hospitalization. . . .

At the hospital the nursing staff sat Harry up in a chair each day and, aided by volunteers, made sure he ate enough. Still, he lost weight and became weaker. He would weep when his wife came to see him, but he did not talk, and he gave no other sign that he recognized her. After a year, even the weeping stopped. Harry's wife could no longer bear to visit. Harry lived on until just after his sixty-fifth birthday, when he choked on a piece of bread, developed pneumonia as a consequence, and soon died.

(Heston, 1992, pp. 87-90)

At any given time, around 3 percent of the entire adult population experience dementia (Muir, 1997; APA, 1994). Its occurrence is very closely related to age (see Figure 17-4). Among people 65 years of age, the prevalence is around 1 to 2 percent, increasing to more than 15 percent for those over the age of 80 (De Leon et al., 1996; Gallagher-Thompson & Thompson, 1995). Around 4 million persons in the United States experience some form of dementia (Alzheimer's Association, 1996; Jenike, 1995).

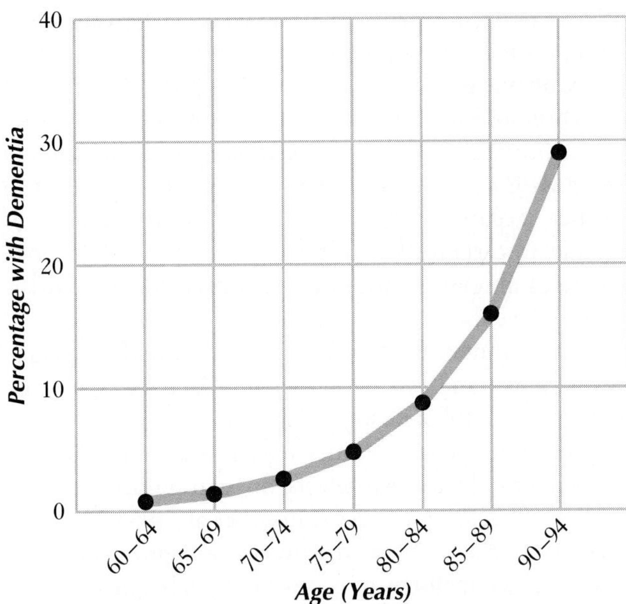

Figure 17-4 *Dementia and age. The occurrence of dementia is closely related to age. Fewer than 1 percent of all 60-year-olds have dementia, compared to 29 percent of those who are 90. After 60, the prevalence of dementia doubles every six years up to age 90, then the increase tapers off. (Adapted from Ritchie et al., 1992.)*

More than 70 forms of dementia have been identified (Noll & Turkington, 1994). Some reflect metabolic, nutritional, or sensory problems that can be corrected when they are identified. Most forms of dementia, however, are caused by neurological problems, such as Alzheimer's disease and stroke, which are currently difficult or impossible to address.

Alzheimer's Disease ***Alzheimer's disease,*** named after Alois Alzheimer, the German physician who first identified it in 1907, is the most common form of dementia, accounting for at least 50 percent of cases (Muir, 1997; Bliwise et al., 1987). This gradually progressive degenerative disease sometimes appears in middle age ***(early onset),*** but most often it occurs after the age of 65 ***(late onset),*** and its prevalence increases markedly among people in their late 70s and early 80s (APA, 1994). Some studies have reported higher rates of this disease in women, but then, women live longer than men on average (Gallagher-Thompson & Thompson, 1995).

The course of Alzheimer's disease ranges from two to as many as twenty years. Dysfunction progresses over time, usually beginning with mild memory problems, lapses of attention, and difficulties in language and communication (Small, Kemper, & Lyons, 1997). These symptoms keep increasing in frequency and severity until at some point it becomes clear that the individual is having difficulty in completing complicated tasks or is forgetting important appointments (Searleman & Herrmann, 1994). Eventually the individual also has difficulty with simple tasks, distant memories are forgotten, and changes in personality often become very noticeable. For example, a man may become uncharacteristically aggressive or amorous.

Although people with Alzheimer's disease initially may deny that they have a problem (Sharkstein et al., 1997), they soon become anxious or depressed about their impaired thinking, and many seem agitated (Devanand et al., 1997). As the dementia progresses still further, however, they show less and less concern about or acknowledgment of their limitations. During the late stages of the disorder, they withdraw socially, become more disoriented as to time and place, wander frequently, and show extremely poor judgment (Gallagher-Thompson & Thompson, 1995). Eventually their cognitive abilities are so severely impaired that they become fully dependent on other people. They may lose virtually all knowledge of the past and fail to recognize the faces of even close relatives. They become increasingly agitated at night and take frequent naps during the day. The late phase of the disorder can last from two to five years, with the individuals requiring constant care and supervision (Mace & Rabins, 1991).

Alzheimer's victims usually remain in fairly good health until the later stages of the disease. As their mental facilities decline, however, their activity level tends to drop off markedly. Eventually they spend much of their time just sitting or lying in bed, and they increasingly develop physical ailments and serious illnesses, such as pneumonia, which can result in death (Gallagher-Thompson & Thompson, 1995). Alzheimer's disease is responsible for 120,000 deaths each year in the United States, making it the fourth leading cause of death among elderly people (Alzheimer's Association, 1996; Jenike, 1995).

In most cases, Alzheimer's disease can be diagnosed with certainty only after death, when the person's brain tissue can be examined and specific structural changes observed. The most notable changes are excessive *neurofibrillary tangles* and *senile plaques* (Iqbal & Grundke-Iqbal, 1996).

Neurofibrillary tangles are twisted protein fibers found *within* the cells of the hippocampus and other brain structures vital to memory and learning. All people form tangles as they age (see Figure 17-5), but people with Alzheimer's disease form an extraordinary number of them (Selkoe, 1992). ***Senile plaques*** are sphere-shaped deposits of a small molecule known as the ***beta-amyloid protein.*** The deposits form in the spaces *between* neurons, particularly those located in the hippocampus, cerebral cortex, and certain other brain regions, as well as in some blood vessels in these areas. As with tangles, the formation of plaques is a normal part of aging, but it is dramatically increased in people with Alzheimer's disease (Lorenzo & Yankner, 1996; Selkoe, 1992). It has been speculated that such plaques may cause interference with exchanges between cells, which in turn leads to cell breakdown or death.

Although excessive numbers of tangles and plaques are clearly present in Alzheimer's disease, we have yet to understand fully why some persons develop these problems and the disease. Research has suggested several possible causes, however, including genetic factors and neurotransmitter abnormalities.

Genetic Causes Research has established that Alzheimer's disease often has a genetic basis. Because many cases seem to run in families, clinicians now distinguish between ***familial*** Alzheimer's disease and ***sporadic*** Alzheimer's disease, which is not associated with a family history of the brain disease (Bergem et al, 1997; Rossor, Kennedy, & Frackowiak, 1996; Gallagher-Thompson & Thompson, 1995).

One line of research has found that a particular gene on chromosome 21 is responsible for the production of a protein called ***beta-amyloid precursor protein (beta-APP).*** A mutated form of this gene may lead to greater accumulations of beta-amyloid protein, or plaque, in certain areas of the brain (Selkoe et al., 1996; Goate et al, 1991; Murrell et al., 1991). Many theorists now believe that in some families genetically transmitted beta-APP mutations heighten the likelihood of plaque formations, and so of familial Alzheimer's disease (Selkoe et al., 1996; Kosik, 1992).

Yet other genetic studies have linked some kinds of Alzheimer's disease to defects on chromosomes 1, 14, and 19 (Higgins et al., 1997; Roses et al., 1996; Wragg et al., 1996). All of these discoveries are promising; but since the vast majority of people with Alzheimer's disease do not have a clear family history of brain dysfunction, scientists still cannot determine the influence of genetic mutations on the disease's development in the popula-

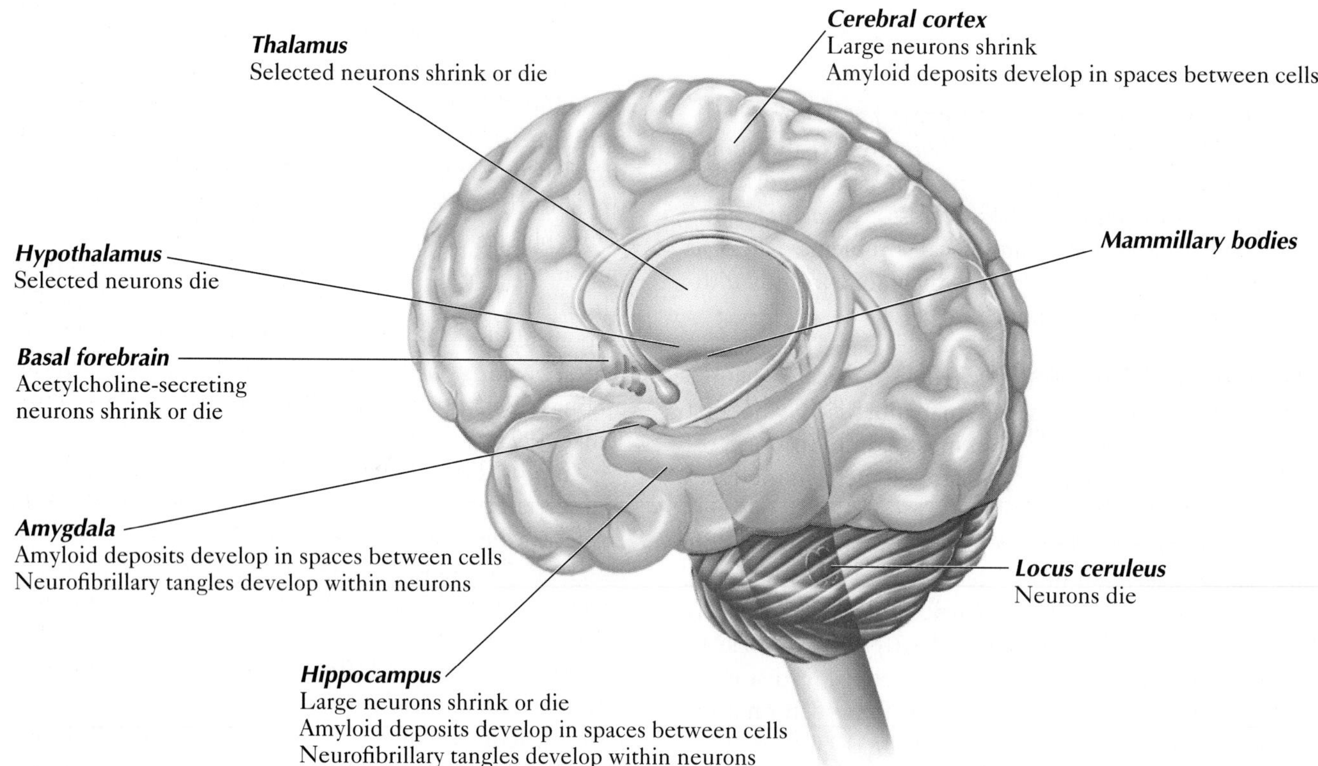

Figure 17-5 *The aging brain. In old age, our brain undergoes structural changes that affect memory, learning, and reasoning to some degree. These same changes occur to an excessive degree in people with Alzheimer's disease. (Adapted from Selkoe, 1992, p. 136.)*

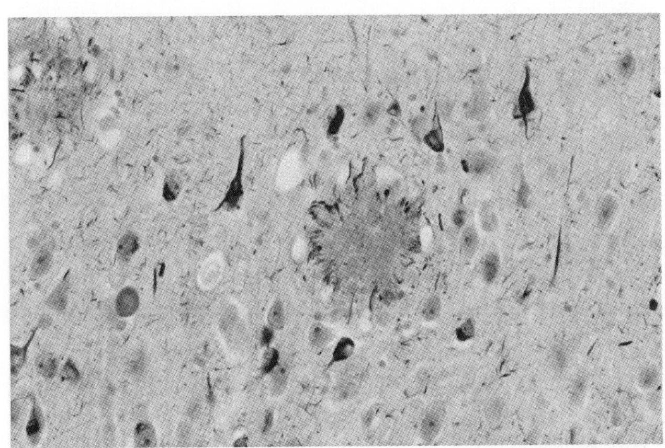

Tissue from the brain of a 69-year-old man with Alzheimer's disease reflects the structural changes characteristic of the disorder, including excessive amounts of plaque (large dark-gold sphere), the clusters of beta-amyloid protein that form outside of cells; and neurofibrillary tangles, the twisted fibers within cells that make the cells appear blackened (small dark blobs).

tion as a whole (Gallagher-Thompson & Thompson, 1995).

Neurotransmitter Abnormalities At least two common neurotransmitters, ***acetylcholine*** and ***glutamate,*** are depleted, or at least act irregularly, in the brains of Alzheimer victims (Bissette et al., 1996; Lee et al., 1996). As we noted earlier, these neurotransmitters play key roles in memory, learning, and abtract thinking, triggering protein production and other cellular activities that are critical to the formation of both short-term and long-term memories.

Other Causes Theorists have also pointed to other possible causes of Alzheimer's disease. Some scientists are looking for a slow-acting *infectious agent* that may help cause the disease (Prusiner, 1991). Others believe the *immune systems* of people who develop the disease may be impaired (Hüll et al., 1996; McGeer & McGeer, 1996). High concentrations of aluminum in the brains of some Alzheimer's victims have led some investigators to look for *heavy metals* or other *toxic substances* in the brains of Alzheimer's patients. Still other researchers have cited elevated levels of *zinc* in the brain as a possible factor in this disease. And it is possible that yet other factors may precipitate the biological changes found in Alzheimer's disease.

Vascular Dementia ***Vascular dementia,*** also known as ***multi-infarct dementia,*** follows a cerebrovascular accident, or stroke, when a loss of blood flow damages specific areas of the brain. The patient may be aware of the stroke, or it may be "silent"—that is, the patient may be unaware that anything has happened. Like Alzheimer's disease, vascular dementia is progressive, but its symptoms develop abruptly rather than gradually. Moreover, some cognitive functioning usually remains intact in parts of the brain that have not been affected by the stroke, whereas Alzheimer's patients are generally impaired in all areas of cognitive functioning (Gallagher-Thompson & Thompson, 1995). Because they cannot discriminate between the kinds of cognitive tasks they perform well and the ones that are significantly impaired, some people with vascular dementia unintentionally place themselves or others at risk. Some people have both Alzheimer's disease and vascular dementia.

Vascular dementia is the second most common type of dementia among the elderly, accounting for 8 to 29 percent of cases (Selkoe, 1992; Katzman, 1981). It occurs more often in men than in women (APA, 1994), a finding consistent with the higher rate of cardiovascular disease and hypertension in men as they age.

Other Dementias Other diseases that may produce the symptoms of dementia include Pick's disease, Creutzfeldt-Jakob disease, Huntington's disease, and Parkinson's disease (see Box 17-3).

Pick's disease is a rare disorder that affects the frontal and temporal lobes. It is difficult to differentiate from Alzheimer's disease clinically, but the distinction becomes clear at autopsy. This disease usually strikes between the ages of 50 and 60 years (APA, 1994).

Creutzfeldt-Jakob disease, another rare progressive dementia, is caused by a slow-acting virus that may live in the body for years before the disease unfolds. The disease has a rapid course, and its symptoms often include spasmodic movements. It typically makes its appearance between 40 and 60 years of age (APA, 1994).

Huntington's disease, an inherited progressive degenerative disease of cognition, emotion, and movement, is usually diagnosed in the late 30s or early 40s, but often begins much earlier (APA, 1994). It has a dramatic effect on personality, and brings on depression, instability, and anxiety (Scourfield et al., 1997). The motor symptoms may initially take the form of increased fidgeting and later progress to general spasmodic twitching. Patients with Huntington's disease show severe retrograde amnesia early on and also are impaired in their ability to learn procedural skills, such as new motor tasks (Butters et al., 1990). Memory problems get worse as the disease progresses. Children of people with Huntington's disease have a 50 percent chance of developing it.

BOX 17-3 "You Are the Music, While the Music Lasts"

Clayton S. Collins

(Excerpted by permission from **Profiles,** *the magazine of Continental Airlines, February 1994.)*

Oliver Sacks danced to the Dead. For three solid hours. At 60. And with "two broken knees."

The Oxford-educated neurologist who likes to say, with an impish grin, that he doesn't like any music after Mozart's *Magic Flute* wasn't particularly taken by the Grateful Dead concert in Friedrich Nietzsche's mnemonic sense, he explains (as only he would), "but in a tonic and dynamic sense they were quite overwhelming. And though I had effusions for a month after, it was worth it."

The power of music—not just to get an aging physician with classical tastes up and rocking, but also to "bring back" individuals rendered motionless and mute by neurological damage and disorders—is what's driving Sacks these days. The . . . best-selling author (*Migraine, A Leg to Stand On, The Man Who Mistook His Wife for a Hat, Seeing Voices* and *Awakenings*—which was made into a 1990 film starring Robin Williams) is working on another case-study book, one that deals in part with the role of music as a stimulus to minds that have thrown up stiff sensory barriers, leaving thousands of victims of stroke, tumors, Parkinson's disease, Tourette's syndrome, Alzheimer's and a wide range of less-publicized ailments alone, debilitated and disoriented.

"One sees how robust music is neurologically," Sacks says. "You can lose all sorts of particular powers but you don't tend to lose music and identity." His conviction regarding the role of music in helping the neurologically afflicted to become mentally "reorganized" runs deep: "Whenever I get out a book on neurology or psychology, the first thing I look up in the index is music," he says. "And if it's not there, I close the book." . . .

Speaking in his distinctive stammer before a gathering of 1,400 music therapists in Toronto, Sacks seems disjointed, his large rumpled form hunched over the podium, squinting in the glare as he fishes for a scrap of paper bearing a relevant quote from a medical text or a favorite philosopher. He drops such provocative phrasings as "kinetic stutter" (in describing Parkinsonism), then recalls all in one breath that the poet Novalis said, "Every disease is a musical disorder. Every cure is a musical solution," basking bemusedly in the appreciative gasps before admitting, "I've never known exactly what it means." . . .

Much of what he has encountered, particularly in working with patients at Beth Abraham Hospital, Bronx, N.Y., . . . relates to music.

"One saw patients who couldn't take a single step, who couldn't walk, but who could dance," he says. "There were patients who couldn't speak, but who could sing. The power of music in these patients was instantaneous . . . from a frozen Parkinsonian state to a freely flowing, moving, speaking state."

Sacks remembers a woman with Parkinson's who would sit perfectly still until "activated" by the music of Chopin, which she loved and knew by heart. She didn't have to hear a tune played. "It was sometimes sufficient to give her an opus number," Sacks says. "You would just say 'Opus 49,' and the F-minor 'Fantasy' would start playing in her mind. And she could move."

Music is certainly cultural, acknowledges the doctor, but it is basically biological. "One listens to music with one's muscles," he says, quoting Nietzsche again. "The 'tonic' [the key] is mostly brainstem, an arousal response." The "dynamic," how loud or forcefully the music is played, registers in the basal ganglia. And the "mnemonic" aspect of songs speaks to the unique memories of individuals: from tribal chant to blare of bagpipes to Bizet. The cliché about music's universality, he says, has merit.

"Deeply demented people respond to music, babies respond to music, fetuses probably respond to music. Various animals respond to music," Sacks says. "There is something about the animal nervous system . . . which seems to respond to music all the way down.

Parkinson's disease, a slowly progressive neurological condition marked by tremors, rigidity, and unsteadiness, causes dementia in 20 to 60 percent of cases, particularly among older people or those whose cases are advanced (APA, 1994). Such patients primarily have problems retrieving long-term memory, but they may also have difficulty learning new information and procedural skills (Harrington et al., 1990). As we noted in Chapters 15 and

"I don't know how it is with invertebrates. I think it's a desperately needed experiment," the grin widens, "to see how squids and cuttlefish respond." . . .

"I think the notion of music as being a prosthesis in a way, for neurological dysfunctions, is very fundamental," Sacks says, citing the case of a patient with damage to the frontal lobes of his brain.

"When he sings, one almost has the strange feeling that [music] has given him his frontal lobes back, given him back, temporally, some function that has been lost on an organic basis," Sacks says, adding a quote from T. S. Eliot: "You are the music, while the music lasts."

The effects of music therapy may not always last. Sacks will take what he can get. "To organize a disorganized person for a minute is miraculous. And for half an hour, more so." . . .

The key, says Sacks, is for patients to "learn to be well" again. Music can restore to them, he says, the identity that predates the illness. "There's a health to music, a life to music." . . .

For Sacks, who's been affiliated with a half-dozen neurological institutes and written dozens of seminal papers, medicine needs to be demonstrable, firmly grounded in physiology. Music's been healing for thousands of years, Sacks says. "It's just being looked at now more systematically and with these special populations."

So if the Grateful Dead moved Sacks to dance, it had been in the name of research. Seeking a clinical application, Sacks returned to Beth Abraham the next day and "kidnapped" one of his patients. "Greg" was an amnesiac with a brain tumor and no coherent memories of life since about 1969—but an encyclopedic memory of the years that came before, and a real love of Grateful Dead tunes.

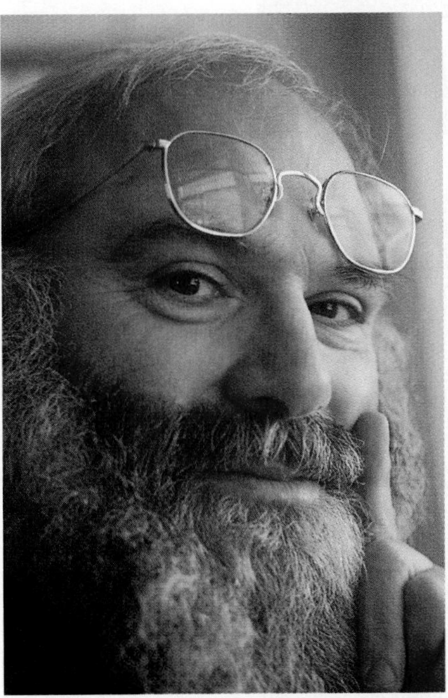

Over the years, the innovative neurologist Oliver Sacks has used treatment techniques that range from the medication L-dopa to the music of the Grateful Dead.

Sacks took Greg to that night's performance. "In the first half of the concert they were doing early music, and Greg was enchanted by everything," Sacks recalls. "I mean, he was not an amnesiac. He was completely oriented and organized and with it." Between sets Sacks went backstage and introduced Greg to band member Micky Hart, who was impressed with Greg's knowledge of the group but quite surprised when Greg asked after Pigpen. When told the former band member had died 20 years before, "Greg was very upset," Sacks recalls. "And then 30 seconds later he asked 'How's Pigpen?'"

During the second half, the band played its newer songs. And Greg's world began to fall apart. "He was bewildered and enthralled and frightened. Because the music for him—and this is an extremely musical man, who understands the idiom of the Grateful Dead—was both familiar and unfamiliar. . . . He said 'This is like the music of the future.'"

Sacks tried to keep the new memories fresh. But the next day, Greg had no memory of the concert. It seemed as if all had been lost. "But—and this is strange—when one played some of the new music, which he had heard for the first time at the concert, he could sing along with it and remember it."

It is an encouraging development. . . . Children have been found to learn quickly lessons that are embedded in song. Sacks, the one-time quiet researcher, is invigorated by the possibilities. He wonders whether music could carry such information, to give his patient back a missing part of his life. To give Greg "some sense of what's been happening in the last 20 years, where he has no autobiography of his own."

That would have Sacks dancing in the aisles.

16, Parkinson's disease is closely tied to a low activity level of the neurotransmitter dopamine in the brain.

Finally, many cases of dementia are caused by viral and bacterial *infectious disorders* such as HIV and AIDs, meningitis, and advanced syphilis. Still others are caused by *epilepsy.* And a number of cases are caused by *substances,* such as abused drugs or toxins (mercury, lead, carbon monoxide).

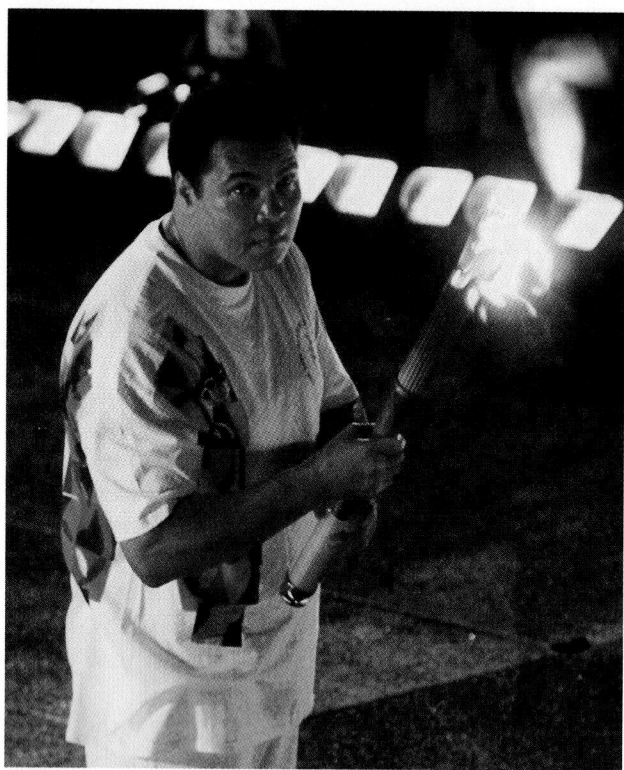

The world cheered when Muhammad Ali, considered the most skilled and influential athlete of his generation, lit the Olympic flame in 1996. At the same time, Ali's slow gait, halting verbal responses, and shaking hands and limbs demonstrated the bodily and psychological debilitation that Parkinson's disease can bring.

Treatments for Amnestic Disorders and Dementias

Treating amnestic disorders and dementias is a frustrating and difficult challenge (see again Box 17-3). Because these disorders affect a variety of brain structures and involve many neurochemical processes, no single approach or set of approaches is effective in all cases. Treatment still offers modest help at best. Recent research on the genetic, biochemical, and anatomical causes of amnestic disorders and dementias, however, has provided hope that these problems may be treated more effectively or even prevented in the years to come.

Currently the most important step in treatment is to identify as clearly as possible the precise type and nature of the disease. Clinicians begin by taking a complete history of the patient; knowing about a person's abuse of alcohol or a family history of Alzheimer's disease, for example, helps narrow the diagnosis. Second, clinicians employ extensive neuropsychological testing (see pp. 133–134) to identify the patient's specific cognitive impairments. Finally, they may employ brain imaging techniques (see pp. 132–133) to help identify the nature and biological causes of the patient's dysfunctioning (Gonzalez, 1996; Jagust, 1996).

In their efforts to find an effective *drug therapy,* researchers have developed the ***nootropics*** ("toward mind"). Most such "smart drugs" alter the activity of memory-linked neurotransmitters, such as glutamate and acetylcholine, in such a way that they are expected to enhance memory (Furey et al., 1997; Hedaya, 1996). So far the effectiveness of most of these drugs has been demonstrated primarily in animals.

One nootropic drug, however, is already approved for use with human patients. The drug ***tacrine*** prevents the breakdown of acetylcholine, the neurotransmitter that is in low supply among people with Alzheimer's disease. Some patients with Alzheimer's disease or other forms of dementia who take high doses of this drug improve slightly in short-term memory and reasoning ability, as well as in their use of language and their coping ability (Davis et al., 1992; Farlow et al., 1992). Although the benefits of tacrine are limited and the risk of adverse effects, such as liver complications, is sometimes high, the drug was approved by the Food and Drug Administration in 1993, under the trade name ***Cognex.*** Most clinicians believe that it may be beneficial for select patients only, particularly those in the early stages of Alzheimer's disease or those with a mild form of dementia, and even then any improvement in function is likely to be limited (Hedaya, 1996; Kumar, 1993).

Tacrine and other nootropic drugs are, obviously, employed after a person has developed Alzheimer's disease. A number of recent longitudinal studies seem to suggest that certain substances may actually help prevent or delay the onset of the disease. For example, one team of researchers has found that taking *estrogen,* the female sex hormone, for years after menopause may decrease a woman's risk of developing Alzheimer's disease by over 50 percent (Kawas et al., 1997). Similarly, long-term use of non-steroid anti-inflammatory drugs such as *ibuprofen* and *naprosyn* (drugs found in Advil, Motrin, Nuprin, and other pain relievers) seems to greatly reduce the risk of Alzheimer's disease.

Behavioral and cognitive interventions have also been tried in cases of amnestic disorder and dementia, with modest success. Some persons with amnestic disorders, particularly those whose amnesia is caused by a head injury, have successfully been taught special methods for remembering new information; in some cases the teachers have been computers (Schacter et al., 1990). Behavioral techniques have also been applied to patients with dementia. Typically, behaviorists identify specific everyday patient actions that are stressful for the family, such as wandering at night, being incontinent, and demanding frequent attention, or deficient behaviors such as inadequate self-care (Fisher &

This 63-year-old man with Alzheimer's disease is being institutionalized after declining for six years. His wife comforts him, and his daughter writes his name on his shoes prior to admission—poignant reminders of the psychological pain and sense of loss felt by the family caretakers of individuals with this disease.

Carstensen, 1990). They then teach family members how and when to apply reinforcement in order to shape positive behaviors, using a combination of role-playing techniques, modeling, and in-home practice (Pinkston & Linsk, 1984). Similar behavioral principles and techniques are often taught to staff members in long-term care facilities and nursing homes.

Caregiving may take a very heavy toll on the close relatives of persons with amnestic disorders or dementia, particularly the latter (Fritz et al., 1997; Kiecolt-Glaser et al., 1996; Gallagher-Thompson & Thompson, 1995). Indeed, one of the most frequent reasons for the institutionalization of Alzheimer's victims is that overwhelmed caregivers can no longer cope with the demands of the situation (Colerick & George, 1986). Many caretakers of Alzheimer's patients report experiencing anger and depression and a deterioration of their own physical and mental health (Fritz et al., 1997; Haley et al., 1995). Clinicians now recognize that one of the most important aspects of treating Alzheimer's disease and other forms of dementia is to reduce caretakers' emotional reactions and difficulties (Zarit et al., 1985). Clinicians have emphasized the need for planned and regular time-out for the caretakers (Berman et al., 1987); offered psychoeducational programs about the relative's disease; and provided psychotherapy for distressed family members. Moreover, some clinicians have developed support groups to meet the needs of caretakers (Gallagher-Thompson et al., 1991).

Rather than being discouraged by the present limitations of treatments for organic disorders of memory and other cognitive functions, researchers are now anticipating significant advances in the understanding, treatment, and prevention of these disorders. The complexity of the biochemical processes and brain structures underlying cognition can be overwhelming, but the coming years are expected to see significant breakthroughs.

Crossroads

Sometimes scientists scoff at a pheomenon that captures the public's interest. Dissociative disorders suffered this fate for many years. The public's interest in dissociative amnesia and fugue was almost insatiable, but investigations into them were limited. Similarly, multiple personality disorder failed to spur much empirical research. However, this scientific skepticism and inattention has changed course during the past few decades. The growing number of reported cases of dissociative disorders, particularly multiple personality disorder, has convinced many researchers that the patterns do exist and can lead to significant dysfunctioning.

The last fifteen years have seen a veritable explosion of research to help clinicians recognize, understand, and treat the dissociative disorders. Not only may disorders be more common than anyone previously believed, but they may have their roots in well-known processes, such as state-dependent learning and self-hypnosis. Still, we do not yet have comprehensive, coherent theories about the causes of dissociative disorders. Nor do we yet understand the relative contributions of sociocultural, psychological, and biological factors. Systematic treatment programs, too, have yet to be fully developed.

Some clinicians worry that the pendulum may, in fact, be swinging too far. They argue, for example, that many current diagnoses have more to do with the increasing popularity of the disorders than with a careful assessment of symptoms. They also worry that at least some of the legal accusations and defenses based on dissociative disorders may be contrived or inaccurate. Such possibilities only underscore the importance of continued investigations.

Less controversial but equally intriguing are the disorders of memory that have organic causes. The enormous complexity of the brain makes it extremely difficult to understand, diagnose, and treat the range of amnestic disorders and dementias. However, exciting research keeps emerging, seemingly daily, and captures the attention of both clinicians and the public. In view of the organic nature of these disorders, the research, as well as its implications for treatment, is largely biological. Once again, however, the disorders have such powerful impacts on patients and their families that psychological and sociocultural investigations are not likely to trail behind for long.

A common thread across the many studies of dissociative disorders and organic memory disorders is the fascination that memory holds for us. Memory is so central to our continuing sense of self that research is of fundamental importance to every person's well-being. We can expect that investigations into the nature of memory and memory disorders will continue to expand in the years to come.

Chapter Review

1. ***Memory*** Memory plays a central role in our functioning by linking us to the past, present, and future.

2. ***Dissociative disorders*** People with dissociative disorders experience significant alterations in memory that are not due to clear physical causes. Typically, one part of the memory is dissociated, or separated, from another.

   A. People with *dissociative amnesia* are suddenly unable to recall important personal information or past events in their lives. There are four kinds of dissociative amnesia: *localized, selective, generalized,* and *continuous.*

   B. People with *dissociative fugue* not only lose their memory of their personal identity but flee to a different location and may establish a new identity.

   C. *Multiple personality disorder* is a rare, dramatic disorder in which a person displays two or more distinct *subpersonalities.*

   (1) A *primary personality* appears more often than the others, but transitions to the other subpersonalities may occur frequently and suddenly.

   (2) Most people with multiple personality disorder have been abused as children.

   (3) The subpersonalities often have complex relationships with one another and usually differ in *vital statistics, abilities and preferences,* and even *physiological responses.*

   (4) The number of people diagnosed with multiple personality disorder has increased in recent years.

3. ***Explanations of dissociative disorders*** Among the factors that have been cited to explain dissociative disorders are extreme *repression, operant conditioning, state-dependent learning,* and *self-hypnosis.*

4. ***Treatments for dissociative disorders*** Dissociative amnesia and fugue may end spontaneously or may require treatment. Multiple personality disorder typically requires treatment for recovery to occur.

   A. Common interventions to help patients recover their lost memories are *psychodynamic therapy, hypnotic therapy,* and *sodium amobarbital* or *sodium pentobarbital.*

   B. Therapists usually try to guide people with multiple personality disorder to recognize the full scope and nature of their disorder, recover the gaps in their memories, and integrate their subpersonalities into one.

5. ***Organic memory disorders*** *Amnestic disorders* and *dementias* are organic disorders that cause problems in memory.

   A. These disorders may be characterized by problems in *short-term memory, long-term memory,* or both.

   B. Often the disorders involve abnormalities in key brain structures, such as the *prefrontal lobes,* the *temporal lobes* (including the *hippocampus* and *amygdala* embedded under them), and the *diencephalon* (including the *mammillary bodies, thalamus,* and *hypothalamus*).

   C. Amnestic disorders, which primarily affect memory, include *Korsakoff's syndrome* and disorders caused by *head trauma, brain surgery, vascular disease, heart attacks,* and certain *infectious diseases.*

   D. Dementias, which affect both memory and other cognitive functions, include *Alzheimer's disease, vascular dementia, Pick's disease, Creutzfeldt-Jakob disease, Huntington's disease,* and *Parkinson's disease.*

6. ***Treatments for amnestic disorders and dementias*** Both drug and behavioral therapies have been applied to organic memory disorders, with limited success. The coming years are expected to see significant treatment breakthroughs.

Thought and Afterthought

Guilty and *Not Guilty*

In 1979, Kenneth Bianchi, one of a pair of men known as the Hillside Stranglers, was accused of raping and murdering several women in the Los Angeles area. Bianchi denied the charges, and during a hypnotic interview another personality named Steve emerged. Steve claimed that he, not Kenneth, had committed the crimes.

Bianchi pleaded not guilty by reason of insanity, but the court refused to accept his claim of multiple personality disorder. The second personality, the prosecution pointed out, emerged only during hypnosis, after the examiner had told Bianchi that the procedure would reveal another part of him. Bianchi was found guilty of the crimes.

Afterthoughts: What would have been an appropriate verdict had Bianchi's disorder been ruled genuine? . . . May highly publicized trials such as this influence other people to believe that they have a multiple personality disorder? . . . Between 23 and 65 percent of accused murderers claim to have no memory of their crimes (Noll & Turkington, 1994). Why might a murderer experience amnesia?

Stricken by Alzheimer's disease, former President Ronald Reagan celebrates his 84th birthday on February 6, 1995.

To Know or Not To Know

For years the only way to diagnose Alzheimer's disease with certainty has been to wait for an autopsy. Today, however, scientists seem close to developing early, definitive tests for the disorder. In fact, diagnosticians may eventually be able to identify victims years or even decades before any noticeable decline in their memory or other cognitive functions (Nash, 1995; Small et al., 1995).

Afterthoughts: Would people be better off not knowing that they will eventually be developing a disease that has no known cure? . . . Are there psychological values to knowing one's fate as soon as possible even when no effective treatment is available? . . . How might the 1980 presidential election have turned out had people known that Ronald Reagan (above) would eventually develop dementia?

Mad Human Disease?

In the 1980s British farmers first observed *bovine spongiform encephalopathy*, or *mad cow disease.* Cows with this disease became disoriented, uncoordinated, and irritable, and eventually died. Autopsies revealed holes and tangles of protein in their brains. Researchers traced the disease to a particular feeding practice and officials promptly banned it. But symptoms of the disease do not appear until years after the infection is contracted, so a continuing epidemic unfolded. Some 160,000 cows have now died of the disease (Sternberg, 1996).

What does all of this have to do with human beings? There is a form of human dementia that is somewhat similar, clinically and biologically, to mad cow disease: *Creutzfeldt-Jakob disease* (CJD). This rare progressive dementia—incurable and fatal—is apparently caused by an infectious protein that stays in the body for decades before producing symptoms (Prusiner, 1995). Normally, one out of a million people develops CJD each year (Pain, 1996). Yet in 1996 ten otherwise healthy young adults in Britain died of a disease that appeared to be a new variant of CJD. Could those individuals have contracted their disease by eating the meat of infected cows?

In short order, panic swept across England and across the world. Most nations banned imports of British beef. Healthy cows could not be distinguished from infected ones, and so the United Kingdom agreed to destroy 4.5 million animals—almost half the nation's herd. Photos of slaughtered cows repelled most people, but few suggested any other solution.

Afterthoughts: Some scientists argue that mad cow disease cannot be transmitted from one species to another, while others counter that it is indeed possible (Aldhous, 1996). When scientists disagree, how should the public proceed? . . . If scientists were to suspect, without certainty, that large numbers of human beings were carrying a deadly contagious disease, how would public officials respond? . . . Are there similarities between the epidemic of mad cow disease and the early stages of the AIDS epidemic, including the public's reaction to the diseases?

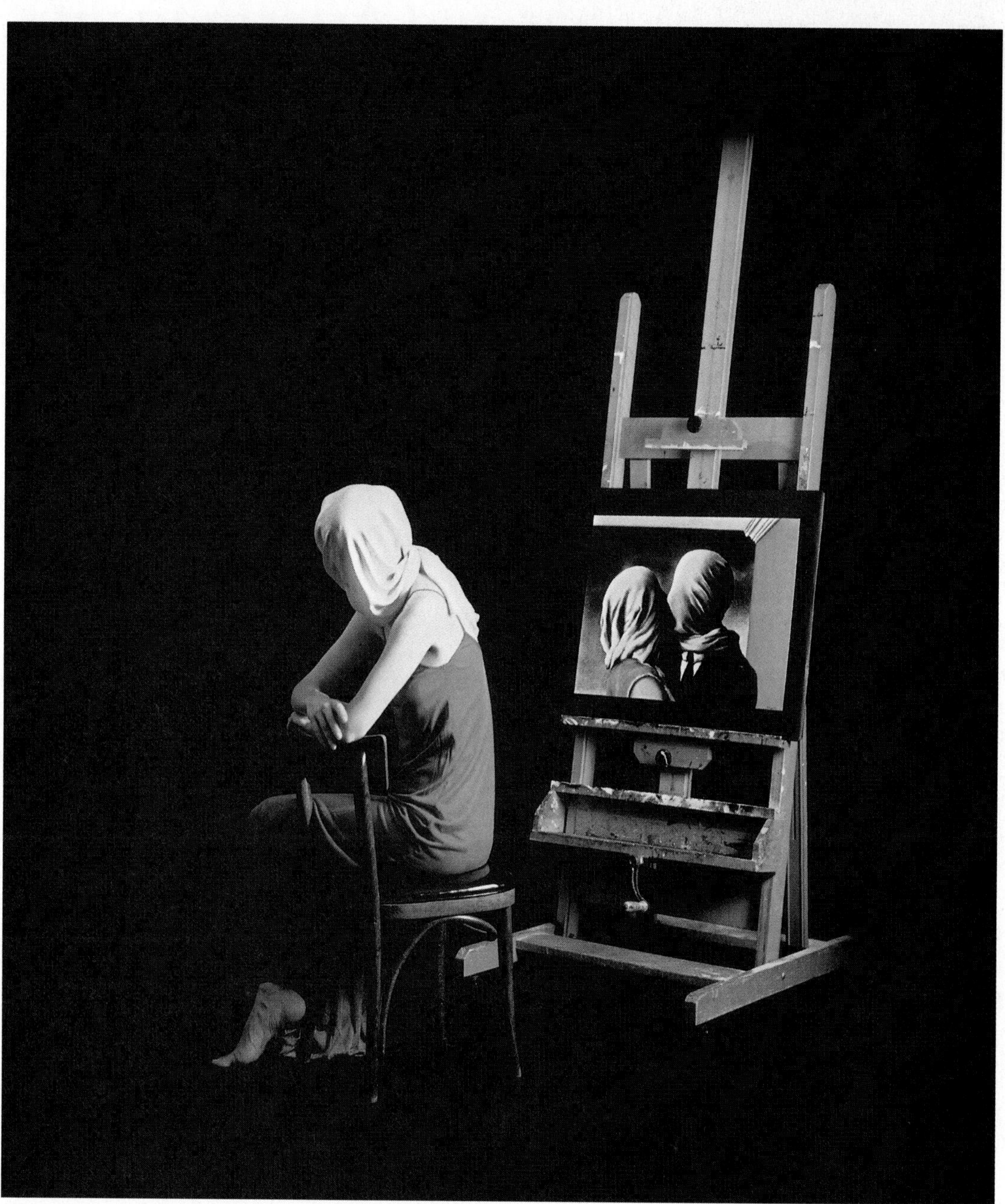

Topic Overview

Chapter 18

Personality Disorders

The maladaptive, enduring, and inflexible patterns of behavior of individuals with personality disorders often lead to psychological pain and to significant problems in relationships. However, like the subject of Eileen Cowin's Untitled, *1988, these individuals have difficulty changing such patterns, avoiding their unpleasant outcomes, or recognizing their role in such outcomes.*

Each of us has a ***personality***—a unique and enduring pattern of inner experience and outward behavior. We tend to react in our own relatively predictable and consistent ways. These enduring consistencies, often called ***personality traits,*** may be the result of intrinsic characteristics, learned responses, or a combination of the two (Watson, Clark, & Harkness, 1994). Yet our personalities are not static. Most of us are also flexible enough to learn from experience. As we interact with our surroundings, we try out various responses to see which are more effective. This is something that people who suffer from a personality disorder are frequently unable to do.

A ***personality disorder*** is an inflexible pattern of inner experience and outward behavior. The pattern is wide-ranging and enduring, and it deviates markedly from the expectations of one's culture. The inflexibility often results in unpleasant experiences, which may cause psychological pain and social or occupational difficulties. Personality disorders typically become recognizable in adolescence or early adulthood, although some start during childhood (APA, 1994).

Although personality disorders vary in the amount of disruption they bring to a person's life, the distress they produce makes for lifelong ordeals. The disorders often cause still more pain to others, and they are among the most difficult psychological disorders to treat. Many people with the disorders are not even aware of their personality problems. They are unable to trace their difficulties in life to their inflexible style of thinking and behaving. The prevalence of personality disorders among adults has been estimated at between 4 and 15 percent (Links, 1997; APA, 1994; Weissman, 1993).

As we saw in Chapter 5, DSM-IV differentiates Axis II disorders, disorders of long standing that usually begin well before adulthood and persist without much change into adult life, from the vivid Axis I disorders, which may emerge and end at various points in the life cycle. The personality disorders are listed on Axis II. Unlike most of the clinical syndromes we have looked at, personality disorders are not marked by periods of significant improvement. They neither vary greatly in intensity nor improve much over time.

Axis I and Axis II disorders often coexist (Flick et al., 1993). It is not at all unusual for a person with a personality disorder to suffer from an acute (Axis I) disorder as well, a relationship called *comorbidity.* Some theorists believe that personality disorders are simply less severe cases of Axis I disorders, and so one disorder almost automatically implies the other. Alternatively, personality

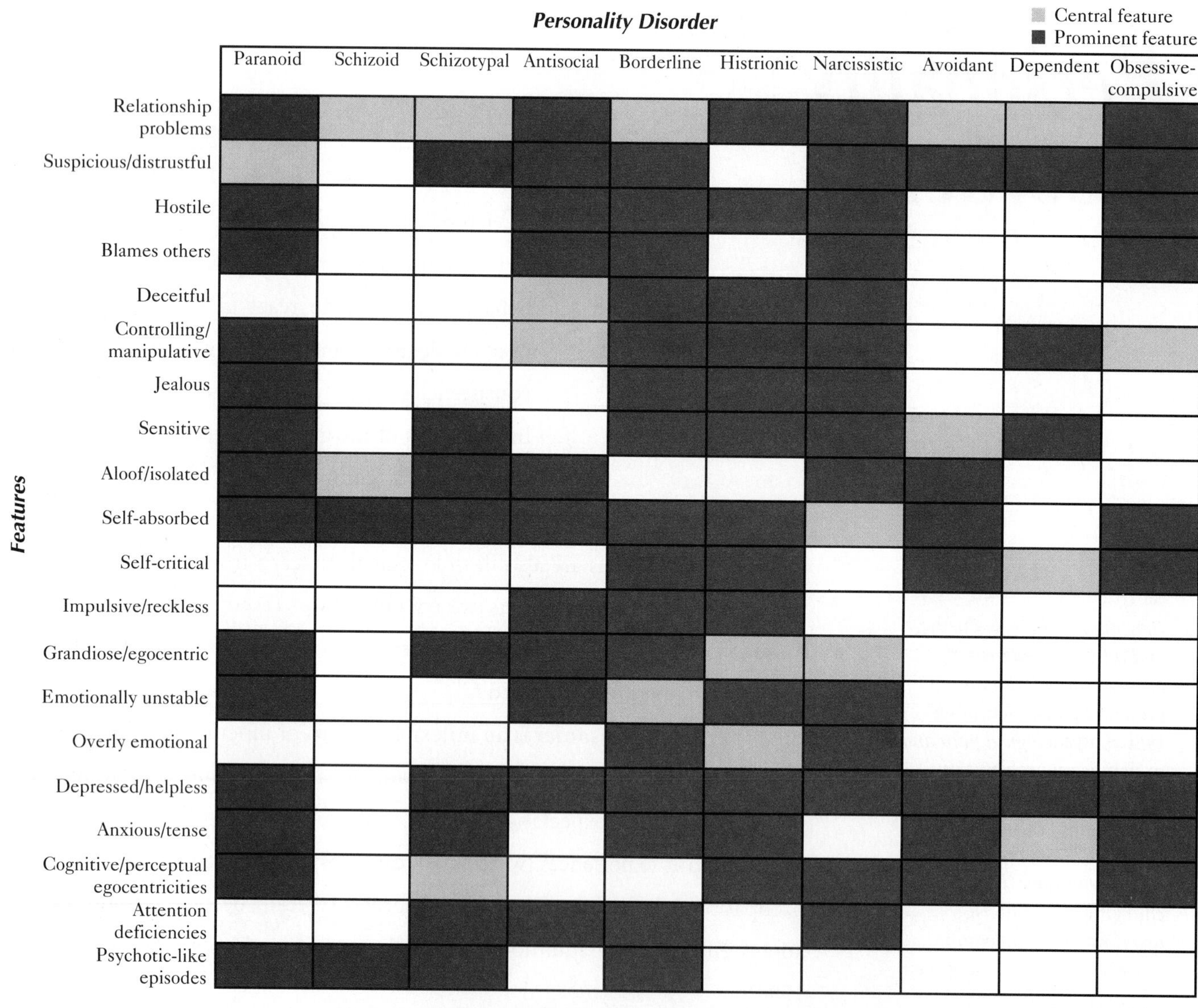

Figure 18-1 *Prominent and central features of ten personality disorders. The symptoms of the various disorders often overlap significantly, leading to frequent misdiagnosis or to multiple diagnoses for a given client. For this reason some clinicians have called for changes in DSM-IV's system of classifying the personality disorders.*

disorders may predispose some people to develop certain Axis I disorders (Johnson & Wonderlich, 1992). For example, people with avoidant personality disorder, who fearfully shun all relationships, may be predisposed to a social phobia. Then again, an Axis I disorder could predispose a person to a personality disorder. Or perhaps some other variable or biological factor creates a predisposition to both. Whatever the reason for the relationship, research indicates that the additional presence of a personality disorder complicates and reduces a client's responses to treatment for an Axis I disorder (Costello, 1996).

DSM-IV distinguishes ten personality disorders and groups them in three clusters (APA, 1994). One cluster, characterized by odd or eccentric behaviors, consists of the *paranoid, schizoid,* and *schizotypal* personality disorders. A second cluster, characterized by dramatic, emotional, or erratic behaviors, consists of the *antisocial, borderline, histrionic,* and *narcissistic* personality disorders. The final cluster, characterized by fearful or anxious behavior, consists of the *avoidant, dependent,* and *obsessive-compulsive* personality disorders.

The various personality disorders often overlap so much that it is difficult to distinguish them (Zimmerman, 1994) (see Figure 18-1). A diagnostician may even assign more than one personality disorder to a given individual (Grove & Tellegen, 1991). In addition, clinicians often disagree as to the correct diagnosis for persons with personality disorders. This lack of consensus has raised serious questions about the *validity* (accuracy) and *reliability* (consistency) of the present DSM categories (Costello, 1996), a concern that we shall return to later.

Finally, these categories can easily be overapplied. We may readily catch glimpses of ourselves or of people we know in the descriptions of these disorders, and be tempted to conclude that pathology is at work (Maher & Maher, 1994; Widiger & Costa, 1994). In the vast majority of cases, such interpretations are unwarranted. We all display personality traits; that is part of being human. Only rarely are they so inflexible, maladaptive, and distressful that they can be considered disorders.

"Odd" Personality Disorders

The cluster of "odd" personality disorders consists of the paranoid, schizoid, and schizotypal personality disorders. People with these disorders typically display the kinds of odd or eccentric behaviors seen in schizophrenia, including extreme suspiciousness, social withdrawal, and cognitive and perceptual peculiarities. Such behaviors often leave a person alone and isolated. Some clinicians believe that these personality disorders are indeed related to schizophrenia and call them *schizophrenia-spectrum disorders* (Battaglia et al., 1997; Siever, 1992). In support of this idea, people with the personality disorders often qualify for an additional diagnosis of schizophrenia or have close relatives with schizophrenia (APA, 1994; Battaglia et al., 1991; Siever et al., 1990). Of course, these findings may simply reflect the difficulty of distinguishing these personality disorders from schizophrenia, rather than some kind of direct relationship between them.

Clinicians have learned much about the *symptoms* of these odd personality disorders, but have not been so successful in determining their causes and treatment. More difficult still, people with these disorders rarely seek treatment (Fabrega et al., 1991).

Paranoid Personality Disorder

People with ***paranoid personality disorder*** display a pattern of pervasive distrust and suspiciousness (APA, 1994). Because they suspect everyone of intending them harm, they shun close relationships. Their trust in their own ideas and abilities can be excessive, though, as we see in the case of Charles.

> Charles, an only child of poorly educated parents, had been recognized as a "child genius" in early school years. He received a Ph.D. degree at 24, and subsequently held several responsible positions as a research physicist in an industrial firm.
>
> His haughty arrogance and narcissism often resulted in conflicts with his superiors; it was felt that he spent too much time working on his own "harebrained" schemes and not enough on company projects. Charles . . . began to feel that both his superiors and his subordinates were "making fun of him" and not taking him seriously. To remedy this attack upon his status, Charles began to work on a scheme that would "revolutionize the industry," a new thermodynamic principle which, when applied to his company's major product, would prove extremely efficient and economical. After several months . . . he presented his plans to the company president. Brilliant though it was, the plan overlooked certain obvious simple facts of logic and economy.
>
> Upon learning of its rejection, Charles withdrew to his home where he became obsessed with "new ideas," proposing them in intricate schematics and formulas to a number of government officials and industrialists. These resulted in new rebuffs which led to further efforts at self inflation.
>
> *(Millon, 1969, pp. 329–330)*

Ever vigilant, cautious, and quick to react to perceived threats, people like Charles continually expect to be the targets of some trickery or exploitation (see Figure 18-2). They find "hidden" meanings everywhere, usually belittling or threatening them. In one study in which subjects were asked to role-play, subjects with paranoia were more likely than controls to interpret the ambiguous actions of others as reflecting hostile intentions. They more often chose anger as the appropriate role-play response (Turkat et al., 1990).

People with paranoid personality disorder approach relationships with skepticism and guardedness. Quick to challenge the loyalty or trustworthiness of acquaintances, they remain cold and distant. A woman might be reluctant to confide in anyone, for example, for fear of being hurt; or a husband might with no justification continually question the fidelity of his wife. Their unwarranted suspicions are not usually delusional; their ideas are not so bizarre or so firmly held that they constitute a clear departure from reality (Fenigstein, 1996).

People with a paranoid personality disorder are critical of weakness and fault in others, particularly in work-related situations. They are unable to recognize their own mistakes, however, and are hypersensitive to criticism. Argumentative and rigid, they often blame others for the things that go wrong in their lives (Fenigstein, 1996; Vaillant, 1994). They persistently bear grudges. Between 0.5 and 2.5 percent of the adult population are believed to manifest this personality disorder, apparently more men than women (APA, 1994).

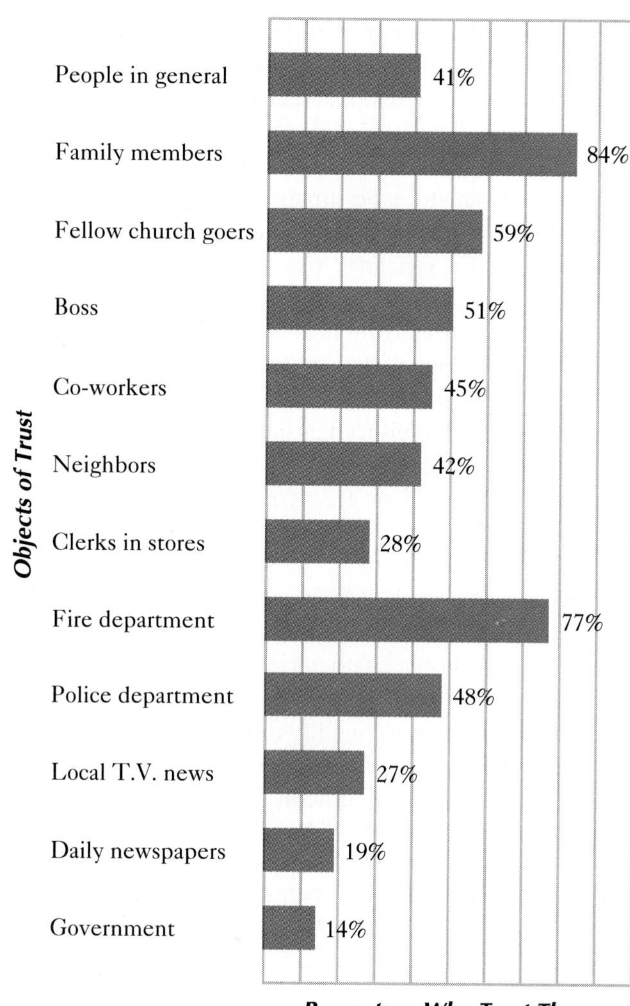

Figure 18-2 *Whom Do You Trust? Although distrust and suspiciousness is the hallmark of paranoid personality disorder, even persons without this disorder are surprisingly untrusting. According to a recent broad survey, only 41 percent of respondents say that they generally trust people. Most respondents do trust their family members and local fire department; however, relatively few trust clerks in stores, daily newspapers, or the government. (Adapted from Pew Research Center for the People and the Press, 1997.)*

Explanations of Paranoid Personality Disorder

The causes of paranoid personality disorder, like those of most other personality disorders, have received little empirical investigation. Psychodynamic theories, the most prominent explanations for this disorder, trace it to early interactions with demanding parents, particularly distant, rigid fathers and overcontrolling, rejecting mothers (Manschreck, 1996). (We shall see that psychodynamic explanations for almost all of the personality disorders begin the same way—with repeated mistreatment during infancy and childhood and lack of love.) According to one psychodynamic view, some individuals come to view their environment as hostile as a result of their demanding upbringing. They become overly vigilant because they cannot trust others (Cameron, 1974). These unfortunate children are also likely to develop excessive hostility and rage. As they project these feelings onto others, they come to feel even more persecuted (Garfield & Havens, 1991).

Other psychodynamic theories propose that such early experiences produce instead feelings of inadequacy. The children view themselves as mistake-prone and different from others as they try to meet their parents' unreasonable expectations (Turkat & Banks, 1987). Increasingly cast out by their peers, they rationalize their social isolation as stemming from others' jealousy.

Some cognitive theorists, too, have pictured paranoid functioning as a set of strategies designed to counter the demanding expectations of others and to cope with feelings of humiliation, shame, and inadequacy (Beck & Freeman, 1990; Colby, 1981). The result can be the adoption of broad maladaptive assumptions, such as "People are evil" and "People will attack you if given the chance" (Freeman et al., 1990).

Biological theorists propose that a genetic factor influences the development of paranoid personality disorder (Fenigstein, 1996). An epidemiologic study that looked at self-reported suspiciousness in 3,810 Australian twin pairs found that if one twin was excessively suspicious, the other had an increased likelihood of also being suspicious (Kendler et al., 1987). Once again, however, such findings alone cannot tell us whether it is genetic factors or common experiences that lead both twins to be overly suspicious.

Treatments for Paranoid Personality Disorder

People with paranoid personality disorder do not typically see themselves as needing help, and so few come to treatment willingly. Moreover, many perceive the role of patient as subordinate, distrust their therapist, and resist treatment (Fenigstein, 1996; Sparr et al., 1986). It is not surprising that therapy for this disorder, as for most other personality disorders, is at best modestly helpful and moves very slowly (Quality Assurance Project, 1990).

Object relations therapists give center stage to relationships in their work. These psychodynamic therapists try to see through the patient's defensive anger and work on what they view as his or her deep wish for a satisfying relationship (Auchincloss & Weiss, 1992). Behavioral and cognitive therapists try instead to help these clients control their anxiety and improve their skills at solving interpersonal problems. Clients are guided to develop more realistic perceptions of what others do and intend and to become more aware of other people's perspectives (Beck & Freeman, 1990). Drug therapy is generally ineffective (Block & Pristach, 1992).

Schizoid Personality Disorder

People with ***schizoid personality disorder*** are detached from social relationships and have a restricted range of emotional expression (APA, 1994). Like those with paranoid personality disorder, these individuals do not have close ties with others. The reason they avoid social contact, however, is that they genuinely prefer to be alone. Other people often view them as "loners," observers rather than participants in the world around them, like Roy:

> Roy was a successful sanitation engineer involved in the planning and maintenance of water resources for a large city; his job called for considerable foresight and independent judgment but little supervisory responsibility. In general, he was appraised as an undistinguished but competent and reliable employee. There were few demands of an interpersonal nature made of him, and he was viewed by most of his colleagues as reticent and shy and by others as cold and aloof.
>
> Difficulties centered about his relationship with his wife. At her urging they sought marital counseling for, as she put it, "he is unwilling to join in family activities, he fails to take an interest in the children, he lacks affection and is disinterested in sex."
>
> The pattern of social indifference, flatness of affect and personal isolation which characterized much of Roy's behavior was of little consequence to those with whom a deeper or more intimate relationship was not called for; with his immediate family, however, these traits took their toll.
>
> *(Millon, 1969, p. 224)*

People like Roy are uninterested in initiating or maintaining acquaintanceships, take little interest in having sexual relationships, and even seem indifferent to their families. They seek out occupations that require little or no contact with others. When necessary, they can form stable, if distant, work relations, but they prefer to keep to themselves, often working alone over the course of the day. They usually live by themselves as well and avoid socializing. As a result, their social skills tend to be limited (Birtchnell, 1996).

These restricted interactions reflect an equally restricted range of emotion and expression. People with schizoid personality disorder are self-absorbed and generally unaffected by praise or criticism. They rarely show their feelings, expressing neither joy nor anger. They seem to have no need for attention or acceptance, are typically viewed as cold, humorless, or dull, and generally succeed in being ignored.

The prevalence of schizoid personality disorder is not known, although it is estimated to be present in fewer than 1 percent of the population (APA, 1994; Weissman, 1993). Slightly more men than women are believed to have the disorder, and men may be more impaired by it (APA, 1994).

Explanations of Schizoid Personality Disorder

Many psychodynamic theorists, particularly object relations theorists, explain schizoid personality disorder as a defensive reaction to an unsatisfied basic need for human contact (Carstairs, 1992; Horner, 1991, 1975). Just as with paranoid personality disorder, psychodynamic theorists see the parents of people with this disorder as having been unaccepting or even abusive. Whereas those with paranoid symptoms react to such parenting with a sense of distrust, these individuals suffer an inability to give or receive love, and they cope by shunning all relationships. Proponents of self theory, another psychodynamic theory, speak of a "self disorder" in schizoid personality disorder, marked by a lack of self-esteem, self-affirmation, or the capacity for "self-soothing" (Cirese, 1993; Gabbard, 1990). Unsure of who they are, the individuals cannot relate to others.

Cognitive theorists propose instead that people with schizoid personality disorder suffer from cognitive deficits. Their thinking tends to be vague and empty and they are unable to scan the environment effectively and arrive at accurate perceptions (Beck & Freeman, 1990).

Unable to interpret subtle emotional cues from others, they simply cannot respond to emotions. As this theory predicts, children with schizoid personality disorder develop language, education, and motor skills unusu-ally slowly, whatever their level of intelligence (Wolff, 1991).

Treatments for Schizoid Personality Disorder

Socially withdrawn already, people with schizoid personality disorder tend to enter therapy only because of some other disorder, such as alcoholism. They often distance themselves from their therapist, seem not to care about their treatment, and make limited progress at best (Quality Assurance Project, 1990; Siever, 1981).

Cognitive therapists have sometimes been able to help clients with this disorder experience more positive emotions (Beck & Freeman, 1990). Their techniques include presenting clients with a list of emotions to think about or having clients record pleasurable experiences. Behavioral therapists have sometimes had success teaching social skills to their clients, using role playing, in vivo exposure, and homework assignments as tools (Beck & Freeman, 1990). Group therapy is apparently useful when it provides a contained, safe setting for social contact (Vaillant & Perry, 1985), although some persons with this disorder feel stifled by any pressure to take part (Gabbard, 1990). As with paranoid personality disorder, drug therapy has offered little help (Liebowitz et al., 1986).

Schizotypal Personality Disorder

People with ***schizotypal personality disorder*** display a pattern of interpersonal deficits marked by acute discomfort in close relationships, cognitive or perceptual distortions, and behavioral eccentricities (APA, 1994). Anxious around others, they seek isolation and have few close friends. Many feel intensely lonely. The disorder is more severe than the paranoid and schizoid personality disorders, as we see in the case of Harold:

> Harold was the fourth of seven children. . . . "Duckie," as Harold was known, had always been a withdrawn, frightened and "stupid" youngster. The nickname "Duckie" represented a peculiar waddle in his walk; it was used by others as a term of derogation and ridicule. Harold rarely played with his sibs or neighborhood children; he was teased unmercifully because of his "walk" and his fear of pranksters. Harold was a favorite neighborhood scapegoat; he was intimidated even by the most innocuous glance in his direction. . . .
>
> Harold's family was surprised when he performed well in the first few years of schooling. He began to falter, however, upon entrance to junior high school. At about the age of 14, his schoolwork became extremely poor, he refused to go to classes and he complained of a variety of vague, physical pains. By age 15 he had totally withdrawn from school, remaining home in the basement room that he shared with two younger brothers. Everyone in his family began to speak of him as "being touched." He thought about "funny religious things that didn't make sense"; he also began to draw "strange things" and talk to himself. When he was 16, he once ran out of the house screaming "I'm gone, I'm gone, I'm gone . . . ," saying that his "body went to heaven" and that he had to run outside to recover it; rather interestingly, this event occurred shortly after his father had been committed by the courts to a state mental hospital. By age 17, Harold was ruminating all day, often talking aloud in a meaningless jargon; he refused to come to the family table for meals.
>
> *(Millon, 1969, pp. 347–348)*

Schizotypal personality disorder is particularly distinguished by cognitive distortions and behavioral eccentricities (Birtchnell, 1996; APA, 1994). The individuals may have *ideas of reference,* believing that unrelated events pertain to them in some important way. They may have bodily *illusions,* such as sensing an external "force" or presence. Some see themselves as having special extrasensory abilities, and some believe that they have magical control over others. They may also display eccentric behavior, such as repeatedly arranging cans to align their labels, organizing closets, or wearing a peculiar assortment of clothing and accessories. Their emotions may be inappropriate or flat, humorless, and bland.

People with schizotypal personality disorder often have great difficulty keeping their attention focused (Lenzenwerger et al., 1991). This problem may partially explain one of their most distinctive characteristics—*digressive speech.* They typically converse in a vague manner, making statements that are inappropriately elaborate. Their loose associations make it difficult to follow their train of thought (Caplan et al., 1990). Unlike the functioning found in schizophrenia, however, these problems in attention and thought do not represent a complete break from reality.

Sometimes the perceptual distortions and magical thinking found in schizotypal personality disorder reflect genuine creative ability (Schuldberg et al., 1988). More often, however, people with this personality disorder drift aimlessly and lead an idle, ineffectual life (Millon, 1990). They are likely to choose undemanding jobs in which they can work below their capacity and have no need to interact with other people.

According to research, the features of this disorder may break down along gender lines. The "positive" symptoms (that is, the excesses), such as magical thinking and ideas of reference, seem to be more common in women, whereas the "negative" symptoms (the deficits),

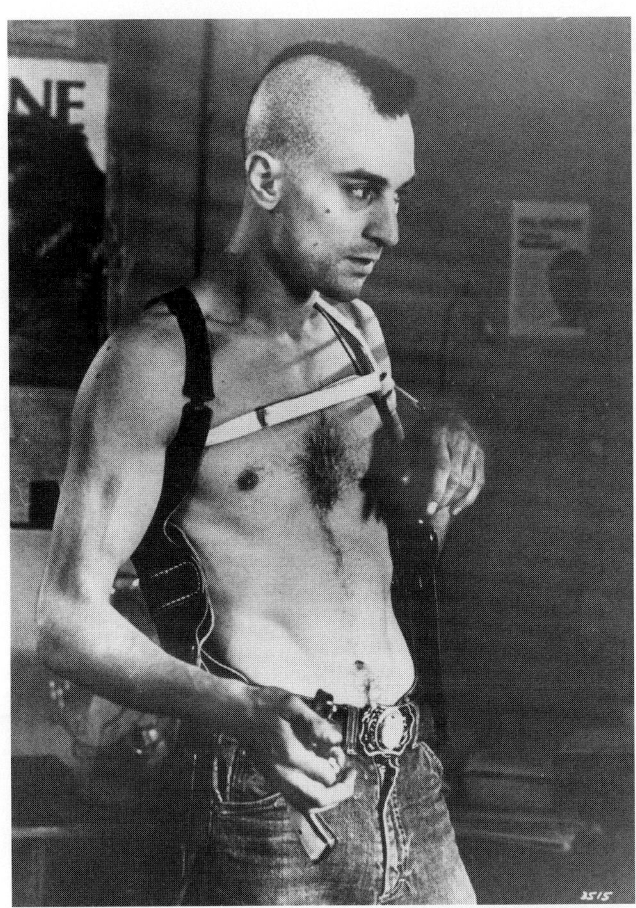

Some of film's most memorable characters have displayed personality disorders. Travis Bickle, of Taxi Driver *fame, seemed to manifest the symptoms of schizotypal personality disorder. His social discomfort and reduced capacity for interpersonal relationships, self-referential interpretations of various events, cognitive eccentricities, highly suspicious nature, grandiosity, emotional flatness, and transient psychotic episodes eventually exploded in a killing rampage.*

such as constricted emotions and lack of friends, appear to be more common among men (Raine, 1992).

People with this disorder are more likely to attempt suicide and to be hospitalized with another mental disorder (Lenzenweger et al., 1991; Bornstein et al., 1988). It has been estimated that around 3 percent of all persons—though slightly more males than females—may have a schizotypal personality disorder (APA, 1994; Weissman, 1993).

Explanations of Schizotypal Personality Disorder Because the symptoms are often so similar (see Table 18-1), researchers have tried to show that factors explaining schizophrenia can also help explain schizotypal personality disorder (Raine et al., 1997). Investigators have found, for example, that schizotypal symptoms, like schizophrenic patterns, are often linked to poor family communication and to psychological disorders in parents (Asarnow et al., 1991; Nagy & Szatmari, 1986). They have also found that defects in attention may contribute to schizotypal personality disorder, just as they apparently do to schizophrenia (Roitman et al., 1997; Weston & Siever, 1993). Both subjects with schizotypal symptoms and those with schizophrenic symptoms perform poorly on a laboratory task of attention called *backward masking.* This task requires subjects to identify a visual stimulus immediately after a previous stimulus has flashed on and off the screen. Both groups of subjects have a hard time shutting out the first stimulus (Weston & Siever, 1993; Braff & Saccuzzo, 1985).

Finally, research has begun to link schizotypal personality disorder to some of the same biological factors tied to schizophrenia, such as high levels of activity of the neurotransmitter *dopamine* and *enlarged brain ventricles* (Trestman et al., 1996; Weston & Siever, 1993; Rotter et al., 1991). There are also some indications that these biological factors may have a genetic base. Schizotypal personality disorder is more prevalent among the close relatives of people with this disorder than in the general population (Carey & DiLalla, 1994; Kendler et al., 1991).

These findings suggest a close relationship between schizotypal personality disorder and schizophrenia. However, the personality disorder has also been linked to mood disorders. Relatives of people with depression have a higher than usual rate of schizotypal personality disorder, and vice versa. Thus, at the very least, schizotypal personality disorder is not tied exclusively to schizophrenia (Schulz et al., 1986).

Treatments for Schizotypal Personality Disorder Therapy is as difficult for persons with schizotypal personality disorder as for those with paranoid and schizoid personality disorders (Stone, 1989; McGlashan, 1986). Most therapists agree on the need to help clients "reconnect" with the world and recognize the limits of their thinking and their powers. The therapists may thus set explicit limits, require punctuality, and distinguish clearly between the patient's views and those of the therapist (Stone, 1989). Other therapy goals are to prevent further social isolation, ease loneliness, avoid overstimulation, and develop self-awareness of personal feelings (Quality Assurance Project, 1990; Walsh, 1990).

Cognitive therapists further try to teach clients to evaluate their unusual thoughts or perceptions objectively and to disregard inappropriate thoughts (Beck & Freeman, 1990). They may keep track of a client's odd or magical predictions, for example, and then point out their invalidity. Or they may have a client who gets caught in loose and abstract verbalizations make summary statements. In addition, specific behavioral methods such as elocution lessons, social skills training, and tips on appropriate dress and manners have on occasion

TABLE 18-1 Comparison of Personality Disorders

	DSM-IV Cluster	*Similar Disorders on Axis I*	*Responsiveness to Treatment*
Paranoid	Odd	Schizophrenia Delusional disorder	Modest
Schizoid	Odd	Schizophrenia Delusional disorder	Modest
Schizotypal	Odd	Schizophrenia Delusional disorder	Modest
Antisocial	Dramatic	Conduct disorder	Poor
Borderline	Dramatic	Mood disorders	Modest
Histrionic	Dramatic	Somatoform disorders Mood disorders	Modest
Narcissistic	Dramatic	Cyclothymic disorder (mild bipolar disorder)	Poor
Avoidant	Anxious	Social phobia	Moderate
Dependent	Anxious	Separation anxiety disorder Dysthymic disorder (mild depressive disorder)	Moderate
Obsessive-compulsive	Anxious	Obsessive-compulsive anxiety disorder	Moderate

helped individuals learn to feel and act less alienated around others (Liebowitz et al., 1986).

Finally, antipsychotic drugs have often been given to patients with schizotypal personality disorder, partly because of the similarities to schizophrenia. These drugs in low doses apparently help some patients, usually by reducing some of their thought problems (Weston & Siever, 1993; Perry et al., 1990). Patients with this disorder may be particularly sensitive to the harmful effects of medication, however, so the dosage must be monitored closely.

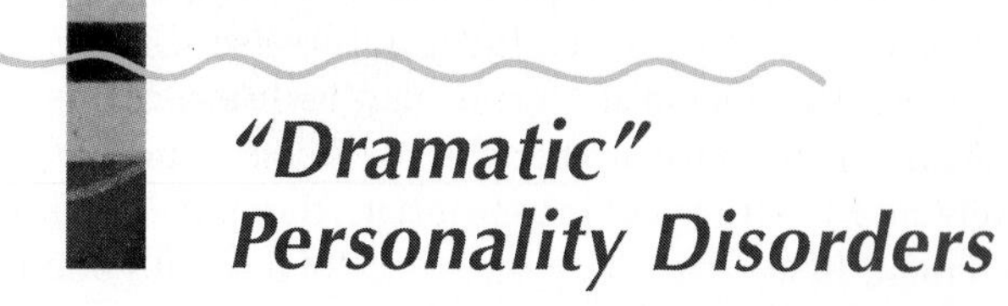

"Dramatic" Personality Disorders

The cluster of "dramatic" personality disorders includes the antisocial, borderline, histrionic, and narcissistic personality disorders. People with these problems often display behaviors that are so highly dramatic, emotional, or erratic that it is almost impossible for them to have reciprocal or normal relationships.

As a group, these personality disorders are more commonly diagnosed than the others (Fabrega et al., 1991). However, only antisocial personality disorder has received much empirical attention over the years, partly because it creates so many problems for society. The causes of the disorders are once again not well understood and treatments range from ineffective to modestly effective.

Antisocial Personality Disorder

Robert Hare (1993), one of the world's leading researchers of antisocial personality disorder, recalls an early professional encounter with Ray, a prison inmate who displayed this disorder:

> In the early 1960s, I found myself employed as the sole psychologist at the British Columbia Penitentiary. . . . I wasn't in my office for more than an hour when my first "client" arrived. He was a tall, slim, dark-haired man in his thirties. The air around him seemed to buzz,

and the eye contact he made with me was so direct and intense that I wondered if I had ever really looked anybody in the eye before. That stare was unrelenting—he didn't indulge in the brief glances away that most people use to soften the force of their gaze.

Without waiting for an introduction, the inmate—I'll call him Ray—opened the conversation: "Hey, Doc, how's it going? Look, I've got a problem. I need your help. I'd really like to talk to you about this."

Eager to begin work as a genuine psychotherapist, I asked him to tell me about it. In response, he pulled out a knife and waved it in front of my nose, all the while smiling and maintaining that intense eye contact.

Once he determined that I wasn't going to push the button, he explained that he intended to use the knife not on me but on another inmate who had been making overtures to his "protégé," a prison term for the more passive member of a homosexual pairing. Just why he was telling me this was not immediately clear, but I soon suspected that he was checking me out, trying to determine what sort of a prison employee I was. Following our session, in which he described his "problem" not once or twice but many times, I kept quiet about the knife. To my relief, he didn't stab the other inmate, but it soon became evident that Ray had caught me in his trap: I had shown myself to be a soft touch who would overlook clear violations of fundamental prison rules in order to develop "professional" rapport with the inmates.

From that first meeting on, Ray managed to make my eight-month stint at the prison miserable. His constant demands on my time and his attempts to manipulate me into doing things for him were unending. On one occasion, he convinced me that he would make a good cook—he felt he had a natural bent for cooking, he thought he would become a chef when he was released, this was a great opportunity to try out some of his ideas to make institutional food preparation more efficient, etc.—and I supported his request for a transfer from the machine shop (where he had apparently made the knife). What I didn't consider was that the kitchen was a source of sugar, potatoes, fruit, and other ingredients that could be turned into alcohol. Several months after I had recommended the transfer, there was a mighty eruption below the floorboards directly under the warden's table. When the commotion died down, we found an elaborate system for distilling alcohol below the floor. Something had gone wrong and one of the pots had exploded. There was nothing unusual about the presence of a still in a maximum-security prison, but the audacity of placing one under the warden's seat shook up a lot of people. When it was discovered that Ray was the brains behind the bootleg operation, he spent some time in solitary confinement.

Once out of "the hole," Ray appeared in my office as if nothing had happened and asked for a transfer from the kitchen to the auto shop—he really felt he had a knack, he saw the need to prepare himself for the outside world, if he only had the time to practice he could have his own body shop on the outside. . . . I was still feeling the sting of having arranged the first transfer, but eventually he wore me down.

Soon afterward I decided to leave the prison to pursue a Ph.D. in psychology, and about a month before I left Ray almost persuaded me to ask my father, a roofing contractor, to offer him a job as part of an application for parole.

Ray had an incredible ability to con not just me but everybody. He could talk, and lie, with a smoothness and a directness that sometimes momentarily disarmed even the most experienced and cynical of the prison staff. When I met him he had a long criminal record behind him (and, as it turned out, ahead of him); about half his adult life had been spent in prison, and many of his crimes had been violent. . . . He lied endlessly, lazily, about everything, and it disturbed him not a whit whenever I pointed out something in his file that contradicted one of his lies. He would simply change the subject and spin off in a different direction. Finally convinced that he might not make the perfect job candidate in my father's firm, I turned down Ray's request—and was shaken by his nastiness at my refusal.

Before I left the prison for the university, I took advantage of the prison policy of letting staff have their cars repaired in the institution's auto shop—where Ray still worked, thanks (he would have said no thanks) to me. The car received a beautiful paint job and the motor and drivetrain were reconditioned.

With all our possessions on top of the car and our baby in a plywood bed in the backseat, my wife and I headed for Ontario. The first problems appeared soon after we left Vancouver, when the motor seemed a bit rough. Later, when we encountered some moderate inclines, the radiator boiled over. A garage mechanic discovered ball bearings in the carburetor's float chamber; he also pointed out where one of the hoses to the radiator had clearly been tampered with. These problems were repaired easily enough, but the next one, which arose while we were going down a long hill, was more serious. The brake pedal became very spongy and then simply dropped to the floor—no brakes, and it was a long hill. Fortunately, we made it to a service station, where we found that the brake line had been cut so that a slow leak would occur. Perhaps it was a coincidence that Ray was working in the auto shop when the car was being tuned up, but I had no doubt that the prison "telegraph" had informed him of the owner of the car.

(Hare, 1993)

Often referred to as "psychopaths" or "sociopaths," persons with ***antisocial personality disorder*** display a

Charles Manson, who directed his followers to kill nine people in 1969, fits many of the criteria of an antisocial personality disorder, including disregard for and violation of others' rights, impulsivity, disregard for truth, and lack of remorse. In a recent interview Manson bragged, "I was crazy when crazy meant something."

pervasive pattern of disregard for and violation of other people's rights (APA, 1994). Outside of substance-related disorders, this is the disorder most closely linked to adult criminal behavior, both minor and major. DSM-IV stipulates that a person must be 18 years of age or older to receive this diagnosis. However, most persons with antisocial personality disorder have displayed some patterns of significant misbehavior before they were 15, including truancy, running away from home, initiating physical fights, physical cruelty to animals or people, deliberate destruction of property, fire setting, and frequent lying and stealing. Some of these youngsters develop ***impulse-control disorders*** (see Box 18-1). Others, however, are well on their way to antisocial personality disorder.

Like Ray, people with this personality disorder are repeatedly deceitful (Seto et al., 1997). Many are unable to work consistently at a job; they have frequent absences and are likely to abandon their jobs altogether (Bland et al., 1988). Usually these individuals are also irresponsible with money, frequently failing to honor financial obligations. They are impulsive, taking action without planning ahead or considering the consequences (Lykken, 1995). They may be irritable and aggressive, and they frequently start fights (Vaillant, 1994). Many travel from place to place. Reckless and egocentric, they have little regard for their own safety or for that of others, even their children. Many also have difficulty maintaining an enduring attachment to another person (Birtchnell, 1996; Whitely, 1994).

People with antisocial personality disorder are very skillful at achieving personal profit by manipulating other people. The pain, loss, or damage they cause seldom distresses them, so they are commonly perceived as lacking moral conscience (Lykken, 1995). They glibly rationalize their actions by characterizing their victims as weak and deserving of being conned or stolen from.

Surveys indicate that up to 3.5 percent of the adult population manifest an antisocial personality disorder (APA, 1994; Kessler et al., 1994; Regier et al., 1993; Sutker, Bugg & West, 1993). The disorder is as much as three times more common among men than among women (APA, 1994), and white Americans are somewhat more likely than African Americans to receive the diagnosis (Robins et al., 1991; Collins et al., 1988).

Because people with this disorder are often arrested, many researchers have looked for patterns of antisocial functioning in prison populations (Lish et al., 1996; Kaplan et al., 1994; Parker, 1991). Among male urban jail detainees, an antisocial personality pattern has been found to be a strong indicator of past arrests for crimes of violence (Abram & Teplin, 1990). Many persons with this disorder display less criminal behavior after 40 years of age; some, however, continue their criminal activities throughout their lives (Arboleda-Florez & Holley, 1991).

Studies and clinical observations also indicate a higher rate of alcoholism among persons with antisocial personality disorder than in the rest of the population (Morgenstern et al., 1997; Sher & Trull, 1994; Lewis & Bucholz, 1991). Other substance-related disorders are also very common (Sher & Trull, 1994; Kosten, 1988). Perhaps early intoxication and substance abuse loosen behavioral inhibitions and thus contribute to the development of antisocial personality disorder (Kaminer, 1991; Newcomb & Bentler, 1988). Alternatively, an antisocial personality disorder may make a person vulnerable to substance abuse (Bukstein et al., 1989). Then again, antisocial personality disorder and substance abuse may have the same cause, such as a deep-seated need to take risks (Sher & Trull, 1994). Interestingly, drug users with the personality disorder specifically cite the recreational aspects of drug use as the reason for initiating and maintaining it (Mirin & Weiss, 1991).

Finally, children with both *conduct disorder* and *attention-deficit hyperactivity disorder* apparently have a heightened risk of developing antisocial personality disorder later (APA, 1994; Hare, 1989). Some clinicians even suggest that these two childhood disorders, which we shall examine in Chapter 19, are sometimes antisocial personality disorders in the making. Like adults with antisocial personality disorder, children with a conduct disorder persistently violate rules and others' rights and are deceitful; and children with attention-deficit hyperactivity disorder display a lack of foresight, an inability to learn from experience, a diminished sense of fear, and poor judgment (Bloomingdale & Bloomingdale, 1989). In fact, however, the precise relationship of all these disorders has been difficult to pinpoint (APA, 1994; Matthys et al., 1988).

Explanations of Antisocial Personality Disorder

Explanations of antisocial personality disorder come primarily from the psychodynamic, behavioral, cognitive, and biological models. Psychodynamic theorists propose that this disorder, like many of the other personality disorders, begins with an absence of parental love during infancy, which leads to a lack of basic trust (Gabbard, 1990). Children who develop antisocial personality disorder respond to such early inadequacies by becoming emotionally detached from all relationships, and attempt to bond with others only through the use of power and destructiveness.

In accord with the psychodynamic explanation, researchers have found that people with this disorder are more likely than others to have experienced childhood stress, particularly in forms such as family poverty, family violence, and parental conflict or divorce (Luntz & Widom, 1994; Farrington, 1991; Emery, 1982). Many persons with antisocial personality disorder have also grown up with parents who themselves had an antisocial personality disorder (Lahey et al., 1988). Such a developmental experience could certainly undermine one's trust in others.

Many behavioral theorists have suggested that antisocial symptoms may be acquired through modeling, or imitation. As evidence, they too point to the heightened rate of antisocial personality disorder among the parents of people with this disorder (Lahey et al., 1988). Other behaviorists have suggested that some parents unwittingly teach antisocial behavior by regularly reinforcing a child's aggressive behavior (Capaldi & Patterson, 1994; Patterson, 1986, 1982). When the child becomes abusive or violent in reaction to the parents' requests or orders, for example, the parents may give in and withdraw their demands in order to restore peace. Inadvertently, however, they may be teaching the child to be stubborn, defiant, and perhaps even violent.

Some cognitive theorists suggest that people with this disorder hold attitudes that trivialize the importance of other persons' needs (Levenson, 1992). Such a philosophy of life, the theorists suggest, may be far more pervasive in our society than people recognize (see Figure 18-3). Cognitive theorists further propose that people with the disorder have genuine difficulty keeping another point of view in mind along with their own.

Finally, research suggests that genetic factors may be at work in the disorder (Zuckerman, 1996; Lykken, 1995; Siever & Davis, 1991). One influential study focused on criminality, a common symptom, by looking at the family lineages of 14,427 adopted persons who had been convicted of crimes in Denmark. The researchers found a significant correlation between the criminal convictions of the adoptees and their biological parents, but not between the convictions of the adoptees and their adoptive parents (Mednick, Gabrielli, & Hutchings, 1987), suggesting that a predisposition to criminality may indeed be inherited.

Genetic factors, if they are operating, may produce biological abnormalities that help to cause antisocial personality disorder. Numerous studies suggest that the autonomic and central nervous systems act more slowly in persons with this disorder than in other persons. Researchers have observed a preponderance of EEG slow waves in subjects with the disorder, decreased skin conductance, and low levels of autonomic arousal (Bloomingdale & Bloomingdale, 1989; Raine, 1989). The

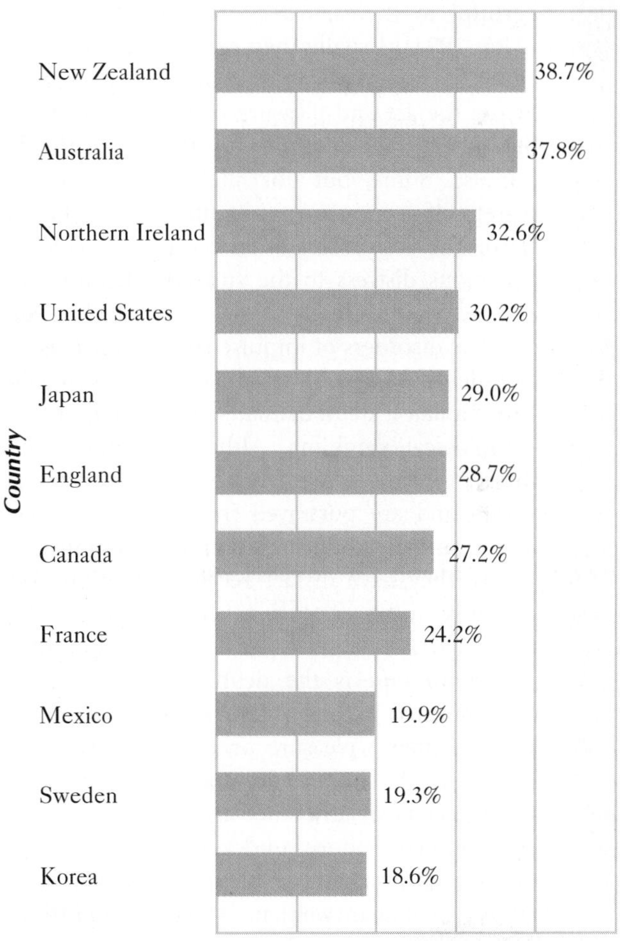

Figure 18-3 *Are some cultures more antisocial than others? In a cross-cultural study, teenagers were asked to write stories about how imaginary characters would respond to various conflicts. About a third of those from New Zealand, Australia, Northern Ireland, and the United States suggested violent responses, compared to less than a fifth of the subjects from Korea, Sweden, and Mexico. (Adapted from Archer & McDaniel, 1995.)*

BOX 18-1 Disorders of Impulse Control Rather than Personality

Impulsivity is a symptom of numerous psychological disorders, including antisocial and borderline personality disorders, bipolar disorders, substance-related disorders, schizophrenia, and paraphilias. DSM-IV also distinguishes several other disorders of which impulsivity is the central disabling feature. People with these ***impulse-control disorders*** fail to resist an impulse, drive, or temptation to perform acts that are harmful to themselves or others (APA, 1994). Usually they experience increasing tension or arousal before the act and pleasure or relief when they succumb to the impulse. Some, but not all, feel regret, self-reproach, or guilt afterward. These disorders often cause enormous distress to the sufferer and the community.

The disorders of impulse control identified by DSM-IV include pyromania, kleptomania, and pathological gambling. Although these problems arouse much curiosity and are portrayed in numerous movies and television programs, they have in fact received relatively little attention from researchers.

Pyromania is the deliberate and repeated setting of fires to achieve intense pleasure or relief from tension. The fires are not set for monetary or any other apparent gain. This poorly understood disorder is much more common among men than women. It may be related to a variety of factors, including poor parental relationships, individual temperament, poor social skills, and possibly a neurochemical predisposition (APA, 1994; Soltys, 1992; Lowenstein, 1989).

Research in this area has been hampered by the difficulty of distinguishing instances of pyromania from those of *arson,* the setting of fires for revenge or gain or because of a psychotic delusion (Puri et al., 1995). The inability of researchers to find more than a few cases of pyromania suggests that the criteria for diagnosis, or perhaps the diagnostic category itself, may not be very useful.

The story is similar with respect to ***kleptomania,*** recurrent failure to resist the impulse to steal. People with kleptomania, which is much more common in women, do not steal for gain. In fact, they often have more than enough money to pay for the articles they steal. Nor do they steal out of anger, out of revenge, or in response to a delusion or hallucination. Apparently, it is again the tension before the act and the sense of relief afterward that drives their behavior. The pattern may appear briefly, recur sporadically, or follow a chronic, fluctuating course (APA, 1994).

What little is known about kleptomania has been drawn largely from case studies of shoplifting and stealing; yet fewer than 5 percent of shoplifters have this disorder. Again, some clinicians question its usefulness as a clinical category (APA, 1994), but others believe it to be more prevalent than previously recognized, especially among persons who also suffer from mood or eating disorders (Gerlinghoff & Backmund, 1997; Goldman, 1992; McElroy et al., 1991).

The most common of the impulse-control disorders is ***pathological gambling,*** persistent and recurrent maladaptive gambling behavior that disrupts personal, family, or vocational pursuits (APA, 1994). It is estimated that between 1 and 3 percent of adults, and many adolescents as well, may suffer from it (Buckley, 1995; APA, 1994; Winters et al., 1993). Clinicians are careful to distinguish pathological from social gambling, for unlike pyromania and kleptomania, this behavior occurs in mild forms that are not only legal but socially approved.

Pathological gambling is defined less by the amount of time or money spent in gambling than by the addictive nature of the behavior. People who manifest pathological gambling are unable to walk away from a wager and are restless and irritable if gambling is denied them. Repeated losses of money lead to more gambling in an effort to win the money back, and the gambling continues even in the face of financial, social, and

---

continual search for excitement by persons with antisocial personality disorder and their disregard for prudence and caution may actually represent attempts to increase their own autonomic and central nervous system activity. As Box 18-2 indicates, researchers have increasingly been closing in on the way biological factors may intersect with behavioral and cognitive factors to bring about some of the symptoms of the disorder.

Treatments for Antisocial Personality Disorder

Approximately a quarter of all people with antisocial personality disorder receive treatment for it (Regier et al., 1993), yet no treatment appears to be effective (Mannuzza & Klein, 1991). A major obstacle is the individuals' lack of conscience or motivation to change (Widiger, Corbitt, & Millon, 1992). Most of those in therapy are acting on an ultimatum from an employer,

health problems. Many individuals go through four progressive phases: winning, losing, desperation, and hopelessness (Rosenthal, 1992).

Pathological gambling differs from the other impulse-control disorders in one very important respect. Because this disorder is more prevalent than the others and because the behavior resembles alcoholism, a great deal of attention has been directed toward its treatment. Treatments that combine approaches and that help build coping skills tend to be the most effective (Echeburúa, Baéz, & Fernandez-Montalvo, 1996; McCormick, 1994; Schwartz & Lindner, 1992). People who join self-help support groups, such as Gamblers Anonymous, a network patterned after Alcoholics Anonymous, seem to have a higher recovery rate, perhaps in part because they have admitted that they have a problem and are seeking to conquer it.

Recently there has been some controversy over the adoption of a disease model of pathological gambling. Journalists and others have asked whether the "medicalization" of gambling too easily excuses irresponsible or illegal behavior (Vatz & Weinberg, 1993). Editorials express dismay at the popularity of public figures who have admitted to powerlessness over gambling impulses. However, several recent studies suggest that a neurochemical factor may in fact be related to pathological gambling and some of the other impulse-control disorders (Stein et al., 1993; McElroy et al., 1992; Moreno et al., 1991), and some case studies indicate that cognitive or behavioral approaches may be effective interventions (Bujold et al., 1994; Hollander et al., 1992).

DSM-IV also distinguishes two other impulse-control disorders. People with ***intermittent explosive disorder,*** a rare disorder more common in men than in women, have periodic aggressive outbursts in which they seriously assault people and destroy property. Their aggressiveness is grossly disproportionate to any provocation. People with ***trichotillomania*** repeatedly pull out hair from various parts of their bodies (particularly the scalp, eyebrows, and eyelashes), with resultant noticeable hair loss. Many clinicians believe that this disorder, which apparently is more common among women, is a compulsion and should be classified as an obsessive-compulsive anxiety disorder (Christenson & MacKenzie, 1995; McElroy et al., 1994). Because it often occurs without accompanying obsessions and without rigid rules, however, DSM-IV contends that it warrants its own category.

As with trichotillomania, it is often very difficult to distinguish the impulse-control disorders from other mental disorders, such as obsessive-compulsive and other anxiety disorders, depression, and personality disorders. Thus theorists commonly explain the impulse-control disorders by referring to the more familiar disorders that they resemble. When they are looked at closely, however, the impulse-control disorders, particularly fire setting, stealing, and pathological gambling, do not fit easily into existing categories of abnormal behavior, and accordingly warrant individual study and perhaps individual explanations.

their school, or the law, or else they have come to the attention of therapists when they also developed another disorder (Fulwiler & Pope, 1987). Not surprisingly, one study found that 70 percent of patients left treatment prematurely (Gabbard & Coyne, 1987).

Some cognitive-behavioral therapists try to move clients with antisocial personality disorder toward thinking about moral issues and about the needs of other people (Beck & Freeman, 1990). Discussions, structured cognitive exercises, and behavioral experiments guide the individual step by step. The success of the approach is uncertain, however.

Some hospitals and prisons have tried to build a therapeutic community for persons with this disorder, a structured environment that emphasizes responsibility toward others (Reid & Burke, 1989; Salama, 1988). An-

BOX 18-2 A Lesson Not Learned

The only personality disorder that has received extensive systematic investigation is antisocial personality disorder, or sociopathy. In one enlightening line of investigation spanning four decades, researchers have built study upon study in an effort to understand why persons with this disorder often seem incapable of learning from experience or weighing possible consequences before they act.

This line of empirical inquiry began in 1957, when the researcher David Lykken hypothesized that people with sociopathy may experience less anxiety than other people and thus may lack an ingredient that is essential for learning a number of important behaviors. He argued that people ordinarily learn socially appropriate behaviors in order to avoid or reduce the anxiety brought on by others' disapproval. People with sociopathy, however, cannot learn from feelings of anxiety, because they do not experience those feelings.

In a clever study, Lykken (1995, 1957) tested the relationship between anxiety and learning in people with antisocial personality disorder. In the first part of the study, Lykken asked whether subjects with sociopathy experience the same anxiety as normal subjects in response to real-life situations. He constructed a questionnaire in which the subjects read thirty-three pairs of activities and were asked which of each pair they would rather do. Both items in each pair described an unpleasant event, but the events differed in the amount of anxiety they provoked. One activity was unpleasant because it was tedious ("cleaning out a cesspool"), the other because it provoked anxiety ("standing on a ledge on the 25th floor"). Lykken reasoned that if subjects with sociopathy were not deterred by anxiety, they would be more likely than the normal subjects to choose the anxiety-producing alternative over the tedious alternative. This was in fact the case. Lykken's findings suggested that people with sociopathy do experience less anxiety than other people.

Next Lykken examined the precise role that anxiety plays in learning for subjects with and subjects without sociopathy. He had subjects try to learn a mental maze that consisted of twenty choice points or steps. At each choice point, the subject was required to press one correct switch out of four choices in order to move to the next step. Subjects were instructed to get through the maze with as few errors as possible. The learning of the twenty correct responses was the *manifest* task. But embedded in this task was an avoidance-learning *latent* task. One of the three incorrect responses at each choice point was paired with an electric shock. That is, when subjects made this incorrect response, they were shocked. Lykken reasoned that in addition to learning correct responses (the manifest task), subjects would learn to avoid shocked incorrect responses (the latent task) and would eventually err only on unshocked responses. Lykken found that subjects with sociopathy learned the manifest task as well as normal subjects, but failed to learn the anxiety-motivated avoidance task—that is, the frequency of their shocked errors did not decrease. So, when learning depended on anxiety, they failed to learn.

Next Lykken placed all of his subjects in a classical conditioning experiment. He paired an unconditioned stimulus (an electric shock) with a conditioned stimulus (the sound of a buzzer), seeking to condition an anxiety response (heightened galvanic skin response) to the sound of the buzzer alone. Lykken was unable to condition an anxiety response in the subjects with sociopathy.

other popular approach uses challenging wilderness programs to build self-confidence, self-esteem, and commitment to others in a group (Reid & Burke, 1989). At least some patients seem to profit from these programs.

Generally, however, most of today's treatment approaches have little or no impact on persons with antisocial personality disorder. Nevertheless, as we noted earlier, some evidence suggests that the criminal features of the disorder may begin to decline on their own around age 40, although the reason is not known. Of course, even then, the individuals may continue to be rather egocentric, callous, and exploitive (Harpur & Hare, 1994; Hare, McPherson, & Forth, 1988).

Borderline Personality Disorder

People with ***borderline personality disorder*** display major shifts in mood, an unstable self-image, and marked impulsivity, which combine to make their relationships very unstable (Barratt & Stanford, 1996; APA, 1994). Some of Ellen Farber's difficulties are typical:

Taken together, these findings support the idea that people with an antisocial personality disorder simply do not feel the normal anxiety needed to learn certain behaviors.

Are people with sociopathy ever capable of learning avoidance responses? Apparently yes. Some years later Frank Schmauk (1970) used Lykken's maze-learning problem and found that subjects with sociopathy did in fact learn to make the avoidance response when failure to do so resulted in a loss of money rather than a shock. This finding suggested to Schmauk that the *type* of punishment was a critical factor in teaching avoidance responses to people with sociopathy.

But the story does not end there. In recent years several researchers have suggested that it is not the type but the *salience* of the punishment that is critical in learning avoidance responses. They claim that in Schmauk's experiment, the loss of money was very salient because the subjects could see the money being taken away in front of them. The shock was not salient because it was a latent punishment that the subjects did not know they could avoid. The researchers found that when subjects with sociopathy were forced to focus their attention on punishments, even little punishments, they performed as well on avoidance learning tasks as subjects without sociopathy (Newman & Kosson, 1986).

Still more recent research has suggested that the learning problems of persons with sociopathy are also related to the difficulty they have *delaying* responses (Newman et al., 1992, 1987). In one experiment subjects played a card game for financial gain in which the probability of punishment (losing 5 cents) increased by 10 percent after each turn, until punishment occurred 100 percent of the time. Therefore, subjects who stopped playing the game the earliest won the most money. When the subjects were allowed to take each turn immediately, those with sociopathy kept choosing to take more turns and lost more money than those without sociopathy. But when the subjects were forced to wait 5 seconds after each turn, subjects with sociopathy did not take more turns than those without sociopathy.

Altogether, these findings suggest that persons with sociopathy can be influenced by anxiety and they can learn to avoid punishment if they are forced to pay attention to the risks involved in a given action, if they are forced to delay responses, or if the punishments are made more meaningful and salient to them (Newman et al., 1987; Newman & Kosson, 1986).

Why should people with antisocial personality disorder experience anxiety less readily than other people? Biological researchers have tried to locate a biological cause for the reactions of these individuals. In a series of studies they have found that subjects with sociopathy often respond to warnings or expectations of stress with physiological responses that collectively indicate low brain and bodily arousal (Patrick et al., 1993, 1990; Hare, 1982, 1978). Such low arousal may lead people with sociopathy to tune out threatening or emotional situations. Consequently, emotional situations may have less impact on them than on people without sociopathy, and failure to learn anxiety-motivated avoidance responses is inevitable (Ellis, 1987; Hare, 1980, 1978).

It could also be argued that chronic underarousal should lead persons with sociopathy to engage in sensation-seeking behavior. Indeed, they may be drawn to antisocial activity precisely because it meets their need for excitement. In support of this idea, researchers have found that antisocial personality disorder often goes hand in hand with sensation-seeking behavior (Hesselbrock & Hesselbrock, 1992; Zuckerman, 1989, 1978; Blackstein, 1975). Simply put, people with this personality pattern generally take risks and seek thrills.

Ellen Farber, a 35-year-old, single, insurance company executive, came to a psychiatric emergency room of a university hospital with complaints of depression and the thought of driving her car off a cliff. . . . Ms. Farber appeared to be in considerable distress. She reported a 6-month period of increasingly persistent dysphoria and lack of energy and pleasure. Feeling as if she were "made of lead," Ms. Farber had recently been spending 15–20 hours a day in her bed. She also reported daily episodes of binge eating, when she would consume "anything I can find," including entire chocolate cakes or boxes of cookies. She reported problems with intermittent binge eating since adolescence, but these had recently increased in frequency. . . .

She attributed her increasing symptoms to financial difficulties. Ms. Farber had been fired from her job two weeks before coming to the emergency room. She claimed it was because she "owed a small amount of money." When asked to be more specific, she reported owing $150,000 to her former employers and another

> $100,000 to various local banks. . . . From age 30 to age 33, she had used her employer's credit cards to finance weekly "buying binges," accumulating the $150,000 debt. [To relieve feelings of distress,] every few days she would impulsively buy expensive jewelry, watches, or multiple pairs of the same shoes. . . .
>
> In addition to lifelong feelings of emptiness, Ms. Farber described chronic uncertainty about what she wanted to do in life and with whom she wanted to be friends. She had many brief, intense relationships with both men and women, but her quick temper led to frequent arguments and even physical fights. Although she had always thought of her childhood as happy and carefree, when she became depressed, she began to recall [being abused verbally and physically by her mother].
>
> *(Spitzer et al., 1994, pp. 395–397)*

Like Ellen Farber, individuals with borderline personality disorder swing in and out of intense depressive, anxious, and irritable states that last anywhere from a few hours to a few days or more. The world around them and their emotions seem to be always in conflict (Perry & Cooper, 1986). They are prone to bouts of anger and hostility (Gardner et al., 1991), sometimes resulting in physical aggression and violent behavior (Lish et al., 1996). Just as often, however, they direct their impulsive anger at themselves, and they are capable of causing significant bodily harm.

Many of the patients in mental health emergency rooms are individuals with borderline personality disorder who have engaged in self-mutilation (Bongar et al., 1990; Margo & Newman, 1989). Their impulsive, self-destructive activities may range from alcohol and substance abuse to delinquency, unsafe sex, irresponsible spending, reckless driving, bloodletting, and other forms of self-mutilation (Morgenstern et al., 1997; Garfinkel & Gallop, 1992; Nace, 1992). Suicidal threats and actions are also common; some studies have found a suicide rate of 6 to 8.5 percent among patients with this disorder (Moskovitz, 1996; APA, 1994; Perry, 1993; Paris, 1990). Many individuals, like Ellen Farber, seem to engage in acts of self-destructiveness as a means of dealing with chronic feelings of emptiness, boredom, and confusion about their identity.

As a result of their distorted sense of self, people with borderline personality disorder frequently seek to identify with others. They form intense, conflict-ridden relationships in which their feelings are not necessarily reciprocated (Modestin & Villiger, 1989). They often overstep their boundaries in relationships (Gunderson, 1996; Melges & Swartz, 1989). They quickly become enraged when others fail to meet their expectations; yet they remain intensely attached to the relationships, paralyzed by their fear of being left alone. Fearing desertion, they frequently resort to self-mutilation or suicidal gestures to prevent the other person from leaving the relationship.

The prevalence of borderline personality disorder has been estimated at 2 percent of the general population (APA, 1994). Around 75 percent of the patients who receive this diagnosis are women (Grilo et al., 1996; APA, 1994; Gibson, 1990). Comparisons of male and female patients indicate that women may be more likely to have coexisting mood disorders and display more self-destructive behavior; men seem more likely to have coexisting conduct, attention-deficit, and antisocial personality disorders (Andrulonis, 1991; Bardenstein et al., 1988).

The course of borderline personality disorder varies from person to person. In the most common pattern, the instability, impairment, and risk of suicide peak during young adulthood, then gradually wane with advancing age (APA, 1994). People with high intelligence or less severe symptoms seem to become increasingly functional over time (McGlashan, 1992).

Explanations of Borderline Personality Disorder Because a fear of abandonment tortures so many people with borderline personality disorder, psychodynamic theorists have looked once again to early parental relationships to explain this disorder (Gunderson, 1996). Object relations theorists, for example, propose that an early lack of acceptance by parents may lead to a loss of self-esteem, heightened dependence, and a lower capacity for coping with separation (Cardasis, Hochman, & Silk, 1997; Richman & Sokolove, 1992; Kernberg, 1984).

Research has found the infancies of many people with borderline personality disorder to be consistent with this view. They are marked by parental neglect and rejection, grossly inappropriate parental behavior, and multiple mother and father substitutes (Ludolph et al., 1990; Paris et al., 1988). Similarly, the childhoods of people with the disorder are often disrupted by divorce or death (Plakun, 1991; Wilson et al., 1986).

A great many studies have also found instances of childhood trauma in people with borderline symptoms, including physical and sexual abuse, sometimes even incest (Spoont, 1996; Atlas, 1995; Beitchman et al., 1992). Just as the disorder is more prevalent among women, more girls than boys are sexually abused. In fact, some theorists believe that the disorder may be an extended form of posttraumatic stress disorder, precipitated by early traumas (Gunderson & Sabo, 1993). Certainly the two disorders share key symptoms, including difficulties controlling one's emotions and troubled interactions (Herman et al., 1989).

Some features of borderline personality disorder have also been linked to biological abnormalities. For example, sufferers who are particularly impulsive, as demonstrated by a suicide attempt or aggression against others, have lower brain serotonin activity (Spoont, 1996; Weston & Siever, 1993; Gardner et al., 1990). People with this disorder also experience abnormalities in REM sleep similar to those of depressed persons (Weston & Siever, 1993; Siever & Davis, 1991). And the transient psychotic symptoms of some individuals have been linked to abnormalities in dopamine activity (Coccaro & Kavoussi, 1991). In accord with such biological findings, close relatives of persons with borderline personality disorder are five times more likely than the general population to have the disorder (APA, 1994; Kendler et al., 1991; Torgersen, 1984).

Finally, some sociocultural theorists suggest that cases of borderline personality disorder are particularly likely to emerge when a culture changes very rapidly. As a culture loses its cohesiveness, it leaves many of its members with problems of identity, a sense of emptiness, heightened anxiety, and fear of abandonment (Paris, 1991). Traditional family structures may come apart and people may be less concerned about social issues. Changes of this kind in contemporary society may in fact explain growing reports of the disorder (Segal, 1988; Millon, 1987).

People around the world felt angry and betrayed in 1994 when they learned that Susan Smith had murdered her two sons by buckling them into the family car and pushing it into a nearby river. For days the woman from South Carolina had tearfully told a story of forced abduction and had begged for the boys' safe return, fooling everyone, including her ex-husband. Some clinicians believe that Smith's impulsive and violent act, her shallow motives, her shifting moods and unstable self-image, and her capacity to convincingly deceive reflect a borderline or antisocial personality disorder.

Treatments for Borderline Personality Disorder

It appears that long-term psychotherapy can eventually lead to some degree of improvement for persons with borderline personality disorder (Moskovitz, 1996; Koenigsberg, 1993; Sansone et al., 1991). Nevertheless, therapists face many challenges in their work. They need, for example, to find a balance between empathizing with clients' dependency and anger and challenging their views (Horton, 1992; Greenberg, 1989). Harder still, attempts to persuade clients to look closely at their own psychological state and at the viewpoints of others may fall flat at first (Fonagy, 1991). Moreover, if patients do make progress in treatment, termination may become difficult because of the patients' problems with attachment and abandonment (Sansone et al., 1991).

Psychodynamic therapy has been somewhat successful when it focuses on the patient's fundamental relationship disturbance, self-identity problems, and pervasive loneliness and emptiness (Gunderson, 1996; Michels, 1992; Egan, 1988). This approach has sometimes been combined with cognitive or behavioral strategies that are designed to improve a patient's awareness of other people's perspectives. The therapist may, for example, model alternative interpretations and reactions to situations (Westen, 1991). Some clinicians also speak with people who are close to the patient as a means of checking his or her perceptions of reality (Rauchfleisch, 1992).

A group format has also been effective in treating some patients with this personality disorder (Moskovitz, 1996; Leszcz, 1992; O'Leary et al., 1991). It offers them an opportunity to form close attachments to several persons rather than investing all of their emotions and hopes in one or two "chosen" relationships. Groups have also been somewhat useful in strengthening the self-image of patients and protecting their self-esteem (Brightman, 1992).

Finally, antidepressant, antibipolar, antianxiety, and antipsychotic drugs have helped some clients to calm their emotional and aggressive storms (Weston & Siever, 1993; Siever & Davis, 1991). One study noted that clinicians were more likely to prescribe antipsychotic drugs for the aggressive outbursts of men with borderline personality disorder, while women were more likely to receive antidepressants (Andrulonis, 1991). Either way, the use of drugs on an outpatient basis in the treatment of this disorder is controversial, given the clients' higher risk for attempting suicide. A combination of drug therapy and psychotherapy has been helpful in some cases (Koenigsberg, 1993; Cowdry & Gardner, 1988).

Patients with this disorder are often hospitalized after self-mutilation or a suicide attempt (Moskovitz, 1996). Despite the risk of further self-harm, some clinicians may place such patients in an unlocked hospital unit where they are given lots of independence and responsibility. This strategy is meant to increase their sense of empowerment and improve their attitude toward treatment (Wester, 1991; Winchel & Stanley, 1991). Some hospital programs also ask patients to sign written contracts, to contain their dangerous behavior and to help keep them on a steady course even in the face of upsetting events (Miller, 1990; Bloom & Rosenbluth, 1989).

Histrionic Personality Disorder

People with ***histrionic personality disorder,*** once called ***hysterical personality disorder,*** display a pattern of excessive emotionality and attention seeking (APA, 1994). Indeed, they are typically described as "emotionally charged." Their exaggerated, rapidly shifting moods can complicate life considerably, as we see in the case of Suzanne:

> Suzanne, an attractive and vivacious woman, sought therapy in the hope that she might prevent the disintegration of her third marriage. The problem she faced was a recurrent one, her tendency to become "bored" with her husband and increasingly interested in going out with other men. She was on the brink of "another affair" and decided that before "giving way to her impulses again" she had "better stop and take a good look" at herself. . . .
>
> Suzanne was quite popular during her adolescent years. . . . Rather than going on to college, Suzanne attended art school where she met and married a fellow student—a "handsome, wealthy ne'er-do-well." Both she and her husband began "sleeping around" by the end of the first year, and she "wasn't certain" that her husband was the father of her daughter. A divorce took place several months after the birth of this child.
>
> Soon thereafter she met and married a man in his forties who gave both Suzanne and her daughter a "comfortable home, and scads of attention and love." It was a "good life" for the four years that the marriage lasted. . . . In the third year of this marriage she became attracted to a young man, a fellow dancing student. The affair was brief, but was followed by a quick succession of several others. Her husband learned of her exploits, but accepted her regrets and assurances that they would not continue. They did continue, and the marriage was terminated after a stormy court settlement.
>
> Suzanne "knocked about" on her own for the next two years until she met her present husband, a talented writer who "knew the scoop" about her past. . . . She had no inclination to venture afield for the next three years. She enjoyed the titillation of "playing games" with other men, but she remained loyal to her husband, even though he was away on reportorial assignments for periods of one or two months. The last trip, however, brought forth the "old urge" to start an affair. It was at this point that she sought therapy.
>
> *(Millon, 1969, p. 251)*

People with histrionic personality disorder are always "on stage," using theatrical gestures and mannerisms and the most grandiose language to describe ordinary everyday events. Like a chameleon, they continually adapt themselves to attract and impress an audience. They change not only their surface characteristics from situation to situation, but their opinions and beliefs; they seem to lack a sense of who they really are. Their speech is actually rather scanty in detail and substance, and they are likely to pursue the latest fads in their efforts to be admired.

The individuals require the constant presence of others to witness their emotionality and to validate their being and their mood states. Approval and praise are their lifeline. They do not tolerate delays in gratification well. Vain, self-indulgent, egocentric, and demanding, they overreact to any minor event that gets in the way of their insatiable quest for attention. Some make suicide attempts, largely as manipulative gestures (Guillard & Guillard, 1987).

People with this disorder may draw attention to themselves by an exaggerated display of physical illness and weakness (Morrison, 1989). Also common are inappropriate provocative behavior and sexual seduction. Most people with the disorder obsess over how they look and how others will perceive them, often wearing bright, eye-catching clothes.

The individuals are also likely to exaggerate the intensity of their relationships. For instance, they may consider themselves to be the intimate confidants of people who actually see them as casual acquaintances. They also tend to gravitate toward inappropriate romantic partners, people who may be exciting but who do not treat them well.

Until recently, this disorder was believed to be more common in women than in men (Reich, 1987). Clinicians long discussed profiles of the "hysterical wife" (Char, 1985). Several studies, however, have uncovered gender bias in past diagnoses. When presented with case studies describing people with various mixtures of histrionic and antisocial traits, clinicians in several studies gave a diagnosis of histrionic personality disorder to more women than men (Ford & Widiger, 1989;

Hamilton et al., 1986). More recent epidemiological studies suggest that 2 to 3 percent of adults have this personality disorder, with males and females equally affected (APA, 1994; Nestadt et al., 1990).

Explanations of Histrionic Personality Disorder

As we saw in Chapter 3, psychodynamic theories have their roots in classic studies of hysteria. Thus it is no surprise that these theorists maintain a strong interest in histrionic personality disorder today. Most psychodynamic theorists believe that as children, persons with this disorder typically experienced unhealthy relationships with one or both of their parents. These parents, often portrayed as cold and controlling, left the children feeling unloved, fearful of abandonment, and extraordinarily needful of nurturance (Gunderson, 1988). To defend against deep-seated fears of loss, the individuals have come to behave emotionally, inventing crises that encourage other people to act protectively (Kuriansky, 1988).

Some psychodynamic explanations focus exclusively on female patients. These theories suggest that a lack of maternal nurturance makes some daughters especially dependent on their father's attention. They engage in flirtatious and dramatic displays of emotion, establishing the histrionic pattern that governs later relationships in their lives (Phillips & Gunderson, 1994; Gabbard, 1990). They enter adulthood as "unhappy little girls," looking to men as idealized fathers and always trying to manipulate them (Char, 1985).

Cognitive explanations look instead at the lack of substance and extreme suggestibility found among persons with histrionic personality disorder. According to these theories, as the individuals become increasingly self-involved and emotional, they have little room left for knowledge of events in the world or intellectual curiosity. Since they have no detailed memories of what they never learned, they must rely on hunches or on others (Hollander, 1988). Other cognitive theorists propose that persons with this disorder have an underlying assumption that they are helpless to care for themselves, and so they constantly seek out others who will meet their needs (Beck & Freeman, 1990).

Finally, sociocultural theorists have suggested that the development of histrionic personality disorder may have roots in society's norms and expectations. Until recent years, our society encouraged girls to hold on to childhood and dependency as they grew up (Hollander, 1988). The vain, self-dramatizing, and selfish histrionic person may actually be an exaggeration of femininity as our culture once defined it (Beck & Freeman, 1990).

Treatments for Histrionic Personality Disorder

People with histrionic personality disorder, unlike those with most other personality disorders, often seek out treatment (Nestadt et al., 1990). Working with them can be very difficult, however, as they commonly bring unreasonable demands, tantrums, and seductiveness into therapy (Phillips & Gunderson, 1994; Gabbard, 1990). They may also grasp at false or premature insights or make superficial pretenses of changing, merely to please the therapist (Chodoff, 1989). To avert these problems, therapists must strike an effective balance between providing support and maintaining strict professional boundaries (Gabbard, 1990; Liebowitz et al., 1986).

Cognitive therapists have tried to help clients with this disorder change their maladaptive beliefs of helplessness and develop precise, systematic ways of thinking and solving problems. Psychodynamic therapy and group therapy formats have also been applied (Phillips & Gunderson, 1994; Winston & Pollack, 1991; Beck & Freeman, 1990). In all such approaches, the ultimate goals are the same: to help the individuals recognize their

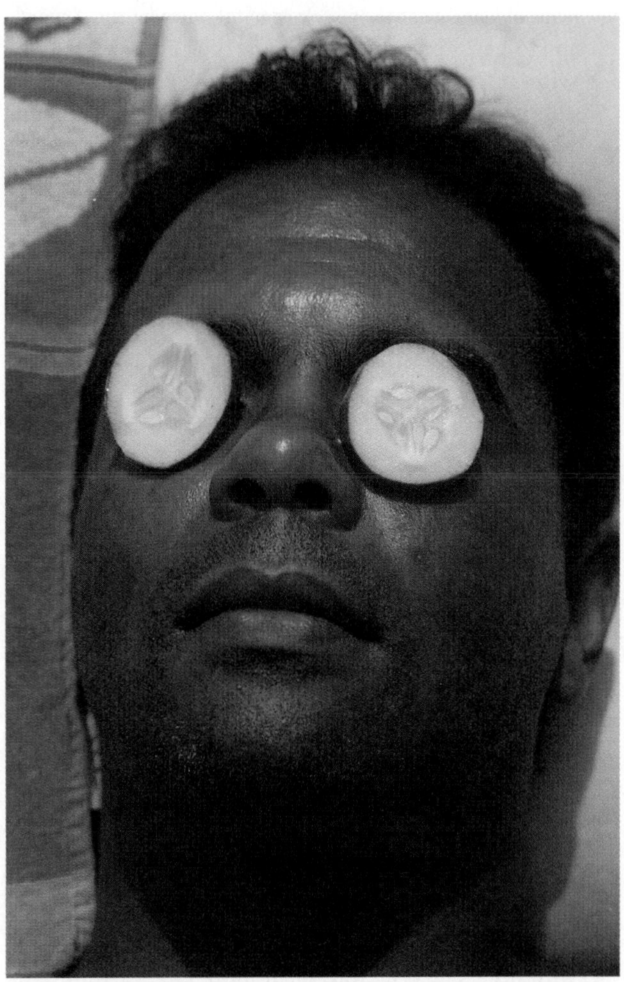

Society today often encourages people to draw attention to themselves, develop a dramatic appearance, and seek the admiration of others. Sociocultural theorists argue that such values may also set the stage for the development of histrionic and narcissistic personality patterns.

excessive dependency (Chodoff, 1989), find an inner source of satisfaction, and achieve a more independent way of life. Clinical case reports suggest that each of the approaches is helpful on occasion. Drug therapy is less useful, except for the depressive symptoms experienced by some of the patients (Liebowitz et al., 1986).

Narcissistic Personality Disorder

People with ***narcissistic personality disorder*** display a chronic and pervasive pattern of grandiosity, need for admiration, and lack of empathy (APA, 1994). Preoccupied with fantasies of unlimited success, power, or beauty, they require the constant attention and admiration of those around them. The disorder can be seen in the case of 30-year-old Steven, an artist who is married and has one child:

> Steven came to the attention of a therapist when his wife insisted that they seek marital counseling. According to her, Steve was "selfish, ungiving and preoccupied with his work." Everything at home had to "revolve about him, his comfort, moods and desires, no one else's." She claimed that he contributed nothing to the marriage, except a rather meager income. He shirked all "normal" responsibilities and kept "throwing chores in her lap," and she was "getting fed up with being the chief cook and bottlewasher, tired of being his mother and sleep-in maid."
>
> On the positive side, Steven's wife felt that he was basically a "gentle and good-natured guy with talent and intelligence." But this wasn't enough. She wanted a husband, someone with whom she could share things. In contrast, he wanted, according to her, "a mother, not a wife"; he didn't want "to grow up, he didn't know how to give affection, only to take it when he felt like it, nothing more, nothing less."
>
> Steve presented a picture of an affable, self-satisfied and somewhat disdainful young man. He was employed as a commercial artist, but looked forward to his evenings and weekends when he could turn his attention to serious painting. He claimed that he had to devote all of his spare time and energies to "fulfill himself," to achieve expression in his creative work. . . .
>
> His relationships with his present co-workers and social acquaintances were pleasant and satisfying, but he did admit that most people viewed him as a "bit self-centered, cold and snobbish." He recognized that he did not know how to share his thoughts and feelings with others, that he was much more interested in himself than in them and that perhaps he always had "preferred the pleasure" of his own company to that of others.
>
> *(Millon, 1969, pp. 261–262)*

The Greek myth has it that Narcissus died enraptured by the beauty of his own reflection in a pool, pining away with longing to possess his own image. His name has come to be synonymous with extreme self-involvement, and indeed people with narcissistic personality disorder have a grandiose sense of self-importance. They exaggerate their achievements and talents, expecting others to recognize them as superior and often appearing arrogant and haughty. They are very choosy about the people and institutions they will associate closely with, believing that their problems are unique and can be appreciated only by other "special" high-status people. Because of their charm, they often make favorable first impressions and gain a wide circle of notable acquaintances. Yet they can rarely maintain stable, long-term relationships.

Persons with narcissistic personality disorder are seldom receptive to the feelings of others. Like Steven, they show a general lack of empathy, an inability or unwillingness to recognize and identify with others' thoughts and needs (Wink, 1996). Many take advantage of others to achieve their own ends, perhaps partly out of envy, usually at the same time that they believe others to be envious of them (Wink, 1996). They are often successful, knowledgeable, and articulate, yet bored and privately doubt-ridden as well (Akhtar, 1989). They seek professional achievement largely to satisfy their need for personal recognition, so it does little to give them a higher sense of purpose or to provide pleasure in and of itself.

While maintaining their grandiosity, some of these individuals react to criticism or frustration with bouts of rage, shame, and humiliation (Gramzow & Tangney, 1992). Others may react with cold indifference (Messer, 1985). And yet others become extremely pessimistic and are pervaded by a sense of futility and depression. Cycles of zest alternating with disappointment are common (Wink, 1996; Svrakic, 1990, 1987).

Probably less than 1 percent of adults manifests narcissistic personality disorder, up to 75 percent of them men (Grilo et al., 1996; APA, 1994; Bourgeois et al., 1993). Narcissistic-type behaviors and thoughts are common and normal among teenagers; they do not usually lead to adult narcissism (APA, 1994).

Explanations of Narcissistic Personality Disorder Again psychodynamic theorists more than others have theorized about narcissistic personality disorder, and again they propose that the disorder is caused by cold, rejecting parents. They argue that some people with this background spend their lives defending against feeling unsatisfied, rejected, unworthy, and wary of the world (Wink, 1996). They repeatedly tell themselves that they are actually perfect and desirable, and seek admiration from others (Vaillant, 1994).

Each psychodynamic theory further explains these dynamics with its own principles. Object relations theorists, who place particular emphasis on early relationships, propose that all children go through a critical process of attachment to their parents. When the attachment process is cut short by negative interactions with the parents, the children may develop a distorted and grandiose self-image that helps them maintain illusions of self-sufficiency and freedom from dependence (Kernberg, 1989; Siomopoulos, 1988). Ignored and rejected by their parents, they also develop an unconscious rage against all others who represent potential sources of gratification and dependence. Along with their rage, they persistently experience envy and develop little empathy for others.

Another group of psychodynamic theorists, self theorists, argue that rejecting parents deprive their children of ***mirroring,*** one of the most important processes in the development of a healthy sense of self (Wink, 1996; Fiscalini, 1993; Kohut, 1971). The parents fail to empathize with and confirm, or *mirror,* the child's innate sense of vigor and uniqueness. As a result, the child's "grandiose" self and "reality-based" self, which normally would merge, remain split throughout life. In fact, the grandiose self, which produces an inflated sense of desirability and power, becomes dominant (Svrakic, 1989; Kohut, 1984).

In support of these psychodynamic theories, research has found that abused children and children of divorce are at greater risk for the development of narcissistic personality disorder. So are children whose mothers or fathers have died or who have been given up for adoption (Kernberg, 1989).

Some behavioral and cognitive theorists propose that persons may develop narcissistic personality disorder as a result of being treated too *positively* rather than too negatively in early life. They hold that individuals may acquire a superior and grandiose posture when their "admiring or doting parents" favor or even idealize them and teach them repeatedly to "overvalue their self worth" (Millon, 1987). In support of these ideas, firstborn and only children, who are indeed often viewed and treated by their parents as having special talents or intelligence, score higher than other children on measures of narcissism (Curtis & Cowell, 1993). Some cognitive theorists further propose that being called "different," even negatively, by parents or others may lead to a similar message of personal uniqueness and in turn to narcissism (Beck & Freeman, 1990).

Finally, many sociocultural theorists link narcissistic personality disorder to "eras of narcissism" in society (Cooper & Ronningstam, 1992; Cooper, 1981; Lasch, 1978). They suggest that periodic breakdowns in family structure and in social ideals produce generations of youth characterized by self-centeredness, a short attention span, and a materialistic outlook. Western cultures in particular, which encourage self-expression, individualism, and competitiveness, are seen as more likely to foster such generational narcissism.

Treatments for Narcissistic Personality Disorder

Narcissistic personality disorder has been characterized as one of the most difficult patterns to treat (Lawrence, 1987). When individuals with the disorder seek treatment, they usually do so because of an associated disorder, most commonly depression (Beck & Freeman, 1990). They are likely to approach therapy with a sense of entitlement and may attempt to manipulate the therapist into supporting their sense of grandiosity. Some clients also seem to project their grandiosity onto therapists and develop a love-hate stance toward them (Uchoa, 1985).

Psychodynamic therapists seek to help the clients uncover their basic insecurities and defenses. A traditional approach relies on gentle interpretation (Masterson, 1990; Spitzer, 1990); others combine

The self-absorption of people with a narcissistic personality is apparent even when they pretend to be interested in others.

confrontation with interpretation (Kernberg, 1989). Cognitive therapists address the specific ways in which clients with this disorder think. The therapists may, for example, try to guide the clients' focus onto other people's opinions, improve the way they interpret and react to criticism, increase their ability to empathize, and change their all-or-nothing categorizations (Beck & Freeman, 1990). All such approaches seem to meet with little success, however.

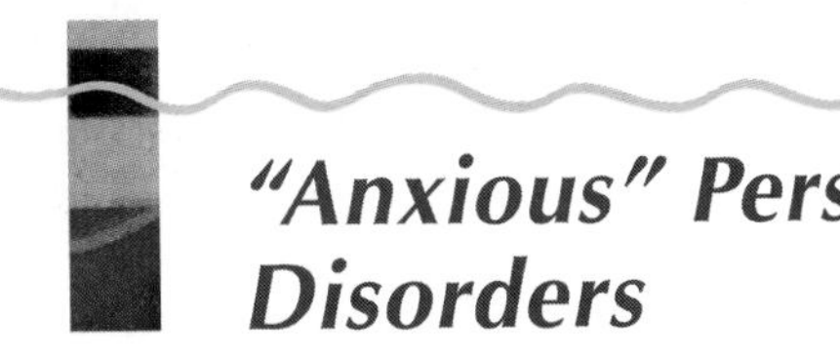

"Anxious" Personality Disorders

The "anxious" cluster of personality disorders includes the avoidant, dependent, and obsessive-compulsive personality disorders. People with these disorders typically display anxious and fearful behavior. Many symptoms of these disorders are similar to those of the anxiety and depressive disorders, but direct links to those Axis I patterns have not been established (Weston & Siever, 1993). As with most of the other personality disorders, empirical support for available explanations is very limited. On the other hand, treatments for these disorders appear to be modestly to moderately helpful—significantly better than for other personality disorders.

Avoidant Personality Disorder

People with ***avoidant personality disorder*** are consistently inhibited in social situations, grapple with feelings of inadequacy, and feel extremely sensitive to negative evaluation (APA, 1994). They are so fearful of being rejected that they give no one an opportunity to reject them—or to accept them either:

> James was a bookkeeper for nine years, having obtained his position upon graduation from high school. He spoke of himself as a shy, fearful and quiet boy ever since early childhood. . . .
>
> James was characterized by his supervisor as a loner, a peculiar young man who did his work quietly and efficiently. They noted that he ate alone in the company cafeteria and never joined in coffee breaks or in the "horsing around" at the office. . . .
>
> As far as his social life was concerned, James had neither dated nor gone to a party in five years. . . . He now spent most of his free time reading, watching TV, daydreaming and fixing things around the house.
>
> James experienced great distress when new employees were assigned to his office section. Some 40 people worked regularly in this office and job turnover resulted in replacement of four or five people a year. . . . In recent months, a clique formed in his office. Although James very much wanted to be a member of this "in-group," he feared attempting to join them because "he had nothing to offer them" and thought he would be rejected. In a short period of time, he, along with two or three others, became the object of jokes and taunting by the leaders of the clique. After a few weeks of "being kidded," he began to miss work, failed to complete his accounts on time, found himself unsure of what he was doing and made a disproportionate number of errors. . . . Although he did not connect his present discomfort to the events in his office, he asked if he could be reassigned to another job where he might work alone.
>
> *(Millon, 1969, pp. 231–232)*

Not surprisingly, people like James strenuously avoid occasions for interpersonal contact. At the center of their social withdrawal lies not so much a low level of social skill as a dread of criticism, disapproval, or rejection. In social situations, their manner is timid and hesitant; they are afraid of saying something foolish or inappropriate or of embarrassing themselves by blushing, crying, or nervousness, and are sensitive to social deprecation. Even in intimate relationships they act and express themselves with restraint, afraid of being shamed or ridiculed.

Individuals with this disorder believe themselves to be personally unappealing or inferior to others. They tend to exaggerate the potential difficulties of new situations, so they seldom take risks or engage in new activities. They usually have few or no close friends, though they actually yearn for intimate relationships, and frequently feel empty, depressed, and lonely. As a substitute, many take refuge in an inner world of fantasy and imagination (Millon, 1990).

Avoidant personality disorder is similar to social phobias (see pp. 179–181). Common symptoms include a fear of humiliation and low confidence, and many people with one of these disorders also experience the other (Fahlen, 1995; Holt et al., 1992; Schneier et al., 1991). People with a social phobia, however, primarily fear *social circumstances,* while persons with the personality disorder largely fear close *social relationships* (Turner et al., 1986). Avoidant personality disorder is also common among people with a chronic depressive disorder (Alnaes & Torgersen, 1989). Indeed, the social withdrawal, low self-esteem, and hypersensitivity to rejection displayed in the personality disorder is also typical of depression.

Between 0.5 and 1.0 percent of adults have avoidant personality disorder, men as frequently as women. Many children and teenagers may also be painfully shy and display avoidant behaviors, but this is usually just a normal part of their development.

Explanations of Avoidant Personality Disorder

Theorists often assume that avoidant personality disorder has the same causes as anxiety disorders—particularly conditioned fears, upsetting thought processes, or biochemical abnormalities. However, direct ties to the Axis I disorders have yet to receive much empirical study (Weston & Siever, 1993). In the meantime, psychodynamic and cognitive theories have received the most clinical attention.

Psychodynamic theorists focus primarily on the pervasive shame experienced by people with avoidant personality disorder. Some trace the shame to childhood experiences such as early bowel and bladder accidents (Gabbard, 1990). If parents repeatedly reprimand or ridicule a child in response to such accidents, the child may internalize the ridicule, in the form of severe self-deprecation. In turn, the individual may feel unlovable throughout life and distrust the professed love of others (Liebowitz et al., 1986). Cognitive theorists agree that strong criticisms and rejections in early childhood may lead persons with avoidant personality disorder to assume that other people are generally critical. They therefore expect and fear rejection, misinterpret the reactions of others, and discount positive feedback. They also develop a negative self-image, and even believe that others are justified in their criticisms. In one study, subjects with avoidant personality disorder recalled childhoods that support both the psychodynamic and cognitive theories. They recalled, for example, unencouraging home climates and few demonstrations of parental love and pride (Arbel & Stravynski, 1991).

Treatments for Avoidant Personality Disorder

Clients with avoidant personality disorder come to therapy in the hope of finding acceptance and affection. Keeping them in therapy can be a challenge, however, for many of them soon begin to avoid the sessions (Beck & Freeman, 1990). Often they distrust the therapist's sincerity and start to fear rejection in the therapeutic relationship. As with several of the other personality disorders, the initial therapeutic task is to build the patient's trust through support and empathy (Gabbard, 1990).

Beyond building trust, therapists tend to treat people with avoidant personality disorder much as they treat persons with social phobias and other anxiety disorders, and their approaches have had at least modest success. Psychodynamic therapists help the patients uncover the origins of their symptoms and resolve the unconscious conflicts that may be operating (Hurt et al., 1991). Cognitive therapists try to help the clients change their distressing beliefs and thoughts, increase their tolerance for emotional discomfort, and build up their self-image (Beck & Freeman, 1990; Alden, 1989). Behavioral therapists provide *social skills training* and *exposure* treatment which require clients gradually to increase their social contacts (Quality Assurance Project, 1991; Stravynski et al., 1987). And antianxiety and antidepressant drugs are sometimes useful in reducing the social anxiety and discomfort of clients, although the symptoms frequently return when medication is stopped (Liebowitz et al., 1991, 1990; Mattick & Newman, 1991).

Many children and teenagers are painfully shy, easily embarrassed, and uncomfortable with people other than their parents, siblings, or close friends. Such reactions are a common and normal part of development and not, by themselves, indicative of an avoidant or dependent personality disorder.

Group therapy also helps many people with avoidant personality disorder, by providing practice in social behaviors. Particularly helpful are groups that use a combination of approaches, such as exposure, behavioral rehearsal, skill building, and support (Azima, 1993; Renneberg et al., 1990; Alden, 1989).

Dependent Personality Disorder

People with ***dependent personality disorder*** have a persistent need to be taken care of (APA, 1994). As a result, they are clinging and submissive and they fear separation from their parent, spouse, or other close relationship. They are so reliant on others that they cannot make the smallest decision for themselves. Mr. G. is a case in point.

> Mr. G.['s] . . . place of employment for the past 15 years had recently closed and he had been without work for several weeks. He appeared less dejected about the loss of his job than about his wife's increasing displeasure with his decision to "stay at home until something came up." She thought he "must be sick" and insisted that he see a doctor. . . .
>
> Mr. G. was born in Europe, the oldest child and only son of a family of six children. . . . His mother kept a careful watch over him, prevented him from engaging in undue exertions and limited his responsibilities; in

> effect, she precluded his developing many of the ordinary physical skills and competencies that most youngsters learn in the course of growth. . . .
>
> A marriage was arranged by his parents. His wife was a sturdy woman who worked as a seamstress, took care of his home, and bore . . . four children. Mr. G. performed a variety of odds-and-ends jobs in his father's tailoring shop. His mother saw to it, however, that he did no "hard or dirty work," just helping about and "overlooking" the other employees. As a consequence, Mr. G. learned none of the skills of the tailoring trade. . . .
>
> During the ensuing years, he obtained employment at a garment factory owned by his brothers-in-law. Again he served as a helper, not as a skilled workman. Although he bore the brunt of essentially good-humored teasing by his co-workers throughout these years, he maintained a friendly and helpful attitude, pleasing them by getting sandwiches, coffee and cigarettes at their beck and call.
>
> He married again to a hard-working, motherly type woman who provided the greater portion of the family income. Shortly thereafter, the son of his first wife emigrated to this country. Although the son was only 19 at the time, he soon found himself guiding his father's affairs, rather than the other way around.
>
> *(Millon, 1969, p. 242)*

It is normal and healthy to depend on others, but those with dependent personality disorder typically need continual reassurance about everyday matters and about their profound feelings of personal inadequacy and helplessness. Afraid that they cannot care for themselves, they cling to friends or relatives with a startling intensity and neediness (see Box 18-3).

We noted earlier that people with avoidant personality disorder have difficulty initiating relationships. In dependent personality disorder the difficulty is instead in *separation.* The individuals feel completely helpless and devastated when close relationships end, and they quickly seek out another relationship to fill the void. Many continue to hold onto relationships with partners who physically or psychologically abuse them.

People with this disorder tend to be submissive. Lacking confidence in their ability and judgment, they allow important decisions to be made for them and seldom disagree with others, no matter what the facts or the consequences may be. They typically depend on a parent or spouse to decide where to live, what job to have, and which neighbors to befriend (Overholser, 1996; APA, 1994). As a result of their profound fear of rejection, the individuals are oversensitive to criticism and disapproval. Skillful social conformists, they adapt themselves to fit others' desires and expectations. Often that means volunteering for unpleasant or even demeaning tasks to win approval.

Many people with dependent personality disorder experience distress, loneliness, depression, self-criticism, and low self-esteem (Overholser, 1996, 1992), so they are at high risk for full depressive disorders and anxiety disorders (Reich, 1996; Bornstein, 1995; APA, 1994). Their separation anxiety and their feelings of helplessness when they anticipate abandonment may leave them particularly susceptible to suicidal thoughts (Kiev, 1989).

It is not known how prevalent dependent personality disorder is in the general population, although some studies suggest that around 2 percent may experience it (Zimmerman & Coryell, 1989). For years clinicians believed that more women than men manifested this pattern (Overholser, 1992), but recent research suggests that the disorder is as common in men (APA, 1994; Reich, 1990). Some studies have found the close relatives of male subjects with this disorder to have more depressive disorders than usual, while the relatives of female subjects have more panic disorders. Perhaps different factors predispose men and women to a dependent personality disorder (Reich, 1990).

Explanations of Dependent Personality Disorder For years psychodynamic theorists have proposed that many of the dynamics that result in depression (see pp. 247–251) are at work in dependent personality disorder as well. Freudian theorists, for example, propose that unresolved conflicts during the oral stage of psychosexual development set the stage for a lifelong need for nurturance and a dependent personality disorder (Greenberg & Bornstein, 1988). Similarly, object relations theorists hold that early parental loss or rejection may disrupt the important developmental processes of attachment and separation, leaving some children with fears of abandonment throughout their lives. Still other psychodynamic theorists suggest that the parents of persons with this disorder were so *overinvolved* and *overprotective* that they inadvertently heightened their child's feelings of dependency, insecurity, and anxiety over separation (Bornstein, 1996, 1992; Gabbard, 1990).

Behaviorists propose that parents of persons with dependent personality disorder unintentionally rewarded the child's clinging and loyal behavior. At the same time, they punished independent actions, perhaps through withdrawal of love. Alternatively, some parents may have modeled their own dependent behavior for their children.

Finally, cognitive theorists believe that persons with this disorder hold two attitudes that help produce and maintain it: (1) they are inadequate and helpless to deal with the world, and (2) they must find another person to provide protection before they can cope (Beck & Freeman, 1990). The individuals also engage in dichotomous thinking: "If one is to be dependent, one must be completely helpless," or "If one is to be independent, one

(A)

(B)

As the technology of film animation has become more complex over time, so have the personality problems of animated characters. (A) Troubled characters of the past were usually defined by a single undesirable personality trait, as demonstrated by Snow White's friend Grumpy, second from left. (B) Today's characters have clusters of self-defeating traits. Beavis and Butt-head, for example, display poor control of impulses, disregard for others' rights, disturbed relationships, emotional and cognitive shallowness, and, in the case of Beavis, submissive and clinging behavior.

must be alone." Such thoughts guide them to avoid any efforts at autonomy.

Treatments for Dependent Personality Disorder

People with dependent personality disorder usually approach therapy passively: they confer all responsibility for their treatment and well-being on the therapist (Perry, 1989). Getting them to accept responsibility for themselves is consequently a central therapeutic concern. Another difficulty is that the needs and behaviors of a spouse or parent may feed into the client's symptoms. Some clinicians, therefore, propose couple therapy as well, or separate therapy for the partner (Liebowitz et al., 1986).

Treatment for dependent personality disorder can be at least modestly helpful. Psychodynamic therapy for these clients focuses on many of the same issues as therapy with depressed persons. In particular, the patient's almost inevitable transference of dependency needs onto the therapist typically becomes a major treatment issue (Perry, 1989). Behavioral therapists often provide assertiveness training to help clients better express their own needs and wishes in relationships. And cognitive therapists try to help the clients challenge and change their assumptions of incompetence and helplessness (Beck & Freeman, 1990).

Finally, as with avoidant personality disorder, a group therapy format is often beneficial. It provides support from numerous peers rather than from a single dominant person (Azima, 1993; Perry, 1989), and it offers peer modeling and practice opportunities for expressing feelings and solving problems (Beck & Freeman, 1990).

Obsessive-Compulsive Personality Disorder

People with ***obsessive-compulsive personality disorder*** are so preoccupied with orderliness, perfectionism, and mental and interpersonal control that they lose their flexibility, openness, and efficiency. Their concern for doing everything "right" impairs their productivity, as in the case of Wayne:

> Wayne was advised to seek assistance from a therapist following several months of relatively sleepless nights and a growing immobility and indecisiveness at his job. When first seen, he reported feelings of extreme self-doubt and guilt and prolonged periods of tension and diffuse anxiety. It was established early in therapy that he always had experienced these symptoms. They were now merely more pronounced than before.
>
> The precipitant for this sudden increase in discomfort was a forthcoming change in his academic post. New administrative officers had assumed authority at the college, and he was asked to resign his deanship to return to regular departmental instruction. In the early sessions, Wayne spoke largely of his fear of facing classroom students again, wondered if he could organize his material well, and doubted that he could keep classes disciplined and interested in his lectures. It was his preoccupation with these matters that he believed was preventing him from concentrating and completing his present responsibilities.

BOX 18-3 Internet Dependence: A New Kind of Problem

There's a new psychological problem going around—an uncontrollable need to be on-line. Sufferers spend up to sixty hours a week surfing the Net, participating in chat groups, e-mailing acquaintances, or playing sophisticated computer games (Murray, 1996). For some, the Internet, a conglomeration of computer networks that spans the world, has become a black hole. Some describe their need to be on-line as an obsession for which they have inadvertently sacrificed their jobs, academic careers, friends, even spouses. University students seem especially vulnerable to the problem:

> I was first introduced while I was studying at the university in '91. I'd send messages to my friends internally and everything was pretty much under control. Then I discovered by accident one day that you could send little messages to people in other universities and even people in America and other exotic places like Mexico and Finland! Well, that was the point of no return for me and I began spending inordinately large periods of time on-line. That was at the beginning of my final year, how I managed to stay on my course right through till the final exams I'm not sure, my attendance record got worse and worse. But I did get through to the end and predictably enough I failed in spectacular fashion. But I didn't mind so much because I had the Net to catch me, I'd made many friends on and off-line through it, including my then girlfriend, so life wasn't that bad really was it? . . .
>
> I've [since] learned to censor out some things, and not to get entwined up to my arse in endless threads of chat. Okay, so this is bad in some ways, but I feel a little more in control of my life. I don't find myself involuntarily glued to my screen at 4 am talking about something that isn't even interesting, begging myself to go to bed.
>
> So, all in all, a big proportion of my life is based around the net. Advantages are: it offers me a creative outlet, disadvantages: it still takes up more time than I have to spare.
>
> *(Anonymous, 1996)*

Like this individual, swelling numbers of users have become attached to the social world of the Internet. Chat rooms allow computer users to converse with other computer users around the world 24 hours a day, 365 days a year. News groups allow users to post messages and receive responses in an ongoing dialogue. These services have allowed people to create social worlds that function exclusively within the digital domain—complete with acquaintances, close friends, and romance.

Clinicians are not sure how to categorize this troublesome pattern of computer use. Noting its similarity to substance-related disorders, many call it "Internet addiction." Others think it has the qualities of an impulse-control disorder, particularly pathological gambling, because it involves a preoccupation with an activity other than an intoxicating substance. Some clinicians note that the pattern also resembles dependent personality disorder: individuals respond to their computer as if it were an important person,

> At no time did Wayne express anger toward the new college officials for the "demotion" he was asked to accept. He repeatedly voiced his "complete confidence" in the "rationality of their decision." Yet, when face-to-face with them, he observed that he stuttered and was extremely tremulous.
>
> Wayne was the second of two sons, younger than his brother by three years. His father was a successful engineer, and his mother a high school teacher. Both were "efficient, orderly and strict" parents. Life at home was "extremely well planned," with "daily and weekly schedules of responsibilities posted" and "vacations arranged a year or two in advance." Nothing apparently was left to chance. . . . Wayne adopted the "good boy" image. Unable to challenge his brother either physically, intellectually or socially, he became a "paragon of virtue." By being punctilious, scrupulous, methodical and orderly, he could avoid antagonizing his perfectionistic parents, and would, at times, obtain preferred treatment from them. He obeyed their advice, took their guidance as gospel and hesitated making any decision before gaining their approval. Although he recalled "fighting" with his brother before he was six or seven, he "restrained his anger from that time on and never upset his parents again."
>
> *(Millon, 1969, pp. 278–279)*

In Wayne's preoccupation with rules and orderliness and doing things right, he has trouble with the larger picture. When confronted with a task, people like him may become so fixated on organization and details that they fail to grasp the point of the activity. As a result, their work is often behind schedule or never completely done, and they may neglect genuine leisure activities and friendships.

clinging to it, fearing separation, ever seeking its guidance and reassurance.

Kimberly S. Young (1995), a psychologist at the University of Pittsburgh in Bradford, investigated 496 people who actively use on-line services. Young classified them as dependent on the Internet if they met four or more of the following criteria over a 12-month-period:

1. Felt preoccupied with the Internet.
2. Needed to spend increasing amounts of time on the Internet to achieve satisfaction.
3. Were unable to control their Internet use.
4. Felt restless or irritable when they tried to cut down or stop Internet use.
5. Used the Internet as a way of escaping from problems or of improving their mood.
6. Lied to family members or friends to conceal the extent of their involvement with the Internet.
7. Risked the loss of a significant relationship, job, or educational or career opportunity because of the Internet.
8. Kept returning to the Internet even after spending an excessive amount of money on on-line fees.
9. Went through withdrawal when off-line.
10. Stayed on-line longer than they originally intended.

Young found that close to 80 percent of the participants were dependent on the Internet. When a problem of that apparent magnitude arises, treatments emerge to help. Workshops and counseling programs, particularly on college campuses, are proliferating. But among the most popular approaches are support groups similar to Alcoholics Anonymous—some of them, ironically, operating on the Internet. The Internet Addiction Support Group, for example, has attracted many subscribers who own up to their problem, support each other, and swap methods for tackling it (Murray, 1996). This sounds to some clinicians "like having an Alcoholics Anonymous meeting in a bar" (Orzack, 1996). Others point out, however, that many dependent Internet users cannot tear themselves away from their computers long enough to visit a traditional treatment center (Belluck, 1996).

People with obsessive-compulsive personality disorder set unreasonably high standards for themselves and others. They can never be satisfied with their performance, but they generally refuse to delegate responsibility or to work with a team, convinced that others are too careless or incompetent to do the job right. Because they are so afraid of making mistakes, they may avoid making decisions.

People with this personality disorder also tend to be inflexible in their morals, ethics, and values. They scrupulously adhere to their own personal code and use it as a yardstick to measure others. Their expressions of affection may be equally restricted, and their relationships are often stilted and superficial. In addition, these individuals are rarely generous with their time or money. And some cannot even throw out things that are worn-out or useless (APA, 1994; Warren & Ostrom, 1988).

Obsessive-compulsive personality disorder has a 1 to 2 percent prevalence in the general population, with white, educated, married, employed men receiving the diagnosis most often (APA, 1994; Weissman, 1993; Nestadt et al., 1991). In general, men are twice as likely as women to receive this diagnosis (APA, 1994).

Clinicians often believe that obsessive-compulsive personality disorder and obsessive-compulsive disorder (the anxiety disorder) are closely related. Some patients do qualify for both diagnoses and the two disorders do share some features (Pollack, 1987). Indeed, obsessive-compulsive personality disorder is present in many patients (perhaps 20 percent) with the anxiety disorder (APA, 1994; Jenike, 1991). Other personality disorders, however (avoidant, histrionic, schizotypal, and dependent), may be even more common among patients with the anxiety disorder (Steketee, 1990). In addition, depression, social phobias, and Type A personality patterns are at least as prevalent as obsessive-compulsive anxiety disorder among people with the personality disorder (Turner et al., 1991; Fulwiler & Pope, 1987).

In fact, no empirical support has been found for the notion of a specific link between the obsessive-compulsive personality and anxiety disorders (Mavissakalian et al., 1990). One of the important differences between them is that the symptoms of obsessive-compulsive anxiety disorder are *ego dystonic;* that is, the person does not want them. The symptoms of obsessive-compulsive personality disorder are *ego syntonic:* the person often embraces them and rarely wishes to resist them (Zohar & Pato, 1991). In addition, the functioning of people with the anxiety disorder is much more likely to be impaired.

Explanations of Obsessive-Compulsive Personality Disorder Most explanations of obsessive-compulsive personality disorder borrow heavily from those of obsessive-compulsive anxiety disorder, despite the imperfect links between the two disorders. As with so many of the personality disorders, psychodynamic explanations dominate, and again empirical evidence is limited at best.

Freudian theorists suggest that people with obsessive-compulsive personality disorder are *anal regressive.* That is, because of overly rigid and punitive toilet training, they become filled with anger, and they remain fixated at the anal stage. They try to contain this anger by persistently resisting both the anger and their instincts to mess, efforts that eventually lead to their resolute orderliness, inhibition, and passion for collecting things. Contemporary psychodynamic theorists suggest that any early struggles with parents over control and independence may set in motion the aggressive impulses (Kuriansky, 1988; Mollinger, 1980).

Cognitive theorists have little to say about the origins of obsessive-compulsive personality disorder, but they do propose that illogical thinking processes help *maintain* it. They point, for example, to black-or-white dichotomous thinking, which may produce rigidity, perfectionism, and procrastination. Individuals with the disorder similarly exaggerate the potential consequences of mistakes or errors. Cognitive theorists also consider some people with this personality disorder to be deficient in the cognitive capacity to reflect on life and the world (Miller, 1988).

Treatments for Obsessive-Compulsive Personality Disorder People with obsessive-compulsive personality disorder do not usually believe there is anything seriously wrong with them. They therefore tend to seek treatment only if they need help for an accompanying Axis I disorder, most frequently anxiety or depression, or if someone close to them insists (Beck & Freeman, 1990). Whereas drug therapy and behavior therapy have been highly effective for patients with obsessive-compulsive anxiety disorder, patients with the personality disorder often respond better to psychodynamic or cognitive therapy (Primac, 1993; Jenike, 1991, 1990; Wells et al., 1990). Psychodynamic therapists typically try to help the patients become more aware of, directly experience, and accept their real feelings; they also may lead patients to overcome their insecurities, take risks, and accept their personal limitations (Salzman, 1989). Cognitive therapists further work on helping clients to correct their dichotomous thinking, perfectionism, indecisiveness, procrastination, and chronic worrying. Over time, both kinds of therapists may also address the clients' tendency to overintellectualize and try to help them loosen up and learn to have fun (Liebowitz et al., 1986).

Personality Disorders: Dilemmas and Confusion

The inclusion of personality disorders in recent versions of the DSM shows that today's clinicians believe them to be important and troubling patterns. Yet they are particularly hard to diagnose—and easy to misdiagnose. As we noted previously, this difficulty indicates serious problems with the *validity* (accuracy) and the *reliability* (consistency) of the DSM categories (Costello, 1996; Zimmerman, 1994).

One problem is that some of the criteria used to identify personality disorders must be inferred rather than directly observed. To distinguish a paranoid from a schizoid personality disorder, for example, clinicians must ask not only about their clients' behavior but *why* they avoid close relationships. In other words, the diagnoses often rely heavily on the impressions of the individual clinician. In a related problem, clinicians tend to vary widely in their judgements about when a normal personality style crosses the line and warrants classification as a disorder (Widiger & Costa, 1994). Some even believe that it is wrong ever to think of personality styles as mental disorders, however counterproductive they may be.

The similarity of personality disorders within a cluster—or even between clusters—poses yet another problem. Within the "anxious" cluster, for example, there is tremendous overlap between the diagnostic criteria for avoidant personality disorder and dependent personality

Different personality disorders often yield similar behaviors, making it difficult for clinicians to distinguish between the disorders. People with schizoid and avoidant personality disorders, for example, may both spend much of their time alone. The former, however, truly want to be alone, whereas the latter yearn for but fear social relationships.

disorder. Faced with similar feelings of inadequacy, fear of disapproval, and the like, is it reasonable for clinicians to consider them independent disorders? Perhaps the disorders within each cluster are but variations of a single deviant personality style (Livesley et al., 1994; Siever & Davis, 1991). Similarly, the prevalence of borderline traits ("dramatic" cluster) among some people with dependent personality disorder ("anxious" cluster) may indicate that these two disorders also represent different degrees of the same pattern (Dolan, Evans, & Norton, 1995; Flick et al., 1993).

An equally troubling problem is that a wide range of people are often assigned the same personality disorder diagnosis (Costello, 1996; Widiger, 1993, 1992). Individuals must meet a certain number of criteria to receive a given diagnosis, but no single feature is essential for any diagnosis. Thus people with very different personalities may meet different sets of criteria for the same disorder, and may receive the same diagnosis.

In response to these problems, the diagnostic criteria for the personality disorders keep undergoing revision. In fact, the categories themselves have changed more than once, and they will no doubt change again. For example, DSM-IV dropped ***passive-aggressive personality disorder,*** a pattern of negative attitudes and passive resistance to the demands of others, because research failed to establish that this was more than a single problematic trait. The pattern is now being studied and considered for inclusion once again in future editions of the DSM, perhaps within a broader category called ***negativistic personality disorder.***

Given these problems, some theorists believe that the personality disorders actually differ more in degree than in type of dysfunction, and have proposed that the disorders be organized by the *severity* of certain central traits rather than by the presence or absence of specific traits (Costello, 1996; Widiger, 1993). It is not yet clear where the arguments will lead, but at the very least, the growing debate indicates once again that more and more clinicians believe personality disorders to be important categories that may have great relevance to their work.

Crossroads

During the first half of this century, clinicians believed deeply in the enduring pattern we call personality, and they tried to identify stable personality traits. They then discovered how readily people can be shaped and even changed by the situations in which they find themselves, and a backlash developed. The concept of personality grew to seem less legitimate, and for a while it almost became an obscene word in some circles. The category of personality disorders traveled a similar road. When psychodynamic and humanistic theorists dominated the clinical field, *neurotic character disorders,* the precursors to personality disorders, were considered useful clinical categories. But the popularity of these categories declined as other models came to the fore.

During the past decade, personality and personality disorders have rebounded. In case after case, clinicians have concluded that rigid personality traits seem to pose special problems for individuals. Consequently, personality disorders are gaining renewed interest and respect. In addition, new objective tests and interview protocols now help clinicians assess these disorders, and have set in motion a wave of systematic research (Loranger et al., 1994; Zimmerman, 1994; Perry, 1992).

So far, only the antisocial and, to a lesser extent, the borderline personality disorders have received much study. As other personality disorders attract research attention as well, however, clinicians should be better able to answer some pressing questions: How prevalent are the various personality disorders? How useful are the present categories? How are the disorders interrelated? And what interventions are most effective?

One of the most important questions is why do people develop these patterns? As we have observed, psychological theories have offered the most answers so far, but these explanations lack precision, and they do not have strong research support. In view of the current enthusiasm for biological insights, genetic and biological factors are likely to receive more and more study in the coming years, helping researchers determine their interaction with psychological causes. Nor should sociocultural factors be overlooked. As we have seen, sociocultural theorists have only occasionally made suggestions about the origins of personality disorders. However, sociocultural factors may well play an important role in personality disorders, and they should be more systematically identified, especially since, by definition, personality disorders must "deviate markedly from the expectations of a person's culture."

The future will undoubtedly bring some significant changes to the field's explanations and treatments for personality disorders. Correspondingly, the current categories of personality disorders will probably undergo change as well. Such changes, however, are now likely to be based on research rather than, as in the past, largely on clinical intuitions, impressions, and biases. For the many people impaired and distressed by inflexible, pervasive, and maladaptive personality traits, these changes and their research foundations should make an important and overdue difference.

Chapter Review

1. ***Personality Disorders*** A *personality disorder* is an inflexible pattern of inner experience and outward behavior. The pattern is wide-ranging and enduring, and it deviates markedly from the expectations of one's culture and leads to distress or impairment. It typically begins in adolescence or early adulthood and makes for a lifelong ordeal. Explanations for most of the personality disorders have received only limited research support. DSM-IV distinguishes ten personality disorders and separates them into three clusters.

2. ***"Odd" Personality Disorders*** Three of the personality disorders are characterized by the kinds of odd or eccentric behavior often seen in the Axis I disorder schizophrenia.

   A. People with *paranoid personality disorder* display a pattern of pervasive distrust and suspiciousness. Those with *schizoid personality disorder* display a pattern of detachment from social relationships and a restricted range of emotional expression. Individuals with *schizotypal personality disorder* display a pattern of interpersonal deficits marked by acute discomfort in close relationships, cognitive or perceptual distortions, and behavioral eccentricities.

   B. People with these disorders usually are resistant to treatment, and treatment gains tend to be modest at best.

3. ***"Dramatic" Personality Disorders*** Four of the personality disorders are marked by highly dramatic, emotional, or erratic symptoms.

   A. Persons with *antisocial personality disorder* display a pervasive pattern of disregard for and violation of the rights of others. No known specific intervention for it is particularly effective.

   B. People with *borderline personality disorder* display a pervasive pattern of instability in interpersonal relationships, self-image, and mood, along with marked impulsivity. Treatment apparently can be effective and lead to sustained, though limited, improvement for some clients with this disorder.

   C. Individuals with *histrionic personality disorder* (once called *hysterical personality disorder*) display a pattern of excessive emotionality and attention seeking. Clinical case reports suggest that treatment is helpful on occasion.

   D. People with *narcissistic personality disorder* display a chronic and pervasive pattern of grandiosity, need for admiration, and lack of empathy. This has been characterized as one of the most difficult disorders to treat.

4. ***"Anxious" Personality Disorders*** Three of the personality disorders are marked by the kinds of symptoms found in Axis I's anxiety and depressive disorders.

   A. People with *avoidant personality disorder* display a chronic and pervasive pattern of inhibition in social situations, feelings of inadequacy, and extreme sensitivity to negative evaluation.

   B. People with *dependent personality disorder* display a pattern of submissive and clinging behavior, fears of separation, and a pervasive and excessive need to be taken care of.

   C. Individuals with *obsessive-compulsive personality disorder* display a pattern of preoccupation with orderliness, perfectionism, and mental and interpersonal control, at the expense of flexibility, openness, and efficiency.

   D. A variety of treatment strategies have been used for people with these disorders and apparently have been modestly to moderately helpful.

5. ***Dilemmas and Confusion*** It appears that personality disorders are commonly misdiagnosed, an indication of some serious problems in the validity and reliability of the diagnostic categories.

Thought and Afterthought

When Life Imitates Art

Oliver Stone's 1994 movie *Natural Born Killers* tells the tale of two sociopathic thrill seekers, Mickey and Mallory, who grow world-famous as they travel the countryside brutally killing people. Stone meant the film to be a satire of our culture's appetite for violence, but it also spawned more copycat killings than any other film ever made (Shnayerson, 1996). Numerous young people went on similar killing sprees, citing the movie as their inspiration.

The copycat phenomenon is not new. When Stanley Kubrick's film *A Clockwork Orange* was released in 1971, critics praised its important social statement. But when some British youths copied the actions of the movie's gang leader and raped a woman to the tune of "Singin' in the Rain," Kubrick had the film banned in Britain (Shnayerson, 1996). It remains so today.

Afterthoughts: Must individuals already be antisocial in order to be influenced by films such as these, or do the films confuse them by glorifying criminal and violent behavior? . . . Should filmmakers and writers consider the possible psychological influence of their work on certain individuals before they undertake such projects?

Distrusting Souls

A recent survey by the Pew Research Center (1997) disclosed just who among us are most distrustful of other people:

1. People whose parents repeatedly warned them against trusting strangers.
2. People under 30 years of age.
3. Individuals who are socially isolated.
4. People who live in the city rather than the suburbs.
5. People who live in poor or crime-ridden neighborhoods.
6. Persons who do not claim a religious affiliation.

Afterthoughts: Why would people in each of these groups feel distrustful of others? . . . Today's young adults received more warnings against trusting strangers as they were growing up than did today's older adults. Is contemporary society unintentionally fostering widespread distrust of others? . . . Is distrust qualitatively different from paranoia, or are the two on a continuum?

"Oh, What a Tangled Web . . . "

One of the most popular movies of 1997 was *Liar, Liar*, starring Jim Carrey. The movie's plot—a notorious liar loses his capacity to deceive—struck a chord in most viewers.

Almost everyone lies from time to time, but many of us know people who, like Carrey's character, lie regularly, almost as if they were driven to do so. They are not necessarily trying to protect themselves, and their lies often get them in trouble (Ford et al., 1988). Interestingly, compulsive lying is not considered a disorder, although it is sometimes characteristic of people with antisocial, histrionic, or narcissistic personality disorder. Nor has lying received much attention from clinical theorists or researchers.

Afterthoughts: What might be the differences between "normal" lying and "pathological" lying? . . . If lying is sometimes pathological, why is it not studied more extensively? . . . How do various institutions in our society—business, academia, science, religion—view lying, and how might these views affect the prevalence and nature of individual deceit? . . . Why do people often admire someone who deceives—a flatterer, an art forger, a jewel thief?

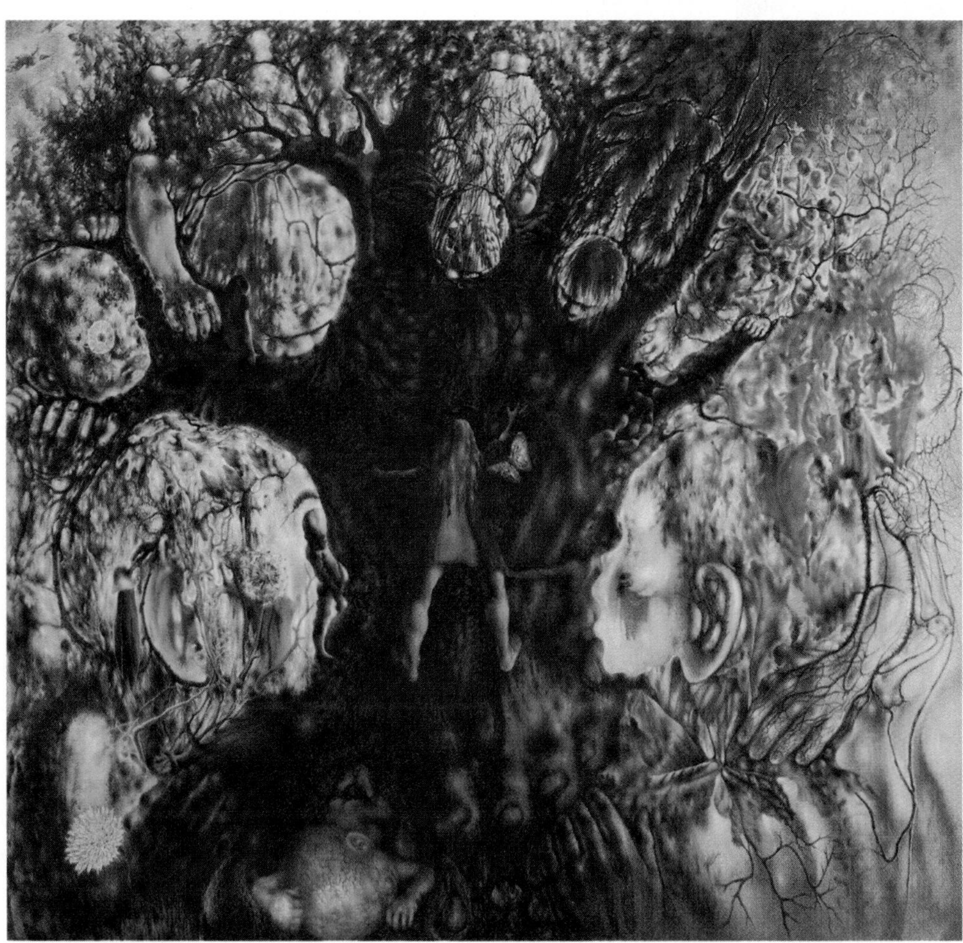

Topic Overview

Chapter 19

Disorders of Childhood and Old Age

Like the children who play hide-and-seek and confront the seasons of life in Pavel Tchelitchew's Hide-and-Seek *{Cache-cache}, 1940–42, people encounter a constant stream of events as they proceed through life. These encounters may feel comforting or frightening, inspiring or disabling, and can lead to growth, regression, or stagnation.*

Most psychological disorders can occur at any time in life. Some, however, are particularly likely to emerge during childhood or at the other end of the spectrum, during old age. Sometimes the special pressures of that age may cause the disorder to emerge. In other cases, unique traumatic experiences or biological abnormalities may be at fault. Some age-related disorders soon subside or can be corrected, but others continue throughout the individual's life. Still others, particularly certain childhood disorders, change form or evolve into different disorders.

Theorists often think of life as a series of stages along the way from birth to death. Most people traverse these stages in the same order, though at their own rates and in their own ways. The stages offer a useful picture of normal development and they often help clinicians detect deviations from the norm.

(*Drawing by Crawford; ©1991 The New Yorker Magazine, Inc.*)

In Chapter 3 we discussed Freud's influential theory of personality development. He proposed that each child passes through the same five psychosexual stages—the oral, anal, phallic, latency, and genital stages. Freud said little about the stages of adulthood, but Erik Erikson (1963), one of the twentieth century's leading psychologists, provided a more comprehensive theory of development. In it Erikson cites old age as one of life's most meaningful stages.

Although theorists may disagree with the details of Freud's or Erikson's scheme, most agree with their belief that we confront key pressures during each stage in life, and we either grow or decline, depending on how we meet these pressures. Each stage offers many opportunities for maladaptiveness, whether because of biological abnormality, psychological inadequacy, or extraordinary environmental stress.

Early in this century, clinicians viewed children as small adults and treated their psychological disorders as extensions of adult problems (Peterson & Roberts, 1991). Worse, they viewed elderly persons merely as survivors of adulthood and rarely treated their psychological disorders at all. Now, however, clinicians recognize that persons in each of these groups have their own issues and problems, and all deserve the possible benefits of treatment.

Disorders of Childhood and Adolescence

People often think of childhood as carefree and happy, yet it can also be a frightening and upsetting time. In fact, most children experience at least some emotional and behavioral problems as they confront new people, situations, and obstacles. They commonly worry, for example; surveys reveal that close to half of all children have multiple fears (Silverman, La Greca, & Wasserstein, 1995) (see Figure 19-1). School, health, and personal safety are their most common areas of concern. Bed wetting, nightmares, temper tantrums, and restlessness are also common among children (King, 1993; Crowther, Bond, & Rolf, 1981).

Nor is adolescence necessarily upbeat. The physical and sexual changes, social and academic pressures, personal doubts, and temptations of adolescence leave many teenagers anxious, confused, and depressed (Petersen et al., 1993; Takanishi, 1993). In fact, their "normal" psychological state seems to be deteriorating in the United States. Today's teenagers, although generally happy, apparently feel less confident and trusting, more sensitive, and less affectionate toward their families than adolescents did several decades ago (Offer et al., 1981).

Beyond these common psychological difficulties, around a fifth of all children and adolescents in the United States experience a diagnosable psychological disorder (Kazdin, 1994; Zill & Schoenborn, 1990). Boys with these disorders outnumber girls, even though most adult psychological disorders are more common among women. This shift may reflect the increased pressures faced by women in Western society, or it may indicate instead biases against women in diagnosis.

Some disorders of children—childhood anxiety disorders, childhood depression, and disruptive disorders—have adult counterparts, although they are also distinct in important ways (Kovacs, 1996). Other childhood disorders—elimination disorders, for example—usually disappear or radically change form by adulthood. Yet a third group often persist in stable forms into adult life. These include mental retardation and autism, disorders involving extensive disturbances in intellect and responsiveness to one's environment, respectively.

Childhood Anxiety Disorders

As in adults, the anxiety disorders experienced by children and adolescents include specific phobias, social phobias, generalized anxiety disorder, and obsessive-compulsive disorder (Murray, 1996; Douglass et al., 1995; APA, 1994; King et al., 1992). However, one form of anxiety in children, ***separation anxiety disorder,*** is different enough from the adult disorders to be listed as a separate category in DSM-IV. Children with this disorder experience excessive anxiety, often panic, whenever they are separated from home or a parent. Carrie, a 9-year-old girl, was referred to a local mental health center by her school counselor when she seemed to become extremely anxious at school for no apparent reason.

> She initially reported feeling sick to her stomach and later became quite concerned over being unable to get her breath. She stated that she was too nervous to stay at school and that she wanted her mother to come get her and take her home. . . . The counselor indicated that a similar incident occurred the next day with Carrie ending up going home again. She had not returned to school since. . . .

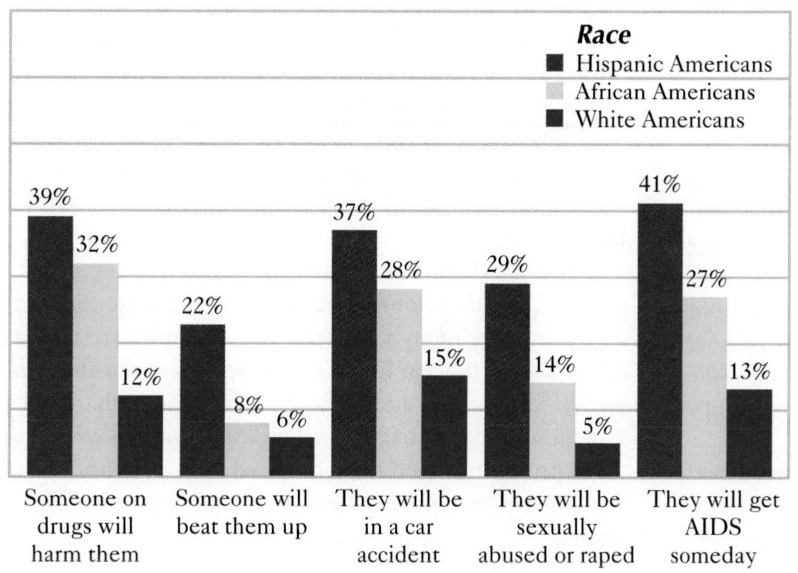

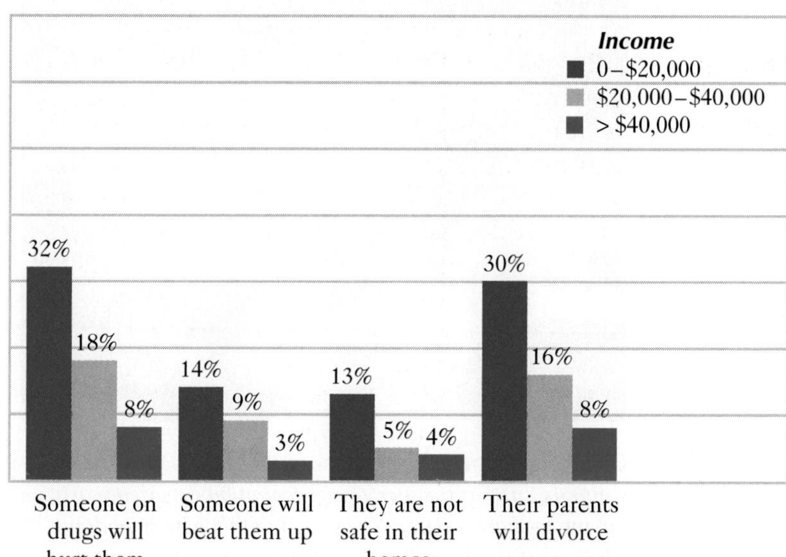

Figure 19-1 *According to a survey of over 900 children and adolescents, Hispanic American and African American children are much more likely than white American children to "worry a lot" about their safety and survival. Similarly, poorer children are more likely to worry about their welfare than wealthier children, irrespective of race, suggesting that the higher anxiety levels of children of racial minorities may be largely a matter of living in poorer, more deprived, or dangerous environments. (Adapted from National Commission on Children, 1991.)*

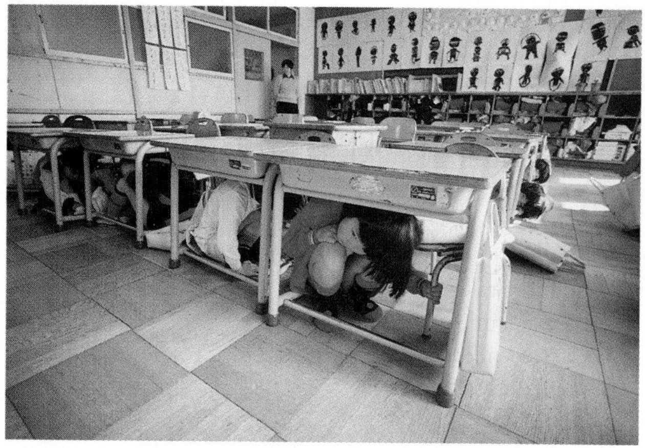

Childhood anxieties can be caused by society's repeated warnings of possible catastrophes. These schoolchildren in Japan dive for cover during an earthquake drill.

> At the time of the intake evaluation the mother indicated that she felt Carrie was just too nervous to go to school. She stated that she had encouraged her daughter to go to school on numerous occasions but that she seemed afraid to go and appeared to feel bad, so she had not forced her. . . . When asked if Carrie went places by herself, the mother stated that Carrie didn't like to do that and that the two of them typically did most everything together. The mother went on to note that Carrie really seemed to want to have her (the mother) around all the time and tended to become upset whenever the two of them were separated.
>
> *(Schwartz & Johnson, 1985, p. 188)*

Children like Carrie have great trouble traveling independently away from home, and they often refuse to visit friends' houses, go on errands, or attend camp or school. Many cannot even stay alone in a room, and cling to their parent around the house. Some also have temper tantrums, cry, or plead with their parents not to leave them. The children may fear that they will get lost when they are separated or that their parent will meet with an accident or illness (APA, 1994).

It has been estimated that about 4 percent of children and young adolescents experience separation anxiety, somewhat more girls than boys (APA, 1994). In many cases it is precipitated by a life stress such as the death of a parent or pet, moving, or a change of schools. The symptoms last at least four weeks, usually much longer, but they may wax and wane over the course of childhood and adolescence.

As in Carrie's case, a separation anxiety disorder sometimes takes the form of a ***school phobia,*** or ***school refusal,*** a common problem in which children experience extreme anxiety about attending school and often stay home for an extended period of time. Many cases of school phobia, however, involve factors other than separation, such as social fears, anxiety about academic performance, depression, and fears of specific objects or persons at school.

Childhood anxiety disorders are generally explained in much the same way as adult anxiety disorders (discussed in Chapters 6 and 7). However, some features unique to childhood can be an important backdrop. First, since children have had fewer experiences than adults, many aspects of their world are new and scary. They may be frightened by common developmental changes, such as a mother's return to work or the beginning of school, or by special traumas, such as moving to a new residence or becoming seriously ill (Tweed, Schoenbach, & George, 1989).

Second, because they are highly dependent on their parents for emotional support and guidance, children may be greatly influenced by parental inadequacies. If, for example, parents themselves react to events with high levels of anxiety or overprotect their child, the child may be more likely to develop anxiety problems (Barrett et al., 1996; Capps et al., 1996). Similarly, if parents repeatedly reject, disappoint, avoid, or abuse their children, the world may become an unpleasant and anxious place for the children.

Finally, their culture often presents children with dark, frightening notions that may set the stage for anxiety disorders. Today's children, for example, are repeatedly warned, both at home and at school, about the dangers of kidnapping and of drugs. They are bombarded by violent and scary images in television shows, movies, and news programs. Even time-honored fairy tales and nursery rhymes contain frightening images that upset many children.

Childhood anxieties may be the result of developmental traumas, such as the increasingly common experience of having to share a parent's affection with a new stepparent. The face of this boy after his mother's remarriage says it all.

Psychodynamic, behavioral, cognitive, and family therapies, or a combination of them, have been used to treat anxiety disorders in children, often with success (Barrett, Dadds, & Rapee, 1996; Kazdin, 1994; Barros, 1992). Drug treatments have also been applied in some cases but have received relatively limited empirical attention (Klein et al., 1992; Simeon et al., 1992).

Because children have a limited capacity for analyzing and reflecting on their feelings and motives, many therapists, particularly psychodynamic therapists, use the technique of ***play therapy*** as part of treatment. They have the children express conflicts and feelings indirectly by playing with toys, drawing, and making up stories. The therapists then interpret these activities and, through continued play and fantasy, try to help the children develop relevant insights, resolve conflicts, and alter their emotions and behavior. Similarly, because children are often excellent hypnotic subjects, some therapists use hypnotherapy to help young clients overcome intense fears (Murray, 1996).

Childhood Depression

Like adults, children may experience a depressive disorder (Kovacs, 1997). Bobby is one such child:

> In observing Bobby in the playroom it was obvious that his activity level was well below that expected for a child of 10. He showed a lack of interest in the toys that were available to him, and the interviewer was unable to get him interested in any play activity for more than a few minutes. In questioning him about home and school, Bobby indicated that he didn't like school because he didn't have any friends, and he wasn't good at playing games like baseball and soccer like the other kids were, stating "I'm not really very good at anything." . . . When asked what he would wish for if he could have any three wishes granted he indicated, "I would wish that I was the type of boy my mother and father want, I would wish that I could have friends, and I would wish that I wouldn't feel sad so much."
>
> In speaking with the parents, the mother reported that she and her husband had become increasingly concerned about their son during the past year. She indicated that he always seemed to look sad and cried a lot for no apparent reason and that he appeared to have lost interest in most of the things that he used to enjoy doing. The mother confirmed Bobby's statements that he had no friends, indicating that he had become more and more of a loner during the past 6 to 9 months. She stated that his schoolwork had also suffered in that he is unable to concentrate on school assignments and seems to have "just lost interest." The mother notes, however, that her greatest concern is that he has recently spoken more and more frequently about "killing himself," saying that the parents would be better off if he wasn't around.
>
> *(Schwartz & Johnson, 1985, p. 214)*

Approximately 2 percent of children under 17 years of age experience a major depressive disorder (Kazdin, 1994). The rate may be 7 percent among adolescents

The death of a parent may lead to childhood depression. Edvard Munch's painting The Dead Mother and the Little Girl *captures the devastating impact of such a loss.*

alone (Petersen et al., 1993, 1991). There appears to be no difference in the rates of depression in boys and girls before the age of 11, but by the age of 16, girls are twice as likely as boys to be depressed (Angold & Rutter, 1992; Kazdin, 1990).

Explanations of childhood depression are similar to those offered for adult depression. Theorists have pointed, for example, to such factors as loss, learned helplessness, negative cognitive bias, and low serotonin or norepinephrine activity (Todd et al., 1996; Petersen et al., 1993). Moreover, like adult depression, many cases of childhood depression seem to be precipitated by a negative life event, major change, rejection, or ongoing abuse (see Box 19-1).

Like depression among adults, childhood depression often responds well to cognitive therapy or interpersonal approaches such as social skills training. In addition, family therapy is often effective (Beardslee et al., 1996; Vostanis et al., 1996; Kazdin, 1994, 1989). Controlled studies, however, have not clearly supported the use of antidepressant medications in treating childhood depression (Ambrosini et al., 1993; Geller et al., 1993). They seem to be of greater help to depressed adolescents (Sallee et al., 1997). Treatments that combine various approaches according to the needs of a particular child are often more helpful than any one of these methods alone (Kazdin, 1989).

Disruptive Behavior Disorders

Children often flout social rules or misbehave (see Figure 19-2). Children who display patterns of extreme hostility and defiance, however, are considered to have either oppositional defiant disorder or conduct disorder.

Children with ***oppositional defiant disorder*** argue repeatedly with adults, lose their temper, and feel great anger and resentment. They frequently defy adult rules and requests, annoy others, and blame others for their own mistakes and problems. The disorder typically begins by 8 years of age and is more common in boys than in girls before puberty, but equally common among boys and girls after puberty. Its prevalence is between 2 and 16 percent, according to various studies (APA, 1994).

Children with ***conduct disorder,*** a more severe pattern, go further and repeatedly violate the basic rights of others. They are often aggressive and may in fact be physically cruel to persons or animals, deliberately destroy others' property, lie and cheat, skip school, or run away from home. Many steal from, threaten, or harm their victims, committing such crimes as shoplifting, forgery, breaking into houses, buildings, or cars, mugging, extortion, and armed robbery. As they get older their physical violence may extend to rape, assault, or in rare cases homicide (APA, 1994).

Conduct disorder usually, but not always, begins before age 10 *(childhood-onset type).* Six to 16 percent of boys and 2 to 9 percent of girls may display this disorder. Many of them also experience additional psychological disorders (Biederman et al., 1996; APA, 1994). Children with a mild conduct disorder may improve over time, but in severe cases the pattern continues into adulthood, when it may lead to an antisocial personality disorder or other psychological problems (Kratzer & Hodgins, 1997).

Many children with conduct disorder are suspended from school, placed in foster homes, or incarcerated. When children between the ages of 8 and 18 break the law, the legal system often labels them ***juvenile delinquents.*** More than half of the juveniles who are arrested each year are ***recidivists,*** or persons who have records of previous arrests. Males are much more involved in juvenile crime than females, although rates for females are on the increase. Females are most likely to be arrested for drug use, sexual offenses, and running away, males for drug use and crimes against property. Arrests of adolescents for serious crimes have at least tripled

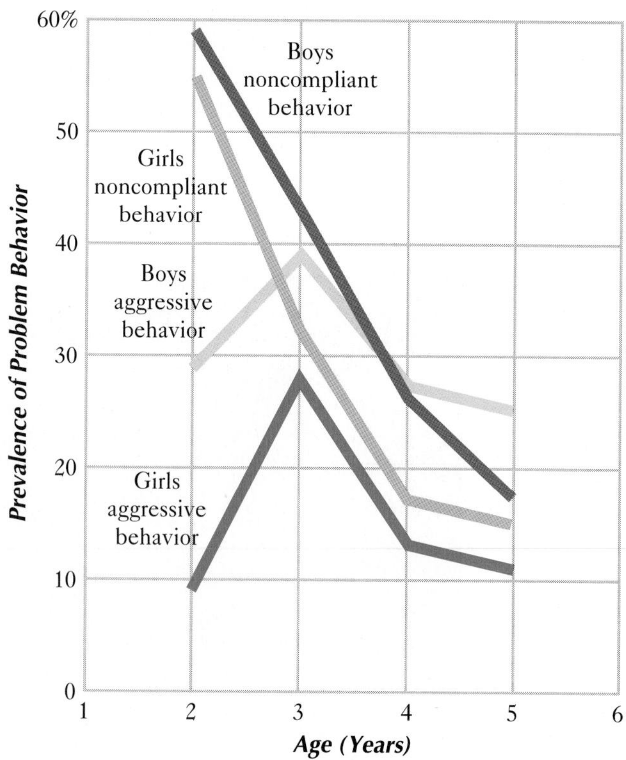

Figure 19–2 *Teachers' evaluations of more than 700 preschoolers indicated that the rates of both noncompliant and aggressive behavior dropped as the children grew older. (Adapted from Crowther, Bond, & Rolf, 1981.)*

"Sam, neither your father nor I consider your response appropriate."

(Drawing by Koren; © 1988 The New Yorker Magazine, Inc.)

during the past twenty years: the juvenile crime rate jumped almost 50 percent just between 1988 and 1992 (U.S. Department of Justice, 1994).

Cases of conduct disorder have been linked to genetic and biological factors, drug abuse, and poverty (Slutske et al., 1997; Needleman et al., 1996; Linz et al., 1990). However, they have most often been tied to parent-child relationships and family dysfunction (Klein et al., 1997; Hoge, Andrews, & Leschied, 1996; Miller & Prinz, 1990). The disorder often emerges in an atmosphere of family conflict and hostility (Dadds et al., 1992; Whittaker & Bry, 1992). Children whose parents reject them, leave them, or fail to provide them with consistent discipline and supervision are apparently more likely to bully others, lie, steal, or run away (Rosenstein & Horowitz, 1996; Seppa, 1996; Staub, 1996). Similarly, when parents display low levels of moral judgment, are themselves antisocial, or have substance-related, mood, or schizophrenic disorders, their children are more likely to display a conduct disorder (APA, 1994; Schachar & Wachsmuth, 1990; Moore & Arthur, 1983).

Generally, treatments for conduct disorder are most effective with children under 13 years of age, as disruptive behavior patterns become more stable with age (Burnette & Murray, 1996; Tate et al., 1995; Loeber, 1991). Given the importance of family factors in this disorder, therapists often use family interventions. In the most successful of these approaches, (1) parents are taught more effective ways to deal with their children (for example, consistently to reward appropriate behaviors) or (2) parents and children meet together in behavior-oriented family therapy (Kazdin, 1997; DeAngelis, 1996; Long et al., 1994; Bank et al., 1991). Sociocultural approaches such as residential programs in the community, interventions at school, and group therapy have also helped some individuals improve (DeAngelis, 1996; Tate et al., 1995).

Individual interventions are sometimes helpful, particularly those that teach the child techniques for coping with anger (Tate et al., 1995; McMahon & Wells, 1989). And recently drug therapy has been tried to help control aggressive outbursts in these children (Donovan et al., 1997; Tate et al., 1995; Kemph et al., 1993).

Institutionalization in so-called *juvenile training centers* has not met with much success (Tate et al., 1995) (see Figure 19-3). In fact, such institutions frequently serve to solidify the delinquent culture rather than resocialize young offenders. While the rate of repeated arrests of adolescents sent to training centers varies with the type of crime and the type of treatment, the overall rate has been estimated to be as high as 80 percent (Erickson, 1992). Immediate probation as an alternative to institutionalization has been more successful in cases involving crimes of a less serious nature, especially when probation officers are sensitive and receive adequate supervision, and when ongoing treatment is available for the individual. Unfortunately, most probation officers are without mental health training and spend an average of one hour per month with each young offender (Erickson, 1992).

Many clinicians claim that the greatest promise for addressing conduct disorders and delinquency lies in ***prevention programs*** that begin in early childhood (Burnette & Murray, 1996). These programs try to

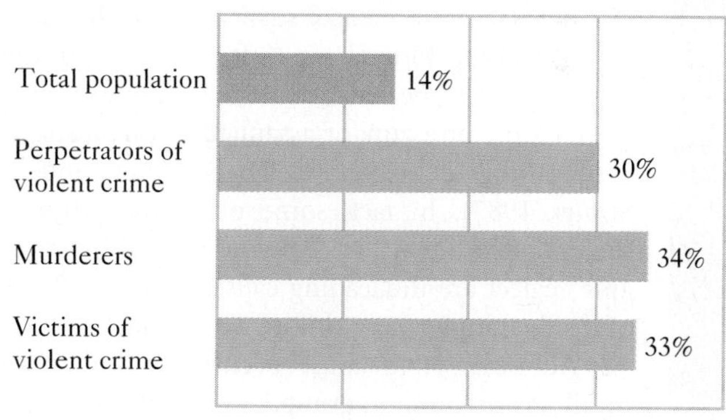

Figure 19-3 *Teenagers in the United States commit crimes at a rate that is disproportionate to their overall population rate. Although they make up only 14 percent of the total population, they commit around 30 percent of all violent crimes and 34 percent of all murders. The number of antisocial acts by teens has increased dramatically since 1980, even though the total number of teenagers has declined during that time. Teenagers are also the victims of 33 percent of all violent crime. (Adapted from Benson, 1996; FBI Uniform Crime Reports, 1996; National Crime Victimization Survey, 1996, 1993.)*

BOX 19-1 Child Abuse

What I remember most about my mother was that she was always beating me. She'd beat me with her high-heeled shoes, with my father's belt, with a potato masher. When I was eight, she black and blued my legs so badly, I told her I'd go to the police. She said, "Go, they'll just put you into the darkest prison." So I stayed. When my breasts started growing at 13, she beat me across the chest until I fainted. Then she'd hug me and ask forgiveness. . . . Most kids have nightmares about being taken away from their parents. I would sit on our front porch crooning softly of going far, far away to find another mother.

(Time, *September 5, 1983, p. 20)*

Child abuse is the intentional use of physical or psychological force by an adult on a child, often aimed at hurting or destroying the child. About 3 million cases of physical child abuse occur each year (Gallup, 1995; McCurdy & Daro, 1993). Surveys suggest that one of every ten children is subjected to severe violence, such as being kicked, bitten, hit (often with an object), beaten, threatened with a knife or a gun, or assaulted with a knife or a gun (Gelles & Straus, 1987). In fact, some observers believe that physical abuse and neglect are the leading causes of death among young children.

Although child abuse occurs in all socioeconomic groups, it is apparently more common among the poor (Gallup, 1995; Gelles, 1992). The abusers are usually the parents. The abuse seems to be more common in one-parent households than in two-parent households. Girls and boys are abused at approximately the same rate. Babies who are fussy and irritable and cry a great deal are apparently at particularly high risk of being abused (Gil, 1970).

Studies suggest that the victims of child abuse may suffer both immediate and long-term psychological effects. Research has revealed, for example, poorer performance and behavioral problems in school among abused children (Eckenrode, Laird, & Doris, 1993). It has also uncovered long-term effects such as lower social acceptance; more psychological problems such as anxiety, misbehavior, aggression, defiance, hyperactivity, and distractibility; more arrests during adolescence and adulthood; a greater risk of becoming criminally violent; a higher unemployment rate, lower-paying jobs, and less education; and a higher suicide rate (Stein et al., 1996; Carrey, 1995; Knutson, 1995; Egeland, 1991; Widom, 1991, 1989). Finally, more than one-third of victims grow up to be abusive, neglectful, or seriously inept parents (Oliver, 1993).

Two forms of child abuse have received special attention in recent years: psychological abuse and sexual abuse. ***Psychological abuse*** may include severe rejection; coercive, punitive, and erratic discipline; scapegoating and ridicule; unrealistic expectations; exploitation and corruption; isolation; and refusal to provide help for a child with psychological problems (Hart & Brassard, 1991, 1987; Hart, Germain, & Brassard, 1987). It probably accompanies all forms of physical abuse and neglect, and occurs by itself in at least 200,000 cases each year (McCurdy & Daro, 1993; AAPC, 1992; Hart & Brassard, 1987).

Child sexual abuse, the use of a child for gratification of adult sexual desires, may occur outside of or in the home (Davidson et al., 1996). Twenty-five percent of all cases occur before age 7 (Wurtele & Schmitt, 1992). In surveys of adult women, around a fifth reported having been forced into sexual contact with an adult male as children, many of them with their father or stepfather (Eisen, 1993; Lloyd, 1992; Green, 1989). Although the majority of victims are girls, boys are also sexually abused (Bolton, Morris, & MacEachron, 1989). In fact, one of every seven men may have been sexually abused as a child (Lloyd, 1992).

Incest, from the Latin *incestus,* "impure," is a particularly damaging type of child sexual abuse. Incest is sexual intercourse between persons closely related by blood or marriage. Its damaging effects may last a lifetime. It is difficult to assess how many cases of child sexual abuse represent father-daughter (or stepfather-stepdaughter) incest, because daughters are reluctant, ashamed, or afraid to tell what has happened to them (Kilpatrick et al., 1987). On the other hand, clinicians have become increasingly aware of the profound feelings of depression, guilt, and shame that many victims of father-daughter incest carry into adulthood, and of the difficulties that these early experiences may pose for later intimacy and interpersonal trust (Karp et al., 1995; Eisen, 1993; Conte, 1991).

Both legal and mental health professionals have become particularly concerned about child sexual abuse because of several highly publicized cases in day-care centers around the United States. Recently the validity of children's testimony in such cases has been debated. Although the trend has been to believe the children, the overturning of a highly publicized conviction in 1993 marked an increasing awareness of the suggestibility of children and the power of interrogators to elicit the testimony they want to hear. A child-care worker at a nursery school had been convicted of 115 charges of sexual abuse of nineteen children and sentenced to forty-seven years in prison. After she had served five years in prison, however, her conviction was overturned on the grounds that she did not receive a fair trial, in part because the judge's questioning of the children was not impartial. Similar cases and overrulings have followed.

Honoré Daumier's Fatherly Discipline.

Before the twentieth century, the legal system tried to avoid intervention in family life, even when a child was being abused (Garrison, 1987). Medical reports of suspected child abuse did not begin to receive widespread attention until the 1960s (Newberger, 1983), and medical and legal professionals did not become actively involved in such cases until 1974, when states and the federal government passed laws requiring physicians to report cases of suspected child abuse (Garrison, 1987). Since then media accounts have kept this staggering social problem in the public eye, courts have become more protective and punitive, and mental health professionals have developed numerous research and therapy programs.

Clinical researchers have learned that a variety of factors may interact to produce child abuse. Abusive parents may have poor impulse control and low self-esteem. Many have been abused themselves as children and have had poor role models. They may be subjected to such situational stresses as marital disputes or family unemployment. Research shows that physically abusive parents also tend to be young and poorly educated, to have low incomes, and to abuse alcohol or drugs (Whipple, Webster, & Stratton, 1991).

Because the causal factors vary from case to case, clinicians must carefully assess the parents, child, and family dynamics before planning a treatment program (Azar & Wolfe, 1989). A variety of interventions have been tried. Parents may develop insight about themselves and their behavior, receive training on alternatives to abuse, and learn parenting skills in groups and classes such as those offered by the national organization known as Parents Anonymous. In groups or in individual treatment, they may learn more effective ways to interact with their children through such behavioral interventions as modeling, role playing, and feedback (Azar & Siegal, 1990; Wolfe et al., 1988; Barth et al., 1983). They may receive cognitive therapy to help correct misperceptions about their children or themselves (Azar & Siegal, 1990; Azar et al., 1984). Many parents who abuse their children believe that their children actually intend to upset them, and some have unrealistic expectations about the children's behavior (Azar & Rohrbeck, 1986; Plotkin, 1983). A number of treatments are also aimed at helping parents deal more effectively with the situational stresses that often trigger their abuse, such as unemployment, marital discord, and depressed feelings (Campbell et al., 1983). The effects of such approaches on the parents' behavior, the child's self-esteem and psychological recovery, and family harmony have yet to be fully determined (Azar & Wolfe, 1989).

Research suggests that the psychological needs of the child victims should also be anticipated and addressed early (Roesler & McKenzie, 1994). It has also occurred to clinicians that the victims themselves may be able to help prevent or mitigate patterns of abuse, and many early detection programs have been launched. The programs typically aim to (1) educate children about the frequency and nature of the child abuse problem; (2) teach skills for avoiding or escaping from abusive encounters; (3) encourage children to tell another adult if they are abused; and (4) assure children that abuse is never their own fault (Finkelhor et al., 1995). Because these programs are aimed at the victims rather than at the abusers, they have not been highly successful at preventing victimization altogether. They do, however, seem to increase the likelihood that children will report abuse, so that they can receive early support or therapy and perhaps escape further victimization. Such programs also seem to decrease children's tendency to blame themselves for abuse and increase their feelings of self-efficacy (Finkelhor et al., 1995).

As we observed previously, the overall effectiveness of the various approaches to child abuse is not clear. However, the relatively recent efforts to understand, treat, and prevent this problem represent a significant improvement over the ignorance and indifference of past times. As such, they offer genuine hope for society's most innocent and helpless victims.

change unfavorable social conditions before they can lead to a case of conduct disorder. Preventive measures include training opportunities for young people who are disaffected by school, recreational facilities, health care, and measures to alleviate the conditions of poverty and improve parents' child-rearing skills. All of the interventions work better when they educate and involve the family (Burnette & Murray, 1996; Zigler et al., 1992).

Attention-Deficit Hyperactivity Disorder

Children who display ***attention-deficit hyperactivity disorder (ADHD)*** attend very poorly to tasks or behave overactively and impulsively, or both. An ADHD pattern often appears before the child starts school, as in the case of Steven, a child who displays poor attention, overactivity, and impulsiveness.

> Steven's mother cannot remember a time when her son was not into something or in trouble. As a baby he was incredibly active, so active in fact that he nearly rocked his crib apart. All the bolts and screws became loose and had to be tightened periodically. Steven was also always into forbidden places, going through the medicine cabinet or under the kitchen sink. He once swallowed some washing detergent and had to be taken to the emergency room. As a matter of fact, Steven had many more accidents and was more clumsy than his older brother and younger sister. . . . He always seemed to be moving fast. His mother recalls that Steven progressed from the crawling stage to a running stage with very little walking in between.
>
> Trouble really started to develop for Steven when he entered kindergarten. Since his entry into school, his life has been miserable and so has the teacher's. Steven does not seem capable of attending to assigned tasks and following instructions. He would rather be talking to a neighbor or wandering around the room without the teacher's permission. When he is seated and the teacher is keeping an eye on him to make sure that he works, Steven's body still seems to be in motion. He is either tapping his pencil, fidgeting, or staring out the window and daydreaming. Steven hates kindergarten and has few long-term friends; indeed, school rules and demands appear to be impossible challenges for him. The effects of this mismatch are now showing in Steven's schoolwork and attitude. He has fallen behind academically and has real difficulty mastering new concepts; he no longer follows directions from the teacher and has started to talk back.
>
> *(Gelfand, Jenson, & Drew, 1982, p. 256)*

The symptoms of ADHD often feed into one another. A child who has trouble focusing attention may be pulled into action in several directions at once. Similarly, a constantly moving child is likely to have difficulty attending to tasks or exercising careful judgment. Often one of these areas of disturbance is much more prominent than the other (Gaub & Carlson, 1997), leading to a precise diagnosis of *ADHD, predominantly inattentive type,* or *ADHD, predominantly hyperactive-impulsive type* (called simply ***hyperactivity*** by many clinicians).

About half of the children with ADHD also experience learning or communication problems, many perform poorly in school, a number have difficulty interacting with other children, and about 80 percent misbehave, often quite seriously (Mariani & Barkley, 1997; Biederman et al., 1996; Greene et al., 1996). The disorder is also common among children with mood and anxiety disorders (APA, 1994).

As many as 5 percent of schoolchildren appear to display ADHD, around 80 percent of them boys. The disorder spans all cultures and usually persists through childhood (APA, 1994; Ross & Ross, 1982). Many children show a lessening of symptoms as they move into late adolescence, but problems remain in a number of cases (Wilson & Marcotte 1996; APA, 1994; Mannuzza et al., 1993). ADHD continues into adulthood for about a third of affected individuals (Lie, 1992). Those whose parents manifested this disorder are more likely than others to develop it (APA, 1994). The prevalence of the disorder is higher than usual among relatives of people with ADHD (Faraone et al., 1996, 1994).

Today's clinicians generally view ADHD as a disorder with multiple and interacting causes, including biological causes (indeed, the disorder was once referred to as ***minimal brain damage***), high levels of stress, and family dysfunctioning (Sherman, McGue, & Iacono, 1997; Needleman et al., 1996; Castellanos et al., 1994; Amsel, 1990). None of these suggested causes taken alone has received clear and consistent support (Anastopoulos & Barkley, 1992).

Sociocultural theorists also point out that ADHD symptoms and a diagnosis of ADHD may create still further interpersonal difficulties and generate additional symptoms in the child. That is, hyperactive children are often viewed more negatively than other children by their peers, their parents, and the children themselves (King & Young, 1981; Arnold, 1973).

There has been heated disagreement about the most effective treatment for ADHD. The most common approach has been stimulant drugs, such as ***methylphenidate (Ritalin)*** (see Figure 19-4 and Box 19-2). These drugs sometimes have a quieting effect on children with ADHD and increase their ability to solve complex problems, perform academically, and control aggressive

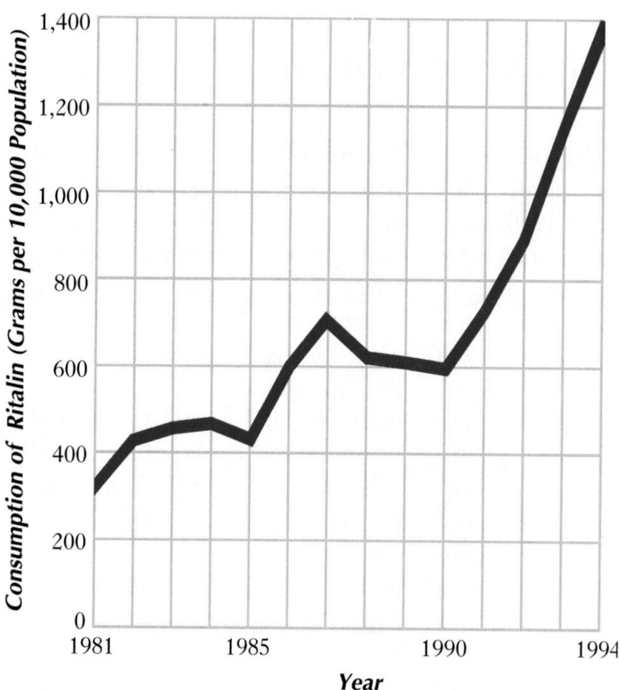

Figure 19-4 *The rise of Ritalin. The use of Ritalin has been increasing since the early 1980s when researchers found that it helped persons with ADHD. Sales have almost tripled during the 1990s alone. (Adapted from Drug Enforcement Administration, 1996.)*

behavior (Hinshaw, 1991; Douglas et al., 1988). However, many clinicians are concerned about the possible long-term effects of these drugs (Greenhill, 1992).

Behaviorists have treated ADHD by teaching parents and teachers how to reinforce the children systematically for paying attention or behaving appropriately at home or school. Such operant conditioning treatments have been relatively successful, especially in combination with drug therapy (Du Paul & Barkley, 1993). Some therapists have further combined behavioral approaches with self-instruction training for children with ADHD, similar to the adult-oriented cognitive approach that we discussed in Chapters 3 and 6 (Hinshaw & Melnick, 1992). However, the effectiveness of this cognitive strategy in treating children with ADHD has yet to be fully demonstrated (Hinshaw & Erhardt, 1991).

Elimination Disorders

Children with elimination disorders repeatedly urinate or pass feces in their clothes, in bed, or on the floor. They already have reached an age at which they are expected to control these bodily functions, and their symptoms are not caused by physical illness.

Enuresis

Enuresis is repeated involuntary (or in some cases intentional) bed wetting or wetting of one's clothes. It typically occurs at night during sleep, but may also occur during the day. Nightly enuresis usually takes place during the first third of the night, when the child is not yet dreaming. Occasionally, however, it occurs while the child dreams that he or she is urinating.

Children must be at least 5 years of age to receive this diagnosis. For some, the disorder represents continuation of wetting behavior from earlier years. Others, however, are dry for years before the onset of the disorder. Their disorder often is precipitated by a stressful event, such as hospitalization, the birth of a sibling, or entrance into school.

The prevalence of enuresis decreases with age. Seven percent of boys and 3 percent of girls who are 5 years old experience this disorder, compared to 3 percent of boys and 2 percent of girls who are 10 years old. At age 18, the pattern is found among 1 percent of males and somewhat fewer females (APA, 1994). Most people with enuresis have a close relative (parent, sibling, or child) who has had or will have the same disorder (APA, 1994).

No single explanation for enuresis has received clear support. Psychodynamic theorists explain it as a symptom of broader underlying conflicts (Olmos de Paz, 1990); family theorists attribute it to disturbed family interactions; behaviorists view it as the result of improperly conducted toilet training; and biological theorists point to delayed development of the physical structure of the urinary system (Erickson, 1992).

Most cases of enuresis correct themselves even without treatment. However, therapy, particularly behavioral therapy, can accelerate the process (Friman & Warzak, 1990; Whelan & Houts, 1990). In a widely used classical conditioning approach, a bell and a battery are wired to a pad consisting of two metallic foil sheets, and the entire apparatus is placed under the child at bedtime (Howe & Walker, 1992; Mowrer & Mowrer, 1938). A single drop of urine acts as an electrolyte that sets off the bell. The child is awakened immediately after he or she starts to wet. Thus the bell (unconditioned stimulus) paired with the sensation of a full bladder (conditioned stimulus) produces the response of waking. Eventually, a full bladder alone awakens the child. Certain cognitive therapies that teach self-control and antidepressant drug therapies have also been used with some success (Fritz et al., 1994; Ronen et al., 1992).

Encopresis

Encopresis, or repeated defecating in inappropriate places, is less common than enuresis and less well researched. This problem seldom occurs at night during sleep (Levine, 1975). As in enuresis, children with encopresis may be continuing the behavior from infancy, or they may be regressing after having mastered bowel

BOX 19-2 Ritalin: Chemical Restraint or Miracle Drug?

When Tom was born, he acted like a "crack baby," his mother, Ann, says. "He responded violently to even the slightest touch, and he never slept." Shortly after Tom turned two, the local day care center asked Ann to withdraw him. They deemed his behavior "just too aberrant," she remembers. Tom's doctors ran a battery of tests to screen for brain damage, but they found no physical explanation for his lack of self-control. In fact, his IQ was high—even though he performed poorly in school. Eventually, Tom was diagnosed with attention-deficit/hyperactivity disorder (ADHD). . . . The psychiatrist told Ann that in terms of severity, Tom was 15 on a scale of one to 10. As therapy, this doctor prescribed methylphenidate, a drug better known by its brand name, Ritalin. Tom is now in fifth grade and lives with his father, Ned, and his problems have worsened. Ned has come to doubt that ADHD exists and took Tom off medication last fall.

(Leutwyler, 1996, p. 13).

Ned is not the only parent to question a diagnosis of ADHD. Many parents also question the safety of its common treatment, the drug ***methylphenidate (Ritalin).*** During the late 1980s, several well-publicized lawsuits were filed against physicians, schools, and even the American Psychiatric Association, alleging misuse of Ritalin (Safer, 1994). Lawyers claimed that it was a dangerous, addictive drug that lazy parents, greedy psychiatrists, and overburdened teachers used indiscriminately to subdue healthy, energetic children (Safer & Kragner, 1993). Most of the lawsuits were dismissed, and at least one was deemed "totally without merit" by the court. Yet the media blitz they generated has had lasting effects on public perceptions (Safer & Kragner, 1992).

In recent years Ritalin has also become a popular drug among teenagers, who snort it to get high; some even become dependent on it (UNINCB, 1996). This development, too, has raised public concerns about its appropriateness and safety.

Methylphenidate has actually been around for decades. In fact, the patent for Ritalin expired a quarter of a century ago, and generic versions of methylphenidate are now widely sold. However, all versions continue to be referred to by the public as Ritalin. In recent decades, researchers have gained a clearer understanding of Ritalin's quieting effect on children and adults with ADHD and its ability to help them focus and solve complex problems, and use of the drug has increased enormously—according to some estimates, as much as 250 percent since 1990 alone (Hancock, 1996). Studies indicate that as many as 10 to 12 percent of all American boys may take Ritalin for ADHD, and the number of girls taking it is growing. During the 1990s, the number of individuals diagnosed with ADHD has increased from 900,000 to over 2 million in the United States, and many of them have been treated with Ritalin (Leutwyler, 1996; UNINCB, 1996). Around 8.5 tons of Ritalin are produced each year, and 90 percent of it is used in the United States.

The explosive increase in Ritalin use has understandably

control. The problem, which is usually involuntary, starts after the age of 4. It affects about 1 percent of 5-year-olds, a rate that drops to near zero by adulthood. It is more common in boys than in girls (APA, 1994).

Encopresis typically causes intense social problems, shame, and embarrassment. Children who suffer from it often try to conceal their condition and try to avoid situations, such as camp or school, in which they might become embarrassed (APA, 1994; Ross, 1981).

Cases of encopresis may stem from constipation, inadequate toilet training, or stress (APA, 1994). The most common and successful treatments for it are behavioral, medical (particularly when constipation is a factor), and combinations of the two (Ronen, 1993; Thapar et al., 1992). Family therapy has also been helpful (Wells & Hinkle, 1990).

Disorders of Learning, Communication, and Coordination

More than 20 percent of children display highly inadequate development and functioning in learning, communication, or coordination (APA, 1994). Such problems may lead to impaired performance in school and daily living (Geisthardt & Munsch, 1996), and typically are more common in boys than in girls. Similar difficulties are often seen in the children's close biological relatives.

One group of such developmental problems are the ***learning disorders.*** Here children's arithmetic, written expression skills, or reading performance are well below their intellectual capacity and cause academic and personal dysfunctioning. *Mathematics disorder,* experienced alarmed both the public and clinicians. Not surprisingly, after conducting an extensive investigation, the United Nations International Narcotics Control Board (1996) recently concluded that ADHD may indeed be overdiagnosed in the United States, and that many children who receive Ritalin have been *inaccurately* diagnosed. ADHD is usually first suspected by teachers or parents and diagnosed by pediatricians, who may not be able to differentiate it from other biological or psychological problems, such as a learning disorder. One study found that only 50 percent of children whom pediatricians diagnosed as having ADHD had undergone any psychological or educational testing to support the diagnosis (Leutwyler, 1996). In fact, ADHD can be reliably diagnosed only after a battery of observations, interviews, psychological tests, and physical exams.

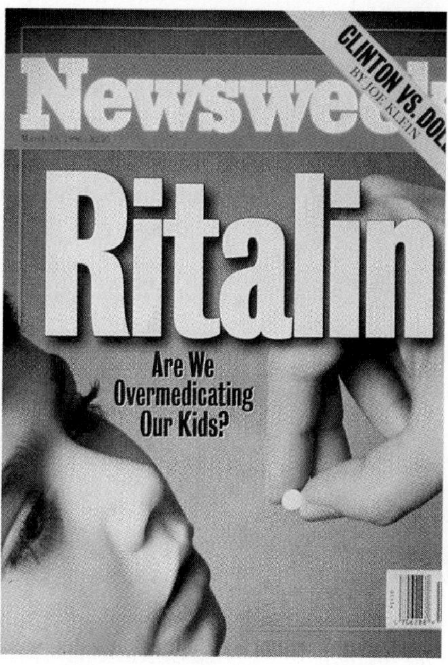

On the positive side, Ritalin is apparently very helpful to children and adults who do suffer from ADHD. Granted, parent training and behavioral programs are also effective in many cases, but not in all. Moreover, the behavioral programs are often more likely to be effective in combination with Ritalin (Vinson, 1994; Du Paul & Barkley, 1993). When children with ADHD are taken off the drug, often because of the drug's negative publicity, many fare badly (Safer & Krager, 1992).

Ritalin also appears to be relatively safe for most persons with ADHD (Leutwyler, 1996; Vinson, 1994; Safer & Krager, 1993). Its undesired effects are typically no worse than insomnia, stomachaches, headaches, or loss of appetite. In a small number of cases, however, it may cause facial tics. And it can affect the growth of some children, thus requiring "drug holidays" during the summer to counter this effect. It does not appear that Ritalin has long-term effects, but more longitudinal studies need to be conducted on this issue. Nevertheless, many members of the medical community believe that it is safe even when taken for years (Vinson, 1994).

The question then is what to do about a drug that is helpful for many people but almost certainly overused and even abused in some cases. The growing answer in the clinical community is to strive for better quality control. Researchers must continue to study the drug to determine its long-term effects. Pediatricians and others who work with children must be better trained in the assessment of ADHD. They must also be required to conduct broader testing before arriving at a diagnosis of ADHD. And they need to be aware of helpful treatments other than Ritalin. Only then will Ritalin fulfill its potential as a truly useful treatment for a serious problem.

by around 1 percent of schoolchildren, is characterized by strikingly impaired mathematical skills. It is usually apparent by the third grade. *Disorder of written expression,* apparent by the second grade, at least in severe cases, is characterized by extreme and repeated errors in spelling, grammar, punctuation, and paragraph organization. *Reading disorder,* also known as *dyslexia,* is marked by impairment of the ability to recognize words and to comprehend what is being read. Children with this disorder may omit, distort, or substitute words when they read, and they typically read slowly and haltingly. The disorder may not be fully apparent until the fourth grade or later. It is estimated that 4 percent of schoolchildren experience dyslexia (APA, 1994).

Another group of developmental problems are the ***communication disorders.*** Children with one such problem, *phonological disorder,* consistently fail to make correct speech sounds at an appropriate age, often giving an impression of baby talk. As many as 3 percent of children under 8 years of age have this problem to a moderate or severe degree, but only 0.5 percent still have it by 17 years of age (APA, 1994). Children with *expressive language disorder,* find it very hard to use language to express themselves. They may, for example, have trouble acquiring new words, regularly shorten sentences, or develop language slowly. As many as 5 percent of all children display this problem, yet almost all of them acquire more or less normal language ability by late adolescence (APA, 1994). Children with *mixed receptive/expressive language disorder* have difficulty comprehending *and* expressing language. Up to 3 percent of schoolchildren display this problem. Many eventually acquire adequate language

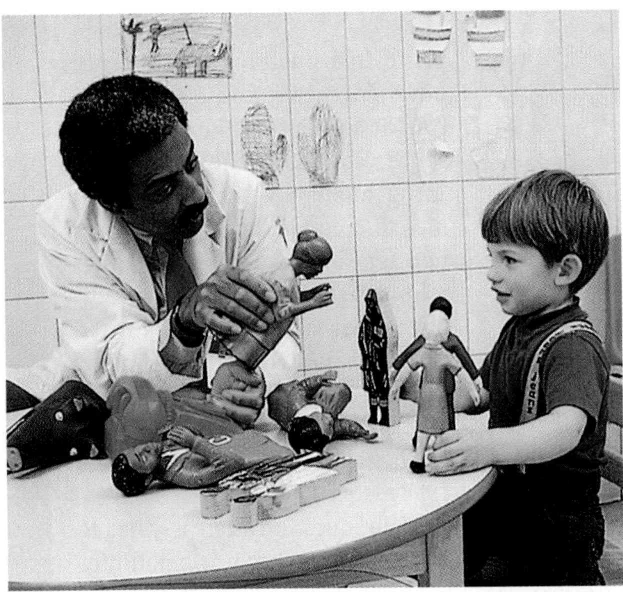

Therapists may use play therapy to assess the functioning of children and to help them express their feelings and thoughts and understand themselves and others.

ability, but some severely affected persons do not. And children who suffer from *stuttering* experience a disturbance in the normal fluency and timing of their speech. They may repeat, prolong, or interject sounds, pause within a word, or experience excessive physical tension when they produce words. Approximately 1 percent of children and adolescents stutter, most of them boys. The problem usually begins between 2 and 7 years of age. As many as 80 percent of children who stutter recover, often without treatment, usually by the age of 16 years.

Finally, children with ***developmental coordination disorder*** perform motor-coordinated activities at a level well below that of others their age. Young children with this disorder are clumsy and show delays in motor activities such as tying shoelaces, buttoning shirts, and zipping pants, while older sufferers may have great difficulty assembling puzzles, building models, playing ball, and printing or writing. As many as 6 percent of children between 5 and 11 years of age may experience the disorder. In some cases the lack of coordination continues into adulthood (APA, 1994).

Studies have linked these various disorders to genetic defects, birth injuries, lead poisoning, inappropriate diet, sensory or perceptual dysfunction, and poor teaching (Erickson, 1997; Gelfand et al., 1982). Research support for each of these factors has been quite limited, however, and the precise causes of the disorders remain unclear.

Some of these disorders respond to special treatment approaches (Merzenich et al., 1996). *Reading therapy,* for example, is very helpful in mild cases of reading disorder, *speech therapy* results in complete recovery in most cases of phonological disorder, and new *computerized language exercises* show considerable promise as a treatment for mixed receptive/expressive language disorder (Merzenich et al., 1996). As we have observed, however, the disorders sometimes disappear before adulthood, even without any treatment.

The classification of learning, communication, and coordination problems as mental disorders is very controversial. Many clinicians view them as primarily educational or social problems, appropriately addressed at school or home. Some further worry that these categories represent a growing trend to label more and more childhood behaviors as abnormal (see Box 19-3). The framers of recent editions of the DSM have reasoned, however, that the dysfunctioning caused by the disorders and by their frequent association with other psychological problems justifies their special clinical classifications (Mishna, 1996). Of special concern are studies that have found an increased risk of depression and even suicide in adolescents with these problems, particularly the learning disorders (Huntington & Bender, 1993).

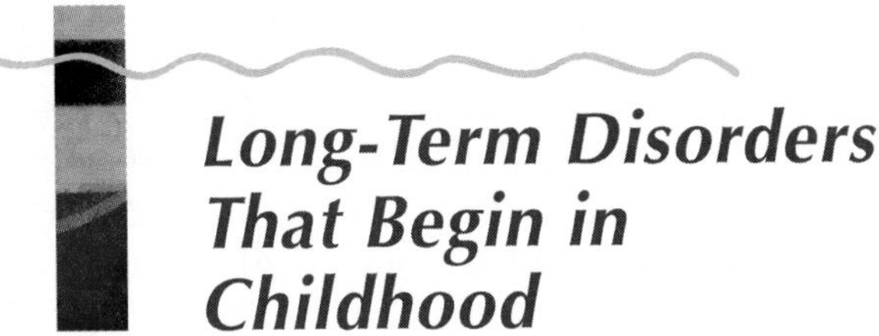

Long-Term Disorders That Begin in Childhood

Most childhood disorders either subside as the person ages or evolve into different disorders. Two disorders that emerge during childhood, however, typically continue unchanged throughout a person's life: autism and mental retardation.

Autism

A little boy named Mark presents a typical picture of autism:

> In retrospect [Susan, Mark's mother] can recall some things that appeared odd to her. For example, she remembers that . . . Mark never seemed to anticipate being picked up when she approached. In addition, despite Mark's attachment to a pacifier (he would complain if it were mislaid), he showed little interest in toys. In fact, Mark seemed to lack interest in anything.

> He rarely pointed to things and seemed oblivious to sounds. . . . Mark spent much of his time repetitively tapping on tables, seeming to be lost in his own world.
>
> After his second birthday, Mark's behavior began to trouble his parents. . . . Mark, they said, would "look through" people or past them, but rarely at them. He could say a few words but didn't seem to understand speech. In fact, he did not even respond to his own name. Mark's time was occupied examining familiar objects, which he would hold in front of his eyes while he twisted and turned them. Particularly troublesome were Mark's odd movements—he would jump, flap his arms, twist his hands and fingers, and perform all sorts of facial grimaces, particularly when he was excited—and what Robert [Mark's father] described as Mark's rigidity. Mark would line things up in rows and scream if they were disturbed. He insisted on keeping objects in their place and would become upset whenever Susan attempted to rearrange the living room furniture. . . .
>
> Slowly, beginning at age five, Mark began to improve. . . . The pronoun in the sentence was inappropriate and the sentence took the form of a question he had been asked previously, but the meaning was clear.
>
> *(Wing, 1976)*

Mark was manifesting an ***autistic disorder,*** also called ***autism,*** a disorder first identified by the American psychiatrist Leo Kanner in 1943. Children with this disorder are extremely unresponsive to others, show poor communication skills, and behave in a highly restricted and repetitive manner. The symptoms of autistic disorder appear very early in life, before 3 years of age. Several other disorders (*Retts, child disintegrative,* and *Asperger's disorders*) are similar to this one, each differing in time of onset or symptoms. Properly speaking, these four disorders are categorized as ***pervasive developmental disorders,*** but most clinicians refer to all of them as "autism," and we shall do the same.

Autism affects only 4 or 5 of every 10,000 persons (Harris, 1995; APA, 1994). Approximately 80 percent of them are boys. Two children with autism in three remain severely impaired into adulthood and are unable to lead independent lives (APA, 1994).

The Clinical Picture of Autism

The cornerstone of the diagnosis of autism has long been ***lack of responsiveness,*** aloofness, and lack of interest in other people (Volkmar et al., 1993). Like Mark, children with autism typically do not reach for their parents during infancy, and many arch their backs when they are held. They often fail to recognize or acknowledge those around them.

Language and communication deficits take various forms in autism. Approximately half of all persons with the disorder fail to speak or develop language skills (Dawson & Castelloe, 1992; Rutter, 1966). Those who do talk may show peculiarities in their speech. One of the most common speech problems is *echolalia,* the exact echoing or parroting of phrases spoken by others. The individuals repeat words with the same accent or inflection, but without comprehension. Some even repeat a sentence hours or days after they have heard it, a pattern called *delayed echolalia.*

People with autism may also display other speech oddities, such as *pronominal reversal,* or confusion of pronouns—the use of "you" instead of "I." When Mark was hungry, he would say, "Do you want dinner?" The individuals may have difficulty naming objects *(nominal aphasia)* or using abstract speech. They may employ incorrect speech inflections, ending statements with a questionlike rise in tone, for example. Most also have difficulty fully understanding speech and using it spontaneously.

Autism is also marked by ***limited imaginative play*** and ***very restricted behavior.*** The individuals often have extreme difficulty playing in a varied, spontaneous way or including others in their play. Typically they become very upset at minor changes in objects, persons, their routine, or ritualistic or repetitive behaviors they may perform. Mark, for example, lined things up and screamed if they were disturbed. Similarly, children with autism may react with tantrums if a parent wears an unfamiliar pair of glasses, a chair is moved to a different part of the room, or a word in a song is changed. Kanner (1943) labeled this characteristic a *perseveration of sameness.* Yet the same children may fail to react at all to changes that make a major difference in their lives.

Many persons with autism become strongly attached to particular objects—plastic lids, rubber bands, buttons, water. They may collect these objects, carry them, or play with them constantly. Some are fascinated by movement and may observe spinning objects, such as fans, for hours.

The ***motor movements*** of people with this disorder may also be unusual. Mark would jump, flap his arms, twist his hands and fingers, and grimace. In addition to such *self-stimulatory behaviors,* some persons perform *self-injurious behaviors,* such as repeatedly lunging or banging their head against a wall, pulling their hair, or biting parts of their body.

These behaviors and limitations seem to reflect a highly disturbed and contradictory pattern of perceptual reactions (Wing, 1976; Wing & Wing, 1971). Sometimes the individuals appear *overstimulated* by sights and sounds and try to block them out, while at other times they seem to be *understimulated* and to perform self-stimulatory actions in compensation. They may fail to react to loud noises, for example, yet turn around when

BOX 19-3 The Etiology and Treatment of Childhood

Jordan W. Smoller

This "clinical review" of the "disorder" called childhood originally appeared in Glen C. Ellenbogen (Ed.), Oral Sadism and the Vegetarian Personality *(New York: Brunner/Mazel, 1986).*

Childhood is a syndrome that has only recently begun to receive serious attention from clinicians. The syndrome itself, however, is not at all recent. As early as the eighth century, the Persian historian Kidnom made reference to "short, noisy creatures," who may well have been what we now call "children." The treatment of children, however, was unknown until this century, when so-called child psychologists and child psychiatrists became common. Despite this history of clinical neglect, it has been estimated that well over half of all Americans alive today have experienced childhood directly (Seuss, 1983). In fact, the actual numbers are probably much higher, since these data are based on self-reports which may be subject to social desirability biases and retrospective distortion. Clinicians are still in disagreement about the significant clinical features of childhood, but the proposed DSM-IV will almost certainly include the following core features:

1. Congenital onset
2. Dwarfism
3. Emotional lability and immaturity
4. Knowledge deficits
5. Legume anorexia

Congenital Onset In one of the few existing literature reviews on childhood, Temple-Black (1982) has noted that childhood is almost always present at birth, although it may go undetected for years or even remain subclinical indefinitely. This observation has led some investigators to speculate on a biological contribution to childhood. As one psychologist has put it, "we may soon be in a position to distinguish organic childhood from functional childhood" (Rogers, 1979).

Dwarfism This is certainly the most familiar clinical marker of childhood. It is widely known that children are physically short relative to the population at large. Indeed, common clinical wisdom suggests that the treatment of the so-called small child (or "tot") is particularly difficult. These children are known to exhibit infantile behavior and display a startling lack of insight (Tom & Jerry, 1967).

Emotional Lability and Immaturity This aspect of childhood is often the only basis for a clinician's diagnosis. As a result, many otherwise normal adults are misdiagnosed as children and must suffer the unnecessary social stigma of being labeled a "child" by professionals and friends alike.

Knowledge Deficits While many children have IQs within or even above the norm, almost all will manifest knowledge deficits. Anyone who has known a real child has experienced the frustration of trying to discuss any topic that requires some general knowledge.

Legume Anorexia This last identifying feature is perhaps the most unexpected. Folk wisdom is supported by empirical observation—children will rarely eat their vegetables (see Popeye, 1957, for review).

Causes of Childhood

Now that we know what it is, what can we say about the causes of childhood? Recent years have seen a flurry of theory and speculation from a number of perspectives. Some of the most prominent are reviewed below.

Sociological Model

Emile Durkind was perhaps the first to speculate about sociological causes of childhood. He points out two key observations about children: (1) the vast majority of children are unemployed, and (2) children represent one of the least educated segments of our society. In fact, it has been estimated that less than 20 percent of children have had more than a fourth-grade education. . . . One promising rehabilitation program (Spanky & Alfalfa, 1978) has trained victims of severe childhood to sell lemonade.

Biological Model

The observation that childhood is usually present from birth has led some to speculate on a biological contribution. An early investigation by Flintstone and Jetson (1939) indicated that childhood runs in families. Their survey of over 8,000 American families revealed that over half contained more than one child. Further investigation revealed that even most nonchild family members had experienced childhood at some point. . . .

Psychological Models

A considerable number of psychologically based theories of the development of childhood exist. They are too numerous to review here. Among the more familiar models are Seligman's "learned childishness" model. According to this model, individuals who are treated like children eventually give up and become children. As a counterpoint to such theories, some experts have claimed that childhood does not really exist. Szasz (1980) has called "childhood" an expedient label. In seeking conformity, we handicap those whom we find unruly or too short to deal with by labeling them "children."

Treatment of Childhood

Efforts to treat childhood are as old as the syndrome itself. Only in modern times, however, have humane and systematic treatment protocols been applied. The overwhelming number of children has made government intervention inevitable. The nineteenth century saw the institution of what remains the largest single program for the treatment of childhood—so-called public schools. Under this colossal program, individuals are placed into treatment groups on the basis of the severity of their condition. For example, those most severely afflicted may be placed in a "kindergarten" program. Patients at this level are typically short, unruly, emotionally immature, and intellectually deficient.

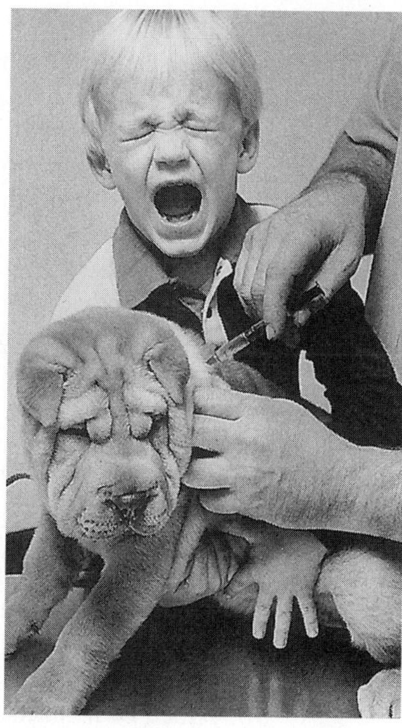

Unfortunately, the "school" system has been largely ineffective. Not only is the program a massive tax burden, but it has failed even to slow down the rising incidence of childhood.

Faced with this failure and the growing epidemic of childhood, mental health professionals are devoting increasing attention to the treatment of childhood. . . . The following case (taken from Gumbie & Pokey, 1957) is typical.

Billy J., age 8, was brought to treatment by his parents. Billy's affliction was painfully obvious. He stood only 4′3″ high and weighed a scant 70 pounds, despite the fact that he ate voraciously. Billy presented a variety of troubling symptoms. His voice was noticeably high for a man. He displayed legume anorexia and, according to his parents, often refused to bathe. His intellectual functioning was also below normal—he had little general knowledge and could barely write a structured sentence. Social skills were also deficient. He often spoke inappropriately and exhibited "whining behavior." His sexual experience was nonexistent. Indeed, Billy considered women "icky." . . .

After years of this kind of frustration, startling new evidence has come to light which suggests that the prognosis in cases of childhood may not be all gloom. . . . Moe, Larrie, and Kirly (1974) began a large-scale longitudinal study. These investigators studied two groups. The first group comprised 34 children currently engaged in a long-term conventional treatment program. The second was a group of 42 children receiving no treatment. . . .

The results . . . of a careful 10-year follow-up were startling. . . . Shemp (1984) found subjects improved. Indeed, in most cases, the subjects appeared to be symptom-free. Moe et al. report a spontaneous remission rate of 95 percent, a finding that is certain to revolutionize the clinical approach to childhood.

These recent results suggest that the prognosis for victims of childhood may not be so bad as we have feared. We must not, however, become too complacent. Despite its apparently high spontaneous remission rate, childhood remains one of the most serious and rapidly growing disorders facing mental health professionals today. And beyond the psychological pain it brings, childhood has recently been linked to a number of physical disorders. Twenty years ago, Howdi, Doodi, and Beauzeau (1965) demonstrated a sixfold increased risk of chickenpox, measles, and mumps among children as compared with normal controls. Later, Barbie and Kenn (1971) linked childhood to an elevated risk of accidents—compared with normal adults, victims of childhood were much more likely to scrape their knees, lose their teeth, and fall off their bikes.

Clearly, much more research is needed before we can give any real hope to the millions of victims wracked by this insidious disorder.

Children with autism are often unresponsive to other people. Yet many of them interact warmly with animals. Regular sessions of stroking and touching this dolphin have helped this young teenager overcome his autistic aversion to touch and have helped him behave more spontaneously.

they hear soda being poured. Similarly, they may fail to recognize that they have reached the dangerous edge of a high place, yet immediately spot a small object that is out of place in their room.

Explanations of Autism

A variety of explanations have been offered for autism. This is one disorder for which sociocultural explanations have probably been overemphasized and have led investigators in the wrong direction. Recent work in the psychological and biological spheres has led clinical theorists to point to cognitive impairments and brain abnormalities as the primary causes of autism.

Sociocultural Views Initially, theorists implicated family dysfunction and social stress as the primary causes of autism. When he first identified autism, for example, Leo Kanner (1954, 1943) argued that particular *personality characteristics of the parents* of children with autism set an undesirable climate for development and thus contributed to the disorder. He saw these parents as very intelligent people, yet obsessive and cold—"refrigerator parents." Such claims had enormous influence on the public and on the self-image of the parents themselves, but research has totally failed to support a picture of rigid, cold, rejecting, or disturbed parents (Roazen, 1992).

Similarly, some other clinicians have proposed that a high degree of *social and environmental stress* helps cause autism. Events that occur very early in life supposedly stifle the emotional development of these individuals and lead them into lives of near-total withdrawal. Once again, however, research has not supported this notion. Researchers who have compared children with autism to children without this disorder have found no differences in the incidence of parental death, divorce, separation, financial problems, or environmental deficits (Cox et al., 1975).

Psychological Views According to some theorists, persons with autism have a primary perceptual or cognitive disturbance that makes normal communication, relationships, and interactions impossible. The leading cognitive explanation holds that individuals with this disorder are unable to develop a "theory of mind"—a realization that other people base their behaviors on their own beliefs, intentions, and other mental states, not on information that they have no way of knowing (Happé, 1997, 1995; Leslie, 1997; Baron-Cohen, 1995; Leslie & Frith, 1990). By the age of 3 to 5, most children can take into account the *perspective* of another person, and they realize that that perspective will enable them to anticipate what that person will do. In a way, they learn to read others' minds.

Let us say that we watch Jane place a marble in a container, and then we observe Frank move the marble to a nearby room while Jane is taking a nap. We know that later Jane will search first in the container for the marble, because she is not aware that Frank moved it. We know that because we take Jane's perspective into account. A normal child would also anticipate Jane's search correctly. A person with autism would not. He or she would expect Jane to look in the nearby room, because that is where the marble actually is. Jane's state of awareness and mental processes would be irrelevant to the person.

Repeated studies show that people with autism have this kind of "mindblindness." Small wonder that they have so much trouble engaging in make-believe play, interacting effectively, using language in ways that include the perspectives of others, and developing relationships. Why do persons with autism have this cognitive impairment? Proponents of this explanation believe that the persons suffer early biological problems that prevent them from developing a theory of mind (Leslie, 1997; Frith, Morton, & Leslie, 1991).

Biological Views For years researchers have tried to determine what biological abnormalities might cause theory-of-mind deficits or the various features of autism. A clear biological explanation has not yet emerged, but some very promising leads are unfolding.

First, examinations of the relatives of people with autism yield results consistent with the possibility of a *genetic factor* in this disorder. The prevalence of autism among their siblings, for example, is as high as 6 to 8 per 100 (Piven et al., 1997), a rate up to 200 times higher than the general population's. Moreover, identical twins of persons with autism display the highest risk of all. In addition, chromosomal abnormalities have been discovered in 10 to 12 percent of persons with this disorder (Sudhalter et al., 1990).

Studies also suggest a link between autism and *prenatal difficulties or birth complications* (Rimland, 1992; Goodman, 1990). The chances of developing the disorder are higher when the mother had rubella (German measles) during pregnancy, was exposed to toxic chemicals before or during pregnancy, or had complications during labor or delivery.

Finally, researchers have identified specific *biological abnormalities* that may underlie autism. Recent studies have strongly implicated the ***cerebellum,*** for example (Courchesne, 1997; Courchesne & Courchesne, 1997; Courchesne et al., 1994). MRI scans and autopsies have revealed that abnormal development occurs in this brain area early in the life of persons with autism. Scientists have known for years that the cerebellum coordinates movement in the body, but they now suspect that it also helps coordinate a person's rapid attention to things. People whose cerebellum develops abnormally will have enormous difficulty adjusting their focus of attention, following verbal and facial cues, and processing social information. These, of course, are among the most prominent features of autism.

Many researchers believe that autism may have multiple biological causes (Gillberg, 1992). Perhaps all of the relevant biological factors (genetic, prenatal, birth, and postnatal) eventually lead to a common problem in the brain—a "final common pathway," such as neurotransmitter abnormalities, that produces cognitive deficits and other autistic patterns of behavior (Martineau et al., 1992; Yuwiler et al., 1992).

Treatments for Autism Treatments can help people with autism adapt better to their environment within their limitations. No treatment now known totally reverses the autistic pattern, but it is possible to help many people attain more effective functioning and contact with the world. Treatments of particular help are behavioral interventions, communication training, parent training, and community integration. In addition, psychotropic drugs and vitamin B6 have sometimes helped when combined with other approaches (Cook et al., 1992; Rimland, 1992, 1988; Todd, 1991). Humanistic interventions, marked by great warmth and unconditional acceptance of persons with autism, were once the leading approach (Bettelheim, 1967). They have not, however, been supported by research and are less popular today.

Behavioral Therapy Behavioral approaches have been applied to persons with autism for more than thirty years. The approaches teach new, appropriate behaviors, including speech, social skills, classroom skills, and self-help skills, while reducing negative, dysfunctional ones. Most often, the therapists employ *modeling* and *operant conditioning.* In modeling, they demonstrate a desired behavior and try to induce persons with the disorder to imitate it. In operant conditioning, they reinforce such behaviors. The desired behaviors must be ***shaped***—broken down and learned step by step—and the reinforcements must be explicit and consistent (Lovaas, 1987; Harris & Milch, 1981). These behavioral procedures are not easy to employ, because people with autism often have difficulty imitating or making connections between behaviors and rewards. Nevertheless, with careful planning and execution, the procedures often produce new behaviors.

A long-term controlled study compared the progress of two groups of children with autism (McEachin et al., 1993; Lovaas, 1987). Nineteen received intensive behavioral interventions, and nineteen formed a control group. The treatment began when the children were 3 years old and continued until they were 7. By the age of 7, the experimental group required less specialized treatment in school and had higher IQs than the control group. Many entered regular classrooms. The gains were still evident in the children at 11 to 19 years of age. In light of such findings, many clinicians now consider early behavioral programs to be the preferred treatment for autism (Harris, 1995; Waters, 1990).

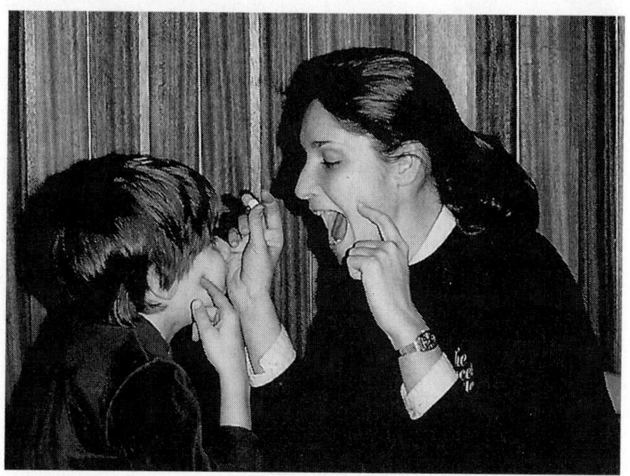

Behaviorists have had considerable success teaching children with autism to speak. The therapist systematically models how to position the mouth and how to make appropriate sounds, and then rewards the child's accurate imitations.

Therapies for people with autism, particularly the behavioral therapies, are ideally conducted in school while the individuals are young. The children attend special classes, often at special schools, where education and therapy can be pursued simultaneously. Specially trained teachers help the children improve their skills, behaviors, and interactions with the world.

Some clinicians suggest that higher-functioning persons with this disorder should be integrated for at least part of the school day into normal classrooms with nonautistic peers (Simpson & Sasso, 1992; Tomchek et al., 1992). These ***integrated education programs*** seem to be especially useful in teaching children with autism how to socialize (Goldstein et al., 1992; Nientimp & Cole, 1992).

Communication Training Despite intensive behavioral treatment, half of persons with autism remain speechless. As a result, many therapists also turn to *nonvocal* modes of communication, including ***sign language*** and ***simultaneous communication,*** a method combining sign language and speech. Other therapists advocate the use of ***augmentative communication systems,*** such as communication boards or computers that use pictures, symbols, or written words to represent objects or needs. A child may point to a picture of a fork to represent "I am hungry," for example, or point to a radio for "I want music."

In "facilitated communication," one of the newest augmentative communication systems, a facilitator gently supports *the hand of a person with autism while he or she points to or strikes letters on an alphabet board or computer keyboard. Recent studies suggest, however, that in many cases facilitators unintentionally influence the person's choice of letters, thus calling into question communications produced by this method.*

Parent Training Treatment programs now typically try to involve parents. Behavioral programs, for example, may include parent-training components to help parents learn and apply behavioral techniques at home (Love, Matson, & West, 1990; Anderson et al., 1989), and some offer instruction manuals for parents and home visits by teachers and other professionals.

Individual therapy and support groups to help parents address their own feelings and needs also are becoming increasingly available. In addition, a number of parent associations and lobbies are providing emotional support and practical help.

Community Integration Many educational and home programs now focus on teaching self-help, self-management, living, social, and work skills as early as possible, so that the children will be better able to live and function in their communities (Koegel et al., 1992; Stahmer & Schreibman, 1992). In addition, carefully run ***group homes*** and ***sheltered workshops*** are becoming increasingly available for adolescents and young adults with autism (Van Bourgondien & Schopler, 1990). These and other community-based programs help integrate the persons into their community and address the concerns faced by aging parents whose children will always need supervision (Pfeiffer & Nelson, 1992).

Mental Retardation

Ed Murphy, aged 26, can tell us what it's like to be diagnosed as retarded:

> What is retardation? It's hard to say. I guess it's having problems thinking. Some people think that you can tell if a person is retarded by looking at them. If you think that way you don't give people the benefit of the doubt. You judge a person by how they look or how they talk or what the tests show, but you can never really tell what is inside the person.
>
> *(Bogdan & Taylor, 1976, p. 51)*

For much of his life Ed was labeled mentally retarded and was educated and cared for in special institutions. During his adult years, his clinicians came to recognize that Ed's intellect in fact surpassed that ordinarily implied by this term. Nevertheless, Ed did live the childhood and adolescence of a person labeled retarded, and his statement illustrates the kinds of difficulties often confronted by persons with mental retardation.

Individuals with ***mental retardation*** are significantly below average in intelligence and adaptive ability. The term has been applied to a broad and varied population, including children in institutional wards who rock vacantly back and forth, young people who work daily in special job programs, and men and women who raise and support their families by working at relatively undemanding jobs (APA, 1994). Approximately one of every 100 persons receives this diagnosis (APA, 1994) (see Table 19-1). Around three-fifths of them are male. As we shall see, the vast majority are considered *mildly* retarded.

In 1905 Alfred Binet developed the first widely used intelligence test and proposed that testing should serve as the first step in treating mental retardation. He wrote, "After the illness, the remedy." Unfortunately, the remedy for this problem proved elusive, and for much of the twentieth century persons with mental retardation were considered beyond help. During the past few decades, professionals have taken a more positive attitude, worked to prevent or alleviate the disorder, and developed special interventions and educational approaches for those with this disorder.

DSM-IV echoes the criteria set forth by the American Association on Mental Retardation (AAMR) in 1992. Mental retardation is diagnosed when people display significant subaverage general *intellectual functioning* (an IQ of 70 or below) and, at the same time, *deficient adaptive behavior* (APA, 1994). That is, beyond having a low IQ, someone with mental retardation must have marked difficulty in areas such as communication, self-care, home living, interpersonal skill, self-direction, work, leisure, health, or safety (APA, 1994). DSM-IV further requires that the symptoms appear before the age of 18. Although the criteria may seem straightforward, they are in fact hard to apply, and scales used to measure them remain controversial.

Intelligence As we observed in Chapter 5, clinicians rely largely on intelligence tests to measure intellectual functioning. These tests consist of questions or tasks that represent different dimensions of intelligence, such as knowledge, reasoning, and judgment. An ***intelligence quotient (IQ)*** score derived from the individual's test performance theoretically indicates overall intellectual capacity.

Many theorists have questioned whether IQ tests are valid. Do they indeed measure and predict what they are supposed to measure and predict? Correlations between IQ and school performance are around .50, indicating that many children with lower IQs do, as one might expect, perform poorly in school, while many of those with higher IQs perform better (Neisser et al., 1996). At the same time, these correlations also suggest that the relationship is far from perfect. A particular child's school performance is often at odds with his or her IQ. IQ scores are correlated less highly still with job productivity and social effectiveness—areas of performance that

TABLE 19-1 Comparison of Childhood Disorders

Disorder	*Usual Age of Identification*	*Prevalence Among All Children*	*Gender with Greater Prevalence*	*Elevated Family History*	*Recovery by Adulthood*
Separation Anxiety Disorder	Before 12 years	4 percent	Females	Yes	Often
Conduct Disorder	Before 12 years	8 percent	Males	Yes	Often
ADHD	Before 12 years	5 percent	Males	Yes	Often
Enuresis	5–8 years	5 percent	Males	Yes	Usually
Encopresis	After 4 years	1 percent	Males	Unclear	Always
Learning Disorders	6–9 years	5 percent	Males	Yes	Often
Autism	0–3 years	0.05 percent	Males	Yes	Sometimes
Mental Retardation	Before 10 years	1 percent	Males	Unclear	Sometimes

Studies suggest that IQ scores and school performances of children from poor neighborhoods can be improved by enriching their daily environments at a young age through programs like "Head Start," thus revealing the powerful effect of the environment on IQ scores and intellectual performance.

often rely on intellectual ability (Neisser et al., 1996; Anastasi, 1982).

Intelligence tests also appear to be socioculturally biased, as we first noted in Chapter 5 (Neisser et al., 1996; Helms, 1992; Puente, 1990). Children reared in households of the middle and upper socioeconomic levels tend to have an advantage on the tests because they are regularly exposed to the kinds of vocabulary, exercises, and challenges that the tests measure. The tests rarely reflect the "street sense" needed for survival by persons who live in poor, crime-ridden areas—a kind of know-how that certainly requires intellectual skills. Similarly, members of cultural minorities and persons for whom English is a second language often appear to be at a disadvantage in taking these tests. People apparently score higher when they are tested in their native language, an opportunity rarely afforded in the United States (Edgerton, 1979).

If IQ tests do not always measure intelligence accurately and objectively, then the diagnosis of mental retardation may reflect biases too (Wilson, 1992; Heflinger, Cook, & Thackrey, 1987). Some persons may receive the diagnosis partly because of test deficiencies, cultural differences, discomfort in the testing situation, or the bias of a tester.

Adaptive Functioning Diagnosticians cannot rely solely on a cutoff IQ score of 70 to determine whether a person suffers from mental retardation, because some people with a low IQ are quite capable of managing their lives and functioning independently.

> Brian comes from a lower-income family. He always has functioned adequately at home and in his community. He dresses and feeds himself and even takes care of himself each day until his mother returns home from work. He also plays well with his friends. At school, however, Brian refuses to participate or do his homework. He seems ineffective, at times lost, in the classroom. Referred to a school psychologist by his teacher, he received an IQ score of 60.

> Jeffrey comes from an upper-middle-class home. He was always slow to develop, and sat up, stood, and talked late. During his infancy and toddler years, he was put in a special stimulation program and given special help and attention at home. Still Jeffrey has trouble dressing himself today and cannot be left alone in the backyard lest he hurt himself or wander off into the street. Schoolwork is very difficult for him. The teacher must work slowly and provide individual instruction for him. Tested at age 6, Jeffrey received an IQ score of 60.

Brian seems well *adapted* to his environment outside of school. He fits the IQ criterion for mental retardation, but perhaps not the adaptive criterion. Jeffrey's limitations are more pervasive. His low IQ score is complemented by poor adaptive behaviors at home and elsewhere. A diagnosis of mental retardation may be more appropriate for Jeffrey than for Brian.

Various scales, such as the *Vineland* and *AAMR adaptive behavior scales,* have been developed to assess adaptive behavior (Leland, 1991; Britton & Eaves, 1986). Here again, however, some persons function better in life than the scales predict, while others fall short. Thus clinicians must observe for themselves the adaptive functioning of every individual, paying attention both to the person's background and to community standards. Unfortunately, such judgments are often subjective, and clinicians are not always familiar with the standards of a particular culture or community.

Characteristics of Individuals with Mental Retardation The most consistent sign of mental retardation is that the person learns very slowly (Kail, 1992; Hale & Borkowski, 1991). Other areas of difficulty are attention, short-term memory, and language (Chamberlain, 1985; Yabe et al., 1985). Limitations in these areas are particularly characteristic of institutionalized persons with mental retardation. It may be that the unstimulating environment and infrequent staff-client interactions in most institutions contribute to the cognitive problems.

Following the tradition of educators and clinicians, DSM-IV distinguishes four levels of mental retardation: *mild* (IQ 50–70), *moderate* (IQ 35–49), *severe* (IQ 20–34), and *profound* (IQ below 20). For its part, the AAMR (1992) prefers to distinguish the different kinds of mental retardation on the basis of the level of support the person needs—"intermittent," "limited," "extensive," or "pervasive"—rather than use the DSM's IQ-based distinctions.

Mild Retardation

Approximately 85 percent of all persons with mental retardation fall into the category of ***mild retardation*** (IQ 50–70) (APA, 1994). They are sometimes called "educably retarded" because they can benefit from an academic education and can support themselves as adults (APA, 1994). Still, they typically need assistance when they are under unusual social or economic stress. Their jobs tend to be unskilled or semiskilled.

Mild mental retardation is not usually detected until a child enters school and is assessed by school evaluators. Interestingly, the intellectual performance of individuals in this category often seems to improve with age; some even seem to leave the label behind them when they leave school and go on to function adequately in the community.

Research has linked mild mental retardation primarily to *sociocultural* and *psychological causes,* particularly impoverished and unstimulating environments, inadequate parent-child interactions, and insufficient early learning experiences. These relationships have been observed in studies comparing deprived and enriched environments (see Figure 19-5). In fact, in some community programs workers have gone into the homes of young children with low IQ scores to help enrich the home environment, and their interventions have often improved the children's functioning (Neisser et al., 1996; Marfo & Kysela, 1985). When continued, programs of this kind also help improve the children's later performance in school (Neisser et al., 1996; Ramey & Ramey, 1992).

Although such factors seem to play the primary causal role in mild mental retardation, at least some *biological factors* also seem to be operating. Studies suggest, for example, that a mother's moderate drinking, drug use, or malnutrition during pregnancy may impair her child's intellectual potential (Neisser et al., 1996; Stein et al., 1972; Harrell et al., 1955). Similarly, malnourishment during childhood hinders intellectual development (Brown & Pollitt, 1996; Davison & Dobbing, 1966), although this effect is at least partly reversible with early intervention (Neisser et al., 1996; Winick, Meyer, & Harris, 1975).

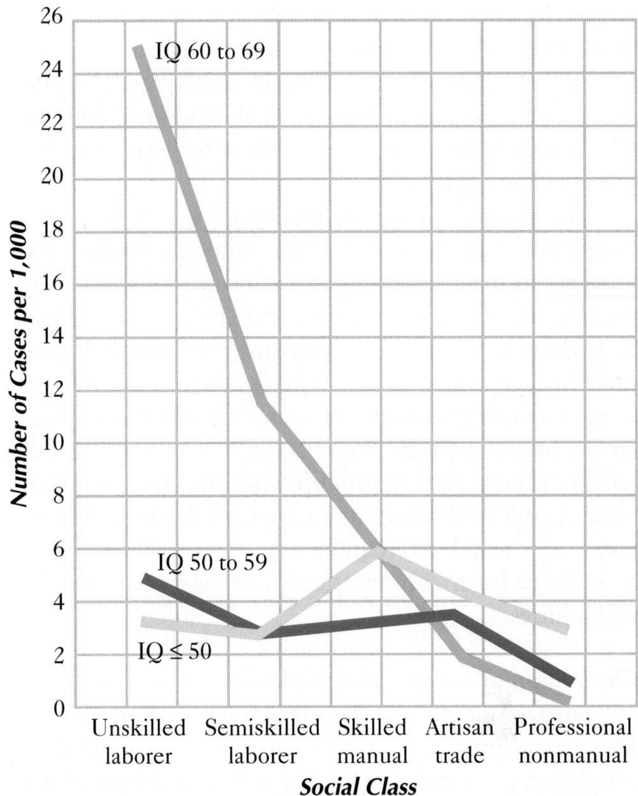

Figure 19-5 *The prevalence of mild mental retardation is much higher in the lower socioeconomic classes than in the upper classes. The forms of mental retardation that result in greater impairment, in contrast, are evenly distributed. (Adapted from Popper, 1988; Birch et al., 1970.)*

Moderate, Severe, and Profound Retardation

Approximately 10 percent of persons with mental retardation function at a level of ***moderate retardation*** (IQ 35–49). They can learn to care for themselves and can profit from vocational training, and many can work in unskilled or semiskilled jobs, usually under supervision. Most persons with moderate retardation adapt well to supervised life in the community (APA, 1994).

Approximately 4 percent of people with mental retardation display ***severe retardation*** (IQ 20–34). They usually require careful supervision, profit somewhat from vocational training, and can perform only basic vocational tasks in structured and sheltered settings. Their understanding of communication is usually better than their speech. Most adapt well to life in the community, in group homes or community nursing homes, or with their families (APA, 1994).

Around 1 percent of all people with mental retardation fall into the category of ***profound retardation*** (IQ below 20). With training they may acquire and improve basic skills such as walking, some talking, and feeding themselves. They require a highly structured environment with close supervision and help and an individual relationship with a caregiver in order to develop to the fullest (APA, 1994).

The primary causes of moderate, severe, and profound retardation are *biological,* although people who function at these levels are also enormously affected by their family and social environment (Bruce et al., 1996). Sometimes genetic factors contribute to these biological problems. In fact, researchers have identified 1,000 genetic causes of mental retardation, although few of these factors have undergone thorough study (Azar, 1995). Often the genetic factors produce chromosomal or metabolic disorders. Other common biological causes of these levels of mental retardation are unfavorable prenatal conditions, birth complications, and postnatal diseases and injuries.

Chromosomal Causes The most common of the chromosomal disorders leading to mental retardation is ***Down syndrome,*** named after Langdon Down, the British physician who first identified it (Evans & Hamerton, 1985). Fewer than 1 of every 1,000 live births results in Down syndrome, but this incidence increases considerably when the mother's age is over 35. Many older expectant mothers are now encouraged to undergo ***amniocentesis,*** testing of the amniotic fluid that surrounds the fetus, during the fourth month of pregnancy to detect Down syndrome and other chromosomal abnormalities.

Until the 1970s, clinicians were pessimistic about the potential of children with Down syndrome. Today these children are viewed as individuals who can learn and accomplish many things in their lives.

Individuals with Down syndrome have a distinctive appearance, with a small head, flat face, slanted eyes, high cheekbones, and, in some cases, a protruding tongue. They may also articulate poorly and be difficult to understand (Mahoney et al., 1981). They are often particularly affectionate with family members, but in general display the same range of personality characteristics as other individuals (Carr, 1994).

Several types of chromosomal aberrations may cause Down syndrome. The most common type (94 percent of the cases) is ***trisomy 21,*** in which the individual has three free-floating twenty-first chromosomes instead of two (Pueschel & Thuline, 1991). In a second type, ***translocation,*** the person has two normal twenty-first chromosomes and a third twenty-first chromosome fused with another chromosome (the fifteenth or thirteenth). And in a third extremely rare type, ***mosaicism,*** cells with two and cells with three twenty-first chromosomes are found in the same person. Most people with Down syndrome range in IQ from 35 to 55. The aging process appears to occur more quickly in people with Down syndrome, and many even show signs of dementia as they approach 40 or so (Zigman et al., 1995; Carr, 1994; Burt et al., 1992) (see Figure 19-6). Studies suggest that Down syndrome and early dementia may occur together because the genes that produce each of them are located close to each other on chromosome 21 (Tanzi et al., 1989).

Fragile X syndrome is the second most common chromosomal cause of mental retardation (Zigler & Hodapp, 1991). Children born with a fragile X chromosome (one with a genetic abnormality) generally have moderate to severe degrees of intellectual dysfunctioning, language impairment, and, in some cases, behavioral problems (McEvoy, 1992). The condition is more common in males. Having only one X chromosome, males are more likely to be affected by genetic abnormalities on the X chromosome.

Metabolic Causes Metabolic disorders that affect intelligence and development are typically caused by the pairing of two defective *recessive genes,* one from each parent. Although one such gene would have no influence if it were paired with a normal dominant gene, its pairing with another defective gene leads to disturbed chemical production in the child and thus to disturbed metabolic processes.

The most common retardation-causing metabolic disorder is ***phenylketonuria (PKU),*** which strikes 1 of every 17,000 children. Babies with PKU appear normal at birth but are unable to metabolize the amino acid *phenylalanine* into *tyrosine.* The phenylalanine accumulates and is converted into substances that poison the system, causing severe retardation and several other symptoms. In-

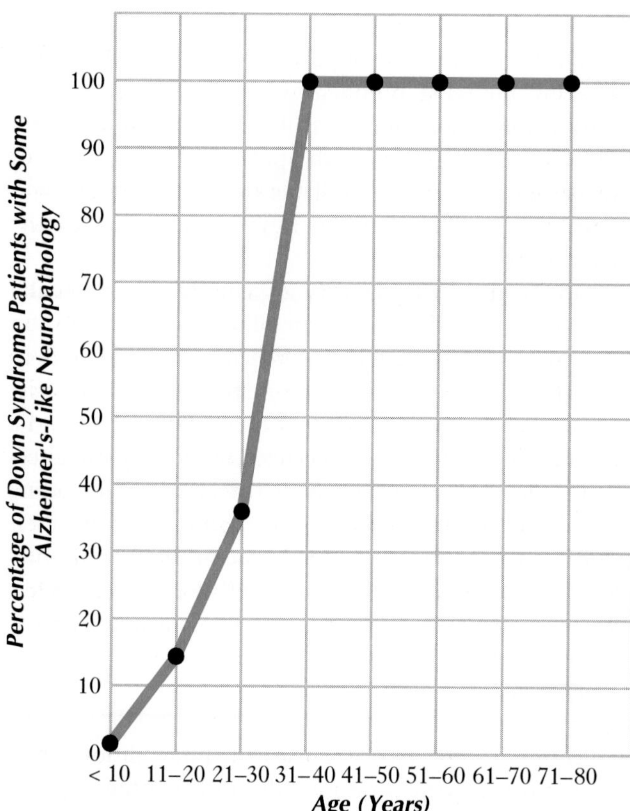

Figure 19-6 *By the age of 35 to 50, many people with Down syndrome show some of the neuropathological changes characteristic of Alzheimer's disease. Both Down syndrome and Alzheimer's disease are linked to abnormalities on chromosome 21. (Adapted from Zigman et al., 1995; Popper, 1988; Wisniewski et al., 1985.)*

fants can now be screened for PKU, and if started on a special low-phenylalanine diet before 3 months of age, they may develop normal intelligence.

In ***Tay-Sachs disease,*** another metabolic disorder resulting from a pairing of recessive genes, an enzyme missing from the infant's nerve cells leads to an excessive accumulation of fats. The result is progressive mental deterioration and loss of visual and motor functioning over the course of two to four years, followed by death. One of every 30 persons of Eastern European Jewish ancestry carries the recessive gene responsible for this disorder, so that one of every 900 Jewish couples is at risk for having a child with Tay-Sachs disease.

Prenatal Causes As a fetus develops, significant physical problems in the pregnant mother can endanger the child's prospects for a normal life (Neisser et al., 1996; Menke et al., 1991). When a pregnant woman has too little iodine in her diet, for example, her child may develop ***cretinism,*** characterized by a defective thyroid gland, slow development, mental retardation, and a dwarflike appearance. The disorder is rare today because the salt in most diets now contains iodine. Also, any infant born with this disorder may quickly be given thyroid extract to bring about a relatively normal development.

Other prenatal problems may also cause mental retardation. As we discussed in Chapter 13, children whose mothers abuse alcohol during pregnancy may be born with ***fetal alcohol syndrome,*** a cluster of very serious problems that includes intellectual deficiencies (Phelps & Grabowski, 1993). In addition, certain maternal infections during pregnancy—***rubella (German measles)*** and ***syphilis,*** for example—may cause childhood abnormalities that include mental retardation.

Birth-related Causes Birth complications can also lead to mental retardation. A prolonged period without oxygen ***(anoxia)*** during or after delivery can cause brain damage and retardation in a baby (Erickson, 1992). Similarly, although premature birth does not necessarily pose problems for children, researchers have found that a birth weight of less than 3.5 pounds may cause some degree of mental retardation (Neisser et al., 1996; Largo et al., 1989).

Childhood Causes After birth, particularly up to age 6, certain injuries and accidents can affect intellectual functioning and in some cases lead to mental retardation. Poisonings, serious head injuries caused by accident or abuse, excessive exposure to X rays, and excessive use of certain drugs pose special dangers. For example, a high degree of ***lead poisoning,*** associated with eating lead-based paints and with inhaling high levels of automobile fumes, can interfere with cellular metabolism and cause retardation in children (Berney, 1993). Mercury, radiation, nitrite, and pesticide poisoning may do the same. In addition, certain infections that fail to receive effective early treatment, such as ***meningitis*** and ***encephalitis,*** can lead to mental retardation (Scola, 1991).

Hereditary, prenatal, birth, and childhood factors may also *combine* to cause certain forms of moderate, severe, or profound mental retardation. For example, a combination of factors contribute to ***microcephaly,*** characterized by a small, unusually shaped head, and ***hydrocephalus,*** marked by an increase in cerebrospinal fluid and resultant head enlargement.

Interventions for People with Mental Retardation

The quality of life achieved by persons with mental retardation is influenced largely by where they live, whom they live with, how they are educated, and the growth opportunities offered at home and in the community. Thus current programs designed to help these individuals place particular emphasis on sociocultural issues—making sure that the individuals reside in desirable places, have social and economic opportunities, and receive a proper education. Once these issues are addressed, psychological or biological treatments are also of help in some cases.

Residential Alternatives Until recent decades, parents of children with mental retardation would send them to live in public institutions—***state schools***—as soon as possible. Unfortunately, in practice these overcrowded institutions provided custodial care only, and these people were neglected, often abused, and isolated from society. Ed Murphy, the misdiagnosed man whom we met earlier, recalls his first day at a state school:

> They had me scheduled to go to P-8—a back ward—when just one man looked at me. I was a wreck. I had a beard and baggy State clothes on. I had just arrived at the place. I was trying to understand what was happening. I was confused. What I looked like was P-8 material. There was this supervisor, a woman. She came on the ward and looked right at me and said: "I have him scheduled for P-8." An older attendant was there. He looked over at me and said, "He's too bright for that ward. I think we'll keep him." . . .
>
> Of course I didn't know what P-8 was then, but I found out. I visited up there a few times on work detail. That man saved my life. Here was a woman that I had never known who they said was the building supervisor looking over me. At that point I'm pretty positive that if I went there I would have fitted in and I would still be there.
>
> *(Bogdan & Taylor, 1976, p. 49)*

During the 1960s and 1970s, the public became increasingly aware of these institutional conditions, and as part of the broader *deinstitutionalization* movement (see pp. 523–530), large numbers of people with mental retardation were released from the state schools (Beyer, 1991). Many had to make the transition to community life without special guidance, even without adequate residential placement. Like deinstitutionalized persons suffering from schizophrenia, they were virtually dumped into the community. Not surprisingly, many failed to adjust and had to be institutionalized once again.

Fortunately, reforms in recent decades have led to the establishment of small institutions that encourage self-sufficiency, devote more staff time to patient care, and offer educational and medical services. Many of these institutions and community residences follow the principles of ***normalization*** first started in Denmark and Sweden. They offer living conditions that closely resemble those of mainstream society, including flexible routines, common developmental experiences, the right to develop a sexual identity, and normal economic freedoms (Baldwin, 1985). Such programs allow those with mental retardation the opportunity to make their own decisions. Growing numbers of group homes, halfway houses, small local branches of larger institutions, and independent residences, each applying the principles of normalization, are now available to assist residents with retardation and teach them how to get along in the community.

Today the vast majority of children with mental retardation live at home rather than in an institution (Erickson, 1992). As they approach adulthood and as their parents age, the family home becomes a less desirable setting for some of them (Krauss et al., 1992) and a community residence may become an appropriate alternative. Most of those with mental retardation, including virtually all with mild mental retardation, now live their adult lives either in the family home or in a community residence (Jacobson & Schwartz, 1991; Repp et al., 1986). Wherever they may live, the family remains important as a source of social support, guidance, and advocacy (Blacher & Baker, 1994, 1992).

Educational Programs Because early intervention seems to offer such great promise, educational programs for children with mental retardation may begin during the child's earliest years. Of course, the appropriate education depends on the severity of retardation (Cipani, 1991).

Educators hotly debate whether special classes or mainstreaming is best once the children enter school (Gottlieb et al., 1991). In ***special education,*** children with mental retardation are grouped together and given a separate, specially designed curriculum. ***Mainstreaming,*** in contrast, puts them in regular classes with nonretarded students. Neither approach seems consistently superior (Gottlieb, 1981). It may well be that mainstreaming is better for some areas of learning and for some children, special classes for others.

Teachers often use operant conditioning principles to teach individuals with mental retardation better self-help skills, proper verbal responding, social responses, and academic skills (Erickson, 1992; Matson & Gorman-Smith, 1986). They break learning tasks down into small steps, giving positive reinforcement as each small step is accomplished. In addition, many institutions, schools, and private homes have instituted *token economy programs*—the operant conditioning programs that have also been used to treat institutionalized patients suffering from schizophrenia.

Therapy Like all other people, those with mental retardation may experience emotional and behavioral problems (Pearson et al., 1996). Perhaps 10 percent of them have an additional psychological disorder (Grizenko et al., 1991). Moreover, some experience low self-esteem, interpersonal difficulties, and difficulty in adjusting to community life (Lubetsky, 1986; Reiss, 1985).

These problems have been addressed with some degree of effectiveness by both individual and group therapies (Hurley & Hurley, 1986; Ginsberg, 1984). In addition, large numbers of persons with retardation are given psychotropic medications (Aman & Singh, 1991). Many clinicians suggest, however, that too often the medications are used simply to keep these individuals docile (Erickson, 1992).

Opportunities for Personal, Social, and Occupational Growth Feelings of self-efficacy and competence are important aspects of personal growth, and people with mental retardation can often achieve them if their communities allow them to grow and to make their own choices in life without undue pressure (Wehmeyer, 1992). Denmark and Sweden, the originators of the normalization movement, have led the way in this area as well, developing youth clubs that encourage persons with mental retardation to take risks and function independently (Perske, 1972).

Socializing, sex, and marriage are difficult issues for persons with mental retardation and their families. The National Association for Retarded Citizens provides guidance in these matters, and some clinicians have developed *dating skills programs* (Valenti-Hein et al., 1994). With proper training and experience, the individuals can usually learn to use contraceptives, carry out responsible family planning, and in many cases rear children effectively (Bakken et al., 1993; Dowdney & Skuse, 1993).

Some states restrict marriage for persons with mental retardation (Levesque, 1996). These laws are rarely enforced, however, and in fact between a quarter and half of all persons with mild mental retardation eventually marry (Grinspoon et al., 1986). Contrary to popular stereotypes, the marriages can be very successful. Moreover, while some individuals may be incapable of raising children, many are quite able to do so, either on their own or with special help and community services (Levesque, 1996; Bakken et al., 1993; Keltner, 1992).

The interpersonal and sexual needs of persons with mental retardation are normal, and many, like this engaged couple, demonstrate considerable ability to express intimacy. Yet most of them receive poor preparation and excessive restriction in these areas.

Finally, adults with all levels of mental retardation need the personal and financial rewards that come with holding a job (AAMR, 1992). Many work in ***sheltered workshops,*** where the pace and type of work are tailored to their skills and where supervision is available. After training in these workshops, many of those with mild or moderate retardation move out into the regular workforce.

Certainly training programs for persons with mental retardation have improved greatly over the past thirty years. Nonetheless, the majority of these individuals fail to receive a full range of educational and vocational training services from which they could profit. Clearly, additional innovative and comprehensive programs are needed. Only then will all persons with mental retardation be able truly to cross the barriers created by their disorder and their label.

Disorders of Later Life

Like childhood, later life brings special pressures, unique traumatic experiences, and biological changes. A number of disorders consequently develop as old age approaches or advances.

"Old age" is arbitrarily defined in our society as referring to the years past age 65. More than 33 million people in the United States are over 65; they account for nearly 13 percent of the total population (Hobbs, 1997) (see Figure 19-7). This figure reflects an eleven-fold increase in the older population since 1900. Older women outnumber older men by 3 to 2.

As people age, they experience many physical, psychological, and sociocultural changes. They become more prone to illness and injury, and they are likely to experience the stress of loss—the loss of spouses, friends, and adult children, and the loss of former activities and roles. Many also lose a sense of purpose in life after they retire. If they live long enough, older persons lose bodily integrity through chronic illness. Even favored pets and possessions may be lost through relocation and the like (Gallagher-Thompson & Thompson, 1995).

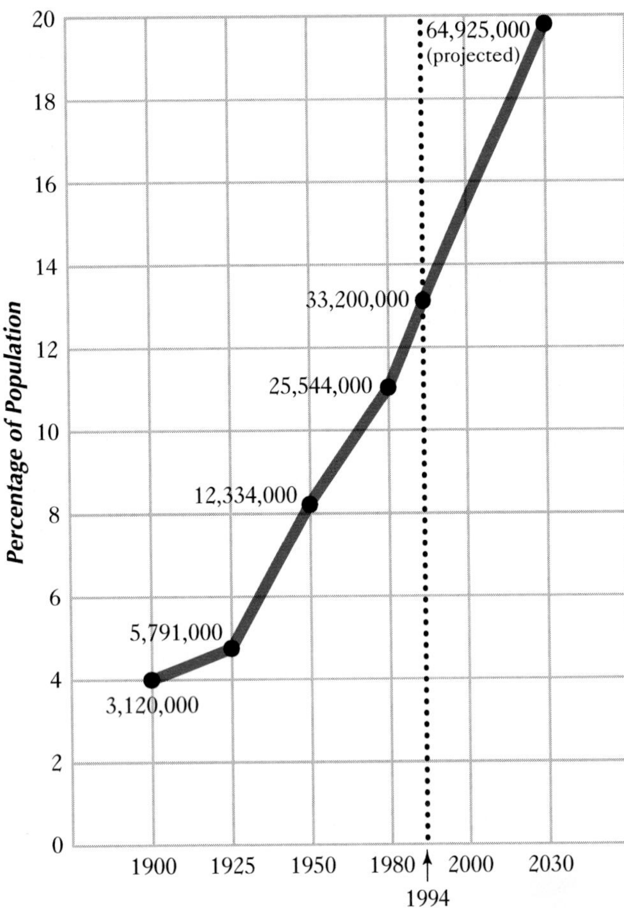

Figure 19-7 *The population of people aged 65 and older in the United States increased eleven-fold during the twentieth century, while the rest of the population grew only three-fold. The percentage of elderly people in the population increased from 4 percent in 1900 to 12.5 percent in 1994 and is expected to be 20 percent in 2030 (Hobbs, 1997; AARP, 1990).*

The stresses of elderly people need not necessarily result in psychological dysfunction (Schultz & Heckhausen, 1996; Lewinsohn et al., 1990). Indeed, some older persons use such situations to learn more about themselves and to grow. For others, however, the stresses of old age do lead to psychological problems (Banerjee & Macdonald, 1996). Studies indicate that as many as 50 percent of elderly people would benefit from mental health services (MacDonald & Schnur, 1987), yet fewer than 20 percent actually receive such help. ***Geropsychology,*** the field concerned with the mental health of elderly people, has developed almost entirely within the last twenty-five years, and at present fewer than 4 percent of all clinical practitioners work primarily with elderly patients (Sleek, 1996; Gallagher-Thompson & Thompson, 1995).

The psychological problems of elderly persons may be divided into two groups. One group consists of disorders that are found in persons of all ages but that often are closely connected to the process of aging when they occur in elderly persons. These include mood, anxiety, and substance-related disorders. The other group consists of disorders that are particularly common among elderly persons, such as delirium and dementia.

Mood, Anxiety, and Substance-Related Disorders

Depression is the most common mental health problem of older adults, especially those who have recently experienced a trauma, such as the loss of a spouse or a serious physical illness, and those with dementia (Krishnan et al., 1996; Philpott, 1990). Overall, as many as 20 percent of the elderly experience it (Koenig & Blazer, 1992; Blazer, 1990). The rate is highest in older women (Fernandez et al., 1995).

Several studies suggest that depression among older persons heightens their chances of developing significant medical problems in addition to causing them enormous psychological distress. For example, older depressed persons with high blood pressure are almost 3 times as likely to suffer a stroke as older nondepressed persons with the same problem (Simonsick et al., 1995). Similarly, elderly persons who are depressed recover more poorly from heart attacks, hip fractures, pneumonia, and other infections and illnesses (Goleman, 1995).

Like younger persons, older individuals who are depressed may be helped by cognitive therapy, antidepressant medications, or a combination of the two (Alexopoulos et al., 1996; Sleek, 1996; Gantz et al., 1991). Between half and 65 percent of older patients with depression improve with such treatments. At the same time, it is sometimes difficult to use antidepressant drugs effectively and safely with older persons because the body breaks them down differently in later life (Blazer, 1990). Finally, group therapy can be a useful format for older patients who are depressed (Finkel, 1991; Yost et al., 1986).

Anxiety is also common among elderly persons. Surveys indicate that generalized anxiety disorder is experienced by about 7 percent of them, agoraphobia by up to 5 percent, specific phobias by as many as 12 percent, obsessive-compulsive disorder by around 3 percent, and panic disorder by 1 percent or less (Schneider, 1996; Flint, 1994). Anxiety in the elderly may be underreported, however (Schneider, 1996; Sleek, 1996). The individual or the clinician may attribute the physical symptoms of anxiety, such as heart palpitations and sweating, to a medical condition.

Older adults with anxiety disorders are often treated with some form of psychotherapy (McCarthy et al., 1991). Many also receive antianxiety medications, particularly benzodiazepines, although those with obsessive-

Staying active, pursuing goals, and seeking stimulation are keys to coping with and enjoying life, particularly old age. In 1997, former president George Bush fulfilled his dream of sky diving from a plane 12,500 feet above the desert. He had wanted to do this since World War II when he had been forced to bail out of his torpedo bomber. After the sky dive, an invigorated Bush said that it was "something I'll carry with me for the rest of my life."

compulsive disorder have, like their younger counterparts, been increasingly treated with fluoxetine (Prozac) and other serotonin-enhancing antidepressant drugs (Jenike, 1991). Again, however, all these drugs must be used cautiously with persons over 60 years of age, because their bodies respond to them quite differently than do the bodies of younger adults (Pomara et al., 1991).

Alcohol abuse and other forms of ***substance abuse*** are another problem for many older persons, although the prevalence of these disorders actually declines among people over 60 (Graham et al., 1996). Changes in health and reduced finances may help account for this decline (Maddox, 1988). Nonetheless, 3 to 5 percent of older persons, particularly men, experience alcohol-related disorders in any given year (Helzer et al., 1991; Maddox, 1988). Researchers often distinguish older problem drinkers who have experienced significant alcohol-related problems for many years, perhaps since their 20s or 30s, from those who do not start the pattern until their 50s or 60s. The latter individuals typically begin their abusive drinking as a reaction to the negative events and pressures of growing older, such as the death of a spouse or retirement.

Alcohol abuse and dependence in elderly people are treated much as among younger adults (see pp. 431–438), with such approaches as detoxification, Antabuse, Alcoholics Anonymous (AA), and cognitive-behavioral therapy (Schiff, 1988). While AA meetings are typically attended by people of varying ages, specialized groups called Golden Years have been organized to attract older adults and make their experience more comfortable (Gallagher-Thompson & Thompson, 1995).

One leading kind of substance-related problem in the elderly is the misuse of prescription drugs (Graham et al., 1996; Gottheil, 1987). Most often it is unintentional. Older persons receive twice as many prescriptions as younger persons, and a quarter take three or more drugs daily (Lipton, 1988). Clearly, the risk of confusing or missing medications under such circumstances is high (Salzman et al., 1995). Thus clinicians, physicians, and pharmacists are increasingly learning to simplify medications and educate older patients about their medications, clarifying directions and teaching them to monitor undesired effects (Gallagher-Thompson & Thompson, 1995).

Delirium and Dementia

Delirium is a clouding of consciousness. As the person's awareness of the environment becomes less clear, he or she has great difficulty concentrating, focusing attention, and maintaining a straightforward stream of thought (APA, 1994). People may think that it is morning during the middle of the night or believe they are home when actually in a hospital room. A state of delirium typically develops over a short period of time, usually hours or days. It may result in misinterpretations, illusions, and, on occasion, hallucinations.

This state of massive confusion may occur in any age group, including children, but it is most common in elderly persons. It is seen in around 10 percent of elderly persons when they enter a hospital to be treated for a general medical condition (APA, 1994). Another 10 to

15 percent develop delirium during their stay in the hospital.

Fever, infections, nutritional imbalances, head injuries, certain neurological disorders, and stress (including that caused by surgery) may all cause delirium. So may intoxication, particularly by illicit or prescription drugs. Partly because older persons experience so many of these problems, they are more likely than younger persons to experience delirium.

If a diagnostician correctly identifies the syndrome, it can often be readily reversed. Practitioners may then treat the underlying infection, for example, or change the patient's drug prescription. Unfortunately, an accurate diagnosis is often elusive. In one study conducted on a medical ward, admitting doctors were found to detect only one of fifteen consecutive cases of delirium (Cameron et al., 1987). Incorrect diagnoses of this kind may contribute to a relatively high mortality rate for older people with delirium (Rabins & Folstein, 1982).

Dementia is a syndrome marked by severe memory impairment and significant deficiencies in at least one other cognitive function, such as abstract thinking, judgment, or language. All people experience some cognitive decline as they age, but only a minority develop dementia (see Figure 19-8). People with this syndrome may also undergo extreme personality and behavioral changes, and they may deteriorate progressively. Some also react to their disorder with anxiety, agitation, or depression (Krishnan et al., 1996; Mintzer & Brawman-Mintzer, 1996). As we observed in Chapter 17, the occurrence of dementia is closely related to age. Its prevalence is around 1 to 2 percent among people 65 years of age and increases to more than 15 percent among those over the age of 80 (DeLeon et al., 1996; Gallagher-Thompson & Thompson, 1995). Dementia is sometimes confused with delirium, and in fact the two may occur together.

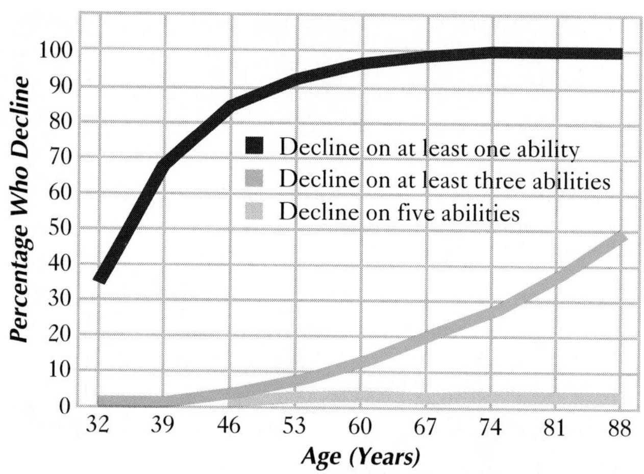

Figure 19-8 *People experience some cognitive decline as a natural part of aging. In one longitudinal study, researchers measured subjects' performance on five primary mental abilities—verbal ability, numeric ability, spatial orientation, reasoning, and verbal memory. By the age of 60 virtually all subjects declined on at least one of these abilities. At the same time, this decline did not reflect dementia in most cases, and in fact, very few subjects declined on all of the mental abilities even by the age of 90. (Adapted from Schaie, 1996, 1989.)*

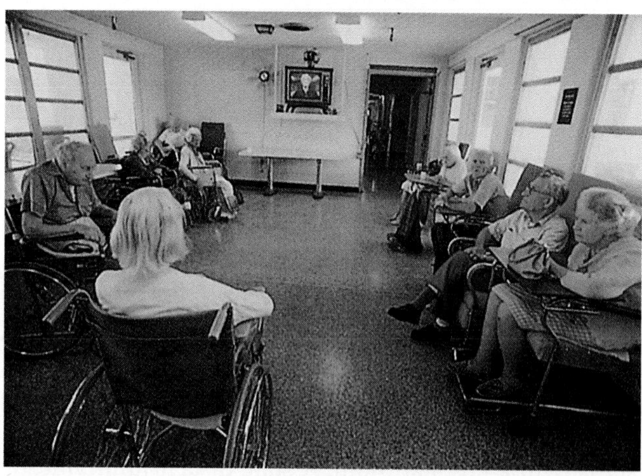

Although only a minority of elderly people actually live in nursing homes, most aging persons fear that they will eventually be forced by poor health to reside in such a setting, separated from their families, friends, and homes. An additional concern is that many of today's nursing homes are unstimulating settings in which residents may be neglected, mistreated, and overmedicated.

Like delirium, dementia sometimes has an underlying cause that is reversible. Some elderly persons, for example, suffer from metabolic or nutritional disorders that can be corrected. Similarly, improving vision and hearing can substantially improve the cognitive performance of some individuals (Gallagher-Thompson & Thompson, 1995). Unfortunately, however, as we saw in Chapter 17, most cases of dementia are caused by neurological problems, such as *Alzheimer's disease* and *stroke*, that are difficult or impossible to address.

Key Factors in the Mental Health of the Elderly

As the field of gerontology has grown, so have concerns about discrimination in mental health care for the elderly, the inadequacies of long-term care, and the necessity of health maintenance in an aging world (Gallagher-Thompson & Thompson, 1995).

As we saw in Chapter 4, discrimination based on ***ethnicity*** has always been a problem in the United States, and many people suffer disadvantages as a result, particularly those who are old (Cavanaugh, 1990). To be simultaneously old and a member of a minority group is con-

sidered a kind of "double jeopardy" by many observers. For older women in minority groups, the difficulties are sometimes termed "triple jeopardy," as many more older women than older men live alone, are widowed, and have incomes below the poverty level (Gallagher-Thompson & Thompson, 1995). Gerontologists warn that clinicians must be aware of their older patients' ethnicity as they try to diagnose and treat their mental health problems (Bazargan, 1996) (see Figure 19-9).

Elderly persons from ethnic minority groups often face language barriers that hinder their medical and mental health care. They may also hold cultural beliefs that prevent them from seeking services. Because many members of minority groups do not trust the establishment, for example, they may rely instead on traditional remedies available in their immediate social network.

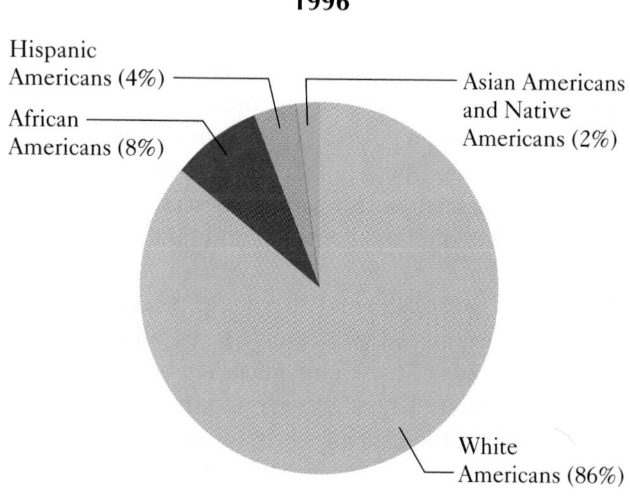

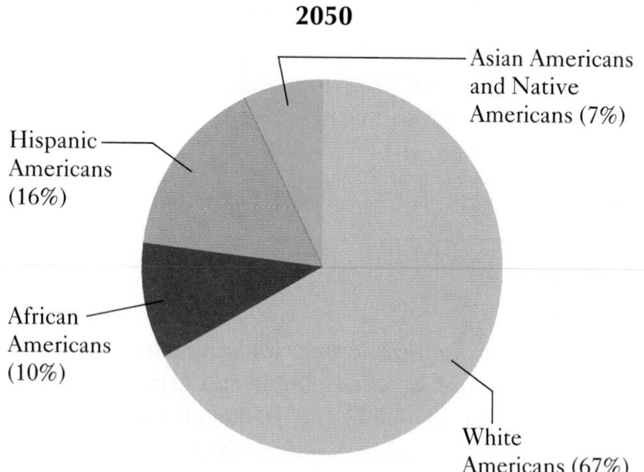

Figure 19-9 *Ethnicity and old age. The elderly population is becoming racially and ethnically more diverse. In the United States today, 86 percent of all persons over the age of 65 are white Americans. By 2050, only 67 percent of the elderly will be from this group. (Adapted from Hobbs, 1997; NIA, 1996.)*

They also may not know about medical and mental health services that are sensitive to their culture and their particular needs (Ralston, 1991; Jackson, 1988).

Many older persons require ***long-term care.*** This term may refer to the services offered in a partially supervised apartment or in a senior housing complex for mildly impaired elderly persons. Or it can mean a nursing home where skilled medical and nursing care are available around the clock. The quality of care provided in such residences varies widely.

At any given time in the United States, about 1.6 million people over the age of 65, that is, only about 5 percent of the elderly population actually reside in nursing homes, but most older adults live with the fear of being "put away" (Hobbs, 1997; NIA, 1996; Butler & Lewis, 1986). They fear having to move, losing independence, and living in an impersonal environment where the emphasis is on disabilities. Many elderly persons know someone who died shortly after being admitted to a long-term care facility, and this increases their fears and pessimism about life in such settings (Gallagher-Thompson & Thompson, 1995).

Many also worry about the cost of moving to a long-term care facility. Families today are trying to keep elderly relatives at home longer and are using a variety of services to help them do so. Most older persons therefore enter nursing homes only in the last stages of a disease and in need of almost total care. Since round-the-clock nursing care is always going to be expensive, nursing home costs will continue to rise. The health insurance plans that are currently available do not even begin to cover the costs of permanent placement (Gallagher-Thompson & Thompson, 1995).

Such issues can significantly harm the mental health of older adults, perhaps leading to depression and anxiety and arousing family conflicts (Banerjee & Macdonald, 1996). Research that focuses on improving the quality of life for both patients and staff in long-term care facilities is sorely needed (Gallagher-Thompson & Thompson, 1995). So is continued training of the staff and management of facilities for the elderly so that advances in knowledge can be quickly shared and implemented (Gallagher-Thompson & Thompson, 1995).

Finally, gerontologists suggest that the current generation of young adults should take a ***wellness*** or ***health-maintenance approach*** to their own aging process. In other words, they should do things that promote physical and mental health—not smoke, eat well-balanced and sensible meals, exercise regularly, and take advantage of psychoeducational, stress management, and other mental health programs. Although research findings are lacking at present, it is reasonable to assume that older adults will adapt more readily to changes and negative events if their physical and psychological health is reasonably good (Gallagher-Thompson & Thompson, 1995).

When long-term care institutions offer stimulating programs, such as this exercise class for people with Alzheimer's disease, allow patients to control their lives, and involve family members and friends, elderly persons are generally happier and show relatively better cognitive functioning.

Crossroads

Early in this century, mental health professionals largely ignored children and elderly persons. Today the problems of these groups have caught the attention of researchers and clinicians. Although all of the current models have been called into action to help explain and treat these problems, the sociocultural perspective—especially the family perspective—has begun to play a special role.

Because both children and the elderly have limited control over their lives and resources, they are particularly subject to the attitudes and reactions of family members. Correspondingly, those attitudes and reactions must be included in efforts to address the problems of the young and the old. Thus it is not surprising that treatments for conduct disorder, ADHD, mental retardation, and other problems of childhood typically fall flat unless clinicians educate and work with the family as well. Similarly, clinicians who treat elderly patients with dementia are most successful when they also consider and address the concerns and needs of the family caregivers.

At the same time, clinicians who work with children, adolescents, and elderly people are again reminded that a narrow focus on any one model can often be problematic. For years autism was explained exclusively by family factors, misleading theorists, researchers, and therapists alike, and compounding the pain of parents already devastated by their child's disorder. In the past, too, the sociocultural model often led professionals to ignore the depression and anxiety of elderly people. Clinicians incorrectly believed that these psychological problems were inevitable in view of the role changes and losses suffered by the elderly.

The increased clinical focus on the young and the elderly has been accompanied by increased advocacy on their behalf. More and more clinicians have enlisted the aid of government agencies to protect the rights and safety of these often powerless populations. They hope to invigorate commitment to fight child abuse and neglect, sexual abuse, malnourishment, and fetal alcohol syndrome, and to address the health and financial needs of the elderly.

As the mistreatment of young persons receives greater attention and as the elderly population grows larger, the needs of these individuals are becoming more and more visible. Thus the study and treatment of their psychological problems are likely to continue at an impressive pace.

As our tongue-in-cheek feature on the "disorder" called childhood implies, childhood, like old age, has been around for a long time. Now that clinicians and public officials have discovered people in these age groups, they are not likely to underestimate their special needs and importance again.

Chapter Review

1. ***Disorders of childhood and old age*** Some problems are particularly likely to emerge during childhood and old age. Such problems may be caused by the special pressures of that stage of life, traumatic or maladaptive experiences, or biological factors.

2. ***Disorders of childhood and adolescence*** Emotional and behavioral problems are common in childhood and adolescence, but a fifth of all children and adolescents in the United States experience a mental disorder.

A. *Anxiety disorders* among children include adult-like disorders such as social phobia and generalized anxiety disorder, as well as the unique childhood pattern of *separation anxiety disorder,* which is characterized by excessive anxiety, often panic, whenever a child is separated from a parent.

B. *Depression* is found among 2 percent of all children under 17 years of age, and among 7 percent of adolescents.

C. Children with *disruptive behavior disorders* exceed the normal breaking of rules and act very aggressively.

(1) Children who display an *oppositional defiant disorder* argue repeatedly with adults, lose their temper, and feel great anger and resentment.

(2) Those with a *conduct disorder,* a more severe pattern, repeatedly violate the basic rights of others. These children often are violent and cruel, and may lie, cheat, steal, and run away.

D. Children who display *attention-deficit hyperactivity disorder (ADHD)* attend poorly to tasks or behave overactively and impulsively, or both.

E. Children with an *elimination disorder—enuresis* or *encopresis*—repeatedly urinate or pass feces in inappropriate places. The behavioral bell-and-battery technique is an effective treatment for enuresis.

F. Highly inadequate functioning in learning, communication, and coordination leads to such diagnoses as *learning disorder, communication disorder,* and *developmental coordination disorder.* More than 20 percent of children may receive one or more of these diagnoses.

3. ***Long-term disorders that begin in childhood*** *Autism* and *mental retardation* are problems that emerge early and typically continue throughout a person's life.

4. ***Autism*** People with autism are unresponsive to others, show poor communication skills (including *echolalia* and *pronominal reversal*), and demonstrate a pattern of restricted and repetitive behaviors (such as *perseveration of sameness, strong attachments to objects, self-stimulatory behaviors,* and *self-injurious behaviors*).

A. The leading explanations of autism point to cognitive deficits, such as failure to develop a *theory of mind,* and biological abnormalities, such as abnormal development of the *cerebellum.*

B. Treatment for autism is designed to help the children adapt to their environment. Although no treatment totally reverses the autistic pattern, significant help has been found through the use of behavioral treatments, communication training, treatment and training for parents, and community integration.

5. ***Mental retardation*** Persons with mental retardation are significantly below average in intelligence (as measured by intelligence tests) and adaptive ability. Approximately one of every 100 persons receives a diagnosis of mental retardation.

A. *Mild retardation,* by far the most common level of mental retardation, has been linked primarily to environmental factors such as understimulation, inadequate parent-child interactions, and insufficient early learning experiences.

B. *Moderate, severe, and profound mental retardation* are caused primarily by biological factors, although individuals who function at these levels are also enormously affected by their environment. The leading biological causes are *chromosomal disorders* (such as *Down syndrome* and *fragile X syndrome*), *metabolic disorders* that typically are caused by the pairing of two defective recessive genes (for example, *phenylketonuria,* or *PKU,* and *Tay-Sachs disease*), disorders related to prenatal problems (*cretinism* and *fetal alcohol syndrome*), disorders related to *birth complications,* such as anoxia or extreme prematurity, and *childhood disease and injuries.*

C. Interventions In recent decades treatment for people with mental retardation has focused on *normalization programs* that offer conditions of everyday life in a community setting or institution. Halfway houses, group homes, and residences of various kinds provide education and training on how to get along in the community.

(1) One of the most intense debates in the field of education centers on whether individuals with mental retardation profit more from *special classes* or *mainstreaming.* Research has not consistently favored one approach over the other.

(2) In general, the use of *operant conditioning* principles has been successful in educating and training individuals with mental retardation.

(3) Persons with mental retardation who also experience emotional or behavioral problems sometimes receive insight, behavioral, or drug therapy.

(4) To enhance opportunities for growth by persons with mental retardation, increasing numbers of programs are offering training in such areas as socializing, sex, marriage, parenting, and vocational skills.

6. ***Disorders of later life*** As many as 50 percent of elderly people would benefit from mental health services. Their problems are often linked to the losses, other stresses, and changes that accompany advancing age.

A. *Depression* is the most common mental health problem of older adults. Cognitive therapy, antidepressant drugs, or both are often used to treat depression among elderly people. However, the drugs are less safe for older depressed patients than for younger ones because the biological mechanisms for the breakdown of the drugs change with age.

B. Many elderly people suffer from *generalized anxiety disorder, agoraphobia, specific phobias,* and *panic disorder.*

C. Between 3 and 5 percent of the older adult population exhibit *alcohol-related problems* in any given year. The *abuse of prescription drugs* is also a significant problem among elderly persons.

D. Older people are more likely than people of other age groups to experience *delirium,* a clouding of consciousness in which a person's awareness of the

environment becomes less clear and he or she has great difficulty concentrating, focusing attention, and maintaining a straightforward stream of thought. The syndrome may be caused by factors that are often quite reversible with proper identification and treatment.

E. *Dementia,* a syndrome characterized by severe memory impairment and other cognitive disturbances, becomes increasingly prevalent in older age groups.

Thought and Afterthought

The Oldest Old

Geropsychologists suggest that aging need not inevitably lead to psychological problems. Nor apparently does it always lead to physical problems. When researchers recently studied people over 95 years of age—often called the "oldest old"—they were surprised to find that the individuals are on average more healthy, cognitively clear, and agile than those in their 80s and early 90s (Perls, 1995). Many, in fact, are still employed, sexually active, and able to enjoy the outdoors and the arts.

John Parrish, a 104-year-old medicine man living in Monument Valley, Arizona.

Some scientists believe that individuals who live this long carry "longevity" genes that make them resistant to disabling or terminal infections (Perls, 1995). The individuals themselves often point to a good frame of mind or regular behaviors that they have maintained for many years—abstinence from smoking, eating healthful food, pursuing regular exercise.

Afterthoughts: People of this age often seem particularly well adjusted. Does their positive frame of mind lead to longevity, or does outstanding health produce greater happiness? . . . Why do many of the oldest old attribute their longevity to psychological factors, while scientists seem to prefer biological explanations?

Power Play Among Kids

Every few years children across the world embrace a new fantasy hero or heroine. Often their preoccupation with the character sparks concern and interest. The Mighty Morphin Power Rangers—both male and female—have been the center of controversy ever since the television show of the same name became popular several years back (Hellmich, 1995). Many clinical theorists and parents worry that the Power Rangers are far too violent, teach children that violence solves problems, and create confusion between fantasy and reality.

Afterthoughts: Could violent action heroes help produce oppositional defiant disorder and conduct disorder? . . . Some experts suggest that superhero play is actually a healthy aspect of development. How might this be so? . . . May concerns about action figures thus be overblown?

A Special Kind of Talent

Most people are familiar with the *savant syndrome*, thanks to Dustin Hoffman's portrayal of a young man with autism in the movie *Rain Man (right)*. The savant skills that Hoffman portrayed—counting 246 toothpicks in the instant after they fall to the floor, memorizing the phone book through the G's, and lightning-fast calculating abilities—were based on the astounding talents of certain real-life people who are otherwise impaired by autism or mental retardation.

A savant (French for "knowing") is a person with a major mental disorder or intellectual handicap who has some spectacular ability, some area of exceptional brilliance. Often these abilities are remarkable only in the context of the handicap, but sometimes they are just plain remarkable (Treffert, 1989).

A common savant skill is calendar calculating, the ability to calculate what day of the week a date will fall on, such as New Year's Day in 2050 (Spitz, 1994). A common musical skill such individuals may possess is the ability to play a piece of classical music flawlessly from memory after hearing it only once. Other individuals can paint exact replicas of scenes they saw years ago.

Some theorists believe that savant skills do indeed represent special forms of cognitive functioning. Others propose that the skills are merely a positive side to certain cognitive impairments. Special memorization skills, for example, may be facilitated by the narrow attention and preoccupation that often characterize autism.

Afterthoughts: Why are people so fascinated by the savant syndrome, and might their fascination predispose them to glamorize it? . . . What hidden reminders of human equality or messages of hope may be derived from observations of savant functioning?

Topic Overview

Clinical Influences on the Criminal Justice System
- Criminal Commitment and Insanity During Commission of a Crime
- Criminal Commitment and Incompetence to Stand Trial

Legal Influences on the Mental Health System
- Civil Commitment
- Protecting Patients' Rights

Other Clinical-Legal Interactions

Self-Regulation: Ethics and the Mental Health Field

Mental Health, Business, and Economics

The Person Within the Profession

Crossroads

Chapter 20

Law, Society, and the Mental Health Profession

Throughout this book we have seen the importance of clinical scientists and practitioners to our society: they gather and impart knowledge about psychological dysfunctioning, and they treat people who are experiencing psychological problems. They do not, however, do these things in a vacuum. Earlier chapters described, for example, how the government has regulated clinicians' use of electroconvulsive therapy. They also noted how clinicians have helped carry out the government's policy of deinstitutionalization and have called to society's attention the psychological ordeal of Vietnam veterans.

Violet Baxter's Spring Trees, *1991, reminds us of the broad social context surrounding the study and treatment of abnormal behavior. The work of clinical scientists and professionals is deeply intertwined with the needs and values of the public and with the legal, business, and economic sectors of society. Each component of society affects and is affected by the others.*

The relationship of clinicians with their science, their clients, and the public unfolds within a complex social system. That system, in fact, assigns clinicians their professional responsibilities and regulates them in the performance of their duties. Just as we must understand the social context of abnormal behavior in order to appreciate its nature and consequences, so must we understand the context in which this behavior is studied and treated.

Two institutions probably have the greatest impact on the mental health profession—the legislative and judicial professions. These institutions have long been charged with promoting and protecting both the public good and the rights of individuals. Sometimes the relationship between the legal field and the mental health field has been harmonious: the two fields have, for example, worked in concert to protect the rights and address the needs of both individuals with psychological problems and society. At other times one field has imposed its will on the other, and the relationship has been stormy.

This relationship has two distinct facets. First, mental health professionals often play a role in the criminal justice system. Clinicians have been called upon to help the courts evaluate the mental stability of people accused of crimes. Second, the legislative and judicial systems regulate some aspects of mental health care. The law may force some individuals to receive psychological treatment, even against their will. It also protects the rights of patients.

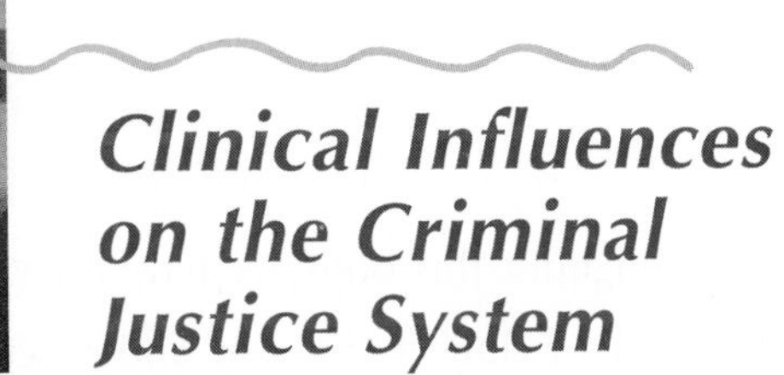

Clinical Influences on the Criminal Justice System

Our courts mete out what they consider just and appropriate punishment. To do that, they must be sure that defendants are *responsible* for their crimes and are *capable* of defending themselves in court. Otherwise it would be inappropriate to find them guilty or punish them in the usual manner. The courts have decided that people who suffer from *mental instability* are not responsible for their actions and not able to defend themselves in court, and should not be punished in the usual way. Although the courts make the final judgment of mental instability, their decisions are guided to a large degree by the opinions of mental health professionals.

When individuals accused of crimes are judged to be mentally unstable, they are typically sent to a mental institution for treatment, a process called ***criminal commitment.*** Actually there are two forms of criminal commitment. In one, individuals are judged *mentally unstable at the time of their crime* and accordingly are found innocent of wrongdoing. They may plead *not guilty by reason of insanity* and bring mental health professionals into court to support their claim. If the individuals are found not guilty on this basis, they are committed for treatment until they improve enough to be released.

In a second form of criminal commitment, individuals are judged *mentally unstable at the time of their trial* and accordingly are considered to be incapable of understanding the procedures and defending themselves in court. They are committed for treatment until they are competent to stand trial. Once again, the testimony of mental health professionals is relied on to help determine the defendant's mental incompetence.

Judgments of mental instability have generated many arguments. Some people consider such judgments unfortunate loopholes in the legal system that allow criminals to escape proper punishment for their wrongdoing. Others argue that a legal system simply cannot be just unless it allows for extenuating circumstances, such as mental instability.

Criminal Commitment and Insanity During Commission of a Crime

In March 1981 the actress Jodie Foster received the following letter:

> Dear Jodie:
>
> There is a definite possibility that I will be killed in my attempt to get Reagan. It is for this very reason that I am writing you this letter now. As you well know by now, I love you very much. The past seven months I have left you dozens of poems, letters and messages in the faint hope you would develop an interest in me. . . . Jodie, I would abandon this idea of getting Reagan in a second if I could only win your heart and live out the rest of my life with you, whether it be in total obscurity or whatever. I will admit to you that the reason I'm going ahead with this attempt now is because I just cannot wait any longer to impress you. I've got to do something now to make you understand in no uncertain terms that I am doing all of this for your sake. By sacrificing my freedom and possibly my life I hope to change your mind about me. This letter is being written an hour before I leave for the Hilton Hotel. Jodie, I'm asking you please to look into your heart and at least give me the chance with this historical deed to gain your respect and love. I love you forever.
>
> JOHN HINCKLEY

Are these the ravings of an insane man? Or are they the heartfelt emotions of a calculating murderer? Soon after writing this letter, John W. Hinckley stood waiting, pistol ready, outside the Washington Hilton Hotel. Moments later, President Ronald Reagan emerged from the hotel, and the popping of pistol fire was heard. As Secret Service men propelled Reagan into the limousine, a policeman and the president's press secretary fell to the pavement. The president had been shot, and by nightfall most of America had seen the face and heard the name of the young man from Colorado.

Few courtroom decisions have spurred as much debate or legislative action as the jury's verdict that John Hinckley, having been captured in the act of shooting President Ronald Reagan, was not guilty by reason of insanity. As a consequence of this verdict, Congress and half of the state legislatures changed their criteria for such a verdict.

Was John Hinckley insane at the time of the shooting? If insane, should he be held responsible for his actions? On June 21, 1982, fifteen months after he shot four men in the nation's capital, a jury pronounced Hinckley not guilty by reason of insanity. Hinckley thus joined Richard Lawrence, a house painter who shot at Andrew Jackson in 1835, and John Schrank, a saloonkeeper who shot former president Teddy Roosevelt in 1912, as a would-be assassin who was found not guilty by reason of insanity.

For most Americans, the Hinckley verdict was a shock. For those familiar with the characteristics of the insanity defense, the verdict was less surprising. In the Hinckley case, as in other federal court cases at that time, the prosecution had the burden of proving that the defendant was sane beyond a reasonable doubt. At that time, many state courts placed a similar responsibility on the prosecution. A clear-cut demonstration of sanity can be a difficult task, especially when the defendant has exhibited bizarre behavior in other domains. In fact, a few years later, Congress passed a law making it the defense's burden in federal cases to prove that defendants are insane, rather then the prosecution's burden to prove them sane. The majority of state legislatures have since followed suit (Steadman et al., 1993).

It is important to recognize that "insanity" is a *legal* term. That is, the definition of "insanity" used to help determine criminal responsibility is set by legislators, not by clinicians. Defendants with mental disorders do not necessarily fulfill the criteria of legal insanity.

A jury's acquittal of a criminal defendant by reason of insanity has been a part of the British legal tradition since 1505 (Robitscher & Haynes, 1982). However, the most important precursor of the modern definition of insanity occurred in 1843, in response to the Daniel M'Naghten murder case. M'Naghten shot and killed Edward Drummond, the secretary to British Prime Minister Robert Peel, while trying to shoot Peel. Because of M'Naghten's apparent delusions of persecution, the jury found him to be not guilty by reason of insanity. The public was appalled by this decision, and their angry outcry forced the British law lords to clarify the insanity defense. This clarification has come to be known as the ***M'Naghten rule:***

> To establish a defense of insanity, it must be proved that at the time of committing the act, the party accused was laboring under such a defect of reason, from disease of the mind, as not to know the nature and quality of the act he was doing, or if he did know it, that he did not know he was doing what was wrong.

In essence, the M'Naghten rule held that a mental disorder at the time of a crime does not by itself constitute insanity. The defendant also had to be unable to know right from wrong. The state and federal courts in the United States adopted this test as well.

In the late nineteenth century some state and federal courts, dissatisfied with the M'Naghten rule, adopted an alternative test—the ***irresistible impulse test.*** This test, which had first been applied in Ohio in 1834, emphasized inability to control one's actions. A person who committed a crime during a "fit of passion" was considered insane and not guilty under this test.

Until recent decades, state and federal courts chose between the M'Naghten test and the irresistible impulse test in determining the sanity of criminal defendants; most courts used the M'Naghten criteria. For a while a third test, called the ***Durham test,*** was popular, but it was soon replaced in most courts. This test, based on a decision handed down by the Supreme Court in 1954 in the case of *Durham v. United States,* stated simply that individuals are not criminally responsible if their "unlawful act was the product of mental disease or mental defect." This test was meant to offer more flexibility in decisions regarding insanity, but the general criterion of "mental disease" or "mental defect" proved too broad. It could refer to such problems as alcoholism or other forms of substance dependence, and conceivably even headaches or ulcers, which were listed as psychophysiological disorders in DSM-I. The Durham test forced courts to rely even more on the interpretations and opinions of clinicians—and these were often contradictory.

In 1955 the American Law Institute (ALI) formulated a test that combined elements of the M'Naghten, irresistible impulse, and Durham tests. The new test indicated that

> A person is not responsible for criminal conduct if at the time of such conduct as a result of mental disease or defect he lacks substantial capacity either to appreciate the criminality (wrongfulness) of his conduct or to conform his conduct to the requirements of law.

The ALI guidelines also established that repeated criminal or antisocial behavior itself could not be cited to demonstrate "mental disease" or "irresistable impulse." There had to be independent indicators of mental instability. Similarly, the Supreme Court ruled in *Barrett v. United States* (1977) that "temporary insanity created by voluntary use of alcohol or drugs" does not relieve an offender of criminal responsibility.

For a time the American Law Institute test became the most widely accepted legal test of insanity. All federal courts, including the court that had jurisdiction over the Hinckley case, and most state courts applied its criteria. After the Hinckley verdict, however, there was a public uproar over the "liberal" ALI guidelines, and a movement to toughen the standards gained momentum. In 1983 the American Psychiatric Association recommended removal of the provision that absolved people of responsibility if they were unable to conform their behavior to the requirements of law. The association advised retention of only the wrongfulness criterion—essentially a return to the M'Naghten standard. It placed renewed emphasis on a defendant's inability to know right from wrong:

> A person charged with a criminal offense should be found not guilty by reason of insanity if it is shown that, as a result of mental disease or mental retardation, he was unable to appreciate the wrongfulness of his conduct at the time of his offense.
>
> *(APA, 1983, p. 685)*

This revised criminal insanity test now applies to all cases tried in federal courts and about half of the state courts (Steadman et al., 1993). The broader ALI standard is still used in the remaining state courts, except those in Idaho, Montana, and Utah, which have abolished the insanity plea altogether. Research has not found, however, that the reform criteria actually diminish the likelihood of verdicts of not guilty by reason of insanity (Ogloff et al., 1992; Finkel, 1991, 1990, 1989).

Obviously, severe and confusing mental disorders may impair individuals' judgments of right versus wrong or their ability to control their behavior (Elliott, 1996). Not surprisingly, then, approximately two-thirds of defendants who are acquitted of a crime by reason of insanity qualify for a diagnosis of schizophrenia (Steadman et al., 1993). The vast majority have a history of past hospitalization, arrest, or both. In addition, about half of the defendants who successfully plead insanity are white, and 86 percent are male. Their mean age is 32 years.

The crimes for which defendants are found not guilty by reason of insanity vary greatly. However, approximately 65 percent are violent crimes of some sort (Steadman et al., 1993). Close to 15 percent of acquitees are accused specifically of murder (see Figure 20-1 and Box 20-1).

Criticisms of the Insanity Defense Despite the revisions of the criteria for a finding of insanity, criticism of the insanity defense continues (Slovenko, 1995). One concern is the seeming incompatibility between the law and the science of human behavior. The law assumes that individuals have free will and are typically responsible for their actions. Several models of human behavior, in contrast, assume that the individual's situation or biological forces act to determine behavior (Winslade, 1983). Inevitably, then, legal views of insanity and responsibility will be more rigid than those implied by clinical research.

A second criticism questions scientific knowledge of abnormal behavior. During a typical insanity defense trial, the testimony of defense clinicians conflicts with the testimony of clinicians hired by the prosecution (Otto, 1989). The jury is faced with "experts" who disagree on their diagnostic assessments. Some people see this lack of professional consensus as evidence that the clinical field may in some areas be too primitive to be influencing important legal proceedings (Slovenko, 1995; Szasz, 1963). Others counter that the field has made great

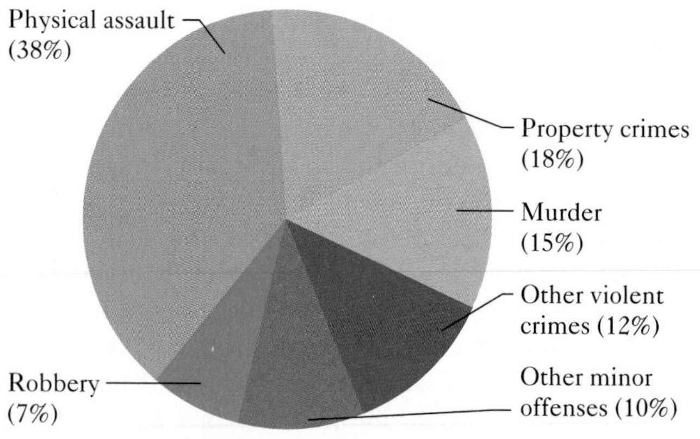

Figure 20-1 *Crimes for which persons are found not guilty by reason of insanity (NGRI). A review of NGRI verdicts in eight states revealed that most persons who were acquitted on this basis had been charged with a crime of violence. This defense is not employed in many cases involving minor offenses. (Based on Steadman et al., 1993; Callahan et al., 1991.)*

strides. In fact, some standardized scales, such as the Rogers Criminal Responsibility Assessment Scales, now help assessors to discriminate sane persons from insane persons according to the M'Naghten standard. The scales are especially useful in applying the standard across genders, races, and ages (Rogers & Ewing, 1992; Rogers, 1987). Moreover, the Council on Psychiatry and the Law (1992) has recommended a system of peer review, to ensure that professional standards are upheld by clinicians in legal cases.

Perhaps the most widespread criticism of the insanity defense is that it systematically allows dangerous criminals to escape punishment. Granted, some people who successfully plead insanity are released from treatment facilities within months of their acquittal. Yet the number of such cases is quite small. According to surveys, the public dramatically overestimates the percentage of defendants who plead insanity, guessing it to be 30 to 40 percent, when in fact it is less than 1 percent (Steadman et al., 1993). Moreover, only a minority fake or exaggerate their psychological symptoms (Fauteck, 1995; Grossman & Wasyliw, 1988), and only a quarter of these defendants are actually found not guilty by reason of insanity (Callahan et al., 1991). On balance, then, less than one of every 400 defendants in the United States is found not guilty by reason of insanity.

During most of U.S. history, a successful insanity plea was the equivalent of a long-term prison sentence. Treatment in a mental hospital often amounted to a longer sentence than a verdict of guilty would have brought (Ogloff et al., 1992; Finkel, 1988). It also brought little, if any, improvement, and mental health professionals were therefore reluctant to assert that the offender was unlikely to commit a crime again. Moreover, tragic cases would occasionally call into question clinicians' ability to make such judgments and to predict dangerousness.

In Idaho, for example, a young man raped two women and was found not guilty by reason of insanity. After receiving less than a year of treatment, he was released. Soon he was arrested again for shooting a nurse, and convicted of assault with intent to kill. The uproar over this 1981 case led the Idaho state legislature to abolish the insanity plea.

Nevertheless, offenders have been released from mental hospitals earlier and earlier in recent years. This trend is the result of the increasing effectiveness of drug therapy in institutions, the growing bias against extended institutionalization, and greater emphasis on patients' rights (Blackburn, 1993). In 1992, in the case of *Foucha v. Louisiana,* the U.S. Supreme Court ruled that the only basis for determining the release of such individuals is whether or not they are still "insane"; they cannot be indefinitely detained in state mental hospitals simply because they are dangerous.

Alternative Verdicts In recent years twelve states have added the option of a verdict of "guilty but mentally ill" when a jury is determining the guilt or innocence of a defendant who has pleaded insanity (Slovenko, 1995; Steadman et al., 1993). Defendants who receive this verdict are found to have had a mental illness at the time of their crimes, but the illness was not sufficiently related to or responsible for the crime to absolve them of responsibility for the offense. The "guilty but mentally ill" option allows jurors to convict a person they perceive as dangerous while attempting also to ensure that the individual's therapeutic needs will be met. Defendants found to be guilty but mentally ill are given a prison term with the proviso that they will also undergo treatment if necessary.

Advocates of this new option see it as a better means of maintaining and defending our society's standards of behavior. In Georgia, juries given the option of declaring a person guilty but mentally ill have, in fact, delivered insanity acquittals less often (Callahan et al., 1992). One study with mock juries found that 86 percent of jurors preferred having a third option and saw it as "moral, just and an adequate means of providing for the treatment needs of mentally ill offenders" (Roberts, Golding, & Fincham, 1987).

Critics of the concept believe that appropriate mental health care should be made available to all prisoners anyway, without any special designation. These critics point out that the prevalence of mental disorders is much higher among prisoners than among the general population (Torrey, 1997; Jordan et al., 1996; Gunn et al., 1991). They argue that the verdict often differs from a guilty verdict in name only (Slovenko, 1995; Tanay, 1992). Critics also argue that the new verdict option may only confuse jurors already faced with an enormously complex task (APA, 1983; Morris, 1983).

Some states allow still another kind of defense, "guilty with diminished capacity." Here a defendant's mental instability is viewed as an extenuating circumstance that should help determine precisely which crime the defendant is guilty of (Slovenko, 1992). The defense lawyer argues that mental dysfunctioning prevented the defendant from having the capacity to harbor the intent required for a particular crime. The accused person can then be found guilty of a lesser crime—of manslaughter (unlawful killing without intent), say, instead of murder in the first degree (planned murder). The case of Dan White, who killed Mayor George Moscone and City Supervisor Harvey Milk of San Francisco in 1978, illustrates the use of this verdict.

> On the morning of November 27, 1978, Dan White loaded his .38 caliber revolver. White had recently resigned his position as a San Francisco supervisor because of family and financial pressures. Now, after a

BOX 20-1 Famous Cases Involving the Insanity Defense

1977 In Michigan, Francine Hughes poured gasoline around the bed where her husband, Mickey, lay in a drunken stupor. Then she lit a match and set him on fire. At her trial she explained that he had beaten her repeatedly for fourteen years, and he had threatened to kill her if she tried to leave him. The jury found her not guilty by reason of temporary insanity, transforming her into a symbol for many abused women across the nation. Some people saw the decision as confirmation of a woman's right to self-defense in her own home.

1978 David "Son of Sam" Berkowitz, a serial killer in New York City, explained that a barking dog had sent him demonic messages to kill. Although two psychiatrists assessed him as psychotic, he was found guilty of his crimes. Long after his trial, he said that he had actually made up the delusions.

1979 Kenneth Bianchi, one of the pair known as the Hillside Stranglers, entered a plea of not guilty by reason of insanity, but was found guilty along with his cousin of sexually assaulting and murdering women in the Los Angeles area in late 1977 and early 1978. He claimed that he had a multiple personality disorder.

1980 In December, Mark David Chapman murdered John Lennon. Chapman later explained that he had killed the rock music legend because he believed Lennon to be a "sell-out." He also described hearing the voice of God, considered himself his generation's "catcher in the rye" (from the J. D. Salinger novel), and compared himself to Moses. Despite clinical testimony that supported Chapman's plea of not guilty by reason of insanity, he himself refused to claim that schizophrenia was at the root of his crime. He was judged competent to stand trial and was ultimately convicted of murder.

1981 In an attempt to prove his love for the actress Jodie Foster, John Hinckley Jr. tried to assassinate President Ronald Reagan. Hinckley was found not guilty by reason of insanity and was committed to St. Elizabeths Hospital for the criminally insane in Washington, where he remains today.

1991 Julio Gonzales stood trial for starting a fire that killed eighty-seven people at a social club in New York. A psychologist testified that Gonzales had suffered from a wide range of personality disorders and "long-standing psychological defects" that led him

change of heart, he wanted his job back. When he asked Mayor George Moscone to reappoint him, however, the mayor refused. Supervisor Harvey Milk was among those who had urged Moscone to keep White out, for Milk was America's first openly gay politician, and Dan White had been an outspoken opponent of measures supporting gay rights.

White avoided the metal detector at City Hall's main entrance by climbing through a basement window after telling construction workers who recognized him that he had forgotten his keys. After they unlocked the window for him, he went straight to the mayor's office. There Moscone greeted him and poured a couple of drinks, perhaps hoping to soothe White's rage at not being reappointed. Neither man had a chance to touch his drink before White pulled out his gun and shot the mayor once in the arm and once in the chest. As Moscone lay bleeding on the floor, White walked over to him and, from only inches away, fired twice into Moscone's head.

White then reloaded his gun, ran down the hall, and spotted Harvey Milk. White asked to talk with him. Right after the two men went into White's former office, three more shots rang out. Milk crumpled to the floor. Once again White from point-blank range fired two more bullets into his victim's head. Shortly afterward he turned himself in to the police. Several months later the jury rendered its verdict: Dan White was not guilty of murder, only voluntary manslaughter.

Murder is the illegal killing of a human being with malice aforethought, that is, with the intent to kill. Manslaughter is the illegal killing of a human being without malice aforethought. The attacker may intend to harm the victim, but not to kill. If the victim nonetheless dies, the crime is voluntary manslaughter. Involuntary manslaughter is an illegal killing from negligence rather than intentional harm.

How could a man who loaded his pistol with cartridges that explode on impact, who made a conscious effort to avoid the metal detector, and who, finally, walked over to the prone, wounded men and shot each one twice more in the head—how could such a man be said to have no murderous intent?

The answer lies in the role psychiatry played in the trial. Defense attorney Douglas Schmidt argued that a to break with reality. The psychologist said that Gonzales started the fire during a brief psychotic episode, after a fight with his girlfriend and his eviction from the club. The jury did not agree, and Gonzales was convicted and sentenced to prison.

1992 Jeffrey Dahmer, a 31-year-old mass murderer in Milwaukee, was tried for the killings of fifteen young men. Dahmer apparently drugged some of his victims and performed crude lobotomies on them in an attempt to create zombielike companions for himself. He also dismembered his victims' bodies and stored their parts to be eaten. Although his defense attorney argued that Dahmer was not guilty by reason of insanity, the jury found him guilty as charged. He was beaten to death by another inmate in 1995.

1994 On June 23, 1993, 24-year-old Lorena Bobbitt cut off her husband's penis with a 12-inch kitchen knife while he slept. During her trial, defense attorneys argued that after years of abuse by John Bobbitt, his wife suffered a brief psychotic episode and was seized by an "irresistible impulse" to cut off his penis after he came home drunk and raped her. On January 23, 1994, the jury acquitted her of the charge of malicious wounding by reason of temporary insanity. She was committed to a state mental hospital for further assessment and treatment and released a few months later.

John Du Pont (left) playfully wrestles with friend and employee Dave Schultz, an Olympic gold medalist. Du Pont murdered Schultz in 1995 and, two years later, was found guilty of third degree murder, but mentally ill.

1997 John E. Du Pont, 57-year-old heir to his family's chemical fortune, shot and killed the Olympic wrestling champion Dave Schultz in January 1995. The murder took place on Du Pont's 800-acre estate, where he had built a sports center for amateur athletes. Schultz, his close friend, had coached wrestlers at the center. In 1997 Du Pont was found *guilty of third degree murder, but mentally ill,* and he was sentenced to prison for 13 to 30 years. He is currently receiving treatment at the mental health unit of a correctional institution.

patriotic, civic-minded man like Dan White—high school athlete, decorated war veteran, former fireman, policeman, and city supervisor—could not possibly have committed such an act unless something had snapped inside him. The brutal nature of the two final shots to each man's head only proved that White had lost his wits. White was not fully responsible for his actions because he suffered from "diminished capacity." Although White killed Mayor George Moscone and Supervisor Harvey Milk, he had not planned his actions. On the day of the shootings, White was mentally incapable of planning to kill, or even of wanting to do such a thing.

Well known in forensic psychiatry circles, Martin Blinder, professor of law and psychiatry at the University of California's Hastings Law School in San Francisco, brought a good measure of academic prestige to White's defense. White had been, Blinder explained to the jury, "gorging himself on junk food: Twinkies, Coca-Cola. . . . The more he consumed, the worse he'd feel and he'd respond to his ever-growing depression by consuming ever more junk food." Schmidt later asked Blinder if he could elaborate on this. "Perhaps if it were not for the ingestion of this junk food," Blinder responded, "I would suspect that these homicides would not have taken place." From that moment on, Blinder became known as the author of the Twinkie defense.

The next psychiatrist, George F. Solomon, further drove home the idea that it was not Dan White but an irritating extraneous influence—something outside himself—that made White do these terrible things. Did White have the capacity to premeditate and deliberate murder? "No," Solomon responded. "Why not?" he was asked. "I don't think that he was capable of permitting himself to plan something so awful." The killings, Solomon told the jury, were the result of "a dissociated state of mind, which means a disruption of the normal integrated functions." White had, Solomon continued, "blocked out of his mind his awareness of his duty to uphold the right."

Dan White was convicted only of voluntary manslaughter, and was sentenced to seven years, eight months. (He was released on parole January 6, 1984.) Psychiatric testimony convinced the jury that White did not wish to kill George Moscone or Harvey Milk.

> The angry crowd that responded to the verdict by marching, shouting, trashing City Hall, and burning police cars was in good part homosexual. Gay supervisor Harvey Milk had worked well for their cause, and his loss was a serious setback for human rights in San Francisco. Yet it was not only members of the gay community who were appalled at the outcome. Most San Franciscans shared their feelings of outrage.
>
> *(Coleman, 1984, pp. 65–70)*

Because of possible miscarriages of justice, many legal experts have argued vociferously against the "diminished capacity" defense (Slovenko, 1992; Coleman, 1984), and a number of states have eliminated it. Some studies find, however, that mock jurors often use the option carefully and appropriately (Finkel & Duff, 1989; Finkel et al., 1985). Jurors have been found to choose this option primarily under two conditions: the jurors generally see some culpability at the time of action, and they believe the defendant was in some way responsible for bringing about his or her own mental condition.

Sex Offender Statutes Ever since 1937, when Michigan enacted the first "sex psychopath" statute, some states have given a special designation to sex offenders (Monahan & Davis, 1983). These states presume that persons who are repeatedly found guilty of certain sex crimes have a mental disorder and categorize them as "mentally disordered sex offenders."

Unlike defendants who have been found not guilty by reason of insanity, people classified as mentally disordered sex offenders have been convicted of a criminal offense and are thus judged to be morally responsible for their actions. Nevertheless, the status of a sex offender, like that of a person found not guilty by reason of insanity, implies that commitment to a mental health facility is a more appropriate sentence than imprisonment (Small, 1992). In part, such statutes reflect society's conception of sex offenders as sick people. On a practical level, the provisions help prevent the physical abuse that sex offenders sometimes face as ostracized members of prison society.

In recent years a growing number of states have modified or abolished these sex offender statutes and programs. There are several reasons for this trend. First, some states have found these statutes difficult to act on. Some state statutes, for example, require that a candidate for sex offender status be found "sexually dangerous beyond a reasonable doubt"—a judgment that often goes beyond the clinical field's expertise (Szasz, 1991). Also, there is evidence that racial bias can significantly affect the assignment of sex offender status (Sturgeon & Taylor, 1980). White Americans are twice as likely to be granted sex offender status as African Americans and Hispanic Americans who have been convicted of similar crimes.

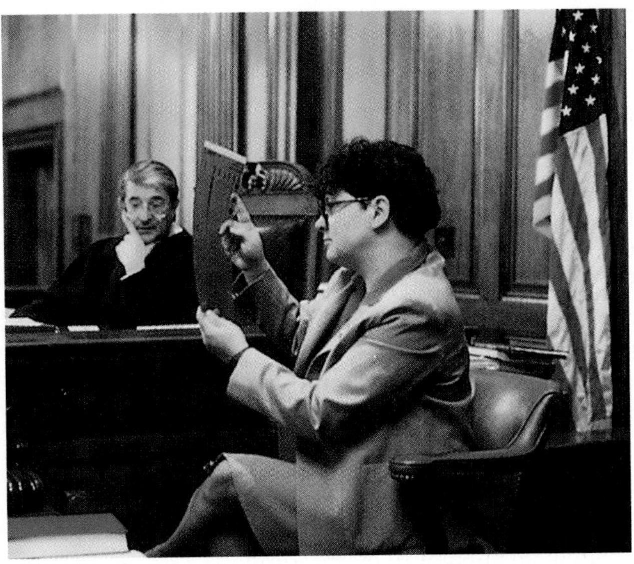

Each segment of the clinical field has its own forensic specialists who represent it in the courts and houses of legislature. Forensic psychologists, psychiatrists, and social workers typically receive special training in such duties as evaluating the functioning of criminal defendants, making recommendations concerning patients' rights, and assessing the psychological trauma experienced by crime victims (Ladds, 1997).

Criminal Commitment and Incompetence to Stand Trial

Regardless of their state of mind at the time of a crime, defendants may be held to be ***mentally incompetent*** to stand trial. The competence provisions have been established to ensure that defendants understand the charges and proceedings they are facing and have "sufficient present ability to consult with" their counsel in preparing and conducting an adequate defense. This minimum standard of competence was specified by the Supreme Court in the case of *Dusky v. United States* (1960).

Competence issues typically are raised by the defendant's attorney, although prosecutors and arresting police officers may bring them before the court as well (Meyer, 1992). All parties (including the presiding judge) are usually careful to recommend a psychological examination for any defendant who seems to exhibit signs of mental dysfunctioning. They prefer to err on the side of caution, because some convictions have been reversed on appeal when a defendant's competence was not initially established. When the issue of competence is raised, the judge orders a psychological evaluation, usually on an inpatient basis. The examiner then presents a written or oral report to the court at a hearing to determine the mental state of the accused person. If the court holds that the defendant is incompetent to participate in his or her defense, the individual is assigned to a mental health facility until he or she is competent to stand trial (Bennett & Kish, 1990).

Many more cases of criminal commitment result from decisions of mental incompetence than from verdicts of not guilty by reason of insanity (Blackburn, 1993). On the other hand, the majority of criminals currently institutionalized for psychological treatment in the United States are not from either of these two groups. Rather, they are convicted inmates whose psychological problems have led officials of correctional institutions to send them for treatment—either to mental health units within the prison or to mental hospitals (Monahan & Steadman, 1983; Steadman et al., 1982).

A risk inherent in competence provisions is that an innocent defendant may spend years in a mental health facility with no opportunity to disprove accusations of criminal conduct in court. Some defendants have served longer "sentences" in mental health facilities awaiting a judgment of competence than they would have in prison if they had been convicted (Meyer, 1992). The possibility of such abuses was curbed when the Supreme Court ruled, in the case of *Jackson v. Indiana* (1972), that a chronically disordered defendant cannot be indefinitely committed under criminal status. After a reasonable amount of time, he or she should be either found competent and tried, set free, or transferred to a mental-health facility under civil commitment procedures.

Until the early 1970s, most states required the commitment of mentally incompetent defendants to maximum security institutions for the "criminally insane" (Winick, 1983). Under current law, the courts have greater flexibility. In some cases, particularly when the charge is a minor one, the defendant may be treated on an outpatient basis.

Legal Influences on the Mental Health System

The legal system also has had a significant impact on clinical professionals. First, courts and legislatures have developed the process of ***civil commitment,*** which forces certain individuals to undergo mental health treatment. Although many persons who show signs of mental disturbance seek treatment voluntarily, a large number are not aware of their problems or are simply not interested in receiving treatment. What are clinicians to do for these people? Should they force treatment upon them? Or do people have the right to feel miserable and function ineffectively? The law has addressed this question by providing civil commitment guidelines under which certain persons can be forced into treatment.

Second, the legal system, on behalf of the state, has also taken on the responsibility of specifying and protecting patients' rights during treatment. It protects not only patients who have been involuntarily committed but also those who voluntarily sought institutionalization or even outpatient therapy.

Civil Commitment

Every year in the United States large numbers of persons with mental disorders are involuntarily committed to mental institutions. These commitments have long been a focus of controversy and debate. In some ways the law provides greater protection for the suspected criminal than for people suspected of displaying psychosis (Burton, 1990).

Why Commit? Generally our legal system permits involuntary commitment of individuals when they are considered to be *in need of treatment* and *dangerous to themselves or others.* The state's authority to commit disturbed individuals rests on its obligations to protect the interests of the individual and of society: the principles of *parens patriae* and *police power* (Wettstein, 1988). Under ***parens patriae*** ("father of the country"), the state can make decisions, including involuntary hospitalization, that promote the patient's best interests and provide protection from self-harm or self-neglect. Conversely, ***police power*** enables the state to protect society from a person who is homicidal or otherwise violent (see Box 20-2). Under these principles, the state provides treatment to those persons whose disabilities are so severe that they are unable to recognize their needs and to seek treatment voluntarily.

Current Procedures and Rights Laws governing the civil commitment process vary from state to state. Some basic procedures and rights, however, are common to most of these laws.

Many formal commitment proceedings are initiated by family members. In response to a son's suicide attempt, for example, his parents may try to persuade him to seek admission to a mental institution. If the son refuses, the parents may go to court and seek an involuntary commitment order. If the son is a minor, the process is simple. The Supreme Court, in the case of *Parham v. J. R.* (1979), ruled that a due process hearing is not necessary in such cases. It need only be demonstrated that a mental health professional considers such commitment warranted. If the son is an adult, however, the process is more elaborate. The court will usually order a mental examination and provide the individual with the opportunity to contest the commitment attempt in court, often with representation by a lawyer (Holstein, 1993).

BOX 20-2 Serial Murderers: Madness or Badness?

His résumé seemed impressive. . . . A shy, brilliant boy, he skipped two grades in school and entered Harvard at age 16. He went on to receive a Ph.D. in mathematics from the University of Michigan in 1967. Securing a highly prestigious position at the University of California, Berkeley, he seemed destined for fame and success. But somewhere along the line, things changed. Two years into his stint at Berkeley, he decided to drop out of society—opting instead for a grubby, Thoreau-like existence in rural Montana.

It was here, alone in a 10-foot-by-12-foot shack, that this reclusive eccentric produced his most renowned works: sixteen bombs, three deaths, twenty-three maimings, several taunting letters to the *New York Times,* and a 35,000-word antitechnology manifesto. By the end of his eighteen-year rampage, "Unabomber"—his FBI code name—had become a household word. On April 3, 1996, federal agents raided Theodore Kaczynski's Montana cabin, and his reign of mail bomb terror, which had captured the attention of a nation, was finally put to an end.

(Duffy, 1996; Thomas, 1996).

Theodore Kaczynski has joined a lengthening list of serial killers who have fascinated and horrified Americans over the years: Ted Bundy, David Berkowitz ("Son of Sam"), Albert DeSalvo, John Wayne Gacy, Jeffrey Dahmer. Serial murderers represent the ultimate extension of violence that one human being can inflict on another—killing only for the sheer thrill of the moment. Clinical theorists do not yet understand these individuals, but they and law officials have gathered information about them, and they are beginning to speculate on the psychology behind such violent patterns.

Although each may have his own modus operandi, serial killers appear to have some characteristics in common. Most are white males between 25 and 34 years old, of average to high intelligence, generally clean-cut, glib, attractive, and skillful manipulators. They select their victims carefully, and though their victims conform to no clear pattern, most are of the same race as their killers. For the most part, these men have no permanent ties to any community, and move from place to place in pursuit of the kill. Many are also fascinated by police work and the popular media and follow their crimes closely in the news (Ressler & Schactman, 1992; Holmes & DeBurger, 1985).

Does serial murder stem from madness or badness—mental dysfunction or sheer deviance (Scarf, 1996)? The answer seems to be that these individuals may indeed have mental disorders, but they do not typically fit the legal criteria of insanity. Park Dietz, a forensic psychiatrist and highly regarded expert on the subject, offers this explanation:

None of the serial killers I've had the occasion to study or examine has been legally insane, but none has been normal, either. They've all been people who've got mental disorders. But despite their mental disorders, which have to do with their sexual interests and their character, they've been people who knew what they were doing, knew what they were doing was wrong, but chose to do it anyway.

(Douglas, 1996, pp. 344–345)

As a result, the plea of not guilty by reason of insanity is generally unsuccessful for serial killers. Communities usually fear that a defendant found not guilty in this way may be released too quickly. Moreover, people typically need to be able to hold someone accountable for the repulsive crimes (Gresham, 1993).

Despite the temptation to consider senseless killers *psychotic,* or out of touch with reality, research indicates otherwise (Carlisle, 1993). Richard Chase, a serial murderer who believed that he needed to drink human blood to stop his own from turning to powder, is one of the few serial killers who are clearly psychotic

Although the Supreme Court has offered few guidelines on the specific procedures of civil commitment, one important decision, rendered in the case of *Addington v. Texas* (1979), has outlined the *minimum standard of proof* necessary for commitment. Before this case was decided, each state developed its own standard of proof for commitment. Many states vaguely required a "preponderance of evidence" that commitment was necessary. Some states, such as Texas, had stricter standards, requiring, for example, the presentation of "clear, unequivocal and convincing evidence" of the necessity of commitment.

(Ressler & Schactman, 1992). Many serial killers seem to display severe personality disorders (Scarf, 1996). Lack of conscience and an utter disregard for people and the rules of society—key features of antisocial personality disorder—seem inherent in the serial killer makeup. Narcissistic thinking is quite common as well. The feeling of being special may even give the killer an unrealistic belief that he won't get caught (Scarf, 1996). Often it is this sense of invincibility that leads to his capture. In the Unabomber case, for instance, it was Kaczynski's moral tirade in support of a return to the state of "wild nature" that led to his downfall. After reading his 35,000-word manifesto—printed, in accordance with his demands, in the *New York Times* and *Washington Post*—his own brother realized that Kaczynski might be the Unabomber.

This 1994 artist's sketch of the Unabomber has become a powerful symbol of serial murder and terror.

Sexual dysfunction and fantasy also seem to be common issues for serial killers (Ressler & Schactman, 1992). Numerous studies have found that vivid fantasies, often sexual and sadistic, are a major driving force behind their behavior (Lachmann & Lachmann, 1995; Ressler & Schactman, 1992). Though the first killing may be an accident, repeated fantasies seem to keep the killers coming back for more. Robert Ressler, an FBI criminal profiler, compares this process to an adventure series, which lures viewers back every week with a cliffhanger ending.

> **T**he very act of killing leaves the murderer hanging, because it isn't as perfect as his fantasy. . . . After a murder, the serial murderer thinks of how the crime could have been bettered. . . . "I killed her too quickly. Didn't take time to have enough fun, to torture her properly." . . . There's an improvement continuum.
>
> *(Ressler & Schactman, 1992, pp. 29–30)*

Some clinicians also believe that the killers may be trying to counteract general feelings of powerlessness by controlling, manipulating, or eliminating those who are momentarily weaker. "Control may be achieved by sadistically inflicting pain or seeking to destroy life—by making others who are incapable of defending themselves suffer" (Levin & Fox, 1985, p. 68). Studies show that the majority of serial killers have endured substantial abuse as children—physically, sexually, and emotionally (Ressler & Schactman, 1992).

Ultimately, clinical theorists do not know why serial killers behave as they do. Some believe that serial murder is a learned response of some sort, through which the killer releases humiliation received during youth (Hale, 1993). Others feel that the killers lack a kind of internal stop mechanism that keeps the rest of us from acting out every violent impulse that comes into our heads (Gelman, 1991). In view of their limited understanding of these individuals, most clinicians and public officials agree with Dietz when he asserts, "It's hard to imagine any circumstance under which they should be released to the public again" (Douglas, 1996, p. 349).

In the case of *Addington v. Texas,* Addington's mother attempted to have her son committed by the state of Texas while he, in turn, argued that Texas' standard of proof for commitment should be even stricter. Addington asked the Supreme Court to mandate that the "beyond a reasonable doubt" standard, the rule employed in criminal cases, should also be applied to his civil commitment case. Addington lost his case. The Court was concerned that the "beyond a reasonable doubt" standard was too strict for civil commitment, given the "fallibility of psychiatric diagnosis." In the course of its decision, however, the Supreme Court established a Texas-style standard as the appropriate minimum standard for *all* states. It ruled that before an individual can be committed, there must be "clear and convincing" proof that he or she is mentally ill and has met the state's criteria for involuntary commitment.

The Court's requirement of "clear and convincing" evidence does not suggest what constitutes such evidence. The criteria are left to each state. The ruling determines only the minimum *standard of proof* that should be applied to whatever commitment criteria the state chooses to enforce.

Emergency Commitment Many situations require immediate action; no one can wait for formal commitment proceedings when a life is at stake. Imagine an emergency room patient who is suicidal or suffering from auditory hallucinations that order hostile actions against others. He or she may need immediate treatment and round-the-clock supervision. If treatment could not be applied in such situations without the patient's full consent, the consequences could be tragic.

Therefore, many states give attending clinicians the right to order temporary commitment and medication of a patient who is behaving in a bizarre or violent manner. Initially these states required certification by two physicians (not necessarily psychiatrists in some of the states). Today some of the states have broadened the procedure to allow certification by other mental health professionals as well. The clinicians must declare that such patients are in a state of mind that makes them dangerous to themselves or others. By tradition, the certifications are often referred to as *two-physician certificates,* or "2 PCs." Limitations on the length of such emergency commitments vary from state to state, but three days is often the limit (Holstein, 1993). Should the clinicians who provide treatment determine that a longer period of commitment is necessary, formal commitment proceedings may be initiated.

Who Is Dangerous? In the past, people with mental disorders were actually less likely than others to commit violent or dangerous acts. This low rate of violence was apparently related to the fact that so many such persons resided in institutions. With the advent of deinstitutionalization, however, hundreds of thousands of people with severe disturbances now live in the community and receive little or no treatment. Some of these individuals are indeed dangerous to others.

Although approximately 90 percent of people with mental disorders are in no way violent or dangerous (Swanson et al., 1990), recent studies suggest at least a modest relationship between severe mental disorders and violent behavior (Eronen et al., 1996; Hodgins et al., 1996; Junginger, 1996). After reviewing a number of studies, the law and psychology professor John Monahan (1993, 1992) concluded that the rate of violent behavior among persons with severe mental disorders, particularly psychotic disorders, is at least somewhat higher than that of people without such disorders:

Approximately 15 percent of patients in mental hospitals have assaulted another person prior to admission.

Around 25 percent of patients in mental hospitals assault another person during hospitalization.

Approximately 12 percent of community residents with schizophrenia, major depression, or bipolar disorder have assaulted other people, compared to 2 percent of persons without a mental disorder. Between 25 and 35 percent of people who display a substance-related disorder have assaulted others.

Approximately 4 percent of persons who report having been violent during the past year suffer from schizophrenia. One percent of nonviolent persons suffer from schizophrenia.

Monahan cautions that the findings do not suggest that people with mental disorders are generally dangerous. Nor do they justify the "caricature of the mentally disordered" that is often portrayed by the media, the "shunning of former patients by employers and neighbors," or the "lock 'em up" laws proposed by some politicians. On the other hand, they do indicate that a severe mental disorder may be more of a risk factor for violence than mental health experts have generally believed.

Because a determination of dangerousness is frequently required for judicial approval of involuntary civil commitment, the reliable and valid determination of who is dangerous is of major importance. But can mental health professionals accurately predict who will commit violent acts? Unfortunately, research suggests that psychiatrists and psychologists are wrong more often than right when they make *long-term* predictions of violence (Buchanan, 1997; Limandri & Sheridan, 1995; Monahan & Walker, 1990). Most frequently they overestimate the likelihood that a patient will eventually engage in violent behavior. Still, studies suggest that *short-term* predictions—that is, predictions of imminent violence—can be more accurate than long-term ones (McNiel & Binder, 1991). Moreover, researchers are now working, with some success, to develop new assessment and prediction techniques that employ statistical approaches and are more accurate (Campbell, 1995; Milner & Campbell, 1995). Their efforts indicate that it may be possible to develop objective assessment techniques that have more predictive power than the subjective judgments of clinicians (Borum, 1996).

Criticisms of Civil Commitment Civil commitment has been criticized on several grounds. First, the criterion of dangerousness is a bone of contention. If judgments of dangerousness are often inaccurate, why should they be used as grounds to deprive someone of liberty? The American Civil Liberties Union has strongly criticized the use of such assessments in commitment cases (Ennis & Emory, 1978).

Second, the legal definitions of "mental illness" and "dangerousness" are vague. The terms may be defined so broadly that they could be applied to anyone the evaluators viewed as undesirable. Indeed, it is not unheard of for mental illness to be imputed to people whose primary offenses have been bouncing checks, spending "too much" money, living unconventional lifestyles, or holding unpopular political opinions (Wexler, 1983) (see Box 20-3).

A third problem with involuntary civil commitment is the sometimes questionable therapeutic value of commitment itself. Research suggests that many persons committed involuntarily do not respond well to therapy (Wanck, 1984). Perceptions of choice and control and personal motivation may be important determinants of a successful outcome in a therapeutic setting (Langer, 1983).

On the basis of these and other arguments, some clinicians argue that involuntary commitment should be abolished (Szasz, 1977, 1963). Moreover, many civil libertarians are worried that involuntary commitment may be abused for purposes of coercive control (Morse, 1982; Ennis & Emory, 1978). In fact, in the former Soviet Union and other countries, mental hospitals have been used routinely to incarcerate political dissidents.

In view of such problems, many clinicians now advocate moving away from a general notion of dangerousness in making decisions about commitment. They suggest instead a concept of *risk assessment:* "The patient is believed to have *X* likelihood of being violent to the following people or under the following conditions over *Y* period of time." Proponents argue that this would be a more useful and appropriate way of deciding where and how persons with psychological disorders should be treated (Snowden, 1997; Monahan & Steadman, 1996; Steadman et al., 1993).

Trends in Civil Commitment The acceptance of broad involuntary commitment statutes probably reached its peak in 1962. In the case of *Robinson v. California,* the Supreme Court ruled that the sentencing of persons with drug addictions to correctional institutions may violate the Constitution's ban on cruel and unusual punishment, and it recommended involuntary civil commitment to a mental hospital as a more reasonable action. This ruling encouraged the application of civil commitment proceedings against many kinds of "social deviants."

In the years that immediately followed this ruling, civil commitment procedures granted far fewer rights to "defendants" than did criminal courts (Holstein, 1993). It was particularly difficult for involuntarily committed patients to obtain their release. Substantial legal assistance was often needed. Clinicians' persistent overprediction of dangerousness exacerbated this problem.

During the late 1960s and early 1970s, the plight of the committed was increasingly publicized. Reporters, novelists, and civil libertarians were convinced that numerous persons were being committed unjustifiably. As the public became more aware of the problems surrounding involuntary commitment, state legislatures started to enact stricter and more precise standards for commitment (Holstein, 1993). Rates of involuntary commitment then declined, release rates increased, and court decisions favored the broadening of patients' rights (Wanck, 1984).

Criticisms of the criteria for dangerousness also increased during this time, and many jurisdictions modified their commitment standards to require the demonstration of *imminent* dangerousness. In addition, many states adopted more specific definitions of dangerousness itself. Some spelled out the specific types of behavior that had to be observed before this assessment could be made.

In a continuation of this trend, fewer people are institutionalized through civil commitment procedures today than in the past. The lower commitment rate has not led to more criminal behavior or more arrests among people who would have been committed under broader criteria (Teplin, Abram, & McClelland, 1994; Hiday, 1992). Nevertheless, some states have become increasingly concerned that commitment criteria are now too narrow, and they are starting to broaden their criteria once again (Beck & Parry, 1992; Belcher & Blank, 1990; Wexler, 1988, 1983). This broadening may or may not lead to a return to the vague commitment procedures of past years. The outcome will become clearer in the coming years.

Protecting Patients' Rights

Over the past two decades the law has significantly expanded the rights of patients with mental disorders. Both court decisions and state and federal legislation have

BOX 20-3 The Separation of Mind and State

During the presidential campaigns of 1992 and 1996, the independent candidate Ross Perot was branded "emotionally unbalanced" by his detractors. Perot reacted to the accusation with good humor and even adopted Willie Nelson's "Crazy" as his theme song. The strategy of questioning the psychological stability of political opponents is not at all new. In the former Soviet Union, for example, particularly under the rule of Josef Stalin, many political dissidents were placed in mental hospitals to get them out of the way and discredit their views.

Abolitionist John Brown's journey to execution is portrayed in Thomas Hovenden's Last Moments of John Brown, *1884.*

Politically motivated labeling was clearly at work during the mid-nineteenth-century debate over slavery in the United States (Gamwell & Tomes, 1995). Proponents of slavery often attacked Abraham Lincoln in the press as "insane" for his antislavery stance. Moreover, many people across the country, even those who were against slavery themselves, feared radical abolitionists and called them mentally unbalanced, blaming them for the upheaval in the nation.

The trial of the abolitionist John Brown brought the issue to life for all to see. Brown, a white opponent of slavery, organized a small force of both African Americans and white Americans to attack the federal armory at Harpers Ferry in Virginia. He was captured after two days and tried for murder and treason.

Many of Brown's supporters, including his own defense attorneys, urged him to plead not guilty by reason of insanity to avoid the death penalty (Gamwell & Tomes, 1995). Some fellow abolitionists, however, were offended by the suggestion that Brown's actions represented insanity, and Brown himself proudly maintained that he was mentally stable. His lawyers tried to introduce a Brown family history of mental disorders into the record, and sympathizers petitioned the governor for clemency on the grounds that Brown suffered from "monomania," obsessive irrationality focused on one issue. Nevertheless, Brown was convicted and executed.

As the historians Lynn Gamwell and Nancy Tomes (1995) point out, it was in the interests of both sides of the case to have Brown declared legally insane. Many people who opposed slavery believed that an insanity verdict would distance Brown's fanaticism from their own efforts in the public's mind, and would calm fears of violent insurrection by abolitionists. Many of those who defended slavery believed that a judgment of insanity would tarnish Brown's reputation and prevent him from becoming a martyred symbol of the abolitionist cause—as in fact he did become. Obviously, neither side was accommodated.

Disparaging people whose opinions differ from one's own is a common strategy in personal arguments. Not surprisingly, then, it has been used throughout the ages for political gain. We may not always be able to stop the practice, but we should at least be aware of it. When we sift through the annals of history, we must employ a sharp eye to isolate mental health terminology that is used correctly and knowingly from imagery that seeks merely to further a political cause.

helped ensure those legal rights, especially the *right to treatment* and *the right to refuse treatment.*

The Right to Treatment If people are committed to mental institutions and then do not receive treatment, the institutions become mere prisons for the unconvicted. To many patients in the late 1960s and the 1970s, large state mental institutions were just that. Some patients and their legal representatives therefore began to demand the treatment they felt the state was obligated to provide. A suit on behalf of institutionalized patients in Alabama led to a landmark decision in the battle for patients' rights. In the 1972 case of *Wyatt v. Stickney*, a federal court ruled that the state was constitutionally obligated to provide "adequate treatment" to all persons who had been committed involuntarily. Because conditions in the state's hospitals were so deplorable, the presiding judge laid out goals that state administrators had to meet. Included were provisions for more therapists, better living conditions, more privacy, opportunities for heterosexual interaction and physical exercise, and a more judicious use of physical restraint and medication. Other court jurisdictions have since adopted many of these standards.

Another important decision was handed down in 1975 by the Supreme Court in the case of *O'Connor v. Donaldson.* After being confined in a Florida mental institution for more than fourteen years, Kenneth Donaldson sued for release. Donaldson had repeatedly sought release and had been overruled by the institution's psychiatrists. He argued that he and his fellow patients were still receiving inadequate treatment, being largely ignored by the staff, and allowed minimal personal freedom. The Supreme Court ruled in his favor, fined the hospital's superintendent, and provided that such institutions must engage in periodic reviews of their patients' cases. The justices also stated unanimously that the state "cannot constitutionally confine . . . a non-dangerous individual who is capable of surviving safely in freedom by himself or with the help of willing and responsible family members or friends." Donaldson did have a friend who had repeatedly agreed to take him into his custody. The Donaldson case attracted a great deal of publicity. In addition to setting an important legal precedent, it helped focus attention on the plight of people committed to mental institutions.

A later case, *Youngberg v. Romeo* (1982), provided support for the right to treatment while cautioning courts against becoming too involved in the exact methods of treatment. The Supreme Court ruled that persons committed involuntarily have a constitutional right to "reasonably nonrestrictive confinement conditions" as well as "reasonable care and safety." In contrast to the earlier lower-court decisions, however, this decision provided only a broad outline of minimum standards for institutions.

Some people feared that the *Youngberg* decision signaled a slowing of the pace of court-mandated reforms and of the Supreme Court's involvement in mental health issues. Noting the expertise of mental health professionals, the Court ruled that treatment decisions must be assumed to be valid until proved otherwise. The justices seemed unwilling to support a significant expansion of the judicial system's involvement in the daily affairs of mental health institutions. The ruling also suggested that mental health professionals could rely largely on their professional judgment when they formulated systematic treatment procedures. To make sure that mental patients did not lose the rights they had gained throughout the 1970s, Congress passed the Protection and Advocacy for Mentally Ill Individuals Act in 1986 (Woodside & Legg, 1990). This law established *protection and advocacy* systems in all states and U.S. territories and gave advocates who worked for patients within the system the power to investigate possible abuse and neglect, and to address these problems legally.

In recent years public advocates have argued that the right to treatment should also be extended to the tens of thousands of persons with severe mental disorders who are repeatedly released from hospitals after too short a stay. Essentially, they are sent to the streets to care for themselves, often winding up homeless or in prisons, where the percentage of inmates who receive treatment is quite low (Torrey, 1997; SAMHSA, 1993) (see Figure 20-2). Many mental health advocates are now suing federal and state agencies across the country, demanding that they fulfill the promises of the community mental health movement.

The Right to Refuse Treatment During the past two decades the courts have also established that patients, particularly those in institutions, have the right to *refuse* certain forms of treatment. The courts have been reluctant to issue a single general ruling on this issue because the range of treatment methods is so broad. A ruling based on one form of treatment would be likely to affect other treatments in unintended ways. Thus specific treatments have been targeted in various court rulings.

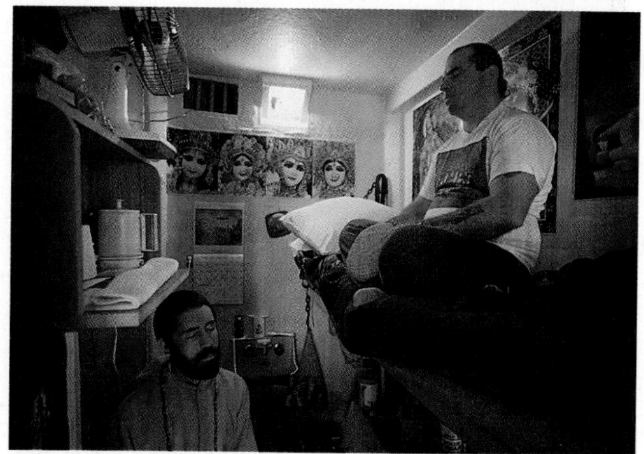

Because mental health care in prisons is typically limited, inmates often seek other avenues for addressing feelings of tension or anger or other psychological problems. Here an inmate (right) meditates with a Hindu minister in order to "leave his prison cell for a peaceful place in the mind" (Swerdlow, 1995, p. 32).

Receive Psychotherapy

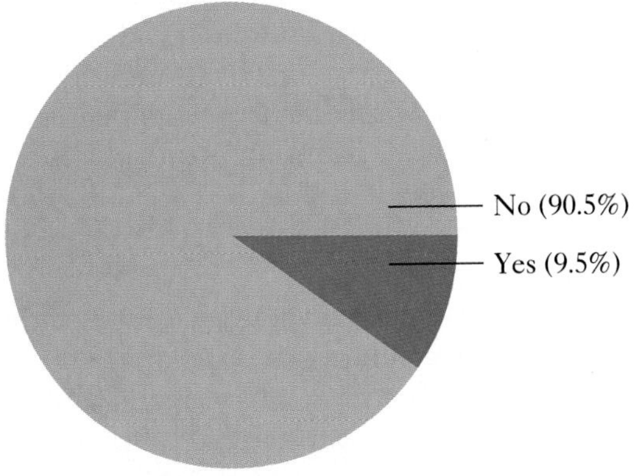

Receive Residential Treatment

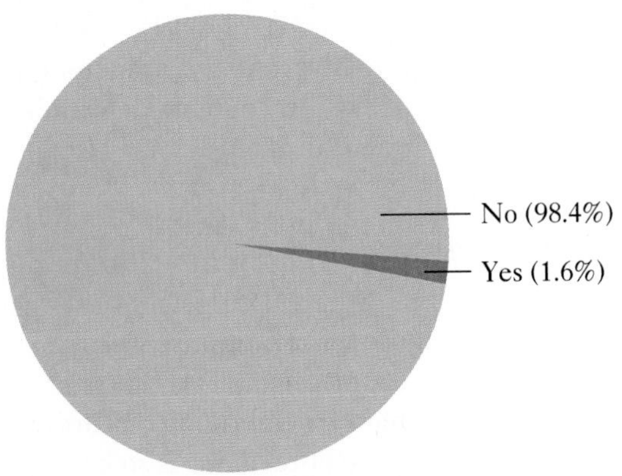

Receive 24-Hour Hospital Mental Health Care

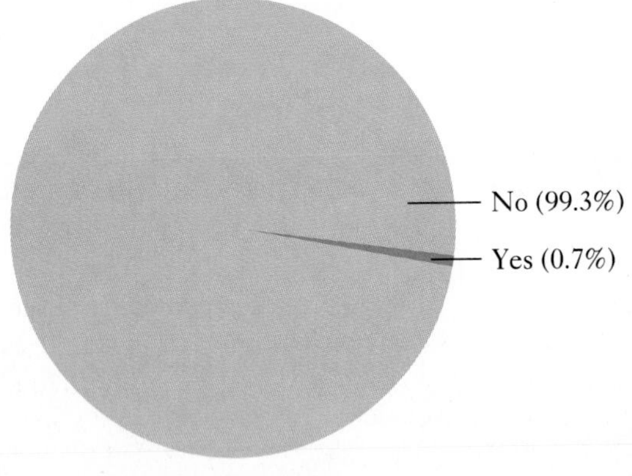

Figure 20-2 *Prisoners who receive treatment. Despite the high prevalence of mental disorders among prisoners, only 9.5 percent of inmates in state prisons in the United States receive psychotherapy, only 1.6 percent receive treatment in a residential treatment program (separate living arrangements), and less than 1 percent receive 24-hour hospital mental health care. More white American and female inmates receive these forms of treatment than African American and male inmates. (Adapted from Swanson et al., 1993; Goldstrom, Manderscheid, & Rudolph, 1992.)*

Most of the "right to refuse treatment" rulings have centered on *biological treatments.* Such treatments are easier to impose on patients without their cooperation than psychotherapy and they often seem more intrusive, aversive, and hazardous. For example, state rulings have consistently granted patients the right to refuse psychosurgery, the most irreversible form of physical treatment—and therefore the most dangerous.

As we saw in Chapter 9, some states have also acknowledged a patient's right to refuse electroconvulsive therapy (ECT), the treatment used in many cases of severe depression. The right-to-refuse issue is much less clear-cut with regard to ECT than with respect to psychosurgery. ECT is highly effective for many persons with severe depression. On the other hand, ECT can cause psychological trauma and can also be misused, as many media reports, books, and movies have made clear. Consider the plight of Nan:

> When her private psychiatrist told her to enter a psychiatric hospital for shock treatment, she reluctantly agreed. After entering the hospital, however, she changed her mind. Despite her protests, she was given shock treatment and experienced the usual effects of confusion and memory loss. After a few shocks, however, her wish to stop the treatment became so strong that she said to a nurse, "I just have to get out of here. I'm leaving no matter what you say." It was then that she escaped.
>
> When the psychiatrist who had sent her to the hospital found out that Nan had run away, he telephoned her at home and said he would call the police if she did not return to the hospital. Under this pressure she returned, telling the nurses, "I really don't want to be here; I feel like I'm being forced to have shock. The doctor said if I didn't come back he'd send the police after me." Despite these events, her readmission was called voluntary, with no mention of her documented fear of shock treatment, of her desire not to be in the hospital, or of the threat of police intervention. She received more shock treatment during her second hospitalization, until she fled once more.
>
> *(Coleman, 1984, pp. 166–167)*

Today states vary in the degree to which they allow patients to refuse ECT. Some continue to permit ECT to be imposed on committed patients, whereas others require the consent of a third party in such cases. Still other states grant patients—particularly voluntary patients—the right to refuse ECT. Usually these patients must also be informed fully about the nature of the treatment and must give their written consent to it.

In the past, patients have not had the right to refuse psychotropic medications. States viewed these drugs as a benign form of treatment that often helped and rarely hurt patients. As we have seen repeatedly, however, many psychotropic drugs are exceedingly powerful. Certain antipsychotic drugs in particular may produce dangerous effects, such as tardive dyskinesia. As these harmful effects have become more apparent, some states have granted patients the right to refuse medication.

Two leading federal cases have led the way on the right to refuse medication—*Rennie v. Klein* (1979, 1981) in New Jersey and *Rogers v. Okin* (1979, 1980, 1981) in Massachusetts. Typically, states that recognize a patient's right to refuse medication require physicians to explain the purpose of the medication to patients and obtain their written consent. If a patient's refusal is considered incompetent, dangerous, or irrational, it can be overturned by an independent psychiatrist, medical committee, or local court (Prehn, 1990; Wettstein, 1988). However, the refusing patient is supported in this review process by a lawyer or a patient advocate.

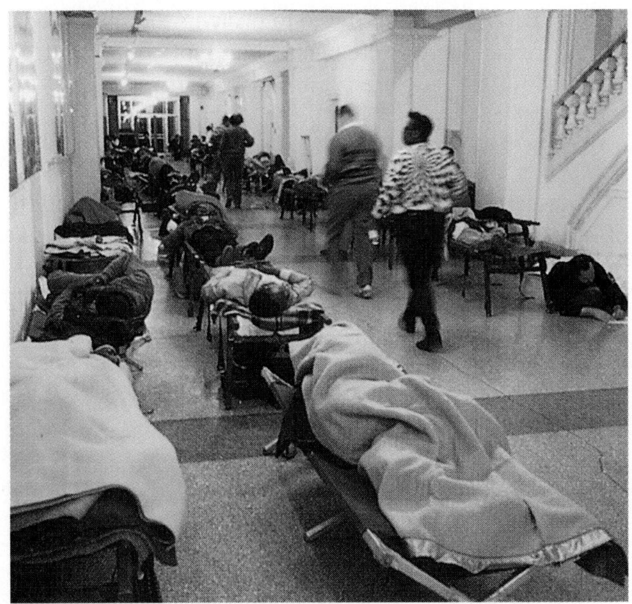

Although "guaranteed" the right to live in community adult homes, chronic mental patients often receive no treatment or guidance and wind up on the streets or in public shelters, such as this shelter for the homeless in Washington, D.C.

Other Rights of Patients Court decisions have safeguarded still other patient rights over the past few decades. In the 1973 case of *Sounder v. Brennan,* for example, a district court ruled that patients who perform work in mental institutions must receive payment in accordance with the Fair Labor Standards Act. Later the Supreme Court ruled that this right applied in private mental institutions but not in state hospitals.

In the 1974 case of *Stoner v. Miller,* a district court ruled that patients released from state mental hospitals have a right to live in community "adult homes." As we discussed earlier, many patients released under the policy of deinstitutionalization have encountered inadequate treatment and poor residential opportunities in the community. As an extension of their guaranteed right to treatment, *Stoner v. Miller* and other court decisions during the 1970s have acknowledged the right of such individuals to aftercare and to an appropriate community residence.

In the 1975 case of *Dixon v. Weinberger,* a district court ruled that individuals whose psychological disorder is not severe enough to require confinement in a mental institution should receive treatment in less restrictive facilities. If an inpatient program at a community mental health center is available, for example, then that is the facility to which such people should be assigned, not a mental hospital.

The "Rights" Debate Few would argue with the intent of the patient rights that are guaranteed today. Obviously, people with psychological disorders do not cease to be human beings: they have civil rights that must be considered and protected at all times. However, many clinicians express concern that these guarantees may inadvertently deprive patients of opportunities for effective recovery.

Consider the right to refuse medication (Appelbaum & Grisso, 1995; Grisso & Appelbaum, 1995; Sheline & Beattie, 1992). If medications can help bring about the recovery of a patient with schizophrenia, does not the patient have the right to that recovery? If confusion causes patients to refuse medication, can clinicians in good conscience go along and delay medication while legal channels are cleared? The psychologist Marilyn Whiteside raises similar concerns in her description of a 25-year-old patient with mental retardation:

> He was 25 and severely retarded. And after his favorite attendant left, he became self-abusive. He beat his fists against the side of his head until a football helmet had to be ordered for his protection. Then he clawed at his face and gouged out one of his eyes.
>
> The institution psychologists began a behavior program that had mildly aversive consequences: they squirted warm water in his face each time he engaged in self-abuse. When that didn't work, they requested permission to use an electric prod. The Human Rights Committee vetoed this "excessive and inhumane form of correction" because, after all, the young man was retarded, not criminal.
>
> Since nothing effective could be done that abridged the rights and negated the dignity of the developmentally disabled patient, he was verbally reprimanded for

> his behavior—and allowed to push his thumb through his remaining eye. He is now blind, of course, but he has his rights and presumably his dignity.
>
> *(Whiteside, 1983, p. 13)*

Similar questions can even be raised about the right of patients to a minimum wage. Although the court ruling correctly tries to protect patients from being taken advantage of by institutions, it may also disrupt helpful token economy programs (Glynn, 1990). As we saw in Chapter 16, these behavioral programs reward patients with hospital privileges, social rewards, and other nonmonetary rewards. While monetary reinforcement may be effective for some patients, nonmonetary rewards may be more effective for others. By depriving such programs of flexibility in determining rewards, a mandated minimum wage may reduce a patient's chances for recovery.

On the other side of the argument, the clinical field has not always monitored itself with respect to patients' rights. Over the years, many treatment programs have administered medications and other biological treatments carelessly, excessively, or harmfully (Crane, 1973). Similarly, many institutions have misused patients' labor. No wonder the courts and state legislatures have stepped in.

One must also ask whether the field's present state of knowledge justifies clinicians in overriding patients' rights. Can clinicians confidently say that certain treatments will indeed help patients? Can they predict the harmful effects of certain treatments? Since clinicians themselves often disagree, it seems appropriate that patients, their advocates, and impartial evaluators play significant roles in decision making.

Other Clinical-Legal Interactions

Mental health and legal professionals may influence each other's work in other ways as well. During the past two decades, their paths have crossed in three new areas: malpractice suits, jury selection, and the scope of clinical practice.

Malpractice Suits

The number of lawsuits against therapists has risen so sharply in recent years that clinicians have coined terms for the fear of being sued—"litigaphobia" and "litigastress." Claims against clinicians have centered on attempted suicide, sexual activity with a patient, failure to obtain informed consent for a treatment, negligent drug therapy, omission of drug therapy that would speed improvement, improper termination of treatment, and wrongful commitment (Smith, 1991; Wettstein, 1989).

The arts are another segment of society with which the mental health field interacts. Therapists have been portrayed in hundreds of novels, movies, and television shows. Like Doctors Frasier Crane and Bob Hartley before him, Dr. Katz, Professional Therapist *enters millions of living rooms each week. These therapists-of-the-arts often greatly affect how people perceive and react to mental health professionals.*

Improper termination of treatment was at issue in one highly publicized case in 1985. A man being treated for alcohol-related depression was released from a state hospital in Alabama. Two and a half months later, he shot and killed a new acquaintance in a motel lounge. He was convicted of murder and sentenced to life in prison. The victim's father, claiming negligence, filed a civil suit against a psychologist, physician, and social worker at the state hospital, and after two years of legal action a jury awarded him a total of almost $7 million. The state supreme court later overturned the verdict, saying that a state hospital is entitled to a certain degree of immunity in such cases.

Two investigators who studied the effects of this case found that the hospital had released 11 percent of its patients during the six months before the lawsuit was filed, 10 percent during the two years it was being litigated, but only 7 percent of its patients during the six months after the verdict (Brodsky & Poythress, 1990). Although judgments about a patient's improvement are supposed to be made on their own merits, they were apparently being affected by a heightened fear of litigation at this hospital. Clearly a malpractice suit, or the fear of one, is capable of having significant effects on clinical decisions and practice, for better or for worse.

Jury Selection

During the past fifteen years more and more lawyers have been turning to clinicians for advice on conducting trials (Gottschalk, 1981). A relatively new breed of clinical specialists, known as "jury specialists," advise lawyers on which prospective jurors are likely to favor their side and on what procedures and strategies are likely to win jurors' support during trials. The jury specialists make their suggestions on the basis of surveys, interviews, correlations between jurors' backgrounds and attitudes, and laboratory simulations of upcoming trials. It is not clear that such clinical advice is more valid than a lawyer's instincts, or indeed that either group's judgments are particularly accurate. Because some lawyers believe that clinical advice is useful, however, clinical professionals are influencing these legal procedures and decisions.

The Scope of Clinical Practice

During the past several years the legislative and judicial systems have also helped to alter the boundaries that distinguish one clinical profession from another. In particular, they have given more authority to psychologists and effectively blurred the line that once separated psychiatry from psychology. Congress, for example, has passed a group of bills that permit psychologists to receive direct reimbursements from Medicare for treating elderly and disabled people. Until recently, only psychiatrists received such payments. Similarly, a growing number of states have ruled that psychologists can admit patients to the state's hospitals, a power previously held only by psychiatrists (Cullen, 1993).

In 1991 Congress empowered the Department of Defense (DOD) to explore the most significant boundary of all between psychiatrists and psychologists—the authority to prescribe drugs, heretofore denied to psychologists. The DOD set up a trial training program for Army psychologists, initially called Cutting Edge (later changed to the Psychopharmacology Demonstration Project), in which the psychologists learned to prescribe drugs for a broad range of psychological problems, under the supervision of physicians (DeLeon, 1992). The program, which consisted of one year of formal medical school and pharmacological training followed by a one-year residency, graduated ten psychologists by its completion in 1997. The program is now being evaluated by the government and may indeed be continued.

The issue of prescription privileges for psychologists is of particular interest to the military, which suffers from a severe shortage of mental health services. From the beginning, however, everyone in the clinical field recognized the much larger implications of the trial program and of Congress's ultimate decision. Indeed, in 1996 the American Psychological Association recommended that a postdoctoral educational program in prescription services be made available to all psychologists and called for the formal certification of those psychologists who receive such training. Such recommendations have stirred heated debate both within and outside of the field (DeLeon & Wiggins, 1996; DeNelsky, 1996; Lorion, 1996; Pachman, 1996).

As the recommendations by the American Psychological Association suggest, the legislative and judicial systems do not simply take it upon themselves to interfere in the affairs of clinical professionals. In fact, psychologists have lobbied in state legislatures across the country for each of the laws and decisions that have increased their power, and psychiatrists have lobbied just as hard against the decisions. In each instance clinicians have sought the involvement of other institutions, demonstrating how intertwined the mental health system is with the various other institutions of society.

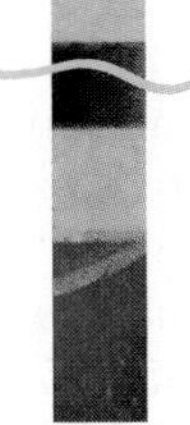

Self-Regulation: Ethics and the Mental Health Field

Discussions of the legal and mental health systems may sometimes give the impression that clinicians are uncaring autocrats who address patients' rights and needs only when they are being monitored by outside forces. This, of course, is not the case. Most clinicians care greatly about their clients and strive to help them and at the same time respect their rights and dignity.

But clinicians do face considerable obstacles in the pursuit of these goals. First, patients' rights and proper care raise complex questions that do not have simple or obvious answers. Different clients and therapists, all guided by their diverse perspectives, may indeed arrive at different answers to such questions. Second, clinicians, like other professionals, often have difficulty appreciating the full impact of their actions or altering the system in which they work. Indeed, thousands of conscientious and caring clinicians contributed to the appalling system of institutional care that marked the first half of the twentieth century—partly because they did not appreciate how misguided the system was and partly because they felt helpless to change it. A third problem is that, like other professions, the clinical field includes at least a few practitioners who place their own needs and wishes before others'. For the integrity of the profession and the

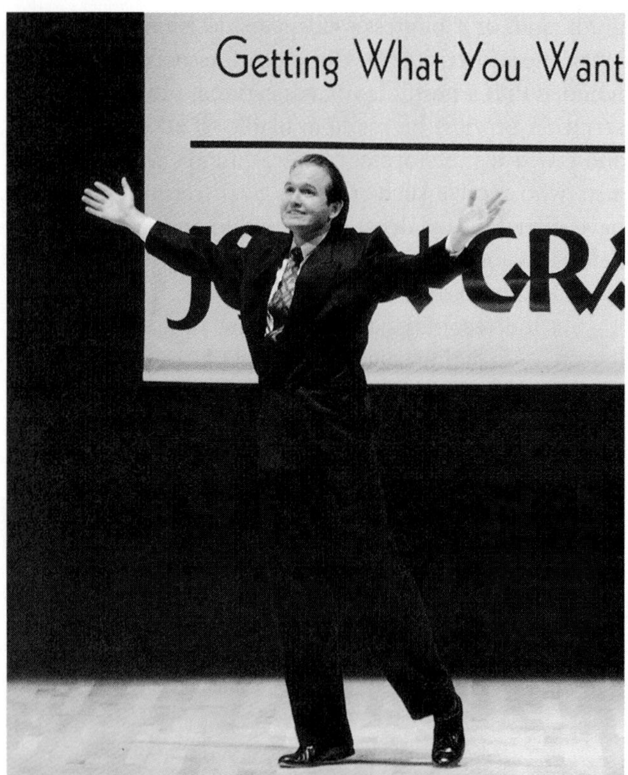

Like John Gray, author of Men Are From Mars, Women Are From Venus, *many of today's clinicians offer insights and advice to millions of people in books, workshops, television and radio programs, and tape packages. Their presentations often affect people greatly, and so they, too, are bound by the field's ethics codes to act responsibly and professionally and to base their presentations on appropriate psychological literature.*

protection of individual clients, such professionals need to be monitored and regulated.

Clinicians do not rely exclusively on the legislative and court systems to address such obstacles to proper and effective clinical practice. They also regulate themselves by continually thinking about, developing, and revising ethical guidelines for members of the field (Bersoff, 1995). Many legal decisions simply place the power of law behind these already-existing professional guidelines.

Each profession within the mental health field has a code of ethics. The code of the American Psychological Association exemplifies the kinds of issues with which the various mental health professions are concerned. It begins with a basic principle, that the goal of psychologists "is to broaden knowledge of behavior and, where appropriate, to apply it pragmatically to improve the conditions of both the individual and society" (APA, 1992). Moreover, because their "judgments and actions may affect the lives of others," the code calls for psychologists to guard against "factors that might lead to misuse of their influence." Some important points addressed by the current code are the following:

1. ***Psychologists are permitted to offer advice*** in self-help books, television and radio programs, newspaper and magazine articles, mailed material, and other nontraditional vehicles and settings, provided they do so responsibly and professionally and base their advice on appropriate psychological literature and practices.
2. ***Psychologists may not engage in fraudulent research, plagiarize the work of others, or publish fabricated data or falsified results.*** During the past two decades cases of scientific fraud or misconduct have been uncovered in all of the sciences, including psychology. These acts have led to misunderstandings of important issues, taken scientific inquiries in the wrong direction, and undermined public trust. Unfortunately, the effects of research misconduct are hard to undo even after a retraction. The impressions created by false findings may continue to influence the thinking of both the public and other scientists for years (Pfeifer & Snodgrass, 1990).
3. ***Psychologists must acknowledge their limitations with regard to patients who are disabled or whose gender, ethnicity, language, socioeconomic status, or sexual orientation differs from that of the therapist.*** This mandate often requires psychotherapists to obtain additional training or supervision, consult with an appropriate colleague, or make appropriate referrals "to ensure the competence of their services."
4. ***Psychologists who make evaluations and testify in legal cases must base their assessments on sufficient information and substantiate their findings appropriately.*** If an adequate examination of the individual in question is not possible, psychologists must make clear the limited nature of their testimony.
5. ***Psychologists are prohibited from exploiting the trust and dependency of clients and students, sexually or otherwise.*** This guideline is meant to address the broad social problem of sexual harassment, as well as the problem of therapists who take sexual advantage of clients in therapy. The current code specifically prohibits psychologists from engaging in sexual intimacies with a present or former therapy client for at least two years after the end of treatment; and even then such conduct is permissible only in "the most unusual circumstances." Moreover, psychologists may not accept as clients people with

whom they have previously engaged in sexual intimacies.

Recent years have seen an increase in the number of clients who have told state licensing boards of sexual misconduct by their therapist or sued their therapist for such behavior (Zamichow, 1993). These increases may reflect not a greater prevalence of such cases but clients' heightened awareness of and anger over the inappropriateness of such behavior. Some cases in point:

> **T**wo women patients brought claims against the same male psychologist in the mid-1980s for having sex during treatment, which he claimed was for "therapeutic benefit." In the first case . . . the patient sued for sexual misconduct, emotional distress, pain and loss of self-esteem. . . . In the second case, the patient sued the therapist for sexual misconduct, breach of contract and assault and battery. The cases were settled out of court.

> **A** woman sued a husband-and-wife psychotherapy team for sexual misconduct and mental and physical discomfort. The patient said sex with the male therapist resulted in a pregnancy and subsequent abortion, and that the woman therapist also inappropriately cuddled her. The case was settled out of court.
>
> *(Youngstrom, 1990, p. 21)*

Clients may suffer extensive emotional damage from such betrayals of trust (Lazarus, 1995; Sherman, 1993). Indeed, a growing number of therapists, perhaps as many as a quarter, are now treating clients whose primary problem is that they have previously been sexually abused in some manner by a therapist (Wincze et al., 1996; Pope & Vetter, 1991). Many such clients experience the symptoms of post-traumatic stress disorder (Hankins et al., 1994).

How many therapists actually have a sexual relationship with a client? A 1977 study found that 12.1 percent of male and 2.6 percent of female psychologists admitted having sexual contact with patients (Holroyd & Brodsky, 1977). A 1989 survey revealed that 0.9 percent of male therapists and 0.2 percent of female therapists had had sexual contact with patients (Borys & Pope, 1989). The decline revealed by these studies may indicate that fewer therapists are in fact having sexual relationships with patients, either because of a growing recognition of the inappropriateness of such behavior or because of growing fear of the legal and professional consequences of such actions (Pope & Bouhoutsos, 1986; Walker & Young, 1986). Alternatively, today's therapists may simply be less willing to admit, even anonymously, the misbehavior that is a felony in a growing number of states. Thus some reviewers conclude that the most accurate estimate of current sexual behavior is around 10 percent by male therapists and 3 percent by female therapists (Hankins et al., 1994).

Although the vast majority of therapists keep their sexual conduct within appropriate professional bounds, their ability to control private feelings and thoughts is apparently another matter (see Figure 20-3). In one survey, 72 percent of therapists reported engaging in sexual fantasy about a client, although most said that this was a rare occurrence (Pope & Brown, 1996; Pope et al., 1987). In other surveys close to 90 percent reported having been sexually attracted to a client, at least on occasion (Pope & Brown, 1996; Pope & Tabachnick, 1993; Pope et al., 1986). Although relatively few of these therapists acted on their feelings, 63 percent felt guilty, anxious, or concerned about the attraction (Pope et al., 1986).

In recent years some consumer-oriented brochures on sexual misconduct in psychotherapy have been developed to equip clients to evaluate the appropriateness of their therapists' behavior (Thorn, Shealy, & Briggs, 1993). Given the potential for damage in a sexual relationship between therapist and client, many clinicians now believe it imperative that clients learn to identify and respond assertively to the early warning signs.

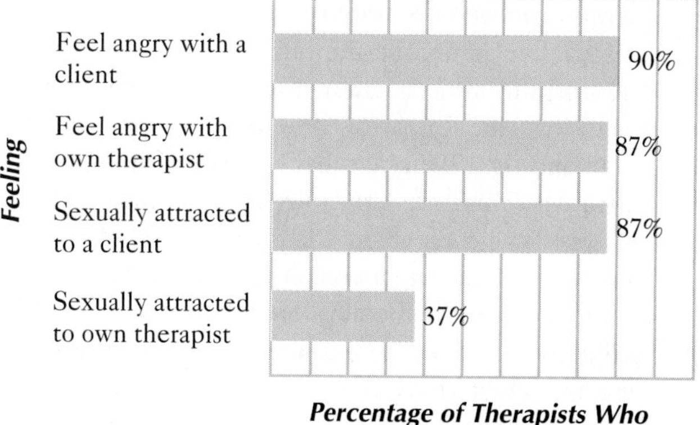

Figure 20-3 *How do therapists feel toward their clients and toward their own therapists? According to surveys, most therapists feel sexually attracted to a client on occasion, but only a minority have such feelings toward their own therapist. In contrast, almost all therapists feel angry on occasion both with clients and with their therapists. (Adapted from Pope & Brown, 1996.)*

6. ***Psychologists must adhere to the principle of confidentiality,*** long one of the most important features of therapy. All of the state courts abide by laws protecting therapist confidentiality, and in the 1996 case of *Jaffee v. Redmond,* the Supreme Court applied this principle to federal courts as well. For peace of mind and to facilitate effective therapy, clients must be able to trust that their private exchanges with a therapist will not be disclosed to others (Smith-Bell & Winslade, 1994). Thus the code of ethics states, "Psychologists have a primary obligation and must take reasonable precautions to respect the confidentiality rights of those with whom they work or consult."

There are times, however, when the principle of complete confidentiality must be compromised. A therapist in training, for example, must discuss cases on a regular basis with a supervisor. Clients, in turn, must be informed when such procedures are in effect. A second exception arises in cases of outpatients who are clearly dangerous, even homicidal. In such cases, a therapist often must breach confidentiality.

A further qualification of the confidentiality principle has been added as a result of a 1976 ruling by the California Supreme Court. The case of *Tarasoff v. Regents of the University of California,* one of the most important cases affecting client-therapist relationships, concerned an outpatient at a University of California hospital. He had confided to his therapist that he wanted to harm his former girlfriend, Tanya Tarasoff. Several days after terminating therapy, the former patient fulfilled his promise. He stabbed Tanya Tarasoff to death.

Should confidentiality have been breached in this case? The therapist, in fact, felt that it should. Campus police were notified, but the patient was released after some questioning. In their suit against the hospital and therapist, the victim's parents argued that the therapist should have also warned them and their daughter that the patient intended to harm Ms. Tarasoff. The court agreed: "The protective privilege ends where the public peril begins." In addition to ordering a breach of confidentiality, this ruling requires the therapist to perform an extremely difficult feat: to determine when "a patient poses a serious danger of violence to others."

In partial concession to the *Tarasoff* ruling, the current code of ethics for psychologists declares that therapists should reveal confidential information, even without the client's consent, when it is necessary "to protect the patient or client or others from harm." Since the *Tarasoff* ruling, California's courts have further held that therapists are obligated to protect persons who are in close proximity to a client's intended victim and thus in danger. A child, for example, is likely to be endangered when a client plans to assault the child's mother. The courts have also held that the *duty to protect* applies only when the intended victim is readily identifiable, as opposed to the public at large. Futhermore, the duty does not apply when violence is unforeseeable or when the object of a client's intended violence is property rather than a person. A number of other states have either adopted these California court rulings or modified them (Bloom, 1990; Pietrofesa et al., 1990). Only a few states have rejected the California principles outright. Moreover, many states have adopted a "duty to protect bill," designed to clarify the standards for confidentiality and action by all mental health professionals and protect them from certain civil suits (Monahan,1993).

Most of today's therapists agree that it is often appropriate to breach confidentiality. In one survey, almost 80 percent of the therapists reported having broken confidentiality when a client was suicidal, 62 percent when child abuse was occurring, and 58 percent when a client was homicidal (Pope et al., 1987).

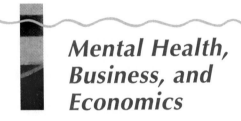

Mental Health, Business, and Economics

The legislative and judicial systems are not the only social institutions with which mental health professionals interact. Among the others that influence and are influenced by clinical practice and study are the business and economic sectors of society. Moreover, health care in all its varieties is itself a business, and many decisions in the clinical field are based on economic considerations.

Business and Mental Health

Psychological disorders are listed among the ten leading work-related disorders and injuries in the United States (Millar, 1984). In fact, almost 12 percent of all employees are said to experience psychological problems that are serious enough to affect their work performance (Kemp, 1994). Psychological problems contribute to 60 percent of all absenteeism from work, up to 90 percent of industrial accidents, and 65 percent of work terminations (Kemp, 1994). Alcohol abuse and other substance-related disorders are particularly damaging, increasing absenteeism by as much as six times, accidents by four times, and workers' compensation claims by five times (Martin, Kraft, & Roman, 1994; Wright, 1984). The business world has turned to clinical professionals to help clarify, prevent, and remedy such problems (Hantula & Reilly, 1996; Millar, 1990, 1984; NIOSH, 1988, 1985). Two programs that have gained broad acceptance in the past two decades are employee assistance programs and stress-reduction and problem-solving seminars.

Employee assistance programs are run either by mental health professionals who are employed directly by a company or by consulting mental health agencies (Canty, 1996). Companies publicize the availability of such services in the workplace, educate workers about psychological dysfunctioning, and teach supervisors how to identify and refer workers who are in psychological distress. Businesses believe that employee assistance programs save them money in the long run by preventing psychological problems from interfering with work performance (Shain, 1994), although this claim has yet to undergo broad, systematic research (Kemp, 1994). Employee assistance programs also appear to help businesses curtail the costs of mental health and substance abuse insurance benefits, which have otherwise risen steadily (Foster-Higgins, 1991).

Stress-reduction and ***problem-solving seminars*** are workshops or group sessions in which mental health professionals teach employees coping, problem-solving, and stress-reduction techniques (Kagan et al., 1995). Programs of this kind are just as likely to be organized for higher-level executives as for mid-level managers and assembly-line workers. Often groups of workers are required to attend such workshops, which may run for several days, and are given time off from their jobs to do so. Again, the expectation is that these programs will save money by helping workers develop coping skills that lead to a healthier state of mind, less dysfunction on the job, and better job performance.

Economics and Mental Health

We have already seen how government-level economic decisions influence the mental health field's treatment of people with severe mental disorders (see Figure 20–4). The desire by state and federal governments to reduce

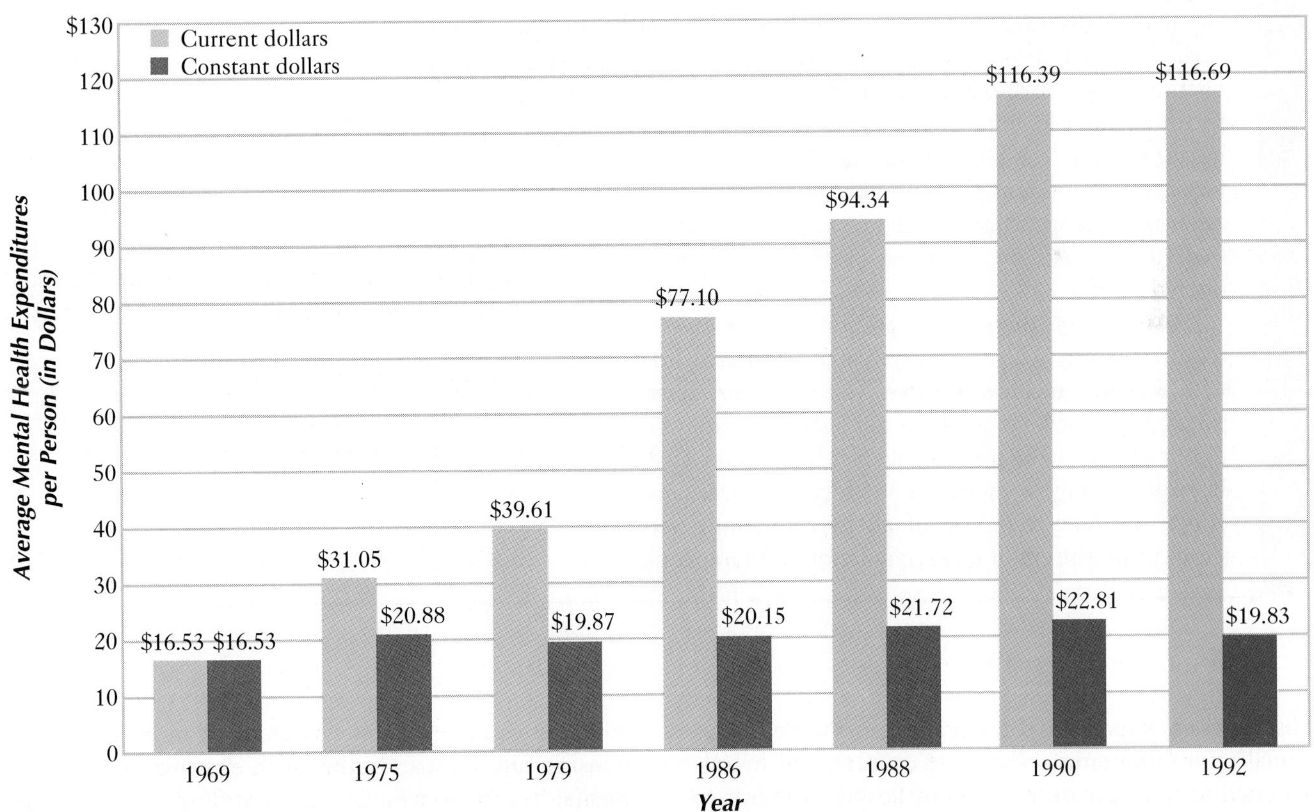

Figure 20-4 *The average amount of money spent for mental health services annually per person in the United States increased sevenfold, from $16.53 in 1969 to $116.69 in 1992. However, a closer look reveals an alarming trend. The amount spent stopped increasing during the 1990s. Moreover, when adjustments are made for inflation and expenditures are stated in 1969 dollars, the amount spent per person actually fell in the 1990s from $22.81 to $19.83, close to the amount back in 1969. (Adapted from Redick et al., 1996, 1992.)*

BOX 20-4 The Itemized Statement in Clinical Psychiatry: A New Concept in Billing

(In this article, by Robert S. Hoffman, M.D., which originally appeared in The Journal of Irreproducible Results, *1980, the psychiatrist's biting wit is equaled only by his sense of outrage over the growing demands made by insurance companies.)*

Due to the rapidly escalating costs of health care delivery, there has been increasing pressure on physicians to document and justify their charges for professional services. This has created a number of serious problems, particularly in the field of psychiatry. Chief among these is the breach of confidentiality that arises when sensitive clinical information is provided to third-party insurance carriers, e.g. the patient's diagnosis or related details about his/her psychiatric disorder. Even when full disclosure of such information is made, insurance carriers frequently deny benefits because the description of the treatment appears imprecise or inadequate. There also has been some criticism of the standard hourly fee-for-service, the argument being that psychiatrists, like other medical specialists, should be required to adjust their fees depending upon the particular treatment offered.

In view of these considerations, a method is required which will bring psychiatric billing in line with accepted medical practice. The procedure illustrated below, which we have successfully employed in our clinic for the past two years, achieves this goal. It requires only a modest investment in time and effort: the tape-recording of all psychotherapy sessions, transcription of tapes, tabulation of therapeutic interventions, and establishment of a relative value scale for the commonly used maneuvers. This can easily be managed by two full-time medical billing personnel per psychiatrist. The method, in our hands, has been found to increase collections from third-party carriers by 65% and to raise a typical psychiatrist's annual net income almost to the level of a municipal street sweeper or plumber's assistant.

Below is a specimen monthly statement illustrating these principles:

CALVIN L. SKOLNIK, M.D., INC.
A Psychiatry Corporation

Jan. 5, 1978

Mr. Sheldon Rosenberg
492 West Maple Dr.
East Orange, N.J.

Dear Mr. Rosenberg:

In response to the request by your insurer, Great Lakes Casualty and Surety Co., for more precise documentation of professional services rendered, I have prepared the enclosed itemization for the month of December. I trust that this will clarify the situation sufficiently for your benefit payments to be resumed.

Until next Tuesday at 11:00, I remain

Cordially,

CALVIN L. SKOLNIK, M.D.

costs was an important consideration in the deinstitutionalization programs around the country, which contributed to the premature release of hospital patients to communities unprepared to provide the needed treatment. Economic considerations by government agencies affect other kinds of clients and forms of treatment as well.

On the one hand, government funding for people with mental disorders has risen sharply over the past three decades, from $3 billion in 1969 to $61 billion today (Torrey, 1997; Redick et al., 1992). On the other hand, much of that money is spent on income support, housing subsidies, and other such expenses, rather than mental health services. Government funding for services may even be decreasing currently. In fact, government funding today covers less than half the cost of all mental health services, leaving much of the expense to individual patients and their private insurance companies (Taube, 1990).

The growing economic role of private insurance companies has a significant effect on the way clinicians go about their work. In an effort to reduce their expendi-

Charges		
140 clarifications	@ .25	35.00
157 restatements	@ .25	39.25
17 broad-focus questions	@ .35	5.95
42 narrow-focus questions	@ .30	12.60
86 reflections of dominant emotional theme	@ .35	30.10
38 resolutions of inconsistencies	@ .45	17.10
22 pointings out of nonverbal communications	@ .40	8.80
187 encouragements to say more	@ .15	28.05
371 sympathetic nods with furrowed brow	@ .10	37.10
517 acknowledgments of information reception (Uh-huhs, Umhmmm, etc.)	@ .08	41.36
24 interpretations of unconscious defense configurations	@ .30	7.20
16 absolution for evil deeds	@ .50	8.00
2 pieces of advice	@ .75	1.50
6 expressions of personal feelings	@ .50	3.00
2 personal reminiscences	@ .65	1.30
35 misc. responses (sighs, grunts, belches, etc.)	@ .20	7.00
7 listening to remarks disparaging therapist's appearance, personal habits, or technique	@ 1.75	12.25
12 listening to sarcastic remarks about psychiatry	@ 1.00	12.00
3 listening to psychiatrist jokes	@ .80	2.40
3 telephone calls to therapist	@ .15	.45
1 telephone call to therapist at especially inopportune moment	@ 10.50	10.50
22 Kleenex tissues	@ .005	.11
1 ashtray	@ 3.50	3.50
1 filling and repainting of 1 ashtray-size dent in wall	@ 27.50	27.50
1 shampooing of soft drink stain on carpet	@ 15.00	15.00
1 letter of excuse from work	@ 2.50	2.50
2 surcharges for unusually boring or difficult sessions	@ 35.00	70.00
Subtotal: charges		$438.52
Credits		
4 unusually interesting anecdotes	@ .45	1.80
3 good jokes	@ .50	1.50
1 item of gossip about another patient which was found useful in her therapy	@ 3.50	3.50
1 apology for sarcastic remark	@ 1.00	1.00
1 use of case history at American Psychiatric Association convention		10.00
1/2 chicken salad sandwich on whole wheat w/mayo	@ 1.75	.88
7 bummed cigarettes (65¢/pack		.23
1 damaged Librium tablet, returned unused		.10
Subtotal: credits		$18.99
Total: **PLEASE REMIT—**		$419.53

tures and to monitor what they are paying for, many of these companies have developed ***managed care systems,*** in which the insurance company often determines such issues as which therapists clients may choose, the cost of sessions, and the number of sessions a client may be reimbursed for.

Many insurance companies, particularly those with managed care systems, have instituted ***peer review procedures,*** in which a panel of clinicians who essentially work for the insurance company periodically review a therapist's report of a client's treatment and recommend that insurance benefits be either continued or terminated. Typically, insurers require details from the therapist's session notes, often including intimate personal information about the patient (Stoline & Sharfstein, 1996; Appelbaum, 1993; Newman & Bricklin, 1991).

Many therapists and clients dislike managed care programs and peer reviews. They claim that the reports that therapists must make breach confidentiality, even when efforts are made to safeguard anonymity, and that the value of therapy in a given case is sometimes difficult to convey in a brief report (see Box 20-4). They also argue that managed care priorities and the peer review process inevitably shorten therapy, even if longer-term treatment would be advisable in particular cases. Indeed, as in the medical arena, some horror stories are now emerging of mental patients who are prematurely cut off from mental health services by their managed care program. Still others worry that the system actually represents a regulation of therapy by insurance companies rather than by therapists.

The Person Within the Profession

The actions and goals of clinical researchers and practitioners not only influence and are influenced by other institutions but are closely tied to their personal needs and goals. Abnormal psychology is a discipline in which the human strengths, imperfections, wisdom, and clumsiness of its professionals combine to influence the effectiveness of the profession as a whole. We have seen that the needs and preferences of these human beings influence their responses to clients' concerns, their theoretical orientations, and the kinds of clients they choose to work with. And we have also noted that personal leanings sometimes overcome professional standards and in extreme cases lead clinical scientists to commit research fraud and clinical practitioners to engage in sexual misconduct with clients.

A national survey on the mental health of therapists found that 84 percent of them reported being in therapy at least once (Pope & Brown, 1996; Pope & Tabachnick, 1994). Their reasons for seeking therapy were largely the same as those of other clients: emotional problems, depression, and anxiety topped the list. In fact, 61 percent of the therapists reported having experienced clinical depression, 29 percent reported having had suicidal feelings, and 4 percent said they had attempted suicide (Pope & Tabachnick, 1994). In related research a number of therapists in treatment reported being brought up in dysfunctional families, sometimes marked by physical and sexual abuse, parental alcoholism, institutionalization of a parent in a mental hospital, or death of a family member (Elliot & Guy, 1993). Many further reported experiencing significant distress in adult life.

Another survey revealed that all therapists feel like imposters at some point in their career. Some 87 percent feel like fakes at least occasionally, and 18 percent feel that way frequently (Gibbs & DeVries, 1987). The survey also seemed to suggest that such feelings are not related to the fact that therapists must appear well adjusted and highly educated. Rather, they stem from personal anxieties and issues.

The science and profession of abnormal psychology has lofty goals: to understand, predict, and change abnormal functioning. But we must not lose sight of the context in which its activities are conducted. Mental health researchers and clinicians are human beings, living within a society of human beings, working to serve human beings. The mixture of discovery, misdirection, promise, and frustration that we have encountered in these chapters is thus to be expected. When one thinks about it, could the study and treatment of human behavior really proceed in any other way?

Crossroads

Clinical researchers and professionals once conducted their work in relative isolation. Today, however, their activities are intimately tied to other institutions, such as the legislative, judicial, and economic systems. One reason for this growing interconnectedness is that the clinical field has achieved a remarkable level of acceptance in our society. Clinicians now provide direct services to millions of people; they have much to say about almost every aspect of society, from education to ecology; and they are widely looked to as sources of expertise. When a field achieves such acceptance, it inevitably influences the way other institutions are run. It also risks becoming so influential that other institutions jump in to monitor and restrict its activities.

Today, when people with psychological problems seek help from a therapist, they are entering a system of interrelated parts. Just as their problems have grown within a social structure, the nature and outcome of their treatment will be affected by all parts of a broader system—the therapist's values and needs, legal and economic forces, societal attitudes, and yet other forces. These many forces influence clinical research as well.

The impact of this broad system on an individual's psychological needs can be positive or negative, like a family's impact on one of its members. When the system protects a client's rights and ensures confidentiality, for example, it is serving the client well. When, however, economic, legal, or other societal forces reduce treatment options, cut off treatment prematurely, or stigmatize a person, the system is exacerbating the person's problems.

The enormous growth and impact of the mental health profession makes it all the more important to hold an accurate perception of its many strengths and weaknesses. As we have seen throughout this book, the field has acquired an impressive body of knowledge, especially during the past several decades. What mental health professionals do not know and cannot do, however, still outweigh what they do know and can do. Everyone who turns to the clinicial field—directly or indirectly—must recognize that it is young and imperfect. Society cannot be faulted for being vastly curious about behavior and regularly seeking information, expertise, and help from this field, as long as its members fully understand that the field is truly at a *crossroads.*

Chapter Review

1. ***The legal system and the mental health field*** The mental health profession interacts with the legislative and judicial institutions in two primary ways. First, clinicians may be called upon to help evaluate the mental stability of people accused of crimes. Second, the legislative and judicial branches of government help regulate mental health care.

2. ***Criminal commitment*** The punishment of persons convicted of crimes depends on the assumption that individuals are *responsible* for their acts and are *capable* of defending themselves in court. Evaluations by clinicians to help judges and juries decide the culpability of defendants often result in *criminal commitment.*

   A. If defendants are judged to have been mentally unstable at the time they committed a crime, they may be found *not guilty by reason of insanity* and placed in a treatment facility rather than a prison.

   (1) "Insanity" is a legal term, defined by legislators, not by clinicians. In federal courts and about half the state courts, insanity is judged in accordance with the *M'Naghten rule.* This standard holds that defendants were insane at the time of a criminal act if they did not know the nature or quality of the act or did not know right from wrong at the time they committed it. Other states use the broader *American Law Institute* test.

   (2) The insanity defense has been criticized on several grounds, and some states have chosen to permit a verdict of *guilty but mentally ill.* Defendants who receive this verdict are sentenced to prison with the proviso that they will also receive psychological treatment. Another verdict option is *guilty with diminished capacity.* And in some states convicted *sex offenders* are considered to have a mental disorder and are assigned to treatment in a mental health facility.

   B. Regardless of their state of mind at the time of the crime, defendants may be *mentally incompetent* to stand trial, that is, incapable of fully understanding the charges or legal proceedings that confront them. If so, they are typically sent to a mental hospital until they are competent to stand trial. A ruling by the Supreme Court ensures that incompetent persons cannot be held in a mental hospital indefinitely.

3. ***Civil commitment*** The legal system also has significant influence on the clinical profession. First, the legal system may be called upon to commit noncriminals to mental hospitals for treatment, a process called *civil commitment.* Society allows involuntary commitment of people considered to be *in need of treatment* and *dangerous to themselves or others.* Statutes governing civil commitment procedures vary from state to state, but a *minimum standard of proof*—clear and convincing evidence of the necessity of commitment—has been defined by the Supreme Court.

4. ***Protecting patients' rights*** The courts and legislatures significantly affect the mental health profession by specifying legal rights to which patients are entitled. The rights that have received the most attention are the *right to treatment* and the *right to refuse treatment.*

5. ***Other clinical-legal interactions*** Mental health and legal professionals also cross paths in three other areas. First, *malpractice suits* against therapists have proliferated

in recent years. Second, lawyers may solicit the advice of mental health professionals regarding the selection of jurors and case strategies. Third, the legislative and judicial systems help define the scope of clinical practice.

6. ***Self-regulation: The code of ethics*** Each clinical profession has a code of ethics. The psychologists' code includes prohibitions against engaging in fraudulent research and against exploiting the trust and dependence of clients and students, sexually or otherwise. It also establishes guidelines for respecting patient *confidentiality.* The case of *Tarasoff v. Regents of the University of California* has determined some of the circumstances in which therapists must break confidentiality in order to protect the public.

7. ***Mental health, business, and economics*** Clinical practice and study also intersect with business and economic institutions.

A. Clinicians are often employed to help identify and address psychological problems in the workplace.

B. Private insurance companies are setting up *managed care programs* whose structure and reimbursement procedures influence, and often reduce, the duration and focus of therapy.

8. ***The person within the profession*** Mental health activities are affected by the personal needs, values, and goals of the human beings who provide the clinical services. These factors inevitably affect the choices, direction, and even quality of their work.

Thought and Afterthought

The Violence of Mice and Men and Women

Is the tendency to be violent inherited? For years, men tended to be more aggressive and to enjoy violence more than women, suggesting that violence may have at least some biological causes. But in recent times violent behaviors and interests have become increasingly common among women, suggesting sociocultural and psychological factors as well. Once Spain's bullfighting academies opened their doors to women, for example, competitors like Cristina Sanchez (*right*) found that they had a great passion and capacity for the violent sport.

A striking new wrinkle on the subject comes from the laboratories at Johns Hopkins University. Investigating the role of *nitric oxide* in the brain damage suffered by stroke victims, researchers created mice who lacked the gene necessary to produce this neurotransmitter (Nelson et al., 1995). The unexpected result: male mice who lacked nitric oxide became violent rapists and mouse murderers. The "monster mice," as they were nicknamed, attacked, bit, wrestled, and chased other mice in their cages. Female mice were unaffected by a lack of nitric oxide. The researchers theorized that nitric oxide probably plays a key role in the regulation of male aggressive behavior.

Afterthoughts: If it turns out that genetic abnormalities also predispose some humans to violent acts, should those people be held responsible for their criminal acts the same as other people are? . . . If culprit genes were found in humans and were clearly linked to aggression, could identified individuals technically be forced into treatment under the present standards of civil commitment?

Therapists Under Attack

(Drawing by W. Miller; ©1983 The New Yorker Magazine, Inc.)

Between 12 and 14 percent of therapists have been attacked by their patients at least once in private therapy, and an even larger percentage have been assaulted in mental hospitals (Tryon, 1987; Bernstein, 1981). One study found that 40 percent of psychiatrists had been assaulted at least once during their career (Menninger, 1993). Patients have used a variety of weapons in their attacks, including such common objects as shoes, lamps, fire extinguishers, and canes. Some have used guns or knives and have severely wounded or even killed a therapist.

Many therapists who have been attacked continue to feel anxious and insecure in their work for a long time afterward. Some try to be more selective in accepting patients and look for cues that signal impending violence. One therapist even studied karate for a year and a half (Tryon, 1987).

Afterthoughts: What do these attacks suggest about therapists' ability to predict dangerousness? . . . Such attacks seem to be on the rise. Why? . . . How might lingering anxiety affect the behavior and effectiveness of clinicians who have been attacked?

Frankly Speaking

When a man says that he is Jesus or Napoleon . . . he is labeled psychotic and locked up in the madhouse. Freedom of speech is only for normal people.

—**Thomas S. Szasz,**
The Second Sin

Afterthoughts: Do people have a right to hold bizarre ideas? . . . How might Szasz be oversimplifying the issue of civil commitment and patients' rights? . . . People do not have the right to yell "Fire" in a public place. What other "rights" are restricted by our society, and how does the right to delusional thought and speech compare to them?

Glossary

Abnormal psychology The scientific study of abnormal behavior in order to describe, predict, explain, and ultimately prevent or alter abnormal patterns of functioning.

Acetylcholine A neurotransmitter that has been implicated in depression and in dementia.

Acute stress disorder An anxiety disorder in which fear and related symptoms are experienced soon after a traumatic event and last less than a month.

Addiction Physical dependence on a substance, marked by such features as tolerance, withdrawal symptoms during abstinence, or both.

Affect A subjective experience of emotion or mood.

Affectual awareness One component of sexual therapy for hypoactive sexual desire or sexual aversion in which the client becomes aware of his or her negative emotions regarding sex.

Aftercare A program of posthospitalization care and treatment out in the community.

Agoraphobia A pervasive and complex phobia that makes people avoid public places or situations in which escape might be difficult or help unavailable should they develop incapacitating or embarrassing paniclike symptoms.

Agoraphobia without history of panic disorder An agoraphobic pattern that does not have its origin in a panic attack.

Akathisia A Parkinsonian symptom consisting of a very high degree of restlessness and agitation and great discomfort in the limbs.

Alarm stage An increase of activity in the sympathetic nervous system in the presence of a perceived threat. See also **General adaptation syndrome.**

Alcohol Any beverage containing ethyl alcohol, including beer, wine, and liquor.

Alcohol dehydrogenase An enzyme that breaks down alcohol in the stomach before it enters the blood. Women have significantly less of this enzyme than men and therefore tend to become more intoxicated after ingesting an equal dose of alcohol.

Alcohol withdrawal delirium A dramatic reaction experienced by some people who are alcohol-dependent. It occurs within three days of cessation or reduction of drinking and consists of mental confusion, clouded consciousness, and terrifying visual hallucinations. Also known as delirium tremens (DTs).

Alcoholics Anonymous (AA) A self-help organization that provides support and guidance for persons with alcohol abuse or dependence.

Alcoholism A pattern of behavior in which a person abuses or develops a dependence on alcohol.

Alogia A symptom in schizophrenia, characterized by a decrease in speech or speech content.

Alpha waves Brain waves characteristic of relaxed wakefulness.

Alprazolam (Xanax) A benzodiazepine drug, also shown to be effective in the treatment of panic disorder.

Altruistic suicide Suicide committed by people very well integrated into the social structure who intentionally sacrifice their lives for the well-being of society.

Alzheimer's disease The most common form of dementia, sometimes occurring before old age.

Amenorrhea The cessation of menstruation. It that often accompanies anorexia nervosa in women.

Amnesia Loss of memory. See also **Anterograde, Dissociative,** and **Retrograde Amnesia.**

Amnestic disorders Organic disorders in which memory impairment is the primary symptom.

Amniocentesis A prenatal procedure used to test the amniotic fluid that surrounds the fetus, in order to detect the possibility of birth defects.

Amphetamine A stimulant drug that is manufactured in the laboratory.

Amphetamine-induced psychotic disorder A syndrome caused by a high dose of amphetamines that closely mimics schizophrenia and includes hallucinations and motor hyperactivity.

Amygdala The structure in the brain's limbic system that gives rise to emotional behavior and that may also regulate the link between arousal and memory.

Anaclitic depression A pattern of symptoms that includes sadness, withdrawal, weight loss, and trouble sleeping and that is associated with separation from one's mother before the age of 6 years.

Anal stage In psychoanalytic theory, the second 18 months of life, during which the child's focus of pleasure shifts to the anus, and libidinal gratification comes from retaining and passing feces.

Analogue experiment An investigation in which the experimenter induces laboratory subjects to behave in ways that resemble real-life abnormal behavior.

Anatomical brain disorders Problems stemming from abnormal size or shape of certain brain regions.

Anesthesia A lessening or loss of sensation for touch or pain.

Anomic suicide (Anomie) Suicide committed by individuals whose social environment fails to provide stability.

Anorexia nervosa A disorder characterized by the relentless pursuit of extreme thinness and by an extreme loss of weight.

Anoxia A complication of birth in which the baby is deprived of oxygen.

Antabuse (Disulfiram) A drug that is relatively benign when taken by itself, but causes intense nausea, vomiting, increased heart rate, and dizziness when taken with alcohol. It is often taken by people who are trying to refrain from drinking alcohol.

Antagonist drug Any drug that blocks or changes the effects of another drug.

Anterograde amnesia The inability to learn and remember new information. It sometimes follows a shock or trauma.

Anthropology The study of human cultures and institutions.

Antianxiety drugs Psychotropic drugs that reduce tension and anxiety.

Antibipolar drug A drug that helps stabilize the moods of people suffering from a bipolar mood disorder. See also **Lithium.**

Antibodies Bodily chemicals that seek out and destroy antigens such as bacteria or viruses.

Antidepressant drugs Psychotropic drugs that lift the mood of depressed people.

Antigens Foreign invaders such as bacteria and viruses that stimulate an immune response.

Antipsychotic drugs Psychotropic drugs that help correct grossly confused or distorted thinking.

Antisocial personality disorder A personality disorder characterized by a pervasive pattern of disregard for and violation of other people's rights.

Anxiety Emotional state characterized by fear, apprehension, and physiological arousal.

Anxiety disorders Disorders in which anxiety is a central symptom.

Anxiety-sensitivity According to cognitive-behavioral theorists, the tendency of certain individuals to become preoccupied with their bodily sensations, lose their ability to assess them logically, and interpret them as potentially harmful, leaving some more likely to develop panic attacks.

Anxiolytics Drugs that reduce anxiety (from "anxiety" and the Greek *lytikos,* able to loosen or dissolve). See also **Antianxiety drugs.**

Aphasia A common symptom in some kinds of dementia, characterized by difficulty producing the names of individuals and objects.

Aphrodisiac A substance that is thought to increase the sex drive. Over the centuries people have considered many substances to be aphrodisiacs, but none has been proven to increase the sex drive.

Arbitrary inference An error in logic in which a person draws negative conclusions on the basis of little or even contrary evidence. It may contribute to some cases of depression.

Assertiveness training A cognitive-behavioral approach to increasing assertive behavior that is socially desirable.

Assessment The collection of relevant information about a client or subject.

Asthma Medical problem marked by constricting of the trachea and bronchi, resulting in shortness of breath, wheezing, coughing, and choking.

Asylum A type of institution first established in the sixteenth century to provide care for persons with mental disorders. Most became virtual prisons in which patients endured degrading conditions.

Attention-deficit/hyperactivity disorder (ADHD) A disorder characterized by a persistent inability to focus attention, overactive and impulsive behavior, or both.

Attribution The explaining of the things we see going on around us as the result of particular causes. The attributions may then influence the way we feel about ourselves and others.

Atypical antipsychotic drugs A new group of antipsychotic drugs (the most common being clozapine and resperidone), which appear to cause few extrapyramidal symptoms. These drugs are labeled "atypical" because they have a different mechanism of action than the traditional drugs.

Auditory hallucination A hallucination in which a person hears sounds and voices that are not actually present.

Augmentative communication systems A method for teaching individuals with autism, mental retardation, or cerebral palsy to communicate by pointing to pictures, symbols, or written words that represent objects or needs.

Aura A warning sensation that may precede a migraine headache.

Autism A pervasive developmental disorder characterized by extreme unresponsiveness to others, poor communication skills, and behavior that is highly restricted and repetitive.

Autoerotic asphyxia A fatal lack of oxygen that people inadvertently self-induce while hanging, suffocating, or strangling themselves during masturbation.

Automatic thoughts Unbidden cognitions that come into the mind, some comforting and some upsetting.

Autonomic learning The inadvertent conditioning of particular responses in the autonomic nervous system.

Autonomic nervous system (ANS) The extensive network of nerve fibers that connects the central nervous system to all the other organs of the body.

Aversion therapy A behavioral technique that helps clients acquire anxiety responses to stimuli that they have been finding too attractive.

Avoidance behavior Behavior that removes or avoids anxiety-producing objects or situations.

Avoidant personality disorder A personality disorder characterized by a chronic and pervasive pattern of inhibition in social situations, feelings of inadequacy, and extreme sensitivity to negative evaluation.

Avolition A symptom in schizophrenia, characterized by apathy, particularly a lack of energy and interest in normal goals.

Axon The long fiber that extends from the body of the neuron. Messages, or impulses, travel down it to the nerve endings.

B-cell Lymphocyte that produces antibodies.

Barbiturates Addictive sedative-hypnotic drugs used to reduce anxiety or to help persons fall asleep.

Baroreceptors Sensitive nerves in the arteries responsible for alerting the brain when blood pressure becomes too high.

Baseline data An individual's initial response level on a test or scale.

Basic irrational assumptions According to rational emotive therapy, inappropriate assumptions guiding the way in which one acts. They may prejudice a person's chances for happiness and success.

Battery A comprehensive group of tests, each of which targets a specific skill area.

Behavioral assessment The collection of information about specific dysfunctional behaviors a person engages in.

Behavioral medicine A field of treatment that combines psychological and physical interventions to treat or prevent medical problems.

Behavioral model A theoretical perspective that emphasizes ingrained behavior and the ways in which it is learned.

Behavioral self-control training (BSCT) An approach to treating alcohol abuse in which clients are taught to monitor their own drinking behavior, set appropriate limits on their drinking, control their rate of drinking, and apply alternative coping behaviors.

Behavioral therapy (Behavior modification) A therapeutic approach that views the goal of therapy as identifying the client's specific problem-causing behaviors and either modifying them or replacing them with more appropriate ones.

Behaviors The responses that an organism makes to its environment.

Bender Visual-Motor Gestalt Test A neuropsychological test in which a subject is asked to copy a set of nine simple designs and later reproduce the designs from memory.

Benzodiazepines The most common antianxiety drugs. The group includes Valium, Xanax, and Librium.

Bereavement The process of working through the grief that one feels when a loved one dies.

Beta-amyloid protein A small molecule that forms sphere-shaped deposits called senile plaques. These deposits collect in excessive numbers in the spaces between neurons in people with Alzheimer's disease, interfering with memory and learning.

Beta blocker A drug that reduces the physical symptoms of anxiety by blocking the reception of norepinephrine in the brain.

Bilateral electroconvulsive therapy (ECT) A form of electroconvulsive therapy in which one electrode is applied to each side of the forehead, and electrical current is passed through the brain's frontal lobes.

Binge-eating disorder A type of eating disorder in which a person displays a pattern of binge eating without accompanying compensatory behaviors. Listed in the DSM-IV appendix, designated for further study.

Binge-eating/purging type anorexia nervosa A type of anorexia nervosa in which people engage in eating binges but still lose excessive weight by forcing themselves to vomit after meals or by abusing laxatives or diuretics.

Biofeedback A treatment technique in which the client is given systematic information about key physiological responses as they occur and learns to control the responses voluntarily.

Biological challenge A procedure used to induce symptoms of panic in subjects or clients by having them exercise vigorously or perform other tasks in the presence of a therapist or researcher.

Biological model The theoretical perspective that cites organic processes as the key to human behavior.

Biological therapy The use of physical and chemical procedures to help people overcome psychological difficulties.

Bipolar disorder A disorder marked by alternating or intermixed periods of mania and depression.

Bipolar I disorder A type of bipolar disorder in which a person experiences manic and major depressive episodes.

Bipolar II disorder A type of bipolar disorder in which a person experiences mildly manic (hypomanic) episodes that alternate with major depressive episodes.

Birth complications Biological conditions during birth, including anoxia and extreme prematurity, that can compromise the physical and psychological well-being of the child.

Blind design An experiment in which subjects do not know whether they are in the experimental or the control condition.

Blocking A symptom associated with schizophrenia in which thoughts seem to disappear from memory and statements end in silence before they can be completed.

Blunted affect A symptom of schizophrenia in which a person displays less emotion—anger, sadness, joy—than other people.

Body dysmorphic disorder (Dysmorphobia) A somatoform disorder marked by excessive worry that some aspect of one's physical appearance is defective.

Borderline personality disorder A personality disorder characterized by a pervasive pattern of instability in interpersonal relationships, self-image, and moods, and marked impulsivity.

Brain stem The region of the central nervous system that connects the spinal cord with the cerebrum.

Brain wave The oscillations of electrical potential, as measured by an electroencephalogram, that are created by neurons in the brain.

Breathing-related sleep disorder A sleep disorder in which sleep is frequently disrupted by a breathing problem, causing excessive sleepiness or insomnia.

Brief psychotic disorder Psychotic symptoms that appear suddenly after a very stressful event or a period of emotional turmoil and last anywhere from a few hours to a month.

Briquet's syndrome See **Somatization disorder.**

Bulimia nervosa A disorder characterized by frequent eating binges, during which the person uncontrollably consumes large quantities of food, followed by forced vomiting or other extreme compensatory behaviors to avoid gaining weight.

Caffeine A stimulant drug that is commonly consumed in the form of coffee, tea, cola, and chocolate.

Cannabis drugs Drugs produced from the different varieties of the hemp plant. They cause a mixture of intoxicating, hallucinogenic, depressant, and stimulant effects.

Case management A full-service form of community treatment that seems to be particularly helpful for persons with schizophrenia. In addition to offering therapy and advice, teaching problem-solving and social skills, and making sure that medications are taken properly, case managers help coordinate community services, guide clients through the community system, and, perhaps most important, act as advocates for the clients.

Case study A detailed account of one person's life and psychological problems.

Catatonia Extreme psychomotor symptoms found in some forms of schizophrenia.

Catatonic excitement A form of catatonia in which a person moves excitedly, sometimes with wild waving of the arms and legs.

Catatonic schizophrenia A type of schizophrenia in which severe psychomotor disturbances dominate.

Catatonic stupor A symptom associated with schizophrenia in which a person becomes almost totally unresponsive to the environment, remaining motionless and silent for long stretches of time.

Catecholamine theory The view that unipolar depression is related to low activity of norepinephrine (a catecholamine) in the brain.

Catharsis In psychodynamic therapy, the reliving of past repressed feelings in order to settle internal conflicts and overcome problems.

Central nervous system The brain and spinal cord.

Cerebral cortex The outer layer of the cerebrum, or upper portion of the brain, also known as the gray matter. It is associated with higher cognitive functions.

Checking compulsion A compulsion in which people feel compelled to check the same things over and over.

Child abuse The intentional, nonaccidental use of physical or psychological force by an adult on a child, often aimed at hurting, injuring, or destroying the child.

Chlorpromazine A phenothiazine drug commonly used for treating schizophrenia. Marketed as Thorazine.

Chromosomes The structures within a cell that contain genes.

Circadian rhythm sleep disorder A sleep disorder in which people experience excessive sleepiness or insomnia as the result of a mismatch between the sleep-wake cycle in their environment and their own circadian sleep-wake cycle.

Circadian rhythms Internal "clocks" consisting of recurrent biological fluctuations.

Cirrhosis A disease of the liver, often caused by excessive drinking, in which the liver becomes scarred, forms fibrous tissue, and begins to change its anatomy and functioning.

Civil commitment The legal process by which individuals can be forced to undergo mental health treatment.

Clang A rhyme used by individuals with schizophrenia as a guide to formulating thoughts and statements.

Classical conditioning A process of learning by temporal association in which two events that repeatedly occur close together in time become fused in a person's mind.

Cleaning compulsion A common compulsion in which people feel compelled to keep cleaning themselves, their clothing, their homes, or anything they might touch.

Client-centered therapy The therapeutic approach developed by Carl Rogers that focuses on a patient's unique subjective perspective rather than on someone's definition of objective reality. Rogers proposed that clients would respond better if therapists showed unconditional positive regard, accurate empathy, and genuineness.

Clinical psychologist A professional who earns a doctorate in clinical psychology by completing four years of graduate training in abnormal functioning and its treatment as well as a one-year internship at a mental hospital or mental health agency.

Clinical psychology The study, assessment, treatment, and prevention of abnormal behavior.

Clitoris The female sex organ located in front of the urinary and vaginal openings. It becomes enlarged during sexual arousal.

Clozapine (Clozaril) A commonly prescribed atypical antipsychotic drug.

Cocaine A drug that is the most powerful natural stimulant known.

Cognition The intellectual capacity to think, remember, and anticipate.

Cognitive behavior Thoughts and beliefs, many of which remain private.

Cognitive-behavioral model A theoretical perspective that attributes psychological problems to cognitive behaviors.

Cognitive model A theoretical perspective that emphasizes the process and content of the thinking that underlies an individuals behavior.

Cognitive therapy A therapeutic system constructed on the premise that abnormal functioning is caused by counterproductive assumptions and thoughts. Its goal is to help people recognize and change their faulty thinking processes.

Cognitive triad The three forms of negative thinking that theorist Aaron Beck says are characteristic of people who are depressed. These persons repeatedly interpret their experiences, themselves, and their future in negative ways.

Cohort A group of people who are born in the same time period or year—that is, people of the same generation.

Coitus Sexual intercourse.

Community mental health A sociocultural treatment approach emphasizing community care, particularly for people with severe psychological disturbances.

Community mental health center A treatment facility for persons with psychological dysfunctions that provides outpatient psychotherapy and medication and, ideally, inpatient emergency care.

Comorbidity The occurrence of two or more disorders in the same individual.

Compulsion A repetitive and rigid behavior or mental act that a person feels compelled to perform in order to prevent or reduce anxiety or distress.

Computerized axial tomography (CAT scan) A composite image of the brain created by compiling X-ray images taken from many angles.

Concordance A statistical measure of the frequency with which family members (often both members of a pair of twins) have the same particular characteristic.

Conditioned response (CR) A response previously associated with an unconditioned stimulus that comes to be elicited by a conditioned stimulus.

Conditioned stimulus (CS) A previously neutral stimulus that comes to be associated with a nonneutral stimulus, and can then elicit responses similar to those elicited by the nonneutral stimulus.

Conditioning A simple form of learning in which a given stimulus comes to evoke a given response.

Conditions of worth According to client-centered theorists, the internal standards by which a person judges his or her own lovability and acceptability, determined by the standards (i.e., conditions of worth) to which the person was held as a child.

Conduct disorder A pathological pattern of childhood behavior in which the child repeatedly violates the basic rights of others or major societal norms or rules, displaying aggression and sometimes destroying others' property, lying, or running away from home.

Confabulation A spontaneously made-up event fabricated to fill in a gap in one's own memory. Characteristic of persons with alcoholism suffering from Korsakoff's syndrome.

Confederate An experimenter's accomplice who plays a role in creating a believable counterfeit situation in an experiment.

Confidentiality The commitment on the part of professionals not to divulge the information they obtain from a client.

Confound In an experiment a variable other than the independent variable that is also acting on the dependent variable.

Conjoint family therapy A family therapy approach in which the therapist focuses primarily on communication within the family system, helping members to recognize harmful patterns of communication, to appreciate the impact of such patterns on other family members, and to change the patterns.

Contingency training A short-term behavioral treatment for drug abuse in which clients receive incentives contingent on submitting drug-free urine samples.

Continuous amnesia A disturbance of memory in which forgetting continues into the present, and new and ongoing experiences fail to be retained.

Control group In an experiment, a group of subjects who are not exposed to the independent variable.

Conversion disorder A somatoform disorder in which a psychosocial conflict or need is converted into dramatic physical symptoms affecting voluntary motor or sensory function.

Coronary heart disease Illness caused by a blocking of the coronary arteries.

Correlation The degree to which events or characteristics vary in conjunction with each other.

Correlational coefficient (r) A statistical expression of the direction and the magnitude of a correlation, ranging from -1.00 to $+1.00$.

Counseling psychology A mental health specialty similar to clinical psychology that requires completion of its own graduate training program.

Countertransference A phenomenon of psychotherapy in which therapists' own feelings, history, and values subtly influence the way they interpret a patient's problems.

Couple therapy A therapeutic approach in which the therapist works with two people who share a long-term relationship. It focuses on the structure and communication patterns in the relationship.

Covert desensitization Desensitization training that focuses on imagining confrontations with the frightening objects or situations while in a state of relaxation. See also **In vivo desensitization.**

Covert sensitization A behavioral treatment for eliminating unwanted behavior by pairing the behavior with unpleasant mental images.

Crack A powerful, ready-to-smoke free-base cocaine. See also **Free-base.**

Cretinism A congenital disorder characterized by mental retardation and physical abnormalities and caused by low levels of iodine in a pregnant woman's diet.

Creutzfeldt-Jakob disease A rare, rapidly progressive dementia caused by a slow-acting virus, that often includes spasmodic movements.

Criminal commitment A legal process by which individuals accused of crimes are judged to be mentally unstable and are sent to a mental institution for treatment.

Crisis intervention See **Suicide prevention programs.**

Cross-tolerance Tolerance for a drug one has never taken, as a result of using another similar drug.

Culture A people's common history, values, institutions, habits, skills, technology, and arts.

Cyclothymic disorder A mood disorder characterized by numerous periods of hypomanic symptoms and mild depressive symptoms.

D_2 receptors The subgroup of dopamine receptors that have been linked most often to schizophrenia. Other subgroups —D_1, D_3, D_4, and D_5 receptors—may, however, turn out to play just as important a role in the disorder.

Date rape Rape by a date or close acquaintance.

Day center (Day hospital) A treatment center that provides daylong therapeutic activity and cure.

Declarative memory Memory for information that is directly accessible to consciousness, such as names, dates, and other learned facts.

Defense mechanisms See **Ego defense mechanisms.**

Deinstitutionalization The practice begun in the mid-twentieth century to release hundreds of thousands of patients from public mental hospitals.

Déjà vu The haunting sense of having previously seen or experienced a new scene or situation.

Delirium A rapidly occurring clouded state of consciousness in which a person experiences great difficulty concentrating, focusing attention, and maintaining a straightforward stream of thought.

Delirium tremens (DTs) See **Alcohol withdrawal delirium.**

Delusion A blatantly false belief firmly held despite evidence to the contrary.

Delusion of control The belief that one's impulses, feelings, thoughts, and actions are being controlled by other people.

Delusion of grandeur The belief that one is a great inventor, historical figure, religious savior, or other specially empowered person.

Delusion of persecution The belief that one is being plotted or discriminated against, spied on, slandered, threatened, attacked, or deliberately victimized.

Delusion of reference A belief that attaches special and personal significance to the actions of others or to various objects or events.

Delusional disorder A disorder consisting of persistent, non-bizarre delusions that are not part of a schizophrenic disorder.

Dementia A syndrome of severe decline of intellectual faculties, marked by an impairment of memory and at least one other cognitive function.

Demonology The belief that abnormal behavior results from supernatural causes such as evil spirits.

Dendrite The extensions, or antennae, located at one end of a neuron that receive impulses from other neurons.

Denial An ego defense mechanism in which a person fails to acknowledge unacceptable thoughts, feelings, or actions.

Dependent personality disorder A personality disorder characterized by a pattern of submissive and clinging behavior and fears of separation related to a pervasive and excessive need to be taken care of.

Dependent variable The variable in an experiment that is expected to change as the independent variable is manipulated.

Depersonalization disorder A disorder characterized by a persistent and recurrent feeling of being detached from one's own mental processes or body; that is, one feels unreal and alien.

Depression A low, sad state in which life seems bleak and its challenges overwhelming.

Derailment (Loose associations) A common formal thought disorder of schizophrenia, characterized by rapid shifts from one topic of conversation to another.

Derealization The feeling that the external world is unreal and strange.

Desire phase The first phase of the sexual response cycle, characterized by an urge to have sex, sexual fantasies, and feelings of sexual attraction to others.

Desynchronization An imbalance between the body's circadian rhythms and the rhythms of the environment.

Detoxification Systematic and medically supervised withdrawal from a drug.

Deviance Variance from accepted patterns of behavior.

Diagnosis The process of determining whether a person's dysfunction constitutes a particular psychological disorder.

Diathesis-stress perspective The view that a person must first have a biological, psychological, or sociocultural predisposition to a disorder and then be subjected to an immediate form of psychosocial stress to develop and maintain it.

Diazepam A benzodiazepine drug marketed as Valium.

Diencephalon A brain structure located below the cerebral cortex, consisting of the mammillary bodies, thalamus, and hypothalamus. Damage to these structures generally results in problems with encoding new information.

Disaster response network A network of thousands of volunteer mental health professionals who mobilize to provide free emergency mental health services at disaster sites throughout North America.

Disorganized schizophrenia A form of schizophrenia characterized by confusion, incoherence, and flat or inappropriate affect.

Displacement An ego defense mechanism that channels unacceptable id impulses toward another, safer substitute.

Disregulation model A theory that explains psychophysiological disorders as breakdowns in the body's negative feedback loops, resulting in an interruption of the body's smooth, self-regulating operation.

Dissociative amnesia A memory disruption in which the inability to recall important personal events and information is not due to organic causes.

Dissociative disorder Disorder characterized by significant alterations in memory without a clear physical cause.

Dissociative fugue A psychologically caused disorder in which a person travels to a new location and may assume a new identity, simultaneously forgetting his or her past.

Dissociative identity disorder (Multiple personality disorder) A disorder in which a person displays two or more distinct personalities.

Dizygotic twins Twins who develop from separate eggs.

Dopamine The neurotransmitter whose high activity has been shown to be related to schizophrenia.

Dopamine hypothesis The theory that schizophrenia results from excessive firing of neurons that use the neurotransmitter dopamine and, hence, from their transmitting too many messages.

Double-bind communication Simultaneous messages that are mutually contradictory.

Double-bind hypothesis A family systems theory that says some parents help cause schizophrenic symptoms in their children by repeatedly engaging in double-bind communications, thus placing the children in the dilemma of being unable to please them.

Double-blind design Experimental procedure in which neither the subject nor the experimenter knows whether the subject has received the experimental treatment or a placebo.

Double depression A sequence in which dysthymic disorder leads to a major depressive disorder.

Down Syndrome A form of mental retardation related to a chromosomal abnormality.

Drapetomania According to a nineteenth-century diagnostic category, an obsessive desire for freedom that drove some slaves to try to flee from captivity.

Drug abuse The ongoing excessive intake of a substance that results in emotional, social, occupational, or functional impairment.

Drug maintenance therapy An approach to treating substance dependence in which clients are given legally and medically supervised doses of a substitute drug with which to satisfy their addiction.

Drug therapy The use of psychotropic drugs to alleviate the symptoms of psychological disorders.

DSM-IV (Diagnostic and Statistical Manual-IV) The current edition of a system for classifying psychological problems and disorders. Developed by the American Psychiatric Association, it is the most widely used system in the United States.

Durham test A legal test for determining the responsibility of a person committing a crime. It asks simply whether the unlawful act is a product of a mental disease or defect. This test was used only for a short period.

Dyslexia (Reading disorder) A disorder characterized by a marked impairment in the ability to recognize words and to comprehend what one reads, not caused by visual or hearing defects, poor schooling, or intellectual deficit.

Dyspareunia Pain in the genitals during sexual activity.

Dyssomnias Sleep disorders in which the amount, quality, or timing of sleep is disturbed.

Dysthymic disorder A mood disorder that is similar to but more chronic and less disabling than major depressive disorder. Periods of normal mood, lasting only days or weeks, may occasionally interrupt the depressed mood.

Dystonia A Parkinsonian symptom in which involuntary muscle contractions cause bizarre and uncontrollable movements of the face, neck, tongue, and back.

Eccentric A person who deviates from an established behavioral pattern, or exhibits odd or whimsical behavior.

Echolalia A symptom of autism or schizophrenia in which a person responds to being spoken to by repeating some of the other person's words.

Educational psychology A mental health specialty that focuses on behavior and problems particularly in educational settings.

Ego One of the three psychological forces proposed by Freud as central to shaping the personality. The ego operates in accordance with the reality principle, employing reason and deliberation to guide us in recognizing when the expression of id impulses would have negative consequences.

Ego defense mechanisms According to psychoanalytic theory, these are strategies developed by the ego to control unacceptable id impulses and to avoid or reduce the anxiety they arouse.

Ego-dystonic homosexuality A past DSM category indicating a homosexual orientation accompanied by extreme distress.

Ego ideal A composite image of the values one has acquired—the kind of person one believes in striving to become.

Ego psychology A psychodynamic theory that focuses on the importance of the ego.

Egoistic suicide Suicide committed by people over whom society has little or no control.

Eidetic imagery A strong visual image of an object or scene that persists in some persons long after the object or scene is removed.

Ejaculation Contractions of the muscles at the base of the penis that cause sperm to be ejected.

Electra complex According to Freud, the pattern of desires all girls experience in which they develop a sexual attraction to their father.

Electroconvulsive therapy (ECT) See **Bilateral ECT** and **Unilateral ECT.**

Electroencephalograph (EEG) A device that records electrical impulses in the brain.

Electromyograph (EMG) A device that provides feedback about the level of muscular tension in the body.

Electrooculograph A device that records the movement of the eyes.

Emergency commitment Temporary commitment to a mental hospital of a patient who is behaving in a bizarre or violent way. See also **Two-physician certificates.**

Employee assistance programs Mental health programs a company offers its employees. They may be run either by mental health professionals employed directly by the company or by consulting mental health agencies.

Encephalitis An early-childhood disease that can sometimes cause serious brain damage if untreated.

Encopresis Childhood disorder characterized by repeated defecation in inappropriate places.

Encounter group A small group guided by a leader through intensive experiences designed to develop participants' self-awareness and, as a consequence, their skills in human relationships.

Endogenous depression A depression that appears to develop without antecedents and is assumed to be caused by internal factors.

Endorphin A neurotransmitter that helps relieve pain and reduce emotional tension. Sometimes referred to as the body's own opioid.

Enmeshed family pattern A family system in which members are overinvolved with each other's affairs and overconcerned about each other's welfare.

Enuresis A pattern of repeated bedwetting or wetting of one's clothes.

Epidemiological study (Epidemiology) An investigation that determines the incidence and prevalence of a disorder in a given population.

Epilepsy (Brain seizure disorder) A disorder of the brain characterized by seizures; alterations in consciousness; and impairment of sensory, mental, or motor skills.

Episodic memory A person's autobiographical memory of personal experiences and other highly personal material.

Ergot alkaloid A naturally occurring compound from which LSD is derived.

Erogenous zones Body areas that Freud considered representative of the child's sexual drives and conflicts at each of the normal stages of development.

Essential hypertension Chronic high blood pressure brought about by a combination of psychological and physiological factors.

Estrogen The primary female sex hormone.

Ethyl alcohol The chemical compound in all alcoholic beverages that is rapidly absorbed into the blood and immediately begins to affect the person's functioning.

Evoked potentials The brain response patterns recorded on an electroencephalograph.

Excitement phase The second phase in the sexual response cycle, characterized by general physical arousal, increases in heart rate, muscle tension, blood pressure, and respiration, and specific changes in the pelvic region.

Exhaustion stage The failure of the parasympathetic nervous system to resist a sustained response of the sympathetic nervous system. It leads to a breakdown in the control of the autonomic nervous system over the organs of the body. See also **General adaptation syndrome.**

Exhibitionism A disorder in which persons have sexually arousing fantasies, sexual urges, or behaviors involving the exposure of their genitals to an unsuspecting stranger, causing significant impairment or distress.

Existential anxiety A pervasive fear of the limits and responsibilities of one's existence.

Existential model The theoretical perspective that human beings are born with the total freedom to either face up to one's existence and give meaning to one's life or to shrink from that responsibility.

Existential therapy Like humanistic therapy, existential therapy emphasizes the validity of the individual's phenomenological world and the importance of the here and now, but it also places great emphasis on making choices and on the relationship between therapist and client.

Exorcism The practice in early societies of treating abnormality by inducing evil spirits to leave the person's body.

Experiment A scientific procedure in which a situation is manipulated and the effect of the manipulation is observed.

Experimental group In an experiment, the group of subjects who are exposed to the independent variable.

Exposure and response prevention A behavioral treatment for obsessive-compulsive disorder in which clients are exposed to anxiety-arousing thoughts or situations and then prevented from performing their compulsive acts.

Exposure treatment Behavioral approaches to treating phobias in which clients are exposed to the dreaded object or situation.

Expressed emotion The level of criticism, emotional overinvolvement, and hostility displayed in a family. High levels of expressed emotion in family members are thought to be associated with a poorer outcome for individuals recovering from schizophrenia.

External validity The degree to which the results of a study may be generalized beyond the immediate investigation.

Extinction The decrease in responding that occurs when an unconditioned stimulus is no longer paired with the conditioned stimulus, or when a response is no longer rewarded.

Extrapyramidal effects Unwanted movements, such as severe shaking, bizarre-looking contractions of the face and body, and extreme restlessness, induced by the traditional antipsychotic drugs. They result from the effect of the drugs on the extrapyramidal areas of the brain.

Facilitated communication A controversial method for teaching individuals with autism to communicate. The therapist or "facilitator" provides physical assistance as the individual types or points to letters on a keyboard or communication board.

Factitious disorder An illness in which the patient intentionally produces or feigns physical symptoms in order to assume a sick role.

Family pedigree study The method used by researchers to see how many and which members of a given patient's family have the same disorder as the patient.

Family systems theory An approach to human behavior that views the family as a system of interacting parts and proposes that members of a given family interact in consistent ways and operate by implicit rules.

Family systems therapy A therapy format in which therapists meet with all members of a family, point out problematic behavior and interactions between the members, and help the whole family to change.

Fantasy An ego defense mechanism in which a person uses imaginary events to satisfy unacceptable impulses.

Fear The central nervous system's physiological and emotional response to danger.

Fear hierarchy A list of the objects or situations that frighten a person, starting with those which are minimally feared and ending with those which are feared the most. Used in desensitization.

Female orgasmic disorder A sexual disorder marked by a woman's inability to reach orgasm despite adequate stimulation.

Fetal alcohol syndrome A cluster of problems in a child, including low birth weight, irregularities in the hands and face, and intellectual deficits, caused by excessive alcohol intake by its mother during gestation.

Fetishism A pattern characterized by recurrent sexual urges, sexually arousing fantasies, or behaviors that involve the use of nonliving objects, causing significant distress or impairment.

Fixation According to Freud, a condition in which the id, ego, and superego do not mature properly and are frozen at an early stage of development.

Flashback (Hallucinogen persisting perception disorder) The recurrence of hallucinogen-induced sensory and emotional changes long after the drug has left the body. Or in posttraumatic stress disorder, the re-experiencing of past traumatic events.

Flat affect A symptom of schizophrenia in which the person shows almost no emotions at all.

Flooding A treatment for phobias in which clients are exposed repeatedly and intensively to the feared object and made to see that it is actually quite harmless.

Folie à deux (Shared psychotic disorder) A psychotic disorder in which a delusion is shared by two people.

Forebrain The top area of the brain, consisting of the cerebrum, thalamus, and hypothalamus.

Forensic science The study of legal issues relating to medicine or psychology.

Formal thought disorders Disturbances in the production and organization of thought, often symptoms in schizophrenia.

Fragile X syndrome A chromosomal disorder characterized by moderate to severe degrees of mental handicap, language impairments, and behavioral problems.

Free association A psychodynamic therapy technique in which the patient describes any thought, feeling, or image that comes to mind, even if it seems unimportant.

Free-base A technique for ingesting cocaine in which the pure cocaine basic alkaloid is chemically separated from processed cocaine, vaporized by heat from a flame, and inhaled with a pipe.

Free-floating anxiety Chronic and persistent feelings of nervousness and agitation that are not clearly attached to a specific, identifiable threat.

Frontal lobe The region of each cerebral hemisphere that helps govern motor function and abstract thinking.

Frotteurism A paraphilia in which recurrent and intense sexual urges, sexually arousing fantasies, or behaviors center on touching and rubbing against a nonconsenting person.

Fugue See **Dissociative fugue.**

Functional mental disorders A term used in the past to indicate abnormal behavior patterns that have no clear link to physical abnormalities in the brain.

GABA The neurotransmitter gamma aminobutyric acid, whose low activity has been linked to generalized anxiety disorder.

Galvanic skin response (GSR) Changes in the electrical resistance of the skin.

Ganja A recreational drug of at least intermediate strength derived from varieties of the hemp plant.

Gender identity disorder (Transsexualism) A disorder in which persons feel uncomfortable about their assigned sex and strongly wish to be a member of the opposite sex. They are often preoccupied with getting rid of their primary and secondary sex characteristics and many find their own genitals repugnant.

Gene A structure within the chromosome that carries a discrete piece of hereditary information.

General adaptation syndrome A three-stage reaction to stress proposed by theorist Hans Selye to describe the relationship between stress and the autonomic nervous system.

General paresis An irreversible, progressive disorder with both physical and mental symptoms, including paralysis and delusions of grandeur.

Generalized amnesia A pattern in which a person forgets both the period beginning with a traumatic event and all other events before the onset of this period.

Generalized anxiety disorder A disorder characterized by general and persistent feelings of anxiety and worry about numerous events or activities.

Genetic linkage study A research approach in which extended families with high rates of a disorder over several generations are observed in order to determine whether the disorder closely follows the distribution pattern of other family traits.

Genital stage In Freud's theory, the stage beginning at approximately 12 years old, when the child begins to find sexual pleasure in heterosexual relationships.

Geropsychology The field of psychology concerned with the mental health of elderly people.

Gestalt therapy A humanistic form of therapy developed by Fritz Perls in which therapists try to move their clients toward self-recognition and self-acceptance.

Glia Brain cells that support the neurons.

Glutamate A common neurotransmitter that is apparently depleted in the brains of Alzheimer's victims.

Grief The reaction one experiences when a loved one is lost.

Group home Special homes where people with disorders or disabilities are taught self-help, living, and working skills.

Group therapy A therapeutic approach in which a group of people with similar problems meet together with a therapist and discuss the problems or concerns of one or more of the members. The therapist usually follows the principles of his or her preferred theoretical model in conducting the group.

Guided participation A modeling technique in which the therapist and client first construct a fear hierarchy and the client then observes and imitates the therapist experiencing the least feared item in the hierarchy, a more feared item, and so on.

Habituation training A cognitive-behavioral therapeutic technique in which a therapist tries to evoke a client's obsessive thoughts again and again with the expectation that the thoughts will eventually lose their threatening meaning and generate less anxiety.

Halcion (Triazolam) An antianxiety drug that is quickly metabolized in the body.

Halfway house A group home that has a live-in staff to offer support, guidance, and practical advice to residents.

Hallucination The experiencing of imagined sights, sounds, or other sensory experiences as if they were real.

Hallucinogen A substance that primarily causes changes in sensory perception.

Hallucinogen persisting perception disorder (Flashback) The recurrence of drug-induced sensory and emotional changes long after a hallucinogenic drug has left the body.

Hallucinosis A state of perceptual distortion and hallucination.

Hardiness A set of positive attitudes in response to stress that enables a person who has been exposed to life-threatening situations to carry on with a sense of fortitude, control, and commitment.

Hashish The most powerful drug produced from varieties of the hemp plant.

Hebephrenic schizophrenia See **Disorganized schizophrenia.**

Helper T-cell A lymphocyte that identifies antigens and then both multiplies and triggers the production of other kinds of immune cells.

Helplessness See **Learned helplessness.**

Heroin A highly addictive substance derived from opium.

High The pleasant feeling of relaxation and euphoria that follows the rush from certain recreational drugs.

High-risk study A study in which people hypothesized to be at greater risk for developing a disorder are followed throughout their childhood and compared with controls who are considered not to be at risk.

Hindbrain The lower rearward portion of the brain comprised of the medulla, pons, and cerebellum.

Hippocampus Part of the limbic system located below the cerebral cortex that is involved in the memory system. Damage to this area can result in severe memory difficulties.

Histrionic personality disorder A personality disorder characterized by excessive emotionality and attention seeking.

Homeostasis A state in which the parts of a system interact in ways that enable the system to maintain itself and survive.

Homosexuality Sexual preference for a person of one's own gender.

Humanistic-existential model A theoretical point of view that stresses the roles of values and choices in determining human individuality and fulfillment.

Humanistic-existential therapy A system of therapy that tries to help clients view themselves and their situations more accurately and acceptingly and move toward actualizing their full potential as human beings.

Humanistic model The theoretical perspective that human beings are born with a natural inclination to be friendly, cooperative, and constructive, and are driven to self-actualize.

Humanistic therapy A system of therapy that tries to help clients look at themselves accurately and acceptingly so that they can fulfill their positive inborn potential.

Huntington's disease An inherited progressive degenerative disease of cognition, emotion, and movement. Its onset, usually during the middle years, is later followed by dementia.

Hydrocephalus A disease characterized by an increase in cerebrospinal fluid and resultant head enlargement.

Hypertension Chronic high blood pressure.

Hypnosis A sleeplike, suggestible state during which a person can be directed to act in unusual ways, to experience unusual sensations, to remember seemingly forgotten events, or to forget remembered events.

Hypnotic amnesia A condition in which a person forgets facts, events, and even his or her identity in obedience to an instruction received under hypnosis.

Hypnotic therapy (Hypnotherapy) A sometimes controversial treatment for psychological problems, such as amnesia and fugue, in which the patient undergoes hypnosis and is then guided to recall forgotten events.

Hypnotism The inducing of a trancelike mental state in which a person becomes extremely suggestible.

Hypoactive sexual desire A lack of interest in sex.

Hypochondriasis A somatoform disorder in which people mistakenly and incessantly fear that minor fluctuations in their physical functioning indicate a serious disease.

Hypocyphilia A form of sexual masochism in which people strangle or smother themselves, or ask their partner to do this, in order to enhance their sexual pleasure.

Hypomanic pattern A pattern in which a person experiences symptoms of mania, but the symptoms are less severe and cause less impairment than a manic episode.

Hypothalamus A part of the brain that helps maintain various bodily functions, including hunger and eating.

Hypothesis A tentative explanation advanced to provide a basis for an investigation.

Hysteria A term once used to describe what are now known as conversion disorder, somatization disorder, and pain disorder associated with psychological factors.

Hysterical disorder A type of somatoform disorder in which physical functioning is altered or lost.

Iatrogenic disorders Disorders that are unintentionally caused by practitioners.

Id One of the three psychological forces proposed by Freud as central to shaping personality. The id is the source of instinctual needs, drives, and impulses.

Identification The unconscious incorporation of parental values and feelings and fusing them with one's identity. Also an ego defense mechanism in which persons take on the values and feelings of the person who is causing them anxiety.

Idiographic understanding An understanding of the abnormal behavior of a particular individual.

Illogical thinking According to cognitive theories, habitual illogical ways of thinking that may lead to self-defeating and even pathological conclusions.

Imipramine A tricyclic drug that has been found to be effective in treating unipolar depression.

Immune system The sum of complex bodily systems that detect and destroy antigens. It serves to prevent physical ailments or help individuals to recover from illness.

Imposter phenomenon A persistent feeling that one does not deserve one's success because it is based solely on hard work or manipulation of others rather than competence.

Impulse-control disorders Disorders in which people repeatedly fail to resist an impulse, drive, or temptation to perform an act that is harmful to themselves or to others.

In vivo desensitization Desensitization training that makes use of actual physical situations, as opposed to imagined ones. See also **Covert desensitization.**

Inappropriate affect A symptom of schizophrenia in which a person expresses emotions that are unsuited to the situation.

Incest Sexual relations between close relatives.

Incidence A statistical measure of the number of new cases of a problem or disorder that occur over a specific period of time.

Independent variable The variable in an experiment that is manipulated to determine whether it has an effect on another variable (the dependent variable).

Individual therapy A therapeutic approach in which a therapist sees a client alone for sessions that may last from fifteen minutes to two hours.

Indoleamine theory The view that unipolar depression is caused by deficiencies in the activity of the neurotransmitter serotonin (an indoleamine).

Informed consent A person's consent to participate in an experiment or procedure, given with full knowledge of the potential benefits and risks.

Inhibited power motive style A personality style characterized by a strong but inhibited need for power. It is linked to a tendency to develop physical illness.

Insanity defense A legal defense in which persons charged with a criminal offense claim to be not guilty by reason of insanity and try to show that, as a result of mental dysfunctioning, they were not legally responsible for their conduct at the time of their offense.

Insight therapy Psychotherapeutic approach that helps the patient primarily achieve a greater understanding of his or her problem and key aspects of his or her functioning.

Insomnia The most common dyssomnia, characterized by difficulties initiating and maintaining sleep.

Instrumental conditioning See **Operant conditioning.**

Integrity test A test that seeks to measure whether the test taker is generally honest or dishonest.

Intelligence quotient (IQ) A score derived from intelligence tests that is designed to represent a person's overall intellectual capacity.

Intelligence test A test designed to measure a person's intellectual ability.

Intermittent explosive disorder An impulse-control disorder in which people periodically fail to resist aggressive impulses, leading to the performance of serious assaults on people or destruction of property.

Internal validity The accuracy with which a study can pinpoint one out of various possible factors as being the cause of a phenomenon.

Interpersonal psychotherapy (IPT) A treatment for unipolar depression. It is based on the premise that because depression occurs in an interpersonal context, clarifying and renegotiating that context is important to a person's recovery.

Intoxication A temporary substance-induced state in which a person exhibits impaired judgment, mood changes, irritability, slurred speech, and loss of coordination.

Introjection The unconscious incorporation of parental values that leads to the development of the superego in the child. Also, according to psychodynamic theory, people who have lost a loved one may introject, or fuse, their own identity with that of the person they have lost.

Irresistible impulse test A legal criterion for determining a person's responsibility for committing a crime. This test asks whether the person was unable to control his or her actions.

Isolation An ego defense mechanism in which people unconsciously isolate and disown undesirable and unwanted thoughts, experiencing them as foreign intrusions from undetermined parts of the mind. This mechanism has been invoked as an explanation of obsessive-compulsive disorder.

Jamais vu The experience of not recognizing a scene or situation that one has previously experienced.

Juvenile delinquents Term often used by the legal system to describe children between the ages of 8 and 18 who break the law.

Killer T-cell A lymphocyte that seeks out and destroys body cells that have been infected by viruses.

Kleptomania An impulse-control disorder characterized by the recurrent failure to resist impulses to steal objects not needed for personal use or monetary value.

Koro A pattern of anxiety found in Southeast Asia in which a man suddenly becomes intensely fearful that his penis will withdraw into his abdomen and that he will die as a result.

Korsakoff's syndrome (alcohol-induced persisting amnestic disorder) An alcohol-related disorder marked by extreme confusion, memory impairment, and other neurological symptoms.

L-dopa A precursor of dopamine, given to patients suffering from Parkinson's disease, a disease in which dopamine is low.

Latency stage In psychoanalytic theory, the stage children enter at 6 years of age in which their sexual desires apparently subside and their libidinal energy is devoted to developing new interests, activities, and skills.

Latent content The symbolic meaning of a dream.

Lateral hypothalamus (LH) The region of the hypothalamus that produces hunger when activated.

Learned helplessness The perception, based on subjective experience, that one has no control over one's reinforcements.

Learning disorder A developmental disorder marked by impairments in cognitive skills such as reading, mathematics, or language.

Lesion Localized damage to tissue.

Lethality scale A scale used by crisis prevention centers to estimate a caller's potential for suicide.

Leveled programs A token economy system that incorporates different levels of difficulty.

Libido In Freudian theory, the sexual energy that fuels the id and other forces of personality.

Life change units (LCUs) A system for measuring the stress associated with various life events.

Light therapy (phototherapy) A treatment for seasonal affective disorder in which patients are exposed to extra light for several hours.

Limbic system Region of the brain at the lower part of the cerebrum that controls bodily changes associated with emotions.

Lithium A metallic element that occurs in nature as a mineral salt and is the most effective antibipolar drug.

Lobotomy Psychosurgery that severs the connections between the cortex of the brain's frontal lobes and the lower centers of the brain.

Localized (circumscribed) amnesia In this, the most common form of dissociative amnesia, a person forgets all events that occurred over a limited period of time.

Logotherapy A treatment that focuses on changing clients' attitudes toward their existence. Developed by Viktor Frankl.

Longitudinal study An investigation in which the characteristics or behavior of the same subjects are observed on different occasions over a long period of time.

Long-term memory The memory system that contains all the information that we have stored over the years.

Loose associations (Derailment) A common thought disorder of schizophrenia, characterized by rapid shifts from one topic of conversation to another.

LSD (lysergic acid diethylamide) A hallucinogenic drug derived from ergot alkaloids that brings on a state in which perceptions in general, but particularly visual perceptions, are intensified.

Lycanthropy A condition in which a person believes himself or herself to be possessed by wolves or other animals.

Lymphocytes White blood cells that are manufactured in the lymph system and circulate throughout the bloodstream. They help the body overcome antigens.

M'Naghten rule A legal test for determining a person's responsibility for committing a crime. First used in the mid-nineteenth century, it is based on whether the person was able to determine right from wrong.

Magnetic resonance imaging (MRI) The use of the magnetic property of certain atoms in the brain to create a detailed picture of the brain's structure.

Mainstreaming An approach to educating persons with mental retardation in which the individuals are placed in regular school classes.

Major depressive episode A severe episode of depressed mood that is significantly disabling and is not caused by such factors as drugs or a general medical condition.

Male erectile disorder A dysfunction of the excitement phase of the sexual response cycle in men, characterized by a persistent or recurrent inability to attain an erection or to maintain an erection until completion of sexual activity.

Male orgasmic disorder A disorder in which a man is repeatedly unable to reach orgasm despite adequate stimulation.

Malingering Intentionally feigning illness to achieve some external gains, such as financial compensation or military deferment.

Managed care system A system of insured health care in which the insurance company may determine such issues as which therapists clients may choose, the cost of sessions, and the number of sessions permitted.

Mania A state or episode of euphoria, frenzied activity, or related symptoms.

Manic-depressive disorder See **Bipolar disorder.**

Manifest content The consciously remembered features of a dream.

Mantra A sound, uttered or thought, used to focus one's attention and to turn away from ordinary thoughts and concerns during meditation.

MAO inhibitor An antidepressant drug that inhibits the action of the enzyme monoamine oxidase.

Marijuana One of the drugs derived from the varieties of the hemp plant.

Marital schism A family situation in which the father and mother are in open conflict, with each trying to undercut the other and compete for the loyalty of the child. Some theorists believe this conflict can lead to schizophrenic behavior in the daughter.

Marital skew A family situation in which a so-called schizophrenogenic mother dominates the family, and the father keeps peace by continually yielding to her wishes. Some theorists believe this conflict can lead to schizophrenic behavior in the son.

Marital therapy A therapeutic approach in which the therapist works with two people who share a long-term relationship. It focuses on the structure and communication patterns in the relationship.

Masochism See **Sexual masochism.**

Masturbation Self-stimulation of the genitals to achieve sexual arousal.

Masturbatory satiation A behavioral treatment for certain paraphilias in which a client masturbates for a prolonged period of time while fantasizing in detail about the paraphiliac object, with the expectation that the procedure will produce a feeling of boredom, which in turn becomes associated with the object.

Mean The average of a group of scores.

Medication-induced movement disorders Disturbing movement abnormalities that are sometimes a side effect of antipsychotic drugs. They include Parkinsonian symptoms, neuroleptic malignant syndrome, and tardive dyskinesia.

Meditation A technique of turning one's concentration inward and achieving a seemingly altered state of consciousness. Often used to relieve emotional and physical stress.

Melancholia A condition described by early Greek and Roman philosophers and physicians as consisting of unshakable sadness. Today it is known as depression.

Melatonin A hormone that appears to have a role in regulating mood. It is secreted when a person's surroundings are dark, but not when they are light.

Meningitis A childhood disease marked by inflammation of the meninges of the brain. It can lead to brain damage and mental retardation if not treated.

Mental age The age level at which a person performs on a test of intellectual skill, independent of his or her chronological age.

Mental retardation A disorder diagnosed when people manifest significant subaverage general intellectual functioning and significant impairment in adaptive functioning.

Mental status exam A set of interview questions and observations designed to reveal the degree and nature of a client's abnormal functioning.

Mentally ill chemical abuser (MICA) A person with a chronic mental disorder who also abuses alcohol or other drugs.

Mescaline A hallucinogenic drug.

Mesmerism The method employed by Austrian physician F. A. Mesmer to treat hysterical disorders. It was a precursor of hypnotism.

Metabolism The chemical and physical processes that go on in any living organism that break down food and convert it into energy. Also, the biochemical transformation of substances in the cells of living things, as when the liver breaks down alcohol into acetylaldehyde.

Metacommunication The context, tone, and gestures attached to any message. See also **Primary communication.**

Methadone A laboratory-made substitute drug for heroin. See also **Drug maintenance therapy.**

Microencephaly A biological disorder characterized by a small, unusually shaped head, resulting from a combination of hereditary, prenatal, birth, and postnatal factors.

Midbrain The middle region of the brain.

Migraine headache An extremely severe headache that occurs on one side of the head and is often immobilizing; often preceded by a warning sensation called an aura.

Milieu therapy A humanistic approach to institutional treatment based on the premise that institutions can help patients recover by creating a climate of self-respect, individual responsibility, and meaningful activity.

Mind-body dualism The view that the mind is a separate entity from the body, totally unable to affect physical matter or somatic processes.

Minnesota Multiphasic Personality Inventory (MMPI) A widely used personality inventory consisting of a large number of statements that subjects mark as being true or false for them.

Minor tranquilizers See **Antianxiety drugs.**

Mitral valve prolapse (MVP) A cardiac malfunction marked by periodic episodes of heart palpitations.

Mixed design A research design in which a correlational analysis is mixed with an experimental analysis. See also **Quasi-experiment.**

Model A set of concepts taken from one domain and applied analogously to another. It helps scientists explain and interpret observations. See also **Paradigm.**

Modeling A form of learning in which an individual acquires responses by observing and imitating others.

Monoamine oxidase (MAO) A body chemical that destroys the neurotransmitter norepinephrine.

Monoamine oxidase (MAO) inhibitors Antidepressant drugs that lower MAO activity and thus increase the level of norepinephrine activity in the brain.

Monozygotic twins Twins who have developed from a single egg.

Mood disorder Disorder affecting one's emotional state, including major depressive disorder and bipolar disorders.

Moral anxiety According to Freud, anxiety that results from being punished or threatened for expressing id impulses rather than following superego standards. A person eventually comes to perceive the id impulses themselves as threatening.

Moral treatment An approach to treating people with mental dysfunction, which was originated by Phillippe Pinel and William Tuke in the early nineteenth century. It emphasized moral guidance, humane and respectful intervention, and kindness.

Morphine A substance derived from opium that is even more effective than opium in relieving pain.

Multiaxial system A classification system in which different "axes," or branches of information, are required from the diagnostician. DSM-IV is a multiaxial system.

Multidimensional risk perspective A theory about the causes of a disorder that identifies several different kinds of risk factors. Presumably, the more factors present, the greater the individual's risk of developing the disorder.

Multiple-baseline design An experimental design in which several behaviors of a single subject are measured and then the experimenter observes the effect that the manipulation of an independent variable has on each of the behaviors.

Multiple personality disorder (Dissociative identity disorder) A dissociative disorder in which a person displays two or more distinct personalities.

Munchausen syndrome An extreme and chronic factitious disorder in which a person travels from hospital to hospital reciting symptoms, gaining admission, and receiving treatment.

Munchausen syndrome by proxy A factitious disorder in which parents fabricate or induce physical illnesses in their children.

Muscle-contraction headache A chronic headache caused by the contraction of muscles surrounding the skull.

Narcissistic personality disorder A personality disorder in which the person displays a chronic and pervasive pattern of grandiosity, need for admiration, and lack of empathy.

Narcolepsy A dyssomnia characterized by sudden onsets of REM sleep during waking hours, generally brought on by strong emotion.

Narcotic Any natural or synthetic derivative of opium.

Narcotic antagonist A substance that counteracts the effects of opioids. See **Antagonist drug.**

Natural experiment An experiment in which nature rather than an experimenter manipulates an independent variable and the experimenter systematically observes the effects.

Naturalistic observation (in vivo observation) A method for observing behavior in which clinicians or researchers observe clients or subjects in their everyday environment.

Negative correlation A statistical relationship in which the value of one variable increases while the other variable decreases.

Negative feedback loops A physiological process in which the brain receives information about external events from the environment, processes this information, and then stimulates body organs into action. Mechanisms in the organs then provide negative feedback, telling the brain that its stimulation has been sufficient and should now stop.

Negative symptoms (of schizophrenia) Symptoms that seem to reflect pathological deficits, that is, characteristics which seem to be lacking—poverty of speech, blunted or flat speech, loss of volition, and social withdrawal.

Neologism A made-up word that has meaning only to the person using it.

Nerve ending The region at the neuron's terminus from which an impulse that has traveled through the neuron is transmitted to a neighboring neuron.

Neurofibrillary tangles Twisted protein fibers found in excessive numbers within certain brain cells of people with Alzheimer's disease, interfering with memory and learning.

Neuroleptic drugs See **Antipsychotic drugs.**

Neuroleptic malignant syndrome A severe, potentially fatal reaction to antipsychotic drugs, marked by muscle rigidity, fever, altered consciousness, and autonomic dysfunction.

Neurological Relating to the structure or activity of the brain.

Neuron A nerve cell. The brain contains billions of neurons.

Neuropsychological test A test that detects brain damage by measuring a person's cognitive, perceptual, and motor performances.

Neurosis Freud's term for disorders characterized by intense anxiety, attributed to failure of a person's ego defense mechanisms to cope with his or her unconscious conflicts.

Neurotic anxiety In Freudian theory, anxiety experienced by people who are repeatedly and excessively prevented, by their parents or by circumstances, from expressing their id impulses.

Neurotransmitter A chemical that, released by one neuron, crosses the synaptic space to be received at receptors on the dendrites of adjacent neurons.

Neutralizing Efforts by persons to eliminate unwanted, intrusive thoughts by thinking or behaving in ways that put matters right internally or that make amends for unacceptable thoughts.

Nicotine patch A patch attached to the skin like a Band Aid, its nicotine content is absorbed through the skin, supposedly easing the withdrawal reaction brought on by quitting cigarette smoking.

Nightmare disorder A common parasomnia in which a person experiences chronic distressful, frightening dreams.

Nomothetic understanding A general truth about the nature, causes, and treatments of abnormality.

Nonpurging type bulimia nervosa A type of bulimia nervosa in which an individual displays compensatory behaviors other than self-induced vomiting or the misuse of laxatives, such as fasting or exercising frantically.

Nootropics Drugs designed to help enhance memory.

Norepinephrine A neurotransmitter whose abnormal activity is linked to depression and panic disorder.

Normalization program A treatment program for persons with mental retardation, which provides everyday conditions that closely resemble life in the mainstream of society.

Norms A given culture's explicit and implicit rules for appropriate conduct.

Object loss The loss of a significant person in one's life. According to psychodynamic theory, the risk of object loss during the oral stage (the loss of the mother who provides food and comfort) makes a child anxious and triggers defense mechanisms.

Object relations theory A psychodynamic theory that views the desire for relatedness with others (objects) as the motivating force in human behavior. It focuses in particular on the processes of attachment and separation.

Observer drift The tendency of an observer who is rating subjects in an experiment to gradually and involuntarily change criteria, thus making the data unreliable.

Obsession A persistent thought, impulse, or mental image that seems to invade a person's consciousness.

Obsessive-compulsive disorder A disorder in which a person experiences recurrent and unwanted thoughts or feels compelled to perform repetitive and rigid behaviors or mental acts, and experiences intense anxiety whenever the behaviors or mental acts are resisted.

Obsessive-compulsive personality disorder A personality disorder characterized by a pattern of preoccupation with orderliness, perfectionism, and mental and interpersonal control, at the expense of flexibility, openness, and efficiency.

Oedipus complex In Freudian theory, the pattern of desires in which boys become attracted to their mother as a sexual object and see their father as a rival they would like to push aside.

Operant conditioning The process of learning through reward.

Operationalization The translating of an abstract variable into discrete, observable entities or events.

Opioid Opium or any of the drugs derived from opium, including morphine, heroin, and codeine.

Opium A highly addictive substance made from the sap of the opium poppy seed. It has been widely used for thousands of years to reduce physical and emotional pain.

Opponent-process theory An explanation for drug addiction based on the interplay of positive, pleasurable emotions that come from ingesting the drug and negative aftereffects that leave a person feeling even worse than usual.

Oppositional defiant disorder A disorder in which children argue repeatedly with adults, lose their tempers, and feel great anger and resentment.

Oral stage In this earliest developmental stage in Freud's conceptualization of psychosexual development, the infant's main libidinal gratification comes from feeding and from the body parts involved in it.

Organic mental disorders A term used in the past to distinguish mental disorders that have clear physical causes.

Orgasm A peaking of sexual pleasure, consisting of rhythmic muscular contractions in the pelvic region. A man's semen is ejaculated, and the outer third of a woman's vaginal wall contracts.

Orgasm phase The third phase in the sexual response cycle, characterized by rhythmic muscular contractions in the pelvic region.

Orgasmic reorientation A procedure for treating pedophilia or certain other paraphilias in which clients are conditioned to new, more appropriate sources of erotic stimuli.

Outpatient A setting for treatment in which persons visit a therapist's office as opposed to remaining in a hospital.

Overt behavior Observable actions or clear verbalizations.

Pain disorder associated with psychological factors A somatoform disorder characterized by severe and prolonged pain in which psychological factors play a significant role in the onset, severity, exacerbation, or maintenance of the pain.

Panic attack Periodic, discrete bouts of panic that occur abruptly and reach a peak within minutes.

Panic disorder An anxiety disorder characterized by recurrent and unpredictable panic attacks that occur without apparent provocation.

Panic disorder with agoraphobia A panic disorder in which panic attacks lead to agoraphobic patterns of behavior.

Panic disorder without agoraphobia A panic disorder in which agoraphobia is absent.

Paradigm An implicit theoretical framework that arises out of an explicit set of basic assumptions. A scientist's paradigm affects the way he or she interprets observations and other data.

Paranoid personality disorder A personality disorder characterized by a pattern of distrust and suspiciousness such that others' motives are interpreted as malevolent.

Paranoid schizophrenia A type of schizophrenia characterized by an organized system of delusions and hallucinations that often guide the person's life.

Paraphilias Disorders in which the person has recurrent and intense sexual urges, sexually arousing fantasies, or behaviors involving either nonhuman objects, children, nonconsenting adults, or the experience of suffering or humiliation.

Paraprofessional A person without previous professional training who provides services under the supervision of a mental health professional.

Parasomnias Sleep disorders characterized by the occurrence of abnormal events during sleep.

Parasuicide A person who attempts suicide and lives.

Parasympathetic nervous system The group of nerve fibers of the autonomic nervous system that helps maintain normal organ functioning. It also slows organ functioning after stimulation and returns other body processes to normal.

Parens patriae The principle by which the state can make decisions—such as to hospitalize a person against his or her wishes—that are believed to promote the individual's best interests and protect him or her from self-harm or neglect.

Parkinsonian symptoms Dystonia, akathisia, tardive dyskinesia, and other symptoms similar to those found in Parkinson's disease. Patients with schizophrenia who take traditional antipsychotic medications may display one or more of these symptoms.

Parkinson's disease A slowly progressive neurological condition marked by tremors, rigidity, and unsteadiness that seems to be caused by decreased dopamine activity.

Passive-aggressive personality disorder A personality disorder characterized by the need to control the lives of people close to oneself by indirect means. Because this problem may reflect a single trait rather than a pervasive personality disorder, the category was dropped from DSM-IV and designated for further study.

Pathological gambling An impulse-control disorder characterized by recurrent and persistent maladaptive gambling behavior that disrupts personal, family, or vocational pursuits.

Pedophilia A disorder in which a person experiences recurrent and intense sexual urges, sexually arousing fantasies, or behaviors involving sexual activity with a prepubescent child.

Peer review system A process in which clinicians review therapist's reports of a client's treatment and recommend that insurance benefits be either continued or terminated.

Penile prosthesis A surgical implantation consisting of a semirigid rod made of rubber and wire that produces an artificial erection.

Penis envy The Freudian theory that girls wish to overcome their feelings of inferiority during the phallic phase by having a penis.

Performance anxiety The fear of performing inadequately and a consequent tension experienced during sex. See also **Spectator role.**

Perseveration The persistent repetition of words and statements often seen in autism or schizophrenia.

Personality The unique and enduring pattern of inner experience and outward behavior displayed by each individual.

Personality assessment The gathering of information about the components of someone's personality and any unconscious conflicts he or she may be experiencing.

Personality disorder A disorder characterized by an inflexible pattern of inner experience and outward behavior. The pattern is wide-ranging and enduring, and it deviates markedly from the expectations of one's culture.

Personality inventory A test designed to measure broad personality characteristics, consisting of statements about behaviors, beliefs, and feelings that people are asked to evaluate as characteristic or uncharacteristic of them.

Personality trait An enduring consistency with which a person reacts to and acts upon his or her surroundings.

Pervasive developmental disorders A broad category of disorders beginning in early childhood, characterized by severe and pervasive impairments in reciprocal social interaction skills, communication skills, or the presence of stereotyped behavior, interests, and activities.

Phallic stage In psychoanalytic theory, the period between the third and fourth years when the focus of sexual pleasure shifts to the genitals.

Phalloplasty A procedure used during sex-reassignment surgery to create a functional penis.

Pharmacotherapist (Psychopharmacologist) A psychiatrist who primarily prescribes medications.

Phenomenology One's personal experiences and perspective on the world.

Phenothiazines A group of antihistamine drugs, originally prescribed for allergic reactions, that were found to be effective antipsychotic medications.

Phenylketonuria (PKU) A metabolic disorder in which the body is unable to metabolize the amino acid phenylalanine into tyrosine. If untreated, the phenylalanine accumulates and is converted into substances that poison the system and cause mental retardation.

Phobia A persistent and irrational fear of a specific object, activity, or situation.

Phototherapy See **Light therapy.**

Pick's disease A degenerative disease of the brain that causes dementia. It particularly affects the frontal and temporal lobes.

Placebo A sham treatment that the subject believes to be genuine.

Play therapy An approach to treating childhood disorders that helps children express their conflicts and feelings indirectly by drawing, playing with toys, and making up stories.

Pleasure principle In Freudian theory, the pursuit of gratification that motivates the id.

Plethysmograph A device used to measure sexual arousal.

Polygraph A test that seeks to determine whether or not the test taker is telling the truth by measuring physiological responses such as respiration level, perspiration level, and heart rate.

Polysubstance use The misuse of combinations of drugs to achieve a synergistic effect.

Positive correlation A statistical relationship in which the values of two variables increase together or decrease together.

Positive symptoms (of schizophrenia) Symptoms that seem to represent pathological excesses or bizarre additions to a normal repertoire of behavior. They include delusions, hallucinations, positive formal thought disorders, and inappropriate affect.

Positron emission tomography (PET scan) A computer-produced motion picture showing rates of metabolism throughout the brain.

Postpartum depression An episode of depression that may begin for some new mothers within four weeks after childbirth. It is different from the more common "baby blues" and the less common postpartum psychosis.

Posttraumatic stress disorder An anxiety disorder in which fear and related symptoms continue to be experienced long after a traumatic event.

Poverty of content A lack of meaning in spite of high emotion that is often found in the speech of people with schizophrenia who display loose associations.

Predisposition An inborn or acquired vulnerability (or inclination or diathesis) for developing certain symptoms.

Premature ejaculation A dysfunction in which a man repeatedly reaches orgasm and ejaculates with minimal sexual stimulation before, on, or shortly after penetration and before he wishes it.

Premenstrual dysphoric disorder A pattern characterized by markedly depressed mood, anxiety, and marked mood changes, and a decreased interest in activities during the last week of the luteal phase. These symptoms remit within a few days after the onset of menses. This pattern is listed in the appendix of DSM-IV as a category provided for further study.

Premorbid The period prior to the onset of an illness.

Preparedness A predisposition to acquire certain fears.

Presenile Occurring in middle age.

Presenile dementia Dementia occurring in middle age. See also **Dementia.**

Prevalence The total number of cases of a problem or disorder occurring in a population over a specific period of time.

Prevention A key aspect of community mental health programs, which strive to prevent or at least minimize psychological disorders.

Primary communication The semantic content in any message. See also **Metacommunication.**

Primary gain In psychodynamic theory, part of a mechanism for explaining hysterical somatoform disorders. The gain that is achieved when hysterical symptoms keep internal conflicts out of awareness.

Primary hypersomnia A sleep disorder in which the predominant problem is excessive sleepiness for at least a month. It takes the form of prolonged sleep episodes or daytime sleep that occurs almost daily.

Primary insomnia A sleep disorder in which the predominant complaint is an inability to initiate or maintain sleep.

Primary personality The subpersonality that appears more often than the others in individuals with multiple personality disorder.

Primary process In Freudian theory, a source of id gratification that consists of activating a memory or image of a desired object.

Primary process gratification In Freudian theory, an indirect source of id gratification. The child receives gratification by activating a memory or image of a desired object. Also called wish fulfillment.

Proband The person who is the focus of a genetic study.

Procedural memory Memory of learned physical or cognitive skills we perform without needing to think about them. These memories are not directly accessible to consciousness.

Prodromal phase The period during which symptoms of schizophrenia are not yet prominent, but the person has begun to deteriorate from previous levels of functioning.

Prognosis A prediction of the course and outcome of a disorder.

Projection An ego defense mechanism in which a person attributes to others undesirable characteristics or impulses in himself or herself.

Projective test A test that consists of unstructured or ambiguous material to which people are asked to respond.

Prolactin A pituitary hormone that can interfere with the sex drive.

Prophylactic drug A drug that actually helps prevent symptoms from developing.

Prospective study A study that predicts future changes on the basis of past and present events.

Protection and advocacy system The system by which lawyers and advocates who work for patients may investigate possible cases of patient abuse and neglect and then address any problems they find.

Prozac (Fluoxetine) A second-generation antidepressant that appears to have fewer undesired side effects than MAO inhibitors and tricyclics. It also appears to be an effective treatment for eating disorders and obsessive-compulsive disorder.

Psychedelic drugs Substances, such as LSD, that cause profound perceptual changes. Also called hallucinogenic drugs.

Psychiatric social worker A mental health specialist who is qualified to conduct psychotherapy upon earning a master's degree or doctorate in social work.

Psychiatrist A physician who in addition to medical school has completed three to four years of residency training in the treatment of abnormal mental functioning.

Psychoanalysis Either the theory or the treatment of abnormal psychological functioning that emphasizes unconscious conflicts as the cause of psychopathology.

Psychodrama A group therapy technique that calls for group members to act out dramatic roles as if they were participating in an improvised play. They express their feelings and thoughts, explore new behaviors and attitudes, and empathize with the feelings and perspectives of others.

Psychodynamic model The theoretical perspective that sees all human functioning as being shaped by dynamic (interacting) psychological forces and looks at people's unconscious internal conflicts in order to explain their behavior.

Psychodynamic therapy A system of therapy whose goals are to help clients uncover past traumatic events and the inner conflicts that have resulted from them; resolve, or settle, those conflicts; and resume interrupted personal development.

Psychogenesis The development of abnormal functioning from psychological causes.

Psychogenic illness An illness caused primarily by psychosocial factors such as worry, family stress, and unconscious needs.

Psychological autopsy A procedure used to analyze information about a deceased person in order to determine whether the person's death was self-inflicted.

Psychoneuroimmunology The study of the connections between stress, illness, and the body's immune system.

Psychopathology Any abnormal pattern of functioning that may be described as deviant, distressful, dysfunctional, or dangerous.

Psychopathy See **Antisocial personality disorder.**

Psychopharmacologist (Pharmacotherapist) A psychiatrist who primarily prescribes medications.

Psychophysiological (psychosomatic) disorders Illnesses believed to result from an interaction of physical and psychosocial factors. DSM-IV uses the label Psychological factors affecting medical condition.

Psychophysiological test A test that measures physical responses (such as heart rate and muscle tension) as possible indicators of psychological problems.

Psychosexual stages The developmental stages defined by Freud in which the id, ego, and superego interact. Each stage is marked by a different source of libidinal pleasure.

Psychosis A state in which an individual loses contact with reality in key ways.

Psychosomatic (psychophysiological) illnesses Illnesses believed to result from an interaction of both physical and psychosocial causes. DSM-IV labels these illnesses Psychological factors affecting medical condition.

Psychotherapy A treatment system in which words and acts are used by a client (patient) and therapist to overcome psychological difficulties.

Psychotropic drugs Drugs that have their dominant effect on emotions or thought processes.

Purging type bulimia nervosa A type of bulimia nervosa in which an individual regularly induces vomiting or misuses laxatives or diuretics.

Pyromania An impulse-control disorder characterized by a pattern of fire setting for pleasure, gratification, or relief from tension.

Quasi-experiment An experiment in which investigators do not randomly assign the subjects to control and experimental groups but instead make use of groups that already exist in the world at large.

Quinine A drug that is often added to heroin to counteract the dangers of infection.

Random assignment A procedure in which subjects are randomly placed either in the control group or in the experimental group in order to reduce the possibility that preexisting differences between the groups will influence the results.

Rape Forced sexual intercourse against the will of the victim.

Rapid eye movement (REM) sleep The period of the sleep cycle during which the eyes move quickly, back and forth, indicating that the person is dreaming.

Rapprochement An effort to delineate a set of "common therapeutic strategies" that characterize the work of all effective therapists.

Rational emotive therapy A therapeutic approach developed by Albert Ellis that helps clients to discover the irrational assumptions governing their behaviors, cognition, and emotions and to change those assumptions into constructive ways of viewing the world and themselves.

Rationalization An ego defense mechanism in which one creates acceptable reasons for unwanted or undesirable behavior.

Reaction formation An ego defense mechanism in which a repressed desire is instead expressed by opposite personality traits (such as when a desire to be messy and rebellious is repressed and expressed as neatness and conformity).

Reactive depression A depression that appears to follow on the heels of clear-cut precipitating events.

Reactivity The extent to which the very presence of an observer affects a person's behavior.

Reality principle In Freudian theory, the knowledge we acquire through experience and from the people around us that it can be dangerous or unacceptable to express our id impulses outright.

Receptor A site on a neuron that receives a neurotransmitter.

Reflex gratification In Freudian theory, a direct source of id gratification, as when an infant seeks and receives milk from the mother's breast to satisfy its hunger.

Regression An ego defense mechanism in which a person returns to a more primitive mode of interacting with the world.

Reinforcement The desirable or undesirable stimuli that follow as a result of an organism's behavior.

Relapse-prevention training A treatment technique in which heavy drinkers are taught to use self-monitoring to identify the situations and emotional changes that place them at high risk for heavy drinking. They then plan ahead for such situations and reactions.

Relaxation training A procedure in which clients are taught to release all the tension in their bodies on cue.

Reliability A measure of the consistency of test or research results.

Repression An ego defense mechanism that prevents unacceptable impulses from reaching consciousness.

Reserpine A drug originally used to treat high blood pressure but later discovered to cause depression in some people.

Residential treatment center A place where persons who have recovered from substance abuse and dependence live, work, and socialize in a drug-free environment. Also called therapeutic communities.

Residual schizophrenia A type of schizophrenia in which the florid symptoms of the disorder have lessened in intensity and number yet remain with the patient in a residual form.

Resistance An ego defense mechanism that blocks a patient's free associations or causes the patient to change subjects to avoid a potentially painful discussion.

Resistance stage The parasympathetic nervous system's attempt to counteract the response of the sympathetic nervous system in the presence of a threat. See also **General adaptation syndrome.**

Resolution phase The fourth phase in the sexual response cycle, characterized by relaxation and a decline in arousal following orgasm.

Resperidone (Risperdole) A commonly prescribed atypical antipsychotic drug.

Response prevention See **Exposure and response prevention.**

Response set A particular way of responding to questions or statements on a test, such as always selecting "true" regardless of the content of the questions.

Restricting type anorexia nervosa A type of anorexia nervosa in which people reduce their weight by restricting their food intake.

Reticular formation The body's arousal center located in the brain.

Retrograde amnesia A lack of memory about events that occurred before the event that caused the amnesia.

Retrospective study (1) A kind of psychological autopsy in which clinicians and researchers piece together data from the past. This type of study is common for studying the past of a person who committed suicide. (2) Also, a kind of research study in which subjects are asked to recall past events.

Reversal design (ABAB) A single-subject experimental design in which behavior is measured to achieve a baseline (A), then again after the treatment has been applied (B), then again after the conditions during baseline have been reintroduced (A), and then once again after the treatment is reintroduced (B).

Reward A pleasurable stimulus given to an organism to encourage a specific behavior.

Ritalin Trade name for methylphenidate, a stimulant drug that is helpful in many cases of attention-deficit/hyperactivity disorder (ADHD).

Role play A therapy technique in which clients are instructed to act out roles assigned to them by the therapist.

Rorschach test A projective test using a subject's reactions to inkblots to help reveal psychological features of the subject.

Rosenthal effect The general finding that the results of any experiment often conform to the expectations of the experimenter. It is attributed to the effects of bias.

Ruminative response Dwelling repeatedly on one's depressive symptoms.

Rush A spasm of warmth and ecstasy that occurs when certain drugs, such as heroin, are ingested.

Sample A group of subjects that is representative of the larger population about which a researcher wishes to make a statement.

Savant A person with a major mental disorder or intellectual handicap who has some extraordinary ability despite his or her handicaps.

Schizoaffective disorder A disorder in which symptoms of both schizophrenia and a mood disorder are prominent.

Schizoid personality disorder A personality disorder characterized by a pattern of detachment from social relationships and a restricted range of emotional expression.

Schizophrenia A psychotic disorder lasting for at least six months in which personal, social, and occupational functioning that were previously adaptive deteriorate as a result of distorted perceptions, disturbed thought processes, deviant emotional states, and motor abnormalities.

Schizophreniform disorder A disorder in which all of the key features of schizophrenia are present but last between one and six months.

Schizophrenogenic mother According to one theory, a mother who is cold, domineering, and impervious to the needs of others. Supposedly, this type of behavior in the mother contributes to schizophrenia in the child; however, research has not supported this theory.

Schizotypal personality disorder A personality disorder characterized by a pattern of acute discomfort in close relationships, cognitive or perceptual distortions, and eccentricities of behavior.

School phobia A childhood anxiety disorder in which children experience extreme anxiety or upset about attending school and often stay home for an extended period of time.

School refusal See **School phobia.**

Scientific method The process of systematically acquiring and evaluating information through observation to gain an understanding of specific phenomena.

Seasonal affective disorder (SAD) A mood disorder in which mood episodes are related to changes in season.

Secondary gain In psychodynamic theory, part of a mechanism for explaining hysterical somatoform disorder. Hysterical symptoms not only keep internal conflicts out of awareness (primary gain) but may also result in the person's receiving kindness or sympathy from others (secondary gain).

Secondary process In Freudian theory, the ego's mode of operation, consisting of assessing new situations, weighing in past experiences, anticipating consequences, and planning how best to obtain gratification.

Second-generation antidepressants New antidepressant drugs that differ structurally from tricyclics and MAO inhibitors.

Sedative-hypnotic drug A drug used in low doses to reduce anxiety and in high doses to help people sleep.

Selective amnesia A disorder in which the person remembers some but not all events occurring over a circumscribed period of time.

Selective serotonin reuptake inhibitors (SSRI) A group of second-generation antidepressant drugs (including fluoxetine, paroxetine, and setraline) that are thought to alter serotonin activity specifically, without affecting other neurotransmitters or biochemical processes.

Self-actualization The humanistic process by which people fulfill their potential for goodness and growth.

Self-efficacy The judgment that one can master and perform needed behaviors whenever necessary.

Self-help group (Mutual help group) A therapy group made up of people who have similar problems and come together to help and support one another without the direct leadership of a professional clinician.

Self-hypnosis The induction by oneself of a hypnotic state.

Self-instruction training A cognitive therapy that helps people solve problems and cope with stress by teaching them to make helpful statements to themselves and to apply such statements in difficult circumstances.

Self-monitoring A technique for monitoring behavior in which subjects or clients observe themselves.

Self psychology A psychodynamic theory developed by Heinz Kohut that focuses on the role of the self.

Self-statements According to some cognitive theorists, statements about oneself, sometimes counterproductive, that come to mind during stressful situations.

Semantic memory A person's memory for abstract, encyclopedic, or categorical information.

Senile Typical of or occurring in people over the age of 65.

Senile dementia See **Dementia.**

Senile plaques Sphere-shaped deposits of beta-amyloid protein that form in excessive numbers in the spaces between certain neurons in people with Alzheimer's disease, interfering with memory and learning.

Sensate focus A treatment for sexual disorders that instructs couples to take the focus away from intercourse and instead spend time concentrating on mutual massage, kissing, and hugging. This approach reduces the pressure to achieve erection and orgasm.

Separation anxiety disorder A childhood disorder characterized by excessive anxiety, even panic, whenever the child is separated from a parent.

Serotonin A neurotransmitter whose abnormal activity is linked to depression, eating disorders, and obsessive-compulsive disorder.

Sex offender statute The presumption by some state legislators that people who are repeatedly found guilty of certain sex crimes have a mental disorder and should be categorized as "mentally disordered sex offenders."

Sexual aversion disorder A disorder characterized by the aversion to and active avoidance of genital sexual contact with a sexual partner.

Sexual dysfunction A disorder in which a person is unable to function normally in some area of the human sexual response cycle.

Sexual masochism A pattern in which a person has repeated and intense sexual urges, fantasies, or behaviors that involve being humiliated, beaten, bound, or otherwise made to suffer.

Sexual pain disorder A dysfunction in which a person experiences pain during arousal or intercourse. See also **Dyspareunia** and **Vaginismus.**

Sexual response cycle The generalized sequence of behavior and feelings that occurs during sexual intercourse, consisting of desire, excitement, orgasm, and resolution.

Sexual sadism A pattern in which a person has repeated and intense sexual urges, fantasies, or behaviors that involve inflicting physical or psychological suffering on others.

Shaping A learning procedure in which successive approximations of the desired behavior are rewarded.

Shared psychotic disorder (Folie à deux) A disorder in which a person embraces delusions held by another individual.

Sheltered workshop A protected and supervised workplace that offers clients occupational training.

Short-term memory The memory system that collects new information.

Shuttle box A box partitioned by a barrier that an animal can jump over in order to escape or avoid shock. Used in learned helplessness and other studies.

Single-subject experimental design A research method in which a single subject is observed and measured both before and after the manipulation of an independent variable.

Situation (or state) anxiety Anxiety experienced in particular situations or environments.

Sleep apnea A disorder in which the person actually stops breathing for up to thirty or more seconds while asleep.

Sleep terror disorder A parasomnia in which persons awaken suddenly during the first third of their major sleep episode, screaming out in extreme fear and agitation.

Sleepwalking disorder A parasomnia in which people repeatedly leave their beds and walk around without being conscious of the episode or remembering it later.

Social breakdown syndrome A pattern of deterioration resulting from institutionalization and characterized by extreme withdrawal, anger, physical aggressiveness, and loss of interest in personal appearance.

Social phobia A persistent fear of social or performance situations in which embarrassment may occur.

Social skills training A therapeutic approach to help people acquire or improve their social skills and assertiveness through the use of role playing and rehearsing of desirable behaviors.

Social therapy (Sociotherapy) An approach to therapy in which the therapist makes practical advice and life adjustment a central focus of treatment for schizophrenia. Therapy also focuses on problem solving, decision making, development of social skills, and management of medications.

Sociocultural model The theoretical perspective that emphasizes the effect of society and culture on individual behavior.

Sociology The study of human relationships and social groups.

Sociopathy See **Antisocial personality disorder.**

Sociotherapy See **Social therapy.**

Sodium amobarbital (Amytal) A drug used to put people into a near-sleep state during which they may recall forgotten events.

Sodium pentobarbital (Pentothal) See **Sodium amobarbital.**

Somatization disorder A somatoform disorder characterized by numerous physical ailments without an organic basis and whose difficulties continue for several years.

Somatoform disorder A physical illness or ailment with predominantly psychosocial causes. It differs from a factitious disorder in that the patient experiences no sense of willing the symptoms or of having control over them.

Somatogenesis The development of abnormal functioning from physical causes.

Specific phobia An intense and persistent fear of a clearly discernible, circumscribed object or situation (excluding social phobia and agoraphobia).

Spectator role A psychological position that some people take during sex in which their focus on their sexual performance is so pronounced that the sexual performance and enjoyment are impeded.

Standardization The process in which a test is administered to a large group of subjects whose performance then serves as a common standard or norm. Also, the process in which the techniques for administering a test are made uniform, so that all subjects are tested under similar conditions.

State dependent learning Learning that becomes associated with conditions in which it occurred, so that it is best remembered under the same conditions. For example, information learned when under the influence of alcohol may be better recalled when the person is again under the influence of alcohol.

State hospital A public mental institution, run by the state.

Statistical analysis The application of principles of probability to the findings of a study in order to learn how likely it is that the findings have occurred by chance.

Statistical significance A measure of the probability that an observed event occurred by chance rather than as the result of a particular relationship or an experimental manipulation.

Statutory rape Sexual intercourse with a minor, under any condition.

Stimulant drug A drug that increases the activity of the central nervous system.

Stimulus generalization A phenomenon in which responses to one stimulus are also elicited by similar stimuli.

Stress inoculation See **Self-instruction training.**

Stress management training An approach to treating generalized and other anxiety problems that focuses on teaching clients to reduce and control stress.

Stressor An event that creates a degree of threat by confronting a person with a demand or opportunity for change of some kind.

Structural family therapy A family systems treatment approach in which the therapist pays particular attention to family structure, including power issues, the role each member plays within the family, and the alliances between family members.

Structured interview An interview format in which clinicians ask prepared questions.

Structured observation A method of observing behavior in which people are monitored in artificial settings created in clinicians' offices or in laboratories.

Stutter A disturbance in the normal fluency and timing of speech. Persons may repeat, prolong, or interject sounds; pause within a word; or experience excessive physical tension when they produce words.

Subintentioned death A death in which the victim plays an indirect, covert, partial, or unconscious causal role.

Subject An individual chosen to participate in a study.

Sublimination In psychoanalytic theory, the rechanneling of impulses into endeavors that are both socially acceptable and personally gratifying. It can also be used as an ego defense mechanism.

Subpersonalities The distinct personalities found in individuals suffering from multiple personality disorder, each with a unique set of memories, behaviors, thoughts, and emotions.

Substance abuse A pattern of behavior in which a person relies on a substance excessively and chronically, allowing it to occupy a central position in his or her life.

Substance dependence A pattern of behavior in which a person relies on a substance excessively and chronically, usually resulting in tolerance to the substance, or withdrawal symptoms upon cessation, or both.

Substance-related disorder A pattern of maladaptive behavior centered around the use of, abuse of, or dependence on certain substances.

Suicide A self-inflicted death in which the person acts intentionally, directly, and consciously.

Suicide prevention programs Programs found in many hospitals and counseling centers that try to identify people who are at the point of killing themselves and to help them perceive their situation more accurately and constructively in order to overcome the crisis.

Superego One of the three psychological forces proposed by Freud as central to shaping the personality. The superego emerges from the ego and embodies the values and ideals taught to us by our parents.

Support group A therapy-like group of people with a common psychological problem who meet and work on their difficulties together.

Supportive nursing care A treatment, applied to anorexia nervosa in particular, in which well-trained nurses conduct a day-to-day hospital program.

Symbolic loss A Freudian concept developed to explain depression in cases where the person has not lost a loved one. In symbolic loss any valued lost object (for example, a loss of employment) may be unconsciously interpreted as the loss of a loved one.

Sympathetic nervous system The nerve fibers of the autonomic nervous system that quicken the heartbeat and produce other changes experienced as fear or anxiety.

Symptom A physical or psychological sign of a disorder.

Symptom substitution The belief held by some psychodynamic therapists that quick symptom reduction is likely to result in the replacement of the old symptoms by new ones.

Synapse The tiny space into which neurotransmitters are released, between the nerve ending of one neuron and the dendrite of another.

Syndrome A cluster of symptoms that usually occur together.

Synergistic effect An enhancement of effects that occurs when more than one drug is having an effect on the body at any one time.

Synesthesia A crossing over of sensory perceptions, caused by LSD and other hallucinogenic drugs. For example, a loud sound may be experienced as visible fluctuation in the air.

Systematic desensitization A treatment procedure in which clients with phobias learn to react calmly instead of with intense fear to the objects or situations they dread.

Tarantism Also known as St. Vitus's dance, this was a disorder that occurred throughout Europe between A.D. 900 and 1800 in which groups of people would suddenly start to jump around, dance, and go into convulsions.

Tardive dyskinesia Extrapyramidal effects, such as involuntary smacking of the lips or wagging of the chin, that appear in some patients after they have taken traditional antipsychotic drugs for an extended time. It is more common in older patients, and it is sometimes difficult or impossible to eliminate. See also **Extrapyramidal effect.**

Tay-Sachs disease A metabolic disorder resulting from a pairing of recessive genes that causes mental deterioration, loss of visual functioning, and death.

Tension headache See **Muscle-contraction headache.**

Testosterone The principal male sex hormone.

Tetrahydrocannabinol (THC) The main psychoactive ingredient of the hemp plant.

Thalamus The region of the brain that acts as a relay station for sensory information, sending it to the cerebrum.

Thanatos According to the Freudian view, thanatos is the basic death instinct that functions in opposition to the life instinct.

Thematic Apperception Test A projective test using pictures that depict people in somewhat unclear situations.

Therapist A person who implements a system of therapy to help a person overcome psychological difficulties.

Therapy A special, systematic process for helping people overcome their psychological difficulties. The process may consist primarily of discussion or action (psychotherapy) or of biological intervention.

Token economy An operant conditioning program in which a person's desirable behaviors are reinforced systematically by the awarding of tokens that can be exchanged for goods or privileges.

Tolerance The adjustment the body makes to the habitual presence of certain drugs so that larger and larger doses are required to achieve the initial effect.

Trait anxiety A person's general level of anxiety.

Tranquilizer A drug that reduces anxiety.

Transference According to psychodynamic theorists, a phenomenon that occurs during psychotherapy, in which the patient acts toward the therapist as he or she did or does toward important figures, particularly parents.

Transsexualism (Gender identity disorder) A disorder in which persons feel uncomfortable about their assigned sex and strongly wish to be a member of the opposite sex. They are often preoccupied with getting rid of their primary and secondary sex characteristics and many find their own genitals repugnant.

Transvestic fetishism (Transvestism, or cross-dressing) A pattern in which a person has recurrent and intense sexual urges, sexually arousing fantasies, or behaviors involving dressing in clothes of the opposite sex, causing significant distress or impairment.

Trephination An ancient operation in which a stone instrument was used to cut away a circular section of the skull. It may have been a Stone Age treatment for abnormal behavior.

Trichotillomania An extremely painful and upsetting impulse-control disorder or compulsion in which people repeatedly pull at and even yank out their hair, eyelashes, and eyebrows.

Tricyclic drug An antidepressant drug such as imipramine that has three rings in its molecular structure.

Trisomy A chromosomal aberration in which an individual has three chromosomes of one kind rather than the usual two.

Tube and intravenous feeding Forced nourishment sometimes provided to sufferers of anorexia nervosa when their condition becomes life-threatening.

Two-physician certificates (2 PCs) A method of emergency involuntary commitment used in some states, marked by certification by two clinicians that a person is in such a state of mind as to be dangerous to himself or herself or to others and may be committed involuntarily.

Type A personality style A personality pattern characterized by hostility, cynicism, drivenness, impatience, competitiveness, and ambition.

Type I schizophrenia A type of schizophrenia that is dominated by positive symptoms, such as delusions, hallucinations, and positive formal thought disorders.

Type II schizophrenia A type of schizophrenia that is dominated by negative symptoms, such as flat affect, poverty of speech, and loss of volition.

Tyramine A chemical that, if allowed to accumulate, can raise blood pressure dangerously. It is found in many common foods and is broken down by MAO. See also **MAO inhibitor.**

Tyrosine The chemical that most people produce by metabolizing the amino acid phenylalanine, a process that fails to occur in children with phenylketonuria.

Ulcer Lesions or holes that form in the wall of the stomach or of the duodenum.

Unconditional positive regard Full, warm acceptance of a person regardless of what he or she says, thinks, or feels; a critical component of client-centered therapy.

Unconditioned response (UCR) The natural, automatic response elicited by an unconditioned stimulus.

Unconditioned stimulus (UCS) A stimulus that elicits an automatic, natural response.

Unconscious The deeply hidden mass of memories, experiences, and impulses that is viewed in Freudian theory as the wellspring of most behavior.

Undifferentiated schizophrenia A diagnosis assigned to people who seem to manifest schizophrenia but who do not fall neatly into one of the other categories of schizophrenia.

Undoing An ego defense mechanism in which a person attempts to atone for an unacceptable desire or act by another act. This concept is sometimes used by some psychodynamic theorists to explain obsessive-compulsive disorder. The compulsive act is thought to implicitly cancel out the person's undesirable impulses.

Unilateral electroconvulsive therapy (ECT) A form of electroconvulsive therapy in which electrodes are attached to the head so that electrical current passes through only one side of the brain. Unilateral ECT causes less confusion and memory loss than bilateral ECT and often appears to be equally effective.

Unipolar depression Depression without a history of mania. It is followed, upon recovery, by a normal or nearly normal mood.

Unstructured interview An interview format in which the clinician asks questions spontaneously, based on issues that emerge during the interview.

Vacuum erection device (VED) A device consisting of a hollow cylinder that is placed over the penis connected to a hand pump. The pump is used to create a partial vacuum around the penis, which fills with blood as a result and becomes erect.

Vaginismus A condition marked by involuntary contractions of the muscles around the outer third of the vagina when penetration is attempted, preventing entry of the penis.

Validity The accuracy of a test's or study's results, that is, the extent to which the test or study actually measures or shows what it claims to. See also **External validity** and **Internal validity.**

Valium (diazepam) An antianxiety drug.

Variable Any characteristic or event that can vary, whether from time to time, from place to place, or from person to person.

Vascular dementia Dementia caused by a cerebrovascular accident, or stroke, that restricted the blood flow to certain areas of the brain.

Ventromedial hypothalamus (VMH) The region of the hypothalamus that when activated depresses hunger.

Vicarious conditioning Acquiring fear or other reactions through modeling.

Visual hallucinations Hallucinations in which a person may either experience vague perceptions, perhaps of colors or clouds, or have distinct visions of people, objects, or scenes that are not there.

Voyeurism A paraphilia in which a person has recurrent and intense sexual desires to observe people in secret as they undress or to spy on couples engaged in intercourse, and acts on these desires.

Waxy flexibility A type of catatonia in which a person will maintain a posture into which he or she has been placed by someone else.

Weight set point The weight level that a person is predisposed to maintain, set up by a "weight thermostat" that is governed by the lateral and ventromedial hypothalamus.

Wernicke's encephalopathy (Alcohol-induced persisting amnestic disorder) A neurological disease characterized by confusion, excitement, delirium, double vision, and other eye-movement abnormalities, and caused by an alcohol-related deficiency of vitamin B. If untreated it progresses into Korsakoff's syndrome.

Windigo An intense fear of being turned into a cannibal by a flesh-eating monster. The disorder was once found among Algonquin Indian hunters.

Wish fulfillment In psychodynamic theory, the gratification of id instincts by primary process thinking.

Withdrawal Unpleasant, sometimes dangerous reactions that occur when individuals who have a physical dependence on a drug suddenly stop taking or reduce their dosage of the drug.

Working through The process during psychoanalysis of confronting repressed conflicts, reinterpreting memories and feelings, and overcoming their negative effects.

References

Journal Abbreviations

Acta Psychiatr. Scandin. *Acta Psychiatrica Scandinavica*
Addic. Behav. *Addictive Behaviors*
Adol. Psychiat. *Adolescent Psychiatry*
Adv. Behav. Res. Ther. *Advances in Behavior Research and Therapy*
Amer. Hlth. *American Health*
Amer. J. Addict *American Journal on Addictions*
Amer. J. Clin. Hyp. *American Journal of Clinical Hypnosis*
Amer. J. Clin. Hypnother. *American Journal of Clinical Hypnotherapy*
Amer. J. Comm. Psych. *American Journal of Community Psychology*
Amer. J. Criminal Justice *American Journal of Criminal Justice*
Amer. J. Ment. Def. *American Journal of Mental Deficiency*
Amer. J. Ment. Retard. *American Journal on Mental Retardation*
Amer. J. Obstet. Gynecol. *American Journal of Obstetrics and Gynecology*
Amer. J. Orthopsychiat. *American Journal of Orthopsychiatry*
Amer. J. Psychiat. *American Journal of Psychiatry*
Amer. J. Psychother. *American Journal of Psychotherapy*
Amer. J. Pub. Hlth. *American Journal of Public Health*
Amer. Psychologist *American Psychologist*
Amer. Sci. *American Scientist*
Amer. Sociol. Rev. *American Sociological Review*
Ann. Behav. Med. *Annals of Behavioral Medicine*
Ann. Clin. Psychiat. *Annals of Clinical Psychiatry*
Ann. Internal Med. *Annals of Internal Medicine*
Annu. Rev. Neurosci. *Annual Review of Neuroscience*
Annu. Rev. Psychol. *Annual Review of Psychology*
Appl. Cog. Psychol. *Applied Cognitive Psychology*
Appl. Prev. Psychol. *Applied and Preventive Psychology*
Arch. Fam. Med. *Archives of Family Medicine*
Arch. Gen. Psychiat. *Archives of General Psychiatry*
Arch. Internal Med. *Archives of Internal Medicine*
Arch. Pediatr. Adoles. *Archives of Pediatric Adolescent Medicine*
Arch. Psychiatr. Nursing *Archives of Psychiatric Nursing*
Arch. Sex. Behav. *Archives of Sexual Behavior*
Austral. Psychologist *Australian Psychologist*
Austral. J. Clin. Exp. Hyp. *Australian Journal of Clinical and Experimental Hypnosis*
Austral. New Zeal. J. Psychiat. *Australian and New Zealand Journal of Psychiatry*

Basic Appl. Soc. Psychol. *Basic and Applied Social Psychology*
Behav. Cog. Psychother. *Behavioral and Cognitive Psychotherapy*
Behav. Genet. *Behavioral Genetics*
Behav. Mod. *Behavior Modification*
Behav. Neurosci. *Behavioral Neuroscience*
Behav. Psychother. *Behavioural Psychotherapy*
Behav. Res. Ther. *Behavior Research and Therapy*
Behav. Sci. *Behavioral Science*
Behav. Sci. Law. *Behavioral Science and the Law*
Behav. Ther. *Behavior Therapy*
Biofeed. Self-Reg. *Biofeedback and Self-Regulation*
Biol. Psychiat. *Biological Psychiatry*
Biol. Psychol. *Biological Psychology*
Brain Res. *Brain Research*
Brit. J. Cog. Psychother. *British Journal of Cognitive Psychotherapy*
Brit. J. Dev. Psychol. *British Journal of Developmental Psychology*
Brit. J. Med. Psychol. *British Journal of Medicinal Psychology*
Brit. J. Psychiat. *British Journal of Psychiatry*

Bull. Amer. Acad. Psychiat. Law *Bulletin of the American Academy of Psychiatry Law*
Bull. Menninger Clin. *Bulletin of the Menninger Clinic*
Bull. Psychosom. Soc. *Bulletin of the Psychosomatic Society*

Canad. J. Psychiat. *Canadian J. Psychiatry*
Child Dev. *Child Development*
Chron. Higher Educ. *Chronicle of Higher Education*
Clin. Pharmacol. Ther. *Clinical and Pharmacological Therapy*
Clin. Rehab. *Clinical Rehabilitation*
Clin. Soc. Work J. *Clinical Social Work Journal*
Child Psychiat. Human Dev. *Child Psychiatry and Human Development*
Cog. Emot. *Cognitive Emotions*
Cog. Ther. Res. *Cognitive Therapy and Research*
Comprehen. Psychiat. *Comprehensive Psychiatry*
Contemp. Hyp. *Contemporary Hypnosis*
Contemp. Psychol. *Contemporary Psychology*
Criminal Justice Behav. *Criminal Justice and Behavior*

Dev. Neuropsychol. *Developmental Neuropsychology*
Dev. Psychopathol. *Developmental Psychopathology*
Dis. Nerv. Syst. *Diseases of the Nervous System*
Dissociat. Prog. Dissociat. Disorders *Dissociation Progress in the Dissociative Disorders*
Drug. Alc. Dep. *Drug and Alcohol Dependence*

Endocrine Res. *Endocrine Research*
Ethics Behav. *Ethics & Behavior*
Eur. Arch. Psychiat. Clin. Neurosci. *European Archives of Psychiatry and Clinical Neuroscience*
Eur. Arch. Psychiat. Neurol. Sci. *European Archives of Psychiatry and Neurological Science*
Eur. J. Pers. *European Journal of Personality*
Eur. J. Psychiat. *European Journal of Psychiatry*
Exp. Clin. Psychopharmacol. *Experimental and Clinical Pharmacology*

Fam. Process *Family Process*
Fed. Probation *Federal Probation*

Gen. Hosp. Psychiat. *General Hospital Psychiatry*

Hlth. Care Women Inter. *Health Care for Women International*
Hlth. Psychol. *Health Psychology*
Hosp. Comm. Psychiat. *Hospital and Community Psychiatry*

Indiv. Psychol. J. Adlerian Res. Prac. *Individual Psychology: A Journal of Adlerian Theory, Research and Practice*
Integ. Physiol. Behav. Sci. *Integrative Physiological and Behavioral Science*
Integ. Psychiat. *Integrated Psychiatry*
Inter. Forum Psychoanal. *International Forum of Psychoanalysis*
Inter. J. Addic. *International Journal of Addiction*
Inter. J. Aging Human Dev. *International Journal of Aging and Human Development*
Inter. J. Behav. Dev. *International Journal of Behavioral Development*
Inter. J. Clin. Exp. Hyp. *International Journal of Clinical and Experimental Hypnosis*
Inter. J. Eat. Disorders *International Journal of Eating Disorders*

Inter. J. Group Psychother. *International Journal of Group Psychotherapy*
Inter. J. Ment. Hlth. *International Journal of Mental Health*
Inter. J. Methods Psychiatr. Res. *International Journal of Methods in Psychiatric Research*
Inter. J. Obesity *International Journal of Obesity*
Inter. J. Offend. Ther. Compar. Crimin. *International Journal of Offender Therapy and Comparative Criminology*
Inter. J. Psychoanal. *International Journal of Psychoanalysis*
Inter J. Psychoanal.-Psychother. *International Journal of Psychoanalytic-Psychotherapy*
Inter. J. Psychosom. *International Journal of Psychosomatics*

J. Abnorm. Child Psychol. *Journal of Abnormal Child Psychology*
J. Abnorm. Psychol. *Journal of Abnormal Psychology*
J. Abnorm. Soc. Psychol. *Journal of Abnormal and Social Psychology*
J. Adolescence *Journal of Adolescence*
J. Affect. Disorders *Journal of Affective Disorders*
J. Amer. Acad. Child Adol. Psychiat. *Journal of the American Academy of Child and Adolescent Psychiatry*
J. Amer. Acad. Psychoanal. *Journal of the American Academy of Psychoanalysis*
J. Amer. Coll. Hlth. *Journal of American College Health*
J. Amer. Ger. Soc. *Journal of the American Geriatric Society*
JAMA *Journal of the American Medical Association*
J. Amer. Psychoanal. Assoc. *Journal of the American Psychoanalytical Association*
J. Anx. Dis. *Journal of Anxiety Disorders*
J. Appl. Behav. Anal. *Journal of Applied Behavior Analysis*
J. Appl. Behav. Sci. *Journal of Applied Behavioral Sciences*
J. Appl. Soc. Psychol. *Journal of Applied Social Psychology*
J. Appl. Soc. Sci. *Journal of Applied Social Sciences*
J. Autism Child. Schizo. *Journal of Autism and Childhood Schizopherenia*
J. Autism Dev. Disorders *Journal of Autism and Developmental Disorders*
J. Behav. Ther. Exp. Psychiat. *Journal of Behavior Therapy and Experimental Psychiatry*
J. Child Psychol. Psychiat. *Journal of Child Psychology and Psychiatry*
J. Child Psychol. Psychiat. Allied Disc. *Journal of Child Psychology, Psychiatry and Allied Disciplines*
J. Clin. Psychiat. *Journal of Clinical Psychiatry*
J. Clin. Psychol. *Journal of Clinical Psychology*
J. Coll. Student Dev. *Journal of College Student Development*
J. Cons. Clin. Psychol. *Journal of Consulting and Clinical Psychology*
J. Couns. Dev. *Journal of Counseling & Development*
J. Couns. Psychol. *Journal of Counseling Psychology*
J. Early Adolescence *Journal of Early Adolescence*
J. Exp. Anal. Behav. *Journal of Experimental Analysis of Behavior*
J. Exp. Child Psychol. *Journal of Experimental Child Psychology*
J. Exp. Psychol. *Journal of Experimental Psychology*
J. Exp. Psychol. Gen. *Journal of Experimental Psychology General*
J. Fam Issues *Journal of Family Issues*
J. Fam. Prac. *Journal of Family Practice*
J. Fam. Psychother *Journal of Family Psychotherapy*
J. Gamb. Stud. *Journal of Gambling Studies*
J. Geriat. Psychiat. Neurol. *Journal of Geriatric Psychiatry and Neurology*
J. Hlth. Soc. Behav. *Journal of Health and Social Behavior*
J. Human. Psychol. *Journal of Humanistic Psychology*
J. Interpers. Violence *Journal of Interpersonal Violence*
J. Learn. Dis. *Journal of Learning Disorders*
J. Marital Fam. Ther. *Journal of Marital and Family Therapy*
J. Ment. Hlth. Admin. *Journal of Mental Health Administration*
J. Ment. Hlth. Couns. *Journal of Mental Health Counseling*
J. Nerv. Ment. Dis. *Journal of Nervous and Mental Diseases*
J. Neurochem. *Journal of Neurochemistry*
J. Neuropsych. Clin. Neurosci. *Journal of Neuropsychiatry and Clinical Neurosciences*
J. Pers. Assess. *Journal of Personality Assessment*
J. Pers. Disorders *Journal of Personality Disorders*
J. Pers. Soc. Psychol. *Journal of Personality and Social Psychology*
J. Pharmacol. Exp. Ther. *Journal of Pharmacology and Experimental Therapeutics*
J. Pineal Res. *Journal of Pineal Research*
J. Psychiat. Neurosci. *Journal of Psychiatry & Neuroscience*
J. Psychiat. Res. *Journal of Psychiatric Research*
J. Psychosom. Med. *Journal of Psychosomatic Medicine*
J. Psychosom. Res. *Journal of Psychosomatic Research*
J. Psychother. Prac. Res. *Journal of Psychotherapy Practice and Research*
J. Rat.-Emot. & Cog.-Behav. Ther. *Journal of Rational-Emotive & Cognitive-Behavior Therapy*
J. Rehab. *Journal of Rehabilitation*
J. Sex Educ. Ther. *Journal of Sex Education and Therapy*
J. Sex Marital Ther. *Journal of Sex and Marital Therapy*
J. Sex Res. *Journal of Sex Research*
J. Soc. Behav. Pers. *Journal of Social Behavior and Personality*
J. Soc. Psychol. *Journal of Social Psychology*
J. Sport Exercise Psychol. *Journal of Sport and Exercise Psychology*
J. Traum. Stress. *Journal of Traumatic Stress*
J. Urology *Journal of Urology*
J. Youth Adolescence *Journal of Youth and Adolescence*

Law Human Behav. *Law and Human Behavior*
Law Psychol. Rev. *Law and Psychology Review*

Marriage Fam. Rev. *Marriage and Family Review*
Med. Aspects Human Sex. *Mental Aspects of Human Sexuality*

N. Engl. J. Med. *New England Journal of Medicine*
Neuropsychiat., Neuropsychol., Behav. Neurol. *Neuropsychiatry, Neuropsychology, and Behavioral Neurology*
NY St. J. Med. *New York State Journal of Medicine*

Obesity Hlth. *Obesity and Health*

Percept. Motor Skills *Perceptual and Motor Skills*
Pers. Individ. Diff. *Personal and Individual Differences*
Pharmacol. Biochem. Behav. *Pharmacological Biochemical Behavior*
Pharmacol. Rev. *Pharmacological Reviews*
Physiol. Behav. *Physiology and Behavior*
Proc. Natl. Acad. Sci. USA *Proceedings of the National Academy of Science*
Profess. Psychologist. *Professional Psychologist*
Profess. Psychol.: Res. Pract. *Professional Psychology: Research and Practice*
Prog. Neuropsychopharmacol. *Progressive Neuropsychopharmacology*
Prog. Neuropsychopharmacol. Biol. Psychiat. *Progressive Neuropsychopharmacological Biological Psychiatry*
Psychiatr. Ann. *Psychiatric Annals*
Psychiatr. Clin. N. Amer. *Psychiatric Clinics of North America*
Psychiatr. Hosp. *Psychiatric Hospital*
Psychiatr. J. Univ. Ottawa *Psychiatric Journal of the University of Ottawa*
Psychiatr. Quart. *Psychiatric Quarterly*
Psychol. Addict. Behav. *Psychology of Addictive Behavior*
Psychol. Aging *Psychology and Aging*
Psychol. Assess. *Psychological Assessment*
Psychol. Bull. *Psychological Bulletin*
Psychol. Med. *Psychological Medicine*
Psychol. Rec. *Psychological Record*
Psychol. Rep. *Psychological Reports*
Psychol. Rev. *Psychological Review*
Psychol. Sci. *Psychological Science*
Psychol. Women Quart. *Psychology of Women Quarterly*
Psychol. Today *Psychology Today*

Psychopharmacol. Bull. *Psychopharmacology Bulletin*
Psychosom. Med. *Psychosomatic Medicine*
Psychother. Priv. Prac. *Psychotherapy in Private Practice*
Psychother. Res. *Psychotherapy Research*
Psychother. Theory Res. Prac. *Psychotherapy: Theory, Research and Practice*

Quart. J. Stud. Alcohol. *Quarterly Journal on the Studies of Alcoholism*

Res. Nursing Hlth. *Research in Nursing and Health*

Scand. J. Work Envir. Hlth. *Scandinavian Journal of Work and Environment Health*
Scientif. Amer. *Scientific American*
Schizo. Bull. *Schizophrenic Bulletin*
Sem. in Neuro. *Seminars in Neurology*
Soc. Behav. Pers. *Social Behavior and Personality*
Soc. Psychiat. *Social Psychiatry*
Soc. Sci. Med. *Social Science and Medicine*
Sex. Disability *Sexual Disability*
Sex. Marital Ther. *Sexual and Marital Therapy*
Soc. Psychiatr. Psychiatr. Epidemiol. *Social Psychiatry & Psychiatric Epidemiology*
Suic. Life-Threat. Behav. *Suicide and Life-Threatening Behavior*

Topics Early Childhood Spec. Ed. *Topics in Early Childhood Special Education*
Trends Neurosci. *Trends in Neuroscience*

Women Hlth. *Women & Health*

APA [American Psychiatric Association] (1968). *Diagnostic and statistical manual of mental disorders* (2nd. ed.). Washington, DC: Author.

APA (1983). APA statement on the insanity defense: Insanity defense work group. *Amer. J. Psychiat., 140*(6), 681–688.

APA (1987). *Diagnostic and statistical manual of mental disorders* (3rd rev. ed.). Washington, DC: Author.

APA (1991). *DSM-IV options book.* Washington, DC.

APA (1993). *Practice Guideline for Major Depressive Disorder in Adults.* Washington, DC: Author.

APA (1994). *Diagnostic and statistical manual of mental disorders* (4th ed.). Washington, DC: Author.

Abadi, S. (1984). Adiccion: la eterna repeticion de un desencuentro (Acerca de la dependencia humana) [Addiction: The endless repetition of a disencounter]. *Revista de Psicoanalisis, 41*(6), 1029–1044.

Abbott, S. (1987). BABES and puppets helping children: Myth Mary & Early Bird teach prevention. *Alcohol. Addic., 8*(2), 17.

Abel, E. L., & Zeidenberg, P. (1985). Age, alcohol and violent death: A postmortem study. *J. Stud. Alc., 46,* 228–231.

Abel, G. G. (1989). Paraphilias. In H. I. Kaplan & B. J. Sadock (Eds.), *Comprehensive textbook of psychiatry* (5th ed., Vol. 1). Baltimore: Williams & Wilkins.

Abel, G. G., Becker, J. V., & Cunningham-Rathner, J. (1984). Complications, consent, and cognitions in sex between children and adults. *Inter. J. Law Psychiat., 7,* 89–103.

Abel, G. G., & Osborn, C. (1992). The paraphilias: The extent and nature of sexually deviant and criminal behavior. *Psychiatr. Clin. N. Amer., 15*(3), 675–687.

Ablow, K. R. (1993, February 9). Being personally touched by mental illness is very different from treating it. *The Washington Post,* p. WH7.

Abou-Saleh, M. T. (1992). Lithium. In E. S. Paykel (Ed.), *Handbook of Affective Disorders.* New York: Guilford.

Abraham, K. (1911). Notes on the psychoanalytic investigation and treatment of manic-depressive insanity and allied conditions. In *Selected papers on psychoanalysis* (pp. 137–156). New York: Basic Books, 1960.

Abraham, K. (1916). The first pregenital stage of the libido. In *Selected papers on psychoanalysis* (pp. 248–279). New York: Basic Books, 1960.

Abraham, S., & Llewellyn-Jones, D. (1984). *Eating disorders: The facts.* New York: Oxford University Press.

Abram, K. M., & Teplin, L. A. (1990). Drug disorder, mental illness, and violence. *Nat. Inst. Drug Abuse Res. Monogr. Ser., 103,* 222–238.

Abramson, E. E., & Valene, P. (1991). Media use, dietary restraint, bulimia and attitudes towards obesity: A preliminary study. *Brit. Rev. of Bulimia Anorexia Nervosa, 5*(2), 73–76.

Abramson, L. Y., Metalsky, G. I., & Alloy, L. B. (1989). Hopelessness depression: A theory-based subtype of depression. *Psychol. Rev., 96*(2), 358–372.

Abramson, L. Y., Metalsky, G. I., & Alloy, L. B. (1989). Hopelessness depression: A theory-based subtype of depression. *Psychol. Rev., 96*(2), 358–372.

Abramson, L. Y., Seligman, M. E., & Teasdale, J. D. (1978). Learned helplessness in humans: Critique and reformulation. *J. Abnorm. Psychol., 87*(1), 49–74.

Ackerman, M. D. (1995). Introduction to the special section on contemporary issues in human sexuality: Research and practice. *J. Cons. Clin. Psychol., 63*(6), 859–861.

Ackerman, M. D. & Carey, M. P. (1995). Psychology's role in the assessment of erectile dysfunction: Historical precedents, current knowledge, and methods. *J. Cons. Clin. Psychol., 63*(6), 862–876.

Ackerman, N. (1965). Interlocking pathologies in family relationships. In S. Rado & G. Daniels (Eds.), *Changing concepts in psychoanalytic medicine.* New York: Grune & Stratton.

Adam, K. S., Bouckoms, A., & Streiner, D. (1982). Parental loss and family stability in attempted suicide. *Arch. Gen. Psychiat., 39*(9), 1081–1085.

Adams, C. E., Pantelis, C., Duke, P. J., & Barnes, T. R. E. (1996). Psychopathology, social, and cognitive functioning in a hostel for homeless women. *Brit. J. Psychiat., 168, 82–86.*

Adams, P. R., & Adams, G. R. (1984). Mount Saint Helen's ashfall: Evidence for a disaster stress reaction. *Amer. Psychologist, 39,* 252–260.

Addington, D. (1995). The use of placebos in clinical trials for acute schizophrenia. *Canad. J. Psychiat., 40*(4), 171–176.

Ader, R., Felten, D. L., & Cohen, N. (Eds). (1991). *Psychoneuroimmunology* New York: Academic Press.

Ader, R., Felten, D., & Cohen, N. (1991). *Psychoneuroimmunology* (2nd ed.). New York: Academic Press.

Adler, A. (1927). *Individual Psychology.* London: Kegan Paul, Trench, Trubner & Co.

Adler, A. (1927). *Understanding human nature.* New York: Premier.

Adler, A. (1931). *What life should mean to you.* New York: Capricorn.

Adler, N. E., Boyce, T., Chesney, M. A., Cohen, S., Folkman, S., Kahn, R. L., & Syme, S. L. (1994). Socioeconomic status and health: The challenge of the gradient. *Amer. Psychologist, 49*(1), 15–24.

Adler, T. (1992). Prenatal cocaine exposure has subtle, serious effects. *APA Monitor, 23*(11), 17.

Advokat, C. & Kutlesic, V. (1995). Pharmacotherapy of the eating disorders: A commentary. *Neurosci. and Biobehav. Rev., 19*(1), 59–66.

Aggleton, J. P., & Shaw, C. (1996). Amnesia and recognition memory: A re-analysis of psychometric data. *Neuropsychology, 34*(1), 51–62.

Agras, W. S. (1984). Behavioral medicine: An overview. In A. J. Frances & R. E. Hales (Eds.), *American Psychiatric Association annual review* (Vol. 5). Washington, DC: American Psychiatric Press.

Agras, W. S. (1984). The behavioral treatment of somatic disorders. In W. D. Gentry (Ed.), *Handbook of behavioral medicine.* New York: Guilford.

Agras, W. S. (1985). *Panic: Facing fears, phobias, and anxiety.* New York: W. H. Freeman.

Agras, W. S., Rossiter, E. M., Arnow, B. et al.. (1992). Pharmacologic and cognitive-behavioural treatment for bulimia nervosa: A controlled comparison. *Amer. J. Psychiat., 149,* 82–87.

Agras, W. S., Rossiter, E. M., Arnow, B., Telch, C. F., et al. (1994). One-year follow-up of psychosocial and pharmacologic treatments for bulimia nervosa. *J. Clin. Psychiat., 55* (5), 179–183.

Agras, W. S., Sylvester, D., & Oliveau, D. (1969). The epidemiology of common fears and phobias. *Comprehen. Psychiat., 10*(2), 151–156.

Agras, W. S., Taylor, O. B., Kraemer, H. C., Allen, R. A., & Schneider, M. S. (1980). Relaxation training: Twenty-four hour blood pressure reductions. *Arch. Gen. Psychiat., 37,* 859–863.

Aguilar, T., & Munson, W. (1992). Leisure education and counseling as intervention components in drug and alcohol treatment for adolescents. *J.of Alc. Drug Educ., 37*(3), 23–34.

Aiken, L. R. (1985). *Psychological testing and assessment* (5th ed.). Boston: Allyn & Bacon.

Akhtar, S. (1989). Narcissistic personality disorder: Descriptive features and differential diagnosis. *Psychiatr. Clin. N. Amer., 12*(3), 505–529.

Akhtar, S., Wig, N. H., Verma, V. K., Pershod, D., & Verma, S. K. (1975). A phenomenological analysis of symptoms in obsessive-compulsive neuroses. *Brit. J. Psychiat., 127,* 342–348.

Akiskal, H. S. (1989). The classification of mental disorders. In H. I. Kaplan & B. J. Sadock (Eds.), *Comprehensive textbook of psychiatry* (5th ed., Vol. 1). Baltimore: Williams & Wilkins.

ADVTP (Alaska Domestic Violence Training Project). (1996). Training the Trainers Workshop.

Albert, M. S., Butters, N., & Levin, J. (1979). Temporal gradients in the retrograde amnesia of patients with alcoholic Korsakoff's disease. *Arch. of Neurol., 36,* 211–216.

Alcoholics Anonymous World Services, Inc. (1994). *Personal communication.* Statistic branch. New York, NY.

Alden, L. (1989). Short-term structured treatment for avoidant personality disorder. *J. Cons. Clin. Psychiat., 57*(6), 756–764.

Alden, L. E., & Wallace, S. T. (1995). Social phobia and social appraisal in successful and unsuccessful social interactions. *Behav. Res. Ther., 33* (5), 497–505.

Aldhous, P. (1996, April 27). Matching proteins raise CJD fears. *New Scientist,* p. 21.

Aleksandrowicz, D. R. (1980). Psychoanalytic studies of mania. In R. H. Belmaker & H. M. van Praag (Eds.), *Mania: An evolving concept.* Jamaica, NY: Spectrum.

Alexander, B. (1981). Behavioral approaches to the treatment of bronchial asthma. In C. K. Prokop & L. A. Bradley (Eds.), *Medical psychology: Contributions to behavioral medicine.* New York: Academic Press.

Alexander, B. K., & Hadaway, P. F. (1982). Opiate addiction: The case for an adaptive orientation. *Psychol. Bull., 92*(2), 367–381.

Alexander, F. (1930). About dreams with unpleasant content. *Psychiatr. Quart., 4,* 447–452.

Alexander, J. F., Holtzworth-Munroe, A., & Jameson, P. (1994). The process and outcome of marital and family therapy: Research review and evaluation. In A. E. Bergin & S. L. Garfiel (Eds.), *Handbook of psychotherapy and behavior change* (4th ed.). New York: Wiley.

Alexopoulos, G. S., Meyers, B. S., Young, R. C., Kakuma, T., et al. (1996). Recovery in geriatric depression. *Arch. Gen. Psychiat., 53,* 305–312.

Allard, R., Marshall, M., & Plante, M. C. (1992). Intensive follow-up does not decrease the risk of repeat suicide attempts. *Suic. Life-Threat. Behav., 22,* 303–314.

Allderidge, P. (1979). Hospitals, madhouses and asylums: Cycles in the care of the insane. *Brit. J. Psychiat., 134,* 321–334.

Allebeck, P., & Bolund, C. (1991). Suicides and suicide attempts in cancer patients. *Psychol. Med., 21*(4), 979–984.

Allen, D., & Lader, M. (1992). The interactions of ethanol with single and repeated doses of suriclone and diazepam on physiological and psychomotor functions in normal subjects. *Eur. J. Clin. Pharmacol., 42.*

Allen, J. G. (1993). Dissociative processes: Theoretical underpinnings of a working model for clinician and patient. *Bull. Menninger Clin., 57*(3), 287–308.

Allen, J. G., & Smith, W. H. (1993). Diagnosing dissociative disorders. *Bull. Menninger Clin., 57*(3), 328–343.

Allen, J. J. B., Law, H. & Laravvso, J. J. (1996). Items for assessing posthypnotic recognition amnesia with the HGSHS:A and the SHSS:C[1]. *Inter. J. Clin. Exper. Hyp., 44*(1), 52–65.

Allison, R. B. (1978). A rational psychotherapy plan for multiplicity. *Svensk Tidskrift Hyp., 3,* 9–16.

Alloway, R., & Bebbington, P. E. (1987). The buffer theory of social support: A review of the literature. *Psychol. Med., 17,* 91–108.

Alloy, L. B., Kelly, K. A., Mineka, S., & Clements, C. M. (1990). Comorbidity of anxiety and depressive disorders: A helplessness-hopelessness perspective. In J. D. Maser & R. Cloninger (Eds.), *Comorbidity of mood and anxiety disorders.* Washington, DC : American Psychiatric Press.

Alnaes, R., & Torgersen, S. (1989). Clinical differentiation between major depression only, major depression with panic disorder and panic disorder only: Childhood and personality disorder. *Psychiatria Fennica, Suppl.,* 58–64.

Aloni, R., Heller, L., Ofer, O., Mendelson, E., & Davidoff, G. (1992). Noninvasive treatment for erectile dysfunction in the neurogenically disabled population. *J. Sex Marital Ther., 18*(3), 243–249.

Alpher, V. S. (1992). Introject and identity: Structural-interpersonal analysis and psychological assessment of multiple personality disorder. *J. Pers. Assess., 58*(2), 347–367.

Altemus, M., Pigott, T., L'Heureux, F., Davis, C. L., Rubinow, D. R., Murphy, D. L., & Gold, P. W. (1993). CSF Somatostatin in obsessive-compulsive disorder. *Amer. J. Psychiat., 150*(3), 460–464.

Althof, S. E. (1995). Pharmacologic treatment of rapid ejaculation. Special issue: Clinical sexuality. *Psychiat. Clin. N. Amer., 18*(1), 85–94.

Althof, S. E., & Seftel, A. D. (1995). The evaluation and management of erectile dysfunction. *Psychiat. Clin. N. Amer., 18*(1), 171–191.

Althof, S. E., Levine, S. B., Corty, E., Risen, C., & Stern, E. (1994, March). *The role of clomipramine in the treatment of premature ejaculation.* Paper presented at the 16th annual meeting of the Society for Sex Therapy and Research.

Althof, S. E., Turner, L. A., Levine, S. B., Risen, C. B., Kursh, E., Bodner, D., & Resnick, M. I. (1991). Long-term use of self-injection therapy of papaverine and phentolamine. *J. Sex Marital Ther., 17,* 101–112.

Altrows, I. F. (1995). The practice of rational emotive and cognitive behavior therapy with offenders. *J. Rat.-Emot. & Cog.-Behav. Ther., 13* (4), 225–241.

Altshuler, L. L., Post, R. M., Leverich, G. S., Mikalauskas, K., Rosoff, A., & Ackerman, L. (1995). Antidepressant-induced mania and cycle acceleration: A controversy revisited. *Amer. J. Psychiat., 152* (8), 1130–1138.

Alvir, J. J., Lieberman, J. A., & Safferman, A. Z. (1995). Do white-cell count spikes predict agranulocytosis in clozapine recipients? *Psychopharmacol. Bull., 31* (2), 311–314.

Alvir, J. M. J., & Lieberman, J. A. (1994). A reevaluation of the clinical characteristics of clozapine-induced agranulocytosis in light of the United States experience. *J. Clin. Psychopharmacol., 14*(2), 87–89.

Aman, M. G., & Singh, N. N. (1991). Pharmacological intervention. In J. L. Matson & J. A. Mulick (Eds.), *Handbook of mental retardation.* New York: Pergamon Press.

Amaral, D. G. (1987). Memory: Anatomical organization of candidate brain regions. In F. Plum (Ed.), *Handbook of Physiology: The nervous system.* New York: Oxford University Press.

Amati, A., Celani, T., del Vecchio, M., & Vacca, L. (1981). Anorexia nervosa: L'iter attraverso la medicina generale e l'approccio differito in psichiatria [Anorexia nervosa: The connection between general medicine and the approach in psychiatry.] *Med. Psicosom., 26*(4), 357–363.

Ambrosini, P. J., Bianchi, M. D., Rabinovich, H., & Elia, J. (1993). Antidepressant treatments in child and adolescents I. Affective disorders. *J. Amer. Acad. Child Adol. Psychiat., 32*(1), 1–6.

Amenson, C., & Lewinsohn, P. (1981). An investigation into the observed sex difference in prevalence of unipolar depression. *J. Abnorm. Psychol., 90,* 1–13.

American Association for Protecting Children (AAPC). (1992). *Highlights of official child neglect and abuse reporting.* Denver, CO: American Humane Society.

American Assoc. of Retired Persons. (1990). *A profile of older Americans.* Washington, DC: Author.

American Assoc. on Mental Retardation. (1992). *Mental Retardation: Definition, Classification, and Systems of Supports* (9th ed.). Washington, D.C.: Author.

American Medical Association (1992). *Diagnostic treatment guidelines on domestic violence.* Washington, DC: Author.

American Psychological Association (1996). Interim report of the working group on investigation of memories of childhood abuse. In K. Pezdek & W. P. Banks (Eds.), *The recovered memory/false memory debate.* San Diego: Academic Press.

Amsel, A. (1990). Arousal, suppression, and persistence: Frustration theory, attention, and its disorders [Special issue]. *Cog. Emot., 4*(3), 239–268.

Ananth, J. (1983). New antidepressants. *Comprehen. Psychiat., 24,* 116–124.

Anastasi, A. (1982). *Psychological testing* (5th ed.). New York: Macmillan.

Anastopoulos, A. D., & Barkley, R. A. (1992). Attention deficit-hyperactivity disorder. In C. E. Walker & M. C. Roberts (Eds.), *Handbook of clinical child psychology* (2nd ed.). New York: Wiley.

Andersen, A. E. (1985). *Practical comprehensive treatment of anorexia nervosa and bulimia.* Baltimore: Johns Hopkins UP.

Andersen, A. E. (1990). Diagnosis and treatment of males with eating disorders. In A. E. Andersen (Ed.), *Males with eating disorders.* New York: Brunner/Mazel.

Andersen, A. E. (1992). Eating disorders in males: A special case? In K. D. Brownell, J. Rodin, & J. H. Wilmore (Eds.), *Eating, body weight, and performance in athletes: Disorders or modern society.* Philadelphia: Lea & Febiger.

Andersen, A. E. (1992). Eating disorders in males: Critical questions. In R. Lemberg (Ed.), *Controlling eating disorders with facts, advice, and resources.* Phoenix, AZ: The Oryx Press.

Andersen, A. E. (1995). Sequencing treatment decisions: Cooperation or conflict between therapist and patient. In G. Szmukler, C. Dare, & J. Treasure (Eds.), *Handbook of eating disorders: Theory, treatment and research.* Chichester, England: Wiley.

Andersen, A. E., Morse, C., & Santmyer, K. (1985). Inpatient treatment for anorexia nervosa. In D. M. Garner & P. Garfinkel (Eds.), *Handbook of psychotherapy for anorexia nervosa and bulimia.* New York: Guilford.

Andersen, B. L., Kiecolt-Glaser, J. K., & Glaser, R. (1994). A biobehavioral model of cancer stress and disease course. *Amer. Psychol., 49*(5), 389–404.

Anderson, D. (1994). *Breaking the tradition on college campuses: Reducing drug and alcohol misuse,* Fairfax, VA.: George Mason University.

Anderson, J. L., Vasile, R. G., Mooney, J. J. & Bloomingdale, K. L. et al. (1992). Changes in norepinephrine output following light therapy for fall/winter seasonal depression. *Bio. Psychiat., 32*(8), 700–704.

Anderson, N. B., McNeilly, M., & Myers, H. F. (1992). A contextual model for research of race differences in autonomic reactivity. In E. H. Johnson, W. D. Gentry, & S. Julius (Eds.), *Personality, Elevated Blood Pressure, and Essential Hypertension.* Washington DC: Hemisphere Publishing Corp.

Anderson, S. C. (1993). Anti-stalking laws: Will they curb the erotomanic's obsessive pursuit? *Law & Psychol. Rev., 17,* 171–191.

Anderson, S. R., Avery, D. L., DiPietro, E. K., Edwards, G. L., et al. (1989). Intensive home-based early intervention with autistic children. *Educ. Treatment Children, 10*(4), 352–366.

Andrade, V. M. (1996). Superego, narcissism and culture. *Revista Brasileira de Psicanalise, 30*(2), 385–405.

Andrasik, F., Blanchard, E. B., & Neff, D. F. (1984). Biofeedback and relaxation training for chronic headaches: A controlled comparison of booster treatments and regular contacts for long-term maintenance. *J. Cons. Clin. Psychol., 52*(4), 609–615.

Andreasen, N. (1987). Creativity and mental illness: Prevalence rates in writers and their first-degree relatives. *Amer. J. Psychiat., 144,* 1288–1292.

Andreasen, N. C. (1980). Mania and creativity. In R. H. Belmaker & H. M. van Praag (Eds.), *Mania: An evolving concept.* New York: Spectrum.

Andreasen, N. C., Hoffman, R. E., & Grove, W. M. (1985). Mapping abnormalities in language and cognition. In M. Alpert (Ed.), *Controversies in schizophrenia: Changes and constancies.* New York: Guilford.

Andreasen, N. C., Rezai, K., Alliger, R., Swayze, V. W., Flaum, M., Kirchner, P., Cohen, G., & O'Leary, D. S. (1992). Hypofrontality in neuroleptic-naïve patients and in patients with chronic schizophrenia: Assessment with xenon 133 single-photon emission computed tomography with the Tower of London. *Arch. Gen. Psychiat., 49,* 943–958.

Andrews, B., Valentine, E., & Valentine, J. (1995). Depression and eating disorders following abuse in childhood in two generations of women. *Brit. J. Clin Psychol., 34,* 37–52.

Andrulonis, P. A. (1991). Disruptive behavior disorders in boys and the borderline personality disorder in men. *Ann. Clin. Psychiat., 3*(1), 23–26.

Angermeyer, K. C., Kuhn, L., & Goldstein, J. M. (1990). Gender and the course of schizophrenia: Differences in treated outcomes. *Schizo. Bull., 16* (2), 293–307.

Angold, A., & Rutter, M. (1992). Effects of age and pubertal status on depression in a large clinical sample. *Development and Psychopathology, 4*(1), 5–28.

Angrist, B., Sathananthan, G., & Gershon, S. (1973). Behavioral effect in schizophrenic patients. *Psychopharmacologia, 31,* 507.

Angst, J. (1995). The epidemiology of depressive disorders. *European Neuropsychopharmacol.,* (Suppl.) pp. 95–98.

Annas, G. J. (1993). Physician-assisted suicide—Michigan's temporary solution. *N. Engl. J. Med., 328*(21), 1573–1574.

Annas, G. J., Glants, L. H., & Katz, B. F. (1977). *Informed consent to human experimentation: The subject's dilemma.* Cambridge, MA: Ballinger.

Annis, H. M., Davis, C. S., Graham, M. et al. (1989). *A controlled trial of relapse prevention procedures based on self-efficacy theory.* Unpublished manuscript. Addiction Research Foundation, Toronto.

Anonymous (1996). First person account: Social, economic, and medical effects of schizophrenia. *Schizo. Bull., 22* (1), 183.

Anslinger, H. J., & Cooper, C. R. (1937). Marijuana: Assassin of youth. *Amer. Ma., 124,* (19) 153.

Anthony, J. C., Arria, A. M., & Johnson, E. O. (1995). Epidemiological and public health issues for tobacco, alcohol, and other drugs. In J. M. Oldham & M. B. Riba (Eds.), *American Psychiatric Press review of psychiatry* (Vol. 14). Washington, DC: American Psychiatric Press.

Anthony, J. C., Warner, L. A., Kessler, R. C. (1994). Comparative epidemiology of dependence on tobacco, alcohol, controlled substances and inhalants: Basic findings from the National Comorbidity Survey. *Clin. Exp. Psychopharmacol., 2,* 244–268.

Appelbaum, P. S. (1993). Legal liability and managed care. *Amer. Psychol., 48,* 251–257.

Appelbaum, P. S., & Grisso, T. (1995). The MacArthur treatment competence study. I. Mental Illness and competence to consent to treatment. *Law Human Behav., 19* (2), 105–126.

Apter, J. T. (1993). Frontiers in biological psychiatry: New drug development. *New Jersey Med., 90*(2), 144–146.

Arbel, N., & Stravynski, A. (1991). A retrospective study of separation in the development of adult avoidant personality disorder. *Acta Psychiatr. Scandin., 83*(3), 174–178.

Arbiter, N. (1991). Residential programs for women. In *National Conference on Drug Abuse Research and Practice Conference Highlights.* Rockville, MD: National Institute on Drug Abuse.

Arboleda-Florez, J., & Holley, H. L. (1991). Antisocial burnout: An exploratory study. *Bull. Amer. Acad. Psychiatr. Law, 19*(2), 173–183.

Archer, D. & McDaniel, P. (1995). Violence and gender: Differences and similarities across societies. In R. B. Ruback & N. A. Weiner (Eds.), *Interpersonal violent behaviors: Social and cultural aspects.* New York: Springer Publishing Company.

Archer, R. P. (1997). Future directions for the MMPI-A: Research and clinical issues. *J. Pers. Assess., 68* (1), 95–109.

Arendt, J. (1994). Clinical perspectives for melatonin and its agonists. *Bio. Psychiat., 35,* 1–2.

Arieti, S. (1974). *Interpretation of schizophrenia.* New York: Basic Books.

Arieti, S., & Bemporad, J. (1978). *Severe and mild depression: The psychotherapeutic approach.* New York: Basic Books.

Arinami, T., Itokawa, M., Komiyama, T., Mitsushio, H., Mori, H. et al. (1993). Association between severity of alcoholism and the A1 allele of the dopamine D2 receptor gene TaqI A RFLP. (in Japanese). *Bio. Psychiat., 33,* 108–114.

Aring, C. D. (1974). The Gheel experience: Eternal spirit of the chainless mind! *JAMA, 230*(7), 998–1001.

Aring, C. D. (1975). Gheel: The town that cares. *Fam. Hlth., 7*(4), 54–55, 58, 60.

Arndt, S., Andreasen, N. C., Flaum, M., Miller, D. et al. (1995). A longitudinal study of symptom dimensions in schizophrenia: Prediction and patterns of change. *Arch. Gen. Psychiat., 52*(5), 352–360.

Arndt, W. B., Jr. (1991). *Gender disorders and the paraphilias.* Madison, CT: International Universities Press.

Arnette, J. (1996). Physiological effects of chronic grief: A biofeedback treatment approach. *Death Stud., 20,* 59–72.

Arnold, L. E. (1973, October). Is this label necessary? *J. School Hlth., 43,* 510–514.

Arnstein, R. L. (1986). Ethical and value issues in psychotherapy with college students. *J. Coll. Student Psychother., 1,* 3–20.

Arntz, A., & Lavy, E. (1993). Does stimulus elaboration potentiate exposure in vivo treatment: Two forms of one-session treatment of spider phobia. *Behav. Psychother., 21,* 1–12.

Asarnow, J. R., Asarnow, R. F., Hornstein, N., & Russell, A. (1991). Childhood-onset schizophrenia: Developmental perspectives on schizophrenic disorders. In E. F. Walker (Ed.), *Schizophrenia: A life-course developmental perspective.* San Diego: Academic Press.

Asarnow, J. R., & Horton, A. A. (1990). Coping and stress in families of child psychiatric inpatients: Parents of children with depressive and schizophrenic spectrum disorders. *Child Psychiat. Human Dev., 21*(2), 145–157.

Asberg, K. H. (1986). Biochemical aspects of suicide. *Clin. Neuropharmacol., 9* Suppl 4: 374–376.

Asberg, M., Nordstrom, P., & Traskman, B. L. (1986). Cerebrospinal fluid studies in suicide. An overview. *Annals of the New York Academy of Sciences, 487:* 168–174.

Asberg, M., Traskman, L., & Thoren, P. (1976). 5 HIAA in the cerebrospinal fluid: A biochemical suicide predictor? *Arch. Gen. Psychiat., 33*(10), 1193–1197.

Aserinsky, E., & Kleitman, N. (1953). Eye movements during sleep. *Fed. Process, 13,* 6–7.

Ashleigh, E. A., & Fesler, F. A. (1992). Fluoxetine and suicidal preoccupation. *Amer. J. Psychiat., 149*(12), 1750.

Ashton, H. (1995). Toxicity and adverse consequences of benzodiazepine use. *Psychiatr. Ann., 25* (3), 158–165.

Ashton, J. R., & Donnan, S. (1981). Suicide by burning as an epidemic phenomenon: An analysis of 82 deaths and inquests in England and Wales in 1978–9. *Psychol. Med., 11*(4), 735–739.

Assalian, P. (1994). Premature ejaculation: Is it really psychogenic? *J. Sex Educ. Ther., 20,* 1–4.

Astin, M. C., Ogland-Hand, S. M., Coleman, E. M., & Foy, D. W. (1995). Posttraumatic stress disorder and childhood abuse in battered women: Comparisons with maritally distressed women. *J. Cons. Clin. Psychol., 63* (2), 308–312.

Atkinson, D. R., Brown, M. T., Parham, T. A., Matthews, L. G., et al. (1996). African American client skin tone and clinical judgments of African Americans and European American psychologists. *Profess. Psychol. Res. Prac., 27* (5), 500–505.

Atkinson, J. M., Coia, D. A., Gilmour, W. H., & Harper, J. P. (1996). The impact of education groups for people with schizophrenia on social functioning and quality of life. *Brit. J. Psychiat., 168,* 199–204.

Atlas, J. A. (1995). Association between history of abuse and borderline personality disorder for hospitalized adolescent girls. *Psychol. Rep., 77,* 1346.

Attie, I. & Brooks-Gunn, J. (1992). Developmental issues in the study of eating problems and eating disorders. In J. H. Crowther, D. L. Tennenbaum, S. E. Hobfoll, & M. A. P. Stephens (Eds.), *The etiology of bulimia nervosa: The individual and familial context.* Washington, DC: Hemisphere.

Auchincloss, E. L., & Weiss, R. W. (1992). Paranoid character and the intolerance of indifference. *J. Amer. Psychoanal. Assoc., 40*(4), 1013–1037.

Avery, D., & Lubrano, A. (1979). Depression treated with imipramine and ECT: The DeCarolis study reconsidered. *Amer. J. Psychiat., 136,* 559–569.

Avia, M. D., Ruiz, M. A., Olivares, E., Crespo, M., et al. (1996). Shorter communications. The meaning of psychological symptoms: Effectiveness of a group intervention with hypochondriacal patients. *Behav. Res. Ther., 34*(1), 23–31.

Ayd, F. J., Jr. (1956). A clinical evaluation of Frenquel. *J. Nerv. Ment. Dis., 124,* 507–509.

Ayllon, T. (1963). Intensive treatment of psychotic behavior by stimulus satiation and food reinforcement. *Behav. Res. Ther., 1,* 53–62.

Ayllon, T., & Azrin, N. H. (1965). The measurement and reinforcement of behavior of psychotics. *J. Exp. Anal. Behav., 8,* 357–383.

Ayllon, T., & Michael, J. (1959). The psychiatric nurse as a behavioural engineer. *J. Exp. Anal. Behav., 2,* 323–334.

Ayllon, T., & Roberts, M. D. (1974). Eliminating discipline problems by strengthening academic performance. *J. Appl. Behav. Anal., 7*(1), 71–76.

Azar, B. (1995). Mental disabilities and the brain-gene link. *APA Monitor, 26* (12), 18.

Azar, B. (1996). Intrusive thoughts proven to undermine our health. *APA Monitor, 27* (10), 34.

Azar, S. T., Fantuzzo, J. W., & Twentyman, C. T. (1984). An applied behavioral approach to child maltreatment: Back to basics. *Adv. Behav. Res. Ther., 8*(1), 3–11.

Azar, S. T., Robinson, D. R., Hekimian, E. E., & Twentyman, C. T. (1984). Unrealistic expectations and problem solving ability in maltreating and comparison mothers. *J. Cons. Clin. Psychol., 52,* 687–691.

Azar, S. T., & Rohrbeck, C. A. (1986). Child abuse and unrealistic expectations: Further validation of the Parent Opinion Questionnaire. *J. Cons. Clin. Psychol., 54,* 867–868.

Azar, S. T., & Siegal, B. R. (1990). Behavioral treatment of child abuse: A developmental perspective. *Behav. Mod., 14* (3), 279–300.

Azar, S. T., & Wolfe, D. A. (1989). Child abuse and neglect. In E. J. Mash & R. Barkley (Eds.), *Treatment of childhood disorders.* New York: Guilford.

Azima, F. J. C. (1993). Group psychotherapy with personality disorders. In H. I. Kaplan & B. J. Sadock (Eds.), *Comprehensive group psychotherapy* (3rd ed.). Baltimore: Williams & Wilkins.

Azrin, N. H., Acierno, R., Kogan, E. S., Donohue, B., Besalel, V. A., & McMahon, P. T. (1996). Follow-up results of supportive versus behavioral therapy for illicit drug use. *Behav. Res. Ther., 34*(1), 41–46.

Baberg, H. T., Nelesen, R. A., Dimsdale, J. E. (1996). Amphetamine use: Return of an old scourge in a consultation psychiatry setting. *Amer. J. Psychiat., 153*(6), 789–793.

Bacon, R. (1995). Paranoid knowledge. *Free Associations, 5* (33, Pt. 1), 10–46.

Bacon, S. D. (1973). The process of addiction to alcohol: Social aspects. *Quart. J. Stud. Alc., 34*(1, Pt. A), 1–27.

Baer, L., Platman, S. R., Kassir, S., & Fieve, R. R. (1971). Mechanisms of renal lithium handling and their relationship to mineralcorticoids: A dissociation between sodium and lithium ions. *J. Psychiat. Res., 8*(2), 91–105.

Bagby, E. (1922). The etiology of phobias. *J. Abnorm. Psychol., 17,* 16–18.

Bagby, R. M., Buis, T., & Nicolson, R. A. (1995) Relative effectiveness of the standard validity scales in detecting fake-bad and fake-good responding: Replication and extension. *Psychol. Assess., 7*(1), 84–92.

Bagley, C. (1991). Poverty and suicide among Native Canadians: A replication. *Psych. Rep., 69*(1), 149–150.

Bailey, J. M., Pillard, R. C., Neale, M. C., et al. (1993). Heritable factors influence sexual orientation in women. *Arch. Gen. Psychiat., 50*(3), 217–223.

Baker, J. E. & Channon, S. (1995). Reasoning in depression: Impairment on a concept discrimination learning task. *Cog. and Emot., 9*(6), 579–597.

Baker, T., & Brandon, T. H. (1988). Behavioral treatment strategies. In *A report of the Surgeon General: The health consequences of smoking: Nicotine addiction.* Rockville, MD: U. S. Dept. of Health and Human Services.

Bakken, J., Miltenberger, R. G., & Schauss, S. (1993). Teaching parents with mental retardation: Knowledge versus skills. *Amer. J. Ment. Retard., 97*(4), 405–417.

Baldwin, S. (1985). Sheep in wolf's clothing: Impact of normalisation teaching on human services and services providers. *Inter. J. Rehab. Res., 8*(2), 131–142.

Balk, D. F. (1995). Bereavement research using control groups: Ethical obligations and questions. [Special issue: Ethics and bereavement research]. *Death Stud. 19* (2), 123–138.

Ball, S. G., Baer, L., & Otto, M. W. (1996). Symptom subtypes of obsessive-compulsive disorder in behavioral treatment studies: A quantitative review. *Behav. Res. Ther., 34*(1), 47–51.

Ballenger, J. C. (1988). The clinical use of carbamazepine in affective disorders. *J. Clin. Psychiat., 49*(Suppl.), 13–19.

Ballenger, J. C. (1995). Benzodiazepines. In A. F. Schatzberg & C. B. Nemeroff (Eds.), *The American Psychiatric Press textbook of psychopharmacology.* Washington, DC: American Psychiatric Press.

Ballenger, J. C. (1997). Panic disorder in the medical setting. *J. Clin. Psychiatr., 38* (Suppl. 2), 13–17.

Ballinger, S. E. (1987). Uses and limitations of hypnosis in treating a conversion overlay following somatic trauma. *Austral. J. Clin. Exp. Hyp., 15*(1), 29–37.

Balshem, M., Oxman, G., Van Rooyen, D., & Girod, K. (1992). Syphilis, sex, and crack cocaine: Images of risk and morality. *Soc. Sci. Med., 35*(2), 147–160.

Baltaxe, C. A. M., & Simmons J. Q., III, (1995). Speech and language disorders in children and adolescents with schizophrenia. *Schizo. Bull., 21* (4), 677–692.

Bancroft, J. (1971). A comparative study of aversion and desensitization in the treatment of homosexuality. In L. Burns & J. Worsley (Eds.), *Behaviour therapy in the 1970s.* Bristol, UK: Wright.

Bancroft, J. (1989). *Human sexuality and its problems.* New York: Churchill-Livingstone.

Bandura, A. (1969). *Principles of behavior modification.* New York: Holt, Rinehart & Winston.

Bandura, A. (1971). Psychotherapy based upon modeling principles. In A. E. Bergin & S. L. Garfield (Eds.), *Handbook of psychotherapy and behavior change.* New York: Wiley.

Bandura, A. (1971). Vicarious and self-reinforcement processes. In R. Glaser (Ed.), *The nature of reinforcement.* New York: Academic Press.

Bandura, A. (1976). *Social learning theory.* Englewood Cliffs, NJ: Prentice Hall.

Bandura, A. (1977). Self-efficacy: Toward a unifying theory of behavioral change. *Psychol. Rev., 84*(2), 191–215.

Bandura, A. (1986). *Social foundations of thought and action: A social cognitive theory.* Englewood Cliffs, NJ: Prentice Hall.

Bandura, A., Adams, N. E., & Beyer, J. (1977). Cognitive processes mediating behavioral change. *J. Pers. Soc. Psychol., 35*(3), 125–139.

Bandura, A., Blanchard, E. B., & Ritter, B. (1969). Relative efficacy of desensitization and modeling approaches for inducing behavioral, affective, and attitudinal changes. *J. Pers. Soc. Psychol., 13,* 173–199.

Bandura, A., & Rosenthal, T. (1966). Vicarious classical conditioning as a function of arousal level. *J. Pers. Soc. Psychol., 3,* 54–62.

Bandura, A., Ross, D., & Ross, S. (1963). Imitation of film-mediated aggressive models. *J. Abnorm. Soc. Psychol., 66,* 3–11.

Banerjee, S., & Macdonald, A. (1996). Mental disorder in an elderly home care population: Associations with health and social service use. *Brit. J. Psychiat., 168,* 750–756.

Banister, P., Burman, E., Parker, I., Taylor, M., & Tindall, C. (1994). *Qualitative methods in psychology: A research guide.* Buckingham: Open University Press.

Bank, L., Marlowe, J. H., Reid, J. B., Patterson, G. R., & Weinrott, M. R. (1991). A comparative evaluation of parent-training interventions for families of chronic delinquents. *J. Abnorm. Child Psychol., 19,* 15–33.

Baraban, J., Worley, P., & Snyder, S. (1989). Second messenger systems and psychoactive drug action: Focus on the phosphoinositide system and lithium. *Amer. J. Psychiat., 146*(10), 1251–1259.

Barahal, H. S. (1958). 1000 prefrontal lobotomies: Five to ten year follow-up study. *Psychiat. Quart., 32,* 653–678.

Barasch, R. (1996). APA false memory group sharply split. *Nat. Psychologist, 5*(4), 1.

Barber, T. X. (1984). Hypnosis, deep relaxation, and active relaxation: Data, theory and clinical applications. In F. L. Woolfolk & P. M. Lehrer (Eds.), *Principles and practice of stress management.* New York: Guilford.

Barber, T. X. (1993). Hypnosuggestive approaches to stress reduction: Data, theory, and clinical applications. In P. M. Lehrer & R. L. Woolfolk (Eds.), *Principles and practice of stress management* (2nd ed.). New York: Guilford.

Bardenstein, K. K., McGlashan, T. H., & McGlashan, T. H. (1988). The natural history of a residentially treated borderline sample: Gender differences. *J. Pers. Disorders., 2*(1), 69–83.

Bardo, M. T., Donohew, R. L., Harrington, N. G. (1996). Psychobiology of novelty seeking and drug seeking behavior. *Behav. Brain Res., 77,* 23–43.

Barker, C., Pistrang, N., & Elliott, R. (1994). *Research methods in clinical and counseling psychology.* Chichester, England: John Wiley & Sons Ltd.

Barker, J. G., & Howell, R. J. (1992). The plethysmograph: A review of recent literature. *Bull. Amer. Acad. Psychiat. Law, 20*(1), 13–25.

Barker, P. R., Manderscheid, R. W., Hendershot, G. E., Jack, S. S., Schoenborn, C. A., & Goldstrom, I. (1992). Serious mental illness and disability in the adult household population: United States, 1989. In R. W. Manderscheid & M. A. Sonnenschein (Eds.), *Mental health, United States, 1992.* Washington, DC: U. S. Department of Health and Human Services.

Barlow, D. H. (1986). Causes of sexual dysfunction: The role of anxiety and cognitive interference. *J. Cons. Clin. Psychol., 54,* 140–148.

Barlow, D. H. (1988). Current models of panic disorder and a view from emotion theory. In A. J. Frances & R. E. Hales (Eds.), *American Psychiatric Press review of psychiatry* (Vol. 7). Washington, DC: American Psychiatric Press.

Barlow, D. H. (1989). Treatment outcome evaluation methodology with anxiety disorders: Strengths and key issues. *Adv. Behav. Res. Ther., 11*(3), 121–132.

Barlow, D. H. (1996). Health care policy, psychotherapy research, and the future of psychotherapy. *Amer. Psychol., 51*(10), 1050–1058.

Barlow, D. H. (1997). Cognitive-behavioral therapy for panic disorder: Current status. *J. Clin. Psychiatr., 58* (Suppl. 2), 32–36.

Barlow, D. H., Rapee, R. M., & Brown, T. A. (1992). Behavioral treatment of generalized anxiety disorder. *Behav. Ther., 23,* 551–570.

Barnard, G. W., Fuller, A. K., Robbins, L., & Shaw, T. (1989). *The child molester: An integrated approach to evaluation and treatment.* New York: Brunner/Mazel.

Barnes, G. E., & Prosen, H. (1985). Parental death and depression. *J. Abnorm. Psychol., 94*(1), 64–69.

Barnett, P. A. & Gotlib, I. H. (1990). Cognitive vulnerability to depressive symptoms among men and women. *Cog. Ther. Res., 14*(1), 47–61.

Baron, M., Barkai, A., Gruen, R., Peselow, E. et al. (1987). Platelet sup 3H imipramine binding and familial transmission of affective disorders. *Neuropsychobiology, 17*(4), 182–186.

Baron-Cohen, S. (1995). *Mindblindness: An essay on autism and theory of mind.* Cambridge, MA: MIT Press.

Barondes, S. H. (1993). *Molecules and mental illness.* New York: Scientific American Library.

Barr, C. E., Mednick, S. A., & Munk-Jorgensen, P. (1990). Exposure to influenza epidemics during gestation and adult schizophrenia: A 40–year study. *Arch. Gen. Psychiat., 47*(9), 869–874.

Barraclough, B. M., Bunch, J., Nelson, B. et al. (1974). A hundred cases of suicide: Clinical Aspects. *Brit. J. Psychiat., 125,* 355–373.

Barratt, E. S. & Stanford, M. S. (1996). Impulsiveness. In C. G. Costello (Ed.), *Personality characteristics of the personality disordered.* New York: Wiley.

Barrett, P. M., Dadds, M. R., & Rapee, R. M. (1996). Family treatment of childhood anxiety: A controlled trial. *J. Cons. Clin. Psychol., 64*(2), 333–342.

Barrett, P. M., Rapee, R. M., Dadds, M. M., & Ryan, S. M. (1996). Family enhancement of cognitive style in anxious and aggressive children. *J. Abnorm. Child Psychol., 24*(2), 187–203.

Barrington, M. R. (1980). Apologia for suicide. In M. P. Battin & D. J. Mayo (Eds.), *Suicide: The philosophical issues.* New York: St. Martin's.

Barros, E. L. (1992). Psychic change in child analysis. *Inter. J. Psychoanal., 73*(2), 303–311.

Barry, H., III. (1982). Cultural variations in alcohol abuse. In I. Al-Issa (Ed.), *Culture and psychopathology.* Baltimore: University Park.

Barsky, A. J. (1992). Amplification, somatization, and the somatoform disorders. *Psychosomatics, 33*(1), 28–34.

Barsky, A. J., & Klerman, G. L. (1983). Overview: Hypochondriasis, bodily complaints and somatic styles. *Amer. J. Psychiat., 140,* 273–283.

Barto, P. E., Pearlson, G. D., Brill, L. B., II, Royall, R. et al. (1997). Planum temporale asymmetry reversal in schizophrenia: Replication and relationship to gray matter abnormalities. *Amer. J. Psychiat., 154* (5), 661–667.

Bartels, S., Teague, G., Drake, R., Clark, R., Bush, P., & Noordsy, D. (1993). Substance abuse in schizophrenia: Service utilization and costs. *J. Nerv. Ment. Dis., 181*(4), 227–232.

Barth, R. P., Blythe, B. J., Schinke, S. P., & Schilling, R. F. (1983). Self-control training with maltreating parents. *Child Welfare, 62,* 313–324.

Bartrop, R. W., Lockhurst, E., Lazarus, L., Kiloh, L. G., & Penny, R. (1977). Depressed lymphocyte function after bereavement. *Lancet, 1,* 834–836.

Basoglu, M. (1992). The relationship between panic disorder and agoraphobia. In G. D. Burrows, S. M. Roth, & R. Noyes, Jr., *Handbook of anxiety* (Vol. 5). Oxford: Elsevier.

Bassett, A. S. (1992). Chromosomal aberrations and schizophrenia: Autosomes. *Brit. J. Psychiat., 161,* 323–334.

Bastiani, A. M., Altemus, M., Pigott, T. A., Rubenstein, C. et al. (1996). Comparison of obsessions and compulsions in patients with anorexia nervosa and obsessive compulsive disorder. *Bio. Psychiat., 39,* 966–969.

Bastiani, A. M., Rao, R., Weltzin, T., & Kaye, W. H. (1995). Perfectionism in anorexia nervosa. *Inter. J. Eat. Disorders, 17*(2), 147–152.

Batchelor, W. F. (1988). AIDS 1988. *Amer. Psychol., 43*(11), 853–858.

Bateson, G. (1978, April 21). The double-bind theory—Misunderstood? *Psychiatr. News,* p. 40.

Bateson, G., Jackson, D., Haley, J., & Weakland, J. (1956). Toward a theory of schizophrenia. *Behav. Sci., 1,* 251–264.

Batki, S. (1988). Treatment of intravenous drug users with AIDS: The role of methadone maintenance. *J. Psychoactive Drugs, 20,* 213–216.

Battaglia, M., Cavallini, M. C., Macciardi, F., & Bellodi, L. (1997). The structure of DSM-III-R schizotypal personality disorder diagnosed by direct interviews. *Schizo. Bull., 23*(1), 83–92.

Battaglia, M., Gasperini, M., Sciuto, G., Scherillo, P. et al. (1991). Psychiatric disorders in the families of schizotypal subjects. *Schizo. Bull., 17*(4), 659–668.

Battin, M. P. (1980). Manipulated suicide. In M. P. Battin & D. J. Mayo (Eds.), *Suicide: The philosophical issues.* New York: St. Martin's.

Battin, M. P. (1980). Suicide: A fundamental human right? In M. P. Battin & D. J. Mayo (Eds.), *Suicide: The philosophical issues.* New York: St. Martin's.

Battin, M. P. (1982). *Ethical issues in suicide.* Englewood Cliffs, NJ: Prentice Hall.

Battin, M. P. (1993). Suicidology and the right to die. In A. A. Leenaars (Ed.), *Suicidology.* Northvale, NJ: Jason Aronson Inc.

Battle, E. K., & Brownell, K. D. (1996). Confronting a rising tide of eating disorders and obesity: Treatment vs. prevention and policy. *Addic. Behav., 32*(6), 755–765.

Bauer, M., & Boegner, F. (1996). Neurological syndromes in factitious disorder. *J. Nerv. Ment. Dis., 184*(5), 281–288.

Bauer, P. J. (1996). What do infants recall of their lives? Memory for specific events by one- to two-year-olds. *Amer. Psychol., 51*(1), 29–41.

Baum, A. (1990). Stress, intrusive imagery, and chronic stress. *Hlth. Psychol., 9,* 653–675.

Baum, A., & Fleming, I. (1993). Implications of psychological research on stress and technological accidents. *Amer. Psychol., 48*(6), 665–672.

Baum, A., Gatchel, R. J., & Schaeffer, M. (1983). Emotional, behavioural and physiological effects of chronic stress at Three Mile Island. *J. Cons. Clin. Psychol., 51,* 565–572.

Bawden, D. L., & Sonenstein, F. L. (1992). Quasi-experimental designs. *Children Youth Serv. Rev., 14*(1–2), 137–144.

Baxter, D. N. (1996). The mortality experience of individuals on the Salford psychiatric case register. I. All-cause mortality. *Brit. J. Psychiat., 168, 772–779.*

Baxter, L. R., Schwartz, J. M., Bergman, K. S., Szuba, M. P., Guze, B. H., Mazziotta, J. C., Alazraki, A., Selin, C. E., Ferng, H. K., Munford, P., & Phelps, M. E. (1992). Caudate glucose metabolic rate changes with both drug and behavior therapy for obsessive-compulsive disorder. *Arch. Gen. Psychiat., 49,* 681–689.

Baxter, L. R., Schwartz, J. M., Guze, B. H., Bergman, K. et al. (1990). PET imaging in obsessive compulsive disorder with and without depression. Symposium: Serotonin and its effects on human behavior (1989, Atlanta, GA). *J. Clin. Psychiat., 51*(Suppl.), 61–69.

Bazargan, M. (1996). Self-reported sleep disturbance among African-American elderly: The effects of depression, health status, exercise, and social support. *Inter. J. Aging Human Dev., 42*(2), 143–160.

Beach, S. R. H., Sandeen, E. E., & O'Leary, K. D. (1990). Depression in marriage: A model for etiology and treatment. In D. H. Barlow (Ed.), *Treatment manuals for practitioners.* New York: Guilford.

Beamish, P. M., Granello, P. F., Granello, D. H., McSteen, P. B. et al. (1996). Outcome studies in the treatment of panic disorder: A review. *J. Couns. Dev., 74,* 460–467.

Beardslee, W. R., Salt, P., Versage, E. M., Gladstone, T. R. G. et al. (1997). Sustained change in parents receiving preventive interventions for families with depression. *Amer. J. Psychiat., 154*(4), 510–515.

Beardslee, W. R., Wright, E., Rothberg, P. C., Salt, P., & Versage, E. (1996). Response of families to two preventive intervention strategies: Long-term differences in behavior and attitude change. *J. Amer. Child Adol. Psychiat., 35*(6), 774–782.

Beasley, C. M., Jr., Tollefson, G., Tran, P., Satterlee, W., Sanger, T., Hamilton, S., & The Olanzapine HGAD Study Group. (1996). Olanzapine versus Placebo and Haloperidol: Acute phase results of the North American Double-Blind Olanzapine Trial. *Neuropsychopharmacology, 14*(2), 111–123.

Beauchemin, K. M., & Hayes, P. (1996). Sunny hospital rooms expedite recovery from severe and refractory depressions. *J. Affect. Disorders., 40,* 49–51.

Beauvais, F. (1992). The consequences of drug and alcohol use for Indian youth. *Amer. Indian Alaska Native Ment. Hlth. Res., 5*(1), 32–37.

Bebbington, P. & Ramana, R. (1995). The epidemiology of bipolar affective disorder. *Soc. Psychiatr. Psychiatr. Epidemiol., 30,* 279–292.

Bech, P. (1995). Social aspects of treatment of depression. BAP Satellite Symposium (1994, Cambridge, England) and at the VIIth Annual Congress of the ECN; Are the newer antidepressants of greater value than the classical ones? Citalopram—a well-documented and novel antidepressant. *Inter. Clin. Psychopharmacol., 10*(Suppl. 1), 11–14.

Beck, A. T. (1967). *Depression: Clinical, experimental and theoretical aspects.* New York: Harper & Row.

Beck, A. T. (1976). *Cognitive therapy and the emotional disorders.* New York: International University Press.

Beck, A. T. (1985). Is behavior therapy on course? *Behav. Psychother., 13*(1), 83–84.

Beck, A. T. (1985). Theoretical perspectives on clinical anxiety. In A. H. Tuma & J. D. Maser (Eds.), *Anxiety and the anxiety disorders.* Hillsdale, NJ: Erlbaum.

Beck, A. T. (1988). Cognitive approaches to panic disorder: Theory and therapy. In S. Rachman & J. Maser (Eds.), *Panic: Psychological perspectives.* Hillsdale, NJ: Erlbaum.

Beck, A. T. (1991). Cognitive therapy: A 30–year retrospective. *Amer. Psychol., 46*(4), 368–375.

Beck, A. T. (1993). Cognitive approaches to stress. In P. M. Lehrer & R. L. Woolfolk (Eds.), *Principles and practice of stress management* (2nd ed.). New York: Guilford.

Beck, A. T. (1997). Cognitive therapy: Reflections. In J. K. Zeig (Ed.), *The evolution of psychotherapy: The third conference.* New York: Brunner/Mazel.

Beck, A. T., & Emery, G., with Greenberg, R. L. (1985). Differentiating anxiety and depression: A test of the cognitive content-specificity hypothesis. *J. Abnorm. Psychol., 96,* 179–183.

Beck, A. T., Emery, G., & Greenberg, R. (1985). *Anxiety disorders and phobias: A cognitive perspective.* New York: Basic Books.

Beck, A. T., et al. (1985). Treatment of depression with cognitive therapy and amitriptyline. *Arch. Gen. Psychiat., 42*(2), 142–148.

Beck, A. T., Freeman, A., & Assoc. (1990). *Cognitive therapy of personality disorders.* New York: Guilford.

Beck, A. T., Laude, R., & Bohnert, M. (1974). Ideational components of anxiety neurosis. *Arch. Gen. Psychiat., 31,* 319–325.

Beck, A. T., Resnik, H., Lettieri, D. (Eds.). (1974). *The prediction of suicide.* Philadelphia: The Charles Press.

Beck, A. T., Rush, A. J., Shaw, B. F., & Emery, G. (1979). *Cognitive therapy of depression.* New York: Guilford.

Beck, A. T., Sokol, L., Clark, D. A., Berchick, R. J., & Wright, F. D. (1992). Focused cognitive therapy of panic disorder: A crossover design and one-year follow-up. *Amer. J. Psychiat., 149*(6), 778–783.

Beck, A. T., Steer, R. A., & Epstein, N. (1992). Self concept dimensions of clinically depressed and anxious outpatients. *J. Clin. Psych., 48*(4), 423–432.

Beck, A. T., Ward, C. H., Mendelson, M., Mock, J. E., & Erbaugh, J. (1962). Reliability of psychiatric diagnosis. 2: A study of consistency of clinical judgments and ratings. *Amer. J. Psychiat., 119,* 351–357.

Beck, A. T. & Weishaar, M. E. (1995). Cognitive therapy. In R. J. Corsini & D. Wedding (Eds.), *Current psychotherapies* (5th ed.). Itasca, IL: Peacock.

Beck, A. T., Weissman, A., Lester, D. et al. (1974). The measurement of pessimism: The hopelessness scale. *J. Cons. Clin. Psychol. 42,* 861–865.

Beck, J. C., & Parry, J. W. (1992). Incompetence, treatment refusal, and hospitalization. *Bull. Amer. Acad. Psychiatr. Law, 20*(3), 261–267.

Beck, J. G. (1995). Hypoactive sexual desire disorder: An overview. *J. Cons. Clin. Psychol., 63*(6), 919–927.

Beck, J. G., & Bozman, A. (1996). Gender differences in sexual desire: The effects of anger and anxiety. *Arch. Sex. Behav., 24*(6), 595–612.

Beck, K., Thombs, D., & Summons, T. (1993). The social context of drinking scales: Construct validation and relationship to indicants of abuse in an adolescent population. *Addic. Behav., 18,* 159–169.

Beck, M., & Cowley, G. (1990, March 26). Beyond Lobotomies. *Newsweek,* p. 44.

Becker, J. V. (1989). Impact of sexual abuse on sexual functioning. In S. R. Leiblum & R. C. Rosen (Eds.), *Principles and practice of sex therapy* (2nd ed.). New York: Guilford.

Becker, J. V. & Segraves, R. T. (1995). Afterword to SectionV. In J. M. Oldham & M. B. Riba (Eds.), *American Psychiatric Press review of psychiatry* (Volume 14). Washington, DC: American Psychiatric Press.

Becker, P., & Comstock, C. (1992, October). *A retrospective look at one MPD/DD group: Recommendations for future MPD/DD groups.* Paper presented at the Ninth International Conference of the International Society for the Study of Multiple Personality and Dissociative Disorders, Chicago.

Becker, W. C. (1964). Consequences of different kinds of parental discipline. In M. L. Hoffman & L. W. Hoffman (Eds.), *Review of child development research* (Vol. 1). New York: Russell Sage Foundation.

Becvar, D. S., & Becvar, R. J. (1993). *Family therapy: A systemic integration* (2nd ed.). Boston: Allyn & Bacon.

Bednar, R. L., & Kaul, T. J. (1994). Experiential group research: Can the canon fire? In A. E. Bergin & S. L. Garfiel (Eds.), *Handbook of psychotherapy and behavior change* (4th ed.). New York: Wiley.

Beebe, D. K. (1991). Emergency management of the adult female rape victim. *Amer. Fam. Physician, 43,* 2041–2046.

Beers, C. W. (1908). *A mind that found itself.* Garden City, NY: Doubleday.

Begley, S. (1989, August 14). The stuff that dreams are made of. *Newsweek,* p. 40.

Begley, S. (1995, Oct. 9). Promises, promises. *Newsweek,* pp. 60–62.

Beidel, D. C., Turner, S. M., & Morris, T. L. (1995). A new inventory to assess childhood social anxiety and phobia: The social phobia and anxiety inventory for children. *Psychol. Assess., 7*(1), 73–79.

Beiser, M., Shore, J. H., Peters, R., & Tatum, E. (1985). Does community care for the mentally ill make a difference? A tale of two cities. *Amer. J. Psychiat., 142,* 1047–1052.

Beitchman, J. H., Zucker, K. J., Hood, J. E., DaCosta, G. A., & Cassavia, E. (1992). A review of the long-term effects of childhood sexual abuse. *Child Abuse Neglect, 16*(1), 101–118.

Beitman, B. D. (1993). Afterward to Section IV. In J. M. Oldham, M. B. Riba, & A. Tasman (Eds.), *Review of psychiatry* (Vol. 12). Washington, DC: American Psychiatric Press.

Beitman, B. D. (1993). Pharmacotherapy and the stages of psychotherapeutic change. In J. M. Oldham, M. B. Riba, & A. Tasman (Eds.), *Review of psychiatry* (Vol. 12). Washington, DC: American Psychiatric Press.

Beitman, B. D. (1996). Integrating pharmacotherapy and psychotherapy: An emerging field of study. *Bull. Menninger Clin., 60*(2), 160–173.

Belcher, J. R. (1988). Defining the service needs of homeless mentally ill persons. *Hosp. Comm. Psychiat., 39*(11), 1203–1205.

Belcher, J. R. (1988). The future role of state hospitals. *Psychiatr. Hosp., 19*(2), 79–83.

Belcher, J. R., & Blank, H. (1990). Protecting the right to involuntary commitment. *J. Appl. Soc. Sci., 14*(1), 95–115.

Belkin, L. (1990, June 6). Doctor tells of first death using his suicide device. *New York Times,* A1, p. 3.

Bell, M. D., Lysaker, P. H., & Milstein, R. M. (1996). Clinical benefits of paid work activity in schizophrenia. *Schizo. Bull., 22*(1), 51–67.

Bellack, A. S., Morrison, R. L., & Mueser, K. T. (1989). Social problem solving in schizophrenia. *Schizo. Bull., 15*(1), 101–116.

Bellafante, G. (1993, June 7). Got a problem? Get in line. *Time*, p. 73.

Belle, D. (1990). Poverty and women's mental health. *Amer. Psychol., 45*(3), 385–389.

Belle, D. (1990). Poverty and women's mental health. *Amer. Psychol., 45*, 385–389.

Belli, R. F., Windschitl, P. D., McCarthy, T. T., & Winfrey, S. E. (1992). Detecting memory impairment with a modified test procedure: Manipulating retention interval with centrally presented event items. *J. Exp. Psychol.: Learn., Memory, Cog., 18*, 356–367.

Bellinger, D. L., Madden, K. S., Felten, S. Y., & Felten, D. L. (1994). Neural and endocrine links between the brain and the immune system. In C. S. Lewis, C. O'Sullivan, & J. Barraclough (Eds.), England. *The psychoimmunology of cancer: Mind and body in the fight for survival.* Oxford: Oxford University Press.

Bellow, S. (1984). *Humboldt's gift.* New York: Penguin.

Belluck, P. (1996, Dec. 1). The symptoms of internet addiction. *The New York Times*, 5.

Belmaker, R. H., Bersudsky, Y., Genjamin, J., Agam, G., Levine, J., & Kofman, O. (1995). Manipulation of Inositol-linked second messenger systems as a therapeutic strategy in psychiatry. In G. Gessa, W. Fratta, L. Pani, & G. Serra (Eds.). *Depression and mania: From neurobiology to treatment.* New York: Raven Press.

Bemporad, J. R. (1992). Psychoanalytically orientated psychotherapy. In E. S. Paykel (Ed.), *Handbook of affective disorders.* New York: Guilford.

Bender, L. (1938). *A visual motor gestalt test and its clinical use.* New York: American Orthopsychiatric Assoc.

Benezech, M., DeWitte, J. J. E., & Bourgeois, M. (1989). A lycanthropic murderer [Letter to the editor]. *Amer. J. Psychiat., 146*(7), 942.

Bennett, G. T., & Kish, G. R. (1990). Incompetency to stand trial: Treatment unaffected by demographic variables. *J. Forensic Sci.,* 35(2), 403–412.

Bennett, M. B. (1987). Afro-American women, poverty and mental health: A social essay. *Women Hlth., 12*(3–4), 213–228.

Benowitz, N. (1990). Clinical pharmacology of caffeine. *Annu. Rev. Med., 41*, 277–288.

Benson, J. (1996, Jan. 15). Crime: Law and order. *Newsweek,* 48–54.

Bergem, A. L., Engedal, K., & Kringlen, E. (1997). The role of heredity in late-onset Alzheimer disease and vascular dementia: A twin study. *Arch. Gen. Psychiat., 54*, 264–270.

Berger, F. M. (1970). The discovery of meprobamate. In F. Ayd & B. Blackwell (Eds.), *Discoveries in biological psychiatry.* Philadelphia: Lippincott.

Bergler, E. (1951). *Neurotic counterfeit sex.* New York: Grune & Stratton.

Berk, S. N., & Efran, J. S. (1983). Some recent developments in the treatment of neurosis. In C. E. Walker et al. (Eds.), *The handbook of clinical psychology: Theory, research, and practice* (Vol. 2). Homewood, IL: Dow Jones-Irwin.

Berkovitz, I. H. (1985). The adolescent, schools, and schooling. *Adol. Psychiat., 12*, 162–176.

Berlin, I. N. (1987). Suicide among American Indian adolescents: An overview. *Suic. Life-Threat. Behav., 17*, 218–232.

Berman, A. L. & Jobes, D. A. (1995). Suicide prevention in adolescents (age 12–18). [Special issue: Suicide prevention: Toward the year 2000.] *Suic. Life-Threat. Behav., 25*(1), 143–154.

Berman, A. L. (1986). Helping suicidal adolescents: Needs and responses. In C. A. Corr & J. N. McNeil (Eds.), *Adolescence and death.* New York: Springer.

Berman, A. L., & Jobes, D. A. (1991). *Adolescent suicide: Assessment and intervention.* Washington, DC: American Psychological Association.

Berman, K. F., Torrey, E. F., Daniel, D. G., & Weinberger, D. R. (1992). Regional cerebral blood flow in monozygotic twins discordant and concordant for schizophrenia. *Arch. Gen. Psychiat., 49*(12), 927–934.

Berney, B. (1993). Round and round it goes: The epidemiology of childhood lead poisoning, 1950–1990. *Milbank Quarterly, 71*(1), 3–39.

Bernstein, D. A., & Carlson, C. R. (1993). Progressive relaxation: Abbreviated methods. In P. M. Lehrer & R. L. Woolfolk (Eds.), *Principles and practice of stress management* (2nd ed.). New York: Guilford.

Bernstein, H. A. (1981). Survey of threats and assaults directed toward psychotherapists. *Amer. J. Psychother., 35*, 542–549.

Berrettini, W. H., Ferraro, T. N., Goldin, L. R., Detera-Wadleigh, S. D. et al. (1997). A linkage study of bipolar illness. *Arch. Gen. Psychiat., 54*, 27–35.

Berry, D. T. R., Wetter, M. W., Baer, R. A., Youngjohn, J. R. et al. (1995). Overreporting of closed-head injury symptoms on the MMPI-2. *Psychol. Assess., 7*(4), 517–523.

Bersoff, D. N. (Ed.). (1995). *Ethical conflicts in psychology.* Washington, DC: American Psychological Association.

Bertani, A., Perna, G., Arancio, C., Caldirola, D., & Bellodi, L. (1997). Pharmacologic effect of imipramine, paroxetine, and sertraline on 35% carbon dioxide hypersensitivity in panic patients: A double-blind, random, placebo-controlled study. *J. Clin. Psychopharmacol. 17*(2), 97–101.

Bertolli, J., Morgenstern, H., & Sorenson, S. B. (1995). Estimating the occurrence of child maltreatment and risk-factor effects: Benefits of a mixed-design strategy in epidemiologic research. *Child Abuse Neglect 19*(8), 1007–1016.

Bettelheim, B. (1967). *The empty fortress: Infantile autism and the birth of the self.* New York: Free Press.

Beutel, M., Deckardt, R., Von Rad, M., & Weiner, H. (1995). Grief and depression after miscarriage: Their separation, antecedents, and course. *Psychosom. Med., 57*, 517–526.

Beutler, L. E. (1979). Toward specific psychological therapies for specific conditions. *J. Cons. Clin. Psychol., 47*, 882–892.

Beutler, L. E. (1991). Have all won and must all have prizes? Revisiting Luborsky et al.'s verdict. *J. Cons. Clin. Psychol., 59*, 226–232.

Beutler, L. E., Machado, P. P. P., & Neufeldt, S. A. (1994). Therapist variables. In A. E. Bergin & S. L. Garfield (Eds.), *Handbook of psychotherapy and behavior change.* New York: Wiley.

Beutler, L. E., Williams, R. E., Wakefield, P. J., & Entwistle, S. R. (1995). Bridging scientist and practitioner perspectives in clinical psychology. *Amer. Psychol., 50*(12), 984–994.

Beutler, L. E., Williams, R. E., Wakefield, P. J., & Entwistle, S. R. (1995). Bridging scientist and practitioner perspectives in clinical psychology. *Amer. Psychol., 50*(12) 984–994.

Beyer, H. A. (1991). Litigation involving people with mental retardation. In J. L. Matson & J. A. Mulick (Eds.), *Handbook of mental retardation* (2nd ed.). New York: Pergamon Press.

Bibring, E. (1953). The mechanisms of depression. In P. Greenacre (Ed.), *Affective disorders.* New York: International Universities Press.

Bickel, W. K. & Amass, L. (1995). Buprenorphine treatment of opioid dependence: A review. *Exp. Clin. Psychopharmacol., 3*(4), 477–489.

Bickman, L., & Dokecki, P. (1989). Public and private responsibility for mental health services. *Amer. Psychol., 44*(8), 1133–1137.

Biederman, J., Faraone, S., Mick, E., Moore, P., & Lelon, E. (1996). Child behavior checklist findings further support comorbidity between ADHD and major depression in a referred sample. *J. Amer. Child Adol. Psychiat., 35*(6), 734–742.

Biederman, J., Faraone, S., Milberger, S., Guite, J. et al. (1996). A prospective 4-year follow-up study of attention-deficit hyperactivity and related disorders. *Arch. Gen. Psychiat., 53*, 437–446.

Biegon, A., Dillon, K., Volkow, N. D., & Fowler, J. S. (1995). Quantitative autoradiographic localization and characterization of cocaine binding sites in the human brain post-moretem. In A. Biegon & N. D. Volkow (Eds.), *Sites of drug action in the human brain.* Boco Raton: CRC Press, Inc.

Biegon, A., & Kerman, I. (1995). Quantitative autoradiography of cannabinoid receptors in the human brain post-mortem. In A. Biegon & N. D. Volkow (Eds.), *Sites of drug action in the human brain.* Boca Raton, FL: CRC Press.

Biegon, A., & Volkow, N. D. (1995). Localization and characterization of drug binding sites in the human brain: Methodological considerations. In A. Biegon & N. D. Volkow (Eds.), *Sites of drug action in the human brain.* Boca Raton, FL: CRC Press.

Biegon, A., & Volkow, N. D. (Eds.), (1995). *Sites of drug action in the human brain.* Boca Raton, FL: CRC Press.

Bierman, K. L., & Furman, W. (1984). The effects of social skills training and peer involvement on the social adjustment of preadolescents. *Child Dev., 55*(1), 151–162.

Bilder, R. M., Lipschutz-Broch, L., Reiter, G., Geisler, S. H. et al. (1992). Intellectual deficits in first-episode schizophrenia: Evidence for progressive deterioration. *Schizo. Bull., 18*(3), 437–448.

Bindrim, P. (1968). A report on a nude marathon: The effects of physical nudity upon the practice interaction in the marathon group. *Psychother. Theory Res. Prac., 5,* 180–188.

Binet, A., & Simon, T. (1916). *The development of intelligence in children (The Binet-Simon Scale).* Baltimore: Williams & Wilkins.

Binik, Y. M., Servan-Schreiber, D., Freiwald, S., & Hall, K. S. (1988). Intelligent computer-based assessment and psychotherapy: An expert system for sexual dysfunction. *J. Nerv. Ment. Dis., 176*(7), 387–400.

Birch, H. G., Richardson, S. A., Baird, D. et al. (1970). *Mental subnormality in the community-A clinical and epidemiological study.* Baltimore: Williams & Wilkins.

Birchwood, M., Smith, J., & Cochrane, R. (1992). Specific and non-specific effects of educational intervention for families living with schizophrenia: A comparison of three methods. *Brit. J. Psychiat., 160,* 806–814.

Bird, J. (1979). The behavioral treatment of hysteria. *Brit. J. Psychiat., 134,* 129–137.

Birtchnell, J. (1996). Detachment. In C. G. Costello (Ed.), *Personality characteristics of the personality disordered.* New York: Wiley.

Bissette, G., Seidler, F. J., Nemeroff, C. B., & Slotkin, T. A. (1996). High affinity choline transporter status in Alzheimer's disease tissue from rapid autopsy. In R. J. Wurtman, S. Corkin, J. H. Growdon, & R. M. Nitsch (Eds.), *The neurobiology of Alzheimer's disease.* New York: New York Academy of Sciences.

Bixler, R. D., Floyd, M. F., & Hammitt, W. E. (1995). Feared stimuli are expected in specific situations: The use of situationalism and fear expectancy in a self-report measurement of fears. *J. Clin. Psychol., 51*(4), 544–547.

Blacher, J., & Baker, B. L. (1992). Toward meaningful involvement in out-of-home placement settings. *Ment. Retard., 30*(1), 35–43.

Blacher, J., & Baker, B. L. (1994). Family involvement in residential treatment of children with retardation: Is there evidence of detachment? *J. Child Psychol. Psychiat. Allied Disc., 35*(3), 505–520.

Black, D. W. & Andreasen, N. C. (1994). Schizophrenia, schizophreniform disorder, and delusional (paranoid) disorder. In R. E. Hales, S. C. Yudofsky, & J. A. Talbott, (Eds.), *The American Psychiatric Press textbook of psychiatry* (2nd ed.). Washington, DC: American Psychiatric Press.

Black, D. W., Kehrberg, L. L. D., Flumerfelt, D. L., & Schlosser, S. S. (1997). Characteristics of 36 subjects reporting compulsive sexual behavior. *Amer. J. Psychiat., 154,* 243–249.

Black, D. W., Monahan, P., & Gabel, J. (1997). Fluvoxamine in the treatment of compulsive buying. *J. Clin. Psychiat., 58*(4), 159–163.

Black, D. W., & Winokur, G. (1990). Suicide and psychiatric diagnosis. In S. J. Blumenthal & D. J. Kupfer (Eds.), *Suicide over the life cycle: Risk factors, assessment, and treatment of suicidal patients.* Washington, DC: American Psychiatric Press, Inc.

Black, D. W., Winokur, G., & Nasrallah, A. (1987). Treatment of mania: A naturalistic study of electroconvulsive therapy vs. lithium in 438 patients. *J. Clin. Psychiat., 48,* 132–139.

Black, S. T. (1993). Comparing genuine and simulated suicide notes: A new perspective. *J. Cons. Clin. Psychol., 61*(4), 699–702.

Black, S. T. (1995). Comparing genuine and simulated suicide notes: Response to Diamond et al. (1995). *J. Cons. Clin. Psychol., 63*(1), 49–51.

Blackburn, R. (1993). *The psychology of criminal conduct: Theory, research, and practice.* New York: Wiley.

Blackstein, K. R. (1975). The sensation seeker and anxiety reactivity. Relationship between sensation-seeking scales and the activity preference questionnaire. *J. Clin. Psychol., 31,* 677–681.

Blackwell, B., Marley, E., Price, J., & Taylor, D. (1967). Hypertensive interactions between monoamine oxidase inhibitors and foodstuffs. *Brit. J. Psychiat., 113,* 349–365.

Blackwood, D. H. R., He, L., Morris, S. W., McLean, A. et al. (1996, April). A locus for bipolar affective disorder on chromosome 4p. *Nature Genetics, 12,* 427–430.

Blair, C. D., & Lanyon, R. I. (1981). Exhibitionism: Etiology and treatment. *Psychol. Bull., 89*(3), 439–463.

Blanchard, E. B. (1994). Behavioral medicine and health psychology. In A. E. Bergin & S. L. Garfield (Eds.), *Handbook of psychotherapy and behavior change.* New York: Wiley.

Blanchard, E. B., & Andrasik, F. (1982). Psychological assessment and treatment of headache: Recent developments and emerging issues. *J. Cons. Clin. Psychol., 50*(6), 859–879.

Blanchard, E. B., & Epstein, L. H. (1978). *A biofeedback primer.* Reading, MA: Addison-Wesley.

Blanchard, E. B., Hickling, E. J., Taylor, A. E., Loos, W. R., et al. (1996). Who develops PTSD from motor vehicle accidents? *Behav. Res. Ther., 34*(1), 1–10.

Blanchard, E. B., Schwarz, S. P., Suls, J. M., Gerardi, M. et al. (1992). Two controlled evaluations of multicomponent psychological treatment of irritable bowel syndrome. *Behav. Res. Ther., 30*(2), 175–189.

Blanchard, E. B. et al. (1982). Biofeedback and relaxation training with three kinds of headache: Treatment effects and their prediction. *J. Cons. Clin. Psychol., 50*(4), 562–575.

Blanchard, R., & Hucker, S. J. (1991). Age, transvestism, bondage, and concurrent paraphilic activities in 117 fatal cases of autoerotic asphyxia. *Brit. J. Psychiat., 159,* 371–377.

Bland, R. C., & Orn, H. (1986). Family violence and psychiatric disorder. *Canad. J. Psychiat., 31*(2), 129–137.

Bland, R. C., Orn, H., & Newman, S. C. (1988). Lifetime prevalence of psychiatric disorders in Edmonton. *Acta Psychiatr. Scandin., 77*(Suppl. 338), 24–32.

Blank, A. S. (1982). Apocalypse terminable and interminable: Operation Outreach for Vietnam veterans. *Hosp. Comm. Psychiat., 33*(11), 913–918.

Blatt, S. J. (1995). The destructiveness of perfectionism. Implications for the treatment of depression. *Amer. Psychol., 50*(12), 1003–1020.

Blatt, S., & Wild, C. (1976). *Schizophrenia: A developmental analysis.* New York: Academic Press.

Blazer, D. (1990). *Emotional problems in later life.* New York: Springer.

Blazer, D. G., George, L. K. & Hughes, D. (1991). The epidemiology of anxiety disorders: An age comparison. In C. Salzman & B. D. Lebowitz (Eds.), *Anxiety in the elderly.* New York: Springer.

Blazer, D. G., Hughes, D., George, L. K., Swartz, M. & Boyer, R. (1991). Generalized anxiety disorder. In L. N. Robins, & D. A. Regier (Eds.), *Psychiatric disorders in America: The epidemiologic catchment area study.* New York: Maxwell Macmillan International.

Blehar, M. C., & Oren, D. A. (1995). Women's increased vulnerability to mood disorders: Integrating psychobiology and epidemiology. *Depression, 3,* 3–12.

Blehar, M. C., Weissman, M. M., & Gershon, E. S. (1988). Family and genetic studies of affective disorders. National Institute of Mental Health: Family and genetic studies of affective disorders. *Arch. Gen. Psychiat., 45*(3), 288–292.

Blier, P., & de Montigny, C. (1994, July). Current advances and trends in the treatment of depression. *TIPS, 15,* 220–226.

Bliss, E. L. (1980). Multiple personalities: A report of 14 cases with implications for schizophrenia and hysteria. *Arch. Gen. Psychiat., 37*(12), 1388–1397.

Bliss, E. L. (1980). *Multiple personality, allied disorders and hypnosis.* New York: Oxford University Press.

Bliss, E. L. (1985). "How prevalent is multiple personality?": Dr. Bliss replies. *Amer. J. Psychiat., 142*(12), 1527.

Bliss, T., & Gardner, M. A. (1973). Long-lasting potentiation of synaptic transmission in the dentate area of unanesthetized rabbit following stimulation of the prerforant path. *J. Physiol., 232,* 357–374.

Bliwise, D. L., Friedman, L., Nekich, J. C., & Yesavage, J. A. (1995). Prediction of outcome in behaviorally based insomnia treatments. *J. Behav. Ther. Exp. Psychiat., 26*(1), 17–23.

Bliwise, N., McCall, M. E., & Swan, S. J. (1987). In E. E. Lurie & J. H. Swan & Assoc. (Eds.), *Serving the mentally ill elderly: Problems and perspectives.* Lexington, MA: Heath.

Bloch, S., Crouch, E., & Reibstein, J. (1982). Therapeutic factors in group psychotherapy: A review. *Arch. Gen. Psychiat., 27,* 216–324.

Bloch, S., Szmukler, G. I., Herrman, H., Benson, A., & Colussa, S. (1995). Counseling caregivers of relatives with schizophrenia: Themes, interventions, and caveats. *Fam. Process, 34,* 413–425.

Block, B., & Pristach, C. A. (1992). Diagnosis and management of the paranoid patient. *Amer. Fam. Physician, 45*(6), 2634–2640.

Bloom, B. L. (1984). *Community mental health: A general introduction* (2nd ed.). Monterey, CA: Brooks/Cole.

Bloom, C., Gitter, A., Gutwill, S., Kogel, L., & Zaphiropoulos, L. (1994). *Eating problems: A feminist psychoanalytic treatment model.* New York: Basic Books.

Bloom, F., Lazerson, A., & Hofstadter, L. (1985). *Brain, mind, and behavior.* New York: W. H. Freeman.

Bloom, H., & Rosenbluth, M. (1989). The use of contracts in the inpatient treatment of the borderline personality disorder. *Psychiat. Quart., 60*(4), 317–327.

Bloom, J. D. (1990). The Tarasoff decision & gun control legislation. *Inter. J. Offend. Ther. Compar. Criminol., 34*(1), v–viii.

Bloomingdale, L., & Bloomingdale, E. (1989). Childhood identification and prophylaxis of antisocial personality disorder. In R. Rosner & H. I. Schwartz (Eds.), *Juvenile psychiatry and the law.* New York: Plenum.

Blum, K., & Noble, E. (1993). Drug dependence and the A1 allele gene. *Drug Alc. Dep., 33*(5).

Blum, K., Noble, E., Sheridan, P., Finley, O., et al. (1991). Association of the A1 allele of the D2 dopamine receptor gene with severe alcoholism. *Alcohol, 8*(5), 409–416.

Blumenthal, S. J. (1996). Women's mental health: The new national focus. In J. A. Sechzer, S. M. Pfafflin, F. L. Denmark, A. Griffin, & S. Blumenthal (Eds.), *Women and mental health (*Annals of the New York Academy of Sciences, *Vol. 789).* New York: New York Academy of Sciences.

Bocker, F. M. (1984). Soziale Integration und Kontakte zu Bezugspersonen des gewohnten sozialen Umfeldes wahrend stationarer Behandlung im psychiatrischen Krankenhaus. Eine prospektive katamnestische Untersuchung an erstmals aufgenommenen Patienten mit schizophrenen und cyclothymen Psychosen [Social integration and contact with people in the normal social environment during treatment in a psychiatric hospital: A follow-up of first-admission inpatients with schizophrenia and affective disorders]. *Eur. Arch. Psychiat. Neurol. Sci., 234*(4), 250–257.

Bockoven, J. S. (1963). *Moral treatment in American psychiatry.* New York: Springer.

Bogdan, R., & Taylor, S. (1976, January). The judged, not the judges: An insider's view of mental retardation. *Amer. Psychol., 31*(1), 47–52.

Bolgar, H. (1965). The case study method. In B. B. Wolman (Ed.), *Handbook of clinical psychology.* New York: McGraw-Hill.

Bolton, D., Luckie, M., & Steinberg, D. (1995). Long-term course of obsessive-compulsive disorder treated in adolescence. *J. Amer. Acad. Child Adol. Psychiat., 34*(11), 1441–1450.

Bolton, F., Morris, L., & MacEachron, A. (1989). *Males at risk: The other side of child abuse.* Newbury Park, CA: Sage.

Bolund, C. (1985). Suicide and cancer: II. Medical and care factors in suicides by cancer patients in Sweden, 1973–1976. *J. Psychol. Oncology, 3*(1), 31–52.

Bongar, B., Peterson, L. G., Golann, S., & Hardiman, J. J. (1990). Self-mutilation and the chronically suicidal patient: An examination of the frequent visitor to the psychiatric emergency room. *Ann. Clin. Psychiat., 2*(3), 217–222.

Bonn, D. (1996). Melatonin's multifarious marvels: Miracle or myth: *Lancet, 347,* 184.

Bonner, R. L. (1992). Isolation, seclusion, and psychosocial vulnerability as risk factors for suicide behind bars. In R. W. Maris, A. L. Berman, J. T. Maltsberger, & R. I. Yufit (Eds.), *Assessment and prediction of suicide.* New York: Guilford.

Borch-Jacobsen, M. (1997). Sybil – The making of a disease: An interview with Dr. Herbert Spiegel. *The New York Review of Books, 44*(7), 60-64.

Borison, R. L. (1995). Clinical efficacy of serotonin-dopamine antagonists relative to classic neuroleptics. *J. Clin. Psychopharmacol., 15*(1, Suppl. 1), 24S–29S.

Borkovec, T. D., & Costello, E. (1992). *Efficacy of applied relaxation and cognitive behavioral therapy in the treatment of generalized anxiety disorder.* Manuscript submitted for publication.

Borkovec, T. D., Lyonfields, J. D., Wiser, S. L., & Deihl, L. (1993). The role of worrisome thinking in the suppression of cardiovascular response to phobic imagery. *Behav. Res. Ther., 31*(3), 321–324.

Borkovec, T. D., Robinson, E., Pruzinsky, T., & Depree, J. A. (1983). Preliminary exploration of worry: Some characteristics and processes. *Behav. Res. Ther., 21,* 9–16.

Bornstein, P. H., Hamilton, S. B., & Bornstein, M. T. (1986). Self-monitoring procedures. In A. R. Ciminero, K. S. Calhoun, & H. E. Adams (Eds.), *Handbook of behavioral assessment* (2nd ed.). New York: Wiley.

Bornstein, R. A., Schwarzkopf, S. B., Olson, S. C., & Nasrallah, H. A. (1992). Third-ventricle enlargement and neuropsy-chological deficit in schizophrenia. *Bio. Psychiat., 31*(9), 954–961.

Bornstein, R. F. (1992). The dependent personality: Developmental, social, and clinical perspectives. *Psychol. Bull., 112*(1), 3–23.

Bornstein, R. F. (1995). Comorbidity of dependent personality disorder and other psychological disorders: An integrative review. *J. Pers. Disorders, 9*(4), 286–303.

Bornstein, R. F. (1996). Dependency. In C. G. Costello (Ed.), *Personality characteristics of the personality disordered.* New York: Wiley.

Bornstein, R. F., Klein, D. N., Mallon, J. C., & Slater, J. F. (1988). Schizotypal personality disorder in an outpatient population: Incidence and clinical characteristics. *J. Clin. Psychiat., 44*(3), 322–325.

Boros, S., Ophoven, J., Anderson, R., & Brubaker, L. (1995). Munchausen syndrome by proxy: A profile for medical child abuse. *Austral. Fam. Physician, 24*(5), 768–773.

Borum, R. (1996). Improving the clinical practice of violence risk assessment. Technology, guidelines, and training. *Amer. Psychol., 51*(9), 945–956.

Borys, D. S., & Pope, K. S. (1989). Dual relationships between therapist and client: A national study of psychologists, psychiatrists and social workers. *Profess. Psychol., 20,* 283–293.

Bose, J. (1995). Depression. In M. Lionells, J. Fiscalini, C. H. Mann, & D. B. Stern (Eds.), *Handbook of interpersonal psychoanalysis.* Hillsdale, NJ: The Analytic Press.

Bose, J. (1992). The difficult patient or the difficult dyad? Stage fright in psychotherapy. Clinical Symposium of the William Alanson White Institute of Psychiatry, Psychoanalysis and Psychology: Interpersonal frontiers in psychoanalytic practice. *Contemp. Psychoanal., 28*(3), 503-512.

Boswell, J. (1933). *The life of Dr. Johnson.* London: J. M. Dent & Sons.

Boswell, J. (1953). *The Life of Samuel Johnson, (Vol 1), The Life (1709–1765).* Oxford: Clarendon Press.

Bott, E. (1928). Teaching of psychology in the medical course. *Bull. Assoc. Amer. Med. Colleges, 3,* 289–304.

Boudewyns, P. A. (1996). Posttraumatic stress disorder: Conceptualization and treatment. In M. Hersen, R. M. Eisler, & P. M. Miller (Eds.), *Progress in behavior modification,* Volume 30. Pacific Grove, CA: Brooks/Cole.

Boudewyns, P. A., Stwertka, S. A., Hyer, L. A., Albrecht, J. W., & Sperr, E. V. (1991). *Eye movement desensitization for PTSD of combat: A treatment outcome pilot study.* Paper presented at the convention of the American Psychological Association, San Francisco.

Boudewyns, P. A., Tanna, V. L., & Fleischman, D. J. A. (1975). A modified shame aversion therapy for compulsive obscene telephone calling. *Behav. Ther., 6,* 704–707.

Bourgeois, J. A., Hall, M. J., Crosby, R. M., & Drexler, K. G. (1993). An examination of narcissistic personality traits as seen in a military population. *Mil. Med., 158*(3), 170–174.

Bourgeois, M. (1991). Serotonin, impulsivity and suicide. *Human Psychopharmacol. Clin. and Exp., 6*(Suppl.), 31–36.

Bourgeois, M. (1995, December). [Importance of DSM IV (APA) and ICD-10 (WHO) in diagnosis and treatment of mood disorders.] *Encephale* (Spec. No. 5), 47–52. [French.]

Bourin, M., Malinge, M., & Guitton, B. (1995). Provocative agents in panic disorder. *Therapie 50*(4), 301–306.

Bourne, P. G. (1970). *Men, stress & Vietnam.* Boston: Little, Brown.

Boutros, N., Bonnet, K., & Mak, T. (1996). Drug abuse: A significant variable in schizophrenia research. *Bio. Psychiat., 39,* 1053–1054.

Bowen, M. A. (1960). A family concept of schizophrenia. In D. D. Jackson (Ed.), *The etiology of schizophrenia.* New York: Basic Books.

Bower, B. (1995, Jul. 15). Deceptive appearances: Imagined physical defects take an ugly personal toll. *Sci. News, 148,* 40–41.

Bower, B. (1995). Moods and the muse. *Sci. News, 147,* 378–380.

Bower, B. (1996, May 18). Trauma syndrome traverses generations. *Sci. News, 149,* 310.

Bower, G. H. (1981). Mood and memory. *Amer. Psychologist, 36*(2), 129–148.

Bowers, K. S., & Woody, E. Z. (1996). Hypnotic amnesia and the paradox of intentional forgetting. *J. Abnorm. Psychol., 105*(3), 381–390.

Bowlby, J. (1969). *Attachment* (Vol. 1). New York: Basic Books.

Bowlby, J. (1980). By ethology out of psychoanalysis: An experiment in interbreeding. *Anim. Behav., 28*(3), 649–656.

Bowman, E. S. & Markand, O. N. (1996). Psychodynamics and psychiatric diagnoses of pseudoseizure subjects. *Amer. J. Psychiat., 153*(1), 57–63.

Boyce, W. T., Chesney, M., Alkon, A., Tschann, J. M., et al. (1995). Psychobiologic reactivity to stress and childhood respiratory illnesses: Results of two prospective studies. *Psychosom. Med., 57,* 411–422.

Boyce, W. T., Chesney, M., Alkon, A., Tschann, J;.M., et al. (1995). Psychobiologic reactivity to stress and childhood respiratory illness: Results of two prospective studies. *Psychosomatic Medicine, 57*(5), 411–422.

Boyd, J. H., Rae, D. S., Thompson, J. W., Burns, B. J. et al. (1990). Phobia: Prevalence and risk factors. *Soc. Psychiat. Psychiatr. Epidemio., 25*(6), 314–323.

Bozman, A., & Beck, J. G. (1991). Covariation of sexual desire and sexual arousal: The effects of anger and anxiety. *Arch. Sex. Behav., 20,* 47–60.

Bracha, H. S., Lange, B., Gill, P. S., Gilger, J. W., et al. (1995). Subclinical microcrania, subclinical macrocrania, and fifth-month fetal markers (of growth retardation or edema) in schizophrenia: A co-twin control study of discordant monozygotic twins. *Neuropsychia., Neuropsychol., and Behav. Neurol., 8*(1), 44–52.

Bracha, H. S., Torey, E. F., Gottesman, I. I., Bigelow, L. B., et al. (1992). Second-trimester markers of fetal size in schizophrenia: A study of monozygotic twins. *Amer. J. Psychiat., 149*(10), 1355–1361.

Bradbury, T. N., & Karney, B. R. (1993). Longitudinal study of marital interaction and dysfunction: Review and analysis. *Clin. Psychol. Rev., 13*(1), 15–27.

Bradford, J. M. W. (1991).*The role of serotonin reuptake inhibitors in forensic psychiatry.* Paper presented at the 4th Congress of the European College of Neuropsychopharmacology, Monte Carlo, Monaco.

Bradford, J. M. W. (1995). Pharmacological treatment of the paraphilias. In J. M. Oldham & M. B. Riba (Eds.), *American Psychiatric Press review of psychiatry,* (Vol. 14). Washington, DC: American Psychiatric Press.

Bradford, J. M. W., & Gratzer, T. G. (1995). A treatment for impulse control disorders and paraphilia: A case report. *Canad. J. Psychiat., 40*(1), 4–5.

Bradley, S. J. (1995). Psychosexual disorders in adolescence. In J. M. Oldham & M. B. Riba (Eds.), *American Psychiatric Press review of psychiatry,* (Vol. 14). Washington, DC: American Psychiatric Press.

Brady, J. P., & Lind, D. L. (1961). Experimental analysis of hysterical blindness: Operant conditioning techniques. *Arch. Gen. Psychiat., 4,* 331–339.

Brady, J. V., Porter, R. W., Conrad, D. G., & Mason, J. W. (1958). Avoidance behavior and the development of gastroduodenal ulcers. *J. Exp. Anal. Behav., 1,* 69–73.

Braff, D. L., & Saccuzzo, D. P. (1985). The time course of information-processing deficits in schizophrenia. *Amer. J. Psychiat., 142*(2), 170–174.

Braginsky, B. M., Braginsky, D. D., & Ring, K. (1969). *Methods of madness: The mental hospital as a last resort.* New York: Holt.

Brandon, S. (1981). The history of shock treatment, in *Electroconvulsive therapy: An appraisal.* Oxford: Oxford University Press.

Braun, B. G., & Sachs, R. G. (1985). The development of multiple personality disorder: Predisposing, precipitating, and perpetuating factors. In R. P. Kluft (Ed.), *Childhood antecedents of multiple personality.* Washington, DC: American Psychiatric Press.

Braun, D. L. (1996, Jul. 28). Interview. In S. Gilbert, More men may seek eating-disorder help. *The New York Times.*

Braun, D. L., Sunday, S. R., & Halmi, K. A. (1995). Psychiatric comorbidity in patients with eating disorders. *Psychol. Med.*

Braun, P., Greenberg, D., Dasberg, H. et al. (1990). Core symptoms of post-traumatic stress disorder unimproved by alprazolam treatment. *J. Clin. Psychiat., 51,* 236–238.

Brawman-Mintzer, O., & Lydiard, R. B. (1997). Biological basis of generalized anxiety disorder. *J. Clin. Psychiat., 58*(Suppl. 3), 16–25.

Bray, G. A., Dahms, W. T., Atkinson, R. L. et al. (1980). Factors controlling food intake: A comparison of dieting and intestinal bypass. *Amer. J. Clin. Nutrition, 33,* 376–382.

Bray, J. H., & Jouriles, E. N. (1995). Treatment of marital conflict and prevention of divorce. Special Issue: The effectiveness of marital and family therapy. *J. Marital. Fam. Ther., 21*(4), 461–473.

Breggin, P. R. (1979). *Electroshock: Its brain-disabling effects.* New York: Springer.

Breier, A. (1995). Serotonin, schizophrenia and antipsychotic drug action. *Schizo. Res., 14*(3), 187–202.

Breier, A., Kelsoe, J. R., Kirwin, P. D. et al. (1988). Early parental loss and development of adult psychopathology. *Arch. Gen. Psychiat., 45,* 987–993.

Breitbart, W., Rosenfeld, B., & Passik, S. (1996). Interest in physician-assisted suicide among ambulatory HIV-infected patients. *Amer. J. Psychiat., 153*(2), 238–242.

Bremner, J. D., Innis, R. B., Chin, K. N., Staib, L. H. et al. (1997). Positron emission tomography measurement of cerebral metabolic correlates of yohimbine administration in combat-related posttraumatic stress disorder. *Arch. Gen. Psychiat., 54,* 246–254.

Bremner, J. D., Licinio, J., Darnell, A., Krystal, J. H. et al. (1997). Elevated CSF corticotropin-releasing factor concentrations in posttraumatic stress disorder. *Amer. J. Psychiat., 154*(5), 624–629.

Bremner, J. D., Southwick, S. M., Johnson, D. R., Yehuda, R., & Charney, D. S. (1993). Childhood physical abuse and combat-related posttraumatic stress disorder in Vietnam Veterans. *Amer. J. Psychiat., 150*(2), 235–239.

Bremner, J. D., Steinberg, M., Southwick, S. M., Johnson, D. R., & Charney, D. S. (1993). Use of the structured clinical interview for DSM-IV dissociative disorders for systematic assessment of dissociative symptoms in posttraumatic stress disorder. *Amer. J. Psychiat., 150*(7), 1101–1014.

Brems, C. (1995). Women and depression: A comprehensive analysis. In W. Beckham & W. Leber (Eds.), *Handbook of depression* (2nd ed.). New York: Guilford.

Brende, J. O., & Parson, E. R. (1985). *Vietnam veterans.* New York: Plenum.

Brende, J. O., & Rinsley, D. B. (1981). A case of multiple personality with psychological automatisms. *J. Amer. Acad. Psychoanal., 9*(1), 129–151.

Brent, D. A., Bridge, J., Johnson, B. A., & Connolly, J. (1996). Suicidal behavior runs in families. A controlled family study of adolescent suicide victims. *Arch. Gen. Psychiat., 53,* 1145–1152.

Brent, D. A., Kupfer, D. J., Bromet, E. J., & Dew, M. A. (1988). The assessment and treatment of patients at risk for suicide. In A. J. Frances & R. E. Hales (Eds.), *American Psychiatric Press review of psychiatry* (Vol. 7). Washington, DC: American Psychiatric Press.

Brent, D. A., Perper, J. A., Moritz, G., Allman, C., Friend, A., Roth, C., Schweers, J., Balach, L., & Baugher, M. (1993). Psychiatric risk factors for adolescent suicide: A case-control study. *J. Amer. Acad. Child Adol. Psychiat., 32*(3), 521–529.

Brent, D. A., Perper, J. A., Moritz, G., Baugher, M., & Allman, C. (1993). Suicide in adolescents with no apparent psychopathology. *J. Amer. Acad. Child Adol. Psychiat., 32*(3), 494–500.

Breslow, N. (1989). Sources of confusion in the study and treatment of sadomasochism. *J. Soc. Behav. Pers., 4*(3), 263–274.

Brewerton, T. D., Lydiard, R. B. & Herzog, D. B., Brotman, A. W., et al. (1995). Comorbidity of Axis I psychiatric disorders in bulimia nervosa. *J. Clin. Psychiat., 56*(2), 77–80.

Briere, J. (1992). *Child abuse trauma: Theory and treatment of the lasting effects.* Newbury Park, CA: SAGE.

Briere, J. (1992). Methodological issues in the study of sexual abuse effects. *J. Cons. Clin. Psychol., 147,* 1398–1390.

Brightman, B. K. (1992). Peer support and education in the comprehensive care of patients with borderline personality disorder. *Psychiatr. Hosp., 23*(2), 55–59.

Brisman, J. (1992). Bulimia in the older adolescent: An analytic perspective to a behavioral problem. In J. D. O'Brien, D. J. Pilowsky, & O. W. Lewis, (Eds.), *Psychotherapies with children and adolescents: Adapting the psychodynamic process.* Washington, DC: American Psychiatric Press.

Bristow, M. & Bright, J. (1995). Group cognitive therapy in chronic depression: Results from two intervention studies. *Behav. Cog. Psychother., 23,* 373–380.

Britton, W. H., & Eaves, R. C. (1986). Relationship between the Vineland Adaptive Behavior Scales-Classroom Edition of the Vineland Social Maturity Scales. *Amer. J. Ment. Def., 91*(1), 105–107.

Brodsky, S., & Pothyress, N. (1990). Presentation. American Psychological Association Convention, Boston.

Brom, D., Kleber, R. J., & Hofman, M. C. (1993). Victims of traffic accidents: Incidence and prevention of post-traumatic stress disorder. *J. Clin. Psychiat., 49*(2), 131–140.

Bromet, E. J., Hough, L., & Connell, M. (1984). Mental health of children near the Three Mile Island reactor. *J. Prev. Psychiat., 2,* 275–301.

Bromet, E. J., Schulberg, H. C., & Dunn, L. (1982). Reactions of psychiatric patients to the Three Mile Island nuclear accident. *Arch. Gen. Psychiat., 39*(6), 725–730.

Brooks, G. R., & Richardson, F. C. (1980). Emotional skills training: A treatment program for duodenal ulcer. *Behav. Ther., 11*(2), 198–207.

Brooks-Gunn, J., & Warren, M. (1989). Biological and social contributions to negative affect in young adolescent girls. *Child Dev., 60,* 40–55.

Brooner, R. K., King, V. L., Kidorf, M., Schmidt, C. W., & Bigelow, G. E. (1997). Psychiatric and substance use comorbidity among treatment-seeking opioid abusers. *Arch. Gen. Psychiat., 54,* 71–80.

Brotman, A. W., Herzog, D. B., & Hamburg, P. (1988). Long-term course in 14 bulimic patients treated with psychotherapy. *J. Clin. Psychiat., 49,* 157–160.

Brown, A. S., Susser, E. S., Butler, P. D., Andrews, R. R., Kaufmann, C. A., & Gorman, J. M. (1996). Neurobiological plausibility of prenatal nutritional deprivation as a risk factor for schizophrenia. *J. Nerv. Ment. Dis., 184*(2), 71–85.

Brown, B. (1974). Depression roundup. *Behav. Today, 5*(17), 117.

Brown, B. S. (1983). The impact of political and economic changes upon mental health. *Amer. J. Orthopsychiat., 53*(4), 583–592.

Brown, E. (1972). Assessment from a humanistic perspective. *Psychother. Theory Res. Prac., 9,* 103–106.

Brown, G. L., Ebert, M., Goyer, P., Jimerson, D. C., Klein, W. J., Bunney, W. E., & Goodwin, F. K. (1982). Aggression, suicide, and serotonin: Relationships to CSF amine metabolites. *Amer. J. Psychiat., 139,* 741–746.

Brown, G. L., Goodwin, F. K., Ballenger, J. C., Goyer, P. F., & Major, L. F. (1979). Aggression in humans correlates with cerebrospinal fluid metabolites. *Psychiatry Research, 1,* 131–139.

Brown, G. L., Linnoila, M. I., & Goodwin, F. K. (1992). Impulsivity, aggression, and associated affects: Relationship to self-destructive behavior and suicide. In R. W. Maris, A. L. Berman, J. T. Maltsberger, & R. I. Yufit (Eds.), *Assessment and prediction of suicide.* New York: Guilford.

Brown, G. W. (1988). Early loss of parent and depression in adult life. In S. Fisher & J. Reason (Eds.), *Handbook of life stress, cognition and health.* Chichester, England: Wiley.

Brown, G. W., Harris, T. O., & Hepworth, C. (1995). Loss, humiliation and entrapment among women developing depression: A patient and non-patient comparison. *Psychol. Med., 25*(1), 7–21.

Brown, G. W. & Harris, T. O. (1978). *Social origins of depression: A study of psychiatric disorder in women.* London: Tavistock.

Brown, G. W., Monck, E. M., Carstairs, G. M., & Wing, J. K. (1962). Influence on family life on the course of schizophrenic illness. *Brit. J. Prev. Soc. Med., 16,* 55–68.

Brown, G. W., Sklair, F., Harris, T. O., & Birley, J. L. T. (1973). Life-events and psychiatric disorders. Part I. Some methodological issues. *Psychol. Med., 3,* 74–87.

Brown, J., Helteleff, P., Barakat, S., & Rowe, C. (1986). Is it normal for terminally ill patients to desire death? *Amer. J. Psychiat., 143,* 208–211.

Brown, J. H., Henteleff, P., Barakat, S., & Rowe, C. J. (1986). Is it normal for terminally ill patients to desire death? *Amer. J. Psychiat., 143*(2), 208–211.

Brown, J. L. (1963). Follow-up of children with atypical development (infantile psychosis). *Amer. J. Orthopsychiat., 33,* 855–861.

Brown, J. L. & Pollitt, E. (1996, February.). Malnutrition, poverty and intellectual development. *Scientif. Amer.*, pp. 38–43.

Brown, L. (1993). Enrollment of drug abusers in HIV clinical trials: A public health imperative for communities of color. *J. Psychoactive Drugs, 25*(1), 45–48.

Brown, P. J., Stout, R. L., & Mueller, T. (1996). Posttraumatic stress disorder and substance abuse relapse among women: A pilot study. *Psychol. Addict. Behav., 10(2),* 124–128.

Brown, T. A., Hertz, R. M. & Barlow, D. H. (1992). New developments in cognitive-behavioural treatment of anxiety disorders. In A. Tasman, & M. B. Riba (Eds.), *Review of Psychiatry* (Vol. 11). Washington, DC: American Psychiatric Press.

Browne, A., & Finklehor, D. (1986). Impact of child sexual abuse: A review of the research. *Psychol. Bull., 99*(1), 66–77.

Brownell, K. D. & Rodin, J. (1995). Medical, metabolic, and psychological effects of weight cycling and weight variability. *Archives of Internal Medicine.*

Brownell, K. D., & Napolitano, M. A. (1995). Distorting reality for children: Body size proportions of Barbie and Ken dolls. *Inter. J. Eat. Disorders., 18*(3), 295–298.

Brownell, K. D., & O'Neil, P. M. (1993). Obesity. In D. H. Barlow (Ed.), *Clinical handbook of psychological disorders: A step-by-step treatment manual* (2nd ed.). New York: Guilford.

Brownell, K. D., & Wadden, T. A. (1992). Etiology and treatment of obesity: Understanding a serious, prevalent, and refractory disorder. *J. Cons. Clin. Psychol., 60*(4), 505–517.

Bruce, E. J., Schultz, C. L., & Smyrnios, K. X. (1996). A longitudinal study of the grief of mothers and fathers of children with intellectual disability. *Brit. J. Med. Psychol., 69,* 33–45.

Bruce, M. L., & Kim, K. M. (1992). Differences in the effects of divorce on major depression in men and women. *Amer. J. Psychiat., 149*(7), 914–917.

Bruce, M. L., Leaf, P. J., Rozal, G. P. M., Florio, L., & Hoff, R. A. (1994). Psychiatric status and 9-year mortality data in the New Haven Epidemiological Catchment Area Study. *Amer. J. Psychiat., 151*(5), 716–721.

Bruch, H. (1962). Perceptual and conceptual disturbances in anorexia nervosa. *Psychosom. Med., 24,* 187–194.

Bruch, H. (1973). *Eating disorders: Obesity, anorexia nervosa and the person within.* New York: Basic Books.

Bruch, H. (1973). Psychiatric aspects of obesity. *Psychiatr. Ann., 3*(7), 6–10.

Bruch, H. (1978). *The golden cage: The enigma of anorexia nervosa.* Cambridge, MA: Harvard University Press.

Bruch, H. (1981). Developmental considerations of anorexia nervosa and obesity. *Canad. J. Psychiat., 26,* 212–217.

Bruch, H. (1982). Anorexia nervosa: Therapy and theory. *Amer. J. Psychiat., 139,* 1531–1538.

Bruch, H. (1986). Anorexia nervosa: The therapeutic task. In K. D. Brownell & J. P. Foreyt (Eds.), *Handbook of eating disorders: Physiology, psychology and treatment of obesity, anorexia and bulimia.* New York: Basic Books.

Bruch, H. (1988). In D. Czyzewski & M. Suhr (Eds.), *Conversations with Anorexics.* New York: Basic Books.

Bruch, H. (1991). The sleeping beauty: Escape from change. In S. I. Greenspan, G. H. Pollock (Eds.), *The course of life: Vol. 4 Adolescence.* Madison, CT: International Universities Press.

Bryant, R. A., & Harvey, A. G. (1995). Posttraumatic stress in volunteer firefighters: Predictors of stress. *J. Nerv. Ment. Dis., 183*(4), 267–271.

Buchan, H., Johnstone, E. C., McPherson, K., Palmer, R. L. et al. (1992). Who benefits from electroconvulsive therapy? Combined results of the Leicester and Northwick Park trials. *Brit. J. Psychiat., 160,* 355–359.

Buchanan, A. (1997). The investigation of acting on delusions as a tool for risk assessment in the mentally disordered. *Brit. J. Psychiat., 170*(Suppl. 32), 12–14.

Buchanan, R. W. (1995). Clozapine: Efficacy and safety. *Schizo. Bull., 21*(4), 579–591.

Buchele, B. J. (1993). Group psychotherapy for persons with multiple personality and dissociative disorders. *Bull. Menninger Clin., 57*(3), 362–370.

Buchkremer, G., Monking, H. S. . Holle, R., & Hornung, W. P. (1995). The impact of therapeutic relatives' groups on the course of illness of schizophrenic patients. *Eur. Psychiat., 10*(1), 17–27.

Buchsbaum, M. S., & Haier, R. J. (1987). Functional and anatomical brain imaging: Impact on schizophrenia research. *Schizo. Bull., 13*(1), 115–132.

Buchwald, A. M., & Rudick-Davis, D. (1993). The symptoms of major depression. *J. Abnorm. Psychol., 102*(2), 197–205.

Buckley, J. T. (1995). Nation raising "a generation of gamblers." *USA Today,* 1A-2A.

Buckley, P., Thompson, P., Way, L., & Meltzer, H. Y. (1994). Substance abuse among patients with treatment-resistant schizophrenia: Characteristics and implications for clozapine therapy. *Amer. J. Psychiat., 151*(3), 385–389.

Buda, M., & Tsuang, M. T. (1990). The epidemiology of suicide: Implications for clinical practice. In S. J. Blumenthal & D. J. Kupfer (Eds.), *Suicide over the life cycle: Risk factors, assessment, and treatment of suicidal patients.* Washington, DC: American Psychiatry Press.

Buffum, J. (1992). Prescription drugs and sexual function. *Psychiatric Med., 10*(2), 181–198.

Bugental, J. F. (1965). The existential crisis in intensive psychotherapy. *Psychother. Theory Res. Prac., 2*(1), 16–20.

Bugental, J. F. T. (1992). The betrayal of the human: Psychotherapy's mission to reclaim our lost identity. In J. K. Zeig (Ed.), *The evolution of psychotherapy: The second conference.* New York: Brunner/Mazel.

Bugental, J. F. T. (1997). There is a fundamental division in how psychotherapy is conceived. In J. K. Zeig (Ed.), *The evolution of psychotherapy: The third conference.* New York: Brunner/Mazel.

Bujold, A., Ladouceur, R., Sylvain, C. & Boisvert J. M. (1994). Treatment of pathological gamblers: An experimental study. *J. Behav. Ther. Exp. Psychiat., 25*(4), 275–282.

Bukstein, O. G., Brent, D. A., & Kaminer, Y. (1989). Comorbidity of substance abuse and other psychiatric disorders in adolescents. *Amer. J. Psychiat., 146*(9), 1131–1141.

Bunney, W. E., & Davis, J. M. (1965). Norepinephrine in depressive reactions: A review. *Arch. Gen. Psychiat., 13*(6), 483–493.

Bunney, W. E., & Garland, B. L. (1981). Receptor function in depression. *Adv. Bio. Psychiat., 7,* 71–84.

Bunney, W. E., & Garland, B. L. (1984). Lithium and its possible modes of actions. In R. M. Post & J. C. Ballenger (Eds.), *Neurobiology of mood disorders: Vol. I, Frontiers of Clinical Neuroscience.* Baltimore: Williams & Wilkins.

Burbach, D. J., & Borduin, C. M. (1986). Parent-child relations and the etiology of depression: A review of methods and findings. *Clin. Psychol. Rev., 6*(2), 133–153.

Burek, D. M. (Ed.). (1990). *Encyclopedia of associations* (25th ed.). Detroit, MI: Gale Research.

Burgess, E., & Haaga, D. A. (1994). The Positive Automatic Thoughts Questionnaire (ATQ-P) and the Automatic Thoughts Questionnaire-Revised (ATQ-RP): Equivalent measures of positive thinking? *Cog. Ther. Res., 18*(1), 15–23.

Burnette, E. (1996). Urban activists call for hands-on community work. *APA Monitor, 27*(10), 30.

Burnette, E. & Murray, B. (1996). Conduct disorders need early treatment. *APA Monitor, 27*(10), 40.

Burns, L. H. (1995). An overview of sexual dysfunction in the infertile couple. *J. Fam. Psychother., 6*(1), 25–46.

Burns, T. P., & Crisp, A. H. (1985). Factors affecting prognosis in male anorexics. *J. Psychiatr. Res., 19*(2–3), 323–328.

Bursztajn, H., Gutheil, T. G., Warren, M. J., & Brodsky, A. (1986). Depression, self-love, time, and the "right" to suicide. *Gen. Hosp. Psychiat., 8*(2), 91–95.

Burt, D. D., Loveland, K. A., & Lewis, K. R. (1992). Depression and the onset of dementia in adults with mental retardation. *Amer. J. Ment. Retard., 96*(5), 502–511.

Burt, D. R., Creese, I., & Snyder, S. H. (1977). Anti-schizophrenic drugs: Chronic treatment elevates dopamine receptor binding in brain. *Science, 196*(4287), 326–328.

Burton, V. S. (1990). The consequences of official labels: A research note on rights lost by the mentally ill, mentally incompetent, and convicted felons. *Comm. Ment. Hlth. J., 26*(3), 267–276.

Busatto, G. F., Pilowsky, L. S., Costa, D. C., Ell, P. J., David, A. S. et al. (1997). Correlation between reduced in vivo benzodiazepine receptor binding and severity of psychotic symptoms in schizophrenia. *Amer. J. Psychiat., 154*(1), 56–63.

Bustillo, J. R., Thaker, G., Buchanan, R. W., Moran, M. et al. (1997). Visual information-processing impairments in deficit and nondeficit schizophrenia. *Amer. J. Psychiat., 154*(5), 647–654.

Butcher, J. N. (Ed.). (1995). *Clinical personality assessment: Practical approaches.* New York: Oxford University Press.

Butler, G., Cullington, A., Hibbert, G., Klimes, I., & Gelder, M. (1987). Anxiety management for persistent generalized anxiety. *Brit. J. Psychiat., 151,* 535–542.

Butler, G., Fennel, M., Robson, P., & Gelder, M. (1991). A comparison of behavior therapy and cognitive behavior therapy in the treatment of generalized anxiety disorder. *J. Cons. Clin. Psychol., 59*(1), 167–175.

Butler, R. N. (1975). Psychiatry and the elderly: An overview. *Amer. J. Psychiat., 132,* 893–900.

Butler, R. W., & Satz, P. (1989). Psychological assessment of personality of adults and children. In H. I. Kaplan & B. J. Sadock (Eds.), *Comprehensive textbook of psychiatry* (5th ed., Vol. 1). Baltimore: Williams & Wilkins.

Butters, N., Delis, D. C., & Lucas, J. A. (1995). Clinical assessment of

memory disorders in amnesia and dementia. *Annu. Rev. Psychol., 46,* 493–523.

Butters, N., Heindel, W. C., & Salmon, D. P. (1990). Dissociation of implicit memory in dementia: Neurological implications. *Bull. Psychon. Soc.,* 28(4), 359–366.

Button, E. (1993). *Eating disorders: Personal construct therapy and change.* Chichester, England: Wiley.

Buysse, D. J., Frank, E., Lowe, K. K., Cherry, C. R., & Kupfer, D. J. (1997). Electroencephalographic sleep correlates to episode and vulnerability to recurrence in depression. *Depression, 41,* 406–418.

Buysse, D. J., Reynolds, C. F., & Kupfer, D. J. (1993). Depression. In M. A. Carsakadon (Ed.), *The Encyclopedia of Sleep and Dreaming.* New York: MacMillan.

Byrne, K., & Stern, S. L. (1981). Antidepressant medication in the outpatient treatment of depression: Guide for nonmedical psychotherapists. *Profess. Psychologist, 12*(3), 302–308.

Byrnes, G., & Kelly, I. W. (1992). Crisis calls and lunar cycles: A twenty-year review. *Psychol. Rep., 71*(3, Pt.1), 779–785.

Cacciola, J. S., Rutherford, M. J., Alterman, A. I., McKay, J. R., & Snider, E. C. (1996). Personality disorders and treatment outcomes in methadone maintenance patients. *J. Nerv. Ment. Dis., 184*(4), 234–239.

Caddy, G. R. (1985). Cognitive behavior therapy in the treatment of multiple personality. *Behav. Mod., 9*(3), 267–292.

Cadoret, R. J., Yates, W. R., Troughton, E., Woodworth, G., & Stewart, M. A. (1995). Adoption study demonstrating two genetic pathways to drug abuse. *Arch. Gen. Psychiat., 52,* 42–52.

Cage, M. C. (1992). 42% of college students engage in "binge drinking," survey shows. *Chron. Higher Educ., 39*(6), S30.

Calahan, D., Cisin, I. H., & Crossley, H. M. (1969). *American drinking practices: A national study of drinking behaviors and attitudes.* New Brunswick, NJ: Rutgers Center of Alcohol Studies.

Calev, A., Gaudino, E. A., Squires, N. K., Zervas, I. M., & Fink, M. (1995). ECT and non-memory cognition: A review. *Brit. J. Clin. Psychol., 34,* 505–515.

Calev, A., Kochav-lev, E., Tubi, N., Nigal, D., et al. (1991). Change in attitude toward electroconvulsive therapy: Effects of treatment, time since treatment, and severity of depression. *Convulsive Therapy,* 7(3), 184–189.

Calev, A., Nigal, D., Shapira, B., Tubi, N., et al. (1991). Early and long-term effects of electroconvulsive therapy and depression on memory and other cognitive functions. *J. Nerv. Ment. Dis., 179*(9), 526–533.

Callahan, L. A., McGreevy, M. A., Cirincione, C., & Steadman, H. J. (1992). Measuring the effects of the GBMI verdict: Georgia's 1982 GBMI reform. *Law and Human Behavior, 16*(4), 447–461.

Callahan, L. A., Steadman, H. J., McGreevy, M. A., & Robbins, P. C. (1991). The volume and characteristics of insanity defense pleas: An eight-state study. *Bulletin of the American Academy of Psychiatry and the Law, 19*(4), 331–338.

Callner, D. A. (1975). Behavioral treatment approaches to drug abuse: A critical review of the research. *Psychol. Bull., 82*(2), 143–164.

Calsyn, D. A., Fleming, C., Wells, E. A., & Saxon, A. J. (1996). Personality disorder subtypes among opiate addicts in methadone maintenance. *Psychol. Addic. Behav., 10*(1), 3–8.

Calvo, M. G., Eysenck, M. W., & Castillo, M. D. (1997). Interpretation bias in test anxiety: The time course of predictive inferences. *Cog. Emot., 11*(1), 43–63.

Camara, W. J., & Schneider, D. L. (1994). Integrity tests: facts and unresolved issues. *Amer. Psychol., 49*(2), 112–119.

Cameron, D. J., Thomas, R. I., Mulvhill, M., & Bronheim, H. (1987). Delirium: A test of the Diagnostic and Statistical Manual III criteria on medical inpatients. *J. Amer. Ger. Soc., 35,* 1007–1010.

Cameron, N. (1974). Paranoid conditions and paranoia. In S. Arieti & E. Brody (Eds.), *American Handbook of Psychiatry.* New York: Basic Books.

Campbell, J. C. (1995). Prediction of homicide of and by battered women. In J. C. Campbell (Ed.), *Assessing dangerousness: Violence by sexual offenders, batterers, and child abusers.* Thousand Oaks, CA: Sage.

Campbell, J. C. (Ed.). (1995). *Assessing dangerousness: Violence by sexual offenders, batterers, and child abusers.* Thousand Oaks, CA: Sage.

Campbell, R. V., O'Brien, S., Bickett, A. D., & Lutzker, J. R. (1983). In-home parent training of migraine headaches and marital counseling as an ecobehavioral approach to prevent child abuse. *J. Behav. Ther. Exp. Psychiat., 14,* 147–154.

Canetto, S. S. (1993). *Women and suicidal behavior.* Unpublished manuscript, Colorado State University, Fort Collins.

Canetto, S. S. (1995). Elderly women and suicidal behavior. In S. S. Canetto & D. Lester (Eds.), *Women and suicidal behavior.* New York: Springer.

Canetto, S. S. (1995). Suicidal women: Prevention and intervention strategies. In S. S. Canetto & D. Lester (Eds.), *Women and suicidal behavior.* New York: Springer Publishing Company.

Canetto, S. S. & Lester, D. (1995). The epidemiology of women's suicidal behavior. In S. S. Canetto & D. Lester (Eds.), *Women and suicidal behavior.* New York: Springer.

Canetto, S. S. & Lester, D. (1995). Gender and the primary prevention of suicide mortality. [Special issue]. *Suic. Life Threat. Behav., 25*(1), 58–69.

Canino, E., Cardona, R., Monsalve, P., Perez, A. F., Lopez, B., & Fragachan, F. (1994). A behavioral treatment program as a therapy in the control of primary hypertension. *Acta Cient. Venez., 45*(1), 23–30.

Cannon, D. S., Baker, T. B., Gino, A., & Nathan, P. E. (1986). Alcohol-aversion therapy: Assessment of conditioning. *J. Cons. Clin. Psychol., 54,* 825–830.

Cannon, D. S., Baker, T. B., & Wehl, W. K. (1981). Emetic and electric shock alcohol aversion therapy: Six and twelve-month follow-up. *J. Cons. Clin. Psychol., 49,* 360–368.

Cannon, T. D., & Marco, E. (1994). Structural brain abnormalities as indicators of vulnerability to schizophrenia. *Schizo. Bull., 20*(1), 89–102.

Cannon, W. (1927). The James-Lange theory of emotions: A critical examination and an alternative. *American Journal of Psychology, 39,* 106–124.

Canter, A., Kondo, C. Y., & Knott, J. R. (1975). A comparison of EMG feedback and progressive muscle relaxation training in anxiety neurosis. *Brit. J. Psychiat., 127,* 470–477.

Canty, G. F. (1996). Therapists at work. *The Institute Notebook, 5*(2), 1,4.

Canty, G. F. (1996). A heart to heart on depression. *The Institute Notebook, 5*(3), 1,4.

Capaldi, D. M., & Patterson, G. R. (1994). Interrelated influences of contextual factors on antisocial behavior in childhood and adoklescence for males. In D. C. Fowles, P. Sutker, & S. H. Goodman (Eds.), *Progress in experimental personality and psychopathology research.* New York: Springer.

Caplan, R., Perdue, S., Tanguay, P. E., & Fish, B. (1990). Formal thought disorder in childhood onset schizophrenia and schizotypal personality disorder. *J. Child Psychol. Psychiat. Allied Disc., 31*(7), 1103–1114.

Capleton, R. A. (1996). Cognitive function in schizophrenia: Association with negative and positive symptoms. *Psychol. Rep., 78,* 123–128.

Capps, L., Sigman, M., Sena, R., Henker, B., & Whalen, C. (1996). Fear, anxiety and perceived control in children of agoraphobic parents. *J. Child Psychol. Psychiat., 37*(4), 445–452.

Cardasis, W., Hochman, J. A., & Silk, K. R. (1997). Transitional objects and borderline personality disorder. *Amer. J. Psychiat, 154*(2), 250–255.

Carey, G., & DiLalla, D. L. (1994). Personality and Psychopathology: Genetic Perspectives. *J. Abnorm. Psychol., 103*(1), 32–43.

Carey, G., & Gottesman, I. I. (1981). Twin and family studies of anxi-

ety, phobic, and obsessive disorders. In D. K. Klein & J. Rabkin (Eds.), *Anxiety: New research and changing concepts.* New York: Raven.

Carey, K. (1989). Emerging treatment guidelines for mentally ill chemical abusers. *Hosp. Comm. Psychiat., 40*(4), 341–342.

Carey, K. B. & Carey, M. P. (1995). Reasons for drinking among psychiatric outpatients: Relationship to drinking patterns. *Psychol. Addic. Behav., 9*(4), 251–257.

Carey, M., Carey, K., & Meisler, A. (1991). Psychiatric symptoms in mentally ill chemical abusers. *J. Nerv. Ment. Dis., 179*(3), 136–138.

Carey, M. P., Wincze, J. P., & Meisler, A. W. (1993). Sexual dysfunction: Male erectile disorder. In D. H. Barlow (Ed.), *Clinical Handbook of Psychological Disorders: A Step-by-Step Treatment Manual* (2nd ed.). New York: Guilford.

Carey, M. P., Wincze, J. P., & Meisler, A. W. (1993). Sexual dysfunction: Male erectile disorder. In H. D. Barlow (Ed.), *Clinical handbook of psychological disorders* (2nd ed., pp. 442–480). New York: Guilford.

Carey, R. J., Pinheiro-Carrera, M., Dai, H., Tomaz, C., & Huston, J. P. (1995). L-Dopa and psychosis: Evidence for L-Dopa-induced increases in prefrontal cortex dopamine and in serum corticosterone. *Bio. Psychiat., 38,* 669–676.

Carlisle, A. L. (1993). The divided self: Toward an understanding of the dark side of the serial killer. *Amer. J. Criminal, Justice, 17*(2), 23–36.

Carlson G. A., Rich, C. L., Grayson, P., & Fowler, R. C. (1991). Secular trends in psychiatric diagnoses of suicide victims. *J. Affect. Disorders, 21,* 127–132.

Carlson, G. A., Fennig, S., & Bromet, E. J. (1994). The confusion between bipolar disorder and schizophrenia in youth: Where does it stand in the 1990s? *J. Amer. Acad. Child Adol. Psychiat., 33*(4), 453–460.

Carlsson, A. (1978). Antipsychotic drugs, neurotransmitters, and schizophrenia. *Amer. J. Psychiat., 135*(2), 104–173.

Carlsson, A. (1978). Does dopamine have a role in schizophrenia? *Bio. Psychiat., 13*(1), 3–21.

Carnahan, H., Elliott, D., & Velamoor, V. R. (1996). Influence of object size on prehension in leukotomized and unleukotomized individuals with schizophrenia. *J. Clin. Exp. Neuropsychol., 18*(1), 136–147.

Carney, P. A., Fitzgerald, C. T., & Monaghan, C. E. (1988). Influence of climate on the prevalence of mania. *Brit. J. Psychiat., 152,* 820–823.

Carpenter, W. T., Conley, R. R., Buchanan, R. W., Breier, A., et al. (1995). Patient response and resource management: Another view of clozapine treatment of schizophrenia. *Amer. J. Psychiat., 152*(6), 827–832.

Carr, A. T., (1979). The psychopathology of fear. In W. Sluckin (Ed.), *Fear in animals and man.* New York: Van Nostrand Reinhold.

Carr, J. (1994). Annotation: Long term outcome for people with Down Syndrome. *J. Child Psychol. Psychiat. Allied Disc, 35*(3), 425–439.

Carr, R. E., Lehrer, P. M., & Cochran, S. M. (1995). Predictors of panic-fear in asthma. Special Section: The interface of mental and physical health. *Health Psychol., 14*(5), 421–426.

Carrera, M. R. A., Ashley, J. A., Parsons, L. H., Wirsching, P. et al. (1995). Suppression of psychoactive effects of cocaine by active immunization. *Nature, 378*(4), 727–730.

Carrey, N. J., Butter, H. J., Persinger, M. A., & Bialik, R. J. (1995). Physiological and cognitive correlates of child abuse. *J. Amer. Acad. Child Adol. Psychiat., 34*(8), 1067–1075.

Carrington, P. (1978). *Clinically standardized meditation (CSM) instructors kit.* Kendall Park, NJ: Pace Educational Systems.

Carrington, P. (1993). Modern forms of meditation. In P. M. Lehrer & R. L. Woolfolk (Eds.), *Principles and Practice of Stress Management* (2nd ed.). New York: Guilford.

Carroll, K. M., & Rounsaville, B. J. (1995). Psychosocial treatments. In J. M. Oldham & M. B. Riba (Eds.), *American Psychiatric Press review of psychiatry, Volume 14.* Washington, DC: American Psychiatric Press.

Carson, N. D., & Johnson, R. E. (1985). Suicidal thoughts and problem-solving preparation among college students. *J. Coll. Stud. Personnel, 26*(6), 484–487.

Carson, R. C., & Sanislow, C. A. (1993). The schizophrenias. In P. B. Sutker & H. E. Adams (Eds.), *Comprehensive handbook of psychopathology.* New York: Plenum Press.

Carstairs, K. (1992). Paranoid-schizoid or symbiotic? *Inter. J. Psychoanal., 73*(1), 71–85.

Carter, C. S., Servan-Schreiber, D., & Perlstein, W. M. (1997). Anxiety disorders and the syndrome of chest pain with normal coronary arteries: Prevalence and pathophysiology. *J. Clin. Psychiat., 58* (Suppl. 3), 70–73.

Cartwright, R. D., & Lamberg, L. (1992). *Crisis Dreaming: Using Your Dreams to Solve your Problems.* New York: Harper Collins.

Cash, T. F., & Henry, P. E. (1995). Women's body images: The results of a national survey in the U. S. A. *Sex Roles, 33*(Nos. 1/2), 19–28.

Casper, R. C. (1995). Biology of eating disorders. In A. F. Schatzberg & C. B. Nemeroff (Eds.), *The American Psychiatric Press textbook of psychopharmacology.* Washington, DC: American Psychiatric Press.

Cassem, N. H. & Hyman, S. E. (1995). Psychological management of grief and serious illness. In *Scientific American Series: Vol. 13, Psychiatry.* New York: Scientific American.

Castellano, T. C., & Soderstrom, I. R. (1992). Therapeutic wilderness programs and juvenile recidivism: A program evaluation. *Journal of Offender Rehabilitation, 17*(3–4), 19–46.

Castellanos, F. X., Giedd, J. N., Eckburg, P., Marsh, W. L. et al. (1994). Quantiative morphology of the caudate nucleus in attention deficit hyperactivity disorder. *Amer. J. Psychiat., 151,* 1791–1796.

Castle, D. J., Abel, K., Takei, N., & Murray, R. M. (1995). Gender differences in schizophrenia: Hormonal effect or subtypes? *Schizo. Bull., 21*(1), 1–12.

Caton, C. L. (1982). Effect of length of inpatient treatment for chronic schizophrenia. *Amer. J. Psychiat., 139*(7), 856–861.

Cattell, H., & Jolley, D. J. (1995). One hundred cases of suicide in elderly people. *Brit. J. Psychiat., 166*(4), 451–457.

Cauchon, D. (1995, December 6). Patients often aren't informed of full danger. *USA Today,* pp. 1A–2A.

Cautela, J. R. (1966). Treatment of compulsive behavior by covert sensitization. *Psych. Rec., 16*(1), 33–41.

Cautela, J. R. (1967). Covert sensitization. *Psych. Rec., 20,* 459–468.

Cauwels, J. M. (1983). *Bulimia: The binge-purge compulsion.* New York: Doubleday.

Cavanaugh, J. C. (1990). *Adult development and aging.* Belmont, CA: Wadsworth.

Centorrino, F., Baldessarini, R. J., Frankenburg, F. R., Kando, J., Volpicelli, S. A., & Flood, J. G. (1996). Serum levels of Clozapine and Norclozapine in patients treated with selective serotonin reuptake inhibitors. *Amer. J. Psychiat., 153*(6), 820–822.

Cerletti, U., & Bini, L. (1938). L'elettroshock. *Arch. Gen. Neurol. Psychiat. & Psychoanal., 19,* 266–268.

Chadwick, P., & Trower, P. (1996). Cognitive therapy for punishment paranoia: A single case experiment. *Behav. Res. Ther., 34*(4), 351–356.

Chaika, E. O. (1990). *Understanding psychotic speech: Beyond Freud and Chomsky.* Springfield, IL: Thomas.

Chait, L. D., Fishman, M. W., & Schuster, C. R. (1985). "Hangover" effects the morning after marijuana smoking. *Drug Alc. Dep., 15*(3), 229–238.

Chakos, M. H., Alvir, J. M. J., Woerner, M. G., Koreen, A., Geisler, S., Mayerhoff, D., Sobel, S., Kane, J. M., Borenstein, M., & Lieberman, J. A. (1996). Incidence and correlates of tardive dyskinesia in first episode of schizophrenia. *Arch. Gen. Psychiat., 53,* 313–319.

Chamberlain, P. (1985). Increasing the attention span of five mentally handicapped children using their parents as agents of change. *Behav. Psychother., 13*(20), 142–153.

Chambless, D. L. (1988). Cognitive mechanisms in panic disorder. In S. Rachman & J. Maser (Eds.), *Panic: psychological perspectives.* Hillsdale, NJ: Erlbaum.

Champion, L. A. & Power, M. J. (1995). Social and cognitive approaches to depression: Towards a new synthesis. *Brit. J. Clin. Psychol., 34,* 485–503.

Char, W. F. (1985). The hysterical spouse. *Med. Aspects Human Sex., 19*(9), 123–133.

Charney, D. S., & Heninger, G. R., (1983). Monoamine receptor sensitivity and depression: Clinical studies of antidepressant effects of serotonin and noradrenergic function. *Psychopharm. Bull., 19,* 490–495.

Charney, D. S., Deutch, A. Y., Krystal, J. H. et al. (1993). Psychobiological mechanisms of posttraumatic stress disorder. *Arch. Gen. Psychiat., 50,* 294–305.

Charney, D. S., Heninger, G. R., & Redmond, D. E. (1983). Yohimbine induced anxiety and increased noradrenergic function in humans: Effects of diazepam and clonidine. *Life Science, 33,* 19–29.

Charney, D. S., Heninger, G. R., & Redmond, D. E. (1984, May). Neurobiological mechanism. From Abstracts of the APA Annual Meeting (Abstract 30C). Los Angeles.

Charney, D. S., Heninger, G. R., & Sternberg, D. E. (1984). The effect of mianserin on alpha 2 adrenergic receptor function in depressed patients. *Brit. J. Psychiat., 144,* 407–418.

Charney, D. S., Woods, S. W., Goodman, W. K., & Heninger, G. R. (1987). Neurobiological mechanisms of panic anxiety: Biochemical and behavioral correlates of yohimbine-induced anxiety. *Amer. J. Psychiat., 144*(8), 1030–1036.

Charney, D. S., Woods, S. W., Krystal, J. H., Nagy, L. M., & Heninger, G. R. (1992). Noradrenergic neuronal dysregulation in panic disorder: The effects of intravenous yohimbine and clonidine in panic disorder patients. *Acta Psychiatr. Scandin., 86,* 273–282.

Charney, D. S., Woods, S. W., Price, L. H., Goodman, W. K., Glazer, W. M., & Heninger, G. R. (1990). Noradrenergic dyssregulation in panic disorder. In J. C. Ballenger (Ed.), *Neurobiology of panic disorder.* New York: Wiley-Liss.

Chase, M. (1993, May 28). Psychiatrists declare severe PMS a depressive disorder. *The Wall Street Journal,* p. B1, B6.

Chase, M. (1996, April 15). If you're considering melatonin, weigh facts against all the hype. *The Wall Street Journal,* pp. B1–B2.

Chatlos, C. (1987). *Crack: What you should know about the cocaine epidemic.* New York: Perigee Books.

Chemtob, C. M., Bauer, G. B., Neller, G., Hamada, R., et al. (1990). Posttraumatic stress disorder among Special Forces Vietnam Veterans. *Military Medicine, 155*(1), 16–20.

Chen, E. Y. H., Lam, L. C. W., Chen, R. Y. L., & Nguyen, D. G. H. (1996). Negative symptoms, neurological signs and neuropsychological impairments in 204 Hong Kong Chinese patients with schizophrenia. *Brit. J. Psychiat., 168,* 227–233.

Chen, W. J., Loh, E. W., Hsu, Y. P., Chen, C., Yu, J., & Cheng, A. T. A. (1996). Alcohol-metabolising genes and alcoholism among Taiwanese Han men: Independent effect of ADH2, ADH3, and ALDH2. *Brit. J. Psychiat., 168,* 762–767.

Chen, X. & Cui, Q. (1995). Effect of biofeedback and relaxation training on patients with 1st or 2nd period primary hypertension. *Chin. Ment. Hlth. J., 9*(3), 126, 125.

Chen, X., Rubin, R. H., & Li, B. (1995). Depressed mood in Chinese children: Relations with school performance and family environment. *J. Cons. Clin. Psychol., 63*(6), 938–947.

Chen, Y. R., Swann, A. C., Burt, D. B. (1996). Stability of diagnosis in schizophrenia. *Amer J. Psychiat., 153*(5), 682–686.

Chen, Z., & Cui, Q. (1995). [Effect of biofeedback and relaxation training on patients with 1st or 2nd period primary hypertension. *Chinese Ment. Hlth. J., 9*(3), 126, 125.

Childress, A. R., McLellan, A. T., & O'Brien, C. P. (1984). Assessment and extinction of conditioned withdrawal-like responses in an integrated treatment for opiate dependence. In L. S. Harris (Ed.), *Problems of drug dependence* (NIDA Research Monograph Series No. 55). Rockville, MD: National Institute on Drug Abuse.

Childress, A. R., McLellan, A. T., & O'Brien, C. P. (1988). Classically conditioned responses in cocaine and opioid dependence: A role in relapse? In B. A. Ray (Ed.), *Learning factors in substance abuse* (NIDA Research Monograph Series No. 84). Rockville, MD: National Institute on Drug Abuse.

Childress, A. R., Hole, A. V., Ehrman, R. N., et al. (1993). Cue reactivity and cue reactivity interventions in drug dependence. In L. S. Onken, J. D. Blaine, & J. J. Boren (Eds.), *Behavioral treatments for drug abuse and dependence* (NIDA Research Monograph Series No. 137). Rockville, MD: National Institute on Drug Abuse.

Chiu, L. H. (1971). Manifested anxiety in Chinese and American children. *J. Psychol., 79,* 273–284.

Chochinov, H., Wilson, K., Enns, M., Mowchum, N., Lander, S., Levitt, M., & Clinch, J. (1995). Desire for death in the terminally ill. *Amer. J. Psychiat., 152,* 1185–1191.

Chodoff, P. (1989). Histrionic personality disorder. In American Psychiatric Association (Eds.), *Treatments of Psychiatric Disorders: A task force report of the American Psychiatric Association.* Washington, DC: American Psychiatric Press.

Chou, T. (1992). Wake up and smell the coffee: Caffeine, coffee, and the medical consequences. *Western Journal of Medicine, 157,* 544–553.

Christensen, A., & Jacobson, N. S. (1994). Who (or what) can do psychotherapy: The status and challenge of nonprofessional therapies. *Psych. Sci., 5*(1), 8–14.

Christenson, G. A., & Mackenzie, T. B. (1995). Trichotillomania, body dysmorphic disorder, and obsessive-compulsive disorder. *J. Clin. Psychiat., 56*(5), 211-212.

Chynoweth, R. (1977). Significance of suicide notes. *Austral. New Zeal. J. Psychiat., 11,* 197–200.

Ciompi, L., Dauwalder, H., Maier, C., Aebi, E., Trutsch, K., Kupper, Z., & Rutishauser, C. (1992). The pilot project 'soteria berne': Clinical experiences and results. *Brit. J. Psychiat., 161*(suppl. 18), 145–153.

Cipani, E. (1991). Educational classification and placement. In J. L. Matson & J. A. Mulick (Eds.), *Handbook of mental retardation.* New York: Pergamon Press.

Cirese, S. (1993). Personal communication.

Cisin, I. H., & Calahan, D. (1970, Jul. 6). The big drinkers. *Newsweek,* 57.

Clark, A. J. (1995). Projective techniques in the counseling process. *J. Counc. Dev., 73*(3), 311–316.

Clark, D. A. (1992). Depressive, anxious and intrusive thoughts in psychiatric inpatients and outpatients. *Behav. Res. Ther., 30,* 93–102.

Clark, D. A., Beck, A. T., & Stewart, B. L. (1990). Cognitive specificity and positive negative affectivity: Complementary or contradictory views on anxiety and depression? *J. Abnorm. Psychiat., 99*(2), 140–155.

Clark, D. A., & deSilva, P. (1985). The nature of depressive and anxious thoughts: Distinct or uniform phenomena? *Behav. Res. Ther., 23,* 383–393.

Clark, D. A., & Purdon, C. (1993). New perspectives for a cognitive theory of obsessions. *Australian Psychologist.*

Clark, D. M. (1993). Cognitive mediation of panic attacks induced by biological challenge tests. *Adv. Behav. Res. Ther., 15,* 75–84.

Clark, D. M., Gelder, M. G., Salkovskis, P. M., Hackman, A., Middleton, H., & Anastasiades, P. (1990, May 15). Cognitive therapy for panic: Comparative efficacy. Paper presented at Annual Conference of American Psychiatric Association, New York.

Clark, L. A., Watson, D., & Reynolds, S. (1995). Diagnosis and classification of psychopathology: Challenges to the current system and future directions. In J.T. Spence, J.M. Darley, & D.J. Foss (Eds.), *Ann. Rev. Psychol., 46,* 121–151.

Clark, L. A., Watson, D., & Mineka, S. (1994). Temperament, personality, and the mood and anxiety disorders. *J. Abnorm. Psychol., 103*(1), 103–116.

Clarke, J. C. & Saunders, J. B. (1988). *Alcoholism and problem drinking: Theories and treatment.* Sydney: Pergamon Press.

Clarkin, J. F., & Kendall, P. C. (1992). Comorbidity and treatment planning: Summary and future directions. *J. Cons. Clin. Psychol., 60*(6), 904–908.

Classen, C., Hermanson, K. S., & Spiegel, D. (1994). Psychotherapy, stress, and survival in breast cancer. In C. E. Lewis, C. O'Sullivan, & J. Barraclough (Eds.), *The psychoimmunology of cancer.* Oxford, England: Oxford University Press.

Classen, C., Koopman, C., & Spiegel, D. (1993). Trauma and dissociation. *Bull. Menninger Clin., 57*(2), 178–194.

Clay, R. A. (1996). Day treatment helps empower patients. *APA Monitor, 26*(5), 31.

Clay, R. A. (1996). Modern hypnosis wins clinical respect, praise. *APA Monitor, 26*(5), 31.

Clay, R. A. (1996). Psychologists' faith in religion begins to grow. *APA Monitor, 27*(8), pg. 1, 48.

Clay, R. A. (1997). Is assisted suicide ever a rational choice? *APA Monitor, 28*(4), 1, 43.

Cleghorn, J. M., Franco, S., Szechtman, B., Kaplan, R. D., et al. (1992). Toward a brain map of auditory hallucinations. *Amer. J. Psychiat., 149*(8), 1062–1069.

Clinton, D. N., & McKinlay, W. W. (1986). Attitudes to food, eating and weight in acutely ill and recovered anorectics. *Brit. J. Clin. Psychol., 25*(1), 61–67.

Clum, G., & Yang, B. (1995). Additional support for the reliability and validity of the Modified Scale for Suicide Ideation. *Psychol. Assess., 7*(1), 122–125.

Clum, G. A., Clum, G. A., & Surls, R. (1993). A meta-analysis of treatment for panic disorder. *J. Cons. Clin. Psychol., 61*(2), 317–326.

Coambs, R. B. & McAndrews, M. P. (1994). The effects of psychoactive substances on workplace performance. In S. Macdonald & P. Roman (Eds.), *Research advances in alcohol and drug problems: Vol. 11. Drug testing in the workplace.* New York: Plenum Press.

Coccaro, E. F., & Kavoussi, R. J. (1991). Biological and pharmacological aspects of borderline personality disorder. *Hosp. Comm. Psychiat., 42*(10), 1029–1033.

Coder, T. L., Nelson, R. E., & Aylward, L. K. (1991). Suicide among secondary students. *School Counselor, 38*(5), 358–361.

Coe, C. L., Rosenberg, L. T., Fischer, M., Levine, S. (1987, December). Psychological factors capable of preventing the inhibition of antibody responses in separated infant monkeys. *Child Dev., 58,* 1420–1430.

Coe, W. C. (1989). Posthypnotic amnesia: Theory and research. In N. P. Spanos & J. F. Chaves (Eds.), *Hypnosis: The cognitive-behavioral perspective.* Buffalo, NY: Prometheus Books.

Cohen, J. D., Dunbar, K. O., Barch, D. M., & Braver, T. S. (1997). Issues concerning relative speed of processing hypotheses, schizophrenic performance deficits, and prefrontal function: Comment on Schooler et al. *J. Exp. Psychol., 126*(1), 37–41.

Cohen, L. H., Sargent, M. M., & Sechrest, L. B. (1986). Use of psychotherapy research by professional psychologists. *Amer. Psychol., 41*(2), 198–206.

Cohen, M. B., Baker, G., Cohen, R. A., Fromm-Reichmann, F., & Weigert, E. V. (1954). An intensive study of twelve cases of manic-depressive psychosis. *Psychiatry, 17,* 103–137.

Cohen, R. M., Semple, W. E., Gross, M., & Nordahl, T. E. (1988). From syndrome to illness: Delineating the pathophysiology of schizophrenia with PET. *Schizo. Bull., 14*(2), 169–176.

Cohen, S. (1980). Coca paste and freebase: New fashions in cocaine use. *Drug Abuse & Alcoholism Newsletter, 9*(3).

Cohen-Kettenis, P. T., & van Goozen, S. H. M. (1997). Sex reassignment of adolescent transsexuals: A follow-up study. *J. Amer. Acad. Child Adol. Psychiat., 36*(2), 263–271.

Cohen, S., & Herbert, T. B. (1996). Health psychology: Psychological factors and physical disease from the perspective of human psychoneuroimmunology. In J. T. Spence, J. M. Darley, & D. J. Foss (Eds.), *Annual review of psychology (Vol. 47).* Palo Alto, CA: Annual Reviews.

Cohen, S., & Williamson, G. M. (1988). Perceived stress in a probability sample of the United States. In S. Spacapan & S. Oskamp (Eds.), *The social psychology of health.* Newbury, CA: Sage.

Cohen-Sandler, R., Berman, A. L., & King, R. A. (1982). A follow-up study of hospitalized suicidal children. *J. Amer. Acad. Child Psychiat., 214,* 398–403.

Cohen-Sandler, R., Berman, A. L., & King, R. A. (1982). Life stress and symptomatology: Determinants of suicidal behavior in children. *J. Amer. Acad. Child Psychiat., 21,* 178–186.

Colahan, M. (1995). Being a therapist in eating disorder treatment trials: Constraints and creativity. Special Issue: Eating disorders. *J. Fam. Ther., 17*(1), 79–96.

Colahan, M. & Senior, R. (1995). Family patterns in eating disorders: Going round in circles, getting nowhere fasting. In G. Szmukler, C. Dare, & J. Treasure (Eds.), *Handbook of eating disorders: Theory, treatment and research.* Chichester, England: Wiley.

Colbach, E. M. (1987). Hysteria again and again and again. *Inter. J. Offend. Ther. Compar. Crimin., 31*(1), 41–48.

Colby, K. M. (1981). Modeling a paranoid mind. *The Behavioral and Brain Sciences, 4,* 515–560.

Colby, K. M., Faught, W. S., & Parkison, R. C. (1979). Cognitive therapy of paranoid conditions: Heuristic suggestions based on a computer simulation model. *Cog. Ther. Res., 3*(1) 55–60.

Cole, D. A., & Turner, J. E., Jr. (1993). Models of cognitive mediation and moderation in child depression. *J. Abnorm. Psychol., 102*(2), 271–281.

Cole, J. O., Klerman, G. L., Goldberg, S. C. et al. (1964). Phenothiazine treatment in acute schizophrenia. *Arch. Gen. Psychiat., 10,* 246–261.

Cole, J. O., & Yonkers, K. A. (1995). Nonbenzodiazepine anxiolytics. In A. F. Schatzberg & C. B. Nemeroff (Eds.), *The American Psychiatric Press textbook of psychopharmacology.* Washington, DC: American Psychiatric Press.

Coleman, L. (1984). *The reign of error: Psychiatry, authority, and law.* Boston: Beacon.

Colerick, E. J., & George, L. K. (1986). Predictors of institutionalization among caregivers of patients with Alzheimer's Disease. *J. Amer. Geriatric Society, 34,* 493–498.

Colligan, R. C., & Offord, K. P. (1992). *The MMPI: A Contemporary Normative Study of Adolescents.* Norwood, NJ: Alex Publishing Corporation.

Collins, E. J., Hogan, T. P., & Awad, A. G. (1992). The pharmacoepidemiology of treatment-refractory schizophrenia. *Canad. J. Psychiat., 37*(3), 192–195.

Collins, J. J., Schlenger, W. E., & Jordan, B. K. (1988). Antisocial personality and substance abuse disorders. *Bull. Amer. Acad. Psychiat. Law, 16*(2), 187–198.

Comer, R. (1973). *Therapy interviews with a schizophrenic patient.* Unpublished manuscript.

Commander, M. J., Dharan, S. P. S., Odell, S. M., & Surtees, P. G. (1997). Access to mental health care in an inner-city health district. II: Association with demographic factors. *Brit. J. Psychiat., 170,* 317–320.

Commander, M. J., Dharan, S. P. S., Odell, S. M., & Surtees, P. G. (1997). Access to mental health care in an inner-city health district: II. Pathways into and within specialist psychiatric servies. *Brit. J. Psychiat., 170,* 312–316.

Compton, A. (1992). The psychoanalytic view of phobias: III. Agoraphobia and other phobias of adults. *Psychoanalytic Quarterly, 61*(3), 400–425.

Compton, W. M., Helzer, J. E., Hwu, H., Yeh, E., McEvoy, L., Tipp, J. E., & Spitznagel, E. L. (1991). New methods in cross-cultural psychiatry: Psychiatric illness in Taiwan and the United States. *Amer. J. Psychiat., 148*(12), 1697–1704.

Condra, M., Morales, A., Surridge, D. H., Owen, J. A., et al. (1986). The unreliability of nocturnal penile tumescence recording as an outcome measurement in the treatment of organic impotence. *J. Urology, 135,* 280–282.

Conrad, N. (1992). Stress and knowledge of suicidal others as factors in suicidal behavior of high school adolescents. *Issues in Mental Health Nursing, 13*(2), 95–104.

Constantino, G., Malgady, R. G., & Vazquez, C. (1981). A comparison of Murray's TAT and a new thematic apperception test for urban

Hispanic children. *Hispanic Journal of Behavioral Sciences, 3,* 291–300.

Conte, J. R. (1991). Overview of child sexual abuse. In A. Tasman & S. M. Goldfinger (Eds.), *American Psychiatric Press Review of Psychiatry (Vol. 10).* Washington, DC: American Psychiatric Press.

Conway, M., Howell, A., & Giannopoulos, C. (1991). Dysphoria and thought suppression. *Cog. Ther. Res., 15,* 153–166.

Conwell, Y., Caine, E. D., & Olsen, K. (1990). Suicide and cancer in late life. *Hosp. Comm. Psychiat., 43,* 1334–1338.

Cook, C. E., Jeffcoat, A. R., & Perez-Reyes, M. (1985. Pharmacokinetic studies of cocaine and phencyclidine in man. In G. Barnett & C. N. Chiang (Eds.), *Pharmacokinetics and pharmacodynamics of psychoactive drugs.* Foster City, CA: Biomedical Publications.

Cook, E. H., Rowlett, R., Jaselskis, C., Leventhal, B. L. (1992). Fluoxetine treatment of children and adults with autistic disorder and mental retardation. J. Amer. Acad. Child Adol. Psychiat., 31*(4),* 739–745.

Cook, E. W., Melamed, B. G., Cuthbert, B. N., McNeil, D. W., & Lang, P. J. (1988). Emotional imagery and the differential diagnosis of anxiety. *J. Cons. Clin. Psychol., 56,* 734–740.

Cookson, M. S., & Nadig, P. W. (1993). Long-term results with vacuum constriction device. *J. Urology, 149,* 290–294.

Cooney, N. L., Kadden, R. M., Litt, M. D., & Getter, H. (1991). Matching alcoholics to coping skills or interactional therapies. Two-year follow-up results. *J. Cons. Clin. Psychol., 59,* 598–601.

Cooney, N. L., Litt, M. D., Morse, P. A., Bauer, L. O., & Gaupp, L. (1997). Alcohol cue reactivity, negative-mood reactivity, and relapse in treated alcoholic men. *J. Abnorm. Psychol., 106*(2), 243–250.

Coons, P. M. (1980). Multiple personality: Diagnostic considerations. J. Clin. Psychiat., 41*(10), 330–336.*

Coons, P. M., Bowman, E. S., & Milstein, V. (1988). Multiple personality disorder: A clinical investigation of 50 cases. *J. Nerv. Ment. Dis., 176*(9), 519–527.

Coons, P. M., & Fine, C. G. (1990, June). Accuracy of the MMPI in identifying multiple personality disorder. *Psych. Rep., 66, 831–834.*

Cooper, A. M. (1981). Narcissism. In S. Arieti & H. K. Brodie (Eds.), *American Handbook of Psychiatry,* Vol. 7. New York: Basic Books.

Cooper, A. M., & Ronningstam, E. (1992). Narcissistic personality disorder. In A. Tasman & M. B. Riba (Eds.), *American Psychiatric Press Review of Psychiatry* (Vol. 11). Washington, DC: American Psychiatric Press.

Cooper, M. L. (1994). Motivations for alcohol use among adolescents: Development and validation of a four-factor model. *Psychol. Assess., 6*(2), 117–128.

Copeland, J., & Hall, W. (1992). A comparison of women seeking drug and alcohol treatment in a specialist women's and two traditional mixed-sex treatment services. *Brit. J. Addic., 87*(9), 1293–1302.

Coppen, A. (1994). Depression as a lethal disease: Prevention strategies. *J. Clin. Psychiat., 55*(Suppl. 4), 37–45.

Cordova, J. V., & Jacobson, N. S. (1993). Couple distress. In D. H. Barlow (Ed.), *Clinical Handbook of Psychological Disorders: A step-by-step treatment manual* (2nd ed.). New York: Guilford.

Corey-Bloom, J., Jernigan, T., Archibald, S., Harris, M. J. et al. (1995). Quantitative magnetic resonance imaging of the brain in late-life schizophrenia. *Amer. J. Psychiat., 152*(3), 447–449.

Corkin, S. (1968). Acquisition of motor skill after bilateral medial temporal-lobe excision. *Neuropsychologia, 6,* 255–264.

Corkin, S. (1984). Lasting consequences of bilateral medial temporal lobectomy: Clinical course and experimental findings in H.M. *Seminars in Neurology, 4,* 249–259.

Cornblatt, B. A., & Erlenmeyer-Kimling, L. (1985). Global attentional deviance as a marker of risk for schizophrenia: Specificity and predictive validity. *J. Abnorm. Psychol., 94*(4), 31–46.

Cornblatt, B. A., & Keilp, J. G. (1994). Impaired attention, genetics, and the pathophysiology of schizophrenia. *Schizo. Bull., 20*(1), 31–46.

Cornelius, J. R., Salloum, I. M., Mezzich, J., Cornelius, M. D., Fabrega, H., Ehler, J. G., Ulrich, R. F., Thase, M. E., & Mann, J. J. (1995). Disproportionate suicidality in patients with comorbid major depression and alcoholism. *Amer. J. Psychiat., 152*(3), 358–364.

Cornell, C. P., & Gelles, R. J. (1983). *Intimate violence in families.* Beverly Hills, CA: Sage.

Cornish, J. W., McNicholas, L. F., & O'Brien, C. P. (1995). Treatment of substance-related disorders. In A. F. Schatzberg & C. B. Nemeroff (Eds.), *The American Psychiatric Press textbook of psychopharmacology.* Washington, DC: American Psychiatric Press.

Corwin, M. (1993, May 8). When the law can't protect. *Los Angeles Times, p.A1.*

Coryell, W., Kelly, M., Perry, P. J. (1990). Haloperidol plasma levels and acute clinical change in schizophrenia. *Journal of Clinical Psychopharmacology, 10,* 397–402.

Coryell, W., Leon, A., Winokur, G., Endicott, J. et al. (1996). Importance of psychotic features to long-term course in major depressive disorder. *Amer. J. Psychiat., 153,* 483–489.

Coryell, W., & Winokur, G. (1992). Course and outcome. In E. S. Paykel (Ed.), *Handbook of Affective Disorders.* New York: Guilford.

Costa, E. (1983). Are benzodiazepine recognition sites functional entities for the action of endogenous effectors or merely drug receptors? *Adv. in Biochem. & Psychopharm., 38,* 249–259.

Costa, E. (1985). Benzodiazepine-GABA interactions: A model to investigate the neurobiology of anxiety. In A. H. Tuma & J. Maser (Eds.), *Anxiety and the anxiety disorders.* Hillsdale, NJ: Erlbaum.

Costa, E., Guidotti, A., Mao, C. C., & Suria, A. (1975). New concepts on the mechanism of action of benzodiazepines. *Life Sciences,* 17(2), 167–185.

Costa, E., Guidotti, A., & Toffano, G. (1978). Molecular mechanisms mediating the action of benzodiazepines on GABA receptors. *Brit. J. Psychiat., 133,* 239–248.

Costa, P., McCrae, R., & Zonderman, A. (1987). Environmental and dispositional influences on well-being: Longitudinal follow-up of an American national sample. *Brit. J. Psychol., 78*(3), 299–306.

Costello, C. G. (1996). The advantages of focusing on the personality characteristics of the personality disordered. In C. G. Costello (Ed.), *Personality characteristics of the personality disordered.* New York: Wiley.

Council on Psychiatry and the Law (1992). Peer review of psychiatric testimony. *Bull. Amer. Acad. Psychiat. Law, 20*(3), 343–352.

Counts, D. A. (1990). Abused women and revenge suicide: Anthropological contributions to understanding suicide. In D. Lester (Ed.), *Current concepts of suicide.* Philadelphia: The Charles Press.

Courchesne, E. (1997, May 23). *The developmental neurobiological approach to understanding autism: From behavioral symptoms to biological explanations.* Keynote address at The Eden Institute Foundation Princeton Lecture Series on Autism.

Courchesne, E., Townsend, J., Akshoomoff, N. A., Saitoh, O. et al. (1994). Impairment in shifting attention in autistic and cerebellar patients. *Behav. Neurosci., 108*(5), 848–865.

Courchesne, R., & Courchesne, E. (1997). From impasse to insight in autism research: From behavioral symptoms to biological explanations. *Dev. Psychopathol.,* Special Issue.

Coursey, R. D. (1975). Electromyograph feedback as a relaxation technique. J. Cons. Clin. Psychol., 43*(6), 825–834.*

Coursey, R. D. (1975). Personality measures and evoked responses in chronic insomniacs. *J. Abnorm. Psychol., 84*(3), 239–249.

Cowdry, R. W., & Gardner, D. L. (1988). Pharmacotherapy of borderline personality disorder. *Arch. Gen. Psychiat., 45,* 111–119.

Cowen, E. L. (1991). In pursuit of wellness. 98th Annual Convention of the American Psychological Association Distinguished Contributions to Psychology in the Public Interest Award Address (1990, Boston, MA). *Amer. Psychol., 46,* 404–408.

Cowley, G. (1995, January 30). A new assault on addiction. *Newsweek,* 51.

Cowley, G., with Holmes, S., Laueman, J. F., & Gordon, J. (1994, February 7). The culture of Prozac. *Newsweek,* p. 41–42.

Cox, A., Rutter, M., Newman, S., & Bartak, L. (1975). A comparative

study of infantile autism and specific developmental receptive language disorder: II. Parental characteristics. *Brit. J. Psychiat., 126,* 146–159.

Cox, B., Fergus, K. & Swinson, R. P. (1993). *Telephone behavior therapy for panic disorder with agoraphobia.* Poster presented at the annual conference of the American Psychological Association, San Francisco.

Cox, B. J. (1996). Invited essay. The nature and assessment of catastrophic thoughts in panic disorder. *Behav. Res. Ther., 34*(4), 363–374.

Cox, B. J., Endler, N. S., & Swinson, R. P. (1995). An examination of levels of agoraphobic severity in panic disorder. *Behav. Res. Ther., 33*(1), 57–62.

Cox, B. J., Endler, N. S., & Swinson, R. P. (1995). Anxiety sensitivity and panic attack symptomatology. *Behav. Res. Ther., 33*(7), 833–836.

Coyne, J. C. (1976). Depression and the response of others. *J. Abnorm. Psychol., 85*(2), 186–193.

Coyne, J. C., Schwenk, T. L., & Fechner-Bates, S. (1995). Nondetection of depression by primary care physicians reconsidered. *Gen. Hosp. Psychiat., 17*(1), 3–12.

Craig, R. J., Cannon, B., & Olson, R. E. (1995). Psychological screening of impotence with Finney's MMPI-derived impotence scale. *Psychol. Rep., 77,* 1019–1026.

Cramer, P. (1996). *Storytelling, narrative, and the thematic apperception test.* New York: Guilford.

Crancer, A., Dille, J., Wallace, J., & Haykin, M. (1969). Comparison of effects of marijuana and alcohol on simulated driving experience. *Science, 164,* 851–854.

Crandall, C. S., Preisler, J. J., & Aussprung, J. (1992). Measuring life events stress in the lives of college students: The Undergraduate Stress Questionnaire (USQ). *Journal of Behavioral Medicine, 15*(6), 627–662.

Crane, G. E. (1973). Persistent dyskinesia. *Brit. J. Psychiat., 122,* 395–405.

Craske, M. G. (1996). An integrated treatment approach to panic disorder. *Bull. Menninger Clin., 60*(2, Suppl. A), A87–A104.

Craske, M. G., & Barlow, D. H. (1993). Panic disorder and agoraphobia. In D. H. Barlow (Ed.), *Clinical Handbook of Psychological Disorders: A Step-by-Step Treatment Manual* (2nd ed.). New York: Guilford.

Craske, M. G., Rowe, M., Lewin, M., & Noriega-Dimitri, R. (1997). Interoceptive exposure versus breathing retraining within cognitive-behavioural therapy for panic disorder with agoraphobia. *Brit. J. Clin. Psychol., 36,* 85–99.

Creed, F., Black, D., & Anthony, P. (1989). Day-hospital and community treatment for acute psychiatric illness: A critical appraisal. *Brit. J. Psychiat., 154,* 300–310.

Creer, C., & Wing, J. K. (1974). *Schizophrenia at home.* London: National Schizophrenia Fellowship.

Creese, I., Burt, D. R., & Snyder, S. H. (1977). Dopamine receptor binding enhancement accompanies lesion-induced behavioral supersensitivity. *Science, 197,* 596–598.

Crino, R. D., & Andrews, G. (1996). Obsessive-compulsive disorder and axis I comorbidity. *J. Anxiety Disorders, 10*(1), 37–46.

Crisp, A. H. (1967). The possible significance of some behavioral correlates of weight and carbohydrate intake. *J. Psychosom. Res., 11,* 117–131.

Crisp, A. H. (1981). Anorexia nervosa at a normal weight?: The abnormal-normal weight control syndrome. *Inter. J. Psychiat. Med., 11,* 203–233.

Crisp, A. H., Harding, B., & McGuinness, B. (1974). Anorexia nervosa: psychoneurotic characteristics of parents: relationship to prognosis. *J. Psychosom. Res., 18,* 167–173.

Crits-Christoph, P. (1992). The efficacy of brief dynamic psychotherapy: A meta-analysis. *Amer. J. Psychiat., 149,* 151–158.

Crits-Christoph, P., Baranackie, K., Kurcias, J. S., Beck, A. T., Carroll, K., Perry, K., Luborsky, L., McLellan, A. T., Woody, G. E., Thompson, L., Gallagher, D. & Zitrin, C. (1991). Meta-analysis of therapist effects in psychotherapy outcome studies. *Psychother. Res., 1*(2), 81–91.

Crocker, P. R. (1989). A follow-up of cognitive-affective stress management training. *Journal of Sport and Exercise Psychology, 11,* 236–242.

Crompton, M. R. (1985). Alcohol and violent accidental and suicidal death. *Med. Sci. Law, 25,* 59–62.

Crook, T., & Eliot, J. (1980). Parental death during childhood and adult depression: A critical review of the literature. *Psychol. Bull., 87*(2), 252–259.

Crow, M. J., Marks, I. M., Agras, W. S., & Leitenberg, H. (1972). Time-limited desensitization implosion and shaping for phobic patients: A cross-over study. *Behav. Res. Ther., 10,* 319–328.

Crow, T. J. (1980). Positive and negative schizophrenic symptoms and the role of dopamine: II. *Brit. J. Psychiat., 137,* 383–386.

Crow, T. J. (1982). Positive and negative symptoms and the role of dopamine in schizophrenia. In G. Hemmings (Ed.), *Biological aspects of schizophrenia and addiction.* New York: Wiley.

Crow, T. J. (1985). The two-syndrome concept: Origins and current status. *Schizo. Bull., 11*(3), 471–486.

Crow, T. J. (1989). A current view of the type ii syndrome: Age of onset, intellectual impairment, and the meaning of structural changes in the brain. *Brit. J. Psychiat., 155*(Suppl. 7), 15–20.

Crow, T. J. (1995). Brain changes and negative symptoms in schizophrenia. 9th World Congress of psychiatry (1993, Rio de Janeiro, Brazil). *Psychopathology, 28*(1), 18–21.

Crowther, J. H., Bond, L. A., & Rolf, J. E. (1981). The incidence, prevalence, and severity of behavior disorder among preschool-age children in day care. *J. Abnorm. Child Psychol., 9,* 23–42.

Culbertson, F. M. (1997). Depression and gender: An international review. *Amer. Psychologist, 52*(1), 25–31.

Cullen, E. A. (1993, August). Iowa becomes the tenth state with a Hospital privileges Statute for psychologists. *Practitioner Focus, 6*(2), p. 6.

Culp, A. M., Clyman, M. M., & Culp, R. E. (1995). Adolescent depressed mood, reports of suicide attempts, and asking for help. *Adolescence, 30*(120), 827–837.

Culver, R., Rotton, J., & Kelly, I. W. (1988). Geophysical variables and behavior: XLIV. Moon mechanisms and myths: A critical appraisal of explanations of purported lunar effects on human behavior. *Psych. Rep., 62*(3), 683–710.

Cumming, J., & Cumming, E. (1962). *Ego and milieu: Theory and practice of environmental therapy.* New York: Atherton.

Cummings, E. M., & Davies, P. T. (1994). Maternal depression and child development. *J. Child Psychol. Psychiat., 35*(1), 73–112.

Curtis, J. M., & Cowell, D. R. (1993). Relation of birth order and scores on measures of pathological narcissism. *Psych. Rep., 72*(1), 311–315.

Custanco, J. (1952). *Wisdom, madness and folly.* New York: Pellegrini & Cudaby.

Cutler, S., & Nolen-Hoeksema, S. (1991). Accounting for sex differences in depression through female victimization: Childhood sexual abuse. *Sex roles, 24,* 425–438.

Cutting, J. (1985). *The psychology of schizophrenia.* Edinburgh: Churchill-Livingstone.

Cutting, J., & Murphy, D. (1988). Schizophrenic thought disorder: A psychological and organic interpretation. *Brit. J. Psychiat., 152,* 310–319.

Cutting, J., & Murphy, D. (1990). Impaired ability of schizophrenics, relative to manics or depressives, to appreciate social knowledge about their culture. *Brit. J. Psychiat., 157,* 355–358.

Cyr, J. J., & Kalpin, R. A. (1988). Investigating the lunar-lunacy relationship: A reply to Rotton and Kelly. *Psych. Rep., 62*(1), 319–322.

Cytryn, L., & McKnew, D. H., Jr. (1996). *Growing up sad: Childhood depression and its treatment.* New York: Norton.

Dadds, M. R., Sanders, M. R., Morrison, M., & Rebgetz, M. (1992). Childhood depression and conduct disorder: II. An analysis of family interaction patterns in the home. *J. Abnorm. Psychol., 101*(3), 505–513.

Darbonne, A. (1969). Study of psychological content in the communications of suicidal individuals. *J. Cons. Clin. Psychol., 33,* 590–596.

Dare, C. & Crowther, C. (1995). Living dangerously: Psychoanalytic psychotherapy of anorexia nervosa. In G. Szmukler, C. Dare, & J. Treasure (Eds.), *Handbook of eating disorders: Theory, treatment and research.* Chichester, England: Wiley.

Dare, C. & Crowther, C. (1995). Psychodynamic models of eating disorders. In G. Szmukler, C. Dare, & J. Treasure (Eds.), *Handbook of eating disorders: Theory, treatment and research.* Chichester, England: Wiley.

Dare, C., & Eisler, I. (1992). Family therapy for anorexia nervosa. In P. J. Cooper & A. Stein (Eds.), *Feeding problems and eating disorders in children and adolescents.* Philadelphia: Harwood Academic Publishers.

Dare, C. & Eisler, I. (1995). Family therapy. In G. Szmukler, C. Dare, & J. Treasure (Eds.), *Handbook of eating disorders: Theory, treatment and research.* Chichester, England: Wiley.

Darvres-Bornoz, J., Lemperiere, T., Degiovanni, A., & Gaillard, P. (1995). Sexual victimization in women with schizophrenia and bipolar disorder. *Soc. Psychiat. Psychiatr. Epidemiol., 30*(2), 78–84.

Dashef, S. S. (1984). Active suicide intervention by a campus mental health service: Operation and rationale. *J. Amer. Coll. Hlth., 33*(3), 118–122.

Davanloo, H. (Ed.). (1980). *Short-term dynamic psychotherapy.* New York: Jason Aronson.

Davidson, J., Hughes, D., George, L., & Blazer, D. (1996). The association of sexual assault and attempted suicide within the community. *Arch. Gen. Psychiat., 53,* 550–555.

Davidson, J. R., Hughes, D., Blazer, D. G., & George, L. K. (1991). Post-traumatic stress disorder in the community: An epidemiological study. *Psychol. Med., 21*(3), 713–721.

Davidson, J. R. T. (1992). Monoamine oxidase inhibitors. In E. S. Paykel (Ed.), *Handbook of affective disorders.* New York: Guilford.

Davidson, J. R. T. (1997). Use of benzodiazepines in panic disorder. *J. Clin. Psychiat., 58*(Suppl. 2), 26–28.

Davies, S., McKenna, L., & Hallam, R. S. (1995). Relaxation and cognitive therapy: A controlled trial in chronic tinnitus. *Psychol. Hlth., 10*(2), 129–143.

Davila, J., Hammen, C., Burge, D., Paley, B., & Daley, S. E. (1995). Poor interpersonal problem solving as a mechanism of stress generation in depression among adolescent women. *J. Abnorm. Psychol., 104*(4), 592–600.

Davis, E. J., Borde, M., & Sharma, L. N. (1992). Tardive dyskinesia and Type II schizophrenia. *Brit. J. Psychiat., 160,* 253–256.

Davis, J. D., Kane, J. M., Marder, S. R., Brauzer, B., Gierl, B., Schooler, N., Casey, D. E., & Hassan, M. (1993). Dose response of propheylatic antipsychotics. *J. Clin. Psychiat., 54*(3, Suppl.), 24–30.

Davis, J. M. (1980). Antidepressant drugs. In H. I. Kaplan, A. M. Freedman, & B. J. Sadock (Eds.), *Comprehensive textbook of psychiatry III.* Baltimore: Williams & Wilkins.

Davis, J. M., Comaty, J. E., & Janicak, P. G. (1988). The psychological effects of antipsychotic drugs. In C. N. Stefanis & A. D. Rabavilis (Eds.), *Schizophrenia: Recent biosocial developments.* New York: Human Sciences.

Davis, J. M., Klerman, G., & Schildkraut, J. (1967). Drugs used in the treatment of depression. In L. Efron, J. O. Cole, D. Levine, & J. R. Wittenborn (Eds.), *Psychopharmacology: A review of progress.* Washington, DC: U. S. Clearinghouse of Mental Health Information.

Davis, J. O., & Phelps, J. A. (1995). Twins with schizophrenia: Genes or germs? *Schizo. Bull., 21*(1), 13–18.

Davis, K., Thal, L., Gamzu, E., et al. (1992). A double-blind, placebo-controlled multicenter study of tacrine for Alzheimer's disease. *N. Eng. J. Med., 327,* 1253–1259.

Davis, K. L., & Greenwald, B. S. (1991). Biology of schizophrenia. In K. Davis, H. Klar, & J. Coyle (Eds.), *Foundations of psychiatry.* Philadelphia: Saunders.

Davis, M. (1992). Analysis of aversive memories using the fear potentiated startle paradigm. In N. Butters & L. R. Squire (Eds.), *The neuropsychology of memory* (2nd ed.). New York: Guilford.

Davis, P. (1989). *In mind of Johnson: A study of Johnson, the Rambler.* London.

Davis, R. (1992, November 19). Canada settles '63 brainwash case. *USA Today*, p. 2A.

Davis, R. C., Brickman, E., & Baker, T. (1991). Supportive and unsupportive responses of others to rape victims: Effects on concurrent victim adjustment. *Amer. J. Comm. Psychol., 19,* 443–451.

Davis, R., Olmsted, M., Rockert, W., Marques, T., & Dolhanty, J. (1997). Group psychoeducation for bulimia nervosa with and without additional psychotherapy process sessions. *Inter. J. Eat. Disorders, 22,* 25–34.

Davis, S. F. (1992). Report to the American Psychological Association. Reported in *Psychol. Today, 25*(6), 9.

Davison, A. N., & Dobbing, J. (1966). Myelination as a vulnerable period in brain development. *Brit. Med. Bull., 22,* 40–44.

DAWN (Drug Abuse Warning Network) (1996). *Highlights from 1995 Report.* Drug Abuse Warning Network.

Dawson, G., & Castelloe, P. (1992). Autism. In C. E. Walker (Ed.), *Clinical psychology: Historical and research foundations.* New York: Plenum Press.

DeAmicis, L., Goldberg, D. C., LoPiccolo, J., Friedman, J., & Davies, L. (1985). Clinical follow-up of couples treated for sexual dysfunction. *Arch. Sex. Behav., 14,* 46–489.

DeBellis, M. D., Chrousos, G. P., Dorn, L. D., et al. (1994). Hypothalamic-pituitary-adrenal axis dysregulation in sexually abused girls. *J. Clin. Endocrinol. Metab., 78,* 249–255.

DeBellis, M. D., Lefter, L., Trickett, P. K., et al. (1994). Urinary catecholamine excretion in sexually abused girls. *J. Amer. Acad. Child Adolesc. Psychiat., 33,* 320–327.

deBeurs, E., van Balkom, A. J. L. M., Lange, A. Koele, P. et al. (1995). Treatment of panic disorder with agoraphobia: Comparison of fluvoxamine, placebo, and psychological panic management combined with exposure and of exposure in vivo alone. *Amer. J. Psychiat., 152*(5), 683–691.

de Castro, J. M., & Pearcey, S. M. (1995). Lunar rhythms of the meal and alcohol intake of humans. *Physiol. Behav., 57*(3), 439–444.

de Groot, J. M., & Kennedy, S. H. (1995). Integrating clinical and research psychiatry. *J. Psychiat. Neurosci., 20*(2), 150–154.

DeLeon, M. J., Convit, A., George, A. E., Golomb., J., De Santi, S., Tarshish, C., Rusinek, H., Bobinski, M., Ince, C., Miller, D., & Wisniewski, H. (1996). *In vivo* structural studies of the hippocampus in normal aging and in incipient Alzheimer's disease. In R. J. Wurtman, S. Corkin, J. H. Growdon, & R. M. Nitsch (Eds.), *The neurobiology of Alzheimer's disease.* New York: New York Academy of Sciences.

de Man, A. F., Ludec, C. P., & Labreche-Gauthier, L. (1993). Correlates of suicidal ideation in French-Canadian adolescents: Personal variables, stress, and social support. *Adolescence, 28*(112), 819–830.

de Man, A. F., Ludec, C. P., & Labreche-Gauthier, L. (1992). Parental control in child rearing and multidimensional locus of control. *Psych. Rep., 70*(1), 320–322.

De Silva, P. (1995). Cognitive-behavioural models of eating disorders. In G. Szmukler, C. Dare, & J. Treasure (Eds.), *Handbook of eating disorders: Theory, treatment and research.* Chichester, England: Wiley.

de Wilde, E. J., Kienhorst, I. C. W. M., Diekstra, R. F. W., & Wolters, W. H. G. (1992). The relationship between adolescent suicidal behavior and life events in childhood and adolescence. *Amer. J. Psychiat, 149,* 45–51.

DeAngelis, T. (1992, December). Illness linked with repressive style of coping. *APA Monitor,* 23(12) 14.

DeAngelis, T. (1992, November). Best psychological treatment for many men: group therapy. *APA Monitor, 23*(11), 31.

DeAngelis, T. (1992, November). Program embodies feminist values to aid women with addictions. *APA Monitor, 23*(11), 29.

DeAngelis, T. (1993, September). Controversial diagnosis is voted into latest DSM. *APA Monitor,* 24(9), 32–33.

DeAngelis, T. (1994, March). Poor kids are focus of asthma studies. *APA Monitor,* 25(3), 26–27.

DeAngelis, T. (1994, May). Vets, minorities, single moms make up homeless population. *APA Monitor, 25*(5), 39.

DeAngelis, T. (1996, October). New interventions address teen-age behavior problems. *APA Monitor,* 42.

DeCubas, M., & Field, T. (1993). Children of methadone-dependent women: Developmental outcomes. *Amer. J. Orthopsychiat., 63*(2), 266–269.

DeFazio, V. J., Rustin, S., & Diamond, A. (1975). Symptom development in Vietnam-era veterans. *Amer. J. Orthopsychiat. 45*(1), 158–163.

Deitch, D., & Solit, R. (1993). International training for drug abuse treatment and the issue of cultural relevance. *J. Psychoactive Drugs, 25*(1), 87–92.

Deitz, S. M. (1977). An analysis of programming DRL schedules in educational settings. *Behav. Res. Ther., 15*(1), 103–111.

Dekker, J. (1993). Inhibited male orgasm. In W. O'Donohue and J. Geer (Eds.), *Handbook of sexual dysfunctions.* Boston: Allyn & Bacon.

Del Monte, M. (1995). Silence and emptiness in the service of healing: Lessons from meditation. *Brit. J. Psychother., 11*(3), 368–378.

Delay, J., & Deniker, P. (1952). Le traitment des psychoses par une methode neurolytique derivee d'hibernotherapie: Le 4560 RP utilise seul en cure prolongee et continuee. *Congres des Medicins Alienistes et Neurologistes de France et des Pays du Langue Francaise, 50,* 503–513.

DeLeon (1992) Cited in Youngstrom, N. Training brings psychologists closer to prescribing drugs. *APA Monitor., 23*(10).

DeLeon, P. H., & Wiggins, J. G. Jr. (1996). Prescription privileges for psychologists. *Amer. Psychol., 51*(3), 225–229.

Delini-Stula, A. & Berdah-Tordjman, D. (1995). Benzodiazepines and GABA hypothesis of schizophrenia. *J. Psychopharmacol., 9*(1), 57–63.

DeLisi, L. E., Crow, T. J., & Hirsch, S. R. (1986). The third biannual winter workshop on schizophrenia. *Arch. Gen. Psychiat., 43*(7), 705–706.

DeLisi, L. E., Hoff, A. L., Kushner, M., Calev, A. et al. (1992). Left ventricular enlargement associated with diagnostic outcome of schizophreniform disorder. *Bio. Psychiat., 32*(2), 199–201.

Delisle, J. R. (1986). Death with honors: Suicide among gifted adolescents [Special issue]. *J. Couns. Dev., 64*(9), 558–560.

Dell, P. F., & Eisenhower, J. W. (1990). Adolescent multiple personality disorder: A preliminary study of eleven cases. *J. Amer. Acad. Child Adol. Psychiat., 29*(3), 359–366.

de Man, A. F. & Leduc, C. P. (1995). Suicidal ideation in high school students: Depression and other correlates. *J. Clin. Psychol., 51*(2), 173–181.

den Boer, J. A., van Vliet, I. M., & Westenberg, H. G. M. (1995). Recent developments in the psychopharmacology of social phobia. [Special issue: Social phobia]. *Eur. Arch. Psychiat. Clin. Neurosci., 244*(6), 309–316.

den Boer, J. A., Westenberg, H. G., & Verhoeven, W. M. (1990). Biological aspects of panic anxiety. *Psychiat. Ann., 20*(9), 494–500, 502.

Dencker, S. J. & Dencker, K. (1995). The need for quality assurance for a better compliance and increased quality of life in chronic schizophrenic patients. XIIth AEP Congress: Improvement of compliance: Quality assurance: Increased quality of life in community care in schizophrenia. *Inter. Clin. Psychopharmacol., 9*(Suppl 5), 35–40.

DeNelsky, G. Y. (1996). The case against prescription privileges for psychologists. *Amer. Psychol., 51*(3), 207–212.

DHHS (Department of Health and Human Services). (1990). *Nutrition and your health: Dietary guidelines for Americans* (3rd ed.) Washington, DC: U. S. Government Printing Office.

Department of Justice. (1994, April 26). Cited in P. Bender, Senate committee praises Delaware Youth Programs. *Gannett News Service,* p. 605.

DeSilva, P., Rachman, S., & Seligman, M. (1977). Prepared phobias and obsessions: Therapeutic outcome. *Behav. Res. Ther., 15,* 65–77.

Devanand, D. P., Jacobs, D. M., Tang, M. X., Del Castillo-Castaneda, C., et al. (1997). The course of psychopathologic features in mild to moderate Alzheimer disease. *Arch. Gen. Psychiat., 54,* 257–263.

DeVeaugh-Geiss, J., Moroz, G., Biederman, J., Cantwell, D. P., et al. (1992). Clomipramine hydrochloride in childhood and adolescent obsessive compulsive disorder. A multicenter trial. *J. Amer. Acad. Child Adol. Psychiat., 31*(1), 45–49.

DeVita, E. (1996, January-February). Melatonin: The hottest hormone of all. *Amer. Hlth.,* pp. 72–73.

Dew, M. A., Bromet, E. J., Brent, D., & Greenhouse, J. B. (1987). A quantitative literature review of the effectiveness of suicide prevention centers. *J. Cons. Clin. Psychol., 55,* 239–244.

Diamond, D. (1987). Psychotherapeutic approaches to the treatment of panic attacks, hypochondriasis and agoraphobia. *Brit. J. Med. Psychol., 60,* 85–90.

DiChiara, T. J., & Reinhart, P. H. (1997). Redox modulation of hslo Ca2+-activated K+ channels. *J. Neurosci., 17*(13), 4942-4955.

Diekstra, R. F. W. (1989). Suicidal behavior in adolescents and young adults: The international picture. *Crisis, 10,* 16–35.

Diekstra, R. F. W. (1989). Suicide and attempted suicide: An international perspective. *Acta Psychiatr. Scandin., 80*(Suppl. 354), 1–24.

Diekstra, R. F., Kienhorst, C. W. M., & de Wilde, E. J. (1995). Suicide and suicidal behaviour among adolescents. In M. Rutter & D. J. Smith, *Psychosocial disorders in young people.* Chichester, England: Wiley.

Diener, E., & Diener, C. (1996). Most people are happy. *Psychol. Sci., 7*(3), 181–185.

Diener, E. (1984). Subjective well-being. *Psychol. Bull, 95,* 542–575.

Diener, E., Sandvik, E., Pavot, W., & Fujita, F. (1992). Extraversion and subjective well-being in a U. S. national probability sample. *J. Res. Pers., 26*(3), 205–215.

Diener, E., Sandvik, E., Seidlitz, L., Diener, M. (1993). The relationship between income and subjective well-being: Relative or absolute? *Soc. Indicators Res., 28*(3), 195–223.

Dietz, P. E., Hazelwood, R. R., & Warren, J. (1990). The sexually sadistic criminal and his offenses. *Bull. Amer. Acad. Psychiat. Law, 18*(2), 163–178.

Dilsaver, S. C., & Swann, A. C. (1995). Mixed mania: Apparent induction by a tricyclic antidepressant in five consecutively treated patients with bipolar depression. *Bio. Psychiat., 37*(1), 60–62.

Dilsaver, S. C. (1990). Onset of winter depression earlier than generally thought? *J. Clin. Psychiat., 51*(6), 258.

DiNardo, P. A., Moras, K., Barlow, D. H., Rapee, R. M., & Brown, T. A. (1993). Reliability of DSM-III-R anxiety disorder categories. *Arch. Gen. Psychiat., 50,* 251–256.

DiPietro, J. A., Suess, P. E., Wheeler, J. S., Smouse, P. H., et al. (1995). Reactivity and regulation in cocaine exposed neonates. *Infant Behavior and Development, 18*(4), 407–414.

Dircks, P., Grimm, F., Tausch, A., & Wittern, O. (1980). Förderung der seelischen Lebensqualitat von Krebspatienten durch personenzentrierte Gruppengesprache. *Z. Klin. Psychol., 9,* 241–251.

di Tomaso, E., Beltramo, M., & Piomelli, D. (1996, August 22). Brain cannabinoids in chocolate. *Nature, 382,* pp. 677–678.

Dixon, L. B. & Lehman, A. F. (1995). Family interventions for schizophrenia. *Schizo. Bull., 21*(4), 631–643.

Dixon, L. B., Lehman, A. F., & Levine, J. (1995). Conventional antipsychotic medications for schizophrenia. *Schizo. Bull., 21*(4), 567–577.

Dixon, W. A., Heppner, P. P., Burnett, J. W., & Lips, B. J. (1993). Hopelessness and stress: Evidence for an interactive model of depression. *Cog. Ther. Res., 17*(1), 39–52.

Doan, B. D. & Bryson, S. E. (1994). Etiological and maintaining factors in multiple personality disorder: A critical review. In R.M. Klein & B.K. Doane (Eds.), *Psychological concepts and dissociative disorders.* Hillsdale, NJ: Erlbaum.

Dobson, D. J. G., McDougall, G., Busheikin, J., & Aldous, J. (1995). Effects of social skills training and social milieu treatment on symptoms of schizophrenia. *Psychiat. Serv., 46*(4), 376–380.

Docherty, N. M., DeRosa, M., & Andreasen, N. C. (1996). Communication disturbances in schizophrenia and mania. *Arch. Gen. Psychiat., 53,* 358–364

Docherty, N. M., Hawkins, K. A., Hoffman, R. E., Quinlan, D. M., Rakfeldt, & Sledge, W. H. (1996). Working memory, attention, and communication disturbances in schizophrenia. *J. Abnorm. Psychol., 105*(2), 212–219.

Dodd, P. R., Kril, J. J., Thomas, G. J., Watson, W. E. J., Johnston, G. A. R., & Harper, C. G. (1996). Receptor binding sites and uptake activities mediating GABA neurotransmission in chronic alcoholics with Wernicke encephalopathy. *Brain Res., 710,* 215–228.

Doghramji, K., Gaddy, J. R., Stewart, K. T., Rosenthal, N. E. et al. (1990). 2– versus 4–hour evening phototherapy of seasonal affective disorder. *J. Nerv. Ment. Dis., 178*(4), 257–260.

Doherty, W. J., & Jacobson, N. S. (1982). Marriage and the family. In B. B. Wolman (Ed.), *Handbook of developmental psychology.* Englewood Cliffs, NJ: Prentice Hall.

Dohrenwend, B. P., Levav, I., Shrout, P. E., Schwartz, S., et al. (1992). Socioeconomic status and psychiatric disorders: The causation-selection issue. *Science, 255*(5047), 946–952.

Dohrmann, R. J., & Laskin, D. M. (1978). An evaluation of electromyographic feedback in the treatment of myofascial pain-dysfunction syndrome. *JADA, 96,* 656–662.

Dolan, B., Evans, C., & Norton, K. (1995). Multiple Axis-II diagnoses of personality disorder. *Brit. J. Psychiat., 166,* 107–112.

Dole, V. P., & Nyswander, M. (1965). A medical treatment for heroin addiction. *JAMA, 193,* 646–650.

Dole, V. P., & Nyswander, M. (1967). Heroin addiction, a metabolic disease. *Arch. Inter. Med., 120,* 19–24.

Domhoff, W. (1996). *Finding meaning in dreams: A quantitative approach.* New York: Plenum Press.

Domino, G. (1985). Clergy's attitudes toward suicide and recognition of suicide lethality. *Death Stud., 2,* 187–199.

Domino, G., & Swain, B. J. (1986). Recognition of suicide lethality and attitudes toward suicide in mental health professions. *Omega: J. Death & Dying, 16*(4), 301–308.

Domino, G., & Takahashi, Y. (1991). Attitudes toward suicide in Japanese and American medical students. *Suic. Life-Threat. Behav., 21*(4), 345–359.

Donaldson, S. K., Klein, D. N., Riso, L. P., & Schwartz, J. E. (1997). Comorbidity between dysthymic and major depressive disorders: A family study analysis. *J. Affect. Disorders, 42,* 103–111.

Donnelly, E. F., Murphy, D. L., & Goodwin, F. K. (1978). Primary affective disorder: Anxiety in unipolar and bipolar depressed groups. *J. Clin. Psychol., 34,* 621–623.

Donohue, B., Thevenin, D. M., & Runyon, M. K. (1997). Behavioral treatment of conversion disorder in adolescence. *Behav. Mod. 21*(2), 231–251.

Donohue, J., & Gebhard, P. (1995). The Kinsey Institute/Indiana University report on sexuality and spinal cord injury. *Sex. Disability, 13*(1), 7–85.

Donovan, S. J., Susser, E. S., Nunes, E. V., Stewart, J. W., et al. (1997). Divalproex treatment of disruptive adolescents: A report of 10 cases. *J. Clin Psychiat., 58*(1), 12–15.

Double, D. B. (1991). A cluster analysis of manic states. *Comprehen. Psychiat., 32*(3), 187–194.

Dougher, M. J. (1997). Cognitive concepts, behavior analysis, and behavior therapy. *J. Behav. Ther. Exp. Psychiat., 28*(1), 65–70.

Douglas, J. (1996). *Mind hunter: Inside the FBI's elite serial crime unit.* New York: Pocket Star.

Douglas, V. I., Barr, R. G., Amin, K., O'Neill, M. E., & Britton, B. G. (1988). Dosage effects and individual responsivity to methylphenidate in attention deficit disorder. *J. Child Psychol. Psychiat. Allied Disc., 29,* 453–475.

Douglass, F. (1855). *My bondage and my freedom.* New York.

Douglass, H. M., Moffitt, T. E., Dar, R., McGee, R., & Silva, P. (1995). Obsessive-compulsive disorder in a birth cohort of 18–year-olds: Prevalence and predictors. *J. Amer. Acad. Child Adol. Psychiat., 34*(11), 1424–1431.

Dowden, S. L., & Allen, G. J. (1997). Relationships between anxiety sensitivity, hyperventilation, and emotional reactivity to displays of facial emotions. *J. Anx. Disorders, 11*(1), 63–75.

Dowdney, L., & Skuse, D. (1993). Parenting provided by adults with mental retardation. *J. Child Psychol. Psychiat. Allied Disc., 34*(1), 25–47.

Downey, A. M. (1991). The impact of drug abuse upon adolescent suicide. *Omega: J. Death & Dying, 22*(4), 261–275.

Doyle, A. C. (1938). The sign of the four. In *The Complete Sherlock Holmes.* Garden City, NY: Doubleday.

Dozier, M. (1996). Personal correspondence. University of Delaware, Newark.

Drake, R., Gates, C., & Cotton, P. G. (1984). Suicide among schizophrenics: Who is at risk? *J. Nerv. Ment. Dis., 172*(10), 813–817.

Drake, R., Gates, C., & Cotton, P. G. (1986). Suicide among schizophrenics: A comparison of attempters and completed suicides. *Brit. J. Psychiat., 149,* 784–787.

Drake, R. E., McHugo, G. J., Becker, D. R., Anthony, W. A., & Clark, R. E. (1996). The New Hampshire study of supported employment for people with severe mental illness. *J. Cons. Clin. Psychol., 64*(2), 391–399.

Drake, R. E., Osher, F., & Wallach, M. (1991). Homelessness and dual diagnosis. *Amer. Psychol., 46*(11), 1149–1158.

Drake, R. E., & Wallach, M. A. (1992). Mental patients' attraction to the hospital: Correlates of living preference. *Comm. Ment. Hlth. J., 28*(1), 5–12.

Drane, J. (1995), Physician-assisted suicide and voluntary active authanasia: Social ethics and the role of hospice. *Amer. J. Hospice & Palliative Care, 12*(6), 3–10.

Drobes, D. J., & Tiffany, S. T. (1997). Induction of smoking urge through imaginal and in vivo procedures: Physiological and self-report manifestations. *J. Abnorm. Psychol., 106*(1), 15–25.

Drug Enforcement Administration (1996). Consumption of ritalin. Washington, DC: Author.

Du Paul, G. J., & Barkley, R. A. (1993). Behavioral contributions to pharmacotherapy: The utility of behavioral methodology in medication treatment of children with attention-deficit hyperactivity disorder. *Behav. Ther., 24,* 47–65.

Dubbert, P. M. (1995). Behavioral (life-style) modification in the prevention and treatment of hypertension. *Clin. Psychol. Rev., 15*(3), 187–216.

Duberstein, P., Conwell, Y., Cox, C., Podgorski, C., Glazer, R., & Caine, E. (1995). Attitudes toward self-determined death: A survey of primary care physicians. *J. Amer. Geriat. Soc., 43,* 395–400.

Dubovsky, S. L., Lee, C., Christiano, J., & Murphy, J. (1991). Elevated platelet intracellular calcium concentration in bipolar depression. *Bio. Psychiat., 29*(5), 441–450.

Dubovsky, S. L., Murphy, J., Christiano, J., & Lee, C. (1992). The calcium second messenger system in bipolar disorders: Data supporting new research direction. *J. Neuropsychiat. Clin. Neurosci., 4*(1), 3–14.

Duffy, B. (1996, April 15). The mad bomber? *U. S. News & World Report,* pp. 29–36.

Duggan, J. P., & Booth, D. A. (1986). Obesity, overeating, and rapid gastric emptying in rats with ventromedial hypothalamic lesions. *Science, 231*(4738), 609–611.

Dugger, C. W. (1996, October 5). Genital ritual is unyielding in Africa. *The New York Times,* pp. 1, 6–7.

Dulloo, A., & Girardier, L. (1990). Adaptive changes in energy expenditure during refeeding following low-calorie intake: Evidence for a specific metabolic component favoring fat storage. *Amer. J. Clin. Nutrition, 52,* 415–420.

Dunbar, F. (1948). *Synopsis of psychosomatic diagnosis and treatment.* St. Louis: Mosby.

Dunner, D. L. & Hall, K. S. (1980). Social adjustment and psychological precipitants in mania. In R. H. Belmaker & H. M. van Praag (Eds.), *Mania: An evolving concept.* New York: Spectrum.

Du Pont, R. L., Rice, D. P., Shiraki, S. et al. (1993). *Anxiety: Economic burden.* Presentation at the annual meeting of the Anxiety Disorders Association of America, Charleston, SC.

Dupont, S. (1995). Multiple sclerosis and sexual functioning: A review. *Clin. Rehab. 9*(2), 135–141.

Dweck, C. S. (1976). Children's interpretation of evaluative feedback: The effect of social cues on learned helplessness. *Merrill Palmer Quart., 22*(2), 105–109.

Dykema, J., Bergbower, K., & Peterson, C. (1995). Pessimistic explanatory style, stress, and illness. *J. Soc. Clin. Psychol., 14*(4), 357–371.

Eakes, G. G. (1995). Chronic sorrow: The lived experience of parents of chronically mentally ill individuals. *Arch. Psychiatr. Nursing. 9*(2), 77–84.

Eaton, W. W., Bilker, W., Haro, J. M., & Herman, H. (1992). Long-term course of hospitalization for schizophrenia: II. Change with passage of time. *Schizo. Bull., 18*(2), 229–241.

Eaton, W. W., Dryman, A., & Weissman, M. M. (1991). Panic and phobia. In L. N. Robins & D. A. Regier (Eds.), *Psychiatric disorders in America: The Epidemiologic Catchment Area Study.* New York: Maxwell Macmillan International.

Eaton, W. W., Kessler, R. C., Wittchen, H. A., & Magee, W. J. (1994). Panic and panic disorder in the United States. *Amer. J. Psychiat., 151*(3), 413–420.

Eaves, L., & Schultz, S. C. et al. (1988). Genetics, immunology, and virology. *Schizo. Bull., 14*(3), 365–382.

Ebihara, S., Marks, T., Hudson, D. J., & Menaker, M. (1986). *Science, 231,* 491–493.

Eccles, J., Miller, C., Tucker, M., Becker, J. et al. (1988, March). *Hormones and affect at early adolescence.* Paper presented at the biennial meeting of the Society for Research on Adolescence, Alexandria, VA.

Echeburúa, E., Báez, C., & Fernández-Montalvo, J. (1996). Comparative effectiveness of three therapeutic modalities in the psychological treatment of pathological gambling: Long-term outcome. *Behav. Cog. Psychother., 24,* 51-72.

Eckenrode, J., Laird, M., & Doris, J. (1993). School performance and disciplinary problems among abused and neglected children. *Dev. Psychol., 29*(1), 54–62.

Eddy, D. M., Wolpert, R. L., & Rosenberg, M. L. (1987). Estimating the effectiveness of interventions to prevent youth suicides. Invitational conference on applications of analytic methods to mental health: Practice, policy, research. *Medical Care, 25*(12), 57–65.

Edelman, R. E., & Chambless, D. L. (1995). Adherence during sessions and homework in cognitive-behavioral group treatment of social phobia. *Behav. Res. Ther., 33*(5), 573–577.

Edelson, J., & Eiskovitz, Z. (1989, September). Intervening with men who batter. *Soc. Serv. Rev.,* pp. 387–414.

Edman, G., & Asberg, M. (1986). Skin conductance habituation and cerebrospinal fluid 5–hydroxyindoleacetic acid in suicidal patients. *Arch. Gen. Psychiat., 43*(6), 586–592.

Edwin, D. H., & Andersen, A. E. (1990). Psychometric testing in 76 males with eating disorders. In A. E. Andersen (Ed.), *Males with eating disorders.* New York: Brunner/Mazel.

Egan, B. M. (1992). Vascular reactivity, sympathetic tone, and stress. In E. H. Johnson, E. D. Gentry, & S. Julius (Eds.), *Personality, elevated blood pressure, and essential hypertension.* Washington, DC: Hemisphere.

Egan, J. (1988). Treatment of borderline conditions in adolescents. *J. Clin. Psychiat., 49*(Suppl. 290), 32–35.

Egeland, B. (1991, February). *Presentation.* American Association for the Advancement of Science.

Egeland, J. A., Gerhard, D. S., Pauls, D. L., Sussex, J. N. et al. (1987). Bipolar affective disorders linked to DNA markers on chromosome 11. *Nature,* 325(6107), 783–787.

Egeland, J. A. et al. (1984). Amish study: V. Lithium sodium countertransport and catechol methyltransference in pedigrees of bipolar probands. *Amer. J. Psychiat., 141*(9), 1049–1054.

Ehlers, A. (1993). Interoception and panic disorder. *Adv. Behav. Res. Ther., 15,* 3–21.

Ehlers, A. (1993). Somatic symptoms and panic attacks: A retrospective study of learning experiences. *Behav. Res. Ther., 31*(3), 269–278.

Ehrman, M. (1995, June 25). Reaching out for virtual therapy. *Los Angeles Times,* pp. E1, E4.

Eich, E. (1995). Mood as a mediator of place dependent memory. *J. Exp. Psychol. Gen. 124*(3), 293–308.

Eich, E. (1995). Searching for mood dependent memory. *Psychol. Sci., 6*(2), 67–75.

Eidelson, J. I. (1985). Cognitive group therapy for depression: Why and what. *Inter. J. Ment. Hlth., 13,* 54–66.

Eigan, L. (1991, February) Alcohol practices, policies, and potentials of American colleges and universities. An OSAP White Paper, Office for Substance Abuse Prevention, Rockville, MD.

Eisen, M. R. (1993). The victim's burden: Guilt, shame and abuse. *Imagination, Cog. and Pers., 12*(1), 69–88.

Eisenberg, L. (1958). School phobia: A study in the communication of anxiety. *Amer. J. Psychiat., 114,* 712–718.

Eisendrath, S. J. (1995). Psychiatric aspects of chronic pain. *Neurology, 45*(Suppl 9), S26–S34.

Eisenthal, S., Koopman, C., & Lazare, A. (1983). Process analysis of two dimensions of the negotiated approach in relation to satisfaction in the initial interview. *J. Nerv. Ment. Dis., 171,* 49–54.

Eisler, I. (1995). Family models of eating disorders. In G. Szmukler, C. Dare, & J. Treasure (Eds.), *Handbook of eating disorders: Theory, treatment and research.* Chichester: John Wiley & Sons, Ltd.

Eitinger, L. (1964). *Concentration camp survivors in Norway and Israel.* New York: Humanities Press.

Eitinger, L. (1969). Psychosomatic problems in concentration camp survivors. *J. Psychosom. Res., 13,* 183–190.

Eitinger, L. (1973). A follow-up study of the Norwegian concentration camp survivors: Mortality and morbidity. *Isr. Ann. Psychiat. Relat. Disciplines, 11,* 199–210.

Ekman, P., Friesen, W. V., & O'Sullivan, M. (1988). Smiles when lying. *J. Pers. Soc. Psychol., 54*(3), 414–420.

El Mallakh, R. S. & Wyatt, R. J. (1995). The Na,K-ATPase hypothesis for bipolar illness. *Bio. Psychiat., 37*(4), 235–244.

Elias, M. (1993, July 15). Poor odds for heroin recovery. *USA Today,* p. 1D.

Elias, M. (1995, April 18). Therapist's program to go on-line. *USA Today,* p. 1D.

Elkin, I. (1994). The NIMH Treatment of Depression Collaborative Research Program: Where we began and where we are. In A. E. Bergin & S. L. Garfiel (Eds.), *Handbook of psychotherapy and behavior change* (4th ed.). New York: Wiley.

Elkin, I., Shea, M. T., Watkins, J. T., Imber, S. D. et al. (1989). National Institute of Mental Health Treatment of Depression Collaborative Research Program: General effectiveness of treatments. *Arch. Gen. Psychiat., 46*(11), 971–982.

Elkins, I. J. & Cromwell, R. L. (1994). Priming effects in schizophrenia: Associative interference and facilitation as a function of visual context. *J. Abnorm. Psychol., 103*(4), 791–800.

Elkins, R. L. (1991). An appraisal of chemical aversion (emetic therapy) approaches to alcoholism treatment. *Behav. Res. Ther., 29,* 387–414.

Ellenberger, H. F. (1972). The story of "Anna O.": A critical review with new data. *J. History Behav. Sci., 8,* 267–279.

Ellenberger, H. F. (1970). *The discovery of the unconscious.* New York: Basic Books.

Elliot, D. M., & Guy, J. D. (1993). Mental health professionals vs. non-mental health professionals: Childhood trauma and adult functioning. *Profess. Psychol. Res. and Prac., 24*(1), 83–90.

Elliott, C. (1996). *The rules of insanity: Moral responsibility and the mentally ill offender.* Albany: State University of New York Press.

Ellis, A. (1962). *Reason and emotion in psychotherapy.* Secaucus, NJ: Lyle Stuart.

Ellis, A. (1977). The basic clinical theory of rational-emotive therapy. In A. Ellis & R. Grieger (Eds.), *Handbook of rational-emotive therapy.* New York: Springer.

Ellis, A. (1979). A note on the treatment of agoraphobics with cognitive modification versus prolonged exposure in vivo. *Behav. Res. Ther., 17,* 162–164.

Ellis, A. (1979). The theory of rational-emotive therapy. In A. Ellis & J. M. Whitely (Eds.), *Theoretical and empirical foundations of rational-emotive therapy.* Monterey, CA: Brooks/Cole.

Ellis, A. (1987). The evolution of rational emotive therapy (RET) and cognitive behavior therapy (BET). In J. K. Zeig (Ed.), *The evolution of psychotherapy.* New York: Brunner/Mazel.

Ellis, A. (1991). The revised ABC's of rational-emotive therapy (RET). *J. Rat.-Emot. & Cog.-Behav. Ther., 9,* 139–172.

Ellis, A. (1992). The revised ABC's of rational-emotive therapy (RET). In J. K. Zeig (Ed.), *The evolution of psychotherapy: The second conference.* New York: Brunner/Mazel.

Ellis, A. (1995). Rational emotive behavior therapy. In R. J. Corsini & D. Wedding (Eds.), Current psychotherapies (5th ed.). Itasca, IL: Peacock.

Ellis, A. (1997). The evolution of Albert Ellis and rational emotive behavior therapy. In J. K. Zeig (Ed.), *The evolution of psychotherapy: The third conference.* New York: Brunner/Mazel.

Ellis, L. (1987). Relationships of criminality and psychopathy with eight other apparent behavioral manifestations of suboptimal arousal. *Per. Indiv. Diff., 8*(6), 905–925.

Elsesser, K., Sartory, G., & Maurer, J. (1996). The efficacy of complaints management training in facilitating benzodiazepine withdrawal. *Behav. Res. Ther., 34*(2), 149–156.

Emery, R. E. (1982). Effects of marital discord on the school behavior of children of schizophrenic, affectively disordered, and normal parents. *J. Abnorm. Child Psychol., 10,* 215–228.

Emmelkamp, P. M. (1982). Exposure in vivo treatments. In A. Goldstein & D. Chambless (Eds.), *Agoraphobia: Multiple perspectives on theory and treatment.* New York: Wiley.

Emmelkamp, P. M. (1982). *Phobic and obsessive-compulsive disorders.* New York: Plenum Press.

Emmelkamp, P. M. (1994). Behavior therapy with adults. In A. E. Bergin & S. L. Garfiel (Eds.), *Handbook of psychotherapy and behavior change* (4th ed.). New York: Wiley.

Emmelkamp, P. M., Van Dyck, R., Bitter, M., Heins, R. et al. (1992). Spouse-aided therapy with agoraphobics. *Brit. J. Psychiat., 160,* 51–56.

Emrick, C. D., & Hansen, J. (1983). Assertions regarding effectiveness of treatment for alcoholism: Fact or fantasy? *Amer. Psychol., 38,* 1078–1088.

Engel, G. L. (1968). A life setting conducive to illness: The giving-up-given-up complex. *Ann. Internal Med., 69,* 293.

Ennis, B. J., & Emery, R. D. (1978). *The rights of patients* (ACLU Handbook Series). New York: Avon.

Enns, M. P., Drewnowski, A., & Grinker, J. A. (1987). Body composition, body size estimation, and attitudes towards eating in male college athletes. *Psychosom. Med., 49*(1), 56–64.

Enright, S. J. (1989). Paedophilia: A cognitive/behavioural treatment approach in a single case. *Brit. J. Psychiat., 155,* 399–401.

Ensminger, M. E. (1995, December). Welfare and psychological distress: A longitudinal study of African American urban mothers. *J. Hlth. Soc. Behav., 36,* 346–359.

Epstein, N., Baucom, D. H., & Rankin, L. A. (1993). Treatment of marital conflict: A cognitive-behavioral approach. *Clin. Psychol. Rev., 13*(1), 45–57.

Epstein, S. (1983). Hypnotherapeutic control of exhibitionism: A brief communication. *Inter. J. Clin. Exp. Hyp., 31*(2), 63–66.

Erdelyi, M. H. (1985). *Psychoanalysis: Freud's cognitive psychology.* New York: W. H. Freeman.

Erdelyi, M. H. (1992). Psychodynamics and the unconscious. *Amer. Psychol., 47*(6), 784–787.

Ereshefsky, L. (1995). Treatment strategies for schizophrenia. New antipsychotic Treatments for Schizophrenia Symposium. *Psychiat. Ann., 25*(5), 285–296.

Erickson, M. T. (1992). *Behavior disorders of children and adolescents.* Englewood Cliffs, NJ: Prentice Hall.

Erikson, E. (1963). *Childhood and society.* New York: Norton.

Ernst, N. D., & Harlan, W. R. (1991). Obesity and cardiovascular disease in minority populations: Executive summary. Conference highlights, conclusions, and recommendations. *Amer. J. Clin. Nutrition, 53*(Suppl.), 1507–1511.

Eron, L. D., & Peterson, R. A. (1982). Abnormal behavior: Social approaches. In M. R. Rosenzweig & L. W. Porter (Eds.), *Annual Review of Psychology.* Palo Alto, CA: Annual Reviews.

Eronen, M., Hakola, P., & Tiihonen, J. (1996). Mental disorders and homicidal behavior in Finland. *Arch. Gen. Psychiat., 53,* 497–501.

Eser, A. (1981). "Sanctity" and "quality" of life in a historical comparative view. In S. E. Wallace & A. Eser (Eds.), *Suicide and euthanasia: The rights of personhood.* Knoxville: University of Tennessee.

Essock, S. M., Hargreaves, W. A., Dohm, F., Goethe, J., Carver, L., & Hipshman, L. (1996). Clozapine eligibility among state hospital patients. *Schizo. Bull., 22*(1), 15–25.

Esterling, B. A., Kiecolt-Glaser, J. K., Bodnar, J. C., & Glaser, R. (1994). Chronic stress, social support and persistent alterations in the natural killer cell response to cytokines in older adults. *Hlth. Psychol., 13,* 291–298.

Etzioni, A. (1973, April) Methadone: Best hope for now. *Smithsonian, 48,* 67–74.

Evans, D. L., Leserman, J., Perkins, D. O., Stern, R. A. et al. (1997). Severe life stress as a predictor of early disease progression in HIV infection. *Amer. J. Psychiat., 154*(5), 630–634.

Evans, J. A., & Hamerton, J. L. (1985). Chromosomol anomalies. In A. M. Clarke, A. D. B. Clarke, & J. M. Berg (Eds.), *Mental deficiency: The changing outlook* (4th ed.). London: Methuen.

Evans, M. D., Hollon, S. D., DeRubeis, R. J., Piasecki, J. M., et al. (1992). Differential relapse following cognitive therapy and pharmacotherapy for depression. *Arch. Gen. Psychiat., 49,* 802–808.

Everson, S. A., Goldberg, D. E., Kaplan, G. A., Cohen, R. D. et al. (1996). Hopelessness and risk of mortality and incidence of myocardial infarction and cancer. *Psychosom. Med., 58,* 113–121.

Ewert, A. (1988). Reduction of trait anxiety through participation in Outward Bound. *Leisure Sci., 10*(2), 107–117.

Exner, J. E. (1993). *The Rorschach: A comprehensive system, Vol. 1: Basic foundations* (3rd ed.). New York: Wiley.

Exner, J. E. (1997). The future of Rorschach in personality assessment. *J. Pers. Assess., 68*(1), 37–46.

FDA [Food and Drug Administration] (1996, March 26). Press release. Cited in A. Manning, Quitter's new tool: Nicotine nasal spray. *USA Today,* p. 1A.

Fabrega, H., Ulrich, R., Pilkonis, P., & Mezzich, J. (1991). On the homogeneity of personality disorder clusters. *Comprehen. Psychiat., 32*(5), 373–386.

Fackelmann, K. (1993, February 6). Marijuana and the brain: Scientists discover the brain's own THC. *Sci. News, 143,* 88–94.

Faedda, G. L., Tondo, L., Teichner, M. H., Baldessarini, R. J., Gelbard, H. A., & Floris, G. F. (1993). Seasonal Mood Disorders: Patterns of seasonal recurrence in mania and depression. *Arch. Gen. Psychiat., 50*(1), 17–23.

Fahlen, T. (1995). Personality traits in social phobia I: Comparisons with healthy controls. *J. Clin. Psychiat., 56*(12), 560–568.

Fahrenberg, J., Foerster, F., & Wilmers, F. (1995). Is elevated blood pressure level associated with higher cardiovascular responsiveness in laboratory tasks and with response specificity? *Psychophysiology, 32*(1), 81–91.

Fahrenberg, J., Franck, M., Baas, U., & Jost, E. (1995). Awareness of blood pressure: Interoception or contextual judgement? *J. Psychosom. Res., 39*(1), 11–18.

Fahy, T. A. (1988). The Diagnosis of multiple personality disorder. *Brit. J. Psychiat., 153,* 597–606.

Fahy, T. A., Eisler, I., & Russell, G. F. M. (1993). A placebo-controlled trial of d-fenfluramine in bulimia nervosa. *Brit. J. Psychiat., 162,* 597–603.

Fairbank, J. A., & Keane, T. M. (1982). Flooding for combat-related stress disorders: Assessment of anxiety reduction across traumatic memories. *Behav. Ther., 13,* 499–510.

Fairburn, C. G. (1985). Cognitive-behavioural treatment for bulimia. In D. M. Garner & P. E. Garfinkel (Eds.), *Handbook of psychotherapy for anorexia nervosa and bulimia.* New York: Guilford.

Fairburn, C. G. (1985). The management of bulimia nervosa. *J. Psychiat. Res., 19,* 465–472.

Fairburn, C. G., Jones, R., Peveler, R. C., Hope, R. A., & O'Connor, M. (1993). Psychotherapy and bulimia nervosa: Longer-term effects of interpersonal psychotherapy behavior therapy, and cognitive behavior therapy. *Arch. Gen. Psychiat., 50,* 419-428.

Fairburn, C. G., Kirk, J., O'Connor, M., & Cooper, P. J. (1986). A comparison of two psychological treatments for bulimia nervosa. *Behav. Res. Ther., 24,* 629–643.

Fairburn, C. G., Norman, P. A., Welch, S. L., O'Connor, M. E. et al. (1995). A prospective study of outcome in bulimia nervosa and the long-term effects of three psychological treatments. *Arch. Gen. Psychiat., 52*(4), 304–312.

Fairweather, G. W., Danders, D. H., Maynard, H., & Cressler, D. L. (1969). *Community life for the mentally ill: An alternative to institutional care.* Chicago: Aldine.

Falloon, I. R. H., Boyd, J. L., & McGill, C. W. (1984). *Family care for schizophrenia: A problem-solving approach to mental illness.* New York: Guilford.

Falloon, I. R. H., Coverdale, J. H., & Brooker, C. (1996). Psychosocial interventions in schizophrenia: A review. *Inter. J. Ment. Hlth., 25*(1), 3–21.

Falloon, I. R. H., & Liberman, R. P. (1983). Behavioral family interventions in the management of chronic schizophrenia. In W. R. McFarlane (Ed.), *Family therapy in schizophrenia.* New York: Guilford.

Fals, S. W., & Schafer, J. (1992). The treatment of substance abusers diagnosed with obsessive-compulsive disorder: An outcome study. *J. Substance Abuse Treatment, 9*(4), 365–370.

Fals-Stewart, W., Marks, A. P., & Schafer, J. (1993). A comparison of behavioral group therapy and individual behavior therapy in treating obsessive-compulsive disorder. *J. Nerv. Ment. Dis., 181,* 189–193.

Faraone, S. V., Biederman, J., & Milberger, S. (1994). An exploratory study of ADHD among second-degree relatives of ADHD children. *Bio. Psychiat., 35*(6), 398–402.

Faraone, S. V., Biederman, J., Mick, E., Wozniak, J. et al. (1996). Attention deficit hyperactivity disorder in a multigenerational pedigree. *Bio. Psychiat., 39,* 906–908.

Faravelli, C., Marinoni, M., Spiti, R., Ginanneschi, A. et al. (1997). Abnormal brain hemodynamic responses during passive orthostatic challenge in panic disorder. *Amer. J. Psychiat., 154*(3), 378–383.

Farberow, N. L. (1991). Adult survivors after suicide: Research problems and needs. In A. A. Leenaars (Ed.), *Life span perspectives of suicide: Time-lines in the suicide process.* New York: Plenum Press.

Farberow, N. L. (1993). Bereavement after suicide. In A. A. Leenaars, A. L. Berman, P. Cantor, R. E. Litman, & R. W. Maris (Eds.), *Suicidology.* Northvale, NJ: Jason Aronson, Inc.

Farberow, N. L., & Litman, R. E. (1970). *A comprehensive suicide prevention program.* Unpublished final report, Suicide Prevention Center of Los Angeles, Los Angeles .

Farde, L., & Nordstrom, A. L. (1992). PET Analysis indicates atypical central dopamine receptor occupancy in clozapine-treated patients. *Brit. J. Psychiat., 160*(Suppl. 17), 30–33.

Farde, L., Nordstrom, A. L., Wiedel, F. A., Pauli, S. et al. (1992). Positron emission tomographic analysis of central D-sub-1 and D-sub-2 dopamine receptor occupancy in patients treated with classical neuroleptics and clozapine: Relation to extrapyramidal side effects. *Arch. Gen. Psychiat., 49*(7), 538–544.

Farina, A. (1976). *Abnormal psychology.* Englewood Cliffs, NJ: Prentice Hall.

Farley, C. J. (1994, April 18). The butt stops here. *Time,* pp. 58–64.

Farlow, M., Gracon, S. I., Hershey, L. A., Lewis, K. W., Sadowsky, C. H., & Dolan-Ureno, J. (1992). A controlled trial of tacrine in Alzheimer's disease. *JAMA, 268*(18), 2523–2529.

Farrell, M. P., Barnes, G. M., & Banerjee, S. (1995). Family cohesion as a buffer against the effects of problem-drinking fathers on psychological distress, deviant behavior, and heavy drinking in adolescents. *J. Hlth. Soc. Behav., 36,* 377–385.

Farrington, D. P. (1991). Psychological contributions to the explanations of offending. *Issues Criminol. & Legal Psychol., 1*(17), 7–19.

Fasko, S. N., & Fasko, D. (1991). Suicidal behavior in children. *Psychology: J. of Human Behav., 27*(4)–28(1), 10–16.

Fauber, R. L., & Long, N. (1992). Parenting in a broader context: A reply to Emery, Finchman, and Cummings. *J. Cons. Clin. Psychol., 60*(6), 913–915.

Fausel, D. F. (1995). Stress innoculation training for stepcouples. *Marriage Fam. Rev., 21*(1–2), 137–155.

Fauteck, P. K. (1995). Detecting the malingering of psychosis in offenders: No easy solutions. *Criminal Justice Behav., 22*(1), 3–18.

Fava, M., Bless, E., Otto, M. W., Pava, J. A., & Rosenbaum, J. F. (1994). Dysfunctional attitudes in major depression. *J. Nerv. Ment. Dis., 182*(1), 45–49.

Fawcett, J., Scheftner, W., Clark, D., Hedeker, D. et al. (1987). Clinical predictors of suicide in patients with major affective disorders: A controlled prospective study. *Amer. J. Psychiat., 144*(1), 35–40.

Fawcett, J. & Busch, K. A. (1995). Stimulants in psychiatry. In A. F. Schatzberg & C. B. Nemeroff (Eds.), *The American Psychiatric Press textbook of psychopharmacology.* Washington, DC: American Psychiatric Press, Inc.

Fawzy, F. I., Fawzy, N. W., Arndt, L. A., & Pasnau, R. O. (1995). Critical Review of psychosocial interventions in cancer care. *Arch. Gen. Psychiat., 52,* 100–113.

Fawzy, F. I., Fawzy, N. W., Hyun, C. S., Elashoff, R., Guthrie, D., et al. (1993). Malignant melanoma: Effects of an early structured psychiatric intervention, coping, and affective state on recurrence and survival six years later. *Arch. Gen. Psychiat., 50,* 681–689.

Fedoroff, J. P. (1993). Serotonergic drug treatment of deviant sexual interests. *Ann. Sex Res., 6,* 105–121.

Fehre, K. & White, B. J. (Eds.) (1996). *The self-help group directory* (14th ed.). Denville, NJ: Northwest Convenant Medical Center.

Feldman, H. A., Goldstein, I., Hatzichristou, D. G., Krane, R. J., & McKinlay, J. B. (1994). Impotence and its medical and psychosocial correlates: Results of the Massachusetts Male Aging Study. *J. Urology, 151,* 54–61.

Feldman, M. D., & Feldman, J. M. (1995). Tangled in the web: Countertransference in the therapy of factitious disorders. *Inter. J. Psychiat. Med., 25*(4), 389–399.

Feldman, M. D. & Ford, C. V. (1994). *Patient or pretender: Inside the strange world of factitious disorders.* New York: Wiley.

Fenichel, O. (1945). *The psychoanalytic theory of neurosis.* New York: Norton.

Fenigstein, A. (1996). Paranoia. In C. G. Costello (Ed.), *Personality characteristics of the personality disordered.* New York: Wiley.

Fenn, D. S., Moussaoui, D., Hoffman, W. F., Kadri, N., Bentounssi, B., Tilane, A., Khomeis, M., Casey, D. E. (1996). Movements in never-medicated schizophrenics: A preliminary study. *Psychopharmacology, 123,* 206–210.

Fennig, S., Schwartz, J. E., & Bromet, E. J. (1994). Are diagnostic criteria, time of episode and occupational impairment important determinants of the female:Male ration for major depression? *J. Affect. Disorders, 30,* 147–154.

Fenton, W. S., & McGlashan, T. H. (1994). Antecedents, symptom progression, and long-term outcome of the deficit syndrome in schizophrenia. *Amer. J. Psychiat., 151*(3), 351–356.

Fenton, W. S., McGlashan, T. H., Victor, B. J., & Blyler, C. R. (1997). Symptoms, subtype, and suicidality in patients with schizophrenia spectrum disorders. *Amer. J. Psychiat., 154*(2), 199–204.

Fernandez, F., Levy, J. K., Lachar, B. L., Small, G. W., et al. (1995). The management of depression and anxiety in the elderly. *J. Clin. Psychiat., 56* [Suppl. 2], 20–29.

Ferrada, N. M., Asberg, M., Ormstad, K., & Nordstrom, P. (1995). Definite and undetermined forensic diagnoses of suicide among immigrants in Sweden. *Acta Psychiatr. Scandin., 91*(2), 130–135.

Fichter, M. (1990). Psychological therapies in bulimia nervosa. In M. M. Fichter (Ed.), *Bulimia nervosa: Basic research, diagnosis and therapy.* Chichester, England: Wiley.

Fichter, M. M. & Pirke, K. M. (1995). Starvation models and eating disorders. In G. Szmukler, C. Dare, & J. Treasure (Eds.), *Handbook of eating disorders: Theory, treatment and research.* Chichester, England: Wiley.

Fichtner, C. G., Kuhlman, D. T., Gruenfeld, M. J., & Hughes, J. R. (1990). Decreased episodic violence and increased control of dissociation in a carbamazepine-treated case of multiple personality. *Bio. Psychiat., 27*(9), 1045–1052.

Field, T. M. (1977). Effects of early separation, interactive deficit, and experimental manipulations on infant-mother face-to-face interaction. *Child Dev., 48*(3), 763–771.

Fields-Meyer, T. & Wagner, J. (1995, November 13). Laugh cure. *People,* pp. 103–104.

Fiester, S. J. (1986). Psychotherapeutic management of gastrointestinal disorders. In A. J. Frances & R. E. Hales (Eds.), *Psychiatric update-American Psychiatric Association annual review* (Vol. 5). Washington, DC: American Psychiatric Press.

Fieve, R. R. (1975). *Moodswing.* New York: Morrow.

Figley, C. R. (1978). Symptoms of delayed combat stress among a college sample of Vietnam veterans. *Military Med., 143*(2), 107–110.

Figley, C. R., & Leventman, S. (1990). Introduction: Estrangement and victimization. In C. R. Figley & S. Leventman (Eds.), *Strangers at home: Vietnam veterans since the war.* New York: Praeger.

Fink, D. (1992). The psychotherapy of multiple personality disorder. A case study. *Psychoanalytic Inquiry, 12*(1), 49–70.

Fink, M. (1978). Efficacy and safety of induced seizures (EST) in man. *Comprehen. Psychiat., 19,* 1–18.

Fink, M. (1978). Is ECT a useful therapy in schizophrenia? In J. P. Brady & H. K. H. Brodie (Eds.), *Controversy in psychiatry.* Philadelphia: Saunders.

Fink, M. (1987). Convulsive therapy in affective disorder: A decade of understanding and acceptance. In H. Y. Meltzer (Ed.), *Psychopharmacology: The third generation of progress.* New York: Raven Press.

Fink, M. (1988). Convulsive therapy: A manual of practice. In A. J. Frances & R. Hales (Eds.), *Review of psychiat.* (Vol. 7). Washington, DC: American Psychiatric Press.

Fink, M. (1992). Electroconvulsive therapy. In E. S. Paykel (Ed.), *Handbook of affective disorders.* New York: Guilford.

Fink, M. (1995). Recognizing NMS as a type of catatonia. *Neuropsychiat., Neuropsychol., and Behav. Neurol., 8*(1), 75–76.

Fink, P. (1995). Psychiatric illness in patients with persistent somatisation. *Brit. J. Psychiat., 166,* 93–99.

Finkel, N. J. (1988). *Insanity on trial.* New York: Plenum Press.

Finkel, N. J. (1989). The Insanity Defense Reform Act of 1984: Much ado about nothing. *J. Behav. Sci. Law, 7*(3), 403–419.

Finkel, N. J. (1990). De facto departures from insanity instructions. *Law Human Behav., 14*(2), 105–122.

Finkel, N. J. (1991). The insanity defense. *Law Human Behav., 15*(5), 533–555.

Finkel, N. J., & Duff, K. (1989). The insanity defense: giving jurors a third option. *Forensic Reports, 1,* 65–70.

Finkel, N. J., Shaw, R., Bercaw, S., & Koch, J. (1985). Insanity defenses: From the juror's perspective. *Law Psychol. Rev., 9,* 97–92.

Finkel, S. (1991). Group psychotherapy in later life. In W. A. Myers (Ed.), *New techniques in the psychotherapy of older patients.* Washington, DC: American Psychiatric Press.

Finkelhor, D., Asdigian, N., & Dziuba-Leatherman, J. (1995). Victimization prevention programs for children: A follow-up. *Amer. J. Pub. Hlth., 85*(12), 1684–1689.

Finkelhor, D., & Dziuba-Leatherman, J. (1995). Victimization prevention programs: A national survey of children's exposure and reactions. *Child Abuse and Neglect, 19*(2), 129–139.

Finkelhor, D., Asdigian, N., & Dziuba-Leatherman, J. (1995). The effectiveness of victimization prevention instruction: An evaluation of children's responses to actual threats and assaults. *Child Abuse and Neglect, 19*(2), 141–153.

Finkelhor, D., Gelles, R., Hotaling, G., & Straus, M. (Eds.). (1983). *The dark side of families.* Beverly Hills, CA: Sage.

Finkelstein, J. R. J., Cannon, T. D., Gur, R. E., Gur, R. C., & Moberg, P. (1997). Attentional dysfunctions in neuroleptic-naive and neuroleptic-withdrawn schizophrenic patients and their siblings. *J. Abnorm. Psychol., 106*(2), 203–212.

First, M. B., Spitzer, R. L., Gibbon, M., & Williams, J. B. W. (1995). The structured clinical interview for DSM-III-R personality disorders (SCID-II): I. Description. *J. Pers. Disorders, 9*(2), 83–91.

Fiscalini, J. (1993). Interpersonal relations and the problem of narcissism. In J. Fiscalini & A. L. Grey (Eds.), *Narcissism and the interpersonal self.* New York: Columbia University Press.

Fischbach, G. D. (1992, September). Mind and brain. *Scientif. Amer.,* p. 48.

Fisher, J. E., & Carstensen, L. L. (1990). Behavior management of the dementias. *Clin. Psychol. Rev., 10,* 611–629.

Fisher, S. (1973). *The female orgasm.* New York: Basic Books.

Fitz, A. (1990). Religious and familial factors in the etiology of obsessive-compulsive disorder: A review. *J. Psychol. Theol., 18*(2), 141–147.

Flament, M. F. (1990). Epidemiologie du trouble obsessionnel-compulsif chez l'enfant et l'adolescent [Epidemiology of obsessive-compulsive disorder during childhood and adolescence] *Encephale, 16,* 311–316.

Flament, M. F., Koby, E., Rapoport, J. L., Berg, C. J. et al. (1991). Childhood obsessive-compulsive disorder: A prospective follow-up study. *Annu. Progr. Child Psychiat. Child Dev.,* 373–394.

Flament, M. F. et al. (1985). Clominpramine treatment of childhood obsessive-compulsive disorder: A double-blind controlled study. *Arch. Gen. Psychiat., 429*(10), 977–983.

Flavin, D. K., Franklin, J. E., & Frances, R. J. (1990). Substance abuse and suicidal behavior. In S. J. Blumenthal & D. J. Kupfer (Eds.), *Suicide over the life cycle: Risk factors, assessment, and treatment of suicidal patients.* Washington, DC: American Psychiatry Press.

Fleer, J., & Pasewark, R. A. (1982). Prior public health agency contacts of individuals committing suicide. *Psychol. Rep., 50*(3, Pt. 2), 1319–1324.

Fleishman, J. A., & Fogel, B. (1994). Coping and depressive symptoms among people with AIDS. *Hlth. Psychol.,* 13(2), 156–169.

Fletcher, J. (1981). In defense of suicide. In S. E. Wallace & A. Eser (Eds.), *Suicide and euthanasia: The rights of personhood.* Knoxville: University of Tennessee.

Flett, G. L., Vredenburg, K., & Krames, L. (1997). The continuity of depression in clinical and nonclinical samples. *Psychol. Bull., 121*(3), 395–416.

Flick, S. N., Roy-Byrne, P. P., Cowley, D. S., Shores, M. M., & Dunner, D. L. (1993). DSM-III-R personality disorders in a mood and anxiety disorders clinic: Prevalence, comorbidity, and clinical correlates. *J. Affect. Disorders, 27,* 71–79.

Flint, A. J. (1994). Epidemiology and comorbidity of anxiety disorders in the elderly. *Amer. J. Psychiat., 151*(5), 640–649.

Floyd, F. J., O'Farrell, T. J., & Goldberg, M. (1987). Comparison of marital observational measures: The Marital Interaction Coding System and the Communications Skills Test. *J. Cons. Clin. Psychol., 55*(3), 2200.

Flynn, T. M., Taylor, P., & Pollard, C. E. (1992). Use of mobile phones in the behavioral treatment of driving phobias. *J. Behav. Ther. Exp. Psychiat., 23*(4), 299–302.

Foa, E. B., & Kozak, M. J. (1995). DSM-IV field trial: Obsessive compulsive disorder. *Amer. J. Psychiat., 152*(1), 90–96.

Foa, E. B., & Riggs, D. S. (1995). Posttraumatic stress disorder following assault: Theoretical considerations and empirical findings. *Current Directions in Psychological Science, 4*(2), 61-65.

Foderaero, L. W. (1993, August 12). Electroshock therapy makes a comeback. *Anchorage Daily News,* p. D3.

Foderaro, L. (1994, March 6). Got problems? Dial a shrink. *The New York Times,* p. B4(L).

Fog, R. (1995). New diagnostic vistas. XIIth AEP Congress: Improvement of compliance: Quality assurance: Increased quality of life in community care in schizophrenia. *Inter. Clin. Psychopharmacol., 9*(Suppl. 5), 71–73.

Fogel, B. S. (1986). ECT versus tricyclic antidepressants. *Amer. J. Psychiat., 143*(1), 121.

Fombonne, E. (1995). Eating disorders: Time trends and possible explanatory mehanisms. In M. Rutter & D. J. Smith, *Psychosocial disorders in young people.* Chichester, England: Wiley.

Fonagy, P. (1991). Thinking about thinking: Some clinical and theoretical considerations in the treatment of a borderline patient. *Inter. J. Psychoanal., 72*(4), 639–656.

Fondacaro, K. M. & Butler, W. M. (1995). Suicidality in female survivors of child sexual abuse. In S. S. Canetto & D. Lester (Eds.), *Women and suicidal behavior.* New York: Springer.

Fontaine, K. R., & Jones, L. C. (1997). Self-esteem, optimism, and postpartum depression. *J. Clin. Psychol., 53*(1), 59–63.

Ford, C. V., King, B. H., & Hollender, M. H. (1988). Lies and liars: Psychiatric aspects of prevarication. *Amer. J. Psychiat., 145*(5), 554–562.

Ford, M. R., & Widiger, T. A. (1989). Sex bias in the diagnosis of histrionic and antisocial personality disorders. *J. Cons. Clin. Psychol., 57*(2), 301–305.

Foreyt, J. P., Poston, W. S. C., & Goodrick, G. K. (1996). Future directions in obesity and eating disorders. *Addic. Behav., 21*(6), 767–778.

Fortmann, S. & Killen, J. (1995). Nicotine gum and self-help behavioral treatment for smoking relapse prevention: Results from a trial using population-based recruitment. *J. Cons. Clin. Psychol., 63*(3), 460–468.

Foster, S. (1995, February 17). The prevalence of "Sex" as a keyword in internet searches. As cited in *USA Today,* p. 1D.

Foster, S. L. & Cone, J. D. (1986). Design and use of direct observation. In A. R. Ciminero, K. S. Calhoun, & H. E. Adams (Eds.), *Handbook of behavioral assessment* (2nd ed.). New York: Wiley.

Foster-Higgins. (1991, June 8) Cited in L. Block "Mental Health Expenses make employers anxious." *Business Insurance,* p. 3.

Fowler, J. S., Volkow, N. D., Logan, J., Wang, G. J., et al. (1994). Slow recovery of human brain MAO B after L-deprenyl (Selegeline) withdrawal. *Synapse, 18*(2): 86–93.

Fowler, J. S., Volkow, N. D., & Wolf, A. P. (1995). PET studies of cocaine in human brain. In A. Biegon & N. D. Volkow (Eds.), *Sites of drug action in the human brain.* Boca Raton, FL: CRC Press, Inc.

Fowles, D. C. (1992). Schizophrenia: Diathesis-stress revisited. *Annu. Rev. Psychol., 43,* 303–336.

Fox, P. (1992). Implications for expressed emotion therapy within a family therapeutic context. *Hlth. Soc. Work, 17*(3), 207–213.

Foy, A., O'Connell, D., Henry, D., Kelly, J., et al. (1995). Benzodiazepine use as a cause of cognitive impairment in elderly hospital inpatients. *J. Gerontol., Series A Bio. Sci. Med Sci., 50A*(2), M99–M106.

Frances, R. J., & Franklin, J. E. (1988). Alcohol and other psychoactive substance use disorders. In J. A. Talbott, R. E. Hales, & S. C. Yudofsky (Eds.), *Textbook of psychiatry.* Washington, DC: American Psychiatric Press.

Franchini, L., Gasperini, M., Perez, J., Smeraldi, E., & Zanardi, R. (1997). A double-blind study of long-term treatment with sertraline or fluvoxamine for prevention of highly recurrent unipolar depression. *J. Clin. Psychiat., 58*(3), 104–107.

Francis, M. E., & Pennebaker, J. W. (1992). Putting stress into words: The impact of writing on physiological, absentee, and self-reported emotional well-being measures. *Amer. J. Hlth. Promotion, 6*(4), 280–287.

Frank, E. (1997). Enhancing patient outcomes: Treatment adherence. *J. Clin. Psychiat., 58*(Suppl. 1), 11–14.

Frank, E., Kupfer, D. J., Perel, J. M., Cornes, C., Jarrett, D. B., Mallinger, A. G. et al. (1990). Three-year outcomes for maintenance therapies in recurrent depression. *Arch. Gen. Psychiat., 47*(12), 1093–1099.

Frank, E., Kupfer, D. J., Wagner, E. F., McEachran, A. B., & Cornes, C. (1991). Efficacy of interpersonal therapy as a maintenance treatment of recurrent depression: Contributing factors. *Arch. Gen. Psychiat., 48,* 1053–1059.

Frank, J. D. (1973). *Persuasion and healing* (Rev. ed.). Baltimore: Johns Hopkins University Press.

Frankel, F. H. (1984). The use of electroconvulsive therapy in suicidal patients. *Amer. J. Psychother., 38*(3), 384–391.

Frankel, F. H. (1993). Adult reconstruction of childhood events in the multiple personality literature. *Amer. J. Psychiat., 150*(6), 954–958.

Frankish, C. J. (1994). Crisis centers and their role in treatment: Suicide prevention versus health promotion. In A. A. Leenaars, J. T. Maltsberger, & R. A. Neimeyer (Eds.), *Treatment of suicidal people.* Washington, DC: Taylor & Francis.

Frankl, V. E. (1963). *Man's search for meaning.* New York: Washington Square.

Frankl, V. E. (1975). Paradoxical intention and dereflection. *Psychother. Theory Res. Prac., 12*(3), 226–237.

Franklin, K. W., & Cornell, D. G. (1997). Rorschach interpretation with high-ability adolescent females: Psychopathology or creative thinking? *J. Pers. Assess., 68*(1), 184–196.

Franko, D. L. (1993). The use of a group meal in the brief group therapy of bulimia nervosa. *Inter. J. Group Psychother., 43*(2), 237–242.

Frasciello, L. M., & Willard, S. G. (1995). Anorexia nervosa in males: A case report and review of the literature. *Clin. Soc. Work J., 23*(1), 47–58.

Frawley, P. & Smith, J. (1992). One-year follow-up after multimodal inpatient treatment for cocaine and methamphetamine dependencies. *J. Substance Abuse Treatment, 9,* 271–286.

Frayn, D. H. (1991). The incidence and significance of perceptual qualities in the reported dreams of patients with anorexia nervosa. *Canad. J. Psychiat., 36*(7), 517–520.

Frederick, C. J. (1969). Suicide notes: A survey and evaluation. *Bull. Suicidol., 8,* 17–26.

Frederiksen, N. (1986). Toward a broader conception of human intelligence. *Amer. Psychol., 41,* 445–452.

Frederiksen, N. (1993). Changing conceptions of intelligence. In G. G. Brannigan & M. R. Merrens (Eds.), *The undaunted psychologist: Adventures in research.* New York: McGraw-Hill.

Fredrikson, M., Annas, P., & Wik, G. (1997). Parental history, aversive exposure and the development of snake and spider phobia in women. *Behav. Res. Ther., 35*(1), 23–28.

Fredrikson, M., Annas, P., Fischer, H., & Wik, G. (1996). Gender and age differences in the prevalence of specific fears and phobias. *Behav. Res. Ther.,* 34(1), 33–39.

Freeman, A., Pretzer, J., Fleming, B., & Simon, K. M. (1990). *Clinical applications of cognitive therapy.* New York: Plenum Press.

Freeman, C. (1995). Cognitive therapy. In G. Szmukler, C. Dare, & J. Treasure (Eds.), *Handbook of eating disorders: Theory, treatment and research.* Chichester, England: Wiley.

Freeston, M. H., & Ladouceur, R. (1997). What do patients do with their obsessive thoughts? *Behav. Res. Ther., 35*(4), 335–348.

Freeston, M., Ladouceur, R., Gagnon, F., & Thibodeau, N. (1992). *Beliefs about obsessional thoughts.* Unpublished manuscript, Laval University, Quebec City, Quebec.

Freiberg, P. (1994, April). Gay-rights position takes on significance. *APA Monitor, 25*(4), 40.

French, O. (1987). More on multiple personality disorder. *Amer. J. Psychiat., 144*(1), 123–124.

Freud, S. (1885). On the general effects of cocaine. *Medicinisch-chirugisches Centralblatt, 20,* 373–375.

Freud, S. (1894). The neuro-psychoses of defense. In J. Strachey (Ed.), *The standard edition of the complete psychological works of Sigmund Freud* (Vol. 3). London: Hogarth Press, 1962.

Freud, S. (1900). *The interpretation of dreams.* J. Strachey (Ed. and Trans.). New York: Wiley.

Freud, S. (1909). Analysis of a phobia in a five-year-old boy. In *Sigmund Freud: Collected Papers.* (Vol. 3). New York: Basic Books.

Freud, S. (1915). A case of paranoia counter to psychoanalytic theory. In *Complete psychological works* (Vol. 14). London: Hogarth, 1957.

Freud, S. (1917). *A general introduction to psychoanalysis.* (J. Riviere, Trans.). New York: Liveright, 1963.

Freud, S. (1917). Mourning and melancholia. In *Collected Papers.* (Vol. 4). pp. 152–172. London: Hogarth Press and the Institute of Psychoanalysis, 1950.

Freud, S. (1924). The loss of reality in neurosis and psychosis. In *Sigmund Freud's Collected papers,* (Vol. 2, pp. 272–282. London: Hogarth Press.

Freud, S. (1933). *New introductory lectures on psychoanalysis.* New York: Norton.

Freud, S. (1955). *Notes upon a case of obsessional neurosis.* London: Hogarth Press.

Frey, K. A., Koeppe, R. A., & Holthoff, V. A. (1995). *In vivo* imaging of benzodiazepine receptors with positron emission tomography. In A. Biegon & N. D. Volkow (Eds.), *Sites of drug action in the human brain.* Boca Raton, FL: CRC Press.

Frick, W. B. (1995). The subpersonalities controversy: A reply to my critics. *J. Human Psychol., 35*(1), 97–101.

Friedberg, J. (1975, August). Electroshock therapy: Let's stop blasting the brain. *Psychol. Today,* 18–23, 98–99.

Friedman, H. R. & Goldman-Rakic, P. S. (1994). Coactivation of prefrontal cortex and inferior parietal cortex in working memory tasks revealed by 2DG functional mapping in the rhesus monkey. *J. Neurosci.,* May 14, 1994 (5 Pt 1), 2775–2788.

Friedman, M., & Rosenman, R. (1959). Association of specific overt behavior pattern with blood and cardiovascular findings. *JAMA, 169,* 1286.

Friedman, M., & Rosenman, R. (1974). *Type A behavior and your heart.* New York: Knopf.

Friedman, M., Thoresen, C., Gill, J. et al. (1984). Alteration of type A behavior and reduction in cardiac recurrences in postmyocardial infarction patients. *Amer. Heart J., 108*(2), 653–665.

Friedman, R. M., Katz-Leavy, J. W., Manderscheid, R. W., & Sondheimer, D. L. (1996). Prevalence of serious emotional disturbance in children and adolescents. In *Mental health, United States, 1996.* R. W. Manderscheid & M. A. Sonnenschein (Eds.), (DHHS Publication No. SMA 96–3098). Washington, DC: U. S. Government Printing Office, Center for Mental Health Services.

Friend, T. (1996, March 4). Alzheimer's deaths "underestimated". *USA Today,* Section D, p. 1.

Friend, T. (1996, March 18). Coffee habit may boost hypertension. *USA Today,* p. 1D.

Friman, P. C., Allen, K. D., Kerwin, M. L. E., & Larzelere, R. (1993). Changes in modern psychology: A citation analysis of the Kuhnian Displacement Thesis. *Amer. Psychol., 48*(6), 658–664.

Friman, P. C., & Warzak, W. J. (1990). Nocturnal enuresis: A prevalent, persistent, yet curable parasomnia. *Pediatrician, 17*(1), 38–45.

Frischholz, E. J., Lipman, L. S., Braun, B. G., & Sachs, R. G. (1992). Psychopathology, hypnotizability, and dissociation. *Amer. J. Psychiat., 149*(11), 1521–1525.

Frith, U., Morton, J., & Leslie, A. M. (1991). The cognitive basis of a biological disorder: Autism. *Trends Neurosci.,* 14, 433–438.

Fritz, C., Farver, T. B., & Kass, P. H. (1997). Correlation among three psychological scales used in research of caregivers for patients with Alzheimer's disease. *Psychol. Rep., 80,* 67–80.

Fritz, G. K., Rockney, R. M., & Yeung, A. S. (1994). Plasma levels and efficacy of imipramine treatment for enuresis. *J. Amer. Acad. Child Adol. Psychiat., 33*(1), 60–64.

Fromm, E., & Nash, M. R., (Eds.) (1992). *Contemporary hypnosis research.* New York: Guilford.

Fromm-Reichmann, F. (1943). Psychotherapy of schizophrenia. *Amer. J. Psychiat., 111,* 410–419.

Fromm-Reichmann, F. (1948). Notes on the development of treatment of schizophrenia by psychoanalytic psychotherapy. *Psychiatry, 11,* 263–273.

Fromm-Reichmann, F. (1950). *Principles of intensive psychotherapy.* Chicago: University of Chicago.

Fromme, K., Katz, E., & D'Amico, E. (1997). Effects of alcohol intoxication on the perceived consequences of risk taking. *Exp. Clin. Psychopharmacol., 5*(1), 14–23.

Frosch, W. A., Robbins, E. S., & Stern, M. (1965). Untoward reactions to lysergic acid diethylamide (LSD) resulting in hospitalization. *N. Engl. J. Med., 273,* 1235–1239.

Frueh, B. C. (1995). Self-administered exposure therapy by a Vietnam veteran with PTSD. *Amer. J. Psychiat., 152*(12), 1831–1832.

Fry, R. (1993). Adult physical illness and childhood sexual abuse. *J. Psychosom. Res., 37*(2), 89–103.

Frye, M. A., Altshuler, L. L., Szuba, M. P., Finch, N. N., & Mintz, J. (1996). The relationship between antimanic agent for treatment of classic or dysphoric mania and length of hospital stay. *J. Clin. Psychiat., 57,* 17–21.

Fuller, R. C. (1982, Fall). Carl Rogers, religion, and the role of psychology in American culture. *J. Human. Psychol., 22,* 21–32.

Fulwiler, C., & Pope, H. G., Jr. (1987). Depression in personality disorder. In O. G. Cameron (Ed.), *Presentations of depression: Depressive symptoms in medical and other psychiatric disorders.* New York: Wiley.

Funari, D. J., Piekarski, A. M., & Sherwood, R. J. (1991). Treatment outcomes of Vietnam veterans with posttraumatic stress disorder. *Psychol. Rep., 68*(2), 571–578.

Furey, M. L., Pietrini, P., et al. (1997). Cholinergic stimulation alters performance and task-specific regional cerebral blood flow during working memory. *Proc. Nat. Acad. Sci., U. S.A., 94.*

Furumoto, L., & Keating, K. M. (1995). Construing anorexia nervosa (1940–1980): The psychoanalysists, the behaviorists, and Hilde Bruch. In I. Lubek, R. van Hezewijk, G. Pheterson, & C. W. Tolman, (Eds), *Trends and issues in theoretical psychology.* New York: Springer.

Gabbard, G. O. (1990). *Psychodynamic psychiatry in clinical practice.* Washington, DC: American Psychiatric Press.

Gabbard, G. O., & Coyne, L. (1987). Predictors of response of antisocial patients to hospital treatment. *Hosp. Comm. Psychiat., 38*(11), 1181–1185.

Gabbard, G. O. & Goodwin, F. K. (1996). Integrating biological and psychosocial perspectives. In L. J. Dickstein, M. B. Riba, & J. M. Oldham (Eds.), *Review of Psychiatry,* (Vol. 15). Washington, DC: American Psychiatric Press.

Gaebel, W. (1995). Is intermittent, early intervention medication an alternative for neuroleptic maintenance treatment? XIIth AEP Congress: Improvement of the quality of life in schizophrenia. *Int. Clin. Psychopharmacol., 9*(Suppl. 5), 11–16.

Galanter, M. (1993). Network therapy for addiction: A model for office practice. *Amer. J. Psychiat., 150*(1), 28–35.

Galanter, M., Talbott, D., Gallegos, K., & Rubenstone, E. (1990). Combined Alcoholics Anonymous and professional care for addicted physicians. *Amer. J. Psychiat., 147*(1), 64–68.

Gallagher-Thompson, D. & Thompson, L. W. (1995). Problems of aging. In R. J. Comer, *Abnormal psychology.* New York: W. H. Freeman.

Gallagher-Thompson, D. (1994). Direct services and interventions for caregivers: A review and critique of extant programs and a look ahead to the future. In M. Cantor (Ed.), *Family caregiving: Agenda for the future.* San Francisco, CA: American Society on Aging.

Gallagher-Thompson, D., Hanley-Peterson, P., & Thompson, L. W. (1989). Maintenance of gains versus relapse following brief psychotherapy for depression. *J. Cons. Clin. Psychol., 58,* 371–374.

Gallagher-Thompson, D., Lovett, S., & Rose, J. (1991). Psychotherapeutic interventions for stressed family caregivers. In W. A. Myers (Ed.), *New techniques in the psychotherapy of older patients.* Washington, DC: American Psychiatric Press.

Gallup Organization (1995). *Child abuse survey.* Princeton, NJ: Author.

Gamwell, L. & Tomes, N. (1995). *Madness in America: Cultural and medical perceptions of mental illness before 1914.* Ithaca, NY: Cornell University Press.

Ganaway, G. K. (1989). Historical versus narrative truth: Clarifying the role of exogenous trauma in the etiology of MPD and its variants. *Dissociation, 2,* 205–222.

Ganley, A. (1981). *A participant and trainer's manual for working with men who batter.* Washington, DC: Center for Women Policy Studies.

Gannon, L., Luchetta, T., Rhodes, K., Pardie, L., & Segrist, D. (1992). Sex bias in psychological research: Progress or complacency? *Amer. Psychol. 47*(3), 389–396.

Gantz, F., Gallagher-Thompson, D., & Rodman, J. (1991). Cognitive-behavioral facilitation of inhibited grief. In A. Freeman & F. Dattilio (Eds.), *Casebook of cognitive-behavior therapy.* New York: Plenum Press.

Ganzach, Y. (1995). Nonlinear models of clinical judgment: Meehl's data revisited. *Psychol. Bull., 118*(3), 422–429.

GAP (Group for the Advancement of Psychiatry). (1947, January 22, p. 18).

Gara, M. A., Woolfolk, R. L., Cohen, B. D., Goldston, R. B., Allen, L. A., & Novalany, J. (1993). Perception of self and other in major depression. *J. Abnorm. Psychol., 102*(1), 93–100.

Garber, J., Weiss, B., & Shanley, N. (1993). Cognitions, depressive symptoms, and development in adolescents. *J. Abnorm. Psychol., 102*(1), 47–57.

Gardner, D. L., Leibenluft, E., O'Leary, K. M., & Cowdry, R. W. (1991). Self-ratings of anger and hostility in borderline personality disorder. *J. Nerv. Ment. Dis., 179*(3), 157–161.

Gardner, D. L., Lucas, P. B., & Cowdry, R. W. (1990). CSF metabolites in borderline personality disorder compared with normal controls. *Bio. Psychiat., 28,* 247–254.

Gardner, F. L., McGowan, L. P., DiGiuseppe, R., & Sutton-Simon, K. (1980, November). *A comparison of cognitive and behavioral therapies in the reduction of social anxiety.* Paper presented to the American Association of Behavior Therapy, New York.

Gardner, J. P. (1996). *The effects of sleep deprivation on serotonergic neuronal activity in the dorsal raphe nucleus of the cat.* Doctoral Dissertation. Princeton University, Princeton, NJ.

Gardner, R. (1984, July 12). Full moon lunacy: Fact or fiction. *Trenton Times,* p. B1.

Gardner, R. M. & Bokenkamp, E. D. (1996). The role of sensory and nonsensory factors in body size estimations of eating disorder subjects. *J. Clin. Psychol., 52*(1), 3–15.

Garety, P. (1991). Reasoning and delusions. *Brit. J. Psychiat., 159*(Suppl. 14), 14–18.

Garfield, D. A. & Havens, L. (1991). Paranoid phenomena and pathological narcissism. *Amer. J. Psychother., 45*(2), 160–172.

Garfield, S. L., & Bergin, A. E. (1994). Introduction and historical overview. In A. E. Bergin & S. L. Garfield (Eds.), *Handbook of psychotherapy and behavior change* (4th ed.). New York: Wiley.

Garfinkel, B. D., Froese, A., & Golombek, H. M. (1979). Suicidal behavior in a pediatric population. In *Proceedings of the 10th International Congress for Suicide Prevention.* Ottawa: International Association for Suicide Prevention.

Garfinkel, P. E. et al. (1978). Body awareness in anorexia nervosa: Disturbances in body image and satiety. *Psychosom. Med., 40*(6), 487–498.

Garfinkel, P. E., & Gallop, R. (1992). Eating disorders and borderline personality disorder. In D. Silver & M. Rosenbluth (Eds.), *Handbook of borderline disorders.* Madison, CT: International Universities Press.

Garfinkel, P. E., & Garner, D. M. (1982). *Anorexia nervosa: A multidimensional perspective.* New York: Brunner/Mazel.

Garland, A. F., Shaffer, D., & Whittle, B. (1989). A national survey of adolescent suicide prevention programs. *J. Amer. Acad. Child Adol. Psychiat., 28,* 931–934.

Garland, A. F., & Zigler, E. (1993). Adolescent suicide prevention: Current research and social policy implications. *Amer. Psychol., 48*(2), 169–182.

Garnefski, N., & Diekstra, R. F. W. (1997). Adolescents from one parent, stepparent and intact families: Emotional problems and suicide attempts. *J. Adolescence, 20,* 201–208.

Garner, D., Cooke, A. K., & Marano, H. E. (1997). The 1997 body image survey results. *Psychol. Today,* pp. 30–44.

Garner, D. M., & Bemis, K. M. (1982). A cognitive-behavioral approach to anorexia nervosa. *Cog. Ther. Res., 6*(2), 123–150.

Garner, D. M., & Bemis, K. M. (1985). Cognitive therapy for anorexia nervosa. In D. M. Garner & P. E. Garfinkel (Eds.), *Handbook of psychotherapy for anorexia nervosa and bulimia.* New York: Guilford.

Garner, D. M., & Garfinkel, P. E. (1978). Sociocultural factors in anorexia nervosa. *Lancet, 2,* 674.

Garner, D. M., & Fairburn, C. G. (1988). Relationship between anorexia nervosa and bulimia nervosa: Diagnostic implications. In D.M. Garner & P.E. Garfinkel (Eds.), *Diagnostic issues in anorexia nervosa and bulimia nervosa. Brunner/Mazel eating disorders monograph series, No. 2.* New York: Brunner/Mazel.

Garner, D. M., Fairburn, C. G., & Davis, R. (1987). Cognitive behavioral treatment of bulimia nervosa: A critical appraisal. *Behav. Mod., 11*(4), 398–431.

Garner, D. M., & Garfinkel, P. E. (1980). Sociocultural factors in the development of anorexia nervosa. *Psychol. Med., 10,* 647–656.

Garner, D. M., & Garfinkel, P. E. (1981). Body image in anorexia nervosa: Measurement, theory and clinical implications. *Inter. J. Psychiat. Med., 11,* 263–284.

Garner, D. M., Garfinkel, P. E., & O'Shaughnessy, M. (1985). The validity of the distinction between bulimia with and without anorexia nervosa. *Amer. J. Psychiat., 142,* 581–587.

Garner, D. M., Garfinkel, P. E., Schwartz, D., & Thompson, M. (1980). Cultural expectations of thinness in women. *Psychol. Rep., 47,* 483–491.

Garner, D. M., Garfinkel, P. E., Stancer, H. C., & Moldofsky, H. (1976). Body image disturbances in anorexia nervosa and obesity. *Psychosom. Med., 38,* 327–336.

Garner, D. M., Olmsted, M. P., & Polivy, J. (1984). *The EDI.* Odessa, FL: Psychological Assessment Resources.

Garner, D. M., Rockert, W., Davis, R., Garner, M. V., Olmsted, M. P., & Eagle, M. (1993). Comparison of cognitive-behavioral and supportive-expressive therapy for bulimia nervosa. *Amer. J. Psychiat., 150*(1), 37–46.

Garner, D. M., & Wooley, S. C. (1991). Confronting the failure of behavioral and dietary treatments for obesity. *Clin. Psychol. Rev., 11*(6), 729–780.

Garofalo, G., Ragusa, R. M., Barletta, C., & Spina, E. (1992). Schizophrenia and chromosomal fragile sites. *Amer. J. Psychiat., 149*(8), 1116.

Garralda, M. E. (1996). Somatisation in children. *J. Child Psychol. Psychiat., 37*(1), 13–33.

Garrison, C. Z., McKeown, R. E., Valois, R. F., & Vincent, M. L. (1993). Aggression, substance use, and suicidal behaviors in high school students. *Amer. J. Pub. Hlth., 83*(2), 179–184.

Garrison, E. G. (1987). Psychological maltreatment of children: An emerging focus for inquiry and concern. *Amer. Psychol., 42*(2), 157–159.

Gatchel, R. J., & Baum, A. (1983). *An introduction to health psychology.* New York: Random House.

Gattaz, W. F. (1995). Does vitamin E prevent tardive dyskinesia? *Bio. Psychiat., 37*(12), 896–897.

Gaub, M., & Carlson, C. L. (1997). Behavioral characteristics of DSM-IV ADHD subtypes in a school-based population. *J. Abnorm. Child Psychol., 25*(2), 103–111.

Gawin, F. H. & Ellinwood, E. H. (1988). Cocaine and other stimulants: actions, abuse, and treatment. *N. Eng. J. Med., 318,* 1173–1182.

Gebhard, P. H. (1965). Situational factors affecting human sexual behavior. In F. Beach (Ed.), *Sex and behavior.* New York: Wiley.

Gebhard, P. H., Gagnon, J. H., Pomeroy, W. B., & Christenson, C. V. (1965). *Sex offenders: An analysis of types.* New York: Harper & Row.

Geisthardt, C., & Munsch, J. (1996). Coping with school stress: A comparison of adolescents with and without learning disabilities. *J. Learn. Disabilities, 29*(3), 287–296.

Gejman, P. V., Ram, A., Gelernter, J., Friedman, E., Cao, Q., et al. (1994). No structural mutation in the Dopamine d-2 receptor gene in alcoholism or schizophrenia. *JAMA, 271*(3), 204–208.

Gelder, M. (1991). Psychological treatment for anxiety disorders: Adjustment disorder with anxious mood, generalized anxiety disorders, panic disorder, agoraphobia, and avoidant personality disorder. In C. Coryell & G. Winokur (Eds.), *The clinical management of anxiety disorders.* New York: Oxford University Press.

Gelfand, D. M., Jenson, W. R., & Drew, C. J. (1982). *Understanding child behavior disorders.* New York: Holt, Rinehart & Winston.

Geller, B., Fox, L. W., & Fletcher, M. (1993). Effect of tricyclic antidepressants on switching to mania and on the onset of bipolarity in depressed 6- to 12-year-olds. *J. Amer. Acad. Child. Adol. Psychiat., 32*(1), 43–50.

Geller, J. L. (1992). A historical perspective on the role of state hospitals viewed from the era of the "revolving door." *Amer. J. Psychiat., 149,* 1526–1533.

Gelles, R. J. (1992). Poverty and violence toward children. *Amer. Behav. Scientist, 35*(3), 258–274.

Gelles, R. J., & Straus, M. A. (1987). Is violence toward children increasing? A comparison of 1975 and 1985 national survey rates. *J. Interpers. Violence, 2,* 212–222.

Gelman, D. (1983, November 7). A great emptiness. *Newsweek,* pp. 120–126.

Gelman, D. (1991, August 15). The secrets of Apt. 213. *Newsweek,* pp. 40–42.

Gelman, D., & Katel, P. (1993, April 5). The trauma after the storm. *Newsweek.*

Gentry, W. D., & Matarazzo, J. D. (1981). Medical psychology: Three decades of growth and development. In L. A. Bradley & C. K. Prokop (Eds.), *Medical psychology: A new perspective.* New York: Academic Press.

Genuis, M. L. (1995). The use of hypnosis in helping cancer patients control anxiety, pain and emesis: A review of recent empirical studies. *Amer. J. Clin. Hyp., 37*(4), 316–325.

George, F. R. (1990). Genetic approaches to studying drug abuse: Correlates of drug self-administration. National Institute on Alcohol Abuse and Alcoholism Neuroscience and Behavioral Research Branch Workshop on the Neurochemical Bases on Alcohol-Related Behavior. *Alcohol, 7*(3), 207–211.

Gerlach, J., Lublin, H., & Peacock, L. (1996). Extrapyramidal symptoms during long-term treatment with antipsychotics: Special focus on Clozapine and D1 and D2 Dopamine Antagonists. *Neuropsychopharmacology, 14,* 35S–39S.

Gerlach, J., & Hansen, L. (1992). Clozapine and D1/D2 antagonism in extrapyramidal functions. *Brit. J. Psychiat., 160*(Suppl.), 34–37.

Gerlach, J. & Peacock, L. (1995). Intolerance to neuroleptic drugs: The art of avoiding extrapyramidal syndromes: Treatment-resistant schizophrenia in perspective: Assessment and management. *Eur. Psychiat., 10*(Suppl. 1), 27S–31S.

Gernsbacher, L. M. (1985). *The suicide syndrome.* New York: Human Sciences.

Gershon, E. S., & Nurnberger, J. I. (1995). Bipolar illness. In J. M. Oldham & M. B. Riba (Eds.), *American Psychiatric Press review of psychiatry,* (Vol. 14). Washington, DC: American Psychiatric Press.

Gershon, E. S. & Rieder, R. O. (1992). Major disorders of mind and brain. *Scientif. Amer.,* 127–133.

Gheorghiu, V. A., & Orleanu, P. (1982). Dental implant under hypnosis. *Amer. J. Clin. Hyp., 25*(1), 68–70.

Ghosh, A., & Greist, J. H. (1988). Computer treatment in psychiatry. *Psychiatr. Ann., 18*(4), 246–250.

Ghosh, A., & Marks, I. M. (1987). Self-treatment of agoraphobia by exposure. *Behav. Ther., 18*(1), 3–16.

Ghubash, R., Hamdi, E., & Bebbington, P. (1992). The Dubai Community Psychiatry Survey: Prevalence and socio-demographic correlates. *Soc. Psychiat. Psychiatr. Epidemiol., 27*(2), 53–61.

Gibbons, F. X., Eggleston, T. J., & Benthin, A. C. (1997). Cognitive reactions to smoking relapse: The reciprocal relation between dissonance and self-esteem. *J. Pers. Soc. Psychol., 72*(1), 184–195.

Gibbs, M. S. (1989). Factors in the victim that mediate between disaster and psychopathology: A review. *J. Traum. Stress, 2,* 489–514.

Gibson, D. (1990). Borderline personality disorder issues of etiology and gender. *Occup. Ther. Ment. Hlth., 10*(4), 63–77.

Gil, D. (1970). *Violence against children.* Cambridge, MA: Harvard, University Press.

Gilbert, K. (1996). "We've had the same loss, why don't we have the same grief?" Loss and differential grief in families. *Death Stud., 20,* 269–283.

Gilbert, P. L., Harris, M. J., McAdams, L. A., & Jeste, D. V. (1995). Neuroleptic withdrawal in schizophrenic patients: Review of the literature. *Arch. Gen. Psychiat., 52*(3), 173–188.

Gilbert, S. (1996, May 1). Estrogen patch appears to lift severe depression in new mothers. *The New York Times,* p. C12.

Gilbert, S. (1996, July 28). More men may seek eating-disorder help. *The New York Times.*

Gill, A. D. (1982). Vulnerability to suicide. In E. L. Bassuk, S. C. Schoonover, & A. D. Gill (Eds.), *Lifelines: Clinical perspectives on suicide.* New York: Plenum Press.

Gillberg, C. (1992). Subgroups in autism: Are there behavioral phenotypes typical of underlying medical conditions? *J. Intellectual Disability Res., 36*(3), 201–214.

Gillberg, C., & Svendsen, P. (1983). Childhood psychosis and computed brain scan findings. *J. Autism Dev. Dis., 13,* 19–32.

Gillham, J. E., Reivich, K. J., Jaycox, L. H., & Seligman, M. E. (1995). Prevention of depressive symptoms in schoolchildren: Two-year follow-up. *Psychol. Sci., 6*(6), 343–351.

Gilmore, K. (1995). Gender identity disorder in a girl: Insights from adoption. *J. Amer. Psychoanal. Assoc., 43*(1), 39–59.

Gilovich, T. et al. (1996). People don't notice you as much as you think they do. *APA Monitor, 27*(10).

Ginns, E. I., Ott, J., Egeland, J. A., Allen, C. R., et al. (1996, April). A genome-wide search for chromosomal loci linked to bipolar affective disorder in the Old Order Amish. *Nature Genetics, 12,* 431–435.

Ginsberg, B. G. (1984). Beyond behavior modification: Client-centered play therapy with the retarded. *Acad. Psychol. Bull., 6*(3), 321–334.

Gladstone, T. R. & Kaslow, N. J. (1995). Depression and attributions in children and adolescents: A meta-analytic review. *J. Abnorm. Child Psychol., 23*(5), 597–606.

Glaser, R., Kiecolt-Glaser, J. K., Bonneau, R. H., Malarkey, W., Kennedy, S., & Hughes, J. (1992). Stress-induced modulation of the immune response to recombinant hepatitis B vaccine. *Psychosom. Med., 54,* 22–29.

Glassman, A. H. et al. (1984). Cigarette craving, smoking withdrawal, and clonidine. *Science, 226*(4676), 864–866.

Glassman, J. N., Rich, C. L., Darko, D., & Clarkin, A. (1991). Menstrual dysfunction in bulimia. *Ann. Clin. Psychiat., 3*(2), 161–165.

Glausiusz, J. (1996, January). The genes of 1995. *Discover,* p. 36.

Glausiusz, J. (1997, January). The genes of 1996. *Discover,* p. 36.

Glazer, S. (1993, February 26). Violence against women: Is the problem more serious than statistics indicate? *CQ Researcher, 3*(8), 169–192.

Gleaves, D. H., Williamson, D. A., & Barker, S. E. (1993). Confirmatory factor analysis of a multidimensional model of bulimia nervosa. *J. Abnorm. Psychol., 102*(1), 173–176.

Gleick, E. (1995, July 10). Sobering times for A. A. *Time,* pp. 49–50.

Gleser, G. C., Green, B. L., & Winget, C. (1981). *Prolonged psychological effects of disaster: A study of Buffalo Creek.* New York: Academic Press.

Glogower, F. D., Fremouw, W. J., & McCroskey, J. C. (1978). A component analysis of cognitive restructuring. *Cog. Ther. Res., 2*(3), 209–223.

Glynn, S. M. (1990). Token economy approaches for psychiatric patients: Progress and pitfalls of chronic psychiatric illness. *Behav. Mod., 14*(4), 383–407.

Glynn, S. M., Eth, S., Randolph, E. T., Foy, D. W. et al. (1995). Behavioral family therapy for Vietnam combat veterans with posttraumatic stress disorder. *J. Psychother. Prac. Res., 4*(3), 214–223.

Goate, A., Chartier, H. M., Mullan, M., et al. (1991). Segregation of a missense mutation in the amyloid precursor protein gene with familial Alzheimer's disease. *Nature, 349*(6311), 704–706.

Goate, A., Chartier-Harlin, M. C., Mullan, M., Brown, J., Crawford, F., Fidani, L., Giuffra, L., Haynes, A., Irving, N., & James, L., (1991). *Nature, 350,* 564.

Goisman, R. M., Goldenberg, I., Vasile, R. G., & Keller, M. B. (1995). Comorbidity of anxiety disorders in a multicenter anxiety study. *Comprehen. Psychiat., 36*(4), 303–311.

Goisman, R. M., Warshaw, M. G., Steketee, G. S., Fierman, E. J. et al. (1995). DSM-IV and the disappearance of agoraphobia without a history of panic disorder: New data on a controversial diagnosis. *Amer. J. Psychiat., 152*(10), 1438–1443.

Gold, E. R. (1986). Long-term effects of sexual victimization in childhood: An attributional approach. *J. Cons. Clin. Psychol., 54,* 471–475.

Gold, M. S. (1986). *The facts about drugs and alcohol.* New York: Bantam.

Gold, M. S., Miller, N. S., Stennie, K., & Populla-Vardi, C. (1995). Epidemiology of benzodiazepine use and dependence. *Psychiatr. Ann., 25*(3), 146–148.

Goldberg, D. (1995). Cost effectiveness studies in the evaluation of mental health services in the community: Current knowledge and unsolved problems. XIIth AEP Congress: Improvement of the quality of life in community care in schizophrenia. *Inter. Clin. Psychopharmacol., 9*(Suppl. 5), 29–34.

Goldberg, J. F., Harrow, M., & Grossman, L. S. (1995). Recurrent affective syndromes in bipolar and unipolar mood disorders at follow-up. *Brit. J. Psychiat., 166,* 382–385.

Goldbloom, D. S., Hicks, L. K., & Garkinkel, P. E. (1990). Platelet serotonin uptake in bulimia nervosa. *Bio. Psychiat., 28*(7), 644–647.

Golden, M. (1964). Some effects of combining psychological tests on clinical inferences. *J. Cons. Clin. Psychol., 28,* 440–446.

Golden, R. N., & Gilmore, J. H. (1990). Serotonin and mood disorders. *Psychiatr. Ann., 20*(10), 580–588.

Goldfried, M. R., & Wolfe, B. E. (1996). Psychotherapy practice and research. Repairing a strained alliance. *Amer. Psychol., 51*(10), 1007–1016.

Goldiamond, I. (1965). Self-control procedures in personal behavior problems. *Psychol. Rep., 17,* 851–868.

Golding, J. M. (1994). Sexual assault history and physical health in randomly selected Los Angeles women. *Hlth. Psychol., 13*(2), 130–138.

Goldman, A., & Greenberg, L. (1992). Comparison of integrated systemic and emotionally focused approaches to couples therapy. *J. Cons. Clin. Psychol., 60*(6), 962–969.

Goldman, J. G. (1995). A mutual story-telling technique as an aid to integration after abreaction in the treatment of MPD. *Dissociat. Prog. Dissociat. Disorders 8*(1), 53–60.

Goldman, M. (1992). Kleptomania: An overview. *Psychiatr. Ann., 22*(2), 68–71.

Goldstein, A. (1994). *Addiction: From biology to drug policy.* New York: W. H. Freeman.

Goldstein, G. (1990). Comprehensive Neuropsychological Assessment Batteries. In G. Goldstein & M. Hersen (Eds.), *Handbook of psychological assessment* (2nd ed.). New York: Pergamon Press.

Goldstein, G., & Hersen, M. (1990). Historical Perspectives. In G. Goldstein & M. Hersen (Eds.), *Handbook of psychological assessment* (2nd ed.). New York: Pergamon Press.

Goldstein, H., Kaczmarek, L., Pennington, R., & Shafer, K. (1992). Peer-mediated intervention: Attending to, commenting on, and acknowledging the behavior of preschoolers with autism. *J. Appl. Behav. Anal., 25*(2), 289–305.

Goldstein, M. J. (1985). Family factors that antedate the onset of schizophrenia and related disorders: The results of a fifteen-year prospective longitudinal study. *Acta Psychiatr. Scandin., Suppl., 319*(71), 7–18.

Goldstein, M. J. (1987). Treatment of families of schizophrenic patients: Theory, practice, and research. *Inter. J. Fam. Psychiat., 8*(2), 99–115.

Goldstein, M. J (1995). Psychoeducation and relapse prevention. XIIth AEP Congress: Improvement of compliance: Quality assurance: Increased quality of life in community care in schizophrenia. *Inter. Clin. Psychopharmacol., 9*(Suppl. 5), 59–69.

Goldstein, M. J. (1991). Psychosocial (nonpharmacologic) treatments for schizophrenia. In A. Tasman & S. M. Goldfinger (Eds.), *American Psychiatric Press review of psychiatry* (Vol. 10). Washington, DC: American Psychiatric Press.

Goldstein, M. J., & Miklowitz, D. J. (1995). The effectiveness of psychoeducational family therapy in the treatment of schizophrenic disorders. [Special issue: The effectiveness of marital and family therapy]. *J. Marital Fam. Ther., 21*(4), 371–376.

Goldstein, M. J., & Palmer, J. O. (1975). *The experience of anxiety: A casebook* (2nd ed.). New York: Oxford University Press.

Goldstein, R. B., Wickramaratne, P. J., Horwath, E., & Weissman, M. M. (1997). Familial aggregation and phenomenology of "early"-onset (at or before age 20 years) panic disorder. *Arch. Gen. Psychiat., 54,* 271–278.

Goldstrom, I. D., Manderscheid, R. W., & Rudolph, L. A. (1992). Mental health services in state adult correctional facilities. In R. W. Manderscheid & M. A. Sonnenschein (Eds.), *Mental health, United States, 1992.* Washington, DC: U. S. Department of Health and Human Services.

Goleman, D. (1995, May 2). Biologists find site of working memory. *The New York Times,* pp. C1, C9.

Goleman, D. (1995, September 6). Depression in the old can be deadly, but the symptoms are often missed. *The New York Times,* p. C10.

Goleman, D. (1995, October 4). Eating disorder rates surprise the experts. *The New York Times,* p. C11.

Goleman, D. (1995, June 13). Provoking a patient's worst fears to determine the brain's role. *The New York Times,* pp. C1, C10.

Goleman, D. (1996, May 1). Higher suicide risk for perfectionists. *The New York Times,* p. C12.

Goleman, D., & Gurin, J. (1993). *Mind/body medicine.* Yonkers, NY: Consumers Union of United States, Inc.

Goleman, D., & Gurin, J. (1993). Mind/body medicine-At last. *Psychol. Today, 26*(2), 16, 80.

Gonzalez, R. G. (1996). Molecular and functional magnetic resonance neuroimaging for the study of dementia. In R. J. Wurtman, S. Corkin, J. H. Growdon, & R. M. Nitsch (Eds.), *The neurobiology of Alzheimer's disease.* New York: New York Academy of Sciences.

Good, M. (1995). A comparison of the effects of jaw relaxation and music on postoperative pain. *Nursing Res., 44*(1), 52–57.

Goodman, B. M., Carnes, M., & Lent, S. J. (1994). Model simulation of ACTH pulsatility. *Life Sciences, 54*(22), 1659–1669.

Goodman, D. (1992). NIMH grantee finds drug responses differ among ethnic groups. *ADAMHA News, 18*(1), p. 5.

Goodman, L. S., & Gilman, A. (Eds.) (1990). *The pharmacological basis of therapeutics* (8th ed.). New York: Pergamon Press.

Goodman, R. (1990). Technical note: Are perinatal complications causes or consequences of autism? *J. Child Psychol. Psychiat. Allied Disc., 31*(5), 809–812.

Goodman, W. K., McDougle, C., & Price, L. H. (1992). Pharmacotherapy of Obsessive Compulsive Disorder. *J. Clin. Psychiat., 53*(Suppl. 4), 29–37.

Goodwin, C. J. (1995). *Research in psychology: Methods and design.* New York: Wiley.

Goodwin, D. W. (1976). *Is alcoholism hereditary?* New York: Oxford University Press.

Goodwin, D. W. (1976). Adoption studies of alcoholism. *J. Operational Psychiat., 7*(1), 54–63.

Goodwin, D. W. (1984). Studies of familial alcoholism: A review. *J. Clin. Psychiat., 45*(12, Sect. 2), 14–17.

Goodwin, D. W., Schulsinger, F., Hermansen, L., Guze, S. B., & Winokur, G. A. (1973). Alcohol problems in adoptees raised apart from alcoholic biological parents. *Arch. Gen. Psychiat., 128,* 239–243.

Goodwin, F. K. (1993). Predictors of antidepressant response. *Bull. Menninger Clin., 57*(2), 146–160.

Goodwin, F. K., & Jamison, K. R. (1984). The natural course of manic-depressive illness. In R. M. Post & J. C. Ballenger (Eds.), *Neurobiology of mood disorders.* Baltimore: Williams & Wilkins.

Goodwin, F. K., & Jamison, K. R. (1990). *Manic-depressive illness.* New York: Oxford University Press.

Goodwin, F. K., Wirz-Justice, A., & Wehr, T. A. (1982). Evidence that pathophysiology of depression and the mechanism of action of antidepressant drugs both involve alterations in circadian rhythms. In E. Costa & G. Racagni (Eds.), *Typical and atypical antidepressants: Clinical practice.* New York: Raven Press.

Goodwin, G. M. (1992). Tricyclic and newer antidepressants. In E. S. Paykel (Ed.), *Handbook of affective disorders.* New York: Guilford.

Goodwin, J. (1980). The etiology of combat-related posttraumatic stress disorders. In T. Williams (Ed.), *Posttraumatic stress disorders of the Vietnam veteran: Observations and recommendations for the psychological treatment of the veteran and his family.* Cincinnati: Disabled American Veterans.

Goodyear-Smith, F. A., Laidlaw, T. M., & Large, R. G. (1997). Surveying families accused of childhood sexual abuse: A comparison of British and New Zealand results. *Appl. Cog. Psychol., 11,* 31–34.

Goodyer, I. M., Herbert, J., Tamplin, A., Secher, S. M., & Pearson, J. (1997). Short-term outcome of major depression: II. Life events, family dysfunction, and friendship difficulties as predictors of persistent disorder. *J. Amer. Acad. Child Adol. Psychiat., 36*(4), 474–480.

Gordis, E. (1991). *Alcohol research: Promise for the decade.* Rockville, MD: National Institute of Alcohol Abuse and Alcoholism.

Gordon, R. A. (1990). *Anorexia and Bulimia.* Cambridge: Basil Blackwell.

Gorelick, P. B., Amico, L. L., Ganellen, R. et al. (1988). Transient global amnesia and thalamic infarction. *Neurology, 38,* 496–499.

Gorenstein, C., Bernik, M. A., Pompéia, S., & Marcourakis, T. (1995). Impairment of performance associated with long-term use of benzodiazepines. *J. Psychopharmacol., 9*(4), 313–318.

Gorman, C. (1995, November 13). Trapped in the body of a man? *Time,* pp. 94–95.

Gorman, J. M., Papp, L. A., & Coplan, J. D. (1995). Neuroanatomy and neurotransmitter function in panic disorder. In S. P. Roose & R. A. Glick (Eds.), *Anxiety as symptom and signal.* Hillsdale, NJ: The Analytic Press.

Gorwood, P., Leboyer, M., Jay, M., Payan, C. et al. (1995). Gender and age at onset in schizophrenia: Impact of family history. *Amer. J. Psychiat., 152*(2), 208–212.

Goshen, C. E. (1967). *Documentary history of psychiatry: A source book on historical principles.* New York: Philosophy Library.

Gossy, M. (1995). *Freudian slips: Woman, writing, the foreign tongue.* Ann Arbor: University of Michigan Press.

Gotlib, I. H., Lewinsohn, P. M., & Seeley, J. R. (1995). Symptoms versus a diagnosis of depression: Differences in psychosocial functioning. *J. Cons. Clin. Psychol., 63*(1), 90–100.

Gotlib, I. H., & Robinson, L. A. (1982). Responses to depressed individuals: Discrepancies between self-report and observer-related behavior. *J. Abnorm. Behav., 91*(4), 231–240.

Gottesman, I. I. (1991). *Schizophrenia genesis.* New York: W. H. Freeman.

Gottfredson, D. C. & Koper, C. S. (1996). Race and sex differences in the prediction of drug use. *J. Cons. Clin. Psychol., 64*(2), 305–313.

Gottheil, E. (1987). Drug use, misuse, and abuse by the elderly. *Med. Aspects Human Sex., 21*(3), 29–37.

Gottlieb, J. (1981). Mainstreaming: Fulfilling the promise? *Amer. J. Ment. Def., 86*(2), 115–126.

Gottlieb, J., Alter, M., & Gottlieb, B. W. (1991). Litigation involving people with mental retardation. In J. L. Matson & J. A. Mulick (Eds.), *Handbook of mental retardation.* New York: Pergamon Press.

Gottschalk, E. C. (1981, April 3). While more firms try jury consultants, debate grows over how much they help. *The Wall St. Journal.*

Gould, M. S., Shaffer, D., & Davies, M. (1990). Truncated pathways from childhood to adulthood: Attrition in follow-up studies due to death. In L. Robins & M. Rutter (Eds.), *Straight and devious pathways from childhood to adulthood.* Cambridge, England: Cambridge University Press.

Gowers, S. G., North, C. D., & Byram, V. (1996). Life event precipitants of adolescent anorexia nervosa. *J. Child Psychol. Psychiat., 37*(4), 469–477.

Graham, J., & Gaffan, E. A. (1997). Fear of water in children and adults: Etiology and familial effects. *Behav. Res. Ther., 35*(2), 91–108.

Graham, J. R. (1977). *The MMPI: A practical guide.* New York: Oxford University Press.

Graham, J. R. (1987). *The MMPI: A practical guide* (2nd ed.). New York: Oxford University Press.

Graham, J. R. (1993). *MMPI-2: Assessing personality and psychopathology* (2nd ed.). New York: Oxford University Press.

Graham, J. R., & Lilly, R. S. (1984). *Psychological testing.* Englewood Cliffs, NJ: Prentice Hall.

Graham, K., Clarke, D., Bois, C., Carver, V., et al. (1996). Addictive behavior of older adults. *Addic. Behav., 21*(3), 331–346.

Gramzow, R., & Tangney, J. P. (1992). Proneness to shame and the narcissistic personality. *Pers. Soc. Psychol. Bull., 18*(3), 369–376.

Graves, J. S. (1993). Living with mania: a study of outpatient group psychotherapy for bipolar patients. *Amer. J. Psychother., 47*(1), 113–126.

Gray, H. (1959). *Anatomy of the human body* (27th ed.). Philadelphia: Lea & Febiger.

Gray, J. A. (1982). *The neuropsychology of anxiety.* New York: Oxford University Press.

Gray, J. A. (1985). Issues in the neuropsychology of anxiety. In A. H. Tuma & J. D. Maser (Eds.), *Anxiety and the anxiety disorders.* Hillside, NJ: Erlbaum.

Gray, J. A. (1987). *The psychology of fear and stress* (2nd ed). Cambridge, England: Cambridge University Press.

Gray, J. A. (1995) Neural systems, emotion and personality. In J. Madden, S. Matthysse, & J. Barchas (Eds.), *Adaptation, learning and affect.* New York: Raven Press.

Gray, J. A. & McNaughton, N. (1996). The neuropsychology of anxiety: Reprise. In D. A. Hope (Ed.), *The Nebraska Symposium on Motivation: Vol. 43.* Lincoln: University of Nebraska Press.

Greeley, A. M. (1991). *Faithful attraction.* New York: Tor Books.

Green, A. H. (1989). Physical and sexual abuse of children. In H. I. Kaplan & B. J. Sadock (Eds.), *Comprehensive textbook of psychiatry/5*–Volume 2 (5th ed.). Baltimore: Williams & Wilkins.

Green, B. L., Grace, M. C., Lindy, J. D., Gleser, G. C. et al. (1990). Risk factors for PTSD and other diagnoses in a general sample of Vietnam veterans. *Amer. J. Psychiat., 147*(6), 729–733.

Green, S. A. (1985). *Mind and body: The psychology of physical illness.* Washington, DC: American Psychiatric Press.

Greenberg, D., & Marks, I. (1982). Behavioral therapy of uncommon referrals. *Brit. J. Psychiat., 141,* 148–153.

Greenberg, E. (1989). Healing the borderline. *Gestalt Journal, 12*(2), 11–55.

Greenberg, L., Elliott, R., & Lietaer, G. (1994). Research on experiential psychotherapies. In A. E. Bergin & S. L. Garfield (Eds.), *Handbook of psychotherapy and behavior change.* New York: Wiley.

Greenberg, R. P., & Bornstein, R. F. (1988). The dependent personality: II Risk for psychological disorders. *J. Pers. Disorders, 2*(2), 136–143.

Greenblatt, M. (1984). ECT: Please, no more regulations! *Amer. J. Psychiat., 14*(11), 1409–1410.

Greene, R. W., Biederman, J., Faraone, S. V., Ouellette, C., et al. (1996). Toward a new psychometric definition of social disability in children with attention-deficit hyperactivity disorder. *J. Amer. Acad. Child Adol. Psychiat., 35*(5), 571–578.

Greenfield, S., Swartz, M., Landerman, L., & George, L. (1993). Long-term psychosocial effects of childhood exposure to parental problem drinking. *Amer. J. Psychiat., 150*(4), 608–619.

Greenhill, L. L. (1992). Pharmacologic treatment of attention deficit hyperactivity disorder. *Psychiatr. Clin. N. Amer., 15*(1), 1–27.

Greenspan, R. J. (1995, April). Understanding the genetic construction of behavior. *Scientif. Amer.*, pp. 72–78.

Greer, S. (1991). Psychological response to cancer and survival. *Psychol. Med., 21,* 43–49.

Greist, J. H. (1990). Treatment of obsessive compulsive disorder: Psychotherapies, drugs, and other somatic treatment. *J. Clin. Psychol., 51*(Suppl. 8), 44–50.

Greist, J. H. (1992). An integrated approach to treatment of obsessive-compulsive disorder. *J. Clin. Psychiat., 53*(Suppl. 4), 38–41.

Greist, J. H., Jefferson, J. W., Kobak, K. A., Katzelnick, D. J., & Serlin, R. C. (1995). Efficacy and tolerability of serotonin transport inhibitors in obsessive-compulsive disorder. *Arch. Gen. Psychiat., 52,* 53–60.

Greist, J. H., Jefferson, J. W., Kobak, K. A., Katzelnick, D. J., et al. (1995). Efficacy and tolerability of serotonin transport inhibitors in obsessive-compulsive disorder: A meta-analysis. *Arch. Gen. Psychiat., 52*(1), 53–60.

Greist, J. H., & Klein, M. H. (1980). Computer programs for patients, clinicians, and researchers in psychiatry. In J. B. Sidowski, J. H. Johnson, & T. A. Williams (Eds.), *Technology in mental health care delivery systems.* Norwood, NJ: Ablex.

Gresham, A. C. (1993). The insanity plea: A futile defense for serial killers. *Law Psychol. Rev., 17,* 193–208.

Gresham, A. C. (1993). The insanity plea: A futile defense for serial killers. *Law Psychol. Rev., 17,* 193–208.

Griffith, J. J., Mednick, S. A., Schulsinger, F., & Diderichsen, B. (1980). Verbal associative disturbances in children at high risk for schizophrenia. *J. Abnorm. Psychol., 89,* 125–131.

Griffiths, A. J. F., Miller, J. H., Suzuki, D. T., Lewontin, R. C., & Gelbart, W. M. (1996). *An introduction to genetic analysis* (6th ed.). New York: W. H. Freeman.

Grigg, J. R. (1988). Imitative suicides in an active duty military population. *Mil. Med., 153*(2), 79–81.

Grilo, C. M., Becker, D. F., Fehon, D. C., Walker, M. L., et al. (1996). Gender differences in personality disorders in psychiatrically hospitalized adolescents. *Amer. J. Psychiat., 153*(8), 1089–1091.

Grinspoon, L., & Bakalar, J. B. (1986). Can drugs be used to enhance the psychotherapeutic process? *Amer. J. Psychother., 40*(3), 393–404.

Grinspoon, L. et al. (Eds.). (1986). Paraphilias. *Harvard Med. School Ment. Hlth. Newsletter, 3*(6), 1–5.

Grinspoon, L. et al. (Eds.). (1986, October) Mental retardation. *Part. I. Ment. Hlth. Letter, 3*(4).

Grisez, G., & Boyle, J. M., Jr. (1979). *Life and death with liberty and justice: A contribution to the euthanasia debate.* Notre Dame, IN: University Notre Dame.

Grisso, T., & Appelbaum, P. S. (1995). The MacArthur treatment competence study. III. Abilities of patients to consent to psychiatric and medical treatments. *Law Human Behav., 19*(2), 149–174

Grizenko, N., Cvejic, H., Vida, S., & Sayegh, L. (1991). Behaviour problems of the mentally retarded. *Canad. J. Psychiat., 36*(10), 712–717.

Grob, G. N. (1966). *State and the mentally ill: A history of Worcester State Hospital in Massachusetts, 1830–1920.* Chapel Hill: University of North Carolina.

Gross-Isseroff, R., Sasson, Y., Voet, H., Hendler, T. et al. (1996). Alternation learning in obsessive-compulsive disorder. *Bio. Psychiat., 39,* 733–738.

Grossman, L. S., & Wasyliw, O. (1988). A Psychometric study of stereotypes: Assessment of malingering in a criminal forensic group. *J. Pers. Assess. 52*(3), 549–563.

Grossman, S. P. (1986). The role of glucose, insulin and glucagon in the regulation of food intake and body weight. *Neurosci. Biobehav. Rev., 10*(3), 295–315.

Grossman, S. P. (1990). Brain mechanisms concerned with food intake and body-weight regulation. In M. M. Fichter (Ed.), *Bulimia nervosa: Basic research, diagnosis and therapy.* Chichester, England: Wiley.

Groth, A. N., & Birnbaum, H. J. (1978). Adult sexual orientation and attraction to under-age persons. *Arch. Sex. Behav., 7,* 175–181.

Grotstein, J. C. (1996). Object relations theory. In E. Nersessian, & R. G. Kopff (Eds.), *Textbook of psychoanalysis.* Washington, DC: American Psychiatric Press.

Grotstein, J. S. (1995). Orphans of the "Real": II. The future of object relations theory in the treatment of the psychoses and other primitive mental disorders. *Bull. Menninger Clin., 59*(3), 312–332.

Grove, W. M. & Tellegen, A. (1991). Problems in the classification of personality disorders. *J. Pers. Disorders, 5,* 31–42.

Gruenberg, E. M. (1980). Mental disorders. In J. M. Last (Ed.), *Maxcy-Rosenau public health and preventive medicine* (11th ed.). New York: Appleton-Century-Crofts.

Guastello, S. J., & Reike, M. L. (1991). A review and critique of honesty test research. *Behav. Sci. Law, 9*(4), 501–523.

Guay, D. R. (1995). The emerging role of valproate in bipolar disorder and other psychiatric disorders. *Pharmacotherapy, 15*(5), 631–647.

Gudjonsson, G. H. (1997). Accusations by adults of childhood sexual abuse: A survey of the members of the British False Memory Society (BFMS). *Appl. Cog. Psychol., 11,* 3–18.

Guerrero, J., & Reiter, R. (1992). A brief survey of pineal gland-immune system interrelationships. *Endocrine Res., 18*(2), 91–113.

Guillard, P., & Guillard, C. (1987). Suicide and attempted suicide in Martinique. *Psychol. Med., 19*(5), 629–630.

Gunby, P. (1981). Many cancer patients receiving THC as antiemetic. *Med. News, 245*(15), 1515.

Gunderson, J. G. (1988). Personality disorders. In A. M. Nicholi Jr. (Ed.), *The new Harvard guide to psychiatry.* Cambridge, MA: Belknap Press.

Gunderson, J. G. (1996). The borderline patient's intolerance of aloneness: Insecure attachments and therapist availability. *Amer. J. Psychiat., 153*(6), 752–758.

Gunderson, J. G. & Sabo, A. N. (1993). The phenomenological and conceptual interface between borderline personality disorder and PTSD. *Amer. J. Psychiat., 150,* 19–27.

Gunn, J., Maden, A., & Swinton, M. (1991). Treatment needs of prisoners with psychiatric disorders. *Brit. Med. J., 303,* 338–341.

Gupta, R. (1988). Alternative patterns of seasonal affective disorder: Three case reports from North India. *Amer. J. Psychiat., 145*(4), 515–516.

Gur, R. C., Skolnick, B. E., & Gur, R. E. (1994). Effects of emotional discrimination tasks on cerebral blood flow: Regional activation and its relation to performance. *Brain Cog., 25*(2), 271–286.

Gur, R. E., & Pearlson, G. D. (1993). Neuroimaging in schizophrenia research. *Schizo. Bull., 19,* 337–353.

Gurling, H. M., Sherrington, R. P., Brynjolfsson, J., Read, T., et al. (1989). Recent and future molecular genetic research into schizophrenia. *Schizo. Bull., 15*(3), 373–382.

Gurman, A., Kniskern, D. P., & Pinsof, W. M. (1986). Research on the process and outcome of marital and family therapy. In S. L. Garfield and A. E. Bergin (Eds.), *Handbook of psychotherapy and behavior change: An evaluative analysis.* (3rd ed.). New York: Wiley.

Gustafson, R. (1992). The relationship between perceived parents' child-rearing practices, own later rationality, and own later depression. *J. Rat. Emot. Cog. Behav. Ther., 10*(4), 253–258.

HEW [Health Education and Welfare]. (1976). *Even my kids didn't know I was an alcoholic: An interview with Dick Van Dyke (ADM* 76–348). Washington, DC: U.S. Government Printing Office.

Haaga, D. A. F., & Beck, A. T. (1992). Cognitive therapy. In E. S. Paykel (Ed.), *Handbook of affective disorders.* New York: Guilford.

Haas, G. L., Radomsky, E. D., Glanz, L., Keshavan, M. S., Mann, J. J., & Sweeney, J. A. (1993, May). *Suicidal behavior in schizophrenia: Course-of-illness predictors.* Presented at the annual meeting of the Society of Biological Psychiatry, San Francisco.

Hackerman, F., Buccino, D., Gallucci, G., & Schmidt, C. W. Jr. (1996). The effect of a split in WAIS-R VIQ and PIQ scores on patients with cognitive impairment and psychiatric illness. *J. Neuropsych. Clin. Neurosci. 8,* 85–87.

Hadley, S. W., & Strupp, H. H. (1976). Contemporary views of negative effects in psychotherapy: An integrated account. *Arch. Gen. Psychiat., 33*(1), 1291–1302.

Haefely, W. (1990). Benzodiazepine receptor and ligands: Structural and functional differences. In I. Hindmarch, G. Beaumont, S. Brandon, & B. E. Leonard (Eds.), *Benzodiazepines: Current concepts* (Pt. 1). Chichester, England: Wiley.

Haefely, W. (1990). The GABA-benzodiazepine receptor: Biology and pharmacology. In G. Burrows, M. Roth, & R. Noyes (Eds.), *Handbook of anxiety* (Vol. 3). Amsterdam: Elsevier Science Publishers.

Hafner, H., & an der Heiden, W. (1988). The mental health care system in transition: A study in organization, effectiveness, and costs of complementary care for schizophrenic patients. In C. N. Stefanis & A. D. Rabavilis (Eds.), *Schizophrenia: Recent biosocial developments.* New York: Human Sciences.

Hagan, T. (1991). Special services for women in treatment. In *National Conference on Drug Abuse Research and Practice Conference Highlights.* Rockville, MD: National Institute on Drug Abuse.

Hage, J. J., & Bouman, F. G. (1992). Silicone genital prosthesis for female-to-male transsexuals. *Plastic Reconstructive Surgery, 90*(3), 516–519.

Halaas, J. L., Gajiwala, K. F., Maffei, M., Cohen, S. L., et al. (1995). Weight-reducing effects of the plasma protein encoded by the obese gene. *Science, 269,* 543–546.

Hale, C. A., & Borkowski, J. G. (1991). Attention, memory and cognition. In J. L. Matson & J. A. Mulick (Eds.), *Handbook of mental retardation.* New York: Pergamon Press.

Hale, E. (1983, April 17). Inside the divided mind. *New York Times Magazine,* pp. 100–106.

Hale, R. L. (1993). The application of learning theory to serial murder: or "You too can learn to be a serial killer." *Amer. J. Criminal Justice, 17*(2), 37–45.

Hales, R. E., Hilty, D. A., & Wise, M. G. (1997). A treatment algorithm for the management of anxiety in primary care practice. *J. Clin. Psychiat., 58*(Suppl. 3), 76–80.

Haley, W. E., West, C. A. C., Wadley, V. G., Ford, G. R. et al. (1995). Psychological, social, and health impact of caregiving: A comparison of black and white dementia family caregivers and noncaregivers. *Psychol. Aging, 10*(4), 540–552.

Hall, C. S. (1951). What people dream about. *Scientif. Amer., 184,* 60–63.

Hall, L. (with L. Cohn). (1980). *Eat without fear.* Santa Barbara, CA: Gurze.

Hall, S. M., Tunstall, C., Rugg, D. et al. (1985). Nicotine gum and behavioral treatment in smoking cessation. *J. Cons. Clin. Psychol., 53,* 256–258.

Hallam, R. S., & Rachman, S. (1976). Current status of aversion therapy. In M. Hersen, R. Eisler, & P. Miller (Eds.), *Progress in behavior modification* (Vol. 2). New York: Academic Press.

Halmi, K. A. (1985). Behavioral management for anorexia nervosa. In D. M. Garner & P. E. Garfinkel (Eds.), *Handbook of psychotherapy for anorexia nervosa and bulimia.* New York: Guilford.

Halmi, K. A. (1985). Classification of the eating disorders. *J. Psychiatr. Res., 19,* 113–119.

Halmi, K. A. (1995). Current concepts and definitions. In G. Szmukler, C. Dare, & J. Treasure (Eds.), *Handbook of eating disorders: Theory, treatment and research.* Chichester, England: Wiley.

Halmi, K. A., Agras, W. S., Kaye, W. H., & Walsh, B. T. (1994). Evaluation of pharmacologic treatments in eating disorders. In R. F. Prien & D. S. Robinson (Eds.), *Clinical evaluation of psychotropic drugs: Principles and guidelines.* New York: Raven Press, Ltd.

Halmi, K. A., Eckert, E., Marchik, P. A., et al. (1991). Comorbidity of psychiatric diagnoses in anorexia nervosa. *Arch. Gen. Psychiat., 48,* 712–718.

Halmi, K. A. & Sunday, S. R. (1991). Temporal patterns of hunger and satiety ratings and related cognitions in anorexia and bulimia. *Appetite, 16,* 219–237.

Halmi, K. A., Sunday, S. R., Puglisi, A., et al. (1989). Hunger and satiety in anorexia and bulimia nervosa. *Ann. NY Acad. Sci., 575,* 431–445.

Halstead, W. C. (1947). *Brain and intelligence: A quantitative study of the frontal lobes.* Chicago: University of Chicago.

Hamilton, M. (1986). Electroconvulsive shock on serotonin activity. In S. Malitz & H. A. Sackeim (Eds.), *Electroconvulsive therapy: Clinical and basic research issues.* New York: Ann. NY Acad. Sci.

Hamilton, N. (1991). Intake and diagnosis of drug-dependent women. In *National Conference on Drug Abuse Research and Practice Conference Highlights.* Rockville, MD: National Institute on Drug Abuse.

Hamilton, S., Rothbart, M., & Dawes, R. N. (1986). *Sex Roles, 15*(5–6), 269–274.

Hammen, C. L., & Glass, D. R. (1975). Expression, activity, and evaluation of reinforcement. *J. Abnorm. Psychol., 84*(6), 718–721.

Hammen, C. L., & Krantz, S. (1976). Effect of success and failure on depressive cognitions. *J. Abnorm. Psychol., 85*(8), 577–588.

Hammer, E. (1981). Projective drawings. In A. I. Rabin (Ed.), *Assessment with projective techniques.* New York: Springer.

Hammer, T. (1993). Unemployment and mental health among young people: A longitudinal study. *J. Adolescence, 16,* 407–420.

Hammond, K. R., & Summers, D. A. (1965). A cognitive dependence on linear and non-linear cues. *Psychol. Rev., 72,* 215–224.

Hancock, L. N. (1996). Mother's little helper. *Newsweek,* March 18, 1996, 51–56.

Hankins, G. C., Vera, M. I., Barnard, G. W., & Herkov, M. J. (1994). Patient-therapist sexual involvement: A review of clinical and research data. *Bull. Amer. Acad. Psychiat. Law., 22*(1), 109–126.

Hantula, D. A., & Reilly, N. A. (1996). Reasonable accommodation for employees with mental disabilities: A mandate for effective supervision? *Behav. Sci. Law, 14,* 107–120.

Happé, F. G. E. (1995). The role of age and verbal ability in the theory of mind task performance of subjects with autism. *Child Devel., 66,* 843–855.

Happe, F. G. E. (1997). Central coherence and theory of mind in autism: Reading homographs in context. *Brit. J. Dev. Psychol., 15,* 1–12.

Harding, C. M., Zubin, J., & Strauss, J. S. (1992). Chronicity in schizophrenia: Revisited. *Brit. J. Psychiat., 161*(Suppl. 18), 27–37.

Hardt, J. V., & Kamiya, J. (1978). Anxiety change through electroencephalographic alpha feedback seen only in high anxiety subjects. *Science, 201*(4350), 79–81.

Hare, R. D. (1978). Electrodermal and cardiovascular correlates of sociopathy. In R. D. Hare & D. Shalling (Eds.), *Psychopathic behaviour: Approaches to research.* New York: Wiley.

Hare, R. D. (1978). Psychopathy and electrodermal responses to nonsignal stimulation. *Biol. Psychol., 6,* 237–246.

Hare, R. D. (1982). Psychopathy and physiological activity during anticipation of an aversive stimulus in a distraction paradigm. *Psychophysiology, 19*(3), 266–271.

Hare, R. D. (1982). Psychopathy and the personality dimensions of psychoticism, extraversion and neuroticism. *Pers. Individ. Diff., 3*(1), 35–42.

Hare, R. D. (1980). A research scale for the assessment of psychopathy in criminal populations. *Pers. Individ. Diff., 1*(2), 111–119.

Hare, R. D. (1993). *Without conscience: The disturbing world of the psychopaths among us.* New York: Pocket Books.

Hare, R. D., McPherson, L. M., & Forth, A. E. (1988). Male psychopaths and their criminal careers. *J Cons. Clin. Psychol., 56,* 710–714.

Harkavy, J. M., & Asnis, G. (1985). Suicide attempts in adolescence: Prevalence and implications. *N. Engl. J. Med., 313,* 1290–1291.

Harlow, H. F., & Harlow, M. K. (1965). The affectional systems. In A. Schrier, H. Harlow, & F. Stollnitz (Eds.), *Behavior of nonhuman primates* (Vol. 2). New York: Academic Press.

Haroutunian, V. (1991). Gross anatomy of the brain. In K. Davis, H.

Klar, & J. T. Coyle (Eds.), *Foundations of psychiatry.* Philadelphia: Saunders.

Harpur, T. J. & Hare, R. D. (1994). Assessment of psychopathy as a function of age. *J. Abnorm. Psychol., 102,* 604–609.

Harrell, R. F., Woodyard, E., & Gates, A. I. (1955). *The effects of mothers' diet on the intelligence of the offspring.* New York: Columbia University Press.

Harrington, D. L. et al. (1990). Procedural memory in Parkinson's disease: impaired motor but not visuoperceptual learning. *J. Clin. Exp. Neuropsych., 12,* 323–339.

Harrington, R. C., Fudge, H., Rutter, M. L., Bredenkamp, D., Groothues, C., & Pridham, J. (1993). Child and adult depression: A test of continuities with data from a family study. *Brit. J. Psychiat., 162,* 627–633.

Harris, A. H., Goldstein, D. S., & Brady, J. V. (1977). Visceral learning: Cardiovascular conditioning in primates. In J. Beatty & H. Legewie (Eds.), *Biofeedback and behavior.* New York: Plenum.

Harris, A., Ayers, T., & Leek, M. R. (1985). Auditory span of apprehension deficits in schizophrenia. *J. Nerv. Ment. Dis., 173*(11), 650–657.

Harris, B. (1979). Whatever happened to Little Albert? *Amer. Psychol., 34,* 151–160.

Harris, E. C., & Barraclough, B. (1997). Suicide as an outcome for mental disorders. *Brit. J. Psychiat., 170,* 205–228.

Harris, F. C., & Lahey, B. B. (1982). Subject reactivity in direct observation assessment: A review and critical analysis. *Clin. Psychol. Rev., 2,* 523–538.

Harris, F. C., & Lahey, B. B. (1986). Condition-related reactivity: The interaction of observation and intervention in increasing peer praising in preschool children. *Education and Treatment of Children, 9*(3), 221–231.

Harris, S. L. (1995). Autism. In M. Hersen & R. T. Ammerman, *Advanced abnormal psychology.* Hillsdale, NJ: Lawrence Erlbaum Associates, Publishers.

Harris, S. L., & Ersner-Hershfield, R. (1978). Behavioral suppression of seriously disruptive behavior in psychotic and retarded patients: A review of punishment and its alternatives. *Psychol. Bull., 85,* 1352–1375.

Harris, S. L., & Milch, R. E. (1981). Training parents as behavior modifiers for their autistic children. *Clin. Psychol. Rev., 1,* 49–63.

Harris, S. M. (1994). Racial differences in predictors of college women's body image attitudes. *Women Hlth., 21*(4), 89–104.

Harrison, P. J., & Roberts, G. W. (1991). "Life, Jim, but not as we know it?" Transmissible dementias and the prion protein. *Brit. J. Psychiat., 158,* 457–470.

Harrow, M. et al. (1988). A longitudinal study of thought disorder in manic patients. *Arch. Gen. Psychiat., 43*(8), 781–785.

Hart, B. (1993). Battered women and the criminal justice system. Special Issue: The impact of arrest on domestic assault. *Amer. Behav. Sci., 36*(5), 624–638.

Hart, B. (1993). The legal road to freedom. In M. Hansen & M. Harway (Eds.), *Battering and family therapy: A feminist perspective.* Newbury Park, CA: Sage.

Hart, B. L. (1985). *The behavior of domestic animals.* New York: W. H. Freeman.

Hart, K. J., & Ollendick, T. H. (1985). Prevalence of bulimia in working and university women. *Amer. J. Psychiat., 142*(7), 851–854.

Hart, K., & Kenny, M. E. (1995, August). *Adherence to the superwoman ideal and eating disorder symptoms among college women.* Paper read at American Psychological Association, New York.

Hart, S. N., & Brassard, M. R. (1987). A major threat to children's mental health: Psychological maltreatment. *Amer. Psychol., 42*(2), 160–165.

Hart, S. N., & Brassard, M. R. (1991). Psychological maltreatment: Progress achieved. *Developmental Psychopathology, 3*(1), 61–70.

Hart, S. N., Germain, R., & Brassard, M. R. (1987). The challenge: To better understand and combat the psychological maltreatment of children and youth. In M. R. Brassard, R. Germain, & S. N. Hart (Eds.), *Psychological maltreatment of children and youth.* New York: Pergamon.

Harter, S. & Marold, D. B. (1994). Psychosocial risk factors contributing to adolescent suicidal ideation. In G.G. Naom & S. Borst (Eds.), *New directions for child development, no. 64—Children, youth, and suicide: Developmental perspectives.* San Francisco, CA: Jossey-Bass.

Harth, S. C., & Thong, Y. H. (1995). Parental perceptions and attitudes about informed consent in clinical research involving children. *Soc. Sci. Med., 40*(11), 1573–1577.

Hartlage, S., Alloy, L. B., Vazquez, C., & Dykman, B. (1993). Automatic and effortful processing in depression. *Psychol. Bull., 113*(2), 247–278.

Hartmann, E. (1996). Who develops PTSD nightmares and who doesn't. In D. Barrett (Ed.), *Trauma and dreams.* Cambridge, MA: Harvard University Press.

Hartmann, U., & Langer, D. (1993). Combination of psychosexual therapy and intrapenile injections in the treatment of erectile dysfunctions: Rationale and predictors of outcome. *J. Sex Educ. Ther., 19,* 1–12.

Harvard School of Public Health (1995). *Binge drinking on American college campuses: A new look at an old problem.* Boston, Massachusetts.

Harvey, P. D. (1991). Cognitive and linguistic functions of adolescent children at risk for schizophrenia. In E. F. Walker (Ed.), Schizophrenia: A life-course developmental perspective. New York: Academic Press.

Hasin, D., Endicott, J., & Lewis, C. (1985). Alcohol and drug abuse in patients with affective syndromes. *Comprehen. Psychiat., 26, 283–295.*

Hatonen, T., Alila, A., & Laakso, M. L. (1996). Exogenous melatonin fails to counteract the light-induced phase delay of human melatonin rhythm. *Brain Res., 710*(1–2), 125–130.

Hauri, P., Chernik, D., Hawkins, D., & Mendels, J. (1974). Sleep of depressed patients in remission. *Arch. Gen. Psychiat., 31,* 386–391.

Hawton, K. (1986). *Suicide and attempted suicide among children and adolescents.* Beverly Hills, CA: Sage.

Hawton, K., & Catalan, J. (1990). Sex therapy for vaginismus: Characteristics of couples and treatment outcome. *Sex. Marital Ther., 5,* 39–48.

Hawton, K., Catalan, J., Martin, P., & Fagg, J. (1986). Long-term outcome of sex therapy. *Behav. Res. Ther., 24,* 665–675.

Hawton, K., Catalan, J., & Fagg, J. (1992). Sex therapy for erectile dysfunction: Characteristics of couples, treatment outcome, and prognostic factors. *Arch. Sex. Behav., 21,* 161–176.

Hawton, K., Cole, D., O'Grady, J., & Osborn, M. (1982). Motivational aspects of deliberate self-poisoning in adolescents. Brit. J. Psychiat., 141, 286–291.

Hawton, K., Fagg, J., Platt, S., & Hawkins, M. (1993). Factors associated with suicide following parasuicide in young people. *Brit. Med. J., 306,* 1641–1644.

Hawton, K., Haigh, R., Simkin, S., & Fagg, J. (1995). Attempted suicide in Oxford University students, 1976–1990. *Psychol. Med., 25*(1), 179–188.

Hawton, K., O'Grady, J., Osborn, M., & Cole, D. (1982). Adolescents who take overdoses: Their characteristics, problems and contacts with helping agencies. *Brit. J. Psychiat., 140,* 118–123.

Haxby, J. (1995, May 2). Cited in D. Goleman, "Biologists find site of working memory." *The New York Times,* pp. C1, C9.

Haxby, J. V., Ungerleider, L. G., Horwitz, B., Maisog, J. M., Rapoport, S. I., & Grady, C. L. (1996). Face encoding and recognition in the human brain. *Proc. Nat. Acad. Sci. USA, 93*(2), 922–927.

Hay, L. R., Hay, W. R., & Angle, H. V. (1977). The reactivity of self-recording: A case report of a drug abuser. Behav. Ther., 8(5), 1004–1007.

Hay, W. M., Hay, L. R., & Nelson, R. Q. (1977). The adaptation of covert modeling procedures to the treatment of chronic alcoholism and obsessive compulsive behavior: Two case reports. *Behav. Ther., 8(1),* 70–76.

Hayes, L. M., & Rowan, J. R. (1988). *National study of jail suicides: seven years later.* Alexandria, VA: National Center for Institutions and Alternatives.

Haynes, S. G., Feinleib, M., & Kannel, W. B. (1980). The relationship of psychosocial factors to coronary heart disease in the Framingham study: III. Eight-year incidence of coronary heart disease. *Amer. J. Epidemiol., 111,* 37–58.

Haynes, S. N. (1990). Behavioral assessment of adults. In G. Goldstein & M. Hersen (Eds.), Handbook of psychological assessment (2nd ed.). New York: Pergamon Press.

Hayward, C., Killen, J. D., Hammer, L. D., Litt, I. F., Wilson, D. M., Simmonds, B., & Taylor, C. B. (1992). Pubertal stage and panic attack history in sixth- and seventh-grade girls. *Amer. J. Psychiat., 149,* 1239–1243.

Hayward, M. D., & Taylor, J. E. (1965). A schizophrenic patient describes the action of intensive psychotherapy. *Psychiat. Quart., 30.*

Haywood, T. W., Kravitz, H. M., Grossman, L. S., Cavanaugh, J. L. et al. (1995). Predicting the "revolving door" phenomenon among patients with schizophrenia, schizoaffective, and affective disorders. *Amer. J. Psychiat., 152*(6), 856–861.

Hazell, P., & Lewin, T. (1993). Friends of adolescent suicide attempters and completers. *J. Amer. Acad. Child Adol. Psychiat., 32*(1), 76–81.

He, H., & Richardson, J. S. (1995). A pharmacological, pharmacokinetic and clinical overview of risperidone, a new antipsychotic that blocks serotonin 5–HT2 and dopamine D2 receptors. *Inter. Clin. Psychopharmacol., 10*(1), 19–30.

Healy, D., & Williams, J. M. (1988). Dysrhythmia, dysphoria, and depression: The interaction of learned helplessness and circadian dysrhythmia in the pathogenesis of depression. *Psychol. Bull., 103*(2), 163–178.

Heather, N., Winton, M., & Rollnick, S. (1982). An empirical test of "a cultural delusion of alcoholics." *Psychol. Rep., 50(2),* 379–382.

Heaton, R. K., Baade, L. E., & Johnson, K. L. (1978). Neuropsychological test results associated with psychiatric disorders in adults. *Psychol. Bull., 85,* 141–162.

Hedaya, R. J. (1996). *Understanding biological psychiatry.* New York: Norton.

Heflinger, C. A., Cook, V. J., & Thackrey, M. (1987). Identification of mental retardation by the System of Multicultural Pluralistic Assessment: Nondiscriminatory or nonexistent? *J. School Psychol., 25*(2), 177–183.

Heider, F. (1944). *Social perception and phenomenal causality. Psychol. Rev., 51,* 358–374.

Heider, F. (1958). *The psychology of interpersonal relations.* New York: Wiley.

Heikkinen, M., Aro, H., & Lonnqvist, J. (1992). Recent life events and their role in suicide as seen by the spouses. *Acta Psychiatr. Scandin., 86*(6), 489–494.

Heilbrun, A. B., & Witt, N. (1990). Distorted body image as a risk factor in anorexia nervosa: Replication and clarification. *Psychol. Rep., 66*(2), 407–416.

Heiman, J. R. (1977). A psychophysiological exploration of sexual-arousal patterns in females and males. *Psychophysiology, 14,* 266–274.

Heiman, J. R., Gladue, B. A., Roberts, C. W., & LoPiccolo, J. (1986). Historical and current factors discriminating sexually functional from sexually dysfunctional married couples. *J. Marital Fam. Ther., 12*(2), 163–174.

Heiman, J. R., & Grafton-Becker, V. (1989). Orgasmic disorders in women. In S. R. Leiblum & R. C. Rosen (Eds.), *Principles and practice of sex therapy: Update for the 1990's.* New York: Guilford.

Heiman, J. R., & LoPiccolo, J. (1988). *Becoming orgasmic: A personal and sexual growth program for women.* New York: Prentice Hall.

Heiman, J. R., LoPiccolo, L., & LoPiccolo, J. (1981). Treatment of sexual dysfunction. In A. S. Gurman & D. P. Kniskern (Eds.), *Handbook of family therapy.* New York: Brunner/Mazel.

Heimberg, R. G., Dodge, C. S., Hope, D. A., Kennedy, C. R. et al. (1990). Cognitive behavioral group treatment for social phobia: Comparison with a credible placebo control. *Cog. Ther. Res., 14*(1), 1–23.

Heimberg, R. G., Liebowitz, M. R., Hope, D. A., & Schneier, F. R. (1995). *Social Phobia: Diagnosis, assessment, and treatment.* New York: Guilford.

Heimberg, R. G., Salzman, D. G., Holt, C. S., & Blendall, K. (1991). *Cognitive behavioral treatment for social phobia: Effectiveness at five-year follow-up.* Manuscript submitted for publication.

Heimberg, R. G., Salzman, D. G., Holt, C. S., & Blendall, K. A. (1993). Cognitive-behavioral group treatment for social phobia: Effectiveness at five-year follow-up. *Cog. Ther. Res., 17,* 325–339.

Heinrichs, D. W., & Carpenter, W. T., Jr. (1983). The coordination of family therapy with other treatment modalities for schizophrenia. In W. McFarlane (Ed.), *Family therapy in schizophrenia.* New York: Guilford.

Heise, L., & Chapman, J. R. (1990). Reflections on a movement: The U.S. battle against women abuse. In M. Schuler (ed.), *Freedom from violence: Women's strategies round the world.* OEF International.

Heller, K. (1996). Coming of age of prevention science: Comments on the 1994 National Institute of Mental Health–Institute of Medicine Prevention Reports. *Amer. Psychologist, 51*(11), 1123–1127.

Hellerstein, D. J., Rosenthal, R. N., & Miner, C. R. (1995). A prospective study of integrated outpatient treatment for substance-abusing schizophrenic patients. *Amer. J. Addic., 4*(1), 33–42.

Hellerstein, D. J., Yanowitch, P., Rosenthal, J., Hemlock, C., et al. (1994). Long-term treatment of double depression: A preliminary study with serotonergic antidepressants. *Prog. Neuro-Psychopharmacol. Biol. Psychiat., 18,* 139–147.

Hellmich, N. (1995, July 21). Power rangers: Negative or empowering? *USA Today,* p. 4D

Hellström, K., & Öst, L.-G. (1996). Prediction of outcome in the treatment of specific phobia. A cross validation study. *Behav. Res. Ther., 34*(5/6), 403–411.

Helms, J. E. (1992). Why is there no study of cultural equivalence in standardized cognitive ability testing? *Amer. Psychol., 47*(9), 1083–1101.

Helzer, J. E., Burnam, A., & McEvoy, L. T. (1991). Alcohol abuse and dependence. In L. N. Robins & D. S. Regier (Eds.), *Psychiatric disorders in America: The epidemiological catchment area study.* New York: Free Press.

Hembree, W. C., Nahas, G. G., & Huang, H. F. S. (1979). Changes in human spermatozoa associated with high dose marihuana-smoking. In G. G. Nahas & W. D. M. Paton (Eds.), *Marihuana: Biological effects.* Elmsford, NY: Pergamon Press.

Henderson, D. J., Boyd, C. J., & Whitmarsh, J. (1995). Women and illicit drugs: Sexuality and crack cocaine. *Hlth. Care Women Inter., 16*(2), 113–124.

Hendin, H. (1987). Youth suicide: A psychosocial perspective. *Suic. Life Threat. Behav., 17*(2), 151–165.

Hendin, H. (1995). Assisted suicide, euthanasia, and suicide prevention: The implications of the Dutch experience. *Suic. Life-Threat. Behav., 25*(1), 193–205.

Hennager, K. (1993). Flying in dreams. In M. A. Carskadon (Ed.), *Encyclopedia of sleep and dreams.* New York: Macmillan.

Henriksson, M. M., Isometsa, E. T., Hietanen, P. S., Aro, H. M., & Lonnqvist, J. K. (1995). Research report. Mental disorders in cancer suicides. *J. Affect. Disorders, 36,* 11–20.

Herbert, J. D. (1995). An overview of the current status of social phobia. *Appl. Prev. Psychol., 4*(1), 39–51.

Herbert, T. B., & Cohen, S. (1993). Stress and immunity in humans: A meta-analytic review. *Psychosom. Med., 55,* 364–379.

Herbert, T. B., & Cohen, S. (1993). Depression and immunity: a meta-analytic review. *Psychol. Bull., 113*(3), 472–486.

Herek, G. M., & Capitanio, J. P. (1993). Public reaction to AIDS in the U.S.: A 2nd generation of stigma. *Amer. J. Pub. Hlth., 83*(4), 574–577.

Herek, G. M., & Glunt, E. K. (1988). An epidemic of stigma: Public reactions to AIDS. *Amer. Psychol., 43*(11), 886–891.

Herman, J. L., Perry, C., & Van Der Kolk, B. A. (1989). Childhood trauma in borderline personality disorder. *Amer. J. Psychiat., 146,* 490–495.

Hermann, C., Kim, M., & Blanchard, E. B. (1995). Behavioral and prophylactic pharmacological intervention studies of pediatric migraine: An exploratory meta-analysis. *Pain, 60*(3), 239–255.

Hermelin, B. (1976). Coding and the sense modalities. In L. Wing (Ed.), *Early childhood autism.* Oxford, England: Pergamon Press.

Hermesh, H., Aizenberg, D., Weizman, A., Lapidot, M., Mayor, C., & Munitz, H. (1992). Risk for definite neuroleptic malignant syndrome: A prospective study in 223 consecutive inpatients. *Brit. J. Psychiat.,* 161, 254–257.

Hernandez, J. (1992). Substance abuse among sexually abused adolescents and their families. *J. Adol. Hlth., 13*(8), 658–662.

Hersen, M., Bellack, A. S., Himmelhoch, J. M., & Thase, M. E. (1984). Effects of social skill training, amitriptyline, and psychotherapy in unipolar depressed women. *Behav. Ther., 15,* 21–40.

Herz, L. R., Volicer, L., Ross, V., & Rhéaume, Y. (1992). A single-case-study method for treating resistiveness in patients with Alzheimer's disease. *Hosp. Comm. Psychiat., 43*(7), 720–724.

Herz, M. I., & Lamberti, J. S. (1995). Prodromal symptoms and relapse prevention in schizophrenia. *Schizo. Bull., 21*(4), 541–551.

Herz, M. I., Endicott, J., & Spitzer, R. L. (1975). Brief hospitalization of patients with families: Initial results. *Amer. J. Psychiat., 132*(4), 413–418.

Herz, M. I., Endicott, J., & Spitzer, R. L. (1977). Brief hospitalization: A two-year follow-up. *Amer. J. Psychiat., 134(5), 502–507.*

Herzog, D. B., Keller, M. B., Lavori, P. W., Bradburn, I. S., & Ott, I. L. (1990). Course and outcome of bulimia nervosa. In M. M. Fichter (Ed.), *Bulimia nervosa: Basic research, diagnosis and therapy.* Chichester, England: Wiley.

Hess, N. (1995). Cancer as a defence against depressive pain. University College Hospital/Middlesex Hospital Psychotherapy Department. *Psychoanalytic Psychother., 9*(2), 175–184.

Hesselbrock, M. N., & Hesselbrock, V. M. (1992). Relationship of family history, antisocial personality disorder and personality traits in young men at risk for alcoholism. *J. Stud. Alc., 53*(6), 619–625.

Heston, L. L. (1992). *Mending Minds: A guide to the new psychiatry of depression, anxiety, and other serious mental disorders.* New York: W. H. Freeman.

Hewitt, P. L., Flett, G. L., & Ediger, E. (1996). Perfectionism and depression: Longitudinal assessment of a specific vulnerability hypothesis. *J. Abnorm. Psychol., 105*(2), 276–280.

Hewitt, P. L., Newton, J., Flett, G. L., & Callander, L. (1997). Perfectionism and suicide ideation in adolescent psychiatric patients. *J. Abnorm. Child Psychol., 25*(2), 95–101.

Hibma, M., & Griffin, J.F.T. (1994). Brief communication: The influence of maternal separation on humoral and cellular immunity in farmed deer. *Brain, Behav., Immun. 8,* 80–85.

Hiday, V. A. (1992). Civil commitment and arrests: An investigation of the criminalization thesis. *J. Nerv. Ment. Dis., 180*(3), 184–191.

Hiday, V. A. (1992). Coercion in civil commitment: Process, preferences, and outcome. *Inter. J. Law Psychiat., 15*(4), 359–377.

Higgins, G. A., Large, C. H., Rupniak, H. T., & Barnes, J. C. (1997). Apolipoprotein E and Alzheimer's disease: A review of recent studies. *Pharmacol. Biochem. Behav., 56*(4), 675–685.

Higgins, S. T., Budney, A. J., Bickel, W. K., Hughes, J., Foerg, F., & Badger, G. (1993). Achieving cocaine abstinence with a behavioral approach. *Amer. J. Psychiat., 150*(5), 763–769.

High, D. M., & Doole, M. M. (1995). Ethical and legal issues in conducting research involving elderly subjects. *Behav. Sci. Law, 13*(3), 319–335.

Higuchi, S., Suzuki, K., Yamada, K., Parrish, K., & Kono, H. (1993). Alcoholics with eating disorders: Prevalence and clinical course, A study from Japan. *Brit. J. Psychiat., 162,* 403–406.

Hilgard, E. R. (1977). Controversies over consciousness and the rise of cognitive psychology. *Austral. Psychol., 12*(1), 7–26.

Hilgard, E. R. (1977). Psychology's influence on educational practices: A puzzling history. *Education, 97*(3), 203–219.

Hilgard, E. R. (1987). Research advances in hypnosis: Issues and methods. *Inter. J. Clin. Exp. Hyp., 35,* 248–264.

Hilgard, E. R. (1992). Dissociation and theories of hypnosis. In E. Fromm & M. R. Nash (Eds.), *Contemporary hypnosis research.* New York: Guilford.

Hill, A. J., & Robinson, A. (1991). Dieting concerns have a functional effect on the behaviour of nine-year-old girls. *Brit. J. Clin. Psychol., 30*(3), 265–267.

Hill, S. Y., & Muka, D. (1996). Childhood psychopathology in children from families of alcoholic female probands. *J. Amer. Acad. Child. Adol. Psychiat., 35*(6), 725–733.

Hill, S. Y., Muka, D., Steinhauer, S., & Locke, J. (1995). P300 amplitude decrements in children from families of alcoholic female probands. *Bio. Psychiat., 38,* 622–632.

Hiller, W., Rief, W., & Fichter, M. M. (1995). Further evidence for a broader concept of somatization disorder using the Somatic Symptom Index. *Psychosomatics, 36*(3), 285–294.

Hilsman, R., & Garber, J. (1995). A test of the cognitive diathesis-stress model of depression in children: Academic stressors, attributional style, perceived competence, and control. *J. Pers. Soc. Psychol., 69*(2), 370–380.

Himelhoch, S., Taylor, S. F., Goldman, R. S., & Tandon, R. (1996). Frontal lobe tasks, antipsychotic medication, and schizophrenia syndromes. *Bio. Psychiat., 39,* 227–229.

Hinshaw, S. P. (1991). Stimulant medication and the treatment of aggression in children with attentional deficits. *J. Clin. Child Psychol., 20,* 301–312.

Hinshaw, S. P., & Erhardt, D. (1991). Attention-deficit hyperactivity disorder. In P. C. Kendall (Ed.), *Child and adolescent therapy: Cognitive-behavioral procedures.* New York: Guilford.

Hinshaw, S. P., & Melnick, S. (1992). Self-management therapies and attention-deficit hyperactivity disorder: Reinforced self-evaluation and anger control interventions. *Behav. Mod., 16*(2), 253–273.

Hiroto, D. S. (1974). Locus of control and learned helplessness. *J. Exp. Psychol., 102*(2), 187–193.

Hiroto, D. S., & Seligman, M. E. (1975). Generality of learned helplessness in man. *J. Pers. Soc. Psychol., 31*(2), 311–327.

Hirsch, A., Gervino, E., Nakao, S., Come, P., Silverman, K., & Grossman, W. (1989). The effect of caffeine on exercise tolerance and left ventricular function in patients with coronary artery disease. *Ann. Interna. Med., 110,* 593–598.

Hirsch, S., Bowen, J., Emami, J., Cramer, P., Jolley, A., Haw, C., & Dickinson, M. (1996). A one year prospective study of the effect of life events and medication in the aetiology of schizophrenic relapse. *Brit. J. Psychiat., 168,* 49–56.

Hirsch, S., & Leff, J. (1975). *Abnormalities in parents of schizophrenics.* Oxford: Oxford University Press.

Hirsch, S. R., Das, I., Garey, L. J., & de Belleroche, J. (1997). A pivotal role for glutamate in the pathogenesis of schizophrenia, and its cognitive dysfunction. *Pharmacol. Biochem. Behav., 56*(4), 797–802.

Hirschfeld, R. M. (1992). The clinical course of panic disorder and agoraphobia. In G. D. Burrows, S. M. Roth, & R. Noyes, Jr. (Eds.), *Handbook of anxiety* (Vol. 5). Oxford: Elsevier.

Hirschfeld, R. M., & Davidson, L. (1988). Clinical risk factors for suicide. [Special issue]. *Psychiatr. Ann., 18*(11), 628–635.

Hirschfeld, R. M., & Davidson, L. (1988). Risk factors for suicide. In A. J. Frances & R. E. Hales (Eds.), *American Psychiatric Press review of psychiatry* (Vol. 7). Washington, DC: American Psychiatric Press.

Hirschfeld, R. M. A. (1996). Placebo response in the treatment of panic disorder. *Bull. Menninger Clin., 60*(2, Suppl. A), A76–A86.

Hirshkowitz, M., Karacan, I., Howell, J. W., Arcasoy, M., & Williams, R. L. (1992). Nocturnal penile tumescence in cigarette smokers with dysfunction. *Urology, 39,* 101–107.

Ho, T. P., Hung, S. F., Lee, C. C., Chung, K. F. et al. (1995). Characteristics of youth suicide in Hong Kong. *Soc. Psychiat. Psychiatr. Epidemiol., 30*(3), 107–112.

Hobbs, F. B. (1997). The elderly population. *U.S. Census Bureau: The official statistics.* Washington, DC: U.S. Census Bureau.

Hoberman, H. M., & Garfinkel, B. D. (1988). Completed suicide in children and adolescents. *J. Amer. Acad. Child Adol. Psychiat., 27,* 689–695.

Hobfoll, S. E., Ritter, C., Lavin, J., Hulsizer, M. R., & Cameron, R. P. (1995). Depression prevalence and incidence among inner-city pregnant and postpartum women. *J. Cons. Clin. Psychol., 63*(3), 445–453.

Hobson, J. A., & McCarley, R. W. (1977). The brain as a dream state generator: An activation-synthesis hypothesis of the dream process. *Amer. J. Psychiat., 134*(12), 1335–1348.

Hodgins, S., Mednick, S. A., Brennan, P. A., Schulsinger, F., & Engberg, M. (1996). Mental disorder and crime. *Arch. Gen. Psychiat., 53,* 489–496.

Hodgson, R., & Rankin, H. (1982). Cue exposure and relapse prevention. In W. Hay & P. Nathan (Eds.), *Clinical case studies in the behavioral treatment of alcoholism.* New York: Plenum Press.

Hodgson, R. J., & Rachman, S. (1972). The effects of contamination and washing in obsessional patients. *Behav. Res. Ther., 10,* 111–117.

Hoebel, B. G., & Teitelbaum, P. (1966). Weight regulation in normal and hypothalamic hyperphagic rats. *J. Compar. Physiol. Psychol., 61*(2), 189–193.

Hoffart, A., Thornes, K., & Hedley, L. M. (1995). DSM-III-R Axis I and II disorders in agoraphobic inpatients with and without panic disorder before and after psychosocial treatment. *Psychiat. Res., 56*(1), 1–9.

Hoffman, R. S. (1980). The itemized statement in clinical psychiatry: A new concept in billing. *J. Irreproducible Results, 26*(3), 7–8.

Hofmann, S. G., Ehlers, A., & Roth, W. T. (1995). Conditioning theory: A model for the etiology of public speaking anxiety? *Behav. Res. Ther., 33*(5), 567–571.

Hogan, R. A. (1968). The implosive technique. *Behav. Res. Ther., 6,* 423–431.

Hogan, R. A., & Kirchner, J. H. (1967). A preliminary report of the extinction of learned fears via a short term implosive therapy. *J. Abnorm. Psychol., 72,* 106–111.

Hogarty, G. E. (1993). Prevention of relapse in chronic schizophrenic patients. *J. Clin. Psychiat., 54*(3, Suppl.), 18–23.

Hogarty, G. E. et al. (1974). Drug and sociotherapy in the aftercare of schizophrenic patients: II. Two-year relapse rates. *Arch. Gen. Psychiat., 31*(5), 609–618.

Hogarty, G. E. et al. (1974). Drug and sociotherapy in the aftercare of schizophrenic patients: III. Adjustment of non-relapsed patients. *Arch. Gen. Psychiat., 31*(5), 609–618.

Hogarty, G. E. et al. (1986). Family psychoeducation, social skills training, and maintenance chemotherapy in the aftercare treatment of schizophrenia: I. One-year effects of a controlled study on relapse and expressed emotion. *Arch. Gen. Psychiat., 43*(7), 633–642.

Hoge, M. A., Farrell, S. P., Munchel, M. E., & Strauss, J. S. (1988). Therapeutic factors in partial hospitalization. *Psychiatry, 51*(2), 199–210.

Hoge, R. D., Andrews, D. A., & Leschied, A. W. (1996). An investigation of risk and protective factors in a sample of youthful offenders. *J. Child Psychiat., 37*(4), 419–424.

Hokkanen, L., Launes, J., Vataja, R., Valanne, L. et al. (1995). Isolated retrograde amnesia for autobiographical material associated with acute left temporal lobe encephalitis. *Psychol. Med., 25*(1), 203–208.

Holaday, J. W., Tortella, F. C., Long, J. B. et al. (1986). Endogenous opioids and their receptors: Evidence for involvement in the postictal effects of electroconvulsive shock. *Ann. NY Acad. Sci., 462,* 124–139.

Holcomb, H. H., Cascella, N. G., Thaker, G. K., Medoff, D. R., Dannals, R. F., & Tamminga, C. A. (1996). Functional sites of neuroleptic drug action in the human brain: PET/FDG studies with and without Haloperidol. *Amer. J. Psychiat., 153,* 41–49.

Holder, H., Longabaugh, R., Miller, W. et al. (1991). The cost effectiveness of treatment for alcoholism: A first approximation. *J. Stud. Alc., 52,* 517–540.

Holinger, P. C. (1988). A prediction model of suicide among youth. *J. Nerv. Ment. Dis., 176*(5), 275–279.

Holinger, P. C., & Offer, D. (1982). Prediction of adolescent suicide: A population model. *Amer. J. Psychiat., 139,* 302–307.

Holinger, P. C., & Offer, D. (1984). Toward the prediction of violent deaths among the young. In Sudak et al. (Eds.), *Suicide among the young.* New York: Wright PSG.

Holinger, P. C., & Offer, D. (1991). Sociodemographic, epidemiologic, and individual attributes. In L. Davidson & M. Linnoila (Eds.), *Risk factors for youth suicide.* New York: Hemisphere.

Holinger, P. C., & Offer, D. (1993). *Adolescent suicide.* New York: Guilford.

Holinger, P. C., Offer, D., & Ostrov, E. (1987). Suicide and homicide in the United States: An epidemiologic study of violent death, population changes, and the potential for prediction. *Amer. J. Psychiat., 144*(2), 215–218.

Holland, J. C. (1996, September). Cancer's psychological challenges. *Scientif. Amer.,* pp. 158–160.

Hollander, E., Frenkel, M., Decaria, C., Trungold, S. et al. (1992). Treatment of pathological gambling with clomipramine. *Amer. J. Psychiat., 149*(5), 710–711.

Hollander, E., Simeon, D., & Gorman, J. M. (1994). Anxiety disorders. In R. E. Hales, S. C. Yudofsky, & J. A. Talbott (Eds.), *The American Psychiatric Press textbook of psychiatry* (2nd ed.). Washington, DC: American Psychiatric Press.

Hollander, M. H. (1988). Hysteria and memory. In H. M. Pettinati (Ed.), *Hypnosis and Memory.* New York: Guilford.

Hollister, L. E. (1986). Health aspects of cannabis. *Pharmacol. Rev., 38*(1), 1–20.

Hollister, L. E. (1986). Pharmacotherapeutic consideration in anxiety disorders. Annual Meeting of the American Academy of Clinical Psychiatrists (1985, San Francisco, CA). *J. Clin. Psychiat., 47*(Suppl.), 33–36.

Hollon, S. D. (1996). The efficacy and effectiveness of psychotherapy relative to medications. *Amer. Psychol., 51*(10), 1025–1030.

Hollon, S. D., & Beck, A. T. (1986). Research on cognitive therapies. In S. L. Garfield & A. E. Bergin (Eds.), *Handbook of psychotherapy and behavior change.* New York: Wiley.

Hollon, S. D., & Beck, A. T. (1994). Cognitive and cognitive-behavioral therapies. In A. E. Bergin & S. L. Garfiel (Eds.), *Handbook of psychotherapy and behavior change* (4th ed.). New York: Wiley.

Hollon, S. D., Evans, M. D., & De Rubeis, R. J. (1985). Preventing relapse following treatment for depression: The cognitive-pharmacotherapy project. In N. Schneiderman & T. Fields (Eds.), *Stress and coping* (Vol. 2). Hillsdale, NJ: Erlbaum.

Hollon, S. D., Shelton, R. C., & Davis, D. D. (1993). Cognitive therapy for depression: Conceptual issues and clinical efficacy. *J. Cons. Clin. Psychol., 61*(2), 270–275.

Hollon, S. D., Shelton, R. C., & Loosen, P. T. (1991). Cognitive therapy and pharmacotherapy for depression. *J. Cons. Clin. Psychol., 59,* 88–99.

Holmes, C. B. (1985). Comment on "Religiosity and U.S. suicide rates, 1972–1978." *J. Clin. Psychol., 41*(4), 580.

Holmes, R. M., & DeBurger, J. E. (1985). Profiles in terror: The serial murderer. *Fed. Probation, 49,* 29–34.

Holmes, T. H., & Rahe, R. H. (1967). The social readjustment rating scale. *J. Psychosom. Res., 11,* 213–218.

Holmes, T. H., & Rahe, R. H. (1989). The social readjustment rating scale. In T. H. Holmes & E. M. David (Eds.), *Life, change, life events, and illness: Selected papers.* New York: Praeger.

Holmes, V. F., & Rich, C. L. (1990). Suicide among physicians. In S. J. Blumenthal & D. J. Kupfer (Eds.), *Suicide over the life cycle: Risk factors, assessment, and treatment of suicidal patients.* Washington, DC: American Psychiatry Press.

Holroyd, J. (1996). Hypnosis treatment of clinical pain: Understanding why hypnosis is useful. *Inter. J. Clin. Exp. Hyp., 54*(1), 33–51.

Holroyd, J. C., & Brodsky, A. M. (1977). Psychologists' attitudes and practices regarding erotic and nonerotic physical contact with patients. *Amer. Psychol., 32,* 843–849.

Holstein, J. A. (1993). *Court-ordered insanity: Interpretive practice and involuntary commitment.* New York: Aldine de Gruyter.

Holt, C. S., Heimberg, R. G., & Hope, D. A. (1992). Avoidant personality disorder and the generalized subtype of social phobia. *J. Abnorm. Psychol., 101*(2), 318–325.

Holzman, P. S. (1986). Quality of thought disorder in differential diagnosis. *Schizo. Bull., 12,* 360–372.

Holzman, P. S., & Matthysse, S. (1990). The genetics of schizophrenia: A review. *Psychol. Sci., 1*(5), 279–286.

Honig, A., Hofman, A., Hilwig, M., Noorthoorn, E., & Ponds, R. (1995). Psychoeducation and expressed emotion in bipolar disorder: Preliminary findings. *Psychiat. Res., 56*(3), 299–301.

Hooley, J. M., Orley, J., & Teasdale, J. D. (1986). Levels of expressed emotion and relapse in depressed patients. *Brit. J. Psychiat., 148,* 642-647.

Hope, D. A., & Heimberg, R. G. (1993). Social phobia and social anxiety. In D. H. Barlow (Ed.), *Clinical handbook of psychological disorders: A step-by-step treatment manual* (2nd ed.). New York: Guilford.

Hope, D. B., Heimberg, R. G., & Bruch, M. A. (1995). Dismantling cognitive-behavioral group therapy for social phobia. *Behav. Res. Ther., 33*(6), 637–650.

Hopkins, J., Marcus, M., & Campbell, S. (1984). Postpartum depression: A critical review. *Psychol. Bull., 95*(3), 498–515.

Hopper, E. (1995). A psychoanalytical theory of 'drug addiction': Unconscious fantasies of homosexuality, compulsions and masturbation within the context of traumatogenic processes. *Inter. J. Psychoanal., 76*(6), 1121–1142.

Hopson, J. L. (1986). The unraveling of insomnia. *Anthropol. Educ. Quart., 20*(6), 42–49.

Horesh, N., Apter, A., Lepkifker, E., Ratzoni, G. et al. (1995). Life events and severe anorexia nervosa in adolescence. *Acta Psychiatr. Scandin., 91*(1), 5–9.

Horgan, J. (1995, November). Gay genes, revisited. *Scientif. Amer.,* p. 26.

Horn, M. (1993, November). Memories lost and found. *U.S. News & World Report,* p. 52–63.

Horner, A. J. (1975). Stages and processes in the development of early object relations and their associated pathologies. *Inter. Rev. Psychoanal., 2,* 95–105.

Horner, A. J. (1991). *Psychoanalytic object relations therapy.* Northvale, NJ: Jason Aronson.

Horney, K. (1937). *The neurotic personality of our time.* New York: Norton.

Horowitz, J., Damato, E., Solon, L., Metzsch, G., & Gill, V. (1995). Postpartum depression: Issues in clinical assessment. *J. Perinatol., 15*(4), 268–278.

Horton, D. (1943). The functions of alcohol in primitive societies: A cross-cultural study. *Quart. J. Stud. Alcohol., 4,* 199–320.

Horton, P. C. (1992). A borderline treatment dilemma: To solace or not to solace. In D. Silver & M. Rosenbluth (Eds.), *Handbook of borderline disorders.* Madison, CT: International Universities Press.

House, J. S., Landis, K. R., & Umberson, D. (1988). Social relationships and health. *Science, 241*(4865), 540–545.

Howe, A., & Walker, C. E. (1992). Behavioral management of toilet training enuresis, encopresis. *Pediat. Clin. N. Amer., 39*(3), 413–432.

Howe, R. & Nugent, T. (1996, April 22). The gory details. *People,* pp. 91–92.

Howells, J. G., & Guirguis, W. R. (1985). *The family and schizophrenia.* New York: International Universities Press.

Howitt, D. (1995). *Paedophiles and sexual offences against children.* Chichester, England: Wiley.

Howitt, D. (1995). Pornography and the paedophile: Is it criminogenic? *Brit. J. Med. Psychol., 68*(1), 15–27.

Hsu, L. K. G. (1980). Outcome of anorexia nervosa: A review of literature (1954–1978). *Arch. Gen. Psychiat., 37,* 1041–1046.

Hsu, L. K. G., Crisp, A. H., & Callender, J. S. (1992). Psychiatric diagnoses in recovered and unrecovered anorectics 22 years after onset of illness: A pilot study. *Comprehen. Psychiat., 33*(2), 123–127.

Hsu, L. K. G., Crisp, A. H., & Harding, B. (1979). Outcome of anorexia nervosa. *Lancet, 1,* 61–65.

Hsu, L. K. G., & Holder, D. (1986). Bulimia nervosa: Treatment and short-term outcome. *Psychol. Med., 16,* 65.

Hu, S., Pattatucci, A. M. L., Patterson, C., Li, L., et al. (1995, November). Linkage between sexual orientation and chromosome Xq28 in males but not in females. *Nature Genetics, 11,* 248–256.

Hubbard, R. W., & McIntosh, J. L. (1992). Integrating suicidology into abnormal psychology classes: The revised facts on suicide quiz. *Teach. Psychol., 19*(3), 163–166.

Hugdahl, K. (1995). *Psychophysiology: The mind-body perspective.* Cambridge, MA: Harvard University Press.

Hughes, C. W. et al. (1984). Cerebral blood flow and cerebrovascular permeability in an inescapable shock (learned helplessness) animal model of depression. *Pharmacol., Biochem. Behav., 21*(6), 891–894.

Hughes, J. R., Oliveto, A. H., Bickel, W. K., Higgins, S. T., & Badger, G. J. (1995). The ability of low doses of caffeine to serve as reinforcers in humans: A replication. *Exp. Clin. Psychopharmacol., 3*(4), 358–363.

Hulbert, D. (1993). A comparative study using orgasm consistency training in the treatment of women reporting hypoactive sexual desire. *J. Sex Marital Ther., 19,* 41–55.

Hulbert, D. F. (1991). The role of assertiveness in female sexuality: A comparative study between sexually assertive and sexually nonassertive women. *J. Sex Marit. Ther., 17,* 183–190.

Hurlbert, D. F., White, L. C., Powell, R. D., & Apt, C. (1993). Orgasm consistency training in the treatment of women reporting hypoactive sexual desire: An outcome comparison of women-only groups and couples-only groups. *J. Behav. Ther. Exp. Psychiat., 24*(1), 3–13.

Hüll, M. Berger, M., Volk, B., & Bauer, J. (1996). Occurrence of interleukin-6 in cortical plaques of Alzheimer's disease patients may precede transformation of diffuse into neuritic plaques. In R. J. Wurtman, S. Corkin, J. H. Growdon, & R. M. Nitsch (Eds.), *The neurobiology of Alzheimer's disease.* New York: New York Academy of Sciences.

Hultman, C. M., Wieselgren, I.-M., & Öhman, A. (1997). Relationships between social support, social coping and life events in the relapse of schizophrenic patients. *Scand. J. Psychol., 38,* 3–13.

Humphrey, D. H., & Dahlstrom, W. G. (1995). The impact of changing from the MMPI to the MMPI-2 on profile configurations. *J. Pers. Assess., 64*(3), 428–439.

Humphreys, K. (1996). Clinical psychologists as psychotherapists. History, future, and alternatives. *Amer. Psychol., 51*(3), 190–197.

Humphreys, K., & Rappaport, J. (1993). From the community mental health movement to the war on drugs: A study in the definition of social problems. *Amer. Psychol., 48*(8), 892–901.

Humphry, D., & Wickett, A. (1986). *The right to die: Understanding euthanasia.* New York: Harper & Row.

Hunt, C., & Andrews, G. (1995). Comorbidity in the anxiety disorders: The use of a life-chart approach. *J. Psychiat. Res., 29*(6), 467–480.

Huntington, D. D., & Bender, W. N. (1993). Adolescents with learning disabilities at risk: Emotional well-being, depression, suicide. *J. Learn. Disabilities, 26*(3), 159–166.

Hurlbert, D., White, C., Powell, D., & Apt., C. (1993). Orgasm consistency training in the treatment of women reporting hypoactive sexual desire. An outcome comparison of women-only groups and couples-only groups. *J. Behav. Ther. Exper. Psychiat.,* 24, 3–13.

Hurley, A. D., & Hurley, F. L. (1986). Counseling and psychotherapy with mentally retarded clients: I. The initial interview. *Psych. Aspects Ment. Retard. Rev., 5*(5), 22–26.

Hurley, J. D., & Meminger, S. R. (1992). A relapse-prevention program: Effects of electromyographic training on high and low levels of state and trait anxiety. *Percep. Motor Skills, 74*(3, Pt. 1), 699–705.

Hurt, R., Offord, K., Lauger, G., Marusic, Z. et al. (1995). Cessation of long-term nicotine gum use: A prospective, randomized trial. *Addiction, 90*(3), 407–413.

Hurt, S. W., Reznikoff, M., & Clarkin, J. F. (1991). *Psychological assessment, psychiatric diagnosis, and treatment planning.* New York: Brunner/Mazel.

Hurwitz, T. D. (1974). Electroconvulsive therapy: A review. *Comprehen. Psychiat., 15*(4), 303–314.

Hutchinson, R. L., & Little, T. J. (1985). A study of alcohol and drug usage by nine- through thirteen-year-old children in Central Indiana. *J. Alc. Drug Educ., 30*(3), 83–87.

Huws, R. (1991). Cardiac disease and sexual dysfunction. *Sex. Marital Ther., 6*(2), 119–134.

Hwu, H. G., Yeh, E. K., & Chang, L. Y. (1989). Prevalence of psychiatric disorders in Taiwan defined by the Chinese Diagnostic Interview Schedule. *Acta Psychiatr. Scandin., 79,* 136–147.

Hyde, A. P., & Goldman, C. R. (1992). Use of a multi-modal family group in the comprehensive treatment and rehabilitation of people with schizophrenia. *Psychosoc. Rehab. J., 15*(4), 77–86.

Hyde, J. (1995). Women and maternity leave: Empirical data and public policy. *Psychol. Women Quart., 19,* 257–285.

Hyde, J. S. (1990). *Understanding human sexuality* (4th ed.). New York: McGraw-Hill.

Hyde, J. S., Klein, M. H., Essex, M. J., & Clark, R. (1995). Maternity leave and women's mental health. *Psychol. Women Quart., 19*(2), 257–285.

Hyde, T. M., Casanova, M. F., Kleinman, J. E., & Weinberger, D. R. (1991). Neuroanatomical and neurochemical pathology in schizophrenia. In A. Tasman & S. M. Goldfinger (Eds.), *American Psychiatric Press review of psychiatry* (Vol. 10). Washington, DC: American Psychiatric Press.

Hyler, S. E., & Spitzer, R. T. (1978). Hysteria split asunder. *Amer. J. Psychiat., 135,* 1500–1504.

Hyman, S. E., & Cassem, N. H. (1994). Psychopharmacologic therapies. In *Scientific American Series: Vol. 13. Psychiatry.* New York: Scientific American.

Iga, M. (1993). Japanese suicide. In A. A. Leenaars (Ed.), *Suicidology.* Northvale, NJ: Jason Aronson.

Iketani, T., Kiriike, N., Nakanishi, S., & Nakasuji, T. (1995). Effects of weight gain and resumption of menses on reduced bone density in patients with anorexia nervosa. *Bio. Psychiat., 37*(80), 521–527.

Inglehart, R. (1990). *Culture shift in advanced industrial society.* Princeton, NJ: Princeton University Press.

Iqbal, K., & Grundke-Iqbal, I. (1996). Molecular mechanism of Alzheimer's neurofibrillary degeneration and therapeutic intervention. In R. J. Wurtman, S. Corkin, J. H. Growdon, & R. M. Nitsch (Eds.), *The neurobiology of Alzheimer's disease.* New York: New York Academy of Sciences.

Ironson, G., Taylor, C. B., Boltwood, M. et al. (1992). Effects of anger on left ventricular ejection fraction in coronary artery disease. *Amer. J. Cardiol., 70*(3), 281–285.

Ishii, K. (1991). Measuring mutual causation: Effects of suicide news on suicide in Japan. *Soc. Sci. Res., 20*(2), 188–195.

Isometsa, E., Heikkinen, M., Henriksson, M., Hillevi, A. et al. (1995). Recent life events and completed suicide in bipolar affective disorder: A comparison with major depressive suicides. *J. Affect. Disorders, 33*(2), 99–106.

Ito, A., Ichihara, M., Hisanaga, N., Ono, Y., et al. (1992). Prevalence of seasonal mood changes in low latitude area: Seasonal Pattern Assessment Questionnaire score of Quezon City workers. *Jpn. J. of Psychiat., 46,* 249.

Iversen, L. L. (1975). Dopamine receptors in the brain. *Science, 188,* 1084–1089.

Iversen, L. L. (1965). *Adv. Drug Res., 2,* 5–23.

Iverson, G. L., Franzen, M. D., & Hammond, J. A. (1995). Examination of inmates' ability to malinger on the MMPI-2. *Psychol. Assess., 7*(1), 118–121.

Jablensky, A. (1995). Kraepelin's legacy: Paradigm or pitfall for modern psychiatry? [Special issue: Emil Kraepelin and 20th century psychiatry]. *Eur. Arch. Psychiat. Clin. Neurosci., 245*(4–5), 186–188.

Jack, R. (1992). *Women and attempted suicide.* Hillsdale, NJ: Erlbaum.

Jackson, J. L., Calhoun, K. S., Amick, A. A., Madever, H. M., & Habif, V. L. (1990). Young adult women who report childhood intrafamilial sexual abuse: Subsequent adjustment. *Arch. Sex. Behav., 19*(3), 211–221.

Jackson, J. S. (Ed.). (1988). *The Black American elderly: Research on physical and psychosocial health.* New York: Springer.

Jacobs, B. L. (1994). Serotonin, motor activity and depression-related disorders. *Amer. Sci., 82,* 456–463.

Jacobs, B. L. (Ed.). (1984). *Hallucinogens: neurochemical, behavioral, and clinical perspectives.* New York: Raven Press.

Jacobs, D., & Klein, M. E. (1993). The expanding role of psychological autopsies. In A. A. Leenaars (Ed.), *Suicidology.* Northvale, NJ: Jason Aronson.

Jacobs, R. (1993). AIDS communication: College students' AIDS knowledge and information sources. *Hlth. Values, J. Hlth., Behav., Educ., Promotion, 17*(3), 32–41.

Jacobsen, F. M. (1992). Fluoxetine-induced sexual dysfunction and an open trial of yohimbine. *J. Clin. Psychiat., 53,* 119–122.

Jacobsen, L. K., Rabinowitz, I., Popper, M. S., Solomon, R. J., Sokol, M. S., & Pfeffer, C. R. (1994). Interviewing prepubertal children about suicidal ideation and behavior. *J. Amer. Acad. Child Adol. Psychiat., 33*(4), 439–452.

Jacobson, B., & Thurman-Lacey, S. (1992). Effect of caffeine on motor performance by caffeine-naive and -familiar subjects. *Percep. Motor Skills, 74,* 151–157.

Jacobson, E. (1971). *Depression.* New York: International Universities Press.

Jacobson, J. W., & Schwartz, A. A. (1991). Evaluating living situations of people with development disabilities. In J. L. Matson & J. A. Mulick (Eds.), *Handbook of mental retardation.* New York: Pergamon Press.

Jacobson, N. S. (1989). The maintenance of treatment gains following social learning-based marital therapy. *Behav. Ther., 20*(3), 325–336.

Jacobson, N. S., & Addis, M. E. (1993). *Research on couple therapy: What do we know? Where are we going?* Submitted for publication.

Jacobson, N. S., & Christensen, A. (1996). Studying the effectiveness of psychotherapy: How well can clinical trials do the job? *Amer. Psychologist, 51*(10), 1031–1039.

Jacobson, N. S., & Margolin, G. (1979). *Marital therapy: Strategies based on social learning and behavior exchange principles.* New York: Brunner/Mazel.

Jacobson, N. S., Dobson, K. S., Truax, P. A., Addis, M. E., et al. (1996). A component analysis of cognitive-behavioral treatment for depression. *J. Cons. Clin. Psychol., 64*(2), 295–304.

Jacobson, N. S., Fruzzetti, A. E., Dobson, K., Whisman, M., & Hops, H. (1993). Couple therapy as a treatment for depression: II. The effects of relationship quality and therapy on depressive relapse. *J. Cons. Clin. Psychol., 61,* 516–519.

Jaffe, J. H. (1985). Drug addiction and drug abuse. In Goodman & Gilman (Eds.), *The pharmacological basis of therapeutic behavior.* New York: Macmillan.

Jagust, W. J. (1996). Functional imaging patterns in Alzheimer's disease: Relationships to neurobiology. In R. J. Wurtman, S. Corkin, J. H. Growdon, & R. M. Nitsch (Eds.), *The neurobiology of Alzheimer's disease.* New York: New York Academy of Sciences.

James, W. (1890). *Principles of psychology* (Vol. 1). New York: Holt, Rinehart & Winston.

James, I. A., & Blackburn, I. M. (1995). Cognitive therapy with obsessive-compulsive disorder. *Brit. J. Psychiat., 166*(4), 444–450.

Jamison, K. (1995, February). Manic-depressive illness and creativity. *Scientif. Amer.,* pp. 63–67.

Jamison, K. R. (1987). Psychotherapeutic issues and suicide prevention in the treatment of bipolar disorders. In R. E. Hales & A. J. Frances (Eds.), *Psychiatric update: American Psychiatric Association annual review* (Vol. 6). Washington, DC: American Psychiatric Press.

Jamison, K. R. (1995). *An unquiet mind.* New York: Vintage Books.

Janca, A., Isaac, M., & Costa-e-Silva, J. A. (1995). World Health Organization International Study of Somatoform Disorders: Background and rationale. *Eur. J. Psychiat., 9*(2), 100–110.

Janowsky, D. S., & Davis, J. M. (1976). Methylphanidate, dextroamphetamine, and levamfetamine: Effects on schizophrenic symptoms. *Arch. Gen. Psychiat., 33*(3), 304–308.

Janowsky, D. S., El-Yousef, M. K., Davis, J. M., & Sekerke, H. J. (1973). Provocation of schizophrenic symptoms by intravenous administration of methylphenidate. *Arch. Gen. Psychiat., 28,* 185–191.

Janus, S. S., & Janus, C. L. (1993). *The Janus report on sexual behavior.* New York: Wiley.

Jarvik, M. E., & Schneider, N. G. (1984). Degree of addiction and effectiveness of nicotine gum therapy for smoking. *Amer. J. Psychiat., 141,* 790–791.

Jay, S. M., Elliot, C. H., Katz, E., & Siegel, S. E. (1987). Cognitive-behavioral and pharmacologic interventions for children's distress during painful medical procedures. *J. Cons. Clin. Psychol., 55,* 860–865.

Jefferson, J. W., & Greist, J. H. (1994). Mood disorders. In R. E. Hales, S. C. Yudofsky, & J. A. Talbott, (Eds.), *The American Psychiatric Press textbook of psychiatry* (2nd ed.). Washington, DC: American Psychiatric Press.

Jefferson, J. W. (1997). Antidepressants in panic disorder. *J. Clin. Psychiat., 58* (Suppl 2), 20–24.

Jefferson, J. W., & Greist, J. H. (1989). Lithium therapy. In H. I. Kaplan & B. J. Sadock (Eds.), *Comprehensive textbook of psychiatry V.* Baltimore: Williams & Wilkins.

Jefferson, J. W., & Greist, J.H. (1996). Mood disorders. In R.E.Hales & S.C. Yudofsky (Eds.), *The American Psychiatric Press Synopsis of Psychiatry.* Washington, DC: American Psychiatric Press.

Jefferson, L. (1948). *These are my sisters.* Tulsa, OK: Vickers.

Jeffries, J. J. (1995). Working with schizophrenia: A clinician's personal experience. *Canad. J. Psychiat., 40*(3, Suppl. 1), S22–S25.

Jemmott, J. B. (1987). Social motives and susceptibility to disease: Stalking individual differences in health risks. *J. Pers., 55*(2), 267–298.

Jemmott, J. B., Borysenko, J. Z., Borysenko, M., McClelland, D. C. et al. (1983). Academic stress, power motivation and decrease in secretion rate of salivary immunoglobulin. *Lancet, 12,* 1400–1402.

Jenike, M. A. (1990). Approaches to the patient with treatment-refractory obsessive compulsive disorder. *J. Clin. Psychiat., 51*(Suppl. 2), 15–21.

Jenike, M. A. (1991). Geriatric obsessive-compulsive disorder. *J. Geriat. Psychiat. Neurol., 4,* 34–39.

Jenike, M. A. (1991). Management of patients with treatment-resistant obsessive-compulsive disorder. In M. T. Pato & J. Zohar (Eds.), *Current treatments of obsessive-compulsive disorder.* Washington, DC: American Psychiatric Press.

Jenike, M. A. (1991). Obsessive-compulsive disorders: A clinical approach. In W. Coryell & G. Winokur (Eds.), *The clinical management of anxiety disorders.* New York: Oxford University Press.

Jenike, M. A. (1992). New Developments in treatment of obsessive-compulsive disorder. In A. Tasman, & M. B. Riba (Eds.), *Review of psychiatry* (Vol. 11). Washington, DC: American Psychiatric Press.

Jenike, M. A. (1995). Alzheimer's disease. In *Scientific American Series: Vol. 13. Psychiatry.* New York: Scientific American.

Jenkins, R. L. (1968). The varieties of children's behavioral problems and family dynamics. *Amer. J. Psychiat., 124*(10), 1440–1445.

Jenkins-Hall, K., & Sacco, W. P. (1991). Effect of client race and depression on evaluations by white therapists. *J. Soc. Clin. Psychol., 10*(3), 322–333.

Jeste, D. V., Eastham, J. H., Lacro, J. P., Gierz, M., Field, M. G., & Harris, M. J. (1996). Management of late-life psychosis. *J. Clin. Psychiat., 57*(Suppl 3), 39–45.

Jimerson, D. C., Lesem, M. D., Kaye, W. H., Hegg, A. P. et al. (1990). Eating disorders and depression: Is there a serotonin connection? *Bio Psychiat., 28*(5), 443–454.

Joffe, R. T., Singer, W., Levitt, A. J., & MacDonald, C. (1993). A placebo-controlled comparison of lithium and triiodothyronine augmentation of tricyclic antidepressants in unipolar refractory depression. *Arch. Gen. Psychiat., 50,* 387–393.

Johnson, C. (1995, February 8). National Collegiate Athletic Association study. In *The Hartford Courant.*

Johnson, C., & Maddi, K. L. (1986). The etiology of bulimia: Bio-psycho-social perspectives. *Ann. Adol. Psychiat., 13,* 253–273.

Johnson, C., & Wonderlich, S. A. (1992). Personality characteristics as a risk factor in the development of eating disorders. In J. H. Crowther, D. L. Tennenbaum, S. E. Hobfoll, & M. A. P. Stephens (Eds.), *The etiology of bulimia nervosa: The individual and familial context.* Washington, DC: Hemisphere.

Johnson, D. R. (1997). An existential model of group therapy for chronic mental conditions. *Inter. J. Group Psychother., 47*(2), 227–250.

Johnson, D. R., Feldman, S., Lubin, H. (1995). Critical interaction therapy: Couples therapy in combat-related posttraumatic stress disorder. *Fam. Process, 34,* 401–412.

Johnson, D. R., Rosenheck, R., Fontana, A., Lubin, H. et al. (1996). Outcome of intensive inpatient treatment for combat-related posttraumatic stress disorder. *Amer. J. Psychiat., 153,* 771–777.

Johnson, E. H., Gentry, W. D., & Julius, S. (Eds.). (1992). *Personality, elevated blood pressure, and essential hypertension.* Washington, DC: Hemisphere.

Johnson, F. A. (1991). Psychotherapy of the elderly anxious patient. In C. Salzman & B. D. Lebowitz (Eds.), *Anxiety in the elderly.* New York: Springer.

Johnson, F. S., Hunt, G. E., Duggin, G. G., Horvath, J. S., & Tiller, D. J. (1984). Renal function and lithium treatment: Initial and follow-up tests in manic-depressive patients. *J. Affect. Disorders, 6,* 249–263.

Johnson, K. (1996, December 31). Medical marijuana rejected as "hoax." *USA Today,* p. 4A.

Johnson, M. E., Jones, G., & Brems, C. (1996). Concurrent validity of the MMPI-2 feminine gender role *(GF)* and masculine gender role *(GM)* scales. *J. Pers. Assess., 66*(1), 153–168.

Johnson, M. R., Lydiard, R. B., Morton, W. A., Laird, L. K., Steele, T. E., Kellner, C. H., & Ballenger, J. C. (1993). Effect of fluvoxamine, imipramine and placebo on catecholamine function in depressed outpatients. *J. Psychiatr. Res., 27*(2), 161–172.

Johnson, S. K., DeLuca, J., & Natelson, B. H. (1996). Assessing somatization disorder in the chronic fatigue syndrome. *Psychosom. Med., 58,* 50–57.

Johnson, W. D. (1991). Predisposition to emotional distress and psychiatric illness amongst doctors: The role of unconscious and experiential factors. *Brit. J. Med. Psychol., 64*(4), 317–329.

Johnson, W. G., Schlundt, D. G., Barclay, D. R., Carr-Nangle, R. E. et al. (1995). A naturalistic functional analysis of binge eating. Special Series: Body dissatisfaction, binge eating, and dieting as interlocking issues in eating disorders research. *Behav. Ther. 26*(1), 101–118.

Johnson, W. G., Schlundt, D. G., Kelley, M. L., & Ruggiero, L. (1984). Exposure with response prevention and energy regulation in the treatment of bulimia. *Inter. J. Eat. Disorders, 3,* 37–46.

Johnson-Greene, D., Fatis, M., Sonnek, K., & Shawchuck, C. (1988). A survey of caffeine use and associated side effects in a college population. *J. Drug Educ., 18*(3), 211–219.

Johnston, D. W. (1992). The management of stress in the prevention of coronary heart disease. In S. Maes, H. Levental, & M. Johnston (Eds.), *International review of health psychology* (Vol. 1). New York: Wiley.

Johnston, L. (1996). *Monitoring the future study.* Rockville, MD: National Institute on Drug Abuse (NIDA).

Johnston, L., Bachman, J., & O'Malley, P. (1996). *Monitoring the future study.* Rockville, MD.: National Institute on Drug Abuse (NIDA).

Johnston, L., Bachman, J., & O'Malley, P. (1995). *Monitoring the future study.* Rockville, MD.: National Institute on Drug Abuse.

Johnston, L. D., Bachman, J. G., & O'Malley, P. M. (1982). *Student drug use, attitudes and beliefs.* Washington, DC: National Institute on Drug Abuse.

Johnston, L. D., O'Malley, P. M., & Bachman, J. G. (1993). *National Survey Results on Drug Use from the Monitoring the Future Study, 1975–1992.* Rockville, MD: National Institute on Drug Abuse.

Joiner, T. E., Heatherton, T. F., Rudd, M. D., & Schmidt, N. B. (1997). Perfectionism, perceived weight status, and bulimic symptoms: Two studies testing a diathesis-stress model. *J. Abnorm. Psychol., 106*(1), 145–153.

Joiner, T. E. Jr. & Blalock, J. A. (1995). Gender differences in depression: The role of anxiety and generalized negative affect. *Sex Roles, 33*(1/2), 91–108.

Joiner, T. E., Metalsky, G. I., & Wonderlich, S. A. (1995). Bulimic symptoms and the development of depressive symptoms: The moderating role of attributional style. *Cog. Ther. Res, 19*(6), 651–666.

Joiner, T. E., Wonderlich, S. A., Metalsky, G. I., & Schmidt, N. B. (1995). Body dissatisfaction: A feature of bulimia, depression, or both? *J. Soc. Clin. Psychol., 14*(4), 339–355.

Jones, A., & Schechter, S. (1992). *When love goes wrong.* New York: HarperCollins.

Jones, F. D., & Koshes, R. J. (1995). Homosexuality and the military. *Amer. J. Psychiat., 152*(1), 16–21.

Jones, G. D. (1997). The role of drugs and alcohol in urban minority adolescent suicide attempts. *Death Stud., 21,* 189–202.

Jones, M. (1994, April 25). The fallout of the burnout: The sad, sordid last days of Kurt Cobain. *Newsweek,* p. 68.

Jones, M. C. (1924). The elimination of children's fears. *J. Exp. Psychol., 7,* 382–390.

Jones, M. C. (1968). Personality correlates and antecedants of drinking patterns in males. *J. Cons. Clin. Psychol., 32,* 2–12.

Jones, M. C. (1971). Personality antecedents and correlates of drinking patterns in women. *J. Cons. Clin. Psychol., 36,* 61–69.

Jones, R. T., & Benowitz, N. (1976). The 30-day trip—clinical studies of cannabis tolerance and dependence. In M. C. Braude & S. Szara (Eds.), *Pharmacology of marijuana.* New York: Raven Press.

Jordan, B. K., Marmar, C. R., Fairbank, J. A., Schlenger, W. E. et al. (1992). Problems in families of male Vietnam veterans with post-traumatic stress disorder. *J. Cons. Clin. Psychol., 60*(6), 916–926.

Jordan, B. K., Schlenger, W. E., Fairbank, J. A., & Caddell, J. M. (1996). Prevalence of psychiatric disorders among incarcerated women. II. Convicted felons entering prison. *Arch. Gen. Psychiat., 53,* 513–519.

Joyner, C. D., & Swenson, C. C. (1993). Community-level intervention after a disaster. In C. F. Saylor (Ed.), *Children and disasters.* New York: Plenum Press.

Judd, L. L. (1995). Depression as a brain disease. *Depression, 3,* 121–124.

Juel-Nielsen, N., & Videbech, T. (1970). A twin study of suicide. *Acta Genet. Med. Gemellol., 19,* 307–310.

Julien, R. M. (1985). *A primer of drug action* (4th ed.). New York: W. H. Freeman.

Julien, R. M. (1988). *A primer of drug action* (5th ed.). New York: W. H. Freeman.

Julius, S. (1992). Relationship between the sympathetic tone and cardiovascular responsiveness in the course of hypertension. In E. H. Johnson, E. D. Gentry, & S. Julius (Eds.), *Personality, elevated blood pressure, and essential hypertension.* Washington, DC: Hemisphere.

Jung, C. G. (1909). *Memories, dreams, and reflections.* New York: Random House.

Jung, C. G. (1967). *The collected works of C. G. Jung.* Princeton, NJ: Princeton University Press.

Junginger, J. (1996). Psychosis and violence: The case for a content analysis of psychotic experience. *Schizo. Bull., 22*(1), 91–103.

Jungman, J. (1985). De l'agir du toxicomane a l'agir du therapeute [From the drug addict's acting out to the therapist's action]. *Information Psychiatr., 61*(3), 383–388.

Just, N., & Alloy, L. B. (1997). The response styles theory of depression: Tests and an extension of the theory. *J. Abnorm. Psychol., 106*(2), 221–229.

Juster, H. R., Heimberg, R. G., & Holt, C. S. (1996). Social phobia: Diagnostic issues and review of cognitive behavioral treatment strategies. In M. Hersen, R. M. Eisler, & P. M. Miller (Eds.), *Progress in behavior modification* (Vol. 30). Pacific Grove, CA: Brooks/Cole.

Kabat-Zinn, J., Massion, A. O., Kristeller, J., Peterson, L. G. et al. (1992). Effectiveness of a meditation-based stress reduction program in the treatment of anxiety disorders. *Amer. J. Psychiat., 149*(7), 936–943.

Kagan, J. (1983). Stress and coping in early development. In N. Garmezy & M. Rutter (Eds.), *Stress, coping, and development in children.* New York: McGraw-Hill.

Kagan, N. I., Kagan, H., & Watson, M. G. (1995). Stress reduction in the workplace: The effectiveness of psychoeducational progams. *J. Couns. Psychol., 42*(1), 71-78.

Kahneman, D., & Tversky, A. (1973). On the psychology of prediction. *Psychol. Rev., 80*(4), 237–251.

Kaij, L. (1960). *Alcoholism in twins: Studies on the etiology and sequels of abuse of alcohol.* Stockholm: Almquist & Wiksell.

Kail, R. (1992). General slowing of information-processing by persons with mental retardation. *Amer. J. Ment. Retard., 97*(3), 333–341.

Kalafat, J., & Elias, M. J. (1995). Suicide prevention in an educational context: Broad and narrow foci [Special issue: Suicide prevention: Toward the year 2000]. *Suic. Life-Threat. Behav., 25*(1), 123–133.

Kalin, N. H. (1993, May). The neurobiology of fear. Scientif. Amer., pp. 94–101.

Kaminer, Y. (1991). Adolescent substance abuse. In R. J. Frances & S. I. Miller (Eds.), *Clinical textbook of addictive disorders.* New York: Guilford.

Kanakis, D. M., & Thelen, M. H. (1995, July/August). Parental variables associated with bulimia nervosa. *Addic. Behav., 20,* 491–500.

Kane, J. M. (1987). Treatment of schizophrenia. *Schizo. Bull., 13*(1), 133–156.

Kane, J. M. (1990). Treatment programme and long-term outcome in chronic schizophrenia. International Symposium: Development of a new antipsychotic: Remoxipride (1989, Monte Carlo, Monaco). *Acta Psychiatr. Scandin., 82*(385, Suppl.), 151–157.

Kane, J. M. (1992). Clinical efficacy of clozapine in treatment-refractory schizophrenia: An overview. *Brit. J. Psychiat., 160*(Suppl. 17), 41–45.

Kanner, L. (1943). Autistic disturbances of affective contact. *Nerv. Child. 2,* 217.

Kanner, L. (1954). To what extent is early infantile autism determined by constitutional inadequacies? *Proceedings of the Assoc. Res. Nerv. Ment. Dis., 33,* 378–385.

Kaplan, H. I., Sadock, B. J., & Greb, J. A. (1994). *Synopsis of psychiatry* (7th ed.). Baltimore: Williams & Wilkins.

Kaplan, H. S. (1974). *The new sex therapy: Active treatment of sexual dysfunction.* New York: Brunner/Mazel.

Kaplan, H. S. (1979). *Disorders of sexual desire.* New York: Brunner/Mazel.

Kaplan, W. (1984). *The relationship between depression and anti-social behavior among a court-referred adolescent population.* Presented to the American Academy of Child Psychiatry, Toronto.

Kapur, S., & Remington, G. (1996). Serotonin-dopamine interaction and its relevance to schizophrenia. *Amer. J. Psychiat., 153*(4), 466–476.

Karasu, T. B. (1992). The worst of times, the best of times. *J. Psychother. Prac. Res., 1,* 2–15.

Kardiner, A. (1977). *My analysis with Freud: Reminiscences.* New York: Norton.

Karel, R. (1992, May 1). Hopes of many long-term sufferers dashed as FDA ends medical marijuana program. *Psychiatr. News.*

Karoly, P., & Lecci, L. (1993). Hypochondriasis and somatization in college women: A personal projects analysis. *Hlth. Psychol., 12*(2), 103–109.

Karon, B. P. (1985). Omission in review of treatment interactions. *Schizo. Bull., 11*(1), 16–17.

Karon, B. P. (1988). Cited in T. De Angelis, "Resistance to therapy seen in therapists, too." *APA Monitor, 19*(11), 21.

Karon, B. P., & Vandenbos, G. R. (1981). *Psychotherapy of schizophrenia: The treatment of choice.* New York: Jason Aronson.

Karp, J. F., & Frank, E. (1995). Combination therapy and the depressed woman. *Depression, 3,* 91–98.

Karp, S. A., Holmstrom, R. W., Silber, D. E., & Stock, L. J. (1995). Personalities of women reporting incestuous abuse during childhood. *Percept. Motor Skills, 81*(3, Pt 1), 955–965.

Kashani, J. H., Goddard, P., & Reid, J. C. (1989). Correlated of suicidal ideation in a community sample of children and adolescents. *J. Amer. Acad. Child. Adol. Psychiat., 28,* 912–917.

Kashden, J., Fremouw, W. J., Callahan, T. S., & Franzen, M. D. (1993). Impulsivity in suicidal and nonsuicidal adolescents. *J. Abnorm. Child Psychol., 21*(3), 339–353.

Kasl, S. V., & Cobb, S. (1970). Blood pressure changes in men undergoing job loss: A preliminary report. *Psychosom. Med., 32*(1), 19–38.

Katel, P., & Beck, M. (1996, March 29). Sick kid or sick Mom? *Newsweek,* p. 73.

Kato, T., Takahashi, S., Shioiri, T., & Inubushi, T. (1993). Alterations in brain phosphorous metabolism in bipolar disorder detected by in vivo 31 P and 7 Li magnetic resonance spectroscopy. *J. Affect. Disorders, 27,* 53–60.

Katon, W., Hollifield, M., Chapman, T., Mannuzza, S., et al. (1995). Infrequent panic attacks: Psychiatric comorbidity, personality characteristics and functional disability. *J. Psychiatr. Res., 29*(2), 121–131.

Katona, C. L. E. (1995). Refractory depression: A review with particular reference to the use of lithium augmentation. *Eur. Neuropsychopharmacol. Suppl.,* 109–113.

Katona, C. L. E., Abou-Saleh, M. T., Harrison, D. A., Nairac, B. A. et al. (1995). Placebo-controlled trial of lithium augmentation of fluoxetine and lofepramine. *Brit. J. Psychiat., 166,* 80–86.

Katzman, R. (1981, June). Early detection of senile dementia. *Hosp. Practitioner,* pp. 61–76.

Kaufman, C. L., & Roth, L. H. (1981). Psychiatric evaluation of patient decision-making: Informed consent to ECT. *Soc. Psychiat., 16*(1), 11–19.

Kaufman, M. Y. (1993, January 27). 'Chutzpah therapy' for New Yorkers. *New York Times,* p. B4.

Kawas, C., Resnick, S., Morrison, A., Brookmeyer, R., Corrada, M., Zonderman, A., Bacal, C., Lingle, D. D., & Metter, E. J. (1997). A prospective study of estrogen replacement therapy and the risk of develoing Alzheimer's disease: The Baltimore Longtitudinal Study of Aging. *Neurology, 48*(6), 1517–1521.

Kaye, W. H., Weltzin, T. E., Hsu, L. G., & Bulik, C. M. (1991). An open trial of fluoxetine in patients with anorexia nervosa. *J. Clin. Psychiat., 52*(11), 464–471.

Kazdin, A. E. (1983). Failure of persons to respond to the token economy. In E. B. Foa & P. M. G. Emmelkamp (Eds.), *Failures in behavior therapy.* New York: Wiley.

Kazdin, A. E. (1989). Childhood depression. In E. J. Mash & R. Barkley (Eds.), *Treatment of childhood disorders.* New York: Guilford.

Kazdin, A. E. (1990). Childhood depression. *J. Child Psychol. Psychiat. Allied Disc., 31,* 121–160.

Kazdin, A. E. (1993). Psychotherapy for children and adolescents: Current progress and future research directions. *Amer. Psychol., 48*(6), 644–657.

Kazdin, A. E. (1994). Methodology, design, and evaluation in psychotherapy research. In A. E. Bergin & S. L. Garfiel (Eds.), *Handbook of psychotherapy and behavior change* (4th ed.). New York: Wiley.

Kazdin, A. E. (1994). Psychotherapy for children and adolescents. In A. E. Bergin & S. L. Garfiel (Eds.), *Handbook of psychotherapy and behavior change* (4th ed.). New York: Wiley.

Kazdin, A. E. (1997). Practitioner review: Psychosocial treatments for conduct disorder in children. *J. Child Psychol. Psychiat., 38*(2), 161–178.

Kazes, M., Danion, J. M., Grange, D., Pradignac, A. et al. (1994). Eating behaviour and depression before and after antidepressant treatment: A prospective, naturalistic study. *J. Affect. Disorders, 30,* 193–207.

Kearney-Cooke, & Steichen-Asch, P. (1990). Men, body image, and eating disorders. In A. E. Andersen (Ed.), *Males with eating disorders.* New York: Brunner/Mazel.

Kebabian, J. W., Petzold, G. L., & Greengard, P. (1972). Dopamine-sensitive adenylate cyclase in caudate nucleus of rat brain and its similarity to the "dopamine receptor." *Proc. Natl. Acad. Sci.* USA, *69,* 2145–2149.

Keefe, R. S. E., Frescka, E., Apter, S. H., Davidson, M., Macaluso, J. M., Hirschowitz, J., & Davis, K. L. (1996). Clinical characteristics of Kraepelinian schizophrenia: Replication and extension of previous findings. *Amer. J. Psychiat., 153*(6), 806–811.

Keel, P. K., & Mitchell, J. E. (1997). Outcome in bulimia nervosa. *Amer. J. Psychiat., 154,* 313–321.

Keen, E. (1970). *Three faces of being: Toward an existential clinical psychology.* By the Meredith Corp. Reprinted by permission of Irvington Publishers.

Keesey, R. E., & Corbett, S. W. (1983). Metabolic defense of the body weight set-point. In A. J. Stunkard & E. Stellar (Eds.), *Eating and its disorders.* New York: Raven Press.

Keitel, M. A., Kopala, M., & Adamson, W. S. (1996). Ethical issues in multicultural assessment. In L. A. Suzuki, P. J. Meller, & J. G. Ponterotto (Eds.), *Handbook of multicultural assessment.* San Francisco: Jossey-Bass.

Keith, S. J., Regier, D. A., & Rae, D. S. (1991). Schizophrenic disorders. In L. N. Robins & D. S. Regier (Eds.), *Psychiatric disorders in America: The epidemiological catchment area study.* New York: Free Press.

Keller, M. B. (1988). Diagnostic issues and clinical course of unipolar illness. In A. J. Frances & R. E. Hales (Eds.), *Review of psychiatry* (Vol. 7). Washington, DC: American Psychiatric Press.

Keller, M., Herzog, D., Lavori, R. et al. (1992). The naturalistic history of bulimia nervosa: extraordinarily high rates of chronicity, relapse, recurrence, and psychosocial morbidity. *Inter. J. Eat. Disorders, 12,* 1–9.

Keller, M. B., Harrison, W., Fawcett, J. A., Gelenberg, A., Hirschfeld, R. M. A., Klein, D., Kocsis, J. H., McCullough, J. P., Rush, A. J., Schatzberg, A., & Thase, M. E. (1995). Treatment of chronic depression with sertraline or imipramine: Preliminary blinded response rates and high rates of under-treatment in the community. *Psychopharacol. Bull., 31*(2), 205–212.

Keller, M. B., Lavori, P. W., Coryell, W., Endicott, J. et al. (1993). Bipolar I: A five-year prospective follow-up. *J. Nerv. Ment. Dis., 181*(4), 238–245.

Keller, R., & Shaywitz, B. A. (1986). Amnesia or fugue state: A diagnostic dilemma. *J. Dev. Behav. Pediatr., 7*(8), 131–132.

Kelley, G. A. (1955). *A theory of personality.* New York: Norton.

Kelly, I. W., Laverty, W. H., & Saklofske, D. H. (1990). Geophysical variables and behavior: LXIV. An empirical investigation of the relationship between worldwide automobile traffic disasters and lunar cycles: No relationship. *Psychol. Rep., 67*(3, Pt.1), 987–994.

Kelly, I. W., Saklofske, D. H., & Culver, R. (1990). Aircraft accidents and disasters and full moon: No relationship. *Psychol: A J. Human Behav., 27*(2), 30–33.

Kelly, J. B. (1982). Divorce: An adult perspective. In B. B. Wolman (Ed.), *Handbook of developmental psychology.* Englewood Cliffs, NJ: Prentice Hall.

Kelly, K. A. (1993). Multiple personality disorders: Treatment coordination in a partial hospital setting. *Bull. Menninger Clin., 57*(3), 390–398.

Kelly, M. P., Strassberg, D. S., & Kircher, J. R. (1990). Attitudinal and experiential correlates of anorgasmia. *Arch. Sex. Behav., 19,* 165–172.

Kelly, V. A., & Myers, J. E. (1996). Parental alcoholism and coping: A comparison of female children of alcoholics with female children of nonalcoholics. *J. of Couns. and Dev., 74*(5), 501–504.

Kelsoe, J. R., Ginns, E. I., Egeland, J. A., Gerhard, D. S. et al. (1989). Reevaluation of the linkage relationship between chromosome 11p loci and the gene for bipolar affective disorder in the Old Order Amish. *Nature, 342*(6247), 238–243.

Keltner, B. R. (1992). Caregiving by mothers with mental retardation. *Fam. Comm. Hlth., 15*(2), 10–18.

Kemp, A., Green, B. L., Hovanitz, C., & Rawlings, E. I. (1995). Incidence and correlates of posttraumatic stress disorder in battered women: Shelter and community samples. *J. Interpers. Violence, 10*(1), 43–55.

Kemp, D. R. (1994). *Mental health in the workplace: An employer's and manager's guide.* Westport, CT: Quorum Books.

Kemph, J. P., DeVane, C. L., Levin, G. M., Jarecke, R., & Miller, R. L. (1993). Treatment of aggressive children with clonidine: Results of an open pilot study. *J. Amer. Acad. Child Adol. Psychiat., 32*(3), 577–581.

Kendall, P. C. (1990). Behavioral assessment and methodology. In C. M. Franks, G. T. Wilson, P. C. Kendall, & J. P. Foreyt (Eds.), *Review of behavior therapy: Theory and practice* (Vol. 12). New York: Guilford.

Kendall, P. C. (1990). Cognitive processes and procedures in behavior therapy. In C. M. Franks, G. T. Wilson, P. C. Kendall, & J. P. Foreyt (Eds.), *Review of behavior therapy: Theory and practice* (Vol. 12). New York: Guilford.

Kendall, P. C. (Ed.). (1990). *Child and adolescent therapy: Cognitive-behavioral procedures.* New York: Guilford.

Kendler, K. S., & Diehl, S. R. (1993). The genetics of schizophrenia: A current, genetic-epidemiologic perspective. *Schizo. Bull., 19,* 261–285.

Kendler, K. S. (1983). Computer analysed EEG findings in children of schizophrenic parents ("high risk" children): Commentary. *Integ. Psychiat., 1*(3), 82–83.

Kendler, K. S. (1997). The diagnostic validity of melancholic major depression in a population-based sample of female twins. *Arch. Gen. Psychiat., 54,* 299–304.

Kendler, K. S., Eaves, L. J., Walters, E. E., Neale, M. C. et al. (1996). The identification and validation of distinct depressive syndromes in a population-based sample of female twins. *Arch. Gen. Psychiat., 53,* 391–399.

Kendler, K. S., Heath, A., & Martin, N. G. (1987). A genetic epidemiologic study of self-report suspiciousness. *Comprehen. Psychiat., 28*(3), 187–196.

Kendler, K. S., Heath, A., Neale, M., Kessler, R., & Eaves, L. (1992). A population-based twin study of alcoholism in women. *JAMA, 268*(14), 1877–1882.

Kendler, K. S., McGuire, M., Gruenberg, A. M., & Walsh, D. (1994). An epidemiological, clinical, and family study of simple schizophrenia in County Roscommon, Ireland. *Amer. J. Psychiat., 151*(1), 27–34.

Kendler, K. S., McGuire, M., Gruenberg, A. M., O'Hare, A., Spellman, M., & Walsh, D. (1993). The Roscommon Family Study. *Arch. Gen. Psychiat., 50,* 527–540.

Kendler, K. S., Neale, M. C., Heath, A. C., Kessler, R. C., & Eaves, L. J. (1994). A twin-family study of alcoholism in women. *Amer. J. Psychiat., 151*(5), 707–715.

Kendler, K. S., Neale, M. C., Kessler, R. C., Heath, A. C., & Eaves, L. J. (1993). Panic disorder in women: A population-based twin study. *Psychol. Med., 23,* 397–406.

Kendler, K. S., Neale, M. C., Kessler, R. C., Heath, A. C., et al. (1992). Generalized anxiety disorder in women: A population-based twin study. *Arch. Gen. Psychiat., 49*(4), 267–272.

Kendler, K. S., Ochs, A. L., Gorman, A. M., Hewitt, J. K., Ross, D. E., & Mirsky, A. F. (1991). The structure of schizotypy: A pilot multitrait twin study. *Psychiat. Res., 36*(1), 19–36.

Kendler, K. S., Walters, E. E., Truett, K. R., Heath, A. C. et al. (1995). A twin-family study of self-report symptoms of panic-phobia and somatization. *Behav. Genet. 25*(6), 499–515.

Kendler, K. S., Walters., E. E., Neale, M. C., Kessler, R. C. et al. (1995). The structure of the genetic and environmental risk factors for six major psychiatric disorders in women: Phobia, generalized anxiety disorder, panic disorder, bulimia, major depression, and alcoholism. *Arch. Gen. Psychiat., 52*(5), 374–383.

Kennedy, J. L., Giuffra, L. A., Moises, H. W. et al. (1988). Evidence against linkage of schizophrenia to markers on chromosome 5 in a northern Swedish pedigree. *Nature, 336,* 167–168.

Kennedy, L. L. (1992). Partial Hospitalization. In A. Tasman & M. B. Riba (Eds.), *Review of psychiatry:* Vol. 11. Washington, DC: American Psychiatric Press.

Kennedy, S. H., Katz, R., Neitzert, C. S., Ralevski, E. et al. (1995). Exposure with response prevention treatment of anorexia nervosa-bulimic subtype and bulimia nervosa. *Behav. Res. Ther., 33*(6), 685–689.

Kent, D. A., Tomasson, K., & Coryell, W. (1995). Course and outcome of conversion and somatization disorders: A four-year follow-up. *Psychosomatics, 36*(2), 138–144.

Kernberg, O. F. (1976). *Object-relations theory and clinical psychoanalysis.* New York: Jason Aronson.

Kernberg, O. F. (1984). *Severe personality disorders.* New Haven, CT: Yale University Press.

Kernberg, O. F. (1997). Convergences and divergences in contemporary psychoanalytic technique and psychoanalytic psychotherapy. In J. K. Zeig (Ed.), *The evolution of psychotherapy: The third conference.* New York: Brunner/Mazel.

Kernberg, P. F. (1989). Narcissistic personality disorder in childhood. *Psychiatr. Clin. N. Amer., 12*(3), 671–694.

Kessler, D. (1995, March 9). In D. Levy. "FDA: Teen smoking is a disease." *USA Today,* p. 1A.

Kessler, R. C., Berglund, P. A., Zhao, S., Leaf, P. J. et al. (1996).The 12-month prevalence and correlates of serious mental illness (SMI). In R. W. Manderscheid & M. A. Sonnenschein (Eds.). *Mental health, United States, 1996.* (DHHS Pub. No. SMA 96–3098). Washington, DC: U. S. Department of Health and Human Services.

Kessler, R. C., Crum, R. M., Warner, L. A., Nelson, C. B., et al. (1997). Lifetime co-occurrence of DSM-III-R alcohol abuse and dependence with other psychiatric disorders in the National Comorbidity Survey. *Arch. Gen. Psychiat., 54,* 313–321.

Kessler, R. C., McGonagle, K. A., Zhao, S., Nelson, C. B., Hughes, M., Eshleman, S., Wittchen, H. U., & Kendler, K. S. (1994). Lifetime and 12-month prevalence of DSM-III-R psychiatric disorders in the United States. *Arch. Gen. Psychiat., 51,* 8–19.

Kessler, R. C., Sonnega, A., Bromet, E., Hughes, M., & Nelson, C. B. (1995). Posttraumatic stress disorder in the National Comorbidity Survey. *Arch. Gen. Psychiat., 52,* 1048–1060.

Ketter, T. A., George, M. S., Kimbrell, T. A., Benson, B. E., & Post, R. (1996). Functional brain imaging, limbic function, and affective disorders. *Neuroscientist, 2*(1), 55–65.

Kety, S. (1974). Biochemical and neurochemical effects of electroconvulsive shock. In M. Fink, S. Kety, J. McGaugh et al. (Eds.), *Psychobiology of convulsive therapy.* Washington, DC: Winston.

Kety, S. S. (1974). From rationalization to reason. *Amer. J. Psychiat., 131*(9), 957–963.

Kety, S. S. (1988). Schizophrenic illness in the families of schizophrenic adoptees: Findings from the Danish national sample. *Schizo. Bull., 14*(2), 217–222.

Kety, S. S., Rosenthal, D., Wender, P. H. et al. (1968). The types and prevalence of mental illness in the biological and adoptive families of schizophrenics. *J. Psychiatr. Res., 6, 345–362.*

Kety, S. S., Rosenthal, D., Wender, P. H. et al. (1975). Mental illness in the biological and adoptive families of adopted individuals who became schizophrenic: A preliminary report based on psychiatric interviews. In R. R. Fieve, D. Rosenthal, & H. Brill (Eds.), *Genetic research in psychiatry.* Baltimore: Johns Hopkins University.

Kety, S. S., Rosenthal, D., Wender, P. H., Schulsinger, F., & Jacobsen, B.

(1978). The biologic and adoptive families of adopted individuals who become schizophrenic: Prevalence of mental illness and other characteristics. In L. C. Wynne, R. L. Cromwell, & S. Matthysse (Eds.), *The nature of schizophrenia: New approaches to research and treatment.* New York: Wiley.

Keys, A., Brozek, J., Henschel, A., Mickelson, O., & Taylor, H. L. (1950). *The biology of human starvation.* Minneapolis: University of Minnesota.

Khalsa, H., Shaner, A., Anglin, M., & Wang, J. (1991). Prevalence of substance abuse in a psychiatric evaluation unit. *Drug Alc. Dep., 28*(3), 215–223.

Khanna, R., Das, A., & Damodaran, S. S. (1992). Prospective study of neuroleptic-induced dystonia in mania and schizophrenia. *Amer. J. Psychiat., 149*(4), 511–513.

Khantzian, E. J. (1985). The self-medication hypothesis of addictive disorders: Focus on heroin and cocaine dependence. *Amer. J. Psychiat., 142*(11), 1259–1264.

Kiecolt-Glaser, J. K. & Glaser, R. (1988). Methodological issues in behavioral immunology research with humans. *Brain Behav. Immun., 2,* 67–68.

Kiecolt-Glaser, J. K., & Glaser, R. (1988). Psychological influences on immunity: Implications for AIDS. *Amer. Psychol., 43*(11), 892–898.

Kiecolt-Glaser, J. K., & Glaser, R. (1992). Psychoneuro-immunology: Can psychological interventions modulate immunity? *J. Cons. Clin. Psychol., 60,* 569–575.

Kiecolt-Glaser, J. K., Dura, J. R., Speicher, C. E., Trask, O. J., & Glaser, R. (1991). Spousal caregivers of dementia victims: Longitudinal changes in immunity and health. *Psychosom. Med., 53,* 345–362.

Kiecolt-Glaser, J. K. et al. (1991). Spousal caregivers of dementia victims: Longitudinal changes in immunity and health. *Psychosom. Med., 53*(4), 345–362.

Kiecolt-Glaser, J. K., Fisher, L., Ogrocki, P., Stout, J. C., Speicher, C. E., & Glaser, R. (1987). Marital quality, marital disruption, and immune function. *Psychosom. Med., 49,* 13–34.

Kiecolt-Glaser, J. K., Garner, W., Speicher, C., Penn, G. M., Holliday, J., & Glaser, R. (1984). Psychosocial modifiers of immunocompetence in medical students. *Psychosom. Med., 46,* 7–14.

Kiecolt-Glaser, J. K., Glaser, R., Gravenstein, S., Malarkey, W. B., & Sheridan, J. (1996). Chronic stress alters the immune response to influenza virus vaccine in older adults. *Proc. Natl. Acad. Sci. U.S.A., 93,* 3043–3047.

Kiecolt-Glaser, J. K., Glaser, R., Shuttleworth, E. C., Dyer, C. S., Ogrocki, P., & Speicher, C. E. (1987). Chronic stress and immunity in family caregivers of Alzheimer's disease victims. *Psychsom. Med., 49,* 523–535.

Kiecolt-Glaser, J. K., Kennedy, S., Malkoff, S., Fisher, L., Speicher, C. E., & Glaser, R. (1988). Marital discord and immunity in males. *Psychosom. Med., 50,* 213–229.

Kiecolt-Glaser, J. K., Ricker, D., Messick, G., Speicher, C. E., Garner, W., & Glaser, R. (1984). Urinary cortisol, cellular immunocompetency and loneliness in psychiatric patients. *Psychosom. Med., 46,* 15–24.

Kienhorst, C. W. M., Wolters, W. H. G., Diekstra, R. F. W., & Otte, E. (1987). A study of the frequency of suicidal behaviour in children aged 5 to 14. *J. Child Psychol. Psychiat. Allied Disc., 28*(1), 151–165.

Kienhorst, I. C., de Wilde, E. J., Diekstra, R. F. W., & Wolters, W. H. G. (1995). Adolescents' image of their suicide attempt. *J. Amer. Acad. Child Adol. Psychiat.,* 34(5), 623–628.

Kiesler, C. A. (1992). U.S. Mental Health Policy: Doomed to fail. *Amer. Psychol., 47*(9), 1077–1082.

Kiesler, D. J. (1966). Some myths of psychotherapy research and the search for a paradigm. *Psychol. Bull., 65,* 110–136.

Kiesler, D. J. (1995). Research classic: "Some myths of psychotherapy research and the search for a paradigm": Revisited. *Psychother. Res.,* 5(2), 91–101.

Kiester, E., & Kiester, S. (1996, July). What we know now about melatonin. *Reader's Digest, pp.* 73–77.

Kiev, A. (1972). *Transcultural psychiatry.* New York: Free Press.

Kiev, A. (1989). Suicide in adults. In J. G. Howells (Ed.), *Modern perspectives in the psychiatry of the affective disorders.* New York: Brunner/Mazel.

Kihlström, J. F., Tataryn, D. J., & Hoyt, I. P. (1993). Dissociative disorders, In P. B. Sucker and H. E. Adams (Eds.) *Comprehensive handbook of psychopathology* (2nd ed.). New York: Plenum Press.

Kilmann, P. R., Sabalis, R. F., Gearing, M. L., Bukstel, L. H., & Scovern, A. W. (1982). The treatment of sexual paraphilias: A review of outcome research. *J. Sex Res., 18,* 193–252.

Kilmann, P. R., Wagner, M. K., & Sotile, W. M. (1977). The differential impact of self-monitoring on smoking behavior: An exploratory study. *J. Clin. Psychol., 33*(3), 912–914.

Kilpatrick, D. G., Best, C. L., Veronen, L. J., Amick, A. E., Vileponteaux, L. A., & Ruff, G. A. (1985). Mental health correlates of criminal victimization: A random community survey. *J. Cons. Clin. Psychol., 53,* 866–873.

Kilpatrick, D. G., Saunders, B. E., Veronen, L. J., Best, C. L., & Von, J. M. (1987). Criminal victimization: Lifetime prevalence, reporting to police, and psychological impact. *Crime & Delinquency, 33,* 479–489.

Kim, S. W., & Hoover, K. M. (1996). Tridimensional personality questionnaire: Assessment in patients with social phobia and a control group. *Psychol. Rep., 78,* 43–49.

Kimball, A. (1993). Nipping and tucking. In Skin Deep: Our national obsession with looks. *Psychol. Today, 26*(3), 96.

Kimzey, S. L. (1975). The effects of extended spaceflight on hematologic and immunologic systems. *J. Amer. Med. Women's Assoc., 30*(5), 218–232.

Kimzey, S. L., Johnson, P. C., Ritzman, S. E., & Mengel, C. E. (1976, April). Hematology and immunology studies: The second manned Skylab mission. *Aviat., Space, Envir. Med.,* pp. 383–390.

Kinard, E. M. (1982). Child abuse and depression: Cause or consequence? *Child Welfare, 61,* 403–413.

Kincel, R. L. (1981). Suicide and its archetypal themes in Rorschach record study of a male attempter. *Brit. J. Projective Psychol. & Pers. Study, 26*(2), 3–11.

Kinderman, P., & Bentall, R. P. (1997). Causal attributions in paranoia and depression: Internal, personal, and situational attributions for negative events. *J. Abnorm. Psychol., 106*(2), 341–345.

King, C. A., & Young, R. D. (1981). Peer popularity and peer communication patterns: Hyperactive vs. active but normal boys. *J. Abnorm. Child Psychol., 9*(4), 465–482.

King, C., Naylor, M., Hill, E., Shain, B., & Greden, J. (1993). Dysthymia characteristic of heavy alcohol use in depressed adolescents. *Bio. Psychiat., 33,* 210–212.

King, D. J., Blomqvist, M., Cooper, S. J., & Doherty, M. M. (1992). A placebo controlled trial of remoxipride in the prevention of relapse in chronic schizophrenia. *Psychopharmacology, 107*(2–3), 175–179.

King, G. A., Polivy, J., & Herman, C. P. (1991). Cognitive aspects of dietary restraint: Effects on person memory. *Inter. J. Eat. Disorders, 10*(3), 313–321.

King, L. W., Liberman, R. P., & Roberts, J. (1974). *An evaluation of personal effectiveness training (assertive training): A behavior group therapy.* Paper presented at the 31st annual conference of American Group Psychotherapy Association, New York.

King, M. B., & Mezey, G. (1987). Eating behaviour of male racing jockeys. *Psychol. Med., 17,* 249–253.

King, M. K., Schmaling, K. B., Cowley, D. S., & Dunner, D. L. (1995). Suicide attempt history in depressed patients with and without a history of panic attacks. *Comprehen. Psychiat., 36*(1), 25–30.

King, N. J. (1993). Simple and social phobias. In T. H. Ollendick & R. J. Prinz (Eds.), *Advances in clinical child psychology* (Vol. 15). New York: Plenum Press.

King, N. J., Gullone, E., & Ollendick, T. H. (1992). Manifest anxiety and fearfulness in children and adolescents. *J. Genet. Psychol., 153*(1), 63–73.

King, N. J., Gullone, E., Tonge, B. J., & Ollendick, T. H. (1993). Self-reports of panic attacks and manifest anxiety in adolescents. *Behav. Res. Ther., 31*(1), 111–116.

Kinsey, A. C., Pomeroy, W. B., & Martin, C. E. (1948). *Sexual behavior in the human male.* Philadelphia: Saunders.

Kinsey, A. C., Pomeroy, W. B., Martin, C. E., & Gebhard, P. H. (1953). *Sexual behavior in the human female.* Philadelphia: Saunders.

Kinzie, J., Leung, P., Boehnlein, J., Matsunaga, D. (1992). Psychiatric epidemiology of an Indian village: A 19-year replication study. *J. Nerv. Ment. Dis., 180*(1), 33–39.

Kipnis, D. (1987). Psychology and behavioral technology. *Amer. Psychol., 42*(1), 30–36.

Kirk, S. A., & Kutchins, H. (1992). *The selling of DSM: The rhetoric of science in psychiatry.* New York: Aldine de Gruyter.

Kirkland, K., & Hollandsworth, J. G. (1980). Effective test taking: Skills-acquisition versus anxiety-reduction techniques. *J. Cons. Clin. Psychol., 48*(4), 431–439.

Kirmayer, L. J., Robbins, J. M., & Paris, J. (1994). Somatoform disorders: Personality and the social matrix of somatic distress. *J. Abnorm. Psychol., 103*(1), 125–136.

Kirsch, I. & Lynn, S. J. (1995). The altered state of hypnosis: Changes in the theoretical landscape. *Amer. Psychol., 50*(10), 846–858.

Kisker, G. W. (1977). *The disorganized personality.* New York: McGraw-Hill.

Kivlaham, D. R., Marlatt, G. A., Fromme, K., Coppel, D. B., & Williams, E. (1990). Secondary prevention with college drinkers: Evaluation of an alcohol skills training program. *J. Cons. Clin. Psychol., 58,* 805–810.

Klass, D. (1997). The deceased child in the psychic and social worlds of bereaved parents during the resolution of grief. *Death Stud., 21,* 147–175.

Klausner, J. D., Sweeney, J. A., Deck, M. D., Haas, G. L. et al. (1992). Clinical correlates of cerebral ventricular enlargement in schizophrenia: Further evidence for frontal lobe disease. *J. Nerv. Ment. Dis., 180*(7), 407–412.

Kleber, H. D. (1981). Detoxification from narcotics. In J. H. Lowinson & P. Ruiz (Eds.), *Substance abuse: Clinical problems and perspectives.* Baltimore: William & Wilkins.

Kleber, H. D. (1995). Afterword to section I. In J. M. Oldham & M. B. Riba (Eds.), *American Psychiatric Press review of psychiatry,* (Vol. 14). Washington, DC: American Psychiatric Press.

Kleber, H. D. (1995). Substance abuse. In J. M. Oldham & M. B. Riba (Eds.), *American Psychiatric Press review of psychiatry* (Vol. 14). Washington, DC: American Psychiatric Press.

Klein, D. F. (1964). Delineation of two drug-responsive anxiety syndromes. *Psychopharmacologia, 5,* 397–408.

Klein, D. F. (1995). What's new in DSM-IV? *Psychiat. Ann., 25*(8), 461, 465–466, 469–474.

Klein, D. F., & Fink, M. (1962). Psychiatric reaction patterns to imipramine. *Amer. J. Psychiat., 119,* 432–438.

Klein, D. F., & Klein, H. M. (1989). The definition and psychopharmacology of spontaneous panic and phobia. In P. Tyrer (Ed.), *Psychopharmacology of anxiety.* Oxford: Oxford University Press.

Klein, D. F., Ross, D. C., & Cohen, P. (1987). Panic and avoidance in agoraphobia. *Arch. Gen. Psychiat., 44,* 377–385.

Klein, D. F., Zitrin, C. M., Woerner, M. G., & Ross, D. C. (1983). Treatment of phobias: II. Behavior therapy and supportive psychotherapy. *Arch. Gen. Psychiat., 40,* 139–145.

Klein, K., Forehand, R., Armistead, L., & Long, P. (1997). Delinquency during the transition to early adulthood: Family and parenting predictors from early adolescence. *Adolescence, 32*(125), 61–80.

Klein, R. G., Koplewicz, H. S., Kaner, A. (1992). Imipramine treatment of children with separation anxiety disorder: Special section: New developments in pediatric psychopharmacology. *J. Amer. Acad. Child Adol. Psychiat., 31*(1), 21–28.

Kleinman, A., & Cohen, A. (1997, March). Psychiatry's global challenge. *Scientif. Amer.,* pp. 86–89.

Klerman, G. L. (1984). Characterologic manifestations of affective disorders: Toward a new conceptualization: Commentary. *Integ. Psychiat., 2*(3), 94–96.

Klerman, G. L. (1984). History and development of modern concepts of affective illness. In R. M. Post & J. C. Ballenger (Eds.), *Neurobiology of affective disorders.* Baltimore: Williams & Wilkins.

Klerman, G. L., & Weissman, M. M. (1989). Increasing rates of depression. *JAMA, 261*(15), 2229–2235.

Klerman, G. L., & Weissman, M. M. (1992). Interpersonal psychotherapy. In E. S. Paykel (Ed.), *Handbook of affective disorders.* New York: Guilford.

Klerman, G. L., Weissman, M. M., Markowitz, J., Glick, I., Wilner, P. J., Mason, B., & Shear, M. K. (1994). Medication and psychotherapy. In A. E. Bergin & S. L. Garfiel (Eds.), *Handbook of psychotherapy and behavior change* (4th ed.). New York: Wiley.

Klerman, G. L., Weissman, M. M., Rounsaville, B., Chevron, E. (1984). *Interpersonal psychotherapy of depression.* New York: Basic Books.

Klieser, E., Lehmann, E., Kinzler, E., Wurthmann, C. et al. (1995). Randomized, double-blind, controlled trial of risperidone versus clozapine in patients with chronic schizophrenia. *J. Clin. Psychopharmacol., 15*(1, Suppl. 1), 45S–51S.

Kline, N. S. (1958). Clinical experience with iproniazid (Marsilid). *J. Clin. Exp. Psychopathol., 19*(1, Suppl.), 72–78.

Kline, P. (1993). *The Handbook of psychological testing.* New York: Routledge.

Klingman, A., & Hochdorf, Z. (1993). Coping with distress and self harm: The impact of a primary prevention program among adolescents. *J. Adolescence, 15,* 121–140.

Klocek, J. W., Oliver, J. M., & Ross, M. J. (1997). The role of dysfunctional attitudes, negative life events, and social support in the prediction of depressive dysphoria: A prospective longitudinal study. *Soc. Behav. Pers., 25*(2), 123–136.

Klopfer, B., & Davidson, H. (1962). *The Rorschach technique.* New York: Harcourt, Brace.

Kluft, R. P. (1983). Hypnotherapeutic crisis intervention in multiple personality. *Amer. J. Clin. Hyp., 26*(2), 73–83.

Kluft, R. P. (1984). Treatment of multiple personality disorder: A study of 33 cases. *Psychiat. Clin. N. Amer., 7*(1), 9–29.

Kluft, R. P. (1985). Hypnotherapy of childhood multiple personality disorder. *Amer. J. Clin. Hyp., 27*(4), 201–210.

Kluft, R. P. (1987). An update on multiple personality disorder. *J. Hosp. Comm. Psychiat., 38*(4), 363–373.

Kluft, R. P. (1987). The simulation and dissimulation of multiple personality disorder. *Amer. J. Clin. Hyp., 30*(2), 104–118.

Kluft, R. P. (1988). The dissociative disorders. In J. Talbott, R. Hales, & S. Yudofsky (Eds.), *Textbook of psychiatry.* Washington, DC: American Psychiatric Press.

Kluft, R. P. (1991). Multiple personality disorder. In A. Tasman & S. M. Goldfinger (Eds.), *American Psychiatric Press review of psychiatry* (Vol. 10). Washington, DC: American Psychiatric Press.

Kluft, R. P. (1992). Discussion: A specialist's perspective on multiple personality disorder. *Psychoanalyt. Inquiry, 12*(1), 139–171.

Kluft, R. P. (1993). Basic principles in conducting the psychotherapy of multiple personality disorder. In R. P. Kluft & C. G. Fine (Eds.), *Clinical perspectives on multiple personality disorder.* Washington, DC: American Psychiatric Press.

Kluft, R. P. (Ed.). (1985). *Childhood antecedents of multiple personality.* Washington, DC: American Psychiatric Press.

Knesper, D. J., Pagnucco, D. J., & Wheeler, J. R. (1985). Similarities and differences across mental health services providers and practice settings in the United States. *Amer. Psychol., 40*(12), 1352–1369.

Knowles, J. A., & Weissman, M. M. (1995). Panic disorder and agoraphobia. In J. M. Oldham & M. B. Riba (Eds.), *American Psychiatric Press review of psychiatry,* (Vol. 14). Washington, DC: American Psychiatric Press.

Knowlton, L. (1995, August 29). Licensed to heal. *Los Angeles Times,* p. E3.

Knox, L. S., Albano, A. M., & Barlow, D. H. (1996). Parental involvement in the treatment of childhood obsessive copulsive disorder: A multiple-baseline examination incorporating parents. *Behav. Ther., 27,* 93–115.

Knutson, J. F. (1995). Psychological characteristics of maltreated children. In J. T. Spence, J. M. Darley, & D. J. Foss (Eds.), *Annu. Rev. Psychol., 46,* 401-431.

Kobak, K. A., Rock, A. L., & Greist, J. H. (1995). Group behavior therapy for obsessive-compulsive disorder. *J. Specialists Group Work 20*(1), 26–32.

Kobasa, S. C. (1979). Stressful life events, personality, and health: An inquiry into hardiness. *J. Pers. Soc. Psychol., 37*(1), 1–11.

Kobasa, S. C. (1982). Commitment and coping in stress resistance among lawyers. *J. Pers. Soc. Psychol., 42,* 707–717.

Kobasa, S. C. (1982). The hardy personality: Towards a social psychology of stress and health. In J. Suls & G. Sanders (Eds.), *Social psychology of health and illness.* Hillsdale, NJ: Erlbaum.

Kobasa, S. C. (1984). Barriers to work stress: II. The "hardy" personality. In W. D. Gentry, H. Benson, & C. J. de Wolff (Eds.), *Behavioral medicine: Work, stress and health.* The Hague: Martinus Nijhoff.

Kobasa, S. C. (1987). Stress responses and personality. In R. C. Barnett, L. Biener, & G. K. Baruch (Eds.), *Gender and stress.* New York: Free Press.

Kobasa, S. C. (1990). Stress resistant personality. In R. E. Ornstein, & C. Swencionis (Eds.), *The healing brain: A Scientific reader.* Oxford, England: Pergamon Press.

Kocsis, J. H., Friedman, R. A., Markowitz, J. C., Miller, N., Gniwesch, L., & Bram, J. (1995). Stability of remission during tricyclic antidepressant continuation therapy for dysthymia. *Psychopharmacol. Bull., 31*(2), 213–216.

Koegel, L. K., Koegel, R. L., Hurley, C., & Frea, W. D. (1992). Improving social skills and disruptive behavior in children with autism through self-management. *J. Appl. Behav. Anal., 25*(2), 341–353.

Koenig, H., & Blazer, D. (1992). Epidemiology of geriatric affective disorders. *Clin. Geriatr. Med., 8,* 235–251.

Koenigsberg, H. W. (1993). Combining psychotherapy and pharmacotherapy in the treatment of borderline patients. In J. M. Oldham, M. B. Riba, & A. Tasman (Eds.), *Review of psychiatry.* Washington, DC: American Psychiatric Press.

Kohlenberg, R. J., Tsai, M., & Kohlenberg, B. S. (1996). Functional analysis in behavior therapy. In M. Hersen, R. M. Eisler, & P. M. Miller (Eds.), *Progress in behavior modification,* (Vol. 30). Pacific Grove, CA: Brooks/Cole.

Kohn, R., & Levav, I. (1994). Jews and their intraethnic differential vulnerability to affective disorders, fact or artifact? I: An overview of the literature. *Isr. J. Psychiat. Relat. Sci., 31*(4), 261–270.

Kohn, R., & Levav, I. (1995, May 23). Jewish depression study. Cited in *USA Today,* p. 1D.

Kohut, H. (1971). *The analysis of the self.* New York: International Universities Press.

Kohut, H. (1977). *The restoration of the self.* New York: International Universities Press.

Kohut, H. (1984). *How does analysis cure?* Chicago: The University of Chicago Press.

Kohut, H., & Wolf, E. S. (1978). The disorders of the self and their treatment: An outline. *Inter. J. Psychoanal., 59*(4), 413–425.

Kolb, B., & Whishaw, I. Q. (1990). *Fundamentals of human neuropsychology* (3rd ed.). San Francisco: W. H. Freeman.

Kolb, L. C. (1956). Psychotherapeutic evolution and its implications. *Psychiatr. Quart., 30,* 1–19.

Kolff, C. A., & Doan, R. N. (1985). Victims of torture: Two testimonies. In E. Stover & E. O. Nightingale (Eds.), *The breaking of bodies and minds: Torture, psychiatric abuse, and the health professions.* New York: W. H. Freeman.

Kolodny, R., Masters, W. H., & Johnson, J. (1979). *Textbook of sexual medicine.* Boston: Little, Brown.

Komaroff, A. L., Masuda, M., & Holmes, T. H. (1986). The Social Readjustment Rating Scale: A comparative study of Negro, White, and Mexican Americans. *J. Psychosom. Res., 12,* 121–128.

Komaroff, A. L., Masuda, M., & Holmes, T. H. (1989). The Social Readjustment Rating Scale: A comparative study of Black, White, and Mexican Americans. In T. H. Holmes and E. M. David (Eds.), *Life change, life events, and illness.* New York: Praeger.

Kondziela, J. R. (1984). Extreme lithium intoxication without severe symptoms. *Hosp. Comm. Psychiat., 35*(7), 727–728.

Koob, G. F. (1992). Drugs of abuse: Anatomy, pharmacology and function of reward pathways. *Trends pharmacol. Sci., 13,* 177–184.

Koopman, C., Classen, C., Cardena, E., & Spiegel, D. (1995). When disaster strikes, acute stress disorder may follow. *J. Traum. Stress., 8*(1), 29–46.

Kopala, L. C., Fredrikson, D., Good, K. P., & Honer, W. G. (1996). Symptoms in neuroleptic-naive, first-episode schizophrenia: Response to resperidone. *Biol. Psychiat., 39,* 296–298.

Kopec, A. M. (1995). Rational emotive behavior therapy in a forensic setting: Practical issues. *J. Rat.-Emot. & Cognit.-Behav. Ther., 13*(4), 243–253.

Kopelman, M. D. (1995). The Korsakoff syndrome. *Brit. J. Psychiat., 166*(2), 154–173.

Kopelman, M. D. (1995). The assessment of psychogenic amnesia. In A. D. Baddeley, B. A. Wilson, F. N. Watts (Eds.), *Handbook of memory disorders.* Chichester, England: Wiley.

Korchin, S. J., & Sands, S. H. (1983). Principles common to all psychotherapies. In C. E. Walker et al. (Eds.), *The handbook of clinical psychology.* Homewood, IL: Dow Jones-Irwin.

Korenman, S. G. & Barchas, J. D. (1993). *Biological basis of substance abuse.* New York: Oxford University Press.

Kornitzer, M., Boutsen, M., Dramaix, M., Thijs, J. et al. (1995). Combined use of nicotine patch and gum in smoking cessation: A placebo-controlled clinical trial. *Prev. Med., 24*(1), 41–47.

Kosik, K. S. (1992). Alzheimer's disease: A cell biological perspective. *Science, 256,* 780–783.

Koss, M. P. (1992). The underdetection of rape: Methodological choices influence incidence estimates. *J. Soc. Issues, 48*(1), 61–75.

Koss, M. P. (1993). Rape: Scope, impact, interventions, and public policy responses. *Amer. Psychol., 48*(10), 1062–1069.

Koss, M. P., Dinero, T. E., Seibel, C., & Cox, S. (1988). Stranger and acquaintance rape: Are there differences in the victim's experience? *Psychol. Women Quart., 12,* 1–23.

Koss, M. P., & Harvey, M. R. (1987). *The rape victim.* Lexington, MA: Stephen Green.

Koss, M. P., & Heslet, L. (1992). Somatic consequences of violence against women. *Arch. Fam. Med., 1*(1), 53–59.

Koss, M. P., Koss, P., & Woodruff, W. J. (1991). Deleterious effects of criminal victimization on women's health and medical utilization. *Arch. Internal Med., 151,* 342–357.

Koss, M. P., Woodruff, W. J., & Koss, P. (1991). Criminal victimization among primary care medical patients: Prevalence, incidence, and physician usage. *Behav. Sci. Law, 9,* 85–96.

Kosten, T. R., & McCance-Katz, E. (1995). New pharmacotherapies. In J. M. Oldham & M. B. Riba (Eds.), *American Psychiatric Press review of psychiatry,* (Vol. 14). Washington, DC: American Psychiatric Press.

Kosten, T. R. (1988). The symptomatic and prognostic implications of psychiatric diagnoses in treated substance abusers. *Nat. Inst. on Drug Abuse Res. Monog. Ser., 81,* 416–421.

Kostlan, A. (1954). A method for the empirical study of psychodiagnosis. *J. Cons. Psychol., 18,* 83–88.

Kovacs, M. (1996). Presentation and source of major depression disorder during childhood and later years of the life span. *J. Amer. Child Adol. Psychiat., 35*(6), 705–715.

Kovacs, M. (1997). Depressive disorders in childhood: An impressionistic landscape. *J. Child Psychol. Psychiat., 38*(3), 287–298.

Kovacs, M., Goldston, D., & Gatsonis, C. (1993). Suicidal behaviors and childhood-onset depressive disorders: A longitudinal investigation. *J. Amer. Acad. Child Adol. Psychiat., 32,* 8–20.

Kraines, S. H., & Thetford, E. S. (1972). *Help for the depressed.* Springfield, IL: Thomas.

Kramer, M. (1989, August 14). Cited in S. Begley, "The stuff that dreams are made of." *Newsweek,* p. 40.

Kramer, M. (1992). Cited in R. D. Cartwright & L. Lamberg, *Crisis dreaming: Using your dreams to solve your problems.* HarperCollins, 1992.

Kramer, P. (1993). *Listening to Prozac-A pychiatrist explores mood-altering drugs and the meaning of the self.* New York: Viking.

Kramer, S. & Akhtar, S. (Eds.). (1994). *Mahler and Kohut: Perspectives on development, psychopathology, and technique.* Northvale, NJ: Jason Aronson.

Krane, R. J., Goldstein, I., & Saenz de Tejada, I. (1989). Impotence. *N. Engl. J. Med., 321,* 1648–1659.

Krantz, L. (1992). *What the odds are.* New York: Harper Perennial.

Kratochwill, T. R. (1992). Single-case research design and analysis: An overview. In T. R. Kratochwill & J. R. Levin (Eds.), *Single-case research design and analysis: new directions for psychology and education.* Hillsdale, NJ: Erlbaum.

Kratochwill, T. R., Mott, S. E., & Dodson, C. L. (1984). Case study and single-case research in clinical and applied psychology. In A. S. Bellack & M. Hersen (Eds.), *Research methods in clinical psychology.* New York: Pergamon Press.

Kratzer, L., & Hodgins, S. (1997). Adult outcomes of child conduct problems: A cohort study. *J. Abnorm. Child Psychol., 25*(1), 65–81.

Krauss, M. W., Seltzer, M. M., Goodman, S. J. (1992). Social support networks of adults with mental retardation who live at home. *Amer. J. Ment. Retard., 96*(4), 432–441.

Krausz, M., Muller-Thomsen, T., & Haasen, C. (1995). Suicide among schizophrenic adolescents in the long-term course of illness. *Psychopathology, 28*(2), 95–103.

Kresin, D. (1993). Medical aspects of inhibited sexual desire disorder. In W. O'Donohue & J. Geer (eds.), *Handbook of sexual dysfunctions.* Boston: Allyn & Bacon.

Kring, A. M. & Neale, J. M. (1996). Do schizophrenic patients show a disjunctive relationship among expressive, experiential, and psychophysiological components of emotion? *J. Abnorm. Psychol., 105*(2), 249–257.

Kripke, D. F., & Robinson, D. (1985). Ten years with a lithium group. *McLean Hosp. J., 10,* 1–11.

Krishnan, K. R. R., Swartz, M. S., Larson, M. J., & Santo-liquido, G. (1984). Funeral mania in recurrent bipolar affective disorders: Reports of three cases. *J. Clin. Psychiat., 45,* 310–311.

Krishnan, K. R. R., Tupler, L. A., Ritchie, J. C., McDonald, W. M. et al. (1996). Brief reports. Apoliprotein E-ε4 frequency in geriatric depression. *Bio. Psychiat., 40,* 69–71.

Kroenke, K., Spitzer, R. L., deGruy, F. V., III, Hahn, S. R., et al. (1997). Multisomatoform disorder. An alternative to undifferentiated somatoform disorder for the somatizing patient in primary care. *Arch. Gen. Psychiat. 54,* 352–358.

Kronenberger, W. G., Laite, G., & Laclave, L. (1995). Self-esteem and depressive symptomatology in children with somatoform disorders. *Psychosomatics, 36,* 564–569.

Krupp, P., & Barnes, P. (1992). Clozapine-associated agranulocytosis: Risk and aetiology. *Brit. J. Psychiat., 160*(Suppl. 17), 38–40.

Krystal, H. (1968). *Massive psychic trauma.* New York: International Universities Press.

Kuch, K., & Cox, B. J. (1992). Symptoms of PTSD in 124 survivors of the Holocaust. *Amer. J. Psychiat., 149*(3), 337–340.

Kuczmarski, R., Fiegal, K., Campbell, S., & Johnson, C. (1994). Increasing prevalence of overweight among U.S. adults: The National Health and Nutrition Examination Surveys, 1960–1991. *JAMA, 272,* 205–211.

Kuhn, R. (1958). The treatment of depressive states with G-22355 (imipramine hydrochloride). *Amer. J. Psychiat., 115,* 459–464.

Kuhn, T. S. (1962). *The structure of scientific revolutions.* Chicago: University of Chicago.

Kulick, A. R., Pope, H. G., & Keck, P. E. (1990). Lycanthropy and self-identification. *J. Nerv. Ment. Dis., 178*(2), 134–137.

Kulkarni, J., de Castella, A., Smith, D., McKenzie, D., Keks, N., Singh, B., & Copolov, D. (1995). Gonadotropin response to naloxone challenge in female and male psychotic patients: A pilot study. *Bio. Psychiat., 38,* 701–703.

Kumar, V. (1993). Editorial Commentary on two studies reporting controlled clinical trials of the use of tacrine in Alzheimer's disease. *Alzheimer's Dis. Relat. Disorders, 7,* 113.

Kupfer, D. J. (1995). Acute continuation and maintenance treatment of mood disorders. *Depression, 3,* 137–138.

Kuriansky, J. B. (1988). Personality style and sexuality. In R. A. Brown & J. R. Field (Eds.), *Treatment of sexual problems in individual and couples therapy.* Costa Mesa, CA: PMA Publishing Corp.

Kurlander, H., Miller, W., & Seligman, M. E. P. (1974). *Learned helplessness, depression, and prisoner's dilemma.* Unpublished manuscript.

Kurtz, D. L., Stewart, R. B., Zweifel, M., Li, T.-K., & Froehlich, J. C. (1996). Genetic differences in tolerance and sensitization to the sedative/hypnotic effects of alcohol. *Pharmacol. Biochem. Behav., 53*(3), 585–591.

Kushner, H. I. (1995). Women and suicidal behavior: Epidemiology, gender and lethality in historical perspective. In S. S. Canetto & D. Lester (Eds.), *Women and suicidal behavior.* New York: Springer.

Kushner, M. G., Riggs, D. S., Foa, E. B., & Miller, S. M. (1992). Perceived controllability and the development of posttraumatic stress disorder (PTSD) in crime victims. *Behav. Res. Ther., 31*(1), 105–110.

Kusumi, I., Ishikane, T., Matsubara, S., & Koyama, T. (1995). Long-term treatment with haloperidol or clozapine does not affect dopamine D_4 receptors in rat frontal cortex. *J. Neural Transmission, 101,* 231–235.

Labbate, L. A., & Snow, M. P. (1992). Posttraumatic stress symptoms among soldiers exposed to combat in the Persian Gulf. *Hosp. Comm. Psychiat., 43*(8), 831–833.

Labbé, E. E. (1995). Treatment of childhood migraine with autogenic training and skin temperature biofeedback: A component analysis. *Headache, 35*(1), 10–13.

Labott, S. M., Preisman, R. C., Popovich, J., & Iannuzzi, M. C. (1995). Health care utilization of somatizing patients in a pulmonary subspecialty clinic. *Psychosomatics, 36*(2), 122–128.

Lachmann, A., & Lachmann, F. M. (1995). The personification of evil: Motivations and fantasies of the serial killer. *Inter. Forum Psychoanal., 4*(1), 17–23.

Lachmann, F. M., & Beebe, B. (1995). Self psychology: Today. *Psychoanal. Dialog., 5*(3), 375–384.

Lachner, G., & Engel, R. R. (1994). Differentiation of dementia and depression by memory tests: A meta-analysis. *J. Nerv. Ment. Dis., 182*(1), 34–39.

Lacks, P. (1984). Bender *Gestalt screening for brain dysfunction.* New York: Wiley.

Ladds, B. (1997). Forensic treatment and rehabilitation: The growing need for more services and more research. *Inter. J. Men. Hlth., 25*(4), 3–10.

Lader, M. (1992). Hazards of benzodiazepine treatments of anxiety. In G. D. Burrows, S. M. Roth, & R. Noyes, Jr., *Handbook of anxiety* (Vol. 5). Oxford, England: Elsevier.

Ladouceur, R., Freeston, M. H., Gagnon, F., Thibodeau, N. et al. (1995). Cognitive-behavioral treatment of obsessions. *Behav. Mod. 19*(2), 247–257.

Ladouceur, R., Rhéaume, J., & Aublet, F. (1997). Excessive responsibility in obsessional concerns: A fine-grained experimental analysis. *Behav. Res. Ther., 35*(5), 423–427.

Ladouceur, R., Rhéaume, J., Freeston, M. H., Aublet, F. et al. (1995). Experimental manipulations of responsibility: An analogue test for models of obsessive-compulsive disorder. *Behav. Res. Ther., 33*(8), 937–946.

Lahey, B. B., Hartdagen, S. E., Frick, P. J., McBurnett, K. et al. (1988). Conduct disorder: Parsing the confounded relation to parental divorce and antisocial personality. *J. Abnorm. Psychol., 97*(3), 334–337.

Lahey, B. B., Piancentini, J. C., McBurnett, K., Stone, P. et al. (1988). Psychopathology in the parents of children with conduct disorder and hyperactivity. *J. Amer. Acad. Child Adol. Psychiat., 27*(2), 163–170.

Lai, J. Y., & Linden, W. (1992). Gender, anger expression style, and opportunity for anger release determine cardiovascular reaction to and recovery from anger provocation. *Psychosom. Med., 54,* 297–310.

Laing, R. D. (1959). *The divided self: An existential study in sanity and madness.* London: Tavistock.

Laing, R. D. (1964). *The divided self* (2nd ed.). London: Pelican.

Laing, R. D. (1967). *The politics of experience.* New York: Pantheon.

Lamb, H. R. (1982). *Treating the long-term mentally ill.* San Francisco: Jossey-Bass.

Lamb, H. R. (1988). When the chronically mentally ill need acute hospitalization: Maximizing its benefits. *Psychiatr. Ann., 18*(7), 426–430.

Lamb, H. R. (1994). Public psychiatry and prevention. In R. E. Hales, S. C. Yudofsky, & J. A. Talbott, (Eds.), *The American Psychiatric Press textbook of psychiatry,* (2nd ed.). Washington, DC: American Psychiatric Press.

Lambert, M. J., & Bergin, A. E. (1994). The effectiveness of psychotherapy. In A. E. Bergin, & S. L. Garfield (Eds.), *Handbook of psychotherapy and behavioral change* (4th ed.). New York: Wiley.

Lambert, M. J., & Hill, C. E. (1994). Assessing psychotherapy outcomes and processes. In A. E. Bergin & S. L. Garfiel (Eds.), *Handbook of psychotherapy and behavior change* (4th ed.). New York: Wiley.

Lambert, M. J., Shapiro, D. A., & Bergin, A. E. (1986). The effectiveness of psychotherapy. In S. L. Garfield & A. E. Bergin (Eds.), *Handbook of psychotherapy and behavioral change* (3rd ed.). New York: Wiley.

Lambert, M. J., Weber, F. D., & Sykes, J. D. (1993, April). *Psychotherapy versus placebo.* Poster presented at the annual meetings of the Western Psychological Association, Phoenix, AZ.

Lamberti, J. S., & Cummings, S. (1992). Hands-on restraints in the treatment of multiple personality disorder. *Hosp. Comm. Psychiat., 43*(3), 283–284.

Landry, D. W. (1997, February). Immunotherapy of cocaine addiction. *Scientif. Amer.,* pp. 42–45.

Landry, D., Zhao, K., Yang, G., Glickman, M., & Georgiadis, T. (1993). Antibody-catalyzed degredation of cocaine. *Science, 259,* 1899–1901.

Landry, M. J. (1994). *Understanding drugs of abuse: The processes of addiction, treatment, and recovery.* Washington, DC: American Psychiatric Press.

Landsbergis, P. A., Schnall, P. L., Warren, K., Pickering, T. G., & Schwartz, J. E. (1994). Association between ambulatory blood pressure and alternative formulations of job strain. *Scand. J. Work Envir. Hlth., 20,* 349–363.

Lang, P. J. (1985). The cognitive psychophysiology of emotion: Fear and anxiety. In A. H. Tuma & J. D. Maser (Eds.), *Anxiety and anxiety disorders.* Hillsdale, NJ: Erlbaum.

Lang, P. J., & Lazovik, A. D. (1963). Experimental desensitization of a phobia. *J. Abnorm. Soc. Psychol., 66,* 519–525.

Langer, E. J. (1983). *The psychology of control.* Beverly Hills, CA: Sage.

Langer, S. Z., & Raisman, R. (1983). Binding of (3H) imipramine and (3H) desipramine as biochemical tools for studies in depression. *Neuropharmacology, 22,* 407–413.

Langevin, R., Bain, J., Wortzman, G., Hucker, S. et al. (1988). Sexual sadism: Brain, blood, and behavior. *Ann. NY Acad. of Sci., 528,* 163–171.

Langwieler, G., & Linden, M. (1993). Therapist individuality in the diagnosis and treatment of depression. *J. Affect. Disorders, 27,* 1–12.

Lanyon, R. I. (1984). Personality assessment. *Annu. Rev. Psychol., 35,* 667–701.

Largo, R. H., Pfister, D., Molinari, L. et al. (1989). Significance of prenatal, perinatal and postnatal factors in the development of AGA preterm infants at five to seven years. *Dev. Med. Child Neurol., 32,* 30–45.

Larsen, R. J. (1993). *Emotional regulation in everyday life: An experience sampling study.* Paper presented at the annual meeting of the American Psychology Association, Toronto.

Lasch, C. (1978). *The culture of narcissism: American life in an age of diminishing expectations.* New York: Norton.

Laumann, E. O., Gagnon, J. H., Michael, R. T., & Michaels, S. (1994). *The social organization of sexuality.* Chicago: University of Chicago Press.

Lawford, B. R., Young, R. McD., Rowell, J. A., Gibson, J. N. et al. (1997). Association of the D_2 dopamine receptor A1 allele with alcoholism: Medical severity of alcoholism and type of controls. *Bio. Psychiat., 41,* 386–393.

Lawrence, C. (1987). An integrated spiritual and psychological growth model in the treatment of narcissism. *J. Psychol. Theol., 15*(3), 205–213.

Lawrence, G. H. (1986). Using computers for the treatment of psychological problems. *Comput. Human Behav., 2*(1), 43–62.

Lawson, D. M. (1995). Conceptualization and treatment for Vietnam veterans experiencing posttraumatic stress disorder. *J. Ment. Hlth. Couns., 17*(1), 31–53.

Lazarus, A. A. (1965). The treatment of a sexually inadequate man. In L. P. Ullman & L. Krasner (Eds.), *Case studies in behavior modification.* New York: Holt, Rinehart, & Winston.

Lazarus, J. A. (1995). Ethical issues in doctor-patient sexual relationships. [Special issue: Clinical sexuality]. *Psychiat. Clin. N. Amer., 18*(1), 55–70.

Lazarus, R. S., & Folkman, S. (1984). *Stress, appraisal, and coping.* New York: Springer.

Leaman, T. L. (1992). *Healing the Anxiety Diseases.* New York: Plenum Press.

Lebegue, B. (1991). Paraphilias in U.S. pornography titles: "Pornography made me do it" (Ted Bundy). *Bull. Amer. Acad. Psychiat. Law, 19*(1), 43–48.

Lebell, M. B., Marder, S. R., Mintz, J., Mintz, L. I., Tompson, M., Wirshing, W., Johnston-Cronk, K., & McKenzie, J. (1993). Patients' perceptions of family emotional climate and outcome in schizophrenia. *Brit. J. Psychiat., 162,* 751–754.

Lebow, J. L., & Gurman, A. S. (1995). Research assessing couple and family therapy. In J. T. Spence, J. M. Darley, & D. J. Foss (Eds.), *Annual review of psychology,* (Vol. 46). Palo Alto, CA: Annual Reviews.

Lecrubier, Y. (1995). Pharmacotherapy and the role of new and classic antidepressants. *Depression, 3,* 134–136.

Ledoux, S., Choquet, M., & Manfredi, R. (1993). Associated factors for self-reported binge eating among male and female adolescents. *J. Adolescence, 16,* 75–91.

Lee, D. E. (1985). Alternative self-destruction. *Percept. Motor Skills, 61*(3, Part 2), 1065–1066.

Lee, K. A., Vaillant, G. E., Torrey, W. C., & Elder, G. H. (1995). A 50-year prospective study of the psychological sequelae of World War II combat. *Amer. J. Psychiat., 152*(4), 516–522.

Lee, P. W. H., Lieh-Mak, Tu, K. K., & Spinks, J. A. (1993). Coping strategies of schizophrenic patients and their relationship to outcome. *Brit. J. Psychiat., 163,* 177–182.

Lee, R. K. K., Jimenez, J., Cox, A. J., & Wurtman, R. J. (1996). Metabotropic glutamate receptors regulate APP processing in hippocampal neurons and cortical astrocytes derived from fetal rats. In R. J. Wurtman, S. Corkin, J. H. Growdon, & R. M. Nitsch (Eds.), *The neurobiology of Alzheimer's disease.* New York: New York Academy of Sciences.

Lee, T., & Seeman, P. (1980). Elevation of brain neuro-leptic/dopamine receptors in schizophrenia. *Amer. J. Psychiat., 137,* 191–197.

Leenaars, A. A. (1989). *Suicide notes: Predictive clues and patterns.* New York: Human Sciences.

Leenaars, A. A. (1991). Suicide in the young adult. In A. A. Leenaars (Ed.), *Life span perspectives of suicide: Time-lines in the suicide process.* New York: Plenum Press.

Leenaars, A. A. (1992). Suicide notes, communication, and ideation. In R. W. Maris, A. L. Berman, J. T. Maltsberger, & R. I. Yufit (Eds.), *Assessment and prediction of suicide.* New York: Guilford.

Leenaars, A. A., & Lester, D. (1992). Facts and myths of suicide in Canada and the United States. *J. Soc. Psychol., 132*(6), 787–789.

Leenaars, A. A. & Wenckstern, S. (1991). *Suicide prevention in the schools.* Washington, DC: Hemisphere.

Leenstra, A. S., Ormel, J., & Giel, R. (1995). Positive life change and recovery from depression and anxiety: A three-stage longitudinal study of primary care attenders. *Brit. J. Psychiat., 166*(3), 333–343.

Leff, J., & Vaughn, C. (1976, November). Schizophrenia and family life. *Psychol. Today,* pp. 13–18.

Lehman, A. F. (1995). Vocational rehabilitation in schizophrenia. *Schizo. Bull., 21*(4), 645–656.

Lehman, A. F., Myers, C. P., Dixon, L. B., & Johnson, J. L. (1996). Detection of substance use disorders among psychiatric inpatients. *J. Nerv. Ment. Dis., 184*(4), 228–233.

Lehman, R. S. (1991). *Statistics and research design in the behavioral sciences.* Belmont, CA: Wadsworth.

Lehmann, H. E. (1967). Psychiatric disorders not in standard nomenclature. In A. M. Freedman, H. I. Kaplan, & H. S. Kaplan (Eds.), *Comprehensive textbook of psychiatry.* Baltimore: Williams & Wilkins.

Lehmann, H. E. (1985). Current perspectives on the biology of schizophrenia. In M. N. Menuck & M. V. Seeman. *New perspectives in schizophrenia.* New York: Macmillan.

Lehrer, P. M., Carr, R., Sargunaraj, D., & Woolfolk, R. L. (1993). Differential effects of stress management therapies in behavioral medicine. In P. M. Lehrer & R. L. Woolfolk (Eds.), *Principles and practice of stress management* (2nd ed.). New York: Guilford.

Leibenluft, E. (1996). Women with bipolar illness: Clinical and research issues. *Amer. J. Psychiat., 153*(2), 163–173.

Leiblum, S. R., & Segraves, R. T. (1995). Sex and aging. In J. M. Oldham & M. B. Riba (Eds.), *American Psychiatric Press review of psychiatry* (Vol. 14). Washington, DC: American Psychiatric Press.

Leiblum, S. R., (1996). Sexual pain disorders. In *Treatment of psychiatric disorders: The DSM-IV edition.* Washington, DC: American Psychiatric Press.

Leipsic, J. S., Abraham, H. D., & Halperin, P. (1995). Neuroleptic malignant syndrome in the elderly. *J. Geriat. Psychiat. Neurol., 8*(1), 28–31.

Leitenberg, H., & Callahan, E. J. (1973). Reinforced practice and reduction of different kinds of fears in adults and children. *Behav. Res. Ther., 11*(1), 19–30.

Leitenberg, H., Rosen, J. C., Wolf, J., Vara, L. S., Detzer, M. J., & Srebnik, D. (1993). Comparison of cognitive-behavior therapy and desipramine in the treatment of bulimia nervosa. *Behav. Res. Ther., 32*(1), 37–45.

Leitenberg, H., Yost, L. W., & Carroll-Wilson, M. (1986). Negative cognitive errors in children: Questionnaire development, normative data, and comparisons between children with and without self-reported symptoms of depression, low self-esteem, and evaluation anxiety. *J. Cons. Clin. Psychol., 54,* 528–536.

Leland, H. (1991). Adaptive behavior scales. In J. L. Matson & J. A. Mulick (Eds.), *Handbook of mental retardation.* New York: Pergamon Press.

LEMAS (Law Enforcement Management and Administrative Statistics Survey). (1990). Cited in U.S. Dept. of Justice (1994) Violence between inmates (Special report).

Lemelin, S., Baruch, P., Vincent, A., LaPlante, L., Everett, J., & Vincent, P. (1996). Attention disturbance in clinical depression: Deficient distractor inhibition or processing resource deficit? *J. Nerv. Ment. Dis., 184*(2), 114–121.

Lemieux, A. M., & Coe, C. L. (1995). Abuse related posttraumatic stress disorder: Evidence for chronic neuroendocrine activation in women. *Psychosom. Med., 57*(2), 105-115.

Leo, R. J., & Kim, K. Y. (1995). Clomipramine treatment of paraphilias in elderly demented patients. *J. Geriatr. Psychiat. Neurol., 8*(2), 123–124.

Leon, G. R. (1977). *Case histories of deviant behavior* (2nd ed.). Boston: Allyn & Bacon.

Leon, G. R. (1984). *Case histories of deviant behavior* (3rd ed.). Boston: Allyn & Bacon.

Leon, R. L., Bowden, C. L., & Faber, R. A. (1989). The psychiatric interview, history, and mental status examination. In H. I. Kaplan & B. J. Sadock (Eds.), *Comprehensive textbook of psychiatry* (5th ed., Vol. 1). Baltimore: Williams & Wilkins.

Leonard, B. E. (1992). Effects of pharmacological treatments on neurotransmitter receptors in anxiety disorders. In G. D. Burrows, S. M. Roth, & R. Noyes, Jr., *Handbook of anxiety* (Vol. 5). Oxford, England: Elsevier.

Leonard, B. E. (1997). Neurotransmitters in depression: Noradrenaline and serotonin and their interactions. *J. Clin. Psychopharmacol., 17*(2, Suppl. 1), 1S.

Lepine, J. P., & Lellouch, J. (1995). Classification and epidemiology of social phobia [Special issue: Social phobia]. *Eur. Arch. Psychiat. Clin. Neurosci. 244*(6), 290–296.

Lerer, B., Shapira, B., Calev, A., Tubi, N., Drexler, H., Kindler, S., Lidsky, D., & Schwartz, J. E. (1995). Antidepressant and cognitive effects of twice- versus three-times-weekly ECT. *Amer. J. Psychiat., 152*(4), 564–570.

Lerner, H. D. (1986). Current developments in the psychoanalytic psychotherapy of anorexia nervosa and bulimia nervosa. *Clin. Psychologist, 39*(2), 39–43.

Lerner, H. D., & Lerner, P. M. (Eds.). (1988). *Primitive mental states and the Rorschach.* Madison, CT: International Universities Press.

Lerner, V., Fotyanov, M., Liberman, M., Shlafman, M., & Bar-El, Y. (1995). Maintenance medication for schizophrenia and schizoaffective patients. *Schizo. Bull., 21*(4), 693–701.

Leroux, J. A. (1986). Suicidal behavior and gifted adolescents. *Roeper Rev., 9*(2), 77–79.

Lesch, K. P., Bengel, D., Heils, A., Sabol, S. Z., Greenberg, B. D., Petri, S., Benjamin, J., Muller, C. R., Hamer, D. H., & Murphy, D. L. (1996). Association of anxiety-related traits with a polymorphism in the serotonin transporter gene regulatory region. *Science, 24*(5292), 1527–31.

Leserman, J., Drossman, D. A., Li, Z., Toomey, T. C., et al. (1996). Sexual and physical abuse history in gastroenterology practice: How types of abuse impact health status. *Psychosom. Med., 58*(1), 4–15.

Leshner, A. I. et al. (1992). *Outcasts on the main street: Report of the Federal Task Force on Homelessness and Severe Mental Illness.* Washington, DC: Interagency Council on the Homeless.

Leslie, A. (1997, May 23). *Theory of mind impairment in autism: Its nature and significance.* Keynote address at The Eden Institute Foundation Princeton Lecture Series on Autism.

Leslie, A. & Frith, U. (1990). Prospects for a cognitive neuropsychology of autism: Hobson's choice. *Psych. Rev., 97,* 122–131.

Lester, D. (1972). Myth of suicide prevention. *Comprehen. Psychiat., 13*(6), 555–560.

Lester, D. (1974). The effects of suicide prevention centers on suicide rates in the United States. *Pub. Hlth. Rep., 89,* 37–39.

Lester, D. (1985). Accidental deaths as disguised suicides. *Psychol. Rep., 56*(2), 626.

Lester, D. (1985). The quality of life in modern America and suicide and homicide rates. *J. Soc. Psychol., 125*(6), 779–780.

Lester, D. (1989). *Can we prevent suicide?* New York: AMS Press.

Lester, D. (1991). Do suicide prevention centers prevent suicide? *Homeostasis Hlth. Dis., 33*(4), 190–194.

Lester, D. (1991). The etiology of suicide and homicide in urban and rural America. *J. Rural Commun. Psychol., 12*(1), 15–27.

Lester, D. (1992). Alcoholism and drug abuse. In R. W. Maris, A. L. Berman, J. T. Maltsberger, & R. I. Yufit (Eds.), *Assessment and prediction of suicide.* New York: Guilford.

Lester, D. (1992). Is there a need for suicide prevention? *Crisis, J. Crisis Intervent. Suic. Prev., 2,* 94.

Lester, D. (1992). Suicide and disease. *Loss, Grief & Care, 6*(2–3), 173–181.

Lester, D. (1994). Involvement in war and suicide rates in Great Britain, 1901–1965. *Psych. Rep., 75*(3, Pt 1), 1154.

Lester, D. (1994). Are there unique features of suicide in adults of different ages and developmental stages? *Omega Journal of Death and Dying, 29*(4), 337–348.

Lester, D. (1994). Motives for suicide in suicide notes from completed and attempted suicides. *Psych. Rep., 75*(3, Pt. 1), 1130.

Lester, D. (1994). Can suicidologists distinguish between suicide notes from completers and attempters? *Percept. Motor Skills, 79*(3, Pt. 2), Spec Issues 1498.

Leszcz, M. (1992). Group psychotherapy of the borderline patient. In D. Silver & M. Rosenbluth (Eds.), *Handbook of borderline disorders.* Madison, CT: International Universities Press.

Letourneau, E., & O'Donohue, W. (1993). Sexual desire disorders. In W. O'Donohue & J. Geer (Eds.), *Handbook of sexual dysfunctions.* Boston: Allyn & Bacon.

Le Unes, A. D., Nation, J. R., & Turley, N. M. (1980). Male-female performance in learned helplessness. *J. Psychol., 104,* 255–258.

Leung, A. W., & Heimberg, R. G. (1996). Homework compliance, perceptions of control, and outcome of cognitive-behavioral treatment of social phobia. *Behav. Res. Ther., 34*(5/6), 423–432.

Leutwyler, K. (1996). Paying attention: The controversy over ADHD and the drug Ritalin is obscuring a real look at the disorder and its underpinnings. *Scientif. Amer., 272*(2), 12–13.

Leutwyler, K. (1996, February). Schizophrenia revisited: New studies focus on malfunctions in the brain. *Scientif. Amer.,* 22–23.

LeVay, S. & Hamer, D. H. (1994). Evidence for a biological influence in male homosexuality. [Review]. *Scientif. Amer., 270*(5), 44–49

Levenson, J. L. (1985). Neuroleptic malignant syndrome. *Amer. J. Psychiat., 142,* 1137–1145.

Levenson, M. R. (1992). Rethinking psychopathy. *Theory Psychol., 2*(1), 51–71.

Levesque, R. J. R. (1996). Regulating the private relations of adults with mental disabilities: Old laws, new policies, hollow hopes. *Behav. Sci. Law, 14,* 83–106.

Levin, B. L. (1992). Managed health care: A national perspective. In R. W. Manderscheid & M. A. Sonnenschein (Eds.), *Mental health, United States, 1992.* Washington, DC: U.S. Department of Health and Human Services.

Levin, H., Chengappa, K. R., Kambhampati, R. K., Mahdavi, N. et al. (1992). Should chronic treatment-refractory akathisia be an indication for the use of clozapine in schizophrenic patients? *J. Clin. Psychiat., 53*(7), 248–251.

Levin, H. S., Mattis, S., Ruff, R. M., Eisenberg, H. M., Marshall, L. F., Tabaddor, K., High, W. M. Jr., & Frankowski, R. F. (1987). Neurobehavioral outcome following minor head injury: A three-center study. *J. Neurosurg., 66,* 234–243.

Levin, J., & Fox, J. A. (1985). *Mass murder.* New York: Plenum Press.

Levine, M. D. (1975). Children with encopresis: A descriptive analysis. *Pediatrics, 56,* 412–416.

Levine, M. D. (1987). *How schools can help combat student eating disorders: Anorexia nervosa and bulimia.* Washington, DC: National Education Assoc.

Levinson, V. R. (1985). The compatibility of the disease concept with a psychodynamic approach in the treatment of alcoholism. Special Issue: Psychosocial issues in the treatment of alcoholism. *Alcohol. Treatment Quart., 2,* 7–24.

Levis, D. J., & Carrera, R. N. (1967). Effects of 10 hours of implosive therapy in the treatment of outpatients: A preliminary report. *J. Abnorm. Psychol., 72,* 504–508.

Levitan, H. L. (1981). Implications of certain dreams reported by patients in a bulimic phase of anorexia nervosa. *Canad. J. Psychiat., 26*(4), 228–231.

Levitt, E. E. (1989). *The clinical application of MMPI Special Scales.* Hillsdale, NJ: Erlbaum.

Levitt, R. (1975). *Psychopharmacology: A biological approach.* New York: Wiley.

Levy, D., Kimhi, R., Barak, Y., Demmer, M. et al. (1996). Brainstem auditory evoked potentials of panic disorder patients. *Neuropsychobiology 33,* 164–167.

Levy, N. B. (1985). Conversion disorder. In R. C. Simons (Ed.), *Understanding human behavior in health and illness* (3rd ed.). Baltimore: Williams & Wilkins.

Levy, N. B. (1985). The psychophysiological disorders: An overview. In R. C. Simons (Ed.), *Understanding human behavior in health and illness* (3rd ed.). Baltimore: Williams & Wilkins.

Levy, R. L., Cain, K. C., Jarrett, M., & Heitkemper, M. M. (1997). The relationship between daily life stress and gastrointestinal symptoms in women with irritable bowel syndrome. *J. Behav. Med., 20*(2), 177–197.

Levy, S. R., Jurkovic, G. L., & Spirito, A. (1995). A multisystems analysis of adolescent suicide attempters. *J. Abnorm. Child Psychol., 23*(2), 221–234.

Levy, S. M., & Roberts, D. C. (1992). Clinical significance of psychoneuroimmunology: Prediction of cancer outcomes. In N. Schneiderman, P. McCabe, & A. Baum (Eds.), *Perspectives in behavioral medicine: Stress and disease processes.* Hillsdale, NJ: Erlbaum.

Lewin, B. D. (1950). *The psychoanalysis of elation.* New York: Norton.

Lewinsohn, P. M. (1975). Engagement in pleasant activities and depression level. *J. Abnorm. Psychol., 84,* 644–654.

Lewinsohn, P. M. (1975). The use of activity schedules in the treatment of depressed individuals. In C. E. Thoresen & J. D. Krumboltz (Eds.), *Counseling methods.* New York: Holt, Rinehart & Winston.

Lewinsohn, P. M. (1988). A prospective study of risk factors for unipolar depression. *J. Abnorm. Psychol., 97*(3), 251–284.

Lewinsohn, P. M., Antonuccio, D. O., Steinmetz, J. L., & Teri, L. (1984). *The coping with depression course.* Eugene, OR: Castalia.

Lewinsohn, P. M., & Arconad, M. (1981). Behavioral treatment of depression: A social learning approach. In J. F. Clarkin & H. I. Glazer (Eds.), *Depression: Behavioral and directive intervention strategies.* New York: Garland STPM.

Lewinsohn, P. M., Biglan, A., & Zeiss, A. M. (1976). Behavioral treatment of depression. In P. O. Davidson (Ed.), *The behavioral management of anxiety, depression and pain.* New York: Brunner/Mazel.

Lewinsohn, P. M., Clarke, G. N., Hops, H., & Andrews, J. (1990). Cognitive-behavioral treatment for depressed adolescents. *Behav. Ther., 21,* 385–401.

Lewinsohn, P. M., Rohde, P., Teri, L., & Tilson, M. (1990, April). *Presentation.* Western Psychological Association.

Lewinsohn, P. M., Sullivan, J. M., & Grosscup, S. J. (1982). Behavioral therapy: Clinical applications. In A. T. Rush (Ed.), *Short-term psychotherapies for the depressed patient.* New York: Guilford.

Lewinsohn, P. M., Youngren, M. A., & Grosscup, S. J. (1979). Reinforcement and depression. In R. A. Depue (Ed.), *The psychobiology of the depressive disorders.* New York: Academic Press.

Lewis, C. E., & Bucholz, K. K. (1991). Alcoholism, antisocial behavior and family history. *Brit. J. Add., 86*(2), 177–194.

Lewis, O., & Chatoor, I. (1994). Eating disorders. In J. M. Oldham & M. B. Riba (Eds.), *Review of psychiatry* (Vol. 13). Washington, DC: American Psychiatric Press.

Lewy, A. J., Ahmed, S., Jackson, J. M., & Sack, R. L. (1992). Melatonin shifts human circadian rhythms according to a phase-response curve. *Chronobiol. Inter., 9*(5), 380–392.

Li, G. (1995). The interaction effect of bereavement and sex on the risk of suicide in the elderly: An historical cohort study. *Social Science and Medicine, 40*(6), 825–828.

Liberman, R. P. (1982). Assessment of social skills. *Schizo. Bull., 8*(1), 82–84.

Liberman, R. P., & Eckman, T. (1981). Behavior therapy vs. insight-oriented therapy for repeated suicide attempters. *Arch. Gen. Psychiat., 38*(10), 1126–1130.

Liberman, R. P., & Raskin, D. E. (1971). Depression: A behavioral formulation. *Arch. Gen. Psychiat., 24,* 515–523.

Libow, J. (1995). Munchausen by proxy victims in adulthood: A first look. *Child Abuse & Neglect, 19*(9), 1131–1142.

Lichtenberg, J. W., & Kalodner, C. (1997, February 28). *The science-based practice of counseling psychology: A case for empirically-vali-*

dated interventions. Paper presented at the midwinter meeting of the Council of Counseling Psychology Training Programs, La Jolla, CA.

Lichtenstein, E. (1980). *Psychotherapy: Approaches and applications.* Monterey, CA: Brooks/Cole.

Lickey, M. E., & Gordon, B. (1991). *Medicine and mental illness: The use of drugs in psychiatry.* New York: W. H. Freeman.

Lidz, T. (1963). *The family and human adaptation.* New York: International Universities Press.

Lidz, T. (1973). *The origin and treatment of schizophrenic disorders.* New York: Basic Books.

Lidz, T., Cornelison, A., & Fleck, S. (1965). *Schizophrenia and the family.* New York: International Universities Press.

Lidz, T., Cornelison, A., Fleck, S., & Terry, D. (1957). The intra-familial environment of the schizophrenic patient: II. Marital schism and marital skew. *Amer. J. Psychiat., 114,* 241–248.

Lidz, T., Cornelison, A. R., Singer, M. T., Schafer, S., & Fleck, S. (1965). In T. Lidz, S. Fleck, & A. R. Cornelison (Eds.), *Schizophrenia and the family.* New York: International Universities Press.

Lie, N. (1992). Follow-ups of children with attention deficit hyperactivity disorder. *Acta Psychiatr. Scandin., 85,* 40.

Lieberman, J. A. (1993). Prediction of outcome in first-episode schizophrenia. *J. Clin. Psychiat., 54*(3, Suppl.), 13–17.

Lieberman, J. A. (1995). Signs and symptoms: What can they tell us about the clinical course and pathophysiologic processes of schizophrenia. *Arch. Gen. Psychiat., 52*(5), 361–363.

Lieberman, J. A., Alvir, J. Ma., Koreen, A., Geisler, S., Chakos, M., Scheitman, B., & Woerner, M. (1996). Psychobiologic correlates of treatment response in schizophrenia. *Neuropsychopharmacology, 14,* 13S–21S.

Liebowitz, M. R. (1992). Diagnostic Issues in Anxiety Disorders. In A. Tasman & M. B. Riba (Eds.), *Review of Psychiatry* (Vol. 11). Washington, DC: American Psychiatric Press.

Liebowitz, M. R., Hollander, E., Schneier, F., Campeas, R. et al. (1990). Reversible and irreversible monoamine oxidase inhibitors in other psychiatric disorders. *Acta Psychiatr. Scandin., 82*(Suppl. 360), 29–34.

Liebowitz, M. R., Schneier, F. R., Hollander, E., & Welkowitz, L. A. et al. (1991). Treatment of social phobia with drugs other than benzodiazepines. *J. Clin. Psychiat., 52*(Suppl.), 10–15.

Liebowitz, M., Stone, M., & Turkat, I. D. (1986). Treatment of personality disorders. In A. Frances & R. Hales (Eds.), *American Psychiatric Association annual review* (Vol. 5). Washington, DC: American Psychiatric Press.

Lifton, R. J. (1973). *Home from the war: Vietnam veterans, neither victims nor executioners.* New York: Simon & Schuster.

Lim, K. O., Harris, D., Beal, M., Hoff, A. L., Minn, K., Csernansky, J. G., Faustman, W. O., Marsh, L., Sullivan, E. V., & Pfefferbaum, A. (1996). Gray matter deficits in young onset schizophrenia are independent of age of onset. *Bio. Psychiat., 40,* 4–13.

Limandri, B. J. & Sheridan, D. J. (1995). Prediction of intentional interpersonal violence: An introduction. In J. C. Campbell (Ed.), *Assessing dangerousness: Violence by sexual offenders, batterers, and child abusers.* Thousand Oaks, CA: Sage.

Lindenmayer, J. P. (1995). New pharmacotherapeutic modalities for negative symptoms in psychosis. *Acta Psychiatr. Scandin. Supple., 91*(388), 15–19.

Lindesmith, A. R. (1968). *Addiction and opiates.* Chicago: Aldine.

Lindholm, C., & Lindholm C. (1981, July). World's strangest mental illnesses. *Sci. Digest.*

Lindner, M. (1968). *Hereditary and environmental influences upon resistance to stress.* Unpublished doctoral dissertation, University of Pennsylvania, Philadelphia.

Lindsay, D. S. (1994). Contextualizing and clarifying criticisms of memory work in psychotherapy. *Consciousness Cog., 3,* 426–437.

Lindsay, D. S. (1996). Contextualizing and clarifying criticisms of memory work in psychotherapy. In K. Pezdek & W. P. Banks (Eds.), *The recovered memory/false memory debate.* San Diego: Academic Press.

Lindsay, D. S., & Read, J. D. (1994). Psychotherapy and memories of childhood sexual abuse: A cognitive perspective. *J. App. Cog. Psychol. 8,* 281–338.

Lindstrom, E. M., Ohlund, L. S., Lindstrom, L. H., & Ohman, A. (1992). Symptomatology and electrodermal activity as predictors of neuroleptic response in young male schizophrenic inpatients. *Psychiat. Res., 42*(2), 145–158.

Lindström, L. H. (1996). Clinical and biological markers for outcome in schizophrenia: A review of a longitudinal follow-up study in Uppsala schizophrenia research project. *Neuropsychopharmacology, 14,* 23S–26S.

Linehan, M. M. (1973). Suicide and attempted suicide: Study of perceived sex differences. *Percep. Motor Skills, 37,* 31–34.

Linehan, M. M., & Nielsen, S. L. (1981). Assessment of suicide ideation and parasuicide: Hopelessness and social desirability. *J. Cons. Clin. Psychol., 49*(5), 773–775.

Links, P. S. (1996). *Clinical assessment and management of severe personality disorders.* Washington, DC: American Psychiatric Press.

Linnoila, V. M., & Virkkunen, M. (1992). Aggression, suicidality, and serotonin. *J. Clin. Psychiat., 53*(10, Suppl.), 46–51.

Linsky, A. S., Strauss, M. A., & Colby, J. P. (1985). Stressful events, stressful conditions and alcohol problems in the United States: A partial test of Bales's theory. *J. Stud. Alc., 46*(1), 72–80.

Linszen, D. H., Dingemans, P. M., Nugter, M. A., Willem, A. J. et al. (1997). Patient attributes and expressed emotion as risk factors for psychotic relapse. *Schizo. Bull., 23*(1), 119–130.

Linz, T. D., Hooper, S. R., Hynd, G. W., Isaac, W. et al. (1990). Frontal lobe functioning in conduct disordered juveniles: Preliminary findings. *Arch. Clin. Neuropsychol., 5*(4), 411–416.

Lipke, H. J., & Botkin, A. L. (1992). Brief case studies of eye movement desensitization and reprocessing (EMD/R) with chronic post-traumatic stress disorder. *Psychotherapy, 29,* 591–595.

Lipowski, Z. J. (1987). Somatization: Medicine's unsolved problem. *Psychosomatics, 28*(6), 294–297.

Lippincott, J. A., & Mierzwa, J. A. (1995). Propensity for seeking counseling services: A comparison of Asian and American undergraduates. *J. Amer. Coll. Hlth., 43*(5), 201–204.

Lipschitz, A. (1995). Suicide prevention in young adults (age 18–30). [Special issue: Suicide prevention: Toward the year 2000]. *Suic. Life-Threat. Behav., 25*(1), 155–170.

Lipton, A. A., & Simon, F. S. (1985). Psychiatric diagnosis in a state hospital: Manhattan State revisited. *Hosp. Comm. Psychiat., 36*(4), 368–373.

Lipton, H. L. (1988). A prescription for change. *Generations, 12*(4), 74–79.

Lisansky-Gomberg, E. (1993). Women and alcohol: Use and abuse. *J. Nerv. Ment. Dis., 181*(4), 211–216.

Lish, J. D., Kavoussi, R. J., & Coccaro, E. F. (1996). Aggressiveness. In C. G. Costello (Ed.), *Personality characteristics of the personality disordered.* New York: Wiley.

Lissner, L., Odell, P. M., D'Agostino, R. B., Stokes, J., Kreger, B. E., Bélanger, A. J., & Brownell, K. D. (1991). Variability of body weight and health outcomes in the Farmingham population. *N. Engl. J. Med., 324,* 1839–1844.

Litman, R. E. (1995). Suicide prevention in a treatment setting. [Special issue: Suicide prevention: Toward the year 2000]. *Suic. Life-Threat. Behav., 25*(1), 134–142.

Litt, M. D. (1996). A model of pain and anxiety associated with acute stressors: Distress in dental procedures. *Behav. Res. Ther., 34*(5/6), 459–476.

Little, K. B., & Shneidman, E. S. (1959). Congruences among interpretations of psychological test and amamnestic data. *Psychol. Monog., 73*(476).

Livesley, W. J. (Ed.). (1995). *The DSM-IV personality disorders.* New York: Guilford.

Livesley, W. J., Schroeder, M. L., Jackson, D. N., & Jang, K. L. (1994). Categorical distinctions in the study of personality disorder: Implications for classification. *J. Abnorm. Psychol., 103*(1), 6–17.

Livingston, M. S. (1995). A self psychologist in Couplesland: Multisubjective approach to transference and countertransference-like phenomena in marital relationships. *Fam. Process, 34,* 427–439.

Livingston, R., Witt, A., & Smith, G. R. (1995). Families who somatize. *J. Dev Behav. Pediat., 16*(1), 42–46.

Lloyd, G. G., & Lishman, W. A. (1975). Effect of depression on the speed of recall of pleasant and unpleasant experiences. *Psychol. Med., 5,* 173–180.

Lloyd, G. K., Fletcher, A., & Minchin, M. C. W. (1992). GABA agonists as potential anxiolytics. (1992). In G. D. Burrows, S. M. Roth, & R. Noyes, Jr., *Handbook of Anxiety* (Vol. 5). Oxford, England: Elsevier.

Lloyd, R. M. (1992). Negotiating child sexual abuse: The interactional character of investigative practices. *Social Problems, 39*(2), 109-124.

Loeb, A., Beck, A. T., & Diggory, J. (1971). Differential effects of success and failure on depressed and nondepressed patients. *J. Nerv. Ment. Dis., 152*(2), 106–114.

Loebel, J. P., Loebel, J. S., Dager, S. R., Centerwall, B. S., et al. (1991). Anticipation of nursing home placement may be a precipitant of suicide among the elderly. *J. Amer. Geriat. Soc., 39*(4), 407–408.

Loeber, R. (1991). Antisocial behavior: More enduring than changeable? *J. Amer. Acad. Child Adol. Psychiat., 30,* 393–397.

Loewenstein, R. J. (1991). Psychogenic amnesia and psychogenic fugue: A comprehensive review. In A. Tasman & S. M. Goldfinger (Eds.), *American Psychiatric Press review of psychiatry* (Vol. 10). Washington, DC: American Psychiatric Press.

Loftus, E. F. (1993). The reality of repressed memories. *Amer. Psychologist, 48,* 518–537.

Loftus, E. F. (1997). Repressed memory accusations: Devastated families and devastated patients. *Appl. Cog. Psychol., 11,* 25–30.

Logue, A. W. (1991). *The psychology of eating and drinking.* New York: W. H. Freeman.

Long, P., Forehand, R., Wierson, M., & Morgan, A. (1994). Does parent training with young noncompliant children have effects? *Behav. Res. Ther., 32*(1), 101–107.

Longshore, D., Hsieh, S. C., Anglin, M. D. et al. (1992). Ethnic patterns in drug abuse treatment utilization. [Special issue: Multicultural mental health and substance abuse services]. *J. Ment. Hlth. Admin. 19*(3), 268–277.

Lonigan, C. J., Shannon, M. P., Taylor, C. M. et al. (1994). Children exposed to disaster: II. risk factors for the development of post-traumatic symptomatology. *J. Amer. Acad. Child Adol. Psychiat., 33,* 94–105.

Loo, H., Poirier-Littre, M.-F., Theron, M., Rein, W., & Fleurot, O. (1997). Amisulpride versus placebo in the medium-term treatment of the negative symptoms of schizophrenia. *Brit. J. Psychiat., 170,* 18–22.

Loomer, H. P., Saunders, J. C., & Kline, N. S. (1957). A clinical and phamacodynamic evaluation of iproniazid as a psychic energizer. *Amer. Psychiat. Assoc. Res. Rep., 8,* 129.

Lopatka, C., & Rachman, S. (1995). Perceived responsibility and compulsive checking: An experimental analysis. *Behav. Res. Ther., 33*(6), 673–684.

LoPiccolo, J. (1985). Advances in diagnosis and treatment of male sexual dysfunction. *J. Sex Marital Ther., 11*(4), 215–232.

LoPiccolo, J. (1990). Treatment of sexual dysfunction. In A. S. Bellak, M. Hersen, & A. E. Kazdin (Eds.), *International handbook of behavior modification and therapy* (2nd ed.). New York: Plenum Press.

LoPiccolo, J. (1991). Post-modern sex therapy for erectile failure. In R. C. Rosen & S. R. Leiblum (Eds.), *Erectile failure: diagnosis and treatment.* New York: Guilford.

LoPiccolo, J. (1992). Paraphilias. *Nord. Sex., 10*(1), 1–14.

LoPiccolo, J. (1995). Sexual disorders and gender identity disorders. In R. J. Comer, *Abnormal psychology* (2nd ed.). New York: W. H. Freeman.

LoPiccolo, J. (1997). Sex therapy: A post-modern model. In S. J. Lynn & J. P. Garske (Eds.), *Contemporary psychotherapies: Models and methods* (2nd ed.).

LoPiccolo, J., & Friedman, J. R. (1988). Broad spectrum treatment of low sexual desire: Integration of cognitive, behavioral, and systemic treatment. In S. Leiblum & R. Rosen (Eds.), *Sexual desire disorders.* New York: Guilford.

LoPiccolo, J., & Stock, W. E. (1987). Sexual function, dysfunction, and counseling in gynecological practice. In Z. Rosenwaks, F. Benjamin, & M. L. Stone (Eds.), *Gynecology.* New York: Macmillan.

Lorand, S. (1950). *Clinical studies in psychoanalysis.* New York: International Universities Press.

Lorand, S. (1968). Dynamics and therapy of depressive states. In W. Gaylin (Ed.), *The meaning of despair.* New York: Jason Aronson.

Loranger, A. W., Sartoruis, N., Andreoli, A., Berger, P. et al. (1994). The International Personality Disorder Examination. *Arch. Gen. Psychiat., 51,* 215–224.

Lorenzo, A., & Yankner, B. A. (1996). Amyloid fibril toxicity in Alzheimer's disease and diabetes. In R. J. Wurtman, S. Corkin, J. H. Growdon, & R. M. Nitsch (Eds.), *The neurobiology of Alzheimer's disease.* New York: New York Academy of Sciences.

Lorion, R. P. (1996). Applying our medicine to the psychopharmacology debate. *Amer. Psychol., 51*(3), 219–224.

Losonczy, M. F. et al. (1986). Correlates of lateral ventricular size in chronic schizophrenia: I. Behavioral and treatment response measures. *Amer. J. Psychiat., 143*(8), 976–981.

Lovaas, O. I. (1987). Behavioral treatment and normal educational/intellectual functioning in young autistic children. *J. Cons. Clin. Psychol., 55,* 3–9.

Love, S. R., Matson, J. L., & West, D. (1990). Mothers as effective therapists for autistic children's phobias. *J. Appl. Behav. Anal., 23*(3), 379–385.

Lovejoy, M. (1982). Expectations and the recovery process. *Schizo. Bull., 8*(4), 605–609.

Lowe, M. R., Gleaves, D. H., DiSimone-Weiss, R. T., Forgueson, C. et al. (1996). Restraint, dieting, and the continuum model of bulimia nervosa. *J. Abnorm. Psychol., 105*(4), 508–517.

Lowenstein, L. F. (1989). The etiology, diagnosis and treatment of the fire-setting behavior of children. *Child Psychiat. Human Dev., 19*(3), 186–194.

Lubetsky, M. J. (1986). The psychiatrist's role in the assessment and treatment of the mentally retarded child. *Child Psychiat. Human Dev., 16*(4), 261–273.

Lubin, B. (1983). Group therapy. In I. B. Weiner (Ed.), *Clinical methods in psychology* (2d ed.). New York: Wiley.

Luborsky, L. (1973). Forgetting and remembering (momentary forgetting) during psychotherapy. In M. Mayman (Ed.), *Psychoanalytic research and psychological issues* (Monograph 30). New York: International Universities Press.

Luborsky, L., Singer, B., & Luborsky, L. (1975). Comparative studies of psychotherapies. *Arch. Gen. Psychiat., 32,* 995–1008.

Luddens, H., & Korpi, E. R. (1995). Biological function of GABA-sub(A)/benzodiazepine receptor heterogeneity. *J. Psychiatr. Res., 29*(2), 77–94.

Ludolph, P. S., Westen, D., Misle, B., Jackson, A. et al. (1990). The borderline diagnosis in adolescents: Symptoms and developmental history. *Amer. J. Psychiat., 147*(4), 470–476.

Ludwig, A. (1994). Creative activity and mental illness in female writers. *Amer. J. Psychiat., 151,* 1650–1656.

Ludwig, A. (1995). Creative activity and mental illness in female writers. *Amer. J. Psychiat., 151,* 1650–1656.

Ludwig, A. M. (1995). *The price of greatness: Resolving the creativity and madness controversy.* New York: Guilford.

Lundholm, J. K., & Waters, J. E. (1991). Dysfunctional family systems: Relationship to disordered eating behaviors among university women. *J. Substance Abuse, 3*(1), 97–106.

Luntz, B. K., & Widom, C. S. (1994). Antisocial personality disorder in abused and neglected children grown up. *Amer. J. Psychiat., 151*(5), 670–674.

Lutgendorf, S. K., Antoni, M. H., Kumar, M., & Schneiderman, N. (1994). Changes in cognitive coping strategies predict EBV-Antibody titre change following a stressor disclosure induction. *J. Psychosom. Res., 38*(1), 63–78.

Lyketsos, C. G., Hoover, D. R., Guccione, M., Dew, M. A., et al. (1996). Changes in depressive symptoms as AIDS develops. *Amer. J. Psychiat., 153*(11), 1430–1437.

Lykken, D. T,. & Tellegen, A. (1996). Happiness is a stochastic phenomenon. *Psychol. Sci., 7*(3), 186–189.

Lykken, D. T. (1957). A study of anxiety in the sociopathic personality. *J. Abnorm. Soc. Psychol., 55,* 6–10.

Lykken, D. T. (1995). *The antisocial personalities.* Hillsdale, NJ: Erlbaum.

Lyman, B. (1982). The nutritional values and food group characteristics of foods preferred during various emotions. *Journal of Psychology, 112,* 121–127.

Lyman, J. L. (1961). Student suicide at Oxford University. *Student Med., 10,* 218–234.

Lyon, K. A. (1992). Shattered mirror: A fragment of the treatment of a patient with multiple personality disorder. *Psychoanal. Quarter., 12*(1), 71–94.

Lyon, L. S. (1985). Facilitating telephone number recall in a case of psychogenic amnesia. *J. Behav. Ther. Exp. Psychiat., 16*(2), 147–149.

Lyon, M., Chatoor, I., Atkins, D., Silber, T. et al. (1977, Spring). Testing the hypothesis of the multidimensional model of anorexia nervosa in adolescents. *Adolescence, 32*(125), 101–111.

Lysaker, P., & Bell, M. (1995). Work and meaning: Disturbance of volition and vocational dysfunction in schizophrenia. *Psychiatry, 58*(4), 392–400.

Lysaker, P. H., Bell, M. D., & Bioty, S. M. (1995). Cognitive deficits in schizophrenia: Prediction of symptom change for participators in work rehabilitation. *J. Nerv. Ment. Dis., 183*(5), 332–336.

M.I.T. (1993). Cited in "Mental depression costs $43.7 billion, study shows. *The Daily News,* December 3, 1993.

Macciardi, G., Kennedy, J. L., Ruocco, L., Guiffra, L. et al. (1992). A genetic-linkage study of schizophrenia to chromosome 5 markers in a northern Italian population. *Bio. Psychiat., 31*(7), 720–728.

MacDonald, M. L., & Schnur, R. E. (1987). Anxieties and American elders: Proposals for assessment and treatment. In L. Michelson & L. M. Ascher (Eds.), *Anxiety and stress disorders: Cognitive behavioral assessment and treatment.* New York: Guilford.

Mace, N., & Rabins, P. (1991). *The 36-hour day* (2nd ed.). Baltimore: Johns Hopkins University.

MacHovek, F. J. (1981). Hypnosis to facilitate recall in psychogenic amnesia and fugue states: Treatment variables. *Amer. J. Clin. Hyp., 24*(1), 7–13.

Machover, K. (1949). *Personality projection in the drawing of the human figure.* Springfield, IL: Thomas.

MacKenzie, K. R. (1996). Time-limited group psychotherapy. *Inter. J. Group Psychother., 46*(1), 41–60.

Madden, P. A. F., Heath, A. C., Rosenthal, N. E., & Martin, N. G. (1996, January). Seasonal changes in mood and behavior. *Arch. Gen. Psychiat., 553,* 47–55.

Maddi, S. R. (1990). Issues and interventions in stress mastery. In H. S. Friedman (Ed.), *Personality and disease.* New York: Wiley.

Maddock, R. J., Carter, C. S., Blacker, K. H., Beitman, B. D., Krishnan, K. R. R., Jefferson, J. W., Lewis, C. P., & Liebowitz, M. R. (1993). Relationship of past depressive episodes to symptom severity and treatment response in panic disorder with agoraphobia. *J. Clin. Psychiat., 54*(3), 88–95.

Maddox, G. L. (1988). Aging, drinking and alcohol abuse. *Generations, 12*(4), 14–16.

Madianos, M. G., & Economou, M. (1988). Negative symptoms in schizophrenia: The effect of long-term, community-based psychiatric intervention [Special issue]. *Inter. J. Ment. Hlth., 17*(1), 22–34.

Madianos, M. G., & Madianou, D. (1992). The effects of long-term community care on relapse and adjustment of persons with chronic schizophrenia. *Inter. J. Ment. Hlth., 21*(1), 37–49.

Maestroni, G. (1993). The immunoneuroendocrine role of melatonin. *J. Pineal Res., 14*(1), 1–10.

Maestroni, G., & Conti, A. (1991). Immuno-derived opioids as mediators of the immuno-enhancing and anti-stress action of melatonin. *Acta Neurologica, 13*(4), 356–360.

Magee, W. J., Eaton, W. W., Wittchen, H.-U., McGonagle, K. A., & Kessler, R. C. (1996). Agoraphobia, simple phobia, and social phobia in the National Comorbidity Survey. *Arch. Gen. Psychiat., 53,* 159–168.

Maher, B. A. (1974). Delusional thinking and perceptual disorder. *J. Individ. Psychol., 30*(1), 98–113.

Maher, B. A., & Maher, W. B. (1994). Personality and psychopathology: A historical perspective. *J. Abnorm. Psychol., 103*(1), 72–77.

Maher, W. B., & Maher, B. A. (1985). Psychopathology: I. From ancient times to the eighteenth century. In G. A. Kimble & K. Schlesinger (Eds.), *Topics in the history of psychology* (Vol. 2). Hillsdale, NJ: Erlbaum.

Mahler, M. (1974). Symbiosis and individuation: The psychological birth of the human infant. *Psychoanalytic Study Child, 29,* 89–106.

Mahoney, G., Glover, A., & Finger, I. (1981). Relationship between language and sensorimotor development of Down syndrome and nonretarded children. *Amer. J. Ment. Def., 86*(1), 21–27.

Maier, S. F., Watkins, L. R., & Fleshner, M. (1994). Psychoneuroimmunology. The interface between behavior, brain and immunity. *Amer. Psychol., 49*(12), 1004–1017.

Maj, M., Satz, P., Janssen, R., Zaudig, M. et al. (1994). WHO neuropsychiatric AIDS study, Cross-sectional Phase II. *Arch. Gen. Psychiat., 51,* 51–61.

Makris, G. S., & Heimberg, R. G. (1995). The scale of maladaptive self-consciousness: A valid and useful measure in the study of social phobia. *Pers. Individ. Diff., 19*(5), 731–740.

Malamud, B. (1979). *Dublin's lives.* New York: Farrar Straus Giroux.

Malcolm, A. H. (1990, Jun. 9). Giving death a hand. *New York Times,* p. A6.

Maletzky, B. M. (1980). Assisted covert sensitization. In D. J. Cox & R. J. Daitzman (Eds.), *Exhibitionism: Description, assessment, and treatment.* New York: Garland STPM.

Maller, R. G., & Reiss, S. (1992). Anxiety sensitivity in 1984 and panic attacks in 1987. *J. Anxiety Disorders, 6*(3), 241–247.

Malmquist, C. P. (1996). *Homicide: A psychiatric perspective.* Washington, DC: American Psychiatric Press.

Mancini, C., Van Ameringen, M., & MacMillan, H. (1995). Relationship of childhood sexual and physical abuse to anxiety disorders. *J. Nerv. Ment. Dis., 183*(5), 309–314.

Mandel, J. L., Monaco, A. P., Nelson, D. L., Schlessinger, D., & Willard, H. (1992). Genome analysis and the human X chromosome. *Science, 258,* 103–109.

Mandell, A. J. & Knapp, S. (1979). Asymmetry and mood, emergent properties of seratonin regulation: A proposed mechanism of action of lithium. *Arch. Gen. Psychiat., 36*(8), 909–916.

Manderscheid, R. W., & Sonnenschein, M. A. (1992). *Mental health, United States, 1992.* Rockville, MD: U.S. Department of Health and Human Services.

Manderscheid, R., & Rosenstein, M. (1992). Homeless persons with mental illness and alcohol or other drug abuse: Current research, policy, and prospects. *Curr. Opin. Psychiat., 5,* 273–278.

Mandler, J. M., & McDonough, L. (1995). Long-term recall of event sequences in infancy. *J. Exp. Child Psychol., 59,* 457–474.

Manley, R. S. & Needham, L. (1995). An anti-bulimia group for adolescent girls. *J. Child Adol. Group Ther., 5*(1), 19–33.

Mann, B. J. (1995). The North Carolina Dissociation Index: A measure of dissociation using items from the MMPI-2. *J. Pers. Assess., 64*(2), 349–359.

Mann, J. J., & Malone, K. M. (1997). Cerebrospinal fluid amines and higher-lethality suicide attempts in depressed inpatients. *Bio. Psychiat., 41,* 162–171.

Mann, J. J., Malone, K. M., Diehl, D. J., Perel, J., Cooper, T. B., & Mintun, M. A. (1996). Demonstration in vivo of reduced serotonin responsivity in the brain of untreated depressed patients. *Amer. J. Psychiat., 153*(2), 174–182.

Manning, A. (1996, January 16). New alcohol programs turn focus to moderation. *USA Today,* p. 6D.

Mannuzza, S., Klein, R. G., Bessler, A., Malloy, P., & LaPadula, M. (1993). Adult outcome of hyperactive boys. *Arch. Gen. Psychiat., 50,* 565–576.

Mannuzza, S., Schneier, F. R., Chapman, T. F., Liebowitz, M. R., Klein, D. F., Fyer, A. J. (1995). Generalized social phobia. *Arch. Gen. Psychiat., 52*(3), 230–237.

Manschreck, T. C. (1996). Delusional disorder: The recognition and management of paranoia. *J. Clin. Psychiat., 57*(Suppl. 3), 32–38.

Manson, J. E., Willett, W. C., Stampfer, M. J., Colditz, G. A., et al. (1995). Body weight and mortality among women. *N. Engl. J. Med., 333*(11), 677–685.

Manson, S. M., & Good, B. J. (1993). *Cultural considerations in the diagnosis of DSM-IV mood disorders. Cultural proposals and supporting papers for DSM-IV.* Submitted to the DSM-IV Task Force by the Steering Committee, NIMH-Sponsored Group on Culture and Diagnosis.

Manuck, S. B., Cohen, S., Rabin, B. S., Muldoon, M. F., & Bachen, E. A. (1991). Individual differences in cellular immune responses to stress. *Psychol. Sci., 2,* 1–5.

Marazziti, D., Toni, C., Bonuccelli, U., Pavese, N. et al. (1995). Headache, panic disorder and depression: Comorbidity or a spectrum? *Neuropsychobiology, 31*(3), 125–129.

March, J. (1992). The stressor "A" criterion in DSM-IV posttraumatic stress disorder. In J. R. Davidson & E. Foa (Eds.), *Posttraumatic stress disorder: DSM-IV and beyond.* Washington, DC: American Psychiatric Press.

Marder, S. R. (1996). Management of schizophrenia. *J. Clin. Psychiat., 57*(Suppl. 3), 9–13.

Marfo, K., & Kysela, G. M. (1985). Early intervention with mentally handicapped children: A critical appraisal of applied research. *J. Pediat. Psychol., 10,* 305–324.

Margo, A., Hemsley, D. R., & Slade, P. D. (1981). The effects of varying auditory input on schizophrenic hallucinations. *Brit. J. Psychiat., 139,* 122–127.

Margo, G. M., & Newman, J. S. (1989). Venesection as a rare form of self-mutilation. *Amer. J. Psycother., 43*(3), 427–432.

Margo, J. L. (1985). Anorexia nervosa in adolescents. *Brit. J. Med. Psychol., 58*(2), 193–195.

Margolin, G., & Weinstein, C. D. (1983). The role of affect in behavioral marital therapy. In M. L. Aronson & L. R. Wolbery (Eds.), *Group and family therapy 1982: An overview.* New York: Brunner/Mazel.

Margraf, J. (1993). Hyperventilation and panic disorder: A psychophysiological connection. *Adv. Behav. Res. Ther., 15,* 49–74.

Margraf, J., Barlow, D. H., Clark, D. M., & Telch, M. J. (1993). Psychological treatment of panic: Work in progress on outcome, active ingredients, and follow-up. *Behav. Res. Ther., 31*(1), 1–8.

Margraf, J., Ehlers, A., Roth, W. T., Clark, D. B. et al. (1991). How "blind" are double-blind studies? *J. Cons. Clin. Psychol., 59*(1), 184–187.

Mariani, M. A., & Barkley, R. A. (1997). Neuropsychological and academic functioning in preschool boys with attention deficit hyperactivity disorder. *Dev. Neuropsychol., 13*(1), 111–129.

Maris, R. W. (Ed.). (1986). *Biology of suicide.* New York: Guilford.

Maris, R. W. (1992). How are suicides different? In R. W. Maris, A. L. Berman, J. T. Maltsberger, & R. I. Yufit (Eds.), *Assessment and prediction of suicide.* New York: Guilford.

Maris, R. W. (1992). Methods of suicide. In R. W. Maris, A. L. Berman, J. T. Maltsberger, & R. I. Yufit (Eds.), *Assessment and prediction of suicide.* New York: Guilford.

Maris, R. W. (1992). Overview of the study of suicide assessment and prediction. In R. W. Maris, A. L. Berman, J. T. Maltsberger, & R. I. Yufit (Eds.), *Assessment and prediction of suicide.* New York: Guilford.

Maris, R. W., & Silverman, M. M. (1995). Postscript: Summary and synthesis [Special issue: Suicide prevention: Toward the year 2000]. *Suic. Life-Threat. Behav., 25*(1), 205–209.

Markman, H. J., & Hahlweg, K. (1993). The prediction and prevention of marital distress: An international perspective. *Clin. Psychol. Rev., 13*(1), 29–43.

Marks, A. (1977). Sex differences and their effect upon cultural evaluations of methods of self-destruction. *Omega, 8,* 65–70.

Marks, I. M. (1977). Phobias and obsessions: Clinical phenomena in search of a laboratory model. In J. Maser & M. Seligman (Eds.), *Psychopathology: Experimental models.* San Francisco: W. H. Freeman.

Marks, I. M. (1986). Genetics of fear and anxiety disorders. *Brit. J. Psychiat., 149,* 406–418.

Marks, I. M. (1987). *Fears, phobias and rituals: Panic, anxiety and their disorders.* New York: Oxford University Press.

Marks, I. M. (1987). Comment on S. Lloyd Williams' "On anxiety and phobia." *J. Anxiety Disorders, 1*(2), 181–196.

Marks, I. M., & Gelder, M. G. (1967). Transvestism and fetishism: Clinical and psychological changes during faradic aversion. *Brit. J. Psychiat., 113,* 711–730.

Marks, I. M., & Swinson, R. (1992). Behavioral and/or drug therapy. In G. D. Burrows, S. M. Roth, & R. Noyes, Jr., *Handbook of Anxiety* (Vol. 5). Oxford, England: Elsevier.

Marlatt, G. A. (1985). Controlled drinking: The controversy rages on. *Amer. Psychol., 40*(3), 374–375.

Marlatt, G. A., & Gordon, J. (Eds.). (1980). Determinants of relapse: Implications for the maintenance of behavior change. In P. Davidson & S. Davidson (Eds.), *Behavioral medicine.* New York: Brunner/Mazel.

Marlatt, G. A., & Gordon, J. R. (1985). *Relapse prevention: Maintenance strategies in the treatment of addictive behaviors.* New York: Guilford.

Marlatt, G. A., Kosturn, C. F., & Lang, A. R. (1975). Provocation to anger and opportunity for retaliation as determinants of alcohol consumption in social drinkers. *J. Abnorm. Psychol., 84*(6), 652–659.

Marmar, C. R., Foy, D., Kagan, B., & Pynoos, R. S. (1993). An integrated approach for treating posttraumatic stress. In J. M. Oldham, M. B. Riba, & A. Tasman (Eds.), *Review of psychiatry* (Vol. 12). Washington, DC: American Psychiatric Press.

Marmor, J. (1987). The psychotherapeutic process: Common denominators in diverse approaches. In J. K. Zeig (Ed.), *The evolution of psychotherapy.* New York: Brunner/Mazel.

Marquis, J. N., & Morgan, W. G. (1969). *A guidebook for systematic desensitization.* Palo Alto, CA: Veterans Administration Hospital.

Marriott, M., Stokes, M., King, P., & French, R. (1995, March 27). Half steps vs. 12 steps. *Newsweek,* p. 62.

Marsella, A. J. (1980). Depressive experience and disorder across cultures. In H. C. Triandis & J. Draguns (Eds.), *Handbook of cross-cultural psychology* (Vol. 6). Boston: Allyn & Bacon.

Marsh, H. W., Richards, G. E., & Barnes, J. (1986). Multidimensional self-concepts: A long-term follow-up of the effect of participation in Outward Bound program. *Pers. Soc. Psychol. Bull., 12*(4), 475–492.

Marshall, J. J. (1997). Private Correspondence.

Marshall, W. L. (1979). Satiation therapy: A procedure for reducing deviant sexual arousal. *J. Appl. Behav. Annal., 12,* 10–22.

Marshall, W. L., & Lippens, K. (1977). The clinical value of boredom: A procedure for reducing inappropriate sexual interests. *J. Nerv. Ment. Dis., 165,* 283–287.

Marston, W. M. (1917). Systolic blood pressure changes in deception. *J. Exp. Physiol., 2,* 117–163.

Martin, G., & Pear, J. (1988). *Behavior modification* (3rd ed.). Englewood Cliffs, NJ: Prentice Hall.

Martin, J. E. (1985). Anorexia nervosa: A review of the theoretical perspectives and treatment approaches. *Brit. J. Occupational Ther., 48*(8), 236–240.

Martin, J. K., Kraft, J. M., & Roman, P. M. (1994). Extent and impact of alcohol and drug use problems in the workplace: A review of the empirical evidence. In S. Macdonald & P. Roman (Eds.), *Research advances in alcohol and drug problems: Vol. 11: Drug testing in the workplace.* New York: Plenum Press.

Martin, R. L. (1995). DSM-IV changes for the somatoform disorders. *Psychiatr. Ann., 25*(1), 29–39.

Martin, S. & Murray, B. (1996). Social toxicity undermines youngsters in inner cities. *APA Monitor, 27*(10), 27.

Martin, S. (1996). Improving lives, not just infrastructures. *APA Monitor, 27*(10), 24.

Martin, W. T. (1984). Religiosity and U.S. suicide rates, 1972–1978. *J. Clin. Psychol., 40*(5), 1166–1169.

Martineau, J., Barthelemy, C., Jouve, J., & Muh, J. P. (1992). Monoamines (serotonin and catecholamines) and their derivatives in infantile autism: Age-related changes and drug effects. *Dev. Med. Child Neurol., 34*(7), 593–603.

Martinez, J. L., Jr. & Derrick, B. E. (1996). Long-term potentiation and learning. In J. T. Spence, J. M. Darley, & D. J. Foss (Eds.), *Annual review of psychology* (Vol. 47). Palo Alto, CA: Annual Reviews.

Martinez, P. & Richters, J. E. (1993). The NIMH community violence project. II. Children's distress symptoms associated with violence exposure. *Psychiatry, 56,* 22–35.

Marzuk, P. M., Tardiff, K., Leon, A. C., Stajic, M., Morgan, E. B., & Mann, J. J. (1992). Prevalence of cocaine use among residents of New York City who committed suicide during a one-year period. *Amer. J. Psychiat., 149*(3), 371–375.

Mason, B. J., Markowitz, J. C., & Klerman, G. L. (1994). Interpersonal psychotherapy for dysthymic disorders. In G. L. Klerman & M. M. Weissman (Eds.), *New applications of interpersonal psychotherapy.* Washington, DC: American Psychiatric Association.

Mason, J., Weizman, R., Laor, N., Wang, S., Schukovitsky, A., Abramovitz-Schneider, P., Feiler, D., & Charney, D. (1996). Serum triodothyronine elevation in Israeli combat veterans with posttraumatic stress disorder: A cross-cultural study. *Bio. Psychiat., 39,* 835–838.

Mason, M. A., & Gibbs, J. T. (1992). Patterns of adolescent psychiatric hospitalization: Implications for social policy. *Amer. J. Orthopsychiat., 62*(3), 447–457.

Mâsse, L. C., & Tremblay, R. E. (1997). Behavior of boys in kindergarten and the onset of substance use during adolescence. *Arch. Gen. Psychiat., 54,* 62–68.

Masters, W. H., & Johnson, V. E. (1966). *Human sexual response.* Boston: Little, Brown.

Masters, W. H., & Johnson, V. E. (1970). *Human sexual inadequacy.* Boston: Little, Brown.

Masterson, J. F. (1990). Psychotherapy of borderline and narcissistic disorders: Establishing a therapeutic alliance. *J. Pers. Disorders, 4*(2), 182–191.

Matarazzo, J. D. (1984). Behavioral health: A 1990 challenge for the health sciences professions. In J. D. Matarazzo, S. M. Weiss, J. A. Herd, N. E. Miller, & S. M. Weiss (Eds.), *Behavioral health: A handbook of health enhancement and disease prevention.* New York: Wiley.

Matarazzo, J. D. (1992). Psychological testing and assessment in the 21st century. *Amer. Psychol., 47*(8), 1007–1018.

Mathew, R., Wilson, W., Blazer, D., & George, L. (1993). Psychiatric disorders in adult children of alcoholics: Data from the epidemiologic catchment area project. *Amer. J. Psychiat., 150*(5), 793–796.

Mathew, R., Wilson, W., Humphreys, D., Lowe, J., & Weithe, K. (1993). Depersonalization after marijuana smoking. *Bio. Psychiat., 33,* 431–441.

Mathews, A. (1984). Anxiety and its management. In R. N. Gaind, F. I. Fawzy, B. L. Hudson, & R. O. Pasnau (Eds.), *Current themes in psychiatry* (Vol. 3). New York: Spectrum.

Mathews, A. (1985). Anxiety states: a cognitive-behavioural approach. In B. P. Bradley & C. T. Thompson (Eds.), *Psychological applications in psychiatry.* Chichester, England: Wiley.

Mathews, A., Mogg, K., Kentish, J., & Eysenck, M. (1995). Effect of psychological treatment on cognitive bias in generalized anxiety disorder. *Behav. Res. Ther., 33*(3), 293–303.

Mathews, A., Whitehead, A., & Hellett, J. (1983). Psychological and hormonal factors in the treatment of female sexual dysfunction. *Psychol. Med., 13,* 83–92.

Mathias, J. L., Mertin, P., & Murray, A. (1995). The psychological functioning of children from backgrounds of domestic violence. *Austral. Psychologist, 30*(1), 47–56.

Matson, J. L., & Gorman-Smith, D. (1986). A review of treatment research for aggressive and disruptive behavior in the mentally retarded. *Appl. Res. Ment. Retard., 7*(1), 95–103.

Matthys, W., Walterbos, W., Njio, L., & Van Engeland, H. (1988). Person perception of children with conduct disorders. *Tijdskr. voor Psychiatr., 30*(5), 302–314.

Mattick, R. P., & Newman, C. R. (1991). Social phobia and avoidant personality disorder. *Inter. Rev. Psychiat., 3*(2), 163–173.

Mattick, R. P., Peters, L., & Clarke, J. C. (1989). Exposure and cognitive restructuring for social phobia: A controlled study. *Behav. Ther., 20*(1), 3–23.

Maugh, T. H., II, (1995, May 31). Researchers hone in on gene that may cause "werewolf" disorder. *Los Angeles Times,* p. A3.

Maurer, D. W., & Vogel, V. H. (1978). *Narcotics and narcotic addiction.* Springfield, IL: Thomas.

Mavissakalian, M. R. (1993). Combined behavioral and pharmacological treatment of anxiety disorders. In A. A. Leenaars (Ed.), *Suicidology.* Northvale, NJ: Jason Aronson.

Mavissakalian, M. R., Hamann, M. S., & Jones, B. (1990). Correlates of DSM III personality disorder in obsessive-compulsive disorder. *Comprehen. Psychiat., 31*(6), 481–489.

Mavissakalian, M. R., Jones, B., & Olson, S. (1990). Absence of placebo response in obsessive-compulsive disorder. *J. Nerv. Ment. Dis., 178,* 268–270.

Mavreas, V. G., Tomaras, V., Karydi, V., Economou, M. (1992). Expressed emotion in families of chronic schizophrenics and its association with clinical measures. *Soc. Psychiat. Psychiat. Epidemiol., 27*(1), 4–9.

Max, J. E., Smith, W. L., Lindgren, S. D., Robin, D. A., et al. (1995). Case study: Obsessive-compulsive disorder after severe traumatic brain injury in an adolescent. *J. Amer. Acad. Child. Adol. Psychiat., 34*(1), 45–49.

May, P. R. A., & Tuma, A. H. (1964). Choice of criteria for the assessment of treatment outcome. *J. Psychiat. Res., 2*(3), 16–527.

May, P. R. A., Tuma, A. H., & Dixon, W. J. (1981). Schizophrenia: A follow-up study of the results of five forms of treatment. *Arch. Gen. Psychiat., 38,* 776–784.

May, R. (1961). *Existential psychology.* New York: Random House.

May, R. (1967). *Psychology and the human dilemma.* New York: Van Nostrand-Reinhold.

May, R. (1987). Therapy in our day. In J. K. Zeig (Ed.), *The evolution of psychotherapy.* New York: Brunner/Mazel.

May, R., Angel, E., & Ellenberger, H. F. (1958). *Existence: A new dimension in psychiatry and psychology.* New York: Basic Books.

May, R., & Yalom, I. (1989). Existential psychotherapy. In R. J. Corsini & D. Wedding (Eds.), *Current psychotherapies.* Itasca, IL: Peacock.

May, R., & Yalom, I. (1995). Existential psychotherapy. In R. J. Corsini & D. Wedding (Eds.), *Current psychotherapies* (5th ed.). Itasca, IL: Peacock.

Mays, D. T., & Franks, C. M. (1985). *Negative outcome in psychotherapy and what to do about it.* New York: Springer.

McCabe, M. P., & Delaney, S. M. (1992). An evaluation of therapeutic programs for the treatment of secondary inorgasmia in women. *Arch. Sex. Behav., 21*(1), 69–89.

McCarroll, J. E., Fullerton, C. S., Ursano, R. J., & Hermsen, J. M. (1996). Posttraumatic stress symptoms following forensic dental identification: Mt. Carmel, Waco, Texas. *Amer. J. Psychiat., 153,* 778–782.

McCarthy, B. W. (1994). Sexually compulsive men and inhibited sexual desire. *J. Sex Marital Ther., 20*(3), 200-209.

McCarthy, B. W. (1994). Etiology and treatment of early ejaculation. *J. Sex Educ. Ther., 20*(1), 5-6.

McCarthy, M. (1990). The thin ideal, depression and eating disorders in women. *Behav. Res. Ther., 28*(3), 205–215.

McCarthy, P. R., Katz, I. R., & Foa, E. B. (1991). Cognitive-behavioral treatment of anxiety in the elderly: A proposed model. In C. Salzman & B. D. Leibowitz (Eds.), *Anxiety in the elderly.* New York: Springer.

McClelland, D. C. (1979). Inhibited power motivation and high blood pressure in men. *J. Abnorm. Psychol., 88*(2), 182–190.

McClelland, D. C. (1985). The social mandate of health psychology. *Amer. Behav. Scientist, 28*(4), 451–467.

McClelland, D. C. (1993). Motives and health. In G. G. Brannigan & M. R. Merrens (Eds.), *The undaunted psychologist.* New York: McGraw-Hill.

McCormack, A., Rokous, F. E., Hazelwood, R. R., & Burgess, A. W. (1992). An exploration of incest in the childhood development of serial rapists. *J. Fam. Violence, 7*(3), 219–228.

McCormick, R. A. (1994). The importance of coping skill enhancement in the treatment of the pathological gambler. Special issue: Pathological gambling: Clinical issues: I. *J. Gamb. Stud., 10*(1), 77–86.

McCoy, S. A. (1976). Clinical judgments of normal childhood behavior. *J. Cons. Clin. Psychol., 44*(5), 710–714.

McCreadie, R. G., Thara, R., Kamath, S., Padmavathy, R., Latha, S., Mathrubootham, N., & Menon, M. S. (1996). Abnormal movements in never-medicated Indian patients with schizophrenia. *Brit. J. Psychiat., 168,* 221–226.

McCurdy, K. & Daro, D. (1993). Current trends: A fifty state survey. Washington, DC: National Committee for the Prevention of Child Abuse.

McDaniel, J. S., Moran, M. G., Levenson, J. L., & Stoudemire, A. (1994). Psychological factors affecting medical conditions. In R. E. Hales, S. C. Yudofsky, & J. A. Talbott, (Eds.), *The American Psychiatric Press textbook of psychiatry* (2nd ed.). Washington, DC: American Psychiatric Press.

McEachin, J. J., Smith, T., & Lovaas, O. I. (1993). Long-term outcome for children with autism who received early intensive behavioral treatment. *Amer. J. Ment. Retard., 97*(4), 359–372.

McElroy, L. P. (1992). Early indicators of pathological dissociation in sexually abused children. *Child Abuse Neglect, 16*(6), 833–846.

McElroy, S. L., Hudson, J. L., Pope, H. G., & Keck, P. E. (1991). Kleptomania: Clinical characteristics and associated psychopathology. *Psychol. Med., 21*(1), 93–108.

McElroy, S. L., Hudson, J. I., Pope, H. G., Keck, P. E., et al. (1992). The DSM-III—R impulse control disorders not elsewhere classified: Clinical characteristics and relationship to other psychiatric disorders. *Amer. J. Psychiat., 149*(3), 318–327.

McEvoy, J. (1992). Fragile X syndrome: A brief overview. *Educ. Psychol. Prac., 8*(3), 146–149.

McFall, M., Mackay, P., & Donovan, D. (1992). Combat-related posttraumatic stress disorder and severity of substance abuse in Vietnam veterans. *J. Stud. Alc., 53*(4), 357–363.

McFarlane, A. C. (1991). Posttraumatic stress disorder. *Inter. Rev. Psychiat., 3*(2), 203–213.

McGeer, P. L., & McGeer, E. G. (1996). Anti-inflammatory drugs in the fight against Alzheimer's disease. In R. J. Wurtman, S. Corkin, J. H. Growdon, & R. M. Nitsch (Eds.), *The neurobiology of Alzheimer's disease.* New York: New York Academy of Sciences.

McGehee, D. S., Heath, M. J. S., Gelber, S., Devay, P., & Role, L. W. (1995). Nicotine enhancement of fast excitatory synaptic transmission in CNS by presynaptic receptors. *Science, 269,* 1692–1696.

McGhie, A., & Chapman, J. S. (1961). Disorders of attention and perception in early schizophrenia. *Brit. J. Med. Psychol., 34,* 103–116.

McGlashan, T. H. (1986). Schizotypal personality disorder: Chestnut Lodge follow-up study: VI. Long-term follow-up perspectives. *Arch. Gen. Psychiat., 43*(4), 329–334.

McGlashan, T. H. (1988). A selective review of recent North American long-term follow-up studies of schizophrenia. *Schizo. Bull., 14*(4), 515–542.

McGlashan, T. H. (1992). The longitudinal profile of borderline personality disorder: Contributions from the Chestnut Lodge Follow-up study. In D. Silver & M. Rosenbluth (Eds.), *Handbook of borderline disorders.* Madison, CT: International Universities Press.

McGorry, P. D., Mihalkopoulos, C., Henry, L., Dakis, J. et al. (1995). Spurious precision: Procedural validity of diagnostic assessment in psychotic disorders. 7th Biennial Winter Workshop on Schizophrenia (1994, Les Diablerets, Switzerland). *Amer. J. Psychiat., 152*(2), 220–223.

McGrady, A., & Roberts, G. (1992). Racial differences in the relaxation response of hypertensives. *Psychosom. Med., 54*(1), 71–78.

McGrath, T., Tsui, E., Humphries, S., & Yule, W. (1990). Successful treatment of a noise phobia in a nine-year-old girl with systematic desensitization in vivo. *Educ. Psychol., 10*(1), 79–83.

McGuffin, P., Katz, R., Watkins, S., & Rutherford, J. (1996). A hospital-based twin register of the heritability of DSM-IV unipolar depression. *Arch. Gen. Psychiat., 53,* 129–136.

McGuire, D. (1982). The problem of children's suicide: Ages 5–14. *Inter. J. Offend. Ther. Compar. Criminol., 26*(1), 10–17.

McGuire, P. K., Shah, G. M. S., & Murray, R. M. (1993). Increased blood flow in Broca's area during auditory hallucinations in schizophrenia. *Lancet, 342,* 703–706.

McGuire, P. K., Silbersweig, D. A., Wright, I., Murray, R. M. et al. (1995). Abnormal monitoring of inner speech: A physiological basis for auditory hallucinations. *Lancet, 346,* 596–600.

McIntosh, J. L. (1987). Suicide: Training and education needs with an emphasis on the elderly. *Gerontol. Geriat. Educ., 7,* 125–139.

McIntosh, J. L. (1991). Epidemiology of suicide in the U.S. In A. A. Leenaars (Ed.), *Life span perspectives of suicide.* New York: Plenum Press.

McIntosh, J. L. (1992). Epidemiology of suicide in the elderly. *Suic. Life-Threat. Behav., 22*(1), 15–35.

McIntosh, J. L. (1992). Methods of suicide. In R. W. Maris, A. L. Berman, J. T. Maltsberger, & R. I. Yufit (Eds.), *Assessment and prediction of suicide.* New York: Guilford.

McIntosh, J. L. (1995). Suicide prevention in the elderly (age 65–99) [Special issue: Suicide prevention: Toward the year 2000]. *Suic. Life-Threat. Behav., 25*(1), 180–192.

McIntosh, J. L. (1996). *U. S. suicide rates 1932–1992.* Washington, DC: National Center for Health Statistics.

McIntosh, J. L., & Santos, J. F. (1982). Changing patterns in methods of suicide by race and sex. *Suic. Life-Threat. Behav., 12,* 221–233.

McIntosh, J. L., Hubbard, R. W., & Santos, J. F. (1985). Suicide facts and myths: A study of prevalence. *Death Stud., 9,* 267–281.

McKay, J. R., Alterman, A. I., McLellan, A. T., Snider, E. C., & O'Brien, C. P. (1995). Effect of random versus nonrandom assignment in a comparison of inpatient and day hospital rehabilitation for male alcoholics. *J. Cons. Clin. Psychol., 63*(1), 70–78.

McKeon, J., McGuffin, P., & Robinson, P. (1984). Obsessive-compulsive neurosis following head injury: A report of four cases. *Brit. J. Psychiat., 144,* 190–192.

McKisack, C., & Waller, G. (1997). Factors influencing the outcome of group psychotherapy for bulimia nervosa. *Inter. J. Eat. Disorders, 22,* 1–13.

McLean, A., Temkin, N. R., Dikmen, S., & Wyler, A. R. (1983). The behavioral sequelae of head injury. *J. Clin. Neuropsychol., 5,* 361–376.

McLean, P. D., & Hakstian, A. R. (1979). Clinical depression: Comparative efficacy of outpatient treatments. *J. Cons. Clin. Psychol., 47*(5), 818–836.

McLellan, A. T., Arndt, I. O., Metzger, D. S. et al. (1993). The effects of psychosocial services in substance abuse treatment. *JAMA, 269,* 1953–1959.

McMahon, R. C., & Richards, S. K. (1996). Profile patterns, consistency, and change in the million clinical multiaxial inventory-II in cocaine abusers. *J. Clin. Psychol., 52*(1), 75–79.

McMahon, R. J., & Wells, K. C. (1989). Conduct disorders. In E. J.

Mash & R. Barkley (Eds.), *Treatment of childhood disorders.* New York: Guilford.

McMinn, M. R., & Wade, N. G. (1995). Beliefs about the prevalence of dissociative identity disorder, sexual abuse, and ritual abuse among religious and nonreligious therapists. *Profess. psychol.: Res. Prac., 26*(3), 257–261.

McNally, R. J. (1986). Behavioral treatment of a choking phobia. *J. Behav. Ther. Exp. Psychiat., 17*(3), 185–188.

McNally, R. J. (1986). Preparedness and phobias: A review. *Psychol. Bull., 101,* 283–303.

McNally, R. J. (1996). *Panic disorder: A critical analysis.* New York: The Guilford.

McNally, R. J., & Lukach, B. M. (1991). Behavioral treatment of zoophilic exhibitionism. *J. Behav. Ther. Exp. Psychiat., 22*(4), 281–284.

McNally, R. J., Hornig, C. D., & Donnell, C. D. (1995). Clinical versus nonclinical panic: A test of suffocation false alarm theory. *Behav. Res. Ther., 33*(2), 127–131.

McNeal, E. T., & Cimbolic, P. (1986). Antidepressants and biochemical theories of depression. *Psychol. Bull., 99*(3), 361–374.

McNeil, E. B. (1967). *The quiet furies.* Englewood Cliffs, NJ: Prentice Hall.

McNew, J. A., & Abell, N. (1995). Posttraumatic stress symptomatology: Similarities and differences between Vietnam veterans and adult survivors of childhood sexual abuse. *Social Work, 40*(1), 115-126.

McNiel, D. E., & Binder, R. L. (1991). Clinical assessment of the risk of violence among psychiatric inpatients. *Amer. J. Psychiat., 148*(10), 1317–1321.

McQuiston, J. T. (1993, February 23). Suffolk mother's illness imperils son, judge rules. *The New York Times,* pp. B1, B2.

McShane, W., & Redoutey, L. J. (1987). Community hospitals and community mental health agencies: Partners in service delivery. Annual Meeting of the Association of Mental Health Administrators (1986, San Francisco, California). *J. Ment. Hlth. Admin., 14*(2), 1–6.

Meana, M., & Binik, Y. M. (1994). Painful coitus: A review of female dysparcunia. *J. Nerv. Ment. Dis., 182,* 264–272.

Mednick, S. A. (1971). Birth defects and schizophrenia. *Psychol. Today, 4,* 48–50.

Mednick, S. A., Gabrielli, W. F., Jr., & Hutchings, B. (1987). Genetic factors in the etiology of criminal behavior. In S. A. Mednick, T. E. Moffitt, & S. A. Stack (Eds.), *The causes of crime: New biological appraoches.* Cambridge, England: Cambridge University Press.

Meehl, P. E. (1951). *Research results for counselers.* St. Paul, MN: State Dept. of Education.

Meehl, P. E. (1960). The cognitive activity of the clinician. *Amer. Psychol., 15,* 19–27.

Meibach, R. C., Mullane, J. F., & Binstok, G. (1987). A placebo-controlled multicenter trial of propranolol and chlordiazepoxide in the treatment of anxiety. *Curr. Ther. Res., 41,* 65–76.

Meichenbaum, D. (1992). Evolution of cognitive behavior therapy: Origins, tenets, and clinical examples. In J. K. Zeig (Ed.), *The evolution of psychotherapy: The second conference.* New York: Brunner/Mazel.

Meichenbaum, D. (1993). Stress inoculation training: A 20-year update. In P. M. Lehrer & R. L. Woolfolk (Eds.), *Principles and Practice of Stress Management* (2nd ed.). New York: Guilford.

Meichenbaum, D. (1997). The evolution of a cognitive-behavior therapist. In J. K. Zeig (Ed.), *The evolution of psychotherapy: The third conference.* New York: Brunner/Mazel.

Meichenbaum, D. H. (1972). Cognitive modification of test-anxious college students. *J. Cons. Clin. Psychol., 39,* 370–380.

Meichenbaum, D. H. (1972). Examination of model characteristics in reducing avoidance behavior. *J. Behav. Ther. Exp. Psychiat., 3,* 225–227.

Meichenbaum, D. H. (1974). *Cognitive behavior modification.* Morristown, NJ: General Learning.

Meichenbaum, D. H. (1974). Self instruction methods. In F. H. Kanfer & A. P. Goldstein (Eds.), *Helping people change.* New York: Pergamon Press.

Meichenbaum, D. H. (1975). A self-instructional approach to stress management: A proposal for stress inoculation training. In I. Sarason & C. D. Spielberger (Eds.), *Stress and anxiety* (Vol. 2). New York: Wiley.

Meichenbaum, D. H. (1975). Enhancing creativity by modifying what subjects say to themselves. *Amer. Educ. Res. J., 12*(2), 129–145.

Meichenbaum, D. H. (1975). Theoretical and treatment implications of development research on verbal control of behavior. *Canad. Psychol. Rev., 16*(1), 22–27.

Meichenbaum, D. H. (1975). Toward a cognitive of self control. In G. Schwartz & D. Shapiro (Eds.), *Consciousness and self regulation: Advances in research.* New York: Plenum Press.

Meichenbaum, D. H. (1977). *Cognitive-behavior modification: An integrative approach.* New York: Plenum Press.

Meichenbaum, D. H. (1977). Dr. Ellis, please stand up. *Couns. Psychologist, 7*(1), 43–44.

Meichenbaum, D. H. (1986). Metacognitive methods of instruction: Current status and future prospects. *Spec. Serv. Schools, 3*(1–2), 23–32.

Meichenbaum, D. H. (1993). The personal journey of a psychotherapist and his mother. In G. G. Brannigan & M. R. Merrens (Eds.), *The undaunted psychologist: Adventures in research.* New York: McGraw-Hill.

Melges, F. T., & Swartz, M. S. (1989). Oscillations of attachment in borderline personality disorder. *Amer. J. Psychiat., 146*(9), 1115–1120.

Melo, J. A., Shendure, J., Pociask, K., & Silver, L. M. (1996, June). Identification of sex-specific quantiative trait loci controlling alcohol preference in C57BL/6 mice. *Nature Genetics, 13,* 147–153.

Meltzer, H. Y. (1987). Biological studies in schizophrenia. *Schizo. Bull., 13*(1), 77–111.

Meltzer, H. Y. (1991). The mechanism of action of novel antipsychotic drugs. *Schizo. Bull., 17*(2), 263–287.

Meltzer, H. Y. (1992). Dimensions of outcome with clozapine. *Brit. J. Psychiat., 160*(Suppl. 17), 46–53.

Meltzer, H. Y. (1992). Treatment of the neuroleptic-nonresponsive schizophrenic patient. *Schizo. Bull., 18*(3), 515–542.

Meltzer, H. Y. (1993). Clozapine: A major advance in the treatment of schizophrenia. *Harvard Ment. Hlth. Letter, 19*(2), 4–6.

Meltzer, H. Y. (1995). Neuroleptic withdrawal in schizophrenic patients: An idea whose time has come. *Arch. Gen. Psychiat., 52*(3), 200–202.

Meltzer, H. Y. (1995). The role of serotonin in schizophrenia and the place of serotonin-dopamine antagonist antipsychotics. *Journal of Clinical Psychopharmacology, 15*(1, Suppl 1), 2S–3S.

Meltzer, H. Y. & Okayli, G. (1995). Reduction of suicidality during clozapine treatment of neuroleptic-resistant schizophrenia: Impact on risk-benefit assessment. *Amer. J. Psychiat., 152*(2), 183–190.

Meltzer, H. Y., Thompson, P. A., Lee, M. A., & Ranjan, R. (1996). Neuropsychologic deficits in schizophrenia: Relation to social function and effect of antipsychotic drug treatment. *Neuropsychopharmacology, 14*(3S), 27S–33S.

Meltzoff, J., & Kornreich, M. (1970). *Research in psychotherapy.* New York: Atherton.

Melville, J. (1978). *Phobias and obsessions.* New York: Penguin.

Mendels, J. (1970). *Concepts of depression.* New York: Wiley.

Mendelson, W. B. (1990). The Stony Brook 600: The experience of a sleep disorder center. *Ann. Clin. Psychiat., 2*(4), 277–283.

Mendlewicz, J., Fleiss, J. L., & Fieve, R. R. (1972). Evidence for X-linkage in the transmission of manic-depressive illness. *JAMA, 222,* 1624–1627.

Mendlewicz, J., Linkowski, P., & Wilmotte, J. (1980). Linkage between glucose-6-phosphate dehydrogenase deficiency in manic depressive psychosis. *Brit. J. Psychiat., 137,* 337–342.

Mendlewicz, J., Simon, P., Sevy, S., Charon, F., Brocas, H., Legros, S., & Vassart, G. (1987). Polymorphic DNA marker on X chromosome and manic depression. *Lancet 1,* 1230–1232.

Menke, J. A., McClead, R. E., & Hansen, N. B. (1991). Perspectives on perinatal complications associated with mental retardation. In J. L. Matson & J. A. Mulick (Eds.), *Handbook of mental retardation.* New York: Pergamon Press.

Menninger, K. (1938). *Man against himself.* New York: Harcourt.

Menninger, W. W. (1993). Management of the aggressive and dangerous patient. *Bull. Menninger Clin., 57,* 209.

Menzies, R. G., & Clarke, J. C. (1993). A comparison of in vivo and vicarious exposure in the treatment of childhood water phobia. *Behav. Res. Ther., 31*(1), 9–15.

Menzies, R. P. D., Federoff, J. P., Green, C. M., & Isaacson, K. (1995). Prediction of dangerous behaviour in male erotomania. *Brit. J. Psychiat., 116*(4), 529–536.

Merikangas, K. R., & Angst, J. (1995). Comorbidity and social phobia: Evidence from clinical, epidemiologic, and genetic studies [Special issue: Social phobia]. *Eur. Arch. Psychiat. Clin. Neurosci., 244*(6), 297–303.

Merikangas, K. R., Stevens, D. E., & Angst, J. (1994). Psychopathology and headache syndromes in the community. *Headache, 34*(8), S17–S22.

Mermelstein, H. T., & Holland, J. C. (1991). Psychotherapy by telephone: A therapeutic tool for cancer patients. *Psychosomatics, 32*(4), 407–412.

Merrill, J., Milner, G., Owens, J., & Vale, A. (1992). Alcohol and attempted suicide. *Brit. J. Addic., 87*(1), 83–89.

Mersch, P. P. (1995). The treatment of social phobia: The differential effectiveness of exposure *in vivo* and an integration of exposure *in vivo,* rational emotive therapy and social skills training. *Behav. Res. Ther., 33*(3), 259–269.

Mersch, P. P. A. (1995). The treatment of social phobia: The differential effectiveness of exposure *in vivo* and an integration of exposure *in vivo,* rational emotive therapy and social skills training. *Behav. Res. Ther., 33*(3), 259–269.

Mersch, P. P., Emmelkamp, P. M., & Lips, C. (1991). Social phobia: Individual response patterns and the long-term effects of behavioural and cognitive interventions. A follow-up study. *Behav. Res. Ther., 29*(4), 357–362.

Merskey, H. (1986). Classification of chronic pain: Descriptions of chronic pain syndromes and definitions of pain terms. *Pain, 3,* 226.

Merskey, H. (1992). The manufacture of personalities: The production of multiple personality disorder. *Brit. J. Psychiat., 160,* 327–340.

Merskey, H. (1995). Multiple personality disorder and false memory syndrome. *Brit. J. Psychiat., 166*(3), 281–283.

Merzenich, M. M., Jenkins, W. M., Johnston, P., Schreiner, C. et al. (1996). Temporal processing deficits of language-learning impaired children ameliorated by training. *Science, 271,* 77–84.

Messer, A. A. (1985). Narcissistic people. *Med. Aspects Human Sex., 19*(9), 169–184.

Messer, S. B., Tishby, O., & Spillman, A. (1992). Taking context seriously in psychotherapy research: Relating therapist interventions to patient progress in brief psychodynamic therapy. *J. Cons. Clin. Psychol., 60*(5), 678–688.

Metalsky, G. I., Joiner, T. E., Jr., Hardin, T. S., & Abramson, L. Y. (1993). Depressive reactions to failure in a naturalistic setting: A test of the hopelessness and self-esteem theories of depression. *J. Abnorm. Psychol., 102*(1), 101–109.

Meyer, B. C., & Weinroth, L. A. (1957). Observations on psychological aspects of anorexia nervosa: Report on a case. *Psychosom. Med., 19,* 389.

Meyer, R. E. (1995). Biology of psychoactive substance dependence disorders: Opiates, cocaine, and ethanol. In A. F. Schatzberg & C. B. Nemeroff (Eds.), *The American Psychiatric Press textbook of psychopharmacology.* Washington, DC: American Psychiatric Press, Inc.

Meyer, R. E., Murray, R. F., Jr., Thomas, F. B. et al. (1989). *Prevention and treatment of alcohol problems: Research opportunities.* Washington, DC: National Academy.

Meyer, R. G. (1992). *Abnormal behavior and the criminal justice system.* New York: Lexington Books.

Meyer, V. (1966). Modification of expectations in cases with obsessional rituals. *Behav. Res. Ther., 4,* 273–280.

Michael, R. T., Gagnon, J. H., Laumann, E. O., & Kolata, G. (1994). *Sex in America: A definitive survey.* Boston: Little, Brown and Company.

Michaelson, R. (1993). Flood volunteers build emotional levees. *APA Monitor, 24*(10), 30.

Michels, R. (1992). The borderline patient: Shifts in theoretical emphasis and implications for treatment. In D. Silver & M. Rosenbluth (Eds.), *Handbook of borderline disorders.* Madison, CT: International Universities Press.

Michelson, L. K., & Marchione, K. (1991). Behavioral, cognitive and pharmacological treatments of panic disorder with agoraphobia: Critique and synthesis. *J. Cons. Clin. Psychol., 59*(1), 100–114.

Mickalide, A. D. (1990). Sociocultural factors influencing weight among males. In A. E. Andersen (Ed.), *Males with eating disorders.* New York: Brunner/Mazel.

Miesel, A. (1989). *The right to die.* New York: Wiley.

Miklowitz, D. J., Goldstein, M. J., & Nuechterlein, K. H. (1995). Verbal interactions in the families of schizophrenic and bipolar affective patients. *J. Abnorm. Psychol., 104*(2), 268–276.

Miles, C. P. (1977). Conditions predisposing to suicide: A review. *J. Nerv. Ment. Dis., 164*(4), 231–246.

Millar, J. D. (1984). The NIOSH-suggested list of the ten leading work-related diseases and injuries. *J. Occup. Med., 26,* 340–341.

Millar, J. D. (1990). Mental health and the workplace: An interchangeable partnership. *Amer. Psychol., 45*(10), 1165–1166.

Millar, M. G., & Millar, K. U. (1996). Effects of message anxiety on disease detection and health promotion behaviors. *Basic Appl. Soc. Psychol., 18*(1), 61–74.

Miller, G. E., & Prinz, R. J. (1990). Enhancement of social learning family interventions for childhood conduct disorder. *Psychol. Bull., 108*(2), 291–307.

Miller, H. L., Coombs, D. W., Leeper, J. D. et al. (1984). An analysis of the effects of suicide prevention facilities on suicide rates in the United States. *Amer. J. Pub. Hlth., 74,* 340–343.

Miller, L. (1988). Neurocognitive aspects of remorse: Impulsivity-compulsivity-reflectivity. *Psychother. Patient, 5,* 63–76.

Miller, L. J. (1990). The formal treatment contract in the inpatient management of borderline personality disorder. *Hosp. Comm. Psychiat., 41*(9), 985–987.

Miller, N. E. (1948). Studies of fear as an acquirable drive. I. Fear as motivation and fear-reduction as reinforcement in the learning of new responses. *J. Exp. Psychol., 38,* 89–101.

Miller, N. S., & Gold, M. S. (1990). Benzodiazepines: Tolerance, dependence, abuse, and addiction. *J. Psychoactive Drugs, 22*(1), 23–33.

Miller, N. S., Klahr, A. L., Gold, M. S., Sweeney, K. et al. (1990). The prevalence of marijuana (cannabis) use and dependence in cocaine dependence. *NY St. J. Med., 90*(10), 491–492.

Miller, N. S., Mahler, J. C., & Gold, M. S. (1991). Suicide risk associated with drug and alcohol dependence. *J. Addic. Dis., 10*(3), 49–61.

Miller, P. M. (1996). Redefining success in eating disorders. *Addic. Behav., 21*(6), 745–754.

Miller, P. M., Ingham, J. G., & Davidson, S. (1976). Life events, symptoms, and social support. *J. Psychiatr. Res., 20*(6), 514–522.

Miller, T. Q., Smith, T. W., Turner, C. W., Guijarro, M. L., & Hallet A. J. (1996). A meta-analytic review of research on hostility and physical health. *Psychol. Bull., 119*(2), 322–348.

Miller, W. R. (1982). Treating problem drinkers: What works? *Behav. Ther., 5,* 15–18.

Miller, W. R. (1983). Controlled drinking, *Quart. J. Stud. Alcohol., 44,* 68–83.

Miller, W. R., & Hester, R. K. (1980). Treating the problem drinker: Modern approaches. In W. R. Miller (Ed.), *The addictive behaviors: Treatment of alcoholism, drug abuse, smoking, and obesity.* Elmsford, NY: Pergamon Press.

Miller, W. R., & Seligman, M. E. (1975). Depression and learned helplessness in man. *J. Abnorm. Psychol., 84*(3), 228–238.

Miller, W. R., Leckman, A. L., Delaney, H. D., & Tinchom, M. (1992).

Long-term follow-up of behavioral self-control training. *J. Stud. Alc., 51,* 108–115.

Millon, T. (1969). *Modern psychopathology: A biosocial approach to maladaptive learning and functioning.* Philadelphia: Saunders.

Millon, T. (1987). *Manual for the MCMI-II* (2nd ed.). Minneapolis, MN: National Computer Systems.

Millon, T. (1987). *Millon Clinical Multiaxial Inventory-II: Manual for the MCMI-II* (2nd ed.). Minneapolis, MN: National Computer Systems.

Millon, T. (1990). *Toward a new personology.* New York: Wiley.

Millon, T. (1990). The disorders of personality. In L. A. Pervin (Ed.), *Handbook of personality theory and practice.* New York: Guilford.

Millstein, R. (1992). The national impact of alcohol and drug problems and HIV infection and AIDS among the poor and underserved. *J. Hlth. Care Poor and Underserved, 3*(1), 21–29.

Millward, D. (1996). Beware of the dog that is being prescribed Prozac. *Electronic Telegraph,* Issue 397, June 3, 1996.

Milner, B. (1971). Interhemispheric difference in the localization of psychological processes in man. *Brit. Med. Bull., 27,* 272–277.

Milner, B., Corkin, S., & Teuber, H. L. (1968). Further analysis of the hippocampal syndrome: 14-year follow-up study of H. M. *Neuropsychologica, 6,* 215–234.

Milner, J. S. & Campbell, J. C. (1995). Prediction issues for practitioners. In J. C. Campbell (Ed.), *Assessing dangerousness: Violence by sexual offenders, batterers, and child abusers.* Thousand Oaks, CA: Sage Publications.

Mineka, S. (1985). Animal models of anxiety-based disorders: Their usefulness and limitations. In A. H. Tuma & J. Maser (Eds.), *Anxiety and the anxiety disorders.* Hillsdale, NJ: Erlbaum.

Mineka, S., Davidson, M., Cook, M., & Keir, R. (1984). Observational conditioning of snake fear in rhesus monkeys. *J. Abnorm. Psychol., 93*(4), 355–372.

Mintzer, J. E., & Brawman-Mintzer, O. (1996). Agitation as a possible expression of generalized anxiety disorder in demented elderly patients toward a treatment approach. *J. Clin. Psychiat., 57*(Suppl. 7), 55–63.

Minuchin, S. (1974). *Families and family therapy.* Cambridge, MA: Harvard University Press.

Minuchin, S. (1987). My many voices. In J. K. Zeig (Ed.), *The evolution of psychotherapy.* New York: Brunner/Mazel.

Minuchin, S. (1992). *Family healing.* New York: Free Press.

Minuchin, S. (1993, March). On family therapy: A visit with Salvador Minuchin. *Psychol. Today, 26*(2), 20–21.

Minuchin, S. (1997). The leap to complexity: Supervision in family therapy. In J. K. Zeig (Ed.), *The evolution of psychotherapy: The third conference.* New York: Brunner/Mazel, Publishers.

Minuchin, S., Rosman, B. L., & Baker, L. (1978). *Psychosomatic families: Anorexia nervosa in context.* Cambridge, MA: Harvard University Press.

Minuchin, S., Rosman, B., & Baker, L. (1978). *Psychosomatic families.* Cambridge, MA: Harvard University Press.

Mirabella, R. F., Frueh, B. C., & Fossey, M. D. (1995). Exposure therapy and antidepressant medication for treatment of chronic PTSD. *Amer. J. Psychiat., 152*(6), 955–956.

Miranda, J., & Persons, J. D. (1988). Dysfunctional attitudes are mood state dependent. Meetings of the Assoc. for Advancement of Behavior Therapy. *J. Abnorm. Psychol., 97*(1), 76–79.

Mirin, S. M., & Weiss, R. D. (1991). Substance abuse and mental illness. In R. J. Frances & S. I. Miller (Eds.), *Clinical textbook of addictive disorders.* New York: Guilford.

Mirowsky, J., & Ross, C. (1995). Sex differences in distress: Real of artifact? *Amer. Sociol. Rev., 60,* 449–468.

Mirsky, A. F., Yardley, S. L., Jones, B. P., Walsh, D., et al. (1995). Analysis of the attention deficit in schizophrenia: A study of patients and their relatives in Ireland. *J. Psychiat. Res., 29*(1), 23–42.

Mirsky, I. A. (1958). Physiologic, psychologic, and social determinants of the etiology of duodenal ulcer. *Amer. J. Digestional Dis., 3,* 285–314.

Mishna, F. (1996). Clinical report. In their own words: Therapeutic factors for adolescents who have learning disabilities. *Inter. J. Group Psychother., 46*(2), 265–273.

Mitchell, J. E., & de Zwaan, M. (1993). Pharmacological treatments of binge eating. In C. G. Fairburn & G. T. Wilson (Eds.), *Binge eating: Nature, assessment, and treatment.* New York: Guilford.

Mitchell, J. E., & Pyle, R. L. (1985). Characteristics of bulimia. In J. E. Mitchell (Ed.), *Anorexia nervosa and bulimia: Diagnosis and treatment.* Minneapolis: University of Minnesota.

Mitchell, J. E., Hatsukami, D., Goff, G., Pyle, R. L., Eckert, E. D., & Davis, L. E. (1985). Intensive outpatient group treatment for bulimia. In D. M. Garner & P. E. Garfinkel (Eds.), *Handbook of psychotherapy for anorexia nervosa and bulimia.* New York: Guilford.

Mitchell, J. E., Pyle, R. L., & Fletcher, L. (1991). The topography of binge eating, vomiting and laxative abuse. Inter. *J. Eat. Disorders, 10*(1), 43–48.

Mitchell, J. E., Pyle, R. L., Eckert, E. D., Hatsukami, D. et al. (1990). Bulimia nervosa in overweight individuals. *J. Nerv. Ment. Disorders, 178*(5), 324–327.

Mitchell, J. E., Pyle, R. L., Miner, R. A. (1982). Gastric dilation as a complication of bulimia. *Psychosomatics, 23,* 96–97.

Mitchell, J. E., Specker, S. M., & de Zwaan, M. (1991). Comorbidity and medical complications of bulimia nervosa. *J. Clin. Psychiat., 52*(Suppl.), 13–20.

Mitchell, S. (Ed.). (1996). *Dramatherapy: Clinical Studies.* London: Kingsley.

Mitchell, T. (1996). Presentation at 11th International Conference on AIDS.

Mizes, J. S. (1995). Eating disorders. In M. Hersen & R. T. Ammerman (Eds.), *Advanced abnormal child psychology.* Hillsdale, NJ: Lawrence Erlbaum Associates, Publishers.

Modestin, J., & Ammann, R. (1996). Mental disorder and criminality: Male schizophrenia. *Schizo. Bull., 22*(1), 69–82.

Modestin, J., & Villiger, C. (1989). Follow-up study on borderline versus nonborderline personality disorders. *Comprehen. Psychiat., 30*(3), 236–244.

Modrow, J. (1992). *How to become a schizophrenic: The case against Bio. Psychiatry,* Everett, WA: Apollyon Press.

Mogg, K., Bradley, B. P., Millar, N., & White, J. (1995). A follow-up study of cognitive bias in generalized anxiety disorder. *Behav. Res. Ther., 33*(8), 927–935.

Mohler, H., & Okada, T. (1977). Benzodiazepine receptor: Demonstration in the central nervous system. *Science, 198*(4319), 849–851.

Mohler, H., Richards, J. G., & Wu, J.-Y. (1981). Autoradiographic localization of benzodiazepine receptors in immunocytochemically identified Y-aminobutyric synapses. *Proc. Natl. Acad. Sci., U.S.A., 78,* 1935–1938.

Mohr, D. C., & Beutler, L. E. (1990). Erectile dysfunction: A review of diagnostic and treatment procedures. *Clin. Psychol. Rev., 10*(1), 123–150.

Mohr, J. W., Turner, R. E., & Jerry, M. B. (1964). *Pedophilia and exhibitionism.* Toronto: University of Toronto.

Möller, H. J. (1990). Suicide risk and treatment problems in patients who have attempted suicide. In D. Lester (Ed.), *Current concepts of suicide.* Philadelphia: The Charles Press.

Mollerstrom, W. W., Patchner, M. A., & Milner, J. S. (1992). Family violence in the Air Force: A look at offenders and the role of the Family Advocacy Program. *Mil. Med., 157*(7), 371–374.

Mollinger, R. N. (1980). Antithesis and the obsessive-compulsive. *Psychoanal. Rev., 67*(4), 465–477.

Monahan, J. (1992). Mental disorder and violent behavior: Perceptions and evidence. *Amer. Psychologist, 47*(4), 511–521.

Monahan, J. (1993). Limiting therapist exposure to Tarasoff liability: Guidelines for risk containment. *Amer. Psychologist, 48*(3), 242–250.

Monahan, J. (1993). Mental disorder and violence: Another look. In S. Hodgins (Ed.), *Mental disorder and crime.* Newbury Park, CA: Sage.

Monahan, J., & Davis, S. K. (1983). Mentally disordered sex offenders.

In J. Monahan & H. J. Steadman (Eds.), *Mentally disordered offenders.* New York: Plenum Press.

Monahan, J., & Steadman, H. J. (Eds.). (1983). *Mentally disordered offenders.* New York: Plenum Press.

Monahan, J., & Steadman, H. J. (1996). Violent storms and violent people. How meteorology can inform risk communication in mental health law. *Amer. Psychol., 51*(9), 931–938.

Monahan, J., & Walker, L. (Eds.). (1990). *Social science in law: Cases and materials* (2nd ed.). Westbury, NJ: Foundation Press.

Moncrieff, J., Drummond, C., Candy, B., Checinski, K., & Farmer, R. (1996). Sexual abuse in people with alcohol problems: A study of the prevalence of sexual abuse and its relationship to drinking behavior. *Brit. J. Psychiat., 169,* 355–360.

Mondimore, F. M. (1993). *Depression, the mood disease.* Baltimore: The Johns Hopkins University Press.

Montgomery, S. A. & Kasper, S. (1995). Comparison of compliance between serotonin reuptake inhibitors and tricyclic antidepressants: A meta-analysis. *Inter. Clinical Psychopharmacology, 9*(Suppl. 4), 33–40.

Montgomery, S. A., Bebbington, P., Cowen, P., Deakin, W., et al. (1993). Guidelines for treating depressive illness with antidepressants. *Journal of Psychopharmacology, 7*(1), 19–23.

Montgomery, S. A., Dufour, H., Brion S., Gailledreau, J. et al. (1988). The prophylactic efficacy of fluoxetine in unipolar depression. *Brit. J. Psychiat., 153*(3, Suppl.), 69–76.

Montorsi, F., Guazzoni, G., Bergamaschi, R., Zucconi, M., Rigatti, P., Pizzini, G., & Pozza, G. (1994). Clinical reliability of multi-drug intracavernous vasoactive pharmacotherapy for diabetic impotence. *Acta Diabetologia, 31,* 1–15.

Moore, D. R., & Arthur, J. L. (1983). Juvenile delinquency. In T. Ollendick & M. Hersen (Eds.), *Handbook of child psychopathology.* New York: Plenum Press.

Moore, M. M. & Freeman, S. J. (1995). Counseling survivors of suicide: Implications for group postvention. *J. for Specialists in Group Work, 20*(1), 40–47.

Morales, A., Condra, M., Heaton, J. P. W., & Varrin, S. (1991). Impotence: organic factors and management approach. *Sex. Marital Ther., 6*(2), 97–106.

Moreno, I., Saiz, R. J., & Lopez, I. J. J. (1991). Serotonin and gambling dependence. *Human Psychopharmacol.-Clin. Exp., 6*(Suppl.), 9–12.

Moreno, J. K., Fuhriman, A., & Hileman, E. (1995). Significant events in a psychodynamic psychotherapy group for eating disorders. *Group, 19*(1), 56–62.

Morgan, A. H., & Hilgard, E. R. (1973). Age differences in susceptibility to hypnosis. *Inter. J. Clin. Exp. Hyp., 21,* 78–85.

Morgan, C. A., Grillon, C., Southwick, S. M., Davis, M., & Charney, D. S. (1996). Exaggerated acoustic startle reflex in Gulf War veterans with posttraumatic stress disorder. *Amer. J. Psychiat., 153,* 64–68.

Morgan, M. J., & London, E. D. (1995). The use of positron emission tomography to study the acute effects of addictive drugs on cerebral metabolism. In A. Biegon & N. D. Volkow (Eds.), *Sites of drug action in the human brain.* Boca Raton: CRC Press, Inc.

Morgenstern, J., Langerbucher, J., Labouvie, E., & Miller, K. J. (1997). The comorbidity of alcoholism and personality disorders in a clinical population: Prevalence rates and relation to alcohol typology variables. *J. Abnorm. Psychol., 106*(1), 74–84.

Morin, C. M., Colecchi, C., Brink, D., Astruc, M. et al. (1995). How "blind" are double-blind placebo-controlled trials of benzodiazepine hypnotics? *Sleep, 18*(4), 240–245.

Morley, S. (1989). Single case research. In G. Parry & N. W. Fraser (Eds.), *Behavioural and mental health research: A handbook of skills and methods.* Hove, UK: Erlbaum.

Morokoff, P. J. (1988). Sexuality in premenopausal and postmenopausal women. *Psychol. Women Quart., 12,* 489–511.

Morokoff, P. J. (1993). Female sexual arousal disorder. In W. O'Donohue and J. Geer (Eds.), *Handbook of sexual dysfunctions.* Boston: Allyn & Bacon.

Morokoff, P. J., & Gillilland, R. (1993). Stress, sexual functioning, and marital satisfaction. *J. Sex Res., 30*(1), 43–53.

Morris, A., Cooper, T., & Cooper, P. J. (1989). The changing shape of female fashion models. *Inter. J. Eat. Disorders, 8*(5), 593–596.

Morris, G. (1983). Acquittal by reason of insanity: Developments in the law. In J. Monahan & H. J. Steadman (Eds.), *Mentally disordered offenders.* New York: Plenum Press.

Morrison, J. (1989). Histrionic personality disorder in women with somatization disorder. *Psychosomatics, 30*(4), 433–437.

Morrow-Bradley, C., & Elliott, R. (1986). Utilization of psychotherapy research by practicing psychotherapists. *Amer. Psychol., 41*(2), 188–197.

Morse, S. J. (1982). A preference for liberty: The case against involuntary commitment of the mentally disordered. *Calif. Law Rev., 70,* 55–106.

Mosak, H. H., & Goldman, S. E. (1995). An alternative view of the purpose of psychoses. *Individual Psychol. J. Adlerian Theory, Res. Prac., 51*(1), 46–49.

Moscicki, E. K. (1995). Epidemiology of suicidal behavior. Special Issue: Suicide prevention: Toward the year 2000. *Suic. Life-Threat. Behav., 25*(1), 22–35.

Moskovitz, R. A. (1996). *Lost in the mirror: An inside look at borderline personality disorder.* Dallas, TX: Tayloir Publishing Company.

Motley, M. T. (1987, February). What I meant to say. *Psychol. Today,* 24–28.

Motto, J. (1967). Suicide and suggestibility: The role of the press. *Amer. J. Psychiat., 124,* 252–256.

Mowrer, O. H. (1939). A stimulus-response analysis of anxiety and its role as a reinforcing agent. *Psychol. Rev., 46,* 553–566.

Mowrer, O. H. (1939). *An experimentally produced "social problem" in rats* [Film]. Bethlehem, PA: Lehigh University, Psychological Cinema Register.

Mowrer, O. H. (1947). On the dual nature of learning: A reinterpretation of "conditioning" and "problem-solving." *Harvard Educ. Rev., 17,* 102–148.

Mowrer, O. H., & Mowrer, W. M. (1938). Enuresis: A method for its study and treatment. *Amer. J. Orthopsychiat., 8,* 436–459.

Mrazek, P. J., & Haggerty, R. J. (Eds.). (1994). *Reducing risks for mental disorders: Frontiers for preventive intervention research.* Washington, DC: National Academy Press.

Muehlenhard, C. L., & Linton, M. A. (1987). Date rape and sexual aggression in dating situations: Incidence and risk factors. *J. Couns. Psychol., 34*(2), 186–196.

Mueser, K. T., Bellack, A. S., & Brady, E. U. (1990). Hallucinations in schizophrenia. *Acta Psychiatr. Scandin., 82*(1), 29–36.

Mueser, K. T., Doonan, R., Penn, D. L., Blanchard, J. J., Bellack, A. S., Nishith, P., & DeLeon, J. (1996). Emotion recognition and social competence in chronic schizophrenia. *J. Abnorm. Psychol., 105*(2), 271–275.

Muir, J. L. (1997). Acetylcholine, aging, and Alzheimer's disease. *Pharmacol. Biochem. Behav., 56*(4), 687–696.

Mulder, A. (1996). *Prevention of suicidal behaviour in adolescents: The development and evaluation of a teacher's education programme.* Leiden: University of Leiden.

Mulkern, V. M., & Manderscheid, R. W. (1989). Characteristics of community support program clients in 1980 and 1984. *Hosp. Comm. Psychiat., 40*(2), 165–172.

Mullins, L. L., Olson, R. A., & Chaney, J. M. (1992). A social learning/family systems approach to the treatment of somatoform disorders in children and adolescents. *Fam. Sys. Med., 10*(2), 201–212.

Munk, J. P., & Mortensen, P. B. (1992). Social outcome in schizophrenia: A 13-year follow-up. *Soc. Psychiat. Psychiat. Epidemiol., 27*(3), 129–134.

Muñoz, R. F., Mrazek, P. J., & Haggerty, R. J. (1996). Institute of Medicine report on prevention of mental disorders. Summary and commentary. *Amer. Psychol., 51*(11), 1116–1122.

Muris, P., Merckelbach, H., & Clavan, M. (1997). Abnormal and normal compulsions. *Behav. Res. Ther. 35*(3), 249–252.

Murphy, C. M., Meyer, S. L., & O'Leary, K. D. (1994). Dependency characteristics of partner assaultive men. *J. Abnorm. Psychol., 103*(4), 729-735.

Murphy, J. B., & Lipshultz, L. I. (1988). Infertility in the paraplegic male. In E. A. Tanagho, T. F. Lue, & R. D. McClure (Eds.), *Contemporary management of impotence and infertility.* Baltimore: Williams & Wilkins.

Murphy, J. M. (1976, March). Psychiatric labeling in cross-cultural perspective: Similar kinds of disturbed behavior appear to be labeled abnormal in diverse cultures. *Science, 101*(4231), 1019–1028.

Murphy, J. M., Sobol, A. M., Neff, R. K., Olivier, D. C., Leighton, A. H. (1984). Stability of prevalence: Depression and anxiety disorders. *Arch. Gen. Psychiat., 41,* 990.

Murphy, S. M. (1990). Rape, sexually transmitted diseases and human immunodeficiency virus infection. *Inter. J. STD AIDS, 1,* 79–82.

Murphy, S. M., Owen, R. T., & Tyrer, P. J. (1984). Withdrawal symptoms after six weeks' treatment with diazepam. *Lancet, 2,* 1389.

Murray, B. (1996). Computer addictions entangle students. *APA Monitor, 27*(6), 38–39.

Murray, B. (1996). Hypnosis helps children address their many fears. *APA Monitor, 27*(10), 46.

Murray, J. B. (1986). Psychological aspects of anorexia nervosa. *Genet., Soc. Genet. Psychol. Monogr., 112*(1), 5–40.

Murray, K. (1993, May 9). When the therapist is a computer. *New York Times,* Section 3, p. 25.

Murrell, J., Farlow, M., Bernardino, G., & Benson, M. D. (1991). A mutation in the amyloid precursor protein associated with hereditary Alzheimer's disease. *Science, 254,* 97–99.

Murstein, B. I., & Fontaine, P. A. (1993). The public's knowledge about psychologists and other mental health professionals. *Amer. Psychol., 48*(7), 839–845.

Mussell, M. P., Mitchell, J. E., de Zwaan, M., Crosby, R. D. et al. (1996). Clinical characteristics associated with binge eating in obese females: A descriptive study. *Inter. J. Obesity, 20,* 324–331.

Muuss, R. E. (1986). Adolescent eating disorder: Bulimia. *Adolescence, 21*(82), 257–267.

Myatt, R. J., & Greenblatt, M. (1993). Adolescent suicidal behavior. In A. A. Leenaars (Ed.), *Suicidology.* Northvale, NJ: Jason Aronson.

Mydans, S. (1996, October 19). New Thai tourist sight: Burmese "giraffe women." *The New York Times,* p. C1.

Myers, D., & Diener, E. (1995). Who is happy? *Psychol. Sci., 6*(1), 10–19.

Myers, D., & Diener, E. (1996). The pursuit of happiness. *Scientif. Amer.* (May, 1996), 70–72.

NAMHC (National Advisory Mental Health Council, Basic Behavioral Science Task Force) (1996). Basic behavioral science research for mental health: Vulnerability and resilience. *Amer. Psychologist, 51*(1), 22–28.

NAMHC (1996). Basic behavioral science research for mental health. *Amer. Psychologist, 51*(3), 181–189.

NAMHC [National Advisory Mental Health Council]. (1996). Basic behavioral science research for mental health. Perception, attention, learning, and memory. *Amer. Psychol. 51*(2), 133–142.

NAMHC (1996). Basic behavioral science research for mental health. Sociocultural and environmental processes. *Amer. Psychol., 51*(7), 722–731.

NAMI [National Alliance for the Mentally Ill]. (1994). Personal communication.

NCHS [National Center for Health Statistics]. (1990). *Vital statistics of the United States, 1987,* Vol. 2. Mortality. Washington, DC: Government Printing Office.

NCHS (1991). *Vital statistics of the United States* (Vol. 2): Mortality - Part A [for the years 1966–1988]. Washington, DC: U. S. Government Printing Office.

NCHS (1993). *Advance report of final mortality statistics, 1991. Monthly Vital Statistics Report,* Vol. 42,(Pt. 2), Hyattsville, MD: US Public Health Service.

NCHS (1995). *Advance report of final divorce statistics.* (Monthly vital statistics report, 43) (9, Suppl) Hyattsville, MD: Public Health Service.

NCHS (1994). *Advance report of final mortality statistics, 1992.* (Monthly vital statistics report, 43). Hyattsville, MD: Public Health Service.

NIA [National Institute on Aging]. (1996). *Aging America poses unprecendented challenge. 65+.* Washington, DC: Office of the Demography of Aging.

NIAAA [National Institute on Alcohol Abuse and Alcoholism]. (1992). *Alcohol alert #15. Alcohol and AIDA.* Rockville, MD: Author.

NIAAA. (1992). *Alcohol alert #16. Moderate Drinking.* Rockville, MD: Author.

NIDA (National Institute on Drug Abuse). (1985). *National household survey on drugs.* Washington, DC: Author.

NIDA. (1987). *Second triennial report to Congress on drug abuse and drug abuse research.* Washington, DC: Author.

NIDA. (1990). *Substance abuse among blacks in the U. S.* Rockville, MD: Author.

NIDA. (1990). *Substance abuse among Hispanic Americans.* Rockville, MD: Author.

NIDA. (1991). *Annual emergency room data, 1991.* Rockville, MD: Author.

NIDA. (1991). *Annual medical examiner data, 1991.* Rockville, MD: Author.

NIDA. (1991). *Third triennial report to Congress on drug abuse and drug abuse research.* Rockville, MD: Author.

NIDA (1995). Facts about teenagers and drug abuse. *NIDA Capsule,* Rockville, MD: Author.

NIDA (1996). *Monitoring the future study, 1975–1996.* Rockville, MD: Author.

NIMH [National Institute of Mental Health]. (1992). Unpublished estimate. Statistical Research Branch.

NIOSH (National Institute for Occupational Safety & Health). (1985). *Proposed national strategies for the prevention of leading work-related diseases and injuries* (Pt. 1, NTIS No. PB87–114740). Cincinnati: Association of Schools of Public Health/NIOSH.

NIOSH. (1988). *Proposed national strategies for the prevention of leading work-related diseases and injuries* (Pt. 2, NTIS No. PB89–130348). Cincinnati: Association of Schools of Public Health/NIOSH.

NVC [National Victims Center]. (1992, April). *Rape in America: A report to the nation.* Arlington, VA: Author.

Nace, E. P. (1992). Alcoholism and the borderline patient. In D. Silver & M. Rosenbluth (Eds.), *Handbook of Borderline Disorders.* Madison, CT: International Universities Press.

Nagy, L. M., Krystal, J. H., Charney, D. S., Merikangas, K. R., & Woods, S. W. (1993). Long-term outcome of panic disorder after short-term imipramine and behavioral group treatment: 2.9-year naturalistic follow-up study. *J. Clin. Psychopharmacol., 13*(1), 16–24.

Nagy, L. M., Morgan, C. A., III, Southwick, S. M., & Charney, D. S. (1993). Open prospective trial of fluoxetine for posttraumatic stress disorder. *J. Clin. Psychopharmacol., 13*(2), 107–113.

Nahas, G. G. (1984). Toxicology and pharmacology. In G. G. Nahas (Ed.), *Marijuana in science and medicine.* New York: Raven Press.

Naring, G. W. B. (1995). The role of biofeedback in the treatment of muscle-contraction headache. *Gedrag and Gezondheid Tijdschrift voor Psychologie and Gezondheid, 23*(1) 12–19.

Narrow, W. E., Regier, D. A., Rae, D. S., Manderscheid, R. W., & Locke, B. Z. (1993). Use of services by persons with mental and addictive disorders: Findings from the National Institute of Mental Health Epidemiologic Catchment Area Program. *Arch. Gen. Psychiat., 50,* 95–107.

Nash, J. M. (1995, April 3). To know your own fate. *Time,* p. 62.

Nash, J. M. (1997, May 5). Addicted. *Time,* p. 68–76.

Nash, M. R., Hulsey, T. L., Sexton, M. C., Harralson, T. L., & Lambert, W. (1993). Long-term sequelae of childhood sexual abuse: Perceived family environment, psycho-pathology, and dissociation. *J. Cons. Clin. Psychol., 61,* 276–283.

National Commission on Children (1991). *Speaking of kids: A national survey of children and parents.* Washington, DC: Author.

National Crime Victimization Survey. (1993). *Highlights from 20 years of surveying crime victims: The National Crime Victimization Survey, 1973–1992.* Washington, DC: Bureau of Justice Statistics.

National Crime Victimization Survey. (1996). Washington, DC: Bureau of Justice Statistics.

National Opinion Research Center (1994). *Survey on extramarital relationships.* Washington, DC: Author.

Needleman, H. O., Riess, J. A., Tobin, M. J., Biesecker, G. E. et al. (1996). Bone lead levels and delinquent behavior. *JAMA, 275*(5), 363–369.

Neimeyer, G. (1996). Glossary of therapists. In R. Comer (Ed.), *Abnormal psychology newsletter* (Issue No. 6).

Neimeyer, R. A., & Bonnelle, K. (1997). The suicide intervention response inventory: A revision and validation. *Death Stud., 21,* 59–81.

Neims, D. M., McNeill, J., Giles, T. R., & Todd, F. (1995). Incidence of laxative abuse in community and bulimic populations: A descriptive review. *Inter. J. Eat. Disorders, 17*(3), 211–228.

Neisser, U. (1985, September). Voices, glances, flashbacks. *Psychol. Today,* pp. 48–53.

Neisser, U., Boodoo, G., Bouchard, T. J. Jr., Boykin, A. W. et al. (1996). Intelligence: Knowns and unknowns. *Amer. Psychol., 51*(2), 77–101.

Nelson, R. O. (1977). Assessment and therapeutic functions of self-monitoring. In M. Hersen, R. M. Eisler, & P. M. Miller (Eds.), *Progress in behavior modification.* New York: Academic Press.

Nelson, R. O. (1981). Realistic dependent measures for clinical use. *J. Cons. Clin. Psychol., 49,* 168–182.

Nelson, R., Demas, G., Huang, P., Fishman, M., Dawson, V., Dawson, T., & Snyder, S. (1995). Behavioral abnormalities in male mice lacking neuronal nitric oxide synthase. *Nature, 378,* 383–386.

Nemecek, S. (1995, April). I get no kick from CH_3CH_2OH: A new treatment for alcoholism receives FDA approval. *Scientif. Amer.,* 24,26.

Nemiah, J. C. (1984). In T. R. Insel (Ed.), *New findings in obsessive compulsive disorder.* Washington, DC: American Psychiatric Press. [7–6]

Nestadt, G., Romanoski, A. J., Brown, C. H., Chahal, R., et al. (1991). DSM-III compulsive personality disorder: An epidemiological survey. *Psychol. Med., 21*(2), 461–471.

Nestadt, G., Romanoski, A. J., Chahal, R., Merchant, A., Folstein, M. F., Gruenberg, E. M., & McHugh, P. R. (1990). An epidemiological study of histrionic personality disorder. *Psychol. Med., 29,* 413–422.

Nestler, E. J., Fitzgerald, L. W., & Self, D. W. (1995). Neurobiology. In J. M. Oldham & M. B. Riba (Eds.), *American Psychiatric Press review of psychiatry,* (Vol. 14). Washington, DC: American Psychiatric Press.

Neugebauer, R. (1978). Treatment of the mentally ill in medieval and early modern England: A reappraisal. *J. Hist. Behav. Sci., 14,* 158–169.

Neugebauer, R. (1979). Medieval and early modern theories of mental illness. *Arch. Gen. Psychiat., 36,* 477–483.

Neumaier, J. F., Petty, F., Kramer, G. L., Szot, P., & Hamblin, M. W. (1997). Learned helplessness increases 5-hydroxytryptamine$_{1B}$ receptor mRNA levels in the rat dorsal raphe nucleus. *Bio. Psychiat., 41,* 668–674.

Neuman, P. A., & Halvorson, P. A. (1983). *Anorexia nervosa and bulimia: A handbook for counselors and therapists.* New York: Van Nostrand-Reinhold.

Newberger, E. H. (1983). The helping hand strikes again: Unintended consequences of child abuse reporting. *J. Clin. Child. Psychol., 12,* 307–311.

Newcomb, M. D. (1994). Predictors of drug use and implications for the workplace. In S. Macdonald & P. Roman (Eds.), *Research advances in alcohol and drug problems: (Vol. 11). Drug testing in the workplace.* New York: Plenum Press.

Newcomb, M. D., & Bentler, P. M. (1988). *Consequences of adolescent drug use: Impact on the lives of young adults.* Newbury Park, CA: Sage.

Newman, J. D., & Farley, M. J. (1995). An ethologically based, stimulus and gender-sensitive nonhuman primate model for anxiety. *Prog. Neuropsychopharmacol. Bio. Psychiat., 19*(4), 677–685.

Newman, J. P., & Kosson, D. S. (1986). Passive avoidance learning in psychopathic and nonpsychopathic offenders. *J. Abnorm. Psychol., 95,* 257–263.

Newman, J. P., Kosson, D. S., & Patterson, C. M. (1987). Response perseveration in psychopaths. *J. Abnorm. Psychol., 96,* 145–149.

Newman, J. P., Kosson, D. S., & Patterson, C. M. (1992). Delay of gratification in psychopathic and nonpsychopathic offenders. *J. Abnorm. Psychol., 101*(4), 630–636.

Newman, R. & Bricklin, P. M. (1991). Parameters of managed mental health care: Legal, ethical, and professional guidelines. *Profess. Psychol.: Res. Prac., 22,* 26–35.

Newman, R. et al. (1996). State leadership conference mobilizes practitioners for community outreach. *Practitioner Update, 4*(1), 1.

Newmann, J. (1986). Gender, life strains, and depression. *J. Hlth. Soc. Behav., 27,* 161–178.

Newsweek Poll (1995). *The state of shame and the union.* Princeton, NJ: Princeton Survey Research Associates.

Newton, J. T. O., Spence, S. H., & Schotte, D. (1995). Cognitive-behavioral therapy versus EMG biofeedback in the treatment of chronic low back pain. *Behav. Res. Ther., 33*(6), 691–697.

Neziroglu, F., McKay, D., Todaro, J., & Yaryura-Tobias, J. A. (1996). Effect of cognitive behavior therapy on persons with body dysmorphic disorder and comorbid axis II diagnoses. *Behav. Ther., 27,* 67–77.

Nichols, M. P. (1984). *Family therapy: concepts and methods.* New York: Gardner Press.

Nichols, M. P. (1992). *The power of family therapy.* New York: Gardner Press.

Nichter, M., & Nichter, M. (1991). Hype and weight. *Med. Anthropol., 13*(3), 249–284.

Nichter, M., & Vuckovic, N. (1994). Fat talk: Body image among adolescent females. In N. Sault (Ed.), *Mirror, mirror: Body image and social relations.* New Brunswick, NJ: Rutgers University Press.

Nickerson, K. J., Helms, J. E., & Terrell, F. (1994). Cultural mistrust, opinions about mental illness, and black students' attitudes toward seeking psychological help from white counselors. *J. Couns. Psychol., 41*(3), 378–385.

Nientimp, E. G., & Cole, C. L. (1992). Teaching socially valid social interaction responses to students with severe disabilities in an integrated school setting. *J. School Psychol., 30*(4), 343–354.

Nietzel, M. T., Bernstein, D. A., & Milich, R. (1994). *Introduction to clinical psychology* (4th ed.). Englewood Cliffs, NJ: Prentice Hall.

Nijinsky, V. (1936). *The diary of Vaslav Nijinsky.* New York: Simon & Schuster.

Niler, E. R., & Beck, S. J. (1989). The relationship among guilt, anxiety and obsessions in a normal population. *Behav. Res. Ther. 27,* 213–220.

Nishino, S., Mignot, E., & Dement, W. C. (1995). Sedative-hypnotics. In A. F. Schatzberg & C. B. Nemeroff (Eds.), *The American Psychiatric Press textbook of psychopharmacology.* Washington, DC: American Psychiatric Press.

Nitenson, N. C., & Cole, J. O. (1993). Psychotropic-induced sexual dysfunction. In D. L. Dunner (ed.), *Current psychiatric therapy.* Philadelphia: Saunders.

Nolan, R. F., Dai, Y., & Stanley, P. D. (1995). An investigation of the relationship between color choice and depression measured by the Beck depression inventory. *Percept. Motor Skills, 81,* 1195–1200.

Nolen-Hoeksema, S. (1987). Sex differences in unipolar depression: Evidence and theory. *Psychol. Bull., 101*(2), 259–282.

Nolen-Hoeksema, S. (1990). *Sex differences in depression.* Stanford, CA: Stanford University Press.

Nolen-Hoeksema, S. (1995). Gender differences in coping with depression across the lifespan. *Depression, 3,* 81–90.

Nolen-Hoeksema, S., & Girgus, J. (1995). Explanatory style and achievement, depression, and gender differences in childhood and early adolescence. In G. Buchanan & M. Seligman (Eds.), *Explanatory style.* Hillsdale, NJ: Erlbaum.

Noll, R., & Turkington, C. (1994). *The encyclopedia of memory and memory disorders.* New York: Facts on File.

Noonan, J. R. (1971). An obsessive-compulsive reaction treated by induced anxiety. *Amer. J. Psychother., 25*(2), 293–299.

Norcross, J. C., & Prochaska, J. O. (1984). Where do behavior (and other) therapists take their troubles? II. *Behav. Therapist, 7*(2), 26–27.

Norcross, J. C., & Prochaska, J. O. (1986). Psychotherapist heal thyself: I. The psychological distress and self-change of psychologists, counselors, and laypersons. *Psychotherapy, 23,* 102–114.

Norcross, J. C., Prochaska, J. O., & Farber, J. A. (1993). Psychologists conducting psychotherapy: New findings and historical comparisons on the psychotherapy division membership. *Psychotherapy, 30*(4), 692–697.

Norcross, J. C., Strausser, D. J., & Missar, C. D. (1988). The process and outcomes of psychotherapists' personal treatment experiences. *Psychotherapy, 25,* 36–43.

Nordstrom, P., Samuelsson, M., & Asberg, M. (1995). Survival analysis of suicide risk after attempted suicide. *Acta Psychiatr. Scandin., 91*(5), 336–340.

Norman, R. M. G., & Malla, A. K. (1995). Prodromal symptoms of relapse in schizophrenia: A review. *Schizo. Bull., 21*(4), 527–539.

Norris, P. A., & Fahrion, S. L. (1993). Autogenic biofeedback in psychophysiological therapy and stress management. In P. M. Lehrer & R. L. Woolfolk (Eds.), *Principles and practice of stress management* (2nd ed.). New York: Guilford.

Norton, G. R., Cox, B. J., Asmundson, G. J. G., & Maser, J. D. (1995). The growth of research on anxiety disorders during the 1980s. *J. Anxiety Disorders, 9*(1), 75–85.

Norton, G. R., Cox, B. J., Hewitt, P. L., & McLeod, L. (1997). Personality factors associated with generalized and non-generalized social anxiety. *Pers. Individ. Diff., 22*(5), 655–660.

Norton, G. R., Dorward, J., & Cox, B. J. (1986). Factors associated with panic attacks in non-clinical subjects. *Behav. Ther., 17,* 239–252.

Norton, G. R., Rockman, G. E., Luy, B., & Marion, T. (1993). Suicide, chemical abuse, and panic attacks: A preliminary report. *Behav. Res. Ther., 31*(1), 37–40.

Novaco, R. W. (1975). *Anger control: The development and evaluation of an experimental treatment.* Lexington, MA: Heath.

Novaco, R. W. (1976). The functions and regulation of the arousal of anger. *Amer. J. Psychiat., 133*(10), 1124–1128.

Novaco, R. W. (1976). Treatment of chronic anger through cognitive and relaxation controls. *J. Cons. Clin. Psychol., 44*(4), 681.

Novaco, R. W. (1977). A stress inoculation approach to anger management in the training of law enforcement officers. *Amer. J. Comm. Psychol., 5*(3), 327–346.

Novaco, R. W. (1977). Stress innoculation: A cognitive therapy for anger and its application to a case of depression. *J. Cons. Clin. Psychol., 45*(4), 600–608.

Nurnberger, J. I., Jr., & Gershon, E. S. (1984). Genetics of affective disorders. In R. M. Post & J. C. Ballenger (Eds.), *Neurobiology of mood disorders:* Vol. 1. Frontiers of clinical neuroscience. Baltimore: Williams & Wilkins.

Nurnberger, J. I., Jr., & Gershon, E. S. (1992). Genetics. In E. S. Paykel (Ed.), *Handbook of affective disorders.* New York: Guilford.

Nye, J. S., Seltzman, H. H., Pitt, C. G., & Snyder, S. H. (1985). High-affinity cannabinoid binding sites in brain membranes labeled with [3H]-5′-trimethylammonium Δ8-tetrahydrocannabinol. *J. Pharmacol. Exp. Ther., 234,* 784–791.

Nye, J. S., Snowman, A. M., Voglmaier, S., & Snyder, S. H. (1989). High-affinity cannabinoid binding site: regulation by ions, ascorbic acid, and nucleotides. *J. Neurochem., 52,* 1892–1897.

Nye, J. S., Voglmaier, S., Martenson, R. E., & Snyder, S. H. (1988). Myelin basic protein is an endogenous inhibitor of the high-affinity cannabinoid binding site in brain. *J. Neurochem., 50,* 1170–1178.

OSAP (Office for Substance Abuse Prevention). (1991). *Children of alcoholics: Alcoholism tends to run in families.* Rockville, MD: Author.

OSAP. (1991). *College youth.* Rockville, MD: Author.

OSAP. (1991). *Crack cocaine: A challenge for prevention.* (R. Dupone, Ed.). Rockville, MD: OSAP.

OSAP. (1991). *Impaired driving.* Rockville, MD: Author.

O'Brien, C. P., O'Brien, T. J., Mintz, J., & Brady, J. P. (1975). Conditioning of narcotic abstinence symptoms in human subjects. *Drug. Alc. Dep., 1,* 115–123.

O'Brien, E. (1993, Oct. 19). Expert sorts out the ways to chase the blues. *The Philadelphia Inquirer,* p. E5.

O'Carroll, R. (1991). Sexual desire disorders: A review of controlled treatment studies. *J. Sex Res., 28,* 607–624.

O'Connell, R. A., Mayo, J. A., Eng, L. K., Jones, J. S., & Gabel, R. H. (1985). Social support and long-term lithium outcome. *Br. J. Psychiat., 147,* 272–275.

O'Donnell, I., & Farmer, R. (1995). The limitations of official suicide statistics. *Brit. J. Psychiat., 166*(4), 458–461.

O'Hare, T. (1992). The substance-abusing chronically mentally ill client: Prevalence, assessment, treatment and policy concerns. *Soc. Work, 37*(2), 185–187.

O'Leary, D., Gill, D., Gregory, S., & Shawcross, C. (1995). Which depressed patients respond to ECT? The Nottingham results. *J. Affect. Disorders, 33*(4), 245–250.

O'Leary, K. D., & Kent, R. (1973). Behavior modification for social action: Research tactics and problems. In L. A. Hamerlynck, L. C. Handy, & E. J. Mash (Eds.), *Behavior change: Methodology, concepts, and practice.* Champaign, IL: Research Press.

O'Leary, K. D., & Wilson, G. T. (1987). *Behavior therapy: Application and outcome* (2nd ed.). Englewood Cliffs, NJ: Prentice Hall.

O'Leary, K. M., Brouwers, P., Gardner, D. L., Cowdry, R. W. (1991). Neuropsychological testing of patients with borderline personality disorder. *Amer. J. Psychiat., 148*(1), 106–111.

O'Leary, K. M., Turner, E. R., Gardner, D., & Cowdry, R. W. (1991). Homogeneous group therapy of borderline personality disorder. *Group, 15*(1), 56–64.

O'Malley, S. S., Jaffe, A. J., Rode, S., & Rounsaville, B. J. (1996). Experience of a "slip" among alcoholics treated with naltrexone or placebo. *Amer. J. Psychiat., 153,* 281–283.

O'Malley, S., Jaffe, A., Chang, G., Schottenfeld, R., Meyer, R., & Rounsaville, B. (1992). Naltrexone and coping skills therapy for alcohol dependence. *Arch. Gen. Psychiat., 49,* 881–888.

O'Rourke, G. C. (1990). The HIV-positive intravenous drug abuser. [Special issue: HIV infection and AIDS]. *Amer. J. Occupational Ther., 44*(3), 280–283.

O'Sullivan, G., & Marks, I. (1991). Follow-up studies of behavioral treatment of phobias and obsessive compulsive neuroses. *Psychiatr. Ann., 21*(6), 368–373.

O'Sullivan, G., & Marks, I. M. (1991). Long-term outcome of phobic and obsessive-compulsive disorders after treatment. In R. Noyes, G. D. Burrows, & M. Roth (Eds.), *Handbook of anxiety* (Vol. 4). Amsterdam: Elsevier Science Publishers.

O'Sullivan, G., Noshirvani, H., Marks, I., Monteiro, W. et al. (1991). Six-year follow-up after exposure and clomipramine therapy for obsessive compulsive disorder. *J. Clin. Psychiat., 52*(4), 150–155.

O'Sullivan, M. J., Peterson, P. D., Cox, G. B., & Kirkeby, J. (1989). Ethnic populations: Community mental health services ten years later. *Amer. J. Comm. Psychol., 17,* 17–30.

Oei, T. P., Lim, B., & Hennessy, B. (1990). Psychological dysfunction in battle: Combat stress reactions and posttraumatic stress disorder. *Clin. Psychol. Rev., 10*(3), 355–388.

Offer, D., Ostrov, E., & Howard, K. I. (1981). The mental health professional's concept of the normal adolescent. *Arch. Gen. Psychiat., 38*(2), 140–152.

Ogden, J., & Ward, E. (1995). Help-seeking behavior in suffers of vaginismus. *Sex Marital Ther., 10*(1), 23–30.

Ogden, J. A. & Corkin, S. (1991). Memories of H. M. In W. C. Abraham, M. C. Corballis, & K. G. White (Eds.), *Memory mechanisms: A tribute to G. V. Goddard.* Hillsdale, NJ: Erlbaum.

Ogles, B. M., Lambert, M. J., & Sawyer, D. (1993, June). *The clinical significance of the NIMH Treatment of Depression Collaborative Research.* Paper presented at the annual meetings of the Society for Psychotherapy Research, Pittsburgh.

Ogloff, J. R. P., Schweighofer, A., Turnbull, S. D., & Whittemore, K. (1992). Empirical research regarding the insanity defense: How much do we really know? In J. R. P. Ogloff (Ed.), *Law and psychology: The broadening of the discipline.*

Ohberg, A., Lonnqvist, J., Sarna, S., Vuori, E. et al. (1995). Trends and availability of suicide methods in Finland: Proposals for restrictive measures. *Brit. J. Psychiat., 166,* 35–43.

Ohman, A. (1993). Stimulus prepotency and fear learning: Data and theory. In N. Birbaumer, & A. Öhman (Eds.), *The organization of emotion: Cognitive, clinical, and psychophysiological perspectives.* Göttingen, FRG: Hogrefe & Huber.

Ohman, A., & Soares, J. J. F. (1993). On the automatic nature of phobic fear: Conditioned electrodermal responses to masked fear-relevant stimuli. *J. Abnorm. Psychol., 102(1*), 121–132.

Ohman, A., Erixon, G., & Lofberg, I. (1975). Phobias and preparedness: Phobic versus neutral pictures as continued stimuli for human autonomic responses. *J. Abnorm. Psychol., 84,* 41–45.

Oldenburg, D. (1995, August 18). Miserable? Check out self-analysis. *The Washington Post,* p. G5.

Olfson, M. (1992). Utilization of neuropsychiatric diagnostic tests for general hospital patients with mental disorders. *Amer. J. Psychiat., 149*(12), 1711–1717.

Olfson, M., & Klerman, G. L. (1993). Trends in the prescription of antidepressants by office based psychiatrists. *Amer. J. Psychiat., 150*(4), 571–577.

Olfson, M., Pincus, H. A., & Dial, T. H. (1994). Professional practice patterns of U. S. Psychiatrists. *Amer. J. Psychiat., 151*(1), 89–95.

Oliver, J. E. (1993). Intergenerational transmission of child abuse: Rates, research and clinical implications. *Amer. J. Psychiat., 150*(9).

Oliver, K. K., & Thelen, M. H. (1996). Children's perceptions of peer influence on eating concerns. *Behav. Ther., 27,* 25–39.

Olmos de Paz, T. (1990). Working-through and insight in child psychoanalysis. *Melanie Klein & Object Relations, 8*(1), 99–112.

Olmsted, M. P., Kaplan, A. S., & Rockert, W. (1994). Rate and prediction of relapse in bulimia nervosa. *Amer. J. Psychiat., 151*(5), 738–743.

Oostveen, T., Knibbe, R., & de Vries, H. (1996). Social influences on young adults' alcohol consumption: Norms, modeling, pressure, socializing, and conformity. *Addic. Behav., 21*(2), 187–197.

Oppenheim, S., & Rosenberger, J. (1991). Treatment of a case of obsessional disorder: Family systems and object relations approaches. *Amer. J. Fam. Ther., 19*(4), 327–333.

Orloff, L. M., Battle, M. A., Baer, L., Ivanjack, L., Pettit, A. R., Buttolph, M. L., & Jenike, M. A. (1994). Long-term follow-up of 85 patients with obsessive-compulsive disorder. *Amer. J. Psychiat., 151*(3), 441–442.

Orsillo, S. M., Weathers, F. W., Litz, B. T., Steinberg, H. R. et al. (1996). Current and lifetime psychiatric disorders among veterans with war zone-related posttraumatic stress disorder. *J. Nerv. Ment. Dis., 184,* 307–313.

Orzack, M. H. (1996, December 1). Interview in P. Belluck, The symptoms of internet addiction, *The New York Times,* p. 5.

Osgood, M. J. (1987). Suicide and the elderly. *Generations, 11*(3), 47–51.

Osgood, N. J., & Eisenhandler, S. A. (1995). By her own hand: The acquiescent suicide of older women. In S. S. Canetto & D. Lester (Eds.), *Women and suicidal behavior.* New York: Springer.

Öst, L.-G., & Westling, B. E. (1995). Applied relaxation vs. cognitive behavior therapy in the treatment of panic disorder. *Behav. Res. Ther., 33*(2), 145–158.

Osterweis, M., & Townsend, J. (1988). *Understanding bereavement reactions in adults and children: A booklet for lay people.* Rockville, MD: U. S. Department of Health and Human Services.

Otto, R. K. (1989). Bias and expert testimony of mental health professionals in adversarial proceedings: A preliminary investigation. *Behav. Sci. Law, 7*(2), 267–273.

Ottosson, J. O. (1960). Experimental studies of the mode of action of electroconvulsive therapy. *Acta Psychiatr. Neurol. Scandin., 35*(145), 141.

Ottosson, J. O. (1985). Use and misuse of electroconvulsive treatment. *Bio. Psychiat., 20*(9), 933–946.

Overholser, J. C. (1992). Interpersonal dependency and social loss. *Pers. Individ. Diff., 13*(1), 17–23.

Overholser, J. C. (1996). The dependent personality and interpersonal problems. *J. Nerv. Ment. Dis., 184*(1), 8–16.

Overmier, J. B. (1992). On the nature of animal models of human behavioral dysfunction. In J. B. Overmier, & P. D. Burke (Eds.), *Animal models of human pathology: A bibliography of a quarter century of behavioral research 1967–1992.* Washington, DC: American Psychological Association.

Overstreet, D. H. (1993). The Flinders sensitive line rats: A genetic animal model of depression. *Neurosci. Biobehav. Rev., 17,* 51–68.

Overton, D. (1964). State-dependent or "dissociated" learning produced with pentobarbital. *J. Compar. Physiol. Psychol., 57,* 3–12.

Overton, D. (1966). State-dependent learning produced by depressant and atropine-like drugs. *Psychopharmacologia, 10,* 6–31.

Owen, F., Crow, T. J., & Poulter, M. (1987). Central dopaminergic mechanisms in schizophrenia. *Acta Psychiatr. Belg., 87*(5), 552–565.

Owen, F., Crow, T. J., Poulter, M. et al. (1978). Increased dopamine receptor sensitivity in schizophrenia. *Lancet, 2,* 223–226.

Owen, M. K., Lancee, W. J., & Freeman, S. J. (1986). Psychological factors and depressive symptoms. *J. Nerv. Ment. Dis., 174*(1), 15–23.

Owen, R. R., Gutierrez-Esteinou, R., Hsiao, J., Hadd, K. et al. (1993). Effects of clozapine and fluphenazine treatment on response to m-chlorophenylpiperazine infusions in schizophrenia. *Arch. Gen. Psychiat., 50,* 636–644.

Oyemade, U. J. (1989). *Parents and children getting a head start against drugs. Fact Sheet 1989.* Alexandria, VA: National Head Start Association.

Özcan, M. E., Taskin, R., Banoglu, R., Babacan, M., & Tuncer, E. (1996). HLA antigens in schizophrenia and mood disorders. *Bio. Psychiat., 39,* 891–895.

Pace, T. M., & Dixon, D. N. (1993). Changes in depressive self-schemata and depressive symptoms following cognitive therapy. *J. Couns. Psychol., 40*(3), 288–294.

Pachman, J. S. (1996). The dawn of a revolution in mental health. *Amer. Psychol. 51*(3), 213–215.

Page, S. (1996). Nationwide hot line to aid abuse victims. *USA Today,* February 21, 1996, 1D.

Pagelow, M. D. (1981). *Family violence.* New York: CBS Education.

Pain, S. (1996, March). Ten deaths that may tell a shocking tale. *New Scientist,* p. 6.

Painter, K. (1992, March 25). Drunken-driving casualties aren't the only victims of alcohol abuse. *USA Today,* p. 5D.

Pajer, K. (1995). New strategies in the treatment of depression in women. *J. Clin. Psychiat., 56*(Suppl. 2), 30–37.

Palacios, J. M., Mengod, G., & Cortés, R. (1995). Autoradiographic localization of benzodiazepine receptors in the human brain postmortem. In A. Biegon & N. D. Volkow (Eds.), *Sites of drug action in the human brain.* Boca Raton, FL: CRC Press.

Palazzoli, M. S. (1985). Anorexia nervosa: A syndrome of the affluent society. *J. Strategic & Systemic Ther. 4*(3), 12–16.

Palmblad, J., Cantell, K., Strander, H., Froberg, J., Karlsson, C., Levi, L., Grnstrom, M., & Unger, P. (1976). Stressor exposure and immunological response in man: Interferon-producing capacity and phagocytosis. *J. Psychosom. Res., 20,* 193–199.

Palosaari, U. K., & Aro, H. M. (1995). Parental divorce, self-esteem and depression: An intimate relationship as a protective factor in young adulthood. *J. Affect. Disorders, 35,* 91–96,

Paradis, C. M., Freidman, S., Hatch, M., & Lazar, R. M. (1992). Obsessive-compulsive disorder onset after removal of a brain tumor. *J. Nerv. Ment. Dis., 180*(8), 535–536.

Paris, J. (1990). Completed suicide in borderline personality disorder. *Psychiatr. Ann., 20*(1), 19–21.

Paris, J. (1991). Personality disorders, parasuicide, and culture. *Transcult. Psychiatr. Res. Rev., 28*(1), 25–39.

Paris, J., Nowlis, D., & Brown, R. (1988). Developmental factors in the outcome of borderline personality disorder. *Comprehen. Psychiat., 29*(2), 147–150.

Parker, G. (1983). Parental 'affectionless control' as an antecedent to adult depression. *Arch. Gen. Psychiat., 48,* 956–960.

Parker, G. (1992). Early environment. In E. S. Paykel (Ed.), *Handbook of affective disorders.* New York: Guilford.

Parker, G., & Hadzi-Pavlovic, D. (1990). Expressed emotion as a predictor of schizophrenic relapse: An analysis of aggregated data. *Psychol. Med., 20,* 961–965.

Parker, G., Hadzi-Pavlovic, D., Brodaty, H., Boyce, P., Mitchell, P., Wilhelm, K., Hickie, I., & Eyers, K. (1993). Psychomotor disturbance in depression: Defining the constructs. *J. Affect. Disorders, 27,* 255–265.

Parker, G., Hadzi-Pavlovic, D., Greenwald, S., & Weissman, M. (1995). Low parental care as a risk factor to lifetime depression in a community sample. *J. Affect. Disorders, 33*(3), 173–180.

Parker, G., Roussos, J., Mitchell, P., Wilhelm, K. et al. (1997). Distinguishing psychotic depression from melancholia. *J. Affect. Dis., 42,* 155–167.

Parker, N. (1991). The Gary David case. *Austral. New Zeal. J. Psychiat., 25*(3), 371–374.

Parker, P. E. (1993). A case report of Munchausen Syndrome with mixed psychological features. *Psychosomatics, 34*(4), 360–364.

Parker, S., Nichter, M., Vuckovic, N., Sims, C., & Ritenbaugh, C. (1995). Body image and weight concerns among African American and White adolescent females: Differences that make a difference. *Human Organization, 54*(2), 103–114.

Parnas, J. (1988). Assortative mating in schizophrenia: Results from the Copenhagen high-risk study. *Psychiatry, 51*(1), 58–64.

Parnas, J., Cannon, T. D., Jacobsen, B., Schulsinger, H., Schulsinger, F., & Mednick, S. A. (1993). Lifetime DSM-III-R diagnostic outcomes in the offspring of schizophrenic mothers. *Arch. Gen. Psychiat., 50,* 707–714.

Parry, B. L. (1995). Sex hormones, circadian rhythms, and depressive vulnerability. *Depression 3,* 43–48.

Partonen, T., Vakkuri, O., Lamberg-Allardt, C., & Lönnqvist, J. (1996). Effects of bright light on sleepiness, melatonin, and 25-hydroxyvitamin D_3 in winter seasonal affective disorder. *Bio. Psychiat., 39,* 865–872.

Patel, A. R., Roy, M., & Wilson, G. M. (1972). Self-poisoning and alcohol. *Lancet, 2,* 1099–1103.

Patel, T. (1996). French crack down on happy pills. *New Scientist,* April 13, 1996, 7.

Patrick, C. J., Bradley, M. M., & Lang, P. J. (1993). Emotion in the criminal psychopath: Startle reflex modulation. *J. Abnorm. Psychol., 102*(1), 82–92.

Patrick, C. J., Cuthbert, B. N., & Lang, P. J. (1990). Emotion in the criminal psychopath: Fear imagery. *Psychophysiology, 27*(Suppl.), 55.

Patterson, G. R. (1982). *Coercive family process.* Eugene, OR: Castalia.

Patterson, G. R. (1986). Performance models for antisocial boys. *Amer. Psychologist, 41,* 432–444.

Paul, G. L. (1967). The strategy of outcome research in psychotherapy. *J. Cons. Psychol., 31,* 109–118.

Paul, G. L., & Lentz, R. (1977). *Psychosocial treatment of the chronic mental patient.* Cambridge, MA: Harvard University Press.

Pauli, P., Dengler, W., Wiedemann, G. Montoya, P. et al. (1997). Behavioral and neurophysiological evidence for altered processing of anxiety-related words in panic disorder. *J. Abnorm. Psychol., 106*(2), 213–220.

Paurohit, N., Dowd, E. T., & Cottingham, H. F. (1982). The role of verbal and nonverbal cues in the formation of first impressions of black and white counselors. *J. Couns. Psychol., 4,* 371–378.

Paxton, S. J., & Diggens, J. (1997). Avoidance coping, binge eating, and depression: An examination of the escape theory of binge eating. *Inter. J. Eat. Disorders, 22,* 83–87.

Paykel, E. S. (Ed.). (1982). *Handbook of affective disorders.* New York: Guilford.

Paykel, E. S. (1991). Stress and life events. In L. Davidson & M. Linnoila (Eds.), *Risk factors for youth suicide.* New York: Hemisphere.

Paykel, E. S. (1995). Clinical efficacy of reversible and selective inhibitors of monoamine oxidase A in major depression. *Acta Psychiatr. Scandin. Suppl., 91*(386), 22–27.

Paykel, E. S. (1995). Psychotherapy, medication combinations, and compliance. Compliance strategies to optimize antidepressant treatment outcomes. *J. Clin. Psychiat., 56*(1), 24–30.

Paykel, E. S., & Cooper, Z. (1992). Life events and social stress. In E. S. Paykel (Ed.), *Handbook of affective disorders.* New York: Guilford.

Paykel, E. S., Rao, B. M., & Taylor, C. N. (1984). Life stress and symptom pattern in outpatient depression. *Psychol. Med., 14*(3), 559–568.

Payne, A. F. (1928). *Sentence completion.* New York: New York Guidance Clinics.

Payte, T. J. (1989). Combined treatment modalities: The need for innovative approaches. Third National Forum on AIDS and Chemical Dependency of the American Society of Addiction Medicine. *J. Psychoactive Drugs, 21*(4), 431–434.

Peach, L., & Reddick, T. L. (1991). Counselors can make a difference in preventing adolescent suicide. *School Counselor, 39*(2), 107–110.

Peachey, J. E., & Franklin, T. (1985). Methadone treatment of opiate dependence in Canada. *Brit. J. Addic., 80*(3), 291–299.

Pearlson, G. D. et al. (1984). Lateral ventricular enlargement associated with persistent unemployment and negative symptoms in both schizophrenia and bipolar disorder. *Psychiat. Res., 12*(1), 1–9.

Pearson, D. A., Yaffee, L. S., Loveland, K. A., & Lewis, K. R. (1996). Comparison of sustained and selective attention in children who have mental retardation with and without attention deficit hyperactivity disorder. *Amer. J. Ment. Retard., 100*(6), 592–607.

Peck, D. L., & Warner, K. (1995). Accident or suicide? Single-vehicle car accidents and the intent hypothesis. *Adolescence, 30*(118), 463–472.

Peck, M. (1982). Youth suicide. *Death Educ., 6*(1), 27–47.

Peele, S. (1992). Alcoholism, politics, and bureaucracy: The consensus against controlled-drinking therapy in America. *Addic. Behav., 17,* 49–62.

Peele, S. (1989). *Diseasing of America: Addiction treatment out of control.* Lexington, MA: Lexington Books/D.C. Heath.

Pekrun, R. (1992). Expectancy-value theory of anxiety: Overview and implications. In D. G. Forgays, T. Sosnowski, & K. Wrzesniewski (Eds.), *Anxiety: Recent developments in cognitive, psychophysiological, and health research.* Washington, DC: Hemisphere.

Pekrun, R. (1992). The impact of emotions on learning and achievement: Towards a theory of cognitive/motivational mediators. *Appl. Psychol.: Inter. Rev., 41*(4), 359–376.

Pendery, M. L., Maltzman, I. M., & West, L. J. (1982). Controlled drinking by alcoholics? New findings and a reevaluation of a major affirmative study. *Science, 217*(4555), 169–175.

Penn, D. L., & Mueser, K. T. (1996). Research update on the psychosocial treatment of schizophrenia. *Amer. J. Psychiat., 153,* 607–617.

Penn, D. L., Corrigan, P. W., Bentall, R. P., Racenstein, J. M., & Newman, L. (1997). Social cognition in schizophrenia. *Psychol. Bull., 121*(1), 114–132.

Pennebaker, J. W., & Beall, S. K. (1986). Confronting a traumatic event:

Toward an understanding of inhibition and disease. *J. Abnorm. Psychol., 95,* 274–281.

Pennebaker, J. W., Colder, M., & Sharpi, L. K. (1990). Accelerating the coping process. *J. Pers. Soc. Psychol., 58*(3), 528–537.

Pennebaker, J. W., Kiecolt-Glaser, J. K., & Glaser, R. (1988). Disclosures of traumas and immune function: Health implications for psychotherapy. *J. Cons. Clin. Psychol., 56,* 239–245.

Perkins, K., Grobe, J., DiAmico, D., Fonte, C., Wilson, A., & Stiller, R. (1996). Low-dose nicotine nasal spray use and effects during initial smoking cessation. *Exp. Clin. Psychopharmacol., 4*(2), 191–197.

Perlick, D., Stastny, P., Mattis, S., & Teresi, J. (1992). Contribution of family, cognitive and clinical dimensions to long-term outcome in schizophrenia. *Schizo. Res., 6*(3), 257–265.

Perls, F. S. (1969). *Gestalt therapy verbatim.* Moab, UT: Real People.

Perls, F. S. (1973). *The Gestalt approach.* Palo Alto, CA: Science Behavior.

Perls, T. T. (1995, January). The oldest old. *Scientif. Amer.,* pp. 70–75.

Perris, C. (1988). Decentralization, sectorization, and the development of alternatives to institutional care in a northern county in Sweden. In C. N. Stefanis & A. D. Rabavilis (Eds.), *Schizophrenia: Recent biosocial developments.* New York: Human Science.

Perry, A., Tarrier, N., & Morriss, R. (1995). Identification of prodromal signs and symptoms and early intervention in manic depressive psychosis patients: A case example. *Behav. Cog. Psychother., 23,* 399–409.

Perry, J. C. (1989). Dependent personality disorder. In American Psychiatric Association (Eds.), *Treatments of psychiatric disorders: A task force report of the American Psychiatric Association.* Washington, DC: American Psychiatric Press.

Perry, J. C. (1992). Problems and considerations in the valid assessment of personality disorders. *Amer. J. Psychiat., 149,* 1645–1653.

Perry, J. C. (1993). Longitudinal studies of personality disorders. *J. Pers. Disorders, 7,* 63–85.

Perry, J. C., & Cooper, S. H. (1986). A preliminary report on defenses and conflicts associated with borderline personality disorder. *J. Amer. Psychoanalyt. Assoc., 34*(4), 863–893.

Perry, J. C., & Jacobs, D. (1982). Overview: Clinical applications of the amytal interview in psychiatric emergency settings. *Amer. J. Psychiat., 139*(5), 552–559.

Perry, J. C., Herman, J. L., & Van der Kolk, B. A. (1990). Psychotherapy and psychological trauma in borderline personality disorder. *Psychiat. Ann., 20*(1), 33–43.

Perry, S., Difede, J., Musngi, G., Frances, A. J., et al. (1992). Predictors of posttraumatic stress disorder after burn injury. *Amer. J. Psychiat., 149*(7), 931–935.

Perske, R. (1972). The dignity of risk and the mentally retarded. *Ment. Retard., 10,* 24–27.

Persons, J. B. (1991). Psychotherapy outcome studies do not accurately represent current models of psychotherapy: A proposed remedy. *Amer. Psychol., 46*(2), 99–106.

Persson, C. (1972). Lithium prophylaxis in affective disorders: An open trial with matched controls. *Acta Psychiatr. Scandin., 48,* 462–479.

Pertschuk, M. J. (1977). Behavior therapy: Extended follow-up. In R. A. Vigersky (Ed.), *Anorexia Nervosa.* New York: Raven Press.

Pertschuk, M. J., Forster, J., Buzby, G., & Mullen, J. L. (1981). The treatment of anorexia nervosa with total parenteral nutrition. *Bio. Psychiat., 16,* 539–550.

Petersen, A. C., Compas, B. E., Brooks-Gunn, J., Ey, S., & Grant, K. E. (1993). Depression in adolescence. *Amer. Psychol., 48*(2), 155–168.

Petersen, A. C., Compas, B., & Brooks-Gunn, J. (1991). *Depression in adolescence: Implications of current research for programs and policy.* Report prepared for the Carnegie Council on Adolescent Development, Washington, D.C.

Petersen, D. (1988). Substance abuse, criminal behavior, and older people. *Generations, 12*(4), 63–67.

Petersen, R. C. (1984). Marijuana overview. In M. D. Glantz (Ed.), *Correlates and consequences of marijuana use. NIDA Research Issues,* No. 34. Washington, DC: U. S. Department of Health and Human Service, U. S. Government Printing Office.

Peterson, A. L., Talcott, G. W., Kelleher, W. J., & Haddock, C. K. (1995). Site specificity of pain and tension in tension-type headaches. *Headache, 35*(2), 89–92.

Peterson, B. D., West, J., Pincus, H. A., Kohout, J. et al. (1996). An update on human resources in mental health. In R. W. Manderscheid & M. A. Sonnenschein (Eds.)., *Mental Health, United States, 1996* (DHHS Publication No. SMA 96–3098) Washington, DC: U. S. Department of Health and Human Services.

Peterson, C. (1993). Helpless behavior. *Behav. Res. Ther., 31*(3), 289–295.

Peterson, C., Colvin, D., & Lin, E. H. (1992). Explanatory style and helplessness. *Soc. Behav. Pers. 20*(1), 1–13.

Peterson, D. R. (1968). *The clinical study of social behavior.* New York: Appleton-Century-Crofts.

Peterson, J. (1996). Healing continues a year after bombing. *APA Monitor, 27*(6), 22.

Peterson, K. S. (1995, October 9). Oddness admired in one offbeat point of view. *USA Today,* p. 4D.

Peterson, K. S. (1996, February 21). Harm of domestic strife lingers. *USA Today,* p. 3D.

Peterson, L., & Roberts, M. C. (1991). Treatment of children's problems. In C. E. Walker (Ed.), *Clinical psychology: Historical and research foundations.* New York: Plenum Press.

Petrella, R. C., Benedek, E. P., Bank, S. C., & Packer, I. K. (1985). Examining the application of the guilty but mentally ill verdict in Michigan. *Hosp. Comm. Psychiat., 36*(3), 254–259.

Peuskens, J., De Hert, M., Cosyns, P., Pieters, G. et al. (1997). Suicide in young schizophrenic patients during and after inpatient treatment. *Inter. J. Ment. Hlth., 25*(4), 39–44.

Pew Research Center for the People and the Press. (1997). *Trust and citizen engagement in metropolitan Philadelphia: A case study.* Washington, DC: Author.

Pfeffer, C. R. (1986). *The suicidal child.* New York: Guilford.

Pfeffer, C. R. (1988). Risk factors associated with youth suicide: A clinical perspective. *Psychiatr. Ann., 18*(11), 652–656.

Pfeffer, C. R. (1990). Clinical perspectives on treatment of suicidal behavior among children and adolescents. *Psychiatr. Ann., 20*(3), 143–150.

Pfeffer, C. R. (1993). Suicidal children. In A. A. Leenaars (Ed.), *Suicidology.* Northvale, NJ: Jason Aronson.

Pfeffer, C. R., Klerman, G. L., Hurt, S. W., Kakuma, T. et al. (1993). Suicidal children grow up: Rates and psychosocial risk factors for suicide attempts during follow-up. *J. Amer. Acad. Child Adol. Psychiat., 30,* 106–113.

Pfeffer, C. R., Zuckerman, S., Plutchik, R., & Mizruchi, M. S. (1984). Suicidal behavior in normal school children: A comparison with child psychiatric inpatients. *J. Amer. Acad. Child Adol. Psychiat., 23,* 416–423.

Pfeifer, M. P., & Snodgrass, G. L. (1990). The continued use of retractable invalid scientific literature. *JAMA, 263*(10), 1420–1427.

Pfeiffer, S. I., & Nelson, D. D. (1992). The cutting edge in services for people with autism. *J. Autism Dev. Disorders, 22*(1), 95–105.

Phares, E. J. (1979). *Clinical psychology: Concepts, methods, and profession.* Homewood, IL: Dorsey.

Phelan, J. (1976). *Howard Hughes: The hidden years.* New York: Random House.

Phelps, L., & Grabowski, J. (1993). Fetal Alcohol Syndrome: Diagnostic features and psychoeducational risk factors. *School Psychol. Quart., 7*(2), 112–128.

Phillips, D. P., & Carstensen, L. L. (1986). Clustering of teenage suicides after television news stories about suicide. *N. Engl. J. Med., 315,* 685–689.

Phillips, D. P., & Carstensen, L. L. (1988). The effects of suicide stories on various demographic groups. *Suic. Life-Threat. Behav., 18,* 100–114.

Phillips, D. P., & Ruth, T. E. (1993). Adequacy of official suicide statistics for scientific research and public policy. *Suic. Life-Threat. Behav., 23*(4), 307–319.

Phillips, D. P. (1974). The influence of suggestion on suicide: Substantive and theoretical implications of the Werther effect. *Amer. Sociol. Rev., 39,* 340–354.

Phillips, D. P., Lesyna, K., & Paight, D. J. (1992). Suicide and the media. In R. W. Maris, A. L. Berman, J. T. Maltsberger, & R. I. Yufit (Eds.), *Assessment and prediction of suicide.* New York: Guilford.

Phillips, K. A., & Gunderson, J. G. (1994). Personality disorders. In R. E. Hales, S. C. Yudofsky, & J. A. Talbott (Eds.), *The American Psychiatric Press textbook of psychiatry* (2nd ed.). Washington, DC: American Psychiatric Press.

Phillips, K. A. (1991). Body dysmorphic disorder: The distress of imagined ugliness. *Amer. J. Psychiat., 148*(9), 1138–1149.

Phillips, K. A., Kim, J. M., & Hudson, J. I. (1995). Body image disturbance in body dysmorphic disorder and eating disorders: Obsessions or delusions? *Psychiat. Clin. N. Amer., 18*(2), 317–334.

Phillips, K. A., McElroy, S. L., Keck, P. E., Pope, H. G. et al. (1993). Body dysmorphic disorder: 30 cases of imagined ugliness. *Amer. J. Psychiat., 150*(2), 302–308.

Philpot, V. D., Holliman, W. B., & Madonna, S., Jr. (1995). Self-statements, locus of control, and depression in predicting self-esteem. *Psychol. Rep., 76*(3 Pt 1), 1007–1010.

Philpott, R. M. (1990). Affective disorder and physical illness in old age. *Inter. Clin. Psychopharmacol., 5*(3), 7–20.

Phinney, J. S. (1996). When we talk about American ethnic groups, what do we mean? *Amer. Psychol., 51*(9), 918–927.

Physicians' Desk Reference (48th ed.). (1994). Montvalle, NJ: Medical Economic Data Production Company.

Piacentini, J., Rotheram-Bors, M. J., Gillis, J. R., Graae, F. et al. (1995). Demographic predictors of treatment attendance among adolescent suicide attempters. *J. Cons. Clin. Psychiat., 63*(3), 469–473.

Pickar, D., Owen, R. R., & Litman, R. E. (1991). New developments in pharmacotherapy of schizophrenia. In A. Tasman & S. M. Goldfinger (Eds.), *American Psychiatric Press Review of Psychiatry* (Vol. 10). Washington, DC: American Psychiatric Press.

Pickens, J., Field, T., Prodromidis, M., Pelaez-Nogueras, M., et al. (1995). Posttraumatic stress, depression and social support among college students after Hurricane Andrew. *J. Coll. Student Dev., 36*(2), 152–161.

Pickens, R., & Fletcher, B. (1991). Overview of treatment issues. In R. Pickens, C. Leukefeld, & C. Schuster (Eds.), *Improving drug abuse treatment.* Rockville, MD: National Institute on Drug Abuse.

Pietrofesa, J. J. et al. (1990). The mental health counselor and "duty to warn." *J. Ment. Hlth. Couns., 12*(2), 129–137.

Pillard, R. C., & Bailey, J. M. (1995). A biologic perspective on sexual orientation. Specific issue: Clinical sexuality. *Psychiat. Clin. N. Amer., 18*(1), 71–84.

Pillow, D. R., Zautra, A. J., & Sandler, I. (1996). Major life events and minor stressors: Identifying mediational links in the stress process. *J. Pers. Soc. Psychol., 70*(2), 381–394.

Pincus, H. A., Henderson, B., Blackwood, D., & Dial, T. (1993). Trends in research in two general psychiatric journals in 1969–1990: Research on research. *Amer. J. Psychiat., 150*(1), 135–142.

Pine, C. J. (1981). Suicide in American Indian and Alaskan native tradition. *White Cloud J., 2*(3), 3–8.

Pinkston, E. M., & Linsk, N. L. (1984). Behavioral family intervention with the impaired elderly. *Gerontologist, 24,* 576–583.

Pinsof, W. M., & Wynne, L. C. (1995). The effectiveness and efficacy of marital and family therapy: Introduction to the special issue. *J. Marital Fam. Ther., 21*(4), 341–343.

Pirke, K. M., Kellner, M., Philipp, E., Laessle, R., Krieg, J. C., & Fichter, M. M. (1992). Plasma norepinephrine after a standardized test meal in acute and remitted patients with anorexia nervosa and in healthy controls. *Bio. Psychiat., 31,* 1074–1077.

Pithers, W. D. (1990). Relapse prevention with sexual aggressors. In W. L. Marshall, D. R. Laws, & H. E. Barbaree (Eds.), *Handbook of sexual assault.* New York: Plenum Press.

Pithers, W. D., & Cumming, G. F. (1989). Can relapses be prevented? Initial outcome data for the Vermont Treatment Program for Sexual Aggressors. In D. R. Laws (Ed.), *Relapse prevention with sex offenders.* New York: Guilford.

Piven, J., Palmer, P., Jacobi, D., Childress, D., & Arndt, S. (1997). Broader autism phenotype: Evidence from a family history study of multiple-incidence autism families. *Amer. J. Psychiat., 154*(2), 185–190.

Plakun, E. M. (1991). Prediction of outcome in borderline personality disorder. *J. Pers. Disorders, 5*(2), 93–101.

Plasse, T. F. et al. (1991). Recent clinical experience with dronabinol. *Pharmacol. Biochem. Behav., 40,* 695.

Plotkin, R. (1983). *Cognitive mediation in disciplinary action among mothers who have abused or neglected their children: Dispositional and environmental factors.* Unpublished doctoral dissertation, University of Rochester, Rochester, NY.

Plous, S. (1996). Attitudes toward the use of animals in psychological research and education: Results from a national survey of psychologists. *Amer. Psychol., 51*(11), 1167–1180.

Polcin, D. (1992). Issues in the treatment of dual diagnosis clients who have chronic mental illness. *Profess. Psychol.: Res. Prac., 23*(1), 30–37.

Polivy, J., & Herman, C. P. (1985). Dieting and bingeing: A causal analysis. *Amer. Psychol., 40,* 193–201.

Polk, W. M. (1983). Treatment of exhibitionism in a 38-year-old male by hypnotically assisted covert sensitization. *Inter. J. Clin. Exp. Hyp., 31,* 132–138.

Pollack, J. M. (1987). Relationship of obsessive-compulsive personality to obsessive-compulsive disorder: A review of the literature. *J. Psychol., 121*(2), 137–148.

Pollack, W. (1989). Schizophrenia and the self: Contributions of psychoanalytic self-psychology. *Schizo. Bull., 15*(2), 311–322.

Pollard, C. A., Tait, R. C., Meldrum, D., Dubinsky, I. H., & Gall, J. S. (1996). Agoraphobia without panic: Case illustrations of an overlooked syndrome. *J. Nerv. Ment. Dis., 184*(1), 61–62.

Pollock, M. H., Kradin, R., Otto, M. W., Worthington, J. et al. (1996). Prevalence of panic in patients referred for pulmonary function testing at a major medical center. *Amer. J. Psychiat., 153,* 110–113.

Polster, E. (1992). The self in action: A gestalt outlook. In J. K. Zeig (Ed.), *The evolution of psychotherapy: The second conference.* New York: Brunner/Mazel.

Pomara, N., Deptula, D., Singh, R., & Monroy, C. (1991). Cognitive toxicity of benzodiazepines in the elderly. In C. Salzman & B. D. Lebowitz (Eds.), *Anxiety in the elderly.* New York: Springer.

Pope, B. (1983). The initial interview. In C. E. Walker (Ed.), *The handbook of clinical psychology: Theory, research, and practice.* Homewood, IL: Dow Jones-Irwin.

Pope, H. G., & Hudson, J. I. (1984). *New hope for binge eaters: Advances in the understanding and treatment of bulimia.* New York: Harper & Row.

Pope, H. G., & Yurgelun-Todd, D. (1996). The residual cognitive effects of heavy marijuana use in college students. *JAMA, 275*(7), 521–527.

Pope, H. G., Herridge, P. L., Hudson, J. I., & Fontaine, R. (1986). Treatment of bulimia with nomifensine. *J. Clin. Psychiat., 143,* 371–373.

Pope, H. G., Hudson, J. I., & Jonas, J. M. (1983). Antidepressant treatment of bulimia: Preliminary experience and practical recommendations. *J. Psychiat., 140,* 554–558.

Pope, H. G., Hudson, J. I., & Jonas, J. M. (1983). Bulimia treated with imipramine: A placebo-controlled, double-blind study. *Amer. J. Psychiat., 140*(5), 554–558.

Pope, K. S., & Brown, L. S. (1996). *Recovered memories of abuse: Assessment, therapy, forensics.* Washington, DC: American Psychological Association.

Pope, K. S., & Tabachnick, B. G. (1994). Therapists as patients: A national survey of pscyhologists' experiences, problems, and beliefs. *Profess. Psychol.: Res. Prac., 25*(3), 247–258.

Pope, K. S., & Bouhoutsos, J. (1986). *Sexual intimacy between therapists and patients.* New York: Praeger.

Pope, K. S., & Tabachnick, B. G. (1993). Therapists' anger, hate, fear, and sexual feelings: National survey of therapist responses, client characteristics, critical events, formal complaints, and training. *Profess. Psychol.: Res. Pract., 24*(2), 142–152.

Pope, K. S., & Vetter, V. A. (1991). Prior therapist-patient sexual involvement among patients seen by psychologists. *Psychotherapy, 28*(3), 429–438.

Pope, K. S., Tabachnick, B. G., & Keith-Spiegel, P. (1986). Sexual attraction to clients: The human therapist and the (sometimes) inhuman training system. *Amer. Psychol., 41*(2), 147–158.

Pope, K. S., Tabachnick, B. G., & Keith-Spiegel, P. (1987). Ethics of practice: The beliefs and behaviors of psychologists as therapists. *Amer. Psychol., 42*(11), 993–1166.

Popper, C. W. (1988). Disorders usually first evident in infancy, childhood, or adolescence. In J. Talbott, R. S. Hales, & S. C. Yudofsky (Eds.), *Textbook of psychiatry.* Washington, DC: American Psychiatric Press.

Poretz, M., & Sinrod, B. (1991). *Do you do it with the lights on?* New York: Ballantine Books.

Porter, S., Kelly, K. A., & Grame, C. J. (1993). Family treatment of spouses and children of patients with multiple personality disorder. *Bull. Menninger Clin., 57*(3), 371–379.

Post, R. M. et al. (1978). Cerebrospinal fluid norepinephrine in affective illness. *Amer. J. Psychiat., 135*(8), 907–912.

Post, R. M., Ballenger, J. C., & Goodwin, F. K. (1980). Cerebrospinal fluid studies of neurotransmitter function in manic and depressive illness. In J. H. Wood (Ed.), *The neurobiology of cerebrospinal fluid,* (Vol. 1). New York: Plenum Press.

Post, R. M., Denicoff, K. D., Frye, M. A., & Leverich, G. S. (1997). Re-evaluating carbamazepine prophylaxis in bipolar disorder. *Brit. J. Psychiat., 170,* 202–204.

Poulos, C. X., Le, A. D., & Parker, J. L. (1995). Impulsivity predicts individual susceptibility to high levels of alcohol self-administration. *Behav. Pharmacol., 6*(8), 810–814.

Poulton, R., Thomson, W. M., Davies, S., Kruger, E. et al. (1997). Good teeth, bad teeth and fear of the dentist. *Behav. Res. Ther., 35*(4), 327–334.

Poulton, R. G., & Andrews, G. (1996). Change in danger cognitions in agoraphobia and social phobia during treatment. *Behav. Res. Ther., 34*(5/6), 413–421.

Powell, J., Bradley, B., & Gray, J. (1992). Classical conditioning and cognitive determinants of subjective craving for opiates: An investigation of their relative contributions. *Brit. J. Addic., 87*(8), 1133–1144.

Powis, T. (1990, March 19). Paying for the past: A brainwashing victim seeks compensation. *Macleans.*

Prange, A. J. et al. (1970). Enhancement of imipramine by thyroid stimulating hormone: Clinical and theoretical implications. *Amer. J. Psychiat., 127*(2), 191–199.

Prange, A. J. et al. (1970). Use of a thyroid hormone to accelerate the action of imipramine. *Psychosomatics, 11*(5), 442–444.

Prange, A. J. et al. (1974). L tryptophan in mania: Contribution to a permissive hypothesis of affective disorders. *Arch. Gen. Psychiat., 30*(1), 56–62.

Prehn, R. A. (1990). Medication refusal: Suggestions for intervention. *Psychiatr. Hosp., 21*(1), 37–40.

Prendergast, P. J. (1995). Integration of psychiatric rehabilitation in the long-term management of schizophrenia. *Canad. J. Psychiat., 40*(3, Suppl. 1), S18–S21.

President's Commission on Mental Health. (1978). *Report to the President.* Washington, DC: U. S. Government Printing Office.

Price, L. H. (1990). Serotonin reuptake inhibitors in depression and anxiety: An overview. *Ann. Clin. Psychiat., 2*(3), 165–172.

Price, R. W., Brew, B., Sidtis, J., Rosenblum, M., Scheck, A. C., & Cleary, P. (1988). The brain in AIDS: Central nervous system HIV-1 infection and AIDS dementia complex. *Science, 239,* 586–592.

Prien, R. F. (1978). Clinical uses of lithium—Part 1: Introduction. In T. B. Cooper, S. Gershon, N. S. Kline, & M. Schou (Eds.). *Lithium: Controversies and unresolved issues.* Amsterdam: Excerpta Medica.

Prien, R. F. (1992). Maintenance treatment. In E. S. Paykel (Ed.), *Handbook of affective disorders.* New York: Guilford.

Prien, R. F., & Potter, W. Z. (1990). NIMH workshop report on the treatment of bipolar disorder. *Psychopharmacol. Bull., 26*(4), 409–427.

Prien, R. F., Caffey, E. M., Jr., & Klett, C. J. (1974). Factors associated with treatment success in lithium carbonate prophylaxis. *Arch. Gen. Psychiat., 31,* 189–192.

Prigerson, H., Frank, E., Kasl, S., Reynolds, C. et al. (1995). Complicated grief and bereavement-related depression as distinct disorders: Preliminary empirical validation in elderly bereaved spouses. *Amer. J. Psychiat., 152*(1), 22–30.

Primac, D. W. (1993). Measuring change in a brief therapy of a compulsive personality. *Psychol. Rep., 72*(1), 309–310.

Primus, R. J., Yu, J., Xu, J., Hartnett, C. et al. (1996). Allosteric uncoupling after chronic benzodiazepine exposure of recombinant γ-aminobutyric $acid_A$ receptors expressed in Sf9 cells: Ligand efficacy and subtype selectivity. *J. Pharmacol. Exp. Ther., 276*(3), 882–890.

Prince, M. (1906). *The dissociation of a personality.* New York: Longmans, Green.

Prince, S. E., & Jacobson, N. S. (1995). A review and evaluation of marital and family therapies for affective disorders. [Special issue: The effectiveness of marital and family therapy]. *J. Marital Fam. Ther., 21*(4), 377–401.

Princeton Survey Research Associates (1996). Adultery in the '90s. In *Newsweek Poll,* New York: Author.

Princeton Survey Research Associates (1996). *Healthy steps for young children: Survey of parents.* Princeton: Author.

Prochaska, J. O. (1984). *Systems of psychotherapy.* Chicago: Dorsey.

Prochaska, J. O., & Norcross, J. C. (1994). *Systems of psychotherapy: A transtheoretical analysis* (3rd ed.). Pacific Grove, CA: Brooks/Cole.

Prochaska, J. O., DiClemente, C. C., & Norcross, J. C. (1992). In search of how people change. *Amer. Psychologist, 47*(9), 1102–1114.

Prusiner, S. (1995, January). The prion diseases. *Scientif. Amer.,* pp. 48–57.

Prusiner, S. B. (1991). Molecular biology of prion diseases. *Science, 252, 1515–1522.*

Prusoff, B. A., Weissman, M. M., Klerman, G. L., & Rounsaville, B. J. (1980). Research diagnostic criteria subtypes of depression: Their role as predictors of differential response to psychotherapy and drug treatment. *Arch. Gen. Psychiat., 37*(7), 796–801.

Prussin, R. A., & Harvey, P. D. (1991). Depression, dietary restraint, and binge eating in female runners. *Addic. Behav., 16*(5), 295–301.

Puente, A. E. (1990). Psychological assessment of minority group members. In G. Goldstein & M. Hersen (Eds.), *Handbook of psychological assessment* (2nd ed., Pergamon General Psychology Series, Vol. 131). New York: Pergamon.

Pueschel, S. M., & Thuline, H. C. (1991). Chromosome disorders. In J. L. Matson & J. A. Mulick (Eds.), *Handbook of mental retardation.* New York: Pergamon.

Puk, G. (1991). Treating traumatic memories: A case report on the eye movement desensitization procedure. *J. Behav. Ther. Exp. Psychiat., 22,* 149–151.

Pulver, A. E., Carpenter, W. T., Adler, L., & McGrath, J. (1988). Accuracy of the diagnoses of affective disorders and schizophrenia in public hospitals. *Amer. J. Psychiat., 145*(2), 218–220.

Puri, B. K., Baxter, R., & Cordess, C. C. (1995) Characteristics of firesetters: A study and proposed multiaxial psychiatric classification. *Brit. J. Psychiat., 166,* 393–396.

Pusakulich, R. L., & Nielson, H. C. (1976). Cue use in state-dependent learning. *Physiol. Psychol., 4*(4), 421–428.

Putnam, F. W. (1984). The psychophysiologic investigation of multiple personality disorder. *Psychiatr. Clin. N. Amer., 7,* 31–40.

Putnam, F. W. (1985). Dissociation as a response to extreme trauma. In R. P. Kluft, *Childhood antecedents of multiple personality.* Washington, DC: American Psychiatric Press.

Putnam, F. W. (1985). Multiple personality disorder. *Med. Aspects Human Sex., 19*(6), 59–74.

Putnam, F. W. (1988). The switch process in multiple personality disorder and other state-change disorders. *Dissociation, 1,* 24–32.

Putnam, F. W. (1992). Are alter personalities fragments of figments? *Psychoanaly. Inquiry, 12*(1), 95–111.

Putnam, F. W. (1996). Posttraumatic stress disorder in children and adolescents. In L. J. Dickstein, M. B. Riba, & J. M. Oldham (Eds.), *Review of psychiatry,* (Vol. 15). Washington, DC: American Psychiatric Press.

Putnam, F. W., Guroff, J. J., Silberman, E. K., Barban, L. et al. (1986). The clinical phenomenology of multiple personality disorder: Review of 100 recent cases. *J. Clin. Psychol., 47*(6), 285–293.

Putnam, F. W., Zahn, T. P., & Post, R. M. (1990). Differential autonomic nervous system activity in multiple personality disorder. *J. Psychiatr. Res., 31*(3), 251–260.

Putnam, K. M., Harvey, P. D., Parrella, M., White, L., Kincaid, M., Powchik, P., & Davidson, M. (1996). Symptom stability in geriatric chronic schizophrenic inpatients: A one-year follow-up study. *Bio. Psychiat., 39,* 92–99.

Quality Assurance Project. (1990). Treatment outlines for paranoid, schizotypal and schizoid personality disorders. *Austral. New Zeal. J. Psychiat., 24,* 339–350.

Quality Assurance Project. (1991). Treatment outlines for antisocial personality disorder. *Austral. New Zeal. J. Psychiat., 25,* 541–547.

Quality Assurance Project. (1991). Treatment outlines for avoidant, dependent and passive-aggressive personality disorders. *Austral. New Zeal. J. Psychiat., 25*(3), 311–313.

Quality Assurance Project. (1991). Treatment outlines for borderline, narcissistic and histrionic personality disorders. Austral. *New Zeal. J. Psychiat., 25,* 392–403.

Quevillon, R. P. (1993). Vaginismus. In W. O'Donohue & J. Geer (eds.), *Handbook of sexual dysfunctions.* Boston: Allyn & Bacon.

Quinsey, V. L., & Earls, G. M. (1990). The modificator of sexual preferences. In W. L. Marshall, D. R. Laws, & H. E. Barbaree (Eds.), *Handbook of sexual assault.* New York: Plenum.

Rabin, B. S., Kusnecov, A., Shurin, M, Zhou, D., & Rasnick, S. (1994). Mechanistic aspects of stressor-induced immune alteration. In R. Glaser & J. K. Kiecolt-Glaser. *Handbook of human stress and immunity.* San Diego: Academic Press.

Rabins, P. V. & Folstein, M. F. (1982). Delirium and dementia: Diagnostic criteria and fatality rates. *Brit. J. Psychiat., 140,* 149-153.

Raboch, J., & Raboch, J. (1992). Infrequent orgasm in women. *J. Sex Marital Ther., 18*(2), 114–120.

Rachman, S. (1966). Sexual fetishism: An experimental analog. *Psychol. Rec., 18,* 25–27.

Rachman, S. (1993). Obsessions, responsibility and guilt. *Behav. Res. Ther., 31*(2), 149–154.

Rachman, S., & deSilva, P. (1978). Abnormal and normal obsessions. *Behav. Res. Ther. 16,* 233–248.

Rachman, S., & Hodgson, R. (1980). *Obsessions and compulsions.* Englewood Cliffs, NJ: Prentice Hall.

Rachman, S., & Hodgson, R. J. (1974). Synchrony and desynchrony in fear and avoidance. *Behav. Res. Ther., 12,* 311–318.

Rachman, S., Hodgson, R., & Marks, I. M. (1971). Treatment of chronic obsessive-compulsive neurosis. *Behav. Res. Ther., 9*(3), 237–247.

Rachman, S., Hodgson, R., & Marzillier, J. (1970). Treatment of an obsessional-compulsive disorder by modelling. *Behav. Res. Ther., 8,* 385–392.

Rada, R. T. (1976). Alcoholism and the child molester. *Ann. NY Acad. Sci., 273,* 492–496.

Raffety, B. D., Smith, R. E., & Ptacek, J. T. (1997). Facilitating and debilitating trait anxiety, situational anxiety, and coping with an anticipated stressor: A process analysis. *J. Pers. Soc. Psychol., 72*(4), 892–906.

Ragin, A. B., Pogue-Geile, M. F., & Oltmanns, T. F. (1989). Poverty of speech in schizophrenia and depression during inpatient and posthospital periods. *Brit. J. Psychiat., 154,* 52–57.

Ragland, J. D., & Berman, A. L. (1991). Farm crisis and suicide: Dying on the vine? *Omega: J. Death & Dying, 22*(3), 173–185.

Raguram, R., Weiss, M. G., Channabasavanna, S. M., & Devins, G. M. (1996). Stigma, depression, and somatization in South India. *Amer. J. Psychiat., 153,* 1043–1049.

Rahe, R. H. (1968). Life-change measurement as a predictor of illness. *Proc. R. Soc. Med., 61,* 1124–1126.

Raine, A. (1989). Evoked potentials and psychopathy. *Inter. J. Psychophysiol., 8*(1), 1–16.

Raine, A. (1992). Sex differences in schizotypal personality in a nonclinical population. *J. Abnorm. Psychol., 101*(2), 361–4.

Raine, A., Benishay, D., Lencz, T., & Scarpa, A. (1997). Abnormal orienting in schizotypal personality disorder. *Schizo. Bull., 23*(1), 75–82.

Raja, M., & Miti, G. (1995). Neuroleptic malignant syndrome. *Neuropsychiat., Neuropsychol., Behav. Neurol., 8*(1), 74.

Raloff, J. (1995). Drug of darkness: Can a pineal hormone head off everything from breast cancer to aging? *Sci. News, 147,* 300–301.

Ralston, P. A. (1991). Senior centers and minority elders: A critical review. *Gerontologist, 31,* 325–331.

Ram, R., Bromet, E. J., Eaton, W. W., & Pato, C. (1992). The natural course of schizophrenia: A review of first-admission studies. *Schizo. Bull., 18*(2), 185–207.

Ramey, C. T., & Ramey, S. L. (1992). Effective early intervention. *Ment. Retard., 30*(6), 337–345.

Ramirez, E., Maldonado, A., & Martos, R. (1992). Attributions modulate immunization against learned helplessness in humans. *J. Pers. Soc. Psychol., 62*(1), 139–146.

Ramirez, S. Z., Wassef, A., Paniagua, F. A., & Linskey, A. O. (1996). Mental health providers' perceptions of cultural variables in evaluating ethnically diverse clients. *Profess. Psychol.: Res. Pract., 27,* 284–288.

Ramm, E., Marks, I. M., Yuksel, S., & Stern, R. S. (1981). Anxiety management training for anxiety states: Positive compared with negative self-statements. *Brit. J. Psychiat., 140,* 397–373.

Rand, C. S., & Kuldau, J. M. (1991). Restrained eating (weight concerns) in the general population and among students. *Inter. J. Eat. Disorders, 10*(6), 699–708.

Randall, L. O. (1982). Discovery of benzodiazepines. In E. Usdin, P. Skolnick, J. F. Tallman, Jr., et al. (Eds.), *Pharmacology of benzodiazepines.* London: Macmillan.

Rao, U., Ryan, N. D., Birmaher, B., Dahl, R. E. et al. (1995). Unipolar depression in adolescents: Clinical outcome in adulthood. *J. Amer. Acad. Child Adol. Psychiat., 34*(5), 566–578.

Rapee, R. M. (1993). Psychological factors in panic disorder. Adv. *Behav. Res. Ther., 15*(1), 85–102.

Rapee, R. M. (1995). Psychological factors influencing the affective response to biological challenge procedures in panic disorder. *J. Anxiety Disorders, 9*(1), 59–74.

Rapee, R. M., & Hayman, K. (1996). The effects of video feedback on the self-evaluation of performance in socially anxious subjects. *Behav. Res. Ther., 34*(4), 315–322.

Raphling, D. L. (1989). Fetishism in a woman. *J. Amer. Psychoanal. Assoc., 37*(2), 465–491.

Rapoport, J. L. (1989, March). The biology of obsessions and compulsions. *Scientif. Amer.,* 82–89.

Rapoport, J. L. (1991). Recent advances in obsessive-compulsive disorder. *Neuropsychopharmacology, 5*(1), 1–10.

Rapoport, J. L., Ryland, D. H., & Kriete, M. (1992). Drug treatment of canine acral lick: An animal model of obsessive-compulsive disorder. *Arch. Gen. Psychiat., 49,* 517–521.

Rapoport, J. L., Swedo, S. E., & Leonard, H. L. (1992). Childhood obsessive compulsive disorder. *J. Clin. Psychiat., 53*(Suppl. 4), 11–16.

Raskin, D. C. (1982). The scientific basis of polygraph techniques and their uses in the judicial process. In A. Trankell (Ed.), *Reconstructing the past: The role of psychologists in criminal trials.* Stockholm: Norstedt & Soners.

Raskin, M., Peeke, H. V. S., Dickman, W., & Pinkster, H. (1982). Panic and generalized anxiety disorders: Developmental antecedents and precipitants. *Arch. Gen. Psychiat., 39,* 687–689.

Raskin, N. H., Hobobuchi, Y., & Lamb, S. A. (1987). Headaches may arise from perturbation of the brain. *Headache 27,* 416–420.

Raskin, N. J., & Rogers, C. R. (1995). Person-centered therapy. In R. J. Corsini & D. Wedding (Eds.), *Current psychotherapies* (5th ed.). Itasca, IL: Peacock.

Rauchfleisch, U. (1992). The importance of different reference groups in the therapy of borderline patients. *Group Anal., 25*(1), 33–41.

Ray, J. M., & Walter, G. (1997). Half a century of ECT use in young people. *Amer. J. Psychiat., 154*(5), 595–602.

Ray, O., & Ksir, C. (1993). *Drugs, society, & human behavior.* St. Louis: Mosby.

Rebert, W. M., Stanton, A. L., Schwarz, R. M. (1991). Influence of personality attributes and daily moods on bulimic eating patterns. *Addic. Behav. 16*(6), 497–505.

Reda, M. A., Carpiniello, B., Secchiaroli, L., & Blanco, S. (1985). Thinking, depression, and antidepressants: Modified and unmodified depressive beliefs during treatment with amitriptyline. *Cog. Ther. Res., 9*(2), 135–143.

Redick, R. W., Witkin, M. J., Atay, J. E., & Manderscheid, R. W. (1992). Specialty mental health system characteristics. In R. W. Manderscheid & M. A. Sonnenschein (Eds.), *Mental health, United States,* 1992. Washington, DC: U. S. Department of Health and Human Services.

Redick, R. W., Witkin, M. J., Atay, J. E., & Manderscheid, R. W. (1996). Highlights of organized mental health services in 1992 and major national and state trends. In R. W. Manderscheid & M. A. Sonnenschein (Eds.), DHHS Publication No. SMA 96-3098. Washington, DC: U. S. Department of Health and Human Services.

Redmond, D. E. (1977). Alterations in the function of the nucleus locus coeruleus: A possible model for studies of anxiety. In I. Hanin & E. Usdin (Eds.), *Animal models in psychiatry and neurology.* New York: Pergamon Press.

Redmond, D. E. (1979). New and old evidence for the involvement of a brain norepinephrine system in anxiety. In W. E. Fann, I. Karacan, A. D. Pokorny, & R. L. Williams (Eds.), *Phenomenology and treatment of anxiety.* New York: Spectrum.

Redmond, D. E. (1981). Clonidine and the primate locus coeruleus: Evidence suggesting anxiolytic and anti-withdrawal effects. In H. Lal & S. Fielding (Eds.), *Psychopharmacology of clonidine.* New York: Alan R. Liss.

Redmond, D. E. (1985). Neurochemical basis for anxiety and anxiety disorders: Evidence from drugs which decrease human fear or anxiety. In A. H. Tuma & J. Maser (Eds.), *Anxiety and the anxiety disorders.* Hillsdale, NJ: Erlbaum.

Rees, L. (1964). The importance of psychological, allergic and infective factors in childhood asthma. *J. Psychosom. Res., 7*(4), 253–262.

Rees, W. D., & Lutkin, S. G. (1967). Mortality of bereavement. *Brit. Med. J., 4,* 13–16.

Regan, P. C. (1996). Sexual outcasts: The perceived impact of body weight and gender on sexuality. *J. Appl. Soc. Psychol., 26,* 1803–1815.

Regier, D. A., Farmer, M. E., Rae, D. S. et al. (1990). Co-morbidity of mental disorders with alcohol and other drug abuse: results from the Epidemiologic Catchment Area (ECA) Study. *JAMA, 264,* 2511–2518.

Regier, D. A., Narrow, W. E., Rae, D. S., Manderscheid, R. W., Locke, B. Z., & Goodwin, F. K. (1993). The de facto US Mental and Addictive Disorders Service System: Epidemiologic Catchment Area prospective 1-year prevalence rates of disorders in services. *Arch. Gen. Psychiat., 50,* 85–94.

Reich, J. (1996). The morbidity of DSM-III-R depedent personality disorder. *J. Nerv. Ment. Dis., 184*(1), 22–26.

Reich, J. H. (1987). Sex distribution of DSM-III personality disorders in psychiatric outpatients. *Amer. J. Psychiat., 144*(4), 485–488.

Reich, J. H. (1990). Comparisons of males and females with DSM-III dependent personality disorder. *Psychiatr. Res., 33*(2), 207–214.

Reid, A. H. (1997). Mental handicap or learning disability: A critique of political correctness. *Brit. J. Psychiat., 170,* 1.

Reid, R., & Lininger, T. (1993). Sexual pain disorders in the female. In W. O'Donohue & J. Geer (eds.), *Handbook of sexual dysfunctions.* Boston: Allyn & Bacon.

Reid, W. H., & Burke, W. J. (1989). Antisocial personality disorder. In American Psychiatric Association (Eds.), *Treatments of Psychiatric Disorders: A task force report of the American Psychiatric Association.* Washington, DC: American Psychiatric Press.

Reik, T. (1989). The characteristics of masochism. *Amer. Imago, 46*(2–3), 161–195.

Reis, B. E. (1993). Toward a psychoanalytic understanding of multiple personality disorder. *Bull. Menninger Clin., 57*(3), 309–318.

Reisman, J. M. (1991). *A history of clinical psychology* (2nd ed.). New York: Hemisphere.

Reiss, S. (1985). The mentally retarded, emotionally disturbed adult. In M. Sigman (Ed.), *Children with emotional disorders and developmental disabilities.* New York: Grune & Stratton.

Reitan, R. M., & Wolfson, D. (1985). *The Halstead-Reitan Neuropsychological Test Battery: Theory and clinical interpretation.* Tucson, AZ: Neuropsychology.

Remington, B., Roberts, P., & Glautier, S. (1997). The effect of drink familiarity on tolerance to alcohol. *Addic. Behav., 22*(1), 45–53.

Remington, G., Pollock, B., Voineskos, G., Reed, K., & Coulter, K. (1993). Acutely psychotic patients receiving high-dose Haloperidol therapy. *J. Clin. Psychopharmacol., 13*(1), 41–45.

Renneberg, G., Goldstein, A. J., Phillips, D., Chambless, D. L. (1990). Intensive behavioral group treatment of avoidant personality disorder. *Behav. Ther., 21*(3), 363–377.

Repp, A. C., Barton, L. E., & Brulle, A. R. (1986). Assessing a least restrictive educational environment transfer through social comparison. *Educ. Training Ment. Retarded, 21*(1), 54–61.

Resnick, H. S., Yehuda, R., Pitman, R. K., & Foy, D. W. (1995). Effect of previous trauma on acute plasma cortisol level following rape. *Amer. J. Psychiat., 152*(11), 1675–1677.

Ressler, R. K. & Schactman, T. (1992). *Whoever Fights Monsters.* New York: St. Martin's Press.

Restak, R. M. (1979). The sex-change conspiracy. *Psychol. Today, 20,* 20–25.

Reyna, L. J. (1989). Behavior therapy, applied behavior analysis, and behavior modification. In J. Hobson (Ed.), *Abnormal states of brain and mind.* Boston: Birkhauser.

Rheaume, J., Ladouceur, R., Freeston, M. H., & Letarte, H. (1995). Inflated responsibility in obsessive compulsive disorders: Validation of an operational definition. *Behav. Res. Ther., 33*(2), 159–169.

Rice, C. A. (1996). Premature termination of group therapy: A clinical perspective. *Inter. J. Group Psychother., 46*(1), 5–23.

Rice, K. M., & Blanchard, E. B. (1982). Biofeedback in the treatment of anxiety disorder. *Clin. Psychol. Rev., 2,* 557–577.

Richardson, S. (1997, January). An ancient immunity. *Discover,* p. 30.

Richardson, S. (1997, January). The second key. *Discover,* pp. 29–30.

Richardson, T. Q., & Molinaro, K. L. (1996). White counselor self-awareness: A prerequisite for developing multicultural competence. *J. Couns. Dev., 74,* 238–242.

Richman, N. E., & Sokolove, R. L. (1992). The experience of aloneness, object representation, and evocative memory in borderline and neurotic patients. *Psychoanalyt. Psychiat., 9*(1), 77–91.

Richters, J. E., & Martinez, P. (1993). The NIMH community violence project: I. Children as victims of and witnesses to violence. *Psychiatry, 56,* 7–21.

Rickels, K. (1978). Use of antianxiety agents in anxious outpatients. *Psychopharmacology, 58*(1), 1–17.

Rickels, K., & Schweizer, E. (1990). The clinical course and long-term management of generalized anxiety disorder. *J. Clin. Psychopharmacol., 10*(Suppl. 3), 101–110.

Rickels, K., Schweizer, E., Weiss, S., & Zavodnick, S. (1993). Maintenance drug treatment for panic disorder II. Short- and long-term outcome after drug taper. *Arch. Gen. Psychiat., 50,* 61–68.

Ricketts, R. W., Singh, N. N., Ellis, C. R., Chambers, S., et al. (1995). Calcium channel blockers and vitamin E for tardive dyskinesia in adults with mental retardation. (Special issue: Pharmacotherapy III). *J. Dev. Phys. Disabilities, 7*(2), 161–174.

Riggs, D. S., & Foa, E. B. (1993). Obsessive compulsive disorder. In D. H. Barlow (Ed.), *Clinical handbook of psychological disorders: A step-by-step treatment manual* (2nd ed.). New York: Guilford.

Rihmer, Z., Rutz, W., & Pihlgren, H. (1995). Depression and suicide on Gotland. An intensive study of all suicides before and after a depression-training programme for general practitioners. *J. Affect. Disorders, 35,* 147–152.

Rimland, B. (1988). Vitamin B6 (and magnesium) in the treatment of autism. *Autism Research Review International, 1*(4).

Rimland, B. (1992). *Form letter regarding high dosage vitamin B6 and magnesium therapy for autism and related disorders.* Autism Research Institute, publication 39E.

Rimland, B. (1992). Leominster: Is pollution a cause of autism? *Autism Res. Rev. Inter., 6*(2), 1.

Rimm, D. C., & Litvak, S. B. (1969). Self-verbalization and emotional arousal. *J. Abnorm. Psychol., 74*(2), 181–187.

Rimm, D. C., & Masters, J. C. (1979). *Behavior therapy: Techniques and empirical findings* (2nd ed.). New York: Academic Press.

Ringuette, E., & Kennedy, T. (1966). *J. Abnorm. Psychol., 71,* 136–141.

Risch, S. C., & Janowsky, D. S. (1984). Cholinergic-Adrenergic balance in affective illness. In R. M. Post & J. C. Ballenger (Eds.), *Neurobiology of mood disorders:* Vol. 1. *Frontiers of clinical neuroscience.* Baltimore: Williams & Wilkins.

Ritchie, E. C. (1992). Treatment of gas mask phobia. *Mil. Med., 157*(2), 104–106.

Ritchie, G. G. (1968). The use of hypnosis in a case of exhibitionism. *Psychother. Theory Res. Prac., 5,* 40–43.

Ritchie, K., Kildea, D., & Robine, J. M. (1992). The relationship between age and the prevalence of senile dementia: A meta-analysis of recent data. *Inter. J. Epidemiol., 21,* 763–769

Ritzler, B. A. & Exner, J. E., Jr. (1995). Special issues in subject selection and design. Issues and methods in Rorschach research. In John E. Exner, Jr., (Ed.), *LEA series in personality and clinical psychology.* Mahwah, NJ: Erlbaum.

Roazen, P. (1992). The rise and fall of Bruno Bettelheim. *Psychohist. Rev., 20*(3), 221–250.

Roberts, A. R. (1979). Organization of suicide prevention agencies. In L. D. Hankoff & B. Einsidler (Eds.), *Suicide: Theory and clinical aspects.* Littleton, MA: PSG Publishing Company.

Roberts, A. R. (1990). *Crisis intervention handbook: Assessment, intervention, and research.* Belmont, CA: Wadsworth.

Roberts, C. F., Golding, S. L., & Fincham, F. D. (1987). Implicit theories of criminal responsibility. *Law Human Behav., 11*(3), 297–232.

Roberts, W. (1995). Postvention and psychological autopsy in the suicide of a 14-year-old public school student. *School Counselor, 42*(4), 322–330.

Robertson, E. (1992). The challenge of dual diagnosis. *J. Hlth. Care Poor Underserved, 3*(1), 198–207.

Robertson, M. (1992). *Starving in the silences: An exploration of anorexia nervosa.* New York: New York University Press.

Robin, A. L., Siegel, P. T., & Moye, A. (1995). Family versus individual therapy for anorexia: Impact on family conflict. Topical Section: Treatment and therapeutic processes. *Inter. J. Eat. Disorders, 17*(4), 313–322.

Robins, L. N. & Regier, D. A. (eds.) (1991). *Psychiatric disorders in America: The epidemiologic catchment area study.* New York: Free Press.

Robins, L. N., & Regier, D. S. (1991). *Psychiatric disorders in America: The epidemiological catchment area study.* New York: Free Press.

Robins, L. N., Locke, B. Z., & Regier, D. A. (1991). An overview of psychiatric disorders in America. In L. N. Robins & D. A. Regier (Eds.), *Psychiatric disorders in America: The Epidemiological Catchment Area Study.* New York: Free Press.

Robitscher, J., & Haynes, A. K. (1982). In defense of the insanity defense. *Emory Law J., 31,* 9–60.

Rodgers, L. N. (1995). Prison suicide: Suggestions from phenomenology. *Deviant Behav., 16*(2), 113–126.

Rodin, J. (1992). Sick of worrying about the way you look? Read this. *Psychol. Today, 25*(1), 56–60.

Rodriguez, O. (1986). *Overcoming barriers to services among chronically mentally ill Hispanics: Lessons from the Project COPA evaluation.* (Research Bulletin 9, 1). Bronx, NY: Fordham University, Hispanic Research Center.

Roehrich, L. & Kinder, B. N. (1991). Alcohol expectancies and male sexuality: Review and implications for sex therapy. *J. Sex Marital Ther., 17*(1), 45–54.

Roemer, L., Borkovec, M., Posa, S., & Borkovec, T. D. (1995). A self-report diagnostic measure of generalized anxiety disorder. *J. Behav. Ther. Exp. Psychiat., 26*(4), 345–350.

Roesler, T. A., & McKenzie, N. (1994). Effects of childhood trauma on psychological functioning adults sexually abused as children. *J. Nerv. Ment. Dis., 182*(3), 145–150.

Rogers, C. R. (1951). *Client-centered therapy.* Boston: Houghton Mifflin.

Rogers, C. R. (1961). *On becoming a person.* Boston: Houghton Mifflin.

Rogers, C. R. (1987). Rogers, Kohut, and Erickson: A personal perspective on some similarities and differences. In J. K. Zeig (Ed.), *The evolution of psychotherapy.* New York: Brunner/Mazel.

Rogers, C. R., & Sanford, R. C. (1989). Client-centered psycho therapy. In H. I. Kaplan & B. J. Sadock (Eds.), *Comprehensive textbook of psychiatry* (5th ed., Vol 1). Baltimore: Williams & Wilkins.

Rogers, J. C., & Holloway, R. L. (1990). Assessing threats to the validity of experimental and observational designs. *Fam. Pract. Res. J., 10*(2), 81–95.

Rogers, J. R. (1992). Suicide and alcohol: Conceptualizing the relationship from a cognitive-social paradigm. *J. Couns. Dev., 70*(4), 540–543.

Rogers, L., Resnick, M. D., Mitchell, J. E., & Blum, R. W. (1997). The relationship between socioeconomic status and eating-disordered behaviors in a community sample of adolescent girls. *Inter. J. Eat. Disorders, 22,* 15–23.

Rogers, R. (1987). Assessment of criminal responsibility: empirical advances and unanswered questions. *J. Psychiat. Law, 51*(1), 73–82.

Rogers, R., & Ewing, C. P. (1992). The measurement of insanity: Debating the merits of the R-CRAS and its alternatives. *Inter. J. Law Psychiat., 15,* 113–123.

Rogers, R., Sewell, K. W., & Ustad, K. L. (1995). Feigning among chronic outpatients on the MMPI-2: A systematic examination of fake-bad indicators. *Assessment, 2*(1), 81–89.

Roggla, H., & Uhl, A. (1995). Depression and relapses in treated chronic alcoholics. *Inter. J. Addic., 30*(3), 337–349.

Rogler, L. H., Malgady, R. G., & Rodriguea, O. (1989). *Hispanics and mental health: A framework for research.* Malabar, FL: Krieger Publishing Company.

Rohde, P., Lewinsohn, P. M., & Seeley, J. R. (1996). Psychiatric comorbidity with problematic alcohol use in high school students. *J. Amer. Acad. Child Adol. Psychiat., 35*(1), 101–109.

Rohsenow, D. J., Smith, R. E., & Johnson, S. (1985). Stress management training as a prevention program for heavy social drinkers: Cognition, affect, drinking, and individual differences. *Addic. Behav., 10*(1), 45–54.

Roitman, S. E. L., Cornblatt, B. A., Bergman, A., Obuchowski, M., et al. (1997). Attention functioning in schizotypal personality disorder. *Amer. J. Psychiat., 154*(5), 655–660.

Rolland, J. S., & Walsh, F. (1994). Family therapy: Systems approaches to assessment and treatment. In R. E. Hales, S. C. Yudofsky, & J. A. Talbott, (Eds.), *The American Psychiatric Press textbook of psychiatry* (2nd ed.). Washington, DC: American Psychiatric Press.

Rollin, H. R. (1980). *Coping with schizophrenia.* London: Burnett.

Rolls, B. J., Fedroff, I. C., & Guthrie, J. F. (1991). Gender differences in eating behavior and body weight regulation. *Hlth. Psychol., 10*(2), 133–142.

Ronen, T. (1993). Intervention package for treating encopresis in a 6–year-old boy: A case study. *Behav. Psychother., 21,* 127–135.

Ronen, T., Wozner, Y., & Rahav, G. (1992). Cognitive intervention in enuresis. *Child Fam. Behav. Ther., 14*(2), 1–14.

Roper, G., Rachman, S., & Hodgson, R. (1973). An experiment on obsessional checking. *Behav. Res. Ther., 11,* 271–277.

Roper, M. (1992). Reaching the babies through the mothers: the effects of prosecution on pregnant substance abusers. *Law Psychol. Rev., 16,* 171–188.

Roscoe, B., Martin, G. L., & Pear, J. J. (1980). Systematic self desensitization of fear of flying: A case study. In G. L. Martin & J. G. Osborne (Eds.), *Helping in the community: Behavioral applications.* New York: Plenum Press.

Rose, S. D. (1990). Group exposure: A method of treating agoraphobia. *Soc. Work with Groups, 13*(1), 37–51.

Rosen, E. F., Anthony, D. L., Booker, K. M., Brown, T. L., et al. (1991). A comparison of eating disorder scores among African American and White college females. *Bull. Psychon. Soc., 29*(1), 65–66.

Rosen, J. C., & Leitenberg, H. (1982). Bulimia nervosa: Treatment with exposure and response prevention. *Behav. Ther., 13*(1), 117–124.

Rosen, J. C., & Leitenberg, H. (1985). Exposure plus response prevention treatment of bulimia. In D. M. Garner & P. E. Garfinkel (Eds.), *Handbook of psychotherapy for anorexia nervosa and bulimia.* New York: Guilford.

Rosen, J. C., Orosan, P., & Reiter, J. (1995). Cognitive behavior therapy for negative body image in obese women. *Behav. Ther., 26,* 25–42.

Rosen, L. N., Targum, S. D., Terman, M., Bryant, M. J., Hoffman, H., Kasper, S. F., Hamovit, J. R., Docherty, J. P., Welch, B., & Rosenthal, N. E. (1990). Prevalence of seasonal affective disorder at four latitudes. *Psychiat. Res., 31,* 131–144.

Rosen, L. W., & Hough, D. O. (1988). Pathogenic weight-control behaviors of female college gymnasts. *Physician Sports Med., 16*(9), 141–144.

Rosen, L. W., McKeag, D. B., Hough, D. O., & Curley, V. (1986). Pathogenic weight-control behavior in female athletes. *The Physician and Sports Medicine, 14*(1), 79–86,

Rosen, M. I., McMahon, T. J., Hameedi, F. A., Pearsall, H. R., Woods, S. W., Kreek, M. J., & Kosten, T. R. (1996). Effect of clonidine pretreatment on naloxone-precipitated opiate withdrawal. *J. Pharmacol. Exp. Thera., 276,* 1128–1135.

Rosen, R. C., & Rosen, L. R. (1981). *Human sexuality.* New York: Alfred A. Knopf.

Rosen, R. C. & Leiblum, S. R. (1993). Treatment of male erectile disorder: Current options and dilemmas. *Sex. Marital Ther., 8*(1), 5–8.

Rosen, R. C., & Leiblum, S. R. (1995). Hypoactive sexual desire. *Psychiat. Clin. N. Amer., 13*(1), 107–121.

Rosen, R. C., & Leiblum, S. R. (1995). Hypoactive sexual desire. [Special issue: Clinical sexuality]. *Psychiat. Clin. N. Amer., 18*(1), 107–121.

Rosen, R. C., & Leiblum, S. R. (1995). Treatment of sexual disorders in the 1990s: An integrated approach. *J. Cons. Clin. Psychol., 63*(6), 877–890.

Rosen, R. C., Leiblum, S. R., & Spector, I. (1994). Psychologically based treatment for male erectile disorder: A cognitive-interpersonal model. *J. Sex Marital Ther., 20,* 78–85.

Rosen, R. C., Taylor, J. F., Leiblum, S. R., & Bachmann, G. A. (1993). Prevalence of sexual dysfunction in women: Results of a survey study of 329 women in an outpatient gynecological clinic. *J. Sex Marital Ther., 19,* 171–188.

Rosenbaum, J. F., Pollock, R. A., Jordan, S. K., & Pollack, M. H. (1996). The pharmacotherapy of panic disorder. *Bull. Menninger Clin., 60*(2, Suppl. A), A54–A75.

Rosenbaum, M. (1980). The role of the term schizophrenia in the decline of diagnoses of multiple personality. *Arch. Gen. Psychiat., 37*(12), 1383–1385.

Rosenbaum, M., & Berger, M. (Eds.). (1963). *Group psychotherapy and group function.* New York: Basic Books.

Rosenberg, H. (1993). Prediction of controlled drinking by alcoholics and problem drinkers. *Psychol. Bull., 113*(1), 129–139.

Rosenfarb, I. S., Goldstein, M. J., Mintz, J., & Nuechterlein, K. H. (1995). Expressed emotion and subclinical psychopathology observable within the transactions between schizophrenic patients and their family members. *J. Abnorm. Psychol., 104*(2), 259–267.

Rosenhan, D. L. (1973). On being sane in insane places. *Science, 179*(4070), 250–258.

Rosenman, R. H. (1990). Type A behavior pattern: A personal overview. *J. Soc. Behav. Pers., 5,* 1–24.

Rosenstein, D. S., & Horowitz, H. A. (1996). Adolescent attachment and psychopathology. *J. Cons. Clin. Psychol., 64*(2), 244–253.

Rosenstein, M. J., Milazzo-Sayre, L. J., & Manderscheid, R. W. (1989). Care of persons with schizophrenia: A statistical profile. *Schizo. Bull., 15*(1), 45–58.

Rosenstein, M. J., Milazzo-Sayre, L. J., & Manderscheid, R. W. (1990). Characteristics of persons using specialty inpatient, outpatient, and partial care programs in 1986. In R. W. Manderscheid & M. A. Sonnenschein (Eds.), *Mental health, United States, 1990* (DHHS Publication No. ADM 90–1708). Washington DC: U. S. Department of Health & Human Services.

Rosenthal, D. (Ed.). (1963). *The Genain quadruplets.* New York: Basic Books.

Rosenthal, N. E., & Blehar, M. C. (Eds.). (1989). *Seasonal affective disorders and phototherapy.* New York: Guilford.

Rosenthal, N. E., Jacobsen, F. M., Sack, D. A., Arendt, J., James, S. P., Parry, B. L., & Wehr, T. A. (1988). Atenolol in seasonal affective disorder: A test of the melatonin hypothesis. *Amer. J. Psychiat., 145,* 52–56.

Rosenthal, R. (1966). *Experimenter effects in behavioral research.* New York: Appleton-Century-Crofts.

Rosenthal, R. J. (1992). Pathological gambling. *Psychiatr. Ann., 22*(2), 72–78.

Rosenzweig, M. R. (1996). Aspects of the search for neural mechanisms of memory. In J. T. Spence, J. M. Darley, & D. J. Foss (Eds.), *Annual review of psychology* (Vol. 47). Palo Alto, CA: Annual Reviews.

Rosenzweig, S. (1933). The recall of finished and unfinished tasks as affected by the purpose with which they were performed. *Psychol. Bull., 30,* 698.

Rosenzweig, S. (1943). An experimental study of repression with special reference to need-persistive and ego-defensive reactions to frustration. *J. Exp. Psychol., 32,* 64–74.

Rosenzweig, S. (1988). The identity and idiodynamics of the multiple personality "Sally Beauchamp": A confirmatory supplement. *Amer. Psychol., 43*(1), 45–48.

Roses, A. D., Einstein, G., Gilbert, J., Goedert, M., Han, S. H., Huang, D., Hulette, C., Masliah, E., Pericak-Vance, M. A., Saunders, A. M., Schmechel, D. E., Strittmatter, W. J., Weisgraber, K. H., & Xi, P. T. (1996). Morphological, biochemical, and genetic support for an apolipoprotein E effect on microtubular metabolism. In R. J. Wurtman, S. Corkin, J. H. Growdon, & R. M. Nitsch (Eds.), *The neurobiology of Alzheimer's disease.* New York: New York Academy of Sciences.

Roskies, E., Seraganian, P., Oseasohn, R., Hanley, J. A., Collu, R., Martin, N., & Smigla, C. (1986). The Montreal Type A Intervention Project: Major findings. *Hlth. Psychol., 5,* 45–69.

Rosmarin, P. (1989). Coffee and coronary heart disease: A review. *Prog. Cardiovasc. Dis., 32*(3), 239–245.

Ross, A. O. (1981). *Child behavior therapy: Principles, procedures and empirical basis.* New York: Wiley.

Ross, C. A., & Gahan, P. (1988). Techniques in the treatment of multiple personality disorder. *Amer. J. Psychother., 42*(1), 40–52.

Ross, C. A., Miller, S. D., Bjornson, L., Reagor, P., Fraser, G. A., & Anderson, G. (1991). Abuse histories in 102 cases of multiple personality disorder. *Canad. J. Psychiat., 36,* 97–101.

Ross, C. A., Miller, S. D., Reagor, P., & Bjornson, L. et al. (1990). Structured interview data on 102 cases of multiple personality disorder from four centers. *Amer. J. Psychiat., 147*(5), 596–601.

Ross, C. A., Norton, G. R., & Wozney, K. (1989). Multiple personality disorder: An analysis of 236 cases. *Canad. J. Psychiat., 34*(5), 413–418.

Ross, D. M., & Ross, S. A. (1982). *Hyperactivity: Current issues, research and theory* (2nd ed.). New York: Wiley.

Ross, S. M., Gottfredson, D. K., Christensen, P., & Weaver, R. (1986). Cognitive self statements in depression: Findings across clinical populations. *Cog. Ther. Res., 10*(2), 159–165.

Rosse, R., Fay-McCarthy, M., Collins, J., Risher-Flowers, D., Alim, T., & Deutsch, S. (1993). Transient compulsive foraging behavior associated with crack cocaine use. *Amer. J. Psychiat., 150*(1), 155–156.

Rosselli, M. & Ardila, A. (1996). Cognitive effects of cocaine and polydrug abuse. *J. Clin. Exp. Neuropsychol., 18*(1), 122–135.

Rossor, M. N., Kennedy, A. M., & Frackowiak, R. S. J. (1996). Clinical and neuroimaging features of familial Alzheimer's disease. In R. J. Wurtman, S. Corkin, J. H. Growdon, & R. M. Nitsch (Eds.), *The neurobiology of Alzheimer's disease.* New York: New York Academy of Sciences.

Rossow, I. & Amundsen, A. (1995). Alcohol abuse and suicide: A 40-year prospective study of Norwegian conscripts. *Addiction, 90*(5), 685–691.

Rothbaum, B. O., Foa, E. B., Riggs, D. S., Murdock, T., & Walsh, W. (1992). A prospective examination of posttraumatic stress disorder in rape victims. *J. Traum. Stress, 5*(3), 455–475.

Rothbaum, B. O., Hodges, L., Watson, B. A., Kessler, G. D., & Opdyke, D. (1996). Shorter Communications. Virtual reality exposure therapy in the treatment of fear of flying: A case report. *Behav. Res. Ther., 34*(5/6), 477–481.

Rothblum, E. D. (1992). The stigma of women's weight: Social and economic realities. *Feminism Psychol., 2*(1), 61–73.

Rotheram-Borus, M. J., Piacentini, J., Miller, S., Graae, F., & Castro-Blanco, D. (1994). Brief cognitive-behavioral treatment for adolescent suicide attempters and their families. *J. Amer. Acad. Child Adol. Psychiat., 33*(4), 508–517.

Rothman, D. (1985). ECT: The historical, social and professional sources of the controversy. In *NIH Consensus Development Conference: Electroconvulsive therapy.* Bethesda, MD: NIH & NIMH.

Rotter, J. B. (1954). *Social learning and clinical psychology.* Englewood Cliffs, NJ: Prentice Hall.

Rotter, M., Kalus, O., Losonczy, M., Guo, L. et al. (1991). Lateral ventricular enlargement in schizotypal personality disorder. *Bio. Psychiat., 29,* 182–185.

Rowe, D. (1978). *The experience of depression.* Chichester, England: Wiley.

Rowland, C. V. (1970). Anorexia nervosa: A survey of the literature and review of 30 cases. *Inter. Psychiat. Clin., 7*(1), 37–137.

Rowlands, P. (1995). Schizophrenia and sexuality. *Sex. Marital Ther. 10*(1), 47–61.

Roy, A. (1982). Suicide in chronic schizophrenics. *Brit. J. Psychiat., 141,* 171–177.

Roy, A. (1992). Genetics, biology, and suicide in the family. In R. W. Maris, A. L. Berman, J. T. Maltsberger, & R. I. Yufit (Eds.), *Assessment and prediction of suicide.* New York: Guilford.

Roy, A. (1992). Suicide in schizophrenia. *Inter. Rev. Psychiat., 4*(2), 205–209.

Roy-Byrne, P. P., & Katon, W. (1997). Generalized anxiety disorder in primary care: The precursor/modifier pathway to increased health care utilization. *J. Clin. Psychiat., 58*(Suppl. 3), 34–38.

Roy-Byrne, P. P., & Wingerson, D. (1992). Pharmacotherapy of Anxiety Disorders. In A. Tasman, & M. B. Riba (Eds.), *Review of psychiatry* (Vol. 11). Washington, DC: American Psychiatric Press.

Rozin, P., & Stoess, C. (1993). Is there a general tendency to become addicted? *Addic. Behav., 18,* 81–87.

Rozynko, V., & Dondershine, H. E. (1991). Trauma focus group therapy for Vietnam veterans with PTSD. *Psychotherapy, 28*(1), 157–161.

Rubonis, A. V., & Bickman, L. (1991). Psychological impairment in the wake of disaster: The disaster-psychopathology relationship. *Psychol. Bull., 109,* 384–399.

Rudolph, J., Langer, I., & Tausch, R. (1980). An investigation of the psychological affects and conditions of person-centered individual psychotherapy. *Z. Klin. Psychol.: Forsch. Praxis, 9,* 23–33.

Ruedrich, S. L., Chu, C., & Wadle, C. V. (1985). The amytal interview in the treatment of psychogenic amnesia [Special issue]. *Hosp. Comm. Psychiat., 36*(10), 1045–1046.

Rupp, A. (1995). The economic consequences of not treating depression. *Brit. J. Psychiat., 166*(Suppl. 27), 29–33.

Rush, A. J., & Watkins, J. T. (1981). Group versus individual cognitive therapy: A pilot study. *Cog. Ther. Res., 5,* 95–103.

Rush, A. J., Weissenburger, J., & Eaves, G. (1986). Do thinking patterns predict depressive symptoms? *Cog. Ther. Res., 10*(2), 225–235.

Rushford, N., & Ostermeyer, A. (1997). Body image disturbances and their change with videofeedback in anorexia nervosa. *Behav. Res. Ther., 35*(5), 389–398.

Russell, G. (1979). Bulimia nervosa: An ominous variant of anorexia nervosa. *Psychol. Med., 9*(3), 429–448.

Russell, G. F. M. (1995). Anorexia nervosa through time. In G. Szmukler, C. Dare, & J. Treasure (Eds.), *Handbook of eating disorders: Theory, treatment and research.* Chichester: John Wiley & Sons Ltd.

Russell, R. J., & Hulson, B. (1992). Physical and psychological abuse of heterosexual partners. *Pers. Individ. Diff., 13*(4), 457–473.

Russell, R. M. et al. (1992). Chapter 12. In K. Halmi (Ed.), *Psychobiology and treatment of anorexia nervosa and bulimia nervosa.* Washington, DC: American Psychiatric Press.

Rutter, M. (1966). Prognosis: Psychotic children in adolescence and early adult life. In J. K. Wing (Ed.), *Childhood autism: Clinical, educational, and social aspects.* Elmsford, NY: Pergamon Press.

Rutter, M., & Garmezy, N. (1983). Developmental psychopathology. In E. M. Hetherington (Ed.), *Handbook of child psychology: Socialization, personality, and social development* (Vol. 4). New York: Wiley.

SAMHSA (Substance Abuse and Mental Health Services Administration). (1996). *Advance Report Number 17: Preliminary estimates from the drug abuse warning network.* Washington, DC: U. S. Department of Health and Human Services.

SAMHSA (1996). *National Household Survey on Drug Abuse, 1994 and 1995.* Office of Applied Studies.

SAMHSA News. (1993, Spring). *Agencies improve mental health services in jails,* (Vol. 1, No. 2.) U. S. Dept. of Health and Human Services.

Sachs, R. G. (1986). The adjunctive role of social support systems. In B. G. Braun (Ed.), *The treatment of multiple personality disorder.* Washington, DC: American Psychiatric Press.

Sackeim, H. A. (1988). Mechanisms of action of electroconvulsive therapy. In A. J. Frances & R. E. Hales (Eds.), *American Psychiatric Press review of psychiatry* (Vol. 7). Washington, DC: American Psychiatric Press.

Sadock, B. J. (1989). Group psychotherapy, combined individual and group psychotherapy, and psychodrama. In H. I. Kaplan & B. J. Sadock (Eds.), *Comprehensive textbook of psychiatry* (5th ed., Vol. 1). Baltimore: Williams & Wilkins.

Sadock, V. A. (1989). Rape, spouse abuse, and incest. In H. I. Kaplan &

B. J. Sadock (Eds.), *Comprehensive textbook of psychiatry* (5th ed., Vol. 1). Baltimore: Williams & Wilkins.

Safer, D. (1994). The impact of recent lawsuits on methylphenidates sales. *Clin. Pediatr.*, 33(3), 166–168.

Safer, D., & Krager, J. (1992). Effect of a media blitz and a threatened lawsuit on stimulant treatment. *JAMA, 268*(8), 1004–1007.

Safer, D., & Krager, J. (1993). Reply to "Treatment of ADHD" (Letter). *JAMA, 269*(18), 2369.

Safferman, A. Z., & Munne, R. (1992). Combining clozapine with ECT. *Convulsive Ther., 8*(2), 141–143.

Safferman, A. Z., Lieberman, J. A., Kane, J. M., Szymanski, S., & Kinon, B. (1991). Update on the clinical efficacy and side effects of clozapine. *Schizo. Bull., 17*(2), 247–261.

Sagawa, K., Kawakatsu, S., Shibuya, I., Oiji, A. et al. (1990). Correlation of regional cerebral blood flow with performance on neuropsychological tests in schizophrenic patients. *Schizo. Res., 3*(4), 241–246.

Sakel, M. (1938). The pharmacological shock treatment of schizophrenia. *Nerv. Ment. Dis. Monogr. Ser., 62,* 136.

Sakheim, D. K., Hess, E. P., & Chivas, A. (1988). General principles for short-term inpatient work with multiple personality-disorder patients. *Psychotherapy, 24,* 117–124.

Salama, A. A. (1988). The antisocial personality (the sociopathic personality). *Psychiat. J. Univ. Ottawa, 13*(3), 149–151.

Sales, E., Baum, M., & Shore, B. (1984). Victim readjustment following assault. *J. Soc. Issues, 40*(1), 117–136.

Salkovskis, P. M. (1985). Obsessional-compulsive problems: A cognitive-behavioural analysis. *Behav. Res. Ther., 23,* 571–584.

Salkovskis, P. M. (1989). Cognitive-behavioural factors and the persistence of intrusive thoughts in obsessional problems. *Behav. Res. Ther., 27,* 677–682.

Salkovskis, P. M., Atha, C., Storer, D. (1990). Cognitive behavioural problem solving in the treatment of patients who repeatedly attempt suicide: A controlled trial. *Brit. J. Psychiat., 157,* 871–876.

Salkovskis, P. M., & Westbrook, D. (1989). Behaviour therapy and obsessional ruminations: Can failure be turned into success? *Behav. Res. Ther., 27,* 149–160.

Salkovskis, P. M., Clark, D. M., & Gelder, M. G. (1996). Cognition-behaviour links in the persistence of panic. *Behav. Res. Ther., 34*(5/6), 453–458.

Salkovskis, P. M., Westbrook, D., Davis, J., Jeavons, A., & Gledhill, A. (1997). Effects of neutralizing on intrusive thoughts: An experiment investigating the etiology of obsessive-compulsive disorder. *Behav. Res. Ther., 35*(3), 211–219.

Sallee, F. R., Vrindavanam, N. S., Deas-Nesmith, D., Carson, S. W., & Sethuraman, G. (1997). Pulse intravenous clomiparamine for depressed adolescents: Double-blind, controlled trial. *Amer. J. Psychiat., 154*(5), 668–673.

Salloway, S., & Cummings, J. (1996). Subcortical structures and neuropsychiatric illness. *Neuroscientist, 2,* 66–75.

Salzman, C., Vaccaro, B., Lieff, J., & Weiner, A. (1995). Clozapine in older patients with psychosis and behavioral disruption. *American J. Geriat. Psychiat., 3*(1), 26–33.

Salzman, L. (1968). *The obsessive personality.* New York: Science House.

Salzman, L. (1980). *Psychotherapy of the obsessive personality.* New York: Jason Aronson.

Salzman, L. (1985). Psychotherapeutic management of obsessive-compulsive patients. *Amer. J. Psychother., 39*(3), 323–330.

Salzman, L. (1989). Compulsive personality disorder. In *Treatments of psychiatric disorders.* Washington, DC: American Psychiatric Press.

Samelson, F. (1980). J. B. Watson's Little Albert, Cyril Burt's twins, and the need for a critical science. *Amer. Psychologist, 35,* 619–625.

Sampath, G., Shah, A., Kraska, J., & Soni, S. D. (1992). Neuroleptic discontinuation in the very stable schizophrenic patient: Relapse rates and serum neuroleptic levels. *Human Psychopharmacol. Clin. Exp., 7*(4), 255–264.

Sanchez-Canovas, J., Botella-Arbona, C., Ballestin, G. P., & Soriano-Pastor, J. (1991). Intervencion comportamental y analisis ipsativo normativo en un trastorno de ansiedad. [Behavioral intervention and ipsative-normative analysis in an anxiety disorder]. *Anal. Modif. Conducta, 17*(51), 115–151.

Sandelowski, M. (1995). Sample size in qualitative research. *Res. Nursing Hlth., 18*(2), 179–183.

Sander, F. M., & Feldman, L. B. (1993). Integrating individual, marital, and family therapy. In J. M. Oldham, M. B. Riba, & A. Tasman (Eds.), *Review of psychiatry* (Vol. 12). Washington, DC: American Psychiatric Press.

Sanderman, R., & Ormel, J. (1992). De Utrechtse Coping Lijst (UCL): Validiteit en betrouwbaarheid [The Utrecht Coping List (UCL): Validity and reliability]. *Gedrag Gezondheid Tijdschr. Psychol. Gezondheid, 20*(1), 32–37.

Sanders, S. K., & Shekhar, A. (1995). Anxiolytic effects of chlordiazepoxide blocked by injection of GABA-sub(A) and benzodiazepine receptor antagonists in the region of the enterior basolateral amygdala of rats. *Biol. Psychiat., 37*(7), 473–476.

Sanders, S. K., & Shekhar, A. (1995). Regulation of anxiety by GABAA receptors in the rat amygdala. *Pharmacol. Biochem. Behav., 52*(4), 701–706.

Sanderson, R. E., Campbell, D., & Laverty, S. G. (1963). An investigation of a new aversive conditioning treatment for alcoholism. *Quart. J. Stud. Alcohol., 24,* 261–275.

Sandler, M. (1990). Monoamine oxidase inhibitors in depression: History and mythology. *J. Psychopharmacol., 4*(3), 136–139.

Sanford, R. C. (1987). An inquiry into the evolution of the client-centered approach to psychotherapy. In J. K. Zeig (Ed.), *The evolution of psychotherapy.* New York: Brunner/Mazel.

Sanftner, J. L., Barlow, D. H., Marschall, D. E., & Tangney, J. P. (1995). The relation of shame and guilt to eating disorder symptomatology. *J. Soc. Clin. Psychol., 14*(4), 315–324.

Sansone, R. A., Fine, M. A., & Dennis, A. B. (1991). Treatment impressions and termination experiences with borderline patients. *Amer. J. Psychother., 45*(2), 173–180.

Saper, Z., Blank, M. K., & Chapman, L. (1995). Implosive therapy as an adjunct treatment in a psychotic disorder: A case report. *J. Behav. Ther. Exp. Psychiat., 26*(2), 157–160.

Sapsford, L. (1995). Surviving the suicidal death of a loved one: Women's experience of grief integration. In S. S. Canetto & D. Lester (Eds.), *Women and suicidal behavior.* New York: Springer.

Satir, V. (1964). *Conjoint family therapy: A guide to therapy and technique.* Palo Alto, CA: Science & Behavior Books.

Satir, V. (1967). *Conjoint family therapy* (Revised Ed.). Palo Alto, CA: Science & Behavior Books.

Satir, V. (1987). Going behind the obvious: The psychotherapeutic journey. In J. K. Zeig (Ed.), *The evolution of psychotherapy.* New York: Brunner/Mazel.

Sato, T., Sakado, K., Uehara, T., Nichioka, K., & Kasahara, Y. (1997). Perceived parental styles in a Japanese sample of depressive disorders. A replication outside Western culture. *Brit. J. Psychiat., 170,* 173–175.

Saunders, D. G. (1982). Counseling the violent husband. In P. A. Keller & L. G. Ritt (Eds.), *Innovations in clinical practice: A source book* (Vol. 1). Sarasota, FL: Professional Resource Exchange.

Saunders, D. G. (1992). A typology of men who batter: Three types derived from cluster analysis. *Amer. J. Orthopsychiat., 62*(2), 264–275.

Saunders, R. (1985). Bulimia: An expanded definition. *Soc. Casework, 66*(10), 603–610.

Saxe, G. N., van der Kolk, B. A., Berkowitz, R., Chinman, G., Hall, K., Lieberg, G., & Schwartz, J. (1993). Dissociative disorders in psychiatric inpatients. *Amer. J. Psychiat., 150*(7), 1037–1042.

Saxe, L., Dougherty, D., & Cross, T. P. (1985). The validity of polygraph testing: Scientific analysis and public controversy. *Amer. Psychol., 40*(3), 355–366.

Sayers, J. (1988). Anorexia, psychoanalysis, and feminism: Fantasy and reality. *J. Adolescence, 11*(4), 361–371.

Sayers, M. D., Bellack, A. S., Wade, J. H., Bennett, M. E. et al. (1995). An empirical method for assessing social problem solving in schizophrenia. *Behav. Mod., 19*(3), 267–289.

Scarf, M. (1996, June 10). The mind of the Unabomber. *New Republic*, pp. 20–23.

Schachar, R. J., & Wachsmuth, R. (1990). Hyperactivity and parental psychopathology. *J. Child Psychol. Psychiat. Allied Disc., 31*, 381–392.

Schacter, D. L. (1989). Autobiographical memory in a case of multiple personality disorder. *J. Abnorm. Psychol., 98*(4), 508–514.

Schacter, D. L., Glisky, E. L., & McGlynn, S. M. (1990). Impact of memory disorder on everyday life: Awareness of deficits and return to work. In D. Tupper & K. Cicerone (Eds.), *The neuropsychology of everyday life: Vol. 1. Theories and Basic Competencies.* Boston: Martinus Nijhoff.

Schacter, D. L., Reiman, E., Curran, T., Yun, L. S., Bandy, D., McDermott, K. B., & Roediger, H. L., 3rd. (1996). Neuroanatomical correlates of veridical and illusory recognition memory: Evidence from positron emission tomography. *Neuron, 17*(2), 267–274.

Schaie, K. W. (1996). Intellectual development in adulthood. In J. E. Birren, K. W. Schaie, R. P. Abeles, M. Gatz, & T. A. Salthouse, (Eds.), *The handbook of aging.* San Diego: Academic Press.

Schaie, K. W. (1989). The hazards of cognitive aging. *Gerontologist, 29*, 484–493.

Schatzberg, A. T. et al. (1982). Toward a biochemical classification of depressive disorders: V. Heterogeneity of unipolar depressions. *Amer. J. Psychiat., 130*(4), 471–475.

Scheff, T. J. (1966). *Being mentally ill: A sociological theory.* Chicago: Aldine.

Scheff, T. J. (1975). *Labeling madness.* Englewood Cliffs, NJ: Prentice Hall.

Scheier, L. M., & Botvin, G. J. (1997). Expectancies as mediators of the effects of social influences and alcohol knowledge on adolescent alcohol use: A prospective analysis. *Psychol. Addic. Behav., 11*(1), 48–64.

Scherling, D. (1994). Prenatal cocaine exposure and childhood psychopathology: A developmental analysis. *Amer. J. Orthopsychiat., 64*(1), 9–19.

Schiavi, R. C., Stimmel, B. B., Mandeli, J., Schreiner-Engel, P. et al. (1995). Diabetes, psychological function and male sexuality. *J. Psychosom. Res., 39*(3), 305–314.

Schiavi, R. C., White, D., Mandeli, J., & Schreiner-Engel, P. (1993). Hormones and nocturnal penile tumescence in healthy aging men. *Arch. Sex. Behav., 22*(2), 207–216.

Schiff, S. M. (1988). Treatment approaches for older alcoholics. *Generations, 12*(4), 41–45.

Schildkraut, J. J. (1965). The catecholamine hypothesis of affective disorders: A review of supporting evidence. *Amer. J. Psychiat., 122*(5), 509–522.

Schleifer, J. S., Keller, S. E., Bartlett, J. A., Eckholdt, H. M., & Delaney, B. R. (1996). Immunity in young adults with major depressive disorder. *Amer. J. Psychiat., 153*, 477–482.

Schlichter, K. J., & Horan, J. J. (1981). Effects of stress innoculation on the anger and aggression management skills of institutionalized juvenile delinquents. *Cog. Ther. Res., 5*(4), 359–365.

Schloss, P. J. & Smith, M. A. (1994). *Applied behavior analysis in the classroom.* Boston: Allyn & Bacon.

Schmauk, F. J. (1970). Punishment, arousal, and avoidance learning in sociopaths. *J. Abnorm. Psychol. 76*(3, Pt. 1), 325–335.

Schmidt, N. B., & Telch, M. J. (1997). Nonpsychiatric medical comorbidity, health perceptions, and treatment outcome in patients with panic disorder. *Hlth. Psychol., 16*(2), 114–122.

Schmidt, U., Tiller, J., Treasure, J. (1993). Self-treatment of bulimia nervosa: A pilot study. *Inter. J. Eat. Dis., 13*(3), 273–277.

Schmidt, U., Tiller, J., Treasure, J. (1993). Psychosocial factors in the origins of bulimia nervosa. *Inter. Rev. Psychiat., 5*(1), 51–59.

Schmidtke, A., & Häfner, H. (1988). The Werther effect after television films: New evidence for an old hypothesis. *Psychol. Med., 18*, 665–676.

Schneider, B. E. (1991). Put up and shut up: Workplace sexual assaults. *Gender and Society, 5*(4), 533–548.

Schneider, L. S. (1996). Overview of generalized anxiety disorder in the elderly. *J. Clin. Psychiat., 57*(Suppl. 7), 34–45.

Schneider, R. H., Alexander, C. N., & Wallace, R. K. (1992). In search of an optimal behavioral treatment for hypertension: A review and focus on transcendental meditation. In E. H. Johnson, W. D. Gentry, & S. Julius (Eds.), *Personality, elevated blood pressure, and essential hypertension.* Washington, DC: Hemisphere.

Schneiderman, L., & Baum, A. (1992). Acute and chronic stress and the immune system. In N. Schneiderman, P. McCabe, & A. Baum (Eds.), *Perspectives in behavioral medicine: Stress and disease processes.* Hillsdale, NJ: Erlbaum.

Schneier, F. R., Spitzer, R. L., Gibbon, M., Fyer, A. J. et al. (1991). The relationship of social phobia subtypes and avoidant personality. *Comprehen. Psychiat., 32*(6), 496–502.

Scholing, A., & Emmelkamp, P. M. G. (1993). Cognitive and behavioral treatments of fear of blushing, sweating or trembling. *Behav. Res. Ther., 31*, 155–170.

Scholing, A., & Emmelkamp, P. M. G. (1993). Exposure with and without cognitive therapy for generalized social phobia: Effects of individual and group treatment. *Behav. Res. Ther. 31*(7), 667–681.

Scholing, A., & Emmelkamp, P. M. G. (1996). Treatment of generalized social phobia: Results at long-term follow-up. *Behav. Res. Ther., 34*(5/6), 447–452.

Schooler, J. W. (1994). Seeking the core: The issues and evidence surrounding recovered accounts of sexual trauma. *Consciousness Cog., 3*, 452–269.

Schooler, J. W. (1996). Seeking the core: The issues and evidence surrounding recovered accounts of sexual trauma. In K. Pezdek & W. P. Banks (Eds.), *The recovered memory/false memory debate.* San Diego: Academic Press.

Schott, R. L. (1995). The childhood and family dynamics of transvestites. *Arch. Sex. Behav., 24*(3), 309–327.

Schou, M. (1997). Forty years of lithium treatment. *Arch. Gen. Psychiat., 54*, 9–13.

Schover, L. R. & Leiblum, S. R. (1994). The stagnation of sex therapy. *J. Psychol. Human Sex., 6*, 5–30.

Schover, L. R., & LoPiccolo, J. (1982). Treatment effectiveness for dysfunctions of sexual desires. *J. Sex and Marital Ther., 8*(3), 179–197.

Schover, L. R., Youngs, D. D., & Gannata, R. (1992). Psychosexual aspects of the evaluation and management of vulvar vestibulitis. *Amer. J. Obstet. Gynecol., 167*, 630–638.

Schreiber, F. R. (1973). *Sybil.* Chicago: Regnery.

Schreier, H., & Libow, J. (1993). Munchausen syndrome by proxy: Diagnosis and prevalence. *Amer. J. Orthopsychiat. 63*(2), 318–321.

Schreier, H., & Libow, J. (1994). Munchausen by proxy syndrome: A clinical fable for our times. *J. Amer. Acad. Child Adol. Psychiat., 33*(6), 904–905.

Schreier, H., & Libow, J. (1994). Munchausen by proxy syndrome: A modern pediatric challenge. *J. Pediatr., 125*(6, Pt. 2), S110–115.

Schuckit, M. A. (1987). Alcohol and alcoholism. In E. Braunwald, K. J. Isselbacher, R. G., Petersdorf, et al. (Eds.), *Harrison's principles of internal medicine,* (Vol. 2). New York: McGraw-Hill.

Schuckit, M. A. (1994). The relationship between alcohol problems, substance abuse, and psychiatric syndromes. In T. A. Widiger, A. J. Frances, H. A. Pincus, et al. (Eds.), *DSM-IV Sourcebook, Volume 1.* Washington, DC: American Psychiatric Association.

Schuckit, M. A., & Schuckit, J. J. (1991). In L. Davidson & M. Linnoila (Eds.), *Risk factors for youth suicide.* New York: Hemisphere.

Schuldberg, D., French, C., Stone, B. L., & Heberle, J. (1988). Creativity and schizotypal traits: Creativity test scores and perceptual aberration, magical ideation, and impulsive nonconformity. *J. Nerv. Ment. Dis., 176*(11), 648–57.

Schultz, R., & Heckhausen, J. (1996). A life span model of successful aging. *Amer. Psychol., 51*(7), 702–714.

Schultz, S. K., Miller, D. D., Arndt, S., Ziebell, S., Gupta, S., & Andreasen, N. (1995). Withdrawal-emergent dyskinesia in patients with schizophrenia during antipsychotic discontinuation. *Bio. Psychiat., 38*, 713–719.

Schulz, P. M. et al. (1986). Diagnoses of the relatives of schizotypal outpatients. *J. Nerv. Ment. Dis., 174*(8), 457–463.

Schwab, R. (1996). Gender differences in parental grief. *Death Stud., 20,* 103–113.

Schwartz, A. J., & Whitaker, L. C. (1990). Suicide among college students: Assessment, treatment, and intervention. In S. J. Blumenthal & D. J. Kupfer (Eds.), *Suicide over the life cycle: Risk factors, assessment, and treatment of suicidal patients.* Washington, DC: American Psychiatry Press.

Schwartz, G. (1977). College students as contingency managers for adolescents in a program to develop reading skills. *J. Appl. Behav. Anal., 10,* 645–655.

Schwartz, G. E. (1977). Psychosomatic disorders and biofeedback: A psychobiological model of disregulation. In J. D. Maser & M. E. P. Seligman (Eds.), *Psychopathology: Experimental models.* San Francisco: W.H. Freeman.

Schwartz, G. E. (1982). Testing the biopsychosocial model: The ultimate challenge facing behavioral medicine? *J. Cons. Clin. Psychol., 50*(6), 1040–1053.

Schwartz, J. M., Stoessel, P. W., Baxter, L. R. Jr., Martin, K. M., & Phelps, M. E. (1996). Systematic changes in cerebral glucose metabolic rate after successful behavior modification treatment of obsessive-compulsive disorder. *Arch. Gen. Psychiat., 53,* 109–113.

Schwartz, S., & Johnson, J. J. (1985). *Psychopathology of childhood.* New York: Pergamon Press.

Schwarz, J., & Lindner, A. (1992). Inpatient Treatment of male pathological gamblers in Germany. *J. Gamb. Stud., 8*(1), 93–109.

Schwarz, K., Harding, R., Harrington, D., & Farr, B. (1993). Hospital management of a patient with intractable factitious disorder. *Psychosomatics, 34*(3), 265–267.

Schweizer, E., & Rickels, K. (1996). The long-term management of generalized anxiety disorder: Issues and dilemmas. *J. Clin. Psychiat., 57*(Suppl 7), 9–12.

Schweizer, E. S., & Rickels, K. (1997). Strategies for treatment of generalized anxiety in the primary care setting. *J. Clin. Psychiat., 58*(Suppl. 3), 27–31.

Scola, P. S. (1991). Classification and social status. In J. L. Matson & J. A. Mulick (Eds.), *Handbook of mental retardation.* New York: Pergamon Press.

Scott, A. (1995). "Reclaimed once more by the realities of life": Hysteria and the location of memory. *Brit. J. Psychother., 11*(3), 398–405.

Scott, J. (1995). Psychotherapy for bipolar disorder. *Brit. J. Psychiat., 167*(5), 581–588.

Scott, J. E., & Dixon, L. B. (1995). Assertive community treatment and case management for schizophrenia. *Schizo. Bull., 21*(4), 657–668.

Scott, J. E., & Dixon, L. B. (1995). Psychological interventions for schizophrenia. *Schizo. Bull., 21*(4), 621–630.

Scott, R. D., Fagin, L., & Winter, D. (1993). The importance of the role of the patient in the outcome of schizophrenia. *Brit. J. Psychiat., 163,* 62–68.

Scourfield, J., Soldan, J., Gray, J., Houlihan, G., & Harper, P. S. (1997). Huntington's disease: Psychiatric practice in molecular genetic prediction and diagnosis. *Brit. J. Psychiat., 170,* 146–149.

Seale, C., & Addington-Hall, J. (1995a). Euthanasia: The role of good care. *Soc. Sci. Med., 40*(5), 581–587.

Seale, C., & Addington-Hall, J. (1995b). Dying at the best time. *Soc. Sci. Med., 40*(5), 589–595.

Sechrest, L., McKnight, P., & McKnight, K. (1996). Calibration of measures for psychotherapy outcome studies. *Amer. Psychol., 51*(10), 1065–1071.

Sederer, L. I. (1992). Brief Hospitalization. In A. Tasman & M. B. Riba (Eds.), *Review of psychiatry* (Vol. 11). Washington, DC: American Psychiatric Press.

Sedvall, G. (1990). Monoamines and schizophrenia. International Symposium: Development of a new antipsychotic: Remoxipride. *Acta Psychiatr. Scandin., 82*(358, Suppl.), 7–13.

Sedvall, G. (1990). PET imaging of dopamine receptors in human basal ganglia: Relevance to mental illness. *Trends Neurosci., 13*(7), 302–308.

Seeman, M. (1982). Gender differences in schizophrenia. *Canad. J. Psychiat., 27,* 108–111.

Seeman, P., Lee, T., Chau Wong, M., & Wong, K. (1976). Antipsychotic drug doses and neurolaptic/dopamine receptors. *Nature, 281*(5582), 717–718.

Segal, B. M. (1988). A borderline style of functioning: The role of family, society, and heredity: An overview. *Child Psychiat. Human Dev., 18*(4), 219–238.

Segal, S. P., Cohen, D., & Marder, S. R. (1992). Neuroleptic medication and prescription practices with sheltered-care residents: A twelve-year perspective. *Amer. J. Pub. Hlth., 82*(6), 846–852.

Segraves, K. B., & Segraves, R. T. (1991). Hypoactive sexual desire disorder: Prevalence and comorbidity in 906 subjects. *J. Sex Marital Ther., 17,* 55–58.

Segraves, R. T. (1993). Treatment-emergent sexual dysfunction in affective disorder: A review and management strategies. *J. Clin. Psychiat., Monogr. Ser. 11,* 7–63.

Segraves, R. T. (1995). Psychopharmacological influences on human sexual behavior. In J. M. Oldham & M. B. Riba (Eds.), *American Psychiatric Press review of psychiatry,* (Vol. 14). Washington, DC: American Psychiatric Press.

Segraves, R. T., Saran, A., Segraves, K., & Maguire, E. (1993). Clomipramine versus placebo in the treatment of premature ejaculation: A pilot study. *J. Sex Marital Ther., 19*(3), 198–200.

Segraves, R. T., & Segraves, K. B. (1991). Diagnosis of female arousal disorder. *Sex. Marital Ther., 6,* 9–13.

Segrin, C., & Abramson, L. Y. (1994). Negative reactions to depressive behaviors: A communication theories analysis. *J. Abnorm. Psychol., 103*(4), 655–668.

Seiden, R. H. (1969, December). *Suicide among youth: A review of the literature, 1900–1967* (NIMH Bulletin of Suicidology (Supplement), PHS Publication No. 1971). Washington, DC: NIMH.

Seiden, R. H. (1981). Mellowing with age: Factors influencing the nonwhite suicide rate. *Inter. J. Aging and Human Devel., 13,* 265–284.

Seidman, L. J. (1990). The neuropsychology of schizophrenia: A neurodevelopmental and case study approach. *J. Neuropsychiat. Clin. Neurosci., 2*(3), 301–312.

Seidman, S. N. & Rieder, R. O. (1995). Sexual behavior through the life cycle: An empirical approach. In J. M. Oldham & M. B. Riba (Eds.), *American Psychiatric Press review of psychiatry,* (Vol. 14). Washington, DC: American Psychiatric Press.

Seligman, M. E. P. (1971). Phobias and preparedness. *Behav. Ther., 2,* 307–320.

Seligman, M. E. P. (1975). *Helplessness.* San Francisco: W. H. Freeman.

Seligman, M. E. P. (1992). Wednesday's children. *Psychol. Today, 25*(1), 61.

Seligman, M. E. P. (1995). The effectiveness of psychotherapy. The *Consumer Reports* study. *Amer. Psychol., 50*(12), 965–974.

Seligman, M. E. P. (1996). A creditable beginning. *Amer. Psychol., 51*(10), 1086–1088.

Seligman, M. E. P., Abramson, L., Semmel, A., & von Baeyar, C. (1984). Depressive attributional style. *Southern Psychol., 2*(1), 18–22.

Seligman, M. E. P., Castellon, C., Cacciola, J., Schulman, P. et al. (1988). Explanatory style change during cognitive therapy for unipolar depression. *J. Abnorm. Psychol., 97*(1), 13–18.

Seligmann, J., Rogers, P., & Annin, P. (1994, May 2). The pressure to lose. *Newsweek,* pp. 60–61.

Selkoe, D. J. (1992). Alzheimer's disease: New insights into an emerging epidemic. *J. Geriat. Psychiat., 25*(2), 211–227.

Selkoe, D. J., Yamazaki, T., Citron, M., Podlisny, M. B., Koo, E. H., Teplow, D. B., & Haass, C. (1996). The role of APP processing and trafficking pathways in the formation of Amyloid ***B***-protein. In R. J. Wurtman, S. Corkin, J. H. Growdon, & R. M. Nitsch (Eds.), *The neurobiology of Alzheimer's disease.* New York: The New York Academy of Sciences.

Selling, L. S. (1940). *Men against madness.* New York: Greenberg.

Selye, H. (1974). *Stress without distress.* Philadelphia: Lippincott.

Selye, H. (1976). *Stress in health and disease.* Woburn, MA: Butterworth.

Semans, J. H. (1956). Premature ejaculation: A new approach. *South. Med. J., 49,* 353–357.

Senter, N. W., Winslade, W. J., Liston, E. H. et al. (1984). *Electroconvulsive therapy.* Bethesda, MD: NIH and NIMH.

Seppa, N. (1996). Bullies spend less time with adults. *APA Monitor, 27*(10), 41.

Seppa, N. (1996). Helping people identify and cope with anxieties. *APA Monitor, 27*(6), 24.

Seppa, N. (1996). Psychologist testifies on handling disasters. *APA Monitor, 27*(11), 38.

Sereno, A. B. & Holzman, P. S. (1995). Antisaccades and smooth pursuit eye movements in schizophrenia. *Bio. Psychiat. 37*(6), 394–401.

Seto, M. C., Khattar, N. A., Lalumière, & Quinsey, V. L. (1997). Deception and sexual strategy in psychopathy. *Pers. Individ. Diff., 22*(3), 301–307.

Settlage, C. F. (1994). On the contribution of separation-individuation theory to psychoanalysis: Developmental process, pathogenesis, therapeutic process, and technique. In S. Kramer & S. Akhtar (Eds.), *Mahler and Kohut: Perspectives on development, psychopathology, and technique.* Northvale, NJ: Jason Aronson.

Shader, R. I., & Greenblatt, D. J. (1993, May 13). Use of benzodiazepines in anxiety disorders. *N. Engl. J. Med.,* pp. 1398–1405.

Shadish, W. R., Montgomery, L. M., Wilson, P., Wilson, M. R., Bright, I., & Okwumakua, T. (1993). The effects of family and marital psychotherapies: A meta-analysis. *J. Cons. Clin. Psychol., 61,* 61.

Shadish, W. R., Ragsdale, K., Glaser, R. R., & Montgomery, L. M. (1995). The efficacy and effectiveness of marital and family therapy: A perspective from meta-analysis. [Special issue: The effectiveness of marital and family therapy]. *J. Marital Fam. Ther., 21*(4), 345–360.

Shafii, M., Carrigan, S., Whittinghill, J. R., & Derrick, A. (1985). Psychological autopsy of completed suicide in children and adolescents. *Amer. J. Psychiat., 142*(9), 1061–1064.

Shaham, Y., Rajabi, H., & Stewart, J. (1996). Relapse to heroin-seeking in rats under opioid maintenance: The effects of stress, heroin priming, and withdrawal. *J. Neurosci., 16*(5), 1957–1963.

Shain, M. (1994). Alternatives to drug testing: Employee assistance and health promotion programs. In S. Macdonald & P. Roman (Eds.), *Research advances in alcohol and drug problems: Vol. 11: Drug testing in the workplace.* New York: Plenum Press.

Shalev, A. Y., Bonne, O., & Eth, S. (1996). Treatment of posttraumatic stress disorder: A review. *Psychosom. Med., 58,* 165–182.

Shalev, A. Y., Peri, T., Canetti, L., & Schreiber, S. (1996). Predictors of PTSD in injured trauma survivors: A prospective study. *Amer. J. Psychiat., 153,* 219–225.

Shaner, A., Khalsa, M., Roberts, L., Wilkins, J., Anglin, D., & Hsieh, S. (1993). Unrecognized cocaine use among schizophrenic patients. *Amer. J. Psychiat., 150*(5), 758–762.

Shapiro, D. A. (1982). Overview: Clinical and physiological comparison of meditation with other self-control strategies. *Amer. J. Psychiat., 139*(3), 267–274.

Shapiro, F. (1989). Efficacy of the eye movement desensitization procedure in the treatment of traumatic memories. *J. Traum. Stress, 2,* 199–223.

Shapiro, F. (1989). Eye movement desensitization: A new treatment for post-traumatic stress disorder. *J Behav. Ther. Exp. Psychiat., 20,* 211–217.

Shapiro, F. (1991). Eye movement desensitization and reprocessing procedure: From EMD to EMD/R – A new model for anxiety and related traumata. *Behav. Therapist, 14,* 133–135.

Shapiro, L. (1996, January 22). To your health? *Newsweek,* pp. 52–53.

Sharan, P., Chaudhary, G., Kavathekar, S. A., & Saxena, S. (1996). Preliminary report of psychiatric disorders in survivors of a severe earthquake. *Amer. J. Psychiat., 153,* 556–558.

Sharp, C. W., & Freeman, C. P. L. (1993). The medical complications of anorexia nervosa. *Brit. J. Psychiat., 162,* 452–462.

Shaunesey, K., Cohen, J. L., Plummer, B., & Berman, A. (1993). Suicidality in hospitalized adolescents: Relationship to prior abuse. *Amer. J. Orthopsychiat., 63*(1), 113–119.

Shaw, B. F. (1976). A systematic investigation of two psychological treatments of depression. *Dissertation Abstr. Inter., 36*(8-B), 4179–4180.

Shaw, B. F. (1977). Comparison of cognitive therapy and behavior therapy in the treatment of depression. *J. Clin. Psychol., 45,* 543–551.

Shaw, J. (1990). Play therapy with the sexual workhorse: Successful treatment with twelve cases of inhibited ejaculation. *J. Sex Marital Ther., 16,* 159–164.

Shea, S. (1990). Contemporary psychiatric interviewing: Integration of DSM-III-R, psychodynamic concerns and mental status. In G. Goldstein & M. Hersen (Eds.), *Handbook of psychological assessment* (2nd ed.). New York: Pergamon Press.

Shedler, J., & Block, J. (1990). Adolescent drug use and psychological health: A longitudinal inquiry. *Amer. Psychol., 45*(5), 612–630.

Shedler, J., Mayman, M., & Manis, M. (1993). The illusion of mental health. *Amer. Psychol., 48*(11), 1117–1131.

Sheehan, M., Oppenheimer, E., & Taylor, C. (1993). Opiate users and the first years after treatment: Outcome analysis of the proportion of follow-up time spent in abstinence. *Addiction, 88,* 1679–1689.

Sheline, Y., & Beattie, M. (1992). Effects of the right to refuse treatment medication in an emergency psychiatric service. *Hosp. Comm. Psychiat., 43*(6), 640–642.

Shelton, R. C., Davidson, J., Yonkers, K. A., Koran, L. et al. (1997). The undertreatment of dysthymia. *J. Clin. Psychiat., 58*(2), 59–65.

Sher, K. J., & Trull, T. J. (1994). Personality and disinhibitry psychopathology: Alcoholism and antisocial personality disorder. *J. Abnorm. Psychol., 103*(1), 92–102.

Sheras, P., & Worchel, S. (1979). *Clinical psychology: A social psychological approach.* New York: Van Nostrand.

Sherbourne, C. D., Hays, R. D., & Wells, K. B. (1995). Personal and psychosocial risk factors for physical and mental health outcomes and course of depression among depressed patients. *J. Cons. Clin. Psychol., 63*(3), 345–355.

Sherbourne, C. D., Jackson, C. A., Meredith, L. S., Camp, P., & Wells, K. B. (1996). Prevalence of comorbid anxiety disorders in primary care outpatients. *Arch. Fam. Med., 5*(1), 27–34.

Sherer, M. (1985). Depression and suicidal ideation in college students. *Psychol. Rep., 57*(3, Pt. 2), 1061–1062.

Sherfey, M. J. (1973). *The nature and evolution of female sexuality.* New York: Vintage.

Sherlock, R. (1983). Suicide and public policy: A critique of the "New Consensus." *J. Bioethics, 4,* 58–70.

Sherman, C. (1993). Behind closed doors: therapist-client sex. *Psychol. Today, 26*(3), 64–72.

Sherman, D. K., McGue, M. K., & Iacono, W. G. (1997). Twin concordance for attention deficit hyperactivity disorder: A comparison of teachers' and mothers' reports. *Amer. J. Psychiat., 154*(4), 532–535.

Sherman, L. W. (1992). *Policing domestic violence.* New York: Free Press.

Sherman, R., & Thompson, R. (1990). *Bulimia: A guide for family and friends.* Lexington, MA: Lexington.

Sherman, R. A., Camfield, M. R., & Arena, J. G. (1995). The effect of presence or absence of low back pain on the MMPI's conversion V. *Mil. Psychol., 7*(1), 29–38.

Sherrington, C. S. (1906). *Integrative action of the nervous system.* New Haven, CT: Yale University Press.

Shi, J., Benowitz, N., Denaro, C., & Sheiner, L. (1993). Pharmacokinetic-pharmacodynamic modeling of caffeine: Tolerance to pressor effects. *Clin. Pharmacol. Ther., 53*(1), 6–15.

Shi, J. M., O'Connor, P. G., Constantino, J. A. et al. (1993). Three methods of ambulatory opiate detoxification. In L. S. Harris (Ed.), *Preliminary results of a randomized clinical trial* (NIDA Res. Monograph Series No. 132, NIH Publication No. 93-3505). Washington, DC: U. S. Government Printing Office.

Shnayerson, M. (1996, July). Natural opponents. *Vanity Fair,* pp. 98–105.

Shneidman, E. S. (1963). Orientations toward death: Subintentioned death and indirect suicide. In R. W. White (Ed.), *The study of lives.* New York: Atherton.

Shneidman, E. S. (1973). Suicide notes reconsidered. *Psychiatry, 36,* 379–394.

Shneidman, E. S. (1979). An overview: Personality, motivation, and behavior theories. In L. D. Hankoff & B. Einsidler (Eds.), *Suicide: Theory and clinical aspects.* Littleton, MA: PSG Publishing Company.

Shneidman, E. S. (1981). Suicide. *Suic. Life-Threat. Behav., 11*(4), 198–220.

Shneidman, E. S. (1985). *Definition of suicide.* New York: Wiley.

Shneidman, E. S. (1987, March). At the point of no return. *Psychol. Today.*

Shneidman, E. S. (1991). *The key to suicide.* In personal correspondence.

Shneidman, E. S. (1993). *Suicide as psychache: A clinical approach to self-destructive behavior.* Northvale, NJ: Jason Aronson.

Shneidman, E. S., & Farberow, N. (1968). The Suicide Prevention Center of Los Angeles. In H. L. P. Resnick (Ed.), *Suicidal behaviors: Diagnosis and management.* Boston: Little, Brown.

Shrivastava, R. K., Shrivastava, S., Overweg, N., & Schmitt, M. (1995). Amantadine in the treatment of sexual dysfunction associated with selective serotonin reuptake inhibitors. *J. Clin. Psychopharmacol., 15*(1), 83–84.

Shtasel, D. L., Gur, R. E., Gallacher, F., Heimburg, C., et al. (1992). Gender differences in the clinical expression of schizophrenia. *Schizo. Res., 7*(3), 225–231.

Shucksmith, J., Glendinning, A., & Hendry, L. (1997). Adolescent drinking behaviour and the role of family life: A Scottish perspective. *J. Adolescence, 20,* 85–101.

Shuller, D. Y., & McNamara, J. R. (1980). The use of information derived from norms and from a credible source to counter expectancy effects in behavioral assessment. *Behav. Assess., 2,* 183–196.

Siegel, K. (1988). Rational suicide. In S. Lesse (Ed.), *What we know about suicidal behavior and how to treat it.* Northvale, NJ: Jason Aronson.

Siever, L. J. (1981). Schizoid and schizotypal personality disorders. In J. R. Lion (Ed.), *Personality disorders—Diagnosis and management.* Baltimore: Williams & Williams.

Siever, L. J. (1992). Schizophrenia spectrum personality disorders. In A. Tasman & M. B. Riba (Eds.), *American Psychiatric Press review of psychiatry* (Vol. 11). Washington, DC: American Psychiatric Press.

Siever, L. J., & Davis, K. L. (1991). A psychobiological perspective on the personality disorders. *Amer. J. Psychiat., 148*(12), 1647–1658.

Siever, L. J., Davis, K. L., & Gorman, L. K. (1991). Pathogenesis of mood disorders. In K. Davis, H. Klar, & J. T. Coyle (Eds.), *Foundations of psychiatry.* Philadelphia: Saunders.

Siever, L. J., Keefe, R., & Bernstein, D. (1990). Eye tracking impairment in clinically-identified patients with schizotypal personality disorder. *Amer. J. Psychiat., 147,* 740–745.

Siever, L. J., Silverman, J. M., Horvath, T. B. et al. (1990). Increased morbid risk for schizophrenia-related disorders in relatives of schizotypal personality disordered patientes. *Arch. Gen. Psychiat., 47*(7), 634–640.

Sifneos, P. E. (1987). *Short term dynamic psychotherapy evaluation and technique* (2nd ed.). New York: Plenum Press.

Sifneos, P. E. (1992). *Short-term anxiety-provoking psychotherapy: A treatment manual.* New York: Basic Books.

Sigerist, H. E. (1943). *Civilization and disease.* Ithaca, NY: Cornell University Press.

Sigmon, S. T. (1995). Ethical practices and beliefs of psychopathology researchers. *Ethics Behav., 5*(4), 295–309.

Silbersweig, D. A., Stern, E., Frith, C., Cahill, C., et al. (1995). A functional neuroanatomy of hallucinations in schizophrenia. *Nature, 378*(6553), 176–179.

Silver, H., Geraisy, N., & Schwartz, M. (1995). No difference in the effect of biperiden and amantadine on parkinsonian- and tardive dyskinesia-type involuntary movements: A double-blind crossover, placebo-controlled study in medicated chronic schizophrenic patients. *J. Clin. Psychiat., 56*(4), 167–170.

Silver, J. M., & Yudofsky, S. C. (1988). Psychopharmacology and electroconvulsive therapy. In J. A. Talbott, R. E. Hales, & S. C. Yudofsky (Eds.), *The American Psychiatric Press textbook of psychiatry.* Washington, DC: American Psychiatric Press.

Silverman, K., Evans, S. M., Strain, E. C., & Griffiths, R. R. (1992). Withdrawal syndrome after the double-blind cessation of caffeine consumption. *N. Engl. J. Med., 327*(16), 1109–1114.

Silverman, M. M. & Felner, R. D. (1995). The place of suicide prevention in the spectrum of intervention: Definitions of critical terms and constructs. [Special issue: Suicide prevention: Toward the year 2000]. *Suic. Life-Threat. Behav., 25*(1), 70–81.

Silverman, P. (1992). An introduction to self-help groups. In B. J. White & E. J. Madara (Eds.), *The self-help sourcebook: Finding & forming mutual aid self-help groups.* Denville, NJ: St. Clares-Riverside Medical Center.

Silverman, W. K., La Greca, A. M., & Wasserstein, S. (1995). What do children worry about? Worries and their relation to anxiety. *Child Dev., 66,* 671–686.

Silverstein, B., Perdue, L., Peterson, B., & Kelly, E. (1986). The role of mass media in promoting a thin standard of bodily attractiveness for women. *Sex roles, 14,* 519–532.

Silverstein, B., Perdue, L., Peterson, B., & Kelly, E. (1986). The role of mass media in promoting a thin standard of bodily attractiveness for women. *Sex roles, 14,* 519–532.

Silverstone, P. H. (1990). Low self-esteem in eating disordered patients in the absence of depression. *Psychol. Rep., 67*(1), 276–278.

Silverstone, T., & Hunt, N. (1992). Symptoms and assessment of mania. In E. S. Paykel (Ed.), *Handbook of affective disorders.* New York: Guilford.

Simeon, J. G., Ferguson, H. B., Knott, V., Roberts, N. et al (1992). Clinical, cognitive, and neurophysiological effects of alprazolam in children and adolescents with overanxious and avoidant disorders. Special section: New developments in pediatric psychopharmacology. *J. Amer. Acad. Child Adol. Psychiat., 31*(1), 29–33.

Simeonsson, N., Lorimer, M., Shelley, B., & Sturtz, J. L. (1995). Asthma: New information for the early interventionist. *Topics Early Childhood Spec. Educ., 15*(1), 32–43.

Simhandl, C., & Meszaros, K. (1992). The use of carbamazepine in the treatment of schizophrenia and schizoaffective psychoses: A review. *J. Psychiat. Neurosci., 17*(1), 1–14.

Simmon (1990). Media and market study. In skin deep: Our national obsession with looks. *Psychol. Today, 26*(3), 96.

Simon, G. E., & Katzelnick, D. J. (1997). Depression, use of medical services and cost-offset effects. *J. Psychosom. Res., 42*(4), 333–344.

Simon, G. E., Maier, W., Ustun, T. B., Linden, M., & Boyer, P. (1995). Research diagnosis of current depressive disorder: A comparison of methods using current symptoms and lifetime history. *J. Psychiatr. Res., 29*(6), 457–465.

Simon, Y., Bellisle, F., Monneuse, M. O., Samuel-Lajeunesse, B., & Drewnowski, A. (1993). *Brit. J. Psychiat., 162,* 244–246.

Simons, L. S. (1989). Privatization and the mental health system: A private sector view. *Amer. Psychol., 44*(8), 1138–1141.

Simons, R. C. (1981). Contemporary problems of psychoanalytic technique. *J. Amer. Psychoanal. Assoc., 29*(3), 643–658.

Simonsick, E. M., Wallace, R. B., Blazer, D. G., & Berkman, L. F. (1995). Depressive symptomatology and hypertension-associated morbidity and mortality in older adults. *Psychosom. Med., 57*(5), 427–435.

Simpson, C. J., Hyde, C. E., & Faragher, E. B. (1989). The chronically mentally ill in community facilities: A study of quality of life. *Brit. J. Psychiat., 154,* 77–82.

Simpson, R. L., & Sasso, G. M. (1992). Full inclusion of students with autism in general education settings: Values versus science. *Focus Autistic Behav., 7*(3), 1–13.

Simpson, R. O., & Halpin, G. (1986). Agreement between parents and teachers in using the Revised Behavior Problem Checklist to identify deviant behavior in children. *Behav. Disorders, 12*(1), 54–58.

Sines, L. K. (1959). The relative contribution of four kinds of data to accuracy in personality assessment. *J. Cons. Psychol., 23,* 483–495.

Singh, A., & Lucki, I. (1993). Antidepressant-like activity of compounds with varying efficacy at 5-HT receptors. *Neuropharmacology, 32*(4), 331–340.

Siomopoulos, V. (1988). Narcissistic personality disorder: Clinical features. *Amer. J. Psychother., 42*(2), 240–253.

Sipprelle, R. C. (1992). A Vet Center experience: Multievent trauma, delayed treatment type. In D. W. Foy (Ed.), *Treating PTSD: Cognitive-behavioral strategies. Treatment manuals for practitioners.* New York: Guilford.

Sizemore, C. C., & Huber, R. J. (1988). The twenty-two faces of Eve. *Individ. Psychol. J. Adlerian Theory Res. Prac., 44*(1), 53–62.

Skau, K., & Mouridsen, S. (1995). Munchausen syndrome by proxy: A review. *Acta Paediatr., 84,* 977–982.

Skelton, M. D., Boik, R. J., & Madero, J. N. (1995). Thought disorder on the WAIS—R relative to the Rorschach: Assessing identity-disordered adolescents. *J. Pers. Assess., 65*(3), 533–549.

Skinner, B. F. (1948). Superstition in the pigeon. *J. Exp. Psychol., 38,* 168–172.

Skoff, B. F., Mirsky, A. F., & Turner, D. (1980). Prolonged brainstem transmission time in autism. *Psychiat. Res., 2,* 157–166.

Slade, P. (1995). Prospects for prevention. In G. Szmukler, C. Dare, & J. Treasure (Eds.), *Handbook of eating disorders: Theory, treatment and research.* Chichester, England: Wiley.

Slater, E., & Shields, J. (1969). Genetical aspects of anxiety. Special Publication No. 3. M. H. Lader (Ed.). *Brit. J. Psychiat.,* pp. 62–71.

Sleek, S. (1995). Online therapy services raise ethical questions. *APA Monitor, 26*(11), 9.

Sleek, S. (1995). Rallying the troops inside our bodies. *APA Monitor, 26*(12), 1, 24.

Sleek, S. (1996). AIDS therapy: Patchwork of pain, hope. *APA Monitor, 27*(6), 1, 31.

Sleek, S. (1996). Practitioners will eventually have to meet steeper criteria to practice geropsychology, experts predict. *APA Monitor, 27*(10), 17.

Slife, B. D., & Weaver, C. A., III. (1992). Depression, cognitive skill, and metacognitive skill in problem solving. *Cog. Emot., 6*(1), 1–22.

Sloane, R. B., Staples, F. R., Cristol, A. H., Yorkson, N. J., & Whipple, K. (1975). *Psychotherapy versus behavior therapy.* Cambridge, MA: Harvard University Press.

Slovenko, R. (1992). Is diminished capacity really dead? *Psychiat. Ann., 22*(11), 566–570.

Slovenko, R. (1995). *Psychiatry and criminal culpability.* New York: Wiley.

Slutske, W. S., Heath, A. C., Dinwiddie, S. H., Madden, P. A. F. et al. (1997). Modeling genetic and environmental influences in the etiology of conduct disorder: A study of 2,682 adult twin pairs. *J. Abnorm. Psychol., 106*(2), 266–279.

Small, G. W., Mazziotta, J. C., Collins, M. T., Baxter, W. R. et al. (1995). Apolipoprotein E type 4 allele and cerebral glucose metabolism in relatives at risk for familial Alzheimer disease. *JAMA, 273*(12), 942–947.

Small, J. A., Kemper, S., & Lyon, K. (1997). Sentence comprehension in Alzheimer's disease: Effects of grammatical complexity, speech rate, and repetition. *Psychol. Aging, 12*(1), 3–11.

Small, M. A. (1992). The legal context of mentally disordered sex offender (MDSO) treatment programs. *Criminal Justice Behav., 19*(2), 127–142.

Smith, A. L., & Weissman, M. M. (1992). Epidemiology. In E. S. Paykel (Ed.), *Handbook of affective disorders.* New York: Guilford.

Smith, E., North, C., & Spitznagel, E. (1993). Alcohol, drugs, and psychiatric comorbidity among homeless women: An epidemiologic study. *J. Clin. Psychiat., 54*(3), 82–87.

Smith, G. R., Rost, K., & Kashner, T. M. (1995). A trial of the effect of a standardized psychiatric consultation on health outcomes and costs in somatizing patients. *Arch. Gen. Psychiat., 52*(3), 238–243.

Smith, H. (1995). *Unhappy children: Reasons and remedies.* London: Free Association Books.

Smith, K. (1991). Comments on "Teen suicide and changing cause-of-death certification, 1953–1987." *Suic. Life-Threat. Behav., 21*(3), 260–262.

Smith, K., & Killam, P. (1994). Munchausen syndrome by proxy. *MCN, 19,* 214–221.

Smith, M. J., Brebion, G., Banquet, J. P., & Cohen, L. (1995). Retardation of mentation in depressives: Posner's covert orientation of visual attention test. *J. Affect. Disorders, 35,* 107–115.

Smith, M. L., & Glass, G. V. (1977). Meta-analysis of psychotherapy outcome studies. *Amer. Psychologist, 32*(9), 752–760.

Smith, M. L., Glass, G. V., & Miller, T. I. (1980). *The benefits of psychotherapy.* Baltimore: Johns Hopkins University.

Smith, R. E. (1988). The logic and design of case study research. *Sport Psychologist, 2*(1), 1–12.

Smith, R. R., & Lombardo, V. S. (1995). Rational cognitive therapy with public offenders. *J. Rat.-Emot. & Cog.-Behav. Ther., 13*(4), 255–260.

Smith, S. (1991). Mental health malpractice in the 1990s. *Houston Law Rev., 28,* 209–283.

Smith, W. H. (1993). Incorporating hypnosis into the psychotherapy of patients with multiple personality disorder. *Bull. Menninger Clin., 57*(3), 344–354.

Smith-Bell, M. & Winslade, W. J. (1994). Privacy, confidentiality, and privilege in psychotherapeutic relationships. *Amer. J. Orthopsychiat., 64,* 180–193.

Smolan, R., Moffitt, P., & Naythons, M. (1990). *The power to heal: Ancient arts & modern medicine.* New York: Prentice Hall.

Smyer, M. A. (1989). Nursing homes as a setting for psychological practice: Public policy perspectives. *Amer. Psychologist, 44*(10), 1307–1314.

Snow, E. (1976, December). In the snow. *Texas Monthly Magazine.*

Snowden, P. (1997). Practical aspects of clinical risk assessment and management. *Brit. J. Psychiat., 170*(Suppl.32), 32–34.

Snyder, C. R. (1955). Studies of drinking in Jewish culture. IV. Culture and sobriety. A study of drinking patterns and sociocultural factors related to sobriety among Jews. *Quart. J. Stud. Alcohol., 16,* 263–289, 700–742.

Snyder, D. K., Wills, R. M., & Grady-Fletcher, A. (1991). Risks and challenges of long-term psychotherapy outcome research: Reply to Jacobson. *J. Cons. Clin. Psychol., 59*(1), 146–149.

Snyder, F. (1970). The phenomenology of dreaming. In L. Madlow & L. Snow (Eds.), *The psychodynamic implications of the physiological studies on dreams.* Springfield, IL: Thomas.

Snyder, M. L. (1992). Unemployment and suicide in Northern Ireland. *Psychol. Rep., 70*(3, Pt. 2), 1116–1118.

Snyder, S. (1976). Dopamine and schizophrenia. *Psychiatr. Ann., 8*(1), 53–84.

Snyder, S. (1976). The dopamine hypotheses of schizophrenia: Focus on the dopamine receptor. *Amer. J. Psychiat., 133*(2), 197–202.

Snyder, S. (1980). *Biological aspects of mental disorder.* New York: Oxford University Press.

Snyder, S. (1986). *Drugs and the brain.* New York: Scientific American Library.

Snyder, S. (1991). Drugs, neurotransmitters, and the brain. In P. Corsi (Ed.), *The enchanted loom: Chapters in the history of neuroscience.* New York: Oxford University Press.

Snyder, S., Burt, D. R., & Creese, I. (1976). The dopamine receptor of mammalian brain: Direct demonstration of binding to agonist and antagonist states. *Neurosci. Symp., 1,* 28–49.

Snyder, W. V. (1947). *Casebook of non-directive counseling,* Boston: Houghton Mifflin.

Sobell, M. B., & Sobell, L. C. (1973). Individualized behavior therapy for alcoholics. *Behav. Ther., 4*(1), 49–72.

Sobell, M. B., & Sobell, L. C. (1976). Second year treatment outcome of alcoholics treated by individualized behavior therapy: Results. *Behav. Res. Ther., 14*(3), 195–215.

Sobell, M. B., & Sobell, L. C. (1984). The aftermath of heresy: A response to Pendery et al.'s (1982) critique of "Individualized Behavior Therapy for Alcoholics." *Behav. Res. Ther., 22*(4), 413–440.

Sobell, M. B., & Sobell, L. C. (1984). Under the microscope yet again: A commentary on Walker and Roach's critique of the Dickens Committee's enquiry into our research. *Brit. J. Addic., 79*(2), 157–168.

Sobin, C., & Sackeim, H. A. (1997). Psychomotor symptoms of depression. *Amer. J. Psychiat., 154,* 4–17.

Sohlberg, S., & Norring, C. (1992). A three-year prospective study of life events and course for adults with anorexia nervosa/bulimia nervosa. *Psychosom. Med., 54*(1), 59–70.

Sokol-Kessler, L., & Beck, A. T. (1987). *Cognitive treatment of panic disorders.* Paper presented at the 140th annual meeting of the American Psychiatric Association, Chicago.

Solomon, D. A., Keitner, G. I., Miller, I. W., Shea, M. T., & Keller, M. B. (1995). Course of illness and maintenance treatments for patients with bipolar disorder. *J. Clin. Psychiat., 56*(1), 5–13.

Solomon, P., Draine, J., Mannion, E., & Meisel, M. (1996). Impact of brief family psychoeducation on self-efficacy. *Schizo. Bull., 22*(1), 41–50.

Solomon, R. L. (1980). The opponent-process theory of acquired motivation: The costs of pleasure and the benefits of pain. *Amer. Psychol., 35,* 691–712.

Solomon, R. L., Kamin, L. J., & Wynne, L. C. (1953). Traumatic avoidance learning: The outcomes of several extinction procedures with dogs. *J. Abnorm. Soc. Psychol., 48,* 291–302.

Soltys, S. M. (1992). Pyromania and firesetting behaviors. *Psychiatr. Ann., 22*(2), 79–83.

Somasundaram, D. J. & Rajadurai, S. (1995). War and suicide in northern Sri Lanka. *Acta Psychiatr. Scandin., 91*(1), 1–4.

Somer, E. (1995). Biofeedback-aided hypnotherapy for intractable phobic anxiety. *Amer. J. Clin. Hypnother., 37*(3), 54–64.

Somova, L. I., Diarra, K., & Jacobs, T. Q. (1995). Psychophysiological study of hypertension in Black, Indian and White African students. *Stress Med., 11*(2), 105–111.

Sorokin, J. E., Giordani, B., Mohs, R. C., Losonczy, M. F. et al. (1988). Memory impairment in schizophrenic patients with tardive dyskinesia. *Bio. Psychiat., 23*(2), 129–135.

Spalter, A. R., Gwirtsman, H. E., Demitrack, M. A., & Gold, P. W. (1993). Thyroid function in bulimia nervosa. *Bio. Psychiat., 33,* 408–414.

Spanier, C., Shiffman, S., Maurer, A., Reynolds, W., & Quick, D. (1996). Rebound following failure to quit smoking: The effects of attributions and self-efficacy. *Exp. Clin. Psychopharmacol., 4*(2), 191–197.

Spanos, N. P., Burgess, C. A., DuBreuil, S. C., Liddy, S., et al. (1995). The effects of simulation and expectancy instructions on responses to cognitive skill training for enhancing hypnotizability. Special Issue: To the memory of Nicholas Spanos. *Contemp. Hyp., 12*(1), 1–11.

Spanos, N. P., & Coe, W. C. (1992). A social-psychological approach to hypnosis. In E. Fromm & M. R. Nash (Eds.), *Contemporary hypnosis research.* New York: Guilford.

Sparr, L. F., Boehnlein, J. K., & Cooney, T. G. (1986). The medical management of the paranoid patient. *Gen. Hosp. Psychiat., 8*(1), 49–55.

Speckens, A. E. M., Hengeveld, M. W., Lycklama-a-Nijeholt, G., van Hemert, A. M., et al. (1995). Psychosexual functioning of partners of men with presumed non-organic erectile dysfunction: Cause or consequence of the disorder? *Arch. Sex. Behav., 24*(2), 157–172.

Spector, I. P., & Carey, M. P. (1990). Incidence and prevalence of sexual dysfunctions: A critical review of the empirical literature. *Archives of Sexual Behavior, 19*(4), 389–408.

Spiegel, D. (1994). Dissociative disorders. In R. E. Hales, S. C. Yudofsky, & J. A. Talbott (Eds.), *The American Psychiatric Press textbook of psychiatry,* (2nd ed.). Washington, DC: American Psychiatric Press.

Spiegel, D., Bloom, J. R., Kraemer, H. C., & Gottheil, E. (1989). The beneficial effect of psychosocial treatment on survival of metastatic breast cancer patients: A randomized prospective outcome study. *Lancet, 2,* 888.

Spiegel, R. (1965). Communication with depressive patients. *Contemp. Psychoanal., 2,* 30–35.

Spielberger, C. D. (1966). Theory and research on anxiety. In C. D. Spielberger (Ed.), *Anxiety and behavior.* New York: Academic Press.

Spielberger, C. D. (1972). Anxiety as an emotional state. In C. D. Spielberger (Ed.), *Anxiety: Current trends in theory and research* (Vol. 1). New York: Academic Press.

Spielberger, C. D. (1972). Conceptual and methodological issues in anxiety research. In C. D. Spielberger (Ed.), *Anxiety: Current trends in theory and research* (Vol. 2). New York: Academic Press.

Spielberger, C. D. (1985). Anxiety, cognition, and affect: A state-trait perspective. In A. H. Tuma & J. Maser (Eds.), *Anxiety and the anxiety disorders.* Hillsdale, NJ: Erlbaum.

Spielrein, S. (1995). [On the psychological content of a case of schizophrenia (dementia praecox).] *Evolution Psychiatr., 60*(1), 69–95. [French.]

Spirito, A., Brown, L., Overholser, J., & Fritz, G. (1989). Attempted suicide in adolescence: A review and critique of the literature. *Clin. Psychol. Rev., 9,* 335–363.

Spitz, H. H. (1994). Lewis Carroll's formula for calendar calculating. *Amer. J. Ment. Retard., 98*(5), 601–606.

Spitz, R. A. (1945). Hospitalization: An inquiry into the genesis of psychiatric conditions of early childhood. In R. S. Eissler, A. Freud, H. Hartman, & E. Kris (Eds.), *The psychoanalytic study of the child* (Vol. 1). New York: International Universities Press.

Spitz, R. A. (1946). *Anaclitic depression. The psychoanalytic study of the child* (Vol. 2). New York: International Universities Press.

Spitzer, J. (1990). On treating patients diagnosed with narcissistic personality disorder: The induction phase. *Issues Ego Psychol., 13*(1), 54–65.

Spitzer, R. L., Gibbon, M., Skodol, A. E., Williams, J. B. W., & First, M. B. (Eds.) (1994). *DSM-IV Casebook: A learning companion to the diagnostic and statistical manual of mental disorders* (4th ed.). Washington, DC: American Psychiatric Press.

Spitzer, R. L., Skodol, A., Gibbon, M., & Williams, J. B. W. (1981). *DSM-III case book* (1st ed.). Washington, DC: American Psychiatric Press.

Spitzer, R. L., Skodol, A. E., Gibbon, M., & Williams, J. B. W. (1983). *Psychopathology: A case book.* New York: McGraw-Hill Book Company.

Spitzer, R. L., Skodol, A., Gibbon, M., & Williams, J. B. W. (1983). *Psychopathology: A case book.* New York: McGraw-Hill.

Sponheim, S. R., Iacono, W. G., Clementz, B. A., & Beiser, M. (1997). Season of birth and electroencephalogram power abnormalities in schizophrenia. *Bio. Psychiat., 41,* 1020–1027.

Spoont, M. R. (1996). Emotional instability. In C. G. Costello (Ed.), *Personality characteristics of the personality disordered.* New York: Wiley.

Spoov, J., Suominen, J. Y., Lahdelma, R. L., Katila, H., Kymalainen, O., Isometsa, E., Liukko, H., & Auvinen, J. (1993). Do reversed depressive symptoms occur together as a syndrome? *J. Affect. Disorders, 27,* 131–134.

Squire, L. R. (1977). ECT and memory loss. *Amer. J. Psychiat., 134,* 997–1001.

Squire, L. R., & Slater, P. C. (1983). Electroconvulsive therapy and complaints of memory dysfunction: A prospective three-year follow-up study. *Brit. J. Psychiat., 142,* 1–8.

Squires, R. F., & Braestrup, C. (1977). Benzodiazepine receptors in rat brain. *Nature, 266*(5604), 732–734.

Stacey, J. (1996, February 12). Family life: A changing national portrait. *USA Today,* p. 6D.

Stack, S. (1981). Comparative analysis of immigration and suicide. *Psychol. Rep., 49*(2), 509–510.

Stack, S. (1987). Celebrities and suicide: A taxonomy and analysis, 1948–1983. *Amer. Sociol. Rev., 52,* 401–412.

Stahl, S. M., & Soefje, S. (1995). Panic attacks and panic disorder: The great neurologic imposters. *Sem. Neurol., 15*(2), 126–132.

Stahmer, A. C., & Schreibman, L. (1992). Teaching children with autism appropriate play in unsupervised environments using a self-management treatment package. *J. Appl. Behav. Anal., 25*(2), 447–459.

Stampfl, T. G., & Levis, D. J. (1967). Essentials of implosive therapy: A learning theory-based psychodynamic behavioral therapy. *J. Abnorm. Psychol., 72,* 496–503.

Stanford, S. C., & Salmon, P. (1993). *Stress: From synapse to syndrome.* London: Academic Press.

Stanley, M. (1991). Post mortem studies of suicide. In L. Davidson & M. Linnoila (Eds.), *Risk factors for youth suicide.* New York: Hemisphere.

Stanley, M. A., & Turner, S. M. (1995). Current status of pharmacological and behavioral treatment of obsessive-compulsive disorder. *Behav. Ther., 26*(1), 163–186.

Stanley, M., Stanley, B., Traskman-Bendz, L., Mann, J. J., & Meyendorff, E. (1986). Neurochemical findings in suicide completers and suicide attempters. In R. W. Maris (Ed.), *Biology of Suicide.* New York: Guilford.

Stanley, M., Virgilio, J., & Gershon, S. (1982). Tritiated imipramine binding sites are decreased in the frontal cortex of suicides. *Science, 216,* 1337–1339.

Staples, S. L. (1996). Human response to environmental noise. *Amer. Psychol., 51*(2), 143–150.

Stapleton, J., Russell, M., Feyerabend, C., Wiseman, S. et al. (1995). Dose effects and predictors of outcome in a randomized trial of transdermal nicotine patches in general practice. *Addiction, 90*(1), 31–42.

Stark-Adamek, C. (1992). Sexism in research: The limits of academic freedom. *Women Ther., 12*(4), 103–111.

Stattin, H., & Magnusson, D. (1980). Stability of perceptions of own reactions across a variety of anxiety-provoking situations. *Percept. Motor Skills, 51,* 959–967.

Staub, E. (1996). Cultural-societal roots of violence. The examples of genocidal violence and of contemporary youth violence in the United States. *Amer. Psychol., 51*(2), 117–132.

Steadman, H. J., Monahan, J., Robbins, P. C., Appelbaum, P., Grisso, T., Klassen, D., Mulvey, E. P., & Roth, L. (1993). From dangerousness to risk assessment: Implications for appropriate research strategies. In S. Hodgins (Ed.), *Mental disorder and crime.* New York: Sage.

Steege, J. F. & Ling, F. W. (1993). Dyspareunia: A special type of chronic pelvic pain. *Obstetrics and Gynecology Clinics of North America, 20,* 779–793.

Steen, S. N., Oppliger, R. A., & Brownell, K. D. (1988). Metabolic effects of repeated weight loss and regain in adolescent wrestlers. *JAMA, 260,* 47–50.

Steiger, H., & Houle, L. (1991). Defense styles and object-relations disturbances among university women displaying varying degrees of "symptomatic" eating. *Inter. J. Eat. Disorders, 10*(2), 145–153.

Stein, D. J., Hollander, E., Anthony, D. T., Schneier, F. R., et al. (1992). Serotonergic medications for sexual obsessions, sexual addictions, and paraphilias. *J. Clin. Psychiat., 53*(8), 267–271.

Stein, D. J., Hollander, E., & Liebowitz, M. R. (1993). Neurobiology of impulsivity and the impulse control disorders. *J. Neuropsychiat. Clin. Neurosci., 5*(1), 9–17.

Stein, G., & Bernadt, M. (1993). Lithium augmentation therapy in tricyclic-resistant depression: A controlled trial using lithium in low and normal doses. *Brit. J. Psychiat., 162,* 634–640.

Stein, L. I. (1993). A system approach to reducing relapse in schizophrenia. *J. Clin. Psychiat., 54*(3 Suppl.), 7–12.

Stein, M. B., & Uhde, T. W. (1995). In A. F. Schatzberg & C. B. Nemeroff (Eds.), *The American Psychiatric Press textbook of psychopharmacology.* Washington, DC: American Psychiatric Press.

Stein, M. B., Walker, J. R., Anderson, G., Hazen, A. L., et al. (1996). Childhood physical and sexual abuse in patients with anxiety disorders and in a community sample. *Amer. J. Psychiat., 153*(2), 275–277.

Stein, M. B., Walker, J. R., & Forde, D. R. (1994). Setting diagnostic thresholds for social phobia: Considerations from a community survey of social anxiety. *Amer. J. Psychiat., 151*(3), 408–412.

Stein, Z., Susser, M., Saenger, G., & Marolla, F. (1972). Nutrition and mental performance. *Science, 178,* 708–713.

Steinberg, J. (1996, March 17). Implant to help dog get over post-neutering trauma. *The Fresno Bee,* p. B1.

Steinberg, M. & Hall, P. (1997). The SCID-D diagnostic interview and treatment planning in dissociative disorders. *Bull. Menninger Clin., 61*(1), 108–120.

Steinbrook, R. (1992). The polygraph test: A flawed diagnostic method. *N. Engl. J. Med., 327*(2), 122–123.

Steiner, H., Smith, C., Rosenkranz, R. T., & Litt, I. (1991). The early care and feeding of anorexics. *Child Psychiat. Human Dev., 21*(3), 163–167.

Steinhausen, H.-C. (1997). Annotation: Outcome of anorexia nervosa in the younger patient. *J. Child Psychol. Psychiat., 38*(3), 271–276.

Steketee, G. (1990). Personality traits and disorders in obsessive-compulsives. *J. Anxiety Disorders, 4*(4), 351–364.

Steketee, G., Chambless, D. L., Tran, G. Q., Worden, H., & Gillis, M. M. (1996). Behavioral avoidance test for obsessive compulsive disorder. *Behav. Res. Ther., 34*(1), 73–83.

Stellar, E. (1954). The physiology of motivation. *Psychol. Rev., 61,* 5–22.

Stengel, E. (1964). *Suicide and attempted suicide.* Baltimore: Penguin.

Stengel, E. (1974). *Suicide and attempted suicide* (2nd ed.). New York: Jason Aronson.

Stephens, R. S., & Curtin, L. (1995). Alcohol and depression: Effects on mood and biased processing of self-relevant information. *Psychol. Addic. Behav., 9*(4), 211–222.

Stern, G., & Kruckman, L. (1983). Multi-disciplinary perspectives on post-partum depression: An anthropological critique. *Soc. Sci. Med., 17,* 1027–1041.

Sternbach, L. H. (1982). The discovery of CNS active 1,4–benzodiazepines (chemistry). In E. Usdin, P. Skolnick, J. F. Tallman, Jr., et al. (Eds.), *Pharmacology of benzodiazepines.* London: Macmillan.

Sternberg, S. (1996). Human version of mad cow disease? *Sci. News, 149,* 228.

Sternberg, S. (1996). Of mad cows and Englishmen. *Sci. News, 150,* 238–239.

Stewart, J. W., Mercier, M. A., Agosti, V., Guardino, M., & Quitkin, F. M. (1993). Imipramine is effective after unsuccessful cognitive therapy: Sequential use of cognitive therapy and imipramine in depressed outpatients. *J. Clin. Psychopharmacol., 13,* 114–119.

Stewart, S. H., Zeitlin, S. B., & Samoluk, S. B. (1996). Examination of a three-dimensional drinking motives questionnaire in a young adult university student sample. *Behav. Res. Ther., 34*(1), 61–71.

Stillion, J. M. (1985). *Death and the sexes: An examination of differential longevity, attitudes, behaviors, and coping skills.* Washington, DC: Hemisphere.

Stillion, J. M. (1995). Through a glass darkly: Women and attitudes toward suicidal behavior. In S. S. Canetto & D. Lester (Eds.), *Women and suicidal behavior.* New York: Springer.

Stillion, J. M. & McDowell, E. E. (1996). *Suicide across the life span: Premature exits* (2nd ed.) Washington, DC: Taylor & Francis.

Stine, O. C., Xu-J., Koskela, R., McMahon, F. J., Gschwend, M., Friddle, C., Clark, C. D., McInnis, M. G., Simpson, S. G., Breschel, T. S. et al. (1995). Evidence for linkage of bipolar disorder to chromosome 18 with a parent of origin effect. *Amer. J. Hum. Genet., 57*(6), 1384–1394.

Stitzer, M. L., Iguchi, M. Y., Felch, L. J. (1992). Contingent take-home incentive: Effects on drug use of methadone maintenance patients. *J. Cons. Clin. Psychol., 60*(6), 927–934.

Stitzer, M. L., Iguchi, M. Y., Kidorf, M., Bigelow, G. E. (1993). Contingency management in methadone treatment: the case for positive incentives. *NIDA Research Monograph, 137,* 19–36.

Stix, G. (1996). Profile: Wayne B. Jonas. Probing medicine's outer reaches [news]. *Scientif. Amer., 275*(4), 52, 56.

Stix, G. (1996). Is genetic testing premature? *Scientif. Amer., 275*(3), 107.

Stix, G. (1996, January). Listening to culture: Psychiatry takes a leaf from anthropology. *Scientific Amer., 274* (1), 16, 21.

St. Lawrence, J. S., & Madakasira, S. (1992). Evaluation and treatment of premature ejaculation: A critical review. *Inter. J. Psychiat. Med., 22,* 77–97.

Stock, W. (1993). Inhibited female orgasm. In W. O'Donohue & J. Geer (eds.), *Handbook of sexual dysfunctions.* Boston: Allyn & Bacon.

Stokes, T. E., & Osnes, P. G. (1989). An operant pursuit of generalization. *Behav. Ther., 20*(3), 337–355.

Stolerman, I., & Jarvis, M. (1995). The scientific case that nicotine is addictive. *Psychopharmacology, 117*(1), 2–10.

Stoline, A. M., & Sharfstein, S. S. (1996). Practice in the eye of a hurricane, or how does the psychiatrist survive in an era of change? In L. J. Dickstein, M. B. Riba, & J. M. Oldham (Eds.), *Review of psychiatry,* (Vol. 15). Washington, DC: American Psychiatric Press.

Stone, A. A., Neale, J. M., Cox, D. S., Napoli, A., Valdimarsdottir, H., & Kennedy-Moore, E. (1994). Daily events are associated with a secretory immune response to an oral antigen in men. *Hlth. Psychol., 13,* 440–446.

Stone, M. H. (1989). Schizoid personality disorder. In American Psychiatric Association (Eds.), *Treatments of psychiatric disorders: A task force report of the American Psychiatric Association.* Washington, DC: American Psychiatric Press.

Stone, W. (1996). *Group psychotherapy for people with chronic mental illness.* New York: Guilford.

Stores, G. (1996). Practitioner review: Assessment and treatment of sleep disorders in children and adolescents. *J. Child Psychol. Psychiat., 37*(8), 907–925.

Stowe, Z., Casarella, J., Landry, J., & Nemeroff, C. (1995). Sertraline in the treatment of women with postpartum major depression. *Depression, 3,* 49–55.

Stoyva, J. M., & Budzynski, T. H. (1993). Biofeedback methods in the treatment of anxiety and stress disorders. In P. M. Lehrer & R. L. Woolfolk (Eds.), *Principles and practice of stress management* (2nd ed.). New York: Guilford.

Strakowski, S. M., Lonczak, H. S., Sax, K. W., West, S. A., Crist, R. M., & Thienhaus, O. J. (1995). The effects of race on diagnosis and disposition from a psychiatric emergency service. *J. Clin. Psychiat., 56*(3), 101–107.

Strange, P. G. (1992). *Brain biochemistry and brain disorders.* New York: Oxford University Press.

Strassberg, D. S., Kelly, M. P., Carroll, C., & Kircher, J. C. (1987). The psychophysiological nature of premature ejaculation. *Archives of Sexual Behavior, 16*(4), 327–336.

Strassberg, D. S., Mahoney, J. M., Schaugaard, M., & Hale, V. E. (1990). The role of anxiety in premature ejaculation: A psychophysiological model. *Arch. Sex. Behav., 15*(4), 251–157.

Strassman, R. J. (1995). Human psychopharmacology of N,N-dimethyltryptamine. Third IUPHAR Satellite Meeting: Clinical and preclinical studies of hallucinogens. *Behav. Brain Res., 73*(1–2) 121–124.

Strassman, R. J. (1995). Hallucinogenic drugs in psychiatric research and treatment: Perspectives and prospects. *J. Nerv. Ment. Dis., 183*(3), 127–138.

Straus, M. A., Gelles, R. J. (1986). Societal change and change in family violence from 1975 to 1985 as revealed by two national surveys. *J. Marriage Family, 48*(3), 465–479.

Strauss, J., & Ryan, R. (1987). Autonomy disturbances in subtypes of anorexia nervosa. *J. Abnorm. Psychol., 96*(3), 254–258.

Strauss, J. S. (1979). Social and cultural influences on psychopathology. *Annu. Rev. Psychol., 30,* 397–415.

Stravynski, A., & Greenberg, D. (1992). The psychological management of depression. *Acta Psychiatr. Scandin., 85*(6), 407–414.

Stravynski, A., Gaudette, G., Lesage, A., Arbel, N. et al. (1997). The treatment of sexually dysfunctional men without partners: A controlled study of three behavioural group approaches. *Brit. J. Psychiat., 170,* 338–344.

Stravynski, A., Grey, S., & Elie, R. (1987). Outline of the therapeutic process in social skills training with socially dysfunctional patients. *J. Cons. Clin. Psychol., 55*(2), 224–228.

Strecher, V., Kreuter, M., & Kobrin, S. (1995). Do cigarette smokers have unrealistic perceptions of their heart attack, cancer, and stroke risk? *J. Behav. Med., 18*(1), 45–54.

Streiner, D. L., & Adams, K. S. (1987). Evaluation of the effectiveness of suicide prevention programmes: A methodological perspective. *Suic. Life-Threat. Behav., 17,* 93–106.

Streissguth, A. P., Aase, J. M., Clarren, S. K., Randels, S. P., LaDue, R. A., & Smith, D. F. (1991). Fetal alcohol syndrome in adolescents and adults. *JAMA, 265,* 1961–1967.

Strelau, J. (1992). Introduction: Current studies on anxiety from the perspective of research conducted during the last three decades. In D. G. Forgays, T. Sosnowski, & K. Wrzesniewski (Eds.), *Anxiety: Recent developments in cognitive, psychophysiological, and health research.* Washington, DC: Hemisphere.

Stricker, G., & Trierweiler, S. J. (1995). The local clinical scientist. A bridge between science and practice. *Amer. Psychologist., 50*(12), 995–1002.

Strickland, B. R., Hale, W. D., & Anderson, L. K. (1975). Effect of induced mood states on activity and self-reported affect. *J. Cons. Clin. Psychol., 43*(4), 587.

Strickland, C. J. (1997). Suicide among American Indian, Alaskan Native, and Canadian Aboriginal youth: Advancing the research agenda. *Inter. J. Ment. Hlth., 25*(4), 11–32.

Striegel-Moore, R. H., Silberstein, L. R., & Rodin, J. (1986). Toward an understanding of risk factors for bulimia. *Amer. Psychol., 41*(3), 246–263.

Striegel-Moore, R. H., Silberstein, L. R., & Rodin, J. (1993). The social self in bulimia nervosa: Public self-consciousness, social anxiety, and perceived fraudulence. *J. Abnorm. Psychol., 102*(2), 297–303.

Strober, M. (1981). The relation of personality characteristics to body image disturbances in juvenile anorexia nervosa: A multivariate analysis. *Psychosom. Med., 43*(4), 323–330.

Strober, M. (1981). The significance of bulimia in juvenile anorexia nervosa: An exploration of possible etiological factors. *Inter. J. Eat. Disorders, 1,* 28–43.

Strober, M. (1983, May). *Familial depression in anorexia nervosa.* Paper presented at the meeting of the American Psychiatric Association, New York.

Strober, M. (1992). Family factors in adolescent eating disorders. In P. J. Cooper & A. Stein (Eds.), *Feeding problems and eating disorders in children and adolescents.* Philadelphia: Harwood Academic Publishers.

Strober, M., & Yager, J. (1985). A developmental perspective on the treatment of anorexia nervosa in adolescents. In D. M. Garner & P. E. Garfinkel (Eds.), *Handbook of psychotherapy for anorexia nervosa and bulimia.* New York: Guilford.

Stroebe, M., Gergen, M. M., Gergen, K. J., & Stroebe, W. (1992). Broken hearts or broken bonds: Love and death in historical perspectives. *Amer. Psychol., 47*(10), 1205–1212.

Strupp, H. H. (1989). Psychotherapy: Can the practitioner learn from the researcher? *Amer. Psychologist., 44,* 717–724.

Strupp, H. H. (1996). The tripartite model and the *Consumer Reports* study. *Amer. Psychologist, 51*(10), 1017–1024.

Stuart, R. B. (1975). Behavioral remedies for marital ills: A guide to the use of operant-interpersonal techniques. In A. S. Gurman & D. G.

Rice (Eds.), *Couples in conflict: New directions in marital therapy.* New York: Jason Aronson.

Stuart, R. B. (1980). *Helping couples change: A social learning approach to marital therapy.* New York: Guilford.

Stuart, S., & O'Hara, M. W. (1995). Interpersonal psychotherapy for postpartum depression: A treatment program. *J. Psychother. Prac.. Res., 4*(1), 18–29.

Stuhr, U., & Meyer, A. E. (1991). Hamburg short psychotherapy comparison experiment. In M. Crago & L. Beutler (Eds.), *Psychotherapy research: An international review of programmatic studies.* Washington, DC: American Psychological Association.

Stunkard, A., Berkowitz, R., Wadden, T., Tanrikut, C., Reiss, E., & Young L. (1996). Binge eating disorder and the night-eating syndrome. *Inter. J. Obesity, 20,* 1–6.

Stunkard, A. J. (1975). From explanation to action in psychosomatic medicine: The case of obesity. *Psychosom. Med., 37,* 195–236.

Stunkard, A. J., Sorenson, T. I. A., Hanis, C., Teasdale, T. W., et al. (1986). An adoption study of human obesity. *N. Engl. J. Med., 314,* 193–198.

Stunkard, A. J., & Wadden, T. A. (1992). Psychological aspects of severe obesity. *Amer. J. Clin. Nutrition, 55*(Suppl.), 524–532.

Sturgeon, V., & Taylor, J. (1980). Report of a five-year follow-up study of mentally disordered sex offenders released from Atascadero State Hospital in 1973. Criminal Justice *J. Western S. Univ., San Diego, 4,* 31–64.

Suddath, R. L., Christison, G. W., & Torrey, E. F. (1990). Anatomical abnormalities in the brains of monozygotic twins discordant for schizophrenia. *New England J. of Medicine, 322*(12), 789–794.

Suddath, R. L., Christison, G. W., Torrey, E. F., Casanova, M. F., & Weinberger, D. R. (1990). Anatomical abnormalities in the brains of monozygotic twins discordant for schizophrenia. *New England Journal of Medicine, 322,* 789–794.

Sudhalter, V., Cohen, I. L., Silverman, W., & Wolf-Schein, E. G. (1990). Conversational analyses of males with Fragile X, Down Syndrome, and autism: Comparison of the emergence of deviant language. *Amer. J. Ment. Retard., 94,* 431–441.

Sue, S. (1991). Ethnicity and culture in psychological research and practice. In L. Garnets, J. M. Jones, D. Kimmel, S. Sue, & C. Tavris (Eds.), *Psychological perspectives on human diversity in America.* Washington, DC: American Psychological Association.

Sue, S. (1991). Ethnicity and culture in psychological research and practice. In J. D. Goodchilds (Ed.), *Psychological perspectives on human diversity.* Washington, DC: American Psychological Association.

Sue, S., Zane, N., & Young, K. (1994). Research on psychotherapy with culturally diverse populations. In A. E. Bergin & S. L. Garfield (Eds.), *Handbook of psychotherapy and behavior change.* New York: Wiley.

Sugar, M. (1995). A clinical approach to childhood gender identity disorder. *Amer. J. Psychother., 49*(2), 260–281.

Sugarman, A., Quinlan, D., & Devenis, L. (1981). Anorexia nervosa as a defense against anaclitic depression. *Inter. J. Eat. Disorders, 1,* 44–61.

Suh, E., Diener, E., & Fujita, F. (1996). Events and subjective well-being: Only recent events matter. *J. Pers. Soc. Psychol., 70*(5), 1091–1102.

Suinn, R., & Richardson, F. (1971). Anxiety management training. A nonspecific behavior therapy program for anxiety control. *Behav. Ther., 2,* 498–510.

Sullivan, C. M., Tan, C., Basta, J., Rumptz, M. et al. (1992). An advocacy intervention program for women with abusive partners: Initial evaluation. *Amer. J. Comm. Psychol., 20*(3), 309–332.

Sullivan, E. V., Shear, P. K., Lim, K. O., Zipursky, R. B., & Pfefferbaum, A. (1996). Cognitive and motor impairments are related to gray matter volume deficits in schizophrenia. *Bio. Psychiat., 39,* 234–240.

Sullivan, H. S. (1953). *The interpersonal theory of psychiatry.* New York: Norton.

Sullivan, H. S. (1954). *The psychiatric interview.* New York: Norton.

Sullivan, H. S. (1962). *Schizophrenia as a human process.* New York: Norton.

Sullivan, M., & Younger, S. (1994). Depression, competence, and the right to refuse lifesaving medical treatment. *Amer. J. Psychiat., 151*(7), 971–978.

Sulser, F., Vetulani, J., & Mobley, P. L. (1978). Mode of action of antidepressant drugs. *Biomed. Pharmacol., 27*(3), 257–261.

Sultenfuss, J., & Geczy, B., Jr. (1996). Group therapy on state hospital chronic wards: Some guidelines. *Inter. J. Group Psychother., 46*(2), 163–176.

Sumiyoshi, T., Stockmeier, C. A., Overholser, J. C., Dilley, G. E., & Meltzer, H. Y. (1996). Serotonin receptors are increased in postmortem prefrontal cortex in schizophrenia. *Brain Res., 708,* 209–214.

Summers, M. (1996, December 9). Mister Clean. *People,* pp. 139–140.

Suokas, J., & Lonnqvist, J. (1991). Selection of patients who attempted suicide for psychiatric consultation. *Acta Psychiatr. Scandin., 83*(3), 179–182.

Suokas, J., & Lonnqvist, J. (1995). Suicide attempts in which alcohol is involved: A special group in general hospital emergency rooms. *Acta Psychiatr. Scandin., 91*(1), 36–40.

Suomi, S. J. (1991). Adolescent depression and depressive symptoms: Insights from longitudinal studies with rhesus monkeys. *J. Youth Adolescence, 20,* 273–287.

Suppes, T., Baldessarini, R. J., Faedda, G. L., & Tohen, M. (1991). Risk of recurrence following discontinuation of lithium treatment in bipolar disorder. *Arch. Gen. Psychiat., 48*(12), 1082–1088.

Suppes, T., Calabrese, J. R., Mitchell, P. B., Pazzaglia, P. J., Potter, W. Z., & Zarin, D. A. (1995). B. Algorithms for the treatment of bipolar, manic-depressive illness. *Psychopharmacol. Bull., 31*(3), 469.

Susnick, L. C., & Belcher, J. R. (1995). Why are they homeless?: The chronically mentally ill in Washington, DC. *Inter. J. Ment. Hlth., 24*(4), 70–84.

Susser, E., Miller, M., Valencia, E., Colson, P. et al. (1996). Injection drug use and risk of HIV transmission among homeless men with mental illness. *Amer. J. Psychiat., 153*(6), 794–798.

Susser, E., Neugebauer, R., Hoek, H. W., Brown, A. S. Lin, S., Labovitz, D., & Gorman, J. M. (1996). Schizophrenia after prenatal famine. *Arch. Gen. Psychiat., 53*(1), 25–31.

Suter, S. (1986). *Health psychophysiology: Mind-body interactions in wellness and illness.* Hillsdale, NJ: Erlbaum.

Sutker, P. B., Allain, A. N., & Winstead, D. K. (1993). Psychopathology and psychiatric diagnoses of World War II Pacific Theater prisoner of war survivors and combat veterans. *Amer. J. Psychiat., 150*(2), 240–245.

Sutker, P. B., Bugg, F., & West, J. A. (1993). Antisocial personality disorder. In P. B. Sutker & H. E. Adams (Eds.), *Comprehensive handbook of psychopathology* (2nd ed.). New York: Plenum Press.

Svartberg, M., & Stiles, T. C. (1991). Comparative effects of short-term psychodynamic psychotherapy: A meta-analysis. *J. Cons. Clin. Psychol., 59,* 704–714.

Svrakic, D. M. (1987). Pessimistic mood in narcissistic decompensation. *Amer. J. Psychoanal., 47*(1), 58–71.

Svrakic, D. M. (1989). Narcissistic personality disorder: A new clinical systematics. *Eur. J. Psychiat., 3*(4), 199–213.

Svrakic, D. M. (1990). Pessimism and depression: Clinical and phenomenological distinction. *Eur. J. Psychiat., 4*(3), 139–145.

Svrakic, D. M. (1990). The functional dynamics of the narcissistic personality. *Amer. J. Psychother., 44*(2), 189–203.

Swanson, J., Holzer, C., Ganju, V., & Jono, R. (1990). Violence and psychiatric disorder in the community: Evidence from the epidemiological catchment area surveys. *Hosp. Comm. Psychiat., 41,* 761–770.

Swanson, J., Morrissey, J. P., Goldstrom, I., Rudolph, L., & Manderscheid, R. W. (1993, August). *Demographic and diagnostic characteristics of inmates receiving mental health services in state adult correctional facilities: United States, 1988.* (Mental Health Statistical Note No. 209). Washington, DC: U. S. Department of Health and Human Services.

Swayze, V. W. (1995). Frontal leukotomy and related psychosurgical procedures in the era before antipsychotics (1935–1954): A historical overview. *Amer. J. Psychiat., 152*(4), 505–515.

Swedo, S. E., Pietrini, P., Leonard, H. L., Schapiro, M. B., et al. (1992). Cerebral glucose metabolism in childhood-onset obsessive-compulsive disorder: Revisualization during pharmacotherapy. *Arch. Gen. Psychiat., 49*(9), 690–694.

Swerdlow, J. L. (1995). Quiet miracles of the brain. *Natl. Geogr., 187*(6), 12–13.

Swoboda, K. J., & Jenike, M. A. (1995). Frontal abnormalities in a patient with obsessive-compulsive disorder: The role of structural lesions in obsessive-compulsive behavior. *Neurology, 45,* 2130–2134.

Swonger, A. K., & Constantine, L. L. (1983). *Drugs and therapy: A handbook of psychotropic drugs* (2nd ed.). Boston: Little, Brown.

Szapocznik, J., & Kurtines, W. M. (1993). Family psychology and cultural diversity: Opportunities for theory, research, and application. *Amer. Psychol., 48*(4), 400–407.

Szasz, T. (1997). The healing word: Its past, present, and future. In J. K. Zeig (Ed.), *The evolution of psychotherapy: The third conference.* New York: Brunner/Mazel.

Szasz, T. S. (1961). *The myth of mental illness: Foundations of a theory of personal conduct.* New York: Harper (Hoeber).

Szasz, T. S. (1963). *Law, liberty, and psychiatry.* Englewood Cliffs, NJ: Prentice Hall.

Szasz, T. S. (1963). *The manufacture of madness.* New York: Harper & Row.

Szasz, T. S. (1977). *Psychiatric slavery.* New York: Free Press.

Szasz, T. S. (1987). Justifying coercion through theology and therapy. In J. K. Zeig (Ed.), *The evolution of psychotherapy.* New York: Brunner/Mazel.

Szasz, T. S. (1991). The medicalization of sex. *J. Human. Psychol., 31*(3), 34–42.

Szmukler, G. I., & Patton, G. (1995). Sociocultural models of eating disorders. In G. Szmukler, C. Dare, & J. Treasure (Eds.), *Handbook of eating disorders: Theory, treatment and research.* Chichester, England: Wiley.

Szymanski, S., Lieberman, J., Alvir, J. M., Mayerhoff, D. et al. (1995). Gender differences in onset of illness, treatment response, course, and biologic indexes in first-episode schizophrenic patients. *Amer. J. Psychiat., 152*(5), 698–703.

Szymanski, S., Lieberman, J., Pollack, S., Kane, J. M., Safferman, A., Munne, R., Umbricht, D., Woerner, M., Masiar, S., & Kronig, M. (1996). Gender differences in neuroleptic nonresponsive clozapine-treated schizophrenics. *Bio. Psychiat., 39,* 249–254.

Szymanski, S. R., Cannon, T. D., Gallacher, F., Erwin, R. J., & Gur, R. E. (1996). Course of treatment response in first-episode and chronic schizophrenia. *Amer. J. Psychiat., 153*(4), 519–525.

Takanishi, R. (1993). The opportunities of adolescence—Research, interventions, and policy. *Amer. Psychol., 48*(2), 85–87.

Takano, Y., Tsukahara, T., Suzuki, T., Hara, T., et al. (1995). The improvement of psychiatric symptoms of schizophrenic patients during day care treatment. *Seishin Igaku (Clin. Psychiat.), 37*(4), 369–376.

Takei, N., van Os, J., & Murray, R. M. (1995). Maternal exposure to influenza and risk of schizophrenia: A 22 year study from the Netherlands. *J. Psychiatr. Res., 29*(6), 435–445.

Tallis, F. (1996). Compulsive washing in the absence of phobia and illness anxiety. *Behav. Res. Ther., 34*(4), 361–362.

Tam, W. C. C., & Sewell, K. W. (1995). Seasonality of birth in schizophrenia in Taiwan. *Schizo. Bull., 21*(1), 117–127.

Tambs, K., Harris, J. R., & Magnus, P. (1995). Sex-specific causal factors and effects of common environment for symptoms of anxiety and depression in twins. *Behav. Genet., 25*(1), 33–44.

Tanay, E. (1992). The verdict with two names. *Psychiatr. Ann., 22*(11), 571–573.

Tanney, B. (1995). Suicide prevention in Canada: A national perspective highlighting progress and problems. Special Issue: Suicide prevention: Toward the year 2000. *Suic. Life-Threat. Behav., 25*(1), 105–122.

Tanzi, R. C., St. George Hyslop, P. H., & Gusella, J. T. (1989). Molecular genetic approaches to Alzheimer's disease. *Trends Neurosci., 12*(4), 152–158.

Tartaglia, L. A., Dembski, M., Weng, X., Deng, N. et al. (1995). Identification and expression cloning of a leptin receptor, OB-R. *Cell, 83,* 1263–1271.

Tate, D. C., Reppucci, N. D., & Mulvey, E. P. (1995). Violent juvenile delinquents. *Amer. Psychol., 50*(9), 777–781.

Taube, C. A. (1990). Funding and expenditures for mental illness. In R. W. Manderscheid & M. A. Sonnenschein (Eds.), *Mental Health, United States, 1990.* (DHHS Publication No. ADM 90–1708). Washington, DC: U. S. Department of Health and Human Services.

Tavris, C. (1993). *Beware the incest-survivor machine.* New York: New York Times Review of Books.

Taylor, C. B., Farquhar, J. W., Nelson, E., & Agras, S. (1977). Relaxation therapy and high blood pressure. *Arch. Gen. Psychiat., 34,* 339–342.

Taylor, E. A., & Stansfeld, S. A. (1984). Children who poison themselves. *Brit. J. Psychiat., 145,* 127–135.

Taylor, E. R., Amodei, N., & Mangos, R. (1996). The presence of psychiatric disorders in HIV-infected women. *J. Couns. Dev., 74,* 345–351.

Taylor, J. R., & Carroll, J. L. (1987). Current issues in electroconvulsive therapy. *Psychol. Rep., 60*(3, Pt. 1).

Taylor, R. (1975). *Electroconvulsive treatment (ECT): The control of therapeutic power.* Exchange.

Taylor, S. (1995). Anxiety sensitivity: Theoretical perspectives and recent findings. *Behav. Res. Ther., 33*(3), 243–258.

Taylor, S., Koch, W. J., & McNally, R. J. (1992). How does anxiety sensitivity vary across the anxiety disorders? *J. Anxiety Disorders, 6*(3), 249–259.

Taylor, S., Woody, S., Koch, W. J., McLeon, P. D., & Anderson, K. W. (1996). Suffocation false alarms and efficacy of cognitive behavioral therapy for panic disorder. *Behav. Ther., 27,* 115–126.

Teichman, Y., Bar-El, Z., Shor, H., Sirota, P. et al. (1995). A comparison of two modalities of cognitive therapy (individual and marital) in treating depression. *Psychiat. Interpers. Biol. Process., 58*(2), 136–148.

Telch, C. F., & Agras, W. S. (1993). The effects of a very low calorie diet on binge eating. *Behav. Ther., 24,* 177–193.

Teller, V., & Dalh, H. (1995). What psychoanalysis needs is more empirical research. In T. Shapiro, & R. N. Emde (Eds.), *Research in psychoanalysis: Process, development, outcome.* Madison, CT: International Universities Press.

Telner, J. I., Lapierre, Y. D., Horn, E., & Browne, M. (1986). Rapid reduction of mania by means of reserpine therapy. *Amer. J. Psychiat., 143*(8), 1058.

Tenenbaum, J. (1983). ECT regulation reconsidered. *Ment. Disability Law Reporter, 7,* 148–157.

Teng, C. T., Akerman, D., Cordas, T. A., Kasper, S. et al. (1995). Seasonal affective disorder in a tropical country: A case report. *Psychiatr. Res., 56*(1), 11–15.

Tennant, C. (1988). Psychological causes of duodenal ulcer. *Austral. N. Zeal. J. Psychiat., 22*(2), 195–202.

Teplin, L. A., Abram, K. M., & McClelland, G. M. (1994). Does psychiatric disorder predict violent crime among released jail detainees? *Amer. Psychol., 49*(4), 335–342.

Teri, L., & Lewinsohn, P. M. (1986). Individual and group treatment of unipolar depression: Comparison of treatment outcome and identification of predictors of successful treatment outcome. *Behav. Ther., 17*(3), 215–228.

Terr, L. (1988). What happens to early memories of trauma? A study of twenty children under age five at the time of documented traumatic events. Annual Meeting of the American Psychiatry Association. *J. Amer. Acad. Child Adol. Psychiat., 27*(1), 96–104.

Terry, D., Mayocchi, L., & Hynes, G. (1996). Depressive symptomatology in new mothers: A stress and coping perspective. *J. Abnorm. Psychol., 105*(2), 220–231.

Thalen, B. E., Kjellman, B. F., Morkrid, L., Wibom, R. et al. (1995). Light treatment in seasonal and nonseasonal depression. *Acta Psychiatr. Scandin., 91*(5), 352–360.

Thapar, A., Davies, G., Jones, T., & Rivett, M. (1992). Treatment of childhood encopresis: A review. *Child Care, Hlth. Dev., 18*(6), 343–353.

Thase, M. E., Buysse, D. J., Frank, E., Cherry, C. R. et al. (1997). Which depressed patients will respond to interpersonal psychotherapy? The role of abnormal EEG sleep profiles. *Amer. J. Psychiat., 154*(4), 502–509.

Thase, M. E., Kupfer, D. J., Buysse, D. J., Frank, E., et al. (1995). Electroencephalographic sleep profiles in single-episode and recurrent unipolar forms of major depression: I. Comparison during acute depressive states. *Bio. Psychiat., 38,* 506–515.

Thase, M. E., Kupfer, D. J., Fasiczka, A. J., Buysse, D. J., et al. (1997). Identifying an abnormal electroencephalographic sleep profile to characterize major depressive disorder. *Bio. Psychiat., 41,* 964–973.

Thase, M. E., Simons, A. D., & Reynolds, C. F. (1996, February). Abnormal electroencephalographic sleep profiles in major depression: Association with response to cognitive behavior therapy. *Arch. Gen. Psychiat., 53,* 99–108.

Thase, M. E., Trivedi, M. H., & Rush, A. J. (1995). MAOIs in the contemporary treatment of depression. *Neuropsychopharmacology, 12*(3), 185–219.

Thayer, J. F., Friedman, B. H., & Borkovec, T. D. (1996). Autonomic characteristics of generalized anxiety disorder and worry. *Bio. Psychiat., 39,* 255–266.

Theander, S. (1970). Anorexia nervosa. *Acta Psychiatr. Scandin., Suppl.,* pp. 1–194.

Thelen, M. H., & Cormier, J. F. (1995). Desire to be thinner and weight control among children and their parents. *Behav. Ther.,* 26, 85–99.

Thelen, M., Lawrence, C. M., & Powell, A. (1992). Body image, weight control, and eating disorders among children. In J. H. Crowther, D. L. Tennenbaum, S. E. Hobfoll, & M. A. P. Stephens (Eds.), *The etiology of bulimia nervosa:* The individual and familial context. Washington, DC: Hemisphere.

Thiel, A., Broocks, A., Ohlmeier, M., Jacoby, G. E. et al. (1995). Obsessive-compulsive disorder among patients with anorexia nervosa and bulimia nervosa. *Amer. J. Psychiat., 154*(1), 72–75.

Thigpen, C. H., & Cleckley, H. M. (1957). *The three faces of Eve.* New York: McGraw-Hill.

Thomas, E. (1996, April 15). What the unabomber did to me. *Newsweek,* pp. 40–41.

Thompson, J. W., Belcher, J. R., DeForge, B. R., Myers, C. P. et al. (1995). Trends in the inpatient care of persons with schizophrenia. *Schizo. Bull., 21*(1), 75–85.

Thompson, P. M., Gillin, J. C., Golshan, S., & Irwin, M. (1995). Polygraphic sleep measures differentiate alcoholics and stimulant abusers during short-term abstinence. *Bio. Psychiat., 38,* 831–836.

Thompson, R. A., & Sherman, R. T. (1993). *Helping athletes with eating disorders.* Champaign, IL: Human Kinetics Publishers.

Thorn, B. E., Shealy, R. C., & Briggs, S. D. (1993). Sexual misconduct in psychotherapy: Reactions to a consumer-oriented brochure. *Profess. Psychol. Res. Prac., 24*(1), 75–82.

Thorpe, S. J., & Salkozskis, P. M. (1995). Phobia beliefs: Do cognitive factors play a role in specific phobias? *Behav. Res. Ther., 33*(7), 805–816.

Tice, D. (1992). *Strategies for changing our emotional states. Conference presentation.* American Psychological Association, Washington, DC.

Tien, H. C. (1975). Pattern of electrotherapy in Michigan. *Michigan Med., 74,* 251–257.

Tiihonen, J., Kuikka, J., Viinamaki, H., Lehtonen, J. et al. (1995). Altered cerebral blood flow during hysterical paresthesia. *Bio. Psychiat., 37*(2), 134–135.

Tiller, J., Schmidt, U., Ali, S., & Treasure, J. (1995). Patterns of punitiveness in women with eating disorders. *Inter. J. Eat. Disorders, 17*(4), 365–371.

Tillich, P. (1952, December). Anxiety, religion, and medicine. *Pastoral Psychol., 3,* 11–17.

Tishler, C. L., McKenry, P. C., & Morgan, K. C. (1981). Adolescent suicide attempts: Some significant factors. *Suic. Life-Threat. Behav., 11*(2), 86–92.

Tobin, D. L., & Johnson, C. L. (1991). The integration of psychodynamic and behavior therapy in the treatment of eating disorders: Clinical issue versus theoretical mystique. In C. L. Johnson (Ed.), *Psychodynamic treatment of anorexia nervosa and bulimia.* New York: Guilford.

Todd, R. D. (1991). Fluoxetine in autism. *Amer. J. Psychiat., 148*(8), 1089.

Todd, R. D., Reich, W., Petti, T., Joshi, P., et al. (1996). Psychiatric diagnoses in the child and adolescent members of extended families identified through adult bipolar affective disorder probands. *Amer. J. Acad. Child Adol. Psychiat., 35*(5), 664–671.

Todd, R. D., Geller, B., Neuman, R., Fox, L. W., et al. (1996). Increased prevalence of alcoholism in relatives of depressed and bipolar children. *Amer. J. Acad. Child Adol. Psychiat., 35*(6), 716–724.

Todd, T. C., & Stanton, M. D. (1983). Research on marital and family therapy: Answers, issues, and recommendations for the future. In B. B. Wolman & G. Stricker (Eds.), *Handbook of family and marital therapy.* New York: Plenum Press.

Toglia, M. P. (1996). Recovered memories: Lost and found? In K. Pezdek & W. P. Banks (Eds.), *The recovered memory/false memory debate.* San Diego: Academic Press.

Tolbert, H. A. (1996). Psychoses in children and adolescents: A review. *J. Clin. Psychiat., 57*(Suppl. 3), 4–8.

Tollefson, G. D., Beasley, C. M., Tran, P. V., Street, J. S. et al. (1997). Olanzapine versus haloperidol in the treatment of schizophrenia and schizoaffective and schizophreniform disorders: Results of an international collaborative trial. *Amer. J. Psychiat., 154*(4), 457–465.

Tollefson, G. D., Holman, S. L., Sayler, M. E., & Potvin, J. H. (1995). Fluoxetine, placebo, and tricyclic antidepressants in major depression with and without anxious features. *J. Clin. Psychiat. Monog. Ser., 13*(2), 13–22.

Tomasson, K., Kent, D., & Coryell, W. (1991). Somatization and conversion disorders: Comorbidity and demographics at presentation. *Acta Psychiatr. Scandin., 84*(3), 288–293.

Tomchek, L. B., Gordon, R., Arnold, M., Handleman, J. (1992). Teaching preschool children with autism and their normally developing peers: Meeting the challenges of integrated education. *Focus Autistic Behav., 7*(2), 1–17.

Toomey, R., Kremen, W. S., Simpson, J. C., Samson, J. A. et al. (1997). Revisiting the factor structure for positive and negative symptoms: Evidence from a large heterogeneous group of psychiatric patients. *Amer. J. Psychiat., 154*(3), 371–377.

Torgersen, S. (1983). Genetic factors in anxiety disorders. *Arch. Gen. Psychiat., 40,* 1085–1089.

Torgersen, S. (1983). Genetics of neurosis: The effects of sampling variation upon the twin concordance ratio. *Brit. J. Psychiat., 142,* 126–132.

Torgersen, S. (1984). Genetic and nosological aspects of schizotypal and borderline personality disorders: A twin study. *Arch. Gen. Psychiat., 41,* 546–554.

Torgersen, S. (1990). Comorbidity of major depression and anxiety disorders in twin pairs. *Amer. J. Psychiat., 147,* 1199–1202.

Torrey, E. F. (1988). *Nowhere to go: The tragic odyssey of the homeless mentally ill.* New York: Harper & Row.

Torrey, E. F. (1991). A viral-anatomical explanation of schizophrenia. *Schizo. Bull., 17*(1), 15–18.

Torrey, E. F. (1992). Are we overestimating the genetic contribution to schizophrenia? *Schizo. Bull., 18*(2), 159–170.

Torrey, E. F. (1997). *Out of the shadows: Confronting America's mental illness crisis.* New York: Wiley.

Torrey, E. F., Bowler, A. E., Rawlings, R., & Terrazas, A. (1993). Seasonality of Schizophrenia and Stillbirths. *Schizo. Bull., 19*(3), 557–562.

Torrey, E. F., Bowler, A. E., Taylor, E. H., & Gottesman, I. I. (1994). *Schizophrenia and manic-depressive disorder.* New York: Basic Books.

Torrey, E. F., Wolfe, S. M., & Flynn, L. M. (1988). *Care of the seriously mentally ill: A rating of state programs* (2nd ed.). Washington, DC: Public Citizen Health Research Group and National Alliance for the Mentally Ill.

Toufexis, A. (1993, October 11). The personality pill. *Time,* pp. 61–62.

Travin, S. (1995). Compulsive sexual behaviors. *Psychiat. Clin. N. Amer., 18*(1), 155–169.

Travis, J. (1996, March 23). AIDS update '96: New drugs, new tests, new optimism mark recent AIDS research. *Science News,* 149, pp. 184–186.

Treaster, J. B. (1992, September 20). After hurricane, Floridians show symptoms seen in war. *The New York Times.*

Treasure, J., Schmidt, U., Troop, N., Tiller, J., Todd, G., & Turnbull, S. (1996). Sequential treatment for bulimia nervosa incorporating a self-care manual. *Brit. J. Psychiat., 168,* 94–98.

Treasure, J. & Szmukler, G. I. (1995). Medical complications of chronic anorexia nervosa. In G. I. Szmukler, C. Dare, & J. Treasure (Eds.), *Handbook on eating disorders: Theory, treatment and research.* Chichester, England: Wiley.

Treasure, J., Todd, G., & Szmukler, G. (1995). The inpatient treatment of anorexia nervosa. In G. Szmukler, C. Dare, & J. Treasure (Eds.), *Handbook of eating disorders: Theory, treatment and research.* Chichester, England: Wiley.

Treffert, D. A. (1989). *Extraordinary People: Understanding Savant Syndrome.* New York: Ballantine Books.

Trestman, R. L., Horvath, T., Kalus, O., Peterson, A. E. et al. (1996). Event-related potentials in schizotypal personality disorder. *J. Neuropsych. Clin. Neurosci., 8,* 33–40.

Troiano, R. P., Frongillo, E. A., Sobal, J., Levitsky, D. A. (1996). The relationship between body weight and mortality: A quantitative analysis of combined information from existing studies. *Inter. J. Obesity, 20,* 63–75.

Tross, S., & Hirsch, D. A. (1988). Psychological distress and neuropsychological complications of HIV infection and AIDS. *Amer. Psychol., 43*(11), 929–934.

Trovato, F. (1987). A longitudinal analysis of divorce and suicide in Canada. *J. Marriage Fam., 49,* 193–203.

True, W., Rice, L., Eisen, S. A. et al. (1993). A twin study of genetic and environmental contributions to the liability for posttraumatic stress symptoms. *Arch. Gen. Psychiat., 50,* 257–264.

Trujillo, K. A., & Akil, H. (1991). The NMDA receptor antagonist MK-801 increases morphine catalepsy and lethality. *Pharmacol. Biochem. Behav., 38*(3), 673–675.

Tryon, G. (1987). *Profess. Psychol., 17,* 357–363.

Tsoi, W. F. (1992). Male and female transsexuals: a comparison. *Singapore Med. J., 33*(2), 182–185.

Tunstall, C. D., Ginsberg, D., & Hall, S. M. (1985). Quitting smoking. *Inter. J. Addic., 20,* 1089–1112.

Turek, F. (1996). Melatonin hype hard to swallow. *Nature, 379,* 295–296.

Turkat, I. D., & Banks, D. S. (1987). Paranoid personality and its disorder. *J. Psychopathol. Behav. Assess., 9*(3), 295–304.

Turkat, I. D., Keane, S. P., Thompson-Pope, S. K. (1990). Social processing errors among paranoid personalities. *J. Psychopathol. Behav. Assess., 12*(3), 263–269.

Turner, E., Ewing, J., Shilling, P., Smith, T., Irwin, M., Schuckit, M., & Kelsoe, J. (1992). Lack of association between an RFLP near the D2 dopamine receptor gene and severe alcoholism. *Bio. Psychiat., 31*(3), 285–290.

Turner, L. A., Althof, S. E., Levine, S. B., Bodner, D. R., Kursh, E. D., & Resnick, M. I. (1991). External vacuum devices in the treatment of erectile dysfunction: A one-year study of sexual and psychosocial impact. *J. Sex Marital Ther., 17*(2), 81–93.

Turner, R. J., & Lloyd, D. A. (1995, December). Lifetime traumas and mental health: The significance of cumulative adversity. *J. Hlth. Soc. Behav., 36,* 360–376.

Turner, S. M., Beidel, D. C., & Nathan, R. S. (1985). Biological factors in obsessive-compulsive disorders. *Psychol. Bull., 97,* 430–450.

Turner, S. M., Beidel, D. C., Borden, J. W., Stanley, M. A. et al. (1991). Social phobia: Axis I and II correlates. *J. Abnorm. Psychol., 100*(1), 102–106.

Turner, S. M., Beidel, D. C., Dancu, C. V., & Keys, D. J. (1986). Psychopathology of social phobia and comparison to avoidant personality disorder. *J. Abnorm. Psychol., 95*(4), 389–394.

Turner, S. M., Beidel, D. C., Long, P. J., & Greenhouse, J. (1992). Reduction of fear in social phobics: An examination of extinction patterns. *Behav. Ther., 23*(3), 389–403.

Turner, S. M., Hersen, M., & Bellack, A. S. (1977). Effects of social disruption, stimulus interference, and aversive conditioning on auditory hallucinations. *Behav. Mod., 1*(2), 249–258.

Turner, W. J. (1995). Homosexuality, Type 1: An Xq28 phenomenon. *Arch. Sex. Behav., 24*(2), 109–134.

Turton, M. D., O'Shea, D., Gunn, I., Beak, S. A., et al. (1996, January 4). A role for glucagon-like peptide-1 in the central regulation of feeding. *Nature, 379,* pp. 69–72.

Twain, M. (1885). *The adventures of Huckleberry Finn.*

Tweed, J. L., Schoenbach, V. J., & George, L. K. (1989). The effects of childhood parental death and divorce on six-month history of anxiety disorders. *Brit. J. Psychiat., 154,* 823–828.

Tyrer, P. (1992). Anxiolytics not acting at the benzodiazepine receptor: Beta blockers. *Prog. Neuropsychopharmacol. Bio. Psychiat., 16*(1), 17–26.

Uchino, B. N., & Garvey, T. S. (1997). The availability of social support reduces cardiovascular reactivity to acute psychological stress. *J. Behav. Med., 20*(1), 15–27.

Uchoa, D. D. (1985). Narcissistic transference? *Rev. Bras. Psicanal., 19*(1), 87–96.

Uhde, T. W. et al. (1984). Fear and anxiety: Relationship to noradrenergic function. 14th Collegium Internationale Neuro-Psychopharmacologicum Congress (Florence, Italy). *Psychopathology, 17*(3, Suppl.), 8–23.

Uhde, T. W. et al. (1984). The sleep of patients with panic disorder: A preliminary report. *Psychiat. Res., 12*(3), 251–259.

Uhde, T. W., Siever, L. J., & Post, R. M. (1984). Clonidine: Acute challenge and clinical trial paradigms for the investigation and treatment of anxiety disorders, affective illness and pain syndromes. In R. M. Post & J. C. Ballenger (Eds.), *Neurobiology of mood disorders.* Baltimore: Williams & Wilkins.

Uhde, T. W., Siever, L. J., Post, R. M., Jimerson, D. C., Boulenger, J. P., & Buchsbaum, M. S. (1982). The relationship of plasma-free MHPG to anxiety and psychophysical pain in normal volunteers. *Psychopharmacol. Bull., 18,* 129–132.

Uhde, T. W., Stein, M. B., Vittone, B. A. et al. (1989). Behavioral and physiologic effects of short-term and long-term administration of clonidine in panic disorder. *Arch. Gen Psychiat., 46,* 170–177.

Uhde, T. W., Vittone, B. J., & Post, R. M. (1984). Glucose tolerance testing in panic disorder. *Amer. J. Psychiatr., 14*(11), 1461–1463.

Uhlenhuth, E. H., Balter, M. B., Ban, T. A., Yang, K. (1995). International study of expert judgement on therapeutic use of benzodiazepines and other psychotherapeutic medications: II. Pharmacotherapy of anxiety disorders. *J. Affect. Disorders, 35,* 153–162.

Uhlenhuth, E. H., Balter, M. B., Ban, T. A., & Yang, K. (1995). International study of expert judgment on therapeutic use of benzodiazepines and other psychotherapeutic medications: III. Clinical features affecting experts' therapeutic recommendations in anxiety disorders. *Psychopharmacol. Bull., 31*(2), 289–296.

Uhlig, R. (1996, October 31). Prosthetics improve a dog's life. *Electronic Telegraph,* Issue 526.

Ullmann, L. P., & Krasner, L. (1975). *A psychological approach to abnormal behavior* (2nd ed.). Englewood Cliffs, NJ: Prentice Hall.

U. S. Dept. of Justice/Bureau of Justice Statistics. (1994). *Violence between inmates: Domestic violence.* Anapolis Junction, MD: Bureau of Justice Statistics Clearinghouse.

U. S. Dept. of Justice/Bureau of Justice Statistics. (1995). *Violence against women: Estimates from the Redesigned National Crime Victimization Survey.* Anapolis Junction, MD: Bureau of Justice Statistics Clearinghouse.

Ursano, R. J., Boydstun, J. A., & Wheatley, R. D. (1981). Psychiatric illness in U. S. Air Force Vietnam Prisoners of war: A five-year follow-up. *Amer. J. Psychiat., 138*(3), 310–314.

U. S. Bureau of the Census. (1988). *Statistical abstract of the United States* (108th ed.). Washington, DC: U. S. Government Printing Office.

U. S. Bureau of the Census. (1990). *Statistical abstract of the United States.* Washington, DC: U. S. Government Printing Office.

Vaillant, G. E. (1983). Natural history of male alcoholism: V. Is alcoholism the cart or the horse to sociopathy? *Brit. J. Addic., 78*(3), 317–326.

Vaillant, G. E., (1992). Prospective evidence for the effects of environment upon alcoholism. In S. Saitoh, P. Steinglass, & M. A. Schuckit (Eds.), *Alcoholism and the family.* New York: Brunner/Mazel.

Vaillant, G. E. (1993). The wisdom of the ego. Cambridge, MA: Harvard University Press.

Vaillant, G. E. (1994). Ego mechanisms of defense and personality psychopathology. *J. Abnorm. Psychol., 103*(1), 44–50.

Vaillant, G. E., & Milofsky, E. S. (1982). Natural history of male alcoholism: IV. Paths to recovery. *Arch. Gen. Psychiat., 39,* 127–133.

Vaillant, G. E., & Perry, J. C. (1985). Personality disorders. In H. I. Kaplan & B. J. Sadock (Eds.), *Comprehensive textbook of psychiatry* (4th ed.). Baltimore: Williams & Wilkins.

Vaillant, P. M., & Antonowicz, D. H. (1992). Rapists, incest offenders, and child molesters in treatment: Cognitive and social skills training. *Inter. J. Offend. Ther. Compar. Criminol., 36*(3), 221–230.

Valenstein, E. S. (1986). *Great and desperate cures.* New York: Basic Books.

Valente, S. M., & Saunders, J. M. (1995). Women, physical illness and suicidal behavior. In S. S. Canetto & D. Lester (Eds.), *Women and suicidal behavior.* New York: Springer.

Valenti-Hein, D. C., Yarnold, P. R., & Mueser, K. T. (1994). Evaluation of the dating skills program for improving heterosocial interactions in people with mental retardation. *Behav. Mod., 18*(1), 32–46.

van Bommel, H. (1992). *Dying for care: Hospice care or euthanasia.* Toronto: NC Press.

Van Bourgondien, M. E., & Schopler, E. (1990). Critical issues in the residential care of people with autism. *J. Autism Dev. Disorders, 20*(3), 391–399.

Van de Castle, R. (1993). Content of dreams. In M. A. Carskadon (Ed.), *Encyclopedia of Sleep and Dreams.* New York: Macmillan.

Van den Berg, J. H. (1971). What is psychotherapy? *Humanitas, 7*(3), 321–370.

VanDerHal, E., Tauber, Y., & Gottesfeld, J. (1996). Open groups for children of Holocaust survivors. *Inter. J. Group Psychother., 46*(2), 193–208.

Van der Ham, T., Meulman, J. J., Van Strien, D. C., & Van Engeland, H. (1997). Empirically based subgrouping of eating disorders in adolescents: A longitudinal perspective. *Brit. J. Psychiat., 170,* 363–368.

Van der Molen, H. T., Nijenhuis, J. T., & Keen, G. (1995). The effects of intelligence test preparation. *Eur. J. Pers., 9*(1), 43–56.

Van Hasselt, V., Null, J., Kempton, T., & Buckstein, O. (1993). Social skills and depression in adolescent substance abusers. *Addic. Behav., 18,* 9–18.

van Kammen, D. P., Kelley, M. E., Gurklis, J. A., Gilbertson, M. W., Yao, J. K., Condray, R., & Peters, J. L. (1996). Predicting duration of clinical stability following haloperidol withdrawal in schizophrenic patients. *Neuropsychopharmacology, 14,* 275–283.

van Oppen, P., & Arntz, A. (1994). Cognitive therapy for obsessive-compulsive disorder. *Behav. Res. Ther., 33,* 79–87.

van Os, J., Fañanas, L., Cannon, M., Macdonald, A., & Murray, R. (1997). Dermatoglyphic abnormalities in psychosis: A twin study. *Bio. Psychiat., 41,* 624–626.

Van Praag, H. M. (1977). The significance of dopamine for the mode of action of neuroleptics and the pathogenesis of schizophrenia. *Brit. J. Psychiat., 132,* 593–597.

Van Praag, H. M. (1982). Depression, suicide and the metabolism of serotonin in the brain. *J. Affect. Disorders, 4,* 275–290.

Van Praag, H. M. (1983). CSF 5-HIAA and suicide in non-depressed schizophrenics. *Lancet,* 2, 977–978.

Van Praag, H. M. (1983). In search of the action mechanism of antidepressants. 5-HTP/tyrosine mixtures in depression. *Neuropharmacology, 22,* 433–440.

Van Praag, H. M. (1986). Affective disorders and aggression disorders: Evidence for a common biological mechanism. In R. W. Maris (Ed.), *Biology of suicide.* New York: Guilford.

van Vliet, I. M., den Boer, J. A., Westenberg, H. G. M., & Pian, K. L. H. (1997). Clinical effects of buspirone in social phobia: A double-blind placebo-controlled study. *J. Clin. Psychiat., 58*(4), 164–168.

VanGent, E. M., & Zwart, F. M. (1991). Psychoeducation of partners of bipolar-manic patients. *J. Affect. Disorders, 21*(1), 15–18.

VandenBos, G. R. (1996). Outcome assessment of psychotherapy. *Amer. Psychologist, 51*(10), 1005–1006.

Vandereycken, W. (1994). Parental rearing behaviour and eating disorders. In C. Perris, W. A. Arrindell, & M. Eisemann (Eds.), *Parenting and psychopathology.* Chichester, England: Wiley.

Vanderlinden, J. & Vandereycken, W. (1991). Guidelines for the family therapeutic approach to eating disorders. *Psychother. Psychosom., 56,* 36–42.

Varis, K. (1987). Psychosomatic factors in gastrointestinal disorders. *Ann. Clin. Res., 19*(2), 135–142.

Varma, V. K., Malhorta, A. K., Dang, R., Das, K., & Nehra, R. (1988). Cannabis and cognitive functions: a prospective study. *Drug Alc. Dep., 21,* 147.

Vatz, R., & Weinberg, L. (1993, January 10). Keno Krazy? *The Washington Post,* p. C5.

Vaughan, K., Doyle, M., McConaghy, N., Blaszcznski, A. (1992). The relationship between relative's expressed emotion and schizophrenic relapse: An Australian replication. *Soc. Psychiat. Psychiatr. Epidemiol., 27*(1), 10–15.

Vega, W., & Rumbaut, R. (1991). Ethnic minorities and mental health. *Annu. Rev. Sociol., 17,* 351–383.

Veiel, H. O., Kuhner, C., Brill, G., & Ihle, W. (1992). Psychosocial correlates of clinical depression after psychiatric in-patient treatment: Methodological issues and baseline differences between recovered and non-recovered patients. *Psychol. Med., 22*(2), 415–427.

Velamoor, V. R., Norman, R. M., Caroff, S. N. et al (1994). Progression of symptoms in neuroleptic malignant syndrome. *J. Nerv. Ment. Dis., 182,* 168–173.

Velleman, R., & Orford, J. (1993). The adult adjustment of offspring of parents with drinking problems. *Brit. J. Psychiat., 162,* 503–516.

Velligan, D. I., Funderburg, L. G., Giesecke, S. L., & Miller, A. L. (1995). Longitudinal analysis of communication deviance in the families of schizophrenic patients. *Psychiat. Interpers. Biol. Process., 58*(1), 6–19.

Venditti, E., Wing, R. Jakicic, J., Butler, B., & Marcus, M. (1996). Weight cycling, psychological health, and binge eating in obese women. *J. Cons. Clin. Psychol., 64*(2), 400–405.

Verburg, K., Griez, E., Meijer, J., & Pols, H. (1995). Respiratory disorders as a possible predisposing factor for panic disorder. *J. Affect Disorders, 33*(2), 129–134.

Verdoux, H., & Bourgeois, M. (1993). A comparison of manic patient subgroups. *J. Affect. Disorders, 27,* 267–272.

Verfaellie, M., Cermak, L. S., Blackford, S. P., et al. (1990). Strategic and automatic priming of semantic memory in alcoholic Korsakoff patients. *Brain Cog., 13*(2), 178–192.

Vernberg, E. M., La Greca, A. M., Silverman, W. K., & Prinstein, M. J. (1996). Prediction of posttraumatic stress symptoms in children after Hurricane Andrew. *J. Abnorm. Psychol., 105*(2), 237–248.

Vetter, H. J. (1969). *Language behavior and psychopathology.* Chicago: Rand McNally.

Vieira, C. (1993). Nudity in Dreams. In M. A. Carskadon (Ed.), *Encyclopedia of Sleep and Dreams.* New York: Macmillan.

Villarreal, G. (1995). Desipramine plasma levels and treatment response in panic disorder. *Canad. J. Psychiat., 40*(2), 110–111.

Viney, W., & Zorich, S. (1982). Contributions to the history of psychology: XXIX. Dorothea Dix and the history of psychology. *Psychol. Rep., 50,* 211–218.

Vinogradov, S. & Yalom, I. D. (1994). Group therapy. In R. E. Hales, S. C. Yudofsky, & J. A. Talbott, (Eds.), *The American Psychiatric Press textbook of psychiatry,* (2nd ed.). Washington, DC: American Psychiatric Press.

Vinson, D. (1994). Therapy for attention-deficit hyperactivity disorder. *Arch. Fam. Med., 3,* 445–451.

Vitousek, K., & Manke, F. (1994). Personality variables and disorders in anorexia nervosa and bulimia nervosa. *J. Abnorm. Psychol., 103*(1), 137–147.

Vlaeyen, J. W. S., Haazen, I. W. C. J., Schuerman, J. A., Kole-Snijders, A. M. J. et al. (1995). Behavioural rehabilitation of chronic low back pain: Comparison of an operant treatment, an operant-cognitive treatment and an operant-respondent treatment. *Brit. J. Clin. Psychol., 34*(1), 95–118.

Vogele, C., & Steptoe, A. (1993). Anger inhibition and family history as modulators of cardiovascular responses to mental stress in adolescent boys. *J. Psychosom. Res., 37*(5), 503–514.

Volavka, J. (1995). *Neurobiology of violence.* Washington, D.C.: American Psychiatric Press.

Volkmar, F. R., Carter, A., Sparrow, S. S., & Cicchetti, D. V. (1993). Quantifying social development in autism. *J. Amer. Acad. Child Adol. Psychiat., 32*(3), 627–632.

Volkow, N. D., Gillespie, H., Tancredi, L., & Hollister, L. (1995). The effects of marijuana in the human brain measured with regional brain glucose metabolism. In A. Biegon & N. D. Volkow (Eds.), *Sites of drug action in the human brain.* Boca Raton, FL: CRC Press.

Volkow, N. D., Wang, G. J., Fowler, J. S., Logan, J., Gatley, S. J., Hitzemann, R., Chen, A. D., Dewey, S. L., & Pappas, N. (1997). Decreased striatal dopaminergic responsiveness in detoxified cocaine-dependent subjects. *Nature, 386*(6627), 830–833.

Volpe, B. T., & Hirst, W. (1983). The characterization of an amnestic syndrome following hypoxic ischemic injury. *Arch. Neurol., 40,* 436–440.

Volpicelli, J., Alterman, A., Hayashida, M., & O'Brien, C. (1992). Naltrexone in the treatment of alcohol dependence. *Arch. Gen. Psychiat., 49,* 876–880.

Von Burg, M., & Hibbard, R. (1995). Munchausen syndrome by proxy: A different kind of child abuse. *Indiana Med., 88*(5), 378–382.

Von Korff, M., Nestadt, G., Romanoski, A. et al. (1985). Prevalence of treated and untreated DSM-III schizophrenia. *J. Nerv. Ment. Dis., 173,* 577–581.

Vonnegut, M. (1974, April). Why I want to bite R. D. Laing. *Harper's Mag., 248*(1478), 80–92.

Vostanis, P., Feehan, C., Grattan, E., & Bickerton, W.-L. (1996). A randomised controlled out-patient trial of cognitive-behavioural treatment for children and adolescents with depression: 9-month follow-up. *J. Affect. Disorders, 40,* 105–116.

Vredenburg, K., Flett, G. L., & Krames, L. (1993). Analogue versus clinical depression: A critical reappraisal. *Psychol. Bull., 113*(2), 327–344.

WHO (World Health Organization). (1992). *World Health Statistics Annual.* Geneva: Author.

Wadden, T. A., & Anderton, C. H. (1982). The clinical use of hypnosis. *Psychol. Bull., 91*(2), 215–243.

Wadden, T. A., Stunkard, A. J., & Liebschutz, J. (1988). Three-year follow-up of the treatment of obesity by very low calorie diet, behavior therapy, and their combination. *J. Cons. Clin. Psychol., 56*(6), 925–928.

Wahl, O. F., & Hunter, J. (1992). Are gender effects being neglected in schizophrenia research? *Schizo. Bull., 18*(2), 313–318.

Wahlberg, K.-E., Wynne, L. C., Oja, H., Keskitalo, P. et al. (1997). Gene-environment interaction in vulnerability to schizophrenia: Findings from the Finnish Adoptive Family Study of Schizophrenia. *Amer. J. Psychiat., 154*(3), 355–362.

Waikar, S. V., & Craske, M. G. (1997). Cognitive correlates of anxious and depressive symptomatology: An examination of the helplessness/hopelessness model. *J. Anxiety. Disorders, 11*(1), 1–16.

Wakeling, A. (1995). Physical treatments. In G. Szmukler, C. Dare, & J. Treasure (Eds.), *Handbook of eating disorders: Theory, treatment and research.* Chichester, England: Wiley.

Waldhauser, F., Saletu, B., & Trinchard, L. (1990). Sleep laboratory investigations on hypnotic properties of melatonin. *Psychopharmcology, 100*(2), 222–226.

Walker, E., & Lewine, R. (1990). Prediction of adult-onset schizophrenia from childhood home movies of the patients. *Amer. J. Psychiat., 147,* 1052–1056.

Walker, E., & Young, T. D., (1986). *A killing cure.* New York: Henry Holt.

Walker, L. E. (1979). *The battered woman.* New York: Harper & Row.

Walker, L. E. (1984). *The battered woman syndrome.* New York: Springer.

Walker, L. E. (1984). Battered women, psychology, and public policy. *Amer. Psychologist, 39*(10), 1178–1182.

Walker, R. D., Howard, M. O., Walker, P. S., Lambert, M. D., Maloy, F., & Suchinsky, R. T. (1996). Essential and reactive alcoholism: A review. *J. Clin. Psychol., 52*(1), 80–95.

Wallace, B. (1993). Cross-cultural counseling with the chemically dependent: Preparing for service delivery within a culture of violence. *J. Psychoactive Drugs, 25*(1), 9–12.

Wallace, S. E. (1981). The right to live and the right to die. In S. E. Wallace & A. Eser (Eds.), *Suicide and euthanasia: The rights of personhood.* Knoxville: University of Tennessee.

Wallen, J. (1992). A comparison of male and female clients in substance abuse treatment. *Journal of Substance Abuse Treatment, 9*(3), 243–248.

Waller, G., & Hodgson, H. (1996) Body image distortion in anorexia and bulimia nervosa: The role of perceived and actual control. *J. Nerv. Ment. Dis., 184,* 213–219.

Walsh, B. T., Wilson, G. R., Loeb, K. L., Devlin, M. J., et al. (1997). Medication and psychotherapy in the treatment of bulimia nervosa. *Amer. J. Psychiat., 154,* 523–531.

Walsh, J. (1990). Assessment and treatment of the schizotypal personality disorder. *J. Independent Soc. Work, 4*(3), 41–59.

Walsh, J., & Engelhardt, C. L. (1993). Myths about dreaming. In M. A. Carskadon (Ed.), *Encyclopedia of Sleep and Dreams.* New York: Macmillan.

Wanck, B. (1984). Two decades of involuntary hospitalization legislation. *Amer. J. Psychiat., 41,* 33–38.

Wang, S., Sun, C., Walczak, C. A., Ziegle, J. S., et al. (1995, May). Evidence for a susceptibility locus for schizophrenia on chromosome 6pter-p22. *Nature Genetics, 10,* 41–46.

Ward, A., Brown, N., & Treasure, J. (1996). Persistent osteopenia after recovery from anorexia nervosa. *Inter. J. Eat. Disorders,* 22, 71–75.

Ward, D. A. (1985). Conceptions of the nature and treatment of alcoholism. *J. Drug Issues, 15*(1), 3–16.

Warga, C. (1988, September). You are what you think. *Psychology Today,* pp. 54–58.

Waring, M., & Ricks, D. (1965). Family patterns of children who become adult schizophrenics. *J. Nerv. Ment. Dis., 140*(5), 351–364.

Warren, G., & Sampson, G. (1995). Medical audit of an assessment clinic for male erectile dysfunction. *Sex. Marital Ther., 10*(1), 39–46.

Warren, L. W., & Ostrom, J. C. (1988). Pack rats: World-class savers. *Psychol. Today, 22*(2), 58–62.

Warwick, H. M. C. (1995). Assessment of hypochondriasis. *Behav. Res. Ther., 33*(7), 845–853.

Washton, A. M., & Stone-Washton, N. (1990). Abstinence and relapse in outpatient cocaine addicts. *J. Psychoactive Drugs, 22*(2), 135–147.

Wasserman, I. M. (1992). The impact of epidemic, war, prohibition and media on suicide: United States, 1910–1920. *Suic. Life-Threat. Behav., 22*(2), 240–254.

Wasylenki, D. (1992). Psychotherapy of schizophrenia revisited. *Hosp. Comm. Psychiat., 43*(2), 123–128.

Waters, L. (1990). Reinforcing the empty fortress: An examination of recent research into the treatment of autism. *Educ. Studies, 16*(1), 3–16.

Watkins, C. E., Campbell, V. L., Nieberding, R., & Hallmark, R. (1995). Contemporary practice of psychological assessment by clinical psychologists. *Profess. Psychol.: Res. Prac., 26*(1), 54–60.

Watkins-Duncan, B. A. (1992). Principles for formulating treatment with Black patients. *Psychotherapy, 29*(3), 452–457.

Watson, C. G. (1987). Recidivism in "controlled drinker" alcoholics: A longitudinal study. *J. Clin. Psychol., 43*(3), 404–412.

Watson, C. G., Hancock, M., Gearhart, L. P. Mendez, C. M., et al. (1997). A comparative outcome study of frequent, moderate, occasional, and nonattenders of Alcoholics Anonymous. *J. Clin. Psychol., 53*(3), 209–214.

Watson, C. G., Tuorila, J., Detra, E., Gearhart, L. P. et al. (1995). Effects of a Vietnam War Memorial pilgrimage on veterans with posttraumatic stress disorder. *J. Nerv. Ment. Dis., 183*(5), 315–319.

Watson, D., Clark, L. A., & Harkness, A. R. (1994). Structures of personality and their relevance to psychopathology. *J. Abnorm. Psychol., 103*(1), 18–31.

Watson, J. B. (1930). *Behaviorism* (Rev. Ed.). Chicago: University of Chicago Press.

Watson, J. B., & Rayner, R. (1920). Conditioned emotional reaction. *J. Exp. Psychol., 3,* 1–14.

Watten, R. G., Vassend, O., Myhrer, T., & Syversen, J.-L. (1997). Personality factors and somatic symptoms. *Eur. J. Pers., 11*(1), 57–68.

Waxer, P. (1974). Nonverbal cues for depression. *J. Abnorm. Psychol., 83*(3), 319–322.

Wechsler, H., Davenport, A., Dowdall, G., Moeykens, B., & Castillo, S. (1994). Health and behavioral consequences of binge drinking in college. *JAMA, 272*(21), 1672–1677.

Wechsler, H., Dowdell, G. W., Davenport, A., & Castllo, S. (1995). Correlates of college student binge drinking. *Amer. J. Pub. Hlth., 85*(7), 921–926.

Wechsler, H., Dowdell, G. W., Davenport, A., & Rimm, E. (1995). A gender-specific measure of binge drinking among college students. *Amer. J. Pub. Hlth., 85*(7), 982–985.

Wechsler, H., & Isaac, N. (1992). "Binge" drinkers at Massachusetts colleges: Prevalence, drinking styles, time trends, and associated problems. *JAMA, 267,* 2929–2931.

Wechsler, H., Grosser, G. H., & Greenblatt, M. (1965). Research evaluating antidepressant medications on hospitalized mental patients: A survey of published reports during a five-year period. *J. Nerv. Ment. Dis., 141,* 231–239.

Wechsler, J. A. (1972). *In a darkness.* New York: Norton.

Weeks, D., & James, J. (1995). *Eccentrics: A study of sanity and strangeness.* New York: Villard.

Wehmeyer, M. L. (1992). Self-determination and the education of students with mental retardation. *Educ. Training Ment. Retard., 27*(4), 302–314.

Weinberg, J., & Levine, S. (1980). Psychobiology of coping in animals: The effects of predictability. In S. Levine & H. Ursin (Eds.), *Coping and health.* New York: Plenum Press.

Weinberger, D. R. (1983). "Imaging of the brain: Aiding the search for physical correlates of mental illness": Comment. *Integ. Psychiat., 1*(4), 146.

Weinberger, D. R. et al. (1982). Computed tomography in schizophreniform disorder and other acute psychiatric disorders. *Arch. Gen. Psychiat., 30*(7), 770–783.

Weiner, H. (1977). *Psychobiology and human disease.* New York: Elsevier.

Weiner, H. (1985). The psychobiology and pathophysiology of anxiety and fear. In A. H. Tuma & J. Maser (Eds.), *Anxiety and the anxiety disorders.* Hillsdale, NJ: Erlbaum.

Weiner, H., Thaler, M., Reiser, M. F., & Mirsky, I. A. (1957). Etiology of duodenal ulcer: I. Relation of specific psychological characteristics to rate of gastric secretion (serum pepsinogen). *Psychosom. Med., 19,* 1–10.

Weiner, I. B. (1995). Methodological considerations in Rorschach research [Special issue: Methodological issues in psychological assessment research]. *Psychol. Assess., 7*(3), 330–337.

Weiner, I. W. (1969). The effectiveness of suicide prevention programs. *Ment. Hyg., 53,* 357–373.

Weiner, R. D. (1984). Does electroconvulsive therapy cause brain damage? *Behav. Brain Sci., 7,* 1–54.

Weiner, R. D., & Coffey, C. E. (1988). Indications for use of electroconvulsive therapy. In A. J. Frances & R. E. Hales (Eds.), *American Psychiatric Press review of psychiatry* (Vol. 7). Washington, DC: American Psychiatric Press.

Weintraub, M., Segal, R. M., & Beck, A. T. (1974). An investigation of cognition and affect in the depressive experience of normal men. *J. Cons. Clin. Psychol., 42,* 911.

Weir, R. F. (1992). The morality of physician-assisted suicide. *Law, Med. Hlth. Care, 20*(1–2), 116–126.

Weishaar, M. E., & Beck, A. T. (1992). Clinical and cognitive predictors of suicide. In R. W. Maris, A. L. Berman, J. T. Maltsberger, & R. I. Yufit (Eds.), *Assessment and prediction of suicide.* New York: Guilford.

Weisheit, R. A. (1990). Domestic marijuana growers: Mainstreaming deviance. *Deviant Behav., 11*(2), 107–129.

Weiss, D. E. (1991). *The Great Divide.* New York: Poseidon Press/Simon & Schuster.

Weiss, D. S., & Marmar, C. R. (1993). Teaching time-limited dynamic psychotherapy for posttraumatic stress disorder and pathological grief. *Psychotherapy.*

Weiss, D. S., Marmar, C. R., Schlenger, W. E., & Fairback, J. A. et al. (1992). The prevalence of lifetime and partial posttraumatic stress disorder in Vietnam theater veterans. *J. Traum. Stress, 5*(3), 365–376.

Weiss, J. M. (1977). Ulcers. In J. D. Maser & M. E. P. Seligman (Eds.), *Psychopathology: Experimental models.* San Francisco: W. H. Freeman.

Weiss, J. M., Glazer, H. I., & Pohorecky, L. A. (1974). Neurotransmitters and helplessness: A chemical bridge to depression? *Psychol. Today, 8*(7), 58–62.

Weiss, J. M., Glazer, H. I., & Pohorecky, L. A. (1976). Coping behavior and neurochemical changes: An alternative explanation for the original "learned helplessness" experiments. In G. Serban & A. Kling (Eds.), *Animal models of human psychobiology.* New York: Plenum Press.

Weiss, R. (1997, January 3). Study takes a new tack on asthma. *The Philadelphia Inquirer,* pp. A1, A22.

Weiss, R. L., Hops, H., & Patterson, G. R. (1973). A framework for conceptualizing marital conflict, a technology for altering it, some data for evaluating it. In L. A. Hamerlynck, L. C. Handy, & E. J. Mash (Eds.), *Behavior change: Methodology, concepts, and practice.* Champaign, IL: Research.

Weissman, M., & Olfson, M. (1995). Depression in women: Implications for health care research. *Science, 269*(5225), 799–801.

Weissman, M. M. (1988). The epidemiology of panic disorder. In A. J.

Frances & R. E. Hales (Eds.), *American Psychiatric Press review of psychiatry* (Vol. 7). Washington, DC: American Psychiatric Press.

Weissman, M. M. (1993, Spring). The epidemiology of personality disorders. A 1990 update. *J. Pers. Disorders,* Suppl., pp. 44–62.

Weissman, M. M. (1995). The epidemiology of psychiatric disorders: Past, present, and future generations. [Special issue: Festschfirt for Ben Z. Locke, MSPH]. *Inter. J. Methods Psychiatr. Res., 5*(2), 69–78.

Weissman, M. M., Bland, R. C., Canino, G. J., Faravelli, C. et al. (1997). The cross-national epidemiology of panic disorder. *Arch. Gen. Psychiat., 54,* 305–309.

Weissman, M. M., & Boyd, J. H. (1984). The epidemiology of mental disorders. In R. M. Post & J. C. Ballenger (Eds.), *Neurobiology of mood disorders.* Baltimore: Williams & Wilkins.

Weissman, M. M., Bruce, M. L., Leaf, P. J., Florio, L. P., & Holzer, C. (1991). Affective disorders. In L. N. Robins & D. A. Regier (Eds.), *Psychiatric disorders in America: The Epidemiologic Catchment Area Study.* New York: Free Press.

Weissman, M. M. et al. (The Cross-national Collaborative Group). (1992). The changing rate of major depression: Cross-national comparisons. *JAMA, 268*(21), 3098–3105.

Weissman, M. M. et al. (1979). The efficacy of drugs and psychotherapy in the treatment of acute depressive episodes. *Amer. J. Psychiat., 136*(4–B), 555–558.

Weissman, M. M. et al. (1982). Short-term interpersonal psychotherapy (IPT) for depression: Description and efficacy. In J. C. Anchin & D. J. Kiesler (Eds.), *Handbook of interpersonal psychotherapy.* New York: Pergamon Press.

Weissman, M. M., Livingston Bruce, M., Leaf, P. J., Florio, L. P., & Hozer III, C. (1991). Affective disorders. In L. N. Robins & D. A. Regier (eds.), *Psychiatric disorders in America: The Epidemiologic Catchment Area Study.* New York: Free Press.

Weissman, M. M., Myers, J. K., & Harding, P. S. (1978). Psychiatric disorders in a U. S. urban community. *Amer. J. Psychiat., 135,* 459–462.

Welldon, E. V. (1995). Female perversion and hysteria. *Brit. J. Psychother., 11*(3), 406–414.

Wells, A., Clark, M. D., Salkovskis, P., Ludgate, J., et al. (1995). Social phobia: The role of in-situation safety behaviors in maintaining anxiety and negative beliefs. *Behav. Ther., 26*(1), 153–161.

Wells, E. A., Peterson, P. L., Gainey, R. R., Hawkins, J. D., & Catalano, R. F. (1994). Outpatient treatment for cocaine abuse: A controlled comparison of relapse prevention and twelve-step approaches. *Amer. J. Drug Alc. Abuse, 20,* 1–17.

Wells, M. C., Glickauf-Hughes, C., & Bruzzell, V. (1990). Treating obsessive-compulsive personalities in psycho-dynamic/interpersonal group ther y. *Psychotherapy, 27*(3), 366–379.

Wells, M. E., Hinkle, J. S. (1990). Elimination of childhood encopresis: A family systems approach. *J. Ment. Hlth. Couns., 12*(4), 520–526.

Wender, P. H., Kety, S. S., Rosenthal, D., Schulsinger, F., Ortmann, J., & Lunde, I. (1986). Psychiatric disorders in the biological and adoptive families of adopted and individuals with affective disorders. *Arch. Gen. Psychiat., 43,* 923–929.

Werder, S. F. (1995). An update on the diagnosis and treatment of mania in bipolar disorder. *Amer. Fam. Physician, 51*(5), 1126–1136.

Wernick, R. L. (1983). Stress inoculation in the management of clinical pain. In D. Meichenbaum & M. E. Jaremko (Eds.), *Stress reduction and prevention.* New York: Plenum Press.

Werth, J. (1995). Rational suicide reconsidered: AIDS as an impetus for change. Annual Conference of the Association for Death Education & Counseling. *Death Stud., 19*(1), 65–80.

Werth, J. (1996). Rational suicide? Implications for mental health professionals. Washington, DC: Taylor and Francis.

Werth, J., & Cobia, D. (1995). Empirically based criteria for rational suicide: A survey of psychotherapists. *Suic. Life-Threat. Behav., 25*(2), 231–240.

West, L. J. (1993). Reflections of the right to die. In A. A. Leenaars (Ed.), *Suicidology.* Northvale, NJ: Jason Aronson.

Westen, D. (1991). Cognitive-behavioral interventions in the psychoanalytic psychotherapy of borderline personality disorders. *Clin. Psychol. Rev., 11*(3), 211–230.

Wester, J. M. (1991). Rethinking inpatient treatment of borderline clients. *Perspect. Psychiatr. Care, 27*(2), 17–20.

Westermeyer, J. (1992). Schizophrenia and substance abuse. In A. Tasman, & M. B. Riba (Eds.), *Review of psychiatry* (Vol. 11). Washington, DC: American Psychiatric Press.

Weston, S. C., & Siever, L. J. (1993, Spring). Biological correlates of personality disorders. *J. Pers. Disorders,* Suppl., pp. 129–148.

Wethington, E., & Kessler, R. C. (1989). Employment, parental responsibility, and psychological distress: A longitudinal study of married women. *J. Fam. Issues, 10,* 527–546.

Wettstein, R. M. (1988). Psychiatry and the law. In J. A. Talbott, R. E. Hales & S. C. Yudofsky (Eds.), *American Psychiatric Press textbook of psychiatry.* Washington, DC: American Psychiatric Press.

Wettstein, R. M. (1989). Psychiatric malpractice. In A. Tasman, R. E. Hales, & A. J. Frances (Eds.), *American Psychiatric Press Review of Psychiatry* (Vol. 8). Washington, DC: American Psychiatric Press.

Wetzel, H., Szegedi, A., Hain C., Wiesner, J. et al. (1995). Seroquel (ICI 203 636), a putative "atypical" antipsychotic, in schizophrenia with positive symptomatology: Results of an open clinical trial and changes of neuroendocrinological and EEG parameters. *Psychopharmacology, 119*(2), 231–238.

Wexler, D. B. (1983). The structure of civil commitment. *Law Human Behav., 7,* 1–18.

Wexler, D. B. (1988). Reforming the law in action through empirically grounded civil commitment guidelines. *Hosp. Comm. Psychiat., 39,* 402–405.

Whelan, J. P., & Houts, A. C. (1990). Effects of a waking schedule on primary enuretic children treated with full-spectrum home training. *Hlth. Psychol., 9,* 164–176.

Whipple, E. E., Webster, S. C., & Stratton, C. (1991). The role of parental stress in physically abusive families. *Child Abuse Neglect: Inter. J., 15*(3), 279.

Whisman, M. A., & McGarvey, A. L. (1995). Attachment, depressotypic cognitions, and dysphoria. *Cog. Ther. Res., 19*(6), 633–650.

Whitacre, C. C., Cummings, S. O., & Griffin, A. C. (1994). The effects of stress on autoimmune disease. In R. Glaser & J. K. Kiecolt-Glaser (Eds.), *Handbook of human stress and immunity.* San Diego: Academic Press.

Whitby, P. (1996). Spider Phobia Control (Spider PC). *Behav. Res. Methods, Instruments, & Computers, 28*(1), 131–133.

Whitehead, W. E., Crowell, M. D., Heller, B. R., Robinson, J. C. et al. (1994). Modeling and reinforcement of the sick role during childhood predicts adult illness behavior. *Psychosom. Med., 56,* 541–550.

Whitehorn, J. C., & Betz, B. J. (1975). *Effective psychotherapy with the schizophrenic patient.* New York: Jason Aronson.

Whitely, J. S. (1994). In pursuit of the elusive category. *Brit. J. Psychiat. Rev. Books, 7,* 14–17.

Whiteside, M. (1983, September 12). A bedeviling new hysteria. *Newsweek.*

Whiting, J. W. et al. (1966). *Six cultures series: I. Field guide for a study of socialization.* New York: Wiley.

Whittaker, S., & Bry, B. H. (1992). Overt and covert parental conflict and adolescent problems: Observed marital interaction in clinical and nonclinical families. *Fam. Ther., 19*(1), 43–54.

Whittal, M. L., & Goetsch, V. L. (1995). Physiological, subjective and behavioral responses to hyperventilation in clinical and infrequent panic. *Behav. Res. Ther., 33*(4), 415–422

Whorley, L. W. (1996). Cognitive ther techniques in continuing care planning with substance-depen t patients. *Addic. Behav., 21*(2), 223–231.

Whybrow, P. (1994). Of the muse and moods mundane. *Amer. J. Psychiat., 151*(4), 477–479.

Widiger, T. A. (1992). Categorical versus dimensional classification: Implications from and for research. *J. Pers. Disorders, 6,* 287–300.

Widiger, T. A., Corbitt, E. M., & Millon, T. (1992). Antisocial personality disorder. In A. Tasman & M. B. Riba (Eds.), *American Psychiatric Press review of psychiatry* (Vol. 11). Washington, DC: American Psychiatric Press.

Widiger, T. A., & Costa, P. T. (1994). Personality and personality disorders. *J. Abnorm. Psychol., 103*(1), 78–91.

Widom, C. S. (1989). The cycle of violence. *Science, 244,* 160–166.

Widom, C. S. (1991, February). *Presentation.* Washington, DC: American Association for the Advancement of Science.

Wiederman, M., & Pryor, T. (1996). Substance use and impulsive behaviors among adolescents with eating disorders. *Addic. Behav., 21*(2), 269–272.

Wiegner, K. (1995, April 19). Shrink software. *The New York Times,* p. D5.

Wiens, A. N. (1990). Structured clinical interviews for adults. In G. Goldstein & M. Hersen (Eds.), *Handbook of psychological assessment* (2nd ed.). New York: Pergamon Press.

Wiggins, J. S., & Trobst, K. K. (1997). Prospects for the assessment of normal and abnormal interpersonal behavior. *J. Pers. Assess., 68*(1), 110–126.

Wikan, U. (1991). *Managing turbulent hearts.* Chicago: University of Chicago Press.

Wilbur, C. B. (1984). Treatment of multiple personality. *Psychiatr. Ann., 14,* 27–31.

Wilcox, J. A. (1990). Fluoxetine and bulimia. *J. Psychoactive Drugs, 22*(1), 81–82.

Wilde, E. J., Kienhorst, I. C. W. M., Diekstra, R. F. W., & Wolters, W. H. G. (1992). The relationship between adolescent suicidal behavior and life events in childhood and adolescence. *Amer. J. Psychiat, 149,* 45–51.

Wilfley, D. E., Agras, W. S., Telch, C. F., Rossiter, E. M., Schneider, J. A., Cole, A. G., Sifford, L., & Raeburn, S. D. (1993). Group cognitive-behavioral therapy and group interpersonal psychotherapy for the nonpurging bulimic individual: A controlled comparison. *J. Cons. Clin. Psychol., 61*(2), 296–305.

Will, O. A. (1961). Paranoid development and the concept of self: Psychotherapeutic intervention. *Psychiatry, 24*(2), 16–530.

Will, O. A. (1967). Psychological treatment of schizophrenia. In A. M. Freedman & H. I. Kaplan (Eds.), *Comprehensive textbook of psychiatry.* Baltimore: Williams & Wilkins.

Willard, W. (1979). American Indians. In L. D. Hankoff & B. Einsidler (Eds.), *Suicide: Theory and clinical aspects.* Littleton, MA: PSG Publishing Company.

Williams, C. C. (1983). The mental foxhole: The Viet Nam veterans' search for meaning. *Amer. J. Orthopsychiat., 53*(1), 4–17.

Williams, L. M. (1996). Cognitive inhibition and schizophrenic symptom subgroups. *Schizo. Bull., 22*(1), 139–151.

Williams, R. B. (1989). *The trusting heart: Great news about Type A behavior.* New York: Times Books.

Williams, R. B. (1989). Biological mechanisms mediating the relationship between behavior and coronary heart disease. In A. W. Siegman & T. M. Dembroski (Eds.), *In search of coronary behavior.* Hillsdale, NJ: Erlbaum.

Williams, S. S., Michela, J. L., Contento, I. R., Gladis, M. M., & Pierce, N. T. (1996). Restrained eating among adolescents: Dieters are not always bingers and bingers are not always dieters. *Hlth. Psychol., 15*(3), 176–184.

Williamson, D. A., Gleaves, D. H., & Lawson, O. J. (1991). Biased perception of overeating in bulimia nervosa and compulsive binge eaters. *J. Psychopathol. Behav. Assess., 13*(3), 257–268.

Williamson, D. A., Netemeyer, R. G., Jackman, L. P., Anderson, D. A. et al. (1995). Structural equation modeling of risk factors for the development of eating disorder symptoms in female athletes. *Inter. J. Eat. Disorders, 17*(4), 387–393.

Wills, T. A., McNamara, G., Vaccaro, D., & Hirky, A. E. (1996). Escalated substance use: A longitudinal grouping analysis from early to middle adolescence. *J. Abnorm. Psychol., 105*(2), 166–180.

Wilmer, H. A. (1996). The healing nightmare: War dreams of Vietnam veterans. In D. Barrett (Ed.), *Trauma and dreams.* Cambridge, MA: Harvard University Press.

Wilson, G. T. (1978). Alcoholism and aversion therapy: Issues, ethics, and evidence. In G. A. Marlatt & P. E. Nathan (Eds.), *Behavioral approaches to alcoholism.* New Brunswick, NJ: Rutgers Center for Alcohol Studies.

Wilson, G. T. (1978). On the much discussed nature of the term "Behavior Therapy." *Behav. Ther., 9,* 89–98.

Wilson, G. T. (1987). Chemical aversion conditioning as a treatment for alcoholism: A re-analysis. *Behav. Res. Ther., 25,* 503–516.

Wilson, G. T. (1994). Behavioral treatment of obesity: Thirty years and counting. *Adv. Behav. Res. Ther., 16,* 31–75.

Wilson, G. T., & Fairburn, C. G. (1993). Cognitive treatments for eating disorders. *J. Cons. Clin. Psychol., 61*(2), 261–269.

Wilson, G. T., & Pike, K. M. (1993). Eating disorders. In D. H. Barlow (Ed.), *Clinical handbook of psychological disorders: A step-by-step treatment manual* (2nd ed.). New York: Guilford.

Wilson, G. T., Heffernan, K., & Black, C. M. D. (1996). Eating disorders In E. J. Mash & R. A. Barkley (Eds.), *Child psychopathology.* New York: Guilford.

Wilson, G. T., Rossiter, E., Kleifield, E. I., & Lindholm, L. (1986). Cognitive-behavioral treatment of bulimia nervosa: A controlled evaluation. *Behav. Res. Ther., 24*(3), 277–288.

Wilson, J. M., & Marcotte, A. C. (1996). Psychosocial adjustment and educational outcome in adolescents with a childhood diagnosis of attention deficit disorder. *J. Amer. Acad. Child Adol. Psychiat., 35*(5), 579–587.

Wilson, K. G., Hayes, S. C., & Gifford, E. V. (1997). Cognition in behavior therapy: Agreements and differences. *J. Behav. Ther. Exp. Psychiat., 28*(1), 53–63.

Wilson, M. R., Greene, J. H., & Soth, N. B. (1986). Psychodynamics of the adopted patient. *Adoption Fostering, 10*(1), 41–46.

Wilson, W. H., Diamond, R. J., & Factor, R. M. (1990). Group treatment for individuals with schizophrenia. *Comm. Ment. Hlth. J., 26*(4), 361–372.

Wilson, W. M. (1992). The Stanford-Binet: Fourth Edition and Form L-M in assessment of young children with mental retardation. *Ment. Retard., 30*(2), 81–84.

Winchel, R. M. & Stanley, M. (1991). Self-injurious behavior: A review of the behavior and biology of self-mutilation. *Amer. J. Psychiat., 148*(3), 306–317.

Wincze, J. P. & Carey, M. P. (1991). *Sexual dysfunction: A guide for assessment and treatment.* New York: Guilford.

Wincze, J. P., & Lange, J. D. (1981). Assessment of sexual behavior. In D. H. Barlow (Ed.), *Behavioral assessment of adult disorders.* New York: Guilford.

Wincze, J. P., Richards, J., Parsons, J., & Bailey, S. (1996). A comparative survey of therapist sexual misconduct between an American state and an Australian state. *Profess. Psychol:. Res. Prac., 27*(3), 289–294.

Wing, L. (1976). *Early childhood autism.* Oxford, England: Pergamon Press.

Wing, L., & Wing, J. K. (1971). Multiple impairments in early childhood autism. *J. Autism Child. Schizo., 1,* 256–266.

Winick, B. J. (1983). Incompetency to stand trial: Developments in the law. In J. Monahan & H. J. Steadman (Eds.), *Mentally disorded offenders.* New York: Plenum Press.

Winick, M., Meyer, K., & Harris, R. C. (1975). Malnutrition and environmental enrichment by early adoption. *Science,* pp. 1173–1175.

Wink, P. (1996). Narcissism. In C. G. Costello (Ed.), *Personality characteristics of the personality disordered.* New York: Wiley.

Winokur, G., Coryell, W., Keller, M., Endicott, J. et al. (1995). A family study of manic-depressive (bipolar I) disease: Is it a distinct illness separable from primary unipolar depression? *Arch. Gen. Psychiat., 52*(5), 367–373.

Winslade, W. J. (1983). *The insanity plea.* New York: Scribner's.

Winslade, W. J. (1988). Electroconvulsive therapy: Legal regulations and ethical concerns. In A. J. Frances & R. E. Hales (Eds.), *American Psychiatric Press review of psychiatry* (Vol. 7). Washington, DC: American Psychiatric Press.

Winslade, W. J., Liston, E. H., Ross, J. W. et al. (1984). Medical, judicial, and statutory regulation of ECT in the United States. *Amer. J. Psychiat., 141,* 1349–1355.

Winson, J. (1990, November). The meaning of dreams. *Scientif. Amer.,* pp. 86–96.

Winston, A., & Pollack, J. (1991). Brief adaptive psychotherapy. *Psychiatr. Ann., 21*(7), 415–418.

Winters, K. C., Stinchfield, R., & Fulkerson, J. (1993). Patterns and characteristics of adolescent gambling. *J. Gamb. Stud., 9*(4), 371–386.

Wirz-Justice, A., Graw, P., Kräuchi, K., Sarrafzadeh, A. et al. (1996). "Natural" light treatment of seasonal affective disorder. *J. Affect. Disorders, 37,* 109–120.

Wise, R. A. (1996). Neurobiology of addiction. *Curr. Opin. Neurobiol., 6,* 243–251.

Wise, T. N. (1985). Fetishism—etiology and treatment: A review from multiple perspectives. *Comprehen. Psychiat., 26,* 249–257.

Wise, T. N., Fagan, P. J., Schmidt, C. W., Ponticas, Y. et al. (1991). Personality and sexual functioning of transvestitic fetishists and other paraphilics. *J. Nerv. Ment. Dis., 179*(11), 694–698.

Wiseman, C. V., Gray, J. J., Mosimann, J. E., & Ahrens, A. H. (1992). Cultural expectations of thinness in women: An update. *Inter. J. Eat. Disorders, 11*(1), 85–89.

Wisniewski, K. E., Wisniewski, H. M., & Wen, G. Y. (1985). Occurrence of neuropathological changes and dementia of Alzheimer's Disease in Down Syndrome. *Ann. Neurol., 17,* 278–282.

Witkin, M. J., Atay, J. E., Fell, A. S., & Manderscheid, R. W. (1990). Specialty mental health system characteristics. In R. W. Manderscheid & M. A. Sonnenschein (Eds.), *Mental health, United States* (DHHS Publication No. ADM 90–1708). Washington, DC: U. S. Department of Health and Human Services.

Wittrock, D. A., & Blanchard, E. B. (1992). Thermal biofeedback treatment of mild hypertension: A comparison of effects on conventional and ambulatory blood pressure measures. *Behav. Mod., 16*(3), 283–304.

Wittrock, D. A., Blanchard, E. B., McCoy, G. C., McCaffrey, R. J. et al. (1995). The relationship of expectancies to outcome in stress management treatment of essential hypertensions: Results from the joint USSR-USA Behavioral Hypertension Project. *Biofeed. Self-Reg., 20*(1), 51–68.

Wlazlo, Z., Schroeder-Hartwig, K., Hand, I., Kaiser, G., & Munchau, N. (1990). Exposure in vivo vs. social skills training for social phobia: Long term outcome and differential effects. *Behav. Res. Ther., 28,* 181–193.

Wolberg, L. R. (1967). *The technique of psychotherapy.* New York: Grune & Stratton.

Wolf, S., & Wolff, H. G. (1947). *Human gastric functions.* New York: Oxford University.

Wolfe, D. A., Edwards, B., Manion, I. & Koverola, C. (1988). Early intervention for parents at risk for child abuse and neglect: A preliminary investigation. *J. Cons. Clin. Psychol., 56,* 40–47.

Wolfe, J. K. L., & Fodor, I. G. (1977). Modifying assertive behavior in women: Comparison of three approaches. *Behav. Ther., 8,* 567–574.

Wolfe, J. L., & Russianoff, P. (1997). Overcoming self-negation in women. *J. Rat.-Emot. & Cog.-Behav. Ther., 15*(1), 81–92.

Wolfe, J., Schnurr, P. P., Brown, P. J., & Furey, J. (1994). Posttraumatic stress disorder and war-zone exposure as correlates of perceived health in female vietnam war veterans. *J. Cons. Clin. Psychol., 62*(6), 1235–1240.

Wolfe, S. M., Fugate, L., Hulstrand, E. P., Kamimoto, L. E. (1988). *Worst pills best pills: The older adult's guide to avoiding drug-induced death or illness.* Washington, DC: Public Citizen Health Research Group.

Wolff, N., Helminiak, T. W., Morse, G. A., Calsyn, R. J. et al. (1997). Cost-effectiveness evaluation of three approaches to case management for homeless mentally ill clients. *Amer. J. Psychiat., 154*(3), 341–348.

Wolff, S. (1991). Schizoid personality in childhood and adult life I: The vagaries of diagnostic labeling. *Brit. J. Psychiat., 159,* 615–620.

Wolpe, J. (1958). *Psychotherapy by reciprocal inhibition.* Stanford, CA: Stanford University Press.

Wolpe, J. (1969). *The practice of behavior therapy.* Oxford, England: Pergamon Press.

Wolpe, J. (1987). The promotion of scientific psychotherapy: A long voyage. In J. K. Zeig (Ed.), *The evolution of psychotherapy.* New York: Brunner/Mazel.

Wolpe, J. (1990). *The practice of behavior therapy* (4th ed.). Elmsford, NY: Pergamon Press.

Wolpe, J. (1997). From psychoanalytic to behavioral methods in anxiety disorders: A continuing evolution. In J. K. Zeig (Ed.), *The evolution of psychotherapy: The third conference.* New York: Brunner/Mazel.

Wolpe, J. The case of Mrs. Schmidt [Transcript and record]. Nashville, TN: Counselor Recording and Tests.

Wolpe, J., Craske, M. G., & Reyna, L. J. (1994). *The comparative efficacy of behavior therapy and psychodynamic methods in the anxiety disorders.* Unpublished manuscript.

Woo, S. M., Goldstein, M. J., & Nuechterlein, K. H. (1997). Relatives' expressed emotion and non-verbal signs of subclinical psychopathology in schizophrenic patients. *Brit. J. Psychiat., 170,* 58–61.

Woodside, M. R., & Legg, B. H. (1990). Patient advocacy: A mental health perspective. *J. Ment. Hlth. Couns., 12*(1), 38–50.

Woodward, B., Duckworth, K. S., & Gutheil, T. G. (1993). The pharmacotherapist-psychotherapist collaboration. In J. M. Oldham, M. B. Riba, & A. Tasman (Eds.), *Review of psychiatry* (Vol. 12). Washington, DC: American Psychiatric Press.

Woodward, S. H., Drescher, K. D., Murphy, R. T., Ruzek, J. I. et al. (1997). Heart rate during group flooding therapy for PTSD. *Integ. Physiol. Behav. Sci., 32*(1), 19–30.

Woody, G. E., McLellan, A. T., & Bedrick, J. (1995). Dual diagnosis. In J. M. Oldham & M. B. Riba (Eds.), *American Psychiatric Press review of psychiatry,* (Vol. 14). Washington, DC: American Psychiatric Press.

Woody, S. R., Chambless, D. L., & Glass, C. R. (1997). Self-focused attention in the treatment of social phobia. *Behav. Res. Ther., 35*(2), 117–129.

Wooley, S. C., & Wooley, O. W. (1979). Obesity and women—I. A closer look at the facts. *Women's Stud. Inter. Quart., 2,* 67–79.

Wooley, S. C., & Wooley, O. W. (1982). The Beverly Hills eating disorder: The mass marketing of anorexia nervosa. *Inter. J. Eat. Disorders, 1,* 57–69.

Wooley, S. C., & Wooley, O. W. (1985). Intensive outpatient and residential treatment for bulimia. In D. M. Garner & P. E. Garfinkel (Eds.), *Handbook of psychotherapy for anorexia nervosa and bulimia.* New York: Guilford.

Woolfolk, R. L., Carr-Kaffashan, L., McNulty, T. F., & Lehrer, P. M. (1976). Meditation training as a treatment for insomnia. *Behav. Ther. 7*(3), 359–365.

Workman, E. A., & Short, D. D. (1993). Atypical antidepressants versus imipramine in the treatment of major depression: A meta-analysis. *J. Clin. Psychiat., 54*(1), 5–12.

Worth, D. (1991). A service delivery system model for AIDS prevention for women. In *National Conference on Drug Abuse Research and Practice Conference Highlights.* Rockville, MD: National Institute on Drug Abuse.

Worthington, J., Fava, M., Davidson, K., Alpert, J., Nierenberg, A. A., & Rosenbaum, J. F. (1995). Patterns of improvement in depressive symptoms with fluoxetine treatment. *Psychopharmacol. Bull., 31*(2), 223–226.

Wragg, M., Hutton, M., Talbot, C., & Alzheimer's Disease Collaborative Group. (1996). Genetic association between intronic polymorphism in presenilin-1 gene and late-onset Alzheimer's disease. *Lancet, 347,* 509–512.

Wright, J. (1984). EAP: An important supervisory tool. *Supervisory Management, 29*(12), 16–17.

Wright, L. S. (1985). High school polydrug users and abusers. *Adolescence, 20*(80), 852–861.

Wright, L. S. (1985). Suicidal thoughts and their relationship to family stress and personal problems among high school seniors and college undergraduates. *Adolescence, 20*(79), 575–580.

Wu, X., & DeMaris, A. (1996). Gender and marital status differences in depression: The effects of chronic strains. *Sex Roles, 34*(5–6), 299–319.

Wulsin, L., Bachop, M., & Hoffman, D. (1988). Group therapy in manic-depressive illness. *Amer. J. Psychother., 42,* 263–271.

Wurtele, S. K., & Schmitt, A. (1992). Child care workers' knowledge about reporting suspected child sexual abuse. *Child Abuse and Neglect, 16*(3) 385–390.

Wurtman, R. (1995). Interview, cited in Roan., S. (1995, October 17). Super pill. *Los Angeles Times,* pp. E1–E5.

Wurtman, R. J., & Wurtman, J. J. (1984). Nutritional control of central neurotransmitters. In K. M. Pirke & D. Ploog (Eds.), *The psychobiology of anorexia nervosa.* Berlin: Springer-Verlag.

Wyatt, R. J. (1995). Risks of withdawing antipsychotic medications. *Arch. Gen. Psychiat., 52*(3), 205–208.

Yabe, K., Tsukahar, R., Mita, K., & Aoki, H. (1985). Developmental trends of jumping reaction time by means of EMG in mentally retarded children. *J. Ment. Def. Res., 29*(2), 137–145.

Yager, J. (1985). The outpatient treatment of bulimia. *Bull. Menninger Clin., 49*(3), 203–226.

Yager, J., Rorty M., & Rossoto E. (1995). Coping styles differ between recovered and nonrecovered women with bulimia nervosa, but not between recovered women and non-eating-disordered control subjects. *J. Nerv. Ment. Dis., 183*(2), 86–94.

Yalom, I. D. (1985). *The theory and practice of group psychotherapy* (3rd ed.). New York: Basic Books.

Yama, M., Fogas, B., Teegarden, L., & Hastings, B. (1993). Childhood sexual abuse and parental alcoholism: Interactive effects in adult women. *Amer. J. Orthopsychiat., 63*(2), 300–305.

Yang B., & Lester, D. (1995). Suicidal behavior and employment. In S. S. Canetto & D. Lester (Eds.) *Women and suicidal behavior.* New York: Springer.

Yang, B., Stack, S., & Lester, D. (1992). Suicide and unemployment: Predicting the smoothed trend and yearly fluctuations. *J. Socioecon., 21*(1), 39–41.

Yank, G. R., Bentley, K. J., & Hargrove, D. S. (1993). The vulnerability-stress model of schizophrenia: advances in psychosocial treatment. *Amer. J. Orthopsychiat., 63*(1), 55–69.

Yap, P. M. (1951). Mental diseases peculiar to certain cultures: A survey of comparative psychiatry. *J. Ment. Sci., 97,* 313–327.

Yarock, S. (1993). Understanding chronic bulimia: A four psychologies approach. *Amer. J. Psychoanal., 53*(1), 3–17.

Yates, A. (1990). Current perspectives on the eating disorders: II. Treatment, outcome, and research directions. *J. Amer. Acad. Child Adol. Psychiat., 29,* 1–9.

Yehuda, R., Giller, E. L., Southwick, S. M. et al. (1994). The relationship between catecholamine excretion and PTSD symptoms in Vietnam combat veterans and Holocaust survivors. In M. M. Marburg, (Ed.), *Catecholamine function in post-traumatic stress disorder.* Washington, DC: American Psychiatric Press.

Yehuda, R., Kahana, B., Binder-Brynes, K., Southwick, S. M. et al. (1995). Low urinary cortisol excretion in Holocaust survivors with posttraumatic stress disorder. *Amer. J. Psychiat., 152*(7), 982–986.

Yehuda, R., Southwick, S., Giller, E. et al. (1992). Urinary catecholamine excretion and severity of PTSD symptoms in Vietnam combat veterans. *J. Nerv. Ment. Dis., 180,* 321–325.

Yehuda, R., Southwick, S. M., & Giller, E. L. (1992). Exposure to atrocities and severity of chronic posttraumatic stress disorder in Vietnam combat veterans. *Amer. J. Psychiat., 149*(3), 333–336.

Yehuda, R., Southwick, S. M., Krystal, J. H. et al. (1993). Enhanced suppression of cortisol following dexamethasone administration in posttraumatic stress disorder. *Amer. J Psychiat., 150,* 83–86.

Yesavage, J. A., Leirer, V. O., Denari, M., & Hollister, L. E. (1985). Carry-over effects of marijuana intoxication on aircraft pilot performance: A preliminary report. *Am. J. Psychiat., 142*(11), 1325.

Yontef, G. M., & Simkin, J. F. (1989). Gestalt therapy. In R. J. Corsini & D. Wedding (Eds.), *Current psychotherapies.* Itasca, IL: Peacock.

Yost, E., Beutler, L., Corbishley, A. M., & Allender, J. (1986). *Group cognitive therapy: A treatment approach for depressed older adults.* New York: Pergamon Press.

Young, J. E., Beck, A. T., & Weinberger, A. (1993). Depression. In D. H. Barlow (Ed.), *Clinical handbook of psychological disorders: A step-by-step treatment manual* (2nd ed.). New York: Guilford.

Young, K. S. (1996). Psychology of computer use: XL. Addictive use of the Internet: A case that breaks the stereotype. *Psych. Rep. 79*(3, Pt 1), 899–902.

Young, K. S. (1996). As cited in "Middle-aged women are more at risk for Internet addiction." *APA Monitor, 27*(10), 10.

Young, L. D., & Allin, J. M. (1992). Repression-sensitization differences in recovery from learned helplessness. *J. Gen. Psychol., 119*(2), 135–139.

Young, M., Benjamin, B., & Wallis, C. (1963). Mortality of widowers. *Lancet, 2,* 454–456.

Young, T. J. (1991). Suicide and homicide among Native Americans: Anomie or social learning? *Psychol. Rep., 68*(3, Pt. 2), 1137–1138.

Young, W. C., Young, L. J., & Lehl, K. (1991). Restraints in the treatment of dissociative disorders: A follow-up of twenty patients. *Dissociation Prog. Dissociative Disorders, 4*(2), 74–78.

Youngren, M. A., & Lewinsohn, P. M. (1980). The functional relation between depression and problematic interpersonal behavior. *J. Abnorm. Psychol., 89*(3), 333–341.

Youngstrom, N. (1990). Six offender types are identified. *APA Monitor, 21*(10), 21.

Youngstrom, N. (1992). Grim news from national study of rape. *APA Monitor, 23*(7), 38.

Youngstrom, N. (1992). Psychology helps a shattered L. A. *The APA Monitor, 23*(7), 1, 12.

Yudofsky, S. (1996). Foreword. In J. H. Bruch, *Unlocking the golden cage: An intimate biography of Hilde Bruch, M.D.* Carlsbad, CA: Gürze Books.

Yudofsky, S., Silver, J., & Hales, R. (1993). Cocaine and aggressive behavior: Neurobiological and clinical perspectives. *Bull. Menninger Clin., 57*(2), 218–226.

Yuen, O., Caligiuri, M. P., Williams, R., & Dickson, R. A. (1996). Tardive dyskinesia and positive and negative symptoms of schizophrenia: A study using instrumental measures. *Brit. J. Psychiat., 168,* 702–708.

Yutzy, S. H., Cloninger, C. R., Guze, S. B., Pribor, E. F. et al. (1995). DSM-IV field trial: Testing a new proposal for somatization disorder. *Amer. J. Psychiat., 152*(1), 97–101.

Yuwiler, A., Shih, J. C., Chen, C., Ritvo, E. R. (1992). Hyperserotoninemia and antiserotonin antibodies in autism and other disorders. *J. Autism Dev. Disorders., 22*(1), 33–45.

Zack, M., & Vogel-Sprott, M. (1995). Behavioral tolerance and sensitization to alcohol in humans: The contribution of learning. *Exp. Clin. Psychopharmacol., 3*(4), 396–401.

Zajecka, J. (1997). Importance of establishing the diagnosis of persistent anxiety. *J. Clin. Psychiat., 58*(Suppl 3), 9–13.

Zaleman, S. (Ed.) (1995). Neural basis of psychopathology. In S. H. Koslow, D. L. Meinecke, I. I. Lederhendler, H. Khachaturian, R. K. Nakamura, D. Karp, L. Vitkovic, D. L. Glanzman, & S. Zaleman (Eds.), *The neuroscience of mental health: II A report on neuroscience research—Status and potential for mental health and mental illness.*

Rockville, MD: National Institutes of Health, National Institute of Mental Health.

Zamichow, N. (1993, February 15). The dark corner of psychology. *Los Angeles Times,* p. A1.

Zarit, S. H., Orr, N., & Zarit, J. M. (1985). *The hidden victims of Alzheimer's disease: Families under stress.* New York: New York University.

Zastowny, T. R., Lehman, A. F., Cole, R. E., & Kane, C. (1992). Family management of schizophrenia: A comparison of behavioral and supportive family treatment. *Psychiatr. Quart., 63*(2), 159–186.

Zax, M., & Cowen, E. L. (1969). Research on early detection and prevention of emotional dysfunction in young school children. In C. D. Speilberger (Ed.), *Current topics in clinical and community psychology* (Vol. 1). New York: Academic Press.

Zax, M., & Cowen, E. L. (1976). *Abnormal psychology: Changing conceptions.* New York: Holt, Rinehart & Winston.

Zelkowitz P., & Milet, T. (1996). Postpartum psychiatric disorders: Their relationship to psychological adjustment and marital satisfaction in the spouses. *J. Abnorm. Psychol., 105*(2), 281–285.

Zeman, N. (1989, October 23). Fear of flying. *Newsweek,* p. 10.

Zemishlany, Z., Alexander, G. E., Prohovnik, I., Goldman, R. G., Mukherjee, S., & Sackeim, H. (1996). Cortical blood flow and negative symptoms in schizophrenia. *Neuropsychobiology, 33,* 127–131.

Zerbe, K. J. (1990). Through the storm: Psychoanalytic theory in the psychotherapy of the anxiety disorders. *Bull. Menninger Clin., 54*(2), 171–183.

Zerbe, K. J. (1993). Whose body is it anyway? Understanding and treating psychosomatic aspects of eating disorders. *Bull. Menninger Clin., 57*(2), 161–177.

Zerssen, D. et al. (1985). Circadian rhythms in endogenous depression. *Psychiat. Res., 16,* 51–63.

Zetin, M., & Kramer, M. A. (1992). Obsessive-compulsive disorder. *Hosp. Comm. Psychiat., 43*(7), 689–699.

Zettle, R. D., Haflich, J. L., & Reynolds, R. A. (1992). Responsivity of cognitive therapy as a function of treatment format and client personality dimensions. *J. Clin. Psychol., 48*(6), 787–797.

Zhou, J.-N., Hofman, M. A., Gooren, L. J. G., & Swaab, D. F. (1995). A sex difference in the human brain and its relation to transsexuality. *Nature, 378,* 68–70.

Zigler, E., & Hodapp, R. M. (1991). Behavioral functioning in individuals with mental retardation. *Annu. Rev. Psychol., 42,* 29–50.

Zigler, E., Taussig, C., & Black, K. (1992). Early childhood intervention: A promising preventative for juvenile delinquency. *Amer. Psychol., 47*(8), 997–1006.

Zigman, W. B., Schupf, N., Sersen, E., & Silverman, W. (1995). Prevalence of dementia in adults with and without Down syndrome. *Amer. J. Ment. Retard., 100*(4), 403–412.

Zilbergeld, B. (1978). *Male sexuality.* Boston: Little, Brown.

Zilboorg, G., & Henry, G. W. (1941). *A history of medical psychology.* New York: Norton.

Zill, N., & Schoenborn, C. A. (1990, November). *Developmental, learning, and emotional problems: Health of our nation's children, United States, 1988* (No. 190). Advance Data: National Center for Health Statistics.

Zima, B. T., Wells, K. B., Benjamin, B., & Duan, N. (1996). Mental health problems among homeless mothers. *Arch. Gen. Psychiat., 53,* 332–338.

Zimbardo, P. (1976). *Rational paths to madness.* Presentation at Princeton University, Princeton, NJ.

Zimmerman, M. (1994). Diagnosing personality disorders: A review of issues and research methods. *Arch. Gen. Psychiat., 51,* 225–245.

Zimmerman, M., & Coryell, W. (1989). DSM-III personality disorder diagnoses in a nonpatient sample: Demographic correlates and comorbidity. *Arch. Gen. Psychiat., 46*(8), 682–689.

Zoellner, L. A., Craske, M. G., & Rapee, R. M. (1996). Stability of catastrophic cognitions in panic disorder. *Behav. Res. Ther., 34*(5/6), 399–402.

Zohar, J., & Pato, M. T. (1991). Diagnostic considerations. In M. T. Pato & J. Zohar (Eds.), *Current treatments of obsessive-compulsive disorder.* Washington, DC: American Psychiatric Press.

Zucker, K. J., Bradley, S. J., & Sullivan, C. B. L. (1996). Traits of separation anxiety in boys with gender identity disorder. *J. Amer. Child Adol. Psychiat., 35*(6), 791–798.

Zucker, K. J., Bradley, S. J., & Sullivan, C. B. L. (1996, April 7). Probing the mind of a killer. *Newsweek,* pp. 30–42.

Zucker, K. J., Bradley, S. J., & Sullivan, C. B. L. (1996, April 15). The mad bomber. *U. S. News & World Report,* pp. 29–36.

Zuckerman, M. (1978). Sensation seeking and psychopathy. In R. D. Hare & D. Schalling (Eds.), *Psychopathic behavior: Approaches to research.* New York: Wiley.

Zuckerman, M. (1996). Sensation seeking. In C. G. Costello (Ed.), *Personality characteristics of the personality disordered.* New York: Wiley.

Zuckerman, M. (1989). Personality in the third dimension: A psychobiological approach. *Pers. Individ. Diff., 10,* 391–418.

Zuger, A. (1993, July). The Baron strikes again. *Discover,* pp. 28–30.

Zwilling, B. S., Brown, D., Feng, N., Sheridan, J., & Pearl, D. (1993). The effect of adrenalectomy on the restraint stress induced suppression of MHC class II expression by murine peritoneal macrophages. *Brain, Behav. Immun., 7,* 29–35.

Sources of Illustrations

Chapter 1, opposite 1: Jan Saunders Van Hemessen, *The Surgeon,* 1530. Museo Nacional del Prado; **3:** Carol Beckwith; **4(t):** Gaye Hilsenrath/ The Picture Cube; **4(b):** Catherine Allemande/ Gamma Liaison; **5:** Thomas Szasz; **6:** Gamma Liaison; **10:** John W. Verano; **11(l/r):** Zentralbibliothek, Zurich; **14:** Corbis-Bettman; **15(t):** The Granger Collection; **15(b):** Bettman Archives; **16:** George Wesley Bellows, *Dance in a Madhouse,* 1907. Black crayon, charcoal, pen and ink on wove paper, 48 × 62.5 cm. Charles H. and Mary F. S. Worcester Collection, 1936.223. Photograph © 1997 The Art Institute of Chicago. All rights reserved; **17:** National Library of Medicine; **19:** Wellcome Institute Library, London; **21:** Bettmann Archives; **22(l):** Jerry Cooke/ Photo Researchers; **23:** Dan McCoy/ Rainbow; **27(t):** Judy Griesedieck, Minneapolis; **27(b):** Gamma Liaison; **Chapter 2, 28:** M. C. Escher, *Relativity,* 1953. © 1997 Cordon Art, Baarn, Holland. All rights reserved; **30:** Sidney Harris; **32:** Edna Morlok; **33:** Edna Morlok; **34:** Joel Gordon, New York, N.Y.; **37:** Rob Nelson/ Picture Group; **39:** Joel Gordon, New York, N.Y.; **40:** Walter Reed, Army Institute of Research; **42:** James Aronovski/ Picture Group; **43:** Cliff Schiappa/ AP/Wide World Photos; **44:** Time-Life Syndicate, photo from *London Daily Mirror;* **49(t):** Rhoda M. Karp; **49(b):** © 1991, *Newsweek,* Inc. All rights reserved. Reprinted by permission. (Artist: Coco Masuda); **Chapter 3, 50:** Richard Bergh, *Hypnotic Seance,* 1887. Nationmuseum, Stockholm; **55:** Mary Evans Picture Library/ Sigmund Freud Copyrights; **56:** Mary Evans Picture Library/ Sigmund Freud Copyrights; **58:** Laura Dwight, New York, N.Y.; **59:** Catherine Karnow/ Woodfin Camp & Associates; **62:** Ursula Edelmann, Frankfurt; **64:** Laura Dwight, New York, N.Y.; **67:** Joseph Wolpe; **68:** Photofest; **69:** The National Broadcasting Company, Inc.; **71(t/m/b):** A. Bandura, Stanford University; **73:** Gary Larson, Universal Press Syndicate; **75:** Leif Skoogsfor/ Woodfin Camp & Associates; **77:** Donald Meichenbaum, Ph.D., University of Waterloo, Ontario, Canada; **80:** G. & V. Chapman, Jonesboro, Georgia; **82:** Leif Skoogfors/ Woodfin Camp & Associates; **84:** Janod Kalmar; **87(t):** Chuck Fishman/ Woodfin Camp & Associates; **87(b):** © 1996 Robert Allison/ Contact Press Images; **Chapter 4, 88:** Karen Poulsen, *Unseeing,* 1992. Acrylic on paper, 15 × 15 inches. Photo, Karen Poulsen, Boulder, Colo.; **91:** Gary Larson, Universal Press Syndicate; **93(t):** Centre National de Recherches Iconographiques; **93(b):** © 1990 Bob Sacha, New York, N.Y.; **94:** Ohio Historical Society; **96:** James D. Wilson; **97:** Washington University School of Medicine; **99:** Courtney Kealy/ Gamma Liaison; **101:** National Library of Medicine; **102:** © 1991 Donna Ferrato/ Domestic Abuse Awareness Project, NYC, from the book *Living with the Enemy,* New York: Aperture; **104:** James Nachtwey/ Magnum Photos; **105:** Peter Turnley/ Black Star; **108(t):** Ralph Crane, *Life* © 1968 Time Warner, Inc.; **108(b):** Alon Reininger/ Contact Press Images; **109:** Avanta Network; **113:** Robert Maass/ Photoreporters; **114:** Alon Reininger/ Woodfin Camp & Associates, **117(l):** Archive Photos; **117(r):** Rick Maiman/ Sygma; **Chapter 5, 118:** M.C. Escher, *Drawing Hands,* 1948. © 1997 Cordon Art, Baarn, Holland. All rights reserved; **121:** *The Palm Beach Post,* photo by Mark Mirko; **124:** Gary Larson, Chronicle Features; **126:** Sidney Harris; **127:** Reprinted by permission of the publishers from Henry A. Murray, *Thematic Apperception Test,* Cambridge, Mass.: Harvard University Press, © 1943 by the President and Fellows of Harvard College, © 1971 by Henry A. Murray; **128:** Rick Friedman/ Black Star; **129(l/r):** Louis Wain; **133(l):** Marcus E. Raichle, MD, Washington University School of Medicine, St. Louis, Mo.; **133(r):** Hans Breiter, Mark S. Cohen, Bruce Rosen, University of California, Los Angeles; **134:** Joe McNally/ Sygma; **136:** Travis Amos; **138:** National Library of Medicine; **141:** © by Doug Milman and Gerlad Mayerhofer, *Are You Normal,* New York: Quill; **143:** Elizabeth Eckert, Middletown, N.Y. From L. Gamwell and N. Tomes, *Madness in America,* 1995, Ithaca, N.Y.: Cornell University Press; **146:** The Kansas State Historical Society, Topeka; **153(t):** Tasso Taraboulsi/ SABA; **153(b):** Fogg Art Museum, Harvard University, Cambridge, Mass.; **Chapter 6, 154:** Diane Kepford, *Alex* # 10, 1996. Oil on linen. 42 × 35 inches. Littlejohn Contemporary Gallery, New York, N.Y.; **156:** Museum of Modern Art Film Stills Archive; **157:** Bill Frakes, Coral Gables, Fla.; **159:** Thomas Ulrich/ Adventure Photo & Film, Ventura, Calif.; **161:** Cynthia Lee Katona, Freeman, Calif.; **162:** *The Miami Herald,* photo by Chuck Fadely; **166:** Drawing by P. Steiner; © 1993 *The New Yorker Magazine,* Inc.; **168:** Karen Kasmauski, Falls Church, Va.; **169:** The Kobal Collection; **170:** Albert Ellis Institute, New York, N.Y.; **172:** Julie Newdoll, Computer Graphics Laboratory, UCSF; **173:** Bella C. Laudauer Collection of Business and Advertising Art, The New York Historical Society; **174:** Julie Newdoll, Computer Graphics Laboratory, UCSF; **175:** Dan McCoy/ Rainbow; **179:** George Tooker, *The Subway,* 1950. Egg tempera on composition board. 18 × 36 inches. Collection of Whitney Museum of American Art. Juliana Force Purchase 50-23. Photograph copyright © 1997: Whitney Museum of Art, New York; **184(t):** Michael Melford; **184(b):** Museum of Modern Art Film Stills Archive; **185:** Ferndinand Hamburger, Jr., Archives of the Johns Hopkins University; **186:** University of Wisconsin Primate Laboratory, Madison; **187:** Torin Boyd Photo, Tokyo, Japan; **189:** Andrew Sacks/ Black Star; **195(t):** US Airways; **195(b):** Paulo Fridman/ Gamma Liaison; **Chapter 7, 196:** George Scholz, *Nightly Noise,* 1919, The Fishmann Collection; **201:** Nick Didlick/Reuters—Bettman Archives; **204:** *Ahab and Moby Dick,* etching by I.W. Taber, in Herman Melville, *Moby Dick,* New York, 1899 edition. Department of Rare Books and Special Collections, Princeton University Libraries, Princeton, N.J.; **207:** Smithsonian Institution/National Air and Space Museum; **211:** Gary Larson, Universal Press Syndicate; **215:** Larry Burrows, *Life* © Time Warner, Inc.; **216:** Christopher Morris/ Black Star; **218:** National Archives; **219:** Alain Keler/ Sygma; **224:** Michael Schumann/ SABA; **225:** Peter Turnley/ Black Star; **227:** J.P. Laffont/ Sygma; **228:** Carol Guzy/ *Washington Post;* **229:** Charles H. Porter IV/ Sygma; **233(t):** Vickie Lewis, © 1996 *People;* **233(b):** Steve Labadessa/ Outline; **Chapter 8, 234:** Jacob Lawrence, *Depression,* 1950. Tempera on paper. 22 × 30 1/2 inches. Collection of Whitney Museum of American Art. Gift of David M. Solinger 66.98. Photograph copyright © 1997: Whitney Museum of Art, New York. Photo by Geoffrey Clements; **236:** George P.A. Healy, 1887, The National Portrait Gallery, Smithsonian Institution; **238:** Edvard Munch, *Melancholia, Laura,* 1899. Oslo kommunes kunstsamlinger Munch-Museet; **240:** John Leongard; **241:** Manfred Reiner/ Black Star; **245:** Mark S. Wexler, Chicago; **246:** Julie Newdoll, Computer Graphics Laboratory, UCSF; **249:** W. Barr/ Gamma Liaison; **250:** Homer Sykes/ Woodfin Camp & Associates; **251:** Barry Jarvinen/ AP/Wide World Photos; **252:** University of Wisconsin Primate Laboratory, Madison; **253:** Dorothea Lange, February 1936, Farm Security Administration, Library of Congress; **255:** PEANUTS by Charles Schulz, © 1956 United Features Syndicate Inc.; **257:** Sidney Harris; **263:** The Lilly Library, Indiana University, Bloomington; **264:** A Knudsen/ Sygma; **265:** Sidney Harris; **268:** Jerry Irwin; **271(t):** Dr. Rubin Gur, University of Pennsylvania Medical School; **271(b):** Steve Labadessa/ Outline; **Chapter 9, 272:** Winsook Kim Linton, *Rowing,* Oil on canvas. Winsook Kim Linton, New York, N.Y.; **274:** Callahan; **275:** Joel Gordon, New

York, N.Y.; **276:** Myrleen Ferguson/ Tony Stone Worldwise; **278:** Rick Rickman/ Matrix; **281:** Joe McNally/ Matrix; **283:** Tom Moran; **286:** Will McIntyre/ Photo Researchers; **290:** Karen Kasmauski, Falls Church, Va.; **294:** Travis Amos; **297:** Phil Huber/ Black Star; **298:** Theo Westenberger/ Gamma Liaison; **Chapter 10, 302:** Frida Kahlo, *The Suicide of Dorothy Hale,* 1938–1939, Phoenix Art Museum, gift of anonymous donor; **304:** Dr. Andrew C. Mason, Section of Neurobiology & Behavior, Cornell University; **308:** Nick Ut/ AP/Wide World Photos; **309:** Pressenbild/ Adventure; **310:** Alex Colville, *Target Pistol and Man,* 1988. Acrylic on wood particle board. 60 × 60 cm. Alex Colville, A. C. Fine Art, Inc., Wolfville, N.S., Canada; **314:** David Woo, *Dallas Morning News/* Sygma; **315:** Everett Collection; **319:** Steve Nickerson/ Black Star; **320:** Grant Haller, *Seattle Post Intelligencer/* Sygma; **321:** R. Brandon/ Alaska Stock Images; **322:** John Kaplan/ Media Alliance; **326:** H. Yamaguchi/ Gamma Liaison; **329:** Lawrence Migdale; **330:** Rob Sollett/ *Staten Island Advance;* **332:** Edward Abbott; **335(t):** Marc C. Biggins/ Gamma Liaison; **335(b):** Karsh/ Woodfin Camp & Associates; **Chapter 11, 336:** Limbourg Brothers, *Très Riches Heures du Jean, Duc de Berry,* Musée Conde, Chantilly, France. Giraudon/ Art Resource, N.Y.; **339:** Sidney Harris; **341:** Frank Holl, *Convalescent,* 1994. Christopher Wood Gallery, London, Bridgeman/ Art Resource, N.Y.; **344:** Steve McCurry/ Magnum Photos; **346:** Mary Evans Picture Library/ Sigmund Freud Copyrights; **348:** Torlin Boyd Photo, Tokyo, Japan; **350:** Lester Sloan/ Woodfin Camp & Associates; **351:** Lionel Cihes/ AP/Wide World Photos; **355:** Lennart Nilsson/ Boehringer Ingelheim International GmbH; **357:** Frank Fournier/ Woodfin Camp & Associates; **358:** Ted Spiegel/ Black Star; **359:** Marc Geller; **362:** Louis Psihoyos/ Matrix; **363:** Joe McNally, *Life* © Time Warner, Inc.; **365:** Ted Spagna; **369(t):** Peter Serling, New York, N.Y.; **369(b):** Rick Rickman/ Matrix; **Chapter 12, 370:** Wayne Thiebaud, *Confections,* 1962. Collection-Byron R. Meyer, San Francisco; **373:** B. Schiffman/ Gamma Liaison; **373(inset):** Steve Schapiro/ Sygma; **375:** J. Polleross/ The Stock Market; **377(t):** David Garner; **377(b):** Wallace Kirkland, *Life* © Time Warner, Inc.; **378:** Donna Terek, Michigan Magazine, *The Detroit News/Free Press;* **380:** Richard Howard, © 1991 *Discover;* **384:** Pierre August Renoir, *Seated Bather,* 1903–1906. Detroit Institute of the Arts, bequest of Robert H. Tannahill; **385:** Claus Meyer/ Black Star; **388:** Ilene Perlman/ Impact Visuals; **389:** Historical Research Center, Houston Academy of Medicine, Texas Medical Center Library; **392(l/r):** John Annerino, Tucson; **393:** Yvonne Hemsey/ Gamma Liaison; **396:** Joseph Neumayer/ Design Conceptions; **401(t):** Marcus/ Sipa Press; **401(b):** AP/Wide World Photos; **Chapter 13, 402:** Joel Gordon, New York, N.Y.; **407(l):** Currier & Ives, *Washington's Farewell to the Officers of His Army,* 1848. The Museum of the City of New York. Gift of Gerald Levino; **407(r):** Currier & Ives, *Washington's Farewell to the Officers of His Army,* 1876. The Museum of the City of New York. Gift of Gerald Levino; **409:** George Steinmetz; **411:** John Chiasson/ Gamma Liaison; **413:** Tony O'Brian/ Picture Group; **417:** Michele McDonald, Arlington, Mass.; **418:** The Granger Collection; **419:** Charlie Steiner/ JB Pictures; **421:** E.T. Archives; **422:** Vaughan Fleming/Science Photo Library/ Photo Researchers; **426(l):** Richard E. Aaron/ Sygma; **426(r):** Stephen Ellison/ Shooting Star; **428:** Liam Longman/Miramax/ The Kobal Collection; **430:** C/B Productions/ The Stock Market; **431:** Jeff Mermelstein, New York, N.Y.; **432:** Culver Pictures; **435:** Ricki Rosen/ SABA; **436:** Layne Kennedy, Minneapolis, **438:** Marc R. Wood, Marinette, Wis.; **441(t):** Steve Sands/ Outline; **441(b):** Bismarck Tribune Photo by Tom Stromme/ AP/Wide World Photos; **Chapter 14, 442:** Marc Chagall, *Birthday* [l'Anniversaire], 1915. Oil on cardboard, 31 3/4 × 39 1/4 inches. The Museum of Modern Art, New York. Acquired through the Lillie P. Bliss Bequest. Photograph © 1994 the Museum of Modern Art, New York; **448:** Callahan; **451:** M. Siluk/ The Image Works; **452:** Joseph LoPiccolo; **454:** From Joseph R. Buchanan, *Outlines of Lectures on the Neurological System of Anthropology,* Cincinnati, 1854. The Oskar Diethelm Library, Department of Psychiatry, Cornell University Medical College and the New York Hospital, New York; **457:** Mariella Furrer/ SABA; **458:** Gilbert Dupuy/ Black Star; **463:** Catherine Karnow/ Woodfin Camp & Associates; **467:** Peter Yates/ Picture Group; **468:** Masny/ Sipa Press; **470:** Joel Gordon, New York, N.Y.; **473:** AP/Wide World Photos; **474(l):** Bettmann Archives; **474(r):** David Levenson/ Rex USA Ltd.; **477(t):** Michael S. Kenner/ Bruce Coleman; **477(b):** Donald C. Roberts/ Gamma Liaison; **Chapter 15, 478:** George Tooker, *Voice 1,* 1963. Egg tempera on gesso panel. 19 1/2 × 17 1/2 inches. Private Collection. Courtesy Chameleon Artworks, Chameleon Books, Chesterfield, Mass.; **480:** Mutter Museum, College of Physicians of Philadelphia; **483:** The Kobal Collection; **485:** David Graham/ Black Star; **487:** Marcus E. Raichle, M.D., Washington University, School of Medicine, St. Louis, Mo.; **488:** D. Silbersweig, M.D. and E. Stern, M.D., Functional Neuroimaging Laboratory, The New York Hospital-Cornell Medical Center, New York, N.Y.; **489:** The Oskar Diethelm Library, History of Psychiatry Section, Department of Psychiatry, Cornell University Medical College and The New York Hospital, New York; **495:** Antoine Weitz, *Hunger, Madness, Crime,* 1864. Royal Museum, Belgium; **497:** Julie Newdoll, Computer Graphics Laboratory, UCSF; **499:** Joe McNally/ Matrix; **501:** NYPL Performing Arts Research Center; **504:** Courtesy of the artist, Gerald Scharfe and Tin Blue Ltd.; **507(t):** Claus Bergmann/ Conti Press, Germany; **507(b):** Milwaukee Sentinel/ SABA; **Chapter 16, 508:** Jean Beraud, *The Asylum,* 1885. Mansell Collection, London; **510:** Temple University Urban Archives, Philadelphia, Pa.; **513:** Bettmann Archives; **514(l):** Francisco Jose de Goya, *The House of the Insane,* Prado, Madrid/ Art Resource, New York; **514(r):** Museum of Modern Art Film Stills Archive; **517:** Lynn Johnson/ Black Star; **519:** Sidney Harris; **525:** Andrew Savulich/ New York Times Pictures; **527:** Christopher Morris/ Black Star; **528:** E. Fuller Torrey; **530:** Dewey Fladd, Canadaigua, N.Y.; **533(b):** Andrew Holbrooke/ Black Star; **Chapter 17, 534:** Self portraits collected by Richard Jung of the University of Freiburg and published through courtesy of Gisele Raderscheidt, the widow of the artist. From Michael I. Posner and Marcus E. Raichle, *Images of Mind,* New York: Scientific American Library, 1994, p. 152; **536:** M. Lerner, W. H. Freeman; **537:** AP/ Wide World Photos; **539:** Eric Reiman, University of Arizona PET Center, Good Samaritan Medical Center; **541:** © 1989 Debra Lex, *People;* **543:** The Kobal Collection; **544:** Thorensen; **546:** Ernest Hilgard, Stanford University; **551:** PEANUTS © 1977 United Features Syndicate, Inc.; **552:** Doug Menuez/ SABA; **556:** Richard Falco/ Black Star; **559:** Dennis Selkoe, Harvard Medical School; **561:** Christopher Little/ Outline; **562:** Doug Mills/ AP/Wide World Photos; **563:** Lynn Johnson, Munhall, Pennsylvania; **565(t):** Mike Guastella/ Star File; **565(b):** Martyn Hayhow/ AP/Wide World Photos; **Chapter 18, 566:** Eileen Cowin, *Untitled,* 1988. **60 × 48** inches. Courtesy of Eileen Cowin, Santa Monica, Calif.; **573:** The Kobal Collection; **576:** AP/ Wide World Photos; **579:** Michael S. Yamashita/ Woodfin Camp & Associates; **583:** Tim Kimzey, *Union Daily Times/* Sipa Press; **585:** Martin/Prism Rogers/ FPG International; **587:** GARFIELD, Jim Davis © 1985 United Features Syndicate, Inc.; **589:** Mark Richards/ PhotoEdit; **591(t):** The Kobal Collection; **591(b):** AP/Wide World Photos; **593:** Randy Jones/ *The New York Times;* **595:** Joel Gordon, New York, N.Y.; **597(t):** W.B. Productions Ltd/ Photofest; **597(b):** Melinda Sue Gordon/ Photofest; **Chapter 19, 598:** Pavel Tchelitchew, *Hide-and-Seek* {Cache-Cache}, 1940–42. Oil on canvas. 6 feet 6 1/2 inches × 7 feet 3/4 inches The Museum of Modern Art, New York. Mrs. Simon Guggenheim Fund. Photograph © 1998 The Museum of Modern Art, New York; **602(t):** Paul Chesley/ Tony Stone Worldwide; **602(b):** April Saul/ *The Philadelphia Inquirer;* **603:** Edvard Munch, *The Dead Mother and the Little Girl,* Munch Museum, Oslo/ Art Resource, New York; **607:** Honore Daumier, *Fatherly Discipline,* 1851. The Art Institute of Chicago, Arthur Heun Fund, 1952.1108; **611:** © 1996, *Newsweek,* Inc. All rights reserved. Reprinted by permission; **612:** Michael Heron/ Woodfin Camp & Associates; **614:** Arthur Pollock, Boston Herald;

615: Janet Kelly/ *Eagle-Times,* Reading, Pa.; **616:** Randy Olson, from Rick Smolan, Phillip Moffitt, and Matthew Naythons, M.D., *The Power to Heal,* New York: Prentice Hall, 1990, p. 95; **617:** The Eden Institute Foundation, Inc.; **618:** Nicholas Lisi/ Syracuse Newspapers; **620:** E. Lee White/ *Newsweek;* **622:** Frank Varney; **625:** Stephanie Maze/ Woodfin Camp & Associates; **627:** United States Parachute Association, Alexandria, Va.; **628:** Michael Heron/ Woodfin Camp & Associates; **630:** Lynn Johnson/ Black Star; **633(t):** Ethan Hoffman/Picture Project, New York, N.Y.; **633(b):** Photofest; **Chapter 20, 634:** Violet Baxter, *Spring Trees,* 1991. Watercolor on paper, 9 × 12 inches. Violet Baxter, New York, N.Y.; **637:** AP/Wide World Photos; **641:** Bill Fitz-Patrick/ Gamma Liaison; **642:** Stephen Ferry/ Gamma Liaison; **645:** FBI/Jeanne Boylan/ AP/Wide World Photos; **648:** Thomas Hovenden, *The Last Moments of John Brown,* 1884. Oil on canvas. 77 3/8 × 63 1/4 inches. The Metropolitan Museum of Art, New York. Gift of Mr. and Mrs. Carl Stoeckel, 1897. (97.5); **649:** Joe McNally/ Matrix; **651:** John Ficara/ Woodfin Camp and Associates; **652:** Comedy Central/ Shooting Star International; **654:** Shonna Valeska, New York, N.Y.; **660:** Drawing by Piraro, © 1991 Chronicle Features; **663(t):** Lucien Clergue/ Contact Press Images

Name Index

Page numbers in *italics* indicate figure captions

Subject Index